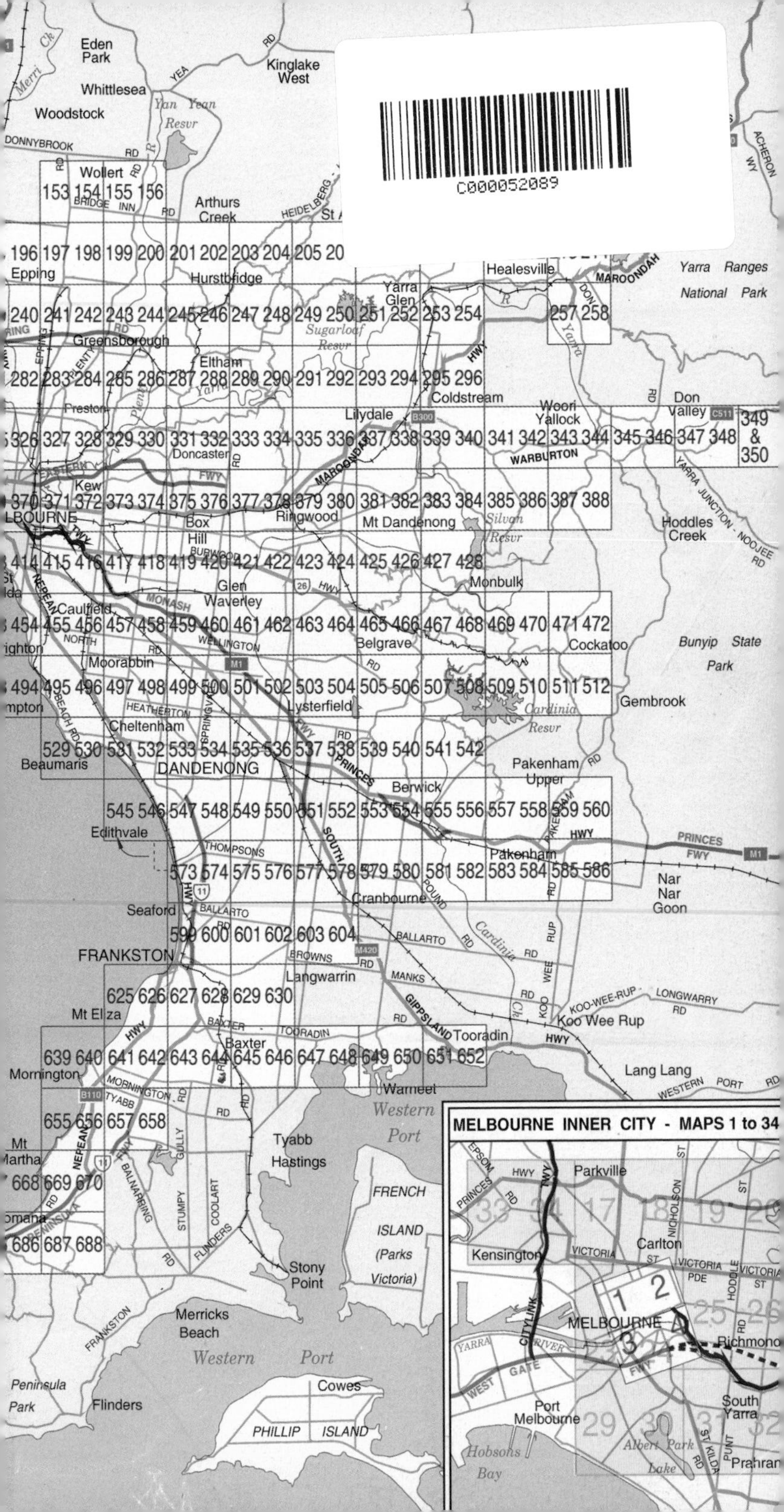

Eden Park
Kinglake West
Whittlesea
Woodstock
Yan Yean Resvr
C000052089
Wollert
153 154 155 156
Arthurs Creek
196 197 198 199 200 201 202 203 204 205
Epping
Hurstbridge
Healesville
Yarra Ranges National Park
Yarra Glen
240 241 242 243 244 245 246 247 248 249 250 251 252 253 254
257 258
Sugarloaf Resvr
Greensborough
Eltham
282 283 284 285 286 287 288 289 290 291 292 293 294 295 296
Coldstream
Preston
Lilydale
Woori Yallock
Don Valley
326 327 328 329 330 331 332 333 334 335 336 337 338 339 340 341 342 343 344 345 346 347 348
349 & 350
Doncaster
WARBURTON
Kew
370 371 372 373 374 375 376 377 378 379 380 381 382 383 384 385 386 387 388
Box Hill
Ringwood
Mt Dandenong
Silvan Resvr
Hoddles Creek
YARRA JUNCTION - NOOJEE RD
414 415 416 417 418 419 420 421 422 423 424 425 426 427 428
Monbulk
Glen Waverley
Caulfield
454 455 456 457 458 459 460 461 462 463 464 465 466 467 468 469 470 471 472
Belgrave
Cockatoo
Bunyip State Park
Moorabbin
494 495 496 497 498 499 500 501 502 503 504 505 506 507 508 509 510 511 512
Lysterfield
Cardinia Resvr
Gembrook
Cheltenham
529 530 531 532 533 534 535 536 537 538 539 540 541 542
Beaumaris
DANDENONG
Pakenham Upper
Berwick
545 546 547 548 549 550 551 552 553 554 555 556 557 558 559 560
Edithvale
PRINCES FWY
Pakenham
573 574 575 576 577 578 579 580 581 582 583 584 585 586
Nar Nar Goon
Seaford
Cranbourne
599 600 601 602 603 604
FRANKSTON
Langwarrin
625 626 627 628 629 630
Mt Eliza
Koo Wee Rup
Baxter
Tooradin
639 640 641 642 643 644 645 646 647 648 649 650 651 652
Mornington
Lang Lang
Warneet
Western Port
655 656 657 658
Tyabb
Hastings
Mt Martha
668 669 670
FRENCH ISLAND (Parks Victoria)
686 687 688
Stony Point
Merricks Beach
Western Port
Peninsula Park
Flinders
Cowes
PHILLIP ISLAND
MELBOURNE INNER CITY - MAPS 1 to 34
Parkville
Carlton
Kensington
MELBOURNE
Richmond
Port Melbourne
South Yarra
Hobsons Bay
Albert Park Lake
Prahran

Produced and published in Australia by UBD Publishing Company
A division of Universal Publishers Pty Ltd
ABN 83 000 087 132
585 Burwood Rd, Hawthorn VIC 3122
Telephone: (03) 9818 4455 Facsimile: (02) 9818 6123

www.ubd-online.com

ISBN 0 7319 1471 6
6th Edition 2004

Printed by Craft Print Pte Ltd

Cover
Design: Designer Graphics
Photo: Luna Park, St Kilda
David B Simmonds / The Urban Image

Cityside Guide
Author: Grant Arnott
Photos: Tourism Victoria, Buzzwords Media, Melbourne Aquarium & Heat Nightclub

The *Cityside Guide* contains only a selection of attractions in and around Melbourne CBD and therefore does not purport to be a comprehensive listing.

How To Find A Street

Look up the street name and suburb in the Street Index.

Example: Amanda Court, Melton
Shown in the Street Index as:

AMANDA	Map	Ref
ct. Melton	268	G1

Turn to map 268 and trace lines downwards from (G) and across from (1) in the map border. Amanda Court will be found at the intersection of the two lines. If the Street Index does not list the street you are seeking under a particular suburb, check to see if the street is actually in an adjoining suburb. Refer to the Suburbs & Localities Index and find on which map the suburb appears. Turn to that map and note the names of surrounding suburbs. Now return to the Street Index and look for the street in one of these suburbs.

Contents

Cityside Guide

on the waterfront

Splash onto Melbourne's exciting aquatic scene. Beaches, boats and boardwalks line the stunning waterways of the city and surrounds, providing a serene, beautiful playground for Melburnians and visitors alike.

Port Phillip Bay is Melbourne's gateway to the rest of the world, and a favourite with locals because of its variety of beaches, scenery and widespread attractions. There's an incredible variety of things to do around this huge body of water. The bay has been amusing Melburnians since the first settlers arrived over 150 years ago.

At the northern end of the bay, the city sits near the mouth of the famous Yarra River. Once bustling with traders, the Yarra is now a peaceful estuary plied by rowers, water taxis, gondolas and scenic cruise vessels. Along its banks, the cyclists, skaters and joggers enjoy the winding trails, while those who just want to relax can settle back on the grassy slopes and watch the world go by.

In the city, at **Southgate Arts & Leisure Precinct (Map 4, Ref C4)** and the **Crown Entertainment Complex (Map 3, Ref B4)**, the Yarra has been turned into a spectacular and exciting waterfront featuring works of art, street theatre and a huge variety of activities.

At the Docklands (Map 368, Ref L14), Melbourne's new 'blue park' is the hottest waterfront attraction in town, boasting waterside restaurants, bars, apartments and stunning views across Victoria Harbour. NewQuay is the hub of entertainment at the Docklands, thriving day and night as locals indulge in exquisite waterfront dining and entertainment. Stunning artworks and visionary architecture enhance the promenade experience.

Beyond the Yarra, the shores of Port Phillip Bay are teeming with picturesque seaside towns like **Brighton (Map 454), Mornington (Map 641)** and **Sorrento (Map 678)**. Brimming with life and atmosphere, every little town along the coast is a great getaway any time of the year. Check out these options!

Arthurs Seat
(Map 685, Ref H14)

Arthurs Seat Road, Dromana
If you want the most breathtaking views of Port Phillip Bay, then Arthurs Seat on the Mornington Peninsula is the number one choice! Treat your honey to the scenic chairlift ride through the treetops to win some serious points. Nearby, cafés, restaurants and wineries beckon for a Sunday afternoon escape.

Brighton (Map 454, Ref L16)

Brighton Beach (Map 494, Ref G5) is famous for its colourful bathing boxes, a remnant of the beach-goer's style from earlier times. Off the sand, Brighton has an excellent seaside atmosphere with a terrific range of cafés. It's easy to get to — from the city, take the Sandringham train line to Brighton Beach Railway Station and you're right there!

Enterprize (Map 411, Ref H15)

Gem Pier, Williamstown

Catch the train from the city to Williamstown for the opportunity to sail on an awesome replica of the ship that brought the first European settlers to Melbourne — the schooner Enterprize. Put yourself in their shoes as you cruise majestically on the glistening waters of Port Phillip Bay and take in the outstanding views of the city skyline. Ph: (03) 9397 3477

Geelong and Bellarine Peninsula

A little further afield, on the western side of the bay, is the city of Geelong. It boasts a spectacular waterfront with a wide range of restaurants, shopping and outdoor activities. Further south is Victoria's surf coast, featuring legendary beach towns like Torquay and Barwon Heads, along with some of the best surfing and most spectacular coastal scenery in Australia. Trains and buses depart regularly from **Spencer Street Station (Map 23, Ref F11)** in the city.

Golf Highlights

If you fancy a hit of stick, some of Melbourne's best sandbelt courses are situated along the shores of Port Phillip Bay, including the **Royal Melbourne Golf Course (Map 529, J2)**, Cheltenham Road, Black Rock (03) 9598 6755 , site of numerous major tournaments. There are some stunning public courses in the area, including **Moonah Links (Map 698, Ref D15),** the **Dunes at Rye (Map 697, Ref G14)** and **Brighton (Map 495, Ref E3)**.

Sorrento–Portsea
(Maps 677 & 678)

Sorrento was one of Melbourne's first seaside resorts, when paddlesteamers used to transport city folk down to the Sorrento Pier for a day on the beach. Over a hundred years later, Sorrento is still a hugely popular destination and neighbouring Portsea is a fabulous holiday place during the summertime.

St Kilda Foreshore
(Map 413)

Vast green gardens, wide beaches and a canopy of palm trees make St Kilda the vogue capital of Melbourne's waterfront. Home to the famous St Kilda Pier, The Esplanade and Luna Park, the foreshore has a well-deserved reputation for outdoor pleasure. Rollerbladers, cyclists and joggers ply the well-maintained boardwalks endlessly. Kitesurfing, sailing, boating and swimming are all popular activities here. Parasailing and jet-skiing are available from St Kilda Marina, Marine Pde, **St Kilda (Map 454, Ref A1)**, plus the hip new sport of kiteboarding is taking off dramatically, with lessons also available at the Marina. The St Kilda Pier, jutting out into Port Phillip Bay, , is a fantastic place to sit and watch the sunset, and the nearby kiosks offer a range of foods to enjoy whilst overlooking the bay.

- **Melbourne River Cruises (Map 4, Ref G3)** Princes Walk, cnr of Princes Bridge and Batman Avenue, City, Ph: (03) 9614 1215
Stuck for a new way to see Melbourne? Relax and soak in the sights of the city with informative commentary in the comfort of a Melbourne River Cruiser. Choose from the 'Scenic River Gardens' upriver cruise, the 'Port & Docklands' downriver cruise, or for the complete city experience, consider the 'Melbourne Highlights' up- and down-river cruise. Cruises depart every half hour daily (except Christmas Day).

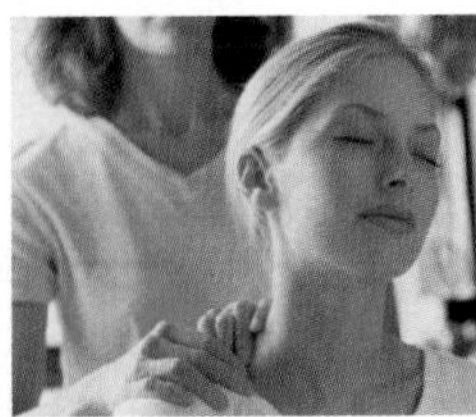

When it comes to spoiling yourself, sometimes dinner for two and a movie is just not enough!

Melburnians love to throw the book of convention out the window. Always creative and constantly innovative, the people of Melbourne dare to be different. The result is a fantastic range of alternative activities for those of us who like to veer off the beaten path once in a while.

Whatever takes your fancy — heart-pumping thrills, mouth-watering delights, spectacular scenery or something completely off the wall — Melbourne's got an idea for you!

Here are a few choices for making a special occasion a little more special.

Balloon Sunrise

See Melbourne come to life from a unique perspective, floating quietly above the skyscrapers as you watch the city awaken below. The view is superb, with spectacular morning vistas of prominent landmarks — including Fitzroy Gardens, Botanical Gardens, the Yarra and MCG — followed by a champagne breakfast in Richmond. Ph: (03) 9427-7596

Chocolate Indulgence Walk

For sheer decadence, Suzie Wharton's Chocolate Indulgence Walk is the ultimate. Tastings at Cadbury's, Myer, New Zealand Ice Creamery, Chocolate Box and Darrell Lea will spoil your tastebuds rotten. Go on, you know you want it! Other tours include the Chocolate & Other Desserts Walk, or if coffee is more your scene, rather than chokky, choose the '2Cs' — Coffee & Cakes Walk — Ph: (03) 9815 1228

Colonial Tramcar Restaurant

The only restaurant in Melbourne where the scenery changes every minute! Dazzle your special someone in style with fine dining on a classic W Class Tram. You'll enjoy fantastic food, great wine and some unique city sights while trundling around town in comfort. The Colonial Tramcar Restaurant is ideal for parties, too - you'll find it a moving experience.
Ph: (03) 9696 4000

Day Spas

Pamper yourself and your partner with a special treat – visit one of Melbourne's acclaimed day spas, where super-friendly, super-handy staff utilise massage and aromatherapy to melt away your daily stresses. One of the finest is **Geisha (Map 2, Ref D14)**, Little Collins St, City, (03) 9663 5544 where gorgeous Japanese décor and soothing Oriental delights enhance the pampering experience.

MCG Tours

Sports fans owe it to themselves to take a tour of Australia's most famous sporting venue, the **Melbourne Cricket Ground (Map 25, Ref F12)**, Jolimont. Inside you'll find heaps of memorabilia from our many sporting legends over the years. Stride in the footsteps of our national heroes as you visit the Long Room, the Players' Change Rooms and even take a walk out onto the hallowed turf.
Ticketmaster Ph: 136 100

Putting Melbourne in Plane View

Soar above magnificent Melbourne and the spectacular Port Phillip Bay in a seaplane. Scenic Seaplane Flights in Williamstown (Map 411, Ref H15) take off and land in Hobsons Bay, Williamstown. Step out of your plane and straight into one of this village's fantastic waterfront cafes for a day's outing you'll never forget.

Scienceworks

This one's not for nerds — a multitude of cool games awaits you at Scienceworks, 2 Booker St, Spotswood (Map 411, Ref D 2). There's a six million dollar planetarium that will blow your mind, plus a machine that lets you race against Cathy Freeman — don't expect to win! You can also take on a friend in a mechanised rowing contest or test your fitness and learn how technology aids survival in the ocean, desert, Antarctica and outer space. Ph: (03) 9392 4800

Skydive City

For the ultimate thrill there's really nothing that quite compares to diving out of a plane at 10 000+ feet! Skydive City offers you the unique opportunity to tandem skydive into the city of Melbourne. Jump start your day and soar above the city for an adrenaline rush you'll never forget. Ph: (0414) 686 722

The Melbourne Ghost Tour

Smiling city by day, ghosts' playground by night! Melbourne is inhabited by a number of ghosts, and this tour will open your eyes to the city's haunted past.

Your guide is an avid ghosthunter! Get a look at the creepiest parts of Melbourne where the city's first and most recent ghosts have been sighted. This tour has converted many a skeptic — who knows, you might get slimed. 'Who you gonna call?' Ph: (03) 9662 9010

Wine On Sunday

Experience wine and food from various Victorian regions, plus guest speakers & entertainment. Around 60 stalls sell some of Victoria's premium wines, local food can be sampled and wine tasting is available through the purchase of a 'Wine on Sunday' glass. Afterwards, you can catch a classic flick at the Kino Cinema. 'Wine on Sunday' is held the first Sunday of every month from 11am-4pm at **Collins Place (Map 24, Ref J7)**, 45 Collins St, City, Ph: (03) 9655 3600.

Village Gold Class Movies

For the ultimate movie experience, this one's in a class of its own! Sink into the luxurious reclining armchairs, kick your feet up and lounge in first class comfort as you enjoy the latest blockbusters on the big screen. Gold Class also has the ultimate in refreshments available, with a wine bar, a great range of light fare and delicious desserts to add to your viewing pleasure.
Ph: 132 929

village treasures

The CBD is the heart of Melbourne, but the soul and spirit of the city is alive in the urban villages clustered around its perimeter. Diversity is truly defined on the city fringe – experience the colour, the music and the life of Melbourne's inner city suburbs.

Since the end of World War II, Melbourne has hosted a steady stream of immigrants, firstly from Europe, and more recently Asia and the Middle East. The eclectic melting pot of cultures that has evolved is a mix of continental flavours blended with the ubiquitous Aussie persona.

What this means for Melbourne is that the surrounding suburbs offer a mix of ideas and cultural influences, each village marking its territory with its own distinct style.

Each of these areas is just a short sojourn from the city centre, by tram, train, bus or taxi-cab. Though the CBD has plenty to offer, the only way to claim a full Melbourne experience is to get out and about in the thriving inner city suburbs.

carlton (Map 17)

When Italian migrants arrived in Melbourne by the thousands in the post-WWII era, they brought a little piece of Italy with them and planted it just north of the city in Carlton. Melbourne's 'Little Italy' has flourished ever since.

From the time University Cafe opened its doors back in 1951, espresso has been an institution on Lygon Street's vibrant cafe strip, and pizza and pasta are never more than a stone's throw away. In fact, Toto's Pizza House, at 101 Lygon Street, lays claim to being the very first pizzeria in Australia. You'll also find a tremendous variety of other national cuisines, including Thai, Afghan, Malay, Caribbean and Greek. For a slightly more serene dining environment, try Rathdowne or Grattan Streets for a further range of top quality restaurants, cafes and bars.

Lygon Street's trendy eateries are complemented by a superb range of shopping outlets, including gourmet delicatessens, bookshops and fashion houses. Elegantly presented shopfronts beckon passers-by with a wide range of temptations, from sugar-dusted Mediterranean sweets to the latest in European and Australian fashion.

The Carlton Gardens are home to the Royal Exhibition Building, IMAX Theatre and the new Melbourne Museum.

fitzroy (Map 19)

The lively village of Fitzroy is an eclectic melting pot of expression, individualism and alternative lifestyles. The eccentric, the artistic, and the extroverted converge here in a parade of colour to eat, shop and consume lattes at a frightening rate. A concentration of the city's trendy Bohemian set can be found on Brunswick Street's lively eatery and entertainment strip. If it's zany or esoteric, you'll find it here – from the incredible range of exotic cuisines to original handmade art, and retro clothing that will ensure you stand out from the crowd. This is a place where green hair and a nipple ring will score you smiles, not scowls.

By day, busking poets roam Brunswick Street while the sidewalk cafes are abuzz with activity. By night, the place comes alive as the pubs, bars and live music take centre stage. The available cuisines are as varied and exotic as the clientele they attract, including the best of Thai, Afghan, French, African, Asian, Scandinavian, Malay and Japanese, as well as the standard 'pizza and pasta' type establishments. Brunswick Street is also renowned for its superb vegetarian cuisine, catering to the strictest vegan diets right through to the 'occasional vegetarian' patron. Another Fitzroy icon is the fantastic cooked breakfasts and brunches – great for revitalisation after a big night out at one of the precinct's many bars, pubs and clubs.

port melbourne (Map 29)

Ever since the city was first settled, Port Melbourne has historically provided the first glimpse of Melbourne for visitors, immigrants and sailors arriving by water from destinations all over the world. Nowadays, the re-invented Port has a new appeal, pioneering a hip beachside ambience that's attracting Melburnians and visitors in droves.

Bay Street is the centrepiece of this historic township, beginning at the beach and stretching east to the city skyline. Once the first port of call for goldrush prospectors, international industrialists and hundreds of thousands of European immigrants, Bay Street is now a slick, fashionable enclave for those seeking chic village shopping, dining and lifestyle close to the city.

Bay Street is a shopper's delight – art galleries, gift shops and boutiques line the historical boulevard, combining the traditional and contemporary in elegant fashion. Recently widened footpaths and striking new décor have lifted Bay Street to the status of one of Melbourne's premier shopping promenades.

Gourmet food and wine have found a bright new home on Bay Street. The conventional rules that stipulate what defines a restaurant, café or bar are ignored here – every venue in Port Melbourne, large or small, casual or formal, promises a range of first class cuisine presented with an artistic flair symbolic of Bay Street's passionate devotion to style. Enjoy a sunny light lunch at a superb street cafe, or linger over a long, elegant evening meal with a bottle of fine wine at a first class establishment. Sample one of the many upbeat local pubs, a fortunate legacy of Bay Street's seaside history.

In the last few years, Port Melbourne has embraced its waterfront more fully than ever before with first class beachside restaurants and taverns propelling the once working class region to prime real estate status.

Port Melbourne is just minutes by car or taxi from the heart of the CBD. Alternatively, catch the 109 tram from Collins Street in the city.

richmond (Map 26)

This is one of Melbourne's oldest villages, renowned for its excellent shopping and South-East Asian cuisine. Bridge Road is the mecca of discerning bargain-hunters, with a high concentration of quality designer factory outlets. The neighbouring thoroughfares of Swan Street and Church Street also offer a great range of top class products. Shopping aside, Richmond boasts a thriving social scene with some of Melbourne's finest venues for dancing, drinking and live music.

Victoria Street is now home for many of the post-70s Vietnamese migrants who came to Australia. You'll find many mid-20s returned backpackers attempting their newly acquired Vietnamese at Thang Phong, Quan 88 or Thy Thy. With delicious soups, rice paper rolls, sticky pork buns plus a host of other entrees and main dishes for around $10, you've just discovered the best cheap eats in Melbourne.

south yarra (Map 31)

From fashion to food and furnishings, South Yarra's dedication to class is unparallelled anywhere else in Melbourne. It is the urban playground of choice for Melbourne's celebrities, sports stars and social elite… the place to be seen. South Yarra is Melbourne's heart of sophistication and style. The Chapel Street and Toorak Road shopping precincts exude elegance with countless boutiques, jewellers and exclusive homeware stores. Outlets of world-class designer labels abound, including the likes of Cose Ipanema, Helmut Lang, Carla Zampatti, Collette Dinnigan and Bettina Liano.

South Yarra's high-class image is matched by its superb cuisine. Not surprisingly, the city boasts more first-rate dining establishments than any other part of Melbourne. The finest ingredients, the most sophisticated techniques and an overwhelming attention to detail distinguish South Yarra as a forerunner in culinary excellence. Glamorous patrons are drawn to the delectable choices of Japanese, French, Spanish and nouveau gourmet food. The guardians of glamour are in their element in South Yarra at night time, when the stylish clubs and exclusive bars are pumping – offering everything from popular modern beats to jazz and blues.

st kilda (Map 414)

St Kilda is one of Melbourne's favourite bayside villages. In summer, its long sandy beach is inundated with Melburnians lapping up the sunshine or splashing in the marine playground of Port Phillip Bay. The many cafes, restaurants and specialty shops in Acland Street and Fitzroy Street give St Kilda its cosmopolitan ambience. Home to the famous St Kilda Pier, The Esplanade and Luna Park, St Kilda has a well-deserved reputation for outdoor pleasure.

Waterfront activities are something of a speciality in St Kilda with the bay, the marina and easy access to Albert Park Lake. Kitesurfing, sailing, boating and swimming are all popular activities here. The St Kilda Pier, jutting out into Port Phillip Bay, offers great panoramic views of the bay. St Kilda's landmarks have been made famous by the successful Australian drama, *The Secret Life Of Us*. On sunny days, you can sit on the pier and watch people playing beach volleyball or rollerblading along the Esplanade. On Sundays, the Upper Esplanade is transformed into an open-air art and craft market. This lively beachfront market specialises in handmade goods such as ceramics, leather goods and jewellery.

Just up from the market is Luna Park, a fun park modelled on New York's Coney Island. Since its opening in 1912, Luna Park's trademark open-mouthed entrance has been a celebrated Melbourne icon, recently refurbished in 2001.

With so much to do, you could almost forget to eat, but that would really be missing out. Fitzroy and Acland Streets are renowned as two of Melbourne's best 'eat streets'. Allow yourself to be tempted by the irresistible aromas of espresso coffee, freshly-baked cakes, breads, muffins and pastries. Pubs and licensed cafes on both Fitzroy and Acland streets ensure that the party continues well after the last dinner guests have left.

williamstown (Map 411)

Williamstown is the oldest continuous post-colonial settlement on the shores of Port Phillip Bay, named in honour of King William IV in 1837. For most of its 150-year history, Williamstown has thrived primarily as a working seaport. Today, however, food, art, gardens, a touch of shopping and weekend tourists lend Williamstown the laid-back ambience of a holiday village.

As is the case with many of Melbourne's eclectic villages, Williamstown has a well-established outdoor cafe culture. 'When in Rome', do as the locals do, enjoying freshly-squeezed juice or lattes over weekend newspapers in the glorious sunshine. Mingle among cyclists, rollerbladers and casual strollers who utilise the gorgeous waterfront. From Williamstown, you have a unique view of Melbourne's skyline and in the late afternoon, the Rialto reflects brilliant sunset colours like a mirror – spectacular hues of pink, red and orange.

Williamstown's dining culture promises an enjoyable outing on any level – a café brunch, elegant fine dining, or a picnic in the park. It's not just the destination, but the journey that matters. If this is true, then Williamstown is an ideal weekend visit. You can choose to drive there, via the panoramic West Gate Bridge, catch a train out of Spencer Street Station, or cruise across the scenic waters of the bay.

The best of the world is on sale in Melbourne's labyrinth of lanes, arcades and major shopping centres. First class international labels including Versace, Cartier, Ferragamo and Max Mara claim retail outlets in Melbourne's CBD. From the Paris end of Collins Street to the Queen Victoria Market, the city is bursting with opportunities. A little exploring divulges a surfeit of options – experience the classic grandeur of the Block and Royal Arcades, or the contemporary elegance of Australia on Collins. Strips of designer boutiques and big brand retailers are peppered with quirky, original and often amusing smaller stores. A day's shopping in Melbourne may reveal many unusual treasures. For instant gratification, you'll soon find everything you need and beyond right in the heart of the city, with three major department stores and several mega-malls offering excellent service, competitive prices and a huge range of merchandise.

One of Melbourne's most exciting new retail precincts is QV (Map 2, Ref H7), occupying the old site of the Queen Victoria Hospital. This monolithic retail, dining and residential centre opened recently and promises to rejuvenate shopping in the heart of the CBD. Remaining true to Melbourne's traditional lanes, arcades and alleyways, QV will service the city's rapidly growing resident population and draw visitors back to the centre of Melbourne with a vibrant new retail complex.

Melbourne Central is the colosseum of the consumer. Over 160 specialty shops plus the Daimaru department store surround one of the city's most impressive landmarks. A 20-storey glass cone stretches skyward to envelope the historic Coop's Shot Tower, a 111-year-old heritage building preserved in its original glory beneath the Melbourne Central dome. Inside the atrium, replicas of a hot air balloon and a vintage bi-plane float timelessly overhead, while a gigantic Marionette fob watch chimes to the tune of Waltzing Matilda every hour.

Stretching from Bourke to Lonsdale Streets, the massive Myer and David Jones department stores offer a world of good buys. Featuring an endless variety of items in a wide range of prices, the retail giants provide friendly service and convenience. Out at ground level, tree-lined Collins Street is king with an abundance of premier vogue retailers, but Little Collins, Flinders Lane and Swanston Street also present a remarkable collection of hip fashion outlets.

Across the Yarra River, Southgate Arts & Leisure Centre promises an exciting array of consumer delights with a waterfront promenade housing a range of boutique stores with exotic wares on offer. A little further west, Crown Entertainment Complex displays the finest international labels in opulent fashion beside the Yarra.

The Queen Victoria Market is the largest undercover market in Australia. Established in 1878, the Market is an historic landmark and a Melbourne institution. The variety is eclectic, and bargain opportunities are endless. Open Tuesday through Sunday at various times, this world class shopping destination boasts a vast collection of items, from fresh produce to first-class fashion, as well as homewares, electronics, gifts and much more. Other open markets operating throughout the metropolitan area offer fresh food, flowers, art, giftware and clothing on various days.

beyond the cbd...

From upmarket shops featuring world famous labels to shopping up at the market for a bargain bracelet, Melbourne's metropolitan area offers a multitude of choices. Bridge Road, Richmond, is popular for the huge number of designer outlets available, featuring select labels and garments at affordable prices. There's a blasé, bohemian atmosphere pervading the area – located close to the city, shopping here is casual and fun. For the vogue shopper with a limited budget, Bridge Road in Richmond is a godsend. On this busy inner-city strip, thousands of shoppers converge daily, seeking wide variety and excellent value for money.

Bridge Road is the acknowledged leader of designer outlets in Melbourne – big name brands at bargain prices, plus up-market fashion boutiques, homewares and gift shops. The neighbouring Swan and Church Streets offer a continuation of trendy retail stores and quality items. Situated just beyond the rim of the Central Business District, Richmond is just a short hop away by tram. Catch the number 48 or 75 tram from Flinders Street, and you'll arrive at Bridge Road within minutes. The chic shopping is well catered for by an abundance of hip cafés, cake shops and restaurants – soak in the casual, laid-back atmosphere while seeking a world full of bargains.

In South Yarra, the sophisticated fashion set have stamped a claim on this trendy shopping precinct. Discerning buyers converge on the area daily, arriving in droves by Mercedes, Range Rover or BMW. Ever in vogue, the streets of Chapel, Greville and Toorak Road are lined with prestigious, high-class stores offering the finest in fashion and jewellery. Renowned Melbourne designers proudly call South Yarra home – shopping here can be quite expensive, but it is certainly the best choice on offer.

The wide variety of shopping available is serviced in every location by quality cafes, bars, and restaurants – complete your day with a latte or glass of wine, soaking up Melbourne's cosmopolitan atmosphere in the style of the elite. From fashion to furniture, electronics to elegance, Melbourne boasts unlimited choices at sensational prices, and visitors converge on the city daily as a shopping mecca.

the colour of melbourne

The city pulsates with colour and culture. From innovative 'buskers' amusing crowds on the street to classic symphonies and world class drama, Melbourne's diverse cultural background supplies an abundance of creativity. Magnificent sculptures adorn our streets, parks and promenades. Footpaths and walkways feature attractive murals, lovingly crafted by free-spirited young artists.

Cosmopolitan, fun-loving, and friendly, Melburnians are indeed a mixed breed that draw appeal from visitors throughout the world. Over a third of Melbourne's population has strong ties abroad, creating a multicultural melting pot of ideas, skills and personalities. Ethnic groups delight in celebrating their backgrounds with events including the Antipodes Festival, Oktoberfest and the Chinese New Year. Jazz, film, art, automobiles, flowers and gardens are all highlighted in their own shows and festivals.

art

• Ian Potter Centre Federation Square (Map 2, Ref J20)

Ph: (03) 9208 0222

The Ian Potter Centre features exclusively Australian exhibits. The gallery includes artwork from Aboriginal and Torres Strait Islanders as well as colonial, Heidelberg school and modern art pieces. Aligned with the National Gallery of Victoria, the Ian Potter Centre is proving a major Melbourne attraction.

• National Gallery of Victoria on St Kilda Road (Map 4, Ref D8)

Ph: (03) 8662 1555

After four years in a temporary locale, the National Gallery has returned to its fabulous home on St Kilda Road, fully redeveloped to provide Australia's finest international art experience.

If you're an art lover, you'll need to explore some of the City's many private galleries, particularly on **Flinders Lane (Map 2, Ref B17-L17)**. This exciting little thoroughfare in the heart of the city reveals a treasure trove of exotic, indigenous and original galleries of painted and sculptured art.

In **South Yarra, Kirkcaldy Davies Galleries (Map 32, Ref G17)**, 467 Malvern Road, Ph: (03) 9827 8790, exhibits a wide variety of works by emerging sculptors, painters and photographers, with solo and group exhibitions changing every month. In **Richmond, Niagara Galleries (Map 25, Ref L12)** at 245 Punt Road, Ph: (03) 9429 3666, showcases some of Australia's greatest modern artists.

If photography is more your style, shoot down to the **Centre for Contemporary Photography (Map 19, Ref B13)**, located in Johnston St, Fitzroy Ph: (03) 9417 1549, highlighting local and international artists.

classic films

Melbourne boasts several independent theatres serving up classic and contemporary films in an intimate atmosphere. **The Lumiere (Map 24, Ref F3)**, 108 Lonsdale St, City, (03) 9639 1055 , carries the friendly ambience of the times before multiplexes took over, while the **Astor Theatre (Map 414, Ref G13)** at 1 Chapel St, St Kilda (03) 9510 1414, is a classic cinema icon. The old-fashioned kiosk and original 1930s décor is perfect for that nostalgic movie experience.

comedy

Melbourne delivers some of Australia's best comedy — this is why we're home to the International Comedy Festival in April each year. The most consistent laughs are served up at **The Comedy Club (Map 18, Ref F10)** 380 Lygon St, Carlton, Ph: (03) 9348 1622 . There's always a good laugh to be had around town — check the Entertainment Guide in The Age every Friday.

culture

The Koori Heritage Trust (Map 2, Ref C17) 234 Flinders Lane, City, Ph: (03) 9639 6555 was established in 1985 with a commitment to protect, preserve and promote the living culture of the indigenous people of south-east Australia, whose heritage spans more than 40,000 years.

Commemorating those who have journeyed to Melbourne from far-off places, the **Immigration Museum (Map 1, Ref F19)** 400 Flinders St, City, Ph: (03) 9927 2700, is located in the Old Customs House on Flinders St. Visitors can wander through interactive displays of Melbourne's migrant history, featuring graphics, videos and models depicting immigrant life.

dance

The internationally acclaimed Australian Ballet floats into your soul with dance and musical performances at the **State Theatre (Map 4, Ref D9)** St Kilda Road, City, Ph: (03) 9281 8000. If you're after some dance with a little more beat, keep an eye out for **Chunky Move (Map 4, Ref A6)** 35 City Road, Southbank, Ph: (03) 9645 5188. Stylish, sexy and provocative, this troupe will blow you away.

theatre

From summer Shakespearean performances in the Royal Botanic Gardens to the latest Andrew Lloyd Webber production and a host of local talent, the Melbourne stage is set for all seasons.

• Victorian Arts Centre (Map 4, Ref D7) 100 St Kilda Road, Melbourne, Ph: 03 9281 8000
Crowned by the magnificent Spire, one of Melbourne's most distinctive icons, the Arts Centre is the city's hub of visual and performing arts. Explore the centre's many theatres and discover the history of the site on a guided tour.

• CUB Malthouse (Map 3, Ref J15)
113 Sturt Street, Southbank
Ph: (03) 9685 5111
A classic venue for contemporary live theatre, this marvellous old brewery sets the stage for you to enjoy the very best in Australian drama, comedy and satire.

• The Athenaeum (Map 2, Ref G15)
188 Collins Street, City, Ph: 9650 1500
This is an intimate venue, popular with the Bell Shakespeare Company, with the unassuming entrance hiding a 'shabby chic' interior.

In the heart of the city, Melbourne's grand old theatres are unbeatable for character and atmosphere, their ageless Victorian opulence sets the stage for major productions into the new millennium. **The Princess, (Map 24, Ref J3); The Regent, (Map 2, Ref F8); Her Majesty's, (Map 24, Ref G4);** and **The Comedy, (Map 24, Ref H5)** are classic beauties that — in the world of live entertainment — never seem to fade from style.
For theatre bookings,
Ph: Ticketmaster Bass on 11 500
or Ticketek on 132 849.

pamper your palate

Eating out in Melbourne is an art form. Native 'foodies' know not all is as it seems. Follow the locals and you'll discover that some of the most humble lanes & the most obscure entrances hide the most exquisite dining havens. To truly indulge in the city's food and wine treasures, one must possess a spirit of adventure and embrace the unusual. The maze of laneways criss-crossing Melbourne offers some supreme opportunities.

Dining in the city is a blend of concepts from around the globe… experience a French café on the Riviera… a serene teahouse in a Japanese village… or a Mediterranean tapas bar. Savour a bottle of wine and a gourmet meal in soft-lit intimacy, or gather with friends at a lively bistro for delicious food and a few laughs. Melbourne's eateries cater for all seasons – enjoy warm, moonlit evenings on a terrace during summer; colourful flowers and upbeat ambience in the spring; and cosy, red leather interiors with crackling log fires beckon for an escape from the winter chill.

chinatown (Map 2, H10)

In the heart of the city, lights, lanterns and exotic Asian symbols transform Chinatown into a slice of the Far East. Succulent Oriental cuisine is served in traditional surrounds, using the freshest ingredients and centuries-old recipes to enhance the joy of eating. Surrounding the nearby theatre district is a range of bistros, brasseries and boutique wine bars serving outstanding cuisine in a variety of settings.

- **Empress Of China**
20 Lt Bourke St, City, Ph: 9663 1883
- **New Lat's**
15-19 Heffernan La, City
Ph: 9663 2848
- **Curry Corner**
Shop 2,188 Russell St, City
Ph: 9663 4040
- **Bamboo House**
47 Lt Bourke St, City, Ph: 9662 1565
- **Empress of China**
120 Lt Bourke St, City, Ph: 9663 1883
- **Jan Bo**
40 Lt Bourke St, City, Ph: 9662 2884
- **Pepper Chilli**
85 Lt Bourke St, City, Ph: 9662 9662

southgate (Map 4, B4)

The Yarra River promenade on the south bank, once devoid of restaurants, has become one of Melbourne's premium dining districts. Between Southgate Arts & Leisure Centre and Crown Entertainment Complex, there's an entire world of first-class establishments overlooking the Yarra River and city skyline beyond. Contemporary European, Asian, and Australian restaurants present exotic décor, excellent service and a delectable choice of dishes.

- **Bearbrass**
Shop GR3A, River Level, Southgate
Ph: 9682 3799
- **Blue Train Café**
Mid Level, Southgate, Ph: 9696 0111
- **Egusto**
Shop GR3B, River Level, Southgate
Ph: 9690 9819
- **Saturne**
Shop G12/13, River Level, Southgate
Ph: 9645 9499
- **The River Seafood Grill**
Shop MR6, Mid Level, Southgate,
Ph: 9690 4699

uptown (Map 2)

In the savvy uptown theatre district on the Spring Street side of town, Melbourne's passion for great food is evident. Local chefs take immense pride in serving up innovative, healthy dishes combining the best international recipes with a touch of Melbourne panache.

- **Becco**
11-25 Crossley St, City,
Ph: 9663 3000
- **Bottega**
74 Bourke St, City, Ph: 9654 2252
- **Café Il Duca**
55 Little Bourke St, City,
Ph: 9639 1993
- **De Lacy**
29 Niagara Ln, City, Ph: 9670 9099
- **Fish Bowl**
575 Flinders Ln, City, Ph: 9612 5788
- **Florentino**
80 Bourke St, City, Ph: 9662 1811
- **Il Bacaro**
168-170 Lt Collins St, Ph: 9654 6778
- **Stella**
159 Spring St, City, Ph: 9639 1555

the villages

On the northern rim of the CBD, Carlton is one of Australia's best-loved dining precincts. The town's centrepiece, Lygon Street, boasts the finest Italian food outside of Rome, a claim endorsed by Melbourne diners with a unanimous 'Bellissimo!' Ribbons of pasta dance around your fork, the hearty aromas of a million different spices fill the air, and an impressive selection of world class wines will satisfy every connoisseur.

Below the river, South Yarra boasts more first class dining establishments than any other part of Melbourne. Restaurants, cafes and bars clamour to be coolest. Along Chapel Street, Toorak Road, Greville and High Streets, many of the nation's top chefs have carved a special niche. The finest ingredients, the most sophisticated techniques and overwhelming dedication to detail distinguish South Yarra as a forerunner in culinary excellence.

On the edge of the bay, Fitzroy Street in St Kilda plays host to exciting, innovative restaurants and bistros oozing with style, plus a number of classic hotels providing sensational meals with a lively pub atmosphere. Casual ambience, Mediterranean flavours and a great mix of cultures score instantly with diners. By day, adjacent Acland Street indulges the senses with the aroma of freshly-baked cakes, breads, muffins and pastries, and by night it transforms into a chic, contemporary dining strip featuring a range of quality international cuisine.

Just across Port Phillip Bay, the seaside village of Williamstown has reinvented itself as one of Melbourne's most attractive dining destinations. Multiple restaurant venues are enjoying success in recent times, capitalising on panoramic views of the city skyline and an alluring bayside ambience.

living for lattes

During the day, the humble café is the heart and soul of Melbourne, a maelstrom of cappuccinos, lattes, muffins, mochas, and pastries. Enjoy a hot chocolate topped with a mountain of whipped cream high enough to ski on! Relax and read a magazine while sipping a latte with a blackberry muffin chaser... Socialise with other like-minded souls... Devour a turkey and avocado focaccia… You can even buy a cup of coffee!

The evolution of the simple sandwich and cuppa have created a thriving culture that has become a trademark of our city — use your UBD Compact to do a little exploring and see for yourself. Discard the diet for a day and you'll be hooked on Melbourne's café scene.

In other parts of the city, DeGraves Street and Block Place are two more exceptional café enclaves, where visitors can enjoy lattes and light fare in true Melbourne style.

Clarendon Street in South Melbourne is a hotbed of latte lifestyle – celebrities mingle with city workers and coffee lovers in a strip of fantastic cafes, including **Chocolat Champagne (Map 30, Ref A3)** 253 Coventry St and the **Old Paper Shop Deli (Map 3, Ref A4)** 266 Clarendon St.

city

Melbourne is peppered with an amazing assortment of cafes, from dingy dreghouses to refined European eateries. Try the **Medallion Cafe (Map 2, Ref G8)** on Lonsdale St for a Greek flavour, or visit **Guggenheim (Map 24, Ref K7)** on Flinders Lane for the best bagels in town. **Mary Martin Bookshop Café (Map 24, Ref G5)** on Bourke St offers great food, coffee and reading, and the **Hairy Canary Map 2, Ref F13)** on Little Collins St is just downright funky.

Hells Kitchen (Map 2, Ref C17) is a small, New York-style café tucked in off Flinders Lane on Centre Place. **The Paris End (Map 24, Ref K6)** of Collins St hosts many European style cafes, and **Pellegrini's (Map 24, Ref J5)** on Bourke St is a Melbourne institution.

city arcades

Buyers and browsers love roaming Melbourne's labyrinth of arcades, lanes and alleyways, and even the die-hard shopaholics need a place to eat. There's an awesome range of hip cafes filling every spare nook and cranny around town. **DeGraves (Map 2, Ref C18)** is dear to the hearts of many Melburnians, **Block Place (Map 2, Ref C14)** exudes café culture, and **Manchester Lane (Map 2, Ref D17)** sets new standards for café dining. The city's maze of arcades is the ultimate place to get lost.

hardware lane
(Map 1, Ref K 10)

For the latte set, Hardware Lane is the 'in' locale of Melbourne. A myriad of groovy cafes line this unusual bluestone laneway in the heart of the city. Jazz tunes lilt across the pavement during summer, creating a lively, New Orleans-style ambience. Hidden between Bourke and Lonsdale Sts, Hardware Lane boasts an awesome variety of cafés, including Alley Blue, Café Max, Hard Bourke Café and many others. There's a distinct aura about the place, an air of nonchalance oblivious to the pandemonium of the busy city just beyond the lane's entrance.

southgate **(Map 4, Ref C4)**

From it's very beginning, Southgate has had café-goers drooling. The stunning Yarra waterfront and the festive atmosphere provided by crazy street performers and amazing artworks are reason enough to visit, but the cafés are in a class of their own. From simple snacks to delicious main dishes, the food is excellent, and the prices won't punish the purse either. The Blue Train Café is always popular, and the unique Llama Bar is Melbourne's only island café, sitting in the middle of the Yarra River. Every place at Southgate is top notch — a little exploring will be well-rewarded.

villages

Melbourne's café culture is very much alive in the surrounding villages, and each community has blended its own style into the mix. From dawn until dusk, the pursuit of a perfect blend of coffee and food is an irresistible pastime for Melburnians and visitors.

On Brunswick Street in Fitzroy, try cult icons like **Marios (Map 19, Ref C13)**, the **Retro Café (Map 19, Ref C9)** and **Vertigo (Map 19, Ref C12)**.

In Carlton, the **Rathdowne Street Food Store (Map 18, Ref H14)** is a hot favourite with locals, along with Tiamo on **Lygon Street (Map 18, Ref E13)** and many others along this famous stretch of taste treats.

St Kilda is full of beans. Check out **Cavalli (Map 414, Ref B14)** at 165 Fitzroy St , and on Acland try **Il Fornaio (Map 414, Ref C18)** and **189 Espresso Bar (Map 414, Ref B18)**. In South Yarra, cafés are all class – sample the best on offer at the **Jam Factory (Map 32, Ref D12)** and all along groovy Chapel Street.

It doesn't matter whether you know the difference between a double decaf French mocha or a plain white tea, every café in Melbourne is a haven where you can sit down with a few friends, relax and simply enjoy the passing parade.

pubs & bars

Step up to any bar in Melbourne, order your first pot or cocktail, and take a look around. Pub culture is as thick in our atmosphere as the air we breathe – if Singapore Slings and sultry lighting get you in the mood, Melbourne has a plethora of hip bars with attitude! Or if tipping a few ales with the boys is more your scene, there's an endless choice of classic hotels that will never, ever go out of style!

No two pubs are alike in Melbourne – there's a broad mix of first class, casual and downright seedy! Whatever appeals, be it cocktails, live music, ambience, or the pursuit of intoxication, you'll find the right venue here!

Only one question left…
'Whose shout?'

a touch of UK

• The Elephant & Wheelbarrow (Map 414, Ref C13)
Fitzroy St, St Kilda
Don't let the name fool you – this pub's full of attractive young people! Friendly, up beat, there's a very English/Irish feel about the place. Knock back a few drinks, then stay while it transforms into a happening dance venue. Also located at 94-96 Bourke St, City (Map 24, Ref H5) and Bay Street, Port Melbourne (Map 412, Ref K7)

• Bridie O'Reilly's (Map 24, Ref J6)
62 Little Collins Street, City
Live bands offer a combination of local music and traditional Irish jigs to set the night's scene.

• Molly Blooms (Map 412, Ref J7)
39 Bay St, Port Melbourne
Sitting pretty, Molly Blooms is a popular Irish pub close to the beach, ideal for a night of tasty lagers and fine music.

classic jazz

• Night Cat (Map 19, Ref A13)
141 Johnston Street, Fitzroy
Enjoy a vibrant scene with the young trendy crowd and live music lovers.

• Purple Emerald (Map 2, Ref G18)
191 Flinders Lane, City
Retro rules at this hip new bar, featuring live acid jazz, classic 70s furnishings, 16 types of beer and a huge range of cigars.

• Tony Starr's Kitten Club (Map 2, Ref D13)
267 Little Collins Street, City
Sip on the latest martini at this popular venue for those who love to relax to the funky tunes of live jazz.

cocktails and class

• Cargo (Map 368, Ref K14)
NewQuay, Melbourne Docklands
On the edge of Victoria Harbour, Cargo is one of Melbourne's hottest new bars - all style and sophistication, frequented by gorgeous ladies and gentlemen enjoying cocktails and fine music.

• One Six One (Map 32, Ref C20)
161 High St, Prahran
As you enter the upper dominion of the bar, the overwhelming glow of red sets the mood whether you seek a sexy place to meet up with friends or a retro bar scene to socialise.

• Gin Palace (Map 2, Ref H13)
190 Lt Collins St, City
A true royal amongst Melbourne's pub scene – sample the 1951 Martini and the industrial revolution, a killer vodka and Sambuca mix!

• Velour (Map 2, Ref L18)
121 Flinders Lane, City
Zone out in the electric blue light of Velour, with killer cocktails and pumping dance music.

designer bars

• Misty (Map 2, Ref H19)
3-5 Hosier Lane, City
Weird, warped and wonderful décor highlight this groovy little hideaway on a cobblestone lane.

• Double O (Map 2, Ref D7)
Sniders Lane, City
The projected logo on the wall is the only external evidence that Double O exists – a cosy, comfortable bar with curvaceous couches, cool cocktails and seductive lighting.

• Troika (Map 24, Ref G2)
106 Lt Lonsdale St, City
It'd make a great 'drop zone' for international spies, yet Troika welcomes everyone to this mysterious cool bar.

• Bond (Map 1, Ref K19)
24 Bond St, City
One of the hottest destinations in Melbourne's bar scene, Bond is slick, cool and a prime venue for both watching and being watched.

live music hotspots

• The Corner Hotel (Map 26, Ref C16)
57 Swan St, Richmond
Specialising in original music from local outfits and overseas bands, the Corner isn't afraid to get a little 'out there'!

• Esplanade Hotel (Map 414, Ref A17)
11 Upper Esplanade, St Kilda
When venturing out of the city grid, the 'Espy' is a Melbourne icon, offering the best local acts in music and comedy and with a prime position overlooking the bay.

• Star Bar (Map 29, Ref L1)
160 Clarendon St, South Melbourne
Best known for fantastic live music, the Star Bar is regularly rocking with a hip young crowd.

• The Punters Club (Map 19, Ref C10)
376 Brunswick St, Fitzroy
Definitely a rocking pub, the 'Punna's' is a cult favourite for Melbourne's alternative live music scene.

on tap

• The Great Britain (Map 26, Ref F18)
447 Church Street, Richmond
From the fireplace in the winter and the textured wall coverings, the 'GB' is an eclectic mix of people just as interesting to be around as the venue itself.

• Island (Map 30, Ref E19)
Cnr Canterbury Rd and Armstrong St, Middle Park
House-brewed beers on tap, a friendly sporty atmosphere and Melbourne's best ventilation make this a popular bayside icon.

• Yelza (Map 19, Ref C19)
245 Gertrude Street, Fitzroy
On the city fringe, with a fabulous outdoor setting for when the temperature rises and a luscious venue indoors, this is a bar for all seasons.

• Provincial Hotel (Map 19, Ref B13)
299 Brunswick St, Fitzroy
Everyone knows the Provincial – when you want to go with an 'old faithful', you're always assured a good night out here.

Locals know it, visitors love it, others envy it — Melbourne's nightlife is the hottest scene around, a funky tribute to our cosmopolitan people and vibrant lifestyle. When daylight disappears, the city ignites into action, and the party doesn't stop until the sun rises to light the way home. Young revellers flood into town for a pumping, thumping good night!

From jazz to jungle techno, blues to ballroom, retro to rap and grunge to gothic, Melbourne has a hotspot with the groove to get you moving.

clubs

• **Candy Bar (Map 32, Ref C18)**
162 Greville St, Prahran
Masterful mixes from dynamic DJs all night long.

• **cbd (Map 1, Ref K13)**
12 McKillop St, City
Casual, bold and dynamic, the ultimate expression venue.

• **Club 383 (Map 1, Ref L9)**
383 Lonsdale St, City
Cutting edge sound with multiple dance levels - lots of '80s hits too.

• **Club UK (Map 24, Ref H5)**
169 Exhibition St, City
The best of British and loads more - a bleedin' good sound and a choice venue.

• **Diva Bar (Map 32, Ref C16)**
153 Commercial Rd, South Yarra
The name says it all - a must for guys and girls who live for a special kind of beat.

• **Felix (Map 414, Ref A15)**
43 Fitzroy St, St Kilda
Plush lounges, surreal lighting and a sensational cocktail range complement the pumping dance floor at Felix.

• **Heat Nightclub (Map 3, Ref B4)**
Level 3, Crown Casino, Southbank
A surreal chic club featuring mezzanine levels where you can dance on the main floor to the backdrop of the Melbourne city skyline.

• **Khokolat (Map 1, Ref K11)**
Hardware Lane, City
A discreet club with a sleek retro interior. Day or night, listen to the grooves of local DJs and bands.

• **Laundry (Map 19, Ref A13)**
50 Johnston St, Fitzroy
Bold and brash, this place is firing every night of the week.

• **Mercury Lounge (Map 3, Ref C5)**
Level 3, Crown Casino, Southbank
Funky and upbeat, the Mercury Lounge continues to set temperatures rising.

• **Metro (Map 24, Ref J4)**
20 Bourke St, City
If bigger is better, the Metro is guaranteed to impress - a staple of the Melbourne nightlife scene for generations.

• **Prince of Wales (Map 414, Ref A15)**
29 Fitzroy Street, St Kilda
The best local and international DJs spin here as gorgeous people lose themselves amongst disco balls, curvaceous bars and the balcony area.

• **QBH (Map 3, Ref F3)**
1 Queensbridge Street, South Melbourne
Said to be the largest club in the Southern Hemisphere, take your pick from the seven bars, two dance floors and five DJ booths.

• **Revolver (Map 32, Ref D14)**
(upstairs) 229 Chapel Street, Prahran
Revolver offers hip-hop, house, UK garage and a concoction of all sorts of beats in the heart of ultra-cool Prahran.

• **Salon Rouge (Map 2, Ref D17)**
Flinders Lane, City
A funky bar with a happening crowd, cool atmosphere and irresistible dance tunes.

• **Silvers (Map 415, Ref C5)**
445 Toorak Rd, Toorak
The tempo's always on the move, from R&B and swing to commercial dance.

• **Tatou (Map 23, Ref H10)**
577 Lt Collins St, City
Classic funky grooves from every era - always a late-night hit.

• **The Club (Map 19, Ref F19)**
132a Smith St, Collingwood
Offering entertainment several nights a week, you can indulge in a variety of music.

• **The Dome (Map 31, Ref J15)**
19 Commercial Road, Prahran
Dome provides deep house music and beautiful people to dance and play with.

• **The Icon (Map 2, J18)**
Flinders La, City
Bright atmosphere, sensational music and an upbeat crowd that loves dancing on the bar.

• **The Viper Room (Map 32, Ref D15)**
371 Chapel St, South Yarra
Style is the domain of the Viper Room - thumbs up from those in the know.

• **Twister (Map 414, Ref A18)**
Lower Esp, St Kilda
A pumping, thumping humongous dance floor makes Twister a hit every time.

late night munchies

When your body's been in motion for more than a few hours, a fast snack is just what the doctor ordered. Melbourne delivers with a sensational variety of places burning the midnight oil to satisfy your late-night cravings…

• **Barflys (Map 24, Ref J5)**
16 Bourke St, City
This place not only serves great food, foccaccias and snacks until 5am, it's also a rocking good licensed bar.

• **China Bar (Map 2, Ref J9)**
235b Russell St, City
Great prices, fast service and a huge menu - the China Bar will fill that hole with great flavours of the Orient.

• **Crown Entertainment Complex (Map 3, Ref B4)**
8 Whiteman St, Southbank.
Chow down at one of the food courts in between hopping around Crown's awesome clubs.

• **The Supper Club (Map 24, Ref J3)**
161 Spring Street, City
If you're looking to indulge and impress, wander uptown to the Supper Club for a fine wine, gourmet tapas treats and lush furnishings.

For the fast food classic like McDonald's, Subway and KFC, swing down Swanston Street on your way to catch a cab to satisfy those after party fast food cravings.

melbourne outdoors

Surrounding the CBD, Melbourne is blessed with a beautiful ring of parkland, an idyllic contrast to the excitement of the city. Constant upkeep ensures the parks are in stunning condition year-round, a menagerie of rich colours and tranquil settings. A variety of native birds and animals have made Melbourne's gardens home, promising sights and sounds to delight those enjoying a stroll, picnic or a quiet, lazy afternoon. Along the Yarra River, the waterfront has been transformed into a spectacular promenade at Southgate and Crown Entertainment Complex, while the Alexandra Gardens and Batman Avenue provide manicured gardens, lawns and trails along the riverbank.

The parks are a haven for recreational activities of all kinds — running, skating, cycling, throwing a frisbee or relaxing the soul through the ancient art of tai chi. If you live in Melbourne and you're not exercising, there's no excuse! Step outside, breathe some fresh air and make the most of our city's green recreational zones.

royal botanic gardens

(Map 31, Ref E2)

At its northern border, South Yarra adjoins the Royal Botanic Gardens and the Yarra River. Established in 1846, Melbourne's Botanic Gardens comprise over 36 hectares of some of the most magnificent landscaped gardens in the world.

Lush green parklands are complemented by marvellous historic buildings, including Government House, the Shrine of Remembrance, the former Melbourne Observatory and La Trobe's cottage. The Royal Botanic Gardens are the emerald jewels of Melbourne. In summer, the Gardens are the site of Melbourne's Moonlight Cinema, an open-air film theatre, featuring classic, cult and arthouse favourites. Visit www.moonlightcinema.com.au . The Royal Botanic Gardens are open every day of the year from 7.30am.

south yarra

Another highlight of South Yarra's parklands is **Fawkner Park (Map 31, Ref F10)** a 19th century landscaped design, featuring shady English Elms and Moreton Bay Fig Trees. Much of the park has been set aside for sporting activities, including tennis. Year-round, cricketers, footballers, softball teams and touch footy players converge on Fawkner Park for both serious and social competition.

carlton

Just a short stroll away from the frenetic activity of Lygon Street is the peaceful **Carlton Gardens (Map 18, Ref H20)** – 16 hectares of landscaped garden featuring floral displays, ornamental lakes and fountains. The centerpiece of the Gardens is the historic Royal Exhibition Building, first built in 1888 and now a splendid backdrop to the ultra-modern Melbourne Museum.

along the yarra banks

Cycling along the Yarra is one of the most relaxing yet exhilarating forms of exercise in Melbourne. The cool breeze, smooth water and green grass generates a sensational feeling of freedom. Whether you're walking, riding or running, the trails winding along the banks of the Yarra River are just a wonderful place to be.

albert park lake

(Map 30, Ref H13)

If you're the type who loves the idea of running but decides they've had enough after a few hundred yards, Albert Park Lake is the place to get you moving! Complete one lap of the lake — 5km — and you'll be taking the first steps towards a healthier lifestyle. You won't be as quick as the Formula One cars in March, but I guarantee you'll feel better.

Located within Albert Park Lake is the **Melbourne Sports and Aquatic Centre**, one of the finest recreational facilities in the city. There's a fantastic pool, plus a gym, numerous basketball courts, table tennis, badminton and much more. It's an outstanding, state-of-the-art venue with just as much emphasis on fun as there is on hardcore training.

city gardens

From the heart of the city, every direction you go will bring you to a haven of greenery in which you can escape for a while. Located close to the CBD, the **Fitzroy and Treasury Gardens (Map 25, Ref D5)** are a popular escape for city workers and students. Possums are everywhere, and while joggers and cyclists plough up-and-down the pathways, the grass areas are a great place to stretch, do a few exercises or throw a frisbee around. In fact, frisbee-golf — the poor-man's version of golf — is a favoured game in the Fitzroy Gardens, where regular 'golfers' have marked out a complex course with pars, tee-off points and obstacles.

Flagstaff Gardens (Map 1, Ref C1) is alive with birds and small animals, while on the banks of the Yarra the **Alexandra Gardens (Map 4, Ref H6)** are the ideal setting for a waterfront picnic, or party central when they host Australia's biggest outdoor festival, Moomba in March. For all their serenity, Melbourne's gardens are a great place to party! Concerts at the **Sidney Myer Music Bowl in Kings Domain (Map 4, Ref L12)** are always a rocking good time too. There's no shortage of great recreational opportunities around here.

Melbourne is a garden city, Melbourne is a sporting city, and Melbourne is a FUN city! If you're not making the most of that, I think it's time you should. Utilise your parks and gardens – call (03) 9658 8713 for more information about Melbourne's parks, including booking areas for functions and events.

Contemporary, protean, always developing and constantly innovating, Melbourne has given rise to an extraordinary number of world class sporting, entertainment, transport, cultural and scientific facilities. Telstra Dome, Federation Square, Docklands and the Melbourne Museum are just some of the recent additions to the city's landscape. The reinvention of Melbourne's tourism identity continues, and several new developments promise to lift the city even further into the world spotlight.

• Melbourne Cricket Ground - MCG (Map 25, Ref G12)
www.mcg.org.au
The 'G', the 'people's ground', is one of Melbourne's proudest icons, and has undergone an enormous refurbishment of its northern side. Home of the AFL Grand Final, the Boxing Day Test, and countless historical sporting moments including the 1956 Olympics, the MCG's new fitout will reestablish the stadium's preeminence as one of the world's greatest sporting venues. Improved seating, advanced technology and new facilities will make the experiences of sports fans at the 'G' all the more memorable.

• QV (Map 2, Ref H7)
This $600 million, 1.8 hectare development on the old Queen Victoria Hospital site has revolutionised shopping and living in the city. The retail mix has been carefully selected to provide a unique offering. QV's design edge and concept of a gritty urban precinct sets it apart from other inner city and suburban shopping centres. QV offers the finest in fashion and retail, and for food lovers it boasts a European style piazza area with cafes, restaurants and bars spilling tables and chairs from laneways and shop fronts onto QV square. BHP Billiton and Sensis have established their global headquarters at this amazing new Melbourne CBD landmark.

• National Gallery of Victoria (Map 4, Ref D8)
www.ngv.vic.gov.au
The National Gallery of Victoria has finally returned home to St Kilda Rd after a four year hiatus for renovations. At Federation Square, the Ian Potter Centre houses Australian artworks exclusively, whilst the brilliantly refurbished NGV is the home to amazing contemporary and classic artworks from every corner of the globe.

• Docklands (Map 369, Ref A16)
www.docklands.vic.gov.au
Covering 200 hectares of land and water, Docklands' eight precincts will ultimately feature a diversity of entertainment, waterfront restaurants, promenade shops, residential apartments and townhouses, technology and business centres. Development is staged to meet market demand, with each precinct planned to complement its neighbour and ensure Docklands offers something for everyone.

Melbourne Docklands promises to be the most exciting development since the city was founded in the 19th century, with a brand new area the size of the existing CBD being constructed on the stunning Yarra River waterfront. The new precinct will provide Victorians with significant economic, social and lifestyle benefits over the coming decades.

Development will not occur overnight, but the success of Telstra Dome has already focused attention on the area. Construction is estimated to take approximately 15 years, spanning a number of economic cycles. Docklands is, after all, six times the size of Sydney's Circular Quay.

Melbourne Docklands will irrevocably change the look and feel of Melbourne. It will become a waterfront destination for an estimated 20 million visitors each year, home for 15,000 people and a workplace for 20,000.

Close monitoring by the government and the critical Melbourne public will ensure good quality design, full public access to Docklands' seven kilometres of waterfront, and integration of public parks, boat moorings, urban art and public transport.

• Eureka Tower (Map 3, Ref K5)
Southbank,
www.eurekatower.com.au

The new Eureka Tower promises to take apartment living to an entirely new level... literally! Rising 88 storeys out of Southbank, Melbourne's premier shopping, dining and entertainment district, Eureka Tower is destined to be the first landmark tower of the 21st century. This exciting development will rank with the construction of the Eiffel Tower or the Empire State Building as a turning point and inspiration for future design ambitions. Eureka Tower will be an extremely high-tech, slick apartment tower designed and built by Australians focusing on quality, technology and environmental responsibility.

Conceptually, the tower is a vertical city. Apartments start on Level 11 and conclude at the penthouses on Level 80 ensuring unimpeded views.

• Federation Square (Map 2, Ref G20)
cnr Swanston & Flinders Streets, City,
Ph: (03) 9639 2800

Federation Square is a $260 million project celebrating the centenary of the federation of Australian states. Situated on the corner of Swanston and Flinders Streets, the bold, striking architecture of the Square will propel Melburnians and visitors into the 21st century. Presenting innovative new concepts and designs, this new public space in the heart of Melbourne is set to create cultural, educational and leisure opportunities of a level unlike anything else in Australia. Federation Square will be complemented by the recently refurbished City Square on Swanston Street.

Federation Square is one of the most ambitious and complex projects ever undertaken in Australia. It involves the development of an entire city block, the first ever to physically connect the Melbourne central business district with its Yarra river waterfront. Situated at the heart of central Melbourne, Federation Square will be a fusion of arts and events, leisure, hospitality and promenading.

Melbourne's reputation as a tourist destination has exploded meteorically in the past 10 years. The number of world class attractions available has risen dramatically, confirming the international notion that the city is a highly developed holiday destination. The temperate climate year-round encourages a great deal of activity both indoors and out.

First settled by Europeans in 1835, Melbourne has been a home to indigenous populations for up to 50,000 years. Within three years of their arrival, the Europeans had established the city's rectangular grid pattern, which eventually became known as 'The Golden Mile'. The Gold Rush of the 1850s brought Melbourne enormous prosperity, and many of the grand old buildings that grace our city were erected as a result of these golden years. The riches were also used to build many of Melbourne's magnificent architectural landmarks, including the Melbourne Town Hall, St Paul's Cathedral and 333 Collins St.

In 1901, Australia's federal government was established here in Melbourne and remained headquartered at Parliament House on Spring Street until 1927, when Canberra took over as the seat of national government.

Nowadays, Melbourne is a thriving, cosmopolitan capital with a population of 3.3 million, and visitors can appreciate the clever blend of impressive modern architecture with classic historical landmarks.

Amiable and unpretentious, Melbourne provides a warm welcome with visitors in mind — you'll be amazed how convenient and easy everything is here. The influence of Melbourne's people is everywhere — in our food, our arts, our events and all our passions.

Centred in Australia's most compact mainland state, Melbourne provides day access to all of Victoria's natural wonders — like rainforests, mountain ranges and snowfields. Anywhere and everywhere you turn, Melbourne has something to appeal.

information

• Melbourne Visitor Centre (Map 2, Ref F20)
Federation Square, City, Ph: (03) 9658 9658
For new visitors, the first port of call should be the Melbourne Visitor Centre, where you can pick up brochures, maps and information on all of Melbourne's secrets.

Friendly staff will gladly answer all your questions - apart from the main headquarters in Federation Square, there are a number of accredited Visitor Information Centres located throughout Melbourne. Look for the yellow 'i ' on signs during your travels for access to information.

city attractions

With the number of fantastic tourist attractions continuing to grow, visitors to Melbourne now have the opportunity to access the very best of these in one affordable pass. The Melbourne Attractions Pass incorporates the best venues in Melbourne, from sport, to the arts, history and heritage.

Passholders gain entry to a minimum of three and a maximum of six of Melbourne's premier attractions, providing an easy and convenient way to experience the finest of Melbourne's attractions. Contact your local travel agent for further details.

• City Circle tram
The City Circle tram is a completely free way to see the City and learn more about Melbourne. This is the perfect first step to seeing what Melbourne's all about. Visitor brochures are available on board, a running commentary is provided and attendants are happy to answer any questions. Running at 10 minute intervals, the City Circle tram operates between 10am and 6pm, daily and travels to the Docklands as well as the CBD.

• Crown Entertainment Complex (Map 3, Ref B4)
8 Whiteman Street, Southbank, Ph: (03) 9292 8888
Crown has become synonymous with entertainment and glamour. There are more than 40 restaurants, bars and cafés to choose from. Add in the casino, cinemas, games arcades, international designer stores, nightclubs, live performance venues, and you've got a cauldron of excitement. Crown hosts film premiers, international conferences and awards ceremonies. Located downstream from Southgate on the banks of the Yarra River, Crown is a world of entertainment.

• Golden Mile Heritage Trail
For a new angle on Melbourne's heritage, the Golden Mile Heritage Trail places the best of Melbourne's historical landmarks on a well-marked path. The trail begins at **Old Customs House (Map 1, Ref F19)**, with decorative plaques set into the pavement marking the route. Along the way, visitors are acquainted with the story of Melbourne's early development and highlighted through a collection of the City's key 'golden era' buildings.

Connect the dots all the way to the **Royal Exhibition Building (Map 18, Ref H18)**, and you'll reveal a marvellous picture of our City's unique historical development, largely thanks to the influx of migrants during the 19th century Gold Rush. Afterwards, the free City Circle tram returns walkers to the city centre.

• IMAX Theatre (Map 18, Ref H17)
Rathdowne Street, Carlton, Ph: (03) 9663 5454
Feel the awe-inspiring convergence of cinema and reality as you watch large format and 3D films on the gargantuan IMAX screen – eight storeys high and 31 metres wide. The visual impact is enhanced by full digital surround sound and hi-tech liquid crystal glasses for 3D movies. Imax films screen daily from 10am until 10pm (late sessions on Fridays and Saturdays).

• Luna Park (Map 414, Ref A18)
Lower Esplanade, St Kilda, Ph: 1902 240 112
Melbourne's Luna Park, based on New York's famous Coney Island, has delighted visitors since its opening in 1912. The bayside theme park has recently undergone a complete refurbishment, and the revamped Luna Park features a host of new state-of-the-art rides and facilities.

Tram No. 96 from Bourke or Spencer Streets, or tram no. 12 from Swanston St, will deliver you from the city to Luna Park and the St Kilda foreshore.

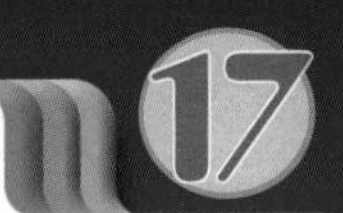

• Melbourne Aquarium (Map 1, Ref B20)
cnr King Street and Queens Wharf Road, City, Ph: (03) 9620 0999
Immerse yourself in the totally interactive marine experience of the Melbourne Aquarium. Travel through billabongs, mangrove swamps, coral atolls, rock pools, a transparent tunnel where sharks and giant stingrays will surround you, and finally right off the deep end into the 2.2 million litre Oceanarium. The City Circle Tram stops right outside.

• Melbourne Museum (Map 18, Ref H17)
Rathdowne Street, Carlton, Ph: 13 11 02 (Map 18, Ref H17)
Walk through a living forest gallery, discover the vibrant story of Melbourne and experience Aboriginal cultural performances in this ultra-modern hands-on museum. Performances, activities and interactive displays make a visit to the Melbourne Museum a truly memorable experience.

• Melbourne Observation Deck (Map 1, Ref B16)
Collins St, City, (03) 9629 8222
For unparalleled views of the City, you naturally have to pick the tallest building in town. The Melbourne Observation Deck offers splendid 360 degree panoramic vistas of the city, Port Phillip Bay, the MCG, Melbourne Park, Colonial Stadium, Southgate and the Crown Entertainment Complex, plus magnificent parkland and beautiful scenery as far as the eye can see.

Up top, a café and bar offer stratospheric dining and drinking while you enjoy the stunning views, and 'Rialto Vision' — a million dollar, award-winning sight and sound extravaganza is free with your Observation Deck admission. Located at the top of Rialto Towers, the Melbourne Observation Deck is near the corner of King and Collins Sts, close to Spencer St railway station and a City Circle tram stop.

• Melbourne Zoo (Map 17, Ref D1)
Elliott Av, Parkville, Ph: (03) 9285 9300
The Melbourne Zoo is world-renowned, and one of the premier features is the amazing gorilla rainforest. In their natural habitat, you'll feel right at home with the gorillas. Or, if you still don't recognize any long-lost family members, try the monkeys, gibbons and orangutans. Plus, there's the tropical butterfly enclosure — just remember to close your mouth. Visit the lions, tigers, bears, reptiles, elephants and giraffes — more creatures than Noah ever dreamed of. The magnificent gardens and scenery are also very attractive.

To get there, take the number 55 tram north from William St in the city.

• Old Melbourne Gaol (Map 2, Ref H2)
Russell St, City, Ph: (03) 9663 7728
Some of Melbourne's most notorious criminals of the past have spent a portion of their lives here, including the legendary bushranger Ned Kelly. The gaol features a fascinating exhibition of 19th century gaol life, and the special night tours with theatrical performances will chill you to the bone.

The free City Circle tram stops at the corner of Russell and La Trobe Streets, very close to the Old Melbourne Gaol.

• Southgate Arts & Leisure Precinct (Map 4, Ref C4)
Southbank, City, Ph: (03) 9699 4311
One of Melbourne's most spectacular showpieces, Southgate is home to more than 20 restaurants, cafés and bars, 41 unique retailers and an innovative food wharf. Lively street theatre, impressive sculptures and artworks, and the magnificent Yarra waterfront make Southgate a wonderful attraction, day or night, year-round.

Southgate is located directly across the Yarra River from Flinders St railway station, with a footbridge conveniently connecting the two.

beyond the city

• Healesville Wildlife Sanctuary (Map 258, Ref C12)
Badger Creek Rd, Healesville, Ph: (03) 5957 2800
Wander among koalas, kangaroos, wombats and countless other native Australian birds and animals at the award-winning Healesville Wildlife Sanctuary. Enjoy a close encounter with an emu, a rare look at a platypus, plus numerous animal presentations by the friendly staff.

If you don't have access to a car, simply catch a train all the way to Lilydale, then jump on a McKenzies coach to Healesville.

• Phillip Island (Maps 725 & 726)
Journey down the Princes Hwy to **Dandenong (Map 536)**, connect with the **South Gippsland Hwy (Map 536, Ref E15)** and follow the signs to Phillip Island — home to the world-famous penguin parade, Seal Rocks Sea Life Centre and numerous other attractions. Check out the fairy penguins as they surf onto the beach and waddle home across the sand every evening. Explore the various wildlife parks on the island that are home to a huge population of fur seals, koalas, kangaroos and other native Australian animals.

• Sovereign Hill
Bradshaw St, Ballarat, Ph: (03) 5331 1944
Follow the Western Freeway through **Melton (Map 269)** all the way to the historic town of **Ballarat** — a 90 minute drive from Melbourne — where you'll see numerous signs guiding you to Sovereign Hill. This living museum is the ultimate goldrush experience, a time warp back to the 1850s, where visitors are immersed in the everyday life at an original gold-mining settlement.

• Victoria's Open Range Zoo (Map 487, Ref J4)
K Rd, Werribee, Ph: (03) 9731 9600
You don't have to go to Africa to enjoy a unique wildlife safari — the Open Range Zoo has an unbelievable range of exotic creatures roaming free within the park. Get up close and personal with rhinos, giraffes, zebras, antelopes, hippos and our own native kangaroos as you tour the savannahs on a special safari bus.

Melburnians love to entertain, and our list of major events is the envy of the world. Roaring crowds... screaming engines... thundering hooves... endless celebrations... experience world-class festivals and events in Melbourne year-round.

Travellers from all over the globe flock to sporting events like the Australian Grand Prix, Australian Open, AFL Grand Final and the Melbourne Cup. Lively festivals adorn the state's calendar throughout the year, including Moomba, the International Comedy Festival, and the Melbourne Festival.

Below is a listing of some of the city's finest, but there's always much more happening each week. For up-to-date information on what's happening in and around the city, visit: www.melbourne.citysearch.com.au.

january

• Australia Day Festival
Various venues, Ph: 9651 5026
In true Aussie fashion, break out the snags and celebrate being part of the greatest country in the world. This fantastic festival will remind you why we're considered the luckiest nation on earth.

• Australian Open Tennis Championships (Map 25, Ref C14)
Melbourne Park, Swan Street, Richmond , Ph: 9286 1175 or visit www.ausopen.org.
The atmosphere is electric and the play is inspirational as the real superstars of tennis put everything on the line for one of the world's biggest Grand Slam tennis competitions. Cheer on your favourite pros, and mingle with one of the biggest international crowds you'll ever see. The combination of Rod Laver Arena and the new Vodafone Arena makes a superb venue.

• Midsumma Festival
Various venues, Ph: 9525 4746 or visit www.midsumma.org.
A gay and lesbian celebration with sensational festivities and art exhibitions — everybody's welcome, gay, straight or just plain curious. There are shows and entertainment to humour all ages, plus a terrific range of stalls offering a collection of the most outrageous products you're ever likely to see in one place.

february

• Woolmark Melbourne Fashion Festival
Various venues, Ph: 9826 9688 or visit www.mff.com.au.
Celebrate style in style with a sensational variety of fashion events and the latest looks for autumn and winter. Gorgeous catwalk models introduce the latest trends, plus there are plenty of social functions and entertainment to amuse even those who can't spot the difference between leather and polyester.

march

• Antipodes Festival
Various city locations, Ph: 9662 2722 or visit ww.antipodesfestival.com.au.
A lively celebration of Melbourne's thriving Greek community, who love to party, love to entertain and love to eat good food. What a combination! Enjoy gourmet Greek cuisine, traditional and contemporary entertainment, and experience the hidden joys of zorba dancing.

• Melbourne Food & Wine Festival
Various venues, Ph: 9628 5008 or visit www.melbfoodwinefest.com.au.
Pay homage to the great tastes of Melbourne and pig out on delicious offerings at this mouth-watering event. Melburnians take enormous pride in their food and wine culture, and this is the occasion where efforts are doubled and competition is fierce to show off the tastiest creations imaginable. Make the most of it - worry about your waistline later!

• Melbourne Moomba Festival (Map 4, Ref L7) Yarra River, Alexandra Gardens and City Ph: 9658 9658 or visit www.moomba.com.au.
This is the biggest outdoor festival in Australia, featuring carnival rides, entertainment and loads of excitement in the city centre and down by the banks of the Yarra. Highlights of the event include the Tram Parade, Garden Party and the awesome River of Light fireworks spectacular. Thrill to the best water-skiers in the world carving up the Yarra River and soaring over 200 feet through the air at the world's biggest tournament, the Melbourne Masters.

• Fosters Australian Grand Prix (Map 30) Albert Park Lake, Albert Park, Ph: Ticketmaster 131 641 or visit www.grandprix.com.au.
The biggest names in the world of Formula One hurtle around Albert Park Lake at insane speeds during this mammoth international event. Grab your earplugs and join the crowd for one of the biggest parties you'll ever see, a Ferrari-fuelled experience you're never going to forget.

april

• Melbourne International Comedy Festival (Map 2, Ref F15)
Melbourne Town Hall, Swanston Walk, City and various City venues, Ph: Ticketmaster 136 100 or visit www.comedyfestival.com.au.
The funniest April fools from all around the world bombard our City with hilarious entertainment during this major comedy extravaganza. There are more than a hundred acts to choose from every evening throughout the whole month. Warning – Attend too many and you risk dying of laughter!

• Melbourne International Flower & Garden Show (Map 18, Ref H18)
Royal Exhibition Building and Carlton Gardens Ph: 9639 2333 or visit www.melbflowershow.com.au.
To stop and smell the flowers here would take a while. Tens of thousands of cut flowers are under one roof, formed in the most amazing displays your eyes (and your nose) will ever experience. Outside, stroll amidst cool and innovative garden displays that will blow you away, and see incredible sculptures and artwork.

may

• Next Wave Festival
Various venues, Ph: 9417 7544 or visit www.nextwave.org.au.
A showcase of the future, the Next Wave Festival is dedicated to nurturing a culture of contemporary ideas into the 21st Century, supporting the work of a new generation of Australian artists, and encouraging young people to engage with the arts.

• St Kilda Film Festival (Map 414, Ref C17)
National Theatre, Barkly St, St Kilda, Ph: 9209 6711 or visit www.stkildafilmfest.com.au.
A great showing of cool, contemporary Australian short films and videos. The National Theatre's laid-back atmosphere is a tribute to the halcyon days of cinema, before multiplexes and blockbuster special effects blew away the intimate romance of the movies. It's a great chance to see rare, hip films that veer off the mainstream.

• Yarra Valley Expo (Map 253, Ref E1)
Yarra Glen Racecourse, Ph: 9730 1722 or visit www.yarra-valley-expo.com.au.
There's something for everyone here. You'll not only enjoy wine, food and jazz – there are world champion axemen, fashion parades, whipcracking and much more on show at the Yarra Valley Expo. Plenty of stalls offering samples of some of Australia's finest wines – make sure you bring a designated driver!

june

• Mind Body Spirit Festival (Map 23, Ref H17)
Melbourne Exhibition Centre, Ph: 9819 0211, or visit www.mindbodyspiritfest.com.
Nourish your soul at the Mind Body Spirit Festival, where exhibitors present a rare view of holistic pursuits such as Chinese medicine and kinesiology. A truly spiritual experience…

july

• Melbourne International Film Festival
Various cinemas, Ph: 9417 2011 or visit www.melbournefilmfestival.com.au.
Movie fans will go crazy over this showcase of the latest and best films. Take the chance to meet filmmakers, mingle with stars and party in the Festival Club.

august

• The Age Melbourne Writers' Festival
CUB Malthouse, Melbourne Town Hall and various venues, Ph: 9261 4500 or visit www.mwf.com.au.
Lectures and seminars galore with successful writers giving talks and tips on how to make it in the world of writing. Gain inspiration from those who've made it, and learn how you can best launch your writing career.

september

• AFL Grand Final (Map 25, Ref F12)
Melbourne Cricket Ground, Jolimont, Ph: 9643 1999 or visit www.afl.com.au.
Up there Cazaly! Take the top two AFL teams of the season, a crowd of almost 100,000 roaring fans, a skyfull of balloons, a fighter jet, and stir everything into a huge pot called the MCG — this is the recipe for Aussie Rules Football's ultimate clash of the year!

• Melbourne Spring Fashion Week
Various venues, visit www.msfw.org.
A sizzling week of shows and parades that feature the hottest new looks for the spring–summer season, plus a variety of entertainment, competitions and cool seminars. If fashion is your thing and style is your friend, you'd better not miss this event.

• Royal Melbourne Show (Map 323, Ref J20)
Royal Melbourne Showgrounds, Ascot Vale, Ph: 9281 7444 or visit www.royalshow.com.au.
An old favourite with Melburnians, there's always something to entertain everyone at 'The Show'. Carnival rides, animal and agricultural exhibitions, plus fireworks and thrilling entertainment in the arena, the Royal Melbourne Show always puts on a great… show!

october

• Lygon Street Festa (Map 18, Ref E17)
Lygon St, Carlton, Ph: 9348 1299.
Pasta lover or not, you'll have the time of your life at this spirited Italian community festival in one of Melbourne's most-loved streets.

• Melbourne Festival
Various venues, Ph: 9662 4242 or visit www.melbournefestival.com.au.
The very best of our creative culture on show, entertaining you with arts, theatre, music and exhibitions.

• Melbourne Fringe Festival
Various venues, Ph: 9534 0722 or visit www.melbournefringe.org.au.
A three week explosion of fringe art encourages newcomers.
Artists devise, produce and finance their own shows, culminating in the colourful spectacle of the Brunswick Street Parade.

• Melbourne Oktoberfest (Map 323, Ref J20)
Royal Melbourne Showgrounds, Ascot Vale, Ph: 9529 5211.
Why travel to Germany, when you can enjoy the great Bavarian tradition of Oktoberfest right here in Melbourne. A favourite with beerlovers across the city, Oktoberfest is a fantastic weekend.

• QANTAS Australian Motorcycle Grand Prix
Phillip Island Motor Sports Centre, Phillip Island, Ph: Ticketmaster 131 641, or visit www.grandprix.com.au.
At this amazing international event, lives are on the line as the world's top motorcycle racers scream around the premier track at Phillip Island.

november

• Melbourne Cup Day (Map 367, Ref K4)
Flemington Racecourse, Ascot Vale, Ph: 9258 4666, or visit www.racingvictoria.com.au.
Held on the first Tuesday of November, this world famous horse race is an odds-on favourite with everyone throughout Australia. Hats, horses, fashions and flowers will add colour to your day. Only one thing's a sure bet – a photo finish!

december

• Carols By Candlelight (Map 4, Ref L12)
Sidney Myer Music Bowl, City, Ph: 9522 5222 or visit www.avib.org.au.
An Aussie tradition since 1937, thousands of people get together to celebrate Christmas under the stars with live music plus lots and lots of candles.

• Melbourne Boxing Day Test Match (Map 25, Ref F12)
Melbourne Cricket Ground, Jolimont, Ph: 9653 1100 or visit www.viccricket.asn.au.
Cheer on the indomitable Aussies as they clash with international opponents at one of the world's finest cricketing venues — the MCG.

show me the way

Your UBD Compact is the ultimate companion for every journey. Use this key information to get where you need to go in the most efficient way possible. Melbourne's road system and public transport network is world class — trams, trains and buses deliver you virtually to the doorstep of your City destination. There's a vast network of rails, including the underground City Loop, that makes getting into and out of Melbourne a very simple prospect. Read on for all the info you need on Melbourne's transport network.

citylink

The CityLink roadway has been the greatest improvement on Melbourne's traffic situation in many years. The high-tech electronic tolling system allows the uninterrupted flow of traffic, and drivers can travel from one side of the city to the other without stopping, via a network of bridges and tunnels including the scenic Bolte Bridge.

For details call CityLink on 132 629. Alternatively, you can purchase an e-TAG or Day Pass from a CityLink Customer Centre, selected Australia Post Offices or Touch Screen machines at selected Shell outlets. Or you can buy online at www.transurban.com.au.

the met

The Met incorporates all of Melbourne's tram, train and bus services. These services extend from the city in all directions to numerous outer suburbs, with plenty of stops in between to ensure that your destination is accessible as conveniently as possible.

Three different fare zones apply to travelling on the Met. Zone 1 covers the majority of the city and inner suburbs, Zone 2 is the mid-range metropolitan area and Zone 3 applies to the outer suburbs. Each time you pass through a different zone, you pay for a ticket accordingly.

The full range of Met tickets may be purchased from train stations, buses, selected retail outlets and the Met Shop at 103 Elizabeth Street in the city. Aboard trams, only short trip, two-hour and 60+ tickets may be purchased from a machine.

Remember, you must validate your Met ticket before you travel, which means sliding it through one of the validating machines at the train station, or on your bus or tram.

The Met system generally operates between 5am and midnight from Monday to Saturday, and between 8am to 11pm on Sundays. For timetables and route information, call 131 638.

taxis

Over 3000 taxis cruise across all parts of Melbourne day and night, so hailing one usually isn't a problem. But if you're not having any luck, try calling one of the taxi phone numbers (see Fast Facts page 23).

the nightrider bus

You've only got five bucks left and the last train's long gone. Don't panic! Departing hourly from the corner of **Swanston and Collins Sts in the city (Map 2, Ref F15)**, the Nightrider Bus operates between 12.30am and 4.30am on weekends, with routes covering most of the metropolitan area. For further information Ph: 131 638.

train routes

Melbourne has an expansive rail network that heads out from the City in all directions to more than 16 outer suburbs. Here are a few key train routes.

• South Yarra (Map 32, Ref C8)
If you're looking to shop and hang out on Chapel St, you can take your pick from Flinders St railway station – the Sandringham, Frankston, Cranbourne and Pakenham trains all stop at South Yarra.

• Williamstown (Map 411, Ref J18)
This is an easy one! Take the Williamstown line all the way to the last station, then hop off and enjoy life on the Strand.

trams

The green tram is a Melbourne icon, and these much-adored steely beasts dart across the city and suburbs, in all directions, from one stop to the next.

Cars and motorcycles must always give way to trams. If a tram is stopped, no overtaking is permitted – pedestrians may step out unexpectedly when a tram is in the vicinity.

In central Melbourne, many intersections require 'hook turns' for vehicles turning right, which are marked by signs overhead. To make a right turn, you must pull over to the left of the intersection, wait for the light to turn red, and then complete your turn. Though it seems unusual, the system is designed to allow the free flow of cars and trams through the city streets. Here are a few key tram route numbers to remember.

• **70** – From Flinders St in the City, this tram takes you between two of Melbourne's biggest sporting and entertainment venues, Melbourne Park and the **MCG (Map 25, Ref F12)**, before continuing on up Swan St, Richmond.

• **79** – Starting at the corner of **Victoria and Church Sts in Abbotsford (Map 26, Ref H 3)**, No. 79 trundles through Richmond and South Yarra all the way to **St Kilda Beach (Map 413, Ref L17)**.

• **96** – This is the fun tram, touring through some of Melbourne's favourite destinations, splitting the popular villages of Carlton and Fitzroy, down through the city and past Albert Park Lake to another popular hangout, **St Kilda Beach (Map 413, Ref L17)**.

v-line

For travelling further afield to Victoria's regional attractions, V-Line provides convenient, comfortable services to a wide range of destinations across the state. For bookings and further information, contact 136 196 or visit www.vline.vic.gov.au.

fast facts

emergency services

• **Ambulance–fire–police** – Ph: 000.

• **Centre Against Sexual Assault**
Ph: (03) 9344 2210 BH or
Ph: (03) 9349 1766 AH.

• **Crisis Line**
24hr general counselling,
Ph: (03) 9329 0300.

• **Direct Line**
24hr drug counselling,
Ph: (03) 9416 1818.

• **Lifeline**
24hr general counselling, Ph: 131 114.

• **Maternal and child health**
After hours service, Ph: (03) 9853 0844.

public hospitals

Each of the hospitals listed below provides 24 Hour Emergency Service.

• **Mercy Hospital for Women (Map 25, Ref G5)**
126 Clarendon Street,
East Melbourne Ph: (03) 9270 2222

• **Royal Children's Hospital (Map 17, Ref E10)**
Flemington Road, Parkville
Ph: (03) 9345 5522

• **Royal Melbourne Hospital (Map 17, Ref H14)**
Grattan Street, Parkville
Ph: (03) 9342 7000

• **Royal Women's Hospital (Map 18, Ref D14)**
132 Grattan Street, Carlton
Ph: (03) 9344 2000

• **Royal Victorian Eye & Ear Hospital (Map 25, Ref A2)**
32 Gisborne Street, East Melbourne
Ph: (03) 9929 8666

internet cafés

Immerse yourself in the online world with a cup of coffee and a snack at any one of these great internet havens, where you can chat, send emails or surf the net at very affordable prices.

• **Café Wired (Map 30, Ref B7)**
363 Clarendon Street, South
Melbourne Ph: (03) 9686 9555

• **Cybernet Café (Map 372, Ref A14)**
789 Glenferrie Road, Hawthorn
Ph: (03) 9818 1288

• **Go Local Internet Lounge (Map 2, Ref E6)**
277 Little Lonsdale Street, City
Ph: (03) 9639 6060

• **Internet Café St Kilda (Map 414, Ref B14)**
9 Grey Street, St Kilda
Ph: (03) 9534 2666

• **Mary Martin Bookshop Café (Map 2, Ref L11)**
108 Bourke St, City,
Ph: (03) 9663 9633

• **Melbourne Central Internet (Map 2, Ref C5)**
Level 2, Melbourne Central, Off
Swanston Walk, City Ph: (03) 9922 1100

• **Myer RMIT Internet Café (Map 2, Ref D9)**
Level 4, 295 Lonsdale Street, City
Ph: (03) 9661 1700

• **Net City (Map 414, Ref G12)**
40 Chapel St, Windsor
Ph: (03) 9529 1937

• **Net City (Map 19, Ref B12)**
404 Brunswick St, Fitzroy
Ph: (03) 9486 0087

• **Net City (Map 414, Ref A15)**
7/63 Fitzroy St, St Kilda
Ph: (03) 9525 3411

lost property

• **Melbourne Town Hall (Map 2, Ref F15)**
Swanston St, City, Ph: (03) 9658 9463
week days or (03) 9658 9774 w'ends.

movies

Movies always make for a great night out, and Melbourne is a breeding ground for state-of-the-art cinemas.

• **Greater Union (Map 2, Ref J13)**
131 Russell Street, City
Ph: (03) 9654 8133

• **IMAX Theatre Melbourne (Map 18, Ref H17)**
Rathdowne Street, Carlton
Ph: (03) 9663 5454

• **Movieline** Ph:(03) 9685 7111
Just call this number, and enter the location code of your choice from the selections below for information, movie session times and credit card bookings.
• Code 341: **Jam Factory (Map 32, Ref E12)**
Chapel Street, South Yarra
• Code 342: **Crown Entertainment Complex (Map 3, Ref C4)** Southbank
• Code 343: **Knox Towerpoint (Map 422, Ref K16)**
Burwood Highway, Wantirna
• Code 344: **Sunshine Megaplex 20 (Map 321, Ref C20)**
cnr Harvester & Hampshire Rds, Sunshine
• Code 346: **Southland (Map 496, Ref H17)**
Nepean Highway, Cheltenham
• Code 347: **City Centre (Map 2, Ref H11)**
206 Bourke Street, City
• Code 348: **Airport West 8 (Map 279, Ref A10)**
Westfield Shoppingtown,
29 Louis Street, Airport West
• Code 357: **Glen Waverley 10 (Map 420, Ref D20)**
256 Springvale Road, Glen Waverley
• Code 371: **Highpoint Shopping Centre (Map 323, Ref B16)**
Rosamond Road, Maribyrnong
• Code 372: **Cinema Centre (Map 2, Ref L11)**
140 Bourke Street, City
• Code 373: **Greensborough (Map 286, Ref B4)**
25 Main Street, Greensborough
• Code 374: **Chadstone Shopping Centre (Map 457, Ref H5)**
1341 Dandenong Road, Chadstone
• Code 375: **Northland Shopping Centre (Map 283, Ref J19)**
50 Murray Road, Preston
• Code 377: **Croydon (Map 380, Ref B4)**
3 Hewish Road, Croydon
• Code 378: **Forest Hill Chase Shopping Centre (Map 420, Ref C2)**
Canterbury Road, Forest Hill
• Code 379: **Broadmeadows (Map 237, Ref L15)**
48-50 Pearcedale Road,
Broadmeadows

taxi cabs

When you're stuck for a ride, call one of these numbers and you'll be on your way in no time.

• **Arrow** Ph: 132 211
• **Black Cabs** Ph: 132 227
• **Dandenong Taxis** Ph: (03) 9791 2111
• **Embassy** Ph: 131 755
• **North Suburban** Ph: 131 119
• **Silver Top** Ph: 131 008
• **West Suburban** Ph: (03) 9689 1144

Useful Numbers

Here's some handy phone numbers to have at all times.

• **Melbourne City Council**
General inquiries, Ph: (03) 9658 9658

• **Directory assistance**
Local, Ph: 12455; International, Ph: 1225

• **Legal Aid Commission**
Ph: (03) 9269 0234

• **Met transport info** Ph: 131 638

• **Relationships Australia**
Counselling, Ph: (03) 9261 8700

• **Reverse charges** from a public telephone Ph: 12550

• **Time** Ph: 1194 & **Weather** Ph: 1196

• **Traffic hazards** (VicRoads)
Ph: 131 170

Useful Websites

Check out these great sites.

• **www.visitmelbourne.com**
Informative Melbourne site with a huge range of info and plenty of links.

• **www.whereis.com.au** Type in an address and whereis shows you the location on a map from UBD Melbourne & Surrounds Street Directory.

• **www.beat.com.au** with a finger on Melbourne's pulse, the Beat Magazine website has the latest info on gigs and hotspots around the City.

MAP SYMBOLS

CltyLink Tollway with electronic toll — CITYLINK Toll 5 TOLLWAY

Freeway or Motorway — CALDER FREEWAY

Proposed Freeway — Proposed Freeway

Primary Arterial Road — MELTON HIGHWAY

Secondary Arterial / Collector Road — SUNSHINE AV

Local Access Road — VERONA DR

Lane with One-way Traffic Route — MILLER LA

Un-trafficable / Proposed Road — SHEOAK CL

Railway Line with Station (distance from Flinders St Stn) — Somerville 55

Tramway

Roundabouts

Traffic Lights and Level Crossing

Road and Rail Bridges & Bridge Clearance Heights — 4.5m

Distance by road from GPO — 22

Victorian Route Numbers — M1 A420 B420 C777

National / Alternative / State & Metropolitan Route Shields — 1 1 180 10

Suburb Name — BURNSIDE

Locality Name — Jolimont

Ferry Route

Walking Track, Cycleway

Park, Reserve, Golf Course, etc (with Oval)

School or Hospital

Caravan Park, Cemetery, Shopping Centre, etc.

Mall, Plaza

Swamp, Land Subject to Inundation

- Caravan Park
- Car Park
- College - Private
- - State
- Golf Course
- Hospital
- Hotel
- Library
- Lookout
- Motel
- Picnic Area
- Place of Worship
- Police Station
- Post Office
- School - Private
- - Public
- Shopping Centre
- Swimming Pool
- Wineries

STREET MAPS overlap on each page to help in re-locating position on an adjoining page.

ADJOINING MAP NUMBERS are shown in the borders and corners of the street maps.

REFERENCE NUMBERS AND LETTERS within the borders of the street maps are the reference co-ordinates given in the indexes, see "How To Find A Street" - inside front cover.

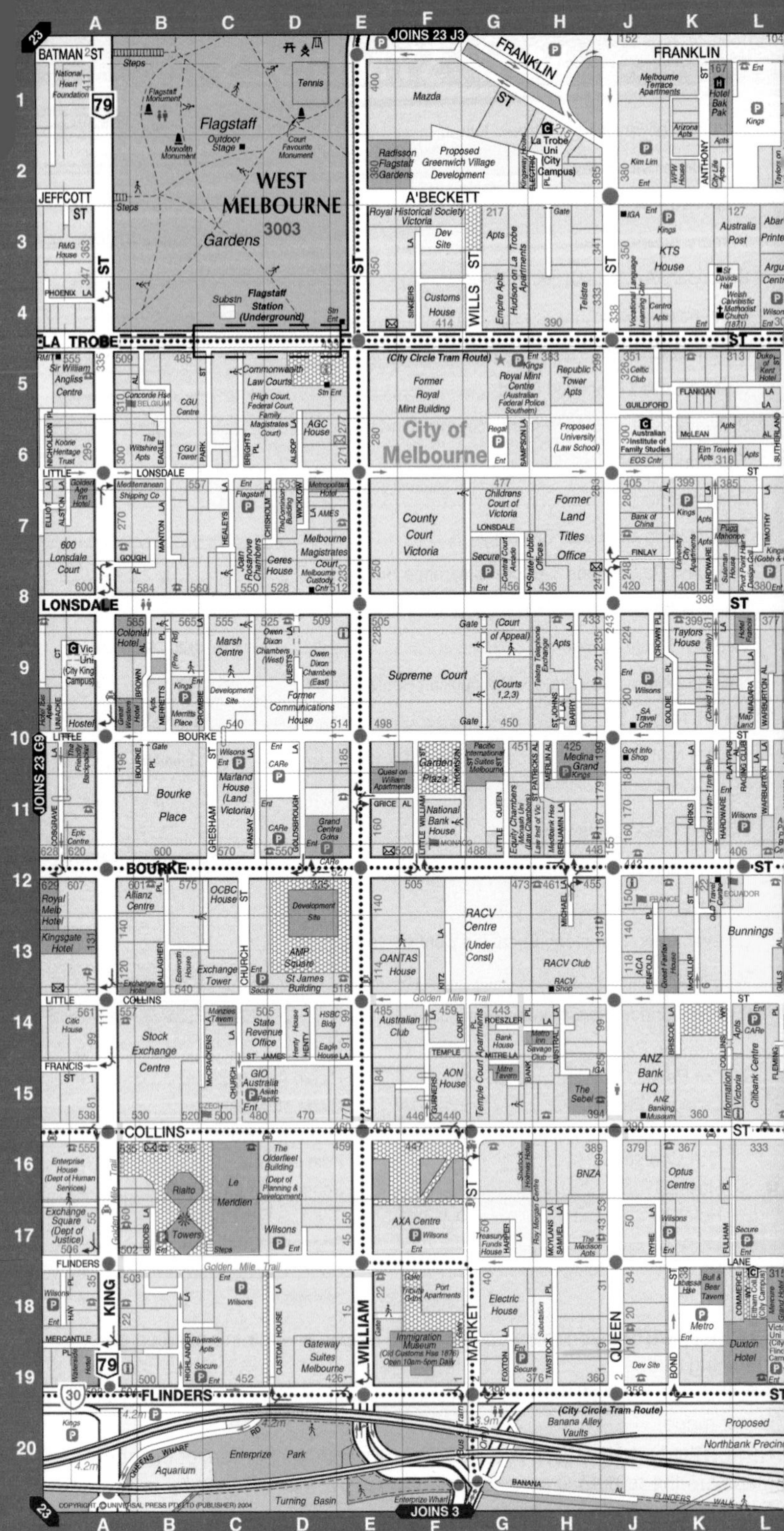
23
JOINS 23 J3
JOINS 23 G9
JOINS 3
BATMAN ST
FRANKLIN ST
FRANKLIN
National Heart Foundation
79
Flagstaff
WEST MELBOURNE 3003
Gardens
Outdoor Stage
Monolith Monument
Court Favourite Monument
Tennis
Steps
Flagstaff Station (Underground)
Substn
Stn Ent
Mazda
Radisson Flagstaff Gardens
Proposed Greenwich Village Development
La Trobe Uni (City Campus)
Melbourne Terrace Apartments
Hotel Bak Pak
Kings
Kim Lim
Arizona Apts
ANTHONY
JEFFCOTT ST
A'BECKETT
RMG House
PHOENIX LA
Royal Historical Society Victoria
Dev Site
Apts
Customs House
WILLS ST
Empire Apts
Hudson on La Trobe Apartments
Telstra
KTS House
Australia Post
Vocational Language Learning Cntr
Centro Apts
St Davids Hall
Welsh Calvinistic Methodist Church (1871)
LA TROBE ST
Sir William Angliss Centre
Commonwealth Law Courts
(High Court, Federal Court, Family Magistrates Court)
AGC House
(City Circle Tram Route)
Former Royal Mint Building
City of Melbourne
Royal Mint Centre
(Australian Federal Police Southern)
Republic Tower Apts
Proposed University (Law School)
Celtic Club
GUILDFORD
FLANIGAN
Australian Institute of Family Studies
EOS Cntr
McLEAN
Elm Towers Apts
Concorde Hse
CGU Centre
CGU Tower
The Wiltshire Apts
Kooie Heritage Trust
NICHOLSON PL
LITTLE LONSDALE
Mediterranean Shipping Co
Golden Age Inn Hotel
600 Lonsdale Court
MANTON
HEALEYS
Joan Rosanove Chambers
Ceres House
Flagstaff
AMES
Melbourne Magistrates Court
Metropolitan Hotel
County Court Victoria
Childrens Court of Victoria
LONSDALE
State Public Offices
Former Land Titles Office
Bank of China
FINLAY
Pugg Mahones
LONSDALE
ST
Colonial Hotel
Marsh Centre
Owen Dixon Chambers (West)
Owen Dixon Chambers (East)
Development Site
Former Communications House
Merritts Place
Vic Uni (City King Campus)
Hostel
Supreme Court
(Court of Appeal)
(Courts 1,2,3)
Telstra Telephone Exchange
Taylors House
SA Travel Cntr
LITTLE BOURKE
Bourke Place
Marland House (Land Victoria)
GRESHAM
GOLDSBROUGH
Grand Central Gdns
Epic Centre
Quest on William Apartments
Garden Plaza
Pacific International Suites Melbourne
National Bank House
Equity Chambers
Medina Grand Kings
Govt Info Shop
BOURKE
ST
Royal Melb Hotel
Kingsgate Hotel
Allianz Centre
OCBC House
Development Site
AMP Square
St James Building
Exchange Tower
CHURCH
QANTAS House
RACV Centre (Under Const)
RACV Club
ACA
Bunnings
LITTLE COLLINS
Golden Mile Trail
Citic House
Stock Exchange Centre
State Revenue Office
HSBC Bldg
Eagle House
GIO Australia
Australian Club
AON House
Temple Court Apartments
Bank House
Mitre Tavern
The Sebel
ANZ Bank HQ
ANZ Banking Museum
Citibank Centre
FRANCIS ST
COLLINS
ST
Enterprise House (Dept of Human Services)
Exchange Square (Dept of Justice)
Rialto
Towers
Le Meridien
The Olderfleet Building (Dept of Planning & Development)
Wilsons
AXA Centre
Treasury Funds House
Roy Morgan Centre
BNZA
Optus Centre
FLINDERS LANE
KING
WILLIAM
MARKET
QUEEN
Gateway Suites Melbourne
CUSTOM HOUSE
Immigration Museum (Old Customs Hse 1876) Open 10am-5pm Daily
Port Apartments
Electric House
Metro
Duxton Hotel
Bull & Bear Tavern
Dev Site
FLINDERS ST
30
Enterprize Park
Aquarium
(City Circle Tram Route)
Banana Alley Vaults
Proposed Northbank Precinct
Turning Basin
BANANA
FLINDERS WALK
COPYRIGHT © UNIVERSAL PRESS PTY LTD (PUBLISHER) 2004

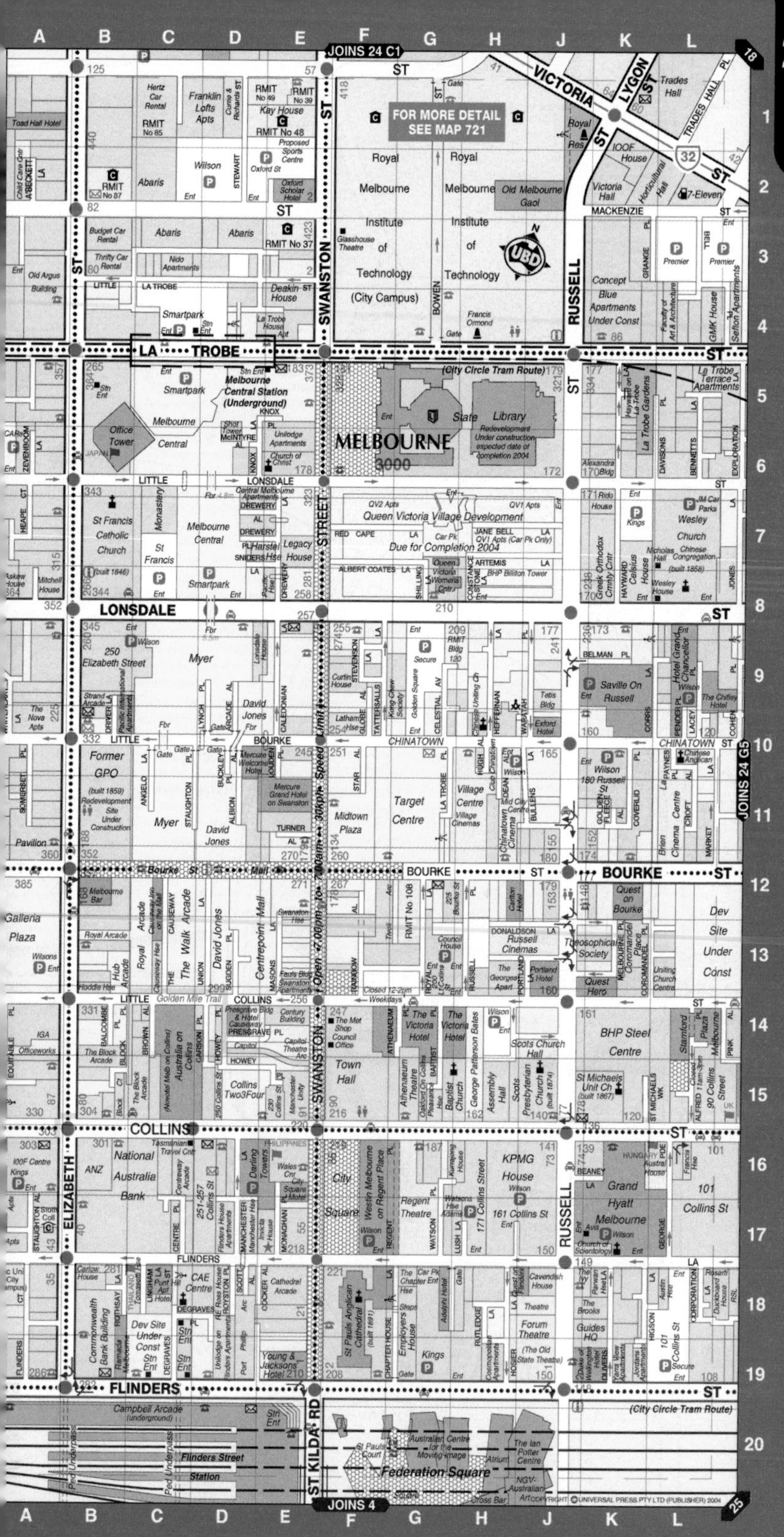

A B C D E F G H J K L
JOINS 24 C1
78
FOR MORE DETAIL SEE MAP 721
VICTORIA
LYGON ST
Trades Hall
TRADES HALL PL
Royal Res
IOOF House
Victoria Hall
Horticultural Hall
7-Eleven
32
Hertz Car Rental
Franklin Lofts Apts
RMIT No 65
RMIT No 49
RMIT No 39
Kay House
RMIT No 48
Proposed Sports Centre
Toad Hall Hotel
Wilson
Abaris
RMIT No 87
Oxford St
Oxford Scholar Hotel
STEWART
Royal Melbourne Institute of Technology (City Campus)
Royal Melbourne Institute of Technology
Glasshouse Theatre
Old Melbourne Gaol
BOWEN
Francis Ormond
Budget Car Rental
Thrifty Car Rental
Nido Apartments
Old Argus Building
RMIT No 37
Deakin House
LITTLE LA TROBE
Smartpark
La Trobe House Apt
LA TROBE ST
SWANSTON ST
RUSSELL ST
MACKENZIE ST
Concept Blue Apartments Under Const
Premier
GRANGE
Faculty of Art & Architecture
GMK House
Sefton Apartments
Melbourne Central Station (Underground)
Melbourne Central
Office Tower
KNOX
Shot Tower
McINTYRE
Unilodge Apartments
Church of Christ
ZEVENBOOM
(City Circle Tram Route)
State Library
Redevelopment Under construction expected date of completion 2004
MELBOURNE 3000
La Trobe Gardens
La Trobe Terrace Apartments
Alexandra Bldg
DAVISONS
BENNETTS
EXPLORATION
LITTLE LONSDALE
Central Melbourne Apartments
DREWERY
St Francis Catholic Church (built 1846)
Monastery
St Francis
Melbourne Central
Legacy House
Harstel Hse
SNIDERS
Mitchell House
HEAPE CT
QV2 Apts
QV1 Apts
Queen Victoria Village Development
Due for Completion 2004
RED CAPE
JANE BELL
ALBERT COATES
SHILLING
Queen Victoria Womens Cntr
CONSTANCE STONE
ARTEMIS
BHP Billiton Tower
Rido House
Greek Orthodox Cmnty Cntr
Kings
Celsius House
HAYWARD
Nicholas Hall
Wesley Church
Wesley House
Chinese Congregation (built 1858)
JM Car Parks
JONES
LONSDALE ST
250 Elizabeth Street
Myer
Lonsdale House
Strand Arcade
DRIVER
Pacific International Apartments
LYNCH
ARCADE
David Jones
CALEDONIAN
Curtin House
STEVENSON
Latham Hse
GLOBE
TATTERSALLS
Kong Chew Society
Golden Square
CELESTIAL AV
RMIT Bldg 120
Secure
Chinese Uniting Ch
HEFFERNAN
WARATAH
Tetis Bldg
Exford Hotel
BELMAN PL
Saville On Russell
CORRS
Hotel Grand Chancellor
PENDER PL
LACEY
The Chifley Hotel
COHEN
The Nova Apts
LITTLE BOURKE
CHINATOWN
CHINATOWN ST
Former GPO (built 1859) Redevelopment Site Under Construction
ANGELO
STAUGHTON
BUCKLEY
ALBION
Mercure Welcome Hotel
Mercure Grand Hotel on Swanston
TURNER
Open 7.00am to 7.00pm 30kph Speed Limit
Midtown Plaza
STAR
Target Centre
LA TROBE
Village Centre
Village Cinemas
Chinatown Cinema
Mid City Centre
BULLENS
Chinese Anglican
180 Russell St
GOLDEN FLEECE
COVERLID
Cinema Centre
CROFT
MARKET
JOINS 24 G5
SOMERSET
Pavilion
Bourke St Mall
BOURKE ST
Galleria Plaza
Melbourne Bar
Royal Arcade
Causeway Inn on the Mall
CAUSEWAY
The Walk Arcade
David Jones
Centrepoint Mall
Swanston Hse
Hub Arcade
SUGDEN
UNION
MASONS
Fauls Bldg Swanston Apartments
Hoddle Hse
Wilsons
RMIT No 108
225 Bourke St
Carlton Hotel
Council House
DONALDSON
Russell Cinemas
The Georges Apart
PORTLAND
Portland Hotel
RAINBOW
Closed 12-2pm Weekdays
Quest on Bourke
Theosophical Society
MELBOURNE PL
Coromandel Place
COROMANDEL
Quest Hero
Dev Site Under Const
Uniting Church Centre
LITTLE COLLINS
Golden Mile Trail
Equitable
IGA
Officeworks
BALCOMBE
The Block Arcade
BROWN
(Novotel Melb on Collins)
Australia on Collins
CARSON
HOWEY
Presgrave Bldg & Hotel Causeway
PRESGRAVE PL
Century Building
Capitol Theatre Arc
Collins Two3Four
Manchester Unity
The Met Shop Council Office
Town Hall
ATHENAEUM
Athenaeum Theatre
The Victoria Hotel
Oxford On Collins
Baptist Church
George Patterson Bates
Assembly Hall
Scots Church Hall
Scots Presbyterian Church (built 1874)
BHP Steel Centre
St Michaels Unit Ch (built 1867)
ST MICHAELS WK
Stamford Plaza
ALFRED
90 Collins Street
PINK
COLLINS ST
IOOF Centre
Kings
ANZ
National Australia Bank
Tasmanian Travel Cntr
Centreway Arcade
251-257 Collins St
Darling Towers
Wales Cnr
City Square Motel
City Square
Westin Melbourne on Regent Place
REGENT
Regent Theatre
Kurrajong House
Watsons Hse
Adams
171 Collins Street
KPMG House
161 Collins St
HUNGARY
BEANEY
Grand Hyatt Melbourne
Church of Scientology
Avis
Austral House
Francis Hse
101 Collins St
ELIZABETH ST
STAUGHTON AL
MANCHESTER
Invicta House
MONAGHAN
WATSON
LUSH
GEORGE
FLINDERS LA
Carlow House
Commonwealth Bank Building
ROTHSAY
THAILAND
Tomasetti Hse
LINGHAM
Punt Hill Apt Hotel
CAE Centre
DEGRAVES
Dev Site Under Const
Unilodge on Flinders
RE Ross House
ROYSTON
SCOTT AL
COCKER AL
Cathedral Arcade
Young & Jacksons Hotel
St Pauls Anglican Cathedral (built 1891)
CHAPTER HOUSE
Employers House
The Chapter Hse
Steps
Adelphi Hotel
Kings
RUTLEDGE
Cosmopolitan Apartments
HOSIER
Quest on Flinders
Cavendish House
Theatre
Forum Theatre (The Old State Theatre)
The Ivy
The Brooks
Guides HQ
Duke of Wellington Hotel
Yarra View Apartments
Jordans Apartments
HIGSON
101 Collins St
CORPORATION
Duckboard House
Rosati
RSL
Secure
FLINDERS ST
Campbell Arcade (underground)
Flinders Street Station
Ped Underpass
ST KILDA RD
St Pauls Court
Australian Centre for the Moving Image
Atrium
The Ian Potter Centre
NGV Australian Art
Federation Square
Cross Bar
JOINS 4
25
1 2 3 4 5 6 7 8 9 10 11 12 13 14 15 16 17 18 19 20

A B C D E F G H J K L
JOINS 1
23
Aquarium
Enterprize Park
Batman Park
Yarra Northbank Turning Basin
Enterprize Wharf
BANANA AL
FLINDERS
QUEENS BRIDGE
KINGS BRIDGE
YARRA
Boat Mooring
Proposed Sandridge Bridge Development
SOUTHBANK PROMENADE
QUEENSBRIDGE (Tunnel) SQUARE
RIVER PROMENADE
Crown Towers Hotel
Queensbridge Hotel
Riverside Quay
Esso House
Riverside Quay Ent
Car Park Entrance
Crown Entertainment Complex
Entrance to Crown Entertainment Complex
RIVERSIDE QY
Freshwater Place Apartments under construction
COOK ST
Eureka Apartments
Travelodge Southbank
SOUTHGATE AV
Riverside Apartments
Wilson
Schiavello
WHITEMAN ST
SOUTHBANK
POWER ST
BMW
CITY RD
55 Southbank Bvd
Southbank Towers
Imperium Tower Development Under Construction
Hanover House
WALKER ST
The Atrium
QUEENSBRIDGE
FAWKNER ST
Southpoint Apartments
FAWKNER LA
Millbank House
Southbank Apartments
KINGS WY
HANNAH ST
99 Queensbridge St
190 City Road
The Summit Apartments
Yarra Apartments
Private Rd
BVD
Southside Gardens Apartments
ABC Cntr 3LO 3RN Triple
Australian Red Cross Society & Blood Bank
BALSTON ST
Coronial Services Centre of Victoria
Stylecraft
Victoria University City South Melbourne Campus
City of Melbourne
Proposed Southbank Office Park
Sutherland Place Apartments
KAVANAGH ST
SOUTHBANK 3006
Brearley Group
CATHERINE ST
MOORE ST
(Private Car Park)
Collins Mitsubishi
Regent House
McGOWAN ST
SES Victoria State Headquarters
STURT ST
HANCOCK ST
M1
GRANT
Contemporary Art Centre
CHESSELL ST
Walkway
Playbox @ The Malthouse
Gate Offices
Private Road
The Keep Southbank Apartments
MARKET ST
MILES ST
Sturt Street
Gate
SOUTH MELBOURNE 3205
Shell
DODDS ST
Southbank Royale Apartments
ROSS ST
Copytone Building
City View Apartments
Maori Chief Hotel
250 Sturt St
Panama Apartments
YORK ST
Mercedes - Benz
Citipower Substation
Southbank Gardens Apartments
AWI House
LITTLE MORAY PL
MORAY ST
TICHBORNE PL
Southside Tower Apartments
Coventry Gardens Apartments
Bells Hotel
COVENTRY ST
TOPE ST
EASTERN RD
HANNA LA
Coventry Square Apartments
(Private Car Park)
HSV7
WELLS ST
Kings Garden Office Park
JOINS 30 E2
JOINS 23 L18
30
COPYRIGHT UNIVERSAL PRESS PTY LTD (PUBLISHER) 2004

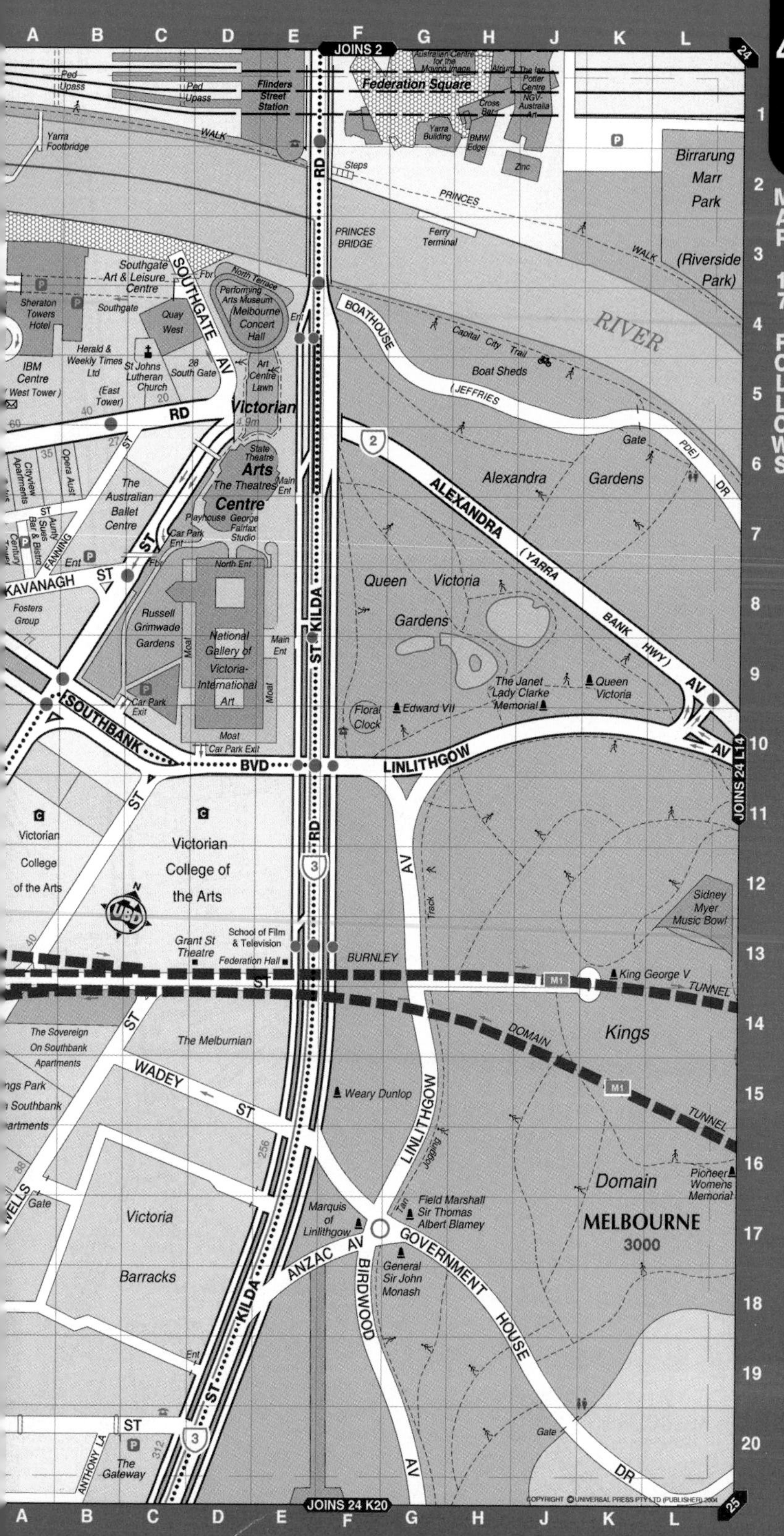

JOINS 2
Flinders Street Station
Federation Square
Australian Centre for the Moving Image
Atrium
The Ian Potter Centre
NGV-Australia Art
Cross Bar
Yarra Building
BMW Edge
Zinc
Ped Upass
Yarra Footbridge
WALK
Steps
PRINCES
PRINCES BRIDGE
Ferry Terminal
Birrarung Marr Park
(Riverside Park)
RIVER
Southgate Art & Leisure Centre
Sheraton Towers Hotel
Southgate
Quay West
SOUTHGATE AV
Performing Arts Museum
Melbourne Concert Hall
North Terrace
Art Centre Lawn
Herald & Weekly Times Ltd
St Johns Lutheran Church
28 South Gate
IBM Centre
(East Tower)
(West Tower)
BOATHOUSE
Capital City Trail
Boat Sheds
(JEFFRIES
Victorian Arts Centre
State Theatre
The Theatres
Main Ent
Playhouse
George Fairfax Studio
Car Park Ent
RD
ALEXANDRA
(YARRA
BANK
HWY)
AV
Alexandra Gardens
Gate
PDE)
DR
The Australian Ballet Centre
Cityview Apartments
Opera Aust
Aunty Sues Bar & Bistro
Century Tower
FANNING ST
Ent
KAVANAGH ST
Fosters Group
North Ent
Russell Grimwade Gardens
National Gallery of Victoria-International Art
Moat
Car Park Exit
SOUTHBANK
BVD
ST KILDA RD
Queen Victoria Gardens
The Janet Lady Clarke Memorial
Queen Victoria
Edward VII
Floral Clock
LINLITHGOW
Victorian College of the Arts
Track
Sidney Myer Music Bowl
School of Film & Television
Grant St Theatre
Federation Hall
BURNLEY ST
King George V
TUNNEL
DOMAIN
M1
Kings Domain
The Sovereign On Southbank Apartments
The Melburnian
WADEY ST
Weary Dunlop
Kings Park
Southbank Apartments
WELLS
Gate
Victoria Barracks
Marquis of Linlithgow
Field Marshall Sir Thomas Albert Blamey
Pioneer Womens Memorial
MELBOURNE 3000
ANZAC AV
BIRDWOOD AV
GOVERNMENT HOUSE DR
General Sir John Monash
Jogging
Tan
Ent
ANTHONY LA
The Gateway
JOINS 24 K20
JOINS 24 L14
MAP 17 FOLLOWS
COPYRIGHT © UNIVERSAL PRESS PTY LTD (PUBLISHER) 2004

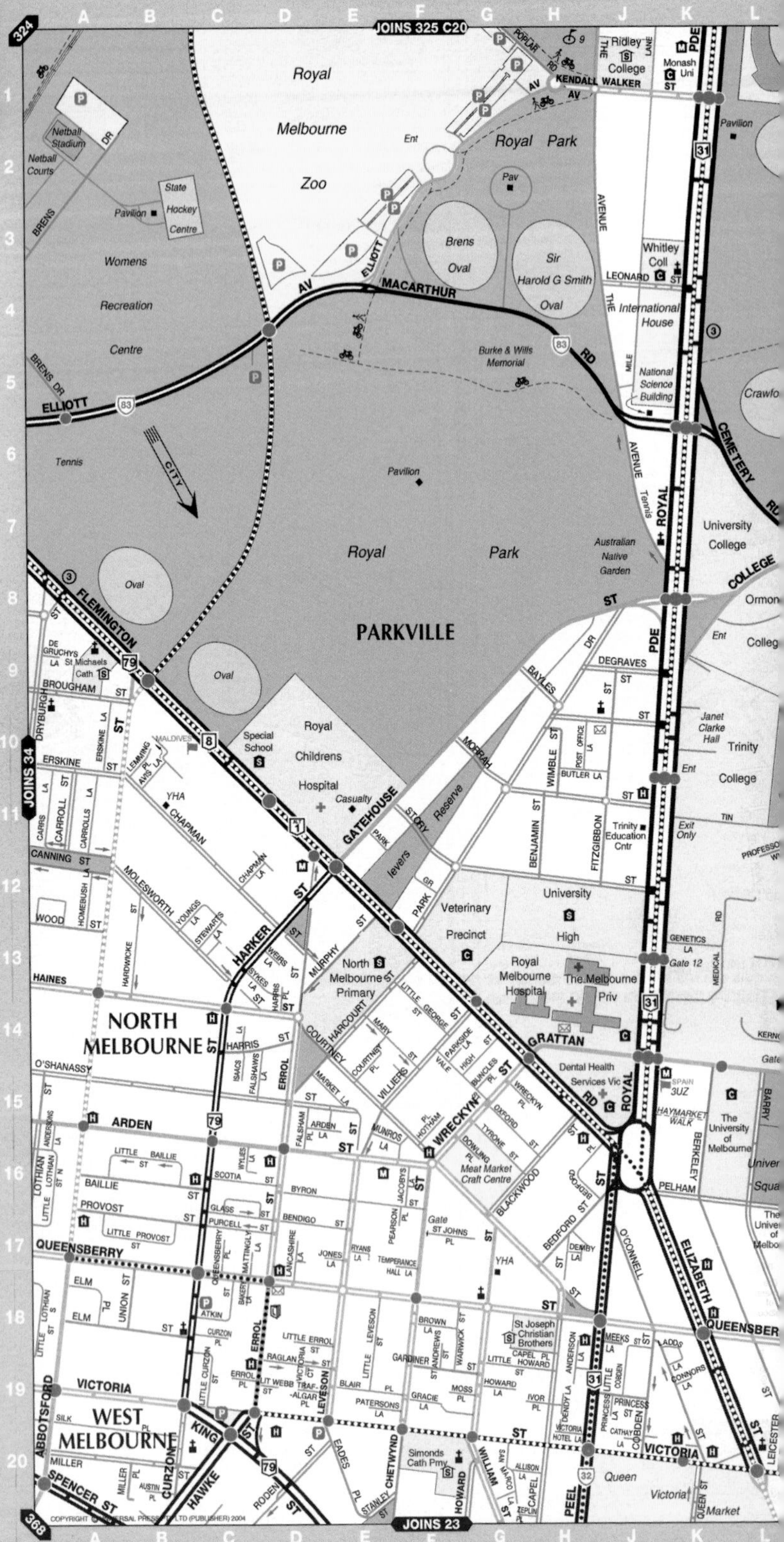

PREVIOUS MAP 4

JOINS 325 J20
326

A B C D E F G H J K L

PRINCES HILL

CARLTON NORTH

CARLTON

FITZROY

Optus Oval
Carlton Cricket Ground
Tennis
Princes Park
Oval
Melbourne General Cemetery
Western Gate
Eastern Gate
Main Entrance
Office
Gate
St Hildas College
Queens College
University Oval
Newman College
Tennis
Athletics
St Marys College
The University of Melbourne
Gate 1
Gate 4
Fbr 5.18m
Frances Perry Priv
Royal Womens Hospital
VicRoads
Victorian College of Optometry
Senior Citizens
Carlton Gardens Primary
Theatre
SPAIN
Nova Cinema & Lygon Court
Theatre
Carlton Moviehouse
La Mama Theatre
Silver Top Taxis
Mosque
Community Centre
Curtain Square
MCH
RSL
Carlton North Primary
VANUATU
SAN MARINO
Child Care
Ministry of Housing
Macarthur Square
AUSTRIA
Victorian Aboriginal Health Service
Murchison Square
Res
Carlton Gardens
Traffic School
Tennis
Carlton Gdns Primary
Corpus Christi College
Melbourne Museum
IMAX Cinema
Ent
Exit
Royal Exhibition Building(1879)
Carlton Gardens
Lincoln Square
Argyle Square
The University of Melbourne
RMIT Future Development Site
Royal Melbourne Institute of Technology
TAFE Sector
SYRIA
City Baths
Cath Academy of Mary Immaculate
St Vincents Hospital
FM 104.3

RICHARDSON ST, ARNOLD ST, WILSON ST, McILWRAITH ST, KEELEY ST, LA, GARTON ST, MACPHERSON ST, Hardy Reserve, PRINCES PARK DR, FLETCHER LA, MACPHERSON, HERBERT ST, FENWICK, SHAKESPEARE ST, DAVIDS LA, DRUMMOND LA, BIRDSALL PL, CURTAIN, RESERVE ST, SUTTON ST, EARL ST, AMESS, TAPLIN, NEWRY, HENRY ST, O'GRADY ST, LEE, RATHDOWNE, DAVIS, CANNING, STATION, NICHOLSON, PRINCES ST, VICTORIA PL, CEMETERY RD E, LYTTON, CR, Ent, ST, DRUMMOND, BONESHAKER PL, O'BRIEN PL, DALGETY PL, BOOM PL, COLEMAN PL, NEILL, Gates, CHARLES ST, KAY, KEPPEL ST, LYGON, WATERLOO ST, PALMERSTON PL, PAINSDALE PL, HOLMWOOD, PALMERSTON, KEPPEL ST, PITT ST, ROSE ST, KERR ST, HENRY ST, ARGYLE ST, SPRING, LITTLE PALMERSTON ST, ASTOR PL, APLIN PL, SUTTON PL, WILLOW LA, DAVID, ALLEY, UNION RD, SPENCER RD, ELGIN PL, UNION PL, ELGIN ST, LITTLE ELGIN, TYNE ST, COURT HOUSE PL, COCHRANE, McGOWANS PL, MASSON RD, MONASH RD, FARADAY, MACARTHUR PL N, MACARTHUR PL S, VICTORIA, FARADAY, DEL MONACO, LA MAMA PL, MOTON PL, CARLOW PL, BARKLY, LITTLE BARKLY ST, UNIVERSITY, POST OFFICE PL, UNIVERSITY ST, GLENNON PL, NAUGHTON LA, REGISTRY PL, YORK PL, BEARD PL, DORRIT ST, GRATTAN LA, DORCHESTER PL, VICTORIA CL, GORDON PL, BAKE HOUSE LA, CARLTON PL, AUSTIN PL, SHIELS LA, SPUR LA, MURCHISON ST, OWEN, BARRUP ST, BELL ST, GARFIELD ST, CREMORNE PL, CREMORNE ST, MOOR ST, BACH LA, KING ST, WILLIAM, HANOVER ST, LITTLE HANOVER ST, COWELL ST, FLEET ST, LITTLE FLEET ST, PALMER ST, LITTLE MARION ST, ROYAL LA, MARION LA, GERTRUDE ST, ALMA ST, PRINCES REGENT ST, FITZROY, WILSON, MALVINA PL, CHURCH, LITTLE GRATTAN ST, GRATTAN, BANBRIDGE PL, SCOTTS PL, LINCOLN, LINCOLN SQ N, LINCOLN SQ S, PELHAM PL, PELHAM ST, MARY ST, ARGYLE, HYAM PL, CHUMMIE PL, LYGON TCE, CARDIGAN, ORMOND PL, O'CONNELL, PELHAM, RODNEY PL, ARGYLE PL S, ARGYLE PL E, FINLAY PL, DRUMMOND PL, YOUNGS PL, GROSVENOR PL, LEICESTER PL, BARKLY PL, CUMBERLAND PL, LINCOLN PL, CARLTON PL, MONAHAN LA, CANADA LA, IEVERS TCE, KELVIN PL, GIBBONS ST, QUEENSBERRY, LITTLE QUEENSBERRY, RUSH PL, MAGENTA PL, MISSION PL, LITTLE CARDIGAN ST, CORNELL PL, ESSEX PL, EARL PL, O'GRADY ST, IEVERS ST, ORR ST, TRADES HALL PL, DRUMMOND, McDONALD LA, ELM TREE PL, HUDSON PL, RATHDOWNE, RENTAL TCE, LANSDOWNE PL, ALMA PL, BOUVERIE PL, BOUVERIE, SWANSTON, CARDIGAN TCE, CARDIGAN, LYGON, ST

FOR MORE DETAIL SEE MAP 715

JOINS 19

1 2 3 4 5 6 7 8 9 10 11 12 13 14 15 16 17 18 19 20

JOINS 24
25

A B C D E F G H J K L

A B C D E F G H J K L
JOINS 326 C20
325
FITZROY NORTH
Edinburgh Gardens
Tennis
MCH
William Peterson Community Oval
John Batman Institute of TAFE Fitzroy Campus
Fitzroy North Pmy
ALFRED
AUSTIN
FERGIE
BEST
MARK
FALCONER
MICHAEL
WOODSIDE
WOODHEAD
DELBRIDGE
ROWE
PARK
PDE
PARK PL
HOWE
RICHARDSON ST
REID
BATMAN
ALFRED ST
SEACOMBE
TRANMERE
EGREMONT
ST GEORGES
RD
SKENE PL
SALISBURY CR
ANNAND ST
HOPETOWN PL
BRUNSWICK
MACPHERSON
WATKINS
BROOKES CR
STATION
TAPLIN
TEMPANY
BOSTON PL
CHURCH
FENWICK ST
RAE
Harold McCracken Nursing Home
CURTAIN ST
FREEMAN
NEWRY
PERCY
San Remo Ballroom
LAURA PL
YORK
COLEMAN ST
GRACE LA
St Brigids Pmy
CURTIN PL
BAKEHOUSE LA
ISABELLA LA
NICHOLSON
QUEENS
GEORGE ST
JAMESON
GROOM LA
REMY LA
Council Depot
GRANT
McKEAN
Child Care
St Johns Catholic Pmy
Croation Cath Centre
Organ Factory Theatre
HILTON
KENT ST
HODGKINSON
PAGE
Clifton Hill Primary
COUNCIL
REEVES ST
NOONE
ALEXANDRA
NAPIER
EASTERN HWY
PDE
Senior Citizens Club
CECIL
WESTGARTH
LEICESTER
Gary Owen Park
ROSE
KERR
HENRY ST
ARGYLE
SPRING
HARRISON PL
JOHNSTON
Stationers Supplies
MATER
EMMA
BLANCHE
HOTHAM
CHARLOTTE
BALLARAT
GOLD
COPPER
FITZROY
KEELE
Child Care Youth Cen
LITTLE
ABBOT
EASEY
RSL
MACROBERTSON LA
SACKVILLE
WELLINGTON
BUDD
VICTORIA
HERTFORD
ROCHESTER
ELLIOT
CHAPEL
Fitzroy Pmy
Pmy
HIGHETT PL
GORE
SMITH
PERRY
Northern Melbourne Institute of TAFE Collingwood Campus
YORK ST
Victorian Aboriginal Health Service
GREEVES
MAHONEY
BELL
CREMORNE
GARFIELD
FITZROY
JOHN
FISHERS LA
ST DAVID
EXHIBITION
RUSSIA
HARGREAVES
OTTER
BEDFORD
TAFE
St Josephs Cath Pmy
EMERALD
LITTLE WELLINGTON
NAPOLEON
MOOR
KENT
YOUNG
NAPIER LA
Whitlam Place
MCH
HODGSON
VERE
PALMER
KING WILLIAM
Sacred Heart Pmy
Civic Cntr
CONDELL
WOOD
STANLEY
Theat
Collingwo
College
McCUTCHEON
St Marys House of Welcome
HANOVER
Nursery
Atherton Gardens Reserve
CHARLES
Youth Centre
LITTLE CHARLES
SANDEMAN
ALBERT PL
CSIRO
COLLINGWOOD
Police Workshop
JOHN
DOWN
DIGHT
SINGLETON
Collingwood Alternative School
CAMPBELL
STURT
LITTLE HANOVER
COWELL
BRUNSWICK PL
JAMES
WEBB
FLEET
PALMER
ETHIOPIA
GIPPS
Ministry of Housing
Child Care
OXFORD
PEEL
Community Health Centre
Brotherhood of St Laurence
MARION
GLASSHOUSE RD
ROBERT
WATERLOO RD
Silvertop Taxis
GERTRUDE
ALMA
St Vincents Hosp
GRAHAM
DUKE ST
PRINCES
LITTLE NAPIER
LITTLE GEORGE
GEORGE
LITTLE GORE
LANGRIDGE
DERBY
CAMBRIDGE
GLASGOW
SILVER
ROKEBY
RUPERT
MONTAGUE
BROWN
CROMWELL
Collingwood English Language
JOINS 18
JOINS 25
24
COPYRIGHT © UNIVERSAL PRESS PTY LTD (PUBLISHER) 2004

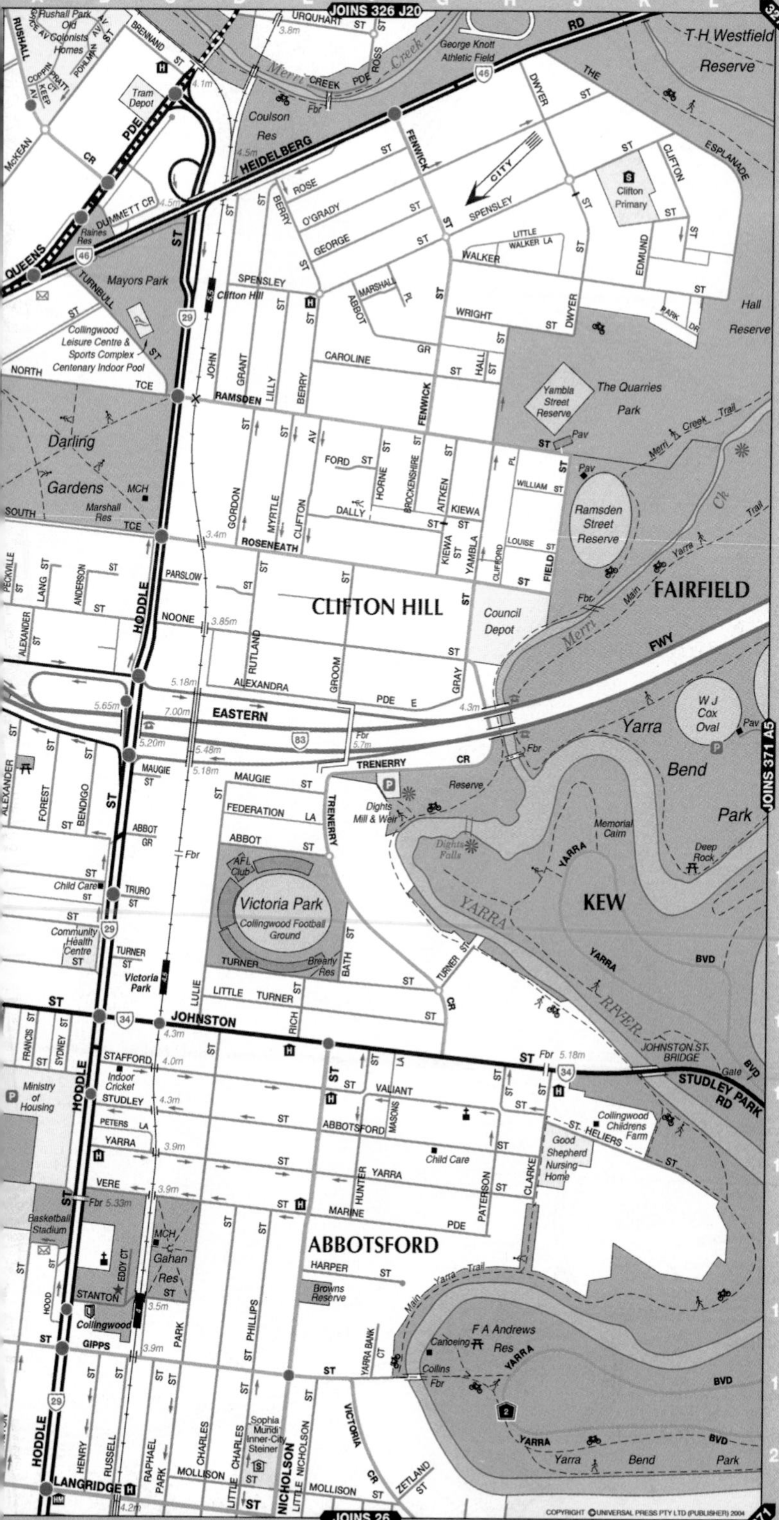

CLIFTON HILL
FAIRFIELD
KEW
ABBOTSFORD

Rushall Park
Old Colonists Homes
George Knott Athletic Field
T H Westfield Reserve
Coulson Res
Tram Depot
Raines Res
Mayors Park
Clifton Hill
Clifton Primary
Collingwood Leisure Centre & Sports Complex Centenary Indoor Pool
Hall Reserve
Yambla Street Reserve
The Quarries Park
Darling Gardens
MCH
Marshall Res
Ramsden Street Reserve
Council Depot
W J Cox Oval
Yarra Bend Park
Reserve
Dights Mill & Weir
Dights Falls
Memorial Cairn
Deep Rock
Victoria Park
AFL Club
Collingwood Football Ground
Brearly Res
Child Care
Community Health Centre
Ministry of Housing
Indoor Cricket
Collingwood Childrens Farm
Good Shepherd Nursing Home
Johnston St Bridge
Basketball Stadium
Gahan Res
Collingwood
Browns Reserve
F A Andrews Res
Canoeing
Collins
Sophia Mundi Inner-City Steiner
Merri Creek
Merri Creek Trail
Main Yarra Trail
Yarra River
Pav

HEIDELBERG RD
QUEENS PDE
HODDLE ST
EASTERN FWY
JOHNSTON ST
NICHOLSON ST
VICTORIA CR
STUDLEY PARK RD
YARRA BVD
THE ESPLANADE
TRENERRY CR
URQUHART ST
MERRI CREEK PDE
ROSS ST
DWYER ST
CLIFTON ST
FENWICK ST
SPENSLEY ST
ROSE ST
O'GRADY ST
GEORGE ST
BERRY ST
WALKER ST
LITTLE WALKER LA
EDMUND ST
PARK DR
MARSHALL PL
ABBOTT ST
WRIGHT ST
CAROLINE GR
HALL ST
RAMSDEN ST
JOHN ST
GRANT ST
LILLY ST
FORD ST
HORNE ST
BROCKENSHIRE ST
AITKEN ST
DALLY ST
KIEWA ST
WILLIAM ST
LOUISE ST
FIELD ST
CLIFFORD ST
YAMBLA ST
GORDON ST
MYRTLE ST
ROSENEATH ST
PARSLOW ST
NOONE ST
RUTLAND ST
GROOM ST
GRAY ST
ALEXANDRA PDE
RUSHALL CR
COPPIN GR
PRATT CT
KEEP AV
POHLMAN ST
BRENNAND ST
McKEAN ST
DUMMETT CR
TURNBULL ST
NORTH TCE
SOUTH TCE
PECKVILLE ST
LANG ST
ANDERSON ST
ALEXANDER ST
FOREST ST
BENDIGO ST
MAUGIE ST
FEDERATION LA
ABBOT GR
TRURO ST
TURNER ST
LITTLE TURNER ST
BATH ST
LULIE ST
RICH ST
FRANCIS ST
SYDNEY ST
STAFFORD ST
STUDLEY ST
PETERS LA
YARRA ST
VERE ST
VALIANT ST
ABBOTSFORD ST
MASONS LA
ST HELIERS ST
HUNTER ST
MARINE PDE
PATERSON ST
CLARKE ST
HARPER ST
EDDY CT
STANTON ST
HOOD ST
GIPPS ST
PHILLIPS ST
PARK ST
YARRA BANK CT
HENRY ST
RUSSELL ST
RAPHAEL ST
CHARLES ST
LITTLE CHARLES ST
MOLLISON ST
LITTLE NICHOLSON ST
ZETLAND ST
LANGRIDGE ST

3.8m 4.1m 4.5m 3.4m 3.85m 5.18m 5.65m 7.00m 5.20m 5.48m 5.7m 4.3m 4.0m 3.9m 5.33m 3.5m 4.2m
Fbr

PREVIOUS MAP 20

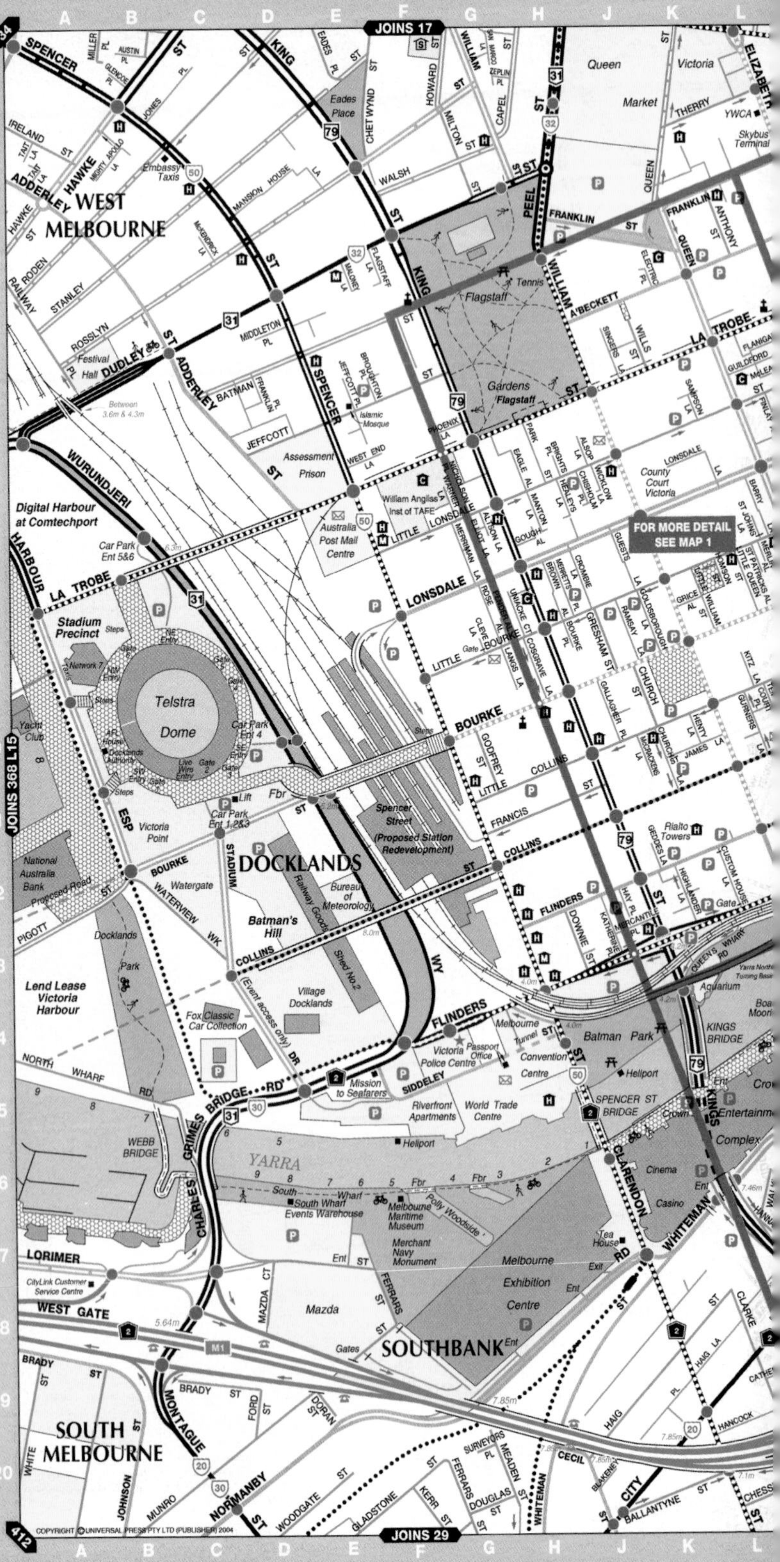

JOINS 17

JOINS 29

JOINS 368 L15

34

412

A B C D E F G H J K L

1 2 3 4 5 6 7 8 9 10 11 12 13 14 15 16 17 18 19 20

WEST MELBOURNE

SPENCER ST
MILLER PL
AUSTIN PL
GLENCOE PL
JONES PL
KING ST
EADES PL
Eades Place
CHETWYND ST
HOWARD ST
WILLIAM ST
MILTON ST
CAPEL ST
ZEPLIN PL
Queen Victoria Market
THERRY ST
YWCA
Skybus Terminal
ELIZABETH ST
IRELAND ST
HAWKE ST
ADDERLEY ST
Embassy Taxis
MANSION HOUSE LA
WALSH ST
PEEL ST
FRANKLIN ST
QUEEN ST
ANTHONY ST
McKENDRICK LA
MALONEY LA
FLAGSTAFF LA
ELECTRIC PL
RODEN ST
RAILWAY PL
STANLEY ST
ROSSLYN ST
DUDLEY ST
MIDDLETON PL
Tennis
Flagstaff Gardens
A'BECKETT ST
SINGERS LA
WILLS ST
LA TROBE ST
FLANIGAN LA
GUILDFORD LA
McLEAN ST
Festival Hall
BATMAN ST
FRANKLIN PL
BROUGHTON PL
JEFFCOTT PL
Islamic Mosque
SAMPSON LA
FINLAY
Between 3.6m & 4.3m
JEFFCOTT ST
Assessment Prison
WEST END LA
PHOENIX LA
PARK ST
EAGLE AL
BRIGHTS PL
ALSOP LA
LONSDALE ST
County Court Victoria
BARRY
WURUNDJERI WY
William Angliss Inst of TAFE
NICHOLSON ST
WARBURTON LA
CHISHOLM PL
HEALEYS LA
WICKLOW LA
MANTON LA
Digital Harbour at Comtechport
Australia Post Mail Centre
LITTLE LONSDALE ST
MERRIMAN LA
ELLIOT LA
ALLISON LA
GOUGH AL
FOR MORE DETAIL SEE MAP 1
GUESTS LA
ST JOHNS LA
HARBOUR ESP
Car Park Ent 5&6
6.3m
LA TROBE ST
ROSE LA
RENDEN LA
UNIACKE CT
BROWN AL
HEFFERNAN LA
CROMBIE LA
THOMSON ST
LITTLE QUEEN ST
ST PATRICKS AL
Stadium Precinct
Steps
NE Entry
CLEVE LA
COSGRAVE LA
BOURKE PL
GRESHAM ST
RAMSAY LA
GOLDSBOROUGH LA
GRICE AL
LITTLE WILLIAM ST
Network 7
Gate 3
NM Entry
Telstra Dome
LITTLE BOURKE ST
LANGS LA
GALLAGHER PL
CHURCH ST
KITZ LA
COURT
Yacht Club
AFL House
Docklands Authority
Live Wire Entry
Gate 2
SE Entry
Car Park Ent 4
Steps
BOURKE ST
GODFREY ST
COLLINS ST
McCRACKENS LA
CHURCH ST
HENTY LA
JAMES LA
GURNERS
SW Entry
Lift
Fbr
LITTLE COLLINS ST
FRANCIS ST
Spencer Street (Proposed Station Redevelopment)
Rialto Towers
GEDDES LA
ESP
Victoria Point
Car Park Ent 1,2&3
STADIUM
DOCKLANDS
National Australia Bank
Proposed Road
BOURKE ST
Watergate
WATERVIEW WK
Bureau of Meteorology
Railway Goods Shed No.2
FLINDERS LA
DOWNIE ST
KATHERINE PL
HAY PL
HIGHLANDER LA
CUSTOM HOUSE LA
MERCANTILE PL
Gate
PIGOTT ST
Docklands Park
Batman's Hill
8.0m
WY
QUEENS WHARF RD
Yarra North Turning Basin
COLLINS ST
Lend Lease Victoria Harbour
Fox Classic Car Collection
(Event access only) DR
Village Docklands
4.0m
4.2m
Aquarium
FLINDERS ST
Melbourne Tunnel
Batman Park
KINGS BRIDGE
Boat Mooring
NORTH WHARF RD
Victoria Police Centre
Passport Office
Convention Centre
Heliport
Crown Entertainment Complex
Mission to Seafarers
SIDDELEY ST
GRIMES BRIDGE RD
Riverfront Apartments
World Trade Centre
SPENCER ST BRIDGE
KINGS WY
WEBB BRIDGE
Heliport
YARRA
CLARENDON ST
Cinema
Ent
South Wharf
South Wharf Events Warehouse
Melbourne Maritime Museum
Polly Woodside
Casino
7.46m
WHITEMAN ST
CHARLES GRIMES BRIDGE
Merchant Navy Monument
Tea House
LORIMER ST
Ent ST
Melbourne Exhibition Centre
Exit
Ent
CityLink Customer Service Centre
MAZDA CT
FERRARS ST
Mazda
WEST GATE FWY
5.64m
M1
Gates
SOUTHBANK
CLARKE ST
HAIG LA
CATHEDRAL
BRADY ST
BRADY ST
FORD ST
DORAN ST
7.85m
HAIG ST
HANCOCK
SOUTH MELBOURNE
MONTAGUE ST
SURVEYORS PL
MEADEN ST
CECIL ST
BLAKENEY
7.1m
WHITE ST
JOHNSON ST
MUNRO ST
NORMANBY ST
WOODGATE ST
GLADSTONE ST
KERR ST
FERRARS ST
DOUGLAS ST
WHITEMAN ST
CITY RD
BALLANTYNE ST
CHESSER ST

JOINS 18
JOINS 25
JOINS 30
FITZROY
St Vincents Hospital
MELBOURNE
Carlton Gardens
Royal Melbourne Institute of Technology (City Campus)
Old Melbourne Gaol
State Library
FOR MORE DETAIL SEE MAP 2
Parliament House
Parliament Gardens
State Government Offices
Treasury Gardens
Collins Place
Town Hall
City Square
Federation Square
Flinders Street
Birrarung Marr Park
Ferry Terminal
PRINCES BRIDGE
Alexandra Gardens
Queen Victoria Gardens
Kings Domain
Sidney Myer Music Bowl
Victorian Arts Centre
National Gallery of Victoria International Art
Victorian College of the Arts
Grant Street Theatre
School of Art
Victoria Barracks
FOR MORE DETAIL SEE MAP 3
FOR MORE DETAIL SEE MAP 4
Victoria University
Red Cross Blood Bank
Coronial Services Centre of Victoria
Playbox Theatre Centre Malthouse
Entrance & Exit to Crown Entertainment Complex Car Park
QUEENS BRIDGE
Riverside Quay
Esso House
Southgate
Sheraton Towers
IBM
Aust Ballet
Concert Hall
Yarra Footbridge
VICTORIA PDE
ALBERT ST
SPRING ST
NICHOLSON ST
EXHIBITION ST
RUSSELL ST
SWANSTON ST
LONSDALE ST
BOURKE ST
COLLINS ST
FLINDERS ST
KING ST
WILLIAM ST
QUEEN ST
ELIZABETH ST
MACARTHUR ST
WELLINGTON PDE S
BATMAN AV
ALEXANDRA AV
ST KILDA RD
SOUTHBANK BVD
CITY RD
KINGSWAY
LINLITHGOW AV
BURNLEY TUNNEL
DOMAIN TUNNEL
GOVERNMENT HOUSE DR
BIRDWOOD AV
ANZAC AV
COPYRIGHT © UNIVERSAL PRESS PTY LTD (PUBLISHER) 2004

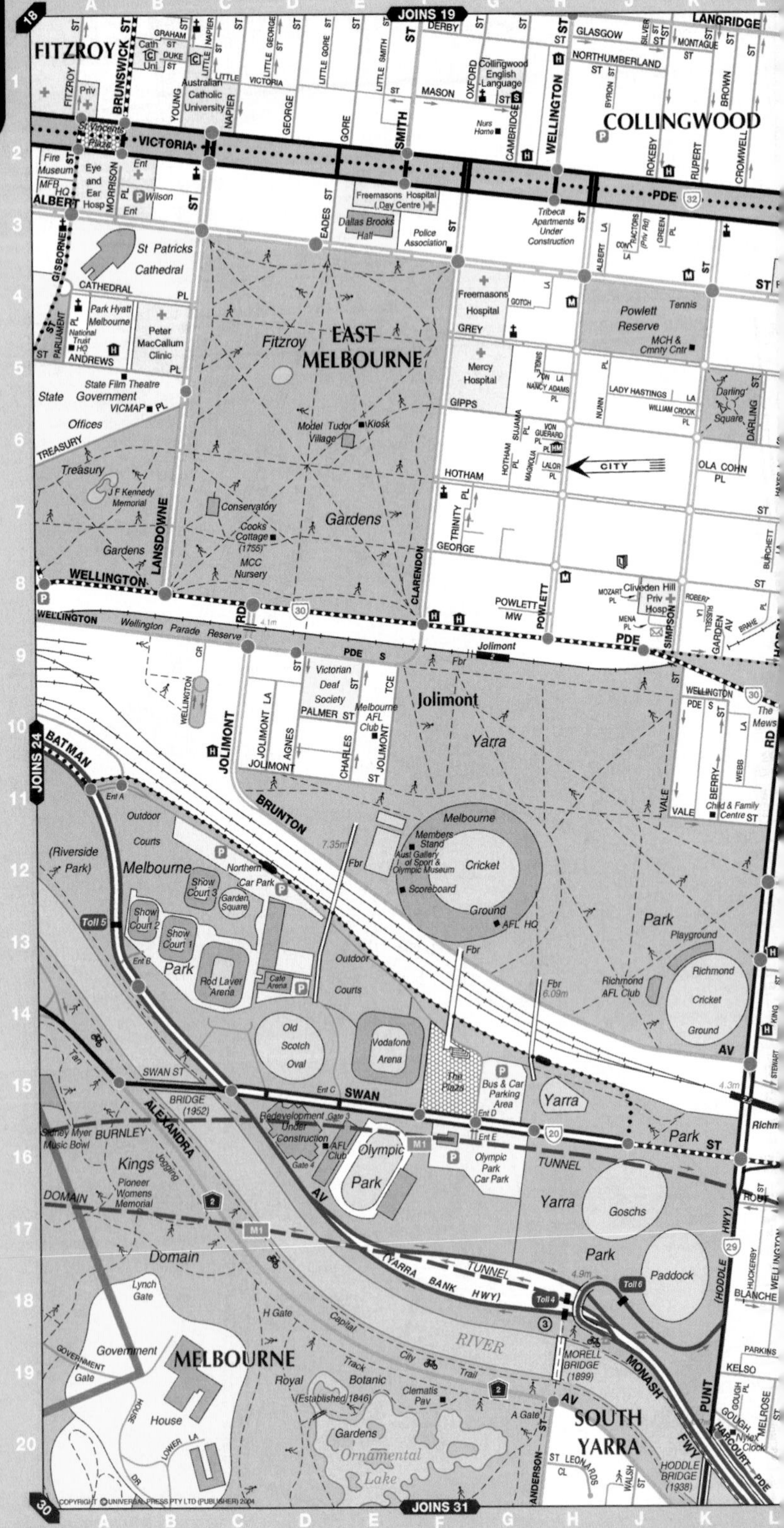

JOINS 19
JOINS 24
JOINS 31
18
30
A B C D E F G H J K L
1 2 3 4 5 6 7 8 9 10 11 12 13 14 15 16 17 18 19 20
FITZROY
COLLINGWOOD
EAST MELBOURNE
Jolimont
MELBOURNE
SOUTH YARRA
LANGRIDGE
GLASGOW
NORTHUMBERLAND
DERBY
MASON
MONTAGUE
GRAHAM
DUKE
BRUNSWICK ST
FITZROY
NAPIER
LITTLE NAPIER
YOUNG
LITTLE GEORGE
GEORGE
LITTLE GORE
GORE
LITTLE SMITH
SMITH ST
VICTORIA
OXFORD
CAMBRIDGE
WELLINGTON
BYRON
SILVER
ROKEBY
RUPERT
BROWN
CROMWELL
Cath Uni
Australian Catholic University
Priv
St Vincent's Plaza
Collingwood English Language
Nurs Home
PDE
Fire Museum
MFB HQ
ALBERT
Eye and Ear Hosp
MORRISON
Wilson
Ent
GISBORNE
EADES
Freemasons Hospital (Day Centre)
Dallas Brooks Hall
Police Association
Tribeca Apartments Under Construction
TRACTORS (Priv Rd)
GREEN
St Patricks Cathedral
CATHEDRAL
PL
Park Hyatt Melbourne
National Trust HQ
PARLIAMENT
ANDREWS
Peter MacCallum Clinic
Freemasons Hospital
GOTCH
GREY
Powlett Reserve
Tennis
MCH & Cmnty Cntr
Fitzroy
Mercy Hospital
GIPPS
NANCY ADAMS
LADY HASTINGS
WILLIAM CROOK
NUNN
Darling Square
DARLING
State Film Theatre
State Government Offices
VICMAP
TREASURY
Model Tudor Village
Kiosk
HOTHAM
SIJUAMA
MAGNOLIA
VON GUERARD
LALOR
CITY
OLA COHN
Treasury
J F Kennedy Memorial
Gardens
Conservatory
Cooks Cottage (1755)
MCC Nursery
LANSDOWNE
TRINITY
GEORGE
CLARENDON
POWLETT
POWLETT MW
BURCHETT
WELLINGTON
MOZART
Cliveden Hill Priv Hosp
MENA
SIMPSON
ROBERT
RUSSELL
GARDEN AV
BRAHE
Wellington Parade Reserve
RD
4.1m
30
Fbr
Victorian Deaf Society
PALMER ST
Melbourne AFL Club
TCE
JOLIMONT
JOLIMONT LA
AGNES
CHARLES
Yarra
The Mews
WEBB
BERRY
VALE
Child & Family Centre
BATMAN
BRUNTON
Ent A
Outdoor Courts
(Riverside Park)
Melbourne Park
Northern Car Park
Show Court 3
Garden Square
Show Court 2
Show Court 1
Rod Laver Arena
Cafe Arena
Toll 5
Ent B
7.35m
Melbourne Cricket Ground
Members Stand
Aust Gallery of Sport & Olympic Museum
Scoreboard
AFL HQ
Park
Playground
Richmond Cricket Ground
Richmond AFL Club
6.09m
Old Scotch Oval
Vodafone Arena
The Plaza
Bus & Car Parking Area
SWAN ST
SWAN
Ent C
Ent D
Ent E
ALEXANDRA
BRIDGE (1952)
Redevelopment Under Construction
AFL Club
Gate 3
Gate 4
Olympic Park
M1
Olympic Park Car Park
TUNNEL
Yarra Park
ST
AV
4.3m
STEWART
KING
Richm
Sidney Myer Music Bowl
BURNLEY
Kings Domain
Jogging
Pioneer Womens Memorial
DOMAIN
Tan
Goschs Paddock
(YARRA BANK HWY)
4.9m
Toll 4
Toll 6
29
(HODDLE HWY)
HUCKERBY
BLANCHE
Lynch Gate
H Gate
Capital City Trail
RIVER
Government House
GOVERNMENT
Gate
MORELL BRIDGE (1899)
MONASH FWY
PARKINS
KELSO
GOUGH PL
MELROSE
PUNT
Royal Botanic Gardens
(Established 1846)
Clematis Pav
A Gate
Ornamental Lake
ANDERSON ST
ST LEONARDS
CL
WALSH
HARCOURT
Nylex Clock
HODDLE BRIDGE (1938)
LOWER LA
DR
HOUSE
COPYRIGHT © UNIVERSAL PRESS PTY LTD (PUBLISHER) 2004

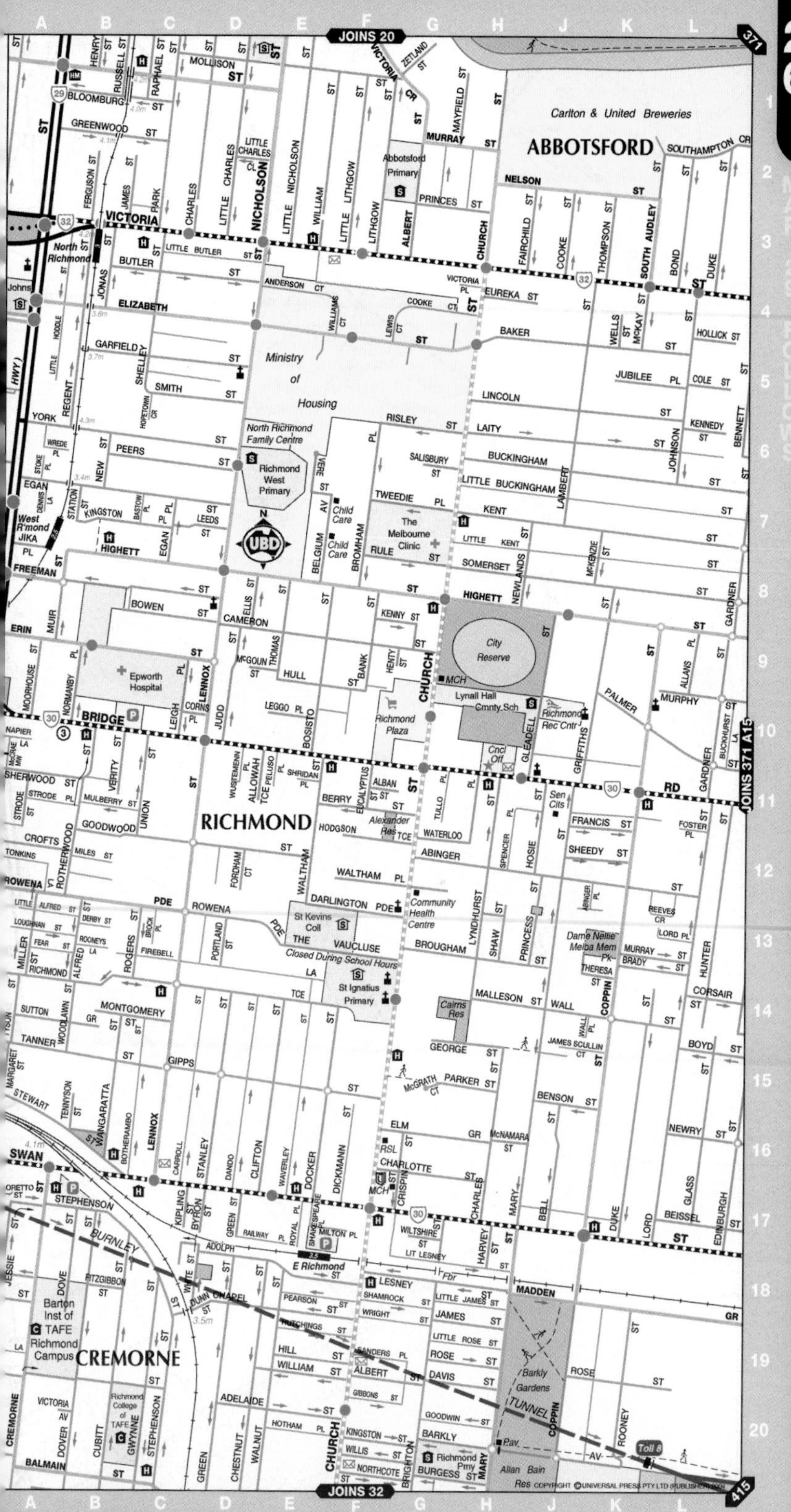

JOINS 20
JOINS 32
JOINS 371 A15
371
415
ABBOTSFORD
RICHMOND
CREMORNE
Carlton & United Breweries
Ministry of Housing
North Richmond Family Centre
Richmond West Primary
Abbotsford Primary
The Melbourne Clinic
City Reserve
Epworth Hospital
Richmond Plaza
Lynall Hall Cmnty Sch
Richmond Rec Cntr
St Kevins Coll
St Ignatius Primary
Community Health Centre
Dame Nellie Melba Mem Pk
Cairns Res
Alexander Res
Barkly Gardens
Allan Bain Res
Barton Inst of TAFE Richmond Campus
Richmond College of TAFE
Richmond Pmy
North Richmond
West R'mond
E Richmond
BURNLEY TUNNEL
Toll 6
Closed During School Hours
COPYRIGHT © UNIVERSAL PRESS PTY LTD (PUBLISHER) 2001
MAP 29 FOLLOWS

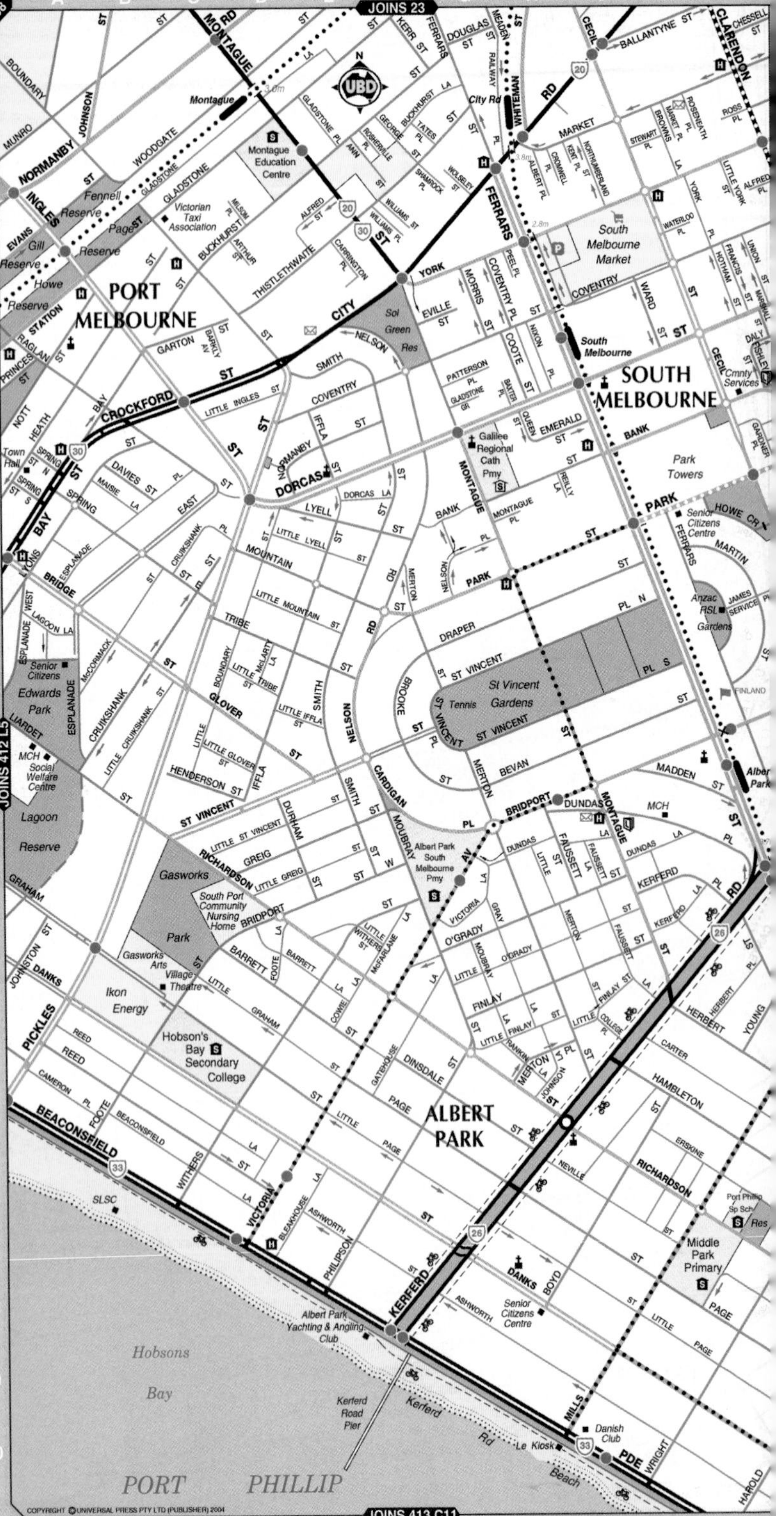

PORT MELBOURNE

SOUTH MELBOURNE

ALBERT PARK

Hobsons Bay

PORT PHILLIP

BOUNDARY ST
JOHNSON ST
MUNRO ST
NORMANBY RD
INGLES ST
EVANS ST
WOODGATE ST
GLADSTONE ST
Fennell Reserve
Gill Reserve
Page Reserve
Howe Reserve
Montague
MONTAGUE RD
Montague Education Centre
Victorian Taxi Association
BUCKHURST ST
NELSON PL
ARTHUR ST
THISTLETHWAITE ST
ALFRED ST
CARRINGTON PL
WILLIAMS ST
GLADSTONE PL
ANN ST
GEORGE ST
ROSHERVILLE PL
BUCKHURST LA
TATES PL
SHAMROCK PL
WOLSELEY ST
KERR ST
FERRARS ST
DOUGLAS ST
MEADEN ST
RAILWAY PL
City Rd
WHITEMAN ST
CITY RD
CECIL ST
BALLANTYNE ST
CLARENDON ST
CHESSELL ST
MARKET ST
ALBERT PL
CROMWELL PL
KENT PL
NORTHUMBERLAND ST
STEWART PL
BROWNS LA
MARKET PL
ROSENEATH PL
ROSS PL
LITTLE YORK ST
ALFRED PL
YORK ST
WATERLOO PL
South Melbourne Market
COVENTRY ST
WARD ST
HOTHAM ST
FRANCIS ST
UNION ST
MARSHALL ST
DALY ST
ASHLEY ST
Cmnty Services
South Melbourne
PEEL PL
MORRIS ST
COVENTRY PL
COOTE ST
NIXON PL
EVILLE ST
Sol Green Res
NELSON RD
PATTERSON PL
GLADSTONE GR
BAXTER PL
STATION ST
RAGLAN ST
PRINCES ST
GARTON ST
BARKLY AV
SMITH ST
COVENTRY ST
LITTLE INGLES ST
CROCKFORD ST
BAY ST
NOTT ST
HEATH ST
Town Hall
SPRING ST N
SPRING ST S
DAVIES ST
MAISIE LA
EAST ST
NORMANBY ST
IFFLA ST
DORCAS ST
DORCAS LA
LYELL ST
LITTLE LYELL ST
EMERALD ST
QUEEN ST
Galilee Regional Cath Pmy
REILLY ST
BANK ST
Park Towers
PARK ST
HOWE CR
Senior Citizens Centre
MARTIN ST
JAMES SERVICE PL
Anzac RSL Gardens
FINLAND
LYONS ST
BRIDGE ST
ESPLANADE WEST
ESPLANADE EAST
LAGOON LA
CRUIKSHANK ST
MOUNTAIN ST
LITTLE MOUNTAIN ST
MERTON ST
NELSON RD
PARK ST
MONTAGUE PL
DRAPER ST
ST VINCENT PL N
ST VINCENT PL S
St Vincent Gardens
Tennis
BROOKE ST
TRIBE ST
LITTLE TRIBE ST
McLARTY LA
BOUNDARY ST
McCORMACK ST
Senior Citizens
Edwards Park
LIARDET ST
MCH
Social Welfare Centre
Lagoon Reserve
GLOVER ST
LITTLE GLOVER ST
LITTLE IFFLA ST
LITTLE CRUIKSHANK ST
HENDERSON ST
CARDIGAN ST
BEVAN ST
MADDEN ST
Albert Park
ST VINCENT ST
LITTLE ST VINCENT PL
DURHAM ST
GREIG ST
LITTLE GREIG ST
RICHARDSON ST
MOUBRAY ST
BRIDPORT ST
DUNDAS PL
DUNDAS LA
FAUSSETT ST
FAUSSETT LA
KERFERD PL
KERFERD RD
Albert Park South Melbourne Pmy
VICTORIA AV
GRAY ST
O'GRADY ST
LITTLE O'GRADY ST
FINLAY ST
FINLAY PL
LITTLE FINLAY ST
RANKIN LA
COLLEGE PL
LITTLE COLLEGE PL
GRAHAM ST
Gasworks Park
South Port Community Nursing Home
Gasworks Arts Village Theatre
BARRETT ST
FOOTE LA
LITTLE WITHERS ST
McFARLANE LA
COWIE LA
Ikon Energy
Hobson's Bay Secondary College
JOHNSTON ST
DANKS ST
PICKLES ST
REED ST
CAMERON PL
BEACONSFIELD PDE
GATEHOUSE ST
DINSDALE ST
PAGE ST
LITTLE PAGE ST
HERBERT ST
YOUNG ST
CARTER ST
HAMBLETON ST
ERSKINE ST
NEVILLE ST
Port Phillip Sp Sch
Res
Middle Park Primary
WITHERS ST
SLSC
BLEAKHOUSE LA
ASHWORTH ST
PHILIPSON ST
BOYD ST
Senior Citizens Centre
Albert Park Yachting & Angling Club
Kerferd Road Pier
Kerferd Rd Beach
MILLS ST
Danish Club
Le Kiosk
WRIGHT ST
HAROLD ST

JOINS 412 L5

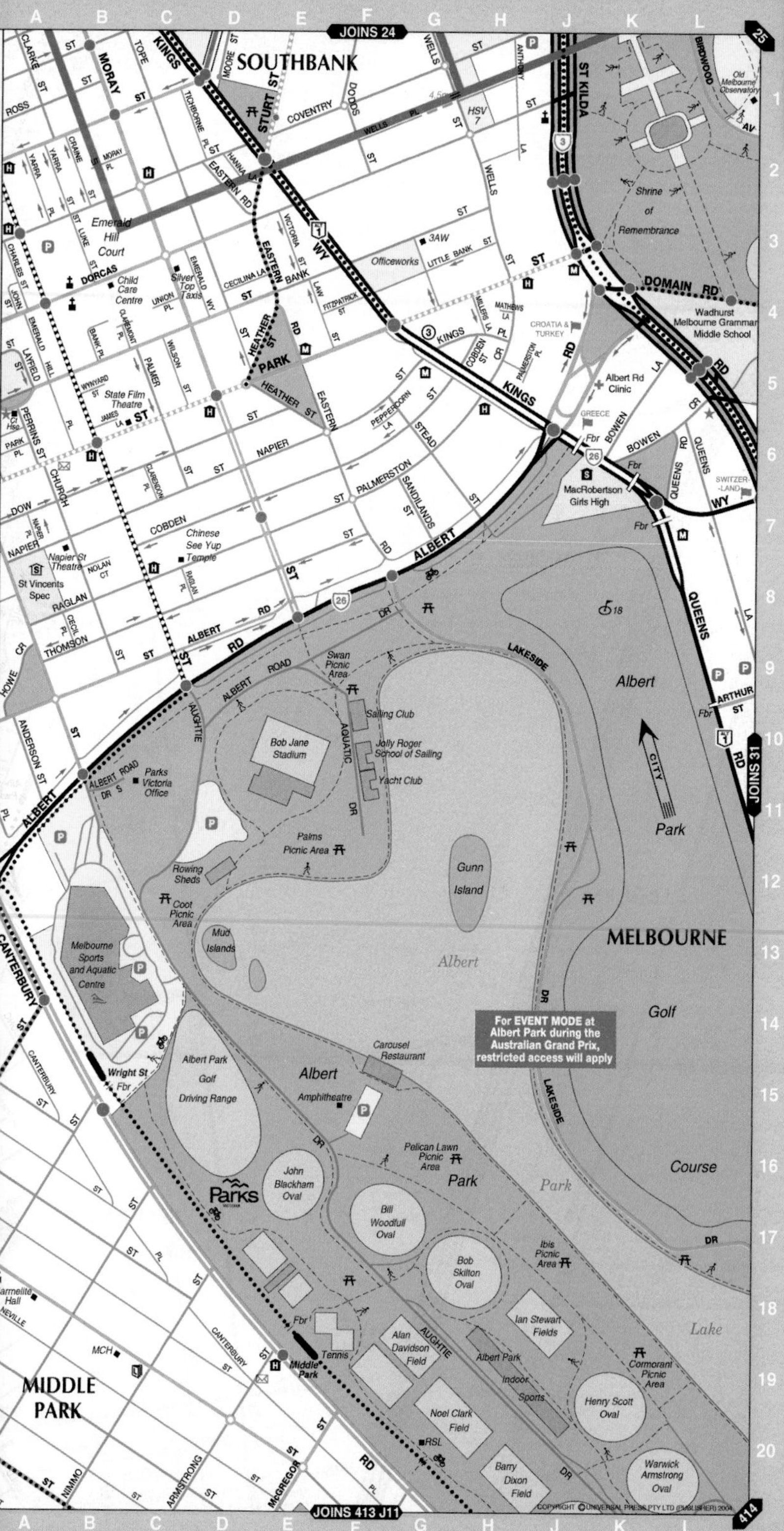
JOINS 24
SOUTHBANK
Emerald Hill Court
Shrine of Remembrance
Old Melbourne Observatory
Wadhurst Melbourne Grammar Middle School
Officeworks
3AW
HSV 7
Child Care Centre
Silver Top Taxis
State Film Theatre
Croatia & Turkey
Greece
Switzerland
Albert Rd Clinic
MacRobertson Girls High
Chinese See Yup Temple
Napier St Theatre
St Vincents Spec
Swan Picnic Area
Sailing Club
Jolly Roger School of Sailing
Yacht Club
Bob Jane Stadium
Parks Victoria Office
Palms Picnic Area
Rowing Sheds
Coot Picnic Area
Mud Islands
Gunn Island
Albert
Melbourne Sports and Aquatic Centre
MELBOURNE
Golf
Course
For EVENT MODE at Albert Park during the Australian Grand Prix, restricted access will apply
Carousel Restaurant
Albert Amphitheatre
Albert Park Golf Driving Range
Wright St
Pelican Lawn Picnic Area
Park
John Blackham Oval
Bill Woodfull Oval
Bob Skilton Oval
Ibis Picnic Area
Ian Stewart Fields
Alan Davidson Field
Albert Park Indoor Sports
Cormorant Picnic Area
Henry Scott Oval
Noel Clark Field
Barry Dixon Field
Warwick Armstrong Oval
Lake
Tennis
Middle Park
MIDDLE PARK
Carmelite Hall
MCH
RSL
KINGS WY
ST KILDA RD
DOMAIN RD
QUEENS RD
ALBERT RD
CITY
LAKESIDE DR
AUGHTIE DR
AQUATIC DR
CANTERBURY RD
JOINS 31
JOINS 413 J11
COPYRIGHT © UNIVERSAL PRESS PTY LTD (PUBLISHER) 2004

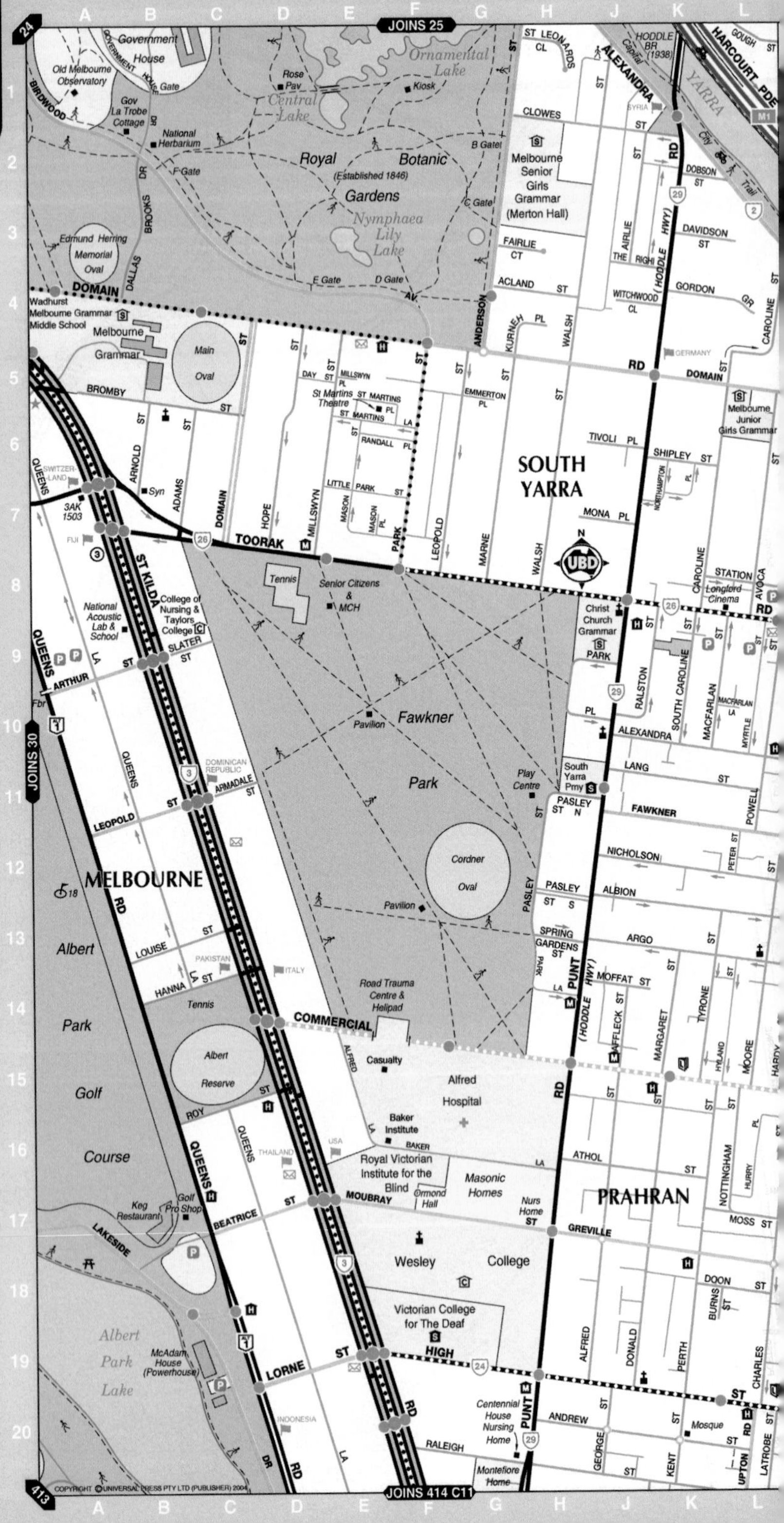

JOINS 25
24

A B C D E F G H J K L

Government House
Government House Gate
Old Melbourne Observatory
Birdwood
Gov La Trobe Cottage
National Herbarium
F Gate
Dallas Brooks Dr
Rose Pav
Central Lake
Ornamental Lake
Kiosk
Royal Botanic Gardens (Established 1846)
B Gate
C Gate
Nymphaea Lily Lake
E Gate
D Gate
Edmund Herring Memorial Oval
Domain Av
Wadhurst Melbourne Grammar Middle School
Melbourne Grammar
Main Oval
Bromby St
Arnold St
Adams St
Syn
Domain St
Hope St
Millswyn St
Day St
Millswyn Pl
St Martins Theatre
St Martins Pl
St Martins La
Randall Pl
Little Park St
Mason St
Mason Pl
Park St
Leopold St
Emmerton Pl
Marne St
Anderson St
Kurneh Pl
Walsh St
St Leonards Cl
Alexandra Av
Capital City Trail
Hoddle Br (1938)
Harcourt Pde
Gough St
Yarra
Syria
M1
Clowes St
Melbourne Senior Girls Grammar (Merton Hall)
Fairlie Ct
Acland St
Airlie St
The Righi
Witchwood Cl
Dobson St
Davidson St
Gordon Gr
Caroline St
Germany
Domain Rd
Melbourne Junior Girls Grammar
Tivoli Pl
Shipley St
Northampton Pl
Mona Pl
SOUTH YARRA
Punt Rd (Hoddle Hwy)
29
2
Queens Rd
Switzerland
3AK 1503
Fiji
3
St Kilda Rd
26
Toorak Rd
Tennis
Senior Citizens & MCH
College of Nursing & Taylors College
National Acoustic Lab & School
Slater St
Arthur St
Queens La
Fbr
Station St
Longford Cinema
Avoca
Christ Church Grammar
Park St
Ralston St
South Caroline St
Macfarlan St
Macfarlan La
Myrtle
Alexandra Pl
Fawkner Park
Pavilion
Play Centre
Cordner Oval
Pavilion
Pasley St
South Yarra Pmy
Pasley St N
Pasley St S
Lang St
Fawkner St
Powell
Nicholson St
Peter St
Albion St
Spring St
Gardens Park La
Argo St
Moffat St
Affleck St
Margaret St
Tyrone St
Hyland
Moore St
Hardy
Dominican Republic
Armadale St
Leopold St
MELBOURNE
Albert Park Golf Course
Louise St
Hanna St
Pakistan
Italy
Tennis
Albert Reserve
Commercial Rd
Road Trauma Centre & Helipad
Alfred St
Casualty
Alfred Hospital
Baker Institute
Baker La
Roy St
Queens Rd
Queens La
Thailand
USA
Royal Victorian Institute for the Blind
Ormond Hall
Masonic Homes
Nurs Home
Athol St
Nottingham St
Hurry Pl
PRAHRAN
Moss St
Keg Restaurant
Golf Pro Shop
Beatrice St
Moubray St
Greville St
Lakeside Dr
Wesley College
Doon St
Burns St
Victorian College for The Deaf
High St
Albert Park Lake
McAdam House (Powerhouse)
Lorne St
Indonesia
Centennial House Nursing Home
Andrew St
Alfred
Donald
Perth
Charles
George St
Kent St
Mosque
Upton Rd
Latrobe St
Raleigh St
Montefiore Home
Queens Dr
Queens La
St Kilda Rd
1
24

JOINS 30
413
JOINS 414 C11

JOINS 26
371
CREMORNE
RICHMOND
Richmond TAFE
BALMAIN
BENT
DOVER
CUBITT
MUNRO
GWYNNE
PALMER
Charles Evans Res
WILLIS
NORTHCOTE
COTTER
GORDON
AMSTERDAM
WILLOW
NEWTON
YORKSHIRE
YARRA
DALE
PRINCE
PATRICK
HOWARD
Richmond Pmy
BURGESS
BARKLY
Allan Bain Reserve
Citipower Terminal
McConchie Res
Ped Upass
BRIGHTON
DURHAM
MARY
Toll 8
Toll 7
FWY
M1
MONASH
CITYLINK
RIVER
Quarry Reserve
Herring Island
Parks
Herring Reserve
Boat Sheds
Thomas Oval
Como Park North
Como Reserve
Jetty
Como Landing
Pavilion
Como Park
ALEXANDRA
AV
Capital City Trail
Darling Gardens
Melbourne High
CLAREMONT
MURPHY
DARLING
South Yarra
YARRA
CLAREMONT
FORREST HILL
DALY
ALMA
ATV Channel 10
Como Centre
Cinema
COPELEN
VICTORIA TCE
MALCOLM
RIVER
ROCKLEY
Rockley Gardens
KENSINGTON
COMO
FULHAM
Como House
LECHLADE
TOORAK
RD
TIVOLI
TIME LA
JOINS 415
PENNY LA
OXFORD
BOND
CHAMBERS
WILLIAM
Reserve
CHAPEL
FORSTER
CUNNINGHAM
CLARA
PALERMO
SURREY
DRAIN RESERVE
CROMWELL
STANLEY
STANHOPE
NORMAN
BUNALBO
Tennis
COOLULLAH
WALTER
HAWKSBURY
QUAMBY
ARTHUR
FITZGERALD
DAVISON
St Josephs
MEDLEY
ROCKY LA
Cinema Jam Factory
Cncl Depot & SES Rubbish Tip
HOPETOUN
THE VAUCLUSE
MAY GR
Hawksburn
CASSELL
WOODSIDE CR
WILLIAMS
GARDEN
WILSON
HOWARD
Grosvenor St Res
SCOTIA
ELLIS
GROSVENOR
RAILWAY
Polyglot Theatre
HAWKSBURN
OBAN
Hawksburn
LUXTON
GORDON
TASHINNY
SMYTH
ASHE
BARRY
HAZELDON
OAK
PALFREYMAN
SIMMONS
PERRY
ELIZABETH
BALMORAL
GREY
Ministry of Housing
SIMMONS
BROWNING
MOTHERWELL
BARNSBURY
JOY
EVELINA
OSBORNE
Prahran Market
MARKET
MALVERN
BRAY
CAVENDISH
HOWITT
McKILLOP
HOBSON
MAY
SAMS WY
Pran Tenpin Central
Rec Centre
Victoria House Private Hospital
WATTLE
CARLTON
Grattan Gardens
CATO
WALKER
Tennis
SUMMERS
CLARKE
FRANCIS
DIXON
MILLER
ROBINSON
GRATTAN
IZETT
CHATHAM
PRINCES
LITTLE CHAPEL
Child Care
Princes Gardens
ESSEX
BELLA
BENDIGO
LEILA
MACKAY
IRENE
ERROL
WESTBOURNE
CONTINENTAL WY
Town Hall
KING
Civic Centre
CECIL
ANCHOR
MURRAY
SPRING
WRIGHTS
YORK
Nurs Home
PORTER
PERCY
EDMONDS
MACQUARIE
MATTHEWS
MAPLES LA
HILLINGDON
CLIFTON
MOUNT
REGENT
BANGS
ST MALO
PRIDHAM
BAYVIEW
Aberdeen Res
ABERDEEN
HIGH
Swinburne University of Technology
THOMAS
VICTORIA
RSL
IVY
LEWISHAM
Victoria Gardens
TRINIAN
JOINS 414 J11
415
COPYRIGHT © UNIVERSAL PRESS PTY LTD (PUBLISHER) 2004

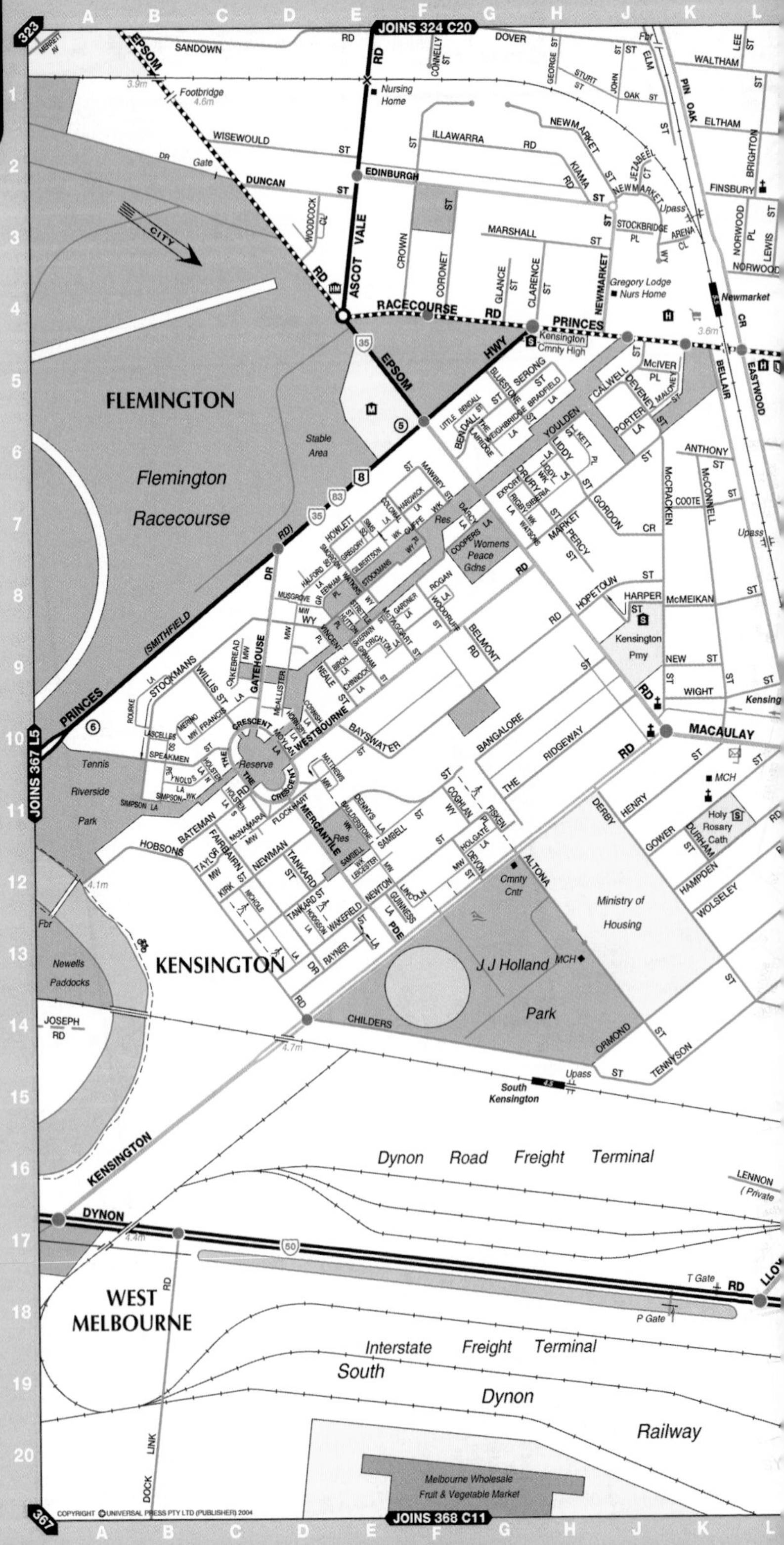
JOINS 324 C20
FLEMINGTON
Flemington Racecourse
KENSINGTON
WEST MELBOURNE
Dynon Road Freight Terminal
Interstate Freight Terminal
South Dynon Railway
Melbourne Wholesale Fruit & Vegetable Market
J J Holland Park
Ministry of Housing
Tennis
Riverside Park
Newells Paddocks
Stable Area
Womens Peace Gdns
Kensington Pmy
Holy Rosary Cath
Gregory Lodge Nurs Home
Nursing Home
Kensington Cmnty High
Cmnty Cntr
South Kensington
Newmarket
PRINCES HWY
RACECOURSE RD
EPSOM RD
ASCOT VALE RD
MACAULAY RD
DYNON RD
KENSINGTON RD
SMITHFIELD RD
JOINS 367 L5
JOINS 368 C11

JOINS 324 J20

PARKVILLE

NORTH MELBOURNE

Royal Park · Debneys Park · Ministry of Housing · Terminal Station · Moonee Ponds Creek · Flemington Bridge · Dynon Bridge · North Melbourne Cricket Ground · National Gallery of Victoria · Womens Recreation Centre · VBA Baseball Ross Straw Field · VAHA Hockey Fields · Netball Stadium · Delhi Reserve · Clayton Res · Gardiner Res · Lost Dogs Home · Council Depot · AFL Club · St Brendans Catholic Pmy · St Aloysius Catholic · Debney Meadows Pmy · AADE & Circus Oz · CityLink · Toll 2

ALEXANDER PDE · FLEMINGTON RD · RACECOURSE RD · MT ALEXANDER RD · ELLIOTT AV · BOUNDARY RD · MACAULAY RD · DYNON RD · ARDEN ST · VICTORIA ST · QUEENSBERRY ST · SPENCER ST · DRYBURGH ST · ABBOTSFORD ST · CANNING ST · ERSKINE ST · MARK ST · SUTTON ST · ALFRED ST · HARDIMAN ST · CHELMSFORD ST · STUBBS ST · WELLINGTON ST · MELROSE ST · HAINES ST · O'SHANASSY ST · LANGFORD ST · BENT ST

JOINS 17

JOINS 368 J11

COPYRIGHT © UNIVERSAL PRESS PTY LTD (PUBLISHER) 2004

41

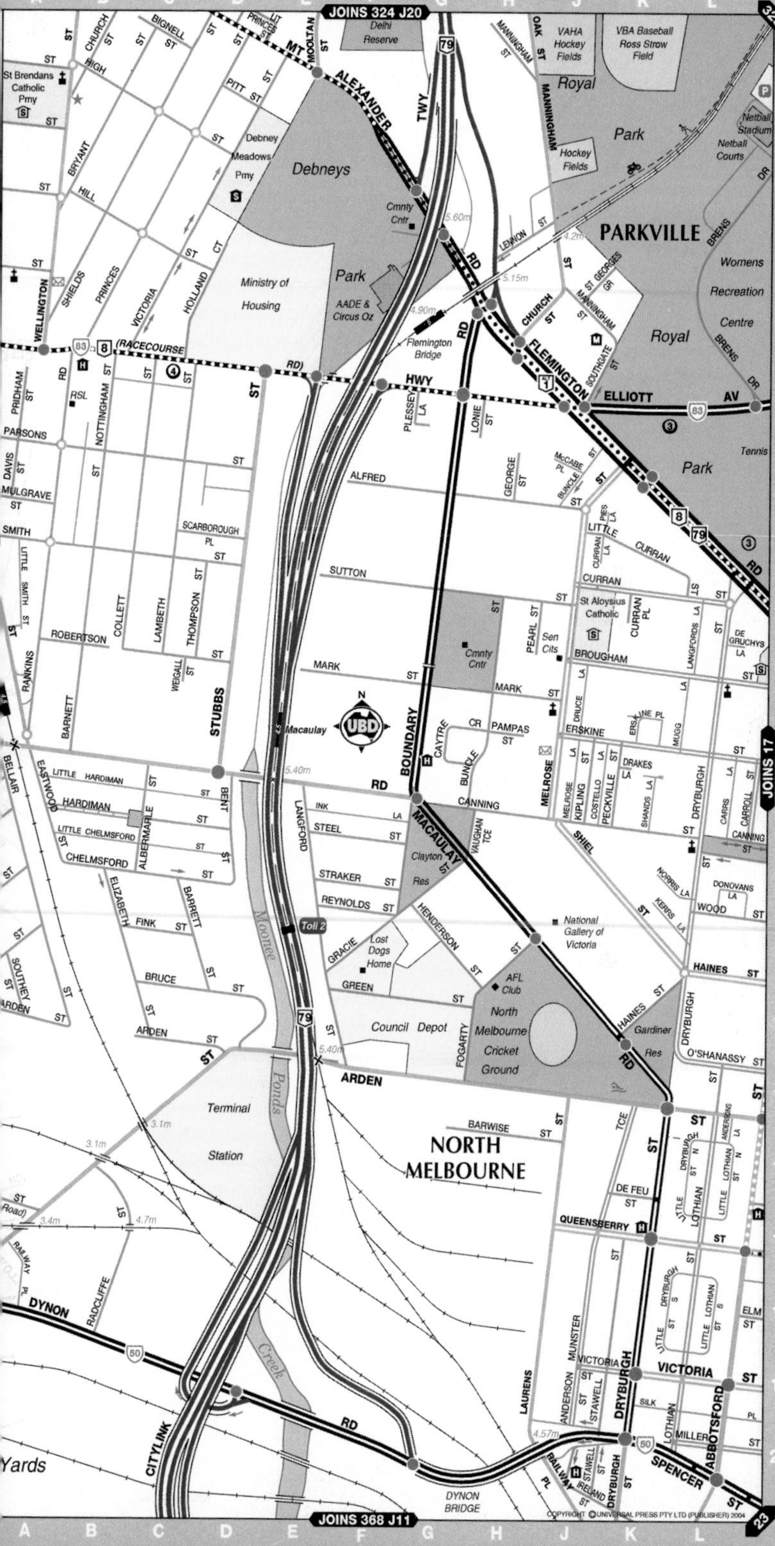

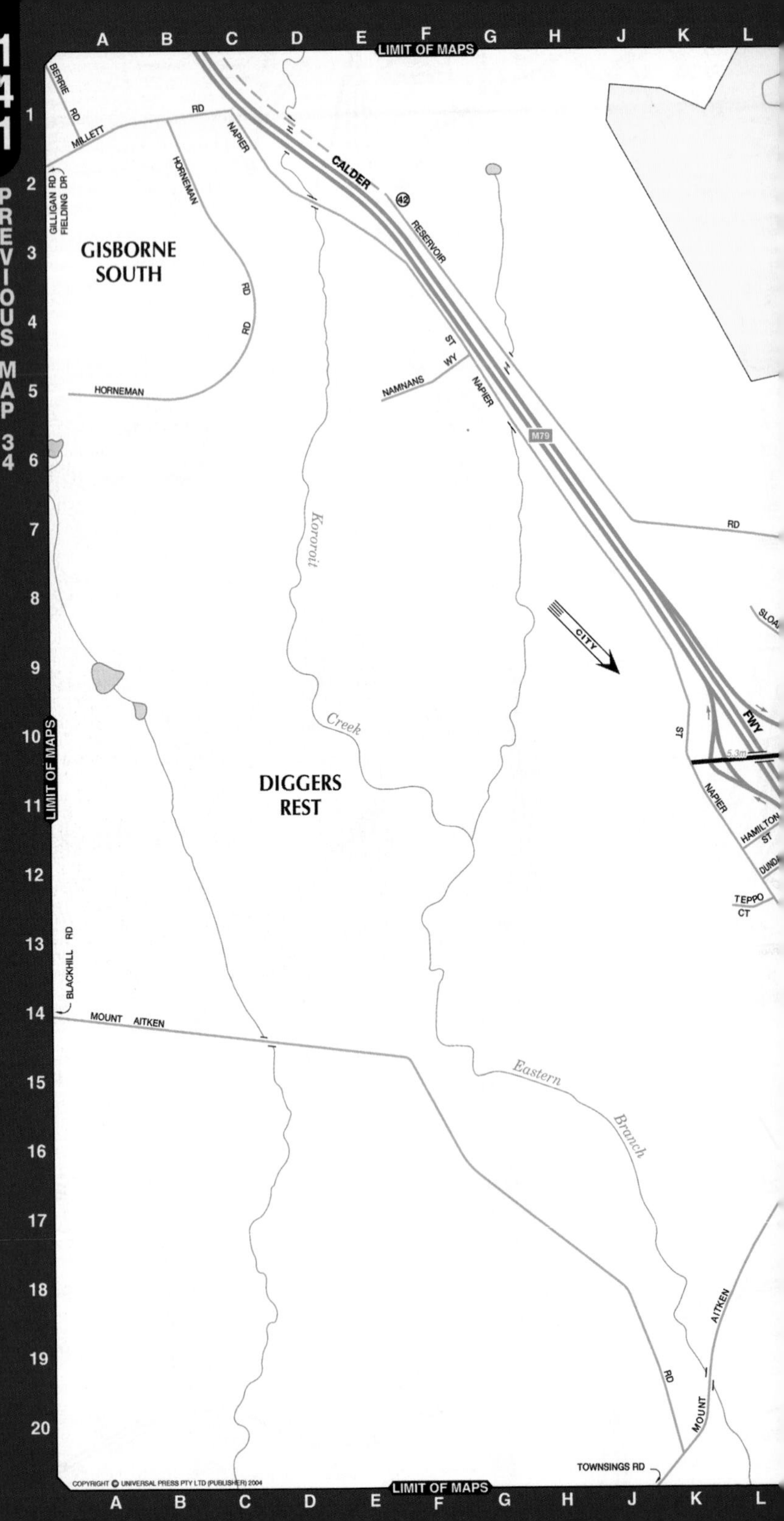
A B C D E F G H J K L
LIMIT OF MAPS
BERRIE RD
MILLETT RD
NAPIER
HORNEMAN
CALDER
42
RESERVOIR
GILLIGAN RD
FIELDING DR
GISBORNE SOUTH
RD
RD
ST
WY
NAMNANS
NAPIER
HORNEMAN
M79
RD
Kororoit
SLOAN
CITY
FWY
Creek
ST
5.3m
NAPIER
DIGGERS REST
HAMILTON ST
DUNDA
TEPPO CT
BLACKHILL RD
MOUNT AITKEN
Eastern
Branch
AITKEN
RD
MOUNT
TOWNSINGS RD
LIMIT OF MAPS
PREVIOUS MAP 34
1 2 3 4 5 6 7 8 9 10 11 12 13 14 15 16 17 18 19 20

Sunbury Landfill & Recycling Centre

SUNBURY

Reserve
Reserve
Reserve
Reservoir
The Common
Killara Primary
Heysen Drive
Reserve
Eric Boardman Memorial Reserve
Pav
Basketball Stadium
Sunbury Heights Primary
Sunbury Downs Sec Coll
Pavilion
Soccer & Hockey Gnds
Langama Park
Jeh Wit
MCH
Res
CFA

Blind Creek

OLD RIDDELL RD
RIDDELL RD
C743
KESWICK
RIVERVIEW TCE
CANTERBURY
POSSUM TAIL RUN
BUNDANOON RI
SAXONWOOD LA
SAXONWOOD DR
WALLABY WK
AV
SMITH CT
MILGATE TCE
GREENHILL CT
DOUTNEY CT
LONG DR
FULLBROOK DR
BATES CT
SOLOMON CT
WESTALL CL
LYNN MW
HAXTON CT
NIMO CT
ISTER CR
LAWRENCE DR
PHILLIP DR
WALKER CT
BANNON AV
JAMES CL
MILAN CT
STEWARTS LA
OFFICER CT
STRACHEN DR
COATES CT
DIDSWELL CT
STREETON CT
REES RD
BRIERLY CT
ALLEN CT
DALKEITH CT
BALMORAL CCT
LONGSTAFF DR
MUNCH PL
MOLVIG RI
WY
NORLING MW
WHEELER CT
HANKE PL
CASSAB MW
FULLWOOD DR
PIDGEON CT
DAWN GR
JELIMAR CT
TRACIE CT
KATHRYN CT
KERRISDALE PL
RESERVOIR RD
CITY VW
VIEW TCE
MOUNT DR
CARLA VW
BAKER RI
OLIVE
ANTHONY ST
ROBERTS CT
DARGIE CT
LA
ATKINSON CL
McGEORGE CT
CONDOR
MELBA
GIBSON CT
RAMSAY CT
HARCOURT CL
BUSH PL
RICHARDSON AV
BLYTON CR
CRAWFORD WY
BLACKMAN CL
TANNER PL
KEMP AV
WRIGHT
HEYSEN DR
MUDIE AV
WITHERS
GRUNER CL
HARCOMBE DR
DYSON
MARTENS CT
OLSON PL
MAY GR
MELBA AV
HERBERT CR
KENDALL CT
BUCKMASTER ST
UNDERHILL CT
SANDLEFORD CT
WINDARRA CT
BARADINE
DRYSDALE ST
FELTON AV
McCUBBIN
MELDRUM CT
ASHTON CT
TIMMS CT
NOLAN AV
WAINEWRIGHT CT
HILL GR
ABELIA CT
DR
DOBELL CT
LINDSAY CT
COUNIHAN CT
ANNOIS CT
DUNDAS AV
LAMBERT
RONALD CT
RESERVOIR RD
CT
WILEMAN
GAP RD
C707
NICHOL ST
REGENT ST
PRESTON ST
GORDON ST
ROVER ST
BOWEN CT
DOWLING CT
ST
FREMANTLE RD
GOSSE CT
COWPER CR
SYME CT
TORRES DR
LANDSBOROUGH DR
DARWIN ST
FORREST ST
KEITH
MARJORIE AV
AV
BENNETT CT
SEVERINO PL
DALY
CHARTER RD
W
CHARTER
AUSTIN CL
TASMAN ST
FITZROY ST
LEARMONTH PEGGY ST
REGHON DR
OVENS CT
RD
39 SOMERSET ST
CALDER
WILSONS
JUNE ST
DOLAN CT
LEICHARDT ST
BURKE CT
LIGHT RD
RAGLAN ST
CHARLES ST
MITCHELLS LA
McCOMB ST
COLLINS ST
GIBBONS ST
MELLON CT
TOWER CT
REGHON CR
SIMPSON DR
ELIZABETH
GREGORY CT
DEAKIN ST
MOORE
BARRINGTON
MITCHELLS DR
PONSFORD PL
O'NEILL PL
BVD
LA
SLATER CT
NOBLE CT
CHAPPELL CT
BRADMAN
ARCHER AV
ALDERMAN
STACKPOLE CR
MARSH CR
RD
WY
BENAUD PL
BRADMAN DR
O'REILLY CT
CL
MORRIS CT
HEALY AV
LA
REDPATH CT
BRA DR
TRUMPER CR
BORDER
MANNING CT
HOBSON CT
DAVENPORT DR
ANGAS CT
LALOR CR
BACKHAUS AV
AGAR PL
M79
FWY
RD

JOINS 143

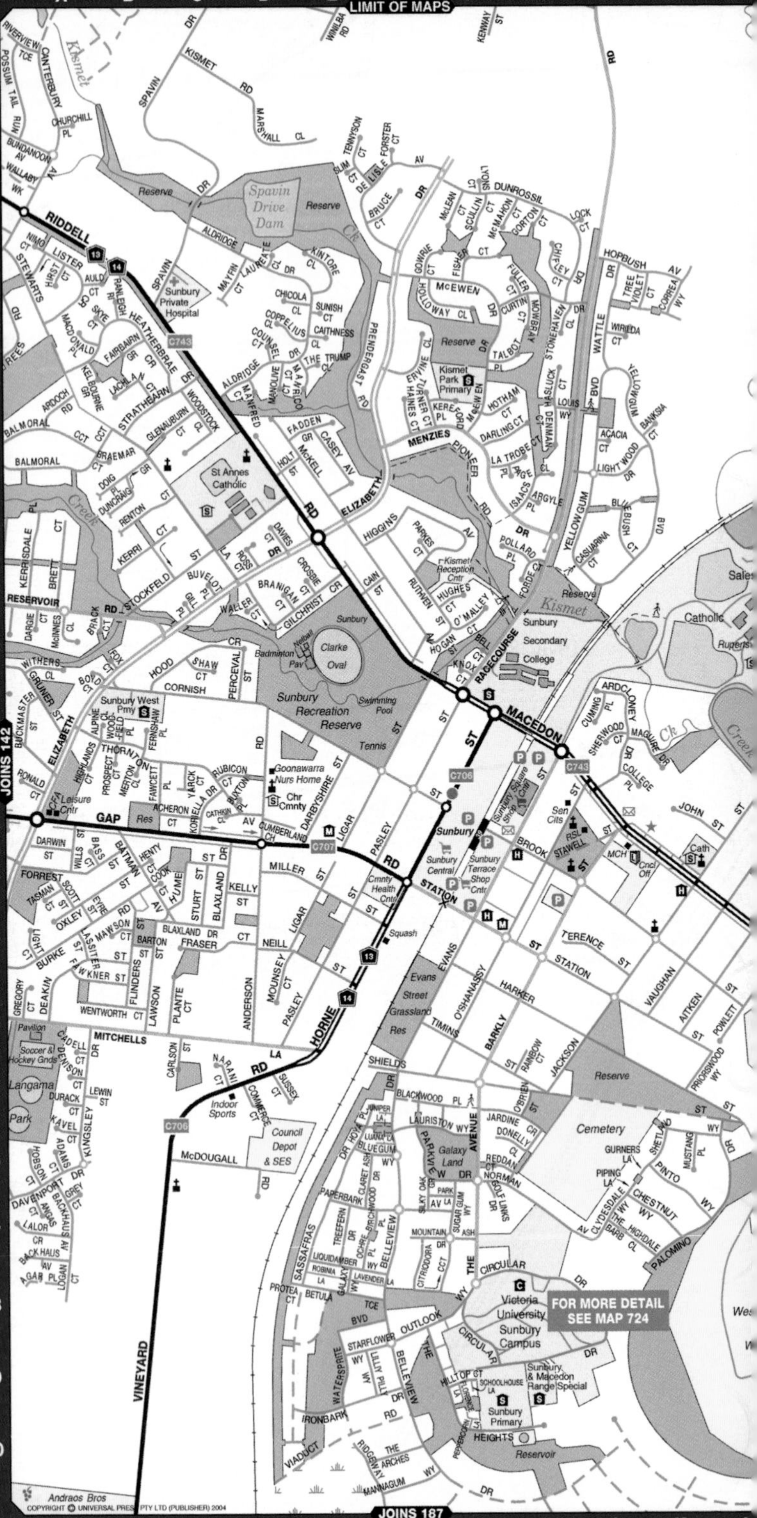

A B C D E F G H J K L

LIMIT OF MAPS

1 2 3 4 5 6 7 8 9 10 11 12 13 14 15 16 17 18 19 20

JOINS 142

RIVERVIEW TCE
POSSUM TAIL RUN
CANTERBURY
CHURCHILL PL
BUNDANOON AV
WALLABY WK
Kismet
SPAVIN DR
KISMET RD
MARSHALL CL
WINILBA RD
KENWAY ST
TENNYSON CT
FORSTER CT
SUM CT
DE LISLE CT
BRUCE CT
Spavin Drive Dam
Reserve
ALDRIDGE
MAYFIN CT
LAUREATE CL
KINTORE DR
CHICOLA CL
SUNISH CT
COPPELIUS CL
CAITHNESS
COUNSEL CT
THE TRUMP CL
PRENDERGAST RD
RIDDELL RD
NIMO CT
LISTER
HIRST CT
STEWARTS RD
AULD CT
RANLEIGH RI
SKYE CT
MACDONALD GR
FAIRBAIRN GR
HEATHERBRAE CR
LACHLAN
KELBOURNE GR
STRATHEARN DR
WOODSTOCK
ARDOCH RD
BALMORAL CCT
GLENAUBURN CT
BRAEMAR CT
DOIG CT
DUNCRAIG CT
RENTON CT
KERRI CT
STOCKFELD
BUVELOT ST
GILL PL
Sunbury Private Hospital
St Annes Catholic
MANFRED
MANOLIVE CT
MANRICO CT
FADDEN GR
CASEY AV
McKELL ST
HOLT ST
ELIZABETH
HIGGINS
DAVIES CT
ROSS CT
CROSBIE CT
BRANIGAN CT
GILCHRIST CR
WALLER CT
CAIN ST
PARKES CT
RUTHVEN
HUGHES CT
O'MALLEY
HOGAN CT
BELL
Kismet Reception Cntr
GOWRIE CT
McEWEN
HOLLOWAY CL
FISHER CT
McLEAN CT
SCULLIN CT
LYONS CT
DUNROSSIL
McMAHON CT
GORTON CT
CHIFLEY CT
FULLER CT
CURTIN CT
MOWBRAY
TALBOT PL
STONEHAVEN CL
HASLUCK CT
DENMAN
LOUIS WY
Kismet Park Primary
ERVINE CL
TURNER CT
HAINES CT
KEREFORD PL
McEWEN
HOTHAM CT
DARLING CT
LA TROBE CT
PAGE CL
ISAACS PL
ARGYLE
MENZIES
PIONEER RD
POLLARD PL
FORDE CT
HOPBUSH
TREE VIOLET CT
CORREA WY
WIRILDA CT
WATTLE BVD
YELLOWGUM
BANKSIA CT
ACACIA CT
LIGHT WOOD DR
BLUE BUSH CT
CASUARINA CT
YELLOW GUM
Sales
Catholic
Rupertswood
Kismet
Reserve
Sunbury Secondary College
RACECOURSE
KNOX CT
MACEDON
ARDCLONEY
CUMING PL
SHERWOOD CT
MAGUIRE DR
COLLEGE PL
Ck
Creek
JOHN ST
KERRISDALE CT
BRETT CT
RESERVOIR RD
DARGIE CT
McINNES CL
BRACK CT
FOX CT
WITHERS CL
GRUNER ST
BOYD CT
HOOD CR
SHAW CT
CORNISH
PERCEVAL ST
Sunbury
Clarke Oval
Badminton
Netball Pav
Sunbury Recreation Reserve
Swimming Pool
Tennis
BUCKMASTER ST
Sunbury West Pmy
ALPINE CT
WOODFIELD CT
FERNSHAW PL
HIGHLANDS
THORNTON
PROSPECT CT
MERTON CT
FAWCETT PL
YARCK CT
RUBICON CT
BUXTON PL
Goonawarra Nurs Home
Chr Cmnty
DARBYSHIRE ST
RONALD CT
CFA
Leisure Cntr
GAP RD
Res
ACHERON CT
KORIELLA DR
CATHKIN PL
AV
CUMBERLAND CH
LIGAR
PASLEY
DARWIN ST
WILLS ST
BASS CT
BATMAN ST
HENTY CT
COOK CT
HUME
STURT ST
BLAXLAND DR
KELLY ST
MILLER ST
FORREST ST
TASMAN CT
SCOTT CT
EYRE ST
OXLEY CT
MAWSON RD
BARTON ST
BLAXLAND DR
FRASER
NEILL
LIGHT CT
BURKE ST
LASSITER ST
FAWKNER ST
FLINDERS ST
GREGORY CT
DEAKIN
WENTWORTH CT
LAWSON
PLANTE CT
ANDERSON
MOUNSEY CT
PASLEY CT
HORNE RD
Cmnty Health Cntr
STATION ST
Squash
Sunbury
Sunbury Central
Sunbury Terrace Shop Cntr
Sunbury Square Shop Cntr
BROOK
STAWELL ST
Sen Cits
RSL
MCH
Cncl Off
Cath
EVANS ST
Evans Street Grassland Res
TIMINS
O'SHANASSY
BARKLY
HARKER
TERENCE ST
STATION ST
VAUGHAN
AITKEN ST
POWLETT ST
RAINBOW CT
JACKSON
Reserve
PRIORSWOOD WY
Pavilion
Soccer & Hockey Gnds
Langama Park
CADELL CT
DENISON CT
MITCHELLS LA
DURACK CT
LEWIN ST
KAVEL CT
ADAMS CT
KINGSLEY DR
HOBSON CT
DAVENPORT DR
BACKHAUS GREY CT
ANGAS CT
LALOR CR
BACKHAUS AV
AGAR PL
LOGAN CT
CARLSON ST
NARANI CT
Indoor Sports
COMMERCE CT
SUSSEX CT
Council Depot & SES
McDOUGALL
VINEYARD
SHIELDS
BLACKWOOD PL
JUNIPER LA
LAURISTON WY
LUANA LA
BLUEGUM WY
HOYA DR
CLARET ASH DR
PARKVIEW DR
Galaxy Land
AVENUE
JARDINE CR
DONELLY CL
REDDAN CT
NORMAN
GOLF LINKS DR
Cemetery
GURNERS LA
PIPING LA
SHETLAND
MUSTANG PL
PINTO
CHESTNUT WY
CLYDESDALE WY
THE HIGHDALE
BARB CL
PALOMINO
PAPERBARK
TREEFERN DR
OCHRE PL
BIRCHWOOD
BELLEVIEW
SILKY OAK
PARK
AV LA
SUGAR GUM
MOUNTAIN ASH
CITRIODORA CCT
SASSAFRAS
LIQUIDAMBER
ROBINIA LA
GALAXY
LAVENDER LA
THE CIRCULAR
PROTEA CT
BETULA TCE
BVD
Victoria University Sunbury Campus

FOR MORE DETAIL SEE MAP 724

STARFLOWER WY
OUTLOOK
LILLY PILLY
WATERSPRITE
BELLEVIEW DR
CIRCULAR DR
HILLTOP CT
SCHOOLHOUSE LA
FLORENCE
Sunbury & Macedon Range Special
Sunbury Primary
HEIGHTS
PEPPERCORN
Reservoir
IRONBARK RD
VIADUCT
RIDGEWAY
THE ARCHES
MANNAGUM WY
DR
Andraos Bros

JOINS 187

A B C D E F G H J K L

LIMIT OF MAPS

MAP 149 FOLLOWS

LIMIT OF MAPS

A B C D E F G H J K L

SUNBURY

BULLA

Goonawarra

Goona Warra Winery & Restaurant

Craiglee

Equestrian Centre

MELBOURNE - LANCEFIELD RD

SUNBURY RD

GELLIES RD

REDSTONE HILL RD

FRANCIS BVD

Melbourne-Bendigo Railway

Jacksons Creek

Emu Ck

Golf Course

Clubhouse

Primary

MCH Tulsa Dr Reserve

Oval

Reserve

CITY

JOINS 188

189

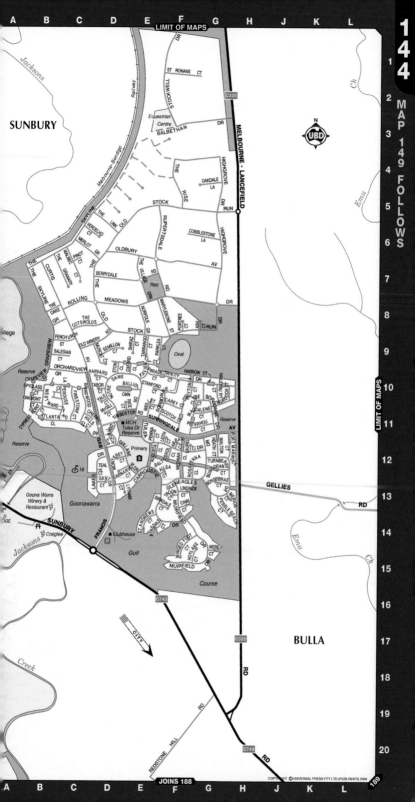

PREVIOUS MAP 144
LIMIT OF MAPS

192
JOINS 193

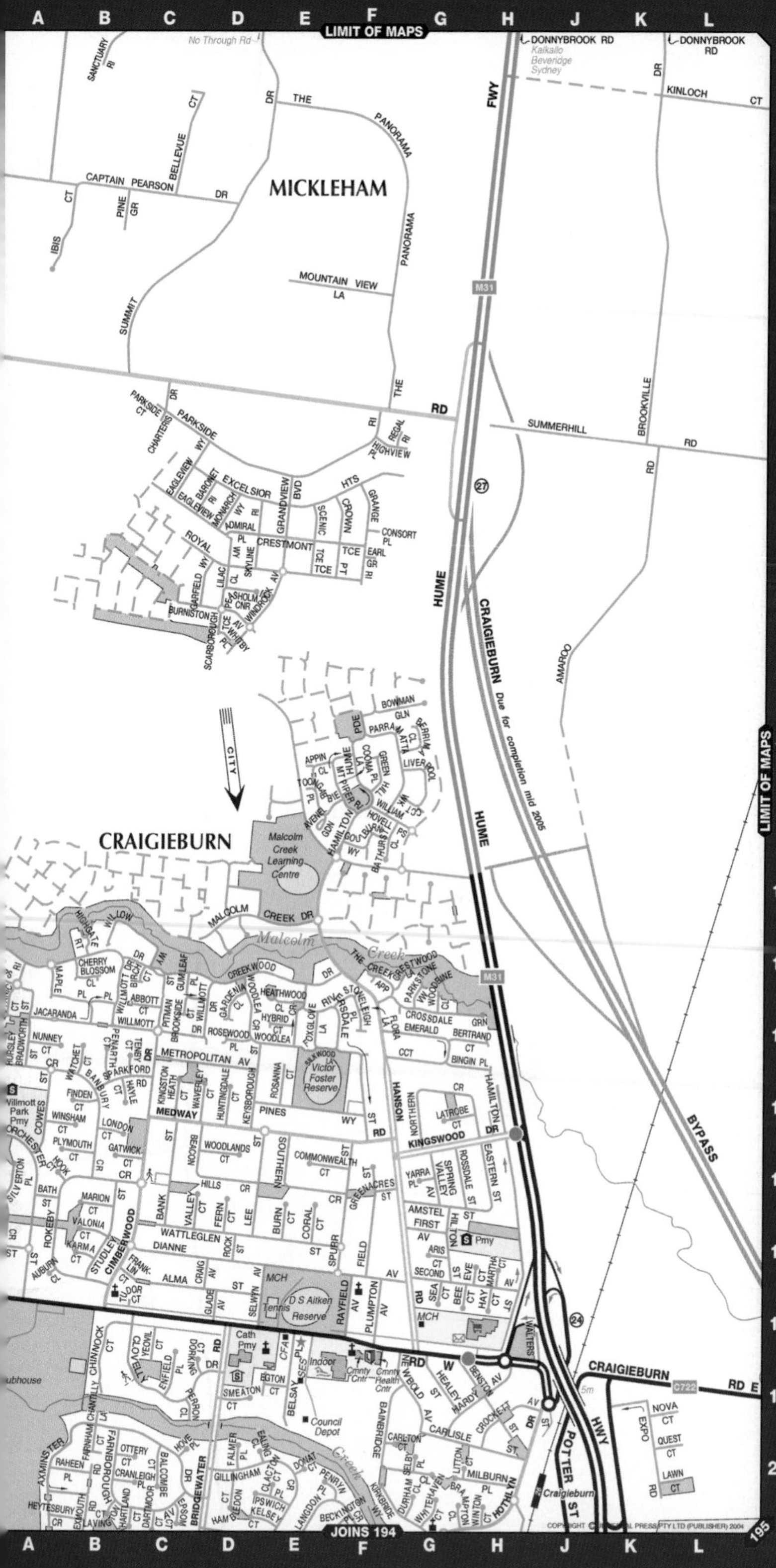

A B C D E F G H J K L

LIMIT OF MAPS

MICKLEHAM

CRAIGIEBURN

DONNYBROOK RD
Kalkallo Beveridge Sydney
HUME FWY
M31
KINLOCH CT
THE PANORAMA
CAPTAIN PEARSON DR
BELLEVUE CT
SANCTUARY RI
IBIS CT
PINE GR
MOUNTAIN VIEW LA
SUMMIT DR
SUMMERHILL RD
BROOKVILLE RD
PARKSIDE WY
HIGHVIEW RI
REGAL
EXCELSIOR HTS
GRANDVIEW BVD
CRESTMONT
CONSORT PL
CRAIGIEBURN BYPASS Due for completion mid 2005
AMAROO
HUME HWY
Malcolm Creek Learning Centre
MALCOLM CREEK DR
Malcolm Creek
Victor Foster Reserve
METROPOLITAN AV
PINES WY
HANSON RD
KINGSWOOD DR
MEDWAY
COMMONWEALTH ST
WATTLEGLEN ST
DIANNE ST
ALMA AV
D S Aitken Reserve
MCH
CIMBERWOOD DR
CRAIGIEBURN RD E
C722
POTTER ST
Craigieburn
Council Depot
Indoor
Cmnty Cntr
Cmnty Health Cntr
Willmott Park Pmy
Cath Pmy

CITY

MAP 153 FOLLOWS

LIMIT OF MAPS

1 2 3 4 5 6 7 8 9 10 11 12 13 14 15 16 17 18 19 20

JOINS 194

PREVIOUS MAP 150
LIMIT OF MAPS

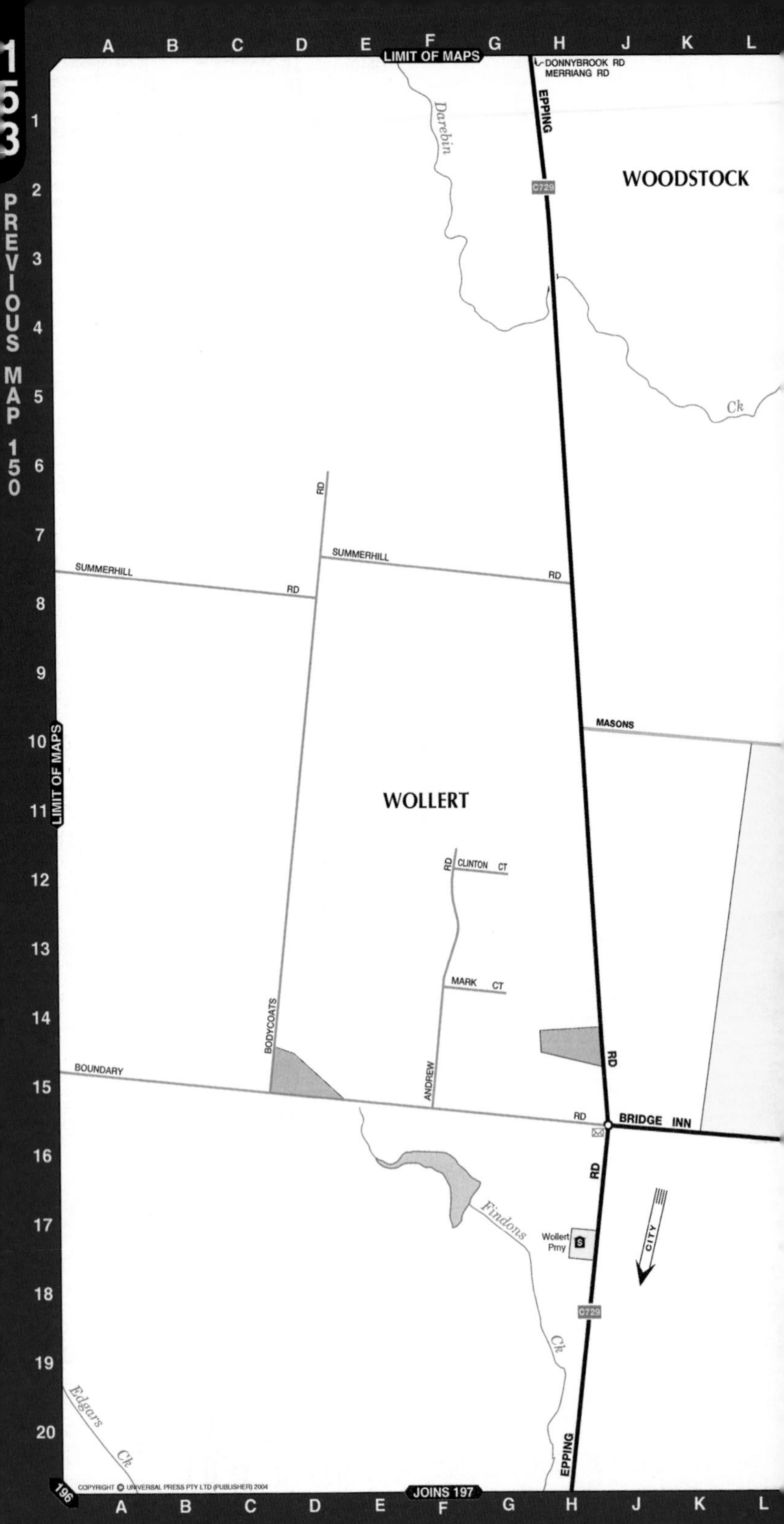

196
JOINS 197

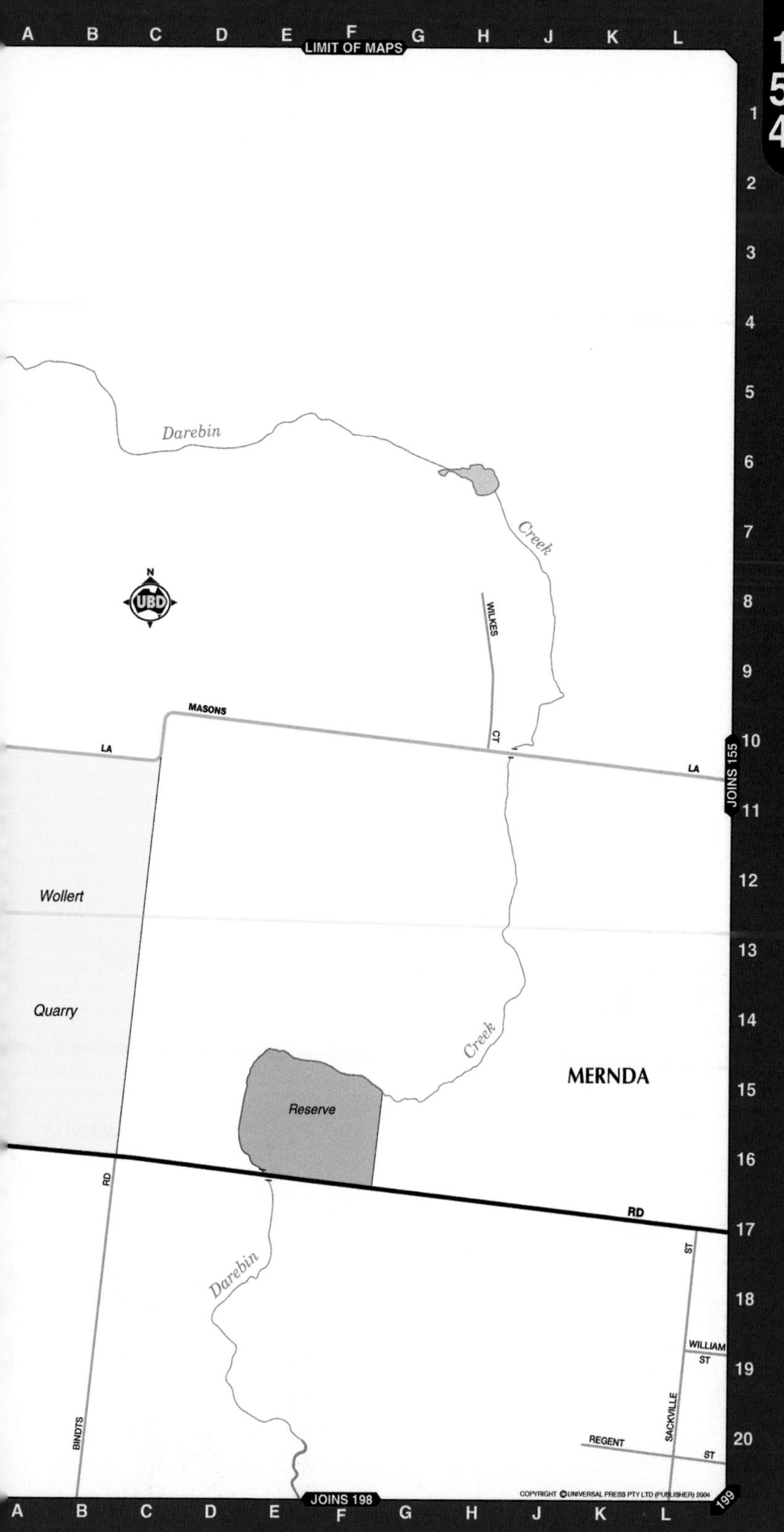
A B C D E F G H J K L
LIMIT OF MAPS
Darebin
Creek
WILKES
CT
MASONS
LA
LA
JOINS 155
Wollert
Quarry
Creek
MERNDA
Reserve
RD
RD
Darebin
ST
WILLIAM
ST
SACKVILLE
REGENT
ST
BINDTS
JOINS 198
199
1 2 3 4 5 6 7 8 9 10 11 12 13 14 15 16 17 18 19 20

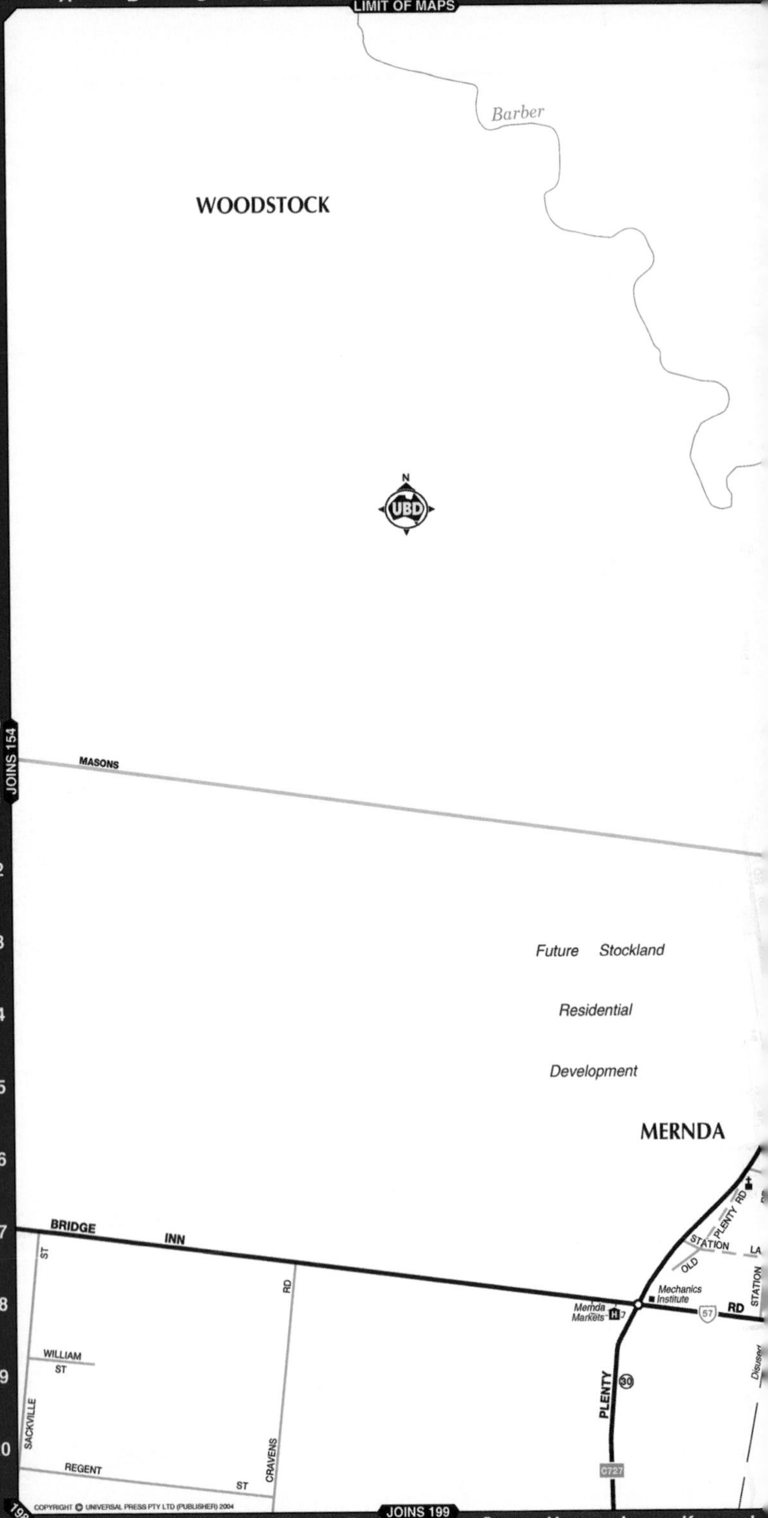

A B C D E F G H J K L

LIMIT OF MAPS

Barber

WOODSTOCK

N

UBD

JOINS 154

MASONS

Future Stockland

Residential

Development

MERNDA

BRIDGE INN

ST

RD

PLENTY RD

STATION

OLD

LA

Mechanics Institute

Mernda Markets

57

RD

STATION

Disused

WILLIAM ST

PLENTY

30

SACKVILLE

CRAVENS

REGENT ST

C727

198

JOINS 199

A B C D E F G H J K L

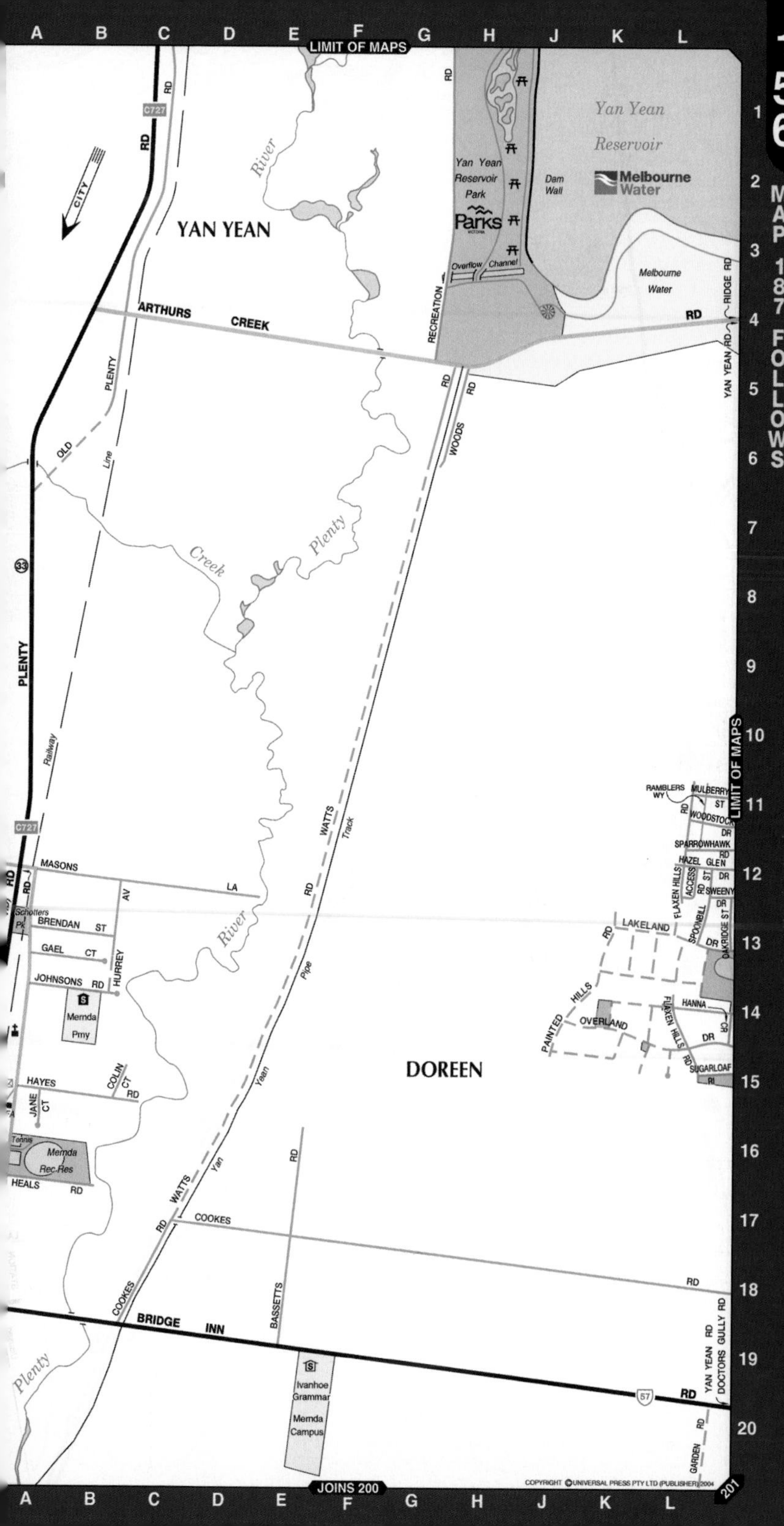

A B C D E F G H J K L
LIMIT OF MAPS
156
MAP 187 FOLLOWS
Yan Yean Reservoir
Melbourne Water
Yan Yean Reservoir Park
Parks VICTORIA
Dam Wall
Overflow Channel
Melbourne Water
YAN YEAN
CITY
C727
PLENTY RD
ARTHURS CREEK RD
RECREATION RD
RIDGE RD
YAN YEAN RD
WOODS RD
OLD PLENTY RD
Railway Line
Plenty River
Creek
WATTS RD
Yan Yean Pipe Track
MASONS RD
LA
Schotters Pl
BRENDAN ST
GAEL CT
JOHNSONS RD
HURREY AV
Mernda Pmy
HAYES RD
COLIN CT
JANE CT
Tennis
Mernda Rec Res
HEALS RD
RAMBLERS WY
MULBERRY ST
WOODSTOCK DR
SPARROWHAWK RD
HAZEL GLEN DR
ACCESS RD
SWEENY DR
FLAXEN HILLS RD
SPOONBILL DR
OAKRIDGE ST
LAKELAND RD
PAINTED HILLS RD
OVERLAND DR
HANNA CR
SUGARLOAF RI
DOREEN
COOKES RD
BASSETTS RD
BRIDGE INN RD
57
Ivanhoe Grammar Mernda Campus
YAN YEAN RD
DOCTORS GULLY RD
GARDEN RD
JOINS 200
COPYRIGHT © UNIVERSAL PRESS PTY LTD (PUBLISHER) 2004
201

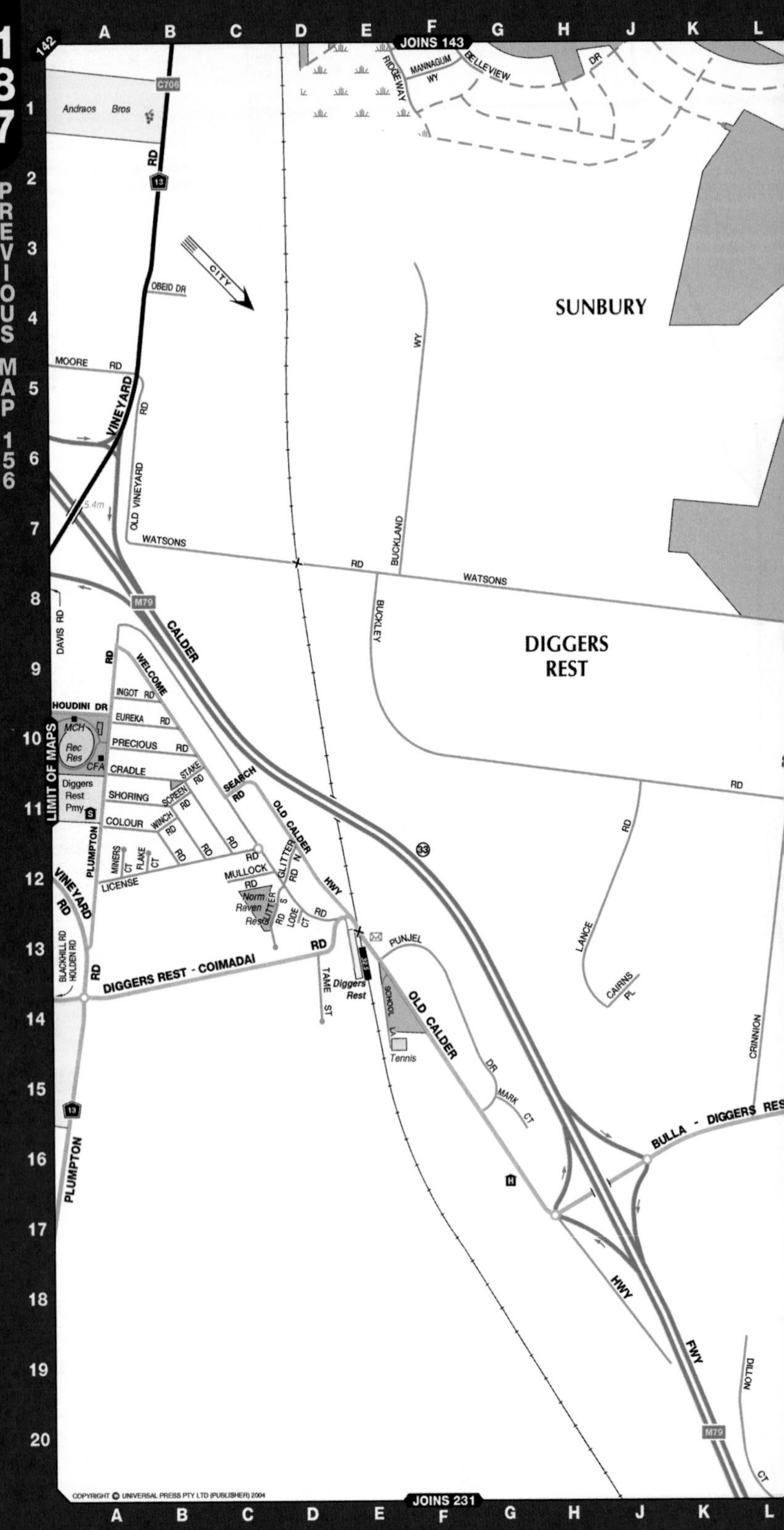
JOINS 143
PREVIOUS MAP 156
142
SUNBURY
DIGGERS REST
Andraos Bros
C706
RD
13
OBEID DR
CITY
MOORE RD
VINEYARD
OLD VINEYARD RD
WATSONS RD
WATSONS
BUCKLAND WY
BUCKLEY RD
RIDGEWAY
MANNAGUM WY
BELLEVIEW DR
M79
CALDER FWY
DAVIS RD
WELCOME RD
INGOT RD
EUREKA RD
PRECIOUS RD
CRADLE
SHORING
COLOUR
STAKE RD
SCREEN RD
WINCH RD
SEARCH RD
OLD CALDER HWY
GLITTER RD N
GLITTER RD S
LODE CT
MULLOCK RD
MINERS CT
FLAKE CT
LICENSE
HOUDINI DR
MCH
Rec Res
CFA
Diggers Rest Pmy
LIMIT OF MAPS
PLUMPTON RD
VINEYARD RD
BLACKHILL RD
HOLDEN RD
Norm Raven Res
DIGGERS REST - COIMADAI RD
TAME ST
Diggers Rest
PUNJEL
SCHOOL LA
Tennis
OLD CALDER DR
MARK CT
LANCE RD
CAIRNS PL
CRINNION
BULLA - DIGGERS RES
33
5.4m
HWY
FWY
DILLON
CT
PLUMPTON
JOINS 231

A B C D E F G H J K L
JOINS 144
SUNBURY
RD
C743
BULLA
REDSTONE
HILL
RD
Jacksons
LA
SHEPHERDS
Holden Flora & Fauna Reserve
RD
LA
Creek
JOINS 189
GLENCOE
DR
DUNCANS
LA
RD
CT
MOREFIELD
DUNCANS
MANINGA PARK
CT
JOINS 232
233
1 2 3 4 5 6 7 8 9 10 11 12 13 14 15 16 17 18 19 20

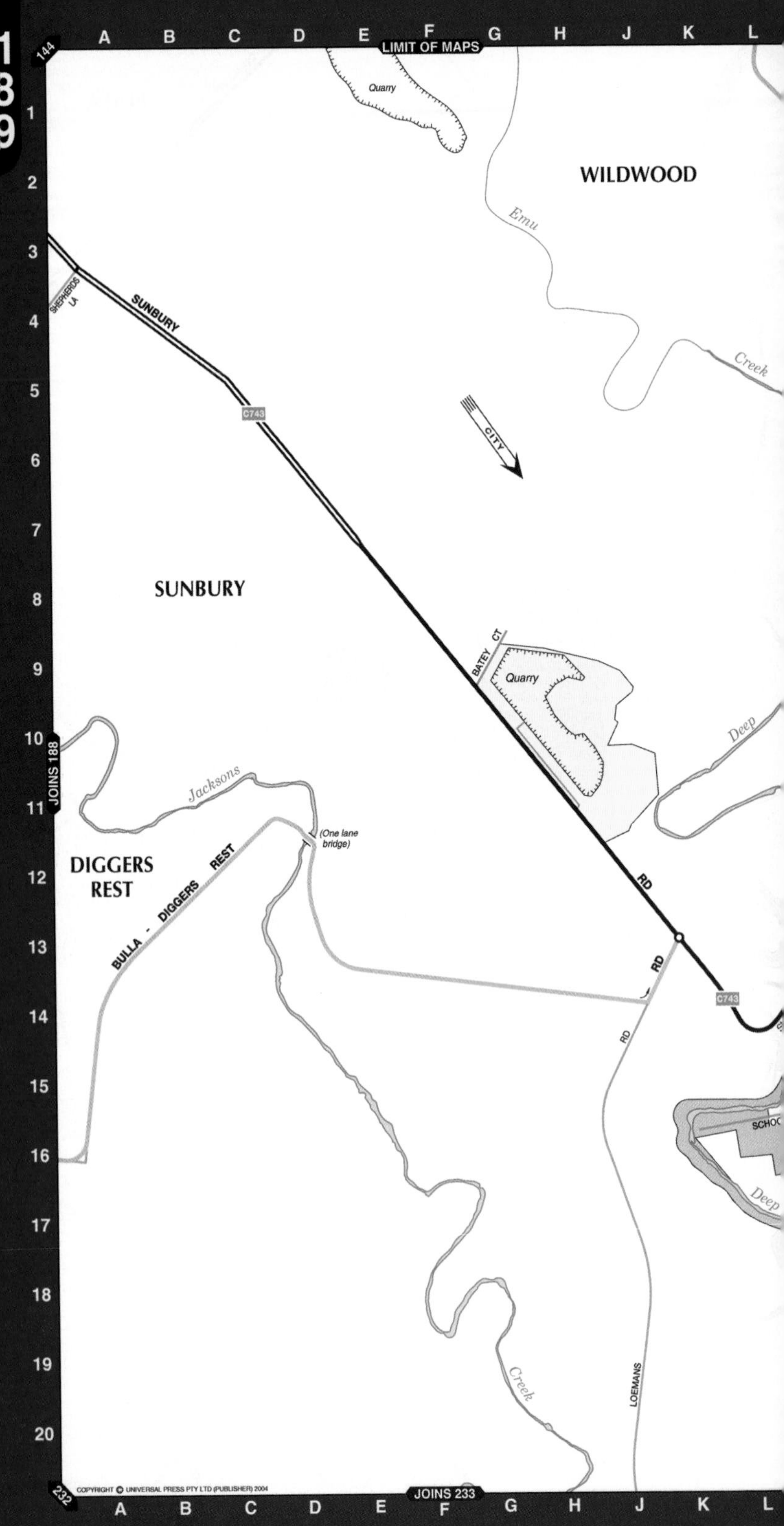
A B C D E F G H J K L
144
LIMIT OF MAPS
1 2 3 4 5 6 7 8 9 10 11 12 13 14 15 16 17 18 19 20
Quarry
WILDWOOD
Emu
Creek
SHEPHERDS LA
SUNBURY
C743
CITY
SUNBURY
BATEY CT
Quarry
Deep
JOINS 188
Jacksons
(One lane bridge)
DIGGERS REST
BULLA - DIGGERS REST
RD
RD
C743
RD
SCHOO
Deep
Creek
LOEMANS
232
JOINS 233

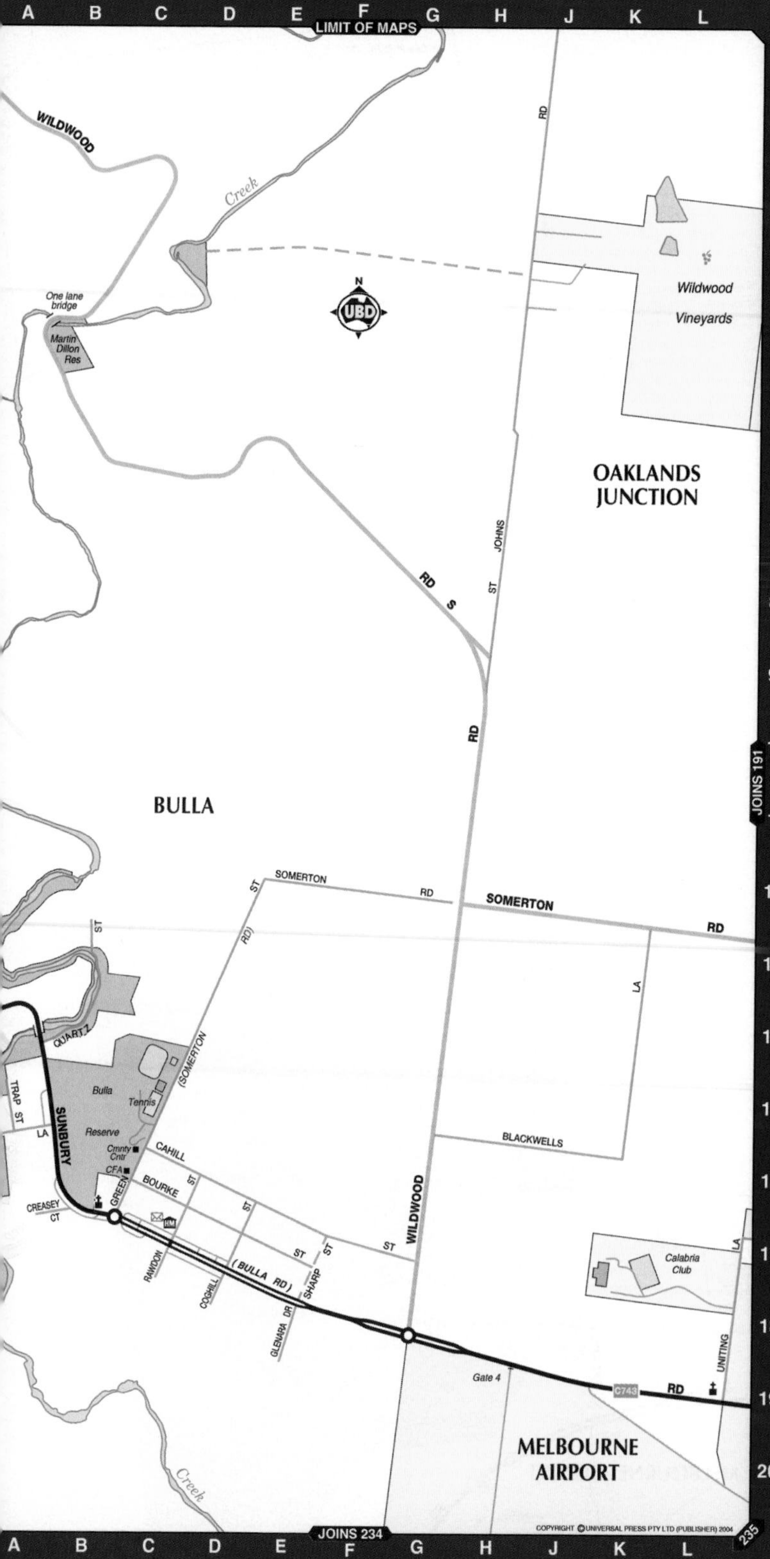

LIMIT OF MAPS

WILDWOOD
Creek
One lane bridge
Martin Dillon Res
RD
Wildwood Vineyards
OAKLANDS JUNCTION
JOHNS ST
RD S
RD
JOINS 191
BULLA
SOMERTON RD
SOMERTON RD
ST
ST
RD)
LA
QUARTZ
(SOMERTON
Bulla
Tennis
Reserve
TRAP ST
LA
SUNBURY
Cmnty Cntr
CFA
CAHILL
BOURKE
ST
GREEN
ST
CREASEY CT
BLACKWELLS
WILDWOOD
ST
ST
ST
(BULLA RD)
SHARP
RAWDON
COGHILL
GLENARA DR
Calabria Club
LA
UNITING
Gate 4
C743
RD
MELBOURNE AIRPORT
Creek

JOINS 234

235

LIMIT OF MAPS

KONAGADERRA RD

CITY

Wildwood Vineyards

Thoroughbred Auctions

Gate

Gate

Quarry

OAKLANDS JUNCTION

DANIEL (Priv Rd) RD

MEEK RD

OAKLANDS RD

SOMERTON RD

Oaklands Hunt Club

Gate

Gate

PROVIDENCE

Ck

Moonee Ponds Ck

Fbr

Fire Access Only TR

LIVINGSTONE DR

"Woodlands" Historic Homestead 1843

Woodlands Historic Park

HOMESTEAD DR

Hume & Hovell Cairn

Cemetery

CEMETERY LA

LA

Calabria Club

UNITING

WOODLANDS

Entrance Gate

Parks

SUNBURY RD

C743

Gate 3

Restricted Area

MELBOURNE AIRPORT

PERIMETER RD

JOINS 190

JOINS 235

234

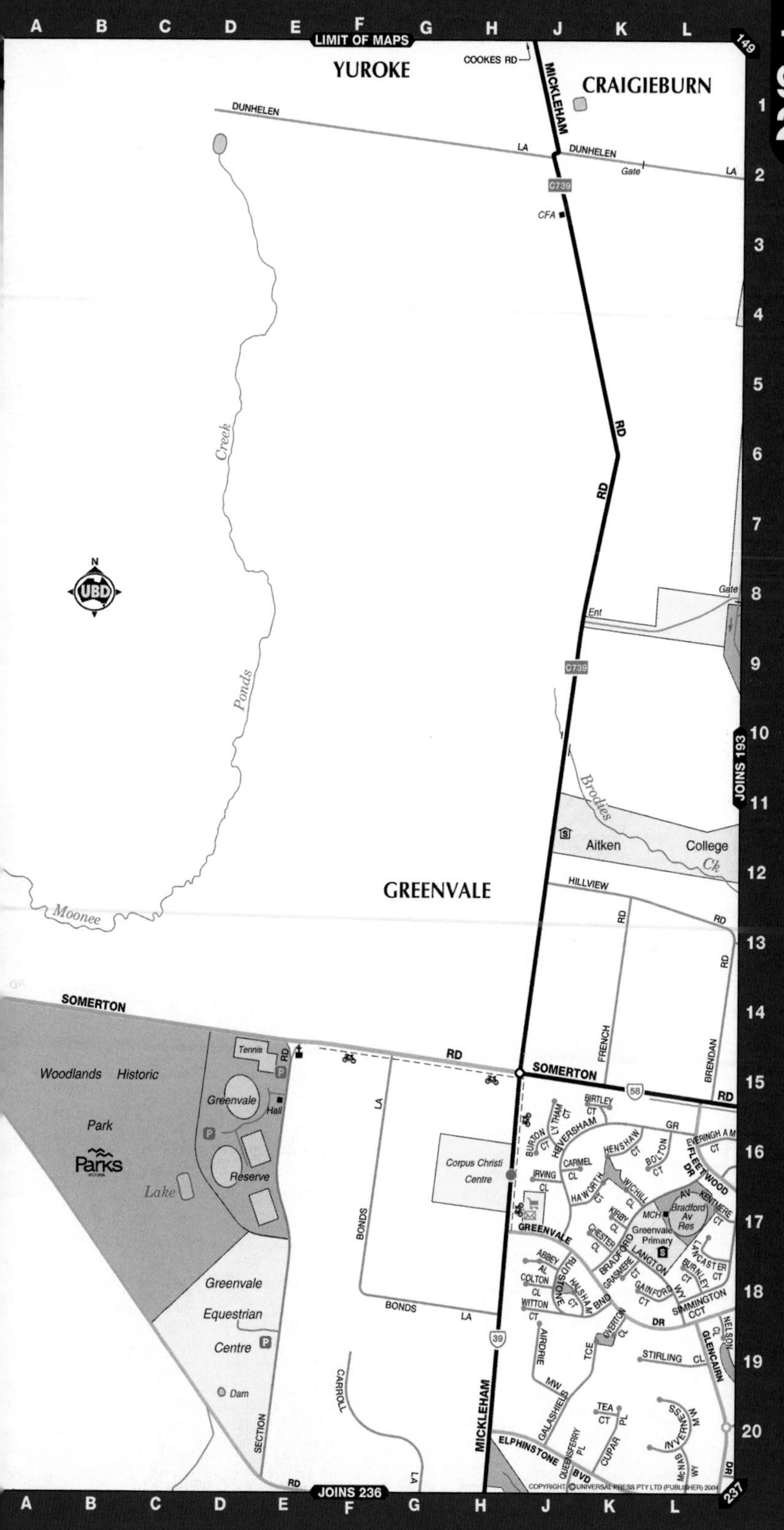
LIMIT OF MAPS
COOKES RD
YUROKE
CRAIGIEBURN
DUNHELEN
LA
DUNHELEN
Gate
LA
MICKLEHAM
C739
CFA
RD
RD
Creek
Ponds
Moonee
Gate
Ent
C739
Brodies
Ck
Aitken
College
JOINS 193
GREENVALE
HILLVIEW
RD
RD
RD
SOMERTON
RD
Tennis
RD
Woodlands Historic
Park
Parks
Lake
Greenvale
Hall
Reserve
SOMERTON
58
RD
FRENCH
BRENDAN
LA
Corpus Christi
Centre
BONDS
BONDS
LA
39
GREENVALE
BIRTLEY
CT
LYTHAM
CT
HEVERSHAM
BURTON
CT
GR
EVERINGHAM
CT
HENSHAW
CT
BOLTON
CT
FLEETWOOD
DR
CARMEL
CL
IRVING
CL
HAWORTH
CT
WICHILL
CL
KIRBY
CL
AV
KENTMERE
CT
MCH
Bradford
Av
Res
Greenvale
Primary
CHESTER
CL
BRADFORD
GRASMERE
CT
LANGTON
LANCASTER
CT
BURNLEY
CT
ABBEY
AL
COLTON
CL
WITTON
CT
RUDSTONE
HALSHAM
CT
BND
GAINFORD
CT
WY
SIMMINGTON
CCT
DR
NELSON
CL
GLENCAIRN
AIRDRIE
TCE
OVERTON
CL
STIRLING
CL
Greenvale
Equestrian
Centre
Dam
SECTION
CARROLL
MICKLEHAM
MW
GALASHIELS
TEA
CT
PL
INVERNESS
MW
CUPAR
PL
QUEENSFERRY
PL
ELPHINSTONE
BVD
McNAB
WY
DR
RD
LA
JOINS 236
COPYRIGHT © UNIVERSAL PRESS PTY LTD (PUBLISHER) 2004
149
237
A B C D E F G H J K L
1 2 3 4 5 6 7 8 9 10 11 12 13 14 15 16 17 18 19 20

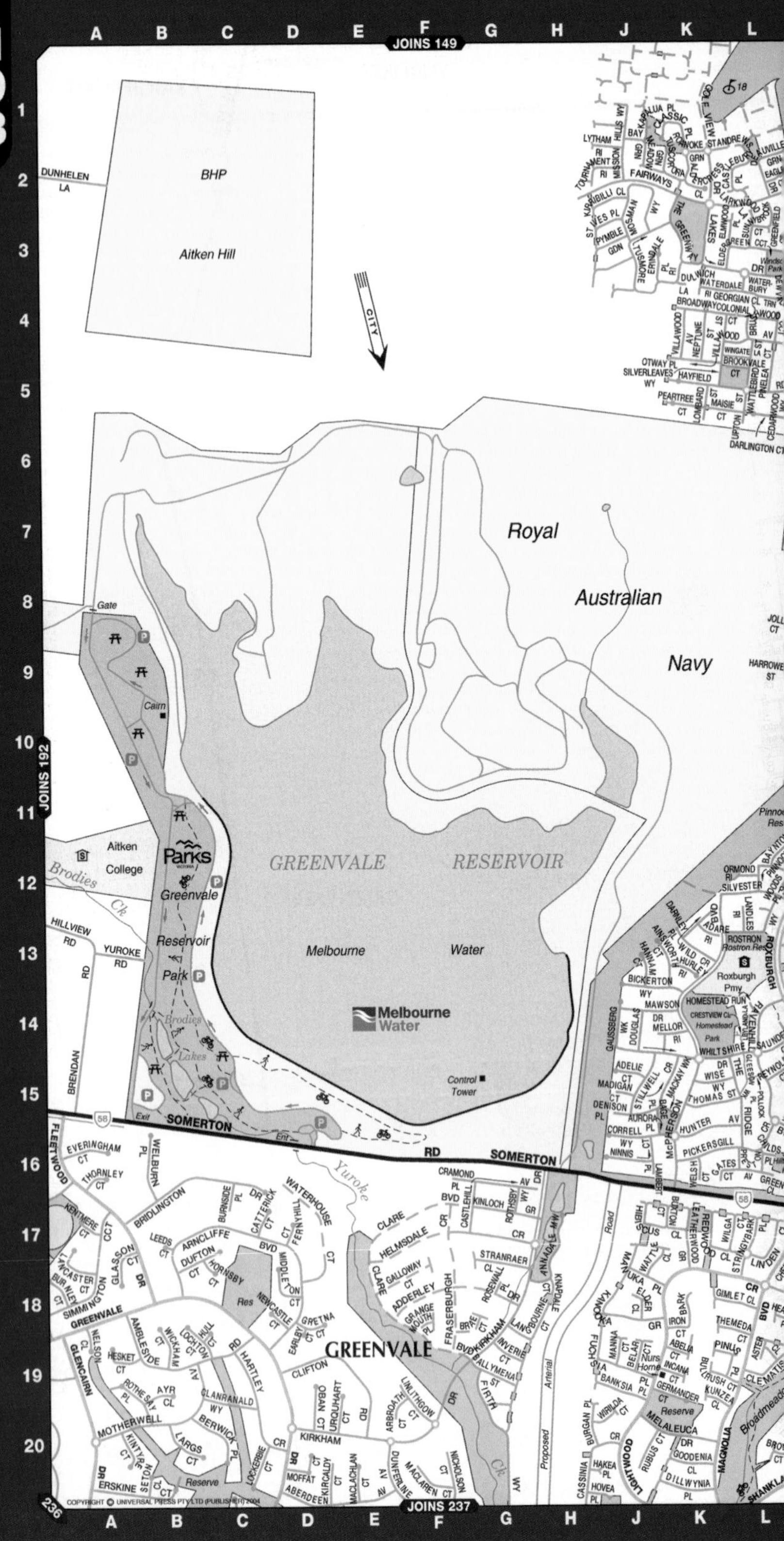

A B C D E F G H J K L
JOINS 149
JOINS 192
JOINS 237
236
BHP
Aitken Hill
DUNHELEN LA
CITY
Royal
Australian
Navy
GREENVALE RESERVOIR
Melbourne Water
Melbourne Water
Control Tower
Parks Victoria
Greenvale Reservoir Park
Brodies Lakes
Aitken College
Brodies Ck
Gate
Cairn
Exit
Ent
HILLVIEW RD
YUROKE RD
BRENDAN RD
SOMERTON RD
SOMERTON RD
58
Yuroke Ck
GREENVALE
FLEETWOOD
EVERINGHAM CT
THORNLEY CT
WELBURN PL
BRIDLINGTON
KENTMERE CT
GLASSON CT
LANCASTER CT
BURNLEY CT
SIMMINGTON CCT
GREENVALE DR
LEEDS CT
ARNCLIFFE CT
DUFTON CT
HORNSBY CT
BURNSIDE PL
CATTERICK DR
WATERHOUSE CT
FERNYHILL CT
MIDDLETON CT
NEWCASTLE CT
Res
GRETNA CT
EARLBY CT
AMBLESIDE
WICKHAM CT
LOCHTON CT
HULL CT
HARTLEY
HESKET CT
ROTHESAY PL
AYR CL
CLANRANALD WY
BERWICK PL
MOTHERWELL
KINTYRE CT
LARGS CT
SETON CT
ERSKINE CT
Reserve
LOCKERBIE CT
GLENCAIRN DR
NELSON
CLIFTON
OBAN CT
URQUHART CT
KIRKHAM DR
MOFFAT CT
ABERDEEN
KIRCALDY CT
MACLACHLAN CT
DUNFERLINE AV
ARBROATH CT
LINLITHGOW CT
MACLAREN CT
NICHOLSON CT
CLARE CR
HELMSDALE
GALLOWAY CT
ADDERLEY CT
GRANGEMOUTH PL
FRASERBURGH
BRAE CT
ROSEWALL DR
KIRKHAM BVD
INVERIE CT
BALLYMENA CT
FIRTH ST
LANGBOURNE CT
ANNADALE MW
KNAPDALE CT
STRANRAER CL
CRAMOND PL
KINLOCH
CASTLEHILL CT
ROTHSBY WY
BVD
GR
CR
Proposed Arterial Road
WY
CASSINIA
BURGAN PL
HAKEA PL
HOVEA
WIRILDA CT
LIGHTWOOD
RUBUS CT
KANOOKA
FUCHSIA
MANNA CT
BELAR CT
BANKSIA PL
Nurs Home
INCANA CT
GERMANDER CT
Reserve
MELALEUCA DR
GOODENIA CL
DILLWYNIA PL
MAGNOLIA
ABELIA CT
IRON BARK
ELDER CL
MALLUKA
WATTLE CL
HIBISCUS
BOXTON
REDWOOD
LEATHERWOOD
WILGA
STRINGYBARK
LINDEN
GIMLET CL
THEMEDA CT
PINUS CT
ASTER
BULLRUSH CT
KUNZEA CL
CLEMATIS
Broadmeadows
SHANKLAND
GAUSSBERG
DOUGLAS
BICKERTON
MAWSON WY
MELLOR DR
ADELIE CT
MADIGAN CT
DENISON PL
STILLWELL CR
AURORA PL
MACKAY WY
BAGE
CORRELL PL
McPHERSON
NINNIS WY
LAMBERT
HUNTER AV
PICKERSGILL
WELSH CT
GATES CT
THOMAS ST
WHILTSHIRE
THE RIDGE
HOMESTEAD RUN
Homestead Park
Roxburgh Pmy
ROSTRON Rostron Res
ROXBURGH
DARNLEY
AINSWORTH
HANNAM
WILD CR
HURLEY
ADARE
ORMOND RI
SILVESTER
LANDLES
Pinnock Res
JOLLY CT
HARROWER ST
LYTHAM
TOURNAMENT RI
MISSION HILLS WY
BAY HILL
KAPALUA PL
CLASSIC
ROANOKE
STANDREWS
TUSCORA
FAIRWAYS
THE GREENWAY
LAKES
KIRRIBILLI CL
ST IVES PL
PYMBLE GDN
MOSMAN WY
TUSMORE
ERINDALE
DULWICH
WATERDALE
WATERBURY
GEORGIAN CL
BROADWAY
COLONIAL
VILLAWOOD
NEPTUNE
BROOKVALE CT
HAYFIELD
OTWAY PL
SILVERLEAVES WY
PEARTREE CT
LOMBARD
MAISIE ST
WATTLEBIRD
PINELEA
UPTON ST
CEDARWOOD
DARLINGTON CT
GOLF VIEW
18
COPYRIGHT © UNIVERSAL PRESS PTY LTD (PUBLISHER) 2004

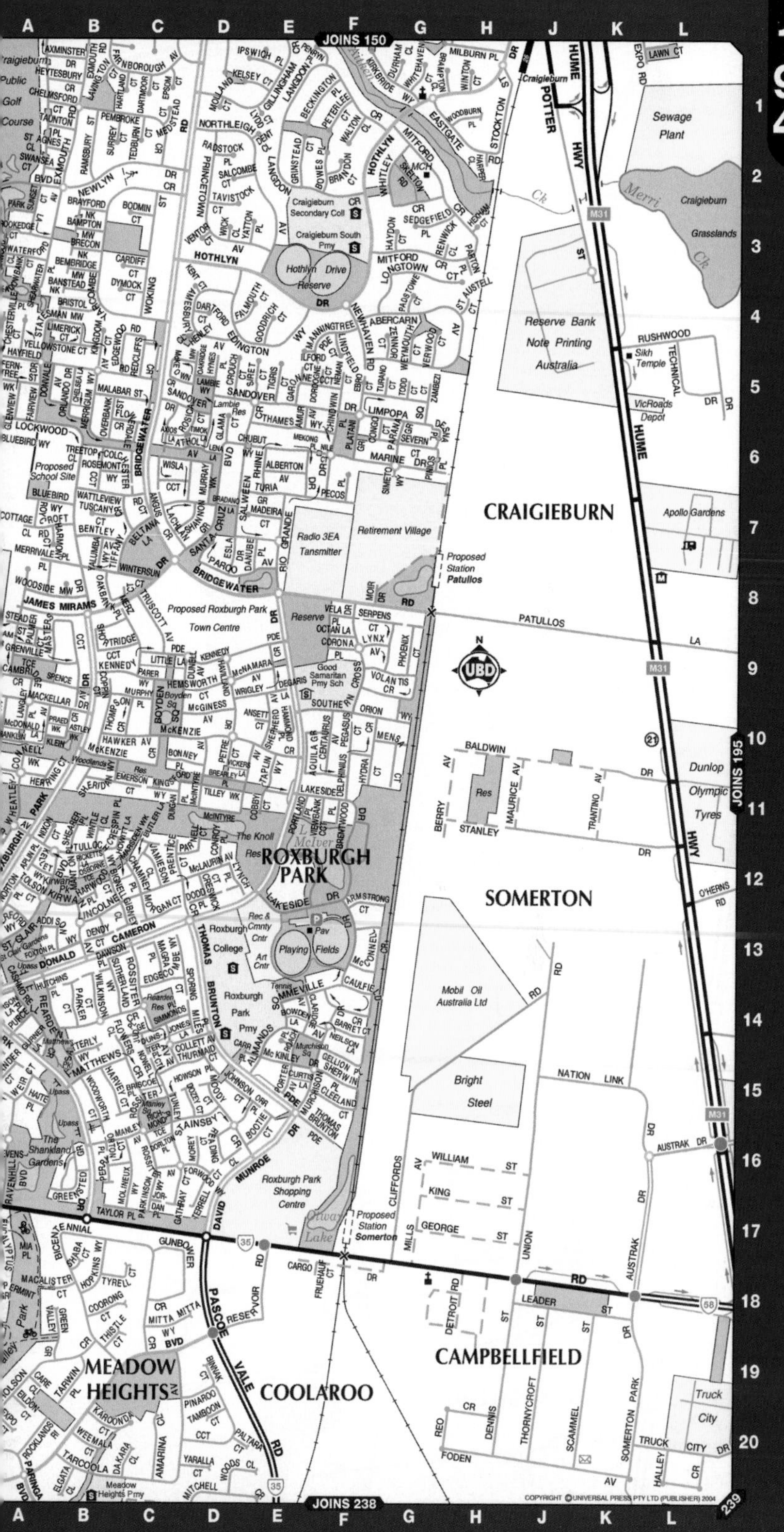

JOINS 150
JOINS 195
JOINS 238
CRAIGIEBURN
ROXBURGH PARK
SOMERTON
CAMPBELLFIELD
MEADOW HEIGHTS
COOLAROO
Craigieburn Public Golf Course
Sewage Plant
Craigieburn Grasslands
Merri Ck
HUME HWY
M31
POTTER ST
Reserve Bank Note Printing Australia
Sikh Temple
VicRoads Depot
Apollo Gardens
Craigieburn Secondary Coll
Craigieburn South Pmy
Hothlyn Drive Reserve
HOTHLYN DR
Radio 3EA Tansmitter
Retirement Village
Proposed Station Patullos
PATULLOS LA
Proposed Roxburgh Park Town Centre
Good Samaritan Pmy Sch
Proposed School Site
BRIDGEWATER
Dunlop Olympic Tyres
The Knoll Res
Lake McIver
Rec & Cmnty Cntr
Roxburgh College
Playing Fields
Art Cntr
Roxburgh Park Pmy
Mobil Oil Australia Ltd
Bright Steel
NATION LINK
The Shankland Gardens
Roxburgh Park Shopping Centre
Proposed Station Somerton
Oliver Lake
SOMERTON RD
PASCOE VALE RD
Truck City
Meadow Heights Pmy
COPYRIGHT © UNIVERSAL PRESS PTY LTD (PUBLISHER) 2004

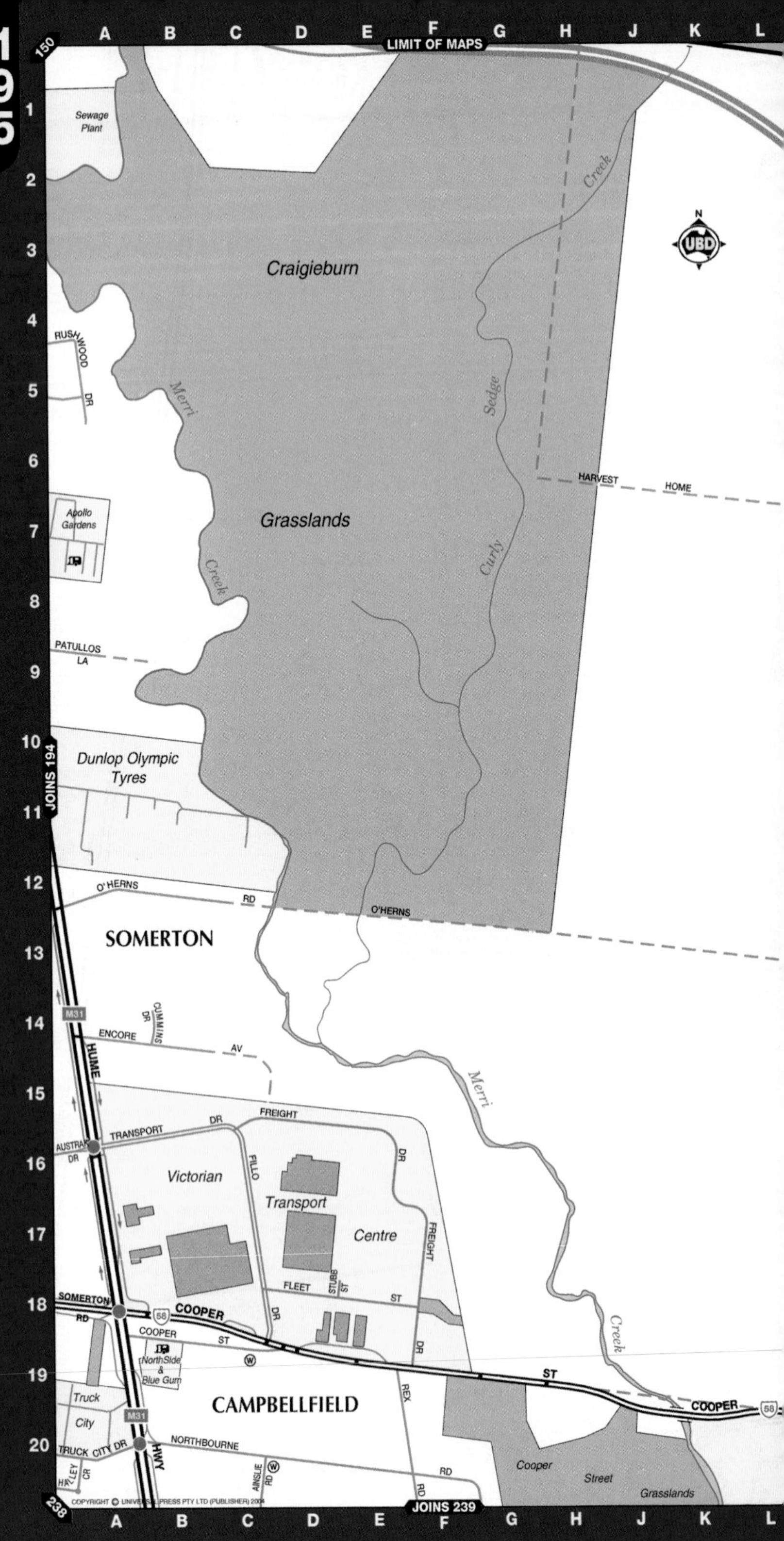

LIMIT OF MAPS
150
Sewage Plant
Craigieburn
Grasslands
Merri Creek
Curly Sedge Creek
RUSHWOOD DR
Apollo Gardens
HARVEST HOME
PATULLOS LA
Dunlop Olympic Tyres
JOINS 194
O'HERNS RD
SOMERTON
ENCORE AV
CUMMINS DR
HUME HWY
M31
TRANSPORT DR
FREIGHT DR
AUSTRAL DR
FILLO DR
Victorian Transport Centre
FLEET ST
STUBB ST
SOMERTON RD
COOPER ST
58
NorthSide & Blue Gum
CAMPBELLFIELD
REX DR
Truck City
TRUCK CITY DR
NORTHBOURNE RD
AINSLIE RD
HAWLEY CR
Cooper Street Grasslands
JOINS 239
238

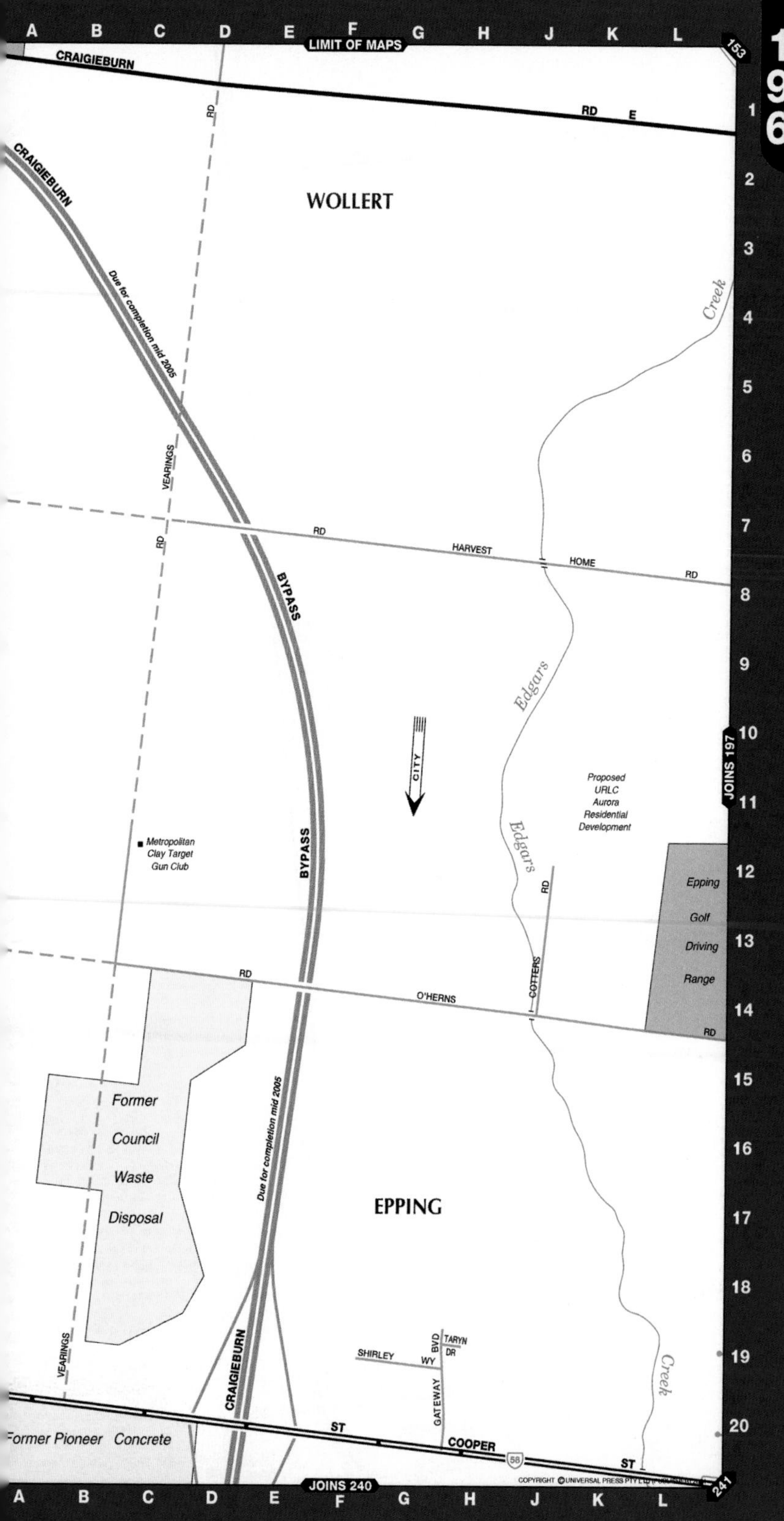

LIMIT OF MAPS
153
196
CRAIGIEBURN RD E
RD
WOLLERT
CRAIGIEBURN
Due for completion mid 2005
Creek
VEARINGS RD
HARVEST HOME RD
RD
BYPASS
Edgars
CITY
JOINS 197
Proposed
URLC
Aurora
Residential
Development
Metropolitan
Clay Target
Gun Club
Edgars
RD
Epping
Golf
Driving
Range
O'HERNS RD
COTTERS
RD
Former
Council
Waste
Disposal
Due for completion mid 2005
EPPING
TARYN DR
SHIRLEY WY
BVD
GATEWAY
VEARINGS
CRAIGIEBURN
Creek
Former Pioneer Concrete
COOPER ST
58
JOINS 240
241

JOINS 153

CRAIGIEBURN RD E
LEHMANNS
Edgars Creek
Findons Creek
HARVEST HOME RD
RSL
National League Soccer Stadium
Epping Golf Driving Range
O'HERNS RD
EPPING RD
EPPING ST
REYNARD ST
BEAGLE ST
JOANNE CT
ALBERT CT
RITA CT
BRUSH
Darebin
FINDON RD
CFA
Cemetery
Casa D'Abruzzo Club
Oval
Epping Rec Res
Pavilion
Tennis
PARK ST
KINLORA
SIMON CT
FRASER
SEBASTION
ROSEN
NICHOLAS
HAMMOND
DEMPSEY
GORHAM AV
NOLAN
DALTON
MELBA
HELPMAN
SUTHERLAND
McCORMACK
LLOYD AV
ACHERON ST
McCARTY
Darebin Creek Res
Epping Sec College
McDONALDS RD
TATLOW
YOUNG ST
HALL ST
DILOP
VIEW RD
MILLER
AMALFI PL
SORRENTO
CORNETTA WY
ORANA PL
Duffy Street Reserve
Epping RSL Memorial Cntr
MEMORIAL
DREAMHAVEN CT
EPPING
Epping Primary
CHURCH ST
DUFFY
Council Depot
HOUSTON
Indoor Tennis
Indoor Sports
RUFUS ST
PINE VALE CT
BROOKGLEN CT
COULSTOCK
MARY CT
WEDGE
HIGH ST
HOWARD
DAVISSON
St Peters Cath
CAMPBELL
LINK CT
GIPPS CT
DEVON CT
HELM CT
YALE
Peppercorn Park
PEPPERCORN PDE
Apex Pk
SUNBIRD GDN
WINTERTON
MASERATI DR
PORSCHE
DAIMLER CT
LANCIA
JAGUAR CT
LOTUS CT
HEALEY
SKEHAN PL
NORTH HAVEN DR
MAHON
CHARTERIS GR
SAUNDERS
EDGWARE
LANARK ST
NORTHUMBERLAND
POLYDOR
WORSLEY
MONTAGUE
GLOUCESTER
ESSEX
PEMBROKE
ROTHWELL CT
RANDWICK
PLYMOUTH
WATFORD
ROXBURGH
CARLISLE
BRISTOL
EALING
FINCHLEY
LAMBETH
CENTURION
SCARBOROUGH RD
KAOLIN
LYNCH
KEITH
TYLER
METCALF
HURST CL
ELLIOTT
DYER
SAVANNAH
McFARLANE
FARRELL
CLUNES
GREENBROOK
DELATITE
BASTINGS
COURTNAY
TOUHEY AV
LETCHWORTH PL
ZIMMER CT
CLELAND

JOINS 196
JOINS 241
240

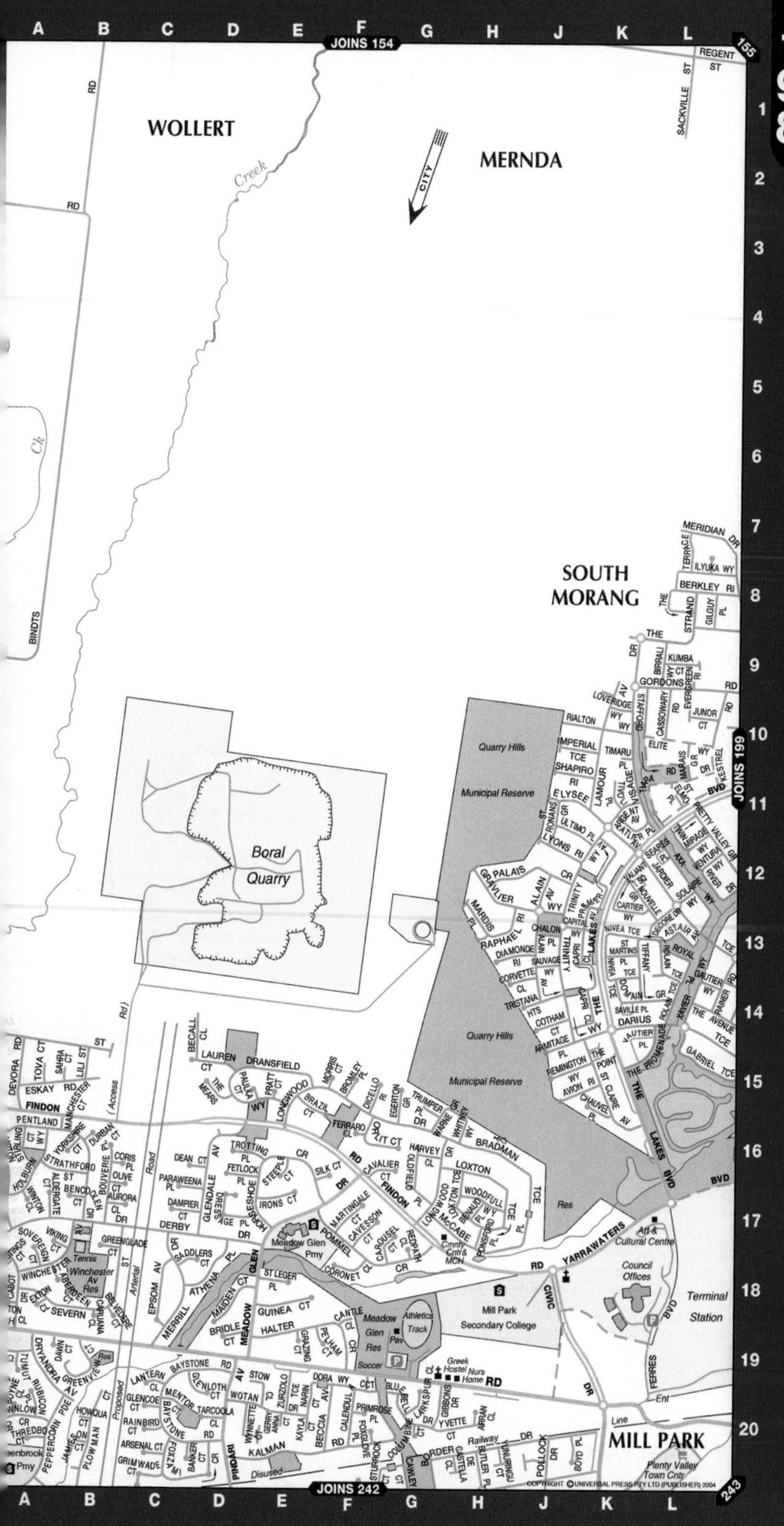

A B C D E F G H J K L
JOINS 154
155
1 2 3 4 5 6 7 8 9 10 11 12 13 14 15 16 17 18 19 20
WOLLERT
MERNDA
CITY
Creek
Ck
RD
BINDTS
REGENT ST
SACKVILLE ST
SOUTH MORANG
MERIDIAN DR
TERRACE
ILYUKA WY
BERKLEY RI
THE STRAND
GILGUY PL
KUMBA
BIRRALI
EVERGREEN
GORDONS RD
JUNOR CT
LOVERIDGE
STAFFORD
CASSOWARY
ELITE
MARAIS
KESTREL
RIALTON
IMPERIAL TCE
SHAPIRO RI
TIMARU
LAMOUR
ELYSEE
ST RONANS
ULTIMO PL
LYONS RI
PALAIS
GRAVLIER
MARDIS PL
ALAIN AV
TRINITY
CHALON
RAPHAEL RI
DIAMONDE
SAUVAGE
CORVETTE CL
TRISTANA HTS
COTHAM CT
ARMITAGE PL
REMINGTON
AVION RI
ST CLAIRE
CHAUVEL
THE POINT
THE PROMENADE
THE LAKES BVD
LAKES AV
CAPRI CL
NIVEA TCE
ST MARTINS PL
TIFFANY
DOMAIN GR
SAVILLE PL
DARIUS
VAUTIER PL
ROLAIN
XAVIER
GAUTIER
RAINIER
THE AVENUE
GABRIEL TCE
ROYAL
ASTAIR
SOLAIRE
SEAPIES
JARDIER
VALIANT
CARTIER
NOUVELLE
DECORE DR
PRETTY VALLEY GR
MIRAGE
VENTURA
RIVER
BVD
JOINS 199
Quarry Hills Municipal Reserve
Boral Quarry
FINDON RD
DEVORA
TOVA CT
SAHRA CT
LILI ST
ESKAY RD
MANCHESTER CT
PENTLAND
STIRLING
YORKSHIRE
DURBAN
STRATHFORD
HOLBURN
ALDERGATE
BENCOOLEN
BOUVERIE
CORIS PL
OLIVE
AURORA
WINTON
SOVEREIGN
VIKING
GREENGLADE
Tennis
Winchester Av Res
WINCHESTER
CABOT
EXTON
ABERDEEN
CARUANA
BELVEDERE
SEVERN
DRYANDRA
DAWN
GREENVIEW
TUMUT
RUBICON
PEPPERCORN PDE
HOWQUA
PLOWMAN
JAMIESON
Pmy
(Access Road)
Arterial Road
Proposed
BECALL CL
LAUREN
DRANSFIELD
THE MEARS
PAULKA CT
PRATT CT
LONGWOOD
MORRIS
BROMLEY
BRAZIL CT
FERRARO CL
DICELLO
EGERTON
TRUMPER
WARNE
WHITNEY
BRADMAN
ORVILT CT
HARVEY
OLDFIELD
LOXTON
WOODFULL
McCABE
PONSFORD
BENAUD
TROTTING PL
DEAN CT
FETLOCK PL
PARAWEENA PL
DAMPIER CT
GLENDALE AV
DRESSAGE
HORSESHOE
STEEPLE CT
IRONS CT
SILK CT
CAVALIER CT
MARTINGALE
CAVESSON
CAROUSEL
REDPATH
DERBY DR
SADDLERS CT
POMMEL
Meadow Glen Pmy
CORONET
Cmnty Cntr & MCH
EPSOM AV
ATHENA PL
MERRILL
MAIDEN CT
MEADOW GLEN
ST LEGER PL
GUINEA CT
HALTER
BRIDLE CT
CANTLE
GRAZING
PELHAM
Meadow Glen Res
Athletics Track
Pav
Soccer
Res
YARRAWATERS RD
CIVIC DR
Art & Cultural Centre
Council Offices
Mill Park Secondary College
Terminal Station
FERRES BVD
BAYSTONE RD
STOW
ZURZOLO
DORA WY
BLUE BELL
Greek Hostel Nurs Home
LANTERN
GLENLOTH
MENTOR
WOTAN
GLENCOE
TARCOOLA
RAINBIRD
ARSENAL CT
FOXZAMI
BANKER
GRIMWADE
PINDARI
WYNNETTE
GERRY
KAYLA
NARIN
BECCIA
CALENDUL
PRIMROSE PL
FOXGLOVE
STURROCK
COLUMBINE
CAWLEY
LARKSPUR
GIBBONS
YVETTE
BORDER
CASTELLA
BUTLER
Railway Line
YUNUPINGU
POLLOCK
BOYD
Ent
MILL PARK
Plenty Valley Town Cntr
KALMAN
Disused
JOINS 242
243
COPYRIGHT © UNIVERSAL PRESS PTY LTD (PUBLISHER) 2004

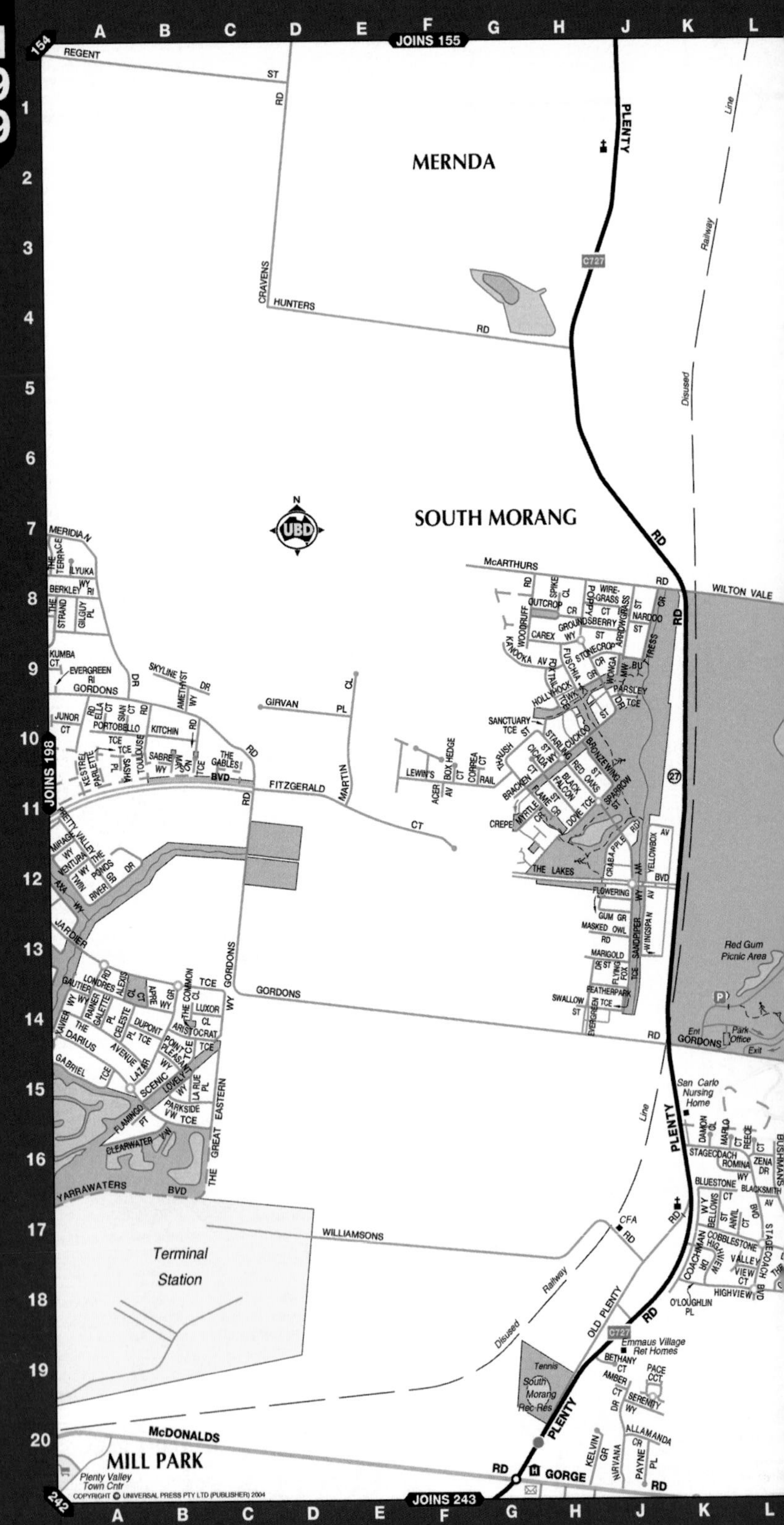
JOINS 155
JOINS 198
JOINS 243
154
242
MERNDA
SOUTH MORANG
MILL PARK
REGENT ST
CRAVENS RD
HUNTERS RD
PLENTY RD
C727
Disused Railway Line
McARTHURS RD
WILTON VALE
GIRVAN PL
MARTIN CL
FITZGERALD RD
GORDONS RD
GORDONS WY
WILLIAMSONS
Terminal Station
Red Gum Picnic Area
Park Office
San Carlo Nursing Home
CFA RD
OLD PLENTY RD
Emmaus Village Ret Homes
Tennis
South Morang Rec Res
McDONALDS
GORGE RD
YARRAWATERS BVD
THE GREAT EASTERN
Plenty Valley Town Cntr
COPYRIGHT © UNIVERSAL PRESS PTY LTD (PUBLISHER) 2004

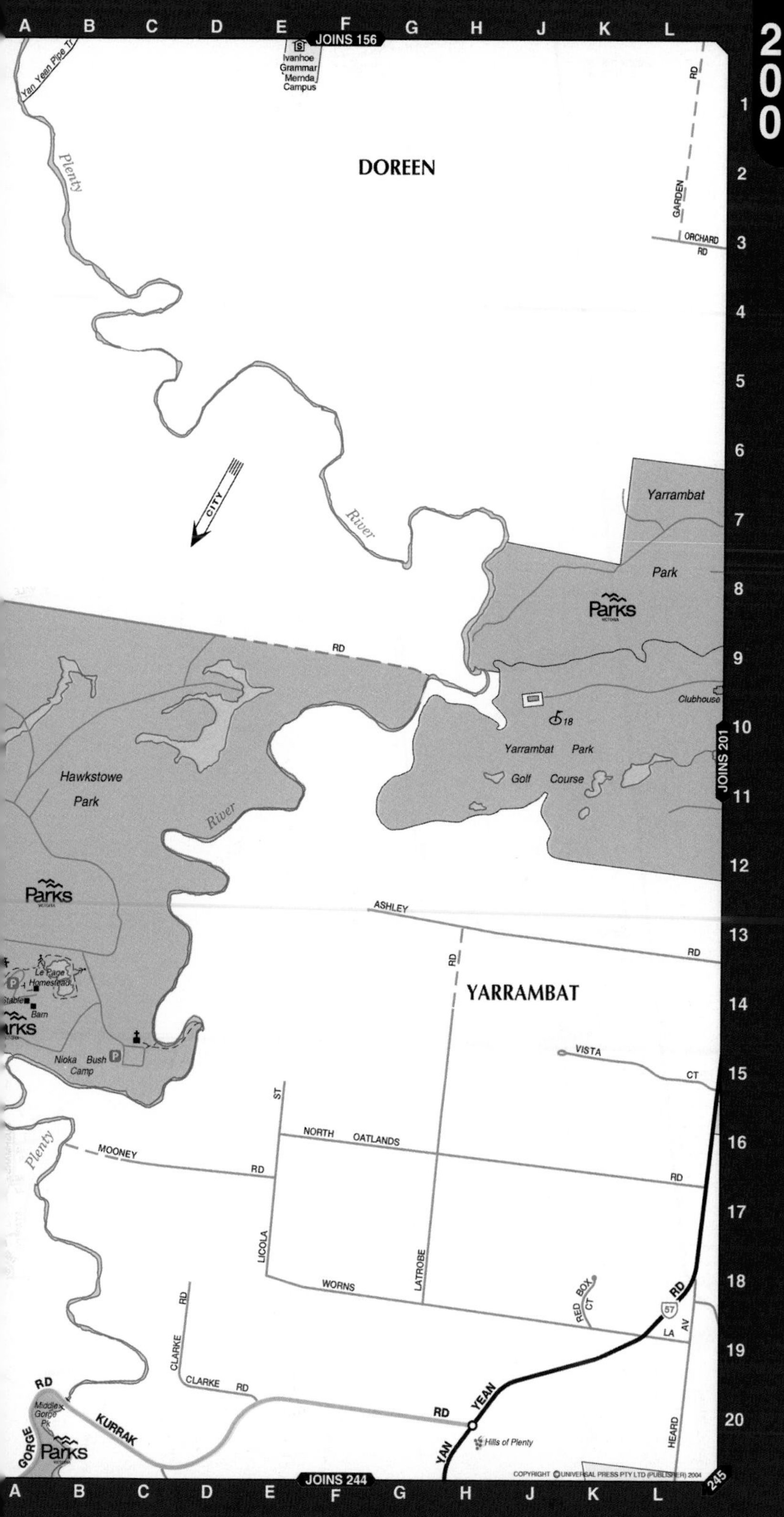
JOINS 156
Ivanhoe Grammar Mernda Campus
Yan Yean Pipe Tr
DOREEN
Plenty
River
CITY
RD
GARDEN
ORCHARD
RD
Yarrambat
Park
Parks
RD
Clubhouse
18
Yarrambat Park
Golf Course
JOINS 201
Hawkstowe
Park
River
Parks
ASHLEY
RD
RD
YARRAMBAT
Le Page Homestead
Stable
Barn
Nioka Bush Camp
VISTA
CT
ST
NORTH OATLANDS
RD
MOONEY
RD
Plenty
LICOLA
LATROBE
WORNS
RED BOX CT
RD
57
LA
AV
CLARKE
RD
CLARKE
RD
RD
Middle Gorge Pk
GORGE
KURRAK
Parks
RD
YAN YEAN
Hills of Plenty
HEARD
JOINS 244
245

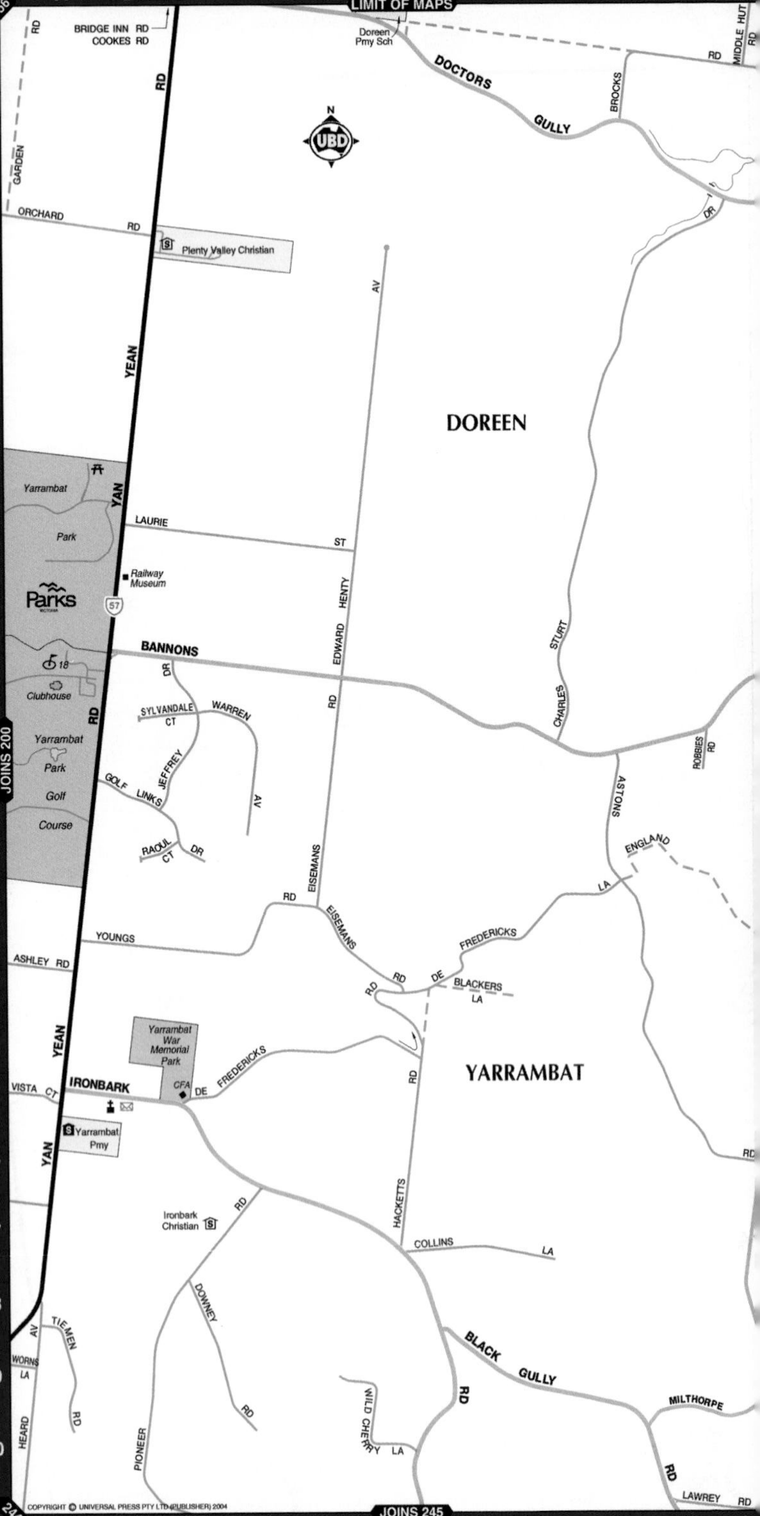

156
LIMIT OF MAPS

DOREEN

YARRAMBAT

BRIDGE INN RD
COOKES RD
GARDEN RD
ORCHARD RD
YEAN RD
YAN YEAN RD
Plenty Valley Christian
Doreen Pmy Sch
DOCTORS GULLY RD
BROCKS
MIDDLE HUT RD
DR
AV
Yarrambat Park
Parks Victoria
Railway Museum
57
LAURIE ST
EDWARD HENTY RD
BANNONS
STURT
CHARLES
ROBBIES RD
ASTONS
ENGLAND
LA
DR
SYLVANDALE CT
WARREN AV
JEFFREY
GOLF LINKS DR
RAOUL CT
Clubhouse
18
Yarrambat Park Golf Course
EISEMANS RD
EISEMANS RD
FREDERICKS DE
BLACKERS LA
YOUNGS RD
ASHLEY RD
Yarrambat War Memorial Park
CFA
IRONBARK RD
FREDERICKS DE
VISTA CT
Yarrambat Pmy
HACKETTS RD
RD
Ironbark Christian
RD
COLLINS LA
DOWNEY RD
TIEMEN RD
AV
WORNS LA
HEARD
PIONEER
WILD CHERRY LA
BLACK GULLY RD
MILTHORPE
RD
LAWREY RD

JOINS 200
JOINS 245
244

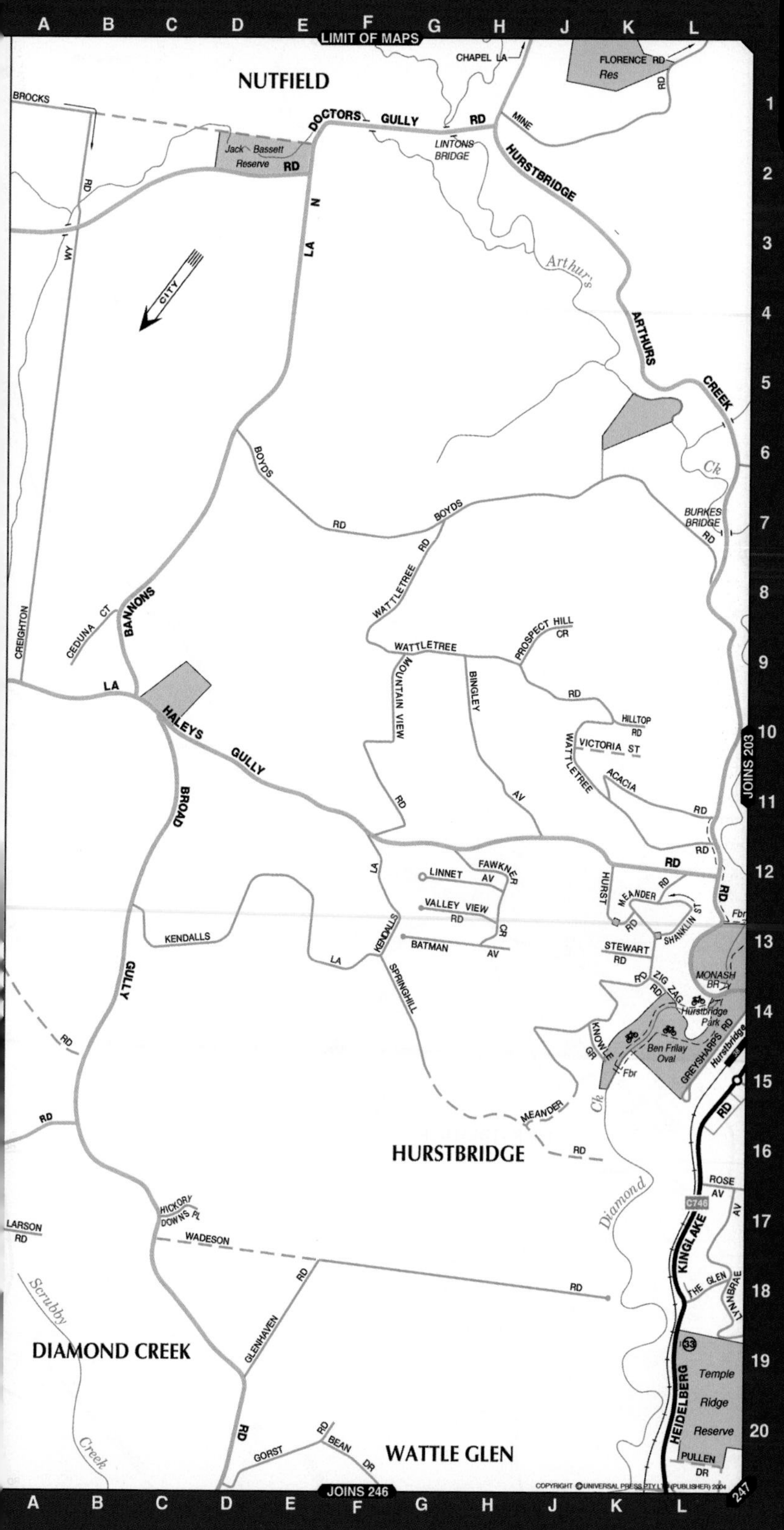

LIMIT OF MAPS
NUTFIELD
HURSTBRIDGE
DIAMOND CREEK
WATTLE GLEN
DOCTORS GULLY RD
Jack Bassett Reserve
BROCKS RD
CREIGHTON WY
CHAPEL LA
FLORENCE RD
Res
MINE RD
LINTONS BRIDGE
HURSTBRIDGE ARTHURS CREEK RD
Arthurs Ck
CITY
BANNONS LA
BOYDS RD
BURKES BRIDGE RD
WATTLETREE RD
PROSPECT HILL CR
CEDUNA CT
MOUNTAIN VIEW RD
BINGLEY AV
HILLTOP RD
VICTORIA ST
ACACIA RD
HALEYS GULLY RD
BROAD GULLY RD
LINNET AV
FAWKNER CR
VALLEY VIEW RD
BATMAN AV
KENDALLS LA
SPRINGHILL
HURST RD
MEANDER RD
SHANKLIN ST
STEWART RD
ZIG ZAG RD
MONASH BR
Fbr
Hurstbridge Park
Ben Frilay Oval
KNOWLE GR
GREYSHARPS RD
Hurstbridge
Diamond Ck
ROSE AV
C746
KINGLAKE RD
THE GLEN
LYNNBRAE
HICKORY DOWNS PL
LARSON RD
WADESON RD
GLENHAVEN RD
Scrubby Creek
33
HEIDELBERG
Temple Ridge Reserve
PULLEN DR
GORST RD
BEAN DR
JOINS 203
JOINS 246

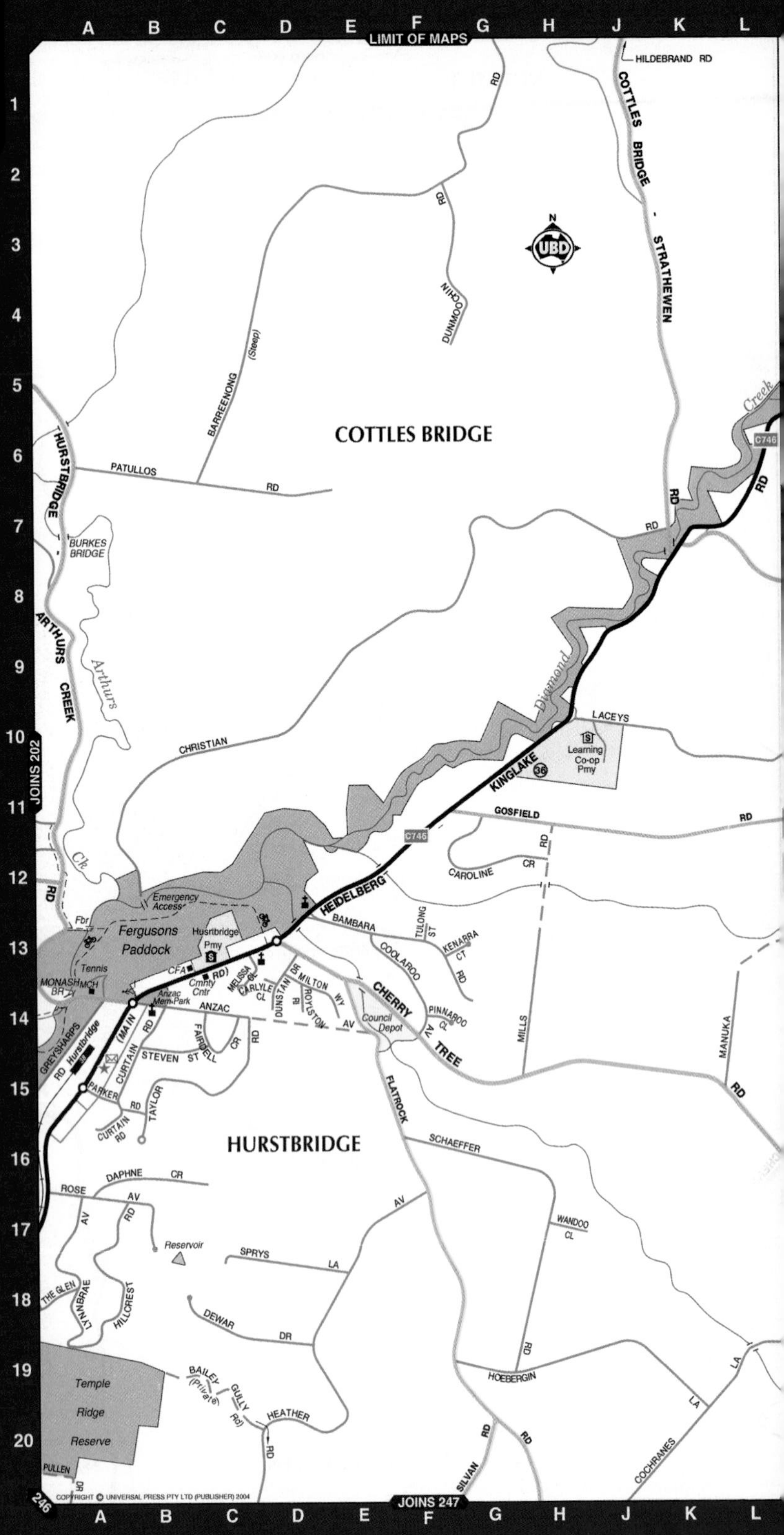
LIMIT OF MAPS
COTTLES BRIDGE
HURSTBRIDGE
COTTLES BRIDGE - STRATHEWEN
HILDEBRAND RD
DUNMOOCHIN
BARREENONG (Steep)
PATULLOS RD
HURSTBRIDGE
BURKES BRIDGE
ARTHURS CREEK
Arthurs Ck
CHRISTIAN
KINGLAKE
HEIDELBERG RD
Diamond Creek
LACEYS
Learning Co-op Pmy
GOSFIELD RD
CAROLINE CR
TULONG ST
KENARRA CT
COOLAROO RD
BAMBARA
CHERRY TREE AV
PINNAROO CL
Council Depot
MILLS
MANUKA RD
Emergency Access
Fergusons Paddock
Hurstbridge Pmy
Tennis
MONASH BR
MCH
CFA
Cmnty Cntr
Anzac Mem Park
ANZAC
MELISSA CL
CARLYLE CL
DUNSTAN
MILTON WY
ROYLSTON
GREYSHARPS RD
Hurstbridge
CURTAIN RD
STEVEN ST
FAIRDELL CR
PARKER
TAYLOR
FLATROCK
SCHAEFFER
DAPHNE CR
ROSE AV
Reservoir
SPRYS LA
WANDOO CL
THE GLEN
LYNNBRAE
HILLCREST
DEWAR DR
HOEBERGIN
Temple Ridge Reserve
BAILEY (Private)
GULLY Rd
HEATHER RD
PULLEN DR
SILVAN RD
COCHRANES
C746
JOINS 202
JOINS 247
246
COPYRIGHT © UNIVERSAL PRESS PTY LTD (PUBLISHER) 2004

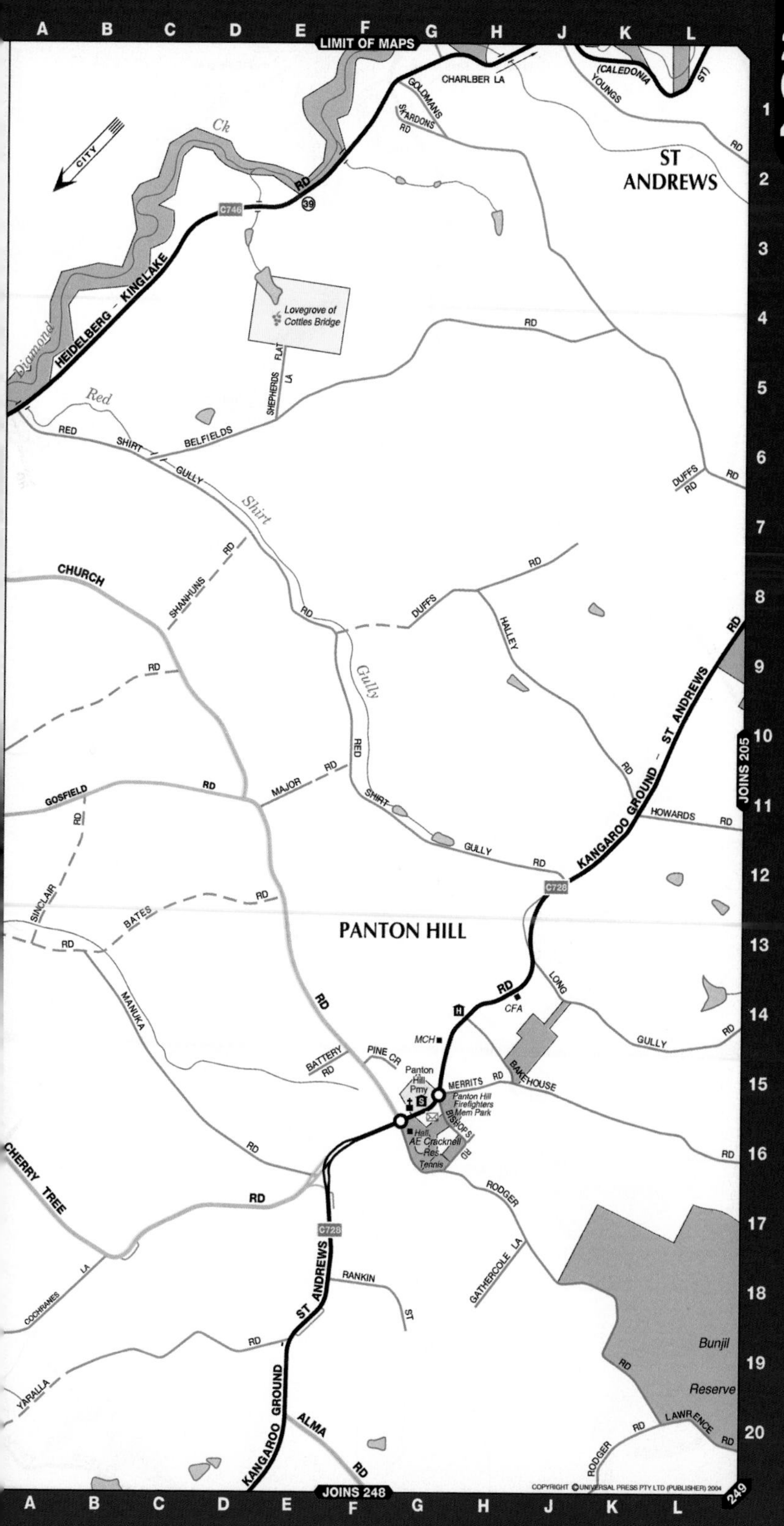

LIMIT OF MAPS
CITY
Ck
Diamond
HEIDELBERG - KINGLAKE
RD
C746
39
CHARLBER LA
GOLDMANS
SHARDONS
RD
(CALEDONIA
YOUNGS
ST)
RD
ST
ANDREWS
Lovegrove of Cottles Bridge
SHEPHERDS FLAT
LA
RD
Red
RED
SHIRT
GULLY
BELFIELDS
Shirt
DUFFS
RD
RD
CHURCH
SHANHUNS
RD
DUFFS
RD
HALLEY
Gully
RD
RED
RD
GOSFIELD
RD
MAJOR
RD
SHIRT
GULLY
RD
KANGAROO GROUND - ST ANDREWS
RD
HOWARDS
RD
C728
RD
SINCLAIR
BATES
RD
RD
PANTON HILL
MANUKA
RD
RD
CFA
LONG
GULLY
RD
MCH
BATTERY
RD
PINE CR
Panton Hill Pmy
MERRITS
RD
BAKEHOUSE
Panton Hill Firefighters Mem Park
BISHOPS
RD
Hall
AE Cracknell Res
Tennis
RD
CHERRY TREE
RD
RD
RODGER
C728
ST ANDREWS
RANKIN
ST
GATHERCOLE LA
COCHRANES
LA
RD
YARALLA
Bunjil
Reserve
RD
KANGAROO GROUND
ALMA
RD
RD
LAWRENCE
RD
RODGER
JOINS 205
JOINS 248

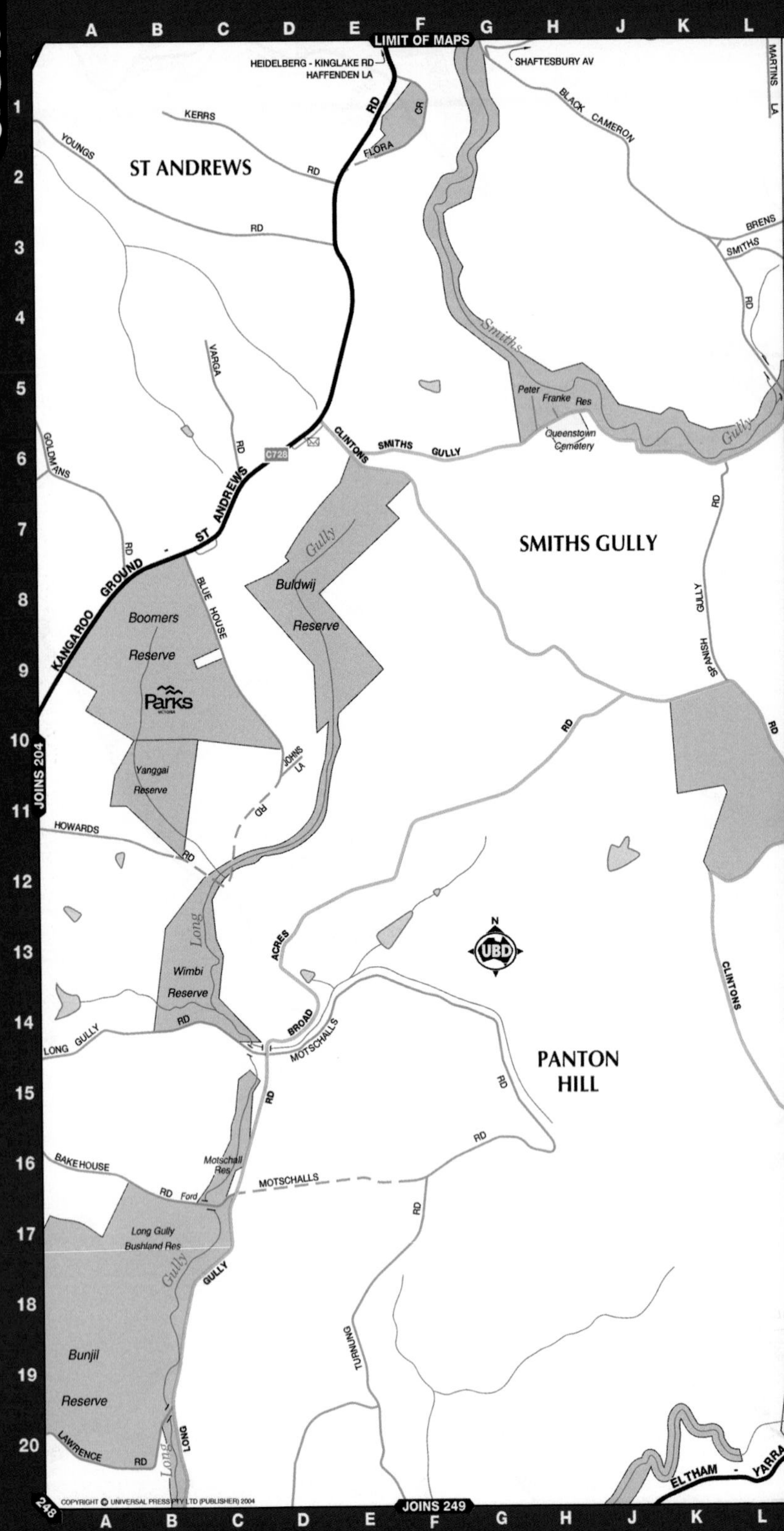
LIMIT OF MAPS
HEIDELBERG - KINGLAKE RD
HAFFENDEN LA
SHAFTESBURY AV
MARTINS LA
KERRS
YOUNGS
ST ANDREWS
RD
FLORA
CR
BLACK CAMERON
BRENS
SMITHS
Smiths
VARGA
Peter Franke Res
Queenstown Cemetery
CLINTONS
SMITHS GULLY
C728
GOLDMANS
ST ANDREWS
KANGAROO GROUND
Gully
Buldwij Reserve
SMITHS GULLY
BLUE HOUSE
Boomers Reserve
Parks
SPANISH GULLY
JOHNS LA
Yanggai Reserve
HOWARDS
Long
Wimbi Reserve
ACRES
BROAD
MOTSCHALLS
LONG GULLY
PANTON HILL
CLINTONS
BAKEHOUSE
Motschall Res
Ford
MOTSCHALLS
Long Gully Bushland Res
Gully
GULLY
TURNING
Bunjil Reserve
LAWRENCE
LONG
ELTHAM - YARRA
JOINS 204
JOINS 249
248

LIMIT OF MAPS

JOINS 207

JOINS 250
251

A B C D E F G H J K L

LIMIT OF MAPS

ST ANDREWS

SMITHS GULLY

CHRISTMAS HILLS

Melbourne Water Catchment Area

Melbourne Water

BUTTERMANS RD
YOW YOW RISING
MARSHALLS RD
RIFLE RANGE RD
Rifle Range
BUTTERMANS TR
WALLACE
DEAN RD (Steep)
BYRON
OSBORNE
REEVES RD
McKINNON
ONE TREE HILL RD
ROBERTS RD
ELTHAM – YARRA GLEN RD
CFA
C726
RIDGE RD
Melbourne Water

JOINS 206

250

JOINS 251

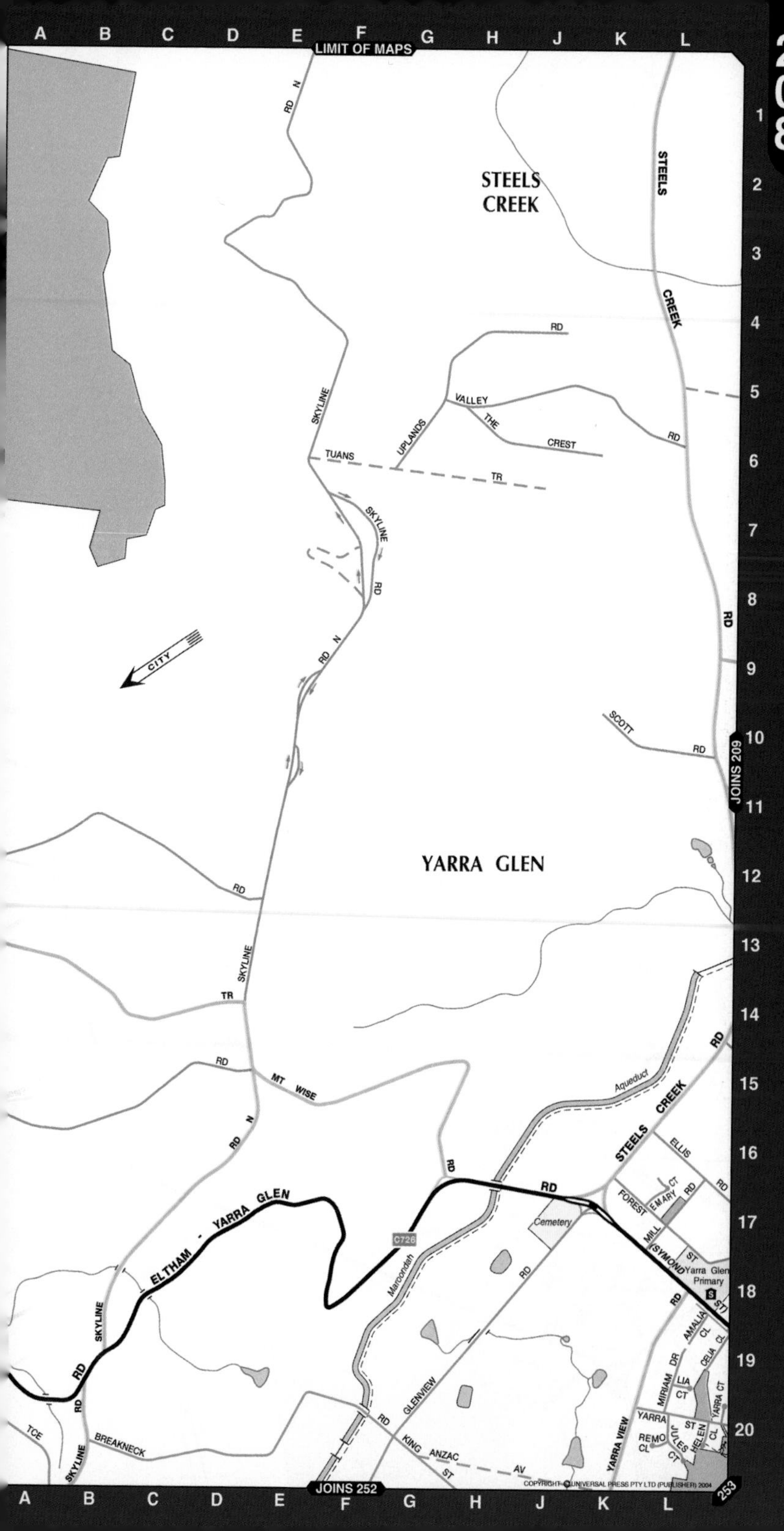

LIMIT OF MAPS
STEELS CREEK
YARRA GLEN
STEELS CREEK RD
SKYLINE RD N
TUANS TR
UPLANDS
VALLEY RD
THE CREST
SCOTT RD
CITY
SKYLINE TR
MT WISE RD
ELTHAM - YARRA GLEN RD
C726
Maroondah Aqueduct
Cemetery
FOREST MILL
EMARY CT
ELLIS RD
SYMOND ST
Yarra Glen Primary
AMALIA CL
CELIA CL
MIRIAM DR
LIA CT
YARRA CT
YARRA ST
REMO CL
JULES CT
HELEN CL
YARRA VIEW
GLENVIEW RD
KING ST
ANZAC AV
BREAKNECK RD
SKYLINE RD
TCE
JOINS 209
JOINS 252
COPYRIGHT © UNIVERSAL PRESS PTY LTD (PUBLISHER) 2004

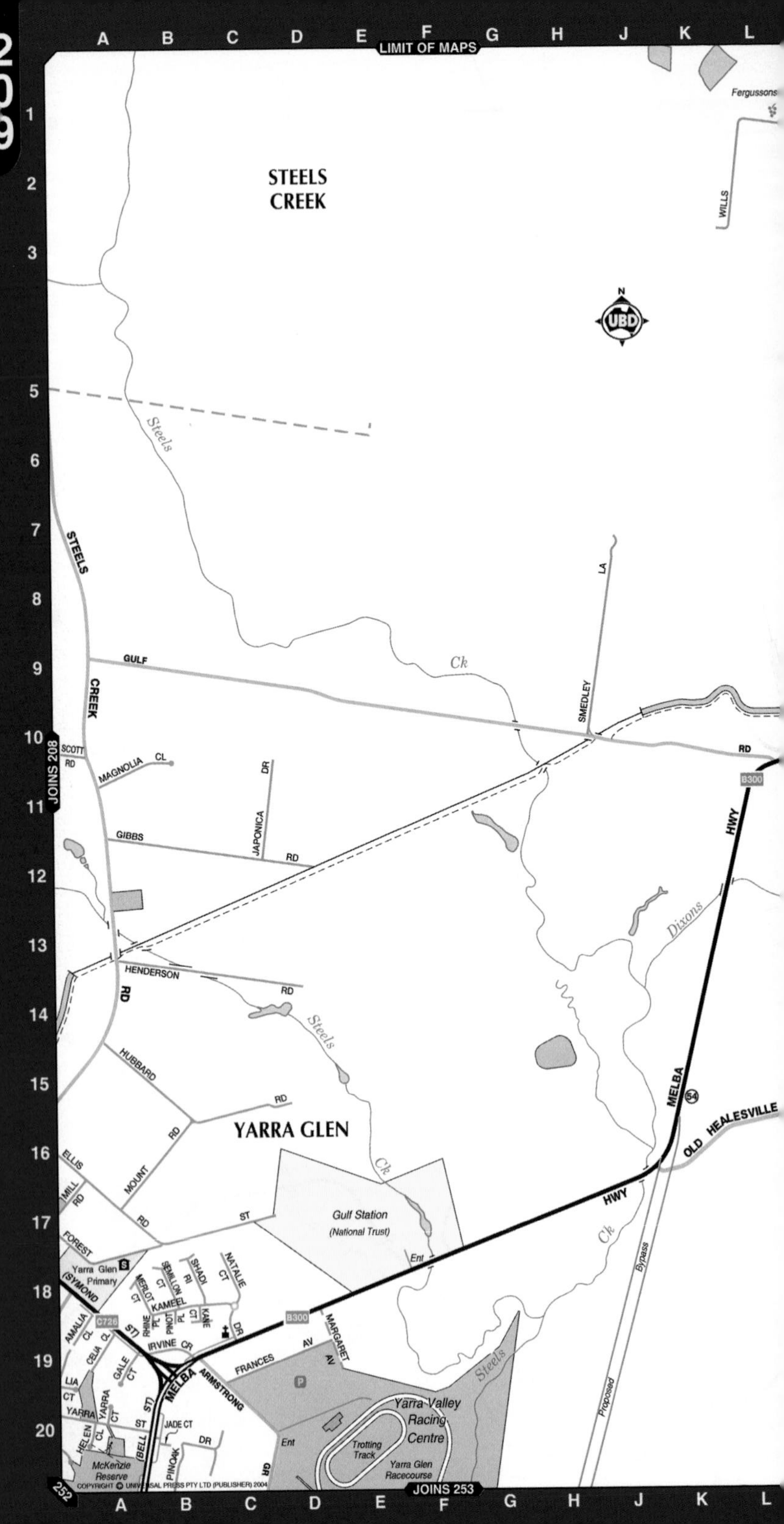
LIMIT OF MAPS
Fergussons
WILLS
STEELS
CREEK
Steels
STEELS
LA
GULF
Ck
SMEDLEY
CREEK
RD
SCOTT
RD
MAGNOLIA
CL
DR
JAPONICA
B300
HWY
GIBBS
RD
Dixons
HENDERSON
RD
RD
Steels
HUBBARD
MELBA
RD
OLD HEALESVILLE
YARRA GLEN
RD
ELLIS
MOUNT
Ck
MILL
RD
HWY
RD
ST
Gulf Station
(National Trust)
Ck
FOREST
Ent
Bypass
Yarra Glen
Primary
(SYMOND
NATALIE
CT
SHADI
RI
SEMILLON
CT
MERLOT
CT
KAMEEL
AMALIA
C726
RHINE
PINOT
PL
CT
KANE
DR
B300
MARGARET
CL
CELIA
ST)
IRVINE
CR
AV
GALE
CT
FRANCES
AV
Steels
LIA
MELBA
ARMSTRONG
Proposed
CT
YARRA
YARRA
CT
ST)
Yarra Valley
Racing
Centre
ST
JADE CT
HELEN
CL
(BELL
DR
Ent
Trotting
Track
Yarra Glen
Racecourse
PINOAK
GR
McKenzie
Reserve
JOINS 208
JOINS 253
252

A B C D E F G H J K L
LIMIT OF MAPS

RD
Henkell
Winery
DIXONS CREEK
HWY
Creek
Creek
Pauls
LA
BOTTINGS
57
BLEASES
Pauls
B300
CITY
MELBA
Creek
JOINS 211
RD
LA
RD
STAG LA
TARRAWARRA
Ck
Pauls
TARRAWARRA
YARRA GLEN RD
C726
HEALESVILLE
RD
TARRAWARRA

1 2 3 4 5 6 7 8 9 10 11 12 13 14 15 16 17 18 19 20

JOINS 254
A B C D E F G H J K L

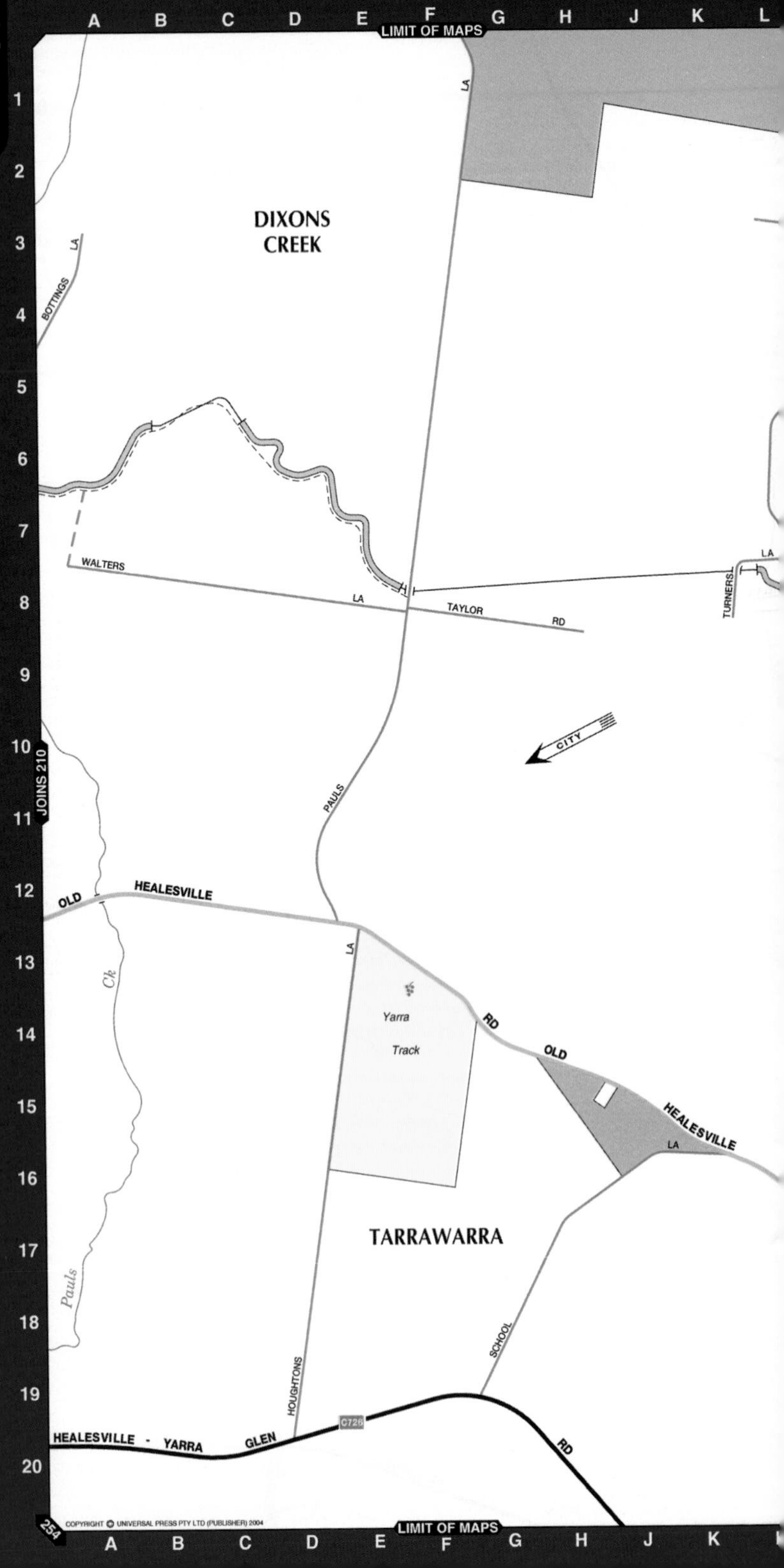

A B C D E F G H J K L

LIMIT OF MAPS

1 2 3 4 5 6 7 8 9 10 11 12 13 14 15 16 17 18 19 20

DIXONS CREEK

BOTTINGS LA

WALTERS LA

TAYLOR RD

TURNERS LA

CITY

JOINS 210

PAULS LA

OLD HEALESVILLE RD

Ck

Yarra Track

OLD HEALESVILLE LA

TARRAWARRA

Pauls

SCHOOL

HOUGHTONS

HEALESVILLE - YARRA GLEN RD

C726

254

LIMIT OF MAPS

A B C D E F G H J K

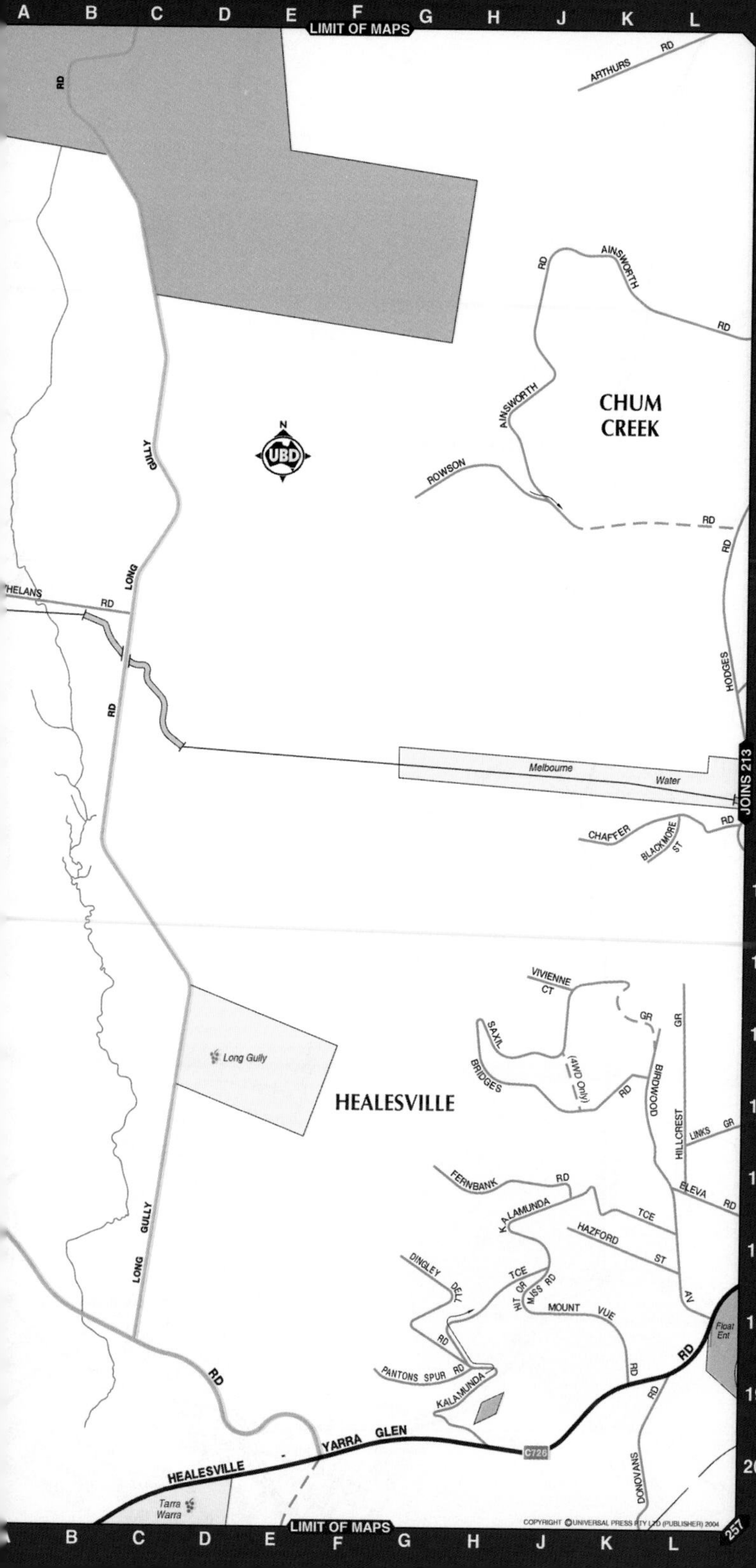
LIMIT OF MAPS
ARTHURS RD
AINSWORTH RD
CHUM CREEK
ROWSON
RD
HODGES
PHELANS RD
LONG GULLY RD
Melbourne Water
JOINS 213
CHAFFER RD
BLACKMORE ST
VIVIENNE CT
SAXIL
BRIDGES RD
(4WD Only)
GR
BIRDWOOD
HILLCREST GR
LINKS GR
Long Gully
HEALESVILLE
FERNBANK RD
ELEVA RD
KALAMUNDA
TCE
HAZFORD ST
DINGLEY DELL
HIT OR MISS RD
MOUNT VUE RD
AV
Float Ent
PANTONS SPUR RD
KALAMUNDA
HEALESVILLE YARRA GLEN RD
C726
DONOVANS RD
Tarra Warra
LIMIT OF MAPS
COPYRIGHT © UNIVERSAL PRESS PTY LTD (PUBLISHER) 2004
257

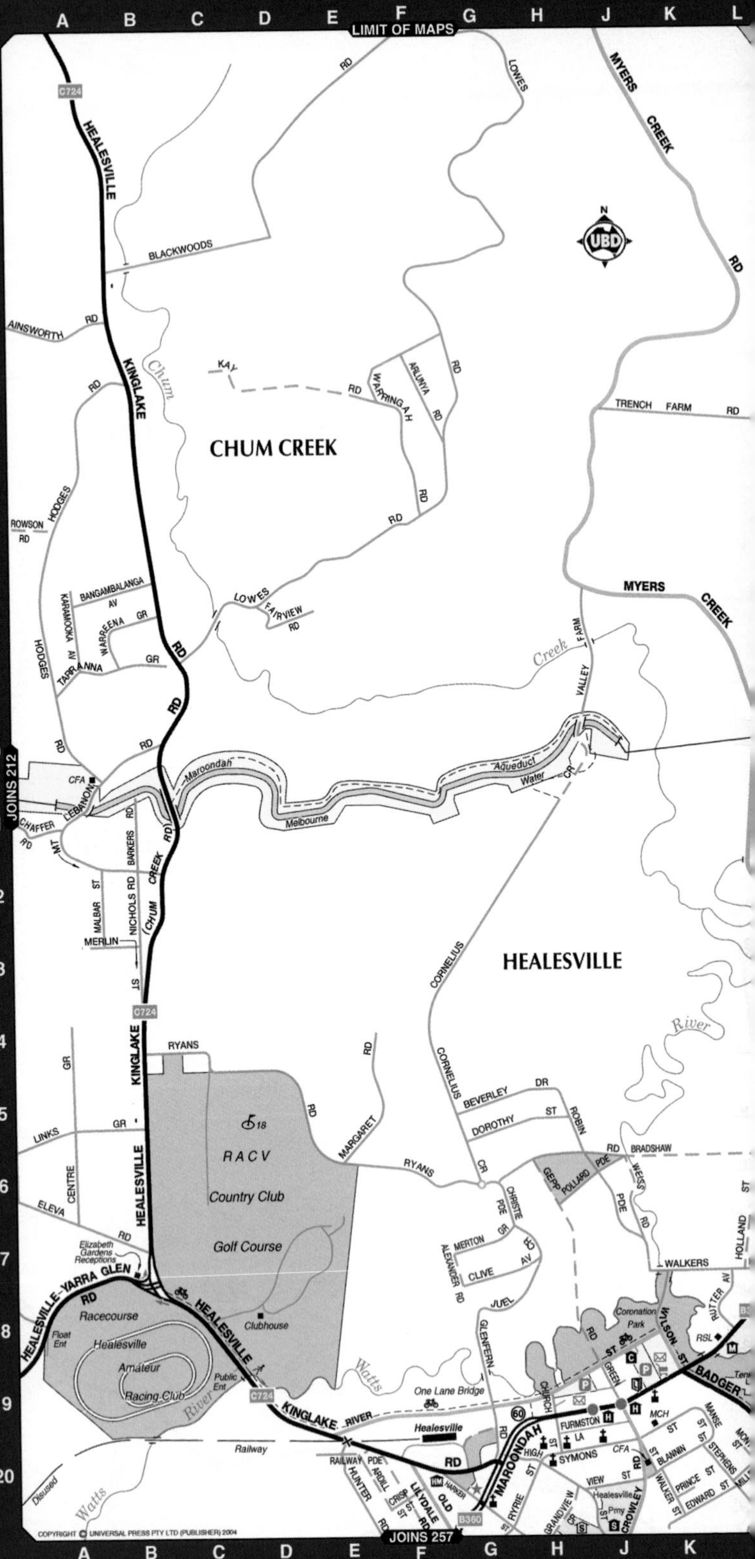

LIMIT OF MAPS

CHUM CREEK

HEALESVILLE

HEALESVILLE RD
KINGLAKE RD
C724
BLACKWOODS
AINSWORTH RD
LOWES RD
MYERS CREEK RD
TRENCH FARM RD
KAY
WARRINGAH RD
ARLUNYA RD
ROWSON RD
HODGES RD
BANGAMBALANGA AV
KARAMOOKA AV
WARREENA GR
TARRANNA GR
LOWES FAIRVIEW RD
VALLEY FARM
Chum Creek
Maroondah Aqueduct
Melbourne Water
CR
CFA
LEBANON
CHAFFER
MT RD
BARKERS RD
MALBAR ST
NICHOLS RD
MERLIN
ST
(CHUM CREEK RD)
CORNELIUS CR
River
RYANS RD
MARGARET
BEVERLEY DR
DOROTHY ST
ROBIN
BRADSHAW RD
GEPP
POLLARD PDE
WEISS PDE
ST
HOLLAND
WALKERS
LINKS GR
CENTRE
ELEVA
RACV Country Club Golf Course
Clubhouse
Elizabeth Gardens Receptions
HEALESVILLE-YARRA GLEN RD
Racecourse
Float Ent
Healesville Amateur Racing Club
Public Ent
Watts River
CHRISTIE PDE
MERTON GR
ALEXANDER RD
CLIVE AV
JUEL
GLENFERN
Coronation Park
WILSON ST
RUTTER AV
RSL
BADGER
One Lane Bridge
KINGLAKE RIVER
Healesville
Railway
Disused
RAILWAY PDE
HUNTER
ARDILL
CRISP ST
LILYDALE OLD RD
HARKER
B360
MAROONDAH
CHURCH
GREEN ST
FURMSTON LA
HIGH ST
SYMONS
RYRIE
GRANDVIEW CR
VIEW ST
Healesville Pmy
CROWLEY RD
CFA
BLANNIN
WALKER ST
MCH
MANSE ST
PRINCE ST
STEPHENS
EDWARD ST
JOINS 212
JOINS 257

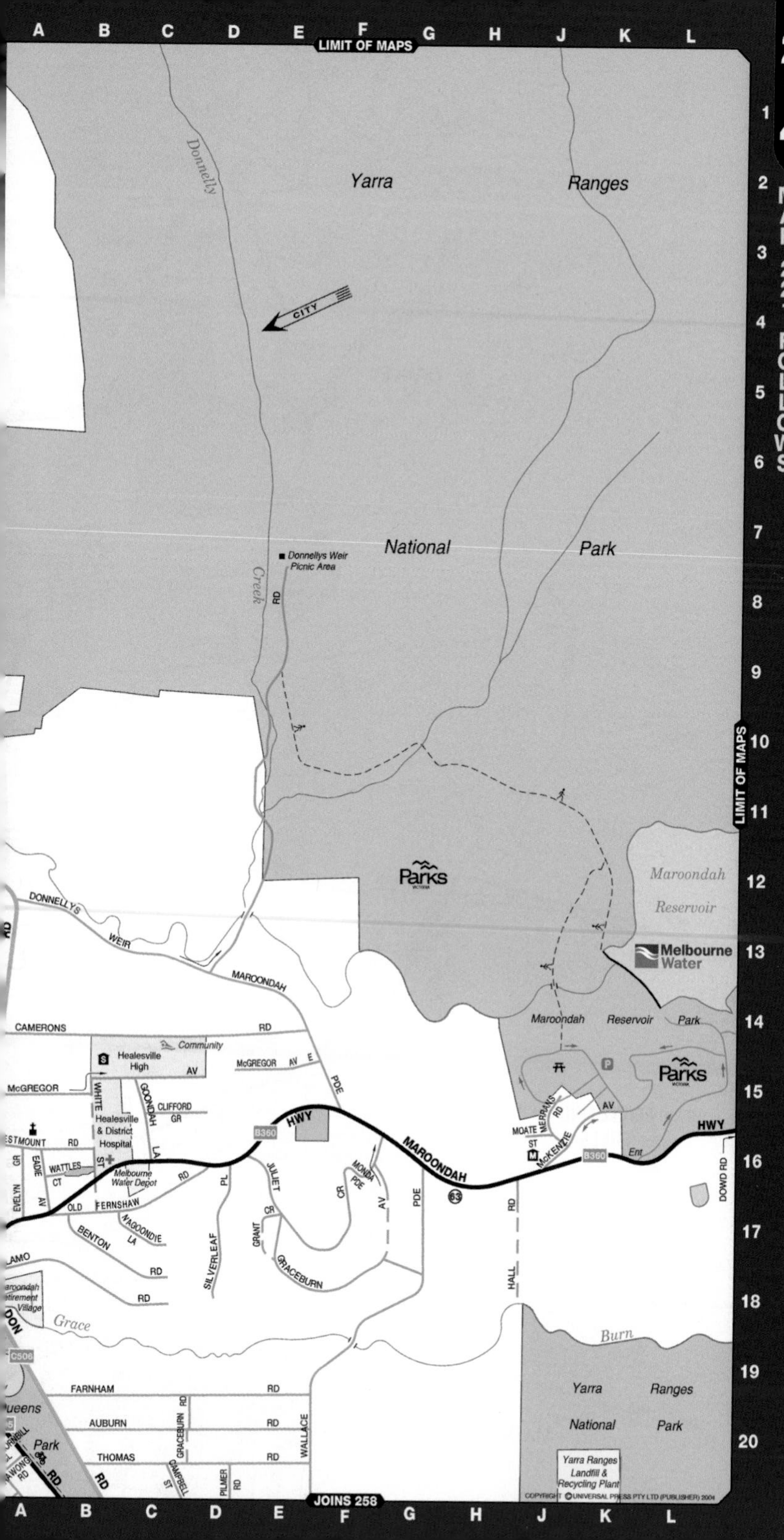

A B C D E F G H J K L
LIMIT OF MAPS
Yarra
Ranges
Donnelly
Creek
CITY
National
Park
Donnellys Weir Picnic Area
RD
LIMIT OF MAPS
Parks
Maroondah
Reservoir
Melbourne Water
DONNELLYS
WEIR
MAROONDAH
CAMERONS
RD
Community
Healesville High
AV
McGREGOR AV E
PDE
McGREGOR
WHITE ST
GOONDAH LA
CLIFFORD GR
Healesville & District Hospital
B360
HWY
MAROONDAH
Maroondah Reservoir Park
MERRANS RD
MOATE ST
McKENZIE
AV
HWY
Ent
B360
DOWD RD
RD
WATTLES CT
Melbourne Water Depot
RD
PL
JULIET
MONDA PDE
CR
AV
PDE
63
RD
EVELYN
EADIE
AV
OLD
FERNSHAW
RD
CR
NAGOONDIE LA
BENTON
RD
SILVERLEAF
GRANT
GRACEBURN
HALL
RD
RD
Grace
Burn
C506
FARNHAM
RD
AUBURN
RD
GRACEBURN RD
THOMAS
RD
WALLACE
Park
CAMPBELL ST
PILMER RD
RD
Yarra Ranges National Park
Yarra Ranges Landfill & Recycling Plant
JOINS 258
MAP 221 FOLLOWS
1 2 3 4 5 6 7 8 9 10 11 12 13 14 15 16 17 18 19 20

PREVIOUS MAP 214

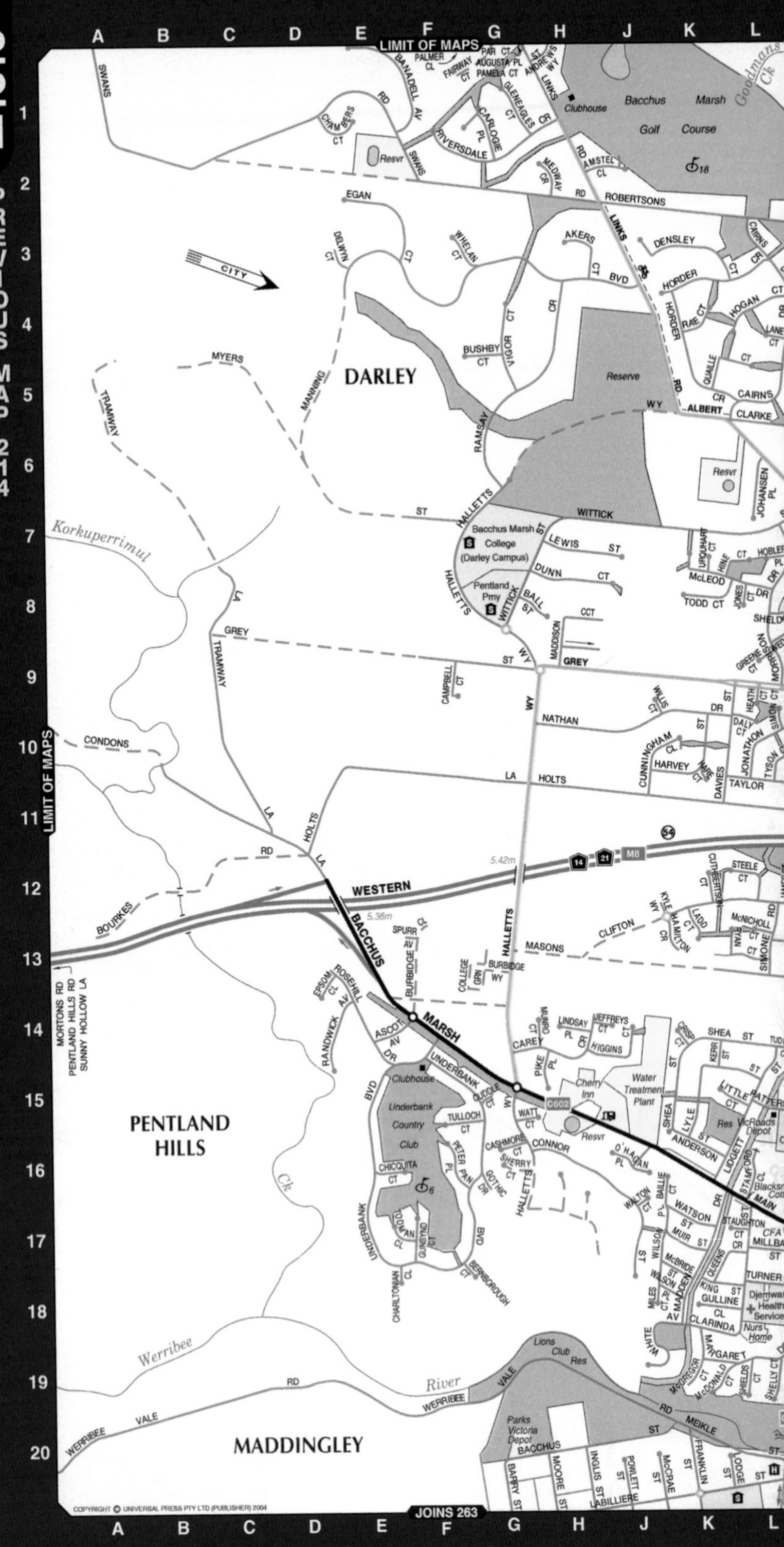

JOINS 263

LIMIT OF MAPS 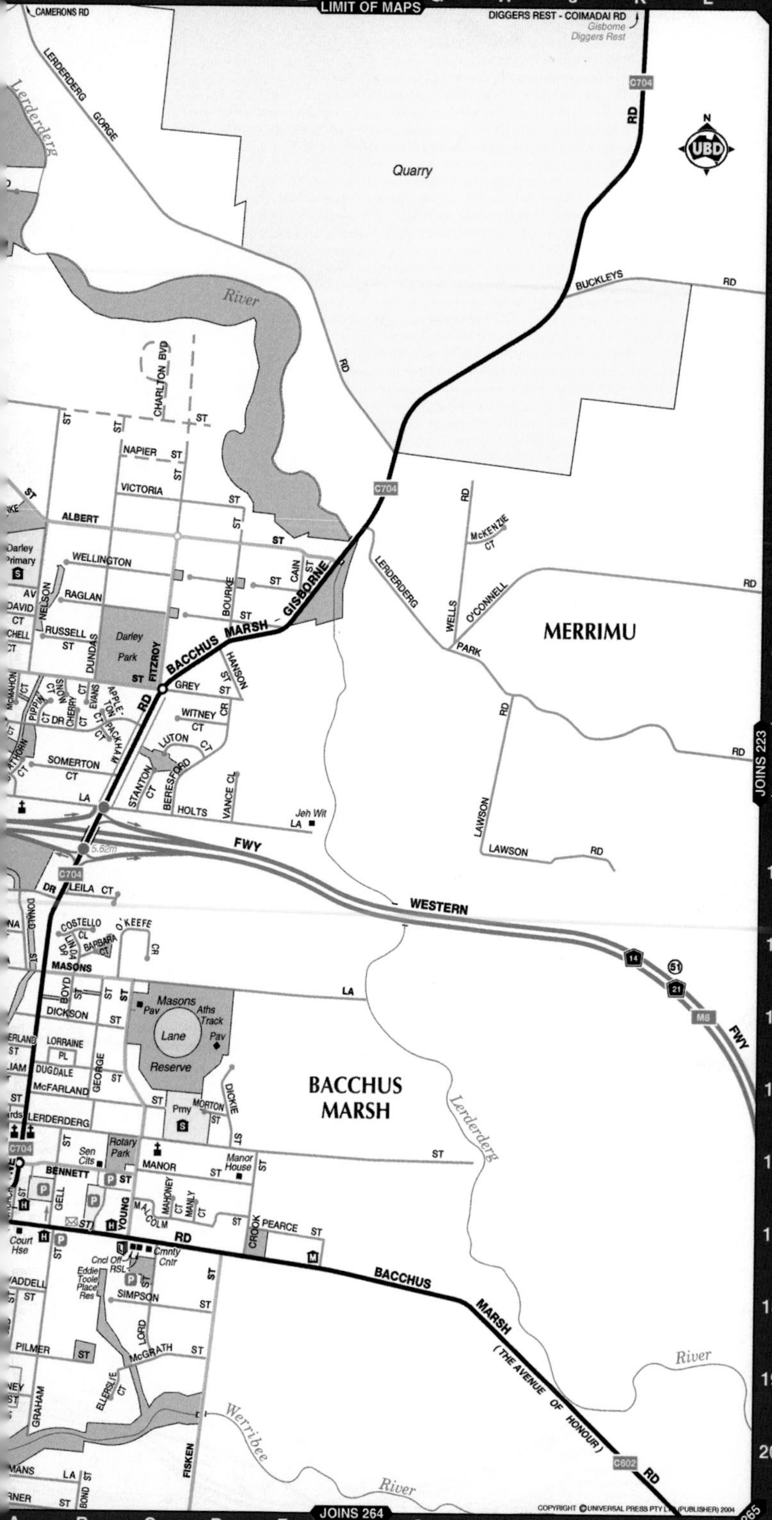
CAMERONS RD
LERDERDERG GORGE RD
DIGGERS REST - COIMADAI RD
Gisborne
Diggers Rest
Quarry
BUCKLEYS RD
Lerderderg River
CHARLTON BVD
NAPIER ST
VICTORIA ST
ALBERT ST
WELLINGTON ST
RAGLAN ST
RUSSELL ST
Darley Primary
Darley Park
BACCHUS MARSH - GISBORNE RD
LERDERDERG PARK
WELLS RD
O'CONNELL
McKENZIE CT
MERRIMU
LAWSON RD
GREY ST
WITNEY CT
LUTON CT
BERESFORD
STANTON CT
HOLTS LA
VANCE CL
Jeh Wit
WESTERN FWY
LEILA CT
COSTELLO CL
O'KEEFE CR
BARBARA CT
MASONS LA
Masons Lane Reserve
Aths Track
DICKSON ST
LORRAINE PL
DUGDALE ST
McFARLAND ST
BACCHUS MARSH
MORTON ST
DICKIE ST
LERDERDERG ST
Rotary Park
Sen Cits
MANOR ST
Manor House
BENNETT ST
MALCOLM
PEARCE ST
CROOK
Court Hse
Cmnty Cntr
Cncl Off
RSL
Eddie Toole Place Res
SIMPSON ST
LORD
McGRATH ST
PILMER ST
ELLERSLIE CT
GRAHAM
FISKEN
Werribee River
BACCHUS MARSH RD (THE AVENUE OF HONOUR)
MERRIMU
JOINS 223
JOINS 264

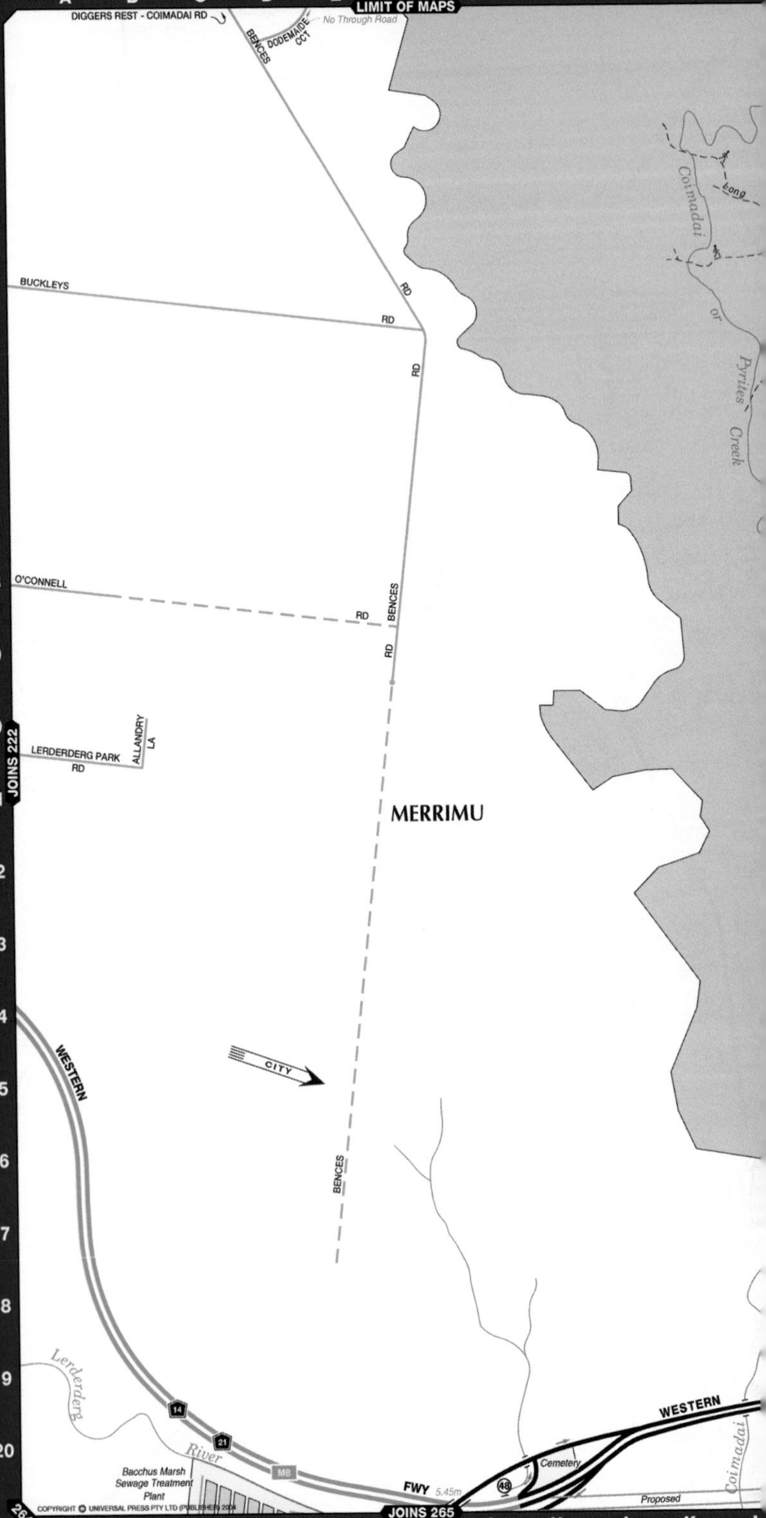
LIMIT OF MAPS
DIGGERS REST - COIMADAI RD
No Through Road
DODEMAIDE CCT
BENCES RD
BUCKLEYS RD
O'CONNELL RD
LERDERDERG PARK RD
ALLANDRY LA
MERRIMU
CITY
Coimadai or Pyrites Creek
Long
WESTERN FWY
Lerderderg River
Bacchus Marsh Sewage Treatment Plant
M8
14
21
48
5.45m
Cemetery
Proposed
Coimadai
JOINS 222
JOINS 265
264

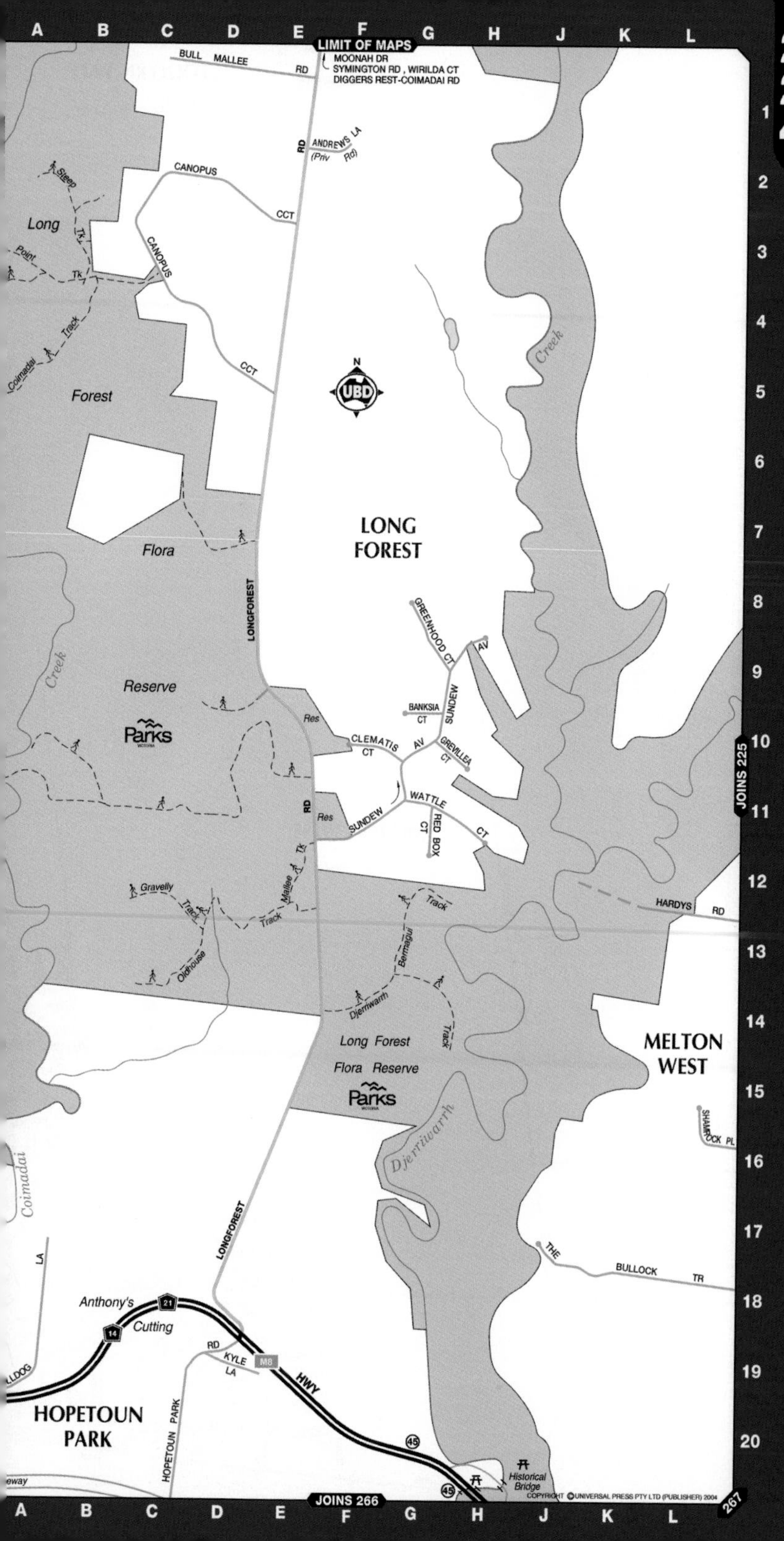

JOINS 225
JOINS 266

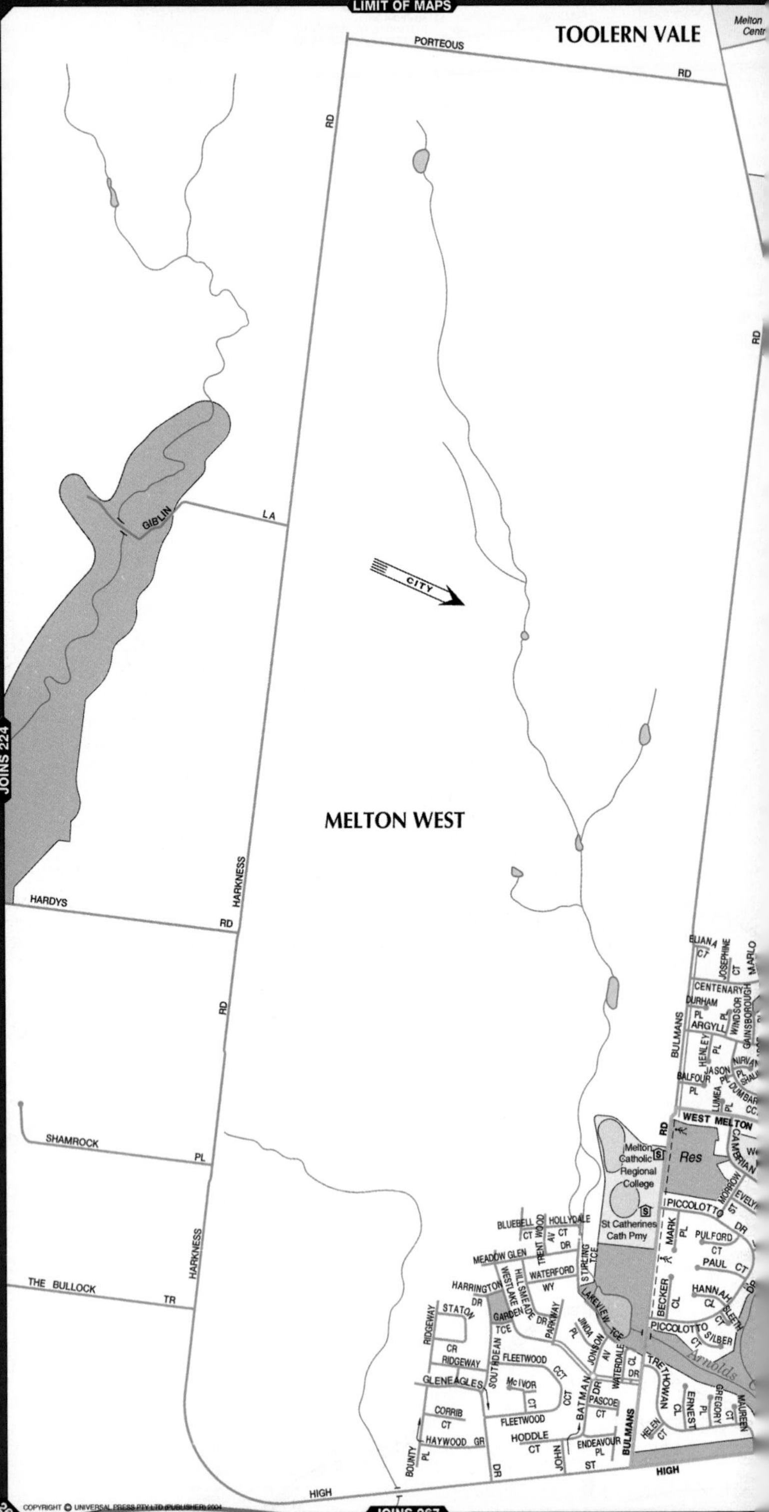
LIMIT OF MAPS
TOOLERN VALE
MELTON WEST
PORTEOUS RD
GIBLIN LA
HARKNESS RD
HARDYS RD
SHAMROCK PL
THE BULLOCK TR
CITY
JOINS 224
JOINS 267
266
HIGH
BULMANS RD
WEST MELTON
Res
Melton Catholic Regional College
St Catherines Cath Pmy
ELIANA CT
JOSEPHINE CT
MARLO
CENTENARY
DURHAM PL
ARGYLL
WINDSOR PL
GAINSBOROUGH
HENLEY PL
JASON PL
BALFOUR PL
LUMEA PL
DUMBAR
CAMBRIAN
MORROW ST
EVELYN
PICCOLOTTO DR
MARK PL
PULFORD CT
PAUL CT
BECKER CL
HANNAH CL
SLEETH
SILBER CT
Arnolds
TRETHOWAN CL
ERNEST PL
GREGORY CT
MAUREEN
HELEN CT
BLUEBELL CT
TRENT WOOD AV
HOLLYDALE CT DR
STIRLING TCE
MEADOW GLEN
WATERFORD WY
HARRINGTON DR
WESTLAKE GARDEN TCE
HILLSMEADE DR
PARKWAY
LAKEVIEW TCE
JINDA PL
JONSON AV
WATERDALE CL DR
STATON
RIDGEWAY CR
RIDGEWAY
SOUTHDEAN
FLEETWOOD CCT
GLENEAGLES
McIVOR CT
BATMAN DR
PASCOE CT
CORRIB CT
FLEETWOOD
HODDLE CT
JOHN
ENDEAVOUR PL
ST
HAYWOOD GR
BOUNTY PL
DR
HIGH
Melton Centr

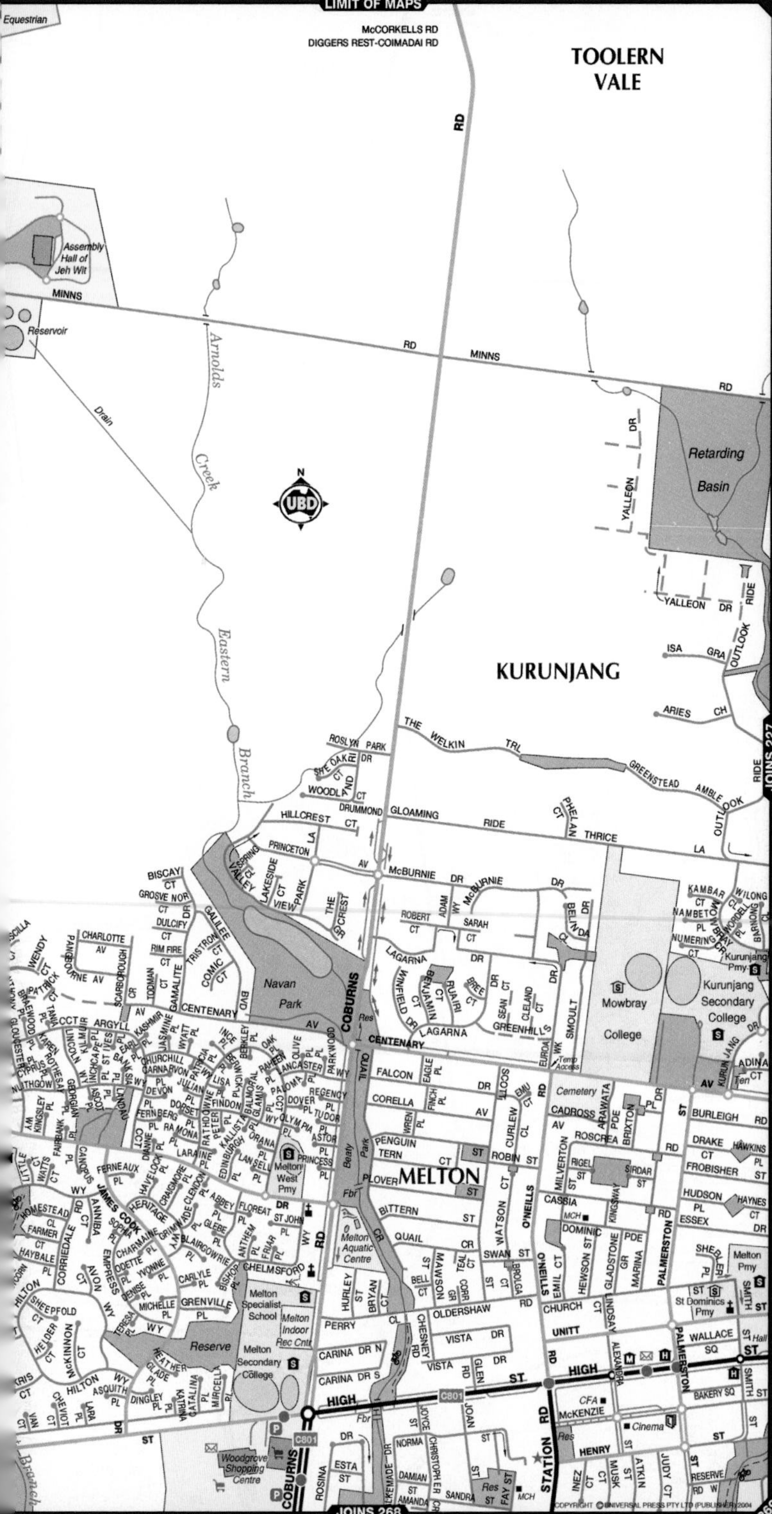

McCORKELLS RD
DIGGERS REST-COIMADAI RD

TOOLERN VALE

KURUNJANG

MELTON

Equestrian
Assembly Hall of Jeh Wit
Reservoir
MINNS RD
Drain
Arnolds Creek
Eastern Branch
Retarding Basin
YALLEON DR
OUTLOOK RIDE
ISA GRA
ARIES CH
THE WELKIN TRL
GREENSTEAD AMBLE
ROSLYN PARK DR
SHE OAK RI
WOODLAND CT
DRUMMOND CT
GLOAMING RIDE
HILLCREST CT
PHELAN CT
THRICE LA
PRINCETON AV
McBURNIE DR
Navan Park
COBURNS RD
CENTENARY AV
Mowbray College
Kurunjang Pmy
Kurunjang Secondary College
KURUNJANG AV
Cemetery
Melton West Pmy
Beaty Park
Melton Aquatic Centre
Melton Specialist School
Melton Indoor Rec Cntr
Melton Secondary College
Reserve
HIGH ST
C801
STATION RD
O'NEILLS RD
PALMERSTON ST
Melton Pmy
St Dominics Pmy
CFA
Cinema
Woodgrove Shopping Centre
HENRY ST
MCH

JOINS 227
JOINS 268
269

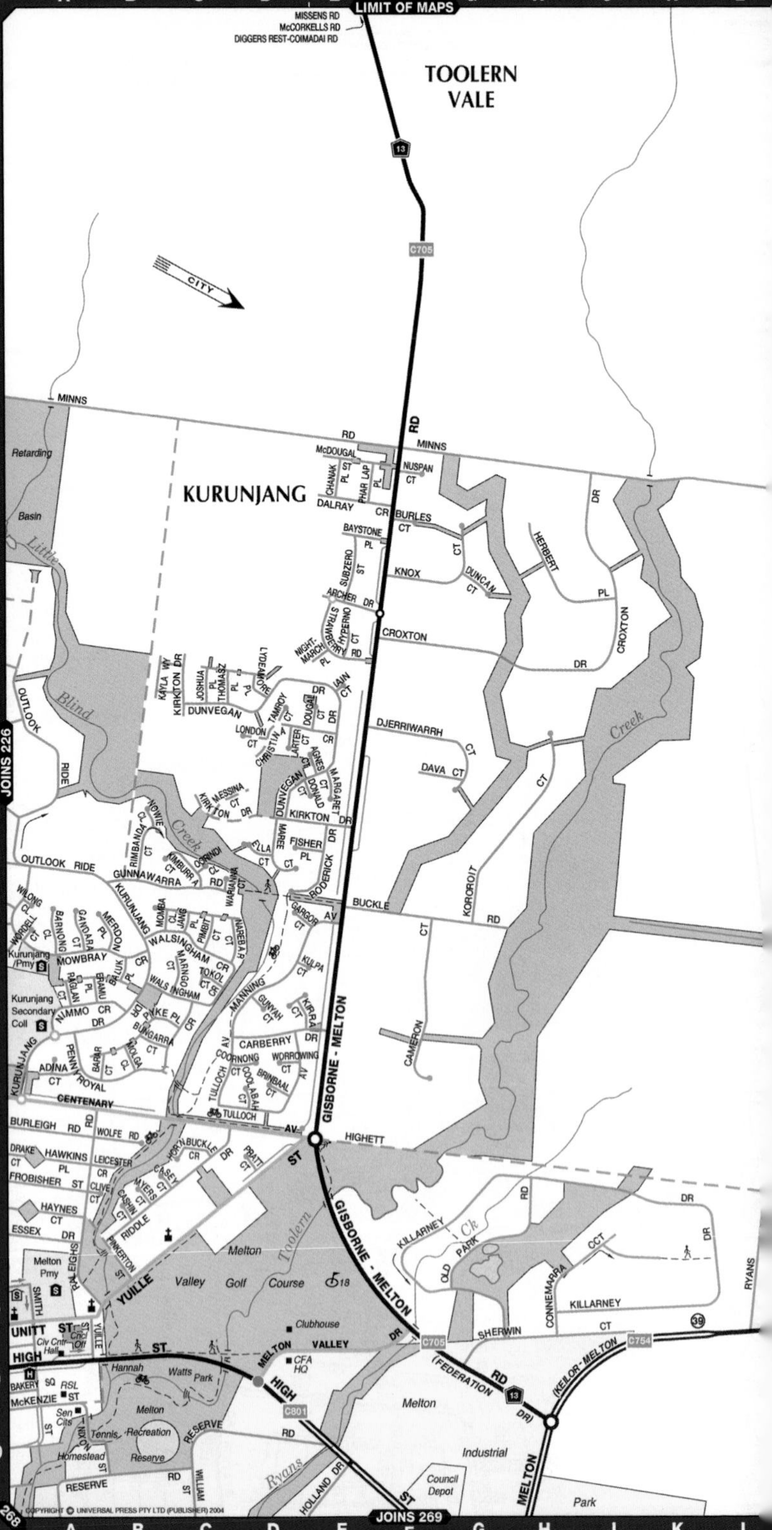

LIMIT OF MAPS
MISSENS RD
McCORKELLS RD
DIGGERS REST-COIMADAI RD
TOOLERN VALE
13
C705
CITY
MINNS
MINNS RD
KURUNJANG
Retarding Basin
Little
Blind Creek
Creek
McDOUGAL
CHANAK ST
THOMAS PL
PHAR LAP PL
NUSPAN CT
DALRAY CR
BURLES CT
BAYSTONE PL
SUBZERO ST
KNOX
DUNCAN CT
HERBERT
PL
CROXTON DR
CROXTON
ARCHER DR
STRAWBERRY
HYPERNO CT
NIGHT-MARCH PL
RD
LYDEAMORE
KAYLA WY
KIRKTON DR
JOSHUA PL
THOMASZ PL
DUNVEGAN
IAIN CT
TAMROY
DOUGAL CT
LONDON CT
CHRISTINA
LARTER
AGNES
DJERRIWARRH CT
DAVA CT
DUNVEGAN CT
DONALD CT
MARGARET CT
MESSINA CT
KIRKTON DR
KIRKTON DR
NOWIE CL
RIMBANDA CT
KIMBURRA
COORINDI CL
ELLA CT
MAREE CT
FISHER PL
RODERICK DR
KOROROIT
CT
OUTLOOK RIDE
OUTLOOK RIDE
GUNNAWARRA RD
WARIANNA
BUCKLE RD
GARGOR AV
WILONG CL
WORDELL CT
BARNONG CL
GANDARA CT
MERDON PL
KURUNJANG
MOMBA CL
JANG
PIMBIT PL
NAREBAR
WALSINGHAM CR
Kurunjang Pmy
MOWBRAY
LUK
RAGLAN
ERAMU
MARINGO
TOKOL CT
WALSINGHAM
KULPA CT
MANNING
GUNYAH CT
KIRRA
CAMERON
Kurunjang Secondary Coll
NIMMO CR DR
PYKE PL
BUNGARRA CT
CARBERRY DR
COORNONG
WORROWING CT
KURUNJANG
ADINA CT
PENNYROYAL
BARAR
TULLOCH
COOLABAH
BRIMBAAL CT
GISBORNE - MELTON RD
CENTENARY AV
TULLOCH
BURLEIGH RD
WOLFE RD
HORN
BUCKLE CR
DR
PRATT CT
HIGHETT
DRAKE CT
HAWKINS PL
LEICESTER CR
FROBISHER ST
CLIVE CT
CASEY CT
MYERS CT
CASHIN CT
ST
HAYNES CT
ESSEX DR
RIDDLE
PINKERTON ST
Melton Valley Golf Course
Toolern
GISBORNE - MELTON RD
KILLARNEY
Ck
OLD PARK
RD
CONNEMARRA
CCT
KILLARNEY CT
DR
DR
RYANS
Melton Pmy
RALEIGHS
SMITH ST
YUILLE ST
YUILLE
Clubhouse
UNITT ST
Civ Cntr Hall
Cncl Off
HIGH ST
MELTON VALLEY DR
C705
SHERWIN
39
C754
(KEILOR-MELTON
(FEDERATION DR)
BAKERY SQ
RSL ST
McKENZIE ST
Hannah Watts Park
MELTON HIGH
CFA HQ
C801
Melton Industrial Park
Sen Cits
NIXON
Tennis
Melton Recreation Reserve
RESERVE RD
Homestead
ST
RESERVE RD
WILLIAM ST
Ryans
HOLLAND DR
ST
Council Depot
MELTON
JOINS 226
JOINS 269
268
COPYRIGHT © UNIVERSAL PRESS PTY LTD (PUBLISHER) 2004

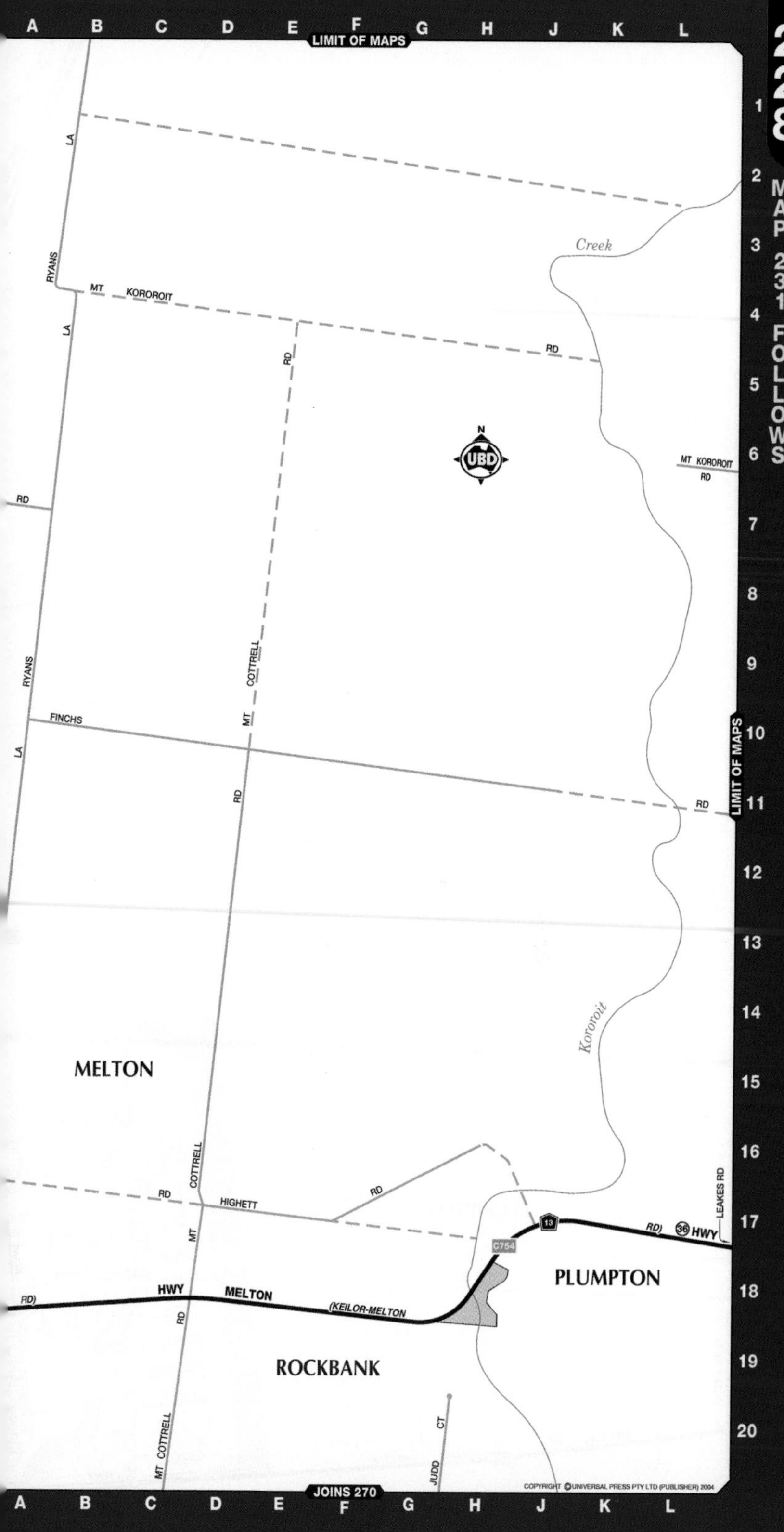

LIMIT OF MAPS
MAP 231 FOLLOWS
RYANS LA
MT KOROROIT RD
MT COTTRELL RD
RD
FINCHS RD
Creek
Kororoit
MT KOROROIT RD
LIMIT OF MAPS
MELTON
HIGHETT RD
RD
MELTON HWY
(KEILOR-MELTON RD)
HWY
C754
13
36
LEAKES RD
PLUMPTON
ROCKBANK
JUDD CT
JOINS 270

PREVIOUS MAP 228
JOINS 187

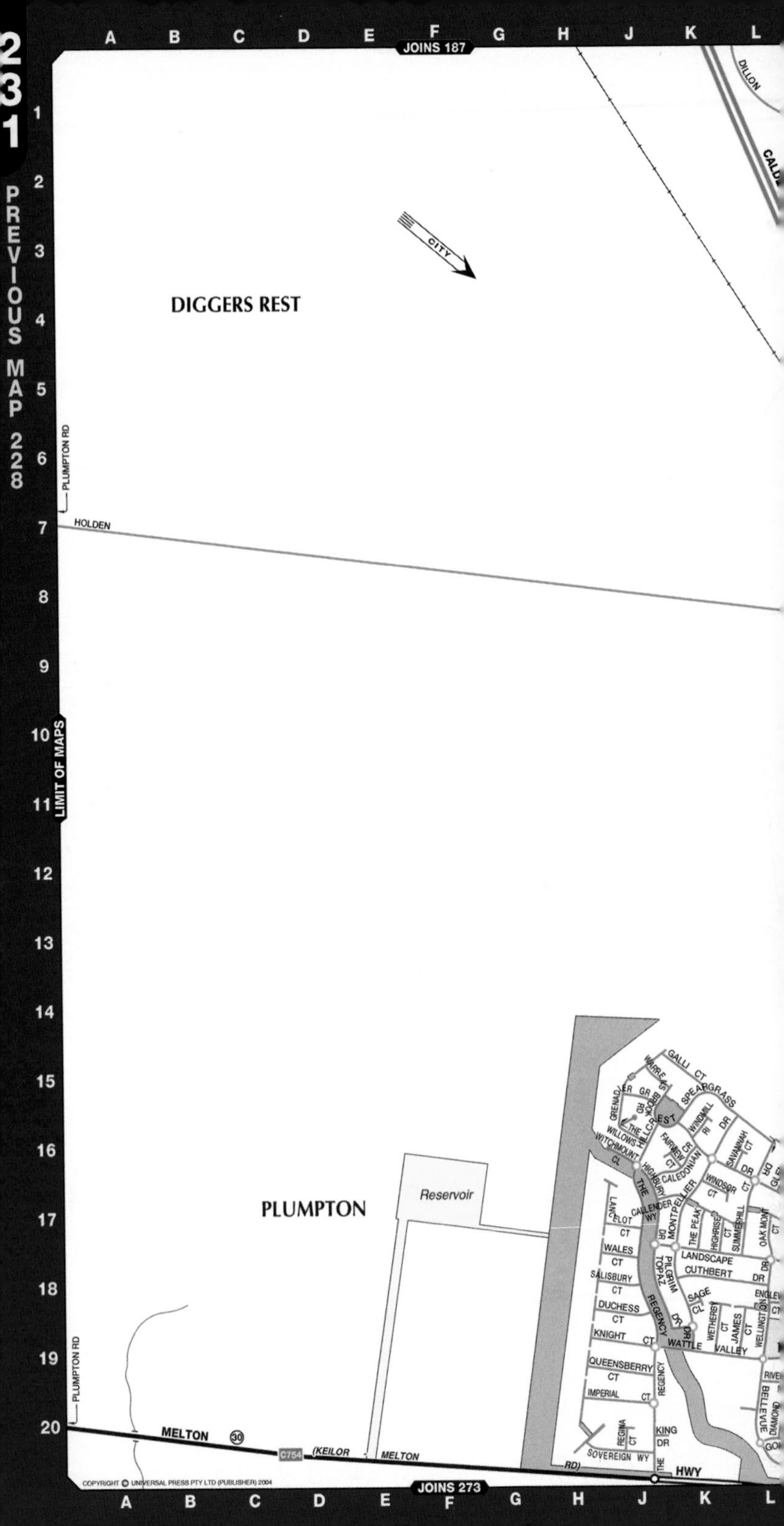

JOINS 273

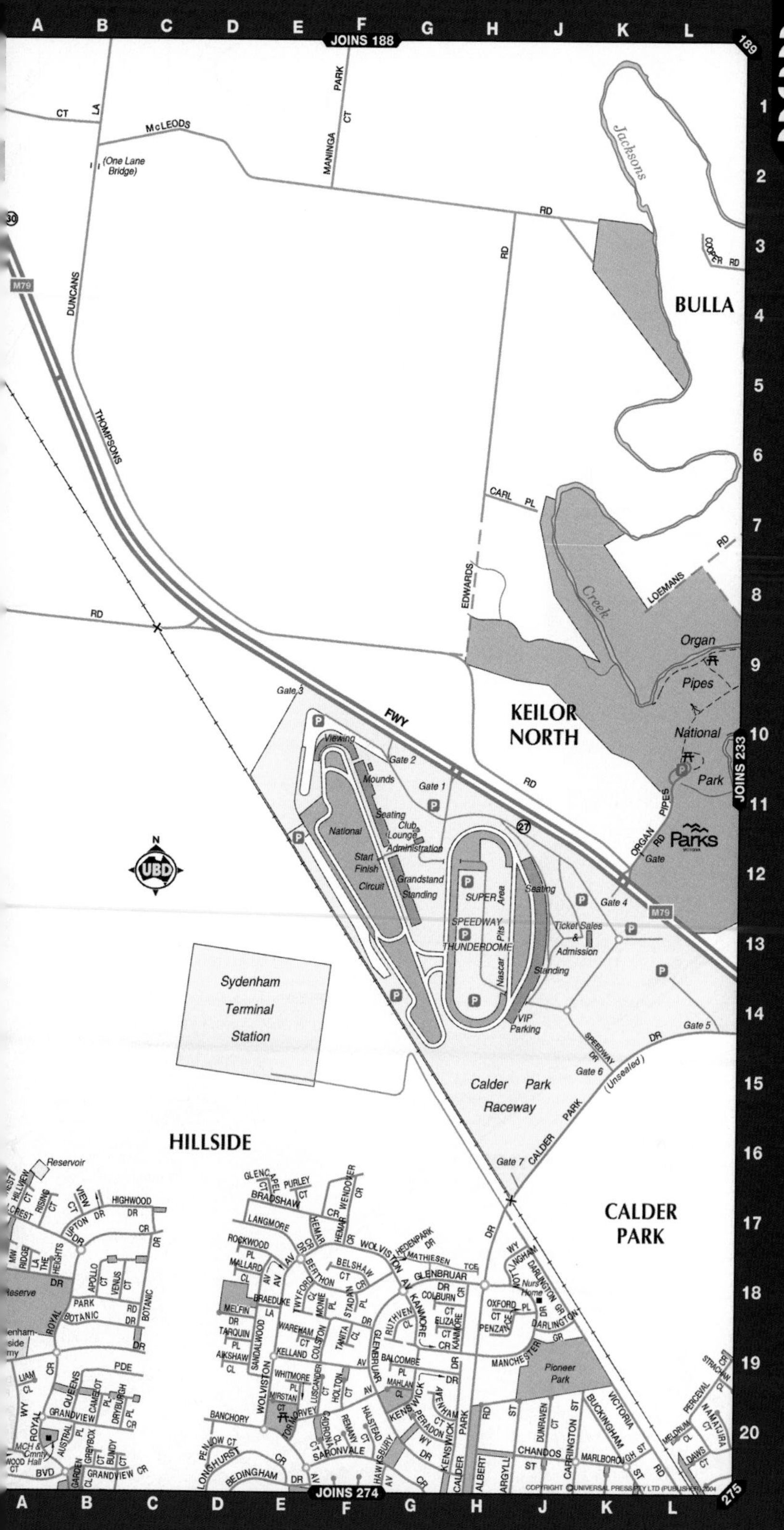
BULLA
KEILOR NORTH
HILLSIDE
CALDER PARK
Sydenham Terminal Station
Calder Park Raceway
Organ Pipes National Park
Jacksons Creek
McLEODS
(One Lane Bridge)
DUNCANS
THOMPSONS
MANINGA CT
PARK
RD
EDWARDS
CARL PL
LOEMANS RD
COOPER RD
FWY
M79
SUPER SPEEDWAY THUNDERDOME
National Circuit
Start Finish
Viewing Mounds
Seating Club Lounge
Administration
Grandstand Standing
Ticket Sales & Admission
VIP Parking
Nascar Pits Area
Gate 1
Gate 2
Gate 3
Gate 4
Gate 5
Gate 6
Gate 7
SPEEDWAY DR
(Unsealed)
CALDER PARK DR
ORGAN PIPES RD
Gate
Parks
Pioneer Park
Reservoir
Nurs Home
MANCHESTER GR
DARLINGTON GR
WOLVISTON AV
GLENBRUAR DR
KANMORE CR
KENSWICK DR
CALDER PARK DR
HIGHWOOD DR
UPTON DR
QUEENS CR
ROYAL CR
BOTANIC DR
GRANDVIEW CR
BEDINGHAM DR
LONGHURST CR
BANCHORY
HAWKSBURY AV
ALBERT RD
ARGYLL ST
CHANDOS ST
MARLBOROUGH ST
CARRINGTON ST
BUCKINGHAM
VICTORIA
DUNRAVEN CT
MELDRUM
PERCEVAL
NAMATJIRA
DAWS CT
STRACHAN CR
COPYRIGHT © UNIVERSAL PRESS PTY LTD (PUBLISHER) 2004

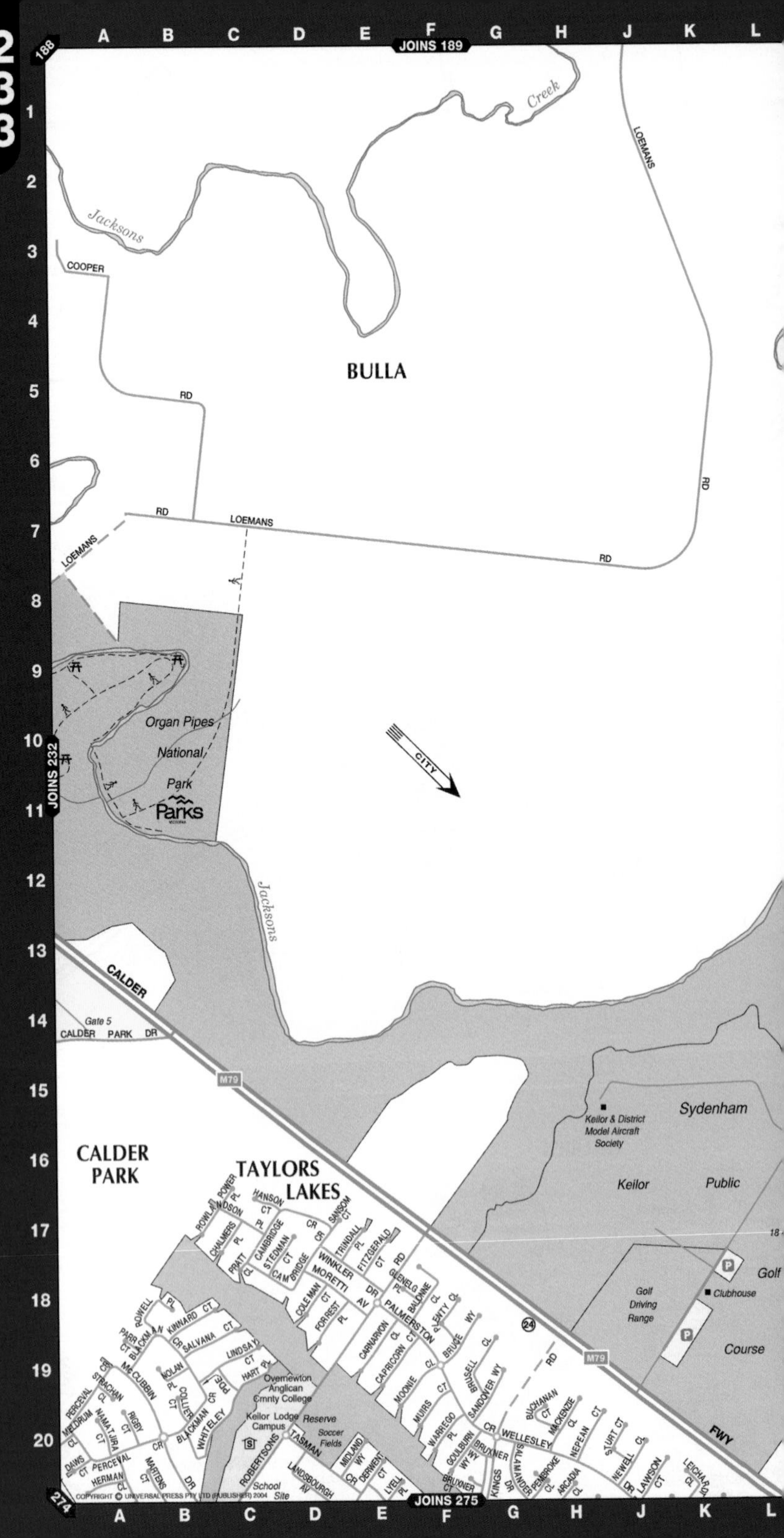
JOINS 189
JOINS 232
JOINS 275
188
274
BULLA
Jacksons
Creek
COOPER
RD
LOEMANS
RD
Organ Pipes
National
Park
Parks
CITY
CALDER
Gate 5
CALDER PARK DR
M79
CALDER
PARK
TAYLORS
LAKES
Keilor & District
Model Aircraft
Society
Sydenham
Keilor
Public
Golf
Clubhouse
Golf
Driving
Range
Course
FWY
Overnewton
Anglican
Cmnty College
Keilor Lodge
Campus
Reserve
Soccer
Fields
School
Site
PALMERSTON
WELLESLEY
WINKLER
MORETTI
ROBERTSONS
TASMAN
LANDSBOROUGH
COPYRIGHT © UNIVERSAL PRESS PTY LTD (PUBLISHER) 2004

MELBOURNE
AIRPORT
Creek
Deep
Creek
Maribyrnong
PERIMETER
Gate 8
RD
Proposed
R
16
09
L
Proposed
Extension
Main East - West Runway No 2
PERIMETER
Future
Gate 11
MANSFIELD
PLANE LA
DR
RD
RD
BASSETT
PANTON
RD
Runway
JOINS 235
RD
BARBISTON
09
R
Proposed
Future
Runway
RD
McNABS
RD
18
34
L
Tullamarine
Country
Club
Park
KEILOR
NORTH
River
KEILOR
OAKBANK RD
KIUNA
RD
McNABS
ARUNDEL
RD

JOINS 191

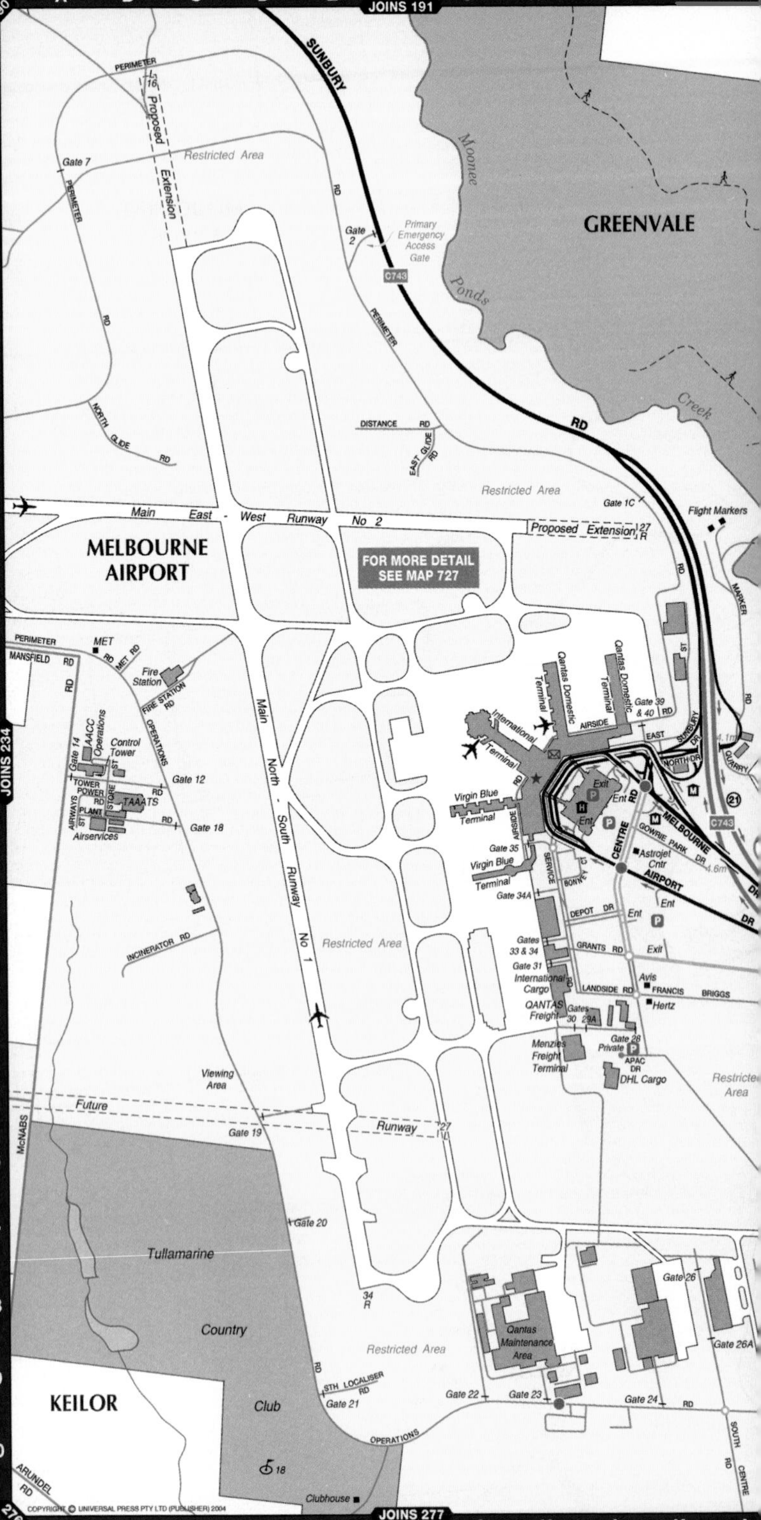

A B C D E F G H J K L

GREENVALE

MELBOURNE AIRPORT

KEILOR

FOR MORE DETAIL SEE MAP 727

SUNBURY RD
PERIMETER RD
Proposed Extension
Restricted Area
Gate 7
Gate 2
Primary Emergency Access Gate
C743
Moonee Ponds Creek
NORTH GLIDE RD
DISTANCE RD
EAST GLIDE RD
Main East - West Runway No 2
Proposed Extension
Gate 1C
Flight Markers
MARKER RD
PERIMETER
MANSFIELD RD
MET RD
MET
Fire Station
FIRE STATION RD
OPERATIONS RD
AACC Operations
Control Tower
Gate 14
TOWER RD
POWER RD
PLANT ST
STORE ST
AIRWAYS ST
TAAATS
Airservices
Gate 12
Gate 18
Main North - South Runway No 1
Qantas Domestic Terminal
Qantas Domestic Terminal
International Terminal
Gate 39 & 40
AIRSIDE
EAST
SUNBURY DR
NORTH DR
QUARRY
MELBOURNE DR
CENTRE RD
GOWRIE PARK DR
Astrojet Cntr
AIRPORT DR
Virgin Blue Terminal
Virgin Blue Terminal
Gate 35
Gate 34A
SERVICE RD
BONNEY CT
DEPOT DR
GRANTS RD
LANDSIDE RD
FRANCIS
BRIGGS
Avis
Hertz
Gates 33 & 34
Gate 31
International Cargo
QANTAS Freight
Gates 30 29A
Gate 28 Private
Menzies Freight Terminal
APAC DR
DHL Cargo
Exit
Ent
INCINERATOR RD
Restricted Area
Viewing Area
Future Runway
Gate 19
McNABS
Gate 20
Tullamarine Country Club
Gate 26
Gate 26A
Qantas Maintenance Area
Gate 22
Gate 23
Gate 24 RD
SOUTH CENTRE RD
STH LOCALISER RD
Gate 21
OPERATIONS
Clubhouse
ARUNDEL RD

JOINS 234

JOINS 277

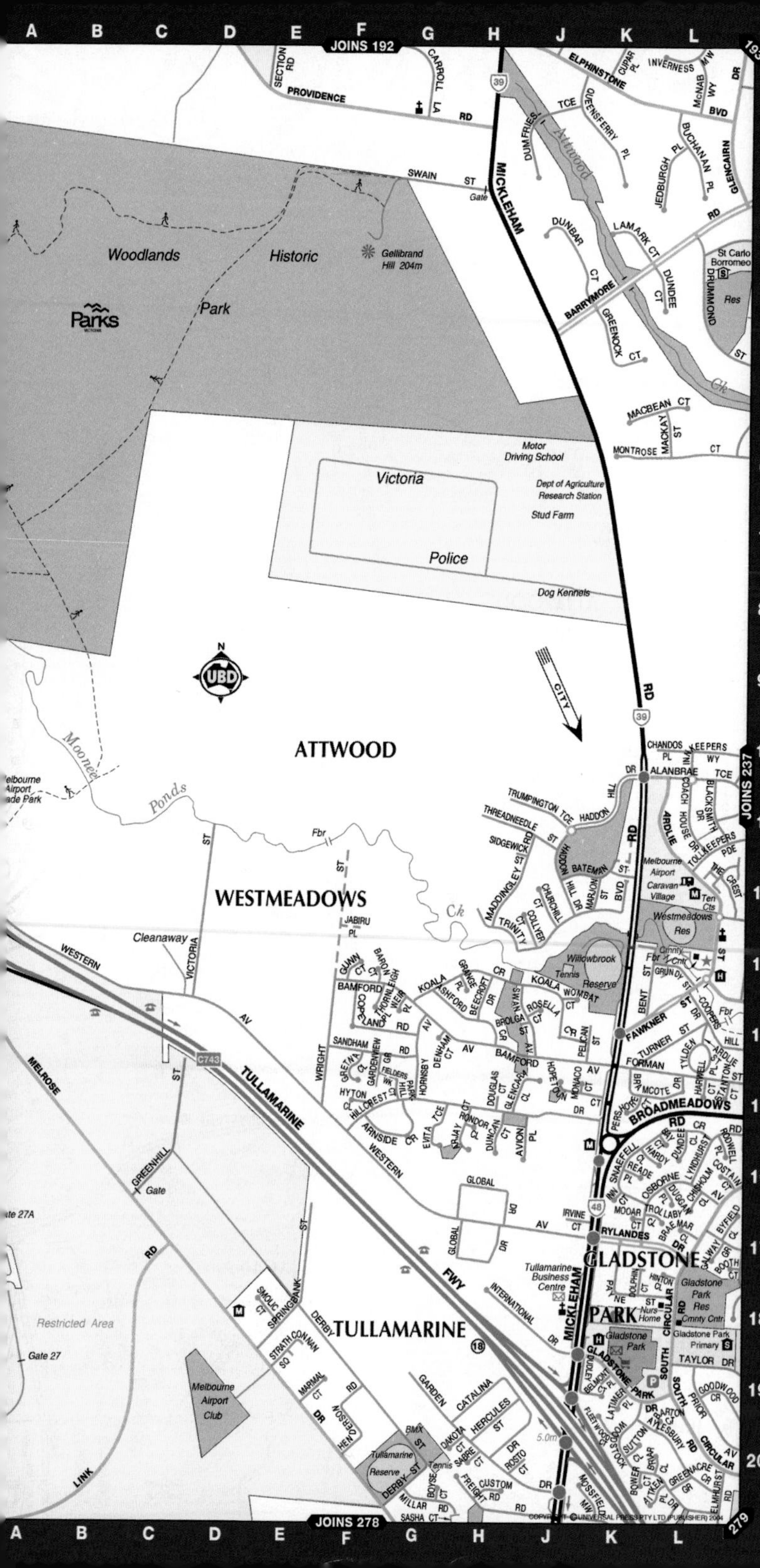
JOINS 192
193
JOINS 237
JOINS 278
279
A B C D E F G H J K L
ATTWOOD
WESTMEADOWS
GLADSTONE PARK
TULLAMARINE
Woodlands Historic Park
Gellibrand Hill 204m
Victoria Police
Motor Driving School
Dept of Agriculture Research Station
Stud Farm
Dog Kennels
MICKLEHAM RD
PROVIDENCE RD
SECTION RD
CARROLL LA
SWAIN ST
Gate
ELPHINSTONE
CUPAR PL
INVERNESS
McNAB MW
WY
BVD
DUMFRIES
TCE
QUEENSFERRY PL
Attwood
BUCHANAN PL
JEDBURGH PL
GLENCAIRN DR
DUNBAR CT
LAMARK CT
DUNDEE CT
BARRYMORE RD
GREENOCK CT
DRUMMOND ST
St Carlo Borromeo
Res
Ck
MACBEAN CT
MACKAY ST
MONTROSE CT
CHANDOS PL
KEEPERS WY
ALANBRAE TCE
TRUMPINGTON TCE
HADDON HILL DR
THREADNEEDLE ST
SIDGEWICK RD
MADDINGLEY ST
BATEMAN ST
MARION
BVD
CHURCHILL DR
COLLYER CT
TRINITY CT
ARDLIE
COACH HOUSE DR
BLACKSMITH DR
TOLLKEEPERS PDE
THE CREST
Melbourne Airport Caravan Village
Ten Cts
Westmeadows Res
Willowbrook Reserve
Tennis
Cmnty Cntr
Fbr
GRUNDY
Moonee Ponds Ck
Melbourne Airport ade Park
JABIRU PL
WESTERN AV
Cleanaway
VICTORIA ST
WRIGHT ST
GUNN CT
BARON CT
BAMFORD CR
HORNLEIGH PL
WEIR PL
COPELAND RD
KOALA CR
GRANGE PL
ASHFORD
BEECROFT DR
SWAN ST
ROSELLA CT
WOMBAT CT
BROLGA CR
EMU
PELICAN ST
FAWKNER ST
TURNER ST
FORMAN ST
BENT ST
COOPERS
SANDHAM CT
GRETNA CL
GARDENVIEW
FIELDERS WK
PARKHILL
HORNSBY
DENHAM CT
HOPETOUN
MONACO CT
GLENCAIRN
DOUGLAS CT
HYTON CL
HILLCREST
ARNSIDE CR
EVITA TCE
KRJAY CT
RONDOR
DUNCAN CT
AVION PL
PERSHORE
MCOTE
BROADMEADOWS RD
TYLDEN PL
HARWELL
STANTON
HILL
SNAEFELL
READE
HARDY
DUNDEE CT
LYNDHURST
RODWELL
COSTAIN
CHISHOLM AV
OSBORNE
DUGGAN
MOOAR CT
TROLLABY
BRAEMAR DR
BYFIELD CL
GALWAY GR
BOOTH CT
IRVINE CT
RYLANDES
GLOBAL DR
Tullamarine Business Centre
INTERNATIONAL DR
DOLPHIN CT
HINTON PL
PAYNE ST
CIRCULAR RD
Gladstone Park Res
Cmnty Cntr
Nurs Home
Gladstone Park Primary
TAYLOR DR
GLADSTONE PARK DR
SOUTH CIRCULAR RD
PRIOR
GOODWOOD CR
DUDLEY
BELMONT
LATIMER
BARTON
AYLESBURY
FLEETWOOD
STOCKPORT
SUTTON
BOWER CL
BRIAR
AYTKEN
GREENACRE CR
ELMHURST
MOSSFIELD MW
TULLAMARINE FWY
C743
MELROSE DR
GREENHILL
Gate
SPRINGBANK ST
SMOLIC CT
DERBY
STRATHCONNAN SQ
MARMAL CT
HENDERSON
GARDEN
CATALINA
HERCULES ST
DAKOTA CT
SABRE CT
ROSTO CT
BMX
Tullamarine Reserve
Tennis
BOYSE CT
FREIGHT
CUSTOM RD
MILLAR RD
SASHA CT
Restricted Area
Gate 27
Gate 27A
Melbourne Airport Club
LINK RD
5.0m
COPYRIGHT © UNIVERSAL PRESS PTY LTD (PUBLISHER) 2004

JOINS 193

GREENVALE

MEADOW HEIGHTS

ATTWOOD

WESTMEADOWS

JACANA

GLADSTONE PARK

400 Acres Reserve

Broadmeadows Valley Park

JOINS 236

JOINS 279

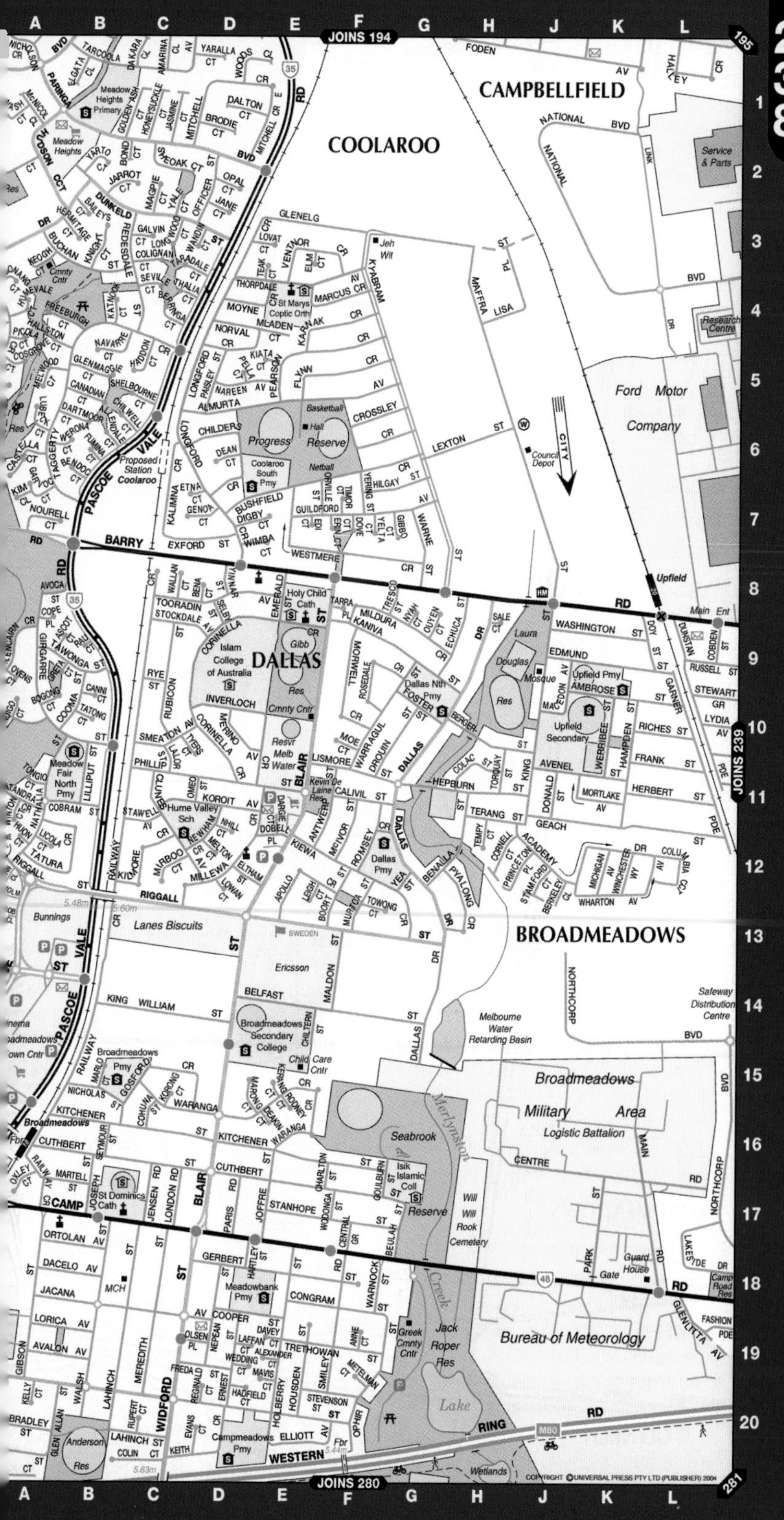

JOINS 194
COOLAROO
CAMPBELLFIELD
DALLAS
BROADMEADOWS
Ford Motor Company
Progress Reserve
Broadmeadows Military Area
Logistic Battalion
Bureau of Meteorology
Jack Roper Res
Seabrook Reserve
Will Will Rook Cemetery
Melbourne Water Retarding Basin
Lanes Biscuits
Bunnings
Ericsson
Safeway Distribution Centre
JOINS 239
JOINS 280
COPYRIGHT © UNIVERSAL PRESS PTY LTD (PUBLISHER) 2004

194
JOINS 195
JOINS 238
JOINS 281
280

A B C D E F G H J K L

1 2 3 4 5 6 7 8 9 10 11 12 13 14 15 16 17 18 19 20

CAMPBELLFIELD

BROADMEADOWS

THOMASTOWN

GLENROY

Cooper Street Grasslands

Lalor

Merri Creek

Galada Tamboore

Ford Motor Company

Service & Parts

Venture Industries

Head Office

Research Centre

Main Assembly Plant

Main Entrance

Ent

Sylvan

Seth Raistrick Reserve

Campbellfield Heights Pmy

Cmnty Cntr Res

Proposed URLC Central Creek Residential Development

Military Area

The Meadows Melbourne Greyhound Racing Association

Council Tip

Broadmeadows Motor Cycle Park

Industrial Area

Indoor Cricket

Pipeworks Fun Market

SES

Camp Road Reserve

Bureau of Meteorology

Sports Centre

Moomba Park Res

HUME HWY (SYDNEY RD)

M31

18

15

48

M80

31

WESTERN RING RD

METROPOLITAN RING RD

NORTHBOURNE RD, REX, AINSLIE RD, MEROLA WY, CAPITAL LINK DR, MEROLA WY, AMCOR WY, FREEMAN ST, REACH ST, FAILLA AV, LARA WY, NATIONAL BVD, HALLEY CR, JESSICA RD, VANESSA RD, ADRIAN RD, KINDER ST, RD, GLENBARRY RD, KILLARA, LARA WY, BARRY RD, MERRI CT, MERRI DR, COBDEN ST, KILBY CT, BRIGHT ST, HUGHES CT, ZIMMER CT, RUSSELL ST, STEWART GR, DUNSTAN PDE, LYDIA AV, AUGUSTA AV, FRANK ST, GENTLES AV, HERBERT ST, GEACH ST, BERWICK RD, COLBERT RD, FORDSON RD, THYME RD, SYCAMORE CR, ROSEMARY CT, ALMOND CT, CEDAR CT, CITRUS CT, LAUREL, MAPLE CT, GUMTREE CT, MIMOSA AV, MASON PL, MONT, COMO, DESI, SYCAMORE, OLIVE CT, WARATAH ST, BLACKWOOD, BEECH CT, CHURCH ST, RESERVE AV, CLARKE ST, CHESTNUT ST, HOLLY CT, PALM CT, MYRTLE ST, POPLAR ST, BIRCH CT, FERN CT, PLANE CT, LUCERNE ST, CAMPBELL ST, CAMBRIDGE CR, CARLISLE CT, BAILEY CT, WY, NORWICH, ALBERT DR, HULL DR, GREENWICH PL, SUFFOLK PL, LEEDS PL, SOPHIA, BYRNE CT, ELMAR CT, SYLVAN WY, HATTY CT, NATALIE CT, FORD, RAINS, JOAN CT, JODIE CT, SUSAN TCE, SAMUEL DR, ARI DR, SARAH ST, PATRICK ST, MALCOLM PL, FABIO CT, SOMERSET RD, DECCO DR, BROOKLYN CT, PAULSON RD, HORNE, OBERON BVD, KEOWN CT, ALBANY CT, MISTY ST, TARONGA CT, LUCY CT, BAMBURY, SHIPTON CT, ST, BANCELL ST, SUNSHINE ST, BOLINDA RD, THOMPSON ST, CENTRE RD, NORTHCORP BVD, LAKESIDE DR, CAMP RD, ELDON ST, FASHION PDE, GLENLITTA AV, ROEBOURNE CR, CHEVIOT CT, JEFFREY ST, KALGOORLIE, KWINANA RD, ONSLOW AV, RIO PL, MAHONEYS RD, OLIVER CT, KATHRYN ST, JANICE CT, RIVIERA CT, TRAWALLA, FAWKNER, TINA CL, EVA CT, ALVA CT, HEDLEY ST, LEIGHTON, SHAW ST, BIRCHWOOD, HONNI CT, GUY CT, IRVIN CT, SARA CT, ALEC, DOROTHY ST, BRIAN ST, HOGAN ST, PALMER ST, SOMERLAYTON CR, JOAN CT, PHILLIP ST, ANSTEY, MOUNTBATTEN CT, HAMERSLEY CT, CHURCHILL, BARRY

5.66m, 5.43m, 5.71m, 5.7m, 5.57m, Fbr

40
EPPING
LALOR
RESERVOIR
CITY
Former
Pioneer
Concrete
Golf
Course
Botanical Gardens
Clubhouse
CRAIGIEBURN BYPASS
Due for completion mid 2005
COOPER ST
CHILDS RD
EDGARS RD
VICTORIA DR
MAIN ST
METROPOLITAN RING RD
MAHONEYS RD
HUGHES PDE
PANDORA AV
ALVARADO RD
MOUNT VIEW RD
THOMAS ST
KINGSWAY DR
ROSEMARY CR
LYNETTE CR
ELIZABETH DR
KATHRYN AV
BENAROON DR
CAMBALA
GILLWELL RD
PADSTUM AV
HERMAN ST
BARRY RD
QUEENSCLIFF
KARINGAL WY
GLADSTONE ST
CATALINA DR
SALAMANDER AV
LINCOLN DR
ROBERT ST
ROSEDALE DR
BROOKLAND
TUSCAN CT
NORWICH AV
LAWSON CR
Lalor West Pmy
Huskisson Avenue Reserve Tennis
St Catherines Cath
Cmnty Cntr
R G C Cook Reserve
Thomastown West Pmy
Thomastown Secondary College
Main Street Rec Res
Sports Centre
St Clares Cath
Thomastown Meadows Pmy
H R Uren Reserve
Cemetery
Indoor Sports
Terminal Station
Edgars Creek
Central Ck
MCH
Res
Pav
Tennis
M80
48
58
1
2
3
4
5
6
7
8
9
10
11
12
13
14
15
16
17
18
19
20
A
B
C
D
E
F
G
H
J
K
L
JOINS 241
JOINS 282
283
COPYRIGHT © UNIVERSAL PRESS PTY LTD (PUBLISHER) 2004

196
JOINS 197

A B C D E F G H J K L

EPPING

The Northern Hospital
Cinema
Epping Plaza Shopping Complex
Bunnings
St Peters Cath
St Monicas Cath Coll Sen
Northern Melb Institute of TAFE Epping Campus
Epping
St Monicas Catholic Coll Junior South Campus
Lowalde Drive Res
Gloria Twins Receptions
Top Kart Racing
Lalor North Secondary College
V R Michael Reserve
Partridge Street Reserve
Soccer
Lalor Nth Pmy
Lalor Park Pmy
Lalor
Lalor Reserve
Pav
Tennis
LALOR
W A Smith Reserve
Marrang Spec Dev
Peter Lalor Sec Coll
Queens Lodge Ret Vill
Lalor Pmy
Lalor Secondary College
St Lukes Cath
Lalor Plaza
Lalor East Pmy
Thomastown East Pmy
Alexander Res
Nurs Home
Thomastown Mosque
Thomastown Pmy
Goodyear Tyres
UBD

COOPER ST
CHILDS RD
HIGH ST
EPPING RD
STATION ST
DALTON RD
MONASH ST
DAREBIN DR
McKIMMIES RD
THE BOULEVARD
METROPOLITAN RING RD
M80

THOMASTOWN

Myer Megamart
Bunnings
SETTLEMENT RD
Terminal Station
Keon Park
Kinetik Energy
Market
WOOD ST
MAHONEYS ROAD
KEON PDE

JOINS 240

282
JOINS 283

A B C D E F G H J K L

MILL PARK

BUNDOORA

CHILDS RD

McKIMMIES RD

METROPOLITAN RING RD

M80

PLENTY RD

CENTENARY DR

MORANG DR

PRINCE OF WALES AV

BOTANICA BVD

BETULA AV

GROVE DR

ROYCROFT AV

REDLEAP AV

Plenty Valley Town Cntr

Greenbrook Pmy

Mill Park Reserve

Aquatic Centre

Cmnty Cntr

Child Care

Mill Park Heights Pmy

Findon Reserve

Findon Primary

St Francis of Assisi Cath

Mill Park Secondary College

Peter Hopper Lake

Redleap Res

Stables

Dr Harry Jenkins Res

Mill Park Pmy

Mimosa Park

Betula Pk

Bus Depot

RMIT Bundoora Campus

Athletics

Hibiscus Av Res

Darebin Creek

Garvey Oval

Northpark Private

Parade College (Christian Brothers)

Villa Madonna Nursing Home

Norris Bank Primary

Norris Bank Reserve

Northside Christian College

CITY

Arterial Road

Proposed

Aqueduct

4.2m

5.25m

27

21

48

198 A B C D E F G H J K L JOINS 199

MILL PARK

SOUTH MORANG

BUNDOORA

WATSONIA NORTH

McDONALDS RD
GORGE RD
PLENTY RD
METROPOLITAN RING RD
M80
GREENSBOROUGH HWY
RIVER AV
MEMORIAL
GOLDSWORTHY
Plenty River
UNIVERSITY DR
DEVELOPMENT BVD
CENTENARY DR
BUSH BVD
JANEFIELD DR
EASTGATE
RICE

Morang South Primary
Nurs Home
MCH
Rivergum Village
THE LINK
Telopea Park Tennis
Plenty Parklands Pmy
Kelynack Pav Reserve
Diosma Res
Yellow Gum Park
Parks VICTORIA
RMIT Bundoora East Campus
Edmund Rice College
Parade College (Christian Brothers)
Admin
Dr J M Wright Oval
Binnak Park
Binnack Park
Res
Fbr
6.0m

UBD

WEALTHILAND DR, ALLWYN CR, ALLWYN, BUSH BVD, HEATHS CT, STILLMAN, BEAN, BENTLEY WY, BENZ CL, BRABHAM DR, ROMEO CT, LUKE, HOWDEN, HICKEY, ATLANTA CT, BREMNER CT, HOPPER CT, BRADLEY DR, MILES CL, RULE CL, CREAN CT, HURLSTONE, EVATT, SCULLIN CT, WALSH, CALWELL CT, CHRISTIE AV, HARPER PL, CHISHOLM, GREENWAY, DAWSON, TRUSCOTT, MACARTHUR, FARRER CT, FLEMING, KELLY, BLACKMAN AV, GARDINER, McCUBBIN, BUVELOT, STREETON CT, CONDOR, SAWREY, ANCONA, YATES, TAREE, WARD DR, TYNDALL, THE GREEN, MERTON PL, CHEVIOT, SHAMROCK, BOTTLEBRUSH, BUNDY, OVINGTON, NOBELIUS, MONTANA, DEAKIN, NAPELLE, EMILY, PARK, HAVEN, FOLEY, RILEY, WESTWOOD, OREGON, ISLAND PL, RESEARCH, SILVERTOP, WOODHILL, AUSTRALIS DR, LATHAM, WY, STOCKDALE, ADAM, TEMPLETON, RENROSE, SELWOOD, INGLEWOOD, RUSHDALE, RIVERGUM DR, EUCALYPTUS, PARKHILL CR, HILLRISE CT, REDGUM CT, WAGSTAFF DR, MANHATTAN, VIEWBANK PL, DIOSMA, LUTEA, TELOPEA, GARDENVIEW CL, MIRBELIA, HOVEA CT, ALBA CT, INCANA CR, REGELIA, VILLOSA CT, TRUNCATA DR, ACMENA CT, OLEA CT, MEDLAR CT, MANUKA CT, BLOSSOM, PARK CR, CASSIA CT, ACONIS, GUNNII, MELIA CT, DAPHNE CL, VERONICA, AZALEA, ROSTRATA, KURRAJONG VW, MANNA WY, VIOLA CT, ZINNEA, CALLISTEMON RI, CANANGA, LAURINA VW, TRN, ASTER, CARLITA, NEWHAVEN, WOOD, WAKEFUL, GREVILLIA, RICANA, HILLIANA, WATERS DR, ISABELLE CT, WILDFIRE CT, GYPSY CT, BLOSSOM PARK DR, JUBILEE CR, COVENTRY CR, CASTLE HILL DR, BENDEMERE DR, GRASSMERE LK, WILLIAMSBROOK TCE, ROSELANDS GR, HENDERSON CT, SPRINGFIELD CT, GREENFIELDS TCE, RIVERS DR, RICHARDS RD, WATTLE DR

KELVIN, GR, NIRVANA DR, PAYNE PL, LANGLEY PL, OBAR CR, JACKSON ST, GEORGE, McGLYNN, ALLAN AV, RONALD AV, KIPPING, REID ST, BRIAR CT, TURNER CT, DOREEN, ECHIDNA, WINIFRED, THOMAS TCE, KANGAROO, WALLABY WK, WOMBAT PL, TEATREE, RIVERSIDE DR, GLIDER, LOBELIA, POSSUM CT, BERRY PL, APPLE, JONES, ROGEN WY, JOHN PL, PLATYPUS, STANLEY, ROSELLA, RYAN, LIGHTWOOD, IBIS, WATTLETREE, MANNA, GUM WK, BLACKWOOD, PEPPERMINT, ANGELA CT, GARRY CT, WILTON CT, CECIL, JOLLY, BUSSELL, LAW CT, GRANT CT, ROBIN, WARBLER, KINGFISHER, KOOKABURRA, KOALA, HONEYEATER, LYREBIRD WK, SILVEREYE, MAGPIE WK, BROLGA, STRINGY BARK, RIVER, REDGUM, DELACOMBE DR, TENNYSON, VANBROOK, YAMBROOK, WINGATE CT

COLLENDINA CR, BRINAWA, WANDA, WANBANNA AV, KARIBOO, MYOORA, KINKA PL, DWYER, GOOLGUNG, JARRAH, NOKUNA, TIRRAY, BOOYAN, BINDI, YONDE, KERTA, VABIRO, SENBIN, NINDA, HEALY CT, TELLIN CT, CHAPPELL, SELWOOD, STALLARD, NAUGHTIN, GLENDALOUGH, LONGFIELD, GUNDRY, VICARAGE WY, EDMUND, EDMOND, RICE PDE, BOOKIN AV, HOLYROOD, DORRINGTON CR, DUNRAVEN, YARRADALE, BERKELEY, STONEHAVEN, HAMILTON, IREDALE, FERNLEA, GILLINGHAM, ALMEIDA, ELTON, BYRNE, DAMIEN, KALISTA, BALFOUR, GERRARD, ATKINS AV, MICHELLE AV, NORMAN AV, BAWDEN, LAWSON, MACORNA, SENIOR CT, HAKEA, SELLARS, NOLAN, CHEADLE, IRVING, CURTIN, ANDERSON, BOSTON, RHONDA, SUSSEX, PAMELA, COLE, LEONARD, JACQUELINE, JOHN, BERRINGA, PAUL, KARU, BALANDA, CANUNGRA, STEVEN, PURCELL, HAYDEN, DAVID, VERONA, FOTINI, TRAFALGAR, NEWTON, CARSON, GRANT, BENTLEY, TONINGTON, LANDRA PL, RENDLE, ARMSTRONG, VINCENT, GILMOUR, NINIAN, PINEHILLS, SIBELLA, ALBERT, HALIDAY, BLANCHARD, AINTREE

JOINS 242

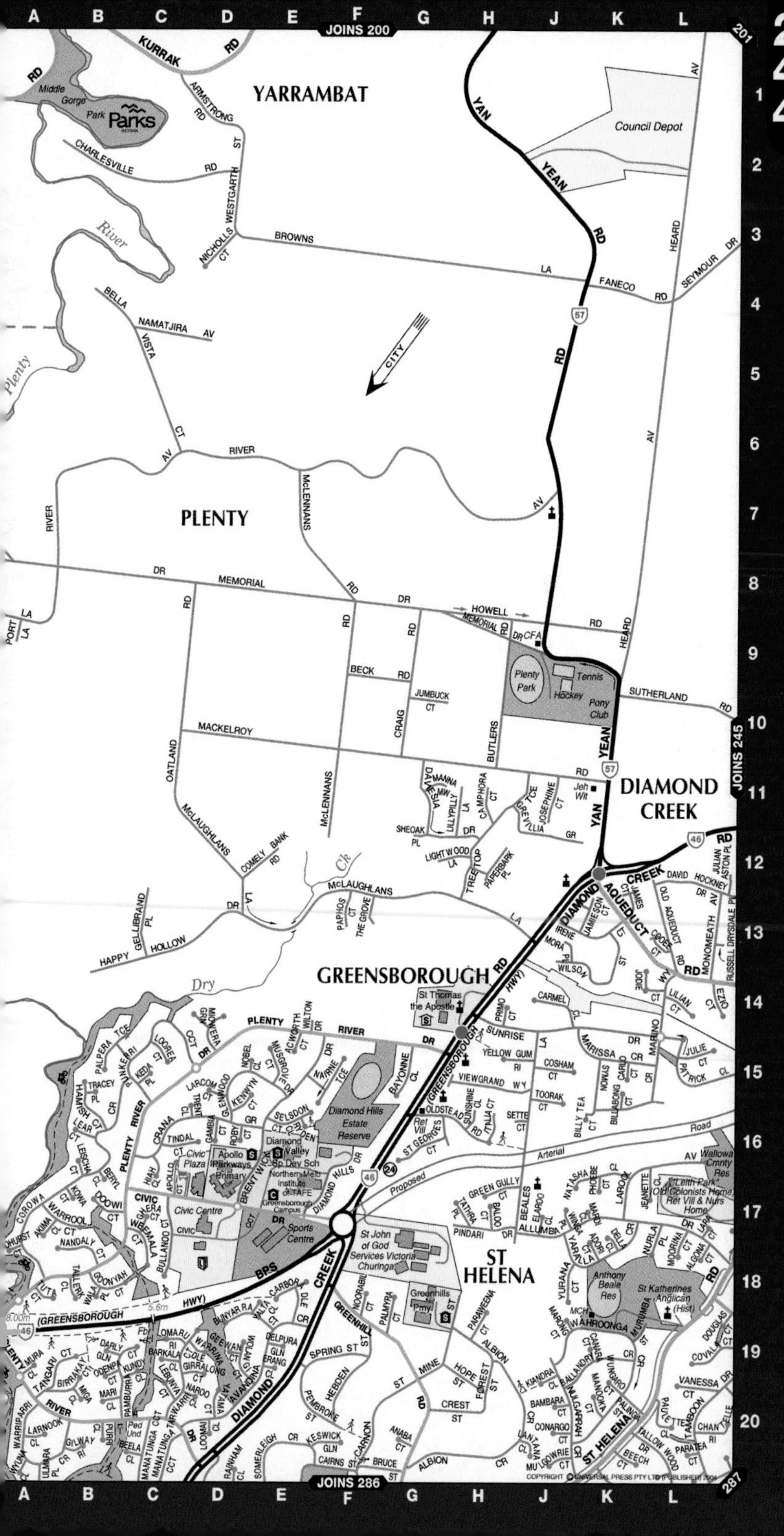

JOINS 200
201
JOINS 245
JOINS 286
287
YARRAMBAT
PLENTY
DIAMOND CREEK
GREENSBOROUGH
ST HELENA
Middle Gorge Park
Parks Victoria
Council Depot
CITY
Plenty River
Dry Ck
KURRAK RD
ARMSTRONG RD
WESTGARTH ST
CHARLESVILLE RD
NICHOLLS CT
BROWNS LA
FANECO RD
SEYMOUR DR
HEARD AV
YAN YEAN RD
57
BELLA VISTA CT
NAMATJIRA AV
RIVER AV
McLENNANS RD
MEMORIAL DR
HOWELL RD
BECK RD
CRAIG RD
JUMBUCK CT
BUTLERS RD
MACKELROY RD
OATLAND RD
SUTHERLAND RD
Plenty Park
Tennis
Hockey
Pony Club
CFA
McLAUGHLANS LA
COMELY BANK RD
GELLIBRAND PL
HAPPY HOLLOW DR
PAPHOS CT
THE GROVE
SHEOAK PL
LIGHTWOOD LA
TREETOP
PAPERBARK PL
CAMPHORA CT
JOSEPHINE CT
GREVILLIA GR
Jeh Wit
DIAMOND CREEK RD
AQUEDUCT RD
DAVID HOCKNEY DR
JULIAN ASTON PL
OLD AQUEDUCT RD
MONOMEATH AV
RUSSELL DRYSDALE PL
46
PLENTY RIVER DR
St Thomas the Apostle
SUNRISE
YELLOW GUM RI
VIEWGRAND WY
COSHAM CT
TOORAK CT
MARISSA CR
JULIE CT
PATRICK CL
Diamond Hills Estate Reserve
Ret Vill
Civic Plaza
Apollo Parkways Primary
Diamond Valley Sp Dev Sch
Northern Melb Institute of TAFE
Greensborough Campus
Civic Centre
Sports Centre
St John of God Services Victoria Churinga
Greenhills Pmy
Arterial Road
Proposed
Wallowa Cmnty Res
"Leith Park" (Old Colonists Home) Ret Vill & Nurs Home
Anthony Beale Res
St Katherines Anglican (Hist)
GREENSBOROUGH HWY
DIAMOND CREEK
GREENHILL RD
SPRING ST
MINE ST
HOPE ST
FOREST ST
CREST ST
ALBION RD
ST HELENA RD
PINDARI DR
ALLUMBA
WAHROONGA CR
TALLOW WOOD DR
VANESSA DR
5.6m
8.00m
COPYRIGHT © UNIVERSAL PRESS PTY LTD (PUBLISHER) 2004

PLENTY

DIAMOND CREEK

ELTHAM NORTH

HEAD AV

PIONEER DR

SEYMOUR RD

CULLEN CR

HILLMARTIN RD

IRONBARK RD

MURRAY RD

BLACK GULLY

LAWREY

ARCHER RD

WESTABY ST

FLAT RD

HARRAP

BROWNLOW DR

HILLINGDON

JONQUIL CL

DAINA CT

SOVEREIGN RI

EVERLEIGH

WAYLAND

MINDARA

UPTON

EATON

PENTON

KINGSBURY

ROCKLEY CL

R A Wadeson Res

RIPON

NEVERN

KALMAINE CT

WEGA CL

GRASSY

DARTAGOOK ST

HIGHBROOK CT

RISDALE CL

LANVOS DR

BROAD

GULLY

STARLING RD

FIELDING RD

ELGATA CT

ARRA WY

KOONAW

PAROOK CT

COLLINS ST

COORAMINTA PL

RYAN ST

HELEN CT

AMAROO CT

Nurs Home

(One Lane Bridge)

NESS ST

CLYDE

EDMONDS ST

MCH

COWIN

Diamond Creek Pmy

CFA

INGLIS CT

Coventry Oval

Nillumbik Pk

ELIZABETH ST

GIPSON ST

Sacred Heart Cath

STATION ST

Diamond Creek

LAMBERT ST

FULLER ST

HAPPY VALLEY RI

STONE

CHUTE ST

HYDE ST

Cmnty Cntr

Marngrook Oval

SUTHERLAND RD

LARCH CR

DIAMOND CREEK (GREENSBOROUGH HWY) RD

57

27

46

OLD DIAMOND CREEK RD

MAIN

Cem

VALLEY CT

BAGE

GALATEA ST

FAIRVIEW

WATKINS CR

DIAMOND ST

Godbers Flat

Reserve

WAIGO WY

BROOKS CR

Diamond Creek Plaza

HALEY ST

NORMA ST

EGAN

WENSLEY ST

Diamond Creek Res

BLUE WREN PL

HONEYEATER CT

JACARANDA

WATTLEBIRD CT

LORIKEET

JUANE PARK DR

EDINBURGH

BOTTE CT

FYFFE ST

PATYAH

KINGFISHER DR

COCKATIEL PL

LA

GREY GUM RI

MORAY ST

Tennis

DERING

FRASER ST

HAGEN CT

PLEDGER CL

HOTHAM CT

CASSINIA CT

PLEASANT VIEW CT

PRICE CT

CAMPBELL

FEATHER CR

TRIDENT CT

STANTON DR

HODDLE PL

JAMES

MITCHELL CT

JULIAN ASTON PL

DAVID

HOCKNEY

FRED McCUBBIN CL

SYDNEY NOLAN PL

TOM ROBERTS GLD

MONOMEATH AV

RUSSELL DRYSDALE PL

LOUIS BUVELOT CT

ARTHUR STREETON

WYN PL

CHALLENGER ST

KIM ST

NICOLE CR

CITRIODORA CT

Diamond

AQUEDUCT RD

EZIO CT

DARIO CT

TETRAGONA WY

CANDLEBARK CL

WINDMILL RI

Arterial Road

Proposed

JULIE CT

PATRICK CL

Plenty Valley Montessori Pmy

St Helena Market Square

SUMMIT CT

LESAY

CATHAY CT

ORONSAY CR

HIMALAYA CT

NANKIN CL

PINJARRA CT

CHITRAL PL

ORMONDE CT

CHUSAN CT

ERINNE

BEN CT

HALSBURY CT

ORCADES PL

SOMALI CL

TYRONE CT

MAXINE DR

WALLOWA RD

LIBERTY CT

HANCOCK CL

STRATHAIRD CL

ALLENDALE

CANTON CT

One Lane Bridge

Wallowa Cmnty Res

KELBOW CL

CHERELLE CT

NIMMARY

St Helena Secondary College

Glen Katherine Primary

SCENIC RI

RYANS RD

MARIAN CT

GREVILLEA CT

LEIGH CT

MICHAEL CT

ORSOVA WY

ORION CT

"Leith Park" (Old Colonists Home) Ret Vill & Nurs Home

ST HELENA RD

MILNE PL

Res

UNGARA CL

PARRY

CHARLES WILSON CL

MOOLTAN PL

DAVELA CT

WEIDLICH

GLENCAIRN AV

ANGELA CL

MURRINDAL

ARCADIA

DOBELL

LANDSCAPE CT

LARA CT

DUGONG

ALGONA CT

BRAE CT

MACDHUI

CASTLE CT

ANGUS

CALENDONIA

LENKUNYA

WATTLETREE RD

SARAH CT

TRISTAN CT

IBERA CT

DRYSDALE AV

HALIDON CL

SOLWAY CT

DUNBARTON DR

SCONE CL

ARGYLL

HIGHLAND CT

GR

JASMINE CT

HONEY MYRTLE RI

RED BOX CL

BURRAWANG RI

MESSMATE

CASUARINA RDG

MURRAYS PL (Priv Rd)

HAWKHURST

GLEN KATHERINE DR

DOUGLAS CT

COVALA

DAINTREE

St Helena Bush Reserve

MELISSA CT

FREDA

BLACKWOOD CL

GULLY

ELMWOOD RI

POLLYOAK

HILL DR

LAUREL

FALCONHURST CT

COTTAGE RI

CREA CT

ESKDALE CT

GREENLEAF CT

GLEN

BANKSIA

CLEMATIS RI

Fbr

Creek

BALMORAL CCT

SANDHURST CT

VANESSA CT

EVELYN WY

SETTLERS WY

ST CLEMS ST

LIDDESDALE

STIRLING

DARWINIA RI

Hall

CEDAR AV

THE EYRIE

TAMBOON

ESKHOLME

HENLEY CL

ST CLEMS ST

BURNS CT

DANDALLO DR

CHANTELLE RI

MOORSIDE RI

OAKBANK CT

DALVIDA CT

ST ANDREWS CT

HILLCREST

BANKS RD

Soccer

GIRRAWEEN

MOOLA PL

PATONGA

STUART

ZIG ZAG

JOINS 244

JOINS 202
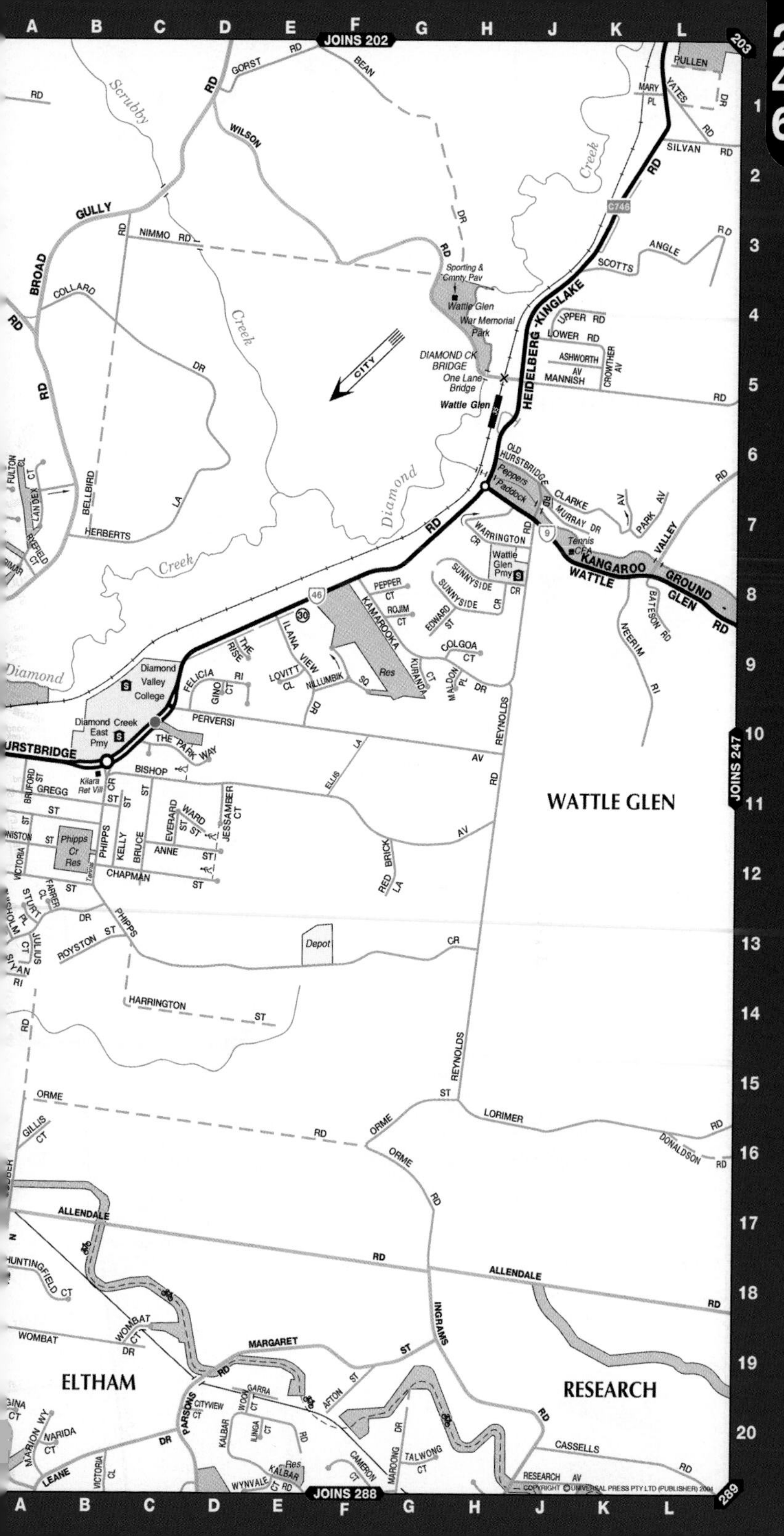

JOINS 247
JOINS 288
203
289

JOINS 203

JOINS 246

JOINS 289

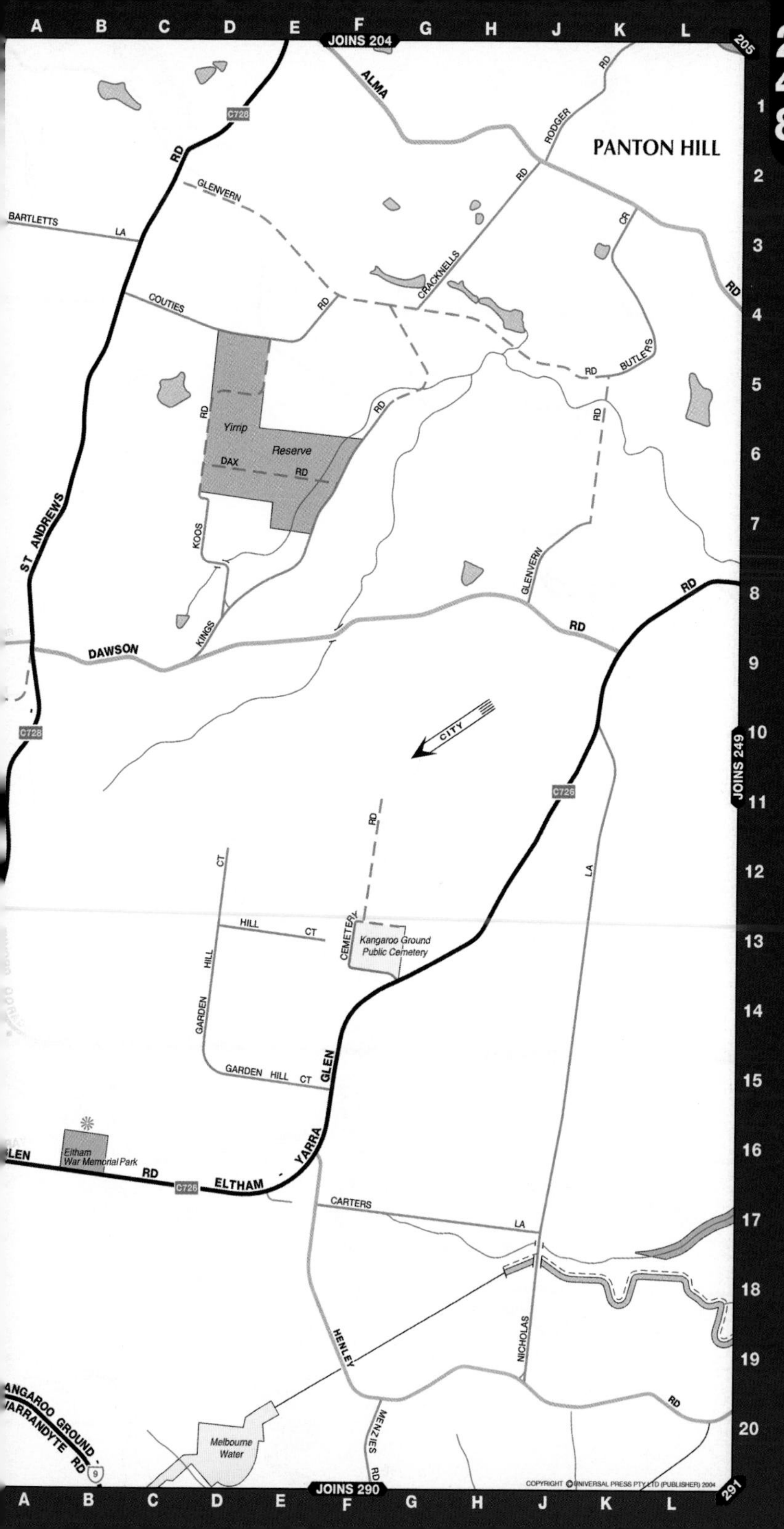

A B C D E F G H J K L
JOINS 204
205
248
1 2 3 4 5 6 7 8 9 10 11 12 13 14 15 16 17 18 19 20
PANTON HILL
ALMA
RODGER RD
RD
CRACKNELLS
CR
RD
BARTLETTS LA
GLENVERN
COUTIES RD
C728
ST ANDREWS RD
BUTLER'S RD
RD
Yirrip Reserve
DAX RD
KOOS RD
KINGS
GLENVERN
DAWSON RD
RD
CITY
JOINS 249
C726
RD
CT
HILL CT
CEMETERY
Kangaroo Ground Public Cemetery
LA
GARDEN HILL
GARDEN HILL CT
GLEN
YARRA
ELTHAM
Eltham War Memorial Park
GLEN RD
C726
CARTERS LA
HENLEY
NICHOLAS
RD
MENZIES RD
KANGAROO GROUND - WARRANDYTE RD
9
Melbourne Water
COPYRIGHT © UNIVERSAL PRESS PTY LTD (PUBLISHER) 2004
JOINS 290
291

A B C D E F G H J K L

JOINS 205

LAWRENCE RD
Wurran Reserve
RD
TURNUNG
Long
GULLY
Gully
RD
GILLS
RD
C726

PANTON HILL

ALMA
LONG

WATSONS CREEK

C726
CITY
RD
GLEN
YARRA
ELTHAM
Gawa Reserve
RIDGE
RD
RIDGE
RD
TR
BILLS
SUGARLOAF
TR

JOINS 248

WESTERING

KANGAROO GROUND

RD
CALWELL
RD
CALWELL
Melbourne Water
HENLEY
HENLEY
Environmental Livin
RD

1 2 3 4 5 6 7 8 9 10 11 12 13 14 15 16 17 18 19 20

204
290
JOINS 291

A B C D E F G H J K L

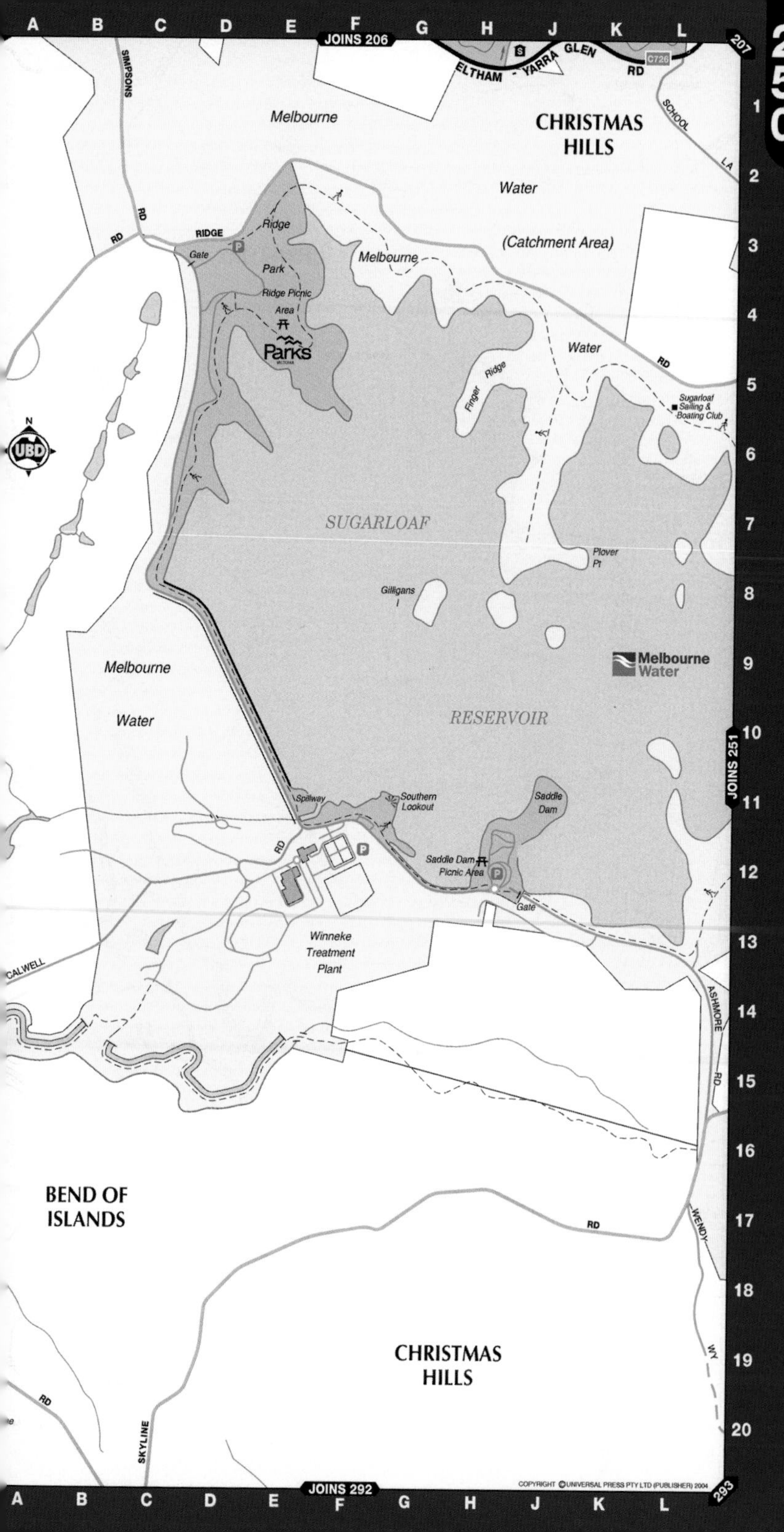

A B C D E F G H J K L
JOINS 206
207
250
ELTHAM - YARRA GLEN RD
C726
SIMPSONS RD
SCHOOL LA
Melbourne
CHRISTMAS
HILLS
Water
(Catchment Area)
RIDGE RD
Gate
Ridge
Park
Ridge Picnic
Area
Parks
Melbourne
Water
RD
Finger Ridge
Sugarloaf Sailing & Boating Club
SUGARLOAF
Plover Pt
Gilligans I
Melbourne Water
Melbourne
Water
RESERVOIR
JOINS 251
Spillway
Southern Lookout
Saddle Dam
Saddle Dam Picnic Area
Gate
RD
Winneke
Treatment
Plant
CALWELL
ASHMORE RD
BEND OF
ISLANDS
RD
WENDY WY
CHRISTMAS
HILLS
RD
SKYLINE
1 2 3 4 5 6 7 8 9 10 11 12 13 14 15 16 17 18 19 20
COPYRIGHT © UNIVERSAL PRESS PTY LTD (PUBLISHER) 2004
JOINS 292
293

A B C D E F G H J K L
206
JOINS 207

Melbourne Water
RD
REEVES
SCHOOL
RD
LA
MUIR
RD

CHRISTMAS HILLS

RIDGE
Melbourne Water
N
UBD
YARRA VIEW
Cockatoo Knoll
SKYLINE
Maroondah
Ashmores Inlet
Eagle Pt
SUGARLOAF
RESERVOIR
Rosella Spur
Melbourne Water
Melbourne Water
Aqueduct
RIVER
RD
Mt Graham
Melbourne Water
ASHMORE
Maroondah
RD
SKYLINE
Melbourne Water
YARRA
WENDY
WY

1 2 3 4 5 6 7 8 9 10 11 12 13 14 15 16 17 18 19 20
JOINS 250

292
JOINS 293
A B C D E F G H J K L

JOINS 208
209
JOINS 253
JOINS 294
295

208
JOINS 209
JOINS 252
JOINS 295
294

A B C D E F G H J K L

YERING

McKenzie Reserve
Tennis
CFA
ANZAC AV
MCH
HERBERT ST
FARRELL AV
BELL ST
JADE CT
PINOAK DR
B300
RSL & Mem Hall
OLIVER ST
Yarra Glen (Disused)
ARMSTRONG GR
Ent
Trotting Track
Yarra Valley Racing Centre
Yarra Glen Racecourse
Steels Ck
C726
HEALESVILLE YARRA GLEN RD
Yarra Glen Rec Reserve & Showgrd
Ent
VASEY HOUGHTON BRIDGE
Bypass
Disused Railway
YARRA RIVER
MELBA (YARRA GLEN RD) HWY
Yering Station
Drain
Proposed
McMEIKANS RD
Railway
Disused
MELBA (YARRA GLEN RD) HWY
LA
Yering (Disused)
Stringybark
ST HUBERTS RD
Yering Farm Wines
Lilydale Airport
MACINTYRE
CAMBUS RD

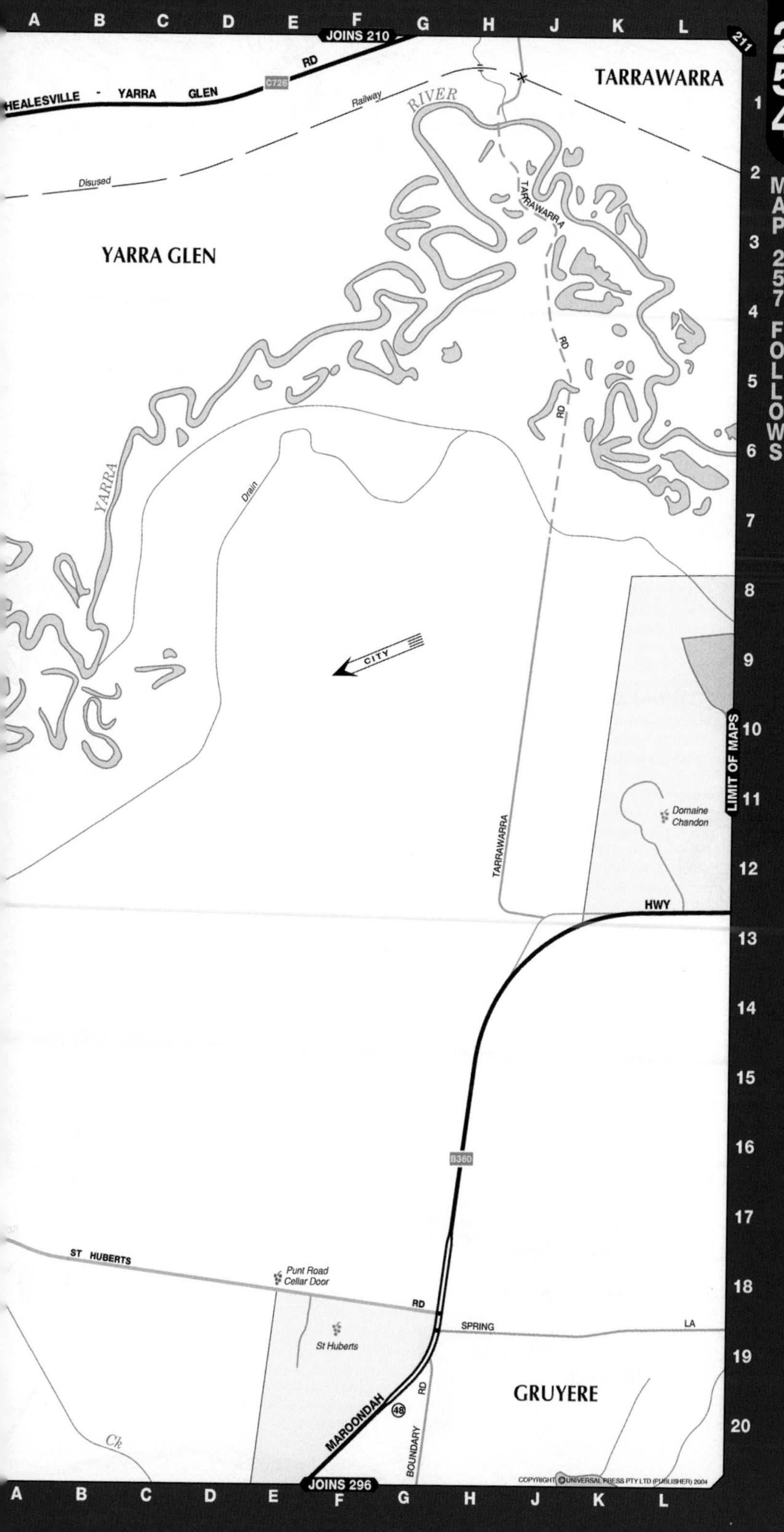
A B C D E F G H J K L
JOINS 210
211
TARRAWARRA
HEALESVILLE - YARRA GLEN RD
C726
Railway
Disused
RIVER
YARRA
TARRAWARRA RD
YARRA GLEN
Drain
CITY
MAP 257 FOLLOWS
LIMIT OF MAPS
Domaine Chandon
TARRAWARRA
HWY
B360
ST HUBERTS RD
Punt Road Cellar Door
St Huberts
SPRING LA
GRUYERE
MAROONDAH
48
BOUNDARY RD
Ck
JOINS 296
1 2 3 4 5 6 7 8 9 10 11 12 13 14 15 16 17 18 19 20
A B C D E F G H J K L

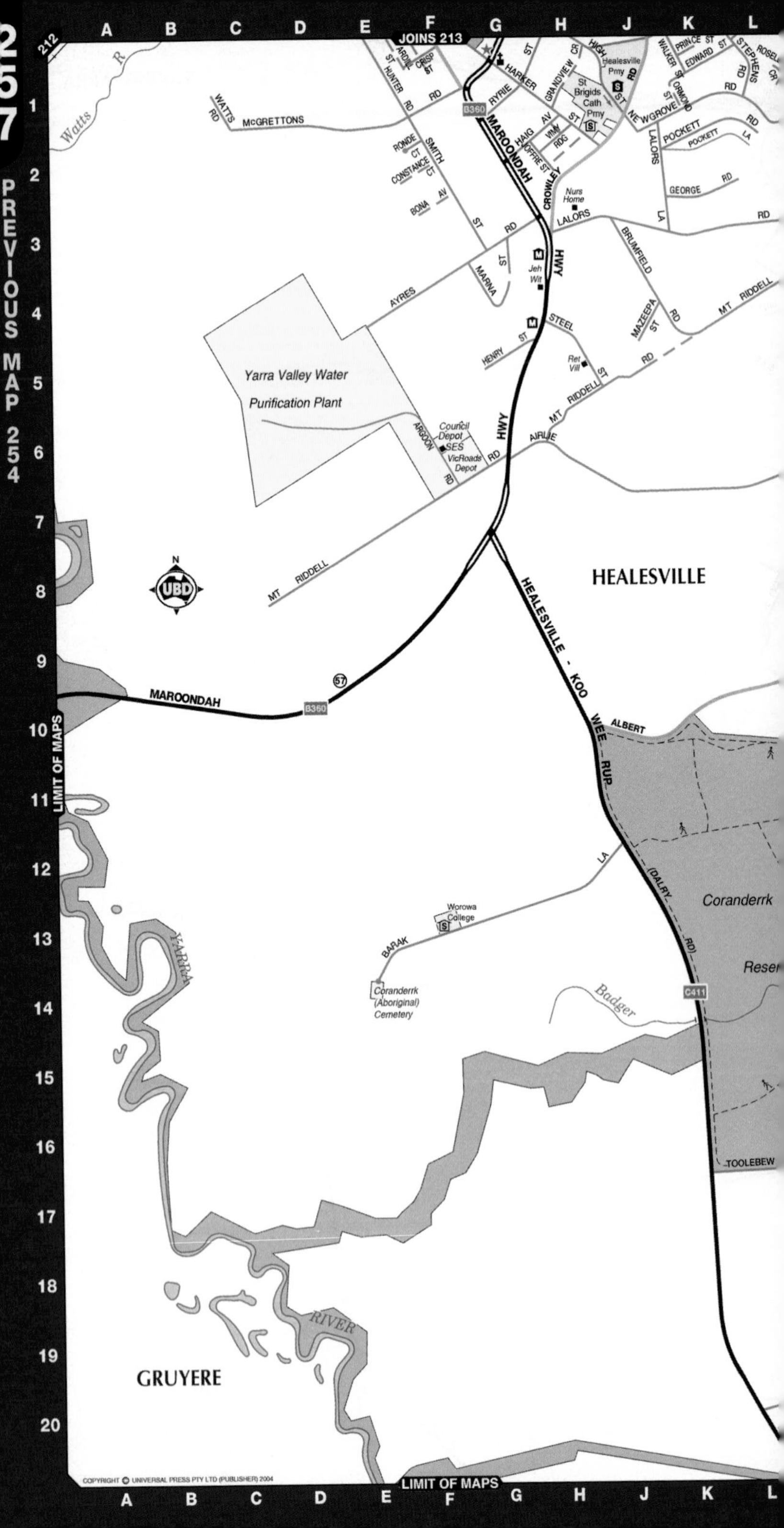
JOINS 213
212
PREVIOUS MAP 254
LIMIT OF MAPS
HEALESVILLE
GRUYERE
Yarra Valley Water
Purification Plant
MAROONDAH HWY
HEALESVILLE - KOO WEE RUP (DALRY RD)
MT RIDDELL RD
McGRETTONS RD
AYRES RD
AIRLIE
ALBERT
BARAK LA
Worowa College
Coranderrk (Aboriginal) Cemetery
Coranderrk Reser
Badger
YARRA RIVER
Watts R
Council Depot
SES
VicRoads Depot
Nurs Home
Ret Vill
Jeh Wit
Healesville Pmy
St Brigids Cath Pmy
LALORS RD
BRUMFIELD RD
MAZEEPA ST
STEEL ST
HENRY ST
MARNA ST
SMITH ST
HUNTER RD
CRISP ST
ARDILL
RONDE CT
CONSTANCE CT
BONA AV
WATTS RD
RYRIE
HARKER
GRANDVIEW CR
HIGH
HAIG AV
VIMY RDG
JOFFRE ST
CROWLEY
NEW GROVE
WALKER ST
ORMOND
PRINCE ST
EDWARD ST
STEPHENS RD
POCKETT RD
GEORGE RD
LALORS LA
ARGOON RD
TOOLEBEW
B360
C411
57
UBD

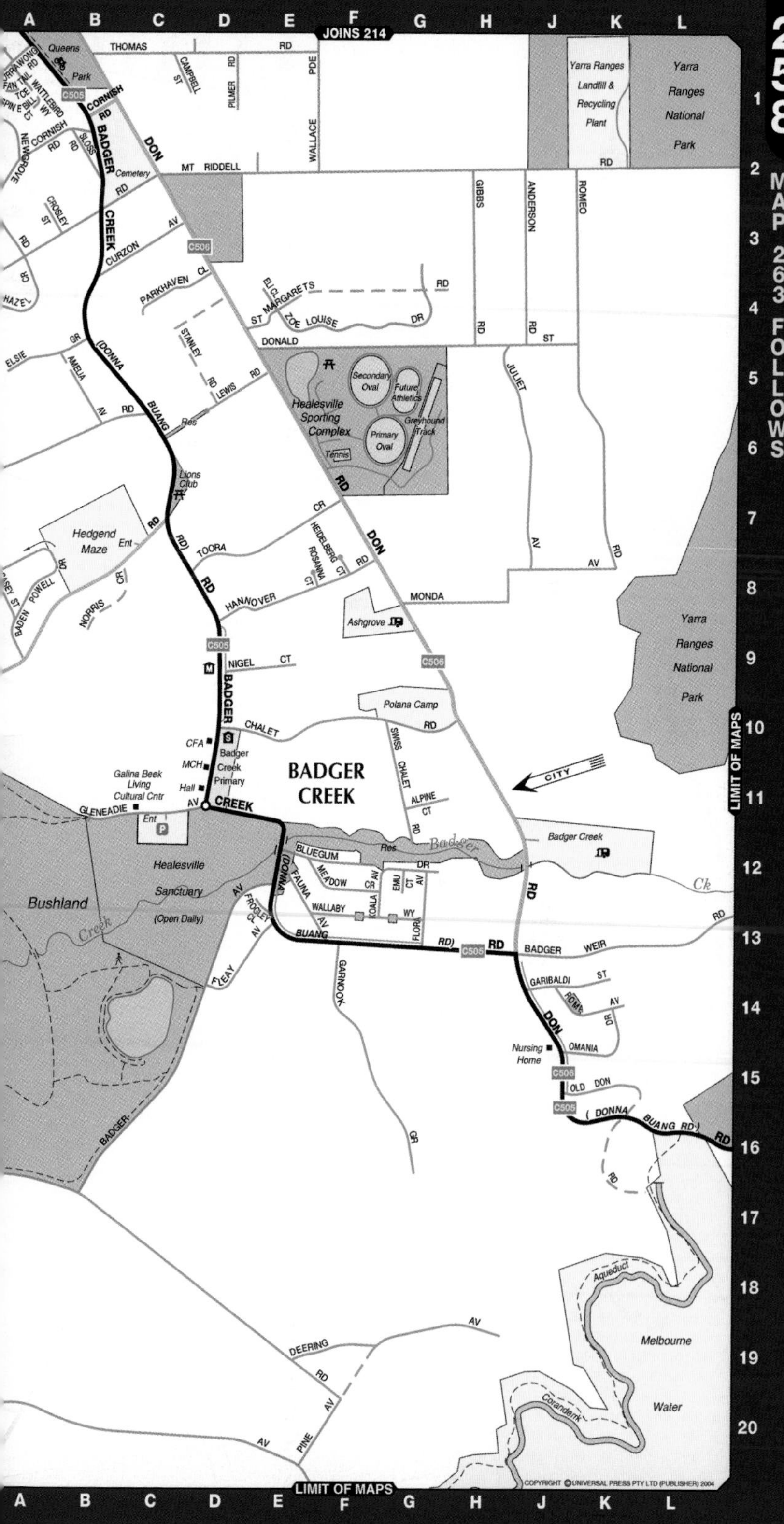
JOINS 214
MAP 263 FOLLOWS
LIMIT OF MAPS
BADGER CREEK
Healesville Sporting Complex
Secondary Oval
Future Athletics
Primary Oval
Greyhound Track
Tennis
Yarra Ranges Landfill & Recycling Plant
Yarra Ranges National Park
Queens Park
Cemetery
Lions Club
Hedgend Maze
Ashgrove
Polana Camp
Badger Creek Primary
CFA
MCH
Hall
Galina Beek Living Cultural Cntr
Healesville Sanctuary (Open Daily)
Bushland
Badger Creek
Nursing Home
Aqueduct
Melbourne Water
Corandenk
CITY
THOMAS RD
MT RIDDELL RD
DON RD
BADGER CREEK RD
(DONNA BUANG RD)
CURZON AV
PARKHAVEN CL
MARGARETS ST
LOUISE DR
DONALD ST
GIBBS RD
ANDERSON RD
ROMEO
JULIET AV
MONDA
HANNOVER
TOORA CR
HEIDELBERG CT
ROSANNA CT
NIGEL CT
CHALET RD
SWISS CHALET RD
ALPINE CT
GLENEADIE AV
BLUEGUM DR
MEADOW CR
FAUNA AV
WALLABY WY
KOALA
EMU CT
FLORA
FROGLEY CL
FLEAY AV
GARNOOK GR
BADGER WEIR RD
GARIBALDI ST
OMANIA
OLD DON
DEERING RD
PINE AV
C505
C506

JOINS 221

PREVIOUS MAP 258

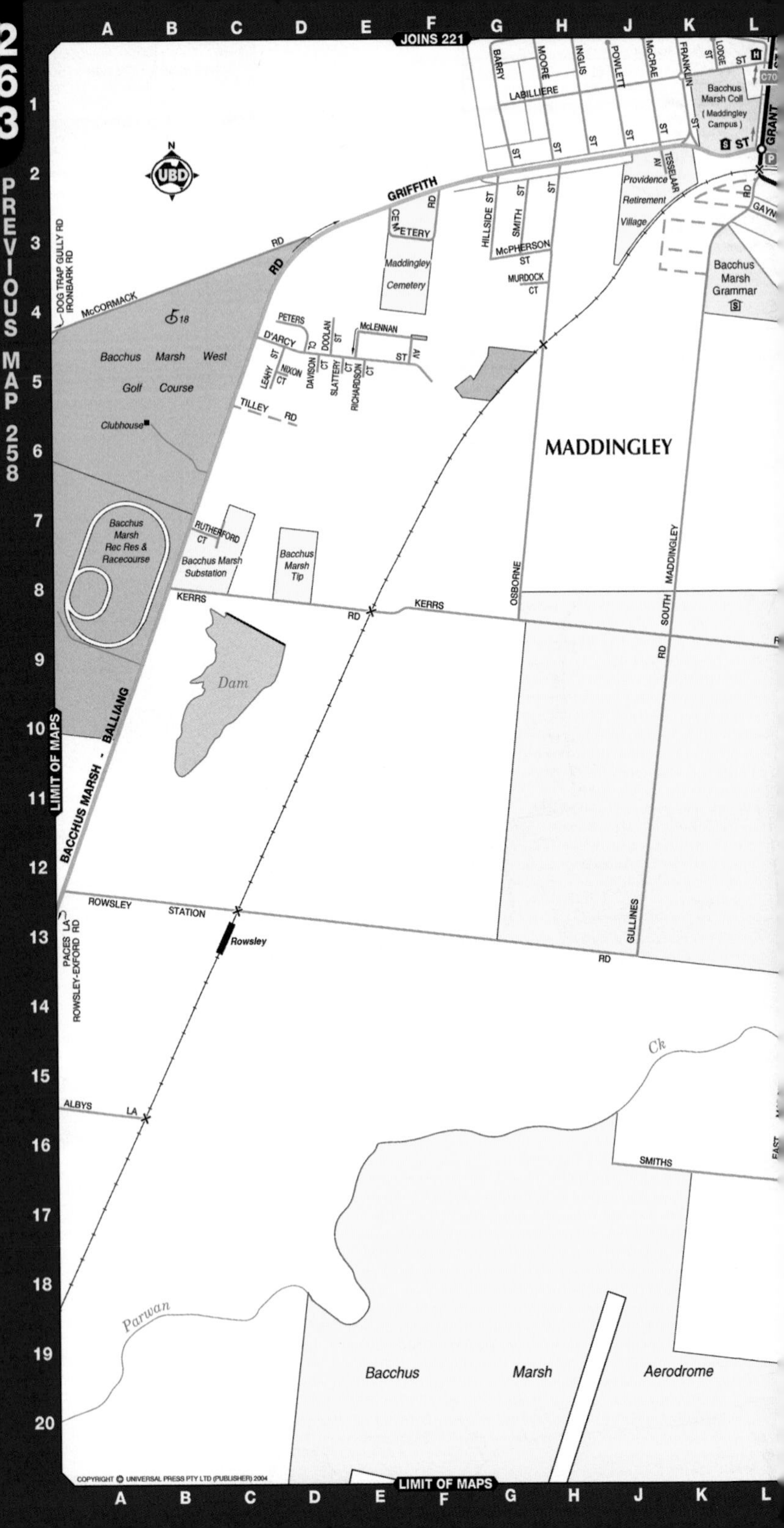

LIMIT OF MAPS

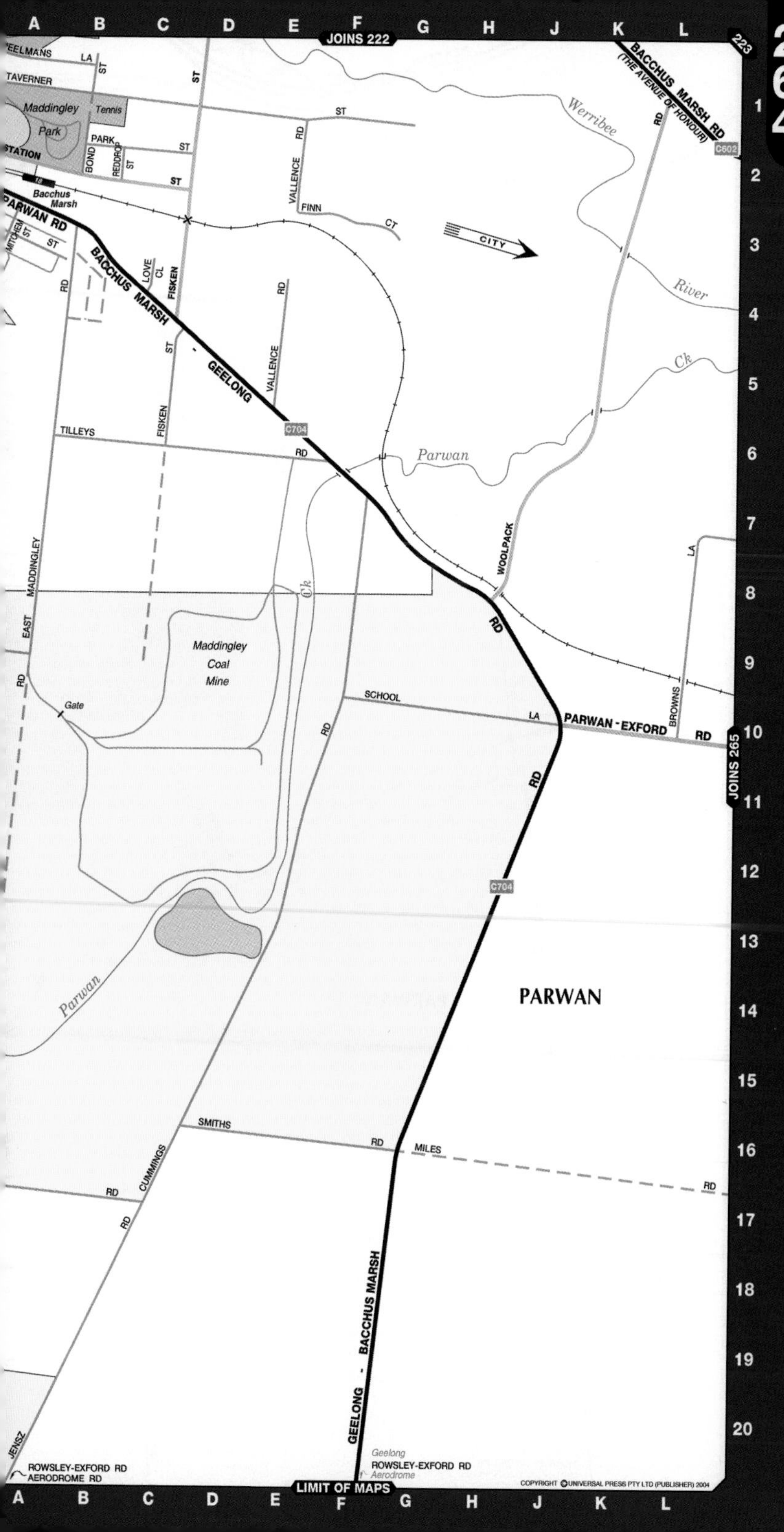
JOINS 222
223
JOINS 265
LIMIT OF MAPS
A B C D E F G H J K L
1 2 3 4 5 6 7 8 9 10 11 12 13 14 15 16 17 18 19 20
PEELMANS LA
TAVERNER
Maddingley Park
Tennis
STATION
PARK
BOND
REDDROP ST
Bacchus Marsh
PARWAN RD
MITCHEM ST
BACCHUS MARSH - GEELONG RD
LOVE CL
FISKEN ST
VALLENCE RD
FINN CT
CITY
Werribee River
BACCHUS MARSH RD (THE AVENUE OF HONOUR)
C602
Ck
Parwan
C704
TILLEYS RD
WOOLPACK RD
EAST MADDINGLEY RD
Maddingley Coal Mine
Gate
SCHOOL LA
PARWAN - EXFORD RD
BROWNS LA
PARWAN
SMITHS RD
MILES RD
CUMMINGS RD
GEELONG - BACCHUS MARSH
JENSZ
ROWSLEY-EXFORD RD
AERODROME RD
Geelong
Aerodrome

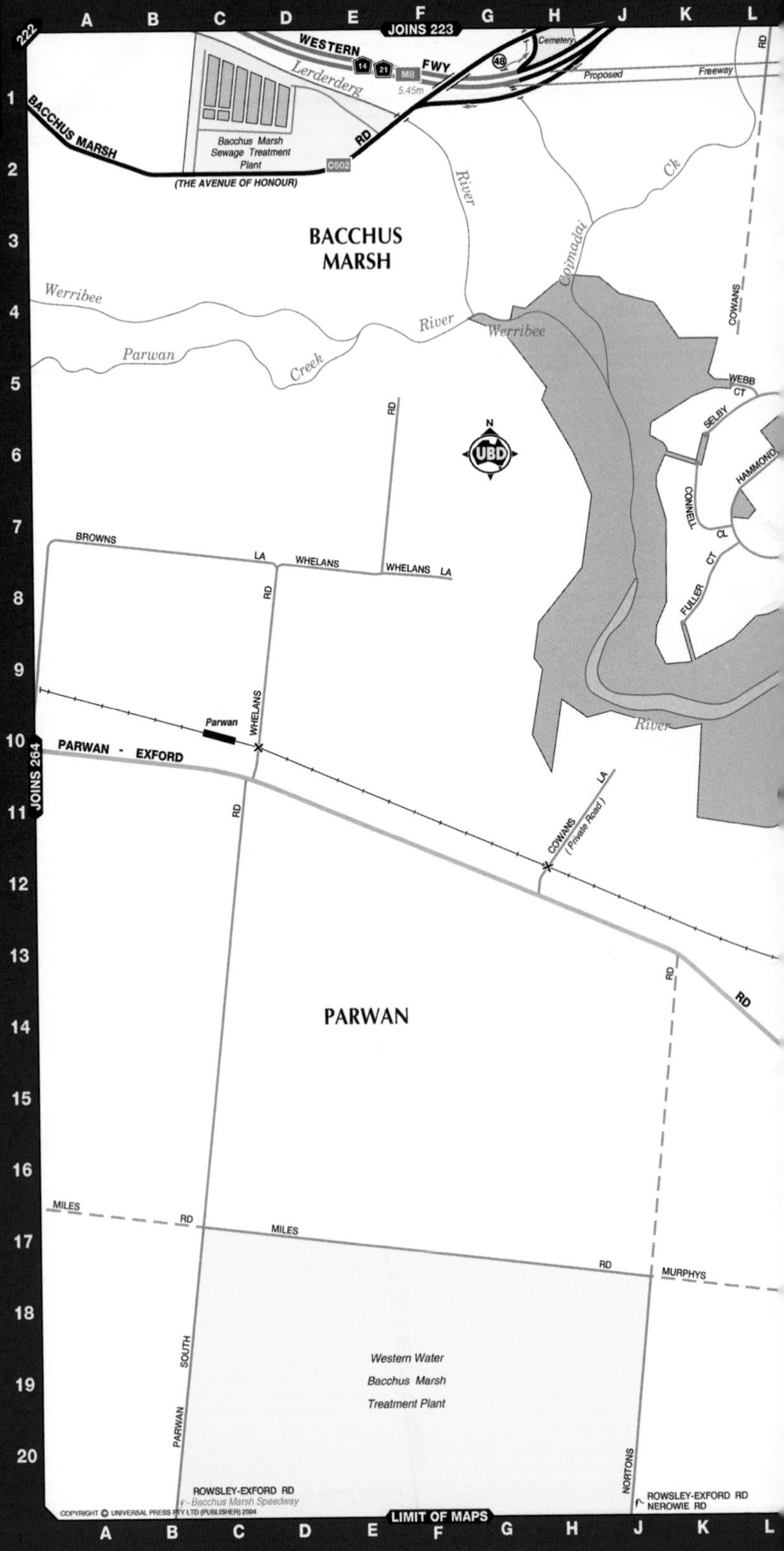

A B C D E F G H J K L
1 2 3 4 5 6 7 8 9 10 11 12 13 14 15 16 17 18 19 20
222
JOINS 223
JOINS 264
LIMIT OF MAPS
WESTERN FWY
14
21
M8
48
Cemetery
Proposed Freeway
Lerderderg
5.45m
RD
BACCHUS MARSH RD
C602
(THE AVENUE OF HONOUR)
Bacchus Marsh Sewage Treatment Plant
River
Ck
Coimadai
BACCHUS MARSH
Werribee
River
Werribee
Parwan
Creek
COWANS
WEBB CT
SELBY
HAMMOND
CONNELL CL
FULLER CT
N
UBD
BROWNS LA
WHELANS
WHELANS LA
RD
WHELANS RD
Parwan
PARWAN - EXFORD RD
River
COWANS LA
(Private Road)
RD
PARWAN
MILES RD
MILES RD
MURPHYS
Western Water
Bacchus Marsh
Treatment Plant
PARWAN SOUTH RD
NORTONS RD
ROWSLEY-EXFORD RD
Bacchus Marsh Speedway
ROWSLEY-EXFORD RD
NEROWIE RD

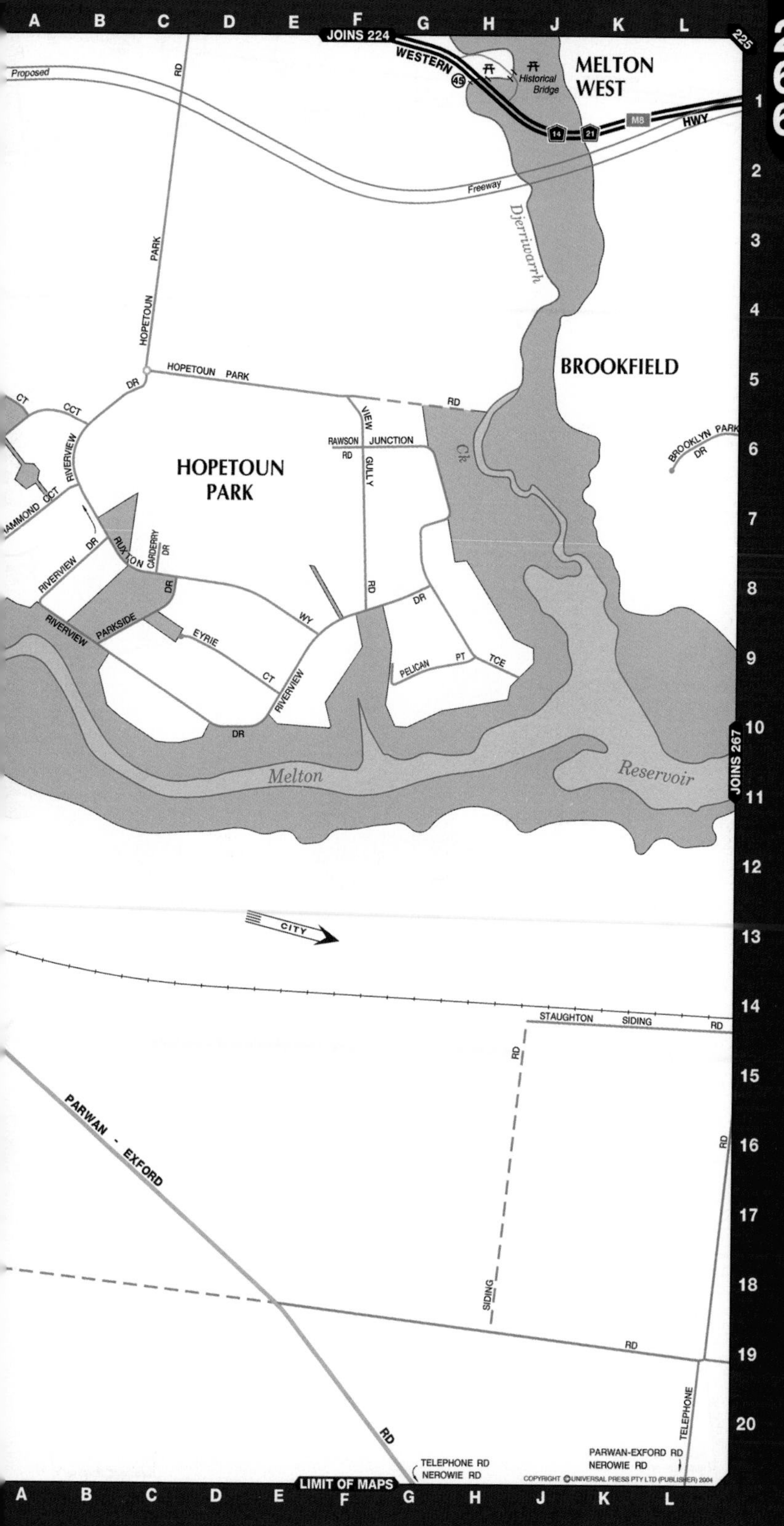

JOINS 224
225
262
WESTERN
HWY
Historical Bridge
MELTON WEST
M8
Proposed
Freeway
Djerriwarrh
Ck
BROOKFIELD
HOPETOUN PARK RD
HOPETOUN PARK
HOPETOUN PARK
RAWSON RD
JUNCTION
VIEW
GULLY RD
BROOKLYN PARK DR
RIVERVIEW
HAMMOND CCT
RIVERVIEW DR
RUXTON
CARDERRY DR
PARKSIDE DR
EYRIE CT
WY
DR
PELICAN PT
TCE
RIVERVIEW DR
Melton
Reservoir
JOINS 267
CITY
STAUGHTON SIDING RD
PARWAN - EXFORD RD
SIDING
RD
TELEPHONE
TELEPHONE RD
NEROWIE RD
PARWAN-EXFORD RD
NEROWIE RD
LIMIT OF MAPS
COPYRIGHT © UNIVERSAL PRESS PTY LTD (PUBLISHER) 2004

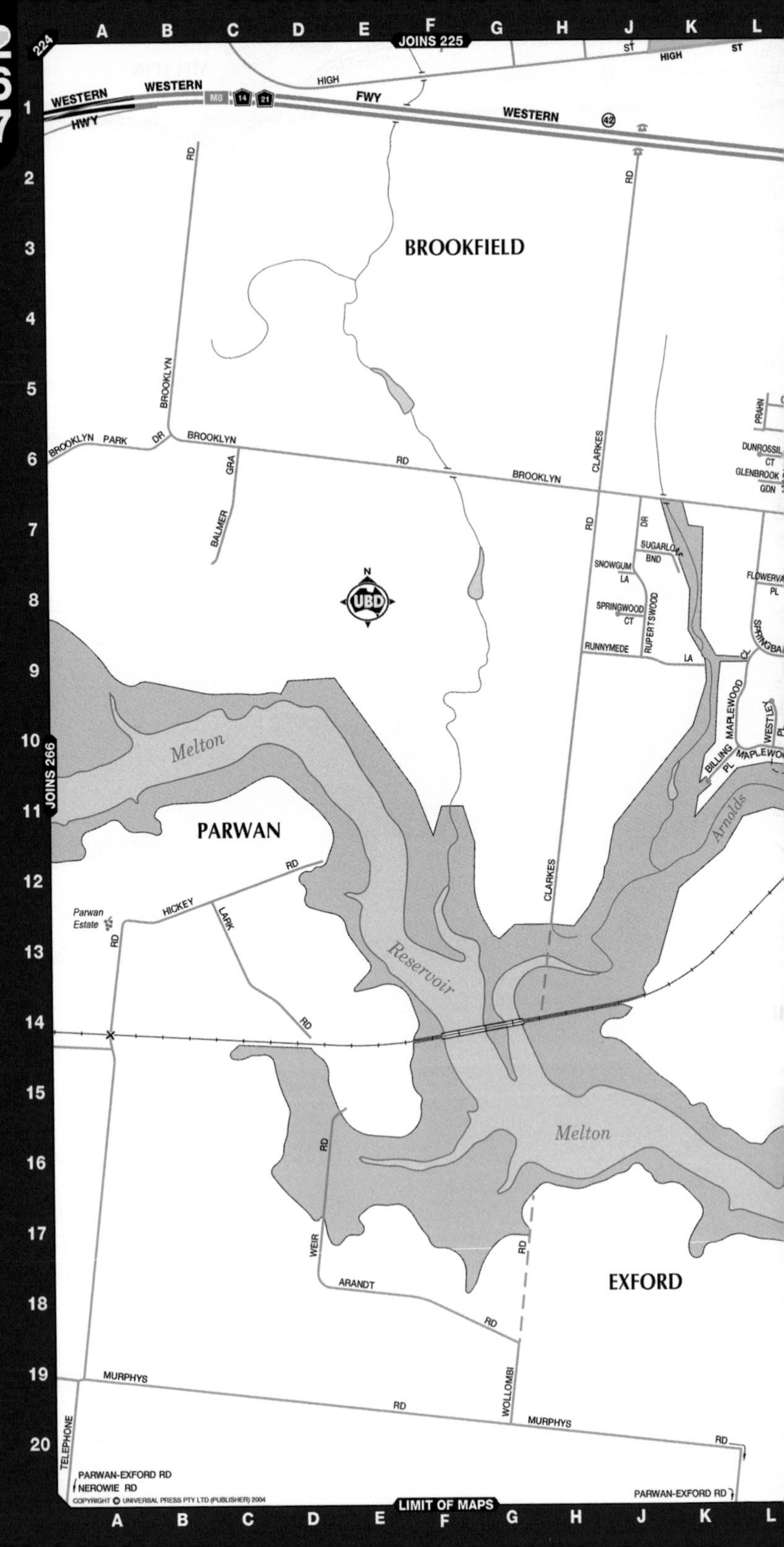
JOINS 225
224
WESTERN HWY
WESTERN FWY
HIGH ST
M8
BROOKFIELD
PARWAN
EXFORD
Melton Reservoir
Arnolds
BROOKLYN RD
BROOKLYN PARK DR
BALMER GRA
CLARKES RD
SUGARLOAF BND
SNOWGUM LA
SPRINGWOOD CT
RUPERTSWOOD DR
RUNNYMEDE LA
PRAHN
DUNROSSIL CT
GLENBROOK GDN
FLOWERVALE PL
MAPLEWOOD CL
WESTLEY PL
BILLING PL
HICKEY RD
LARK RD
Parwan Estate
WEIR RD
ARANDT RD
WOLLOMBI RD
MURPHYS RD
TELEPHONE RD
PARWAN-EXFORD RD
NEROWIE RD
JOINS 266
LIMIT OF MAPS

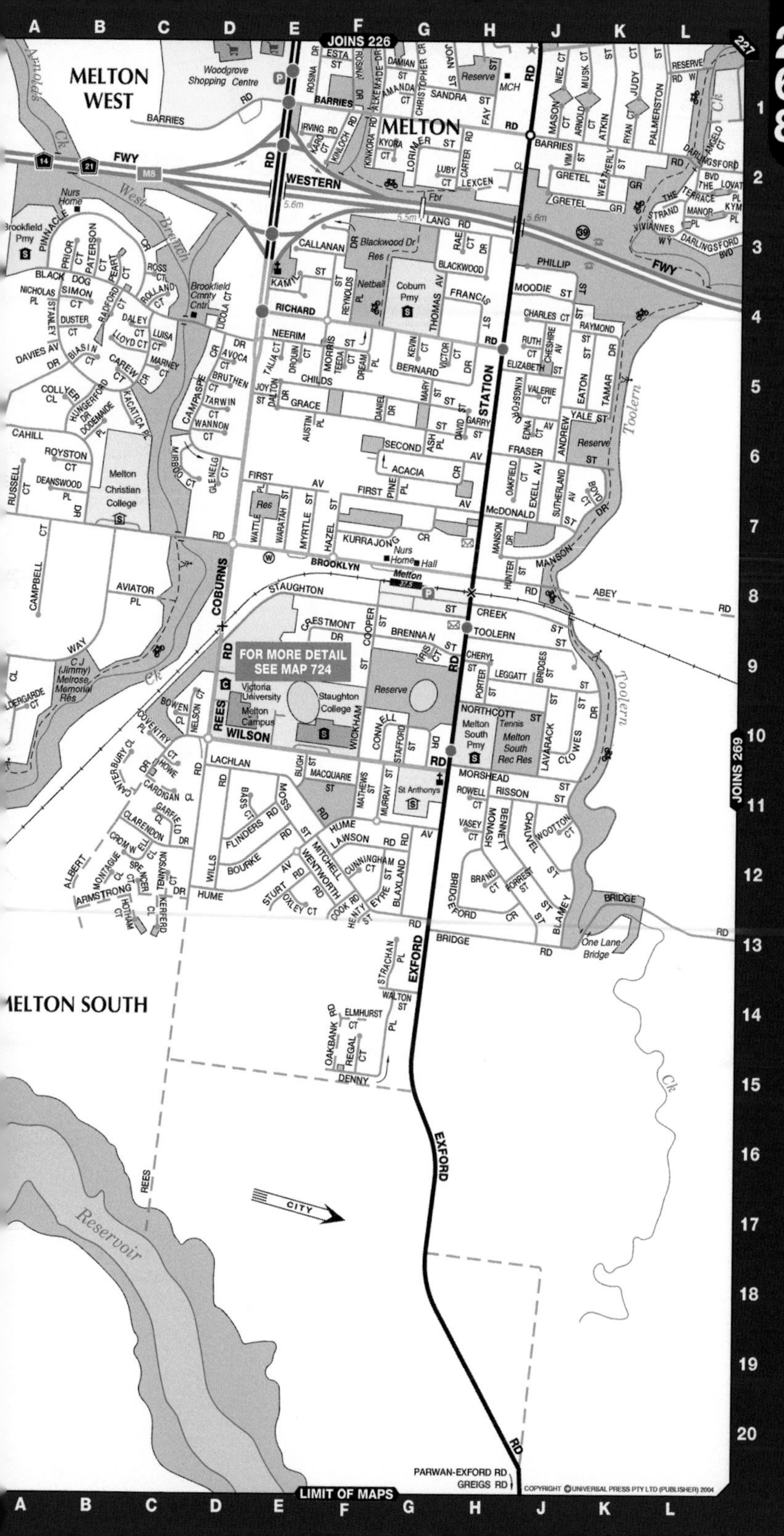

JOINS 226
JOINS 269
LIMIT OF MAPS
227
MELTON WEST
MELTON
MELTON SOUTH
Woodgrove Shopping Centre
WESTERN FWY
M8
FOR MORE DETAIL SEE MAP 724
Blackwood Dr Res
Coburn Pmy
Brookfield Pmy
Brookfield Cmnty Cntr
Nurs Home
Melton Christian College
C J (Jimmy) Melrose Memorial Res
Victoria University Melton Campus
Staughton College
Reserve
Melton South Pmy
Melton South Rec Res
Tennis
St Anthonys
One Lane Bridge
MCH
Melton
Nurs Home
Hall
Toolern Ck
Reservoir
CITY
COBURNS RD
STATION RD
EXFORD RD
REES RD
BRIDGE RD
ABEY RD
PARWAN-EXFORD RD
GREIGS RD
BARRIES RD
BROOKLYN RD
STAUGHTON
RICHARD
NEERIM
HUME
LACHLAN
MORSHEAD
TOOLERN ST
CREEK ST
WILSON
COPYRIGHT © UNIVERSAL PRESS PTY LTD (PUBLISHER) 2004

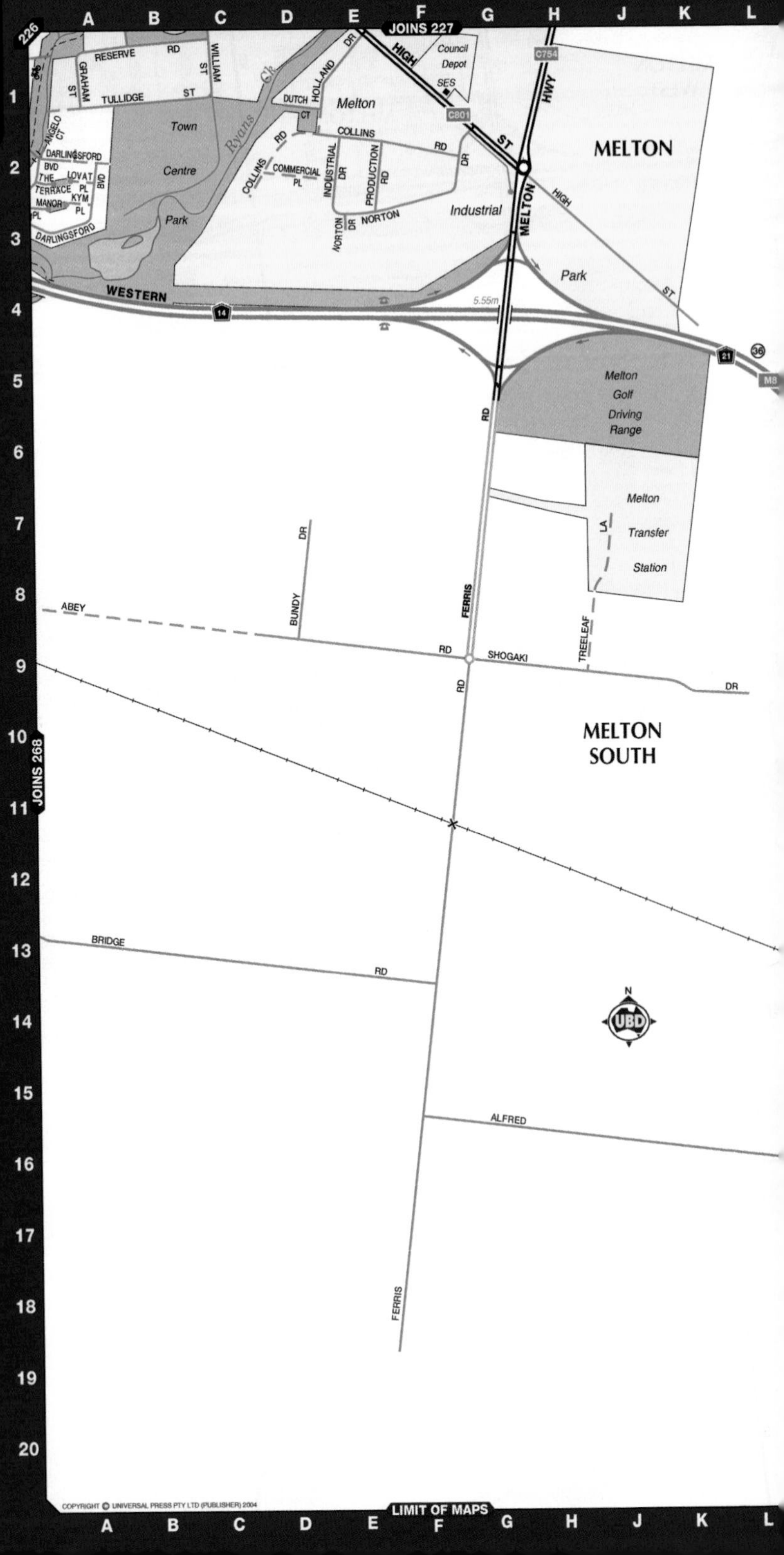
A B C D E F G H J K L
1 2 3 4 5 6 7 8 9 10 11 12 13 14 15 16 17 18 19 20
226
JOINS 227
JOINS 268
LIMIT OF MAPS
MELTON
MELTON SOUTH
Melton Industrial Park
Town Centre Park
Council Depot
SES
C801
C754
HIGH ST
MELTON HWY
RESERVE RD
WILLIAM ST
GRAHAM ST
TULLIDGE ST
Ryans Ck
DUTCH CT
HOLLAND DR
COLLINS RD
COLLINS PL
COMMERCIAL PL
INDUSTRIAL DR
PRODUCTION RD
NORTON DR
NORTON DR
ANGELO CT
DARLINGSFORD BVD
THE TERRACE
LOVAT PL
KYM PL
MANOR PL
BVD
DARLINGSFORD
WESTERN
14
5.55m
21
36
M8
Melton Golf Driving Range
Melton Transfer Station
LA
TREELEAF
ABEY RD
BUNDY DR
FERRIS RD
SHOGAKI DR
BRIDGE RD
ALFRED
FERRIS
N
UBD

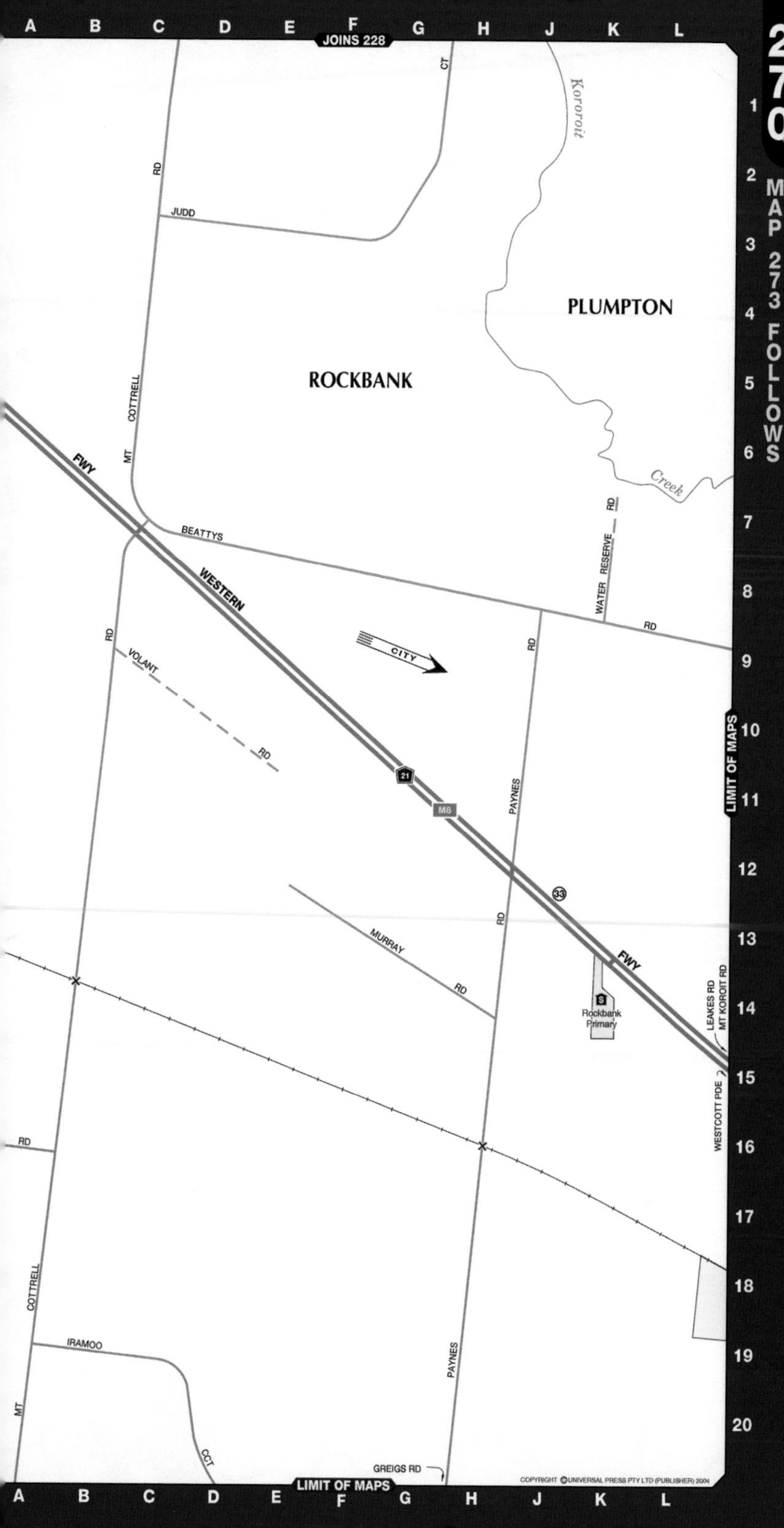
270
MAP 273 FOLLOWS
JOINS 228
LIMIT OF MAPS
ROCKBANK
PLUMPTON
Kororoit Creek
MT COTTRELL RD
JUDD
CT
BEATTYS RD
WATER RESERVE RD
WESTERN FWY
CITY
VOLANT RD
PAYNES RD
MURRAY RD
Rockbank Primary
LEAKES RD
MT KOROIT RD
WESTCOTT PDE
RD
IRAMOO CCT
GREIGS RD
21
M8
33
COPYRIGHT © UNIVERSAL PRESS PTY LTD (PUBLISHER) 2004

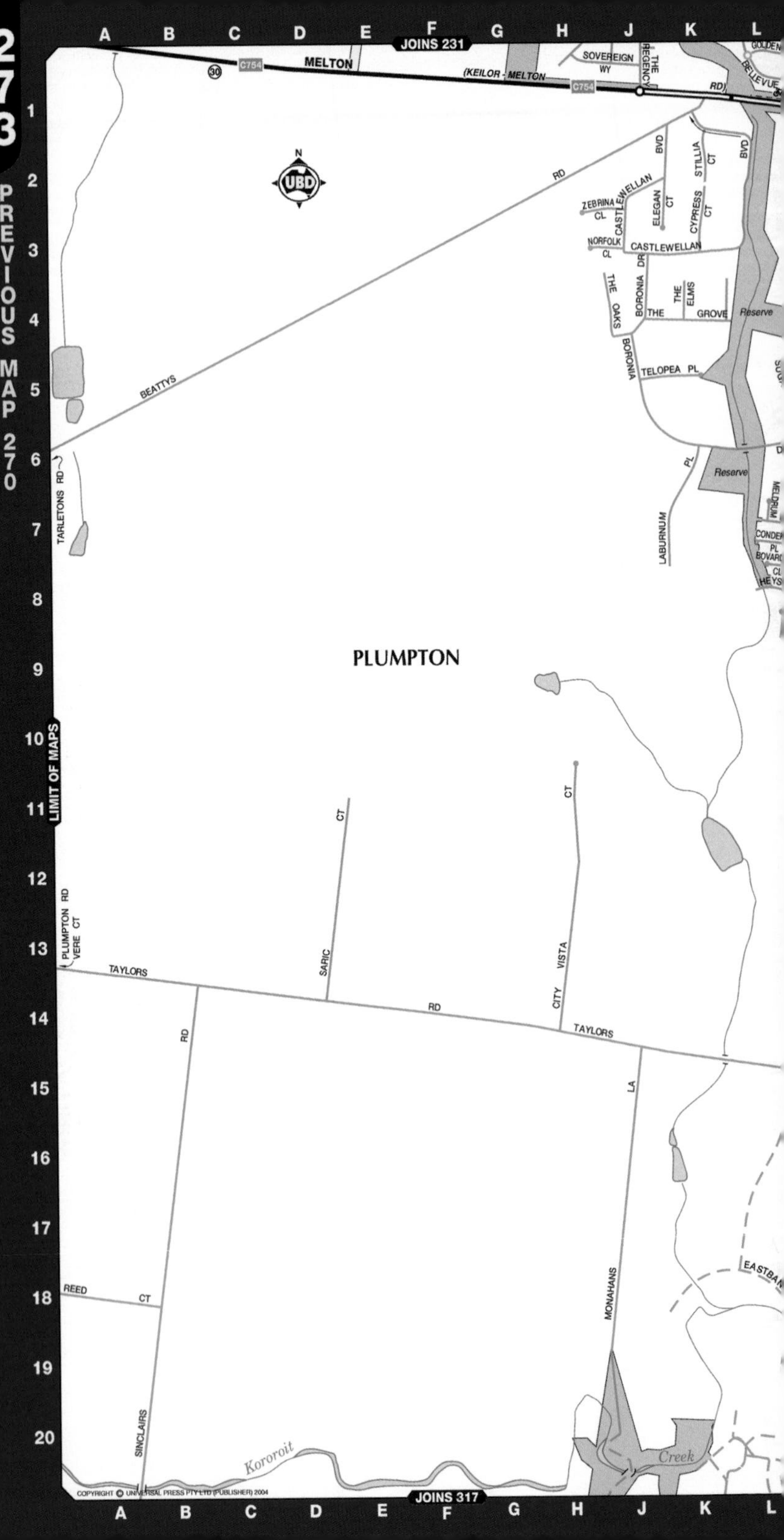

JOINS 231
PREVIOUS MAP 270
MELTON
(KEILOR - MELTON RD)
C754
30
SOVEREIGN WY
THE REGENCY
GOLDEN
BELLEVUE
BVD
STILLIA CT
CASTLEWELLAN
ZEBRINA CL
ELEGAN CT
CYPRESS CT
NORFOLK CL
BORONIA DR
THE OAKS
THE ELMS
THE GROVE
Reserve
TELOPEA PL
BEATTYS RD
TARLETONS RD
LABURNUM PL
MELDRUM
BOVARD
HEYS
PLUMPTON
LIMIT OF MAPS
SARIC CT
CITY VISTA CT
PLUMPTON RD
VERE CT
TAYLORS RD
TAYLORS
MONAHANS LA
REED CT
SINCLAIRS RD
EASTBA
Kororoit Creek
JOINS 317

JOINS 232
233
JOINS 275

HILLSIDE

SYDENHAM

TAYLORS HILL

CAROLINE SPRINGS

BURNSIDE

MELTON HWY

CALDER PARK DR

HUME DR

TAYLORS RD

GOURLAY RD

CAROLINE SPRINGS BVD

Copperfield College

Sydenham Hillside Pmy

Reservoir HARDWARE

Homestead Park

Proposed School

Proposed Retirement Village

Primary School Site

Proposed URLL Tenterfield Residential Development

Gilson College

Delbridge Gardens Ret Vill

Nursing Home

CITY

JOINS 318
319

JOINS 233

JOINS 274

JOINS 319

A B C D E F G H J K L

SYDENHAM

DELAHEY

KINGS PARK

ST ALBANS

Overnewton Anglican Cmnty College Keilor Lodge Campus

Soccer Fields

School Site

Bunnings

Watergardens Shopping Centre

Cinema

The Lakes Ret Vill

Nursing Home

CFA

Sydenham Regional Cath Coll & Emmaus Cath Pmy

Watergardens

Jeh Wit

Stagecoach Res

Nurs Hm

Taylors Lake

Reception Centre

Taylors Lakes Secondary College

Tennis

Taylors Lakes Pmy

Monmia Pmy

Reserve

Soccer Reserve

Cmnty Cntr

Copperfield College Senior Campus

Mackellar Pmy

Tennis Reserve

Radio Mast

Ukrainian Elderly Peoples Home

Hume & Hovell Cairn

Melbourne Water

Copperfield College Junior Campus

Primary

MCH

Resurrection Catholic

Nestlé

Res

MELTON HWY (KEILOR - MELTON RD)

KINGS RD

HUME DR

SYDENHAM RD

TAYLORS RD

GILLESPIE RD

CALDER

C754

M79

24

40

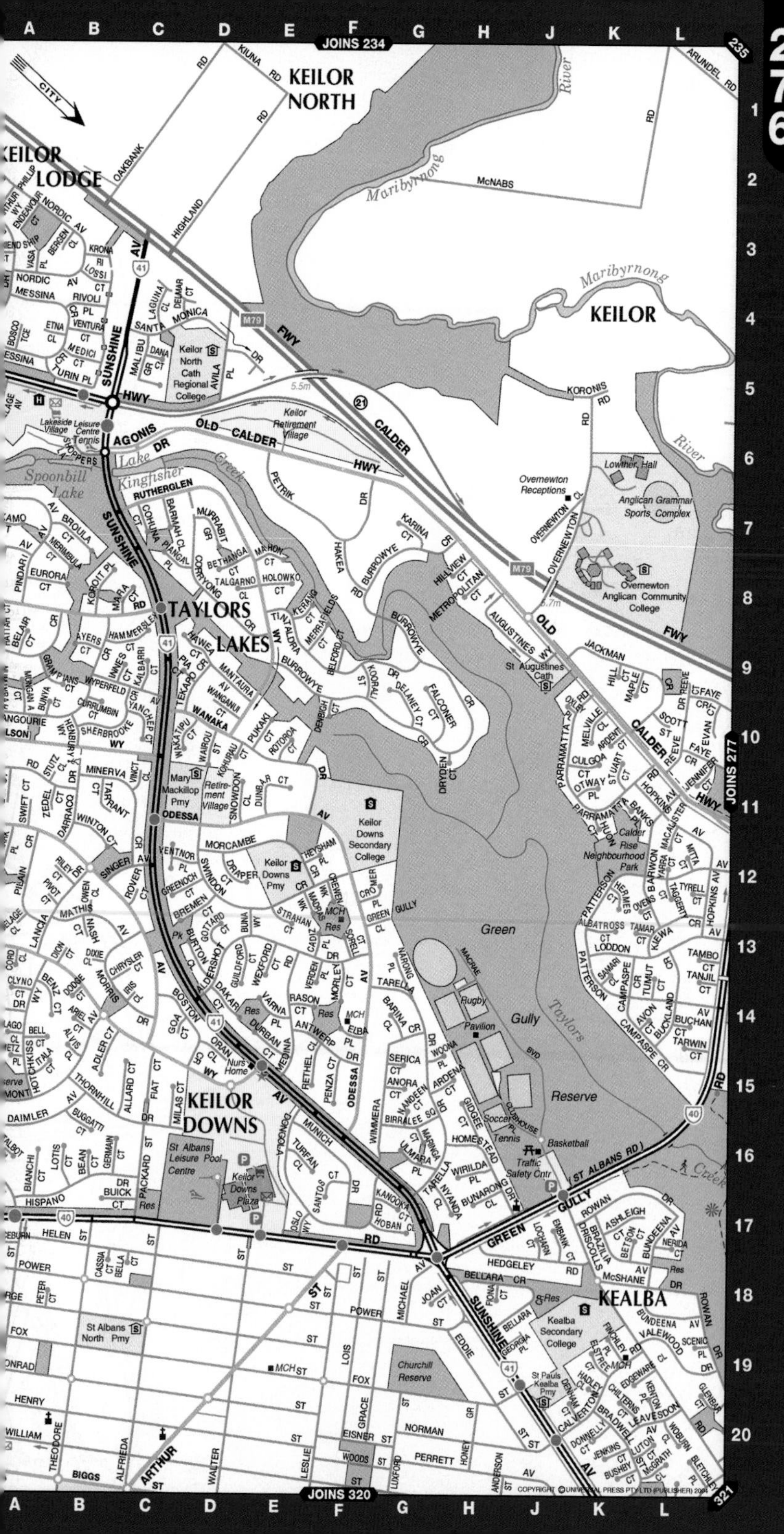
JOINS 234
235
KEILOR NORTH
KEILOR LODGE
KEILOR
TAYLORS LAKES
KEILOR DOWNS
KEALBA
CITY
Maribyrnong River
Taylors Creek
Green Gully Reserve
Spoonbill Lake
Kingfisher Lake
CALDER FWY
SUNSHINE AV
OLD CALDER HWY
CALDER HWY
ST ALBANS RD
GREEN GULLY RD
SUNSHINE HWY
McNABS
KORONIS RD
OVERNEWTON RD
Keilor North Cath Regional College
Keilor Retirement Village
Lakeside Village
Leisure Centre Tennis
Lowther Hall Anglican Grammar Sports Complex
Overnewton Receptions
Overnewton Anglican Community College
St Augustines Cath
Calder Rise Neighbourhood Park
Mary Mackillop Pmy
Retirement Village
Keilor Downs Secondary College
Keilor Downs Pmy
Rugby Pavilion
Soccer Tennis
Basketball
Traffic Safety Cntr
Nurs Home
St Albans Leisure Pool Centre
Keilor Downs Plaza
St Albans North Pmy
Churchill Reserve
Kealba Secondary College
St Pauls Kealba Pmy
JOINS 277
JOINS 320
321
COPYRIGHT © UNIVERSAL PRESS PTY LTD (PUBLISHER) 2004

A B C D E F G H J K L

1 2 3 4 5 6 7 8 9 10 11 12 13 14 15 16 17 18 19 20

MELBOURNE AIRPORT

KEILOR

KEILOR PARK

KEALBA

Tullamarine Country Club
Clubhouse
Quarry
Radio Mast
Maribyrnong
Steele Ck
ARUNDEL RD
BROWNS RD
ANNANDALE RD
MILBURN RD
CALDER FWY
OLD CALDER HWY
MACEDON
ST ALBANS RD
GREEN GULLY RD
KEILOR PARK DR
FULLARTON RD
WESTERN RING RD
International Basketball Centre
Council Depot
SES
Keilor Engineering Services Centre
Athletics Club
Keilor Park Recreation Reserve
Pavilion
Soccer
Pav
Keilor Primary
Tennis
Keilor Res
Caroline Chisholm Park
Lagoon Res
Bonfield Reserve
Gumms Corner
Calder Rise Pmy
Reserve
Visitors Centre
Purification Plant
Oval
Brimbank Park
Horseshoe Bend Farm
Office
Field Centre
Maribyrnong Valley Parklands
Keilor Cemetery
Prop Cem Extension
Terminal Station
Parks
CITY
5.6m
5.4m
5.5m
M79
M80
40
18

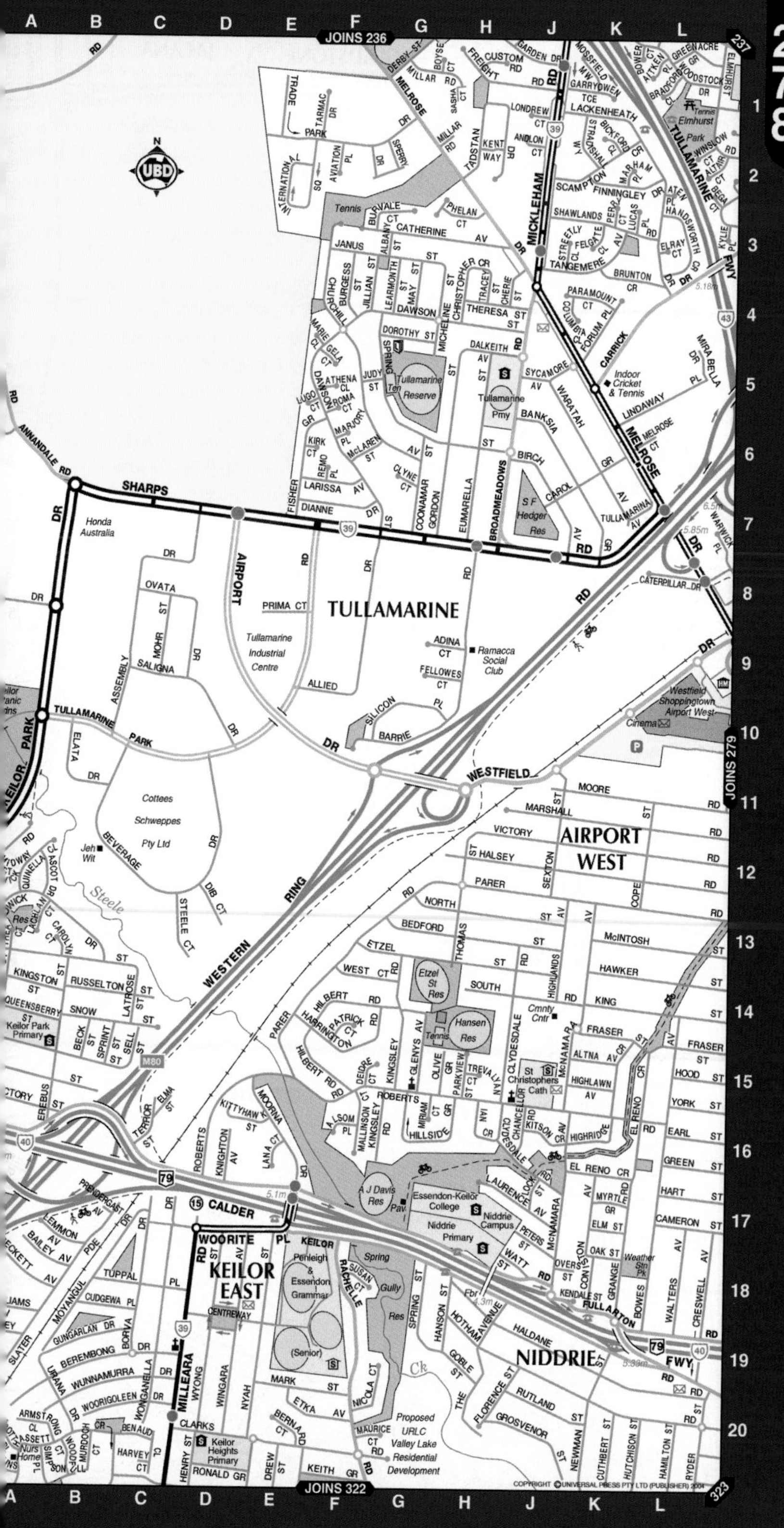

278
JOINS 236
JOINS 279
JOINS 322
237
323
TULLAMARINE
AIRPORT WEST
KEILOR EAST
NIDDRIE
SHARPS RD
MICKLEHAM RD
MELROSE DR
TULLAMARINE FWY
WESTERN RING RD
CALDER FWY
AIRPORT DR
BROADMEADOWS RD
ANNANDALE RD
KEILOR PARK DR
TULLAMARINE PARK RD
WESTFIELD DR
FULLARTON RD
MILLEARA RD
McNAMARA AV
HOTHAM AVENUE
Honda Australia
Tullamarine Industrial Centre
Tullamarine Reserve
Tullamarine Pmy
S F Hedger Res
Indoor Cricket & Tennis
Ramacca Social Club
Westfield Shoppingtown Airport West
Cottees Schweppes Pty Ltd
Etzel St Res
Hansen Res
St Christophers Cath
Essendon-Keilor College Niddrie Campus
Niddrie Primary
A J Davis Res
Penleigh & Essendon Grammar (Senior)
Spring Gully Res
Keilor Heights Primary
Keilor Park Primary
Proposed URLC Valley Lake Residential Development
COPYRIGHT © UNIVERSAL PRESS PTY LTD (PUBLISHER) 2004

GLADSTONE PARK

JACANA

GOWANBRAE

STRATHMORE HEIGHTS

AIRPORT WEST

OAK PARK

STRATHMORE

ESSENDON NORTH

Essendon Airport

WESTERN RING RD

TULLAMARINE FWY

PASCOE VALE RD

MATTHEWS AV

KEILOR RD

BULLA RD

Moonee Ponds Creek

Kingsford Smith Ulm Res

Collier Park

Boeing Res

Strathnaver Res

J P Fawkner Res

Alf Pearce Park

Westfield Shoppingtown Airport West

Melbourne Water Corp Resvr

Passenger Terminal

Control Tower

Administration

Glenroy West Pmy

Oak Park Pmy

Penola Cath Coll Glenroy Campus

JOINS 278

JOINS 323

JOINS 238
239
JOINS 281
JOINS 324
325
A B C D E F G H J K L
1 2 3 4 5 6 7 8 9 10 11 12 13 14 15 16 17 18 19 20
GLENROY
HADFIELD
Westbreen
PASCOE VALE
PASCOE VALE SOUTH
Bureau of Meteorology
Northern Memorial Park
Northern Golf Club
CITY
Anderson Reserve
Wallace Reserve
Wetlands
Merlynston Ck
Cook Res
Tennis
Box Forest Secondary College
Glenory Junior Campus
Glenroy North Pmy
Belle Vue Park Pmy
Corpus Christi Cath
Box Forest Sec Coll
Glenory Senior Campus
Frank Mott Res
RSL
MCH
Glenroy Pmy
St Thomas More Cath
Clubhouse
S G Sewell Reserve
Cmnty Hall
Council Depot
Westbreen Primary
Pascoe Vale Gardens
H M Dowd Res
Pascoe Vale Girls Sec Coll
K W Joyce Reserve
Hallam Res
Oak Park
St Francis de Sales
Rayner Res
S Cole Reserve
Pascoe Vale Nth Pmy
Dorset Priv Hosp
Oak Park Res
Waterslide
Herbert Res
Lebanon Reserve
Austin Crescent Res
Gavin Pk
Dorothy Nurs Home
Spastic Centre
G A James Res
Rogers Res
Raeburn Res
St Oliver Plunket Pmy
H Payne Res
Esslemont Reserve
Pascoe Vale Pmy
Pascoe Vale
Max Johnston Res
Kelvin Thompson Park
Strathmore Sec Coll
Melb Coll of Textiles Pascoe Vale Campus
Brearley Res
WESTERN RING M80
FWY
HILTON ST
GLENROY RD
WHEATSHEAF RD
PLUMPTON AV
CARDINAL RD
WEST ST
BOUNDARY RD
PASCOE ST
RHODES PDE
PASCOE VALE RD
STEWART ST
CUMBERLAND RD
NORTHUMBERLAND RD
GAFFNEY ST
DEVON RD
KENT RD
DERBY ST
BELL ST
O'HEA ST
TURNER ST
WIDFORD ST
5.63m
5.44m
5.33m
5.71m
5.48m
6.09m
COPYRIGHT © UNIVERSAL PRESS PTY LTD (PUBLISHER) 2004

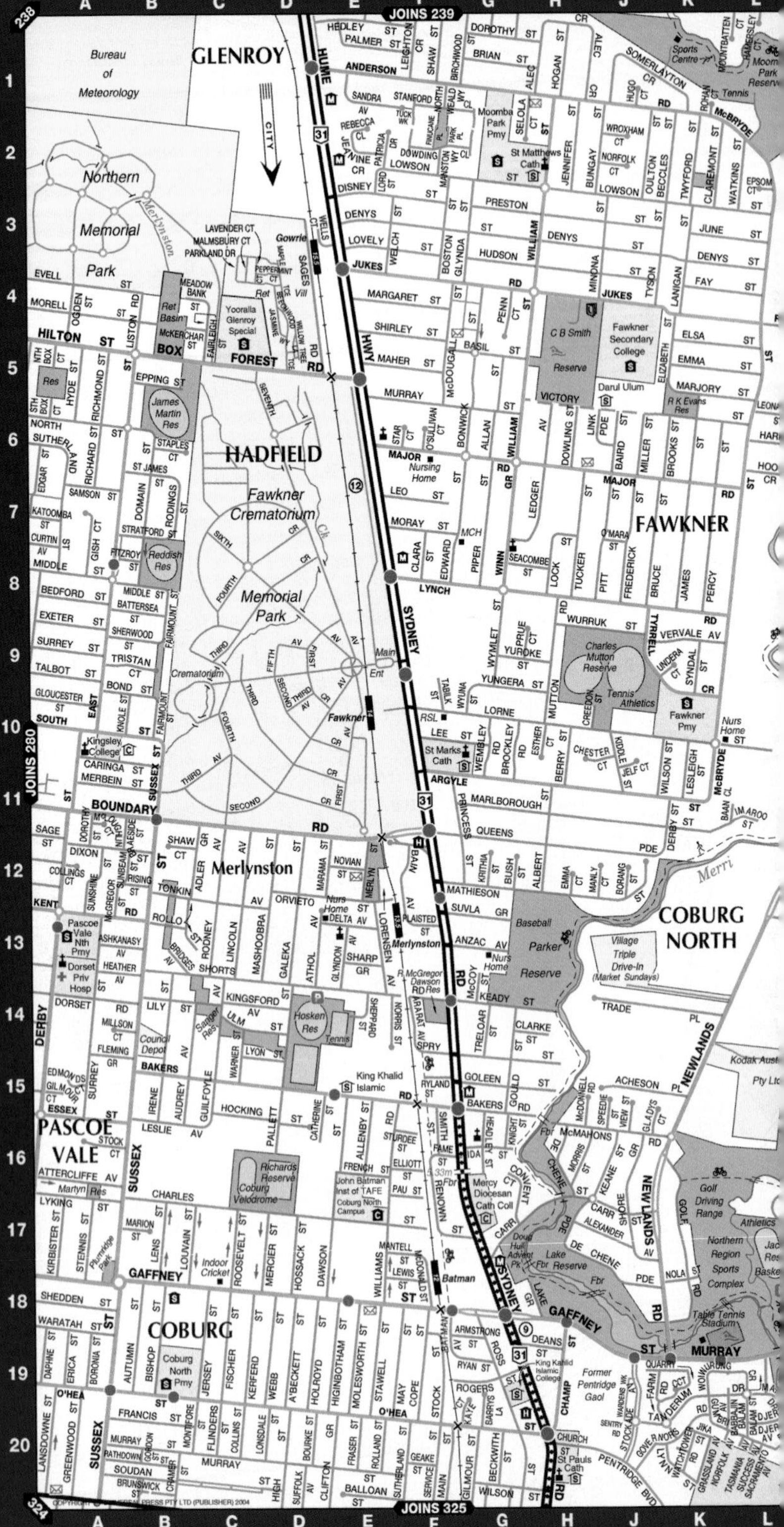

238
JOINS 239
JOINS 280
JOINS 325
324

A B C D E F G H J K L

GLENROY

HADFIELD

Merlynston

FAWKNER

COBURG NORTH

PASCOE VALE

COBURG

Bureau of Meteorology

Northern Memorial Park

Fawkner Crematorium

Memorial Park

C B Smith Reserve

Fawkner Secondary College

Charles Mutton Reserve

Parker Reserve

Village Triple Drive-In (Market Sundays)

Hosken Res

Richards Reserve Coburg Velodrome

Lake Reserve

Northern Region Sports Complex

Golf Driving Range

Former Pentridge Gaol

HUME HWY

SYDNEY RD

BOUNDARY RD

GAFFNEY ST

A
B
C
D
E
F
G
H
J
K
L
JOINS 240
241
JOINS 283
JOINS 326
327
1
2
3
4
5
6
7
8
9
10
11
12
13
14
15
16
17
18
19
20
RESERVOIR
PRESTON
MAHONEYS RD
Merrilands College
MERRILANDS RD
HUGHES PDE
L E Cotchin Reserve
Pavilion
MASSEY AV
DAVIDSON ST
BARTROP ST
Central Ck
Edgars Creek
St Joseph The Worker Catholic
Ruthven Pmy
Tennis Res
BOTHA AV
McFADZEAN AV
ROSENTHAL AV
GELLIBRAND AV
B T Connor Reserve
Soccer
GLASGOW AV
BROADHURST AV
Macedonian Social Club
Linkson Buddhist Temple
Lakeside Sec Coll
RADFORD RD
BANBURY RD
LEAMINGTON ST
Leamington Tennis
Edwardes Park
Preston Yacht Club
Edwardes Lake
Athletics
EDWARDES ST
J E Moore Park
Pav
Reservoir Private Hosp
St Gabriel Cath
RSL
Reservoir
Bus Depot
HIGH ST
HENTY ST
Waste Transfer Station (Open 7 days)
Park WRIGHT
RESERVOIR
Melbourne Reservoirs No 1
No 2 Water
Crispe Park
Melbourne C'van Park
Reservoir West Pmy
CARRINGTON RD
GILBERT RD
SPRING ST
G E Robinson Park Tennis
Cash Reserve
Kodak Australia Pty Ltd
Newlands Pmy
REGENT ST
J S Grey Res
Regent
W-K-Larkins Res Tennis
L W Williams Res
F G Cox Res
Nursing Home
Cath
Nurs Home
E G Pike Res
TYLER ST
MURRAY RD
Preston West Pmy
Preston Market
Preston
Sen Cits
Mosque
Court House
ELIZABETH ST
BELL ST
COPYRIGHT © UNIVERSAL PRESS PTY LTD (PUBLISHER) 2004

A B C D E F G H J K L

JOINS 241

THOMASTOWN

RESERVOIR

KINGSBURY

PRESTON

1 2 3 4 5 6 7 8 9 10 11 12 13 14 15 16 17 18 19 20

J.C. Donath Reserve

I W Dole Res

D R Atkinson Reserve

Keon Park Pmy

H H Leslie Res

St Stephens Cath

John Hall Res

Arch Gibson Res

C W Kirkwood Res

Leisure Cntr

T W Andrews Park

Kevin P Hardiman Reserve

Our Lady of the Way Cath

Kingsbury Pmy

Reservoir East Pmy

Reservoir District Sec Coll

Ford / Hockey

C T Barling Park

Melbourne Water Reservoirs No 2 No 3

Summerhill Retirement Village

Latrobe Village

C H Sullivan Memorial Park

Preston Pmy

Holy Name Cath

W Ruthven VC Reserve

Cmnty Health

Preston Sp Sch

Preston Nth East Pmy

A J Davis Res

Pleasant View

East Preston Pmy

Northland Secondary College

Northland Shopping Centre

Olympic Park

JOINS 282

JOINS 327

240

326

A B C D E F G H J K L

JOINS 242

243

A B C D E F G H J K L

1 2 3 4 5 6 7 8 9 10 11 12 13 14 15 16 17 18 19 20

BUNDOORA

Bundoora Park

Bundoora Reserve

Heritage Village

Coopers Settlement

Urban Farm

Wildlife

Kite Run Reserve

City View Picnic Res

Mount Cooper

Driving Range

Clubhouse

Fitness Track

Golf Course

Norris Bank Reserve

Yulong Park

Bundoora Extended Care Centre

St Damians Catholic

N J Telfer Reserve

Tennis

Bundoora Secondary College

Greenwood Pmy

Gresswell Forest Wildlife Reserve

Habitat Link

Strathallan Golf Course

Clubhouse

Agriculture Reserve

Zoology Reserve

Wildlife Reserve

La Trobe University

North Entry

Exit Only

Agora Cinema

Bundoora Campus

West Entry

South Entry

Preston Cemetery

FOR MORE DETAIL SEE MAP 716

Victoria Forensic Science Centre

La Trobe Sec Coll

Hellenic Cntr

BM Guest House

Cmnty Cntr

Village Hub

MACLEOD

Retirement Village

Uni Lodge

Harry Pottage Reserve

Nurs Home

Sen Cits YMCA

Macleod

Tennis

Macleod Park

HEIDELBERG WEST

HEIDELBERG HEIGHTS

Heidelberg Heights Business Park

Ramu Pde Reserve

Shelley Park

Johnson Res

ROSANNA

Rosanna Primary

Rosanna Parklands

SETTLEMENT RD · BENT ST · GRIMSHAW ST · PLENTY RD · MAIN DR · KINGSBURY DR · DUNNE ST · WATERDALE RD · WAIORA RD · RUTHVEN ST · DAVIES ST · DOUGHARTY RD · DARVALL ST · McNAMARA ST · CHERRY ST · WARRAMUNGA RD · GREENWOOD DR · MORETON ST · WALLARA AV · CAMERON PDE · GRANGE BVD · NORTHERN RD · CRISSANE RD · BARNES WY · ORR ST · BEATRICE AV · PERCY ST · VERNON ST · ORTHLA AV · LILLIMUR AV · PERTH ST · SETANI PDE · COLLINS ST · FLINDERS ST · TERRY ST · OUTHWAITE RD · NORTH CR · MOUNTAIN VIEW RD · GRANDVIEW GR · BELLEVUE AV · ELLESMERE PDE · FINLAYSON ST

JOINS 285

JOINS 328

329

JOINS 243
JOINS 284
JOINS 329
242
328

A B C D E F G H J K L

1 2 3 4 5 6 7 8 9 10 11 12 13 14 15 16 17 18 19 20

WATSONIA NORTH

BUNDOORA

GREENSBOROUGH

WATSONIA

MACLEOD

YALLAMBIE

ROSANNA

Binnak Park

Kalparrin Gardens

Watsonia North Pmy

Concord Sch

Loyola Res

Loyola College

A K Lines Res

St Marys Catholic

R W Fell Reserve

Watsonia Pmy

John Batman Inst of TAFE Watsonia Campus

Greensborough Secondary College

Gresswell Forest Wildlife Reserve

Aminya Res

Gabonia Avenue Res

Elder Street Reserve

Dunvegan Parkland

Winsor Reserve

Nurs Home

Ped U'pass

Soldiers Mess

Military Police HQ 3 MP

Sgts Mess

Officers Mess

Macleod Coll

Sen Cits YMCA

Macleod Park

Strathalan Baptist Home

Res

Rosanna Parklands

Rosanna Golf Links Primary

St Martins Cath

Borlasse Res

Viewbank Pmy

Radio 3TT

Price Park

Tennis Viewbank Reserve

Viewbank Sec College

Retirement Village

Reserve

GREENSBOROUGH HWY

GRIMSHAW ST

LOWER PLENTY RD

ROSANNA RD

GREENSBOROUGH RD

YALLAMBIE RD

CITY

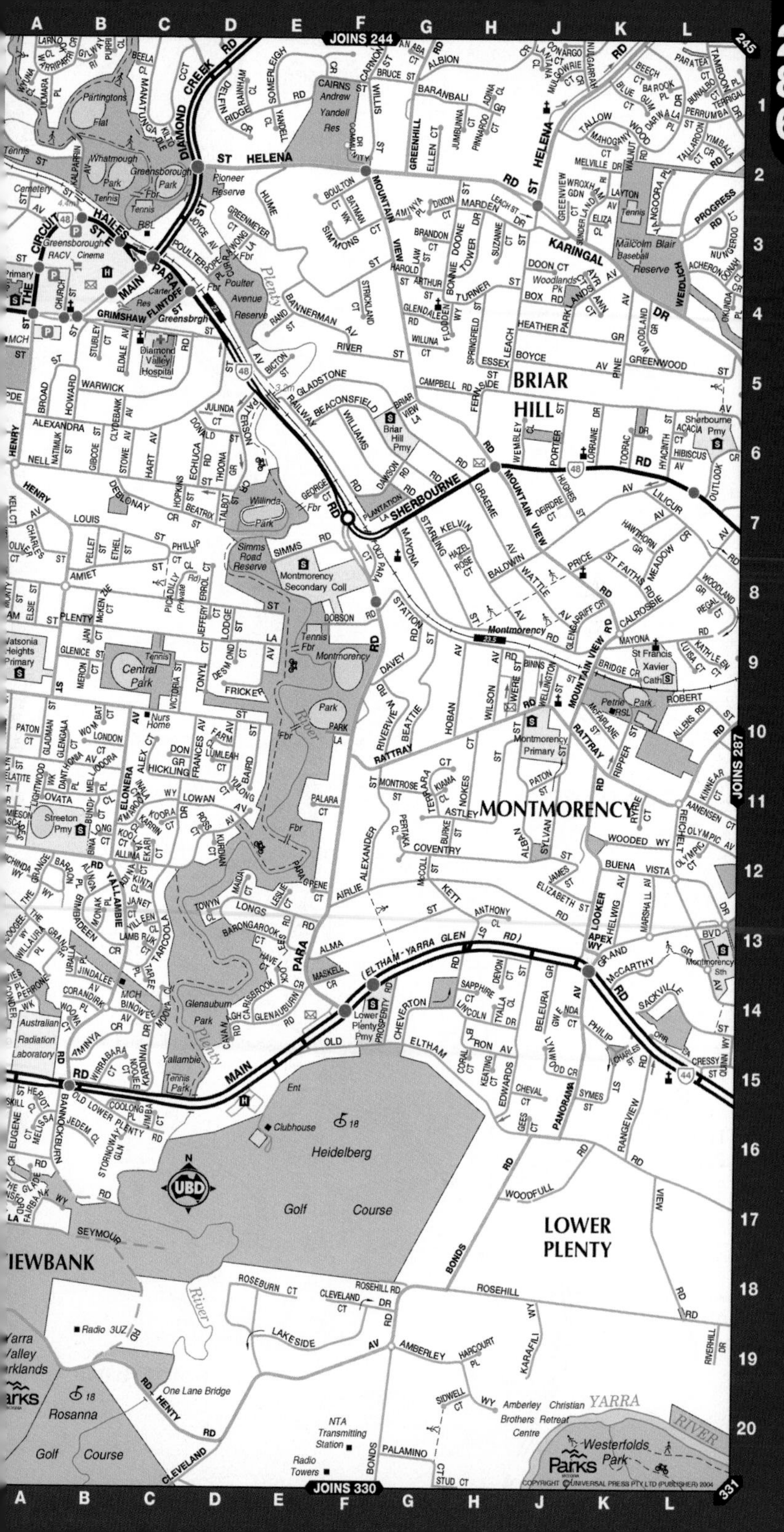

A B C D E F G H J K L
JOINS 244
245
JOINS 287
JOINS 330
331
1 2 3 4 5 6 7 8 9 10 11 12 13 14 15 16 17 18 19 20
BRIAR HILL
MONTMORENCY
LOWER PLENTY
VIEWBANK
DIAMOND CREEK RD
ST HELENA RD
MOUNTAIN VIEW RD
SHERBOURNE RD
KARINGAL DR
MAIN RD
GRIMSHAW ST
HAILES ST
THE CIRCUIT
PARA RD
RATTRAY RD
(ELTHAM - YARRA GLEN RD)
OLD ELTHAM RD
BONDS RD
ROSEHILL RD
LOOKER AV
PROGRESS RD
Partingtons Flat
Whatmough Park
Greensborough Park
Pioneer Reserve
Greensborough
Diamond Valley Hospital
Cairns Andrew Yandell Res
Poulter Avenue Reserve
Malcolm Blair Baseball Reserve
Woodlands Pk
Briar Hill Pmy
Willinda Park
Simms Road Reserve
Montmorency Secondary Coll
Central Park
Watsonia Heights Primary
Streeton Pmy
Montmorency Primary
St Francis Xavier Cath
Petrie Park
Sherbourne Pmy
Lower Plenty Pmy
Montmorency Sth
Australian Radiation Laboratory
Glenauburn Park
Yallambie
Tennis Park
Plenty River
Heidelberg Golf Course
Clubhouse
Radio 3UZ
Yarra Valley Parklands
Rosanna Golf Course
One Lane Bridge
NTA Transmitting Station
Radio Towers
Amberley Christian Brothers Retreat Centre
Westerfolds Park
YARRA RIVER
COPYRIGHT © UNIVERSAL PRESS PTY LTD (PUBLISHER) 2004

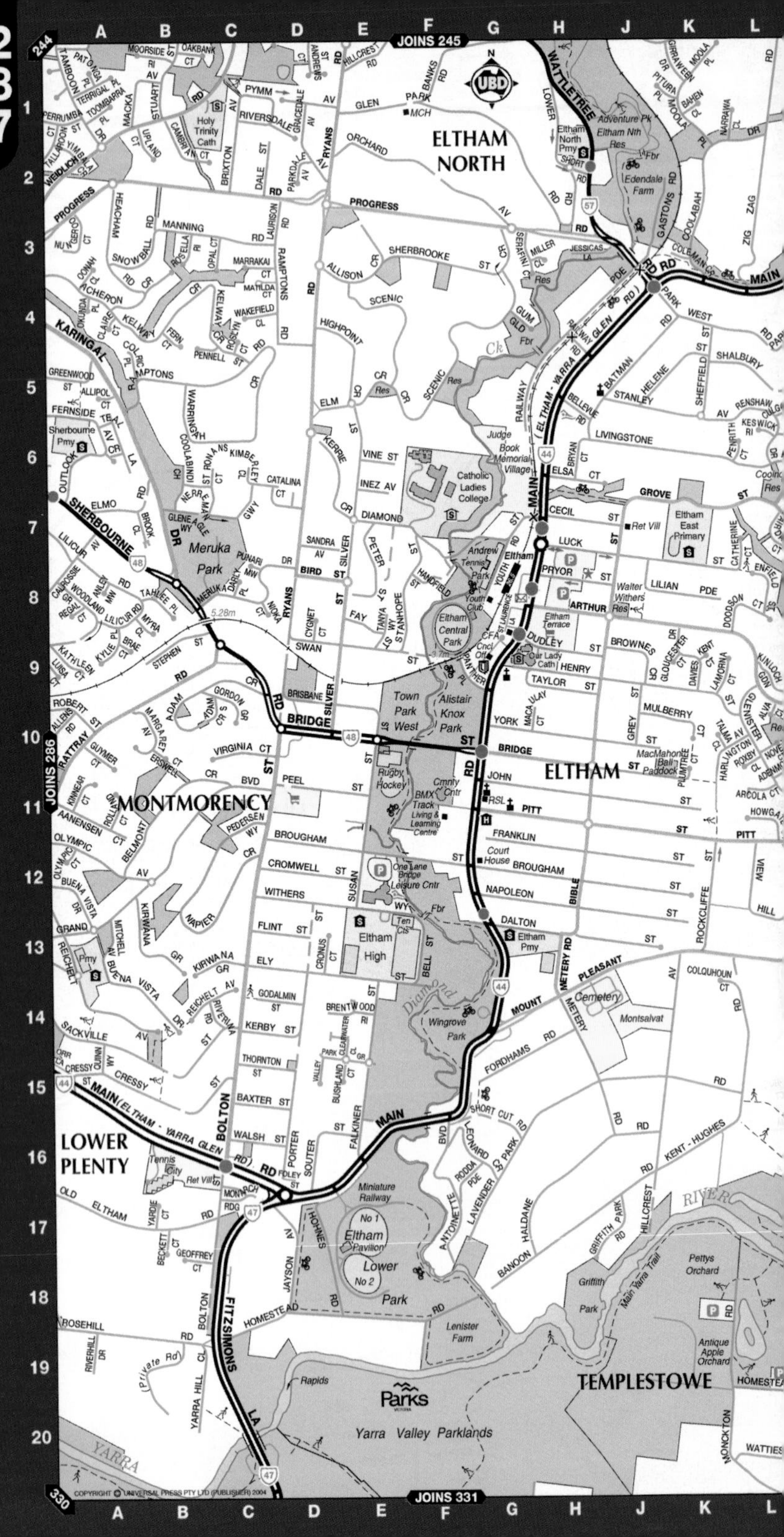
287
JOINS 245
JOINS 286
JOINS 331
244
330
A B C D E F G H J K L
1 2 3 4 5 6 7 8 9 10 11 12 13 14 15 16 17 18 19 20
UBD
ELTHAM NORTH
ELTHAM
MONTMORENCY
LOWER PLENTY
TEMPLESTOWE
Holy Trinity Cath
Eltham North Pmy
Adventure Pk
Eltham Nth Res
Edendale Farm
Sherbourne Pmy
Meruka Park
Catholic Ladies College
Judge Book Memorial Village
Andrew Tennis Park
Youth Club
Eltham Central Park
Eltham Terrace
Walter Withers Res
Eltham East Primary
Our Lady Cath
Town Park West
Alistair Knox Park
Rugby Hockey
Cmnty Cntr
BMX Track
Living & Learning Centre
Court House
One Lane Bridge
Leisure Cntr
Eltham High
Eltham Pmy
MacMahon Ball Paddock
Cemetery
Montsalvat
Wingrove Park
Miniature Railway
Eltham Lower Park
Eltham Pavilion
Lenister Farm
Griffith Park
Pettys Orchard
Antique Apple Orchard
Main Yarra Trail
Rapids
Parks
Yarra Valley Parklands
YARRA
RIVER
Diamond Ck
WATTLETREE RD
MAIN RD
(ELTHAM - YARRA GLEN RD)
SHERBOURNE RD
BRIDGE ST
BOLTON ST
FITZSIMONS LA
KARINGAL DR
PROGRESS RD
RYANS RD
SILVER ST
MAIN RD
KENT - HUGHES RD
MOUNT PLEASANT RD
COPYRIGHT © UNIVERSAL PRESS PTY LTD (PUBLISHER) 2004

RESEARCH

WARRANDYTE

Research Park

Research Primary

Theatre

MCH

CFA

Alan Marshall Res

Child Care

Yarramie Park

Melb Water

Linear Park

Pauline Toner Butterfly Res

Eltham Christian School

Arthur Bird Res

(Very Steep 4 Wheel Drive Only)

CITY

Proposed Yarra Valley Parklands

Longridge Park

Longridge Pk

(Entry by appointment Phone 131 963 - Parks Victoria)

Tikalara Park

Parks Victoria

YARRA RIVER

Mullum Mullum Ck

Yarra Trail

(Priv Rds)

MAIN RD

RESEARCH WARRANDYTE RD

MOUNT PLEASANT RD

GUM TREE RD

REYNOLDS RD

EUCALYPTUS RD

LAUGHING WATERS RD

OVERBANK RD

YARRA BRAES RD

KEARNEY DR

TARGET RD

ALEXANDER RD

HOMEWOOD RI

RIVULET PL

ARLUNYA PL

THE RIDGE

SWEENEYS LA

WILD CHERRY DR

MAYS RD

KAPILI WY

STRINGYBARK RD

KING ST

WATTLE GR

NICHOLSON ST

THOMPSON CR

BRINKKOTTER RD

NORMAN RD

MORELLE ST

EVA ST

BELINDA CR

BRENDA CT

WOODHILL CL

KEITH CT

ASHLEY CT

DUKE RT

CROWE CT

GOOD-LET PL

LYONS RI

GRIFFIN CT

KYNE PL

BOOTH CT

RESEARCH AV

CASSELLS RD

TALWONG CT

CAMERON CT

TYRONE DR

CALTOWIE CT

MAROONG DR

KILANI CT

ECHIDNA RD

TROODOS RI

ENGLEWOOD DR

NATALIE MW

KALBAR CR

DARKAN CT

WYNVALE CT

PARSONS RD

PIPER CR

ARTISTS HILL

VICTORIA CL

KIRWIN AV

CLEARVIEW CT

CLOUD CT

RIDGEVIEW CT

BROOKE CT

MARION WY

NATHAN RD

STOREY RD

PICKWOOD RI

CUDGEE CT

AMBASSADOR RI

THE ESPLANADE

CONTOUR CL

CANDLEBARK CT

VALLEY RD

HEMSLEY CR

INGRAMS RD

RAGLAN CT

KANANDAH CT

LINDON STRIKE CT

HOWELL CL

BEDDOE ST

FINNIGAN ST

BRONWYN CT

MARCONI CT

FLEMING CT

BONDS CT

MILBORNE CR

BAYFIELD DR

FLORISTON CT

HEDDON CT

STAMFORD CT

MORDEN PL

CROFTON MW

ASHDALE GR

FRANK AV

IBSLEY SQ

APREY PL

ARCONIA CT

FOSTER RD

ABERSHAM CT

GLADWYN CT

HARMAN AV

THOMAS ST

ANDREWS ST

BEARD ST

MUIR CL

DEV WY

OTIS PL

ORBEL CT

QUENTIN CT

WYNTON CT

EURABBIE CT

ARUNTA CT

GOROKE CT

VALONIA AV

TADEMA WY

BARINGA CL

JINKANA GR

EURAH PL

ELOUERA CL

AMAROO CT

ALLAMBIE DR

NUNDAH DR

ONKARA CT

PALTARA CT

KIAH MW

CHRISTINE AV

MADINE CT

JUDI CT

WOODRIDGE CT

SUNRAY CT

GUMHILL CT

DIOSMA RD

VIEW MOUNT CT

LEXHAM SQ

MARLOW CT

BARRIEDALE WY

HARTLAND WY

MONCLAIRE CR

POKOLO MW

PEPPERMINT GR

IRONBARK CL

SCARLET ASH CT

STOKES PL

NYORA ST

AVARN CT

RUSKIN CR

VENUE CT

JOINS 289

JOINS 247

JOINS 288

JOINS 333

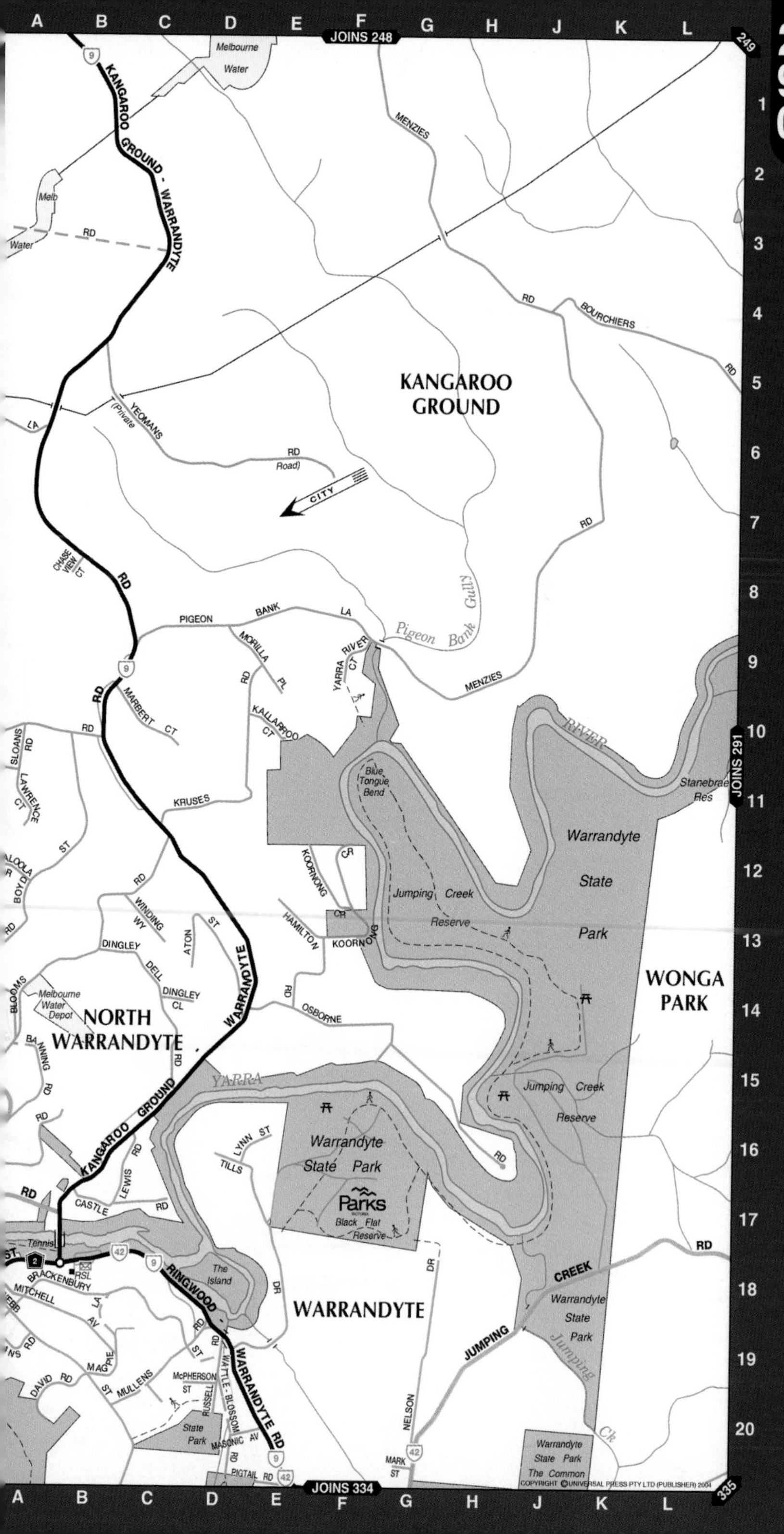

JOINS 248
249
Melbourne Water
KANGAROO GROUND - WARRANDYTE RD
MENZIES RD
BOURCHIERS RD
KANGAROO GROUND
YEOMANS RD
(Private Road)
CITY
CHASE VIEW CT
PIGEON BANK LA
Pigeon Bank Gully
MORILLA PL
YARRA RIVER CT
MARBERT CT
KALLAROO CT
SLOANS RD
LAWRENCE CT
KRUSES RD
Blue Tongue Bend
RIVER
Stanebrae Res
JOINS 291
Warrandyte State Park
KOORNONG CR
Jumping Creek Reserve
HAMILTON RD
WINDING WY
ATON ST
DINGLEY DELL
DINGLEY CL
OSBORNE RD
WONGA PARK
Melbourne Water Depot
NORTH WARRANDYTE
BLOOMS RD
BANNING RD
YARRA
LYNN ST
TILLS DR
LEWIS RD
CASTLE RD
Parks
Black Flat Reserve
Tennis
RSL
BRACKENBURY ST
MITCHELL AV
The Island
RINGWOOD - WARRANDYTE RD
WARRANDYTE
JUMPING CREEK RD
Jumping Ck
MAGPIE ST
DAVID RD
MULLENS ST
McPHERSON ST
RUSSELL ST
WATTLE - BLOSSOM RD
MASONIC AV
State Park
NELSON DR
MARK ST
PIGTAIL RD
Warrandyte State Park The Common
JOINS 334
335
COPYRIGHT © UNIVERSAL PRESS PTY LTD (PUBLISHER) 2004

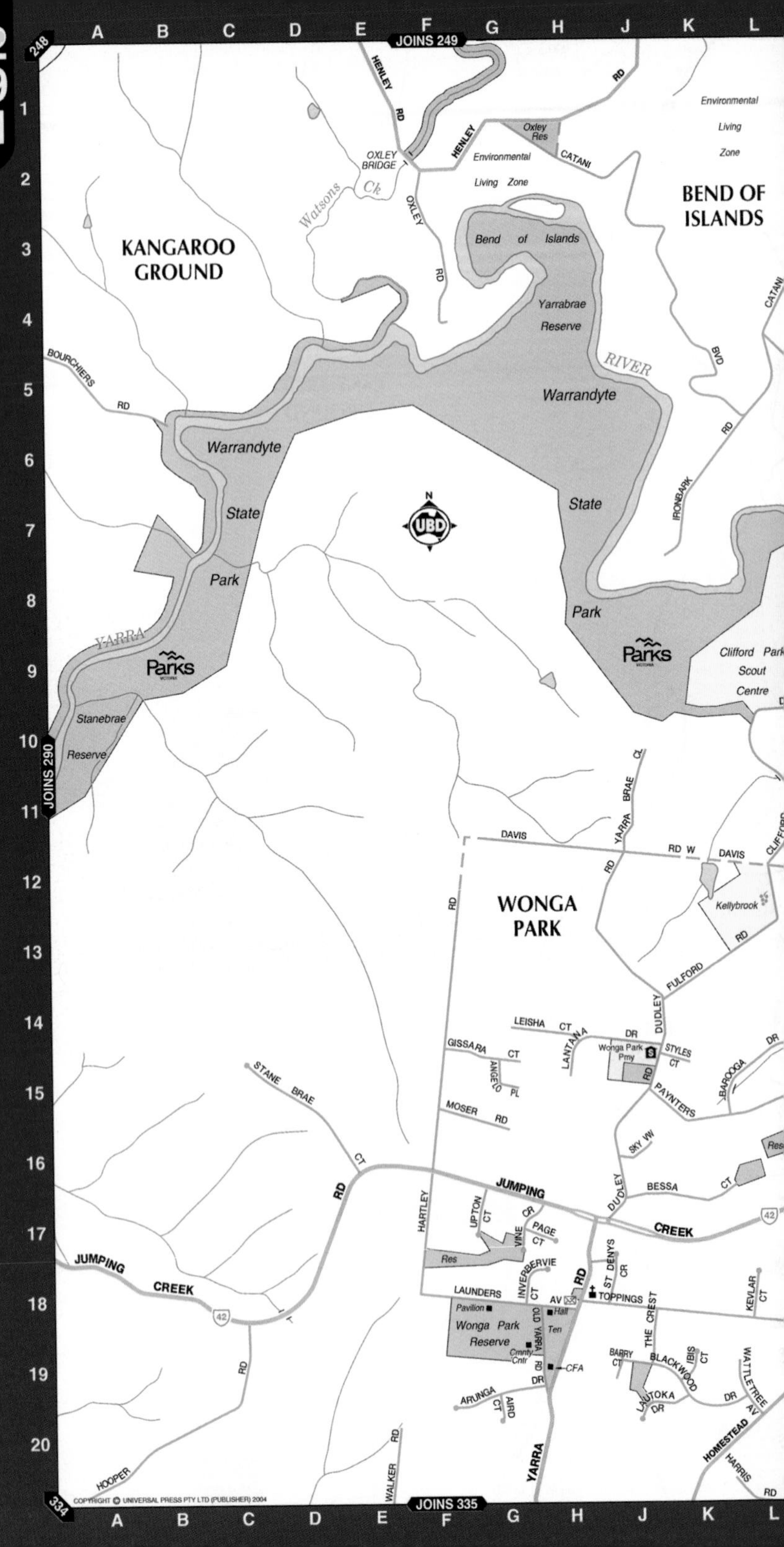
291
JOINS 249
JOINS 290
JOINS 335
248
334
KANGAROO GROUND
BEND OF ISLANDS
WONGA PARK
Warrandyte State Park
Bend of Islands
Yarrabrae Reserve
Stanebrae Reserve
Oxley Res
Environmental Living Zone
OXLEY BRIDGE
Watsons Ck
YARRA RIVER
HENLEY RD
OXLEY RD
CATANI BVD
BOURCHIERS RD
IRONBARK RD
Clifford Park Scout Centre
Parks
DAVIS RD W
YARRA BRAE CL
HARTLEY RD
Kellybrook
FULFORD RD
DUDLEY RD
LEISHA CT
LANTANA DR
GISSARA CT
ANGELO PL
STYLES CT
Wonga Park Pmy
PAYNTERS RD
BAROOGA DR
MOSER RD
STANE BRAE CT
SKY VW
BESSA CT
JUMPING CREEK RD
UPTON CT
VINE CR
PAGE CT
INVERBERVIE CT
ST DENYS CR
LAUNDERS AV
TOPPINGS RD
THE CREST
KEVLAR CT
Pavilion
Hall
Ten
Wonga Park Reserve
Cmnty Cntr
OLD YARRA RD
CFA
BARRY CT
BLACKWOOD DR
IBIS CT
WATTLETREE AV
LAUTOKA DR
ARUNGA CT
AIRD DR
YARRA RD
HOMESTEAD RD
HARRIS RD
WALKER RD
HOOPER RD
Res
42
COPYRIGHT © UNIVERSAL PRESS PTY LTD (PUBLISHER) 2004

HENLEY
SKYLINE RD
CFA
RD
HENLEY
BVD
YARRA

CHRISTMAS HILLS

STEPHEN
Mount Lofty
Park
Parks
VICTORIA
Environmental
Living
Zone
RD
GONGFLERS
Proposed
Golf
Course
RD
RD
WAYNE
RD
DR
RIVER
The Heritage
Golf & Country Club
Project
Management
Office
Clubhouse
HERITAGE CT
ST ANDREWS
Heritage Lodge
ST JOHN
NICKLAUS PL
CIR
HENLEY AV
PINEHURST PL
CARNOUSTIE CR
MUIRFIELD MW
AV
CT
TURNBERRY LA
HERITAGE AV
Wittons
Reserve
RD
Brushy
RD E
HOMESTEAD
HUGHES
RD
WOORARA
YARRAVIEW
RD
CITY
VIOLET CT
LOWER
RD
RESERVE
LOWER HOMESTEAD RD
PAYNES
PENDEREL CT
RD
RD
RD
Creek
Lirralirra
Estate
HOMESTEAD
RD CT
RD
RD

CHIRNSIDE PARK

BRUSHY
PARK
RD
Halcyon Daze
RD
UPLANDS
STANLEY ST

1 2 3 4 5 6 7 8 9 10 11 12 13 14 15 16 17 18 19 20

JOINS 293

250
JOINS 251

CHRISTMAS HILLS

YARRA RIVER

DAVISON (Private

COLDSTREAM WEST

DEVON CL (Private Rd)

RD

Yarra Edge

Bianche

JOINS 292

CITY

CHIRNSIDE PARK

EDWARD RD

PAYNES RD

MEADOW FAIR WY

CHERRY HILL WY

HONEYSUCKLE WY

Reserve

VICTORIA

WOT

KINGSB

VITTORIO

HAR

COT

CHEST

GR

WARR

CT

ZULU

MENTOR

CL

RUSSIA

MWL

SWITCHBACK RD

ROLLING HILLS RD

Chirnside Park

LANCASTER PL

POLARIS WY

BRENTWOODS THE

336
JOINS 337

JOINS 252
YERING
BENSON DR
VICTORIA RD
DR
Road)
Drain
Railway
Disused
LAWLER LA
COLDSTREAM WEST RD
COLDSTREAM
FLOWERFIELD DR
UBD
JOINS 295
Coldstream (Disused)
Crematorium
Lilydale
morial Park
Quarry
Melbourne Water
Melbourne Water Yarra Valley Water Treatment Works
Disused
Quarry
LILYDALE
LA
LANTERN PL
KINGSBURGH LA
GLENLOTH
NIMBLEFOOT WY
REVENUE PL
BRAVO CT
AV
GLENCOE PL
BANKER CT
GATEWAY
THE GATEWAY
NIMBLEFOOT
COMIC CT
DELTA CL
NEWHAVEN CT
RIMFIRE CT
BAYSTONE PL
ARCHER CL
ARWON CT
DALRAY PL
Gateway Res
THE
ARIES CT
RD
TRAFALGAR CT
TONNANT CT
BADGER CT
NEPTUNE CT
BERRY CT
ADMIRAL CT
Melbourne Water
QUARRY
COMO RD
JOINS 338
253
339

JOINS 253

JOINS 339

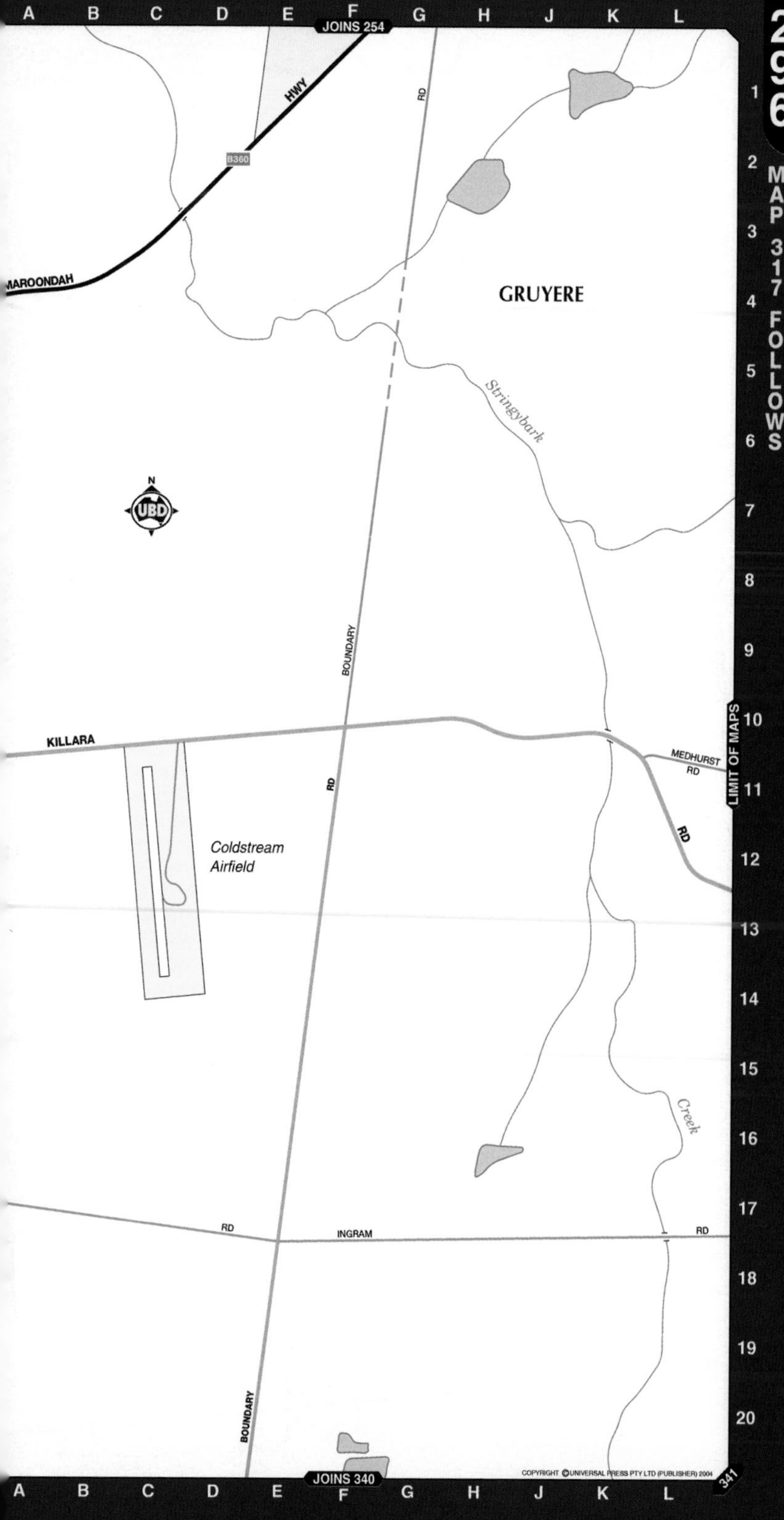

296
MAP 317 FOLLOWS
JOINS 254
JOINS 340
341
GRUYERE
MAROONDAH
HWY
B360
RD
BOUNDARY
RD
Stringybark
Creek
KILLARA
RD
MEDHURST
RD
LIMIT OF MAPS
Coldstream
Airfield
RD
INGRAM
RD
BOUNDARY
UBD
N
COPYRIGHT © UNIVERSAL PRESS PTY LTD (PUBLISHER) 2004

PREVIOUS MAP 296
JOINS 273

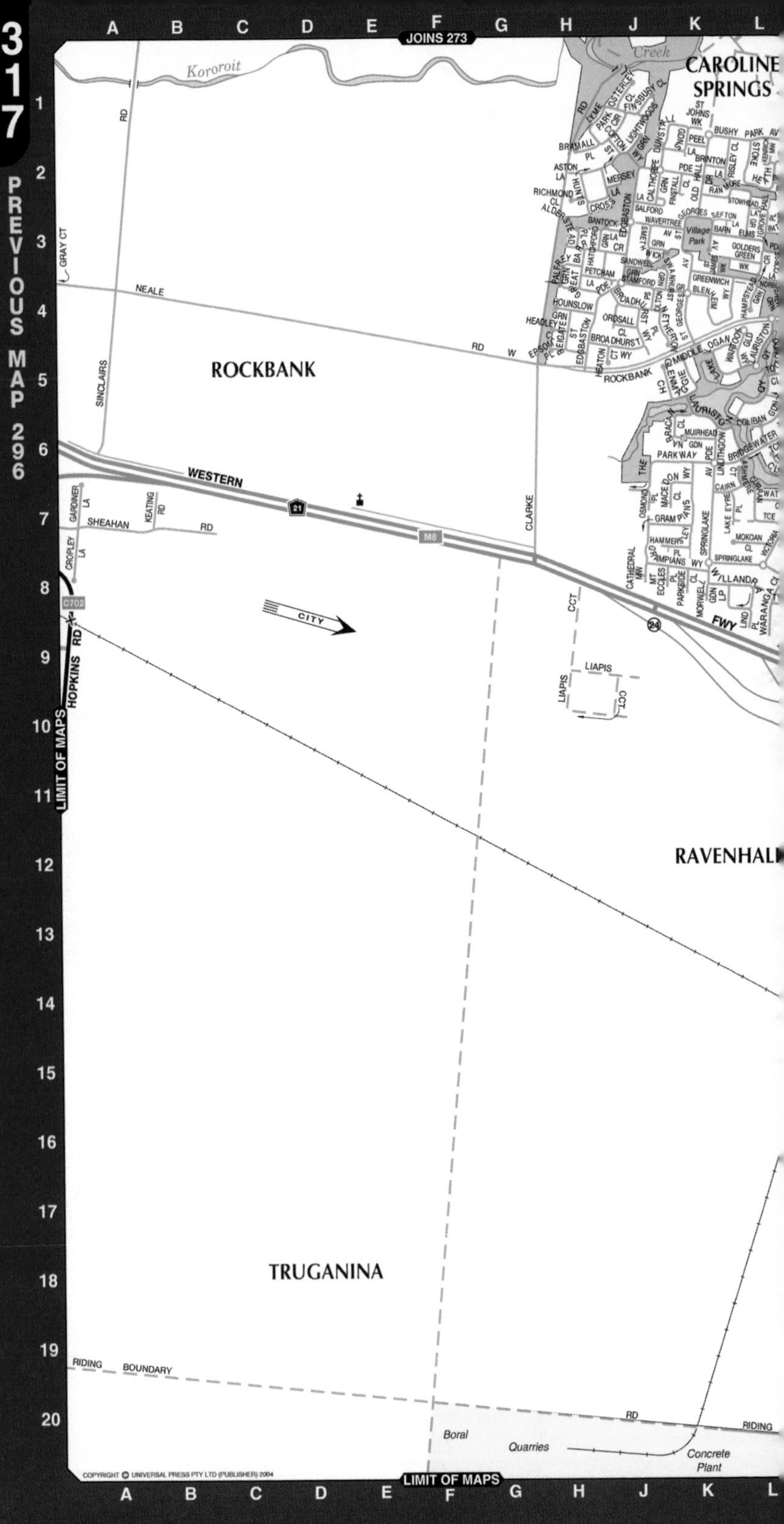

LIMIT OF MAPS

JOINS 274
BURNSIDE
ALBANVALE
DEER PARK
Kororoit Ck
CAROLINE SPRINGS BVD
ROCKBANK MIDDLE RD
WESTWOOD DR
WESTERN (BALLARAT RD) HWY
ROBINSONS RD
Retirement Village
Burnside Shopping Centre
Proposed Commercial Development
Future Hotel
Proposed Shopping Centre
Aboriginal Reserve
Tamar Reserve
Deer Park Secondary College
Evergreen Av Res
Deer Park West Pmy
Bon Thomas Reserve
Brookside Pmy
Playing Field
Lake
Linear Park
Billingham Res
Rotary Pk
(Womens Prison)
Disused Railway
Proposed Fwy
JOINS 319
LIMIT OF MAPS
FOLEYS RD
COPYRIGHT © UNIVERSAL PRESS PTY LTD (PUBLISHER) 2004

274

A B C D E F G H J K L

JOINS 275

KINGS PARK

ALBANVALE

CAIRNLEA

DEER PARK

Protected Native Grassland Reserve

Orica Factories & Explosives Reserve

Orica Commercial Services

Initiating Explosives Systems P/L

Plastics Factory

Explosives Factory

Visqueen Factory

Brimbank College

Brimbank Central RACV

Deer Park Secondary College

Deer Park North Primary

Deer Park West Primary

Deer Park Primary

Resurrection Cath

Cyril Clements Reserve

Diamond Reserve

Robert Bruce Reserve

Sassella Reserve

Bon Thomas Reserve

Waterfield Park

Shearwater Meadow

Jamieson Street Reserve

Rotary Park

Kororoit Creek

Station Waters

Proposed Shopping Centre

Private Rd - No Through Traffic

1 2 3 4 5 6 7 8 9 10 11 12 13 14 15 16 17 18 19 20

JOINS 318

JOINS 363

A B C D E F G H J K L

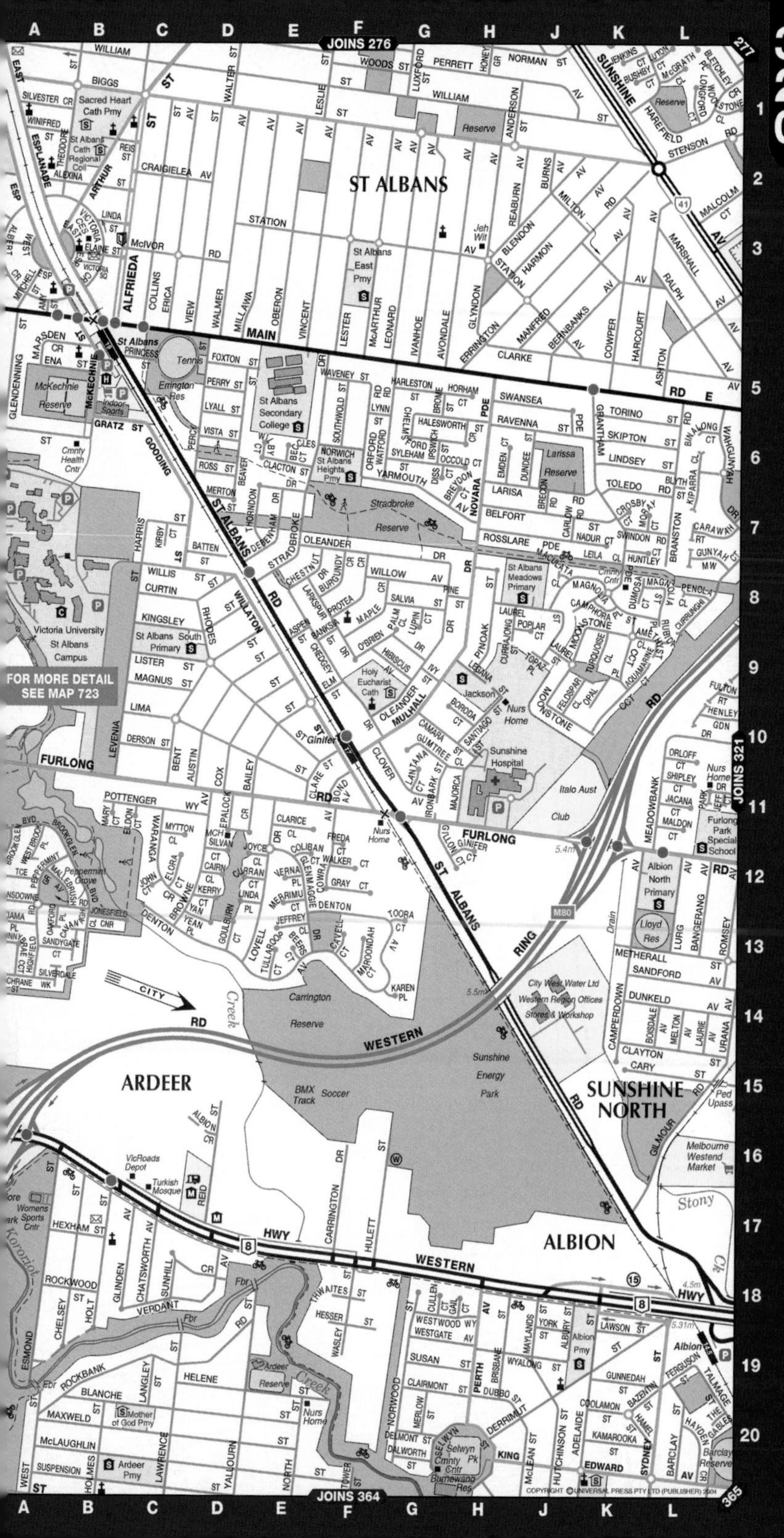

A B C D E F G H J K L
JOINS 276
277
ST ALBANS
Sacred Heart Cath Pmy
St Albans Cath Regional Coll
St Albans East Pmy
Jeh Wit
WILLIAM
BIGGS
SILVESTER CR
WINIFRED
ESPLANADE
ALEXINA
ARTHUR
CRAIGIELEA AV
STATION
McIVOR
ALFRIEDA
COLLINS
ERICA
VIEW
WALMER
MILLAWA
OBERON
VINCENT
LESTER
McARTHUR
LEONARD
IVANHOE
AVONDALE
GLYNDON
ERRINGTON
MANFRED
BERNBANKS
COWPER
HARCOURT
ASHTON
MAIN
RD E
CLARKE
WOODS ST
PERRETT ST
NORMAN ST
LUXFORD
LESLIE
ANDERSON
REABURN
BURNS
MILTON
BLENDON
HARMON
MARSHALL
RALPH
MALCOLM CT
SUNSHINE
STENSON
HAREFIELD
41
St Albans
PRINCESS
Tennis
Errington Res
FOXTON ST
PERRY ST
LYALL ST
VISTA ST
ROSS ST
MERTON ST
St Albans Secondary College
NORWICH St Albans Heights Pmy
McKechnie Reserve
Indoor Sports
GRATZ ST
GOODING
Cmnty Health Cntr
GLENDENNING
MARSDEN
ENA
McKECHNIE
WAVENEY ST
HARLESTON
HORHAM
SOUTHWOLD
LYNN
ORFORD
WATFORD
SYLEHAM
HALESWORTH
IPSWICH
OCCOLD CT
YARMOUTH
BREYDON
NOVARA
SWANSEA
RAVENNA
LARISA
EMDEN
DUNDEE
Larissa Reserve
BELFORT
ROSSLARE PDE
GRANTHAM
TORINO
SKIPTON
LINDSEY
TOLEDO
SWINDON RD
BRANSTON
WAHGUNYAH
Stradbroke Reserve
OLEANDER
STRADBROKE
ST ALBANS
THORNDON
DEBENHAM
HARRIS
KIRBY
BATTEN
WILLIS
CURTIN
KINGSLEY
St Albans South Primary
LISTER ST
MAGNUS ST
LIMA
DERSON ST
FURLONG
LEVENIA
RHODES
WILLATON
Victoria University St Albans Campus
FOR MORE DETAIL SEE MAP 723
CHESTNUT
BURGUNDY
WILLOW
SALVIA
PINE
PROTEA
MAPLE
PALM
LUPIN
O'BRIEN
HIBISCUS
Holy Eucharist Cath
OLEANDER
MULHALL
St Albans Meadows Primary
MAGNOLIA
CAMPHORA
LAUREL
POPLAR
PINOAK
LEGANA
Jackson
Nurs Home
MOONSTONE
TURQUOISE
AMETHYST
AQUAMARINE
OPAL
FELDSPAR
TOPAZ
CURRAJONG
RUBY
PENOLA
CURRUNGHI
GUNYAH
CARAWAH
Ginifer
CLOVER
BONFIELD
LANTANA
GUMTREE
CAMARA
SANTIAGO
BORODA
IRONBARK
MAJORCA
Sunshine Hospital
Italo Aust Club
FULTON
HENLEY
ORLOFF
SHIPLEY
JACANA
MALDON
MEADOWBANK
Nurs Home
Furlong Park Special School
JOINS 321
Albion North Primary
Lloyd Res
LURG
BANGERANG
ROMSEY
METHERALL
SANDFORD
DUNKELD
CAMPERDOWN
BOISDALE
MELTON
LAURIE
URANA
CLAYTON
CARY
Drain
POTTENGER WY
MARY
ELDON
WARANGA
MYTTON
LEPALOCK
SILVAN
JOYCE
CLARICE CL
COLIBAN
FREDA
WALKER
VERNA
GLENMAGGIE
COWRA
GRAY
MERRIMU
DENTON
JEFFREY
TOORA
MAROONDAH
KAREN PL
CAIRN
CURRAN
KERRY
LINDA
GOULBURN
LOVELL
TULLAROOP
BEERS
CAVELL
ELORA
BROWNE
YEAN
JOHN
Peppermint Grove
BROOKLEIGH
WESTBROOK
PEPPERMINT
MALLEBRUSH
JONESFIELD
SANDYGATE
SILVERDALE
HIGHFIELD
OAKFORD
CHRANE
Carrington Reserve
Creek
CITY
WESTERN RD
RING RD
M80
5.4m
5.5m
City West Water Ltd Western Region Offices Stores & Workshop
Sunshine Energy Park
BMX Track
Soccer
ARDEER
SUNSHINE NORTH
ALBION
GILMOUR
Ped Upass
Melbourne Westend Market
Stony Ck
VicRoads Depot
Turkish Mosque
REID
Womens Sports Cntr
Kororoit
HEXHAM ST
CHATSWORTH AV
CARRINGTON DR
HULETT
WESTERN HWY
8
15
4.5m
5.31m
ROCKWOOD
GLINDEN
SUNHILL
VERDANT
CHELSEY
HOLT
ESMOND
ROCKBANK
BLANCHE
LANGLEY
HELENE
Ardeer Reserve
Nurs Home
MAXWELD
Mother of God Pmy
McLAUGHLIN
SUSPENSION
Ardeer Pmy
LAWRENCE
YALLOURN
NORTH
TOWER
THWAITES
HESSER
WASLEY
NORWOOD
CULLEN
WESTWOOD WY
WESTGATE AV
SUSAN ST
CLAIRMONT
MERLOW
DELMONT
DALWORTH
SELWYN
Selwyn Pk
Cmnty Cntr
Burnewang Res
PERTH
BRISBANE
DUBBO
MAYLANDS
YORK
ALBURY
WYALONG
DERRIMUT
KING
McLEAN
HUTCHINSON
ADELAIDE
EDWARD
Albion Pmy
LAWSON ST
GUNNEDAH
COOLAMON
BAZENTIN
HAMEL
KAMAROOKA
SYDNEY
FERGUSON
Albion
TALMAGE
THE GABLES
HAYDEN
BARCLAY
Barclay Reserve
JOINS 364
365
COPYRIGHT © UNIVERSAL PRESS PTY LTD (PUBLISHER) 2004

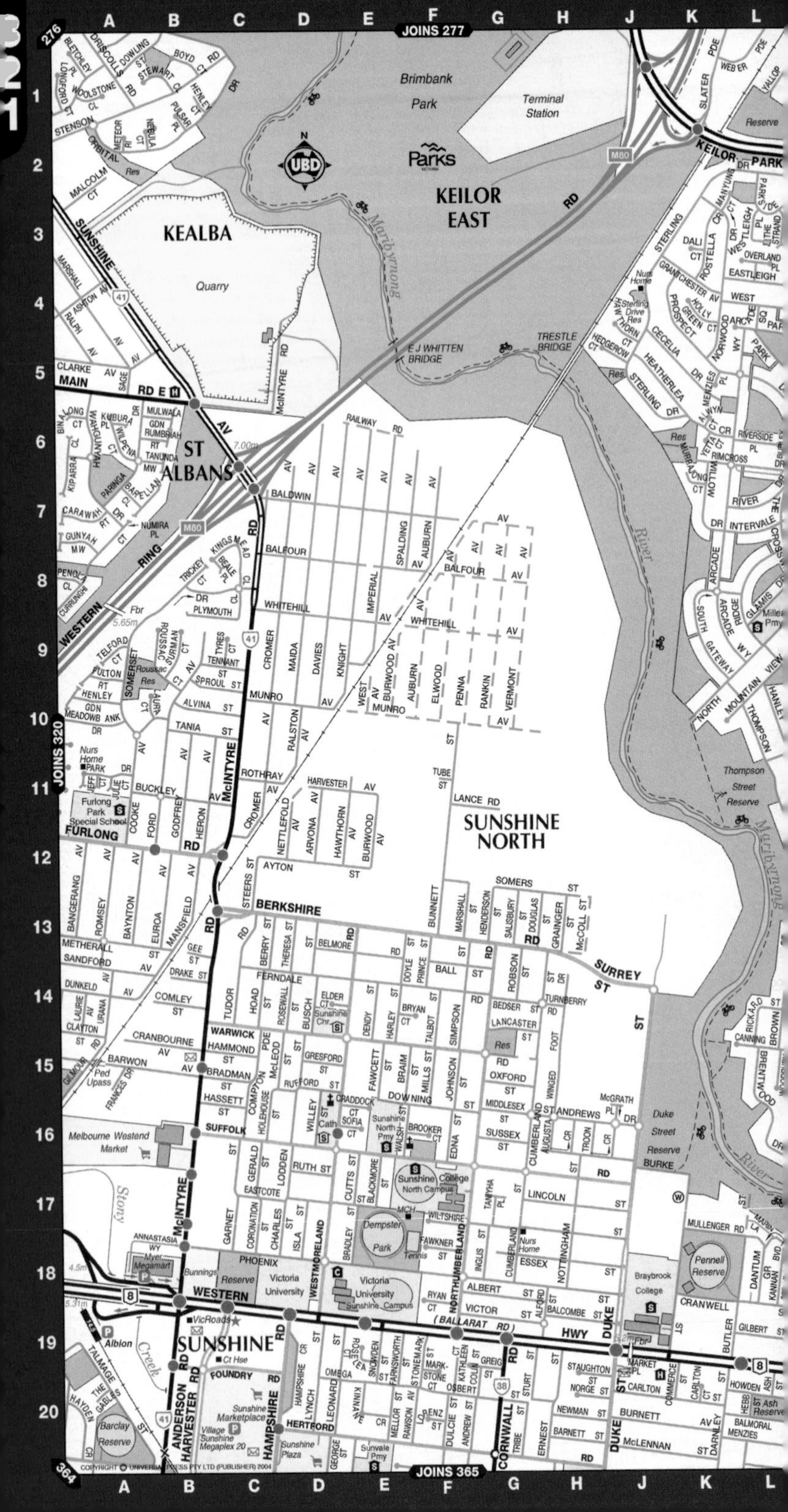

A B C D E F G H J K L

JOINS 277
276

KEALBA

KEILOR EAST

ST ALBANS

SUNSHINE NORTH

SUNSHINE

Brimbank Park

Terminal Station

Parks VICTORIA

Quarry

E J WHITTEN BRIDGE

TRESTLE BRIDGE

Maribyrnong River

Thompson Street Reserve

Duke Street Reserve

Furlong Park Special School

Melbourne Westend Market

Myer Megamart

Bunnings

Phoenix Reserve

Victoria University

Victoria University Sunshine Campus

Dempster Park

Sunshine College North Campus

Sunshine North Pmy

Braybrook College

Pennell Reserve

Barclay Reserve

Sunshine Marketplace

Village Sunshine Megaplex 20

Sunshine Plaza

Sunvale Pmy

Millers Pmy

Stony Creek

Albion

VicRoads

Ct Hse

WESTERN RING RD (M80)

SUNSHINE AV

McINTYRE RD

MAIN RD E

BALLARAT RD

WESTERN HWY

FURLONG RD

BERKSHIRE RD

SURREY ST

DUKE ST

HAMPSHIRE RD

CORNWALL RD

KEILOR PARK DR

1 2 3 4 5 6 7 8 9 10 11 12 13 14 15 16 17 18 19 20

JOINS 320
JOINS 365
364

A B C D E F G H J K L

JOINS 278
279

Proposed URLC Valley Lake Residential Development

Steele

Keilor Heights Pmy
Quinn Reserve
Tennis
Essendon-Keilor College East Keilor Campus
Cmnty Cntr
Overland Reserve
St Peters Cath
Allen Reserve
Hostel for The Aged
Milleara Mall
Western Autistic School

NIDDRIE

Niddrie Sec Coll
St Bernards Catholic College
Senior School
Baronor Priv Hosp
Ian J McWilliams Park
Rosehill Park
MCH
Reserve

ESSENDON WEST

Steele Creek Res
Ck
River
Monte Carlo Res

AVONDALE HEIGHTS

St Martin de Porres Cath
Avondale Heights Reserve
Tennis
Kangan Inst of TAFE Avondale Heights / Brimbank Campus
Avondale Pmy
Reserve

Commonwealth of Australia Department of Defence

MARIBYRNONG

CITY

Department of Defence Explosive Factory
Materials Research Laboratory
Engineering Development Establishment
Canning Reserve
Ent
Homemaker Centre
Village Green Res

Maribyrnong
Reserve
Medway Golf Course
Clubhouse
Telstra Centre
Victoria University Student Village
Immigration Detention Centre
Footscray W Mail Centre

MAIDSTONE

RAYBROOK

Cranwell Park
Vic Roads
Tennis

MILLEARA RD, MILITARY RD, BUCKLEY ST, ROSEHILL RD, CORDITE AV, CANNING ST, RALEIGH RD, WESTS RD, HAMPSTEAD RD, ROSAMOND RD, WESTERN (BALLARAT RD) HWY, ASHLEY ST, DINAH PDE, RACHELLE RD, MEDWAY RD, RIVER ST, MITCHELL ST

JOINS 323

NIDDRIE

ESSENDON

ESSENDON WEST

ABERFELDIE

MOONEE PONDS

MARIBYRNONG

KEILOR RD
BULLA RD
WOODLAND ST
ROSEHILL RD
BUCKLEY ST
MOUNT ALEXANDER RD
LINCOLN RD
WAVERLEY ST
SCOTIA ST
RALEIGH RD
MARIBYRNONG RD
EPSOM RD
VAN NESS AV
THE BOULEVARD
RIVER ST
MILITARY RD

Buckley Park
Clifton Park
Aberfeldie Park
Woodlands Park
Lincoln Park
Riverside Park
E A Coulson Gdns
Fairbairn Park
Pipemakers Park
D F Thompson Res
Essendon Municipal Golf Course
Highpoint City Shopping Centre
Maribyrnong River
Jacks Canal
Jacks Magazine
RAS Showgrounds
Orica Australia Laboratories
Walter Street Reserve

JOINS 322
JOINS 367
366

JOINS 280
281
JOINS 325
JOINS 368
369
STRATHMORE
PASCOE VALE SOUTH
BRUNSWICK WEST
ASCOT VALE
PARKVILLE
TRAVANCORE
CITYLINK
PASCOE VALE RD
MORELAND RD
COONAN'S RD
BELL ST
WOODLAND ST
BUCKLEY ST
ALBION ST
FLETCHER ST
NAPIER ST
MELVILLE RD
REYNOLDS RD
BRUNSWICK RD
ORMOND RD
MOUNT ALEXANDER RD
ASCOT VALE RD
VICTORIA ST
PUCKLE ST
Napier Park
Cross Keys Reserve
Morris Reserve
Government Reserve
Essendon Cricket Ground
Essendon AFL Club
Montgomery Park
Dunstan Reserve
Queens Park
Moonee Valley Racecourse
Trotting Track
Ormond Park
Travancore Park
Royal Park
Moonee Ponds Ck
Essendon Hockey Cntr
Reggio Calabria Club
Parkville Youth Residential Centre
Melbourne Juvenile Justice Centre
Commonwealth Serum Laboratories
Northern Melbourne Inst of TAFE Parkville Campus
Horticulture School
VBA Baseball Ross Straw Field
VAHA Hockey Fields
Kangan Inst of TAFE Moonee Valley Campus
COPYRIGHT © UNIVERSAL PRESS PTY LTD (PUBLISHERS) 2004

JOINS 281

280

A B C D E F G H J K L

1 2 3 4 5 6 7 8 9 10 11 12 13 14 15 16 17 18 19 20

COBURG

Coburg East

BRUNSWICK WEST

BRUNSWICK

BRUNSWICK EAST

PARKVILLE

CARLTON NORTH

PRINCES HILL

Moreland City College

Bridges City Oval Reserve

Bush Reserve

Anderson Res

Alex.G.Gillion Oval

Clifton Tennis Park

Gilpin Park

Temple Park

Barkly Square Shopping Centre

Brunswick Sec Coll

(RMIT) Brunswick Campus

Vic Police Traffic Cntr

John Fawkner Hospital

Vaucluse Hospital

Melbourne Juvenile Justice Centre

Commonwealth Serum Laboratories

Psychiatric Unit

Royal Park

Royal Melbourne Zoo

Golf Course

Princes Park

Carlton Cricket Club Ground

Optus Oval

JOINS 324

368

JOINS 369

A B C D E F G H J K L

JOINS 282

283

PRESTON

THORNBURY

NORTHCOTE

FITZROY NORTH

Coburg Cemetery

HP Zwar Reserve

Institute of TAFE

Preston Market

Cramer Park

Tram Depot

Ray Bramham Gdns

Tate Reserve

WH Robinson Res

H Swain Res

A.H.Capp Res

Egan Res

Sir D Nicholls Sporting Complex

Henderson Pk

Mayer Park

Northcote Municipal Golf Course

Allard Park

Jones Park

Energy Park

Baltara Sch

Batman Pk

All Nations Park

Northcote Shopping Centre

Santa Maria Cath Coll

Merri Park

Baseball

St Josephs Home for Aged

Monastery

Northcote High

Terminal Station

Sumner Park

Merri Creek

Penders Park

Northcote Park

Oldis Gardens

Athletic Field

T.H Westfield Reserve

Balfe Park

Rushall Park

ELIZABETH ST

BELL ST

ST GEORGES RD

HIGH ST

PLENTY RD

GILBERT RD

NORMANBY AV

DAREBIN RD

SEPARATION ST

ARTHURTON RD

HOLDEN ST

NICHOLSON ST

WESTGARTH ST

HEIDELBERG RD

MERRI PDE

SCOTCHMER ST

DUNDAS ST

MILLER ST

1 2 3 4 5 6 7 8 9 10 11 12 13 14 15 16 17 18 19 20

JOINS 327

JOINS 370

371

JOINS 283

282

A B C D E F G H J K L

1 2 3 4 5 6 7 8 9 10 11 12 13 14 15 16 17 18 19 20

PRESTON

THORNBURY

NORTHCOTE

FAIRFIELD

ALPHINGTON

Northland Shopping Centre

Northland Home Centre

T W Blake Park

Commonwealth Industrial Gases Limited

H L T Oulton Park

Darebin Creek Forest Park

Cyril Cummins Reserve

Thornbury-Darebin Secondary College

Hayes Park

John Cain Memorial Park

Cartledge Reserve

Seddon Reserve

All Nations Park

Aquatic & Rec Centre

McDonnell Park

R Thompson Reserve

Pitcher Park

Darebin Parklands

Johnson Park

Council Depot

Fairfield Park

T H Westfield Reserve

AMCOR Packaging

Coate Park

Alphington Park

Murray Rd, Plenty Rd, Bell St, Albert St, Chifley Dr, Victoria Rd, High St, Station St, Livingstone Pde, Separation St, Heidelberg Rd, Chandler Hwy, Grange Rd, Darebin Rd, Wingrove St, Westgarth St

JOINS 326

JOINS 371

370

JOINS 284
285
JOINS 329

A B C D E F G H J K L

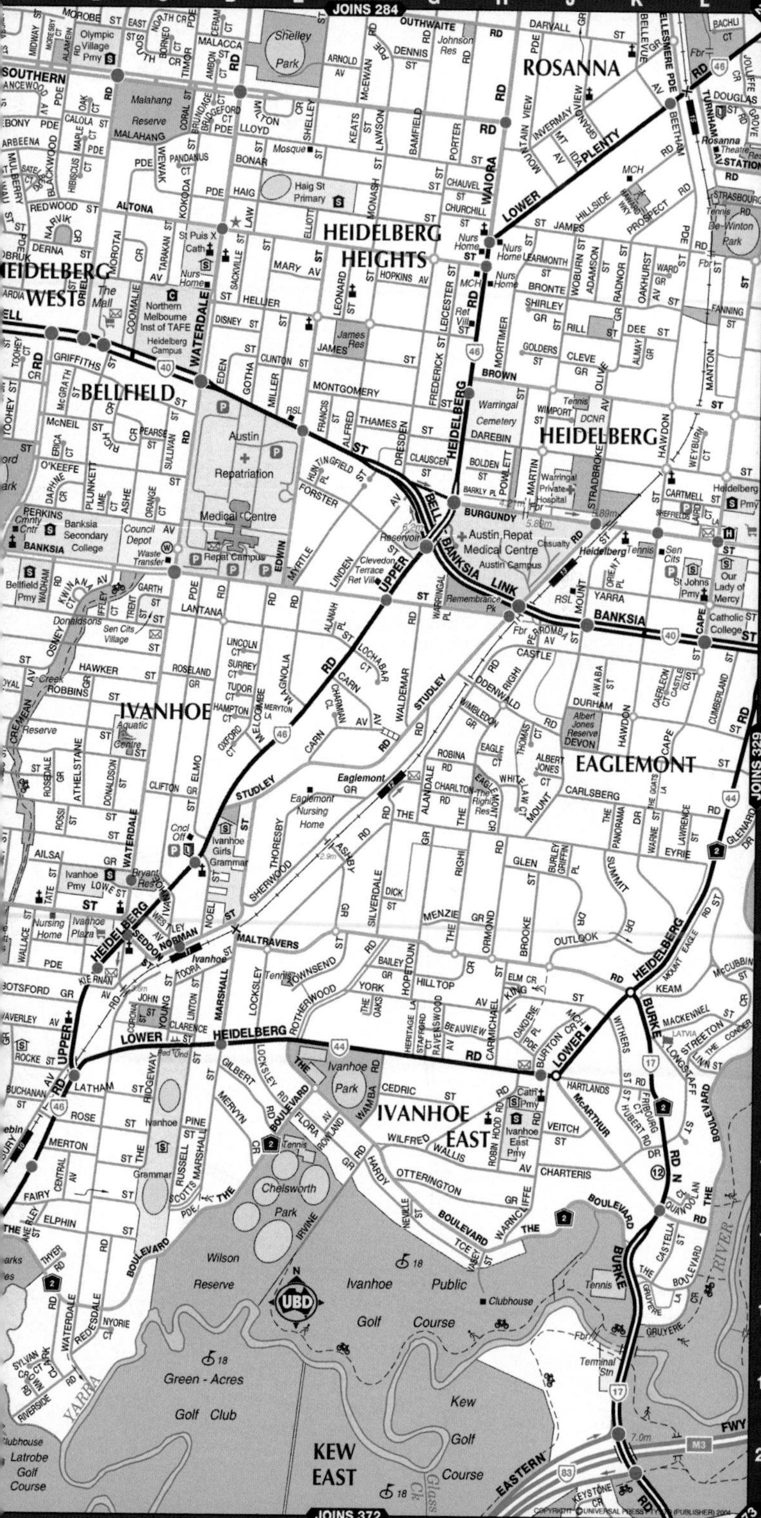

ROSANNA

HEIDELBERG HEIGHTS

HEIDELBERG WEST

BELLFIELD

HEIDELBERG

IVANHOE

EAGLEMONT

IVANHOE EAST

KEW EAST

Shelley Park

Malahang Reserve

Olympic Village Pmy

Haig St Primary

Johnson Res

James Res

Warringal Cemetery

Austin Repatriation Medical Centre

Austin Repat Medical Centre

Repat Campus

Austin Campus

Warringal Private Hospital

Northern Melbourne Inst of TAFE Heidelberg Campus

Banksia Secondary College

Council Depot

Bellfield Pmy

Sen Cits Village

Ivanhoe Aquatic Centre

Ivanhoe Girls Grammar

Ivanhoe Pmy

Ivanhoe Plaza

Eaglemont Nursing Home

Albert Jones Reserve

Our Lady of Mercy Catholic College

Heidelberg Pmy

Rosanna Theatre

De-Winton Park

Ivanhoe Park

Ivanhoe Grammar

Chelsworth Park

Wilson Reserve

Ivanhoe Public Golf Course

Green - Acres Golf Club

Latrobe Golf Course

Kew Golf Course

YARRA RIVER

EASTERN FWY

A B C D E F G H J K L

JOINS 372
373

A B C D E F G H J K L

284
JOINS 285

ROSANNA

VIEWBANK

HEIDELBERG

Banyule Flats Reserve

Yarra Valley Parklands

EAGLEMONT

Yarra Valley Parklands

Bolin Bolin Billabong

BULLEEN

IVANHOE EAST

Bulleen Park

Trinity Grammar Sporting Complex

Marcellin College

Carey Grammar Sportsgrounds

Camberwell Golf Course (Freeway Golf)

Koonung Creek Reserve

BALWYN NORTH

JOINS 328

JOINS 373
372

A B C D E F G H J K L

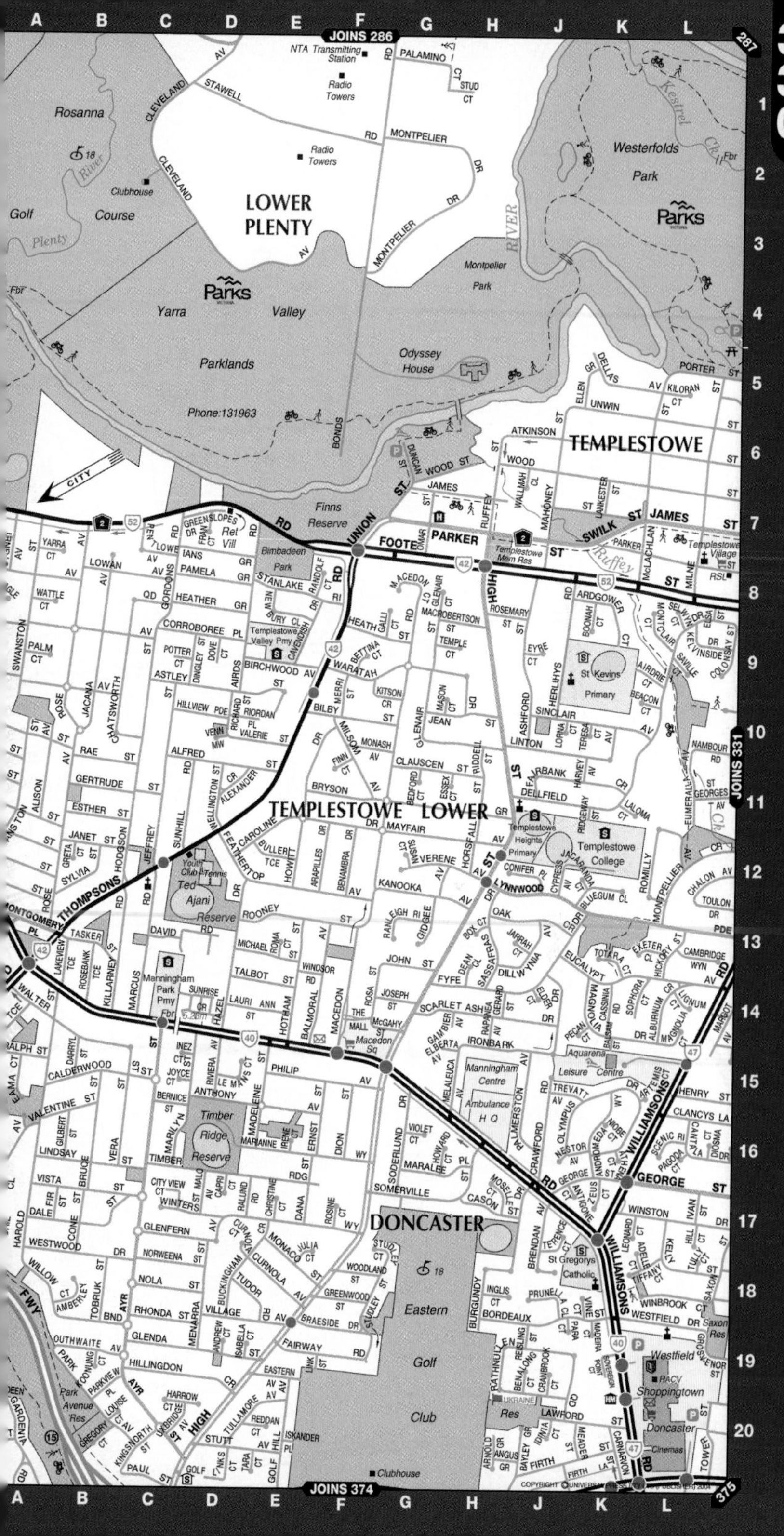

JOINS 286
JOINS 331
JOINS 374
287
375
LOWER PLENTY
TEMPLESTOWE
TEMPLESTOWE LOWER
DONCASTER
Yarra Valley Parklands
Phone:131963
Rosanna Golf Course
Westerfolds Park
Montpelier Park
Odyssey House
Finns Reserve
Bimbadeen Park
Ted Ajani Reserve
Timber Ridge Reserve
Eastern Golf Club
Clubhouse
NTA Transmitting Station
Radio Towers
Templestowe Valley Pmy
St Kevins Primary
Templestowe Heights Primary
Templestowe College
Manningham Park Pmy
Manningham Centre
Ambulance HQ
Aquarena Leisure Centre
Macedon Sq
St Gregorys Catholic
Westfield Shoppingtown Doncaster
Cinemas
RACV
Ukraine Res
Park Avenue Res
Saxon Res
Templestowe Mem Res
Templestowe Village
RSL
Ret Vill
Youth Club
Tennis
UNION RD
FOOTE ST
PARKER ST
HIGH ST
THOMPSONS RD
WILLIAMSONS RD
GEORGE ST
DONCASTER RD
MONTPELIER DR
BONDS RD
PORTER ST
JAMES ST
SWILK ST
MACEDON RD
CITY
COPYRIGHT © UNIVERSAL PRESS PTY LTD (PUBLISHER) 2004

JOINS 287
286

YARRA RIVER
Victorian Board of Canoe Ed
Park Office
Kestrel Ck
Fbr
Westerfolds Park
Parks
Manor House
Ent
Yarra Valley Parklands
Parks
WATTIES
BRIAR LA
TIMOTHY CT
WEBSTERS
MONCKTON
KERRINS LA
RD
NEWMANS
FITZSIMONS LA
47
SUMMERHILL RD
LEMPRIERE CL
BOSC CT
GLENDENNING RI
ST
Templestowe Retirement Village
WINIFRED CT
HERMANN CT
EDWIN
DORA CT
ANNETTE PL
RD
ANGEL TOP TCE
TUSCANY
RI
COTTONWOOD CT
O'BRIENS
NEWMANS RD
HEIDELBERG
DEWPOND AV
SUNSET AV
SPRING VALLEY
Nurs Home
INNISFALLEN AV
AZURE CT
AUGUSTUS RI
PORTER
PARKWOOD PL
PORTER ST
PORTER ST
FULVIEW CT
UNWIN
ANDERSON ST
HEYSHAM WY
REARK CT
MORECAMBE CT
CLARKE ST
CAROLE ST
Tennis
Templestowe Reserve
42
WAKEFIELD PL
CARLTON CT
READ
2
ST
TEMPLESTOWE
ATKINSON
MILAND
Templestowe Park Pmy
RD
WYNNEWOOD CT
CHAPLIN CT
DALE PL
WOOD ST
HAKEA
STRADMORE
SHAUN CT
BEALE AV
YOLANDE CT
JACOBENA PL
MILNER CL
MERNA
PRINCELY
TCE
DENA CT
ENNERSDALE CT
JAMES ST
VERBENA ST
ST
RUTLAND AV
MERRYN CT
McDONALD
ALBERT ST
BARNACLE MW
WARRICK GR
MILNE
PARKER ST
HOVEA
ST
MANDELLA
DURKIN CT
LIBRA CT
PINEWOOD DR
DR
OLIVER
BEBS CT
VALENCIA TCE
LOUISA PL
RSL
Mem Hall
GLENDALE
Templestowe Art Cntr
DES CT
HAWTIN AV
WAITES CT
Templestowe Cemetery
CHURCH
KENMAN CL
MIRIAM CT
LUCIEER CT
TIFFANY GR
Pettys Reserve
AUMANN
52
42
ELSA ST
FOOTE
JUNE CR
REYNOLDS
ST
SMITHS
MEADOW PL
KERYN CL
FIELD
KELVINSIDE DR
COLONSAY ST
DUXSON DR
SERPELLS RD
LITTLE VALLEY RD
RD
SARAH
ROBHILL RI
CR
BERKEFELD CT
WILLOWBANK CT
ALOHA GDN
KEN
BVD
SERPELLS
RD
MT VIEW
JACOV GDN
CR
CR
BERWYN
KILLIBURY CT
VALLEY WY
NAMBOUR
PINE
RD
RASMUSSEN
CIPORA CT
RD
SERPELLS
SARAH
SMITHS
Holy Cross Retreat
BALI HI
WAHINE CT
TATTER
MALEI CT
TENNY
LALANI TCE
PAOA PL
COLER
ST GEORGES AV
EUMERALLA AV
DR
BAMFIELD
CL
CAPRICE CT
COUNTY TCE
PIONEER
WAYAMBA PL
DR
RD
Ruffey
MONTPELLIER
CHALON AV
TOULON DR
CR
WILLIAMSONS
GLEN CT
LAWANNA
HILLCROFT
CLAYS CT
GARDENVIEW CT
DR
HAMPDEN CT
GRANGE
THE
DENHAM CT
St Charles Boromeo Catholic Pmy
RD
SERPE
PR
LYNNWOOD
PDE
47
BRENTVALE CT
MYRON PL
HARVELL BALLAMORE
KERSEY PL
KING
CR
FERNBROOK WY
BRIARFIELD CT
AMBERWOOD
NEWLYN CL
DR
THE MOSSDALE CT
CHIPPENDALE
DELLWOOD CT
CASTLEWOOD PL
MILLWOOD CT
CR
SAMANTHA CT
REBECCA CT
DONHAVEN CT
Serpell Community Reserve
Tennis
Serpell Pmy
LARNA CT
BURLEIGH DR
TAPAROO
CAMBRIDGE WYN
EUCALYPT AV
GAIRLOCK CT
AV
NETLEY
ALTHEA PL
BIRBANK CT
PENDA CL
BOULEVARDE
VEDA CT
BIRCHGROVE
BEECROFT
CHELMSFORD AV
THORNLEIGH
PETER BPL
PARKLEA CL
EDGE AV
GRANGE
FERNDELL CR
TREVINDEN CT
NORAL CL
BEAVIS CT
PLANE CT
OAKWOOD
ELM CT
MARGOT
MURILLO CT
VISCOUNT DR
PARK HILL WY
MINTARO CT
GLOUCESTER CT
RI
GREENRIDGE
ASH CROFT AV
NORWICK
BERWICK
COTSWOLD ST
KING
TUCKERS
STANLEY
ROBIN CT
DONALD CT
GRAEME PL
DR
ST
CROUCH CT
MARTIN CT
Ruffey
KOLOR WY
NOORILIM CL
CHISWICK CT
GREENOCK PL
ST
TYSSEN CT
FARRER CT
INGLEWOOD CL
GAUDION
LYROOL CT
CAWARRA CT
LAUTREC CT
CR
TO
MAVERICK CL
HENRY
Lake
CHURCH
CRICKLEWOOD DR
LOXLEY CT
BERESFORD
CRAIGIEA
LEAWARRA
TAUNT
CLANCYS LA
DONCASTER
TYROL CT
CHILTERN CT
WONUKA CT
MONET CT
BARRENA CT
RUSKIN CT
CANTLA
DIOSMA CT
LEYTE CL
DR
THE
Park
Fbr
Creek
OWENS
ST
HONNI MW
RANDELL CT
CAME
Schramms Cottage
SKYE
AIRLIE CT
LEROY PL
GLENDORA
LA
McCALLUM
RD
RIESCHIECKS Reserve
Athletics
Pav
KIRRABOOL
OTWAY CT
MARSDEN
JARMA
HERTFORD CT
GEORGE
ASTRAN PL
BOTANIC
MILLER PL
DR
RD
DUNDAS CT
RODEN CT
ELRON
IVAN ST
WINSTON
DR
ROSELAND GR
ANARTH ST
EARL ST
WALDAU CT
ST
GEORGE
YALLAROO
ROWAN
TOWONG CT
CRELLIN
SAXONWOOD
DOMAIN
BARTON
REGENCY
HILL CT
TULLY CT
BOARD
JUDITH CT
ST
LANSELL
BENTON CT
OLD ORCHARD
GROVER RD
BEMBOOKA CT
RYALL CT
SANDHURST CT
AV
KIANDRA CT
LATHAM CT
Islamic Centre
GRASMERE
KELLY ST
SAXON
ERIN DR CT
KIRTON ST
THE GLADES
Schramms
AMBROSE
ANTON CT
ALMA CT
ST
FROMHOLD
MERRIGUM CT
DEBRA WY
ROMSEY RI
Doncaster Gardens Pmy
WORTHING
TUSANNE PL
GAINSBOROUGH
SHEF
Saxon
WESTFIELD DR
Res
TONI ST
CORELLA
Doncaster Secondary College
GOLDEN CT
DAWSON ST
DR
Domaine Ret Vill
BELINDA
MOORE DR
KEIR AV
CR
SILVERDALE CT
MONICA CT
TRACEY
DAWS
FRIARS
NOT TINGWOOD ST
Westfield Shoppingtown Doncaster
GROSVENOR ST
ROSEVILLE
ROBYN ST
Reserve
DIANELLA CT
CHAPEL CT
SHARON
ST
KERRY CL
JOCELYN
SIERRA PL
BELVEDERE AV
CAVALIER ST
GOODSON
TURANA
DR
KALIMNA
IBIS
PERSIMMON CT
NATHAN
UBERE CT
MURPHY ST
ST
RD
CELESTE
ST
P
TOWER ST
BERKELEY ST
Doncaster Pmy
Playhouse
HUMMELL WY
Council Offices
JJ TULLY DR
CURLEW CT
THIELE CT
ZANDER CT
CHURCH
LAUER
DONCASTER
VICTORIA
DAPHNE
ACACIA
NORMAN ST
DEHNERT
CHAMPION
MAJOR ST
RODERICK
KENNON
BELVS
COUNCIL
MCH
40
36
Ret Vill AV
QUEENS
Tennis
40
36
RD

JOINS 330
JOINS 375
374

WARRANDYTE

DONCASTER EAST

DONVALE

Tikalara Park
(Access by Arrangement)
Parks Victoria
Templestowe Terminal Station
Templestowe Delivery Cntr
Council SES Depot
Quarry
Deep Ck Res
Baseball
Box Hill Institute of TAFE Doncaster Campus
Warrandyte High
Currawong Bush Park
The Pines
Andersons Park
Onemda Training Centre
Retirement Village
Green Gully Park
MCH
Indoor Sport
Zerbes Reserve
Milgate Pmy
Our Lady of the Pines Cath
Cat Jump Park
Donvale Retirement Village
Carey Baptist Grammar Donvale Campus
Mullum Mullum Reserve
Hockey
Tennis
Pony Club
Buck Reserve
Donburn Pmy
Mullum Mullum Creek
Deep Creek

HEIDELBERG-WARRANDYTE RD
WARRANDYTE RD
REYNOLDS RD
BLACKBURN RD
ANDERSONS CREEK RD
SPRINGVALE RD
OLD WARRANDYTE RD
MULLUM MULLUM RD
TIKALARA PL
THE RIDGE
KEARNEY DR
ARLUNYA PL
STILLWELL PL
SANCTUARY PL
PARKWAY
CLIVEDEN CL
OXFORD CT
CONCORD RI
SUNNY RI
MARGARET CT
SPEERS CT
PAMELA CT
GRIFFITHS LA
ALEXANDER CT
OAKLAND CT
SWANSFIELD CT
RIVULET PL
ROSELILLIAN CT
BELLBIRD
ORCHARD GR
ST MUIR
LOMOND CT
THE RISE
BEAUFORT RI
ANTIGONI CT
MEAKA CT
LOMIC CT
ATHENRY TCE
TEMPLEMORE CR
MAYO CL
PRINCETON PL
MAPLEDENE CT
ROSCOE DR
CLONTARF CL
DERRANE PL
TRAMORE CL
DUNLOE RI
BANTRY GR
KELL PL
LAVIAH CT
RAINTREE RD
DONEGAL CT
CAMINOLE WYN
REGINA CT
FERNLEA CR
BEECHWOOD CT
EDMONTON CT
NEWSTEAD CR
MONTREAL CT
KELVAN GR
TIMMS CT
HOPE CT
ORAN CT
PALTARRA CT
SIMONE CT
GINA CT
DEEP CREEK DR
LEANNE CT
SILVANA CT
DEEP HAY CT
CREEK CT
LYNDAL CT
VIVIENNE CT
MARLENE CT
JULIENNE CT
KRIS CT
LISA CT
HARMAN CL
LARNOO
LYNDA CT
ANGELA CT
HOLLYWOOD CL
BEVERLY HILLS DR
WOODLANDS EDG
HILLHOUSE CL
CLENDON CT
HUTCHINS TCE
MORLBOROUGH CT
SAVERNAKE CT
THE PINES
TIDCOMBE CR
KENT CT
BROOKE DR
WILLORNA CT
JOHNS
LAWSONS CT
GLEN WILL CT
GLENMANOR CT
GLENVISTA CT
JANINE CT
DELORAINE CT
ASHTON RI
LUTON CT
CORSICAN CT
BERNADETTE AV
AIDA CT
CELIA CT
HALDANE CT
MIRA CT
TERINGA CT
HALIFAX CT
LARKIN DR
DILKARA CT
NAVARRE CT
GALWAY CL
CASTLEBAR WY
WAGON RD
BRAY CT
GLENDARRAGH RD
RENOIR CR
HELMSDALE RT
DUNDEE CT
PAISLEY
ANNAN PL
RUBENS GR
MATISSE CL
VERDI CT
VIVALDI CT
MONOMEATH CL
CRESTMONT CT
GUILDFORD CT
VIEWMONT CT
SCHAFTER DR
VAN UNEN CT
RYDER CT
CUMBERLAND CL
WALLARA CT
BALINGA CT
KATANDRA CT
RIDLEY CT
MULLUM PL
NARTANDA CT
REEDPOLOCK DR
LIMASSOL CT
AUSTIN PL
VERNE CT
SHUTE CL
SHAKESPEARE
BLYTON CT
BRONTE RI
KEATS CT
RUSKIN CL
BYRON CT
THOMAS DICKENS CT
HARDY
HAILEY DR
SHELLEY CT
HATHAWAY CL
WIMBLEDON CT
ST JAMES CT
CHESTNUT CT
CHERRY CT
BLOSSOM CT
PEARTREE CT
LAURIE CT
SANTA ROSA
WOGENS CT
HAPPY VALLEY CT
MOOR PARK CT
PICKERING CT
YATES WYN
DEVLAW GR
WHICKSON CT
RED PLUM CT
DARREN RI
APPLE GUM GR
PEACHWOOD DR
LONG VALLEY WY
PINE PL
JEFFERSON GR
CROFTON TCE
CARMEN CL
LISBON CT
DIAMOND CT
RIMMER GR
FIVE CROWN GR
HOWELL CL
HARRINGTON PL
TWYFORD CL
BVD
LYONS CT
PARKLANDS CL
JOLEN CT
ROCHELLE CT
NEWLANDS
ERA CT
HILLCREST CT
FALFIELD PL
WHITEHALL CT
BURNS CT
SCOTT DR
ROTHESAY CL
APPLEWOOD CT
WHISTLEWOOD CL
BRIARWOOD CT
ROBERTSWOOD CL
HALSBURY CT
SERPELLS RD
NOOK CT
TULIP CT
NARCISSUS CT
COSMOS CT
NAVEL ROW
SHORE NK
FOREST CT
FOREST PL
RAVENSWOOD DR
GLEN ORCHARD CL
PEACH WY
HOUNDSWOOD CL
MONTEATH PL
JONQUIL CT
IRIS CT
CATHERINE CT
THORNCOMBE WK
ZERBE CT
HUNTINGFIELD DR
BINDI CT
OWNING CT
MOONBRIA WY
McGAHY CT
ORAMA CL
PEPPER CT
APPLE BLOSSOM RD
DARNLEY DR
HAVELOCK CT
HARKAWAY RI
ALBANY WY
LLOYD CT
ANTHLIN CT
KINGSBURN CT
REFUGE CL
LANDSCAPE DR
REDDINGTON TCE
BUTTERFLY GDN
MARONEY CT
BRENT CT
BICENTENNIAL CT
DELLVIEW CT
BARADINE TCE
WIARANDO CT
ROPER PL
LAMBERT PL
DOWLING GR
FULLWOOD PDE
POWERS LA
THE ELMS
ALLARA CT
ALLINGA PL
SPRINGWOOD CL
BAYLES CT
BARWON CT
BALCOMBE CT
HALCYON CT
PEPPERMINT CT
WENKE CT
NEDLANDS CT
COTSWOLD CT
DALKEITH CT
LONGSTAFF CT
RAMSAY CT
DORELL CT
STREETON LA
CAMELOT WYN
WATLING TCE
PERCEVAL WY
GALOVAC CL
MANOR CT
VALEPARK DR
AKOONAH CL
WALLACE CT
BULLOCK CT
DWYER CT
McCUBBIN TCE
HEYSEN GR
MELDRUM CL
DRYSDALE PL
MIRAMAR CT
NOLAN CT
APOLLO CT
FRATER CT
ROBERTS WY
ELLERTON CT
JASON CT
CRESTHAVEN CT
TAURUS RD
OCTANTIS CT
PHOENIX CT
POLARIS DR
SATURN TCE
CARBINE CT
CAMERON CL
SANDRA CT
DREWE CT
EMPERY CT
RUGBY CT
ROBIN HOOD CR
WINDERMERE AV
MOWBRAY CT
STAFFORD CT
CANOPUS CT
ORION PL
GEMINI CT
CAPRICORN CT
CENTAUR CT
CORONA CT
CAPELLA CT
TELOPEA AV
MIMOSA AV
LESLIE ST
KERN PL
STRINGERS RI
ST CLAIRE
WK
NONDA AV
McKENZIE ST
CASSIA CT
CALLISTEMON CT
BURGESS CT
STANDRING CT
VISTAWAY CT
MICHELLAN CT
MEWISSA CT
MOANA CT
ECUADOR
BELLEVUE
MAY ST
WOORARRA AV
JILPANGER RD
CLARICE CT
ONE TREE HILL
ABELIA ST
GUM RD
KALINDUR CT
PARKVILLE PL
FAHEY CT
BANOOL CT
BAMBRA CT
BEENAK CT
BOGONG CT
LANTANA ST
CORREA CT
CURRAJONG CT
SNOW CT
SANDERS RD
PAGO CT
DANIEL ST
NIGHTINGALE
ILLAWONG CT
OPALA CT
QUAMBY PL
BERRIMA
ASCOT ST
WOODHOUSE CT
MINAKI AV
ROSAMOND CR
CARISBROOK CT
ROWALLAN CT
ARGUS CR
SABASON CT
HUNT CT
EVA CT
BENCIR CT
MELISSA ST
BARRINGTON RI
LEURA ST
DRYDEN CT
CHURCHILL ST
COLCHESTER RD
AZALEA AV
HIGHFIELD RD
AINTREE AV
WOODHOUSE RD
MOZART CIR
CAT JUMP RD
GARDEN RD
MONTGOMERY ST

JOINS 333
JOINS 376
377

A B C D E F G H J K L

1 2 3 4 5 6 7 8 9 10 11 12 13 14 15 16 17 18 19 20

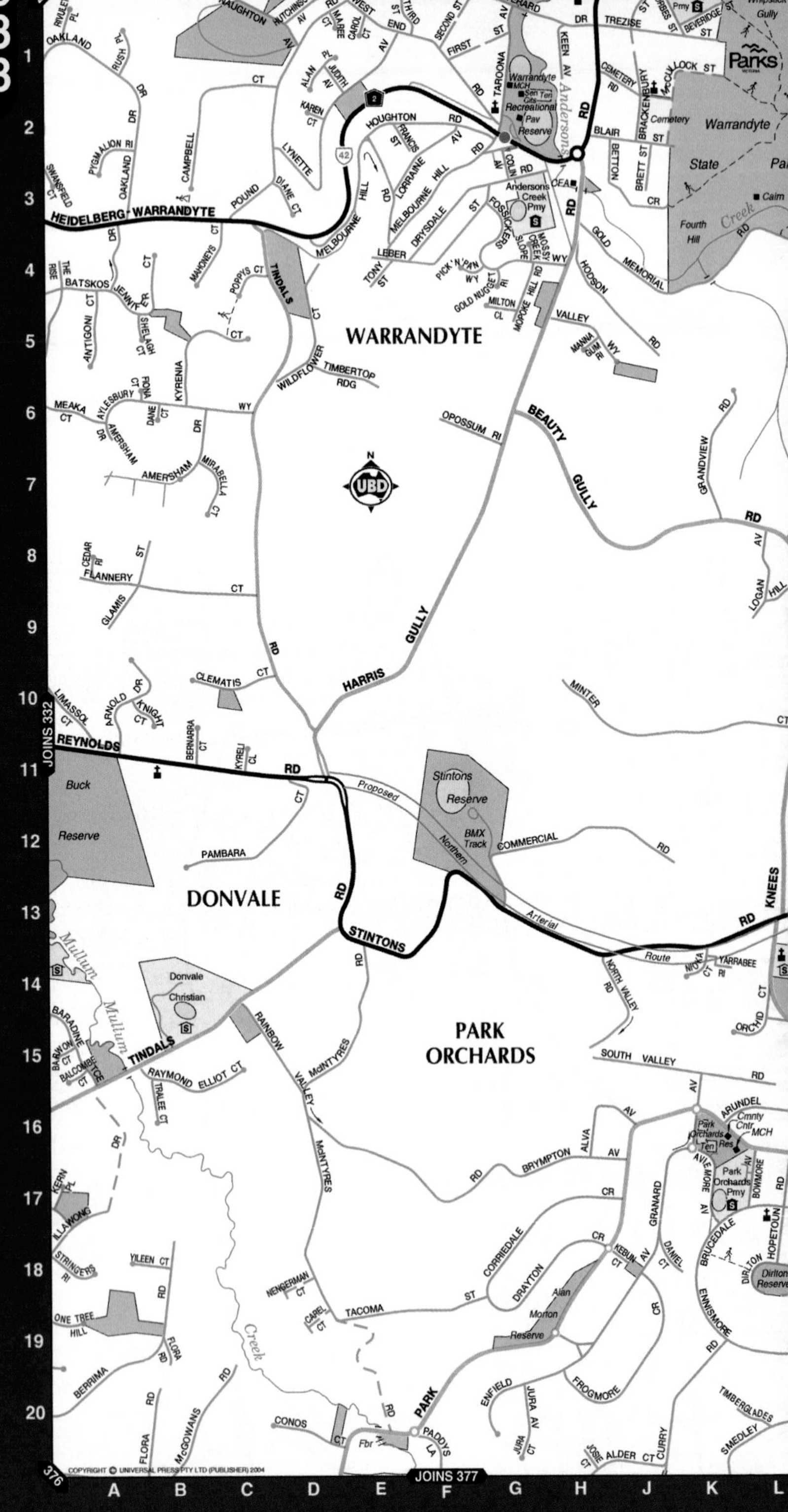
WARRANDYTE
DONVALE
PARK ORCHARDS
HEIDELBERG-WARRANDYTE
REYNOLDS RD
HARRIS GULLY RD
TINDALS RD
STINTONS RD
KNEES RD
Proposed Northern Arterial Route
BEAUTY GULLY RD
WARRANDYTE RD
COMMERCIAL RD
SOUTH VALLEY RD
PARK RD
Buck Reserve
Stintons Reserve
BMX Track
Donvale Christian
Alan Morton Reserve
Warrandyte State Park
Fourth Hill
Cemetery
Warrandyte MCH
Sen Cits
Ten
Recreational Reserve
Pav
Andersons Creek Pmy
Andersons Creek
Park Orchards Cmnty Cntr
MCH
Res
Park Orchards Pmy
Dirlton Reserve
Mullum Mullum Creek
Whipstick Gully
Parks VICTORIA
Cairn
Fbr
UBD
N
JOINS 332
JOINS 377
376
1
2
3
4
5
6
7
8
9
10
11
12
13
14
15
16
17
18
19
20
A
B
C
D
E
F
G
H
J
K
L
COPYRIGHT © UNIVERSAL PRESS PTY LTD (PUBLISHER) 2004

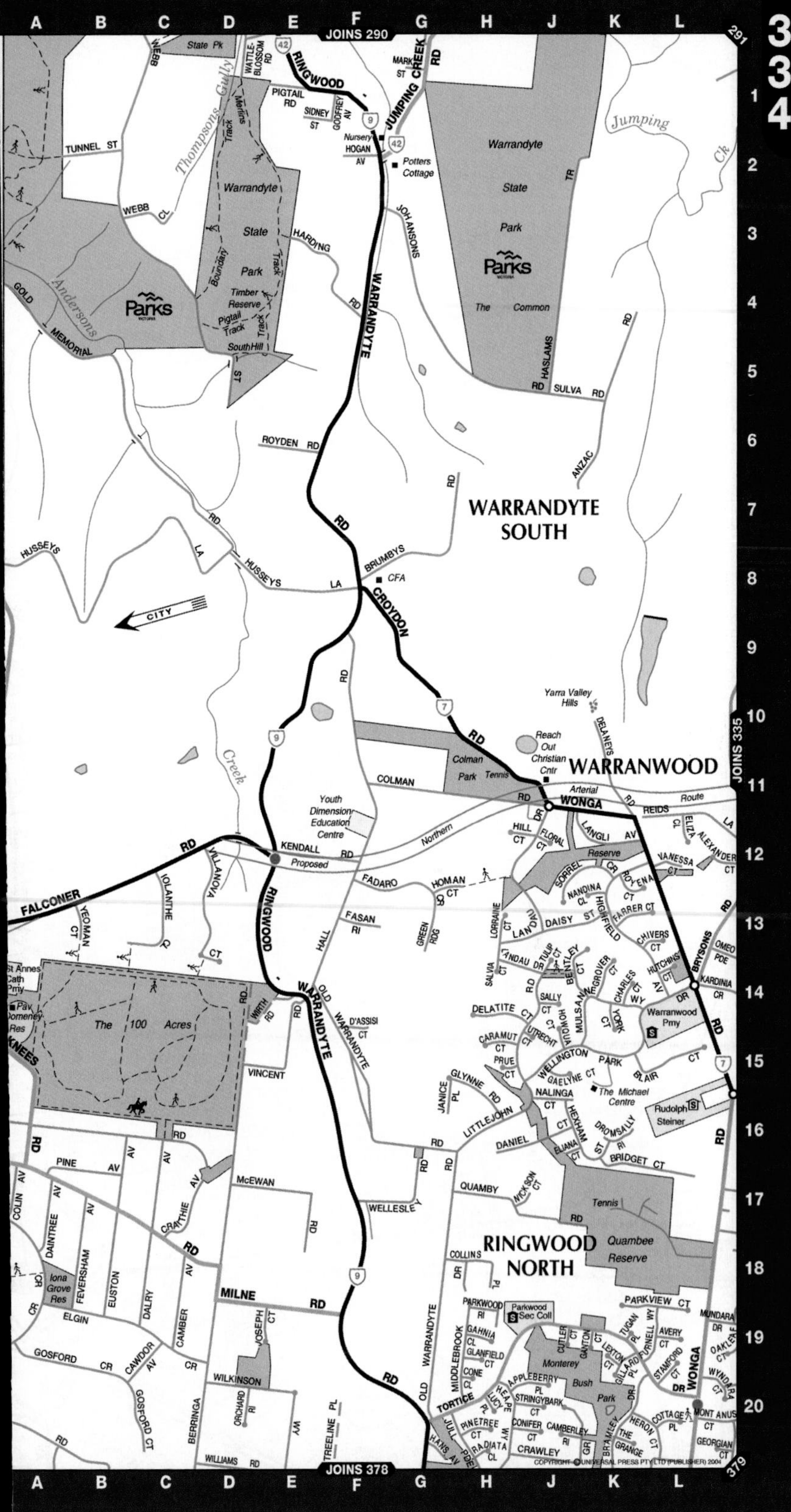

JOINS 290
JOINS 335
JOINS 378
291
379
WARRANDYTE SOUTH
WARRANWOOD
RINGWOOD NORTH
Warrandyte State Park
The Common
The 100 Acres
Monterey Bush Park
Quambee Reserve
RINGWOOD RD
WARRANDYTE RD
CROYDON RD
FALCONER RD
KENDALL RD
WONGA RD
BRYSONS RD
HUSSEYS LA
COLMAN RD
MILNE RD
CITY
COPYRIGHT © UNIVERSAL PRESS PTY LTD (PUBLISHER) 2004

290

A B C D E F G H J K L

JOINS 291

1 2 3 4 5 6 7 8 9 10 11 12 13 14 15 16 17 18 19 20

WARRANDYTE SOUTH

RINGWOOD NORTH

CROYDON HILLS

WARRANWOOD

RINGWOOD

HOOPER RD
HARRIS
DAWES RD
WALKER RD
YARRA RD
HOMESTEAD RD
JAMIESON RD
KENILWORTH
VALERIE AV DR
FREYNE ST
BRYSONS RD
ST JOHNS RD
CLEMENTINE CL
GATTERS RD (Fire Access Only)
EDGAR AV
HILLCREST RD
HOLLOWAY RD
Northern Arterial Route
Proposed
Jumping Creek
GIBSON RD
LANIER
JANSON CT
KEMPSTON
PANORAMA DR
Yarra Road Primary
MOUNTAINVIEW RD
CROYDON HILLS DR
NARR-MAEN DR
KERRY
MERRILL
Warranwood Reserve
Yarrunga Reserve
Croydon Hills Primary
Good Shepherd Lutheran Primary
Luther College
Yarra Valley Anglican Co-Educational
Lipscombe Park
Cherry Tree Grove Retirement Village
Croydon Hotel
Kalinda Pmy
PLYMOUTH RD
WARRANWOOD RD
WONGA RD
MAROONDAH
KENT AV
BEMBOKA RD
NANGATHAN
LEHMANN
RICHARDSON
CHERRY
NURSERY
HIGHLAND

JOINS 334

378

A B C D E F G H J K L

JOINS 379

JOINS 292
293
JOINS 337
JOINS 380
381

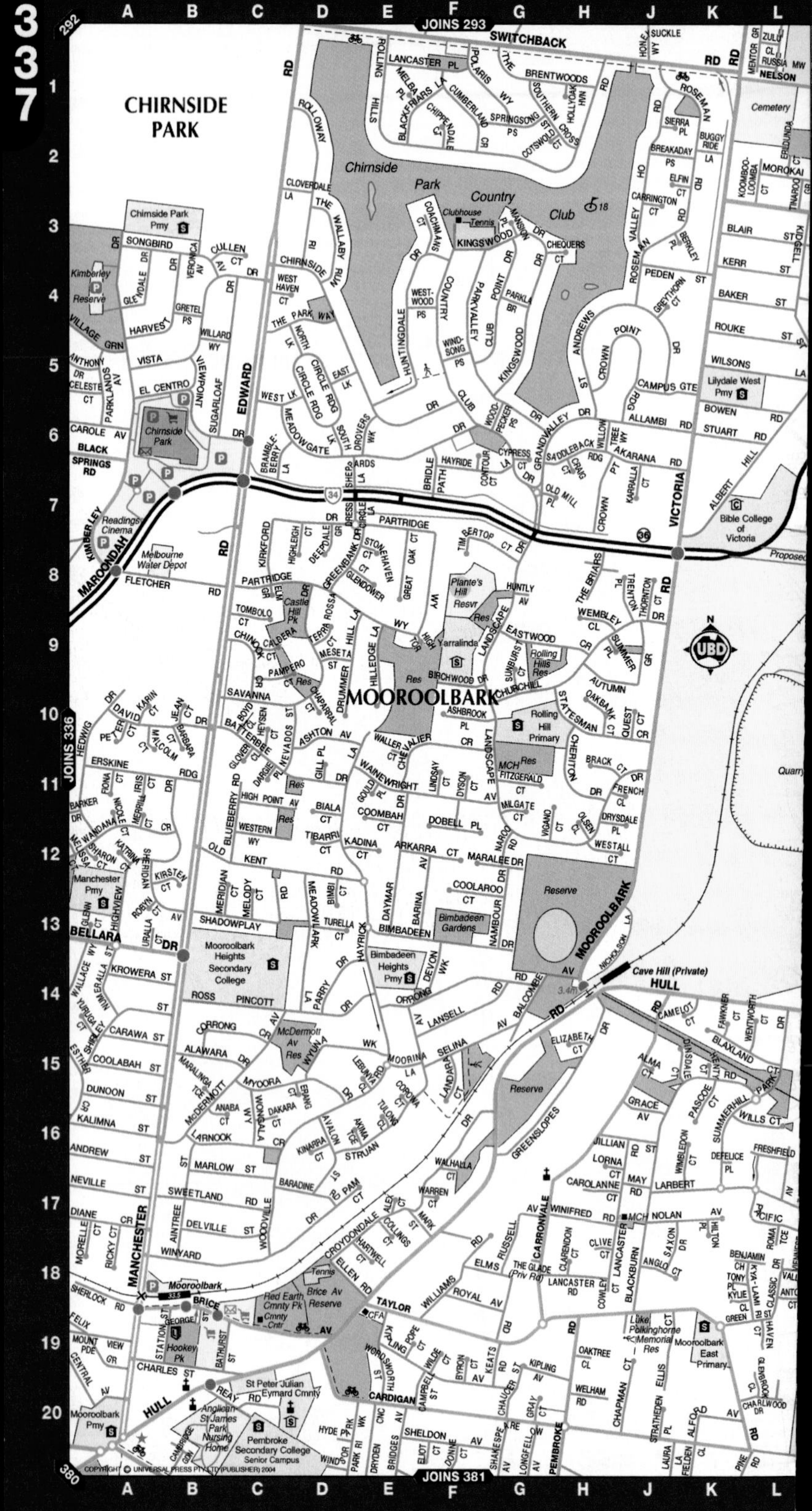

JOINS 293

292

A B C D E F G H J K L

1 2 3 4 5 6 7 8 9 10 11 12 13 14 15 16 17 18 19 20

CHIRNSIDE PARK

MOOROOLBARK

Chirnside Park Country Club

SWITCHBACK RD
HONEYSUCKLE WY
NELSON RD
LANCASTER PL
ROLLING HILLS
MELBA PL
BLACKFRIARS LA
CHIPPENDALE CT
CUMBERLAND CR
POLARIS WY
THE SPRINGSONG PS
BRENTWOODS RD
SOUTHERN CROSS
HOLLYOAK HWY
COTSWOLD CT
ROLLOWAY
ROSEMAN RD
SIERRA PL
BUGGY RIDE LA
BREAKADAY PS
ELFIN CT
CARRINGTON CT
BERKLEY PL
Cemetery
KOOMBOOLOOMBA CT
MOROKAI
TINAROO CT
ERIDUNDA
MENTOR GR
ZULU CL
RUSSIA MW
CLOVERDALE LA
THE WALLABY RUN
COACHMANS CT
Clubhouse
Tennis
KINGSWOOD DR
MANSION PL
CHEQUERS CT
VALLEY HO
BLAIR ST
KIDGELL ST
Chirnside Park Pmy
SONGBIRD DR
CULLEN CT
VERONICA AV
CHIRNSIDE DR
WEST HAVEN CT
PEDEN ST
KERR ST
Kimberley Reserve
GLENDALE DR
GRETEL PS
POINT DR
PARKLA BR
WESTWOOD PS
GREYTHORN CT
BAKER ST
HARVEST
THE PARK WAY
ROUKE ST
VILLAGE GRN
WILLARD WY
NORTH LK
HUNTINGDALE
COUNTRY CLUB DR
PARKVALLEY DR
WINDSONG PS
KINGSWOOD
ANDREWS ST
CROWN POINT RDG
WILSONS LA
VISTA
VIEWPOINT
CIRCLE RDG
EAST LK
CAMPUS GTE
Lilydale West Pmy
ANTHONY DR
CELESTE CT
PARKLANDS AV
EL CENTRO
SUGARLOAF
EDWARD RD
WEST LK
BOWEN RD
ALLAMBI RD
STUART RD
CAROLE AV
Chirnside Park
BRAMBLEBERRY LA
MEADOWGATE
SOUTH LK
DROVERS WK
WOODPECKER PS
GRANDVALLEY DR
SADDLEBACK CT
WILLOW RDG
TREE WY
AKARANA RD
BLACK SPRINGS RD
SHEPHERDS LA
HAYRIDE
BRIDLE PATH
CONTOUR CT
CYPRESS LA
CRAIG CT
KARRALLA CT
HILL
OLD MILL PL
ALBERT
Bible College of Victoria
VICTORIA RD
KIMBERLEY
Readings Cinema
MAROONDAH
DRESSAGE CT
CIRCLE
PARTRIDGE
Melbourne Water Depot
FLETCHER RD
KIRKFORD
HIGHLEIGH CT
DEERDALE GR
GREENBANK DR
STONEHAVEN CT
GLENDOWER
GREAT OAK CT
TIMBERTOP CT
CROWN
Proposed
THE BRIARS
TRENTON PL
THORNTON CT
PARTRIDGE
ELM
Castle Hill Pk
TERRA ROSSA
HUNTLY AV
Plante's Hill Resvr
Res
LANDSCAPE
EASTWOOD
WEMBLEY CL
CR
TOMBOLO CT
CHINOOK CT
CALDERA
MESETA ST
HILL LA
HILLEDGE LA
HIGH TOR WY
Yarralinda
SUNBURST CT
Rolling Hills Res
SUMMER PL
GR
PAMPERO CT
Res
BIRCHWOOD DR
CHURCHILL
AUTUMN
SAVANNA
CHAPARRAL
DRUMMER
ASHBROOK PL
Rolling Hill Primary
STATESMAN CT
OAKBANK CT
QUEST CT
CR
DAVID
KARIN CT
JEAN CT
BOYD CT
HEYSEN
BATTERBEE
NEVADOS ST
ASHTON AV
WALLER CT
CHEVALIER
HEDWIG
PETER CT
MALCOLM CT
BARBARA
GLOVER
DARGIE PL
GILL PL
WAINEWRIGHT
LINDSAY CT
DYSON CT
MCH
FITZGERALD CT
CHERITON
BRACK CT
DR
FRENCH CL
ERSKINE RDG
FIONA CT
IRIS CT
BLUEBERRY RD
HIGH POINT AV
GOULD PL
COOMBAH CT
DOBELL PL
MILGATE CT
VIGANO CT
OLSEN CT
DRYSDALE PL
Quarry
BARKER DR
NICOLE CT
MERRILL CT
WESTERN WY
Res
BIALA CT
TIBARRI CT
KADINA CT
ARKARRA CT
NAROO RD
WESTALL CT
WANDANA
KATRINA
SHERIDAN
MELISSA
SHARON CT
OLD KENT RD
MARALEE DR
Manchester Pmy
KIRSTEN CT
MERIDIAN CT
MELODY CT
MEADOWLARK
BIMBI CT
DAYMAR
BARINA AV
COOLAROO CT
Reserve
MOOROOLBARK LA
GLENIN CT
HIGHVIEW
ROBYN CT
URALLA CT
SHADOWPLAY
TURELLA CT
HAYRICK
BIMBADEEN
Bimbadeen Gardens
NAMBOUR DR
BELLARA DR
WALLACE WY
Mooroolbark Heights Secondary College
Bimbadeen Heights Pmy
DEVON WK
NICHOLSON
Cave Hill (Private)
KROWERA ST
NUMERALLA
ROSS
PINCOTT
PARRY LA
ORRONG
BALCOMBE
3.4m
HULL
YURUGA CT
SHIRLEY CT
CARAWA ST
CORRONG CR
McDermott Av Res
WYUNA WK
LANSELL AV
ELIZABETH CT
CAMELOT CT
FAWKNER CT
WENTWORTH CT
ESTHER
ALAWARA DR
MOORINA LA
SELINA
BLAXLAND
COOLABAH ST
MARALINGA TCE
McDERMOTT
MYOORA
LEBUNYA CT
CORONA
LANDARA CT
Reserve
ALMA CT
DINSDALE CT
KENT RD
PARK
DUNOON ST
ANABA CT
WONGALA WY
DAKARA CT
EPANG CT
TULONG
GRACE AV
PASCOE CT
SUMMERHILL
WILLS CT
KALIMNA ST
LARNOOK
KINARRA CT
AVALON CT
AKIMA
STRUAN
GREENSLOPES DR
JILLIAN RD
LORNA CT
ANDREW ST
MARLOW ST
BARADINE
PAM CT
WALHALLA CT
MAY RD
WIMBLEDON CT
DEFELICE PL
FRESHFIELD
NEVILLE ST
SWEETLAND RD
WOODVILLE
WARREN CT
CAROLANNE CT
LARBERT
DIANE CR
ALEXANDRA
COLLINGS ST
MARK
CARRONVALE
WINIFRED RD
MCH
NOLAN AV
HILTON PL
PACIFIC
MORELLE CT
RICKY CT
AINTREE
DELVILLE ST
CROYDONDALE
HARTWELL
RUSSELL
CLARENDON CT
CLIVE CT
SAXON DR
ROMA TCE
BENJAMIN CH
WINYARD
ELMS
THE GLADE (Priv Rd)
LANCASTER CT
BLACKBURN
ANGLO CT
TONY PL
KYLIE CL
KYA-LAMI RD
CLASSIC CT
VALLEY
ANTON
MANCHESTER
Mooroolbark
ELLEN RD
Tennis
Brice Av Reserve
WILLIAMS
ROYAL AV
LANCASTER RD
COWLEY
GREEN
SHERLOCK RD
BRICE
TAYLOR
CFA
Red Earth Cmnty Pk
Cmnty Cntr
AV
FELIX
MOUNT VIEW PDE
GR
GEORGE
STATION
Hookey Pk
BATHURST
KIPLING
POPE CT
WILDE CT
BYRON CT
KEATS RD
OAKTREE CL
Luke Polkinghorne Memorial Res
Mooroolbark East Primary
HAVEN
CENTRAL AV
CHARLES ST
WORDSWORTH ST
CHAUCER ST
KIPLING AV
WELHAM RD
CHAPMAN CT
ELLIS
GLENBROOK CL
REAY RD
St Peter Julian Eymard Cmnty
CAMPBELL ST
CARDIGAN
GRAY CT
STRATHEDEN PL
ALFORD AV
CHARLWOOD DR
HULL
Anglican St James
Park Nursing Home
CAMBRIDGE
OXFORD
Pembroke Secondary College Senior Campus
HYDE PARK
CNC
SHELDON AV
SHAKESPEARE
LONGFELLOW
PEMBROKE RD
LAURA LA
FIELDEN CL
PINE RD
Mooroolbark Pmy
WINDSOR
PARK RI
DRYDEN
BRIDGES
ELIOT CT
DONNE CT

34
36

UBD

JOINS 336

380

JOINS 381

JOINS 294

JOINS 339

JOINS 382

295

383

A B C D E F G H J K L

1 2 3 4 5 6 7 8 9 10 11 12 13 14 15 16 17 18 19 20

INDEX A

1 CHELSWORTH PARK LA
2 GROSVENOR WK
3 HAMPTON CT
4 MANORHOUSE WK
5 OTTERINGTON WY
6 ST AMBROSE GR
7 ST PATRICKS PL
8 SALISBURY BND
9 SHERBROOK TCE
10 STRATHAVEN PL
11 THE CHANCERY
12 TRAFFORD CL
13 WHITEFRIARS RI

LILYDALE

MOUNT EVELYN

Lilydale Heights Sec Coll

Gateway Res

Melbourne Water Council Depot

Yarra Valley Water Depot

Treatment

Industrial Park

Works

Mt Lilydale Catholic College

Cave Hill Industrial Park

St Patricks Cath

Lilydale Pmy

Court Hse

International Functions Centre

Hist Society Theatre

Melba Pk

Cmnty Youth Cntr

Yarra Valley RSL

Lilydale High

Lilydale Marketplace

Sen Cits

Cncl Off

Tennis

Lilydale Cmnty Hosp (Private)

Swinburne University of Technology (& TAFE) Lilydale Campus

Reserve

Lillydale Lake

Yarra Valley Quarter Horse Assoc

Birmingham Primary

Adventist Academy

Edinburgh Adventist Pmy

Wishart Lodge Scout Camp

Olinda Reservoir

Quinn Reserve

Trail

CITY

MAROONDAH HWY (MAIN ST)

SWANSEA RD

HEREFORD RD

OLD GIPPSLAND RD

HULL RD

BIRMINGHAM RD

MELBA AV

Bypass

O'Shannassy Pipeline

Olinda Creek

Warburton

Disused

Railway

GARDINER ST

BERESFORD RD

NELSON RD

294
JOINS 295
JOINS 338
JOINS 383
382

A B C D E F G H J K L

MOUNT EVELYN

INDEX A

1 CHELSWORTH PARK LA
2 GROSVENOR WK
3 HAMPTON CT
4 MANORHOUSE WK
5 OTTERINGTON WY
6 ST AMBROSE GR
7 ST PATRICKS PL
8 SALISBURY BND
9 SHERBROOK TCE
10 STRATHAVEN PL
11 THE CHANCERY
12 TRAFFORD CL
13 WHITEFRIARS RI

MAROONDAH (MAIN ST) HWY
B300
ROSEMONT RD
COMO RD
WARBURTON HWY
B380
Tudor Village Mews Ret Village
SEE INDEX A
VicRoads Depot
Kyarra Business Retreat
TUDOR VILLAGE DR
GLENSIDE CL
LILY RD
O'SULLIVANS RD
LEONARD RD
HEATHCOTE
STANTON GR
Pine Hill
McNEIL AV
42
HYNE RD
NORTH RD
PANORAMA RI
TAURUS CT
ALEXANDRA RD
AQUARIUS CT
PISCES CT
MANGANS RD
ROACH AV
ANNE ST
JURAT
CITY
OLD GIPPSLAND RD
PARKSIDE CL
VALENCIA RD
CARMEN CT
BRAMWELL ST
FORTUNE
HEREFORD RD
OLD HEREFORD RD
SEPIK VA
KOOKABURRA LA
JITSU RD
MIKADO RD
BRIGHTWELL RD
MITCHELL RD
GARY CT
ATHLONE ST
Morrison House
Morrison Reserve
Pembroke Sec Coll (Mt Evelyn Campus)
Tennis
Spec Dev Sch
MCH
FERNHILL
DAVID RD
(Fire Access Only) RD
HAIG
FULLER RD
EVERTON RD
HARVEY ST
BRADMAN AV
NEWTON AV
MUIR SMYTH PL
WAYCOTT WY
O'CONNOR AV
WATTLE VALLEY RD
KING ST
McGREGOR CT
HEATH AV
ADAMS LA
KEMP
STUBBS
Birmingham Primary
EBBYS WK
Warburton
C404
FORGE
BOURKE ST
WRIGHT ST
MITARM CL
KATHERINE PL
MICHAEL
PAUL CL
CORLESS CL
RUSSELL
POLAT CT
ISABEL CT
STRINGYBARK BVD
SETH PL
RACHAL CL
PEARL CT
IRVINE AV
PDE
DAWN ST
RANGEVIEW
BUCKMASTER DR
WINGARA PL
SPRING ST
BIRMINGHAM
HILL DR
ELIZABETH ST
LOUISA ST
ALICE ST
GARDNER RD
GLENVIEW RD
CAMRIC CT
BAILEY
LITTLEBROOK CL
LONGVIEW RD
ROLAND AV
CRESCENT
DR
WEST GR
GEORGE
WEDDERBURN
Hall
CR
SNOWBALL AV
STATION ST
WRAY CR
MCH
Tennis
GRANTULLY ST
HORDERN RD
MARSHALL ST
JUNCTION RD
THE
ELSIE RD
CHANNEL
CLEMATIS
QUINN CR
MARCUS
C402
CFA
GEAR AV
MONBULK RD
CLANCY
LEGGETT
YORK
NORTH VIEW
ST
OLINDA RD
MACE CT
HILLTOP CR
FALKINGHAM
WATTLE AV
RAILWAY RD
(Steep)
EAST AV
JOY AV
AQUEDUCT AV
BORANG AV
(SILVAN RD)
CLEGG RD
Mt Evelyn Pmy
TRUDY PL
St Marys Cath Pmy
Mt E Gra Ret
Tra

A B C D E F G H J K L

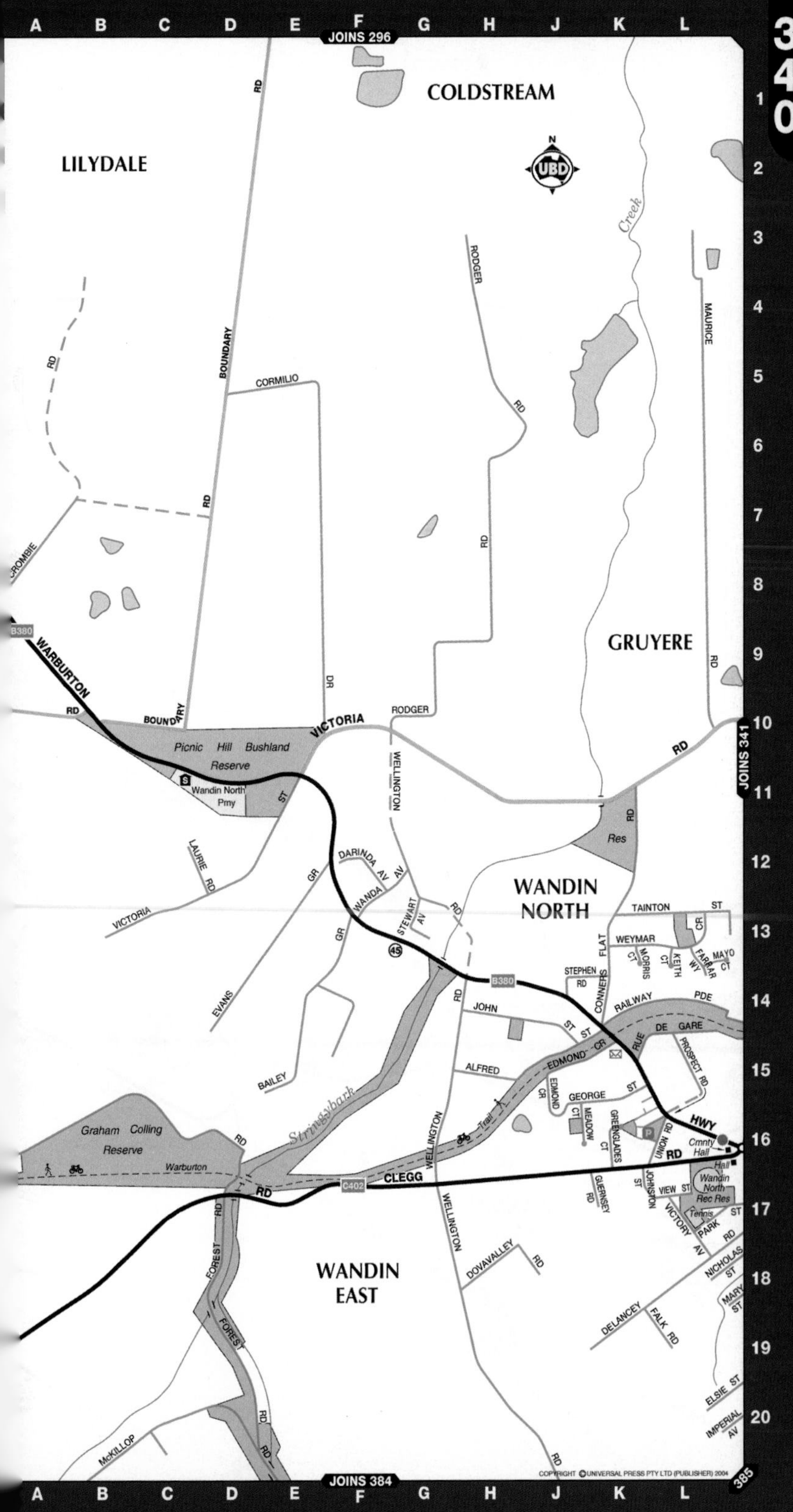
JOINS 296
COLDSTREAM
LILYDALE
GRUYERE
WANDIN NORTH
WANDIN EAST
WARBURTON
HWY
Picnic Hill Bushland Reserve
Wandin North Pmy
Graham Colling Reserve
Warburton Trail
Stringybark Creek
VICTORIA RD
CLEGG RD
BOUNDARY RD
CORMILIO DR
RODGER RD
MAURICE RD
WELLINGTON RD
LAURIE RD
EVANS GR
BAILEY
DARINDA AV
WANDA AV
STEWART AV
JOHN ST
ALFRED
EDMOND CR
GEORGE ST
MEADOW CT
GREENGLADES CT
GUERNSEY RD
UNION RD
JOHNSTON ST
VIEW ST
VICTORY AV
PARK RD
NICHOLAS ST
MARY ST
DELANCEY
FALK RD
ELSIE ST
IMPERIAL AV
DOVAVALLEY RD
FOREST RD
McKILLOP
RUE DE GARE
PROSPECT RD
RAILWAY PDE
CONNERS FLAT RD
STEPHEN RD
WEYMAR CT
MORRIS CT
KEITH CT
FARRAR WY
MAYO CT
TAINTON ST
Res
Cmnty Hall
Hall
Wandin North Rec Res
Tennis
B380
C402
45
JOINS 341
JOINS 384
385
COPYRIGHT © UNIVERSAL PRESS PTY LTD (PUBLISHER) 2004

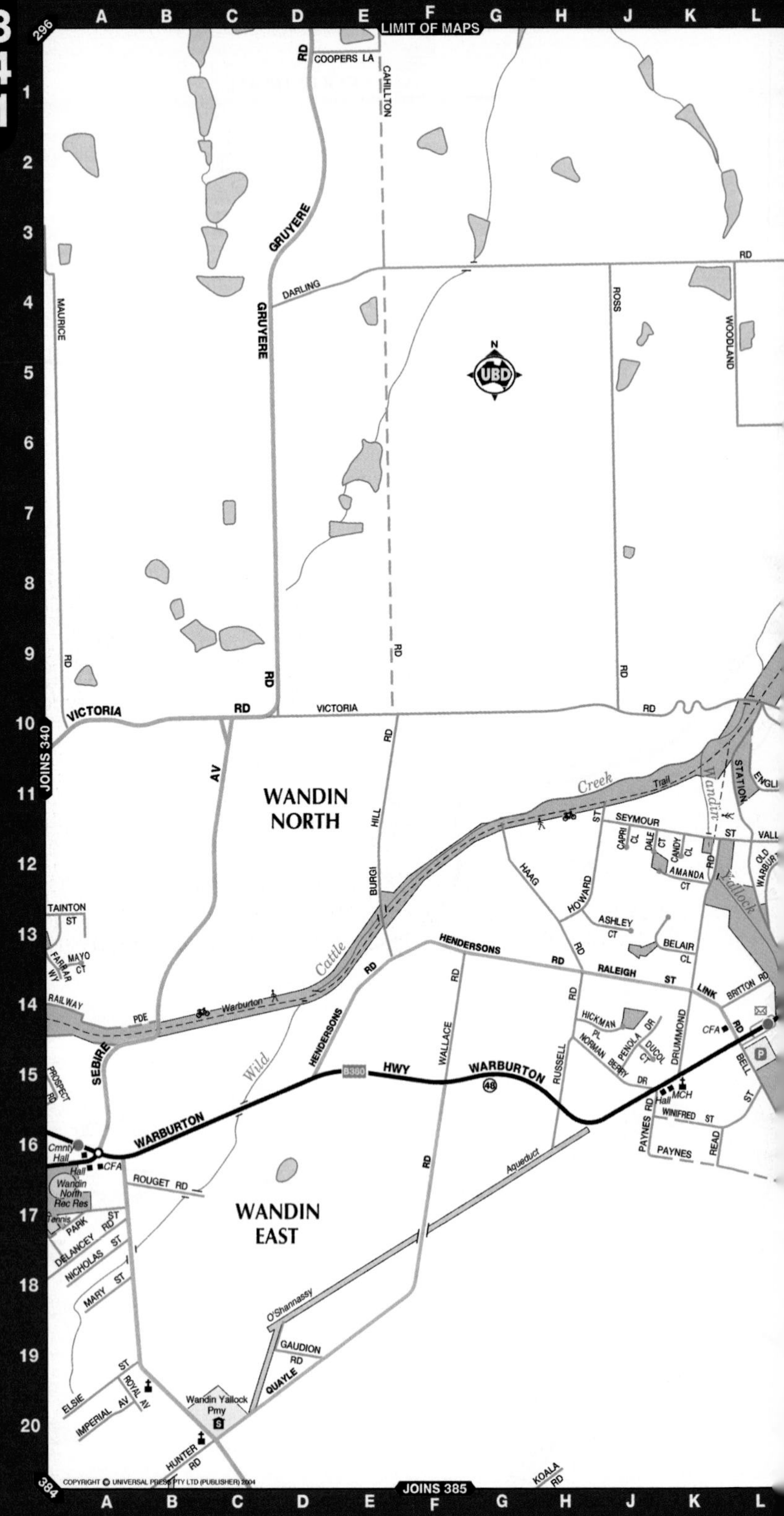

LIMIT OF MAPS
296
COOPERS LA
CAMILLTON
GRUYERE RD
DARLING
RD
MAURICE RD
ROSS RD
WOODLAND
VICTORIA RD
VICTORIA
RD
JOINS 340
AV
WANDIN NORTH
BURGI HILL RD
Creek
Trail
Wandin Yallock
STATION
ENGLI
SEYMOUR ST
VALL
CAPRI CL
DALE CT
CANDY CL
AMANDA CT
OLD WARBURTON
HAAG
HOWARD RD
ASHLEY CT
BELAIR CL
TAINTON ST
FARRAR WY
MAYO CT
Cattle
HENDERSONS RD
RALEIGH ST
LINK RD
BRITTON RD
RAILWAY PDE
Warburton
HENDERSONS
WALLACE RD
RUSSELL
HICKMAN PL
NORMAN
PENOLA DR
DUCOL CT
BERRY DR
DRUMMOND
CFA
BELL ST
SEBIRE
Wild
B380
WARBURTON HWY
48
PROSPECT RD
MCH
Hall
PAYNES RD
WINIFRED ST
PAYNES
READ
Cmnty Hall
Hall
CFA
Wandin North Rec Res
ROUGET RD
Aqueduct
WANDIN EAST
Tennis
PARK ST
RD
DELANCEY ST
NICHOLAS ST
MARY ST
O'Shannassy
GAUDION RD
QUAYLE
ELSIE ST
ROYAL AV
IMPERIAL AV
Wandin Yallock Pmy
HUNTER RD
KOALA RD

LIMIT OF MAPS

JOINS 343

JOINS 386

387

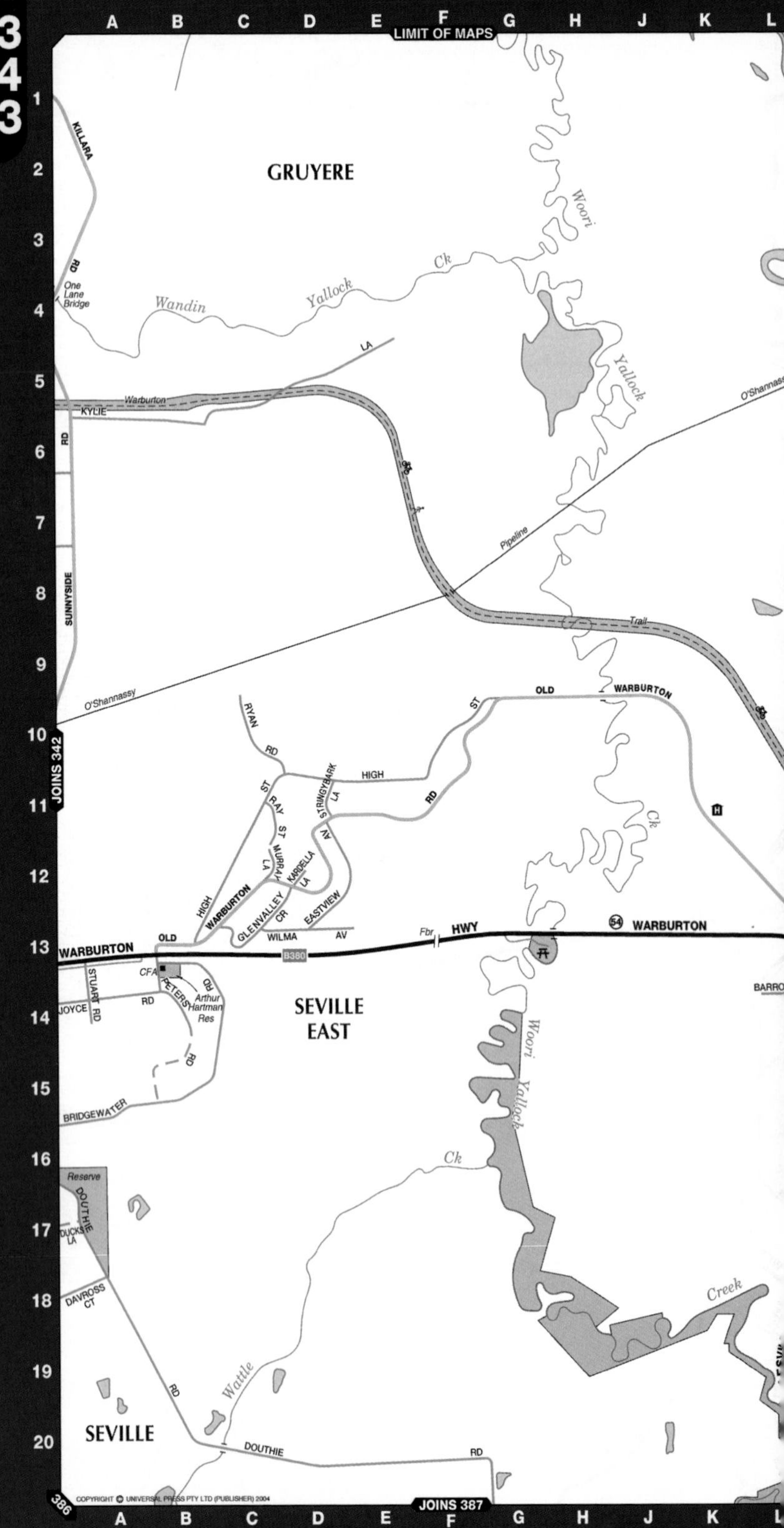

JOINS 342
JOINS 387
386

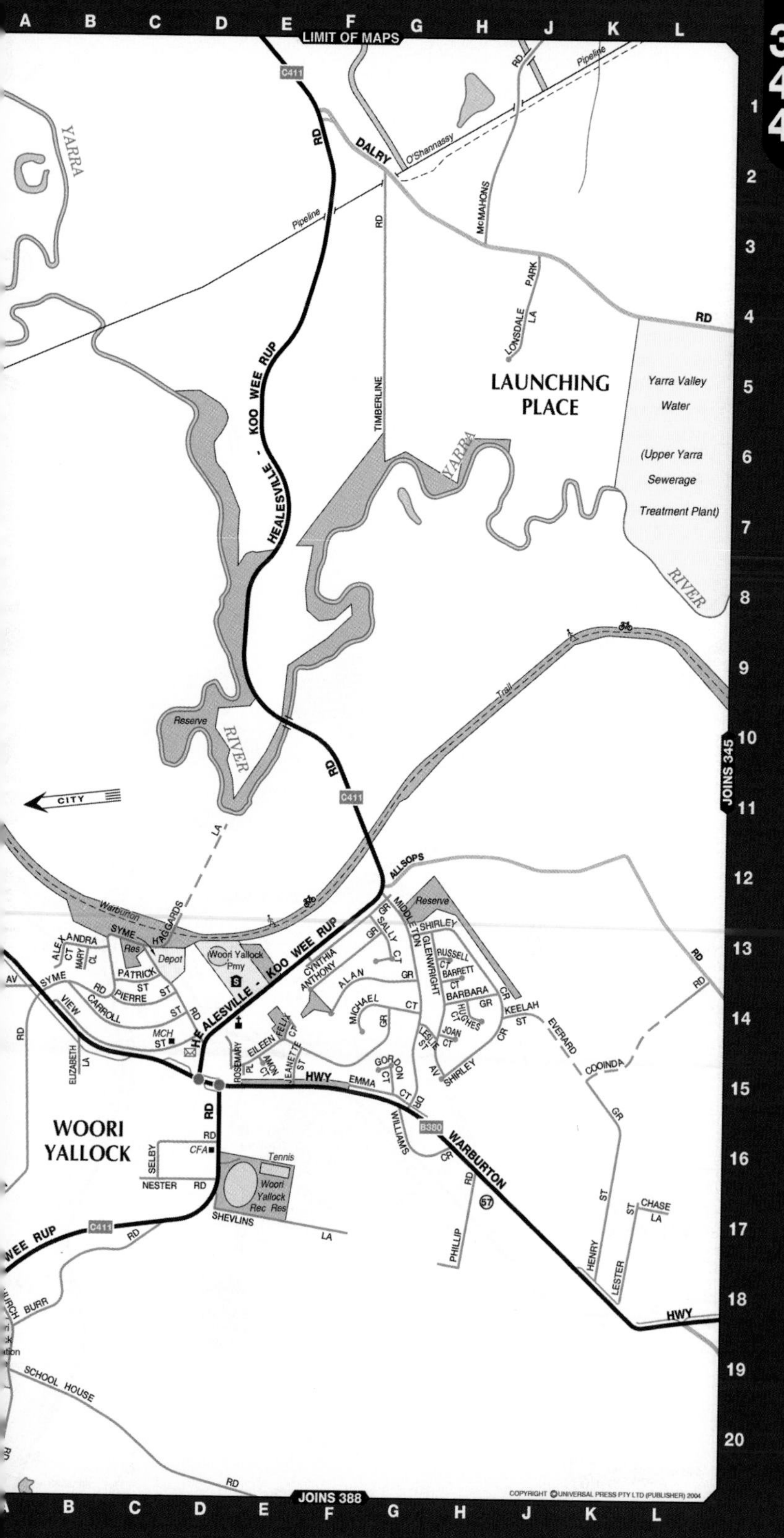

LIMIT OF MAPS
LAUNCHING PLACE
WOORI YALLOCK
HEALESVILLE - KOO WEE RUP RD
C411
DALRY
O'Shannassy
Pipeline
McMAHONS
TIMBERLINE RD
LONSDALE LA
PARK RD
YARRA RIVER
Yarra Valley Water (Upper Yarra Sewerage Treatment Plant)
Reserve
Trail
Warburton
CITY
ALLSOPS
MIDDLETON
SHIRLEY
GLENWRIGHT
RUSSELL CT
BARRETT CT
BARBARA GR
HUGHES CT
KEELAH ST
EVERARD
COOINDA
JOAN CT
LESLIE ST
CYNTHIA
ANTHONY
SALLY CT
ALAN GR
MICHAEL CT
GORDON CT
EMMA CT
HWY
WILLIAMS CR
B380
WARBURTON HWY
PHILLIP RD
HENRY ST
LESTER ST
CHASE LA
SYME
HAGGARDS
ALEXANDRA
MARY CL
PATRICK ST
PIERRE ST
CARROLL RD
VIEW
Res
Depot
Woori Yallock Pmy
MCH ST
ELIZABETH LA
EILEEN
FELIX CT
JEANETTE ST
ROSEMARY PL
AMON CT
SELBY
CFA
NESTER RD
Tennis
Woori Yallock Rec Res
SHEVLINS LA
BURR
SCHOOL HOUSE
JOINS 345
JOINS 388

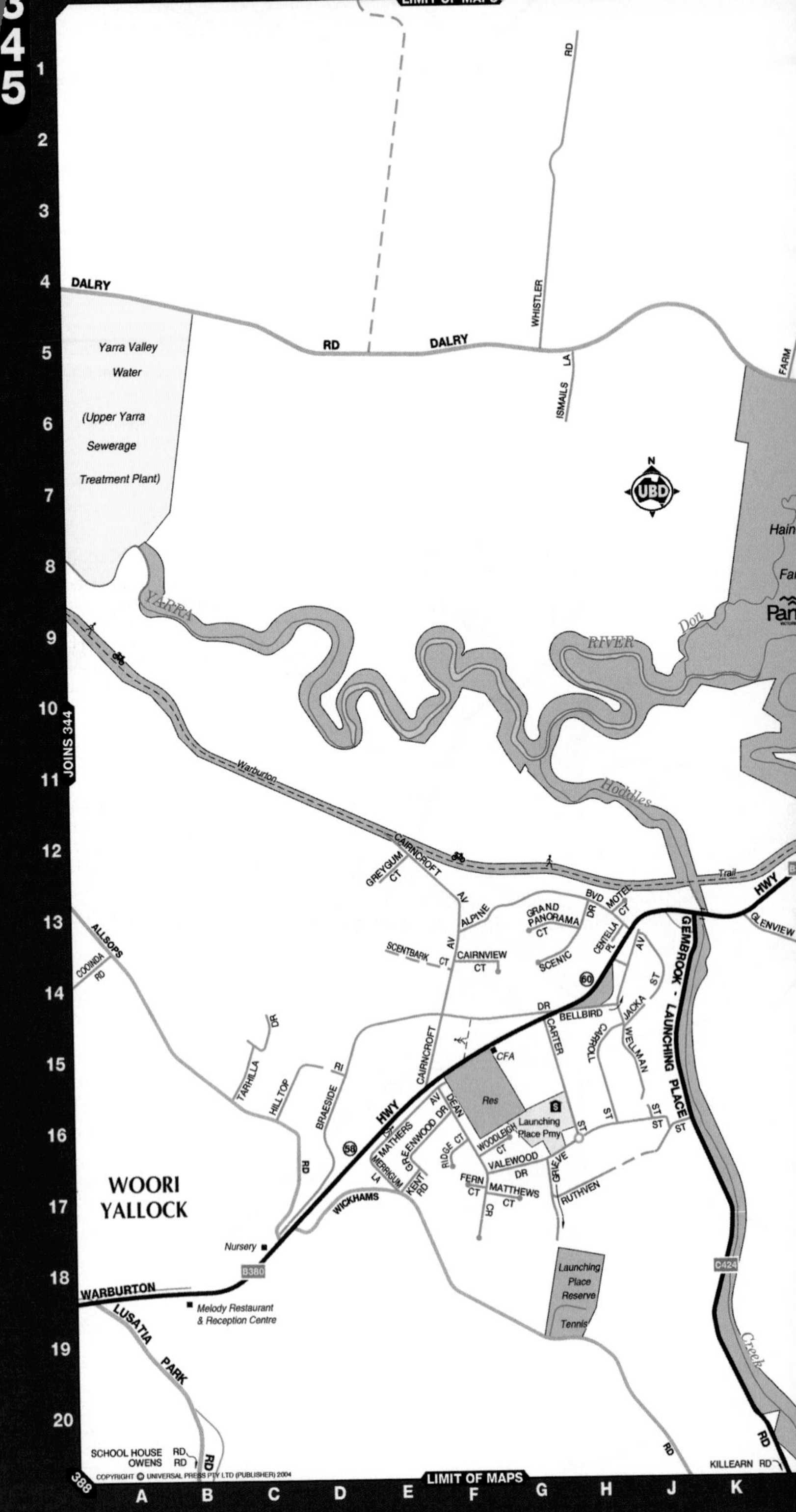
LIMIT OF MAPS
DALRY
RD
DALRY
WHISTLER
RD
ISMAILS LA
FARM
Yarra Valley Water (Upper Yarra Sewerage Treatment Plant)
UBD
YARRA
RIVER
Don
Hoddles
Warburton
Trail
CAIRNCROFT
GREYGUM CT
AV
ALPINE
GRAND PANORAMA CT
BVD
DR
MOTEL CT
CENTELLA PL
AV
HWY
GLENVIEW
GEMBROOK - LAUNCHING PLACE
SCENTBARK CT
CAIRNVIEW CT
SCENIC
ST
ALLSOPS
COOINDA RD
DR
BELLBIRD
JACKA
CARTER
CARROLL
WELLMAN
CFA
Res
CAIRNCROFT
TARHILLA
DR
HILLTOP
BRAESIDE
RI
HWY
AV
DEAN
Launching Place Pmy
ST
ST
ST
ST
MATHERS
GREENWOOD DR
RIDGE CT
WOODLEIGH CT
VALEWOOD DR
GRIEVE
RUTHVEN
MERRIGUM LA
KENT RD
FERN CT
MATTHEWS CT
CR
WICKHAMS
RD
WOORI YALLOCK
Nursery
B380
WARBURTON
Melody Restaurant & Reception Centre
LUSATIA PARK
RD
Launching Place Reserve
Tennis
C424
Creek
RD
RD
SCHOOL HOUSE RD
OWENS RD
KILLEARN RD
JOINS 344
LIMIT OF MAPS
388
1
2
3
4
5
6
7
8
9
10
11
12
13
14
15
16
17
18
19
20
A
B
C
D
E
F
G
H
J
K

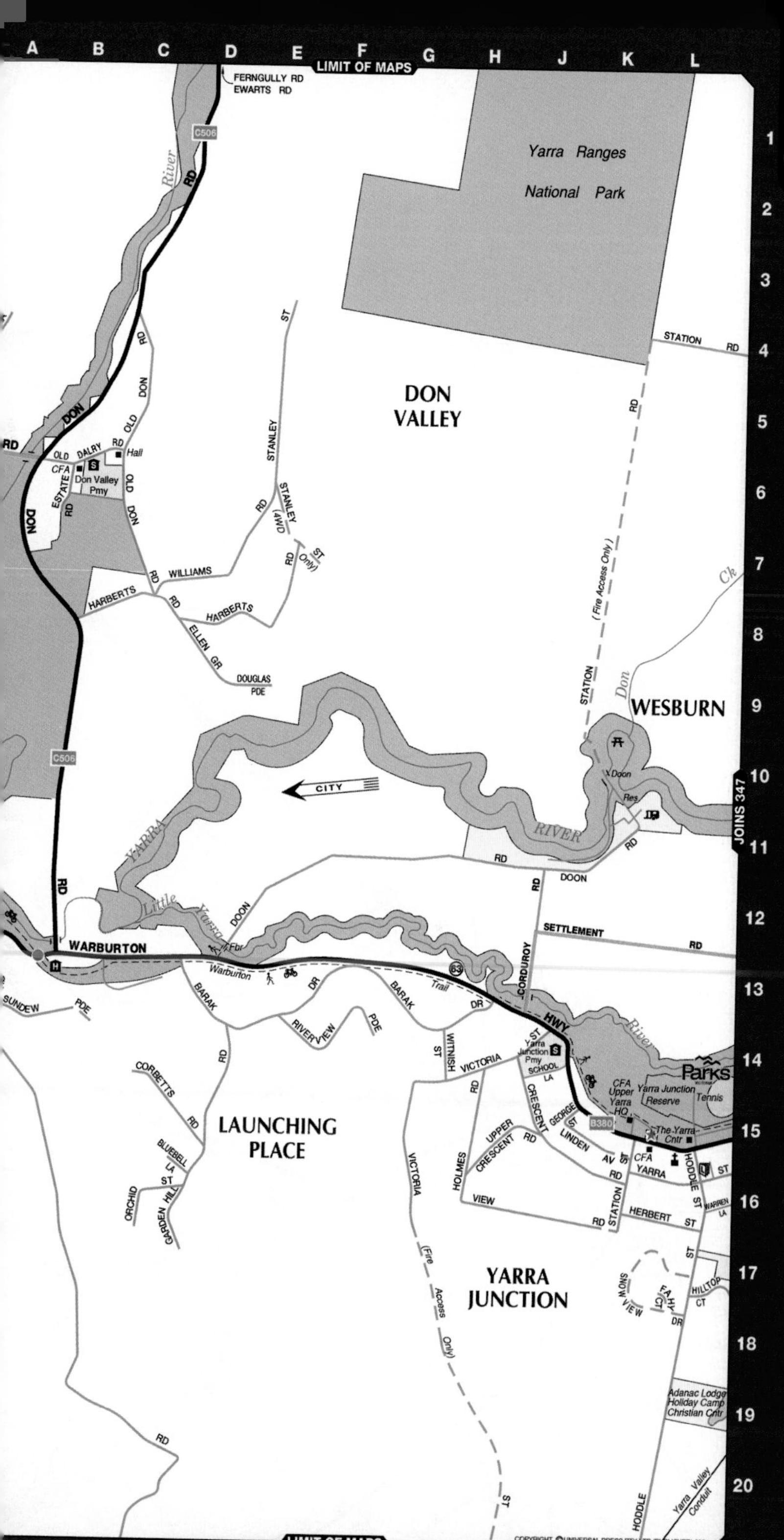
LIMIT OF MAPS
A B C D E F G H J K L
1 2 3 4 5 6 7 8 9 10 11 12 13 14 15 16 17 18 19 20
FERNGULLY RD
EWARTS RD
C506
Yarra Ranges National Park
DON VALLEY
STATION RD
DON RD
OLD DON RD
OLD DALRY RD
ESTATE RD
CFA
Don Valley Pmy
Hall
STANLEY RD
STANLEY ST (4WD Only)
WILLIAMS RD
HARBERTS RD
ELLEN GR
DOUGLAS PDE
STATION RD (Fire Access Only)
Don
Ck
WESBURN
Doon Res
CITY
YARRA RIVER
Little Yarra
DOON RD
SETTLEMENT RD
CORDUROY RD
WARBURTON HWY
Warburton Trail
BARAK DR
RIVERVIEW PDE
SUNDEW PDE
CORBETTS RD
BLUEBELL LA
GARDEN HILL ST
ORCHID
LAUNCHING PLACE
WITNISH ST
VICTORIA RD
Yarra Junction Pmy
SCHOOL LA
CRESCENT RD
UPPER CRESCENT
GEORGE ST
LINDEN AV
HOLMES
VIEW RD
Parks
CFA Upper Yarra HQ
Yarra Junction Reserve
Tennis
The Yarra Cntr
B380
CFA
YARRA ST
HODDLE ST
WARREN LA
STATION
HERBERT ST
YARRA JUNCTION
MONS VIEW
FAHY CT DR
HILLTOP CT
Adanac Lodge Holiday Camp Christian Cntr
Yarra Valley Conduit
JOINS 347
COPYRIGHT © UNIVERSAL PRESS PTY LTD (PUBLISHER) 2004

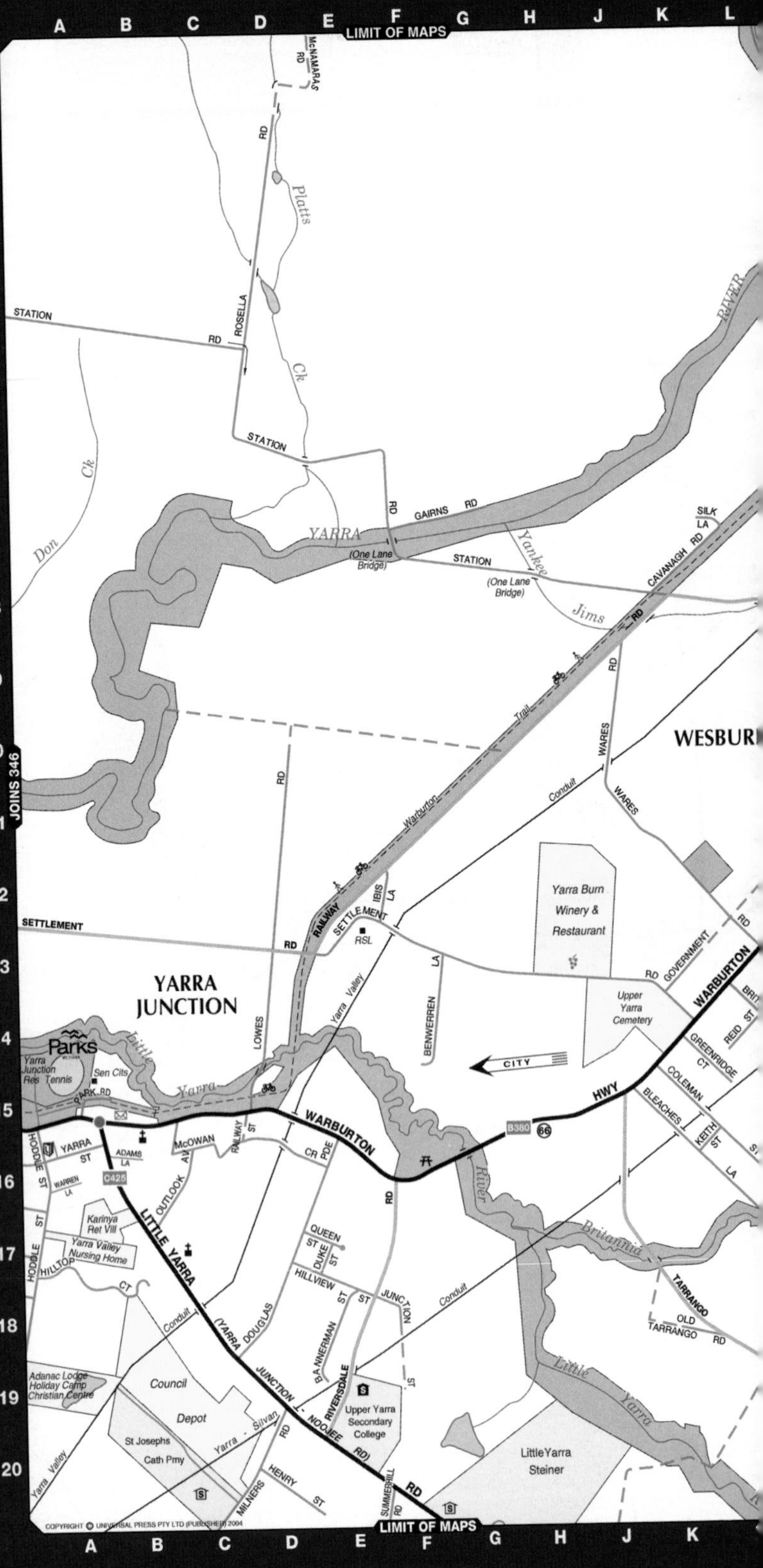

A B C D E F G H J K L

LIMIT OF MAPS

JOINS 346

LIMIT OF MAPS

A B C D E F G H J K

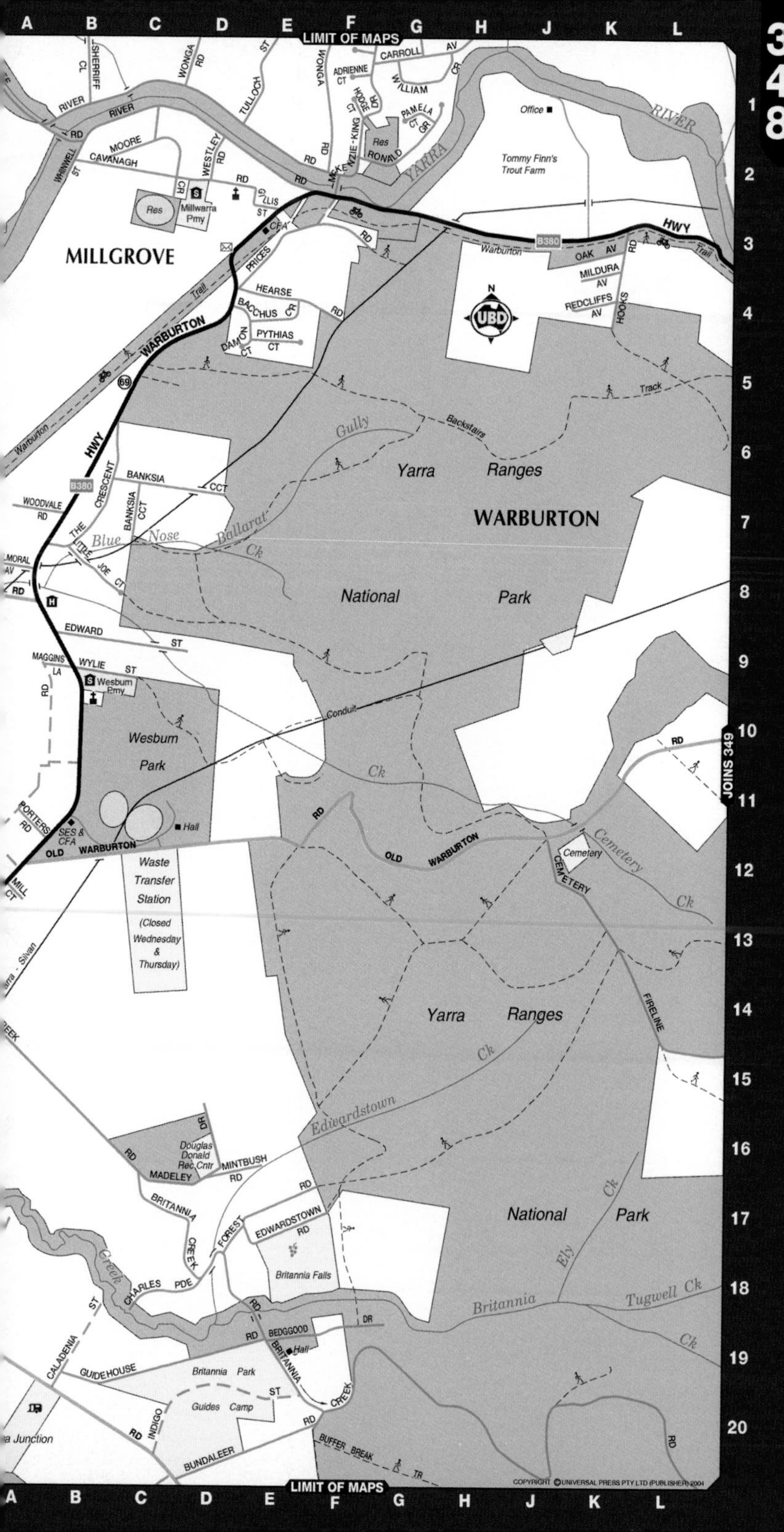
LIMIT OF MAPS
MILLGROVE
WARBURTON
Yarra Ranges National Park
Tommy Finn's Trout Farm
Office
YARRA RIVER
WARBURTON HWY
B380
Warburton Trail
Millwarra Pmy
Res
CFA
Wesburn Park
Wesburn Pmy
SES & CFA
Hall
Waste Transfer Station (Closed Wednesday & Thursday)
OLD WARBURTON RD
Cemetery
CEMETERY RD
Cemetery Ck
Conduit
Backstairs Track
Gully
Ballarat Ck
Blue Nose
Edwardstown Ck
Britannia Ck
Tugwell Ck
Ely Ck
FIRELINE
Douglas Donald Rec Cntr
MINTBUSH RD
MADELEY RD
BRITANNIA CREEK
FOREST RD
EDWARDSTOWN RD
Britannia Falls
CHARLES PDE
BEDGGOOD RD
BRITANNIA CREEK RD
Britannia Park
Guides Camp
GUIDEHOUSE
CALADENIA ST
INDIGO RD
BUNDALEER
BUFFER BREAK TR
JOINS 349
COPYRIGHT © UNIVERSAL PRESS PTY LTD (PUBLISHER) 2004

LIMIT OF MAPS

JOINS 348

WARBURTON

WESBURN

Yarra

National

Warburton Golf Course

Clubhouse

Warburton Chalet

Dolly Grey Park

St Josephs Cemi Cntr

Warburton Pmy

SDA Pmy

Cinema

Hall

CFA

RSL

Pav

YARRA RIVER

Scotchmans Ck

Strathbaan Ck

Backstairs Ck

Dirty Gully

Four Mile

Backstairs Track

Cemetery Track

Justice Track

MOUNT BRIDE RD

OLD WARBURTON RD

WARBURTON HWY

B380

72

STATION ST

DAMMANS RD

HIGHFIELD RD

CROOM ST

ALPINE ST

GLENBROOK RD

CECIL ST

SCOTCHMANS CREEK

MADELINE ST

WELLINGTON RD

WATERLOO AV

MARLINO

MARTYR RD

JOHNS RD

THOMAS AV

BRETT AV

HILL RD

HAND ST

RICHARDS RD

BRISBANE

GIBSONS PDE

WEBB ST

HILL RD

GRANT ST

CORNISH RD

BLACKWOOD

KELLYS

PARK RD

LALA

GABLE LA

FANTAIL RI

LEILA

STORY RD

CLARK

CLARKE AV

SYLVAN AV

UNITY CT

AZALEA CT

ANNE CR

BORONIA RD

IRRUKA RD

HORNERS RD

OLD WARBURTON

PROSPECT

RIVERSIDE

ESSEX ST

DERBY ST

LINCOLN

DAMMANS

SURREY

Gate

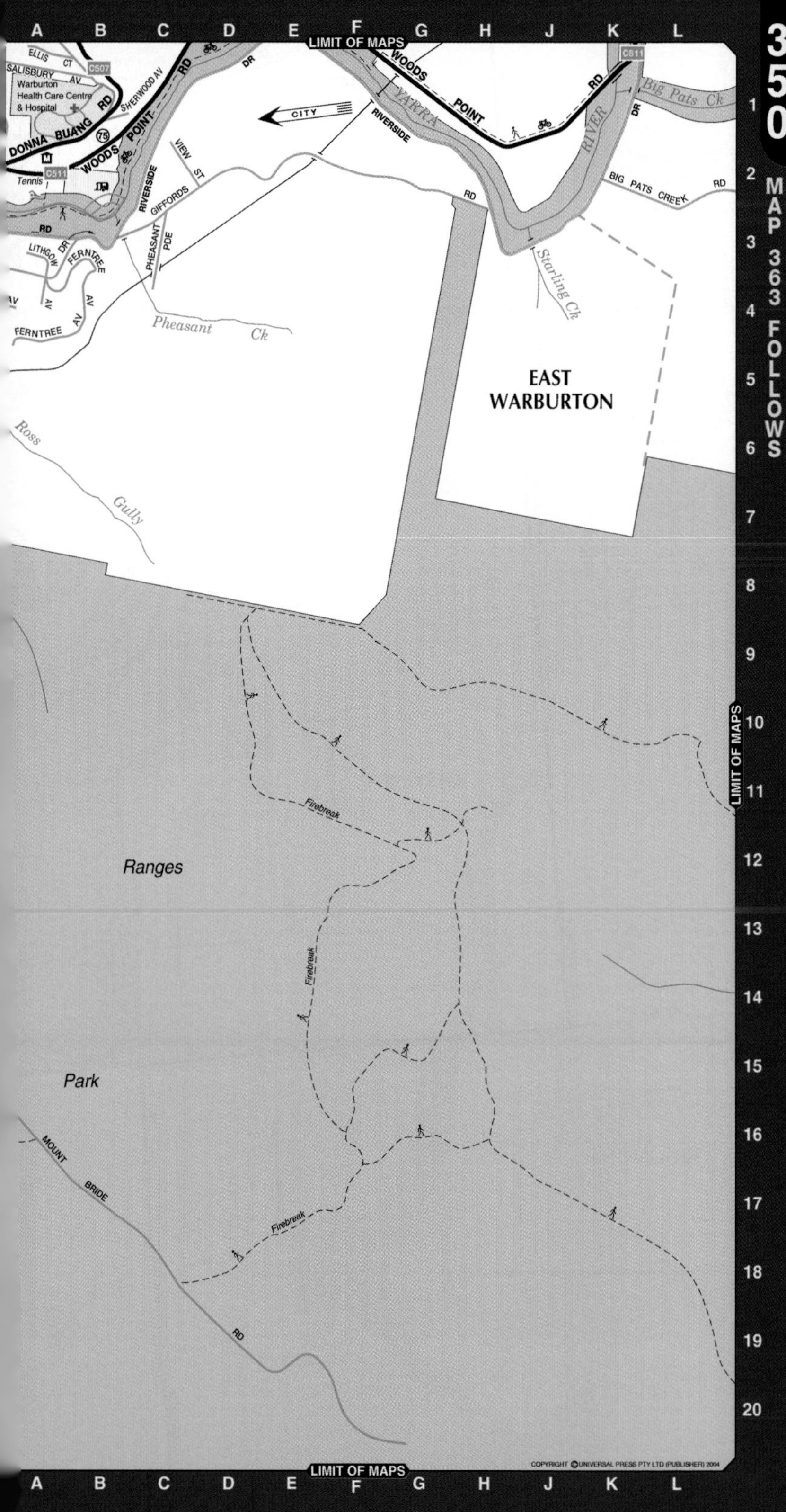
LIMIT OF MAPS
ELLIS CT
SALISBURY AV
C507
Warburton Health Care Centre & Hospital
DONNA BUANG RD
75
WOODS POINT RD
SHERWOOD AV
C511
Tennis
RIVERSIDE DR
VIEW ST
GIFFORDS
PHEASANT PDE
LITHGOW DR
FERNTREE AV
CITY
YARRA RIVER
Big Pats Ck
BIG PATS CREEK RD
Starling Ck
Pheasant Ck
EAST WARBURTON
Ross Gully
Firebreak
Ranges
Park
MOUNT BRIDE RD
MAP 363 FOLLOWS

PREVIOUS MAP 350

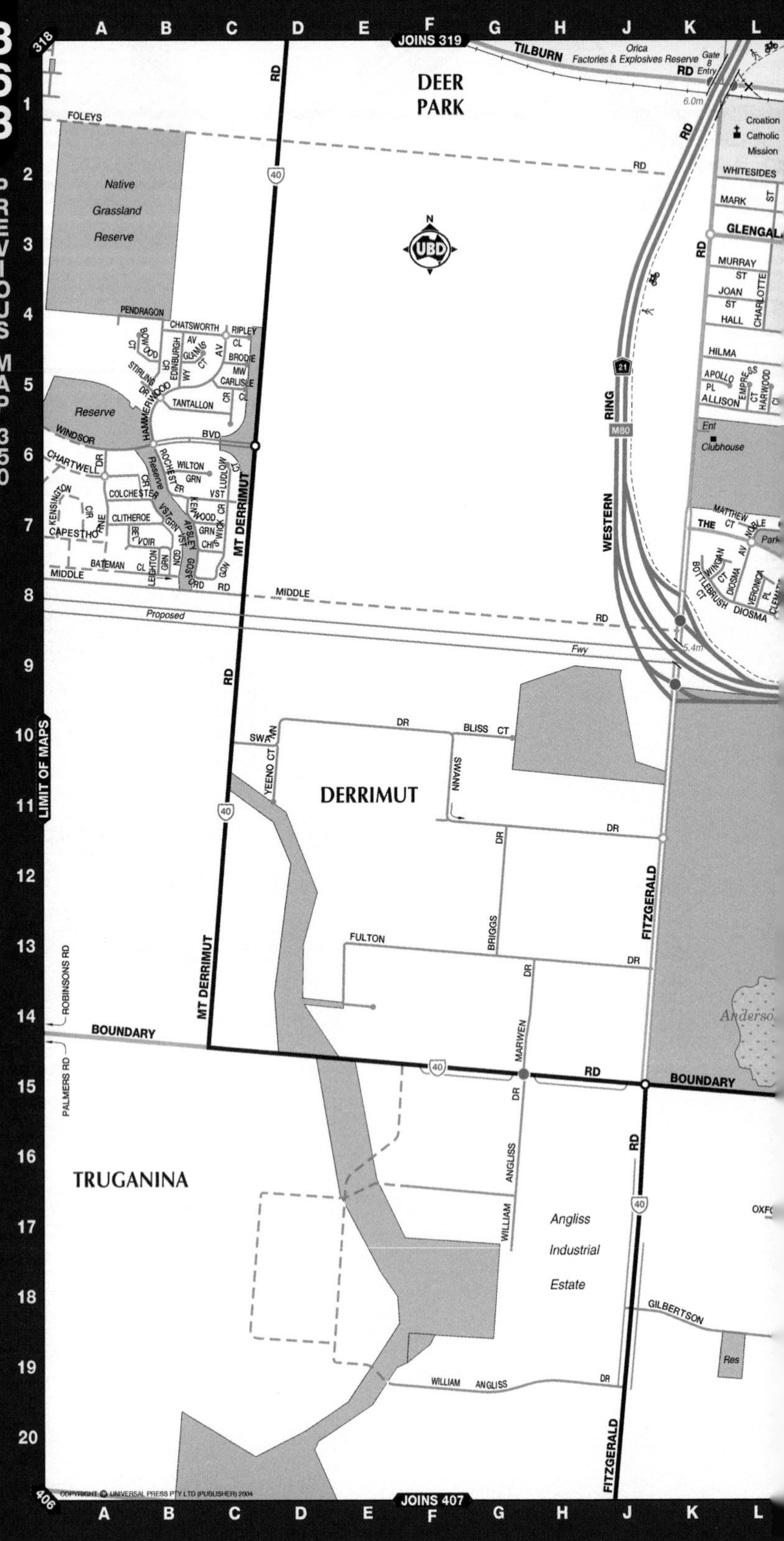

ALBION
SUNSHINE WEST
LAVERTON NORTH

McLAUGHLIN ST
SUSPENSION ST
WEST ST
HOLMES ST
LAWRENCE ST
Ardeer Primary
FORREST
YALLOURN ST
NORTH ST
TOWER ST
Ardeer Cmnty Pk
Ardeer
16.5
FORREST ST
DALWORTH ST
Selwyn Pk
Cmnty Cntr
Burnewang Res
BRUCE ST
McLEAN ST
BURNEWANG
KING ST
HUTCHINSON
ADELAIDE
EDWARD
St Theresas Cath Pmy
DRUMMARTIN ST
SYDNEY
RIDLEY
KOROROIT
BARCLAY
HAYDEN
ST
CR
AV
RIDGEWAY
NANCY ST
DAPHNE ST
FERN ST
MCH
CHANDLER ST
FRANK
ALDEN ST
NORTON ST
MENTHA ST
DALEY ST
PDE
RIDGEWAY
DAVEY
ARNOLD
SMART ST
Fbr
FRASER
ETHEL ST
RIPON ST
LORRAINE CT
Jeh Wit
AV
JAMES
EVELYN
WHITESIDES
AV
McINTOSH ST
Kororoit Ck
Benlynne Pk Nurs Home
MERNDA
LORNA
VERNON
Ainsworth Res
CR
RD
Cmnty Cntr
Marian Cath Coll
St Pauls Cath Pmy
ESTELLE ST
YOUNG
BELL
HENDRY
ANGUS
AINSWORTH
KEON ST
KOROWA
KRAMBRUK
KOSKY
KILLARA
RD
Sunshine College Ardeer Campus
MURRAY
JOAN ST
Ardeer South Primary
JOAN
NINA
EVA
COLLENSO
RAYMOND ST
GLENGALA
DAY
CARTER
GUM
ST ANDREW
RYDER ST
ARMSTRONG
BARDSLEY
MARCIA
MYERS
PELLEW
MCH
SIMMIE
GREGORY
OLDFIELD
Castley Res
ALLISON
MAILEY
LINKS
LACHLAN
HEATON CL
GOTHIC CT
MERRIVALE AV
STANBURY CT
Ralph Res
WRAY CT
COV
CORELLA
BRENT
FERNLEA
MAPLEDENE
LISBAN
Sunshine Heights Pmy
MAYNE
BERWICK
CALDER
LAROO
BEELA
ATUNGA
PINAROO
Sunshine College West Campus
WENDY WY
SANDERS
BEECH CT
THYRA
HAVEN CL
THE MEWS
ILUKA
AUSTRAL
DINNELL
MENTMORE
CL
WRIGHT
CAREN CT
WRIGHT ST
18
Sunshine Golf Club
SHELDON
MALABAR
BOA CT
LK
ADINA
YARALLA CR
ORANA
DELLA
NURLA
MIA CT
BAMBRA
MOIRA ST
BINYA
FREMONT
DALTON
DALPURA
Dalton Reserve
BOORAL DR
DAKARA
TEASDALE CT
Fbr
Arthur Beachley Res
CL
McGREGOR CT
KUTCHER
SALUATORE CT
DRESDEN WY
EUCALYPTUS CT
MAGENTA CT
SALTBUSH
DARWINIA
MARIT
ROAD
INGRAM
GUYS
DRINKWATER
KENNEY
HIBBS
McELROY
KILLEEN
Killeen Res
MAYO
DUNDALK ST
ANGUS
COUPER GR
BOREHAM
CLUES
KIM CT
DEN WY
BRIAR
CORELLA RD
THE AVENUE
DEAN CT
KERMEEN
FOX
MALONEY
WAITE
MUDFORD
SALIBA
LEWIS
CR
Cmnty Cntr
Glengala Primary
Tennis
Tallintyre Res
HUNT CT
AVENUE
GRESHAM WY
ANN
DIOSMA
WIRINGA
PAULA
LORETTA
YOLANTA
PETINA
TAMILYN
KATE
SUNRISE DR
LUCAS CT
HYETT
TALLINTYRE
EMSLIE
ARMOUR CT
JOWETT
St Peters Cath
PICKERSGILL
Pickersgill Res
FOXCROFT CT
GRESHAM WY
FEDERATION
NICHOLSON
LILLIS CT
CR
DR
BARNES CR
PATTEN
NAPIER
ROBERTS
PRESCOTT
HOWITT
BOOTH
WESTERN RING
MARCHANT CT
ROOKE CT
CAWOOD
MOURELL ST
FELSTED
BENNETT
KAY
BOYLE
DEED
WARMINGTON
MOUNSEY ST
McCOUBRIE
MORRISON
OAKES CT
VALENTINE
JONES
NASH CT
IVORY CT
Glengala Park Primary
Sunshine Spec Dev Sch
Service Centre
GLENGALA DR
WEST CCT
EAST CCT
SOMERVILLE RD
LAW CT
FAIRBAIRN
SOMERVILLE RD
32
Derrimut Native Grasslands
Service Centre
CITY
STREZLECKI AV
Parks
Australia Post Parcel Distribution Centre
INDUSTRIAL DR
NORMANBY AV
OVENS CT
COOK ST
Parkwest Industrial Estate
PARK WEST DR
SPENCER ST
FAIRBAIRN RD
5.35m
32
RD
BOUNDARY RD
PROGRESS CT
SILVERTON CL
CAMBRIDGE ST
RD
PLUMMER
SOMERLEIGH RD
LESLIE RD
LITTLE BOUNDARY RD
WESTSIDE
WESTSIDE DR
BURR CT
RAYMOND
HOLCOURT RD
RD
21
M80
THOMAS RD
STANLEY RD
ST
5.25m
MERINO ST
LINCOLN ST
Trail
RD
PIPE
HUME
Federation
15
5.2m
6.42m

JOINS 321

JOINS 364

320

A B C D E F G H J K L

SUNSHINE

SUNSHINE WEST

BROOKLYN

Village Sunshine Megaplex 20

Sunshine Marketplace Shopping Centre

Sunshine Plaza

Sunvale Primary

Sunshine East Primary

K G Chaplin Reserve

Barclay Res

Sunshine College Sen Campus

Sunshine Primary

Kevin Wheelahan Gardens

Caroline Chisholm Cath Coll

Kinder Smith Res

Cmnty Health Cntr

O'Brien Park

Hill Reserve

Parsons Res

Dept of Admin Services

Transport & Storage Group

Arthur Beachley Res

Buckingham Reserve

Dalgety and Elders Wool Handling Centre

Simsmetal

Brooklyn Landfill & Waste Recycling

Brooklyn Industrial Estate

DN Duanne Reserve

Brooklyn Res

Federation Trail

The Memorial Park Crematorium and Floral Lawn Cemetery

Urban Forest Res

W L J Crofts Res

A W Bond Res

HARVESTER RD

HAMPSHIRE RD

ANDERSON RD

FORREST ST

DURHAM RD

WRIGHT ST

SUNSHINE RD

SOMERVILLE RD

MARKET RD

McDONALD RD

PRINCES HWY

WEST GATE FWY

MILLERS RD

GRIEVE PDE

CORNWALL RD

DUKE ST

STATION PL

DEVONSHIRE RD

MONASH ST

SOUTH RD

HERTFORD RD

OLD GEELONG RD

BOUNDARY RD

408

JOINS 409

A B C D E F G H J K L

JOINS 322

323

A B C D E F G H J K L

BRAYBROOK

MAIDSTONE

WEST FOOTSCRAY

KINGSVILLE

TOTTENHAM

YARRAVILLE

JOINS 367

JOINS 410

411

A B C D E F G H J K L

322 JOINS 323

KELLAWAY AV
MITCHELL ST
VALNERE ST
MERLYN ST
PRINCE ST
MONASH ST
BIRDWOOD ST
MEPHAN ST
Jacks Magazine
MARIBYRNONG
Edgewater Lake
Thornbury Pk
MONASH ST
DUMBLANE AV
LANGS RD
RAS Showgrounds
PLUMMER ST
LENNON ST
Showgrounds
PDE
LEONARD CR
Members Car Park
Flemington Racecourse
FLEMINGTON
FOOTSCRAY
Footscray Res
Mervyn G Hughes Oval
Jensen Res
FARNSWORTH AV
FISHER PDE
FOR MORE DETAIL SEE MAP 725
Flemington Racecourse
Henry Turner Memorial Res
Footscray City Coll
Western Hospital
GORDON ST
WESTERN HWY
DROOP ST
Victoria University Footscray Park Campus
Footscray Park
A E Shepherd Oval
MARIBYRNONG BVD
WESTERN (BALLARAT RD) HWY
STIRLING ST
LYNCH ST
NEWELL ST
BEEVERS ST
MARKS LA
Newells Paddock
JOHNSON ST
CATHERINE ST
HOPKINS ST
HOPETOUN BRIDGE
DYNON
BARKLY ST
PRINCES HWY
Whitten Oval
West Footscray
Middle Footscray
Footscray
Gilmore Coll for Girls
Footscray Market
PAISLEY ST
FRENCH ST
IRVING ST
McNAB AV
Railway Res
BUNBURY ST
NAPIER ST
BUCKLEY ST
SEDDON
Victoria University Nicholson Campus
Footscray City Pmy
CHARLES ST
WILLIAMSTOWN RD
STATION RD
FOOTSCRAY RD
Wharves
P&O Ports
CODE ST
No 4 West
DOCK
SOMERVILLE RD
HYDE ST
WHITEHALL ST
MORELAND ST
DOCKLANDS HWY
Hammer Res
Yarraville Gardens
Victoria University Yarraville Campus
Melbourne Terminals
GIBBONS ST
OLIPHANT ST
No 3 West
No 2 West
SWANSON
Yarraville Oval
Yarraville
Theatre
ANDERSON ST
Beaton Res
Yarraville Wharves
No 1 Berth
MACKENZIE RD
No 1 West
RONA AV
LYELL ST
Orica Australia
Holden Swinging Basin
FRANCIS ST
Anderson Reserve
Westgate Golf Course
Mobil Oil Terminal
Holden Oil Dock
YARRA
YARRAVILLE
WEST GATE FWY
Stoney Creek Backwash
Spotswood Oval
SPOTSWOOD
Esso
RMIT Fishermans Bend Campus
Hawker de Havilland
Herald & Weekly Times
TODD RD
LORIMER ST
WHARF RD
Dept Defence Aeronautical Research Laboratory
JOINS 366

410 JOINS 411

A B C D E F G H J K L

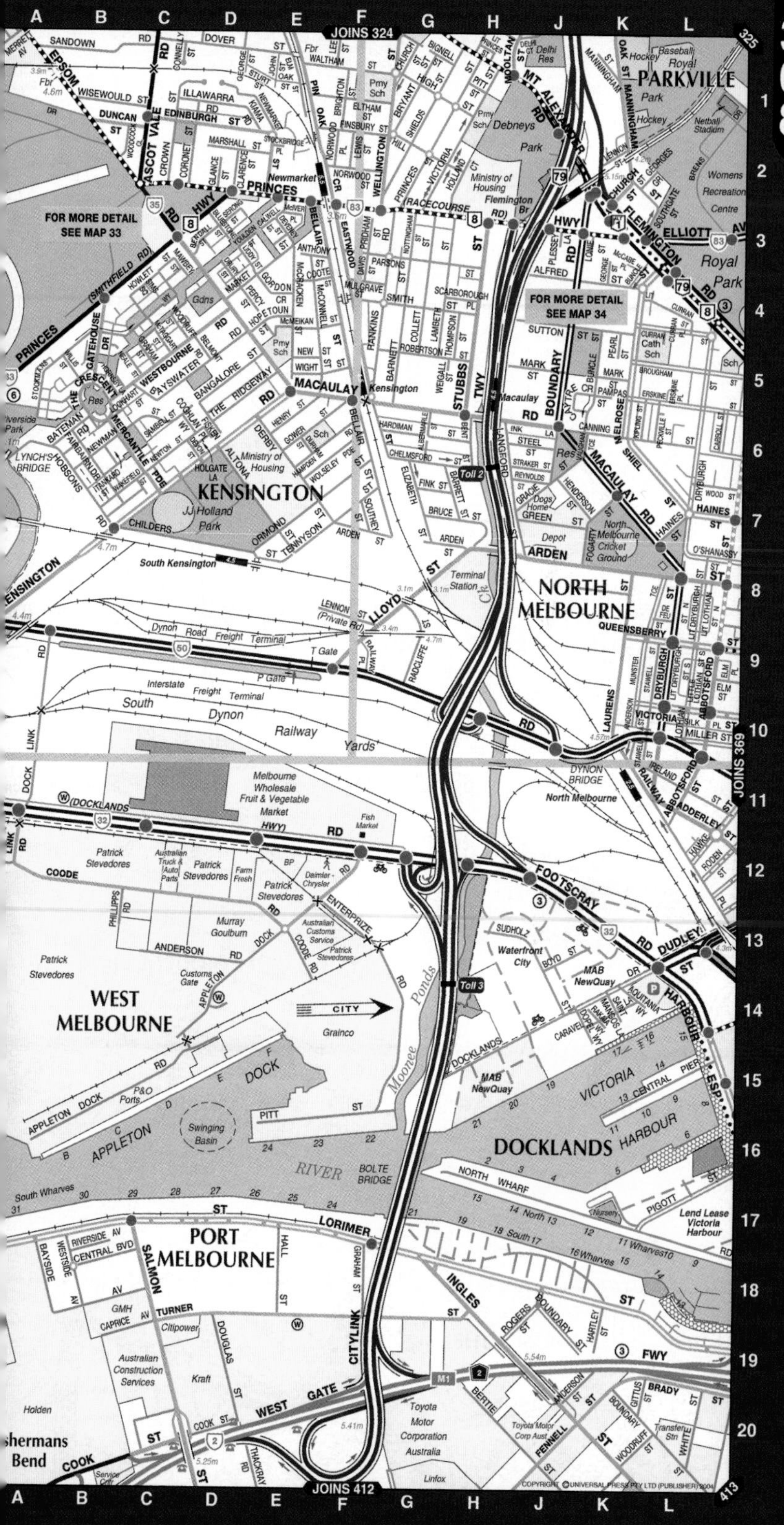

A B C D E F G H J K L
JOINS 324
325
1 2 3 4 5 6 7 8 9 10 11 12 13 14 15 16 17 18 19 20
PARKVILLE
Royal Park
Debneys Park
Ministry of Housing
Flemington Br
FOR MORE DETAIL SEE MAP 33
FOR MORE DETAIL SEE MAP 34
KENSINGTON
JJ Holland Park
Ministry of Housing
NORTH MELBOURNE
North Melbourne Cricket Ground
Arden Depot
Terminal Station
South Kensington
Dynon Road Freight Terminal
Interstate Freight Terminal
South Dynon Railway Yards
Melbourne Wholesale Fruit & Vegetable Market
DYNON BRIDGE
North Melbourne
JOINS 369
Patrick Stevedores
Australian Customs Service
Waterfront City
MAB NewQuay
WEST MELBOURNE
CITY
Grainco
Moonee Ponds
Swinging Basin
APPLETON DOCK
VICTORIA HARBOUR
DOCKLANDS
RIVER
BOLTE BRIDGE
NORTH WHARF
Lend Lease Victoria Harbour
PORT MELBOURNE
Australian Construction Services
Kraft
Holden
Fishermans Bend
Toyota Motor Corporation Australia
Toyota Motor Corp Aust
Transfer Stn
Linfox
JOINS 412
413
COPYRIGHT © UNIVERSAL PRESS PTY LTD (PUBLISHER) 2004

CARLTON NORTH

PARKVILLE

NORTH MELBOURNE

CARLTON

WEST MELBOURNE

MELBOURNE

DOCKLANDS

SOUTHBANK

Royal Park

Royal Melbourne Zoo

Princes Park

Melbourne General Cemetery

The University of Melbourne

Queen Victoria Market

Flagstaff Gardens

Carlton Gardens

Royal Exhibition Building

Telstra Dome

Federation Square

Melbourne Exhibition Centre

FOR MORE DETAIL SEE MAP 17

FOR MORE DETAIL SEE MAP 18

FOR MORE DETAIL SEE MAP 23

FOR MORE DETAIL SEE MAP 24

JOINS 368

JOINS 413

412

JOINS 326
327
FITZROY NORTH
Edinburgh Gardens
CLIFTON HILL
The Quarries Park
Darling Gardens
COLLINGWOOD
FOR MORE DETAIL SEE MAP 19
FOR MORE DETAIL SEE MAP 20
KEW
Victoria Park
ABBOTSFORD
FITZROY
Yarra Bend Park
JOINS 371
Carlton & United Breweries
EAST MELBOURNE
Fitzroy Gardens
Jolimont
FOR MORE DETAIL SEE MAP 25
FOR MORE DETAIL SEE MAP 26
RICHMOND
Melbourne Cricket Ground
Yarra Park
Melbourne Arena
Olympic Park
Gosch's Paddock
Royal Botanic Gardens
Government House
CREMORNE
JOINS 414
415
HEIDELBERG RD
ALEXANDRA PDE
EASTERN FWY
HODDLE ST
PUNT RD
VICTORIA PDE
VICTORIA ST
SWAN ST
BRIDGE RD
JOHNSTON ST
SMITH ST
NICHOLSON ST
CHURCH ST
A B C D E F G H J K L
1 2 3 4 5 6 7 8 9 10 11 12 13 14 15 16 17 18 19 20

326 JOINS 327 JOINS 370 JOINS 415 414

A B C D E F G H J K L

ALPHINGTON

FAIRFIELD

ABBOTSFORD

RICHMOND

HAWTHORN

BURNLEY

T H Westfield Reserve
Fairfield Park
Hall Reserve
The Quarries Park
Northern Melbourne Institute of TAFE (Fairfield Campus)
Thomas Embling Hospital (Victorian Institute of Forensic Mental Health)
Westfield North Oval
Westfield South Oval
Fairlea West Oval
Fairlea East Oval
Yarra Bend Park
Sir Herbert Olney Oval
W T Long Oval
Parks Victoria
Yarra Bend Public Golf Course
Corben Oval
Studley Park Boathouse
Studley Park
Boulevard Restaurant
Studley Park Golf Course
Dickinson Res
Norris Res
Canoeing
Caritas Christi Hospice
Xavier Prep
Xavier Coll
Austin Hospital
Royal Talbot Rehabilitation Centre
Royal Guide Dogs Association of Aust
AMCOR Packaging
Alphington Park
Latrobe Golf Course
Kate Campbell Res
Council & Recycling Depot
Willsmere Development
Kew Cottages
Mt Scopus Mem Coll
Nurs Home
Kew Pmy
Xavier College
Roche Oval
Plunkett Field
Foley Reserve
Tram Depot
Victoria Gdn Shop Cntr
Pridmore Park
St James Park
Grace Park
Glenferrie Sportsground
Melbourne Girls Sec Coll
Strathcona Girls
Burnley Oval
Richmond Public Golf Course
University of Melbourne Burnley Campus
Wallen Rd Res
Fairview Park
Survey Park
Glenferrie Sch
St Joseph's Cath
Erasmus Pmy Sch
GTV 9
Officeworks
Hawthorn

EASTERN FWY
CHANDLER HWY
PRINCESS ST
EARL ST
WILLSMERE RD
STUDLEY PARK RD
HIGH ST
COTHAM RD
BARKERS RD
DENMARK ST
CHURCH ST
BURWOOD RD
BRIDGE RD
SWAN ST
WALLEN RD
RIVERSDALE RD
POWER ST
BURNLEY ST
BARKLY AV
MADDEN GR
YARRA BVD
BOULEVARD
YARRA RIVER
WELLINGTON ST
HAWTHORN RD
GLENFERRIE RD
JOHNSTON ST
VICTORIA ST
HODDLE ST
WALMER ST
HODGSON ST
EGLINTON ST
MALMSBURY ST
FELLOWS ST
MOLESWORTH ST
STEVENSON ST
CARSON ST
FINDON ST
LIT CHURCH ST
GROVE RD
MANNINGTREE RD
LYNCH ST
LENNOX ST
ISABELLA GR
ELGIN ST
BARTON ST
DENHAM ST
HILL ST
CONNELL ST
KINKORA RD
MARY ST
CHRYSTOBEL CR
LUCERNE CR
ROEMER CR
DUKE ST
YARRA ST

JOINS 328

329

A B C D E F G H J K L

KEW EAST

KEW

BALWYN NORTH

BALWYN

CANTERBURY

CAMBERWELL

HAWTHORN EAST

Green - Acres Golf Club

Kew Golf Club

Willsmere Park

Hays Paddock

Boroondara Cemetery

Victoria Park

Stradbroke Park

Kew High

St Georges Hospital

Genazzano College

Methodist Ladies College

Carey Baptist Grammar Kew Campus

Preshil Sch

Ruyton Girls

Camberwell Anglican Girls Gram

Auburn Pmy

Kew East Pmy

Deepdene Pmy

Our Lady of Good Counsel Cath

Sacred Heart Cath

Childrens Traffic School (MPW)

Reservoir Reserve

Monastery

Outer Circle Linear Pk

Hawthorn East Tennis Reserve

Read Gdns

Delivery Centre

Priv Hosp

Glenferrie

Auburn

Camberwell

Swinburne Uni of Tech

Swinburne Sec Coll

Universal Press

EASTERN FWY

HIGH ST

HARP RD

BURKE RD

BELMORE RD

WHITEHORSE RD

BARKERS RD

MONT ALBERT RD

RATHMINES ST

CANTERBURY RD

VICTORIA ST

CAMBERWELL RD

RIVERSDALE RD

TOORONGA RD

AUBURN RD

GLENFERRIE RD

FOR MORE DETAIL SEE MAP 722

JOINS 373

JOINS 416

417

A B C D E F G H J K L

A B C D E F G H J K L

JOINS 329

JOINS 372

JOINS 417

328 416

BALWYN NORTH

BALWYN

CANTERBURY

SURREY HILLS

THE MUSCA ST, LIBRA ST, AQUILA, TAURUS ST, CAPELLA ST, VEGA, PAVO ST, URSA, BULLEEN RD, BERNARD, NEVADA, TURNLEY ST, ECHO, LUCIFER, AJAX, MINERVA, SATURN, HELSTON, FAY ST, FINTONIA, KAWARREN, ORAVEL ST, CORONA ST, KYORA, MT VIEW PDE, CASCADE, RIVERSIDE GR, WATTLE, INVERNESS, WALBUNDRY AV, BOULEVARD, WAY, THE MOOR, TOORANG AV, THE NOOK, RIVERVIEW, CITY, Child Care, Res, RUTH, Boroondara Pk Primary, VICARS, Leigh Park, PENN, MIDVALE, ELLENDALE, DUMBLANE, WOODVILLE, SYLVANDER, TANNOCK, MCH, RSL, CENTRE, LYNNE CT, ARDGOUR, AGNES, HARRINGTON, JASERFOLD, CORBY, ROOKWOOD, WILLIS, DONCASTER RD, Cmnty Cntr, MACEDON, St Bede Cath, SUNBURST, FORTUNA, LONGVIEW, CITYVIEW, PANORAMIC, MOUNTAIN VIEW, HILL, BALWYN RD, BOLINDA, ALMOND, VIEWHILL, WALNUT, FERDINAND, DEMPSTER, TUXEN, CHELMSFORD, TORMEY, JOINT, MAUD, HATFIELD, MARWAL, HIGHBURY ST, OSBURN, THACKRAY, HOUGHTON, SUTTON, Child Care, STEPHENS, DUGGAN, FRANK, ELLSA, RANGEVIEW, ASHBY, MCH, Balwyn North Pmy, LANSDOWN, MADDEN, MCSHANE, Greythorn Park, Tennis, MAUGHAN PDE, MOODY, DOUGLAS, GARDNER CT, EUROLIE, BOORAHMAN, HOSKEN, GREIVE, ROBERT, MAYLANDS AV, HOOD, COBHAM, Balwyn High, SYLVAN, DIGHT, ILLAWARRA, ALBURY, NIXON, ALPHA, GAMA, ROEHAMPTON, AYLMER, SEVERN, GILDAN, Myrtle Park, Baseball, Macleay Park, Tennis, LLOYD, Hislop Reserve, DON, TOVEY, KENNY, READING, Gordon Barnard Reserve, Aquatic & Leisure Centre, CARRINGTON, Res, RENOWN, JUNE, Grey Pmy, LEXTON, LAWSON, HUNT ST, MACASSAR, KENDARI, TOWER, BUCHANAN, MORRIS, HUGHES, PAGE, HEATHER, KELBA, DUNSTAN ST, BURTON ST, WANBROW, LOMA LINDA, WYNYARD CR, BELMORE RD, BIRTLES, PAISLEY ST, PARA ST, BIRDWOOD, HENDER, LYNCH CT, BERNBOROUGH, STROUD, DEE, Bellmore Sch, KALENO, ALANDALE, WOODS, JACKA, PALMER, TIVEY, RUBY, HIGHLAND, TONKIN AV, RAYNES, COLLINS, ETON CT, GLENLUSS, Nurs Home, CLAYTON RD, NAROO, Tennis, Res, CANYON, WYNETTE, ROPLEY, KING, NUNGERNER, METUNG, MONASH, ELLIOTT, SEVENOAKS, HILDA, HENLEY, YONGALA, FREDERICK, BELGROVE, WINMALEE, DUNURE, ROGERSON, HILARY, MARITANA, MELBA, BRUCE, BURROUGHS, PORTER, GORDON, FREEMAN, GROSVENOR PDE, EDAM CT, DUNDEE, MARION, WALLACE, LINCKENS, KALGURLI, DELFI, LIBORIA, PARKDALE AV, BECKETT, CARMEL, BENNETT, HAIG, KITCHENER, NOTT, A.I.F., HAMILTON, IAN ST, YARRBAT, Arthur Preston Cntr, SANCTUARY CR, Maranoa Gardens, Beckett Park, YONGA RD, PRETORIA, MEADOW, LEONARD, TERRY, MAY, HARDWICKE, PERCY, NORBERT, AUSTIN, WALKER, EDMOND, CREMORNE, KALIMNA, ELLEN ST, HENRY ST, JURANG, MANGAN, YERRIN, IRAMOO, All Hallows Cath Pmy, BRENBEAL, KIREEP, PARRING, BANOOL, HERTFORD CR, KAARA, NARRAK, WHITEHORSE RD, Delivery Centre, Deepdene Park, PARKSIDE AV, BELMONT AV, LYDIA, MALEELA, Balwyn Manor Ret Vill, Cinema, TEDSTONE, WESTON, JOHN, POWER, Balwyn Park, MCH, Balwyn Pmy, Fintona Girls, Ret Vill, CONNELL CT, CREST, CHATFIELD, REID, BEVAN, GRANT, GEORGIAN, PROWSE, JERSEY, BOSTON, CHERRY, TALBOT AV, CONWAY CR, Balwyn Cmnty Cntr, SHEPRETH, PALM GR, WALSH, HIGHTON, OAKDALE, Belmont Pk, BOWLEY, RUHBANK, MILLAH RD, ROCHESTER, WEIR, Res Sen Cits, COMO AV, MELDRETH, THORNTON, CLYDE, WHARTON, Chatham Pmy, BANOOL, ROSS, GROVEDALE, Camberwell Grammar, MYAMBERT, SALISBURY, REUMAH CT, KNUTSFORD, CARRONSHORE CL, MARROCK PL, SALFORD, PEMBROKE, VAUXHALL, John August Res, EVERGREEN, NORTHCOTE, NORRIS, WELLS ST, NEATH ST, WEYBRIDGE, MONT ALBERT RD, ATHOL, IRILBARRA, GRANGE AV, WINSON GREEN, BENSON, WANDSWORTH, STANLEY, KNOX, Shierlaw, AVENUE, MANGARRA, Canterbury Girls, MALACCA, WENTWORTH, VIEW, St Johns Home for Boys & Girls, EMPRESS, SIR GARNET, JOCELYN, SURREY RD, RUBENS, GWENDA, ALEXANDRA, MONOMEATH, SNOWDEN, VICTORIA, HOPETOUN, DAPHNE, ERICA, Cmnty Cntr, Nursing Home, FLINDERS AV, VAUGHAN AV, FAVERSHAM, GUILDFORD, Canterbury Sportsground, CROYDON, Grnd, Boroondara Pk, CANTERBURY RD, BEAUMONT ST, MYRTLE, CHAUCER CR, MARLOWE ST, KEATS, BORONIA, BALWYN, DELANY, Canterbury Gdns MCH, SHIERLAW, Colville Res, CHATHAM AV, WEST, JUNCTION, KINGSTON, Chatham, ROBINSON, SUNBURY, Nurs Home, STANLEY, TCE, Tennis, SEFTON PL, BROADWAY, DUDLEY, KENDALL ST, PDE, Canterbury, THEATRE, MALING RD, WILLANDRA AV, MARGARET, REDVERS, East Camberwell, WARBURTON, CHURCH ST, LEURA ST, St Andrews Pmy, Mary McKillop Res, KENT, NORFOLK, STANHOPE, KINGSLEY, MOORHOUSE, BOW, SPENCER, MARDEN ST, MATLOCK, CROSS, GOLDING ST, SHORT, McGREGOR, PAYNE, DENMARK, Matlock Res, MORESBY, CARINDA, DRYDEN, MILTON, CLAREMONT CR, Strathcona Girls Grammar, BRYSON, WATTLE VALLEY RD, SELWYN, TYNDALL, KENNEALY, MIDDLESEX, PROSPECT HILL, Nurs Home, SCOTT, FELIX, AUSTRAL, SUFFOLK, KASOUKA RD, DERBY, PALMERSTON, BRINSLEY ST, WANDIN, Camberwell High, BYRON, BURNSIDE, ALTA, QUANTOCK, HASSETT, LOGAN, GRIOTTE, MOLESWORTH, LEEDS, Canterbury Pmy, HIGHFIELD, ALBION, Tennis, DOME, DURHAM, THAMES, ESSEX, ARUNDEL CR, YORK

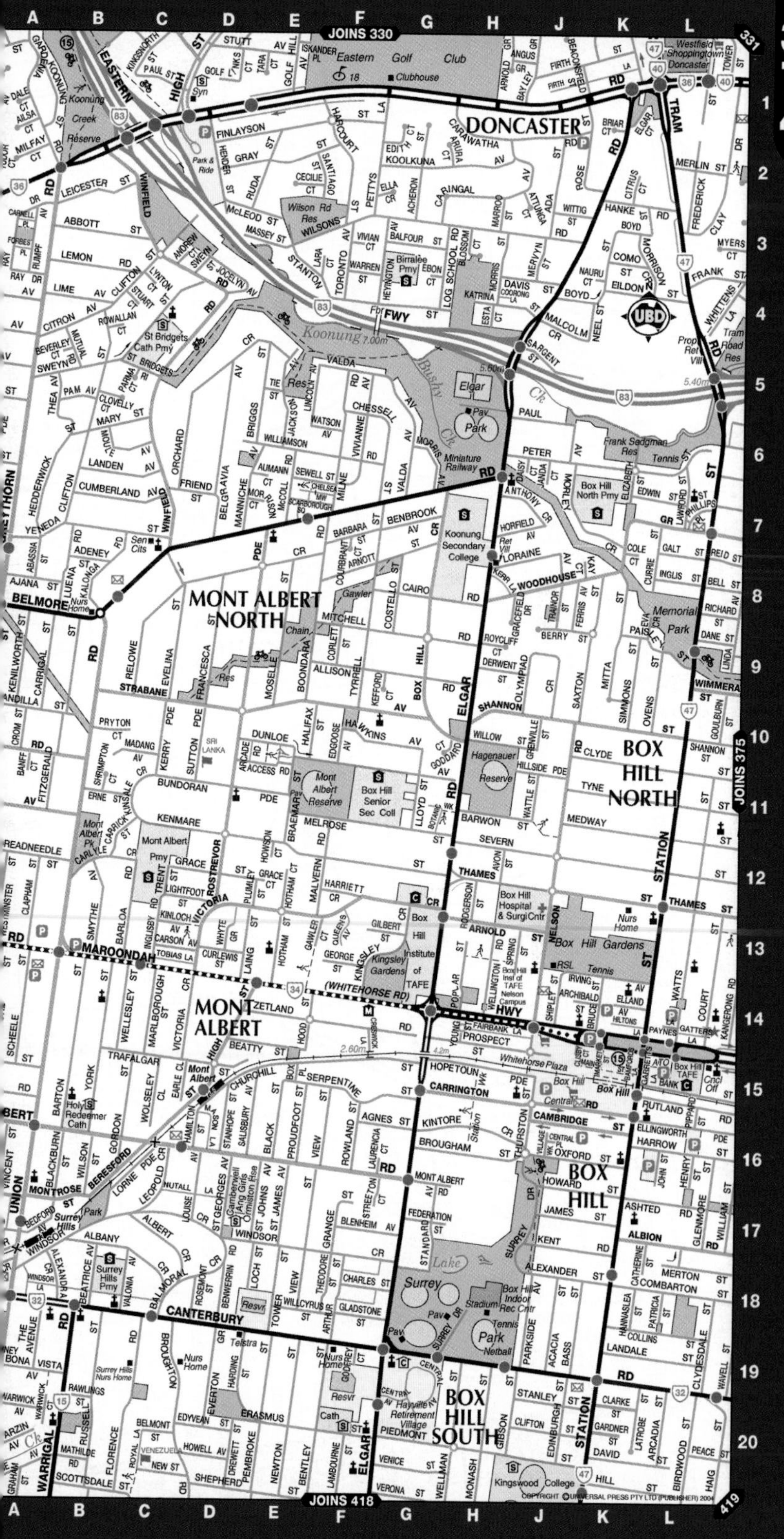

A B C D E F G H J K L
JOINS 330
331
Eastern Golf Club
Clubhouse
Westfield Shoppingtown Doncaster
DONCASTER
Koonung Creek Reserve
EASTERN
HIGH ST
FINLAYSON
Park & Ride
LEICESTER ST
Wilson Rd Res
WILSONS
McLEOD ST
MASSEY ST
STANTON
Birralee Pmy
LOG SCHOOL RD
ABBOTT
LEMON RD
LIME AV
CITRON AV
St Bridgets Cath Pmy
FWY
Koonung 7.00m
Bushy Ck
Elgar Park
Miniature Railway
VALDA
CHESSELL
Frank Sedgman Res
Tennis
Box Hill North Pmy
Koonung Secondary College
Memorial Park
BELMORE RD
MONT ALBERT NORTH
Gawler Chain
STRABANE
SRI LANKA
Mont Albert Reserve
Box Hill Senior Sec Coll
Hagenauer Reserve
BOX HILL NORTH
JOINS 375
Mont Albert Pk
Mont Albert Pmy
ELGAR RD
BOX HILL
STATION ST
Box Hill Hospital & SurgiCntr
Box Hill Institute of TAFE
Kingsley Gardens
Box Hill Gardens
Tennis
MAROONDAH
(WHITEHORSE RD)
HWY
MONT ALBERT
Whitehorse Plaza
Box Hill Central
Box Hill TAFE
Holy Redeemer Cath
CARRINGTON
MONT ALBERT RD
Surrey Hills
UNION
Camberwell Ang Girls Grammar School
Surrey Hills Pmy
Resvr
Surrey Lake
Box Hill Indoor Rec Cntr
Stadium
Tennis
Park
Netball
CANTERBURY RD
Surrey Hills Nurs Home
Nurs Home
Telstra
Hayville Retirement Village
BOX HILL SOUTH
Kingswood College
WARRIGAL RD
VENEZUELA
JOINS 418
COPYRIGHT © UNIVERSAL PRESS PTY LTD (PUBLISHER) 2004
419
1 2 3 4 5 6 7 8 9 10 11 12 13 14 15 16 17 18 19 20

JOINS 331

330

A B C D E F G H J K L

DONCASTER

DONCASTER EAST

BLACKBURN NORTH

BOX HILL NORTH

BOX HILL

THE BLACKBURN

BOX HILL SOUTH

DONCASTER RD

EASTERN FWY

WETHERBY RD

MIDDLEBOROUGH RD

SPRINGFIELD RD

WHITEHORSE RD

MAROONDAH HWY

CANTERBURY RD

STATION ST

BLACKBURN RD

Koonung Creek

Gardiners Creek

Bushy Creek

Eram Park

Tram Road Reserve

Springfield Park

Bolton Park

City Oval

Box Hill Cemetery

Blacks Walk Reserve

Kalang Park

RHL Sparks Reserve

Koonung Reserve

Furness Park

Blackburn High

Box Hill High

Doncaster Community Centre

National Bus Company

Hewlett Packard

JOINS 374

JOINS 419

418

JOINS 332
333
DONVALE
OLD WARRANDYTE RD
MITCHAM RD
SPRINGVALE RD
BLACKBURN RD
TUNSTALL RD
Donburn Pmy
Devon Plaza
Donvale Rehab
Tunstall Square
Haggar Res
Perpetua Nursing Home
Shirvington Ret Vill
Pinetree Retirement Village
Donvale Reserve
Beverley Hills Pmy
Nurs Home and Ret Vill
Donvale Pmy
Manningham Donvale Indoor Sports Centre
Mullum Creek
FWY
Proposed Freeway Due for Completion Mid 2005
Slater Reserve
Springvale Rd Reserve
Proposed Development
Ronald E Gray Reserve
St Philips Cath
Springview Pmy
Nicoll Park
Warekila Res
Linvale Walk Res
JUNCTION RD
SPRINGFIELD RD
JOINS 377
Ashlar Ct Res.
Jeh Wit
Tunstall Park
Nunawading Pmy
Feiglin Reserve
Arts Theatre Centre
Whitehorse Civic Centre
Walker Park
Wirilda Park Res
MAROONDAH HWY
NUNAWADING
Nunawading
Wood Park
Sen Cits
Rec Cntr
SDA Convent Ground
SDA Pmy & Coll
Nurs Home
Eastern Mall Centre
Victoria Deaf Society Nursing Home
Blackburn Lake Sanctuary
Blackburn Lake
Blackburn Lake Pmy
Retirement Village
Erskine Walk
Reserve
Charles Rooks Reserve
Nunawading South Pmy
Glen Valley Rd Res
JOINS 420
421
COPYRIGHT © UNIVERSAL PRESS PTY LTD (PUBLISHER) 2004

JOINS 333

PARK ORCHARDS

DONVALE

MITCHAM

VERMONT

JOINS 376

JOINS 421

JOINS 334
335

A B C D E F G H J K L

1 2 3 4 5 6 7 8 9 10 11 12 13 14 15 16 17 18 19 20

RINGWOOD NORTH

RINGWOOD

RINGWOOD EAST

HEATHMONT

WARRANDYTE RD

RINGWOOD ST

WANTIRNA RD

MAROONDAH HWY

MOUNT DANDENONG RD

OBAN RD

WONGA RD

BEDFORD RD

GREAT RYRIE ST

DUBLIN RD

HEATHMONT RD

RINGWOOD BPS

(WHITEHORSE RD)

Tabor College

Nth Pmy

Nursing Home

Community Centre

Holy Spirit

Mahon Res

McAlpin Reserve

North Ringwood Res

B J Hubbard Reserve

Mullum Pmy

Norwood Secondary College

Child Care

Norwood Reserve

Sen Cits

Nurs Home

Mullum Mullum Reserve

Notlen St Res

Manvantara Hospital

Karralyka Theatre

East Ringwood Res

Ringwood Civic & Cultural Centre

Cncl Off

Amaroo Private Nurs Home

Ringwood Private Hosp

Cinema

Eastland

Court House

Ringwood Market

Ringwood Square

RACV

Ringwood Lake Park

Bedford Park

Ringwood Secondary College

Our Ladys Cath

RSL

Greenwood Park

Ringwood Ret Vill

Knaith Rd Res

A F Bloing Res

Good Shepherd Ret Vill

Croquet Tennis

Jubilee Park

Ringwood Aquatic Centre

Soccer

Aquinas Cath Sec College

Retarding Basin

Great Ryrie Pmy

Herman Pump Res

Leoni Park

A C Robertson Field

Pav

Baseball

Proclamation Park

Southwood Boys Grammar

Cadbury Schweppes

Heathmont Park Tennis

Ringwood Municipal Golf Course

Clubhouse

Mullum Mullum Ck

JOINS 379

JOINS 422

423

A B C D E F G H J K L

A B C D E F G H J K L

334
JOINS 335

1 2 3 4 5 6 7 8 9 10 11 12 13 14 15 16 17 18 19 20

CROYDON

RINGWOOD

CROYDON SOUTH

RINGWOOD EAST

HEATHMONT

Kalinda Urban Forest

Kalinda Primary

Cherry Tree Grove Retirement Village

Croydon Hotel

Douglas Maggs Res

Alto Flora Res

Nurs Home

Croydon West Pmy

Maroondah Secondary College

Cmnty Cntr

Ainslie Park

Grandfill Res

Peter Vergers Res

Tennis

Sacred Heart Monastery

Mingarra Ret Vill

Don-Wood Nursing Home

Res

Maroondah Hospital

Cheong Sanc

Cheong Park

Netball

Pony Club

MCH

Ringwood East

Knaith Rd Res

Tintern Anglican Girls Grammar

Tinternvale Pmy

Eastwood Pmy

Irabina Special Development Sch

Herman Pump Res

Wombolano Park

Gracedale Park

Tennis

Jeh Wit

Dupont Australia

CITY

Heathmont East Pmy

Heathmont Golf Park (Par 3)

H E Parker Reserve

Glen Park

Cmnty Cntr

MAROONDAH HWY

MOUNT DANDENONG RD

EASTFIELD RD

CANTERBURY RD

BAYSWATER RD

WICKLOW AV

JOINS 378
JOINS 423
422

CROYDON
BAYSWATER NORTH
KILSYTH
KILSYTH SOUTH
BAYSWATER
BORONIA

Croydon Park
Dorset Gardens
Dorset Recreational Reserve
Dorset Golf Course
Metropolitan Traffic Education Centre
Maroondah Cycle Training Centre
Bungalook Creek Retarding Basin
Melb Water
Bungalook Conservation Reserve
Kilsyth Oval
Town Park
Swinburne Uni of Tech TAFE Croydon Campus
Australian Auto Air
Arrabri Cmnty Centre

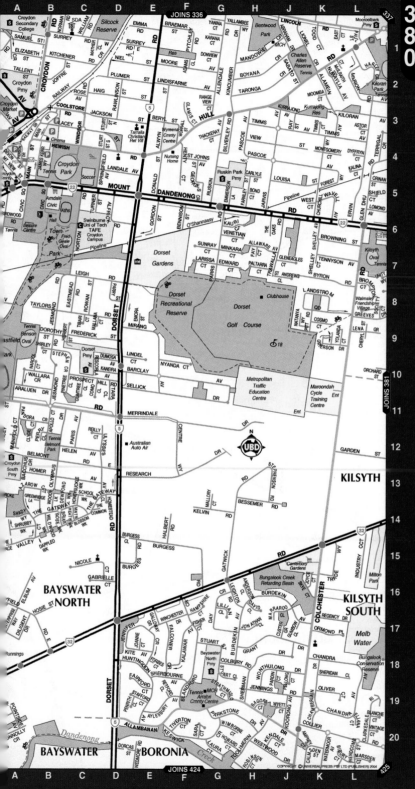

A B C D E F G H J K L

336 JOINS 337

KILSYTH

KILSYTH SOUTH

CAMBRIDGE RD · MOUNT DANDENONG RD · LIVERPOOL RD · CANTERBURY RD · GLASGOW RD · SHEFFIELD RD · DURHAM RD · PEMBROKE RD · LONGFELLOW AV · MOUNTAIN VIEW RD · HAWTHORY RD · CARDIGAN RD · PINE RD · ZINA GR · O'Shannassy Pipeline

Pembroke Secondary College Senior Campus · Nursing Home · Peter James Centre · Mooroolbark Heights Reserve · Kiloran Tennis Park · Centenary · Pembroke Pmy · Pembroke Secondary College Cambridge Campus · Elizabeth Bridge Res · Kilsyth Primary · Sen Cits Hansen Park · Kilsyth Oval · Tennis · Walmsley Friendship Village · MCH · St Richards Cath Pmy · Nursing Home · Wirraminna Reserve · Montrose Reservoir · Melbourne Water · Kirkbrae Presbyterian Ret Vill & Nurs Home · Hazelmere Nursing Home · Kilsyth Sports Centre · Pinks Reserve · Gladesville Pmy · Park · Quarry · Park · Chaucer Park · Eastwood Plaza · Milton Park · Melb Water · Melbourne Water · Bungalook Conservation Res · Ghilgai · Eastwood Golf Course 18 · Res · Billar P

HIGHLAND · CAMBRIDGE GDN · HARLEY CT · MACMILLAN ST · GREENVILLE ST · MARION AV · KILORAN AV · ASTOR CT · TERRIGAL · IDINIA ST · CRINAN ST · ERVIN · GLEN DHU · SHIELD CT · LOMOND · LOCH ST · AMELIA CT · MARGARET · CATHERINE CT · CAMERON · HYDE PL · WINDSOR · ST JAMES · KENSINGTON PL · HOLMES RD · DRYDEN · SHELDON AV · ELIOT CT · DONNE CT · BROOKES CT · SHAKESPEARE AV · MASEFIELD AV · SWINBURNE AV · BRIDGES AV · DENNIS CT · YATES CT · MILTON CNC · GORDON CT · LAWSON · BALLANTYNE · DUNROSSIL DR · CRADLEY CT · BAINBRIDGE CT · ALASTAIR CT · OSWIN CT · PICCADILLY CT · DALLAS CT · FLORENCE ST · BIRKENHEAD · MOUNTFIELD RD · COLEBROOK RD · FERGUSON · MORRISON CR · CAROLINE ST · BEATRICE · ANITA · BICKLEIGH-VALE RD · EDNA WALLING LA · LAURA LA · FIELDEN CL · GREENWOOD LA · FERN LEIGH · VILLAGE WK · COTTAGE CL · LOUPIE ST · ROSNY PL · DYSART DR · DELMONT CT · LUTANA CT · RACHAEL CT · LEVENDALE AV · PENALGA RD · MACDONNELL CT · MAPLE CT · WILLOW CT · HAMMERSLEY CT · JACARANDA AV · ACACIA AV · AMBER CT · TI-TREE CT · BEECH CT · ERICA CR · BRISTOL CT · MILFORD · SENAR ST · STRZELECKI CT · HILDEGARD CT · REGINA · CARINA CT · TREETOP DR · EDENHOPE · PENDLE PL · EDEN WY · CORNELIA CL · WALNUT CT · FIR CT · STRATHBOGIE CT · ATHERTON CT · Mt Waverley · CHESTNUT · STIRLING CT · FLINDERS CT · ALPINE · BRETBY WY · WINTON CT · BANKSIA · DOREEN · TOWER ST · HANSEN RD · EOTHEN · NORTH RD · CHARLES ST · COLLINS PL · MOIRA · DERBY · BELVOIR CT · ASHBY · DENMAN ST · TAMWORTH · BALMORAL · SOPHIE ST · DEBORAH ST · ARNOLD ST · HAYES CT · KILBORN CT · GLENDALE CT · CHERYLNNE · PALM GR · WANNAN CT · KILSYTH AV · MIMOSA AV · HILLVIEW DR · GEOFFREY · LOCKHART CT · GLADESVILLE · HAMILTON CR · HANSFORD CL · DONALD CL · DAVID CL · FERNBANK CT · BUTTLER ST · LANDY CT · TWOBAR PL · URANA ST · ORCHARD ST · RUSSO PL · CHURCH ST · LEONARD RD · PLEASANT ST · AARON PL · LUSCOMBE CT · KEVIN CT · GRAHAM AV · UNITY WY · FRIENDLY CT · BROMPTON CT · SOCIETY CT · GREEVES GR · FELLOWSHIP · LENA ST · CHERYL ST · BELINDA CL · EVA CT · PARAMOUNT AV · TINARRA CT · LUCAS AV · LADE AV · GARDEN ST · MERSEY RD · JANE CT · PAM CT · LEEDS DR · SOUTHFORK DR · EAST SPUR CT · INDUSTRY CCT · SUNSET DR · JEANETTE MAREE CT · CLOVERLEA DR · TEREDDAN DR · ARLIE CR · WOODRIDGE CL · ROSLYN ST · ASH GR · KIRKWOOD CT · CRESTVIEW CL · ACTOAL CT · MAYFIELD CT · CLAIRE CT · SMITHACRES · MAGNOLIA GR · SARAH · GRATTEN · FUSSELL RD · BRIGHT · HAKEA · RUBICON VALLEY · ROWE CT · JUBILEE · EUNICE CT · CHLOE CL · CLARKEDALE RI · BLANCHE CT · VINTAGE CT · JODIE PL · SANDY WYN · PIONEER · COLLIER RD · INDEPENDANCE RI · MARSDEN CT · LOBOSCO CT

CITY

22 · 32

JOINS 380

424 JOINS 425

A B C D E F G H J K L

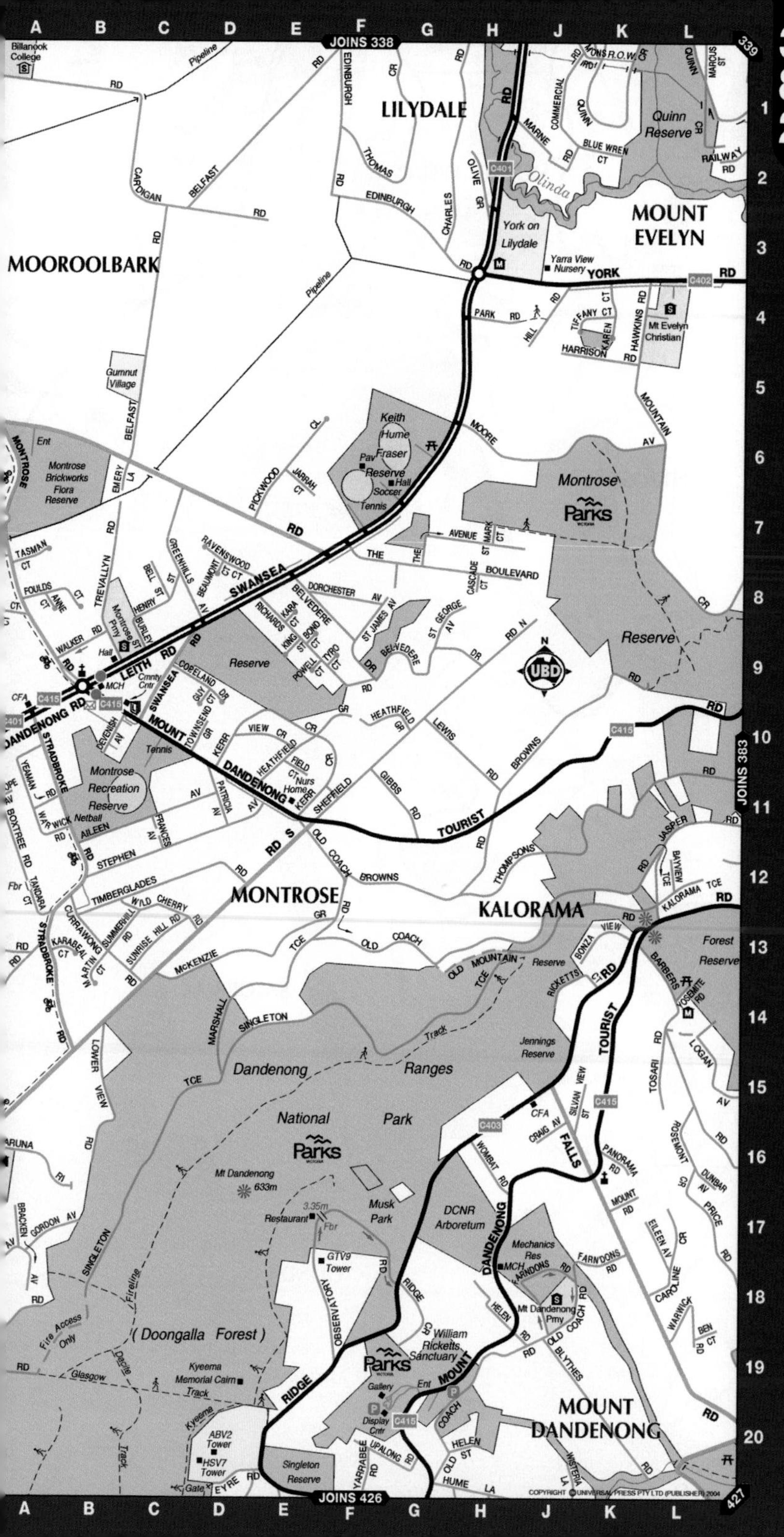

JOINS 338
JOINS 383
JOINS 426
339
427
LILYDALE
MOUNT EVELYN
MOOROOLBARK
MONTROSE
KALORAMA
MOUNT DANDENONG
Billanook College
Quinn Reserve
York on Lilydale
Yarra View Nursery
Mt Evelyn Christian
Gumnut Village
Keith Hume Fraser Reserve
Montrose Brickworks Flora Reserve
Montrose
Parks
Reserve
Montrose Recreation Reserve
Dandenong Ranges
National Park
Mt Dandenong 633m
Musk Park
DCNR Arboretum
Jennings Reserve
Forest Reserve
William Ricketts Sanctuary
(Doongalla Forest)
Kyeema Memorial Cairn
Singleton Reserve
ABV2 Tower
HSV7 Tower
GTV9 Tower
Restaurant
Mt Dandenong Pmy
Montrose Pmy
Mechanics Res
Olinda
COPYRIGHT © UNIVERSAL PRESS PTY LTD (PUBLISHER) 2004

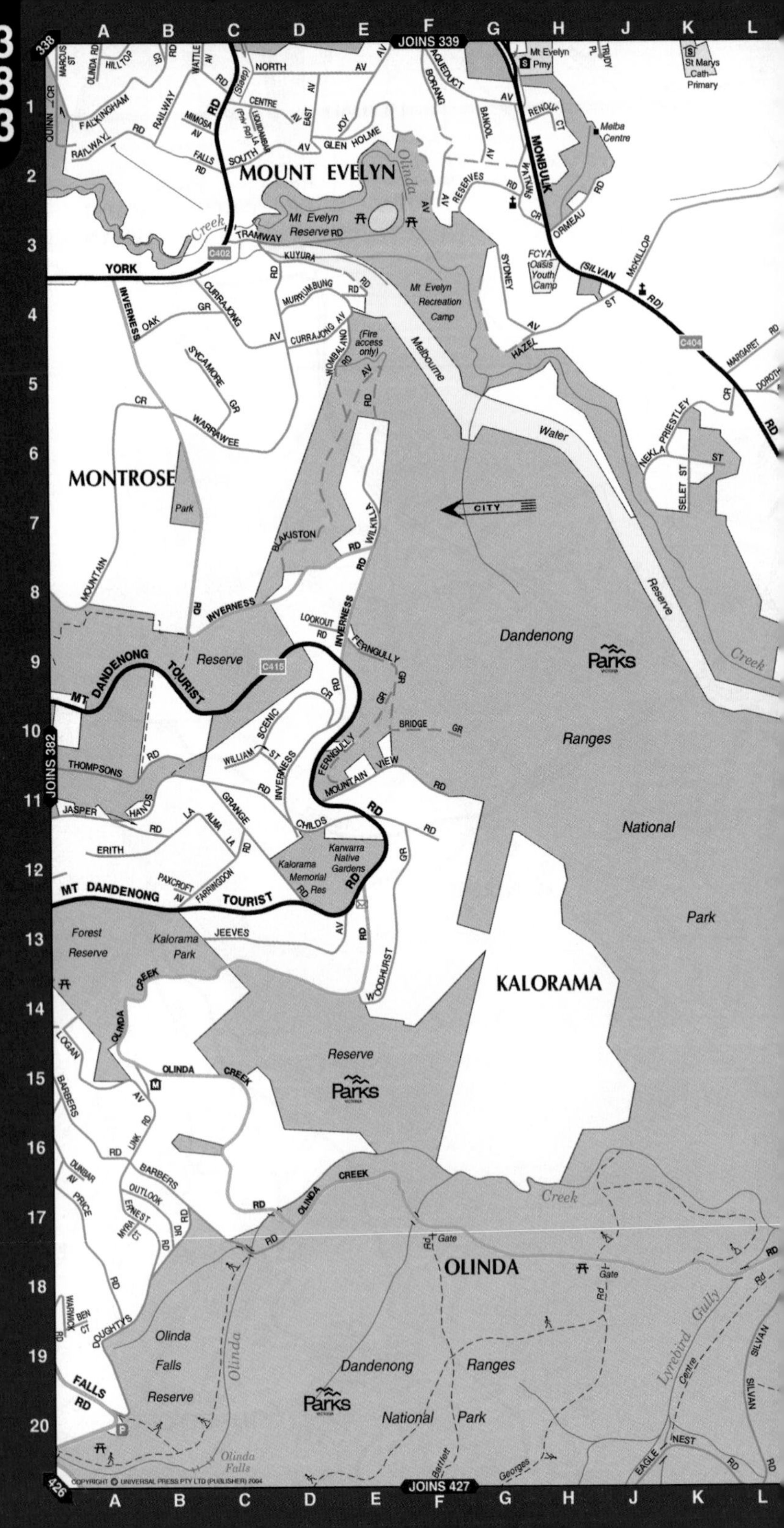
A B C D E F G H J K L
1 2 3 4 5 6 7 8 9 10 11 12 13 14 15 16 17 18 19 20
JOINS 339
JOINS 382
JOINS 427
338
426
MOUNT EVELYN
MONTROSE
KALORAMA
OLINDA
Mt Evelyn Reserve
Mt Evelyn Recreation Camp
(Fire access only)
Melbourne Water Reserve
CITY
Dandenong Ranges National Park
Parks
Reserve
Park
Kalorama Memorial Res
Karwarra Native Gardens
Forest Reserve
Kalorama Park
Olinda Falls Reserve
Olinda Falls
Mt Evelyn Pmy
St Marys Cath Primary
Melba Centre
FCYA Oasis Youth Camp
C402
C404
C415
YORK
MONBULK
(SILVAN RD)
MT DANDENONG TOURIST RD
INVERNESS RD
FALLS RD
OLINDA CREEK RD
Olinda Creek
Lyrebird Gully
Gate
Georges
Bartlett
EAGLE NEST RD
SILVAN
COPYRIGHT © UNIVERSAL PRESS PTY LTD (PUBLISHER) 2004

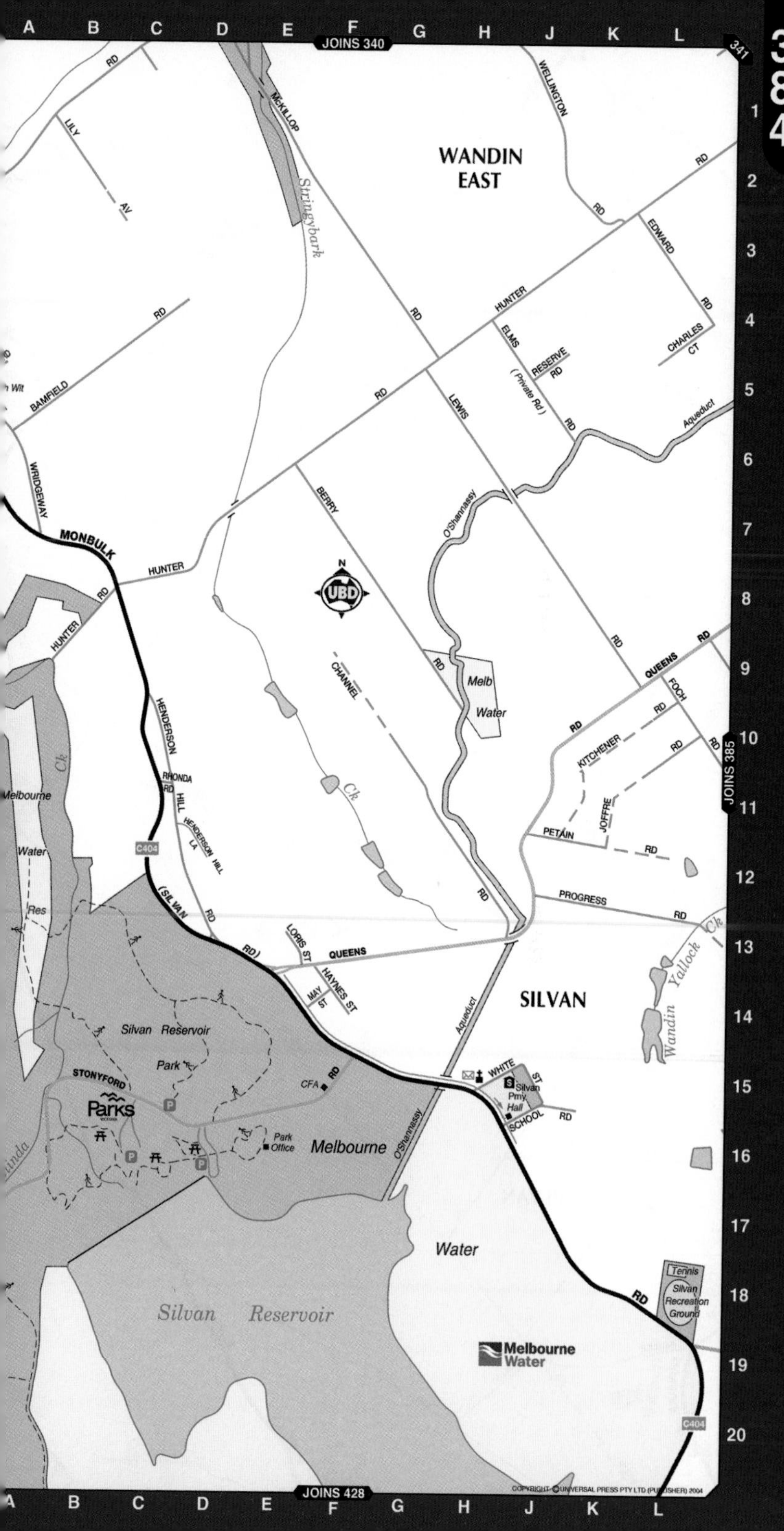

JOINS 340
341
WANDIN EAST
SILVAN
MONBULK
HUNTER RD
BAMFIELD
WRIDGEWAY
LILY AV
MCKILLOP RD
Stringybark
WELLINGTON RD
EDWARD RD
CHARLES CT
ELMS
RESERVE RD
(Private Rd)
LEWIS RD
BERRY RD
CHANNEL
O'Shannassy
Aqueduct
Melb Water
QUEENS RD
FOCH RD
KITCHENER RD
JOFFRE
PETAIN
PROGRESS RD
HENDERSON RD
RHONDA RD
HILL
HENDERSON HILL LA
C404
(SILVAN RD)
LORIS ST
HAYNES ST
MAY ST
Silvan Reservoir Park
STONYFORD RD
CFA
Park Office
Melbourne Water
WHITE ST
Silvan Pmy Hall
SCHOOL RD
Wandin Yallock Ck
Tennis
Silvan Recreation Ground
Silvan Reservoir
Melbourne Water
JOINS 385
JOINS 428

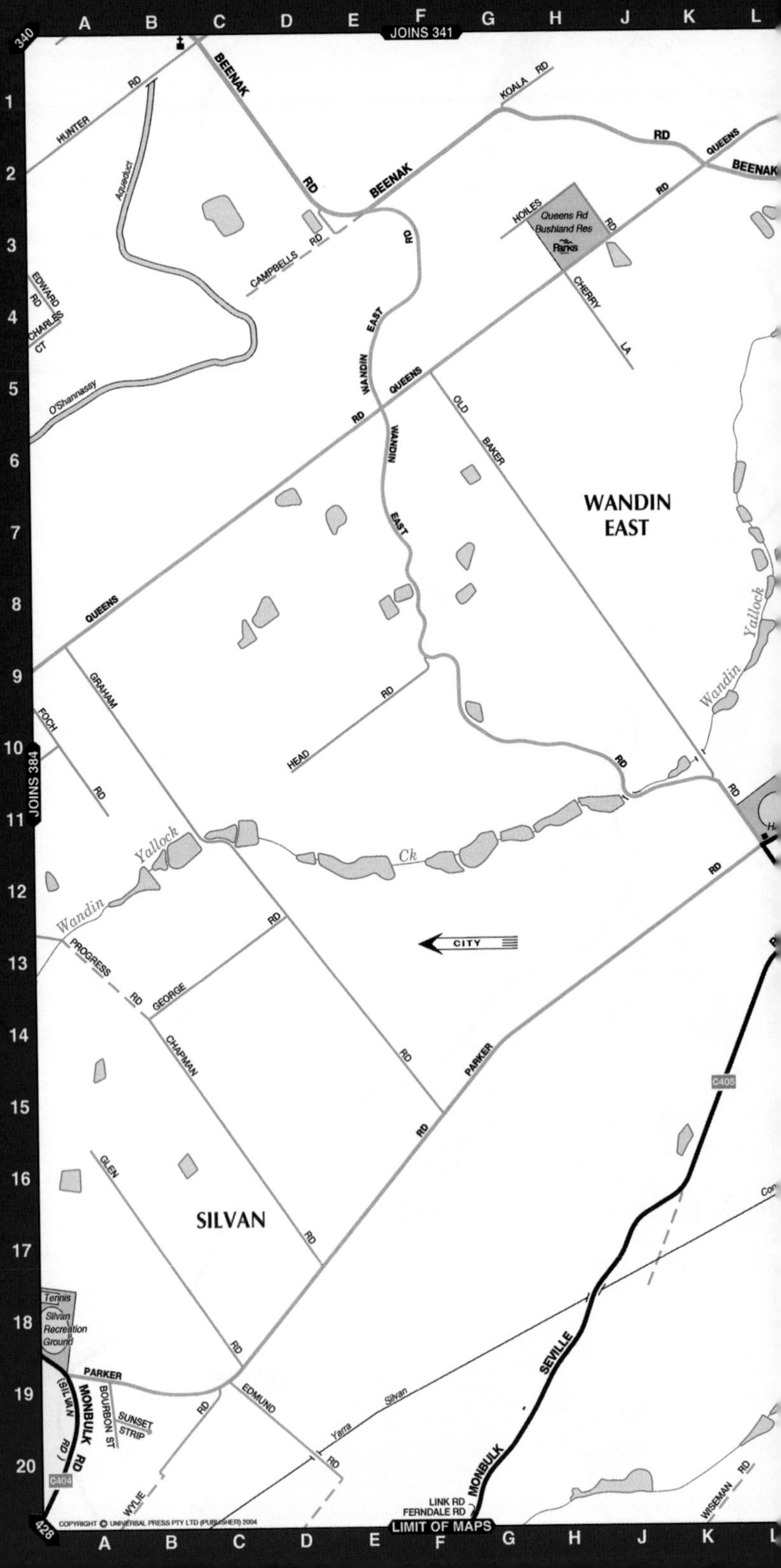

A B C D E F G H J K L

340 JOINS 341

BEENAK RD
HUNTER RD
Aqueduct
KOALA RD
QUEENS RD
BEENAK
BEENAK
CAMPBELLS RD
HOILES RD
Queens Rd Bushland Res
Parks
CHERRY LA
EDWARD RD
CHARLES CT
O'Shannassy
WANDIN EAST RD
QUEENS RD
OLD BAKER
WANDIN EAST
QUEENS
GRAHAM
HEAD RD
FOCH RD
Wandin Yallock Ck
RD
PROGRESS RD
GEORGE RD
CHAPMAN
RD
PARKER RD
CITY
C405
GLEN
SILVAN
RD
Tennis
Silvan Recreation Ground
PARKER
MONBULK RD (SILVAN RD)
BOURBON ST
SUNSET STRIP
EDMUND RD
RD
WYLIE
Yarra Silvan
SEVILLE
MONBULK
LINK RD
FERNDALE RD
C404
WISEMAN RD
Con

JOINS 384

428 LIMIT OF MAPS

A B C D E F G H J K L

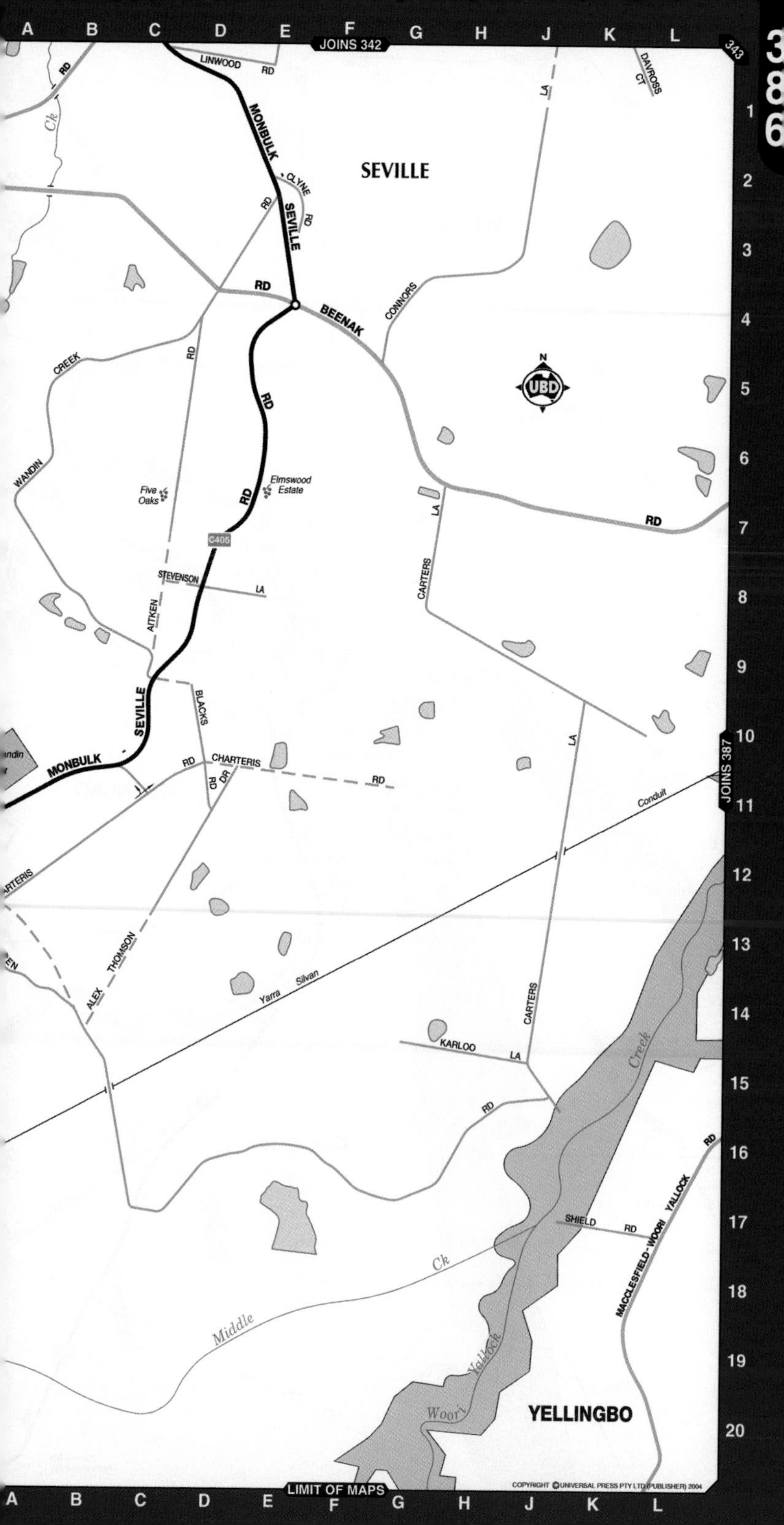

A B C D E F G H J K L
JOINS 342
343
1 2 3 4 5 6 7 8 9 10 11 12 13 14 15 16 17 18 19 20
JOINS 387
LIMIT OF MAPS
SEVILLE
YELLINGBO
LINWOOD RD
DAVROSS CT
MONBULK
SEVILLE
CLYNE RD
RD
BEENAK
RD
CONNORS
LA
CREEK
WANDIN
RD
Five Oaks
Elmswood Estate
C405
STEVENSON LA
AITKEN
CARTERS LA
BLACKS RD
CHARTERIS RD
DR
MONBULK
SEVILLE
CHARTERIS
THOMSON
ALEX
Yarra Silvan Conduit
KARLOO LA
CARTERS
Creek
Ck
Middle
Woori Yallock
SHIELD RD
MACCLESFIELD-WOORI YALLOCK RD

342
JOINS 343

A B C D E F G H J K L

SEVILLE

SEVILLE EAST

YELLINGBO

DOUTHIE RD
RD
CARSON RD
GARDINER RD
McQUIES RD
RIVERDALE RD
BEENAK RD
DOUTHIE
Creek
Yallock
Woori
HEALESVILLE - KOO WEE RUP
THEXTONS RD
C411
CENTRE RD
MIDDLE WY
PARSLOWS RD
RD
Yellingbo Pmy
TUDOR COURT RD
Hall
CFA
Yarra - Silvan
Creek
ANGUS
FOY LA
Yallock
Woori
Creek
HEALESVILLE - KOO WEE RUP
McCrae Ck
Lake Yellingbo
MACCLESFIELD - WOORI YALLOCK
CITY
OLD BEENAK
Cockatoo
Cockatoo
Ck
KOOKABURRA LA
C411
Macclesfield
Ck
Yarra Valley
RD
SMITHS RD
LEMONGUM RD

JOINS 386

1 2 3 4 5 6 7 8 9 10 11 12 13 14 15 16 17 18 19 20

A B C D E F G H J K L

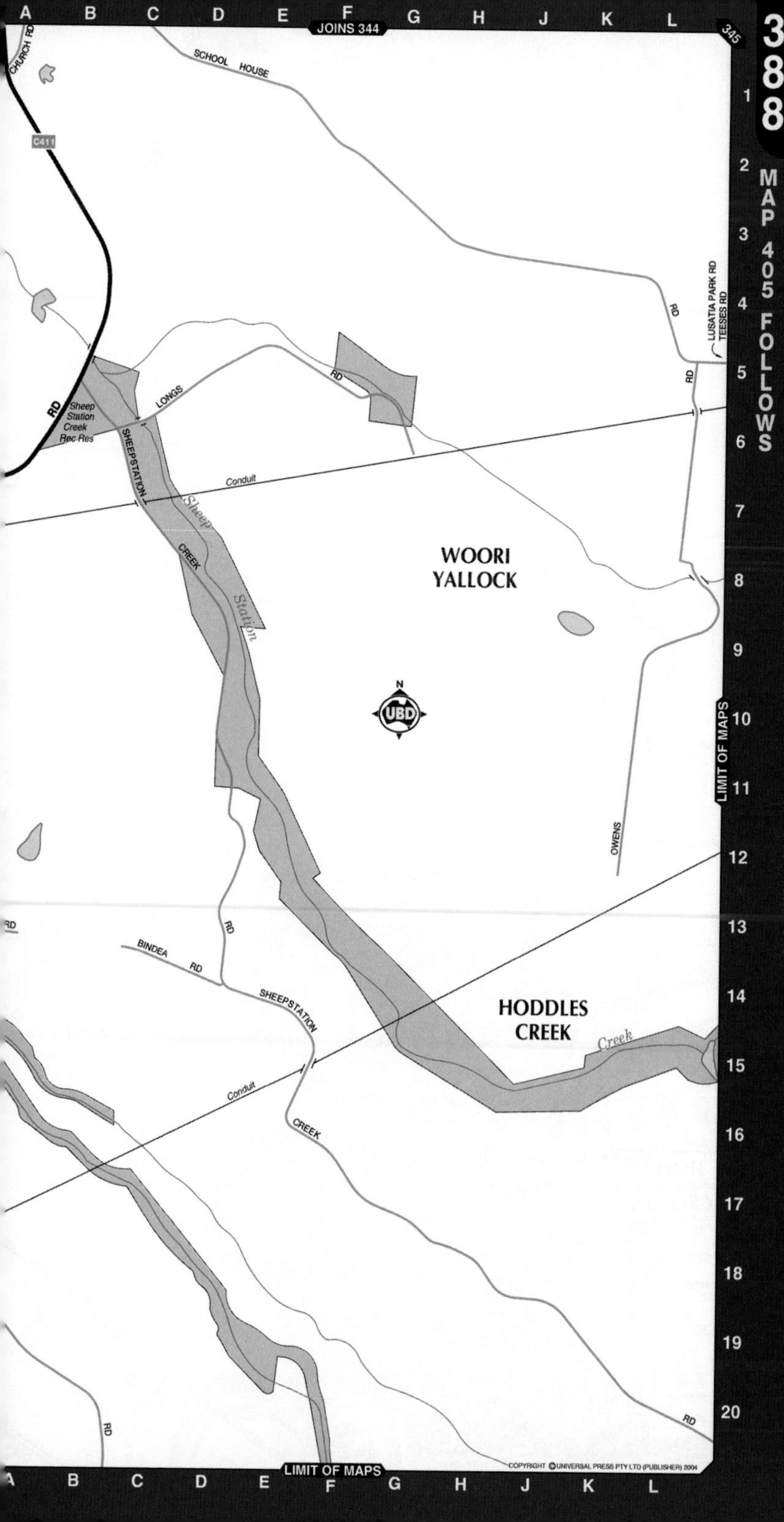
JOINS 344
345
SCHOOL HOUSE
CHURCH RD
C411
RD
LUSATIA PARK RD
TEESES RD
RD
LONGS
RD
Sheep Station Creek Rec Res
SHEEPSTATION
CREEK
Conduit
Sheep
Station
WOORI YALLOCK
LIMIT OF MAPS
OWENS
RD
BINDEA RD
SHEEPSTATION
HODDLES CREEK
Creek
Conduit
CREEK
RD
RD
LIMIT OF MAPS

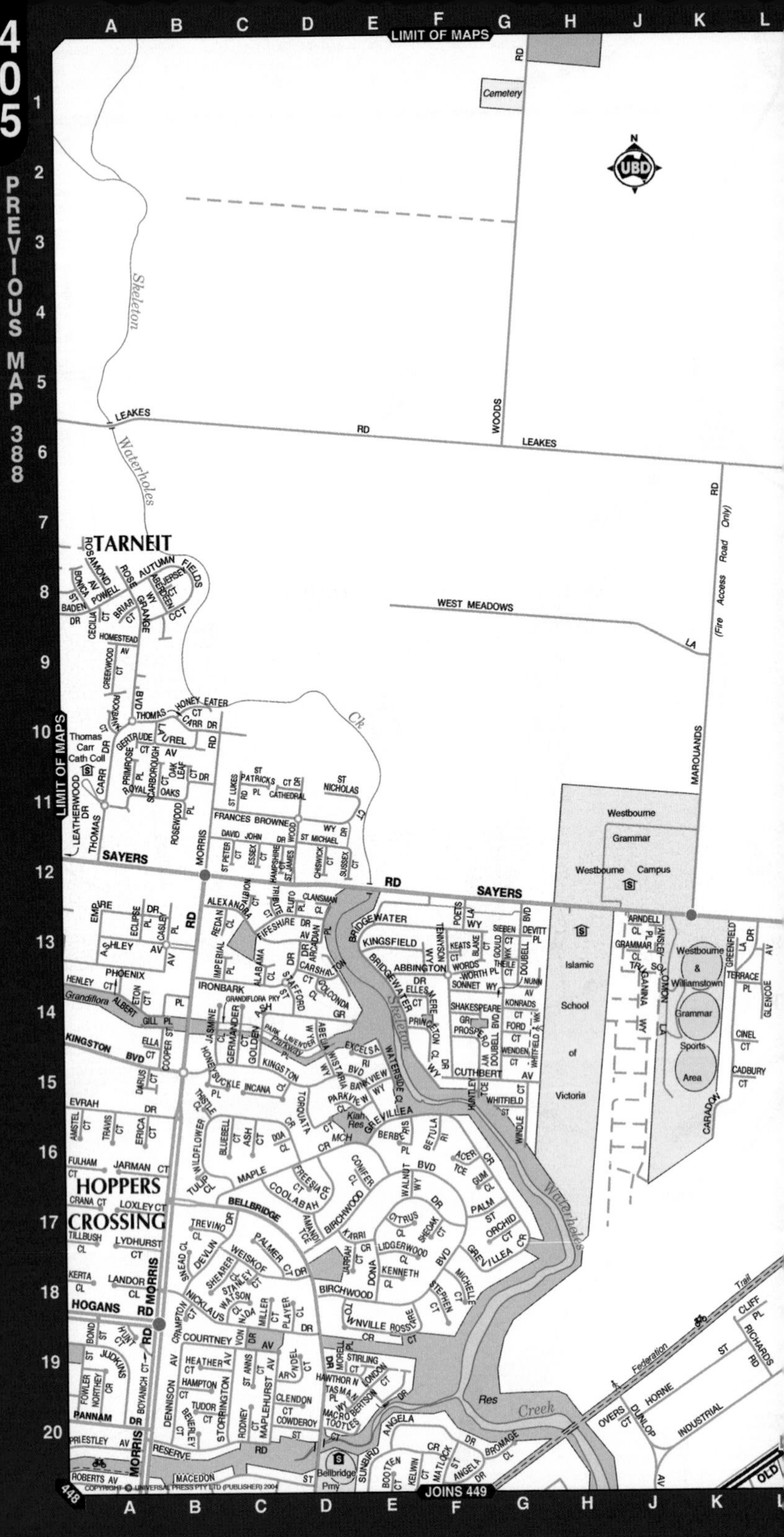

405
PREVIOUS MAP 388
LIMIT OF MAPS
JOINS 449
448
Cemetery
UBD
Skeleton
Waterholes
Ck
Creek
TARNEIT
HOPPERS
CROSSING
LEAKES RD
WOODS RD
WEST MEADOWS LA
MARQUANDS RD (Fire Access Road Only)
SAYERS RD
MORRIS RD
Thomas Carr Cath Coll
Westbourne Grammar Westbourne Campus
Islamic School of Victoria
Westbourne & Williamstown Grammar Sports Area
Kiah Res
Res
Bellbridge Prmy
Federation Trail
KINGSTON BVD
BELLBRIDGE DR
HOGANS RD
INDUSTRIAL
COPYRIGHT © UNIVERSAL PRESS PTY LTD (PUBLISHER) 2004

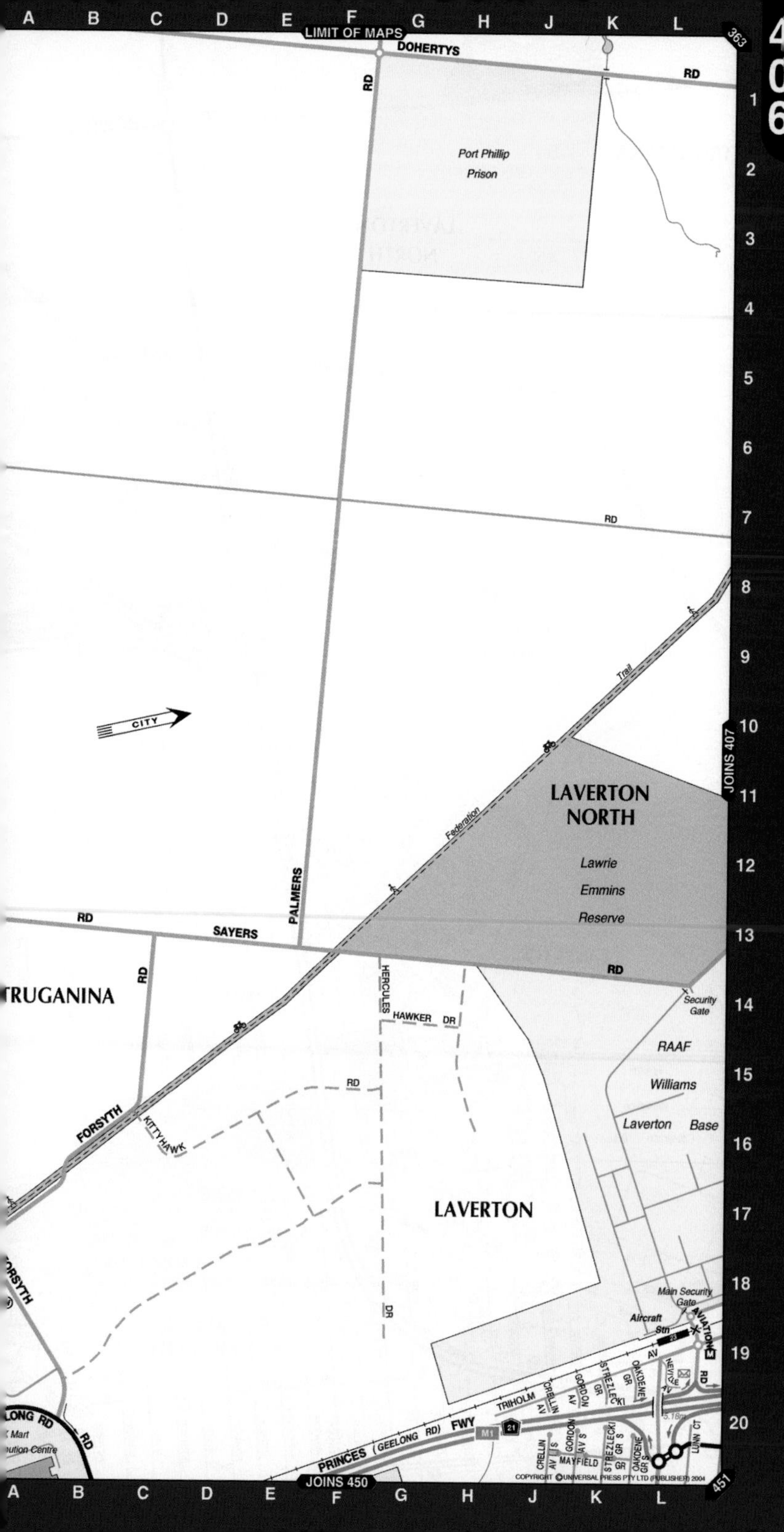
LIMIT OF MAPS
363
DOHERTYS
RD
RD
Port Phillip
Prison
RD
CITY
Trail
Federation
JOINS 407
LAVERTON
NORTH
Lawrie
Emmins
Reserve
RD
SAYERS
PALMERS
RD
RD
TRUGANINA
HERCULES
HAWKER
DR
Security
Gate
RAAF
Williams
Laverton
Base
RD
FORSYTH
KITTYHAWK
LAVERTON
FORSYTH
DR
Main Security
Gate
Aircraft
AVIATION
AV
RD
TRIHOLM
CRELLIN
AV
GORDON
AV
GR
STREZLECKI
GR
OAKDENE
NEVILLE
AV
LUNN CT
PRINCES
(GEELONG
RD)
FWY
M1
21
CRELLIN
AV S
GORDON
AV S
MAYFIELD
STREZLECKI
GR S
GR
OAKDENE
GR S
GEELONG RD
K Mart
Distribution Centre
RD
COPYRIGHT © UNIVERSAL PRESS PTY LTD (PUBLISHER) 2004
JOINS 450
451

A B C D E F G H J K L

JOINS 363

1 2 3 4 5 6 7 8 9 10 11 12 13 14 15 16 17 18 19 20

JOINS 406

TRUGANINA

LAVERTON NORTH

LAVERTON

ALTONA MEADOWS

DOHERTYS RD
DOHERTYS
RD
40
56
FITZGERALD
40
Trail
SCOTT
Federation
Federation
MARIA
EVERAISE CT
Altona Terminal Station
WESTGATE DR
Kayes
CHERRY
PRINCES
LEAKES RD
Rubble & Riches Laverton Market
Honey Hush
FLEET ST
Native Grassland Reserve
KORORO
5.18m
35
18
Orica Aust Ltd
RD
Laverton
CITY
CLIFF CR
TARRAN ST
CROPLEY ST
ROBERTSON CR
HENDERSON ST
BLADIN
CHIRNSIDE CR
Laverton Plains Primary
JONES CT
BURNLEY ST
HILLMAN ST
M1
21
FWY
HARCOURT RD
BURNS RD
CT
GEELONG
OLD
WHITTAKER
KAYE CR
THOMSON AV
WACKETT
BUTCHER CR
PARKSIDE WK
ISAACS ST
MCH
AV
BARWISE ST
BRIGGS ST
PEARCE ST
COLE
EATON PDE
BELLIN ST
St Martin de Porres
CAMPBELL ST
McNAMARA RD
NEWMARKET RD
Lawrie Emmins Reserve
SNOWDEN ST
BLADIN
ORR CT
CRESWICK ST
EVANS CR
EADES ST
TYQUIN
DUNKLEY RD
WESTLINK
Security Gate
CHAYE CT
JENNINGS ST
Laverton Secondary College
McCormack Park
RD)
CORA
HENTY
ALBURY
MANSFIELD
DANGLOW
Ck
RAAF Williams Laverton Base
ULM
ST
COBBY ST
DE BRUN CT
KINGSFORD
CHARLESWORTH
MERTON
Victorian Baseball & Softball Centre
SUMERS ST
BADGE CT
CARTLEDGE
Frank Gibson Res
ARMSTRONG ST
WILLIAMS RD
WRIGHT
Woods St Res
BURTON AV
WATTS
Low Bridge 2.6 Metres
Laverton
ALLEN
BURKE CT
WOODS
THOMAS
LOHSE ST
HICKEY
AV
Little Athletics
Soccer
Softball
STUDLEY CT
HEFFERNAN ST
GOBLE
Laverton RD
4.44m
22
Laverton Park
AB Shaw Reserve
MAHER
Fbr
JAMISON
(GEELONG
HIBISCUS CT
VALENTE ST
RESCHKE CT
NORTH AV
HALL AV
Main Security Gate
MAHER
Hall
Civic Cntr
HIGH ST
GRACE ST
FITZROY ST
Laverton Primary
NEWLAND ST
Altona Meadows Pmy
CLOVER CT
PINE CT
DR
J J Stewart Res
RAILWAY
Cmnty Cntr
MCH
AVIATION RD
AILSA ST
ASCOT ST
BALMORAL ST
BRUCE ST
CROWN ST
DONALD ST
EPSOM
5.48m
ST S
CAMERON
AV
ALMA
21
ALMA
PEPPERMINT CT
KURRAJONG
EUCALYPTUS
HEATH
HAKEA CT
M1
PRINCES
LUNN CT
ST S
ASCOT ST
BALMORAL ST
BRUCE ST
CROWN ST
DONALD ST
Chr Cmnty Cntr
EPSOM ST
FITZROY ST
GRACE ST
HIGH ST
JAMISON
KIORA
LINDEN
MERTON
NICHOLSON
ORVILLE
POWLETT
HOOK
ROSEBERY
SHIRLEY
TALBOT
VICTORIA
HONEYSUCKLE CT
GREVILLIA CT
CENTRAL
MCH
41
AV
MCH

450

JOINS 451

A B C D E F G H J K L

A B C D E F G H J K L
JOINS 364
365
408
The Memorial Park Crematorium and Floral Lawn Cemetery
DOHERTYS RD
FWY
HUME RD
PIPE RD
Trail
JAMES ST
JON ST
CYANAMID ST
LA
TEREX DR
GORDON LUCK AV
(GEELONG RD)
Coles-Myer Distribution Warehouse
Fowles Auction Centre
Bunge Bio Products
WESTGATE DR
Westgate Transport
ALTONA NORTH
PINNACLE RD
STUBER RD
IVES RD
BALDWIN
Gate
CLIFT CT
KEARSLEY CT
Calleja Transport
Dow Irrigated Tree Plantation
SALTA DR
Target Distribution Centre
TARAS AV
Parks
CREEK RD
Ent
GRIEVE PDE
JOINS 409
Hoechst Chemicals
Geon Australia
Dow Chemicals
BASF
Powercor
Kemcor Elastomers
MAIDSTONE ST
Kemcor Olefins
CIG
Nippondenso
Kemcor Plastics
Drain
ALTONA
LIME ST
CHARLES
LUGG ST
F Rush Reserve
DEAVEY CT
FINLEY RD
FORD RD
GREENEY ST
MERRITT CT
SPEAR CT
KEESHAN CT
BROOK AV
HAMMOND ST
KIM CT
CHORLEY AV
FRAZER AV
KEARNEY AV
McINTYRE DR
LOGAN AV
RUSH CT
LOWE AV
AJAX RD
MALTON CT
SLOUGH
ABERDEEN RD
MORROW ST
GALVIN PDE
CHESTER RD
PARK
BELMAR
MERLOW ST
FENFIELD ST
A H Ford Reserve
DELMONT ST
MEDFORD
Altona West Pmy
Altona Sec Coll
LINDWOOD AV
CIVIC PDE
McALPINE
EMERY CT
GREEN CT
FEDERATION CT
HERITAGE CT
CAMPBELL CT
BURT
GLENWOOD AV
PHAIR CT
KARINGAL ST
ILUKA CT
COWRA ST
FLEMING
AKUNA ST
Mt St Joseph Cath Girls
HARRINGTON ST
LELAND
ROSE ST
RAYNER ST
HANCOCK ST
RAILWAY
Westona
WREN ST
BOYD ST
ST N
ST S
Altona Primary
Melbourne Water
Sewage Treatment Plant
Pondage
PURNELL
SEAGULL AV
DOVE
CURLEW AV
LINNET
ROBIN ST
EMU
LARK ST
KOOKABURRA ST
STANLEY
MULGA
RANKIN ST
BLYTH
MANNING GR
GR
GRIEVE
WEBB ST
UPTON ST
QUEEN ST
ESPLANADE
GRANT AV
BELL CT
CROFTS
COBHAM
FINCH ST
SOMERS
Den Dulk Res
BLYTH
BRACKEN
MYRTLE
STEWART AV
Port Phillip Ret Vill
JOINS 452
COPYRIGHT © UNIVERSAL PRESS PTY LTD (PUBLISHER) 2004

1 2 3 4 5 6 7 8 9 10 11 12 13 14 15 16 17 18 19 20

ALTONA NORTH

ALTONA

SEAHOLME

The Memorial Park Crematorium and Floral Lawn Cemetery
Urban Forest Res
G J Hosken Reserve
Tennis
W L J Crofts Reserve
Altona Gate Pmy
A W Bond Reserve
Altona Gate
Indoor Sport & Leisure Centre
Harris Reserve
Bocce Club
Nurs Home
St Pauls Cath College
Hearne Res
MCH
Toyota Engine Plant
Westgate Transport
Kororoit Creek
Bayside Sec Coll Altona Nth Campus
Langshaw Reserve
Cmnty Cntr
Altona North Primary
J J Ginifer Reserve
St Leo The Great Cath Pmy
Irwin Res
Cabot Australasia Pty Ltd
St Clements Reserve
Bus Interchange
5.26m
Mobil
Altona Refinery
Mobil Training Centre
Mobil Altona Refinery
6.3m
Paktank
Cherry Lake
J K Grant Reserve
Little Athletics
Hockey
F J Kirk Oval
Council Depot
SES
Tennis
Youth Centre
Cncl Office
Tennis
Cherry Lake Res
HC Kim Res
McIntyre Res
Pines Scout Camp
P A Burns Reserve
Seaholme Primary
Altona Workers Sports Club
W G Drain
Drain
New Altona Harbour
Altona Yacht Club
Cresser Res
Altona Boatowners Club
St Marys Cath
Altona Primary
MCH
RSL
Mambourin Centre
R J Logan Res
Altona LSC
Frazer Res
Altona
Seaholme
Altona Bay
Pier

DOHERTYS RD, DOHERTYS, GRIEVE PDE, BLACKSHAWS RD, PINNACLE RD, IVES RD, CLIFT CT, KEARSLEY CT, TARAS AV, BARNES RD, LOGISTICS WY, DR, KOROROIT CREEK RD, TOLL, CITY, KNAPP ST, HARRIS ST, GADSDEN ST, CARTHY ST, BINNS ST, MACLEAN CT, MEDDINGS CT, MURDOCH CT, FREEMANS RD, MISTEN AV, ROSALA AV, GLADE AV, IRWIN AV, DUOSA RD, BEURON RD, ESTELLE CT, EDWARD CT, CONWAY CT, JOHN CT, CRAIG CT, DEAN CT, HILL ST, MARSH ST, RYMILL CT, LAWRENCE CT, NEAL CT, WALKER CL, CHERRY AV, MURPHY ST, DUKE ST, BORRACK SQ, McARTHURS RD, CHAMBERS RD, GINIFER AV, BLAIR CT, LULY CT, BUNTING CT, COOPER AV, JOEL AV, BLOMBERG RD, ROSS RD, MILLERS RD, MARIGOLD, CYCLAMEN, CYCADE, VALERIAN AV, MAHON AV, HUXTABLE AV, DELPHIN AV, MAY, MARION, SIXTH, SEVENTH, FIFTH, FOURTH, THIRD, MASON, CRESSER, HENDREN, HOBBS, DOUGLAS ST, RONALD, WINDSOR, PARROTH, McINTOSH, HATHERLEY, BRYAN AV, BERKELEY CR, GILLIGAN, RD, Ped Upass

LUGG ST, KIM CT, CHORLEY AV, McINTYRE, FRAZER AV, KEARNEY AV, RANSOM, LOGAN AV, RUSH CT, LOWE, FEDERATION, CARRUTHERS CT, HERITAGE CT, CAMPBELL CT, BURT ST, CIVIC PDE, SUGARGUM DR, BLUEGUM DR, FRESNO ST, WATSON ST, FISHER CT, SCULLIN CT, CHIFLEY, CURTIN CT, POLLARD CT, CAIN CT, IRVINGTON AV, WATERS, NEWTON, TWENTYMAN CT, NOORDENNE, MARTIN CT, NISSEN, MOORE CT, JURGA CT, JAMES AV, SIMMONS, DENBIGH ST, LEICESTER SQ, STIRLING AV, CAMBRIDGE ST, SUSSEX, SEAHOLME AV, GLOUCESTER, PARKSIDE CR, McIntosh Res, ALTONA DR, HANCOCK ST, UPTON ST, ROMAWI ST, DAVID ST, McBAIN ST, SARGOOD ST, BENT ST, DAVIES ST, MOUNT ST, BAYVIEW ST, SEVES ST, RAILWAY ST, RAILWAY ST N, RAILWAY ST S, RYAN LA, MCH ST, FINDLAY LA, EDWARDS ARC, BLYTH ST, QUEEN ST, ESPLANADE, WEBB ST, PIER ST, WARATAH ST, WATTLE GR, ACACIA AV, CENTRAL AV, GARDEN GR, BEACH ST, HIGH ST, JOINER LA, SEAVIEW CR, SURF ST, STATION

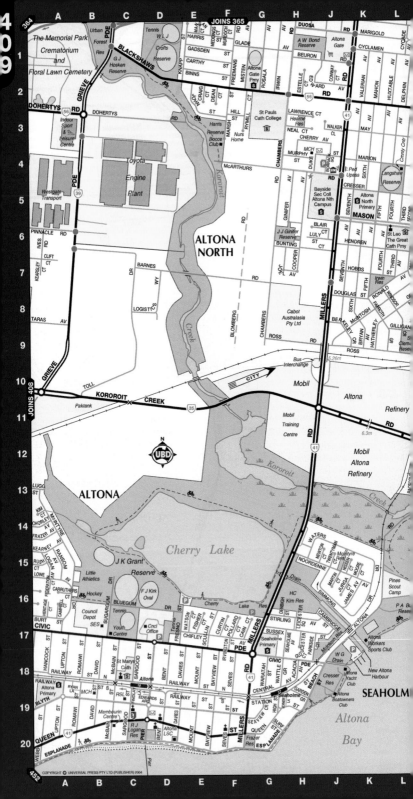

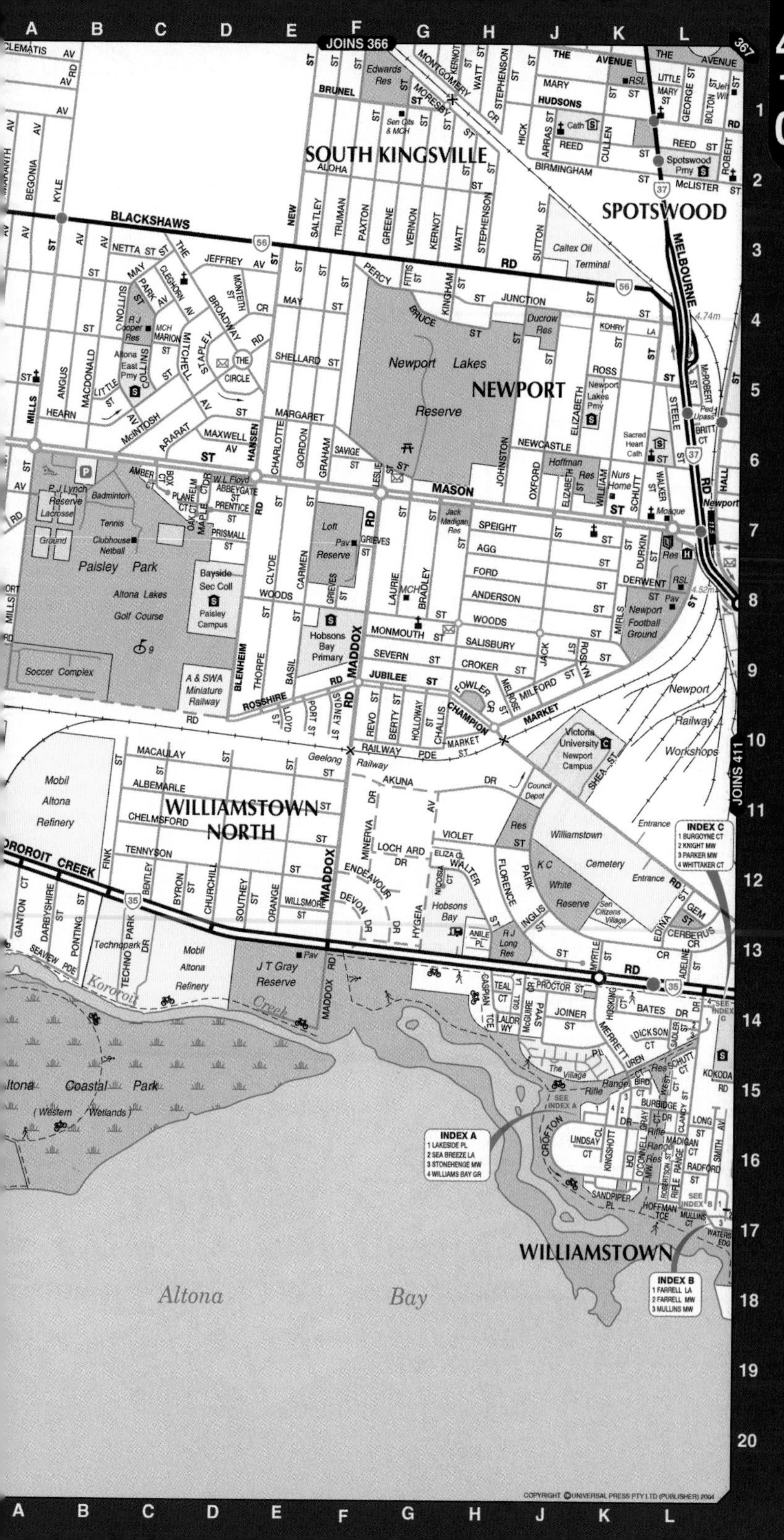

JOINS 366
SOUTH KINGSVILLE
SPOTSWOOD
NEWPORT
WILLIAMSTOWN NORTH
WILLIAMSTOWN
Newport Lakes Reserve
Paisley Park
Altona Lakes Golf Course
Mobil Altona Refinery
Altona Coastal Park (Western Wetlands)
Altona
Bay
Williamstown Cemetery
Newport Railway Workshops
JOINS 411
INDEX A
1 LAKESIDE PL
2 SEA BREEZE LA
3 STONEHENGE MW
4 WILLIAMS BAY GR
INDEX B
1 FARRELL LA
2 FARRELL MW
3 MULLINS MW
INDEX C
1 BURGOYNE CT
2 KNIGHT MW
3 PARKER MW
4 WHITTAKER CT

366
JOINS 367
JOINS 410

SPOTSWOOD

NEWPORT

WILLIAMSTOWN

INDEX D
1 APHRASIA LA
2 BOND LA
3 BREADALBANE PL
4 GARNSWORTHY PL
5 HARTLEY LA
5a JAMES DEANE PL
5b JOAN KIRNER DR
6 JOHN LISTON DR
6a JOHN LISTON LA
7 LILEY LA
8 LILEY ST
9 OBERON WY
10 SIROCCO LA
11 THAMES PL
12 TREGUTHA WY
13 VESTA LA

INDEX C
1 BURGOYNE CT
2 KNIGHT MW
3 PARKER MW
4 WHITTAKER CT

INDEX B
1 FARRELL LA
2 FARRELL MW
3 MULLINS MW

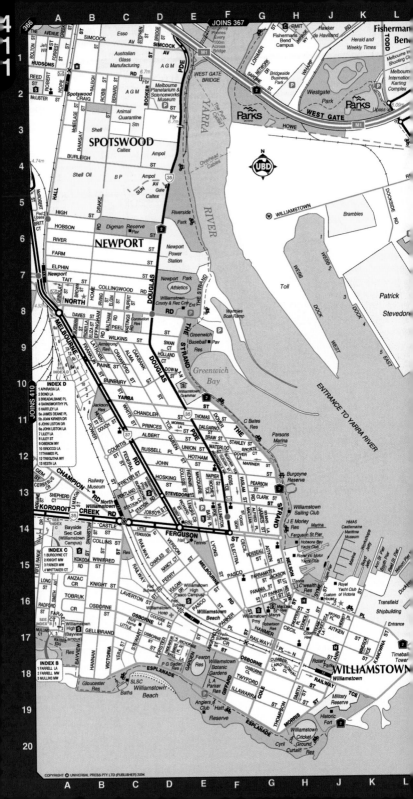

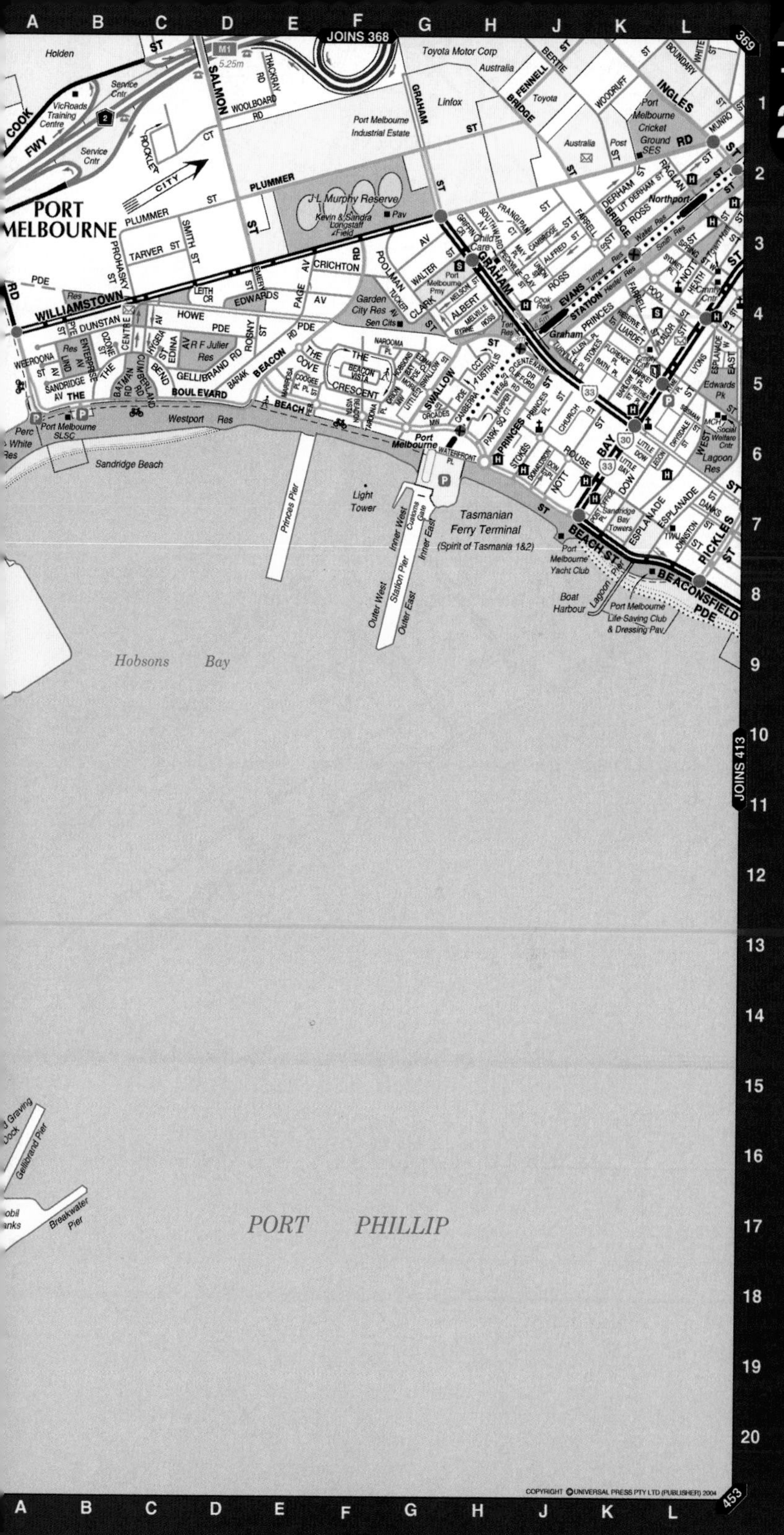
JOINS 368
PORT MELBOURNE
Holden
Toyota Motor Corp Australia
Linfox
Port Melbourne Industrial Estate
J.L. Murphy Reserve
Kevin & Sandra Longstaff Field
Garden City Res
R F Julier Res
Westport Res
Port Melbourne SLSC
Sandridge Beach
Princes Pier
Light Tower
Station Pier
Tasmanian Ferry Terminal
(Spirit of Tasmania 1&2)
Port Melbourne Yacht Club
Boat Harbour
Lagoon Pier
Port Melbourne Life Saving Club & Dressing Pav
Port Melbourne Cricket Ground
Edwards Pk
Lagoon Res
Hobsons Bay
PORT PHILLIP
Gellibrand Pier
Breakwater Pier
JOINS 413
PLUMMER ST
WILLIAMSTOWN RD
GRAHAM ST
BAY ST
BEACH ST
BEACONSFIELD PDE
INGLES ST
BOULEVARD
BEACH
369
453

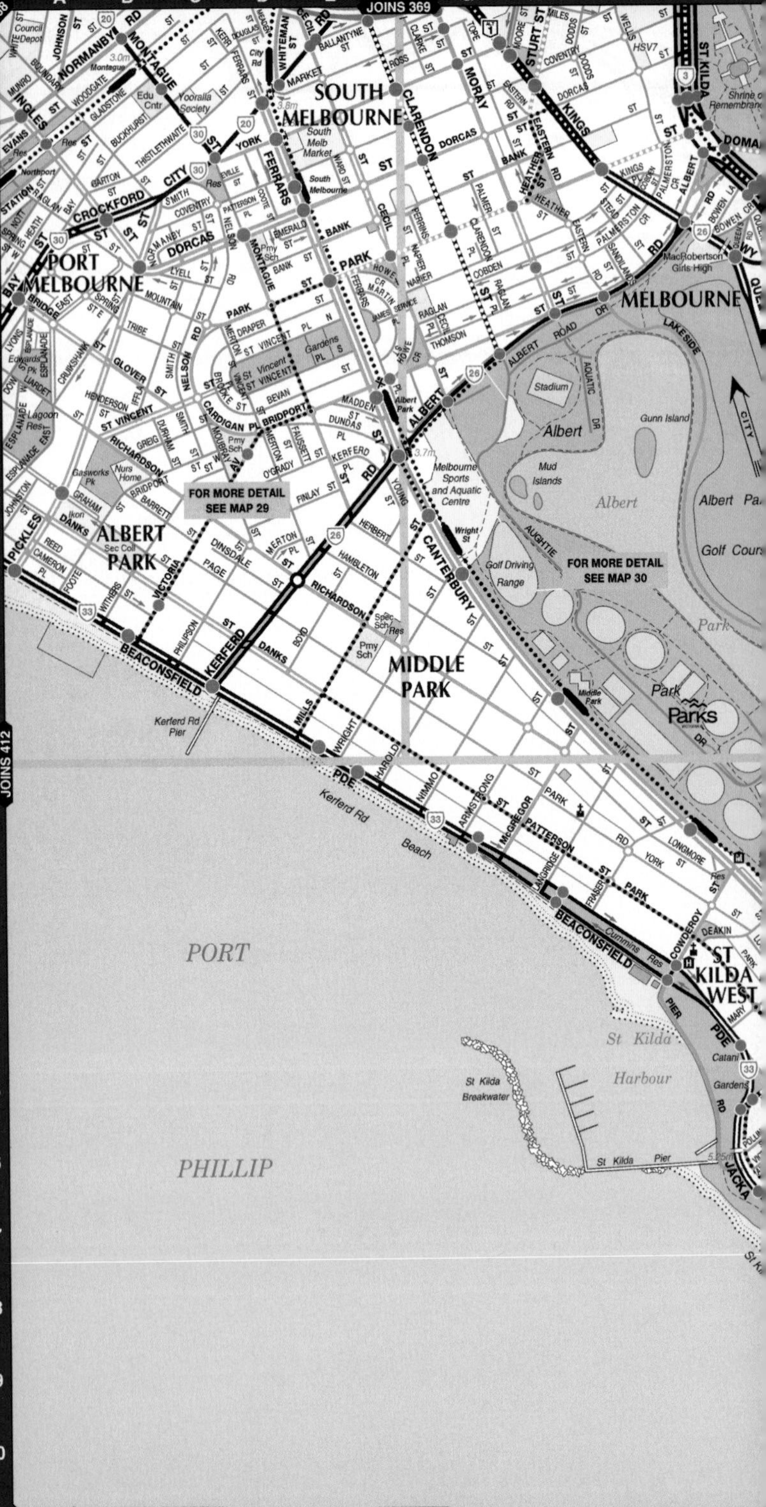

368
JOINS 369
JOINS 412
JOINS 453

A B C D E F G H J K L

SOUTH MELBOURNE

PORT MELBOURNE

ALBERT PARK

MIDDLE PARK

MELBOURNE

ST KILDA WEST

FOR MORE DETAIL SEE MAP 29

FOR MORE DETAIL SEE MAP 30

Council Depot
Edu Cntr
Yooralla Society
South Melb Market
South Melbourne
Northport
Pmy Sch
St Vincent Gardens
Lagoon Reserve
Gasworks Pk
Nurs Home
Ikon
Sec Coll
Albert Park
Melbourne Sports and Aquatic Centre
Stadium
Albert
Mud Islands
Gunn Island
Albert Park Golf Course
Golf Driving Range
Wright St
Middle Park
Spec Sch
Parks
MacRobertson Girls High
Shrine of Remembrance
Kerferd Rd Pier
Kerferd Rd Beach
Cummins Res
Catani Gardens
St Kilda Harbour
St Kilda Breakwater
St Kilda Pier

PORT PHILLIP

NORMANBY RD
MONTAGUE ST
CITY RD
CLARENDON ST
FERRARS ST
KINGS WAY
ST KILDA RD
ALBERT RD
PARK ST
BRIDPORT ST
KERFERD RD
CANTERBURY RD
BEACONSFIELD PDE
MILLS ST
PATTERSON ST
PARK ST
FITZROY ST
JACKA BLVD

1 2 3 4 5 6 7 8 9 10 11 12 13 14 15 16 17 18 19 20

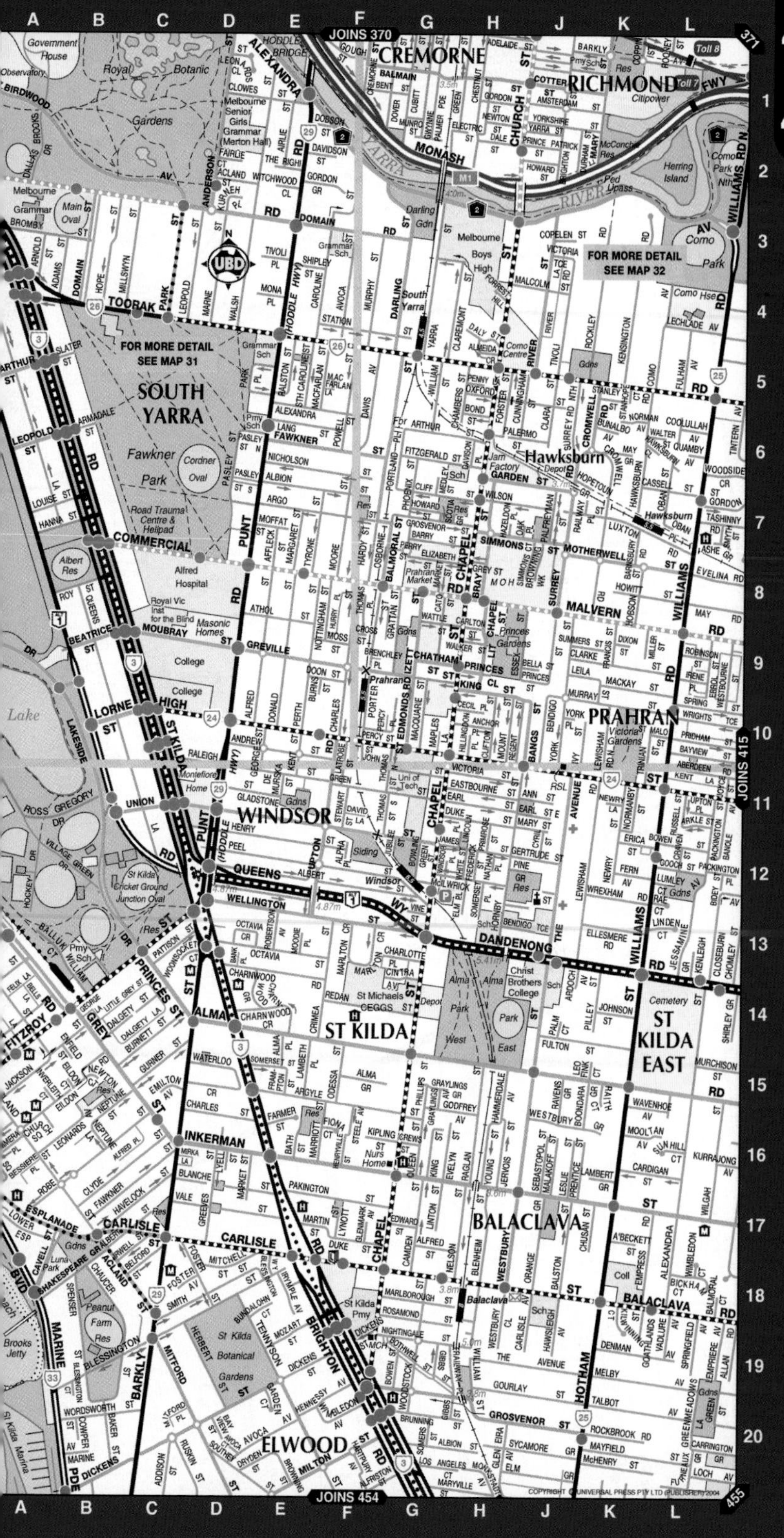

A B C D E F G H J K L
JOINS 370
371
CREMORNE
RICHMOND
Citipower
Government House
Observatory
Royal Botanic Gardens
Melbourne Senior Girls Grammar (Merton Hall)
Melbourne Grammar
Main Oval
HODDLE BRIDGE
ALEXANDRA
YARRA RIVER
MONASH FWY
Herring Island
Como Park Nth
Darling Gdn
Melbourne Boys High
FOR MORE DETAIL SEE MAP 32
Como Park
Como Hse
FOR MORE DETAIL SEE MAP 31
SOUTH YARRA
Fawkner Park
Cordner Oval
Road Trauma Centre & Helipad
Alfred Hospital
Albert Res
Royal Vic Inst for the Blind
Masonic Homes
College
Lake
Como Centre
South Yarra
Hawksburn
Jam Factory
Prahran Market
Princes Gardens
PRAHRAN
Victoria Gardens
Prahran
Montefiore Home
WINDSOR
Uni of Tech
Windsor
Siding
St Kilda Cricket Ground Junction Oval
St Michaels CEGGS
ST KILDA
Alma Park West
Alma Park East
Christ Brothers College
Cemetery
ST KILDA EAST
Peanut Farm Res
Luna Park
Brooks Jetty
St Kilda Marina
St Kilda Botanical Gardens
BALACLAVA
Balaclava
ELWOOD
JOINS 415
JOINS 454
455
TOORAK RD
PUNT RD
CHAPEL ST
CHURCH ST
WILLIAMS RD
DANDENONG RD
COMMERCIAL RD
HIGH ST
GREVILLE ST
MALVERN RD
QUEENS WY
ST KILDA RD
FITZROY ST
GREY ST
ALMA RD
INKERMAN ST
CARLISLE ST
BALACLAVA RD
BRIGHTON RD
HOTHAM ST
MARINE PDE
BARKLY ST
GROSVENOR ST
1 2 3 4 5 6 7 8 9 10 11 12 13 14 15 16 17 18 19 20
COPYRIGHT © UNIVERSAL PRESS PTY LTD (PUBLISHER) 2004

JOINS 371
JOINS 414
JOINS 455
370
454
BURNLEY
TOORAK
ARMADALE
PRAHRAN
ST KILDA EAST
CAULFIELD NORTH
Yarra River
Survey Park
Richmond Golf Course
Uni of Melb
Bastow Oval
Loughnan Oval
Kevin Bartlett Sporting & Recreation Complex
Fletcher Oval
Fairview Park
Loys Paddock Res
Como Park Nth
Como Park
Scotch College
Junior School
Senior School
H A Smith Reserve
St Kevins Coll
Kooyong Lawn Tennis Club
Vision Australia Foundation
Heyington
Kooyong
Toorak
Armadale
Malvern
St Catherines Sch
Grammar Sch
Loreto Coll
Toorak Pmy
Brookville Gdns
Orrong Park
Toorak Park
Victory Sq
Lauriston Girls
Deakin Uni Toorak Campus
Kids Hospice
Malvern Recreation Reserve
St Josephs Cath Pmy
De La Salle Cath Coll
Tram Depot
Malvern Central
Caulfield Park
Caulfield Cricket Ground
Labassa House
Melb Grammar (Grimwade Hse)
Ripponlea Pmy
King David
MONASH FWY
YARRA BVD
TOORAK RD
MALVERN RD
HIGH ST
DANDENONG RD
WATTLETREE RD
ALMA RD
INKERMAN RD
BALACLAVA RD
PRINCES HWY
GLENFERRIE RD
KOOYONG RD
ORRONG RD
WILLIAMS RD
CHAPEL ST
GRANGE RD
TOORONGA RD
HAWTHORN RD
NORMANBY RD
UBD
COPYRIGHT © UNIVERSAL PRESS PTY LTD (PUBLISHER) 2004

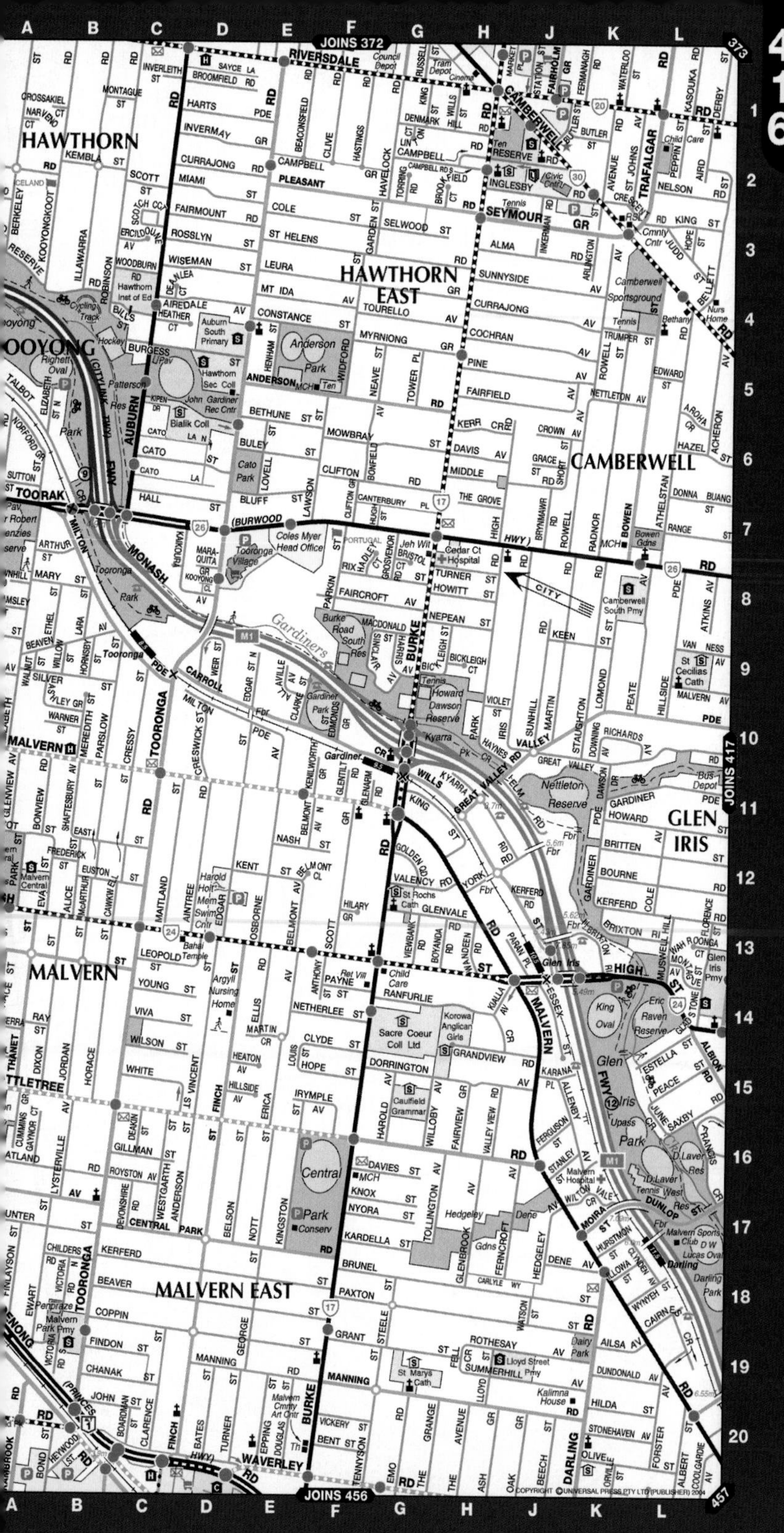

416
JOINS 372
373
JOINS 417
JOINS 456
457
HAWTHORN
HAWTHORN EAST
CAMBERWELL
GLEN IRIS
MALVERN
MALVERN EAST
TOORAK
RIVERSDALE
CAMBERWELL
BURKE
AUBURN
TOORONGA
(BURWOOD
HWY)
MONASH
FWY
MALVERN
HIGH
ST
WAVERLEY
(PRINCES
HWY)
DARLING
GLEN IRIS
WILLS
CARROLL
Gardiners
Anderson Park
Central Park
Burke Road South Res
Howard Dawson Reserve
Nettleton Reserve
King Oval
Glen Iris Park
Camberwell Sportsground
Coles Myer Head Office
Caulfield Grammar
Sacre Coeur Coll Ltd
Hawthorn Sec Coll
John Gardiner Rec Cntr
Malvern Central
COPYRIGHT © UNIVERSAL PRESS PTY LTD (PUBLISHER) 2004

JOINS 373

372

A B C D E F G H J K L

SURREY HILLS

CAMBERWELL

GLEN IRIS

ASHBURTON

MALVERN EAST

RIVERSDALE RD
TOORAK RD
(BURWOOD HWY)
HIGH ST RD
WARRIGAL RD
MONASH FWY
CAMBERWELL RD
GLEN IRIS RD
HIGHFIELD RD
WATTLE VALLEY RD
SUMMERHILL RD
GARDINER PDE
HOLMESGLEN BOULEVARD
GLOUCESTER AV
WARNER AV
VICTORY BVD

Riversdale
Willison
Hartwell
Burwood
Ashburton
Alamein
Holmesglen

Camberwell High
Canterbury Primary
Siena College
Riversdale Park
Council Depot & Transfer Station
Highfield Park
Frog Hollow Res
Willison Park
Council Nursery
St Dominics Cath
Hartwell Private Hospital
Nazareth House Home for Aged
Lynden Nursing Home
Lynden Park
Back Creek
Fordham Gdns
Toorak House Nursing Home
Hartwell Pmy
Back Creek Res
St Cecilias Cath
Ferndale Park
Bus Depot
Hartwell Sportsground
Burwood Reserve
Delmont Private Hospital
Hill & Dale Pk
Summerhill Park
Glen Iris Pmy
Ashburton Primary
Ashburton Park
St Michaels Catholic
Ashburton Recreation Centre
Warner Reserve
Cmnty Centre
D.Laver Res
Malvern Sports Club
D W Lucas Oval
Darling Park
Watson Park
Solway Pmy
Gardiners Creek
Malvern Valley Golf Course
Clubhouse
Holmesglen Inst of TAFE Chadstone Campus
Holmesglen Reserve

JOINS 416

1 2 3 4 5 6 7 8 9 10 11 12 13 14 15 16 17 18 19 20

456

JOINS 457

A B C D E F G H J K L

418
JOINS 374
JOINS 419
JOINS 458
375
459
BOX HILL SOUTH
BURWOOD
MOUNT WAVERLEY
ASHWOOD
JORDANVILLE
INDEX A
1 CARLOGIE CT
2 EAGLE RIDGE RI
3 GLEN EAGLES CT
4 HUNTINGTON TCE
5 IRVINE CT
6 METROPOLITAN CT
7 MUIRFIELD CT
8 ROYAL MELB BVD
9 ROYAL PINES PL
10 ST ANDREWS CT
11 SPEARWATER WY
12 YARRAWONGA WY
Wattle Park
Public Golf Course
Chalet
Kingswood College
Box Hill Golf Course
Gardiners Creek Reserve
FOR MORE DETAIL SEE MAP 718
Deakin University Melbourne Campus
Mt Scopus Memorial College
Presbyterian Ladies College
Burwood Cemetery
Electricity Supply Corporation
Fountain Court Retirement Village
Royal Victorian Inst for the Blind
Greenwood Office Park
Bennettswood Tennis Club
Lundgren Reserve
Gardiners Ck Reserve
Gordon & Gotch Ltd
Federal Reserve
Essex Heights Reserve
Ashwood Secondary College
Damper Creek Reserve
Riversdale Golf Course
Clubhouse
Ashwood Reserve
Jingella Reserve
Electra Reserve
Batesford Reserve
Jordan Reserve
RIVERSDALE RD
BURWOOD HWY
HIGHBURY RD
WARRIGAL RD
ELGAR RD
STATION ST
HUNTINGDALE RD
HIGH STREET RD
COPYRIGHT © UNIVERSAL PRESS PTY LTD (PUBLISHER) 2004

374

JOINS 375

A B C D E F G H J K L

1 2 3 4 5 6 7 8 9 10 11 12 13 14 15 16 17 18 19 20

BOX HILL SOUTH

BLACKBURN SOUTH

BURWOOD EAST

BURWOOD

MOUNT WAVERLEY

St Leos International College

Box Hill Golf Course

Carver Holt Harvey

Council Depot

Salvation Army Inala Village

Fulton Reserve

Wurundjeri Walk

Orchard Grove Reserve

Orchard Grove Pmy

St Lukes Cath

Hunter Knoll

Wandinong Sanctuary

Bellbird Hosp

Artists Pk

Roberts McCubbin Pmy

Indoor Cricket

Crawfords

Gardiners Creek

Eley Park

Cmnty Cntr

Donaldsons Res

Nurs Home

English Language Sch

Royal Victorian Inst for the Blind

Animal Welfare Centre RSPCA

Benwerrin Res

Witchwood Gully

K-Mart

St Scholasticas Cath

Lundgren Res

Mudgee Flat

Bally Shannassy Park

Lawrence Res

Burwood East Sp Sch

Highbury Park

Burwood East Pmy

Tally Ho Reserve

Mt Waverley Sec Coll Junior Campus

Mt Waverley Sec College Senior Campus

Mt Waverley North Pmy

Yernga Ret Vill

Damper Creek Reserve

Mt Waverley Res

Mt Waverley Reservoir

Holy Family Cath Pmy

Avila Cath Coll

Huntingtower Pmy & Sec

St Christophers Cath

Mt Waverley

Syndal

ELEY RD

BURWOOD HWY

HIGHBURY RD

HIGH STREET RD

MIDDLEBOROUGH RD

STEPHENSONS RD

BLACKBURN RD

JOINS 418

JOINS 459

458

420
JOINS 376
JOINS 421
JOINS 460
377
461
A B C D E F G H J K L
1 2 3 4 5 6 7 8 9 10 11 12 13 14 15 16 17 18 19 20
FOREST HILL
VERMONT SOUTH
GLEN WAVERLEY
CANTERBURY RD
BURWOOD HWY
HIGHBURY RD
SPRINGVALE RD
HAWTHORN RD
CITY
Forest Hill Chase
Forest Hill Reserve
Mahoneys Reserve
Global Television Studios
Burwood Heights Pmy
Forest Hill Sec Coll
Emmaus Catholic College
Junior Campus
Parkmore Primary
Whitehorse Horticultural Centre
Strathdon Nursing Home
Vermont South Sp Sch
Livingstone Pmy
Livingstone Road Res
The Peter James Centre
Hewlett Packard
Nunawading Basketball Stadium
East Burwood Res
Oval
Optus Satellite Services
Tally Ho Business Park
Billabong Park
Australian Road Research Board
Holy Saviour Parish
Licola Res
Highview Park
Highvale Primary
Highvale Sec Coll
Highvale Retirement Village
Glendal Primary
Glen Waverley North Reserve
Larpent Res
Capital Reserve
Glen Waverley Pmy
The Glen Shop Cntr
Glen Waverley Sec Coll
COPYRIGHT © UNIVERSAL PRESS PTY LTD (PUBLISHER) 2004

376
JOINS 377
JOINS 420
JOINS 461
460

A B C D E F G H J K L

VERMONT

VERMONT SOUTH

WANTIRNA SOUTH

GLEN WAVERLEY

1
MALVERN ST
Buckanbe Park
GLENBURNIE RD
ERILYN CT
SCOTT ST
BARBARA ST
ADELE ST
Eastmont Res
RD
LIDDLE WY
BELGRAVE RD
ROOKS RD
CARINYA RD
WILLIS CT
PARK DR
MITCHAM RD
GREY ST
FARLEY GREEN CT
GROVE ST
Ten Cts
ARMSTRONG CT
BEDDOE AV
BLANCHE DR
AUBREY CT
Nurs Home
IDA ST
TWEED ST
CALDWELL RD
WK
SMITHFIELD
MANHATTAN SQ
HEATHERDALE RD
RAHNSTON CT
BRAMPTON CT
RACV Accident Repair Centre
TILSON DR
PARK CL
GRIGG AV
FRANK ST
Frank Way
ROWAN ST
OSPREY ST
ARLINGTON WK

2
TRADE PL
CANTERBURY RD
SHORT ST
FRANCES AV
VIEW ST
ELLAD CL
EVANS CT
KAY CT
St James Cath
PHYLLIS CT
McDONOUGH LA
SHIBOR DR
ORBOST CT
JUDY CT
Stevens Reserve
Vermont Rec Res
Vermont Pmy
WEBB ST
BEAUMONT ST
KINGSCLERE ST
BORONIA RD
VERMONT
HAYWARD CT
ALLISON CT
COSGROVE ST
GRAEME AV
PARANDA CT
ADOBE CT
TULKARA GR
CULBARA DR
CRISP CT

3
McARTHUR RD
MASARYK CT
BAHAMA CT
WOORILL CT
CANTLEY LA
TROVE PL
PARK DR
NURLENDI RD
KARWITHA ST
TRINIAN ST
LUSK DR
GALLUS CL
URALLA CT
CENTRE RD
CARDIFF ST
THE MEWS
LONGSTAFF
Culbara Res
WALK
Creek

4
NUNKERI ST
RICKSON PL
SARAH CT
CONDEN CT
LOCKSLEY CH
DUNWOLD WY
MALASET PL
BARNESDALE DR
HELENS CT
LUCERNE CR
CLEMATIS ST
LUNAR CR
MAWSON CT
CARLINGA DR
BARTON CT
PENLYNNE AV
AVILA CT
HOLYROOD DR
PADUA CT
ARCADY GR
LITTLE CT
JOHN CT
Abbey Walk
ABBEY WK
Fbr
CLARENCE
Wetlands Habitat
BARNABY
MARINA ST
BATMAN ST
DEVLIN ST
OLINDA CR
DR

5
HINDLE DR
TIMBERTOP CT
DELATITE CT
BAGLEYS LA
PERITON
TUCKER RD
CAROBEN AV
Vermont Sec Coll
COWRA ST
BELEURA AV
MOORE RD
MADONNA CT
COTSWOLD CL
Campbells Croft
McCLARES PL
SNOWDEN PL
HOWQUA CT
RYECROFT CT
BOLINDA
WINCOTT CT
BELLBIRD CT
PHILIP CR
RHODES CT
OLANDA CT
NARAMBI DR
Cobradah Res

6
JOLIMONT RD
BELLARA ST
KOOROORA CT
NOWINGI CT
BAYLISS PL
LEVEN CT
DALE
GLENORA DR
MYUNA CT
CAPRAMARA CT
MORACK RD
NURLENDI RD
RD
Ent
Proposed Realignment

7
HAWTHORN RD
PECK ST
NOLAN CL
GWYN RI
FELGATE CL
CHADWICK PL
CANOWINDRA CL
VILLAGE WK
KARA WK
NADIA PL
WINSWOOD CL
VERONA ST
LIVERMORE CL
Bellbird Dell
TALARNO CT
Morack Public Golf Course
Trail

8
NGUMBY CT
TERRARA RD
CITRON CT
COLTAIN CT
PDE
TAHLEE CT
KARINA LA
MINDAH AV
WYNNE CT
MURCHISON AV
DANIELLE CT
KATUPNA CT
TARNOOK ST
DELACOMBE DR
ARGYLE CT
KALTARA CL
YAMBUK CT
WINJALLOCK
CR
EAST RD
Dandenong
Koomba Park
Parks
MORACK RD
Clubhouse
ST Res
HANOVER RD

9
GEORGE ST
GREAT WESTERN DR
CHABLIS CR
RENMARK CT
GELEA CR
MILDARA CT
RUTHERGLEN RD
MOYSTON CL
ARAWATTA ST
MINCHINBURY DR
TAHBILK CT
COONAWARRA ST
Ent
18
WILPENA PL
MYRIONG AV
MELISSA GR
HEAD CT
BRACKNELL CT
CRAWLEY CT
STEVENAGE CT
Creek

10
MINNATA WK
WOODLEIGH CR
Terrara Park
MITCHELTON CT
WENDOUREE CT
YALUMBA CT
AULDANA CT
TANUNDA CT
REYNELLA CT
EDEN VALLEY CL
Wantirna Recreation Reserve
Freeway

11
CORNUTA WK
SALIGNA WK
MACULATA WK
NICHOLL WK
Priv Rds
HATFIELD CT
HEMEL CT
HEMPSTEAD AV
WARRINGTON AV
BAROSSA CL
WARWICK CT
HUNTER CT
VALLEY RD
Vermont
SILVERENE CT
QUELLTALER PL
ANGASTON CT
BUNDARRA CT
DALWOOD CT
MORACK RD
Nunawading Park
Fbr
Tennis
MOUNTAIN HWY
28
AUGHTON
KEW

12
BURWOOD RD
EXPLORERS CT
STOCKMANS DR
SETTLERS CT
COACHMANS CT
DROVERS CT
Vermont Retirement Village
MONT CT
(BURWOOD RD)
Golf Driving Range
26
Nutri-Metics HQ
SOUTH
Proposed

13
SHEARERS CT
COLONIAL DR
MUSTER CT
WEEDEN CT
SEWART CL
PIONEER CL
LASCELLE DR
Tyrol Park
RAHEEN CT
Proposed Bushy Park
Whitehorse Transfer & Recycling Centre
Parks

14
OVERLAND DR
SALLURN CT
LINDAU CT
GLENWERRI CT
DONBIRN CT
AKPANA CT
SALSBURG CT
LATURNS CT
CLENDON CT
WY
HIGHBURY RD
Bushy Park
JESSICA CL
CORREA CL

15
GALAHAD CR
DR
RD
ARMOUR CL
AVALON AV
Camelot Rise Pmy
CITY
DAMIAN PL
MIRIAM CL
REN
LESTWICK
JADE CT
ALEXIS CT
CATHIES

16
CHIVALRY AV
DINADAN CT
VALIANT CT
SAGRAMORE CT
MORGAN CT
PDE
Dandenong
PUMPS LA
AXFORD RD
RD

17
GUINEVERE AV
PERCIVALE
ARTHUR
KING
PLUME CT
KNIGHTS DR
PUMPS RD
SYL
BILL
Proposed
Freeway

18
HECTOR CT
SHIELD CT
CHAMPION CR
Proposed Dandenong Valley Metropolitan Park
Parks
BUSHY PARK
RICHARDSON RI
ORLANDO CL
LAMONT CT

19
BANNER CL
EXCALIBUR AV
CASTLE CT
MELROSE CT
LENNOX CT
POETS CT
CAPITAL AV
Pony Club
Drummies Bridge Reserve
Wantirna Estate
Dandenong Valley Parklands
GERA CT
TANDRAGEE

20
HIGH STREET RD
DR
24
GLEN TOWER DR
KRISTEN CL
KYMME CT
Nurs Home
ALMRAY PL
Baseball
Fbr
Napier Park
Shepherds Bush
Parks
Nortons Park
NORTONS LA
Parks
Knox Golf Driving Range
CATHIES LA

A B C D E F G H J K L

JOINS 378
379
JOINS 423
JOINS 462
463

A B C D E F G H J K L

1 2 3 4 5 6 7 8 9 10 11 12 13 14 15 16 17 18 19 20

RINGWOOD

Ringwood Municipal Golf Course

HEATHMONT

WANTIRNA

Clubhouse
Dandenong Ck
Heathmont Park Tennis
Marlborough Primary
Heathmont College Junior Campus
Tennis Res
J W Manson Reserve
Ret Vill
Hungarian Cmnty Cntr
Knox Centre
Trash & Treasure Market
Knox Private Hospital
Wantirna Mall
Wantirna Heights
Schultz Res
Wantirna Park
Salford Park Retirement Village
Nurs Home
Oval
Wantirna College
St Lukes Cath Primary
Regency Park Prmy
William Morris Reserve
Templeton Res
Tennis
Milpera Res
Templeton Primary
Billoo Pk
Knox Club
Knoxfield College
Flamingo Reserve
Wantirna Village
Collier Res
Knox City
Cinemas
Knox Tower Point
RACV
Regional Library HQ
SES Council Depot
Knox Cncl Off
Lewis Park
Skateboard Bowl
Blind Ck
Coleman Road Res
Villa Maria Society
Wantirna South Primary
Swinburne University of Technology (&TAFE) Wantirna Campus
Walker Res
Knox Ret Vill
Curanda Nurs Home
Holy Trinity Primary & St Marys Spec Schs
Latvian Ret Vill
Res

MOUNTAIN HWY
BORONIA RD
WANTIRNA RD
WANTIRNA-SASSAFRAS RD
STUD RD
BURWOOD HWY
HIGH STREET RD
DANDENONG VALLEY HWY
HAROLD ST
TEMPLETON ST
WALLACE RD
PLAZA
COLEMAN
UNIVERSITY
Proposed Realignment

MUIR CT, CARRUTHERS CT, MARLBOROUGH, CUMMING ST, BLIGH CT, WATERLOO, SUNSET, CRAIG CT, LOWEN AV, MOUNTAIN VIEW RD, DICKASONS, BENNETT AV, ORCHID ST, THE OUTLOOK, BELLBIRD CT, CLARKE DR, CUTHBERT CR, HARDEEP PL, PORTSMOUTH ST, YORK CT, HARDY, MARKHILL PL, PARKHAVEN DR, WALLIS CT, WASHUSEN AV, EDEN, ORCHARD GR, SIMLA, MULLER CT, KENBRY RD, BARNIC, POSSUM LA, GORDON CT, BAYLEY CL, ILFORD RD, BLENHEIM ST, JANET CT, KAREN CT, BARROW DR, DIRKALA, BANGOR, SCOTT ST, WATERS GR, SIMPSONS CT, MAGNOLIA ST, EDNA, JUNIPER, MINT, BELLBIRD, HIBISCUS ST, LANTANA CT, CASH FUES PL, CASSIA CT, TONI CT, SWAN CT, ROBIN CT, HOAD AV, BOTANY CT, DUDLEY AV, ANGUS CL, CASEY CT, SELKIRK, DAVIDS, THOMAS AV, INCHCAPE, SANDRINGHAM, BATEMAN, TI TREE AV, CHERRY AV, APPLE GR, LINCOLN RD, FIGTREE GR, CUMBERLAND, MICHELLAN, HAVELOCK, KAREN, DEAN, NORTHAM RD, RACHELLE, TABILK CT, GLEBE, SULLIVAN, MILAN, ELDALE CT, LOTUS, TARA CT, ASHLEY ST, GARRISON GR, OAK TREE, BENMORE PL, DUMFRIES WY, GLENBARRY, DUNBARTON, CHEVIOT, KELSO PL, KINGLOCH, HADLOW, THAXTED, BENTLEY, GRESFORD, SHETLAND, DALKEITH, DUNDEE, PHYLLIS, LEONARD ST, NAOMI CT, TAMAR, PRINCESS ST, RYLANDS PL, CARRICK, DOWNE PL, SKYE, ROXBURGH, WHITEHAVEN CR, GREENOCK, BADMINTON, BARNSDALE, AINSDALE, CHESTER SQ, CHELSEA, NAPIER, KIDDERMINSTER, PUTNEY, WARWICK, KELLAWAY, NESTON, HESWALL, PRENTON, YORKMINSTER, NIZAM, IPSWICH, ASHWOOD, STOKES, NEPAL, ALBANY, BURLINGTON, ETON, CHARTWELL, KINGSFORD, RUTH, DENNIS, JUNE, WEEMALA, NEWLANDS, HAILEYBURY, SMITHFIELD, BELEURA, CLOVERLEA, AMBERLEY, CHESHIRE, SEYMOUR, BARRINGTON, NEWMAN, BILLARA, ST CLAIR, IRELAND, NORFOLK, YORK, LINSLEY, WATERMAN, STRATFORD, HARMSWORTH, HAROLD, COURTNEY, MERIVALE, ASQUITH, DEWSBURY, BAUDELAIRE, FORTESCUE, AMESBURY, MARIEMONT, BIRKENHEAD, CHESTERFIELD, NOTTINGHAM, TELFORD, ROEHAMPTON, BLACKFRIARS, TEDDINGTON, ATTENBOROUGH, MOONAH, COLOMONI, WARRAWEE, KIRRAWEE, DON, MINGANA, ARBROATH, SOMERSET, TATE, AISBETT, BIRRALEE, TELOPEA, CARINA, BINDI, ALLENBY, PESCARA, PETALNINA, MINKELL, DEFELICE, FRESHFIELD, CASTLEFIELD, EGANLEE, CROXTETH, GARSTON, FORMBY, AMERSHAM, BARMAH, QUIXLEY, ADAIR, ABBEY, BROADGREEN, KNOWSLEY, BIRKDALE, DANIELLE, PACIFIC, TANDERRA, ALKIRA, KALINYA, MILPERA, BLUE HILLS, NEWELL, SKIPTON, PRISCILLA, CLEARVIEW, GUY, MARLO, LABUAN, DAVIES, NINA, WINTERTON, GEORGIAN, ROTHERWOOD, CRESTDALE, TRENTHAM, SAXON, TUDOR, KAISMAN, JENKINS, CAMERON, MAIN, REX, COBAIN, BRENTWOOD, DEAUVILLE, CHERRINGTON, BISHOP, MINOR, RAHEEN, MANNIX, BALLARD, SANDHURST, HARROW GDN, BIRCHFIELD, CARISBROOKE, WINBOURNE, CORNELLA, PICCADILLY, LEICESTER, REGENT, HERTFORD, PAUL, SUFFOLK, BERKLEY, COORONG, AMINYA, WINYARRA, PIMPALA, BENWERRIN, CHALICE, BAMBARA, KARA, COACHMANS, CHEQUERS, DUNTROON, TYLOID, CAVENDISH, EDGEWARE, ROTHBURY, MARLESFORD, CARNABY, DAVINGTON, ORMISTON, ELLERTON, GRASMERE, BLADON, GROSVENOR, DEANSWOOD, SNOWDEN, JAMES, HARTINGTON, HAMSTERLEY, ALVASTON, SALISBURY, KINTBURY, ALDERFORD, PINEWOOD, COTTSWOLD, GATESHEAD, HELSAL, APOLLO, MATILDA, MARIPOSA, HEWSON, ORCHARD, OLD, AVOCA, RISDON, SIMMONDS, BURNSIDE, COLLEGE, MARA, MERRYN, CEDUNA, MARINGA, TUMUT, FINLEY, CHARLES, PARKHILL, DUNNS, GLENYS, GIVVENS, LAINIE, GEDYE, FLAMINGO, DAYAN, DRURY, SALLY, ROSALIE, TIMMOTHY, OLD ORCHARD, JONATHON, JACKSON, WHITE, HENRY, LYNNE, MAURICE, SOVEREIGN, EARLS, RIVERPARK, KENSINGTON, MENDORA, ALIKI, LYDIA, TOVA, CAITLYN, JENOLA, CONDOS, LANDSDALE, BUCHAN, HUNTINGDON, AVONWOOD, NEWBURY, RAVENHILL, TYNER, CORNELIUS, LIBRA, VIRGO, ST BERNARDS, SCOTT, BEMBOKA, HILSON, KINGS, ARMAGH, MERIDIAN, MOSMAN, MOONSTONE, WAORA, JEANBART, JULIE, WOLF, NEWSTEAD, HAWKSBURN, DENSHAM, EDGEWOOD, EXELL, WHITING, RIDDELL, JUSTIN, GLENMAGGIE, FONTEYN, GISELLE, ROWENA, ROYCROFT, FRASER, PONSFORD, TYSON, HOGAN, ENDEAVOUR, TAMARA, GORRIE, HASSETT, BLIND CREEK, TOWNVIEW, ROCHELLE, MYALLA, DOWNSHIRE, REITA, KIRRUM, WITKEN, McLEAN, KEYES

JOINS 379

A B C D E F G H J K L

BAYSWATER NORTH

HEATHMONT

BAYSWATER

WANTIRNA SOUTH

KNOXFIELD

FERNTREE GULLY

H-E Parker Reserve
Netball
Tennis
Heathmont Golf Park (Par 3)
Dandenong
Bayswater Tennis Sec College
Bayswater Park
Cmnty Cntr
Glen Park
Pacific
Bayswater
RSL
Bayswater Primary
Guy Turner Res
MCH
Bayswater West Primary
Our Lady of Lourdes Cath
Sasses Av Res
Bayswater South Primary
Tabulam Nursing Home
Mountain Dist Priv Hosp
Nurs Home
Yawarra Pmy
Arthur Kleinert Res
MCH Coleman Road Res
Lewis Park Skateboard Bowl
SES Council Depot
Regional Library HQ
Knox Cncl Off
Knox Cmnty Gardens & Vineyard
Institute For Horticultural Development
Fairhills High
Fairpark
Fairhills Primary
Child Care Cntr
Reservoir
Lakewood Nature Res
Wiluna Pk
Blind Ck

MOUNTAIN HWY
BORONIA RD
SCORESBY RD
STUD RD
BURWOOD HWY
HIGH STREET RD
MOUNTAIN HWY (WANTIRNA - SASSAFRAS RD)
STATION ST
POWER RD
LEWIS RD
COLEMAN RD
McMAHONS RD
DANDENONG CK

1 2 3 4 5 6 7 8 9 10 11 12 13 14 15 16 17 18 19 20

JOINS 422

378

462

JOINS 463

A B C D E F G H J K

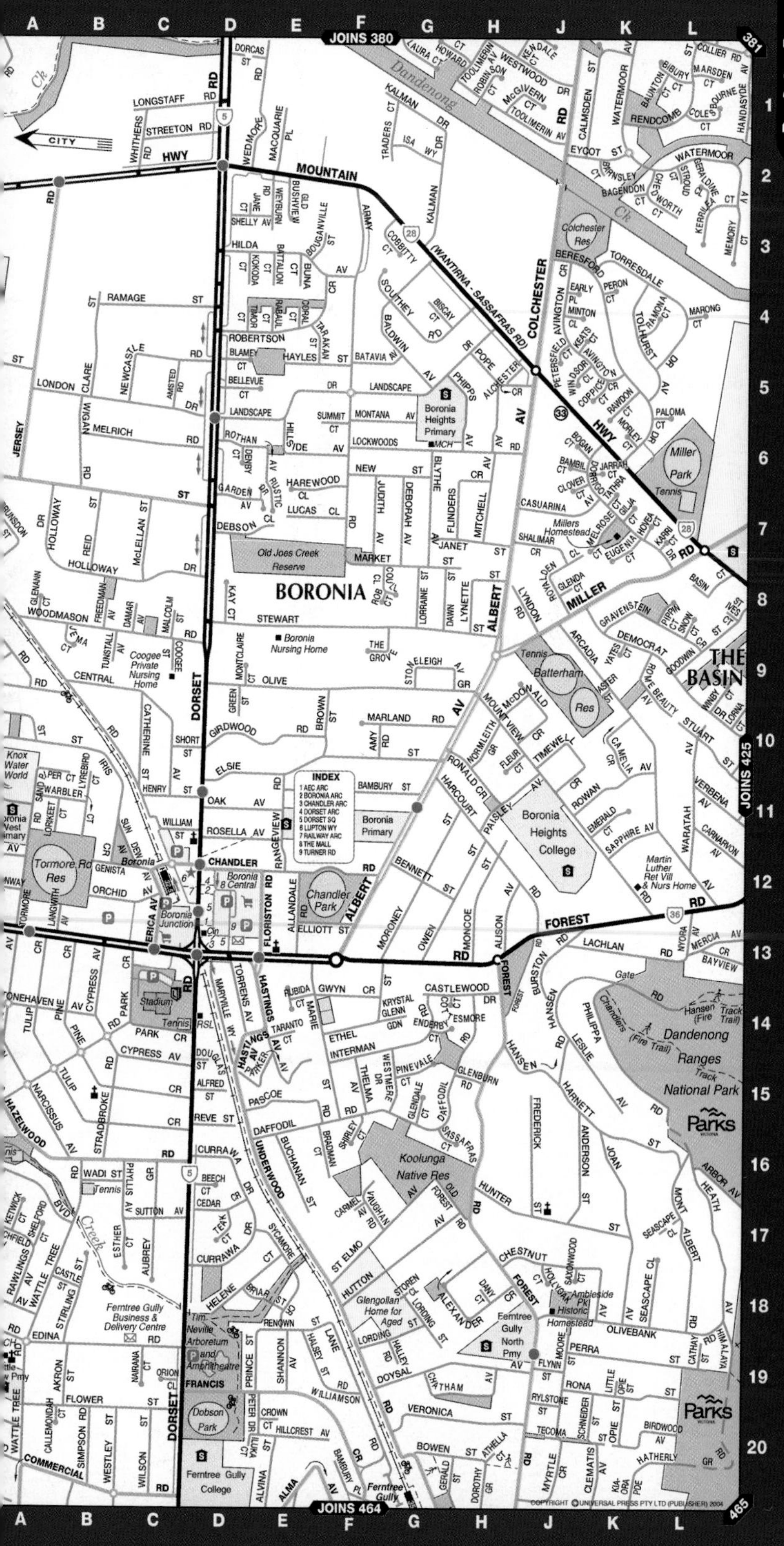
A B C D E F G H J K L
1 2 3 4 5 6 7 8 9 10 11 12 13 14 15 16 17 18 19 20
JOINS 380
381
JOINS 425
JOINS 464
465
CITY
BORONIA
THE BASIN
MOUNTAIN HWY
(WANTIRNA - SASSAFRAS RD)
DORSET RD
COLCHESTER RD
ALBERT AV
FOREST RD
BORONIA RD
MILLER RD
Dandenong Ck
LONGSTAFF RD
STREETON RD
WHITHERS RD
DORCAS ST
WEDMORE RD
MACQUARIE PL
KALMAN DR
TRADERS CT
ISA WY
LAURA CT
HOWARD CT
TOOLIMERIN AV
ROBINSON CT
WESTWOOD DR
McGIVERN CT
KENDALE CT
CALMSDEN CT
WATERMOOR AV
EYCOT ST
BIBURY CT
BAUNTON CT
RENDCOMB CT
COLLIER RD
MARSDEN CT
BOURNE CT
COLES CT
HANDASYDE AV
WATERMOOR
BARNSLEY CT
BAGENDON CT
CHEDWORTH CT
STROUD CT
GERALDINE CT
KERRILEA CT
MEMORY CT
JANE CT
WEYBURN CT
BUSHVIEW GLD
BOUGANVILLE ST
SHELLY AV
HILDA
KOKODA CT
BATTALION CT
BUNA CT
CORAL CT
TIMOR CT
RABAUL CT
TARAKAN ST
ROBERTSON
BLAMEY CT
HAYLES ST
BELLEVUE CT
LANDSCAPE DR
ARMY
COBBITTY CT
SOUTHEY CT
BISCAY CT
BALDWIN AV
BATAVIA
POPE CT
PHIPPS
ALCHESTER CR
SUMMIT CT
MONTANA AV
LOCKWOODS
Boronia Heights Primary
MCH
Colchester Res
BERESFORD CR
TORRESDALE
EARLY PL
PERON CT
MINTON CT
AVINGTON CR
PETERSFIELD
KEATS CT
WINDSOR CT
COPPICE CT
RAWDON CT
TOLHURST DR
RAMONA CT
MARONG CT
PALOMA CT
MORLEY CT
BOGAN CT
BAMBIL CT
JARRAH CT
DORRIGO CT
TATHRA CT
CLOVER CT
CASUARINA
MELROSE CT
GILJA CT
HOVEA CT
KARRI CT
EUGENIA CT
Millers Homestead
Miller Park
Tennis
SHALIMAR CR
RAMAGE ST
ST
LONDON
CLARE
NEWCASTLE
AMSTED RD
WIGAN
MELRICH RD
JERSEY
ROTHAN
DENBY CT
HILLSIDE AV
RUSTIC AV
NEW ST
JUDITH AV
DEBORAH AV
BLYTHE AV
FLINDERS CR
MITCHELL
HAREWOOD CL
LUCAS CL
GARDEN AV
DEBSON CL
HOLLOWAY DR
REID
McLELLAN ST
Old Joes Creek Reserve
MARKET
JANET ST
ROB CL
LORRAINE ST
DAWN
LYNETTE CT
GLENANN CT
FREEDMAN
DAMAR
MALCOLM
WOODMASON
JEMA CT
TUNSTALL AV
KAY CT
STEWART
Boronia Nursing Home
THE GROVE
STONELEIGH AV
Coogee Private Nursing Home
COOGEE
CENTRAL
MONTCLAIRE CT
OLIVE
GREEN ST
BROWN ST
MARLAND RD
AMY RD
LYNDON RD
ROYALDEN
GLENDA CT
GRAVENSTEIN
PIPPIN CT
SNOW CT
DEMOCRAT
ARCADIA
YATES CT
GOODWIN
Tennis
Batterham Res
McDONALD
MOUNT VIEW
JASTER
ROWE BEAUTY
STUART
WINBY
DR LORNA
CATHERINE ST
SHORT ST
GIRDWOOD
ELSIE
HENRY ST
OAK AV
WILLIAM
ROSELLA AV
CHANDLER
Knox Water World
SANDY
JUNIPER CT
LYREBIRD
WARBLER
LORIKEET
IRIS
Boronia West Primary
Tormore Rd Res
GENISTA
ORCHID AV
SUNDEW
Boronia
Boronia Central
Boronia Junction
ERICA AV
INDEX
1 AEC ARC
2 BORONIA ARC
3 CHANDLER ARC
4 DORSET ARC
5 DORSET SQ
6 LUPTON WY
7 RAILWAY ARC
8 THE MALL
9 TURNER RD
BAMBURY ST
Boronia Primary
RANGEVIEW
FLORISTON RD
ALLANDALE
Chandler Park
ELLIOTT ST
NORMLEITH GR
FLEUR CT
TIMEWELL
RONALD CR
HARCOURT
PAISLEY AV
Boronia Heights College
ROWAN
EMERALD
SAPPHIRE AV
CAMELIA AV
VERBENA AV
WARATAH
CARNARVON AV
Martin Luther Ret Vill & Nurs Home
BENNETT ST
MORONEY
OWEN
MONCOE
ALISON AV
LACHLAN
NYORA
MERCIA AV
BAYVIEW
TORMORE
LANGWITH
CYPRESS AV
STONEHAVEN
PARK
Stadium
Tennis
RSL
TORRENS AV
HASTINGS AV
MARYVILLE WY
RUBIDA
GWYN CR
MARIE
CASTLEWOOD
KRYSTAL GLENN
ENDERBY
TESMORE
TARANTO
ETHEL
INTERMAN
THELMA
WESTMERE DR
PINEVALE
GLENBURN
BURSTON
HANSEN
PHILIPPA
LESLIE
Gate
Chandlers (Fire Trail)
Hansen (Fire Trail)
Dandenong Ranges National Park
Parks
TULIP
PINE
NARCISSUS
STRADBROKE
HAZELWOOD
DOUGLAS
ALFRED
PARKER
PASCOE
REVE ST
DAFFODIL
GLENDALE
SASSAFRAS
FREDERICK
HARNETT
ANDERSON
JOAN
CURRAWA
BUCHANAN ST
BRADMAN
SHIRLEY
UNDERWOOD
Koolunga Native Res
CARMEL
VAUGHAN
OLD FOREST
HUNTER
WADI ST
PHYLLIS
Tennis
SUTTON AV
BEECH CT
CEDAR
TEAK CT
SYCAMORE
ST ELMO
ALEXANDER
DAVY CT
CHESTNUT
HOLLYOAK
SAXONWOOD
SEASCAPE CL
MONT ALBERT
ARBOR AV
HEATH
KETWICK
CHFIELD
SHELFORD
RAWLINGS
WATTLE TREE
CASTLE ST
STIRLING
Creek
ESTHER
AUBREY
Ferntree Gully Business & Delivery Centre
HELENE
BRIAR
Tim Neville Arboretum and Amphitheatre
RENOWN
HUTTON
Glengollan Home for Aged
STOREN
LORDING
HALLEY
Ferntree Gully North Pmy
Ambleside Pk
Historic Homestead
OLIVEBANK
PERRA
CATHAY
HIMALAYA
EDINA
AKRON
NAIRANA
ORION
FRANCIS
PRINCE
SHANNON
HALSEY
LANE
DOYSAL
CHATHAM
FLYNN
RONA
LITTLE OPIE
FLOWER
Dobson Park
CROWN
WILLIAMSON
VERONICA
RYLSTONE
SCHNEIDER
OPIE
BIRDWOOD
CALLEMONDAH
SIMPSON
WESTLEY
WILSON
COMMERCIAL
PETER
ILUKA
HILLCREST
BOWEN
ATHELLA
TECOMA
MYRTLE
CLEMATIS
KIA-ORA
POE
HATHERLY
Ferntree Gully College
ALVINA
ALMA
BAMBURY
Ferntree Gully
GERALD
DOROTHY
COPYRIGHT © UNIVERSAL PRESS PTY LTD (PUBLISHER) 2004

1 2 3 4 5 6 7 8 9 10 11 12 13 14 15 16 17 18 19 20

JOINS 424

COLLIER RD
INDEPENDANCE RI
MARSDEN CT
MAYGRAND CL
COLES-BOURNE CT
HANDASYDE AV
ILLUMINATE CT
WATERMOOR AV
GERALDINE CL
KERRILEA CT
MEMORY CT
KILSYTH SOUTH
LILLYPILLY LA
18 Clubhouse
Eastwood Golf Course
RD
LOBOSCO CT
KILSYTH
RD
CHANDLERS LA
CITY
MONTROSE
Doongalla Pony Club
Edgar Track
Bills
Doongalla Reserve
BORONIA
PAVITT
Dandenong
SHEFFIELD RD
LA
Salvation Army Mountain Valley Youth Camp & Conference Centre
Liverpool Road Retarding Basin Reserve
LIVERPOOL
DOBSON LA
Gate
Ridge
Banks
The Basin Pmy
ACADEMY
CREST CT
FESTIVAL PL
LYRIC DR
CT
Melb Water
BASIN CT
ST INES CT
ST
GOODWIN
MOUNTAIN
STANLEY ST
St Bernadettes Cath Pmy
THE BASIN
Salvation Army Youth Training Centre
Dobsons
MILLEARA ST
RD
RD
SIMPSONS
The Basin Theatre
DOONGALLA
WINBY CT
LORNA CT
DEMOCRAT DR
CHRISTOPHER AV
THORNTON
SUZANNE CT
RD
BASIN - OLINDA
SHEFFIELD
(Unsealed Rd)
OLD COACH RD
GRUMONT RD
MCH
ST
Sen Cits
CFA
(WANTIRNA
STUART AV
NORMAN ST
AUGUSTA
CONYERS
RD
CHURCH ST
RD
Wicks Res
RD
OLD
VERBENA
FRANCES ST
Mortiboy Res
36
VIEW
WALKER ST
WICKS
CLEVE AV
ROSS AV
CLEVEDON
WARATAH
CARNARVON AV
ST
AV
HARRISON ST
SASSAFRAS
RD
Clevedon Camp & Conference Centre
ARCADIA AV
FOREST
OLD FOREST
RD
TOORAK
AV
RD
AV
GOLDEN
CORSAIR RD
CLAREMONT
CLAREMONT GR
BOWEN AV
FERNDALE
MERCIA ST
WRIGHT ST
BAYVIEW CR
CR
BAYVIEW
SHORT CR
CR
CLAREMONT
INVERNESS
FERN ST
MOUNTAIN 39
Gate
CRETE RD
Gate
AV
INVERNESS
AV
FERNDALE
STEWART
EDITH RD
HELEN
Hansen (Fire Track Trail)
GOVERNMENT
28
28
RD)
RD
DANIEDA
MYSTIC RD
Alamein
AV
Chandlers (Fire Trail) Track
TOBRUK (Fire Access Track)
AV Gate
RD
HWY
Gate
Tyson (Fire Trail) Track
Gate
OUTLOOK
RD
FERN CREE
ARBOR HEATH AV
Track
(Fire Trail)
One Tree Hill 500m
Ranges
RD
ALPINE
Dandenong
Trail)
TREMONT
JANESDELL
MOUNT VIEW
ALPINE (Fire Access Track)
Gate
Gate
AV
View (Fire Track)
Macedon
Access Track
HILL ST
Gate
LORD SOMERS
MOUNT ERIN
SEABREEZE
AV
RD
ALPINE
RD
OLIVEBANK
RD
Parks
Arbor Track
Gate
Gate RD
Track
HIGHVIEW
CATHAY ST
RD
(Fire
RD
RAMU
Poachers Track
CHURCHILL
ONE TREE HILL
CORNER AV
RD
Telstra Tower
PERRA ST
Stony Rise (Fire Trail) Track
National
Gate
Park
TITANIA
AV
RD
HIMALAYA
Feather (Fire Trail) Track
Trail)
Ramu Link Track
Track Trail)
Gully Track
Fern Tree
DR
DUNCANS LA
ALPINE
MERIMBULA
Reservoir
Lyrebird (Fire
CR
DUNN AV
SCHOOL RD

A B C D E F G H J K L

JOINS 382

383

1 2 3 4 5 6 7 8 9 10 11 12 13 14 15 16 17 18 19 20

MOUNT DANDENONG

OLINDA

SASSAFRAS

SHERBROOKE

Doongalla Forest)

Dandenong Ranges National Park

Dandenong Ranges National Park (Sherbrooke Forest)

ABV2 Tower
HSV7 Tower
ATV10 Tower
Burkes 630m
Singleton Reserve

RIDGE RD
EYRE RD
ORNATA RD
BONNIE VIEW RD
PRION
RAMAGE RD
TOROA RD
UPALONG RD
SELWYN LA
YARRABEE
TOORAK RD
CAMBRIDGE RD
CLAVERTON AV
CAMPBELL
GLADYS CT
YVONNE AV
RADNOR CT
VIOLA AV
EDITH CT
OLD COACH RD
HELEN ST
HUME
THE GROVE
ANN CT
FERNGLEN AV
WISTERIA LA
BLYTHES RD
FALLS
DINGLEY LA
MOUNT DANDENONG TOURIST RD
SUMMERLEA AV
FENTON ST
FORDYCE
FAIRHAVEN RD
DICKENS
STANLEY ST
DULCIE DOMUM RD
OAKLEY ST
ILLOURA CT
WILLIAMS
SUNSET AV
Edward Henty Cottage
Res

Rankin Track
Camellia Track
Dacite Track
Kyeema Track
Channel Ten
Dodds Gate
Dandenong Creek
Track
BASIN - OLINDA (Unsealed) Gravel Road
RANGE RD (Fire Access Road Only)
Bradley Track
School Track
Dog Track (Fire Access Rd)
Gate

MONASH AV
CARDS LA
FALLS
CHARLEMONT
National Rhododendron Garden
Reservoir
SCHOOL RD
Hall
PARSONS LA
Olinda Pmy
OLINDA - MONBULK RD
Res
CFA
GEORGE ST
DODDS
DANDENONG
GAYNERS RD
OLINDA AV
HAROLD ST
NICHOLSON ST
Resvr
RANGE
LUMEAH AV
OLINDA
EVEREST
BEAUMONT ST
BELLA VISTA CR
VISTA
VICTOR
Kenloch Function Centre
C415

JOINS 427

AURORA RI
MASON GR
CHUDLEIGH CR
Sassafras Pmy
DRIFFIELD CR
MILLS AV
PERRINS CREEK RD
Reserve
Hall
LENNOX GR
GUILFOYLE DR
COLEHURST CR
LYLE RD
WOODLANDS
Sassafras Creek
SASSAFRAS CREEK
LYNN ST
COLEHURST CR
ALLISON AV
WARWICK FARM RD
WARWICK RD

MONBULK - SASSAFRAS
SASSAFRAS
HILTON RD
HWY 26
PRINCE ST
WALLABY AV
WANNAWONG
YARILLA RD
COOLOONGATTA RD
GRANDVIEW GR
FLORENCE AV
Sherbrooke Community
GWENNETH CR
KENNETH AV
WILTON GR
THE CRESCENT
Fire Access Track
TRACEY CT
CLARKE
BREEN
MARY ST
WOODS LA
ALICE
HETHERSETT
ROBERT ST
MYRTLE RD
TCE
TOURIST RD
PANTEG
ELLIS AV
HILTON
Ferny Ck Horticultural Society
Burnham Beeches Estate
Alfred Nicholas Memorial Gardens
Dandenong Ranges Gardens Regional Off
Ent
Parks
COLSTON AV
VISTA GR
CLARKMONT RD
Ferny Creek Reserve
CFA
SHERBROOKE RD
Ferny Creek Picnic Ground
MOUNT DANDENONG RD
Monument Track
Hackett Track
Moore Track
Wattle Track
Main Ent
NOBLES
MIZMAZE RD
LA
POETS
George Tindale Memorial Gardens
BRAESIDE
BRAE CT
SAVILLE ST
GREVILLE RD
OLD MONBULK RD

JOINS 383
382
JOINS 426
JOINS 467
466

Dandenong Ranges National Park

Olinda State Forest Reserve

Eagle Nest Picnic Ground

Valley Picnic Ground

National Rhododendron Garden

Olinda Public Golf Course

Clubhouse

R J Hamer Forest Arboretum

Woolrich Lookout

SILVAN

OLINDA

Life Ministry Bible College

Churches of Christ Waterman Camp

Pirianda Garden

KALLISTA

Lyrebird Haunt Res

Kensleys Picnic Gnd

Olympic Picnic Gnd

Reserve

Sen Cits

Hall

CITY

MONBULK RD · OLINDA MONBULK RD · CHALET RD · SILVAN RD · MT DANDENONG TOURIST RD · THE GEORGIAN RD · FALLS RD · PERRINS CREEK RD · SASSAFRAS CREEK RD · UPPER COONARA RD · HOWARD RD · McCARTHY RD · WOOLRICH RD · OLD COONARA RD · OLD RD · PLOWMAN ST · BROOMPARK CR · YURINGA AV · SPENCER RD · INVERMAY AV · REDHILL RD · THOMSON RD · COONARA CT · LAUREL CT · MERNDA RD · GREENTHORPE RD · ROY RD · IDA GR · SEDDON ST · HACKETTS RD (Dry Weather Only) · SKIPTON RD · STEWART RD · FOSTER RD · LYNWOOD AV · HUNTER RD · HOLDEN RD · BEAGLEYS BR · CROOKS RD · SUNNYSIDE AV · WEMBLEY ST · BEAGLEY ST · BRAE CT · BRAESIDE AV · OWEN HILL RD · RIVINGTON ST · ST JAMES AV · ADELAIDE AV · EBBELS PDE · SCHOOL RD · WILLIAMS RD · DINGLEY LA · BELLA VISTA CR · WARWICK · BOUNDARY RD · EAGLE NEST RD · SILVAN RD · MATHIAS (Walkers & Management Tr) · Vehicles Only · Gate

Olinda Falls · Olinda Ck · Perrins Creek · Emerald Ck · Sassafras Ck

Bartlett Track · Barges Road · Bobcat Track · Rifle Range Road · Georges Road · Hermon Road · Gully Road · Chamberlain Road · Prices Road · Prices Track · Bulldog Av · K.C. Track · Black Hole Tr · Lyrebird Track · Yallambee Rd · Gingko Av · Cornus Tr · Fraxinus Track · Simmons Track · Sequoia Tr · Manna Gum Track · Loop Rd · Way Rd · Poplar Rd · Dam Road · Rock Track · Valley Track · Bridge Rd

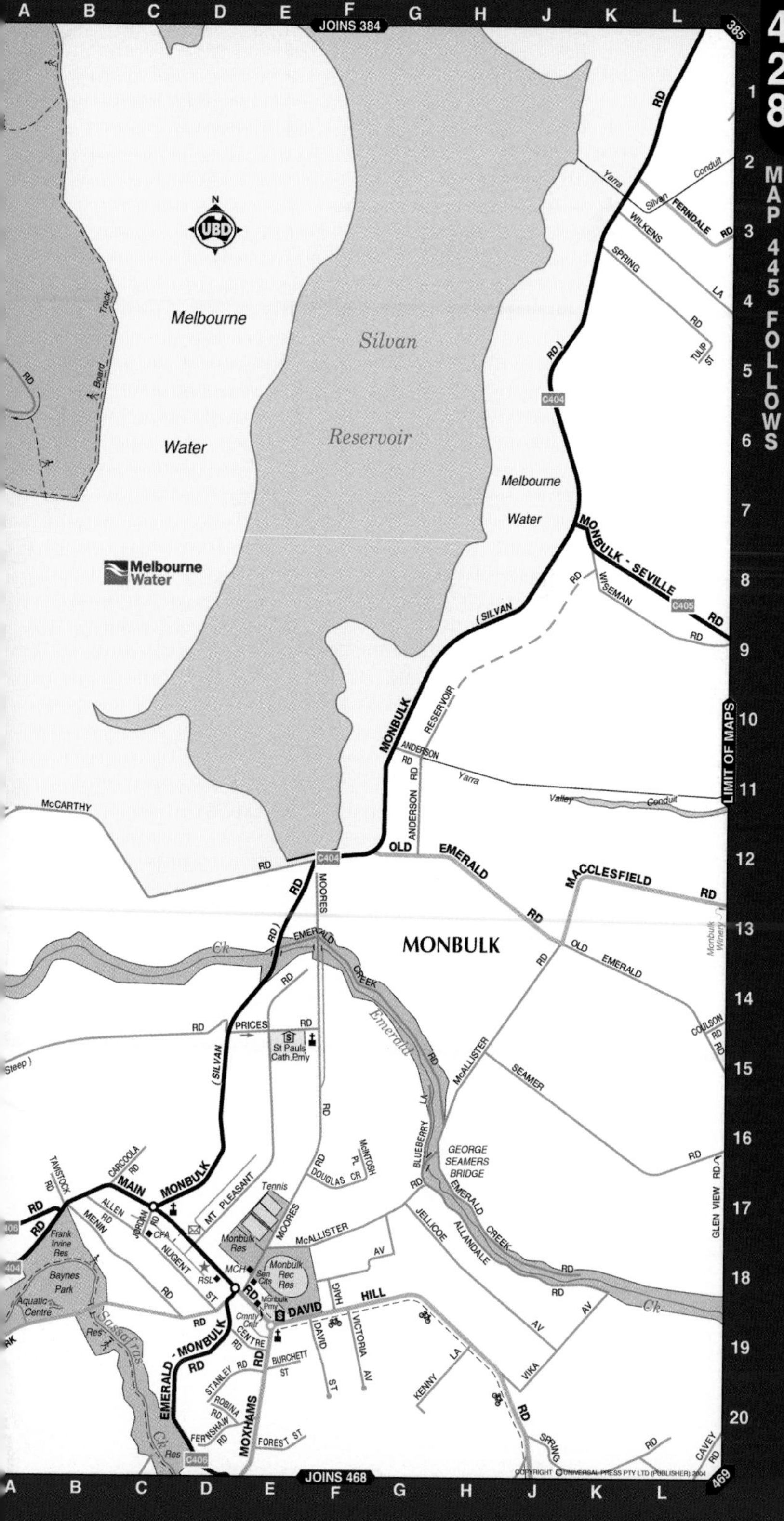
JOINS 384
385
Melbourne
Water
Silvan
Reservoir
Melbourne
Water
Melbourne Water
MONBULK
LIMIT OF MAPS
JOINS 468
469

PREVIOUS MAP 428

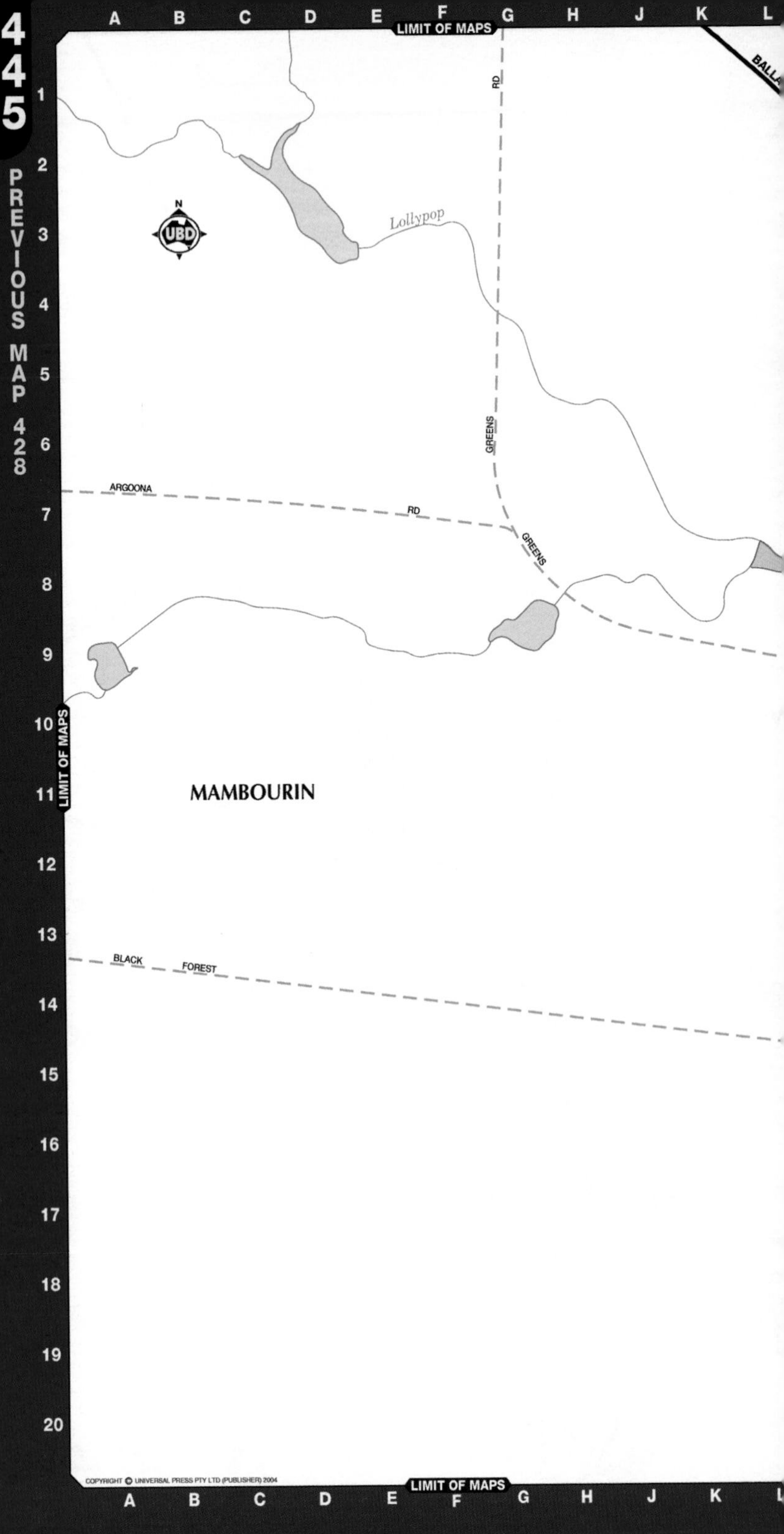

LIMIT OF MAPS
C703
(BACCHUS MARSH - WERRIBEE RD)
WOLLAHRA
CITY
RD
MANOR LAKES DR
EPPALOCK DR
BULOKE DR
CONNEWARRE AV
MULWALA CT
GLEN MAGGIE PL
TYRRELL PL
HINDMARSH
EILDON
McCLARENS
HINDMARSH AV
DARTMOUTH CT
VARSITY MW
BONNEY ST
BALMORAL
MALTRAVERS
STRETTON PL
HERIOT CT
CHYSHOLM
EVERGREEN
CASTLE ROCK
KINLOCH
WHITMORE PL
LAKEVIEW
Creek
BRIGHTON
PELHAM
CHATSWOOD PL
HYDEFIELD
CREEKVIEW
OAKTREE DR
Village
Park
Tennis
GREENGABLES
AMBER
ELM CT
LOLLIPOP
FINCH CL
EAGLE
WYNDHAM BVD
VALLEY MW
GREENS RD
WYNDHAM VALE
LANSELL
CASCADE DR
OLYMPIC
BROADWAY
CHARLOTTE
NEPTUNE
FARMYTAGE WY
BELLARINE
TCE
LADY PENRHYN DR
HALLADALE AV
MACQUARIE
WENTWORTH
DAMPIER CT
BASS CT
FLINDERS
BLIGH
FRANKLAND
TASMAN PL
OXLEY CT
CR
AV
McGRATH
GREENWICH
BLOOMSBURY
CHESTERFIELD
BURLINGTON
MAYFAIR
PEMBROKE
BROMLEY
LEICESTER
BIRCH ST
CHARING CROSS
BYRON CT
BIRCH CT
ALOMA AV
WHITTON
BOLTON RD
BLAXLAND
WINDSOR CT
CASHMERE
BURGUNDY DR
WINSTON
BORONIA
C703
HARCOURT
SQ
MARLO
CAMDEN
HEATHS RD
PRESIDENTS
Softball
Presidents
Park
Gate
Pavilion
Hockey
Baseball
Dog Obedience
TARWIN
TORQUAY
ROSEDALE
NEPEAN CT
Floodway
SOLWAY GDN
ROWES
NICHOLSON CL
BEMM
JAMIESON
ROBINIA
GREAVES ST
RORY
JOINS 447
MALVERN
STRATHFORD AV
ENFIELD
QUEENSBURY
RIVERGLEN DR
SASHA
GERALD
EDINBURGH DR
BEXLEY
STANFORD
ADAM
SONIA
KENT
HERITAGE
CANTERBURY
BUCKINGHAM
WHITEHALL
REGIS
CAREY
WESTMINSTER
GLOUCESTER
COVENTRY
RALEIGH
SOMERSET
GLAMORGAN
NORFOLK
CUMBERLAND
HOOKER
GREENWOOD
VALEWOOD DR
WEMBLEY
ELDORADO
BOTANIC
CYPRUS
ACACIA
STRADBROKE
CROXLEY
SUNRISE
HONOUR
EAST
WHITEHAVEN ST
INTERVALE
Wyndham Vale Shopping Cntr
CHILDERS
MILLEWA
HIGHGATE
ACTON
WESTBOURNE
WEST COUNTY
WOORITE
DRAYTONS
EARLING
HONOUR AV
Iramoo Primary
CARRINGTON
CAMBRIDGE
DERBY
CHESTER
AVENEL
JACKMAN
DAKARA
LENTARA
BALLAN
NEWARK
TYBURN
LYDFORD
LOMOND
TORBAY
KIMBERLEY
LEGANA
NEBO
TANILBA
MOOLONG
ELAROO
TERRIGAL
CHARINGA DR
Mambourin Cntr
Mambourin Sensory Gardens
Netball
Tennis
MCH
BELAIR
VISION
HAVELOCK PL
ORANA ST
FEATHERTOP
MELVIEW
EAGLE
PLEASANT
VISTA
GREENHILL
CAIRN
RIBBLESDALE
BRETT PL
BROUGHAM
OXFORD
MILTON
DOWNHAM
SAWLEY
GEM
WILTON
WEST
PENOLE
ENDEAVOUR
BRIMPTON
THE RIGHT
CLITHEROE
MARNE
TOPAZ
ZIRCON
BLACK
FOREST ST
YANDO PL
OLIVE WY
BVD
RIDGE
Wyndham Vale
Res
Pav
FERRY
PROVAN
GRACE
GENTZEN
McGRATH
KIANDRA
PINAROO
ALKIRA
YALTARA
OPALA
WARRAN
ILUKA
MEMBREY
CAMBRIDGE
BEMBOKA
ILLAWONG
QUAMBY
DALPURA
LOWAN
JIKA CT
DANIEL
WALLS
MONTANA
HEPBURN
HENDRIKS
OZZIMO WY
RACECOURSE
Gordon O'Keeffe Reserve
BUTMAR
FOSTER
FRAN CT
Thomas Chirnside Primary
CALVO
HAVEAUX
SIMPSON
MOLLOY
DALVISTA
ANDREWS
BAY
BEVERSTONE
HOLMESDALE
DONG
DENHOLME
WYCOMBE
BRIARDALE
CARMARTHEN
GAUDIN CT
FLEMINGTON
ALASKA
DIEMA
BONUS
FOUNTAIN
FLEMINGTON
TAISHO
ENGLEFIELD
GAYNESS
THOROUGHBRED
SAVAGE
PLEONE
WERRIBEE
Drain
McGRATH
Res
BULBAN
GALVIN
BELMARINO
LEXINGTON
NOELHURST
WESTLEIGH
HOPETOUN
COULTON CT
BELDALE
DELTA
DELMONT AV
HARTWELL
HENSHAW
KILLARA
LYALL
BROWNS RD
ALFRED RD

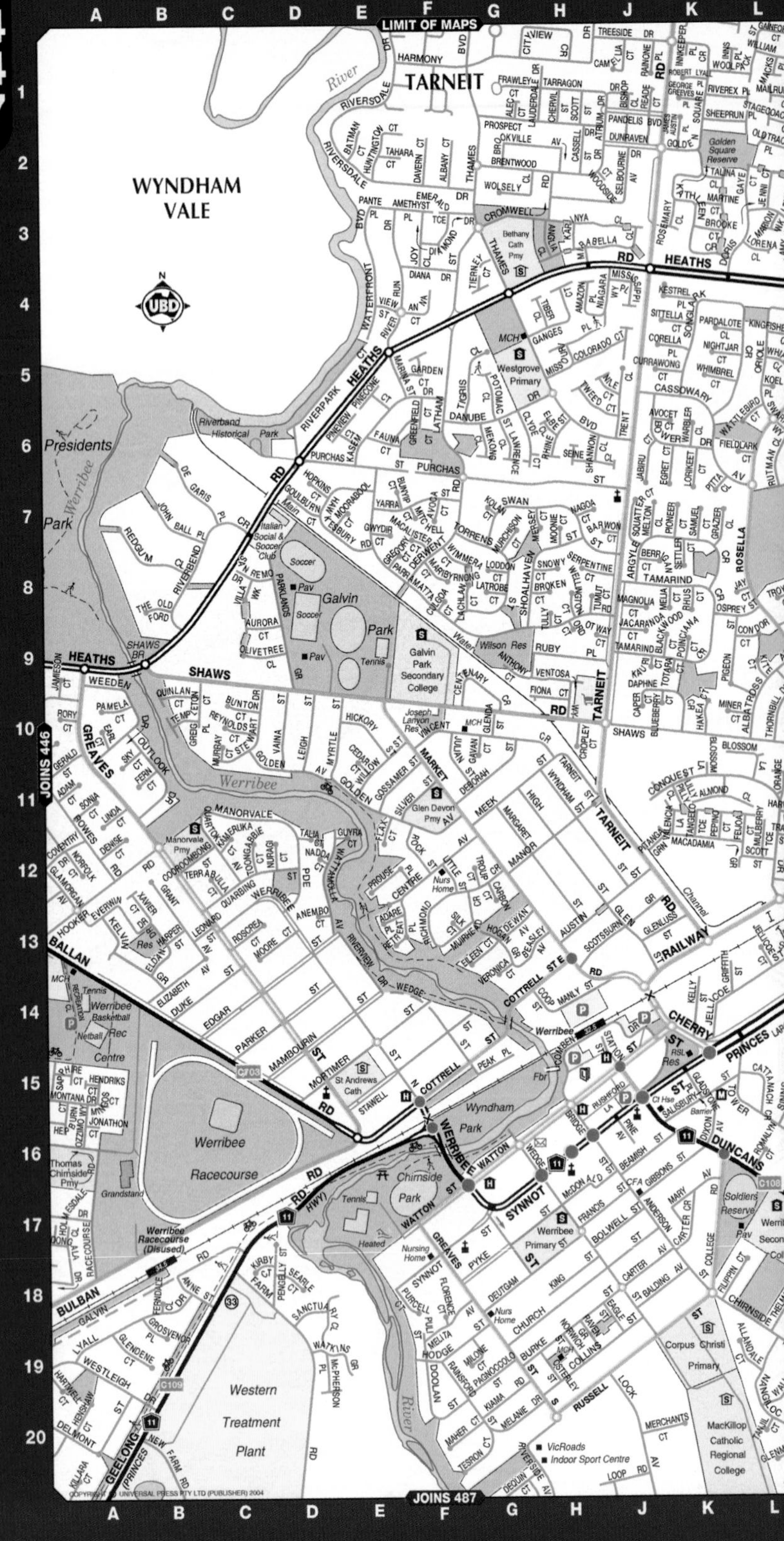
A B C D E F G H J K L
LIMIT OF MAPS
1 2 3 4 5 6 7 8 9 10 11 12 13 14 15 16 17 18 19 20
TARNEIT
WYNDHAM VALE
UBD
N
Werribee River
HEATHS RD
SHAWS RD
TARNEIT RD
PRINCES HWY
GEELONG RD
BALLAN RD
RAILWAY AV
CHERRY ST
DUNCANS RD
JOINS 446
Presidents Park
Riverbend Historical Park
Italian Social & Soccer Club
Galvin Park
Galvin Park Secondary College
Westgrove Primary
Bethany Cath Pmy
Wilson Res
Joseph Lanyon Res
Glen Devon Pmy
Manorvale Pmy
Werribee Basketball Rec Centre
Werribee Racecourse
Thomas Chirnside Pmy
Grandstand
Werribee Racecourse (Disused)
Western Treatment Plant
Chirnside Park
Wyndham Park
St Andrews Cath
Werribee Primary
Soldiers Reserve
Corpus Christi Primary
MacKillop Catholic Regional College
Golden Square Reserve
Nurs Home
Nursing Home
VicRoads
Indoor Sport Centre
Werribee
Main Channel
C703
C109
C108
JOINS 487
COPYRIGHT © UNIVERSAL PRESS PTY LTD (PUBLISHER) 2004

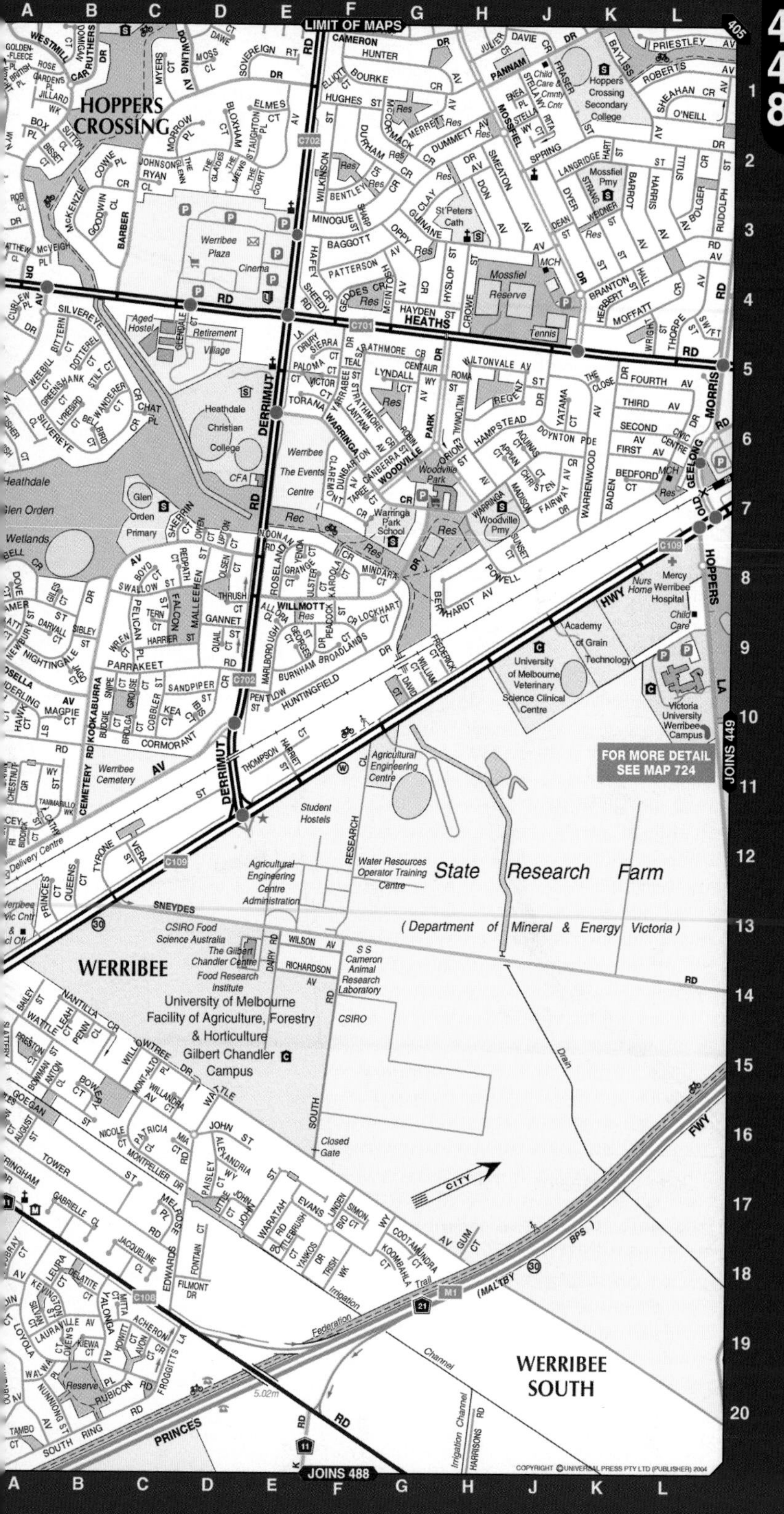

JOINS 449
JOINS 488

JOINS 405

A B C D E F G H J K L

HOPPERS CROSSING

WERRIBEE

WERRIBEE SOUTH

State Research Farm (Department of Mineral & Energy Victoria)

Council Depot

Telstra Depot

Gas & Fuel Corp

Bellbridge Primary

Hoppers Crossing Delivery Cntr

Melbourne Water Pumping Station

Office

Golf Driving Range

Victoria University Industrial Skills

Driver Training Track

Child Care

School Site

Hoppers Crossing

PRINCES FWY

OLD GEELONG RD

HEATHS RD

SNEYDES RD

HACKETTS LA

HOPPERS LA

OLD SNEYDES RD

DUNNINGS

Federation Trail

(MALTBY BPS)

Skeleton Waterholes

Drain

AVIATION RD

JOINS 448

LIMIT OF MAPS

488

JOINS 406
K Mart Distribution Centre
FORSYTH RD
FWY
M1
Westside Industrial Estate
LINMAX CT
WALLACE
MACHINERY DR
THE BOULEVARD
PROMEN ADE
DOLPHIN CR
IRVING ST
WILLOWGREEN WY
MAYFIELD GR
CRELLIN AV
GORDON AV
STREZLECKI GR
OAKDENE GR
CARINZA CT
FITZPATRICK DR
AILSA ST
Creek
SEABROOK BVD
ATTILIO WY
CATHERINE RD
SEABROOK
Seabrook Pmy
THE ROBBINS
SHANE AV
SEABROOK BVD
DANIELA
ALLINGTON PL
STRAND
LANCASTER DR
BALFOUR CL
FOXWOOD
STANTON CT
EVA CT
CAROLE
HOPE PL
ANCHORAGE
COPELAND CR
INVERLOCH DR
Proposed Catholic High Sch
Boardwalk Pmy
Park Ten
Central Park Wetlands
BOARDWALK BVD
Proposed
Murnong Town Centre
DUNNINGS RD
KINGSLEY
Sandstone Pt Res
OCEAN GR
NEWBURGH
WALDSAY RD
SHAFTSBURY BVD
LIVORNO
FRIAR PARK
LICODIA AV
SALERINO
TOURNAMENT DR
DALKEITH
POINT COOK
Sanctuary Lakes
Golf Course
Lumen Christi Catholic Primary
Sanctuary Lakes
JAMIESON WY
SANCTUARY LAKES
JOINS 451
SNEYDES RD
SANDY POINT RD
PANORAMA WY
SOUTH SHORE AV
WATER SUN CT
LINCOLN
YURUGA BVD
HIBISCUS CR
DAISY DR
PARKWOOD TCE
POINT COOK RD
POINT COOK HOMESTEAD RD
Point Cook RAAF Base
UBD

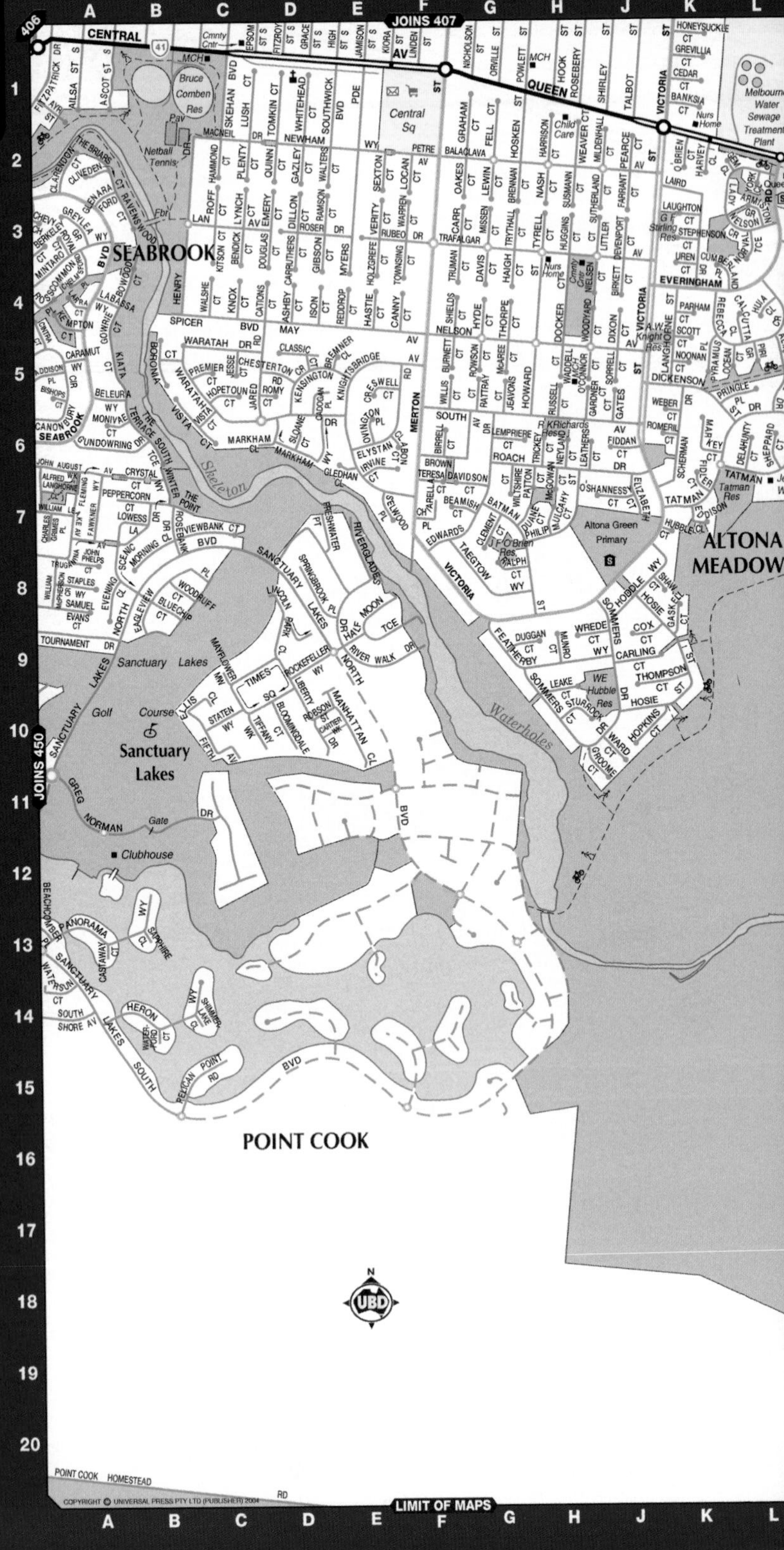

JOINS 407
JOINS 450
406
LIMIT OF MAPS
A B C D E F G H J K L
1 2 3 4 5 6 7 8 9 10 11 12 13 14 15 16 17 18 19 20
SEABROOK
ALTONA MEADOWS
POINT COOK
Sanctuary Lakes
Sanctuary Lakes Golf Course
Central Sq
Melbourne Water Sewage Treatment Plant
Altona Green Primary
Bruce Comben Res
Netball Tennis
Clubhouse
Skeleton
Waterholes
CENTRAL AV
QUEEN ST
VICTORIA ST
MERTON ST
SPICER BVD
NELSON AV
SOUTH AV
SANCTUARY LAKES NORTH
SANCTUARY LAKES SOUTH
GREG NORMAN DR
POINT COOK HOMESTEAD RD
UBD

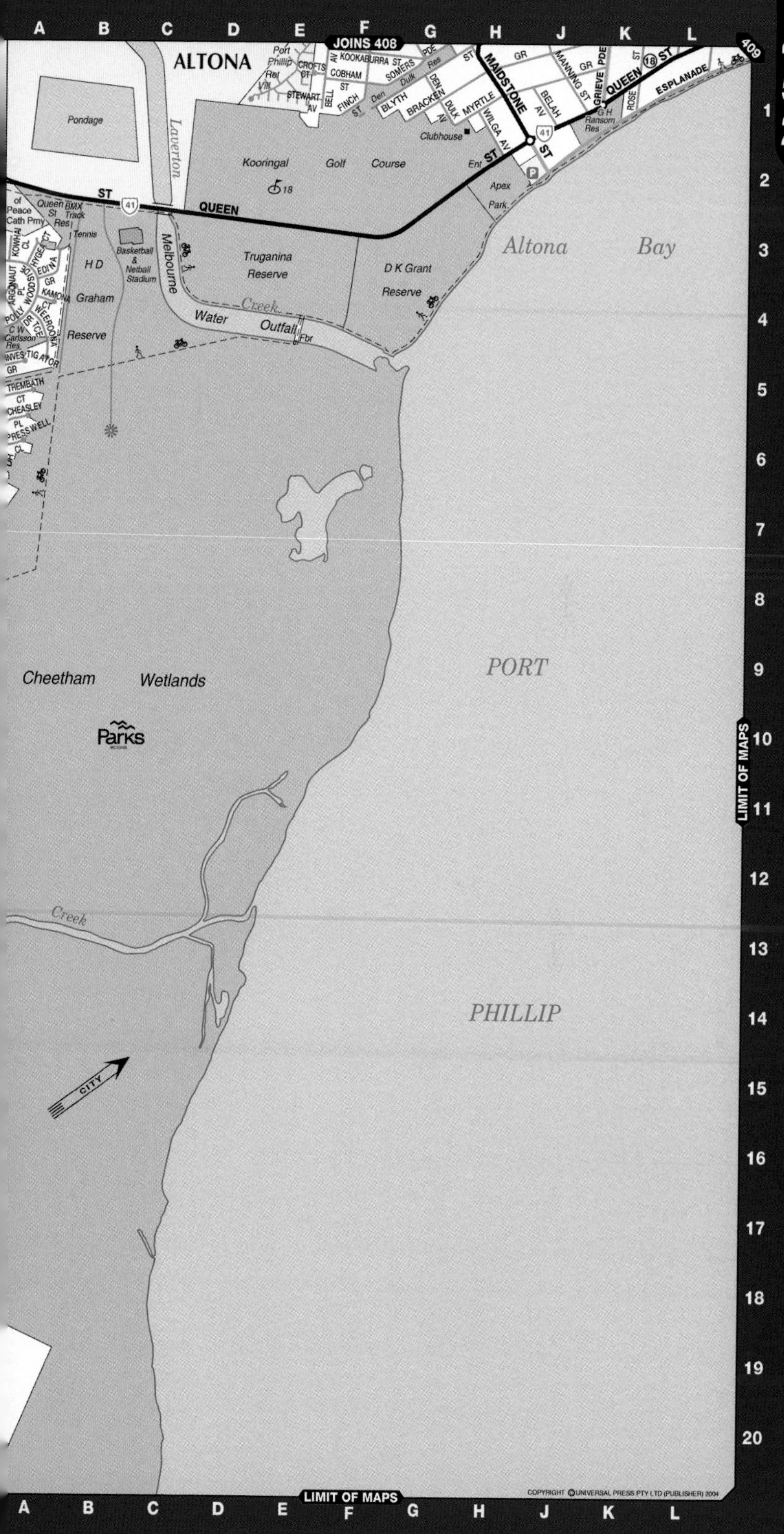

JOINS 408
409
ALTONA
Pondage
Laverton
Kooringal Golf Course
Truganina Reserve
D K Grant Reserve
Apex Park
Altona Bay
H D Graham Reserve
Basketball & Netball Stadium
Tennis
BMX Track
Melbourne Water Outfall
Creek
QUEEN ST
MAIDSTONE ST
ESPLANADE
Clubhouse
G H Ransom Res
Port Phillip Ret Vill
KOOKABURRA ST
COBHAM
SOMERS
BLYTH
BRACKEN
MYRTLE
WILGA AV
BELAH AV
MANNING ST
GRIEVE PDE
ROSE ST
C W Carlsson Res
INVESTIGATOR
TREMBATH
CHEASLEY
PRESSWELL
Cheetham Wetlands
Parks
PORT PHILLIP
CITY
LIMIT OF MAPS

ST KILDA

PORT

PHILLIP

A B C D E F G H J K L

JOINS 414

415

1 2 3 4 5 6 7 8 9 10 11 12 13 14 15 16 17 18 19 20

ELWOOD

RIPPONLEA

ELSTERNWICK

BRIGHTON

Elsternwick Golf Course

Elsternwick Park

Elwood Park

Beach

CITY

Middle Brighton Pier

Marina

Middle Brighton Municipal Baths & Kiosk

Dendy Street Beach

Bayside City Council Car Park Emergency Locators

JOINS 455

JOINS 494

495

JOINS 415

414

A B C D E F G H J K L

CAULFIELD NORTH

CAULFIELD

CAULFIELD SOUTH

ELSTERNWICK

GARDENVALE

BRIGHTON EAST

BRIGHTON

McKINNON

BENTLEIGH

Caulfield General Medical Centre

Princes Park

Brighton Cemetery

Landcox Park

Hurlingham Park

Hopetoun Gdns

JOINS 454

494

JOINS 495

A B C D E F G H J K

A B C D E F G H J K L

JOINS 416

417

1 2 3 4 5 6 7 8 9 10 11 12 13 14 15 16 17 18 19 20

CAULFIELD EAST

Caulfield Racecourse

MALVERN EAST

GLEN HUNTLY

CARNEGIE

ORMOND

BENTLEIGH EAST

JOINS 457

JOINS 496

497

A B C D E F G H J K L

JOINS 417

A B C D E F G H J K L

1
Malvern Valley Golf Course Clubhouse GOLFERS
MONASH
Holmesglen Inst of TAFE Chadstone Campus
BATESFORD
MALVERN RD
SHORT ST
SYLVESTER CR
East Malvern
ALBERT AV
COOLGARDIE AV
MELROSE AV
CAMINO TCE
RAMONA AV
GABRIEL AV
CARMELO AV
ALCALA TCE
ERRESIDE
LOMOND TCE
ARGYLL ST
WAVERLEY RD
BATESFORD RD
MOUNTFIELD AV
JAMES PDE
GREEN GABLES AV
LLANOS AV
THURL
Powernet Malvern Terminal Station
IVANHOE
ROTHERWOOD DR
ANFIELD CT
SHREWSBURY
M1

2
Waverley Oval
Outer Circle Linear Pk
THE RIALTO WEST
O-T Flight Res
RIALTO
Ret Vill
WARIDA AV
COOINDA PL
SLOVAKIA
WAVERLEY
Phoenix Pk Cmnty Cntr
Malvern Valley Pmy
ROB ROY RD
PEVERILL
PEAK ST
COLLINS ST
IPYD CT
ITHACA CT

3
MALVERN EAST
PAUL ST
LANG CT
ARMSTRONG CT
ABBOTSFORD
HILLARD ST
EDNA ST
SYCAMORE
SUTHERLAND
MCH
Tennis
Percy Treyvaud Mem Park
QUENTIN
DURWARD
REBECCA
ROWENA
GAUNTLET
PRIOR
Peverill Park
TUHAN ST
WESTBROOK CT
DRUMMOND
TIMMINS
FOUNTAINE ST
Urban Forest
ALVIE ST
FENWICK ST
GARDEN AV
BERRIMA AV
NIRVANA
KARMA
MERVILLE

4
GOODE ST
Holy Eucharist Cath
BRUCE
THOMAS
HYSLOP
SYDARE
MILLEWA
ALMA
GORDON ST
BELLEVUE AV
MIDLOTHIAN
CHAPMAN ST
RANGEVIEW
VIRGINIA GR
Central Gippsland Inst of TAFE Chadstone Campus
BELGRAVE RD
DANDENONG
BOWEN
KELLY
CHADSTONE

5
ANZAC ST
BRISBANE ST
Murrumbeena Pmy
NANGANA
PERTH ST
ADELAIDE ST
WEEROONA
WILSON
NARBETHONG
Chadstone Shopping Centre
RACV Cinemas
Tenpin Bowl
MIDDLE RD
RAE CT
COLE
NEWTON
ACACIA
BLACKWOOD ST
OAKDENE
WAHROONGA
Nurs Home
WEBSTER

6
SYDNEY ST
MELBOURNE
LOOKER
GILSLAND
CLIVE
HOOPER
MERRIMU
FELLOWS
CASTLEBAR
Ret Vill
WOODLANDS
CAPON
ALLEN
DUNDEE
Nursing Home
BEENA AV
HOBART
OMAMA
JOYOUS
GARD CT
ASTOLAT
LAWRENCE ST
MAROO
WARRIGAL

7
NEERIM
Nursing Home
Springthorpe Gardens
RILEY
PACKER ST
BUSH
PROSPECT WK
CALOOLA AV
Soccer Caloola Reserve Pav
Yasmar Nurs Home
DALGETY
RAILWAY
Murrumbeena
TUCKETT
Riley Res
ELLA
SHORT
RICOURT AV
MONTROSE
FEDERATION
RENDELL CT
ARCADIA
CARRUM
CAMIRA

8
EMILY
ELBENA GR
McLAURIN RD
DUNOON
TOWARD
Nursing Home
ROSELLA
KITMONT
WILLIAM
PAGET
WILBUR CR
(PRINCES HWY)
RUGBY
LOGIE
EUSTON
INNELLAN
FROGMORE RD

9
WILLESDEN
Hughesdale
ARIADNE AV
BUTE
WALKER
HOWE
LYDSON
ARTHUR
CORR ST
BLETCHLEY
CLAPHAM
PADDINGTON
CREWE
Oakleigh Pmy
TAYLOR ST
WAHGOO
HETHERSETT RD
GR
COORIGIL RD
BURNS AV
THOMSON AV
ERINDALE
Murrumbeena Park
STEWART
FREDA
Galbally Res
RSL Warrawee Park Oval
PALMER ST
SWINDON
Hall

10
MOONYA
KANGAROO
ARDYNE
GERALD
CARLISLE
Cmnty Cntr
Pioneer Cem
ATHERTON
ATKINSON
PALMERSTON GR
RD
FIRST AV
SECOND AV
THAXTED RD
PELLING RD
PRESTON
SKIPTON
DALSTON

11
MURRUMBEENA
HENTY
KATRINA
SPARK
ARGGOUR
KELVINSIDE
KANGAROO
CAMDEN
RICHARDSON
EARLSTOWN
STATION
CHESTER ST
PORTMAN
EATON
LINDSAY
DORIS
BOWMORE
CALLANDER
Oakleigh Central
HAUGHTON
MILL RD
HANOVER

12
WILMOTH
BEAUVILLE
St Patricks Catholic
GLOUCESTER
DALNY
MARMA
SWAN
KIRKHAM
MAUDE
DAISY ST
BELVOIR
BLYTHE ST
DUMBLANE ST
ELLENDALE
HUGHESDALE
Sacred Heart Cath
JOHNSON
MORA AV
DAVEY
OXFORD
BARKLY
LEURA
MONA
QUEENS
DOWNING

13
VICTORY
CROSBIE
ATKINSON
ADAMS ST
VERA
HALLIDAY
FINTONIA
HOTHAM
DARLING
CANTERBURY
BOWEN
NORMANBY
LATROBE
WARRIGAL
MURRUMBEENA
Duncan Mackinnon Park
Athletics Track
KINLOCK
WALLACE
GEORGE ST
ARGYLE CL
DALLAS
PRINCES
WILLGILSON CT
Cmnty Cntr

14
GUNN
IRVING AV
STRATHEARN
MARGARETTA AV
DONAL ST
Hughesdale Pmy
SIMMONDS
CALEMBEENA
MOOROOKYLE
ELEEBANA
SCHOOLHALL
MEAD CT
WILSON
Child Care
KINRADE
BRINE
AUSTIN
NORTH
BAKER
REID
VELRA
POATH
BRETT
MURRA
CAREY
COBAR

15
GRIFFITH AV
WONGA CT
WATT
MULSANNE
ANARTH
Jeh Wit
NORTH
WESTGATE
HATTER
EASTGATE
ABBEYGATE
GOLF
BEST
LINKS
BLENHEIM
MAJDAL
BIRDWOOD
DROMANA

16
ARGYLE
POET
MELVA
JASSA
HALLOW
PELL
JULIS
KADIR
CHAUVEL
WHITE
MONASH
REID
LOREEN ST
Clubhouse
KESWICK
Tennis Marlborough Street Res
GOODRICH
WARATAH
BARRANI
BARRINGTON

17
Virginia Park
FORSTER CT
FISHER CT
CURTIN
LATHAM
BENTLEIGH EAST
BANKSIA
BORONIA
KURRAJONG
CAVALIER
KASHMIRA
SANTARAM
THANA
PICADILLY
CLEEK
WARD AV
DEAKIN
PARKMORE
PALOMA
GOWRIE
ALLEFORD

18
CASTLEWOOD
HUGHES
LYONS
FORREST
MANUKA
SELWORTHY
SUMERSETT
TAUNTON
Metropolitan
CITY
STOCKDALE
SIMMONDS CT
MARLBOROUGH
EDINBURGH
BOSSINGTON
DEVOY
BROOKS

19
FRASER ST
STRATFORD
BRAY
BEDDOE
TAMBET
Mackie Ten Pav
Road Ten Reserve
ORANGE
MACKIE
TUDOR
KENNEDY
DALGAN
DERMOT
DELOS
GOLF
Golf
BARHOLME
LANGSLOW
LONGVIEW AV

20
CARDIFF
PLYMOUTH
YORK
HULL
LIVERPOOL
SHEFFIELD
Syn
CECIL
Coatesville Pmy
GARVEY
RICHARD
BRIAR
CONNIE
BEGG
WOLAI
CARINYA
YARALLA
MAGNOLIA
REBECCA
HAVANA
Reservoir
DELIA
PITT
Progress Play Park
CAMERON
Stan Riley Reserve
Oakleigh South Pmy
BERYL
BAKERS
JOYCE
South Oakleigh Sec Coll
Monash Medical Centre Moorabbin Campus
WARWICK
CARLOW
DOVER
BRISTOL

JOINS 456

416
496
JOINS 497

A B C D E F G H J K L
JOINS 418
JOINS 459
JOINS 498
419
499
MOUNT WAVERLEY
CHADSTONE
OAKLEIGH
OAKLEIGH EAST
HUNTINGDALE
OAKLEIGH SOUTH
CLAYTON
WAVERLEY RD
HUNTINGDALE RD
FERNTREE GULLY RD
PRINCES HWY
DANDENONG RD
MONASH FWY
CLAYTON RD
STEPHENSONS RD
NORTH RD
FWY
Tunnel
M1
Salesian Catholic College
Salesian College Playing Fields
Jordan Reserve
Mayfield Park
Sussex Hts Pmy
Public Golf Course
Oakleigh Recreation Centre
Army Res Monash Uni Regiment
Nursing Homes
Industrial Estate
Reg Harris Reserve
Amsleigh Park Pmy
Hunt Reserve
Neighbourhood House & Cmnty Cntr
Princes Highway Reserve
Jack Edwards Res
Indoor Cricket
Army Oakleigh Barracks
Huntingdale Pmy
Huntingdale Golf Course
Davies Reserve
Clayton West Pmy
Quarry
Clayton North Primary
Monash Medical Centre
Clayton Campus
Youth Club Fregon Reserve
Carlson Avenue Res
Bayview Conference Centre
Mount Waverley Pmy
St Mary Magdalens Cath Pmy
APPM
Tennis
Clubhouse
Reserve
UBD
COPYRIGHT UNIVERSAL PRESS PTY LTD (PUBLISHER) 2004

418 JOINS 419

JOINS 458

MOUNT WAVERLEY

Industrial Estate

NOTTING HILL

CLAYTON

Valley Reserve

Melbourne Water Retarding Basin

Pinewood Reserve

Monash University Clayton Campus

CSIRO

Deakin University Rusden Campus

FOR MORE DETAIL SEE MAPS 719-720

498 JOINS 499

A B C D E F G H J K L
JOINS 420
421
1 2 3 4 5 6 7 8 9 10 11 12 13 14 15 16 17 18 19
GLEN WAVERLEY
WHEELERS HILL
MULGRAVE
Wesley College
Glen Waverley Sec Coll
The Glen
Glen Waverley
Australian Unity Nursing Home
Cmnty Health Cntr
Bogong Res
Civic Cntr
Cncl Off
Century City
Tennis
Mount View Pmy
Hinkler Res
Carronbank Sch
Glen-allen Sch
St Leonards Cath
Blackflat Cmnty Centre
Monash Aquatic & Recreation Centre
Central Res
Glen Waverley Res
Waverley Football Ground
Athletics Track
Melbourne Water Corporation Resvr
Victoria Police Training Academy
Oak Tree Hill Retirement Village
Glen Waverley South Primary
Brentwood Secondary College
The Victorian Rehabilitation Centre
Brandon Office Park
Brandon Park Res
Brentwood Reserve
Berengarra Sch & Educat Cntr
Wheelers Hill Pmy
Brandon Park Secondary College
Good Shepherd Cath
Wheelers Hill Secondary College
Lum Reserve
Brandon Park Primary
Mazenod Catholic College
Monash Gardens Units & Hostel
Freeway Reserve
Cmnty Cntr & Sen Cits
Waverley Meadows Primary
Columbia Park
Glenvale Industrial Estate
Ensign Lab
Bayer Aust Ltd
Renold Aust
Safeway Stores
SPRINGVALE RD
WAVERLEY RD
FERNTREE GULLY RD
WELLINGTON RD
MONASH FWY
BRANDON PARK DR
JOINS 461
JOINS 500
501
UBD
COPYRIGHT © UNIVERSAL PRESS PTY LTD (PUBLISHER) 2004

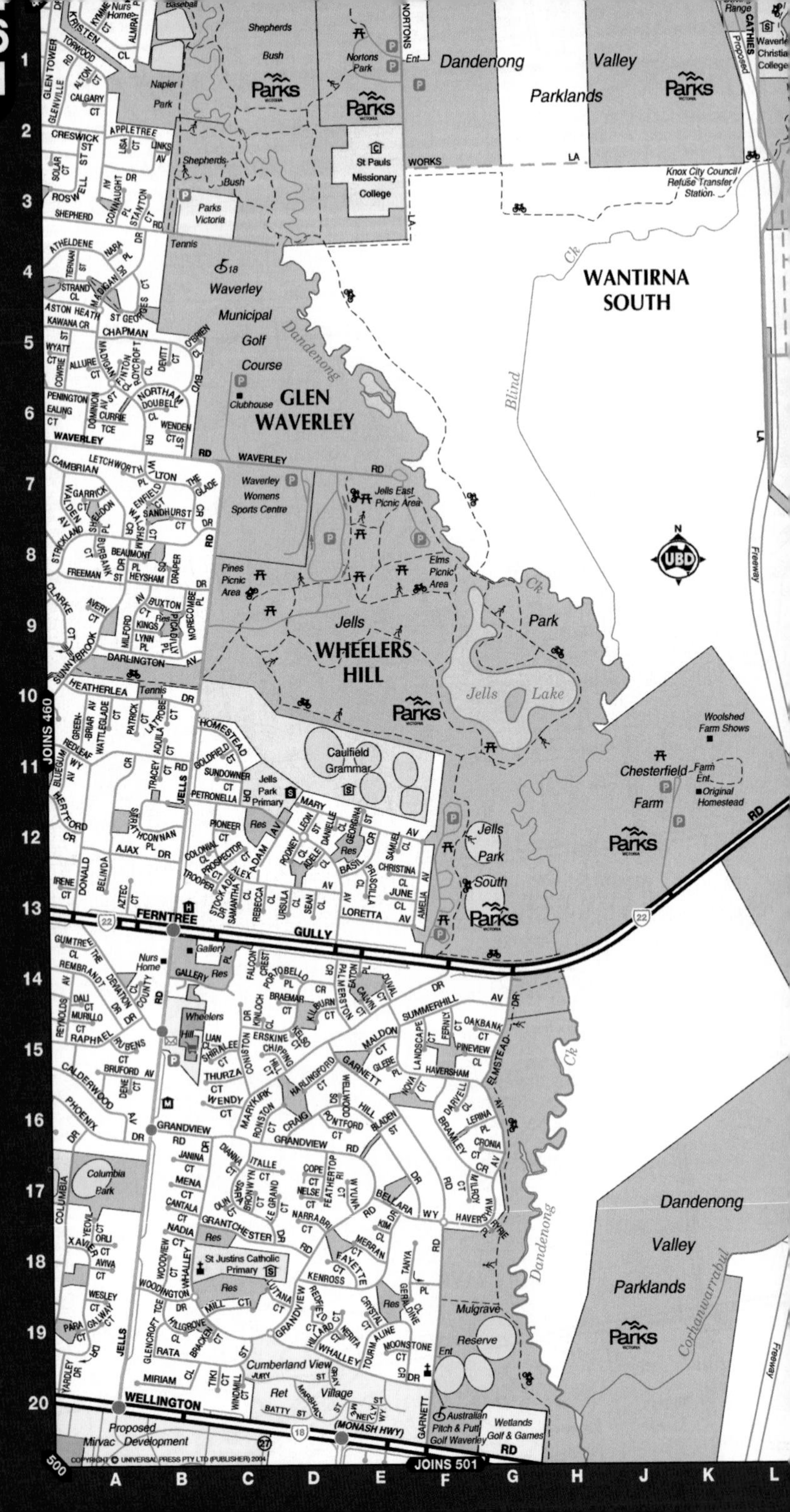

GLEN WAVERLEY
WHEELERS HILL
WANTIRNA SOUTH
Dandenong Valley Parklands
Shepherds Bush
Napier Park
Nortons Park
St Pauls Missionary College
Knox City Council Refuse Transfer Station
Waverley Municipal Golf Course
Waverley Womens Sports Centre
Jells East Picnic Area
Elms Picnic Area
Pines Picnic Area
Jells Park
Jells Lake
Caulfield Grammar
Jells Park Primary
Woolshed Farm Shows
Chesterfield Farm
Original Homestead
Jells Park South
Columbia Park
St Justins Catholic Primary
Mulgrave Reserve
Cumberland View Ret Village
Australian Pitch & Putt Golf Waverley
Wetlands Golf & Games
Proposed Mirvac Development
FERNTREE GULLY RD
WELLINGTON RD
(MONASH HWY)
JOINS 460
JOINS 501
COPYRIGHT © UNIVERSAL PRESS PTY LTD (PUBLISHER) 2004

A B C D E F G H J K L

JOINS 422
423

MILBREY CL
CT
GISELLE AV
ROWENA RI
ROYCROFT AV
PONSFORD
CR
TYSON CT
Latvian Ret Vill
ROCHELLE CT
MYALLA CT
REITA
WALLACE
KIRRUM CL
AV
RIDDELL
McLEAN CT
KEYES CT
HEDGELEY CL
GLENMAGGIE PL
ENDEAVOUR PL
FONTEYN
TAMARA ST
SYLPHIDE ST
MCH
GORRIE CT
HASSETT
HOGAN CT
FRASER
BOYLE CL
GOULD CT
STUD (DANDENONG VALLEY HWY)
GEORDY CL
REBECCA CT
COPPELIA
MOWBRAY
ARGYLE
AV
LANCELOT CT
RD
DEAKON CT
MELANIE CL
LIND CREEK
ARMISTON GR
TASMAN CL
FINDON CT
LOXTON
Knox Gardens Reserve
Tennis
FRASER
HOPMAN CL
CHAPPELL
WITKEN
DUBIN CT
KERGO PL
Llewellyn Park
TATIANA ST
PARFAIT CT
AMOUR CT
FEWSTER
CUTHBERT CT
Knox Gardens Primary
DR
WY
OBERON CT
Nubrik Scoresby Display Centre
NEWRY
DAVALE
OLNEY CT
ALLISTER
R D Egan Lee Reserve
ATTLEY
BLACKHAM
DR
WY
MAWSON CL
HELPMANN
ST
CLARKE
CAWLEY CT
CERUTTY WY
LANDY CT
FROMELLES CT
CHARLTON ST
BELN
NARONG CT
ELLIOT
ST
FOSTER RD
CR
ONASTERY
ST PAULS
BROMAGE CT
APLIN PL
CR
PLAYER CT
ARGYLE WY
MOCKRIDGE
RODNEY
NARONG CR
RD
PHILLIP RD
NOEL CT
LARTER CT
CLEREHAN CT
VIDA CT
TINTERN
LEE CL
DR
NEWCOMBE CT
Balmoral Gardens Retirement Village
RD
RIDGE
ANDERSON
FRUDAL CR
HARLEY
SOMES
BRENNAN
MEAD CT
HORNER CT
JOSEPH CT
SARAH CT
ST MARY
HUNT CT
MARSH CT
ROSEWALL CT
SANDRA CL
TOWNER AV
HAIDEH PL
HAYGARTH CT
RIDGE
MANDALAY
SEBAN
BORDER
Scoresby Secondary College
WATTLEVIEW RI
O'CONNOR
FRUDAL CR
DR
RD
ANNE RD
GEORGE
ST
ST
ARMIN ST
CAVELL ST
ARNOLD
ST N
PAULETTE
WALSH CT
MILLGROVE
NARDU CT
NOLA CT
BROTHERS
St Jude Cath Pmy
Ten
MICHELE DR
ZERFAS
ANNE
OTIRA
LATONA
GRAHAM RD
ALLISTER
Res
VINEN
JENNY CT
COLLENDINA
SEMINARY
MICHELE DR
ZARRO
ROMA
ELM CT
EVANS ST
RIVETTE ST
ROSEHILL
GOLDING CT
GRAYSON
O'CONNOR
LAURA RD
Carrington Pmy
WESTBURN GR
JULIAN AV
KIAMA
BROOKE
TOWNSVILLE CT
NEVANA
MCH
BARRY CT
BENEDIKT
BAMBA CT
KALBAR
YARRABURN
WILUNA CT
COLLENDINA
CR
QUENTIN
Benedikt Res
OLGA CT
BLAKE CT
SEVILLE GR
BERRABRI
PARKSIDE
BEWSELL ST
AV
ROSA ST
GILBERT CT
LAURA
CHRISTIE
WINNIFRED CL
CONSTABLE
DR
Scoresby Pmy
ORSON
SHEPPARD DR
RUMANN AV
LEIGH CT
Carrington Family Leisure Centre
Tennis
Park
RICKARDS AV
BOYD
GRECO CT
INGRID ST
PAMELA
DR
DORIS
JOHANN AV
Redcourt Res
TAUNTON
RUBENS
HILARY CT
FAY CT
NIGEL CT
ENGLISH
ROXANNE CL
CT
LAURENT
DOBELL
CHAGALL
DRYSDALE
BORG
DELLA ST
DALE
GRETEL
THE CLOSE
GLENIFER
AV
McCRAE CL
Pav
ROCCO
JELLICO
LINDSAY
SANDYKE
HOLBEIN
IMPARA CT
BEVERLEY ST
PARKWAY
Scoresby Rec Res
Tennis
SARA
RAY CT
COLLINS CL
GERDA
RD
ST
CAROL
LENNOX
KARABIL
AVRIL ST
LINTON
DARRYL ST
CFA
22
MILLENNIUM CT
BORG
DENHAM
CT
CR
DR
SALLY
FRANCIS
CR
Avis
NYADALE
DR
GULLY
Entrance to Caribbean Gardens
Gate
Caribbean Rollerama
KOORNANG
JANINE ST
Amcor Packaging
STUD
KNOXFIELD
KEITH
CAMPBELL CT
FERNTREE
CARIBBEAN
INTERNATIONAL CT
ELMDON DR
EAST BOUNDARY RD
Scoresby Industry Park
CENTRE RD
CITY
Entrance to Caribbean Gardens
Gate
ALLA PL
RD
DR
Reserve
RD
Ck
LAKEVIEW DR
DR
HENDERSON RD
SCORESBY
Caribbean Gardens
TAMPE
MOSRAEL PL
NEUTRON PL
DALMORE
Fbr
RD
ROWVILLE
SEISMIC CT
Kiosk
Chair Lift
KINGSLEY CL
Wed 8.30am - 3pm
Sun 8.30am - 4.30pm
HENDERSON RD
MACRO CT
Caribbean Gardens Markets
KELLETTS
LASER
HI-TECH PL
Caribbean Lake
CAIRN CL
CURREN
TALI-K CL
ARNG
WINNIPEG ST
ERIE
RD
ONTARIO PL
Cogley Lake
LAKESIDE
HURON
WANAKA CL
ORD PL
HOPKINS CL
SUPERIOR
Sutton Lake
MICHIGAN BVD
Hill Lake
THOMSON CT
AV
LA
COTTER CT
MISSISSIPPI CL
YUKON CT
YELLOWSTONE CL
GLENELG CT
LADONGA PL
AV
WY
AMAZON CT
(DANDENONG VALLEY HWY)
BRIDGEWATER
ST JOHN PL
CORHANWARRABUL CL
OLIVIA CT
STEVENS PL
MAHONGA DR
DENISE CT
MANTUNG CT
AUGUSTA CT
LAKEVIEW
2ND AV
CR
CR
FULHAM
Peppertree Hill Retirement Village
TALIA CT
RD
JINDALEE CR
WARADGERY
TROON CT
GLENEAGLES CT
DR
3RD AV
ELIZABETH CT
9
Cmnty Cntr
Tennis
Netball
KIAKA LA
CL
NATTAI CT
MANTUNG
Clubhouse
CARNOUSTIE CT
DRUMMOND
4TH AV
HILLVIEW AV
Stud Park
BARELLAN CT
DR
Kingston Links
TUNBERRY CT
WATSON CT
THE FAIRWAY
SUNNINGDALE CT
5TH AV
DENVER
DESCHAMP
LIDGATE AV
STAMFORD
Stud Park Reserve
TANYA CT
CR
TAYLORS
Golf Course
MERION CT
MUIRFIELD CT
Row Reserve
PALMER CL
LUTON CT
SELWOOD CT
NIOKA PL
SIMONS
BRIDGEWATER WY
WARADGERY
AVALON
RD
BRUSCO PL
Rowville Primary
FILMER CT
AV
18
SANTED CT
DESCHAMP CT
BICKERTON CT
STUD
PARATEA DR
Rowville Secondary
RICHARD CT
TURRAMURRA
BERNARD
HAMILTON WY
McKAY RD
CORPORATE AV
DR
TOWT CT
CT
LEHONG CL
SOKLENG CL

JOINS 463
JOINS 502
503

1 2 3 4 5 6 7 8 9 10 11 12 13 14 15 16 17 18 19 20

A B C D E F G H J K L

A B C D E F G H J K L

422

JOINS 423

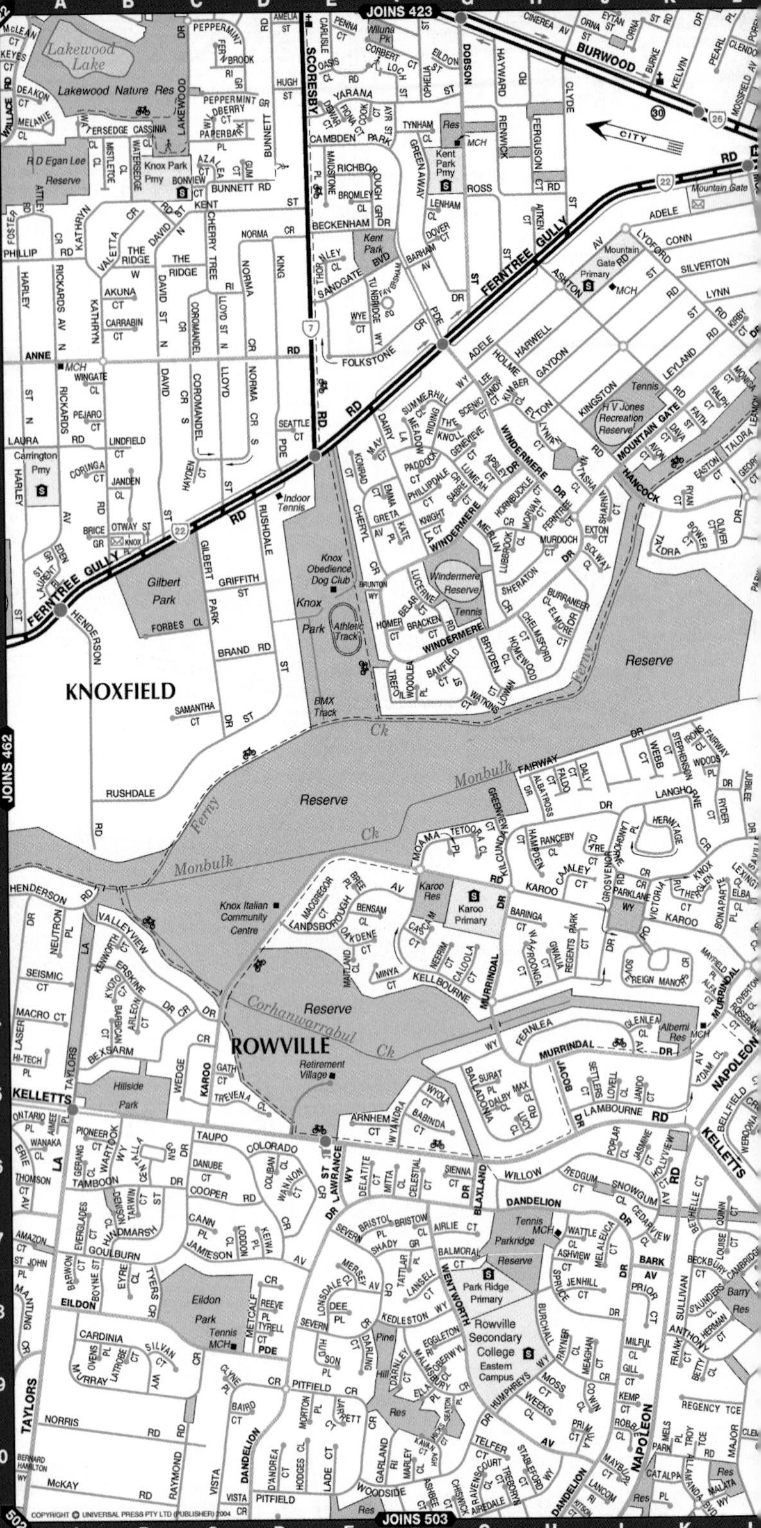

Lakewood Lake

Lakewood Nature Res

R D Egan Lee Reserve

Knox Park Pmy

Kent Park Pmy

Mountain Gate Primary

Mountain Gate

H V Jones Recreation Reserve

Carrington Pmy

Indoor Tennis

Knox Obedience Dog Club

Knox Park

Athletic Track

BMX Track

Gilbert Park

Windermere Reserve

Tennis

KNOXFIELD

Reserve

Ferny Ck

Monbulk Ck

Knox Italian Community Centre

Karoo Res

Karoo Primary

Corhanwarrabul Ck

ROWVILLE

Retirement Village

Hillside Park

Albemi Res

Eildon Park

Parkridge Reserve

Park Ridge Primary

Rowville Secondary College Eastern Campus

Pine Hill Res

Barry Res

CITY

BURWOOD HWY

FERNTREE GULLY RD

SCORESBY RD

KELLETTS RD

NAPOLEON RD

TAYLORS LA

WENTWORTH AV

STUD RD

DANDELION DR

MOUNTAIN GATE DR

WINDERMERE DR

MURRINDAL DR

JOINS 462

1 2 3 4 5 6 7 8 9 10 11 12 13 14 15 16 17 18 19 20

502

JOINS 503

A B C D E F G H J K L

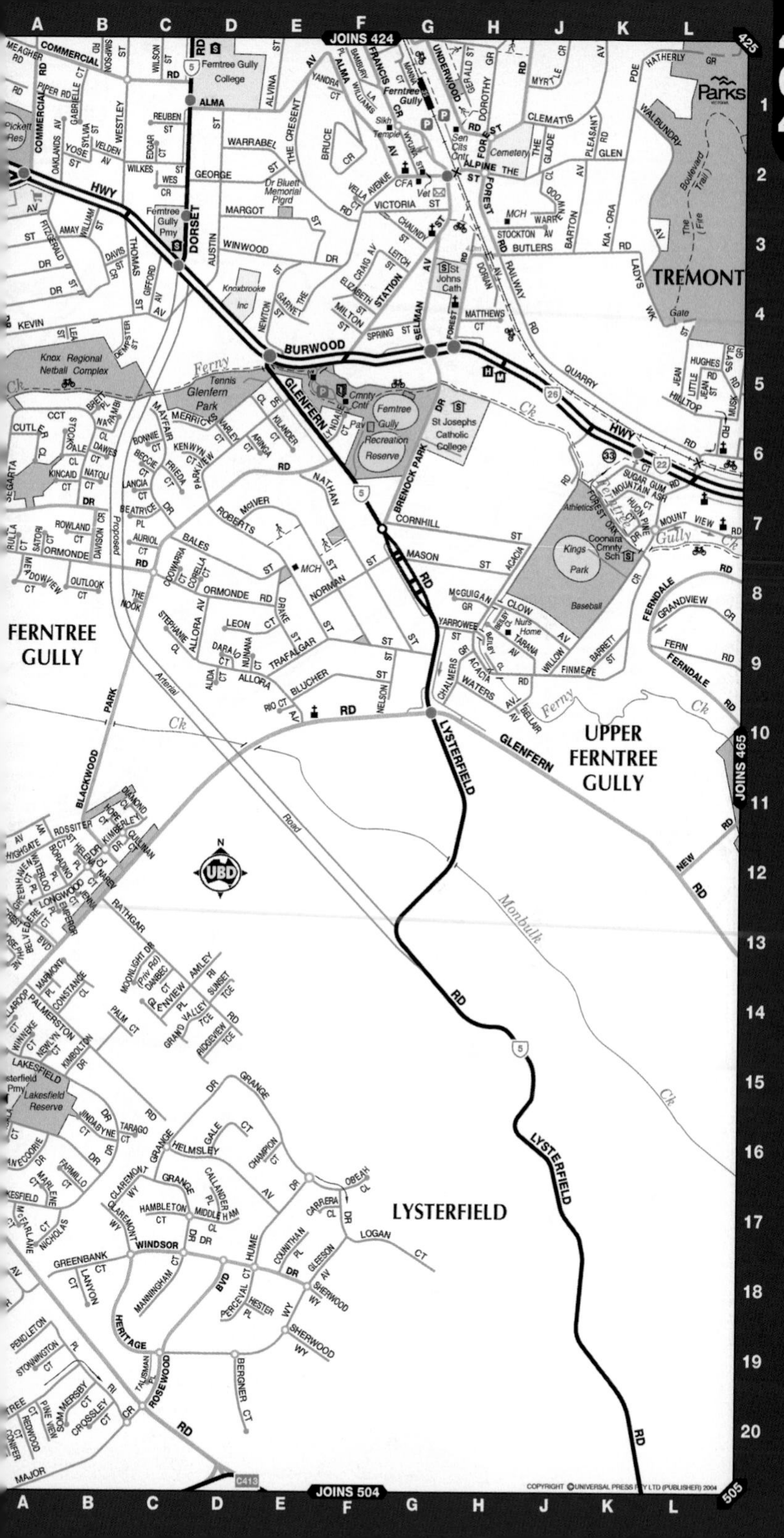

JOINS 424
425
FERNTREE GULLY
UPPER FERNTREE GULLY
TREMONT
LYSTERFIELD
Ferntree Gully College
Knox Regional Netball Complex
Glenfern Park
Ferntree Gully Recreation Reserve
St Josephs Catholic College
Kings Park
Coonara Cmnty Sch
Lakesfield Reserve
Dr Bluett Memorial Plgrd
Knoxbrooke Inc
St Johns Cath
Cemetery
BURWOOD HWY
GLENFERN RD
LYSTERFIELD RD
DORSET RD
Arterial Road
Proposed
Ferny Ck
Monbulk Ck
Gully Ck
JOINS 465
JOINS 504
505
C413
COPYRIGHT © UNIVERSAL PRESS PTY LTD (PUBLISHER) 2004

JOINS 425

A B C D E F G H J K L

1 2 3 4 5 6 7 8 9 10 11 12 13 14 15 16 17 18 19 20

424

JOINS 464

FERNY CREEK

TREMONT

UPPER FERNTREE GULLY

UPWEY

LYSTERFIELD

Dandenong Ranges National Park (Parks Victoria)

Parks Victoria

Ferntree Gully

Reservoir

Feather (Fire Trail) Track

Stony Rise (Fire Trail) Track

The Lantern (Fire Trail) Track

Lyrebird Track (Fire Trail)

Tree Fern Gully Track

Ferntree Gully

Musk Av

Boulevard

Belview (Fire Trail)

Belview Tce

Tce Trail

Acacia Picnic Ground

Acacia Track

Janesleigh Dell Picnic Area

Creek

Devil's Elbow

Tremont (Fire Trail) Hughes Hill Track

Reserve

SAYERS

DEALBATA RD (Fire Access)

MOUNT DANDENONG TOURIST RD

MOUNT DANDENONG RD C415

BURWOOD HWY 26

ONE TREE HILL RD

TITANIA

DUNCANS LA

CHURCHILL

SCHOOL

DUNN AV

JOHNSTON PDE

CR TITANIA TCE

OBERON AV

HOSKINS ST

TITANIA DR

WONDOORA AV

CATON ST

Ferny Creek Primary

BONVIEW RD

SCHOOL RD

LAURES

KALLAMONDAH RD

TREWEEK PDE

WEBB

DUNSTAN CR

ST

GLASS GR

HUGHES RD

JEAN

LITTLE MUSK

BARCLAY AV

LYONES PDE

SEABY AV

HILL RD

RAILWAY

Upper Ferntree Gully

SCHOOL RD

CFA

4.85km

JANIESLEIGH

FERNY CREEK

SALISBURY ST

DAWN ST

LITTLE ST

JENSEN RD

BATES AV

BALDWIN

DARLEY ST

KENSLEY ST

GLASSFORD RD

CURRAWONG CT

JONES

OLIVETTE AV

VERNON ST

IRENE AV

HUGHES ST

KEMP

EARL ST

BELBROOK

WRIGHT

WELDON GR

CARWEEN AV

JULIE CT

GERRATT

THE HIGHWAY

GULLY RD

MAST

KILDA

THE AVENUE

KOOKABURRA

DELL

PIONEER

DARLING

BRUNNING ST

ALEXANDER

Thompson Res

Upwey Primary

Upwey High

ARGYLE

RSL

Cmnty Cntr

MCH

CFA

Upwey

MAIN

4.6km

MAHONY

DAWSON

Theatre

MOUNT VIEW RD

ROSE

WILLIAM

ALFRED ST

Upper Ferntree Gully Pmy

Talaskia Res Tennis

FERNDALE

GRANDVIEW

ROLLINGS

JOHNS ST

TOWNLEY PL

ALBERT

Chandler House

EDWARD

Angliss Health Service

Nursing Home

FERN

ALEXANDRIA ST

VICTORIA

CR

Gate

TALASKIA

WYNETTE AV

ROYAL

OLD BELGRAVE RD

BELGRAVE GRA

Steps

GEORGE

MARY

OAKDALE

ROW

ROPLEY

HIGHCLIFF

BELMONT

Belmont Tower

FERGUSON

TERNES

LEONARD

GUY

PDE

ROMA

Roma Reserve

CALLANDRA WYN

BIRDWOOD

VIEW ST

YERONGA AV

IEVERS ST

IRVINE ST

KIA ORA AV

McLAREN ST

STANHOPE

WAVERLEY ST

BAYVIEW

THOMPSON RD

MORRIS RD

Gilmour Park

Archery Club

NEW

FERNDALE

Ferny

GLENFERN

FOREST

PARK

HUME

TASMAN AV

KOORINGAL

KOORINGAL RD

Res

GRIFFITHS

ST

HILL

HENDERSON ST

TORRY

Ferny

LILIAN ST

RITA ST

TREVOR ST

PALMER ST

MATSON

LEAH

BROOKING

FERNERY RD

GLENFERN

FERNDALE

Upwey South Pmy

RILEY

HUME

Creek

DEANS

Tennis

Upwey South Reserve

CREEKBANK ST

BROOKSIDE ST

MCH

MORRIS

MELALEUCA

PHOTINIA CT

ELOERA ST

GLENFERN

WARRA

Monbulk

CITY

RD

Locked Gate

NIXON

Monbulk Creek Retarding Basin

Dargon Track

Lysterfield Lake Park

504

JOINS 505

A B C D E F G H J K L

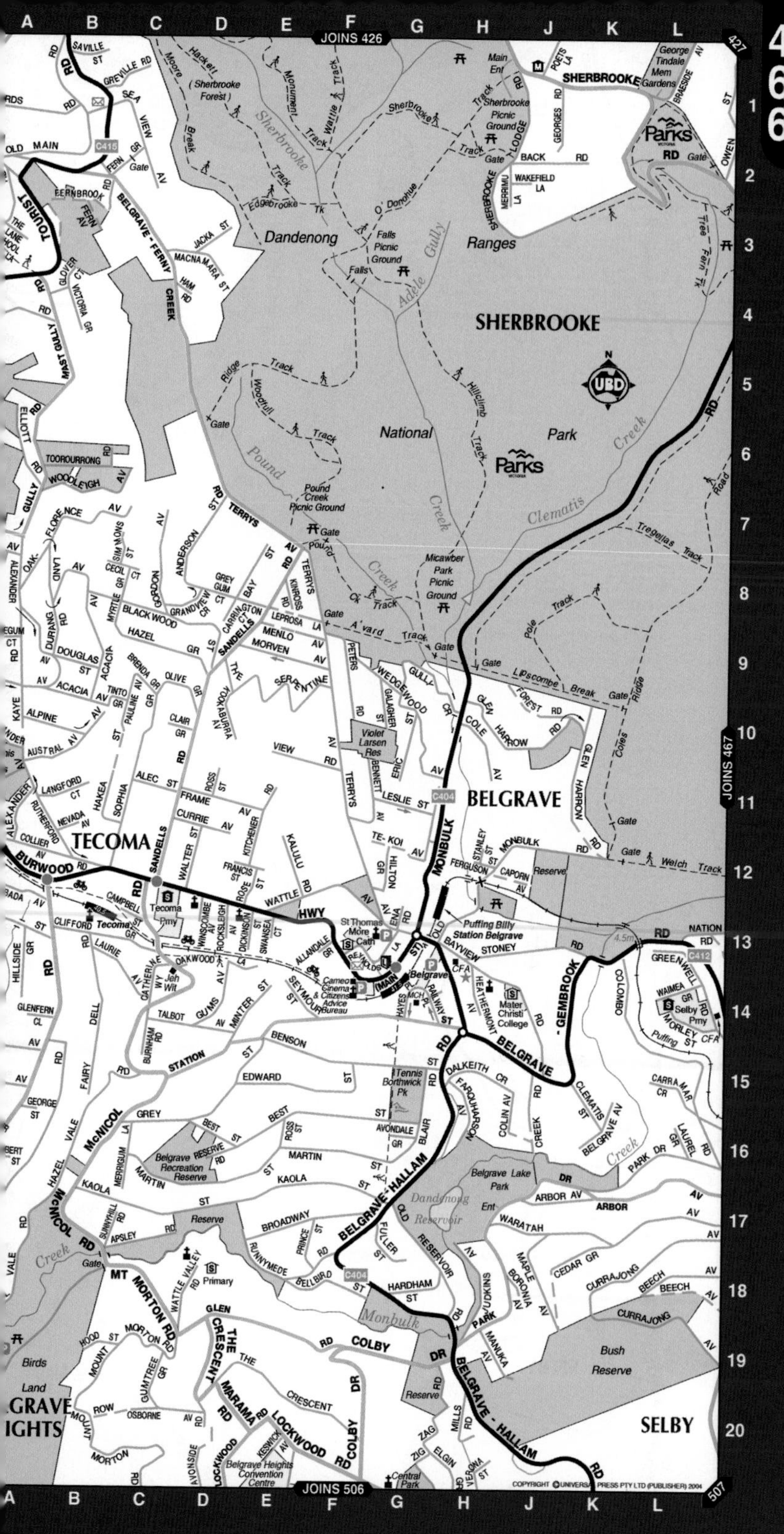
JOINS 426
427
JOINS 467
JOINS 506
507
A B C D E F G H J K L
1 2 3 4 5 6 7 8 9 10 11 12 13 14 15 16 17 18 19 20
SHERBROOKE
Dandenong Ranges National Park
Parks
UBD
George Tindale Mem Gardens
Main Ent
Sherbrooke Picnic Ground
Falls Picnic Ground
Pound Creek Picnic Ground
Micawber Park Picnic Ground
Hackett (Sherbrooke Forest) Break
Moore Break
Monument Track
Wattle Track
Sherbrooke Track
Edgebrooke Tk
O' Donohue Track
Adele Gully
Sherbrooke Creek
Ridge Track
Woodhull Track
Hillclimb Track
Pound Creek
Clematis Creek
Tregellas Track
Pole Track
A'vard Track
Lipscombe Break
Coles Ridge
Welch Track
Gate
BELGRAVE
TECOMA
SELBY
GRAVE IGHTS
Violet Larsen Res
Puffing Billy Station Belgrave
Mater Christi College
St Thomas More Cath
Cameo Cinema & Citizens Advice Bureau
Tecoma Pmy
Selby Pmy
Tennis Borthwick Pk
Belgrave Recreation Reserve
Belgrave Lake Park
Dandenong Reservoir
Monbulk Creek
Bush Reserve
Birds Land
Primary
Belgrave Heights Convention Centre
Central Park
Reserve
CFA
BURWOOD HWY
MONBULK RD
BELGRAVE - GEMBROOK RD
BELGRAVE - HALLAM RD
BELGRAVE - FERNY CREEK RD
MT DANDENONG TOURIST RD
SHERBROOKE RD
TERRYS AV
SANDELLS RD
STATION ST
McNICOL RD
MT MORTON RD
COLBY DR
LOCKWOOD RD
THE CRESCENT
C415
C404
C412
COPYRIGHT © UNIVERSAL PRESS PTY LTD (PUBLISHER) 2004

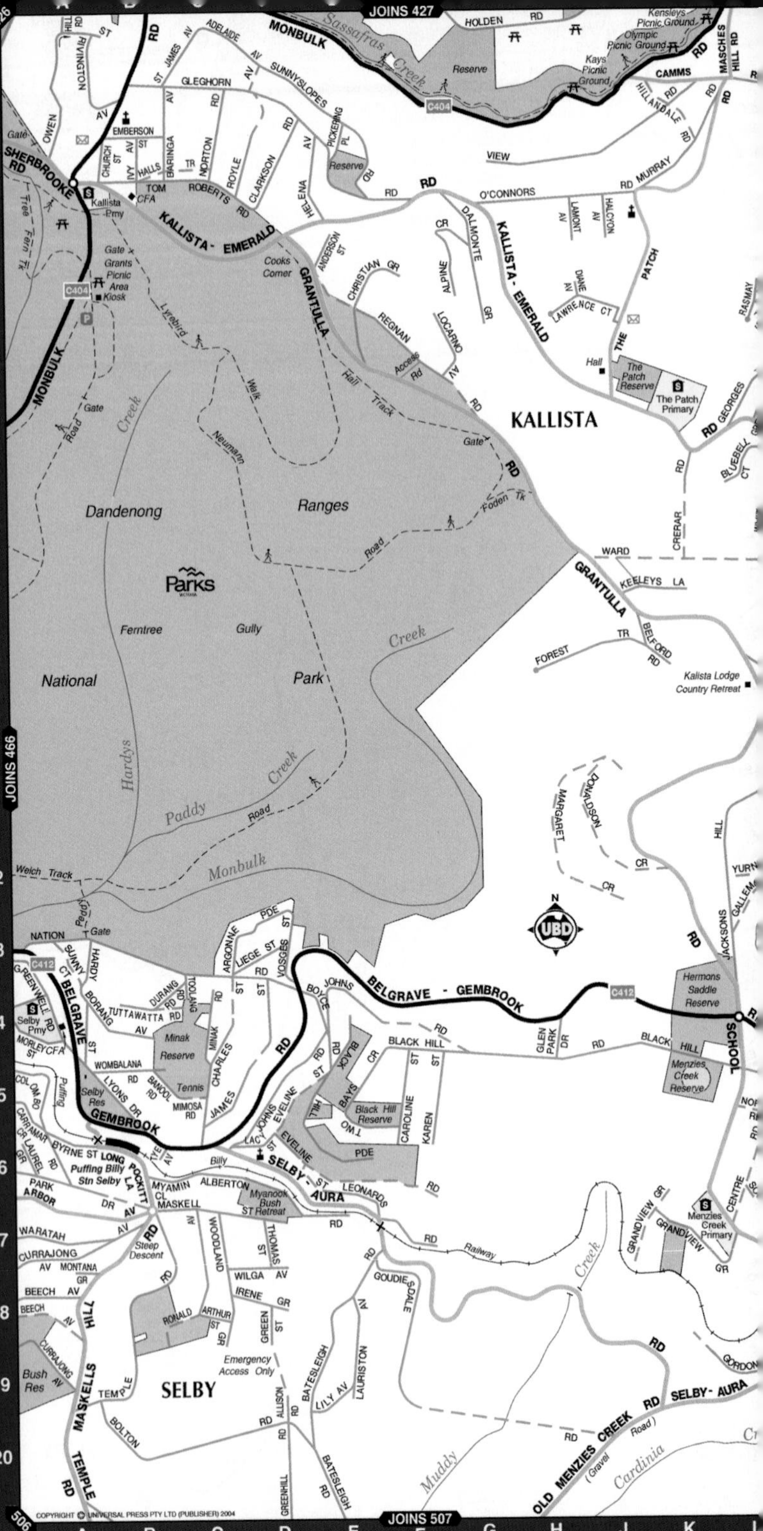

426
JOINS 427
JOINS 466
JOINS 507
506

KALLISTA

SELBY

Dandenong Ranges National Park

Ferntree Gully

Parks

MONBULK RD
SHERBROOKE RD
KALLISTA - EMERALD RD
GRANTULLA RD
O'CONNORS RD
THE PATCH RD
MURRAY RD
CAMMS RD
MASCHES HILL RD
HOLDEN RD
BELGRAVE - GEMBROOK RD
BLACK HILL RD
SCHOOL RD
JACKSONS HILL RD
SELBY - AURA RD
OLD MENZIES CREEK RD
MASKELLS HILL RD
TEMPLE RD
GLEGHORN RD
SUNNYSLOPES RD
ADELAIDE AV
ROBERTS RD
TOM ROBERTS RD
EMBERSON
CHRISTIAN GR
REGNAN
LOCARNO AV
ALPINE CR
DALMONTE GR
LAMONT AV
HALCYON AV
DIANE AV
LAWRENCE CT
WARD
KEELEYS LA
BELFORD RD
FOREST TR
DONALDSON CR
MARGARET CR
GLEN PARK DR
LONG POCKITT LA
MYAMIN CL
ALBERTON
MASKELL
WOODLAND AV
THOMAS ST
WILGA AV
IRENE GR
RONALD
ARTHUR ST
GREEN ST
BATESLEIGH RD
LAURISTON AV
GOUDIE
GRANDVIEW GR
ALLISON RD
GREENHILL RD
WARATAH AV
CURRAJONG AV
MONTANA GR
BEECH AV
BOLTON
TEMPLE

Sassafras Creek
Reserve
Kensleys Picnic Ground
Olympic Picnic Ground
Kays Picnic Ground
Kallista Pmy
CFA
Grants Picnic Area
Kiosk
Cooks Corner
Lyrebird Walk
Hall Track
Neumann Track
Foden Tk
Welch Track
Hardys Creek
Paddy Creek
Monbulk Creek
The Patch Reserve
The Patch Primary
Kalista Lodge Country Retreat
Hermons Saddle Reserve
Menzies Creek Reserve
Menzies Creek Primary
Selby Pmy
Minak Reserve
Tennis
Black Hill Reserve
Puffing Billy Stn Selby
Myanook Bush Retreat
Steep Descent
Emergency Access Only
Bush Res
Railway
Muddy Creek
Cardinia Creek

JOINS 428

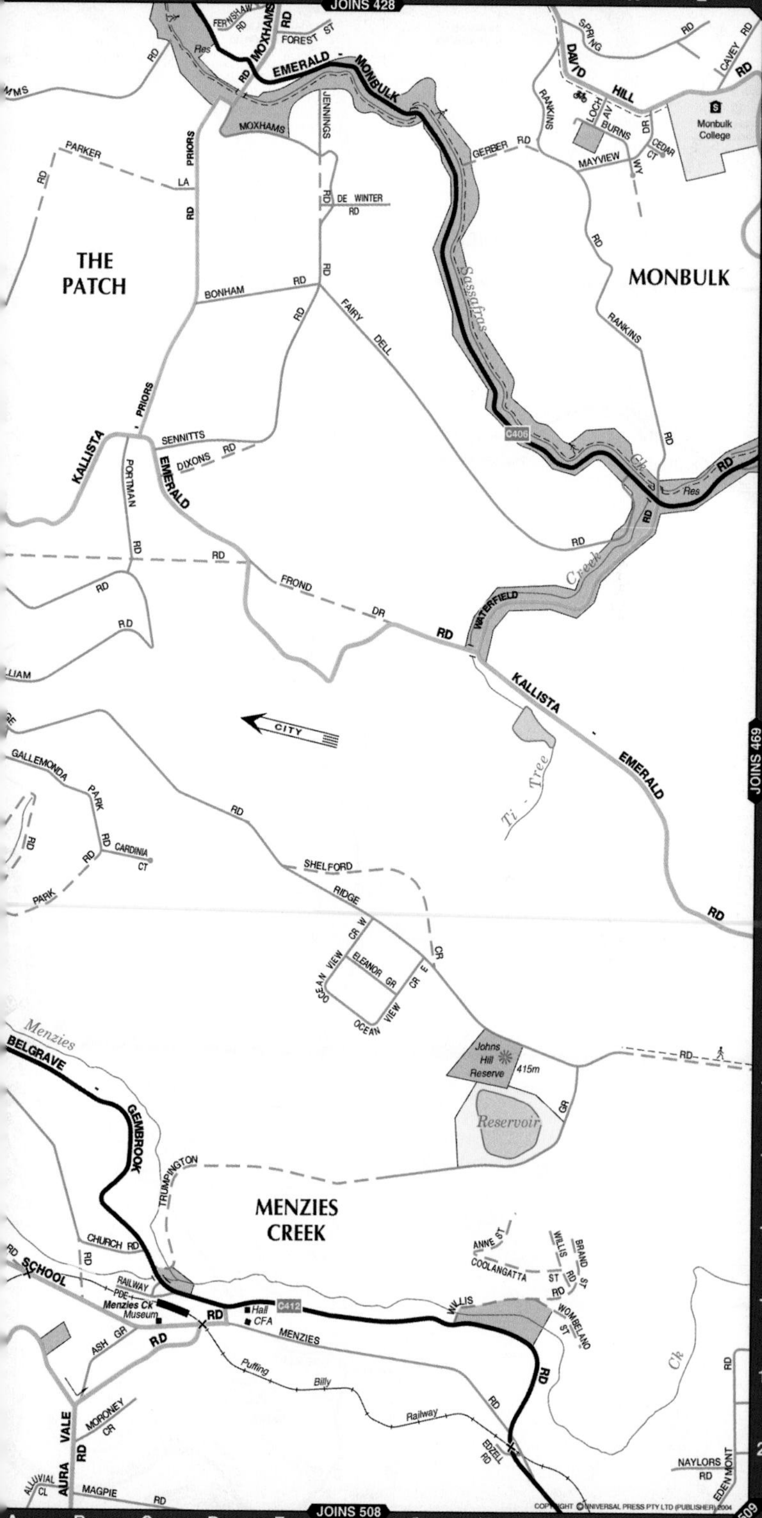

THE PATCH

MONBULK

MENZIES CREEK

EMERALD - MONBULK RD
MOXHAMS RD
FERNSHAW RD
FOREST ST
PRIORS RD
PARKER LA
JENNINGS RD
DE WINTER RD
BONHAM RD
FAIRY DELL RD
SENNITTS RD
DIXONS RD
KALLISTA - EMERALD RD
PORTMAN RD
FROND DR
WATERFIELD RD
SPRING RD
DAVID HILL RD
CAVEY RD
RANKINS RD
LOCH AV
BURNS DR
CEDAR CT
MAYVIEW WY
GERBER RD
Monbulk College
Sassafras Ck
Creek
Res
C406
CITY
Ti - Tree
GALLEMONDA PARK RD
CARDINIA CT
SHELFORD RD
RIDGE CR
OCEAN VIEW CR W
OCEAN VIEW CR E
ELEANOR GR
Johns Hill Reserve
415m
Reservoir
GR
Menzies
BELGRAVE - GEMBROOK RD
TRUMPINGTON
CHURCH RD
SCHOOL RD
RAILWAY PDE
Menzies Ck Museum
Hall
CFA
C412
MENZIES RD
ASH GR
Puffing Billy Railway
MORONEY CR
AURA VALE RD
ALLUVIAL CL
MAGPIE RD
ANNE ST
WILLIS RD
BRAND ST
COOLANGATTA RD
WILLIS ST
WOMBELANO ST
EDZELL RD
NAYLORS RD
EDENMONT RD
Ck

JOINS 469

JOINS 508

509

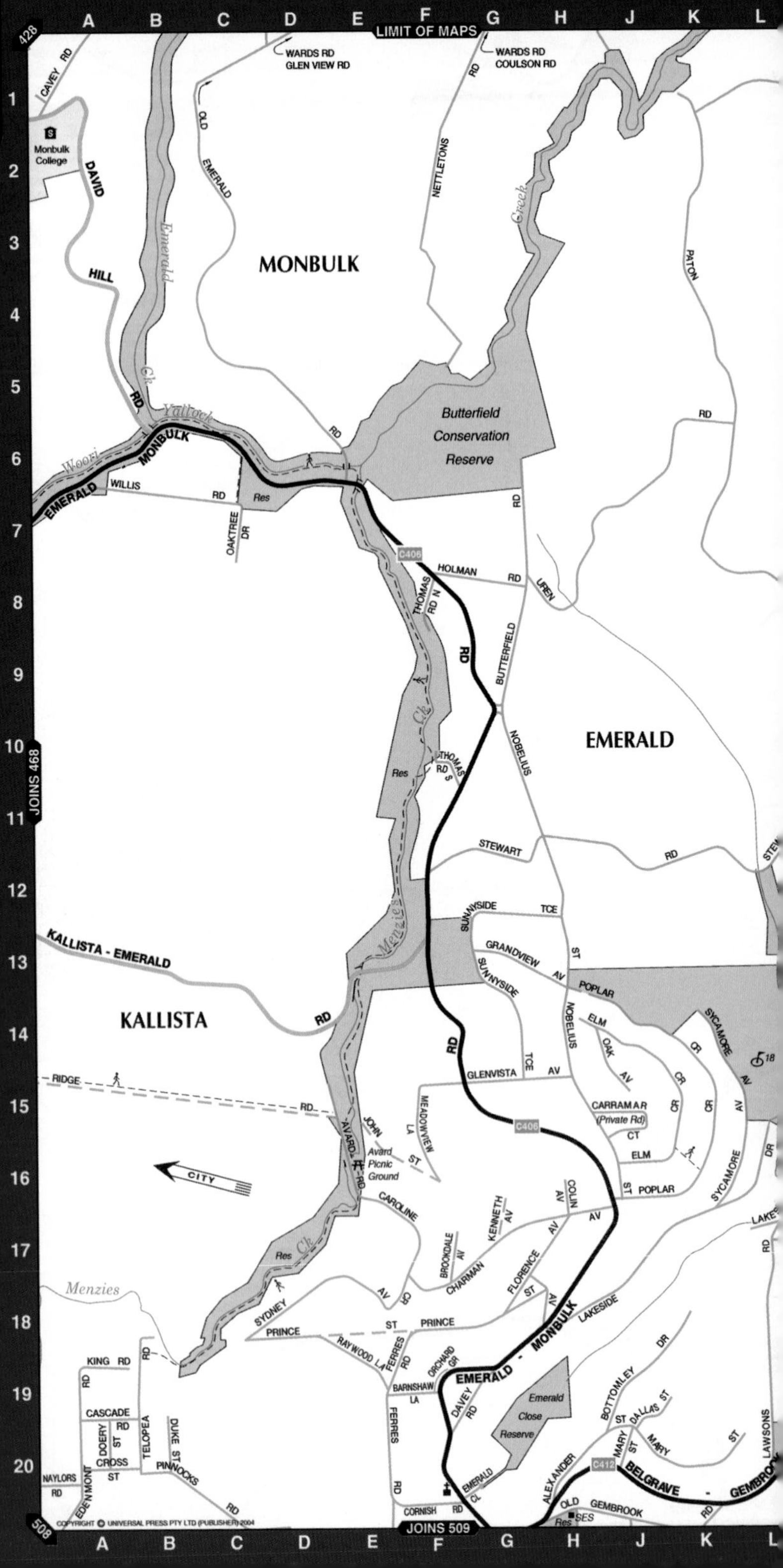

LIMIT OF MAPS

WARDS RD GLEN VIEW RD

WARDS RD COULSON RD

MONBULK

EMERALD

KALLISTA

Monbulk College

Butterfield Conservation Reserve

Avard Picnic Ground

Emerald Close Reserve

CAVEY RD
DAVID HILL RD
OLD EMERALD RD
NETTLETONS RD
PATON RD
MONBULK - EMERALD RD
WILLIS RD
OAKTREE DR
THOMAS RD N
THOMAS RD S
HOLMAN RD
UREN
BUTTERFIELD RD
NOBELIUS ST
STEWART RD
SUNNYSIDE TCE
GRANDVIEW AV
POPLAR
ELM
OAK AV
SYCAMORE AV
CARRAMAR (Private Rd) CT
KALLISTA - EMERALD RD
RIDGE RD
GLENVISTA AV
MEADOWVIEW LA
JOHN ST
AVARD RD
CAROLINE AV
COLIN AV
KENNETH AV
BROOKDALE AV
CHARMAN AV
FLORENCE ST
SYDNEY AV
PRINCE ST
RAYWOOD LA
FERRES RD
ORCHARD GR
BARNSHAW LA
EMERALD - MONBULK RD
LAKESIDE DR
DAVEY RD
BOTTOMLEY ST
DALLAS ST
MARY ST
ALEXANDER
BELGRAVE - GEMBROOK
OLD GEMBROOK RD
LAWSONS
EMERALD CL
CORNISH RD
KING RD
CASCADE RD
DOERY ST
CROSS ST
TELOPEA
DUKE ST
PINNOCKS RD
NAYLORS RD
EDENMONT
Emerald Ck
Yallock
Woori
Creek
Menzies Ck
Res
SES
C406
C412
CITY

JOINS 468
JOINS 509
428
508

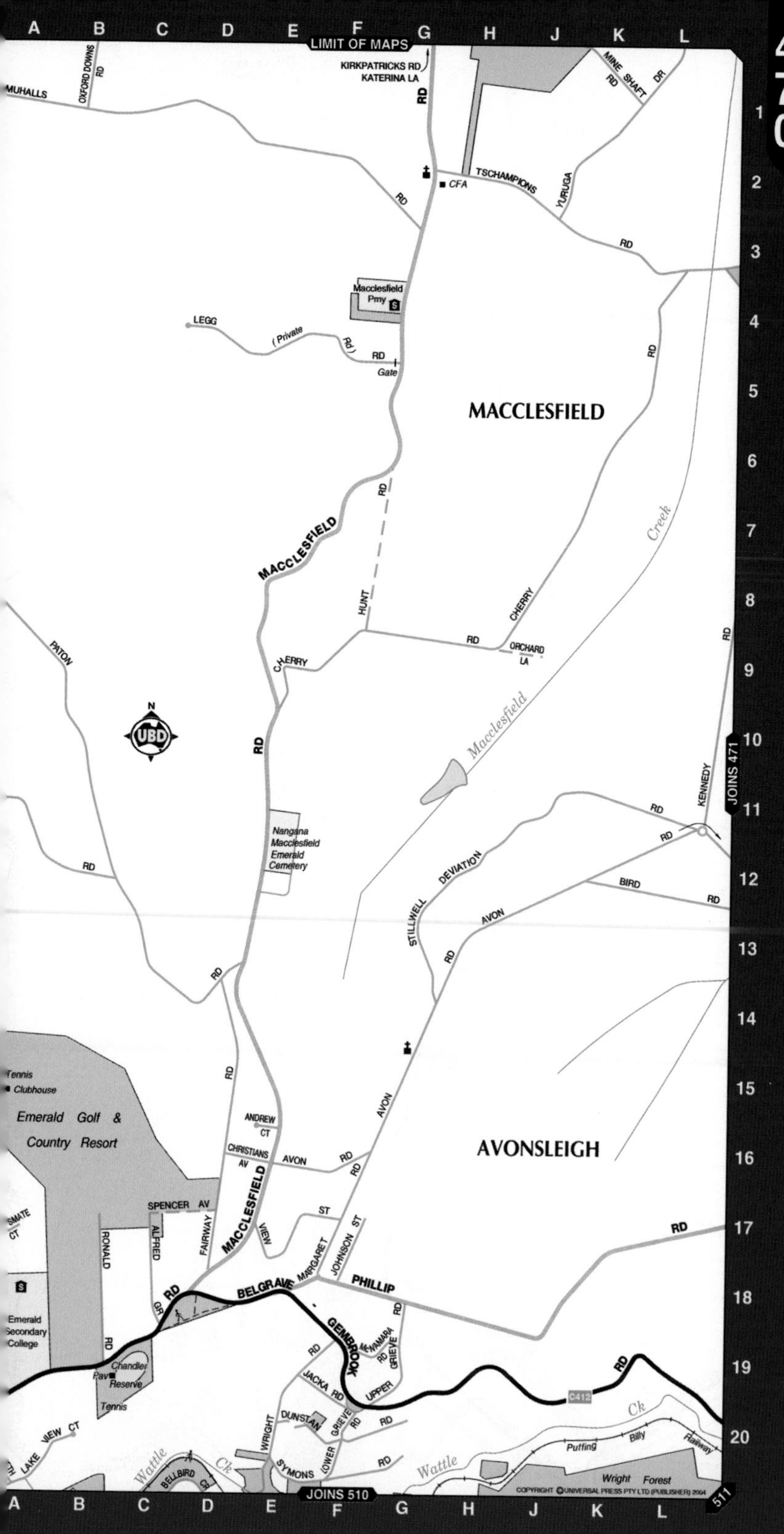

LIMIT OF MAPS
KIRKPATRICKS RD
KATERINA LA
MUHALLS
OXFORD DOWNS RD
MINE SHAFT RD
DR
TSCHAMPIONS
YURUGA
CFA
RD
Macclesfield Pmy
LEGG
(Private Rd)
Gate
MACCLESFIELD
HUNT
CHERRY
ORCHARD LA
Creek
Macclesfield
PATON
KENNEDY
JOINS 471
Nangana Macclesfield Emerald Cemetery
DEVIATION
STILLWELL
BIRD
AVON
Tennis
Clubhouse
Emerald Golf & Country Resort
ANDREW CT
CHRISTIANS AV
AVONSLEIGH
SPENCER AV
ALFRED GR
FAIRWAY
RONALD RD
VIEW
ST
JOHNSON ST
MARGARET
PHILLIP
BELGRAVE
GEMBROOK
McNAMARA RD
GRIEVE
UPPER
JACKA RD
Emerald Secondary College
Chandler Reserve
Pav
Tennis
C412
DUNSTAN
WRIGHT
LOWER
SYMONS
LAKE VIEW CT
BELLBIRD CR
Wattle Ck
Puffing Billy Railway
Wright Forest
JOINS 510
COPYRIGHT © UNIVERSAL PRESS PTY LTD (PUBLISHER) 2004
511
A B C D E F G H J K L
1 2 3 4 5 6 7 8 9 10 11 12 13 14 15 16 17 18 19 20

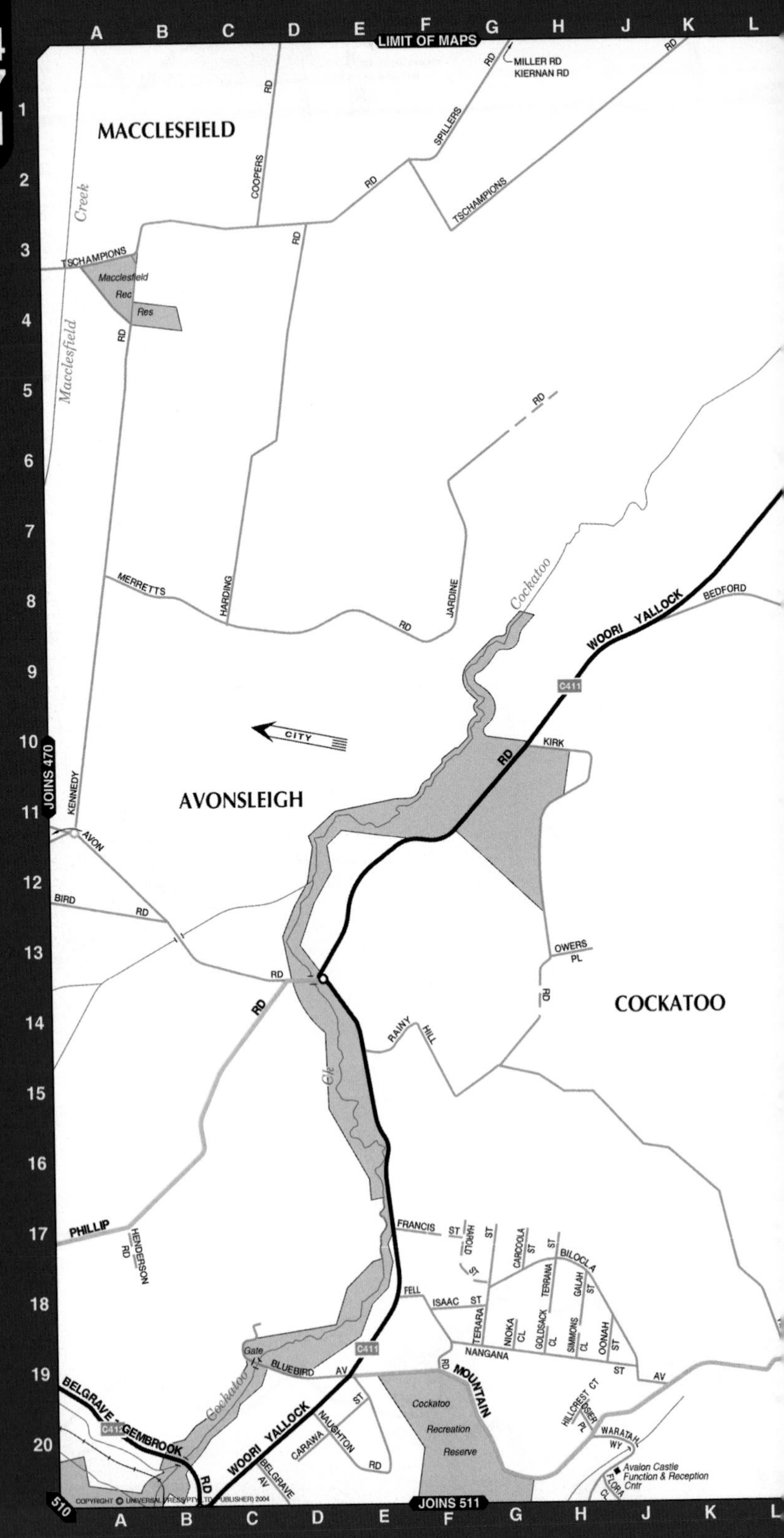

LIMIT OF MAPS
MILLER RD
KIERNAN RD
MACCLESFIELD
COOPERS RD
SPILLERS RD
TSCHAMPIONS
Macclesfield Creek
Macclesfield Rec Res
MERRETTS RD
HARDING
JARDINE
Cockatoo Ck
WOORI YALLOCK RD
BEDFORD
C411
KIRK
CITY
AVONSLEIGH
JOINS 470
KENNEDY
AVON
BIRD RD
OWERS PL
COCKATOO
RAINY HILL
PHILLIP
HENDERSON RD
FRANCIS ST
HAROLD ST
CARCOOLA ST
BILOCLA
TERRANA
GALAH ST
FELL
ISAAC ST
TERARA
NIOKA CL
GOLDSACK CL
SIMMONS CL
OONAH ST
NANGANA ST
AV
Gate
BLUEBIRD AV
MOUNTAIN RD
BELGRAVE - GEMBROOK RD
C412
CARAWA
NAUGHTON ST
BELGRAVE AV
Cockatoo Recreation Reserve
HILLCREST CT
OSIER PL
WARATAH WY
Avalon Castle Function & Reception Cntr
FLORA CL
JOINS 511
510

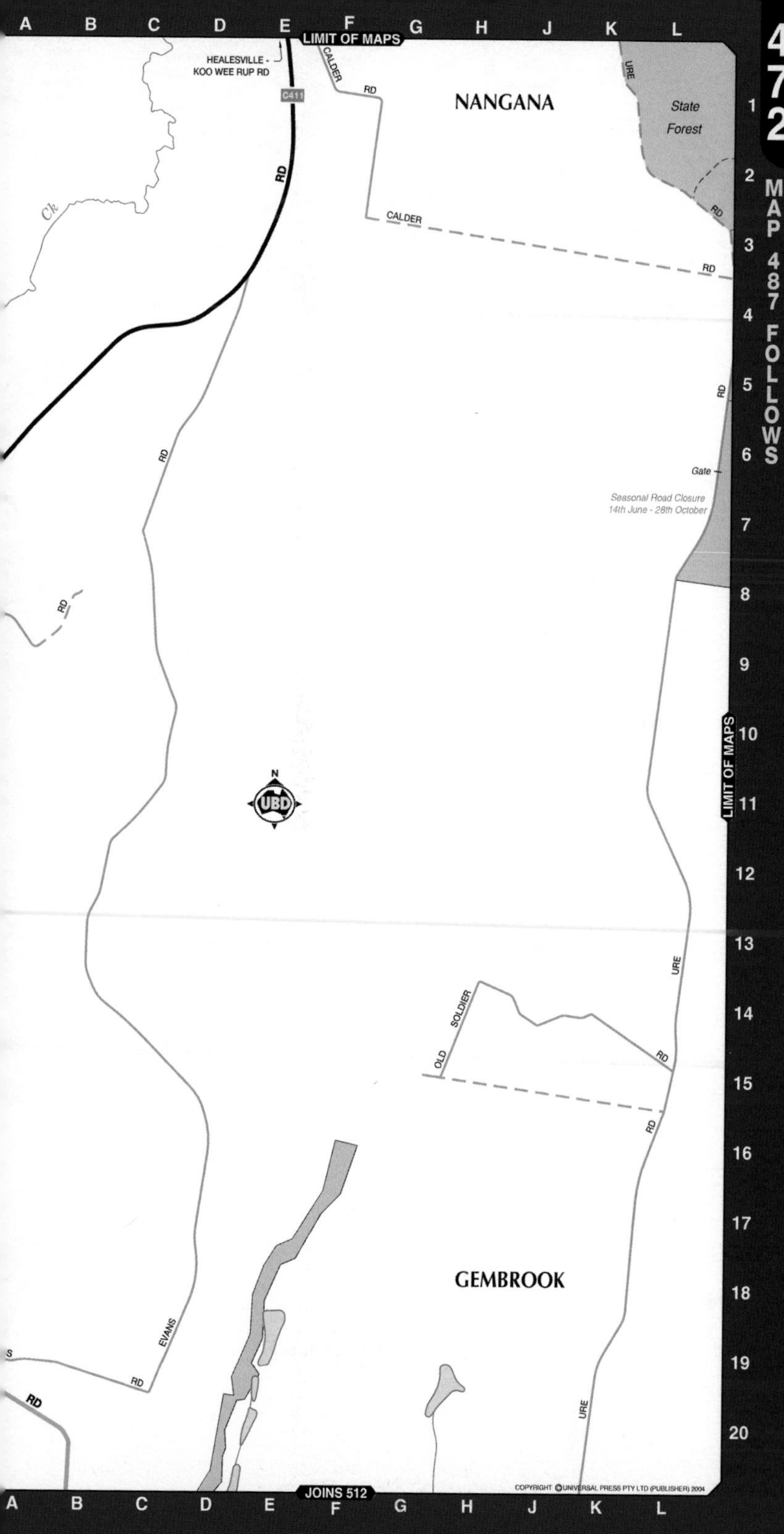

A B C D E F G H J K L
LIMIT OF MAPS
472
HEALESVILLE - KOO WEE RUP RD
C411
RD
CALDER
RD
NANGANA
URE
State Forest
CALDER
RD
RD
Ck
1
2
3
4
5
6
7
8
9
10
11
12
13
14
15
16
17
18
19
20
MAP 487 FOLLOWS
RD
Gate
Seasonal Road Closure
14th June - 28th October
RD
LIMIT OF MAPS
UBD
N
URE
OLD SOLDIER
RD
RD
GEMBROOK
EVANS
RD
RD
URE
JOINS 512
COPYRIGHT © UNIVERSAL PRESS PTY LTD (PUBLISHER) 2004
A B C D E F G H J K L

PREVIOUS MAP 472

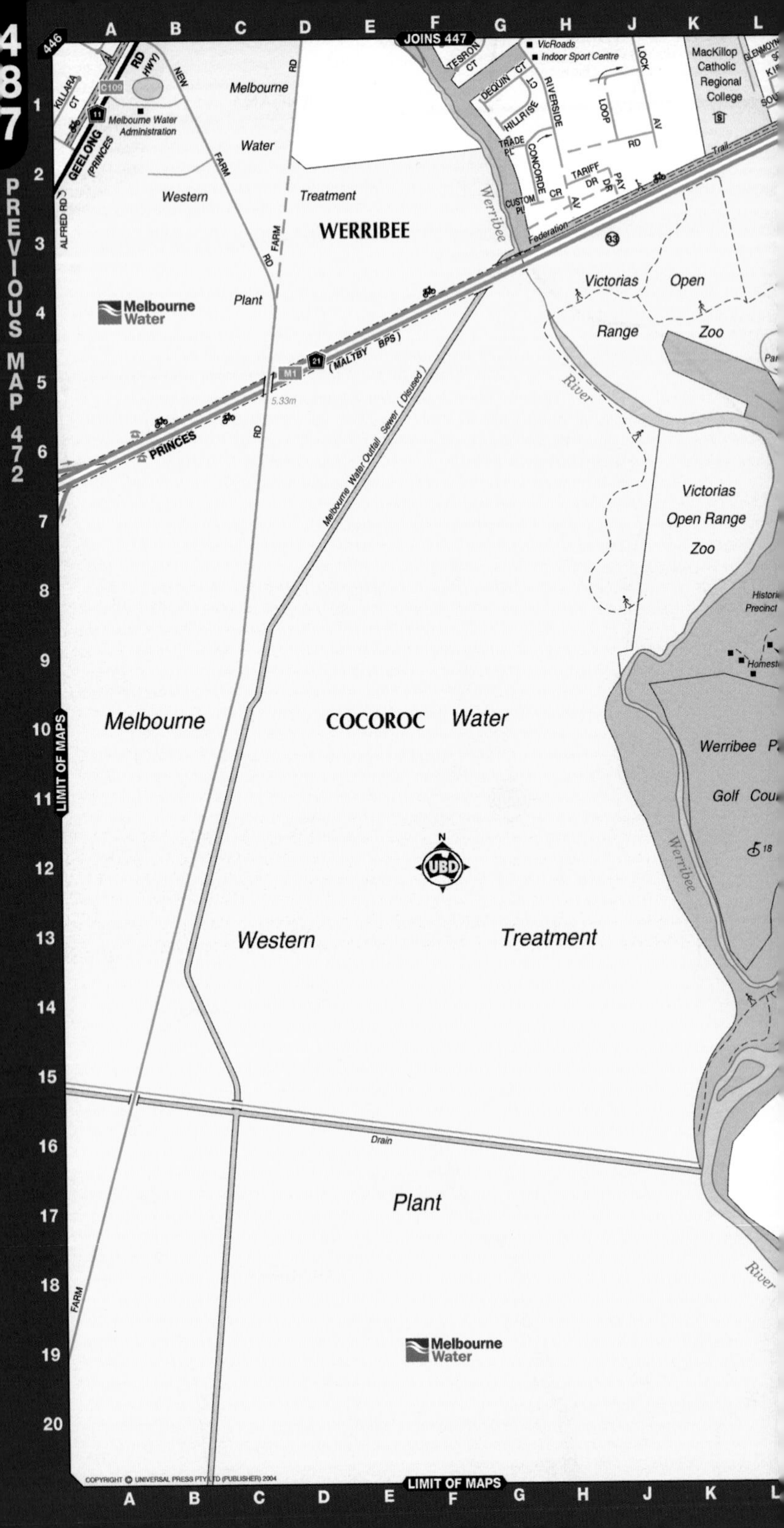

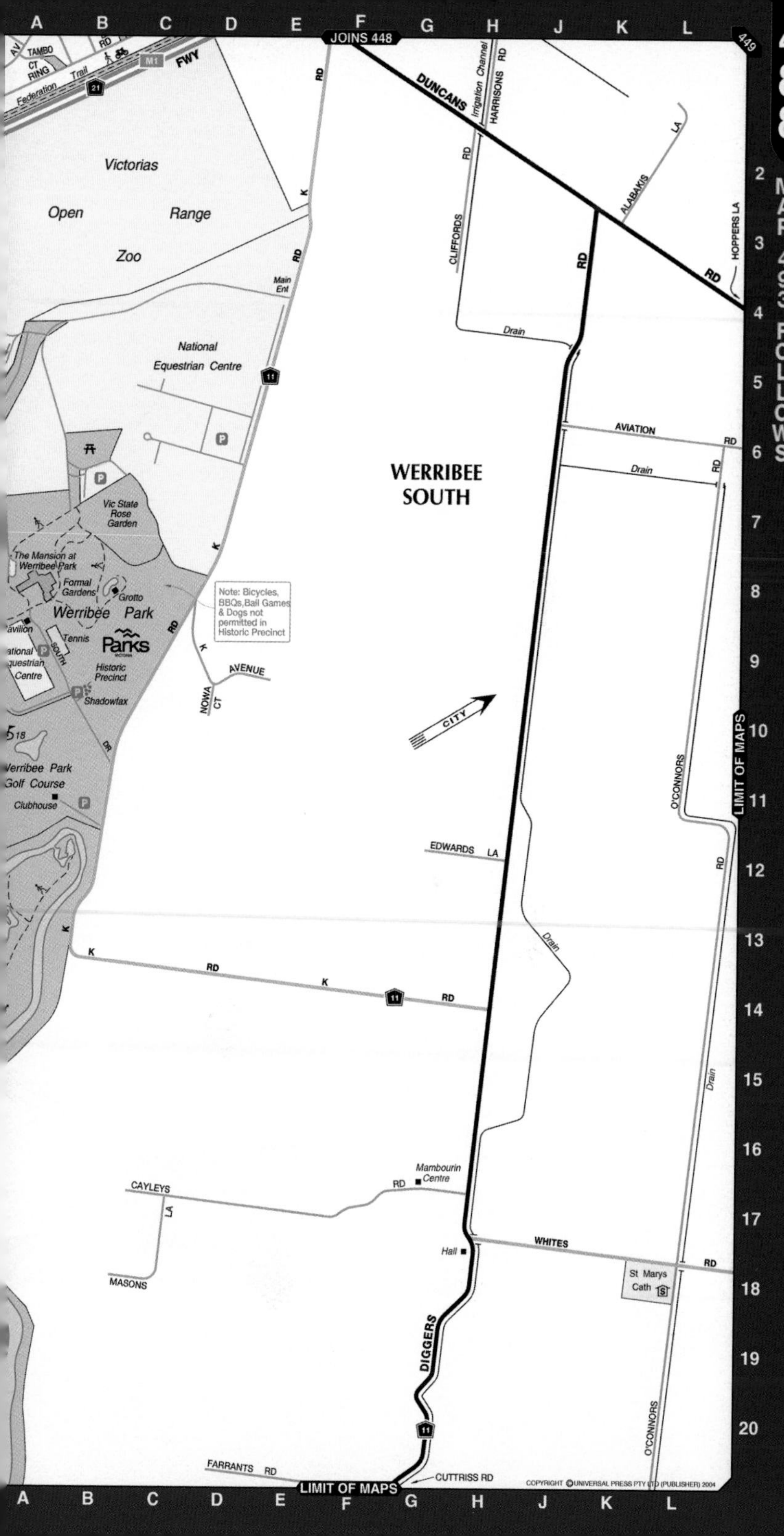

JOINS 448
449
WERRIBEE SOUTH
Victorias Open Range Zoo
National Equestrian Centre
Main Ent
Vic State Rose Garden
The Mansion at Werribee Park
Formal Gardens
Grotto
Werribee Park
Tennis
Historic Precinct
Shadowfax
Werribee Park Golf Course
Clubhouse
Note: Bicycles, BBQs, Ball Games & Dogs not permitted in Historic Precinct
Federation Trail
FWY
DUNCANS RD
Irrigation Channel
HARRISONS RD
CLIFFORDS RD
ALABAKIS LA
HOPPERS LA
Drain
AVIATION RD
K RD
AVENUE
NOWA CT
CITY
EDWARDS LA
O'CONNORS RD
Mambourin Centre
CAYLEYS RD
LA
MASONS
Hall
WHITES RD
St Marys Cath
DIGGERS RD
FARRANTS RD
CUTTRISS RD
LIMIT OF MAPS
MAP 493 FOLLOWS
COPYRIGHT © UNIVERSAL PRESS PTY LTD (PUBLISHER) 2004

PREVIOUS MAP 488

PORT

PHILLIP

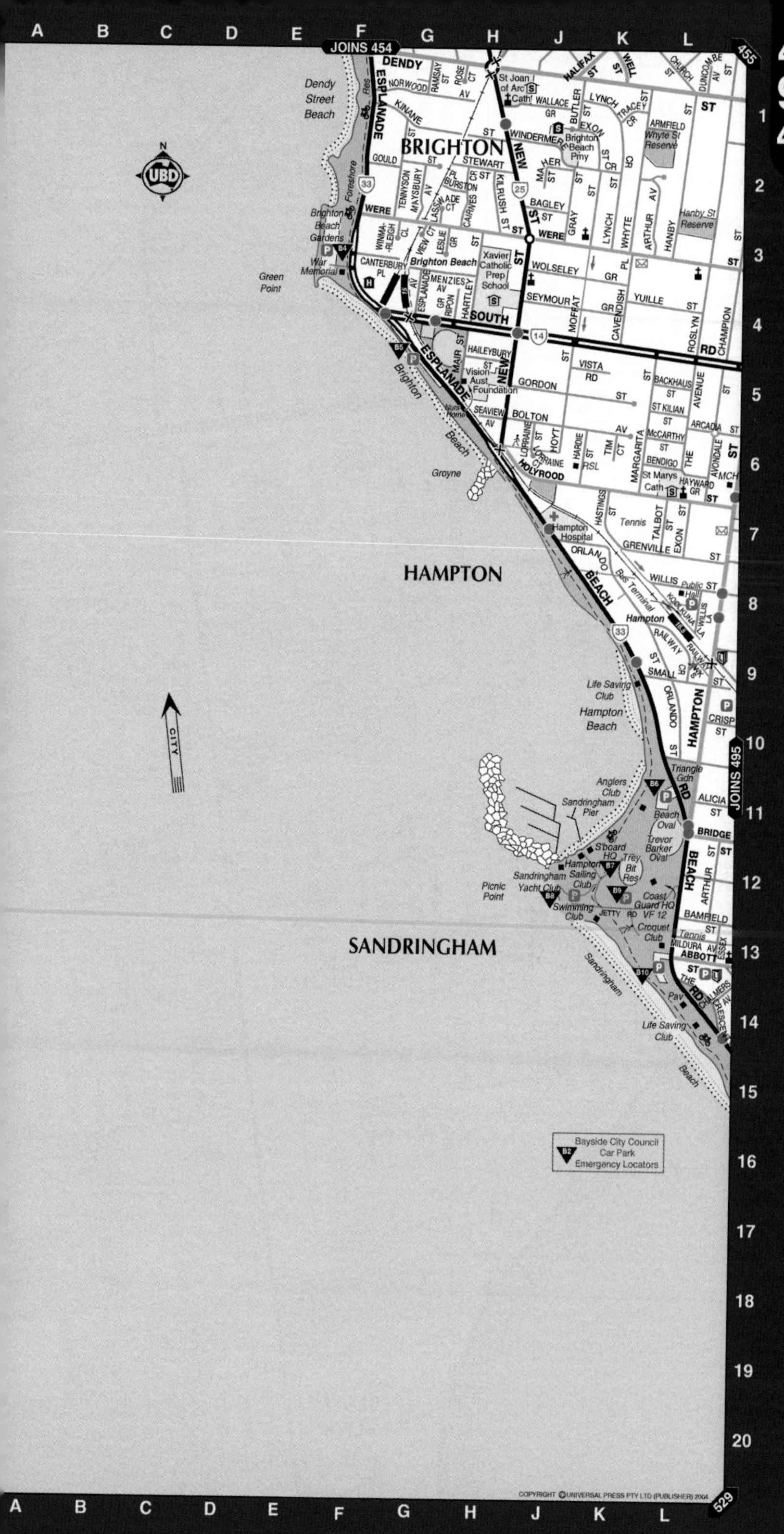

JOINS 454
455
BRIGHTON
HAMPTON
SANDRINGHAM
Dendy Street Beach
Brighton Beach Gardens
War Memorial
Green Point
Brighton Beach
Groyne
Hampton Hospital
Life Saving Club
Hampton Beach
Anglers Club
Sandringham Pier
Sandringham Yacht Club
Hampton Sailing Club
Swimming Club
Picnic Point
Coast Guard HQ VF 12
Croquet Club
Sandringham Beach
Xavier Catholic Prep School
Vision Aust Foundation
Brighton Beach Pmy
Whyte St Reserve
Hanby St Reserve
Beach Oval
Trevor Barker Oval
Triangle Gdn
CITY
JOINS 495
Bayside City Council Car Park Emergency Locators
COPYRIGHT © UNIVERSAL PRESS PTY LTD (PUBLISHER) 2004
529

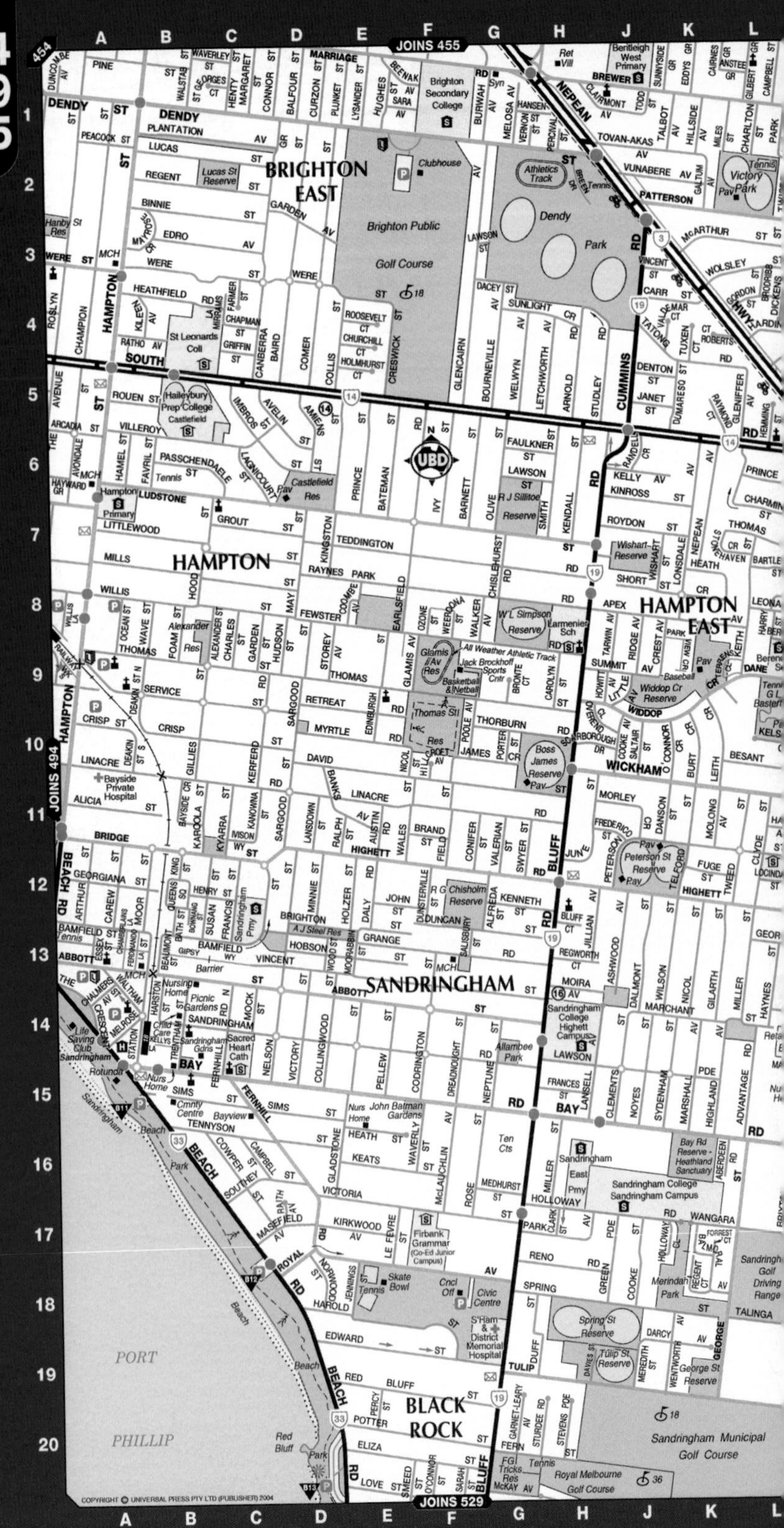

A B C D E F G H J K L
JOINS 455
454
1 2 3 4 5 6 7 8 9 10 11 12 13 14 15 16 17 18 19 20
BRIGHTON EAST
HAMPTON
HAMPTON EAST
SANDRINGHAM
BLACK ROCK
PORT
PHILLIP
JOINS 494
JOINS 529
DENDY ST
PLANTATION
SOUTH RD
NEPEAN HWY
CUMMINS RD
BLUFF RD
HAMPTON ST
BEACH RD
BAY RD
HIGHETT RD
WICKHAM RD
Brighton Public Golf Course
Clubhouse
Dendy Park
Athletics Track
Victory Park
Brighton Secondary College
St Leonards Coll
Haileybury Prep College Castlefield
Castlefield Res
Lucas St Reserve
Hampton Primary
Alexander Res
Bayside Private Hospital
W L Simpson Reserve
Larmenier Sch
R J Sillitoe Reserve
Wishart Reserve
Glamis Av Res
All Weather Athletic Track
Jack Brockhoff Sports Cntr
Basketball & Netball
Thomas St Res
Boss James Reserve
Widdop Cr Reserve
Peterson St Reserve
R G Chisholm Reserve
A J Steel Res
Sandringham Pmy
Sandringham College Highett Campus
Allambee Park
Picnic Gardens
Sandringham Gdns
Sacred Heart Cath
Nursing Home
Life Saving Club Sandringham
Rotunda
Sandringham Beach Park
John Batman Gardens
Ten Cts
Sandringham East Pmy
Sandringham College Sandringham Campus
Bay Rd Reserve - Heathland Sanctuary
Firbank Grammar (Co-Ed Junior Campus)
Skate Bowl
Cncl Off
Civic Centre
S'Ham & District Memorial Hospital
Spring St Reserve
Tulip St Reserve
George St Reserve
Merindah Park
Sandringham Golf Driving Range
Sandringham Municipal Golf Course
Royal Melbourne Golf Course
FG Tricks Res McKAY
Red Bluff
UBD
COPYRIGHT © UNIVERSAL PRESS PTY LTD (PUBLISHER) 2004

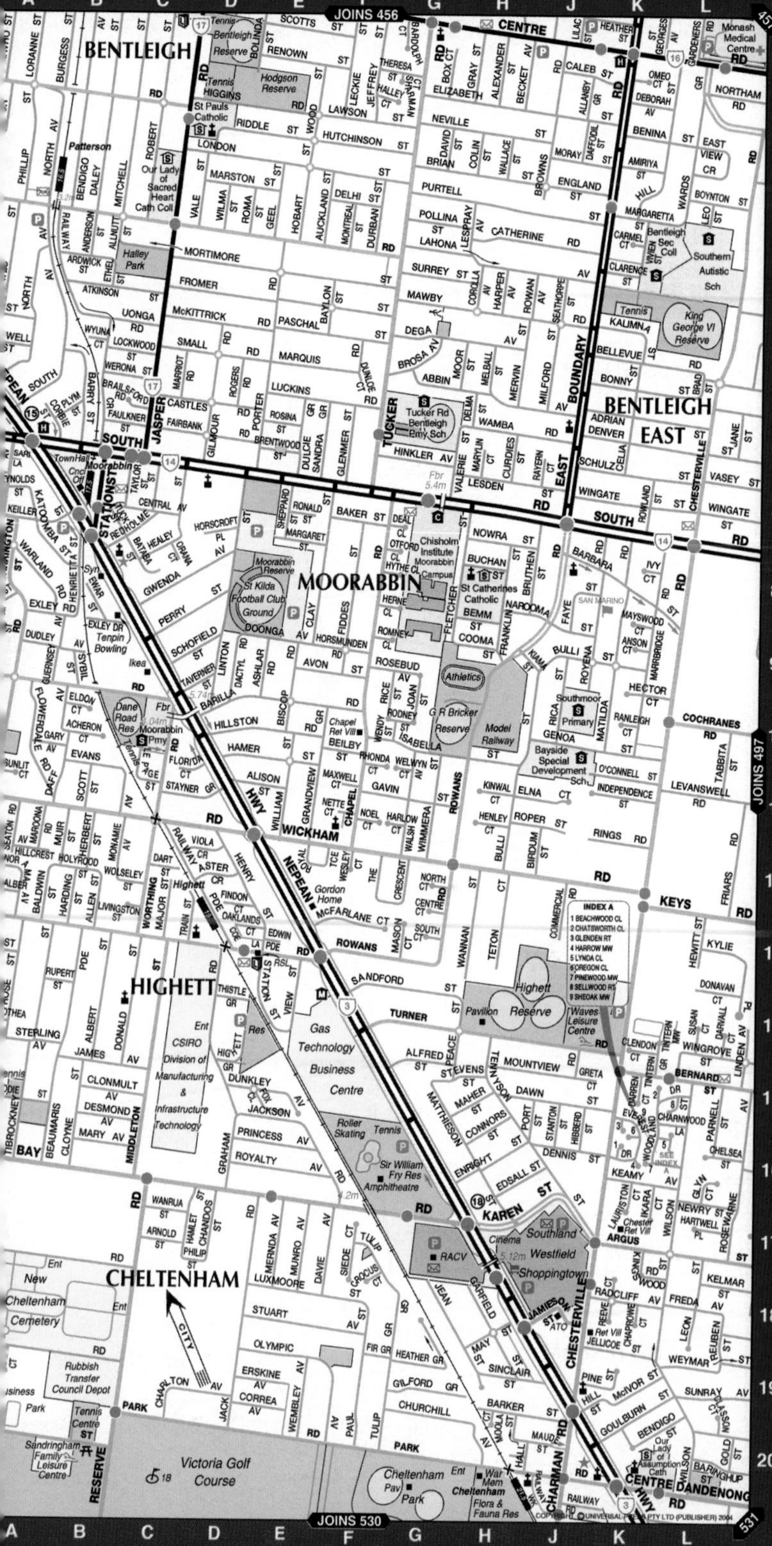

JOINS 456
457
JOINS 497
JOINS 530
531

A B C D E F G H J K L

1 2 3 4 5 6 7 8 9 10 11 12 13 14 15 16 17 18 19 20

BENTLEIGH

BENTLEIGH EAST

MOORABBIN

HIGHETT

CHELTENHAM

Monash Medical Centre

Hodgson Reserve

St Pauls Catholic

Our Lady of Sacred Heart Cath Coll

Halley Park

Bentleigh Sec Coll

Southern Autistic Sch

King George VI Reserve

Tucker Rd Bentleigh Prmy Sch

Moorabbin Reserve

St Kilda Football Club Ground

Chisholm Institute Moorabbin Campus

St Catherines Catholic

Athletics

G R Bricker Reserve

Model Railway

Southmoor Primary

Bayside Special Development Sch

Tenpin Bowling

Ikea

Dane Road Res

Moorabbin Prmy

Chapel Ret Vill

Gordon Home

Highett Reserve

Pavilion

Waves Leisure Centre

Gas Technology Business Centre

CSIRO Division of Manufacturing & Infrastructure Technology

Roller Skating

Sir William Fry Res Amphitheatre

RACV

Southland Westfield Shoppingtown

Cinema

Chester Ret Vill

New Cheltenham Cemetery

Rubbish Transfer Council Depot

Sandringham Family Leisure Centre

Victoria Golf Course

Cheltenham Park

War Mem

Cheltenham Flora & Fauna Res

Our Lady of Assumption Cath

INDEX A

1 BEACHWOOD CL
2 CHATSWORTH CL
3 GLENDEN RT
4 HARROW MW
5 LYNDA CL
6 OREGON CL
7 PINEWOOD MW
8 SELLWOOD RT
9 SHEOAK MW

CITY

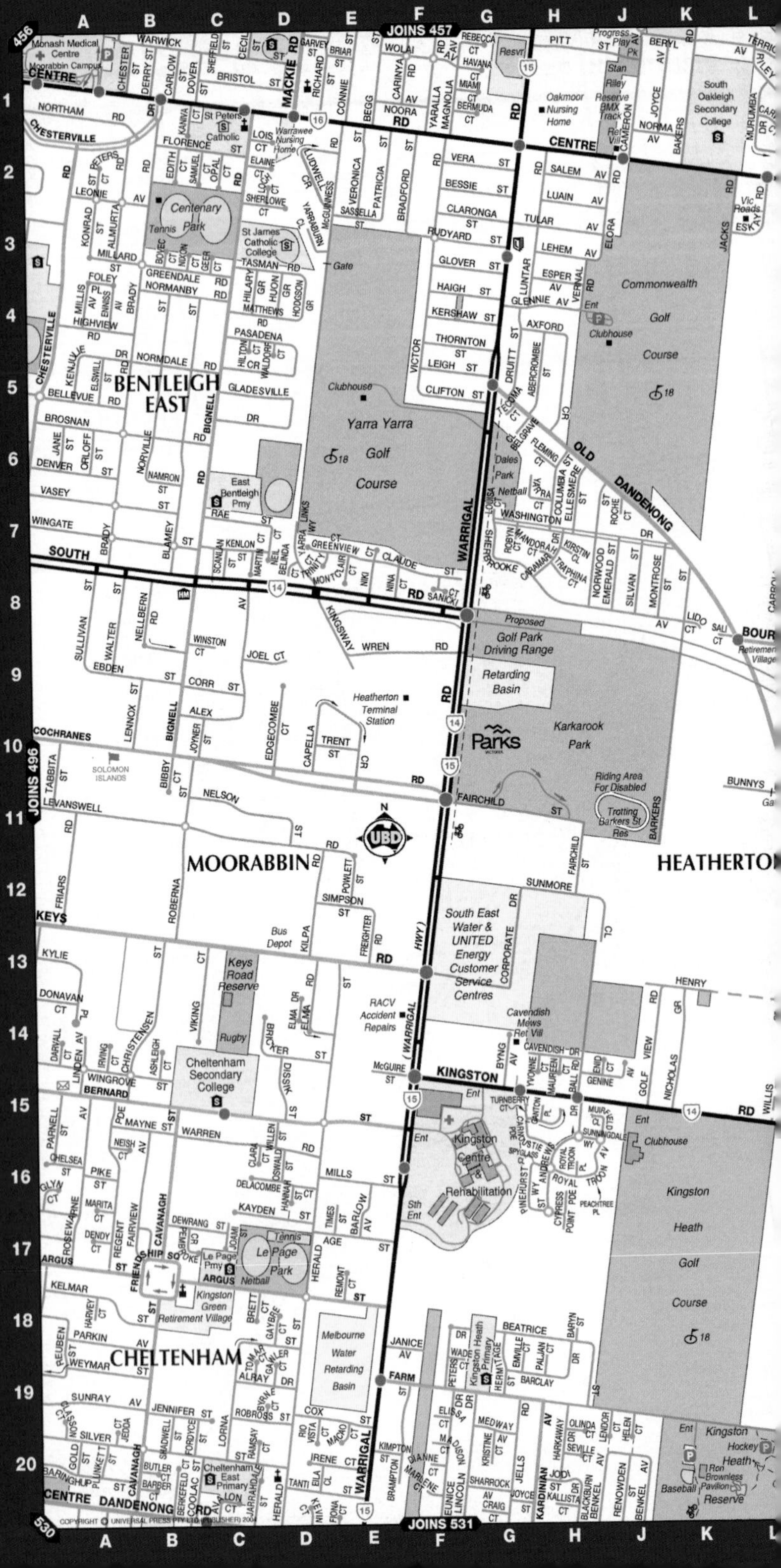

A B C D E F G H J K L

JOINS 457

456

BENTLEIGH EAST

MOORABBIN

HEATHERTON

CHELTENHAM

Monash Medical Centre
Moorabbin Campus
CENTRE
WARWICK
CHESTER
DERRY ST
CARLOW
DOVER
SHEFFIELD
CECIL
BRISTOL
MACKIE RD
GARVEY ST
BRIAR
RICHARD
CONNIE
BEGG
WOLAI
CARINYA
NOORA RD
YARALLA
MAGNOLIA
REBECCA
HAVANA CT
MIAMI CT
BERMUDA CT
Resvr
PITT
Progress Play Pk
BERYL
JOYCE
NORMA
BAKERS
South Oakleigh Secondary College
MURUMBA
RYLEY
NORTHAM RD
CHESTERVILLE
St Peters Catholic
LOIS
FLORENCE
Warrawee Nursing Home
ELAINE
LIDWELL
VERONICA
PATRICIA
BRADFORD
VERA
Oakmoor Nursing Home
Stan Riley Reserve BMX Track
Ret Vill
CAMERON
CENTRE
ST PETERS
LEONIE
EDITH
SAMUEL
OPAL
LOCH
SHERLOWE CT
YARRABURN CL
McGUINNESS
SASSELLA
BESSIE
CLARONGA
SALEM AV
LUAIN AV
TULAR
Vic Roads
ESK
Centenary Park
Tennis
KONRAD
ALMURTA
MILLARD
BOVEC
NIXON
GEER
St James Catholic College
TASMAN RD
Gate
RUDYARD
GLOVER
HAIGH
KERSHAW
THORNTON
LEIGH
CLIFTON
LUNTAR
LEHEM AV
ESPER
VERNAL
ELORA
JACKS
Commonwealth Golf Course
Clubhouse
Ent
FOLEY
GREENDALE
NORMANBY
HILARY
HUON
HODGSON
MATTHEWS
MILLIS
ENNISS
BRADY
HIGHVIEW
PASADENA
HILTON
WALDORF
NORMDALE
GLENNIE AV
AXFORD
DRUITT
ABERCROMBIE
KENJULIE
ELSWELL
BELLEVUE
GLADESVILLE
BIGNELL
Clubhouse
Yarra Yarra Golf Course
VICTOR
TECOMA
BELGRAVE
FLEMING
OLD DANDENONG
BROSNAN
JANE
ORLOFF
DENVER
NORVILLE
NAMRON
Dales Park
Netball
COLUMBIA
ELLESMERE
ROCHE
VASEY
East Bentleigh Pmy
RAE
LOUISA
WASHINGTON
WINGATE
BLAMEY
KENLON
SCANLAN
MARTIN
NEIL
BELINDA
YARRA LINKS WY
GREENVIEW
CLAUDE
MANDORAH
ROBYN
SHERBROOKE
KIRSTIN
TRAPHINA
NORWOOD
EMERALD
SILVAN
MONTROSE
SOUTH
TRINITY
MONTCLAIR
NIKI
NINA
SANICKI
WARRIGAL RD
SULLIVAN
WALTER
NELLBERN
WINSTON CT
JOEL CT
KINGSWAY
WREN RD
Proposed
Golf Park Driving Range
LIDO
SALI CT
BOURKE
Retirement Village
EBDEN
CORR
LENNOX
ALEX
Retarding Basin
Heatherton Terminal Station
EDGECOMBE
CAPELLA
TRENT
Karkarook Park
Parks Victoria
COCHRANES
JOYNER
SOLOMON ISLANDS
TABBITA
BIBBY
NELSON
FAIRCHILD ST
Riding Area For Disabled
Trotting
Barkers St Res
BARKERS
BUNNYS
LEVANSWELL
FRIARS
ROBERNA
POWLETT
SIMPSON
SUNMORE
KEYS
Bus Depot
KILPA
FREIGHTER
South East Water & UNITED Energy Customer Service Centres
CORPORATE
KYLIE
Keys Road Reserve
VIKING
ELMA
RACV Accident Repairs
(WARRIGAL HWY)
Cavendish Mews Ret Vill
CAVENDISH DR
HENRY
GOLF VIEW
NICHOLAS
WILLIS
DONAVAN
DARVALL
LINDEN AV
IRVING
CHRISTENSEN
ASHLEIGH
Rugby
BRIXTER
Cheltenham Secondary College
DISSIK
McGUIRE ST
BYNG
YVONNE
MAUREEN
BALL RD
ENID
GENINE
KINGSTON
WINGROVE
BERNARD
PARNELL
PDE
MAYNE ST
WARREN
CLARA
WILLEN
OSWALD
MILLS
TURNBERRY CT
CARNOUSTIE
SPYGLASS
MUIRFIELD
SUNNINGDALE WY
Clubhouse
NEISH
CHELSEA
PIKE
GLYN
MARITA
DELACOMBE
HANNAH
KAYDEN
Kingston Centre Rehabilitation
Sth Ent
PINEHURST
ANDREWS
ROYAL TROON
CYPRESS POINT PDE
PEACHTREE PL
Kingston Heath Golf Course
ROSEWARNE
DENDY
REGENT
FAIRVIEW
CAVANAGH
DEWRANG
PEMBROKE
JOAMI
TIMES
BARLOW
Tennis
Le Page Park
Le Page Pmy
Netball
AGE
HERALD
REMONT
FRIENDSHIP SQ
ARGUS
KELMAR
HARVEY
Kingston Green Retirement Village
BRETT
GAYBRE
Melbourne Water Retarding Basin
JANICE AV
WADE
Kingston Heath Primary
HERMITAGE
EMVILLE
PALJAN
BEATRICE
BARYN
BARCLAY
REUBEN
PARKIN
WEYMAR
TOMAR
GAWLER
ALRAY
SUNRAY AV
JENNIFER ST
ROBROSS
BYRNE
COX
FARM
PETERS
ELISSA
MADISON
MEDWAY
KRISTINE
HARKAWAY
OLINDA
SEVILLE
LENDOR
HELEN
Kingston Heath Hockey
CLASSON
GOLD
SILVER
PLUNKETT
JEDDA
SHADWELL
FORDYCE
LORNA
RAMSAY
RIO VISTA
MACKO
IRENE CT
KIMPTON
BRAMPTON
DIANNE
MARLENE
EUNICE
LINCOLN
SHARROCK
AV CRAIG
JELLS
JOYCE
KARDINIAN
JODI
KALLISTA
BLACKBURN
BENKEL
RENOWDEN
Baseball
Ron Brownless Pavilion
Reserve
BARINGHUP
BUTLER
BARBER
BERKEFELD
COOLAC
Cheltenham East Primary
LON
JARRAHDALE
TANTI
EILA
KEVIN
FIONA
CENTRE DANDENONG RD

JOINS 496

JOINS 531

530

A B C D E F G H J K L

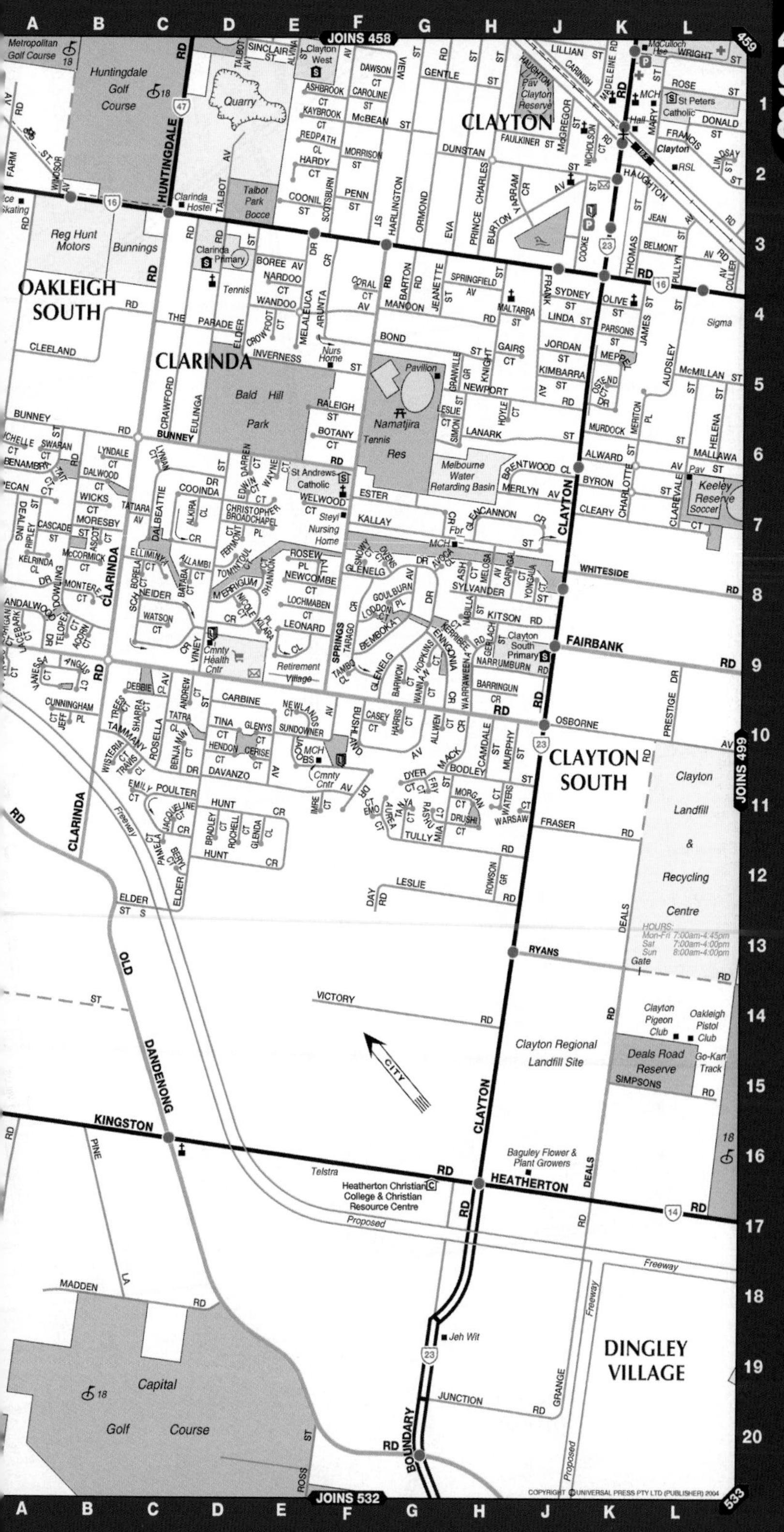

JOINS 458
JOINS 499
JOINS 532
459
533
CLAYTON
OAKLEIGH SOUTH
CLARINDA
CLAYTON SOUTH
DINGLEY VILLAGE
Metropolitan Golf Course
Huntingdale Golf Course
Quarry
Clarinda Hostel
Talbot Park Bocce
Reg Hunt Motors
Bunnings
Clarinda Primary
Tennis
Clayton West
Bald Hill Park
Namatjira Tennis Res
Pavilion
Nurs Home
St Andrews Catholic
Steyl Nursing Home
Melbourne Water Retarding Basin
Clayton Reserve
St Peters Catholic
Clayton RSL
Hall
Sigma
Keeley Reserve Soccer
Clayton South Primary
Cmnty Health Cntr
Retirement Village
Cmnty Cntr
Clayton Landfill & Recycling Centre
HOURS:
Mon-Fri 7:00am-4:45pm
Sat 7:00am-4:00pm
Sun 8:00am-4:00pm
Gate
Clayton Pigeon Club
Oakleigh Pistol Club
Clayton Regional Landfill Site
Deals Road Reserve
SIMPSONS
Go-Kart Track
Baguley Flower & Plant Growers
Telstra
Heatherton Christian College & Christian Resource Centre
Proposed
Freeway
Jeh Wit
Capital Golf Course
CITY
HUNTINGDALE RD
CLAYTON RD
CENTRE DANDENONG RD
HEATHERTON RD
KINGSTON RD
OLD DANDENONG RD
BOUNDARY RD
DEALS RD
RYANS RD
VICTORY RD
FAIRBANK RD
WHITESIDE RD
OSBORNE AV
LESLIE RD
ELDER ST S
MADDEN RD
JUNCTION RD
GRANGE RD
COPYRIGHT © UNIVERSAL PRESS PTY LTD (PUBLISHER) 2004
A B C D E F G H J K L
1 2 3 4 5 6 7 8 9 10 11 12 13 14 15 16 17 18 19 20

CLAYTON

CLAYTON SOUTH

DINGLEY VILLAGE

Monash Med Cntr
WRIGHT ST
ROSE ST
St Peters Cath
DONALD ST
FRANCIS ST
LINDSAY
KANOOKA
CARINISH
HAUGHTON RD
BELMONT AV
COLLIER AV
IONA ST
LUKE ST
PANORAMA
EVELYN
ADALEIGH CT
TREFO
CREST DR
DOOGA ST
WINTERTON RD
WHITE TON RD
Clayton Pmy
BROWNS ST
BIMBI ST
BENDIX DR
MORIAH
KIONGA
JAGUAR
BUCKLAND
Regency
TORTEVAL PL
McNAUGHTON RD
PRINCES
CAMBRO RD
RENVER RD
SARTON RD
Proposed Arterial Rd
GARDEN RD
ANZED CT
MILES
PETERS AV
HARTNETT CL
BASTOW PL
HIGHFIELD
ROBERTS AV
KALIMNA
MONTANA
WILMA AV
GRANDVIEW AV
WILMA
ALBERT CR
(DANDENONG RD)
LONGFORD CT
CENTRE
Sigma
RAYHUR
LIAM
KEOL ST
AONACH
THIRD ST
SECOND
FIRST ST
TIPPET
KOMBI
Bosch
Linfox
YIANNIS CT
McMILLAN ST
CLAREVALE ST
HELENA
LAURA ST
HADKINSON ST
MALLAWA
OAKES ST
Keeley Reserve
Pav
Soccer
CLEARY CT
BEVAN
TENNYSON
MILTON
WORDSWORTH
BROWNING
BURNS
MOORE
Westall
WESTALL
ST
GLENDALE
LEWIS
ASHDALE CT
BIRCH
Glendale Res
WHITWORTH
AVONDALE
OAKDALE CT
SULLIVAN
LOLLER
Mile
FAIRVIEW
CLIVE
JOYCE
HOPE
BLISSINGTON
PEACE
WHITESIDE RD
ROSEBANK
MAIN
FAIRBANK
Australia Post SE Region Office
Westall Secondary College
Arts & Language Centre
Westall Primary
BRADY
SAUNDERS
IDA ST
BESWICK
STEPHENSON
BURDEN
McLEOD
HARRIS ST
ERICKSEN
NEWCOMEN
Springvale Reserve
TREVETHIN
BESSEMER
WATT
BOULTON
PARSONS
REGAL
QUEENS
FURY CT
MONASH CR
RICKI
SHELDON
DURHAM
LUTON PL
ANDLEON
MONASH
OSBORNE
BRANDON
WORSLEY
CULSHAW
BREAR
BOOLOORA
BANDO
AWUN CT
OSBORNE
Clayton Landfill & Recycling Centre
Pav Soccer
The Grange Reserve
Ten Cts
RANDA
KOOLENA CL
MURCHISON
SPRING VALLEY
BELLBROOK
VILLA
MCH SCOTT
GLENMORGAN CL
Lexington Gardens Ret Vill
BALMORAL
RSL
Cmnty Cntr
Court Hse
Child Care
Spring Valley Golf Course
Clubhouse
EILEEN RD
WINDSOR
METYLENE
SOUTER
WILBERTON
RYANS RD
LIBBETT
GRAHAM
THAMES
CHRISTOPHER
KAY
JAMES
VICTORIA
ST JOHNS
St Josephs Cath
BUCKINGHAM
Oakleigh Pistol Club
Go-Kart Track
SIMPSONS RD
Valgunera Social Club
BELLAVISTA
SARAH CL
JEFFREY
KATHRYN
GLENN CT
NETTELBECK
YALTA
Norman Luth Reserve
HERITAGE DR
REGENT
PRINCESS
ALBERT
ROYAL
ALMA CT
JOHNS
THE CRESCENT
LUXFORD
BOONAH GR
MAINE
BRON CT
IRELAND
TADSTAN
GAYLE
HAYDEN
AMOS
DOROTHY
BERTHA
McKIRDY
LARGE
ELLEN
BOURNEMOUTH
KALLISTA
EMERALD
TRICIA
STEVENS
ROSEMARY
ARMSTRONG
ANDREW
Heatherton Park
ERICA
EGAN
Springvale West Pmy
HOOKER AV
DONALD
HILTON
MCH
OLINDA
SILVAN
UPWEY
COMO CT
GUILDFORD
MONCUR
HILL
SHAUN
CLAPHAM
BAILEY
HEATHERTON
Sara Lee
ORLOFF CL
MAHALA
WESTALL EXTENSION
GAVAN DR
HANLETH
Proposed
HOLT
CORIO
LALOR CT
CASEY CL
CHISHOLM
MONTCLAIR DR
JUDITH
NICOLE
CLARKE
FRANCES
RUTH
Springvale Plaza
SPRINGFIELD
JOSHUA
BINDI
ORION
BARTLEY PL
AMERSHAM
SPRINGVALE
Croquet Club
Burden
Christian Centre
LONDREW
MERVIEW
FLINDERS
JUTTER
JANELAINE
CAMELOT
CHATSWORTH
Spring Valley Primary
GOLDING
ALTAIR
TINTERN
ETON
EALING
WALDEN
HUME
Amersham Av Res
EUSTON
WEMBLEY
FINCHLEY
GLENWOOD
CORINNE
DANGERFIELD
PAMELA
EMILY
DORRIT
ELISABETH
Tootal Rd Tip
TOOTAL
JOLIMONT PL
BLYTHE CT
LOUISE
VELLA
EFFIE
KIRRA
ARUNDEL
CARNABY
BERNAY
FOLKESTONE CR
BRANDON
BMX Track
Spring Valley Park
SPRING
DIGBY
RUSSO

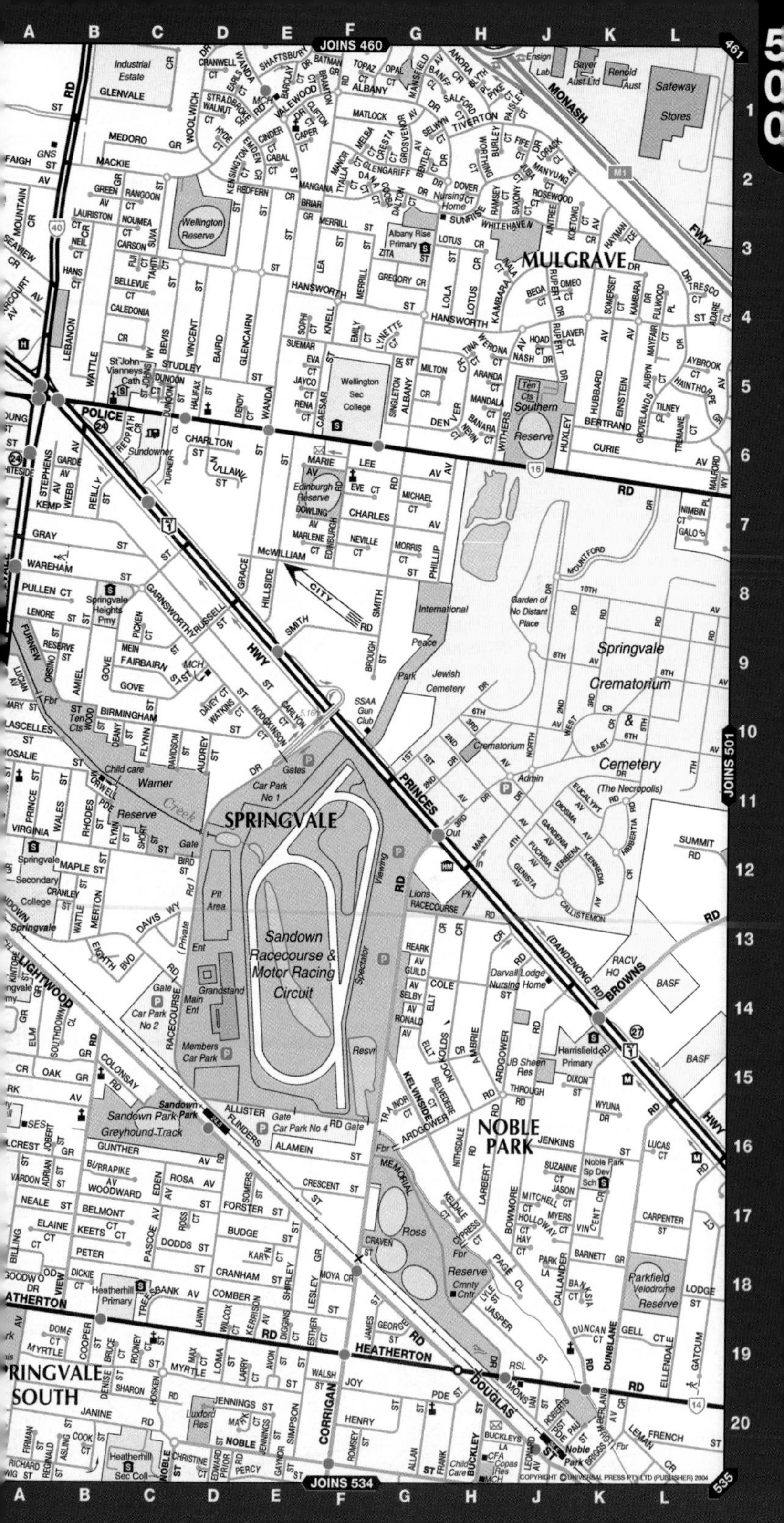

A B C D E F G H J K L
JOINS 460
461
500
1 2 3 4 5 6 7 8 9 10 11 12 13 14 15 16 17 18 19 20
Industrial Estate
GLENVALE
MEDORO
MACKIE
MOUNTAIN
SEAVIEW
LAURISTON
NOUMEA
CARSON
RANGOON
GREEN
Wellington Reserve
KENSINGTON
REDFERN
SHAFTSBURY
BATMAN
CRANWELL
WANDA
STRADBROKE
WALNUT
VALEWOOD
CLIFTON
CAPER
CINDER
CABAL
EMDEN
HYDE
WOOLWICH
TOPAZ
OPAL
ALBANY
MANSFIELD
ANORA
BANFF
BLYTH
SALFORD
PYKE
PAISLEY
TIVERTON
MATLOCK
MELBA
CRESTA
GROSVENOR
SELWYN
GLENGARIFF
DANA
BENTLEY
DOVER
Nursing Home
SUNRISE
RAMSEY
SAXONY
WHITEHAVEN
AINTREE
KOETONG
HAYMAN
ROSEWOOD
MANYUNG
LORACK
FIFE
WORTHING
BURLEY
MONASH
FWY
M1
Ensign Lab
Bayer Aust Ltd
Renold Aust
Safeway Stores
MANGANA
BRIAR
MERRILL
Albany Rise Primary
ZITA
LOTUS
GREGORY
HANSWORTH
LOLA
MULGRAVE
KAMBARA
BEGA
OMEO
RUPERT
SOMERSET
FULWOOD
TRESCO
ADARE
CALEDONIA
BELLEVUE
HANS
NEIL
LEBANON
WATTLE
BEVIS
VINCENT
BAIRD
GLENCAIRN
STUDLEY
St John Vianneys Cath
DUNOON
HALIFAX
SOPHI
KNELL
EMILY
LYNETTE
SUEMAR
EVA
JAYCO
RENA
CAESAR
Wellington Sec College
SINGLETON
MILTON
DENVER
TINA
WERONA
ARANDA
MANDALA
BANARA
NEVIN
NASH
HOAD
LAVER
HUBBARD
EINSTEIN
AUBYN
MAYFAIR
AYBROOK
HAINTHORPE
GROVELANDS
TILNEY
TREMAINE
Ten Cts
Southern Reserve
WITHERS
HUXLEY
BERTRAND
CURIE
MALFORD
POLICE
REDPATH
Sundowner
CHARLTON
DENDY
TURNER
STEPHENS
GARDE
WEBB
KEMP
REILLY
MARIE
LEE
Edinburgh Reserve
EVE
DOWLING
MICHAEL
CHARLES
MARLENE
EDINBURGH
NEVILLE
MORRIS
PHILLIP
GRAY
WAREHAM
PULLEN
LENORE
Springvale Heights Pmy
GARNSWORTH
RUSSELL
GRACE
HILLSIDE
McWILLIAM
CITY
SMITH
BROUGH
International
Peace
Park
Jewish Cemetery
Garden of No Distant Place
MOUNTFORD
10TH
8TH
6TH
Springvale Crematorium & Cemetery
(The Necropolis)
Crematorium
Admin
NORTH
WEST
EAST
EUCALYPT
DIOSMA
GARDENIA
VERBENA
FUCHSIA
KENNEDIA
HIBBERTIA
GENISTA
CALLISTEMON
NIMBIN
GALO
FURNEW
RESERVE
ORSINO
AMIEL
GOVE
MEIN
FAIRBAIRN
PICKEN
MCH
DAVEY
WATKINS
HODGKINSON
CARLYON
BIRMINGHAM
LASCELLES
ROSALIE
DENNY
FLYNN
DAVIDSON
AUDREY
Warner Reserve
Creek
MORWELL
PRINCE
WALES
RHODES
VIRGINIA
SHORT
BIRD
Springvale Secondary College
MAPLE
CRANLEY
MERTON
DAVIS
EIGHTH
BVD
SSAA Gun Club
PRINCES
HWY
Gates
Car Park No 1
SPRINGVALE
Pit Area
Sandown Racecourse & Motor Racing Circuit
Viewing
Spectator
Grandstand
Main Ent
Members Car Park
Car Park No 2
RACECOURSE
Resvr
Lions RACECOURSE Pk
MAIN
Out
In
SUMMIT
DANDENONG
BROWNS
RACV HQ
BASF
REARK
GUILD
SELBY
RONALD
COLE
ELLT
NOCKOLDS
AMBRIE
ARDGOWER
Darvall Lodge Nursing Home
Harrisfield Primary
JB Sheen Res
DIXON
THROUGH
WYUNA
KELVINSIDE
BELVEDERE
TRAINOR
NOBLE PARK
JENKINS
LUCAS
Noble Park Sp Dev Sch
SUZANNE
JASON
MITCHELL
HOLLOWAY
MYERS
VINCENT
BOWMORE
LARBERT
NITHSDALE
KELDALE
CYPRESS
CARPENTER
BARNETT
PAGE
CALLANDER
BANKSIA
Parkfield Velodrome Reserve
LODGE
GELL
ELLENDALE
GATCUM
DUNBLANE
DUNCAN
LIGHTWOOD
SOUTHDOWNE
ELM
OAK
COLONSAY
Sandown Park
Sandown Park Greyhound Track
ALLISTER
FLINDERS
Car Park No 4
ALAMEIN
GUNTHER
BURRAPIKE
WOODWARD
EDEN
ROSA
CRESCENT
MEMORIAL
Ross Reserve
Cmnty Cntr
CRAVEN
NEALE
BELMONT
ELAINE
KEETS
PASCOE
DODDS
FORSTER
BUDGE
SOMERS
PETER
DICKIE
Heatherhill Primary
TREES
BANK
COMBER
CRANHAM
SHIRLEY
LESLEY
MOYA
HEATHERTON
DOME
MYRTLE
COOPER
BRUCE
RODNEY
LAWN
WILCOX
KERRISON
DIGGINS
ESTHER
JAMES
GEORGE
JASPER
LYLE
RSL
DOUGLAS
MONS
IAN
SPRINGVALE SOUTH
DENISE
SHARON
HOSKEN
JENNINGS
LOMA
LARRY
AVON
WALSH
JOY
PDE
CORRIGAN
HENRY
ROBERTS
POST
PAU
Noble Park
BRIGGS
CUMBERLAND
LEMAN
FRENCH
JANINE
FIRMAN
ASLING
COOK
Heatherhill Sec Coll
NOBLE
CHRISTINE
EDWARD
PRIOR
PERCY
Luxford Res
SIMPSON
GAYNOR
ROMSEY
ALLAN
FRANK
Child Care
BUCKLEY
BUCKLEYS
CFA
Copas Res
MCH
LEONARD
JOINS 534
JOINS 501
535
COPYRIGHT © UNIVERSAL PRESS PTY LTD (PUBLISHER) 2004

A B C D E F G H J K L

JOINS 461

460

MULGRAVE

ROWVILLE

DANDENONG NORTH

NOBLE PARK NORTH

NOBLE PARK

Waverley Park

Proposed Mirvac Development

Dandenong Valley Parklands

Springvale Crematorium & Cemetery

Jewish Cemetery

St Marys Catholic Seminary

Mulgrave Primary

Gladeswood Reserve

Cinema Waverley Gardens

Nazareth College

Carwatha College P-12

St Elizabeths Cath

G J Duggan Res

W J Turner Reserve

Silverton Pmy

B J Powell Reserve

Aged Care Waverley Gardens

Eleanora Rd Retarding Basin

BASF

Oakwood Park Pmy

Oakwood Park

Lyndale Secondary College

Lyndale Pmy

Menzies Res

The Dandenong Valley Private Hosp

Trewint Nursing Home

S E Priv Hosp

Australian Pitch & Putt

Wetlands Golf & Games

WELLINGTON RD (MONASH HWY)

MONASH FWY

POLICE RD

JACKSONS RD

HEATHERTON RD

PRINCES HWY

BRADY RD

GLADSTONE RD

CHANDLER RD

BROWNS RD

DANDENONG BVD

JOINS 500

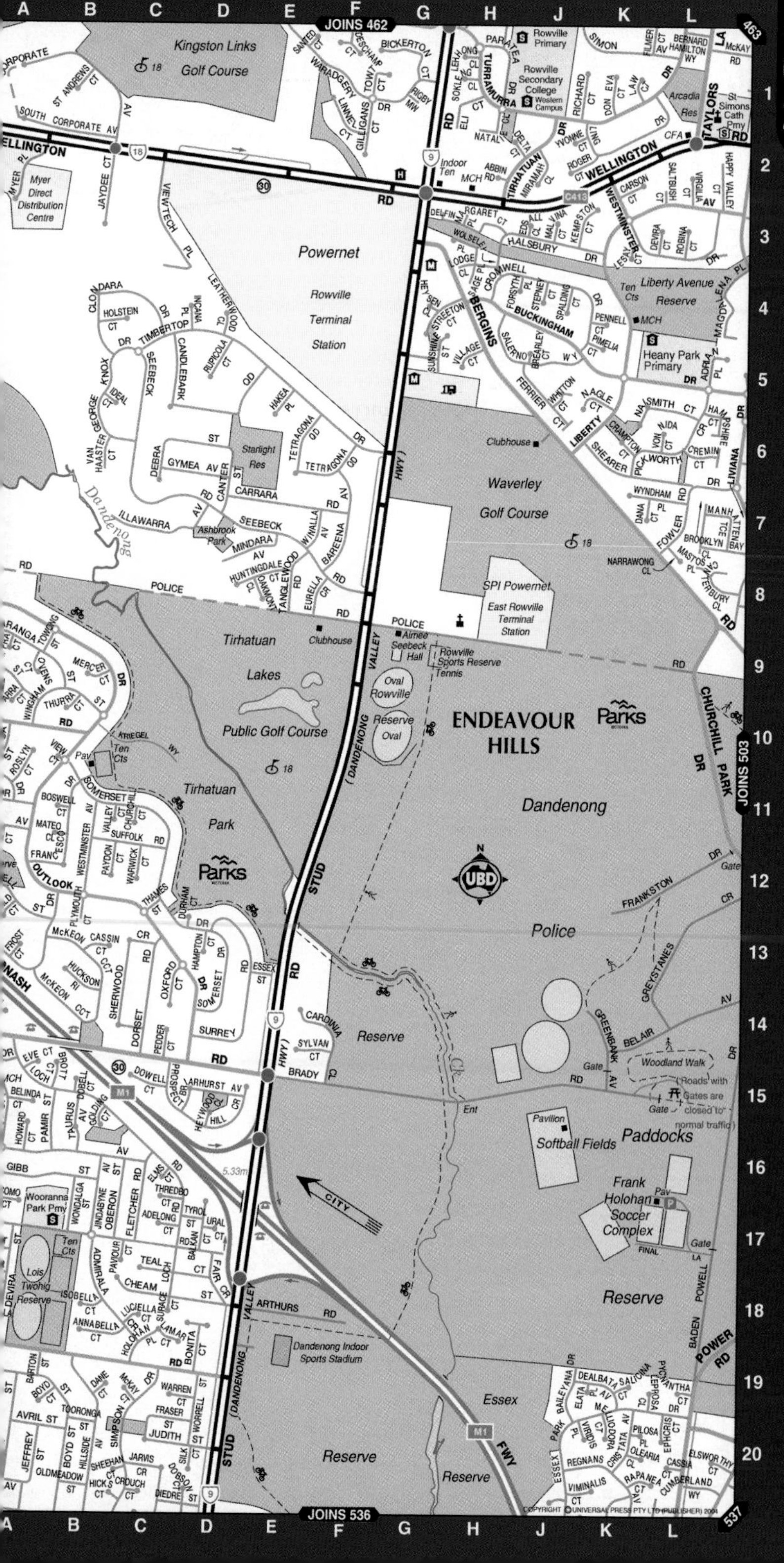

502
JOINS 462
JOINS 463
JOINS 503
JOINS 536
JOINS 537
Kingston Links Golf Course
Rowville Primary
Rowville Secondary College
Western Campus
Arcadia Res
St Simons Cath Pmy
WELLINGTON RD
Myer Direct Distribution Centre
Powernet Rowville Terminal Station
Indoor Ten
MCH
Liberty Avenue Reserve
Ten Cts
Heany Park Primary
Starlight Res
Ashbrook Park
Dandenong
Clubhouse
Waverley Golf Course
SPI Powernet East Rowville Terminal Station
POLICE RD
Tirhatuan Lakes
Public Golf Course
Aimee Seebeck Hall
Rowville Sports Reserve
Tennis
Oval Rowville Reserve Oval
ENDEAVOUR HILLS
Parks
Dandenong Police Paddocks Reserve
Tirhatuan Park
CHURCHILL PARK DR
FRANKSTON
STUD RD
(DANDENONG VALLEY HWY)
GREYSTANES AV
BELAIR
Woodland Walk
Roads with Gates are closed to normal traffic
Pavilion
Softball Fields
Frank Holohan Soccer Complex
Wooranna Park Pmy
Lois Twohig Reserve
CITY
Dandenong Indoor Sports Stadium
ARTHURS RD
Essex Reserve
Reserve
M1 FWY
BADEN POWELL
POWER RD
5.33m
COPYRIGHT © UNIVERSAL PRESS PTY LTD (PUBLISHER) 2004

A B C D E F G H J K L

462

JOINS 463

ROWVILLE

LYSTERFIELD SOUTH

ENDEAVOUR HILLS

WELLINGTON RD

C413

NAPOLEON RD

CHURCHILL PARK DR

POWER RD

KENNINGTON PARK DR

GLENEAGLES DR

MOSSGIEL PARK DR

HEANY PARK RD

GEARON AV

CLAUSCEN DR

LIVIANA DR

BERGINS RD

PIA DR

QUAIL WY

DANDELION DR

DANDELION WY

SILKWOOD WY

TAYLORS LA

McKAY RD

AMES ST

LE JOHN ST

RAYMOND RD

St Simons Cath Pmy

Reserve

Mosque

Res

Quarry

Gate

SUMMIT (Private)

Heany Park

Knox District Scout & Guide Camp

Churchill National Park

Parks Victoria

North Boundary Track

Link Track

Army Channel Walk

Bellbird Track

Ridge Track

Stonemasons Track

Bayview Track

Shelter Track

Army Channel Track

Syphon Walk

Lysterfield Hills Track

Lysterfield Hills Lookout

Grassy Spur

Woodland Walk

Albert E Temple Reserve

Police Paddocks

(Roads with Gates are closed to normal traffic)

Main Gate

Churchill Park Golf Course

Clubhouse

John Strover Res

Sydney Pargeter Rec Res

Ross Weeding

Grant Tierney

Greg Durham

Ray Evans

Pavilion

Cath Primary

Barry Simon Reserve

Mossgiel Park Pmy

Chalcot Lodge Reserve

CHURCHILL PARK DR

LANSDOWNE RD

CLIFFORD PARK RD

BELAIR AV

BADEN POWELL DR

PARKVIEW DR

PANORAMA DR

FORREST DR

THE OUTLOOK

HILLSIDE CT

PARKSIDE TCE

HILL RD

1 2 3 4 5 6 7 8 9 10 11 12 13 14 15 16 17 18 19 20

JOINS 502

536

JOINS 537

A B C D E F G H J K L

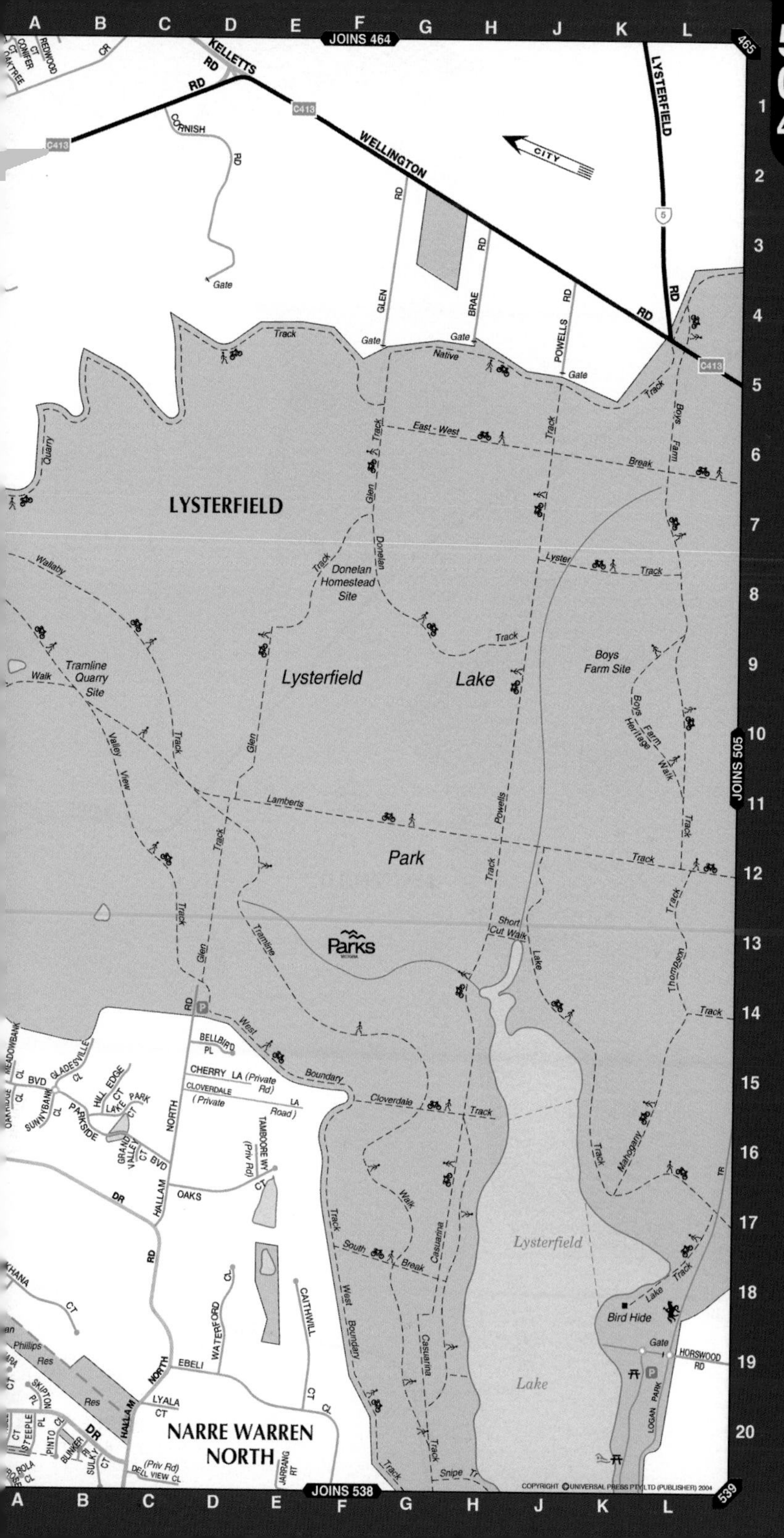

JOINS 464
465
KELLETTS RD
WELLINGTON RD
LYSTERFIELD RD
CORNISH RD
GLEN RD
BRAE RD
POWELLS RD
CITY
Gate
Track
Native
East - West
Break
Boys Farm
Quarry
LYSTERFIELD
Wallaby
Donelan Homestead Site
Lyster
Tramline Quarry Site
Walk
Valley View
Lysterfield Lake Park
Boys Farm Site
Boys Farm Heritage Walk
Lamberts
Short Cut Walk
Tramline
Parks
Thomson
West Boundary
Cloverdale
Mahogany
Casuarina
South Break
Lysterfield Lake
Bird Hide
HORSWOOD RD
LOGAN PARK
Snipe Tr
JOINS 505
JOINS 538
539
NARRE WARREN NORTH
HALLAM NORTH RD
BELLBIRD PL
CHERRY LA (Private Rd)
CLOVERDALE LA (Private Road)
TAMBOORE WY (Priv Rd)
OAKS CT
HALLAM DR
WATERFORD CL
CAITHWILL CT
EBELI
LYALA CT
JARRANG RT
DELL VIEW CL
PARKSIDE BVD
GLADESVILLE CL
SUNNYBANK CL
HILL EDGE CT
LAKE PARK CT
GRAND VALLEY CT
MEADOWBANK CL
OAKRIDGE CL
PHILLIPS RES
SKIPTON PL
STEEPLE PL
PINTO CL
BUNKER PL
SULKY CT
REDWOOD
CONIFER CT
OAKTREE
COPYRIGHT © UNIVERSAL PRESS PTY LTD (PUBLISHER) 2004

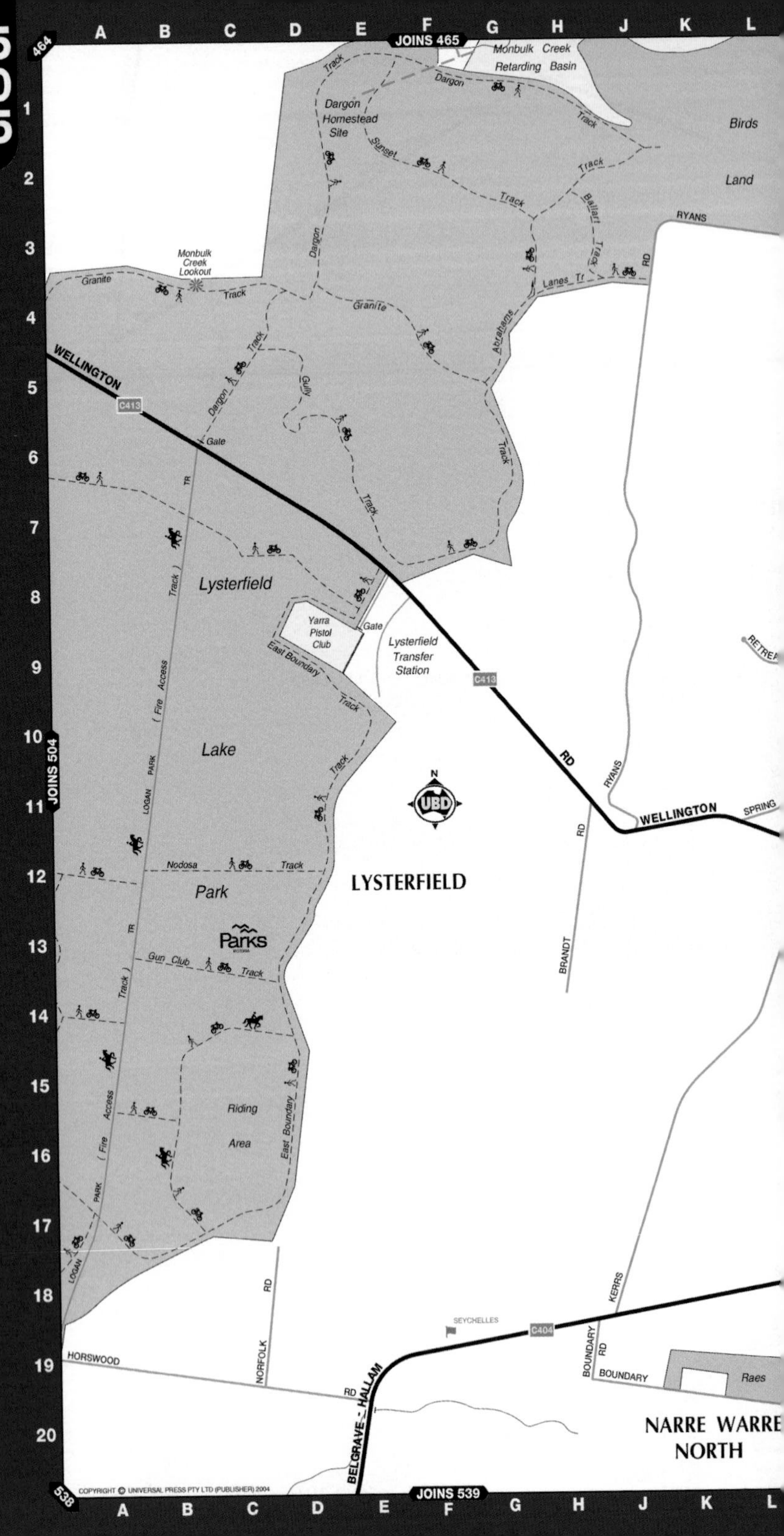

JOINS 465
Monbulk Creek
Retarding Basin
Dargon
Track
Dargon Homestead Site
Sunset
Birds
Land
RYANS
Ballart
Lanes Tr
RD
Monbulk Creek Lookout
Granite
Abrahams
Gully
WELLINGTON
C413
Gate
TR
Lysterfield
Yarra Pistol Club
East Boundary
Lysterfield Transfer Station
RETREAT
Lake
Fire Access
LOGAN
PARK
JOINS 504
UBD
WELLINGTON
SPRING
Nodosa
Park
LYSTERFIELD
Parks
Gun Club
BRANDT
Riding Area
KERRS
SEYCHELLES
C404
HORSWOOD
NORFOLK
BELGRAVE - HALLAM
BOUNDARY
Raes
NARRE WARRE
NORTH
JOINS 539
COPYRIGHT © UNIVERSAL PRESS PTY LTD (PUBLISHER) 2004

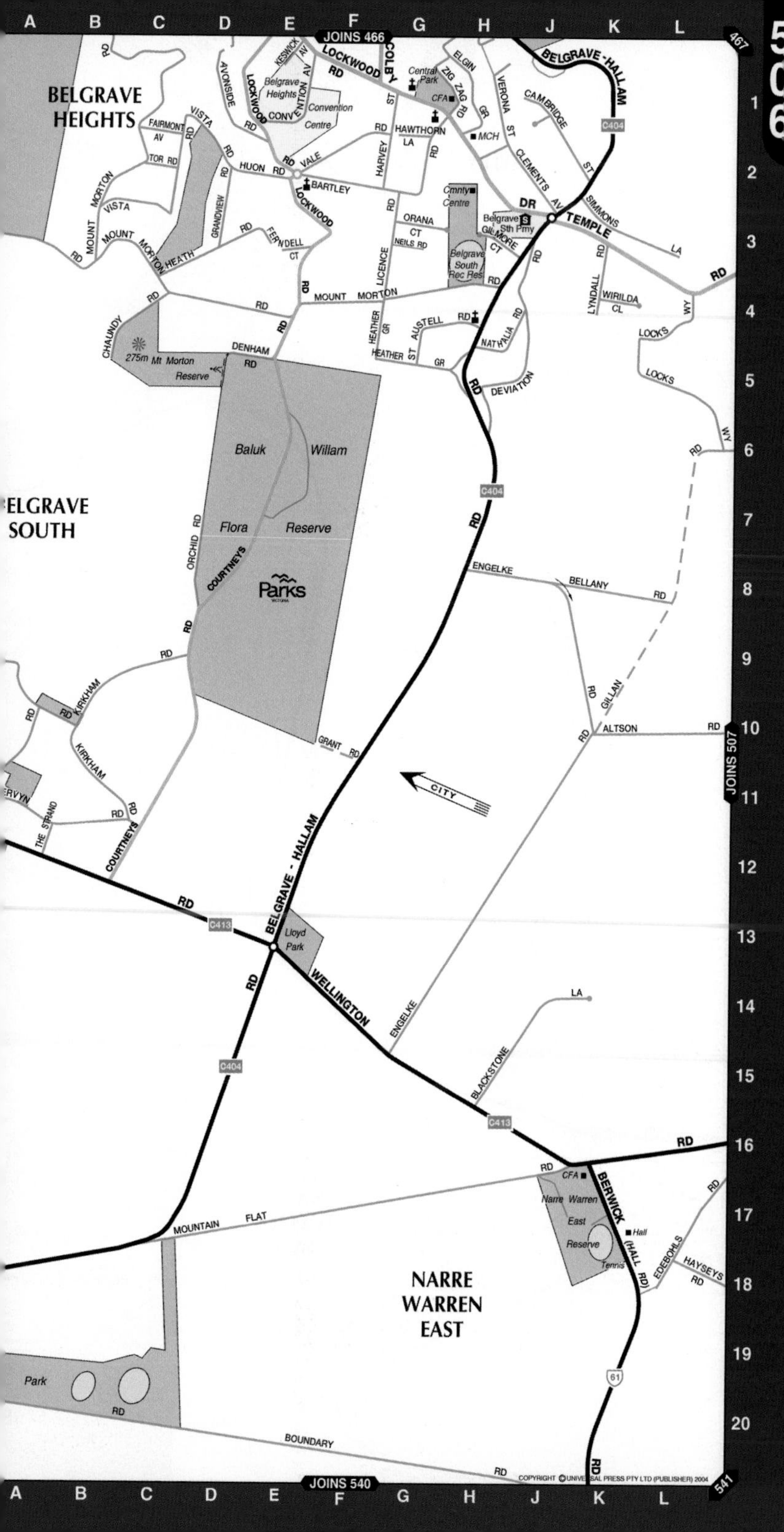

506
JOINS 466
JOINS 540
JOINS 507
467
541
BELGRAVE HEIGHTS
BELGRAVE SOUTH
NARRE WARREN EAST
BELGRAVE - HALLAM RD
C404
C413
61
LOCKWOOD RD
COLBY
KESWICK AV
AVONSIDE
CONVENTION AV
Belgrave Heights Convention Centre
Central Park
CFA
ZIG ZAG RD
ELGIN GR
VERONA ST
CAMBRIDGE ST
CLEMENTS AV
MCH
HAWTHORN LA
HARVEY RD
VISTA RD
FAIRMONT AV
TOR RD
HUON RD
VALE RD
BARTLEY
GRANDVIEW RD
MOUNT MORTON VISTA
MOUNT MORTON RD
HEATH RD
FERNDELL CT
ORANA CT
NEILS RD
LICENCE RD
Cmnty Centre
Belgrave Sth Pmy
GILMORE CT
Belgrave South Rec Res
TEMPLE DR
SIMMONS LA
LYNDALL RD
WIRILDA CL
RD
LOCKS WY
MOUNT MORTON RD
CHAUNDY RD
275m Mt Morton Reserve
DENHAM RD
HEATHER GR
HEATHER ST
AUSTELL GR
NATHALIA RD
DEVIATION RD
Baluk Willam Flora Reserve
Parks VICTORIA
ORCHID RD
COURTNEYS RD
ENGELKE RD
BELLANY RD
GILLAN RD
ALTSON RD
GRANT RD
KIRKHAM RD
THE STRAND
ERVYN
CITY
Lloyd Park
WELLINGTON RD
BLACKSTONE LA
MOUNTAIN FLAT RD
CFA
Narre Warren East Reserve
Tennis
Hall
BERWICK (HALL RD) RD
EDEBOHLS
HAYSEYS RD
Park
BOUNDARY RD
COPYRIGHT © UNIVERSAL PRESS PTY LTD (PUBLISHER) 2004
A B C D E F G H J K L
1 2 3 4 5 6 7 8 9 10 11 12 13 14 15 16 17 18 19 20

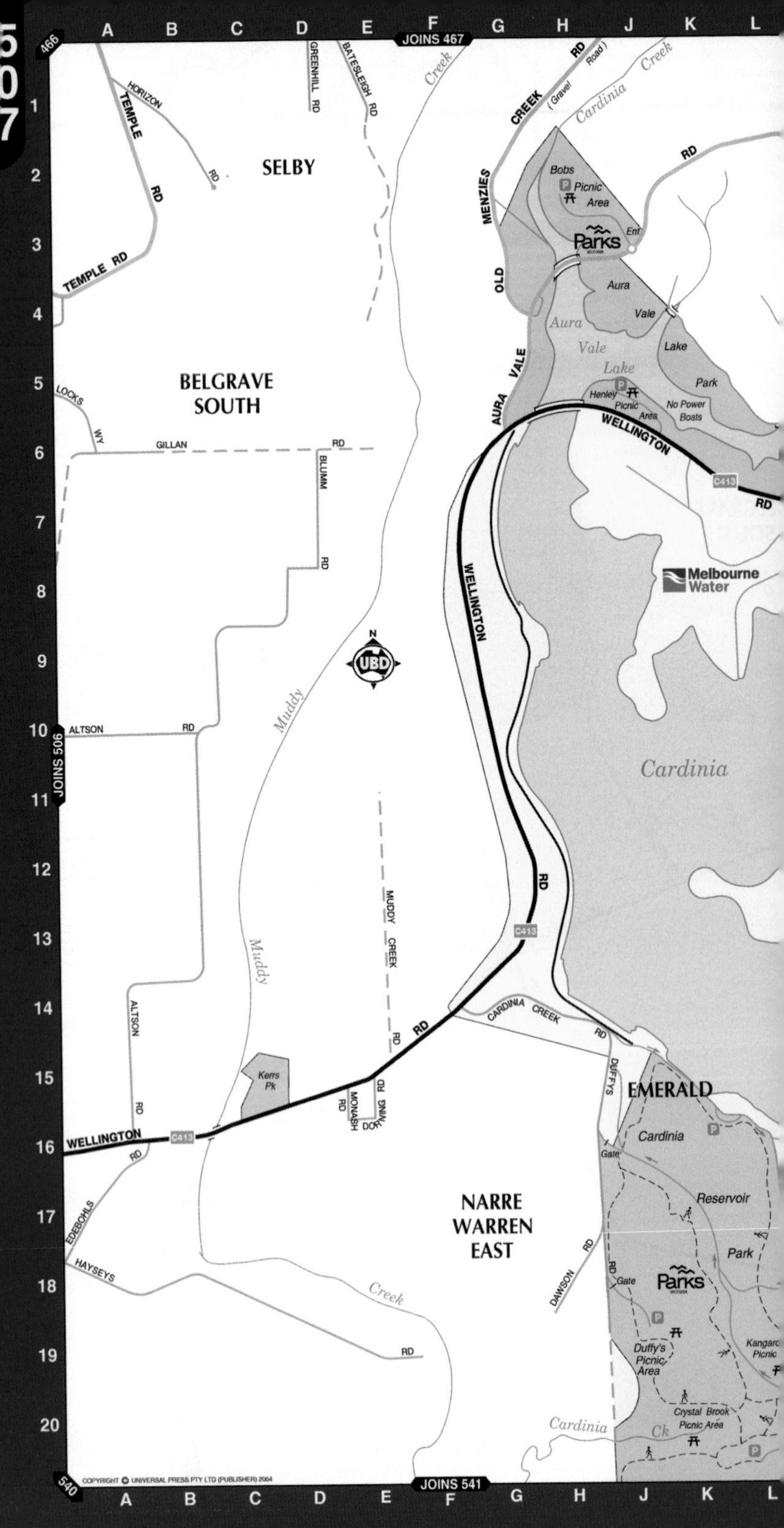

JOINS 467
JOINS 506
JOINS 541
466
540
SELBY
BELGRAVE SOUTH
NARRE WARREN EAST
EMERALD
TEMPLE RD
HORIZON RD
GREENHILL RD
BATESLEIGH RD
OLD MENZIES CREEK RD (Gravel Road)
Cardinia Creek
Bobs Picnic Area
Parks
Ent
Aura Vale Lake Park
Aura Vale Lake
AURA VALE RD
Henley Picnic Area
No Power Boats
WELLINGTON RD
C413
LOCKS WY
GILLAN RD
BLUMM RD
Melbourne Water
Cardinia
Muddy Creek
ALTSON RD
MUDDY CREEK RD
CARDINIA CREEK RD
DUFFYS RD
Kerrs Pk
MONASH RD
DORNING RD
EDEBOHLS RD
HAYSEYS RD
DAWSON RD
Gate
Cardinia Reservoir Park
Duffy's Picnic Area
Kangaroo Picnic
Crystal Brook Picnic Area
Cardinia Ck

JOINS 468
NAYLORS RD
469
Puffing Billy Rly
BELGRAVE - GEMBROOK RD
Clematis
EDENMONT
C412
ALBERT RD
VICTOR RD
CFA
Clematis Reserve
WOODLANDS ST
BELL ST
RONALD ST
RONALD ST
LORNA ST
JAMES ST
PARADISE AV
CLEAR BROOK RD
GLENBROOK RD
KITTY ST
GOWRIE RD
CLEMATIS
MENZIES CREEK
CITY
ALLUVIAL CL
MAGPIE
AURA VALE RD
C413
WELLINGTON
ura Vale Lake Park
Melbourne Water
Reservoir
JOINS 509
JOINS 542
COPYRIGHT © UNIVERSAL PRESS PTY LTD (PUBLISHER) 2004

468
JOINS 469
JOINS 508
542
LIMIT OF MAPS

A B C D E F G H J K L

1 2 3 4 5 6 7 8 9 10 11 12 13 14 15 16 17 18 19 20

CLEMATIS

EMERALD

Reservoir

Melbourne Water

PINNOCKS RD
EDENMONT RD
BELGRAVE - GEMBROOK RD
C412
OGILVY ST
RONALD
CLEMATIS PARK
Clematis Park Reserve
CHURCH ST
Railway
PINNOCKS RD
WALNUT AV
PARADISE GR
BERRYS RD
FERRES RD
ANNE ST
COMO ST
MEMORIAL
CORNISH RD
EMERALD - MONBULK RD
EMERALD CL
ALEXANDER ST
BELGRAVE - GEMBROOK RD
OLD GEMBROOK RD
SES
Pav
Tennis
Emerald Reserve
SHERRIFF RD
DURBAN
LAKE RD
EMERALD LAKE RD
CFA
EMERALD
Hall
(MAIN ST)
Cmnty Centre
Nursing Home
KINGS AV
BEACONSFIELD
PRINCESS AV
Nobelius Heritage Park
CRICHTON RD
Emerald Museum
Puffing Billy
Emerald Lake Park
Nobelius
ALBERT
EMERALD
RD
WESTLANDS RD
WOODLANDS AV
LEIGHTON AV
BAYVIEW RD
RUSSELL ST
Emerald PUFFING BILLY PL
KILVINGTON
MURPHYS WY
HEROES
Emerald Pmy
RAILWAY RD
RSL
PEPPERMINT CT
BENSON ST
Hogan Park
BOUNDARY RD W
BOUNDARY RD E
UPTON RD
LEGG RD
DR
HAMILTON RD
CLOVERLEIGH AV
STATION
AMBROSE
WATTLE AV
BIRCH AV
CURTIS RD
MAISIE RD
NOLAN RD
OLD BEACONSFIELD
OUTLOOK RD
STEEL RD
KILVINGTON
DEWHURST RD
C404
WESTLANDS
RAWHITI
WINTLE RD
DIXON RD
TORLEY RD
LAVENDER FARM RD
DR
RD
WONG HEE RD W
WONG HEE (Steep) RD
DEERY

A B C D E F G H J K L

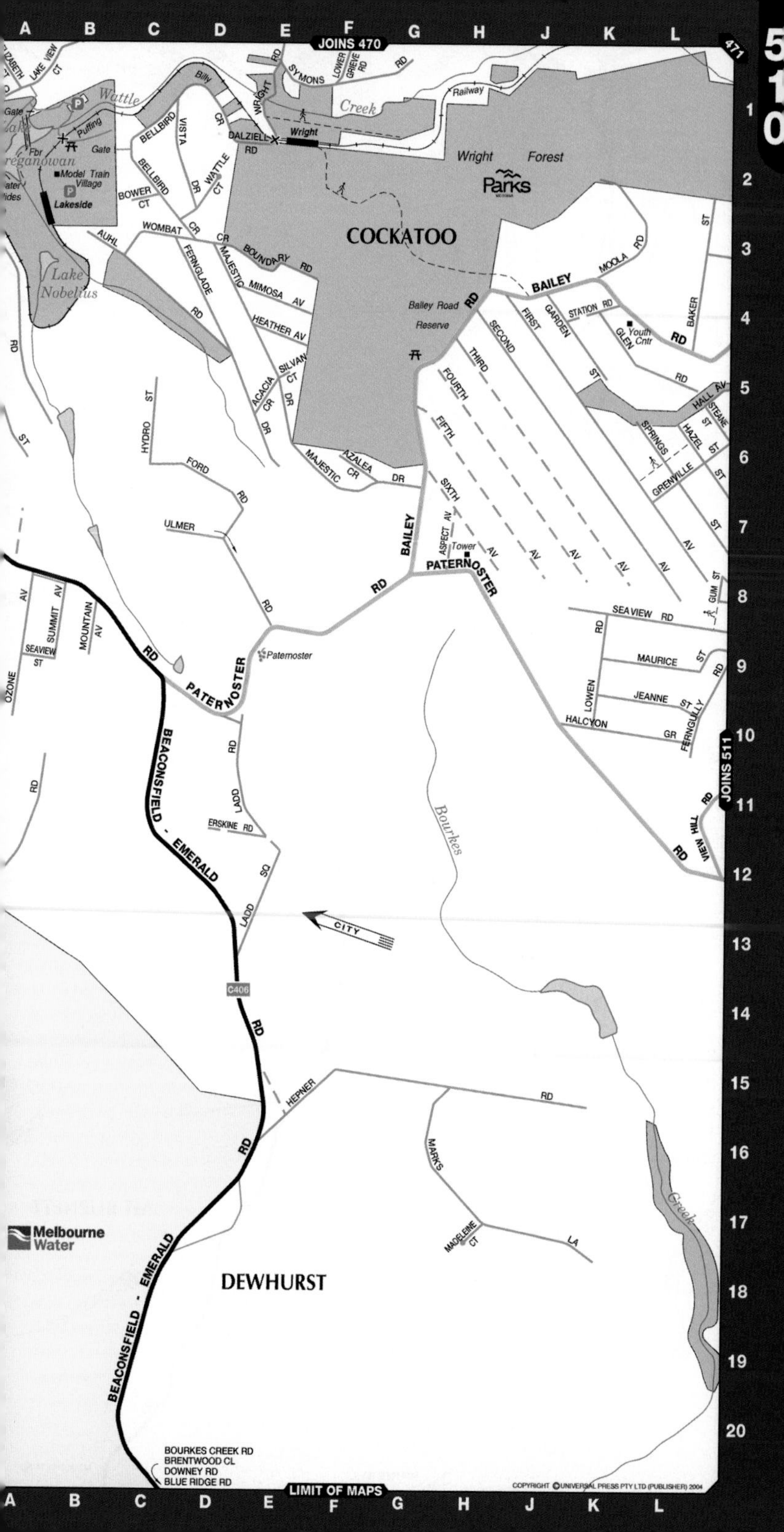
JOINS 470
471
COCKATOO
Wright Forest
Parks
Lake Nobelius
Lakeside
Model Train Village
Wright
Bailey Road Reserve
Paternoster
Tower
Youth Cntr
BAILEY RD
PATERNOSTER RD
BEACONSFIELD - EMERALD RD
C406
HEPNER RD
MARKS
MADELEINE CT
LA
LADD RD
LADD SQ
ERSKINE RD
ULMER
FORD RD
HYDRO ST
SEAVIEW RD
MAURICE ST
JEANNE ST
HALCYON GR
LOWEN
FERNGULLY RD
VIEW HILL RD
Bourkes Creek
CITY
JOINS 511
DEWHURST
Melbourne Water
BOURKES CREEK RD
BRENTWOOD CL
DOWNEY RD
BLUE RIDGE RD
LIMIT OF MAPS

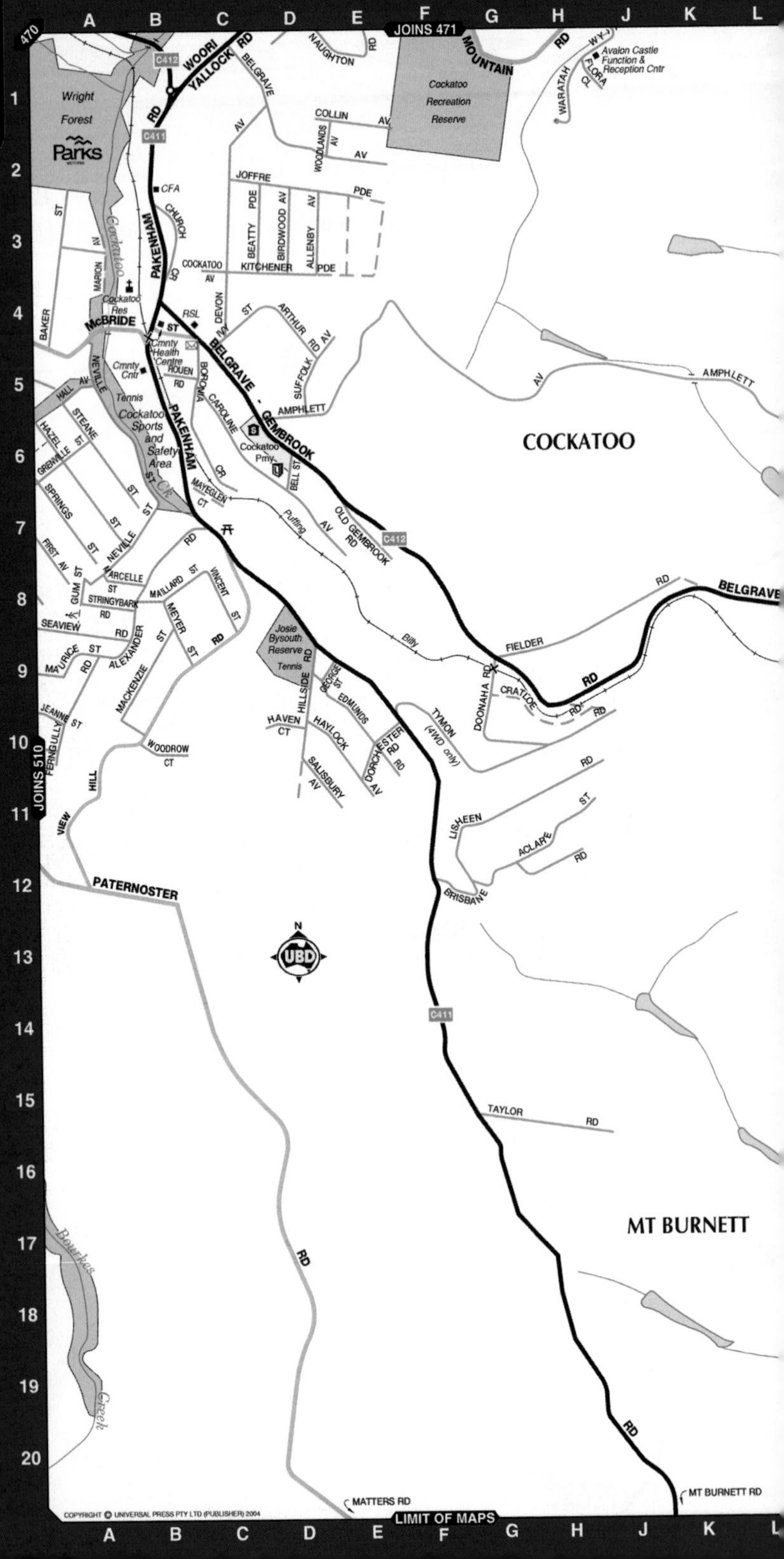

A B C D E F G H J K L

470

JOINS 471

1 2 3 4 5 6 7 8 9 10 11 12 13 14 15 16 17 18 19 20

JOINS 510

Wright Forest
Parks
Cockatoo Recreation Reserve
Avalon Castle Function & Reception Cntr
MOUNTAIN RD
WOORI YALLOCK RD
NAUGHTON RD
BELGRAVE AV
COLLIN AV
WOODLANDS AV
JOFFRE PDE
BEATTY PDE
BIRDWOOD AV
ALLENBY PDE
COCKATOO AV
KITCHENER
WARATAH
FLORA CL
CFA
CHURCH CR
PAKENHAM RD
Cockatoo Res
McBRIDE ST
MARION AV
BAKER ST
RSL
DEVON
IVY ST
ARTHUR RD
SUFFOLK AV
AMPHLETT AV
AMPHLETT
Cmnty Health Centre
Cmnty Cntr
ROUEN RD
BORONIA
CAROLINE CR
BELGRAVE - GEMBROOK
Cockatoo Pmy.
BELL ST
HALL AV
NEVILLE ST
STEANE ST
HAZEL ST
GRENVILLE
SPRINGS ST
Tennis
Cockatoo Sports and Safety Area
MAYEGLEN CT
Puffing Billy
OLD GEMBROOK RD
COCKATOO
FIRST AV
GUM ST
MARCELLE ST
STRINGYBARK RD
MAILLARD ST
VINCENT ST
MEYER ST
SEAVIEW RD
ALEXANDER
MAURICE ST
MACKENZIE
Josie Bysouth Reserve
Tennis
HILLSIDE RD
GEORGE ST
EDMUNDS
HAVEN CT
HAYLOCK
DORCHESTER RD
SALISBURY AV
TYMON (4WD only)
FIELDER RD
DOONAHA RD
CRATLOE RD
BELGRAVE RD
JEANNE ST
FERNGULLY
WOODROW CT
HILL
VIEW
LISHEEN RD
ACLARE ST
BRISBANE
PATERNOSTER RD
C411
C412
TAYLOR RD
MT BURNETT
Cockatoo Ck
Bourkes Creek
MATTERS RD
MT BURNETT RD

LIMIT OF MAPS

512
JOINS 472
MAP 529 FOLLOWS
LIMIT OF MAPS
GEMBROOK
MOUNTAIN
AV
RD
URE
RD
URE
GEMBROOK
C412
RD
Gembrook Sportsground
Ten Cts
Railway
STATION
MAIN
RD
C412
ANZAC AV
HEROES AV
Gembrook Pmy
BROMBY ST
TOWN
RD
KNIGHTS RD
RSL
REDWOOD RD
CITY
ORCHARD
PLUM CT
West Branch
Creek
Shepherd
Gembrook
Park
Fbr
Fbr
RD
RD
HAREWOOD
PARK
RD
PARK
HAREWOOD
WATKINS LA
RAMAGE LA
WILLIAMSON
RITCHIE ST
C424
RD
MAISEY
RD
BOYD RD
RED RD
GEMBROOK
MT EIRENE
RD
BESSIE CREEK RD
LIMIT OF MAPS

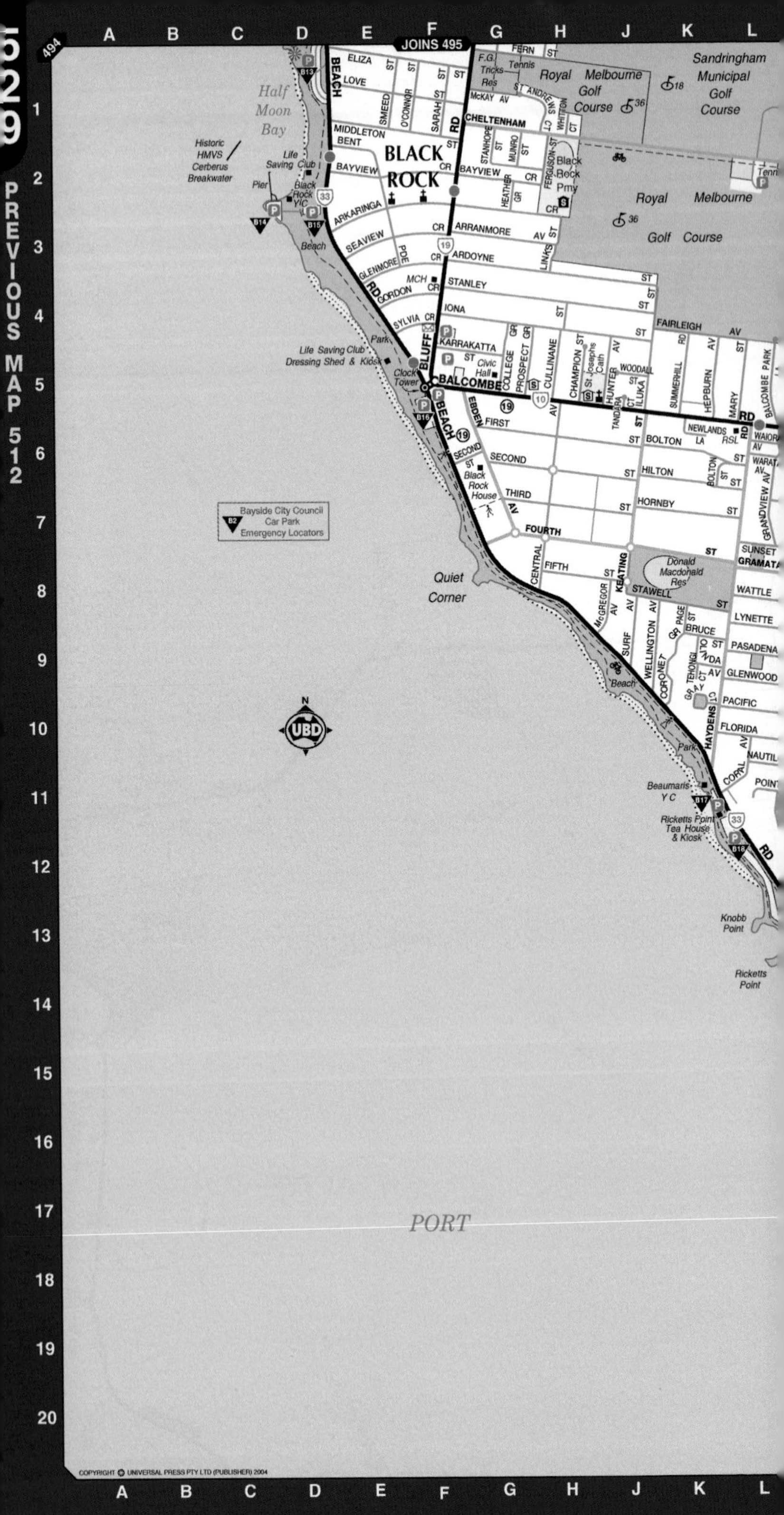
529
PREVIOUS MAP 512
494
JOINS 495
A B C D E F G H J K L
1 2 3 4 5 6 7 8 9 10 11 12 13 14 15 16 17 18 19 20
Half Moon Bay
Historic HMVS Cerberus Breakwater
Life Saving Club
Pier
Black Rock YC
Beach
BLACK ROCK
ELIZA ST
LOVE ST
SMEED ST
O'CONNOR ST
SARAH ST
MIDDLETON ST
BENT ST
BAYVIEW CR
ARKARINGA CR
SEAVIEW CR
GLENMORE CR
GORDON CR
SYLVIA CR
PDE
MCH
STANLEY ST
IONA ST
ARRANMORE AV
ARDOYNE ST
LINKS ST
FERN ST
F.G. Tricks Res
Tennis
McKAY AV
ST ANDREWS CT
WHITTON CT
CHELTENHAM RD
STANHOPE ST
MUNRO ST
HEATHER GR
FERGUSON ST
Black Rock Pmy
Royal Melbourne Golf Course
Sandringham Municipal Golf Course
Tennis
FAIRLEIGH AV
KARRAKATTA ST
Civic Hall
COLLEGE GR
PROSPECT GR
CULLINANE AV
CHAMPION ST
St Josephs Cath
HUNTER AV
WOODALL ST
ILUKA CT
TANDARA
SUMMERHILL RD
HEPBURN AV
MARY ST
BALCOMBE PARK
BALCOMBE RD
NEWLANDS LA
RSL
WAIORA AV
WARATAH AV
Life Saving Club Dressing Shed & Kiosk
Park
Clock Tower
BLUFF RD
BEACH RD
EBDEN AV
FIRST ST
SECOND ST
THIRD ST
FOURTH ST
FIFTH ST
Black Rock House
BOLTON ST
HILTON ST
HORNBY ST
BOLTON ST
GRANDVIEW AV
SUNSET ST
GRAMATAN
CENTRAL AV
KEATING ST
Donald Macdonald Res
STAWELL ST
WATTLE
LYNETTE
PASADENA
GLENWOOD
PACIFIC
FLORIDA
NAUTILUS
POINT
McGREGOR AV
SURF AV
WELLINGTON AV
CORONET GR
PAGE ST
BRUCE ST
OLINDA AV
TEHONGI CT
GRAY CT
HAYDENS RD
CORAL AV
Quiet Corner
Beach
Park
Beaumaris YC
Ricketts Point Tea House & Kiosk
Knobb Point
Ricketts Point
Bayside City Council Car Park Emergency Locators
B2 B13 B14 B15 B16 B17 B18
19 33 10
PORT
COPYRIGHT © UNIVERSAL PRESS PTY LTD (PUBLISHER) 2004

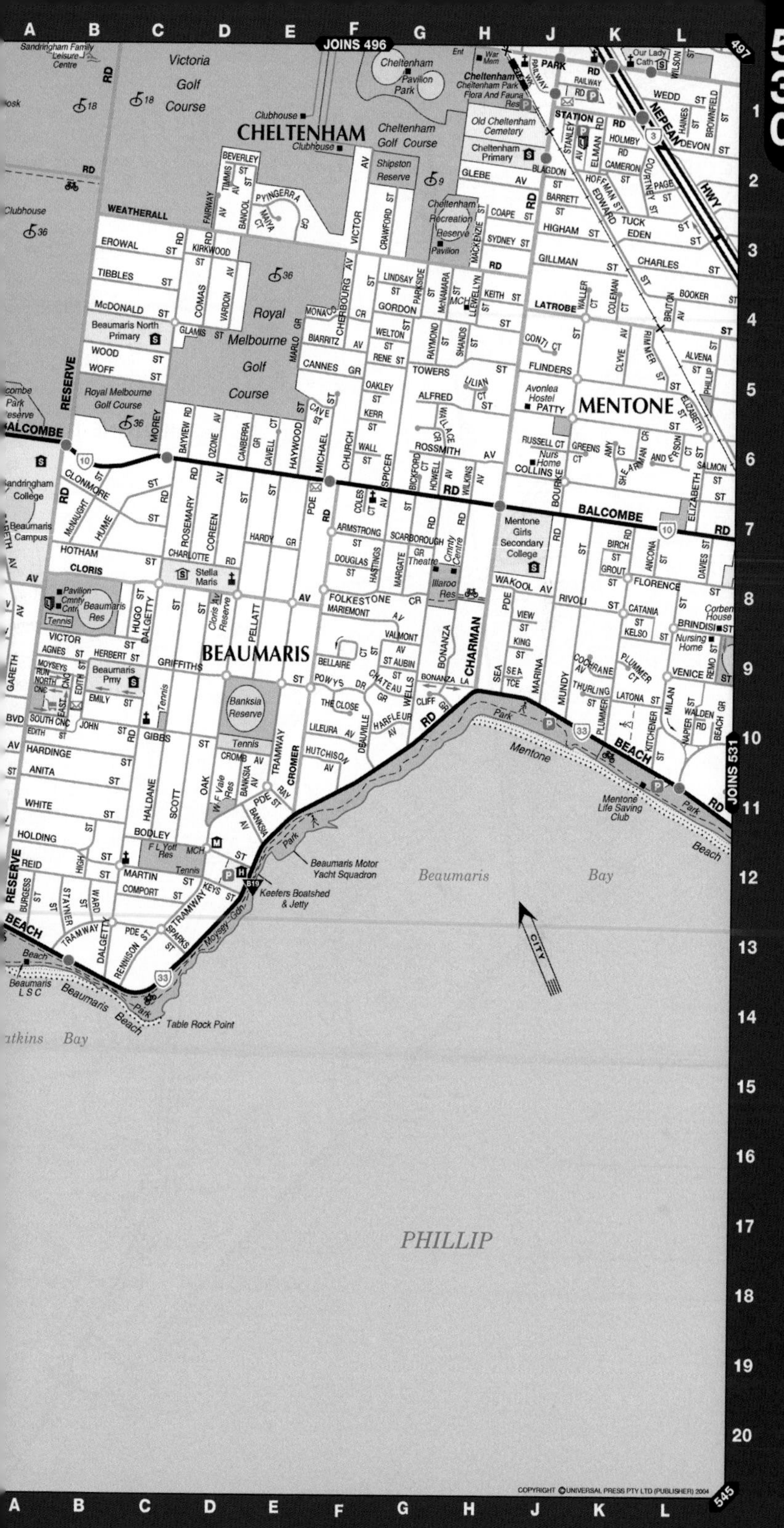
JOINS 496
CHELTENHAM
BEAUMARIS
MENTONE
Victoria Golf Course
Royal Melbourne Golf Course
Beaumaris Bay
PHILLIP
Mentone
Table Rock Point
Beaumaris Beach
JOINS 531
CITY
530
COPYRIGHT © UNIVERSAL PRESS PTY LTD (PUBLISHER) 2004

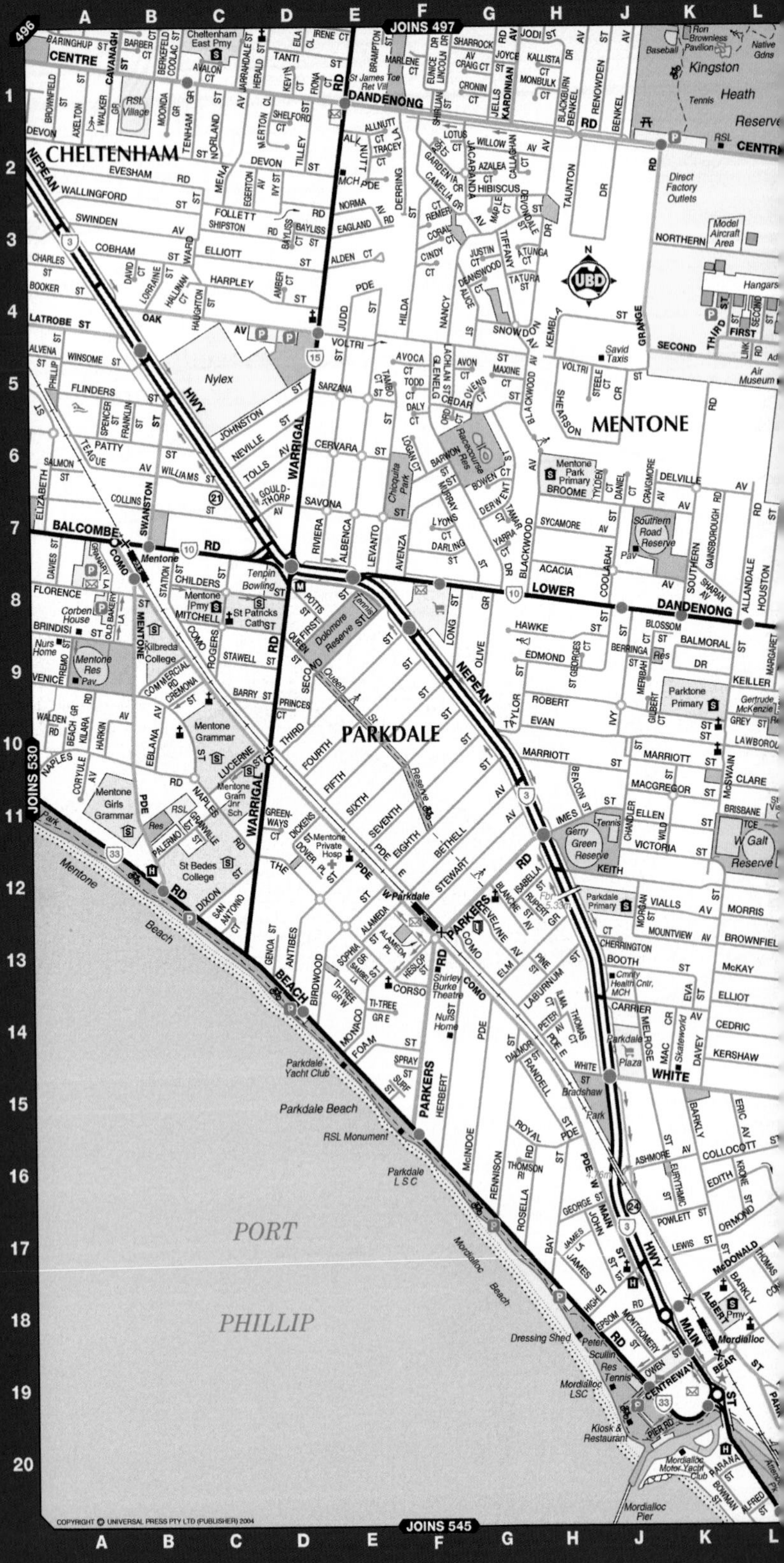

496

A B C D E F G H J K L

JOINS 497

1 2 3 4 5 6 7 8 9 10 11 12 13 14 15 16 17 18 19 20

JOINS 530

CHELTENHAM

MENTONE

PARKDALE

PORT PHILLIP

Kingston Heath Reserve

Direct Factory Outlets

Nylex

Mentone Grammar

Mentone Girls Grammar

St Bedes College

Kilbreda College

Dolomore Reserve

Mentone Res

Southern Road Reserve

Gerry Green Reserve

W Galt Reserve

Parkdale Plaza

Bradshaw Park

Peter Scullin Res

Mentone Beach

Parkdale Beach

Parkdale Yacht Club

RSL Monument

Parkdale LSC

Mordialloc Beach

Mordialloc LSC

Mordialloc Motor Yacht Club

Mordialloc Pier

Kiosk & Restaurant

Dressing Shed

JOINS 545

A B C D E F G H J K L

A B C D E F G H J K L

JOINS 498

499

HEATHERTON

DINGLEY VILLAGE

MOORABBIN AIRPORT

Moorabbin Airport

(Harry Hawker Airport)

Chifley Industry Park

City of Kingston Municipal Golf Course

Capital Golf Course 18

Heatherton Recreation Reserve

Melb Golf Academy & Driving Range

Gate

CITY

DANDENONG RD

OLD DANDENONG RD

BOUNDARY RD

CENTRE DANDENONG RD

TOOTAL RD

FEDERATION ST

CHIFLEY DR

WY

Road

Perimeter Road

Emergency Ent

CAA Operations & Fire Stn

Royal Victorian Aero Club

Control Tower

Maintenance Centre

Clubhouse

Moorabbin Golf Range

CHESTNUT CT

PLANE TREE AV

GARDEN

ALMOND TCE

LARCH LA

CONIFER

SILVER BIRCH AV

FIR ST

HOLLY DR

LAKE DR

OAK ST

WILLOW

ELM TREE

GARDEN BVD

REDWOOD

Proposed

Tennis

LUMEAH CT

CARDINAL CT

MARTENS PL

EMMA PL

GAIL CT

FERNHILL

RIDDER CT

JASMINE CT

BARDOEL CT

ATTENBOROUGH

AUSTRALIS CT

LOBELIA CT

JOHANNA CT

JETSKE

KINGSTON

LAUREN CL

ORLOO CT

FREDMAN CT

FERNDALE CL

ARLINGTON

HARRY CT

GLEN AVIS GR

ALBERT PL

GLENELG

TORQUAY PL

VILLAGE CL

SHERIDAN CT

RIVOLI

SIDELEY CT

GUMLEY CT

RAINSFORD

WESTBURY

DONHAVEN

CREMORNE ST

EARLWOOD

CORMORANT

HERON CT

METUNG

MANUELA

CHIPP

DEBBIE CT

KUBIS CT

CAMPBELL

TIMMS CR

LIBERTY

ROOSEVELT

GLENWAY

EAGLE CT

BISCAY CT

PLAZA

Chadwick Reserve

TWOFOLD CL

SHOAL CT

BRIDGEWATER

CASCO PL

HOWARD RD

BALCOMBE

BAYVILLE

HOBSONS

BOTANY CT

VENUS

SWAN

DR

Braeside Parks Park

Howard Road Trail

Freeway Proposed

JOINS 533

EWEN ST

TEMORA ST

SUSAN ST

KEEFER ST

DE HAVILLAND

SIBTHORPE ST

JAPADDY

Drain

RD

USA CT

RIVETTE

STEVEN CT

ANITA CT

DUGGAN ST

RICHARD

Res

SCARLET

Parkdale Secondary College

HINKLER

BOND ST

RD

ST W

FONCECA ST

Recycling Centre

NICHOLLS CT

BOND ST

TARNARD

BELL GR

DR

WOODLANDS DR

CITRUS ST

HALL ST

DOWNARD

MILLS

CAPITAL CT

KEVLAR CL

MAGNOLIA

FELICIA

WARATAH

VERBENA

BELLE CR

KINGSTON AV

MORDIALLOC

BRAESIDE

Woodlands Golf Course 18

Clubhouse

Indoor Cricket

PHOENIX CT

WALKER ST

CHEFS LA

URBAN ST

MASON DR

BRAESIDE DR

PARK WY

ELLIOT DR

VENTURE

WOODLANDS

CHUTE

BRADSHAW

MALCOLM RD

McDONALD

MANIKATO

EDWARD ST

HALLMARK

GALA

SUPREME

BLACK

MYRTLE ST

NIGHT

RECKLESS

PIPING LA

AFFINITY

HYLAND

PURTEL CL

WILLIAMSON

JARRAH DR

MACBETH

LAKEWOOD

ENDEAVOUR WY

BVD

CENTURY

ARWON ST

POOLEY BRIDGE RD

TREEBY

REYS

JARMAN

WINTERSET

ODWYER ST

JENKINS

BAMBER

HANLON CL

HOYSTED

MANNING

INDUSTRIAL

BAXTER DR

CRAWFORD ST

WOODS AV

Doug Denyer Reserve

Kevin Hayes Res

Ben Kavanagh Reserve

PARSONS ST

STEEDMAN ST

CROWN

PERCY

AVLONA

KAREELA

LAMANA

HUTCHINS CL

JACK BESANKO CL

HOLT

MOLONEY

GOVERNOR RD

GIPPS AV

BERTRAM ST

Jack Grut Reserve

Skateboard Track

G Woods Res

BEACH AV

SPRAY

WELLS RD

CANTERBURY RD

HAYMER CT

Drain

BATE DR

BRADY CL

DARLING

WATERWAYS

Mordialloc Ck

Mordialloc College

PINE CR

PINE CT

Browns Reserve

Pav

Mordialloc Creek Drain

COPYRIGHT © UNIVERSAL PRESS PTY LTD (PUBLISHER) 2004

JOINS 546

547

A B C D E F G H J K L

1 2 3 4 5 6 7 8 9 10 11 12 13 14 15 16 17 18 19 20

498
JOINS 499
JOINS 532
JOINS 547
546

A B C D E F G H J K L

1 2 3 4 5 6 7 8 9 10 11 12 13 14 15 16 17 18 19 20

SPRINGVALE SOUTH

DINGLEY VILLAGE

BRAESIDE

WATERWAYS

JOUMONT PL
BLYTHE CT
WHEATLAND RD
Swallow Res
McCLURE CT
EVELYN CT
JUAN CT
CARUANA DR
RYAN MW
JULIUS AV
AISHA RD
LAKELAND CT
NICKSON CL
Res
WYNDARRA CL
CHALDRON PL
NEWBRIDGE CL
HIGGINS
TOOTAL RD
LUMEAH CT
CARDINAL GR
MARTENS PL
BOGART CL
SADLER CT
WAKEMAN TCE
EMMA CT
REX CT
FERNHILL PL
DONNA CT
GAIL CT
RUBY PL
CHRISTINA
Kingswood Golf Club
Clubhouse
HAMLET CL
VERDANT PL
KINGSMEAD CT
GREENWOODS CL
LACKENHEATH CT
DOWNLAND PL
SPRING RD
Proposed Fwy
VELLA CT
EFFIE CT
WESTALL ROAD EXTENSION
CLARKE RD
Clarke Rd Tip
Spring Valley Park
BMX Track
DORRIT ST
ELISABETH ST
DIGBY CT
RUSSO ANN DR
DEVON
MONTANA
BERRY AV
Springvale South Pmy
KERRIE
DIANNE CT
LORIS
ATHOL
MACKAY
CFA
CONISTON CT
MCH Springvale Sth Res
Tennis
Alex Nature
Temple
Indoor Cricket
NRCL
HAROLD
WIRILDA CT
TERRY CT
LINDY CT
WYTON CR
REGINA CT
ELKA RD
CHARLOTTE
KEAL
WADDINGTON CT
KINARRA CT
GLASSFORD
RICKSON CT
LEONS RD
PATERSON
ROWAN RD
LANDO PL
VISTULA WY
LANSOR ST
WESTVIEW CT
CECILY
GWENT DR
KOVAL CT
ANDLEON CT
CAMBRIDGE
SOLSON CT
NORTHGATE CR
TEDDY CT
COOMOORA
Coomoora Road Reserve
SLOANE
SERPENTINE
PONT CT
Proposed
RIVERGUM
CENTRE DANDENONG RD
HOWARD RD
MANUELA CT
RUDOLF CT
CHIPP CT
SNEAD CT
PICKWORTH DR
KUBIS
DEBBIE CT
VON NIDA CT
CAMPBELL
WILLY CT
KIMBER CT
GOLFWOOD
LEE-ANDY CT
McGREGOR CT
GREENVIEW CL
NAMBROK CL
WOLBERS
SEATON DR
PICOLA
MUNGARI ST
MINJAH CT
TARNOOK CT
SHEPHERD CT
WOODLAND
TOORAK RD
KATHRIN AV
WENDON CT
HILLINGDON
KINGSWOOD DR
IMLACH CT
ROWAN RD
Pav
Netball Complex
DORRINGTON CT
Rowan Road Reserve
Tennis
TERWALLA
TIMMS
LIBERTY CT
ROOSEVELT CT
CR
CHIFLEY CT
ELY GR
SHARROCK
SHELFORD GR
JULIE CT
JANE CT
LORD AV
CANNERY PL
MARJORIE AV
Dingley Primary
MARCUS
Harold Box Cmnty Hall
MCH
ST MARKS CL
PETHYBRIDGE CL
Dingley Reserve
BUNKER CT
CLUB CT
SOUTHERN DR
GLENWAY
DRE
EAGLE CT
Kingswood Pmy
BISCAY CT
TAMBO CT
PLAZA
FLORIDA AV
BRIAN CT
DOUGAND CT
JACKS
FOREST PARK
MUSSERT AV
ANITA AV
CONNELL CL
PAULINE AV
HUNTLEY CL
ST CUTHBERTS
CHADREE CT
BOGEY CT
HARLEY CT
DINGLEY CT
LINKS CT
ST
RD
BOTANY CT
VENUS CT
BAYVILLE
HOLLAND AV
RHODA
ST
BALCOMBE
HOBSONS PL
DR O'BRIEN CT
SWAN CT
GLENCT
SANDLEFORD
ABBOTTSWOOD
PRIORSWOOD
HAZELWOOD
ROBINA
WATTLEBIRD
HARRIER
St Marks Cath Pmy
DIMAR
MEADOW CT
McARDLE
SUNVIEW CT
ELLIOTT
LOCKSLEY
CASSAVA
DELAWARE
ASHBOURNE
COLIN CT
NURSERY
ORA CT
JANNALI DR
PANKINA
WILLIAMS CL
EMERY
PENN PL
GRANDIFLORA CT
CHIVERS CT
Five Ways
Greenwood Mews Ret Village
KINGSLAND CL
GOLF
FAIRWAY
FAUNA AV
Spring Park Public Golf Course
SOUTH PARK
FAIRBOURNE WY
FIVEWAYS
GLEN ALVIE AV
KEYSBOROUGH
CARSON
ANDERSON
RD
BVD
LAKE VIEW BVD
SPRINGVALE RD
LOWER DANDENONG RD
Ent
24 hr Parking
Shelter
Fire Access Only
Visitor Centre
Shelter
Heathland Restricted Access
Clubhouse
CHELTENHAM
Southern Golf Club
Halleybury College
Howard Road Trail
Proposed Freeway
Authorised Access Only
Braeside Park
Red Gum Trail
Info Shelter
Racecourse Dam
Rangers Office
Parks
Mentone Grammar Sportsground
PRINCETON
LATROBE CR
DR
TRINITY LA
STANFORD AV
HARVARD GR
WESLEY
CT
Lighthouse Christian College
Bird Hide
Authorised Access Track
Spoonbill Dam
GRAGWEN CT
CITY
Wetlands Trail
Info Shelter
Daffy Duck Dam
Shelter
Wetlands
Keysborough Golf Course
Clubhouse
Golf Driving Range
GOVERNOR RD
HUTTON
Ent
BLUEGRASS CL
SHOALWATER DR

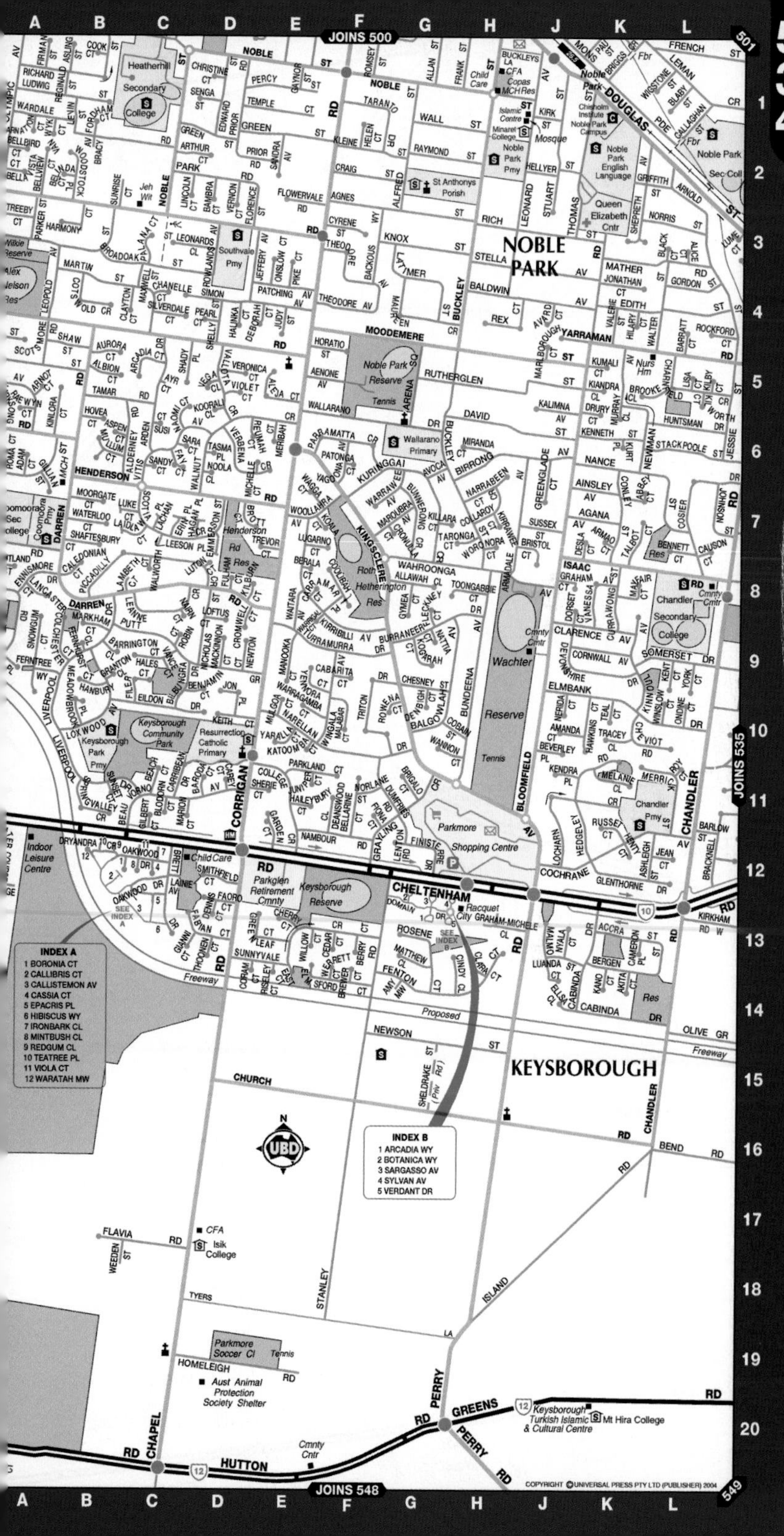

534
JOINS 500
501
JOINS 535
JOINS 548
549
NOBLE PARK
KEYSBOROUGH
Heatherhill Secondary College
Southvale Pmy
St Anthonys Parish
Noble Park Pmy
Noble Park English Language
Chisholm Institute Noble Park Campus
Queen Elizabeth Cntr
Noble Park Reserve
Wallarano Primary
Roth Hetherington Res
Henderson Rd Res
Wachter Reserve
Chandler Secondary College
Keysborough Community Park
Resurrection Catholic Primary
Keysborough Park Pmy
Parkmore Shopping Centre
Parkglen Retirement Cmnty
Keysborough Reserve
Racquet City
Chandler Pmy
Indoor Leisure Centre
Isik College
Parkmore Soccer Cl
Aust Animal Protection Society Shelter
Keysborough Turkish Islamic & Cultural Centre
Mt Hira College
NOBLE ST
DOUGLAS PDE
CORRIGAN RD
BUCKLEY ST
CHELTENHAM RD
CHANDLER RD
CHAPEL RD
HUTTON RD
GREENS RD
PERRY RD
BEND RD
CHURCH RD
NEWSON ST
STANLEY RD
ISLAND RD
KINGSCLERE AV
BLOOMFIELD RD
MOODEMERE ST
RUTHERGLEN ST
DAVID ST
Freeway
Proposed Freeway
INDEX A
1 BORONIA CT
2 CALLIBRIS CT
3 CALLISTEMON AV
4 CASSIA CT
5 EPACRIS PL
6 HIBISCUS WY
7 IRONBARK CL
8 MINTBUSH CL
9 REDGUM CL
10 TEATREE PL
11 VIOLA CT
12 WARATAH MW
INDEX B
1 ARCADIA WY
2 BOTANICA WY
3 SARGASSO AV
4 SYLVAN AV
5 VERDANT DR

JOINS 501

A B C D E F G H J K L

NOBLE PARK

KEYSBOROUGH

DANDENONG SOUTH

JOINS 534

HEATHERTON RD — PRINCES HWY — DOUGLAS ST — RAILWAY PDE — CHELTENHAM RD — GREENS RD — KIRKHAM RD — GLADSTONE RD — DAVID ST — JAMES ST — JONES RD — BENNET ST — FOSTER ST — WEBSTER ST — HAMMOND RD — CHANDLER RD — BRIDGE RD — TOWER CT — DANDENONG — BRIGHTON RD — BRADLAWN — SOUTHBOURNE — CANBERRA AV — ATTENBOROUGH PDE — GOODMAN — YARRAMAN RD — FRENCH ST — MENZIES AV

Yarraman Creek — Mile Creek — Dandenong Creek

Fotheringham Res — Greaves Reserve — Showground — Hemmings Park — Noble Park Sec College — Yarraman Primary — Maralinga Pmy — St Gerards Catholic — Emerson Sch — High School — Dandenong W Pmy — Dandenong Sth Pmy — George Andrews Reserve — Council Depot — DMG Industries — Melbourne Water — Melb Water — Visy Board — Terminal Station — Trewint Nursing Home — Jeh Wit — Cmnty Cntr — MCH

Proposed Freeway — CITY

JOINS 549

A B C D E F G H J K L

JOINS 502

DANDENONG NORTH

DANDENONG

DOVETON

Dandenong Club
Essex Reserve
Essex Res
J C Mills Reserve
Heated
Pav
Hockey
Chisholm Institute
Mosque
Hospital
Pmy Sch
Sec Coll
Retirement Village
Reserve
Dandenong Creek
Little Athletics Pavilion
Baseball
Robert Booth Reserve
Pavilion
Dandenong Rec Club
Market
Cncl Off
Cinemas
RSL
Dandenong Plaza
Dandenong Pmy Sch
St Johns Regional College
Betula Reserve
St Marys School for Children with Impaired Hearing (Dandenong Campus)
Cath Sch
Dandenong Workers Golf Course
(K Wishart Reserve)
Dandenong Park
Shepley Oval
Thomas P Carroll Reserve
Doveton Secondary College
Skate Centre
Myuna Farm
Ray Giles Res
Doveton North Pmy
MCH
Rowans Reserve
Maranatha Sch
Holy Family Cath
Senior Cits Hall
Kanooka Plgrd
Eumemmering Sec Coll
Endeavour Hills Campus
Power Reserve
Doveton Heights Pmy
A J Robinson Oval
Eumemmering Park
L S Reid Oval
Eumemmering Ck
Res
Essex Park Homestead
VicRoads
Tenpin Bowl
Indoor Cricket
Iveco
Heinz Plant
Shawlands
Vic Roads Driver Licence Testing Complex
Lunar Drive-In
Pilkington ACI
Dandenong Cemetery
Proposed Freeway

HEATHERTON RD, PRINCES HWY, DANDENONG VALLEY HWY, STUD RD, MONASH FWY, SOUTH GIPPSLAND HWY, FRANKSTON DANDENONG RD, KIDDS RD, POWER RD, BOX ST, FOSTER ST, McCRAE ST, CLOW ST, LONSDALE ST, CLEELAND ST, WALKER ST, LANGHORNE ST, PULTNEY ST, WILSON ST, POWER ST, WEDGE ST, BALMORAL AV, PLUNKETT RD, QUINN ST, HILTON ST, PATRONA ST, GREEN ST, WINDALE ST, CLAREDALE ST, LINLEY ST, DENNIS ST, COOPER CT, PODMORE ST, FREDERICK ST, JOHN ST, RUSSELL CT, MAXWELL ST, AMBERLEY CR, PALOMAR CT, JOHNSTON CT, DUNLOPILLO DR, WILLIAMS RD, FOWLER RD, NATHAN RD, PROGRESS ST, LACE ST, HALLAM VALLEY RD, ROUND TOWER RD, HEDDERWICK RD, DAVID ST, BRUCE ST, ANN ST, OLIVE ST, HERBERT ST, EDITH ST, KING ST, MARKET ST, ROBERT ST, STUART ST, SLEETH AV, GRACE AV, BURROWS AV, CARROLL AV, GRANDVIEW AV, SUNNYSIDE AV, CLEMENT ST, ARATULA ST, GRANT ST, ROSS ST, LEBANON ST, IRENE CT, SARONA ST, BESS CT, VAL CT, JESSON CR, GARSIDE ST, ETON CT, OAKS CT, COOMA CT, ESK CT, PARKVIEW CL, HILDEN CT, FALKINER CR, GOODING CT, TURNER ST, LEONARD ST, LOUIS AV, LEED ST, CORNELIUS ST, PETER CT, MAY CT, AXEL ST, INGRID ST, OSWALD ST, HEALES ST, GODFREY CR, HOPKINS ST, HOWARD AV, SUZANNE ST, VIZARD ST, BOYD ST, JEFFREY ST, HILLSIDE AV, OLD-MEADOW ST, SIMPSON DR, HICKS CT, CROUCH CT, WOODCOCK CT, JARVIS CR, McALPINE CT, MILLER CT, DIEDRE ST, DOBSON CT, KHALIL, NORISHA AV, RONALD ST, MACPHERSON ST, BESLEY ST, GARDE CT, ARNOLD CT, NOVA DR, TANIA CT, MASTERS ST, ECKFORD ST, CAROLINE ST, ORGILL ST, GLADE ST, FOX ST, NEW ST, CRUMP LA, BETULA AV, BLOSSOM ST, PEPPERMINT ST, ROSE ST, STENOCARPUS DR, CLARET ST, HAKEA ST, FICIFOLIA DR, MELIA ST, KANOOKA GR, WATTLE ST, GREVILLEA ST, CERCIS CT, MAPLE CT, VIRGILIA ST, OLEANDER ST, CHESTNUT DR, PHOTINIA ST, CEDAR ST, CATALPA ST, MATIPO ST, THE PINES GR, CAMELIA CT, MAGNOLIA ST, PEACE CT, BAMBOO CT, WEIGELA CT, CASSIA ST, HEATH CT, JACARANDA CT, WIRILDA CT, PITTOSPORUM ST, BOOBYALLA ST, BOTTLE BRUSH DR, ORANGE CT, AUTUMN PL, PAPERBARK ST, THE BIRCHES, PRUNUS GR, FUGOSIA ST, OAK ST, TARATA DR, NIGRA ST, ASH ST, EUGENIA ST, HAWTHORN RD, TRISTANIA ST, TI TREE GR, HIBISCUS CT, LILLY PILLY AV, CHERRY GR, LAUREL AV, MYRTLE GR, CRIMSON DR, PYRUS CT, PEACH CT, BERRY CT, LAURINA CT, ROWAN ST, AGONIS ST, GUM CT, JUDAS CT, ACER ST, LINDEN PL, LIQUIDAMBER ST, CONFERTA ST, PLUM ST, SPRING ST, PRIVET CT, CAMPHOR CT, COOTAMUNDRA DR, GOLDEN CT, SCARLET ST, BANKSIA ST, BOTANICAL DR, GREEN GR, RIMU CT, RED START CL, DOTTEREL CL, FLORIANA AV, PISA CT, ROBIN CL, KINGFISHER DR, STREET ST, CARDIGAN ST, GRIFFITH ST, CAINE CT, ALDRIDGE ST, DELOS CT, AMALFI CL, BITTERN DR, PIEDMONT CL, NADIA CT, CORMORANT CL, CLANGULA CT, LEIGH CT, JODIE CL, DONNA WY, JACINTA CT, DEBBIE CL, KATHRYN ST, WARATAH ST, LACEY RAIN CT, MIMOSA ST, APPLE CT, BARK ST, ACACIA ST, MARIE ST, KIDDS RD, TEMPLE LA, MELBE CR, FARLANE CR, PALM PL, BOUNDARY WAY, STAFF ST, THEYER ST, McLENNAN ST, STANIS ST, CULLIVER AV, COULSON AV, ROGERS ST, JOHNSTON ST, REDFERN CR, REGNANS CT, VIMINALIS CT, GRACILIS CT, CELTIS PL, RHUS CL, RUBIDA CT, AQUILA CR, ARDEA CT, CORREA PL, SORBUS CL, RAPANEA CT, SPINOSA CL, BELAH PL, MACULOSA CT, CHALCOT RD, CUMBERLAND WY, FITZROY CT, HANOVER CT, ALBANY CT, BEDFORD CT

JOINS 537

JOINS 550

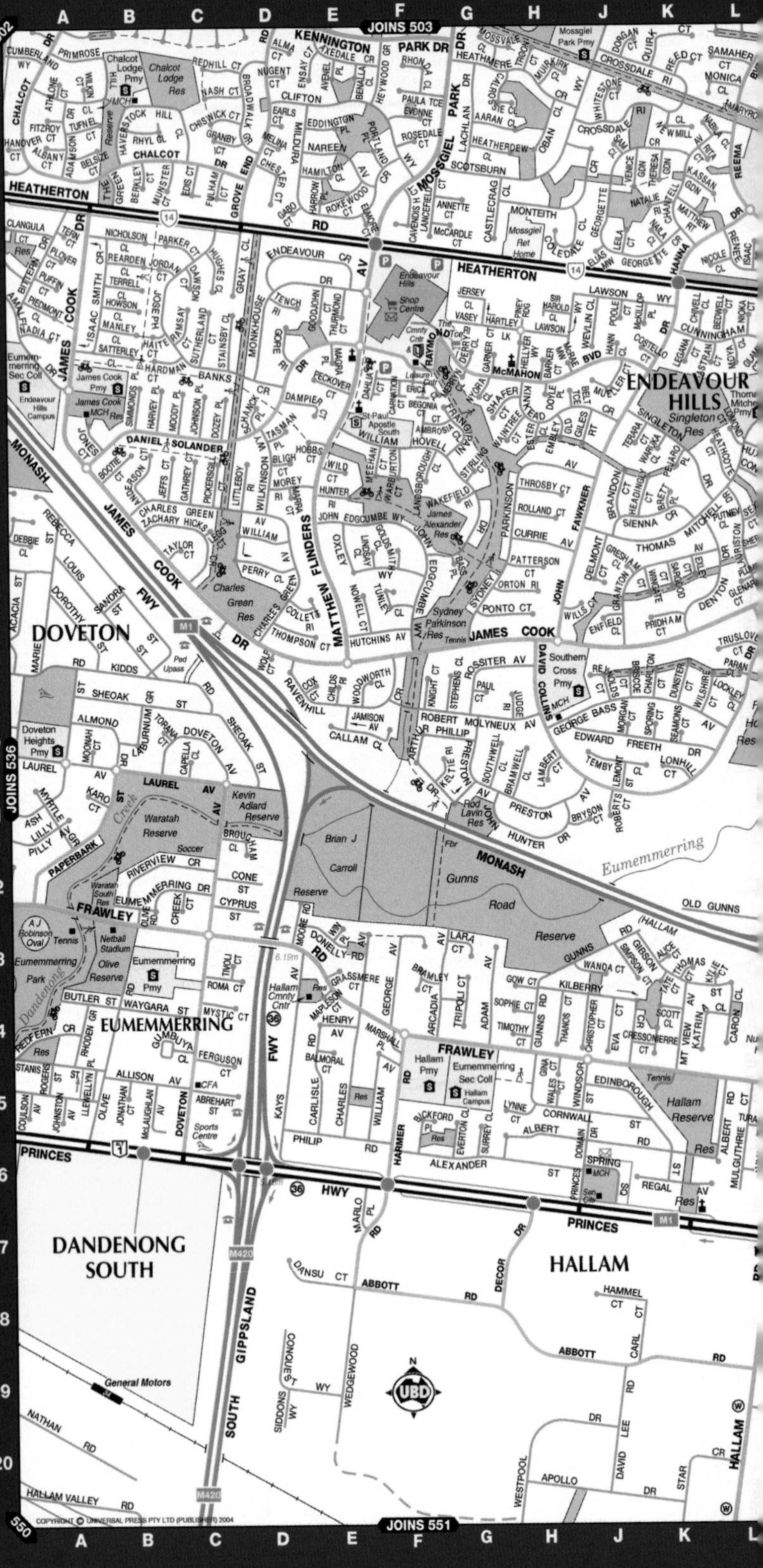

JOINS 503

502

A B C D E F G H J K L

ENDEAVOUR HILLS

DOVETON

EUMEMMERRING

DANDENONG SOUTH

HALLAM

HEATHERTON RD

MOSSGIEL PARK DR

KENNINGTON PARK DR

CHALCOT DR

GROVE END RD

JAMES COOK DR

MATTHEW FLINDERS AV

JOHN EDGCUMBE WY

JOHN FAWKNER DR

DAVID COLLINS DR

MONASH FWY

SOUTH GIPPSLAND FWY

PRINCES HWY

FRAWLEY RD

DONELLY RD

GUNNS RD

OLD GUNNS RD

ABBOTT RD

DAVID LEE RD

HALLAM VALLEY RD

NATHAN RD

HALLAM RD

Endeavour Hills Shop Centre

Endeavour Hills Campus

James Cook Pmy

Doveton Heights Pmy

Southern Cross Pmy

Hallam Pmy

Eumemmerring Sec Coll

Hallam Campus

Mossgiel Park Pmy

Chalcot Lodge Pmy

Chalcot Lodge Res

Mossgiel Ret Home

Singleton Res

James Alexander Res

Charles Green Res

Sydney Parkinson Res

Rod Lavin Res

Waratah Reserve

Kevin Adlard Reserve

Brian J Carroll Reserve

Gunns Road Reserve

Hallam Reserve

Olive Reserve

A J Robinson Oval

Eumemmerring Park

Dandenong Creek

Eumemmerring Creek

General Motors

JOINS 536

1 2 3 4 5 6 7 8 9 10 11 12 13 14 15 16 17 18 19 20

550

JOINS 551

A B C D E F G H J K L

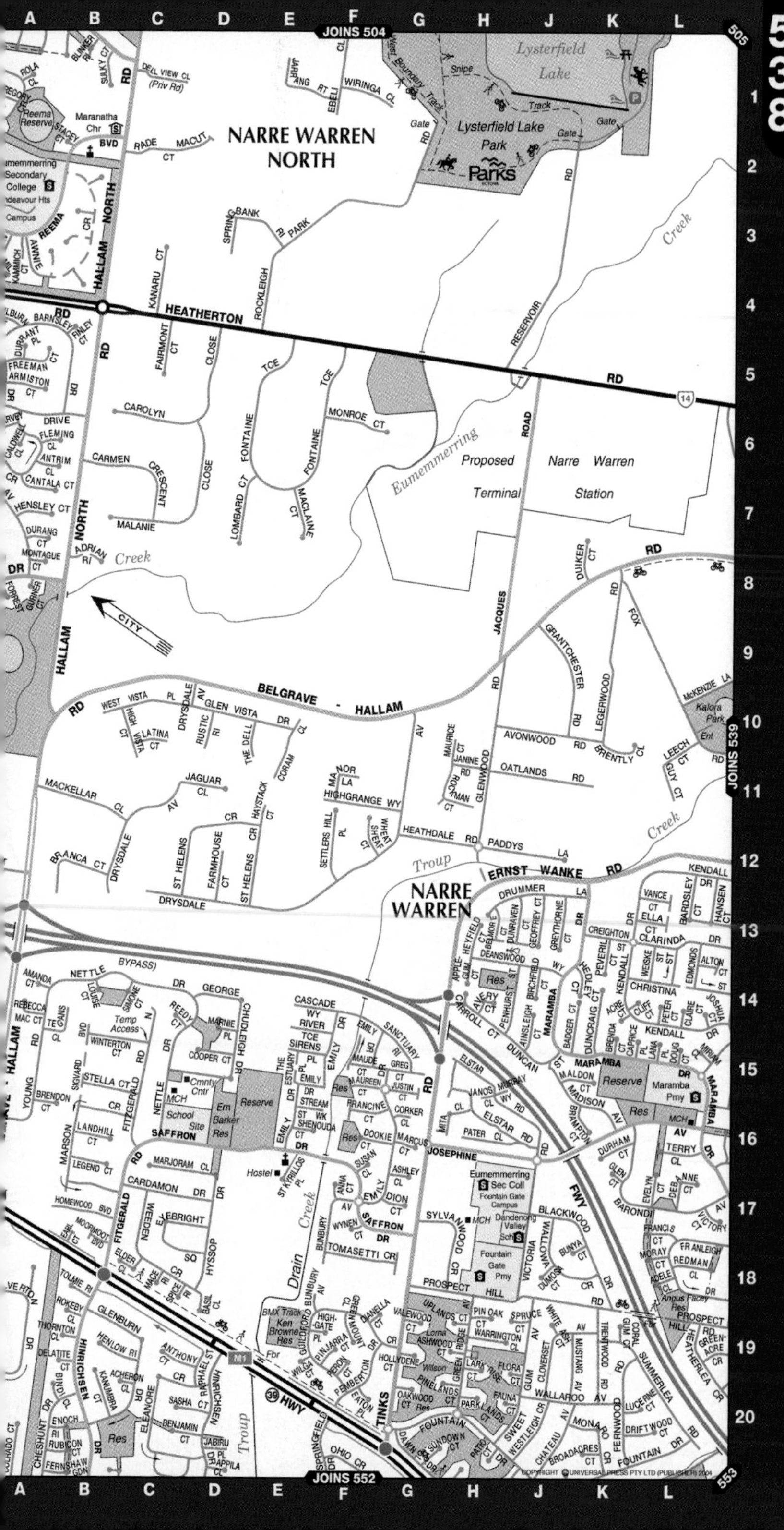
538
JOINS 504
505
JOINS 539
JOINS 552
553
NARRE WARREN NORTH
NARRE WARREN
Lysterfield Lake
Lysterfield Lake Park
Parks
Snipe
Track
West Boundary Track
Gate
Reema Reserve
Maranatha Chr
Eumemmerring Secondary College
Endeavour Hts Campus
HALLAM NORTH RD
HEATHERTON RD
BELGRAVE - HALLAM RD
HALLAM RD
RESERVOIR RD
JACQUES RD
ERNST WANKE RD
PADDYS LA
HEATHDALE RD
TINKS RD
SAFFRON DR
JOSEPHINE AV
PROSPECT HILL RD
FOUNTAIN DR
NETTLE DR
Proposed Terminal
Narre Warren Station
Eumemmerring Creek
Troup Creek
Drain Creek
CITY
Kalora Park
Ern Barker Res
Reserve
Maramba Reserve
Maramba Pmy
Eumemmerring Sec Coll Fountain Gate Campus
Dandenong Valley Sch
Fountain Gate Pmy
Ken Browne Res
Lorna Ashwood Res
Angus Facey Res
School Site
Cmnty Cntr
MCH
Hostel
BMX Track
BYPASS
FWY
HWY
M1
14
39
COPYRIGHT © UNIVERSAL PRESS PTY LTD (PUBLISHER) 2004

JOINS 505

JOINS 538

NARRE WARREN NORTH

NARRE WARREN

Campbelltown Miniature Rly Park

Narre Warren North Road Retarding Basin

Pony Club Iven's Reserve

Kalora Park

Jack Thomas Reserve

Mary McKillop Cath Pmy

BMX Track

Rose Farm

Kurll Park

Oatlands Primary

Prospect Hill

Troup Retarding Basin

Harry Oakes Res

Timbarra Pmy Sch

Maramba Pmy

JOINS 553

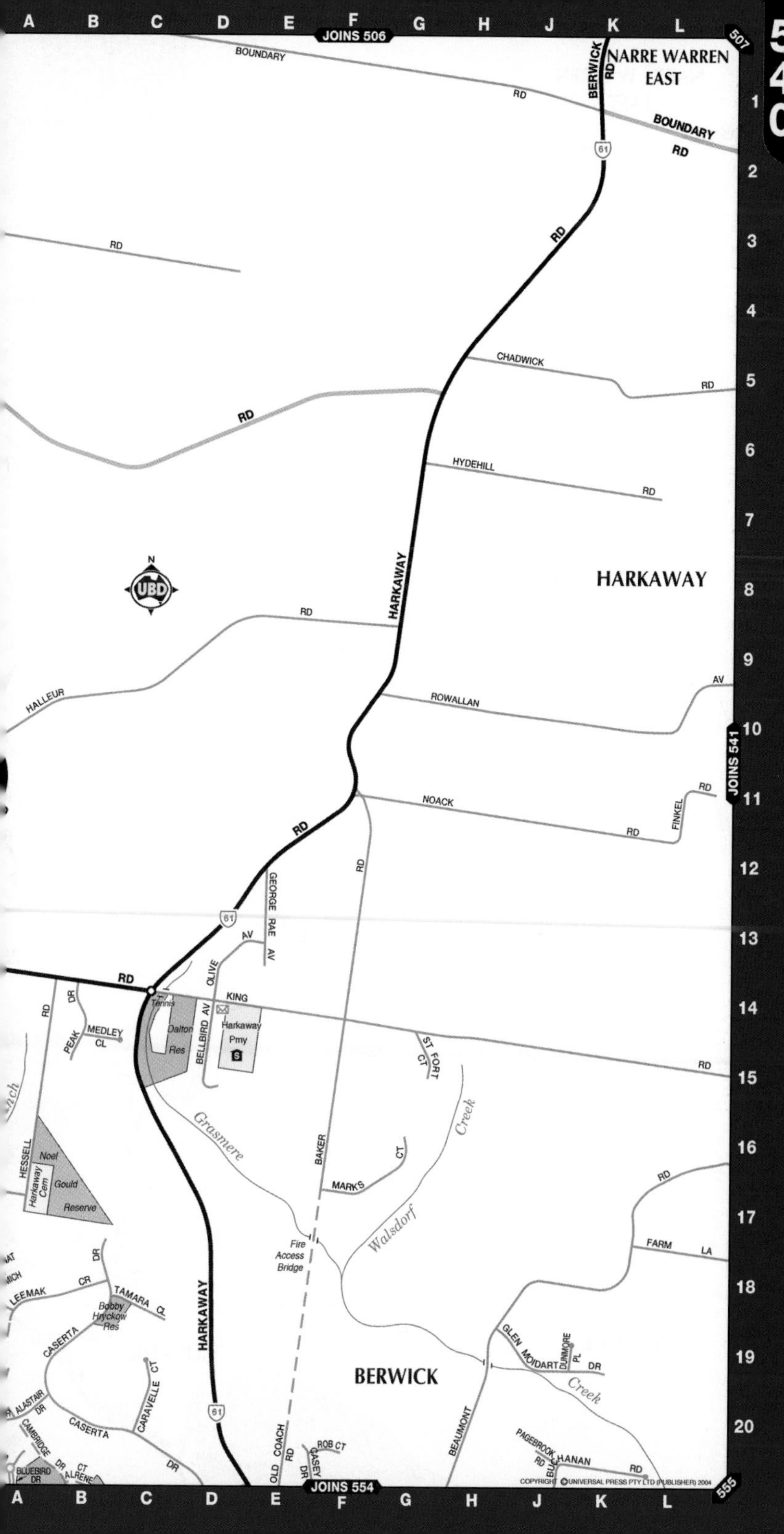
540
JOINS 506
507
NARRE WARREN EAST
BERWICK RD
BOUNDARY RD
BOUNDARY RD
61
RD
HARKAWAY RD
CHADWICK RD
RD
HYDEHILL RD
HARKAWAY
RD
HALLEUR
ROWALLAN AV
NOACK RD
FINKEL RD
JOINS 541
GEORGE RAE AV
OLIVE AV
RD
KING RD
Tennis
Dalton Res
BELLBIRD AV
Harkaway Pmy
PEAK DR
MEDLEY CL
ST FORT CT
HESSELL RD
Noel Gould Reserve
Harkaway Cem
Grasmere
BAKER RD
MARKS CT
Walsdorf Creek
Fire Access Bridge
FARM LA
LEEMAK CR
TAMARA CL
Bobby Hryckow Res
CASERTA
GLEN MOIDART DR
DUNMORE PL
Creek
BERWICK
CARAVELLE CT
ALASTAIR DR
CAMBRIDGE DR
BLUEBIRD DR
ALRENE CT
OLD COACH RD
CASEY DR
ROB CT
BEAUMONT
PAGEBROOK RD
BUCHANAN RD
JOINS 554
555

JOINS 507

NARRE WARREN EAST

HARKAWAY

BERWICK

GUYS HILL

BOUNDARY RD
Muddy Creek Rest
GREENWOOD RD
TANGARA LA
BILLAROY RD
MANESTAR
Cardinia Reservoir Park
Parks Victoria
Cardinia
CHADWICK RD
Harkaway Scout Camping Area
MORRIS DR
FOOTT
JURY ST
Creek
ST GEORGES
ROWALLAN AV
Stoney
KNAPTON AV
FRASER AV
Reserve
AV
BRENNAN
FINKEL RD
KING RD
HILDEN
DR
SEWELL DR
BORCHART ST
ST
Critchley Park Junior Reserve
Creek
HIGH
HIGH
FARM LA
ST
BARNES
C406
BEACONSFIELD - EMERALD
Montuna Golf Course
18
Sanctuary
MONTUNA GR
VICTOR AV
LUKE PL

JOINS 540

JOINS 555

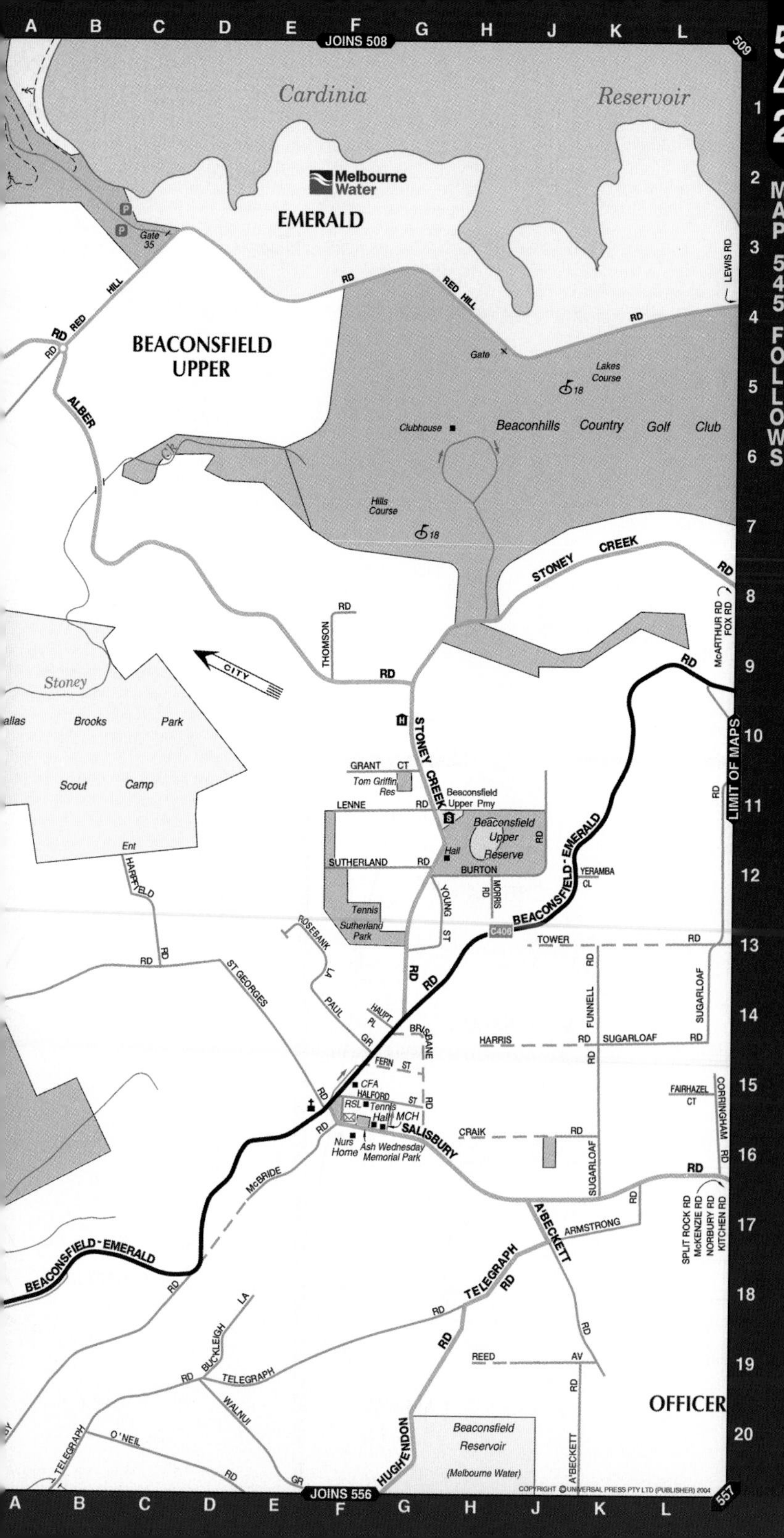

A B C D E F G H J K L
JOINS 508
509
Cardinia Reservoir
Melbourne Water
EMERALD
Gate 35
RED HILL RD
LEWIS RD
BEACONSFIELD UPPER
ALBER
Gate
Lakes Course
18
Clubhouse
Beaconhills Country Golf Club
Ck
Hills Course
18
STONEY CREEK RD
McARTHUR RD
FOX RD
THOMSON RD
CITY
Stoney
allas Brooks Park Scout Camp
Ent
STONEY CREEK RD
GRANT CT
Tom Griffin Res
LENNE RD
Beaconsfield Upper Pmy
Beaconsfield Upper Reserve
Hall
SUTHERLAND RD
BURTON RD
YERAMBA CL
MORRIS RD
YOUNG ST
Tennis
Sutherland Park
BEACONSFIELD - EMERALD
C406
TOWER RD
LIMIT OF MAPS
HARPFIELD RD
ROSEBANK LA
ST GEORGES RD
PAUL GR
HAUPT PL
BRISBANE
FUNNELL RD
SUGARLOAF RD
HARRIS RD
FERN ST
CFA
HALFORD ST
RSL
Tennis
Hall
MCH
Nurs Home
Ash Wednesday Memorial Park
SALISBURY RD
CRAIK RD
FAIRHAZEL CT
CORRINGHAM RD
McBRIDE
A'BECKETT RD
ARMSTRONG RD
SPLIT ROCK RD
McKENZIE RD
NORBURY RD
KITCHEN RD
BEACONSFIELD - EMERALD
TELEGRAPH RD
BUCKLEIGH LA
REED AV
TELEGRAPH RD
WALNUT
OFFICER
O'NEIL RD
TELEGRAPH
HUGHENDON RD
Beaconsfield Reservoir (Melbourne Water)
A'BECKETT RD
GR
JOINS 556
557
1 2 3 4 5 6 7 8 9 10 11 12 13 14 15 16 17 18 19 20

PREVIOUS MAP 542

JOINS 531

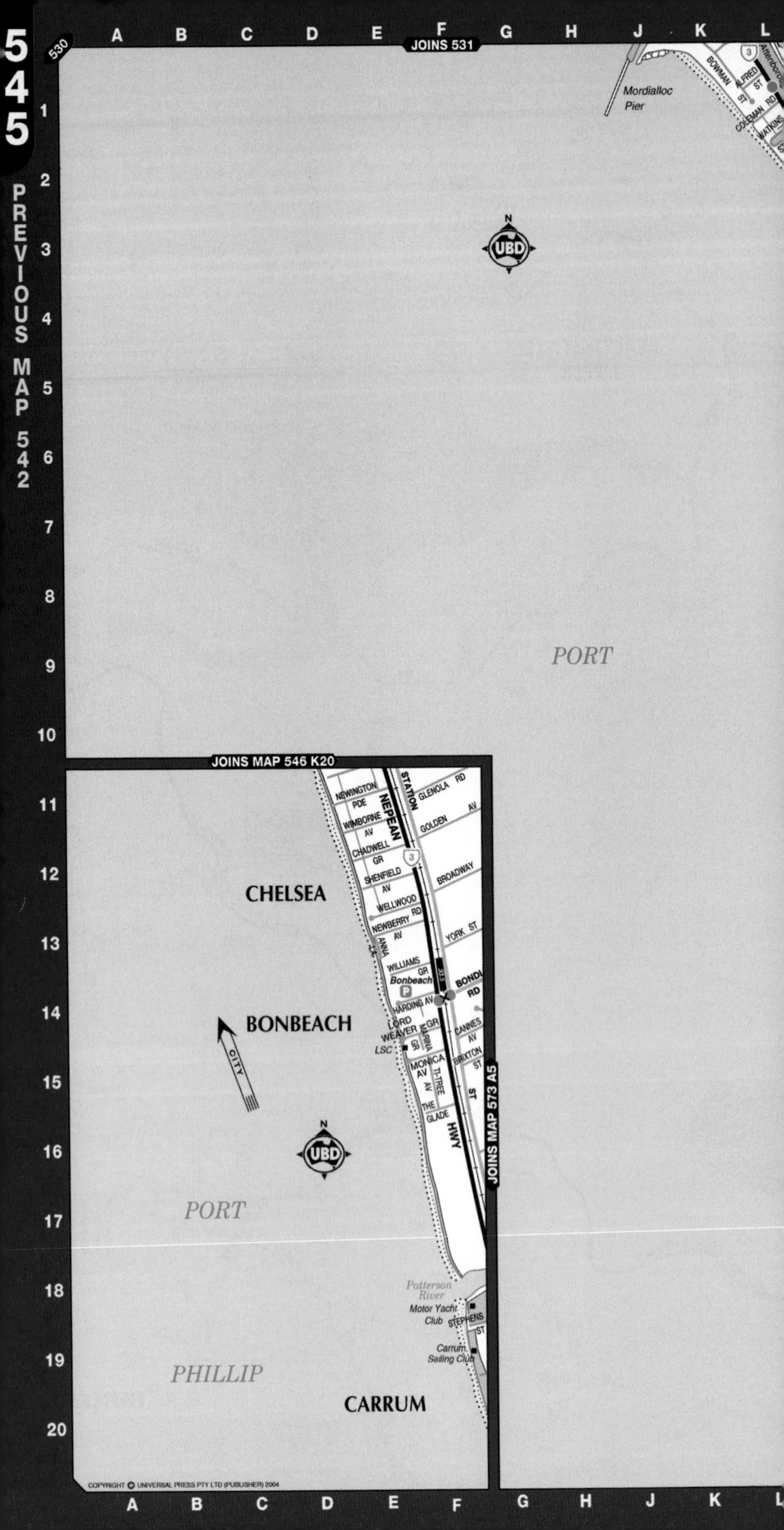

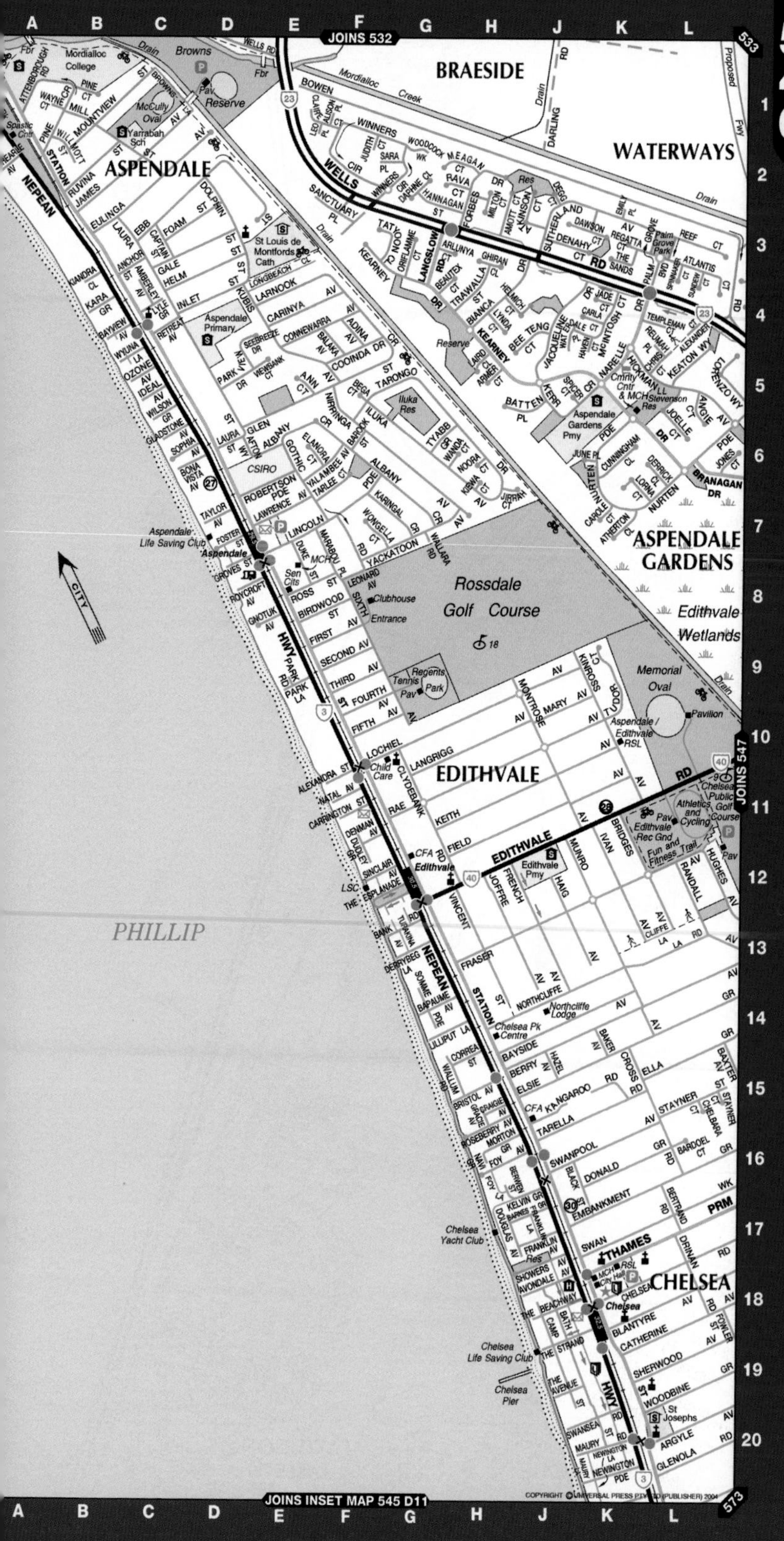

A B C D E F G H J K L
JOINS 532
533
546
BRAESIDE
WATERWAYS
ASPENDALE
ASPENDALE GARDENS
EDITHVALE
CHELSEA
PHILLIP
CITY
Mordialloc College
Browns Reserve
Mordialloc Creek
McCully Oval
Yarrabah Sch
Spastic Cntr
St Louis de Montfords Cath
Aspendale Primary
CSIRO
Iluka Res
Aspendale Life Saving Club
Aspendale
Rossdale Golf Course
Clubhouse
Entrance
Regents Park
Tennis Pav
Edithvale Wetlands
Memorial Oval
Pavilion
Aspendale / Edithvale RSL
Aspendale Gardens Pmy
Cmnty Cntr & MCH
Stevenson Res
Palm Grove Park
Chelsea Public Golf Course
Athletics and Cycling
Edithvale Rec Gnd
Fun and Fitness Trail
Edithvale Pmy
Edithvale
Child Care
Sen Cits
LSC
Northcliffe Lodge
Chelsea Pk Centre
Chelsea Yacht Club
Chelsea Life Saving Club
Chelsea Pier
Chelsea
City Hall
RSL
St Josephs
NEPEAN HWY
WELLS RD
EDITHVALE RD
STATION ST
JOINS 547
JOINS INSET MAP 545 D11
573
1 2 3 4 5 6 7 8 9 10 11 12 13 14 15 16 17 18 19 20
COPYRIGHT © UNIVERSAL PRESS PTY LTD (PUBLISHER) 2004

532
JOINS 533
JOINS 546
JOINS 573

A B C D E F G H J K L

KEYSBOROUGH

WATERWAYS

ASPENDALE GARDENS

Edithvale Wetlands

CHELSEA HEIGHTS

Wetlands

EDITHVALE

CHELSEA

BONBEACH

PATTERSON LAKES

Chelsea Public Golf Course

Bicentennial Park

Chelsea Sportswomens Park

Beazley Res

Chelsea Pony Club

Blue Gum Park

The Heights Park

Southern Obedience Dog Club

SPRINGVALE RD

WELLS RD

EDITHVALE RD

MORNINGTON PENINSULA FWY

THAMES PRM

INDEX
1 BANKSIA CT
2 BLUE GUM CT
3 CARPENTER CT
4 CUTHBERTSON CT
5 CYPRESS CT
6 HUTCHINGS CT
7 KYBERD CT
8 MALCOLM DR
9 MANNA GUM CT
10 PARKLAND DR

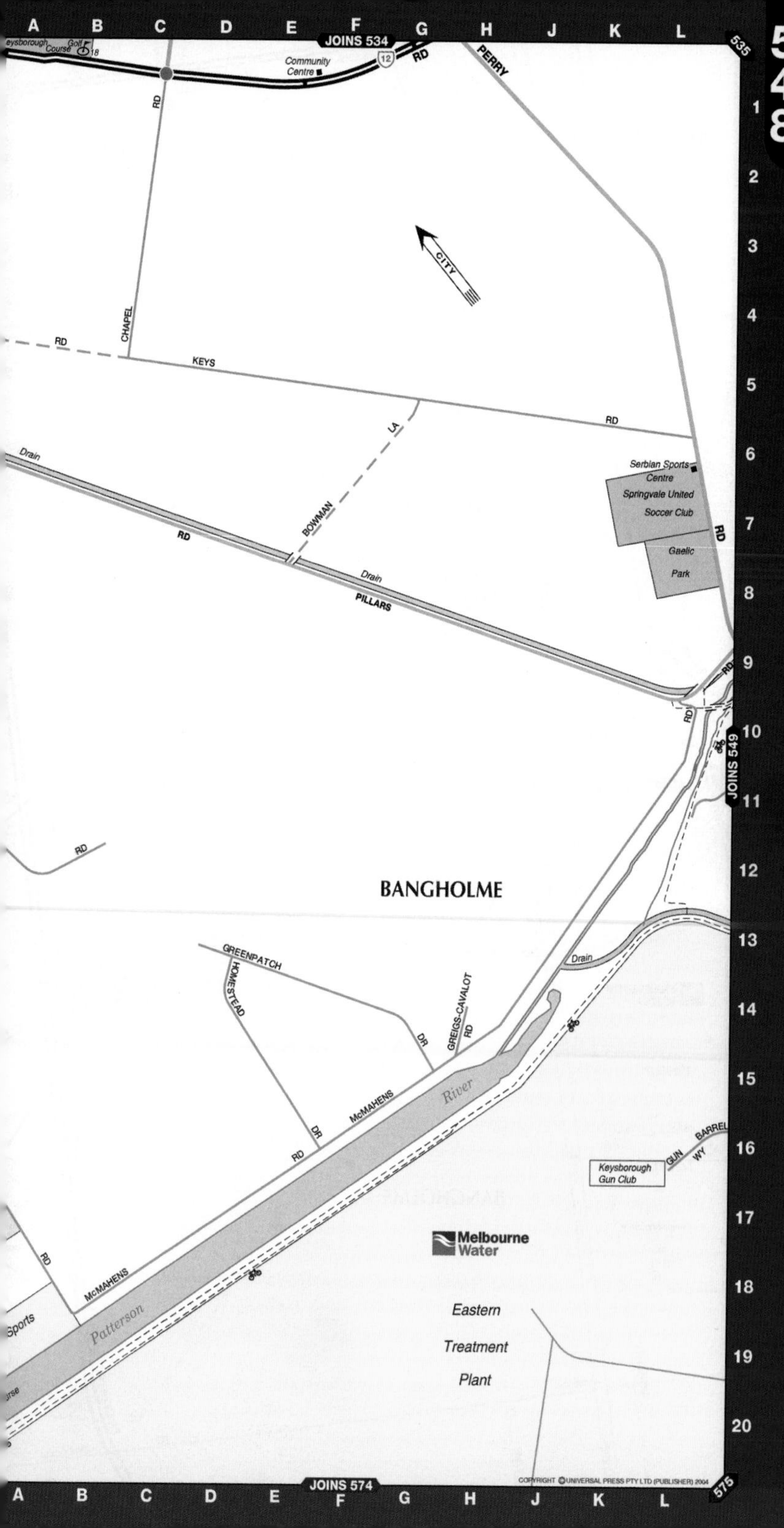
JOINS 534
535
Keysborough Golf Course
Community Centre
12
RD
PERRY
RD
CHAPEL
CITY
RD
KEYS
RD
LA
BOWMAN
Drain
RD
Drain
PILLARS
Serbian Sports Centre
Springvale United Soccer Club
RD
Gaelic Park
RD
RD
JOINS 549
RD
BANGHOLME
Drain
GREENPATCH
HOMESTEAD
GREIGS-CAVALOT
RD
DR
River
McMAHENS
DR
RD
GUN
BARREL
WY
Keysborough Gun Club
Melbourne Water
RD
McMAHENS
Sports
Patterson
Eastern
Treatment
Plant
JOINS 574
575

534
JOINS 535

A B C D E F G H J K L

1 2 3 4 5 6 7 8 9 10 11 12 13 14 15 16 17 18 19 20

KEYSBOROUGH

DANDENONG SOUTH

BANGHOLME

GREENS RD
TATTERSON RD
SOUTH PARK DR
Terminal Station
Melbourne Water
Creek
GPU Gas Network
KILKENNY CT
BROOKS DR
ELLIOTT RD
GUM DR
QUALITY
CAHILL ST
ORDISH
RED
PERRY
Nissan Head Office
Drain
MARNI ST
MICKLE ST
BERENDS DR
KIMBERLY RD
SONIA ST
SUPERIOR DR
Gaelic Park
Dandenong
PILLARS RD
Proposed
Freeway
LICOLA CT
MARK ANTHONY DR
ANTONELLA CT
SWIFT WY
ST
AV
LUISA
APOINGA
NICHOLAS
BUNGALEEN CT
HAMMOND RD
BANGHOLME RD
PERRY RD
Tennis Courts
Creek
Drain
Twin Bridge
Eumemmerring
Willow Lodge Mobile Homes
WILLOW
BIRCH CT
MATLOCK CT
TEEWAH CT
GLENBURN CT
POKOLBIN CT
EUREKA CT
BOGONG CT
BREEZEWAY DR
WAY DR
TRAIN DR
GREEN DR
EVERGREEN DR
WARRICK DR
WAYSIDE DR
BRAYWOOD DR
BRUSHWOOD DR
GENOA CT
FERNY CT
CELIA CT
WINGARA CT
GRAND CT
TANDARA CT
HOLLYDENE DR
NATHAM DR
CONSERVATION DR
QUIET DR
TRANQUILITY DR
GLADE DR
COLONIAL DR
ROYAL DR
RUSTIC DR
Ret Vill
RD
Melbourne Water
Eastern
GUN BARREL WAY
Gate
Treatment
Scoresby
Bangholme Hall
Plant
(DANDENONG VALLEY HWY)
FRANKSTON-DANDENONG RD
WORSLEY
HARWOOD RD
ELMS RD
GLASSCOCKS
Carrum United Soccer Club
Italio Australian Club
Tennis

JOINS 548
574
JOINS 575

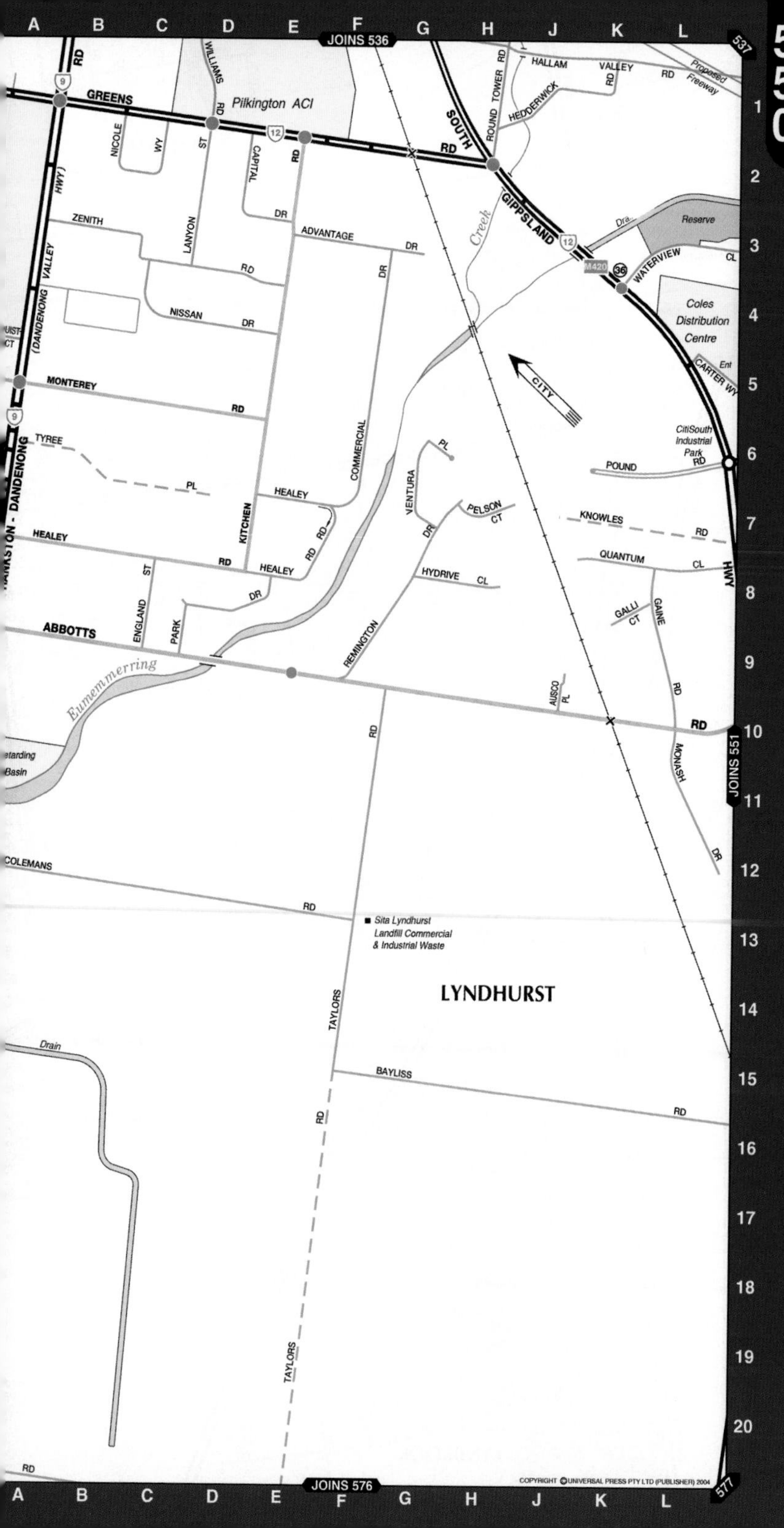
JOINS 536
537
GREENS RD
Pilkington ACI
WILLIAMS RD
NICOLE WY
ST
CAPITAL DR
LANYON
RD
ZENITH RD
ADVANTAGE DR
DR
NISSAN DR
SOUTH GIPPSLAND HWY
ROUND TOWER RD
HALLAM VALLEY RD
HEDDERWICK
Proposed Freeway
Creek
Reserve
WATERVIEW CL
M420
Coles Distribution Centre
CARTER WY
Ent
CITY
CitiSouth Industrial Park
POUND RD
KNOWLES RD
QUANTUM CL
GALLI CT
GAINE RD
(DANDENONG VALLEY HWY)
MONTEREY RD
TYREE PL
HEALEY RD
COMMERCIAL DR
KITCHEN RD
VENTURA DR
PL
PELSON CT
HYDRIVE CL
HEALEY
ENGLAND ST
PARK DR
ABBOTTS RD
REMINGTON
Eumemmerring
AUSCO PL
Retarding Basin
MONASH DR
JOINS 551
COLEMANS RD
Sita Lyndhurst Landfill Commercial & Industrial Waste
LYNDHURST
TAYLORS RD
BAYLISS RD
Drain
JOINS 576
577

JOINS 537

536

A B C D E F G H J K L

HALLAM

HALLAM VALLEY
Proposed
Freeway
RD
FWY
O'GRADY
APOLLO
DR
CR
WESTPOOL DR
STAR
CR
STAR
EMPIRE
WY
KEPPEL
RD
Hallam
BANNON CT
RD
Reserve
WATERVIEW CL
M420
KM Reedy Reserve
Hockey
Football-Cricket Pav
Soccer
Football-Cricket Pav
Hockey & Soccer
Soccer
Hockey
Tennis
Drain
Coles Distribution Centre
Ent
CARTER WY
GIPPSLAND
SOUTH
POUND
5.38m
6.3m
TELFORD
BRUNEL
LONGFORD CT
ROWLAND CL
CONIFER CT
DR
RUDLOE PL
HARBURY MW
ADLEY PL
DULNAIN CT
EDGERTON CT
CHANNELLE CL
KENSINGTON CT
GARFIELD CT
MUNRO CT
DARLING CT
CAROLINE PL
WILLOW
DRIVE
OAKTREE
AFFRA
FULHAM
CHISWICK CT
ASHFORD CL
EDSALL CL
DALVANA
VERONA
HAZELDEAN CT
NARELLAN
MILLS
ELLASWOOD
BARNSBURY
AVOCA
PEPPERMINT CT
Res
HARCOURT
BLACKWOOD
HIGHTON CL
BARRINGTON PL
CASUARINA CT
WYCOMBE
RIMINGTON CT
POLLINA
ASHDALE CT
BECKINGTON DR
CR
DR
THE
COTHAM SQ
GRANGE
COPPIN CL
URQUHART
MANNING
TRAWALLA
AV
BUNYA PL
JUSTIN
GABRIELLE CL
CCT
CANDLE
FAYE
JOEL WY
JUSTIN
SOUTH GIPPSLAND
12
39
MARY
KAROL CT
ST
MARSHALL
SINCLAIR
JAMBE
RD
WAYSIDE CT
AV
HAMPTON
ANDERSON
Sen Cits
GREEN
VALLEY
VILLAGE
DR
GARNET CT
Res
WILLIS CL
VANESSA
George Knowles Res
MARK CT
BELVEDERE CT
HAYES RD
ALMA
WINNIMA
BRIDE
Res
GLEN CT
HIGHLAND
SUNNYVALE CT
BROOK CT
Hampton Park Rec Res
Tennis
Reserve
HALLAM
DELACOMBE
ROHAN
BRADLEY
TARELLA ST
LAUREN
ROSALIE CT
KNOWLES
RD
SOMERVILLE RD
SOMERVILLE
ROBJANT
JENNER
ST
Hampton Park Pmy
BRENTNALL CT
HUGHES CT
FAIRWAY
CFA
BELLVUE
OUTLOOK
COTTAGE AV
DEANSWOOD
SILVAN
LEONNE CT
WARANA
MCH
Marjorie Eastick Res
RD
TADSTAN DR
CLIVE
NOLA CT
REGANS
KERRISON
CODY
MARLENE
PARKLAND
ORA
WREN
ST
DR
ROBINSON
DORTAD
CR
AV
Hampton Park
CRAIGIE CT
HEDLEY
STRONG
JAYNE CT
KELLIE CT
FOX CL
PITMAN CT
FORDHOLM
VIEW
THE
River Gum Pmy
TATTERSON ST
Cmnty Hall
MERCE DR
JASPER CT
TOPAZ WY
LILLIAN
JEFFREY
TALBOT
LORRAINE
MATTHEW
ROBB CT
STUART
ENTERPRISE
COMM
AV
CLIVE ST
EMERALD
GEORGE
KATHLEEN
Res
ANDREW CT
Hampton Park Secondary College
RD
CORAL
Reserve
HWY
ABBOTTS
RD
JADE CT
SAPPHIRE DR
MARGARET CT
ROBYN
VALERIE
DAVID
PAUL
TYALLA
KING DAVID CT
DR
JOSHUA
THANOS CT
ROAD
Retirement Village
CLAUDE
LINDA
AQUAMARINE ST
ST
SHELLEY
EVELYN
STANLEY ST
GENERAL
PRINCESS PL
KOOYONG
ISAAC
5.45m
CAIRNS
NAJA
ALASTER
FEENEY
CT
SUSAN
DOROTHY
Res
Reserve
CAMPBELL
IVAN
MARIA
CRESCENT
EDEYS
WEST
BRANTON DR
MOSIG CT
LUKE CT
BERRIDALE
WY
CAIRNS
HAWKING
RILEY
ROBBINS
WYNETTE
St Kevins Cath Pmy
MOLLISONS
HILL
MAYRUCK
RISE
PIONEER
EDEY
FWY
RD
JASON
RD
THE CLOSE
ALPINE WK
PARKES
UNGARIE
GREENLEE
REEVES
CHESTER
OWENS
PRIDE
CASH CL
CLINE
CONWAY
DENVER
RD
KYLIE CT
SPRINGFIELD
CR
BRANT ON
McDOWALL
ELANORA
THE EYRIE
GUMTREE
STRABANE
INSAF CT
STRABANE
BAEZ
RENDELL PL
KELLER CT
CHERYL
KATHERINE
SOUTH
CENTRAL
FARSKIENE PL
TULSK CT
DONEGAL WY
HUNTINGTON
THE RETREAT
YARRAN
BATEMAN
BRUTUS
OAKLAND DR
HORTON
RD
YASMIN
RD
WENDY CT
TERRY
GRAHAM
PATRICIA
HAZEL
ROBERT
MICHELLE
UBD
ORMOND
THE GLADE
BATEMAN
GR
SHORT
RD
LEOPOLD
Res
BVD
GIPPSLAND
39
TOOHEY CL
SUMMIT
HORIZON
SUNRISE
HWY
RD
SUNSET
RIDGE CT
PINNACLE
THE SPUR
DEW
ALPHA POINT
DUTTON CT
OLIVE
SILVER CREEK
GLENSHEE
PARK CITY
MERIBEL
SUN VALLEY
SUGAR BUSH
WYNDHAM
ARGYLE
PLATEAU
CR
ORMOND
STELLATO PL
ELPARA
CUSH
KAROONDA WY
SEVILLA
CASTELLA PL
RATCLIFFE WY
Mackellar Park
GILMORE CL
Lyndhurst
BAYLISS
ASTLEY
DR
DOBSON
BUCKLEY
TRANTER
BRADY CL
DR
BROOME
DERBY
BVD
WYN
DURACK
HUTCHINSON
FORBES
SLESSOR AV
KEYSTONE CT
LYNBROOK
SUGARLOAF
SILVERTOP
MACLEOD
CARBONI CR
LINDSAY
LITCHFIELD
DYSON
WY
BVD
TOWERHILL
BLUE RANGE
CAVERSHAM
MERCER PL
LIVINGSTONE
RONANS
O'REILLY WY
CHAUNCY
LAWSON
COBBLER RI
RTN
PATERSON
HENRY
(WESTERN PORT HWY)
M420
NUGONG
PARSLOW
COBBLER GRA
Commercial Sands (Private Waste Disposal)
A780
42
MAY GIBBS
GUMNUT LA
PATERSON
LYNBROOK
Proposed Pmy Sch
DR
CAMPION WK
CILENTO CR
DENNIS CL
O'DOWD PL
ST BERNARDS
TEMBIE RI
TCE
SELMA
HALLAM
AMY MACK WK
Banjo Paterson Park
ELDERSHAW
HASLUCK CR
FRANKLIN
ROWCROFT
PEDLEY WY
LOUISE MACK WK
HARFORD CL
DARCY NILAND
SATINWOOD WY
PYRAMID
MORETON BAY
CARABEEN WY
WATERGUM AV
CUDOTTA LA
CATO
PKY
TENNANT
PDE
DANDENONG - HASTINGS
BRAMBLE CL
WATERBUSH CR
RED OAK
TCE
MARIGOLD
BRACKEN
AYLMER
BVD
WATTLE RD
SILVER
Proposed Lynbrook Station
AYLMER
PDE
ELLIOTT
Proposed Retirement Village RD

LYNBROOK

YELLOWBOX
Res

576

JOINS 577

JOINS 550

A B C D E F G H J K L

A B C D E F G H J K L

JOINS 538
539

NARRE WARREN

NARRE WARREN SOUTH

HAMPTON PARK

PRINCES HWY
CENTRE ROAD
SHRIVES RD
POUND RD
NARRE WARREN - CRANBOURNE RD
ORMOND RD
WEBB ST
FULLARD RD
WARREN PARK
BARINGA PARK
GREAVES RD

Fountain Gate Shopping Cntr
City of Casey Services Complex
Max Pawsey Reserve
Patrick Northeast Res Aquatic & Leisure Cntr
Homemaker Centre
Narre Warren Leisure Cntr
Kilberry Valley Pmy
Coral Park Pmy
Narre Warren South P-12 College
Trinity Cath Pmy Sch
Retarding Basin

JOINS 553

1 2 3 4 5 6 7 8 9 10 11 12 13 14 15 16 17 18 19 20

JOINS 578
579

A B C D E F G H J K L

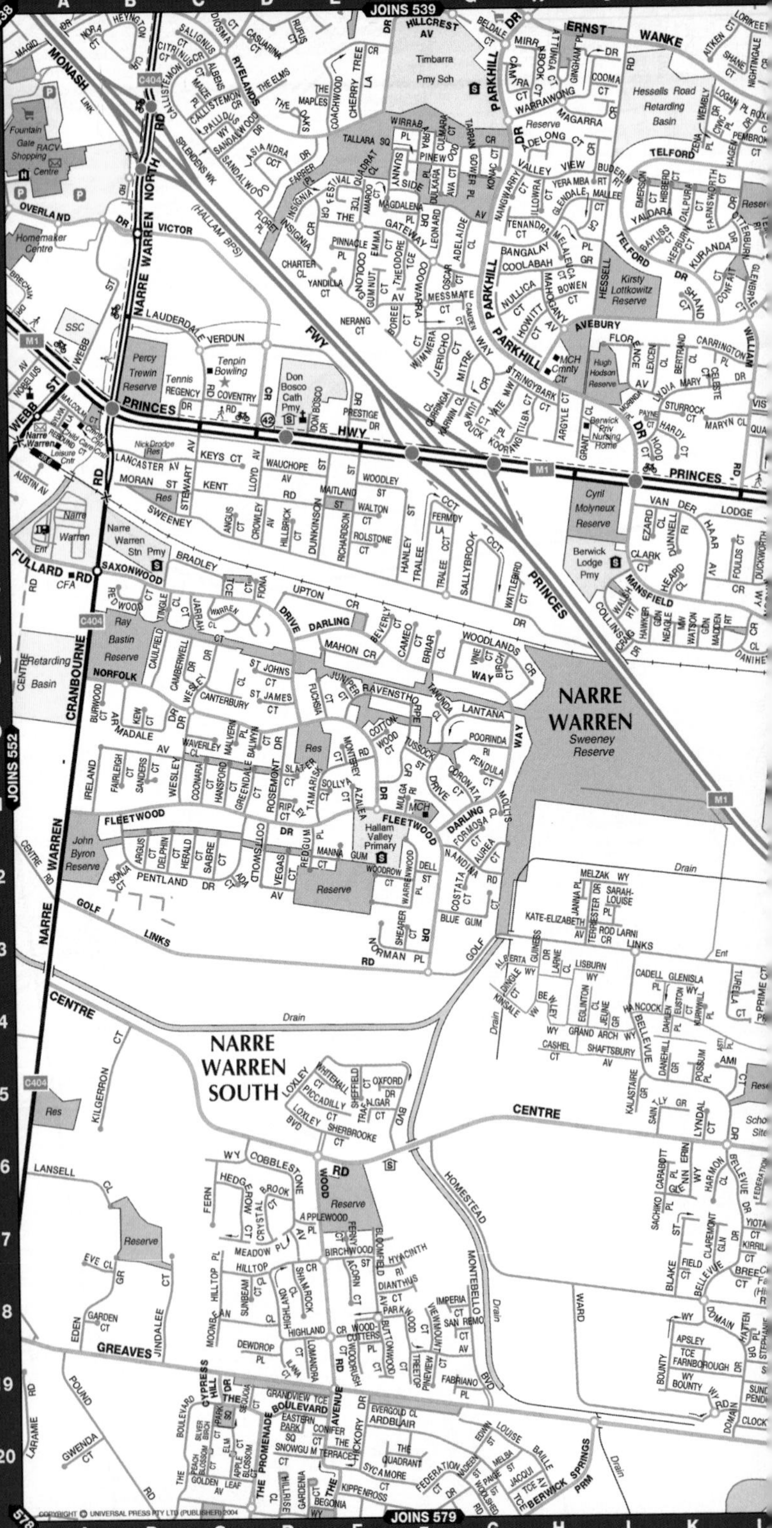

JOINS 552

NARRE WARREN

Sweeney Reserve

NARRE WARREN SOUTH

Fountain Gate Shopping Centre
RACV
Homemaker Centre
SSC
Percy Trewin Reserve
Tenpin Bowling
Don Bosco Cath Pmy
Timbarra Pmy Sch
Hessels Road Retarding Basin
Kirsty Lottkowitz Reserve
Hugh Hodson Reserve
MCH Cmnty Ctr
Berwick Priv Nursing Home
Cyril Molyneux Reserve
Berwick Lodge Pmy
Narre Warren Stn Pmy
Nick Drodge Res
Ray Bastin Reserve
Retarding Basin
John Byron Reserve
Hallam Valley Primary
Reserve
Narre Warren Leisure Cntr
Child Care Cntr
CFA

MONASH FWY
PRINCES HWY
PRINCES FWY
NARRE WARREN NORTH RD
CRANBOURNE RD
NARRE WARREN CRANBOURNE RD
(HALLAM BPS)
M1
C404
PARKHILL DR
TELFORD DR
WEBB ST
OVERLAND DR
VICTOR
LAUDERDALE
VERDUN
REGENCY
COVENTRY
PRESTIGE
KEYS CT
WAUCHOPE
KENT
LANCASTER AV
MORAN ST
SWEENEY
BRADLEY
SAXONWOOD
FULLARD RD
UPTON CR
DARLING DR
MAHON CR
WOODLANDS WAY
RAVENSTHORPE
LANTANA
NORFOLK
CANTERBURY
ARMADALE AV
FLEETWOOD DR
PENTLAND DR
GOLF LINKS RD
CENTRE RD
LANSELL
COBBLESTONE
WOOD RD
HOMESTEAD
MONTEBELLO
BELLEVUE
GREAVES
CYPRESS HILL DR
THE BOULEVARD
THE PROMENADE
AVENUE
ARDBLAIR
BERWICK SPRINGS PRM
KINGS ... LANSELL
WARD
Drain

JOINS 540
541

A B C D E F G H J K L

1
CAMBRIDGE ALRENE CT, CASERTA, HARKAWAY, OLD COACH RD, ROB CT, CASEY DR, PAGEBROOK RD, RD, Grasmere
PHEASANT CT, BLUEBIRD DR, Reserve, DR, BURNVILLE CL, CLOVELLY PL, ALDERFORD CT, DR

2
GLOVER CT, LAWRENCE RD, ASHFORD CT, BALFOUR CT, WERONA CT, SELWOOD CT, MATHESON CT, TRINITY CT, NEVADA CT, HARCOURT WY, DENHAM PL, CASEY, 61, CLOVERFIELD CT
TRAVIS CT, ROYSTON, DR, ANSTEY, Warwick Glendenning Res, CAMDON

3
DR, BARELLAN, DIRKALA, GDN RT, MW, AVEBURY, CHRISTINE, BOURNEVALE, SAVANNA CT, COWPER RI, CHILTERN CT, AV, Ck

4
ALMAIN, HARLEY CT, GAYLARD CT, HASKEN CT, NEWSOM CT, DEAUVILLE CT, BARINA CT, DR, RYDALDENE WY, NYON PL, CAMLEY CT, GARDINER ST, BEAUMONT, BUCHANAN
ANSELL CT

5
Wilson Botanic Park, OUTLOOK DR, HAZELDENE CT, LYALL RD, GRANEEL GR, INGLIS, Berwick Cemetery RD, Tennis, RD
Neville Hamilton Res AV, SHUTE, RUSSELL, KRAMER, MILLER, KIRKHAM, KERRY CT, LIGHTWOOD, AWARD CT, CARA CR, CARA CT
Office & Info Cntr, ROUNDHAY, LINTON CT, Arch Brown Reserve, ST, DR

6
RHEANVA, BRISBANE, Berwick Pmy, RD, HOWELL, JESSICA MW, MICHAEL, Edwin Flack Reserve, Oval, Athletics Track, REGINALD
Berwick Brae Ret Village, QUEENS CT, AYR CT, YORK, RD, McNABB, LYALL RD, PEEL, BURR HILL CT, BUCHANAN, SHANNON CL, WY

7
ANNE ST, WILSON, BLACKBURNE SQ, PATERNOSTER LA, LOVERIDGE WK, WHEELER ST, CAMERON CT, MCH, ST, PALMERSTON, ASCOT PL, KILLARNEY, GRETEL PL, BETTINA CT, Berwick Secondary College
PENRITH, (HIGH ST), ADAMS LA, KEMPSON WK, RUTLAND, EDWARDES, PEEL, CHURCH, SANDGATE, VALDA CL

8
CONISTON, THIRLMERE CT, MILLWOOD AV, PATRICIA CT, RICHARDSON GR, AV, RSL, 45, HWY, MARYGATE PL, SCANLAN, ELGIN, CAMPBELL, CLOVER CT, MARY CL, BEAVIS CT
WINDERMERE, ST, Bill Hudson Res, MARGARET ST, EVAN ST, LANGMORE, LA, STEW WY, BAIN ST, St Michaels Cath, WILLIAMSON, WARNE PL, SCOTSGATE WY, RIDGE RD, RD

9
AMBLESIDE, JANE, DERWENT CT, RD, KEITH TAYLOR DR, Berwick Hosp, GIBB, Stephenson House Nursing Home, GLOUCESTER, St Margarets, ST, HAVELOCK PL, FRITZLAFF CT, ST
ENTERPRISE, ST, RESERVE, NEWMAN, CORO, RENWARL CL, DR, Ent

10
INTREPID, ST, Gate, VENTURE DR, AV, CFA, ST, Fiddlers Green Retirement Village, JOMARY CT, PRINCES, Jack Kirkham Res, TURNER, EXELL MW, NEILL, ST, MANUKA, ST, GAMBLE AV, FUNSTON ST
Buchanan Park, ST MARGARETS, Edrington Park Retirement Village

JOINS 555

11
Monash University Berwick Campus, C407, Berwick, 435, MELVILLE, GRANTHAM, FYFFE ST, BIRALEE CT, ANDVAL CT, AUSOP LA, McKAY CL, (HIGH ST), KILVINGTON CT, ST
MAIN BVD, KANGAN, FURNESS CT, PARK, MILPARINKA, PARK, JANCOL CT, SUMNER CT, Temp Access, CARDINIA, Akoonah Park

12
GRANTHAM, DR, MELVILLE, FAIRHOLME, EDRINGTON, RYAN CT, PARK, DR, HWY
Entrance, Ret Vill, NORMANTON, JOHN FISHER DR, SHERMAN, BVD, ASTRID CT, DR, Haileybury Coll, Ent, Junior Sch
Drain, FWY, 45

13
Chisholm Institute Berwick Campus, FAIRHOLME BVD, SIANDRA PL, CANNING CT, BERWICK
5.6m, Spash's Swimming Sch, WILONA WY, Berwick Pmy Sch Under Constr

14
RD, COUNTY, MURNDAL CT, MALANDA CT, LILY VALE, ESCOTT CT, DR, Proposed Berwick Community Hospital, CITY, NORHAM CT

15
TOTTINGTON RI, HOLLYDALE CL, GR, WARROCK CT, MARIDA CT, CHEVIOT, MELROSE CT, KELSO PL, Eddie Baron Reserve, AV, KANGAN, PRINCES, Beaconhills College Village Campus
GREENLAW, Cmnty Cntr, BEMERSYDE, LAUDER PL, ETTRICK PL, BROXBURN CT

16
RD, TYNT, DR, CARLUKE CT, SELKIRK CT, AV, GIFFORD CL, STRATHAVAN, EARLSTON SQ, FISHER CL, BRUCE CT, DR, M1, HAIR CT, ADAMSON RD, SLINGSBY AV, DRURY ST, 2.2m, RD
DEBRA CT, HARWOOD, PIONEER CT, MARTIN, Chirnside, MCH, Walk, SUGARLOAF LA, 7.0m, 5.7m, SOLDIERS

17
VENABLES CT, ASHFIELD, JACQUELINE, YARROW CT, NEILIAN RT, Brentwood Park Pmy, DR, CHIRNSIDE, RD, CONSTITUTION RI, HIGGINBOTHAM, RI, INNES CT, HUDSON ST, KEVIN CL, Ent, BROOKVALE
Res, HILLMAN, MARGARITA, Reserve, Kambrya College, HALL CT, ALBRECHT, SPENCER CT, DAVISON WY, STREETON, REID MW, DEAKIN, AV, BARTON MW, CHIRNSIDE, RD, CL

18
COONEY, JASON CL, FUSCO, TCE, WILLSLIE, KIMBERLY, BOSWELLS, MARLESFORD, KINTA CL, BARBER CT, VIVIENNE WY, CUMEEN, HOLDER CT, CT, PLAYFORD CT, CHARLES CT, CONDER PL, INNES, JARRYD CL, ALLIRA, JAMIE MW, SUE, KELLY MW, FWY
BENNY, SOUHAIL CT, MOLONEY, DR, LISA, KINGSMILL, EDGBASTON CCT, MARINA CT, FURPHY, McCUBBIN, DICKSON MW, DUFFY CT, BRENT CL, JAY PL

19
BALMACEDA, JIM CT, MICHELLE, BANEEN PL, MONDOUS, GROVE GDN, JOHNS WOOD, OLD TRAFFORD, FROGNAL MW, THE OVAL, WARWICK CT, CR, NNES, THORNLEY, LISSON CT, CRESTA CT, Res, FINDON WY, DR, MARISA, WY, McILWRAITH, KINGSMERE, BOYNTON CR, EARLSFIELD CR, EDWARD CT
Temp Access, MILLGROVE, EDGBASTON CT, LORDS, LENA CT, CR, INGA CT, DRYDEN, FERNCROFT CT, ROXY CL, ABBEY CT, DALE, GEORGINA PL

20
RD, C407, TUMUT CT, RENMARK WY, MARALEE, BEMERSYDE DR, AKITA CT, SELBY CT, KIMBARRA CT, YALUMBA, ZOLA CT, CASHMERE CR, ANNE CT, LANDRA CT, MARISA CR, LYNETTE CT, CARA CT, NIKKI PL, Temp Access, SOLDIERS, MAYBURY CT, EXFORD, REDMORE CT, DR, CORY PL, CR
TARAGO, MAGGIE, RIVERGLEN, HEDGELEY, DR, AUGUSTUS, HILDA CT, NAURU, GOODALL CT, YARDLEY CT, BALANKA CT, RIVIERA DR, ELLESSE, GRAYDEN, SALTAIR CT, GLADE CT, MARISA CT, MARISA PL, DAVENTRY, EARLSFIELD, HOLLINGTON DR, PAXTON CL
O'SHEA, RD, CLYDE

JOINS 580
581

A B C D E F G H J K L

A B C D E F G H J K L

JOINS 541

1 2 3 4 5 6 7 8 9 10 11 12 13 14 15 16 17 18 19 20

BERWICK

GUYS HILL

BEACONSFIELD

Montuna Golf Course
Sanctuary
Clubhouse
LUKE PL
C406
QUAMBY
QUAMBY
MYRTLE GR
Berwick-Beaconsfield Golf Driving Range & Mini Golf
Grasmere
Ck
RD
INGLIS RD
CARA
CR
PL
VINTON
RD
Edwin Flack Reserve
Oval
Craft Market
Leisure Ctr
Berwick Sec Coll
CLOVER
MARY CT
CL
Clover Cottage Restaurant
RIDGE RD
ALLAN ST
MANUKA
CASTLEGATE PL
GAMBLE AV
Cardinia Ck
Sanctuary For Flora and Fauna
Gate
LUKEDENN DR
C406
PAYNE RD
PAYNE
COOINDA AV
WARRAWEE AV
KEITH
MAVIS
RD
VERNON
COOINDA
RD
BEACONSFIELD - EMERALD RD
ST

JOINS 554

HOLM PARK RD
LAKEVIEW TCE N
LAKEVIEW TCE
DOMAIN
CCT
GRANGE
VIEWBANK RI
HIGHTON CT
CCT
SCENIC
SCENIC
PYRENEES CT
DR
MOUNTAIN VIEW CCT
BVD
GUMVIEW
SNOWGUM LA
AIDENS
NORTHVIEW
ISOBEL PDE
CT
WY
CITY
Berwick Showgrds
CARDINIA
Akoonah Park
Tennis
Beaconsfield Rec Res
FIELDSTONE
MANOR WY
PRINCES HWY
HIGH ST
Ent
Haileybury Coll
Junior Sch
SANCTUARY WY
SUNHILL CT
RETREAT CT
CCT
HARBOUR ST
SANCTUARY
CASTLE WY
CT
DR
TIMBERSIDE
WILD DUCK WY
TRANQUILITY PL
HIDDEN VALLEY CCT
VISTA PL
SANCTUARY
Kath Roberts Res
KATHLEEN CT
IVY CT
ST
THELMA
AMELIA CL
WILMA CT
SYLVIA RD
PATRICK PL
CCT
PARKVIEW DR
NORTH DR
CRESTVIEW CCT
SOUTH HIDDEN VALLEY
OLD
MCH
STELLA ST
GEORGE ST
WALLACE
ANN AV
ST
MAHON AV
RD
WESTVIEW LK
POINT
SOUTH RIDGE CT
WALHALLA CT
BVD
GOLDRUSH
CFA
AV
ST
LYLE
Occasional Care
Beaconsfield Pmy
ARTHUR ST
TRYTHALL
BRISBANE ST
WOOD
RAILWAY
SOUTER ST
HORNER ST
ST
PRINCES
48
GLISMANN
WOODS
BOWMAN
JONES CT
DIGGERS
CT
JORDAN CT
JANET
O'NEIL
BEACONHILL DR
SCOTT
WHITAKER PL
LEE DR
RD
GORDON ST
ADAMSON
RD
BEACONSFIELD AV
Beaconsfield
Cmnty Cntr
GOFF
STATION ST
St Francis Xavier Catholic
2.2 m
KENILWORTH AV
Cardinia
SOLDIERS
Ent
KENILWORTH
HWY
Proposed Beaconsfield Community Complex
MAY
DESMOND CT
Retarding Basin
BROOKVALE
PRINCES FWY
HWY
PRINCES
WHITESIDE
RD
M1
WINDSOR DR
AV
ROYAL CR W
CR E
GLAMIS RI
CARLISLE DR
PANORAMA
LUDLOW CT
HAMPTON CT
Blue Gum Eastside
ROYAL
PORCHESTER
ROCHESTER
VST
BVD
STIRLING CCT
EDINBURGH
TANTALLON
WILTON GRN
CHATSWORTH CT
DR
BRODIE MW
BVD
HAMMERWOOD
GRN
EDWARD CT
EARLSFIELD
GEORGINA PL
REDMORE CT
MITCHELL
CORY PL
DR
CL
Ck
48
PRINCES
M1
Proposed Pakenham Bypass
WATER RD
THOMAS ST
AV
BRUNT
PAXTON CL

JOINS 581

A B C D E F G H J K L

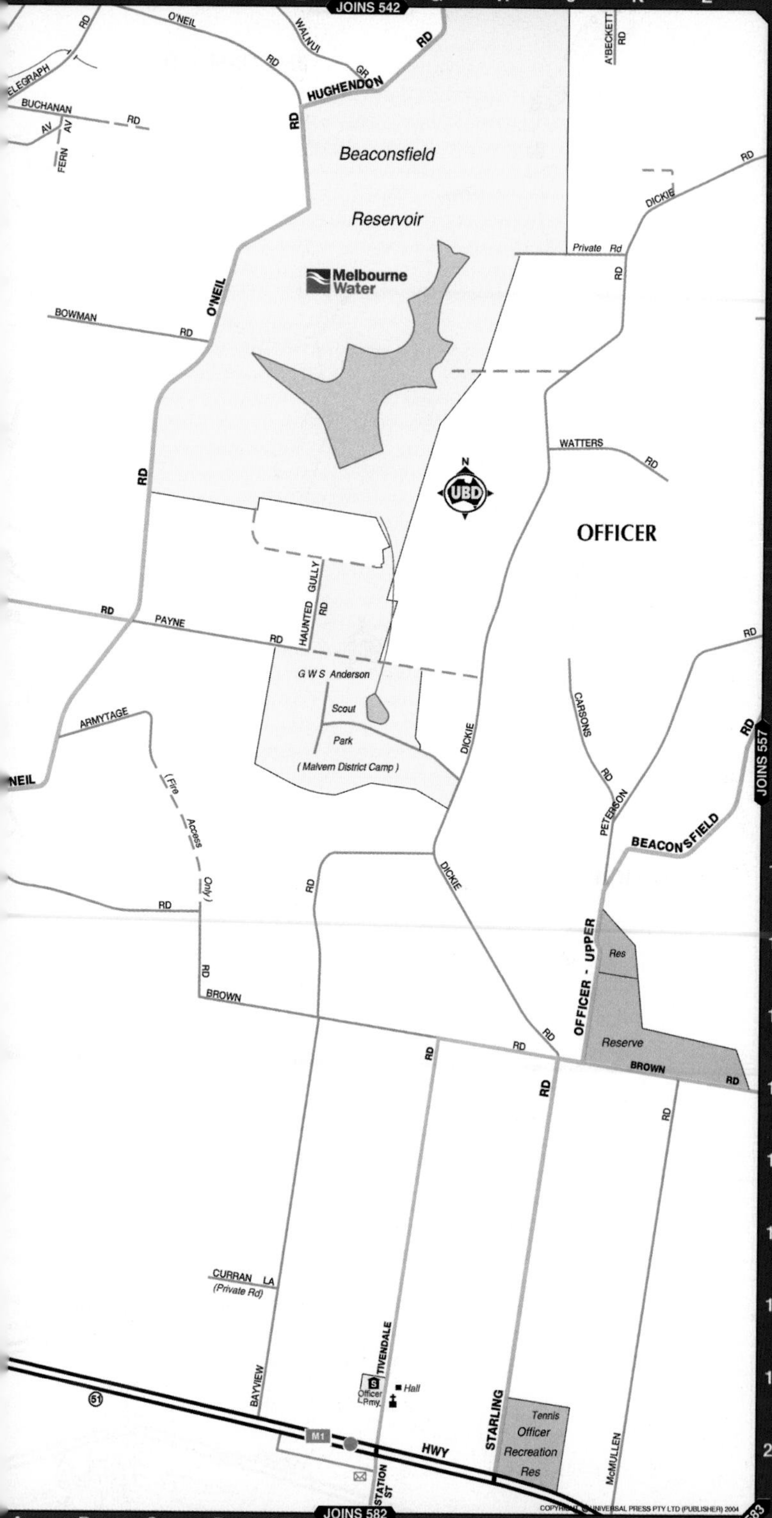

JOINS 542
JOINS 557
JOINS 582
583
O'NEIL RD
WALNUT GR
HUGHENDON RD
TELEGRAPH RD
BUCHANAN RD
FERN AV
A'BECKETT RD
Beaconsfield Reservoir
Melbourne Water
DICKIE RD
Private Rd
BOWMAN RD
O'NEIL RD
WATTERS RD
OFFICER
PAYNE RD
HAUNTED GULLY RD
G W S Anderson Scout Park
(Malvern District Camp)
ARMYTAGE
CARSONS RD
PETERSON
BEACONSFIELD RD
O'NEIL
(Fire Access Only)
RD
DICKIE RD
RD
Res
Reserve
OFFICER - UPPER
BROWN RD
BROWN RD
RD
RD
RD
CURRAN LA
(Private Rd)
BAYVIEW
TIVENDALE
Hall
Officer Prmy.
51
M1
HWY
STARLING
Tennis
Officer Recreation Res
McMULLEN
STATION ST
COPYRIGHT © UNIVERSAL PRESS PTY LTD (PUBLISHER) 2004

542
LIMIT OF MAPS

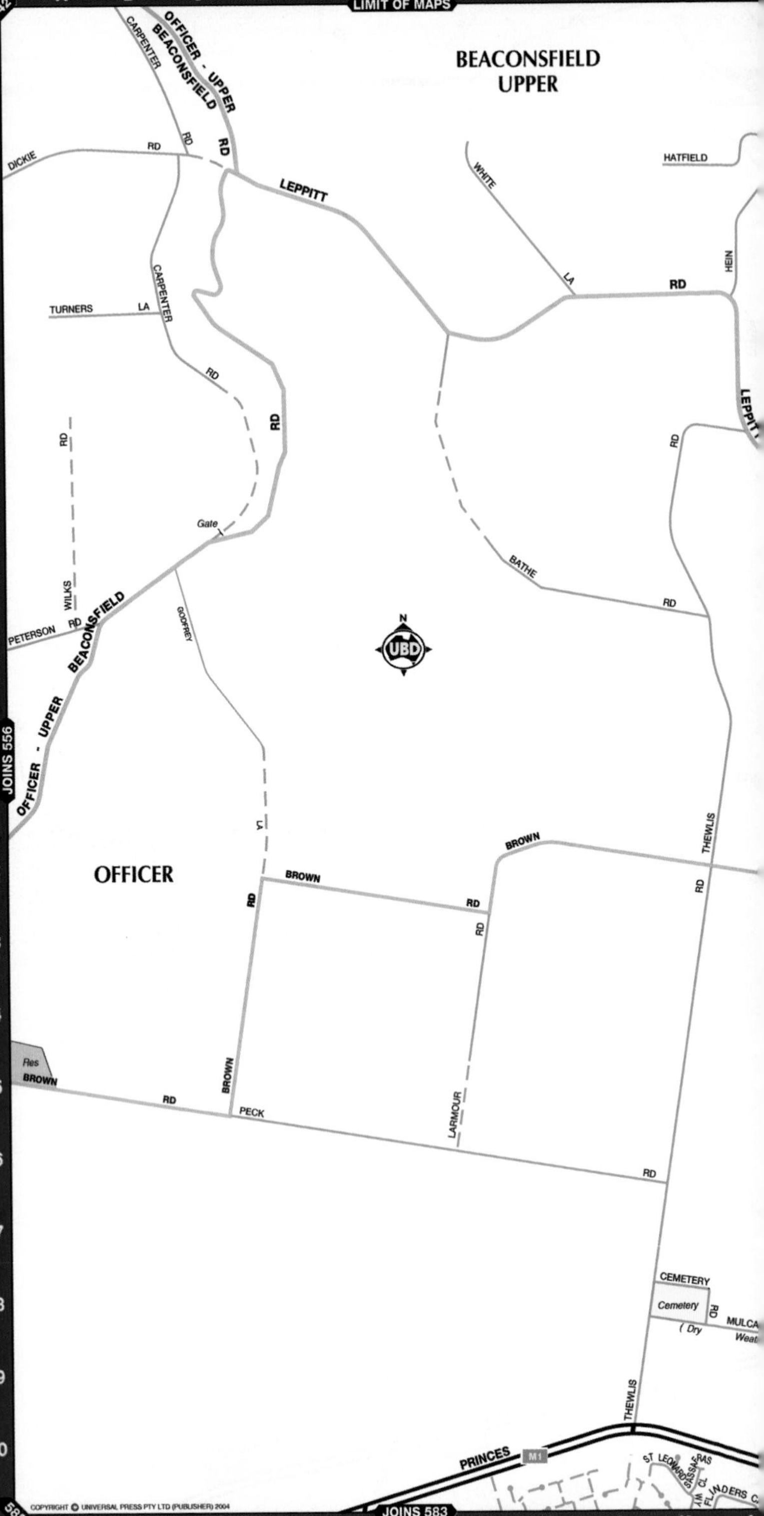

BEACONSFIELD UPPER

OFFICER - UPPER BEACONSFIELD RD
CARPENTER RD
DICKIE RD
LEPPITT RD
WHITE LA
HATFIELD
HEIN
TURNERS LA
WILKS RD
Gate
PETERSON RD
GODFREY LA
BATHE RD
THEWLIS RD
BROWN RD
LARMOUR RD
PECK RD
Res
OFFICER
CEMETERY RD
Cemetery
MULCA
(Dry Weat
PRINCES M1
ST LEONARDS
SASSAFRAS
CL
WY
FLINDERS

JOINS 556
JOINS 583
582

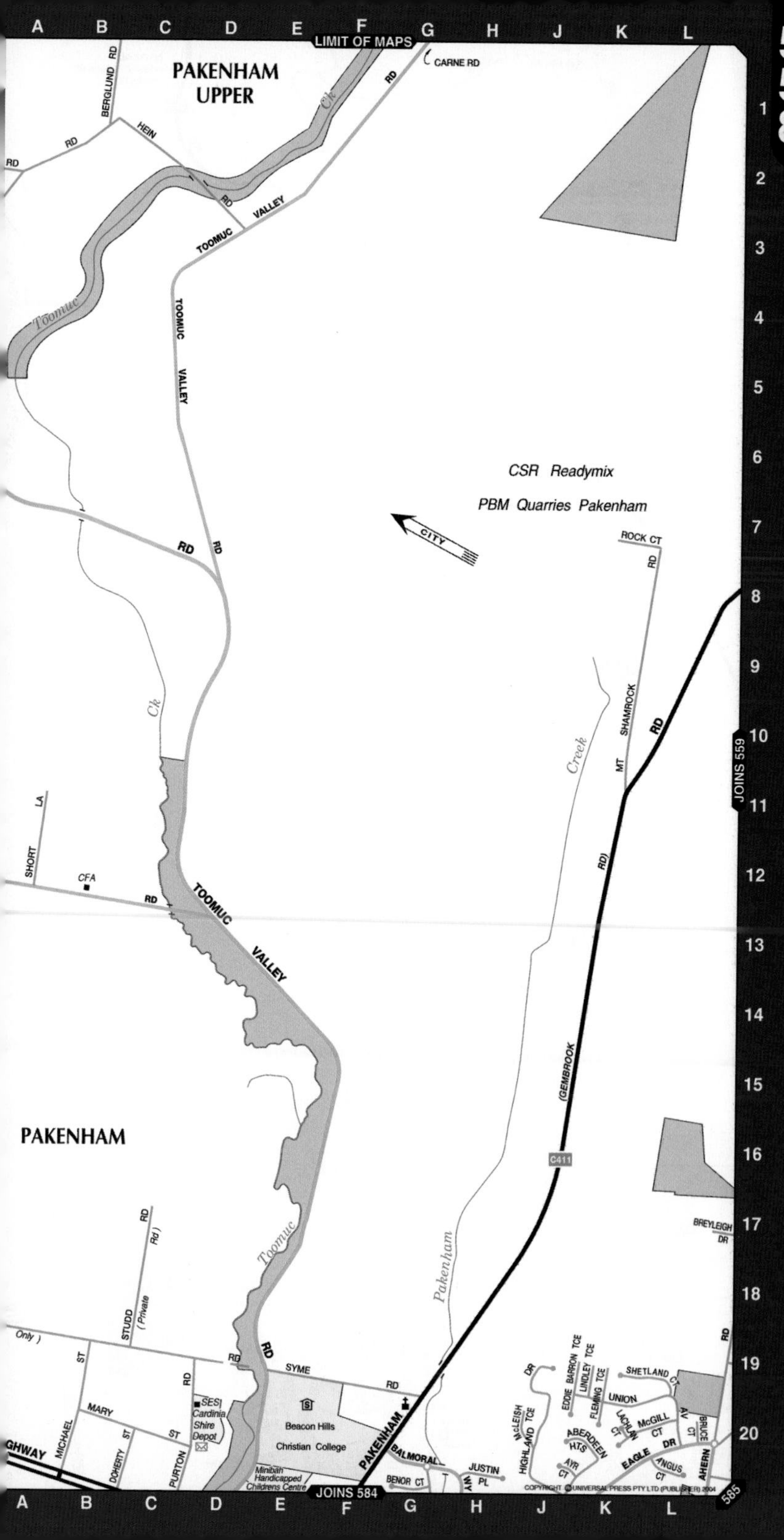

A B C D E F G H J K L
LIMIT OF MAPS
PAKENHAM UPPER
BERGLUND RD
HEIN RD
CARNE RD
Toomuc Ck
TOOMUC VALLEY RD
CSR Readymix
PBM Quarries Pakenham
CITY
ROCK CT
MT SHAMROCK RD
Creek
(GEMBROOK RD)
C411
JOINS 559
SHORT LA
CFA
PAKENHAM
Toomuc
Pakenham
BREYLEIGH DR
STUDD RD (Private Rd)
Only)
SYME RD
ST
MARY ST
MICHAEL
DOHERTY ST
PURTON RD
SES Cardinia Shire Depot
Beacon Hills Christian College
Minibah Handicapped Childrens Centre
PAKENHAM
BALMORAL WAY
BENOR CT
JUSTIN PL
McLEISH DR
HIGHLAND TCE
EDDIE BARRON TCE
LINDLEY TCE
FLEMING TCE
SHETLAND CT
UNION
LACHLAN CT
McGILL CT
AV
BRUCE CT
ABERDEEN
H.T.S.
AYR CT
EAGLE DR
ANGUS CT
AHERN RD
GHWAY
JOINS 584
COPYRIGHT © UNIVERSAL PRESS PTY LTD (PUBLISHER) 2004
1 2 3 4 5 6 7 8 9 10 11 12 13 14 15 16 17 18 19 20

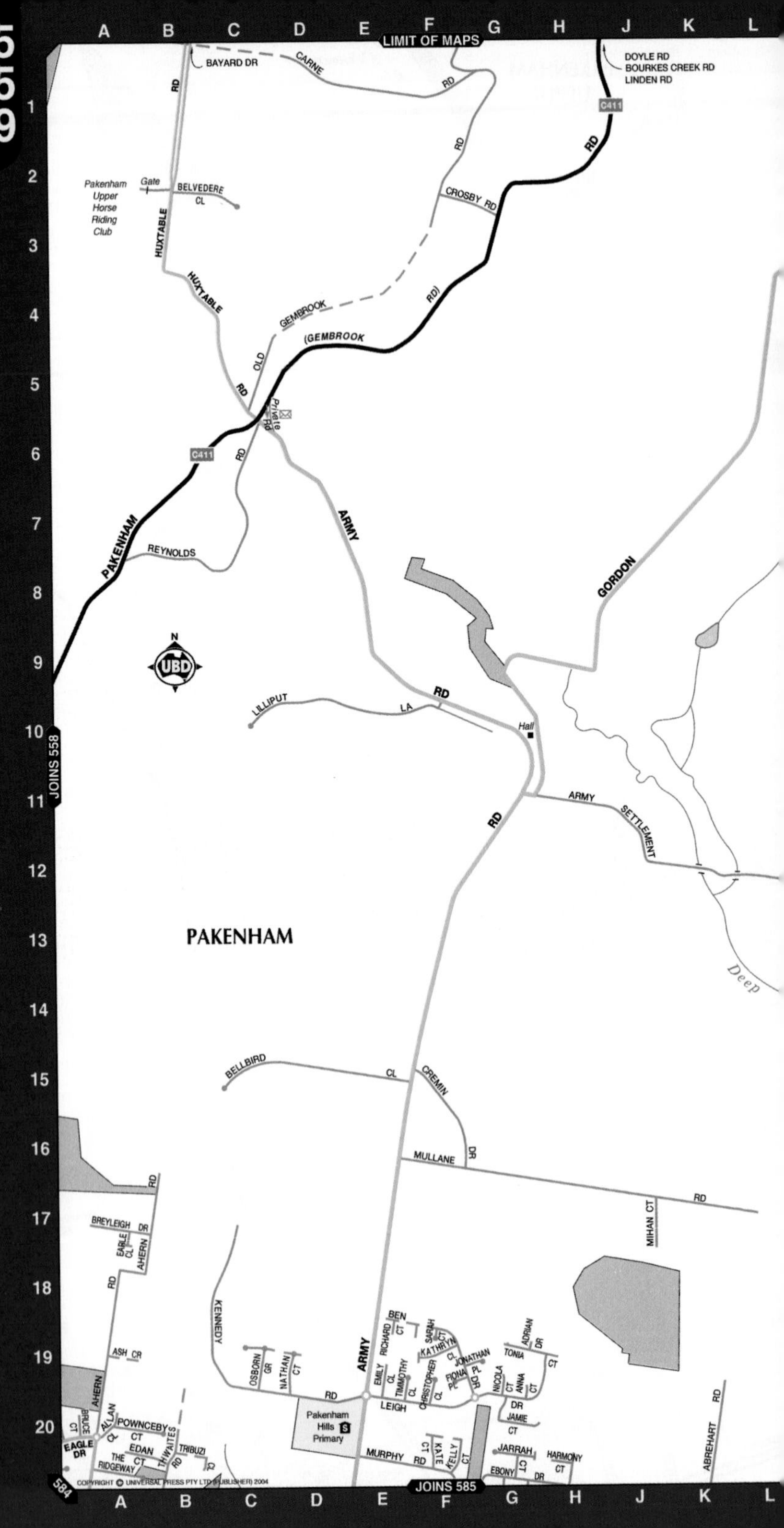

JOINS 558
584
JOINS 585

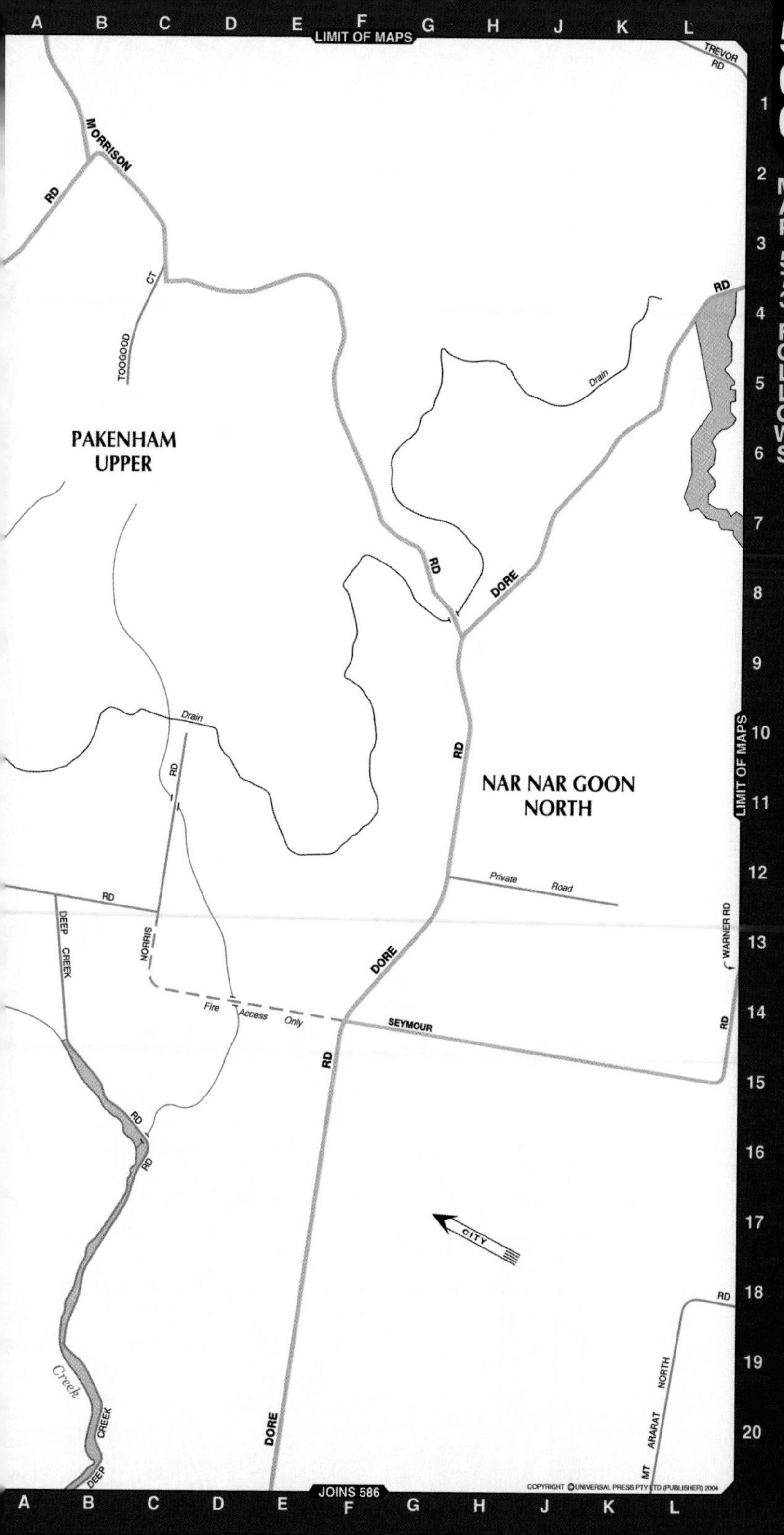

A
B
C
D
E
F
G
H
J
K
L
LIMIT OF MAPS
TREVOR RD
MORRISON
RD
CT
TOOGOOD
RD
Drain
PAKENHAM UPPER
RD
DORE
Drain
RD
RD
NAR NAR GOON NORTH
Private Road
RD
DEEP CREEK
NORRIS
WARNER RD
DORE
Fire Access Only
SEYMOUR
RD
RD
RD
RD
CITY
RD
Creek
CREEK
DEEP
DORE
NORTH
ARARAT
MT
LIMIT OF MAPS
MAP 573 FOLLOWS
1
2
3
4
5
6
7
8
9
10
11
12
13
14
15
16
17
18
19
20

JOINS 586

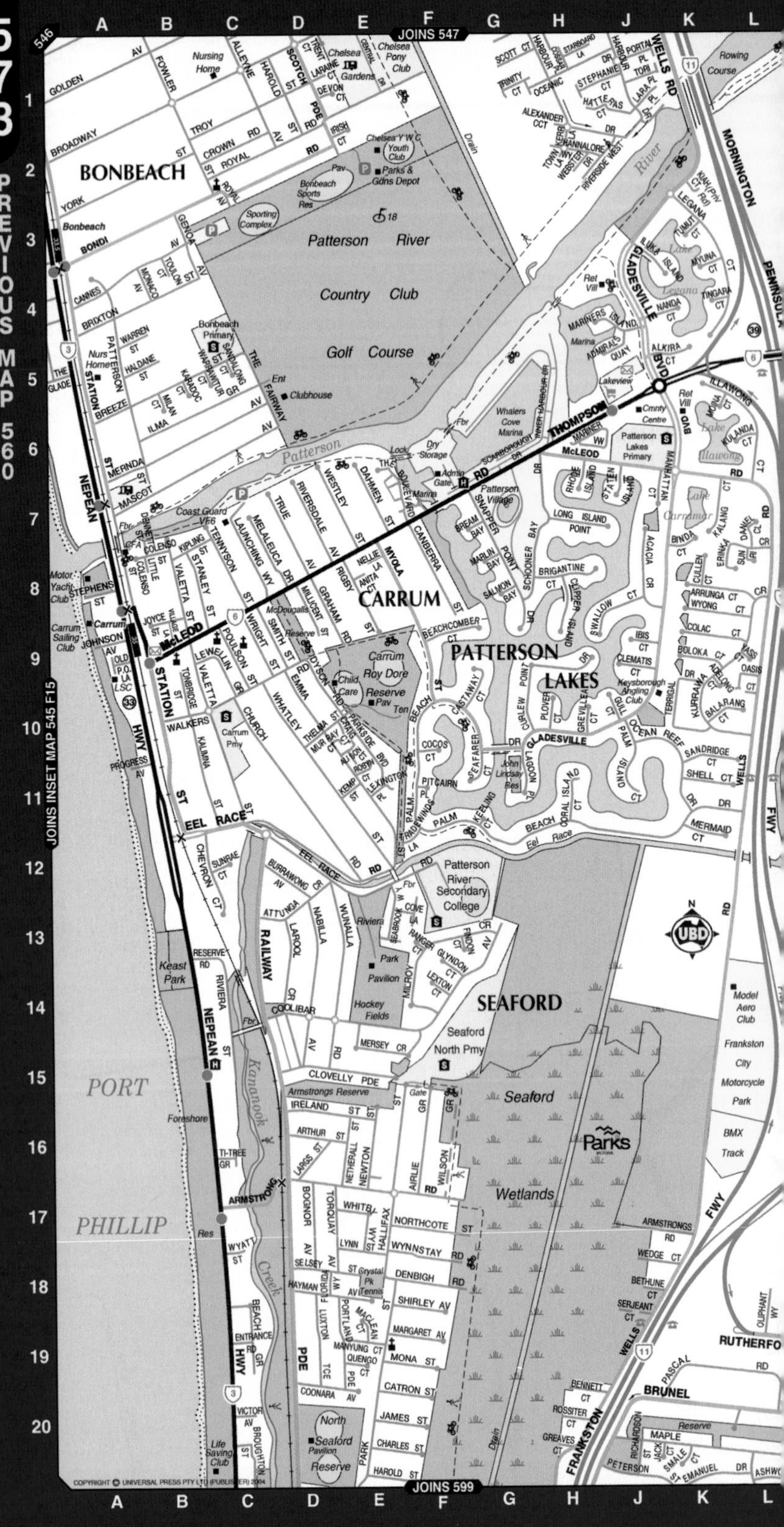

573
PREVIOUS MAP 560
JOINS INSET MAP 545 F15
JOINS 547
JOINS 599
546
A B C D E F G H J K L
1 2 3 4 5 6 7 8 9 10 11 12 13 14 15 16 17 18 19 20
BONBEACH
CARRUM
PATTERSON LAKES
SEAFORD
PORT PHILLIP
Patterson River Country Club Golf Course
Chelsea Pony Club
Chelsea Gardens
Nursing Home
Chelsea Y W C Youth Club
Parks & Gdns Depot
Bonbeach Sports Res
Sporting Complex
Bonbeach Primary
Nurs Home
Clubhouse
Coast Guard VF6
Motor Yacht Club
Carrum Sailing Club
LSC
Carrum Pmy
McDougalls Reserve
Carrum Roy Dore Reserve
Child Care
Whalers Cove Marina
Dry Storage
Admin Gate
Marina
Patterson Village
Patterson Lakes Primary
Cmnty Centre
Ret Vill
Marina
Lakeview
Keysborough Angling Club
John Lindsay Res
Patterson River Secondary College
Riviera
Park Pavilion
Hockey Fields
Seaford North Pmy
Armstrongs Reserve
Keast Park
Foreshore
Seaford Wetlands
Parks
Model Aero Club
Frankston City Motorcycle Park
BMX Track
North Seaford Reserve Pavilion
Life Saving Club
Crystal Pk Tennis
Patterson River
Kananook Creek
Eel Race
Lake Legana
Lake Illawong
Lake Carramar
NEPEAN HWY
McLEOD RD
THOMPSON RD
WELLS RD
MORNINGTON PENINSULA FWY
FRANKSTON FWY
GLADESVILLE BVD
EEL RACE RD
STATION ST
RAILWAY PDE
BEACH RD
PATTERSON
RUTHERFORD RD
BRUNEL
UBD
COPYRIGHT © UNIVERSAL PRESS PTY LTD (PUBLISHER) 2004

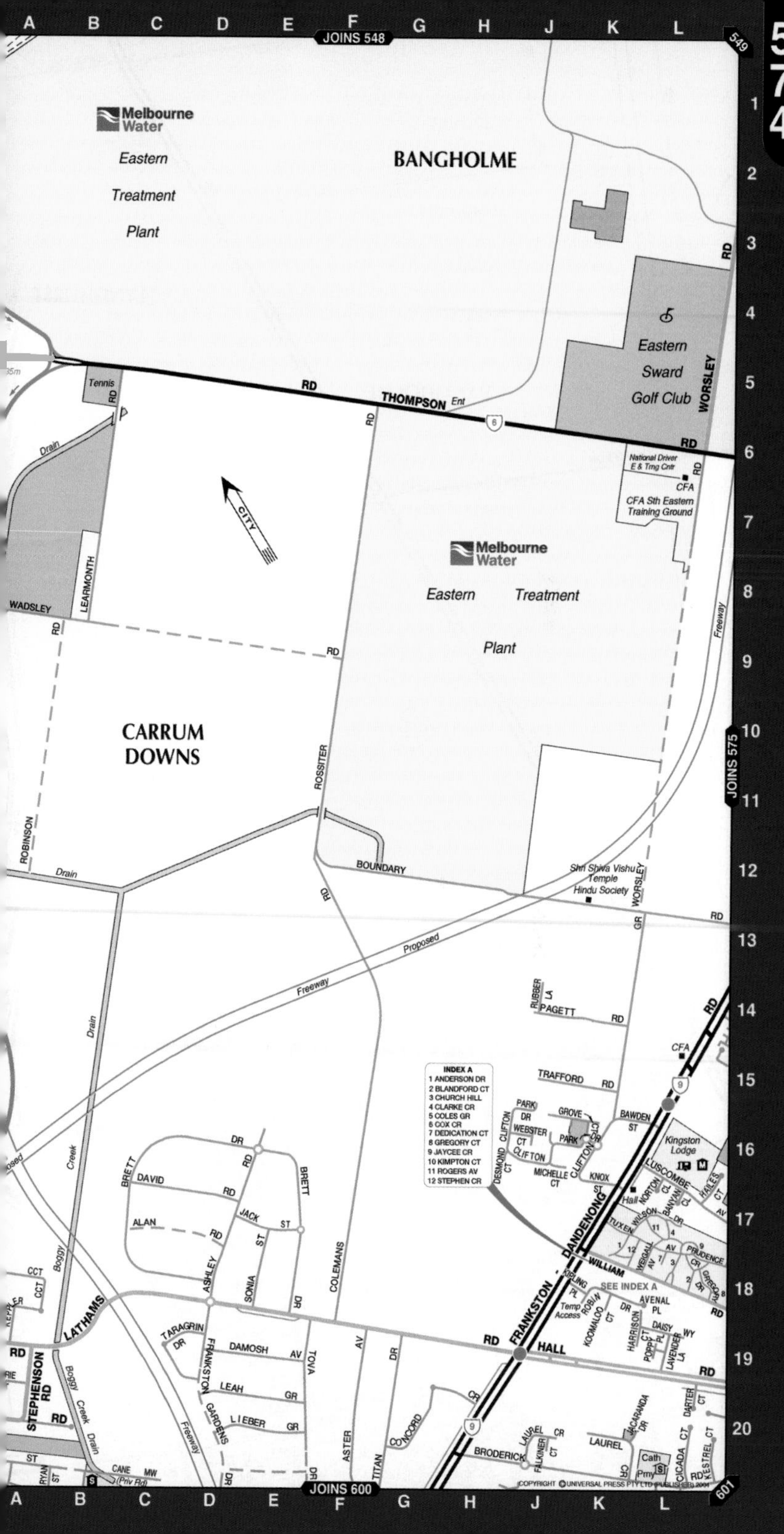

JOINS 548
549
Melbourne Water
Eastern Treatment Plant
BANGHOLME
Eastern Sward Golf Club
WORSLEY RD
THOMPSON RD
Tennis
National Driver E & Trng Cntr
CFA
CFA Sth Eastern Training Ground
Melbourne Water
Eastern Treatment Plant
WADSLEY RD
LEARMONTH
CITY
CARRUM DOWNS
ROSSITER RD
ROBINSON RD
BOUNDARY RD
Shri Shiva Vishu Temple Hindu Society
WORSLEY GR
Freeway Proposed
JOINS 575
INDEX A
1 ANDERSON DR
2 BLANDFORD CT
3 CHURCH HILL
4 CLARKE CR
5 COLES GR
6 COX CR
7 DEDICATION CT
8 GREGORY CT
9 JAYCEE CR
10 KIMPTON CT
11 ROGERS AV
12 STEPHEN CR
RUBBER LA
PAGETT RD
TRAFFORD RD
PARK DR
GROVE
WEBSTER CT
CLIFTON CT
DESMOND CT
MICHELLE CT
BAWDEN ST
KNOX ST
Kingston Lodge
LUSCOMBE
Hall
NORTON CL
BANYAN CL
HAKES
TUXEN
WILSON
WEEGALL AV
PRUDENCE
WILLIAM
SEE INDEX A
AVENAL PL
DAISY WY
LAVENDER LA
FRANKSTON - DANDENONG RD
KIPLING PL
ROBIN
KOOMALOO CT
HARRISON
POPPY PL
HALL RD
BRETT DR
DAVID RD
ALAN RD
JACK ST
SONIA ST
ASHLEY
COLEMANS
Boggy Creek Drain
LATHAMS RD
TARAGRIN DR
DAMOSH AV
TOVA
FRANKSTON GARDENS DR
LEAH GR
LIEBER GR
STEPHENSON RD
ASTER AV
TITAN DR
CONCORD CR
BRODERICK
LAUREL CR
FALKINER CT
LAUREL
JACARANDA DR
DARTER CT
CICADA CT
KESTREL CT
Cath
Pmy
CANE MW
RYAN ST
JOINS 600
601

JOINS 549

JOINS 574

BANGHOLME

LYNDHURST

CARRUM DOWNS

SKYE

Bunurong Memorial Park

Eastern Sward Golf Club

Sandhurst Club North

Maybanke Rk

Proposed Sandhurst Golf & Residential Development

Carrum Downs Recreation Reserve

Tennis

Oval

Ret Village Nursing Home

Nursing Home

Retarding Basin

Kingston Lodge

Carrum Downs Pmy

Banyan Res

Brotherhood of St Laurence

G K Tucker Res MCH

Cmnty Cntr

Carrum Downs Secondary College Under Construction

The Downs Carrum Downs Regional Shopping Centre

Temp Access RD

For street names, see INDEX A on Map 574, Ref H15

JOINS 601

A B C D E F G H J K L
JOINS 550
551
GLASSCOCKS RD
TAYLORS RD
CITY
Proposed Lyndhurst EASTERN Energy Terminal Station
DANDENONG - HASTINGS RD
A780
6
RD
Golf Course
Course
lubhouse
Horse Hospital
45
JOINS 577
WESTERN PORT HWY
WEDGE RD
Kennel Control Council Park
Meeting Room
Judging Rings
Dam
Canine Sporting Complex
CRANBOURNE WEST
1 2 3 4 5 6 7 8 9 10 11 12 13 14 15 16 17 18 19 20
JOINS 602
603
COPYRIGHT ©UNIVERSAL PRESS PTY LTD (PUBLISHER) 2004

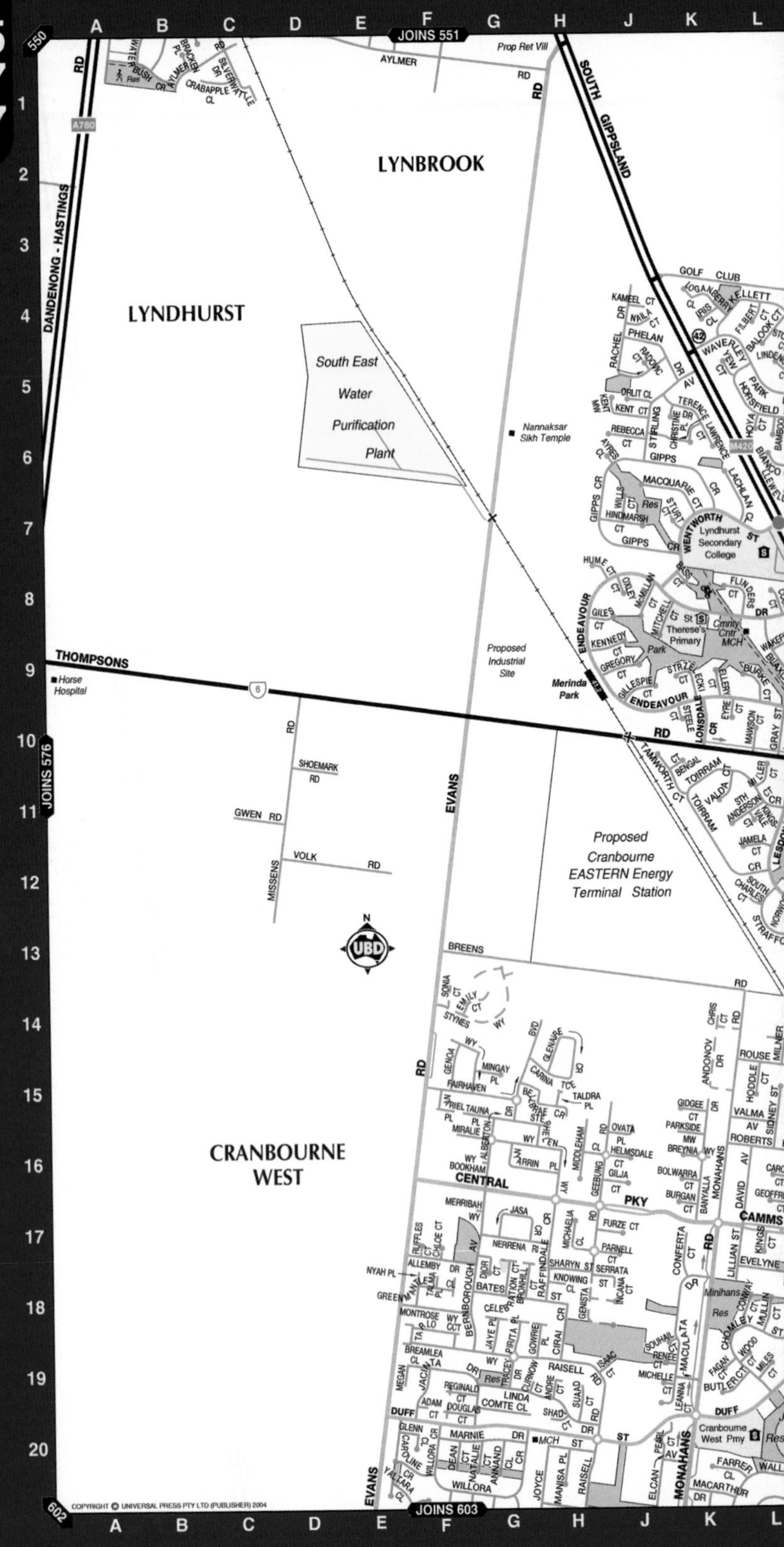

JOINS 551
LYNBROOK
LYNDHURST
South East Water Purification Plant
Nannaksar Sikh Temple
DANDENONG - HASTINGS RD
SOUTH GIPPSLAND
THOMPSONS
Horse Hospital
Proposed Industrial Site
Merinda Park
Proposed Cranbourne EASTERN Energy Terminal Station
EVANS
SHOEMARK RD
GWEN RD
VOLK RD
MISSENS
BREENS
CRANBOURNE WEST
CENTRAL PKY
CAMMS
MONAHANS
DUFF
Lyndhurst Secondary College
St Therese's Primary
Cranbourne West Pmy
JOINS 576
JOINS 603
COPYRIGHT © UNIVERSAL PRESS PTY LTD (PUBLISHER) 2004

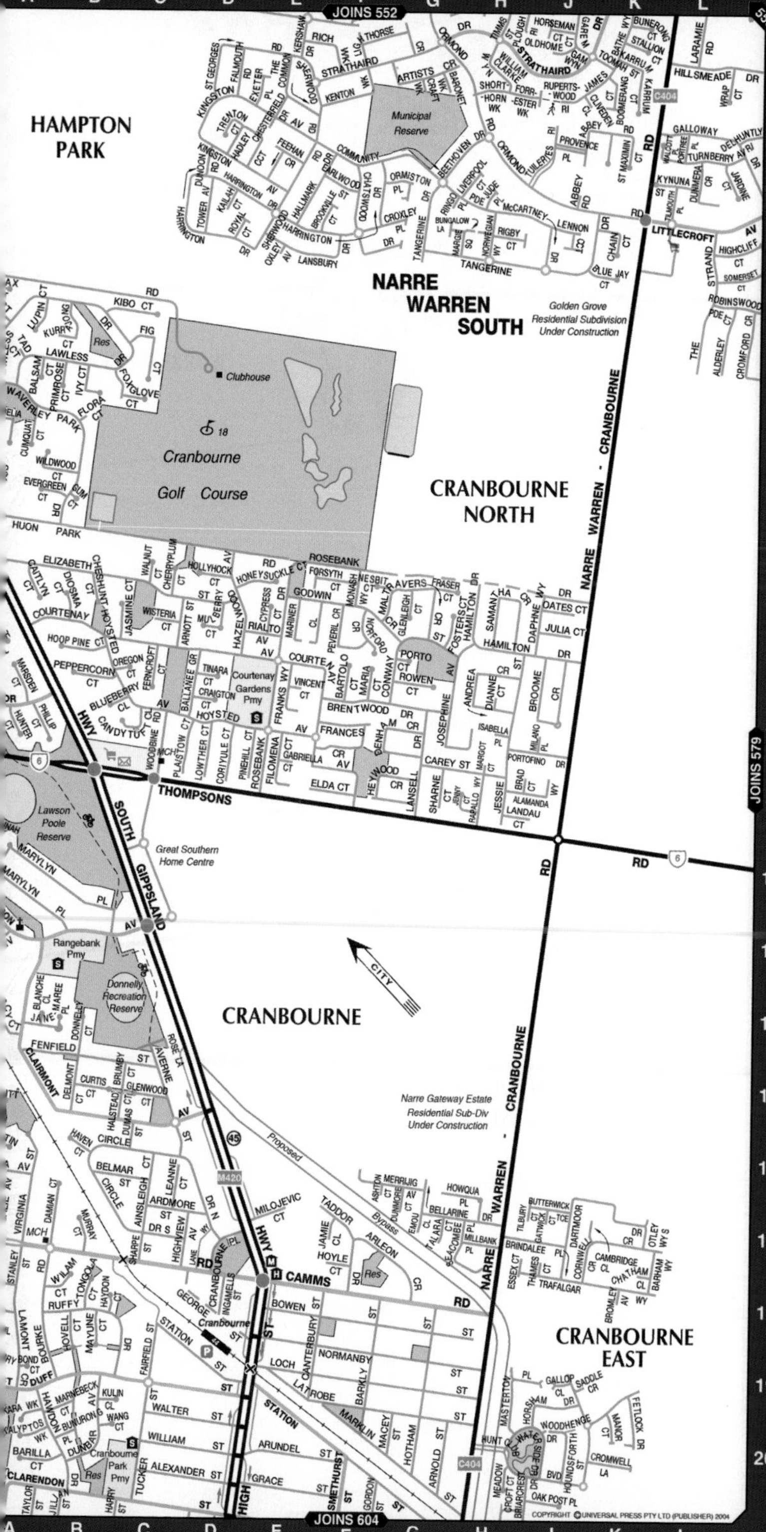

JOINS 552

553

A B C D E F G H J K L

1 2 3 4 5 6 7 8 9 10 11 12 13 14 15 16 17 18 19 20

HAMPTON PARK

NARRE WARREN SOUTH

Municipal Reserve

Golden Grove Residential Subdivision Under Construction

Clubhouse

Cranbourne Golf Course

CRANBOURNE NORTH

NARRE WARREN - CRANBOURNE RD

Courtenay Gardens Pmy

JOINS 579

THOMPSONS RD

SOUTH GIPPSLAND HWY

Lawson Poole Reserve

Great Southern Home Centre

Rangebank Pmy

Donnelly Recreation Reserve

CITY

CRANBOURNE

Narre Gateway Estate Residential Sub-Div Under Construction

Proposed Bypass

CAMMS RD

Cranbourne

CRANBOURNE EAST

Cranbourne Park Pmy

HIGH ST

JOINS 604

JOINS 553
552
JOINS 578

NARRE WARREN SOUTH

CRANBOURNE NORTH

CRANBOURNE EAST

THOMPSONS RD

BERWICK - CRANBOURNE

GARDEN ST

MAYFIELD RD

COLLISON RD

HEATHER GR

PATTERSONS RD

LIMIT OF MAPS
604

JOINS 554

555

A B C D E F G H J K L

BERWICK

The Chase at Berwick
Residential Subdivision
Under Construction

CLYDE NORTH

GREAVES RD
O'SHEA
HEDGELEY
CLYDE RD
SOLDIERS RD
Private Rd
GRICES RD
POUND RD
THOMPSONS RD
HARDYS RD
TUCKERS RD
Drain
St Catherines Cath Pmy
C407
CITY

JOINS 581

1 2 3 4 5 6 7 8 9 10 11 12 13 14 15 16 17 18 19 20

LIMIT OF MAPS

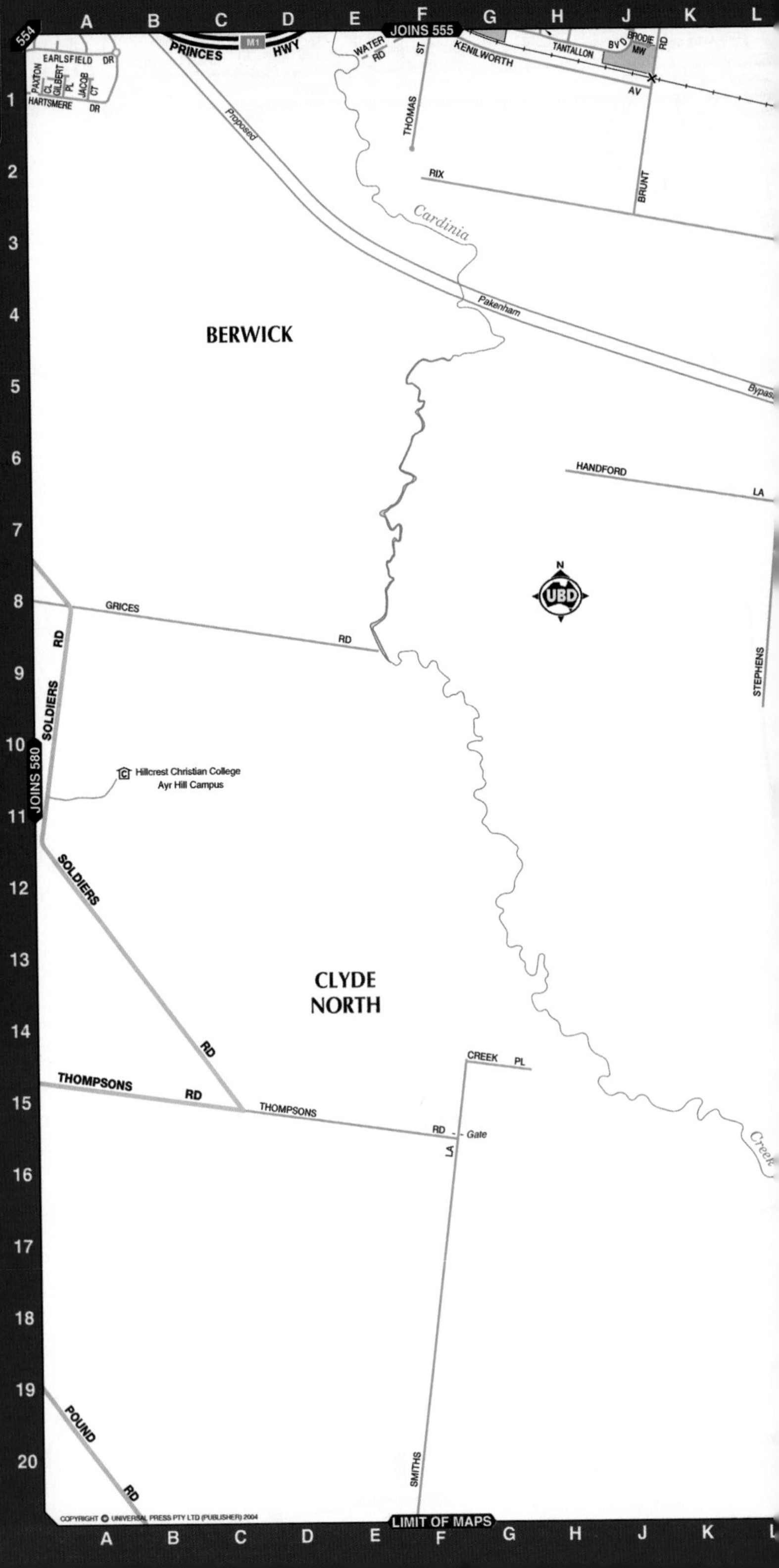

JOINS 555

554

EARLSFIELD DR
PAXTON CL
GILBERT PL
JACOB CT
HARTSMERE DR
PRINCES HWY
M1
WATER RD
THOMAS ST
KENILWORTH AV
TANTALLON BVD
BRODIE MW
BRUNT RD
RIX
Cardinia
Proposed Pakenham Bypass
BERWICK
HANDFORD LA
GRICES RD
SOLDIERS RD
STEPHENS
Hillcrest Christian College Ayr Hill Campus
CLYDE NORTH
THOMPSONS RD
CREEK PL
LA
Gate
Creek
POUND RD
SMITHS

JOINS 580

LIMIT OF MAPS

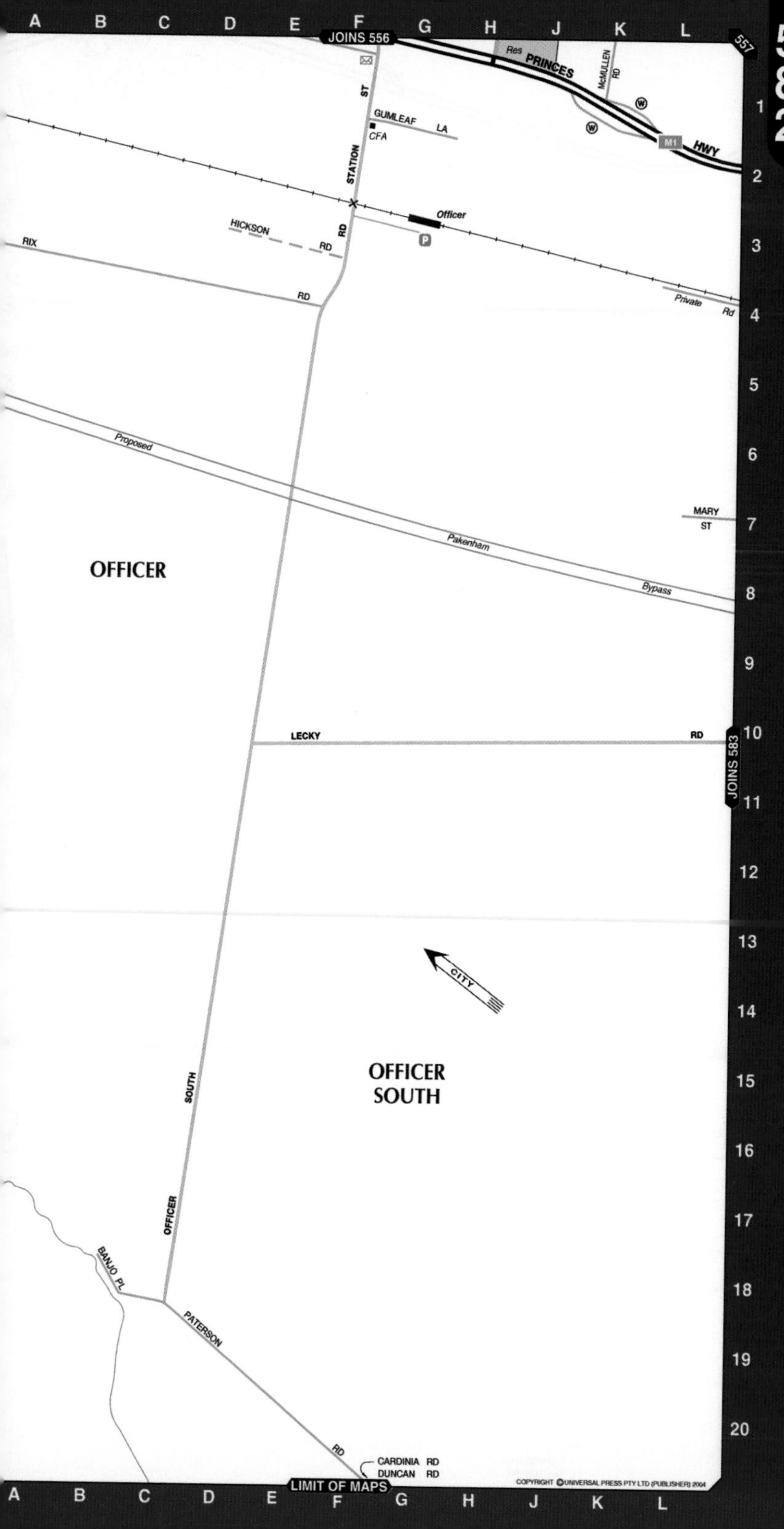
A B C D E F G H J K L
JOINS 556
557
Res
PRINCES
HWY
M1
McMULLEN RD
STATION ST
GUMLEAF LA
CFA
STATION RD
Officer
HICKSON RD
RIX RD
Private Rd
Proposed
Pakenham
Bypass
MARY ST
OFFICER
LECKY RD
JOINS 583
CITY
OFFICER SOUTH
SOUTH
OFFICER
BANJO PL
PATERSON RD
CARDINIA RD
DUNCAN RD
LIMIT OF MAPS
COPYRIGHT © UNIVERSAL PRESS PTY LTD (PUBLISHER) 2004
1 2 3 4 5 6 7 8 9 10 11 12 13 14 15 16 17 18 19 20

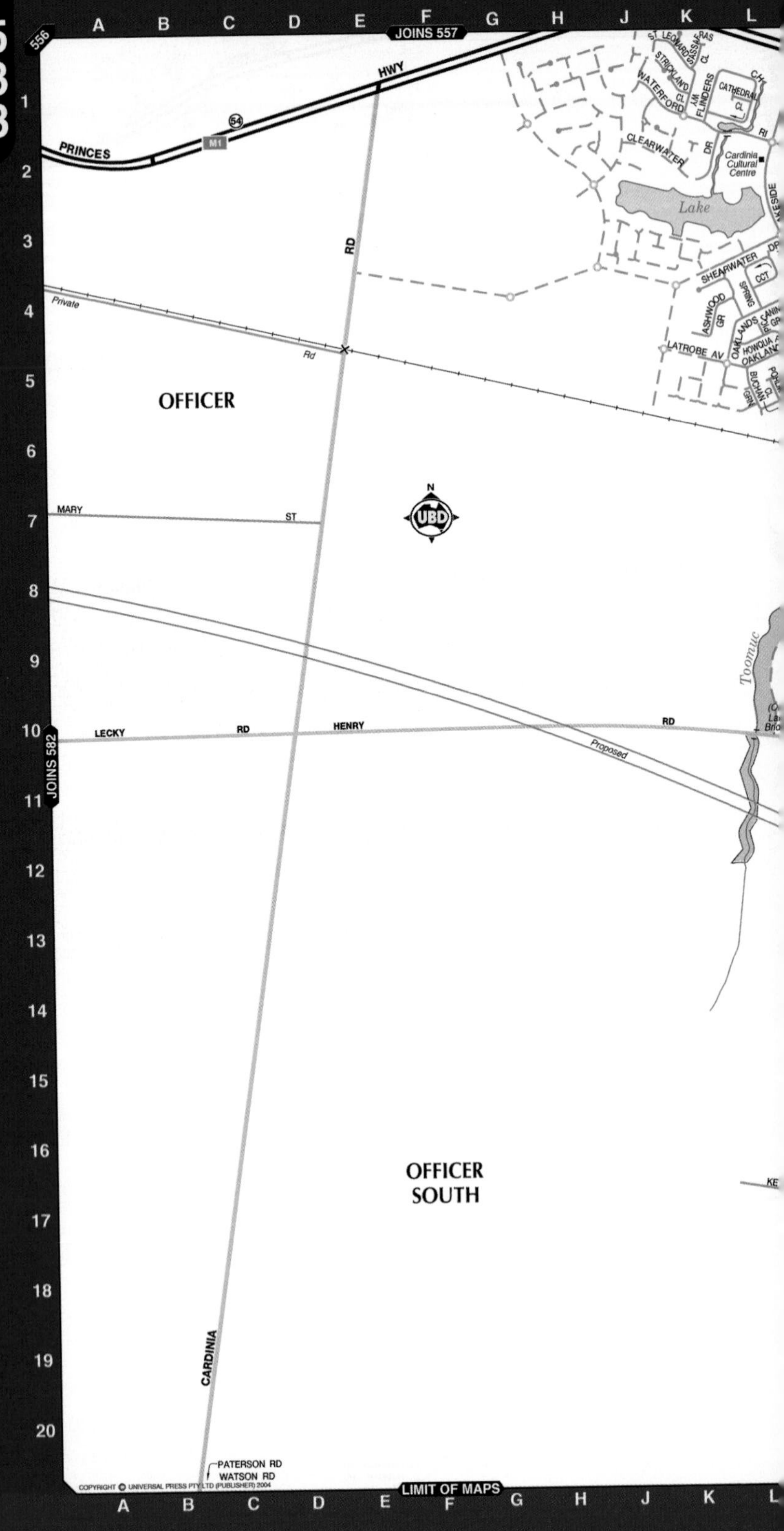
JOINS 557
556
PRINCES
HWY
M1
54
RD
Private
Rd
OFFICER
MARY
ST
LECKY
RD
HENRY
RD
Proposed
JOINS 582
OFFICER
SOUTH
CARDINIA
PATERSON RD
WATSON RD
LIMIT OF MAPS
ST LEONARDS
STRICKLAND
WATERFORD
CL
WY
FLINDERS
CATHEDRAL
CL
CLEARWATER
DR
Cardinia
Cultural
Centre
Lake
SHEARWATER
SPRING
CCT
ASHWOOD
GR
OAKLANDS
LATROBE AV
BUCHAN
Toomuc

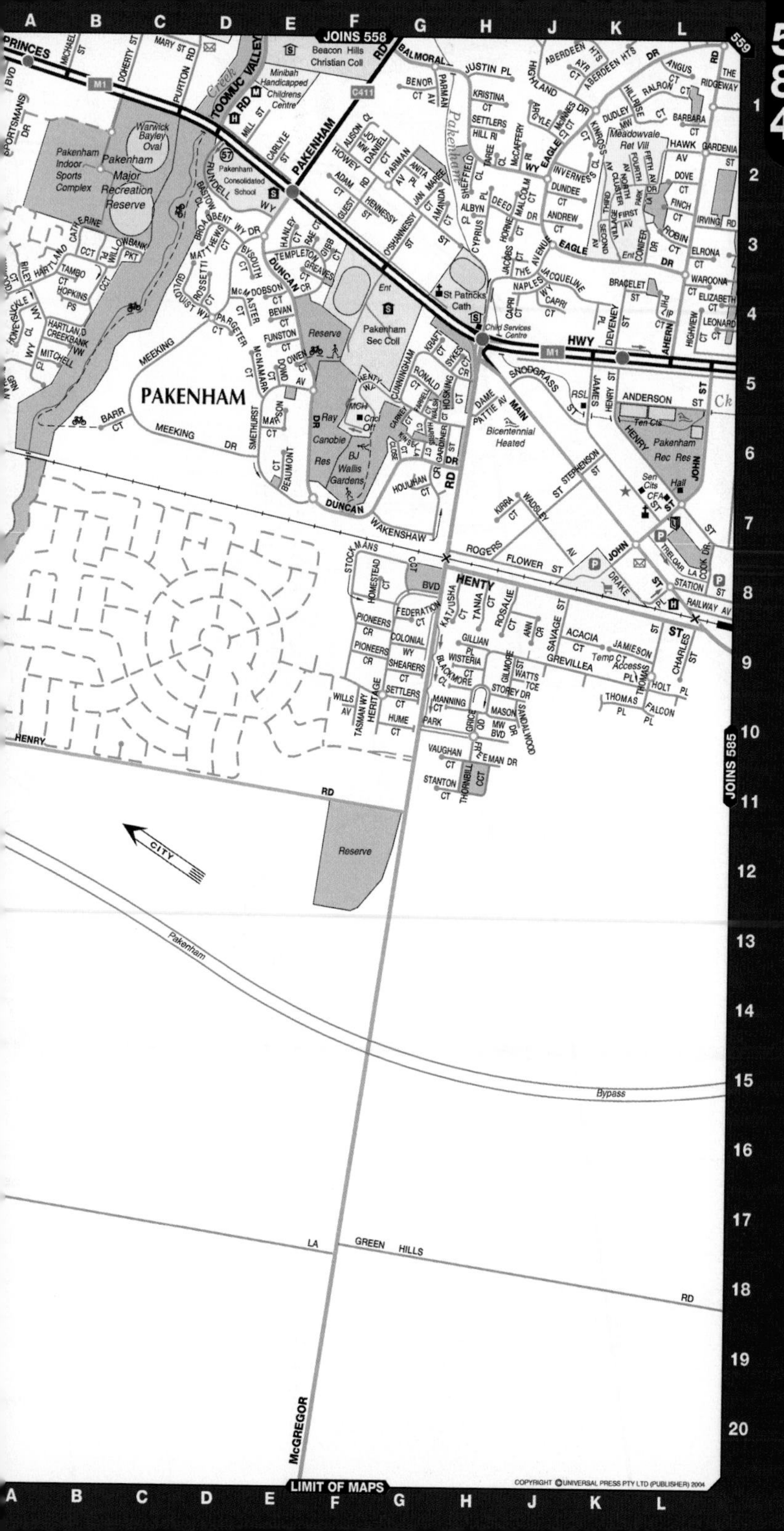

584
JOINS 558
559
JOINS 585
LIMIT OF MAPS
PAKENHAM
PRINCES
HWY
M1
C411
PAKENHAM RD
TOOMUC VALLEY RD
Beacon Hills Christian Coll
Minibah Handicapped Childrens Centre
Warwick Bayley Oval
Pakenham Indoor Sports Complex
Pakenham Major Recreation Reserve
Pakenham Consolidated School
Pakenham Sec Coll
St Patricks Cath
Child Services Centre
Reserve
Ray Canobie Res
BJ Wallis Gardens
MCH
Cncl Off
Bicentennial Heated
RSL
Ten Cts
Pakenham Rec Res
Hall
Sen Cits
CFA
Meadowvale Ret Vill
Temp Ct Access
MAIN
McGREGOR RD
DUNCAN DR
MEEKING DR
HENRY RD
GREEN HILLS RD
CITY
Pakenham Bypass
A B C D E F G H J K L
1 2 3 4 5 6 7 8 9 10 11 12 13 14 15 16 17 18 19 20

1 2 3 4 5 6 7 8 9 10 11 12 13 14 15 16 17 18 19 20

Pakenham Hills Pmy
MURPHY
EDAN CT
TRIBU CL
THE RIDGEWAY
THWAITES
BARBARA CT
MARTIN PL
GARDENIA
KATE CT
KELLY CT
KARA CT
CONRAD CT
CLAIRE CL
BALTASER DR
WYNEN CT
EBONY RD
ARMY RD
JARRAH
HARMONY CT
EBONY
IVORY DR
MAHOGANY CT
COBRAM CT
DR
ABREHART RD
M1
Clubhouse
JOHANNA CT
AHERN RD
IRVING
DAMIEN CT
GERARD CT
RACHAEL CT
CT RD
ELRONA CT
MIKKELL CT
KYLIE CT
WAROONA CT
GREGORY CT
ELIZABETH CT
PETER CT
HIGHVIEW CT
LEONARD CT
SUZANNE CT
ATKINS
Kennedy Creek
PRINCES
60
DARVELL CT
RD N DR
SIR THOMAS DR
BROOKE CT
MONTCLAIRE CT
POMMEL ST
BROADHURST RD
FINTON WY CT
NABILLA CT
RACECOURSE
DALMOR CT
Cmnty Cntr & MCH
HEIDI CT ST
NICHOLAS CT
MARTINGALE PL
OAKTREE DR
FAIRWAY CT
JOHN ST
ST
STELLA PL
MARIA CR
AMY CL
DIANE CL
PARAMOUNT AV
DUNBARTON DR
CANTLE CL
POMMEL DR
BARRINGTON
SIMON
SHE
PRIFF RI
JOSEPH CT
ELEANOR CT DR
ASHTON PL
HARNESS PL
18
Pakenham & District Golf Course
DR
Hall
ISAAC CT
SIMON
P
Pakenham
LORRAINE CT
BLUEGRASS CR
BRIDLE PL
KINGSTON
STIRRUP CT
BLUEGRASS CR
BARRINGTON WY
Grandstand
CAMERON
HENRY
KING ST
DERHAM DR
Reserve
Deep
CONE PL
COOK DR
P
Pakenham Racecourse & Showground
STATION ST
HENRY ST
RAILWAY
AV
P
PINEHILL
56
Pakenham
CHARLES ST
BALD HILL
RACECOURSE
CAMPBELL ST
The Nestle Company
Industrial Park
Creek
PINEHILL DR
EMBREY CT
RD
O'SULLIVAN ST
HILL ST
Deep
PEET ST
RYAN
RD
C422
Proposed
RD
LIVESTOCK RD
EXCHANGE DR
Victorian Livestock Exchange
Creek
GREEN HILLS RD
KOO WEE RUP
McDONALDS DRAIN
BOURKE

JOINS 584

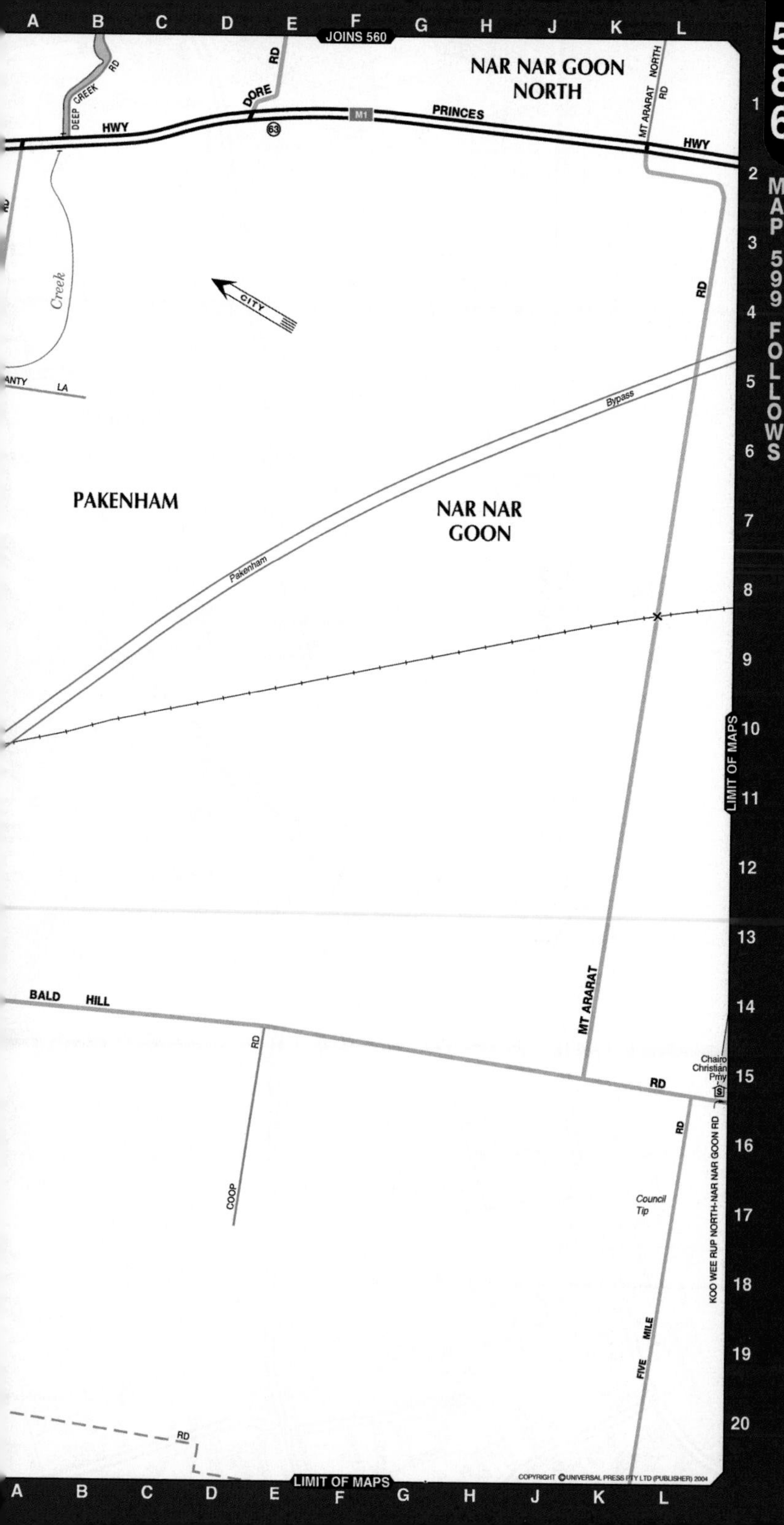

586
JOINS 560
NAR NAR GOON NORTH
DEEP CREEK RD
DORE RD
PRINCES HWY
M1
63
MT ARARAT NORTH RD
HWY
Creek
CITY
RD
ANTY LA
Pakenham Bypass
PAKENHAM
NAR NAR GOON
MAP 599 FOLLOWS
LIMIT OF MAPS
BALD HILL RD
MT ARARAT
COOP RD
Chairo Christian Pmy
FIVE MILE RD
Council Tip
KOO WEE RUP NORTH-NAR NAR GOON RD
RD
LIMIT OF MAPS
COPYRIGHT © UNIVERSAL PRESS PTY LTD (PUBLISHER) 2004

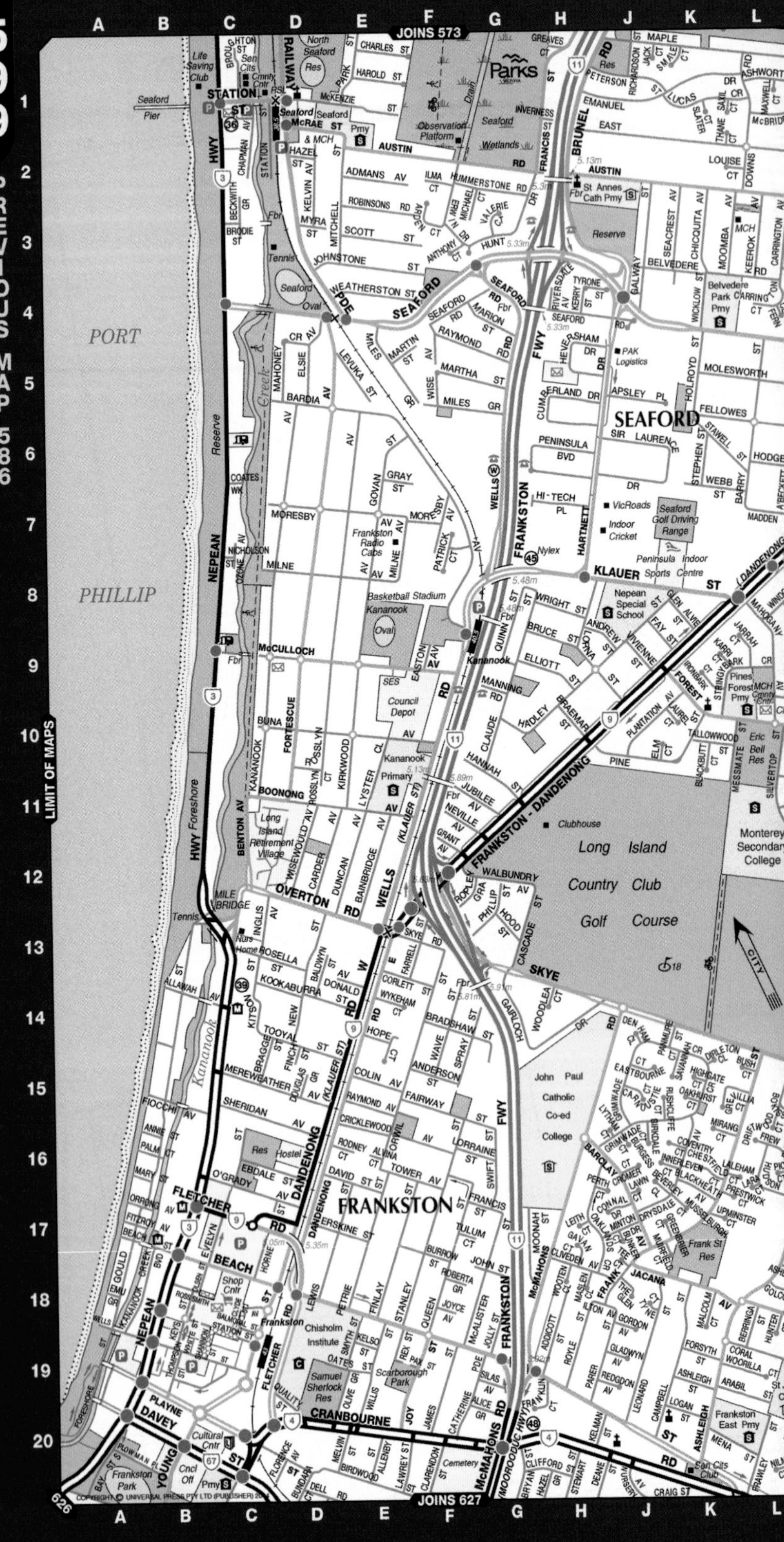

A B C D E F G H J K L
JOINS 573
PREVIOUS MAP 586
LIMIT OF MAPS
PORT
PHILLIP
SEAFORD
FRANKSTON
Long Island
Country Club
Golf Course
Seaford Wetlands
Observation Platform
Seaford Pier
Life Saving Club
STATION ST
NEPEAN HWY
FRANKSTON FWY
WELLS RD
FRANKSTON - DANDENONG RD
KLAUER ST
SEAFORD RD
OVERTON RD
SKYE RD
CRANBOURNE RD
McMAHONS RD
MOOROODUC HWY
BEACH ST
FLETCHER RD
DAVEY ST
YOUNG ST
PLAYNE ST
AUSTIN RD
BRUNEL RD
McCULLOCH ST
Kananook
Frankston
Kananook Creek
Mile Bridge
Basketball Stadium
Kananook Oval
Council Depot
Kananook Primary
Monterey Secondary College
John Paul Catholic Co-ed College
Chisholm Institute
Samuel Sherlock Res
Scarborough Park
Frankston Park
Cultural Cntr
Frankston East Pmy
Nepean Special School
Seaford Golf Driving Range
Peninsula Indoor Sports Centre
Long Island Retirement Village
Belvedere Park Pmy
CITY
JOINS 627
626
COPYRIGHT © UNIVERSAL PRESS PTY LTD (PUBLISHER)

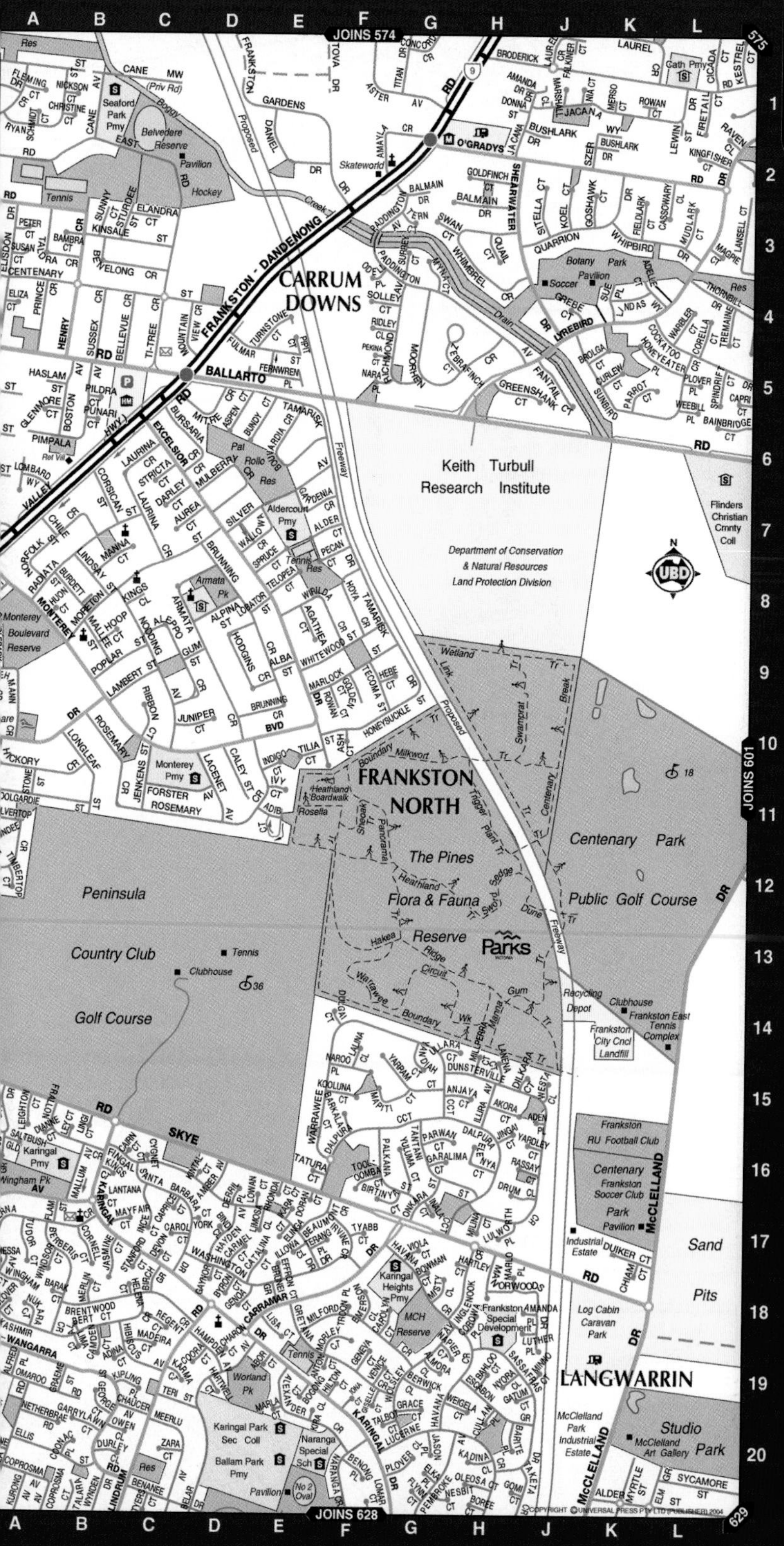

JOINS 574
JOINS 601
JOINS 628
575
629
CARRUM DOWNS
FRANKSTON NORTH
LANGWARRIN
FRANKSTON - DANDENONG RD
BALLARTO RD
SKYE RD
McCLELLAND DR
KARINGAL DR
CARRAMAR DR
WASHINGTON DR
DUIKER RD
Keith Turbull Research Institute
Department of Conservation & Natural Resources Land Protection Division
Flinders Christian Cmnty Coll
Peninsula Country Club Golf Course
Tennis
Clubhouse
The Pines Flora & Fauna Reserve
Parks
Centenary Park Public Golf Course
Recycling Depot
Frankston East Tennis Complex
Frankston City Cncl Landfill
Frankston RU Football Club
Centenary Frankston Soccer Club Park
Pavilion
Industrial Estate
Sand Pits
Log Cabin Caravan Park
McClelland Park Industrial Estate
Studio Park
McClelland Art Gallery
Botany Park
Pavilion
Soccer
Belvedere Reserve
Seaford Park Pmy
Hockey
Tennis
Skateworld
O'GRADYS
Cath Pmy
Pat Rollo Res
Aldercourt Pmy
Armata Pk
Monterey Boulevard Reserve
Monterey Pmy
Heathland Boardwalk
Karingal Pmy
Wingham Pk
Karingal Heights Pmy
MCH Reserve
Frankston Special Development
Worland Pk
Karingal Park Sec Coll
Ballam Park Pmy
Naranga Special Sch
No 2 Oval
Pavilion
Res
Freeway Proposed
COPYRIGHT © UNIVERSAL PRESS PTY LTD (PUBLISHER) 2004

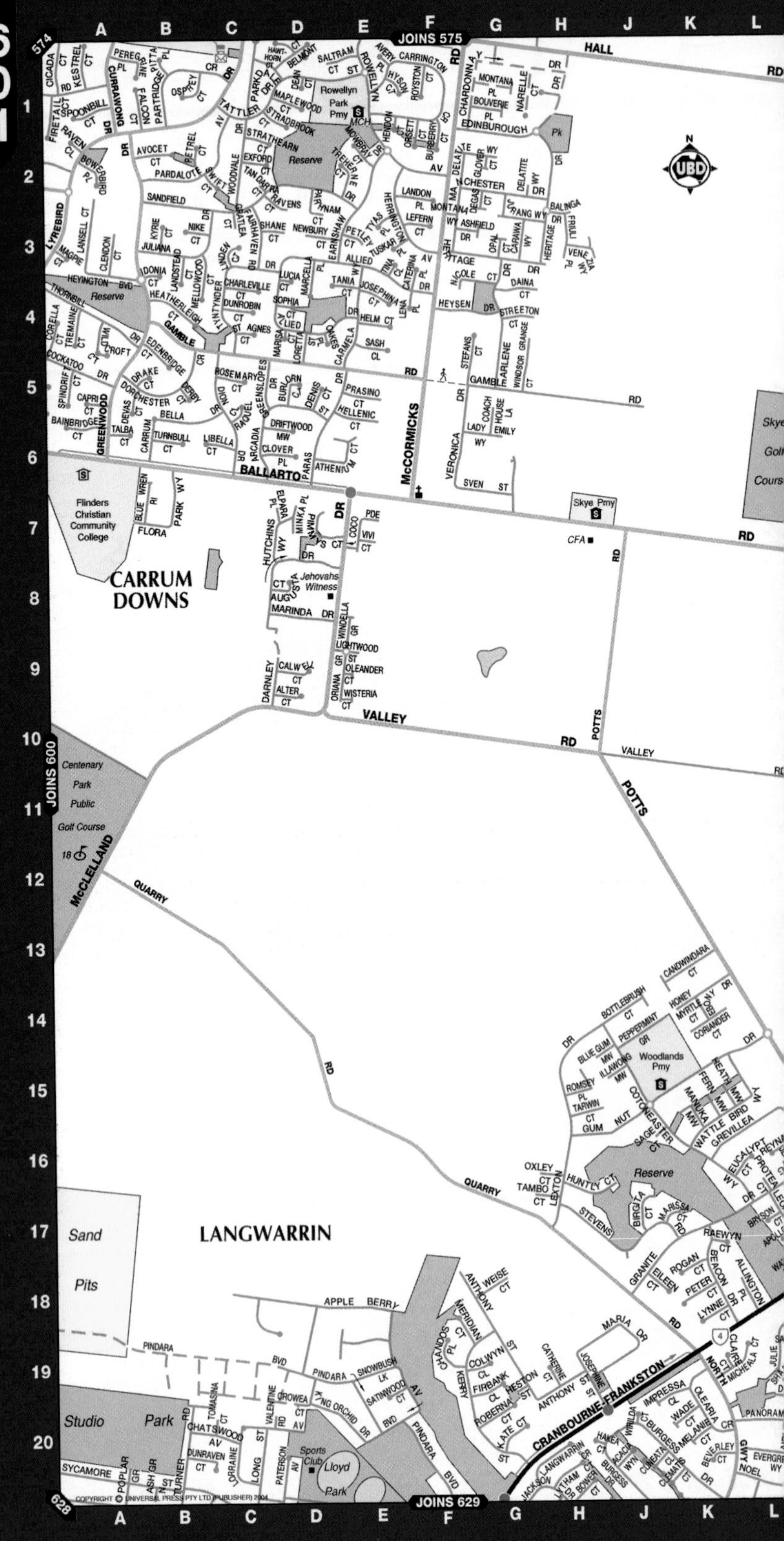

JOINS 575
JOINS 600
JOINS 629
574
628
CARRUM DOWNS
LANGWARRIN
HALL RD
McCORMICKS RD
BALLARTO RD
GAMBLE RD
VALLEY RD
POTTS RD
QUARRY RD
McCLELLAND DR
CRANBOURNE - FRANKSTON RD
PINDARA BVD
Rowellyn Park Pmy
Reserve
Heyington Reserve
Flinders Christian Community College
Skye Pmy
CFA
Jehovahs Witness
Centenary Park Public Golf Course
Woodlands Pmy
Sand Pits
Studio Park
Sports Club
Lloyd Park
Skye Golf Course
UBD
COPYRIGHT © UNIVERSAL PRESS PTY LTD (PUBLISHER) 2004

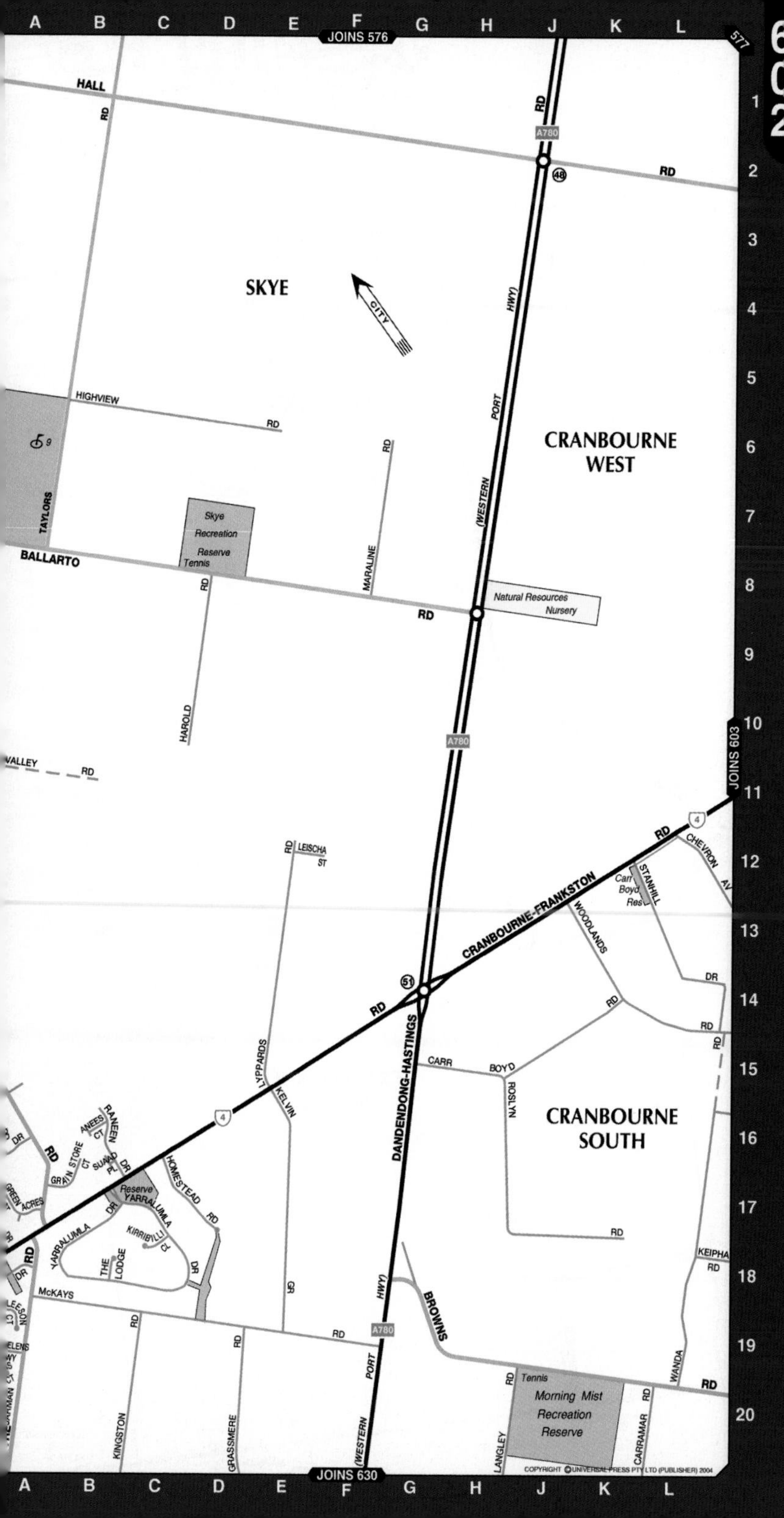

602
JOINS 576
577
JOINS 603
JOINS 630
SKYE
CITY
CRANBOURNE WEST
CRANBOURNE SOUTH
HALL RD
RD
WESTERN PORT HWY
A780
48
51
HIGHVIEW RD
TAYLORS
BALLARTO RD
Skye Recreation Reserve
Tennis
HAROLD RD
MARALINE RD
Natural Resources Nursery
VALLEY RD
LEISCHA ST
LYPPARDS RD
KELVIN GR
CRANBOURNE-FRANKSTON RD
4
CHEVRON AV
STANHILL DR
WOODLANDS RD
DANDENDONG-HASTINGS RD
CARR RD
BOYD
ROSLYN RD
HOMESTEAD RD
RANEEN DR
ANEES CT
STORE CT
SUAAD PL
GRAIN
GREEN ACRES
YARRALUMLA DR
Reserve
KIRRIBILLI CL
THE LODGE
McKAYS RD
KINGSTON RD
GRASSMERE RD
BROWNS RD
Tennis
Morning Mist Recreation Reserve
LANGLEY RD
CARRAMAR RD
WANDA
KEIPHA RD
LEESON CT
ELENS
COPYRIGHT © UNIVERSAL PRESS PTY LTD (PUBLISHER) 2004

JOINS 577

CRANBOURNE WEST

CRANBOURNE

Amstel Golf Course

Clubhouse

Ranfurlie Golf Course

CRANBOURNE SOUTH

HALL RD

EVANS RD

SLADEN RD

MONAHANS RD

CRANBOURNE - FRANKSTON

BALLARTO RD

STEVENSONS RD

PEARCEDALE RD

BROWNS RD

SMITHS LA

CHEVRON AV

STANHILL DR

WOODLANDS RD

SURREY RD

KEIPHA RD

WANDA

VAIL PL

St Peters College

Transfer Stn & Recycling Depot

Stevensons Rd Landfill

Depot

Royal

Native Botanic Garden

Wylies

Cranbourne South Pmy

WATERDALE DR

SCOTT RD

MADELYN CT

FLETCHER RD

KELLY RD

FIONA DR

JOINS 602

LIMIT OF MAPS

JOINS 578

579

MAP 625 FOLLOWS

CRANBOURNE EAST

JUNCTION VILLAGE

DEVON MEADOWS

Cranbourne Recreation Reserve

Botanic Gardens

Cranbourne Secondary College

Cranbourne Christian Cmnty College

Chisholm Institute Cranbourne Campus

Casey City Council (The Complex)

Cranbourne Park Shopping Centre

Cranbourne Primary

St Agathas Catholic

Cranbourne Soccer & Cricket

Racecourse

Stringybark Picnic Area

Botanic Gardens Retirement Village

BERWICK - CRANBOURNE RD

SOUTH GIPPSLAND HWY

CAMERON ST

BALLARTO RD

CRAIG RD

HIGH ST

LIMIT OF MAPS

BROWNS RD
FINSBURY RD
WORTHING RD

PREVIOUS MAP 604

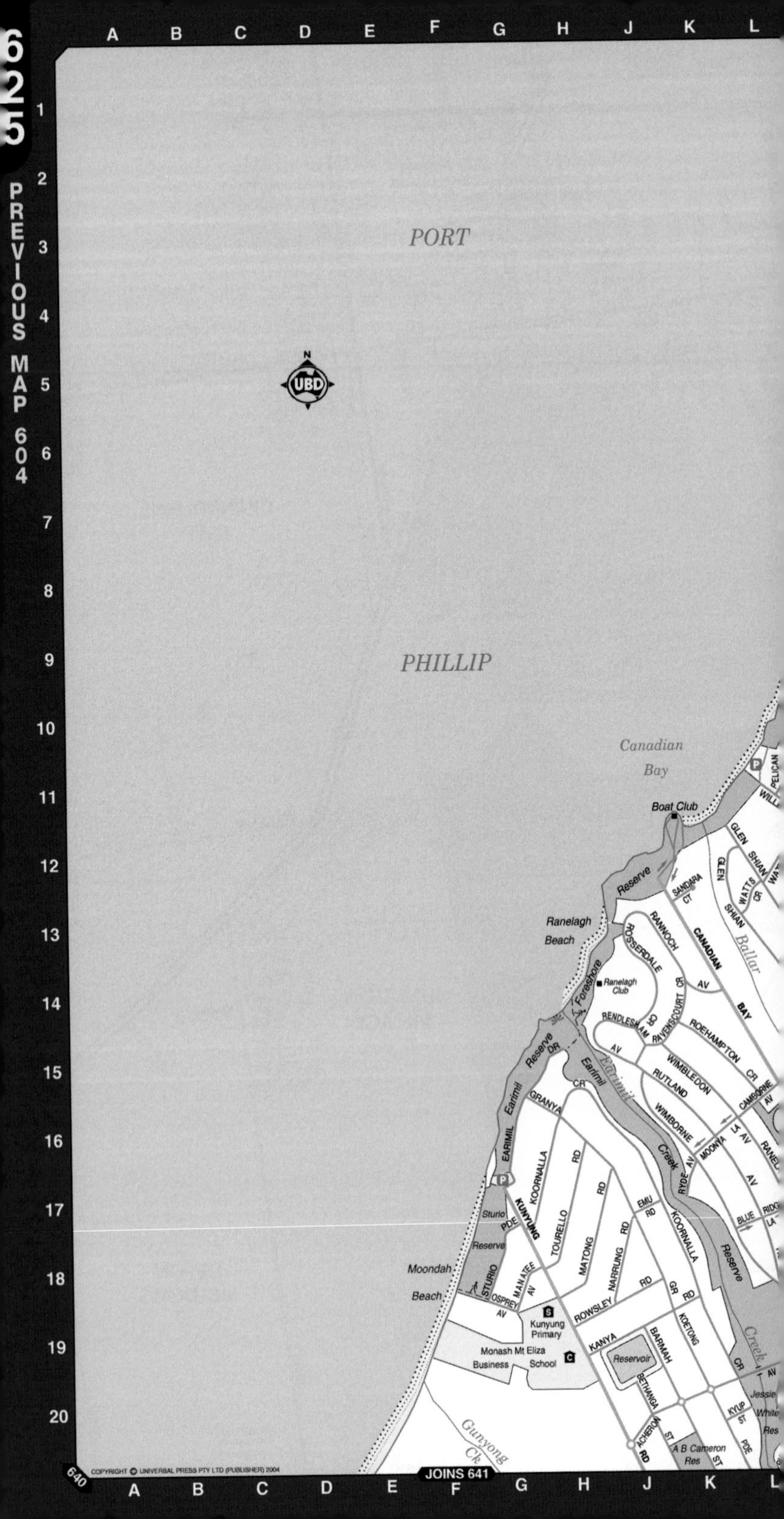

640
JOINS 641

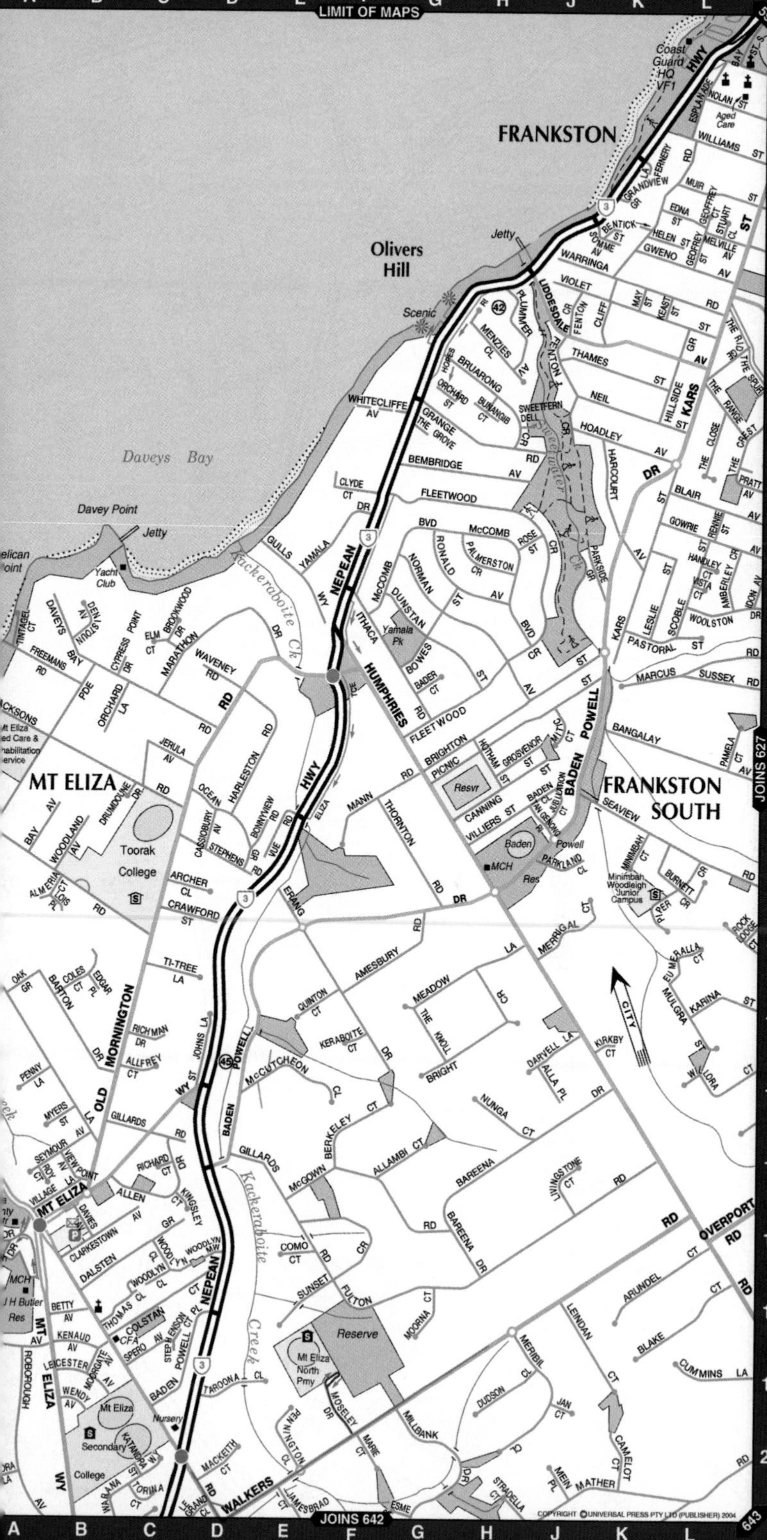

LIMIT OF MAPS

FRANKSTON

Olivers Hill

Daveys Bay

Davey Point

MT ELIZA

FRANKSTON SOUTH

Toorak College

Coast Guard HQ VF1

Yacht Club

Mt Eliza Aged Care & Rehabilitation Service

Minimbah Woodleigh Junior Campus

Mt Eliza North Pmy

Mt Eliza Secondary College

Reserve

Resvr

Baden Powell Res

MCH

J H Butler Res

Nursery

Kackeraboite Ck

Kackeraboite Creek

Sweetwater Ck

NEPEAN HWY

MORNINGTON OLD DR

HUMPHRIES RD

BADEN POWELL DR

KARS ST

WALKERS RD

OVERPORT RD

CITY

JOINS 627

JOINS 642

599

643

JOINS 599

JOINS 626

FRANKSTON

FRANKSTON SOUTH

Frankston Park
Council Off
Victoria Park
Frankston Hospital
George Pentland Botanic Gardens
Cemetery
Monash University Peninsula Campus
Jubilee Park
Pavilion
Frankston RSL
Netball Stadium
Indoor Centre
Montague Park
Overport Pmy
Frankston High
Delacombe Park
Heatherhill Reserve
Bruce Park
Tennis Hall
MCH
Frankston Heights Pmy
RSL
War Veterans Homes Park
Frankston Resvr
Melbourne Water
St Augustines Cath Pmy
Mount Erin Secondary College
Frankston Holiday Village
The Baxter Nursing
Derinya Pmy
Peninsula Light Operatic Society
Tennis
Peninsula Art Society
Pav
Overport Oval Park
Oval
Resvr
Reservoir
Paratea Flora & Fauna Reserve
Reserve
Baxter Park
Pavilion
Archery
Soccer 4
Soccer 5
Nurs Home
Leawarra
Sweetwater Ck
CITY
Clubhouse

Streets: Cranbourne Rd, Beach St, Hastings Rd, McMahons Rd, Moorooduc Hwy, Frankston - Flinders Rd, Golf Links Rd, Robinsons Rd, Bartlett St, Towerhill Rd, Overport Rd, Foot St, Poinciana Rd, Heatherhill Rd, Yuille St, Young St, Baxter St, High St, Nolan St, Williams St, Muir St, Denbigh St, Stuart Cl, George St, Melville Av, Gweno Av, Woodlands Gr, Kars St, Jasper Tce, The Ridge, The Crest, Spur, The Heights, The Range, The Close, Pratt St, Blair St, Gowrie Av, Handley Cr, Woolston Dr, Marcus Rd, Sussex Rd, Pamela Ct, Bangalay Av, Bellbrook Ct, Seaview Dr, Rock Lodge Ct, Karina St, Willora Rd, Ambleside Cl, Humphries Rd, Blake Ct, Cummins La, Mather Rd, Bellbird Rd, Derinya Dr, Wandana Ct, Fontayne Ct, Man Chelle Cl, Innichen Cl, The Helm, Somerset Rd, Armagh Rd, St Ives Av, Chetwyn Ct, Ajana La, Kirkstall Cl, Sibyl Rd, Rosedale Av, Paratea Av, Kristen Cl, Merilyn Wy, McLean Ct, Balamara Ct, Tetragona Pl, Cassinia Pl, Kilmiston Ct, Barriedale Gr, Ellisyum Wy, Harrow Hill Ct, Glenbrook Cl, Maberley Av, Rinella Ct, Lipari Ct, Alioudi Ct, Tindal Ct, Ablett Ct, Jinchilla Av, Rosedale Gr, Shelbury Pl, Brompton Cl, Rylett Ct, Abram Ct, Arkindale Ct, Angala Ct, Kiari Ct, Christopher Dr, Paul Ct, Dowd Pl, Charlotte Ct, Conifer Ct, Woodside Av, Tintern Ct, Blackwood Ct, Lilac Ct, Lauren Cl, Leatherwood St, Sheoak St, Highland Av, Manuka Dr, Sundown Wk, Crestview Ct, Escarpment Dr, Palma Ct, Kara St, Barmah Ct, Casuarina Dr, Burramine Ct, Bacchus Ct, Burswood Ct, Maretimo Ct, Heritage Ct, Banyule Ct, Goldborough Ct, Smeaton Ct, Murindal Ct, Erutta Pl, Warrock Pl, Verbena Ct, Kurrajong Dr, Banksia Ct, Sanders Rd, Harry Ct, Kim Rd, Port Phillip Vw, Water Wy, Sturt Pl, Bolte Ct, Mt Erin Rd, Wentworth Av, Blaxland Av, Giles Ct, Hume Ct, Gregory Av, Eyre Ct, Culcairn Dr, Koala Ct, Lawson Av, Sweetwater Dr, Caladenia Cct, Carnea Cl, Sage Dr, Sycamore St, Tristania St, Genista St, Corinbough Ct, Fulham Pl, Albany Pl, Nareen Ct, Watson St, Tavistock Ct, Baileyana Gr, Japonica Ct, Diosma Ct, Idon Ct, Yuille Av, Stradbroke Av, Wakefield Av, Hamilton Gr, Torrbay Ct, Parva Av, The Mall, Tara Av, Ian Ct, Lyons Rd, Jamboree Av, Kylla Ct, Myall Ct, Warnoo Ct, Cooinda Ct, Marina Ct, Summit Rd, Sebroff Ct, Bayview Rd, Frome Av, Erin Ct, Glen Ct, Eton Av, Victoria Av, Argyle Ct, Oban St, Cecil Ct, Pde, Mountview Ct, Balcombe Ct, Reid St, Winifred St, Vera St, Cambridge St, Oxford St, Macorna St, Warrain St, Murawa St, Mincha St, Verner St, Fenwick St, Winton Av, Corio Av, Helvetia Ct, Tarook Ct, Munica Ct, Banool Ct, Oakfield Ct, Bruce Rd, Burleigh Ct, Rosewood Ct, Brooklyn Av, Grady Ct, Shearer Ct, Sarah Pl, Cadby Pl, Polly Kelly Cl, Octavius Cl, Miranda Cl, Netherplace Cl, Columbans Wy, Raleon Av, Buckingham Cl, Settlers Ct, Sewell Ct, Cozens Cl, Donnelly Rd, Correa Gr, Luke Ct, McMurtry Wy, Putney Av, La Lansvale, Bardwell Ct, Crathie Ct, Wettenhall Rd, Guildford Ct, Robinia Ct, Kalmia St, Erica, Melaleuca, Glenelg Ct, Morris Ct, Sandgate Av, Margate St, Manly Av, Coogee Av, Bondi Av, Hillcrest Rd, Cassia Gr, Wandella Rd, Kiandra Ct, Meribah Ct, Pericoe Ct, Outlook Rd, Barwon Av, Highview Rd, Kent Gr, Wallace Rd, Kenilworth Av, Leawarra, Screen St, Roberts St, Lardner St, St Johns Av, Shaftesbury Av, Anita St, Beaconsfield Av, Holmes St, Samada St, Melva Ct, Millard St, Long St, Bloom St, Randle St, Deane St, Hill St, Burnley St, Gertrude St, Reservoir Rd, Stewart St, Glennis Ct, Hazel Gr, Clifford St, Bryan St, Burns Gr, Clarendon St, Dundas St, Government Rd, Lawrey St, Heath Av, Dingle Av, Nott St, Elizabeth St, Bundara St, Florence St, Playne St, Melvin St, Allenby St, Birdwood Av, Dell St, Plowman Pl, Bay St, Spring St, Bell St, Bentley Pl, Friswell Av, Charlton St, Waterman St, Callaghan Av, Beauty Park St, Nursery Rd, Craig St, Mena St, Frawley St, Nilma Ct, Paisley Av, Sen Cits

JOINS 643

642

JOINS 600
601
JOINS 629
JOINS 644
645

LANGWARRIN

LANGWARRIN SOUTH

BAXTER

Ballam Park

Bunarong Park

Robinsons Reserve

Frankston Golf Course

Langwarrin Flora and Fauna Reserve

Karingal Hub Shopping Centre

Golf Driving Range

Dame Elisabeth Murdoch Arboretum

Peninsula Priv Hosp

CPI Powernet Terminal

Telstra

Kingsley Park Pmy

Bayside Christian College

Lawton Reserve Soccer

Mulberry Hill (National Trust)

Woodleigh St Pauls Anglican Secondary

Village Home Retirement Village

CRANBOURNE - FRANKSTON RD

McCLELLAND DR

ROBINSONS RD

GOLF LINKS RD

NORTH RD

LIPTON DR

Parks Victoria

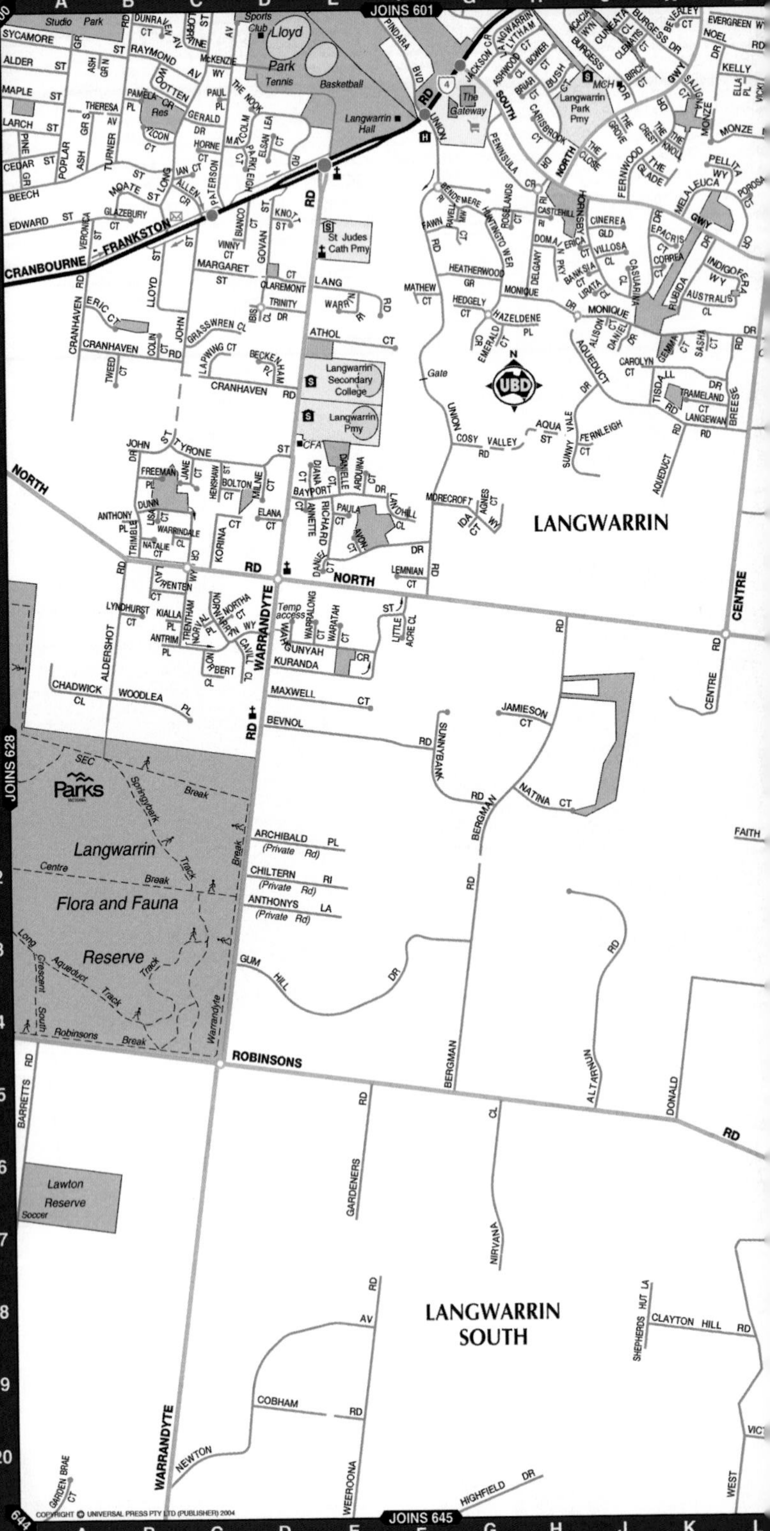

A B C D E F G H J K L

600
JOINS 601
JOINS 628
JOINS 645
644

1 2 3 4 5 6 7 8 9 10 11 12 13 14 15 16 17 18 19 20

Studio Park
Sports Club
Lloyd Park
Tennis
Basketball
Langwarrin Hall
The Gateway
Langwarrin Park Pmy
St Judes Cath Pmy
Langwarrin Secondary College
Langwarrin Pmy
CFA
Res
MCH
Gate
Temp access

SYCAMORE
ALDER ST
MAPLE ST
LARCH ST
CEDAR ST
BEECH
EDWARD ST
PINE
POPLAR
ASH
GR
THERESA AV
TURNER
PAMELA CR
RICON CT
DUNRAVEN AV
LORRAINE
RAYMOND AV
WOOTTEN
GERALD DR
HORNE CT
MCKENZIE WY
PAUL PL
THE NOOK
MALCOLM
ELSAN LEA
PARKLEIGH
MOATE ST
LONG ST
IAN CT
ALLEN CR
GLAZEBURY CT
VERONICA
PATERSON
FRANKSTON
CRANBOURNE
VINNY CT
BIANCO
GOVAN
KNOTT ST
MARGARET ST
CLAREMONT
TRINITY DR
IBIS
LANG
WARRAN RI
ATHOL CT
ERIC CT
CRANHAVEN RD
LLOYD
JOHN ST
GRASSWREN CL
COLIN CT
TWEED CT
LAPWING CT
BECKENHAM PL
CRANHAVEN RD
TYRONE
JOHN DR
FREEMAN PL
JANE
HENSHAW
BOLTON CT
MILNE
DUNN
LISA
ANTHONY PL
WARRINDALE
NATALIE CT
TRIMBLE
ELANA CT
KORINA
DIANA CT
DANIELLE
ARDUINA
BAYPORT
ANNETTE
RICHARD
PAULA CT
AVON CT
LANDHILL CL
DANIEL CT
PINDARA BVD
UNION RD
JACKSON CR
LANGWARRIN LYTHAM CT
ASHWOOD CT
BRIAR CL
BOWER CT
BUSH CT
SOUTH
CARISBROOK CT
PENINSULA CR
ACACIA WYN
CUNEATA CL
BURGESS DR
BEVERLEY CT
CLEMATIS
BIRCH
GWY
SALIGNA
MONZE
EVERGREEN WY
NOEL DR
KELLY
ELLA PL
THE GROVE
THE CREST
THE KNOLL
THE CLOSE
THE GLADE
FERNWOOD
NORTH
PELLITA WY
MELALEUCA
POROSA
BENDEMERE RI
FAWN
RAVELL
HUNTINGTOWER
ROSELANDS
CASTLEHILL
HORNSBY
CINEREA GLD
DOMAIN PKY
ERICA CT
VILLOSA CL
EPACRIS
CORREA
INDIGOFERA
HEATHERWOOD GR
MONIQUE
DELGANY
BANKSIA CT
LIRATA CT
CASUARINA
RUBIDA
AUSTRALIS CL
MATHEW CT
HEDGELY CT
HAZELDENE PL
EMERALD CR
ALISON CT
DANIEL
AQUEDUCT
CAROLYN CT
GEMMA
SASHA CT
TISDALL
TRAMELAND DR
LANGEWAN CT
BREESE
COSY VALLEY RD
AQUA ST
SUNNY VALE
FERNLEIGH CT
MORECROFT
AGNES CT
IDA CT
LANGWARRIN
LEMNIAN CT
NORTH RD
WARRANDYTE RD
LAURENTEN WY
LYNDHURST CT
KIALLA PL
TRENTHAM
NORVAL
NORNABY
NORTHA CT
ANTRIM PL
ROBERT
CAVILL CL
WARRALONG CT
WARATAH CT
GUNYAH
KURANDA
CR
LITTLE ACRE CL
ALDERSHOT
CHADWICK CL
WOODLEA PL
MAXWELL CT
BEVNOL RD
SUNNYBANK
JAMIESON CT
NATINA CT
BERGMAN RD
CENTRE RD
FAITH

Parks
SEC Break
Springbark Track
Langwarrin
Flora and Fauna
Reserve
Centre Break
Long Crescent South
Aqueduct Track
Robinsons Break
Warrandyte
ARCHIBALD PL (Private Rd)
CHILTERN RI (Private Rd)
ANTHONYS LA (Private Rd)
GUM HILL DR
ROBINSONS RD
BARRETTS RD
ALTARNUN RD
DONALD
Lawton Reserve
Soccer
GARDENERS RD
NIRVANA CL
LANGWARRIN SOUTH
AV
SHEPHERDS HUT LA
CLAYTON HILL RD
COBHAM RD
NEWTON
WARRANDYTE
WEEROONA
HIGHFIELD DR
GARDEN BRAE CT
WEST
VIC

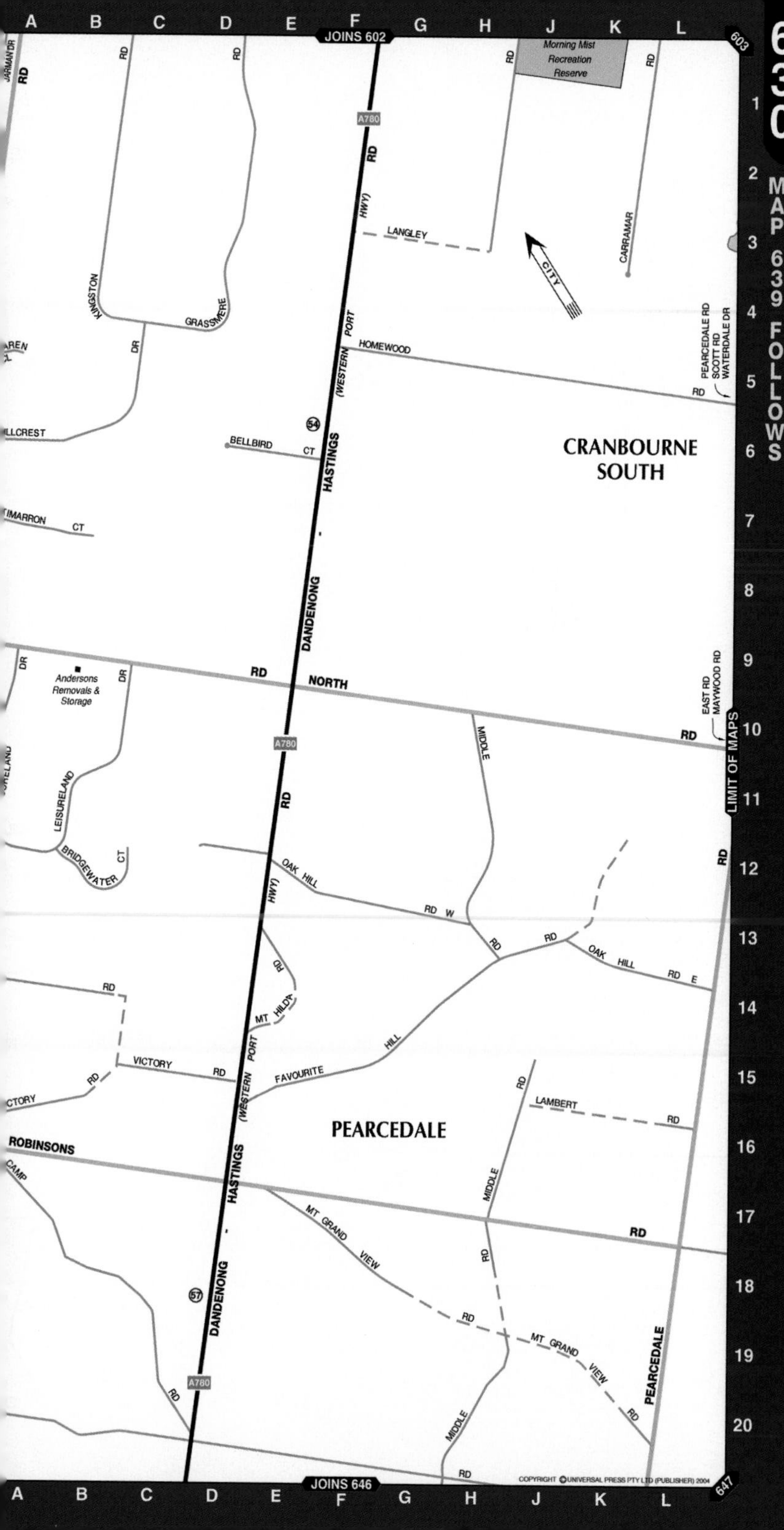
JOINS 602
603
MAP 639 FOLLOWS
Morning Mist Recreation Reserve
A780
DANDENONG - HASTINGS RD (WESTERN PORT HWY)
LANGLEY
CITY
CARRAMAR RD
KINGSTON DR
GRASSMERE RD
HOMEWOOD RD
PEARCEDALE RD
SCOTT RD
WATERDALE DR
HILLCREST
BELLBIRD CT
CRANBOURNE SOUTH
TIMARRON CT
Andersons Removals & Storage
NORTH RD
EAST RD
MAYWOOD RD
MIDDLE RD
LIMIT OF MAPS
LEISURELAND DR
BRIDGEWATER CT
OAK HILL RD W
OAK HILL RD E
MT HILDA RD
VICTORY RD
FAVOURITE HILL RD
LAMBERT RD
PEARCEDALE
ROBINSONS RD
CAMP RD
MT GRAND VIEW RD
PEARCEDALE RD
54
57
JOINS 646
647

639
PREVIOUS MAP 630
628
PORT
JOINS 655

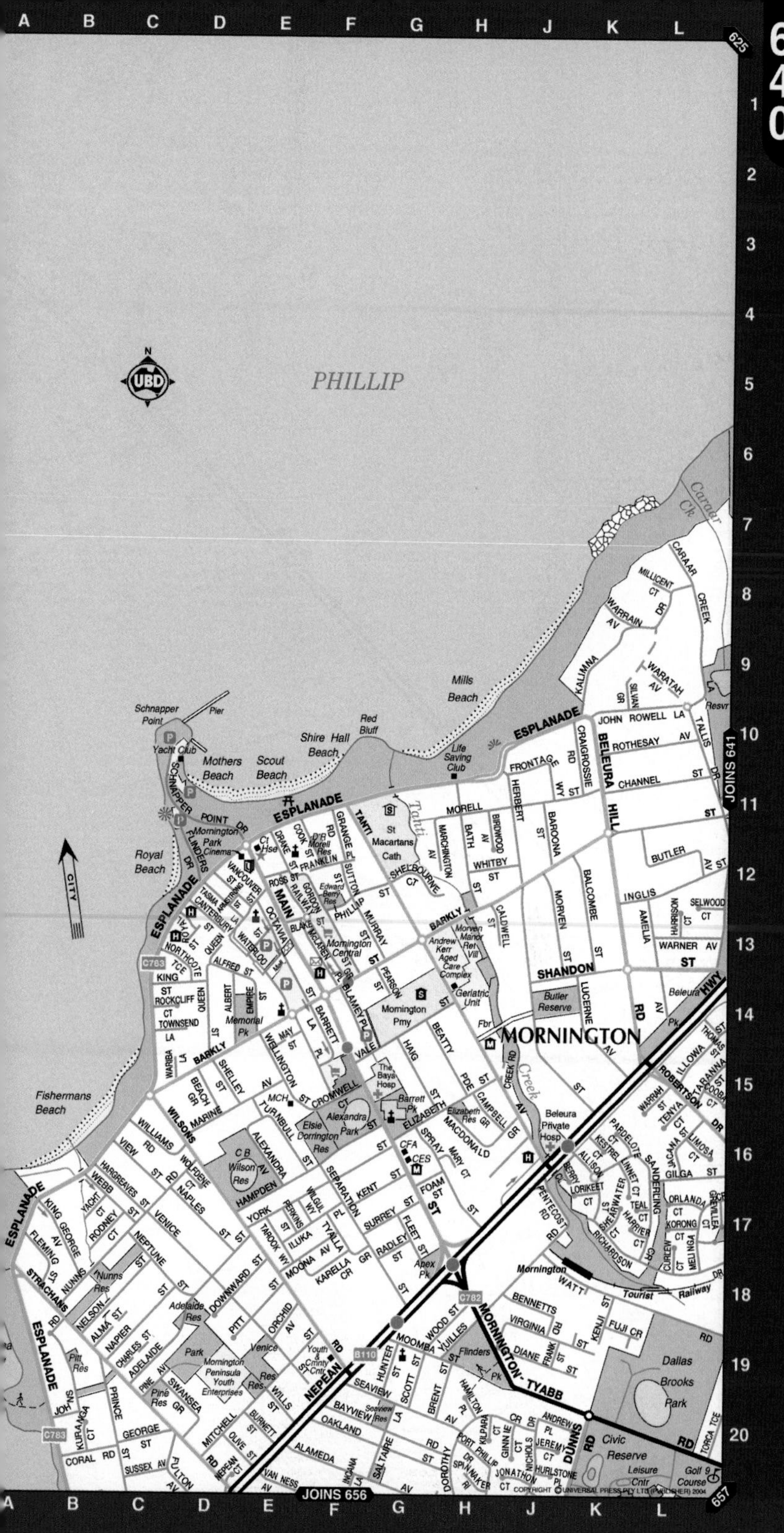
A B C D E F G H J K L
1 2 3 4 5 6 7 8 9 10 11 12 13 14 15 16 17 18 19 20
625
PHILLIP
UBD
N
Caraar Ck
CARAAR CREEK
MILLICENT CT
WARRAIN AV
DR
KALIMNA
WARATAH AV
SILVAN GR
Mills Beach
Schnapper Point
Pier
Yacht Club
Mothers Beach
Scout Beach
Shire Hall Beach
Red Bluff
Life Saving Club
ESPLANADE
JOHN ROWELL LA
TALLIS DR
Resvr
BELEURA HILL
CRAIGROSSIE RD
ROTHESAY AV
FRONTAGE WY
CHANNEL ST
JOINS 641
SCHNAPPER POINT DR
Mornington Park Cinema
FLINDERS DR
Royal Beach
CITY
Ct Hse
TANTI
St Macartans Cath
MORELL ST
MARCHINGTON AV
BATH ST
BIRDWOOD AV
HERBERT ST
BAROONA
BUTLER AV
WHITBY ST
SHELBOURNE CT
BARKLY ST
INGLIS ST
SELWOOD CT
HARRISON CT
MORVEN ST
BALCOMBE ST
AMELIA AV
CALDWELL
Morven Manor Ret Vill
Andrew Kerr Aged Care Complex
WARNER AV
SHANDON ST
MAIN ST
OCTAVIA
VANCOUVER ST
TASMA ST
CANTERBURY ST
WATERLOO
QUEEN ST
NORTHCOTE TCE
ALFRED ST
KING ST
ROCKCLIFF CT
TOWNSEND LA
ALBERT ST
EMPIRE ST
Memorial Pk
DRAKE ST
COOK ST
D'R Morell Res
GRANGE RD
FRANKLIN
SUTTON
ROSS ST
GORDON ST
RAILWAY
Edward Barry Res
PHILLIP ST
MURRAY ST
BLAKE ST
McLAREN ST
Mornington Central
PEARSON ST
BLAMEY PL
Mornington Pmy
Geriatric Unit
Butler Reserve
LUCERNE AV
RD
Beleura
HWY
MORNINGTON
Creek
Fbr
CREEK RD
BARRETT
VALE
MAY ST
WELLINGTON ST
LA
PL
HAIG ST
BEATTY PDE
The Bays Hosp
Barrett Pk
CROMWELL CT
Alexandra Park
Elsie Dorrington Res
ELIZABETH ST
Elizabeth Res
CAMPBELL GR
MACDONALD
SPRAY ST
MARY CT
CFA
CES
Beleura Private Hosp
ROBERTSON DR
ILLOWA ST
TARANNA CT
THOMAS ST
WARRAH
TENYA
COOBA CT
JACANA ST
LIMOSA CT
GILGA ST
PARDELOTE CT
KESTREL CT
LINNET CT
SANDERLING
ALLISON
BERRY CL
LORIKEET CT
SHEARWATER
TEAL CT
HARRIER CT
ORLANDA CT
GREVILLEA CT
KORONG CT
CURLEW CT
MELINGA CT
RICHARDSON
PENTECOST RD
Fishermans Beach
WARIBA LA
SHELLEY ST
BARKLY
BEACH GR
MARINE
WILSONS
MCH
TURNBULL
WILLIAMS RD
VIEW
WOLFDENE CT
C B Wilson Res
ALEXANDRA
HAMPDEN
SEPARATION
KENT ST
FOAM ST
HARGREAVES ST
WEBB
YACHT CT
RODNEY CT
NAPLES
VENICE
NEPTUNE
KING GEORGE AV
FLEMING ST
STRACHANS
NUNNS
YORK
PERKINS
WILGUL WY
TAROOK WY
ILUKA
TYALLA
SURREY
FLEET ST
RADLEY
MOONA AV
KARELLA CR
Apex Pk
Nunns Res
NELSON
ALMA ST
DOWNWARD ST
Adelaide Res
NAPIER
CHARLES ST
ADELAIDE
PITT
ORCHID AV
Venice
Youth Cmnty Cntr
Park
Mornington Peninsula Youth Enterprises
Pitt Res
PINE AV
Pine Res
SWANSEA GR
Res
WILLS
ESPLANADE
JOHNS
KURANGA CT
PRINCE
GEORGE ST
CORAL RD
SUSSEX AV
FULTON AV
MITCHELL
OLIVE ST
BURNETT
NEPEAN CT
NEPEAN
MOOMBA
WOOD ST
YUILLES
HUNTER ST
SCOTT ST
BRENT ST
Flinders
Pk
SEAVIEW
BAYVIEW
Seaview Res
OAKLAND
ALAMEDA
VAN NESS AV
IKOANA LA
SALTAIRE ST
DOROTHY
HAMILTON PL
KILPARA CT
PORT PHILLIP DR
SPINNAKER RI
GINNIE CT
NICHOLS CT
JEREMY CT
JONATHON CT
HURLSTONE PL
ANDREWS CR
DUNNS RD
Civic Reserve
Leisure Cntr
Golf Course
Dallas Brooks Park
TORCA TCE
MORNINGTON-TYABB RD
BENNETTS
VIRGINIA
DIANE
FRANK ST
KENJI
FUJI CR
Mornington
WATT
Tourist Railway
C783
C782
B110
JOINS 656
657

JOINS 625
JOINS 640

North Sunnyside Beach
Sunnyside Beach
Mornington Country Golf Course
Clubhouse
Resvr
Camp Manyung
Morning Star Estate
Mt Eliza Estate
Vintina Estate
Vision Australia Foundation - George Vowell Centre
Melbourne Water Mornington Service Reservoir
Cobblestone Manor Receptions
Bata
Mornington Secondary College
Tallis Park
Mornington Industrial Park
Padua Catholic College
Reserve
Beleura Pk
Taranna Res
Cmnty Cntr
Tanti
Mornington Gardens
Mornington Sp Dev Sch
Mornington Park Pmy
Pavilion
Narambi Reserve
MORNINGTON
Origin Energy Comdain Gas
Dallas Brooks Park
Indoor Cricket Centre
Razor Blades Roller Skating
Dog Pound
Transfield Depot & Mornington Waste Disposal Centre
Kankama Adult Cntr
Mornington Racecourse
Grandstand
A B Cameron Res
Jessie White Res
Balcombe
NEPEAN HWY
BUNGOWER RD
RACECOURSE RD
ROBERTS RD
MORNINGTON-TYABB RD
SHOTTON RD
COBB RD
OAKBANK RD
TOWER RD
BALDOCK RD
GRANT RD
SUNNYSIDE RD

JOINS 657
656

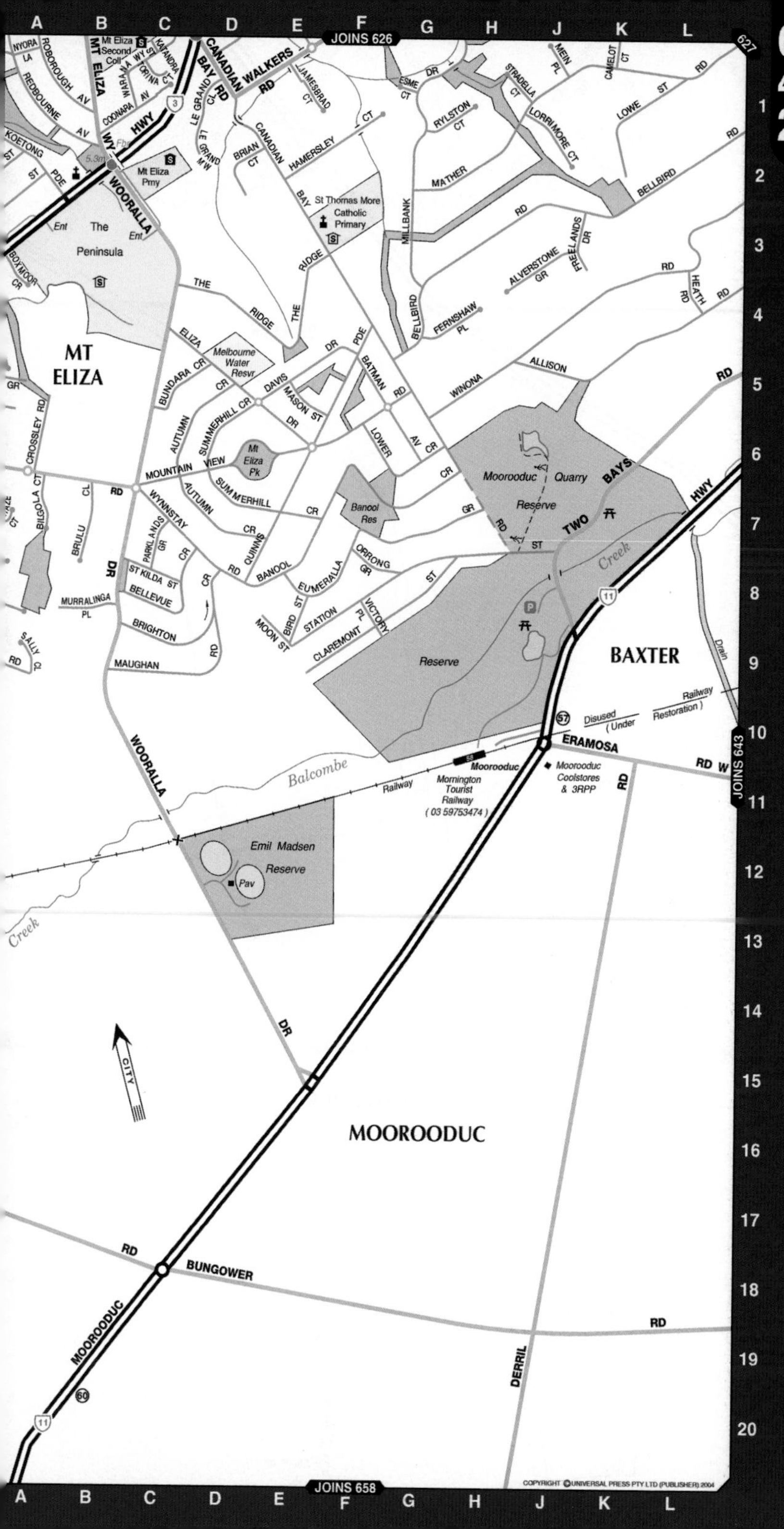

JOINS 626
627
JOINS 643
JOINS 658
MT ELIZA
BAXTER
MOOROODUC
Mt Eliza Second Coll
Mt Eliza Pmy
The Peninsula
St Thomas More Catholic Primary
Melbourne Water Resvr
Mt Eliza Pk
Banool Res
Mooroduc Quarry Reserve
Reserve
Emil Madsen Reserve
Pav
Balcombe Creek
Disused (Under Railway Restoration)
Mooroduc
Mornington Tourist Railway (03 59753474)
Mooroduc Coolstores & 3RPP
NEPEAN HWY
CANADIAN BAY RD
WALKERS RD
WOORALLA DR
MOUNTAIN VIEW RD
TWO BAYS RD
MOOROODUC HWY
ERAMOSA RD W
BUNGOWER RD
DERRIL RD
WINONA RD
BATMAN RD
BELLBIRD RD
MATHER RD
HEATH RD
ALLISON RD
LOWE ST
THE RIDGE
CITY
COPYRIGHT © UNIVERSAL PRESS PTY LTD (PUBLISHER) 2004

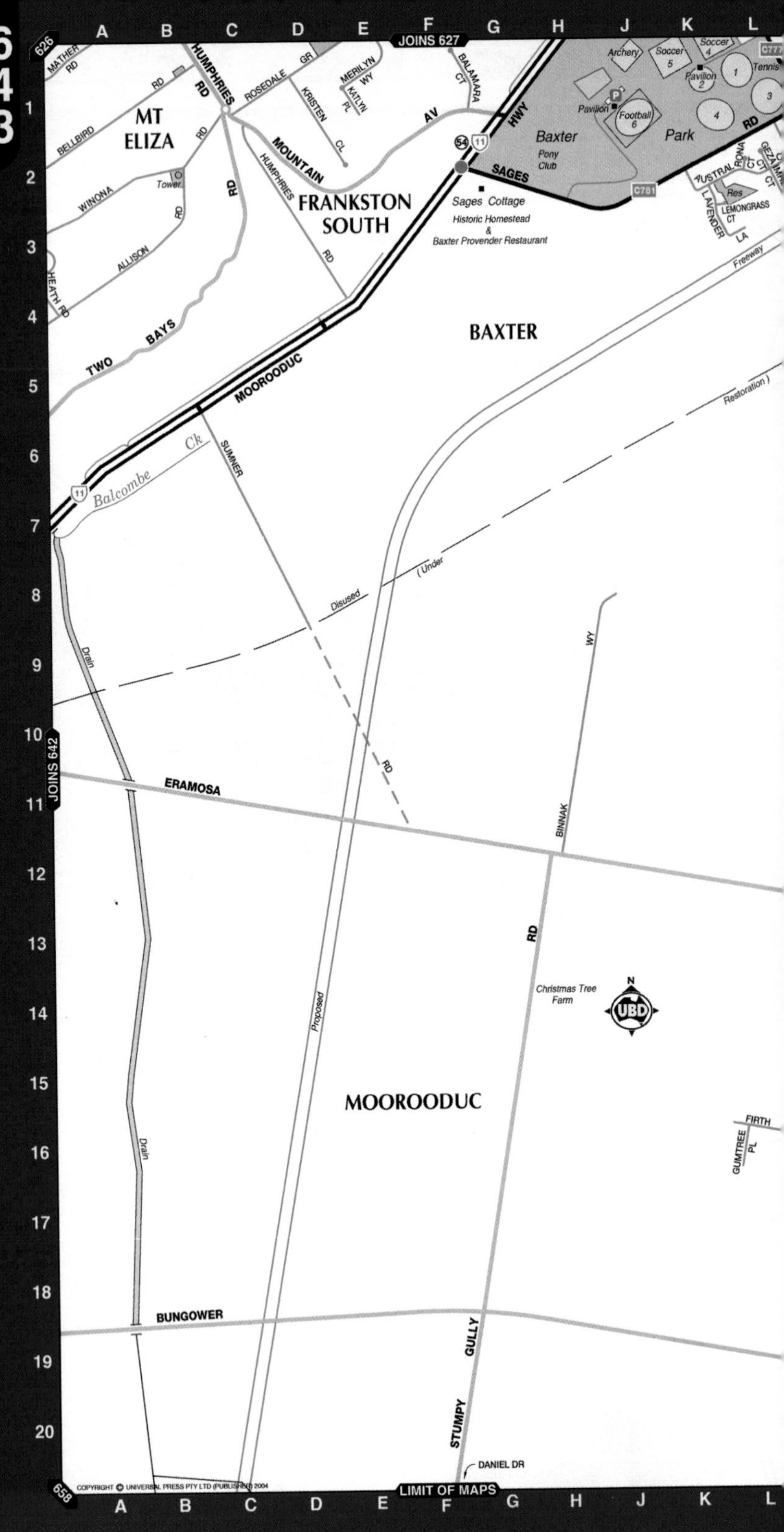
A B C D E F G H J K L
1 2 3 4 5 6 7 8 9 10 11 12 13 14 15 16 17 18 19 20
626
JOINS 627
JOINS 642
658
LIMIT OF MAPS
MATHER RD
BELLBIRD RD
MT ELIZA
WINONA RD
Tower
ALLISON
HEATH RD
TWO BAYS RD
HUMPHRIES RD
ROSEDALE GR
KRISTEN CL
MERILYN WY
KATLYN PL
BALAMARA CT
MOUNTAIN AV
HUMPHRIES RD
FRANKSTON SOUTH
HWY
MOOROODUC
SAGES RD
Sages Cottage
Historic Homestead & Baxter Provender Restaurant
Baxter Pony Club
Baxter Park
Archery
Soccer 5
Soccer 4
Pavilion 2
Pavilion
Football 6
Tennis
C777
C781
AUSTRAL
RONA CT
GEZA CT
LAVENDER LA
LEMONGRASS CT
Res
BAXTER
Freeway
Restoration)
(Under
Disused
Balcombe Ck
SUMMER RD
Drain
ERAMOSA
BINNAK WY
RD
Christmas Tree Farm
UBD
N
Proposed
MOOROODUC
FIRTH
GUMTREE PL
BUNGOWER
STUMPY GULLY
DANIEL DR

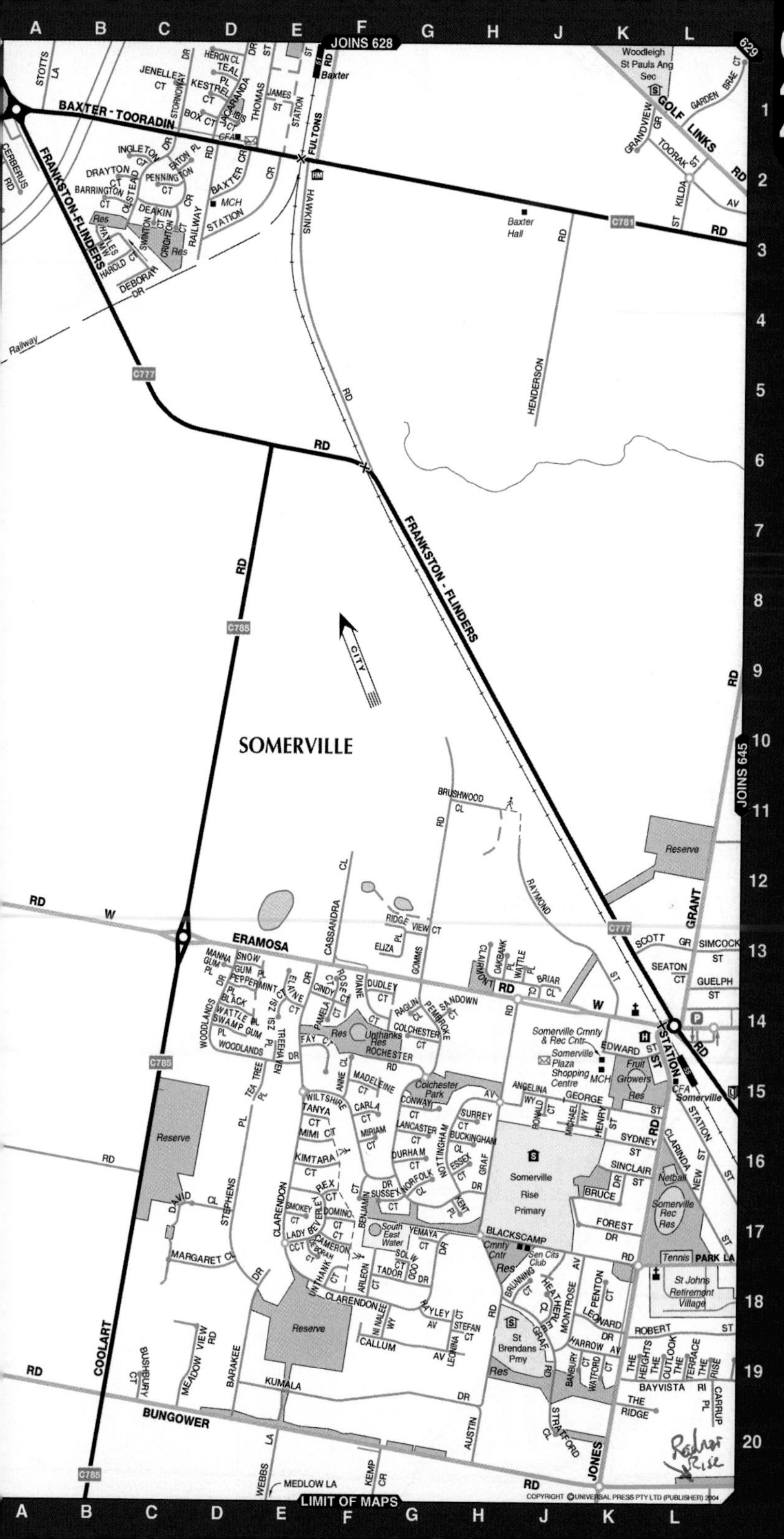
JOINS 628
629
JOINS 645
LIMIT OF MAPS
SOMERVILLE
Baxter
BAXTER - TOORADIN
FRANKSTON-FLINDERS
FRANKSTON - FLINDERS
FULTONS RD
HAWKINS
GOLF LINKS RD
Woodleigh St Pauls Ang Sec
Baxter Hall
HENDERSON RD
COOLART RD
ERAMOSA RD W
BUNGOWER RD
JONES RD
STATION ST
GRANT RD
Railway
CITY
Somerville Cmnty & Rec Cntr
Somerville Plaza Shopping Centre
Fruit Growers Res
Colchester Park
Somerville Rise Primary
South East Water
St Brendans Pmy
St Johns Retirement Village
Somerville Rec Res
Netball
Tennis
PARK LA
Reserve
COPYRIGHT © UNIVERSAL PRESS PTY LTD (PUBLISHER) 2004

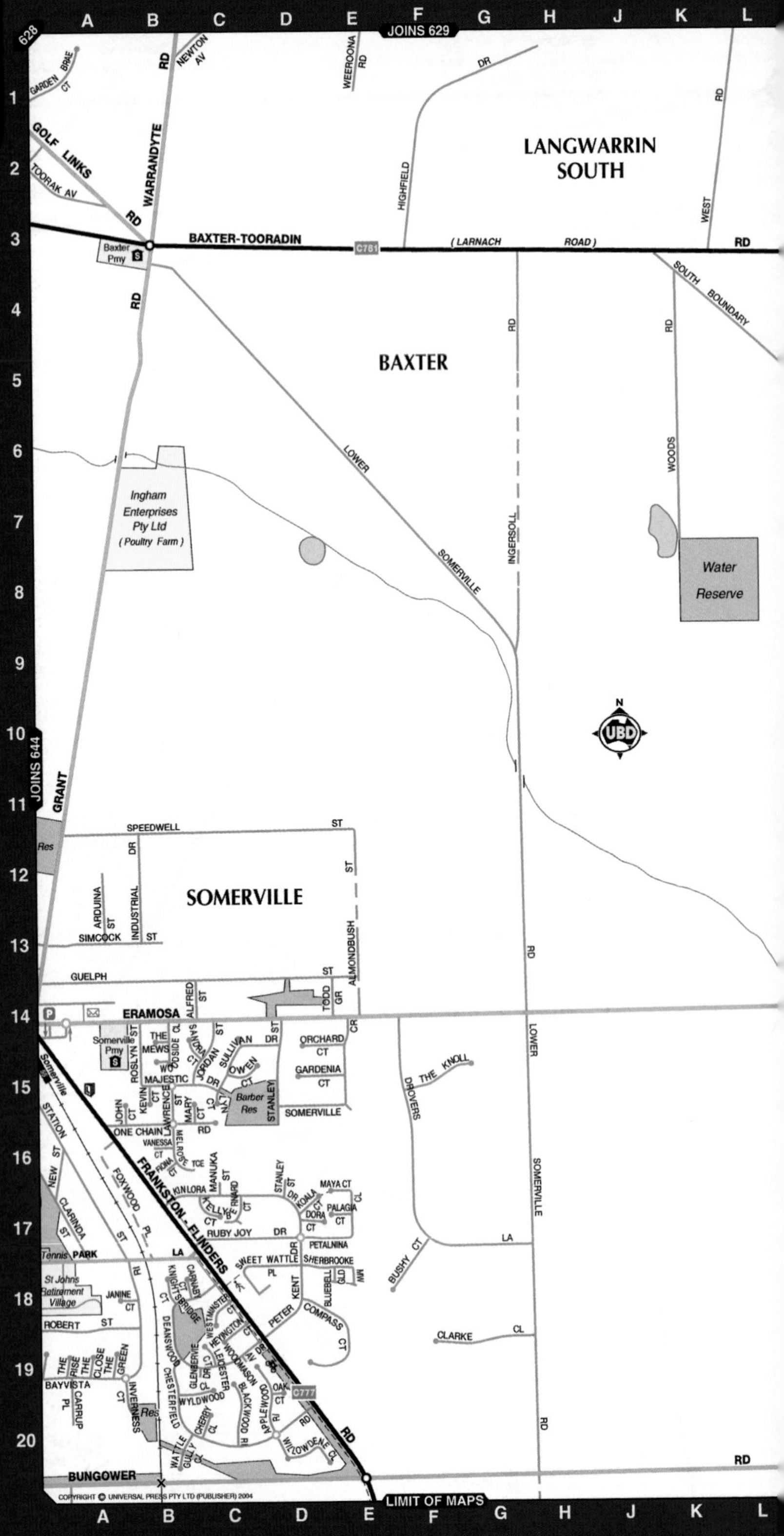

A B C D E F G H J K L

JOINS 629

628

1 2 3 4 5 6 7 8 9 10 11 12 13 14 15 16 17 18 19 20

LANGWARRIN SOUTH

BAXTER

SOMERVILLE

GARDEN BRAE CT
GOLF LINKS RD
TOORAK AV
WARRANDYTE RD
NEWTON AV
WEEROONA RD
HIGHFIELD DR
WEST RD
BAXTER-TOORADIN RD
C781
(LARNACH ROAD)
Baxter Pmy
SOUTH BOUNDARY RD
INGERSOLL RD
WOODS RD
LOWER SOMERVILLE RD
Ingham Enterprises Pty Ltd (Poultry Farm)
Water Reserve
GRANT RD
Res
SPEEDWELL ST
INDUSTRIAL DR
ARDUINA ST
SIMCOCK ST
ALMONDBUSH ST
GUELPH ST
ALFRED ST
TODD GR
ERAMOSA RD
Somerville Pmy
THE MEWS
WOODSIDE CL
SANDS CT
JORDAN ST
SULLIVAN DR
OWEN CT
ROSLYN ST
MAJESTIC DR
ORCHARD CT
GARDENIA CT
CR
KEVIN CT
JOHN CT
LAWRENCE ST
MARY ST
Barber Res
STANLEY ST
SOMERVILLE RD
ONE CHAIN RD
MELROSE TCE
VANESSA CT
FIONA CT
MANUKA ST
KINLORA
KELLY CT
FENDRO CT
STANLEY ST
KOALA CT
MAYA CT
PALAGIA CL
DORA CT
RUBY JOY DR
PETALNINA
SWEET WATTLE PL
SHERBROOKE MW
BLUEBELL GLD
KENT DR
PETER CT
COMPASS CT
DROVERS
THE KNOLL
BUSHY CT
LA
CLARKE CL
Somerville STATION
NEW ST
CLARINDA ST
FOXWOOD PL
FRANKSTON - FLINDERS RD
C777
Tennis PARK LA
St Johns Retirement Village
JANINE CT
ROBERT ST
THE RISE
THE CLOSE
THE GREEN
BAYVISTA PL
CARRUP
INVERNESS CT
Res
KNIGHTSBRIDGE
CARNABY CT
DEANSWOOD
CHESTERFIELD
GLENBERVIE DR
WESTMINSTER
HEYINGTON
LEICESTER
WOODMASON
BLACKWOOD RI
APPLEWOOD RI
OAK CT
WYLDWOOD
CHERRY CL
WATTLE GULLY CL
WINZOWDENE CL
RD
BUNGOWER RD

JOINS 644

LIMIT OF MAPS

A B C D E F G H J K L

JOINS 630

PEARCEDALE

VICTORIA RD
BAXTER - TOORADIN (LARNACH RD) C781
DANDENONG - HASTINGS RD A780
MEDLAR ST
FERN ST
MIDDLE RD
PEACH ST
NATHANIAL ST
CHERRY ST
COLLEY ST
Colley St Bushland Reserve
BELLTREES CT
MONAVALE CL
NOORILIM WY
GRACEMERE DR
HATCH ST
ELWOOD DR
ERIC CT
RAINBOW CT
ROSELLA CT
DOVE CT
PEARCEDALE RD
EVANS ST
OAKDEN ST
APPLE ST
LEWIS ST
BAYLISS CT
KENNETH CT
BRICK CT
PADLEY
CFA
Pearcedale Rec Res
Tennis
Pearcedale Primary
PERYMAN ST
CLAREMONT ST
Hall
MCH
CHARLES DR
FELTHAM ST
TROEDEL ST
DERHAM
TERRY
HASTINGS ST
SOUTH BOUNDARY RD W
QUEENS RD
(WESTERN PORT HWY) 60
CITY
PEARCEDALE RD E
RD E
Bembridge Golf Course 9
BEMBRIDGE RD
TYABB - TOORADIN RD
BUNGOWER RD
(Fire Access Only)
WHITNEYS RD
Treehaven Equestrian Centre 500m

JOINS 647

LIMIT OF MAPS

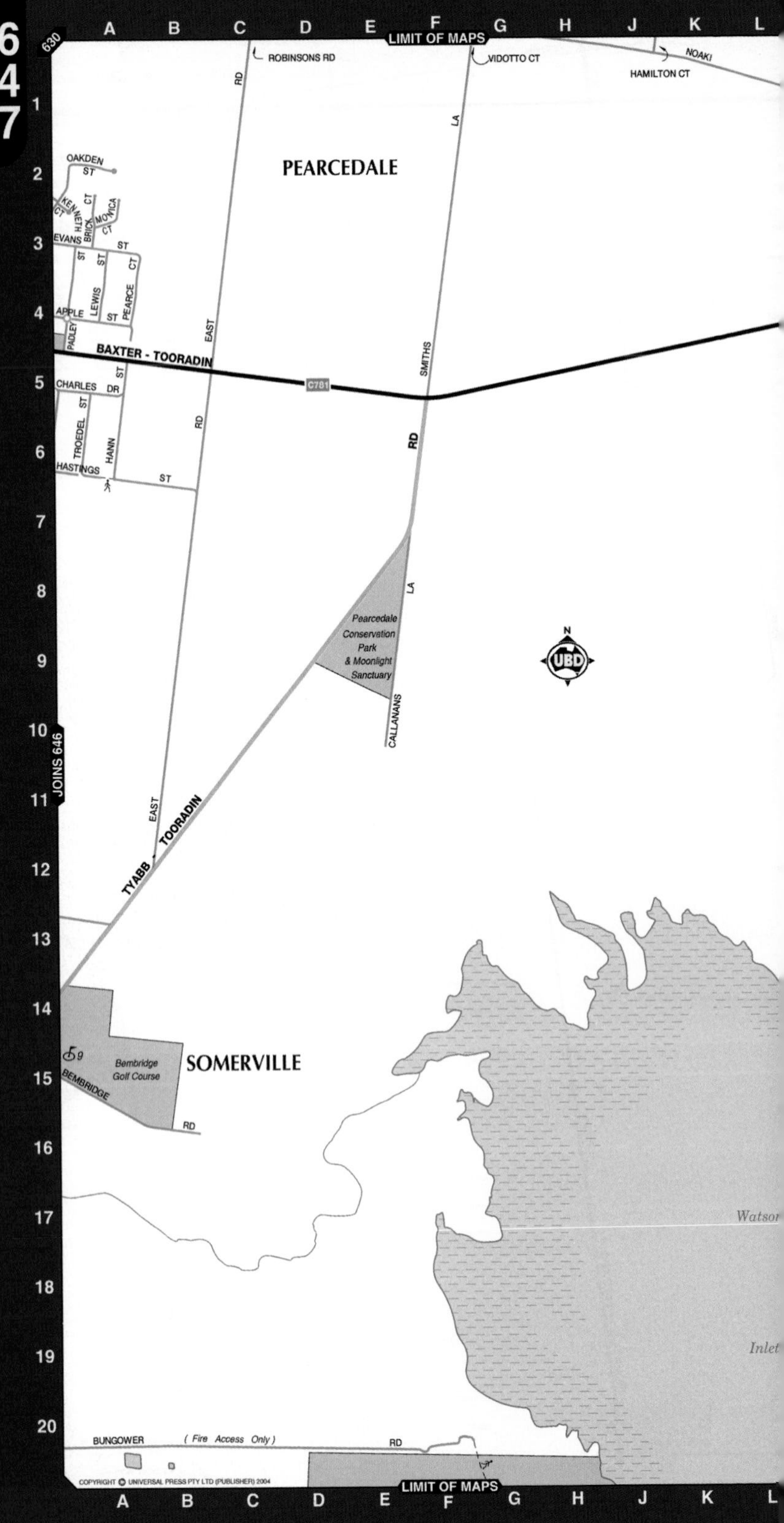
LIMIT OF MAPS
630
ROBINSONS RD
VIDOTTO CT
NOAKI
HAMILTON CT
PEARCEDALE
OAKDEN ST
KENNETH CT
BRICK CT
MONICA CT
EVANS ST
LEWIS ST
PEARCE CT
APPLE
PADLEY
BAXTER - TOORADIN
EAST RD
SMITHS LA
C781
CHARLES DR
TROEDEL ST
HANN ST
HASTINGS ST
RD
Pearcedale Conservation Park & Moonlight Sanctuary
LA
CALLANANS
UBD
N
JOINS 646
EAST
TYABB - TOORADIN
SOMERVILLE
Bembridge Golf Course
BEMBRIDGE RD
Watson
Inlet
BUNGOWER
(Fire Access Only)
RD
LIMIT OF MAPS

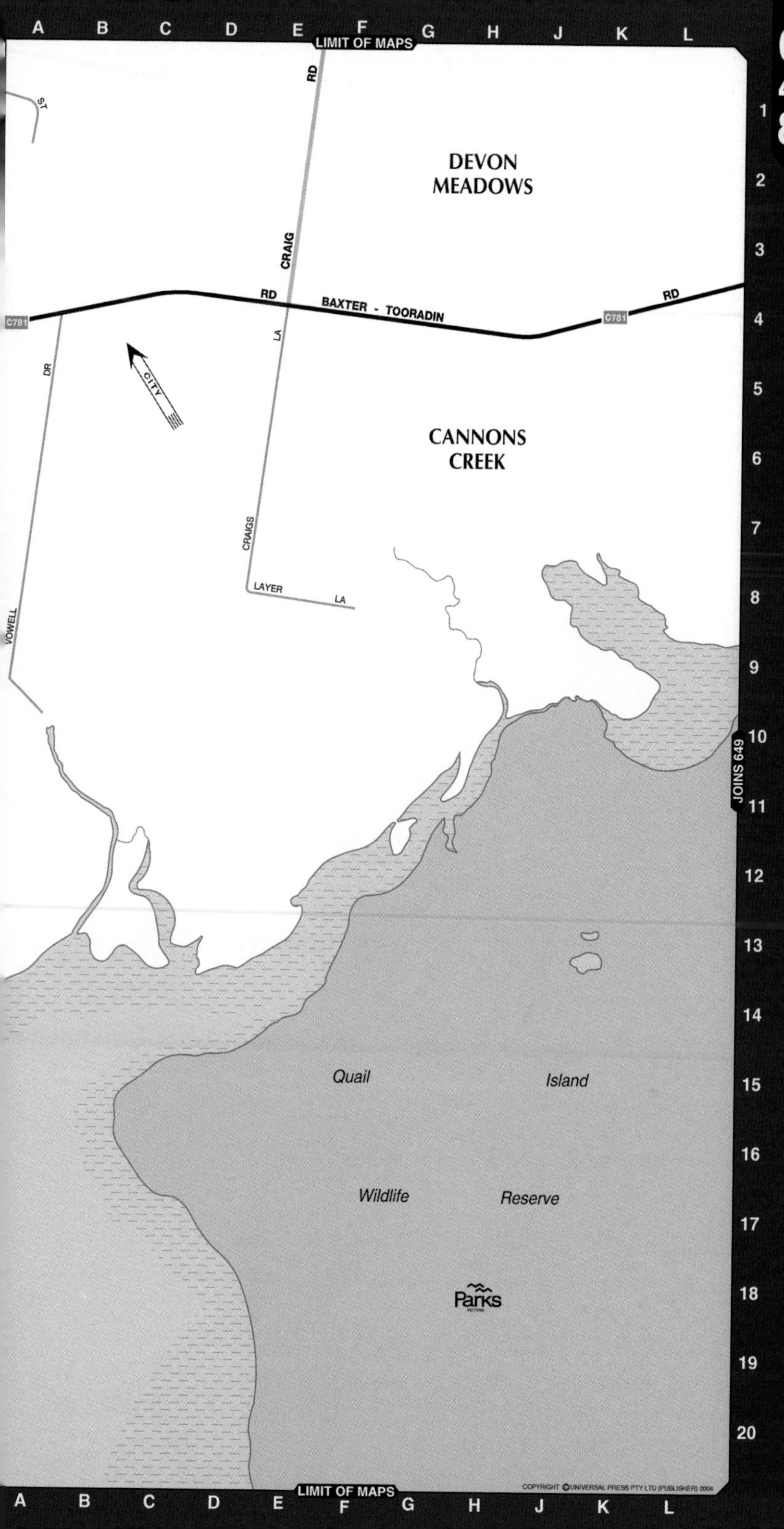

A B C D E F G H J K L
LIMIT OF MAPS
ST
RD
CRAIG
DEVON
MEADOWS
RD
BAXTER - TOORADIN
RD
C781
C781
LA
DR
CITY
CANNONS
CREEK
CRAIGS
LAYER
LA
VOWELL
JOINS 649
Quail
Island
Wildlife
Reserve
Parks
1 2 3 4 5 6 7 8 9 10 11 12 13 14 15 16 17 18 19 20
LIMIT OF MAPS
A B C D E F G H J K L

LIMIT OF MAPS

JOINS 648

A B C D E F G H J K L

1 2 3 4 5 6 7 8 9 10 11 12 13 14 15 16 17 18 19 20

DEVON MEADOWS

CANNONS CREEK

WARNEET

BAXTER - TOORADIN RD

C781

FISHERIES RD

CANNONS CREEK RD

Private Road

IBIS WY

GR

BRONZE WING CT

CURRAWONG

ALBATROSS CT

GLENALVA PDE

PETERS ST

SANDY CT

BLUFF RD

IRIS CT

IRENE

PIVATO CT

DALY DR

HARDY

MAY ST

HARDY AV

AV

CFA

Cannons Creek Foreshore Res

RD PDE

ADENEYS

Rutherford

Jetty

Warneet Nature Reserve

Parks Victoria

Warneet Reserve

Ten Cts

Oval

RUTHERFORD PDE

AKUNA ST

GILGANDRA ST

ARUMA ST

CORANDIRK ST

WARNEET RD

PDE

CFA

ILUKA ST

COOINDA ST

ANEBO ST

ST

RIGBY

GNOORONG

CULGOA

ELIMATTA ST

BUNGADOOL ST

KALLARA PDE

ST

RUTHERFORD

BANKS ST

BALAKA ST

RUTHERFORD

Warneet North Boat Club

P

Jetty

Rutherford Inlet

Quail Island Wildlife Reserve

Parks Victoria

Chinaman Island

China Bay

N

UBD

LIMIT OF MAPS

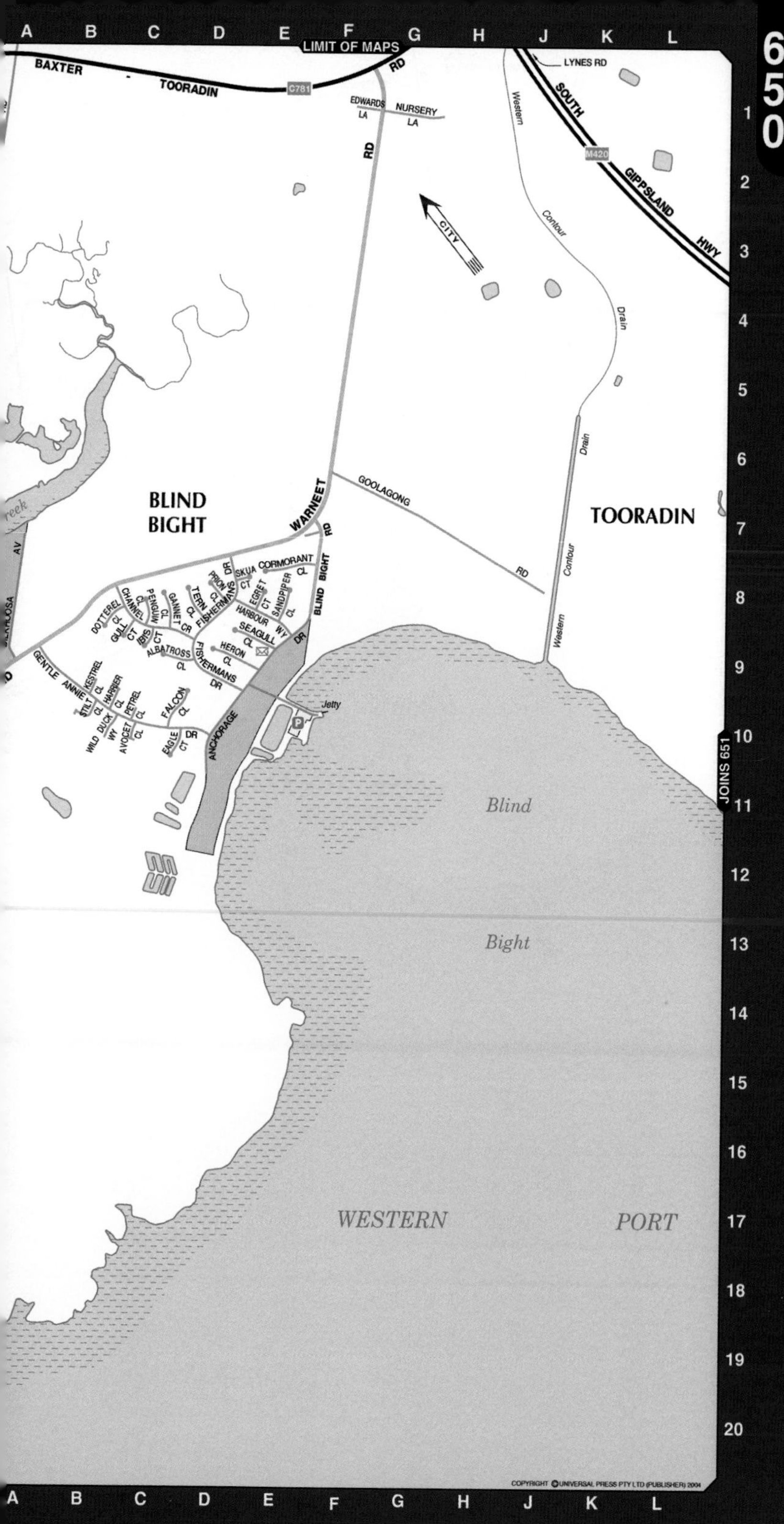
A B C D E F G H J K L
LIMIT OF MAPS
BAXTER
TOORADIN
RD
C781
LYNES RD
SOUTH
GIPPSLAND
HWY
M420
EDWARDS LA
NURSERY LA
Western
Contour
Drain
CITY
BLIND BIGHT
WARNEET
RD
GOOLAGONG
RD
TOORADIN
CORMORANT CL
SKUA CT
PRION CL
TERN CL
FISHERMANS DR
EGRET CT
SANDPIPER CL
HARBOUR WY
SEAGULL CL
HERON CL
BLIND BIGHT DR
CHANNEL CL
PENGUIN CL
GANNET CR
DOTTEREL CL
GULL CT
IBIS CT
ALBATROSS CL
GENTLE ANNIE
KESTREL CL
HARRIER CL
PETREL CL
STILT CL
WILD DUCK WY
AVOCET CL
FALCON CL
EAGLE CT
ANCHORAGE
Jetty
Blind
Bight
WESTERN
PORT
JOINS 651
1 2 3 4 5 6 7 8 9 10 11 12 13 14 15 16 17 18 19 20

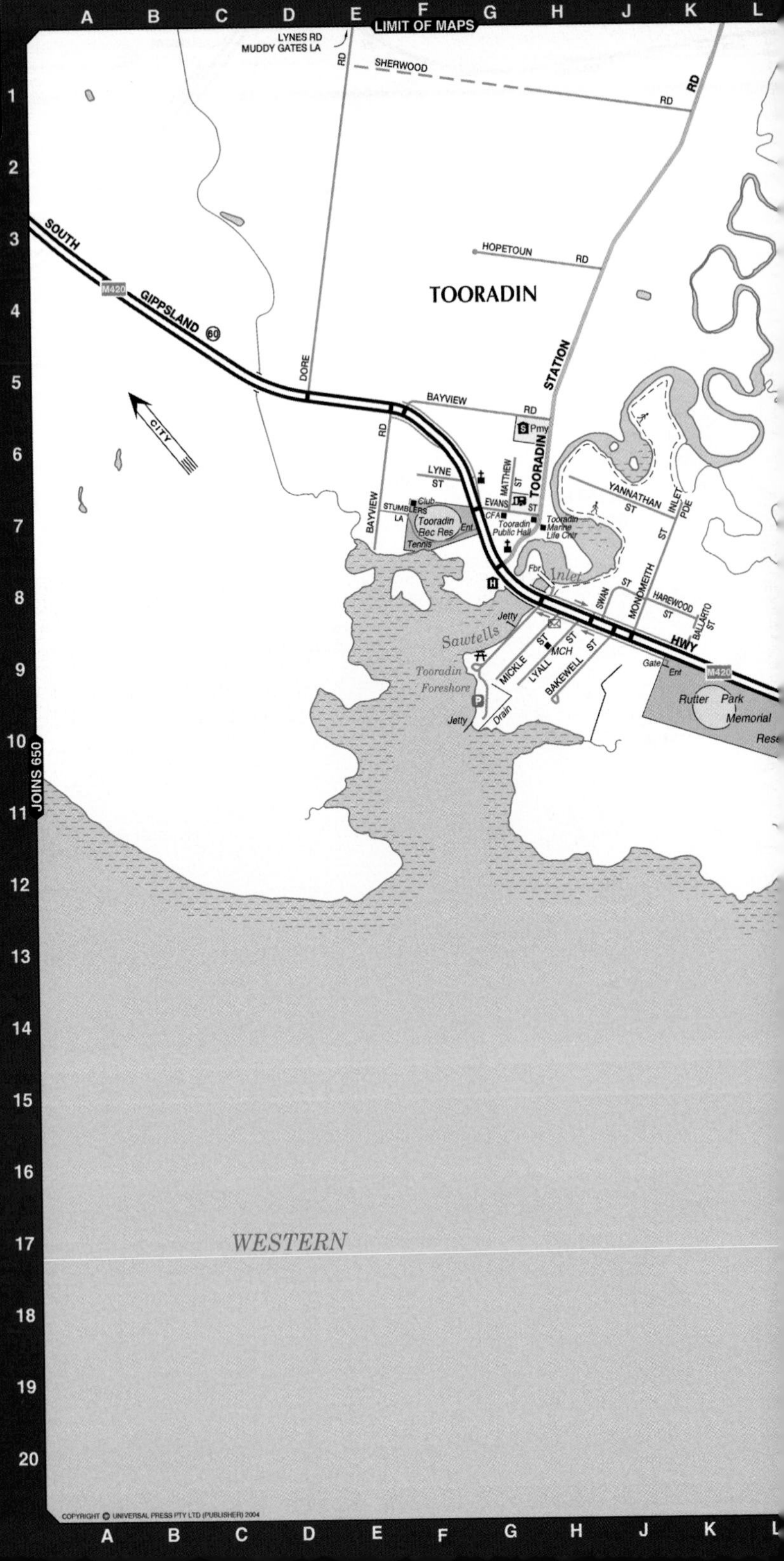
LIMIT OF MAPS
LYNES RD
MUDDY GATES LA
SHERWOOD RD
HOPETOUN RD
TOORADIN
SOUTH GIPPSLAND HWY
M420
60
DORE RD
CITY
BAYVIEW RD
STATION RD
TOORADIN
Pmy
LYNE ST
MATTHEW ST
EVANS ST
YANNATHAN ST
INLET PDE
BAYVIEW
STUMBLERS LA
Club
Tooradin Rec Res
Ent
Tennis
CFA
Tooradin Public Hall
Tooradin Marine Life Cntr
Fbr
Inlet
ST
SWAN
MONDMEITH
HAREWOOD ST
BALLARTO ST
Jetty
Sawtells
MICKLE ST
LYALL ST
MCH
BAKEWELL ST
Tooradin Foreshore
Jetty
Drain
Gate
Ent
M420
Rutter Park Memorial Rese
JOINS 650
WESTERN

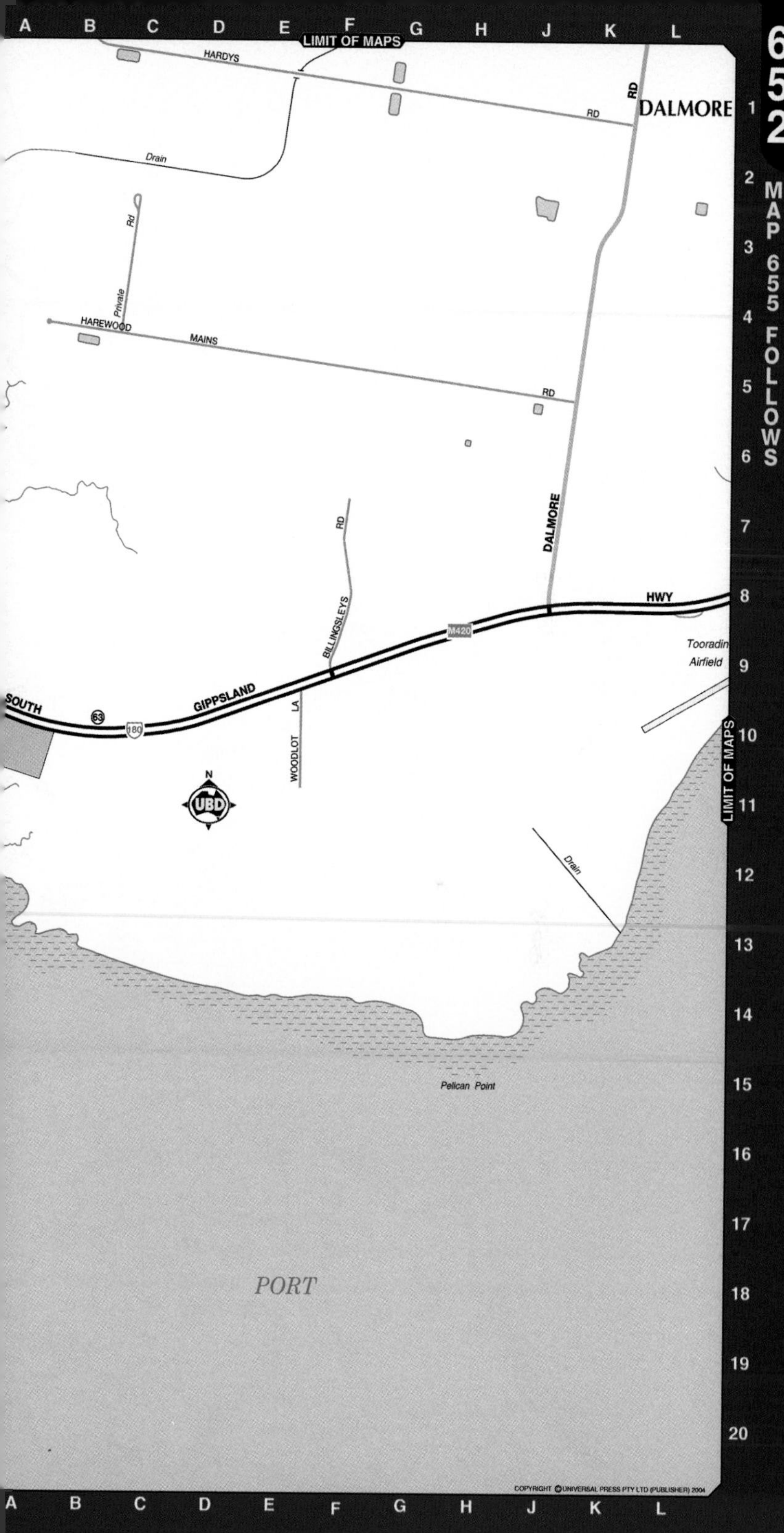
LIMIT OF MAPS
HARDYS
RD
RD
DALMORE
Drain
Rd
Private
HAREWOOD
MAINS
RD
RD
DALMORE
BILLINGSLEYS
HWY
M420
Tooradin
Airfield
SOUTH
63
GIPPSLAND
180
WOODLOT
LA
LIMIT OF MAPS
N
UBD
Drain
Pelican Point
PORT
MAP 655 FOLLOWS

PORT
PHILLIP
Hawker Beach
Mt Martha Beach North
ESPLANADE
C783
ALICE
OSBORNE
Foreshore Res
COOLANGATTA RD
Osborne Park
TAYLOR
ERNEST ST
MAUDE
CR
VICTORIA
LOTRIEL CT
Victoria Park
Balcombe Ck
Life Saving Club
Yacht Club
Mt Martha Beach South
MIRANG AV
RATHGAEL AV
WATSON
WATTLE AV
HENLEY AV
LOCHEL AV
HOWEY RD
LANGRIGG AV
BLENCAIRN AV
Tennis & Netball
MCH
RD
Foreshore Res
BAY
ST
REEVE
MOORE ST
BYRON ST
AILSA ST
DOMINION
Cmnty Cntr
Tennis
TCE
KILBURN
ELMIE
GREENSLADE CT
SINCLAIR CT
DR
JAMES CT
BUXTON
Balcombe Pt
PLEASANT VIEW CT
CR
AV
J/E Dowdle Res
CR
AV
AV
AVOCA
ELLESMERE AV
PRESCOTT
NORMANBY TCE
RD
BRAD
DOMINION
BUXTON CT S
TWO BAYS
LEMPRIERE
AMANDA CT
GR
GLENISLA
RAMSAY CT
DR
WINSTON CT
FAIRVIEW AV
DR
DR
PEN
Mt Martha Pmy
MELROSE
GLENISLA
PINDARI ST
DR
FERRERO GR
DR
GLA
LEGGATT CR
AV
IRVINE
DEAKIN
Foreshore
C783
Res
WALARA
DR
WALARA
KINROSS ST
Res ST
ORANA
LEGACY
DORSET
CORYULE
ROSLYN
MANKINA CT
GLAM
GR
ILARI CT
SOMERS
MARGUERITA
DR
FERNE PL
LABRENT CT
DICKINSON
RD
DR
SOMERSET
DR
ESPLANADE
EDWARD GR
ALEXANDRINA
DR
AV
JASPER CT
HOOPER
PANORAMA DR
GR
AV
Res CR
CORNWALL RD
CAMBRIDGE RD
Res
DEVON CT
SUNSHINE
RD

JOINS 640
641
JOINS 657
JOINS 670

A B C D E F G H J K L

1 2 3 4 5 6 7 8 9 10 11 12 13 14 15 16 17 18 19 20

MORNINGTON

MT MARTHA

Mornington Peninsula Regional Gallery
Leisure Cntr
Golf Course
Civic Res
Golf Driving Range
Bentons Square
Fossil Beach
Foreshore
Dava Beach
Bird Rock Beach
Craigie Beach
Koorootang Ret Vill
Lawton Lodge Conference Centre
Jeh Wit
Fitness Centre
Nursing Home
Reserve
Dava Lodge Nurs Home
Cemetery
J R Anderson Res
Osborne Prmy
Citation Reserve
Pistol Club
Balcombe Res
Balcombe Creek
"The Briars" Historic Property
Wetland Wk
Visitor Centre
Homestead
Josephines Restaurant
(Cellar door sales)
Briar Creek
Weber Res
Warilda Res
Campbell Res

NEPEAN HWY
ESPLANADE
BENTONS RD
CRAIGIE RD
DUNNS RD
GREEN ISLAND AV
RACECOURSE RD
URALLA DR
HOPETOUN AV
NORFOLK RD

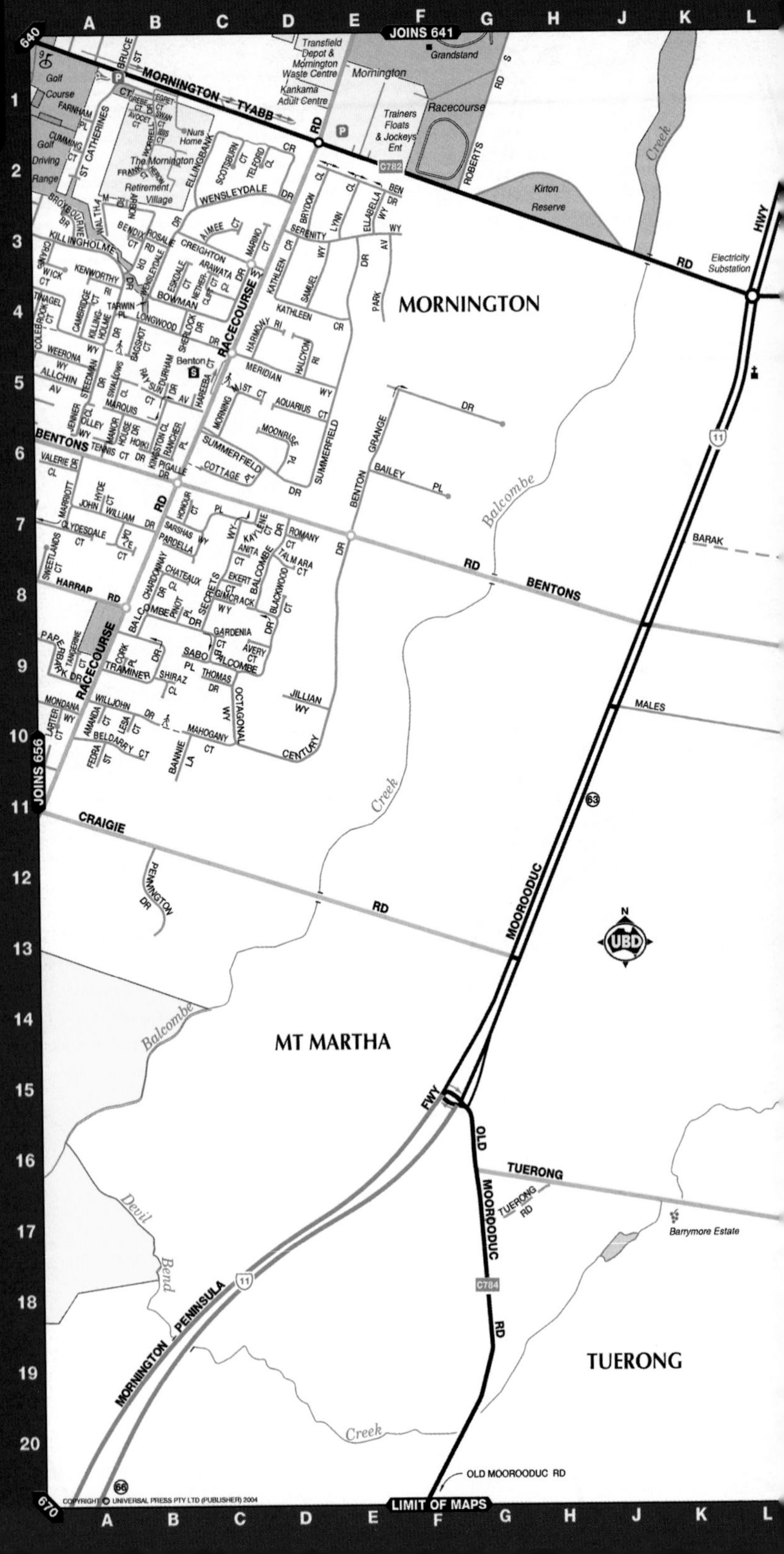

A B C D E F G H J K L
JOINS 641
640
Golf Course
Golf Driving Range
FARNHAM PL
CUMMING CT
ST CATHERINES
BRUCE ST
MORNINGTON - TYABB RD
Transfield Depot & Mornington Waste Centre
Kankama Adult Centre
Mornington
Grandstand
Racecourse
Trainers Floats & Jockeys Ent
C782
ROBERTS RD
Kirton Reserve
Creek
Electricity Substation
HWY
The Mornington Retirement Village
Nurs Home
ELLINGBANK
SCOTSBURN CT
TELFORD CL
CR
WENSLEYDALE DR
BRYDON CL
LYNN CL
ELLABELLA WY
BEN DR
WY
SERENITY
KILLINGHOLME
BROXBOURNE GR
WALTHAM
BENDIX
ROSALIE
CREIGHTON
AIMEE CT
MARINO
ARAWATA DR
KENWORTHY RI
WICK CT
TINAGEL
COLEBROOK CT
CAMBRIDGE CT
KILLINGHOLME
TARWIN PL
ESKDALE CT
NETHERCLIFT CT
BOWMAN
LONGWOOD DR
SHERLOCK DR
RACECOURSE
KATHLEEN CR
SAMUEL WY
HARMONY RI
HALCYON RI
MERIDIAN
PARK DR
AV
MORNINGTON
WEERONA WY
ALLCHIN AV
STEEDMAN DR
SWALLOWS CL
BAGSHOT CT
RAYSUN CT
DURHAM
Benton
HAREEBA CT
MIST CT
AQUARIUS CT
WY
MARQUIS
MANOR
HOUSE DR
HOIKI
KINGSTON CL
RANCHER PL
MORNING
MOONRISE PL
SUMMERFIELD DR
SUMMERFIELD
GRANGE
DR
BENTON
BAILEY PL
BENTONS
TENNIS CT DR
PIGALLE
COTTAGE
VALERIE CL
MARRIOTT
HYDE CT
JOHN
WILLIAM DR
HONOUR CT
PL
Balcombe
CLYDESDALE CT
SARSHAS WY
PARDELLA
KAYLENE CT
ANITA CT
ROMANY CT
TALMARA CT
BARAK
SWEETLANDS CT
CHARDONNAY DR
CHATEAUX
SECRETS
EKERT CT
GIMCRACK WY
BALCOMBE
BLACKWOOD CT
RD
BENTONS
HARRAP RD
PINOT PL
BALCOMBE DR
GARDENIA
AVERY CT
PAPE
TANGERINE
CORK PL
TRAMINER
SABO PL
BALCOMBE
SHIRAZ CL
THOMAS DR
OCTAGONAL WY
JILLIAN WY
MALES
MONDANA WY
LARTER CT
WILLJOHN
AMANDA CT
LESA CT
MAHOGANY CT
BELDARRY CT
FEDRA ST
BANNIE LA
CENTURY
JOINS 656
Creek
63
11
CRAIGIE
PENNINGTON DR
RD
MOOROODUC
Balcombe
MT MARTHA
FWY
OLD MOOROODUC RD
TUERONG
TUERONG RD
Barrymore Estate
Devil Bend
MORNINGTON PENINSULA
C784
TUERONG
Creek
OLD MOOROODUC RD
66
670
LIMIT OF MAPS

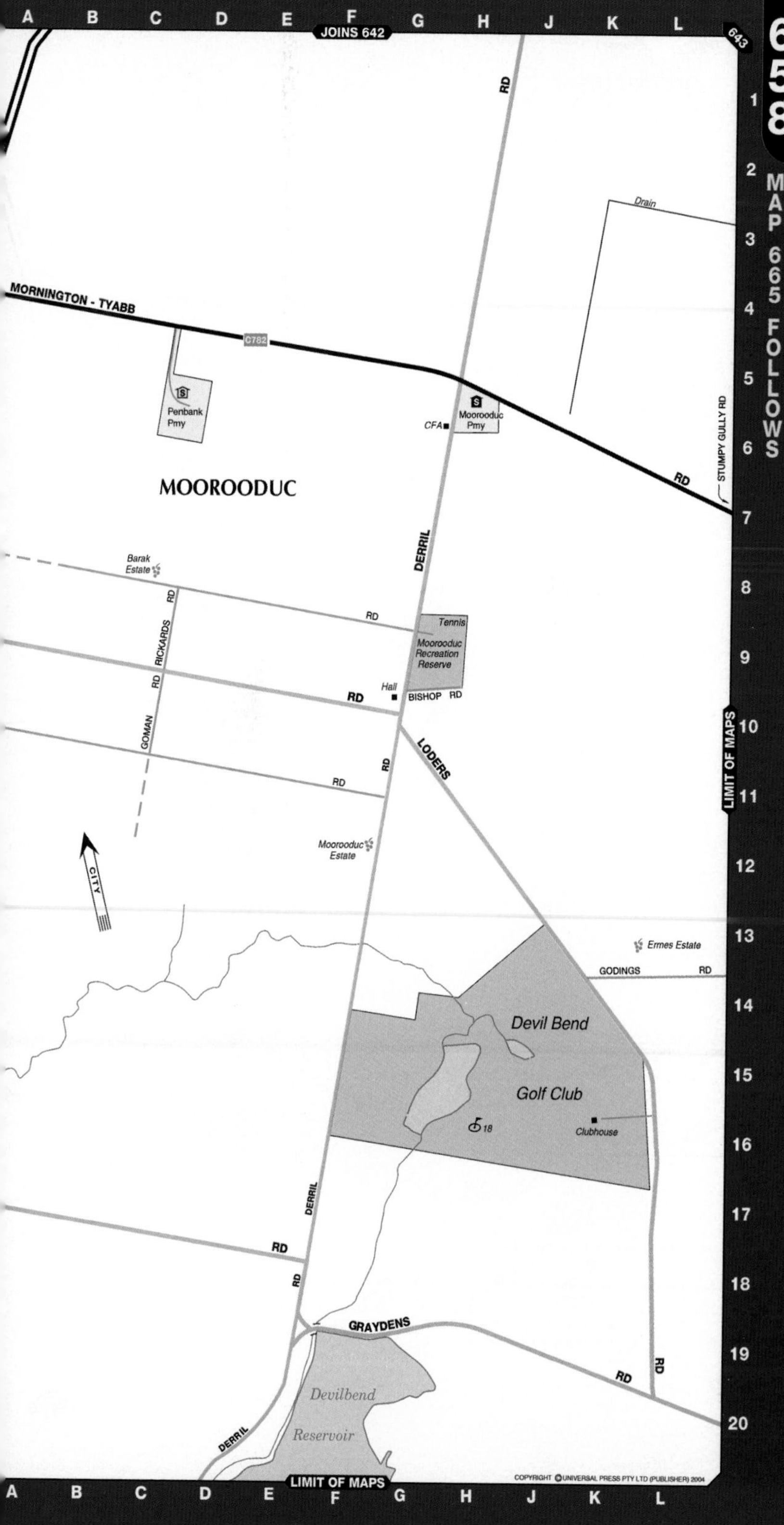

A
B
C
D
E
F
G
H
J
K
L
JOINS 642
643
1
2
3
4
5
6
7
8
9
10
11
12
13
14
15
16
17
18
19
20
MAP 665 FOLLOWS
LIMIT OF MAPS
MORNINGTON - TYABB
C782
RD
Penbank Pmy
Moorooduc Pmy
CFA
Drain
STUMPY GULLY RD
MOOROODUC
DERRIL
RD
Barak Estate
RICKARDS
RD
GOMAN
RD
Tennis
Moorooduc Recreation Reserve
Hall
BISHOP
RD
LODERS
Moorooduc Estate
CITY
Ermes Estate
GODINGS
RD
Devil Bend
Golf Club
18
Clubhouse
DERRIL
RD
GRAYDENS
RD
Devilbend
Reservoir
DERRIL
LIMIT OF MAPS

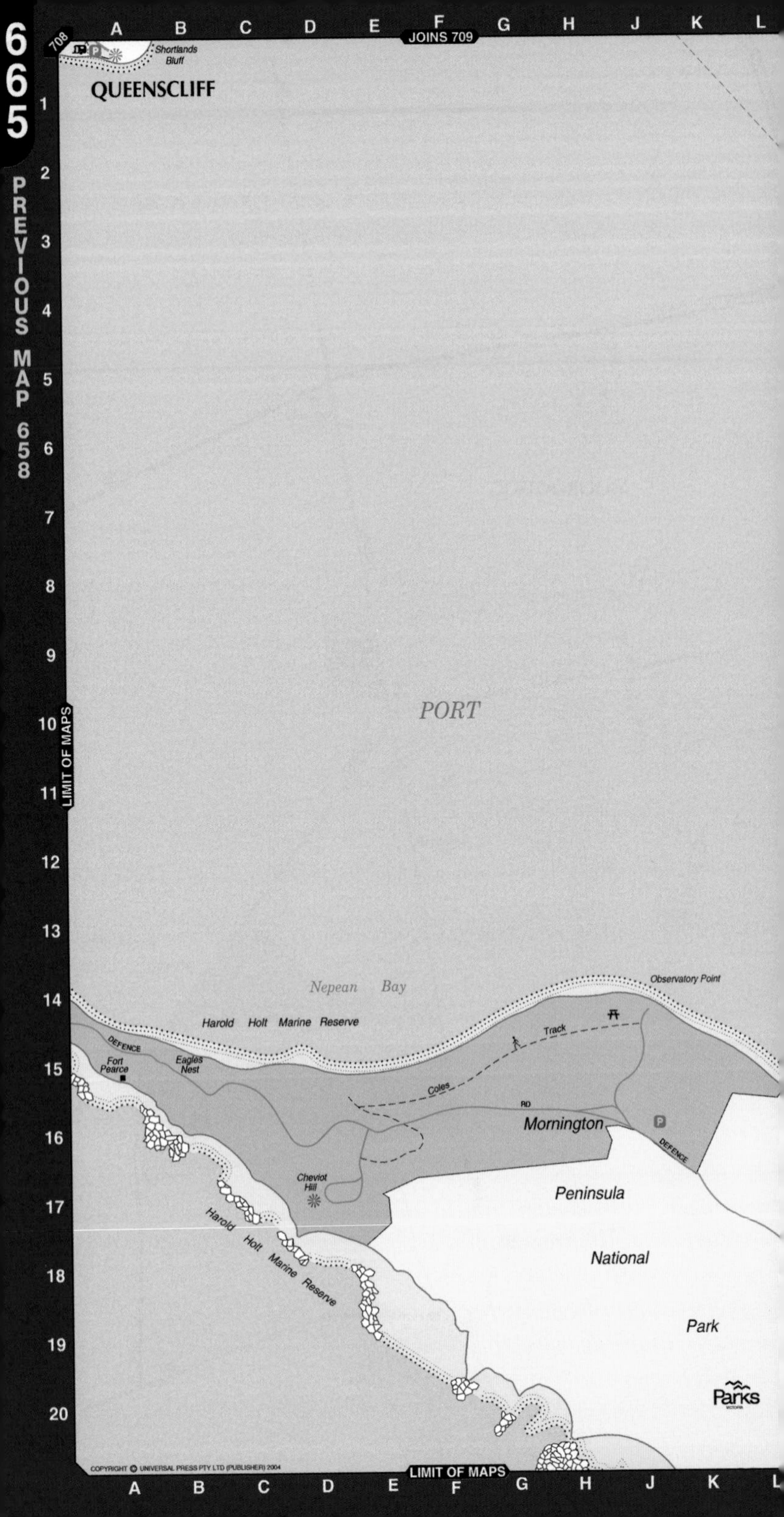
665
PREVIOUS MAP 658
JOINS 709
708
LIMIT OF MAPS
QUEENSCLIFF
Shortlands Bluff
PORT
Nepean Bay
Observatory Point
Harold Holt Marine Reserve
DEFENCE
Fort Pearce
Eagles Nest
Track
Coles
RD
Mornington
Peninsula
National
Park
Cheviot Hill
Harold Holt Marine Reserve
Parks
LIMIT OF MAPS
COPYRIGHT © UNIVERSAL PRESS PTY LTD (PUBLISHER) 2004

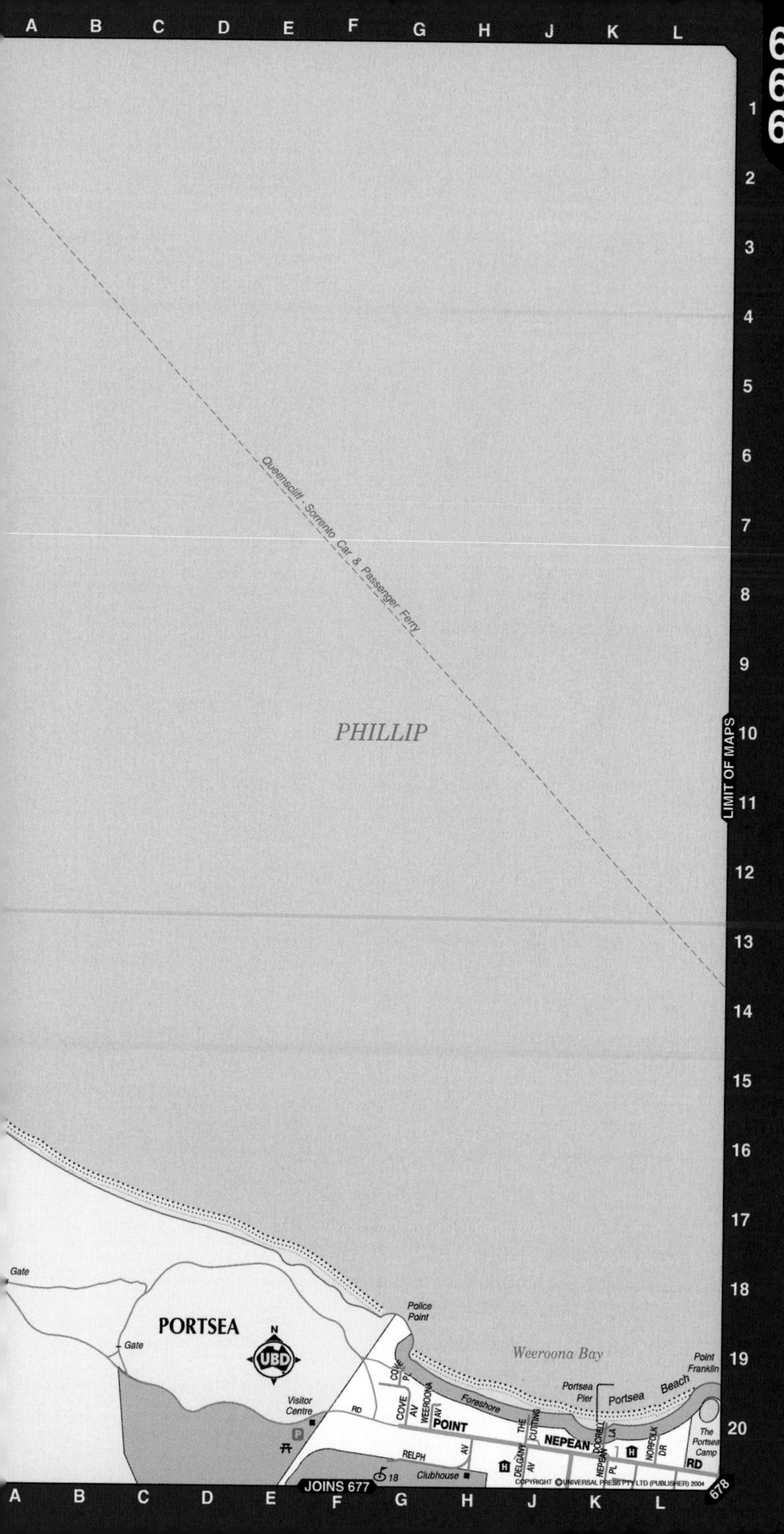

A
B
C
D
E
F
G
H
J
K
L
666
1
2
3
4
5
6
7
8
9
10
11
12
13
14
15
16
17
18
19
20
LIMIT OF MAPS
Queenscliff - Sorrento Car & Passenger Ferry
PHILLIP
Gate
PORTSEA
Gate
Police Point
Weeroona Bay
Point Franklin
Portsea Pier
Portsea Beach
Foreshore
Visitor Centre
COVE PL
COVE AV
WEEROONA AV
POINT
THE CUTTING
DELGANY AV
NEPEAN
DOCRELL LA
NEPEAN PL
NORFOLK DR
RD
RELPH AV
Clubhouse
18
The Portsea Camp
JOINS 677
678
COPYRIGHT © UNIVERSAL PRESS PTY LTD (PUBLISHER) 2004

PORT

JOINS 685

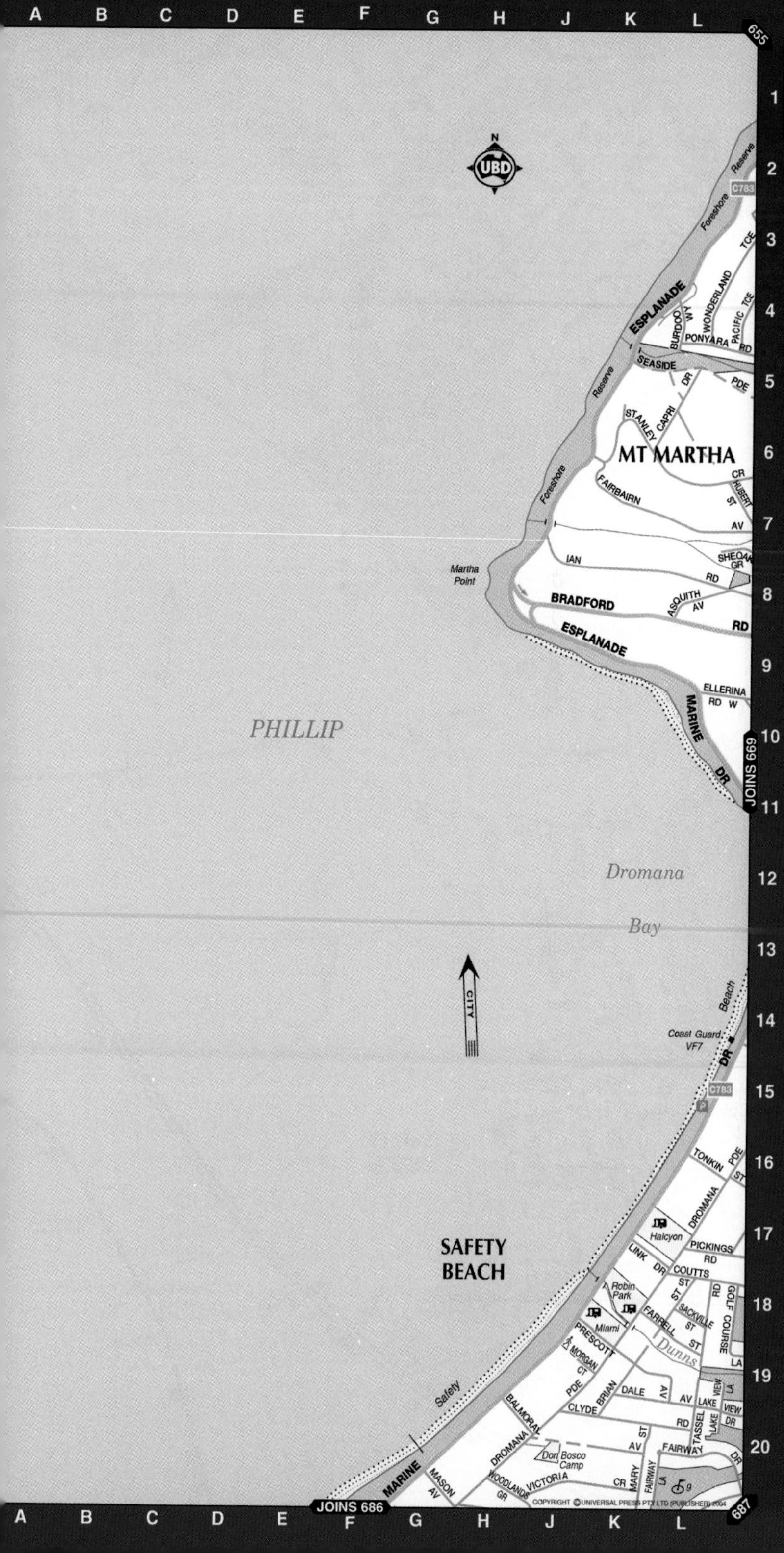

PHILLIP
Dromana
Bay
MT MARTHA
SAFETY BEACH
Martha Point
Coast Guard VF7
CITY
ESPLANADE
Foreshore Reserve
C783
TCE
WONDERLAND
BURDOO WY
PACIFIC TCE
PONYARA RD
SEASIDE PDE
DR
CAPRI
STANLEY
FAIRBAIRN
CR
HUBERT ST
AV
IAN RD
SHEOAK GR
BRADFORD RD
ASQUITH AV
ESPLANADE
ELLERINA RD W
MARINE DR
Beach
DR
TONKIN PDE
ST
DROMANA
Halcyon
PICKINGS RD
LINK DR
COUTTS ST
Robin Park
ST
RD
SACKVILLE ST
GOLF COURSE
FARRELL ST
Miami
PRESCOTT
Dunns
MORGAN CT
PDE
LA
BRIAN
DALE AV
AV
LAKE VIEW LA
Safety
BALMORAL
CLYDE
RD
TASSEL
LAKE VIEW DR
DROMANA
ST
AV
FAIRWAY
Don Bosco Camp
DR
MARINE
MASON AV
WOODLANDS GR
VICTORIA
CR
MARY
FAIRWAY
LA
9

JOINS 669
JOINS 686
687

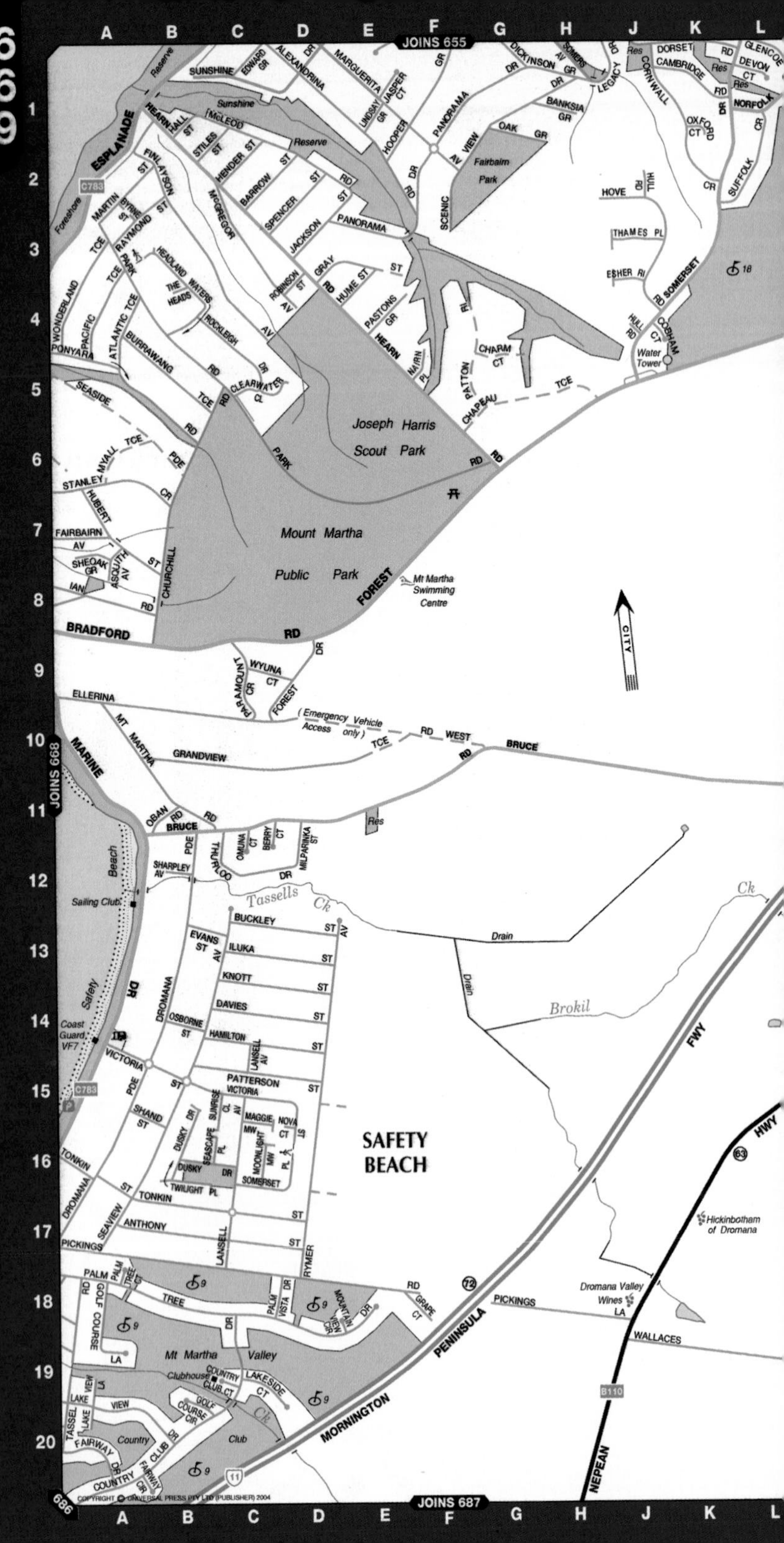

A B C D E F G H J K L
1 2 3 4 5 6 7 8 9 10 11 12 13 14 15 16 17 18 19 20
JOINS 655
JOINS 668
JOINS 687
686
SUNSHINE
EDWARD GR
ALEXANDRINA DR
MARGUERITA
JASPER CT
LINDSAY GR
HOOPER DR
PANORAMA
SCENIC
VIEW AV
Fairbairn Park
OAK GR
DICKINSON GR
SOMERS AV
BANKSIA GR
LEGACY DR
Res
DORSET RD
CAMBRIDGE
CORNWALL
GLENCOE
DEVON CT
NORFOLK DR
OXFORD CT
SUFFOLK CR
HOVE RD
HULL
THAMES PL
ESHER RI
SOMERSET
HULL CT
COBHAM
Water Tower
Reserve
Sunshine
ESPLANADE
HEARN
HALL ST
McLEOD
STILES ST
HENDER ST
BARROW ST
SPENCER ST
JACKSON ST
RD
C783
Foreshore
FINLAYSON ST
MARTIN TCE
BYRNE ST
RAYMOND ST
PARK
McGREGOR RD
HEADLAND
THE HEADS
WATERS
ROCKLEIGH
ROBINSON AV
GRAY RD
HUME ST
PASTONS GR
HEARN RD
NAIRN PL
RI
CHARM CT
PATTON
CHAPEAU
TCE
WONDERLAND
PACIFIC
ATLANTIC TCE
PONYARA
BURRAWANG
CLEARWATER CL
DR
SEASIDE
Joseph Harris Scout Park
MYALL TCE
PDE
STANLEY
CR
HUBERT
FAIRBAIRN AV
SHEOAK GR
ASQUITH AV
IAN
CHURCHILL
Mount Martha Public Park
FOREST RD
Mt Martha Swimming Centre
BRADFORD
CITY
PARAMOUNT CR
WYUNA CT
FOREST DR
ELLERINA
(Emergency Vehicle Access only)
MT MARTHA
GRANDVIEW
TCE
RD WEST
BRUCE RD
MARINE
OBAN RD
BRUCE
THURLOO DR
OMUNA CT
BERRY CT
MILPARINKA ST
SHARPLEY AV
Beach
Sailing Club
Tassells Ck
Drain
BUCKLEY ST
EVANS ST
AV
ILUKA ST
KNOTT ST
DAVIES ST
OSBORNE ST
HAMILTON ST
LANSELL AV
Safety
Coast Guard VF7
VICTORIA
PATTERSON ST
Brokil
FWY
Ck
SHAND ST
DUSKY DR
SEASCAPE PL
SUNRISE CL
MAGGIE MW
MOONLIGHT MW
NOVA CT
TWILIGHT PL
SOMERSET
SAFETY BEACH
HWY
63
TONKIN
DROMANA
SEAVIEW
ANTHONY ST
PICKINGS
LANSELL
RYMER
Hickinbotham of Dromana
PALM
TREE
GOLF COURSE RD
VISTA DR
MOUNTAIN VIEW CIR
GRAPE CT
72
PICKINGS LA
Dromana Valley Wines
WALLACES
PENINSULA
LA
Mt Martha Valley
Clubhouse
COUNTRY CLUB CT
LAKESIDE CT
LAKE VIEW
TASSEL
FAIRWAY DR
GOLF COURSE CIR
Country Club
COUNTRY CLUB DR
MORNINGTON
B110
NEPEAN
11

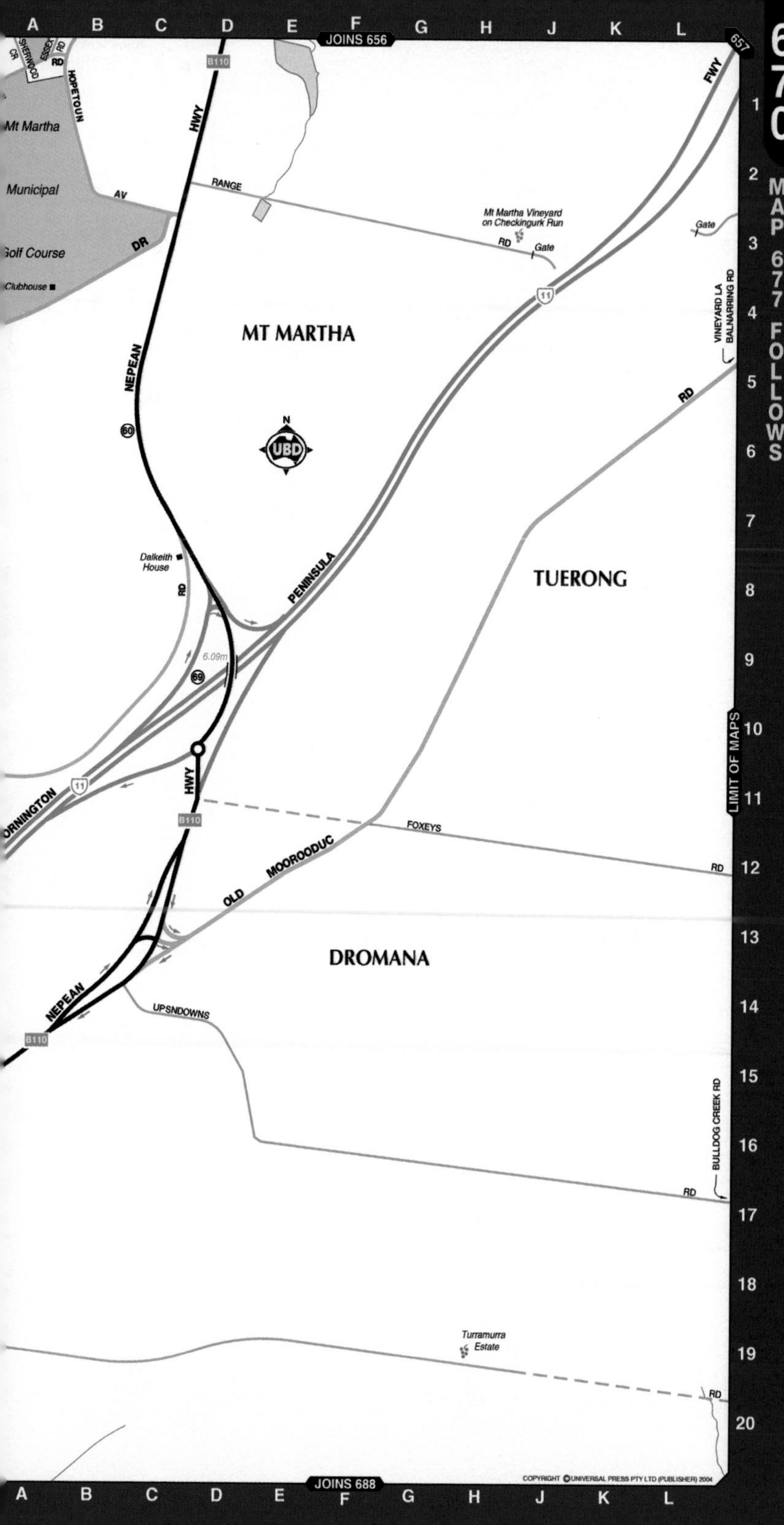

MAP 677 FOLLOWS

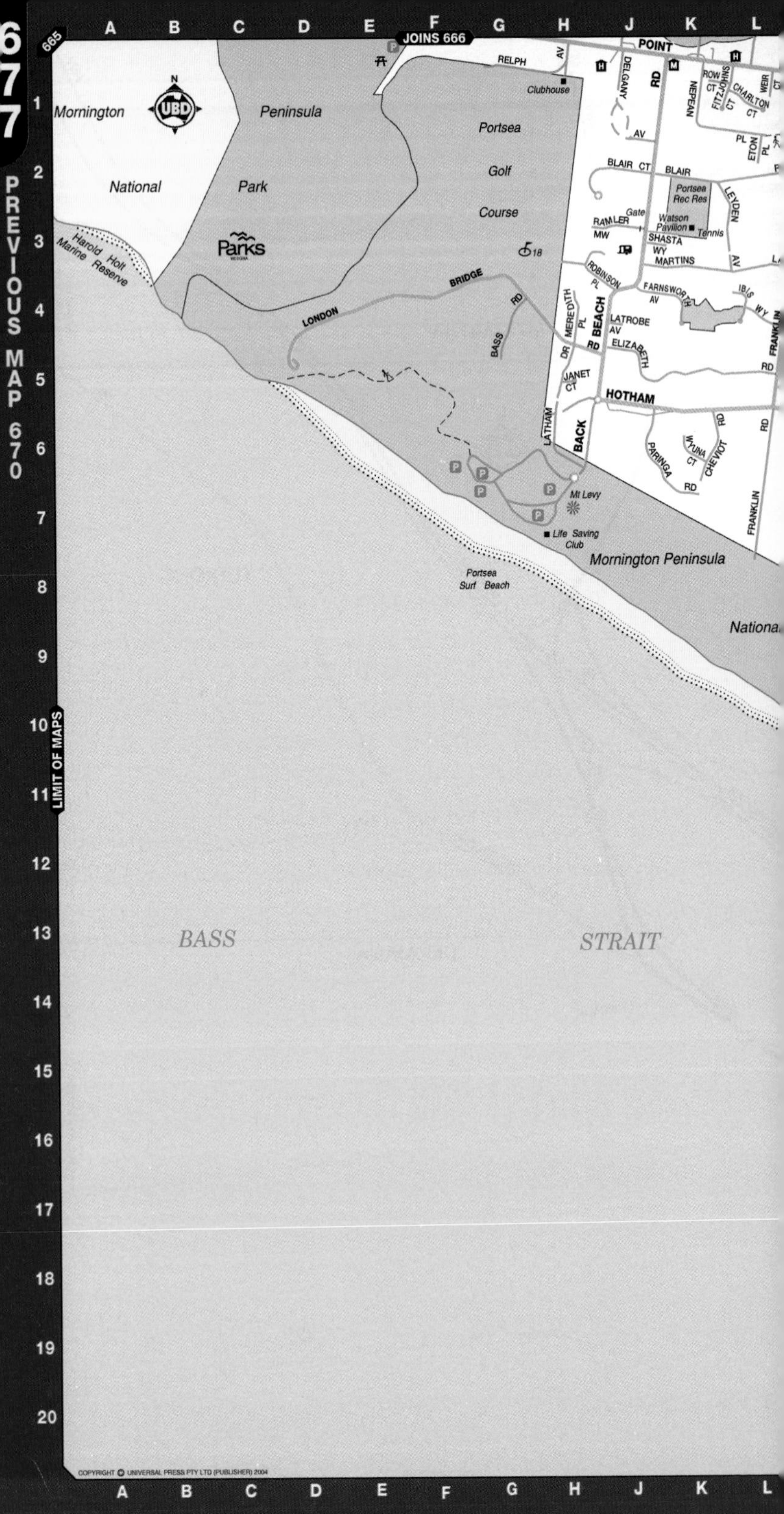

677
PREVIOUS MAP 670
665
JOINS 666
LIMIT OF MAPS
Mornington
Peninsula
National
Park
Parks
Harold Holt Marine Reserve
Portsea
Golf
Course
Clubhouse
RELPH
POINT
RD
DELGANY
AV
NEPEAN
ROW CT
FITZJOHNS CT
CHARLTON CT
WEIR
EATON
PL
BLAIR CT
BLAIR
Portsea Rec Res
LEYDEN
AV
Gate
RAMLER MW
Watson Pavilion
Tennis
SHASTA WY
MARTINS
ROBINSON PL
FARNSWORTH AV
IBIS WY
FRANKLIN
LONDON
BRIDGE
RD
BASS
MEREDITH DR
PL
BEACH RD
LATROBE AV
ELIZABETH
RD
JANET CT
HOTHAM
LATHAM
BACK
PARINGA
W'PUNA CT
CHEVIOT
RD
Mt Levy
Life Saving Club
Mornington Peninsula
National
Portsea Surf Beach
BASS
STRAIT

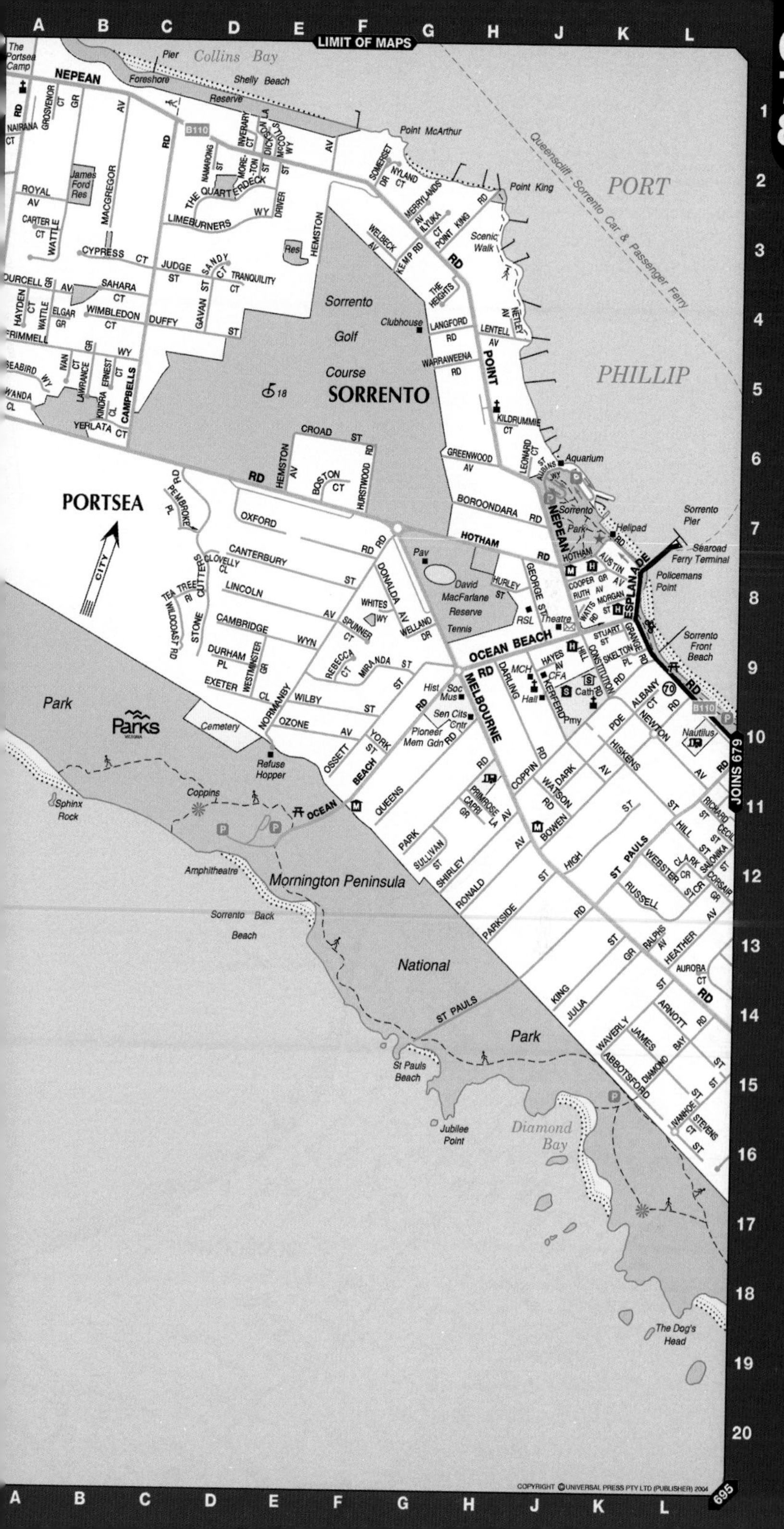
LIMIT OF MAPS
The Portsea Camp
Pier
Collins Bay
Foreshore Reserve
Shelly Beach
NEPEAN
Point McArthur
Point King
PORT
PHILLIP
Queenscliff - Sorrento Car & Passenger Ferry
Scenic Walk
James Ford Res
THE QUARTERDECK
LIMEBURNERS
ROYAL AV
CYPRESS CT
JUDGE ST
SANDY CT
TRANQUILITY CT
SAHARA CT
WIMBLEDON CT
DUFFY
GAVAN ST
Sorrento Golf Course
Clubhouse
LANGFORD RD
WARRAWEENA RD
LENTELL AV
POINT
KILDRUMMIE CT
SORRENTO
CROAD ST
HEMSTON AV
BOSTON CT
HURSTWOOD RD
GREENWOOD AV
Aquarium
BOROONDARA RD
PORTSEA
CITY
OXFORD
HOTHAM RD
CANTERBURY ST
LINCOLN AV
CAMBRIDGE WYN
DURHAM PL
EXETER CL
WILBY ST
OZONE AV
Sorrento Park
Helipad
Sorrento Pier
Searoad Ferry Terminal
Policemans Point
ESPLANADE
David MacFarlane Reserve
Tennis
Pav
RSL
Theatre
OCEAN BEACH RD
MELBOURNE
Sorrento Front Beach
Nautilus
Hist Soc Mus
Sen Cits Cntr
Pioneer Mem Gdn
CFA
MCH
Hall
Cath
Pmy
B110
JOINS 679
Park
Parks
Cemetery
Refuse Hopper
Sphinx Rock
Coppins
OCEAN
Amphitheatre
Mornington Peninsula
Sorrento Back Beach
National
ST PAULS
Park
St Pauls Beach
Jubilee Point
Diamond Bay
The Dog's Head
QUEENS
PARK
SULLIVAN
SHIRLEY
RONALD
PARKSIDE
HIGH
ST PAULS
WEBSTER
RUSSELL
HEATHER
AURORA CT
KING
JULIA
WAVERLY
JAMES
ARNOTT
DIAMOND BAY
ABBOTSFORD
IVANHOE
STEVENS
COPYRIGHT © UNIVERSAL PRESS PTY LTD (PUBLISHER) 2004

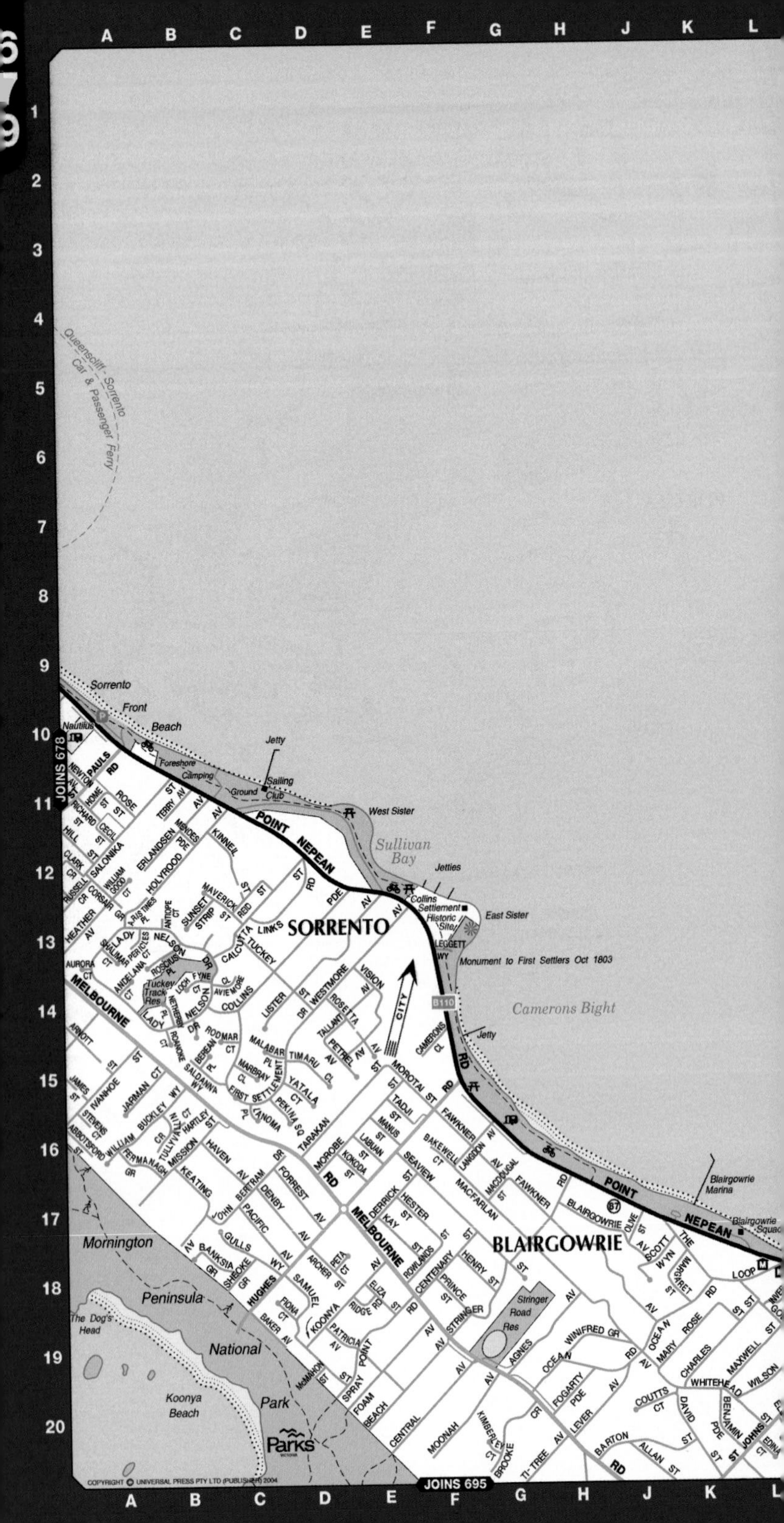

A B C D E F G H J K L
1 2 3 4 5 6 7 8 9 10 11 12 13 14 15 16 17 18 19 20
Queenscliff - Sorrento Car & Passenger Ferry
Sorrento Front Beach
Nautilus
Foreshore Camping Ground
Sailing Club
Jetty
West Sister
Sullivan Bay
Jetties
Collins Settlement Historic Site
East Sister
LEGGETT WY
Monument to First Settlers Oct 1803
Camerons Bight
Jetty
SORRENTO
POINT NEPEAN RD
B110
CITY
Tuckey Track Res
MELBOURNE RD
Stringer Road Res
BLAIRGOWRIE
Blairgowrie Marina
Blairgowrie Squadron
B7
Mornington Peninsula National Park
The Dog's Head
Koonya Beach
Parks Victoria
JOINS 678
JOINS 695
COPYRIGHT © UNIVERSAL PRESS PTY LTD (PUBLISHER) 2004

PORT
PHILLIP
680
MAP 683 FOLLOWS
LIMIT OF MAPS
RYE
NEPEAN
POINT
RD
Blairgowrie
Clayton Pk
Harry Blythe Plgrd
Foreshore
Reserve
Tyrone
JOINS 696
697
COPYRIGHT © UNIVERSAL PRESS PTY LTD (PUBLISHER) 2004

683
PREVIOUS MAP 680
LIMIT OF MAPS
PORT
ROSEBUD WEST
POINT NEPEAN RD
Rosebud Foreshore Reserve
Rotary Park
Foreshore Ranger
Lotus Lodge Hostel For Aged
Nursing Home
Rosebud Hospital
Port Phillip Plaza
Cath Prmy
Navarac
Chinamans Ck
Nurs Home
Sundowner Willows
The Village Glen (Ret Village)
Rosebud Secondary College
Hillview Stadium
Res
Rosebud Cmnty Rehab Service
Parks Victoria
Olympic Park
EASTBOURNE RD
BONEO RD
MOUNT
CLACTON
JOINS 699
698
COPYRIGHT © UNIVERSAL PRESS PTY LTD (PUBLISHER) 2004

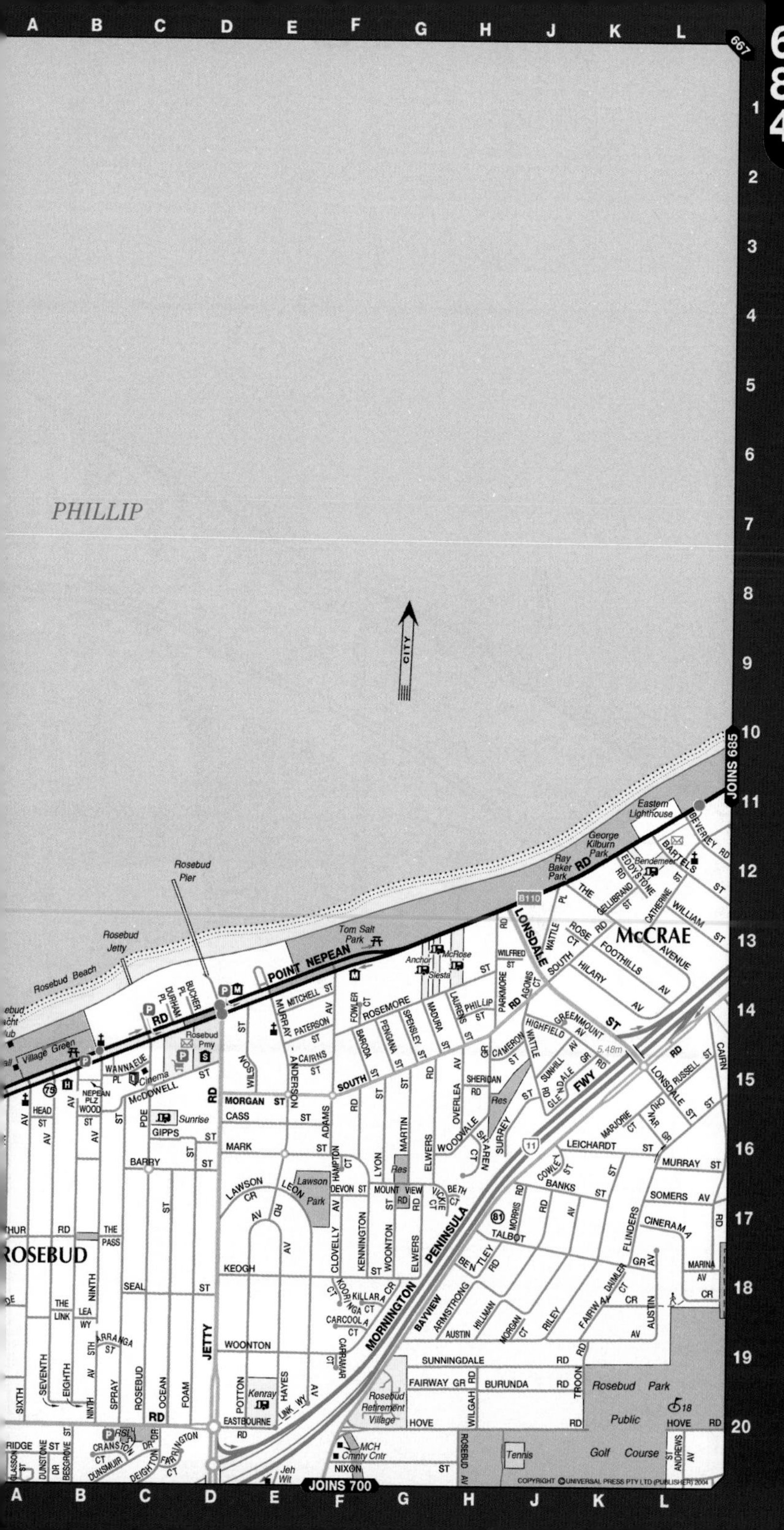

A B C D E F G H J K L
667
1 2 3 4 5 6 7 8 9 10 11 12 13 14 15 16 17 18 19 20
PHILLIP
CITY
JOINS 685
JOINS 700
Rosebud Pier
Rosebud Jetty
Rosebud Beach
Eastern Lighthouse
George Kilburn Park
Ray Baker Park
Tom Salt Park
McCRAE
ROSEBUD
POINT NEPEAN RD
LONSDALE ST
MORNINGTON PENINSULA FWY
JETTY RD
Rosebud Park Public Golf Course
Lawson Park
Rosebud Retirement Village
MCH
Cmnty Cntr
Tennis
COPYRIGHT © UNIVERSAL PRESS PTY LTD (PUBLISHER) 2004

PORT
PHILLIP
Anthonys Nose
NEPEAN
POINT
LATROBE
MORNINGTON
PENINSULA
McCRAE
ROSEBUD
Arthurs Seat State Park
Dromana Cemetery
Bowens Pt 145m
Franklin Pt 195m
Murrays Lookout 245m
Chapmans Pt 271m
McCrae Homestead
Heronswood
MATTHEW FLINDERS BRIDGE
Arthurs Peak Restaurant
Tower
Fauna Pk
Arthurs Seat Maze
Seawinds Park
Dam
McKellar Flora Reserve
Rosebud Park Public Golf Course
Two Bays Walking Track
Dromana Pmy
Cmnty Hall
Ct Hse Res
Foreshore
Splitters
Waterfall Ck
WATERFALL GULLY RD
PURVES RD
ARTHURS SEAT RD
Chairlift
3.5m Clearance to Road
CITY
Parks

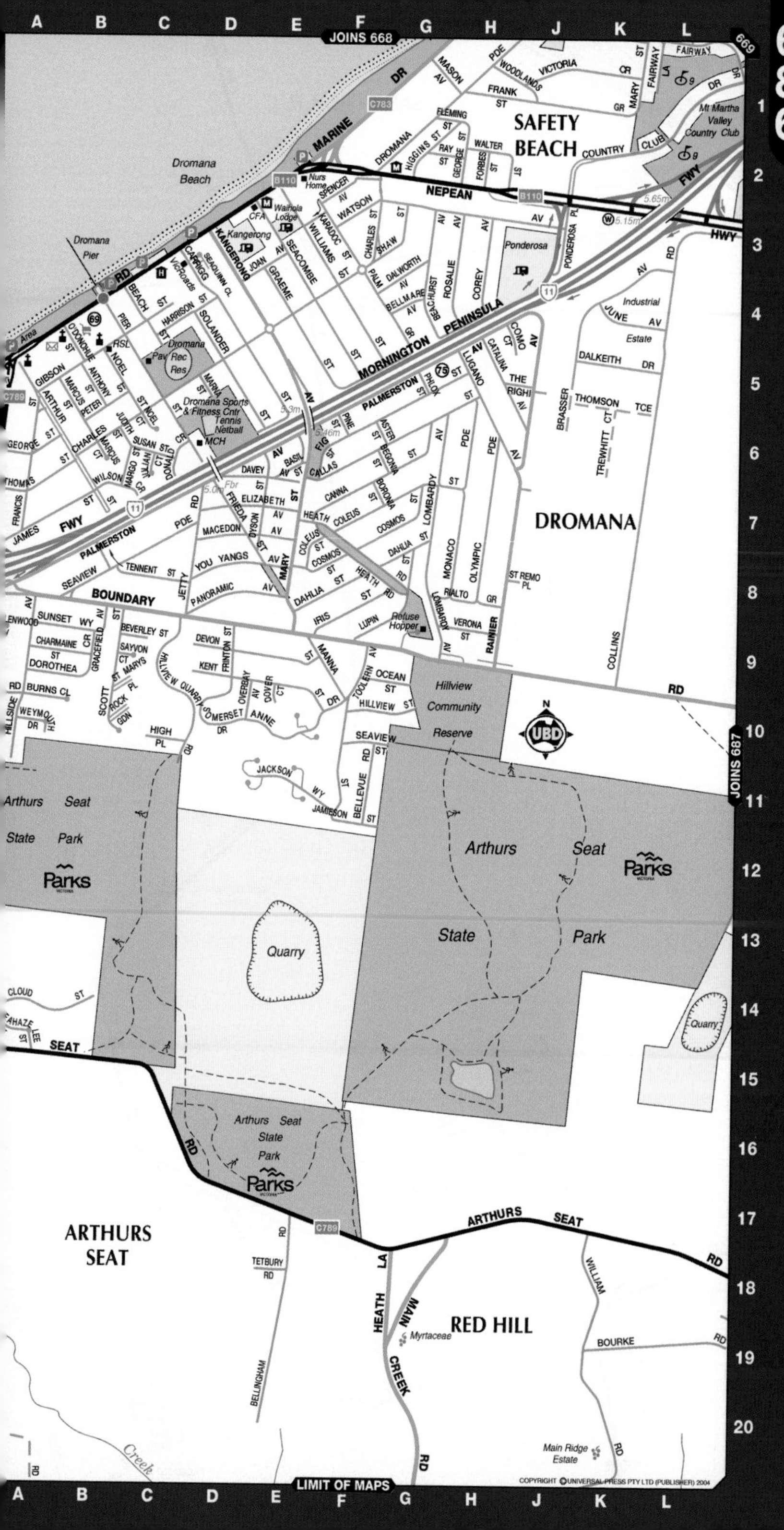

JOINS 668
669
SAFETY BEACH
Dromana Beach
Dromana Pier
Mt Martha Valley Country Club
MARINE DR
NEPEAN HWY
MORNINGTON PENINSULA FWY
PALMERSTON AV
BOUNDARY RD
Dromana Rec Res
Dromana Sports & Fitness Cntr
Industrial Estate
Ponderosa
DROMANA
Hillview Community Reserve
Refuse Hopper
JOINS 687
Arthurs Seat State Park
Parks VICTORIA
Quarry
ARTHURS SEAT RD
ARTHURS SEAT
RED HILL
MAIN CREEK RD
HEATH LA
Myrtaceae
Main Ridge Estate
LIMIT OF MAPS

668
JOINS 669

A B C D E F G H J K L

SAFETY BEACH

FAIRWAY DR
COUNTRY CLUB DR
FAIRWAY CIR
MORNINGTON PENINSULA FWY
11
Mt Martha Valley Country Club
Dromana Golf Course
Dromana
Dromana Twin Drive-in Theatre
Dunns
Bald Hill
Drain
NEPEAN HWY
B110
Moats Corner
COLLINS RD
MARYFIELD LA
DUNNS CREEK RD
C788
Creek
Drain
LA
RD
Dromana Estate
Karina
C787
Drain
WHITE HILL (MORNINGTON - FLINDERS RD)
Recreation Reserve
RD
Wildlife Sanctuary
Dromana Secondary College
Peninsula Special Dev
OLD WHITE HILL
Dromana Reservoir
CITY
SHERGOLDS
Bald Hill Creek
BOUNDARY RD
Gate
Road
EATONS CUTTING
(Fire
LUTON AV
HARRISONS
Private
RD
Access
Tracks)
Marion Rosetzky Gallery
McILROYS
RD
Quarry
Arthurs Seat State Park
Circuit Walk
EATONS CUTTING RD
LOOKOUT RD
Parks VICTORIA
Gate
HOLMES RD
Arthurs Seat State Park
RD
LA
ARTHURS SEAT RD
C789
EATONS CUTTING
COLLINS ST
BOURKE RD
ELIZABETH RD
Red Hill Consolidated Pmy
SHEEHANS
ARKWELLS
Red Hill Recreation Reserve
Showground & Market
Tennis
MCH
LA
ANDREWS
PROSSORS LA

JOINS 686
LIMIT OF MAPS

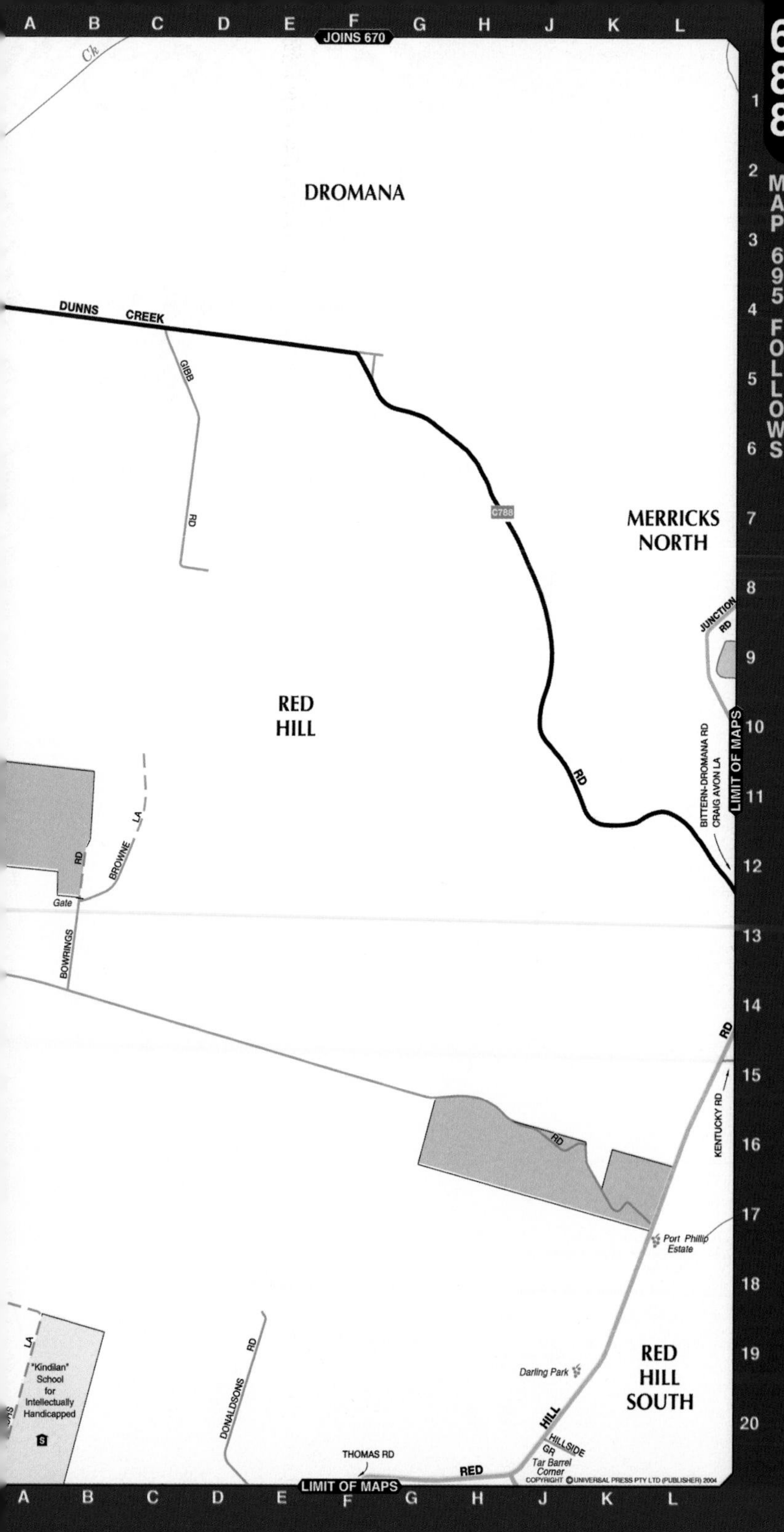
A B C D E F G H J K L
JOINS 670
MAP 695 FOLLOWS
Ck
DROMANA
DUNNS CREEK
GIBB RD
C788
RD
MERRICKS NORTH
JUNCTION RD
RED HILL
LIMIT OF MAPS
BITTERN-DROMANA RD
CRAIG AVON LA
RD
BROWNE LA
Gate
BOWRINGS
RD
KENTUCKY RD
RD
Port Phillip Estate
LA
"Kindilan" School for Intellectually Handicapped
DONALDSONS RD
Darling Park
RED HILL SOUTH
HILL
HILLSIDE GR
Tar Barrel Corner
THOMAS RD
RED
LIMIT OF MAPS
1 2 3 4 5 6 7 8 9 10 11 12 13 14 15 16 17 18 19 20

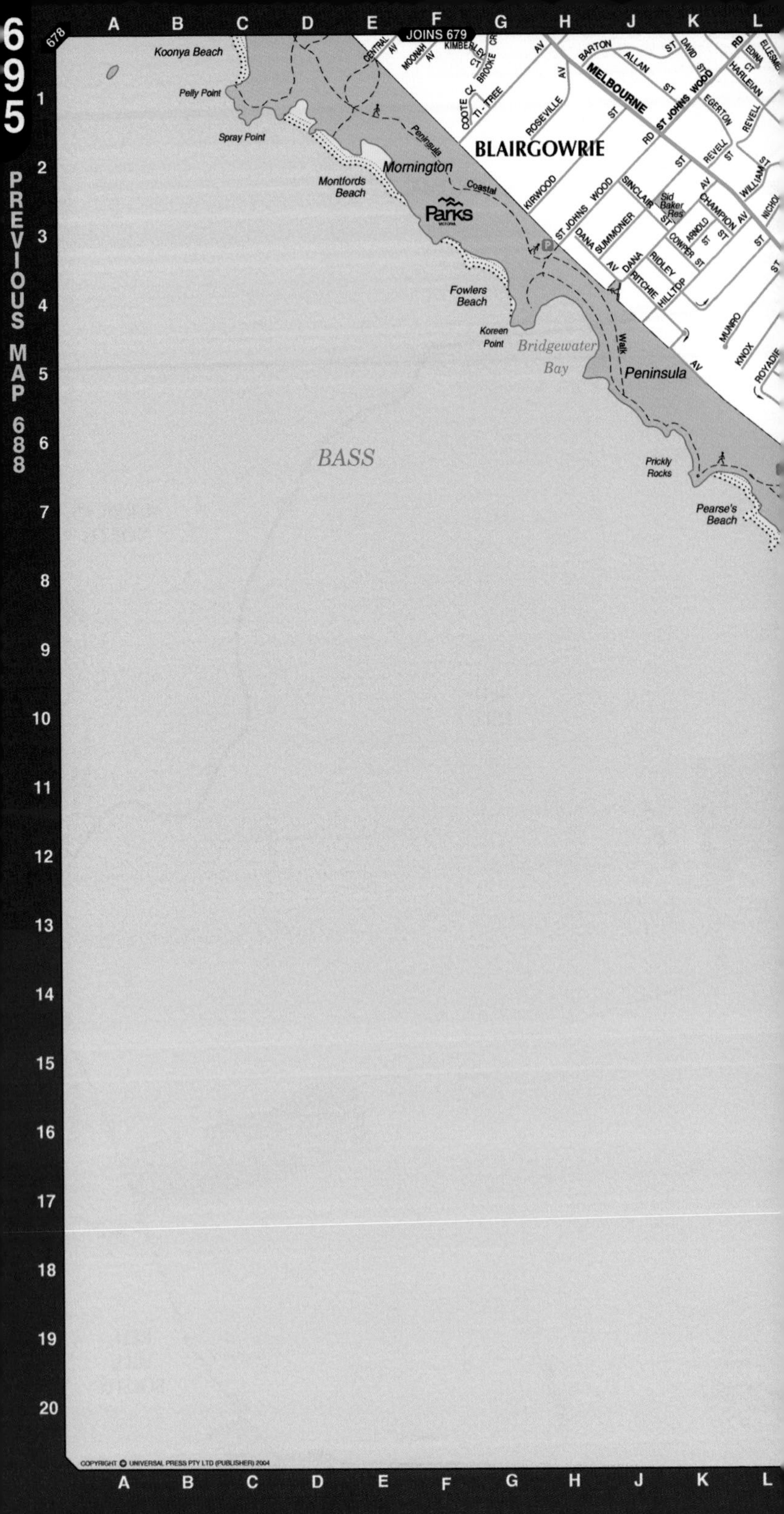
JOINS 679
678
PREVIOUS MAP 688
BLAIRGOWRIE
Koonya Beach
Pelly Point
Spray Point
Montfords Beach
Mornington Peninsula
Parks
Peninsula Coastal Walk
Fowlers Beach
Koreen Point
Bridgewater Bay
Peninsula
Prickly Rocks
Pearse's Beach
BASS
MELBOURNE RD
ST JOHNS WOOD RD
ROSEVILLE AV
KIRWOOD
SINCLAIR ST
Sid Baker Res
CHAMPION AV
SUMMONER
RIDLEY
RITCHIE
HILLTOP
MUNRO
KNOX
BARTON
ALLAN ST
EGERTON
REVELL ST
HARLEIAN
WILLIAM ST
COOTE CL
TI-TREE
BROOKE CR
KIMBERLEY CT
MOONAH AV
CENTRAL AV
ARNOLD ST
COWPER ST
DANA AV
COPYRIGHT © UNIVERSAL PRESS PTY LTD (PUBLISHER) 2004

A B C D E F G H J K L
JOINS 680
JOINS 697
1 2 3 4 5 6 7 8 9 10 11 12 13 14 15 16 17 18 19 20
RYE
Blairgowrie
STRAIT
National Park
Peninsula Coastal Walk
Dimmicks Beach
The Divide
Number Sixteen Beach
Parks
Proposed Freeway
CITY
UBD
POINT NEPEAN RD
B110
Reserve
Harry Blythe Plgrd
GR Res
MELBOURNE RD
CANTERBURY JETTY RD
TASMAN DR
BROWNS RD
GLENVUE RD
LANDSDOWNE
GRANT
KENNEDY
ADELAIDE
MADELEINE
DUNTROON AV
AUSTIN ST
GORDON ST
JOHNSON AV
EDGAR
ROSLYN
ALEXANDER AV
MILTON
FERN GR
PARSON ST
BECKET ST
VALENTINE
HOLDEN
WILDCOAST
WALBROOK
DOE
FLORENCE
PRESTON
HOGAN
LOUISE ST
WAGSTAFF ST
HACKWORTH RD
BELINDA ST
MARCIA
BRUCE AV
LANDRA
DRUM ST
MENZIES
SARA
MARMION ST
MERNDA
GERALDINE
JAMES
HEYFIELD
HAY
STRATFORD RD
COORAMINTA RD
ROLLS CT
AVON
BREWSTER
FRANCIS
EVANS
SABATO
HOWELL
PASADENA
NIBLICK
FAIRWAY DR
BACHLI
ST ANDREWS DR
SARAZEN
THOMSON
FLINDERS
PENINSULA AV
FRENCH ST
WOOMERA
SHERWOOD FOREST DR
GLADWELL
TANYA ST
LUCIEN
WHITE CLIFFS
BIMBIANG CR
ARUNTA CT
JEDDA ST

A B C D E F G H J K L

PORT

Rye Pier

Rye Beach

POINT NEPEAN RD

Foreshore Reserve

Rye Yacht Club

Rye Bicentennial Park

R J Rowley Recreation Reserve

Cmnty Hse

MCH Civic Hall

Snr Cits

RSL

CFA

Rye Pmy

Kanasta Karavan Kamp

Cemetery

Glenvue Holiday Park

RYE

The Dunes Golf Course

Clubhouse

Mornington Peninsula National Park

Peninsula Coastal Walk

BASS STRAIT

ST ANDREWS BEACH

JOINS 696

680

LIMIT OF MAPS

A B C D E F G H J K L

LIMIT OF MAPS
683

JOINS 699

LIMIT OF MAPS

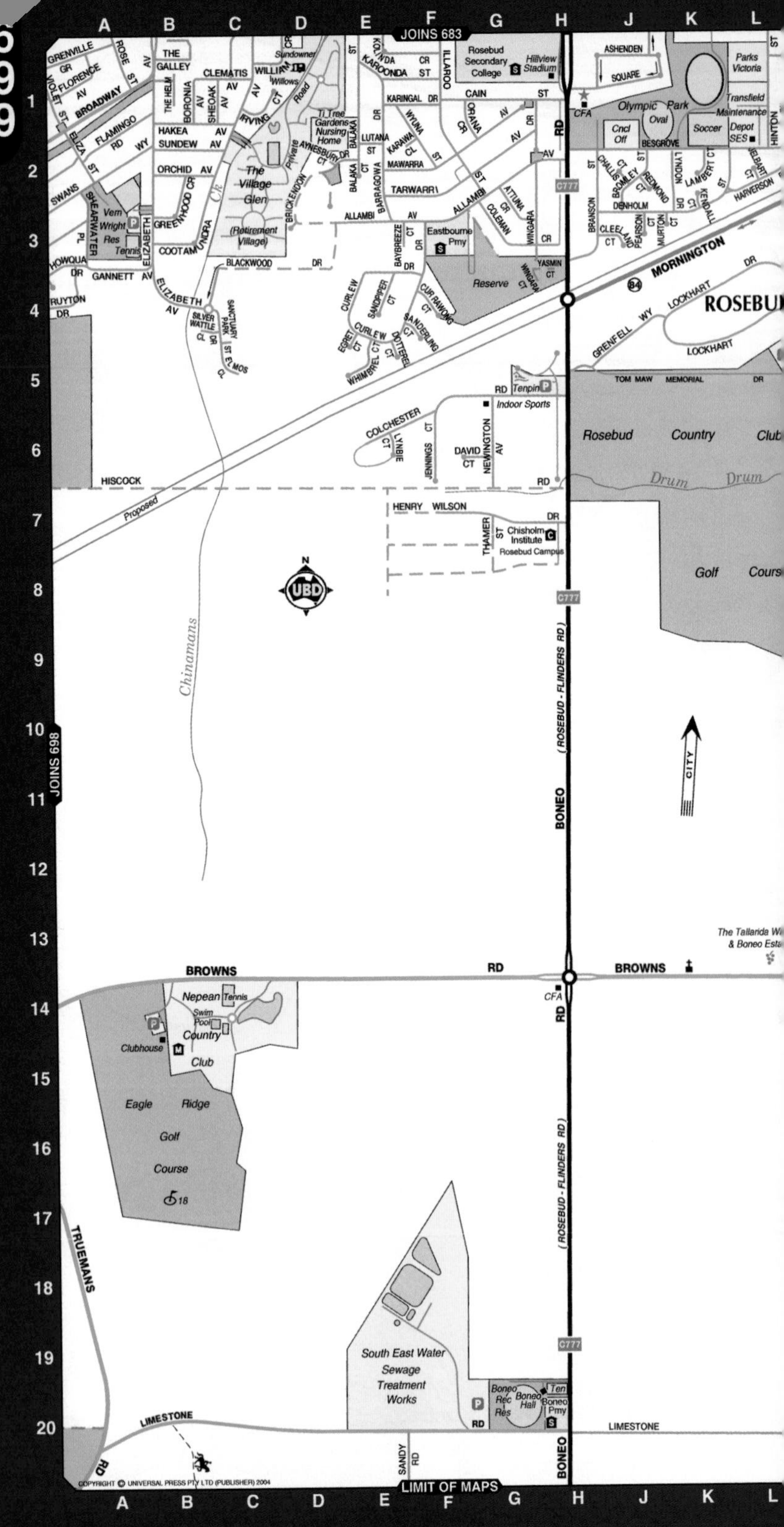
JOINS 683
JOINS 698
LIMIT OF MAPS
ROSEBUD
MORNINGTON
BONEO
(ROSEBUD - FLINDERS RD)
BROWNS RD
LIMESTONE
TRUEMANS RD
SANDY RD
HISCOCK RD
HENRY WILSON DR
Rosebud Secondary College
Hillview Stadium
Olympic Park
Parks Victoria
Transfield Maintenance Depot
SES
CFA
The Village Glen (Retirement Village)
Eastbourne Pmy
Reserve
Rosebud Country Club
Drum Drum
Golf Course
Tenpin
Indoor Sports
Chisholm Institute Rosebud Campus
Chinamans Ck
Proposed
Nepean Country Club
Clubhouse
Eagle Ridge Golf Course
South East Water Sewage Treatment Works
Boneo Rec Res
Boneo Hall
Boneo Pmy
The Tallarida W
& Boneo Esta
CITY
Vern Wright Res
Ti Tree Gardens Nursing Home
Sundowner Willows

A B C D E F G H J K L
1 2 3 4 5 6 7 8 9 10 11 12 13 14 15 16 17 18 19 20
PENINSULA FWY
Freeway
Rosebud Park Public Golf Course
Tennis
Pavilion
Pony Club
MCH
Cmnty Cntr
Padua College
Carrington
Reserve
Clubhouse
Amberlee
Tudor
Res
Arthurs Seat State Park
Rosebud Golf Course
Peninsula Function Centre
Waterfall
Alloc
Ck
JETTY RD
BAYVIEW RD
CAPE SCHANCK RD
OLD CAPE SCHANCK RD
GRASSLANDS RD
BROWNS RD
KINWENDY RD
LIMESTONE RD
HYSLOPS RD
ROGERS RD
ELIZABETH ST
WATERFALL GULLY RD
SHERWOOD AV
DUELLS RD
WAKOOL AV
MURAWA DR
AVALON AV
WIDDOP AV
INGLEWOOD CR
WEDGEWOOD DR
CLEEK CT
MASHIE CT
BOONEO
Mornington Peninsula National Park
LIMIT OF MAPS

BONEO

A B C D E F G H J K L

LIMIT OF MAPS

1 2 3 4 5 6 7 8 9 10 11 12 13 14 15 16 17 18 19 20

UBD

FYANSFORD

HIGHTON

WANDANA HEIGHTS

HERNE HILL

Freeway
Proposed
Moorabool
Moorabool River Reserve
Geelong Cement
7.3m
HAMILTON HWY
B140
HYLAND ST
DEVIATION RD
McCURDY RD
CLARKES RD
UPPER PAPER MILLS RD
LOWER PAPER MILLS RD
CARROLLS RD
DEGOLDIS RD
Fyansford Common
River
Ford
Billabong Wildlife Park
Weir
Buckley Weir
Paper Mills
Falls
Barwon
BUCKLEY FALLS RD
Zillah Crawcour Park
Aqueduct
Queens Park
Public Golf Course
Pavillion
Clubhouse
Parks Depot
QUEENS PARK RD
QUEENS BRIDGE
One lane 4.2m Clearance
Kevin Kirby Reserve
Herne Hill Reserve
Walker Oval
Elderslie Reserve
Geelong College Preparatory School
Windmill Reserve
Fyans Park Pmy
Newtown Park
Fyans Park
Foreshore
Barwon River Reserve

MATLOCK, BAKEWELL, BONVIEW, JOYCE, DERBY RD, ASHBOURNE, GRAYLEA, HENNESSEY, BECKLEY ST, POD, ROD, ITKESTON, CASTLETON, BUXTON, INGRID, OAK, HUNT, GREAT BRITAIN, KAROOMBA AV, MARLBOROUGH ST, LEAN, FRASER, HEYTESBURY, STAFFORD ST, FINCHAVEN, KNIGHT AV, AUTUMN, CHELMSFORD, CARMICHAEL, STEWART, NORWOOD, BOSANQUET, DUDLEY, CHESTER ST, SHERBOURNE ST, CORONAL AV, RAITH, READ, PATTEN, BAYLARD, GARLICK, WARWICK, WIRKSWORTH, COLVILLE, DOUGLAS, KEDLESTON, ATKINS ST, FYANS ST

MAIDIE, CLOUD, TUXEN, MANOR, WATERSEDGE TCE, TRENTWOOD CT, WILLOWFIELD CT, DESMOND ST, CANNES, ADMIRAL, KOOYONG PL, HIGHETT RD, CARROLL, OLD FLOUR MILL, TARA LA, VALLEY, LEYLANI CT, MERRIGUM CT, NOMAD LA, LOCHGOIN MW, NEVAIR CT, SCENIC RD, HORIZON, WALLAROO, BOUNTY CL, GREENWICH GRA, GLENVALE, BILBY LA, MONTROSE, ORANA, HEATHFIELD, NOBLE ST, CHESTER, MAYFAIR, SYLVAN CT, JACKMAN RD, CAMDEN, BALLATER, ARDLUI, CRAIGIE, GAIRLOCH, DUNDEE, WEST FYANS, BUCKINGHAM, GLAMIS, SANDRINGHAM, BALCOMBE, PINNACLE CL, WYNDABANK, HIGHRISE CT, WYNFIELD, CREST, THE, CHALLAMBRA CR, BARWON BVD, TEASDALE CT, BRENDAN CT, LINTON RD, JINJELLA RD

Montpellier Service Basins
Barwon Water
GEELONG

THE WESTBURY TCE, DENHAM, HUXLEY CT, BEVINGTON, RIVINGTON, MONTPELLIER CR, THE RIDGE, HILLARY CT, Monpellier Park, CULZEAN DR, HARVELL CT, LANSBURY, TUNBURY, GIVERNY CL, VAUCLUSE, PALMERSTON PL, Private RD, LEIGH, EXMOOR, TIMOR, PINTO, LIPIZZANER, GALLOWAY, BAYVIEW, VICTORY WY, WALER, SHIRE CT, DARTMOOR, CLYDESDALE, KYEEMA, HILLCREST, BADENOCH CT, ST GABRIELS, HIGHLAND WY, CONNEMARA CL, WELSH, SHETLAND, THOROUGHBRED, DALE, ALAMO, TRIUMPH PL, VICTORY, PREMIER, REIGATE RD, LAMBHILL, MT PLEASANT, MERINO, MONTPELLIER, HIGHTON CR, EWWICK, CHEAM, THORNBURY LA, MELROSE AV, MONTD'OR PDE, MAWARRA CT, BAUM AV, GWENETH, VALLEY, Montpellier Pmy, Highton Cemetery, MURRAY ST, MARCUS, BENNETT ST, WOODLEY CT, ADELAIDE ST, ARKANA, WAHRONGA, RONCLIFFE, NORTH, GRETTON CT, ELIZABETH ST, MONTAGUE ST, MARLYN CT, LICHEN CT, REYFERN CT, FERNDALE, BRUTHEN, CARA RD, CEDAR, FERNHILL

BARRABOOL RD
C136
THE GROSVENOR, TRAFALGAR SQ, STRAND, PALL ML, SCENIC RD, ST ELMO CR, ROSLYN RD, GLENMIRE ST, TARRING CT, CFA, Tennis, Highton Pmy, BRACKEN CT, Highton Rec Res, DUGGAN CT, HARRISON, TAY
BARRABOOL, CHRISTIE CT, GROSVENOR, EBONY CL, HIGH VIEW, NOBLE CT, HENDERSON, EUCALYPTUS CT, STIRLING, BENT, REGENCY CL, ATTUNGA, ST GEORGES CT, BUCHAN CT, CROMWELL, CATHERINES CT, LASCELLES, THORNHILL RD, CARRAMAR CT, DOUGLAS CT, KERAM, MCH, NORMAN CT, PATERN ST, SOUTH VALLEY RD, C133, NELSON AV
Drewan Park, Brownhill Heights Lookout, Tim Hill Res, Tennis, Hockey Res, KENT-HILL, CANTERBURY, LEONARD, FLORENCE CL, KIRAMI, BROLGA, KNOLLBROOK CL, CHANCELLOR, LANSELL, MERCIA, SHOUBRA, TANIA DR, REMONY, DUNSMORE, JALANA, MORVEN CT, VANESSA, COBDEN ST, LARCOMBE, CAROLINE ST, HELENA, MAUS ST, VUE, BELLE, SANGLEN, SAVAGE ST, WHITE, VIOLA, NIREEDA CT, WANDANA, SUNDERLAND RD, Proposed Fwy

JOINS 705

A B C D E F G H J K L

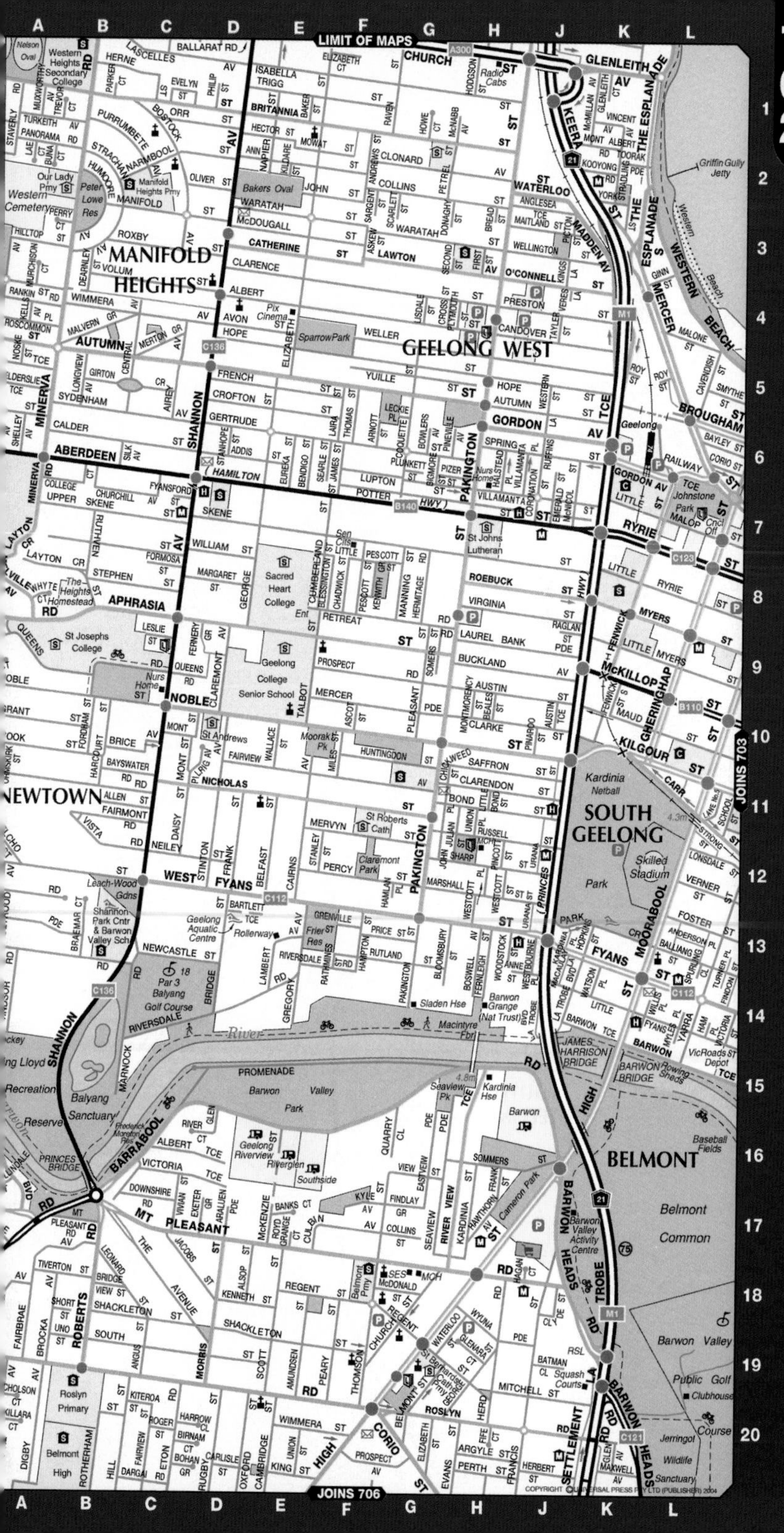

LIMIT OF MAPS
JOINS 703
JOINS 706
MANIFOLD HEIGHTS
GEELONG WEST
NEWTOWN
SOUTH GEELONG
BELMONT
Western Heights Secondary College
Western Cemetery
Peter Lowe Res
Bakers Oval
Sparrow Park
Pix Cinema
Sacred Heart College
St Josephs College
Geelong College Senior School
St Johns Lutheran
Kardinia Netball
Skilled Stadium
Kardinia Park
Johnstone Park
Leach-Wood Gdns
Shannon Park Cntr & Barwon Valley Sch
Geelong Aquatic Centre
Par 3 Balyang Golf Course
Balyang Sanctuary
Barwon Valley Park
Geelong Riverview
Riverglen
Southside
Cameron Park
Barwon Valley Activity Centre
Belmont Common
Barwon Valley Public Golf Course
Jerringot Wildlife Sanctuary
Roslyn Primary
Belmont High
Sladen Hse
Barwon Grange (Nat Trust)
Kardinia Hse
Macintyre Br
James Harrison Bridge
Barwon Bridge
Princes Bridge
VicRoads Depot
Griffin Gully Jetty
Western Beach
Geelong
SHANNON AV
ABERDEEN ST
PAKINGTON ST
LATROBE TCE
PRINCES HWY
BARRABOOL RD
BARWON HEADS RD
HIGH ST
THE ESPLANADE
WESTERN BEACH
MOORABOOL ST
COPYRIGHT © UNIVERSAL PRESS PTY LTD (PUBLISHER) 2004

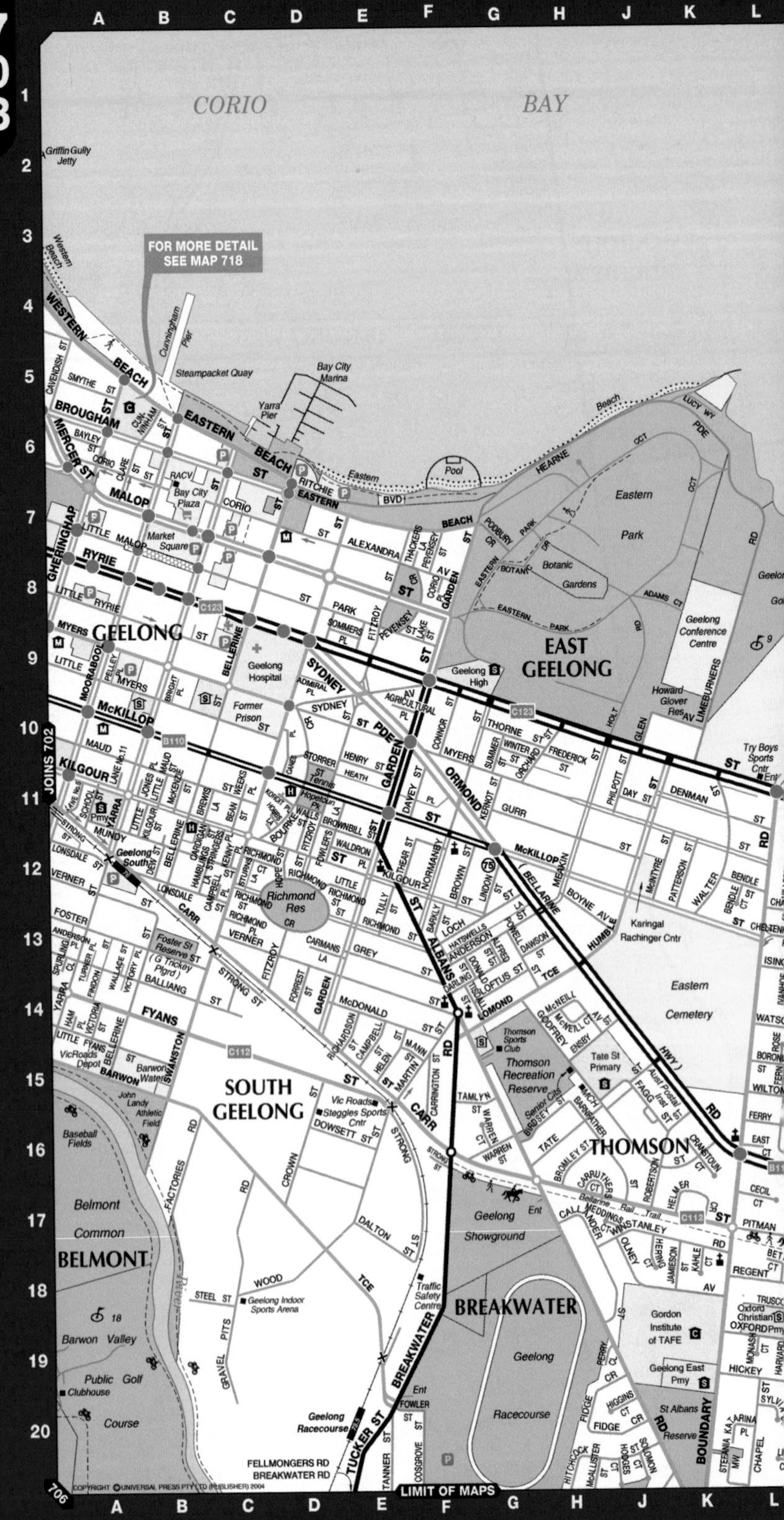
A B C D E F G H J K L
CORIO
BAY
Griffin Gully Jetty
Western Beach
FOR MORE DETAIL SEE MAP 718
Cunningham Pier
Steampacket Quay
Bay City Marina
Yarra Pier
Pool
Eastern Beach
Eastern Park
Botanic Gardens
Geelong Conference Centre
GEELONG
EAST GEELONG
Geelong Hospital
Former Prison
Geelong High
Howard Glover Res
Try Boys Sports Cntr
Market Square
Bay City Plaza
RACV
Hopetoun Pk
St Tennis
Richmond Res
Karingal Rachinger Cntr
Eastern Cemetery
Geelong South
Foster St Reserve (G Trickey Plgrd)
VicRoads Depot
Barwon Water
John Landy Athletic Field
SOUTH GEELONG
Vic Roads Steggles Sports Cntr
Thomson Sports Club
Thomson Recreation Reserve
Tate St Primary
THOMSON
Senior Cits
Baseball Fields
Belmont Common
BELMONT
Barwon Valley Public Golf Course
Clubhouse
Geelong Indoor Sports Arena
Traffic Safety Centre
Geelong Showground
BREAKWATER
Geelong Racecourse
Gordon Institute of TAFE
Geelong East Pmy
St Albans Reserve
Oxford Christian Pmy
Bellarine Rail Trail
JOINS 702
LIMIT OF MAPS
706
WESTERN BEACH
EASTERN BEACH
MALOP
RYRIE
MYERS
McKILLOP
KILGOUR
MOORABOOL
BELLERINE
YARRA
GHERINGHAP
SYDNEY PDE
GARDEN ST
ST ALBANS RD
BELLARINE HWY
BOUNDARY RD
BREAKWATER RD
TUCKER ST
CARR ST
FYANS
BARWON
FELLMONGERS RD
BREAKWATER RD

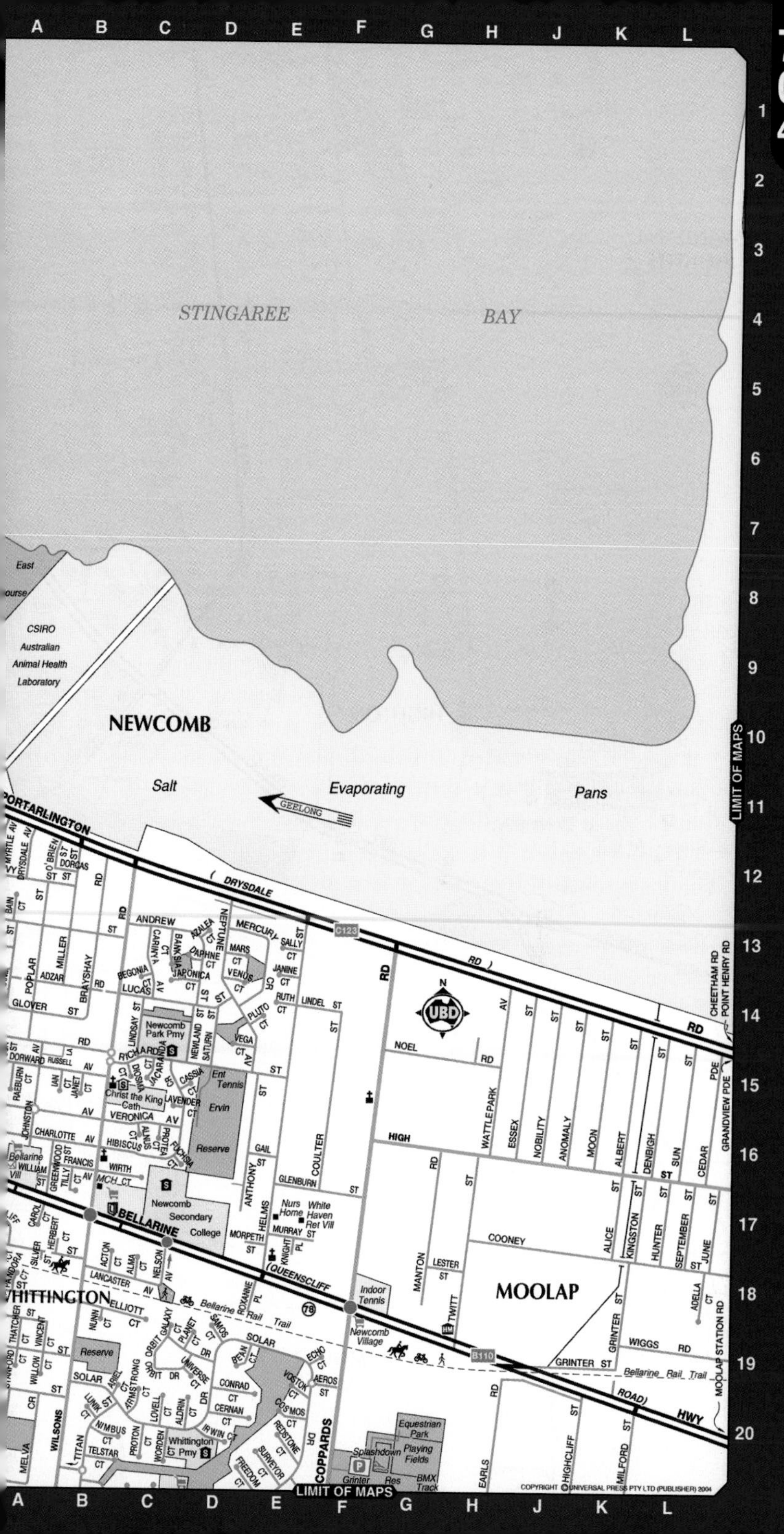
STINGAREE
BAY
East
CSIRO
Australian
Animal Health
Laboratory
NEWCOMB
Salt
Evaporating
Pans
GEELONG
PORTARLINGTON
DRYSDALE
RD
C123
MOOLAP
WHITTINGTON
BELLARINE
(QUEENSCLIFF
ROAD)
HWY
B110
Bellarine Rail Trail
Newcomb Park Pmy
Christ the King Cath
Ent Tennis
Ervin
Reserve
Newcomb Secondary College
Nurs Home
White Haven Ret Vill
Indoor Tennis
Newcomb Village
Whittington Pmy
Equestrian Park
Playing Fields
Splashdown
Grinter Res
BMX Track
LIMIT OF MAPS
COPPARDS
HIGH
NOEL
COONEY
GRINTER
WIGGS
MOOLAP STATION RD
CHEETHAM RD
POINT HENRY RD
GRANDVIEW PDE
COPYRIGHT © UNIVERSAL PRESS PTY LTD (PUBLISHER) 2004

WANDANA HEIGHTS

HIGHTON

WAURN PONDS

MOUNT DUNEED

Deakin University
Geelong Campus
FOR MORE DETAIL SEE MAP 717

Marcus Oldham Farm Management College

Christian College Senior Campus

Christian College Highton Campus Middle School

Highton Basins

Bellaire Primary

McDonald Reserve

Clairvaux Cath Pmy

Tenpin Bowls

Christian College Junior Sch

Retarding Basin

Waurn Ponds Valley Parklands

Geelong Regional Baseball Cntr

Skate Ramp

Tennis

Nursery

Town & Country Shop Centre

Baseball & Football Fields

Jarvis Oval

Coolabah Park

Reserve

Prince Albert Winery

Waurn Ponds

SUNDERLAND, GROSVENOR, SHOLDEN CT, STANFIELD DR, XAVIER CT, MADELINE DR, KIRAMI, NIREEDA CT, BROLGA, FARRER CL, CHISHOLM CL, HARGRAVE CR, SUNHILL CT, GREENFINCH WY, JAMES COOK, GREENWAY CT, WANDANA, Proposed, CHANCELLOR CL, HUNTLEY PL, LANSELL, KNOLLBROOK DR, THE MEWS, PARKLAND, WY, PEPPERDINE, SUNSET CT, SUMMER HILL TCE, TUMBLE TREE, HOMESTEAD CT, SHEOAK CT, THORNHILL RD, AUGUSTINES RD, DUNSMORE RD, JALANA CT, VANESSA AV, BRASSEY AV, CEDMAR, MORTON BAY DR, CEMALOMA AV, BONSEY RD, ARINGA AV, LINTHWAITE CL, SHERWOOD CT, BUNDOORA CR, SUTCLIFFE CT, KINTHER CT, GWYTHER RD, VILLAWOOD CT, BURDEKIN, KOORONG CT, PINEHILL CT, MERRICK CT, BALLARA CT, PERCY JONES CT, CON WAY, KERRINS, MULQUINEY CR, KEATING, WEBSTER CT, BUTLER CT, O'DRISCOLL CT, WHITTEN CT, BILSTON CR, HAYES CT, AUGUSTINE DR, SWEENEY CT, OAKVIEW DR, GUMTREE CT, CEDARVILLE CL, ELMSFORD CT, PARKWOOD, Geelong, Freeway

COBDEN ST, HELENA, CAROLINE ST, HUTCHESON AV, TORULOSA CT, KENNEDY, AMBERLEY CT, HOLLAND CT, LARCOMBE, CUTHBERT, PORTER AV, LANDY, STRICKLAND AV, BERRY CT, LUND CT, MASON CT, ROYCROFT AV, ELLIOTT AV, MADIGAN CR, KONRAD, HENDRIKS CT, BELLE VUE, NORTHAM AV, AMOORE AV, FRYERS RD, CREST MOOR, PINOAK, CORONADO, WOODFERN DR, DONNINGTON, FENLAND CT, PINECREST, GRENOBLE CT, MARFELL, CHADREE CT, GLASTONBURY DR, BELVEDERE, CORTLAND, RESTON, LINDHOLME, DUMFRIES, KINDALE CT, HOMEWOOD LA, BINBROOK, WADDINGTON CT, HEMSWELL, GAMSTON, FRAYNE CT, WICKENBY, SCAMPTON, EAST KIRKBY CT, MOLESWORTH, BROUGHTON, FINNINGLEY, GRANBY, IDWALL, SANDTOFT, BLYTON, CRANWELL, KELSTERN, SOUTH VALLEY RD, HELENA, WHITE, LAURA, PAVO, APEX, IONA, REYNOLDS, WAURNVALE, TETTENHALL, WAURN PARK

UNIVERSITY DR, FOGARTY AV, DALY BVD, McEVOY CL, LYNCH CT, TIERNEY, CAHILL CT, PIGDONS RD, NICOL DR, KINGS WY, LAKE DR, DEAKIN AV, BAXTER DR, RESIDENCE RD, GORDON BVD, JARVIS RD

COLAC HWY, PRINCES HWY, A1, M1, 81, ROSSACK DR, BINALONG CT, HYATT CT, AMARINA, GLOUCESTER, PIONEER RD, C133, C134

MEADOWVALE, CHENIN MW, ELLETT CT, CLOVER CT, GROSS CT, TUFFS GR, STRAWBERRY, PERENNIAL RI, MOATA CT, TAMA CT, MANET AV, TETILA AV, JEAN PL, AUSTIN PL, PETHAJOHN PDE, PITT ST, JAMMAR CT, EMMY CT, POLLEY CT, KERGER CT, PANNELL CT, HARTWICK CT, COROWA CT, COOLALIE CT, DUBLIN, BAMBRA CT, BOORAL CT, ALLAMBEE AV, TITIAN CT, HOLBEIN CT, VERMEER CT, BELLINI CT, RUBENS CT, COOLABAH, MARAMBA, MORUYA, HEYERS, RAPHAEL CT, YONGALA CT, SHERINGA CR, SMART CT, NIBLETT CT, SKINNER CT, VILLEA AV, LEHMANN AV, WINGARRA, ELLIS CT, DUNOWIE CT, MULHOLLAND, CHILLER CT, EUROKA, LANDRA CT, SPRINGHURST

CARRADALE ST, RESOLUTE, BURGUNDY DR, ALVA CT, JASMIN CT, CABERNET DR, VINTAGE CT, SHIRAZ CT, LEXIA PL, MONTEREY, BANYAN CT, KINSMEAD ST, CHARDONNAY, BORDEAUX DR, DEAKINWOOD DR, MERRIBELL DR, MOET CT, MUSKET PL, MERLOT CT, PINOT ST, THE VINEYAR, WILLESDEN, OAKWOOD CR, JARRAH PL, MAPLE PL, ELM, PINE, ASH, ACACIA LA, IRONBARK ST, OAKWOOD, HUON, TREE ST, BOURBON WY, RD, ROSSACK ST

MARENDAZ RD, LEMINS RD, ANGLESEA RD, TUSCAN CT, BRENTWOOD WY, PARK DR, BAROSSA CT, MOYSTON LA, CHANDON CT, GRANGE CT, HAMS RD, BOUNDARY, GHAZEEPORE, WHITES RD, AIRPORT RD

LIMIT OF MAPS

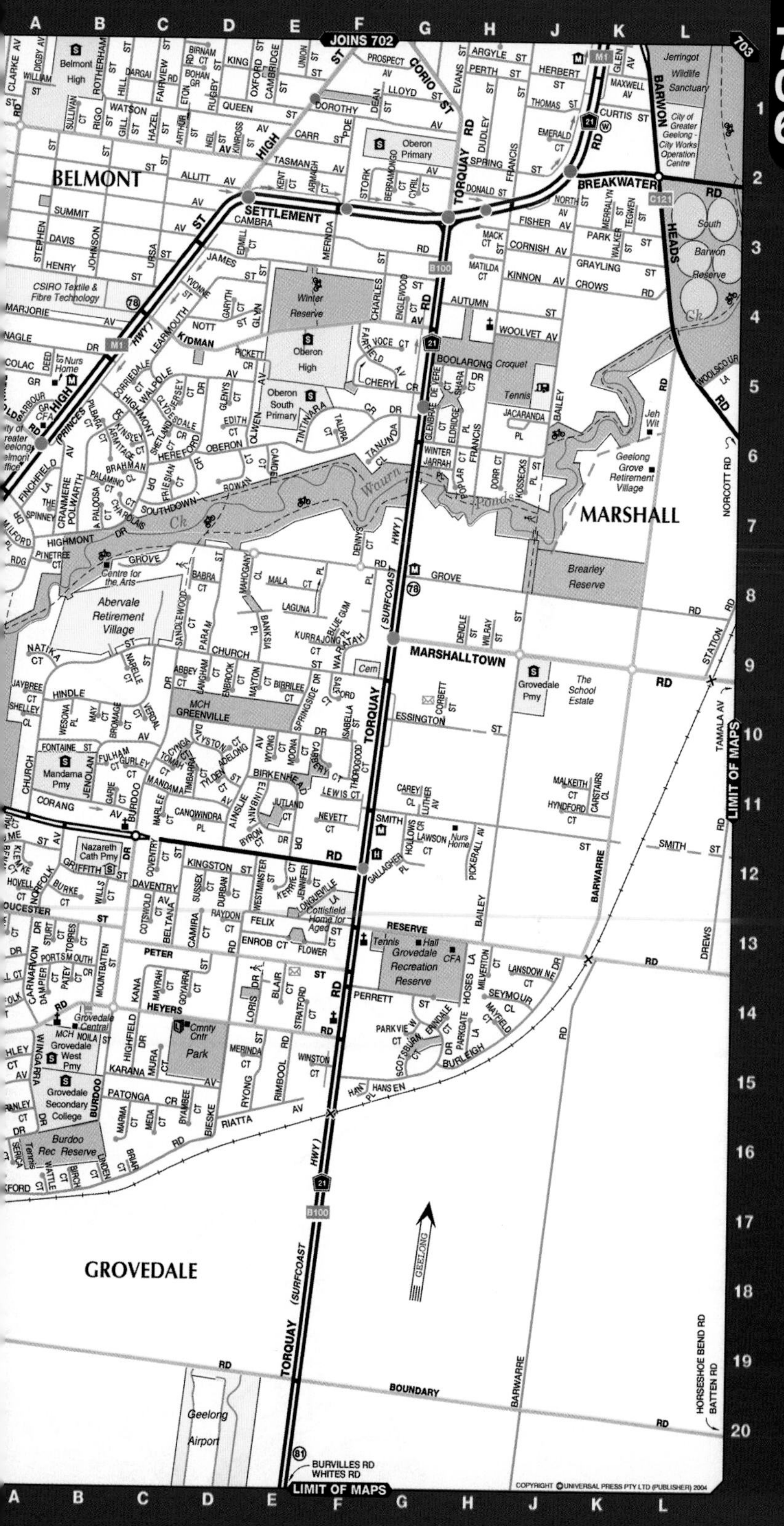

A B C D E F G H J K L
JOINS 702
703
1 2 3 4 5 6 7 8 9 10 11 12 13 14 15 16 17 18 19 20
BELMONT
MARSHALL
GROVEDALE
Belmont High
Oberon Primary
Jerringot Wildlife Sanctuary
City of Greater Geelong - City Works Operation Centre
South Barwon Reserve
CSIRO Textile & Fibre Technology
Winter Reserve
Oberon High
Oberon South Primary
Croquet
Tennis
Jeh Wit
Geelong Grove Retirement Village
Waurn Ponds Ck
Centre for the Arts
Abervale Retirement Village
Brearley Reserve
Grovedale Pmy
The School Estate
Cem
MCH GREENVILLE
Mandama Pmy
Nazareth Cath Pmy
Cottisfield Home for Aged
Grovedale Recreation Reserve
Hall
CFA
Grovedale Central
MCH NOILA
Grovedale West Pmy
Cmnty Cntr
Park
Grovedale Secondary College
Burdoo Rec Reserve
Geelong Airport
SETTLEMENT RD
BREAKWATER RD
HIGH ST
TORQUAY RD
CORIO ST
BARWON HEADS RD
PRINCES HWY
TORQUAY (SURFCOAST) HWY
MARSHALLTOWN RD
GROVE RD
BOUNDARY RD
BARWARRE RD
CHURCH ST
SMITH ST
RESERVE RD
HEYERS RD
ANGLESEA RD
BAILEY ST
STATION RD
DREWS RD
NORCOTT RD
TAMALA AV
HORSESHOE BEND RD
BATTEN RD
BURVILLES RD
WHITES RD
GEELONG
LIMIT OF MAPS
M1
B100
C121
21
78
81
COPYRIGHT © UNIVERSAL PRESS PTY LTD (PUBLISHER) 2004

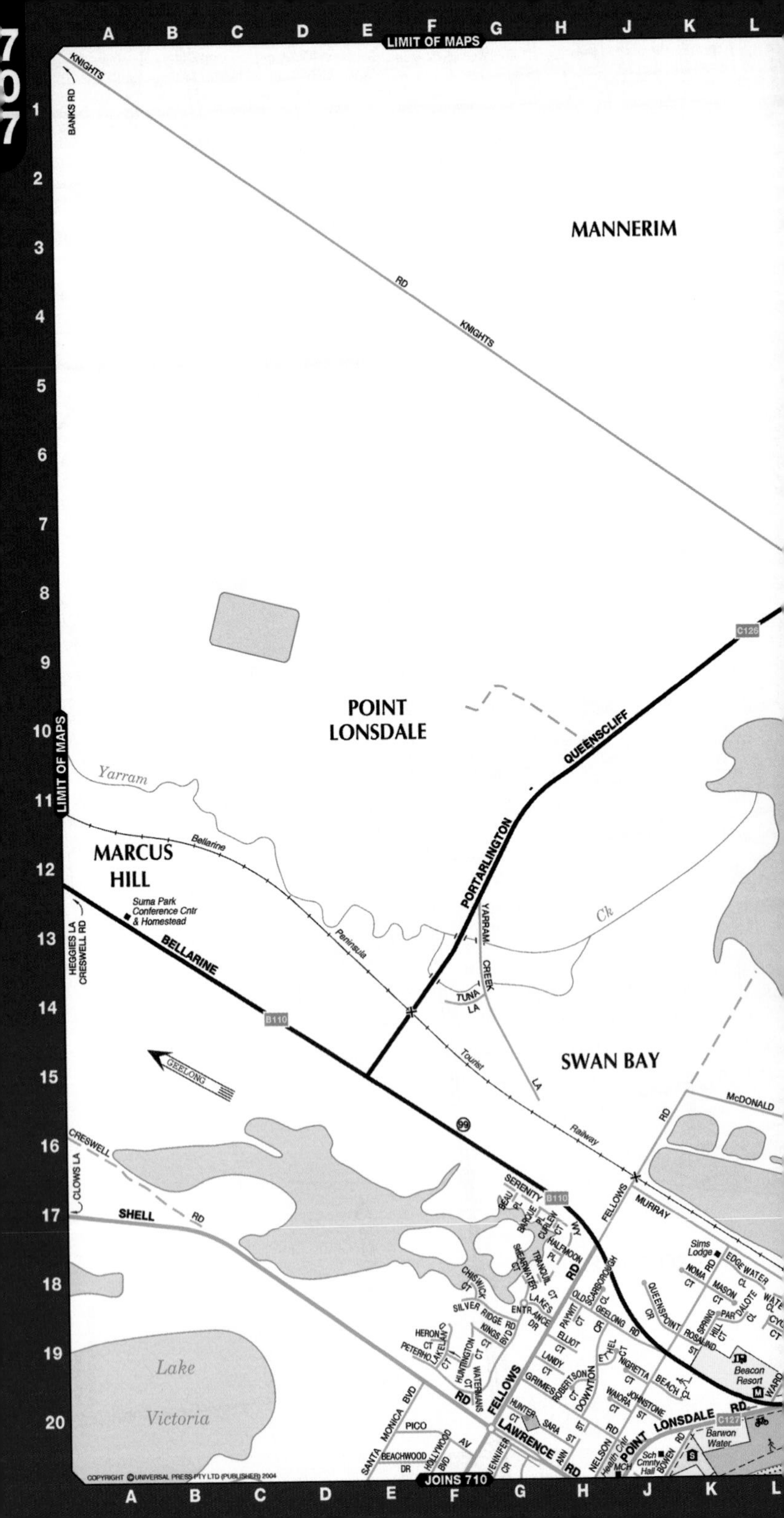
LIMIT OF MAPS
KNIGHTS RD
BANKS RD
MANNERIM
POINT LONSDALE
MARCUS HILL
SWAN BAY
Yarram Ck
Bellarine Peninsula Tourist Railway
PORTARLINGTON
QUEENSCLIFF
C126
BELLARINE
B110
Suma Park Conference Cntr & Homestead
HEGGIES LA
CRESWELL RD
YARRAM CREEK
TUNA LA
GEELONG
99
McDONALD RD
MURRAY
FELLOWS
CRESWELL
CLOWS LA
SHELL RD
SERENITY
Lake Victoria
Sims Lodge
EDGEWATER
NOMA CT
MASON CT
QUEENSPOINT CR
ROSALIND ST
SPRING HILL CT
PARDALOTE CL
Beacon Resort
NIGRETTA
BEACH CL
JOHNSTONE ST
WAIORA CT
POINT LONSDALE RD
C127
Barwon Water
Sch Cmnty Hall
Health Cntr MCH
BOWEN RD
NELSON RD
LAWRENCE RD
FELLOWS RD
HUNTER CT
SARA ST
ANN ST
JENNIFER CR
SANTA MONICA BVD
PICO
BEACHWOOD DR
HOLLYWOOD BVD
AV
HERON CT
PETERHO CT
LAKELAND
HUNTINGTON CT
WATERMANS
KINGS BVD
SILVER RIDGE RD
CHISWICK CT
ENTRANCE DR
LAKES CT
SHEARWATER
TRINDALL CL
HALFMOON PL
CURLEW CT
BARQUE PL
BEAU CT
WY
OLD SCARBOROUGH CL
GEELONG RD
PAYWIT CT
ELLIOT CT
LANDY CT
GRIMES CT
ROBERTSON CT
DOWNTON ST
ETHEL CT
COPYRIGHT © UNIVERSAL PRESS PTY LTD (PUBLISHER) 2004
JOINS 710

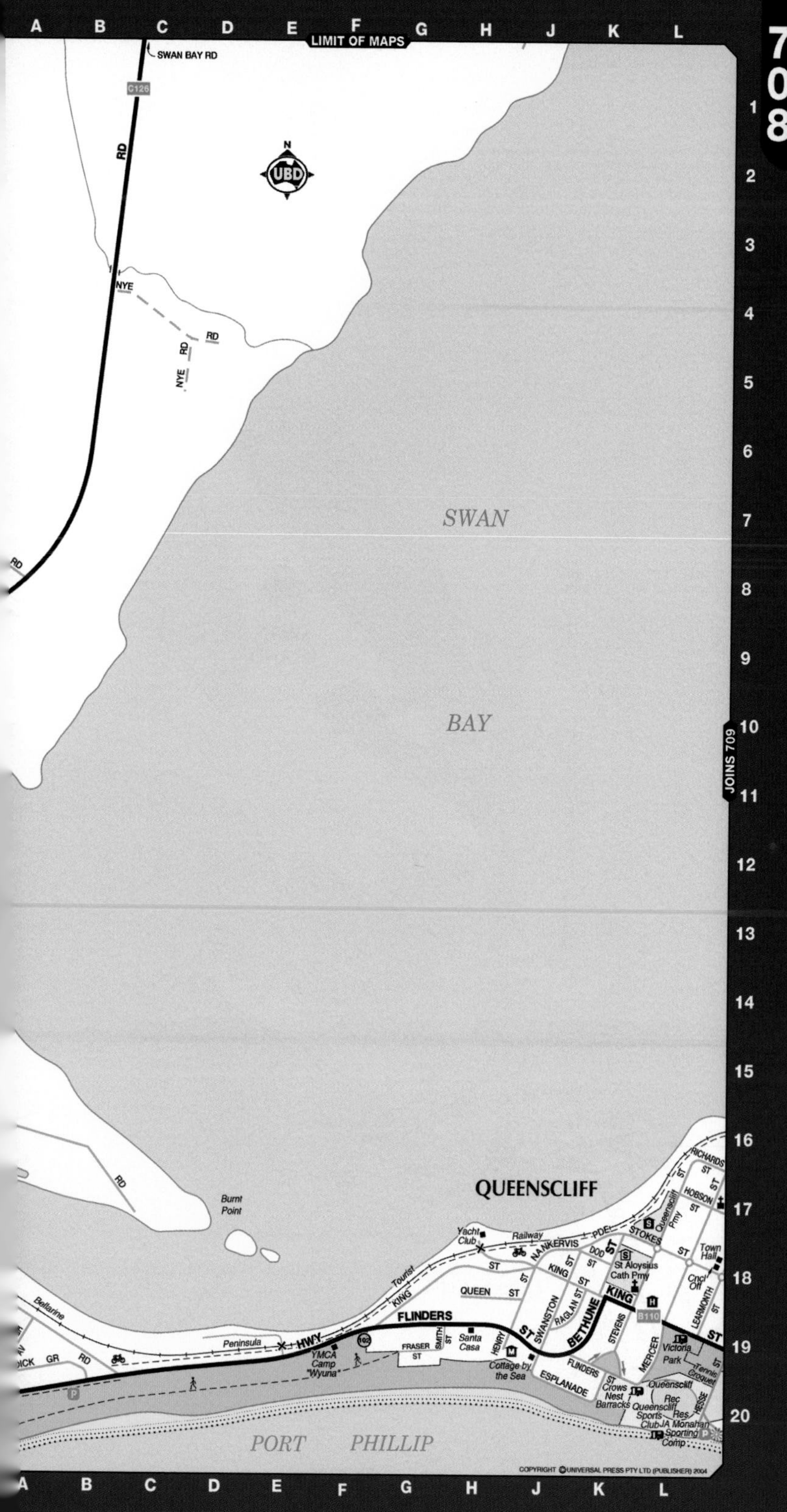

LIMIT OF MAPS
SWAN BAY RD
C126
RD
NYE
RD
RD
NYE
SWAN
BAY
JOINS 709
RD
Burnt Point
QUEENSCLIFF
Yacht Club
Railway
NANKERVIS
PDE
STOKES
Queenscliff Pmy
HOBSON
RICHARDS
ST
DOD
KING
St Aloysius Cath Pmy
Town Hall
Cncl Off
Tourist
KING
QUEEN
ST
BETHUNE
STEVENS
MERCER
LEARMONTH
B110
FLINDERS
HWY
Peninsula
Bellarine
DICK
GR
RD
YMCA Camp "Wyuna"
FRASER
ST
SMITH
Santa Casa
HENRY
SWANSTON
RAGLAN ST
Cottage by the Sea
ESPLANADE
Crows Nest Barracks
Queenscliff Sports Club
Rec Res
JA Monahan Sporting Comp
HESSE
Victoria Park
Tennis Croquet
PORT
PHILLIP

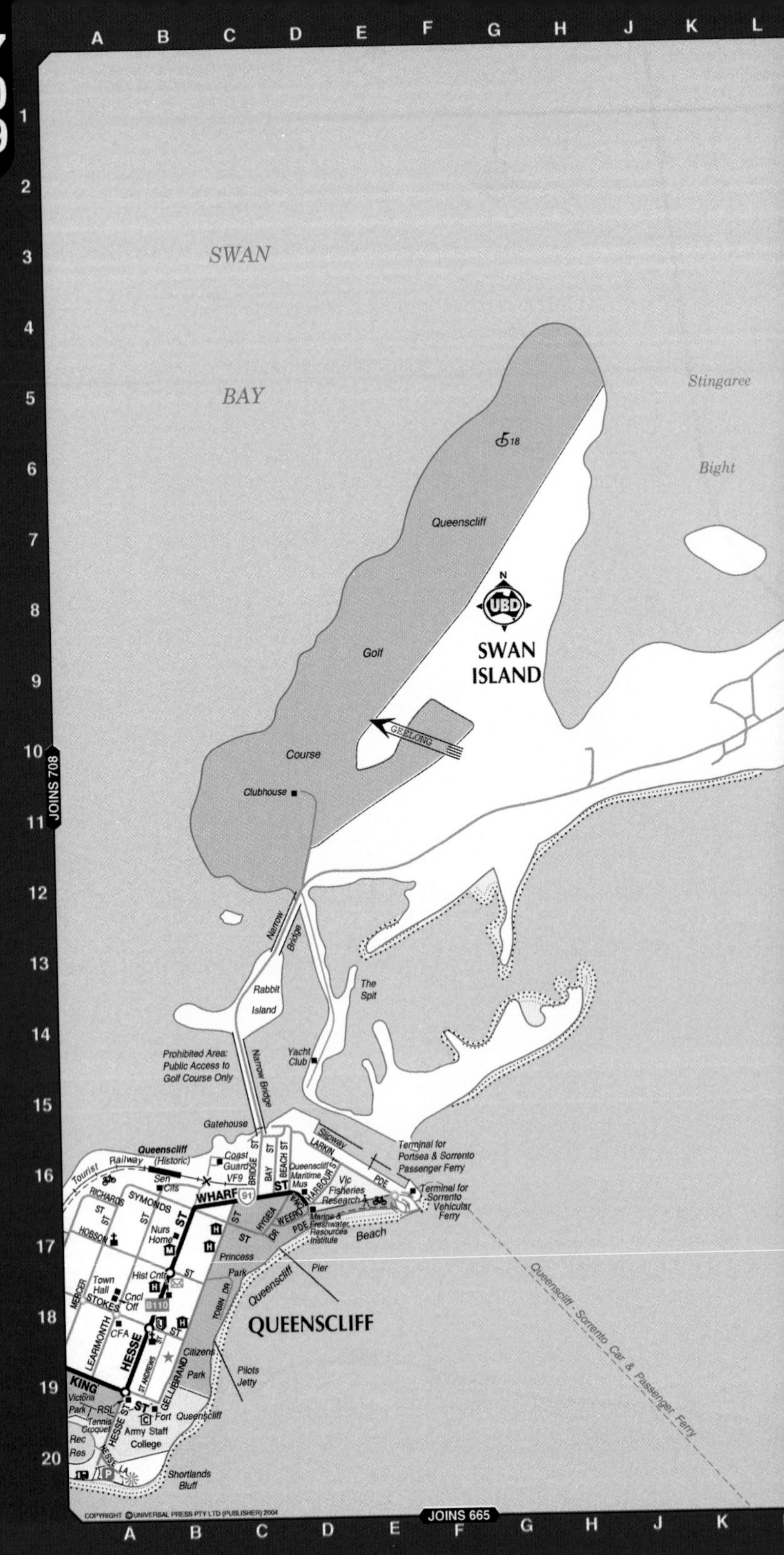

SWAN
BAY
Stingaree
Bight
Queenscliff
Golf
Course
Clubhouse
SWAN
ISLAND
GEELONG
Narrow
Bridge
Rabbit
Island
The
Spit
Yacht
Club
Prohibited Area:
Public Access to
Golf Course Only
Narrow Bridge
Gatehouse
Slipway
LARKIN
PDE
Terminal for
Portsea & Sorrento
Passenger Ferry
Terminal for
Sorrento
Vehicular
Ferry
Queenscliff
Railway
(Historic)
Tourist
Coast
Guard
VF9
Sen
Cits
RICHARDS
SYMONDS
WHARF
ST
HYGEIA
DR
WEERONA
PDE
HARBOUR ST
BAY ST
BEACH ST
BRIDGE ST
Queenscliff
Maritime
Mus
Vic
Fisheries
Research
Marine &
Freshwater
Resources
Institute
Beach
HOBSON
Nurs
Home
Princess
Park
Pier
Queenscliff
Town
Hall
Hist Cntr
Cncl
Off
MERCER
STOKES
B110
TOBIN DR
QUEENSCLIFF
LEARMONTH
CFA
HESSE
ST ANDREWS
GELLIBRAND
Citizens
Park
Pilots
Jetty
KING
Victoria
Park
RSL
Tennis
Croquet
Army Staff
College
Fort Queenscliff
Rec
Res
HESSE LA
Shortlands
Bluff
Queenscliff - Sorrento Car & Passenger Ferry
JOINS 708

JOINS 665

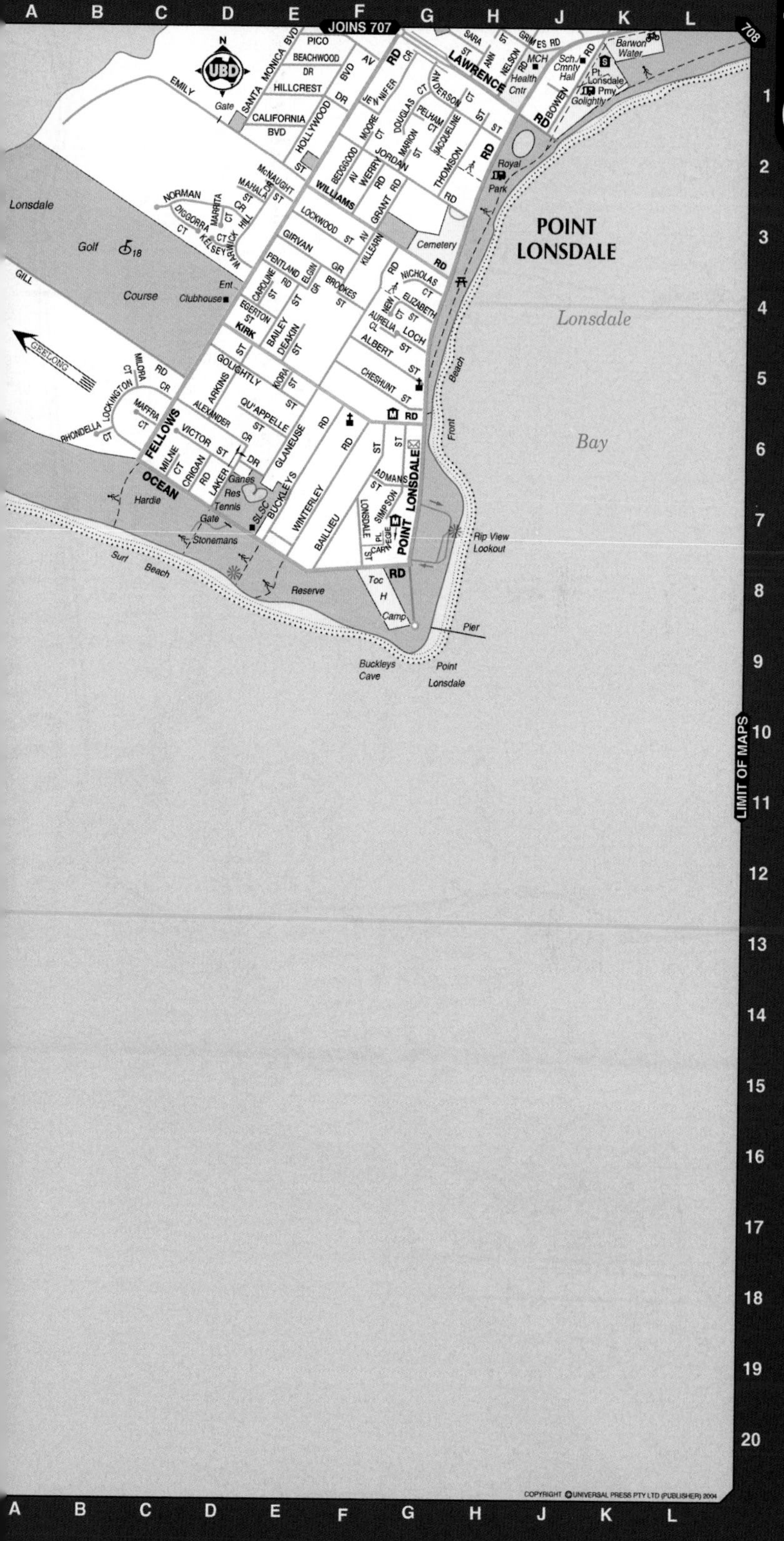

A B C D E F G H J K L

JOINS 707

708

POINT LONSDALE

Lonsdale Bay

PICO
BEACHWOOD DR
HILLCREST
CALIFORNIA BVD
SANTA MONICA BVD
HOLLYWOOD DR
BVD
AV
RD
JENNIFER CR
MOORE CT
DOUGLAS CT
ANDERSON CT
PELHAM CT
JACQUELINE ST
MARION ST
JORDAN
THOMSON RD
BEDGGOOD AV
WERRY RD
GRANT RD
WILLIAMS
LOCKWOOD ST
KILLEARN AV
Cemetery
RD
GIRVAN
PENTLAND RD
ELGIN GR
GR
BROOKES ST
CAROLINE ST
EGERTON ST
KIRK
BAILEY ST
DEAKIN ST
NICHOLAS CT
ELIZABETH
NEW ST
CT
AURELIA CL
LOCH
ALBERT ST
CHESHUNT ST
ST
RD
GOLIGHTLY
KOPA ST
ARKINS ST
QU'APPELLE ST
ALEXANDER ST
GLANEUSE
VICTOR CR
DR
WINTERLEY RD
BAILLIEU RD
ST
ST
ADMANS ST
SIMPSON
LONSDALE ST
PL
CARNEGIE
POINT LONSDALE RD
Toc H Camp
Pier
Buckleys Cave
Point Lonsdale
Rip View Lookout
Front Beach
SARA ST
ANN ST
NELSON RD
GRIMES RD
LAWRENCE
MCH
Health Cntr
Sch. Cmnty Hall
RD
BOWEN RD
Barwon Water
Pt. Lonsdale Pmy
Golightly
Royal Park
EMILY
Gate
Lonsdale Golf 18 Course
Ent.
Clubhouse
GILL
GEELONG
NORMAN
DIGGORRA CT
MARRITA CT
CR
KELSEY CT
WARWICK HILL
MAHALA ST
McNAUGHT DR
ST
MILORA CT
RD
LOCKINGTON CR
MAFFRA CT
RHONDELLA CT
FELLOWS
MILNE CT
CRIGAN RD
LAKER ST
OCEAN
Ganes Res
Tennis
SLSC
BUCKLEYS
Hardie
Gate
Stonemans
Surf Beach
Reserve

LIMIT OF MAPS

1 2 3 4 5 6 7 8 9 10 11 12 13 14 15 16 17 18 19 20

A B C D E F G H J K L

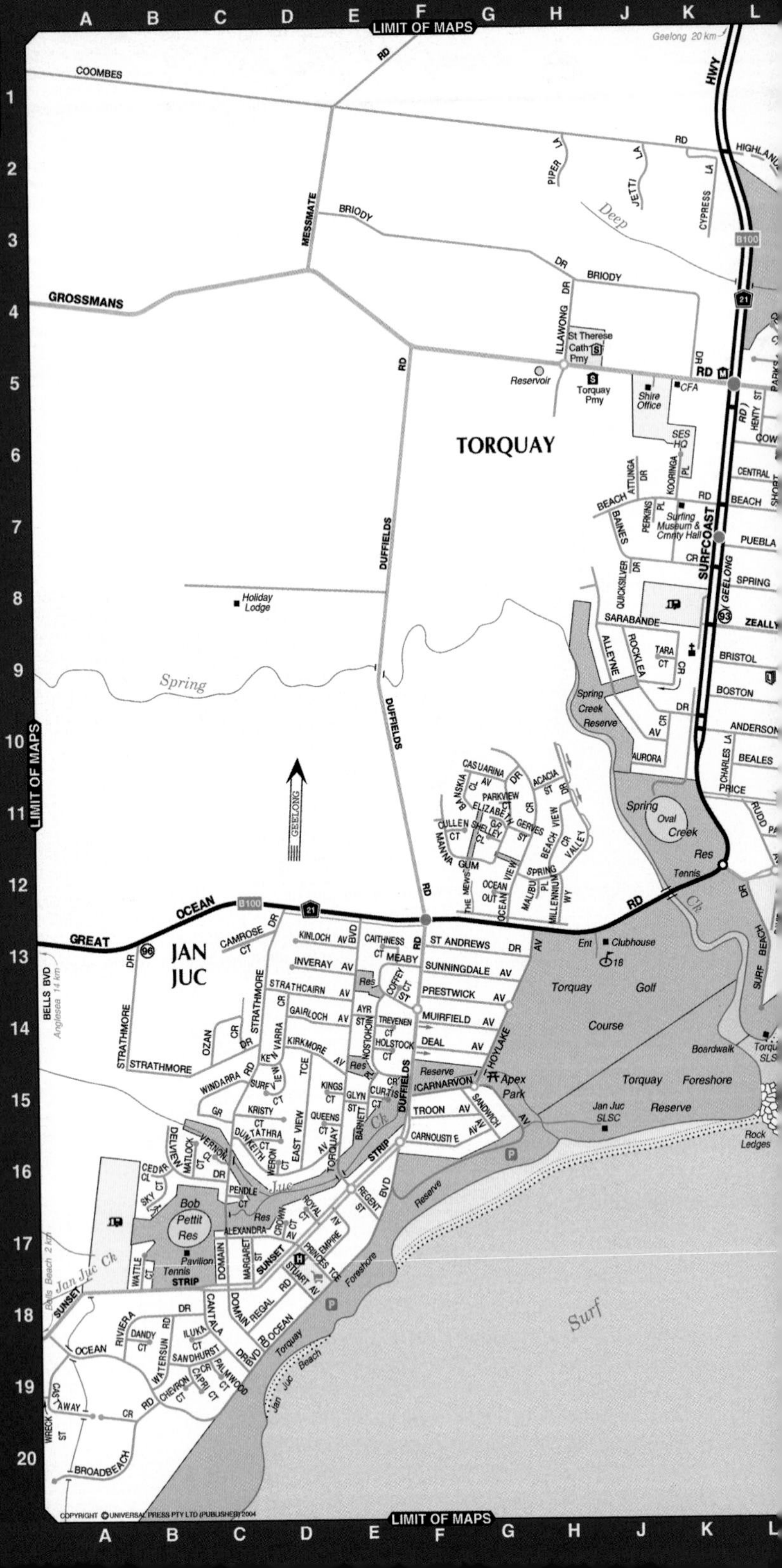

LIMIT OF MAPS
Geelong 20 km
COOMBES
RD
HWY
HIGHLAND
PIPER LA
JETTI LA
CYPRESS LA
MESSMATE
BRIODY
Deep
B100
BRIODY
DR
ILLAWONG DR
GROSSMANS
St Therese Cath Pmy
Reservoir
Torquay Pmy
RD
Shire Office
CFA
SES HQ
TORQUAY
ATTUNGA DR
KOORINGA PL
BEACH
PERKINS PL
Surfing Museum & Cmnty Hall
BAINES
SURFCOAST
GEELONG
PUEBLA
SPRING
CENTRAL
BEACH
QUICKSILVER DR
SARABANDE
ZEALLY
ALLEYNE
ROCKLEA
TARA CT
BRISTOL
BOSTON
DUFFIELDS
Holiday Lodge
Spring
Spring Creek Reserve
ANDERSON
AURORA
BEALES
CHARLES LA
PRICE
RUDD
CASUARINA DR
BANKSIA CL
PARKVIEW CT
ACACIA ST
ELIZABETH CR
GERVES ST
CULLEN CT
SHELLEY CL
BEACH VIEW
VALLEY CR
MANNA GUM
THE MEWS
OCEAN OUT
OCEAN VIEW
MALIBU PL
SPRING
MILLENNIUM WY
Spring Creek Oval
Res
Tennis
Ck
GREAT OCEAN RD
B100
JAN JUC
CAMROSE CT
KINLOCH AV
CAITHNESS CT
MEABY
ST ANDREWS DR
SUNNINGDALE AV
Ent
Clubhouse
18
Torquay Golf Course
INVERAY AV
STRATHCAIRN AV
COFFEY ST
PRESTWICK AV
GAIRLOCH AV
AYR ST
TREVENEN CT
MUIRFIELD AV
HOLSTOCK CT
DEAL AV
KIRKMORE AV
BELLS BVD
Anglesea 14 km
STRATHMORE DR
OZAN CR
WINDARRA RD
KEW
YARRA
CARNARVON
Reserve
HOYLAKE
Apex Park
Torquay Foreshore Reserve
Boardwalk
Torquay SLSC
SURF BEACH
KINGS CT
GLYN ST
CURTIS CT
SURF CT
KRISTY CT
TATHRA CT
DUNKEITH CT
WERON
EAST VIEW
QUEENS CT
TROON AV
SANDWICH AV
CARNOUSTIE AV
Jan Juc SLSC
Rock Ledges
DELVIEW
MATLOCK
VERNON CT
CEDAR CL
SKY CT
PENDLE CT
Bob Pettit Res
ALEXANDRA
CROWN CT
ROYAL CT
EMPIRE
REGENT ST
BVD
STRIP
Reserve
Foreshore
Res
Juc
Pavilion
Tennis
STRIP
WATTLE CT
DOMAIN
MARGARET ST
SUNSET
STUART AV
PRINCES TCE
Jan Juc Ck
Bells Beach 2 km
SUNSET
RIVIERA
DANDY CT
WATERSUN RD
ILUKA CT
CANTALA DR
REGAL RD
OCEAN
DRBVD
OCEAN
SANDHURST
PALMWOOD
CHEVRON CT
CAPRI CT
CR
Torquay
Jan Juc Beach
Surf
CASTAWAY
CR
RD
WRECK ST
BROADBEACH
LIMIT OF MAPS

A B C D E F G H J K L

LIMIT OF MAPS

Torquay Sands Golf Course
Clubhouse
18

BLACKGATE RD
CEDUNA PL
NORFOLK CT
TIDAL BVD
ISLAND DR
SAND DUNE RI
OCEAN MW
ISLAND DR
HANI CT
HALLIS CT
GOLDEN BEACH ESPLANADE
FATIMAH CT
AFZAN WY
SHAH CT
LESSEY CL
THE ESPLANADE
HORSESHOE BEND
BOSCARNE AV
FLINDERS LA
AV
JOANNA CT
COLINA CR
PENOLA ST
GLANEUSE DR
KOOMEELA
BYDEN CT
DR
POMORA
GLENGARRY CR
WY
ARTISAN CL
PETREL CL
CASINO CT
ST
DUMFRIES CT
HETTIE CT
NEVA CT
AV
GLANEUSE CT
GRANGE
MADINA PL
LOCHARD DR
INSIDE
LUNE CT
DR
FOAM AV
EMPIRE CT
BULLI CT
ELM GROVE CT
CORSAIR CT
RIO CT
RAYVILLE AV
NESTOR CT
ENDEAVOUR DR
ELANORA CT
TIME CT
PETRIANA CT
DR
ANTARES CT
SCAMMELL
CR
ST
AQUILLA
ROMEO CT
HOLYHEAD
LYDIA CT
OSPREY CT
SEABIRD CT
ORUNGAL CT
ORUNGAL CT
ROSNEY CT
EDINA PL
PL
MIRANDA CL
AV
ESPLANADE
Recreation Reserve
CR
HAVEN
RIVERSIDE
GRANDVIEW
DR
Tennis
Ch
THE
Foreshore
Reserve
MARIAN
FISCHER
RD
RD
BOLL CR
VARYDALE AV
ST
FOLLET ST
NEW ST
CR
RD
Reserve
AV
FELIX
RD
Beach
ST
ST
Taylor Park
ESPLANADE
FISCHER
RD
WALKER ST
ST CLIFF
ST
Foreshore
Yellow Bluff
Fishermans
Zeally
Bay
RD
PEARL
GILBERT ST
RD
PATRE ST
PEARL ST
ST
ST
ST
CH
ST
ST
MUNDAY
PRIDE
ST
Beach
Front
PARK LA
THE ESPLANADE
Point Danger
Beach
Surf
Coast
BASS STRAIT

1 2 3 4 5 6 7 8 9 10 11 12 13 14 15 16 17 18 19 20

A B C D E F G H J K L

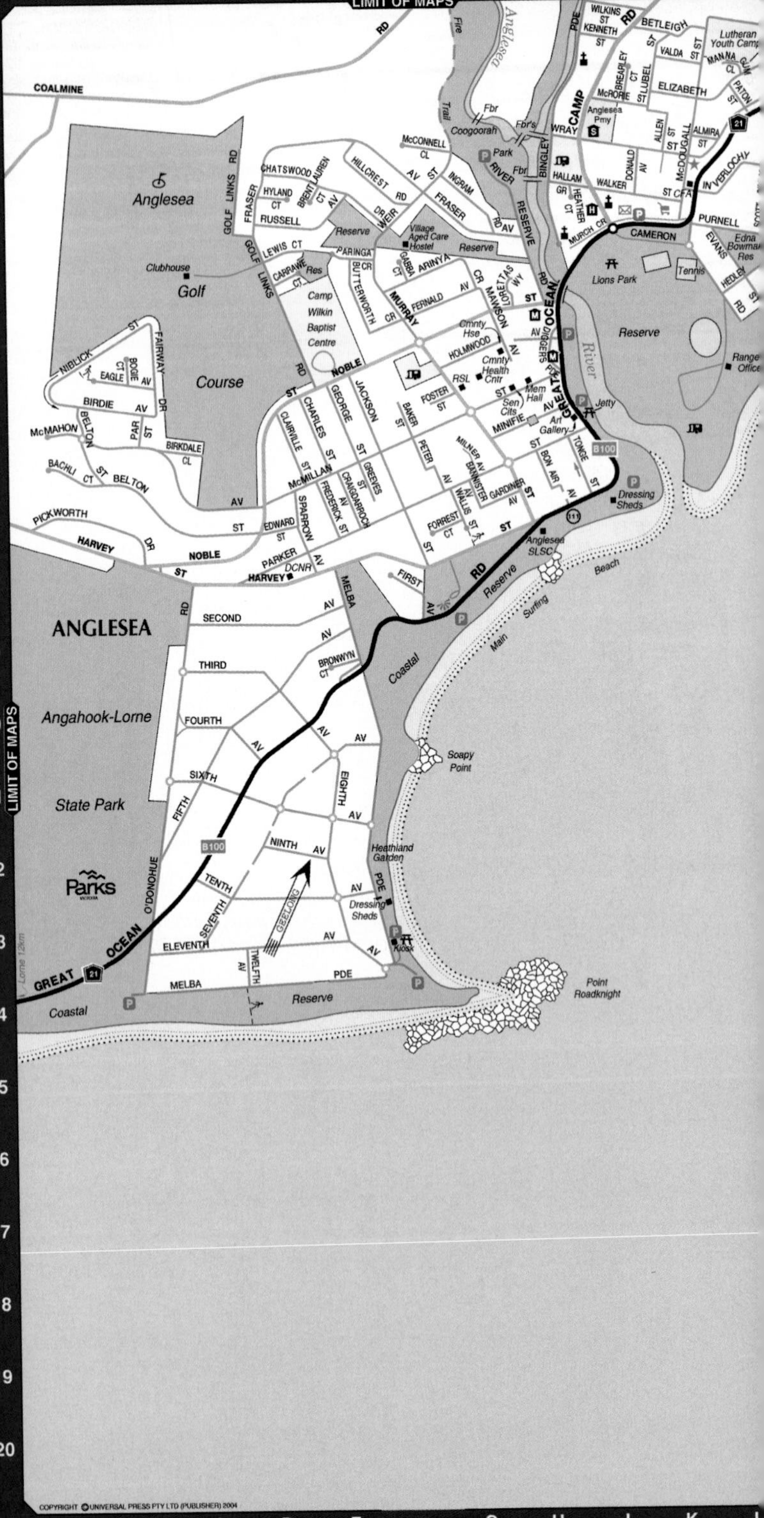
LIMIT OF MAPS
COALMINE RD
Anglesea
Golf
Course
Clubhouse
GOLF LINKS RD
FRASER ST
CHATSWOOD
LAUREN
HYLAND CT
BRENT CT
RUSSELL
LEWIS CT
CARRAWE CT
Res
Reserve
PARINGA
HILLCREST RD
WEIR DR
McCONNELL CL
INGRAM
FRASER RD
Village Aged Care Hostel
BUTTERWORTH CR
GABBA
ARINYA
MURRAY
FERNALD
MAWSON CR
GRETTAS WY
Camp Wilkin Baptist Centre
NOBLE ST
CHARLES
GEORGE
JACKSON
CLAIRVILLE
McMILLAN
SPARROW AV
FREDERICK ST
CRAIGDARROCH
GREEVES
BAKER
PETER
FOSTER ST
HOLMWOOD
Cmnty Hse
Cmnty Health Cntr
RSL
Sen Cits
Mem Hall
MINIFIE
Art Gallery
MILNER AV
BANNISTER
WALLIS
GARDINER
BON AIR AV
TONGE ST
FORREST CT
EDWARD ST
PARKER ST
DCNR
HARVEY
FIRST AV
MELBA
NIBLICK
FAIRWAY
EAGLE CT
BOGIE AV
BIRDIE AV
PAR ST
BIRKDALE CL
McMAHON
BELTON
BACHLI CT
BELTON ST
PICKWORTH
HARVEY DR
NOBLE ST
ANGLESEA
Angahook-Lorne
State Park
Parks
SECOND AV
THIRD AV
BRONWYN CT
FOURTH AV
SIXTH
FIFTH
EIGHTH AV
NINTH AV
TENTH
SEVENTH
ELEVENTH AV
TWELFTH AV
MELBA PDE
O'DONOHUE RD
GEELONG
GREAT OCEAN RD
B100
21
111
Coastal Reserve
Heathland Garden
Dressing Sheds
Kiosk
Soapy Point
Point Roadknight
Main Surfing Beach
Anglesea SLSC
Dressing Sheds
Jetty
Lions Park
Reserve
Range Office
River
Anglesea River
Fire Trail
Fbr
Coogoorah Park
RIVER RESERVE RD
BINGLEY PDE
CAMP RD
WRAY
HALLAM
HEATHER CT
MURCH CR
WALKER
DONALD AV
ALLEN ST
McDOUGALL
BREARLEY CT
LUBEL ST
McRORIE
Anglesea Pmy
WILKINS ST
KENNETH ST
BETLEIGH
VALDA ST
ELIZABETH
MANNA CL
PATON
ALMIRA
INVERLOCHY
CFA
CAMERON
PURNELL
EVANS
HEDLEY RD
Edna Bowman Res
Tennis
Lutheran Youth Camp
DIGGERS PDE
Lorne 12km

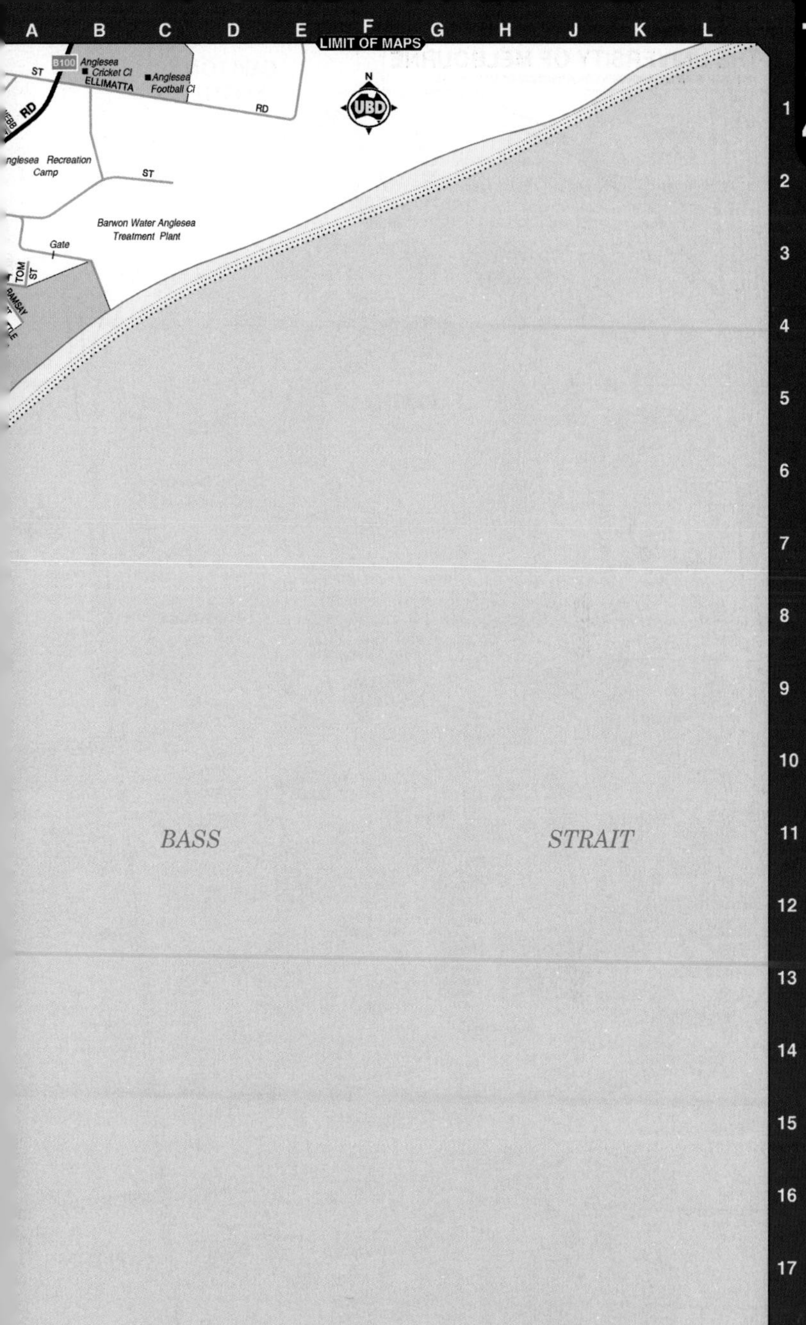

LIMIT OF MAPS
B100
Anglesea Cricket Cl
Anglesea Football Cl
ELLIMATTA
RD
ST
nglesea Recreation Camp
ST
Barwon Water Anglesea Treatment Plant
Gate
TOM
ST
RAMSAY
BASS
STRAIT

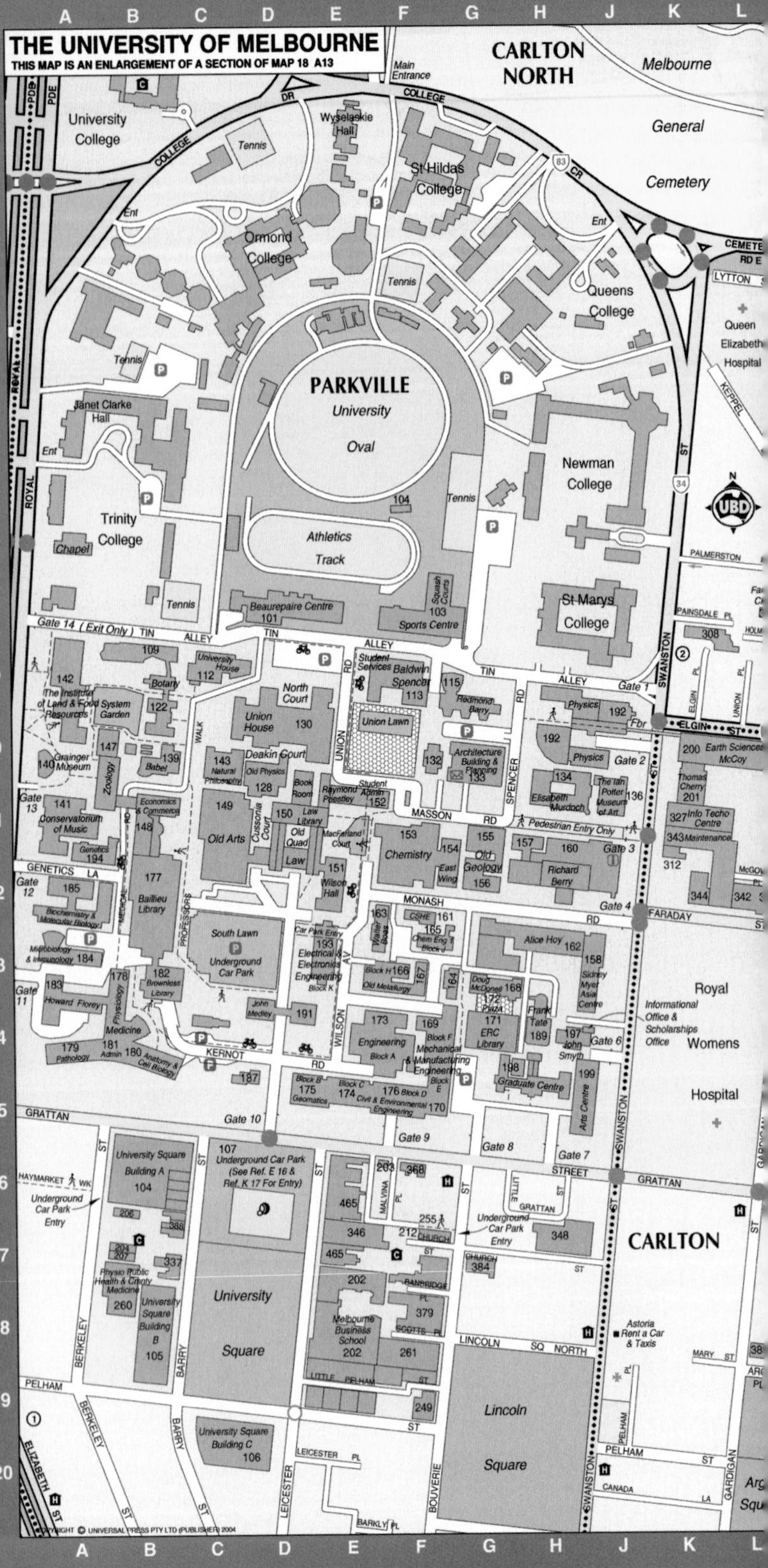

THE UNIVERSITY OF MELBOURNE

THIS MAP IS AN ENLARGEMENT OF A SECTION OF MAP 18 A13

CARLTON NORTH

Melbourne General Cemetery

Main Entrance

COLLEGE DR

COLLEGE CR

University College

Tennis

Wyselaskie Hall

St Hildas College

Ormond College

Queens College

Queen Elizabeth Hospital

KEPPEL

LYTTON

CEMETERY RD E

Janet Clarke Hall

PARKVILLE

University Oval

Athletics Track

Newman College

Trinity College

Chapel

St Marys College

Beaurepaire Centre 101

Squash Courts 103 Sports Centre

104

Gate 14 (Exit Only) TIN ALLEY

ROYAL PDE

PALMERSTON

PAINSDALE PL

308

SWANSTON ST

ELGIN ST

109 Botany

112 University House

142 The Institute of Land & Food Resources

System Garden 122

North Court

Union House 130

Student Services Baldwin Spencer 113

115 Redmond Barry

Union Lawn

Physics 192

Gate 1

Fbr

200 Earth Sciences McCoy

140 Grainger Museum

147 Zoology

139 Babel

143 Natural Philosophy

Deakin Court

128 Old Physics

Book Room

Raymond Priestley

Student Admin 152

132

Architecture Building & Planning 133

Physics Gate 2

134 Elisabeth Murdoch

The Ian Potter Museum of Art 136

Thomas Cherry 201

327 Info Techo Centre

343 Maintenance

312

Gate 13

141 Conservatorium of Music

Economics & Commerce 148

149 Old Arts

Cussonia Court 150

Law Library

Old Quad

Law

MacFarland Court

151 Wilson Hall

MASSON RD

Pedestrian Entry Only

153 Chemistry

154 East Wing

155 Old Geology 156

157

160 Richard Berry

Gate 3

194 Genetics

GENETICS LA

Gate 12

185

Biochemistry & Molecular Biology

177 Baillieu Library

MEDICAL

PROFESSORS WALK

MONASH RD

163 Walter Boas

CSHE 161

165 Chem Eng 1 Block J

Alice Hoy 162

158 Sidney Myer Asia Centre

Gate 4

FARADAY ST

344

342

Microbiology & Immunology 184

South Lawn Underground Car Park

Car Park Entry

193 Electrical & Electronics Engineering Block K

Block H 166

167

Old Metallurgy

164

Doug McDonell 168

172 Plaza

171 ERC Library

Frank Tate 189

197 John Smyth

Gate 6

Gate 11

183 Howard Florey

178 Physiology

182 Brownless Library

John Medley

191

WILSON AV

173 Engineering Block A

169 Block F Mechanical & Manufacturing Engineering

Block E

198 Graduate Centre

199 Arts Centre

Royal Womens Hospital

Informational Office & Scholarships Office

Medicine

179 Pathology

181 Admin

180 Anatomy & Cell Biology

KERNOT RD

187

Block B 175 Geomatics

Block C 174

176 Block D Civil & Environmental Engineering

170

GRATTAN ST

Gate 10

Gate 9

Gate 8

Gate 7

University Square Building A 104

107 Underground Car Park (See Ref. E 16 & Ref. K 17 For Entry)

203

368

MALVINA PL

LITTLE GRATTAN ST

HAYMARKET WK

Underground Car Park Entry

206

388

465

346

255

212

CHURCH ST

Underground Car Park Entry

348

CARLTON

204

207

337

465

384

Physio Public Health & Cmnty Medicine

260

University Square Building B 105

University Square

202

BARRIDGE PL

379

Melbourne Business School 202

SCOTTS PL

LINCOLN SQ NORTH

Astoria Rent a Car & Taxis

MARY ST

BERKELEY ST

BARRY ST

261

LITTLE PELHAM ST

PELHAM ST

249

Lincoln Square

PELHAM ST

University Square Building C 106

LEICESTER PL

LEICESTER ST

BOUVERIE ST

CANADA LA

GARDIGAN ST

ELIZABETH ST

BARKLY PL

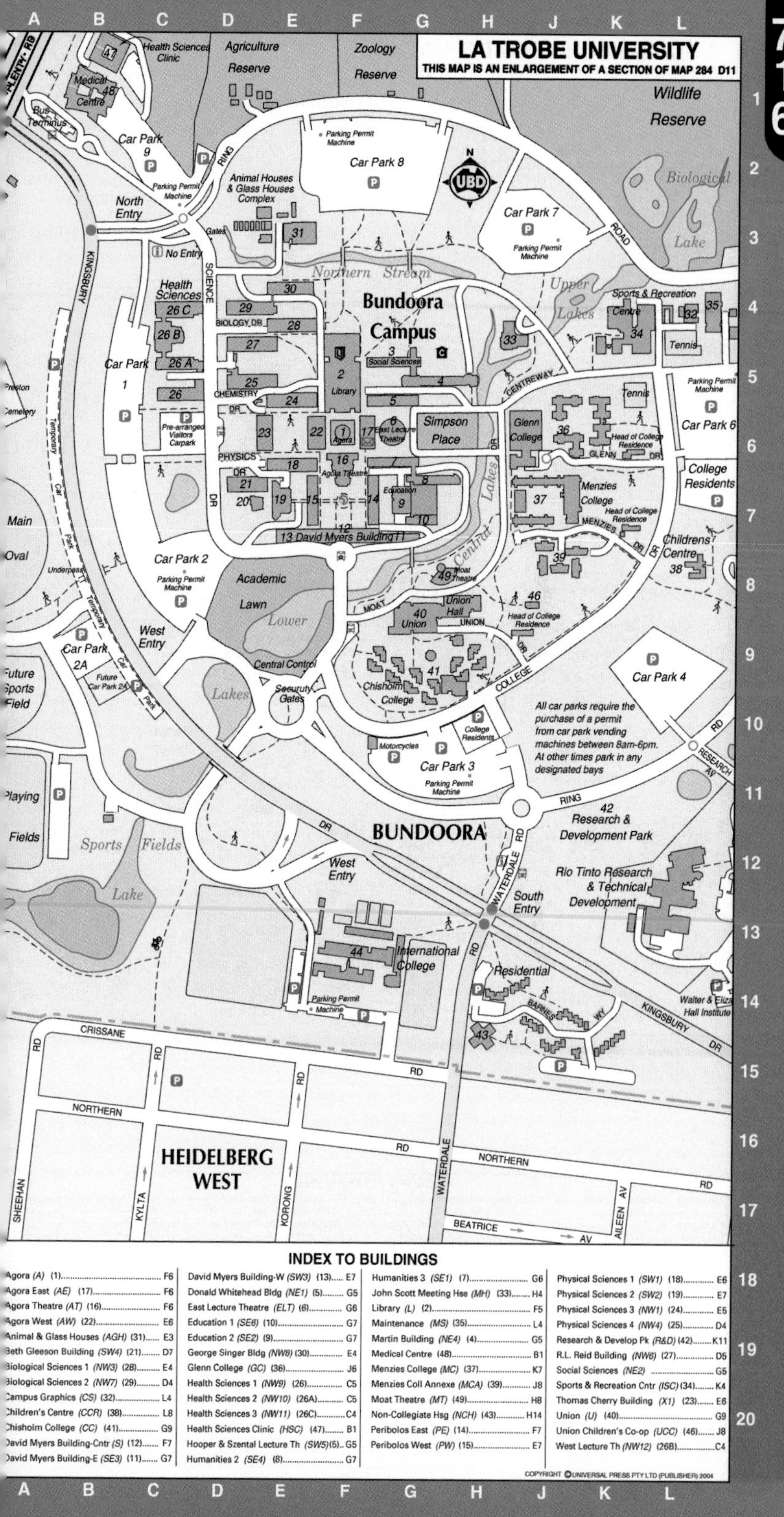
LA TROBE UNIVERSITY
THIS MAP IS AN ENLARGEMENT OF A SECTION OF MAP 284 D11
Bundoora Campus
BUNDOORA
HEIDELBERG WEST
Agriculture Reserve
Zoology Reserve
Wildlife Reserve
Health Sciences Clinic
Medical Centre
Bus Terminus
Car Park 9
North Entry
Parking Permit Machine
Animal Houses & Glass Houses Complex
Car Park 8
Car Park 7
Biological Lake
Northern Stream
Upper Lakes
Sports & Recreation Centre
Tennis
Health Sciences
Car Park 1
No Entry
Pre-arranged Visitors Carpark
Social Sciences
Library
Agora
East Lecture Theatre
Agora Theatre
Education
Simpson Place
Glenn College
Head of College Residence
Car Park 6
College Residents
Menzies College
Childrens Centre
13 David Myers Building
Central Lakes
Moat Theatre
Main Oval
Car Park 2
Academic Lawn
Lower Lakes
Union
Union Hall
Car Park 2A
Future Car Park 2A
Future Sports Field
West Entry
Central Control
Security Gates
Chisholm College
Car Park 4
All car parks require the purchase of a permit from car park vending machines between 8am-6pm. At other times park in any designated bays
Motorcycles
Car Park 3
Playing Fields
Sports Fields
Lake
Research & Development Park
Rio Tinto Research & Technical Development
South Entry
International College
Residential
Walter & Eliza Hall Institute
KINGSBURY DR
SCIENCE DR
RING RD
BIOLOGY DR
CHEMISTRY DR
PHYSICS DR
CENTREWAY
GLENN DR
MENZIES DR
MOAT DR
UNION DR
COLLEGE DR
RESEARCH AV
WATERDALE RD
BARNES WY
CRISSANE RD
NORTHERN RD
BEATRICE AV
SHEEHAN RD
KYLTA RD
KORONG RD
AILEEN AV
PLENTY RD
Preston Cemetery
Temporary Car Park
Underpass

INDEX TO BUILDINGS
Agora (A) (1) F6
Agora East (AE) (17) F6
Agora Theatre (AT) (16) F6
Agora West (AW) (22) E6
Animal & Glass Houses (AGH) (31) E3
Beth Gleeson Building (SW4) (21) D7
Biological Sciences 1 (NW3) (28) E4
Biological Sciences 2 (NW7) (29) D4
Campus Graphics (CS) (32) L4
Children's Centre (CCR) (38) L8
Chisholm College (CC) (41) G9
David Myers Building-Cntr (S) (12) F7
David Myers Building-E (SE3) (11) G7
David Myers Building-W (SW3) (13) E7
Donald Whitehead Bldg (NE1) (5) G5
East Lecture Theatre (ELT) (6) G6
Education 1 (SE6) (10) G7
Education 2 (SE2) (9) G7
George Singer Bldg (NW8) (30) E4
Glenn College (GC) (36) J6
Health Sciences 1 (NW9) (26) C5
Health Sciences 2 (NW10) (26A) C5
Health Sciences 3 (NW11) (26C) C4
Health Sciences Clinic (HSC) (47) B1
Hooper & Szental Lecture Th (SW5)(5) G5
Humanities 2 (SE4) (8) G7
Humanities 3 (SE1) (7) G6
John Scott Meeting Hse (MH) (33) H4
Library (L) (2) F5
Maintenance (MS) (35) L4
Martin Building (NE4) (4) G5
Medical Centre (48) B1
Menzies College (MC) (37) K7
Menzies Coll Annexe (MCA) (39) J8
Moat Theatre (MT) (49) H8
Non-Collegiate Hsg (NCH) (43) H14
Peribolos East (PE) (14) F7
Peribolos West (PW) (15) E7
Physical Sciences 1 (SW1) (18) E6
Physical Sciences 2 (SW2) (19) E7
Physical Sciences 3 (NW1) (24) E5
Physical Sciences 4 (NW4) (25) D4
Research & Develop Pk (R&D) (42) K11
R.L. Reid Building (NW6) (27) D5
Social Sciences (NE2) G5
Sports & Recreation Cntr (ISC) (34) K4
Thomas Cherry Building (X1) (23) E6
Union (U) (40) G9
Union Children's Co-op (UCC) (46) J8
West Lecture Th (NW12) (26B) C4
COPYRIGHT © UNIVERSAL PRESS PTY LTD (PUBLISHER) 2004

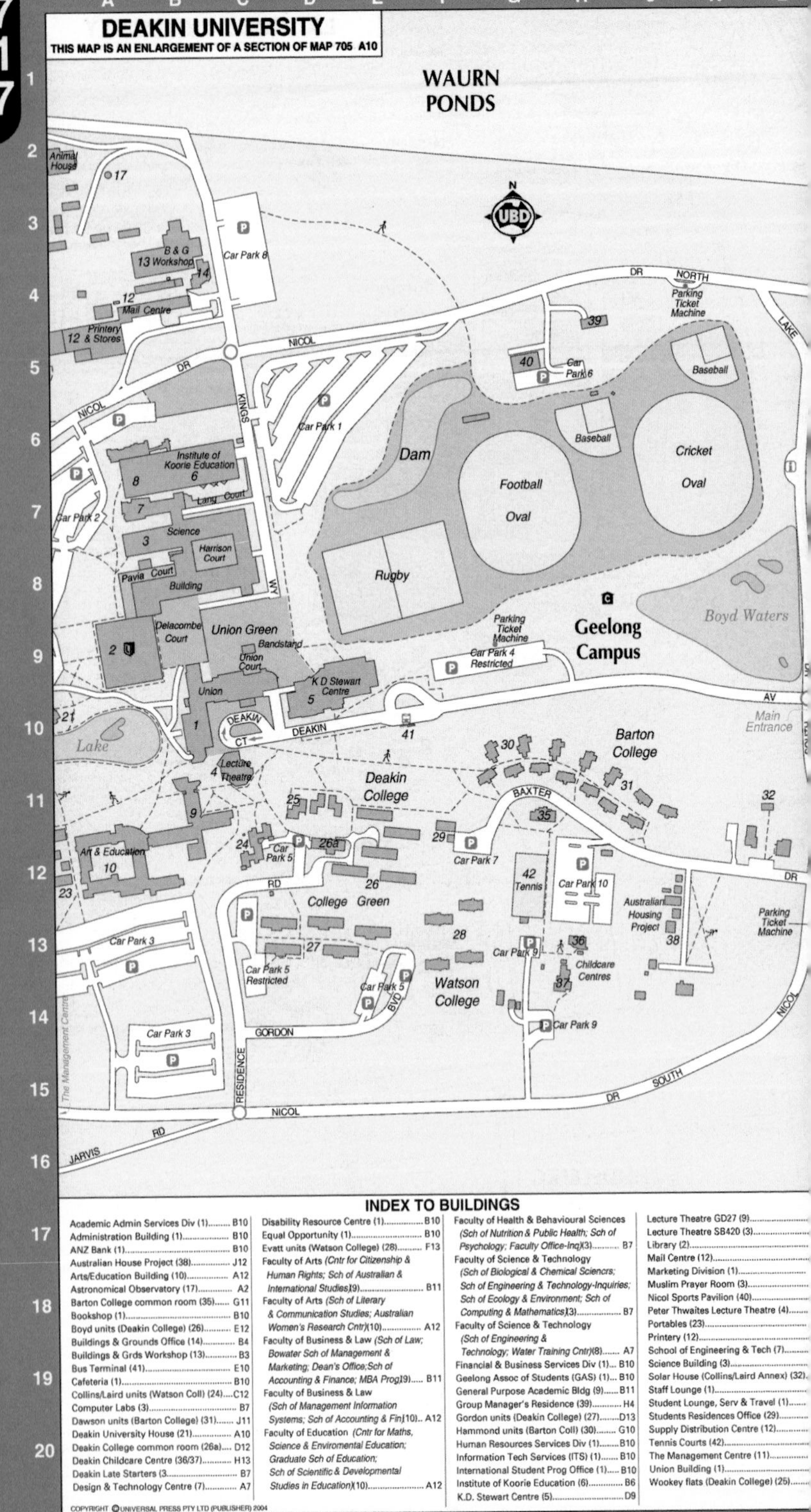

INDEX TO BUILDINGS

DEAKIN UNIVERSITY

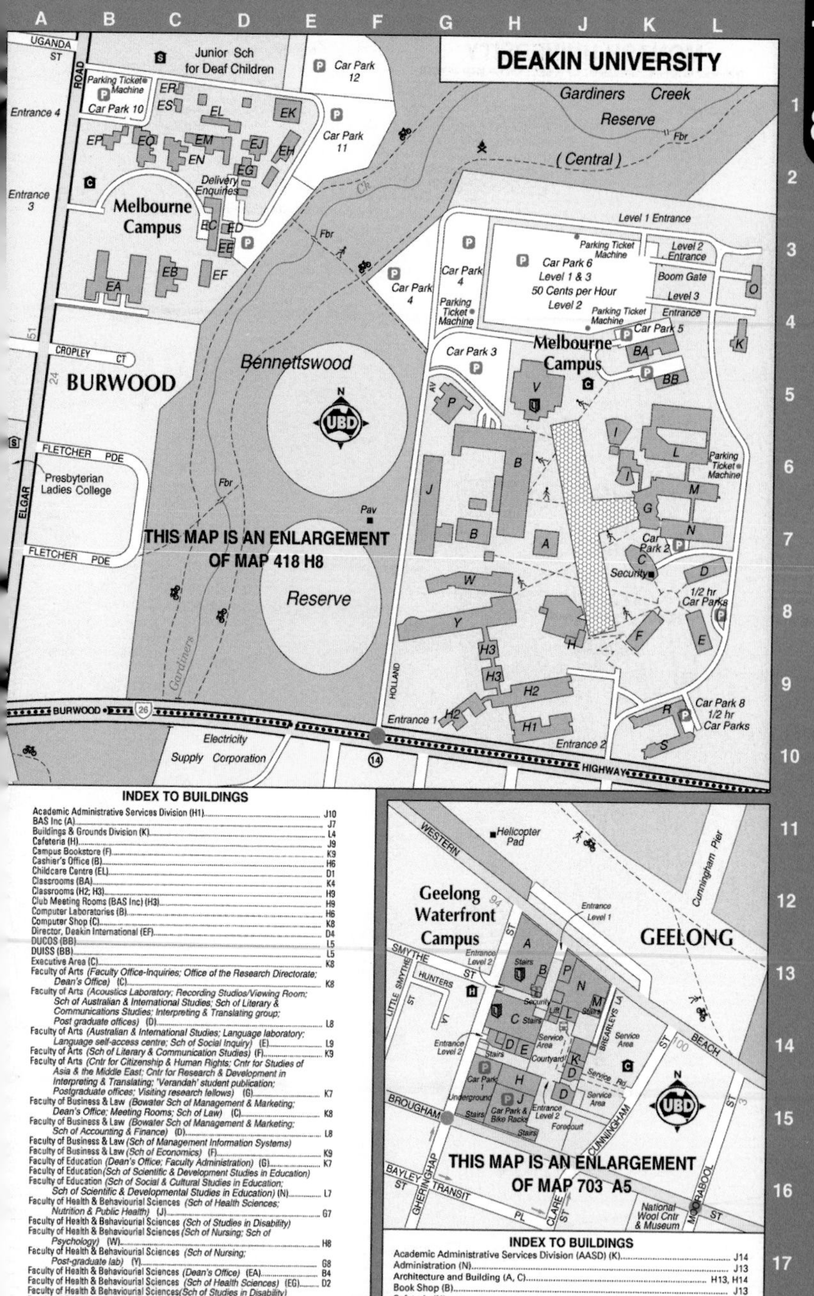

INDEX TO BUILDINGS

Academic Administrative Services Division (H1) ... J10
BAS Inc (A) ... J7
Buildings & Grounds Division (K) ... L4
Cafeteria (H) ... J9
Campus Bookstore (F) ... K9
Cashier's Office (B) ... H6
Childcare Centre (EL) ... D1
Classrooms (BA) ... K4
Classrooms (H2; H3) ... H9
Club Meeting Rooms (BAS Inc) (H3) ... H9
Computer Laboratories (B) ... H6
Computer Shop (C) ... K8
Director, Deakin International (EF) ... D4
DUCOS (BB) ... L5
DUISS (BB) ... L5
Executive Area (C) ... K8
Faculty of Arts *(Faculty Office-Inquiries; Office of the Research Directorate; Dean's Office)* (C) ... K8
Faculty of Arts *(Acoustics Laboratory; Recording Studios/Viewing Room; Sch of Australian & International Studies; Sch of Literary & Communications Studies; Interpreting & Translating group; Post graduate offices)* (D) ... L8
Faculty of Arts *(Australian & International Studies; Language laboratory; Language self-access centre; Sch of Social Inquiry)* (E) ... L9
Faculty of Arts *(Sch of Literary & Communication Studies)* (F) ... K9
Faculty of Arts *(Cntr for Citizenship & Human Rights; Cntr for Studies of Asia & the Middle East; Cntr for Research & Development in Interpreting & Translating; 'Verandah' student publication; Postgraduate offices; Visiting research fellows)* (G) ... K7
Faculty of Business & Law *(Bowater Sch of Management & Marketing; Dean's Office; Meeting Rooms; Sch of Law)* (C) ... K8
Faculty of Business & Law *(Bowater Sch of Management & Marketing; Sch of Accounting & Finance)* (D) ... L8
Faculty of Business & Law *(Sch of Management Information Systems)*
Faculty of Business & Law *(Sch of Economics)* (F) ... K9
Faculty of Education *(Dean's Office; Faculty Administration)* (G) ... K7
Faculty of Education *(Sch of Scientific & Development Studies in Education)*
Faculty of Education *(Sch of Social & Cultural Studies in Education; Sch of Scientific & Developmental Studies in Education)* (N) ... L7
Faculty of Health & Behavioural Sciences *(Sch of Health Sciences; Nutrition & Public Health)* (J) ... G7
Faculty of Health & Behavioural Sciences *(Sch of Studies in Disability)*
Faculty of Health & Behavioural Sciences *(Sch of Nursing; Sch of Psychology)* (W) ... H8
Faculty of Health & Behavioural Sciences *(Sch of Nursing; Post-graduate lab)* (Y) ... G8
Faculty of Health & Behavioural Sciences *(Dean's Office)* (EA) ... B4
Faculty of Health & Behavioural Sciences *(Sch of Health Sciences)* (EG) ... D2
Faculty of Health & Behavioural Sciences*(Sch of Studies in Disability)*
Faculty of Science & Technology *(Burwood Science & Technology Centre; Dean's Office; Ecology & Environment; Mathematics Research)*
Faculty of Science & Technology (M) ... L6
Financial & Business Services Division (EF) ... D4
Indoor Sporting Facilities (B) ... H6
Information Technology Services (ITS) (EC) ... D3
Laundry (ED) ... D3
Learning Resources Services (H2) ... J9
Lecture Theatres 1 & 2 (I) ... K6
Lecture Theatres 3, 4 & 5 (B) ... H6
Library (V) ... J5
Mature-age Students Lounge (BAS Inc) (H3) ... H9
Muslim Prayer Room (BB) ... L5
Noodle Shop (G) ... K7
Our Restaurant & Bar (BAS Inc) (H) ... J9
Phoenix Theatre (B) ... H7
Plateau Cafe (G) ... K7
Printery (O) ... L4
Residential Accommodation (ER, ES) ... C1
Security ... K8
Staff Training Laboratory (EM) ... C2
Student Games Room & Student Radio (BAS Inc) (H) ... J9
Student Residences (EB, EK, EN) ... C3,E1,C2
University Childcare Centre (R) ... K9

INDEX TO BUILDINGS

Academic Administrative Services Division (AASD) (K) ... J14
Administration (N) ... J13
Architecture and Building (A, C) ... H13, H14
Book Shop (B) ... J13
Cafeteria (N) ... J13
Cashier (N) ... J13
COSTA Theatre (H) ... H14
Deakin Centre for Academic Development (DCAD) (A) ... H13
Gallery (N) ... J13
Geelong Association of Students (GAS) (P) ... J13
Geelong Science and Technology Centre (GSAT) (A) ... H13
Information (B) ... J13
Information Technology Services (ITS) (C) ... H14
Learning Resources Services (LRS) (A) ... H13
Lecture Rooms (D) ... H14
Library (C) ... H14
Loading Platform (L) ... J14
Main Library (A) ... H13
Meeting Room (M) ... H14
Percy Baxter Lecture Theatre (E) ... H14
Security (B) ... J13
Student Services (N) ... J13
Technical Services (C) ... H14
The Chancellery (N) ... J13
The COSTA Hall (J) ... H15

A B C D E F G H J K L

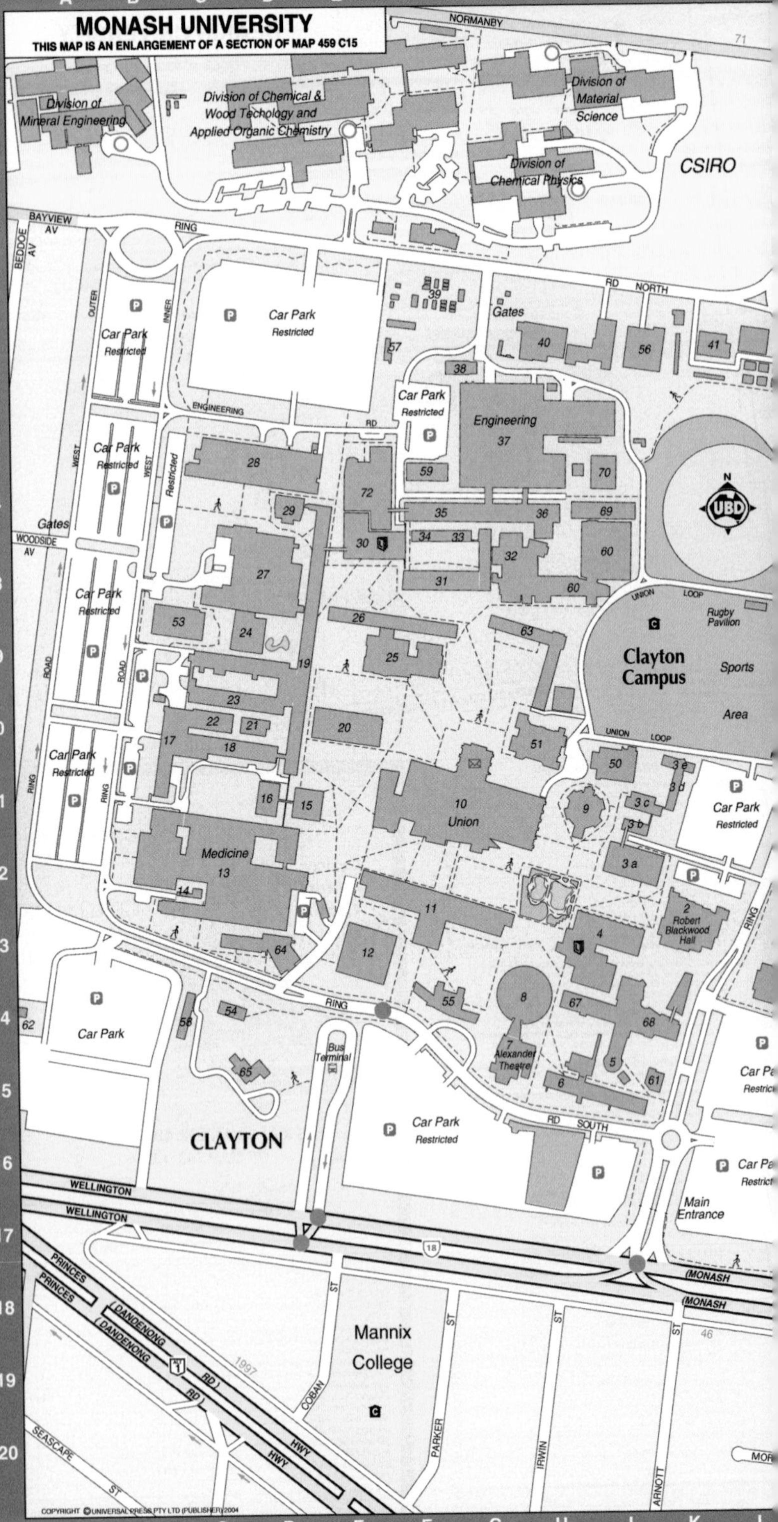

MONASH UNIVERSITY

THIS MAP IS AN ENLARGEMENT OF A SECTION OF MAP 459 C15

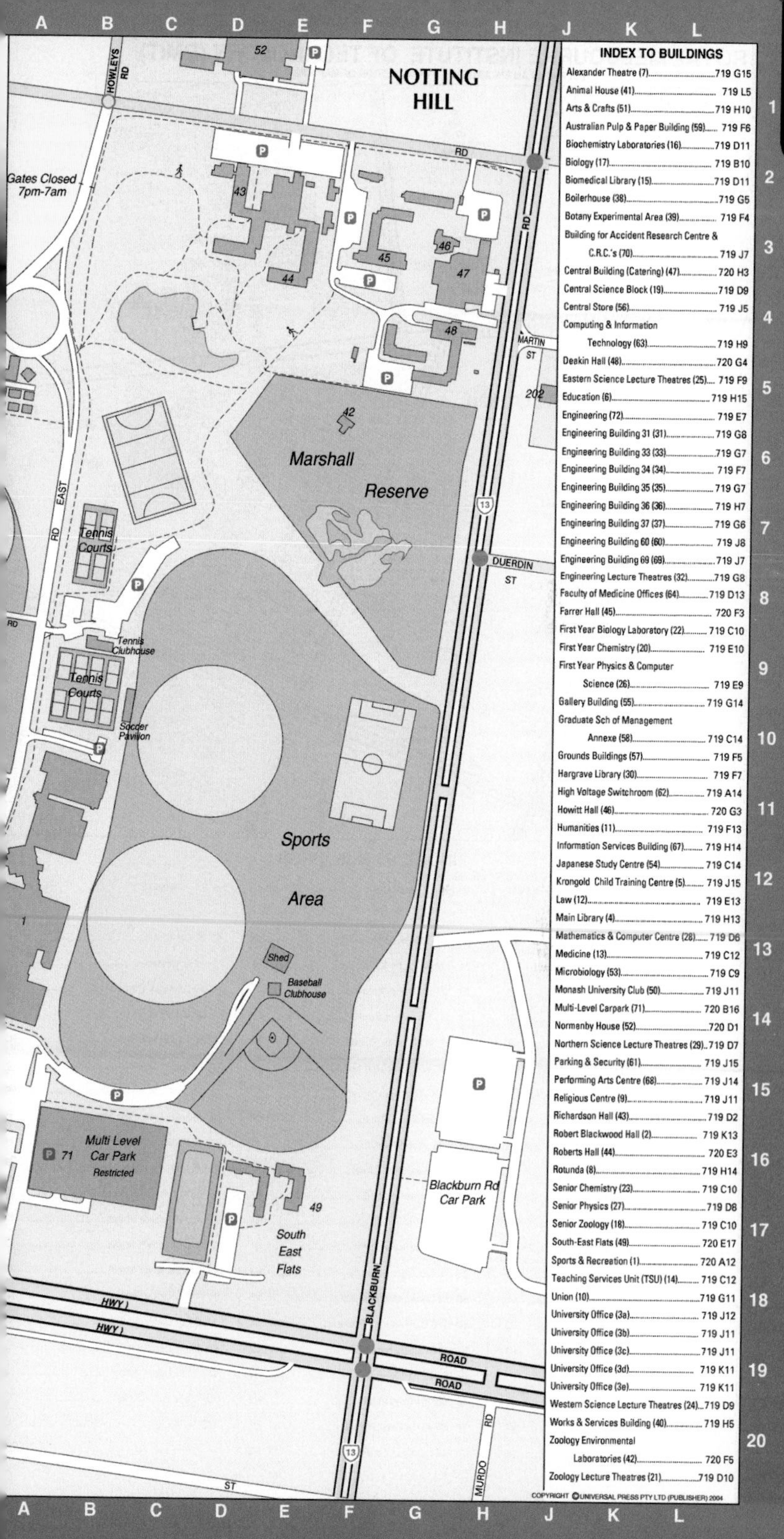

A B C D E F G H J K L
NOTTING HILL
HOWLEYS RD
RD
Gates Closed 7pm-7am
52
43
44
45
46
47
48
42
MARTIN ST
202
Marshall
Reserve
13
DUERDIN ST
EAST RD
Tennis Courts
Tennis Clubhouse
Tennis Courts
Soccer Pavilion
RD
Sports
Area
1
Shed
Baseball Clubhouse
Multi Level Car Park Restricted
71
49
South East Flats
Blackburn Rd Car Park
HWY
HWY
BLACKBURN
ROAD
ROAD
MURDO RD
ST
13
INDEX TO BUILDINGS
Alexander Theatre (7) 719 G15
Animal House (41) 719 L5
Arts & Crafts (51) 719 H10
Australian Pulp & Paper Building (59) 719 F6
Biochemistry Laboratories (16) 719 D11
Biology (17) 719 B10
Biomedical Library (15) 719 D11
Boilerhouse (38) 719 G5
Botany Experimental Area (39) 719 F4
Building for Accident Research Centre & C.R.C.'s (70) 719 J7
Central Building (Catering) (47) 720 H3
Central Science Block (19) 719 D9
Central Store (56) 719 J5
Computing & Information Technology (63) 719 H9
Deakin Hall (48) 720 G4
Eastern Science Lecture Theatres (25) 719 F9
Education (6) 719 H15
Engineering (72) 719 E7
Engineering Building 31 (31) 719 G8
Engineering Building 33 (33) 719 G7
Engineering Building 34 (34) 719 F7
Engineering Building 35 (35) 719 G7
Engineering Building 36 (36) 719 H7
Engineering Building 37 (37) 719 G6
Engineering Building 60 (60) 719 J8
Engineering Building 69 (69) 719 J7
Engineering Lecture Theatres (32) 719 G8
Faculty of Medicine Offices (64) 719 D13
Farrer Hall (45) 720 F3
First Year Biology Laboratory (22) 719 C10
First Year Chemistry (20) 719 E10
First Year Physics & Computer Science (26) 719 E9
Gallery Building (55) 719 G14
Graduate Sch of Management Annexe (58) 719 C14
Grounds Buildings (57) 719 F5
Hargrave Library (30) 719 F7
High Voltage Switchroom (62) 719 A14
Howitt Hall (46) 720 G3
Humanities (11) 719 F13
Information Services Building (67) 719 H14
Japanese Study Centre (54) 719 C14
Krongold Child Training Centre (5) 719 J15
Law (12) 719 E13
Main Library (4) 719 H13
Mathematics & Computer Centre (28) 719 D6
Medicine (13) 719 C12
Microbiology (53) 719 C9
Monash University Club (50) 719 J11
Multi-Level Carpark (71) 720 B16
Normanby House (52) 720 D1
Northern Science Lecture Theatres (29) 719 D7
Parking & Security (61) 719 J15
Performing Arts Centre (68) 719 J14
Religious Centre (9) 719 J11
Richardson Hall (43) 719 D2
Robert Blackwood Hall (2) 719 K13
Roberts Hall (44) 720 E3
Rotunda (8) 719 H14
Senior Chemistry (23) 719 C10
Senior Physics (27) 719 D8
Senior Zoology (18) 719 C10
South-East Flats (49) 720 E17
Sports & Recreation (1) 720 A12
Teaching Services Unit (TSU) (14) 719 C12
Union (10) 719 G11
University Office (3a) 719 J12
University Office (3b) 719 J11
University Office (3c) 719 J11
University Office (3d) 719 K11
University Office (3e) 719 K11
Western Science Lecture Theatres (24) 719 D9
Works & Services Building (40) 719 H5
Zoology Environmental Laboratories (42) 720 F5
Zoology Lecture Theatres (21) 719 D10
COPYRIGHT © UNIVERSAL PRESS PTY LTD (PUBLISHER) 2004
1 2 3 4 5 6 7 8 9 10 11 12 13 14 15 16 17 18 19 20
A B C D E F G H J K L

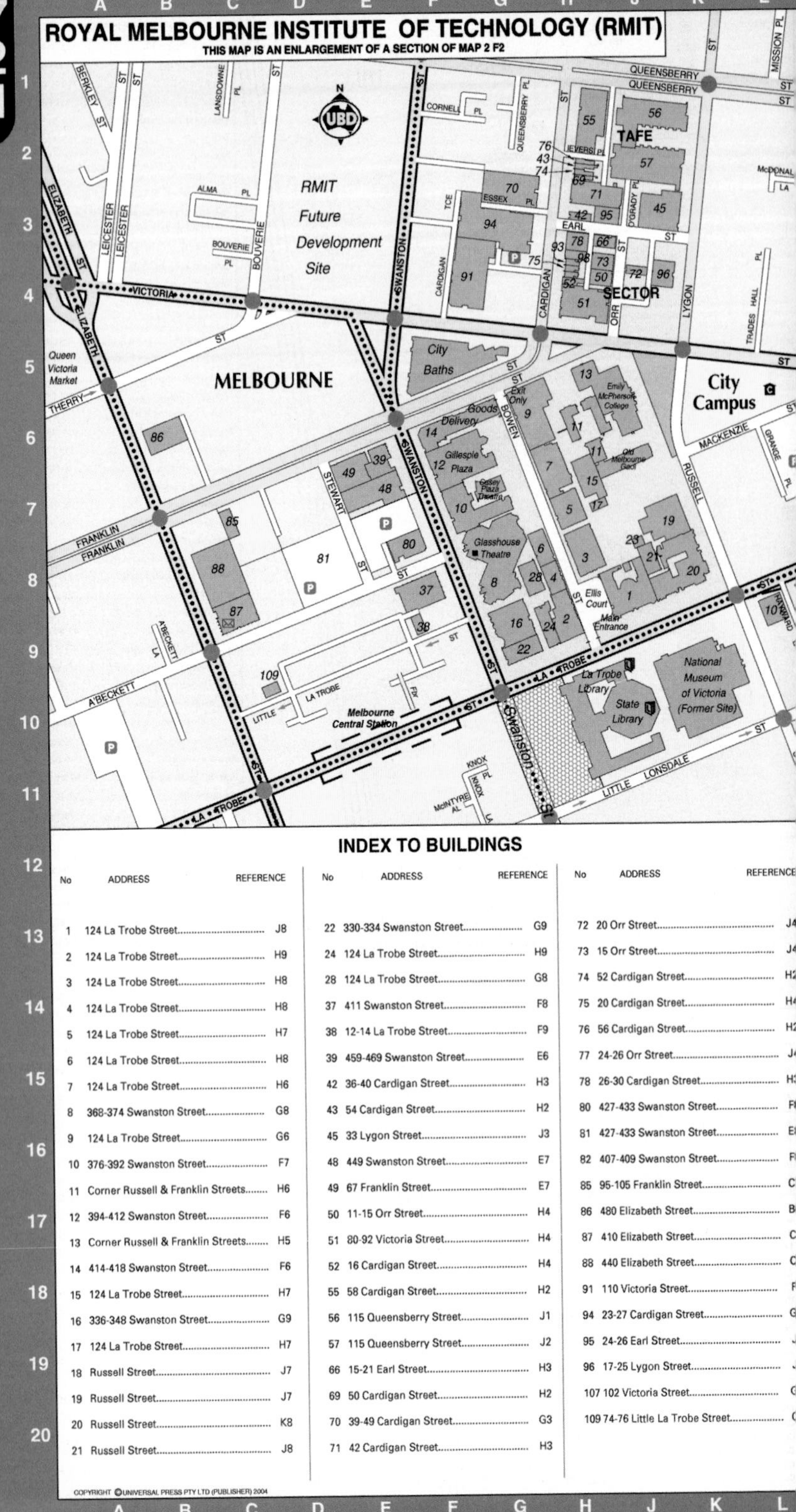

INDEX TO BUILDINGS

No	ADDRESS	REFERENCE
1	124 La Trobe Street	J8
2	124 La Trobe Street	H9
3	124 La Trobe Street	H8
4	124 La Trobe Street	H8
5	124 La Trobe Street	H7
6	124 La Trobe Street	H8
7	124 La Trobe Street	H6
8	368-374 Swanston Street	G8
9	124 La Trobe Street	G6
10	376-392 Swanston Street	F7
11	Corner Russell & Franklin Streets	H6
12	394-412 Swanston Street	F6
13	Corner Russell & Franklin Streets	H5
14	414-418 Swanston Street	F6
15	124 La Trobe Street	H7
16	336-348 Swanston Street	G9
17	124 La Trobe Street	H7
18	Russell Street	J7
19	Russell Street	J7
20	Russell Street	K8
21	Russell Street	J8
22	330-334 Swanston Street	G9
24	124 La Trobe Street	H9
28	124 La Trobe Street	G8
37	411 Swanston Street	F8
38	12-14 La Trobe Street	F9
39	459-469 Swanston Street	E6
42	36-40 Cardigan Street	H3
43	54 Cardigan Street	H2
45	33 Lygon Street	J3
48	449 Swanston Street	E7
49	67 Franklin Street	E7
50	11-15 Orr Street	H4
51	80-92 Victoria Street	H4
52	16 Cardigan Street	H4
55	58 Cardigan Street	H2
56	115 Queensberry Street	J1
57	115 Queensberry Street	J2
66	15-21 Earl Street	H3
69	50 Cardigan Street	H2
70	39-49 Cardigan Street	G3
71	42 Cardigan Street	H3
72	20 Orr Street	J4
73	15 Orr Street	J4
74	52 Cardigan Street	H2
75	20 Cardigan Street	H4
76	56 Cardigan Street	H2
77	24-26 Orr Street	J
78	26-30 Cardigan Street	H
80	427-433 Swanston Street	F
81	427-433 Swanston Street	E
82	407-409 Swanston Street	F
85	95-105 Franklin Street	C
86	480 Elizabeth Street	B
87	410 Elizabeth Street	C
88	440 Elizabeth Street	C
91	110 Victoria Street	F
94	23-27 Cardigan Street	G
95	24-26 Earl Street	J
96	17-25 Lygon Street	J
107	102 Victoria Street	C
109	74-76 Little La Trobe Street	C

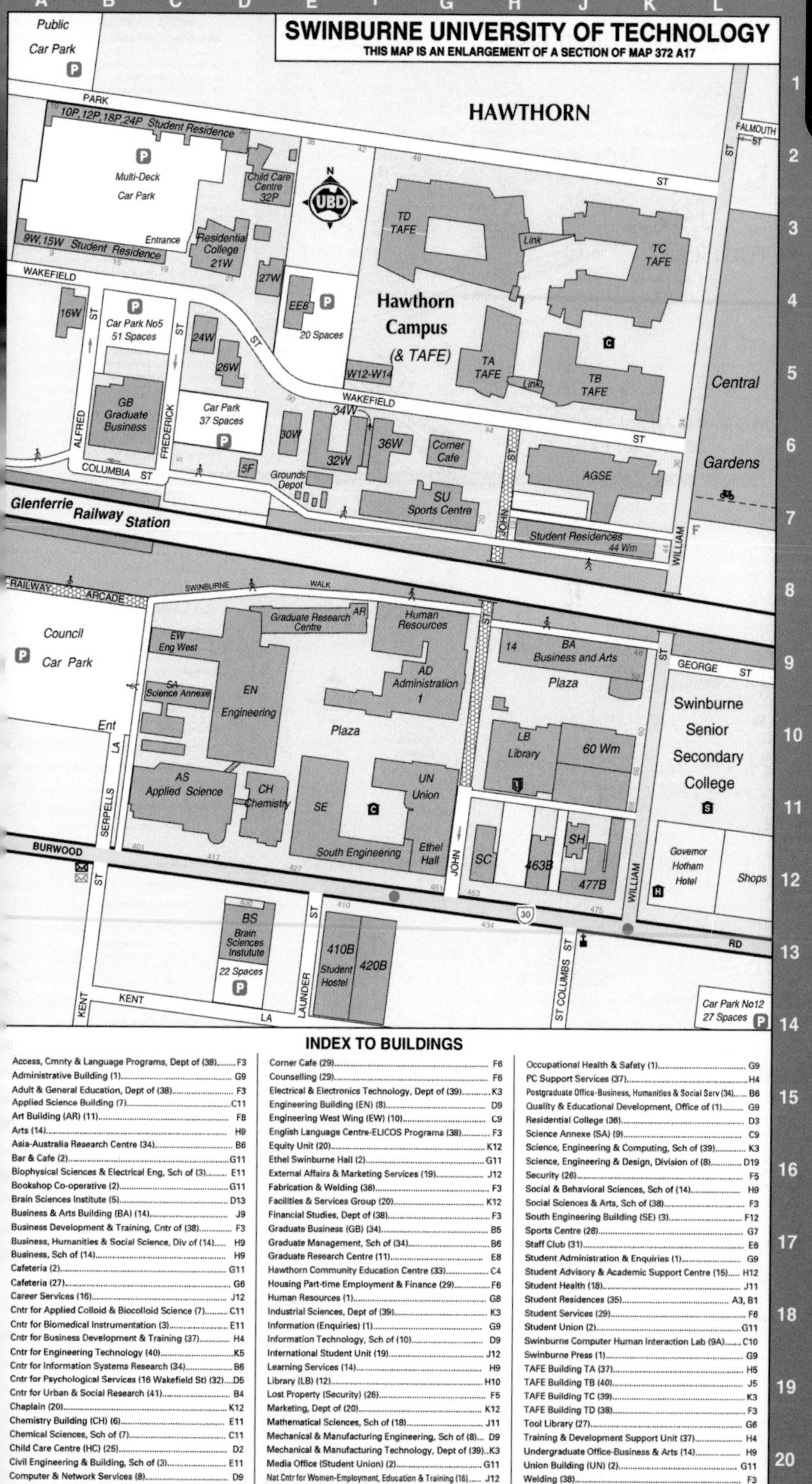

INDEX TO BUILDINGS

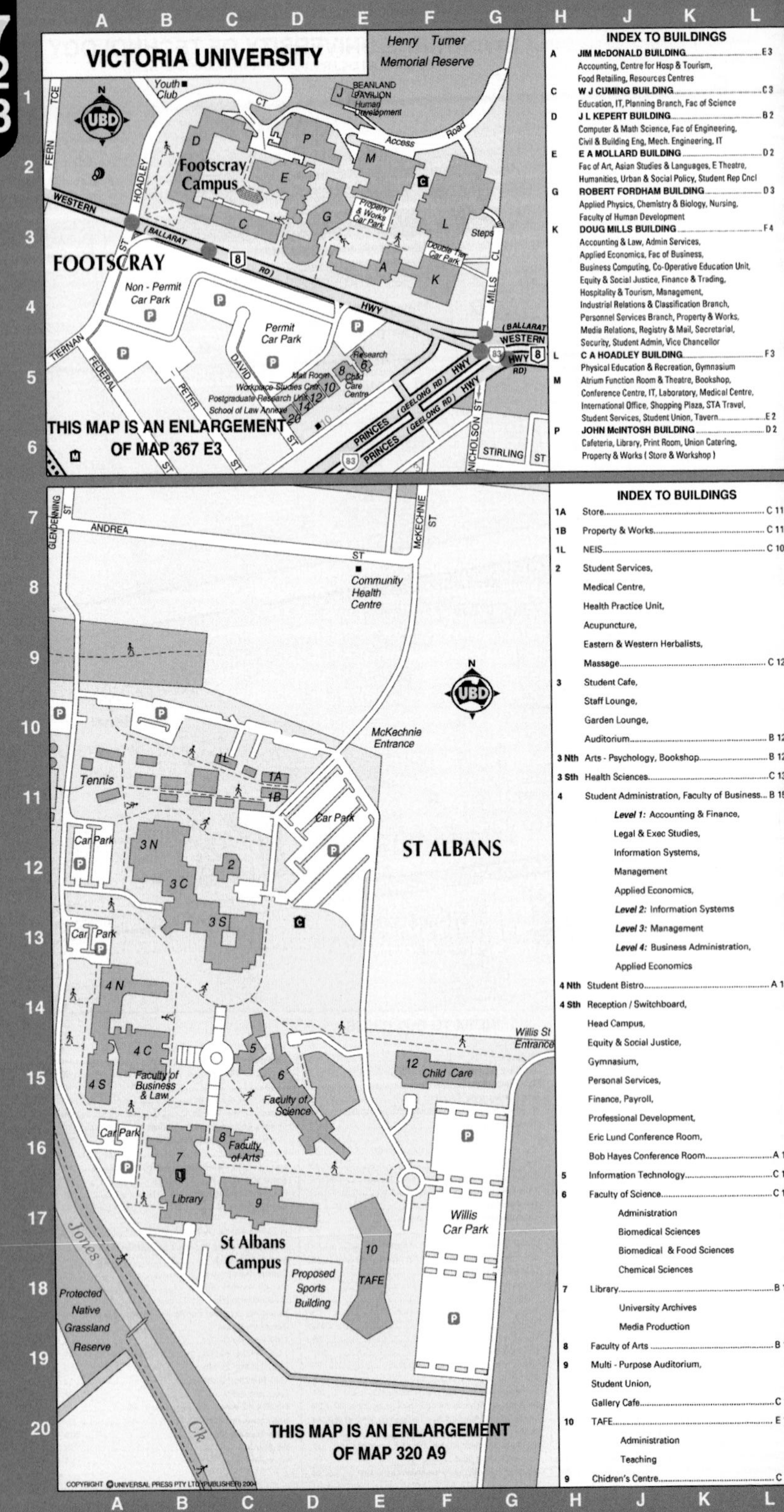
VICTORIA UNIVERSITY
Henry Turner Memorial Reserve
Youth Club
BEANLAND PAVILION
Human Development
Footscray Campus
Access Road
Property & Works Car Park
Double Tier Car Park
Steps
FOOTSCRAY
WESTERN (BALLARAT RD) HWY
Non - Permit Car Park
Permit Car Park
Research
Mail Room
Workplace Studies Cntr
Postgraduate Research Unit
School of Law Annexe
Child Care Centre
PRINCES (GEELONG RD) HWY
HOADLEY ST
MILLS CL
NICHOLSON ST
STIRLING ST
TIERNAN ST
FEDERAL ST
PETER ST
DAVID ST
FERN TCE
THIS MAP IS AN ENLARGEMENT OF MAP 367 E3
INDEX TO BUILDINGS
A JIM McDONALD BUILDING E 3
Accounting, Centre for Hosp & Tourism, Food Retailing, Resources Centres
C W J CUMING BUILDING C 3
Education, IT, Planning Branch, Fac of Science
D J L KEPERT BUILDING B 2
Computer & Math Science, Fac of Engineering, Civil & Building Eng, Mech. Engineering, IT
E E A MOLLARD BUILDING D 2
Fac of Art, Asian Studies & Languages, E Theatre, Humanities, Urban & Social Policy, Student Rep Cncl
G ROBERT FORDHAM BUILDING D 3
Applied Physics, Chemistry & Biology, Nursing, Faculty of Human Development
K DOUG MILLS BUILDING F 4
Accounting & Law, Admin Services, Applied Economics, Fac of Business, Business Computing, Co-Operative Education Unit, Equity & Social Justice, Finance & Trading, Hospitality & Tourism, Management, Industrial Relations & Classification Branch, Personnel Services Branch, Property & Works, Media Relations, Registry & Mail, Secretarial, Security, Student Admin, Vice Chancellor
L C A HOADLEY BUILDING F 3
Physical Education & Recreation, Gymnasium
M Atrium Function Room & Theatre, Bookshop, Conference Centre, IT, Laboratory, Medical Centre, International Office, Shopping Plaza, STA Travel, Student Services, Student Union, Tavern E 2
P JOHN McINTOSH BUILDING D 2
Cafeteria, Library, Print Room, Union Catering, Property & Works (Store & Workshop)
GLENDENNING ST
ANDREA ST
McKECHNIE ST
Community Health Centre
McKechnie Entrance
Tennis
Car Park
ST ALBANS
Willis St Entrance
Child Care
Faculty of Business & Law
Faculty of Science
Faculty of Arts
Library
Willis Car Park
St Albans Campus
Proposed Sports Building
TAFE
Jones Ck
Protected Native Grassland Reserve
THIS MAP IS AN ENLARGEMENT OF MAP 320 A9
COPYRIGHT © UNIVERSAL PRESS PTY LTD (PUBLISHER) 2004
INDEX TO BUILDINGS
1A Store C 11
1B Property & Works C 11
1L NEIS C 10
2 Student Services, Medical Centre, Health Practice Unit, Acupuncture, Eastern & Western Herbalists, Massage C 12
3 Student Cafe, Staff Lounge, Garden Lounge, Auditorium B 12
3 Nth Arts - Psychology, Bookshop B 12
3 Sth Health Sciences C 13
4 Student Administration, Faculty of Business B 15
Level 1: Accounting & Finance, Legal & Exec Studies, Information Systems, Management, Applied Economics,
Level 2: Information Systems
Level 3: Management
Level 4: Business Administration, Applied Economics
4 Nth Student Bistro A 1
4 Sth Reception / Switchboard, Head Campus, Equity & Social Justice, Gymnasium, Personal Services, Finance, Payroll, Professional Development, Eric Lund Conference Room, Bob Hayes Conference Room A 1
5 Information Technology C 1
6 Faculty of Science C 1
Administration, Biomedical Sciences, Biomedical & Food Sciences, Chemical Sciences
7 Library B 1
University Archives, Media Production
8 Faculty of Arts B 1
9 Multi - Purpose Auditorium, Student Union, Gallery Cafe C
10 TAFE E 1
Administration, Teaching
9 Chidren's Centre C

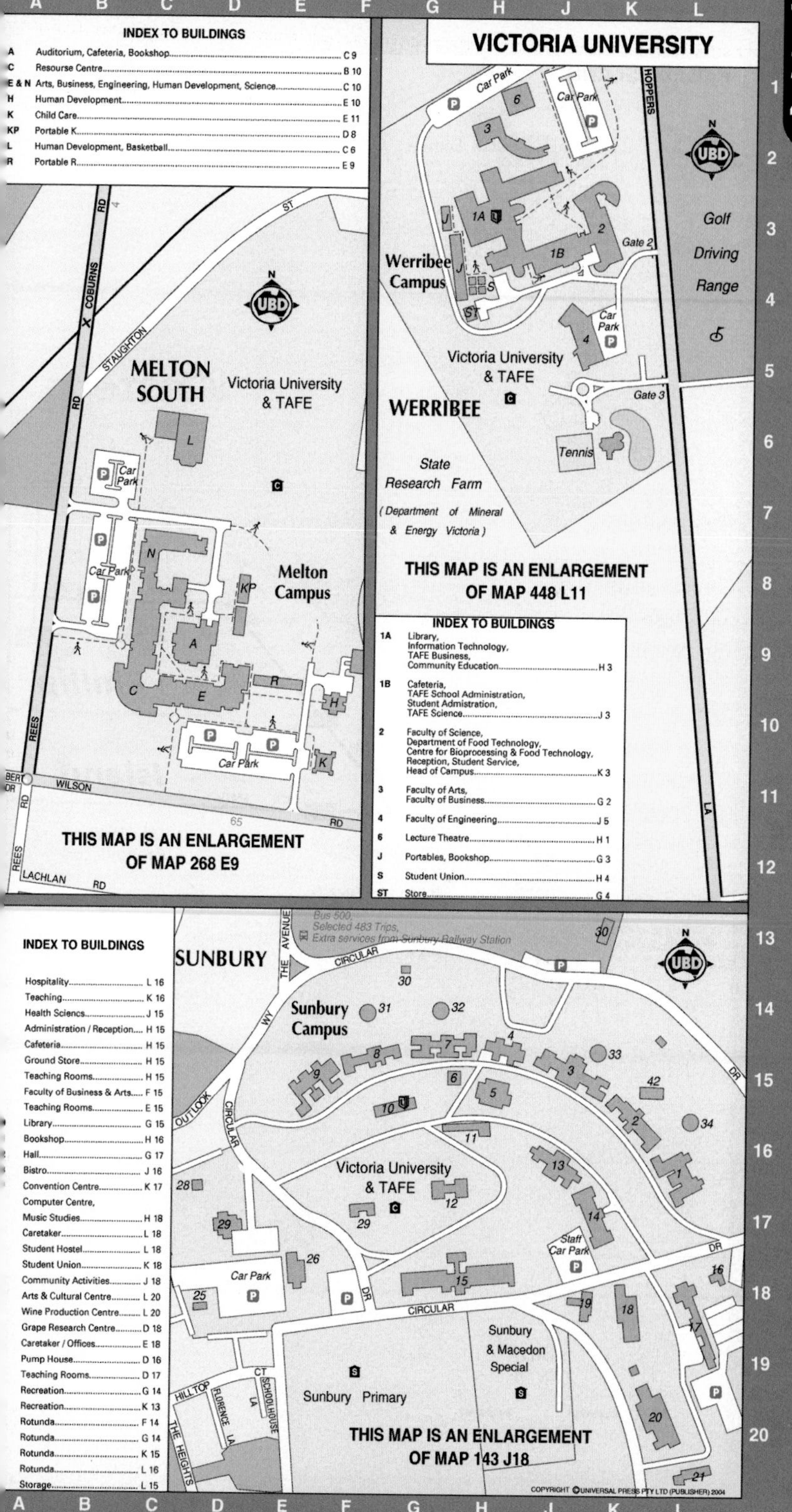

INDEX TO BUILDINGS
A Auditorium, Cafeteria, Bookshop........ C 9
C Resourse Centre........ B 10
E & N Arts, Business, Engineering, Human Development, Science........ C 10
H Human Development........ E 10
K Child Care........ E 11
KP Portable K........ D 8
L Human Development, Basketball........ C 6
R Portable R........ E 9
MELTON SOUTH
Victoria University & TAFE
Melton Campus
COBURNS RD
STAUGHTON ST
REES RD
WILSON RD
LACHLAN RD
Car Park
THIS MAP IS AN ENLARGEMENT OF MAP 268 E9
VICTORIA UNIVERSITY
Car Park
HOPPERS LA
Golf Driving Range
Gate 2
Gate 3
Werribee Campus
Victoria University & TAFE
WERRIBEE
Tennis
State Research Farm
(Department of Mineral & Energy Victoria)
THIS MAP IS AN ENLARGEMENT OF MAP 448 L11
INDEX TO BUILDINGS
1A Library, Information Technology, TAFE Business, Community Education........ H 3
1B Cafeteria, TAFE School Administration, Student Admistration, TAFE Science........ J 3
2 Faculty of Science, Department of Food Technology, Centre for Bioprocessing & Food Technology, Reception, Student Service, Head of Campus........ K 3
3 Faculty of Arts, Faculty of Business........ G 2
4 Faculty of Engineering........ J 5
6 Lecture Theatre........ H 1
J Portables, Bookshop........ G 3
S Student Union........ H 4
ST Store........ G 4
INDEX TO BUILDINGS
Hospitality........ L 16
Teaching........ K 16
Health Sciencs........ J 15
Administration / Reception........ H 15
Cafeteria........ H 15
Ground Store........ H 15
Teaching Rooms........ H 15
Faculty of Business & Arts........ F 15
Teaching Rooms........ E 15
Library........ G 15
Bookshop........ H 16
Hall........ G 17
Bistro........ J 16
Convention Centre........ K 17
Computer Centre, Music Studies........ H 18
Caretaker........ L 18
Student Hostel........ L 18
Student Union........ K 18
Community Activities........ J 18
Arts & Cultural Centre........ L 20
Wine Production Centre........ L 20
Grape Research Centre........ D 18
Caretaker / Offices........ E 18
Pump House........ D 16
Teaching Rooms........ D 17
Recreation........ G 14
Recreation........ K 13
Rotunda........ F 14
Rotunda........ G 14
Rotunda........ K 15
Rotunda........ L 16
Storage........ L 15
SUNBURY
Bus 500, Selected 483 Trips, Extra services from Sunbury Railway Station
Sunbury Campus
Victoria University & TAFE
CIRCULAR DR
OUTLOOK WY
THE AVENUE
Car Park
Staff Car Park
Sunbury Primary
Sunbury & Macedon Special
HILLTOP CT
FLORENCE LA
SCHOOLHOUSE LA
THE HEIGHTS
THIS MAP IS AN ENLARGEMENT OF MAP 143 J18
COPYRIGHT © UNIVERSAL PRESS PTY LTD (PUBLISHER) 2004

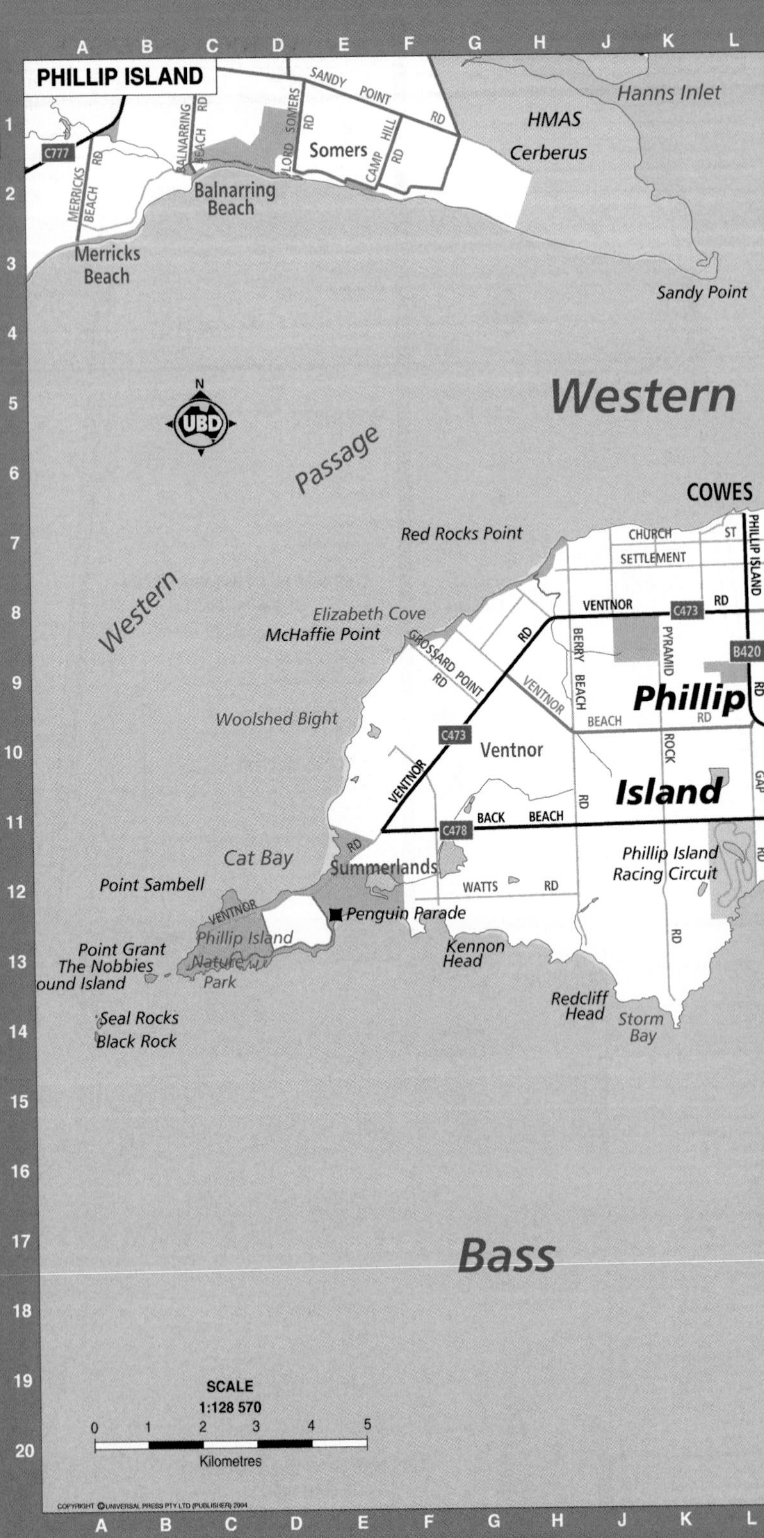

PHILLIP ISLAND
A B C D E F G H J K L
1 2 3 4 5 6 7 8 9 10 11 12 13 14 15 16 17 18 19 20
Hanns Inlet
HMAS
Cerberus
SANDY POINT RD
Somers
SOMERS RD
CAMP HILL RD
LORD
BALNARRING BEACH RD
MERRICKS BEACH RD
C777
Balnarring
Beach
Merricks
Beach
Sandy Point
Western
Passage
Western
N
UBD
COWES
CHURCH ST
SETTLEMENT
PHILLIP ISLAND
VENTNOR RD
C473
B420
RD
BERRY BEACH RD
PYRAMID ROCK RD
Phillip
Island
Red Rocks Point
Elizabeth Cove
McHaffie Point
GROSSARD POINT RD
VENTNOR
BEACH RD
GAP RD
Woolshed Bight
C473
Ventnor
VENTNOR RD
BACK BEACH
C478
Cat Bay
Summerlands
Phillip Island
Racing Circuit
WATTS RD
Point Sambell
VENTNOR
Penguin Parade
Phillip Island
Nature
Park
Point Grant
The Nobbies
ound Island
Kennon
Head
Redcliff
Head
Storm
Bay
Seal Rocks
Black Rock
Bass
SCALE
1:128 570
0 1 2 3 4 5
Kilometres

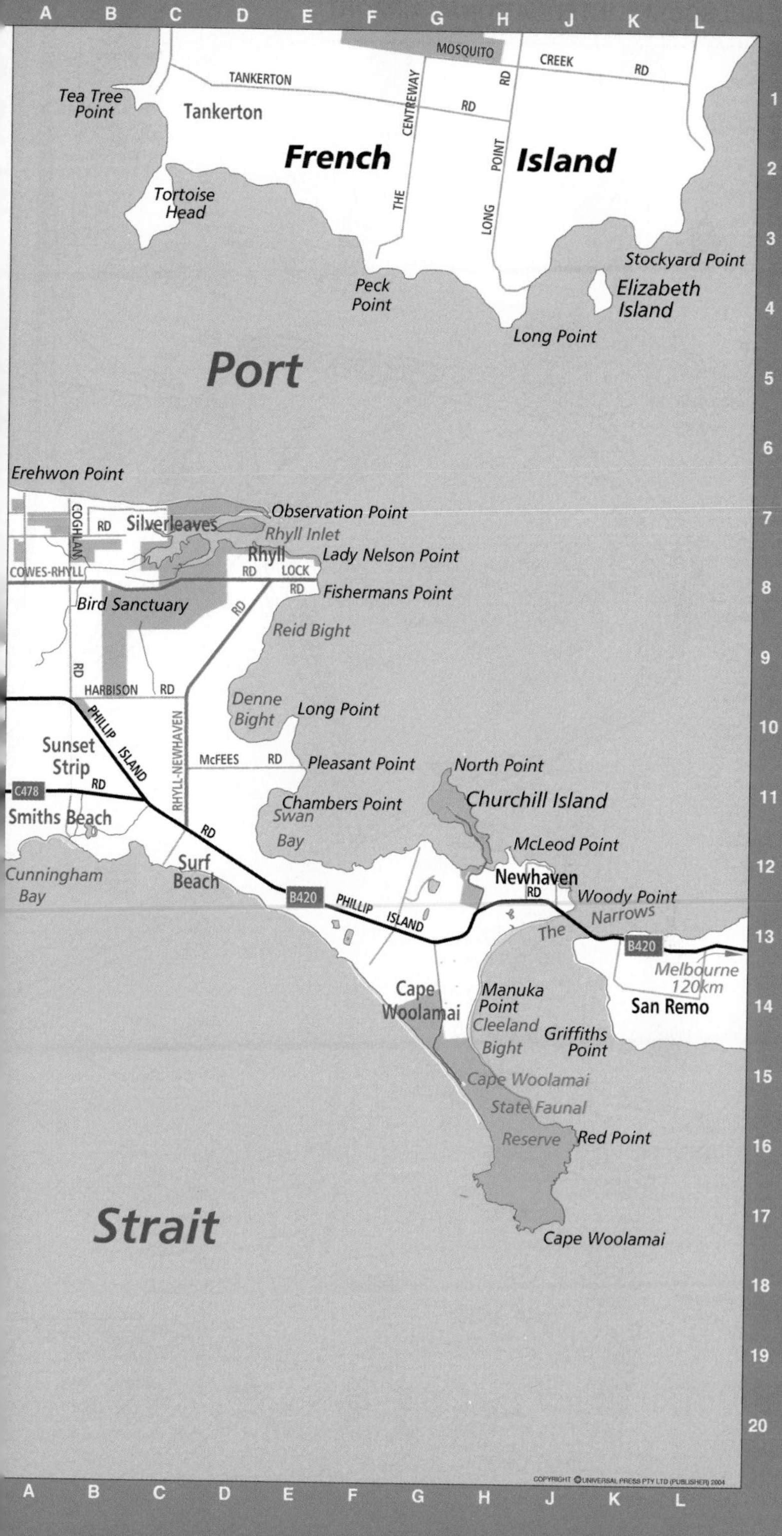

A B C D E F G H J K L
1 2 3 4 5 6 7 8 9 10 11 12 13 14 15 16 17 18 19 20
MOSQUITO CREEK RD
TANKERTON RD
THE CENTREWAY
LONG POINT RD
Tea Tree Point
Tankerton
French Island
Tortoise Head
Stockyard Point
Elizabeth Island
Peck Point
Long Point
Port
Erehwon Point
Observation Point
COGHLAN RD
Silverleaves
Rhyll Inlet
Rhyll
Lady Nelson Point
COWES-RHYLL RD
LOCK RD
Fishermans Point
Bird Sanctuary
Reid Bight
HARBISON RD
Denne Bight
Long Point
PHILLIP ISLAND RD
RHYLL-NEWHAVEN RD
Sunset Strip
McFEES RD
Pleasant Point
North Point
C478
Smiths Beach
Chambers Point
Churchill Island
Swan Bay
McLeod Point
Surf Beach
Cunningham Bay
Newhaven
Woody Point
The Narrows
B420
B420
Melbourne 120km
Cape Woolamai
Manuka Point
San Remo
Cleeland Bight
Griffiths Point
Cape Woolamai State Faunal Reserve
Red Point
Strait
Cape Woolamai

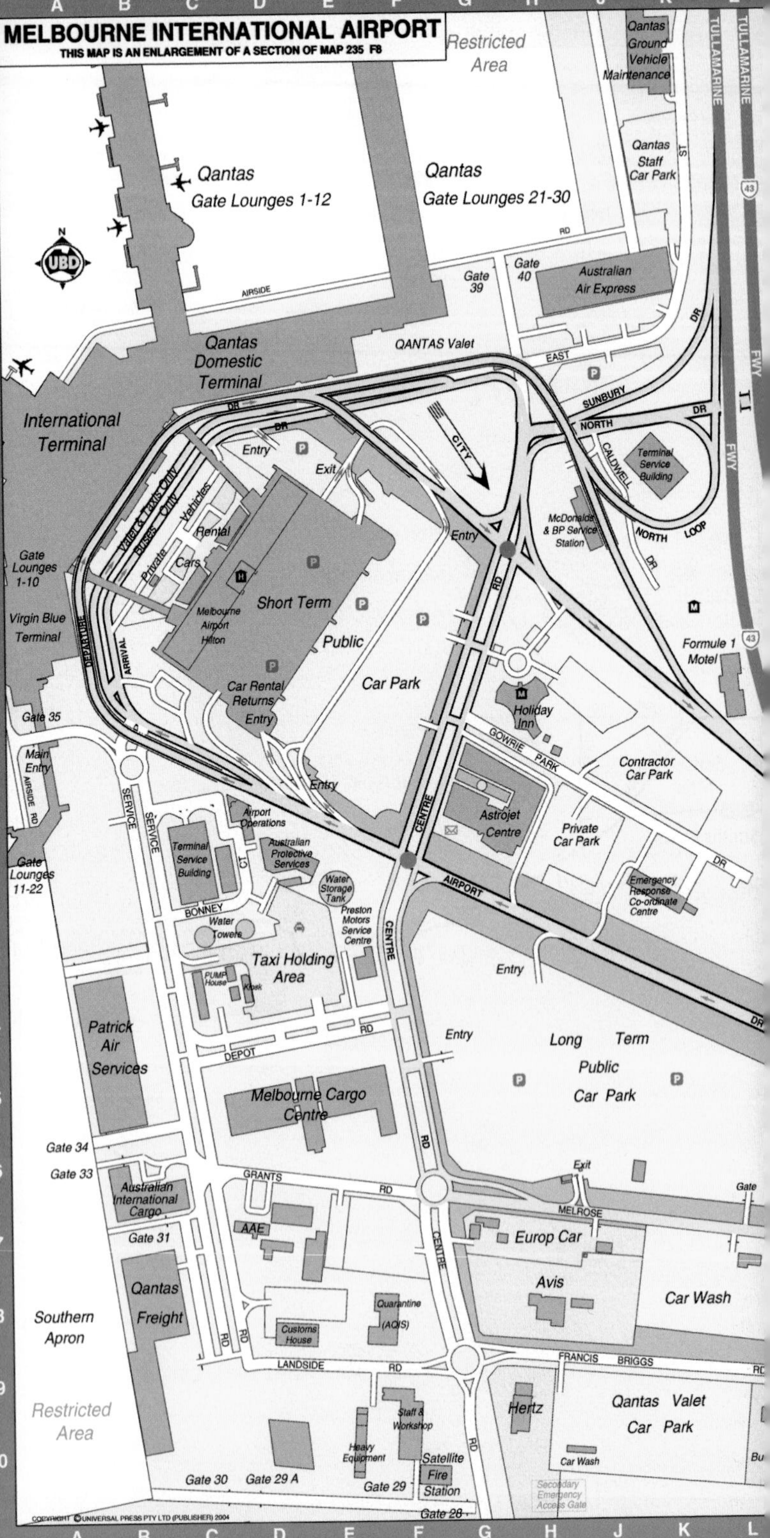

MELBOURNE INTERNATIONAL AIRPORT

THIS MAP IS AN ENLARGEMENT OF A SECTION OF MAP 235 F8

Restricted Area
Qantas Ground Vehicle Maintenance
Qantas Staff Car Park
Qantas Gate Lounges 1-12
Qantas Gate Lounges 21-30
Gate 39
Gate 40
Australian Air Express
AIRSIDE
Qantas Domestic Terminal
QANTAS Valet
International Terminal
Entry
Exit
City
Valet & Taxis Only
Buses Only
Private Vehicles
Rental Cars
Melbourne Airport Hilton
Short Term Public Car Park
Gate Lounges 1-10
Virgin Blue Terminal
DEPARTURE
ARRIVAL
Car Rental Returns
Terminal Service Building
McDonalds & BP Service Station
Formule 1 Motel
Holiday Inn
Contractor Car Park
Gate 35
Main Entry
AIRSIDE RD
SERVICE
Airport Operations
Australian Protective Services
Water Storage Tank
Preston Motors Service Centre
Astrojet Centre
Private Car Park
Emergency Response Co-ordinate Centre
Gate Lounges 11-22
Terminal Service Building
BONNEY CT
Water Towers
Taxi Holding Area
PUMP House
Kiosk
Patrick Air Services
DEPOT RD
Melbourne Cargo Centre
Long Term Public Car Park
Gate 34
Gate 33
Australian International Cargo
GRANTS RD
MELROSE
Gate
Gate 31
AAE
Europ Car
Avis
Car Wash
Qantas Freight
Southern Apron
Quarantine (AQIS)
Customs House
LANDSIDE RD
FRANCIS BRIGGS RD
Hertz
Qantas Valet Car Park
Restricted Area
Staff & Workshop
Heavy Equipment
Satellite Fire Station
Car Wash
Gate 30
Gate 29 A
Gate 29
Gate 28
Secondary Emergency Access Gate
SUNBURY RD
EAST
NORTH DR
CALDWELL
NORTH LOOP DR
CENTRE RD
GOWRIE PARK DR
AIRPORT DR
TULLAMARINE FWY
ST

STREET INDEX

[ABBREVIATIONS USED IN THE STREET INDEX]

ABBREVIATIONS FOR DESIGNATIONS

Alley	al	Cross	cs	Junction	jnc	Return	rtn
Approach	app	Crossing	csg	Key	key	Ridge	rdg
Arcade	arc	Curve	cve	Lane	la	Rise	ri
Avenue	av	Dale	dle	Link	lk	Road	rd
Bend	bnd	Down/s	dn	Loop	lp	Roadway	rdy
Boulevard	bvd	Drive	dr	Mall	ml	Route	rte
Bowl	bl	Driveway	dwy	Mead	md	Row	row
Brace	br	East	e	Meander	mdr	Serviceway	swy
Brae	br	Edge	edg	Mews	mw	South	s
Break	brk	Elbow	elb	Motorway	mwy	Square	sq
Brook	brk	End	end	Nook	nk	Strand	sd
Broadway	bwy	Entrance	ent	North	n	Street	st
Brow	brw	Esplanade	esp	Outlook	out	Tarn	tn
Bypass	bps	Expressway	exp	Parade	pde	Terrace	tce
Centre	ctr	Fairway	fy	Park	pk	Tollway	twy
Chase	ch	Freeway	fwy	Parkway	pky	Top	top
Circle	cir	Frontage	fr	Pass	ps	Tor	tor
Circuit	cct	Garden/s	gdn	Pathway	pwy	Track	tr
Circus	crc	Gate/s	gte	Place	pl	Trail	trl
Close	cl	Gateway	gwy	Plaza	plz	Turn	trn
Common	cmn	Glade	gld	Pocket	pkt	Underpass	ups
Concourse	cnc	Glen	gln	Point/Port	pt	Vale	va
Copse	cps	Grange	gra	Promenade	prm	View	vw
Corner	cnr	Green	grn	Quadrant	qd	Vista	vst
Corso	cso	Grove	gr	Quay/s	qy	Walk	wk
Court	ct	Grovet	gr	Ramble	ra	Walkway	wky
Courtyard	cyd	Haven	hvn	Reach	rch	Way	wy
Cove	cov	Heights	hts	Reserve	res	West	w
Crescent	cr	Highway	hwy	Rest	rst	Wynd	wyn
Crest	cst	Hill	hill	Retreat	rt		

ABBREVIATIONS FOR SUBURB NAMES

Where it has been necessary to abbreviate the suburb names in the street index the following conventions have been used.
If any difficulty is experienced with the suburban names refer to the SUBURBS and LOCALITIES index.

Airport	Aprt	Forest	Frst	Lower	Lr	River	R
Basin	Bsn	Garden/s	Gdn	Meadows/s	Mdw	Rocks	Rks
Bay	B	Grove	Gr	Mount	Mt	Saint	St
Beach	Bch	Gully	Gly	Mountain/s	Mtn	South	S
Bridge	Br	Harbor/our	Hbr	North	N	Terminal	Term
Brook	Brk	Head/s	Hd	Paradise	Pdse	University	Uni
Central	Ctrl	Headland	Hd	Park	Pk	Upper	Up
Chase	Ch	Heights	Ht	Plain/s	Pl	Valley	Vy
Corner	Cnr	Hill/s	Hl	Plateau	Plat	Vale	Va
Creek	Ck	Island	I	Pocket	Pkt	Village	Vill
Crossing	Csg	Junction	Jctn	Point/Port	Pt	Waters	Wtr
Down/s	Dn	Lagoon	Lgn	Range	Rge	West	W
East	E	Lakes	L	Reach	Rch		
Field/s	Fd	Lodge	Ldg	Reserve	Res		
Flat	Fl	Lookout	Lkt	Ridge	Rdg		

NON-STANDARD ABBREVIATIONS FOR SUBURB NAMES

Bacchus Marsh	Bacchus Msh	**Moonee Ponds**	Moonee Pnd	**Narre Warren South**	Nar Warrn S
Beaconsfield Upper	Beaconsfld Up	**Nar Nar Goon**	Nr Nr Goon	**Port Melbourne**	Port Melb
Caroline Springs	Caroline Spr	**Nar Nar Goon North**	Nr Nr Goon N	**Strathmore Heights**	Strathmr Ht
Kangaroo Ground	Kangaroo Grnd	**Narre Warren East**	Nar Warrn E	**Templestowe Lower**	Templstw Lr
Launching Place	Launching Pl	**Narre Warren North**	Nar Warrn N	**Upper Ferntree Gully**	Up Fntree Gly
Melbourne Airport	Melb Airport			**Williamstown North**	Williamstn N

SPECIAL NOTE
The LANES shown in *italics* in the street index are not chartered on the street maps.
For reasons of clarity it is not practical to show them.

A

ENSEN
Montmorency 287 A11
AN
Endeavour Hl 537 G1
ON
Kilsyth 381 B8
SSIA
Balwyn N 374 A8
EY
Greenvale 192 J18
Kings Park 319 C2
Frankston S 628 C15
Gladstone Pk 237 B20
Grovedale 706 C9
Noble Park 534 K7
Ringwood 379 A3
Wantirna 422 B11
McCrae 685 A14
Edithvale, off
The Esplanade 546 G12
Eltham 288 A7
Melton W 226 D17
Nar Warrn S 578 J3
Point Cook 450 F5
Vermont 421 K5
EY DALE
Berwick 554 L19
EYDALE
Mulgrave 501 B5
EYGATE
Frankston 628 B8
Altona North 410 D7
Oakleigh 457 K15
N
Bentleigh E 496 G5
Rowville 502 H2
INGTON
Caroline Spr 318 D4
Truganina 405 F13
OT
Albanvale 319 E4
Glen Waverley 459 H8
Abbotsford 20 C11
Clifton Hill 20 F4
Abbotsford 20 D12
OTSFORD
Malvern East 457 F3
Ivanhoe 328 A14
Abbotsford 20 F16
N Melbourne 17 A20
N Melbourne 34 L20
Sorrento 678 K15
W Melbourne 17 A19
OTT
Craigieburn 150 C14
Taylors L 275 J3
Hallam 537 E18
Alphington 327 H14
Balwyn N 374 B3
Dandenong 535 J9
Sandringham 494 L13
Sandringham 495 A13
Spotswood 366 G19
OTTS
Dandenong S 550 B9
Lyndhurst 550 B9
OTTSWOOD
Dingley Vill 533 B9
ECKETT
Mt Martha 656 C15
Melbourne 2 A2
Beaconsfld Up 542 J17
Beaconsfld Up 556 K1
Nar Warrn N 539 E4
Officer 542 K20
Coburg 281 D19
Kew 371 J8
Melbourne 1 F2
Melbourne 23 J4
Prahran 415 B10
St Kilda E 414 K17
Seaford 599 L7
LIA
Bundoora 284 K5
Hillside 274 D3
Meadow Ht 193 K19
Sunbury 142 G10
Narre Warren 539 D19
Doncaster E 332 D19
Forest Hill 376 J20
Nunawading 376 J20
Hoppers Csg 405 D14
RCAIRN
Deer Park 318 J11
RCARN
Craigieburn 194 G4
RCORN
Ivanhoe 327 K14

ABERCROMBIE
st. Balwyn 372 K10
st. Berwick 579 L2
st. Oakleigh S 497 H5
ABERCROMBY
rd. Blackburn S 419 G2
ABERDEEN
av. Greenvale 237 D1
cr. Essendon 323 F8
ct. Epping 198 A18
ct. Narre Warren 539 B18
ct. Wheelers Hl 460 G14
dr. Dandenong N 501 F13
dr. Lilydale 338 J9
gr. Northcote 326 F16
hts. Pakenham 584 K1
rd. Altona 408 F15
rd. Blackburn S 375 E20
rd. Blackburn S 419 E2
rd. Macleod 285 A15
rd. Prahran 32 K20
rd. Prahran 414 L10
rd. Prahran 415 A11
rd. Sandringham 495 K16
st. Aberfeldie 323 F10
st. Brunswick 325 J13
st. Geelong West 702 A6
st. Hawthorn E 372 E20
st. Herne Hill 702 B6
st. Manifold Ht 702 B6
st. Newtown 702 B6
st. Pascoe Vale S 324 L5
st. Reservoir 283 D4
wy. Tarneit 405 B8
ABERFELDIE
st. Aberfeldie 323 G11
st. Moonee Pnd 323 G11
ABERGELDIE
av. Bentleigh 456 F18
av. McKinnon 456 F18
ABERSHAM
ct. Eltham 288 B5
ABEY
rd. Melton S 268 K8
rd. Melton S 269 A8
ABINGER
ct. Gladstone Pk 237 C19
pl. Richmond 26 J12
st. Richmond 26 G12
ABLETT
ct. Frankston S 627 G17
ABOR
ct. Frankston 600 E19
pl. Melton W 225 L15
ABOYNE
cl. Mulgrave 501 H5
ABRAHAM
dr. Croydon 380 J1
ABRAHAMS
ct. Burwood 419 B7
tr. Lysterfield 505 G4
ABRAM
ct. Frankston S 627 H17
ABREHART
rd. Pakenham 585 K1
st. Eumemmerring 537 C15
ABRUZZO
cr. Thomastown 241 B18
ACACIA
av. Blackburn 375 G17
av. Kilsyth 381 L6
av. Mentone 531 H8
av. Oakleigh S 458 A17
av. Seaholme 409 H18
av. Upwey 466 B9
av. Watsonia 285 C8
cl. Meadow Ht 237 J1
cl. Sunshine W 364 A7
cr. Emerald 510 E5
cr. Melton S 268 G6
cr. Patterson L 573 J8
ct. Briar Hill 286 L6
ct. Bundoora 284 H6
ct. Croydon S 379 F11
ct. Delahey 275 C9
ct. Frankston 628 C4
ct. Pakenham 584 K9
ct. Ringwood 378 C11
ct. Sunbury 143 J6
ct. W Footscray 366 F10
ct. Wyndham Va 446 E12
ct. Dandenong, off
David St 536 D4
gr. Glen Waverley 420 B14
gr. Pascoe Vale S 324 E5
la. Waurn Ponds 705 D16
pl. Burwood 418 C5
rd. Ferntree Gly 464 H8
rd. Hurstbridge 202 K11
rd. Up Fntree Gly 464 H8
rd. Up Fntree Gly 464 H9
st. Box Hill 374 J19
st. Cairnlea 319 F9
st. Camberwell 417 G5
st. Carnegie 456 L5
st. Doncaster E 331 G20
st. Doveton 536 L8
st. Doveton 537 A8
st. Elsternwick 454 K2
st. Glenroy 280 C7
st. Mt Martha 656 F8
st. Thomastown 241 F14
st. Torquay 711 H11
wyn. Langwarrin 601 J20
ACADEMY
av. Reservoir 282 F13
av. Wheelers Hl 460 D14
dr. Broadmeadows 238 J12
dr. The Basin 425 B7
ACCESS
rd. Doreen 156 L12
rd. Mont Albert N 374 D11
ACCRA
st. Keysborough 534 K13
ACER
av. S Morang 199 F11
cl. Broadmeadows 237 L12
st. Doveton 536 K8
tce. Hoppers Csg 405 F16
ACFOLD
ct. St Albans 275 G17
ACHERON
av. Camberwell 416 L6
av. Camberwell 417 A6
av. Mt Eliza 625 J20
av. Reservoir 283 D13
cl. Hallam 538 C19
cr. Eltham North 287 A4
cr. Werribee 448 C19
ct. Hampton E 496 B10
ct. Sunbury 143 C11
st. Doncaster 374 G2
st. Epping 197 G19
st. Tootgarook 698 C5
ACHESON
pl. Coburg N 281 J15
ACHILLES
ct. Lilydale 338 J1
st. Heidelberg W 284 C18
ACLAND
cl. Mulgrave 501 F5
ct. Bundoora 285 D1
ct. Noble Park 535 B6
st. Albanvale 319 D5
st. St Kilda 414 A15
st. St Kilda 414 B18
st. South Yarra 31 H4
st. South Yarra 414 D2
ACLARE
st. Cockatoo 511 H11
ACMENA
ct. Mill Park 243 B8
ACOL
ct. Mulgrave 501 A5
ACORN
ct. Nar Warrn S 553 E18
ct. Oakleigh S 498 B9
wy. Baxter 628 D20
ACRE
ct. Narre Warren 538 K14
pl. Malvern 415 L10
ri. Hampton Pk 552 D12
ACTION
st. Braybrook 366 B6
ACTOAL
dr. Montrose 381 K11
ACTON
cl. Frankston 628 F4
ct. Newcomb 704 B18
pl. Wyndham Va 446 G13
st. Mt Waverley 458 J8
st. Seddon 367 A12
ACUBA
cl. St Albans 275 J18
ACUNHA
st. Mt Eliza 641 H3
ACWORTH
ct. Greensbrgh 244 E15
ADA
ct. Narre Warren 553 C12
ct. Noble Park 535 D3
ct. Sunshine W 364 A5
st. Camberwell 417 G5
st. Doncaster 374 J2
st. Glen Waverley 460 B5
st. Preston 282 C20
st. Rowville 503 C4
ADAIR
ct. Wantirna 422 B12
pl. Sunshine W 364 C6
ADALEIGH
ct. Clayton 459 C20
st. Yarraville 366 H14
ADAM
av. Hallam 537 G14
av. Wheelers Hl 461 C12
cl. Rowville 463 K15
cr. Montmorency 287 B10
cr. Roxburgh Pk 194 A9
cr.s. Montmorency 287 C10
ct. Cranbourne W 577 F19
ct. Gladstone Pk 237 E18
ct. Pakenham 584 F2
ct. Reservoir 282 B2
ct. Ringwood N 378 A6
ct. Springvale S 534 A6
ct. Viewbank 285 J19
ct. Werribee 446 L11
ct. Werribee 447 A11
pl. Mill Park 243 E6
st. Bentleigh 455 J19
st. Burnley 371 A20
st. Nunawading 376 J11
st. Rye 696 E5
wy. Kurunjang 226 G13
ADAMS
av. Rosebud 684 F16
cl. Croydon 380 F1
ct. Dandenong N 501 J9
ct. E Geelong 703 J8
ct. Sunbury 143 A16
la. Berwick 554 D8
la. Mt Evelyn 339 E15
la. Yarra Jctn 347 B16
pl. Glen Waverley 420 B19
pl. Mt Evelyn 338 L14
pl. Port Melb, off
Dow St 412 L5
pl. Geelong, off
Little Ryrie St 703 B9
st. Alphington 327 K20
st. Murrumbeena 457 D12
st. Preston 327 E7
st. St Albans 319 F5
st. South Yarra 31 B7
st. South Yarra 414 A3
ADAMSON
dr. Endeavour Hl 537 A2
rd. Beaconsfield 554 L16
st. Braybrook 366 A3
st. Brighton 454 K19
st. Heidelberg 328 J4
ADARE
cl. Mulgrave 500 L4
cl. Mulgrave 501 A4
pl. Werribee 447 E13
ri. Roxburgh Pk 193 K13
ADDERLEY
ct. Point Cook 450 G4
dr. Greenvale 193 F18
st. Docklands 23 C5
st. W Melbourne 23 A2
ADDICOTT
st. Frankston 599 G19
ADDIS
st. Geelong West 702 D6
ADDISON
ct. Mulgrave 501 H5
pl. Seabrook 450 L5
st. Elwood 454 C3
st. Moonee Pnd 324 E15
wy. Roxburgh Pk 194 A13
ADDLINGTON
ct. Nar Warrn S 552 K20
ADECROFT
ct. Eltham 288 A8
ADELA
ct. Mulgrave 501 F5
ct. Mulgrave 501 G5
ADELAIDE
av. Kallista 467 C1
av. Mt Waverley 458 H1
bvd. Gowanbrae 279 E7
cl. Berwick 553 G3
st. Albion 364 J1
st. Armadale 415 J11
st. Ascot Vale 324 F16
st. Blairgowrie 696 C1
st. Cremorne 26 D20
st. Dandenong 535 G2
st. Footscray 367 A7
st. Highton 701 H17
st. McKinnon 456 D17
st. Mornington 640 C19
st. Murrumbeena 457 B5
st. Pascoe Vale 280 B15
st. St Albans 319 J3
st. Wantirna S 422 K16
ADELE
av. Ferntree Gly 463 G5
cl. Narre Warren 538 L18
cl. Wheelers Hl 461 D12
ct. Hoppers Csg 449 B1
ct. Ringwood 379 A2
ct. Rye 696 K5
st. Vermont 377 G20
ADELIE
ct. Roxburgh Pk 193 J15
ADELINE
ct. Deer Park 318 L17
st. Greensbrgh 285 J6
st. Preston 326 J4
st. Williamstn N 410 L13
ADELLA
ct. Moolap 704 L18
pl. Templestowe 332 A10
ADELLE
ct. Carrum Downs 600 K3
ct. Doncaster 330 L18
ADELONG
ct. Berwick 553 H2
ct. Dandenong N 502 C17
ct. Grovedale 706 D10
ct. Patterson L 573 K9
ADELYN
av. Donvale 376 J7
ADEN
ct. Thomastown 240 K11
ct. Tootgarook 698 C9
pl. Frankston 600 J15
ADENEY
av. Kew 372 E10
st. Balwyn N 374 B7
st. Yarraville 366 D15
ADENEYS
rd. Cannons Creek 649 L5
ADENMORE
ct. Eltham 287 L10
ADIB
ct. Frankston N 600 E11
ADINA
av. Aspendale 546 F4
cl. Bayswater N 379 L15
cl. Greensbrgh 286 H1
ct. Frankston 600 B19
ct. Kurunjang 227 A15
ct. Sunshine W 364 F7
ct. Tullamarine 278 H9
ct. Yallambie 286 C12
pl. Delahey 275 B9
pl. Mornington 641 C15
st. Blackburn N 375 J9
st. Rye 697 A9
ADIOS
pl. Keilor Dn 275 H11
ADLER
ct. Keilor Dn 276 B15
gr. Coburg N 281 C12
ADLEY
ct. Vermont S 420 G10
pl. Hampton Pk 551 G4
ADMANS
av. Seaford 599 E2
st. Pt Lonsdale 710 G6
ADMIRAL
ct. Highton 701 H10
ct. Lilydale 338 J1
pl. Craigieburn 150 D7
pl. Geelong 703 D9
st. Seddon 367 D10
ADMIRALA
cr. Dandenong N 502 B18
ADMIRALS
cr. Taylors L 275 G9
ct. Frankston 628 E7
qy. Patterson L 573 J5
ADNETTE
ct. Coburg N 282 B14
ADOBE
ct. Vermont 421 J3
ADOLPH
st. Cremorne 26 D17
ADOLPHSON
av. Ringwood N 378 B6
ADORI
ct. St Helena 244 K18
ADRIAN
av. Blackburn S 419 L6
av. Vermont S 420 G8
ct. Braybrook 366 A4
ct. Bundoora 284 H5
ct. Gladstone Pk 237 B18
ct. Heathmont 378 F18
dr. Pakenham 559 G19
pl. Rowville 502 L5
pl. Rowville 503 A5
rd. Campbellfield 239 E7
ri. Nar Warrn N 538 B8
st. Bentleigh E 496 K6
st. Chadstone 458 C5
st. Cranbourne E 604 K11
st. Glen Iris 417 E10
st. Springvale 500 A16
ADRIENNE
cl. Keilor Park 277 K13
cr. Mt Waverley 458 H9
ct. Millgrove 348 F1
ADVANTAGE
dr. Dandenong S 550 F3
rd. Highett 495 L15

ADZAR
rd. Newcomb 704 A14
AEC
arc. Boronia 424 E11
AENONE
av. Noble Park 534 F5
AERODROME
rd. Parwan 264 A20
AEROLINK
dr. Tullamarine 277 K8
AEROS
st. Whittington 704 F19
AFFINITY
cl. Mordialloc 532 D16
AFFLECK
st. South Yarra 31 J15
st. South Yarra 414 E7
wy. Rowville 503 H1
AFFRA
pl. Hampton Pk 551 D4
AFTON
ct. Glen Waverley 460 A10
st. Aberfeldie 323 B10
st. Essendon W 323 B10
st. Research 246 F20
wy. Aspendale 546 D6
AFZAN
ct. Torquay 712 H2
AGANA
av. Noble Park 534 K7
AGAR
pl. Sunbury 142 L18
pl. Sunbury 143 A18
AGATHA
st. Essendon 324 C8
AGATHEA
ct. Frankston N 600 E8
AGE
st. Cheltenham 497 D17
AGG
st. Newport 410 H7
st. Thornbury 327 F11
AGNES
av. Balwyn N 373 L3
av. Blairgowrie 679 G19
ct. Glen Waverley 460 B9
ct. Kurunjang 227 E11
ct. Langwarrin 629 G7
st. Beaumaris 530 A9
st. Bentleigh E 456 H20
st. E Melbourne 25 D10
st. Mont Albert 374 F15
st. Noble Park 534 F2
st. St Albans 319 F2
st. Thornbury 326 L11
st. Yarraville 367 A13
AGNEW
st. Blackburn S 375 D20
st. Blackburn S 419 D1
st. Brighton East 455 C17
AGONIS
ct. McCrae 684 J14
ct. Mill Park 243 C10
ct. Mt Martha 656 G7
dr. Keilor 276 C6
st. Doveton 536 J8
AGORA
bvd. Ferntree Gly 423 L16
AGRA
st. Mitcham 377 B15
AGRICULTURAL
pl. Geelong 703 F10
A'HERN
pl. Avondale Ht 322 E16
AHERN
rd. Pakenham 584 L4
st. Noble Park N 501 D10
AHMET
pl. Hillside 274 F3
AIDA
ct. Doncaster E 332 G8
AIDENS
wy. Beaconsfield 555 F12
A I F
st. Balwyn 373 E10
AIKMAN
cr. Chadstone 458 A6
AIKSHAW
cl. Hillside 232 D19
AILEEN
av. Caulfield S 455 E8
av. Heidelberg W 284 F16
av. Montrose 382 B11
ct. Hallam 552 C1
AILSA
av. Malvern East 416 K19
ct. Balwyn N 374 A1
ct. Ringwood 379 B3
ct. Sunbury 144 F12
gr. Ivanhoe 328 A12
st. Ascot Vale 324 F19
st. Box Hill S 419 C3
st. Dandenong N 501 L16
st. Keilor 277 D12
st. Laverton 407 A19
st. Mt Martha 655 L16
st.s, Altona Mdw 451 A1
AIMEE
ct. Mornington 657 C3
pl. Rowville 463 A15
AINSDALE
av. Wantirna 422 E8
ct. Sunbury 144 E14
AINSLEIGH
ct. Cranbourne 578 C17
ct. Narre Warren 538 J14
AINSLEY
av. Noble Park 534 K6
AINSLIE
av. Grovedale 706 D11
dr. Wheelers Hl 460 J14
rd. Campbellfield 239 B1
AINSLIE PARK
av. Croydon 379 G3
AINSWORTH
ct. Roxburgh Pk 193 K13
rd. Chum Creek 212 H5
st. Sunshine W 364 H3
AINTREE
av. Doncaster E 376 D1
av. Mulgrave 500 J3
av. Point Cook 450 J9
ct. Greensbrgh 243 L20
ct. Noble Park N 501 A8
rd. Glen Iris 416 D12
st. Brunswick E 326 A14
st. Mooroolbark 337 B17
AINWICK
cr. Thomastown 240 L11
AIRD
ct. Wonga Park 291 G20
st. Camberwell 416 L2
st. Camberwell 417 A2
st. Ringwood 378 F11
AIRDRIE
ct. Templstw Lr 330 L9
mw. Greenvale 192 J19
rd. Caulfield N 415 F20
AIRDS
rd. Templstw Lr 330 D9
AIREDALE
av. Hawthorn E 416 C4
wy. Rowville 503 F1
AIREY
av. Manifold Ht 702 C5
AIR FORCE
av. Braybrook 366 C6
AIRLEY
ct. Meadow Ht 237 J5
rd. Glen Iris 417 C11
AIRLIE
av. Dandenong 535 G3
av. Prahran 415 B12
ct. Doncaster E 331 J16
ct. Langwarrin 601 L20
ct. Rowville 463 G17
gr. Seaford 573 F16
rd. Healesville 257 H6
rd. Montmorency 286 F12
st. Brighton 454 J7
st. South Yarra 31 J3
st. South Yarra 414 E2
AIRPORT
dr. Melb Airport 235 K12
dr. Tullamarine 278 D8
rd. Mt Duneed 705 J20
AIRSIDE
rd. Melb Airport 235 H11
rd. Melb Airport 235 J10
AIRWAYS
st. Melb Airport 235 A11
AISBETT
av. Camberwell 417 J8
av. Wantirna S 422 K12
AISHA
cr. Dingley Vill 533 D2
AITCHISON
av. Ashburton 417 E14
pl. Geelong, off Fenwick St 702 L7
AITKEN
av. Hoppers Csg 449 A2
bvd. Craigieburn 149 E16
cl. Caroline Spr 318 C8
ct. Berwick 553 L1
ct. Ferntree Gly 463 H3
dr. Delahey 275 A12
pl. Gladstone Pk 236 L20
rd. Seville 386 C8
rd. Wandin East 386 C8
st. Clifton Hill 20 G7
st. Sunbury 143 K14
st. W Footscray 366 H9
st. Williamstown 411 G15
AJANA
ct. Dandenong N 501 G13
ct. Wheelers Hl 460 H14
la. Frankston S 627 C18
st. Balwyn N 374 A8
AJAX
cl. Keilor Dn 275 L14
ct. Heidelberg W 284 B19
ct. Lilydale 338 J2
ct. Mill Park 242 J12
dr. Wheelers Hl 461 A12
rd. Altona 408 D14
st. Balwyn N 373 G1
AKARANA
dr. Lilydale 338 G13
rd. Chirnside Pk 337 J6
AKEROA
av. Brunswick E 326 A12
AKERS
ct. Darley 221 H3
AKIMA
cl. Greensbrgh 244 A17
tce. Mooroolbark 337 E16
AKITA
ct. Berwick 554 D20
ct. Keysborough 534 K14
AKMA
ct. Taylors L 275 L8
AKOONAH
cl. Donvale 332 J15
ct. Burnside 318 H9
AKORA
ct. Frankston 600 H15
AKRANA
ct. Vermont S 421 C14
AKRON
st. Ferntree Gly 424 B19
AKUNA
av. Notting Hill 459 H14
ct. Knoxfield 463 B4
dr. Williamstn N 410 G11
st. Altona 408 K17
st. Warneet 649 G11
ALABAKIS
la. Werribee S 488 K2
ALABAMA
cl. Hoppers Csg 405 C13
ALAIN
av. S Morang 198 J12
ALAMANDA
wy. Cranbourne N 578 J11
ALAMAR
av. Glen Huntly 456 B6
ALAMEDA
av. Maribyrnong 323 C15
av. Mornington 656 F1
pl. Parkdale 531 E13
st. Parkdale 531 E13
ALAMEIN
av. Ashburton 417 F17
av. Croydon 380 K2
av. Kilsyth 380 K2
rd. Heidelberg W 284 B20
st. Noble Park 500 E16
ALAMO
cl. Highton 701 D17
rd. Reservoir 282 D13
ALAN
ct. Alphington 327 J13
ct. Bundoora 285 B2
ct. Noble Park N 501 D8
gr. Woori Yall 344 F13
pl. Rowville 503 A6
pl. Warrandyte 333 D1
rd. Carrum Downs 574 C17
st. Blackburn S 419 L1
st. Box Hill N 375 C8
st. Croydon 379 L7
st. Kings Park 275 E17
ALANA
ct. Wantirna S 421 L18
ALANAH
pl. Ivanhoe 328 F9
ALANBRAE
tce. Attwood 236 L10
tce. Attwood 237 A10
ALANDALE
av. Balwyn 373 H9
ct. Blackburn 375 L18
rd. Blackburn 375 L18
rd. Eaglemont 328 G11
st. Surrey Hills 418 D3
ALASKA
ct. Werribee 446 H18
ALASTAIR
ct. Kilsyth 381 D3
ct. Surrey Hills 373 L20
dr. Berwick 540 A20
ALASTER
ct. Hampton Pk 551 D11
ALATHEA
ct. Rye 697 E4
ALAWA
ct. Keilor Dn 275 H10
ALAWARA
ct. Burwood E 419 F10
dr. Mooroolbark 337 B15
ALAWARRA
ct. Ringwood N 378 E3
ALBA
ct. Mill Park 243 C8
st. Frankston N 600 E9
wk. Cairnlea 319 F12
ALBAN
st. Montmorency 286 J12
st. Richmond 26 F11
ALBANY
cl. Ringwood N 378 D5
cr. Aspendale 546 E6
cr. Surrey Hills 374 B17
ct. Campbellfield 239 G15
ct. Caulfield N 415 B20
ct. Endeavour Hl 536 L2
ct. Endeavour Hl 537 A2
ct. Macleod 285 J11
ct. Noble Park N 501 D16
ct. Sorrento 678 K9
ct. Taylors Hill 274 C9
ct. Taylors L 275 F1
ct. Wantirna 422 H8
ct. Werribee 447 F2
dr. Mulgrave 500 G5
pl. Bulleen 329 G13
pl. Frankston S 627 F9
pl. Mt Martha 656 D8
rd. Oakleigh E 458 H12
rd. Oakleigh E 458 J12
rd. Toorak 415 F7
st. Tullamarine 278 G3
wy. Doncaster E 332 C14
wy. Mornington 641 D19
ALBATROSS
av. Mt Eliza 641 H2
av. Werribee 447 L10
cl. Blind Bight 650 C9
ct. Cannons Creek 649 C8
ct. Keilor 276 K13
dr. Rowville 463 H11
ALBEMARLE
ct. Glen Iris 417 J9
st. Williamstn N 410 C11
ALBENCA
st. Cheltenham 531 E7
st. Mentone 531 E7
ALBENS
st. Narre Warren 553 C1
ALBER
rd. Beaconsfld Up 542 B6
ALBERMARLE
st. Kensington 34 C12
ALBERT
av. Boronia 424 F12
av. Oakleigh 457 L10
av. Rye 696 K2
av. Springvale 499 H15
cr. Mulgrave 499 L4
cr. St Albans 320 A3
cr. Surrey Hills 374 C17
ct. Dromana 685 L10
ct. Epping 197 G14
ct. Frankston 600 B18
ct. Greensbrgh 243 L20
ct. Greensbrgh 285 L1
dr. Melton S 268 B12
la. E Melbourne 25 J3
pl. Dingley Vill 532 K7
pl. Fitzroy 19 E17
pl. Hoppers Csg 405 A14
pl. S Melbourne 29 H2
pl. Burnley, off Bendigo St 371 C18
rd. Badger Creek 257 J10
rd. Carnegie 456 G12
rd. Clematis 508 J2
rd. Emerald 509 J3
rd. Hallam 537 H15
rd. Healesville 257 J10
rd. Lilydale 338 H7
rd. Melbourne 30 G7
rd. Melbourne 413 K2
rd. N Warrandyte 289 H14
rd. S Melbourne 30 A11
rd. S Melbourne 30 D9
rd. S Melbourne 30 G7
rd. S Melbourne 413 F6
rd. Sydenham 274 H2
st. Abbotsford 26 G3
st. Bayswater 423 D4
st. Blackburn 375 K15
st. Brighton 454 F18
st. Brunswick 325 B13
st. Brunswick E 325 L14
st. Brunswick E 326 B14
st. Brunswick W 325 A13
st. Caulfield N 415 H18
st. Coburg N 281 H12
st. Dandenong S 535
st. Darley 221
st. Darley 222
st. E Melbourne 24
st. E Melbourne 25
st. Fawkner 281
st. Footscray 367
st. Geelong West 702
st. Hawthorn E 372
st. Highett 496
st. Malvern East 456
st. Mitcham 377
st. Moolap 704
st. Moonee Pnd 324
st. Mordialloc 531
st. Mornington 640
st. Mt Waverley 459
st. Niddrie 322
st. Northcote 327
st. Oak Park 280
st. Pt Lonsdale 710
st. Port Melb 412
st. Preston 327
st. Reservoir 283
st. Richmond 26
st. Ringwood 378
st. St Kilda 414
st. Seddon 367
st. Sunshine N 321
st. Surrey Hills 417
st. Templestowe 331
st. Up Fntree Gly 465
st. Williamstown 411
st. Windsor 414
tce. Belmont 702
ALBERTA
av. Box Hill N 375
st. W Footscray 366
wy. Berwick 553
ALBERT COATES
la. Melbourne 2
ALBERT FACEY
st. Maidstone 366
ALBERT HILL
rd. Lilydale 337
ALBERTINE
cr. Sydenham 275
ALBERT JONES
ct. Eaglemont 328
ALBERTON
av. Roxburgh Pk 194
dr. Cranbourne W 577
rd. Selby 467
ALBERT ROAD
dr. Albert Park 30
dr. Albert Park 413
dr.s, Albert Park 30
ALBION
al. Melbourne 2
al. Melbourne 24
cr. Ardeer 320
cr. Greensbrgh 244
ct. Hoppers Csg 405
ct. Springvale S 534
pl. Mulgrave 501
rd. Ashburton 417
rd. Box Hill 374
rd. Glen Iris 417
st. Balaclava 414
st. Brunswick 325
st. Brunswick E 325
st. Brunswick W 324
st. Caulfield S 455
st. Essendon 324
st. Kingsville 366
st. South Yarra 31
st. South Yarra 32
st. South Yarra 414
st. Surrey Hills 373
st. Surrey Hills 417
ALBRECHT
av. Berwick 554
ALBURNUM
cr. Templstw Lr 330
ALBURY
av. Altona 407
ct. Croydon N 336
rd. Balwyn N 373
st. Albion 320
ALBYN
cl. Pakenham 584
ct. Mill Park 242
ALBYS
la. Maddingley 263
ALCALA
av. Malvern East 457
ALCHESTER
cr. Boronia 424
cr. Thomastown 240
ALCOCK
st. Reservoir 240

ALMA
av. Altona Mdw 407 G19
av. Ferntree Gly 464 D1
av. Laverton 407 A19
cl. Mulgrave 501 H7
cr. Noble Park 535 D3
ct. Doncaster 331 D18
ct. Endeavour Hl 537 D1
ct. Mooroolbark 337 J15
ct. Newcomb 704 C18
ct. Ringwood 378 J6
ct. Springvale 499 J15
gr. St Kilda 414 F15
la. Caroline Spr 274 D16
la. Kalorama 383 C11
pl. Carlton 18 A20
pl. St Kilda 414 E15
rd. Bundoora 284 H2
rd. Camberwell 416 H3
rd. Caulfield N 415 A15
rd. Caulfield N 415 C15
rd. Hampton Pk 551 E7
rd. Panton Hill 204 E20
rd. Parkdale 532 A10
rd. St Kilda 414 D14
rd. St Kilda E 414 D14
rd. Watsons Ck 249 A4
st. Aberfeldie 323 E9
st. Craigieburn 150 C17
st. Fitzroy 18 L20
st. Lower Plenty 286 F13
st. Maidstone 366 F1
st. Malvern East 457 E4
st. Mornington 640 B19
st. Tootgarook 698 C4
st. W Footscray 366 D5
tce. Newport 411 C9
tce. Williamstown 411 C9
ALMA DOEPEL
dr. Altona Mdw 451 L5
ALMANDS
av. Roxburgh Pk 194 E14
ALMAY
gr. Heidelberg 328 K5
ALMEIDA
cr. South Yarra 32 D8
cr. South Yarra 414 H5
ct. Watsonia N 243 G19
ALMER
av. Blackburn 376 D12
av. Nar Warrn S 579 D1
av. Nunawading 376 D12
ALMERIA
ct. Mt Eliza 626 A12
ALMERTA
pl. Bulleen 329 K9
ALMIRA
st. Anglesea 713 K2
ALMOND
av. Brooklyn 365 F18
cl. Werribee 447 K11
ct. Campbellfield 239 F11
ct. Thomastown 240 K14
dr. Doveton 537 A10
st. Balwyn N 373 H3
st. Caulfield S 455 G7
tce. Dingley Vill 532 H4
ALMONDBUSH
st. Somerville 645 E13
ALMONDSBURY
ct. Blackburn 376 C12
ALMORA
cl. Frankston 600 G19
ALMRAY
pl. Glen Waverley 421 B20
ALMURTA
av. Coolaroo 238 D5
rd. Bentleigh E 497 A3
ALNUS
ct. Newcomb 704 C16
ALOAH
st.e, Bayswater N 379 H18
st.w, Bayswater N 379 G19
ALOCASIA
cl. Lysterfield 503 L1
ALOHA
gdn. Templestowe 331 K10
st. S Kingsville 410 F2
ALOMA
av. Wyndham Va 446 F10
ALONSO
st. Glen Iris 417 H11
ALONZO
ct. Frankston 628 F2
ALOOMBA
st. Chadstone 458 B2
ALOYSIUS
st. Braybrook 322 C19
ALPHA
cl. Hampton Pk 551 K15
ct. Mitcham 377 F10
pl. Windsor 414 F12
st. Balwyn N 373 J6
ALPHINGTON
st. Alphington 327 F20
st. Northcote 327 A16
ALPINA
st. Frankston N 600 D8
ALPINE
av. Upwey 466 A10
bvd. Launching Pl 345 F13
cl. Sunbury 143 A10
cr. Kallista 467 G4
cr. Noble Park N 501 E10
ct. Badger Creek 258 G11
ct. Lalor 240 J10
ct. Vermont S 420 H9
gr. Pascoe Vale 280 G15
rd. Ferny Creek 425 J17
rd. Ferny Creek 425 J20
st. Ferntree Gly 464 H2
st. Warburton 349 E4
wk. Hampton Pk 551 E12
wy. Kilsyth 381 H8
ALRAY
dr. Cheltenham 497 C19
ALRENE
ct. Berwick 554 B1
ct. Vermont S 420 K8
ALSACE
st. Brunswick E 325 L10
st. Dandenong 535 E4
ALSOM
pl. Airport W 278 F16
ALSOP
la. Berwick 554 J11
la. Melbourne 1 D6
la. Melbourne 23 J6
st. Belmont 702 D18
ALSTON
ct. Nar Warrn S 552 F19
ct. Thornbury 327 F7
gr. St Kilda E 415 A19
st. Thornbury 327 D7
ALTA
st. Canterbury 373 D20
ALTAIR
cl. Frankston 628 F5
ct. Gladstone Pk 278 L2
ct. Gladstone Pk 279 A2
ct. Lilydale 338 L6
st. Springvale S 499 G19
ALTARNUN
rd. Langwarrin 629 J15
ALTER
ct. Skye 601 D9
ALTHEA
pl. Doncaster 331 B14
ALTNA
av. Airport W 278 K15
ALTO
av. Croydon 379 H1
cl. Bundoora 242 G18
ALTON
av. Brighton 454 G15
ct. Glen Waverley 461 A1
ct. Narre Warren 539 A13
ALTONA
ct. Doncaster E 375 G2
rd. Altona 409 K17
rd. Seaholme 409 K17
st. Heidelberg Ht 328 B3
st. Heidelberg W 328 C3
st. Kensington 33 H12
ALTSON
la. Melbourne 1 A7
la. Melbourne 23 G7
rd. Belgrave S 506 K10
rd. Belgrave S 507 A10
rd. Belgrave S 507 A14
ALTYRE
ct. St Albans 275 J18
ALUMNUS
ct. Wheelers Hl 460 D14
ALVA
av. Pk Orchards 333 H16
cl. Eltham 287 L10
ct. Fawkner 239 E20
ct. Waurn Ponds 705 E14
gr. Coburg 325 K2
ALVANLEY
ct. Mulgrave 501 G5
ALVARADO
av. Thomastown 240 F18
ALVASTON
av. Wantirna 422 G15
ALVENA
cr. Heathmont 378 L16
cr. Heathmont 379 A16
st. Mentone 530 L5
st. Mentone 531 A5
ALVERNA
cl. Greensbrgh 285 L8
gr. Brighton 454 L17
gr. Brighton 455 A17
ALVERSTONE
gr. Mt Eliza 642 J3
ALVIE
ct. Westmeadows 237 G10
rd. Mt Waverley 418 K19
st. Malvern East 457 D3
ALVINA
ct. Frankston 599 E16
st. Ferntree Gly 464 E1
st. Oakleigh S 458 E20
st. Sunshine N 321 B10
ALVIS
cl. Keilor Dn 276 B14
ALWARD
av. Clayton S 498 K6
ALWYN
ct. Braybrook 366 B3
ct. Keilor East 321 K6
ct. Mitcham 377 C18
st. Bayswater 423 F4
st. Croydon 380 E4
st. Mitcham 377 A18
st. Pascoe Vale 280 K14
st. Rye 697 B12
AMALFI
dr. Endeavour Hl 536 L4
dr. Endeavour Hl 537 A4
pl. Epping 197 E17
AMALIA
cl. Yarra Glen 208 L19
cl. Yarra Glen 209 A19
AMANDA
ct. Hallam 538 A14
ct. Keysborough 534 J10
ct. Melton 268 G1
ct. Mt Martha 655 E18
ct. Mt Martha 657 A10
ct. Pakenham 584 G3
ct. Rowville 503 B8
ct. Seville 341 K12
ct. Yallambie 285 F16
dr. Carrum Downs 600 H1
pl. Frankston 600 J18
rd. Tottenham 365 K10
AMANDI
tce. Hoppers Csg 405 D17
AMAR
st. Strathmore 279 L15
AMARANTH
av. Altona North 410 A2
AMARINA
cl. Meadow Ht 194 C20
cr. Grovedale 705 K12
AMAROO
ct. Berwick 553 E3
ct. Box Hill N 375 B6
ct. Burwood E 419 F10
ct. Diamond Ck 245 K8
ct. Eltham 288 D6
dr. Chelsea Ht 547 D11
gr. Burnside 318 G8
rd. Craigieburn 150 J9
st. Chadstone 458 B2
wy. Yallambie 286 C11
AMAY
cr. Ferntree Gly 464 B3
AMAYLA
cr. Carrum Downs 600 F2
AMAZON
ct. Rowville 462 L17
ct. Rowville 463 A17
pl. Werribee 447 H4
AMBASSADOR
ri. Research 288 J1
AMBER
av. Frankston 600 D16
cl. Brighton 454 J13
cr. Narre Warren 539 D13
ct. Altona North 410 C6
ct. Bundoora 284 H5
ct. Cheltenham 531 D4
ct. Kilsyth 381 K7
ct. Pascoe Vale 280 K11
ct. S Morang 199 J19
dr. Hampton Pk 551 L14
gr. Mt Waverley 419 B20
pl. Wyndham Va 446 E9
st. Bayswater 423 C6
st. Forest Hill 420 H3
wy. Taylors Hill 274 H12
AMBERLEY
av. Aspendale 546 C4
cr. Dandenong S 536 A15
cr. Frankston S 626 L8
ct. Bulleen 330 B18
ct. Highton 705 K1
ct. Wantirna 422 H10
dr. Mt Martha 656 K9
wy. Lower Plenty 286 G19
AMBERLY PARK
dr. Nar Warrn S 552 F15
AMBERWOOD
ct. Templestowe 331 D13
AMBLECOTE
cr. Mulgrave 501 F5
AMBLESIDE
cl. Frankston S 627 A15
cl. Mooroolbark 338 A15
cr. Berwick 554 A9
pl. Cairnlea 319 J11
rd. Greenvale 193 B19
AMBOINA
av. Mitcham 377 E16
AMBON
av. Deer Park 319 C9
ct. Heidelberg W 328 D1
ri. Croydon N 335 K15
st. Ashburton 417 F18
st. Preston 283 H18
AMBRIDGE
gr. Sydenham 275 B9
AMBRIE
av. Ringwood 378 K4
cr. Noble Park 500 H15
AMBROSE
av. Malvern East 417 H20
st. Dallas 238 K9
st. Doncaster 331 D18
st. Emerald 509 L5
st. Ivanhoe 327 J10
AMBROSIA
ct. Endeavour Hl 537 F6
AMCOR
wy. Campbellfield 239 D3
AMDURA
rd. Doncaster E 376 E3
AMEILY
cr. Reservoir 282 G8
AMELIA
av. Deer Park 319 D9
av. Essendon 324 C4
av. Healesville 258 B5
av. Mornington 640 L13
av. Rye 697 K5
av. Wheelers Hl 461 F13
cl. Beaconsfield 555 D13
cr. Doncaster E 376 D3
ct. Kilsyth 381 B5
st. Camberwell 417 G4
st. Caulfield S 455 L7
st. Knoxfield 423 D20
st. McKinnon 455 K16
AMERSHAM
av. Springvale S 499 K19
dr. Wantirna 422 C11
dr. Warrandyte 333 A6
dr. Warrandyte 333 B7
AMERY
av. Blackburn 375 E20
st. Ashburton 417 B16
st. Reservoir 282 D1
AMES
av. Carnegie 456 L8
st. Rowville 503 A1
AMESBURY
av. Craigieburn 194 C4
av. Wantirna 422 F11
ct. Mt Waverley 458 H4
rd. Mt Eliza 626 F13
AMESS
st. Brunswick E 325 L20
st. Carlton N 18 K3
AMETHYST
av. Glen Waverley 420 G18
cl. St Albans 320 L9
pl. Werribee 447 F3
wk. Bundoora 284 G7
wy. S Morang 199 B9
AMI
ct. Berwick 553 L15
AMIEL
ct. Springvale 500 B9
AMIENS
st. Hampton 495 D5
st. Surrey Hills 417 L1
AMIET
st. Greensbrgh 286 B8
AMINGA
av. Doncaster E 376 E1
ct. Croydon 336 D18
AMINYA
cr. Yallambie 286 B15
ct. Wantirna 422 C13
pl. Briar Hill 286 G3
pl. Camberwell 417 L3
AMIRIYA
st. Bentleigh E 496 K2
AMIS
cr. Avondale Ht 322 B7
cr. Keilor East 322 B7
AMLEY
ct. Wonga Park 336 E7
ri. Lysterfield 464 D13
AMON
ct. Woori Yall 344 E15
AMOORE
av. Highton 705
AMOS
ct. Clayton S 499
ct. Nar Warrn S 552
AMOTT
ct. Aspendale Gdn 546
AMOUR
ct. Wantirna S 462
AMPHLETT
av. Cockatoo 511
av. Gembrook 511
AMRON
st. Chelsea Ht 547
AMSTED
rd. Bayswater 424
AMSTEL
cl. Darley 221
ct. Hoppers Csg 405
ct. Meadow Ht 237
ct. Mt Waverley 458
st. Craigieburn 150
AMSTERDAM
st. Richmond 32
st. Richmond 414
AMUNDSEN
st. Belmont 702
AMUR
av. Roxburgh Pk 194
AMY
cl. Hoppers Csg 447
cl. Pakenham 585
ct. Hampton Pk 552
ct. Mentone 530
mw. Keysborough 534
rd. Boronia 424
st. Camberwell 417
st. St Albans 320
AMY MACK
wk. Lynbrook 551
AMYS
gr. Donvale 377
ANABA
ct. Greensbrgh 244
ct. Mooroolbark 337
st. Bayswater 423
ANACONDA
rd. Narre Warren 539
rd. Narre Warren 539
ANAKIE
ct. Rosebud 700
wk. Delahey 275
ANAMA
st. Greensbrgh 285
ANANDA
ct. Donvale 376
ct. Watsonia 285
ANARTH
st. Bentleigh E 457
st. Doncaster 331
ANCHOR
ct. Seabrook 450
pl. Prahran 32
pl. Prahran 414
st. Aspendale 546
ANCHORAGE
av. Williamstown 411
dr. Blind Bight 650
st. Point Cook 450
ANCONA
ct. Eltham 288
ct. Point Cook 450
dr. Mill Park 243
pl. Keilor Ldg 275
st. Mentone 530
ANDACANI
ct. Mt Eliza 641
ANDELANA
av. Wheelers Hl 460
ct. Sorrento 679
ANDENE
dr. Narre Warren 539
ANDERSON
av. Bentleigh E 456
av. Caroline Spr 318
cl. Bayswater N 380
cl. Hampton Pk 551
ct. Endeavour Hl 537
ct. Mentone 530
ct. Richmond 26
ct. Wantirna S 462
dr. Carrum Downs 574
la. N Melbourne 17
pde. Bundoora 285
pl. S Geelong 702
rd. Albion 365
rd. Fawkner 281
rd. Hawthorn E 416
rd. Healesville 258
rd. Keysborough 533
rd. Monbulk 428
rd. Sunbury 143
rd. Sunshine 365

Thornbury...326 B8
W Melbourne...368 C13
Ascot Vale...323 H20
Bacchus Msh...221 K16
Bentleigh...496 B3
Caulfield...455 H3
Clifton Hill...20 B8
E Geelong...703 F13
Ferntree Gly...424 K16
Frankston...599 F15
Heidelberg...329 C4
Kallista...467 E3
Lalor...241 D7
Lilydale...338 F7
Malvern East...416 C17
Melbourne...31 G4
Newport...410 H8
Pakenham...584 L5
Pascoe Vale S...280 G20
Pt Lonsdale...710 G1
Port Melb...368 J19
St Albans...320 H1
S Melbourne...30 A10
South Yarra...31 G4
South Yarra...414 D2
Surrey Hills...373 L20
Tecoma...466 D7
Templestowe...331 A7
Torquay...711 L10
Warrandyte...289 K19
Werribee...447 J17
W Melbourne...34 J19
Yarraville...366 K15
Geelong West, off Emerald St...702 J7
)ERSONS
N Melbourne...17 A15
)ERSONS CREEK
Doncaster E...332 C16
)ES
Lalor...240 H7
)LEIGH
Mulgrave...501 E2
)LEON
Clayton S...499 C10
Springvale S...533 K7
)LON
Tullamarine...278 J2
)ONOV
Cranbourne W...577 K15
)OVER
Mitcham...377 A8
Hampton Pk...552 B9
Mulgrave...501 A6
RE
Cranbourne W...577 H19
REA
Cranbourne N...578 H9
Taylors L...275 F5
. Ringwood N...378 J2
Rye...696 G10
St Albans...319 L6
REA CLAIRE
Skye...575 H18
REW
Croydon S...379 E11
Tootgarook...698 G6
Balwyn N...374 C3
Clarinda...498 C9
Doncaster...330 D19
Emerald...470 E16
Narre Warren...539 C17
Pakenham...584 J3
Rowville...503 D2
Bundoora...285 B3
Mornington...640 J20
St Albans...275 G20
Wollert...153 F15
Forest Hill...376 H20
Glenroy...280 K1
Hampton Pk...551 F10
Melton S...268 J6
Mooroolbark...337 A16
Mt Waverley...418 L12
Newcomb...704 C13
Northcote...326 K16
Oakleigh...457 L15
Ringwood...378 B10
Seaford...599 J9
Springvale...499 K17
Sunshine...321 F20
Sunshine...365 F1
Vermont...377 H20
Windsor...31 H20
Windsor...414 D10
REW CHIRNSIDE
Seabrook...450 L6
REWS
Reservoir...283 H16
Long Forest...224 F2
Red Hill...687 K20
Burwood...419 A9
Eltham...288 A4
Geelong West...702 F2

st. Heidelberg...329 A5
st. Spotswood...366 H20
ANDROMEDA
wy. Templstw Lr...330 K16
ANDVAL
ct. Berwick...554 G11
ANDY
cl. Lilydale...294 A19
ANEBO
st. Warneet...649 E13
ANEES
ct. Langwarrin...602 B16
ANELIDA
st. Rye...696 D5
ANEMBO
ct. Doncaster...375 D2
ct. Werribee...447 D13
ANERLEY
st. Ivanhoe...328 A17
ANETA
av. Hillside...274 E6
ANFIELD
ct. Malvern East...457 J1
ANGALA
ct. Frankston S...627 H16
ANGAS
ct. Sunbury...142 L17
ct. Sunbury...143 A17
ANGASTON
ct. Vermont S...421 D11
ANGEL
cl. Nar Warrn S...552 H16
ANGELA
cl. Eltham North...245 C17
ct. Doncaster E...332 G7
ct. Nar Warrn N...539 J9
ct. Rye...696 K4
ct. S Morang...243 H3
dr. Hoppers Csg...405 E20
ANGELICA
cr. Croydon Hl...335 E15
ANGELINA
wy. Somerville...644 J15
ANGELIQUE
gr. Albanvale...319 B7
ANGELO
ct. Melton...268 L1
la. Melbourne...2 C11
la. Melbourne...24 C6
pl. Wonga Park...291 G15
ANGELTOP
tce. Templestowe...331 G5
ANGIE
ct. Aspendale Gdn...546 L5
ANGLE
rd. Balwyn...372 J14
ANGLEMERE
cr. Donvale...376 L5
ANGLER
pde. Ascot Vale...323 G20
ANGLERS
ct. Seabrook...450 H6
ANGLESEA
rd. Waurn Ponds...705 A16
tce. Geelong West...702 J2
ANGLESEY
ct. Mulgrave...501 G5
ANGLIA
cl. Werribee...447 H3
ANGLISS
st. Yarraville...366 E16
ANGLO
ct. Mooroolbark...337 J18
ANGOURIE
cr. Taylors L...276 A10
ANGUS
av. Altona North...410 B5
av. Croydon...379 E8
av. Ringwood E...379 E8
cl. Wantirna...422 F4
ct. Dandenong N...501 F13
ct. Eltham North...245 C18
ct. Mt Eliza...641 J7
ct. Narre Warren...553 C7
ct. Oakleigh S...498 B9
ct. Pakenham...558 L20
ct. Roxburgh Pk...194 C7
dr. Glen Waverley...420 C17
gr. Doncaster...374 H1
pl. Lilydale...338 J10
rd. Yellingbo...387 G12
st. Belmont...702 C19
st. Hadfield...280 K7
st. Sunshine W...364 G3
ANILE
pl. Williamstn N...410 H13
ANITA
av. Dingley Vill...533 C8
ct. Carrum...573 E8
ct. Doncaster E...376 E1
ct. Frankston...627 H4
ct. Mordialloc...532 B10
ct. Mt Martha...657 C7

ct. Taylors L...275 E6
pl. Pakenham...584 G2
st. Beaumaris...530 A11
st. Kilsyth...381 D6
ANJAYA
ct. Blackburn...376 C20
ct. Frankston...600 H15
ANKA
cl. Eltham...288 C7
ANKETELL
st. Coburg...325 D3
ANLEY
mw. Montmorency...287 A8
pl. Sunshine W...364 A6
ANN
cr. Pakenham...584 J9
ct. Aspendale...546 E5
ct. Briar Hill...286 K4
ct. Bundoora...242 C18
ct. Mt Dandenong...426 H1
ct. Mt Waverley...458 J2
ct. Sunshine W...364 D9
pl. Seabrook...450 J4
st. Bayswater...423 G11
st. Beaconsfield...555 C14
st. Brunswick...325 K14
st. Croydon...336 A18
st. Dandenong...535 L5
st. Footscray...367 C9
st. Geelong West...702 D2
st. Pascoe Vale...280 G17
st. Pt Lonsdale...707 H20
st. S Melbourne...29 E2
st. Springvale...499 L17
st. Williamstown...411 J18
st. Windsor...414 J11
ANNA
ct. Narre Warren...538 F17
ct. Pakenham...559 G19
ct. Werribee...447 F4
la. Bonbeach...545 E13
st. Bundoora...242 F16
st. Glen Huntly...456 B7
st. St Albans...319 J5
ANNABELLA
ct. Dandenong N...502 B18
ANNADALE
mw. Greenvale...193 H17
st. Kew...372 D11
ANNAN
ct. Greenvale...237 B3
pl. Templestowe...332 B9
ANNAND
cl. Cranbourne W...577 G20
st. Fitzroy N...19 C2
ANNANDALE
cr. Glen Waverley...420 K19
mw. Point Cook...450 G5
rd. Keilor...277 F4
rd. Melb Airport...277 F4
rd. Melb Airport...278 A6
rd. Tullamarine...277 F4
ANNASTASIA
wy. Sunshine N...321 B17
ANNE
cl. Somerville...644 F15
cr. Brighton...454 K15
cr. Warburton...349 L6
ct. Berwick...554 G20
ct. Cranbourne...603 L3
ct. Heathmont...379 B20
ct. Montrose...382 A8
ct. Tootgarook...698 B8
ct. Yallambie...285 F16
dr. Dromana...686 E10
rd. Knoxfield...462 J6
st. Berwick...554 D7
st. Blackburn N...375 K8
st. Broadmeadows...238 F19
st. Diamond Ck...246 C12
st. Emerald...509 C3
st. Lilydale...339 E9
st. McKinnon...455 L16
st. Menzies Ck...468 H17
st. Newtown...702 H13
st. Reservoir...283 E2
st. Rosebud...700 E3
st. Werribee...447 B18
ANNESLEY
av. Mt Waverley...458 K3
st. Braybrook...322 A19
ANNETTA
av. Ashburton...417 B18
ct. Albanvale...319 C4
ct. Wheelers Hl...460 H7
ANNETTE
ct. Avondale Ht...322 A16
ct. Endeavour Hl...537 G3
ct. Langwarrin...629 E7
gr. Boronia...423 C14
pl. Templestowe...331 F5
ANNIBA
ct. Melton W...226 B17

ANNIE
ct. Croydon...336 J16
st. Frankston...599 B16
wy. Lilydale...338 H10
ANNIE BORAT
cl. Brunswick, off Eveline St...325 G14
ANNINGIE PARK
cl. Croydon N...336 A13
ANNIVERSARY
pl. Rowville...503 C8
ANNOIS
ct. Sunbury...142 K10
ANOMALY
st. Moolap...704 J16
ANORA
cr. Mulgrave...460 G20
ct. Keilor Dn...276 G15
ANSELM
gr. Glenroy...279 J4
ANSETT
cr. Forest Hill...420 E8
ct. Roxburgh Pk...194 E10
ANSLEY
pl. Truganina...405 J13
ANSON
ct. Ashburton...417 K17
ct. Moorabbin...496 K9
ANSTEE
gr. Bentleigh...455 L20
ANSTEL
mw. Cranbourne...603 E6
ANSTEY
av. Reservoir...239 L20
rt. Berwick...554 A3
ANSWER
cl. Sydenham...274 H4
ANTARES
ct. Aberfeldie...323 E11
ct. Torquay...712 D3
ANTHEM
pl. Melton W...226 D17
ANTHLIN
ct. Templestowe...332 B14
ANTHONY
av. Doncaster...330 D15
cl. Lower Plenty...286 H13
cr. Box Hill N...374 J7
ct. Burwood E...419 L8
ct. Hallam...538 C19
ct. Keilor East...322 B6
ct. Kingsbury...283 G9
ct. Melton W...226 A14
ct. Ringwood...378 J7
ct. Rosanna...329 D2
ct. Rye...696 F1
ct. Seaford...599 F3
ct. Werribee...447 G9
dr. Chirnside Pk...336 L5
dr. Mt Waverley...459 D6
dr. Rowville...463 K18
gr. Woori Yall...344 F14
la. Southbank...4 B20
la. Southbank...30 H1
la. S Melbourne...30 H1
pl. Langwarrin...629 B7
st. Croydon...379 G3
st. Dandenong N...502 A20
st. Dromana...686 B5
st. Glen Iris...416 F13
st. Kensington...33 K6
st. Langwarrin...601 G18
st. Melbourne...1 K2
st. Melbourne...23 L3
st. Newcomb...704 E17
st. Ormond...456 B14
st. Safety Bch...669 A17
st. Sunbury...142 K8
ANTHONYS
la. Langwarrin...629 D12
ANTIBES
st. Parkdale...531 D13
wy. Point Cook...450 G11
ANTIGONE
ct. Templstw Lr...330 K17
ANTIGONI
ct. Warrandyte...333 A5
ANTILL
ct. Mulgrave...460 D16
ANTIOCH
ct. Albanvale...318 L7
ANTIONETTA
wy. Hillside...274 G2
ANTIOPE
ct. Sorrento...679 B13
ANTOINETTE
bvd. Eltham...287 F17
ct. Mt Waverley...458 K2
ANTON
cl. Werribee...448 B15
ct. Chelsea Ht...547 F16
ct. Doncaster...331 D18
ct. Frankston...600 F19

ct. Mooroolbark...337 L18
ct. Nar Warrn S...552 E17
gr. Flemington...324 C20
ANTONELLA
ct. Dandenong S...549 J9
ANTONIE
av. Delahey...275 E10
ANTONIETTA
pl. Narre Warren...539 F16
ANTONY
cl. Mill Park...241 L6
dr. Mornington...641 C19
ANTRIM
cl. Endeavour Hl...538 A6
ct. Deer Park...318 K10
pl. Langwarrin...629 B9
ANTWERP
dr. Keilor Dn...276 F14
st. Dallas...238 E11
ANVIL
ct. S Morang...199 K17
pl. Attwood...237 A10
ANZAC
av. Coburg N...281 G13
av. Gembrook...512 K10
av. Hurstbridge...203 C14
av. Melbourne...4 E18
av. Melbourne...24 J18
av. Yarra Glen...208 H20
av. Yarra Glen...252 H1
av. Yarra Glen...253 A1
cr. Williamstown...411 A15
rd. Warrandyte S...334 J6
st. Carnegie...457 A5
st. Croydon...379 L4
ANZED
ct. Mulgrave...499 K1
AONACH
st. Clayton S...499 C5
APAC
dr. Melb Airport...235 J15
APALOOSA
ct. Belmont...706 B7
APEX
av. Belmont...705 L2
av. Hampton E...495 J8
cr. Bulleen...329 J13
ct. Thomastown...283 K1
st. Dandenong N...502 A16
wy. Montmorency...286 K13
APHRASIA
la. Newport...411 A10
st. Newtown...702 C8
APLIN
pl. Carlton...18 G12
pl. Roxburgh Pk...194 A12
pl. Wantirna S...462 C3
APOINGA
st. Dandenong S...549 J11
APOLLO
cr. Dallas...238 E12
ct. Aspendale Gdn...547 C6
ct. Blackburn...376 B15
ct. Croydon S...380 B11
ct. Doncaster E...332 D17
ct. Frankston...628 F9
ct. Greensbrgh...244 C17
ct. Hillside...232 B18
ct. Keysborough...535 A8
ct. Langwarrin...601 L17
ct. Wantirna S...422 B15
dr. Hallam...537 H20
pl. Sunshine W...363 K5
rd. Taylors L...275 L8
APPERLY
st. Fitzroy N...326 D19
APPIAN
ct. Hoppers Csg...448 H6
dr. Albanvale...319 C6
APPILA
cl. Hallam...538 D20
cl. Hallam...552 D1
APPIN
cl. Craigieburn...150 E10
ct. Meadow Ht...237 J4
APPLE
ct. Burwood E...419 J8
ct. Doveton...536 K8
gr. Bayswater...422 J4
st. Pearcedale...646 L4
st. Pearcedale...647 A4
APPLE BERRY
av. Langwarrin...601 D18
APPLEBERRY
cl. Knoxfield...423 A19
pl. Ringwood N...334 J20
pl. S Morang...243 L2
APPLE BLOSSOM
ct. Nar Warrn S...553 C20
ct. Templestowe...332 B14
APPLEBLOSSOM
ct. Viewbank...329 K1

APPLEBY
cr. Brunswick W 325 A8
ct. Sunshine 365 H2
APPLEGUM
cl. Croydon Hl 335 F17
cr. Ferntree Gly 423 E19
ct. Narre Warren 538 H14
gr. Doncaster E 332 F12
APPLETON
ct. Darley 222 B10
st. Richmond 371 B14
APPLETON DOCK
rd. W Melbourne 368 A16
rd. W Melbourne 368 D14
APPLETREE
dr. Glen Waverley 461 A2
dr. Mill Park 242 D9
gr. Cairnlea 319 K12
APPLEWOOD
ct. Doncaster E 332 C12
dr. Knoxfield 423 B20
pl. Nar Warrn S 553 E17
ri. Somerville 645 C20
APRE
ct. S Morang 199 B14
APREY
pl. Eltham 288 C5
APRIL
cl. Albanvale 319 C7
APSLEY
ct. Ferntree Gly 463 G6
ct. Mill Park 242 K12
pl. Seaford 599 J5
rd. Belgrave 466 C17
st. Glenroy 280 D7
st. Mt Waverley 459 C7
tce. Berwick 553 K19
vst. Derrimut 363 B7
AQUA
st. Langwarrin 629 H6
AQUAMARINE
ct. Hampton Pk 551 C10
ct. St Albans 320 K9
AQUANITA
cr. Keilor Dn 275 L12
AQUARIUS
ct. Donvale 377 F2
ct. Lilydale 338 L7
ct. Lilydale 339 A7
ct. Mornington 657 D5
ct. Wheelers Hl 460 J10
dr. Frankston 628 D7
AQUATIC
dr. Albert Park 30 F10
dr. Albert Park 413 J5
AQUEDUCT
av. Mt Evelyn 339 F20
la. Diamond Ck 245 C14
rd. Diamond Ck 244 K13
rd. Langwarrin 629 J5
rd. Langwarrin 629 K6
tr. Langwarrin 629 A13
AQUILA
cr. Endeavour Hl 536 J2
ct. Wheelers Hl 461 B11
gr. Roxburgh Pk 194 E10
pl. Carrum Downs 575 B14
st. Balwyn N 329 A20
st. Balwyn N 373 A1
AQUILLA
av. Torquay 712 C4
ct. Chelsea Ht 547 D10
AQUINAS
ct. Hoppers Csg 448 J6
AQUITANIA
wy. Docklands 368 K14
ARABIL
st. Frankston 599 K19
ARABIN
st. Keilor 277 C13
ARALUEN
dr. Croydon 380 A10
pde. Belmont 702 D17
ARAMA
st. Balwyn N 329 L19
ARANDA
ct. Mulgrave 500 H5
pl. Epping 241 K3
ARANDT
rd. Exford 267 E18
ARANGA
cr. Donvale 376 F6
ARANMORE
cr. Nar Warrn N 539 K9
ARAPILLES
dr. Templstw Lr 330 E12
ARARAT
av. Coburg N 281 F14
st. Altona North 410 C6
ARATULA
st. Dandenong 536 D8
ARAWATA
cl. Mornington 657 C3
dr. Doncaster E 376 D1
pde. Melton 226 J16
ARAWATTA
st. Carnegie 456 K5
st. Vermont S 421 E8
ARBON
rd. Mornington 657 A2
ARBOR
av. Belgrave 466 J17
av. Ferntree Gly 424 L16
av. Nunawading 376 K12
av. Reservoir 282 E13
av. Tremont 425 A16
st. Alphington 327 K18
tce. Avondale Ht 322 D13
ARBOUR
gr. Belmont 706 A5
ARBROATH
ct. Greenvale 193 E20
rd. Wantirna S 422 K12
rd. Wantirna S 423 A12
ARCADE
al. Melbourne 2 D10
al. Melbourne 24 C5
rd. Mont Albert N 374 E10
sq. Keilor East 321 L4
wy. Avondale Ht 321 K8
wy. Keilor East 321 K8
ARCADIA
av. Hallam 537 F14
av. Malvern East 457 H7
av. Mickleham 149 D3
av. Reservoir 283 F10
av. The Basin 424 J9
cl. Ringwood N 378 F3
cl. Taylors L 275 H1
ct. Glen Waverley 419 L14
ct. Noble Park 534 C5
st. Box Hill S 374 L20
st. Carrum Downs 601 C6
st. Hampton 494 L5
st. Hampton 495 A5
wy. Eltham North 245 G17
wy. Keysborough 534 G16
ARCADIAN
pl. Hoppers Csg 405 D13
ARCADY
gr. Vermont 421 J4
ARCHBOLD
st. Thornbury 326 K7
ARCHER
av. Ascot Vale 323 H19
av. Sunbury 142 G15
cl. Lilydale 294 B20
cl. Mt Eliza 626 C12
ct. Brighton East 455 D18
ct. Gladstone Pk 279 B1
dr. Kurunjang 227 E8
dr. Mornington 641 D17
pl. Keilor Dn 275 K13
pl. Mill Park 242 L10
rd. Diamond Ck 245 K2
st. Blairgowrie 679 D18
ARCHERON
ct. Caroline Spr 318 C6
ARCHIBALD
av. Narre Warren 539 E18
pl. Langwarrin 629 D11
st. Box Hill 374 K14
st. Elsternwick 455 A6
st. Pascoe Vale 280 F17
ARCH WRIGHT
dr. Reservoir 282 G5
ARCOLA
ct. Eltham 287 L11
ARDBLAIR
tce. Nar Warrn S 553 E20
ARDCLONEY
dr. Sunbury 143 J10
ARDEA
ct. Endeavour Hl 536 K2
ARDEER
ct. Meadow Ht 237 K4
ARDEL
st. Croydon 335 D20
st. Croydon 379 E1
ARDEN
cr. Rosanna 285 B20
ct. Kew East 372 H3
ct. Seaford 599 F3
dr. Noble Park 534 C6
la. N Melbourne 17 D15
st. Croydon 336 G19
st. Kensington 34 A14
st. Kensington 34 C14
st. N Melbourne 34 F15
ARDENA
ct. Bentleigh E 456 K18
ct. Keilor Dn 276 H15
ARDENE
ct. Hawthorn 371 K18
ARDENNE
ct. Nar Warrn S 579 G4
ARDENT
ct. Keilor 276 K10
ARDGOUR
st. Balwyn N 373 J3
st. Hughesdale 457 E11
ARDGOWER
ct. Templstw Lr 330 K8
rd. Noble Park 500 G16
ARDILL
st. Healesville 213 E20
st. Healesville 257 F1
ARDLIE
st. Attwood 236 L11
st. Attwood 237 A12
st. Westmeadows 236 L14
st. Westmeadows 237 A14
ARDLUI
dr. Newtown 701 K11
ARDMERE
pl. Eltham 288 A6
ARDMILLAN
rd. Moonee Pnd 323 J12
ARDMORE
ct. Macleod 284 L11
st. Cranbourne 578 C17
st. Mitcham 376 L9
ARDOCH
av. St Kilda E 414 J14
av. Thomastown 240 G14
ct. Gladstone Pk 237 B17
rd. Sunbury 143 A6
st. Essendon 324 B6
ARDOYNE
st. Black Rock 529 G3
st. Sunshine 365 A8
ARDRIE
rd. Malvern East 456 F1
ARDUINA
ct. Langwarrin 629 E6
st. Somerville 645 A13
ARDWELL
ct. St Albans 275 G19
ARDWICK
st. Bentleigh 496 B4
ARDYNE
st. Murrumbeena 457 B10
ARENA
cl. Flemington 33 K3
sq. Noble Park 534 G5
ARGENT
av. S Morang 198 K11
pl. Ringwood 377 K18
ARGO
st. South Yarra 31 J13
st. South Yarra 414 E7
ARGONAUT
pl. Altona Mdw 452 A4
ARGONNE
pde. Selby 467 C13
ARGOON
rd. Healesville 257 F6
ARGOONA
rd. Mambourin 445 A7
rd. Wyndham Va 445 A7
ARGUS
cr. Doncaster E 332 E20
ct. Narre Warren 553 B12
st. Cheltenham 496 K17
ARGYLE
av. Chelsea 547 A20
av. Upwey 465 K10
cl. Hughesdale 457 E13
cr. Werribee 447 J8
ct. Berwick 553 H6
ct. Glen Waverley 420 F15
ct. Pakenham 584 J1
ct. Vermont S 421 F8
pl. Fitzroy 19 C12
pl. Lynbrook 551 H15
pl. Sunbury 143 H7
pl.e, Carlton 18 E18
pl.n, Carlton 18 D16
pl.s, Carlton 18 D17
rd. Kew 372 F8
st. Belmont 702 H20
st. Bentleigh E 457 C16
st. Donvale 376 E5
st. Fawkner 281 F11
st. Fitzroy 19 A12
st. Frankston 627 C4
st. Glenroy 280 A6
st. Macleod 285 B15
st. Moonee Pnd 323 H14
st. Reservoir 283 F5
st. St Kilda 414 E15
st. St Kilda E 414 E15
st. W Footscray 366 H7
st. Geelong, off Little Ryrie St 703 C9
wy. Wantirna S 462 D1
ARGYLL
cct. Melton W 225 K14
cl. Epping 197 L16
ct. Eltham North 245 C18
st. Malvern East 417 G20
st. Sydenham 274 H1
ARI
dr. Campbellfield 239 G10
ARIADNE
av. Murrumbeena 457 A9
ARIANNE
rd. Glen Waverley 420 G20
ARIEL
av. Glen Iris 417 E11
ct. Keilor Dn 276 B14
ct. Whittington 704 B19
wy. Patterson L 547 G20
ARIES
ch. Kurunjang 226 L10
ct. Lilydale 294 H19
ARILPA
ct. Ashwood 418 C19
ARINGA
av. Highton 705 G3
ct. Ferntree Gly 464 E6
ct. Heathmont 379 B17
ARINYA
cr. Anglesea 713 F4
ARIS
ct. Craigieburn 150 G17
ARISTINES
pl. Sorrento 679 A13
ARISTOC
rd. Glen Waverley 460 A5
ARISTOCRAT
tce. S Morang 199 B14
ARISTOTLE
ct. Narre Warren 539 E16
ARJAY
ct. Westmeadows 236 H15
ARKANA
av. Highton 701 H17
ARKARINGA
cr. Black Rock 529 E3
ARKARRA
ct. Croydon N 336 C15
ct. Mooroolbark 337 E12
ARKINDALE
pl. Frankston S 627 H17
ARKINS
st. Pt Lonsdale 710 D5
ARKLE
st. Prahran 414 L11
st. Prahran 415 A11
ARKLEY
dr. Greenvale 237 E1
ARKWELLS
la. Red Hill 687 H19
ARKWRIGHT
ct. Noble Park N 501 D14
ARLENE
dr. Skye 601 G5
ARLEON
cr. Cranbourne 578 F17
ct. Rowville 463 B14
ct. Somerville 644 F18
ARLIE
cr. Montrose 381 J10
ARLINGTON
ct. Dingley Vill 532 K6
dr. Glen Waverley 460 J4
pl. Nar Warrn S 579 B3
st. Camberwell 416 K3
st. Reservoir 282 L16
st. Ringwood 378 B14
wk. Vermont 421 K2
wy. Point Cook 450 G12
ARLUNYA
ct. Aspendale Gdn 546 G3
pl. Templestowe 288 E20
pl. Templestowe 332 E1
rd. Chum Creek 213 F5
ARMADALE
av. Noble Park 534 H8
dr. Narre Warren 553 B10
st. Armadale 415 F13
st. Melbourne 31 C11
st. Melbourne 414 B6
st. Thornbury 326 J10
ARMAGH
ct. Belmont 706 E2
pl. Wantirna S 422 C19
rd. Frankston S 627 A17
ARMAO
ct. Noble Park 534 K7
ARMATA
cr. Frankston N 600 C8
ARMER
ct. Aspendale Gdn 546 H5
ARMFIELD
st. Brighton 494 L1
ARMIN
st. Scoresby 462 G5
ARMISTAN
cr. Chelsea Ht 547
ARMISTON
ct. Endeavour Hl 538
gr. Altona Mdw 451
gr. Wantirna S 462
ARMITAGE
ct. Belmont 706
dr. Nar Warrn S 579
pl. S Morang 198
ARMOUR
cl. Glen Waverley 420
ct. Sunshine W 364
ARMSTEAD
av. Coburg 325
ARMSTRONG
cl. Keilor East 278
ct. Malvern East 457
ct. Roxburgh Pk 194
ct. Vermont 421
ct. Whittington 704
dr. Melton S 268
dr. Rowville 503
gr. Yarra Glen 209
rd. Bayswater 423
rd. Beaconsfld Up 542
rd. Heathmont 379
rd. McCrae 684
rd. Seaford 573
rd. Yarrambat 244
st. Beaumaris 530
st. Coburg 281
st. Greensbrgh 243
st. Laverton 407
st. Middle Park 30
st. Middle Park 413
st. Mornington 640
st. Mt Waverley 418
st. Reservoir 282
st. Springvale 499
st. Sunshine W 364
wy. Dandenong N 501
ARMSTRONGS
rd. Seaford 573
ARMY
av. Reservoir 282
rd. Boronia 424
rd. Lysterfield S 503
rd. Pakenham 559
rd. Pakenham 585
rd. Pakenham Up 559
tr. Lysterfield S 503
ARMY SETTLEMENT
rd. Pakenham 559
rd. Pakenham Up 559
ARMYTAGE
rd. Officer 556
wy. Wyndham Va 446
ARNA
st. Blackburn 375
ARNCLIFFE
bvd. Greenvale 193
ARNDELL
cl. Truganina 405
st. Thomastown 241
ARNDT
rd. Pascoe Vale 280
ARNHEM
ct. Rowville 463
ARNICA
cl. Hampton Pk 552
ARNOLD
av. Heidelberg Ht 328
ct. Bundoora 242
ct. Dandenong 536
ct. Hoppers Csg 449
ct. Melton 268
ct. Pascoe Vale 280
dr. Chelsea 547
dr. Donvale 333
dr. Scoresby 462
gr. Doncaster 374
rd. Brighton East 495
st. Blairgowrie 695
st. Box Hill 374
st. Brunswick E 325
st. Cheltenham 496
st. Cranbourne 578
st. Kilsyth 381
st. Melbourne 31
st. Melbourne 414
st. Mt Waverley 418
st. Noble Park 534
st. Preston 282
st. Princes Hill 18
st. Princes Hill 325
st. Ringwood 378
st. South Yarra 31
st. South Yarra 414
st. Sunshine W 364
ARNOT
ct. Springvale S 534
st. Brighton East 455

ATLANTIC
pl. *Berwick, off Lyrebird Gdn 539 H19*
st. Clayton 459 B19
st. Mooroolbark 338 A17
tce. Mt Martha 669 A4
ATLANTIS
ct. Aspendale Gdn 546 L3
ct. Aspendale Gdn 547 A3
ATLIER
pl. S Morang 198 K11
ATON
st. N Warrandyte 290 D13
ATRIUM
dr. Tarneit 447 J2
ATTENBOROUGH
ct. Dingley Vill 532 K4
rd. Aspendale 546 A1
sq. Wantirna 422 J11
st. Dandenong 535 G8
ATTERCLIFFE
av. Pascoe Vale 281 A16
ATTILIO
wy. Seabrook 450 H4
ATTLEY
ct. Keilor Dn 276 A11
gr. St Kilda E 454 K1
rd. Knoxfield 462 L3
rd. Knoxfield 463 A3
ATTUNA
cr. Rosebud W 699 G2
ATTUNGA
cr. Seaford 573 D13
ct. Berwick 553 H1
ct. Doncaster 374 J3
ct. Highton 701 F19
dr. Torquay 711 J6
st. Blackburn 375 E14
st. Chadstone 458 E2
wy. Mt Eliza 641 K8
ATTWELL
cl. Bundoora 242 K15
ATTWOOD
ct. Viewbank 285 L16
ATUNGA
ct. Cheltenham 531 H3
ct. Heathmont 379 F19
ct. Sunshine W 364 G6
tce. Dromana 685 K9
AUBIN
ct. Keysborough 535 B10
AUBREY
gr. Boronia 424 C17
st. Armadale 415 D11
st. Vermont 421 H1
AUBURN
av. Northcote 326 D13
av. Sunshine N 321 F10
av. Sunshine N 321 F7
cl. Craigieburn 150 A17
ct. Rowville 503 D6
gr. Armadale 415 D12
gr. Hawthorn E 372 D18
pde. Hawthorn E 372 G18
rd. Hawthorn 372 C20
rd. Hawthorn 416 C6
rd. Healesville 214 B20
AUBYN
ct. Mulgrave 500 L5
AUCKLAND
st. Bentleigh 496 E3
AUDLEY
st. Coburg 325 F6
AUDREY
av. Coburg N 281 B15
cr. Glen Iris 417 E12
st. Springvale 500 D10
AUDSLEY
st. Clayton S 498 L5
AUGHTIE
dr. Albert Park 30 D10
dr. Albert Park 413 H7
dr. Melbourne 30 G19
dr. Melbourne 413 H7
AUGHTON
ct. Wantirna 421 L11
AUGUST
st. Werribee 448 A16
AUGUSTA
av. Campbellfield 239 A10
cl. Cranbourne 603 J4
cl. Sunbury 144 E12
cr. Sunshine N 321 H16
ct. Rowville 462 D18
ct. Skye 601 D8
pl. Darley 221 G1
rd. The Basin 425 B11
st. Glen Huntly 456 B8
st. Mt Martha 656 A11
AUGUSTINE
dr. Highton 705 G7
tce. Glenroy 279 J2
AUGUSTINES
rd. Highton 705 E5
wy. Keilor 276 J9
AUGUSTUS
dr. Berwick 554 E20
ri. Templestowe 331 K6
AUHL
rd. Emerald 510 B3
AULD
ct. Sunbury 143 A4
AULDANA
ct. Vermont S 421 D10
AUMANN
ct. Croydon N 335 L12
ct. Mont Albert N 374 E6
dr. Templestowe 331 K9
st. Heathmont 379 A17
AURARIA
cl. Nar Warrn S 579 F4
AURA VALE
rd. Belgrave S 507 G5
rd. Menzies Ck 507 G5
rd. Menzies Ck 508 A2
AUREA
ct. Clarinda 498 G11
ct. Frankston N 600 C7
ct. Narre Warren 553 G12
AURELIA
cl. Pt Lonsdale 710 F4
AURIOL
ct. Ferntree Gly 464 C7
ct. Greensbrgh 243 L20
AURISCH
av. Glen Waverley 420 D17
dr. Nar Warrn N 539 G3
AURORA
cl. Epping 198 B17
cr. Torquay 711 J10
ct. Glen Waverley 460 K2
ct. Sorrento 679 A13
ct. Springvale S 534 B5
ct. Werribee 447 C9
pl. Roxburgh Pk 193 J15
ri. Sassafras 426 G11
AURUM
cr. Ringwood N 377 L8
AUSCO
pl. Dandenong S 550 J9
AUSTARC
av. Thomastown 241 A17
AUSTIN
av. Elwood 454 F4
av. McCrae 684 H19
av. Narre Warren 552 L6
av. Sorrento 678 K8
cl. Noble Park N 501 D12
cr. Pascoe Vale 280 E15
cr.e, Yarraville 366 J15
cr.w, Yarraville 366 F14
ct. Sunbury 142 L12
pl. Carlton 18 H15
pl. Grovedale 705 H14
pl. Melton S 268 E6
pl. Templestowe 332 B10
pl. W Melbourne 17 B20
rd. Hampton 495 E11
rd. Seaford 599 E2
rd. Seaford 599 J2
rd. Somerville 644 H20
st. Alphington 327 E20
st. Balwyn 373 D12
st. Bentleigh 456 C18
st. Bulleen 329 F11
st. Fairfield 327 E20
st. Ferntree Gly 464 D3
st. Hughesdale 457 F15
st. Mitcham 377 E12
st. Newtown 702 H9
st. Preston 327 D6
st. Rye 680 F20
st. St Albans 320 D10
st. Seddon 367 D11
st. Werribee 447 H13
st. *Hawthorn, off Majore St 371 G17*
tce. Brunswick 325 H10
tce. Newtown 702 J10
wy. Fitzroy N 19 F1
wy. Fitzroy N 326 C20
AUSTRAK
dr. Somerton 194 K17
dr. Somerton 194 L16
dr. Somerton 195 A16
AUSTRAL
av. Brunswick 325 D11
av. Preston 326 F4
av. Upwey 466 A10
cr. Baxter 643 K2
ct. Heidelberg 329 E1
ct. Wheelers Hl 460 G17
la. Melbourne 1 H14
la. Melbourne 24 A9
pl. Hillside 232 B20
pl. Sunshine W 364 E6
st. Surrey Hills 373 L20
AUSTRALIA
dr. Taylors L 275 F8
AUSTRALIS
cct. Port Melb 412 H5
cl. Langwarrin 629 L4
ct. Dingley Vill 532 K4
dr. Mill Park 243 C6
AUTUMN
cl. Point Cook 450 L10
cr. Mt Eliza 642 C6
ct. Glen Waverley 459 K2
gr. Cairnlea 319 F12
gr. Mitcham 377 A16
gr. Mooroolbark 337 H10
pl. Doveton 536 K12
ri. Bundoora 284 F7
st. Belmont 706 H4
st. Coburg 281 A19
st. Geelong West 702 B4
st. Herne Hill 701 H4
st. Manifold Ht 702 B4
st. Newtown 701 H4
AUTUMNDALE
av. Reservoir 283 L15
ct. Nar Warrn N 539 F9
AUTUMN FIELDS
cct. Tarneit 405 B8
AVA
ct. Berwick 553 G3
AVALON
av. Broadmeadows 238 A19
av. Glen Waverley 421 A15
ct. Avondale Ht 322 G7
ct. Cheltenham 497 C20
dr. Rosebud 700 K6
gr. Ringwood N 378 C8
rd. Armadale 415 C13
rd. Rowville 462 E20
st. Mooroolbark 337 D16
wy. Thomastown 240 F13
AVANDEL
pl. Sydenham 275 B9
AVANDINA
cr. Greensbrgh 244 D19
AVARD
ct. Berwick 554 L5
ct. Noble Park 534 J4
rd. Emerald 469 E15
AVARN
ct. Eltham 288 A10
AVEBURY
dr. Berwick 553 J4
dr. Berwick 554 B3
AVELIN
st. Hampton 495 D5
AVENAL
pl. Carrum Downs 574 L18
AVENDER
ct. Ashwood 418 C16
AVENDON
bvd. Glen Waverley 459 K2
bvd. Glen Waverley 459 K3
ct. Nar Warrn S 579 G3
AVENEL
ct. Thomastown 240 F13
ct. Wyndham Va 446 H13
gdn. Craigieburn 150 E11
pl. Endeavour Hl 537 E1
rd. Kooyong 416 A6
st. Dallas 238 J11
AVENHAM
ct. Hillside 232 H20
AVENUE
rd. Camberwell 416 K2
AVENUE ATHOL
Canterbury 373 A16
AVENUE VICTORIA
Hawthorn E 372 F17
AVENZA
st. Mentone 531 F7
AVERNE
st. Cranbourne 578 C15
AVERY
ct. Mt Martha 657 C9
ct. Narre Warren 538 H14
ct. Ringwood N 334 L19
ct. Wheelers Hl 461 A9
pl. Carrum Downs 601 E1
AVIATION
pl. Tullamarine 278 F2
rd. Laverton 407 A19
rd. Werribee S 449 F20
rd. Werribee S 488 K6
AVIATOR
pl. Brookfield 268 C8
AVIEMORE
av. Pk Orchards 333 K17
cl. Sorrento 679 C14
wy. Point Cook 450 G7
AVILA
ct. Vermont 421 H4
pl. Keilor Ldg 276 D5
st. Coldstream 295 F14
AVINGTON
cr. Boronia 424 J4
AVION
pl. Westmeadows 236 J16
ri. S Morang 198 J15
AVIS
ct. Forest Hill 420 C7
ct. Ringwood 379 A1
la. N Melbourne 17 B10
AVIVA
ct. Wheelers Hl 460 L18
ct. Wheelers Hl 461 A18
AVLONA
st. Mordialloc 532 B18
AVOCA
av. Elwood 414 E20
av. Mt Martha 655 E17
av. Noble Park 534 G6
cl. Clayton S 498 G8
cl. Hampton Pk 551 H5
cr. Pascoe Vale 280 D18
ct. Ashwood 418 B14
ct. Brookfield 268 D5
ct. Croydon N 336 D10
ct. Dandenong N 501 K9
ct. Elwood 414 D20
ct. Mentone 531 F5
ct. Werribee 447 F7
gr. Caulfield N 455 B1
pl. Taylors Hill 274 J13
pl. *Geelong, off Malop St 703 E8*
st. Broadmeadows 238 A8
st. Brunswick 325 K8
st. Camberwell 372 J18
st. Heidelberg 329 C4
st. Highett 496 A15
st. South Yarra 31 L8
st. South Yarra 414 F4
st. Yarraville 367 B14
st. Yarraville 367 C14
wy. Wantirna S 422 D16
AVOCET
cl. Blind Bight 650 C10
ct. Carrum Downs 601 B2
ct. Mornington 657 B1
ct. Tootgarook 698 E9
ct. Werribee 447 J6
st. Doncaster E 375 L4
AVON
av. Mitcham 377 F16
ct. Berwick 579 L2
ct. Bundoora 284 G5
ct. Chirnside Pk 336 G7
ct. Croydon Hl 335 J17
ct. Dandenong N 501 G15
ct. Ferntree Gly 463 K6
ct. Glen Waverley 459 J11
ct. Keilor 276 L14
ct. Langwarrin 629 E7
ct. Melton W 226 B18
ct. Mentone 531 G5
ct. Werribee 448 C19
pl. Deer Park 318 L14
pl. Epping 242 B1
rd. Avonsleigh 470 E16
rd. Rye 696 J14
st. Box Hill N 374 H12
st. Bulleen 329 F11
st. Geelong West 702 D4
st. Moorabbin 496 E9
st. Noble Park 500 E19
wk. Taylors Hill 274 L13
AVONBURY
ct. Brighton 454 F13
AVONDALE
av. Chelsea 546 J18
av. St Albans 320 G4
ct. Gladstone Pk 279 C1
ct. Rye 698 A8
gr. Belgrave 466 G16
gr. Mt Waverley 418 L19
rd. Armadale 415 D12
rd. Lalor 241 C7
rd. Preston 327 B1
st. Hampton 494 L6
st. Hampton 495 A6
st. Springvale 499 L8
AVONHURST
dr. Glen Waverley 459 H9
AVONMORE
cl. Mill Park 242 G9
AVONSIDE
rd. Belgrave Ht 506 D1
AVONSLEIGH
cl. Warranwood 335 B11
AVONWOOD
cl. Wantirna S 422 K19
rd. Nar Warrn N 538 J10
AVRIL
st. Dandenong N 502 A2
st. Scoresby 462 E
AVRO
ct. Strathmr Ht 279 D
AWABA
st. Eaglemont 328 K
AWETA
st. Ashwood 418 D1
AWNIE
cr. Endeavour Hl 538 A
AWUN
ct. Springvale 499 H1
AXA
wy. S Morang 198 L1
AXEDALE
cr. Endeavour Hl 537 E
AXEL
st. Dandenong 536 C
AXELTON
st. Cheltenham 531 A
AXFORD
cr. Oakleigh S 497 H
rd. Kings Park 318 L
rd. Wantirna S 421 G1
AXIOS
la. Roxburgh Pk 194 C
AXMINSTER
dr. Craigieburn 150 A2
AYBROOK
ct. Mulgrave 500 L
ct. Mulgrave 501 A
AYCLIFFE
dr. Deer Park 318 L
AYERS
ct. Epping 241 C
ct. Taylors L 276 E
AYLESBURY
av. Bayswater N 380 E1
cr. Gladstone Pk 236 L2
wy. Warrandyte 333 A
AYLMER
rd. Lynbrook 577
rd. Lyndhurst 551 C2
st. Balwyn N 373 A
AYLWARD
av. Thomastown 240 F
AYLWIN
av. Burwood 418
AYNES
ct. Point Cook 450
AYNESBURY
ct. Rosebud W 699
AYR
av. Malvern East 417 J
cl. Greenvale 193 B
ct. Berwick 554
ct. Briar Hill 286
ct. Glen Waverley 420 K
ct. Noble Park 534
ct. Pakenham 584
st. Altona Mdw 450
st. Ascot Vale 324 F
st. Blackburn S 419
st. Doncaster 330 C
st. Ferntree Gly 463
st. Jan Juc 711 E
st. Macleod 285 D
st. Reservoir 283
AYRES
cl. Cranbourne N 577
rd. Healesville 257
AYTON
ct. Noble Park N 501
st. Ivanhoe 327
st. Sunshine N 321
AZALEA
av. Brooklyn 365
av. Doncaster E 376
av. Mill Park 243 E
cr. Dandenong N 501 H
cr. Emerald 510
ct. Cheltenham 531
ct. Croydon N 335
ct. Knoxfield 463
ct. Narre Warren 553
ct. Newcomb 704
ct. Warburton 349
ct. Wheelers Hl 460
ct. *Dandenong, off David St 536*
st. Forest Hill 420
st. Vermont 420
AZAROW
cct. Croydon S 380
AZTEC
ct. Wheelers Hl 461
pl. Thomastown 240
AZURE
ct. Templestowe 331

B

AN
Fawkner 281 K11
BB
Maidstone 366 G3
BBAJIN
Coburg 281 L20
BINDA
Rowville 463 F15
BRA
Grovedale 706 D8
CCHUS
Millgrove 348 E4
Frankston S 627 F13
Croydon S 380 A13
Maddingley 221 G20
CCHUS MARSH
Bacchus Msh 221 E13
Bacchus Msh 265 A1
CCHUS MARSH-LIANG
Maddingley 263 A11
CCHUS MARSH-ELONG
Maddingley 264 B3
Maddingley 264 B3
CCHUS MARSH-BORNE
Darley 222 C9
Merrimu 222 C9
CCHUS MARSH-RRIBEE
Wyndham Va 446 A2
CH
Fitzroy 18 L16
HLI
Mill Park 242 C5
Anglesea 713 A6
Rosanna 284 L20
Rosanna 285 A20
Rye 696 J5
K
Sherbrooke 466 J2
K BEACH
Portsea 677 H6
KHAUS
Sunbury 142 L17
Sunbury 143 A17
Hampton 494 L5
KOUS
Noble Park 534 F3
KSTAIRS
Warburton 348 H6
Warburton 349 A5
KWELL
Geelong, off Maud St 703 A10
EN
Frankston S 626 J11
Torquay 712 C1
Hoppers Csg 448 K7
ENOCH
Highton 701 E16
Blackburn 376 C14
EN POWELL
Endeavour Hl 502 L18
Endeavour Hl 503 A18
Frankston S 626 J11
Healesville 258 A9
Mt Eliza 626 D15
Tarneit 405 A8
Mt Eliza 626 C19
ER
Nunawading 376 K12
Frankston S 626 G9
Ringwood 378 L2
GE
Laverton 407 B16
GER
Badger Creek 258 B16
Lilydale 294 J20
Narre Warren 538 J14
Thomastown 240 H14
Mulgrave 501 E5
GER CREEK
Badger Creek 258 D10
Healesville 213 K19
Healesville 258 B2
GER WEIR
Badger Creek 258 J13
MINTON
Wantirna 422 E8
Z
Hampton Pk 551 H12
E
Roxburgh Pk 193 J15
Diamond Ck 245 H10
ENDON
Kilsyth S 424 K2

BAGGOTT
dr. Hoppers Csg 448 F3
BAGLEY
st. Brighton 494 J2
BAGLEYS
la. Vermont 421 B5
BAGORA
ct. Bayswater N 380 H19
BAGSHOT
ct. Mornington 657 B4
BAGULEY
cr. Kings Park 275 B20
BAHAMA
ct. Vermont 420 L3
ct. Vermont 421 A3
BAHEN
cl. Eltham 287 K1
ct. Watsonia 285 E8
BAHLOO
ct. Frankston 600 H19
BAILEY
av. Armadale 415 H15
av. Keilor East 278 A17
av. Preston 327 B5
av. St Kilda E 454 K1
ct. Campbellfield 239 G14
ct. Springvale 499 L18
gr. Ivanhoe East 328 G13
gr. Wandin N 340 E15
pl. Mornington 657 E6
rd. Cockatoo 510 J4
rd. Emerald 510 G7
rd. Mt Evelyn 339 E18
rd. Nar Warrn N 539 H4
st. Belmont 706 J5
st. Boronia 423 L14
st. Grovedale 706 H12
st. Pt Lonsdale 710 E4
st. St Albans 320 D11
st. Werribee 448 A14
BAILEYANA
dr. Endeavour Hl 502 J19
st. Frankston S 627 D8
BAILEY GULLY
rd. Hurstbridge 203 C19
rd. Hurstbridge 247 B1
BAILEY JAMES
ct. Rowville 503 C7
BAILEYS
ct. Meadow Ht 238 B3
BAILLIE
ct. Bacchus Msh 221 J16
ct. Frankston 628 C6
st. N Melbourne 17 A16
BAILLIEU
st. Pt Lonsdale 710 F7
BAILY
st. Mt Waverley 419 G17
BAIN
av. Coburg N 281 F12
ct. Newcomb 704 A13
st. Berwick 554 G8
BAINBRIDGE
av. Seaford 599 E12
cl. Craigieburn 150 F20
ct. Carrum Downs 600 L6
ct. Carrum Downs 601 A6
ct. Kilsyth 381 C3
dr. Eltham 288 A7
BAINES
cr. Torquay 711 J7
BAIRD
ct. Blackburn S 419 G2
ct. Rowville 463 C19
st. Ashburton 417 B17
st. Brighton East 495 D5
st. Fawkner 281 J6
st. Greensbrgh 286 D11
st. Maidstone 366 G3
st. Mulgrave 500 D5
st.e, Doncaster 375 C3
st.n, Doncaster 375 B2
st.s, Doncaster 375 B3
BAKE HOUSE
la. Carlton 18 J15
BAKEHOUSE
la. Fitzroy N 19 C8
rd. Panton Hill 204 J15
BAKER
av. Blairgowrie 679 C19
av. Edithvale 546 K14
av. Glen Waverley 459 K9
av. Kew East 372 B4
ct. Burwood E 419 L11
ct. Meadow Ht 237 L6
la. Melbourne 31 F16
pde. Ashburton 417 G13
rd. Bayswater N 379 J15
rd. Harkaway 540 F16
ri. Sunbury 142 G8
st. Anglesea 713 F6
st. Brighton 454 K17
st. Cockatoo 510 L4
st. Geelong West 702 E1
st. Lilydale 337 K4
st. Malvern East 456 K2
st. Moorabbin 496 F7
st. Murrumbeena 457 C14
st. Richmond 26 H4
st. St Kilda 414 B20
st. Sunshine 365 G3
BAKERS
pde. Brunswick W 324 K7
rd. Coburg N 281 B15
rd. Dandenong N 501 E13
rd. Oakleigh S 497 K2
BAKERY
la. N Melbourne 17 C18
sq. Melton 226 L19
st. Brunswick 325 E17
BAKEWELL
ct. Blairgowrie 679 F16
st. Cranbourne 604 E3
st. Tooradin 651 H9
BALACLAVA
av. Altona Mdw 451 G2
rd. Caulfield N 415 F19
rd. St Kilda E 414 L18
rd. St Kilda E 415 A18
BALAKA
av. Aspendale 546 F4
ct. Delahey 275 B11
ct. Rosebud W 699 E2
pl. Bundoora 284 K3
st. Rosebud W 699 E2
st. Warneet 649 D14
BALAM
grn. Sydenham 274 K6
BALAMARA
ct. Frankston S 643 G1
pl. Mornington 641 C16
BALAM BALAM
st. Coburg 281 L20
BALANDA
ct. Bundoora 243 A20
BALARANG
ct. Patterson L 573 K10
BALBETHAN
dr. Sunbury 144 F3
BALCOMBE
av. Mooroolbark 337 G14
ct. Craigieburn 150 C20
ct. Croydon 379 H6
ct. Donvale 332 L15
ct. Narre Warren 552 G2
ct. Thomastown 240 G14
dr. Mt Martha 657 B8
dr. Mt Martha 657 C8
pl. Dingley Vill 532 L9
pl. Hillside 232 G19
pl. Melbourne 2 B14
pl. Melbourne 24 D8
rd. Beaumaris 529 G5
rd. Black Rock 529 G5
rd. Mentone 530 K7
rd. Newtown 701 L13
st. Frankston 627 E4
st. Mornington 640 K13
st. Sunshine N 321 H19
BALCOMBE CREEK
cl. Mt Martha 656 B14
BALCOMBE PARK
la. Beaumaris 529 L5
BALD HILL
rd. Pakenham 585 A9
rd. Pakenham 586 A14
BALDING
av. Werribee 447 J18
BALDOCK
rd. Mornington 641 J13
BALDWIN
av. Boronia 424 G4
av. Montmorency 286 H8
av. Noble Park 534 H4
av. Sunshine N 321 D7
av. Up Fntree Gly 465 E7
dr. Somerton 194 H10
rd. Altona North 408 K6
rd. Blackburn 375 H20
st. Armadale 415 G12
st. Highett 496 A12
BALDWYN
st. Frankston 599 D13
BALES
st. Ferntree Gly 464 D7
st. Mt Waverley 458 K6
BALFE
cr. Brunswick W 324 J14
BALFOUR
av. Heathmont 378 J17
av. Sunshine N 321 D8
cl. Point Cook 450 F4
cl. Watsonia N 243 H19
ct. Berwick 554 B2
ct. Glen Waverley 420 D15
pl. Melton W 225 K15
pl. Noble Park N 501 A7
st. Brighton East 495 D1
st. Doncaster 374 G3
st. Reservoir 282 K1
st. Toorak 415 G3
BALGONIE
pl. Northcote 326 J14
BALGOWLAH
av. Keysborough 534 G10
BALI
pl. Lalor 241 H7
BALI HI
bvd. Templestowe 331 K11
BALINGA
ct. Doncaster E 332 H10
dr. Skye 601 H3
BALKAN
ct. Dandenong N 502 D17
BALL
rd. Heatherton 497 H15
st. Darley 221 H8
st. Sunshine N 321 F14
BALLABIL
st. Rye 697 F4
BALLADONIA
rd. Rowville 463 G15
BALLAM
cl. Frankston 628 F2
BALLAMORE
cr. Doncaster 331 B13
BALLAN
rd. Werribee 446 J12
rd. Werribee 447 A13
rd. Wyndham Va 445 L1
st. Reservoir 282 E1
st.s, Reservoir 282 E1
BALLANDRY
cr. Greensbrgh 244 K19
BALLANEE
gr. Cranbourne N 578 D9
BALLANTYNE
cr. Kilsyth 381 C3
st. Burwood E 420 B8
st. Southbank 23 J20
st. Southbank 29 K1
st. Southbank 413 E1
st. Thornbury 326 E8
BALLARA
av. Glen Waverley 459 L11
ct. Brighton 454 G13
ct. Highton 705 H5
BALLARAT
rd. Ardeer 319 K16
rd. Braybrook 322 B20
rd. Burnside 318 G12
rd. Cairnlea 319 K16
rd. Deer Park 319 J16
rd. Footscray 367 J6
rd. Maidstone 366 J2
rd. Ravenhall 318 G12
rd. Sunshine 321 F19
rd. Sunshine N 321 F19
st. Brunswick 325 F12
st. Collingwood 19 L11
st. Lalor 241 E6
st. Yarraville 367 C17
BALLARD
av. Coburg N 282 A17
cl. Gladstone Pk 279 D1
ct. Wantirna 422 E13
st. Yarraville 366 E16
BALLART
tr. Lysterfield 505 H2
BALLARTO
rd. Carrum Downs 600 D5
rd. Cranbourne 603 D9
rd. Cranbourne 604 G11
rd. Cranbourne E 604 J11
rd. Cranbourne S 603 D9
rd. Frankston N 600 D5
rd. Junction Vill 604 G11
rd. Skye 601 C6
st. Tooradin 651 K8
BALLATER
av. Newtown 701 K11
st. Essendon 323 G6
BALLIANG
st. S Geelong 702 L13
st. S Geelong 703 B14
BALLIN
st. Kings Park 319 E1
BALLINA
ct. Deer Park 318 K12
pl. Hampton Pk 552 B9
tce. Vermont S 420 L14
BALLINAMONA
st. Fairfield 327 G17
BALLIOL
cmn. Sunbury 144 E10
BALLOAN
st. Coburg 325 E1
BALLUK WILLIAM
ct. St Kilda 414 A13
BALLYMENA
st. Greenvale 193 G19
BALLYMORE
ct. Frankston 628 B5
BALMACEDA
ct. Berwick 554 A19
BALMAIN
ct. Lalor 240 K8
ct. Wantirna 422 F12
dr. Berwick 554 A4
dr. Carrum Downs 600 H2
st. Cremorne 26 A20
st. Cremorne 32 A1
st. Glen Waverley 460 F12
BALMANNO
cr. Strathmore 323 L2
BALMER
gra. Brookfield 267 C7
st. Brunswick 325 H12
BALMERINO
av. Toorak 415 B3
sq. Frankston 628 D8
BALMORAL
av. Bentleigh 456 E20
av. Brunswick E 325 L10
av. Bundoora 284 J6
av. Dandenong 536 D13
av. Kew 372 J13
av. McKinnon 456 E20
av. Pascoe Vale S 324 J3
av. Safety Bch 668 J20
av. Sandringham 495 K17
av. Springvale 499 H12
av. Strathmore 279 H20
av. Templstw Lr 330 E14
av. Wesburn 348 A8
cct. Eltham 245 J19
cct. Sunbury 142 L6
cct. Sunbury 143 A6
cl. Hillside 274 D7
cl. Kings Park 318 L1
cl. Wyndham Va 446 C7
cr. Surrey Hills 374 C18
ct. Burwood E 420 A9
ct. Frankston S 628 C15
ct. Glen Waverley 459 H10
ct. Hallam 537 E14
ct. Rowville 463 G17
ct. St Kilda E 414 L18
ct. St Kilda E 415 A18
dr. Parkdale 531 K9
pl. Melton W 226 D15
pl. South Yarra 32 B15
rd. Ringwood N 378 E4
st. Braybrook 321 L20
st. Braybrook 365 L1
st. Essendon 323 H6
st. Frankston 599 C18
st. Kilsyth 381 G7
st. Laverton 407 B19
st. South Yarra 32 A15
st. South Yarra 414 G7
st.s, Altona Mdw 407 B20
wy. Pakenham 584 G1
BALNARRING
dr. Kings Park 319 A2
rd. Tuerong 670 L4
BALONNE
cl. Taylors L 233 F18
BALOO
ct. St Helena 244 H17
BALOOK
ct. Cranbourne N 577 L4
ct. Meadow Ht 237 K6
st. Rye 697 B8
BALSAM
ct. Cranbourne N 578 A5
st. Templstw Lr 330 K15
BALSTON
st. Balaclava 414 J18
st. Southbank 3 C10
st. Southbank 24 B17
BALTASER
dr. Pakenham 585 E2
BALTIMORE
dr. Point Cook 449 K6
BALTUSROL
cl. Sunbury 144 F12
BALUK
pl. Kurunjang 227 B13
BALWYN
ct. Narre Warren 553 D10
rd. Balwyn 373 E17
rd. Balwyn N 373 G4
rd. Bulleen 329 H17
rd. Canterbury 373 E17
BALYARTA
ct. Forest Hill 420 E6
BAMBA
ct. Scoresby 462 H6
BAMBARA
ct. Greensbrgh 244 J20
ct. Sunshine W 364 K7

rd. Hurstbridge 203 E13
st. Wantirna 422 C14
BAMBER
cl. Mordialloc 532 E17
BAMBIL
ct. Boronia 424 J6
st. Chadstone 458 B2
BAMBOO
ct. Cranbourne N 577 L6
ct. Doveton 536 H9
ct. Mill Park 242 D11
BAMBRA
ct. Doncaster E 332 C19
ct. Grovedale 705 L14
ct. Mt Waverley 419 E12
ct. Noble Park 534 D2
ct. Seaford 600 B3
ct. Tootgarook 698 F8
ct. Vermont 420 L5
rd. Caulfield 455 K5
rd. Caulfield N 415 K20
rd. Caulfield S 455 J12
st. Croydon 336 J15
st. Mt Eliza 641 L3
st. Geelong, off McKillop St 703 A9
BAMBURGH
st. Jacana 237 J18
BAMBURY
ct. Campbellfield 239 H14
pl. Ferntree Gly 464 F1
st. Boronia 424 F11
BAMFIELD
cl. Templestowe 331 C11
rd. Heidelberg Ht 328 G2
rd. Heidelberg W 284 G20
rd. Mt Evelyn 384 A5
st. Sandringham 494 L12
st. Sandringham 495 A13
st. Sandringham 495 B13
BAMFORD
av. Westmeadows 236 F13
BAMFORDS
la. Box Hill 374 K15
BAMPTON
mw. Craigieburn 194 B3
BANADELL
av. Darley 221 F1
BANANA
al. Melbourne 1 G20
al. Melbourne 24 B12
BANARA
ct. Mulgrave 500 H6
BANBRIDGE
pl. Carlton 18 B16
BANBURY
cr. Craigieburn 149 L15
ct. Somerville 644 J19
rd. Reservoir 282 D9
st. Burwood E 419 L11
BANCELL
st. Campbellfield 239 F16
BANCHORY
av. Hillside 232 D20
st. Essendon 323 H6
BANCROFT
av. Nar Warrn S 579 B5
BANDA
ct. Rye 697 C9
BANDALONG
ct. Bundoora 285 A1
BANDO
rd. Springvale 499 G11
BANEEM
ct. Sydenham 275 A8
BANFF
cl. Mulgrave 500 G1
ct. Balwyn 374 A11
st. Reservoir 283 F5
BANFIELD
ct. Ferntree Gly 463 G9
sq. Mt Waverley 419 D20
BANGALAY
av. Frankston S 626 K10
pl. Berwick 553 H3
BANGALORE
st. Kensington 33 G10
BANGALOW
wy. Aspendale Gdn 547 B4
BANGAMBALANGA
av. Chum Creek 213 A8
BANGERANG
av. Sunshine N 320 L13
av. Sunshine N 321 A13
BANGHOLME
rd. Bangholme 549 C11
rd. Dandenong S 549 A11
BANGOR
ct. Heathmont 422 G2
dr. Frankston 628 E3
BANGS
st. Prahran 32 F20
st. Prahran 414 J10
BANHUL
pl. Bundoora 284 E3
BANJO
bvd. Carrum Downs 575 F18
pl. Officer S 582 B18
BANJO PATERSON
av. Oakleigh E 458 J12
cir. Point Cook 449 K8
BANJORA
cl. Croydon Hl 335 H15
BANK
la. Edithvale, off Bank Rd 546 G13
pl. Melbourne 1 G15
pl. Melbourne 24 A9
pl. St Kilda 414 D13
pl. S Melbourne 30 B4
pl. Taylors Hill 274 G9
pl. Geelong, off Little Malop St 703 B8
rd. Edithvale 546 G13
st. Alphington 327 K18
st. Ascot Vale 324 D16
st. Box Hill 374 L15
st. Braybrook 366 C5
st. Brunswick 325 H16
st. Bundoora 284 A1
st. Craigieburn 150 C16
st. Northcote 327 C17
st. Oakleigh 457 K13
st. Richmond 26 F9
st. S Melbourne 29 G7
st. S Melbourne 413 E3
st. S Melbourne 413 H2
BANKER
ct. Epping 198 D20
ct. Epping 242 C1
ct. Lilydale 294 A19
BANKS
av. Hampton 495 D11
ct. Belmont 702 E17
pl. Gladstone Pk 237 E16
pl. Keilor 276 L11
rd. Cranbourne 604 A5
rd. Eltham North 287 F1
rd. Mannerim 707 A1
st. McCrae 684 J17
st. Warneet 649 D14
BANKSIA
av. Beaumaris 530 E11
av. Thomastown 240 G14
cct. Wesburn 348 C6
ct. Altona Mdw 451 K1
ct. Bayswater 423 G5
ct. Chelsea 547 B19
ct. Croydon S 379 E11
ct. Frankston S 627 H12
ct. Heathmont 379 B18
ct. Langwarrin 629 J4
ct. Long Forest 224 G10
ct. Newcomb 704 C13
ct. Noble Park 500 K18
ct. Sunbury 143 K6
ct. W Footscray 366 F11
ct. Wheelers Hl 460 E13
ct. Dandenong, off David St 536 D4
gr. Mt Martha 669 H1
gr. Sorrento 679 B18
gr. Tullamarine 278 J6
pl. Grovedale 706 E9
pl. Meadow Ht 193 J19
pl. Melton W 226 B15
pl. Rosebud 683 L20
pl. Rosebud 684 A20
rd. Caulfield S 455 F9
ri. Eltham North 245 F19
st. Bellfield 327 L7
st. Bentleigh E 457 E17
st. Blackburn 375 F20
st. Burwood 418 A6
st. Clayton 458 J18
st. Doveton 536 J6
st. Eaglemont 328 A8
st. Eaglemont 328 K8
st. Heidelberg 328 A8
st. Heidelberg 328 K8
st. Heidelberg 329 B9
st. Heidelberg Ht 328 A8
st. Ivanhoe 328 A8
st. Montrose 381 L9
st. St Albans 320 F8
BANKVIEW
wy. Hoppers Csg 405 E15
BANNER
ct. Glen Waverley 420 L18
BANNERMAN
av. Greensbrgh 286 E4
st. Yarra Jctn 347 E18
BANNES
rd. Cairnlea 319 K14
BANNIE
la. Mt Martha 657 B10
BANNING
rd. N Warrandyte 290 A15
BANNISTER
av. Anglesea 713 G7
st. Jacana 237 H19
BANNOCKBURN
rd. Viewbank 286 B16
BANNON
av. Sunbury 142 H4
ct. Hallam 551 J3
BANNONS
la. Yarrambat 201 B9
la.n, Doreen 202 C8
la.n, Yarrambat 202 B8
BANOLE
av. Prahran 414 L12
av. Prahran 415 A12
BANOOL
av. Kew 371 H10
av. Mt Evelyn 383 G1
av. Yarraville 367 B18
cr. Mt Eliza 642 E8
ct. Blackburn S 419 J3
ct. Croydon 379 H3
ct. Frankston S 627 E8
qd. Doncaster E 332 C19
rd. Balwyn 373 K12
rd. Selby 467 B15
st. Cheltenham 530 D3
st. Preston 327 D1
st. Surrey Hills 373 K14
BANOON
rd. Eltham 287 G18
BANSKIA
cl. Torquay 711 F11
BANSTEAD
nk. Craigieburn 194 B4
BANTOCK
la. Caroline Spr 317 J3
BANTRY
gr. Templestowe 332 D5
BANYALLA
dr. Cranbourne W 577 K16
BANYAN
cl. Carrum Downs 574 L17
ct. Waurn Ponds 705 D15
dr. Frankston 628 C1
st. Chelsea 547 B14
st. St Andrews Bch 697 F20
BANYULE
ct. Frankston S 627 G13
rd. Heidelberg 329 D1
rd. Rosanna 329 C1
rd. Viewbank 329 G2
BAPAUME
av. Edithvale 546 G14
BAPTIST
pl. Melbourne 2 G15
pl. Melbourne 24 F7
BARADINE
ct. Sunbury 142 G10
rd. Mooroolbark 337 D17
st. Chadstone 458 C2
tce. Donvale 332 L14
BARAK
ct. Frankston 600 B18
ct. Glenroy 280 D10
dr. Launching Pl 346 D13
dr. Yarra Jctn 346 G13
la. Healesville 257 E13
rd. Mooroduc 657 K7
rd. Port Melb 412 D5
st. Bulleen 329 G16
BARAKEE
dr. Somerville 644 D19
BARANBALI
dr. Vermont S 420 E12
gr. Greensbrgh 286 G1
BARAR
ct. Kurunjang 227 A15
BARATTA
st. Blackburn S 419 E3
st. Doncaster E 375 K5
BARB
st. Maribyrnong 323 C14
BARBARA
av. Boronia 423 J11
av. Dandenong N 501 E20
av. Glen Iris 417 J9
av. Glen Waverley 420 C19
cr. Avondale Ht 322 A17
ct. Bacchus Msh 222 B13
ct. Bundoora 285 B2
ct. Heathmont 379 C18
ct. McCrae 685 A14
ct. Mooroolbark 337 B10
ct. Pakenham 584 L1
ct. Thomastown 241 K13
gr. Woori Yall 344 H14
st. Braybrook 322 C19
st. Doncaster E 375 J3
st. Hadfield 280 J8
st. Mont Albert N 374 F7
st. Moorabbin 496 J8
st. Vermont 377 G20
BARBARY
cr. Taylors L 275 J10
BARBER
ct. Berwick 554 D18
ct. Cheltenham 497 B20
dr. Hoppers Csg 448 C3
BARBERS
rd. Kalorama 382 L13
rd. Kalorama 383 A15
BARBICAN
ct. Rowville 463 B14
BARBISTON
rd. Melb Airport 234 E14
BARCE
pl. Heidelberg W 283 L19
BARCELONA
av. Keilor 277 C11
cl. Thomastown 240 E14
st. Box Hill 375 B17
BARCLAY
av. Croydon 380 E10
av. Frankston 599 H16
av. Up Fntree Gly 465 A5
cl. Gladstone Pk 237 A18
ct. Mulgrave 460 E20
dr. Cheltenham 497 G19
st. Albion 320 L20
st. Albion 364 L1
BARDEN
pl. Thomastown 240 E17
BARDIA
av. Ashburton 417 J15
av. Seaford 599 D5
st. Heidelberg W 328 A4
st. Ringwood 378 F11
BARDOEL
ct. Chelsea 546 L16
ct. Dingley Vill 532 J4
BARDOLPH
ct. Bentleigh 456 G20
st. Glen Iris 417 F10
BARDSLEY
ct. Narre Warren 539 A13
st. Sunshine W 364 K5
BARDWELL
av. Frankston 627 K9
BAREENA
av. Rowville 502 F7
ct. Mornington 641 D19
dr. Mt Eliza 626 H16
gr. Doncaster E 331 K16
BARELLAN
cl. Rowville 462 K19
cl. St Albans 321 A7
mw. Berwick 554 A3
BARENYA
ct. Kew 372 B11
BARFORD
ct. Sunshine W 363 L5
BARGES
rd. Olinda 427 D1
BARGROVE
ct. Thomastown 240 G11
BARHAM
av. Ferntree Gly 463 F3
wy. Cranbourne E 578 L17
BARHOLME
ct. Oakleigh S 457 K19
BARILLA
ct. Burwood E 419 H12
ct. Cranbourne 578 A20
rd. Moorabbin 496 D10
BARINA
av. Mooroolbark 337 E13
cl. Keilor Dn 276 G14
cr. Croydon 336 A20
ct. Berwick 554 C4
rd. Glen Iris 417 A14
rd. Glenroy 280 B10
wy. Mill Park 242 K2
BARINGA
av. Kallista 467 C2
ct. Rowville 463 H13
pl. Eltham 288 C6
rd. Croydon N 336 A15
st. Mt Waverley 419 F19
BARINGA PARK
dr. Nar Warrn S 552 H18
BARINGHUP
st. Cheltenham 496 L20
BARITE
pl. Frankston 600 J20
BARK
av. Rowville 463 K17
BARKALA
cl. Greensbrgh 244 C19
ct. Frankston 600 F15
st. Rye 697 D8
BARKER
ct. Endeavour Hl 537 H5
dr. Mooroolbark 336 K12
st. Blackburn S 419
st. Cheltenham 496
BARKERS
rd. Chum Creek 213
rd. Hawthorn 371
rd. Hawthorn E 372
rd. Kew 371
st. Heatherton 497
st. Oakleigh S 497
BARKLY
av. Armadale 415
av. Burnley 371
av. Port Melb 29
av. Richmond 26
ct. Brunswick 325
pl. Carlton 18
pl. Footscray 367
pl. Heidelberg 328
st. Box Hill 375
st. Brighton 454
st. Brunswick 325
st. Brunswick E 325
st. Camberwell 417
st. Carlton 18
st. Cranbourne 578
st. E Geelong 703
st. Elwood 454
st. Fitzroy N 326
st. Footscray 366
st. Footscray 367
st. Hughesdale 457
st. Mordialloc 531
st. Mornington 640
st. Mornington 641
st. Ringwood 378
st. St Kilda 414
st. Sunbury 143
st. W Footscray 366
tce. Mitcham 377
BARLBY
ct. Greenvale 237
BARLEY
ct. Delahey 275
BARLEYCORN
pl. Melton W 226
BARLOA
rd. Balwyn 374
rd. Mont Albert 374
BARLOW
av. Cheltenham 497
cl. Caroline Spr 318
st. Keysborough 534
st. Keysborough 535
st. Port Melb 412
BARLYN
rd. Mt Waverley 418
BARM
cl. Sydenham 275
BARMAH
cl. Taylors L 276
ct. Frankston S 627
dr. Wantirna 422
st. Mt Eliza 625
BARNABY
pl. Vermont 421
BARNACLE
mw. Templestowe 331
BARNARD
cr. Croydon N 335
ct. Epping 197
ct. Sunshine 365
gr. Kew 371
rd. Toorak 415
BARNATO
gr. Armadale 415
BARN ELMS
pde. Caroline Spr 317
BARNES
av. Burwood 418
cr. Sunshine W 364
dr. Guys Hill 541
gr. Chelsea 546
rd. Altona North 409
wy. Bundoora 284
BARNESDALE
dr. Vermont 421
BARNET
st. Highett 495
st. Yarraville 367
BARNETT
gr. Noble Park 500
pl. Jan Juc 711
pl. Mt Martha 656
st. Hampton 495
st. Kensington 34
st. Sunshine 321
st. Sunshine 365
BARNETTS
pl. Hawthorn 372
BARNEY
ct. Rye 696
BARNFATHER
st. Thomson 703

RNHILL
Viewbank..........329 K1
RNIC
Heathmont.........422 K1
RNINGHAM
Brunswick..........325 G13
RNONG
Kurunjang..........227 A13
RNS
Blackburn S.......375 J20
Blackburn S.......419 J1
RNSBURY
Hampton Pk.......551 H5
Balwyn 372 L13
Balwyn 372 L12
South Yarra 32 J14
South Yarra 414 K7
RNSDALE
Wantirna...........422 F8
Ringwood N........377 L3
RNSHAW
Emerald............469 F19
RNSLEY
Kilsyth S...........424 K2
Endeavour Hl.....538 A4
. Westmeadows...237 H12
Nunawading 376 E10
RNSTON
Ringwood..........335 C20
RODA
Glen Waverley....460 A10
Keysborough 534 D11
Rosebud............684 F15
Travancore 324 F18
RON
Kings Park.........318 L2
Ringwood..........378 L3
Ringwood..........379 A3
Westmeadows....236 F13
RONDI
Narre Warren.....538 K17
RONET
Craigieburn........150 D6
Nar Warrn S.......578 G1
RONGAROOK
Lower Plenty......286 D13
ROOGA
Wonga Park.......291 K15
ROOK
Ringwood N.......378 D3
Greensbrgh........286 L1
Aspendale..........546 F6
ROONA
Brighton 454 K12
Mornington........640 J11
ROSSA
Vermont S 421 C10
Mt Martha..........656 A15
Waurn Ponds......705 A17
RQUE
Pt Lonsdale.......707 G17
RR
Pakenham 584 B6
Brighton East.....495 L6
RRABOOL
Belmont............702 C16
Highton 701 G17
Wandana Ht.......701 A18
Doncaster E 331 J17
RRADINE
Vermont S 420 K9
RRAGOWA
Rosebud W........699 E2
RRANI
Bentleigh E 457 C16
RRATT
Noble Park.........534 L5
RREENONG
Cottles Br...........203 C5
Hurstbridge 203 C5
RRELL
Delahey 275 E12
RRETT
Roxburgh Pk......194 F14
Woori Yall..........344 H13
Yarraville 366 J15
Albert Park...........29 D13
Mornington........640 F14
Albert Park...........29 D13
Albert Park.........413 B7
Cheltenham 530 J2
Kensington 34 C13
Maidstone..........366 E2
Up Fntree Gly.....464 K9
RRETTS
Langwarrin S 628 J19
RRIE
Braybrook..........366 A1
Tullamarine........278 G10
RRIEDALE
Eltham...............288 A8
Frankston S 627 H19

BARRIES
rd. Melton..............268 F1
rd. Melton W..........268 C1
BARRIMAL
wy. Bundoora..........284 F3
BARRINA
st. Blackburn S......419 E2
BARRINE
wy. Taylors L 275 L10
BARRINGTON
av. Kew..................372 C10
cl. Keysborough.....534 B9
cr. Gladstone Pk.....237 C19
ct. Baxter...............644 B2
ct. Wantirna............422 J10
dr. Ashwood............418 B16
dr. Pakenham 585 D5
la. Sunbury 142 E14
pl. Hampton Pk.......551 D6
ri. Donvale 332 H20
st. Bentleigh E 457 C17
tce. Point Cook.........450 H9
BARRINGUN
cr. Clayton S...........498 H9
BARRON
av. Braybrook..........366 A7
ct. Dandenong N.....501 F8
st. Reservoir...........282 C6
wy. Yallambie..........286 B12
BARROT
av. Hoppers Csg......448 K2
BARROW
dr. Heathmont.........422 K2
pl. Burnley..............371 C20
st. Brunswick..........325 J9
st. Coburg..............325 J9
st. Mt Martha..........669 C2
BARROWBY
av. Woori Yall..........343 L14
BARRUP
st. Carlton 18 K15
BARRY
av. Burwood............418 J8
ct. Scoresby 462 F6
ct. Wonga Park.......291 J19
la. Melbourne.............1 H10
la. Melbourne............23 L7
rd. Broadmeadows..238 B7
rd. Burwood E.........419 K11
rd. Campbellfield.....239 A8
rd. Dallas 238 B7
rd. Lalor..................239 L10
rd. Meadow Ht........237 H7
rd. Thomastown......239 L10
rd. Westmeadows...237 H7
st. Bayswater..........423 L6
st. Bentleigh 496 B5
st. Brunswick..........325 C16
st. Carlton 17 L15
st. Kew...................371 H9
st. Macleod 285 H10
st. Maddingley.........263 G1
st. Mentone.............531 C9
st. Northcote 326 G18
st. Reservoir............282 H7
st. Rosebud.............684 C16
st. Seaford..............599 L7
st. South Yarra 32 C14
st. South Yarra 414 G7
st. Tootgarook.........698 H2
st. Watsonia 285 H10
BARRYMORE
rd. Greenvale 236 K4
rd. Greenvale 237 A2
BARRYS
la. Coburg 281 G20
BARTELS
st. McCrae..............684 L12
BARTER
cr. Forest Hill 420 D5
BARTLETT
av. Croydon 336 E18
rd. Olinda...............427 B1
st. Frankston S 627 J13
st. Hampton E.........495 L8
st. Preston..............282 F17
tce. Newtown 702 D13
BARTLETTS
la. Hurstbridge 247 J2
la. Kangaroo Grnd ..247 J2
la. Panton Hill 247 J2
la. Panton Hill 248 A3
BARTLEY
pl. Springvale S 499 J18
rd. Belgrave Ht........506 F2
rd. Belgrave S 506 F2
BARTOK
ct. Nar Warrn S.......552 G11
BARTOLO
ct. Cranbourne N 578 F9
BARTON
av. Ferntree Gly 464 J3
ct. Bundoora............284 J4
ct. Gladstone Pk 236 L19
ct. Vermont 421 F4
dr. Mt Eliza.............626 B14
mw. Berwick 554 H18
rd. Clayton S...........498 G4
st. Blairgowrie 679 J20
st. Dandenong N.....502 A19
st. Doncaster E 331 L17
st. Hawthorn...........371 F16
st. Mt Waverley 418 L14
st. Reservoir............282 H8
st. Sunbury 143 B13
st. Surrey Hills.........374 B15
st. W Footscray 366 G5
BARTRAM
ri. Viewbank...........329 J1
BARTROP
st. Reservoir...........282 B2
BARUNAH
ct. Narre Warren.....539 A13
st. Hadfield.............280 J5
BARWARRE
rd. Grovedale 706 J19
rd. Marshall 706 K12
rd. Marshall 706 J19
BARWISE
st. Laverton 407 E13
st. N Melbourne........34 H15
BARWON
av. Frankston 627 L5
av. Keilor.................276 L12
av. Reservoir............283 F13
av. Sunshine N.........321 A15
bvd. Highton 701 J12
ct. Clayton S............498 G9
ct. Croydon Hl 335 H14
ct. Donvale 332 L15
ct. Rowville..............463 A17
ct. Werribee.............447 J7
st. Box Hill N 374 H11
st. Glenroy..............279 L7
st. Mentone 531 F6
st. Taylors Hill.........274 J15
tce. S Geelong..........702 L14
BARWON HEADS
rd. Belmont.............702 J17
rd. Marshall 706 L1
BARYN
st. Ashwood 418 C13
st. Cheltenham 497 H18
BASALT
ct. Delahey 275 A15
BASANO
rt. Berwick 539 H18
BASIL
cl. Hallam...............538 D18
cr. Wheelers Hl.......461 E12
st. Bayswater..........423 B8
st. Dromana 686 E6
st. Fawkner.............281 G5
st. Malvern East......417 A18
st. Newport 410 E9
BASIN
ct. The Basin...........424 L8
BASINGSTOKE
rd. Mitcham 376 L9
BASIN-OLINDA
rd. Olinda...............426 C8
rd. Sassafras...........426 C8
rd. The Basin...........425 D10
BASS
av. Rosebud............700 E1
ct. Cranbourne N 577 K8
ct. Heathmont..........378 D18
ct. Melton S.............268 D11
ct. Mt Waverley 419 D12
ct. Sunbury 143 A12
ct. Taylors L 275 J3
ct. Wyndham Va 446 F8
pl. Endeavour Hl 537 G8
rd. Portsea..............677 G4
st. Box Hill.............374 J19
st. McCrae..............685 A16
st. Pascoe Vale 280 C16
BASSETT
rd. Melb Airport........234 G11
BASSETTS
rd. Doreen 156 E18
BASTINGS
ct. Epping...............197 K19
st. Northcote 326 J16
BASTOW
cl. Pakenham 584 D2
pl. Mulgrave 499 K1
pl. Richmond............26 C7
rd. Lilydale..............338 J6
BATAAN
ct. Lalor..................241 H6
BATABA
ct. Clarinda..............498 C8
st. Moorabbin..........496 C8
BATAVIA
av. Boronia..............424 F5

BATE
dr. Waterways.........532 K20
BATEMAN
cl. Derrimut............363 A8
ct. Coburg..............282 B19
gr. Hampton Pk.......551 E13
gr. Hampton Pk.......551 E14
rd. Kensington 33 B11
st. Attwood.............236 K12
st. Hampton 495 E7
st. Wantirna............422 B5
BATES
av. Thomastown......241 K14
av. Up Fntree Gly.....465 E7
ct. Jacana...............237 J20
ct. Sunbury 142 K3
dr. Williamstown.....410 L14
rd. Panton Hill.........204 C13
st. Cranbourne W ...577 G18
st. Malvern East......416 D20
BATESFORD
rd. Chadstone 417 L20
rd. Malvern East......457 J1
BATESLEIGH
rd. Selby.................467 D19
BATESON
rd. Wattle Glen........246 L8
BATEY
ct. Bulla..................189 G9
BATH
pl. Port Melb...........412 K5
pl. Williamstown.....411 E14
rd. Glen Iris.............417 G11
st. Abbotsford 20 F13
st. Blairgowrie 696 A4
st. Chelsea.............546 J18
st. Craigieburn........150 A16
st. Mornington.........640 H11
st. St Kilda..............414 E16
st. Sandringham 495 B13
wk. Nar Warrn S.......552 G20
BATHE
rd. Pakenham 557 H8
BATHURST
cl. Craigieburn........150 F11
st. Broadmeadows..237 J13
st. Mooroolbark......337 B19
BATMAN
av. Coburg..............281 F18
av. Hurstbridge 202 G13
av. Keilor Park.........277 J15
av. Melbourne...........24 L10
av. Melbourne...........25 A10
av. Mt Eliza.............642 F5
av. Sunbury 143 B12
cl. Belmont.............702 J19
ct. Vermont 421 F5
ct. Werribee.............447 E2
gr. Mulgrave 460 F20
rd. Eltham...............287 J5
rd. Port Melb...........412 B5
st. Aberfeldie 323 C8
st. Altona Mdw 451 G7
st. Fitzroy N..............19 C1
st. Footscray...........367 B8
st. W Melbourne.........1 A1
st. W Melbourne.......23 C5
wk. Greensbrgh........286 F3
BATSKOS
dr. Warrandyte........333 A4
BATTALION
ct. Boronia..............424 E3
BATTEN
pl. Aspendale Gdn...546 J5
rd. Marshall 706 L19
st. Glen Waverley....460 B4
st. St Albans...........320 C7
BATTERBEE
cr. Caroline Spr.......274 B8
dr. Mooroolbark......337 C10
BATTERSEA
la. Caroline Spr, off Grove Hall Pl......317 L3
st. Hadfield.............281 B8
BATTERY
rd. Panton Hill.........204 E15
BATTY
st. Wheelers Hl 461 C20
BAUDELAIRE
av. Wantirna............422 F10
BAULDERSTONE
wk. Kensington 33 E11
BAUM
cr. Highton 701 J16
BAUNTON
ct. Kilsyth S 424 K1
BAWDEN
cl. Watsonia N........243 H20
ct. Pascoe Vale 280 L12
st. Carrum Downs...574 K16
BAWKER
pl. Epping...............197 L19

BAXTER
av. Chelsea.............547 A15
cl. Gladstone Pk 237 C20
cr. Baxter................644 D2
ct. Chelsea..............547 A15
ct. Mt Waverley 418 K14
ct. Thomastown.......240 D13
dr. Braeside 532 G17
dr. Waurn Ponds.....705 C11
pl. S Melbourne........29 H5
st. Coburg..............325 G4
st. Elsternwick 455 D6
st. Eltham...............287 C15
st. Frankston 627 C1
st. Toorak...............415 C8
BAXTER-TOORADIN
rd. Baxter...............644 B1
rd. Blind Bight.........650 B1
rd. Cannons Creek...649 B3
rd. Devon Mdw 648 F4
rd. Frankston S 644 B1
rd. Langwarrin S 645 C3
rd. Langwarrin S 646 A3
rd. Pearcedale 645 C3
rd. Pearcedale 646 A3
rd. Warneet.............650 B1
BAY
av. Mt Eliza..............626 A12
ct. Gladstone Pk 236 L15
rd. Cheltenham 496 A16
rd. Mt Martha..........655 J15
rd. Mt Martha..........656 B16
rd. Sandringham 495 B15
st. Brighton 454 E13
st. Brighton 455 A14
st. Mordialloc 531 H17
st. Parkdale 531 H17
st. Port Melb 29 A7
st. Port Melb...........412 K6
st. Port Melb...........413 A3
st. Queenscliff.........709 C16
st. Tecoma 466 E8
st.s, Frankston 627 A1
BAYARD
dr. Pakenham Up 559 C1
BAYBREEZE
ct. Rosebud W........699 E3
BAYFIELD
ct. Mt Martha..........656 J5
dr. Eltham...............288 C3
rd.e, Bayswater N 380 A16
rd.w, Bayswater N 379 J16
BAYLES
ct. Donvale 332 L15
st. Parkville..............17 H9
BAYLEY
cl. Heathmont..........422 H1
gr. Doncaster..........330 J20
gr. Doncaster..........374 J1
st. Geelong.............703 A6
BAYLIE
pl. Geelong, off Myers St...........703 A9
BAYLISS
av. Hoppers Csg......448 K1
ct. Berwick 553 K3
ct. Cheltenham 531 D3
ct. Pearcedale 646 L2
pl. Vermont 421 B6
rd. Deer Park..........318 J17
rd. Lyndhurst..........550 G15
rd. Lyndhurst..........551 A16
st. Cheltenham 531 D3
st. Preston..............282 G17
BAYLON
st. Bentleigh 496 E4
BAY MEADOW
grn. Craigieburn........193 J1
BAYNES PARK
rd. Monbulk 427 L19
BAYNTON
av. Sunshine N........321 A13
cr. Roxburgh Pk......193 L12
st. Oakleigh E 458 H12
BAYONNE
cl. Greensbrgh........244 G15
BAYPORT
dr. Langwarrin 629 E7
BAY RISE
dr. Mornington........656 H2
BAYSIDE
av. Edithvale............546 J14
av. Port Melb...........368 A18
cr. Hampton 495 B11
BAYSTONE
ct. Mt Martha..........656 H8
dr. Cranbourne........604 B5
pl. Kurunjang...........227 E7
pl. Lilydale..............294 B20
rd. Epping...............198 C20
BAYSWATER
rd. Bayswater..........423 J1
rd. Bayswater N 379 H17

rd. Bayswater N 423 J1
rd. Croydon 379 J9
rd. Croydon S 379 H17
rd. Kensington 33 E10
rd. Newtown 702 C11
BAY VIEW
rd. Seddon 367 A14
rd. Yarraville 367 A14
st. Elwood 414 D20
BAYVIEW
av. Aspendale 546 B4
av. Clayton 459 A14
av. Hawthorn E 372 E15
av. Rosebud 700 F4
av. Upwey 465 J13
cr. Black Rock 529 E2
cr. Hoppers Csg 449 B2
cr. The Basin 425 A13
cr. Tremont 425 C13
ct. Highton 701 D15
la. Aspendale, off Bayview Av 546 B4
rd. Beaumaris 530 C6
rd. Belgrave 466 H13
rd. Brighton East 455 H14
rd. Emerald 509 C4
rd. Frankston 627 C5
rd. Glenroy 280 C8
rd. McCrae 685 A14
rd. Mornington 640 F20
rd. Officer 556 E19
rd. Rosebud 700 E2
rd. Tooradin 651 E7
st. Altona 409 E20
st. Bentleigh E 456 K15
st. Elsternwick 455 C3
st. Northcote 326 J17
st. Prahran 32 L20
st. Prahran 414 L10
st. Prahran 415 A10
st. Williamstown 411 A18
tce. Ascot Vale 324 B16
tce. Kalorama 382 L12
tr. Lysterfield S 503 E13
BAYVILLE
dr. Dingley Vill 532 L9
BAYVISTA
ri. Somerville 644 L19
ri. Somerville 645 A19
BAZENTIN
st. Albion 320 K19
BEACH
av. Blairgowrie 679 E20
av. Elwood 454 E5
av. Mordialloc 532 D20
cl. Pt Lonsdale 707 J20
ct. Keysborough 534 C11
gr. Mentone 530 L10
gr. Mentone 531 A10
gr. Mornington 640 D15
gr. Seaford 573 C19
rd. Beaumaris 529 F6
rd. Black Rock 495 D19
rd. Hampton 494 K8
rd. Mentone 530 K10
rd. Mordialloc 531 D13
rd. Parkdale 531 D13
rd. Sandringham 494 L12
rd. Sandringham 495 A12
rd. Torquay 711 J7
st. Dromana 686 C4
st. Frankston 599 A17
st. Frankston 599 C18
st. Port Melb 412 E5
st. Queenscliff 709 C16
st. Seaholme 409 H18
BEACHCOMBER
ct. Patterson L 573 F9
pl. Point Cook 450 L13
BEACHLEY
st. Braybrook 365 K6
BEACHURST
av. Dromana 686 G4
BEACH VIEW
cr. Torquay 711 H11
BEACHWOOD
cl. Cheltenham 496 J13
dr. Pt Lonsdale 710 E1
BEACON
av. Point Cook 449 L6
ct. Templstw Lr 330 K10
dr. Langwarrin 601 K18
la. Caroline Spr 317 L2
rd. Port Melb 412 E5
st. Glen Waverley 460 C4
st. Parkdale 531 H11
st. Vermont S 420 J10
BEACONHILL
dr. Beaconsfield 555 G16
BEACON HILLS
cr. Craigieburn 150 C15
BEACONSFIELD
av. Beaconsfield 555 B16
av. Frankston 627 H4
la. Albert Park 29 B16
pde. Albert Park 29 A15
pde. Albert Park 412 L8
pde. Albert Park 413 B9
pde. Middle Park 29 A15
pde. Middle Park 413 J13
pde. Northcote 326 E11
pde. Port Melb 412 L8
pde. St Kilda W 413 J13
rd. Briar Hill 286 F5
rd. Hawthorn E 416 E1
st. Doncaster 374 J1
BEACONSFIELD-EMERALD
rd. Beaconsfield 555 B11
rd. Beaconsfld Up 542 B17
rd. Dewhurst 510 C18
rd. Emerald 509 G3
rd. Emerald 510 C18
rd. Guys Hill 555 B11
BEACON VISTA
Port Melb 412 F5
BEAGLE
st. Epping 197 G13
BEAGLEY
st. Kallista 427 A20
BEAL
pl. Mornington 656 J3
st. Mt Waverley 419 F19
BEALE
ct. Templestowe 331 D7
pl. Sunshine N 321 C8
BEALES
la. Greensbrgh 244 J17
la. St Helena 244 J17
st. Newtown 702 H10
st. Torquay 711 L10
BEALIBA
rd. Caulfield S 455 K8
BEAMISH
ct. Altona Mdw 451 F7
st. Werribee 447 J16
BEAMOND
cl. Langwarrin S 628 K17
BEAMSLEY
st. Malvern 416 A8
BEAN
ct. Keilor Dn 276 B16
ct. Mill Park 243 A2
ct. Whittington 704 D19
dr. Hurstbridge 246 F1
dr. Wattle Glen 202 F20
st. Geelong 703 C11
BEANEY
la. Melbourne 2 K16
la. Melbourne 24 G8
BEAR
st. Mordialloc 531 K19
BEARD
ct. Heathmont 378 G19
pl. Carlton 18 F15
st. Eltham 288 A6
BEARDSWORTH
av. Chelsea 547 A17
BEASLEY
av. Werribee 447 G13
BEATRICE
av. Aberfeldie 323 B8
av. Heidelberg W 284 E16
av. Surrey Hills 374 B18
ct. Blackburn 376 C20
pl. Ferntree Gly 464 C7
st. Chadstone 418 E19
st. Cheltenham 497 G18
st. Glen Iris 417 G10
st. Kew 371 J9
st. Kilsyth 381 D5
st. Melbourne 31 C17
st. Melbourne 414 B9
st. Noble Park 535 B7
st. Preston 283 G19
st. Yarraville 367 A17
BEATRIX
st. Greensbrgh 286 D7
BEATTIE
st. Montmorency 286 G10
BEATTY
av. Armadale 415 D9
av. Glenroy 280 C5
cr. Ashburton 417 D17
cr. Ormond 456 B10
pde. Cockatoo 511 C3
pde. Mornington 640 H14
st. Ivanhoe 327 K9
st. Mont Albert 374 D14
st. Reservoir 282 F15
BEATTYS
rd. Hillside 273 B5
rd. Plumpton 273 B5
rd. Rockbank 270 C7
BEAU
pl. Pt Lonsdale 707 G17
BEAUCHAMP
st. Preston 282 L19
BEAUFORD
av. Nar Warrn S 579 G4
st. Huntingdale 458 E14
BEAUFORT
ct. Ashburton 417 J16
rd. Croydon 379 D4
rd. Ringwood E 379 D4
ri. Warrandyte 332 L5
st. Mitcham 377 D8
st. Mt Waverley 419 C17
st. Point Cook 450 A5
st. Preston 327 H7
BEAULIEU
av. Lilydale 338 C15
av. Mooroolbark 338 C15
BEAUMARIS
pde. Highett 496 B16
BEAUMONDE
st. Coburg 326 A7
BEAUMONT
cr. Frankston 600 E17
cr. Lalor 241 K6
ct. Montrose 382 D8
ct. Pakenham 584 E6
ct. Sydenham 274 J1
dr. Point Cook 450 E5
pde. W Footscray 366 E12
pl. Wheelers Hl 461 A8
rd. Berwick 554 G4
st. Canterbury 373 B17
st. Olinda 426 K11
st. Sandringham 495 B13
st. Vermont 421 D3
st. Watsonia 285 C8
BEAUNA VISTA
dr. Rye 697 K5
BEAUTEX
ct. Aspendale Gdn 546 G4
BEAUTY GULLY
rd. Warrandyte 333 H6
BEAUTY POINT
rd. Research 289 B10
BEAUVIEW
pde. Ivanhoe East 328 H14
BEAUVILLE
av. Murrumbeena 457 A12
BEAU VORNO
av. Keysborough 534 B11
BEAVEN
av. Malvern 416 A9
BEAVER
ct. Wheelers Hl 460 J11
pl. Point Cook 450 A7
st. Aberfeldie 323 F10
st. Box Hill S 419 B2
st. Malvern East 416 C18
st. St Albans 320 D6
BEAVERS
rd. Northcote 326 D12
BEAVIS
ct. Berwick 554 L8
ct. Templestowe 331 K14
st. Elsternwick 455 B5
BEBINGTON
cl. Ringwood 335 B19
BEBS
ct. Templestowe 331 K8
BECALL
cl. Epping 198 C14
BECCIA
av. Epping 198 F20
BECCIE
ct. Ferntree Gly 464 C6
BECCLES
ct. St Albans 320 E6
st. Fawkner 281 K2
BECK
ct. Noble Park 501 C20
rd. Plenty 244 F9
st. Blackburn 375 E19
st. Keilor Park 278 B14
BECKBURY
ct. Rowville 463 K17
BECKENHAM
dr. Ferntree Gly 463 E3
pl. Langwarrin 629 D5
BECKER
cl. Melton W 225 K18
BECKET
av. Bentleigh E 496 H1
st. Glenroy 279 K2
st. Glenroy 279 K4
st. Rye 696 D4
st.n, Glenroy 279 K2
BECKETT
av. Keilor East 278 A18
cr. Caroline Spr 274 D17
ct. Lower Plenty 287 B17
rd. Donvale 377 G8
st. Balwyn 373 K10
st. Chadstone 458 A3
BECKINGTON
cr. Hampton Pk 551 F6
pl. Craigieburn 194 E1
BECKLEY
st. Coburg 326 A5
st. Herne Hill 701 H1
BECKWITH
ct. Taylors L 275 G7
gr. Seaford 599 C2
st. Coburg 325 G1
BEDDOE
av. Bentleigh E 457 B19
av. Brighton East 455 F16
av. Clayton 459 B16
rd. Vermont 421 G2
st. Research 288 H4
BEDDOWS
st. Burwood 418 H10
BEDE
av. Coldstream 295 F15
ct. Gladstone Pk 237 C17
BEDERVALE
dr. Templestowe 331 L7
BEDFORD
av. Surrey Hills 374 A17
ct. Endeavour Hl 536 L2
ct. Heathmont 378 L15
ct. Heidelberg 329 G2
ct. Hoppers Csg 448 K7
ct. Templstw Lr 330 G11
pl. Mornington 656 F1
pl. N Melbourne 17 H16
rd. Cockatoo 471 K8
rd. Heathmont 378 L14
rd. Ringwood 378 F13
rd. Ringwood E 378 L14
rd. Ringwood E 379 A15
st. Airport W 278 G13
st. Box Hill 375 B19
st. Collingwood 19 G15
st. Hadfield 281 A8
st. N Melbourne 17 H17
st. Reservoir 283 A11
BEDGGOOD
av. Pt Lonsdale 710 F2
dr. Wesburn 348 E19
BEDINGHAM
dr. Hillside 274 D1
BEDSER
st. Sunshine N 321 G14
BEDWELL
av. Dandenong 535 L3
ct. Endeavour Hl 537 L4
st. Reservoir 240 E20
BEE
ct. Craigieburn 150 H18
BEECH
av. Selby 466 L18
av. Selby 467 A18
ct. Boronia 424 D16
ct. Campbellfield 239 G13
ct. Greensbrgh 244 K20
ct. Greensbrgh 286 K1
ct. Sunshine W 364 K6
pl. Hallam 552 C2
st. Bentleigh 455 K17
st. Camberwell 417 G5
st. Caulfield S 455 G8
st. Kilsyth 381 L7
st. Langwarrin 628 K3
st. McKinnon 455 K17
st. Malvern East 456 J1
st. Nunawading 376 L20
st. Surrey Hills 418 E2
st. Thomastown 241 D14
BEECHER
st. Preston 327 G7
BEECHWOOD
cl. Doncaster E 332 E6
tce. Ashwood 418 C15
tce. Glenroy 281 D4
BEECROFT
cr. Templestowe 331 G13
dr. Westmeadows 236 H13
BEELA
cl. Greensbrgh 244 C20
cl. Greensbrgh 286 C1
ct. Sunshine W 364 F6
BEENA
av. Carnegie 456 L6
ct. Glen Waverley 460 G12
BEENAK
av. Brighton East 495 F1
ct. Doncaster E 332 C19
ct. Forest Hill 420 F4
rd. Seville 385 L2
rd. Seville E 387 A6
rd. Wandin East 341 A17
rd. Wandin East 385 L2
st. Reservoir 283 G7
BEERS
ct. St Albans 320 E13
BEESLEY
pl. Gladstone Pk 237
BEE TENG
ct. Aspendale Gdn 546
BEETHAM
pde. Rosanna 328
BEETHOVEN
ct. Bundoora 242
ct. Mt Martha 656
dr. Nar Warrn S 578
BEEVERS
st. Altona North 365
st. Footscray 367
BEEWAR
st. Greensbrgh 285
BEGA
ct. Aspendale 546
ct. Gladstone Pk 278
ct. Gladstone Pk 279
ct. Lalor 240
ct. Lalor 241
ct. Mulgrave 500
ct. Ringwood 379
st. Chadstone 458
BEGG
st. Oakleigh S 497
BEGGS
pl. Rowville 503
BEGONIA
av. Altona North 410
av. Bayswater 423
av. Bayswater 423
ct. Blackburn N 375
ct. Endeavour Hl 537
ct. Lalor 240
ct. Newcomb 704
rd. Gardenvale 455
st. Box Hill S 418
st. Dromana 686
wy. Nar Warrn S 579
BEILBY
cl. Up Fntree Gly 464
st. Bayswater 423
st. Moorabbin 496
BEISSEL
st. Richmond 26
st. Richmond 371
BEITH
st. Brunswick 325
BELAH
av. Altona 452
pl. Endeavour Hl 536
st. Thomastown 241
BELAIR
av. Endeavour Hl 502
av. Endeavour Hl 503
av. Glenroy 279
cl. Seville 341
ct. Bundoora 284
ct. Taylors L 276
ct. Wyndham Va 446
BELALIE
cl. Hampton Pk 552
BELANDRA
dr. Wheelers Hl 460
BELAR
av. Frankston 600
ct. Ferntree Gly 463
ct. Meadow Ht 193
rd. Tootgarook 698
BELBIN
ct. Mill Park 242
BELBROOK
rd. Upwey 465
BELCHER
arc. Geelong, off Little Ryrie St 703
BELCHESTER
av. Coldstream 295
BELDALE
av. Werribee 446
ct. Berwick 539
ct. Berwick 553
BELDARRY
ct. Mt Martha 657
BELEURA
av. Vermont 421
ct. Taylors L 275
ct. Wantirna 422
gr. Clayton 458
gr. Lower Plenty 286
wy. Seabrook 451
BELEURA HILL
rd. Mornington 640
BELFAST
rd. Brunswick 325
rd. Montrose 382
rd. Mooroolbark 382
st. Broadmeadows 238
st. Newtown 702
BELFIELDS
rd. Cottles Br 204

BENMORE
pl. Wantirna 422 K6
BENNET
st. Dandenong 535 F9
BENNETT
av. Belgrave 466 G11
av. Heathmont 378 L20
av. Mt Waverley 419 H13
ct. Noble Park 534 L7
ct. Seaford 573 H19
ct. Sunbury 142 H12
ct. Fitzroy N, off Bennett St 326 E19
pde. Kew East 372 J7
pl. Sunshine 365 C2
st. Alphington 327 J16
st. Bacchus Msh 222 B16
st. Balwyn 372 L11
st. Balwyn 373 A11
st. Boronia 424 G12
st. Burwood 418 H10
st. Fitzroy N 326 E20
st. Forest Hill 420 B3
st. Highton 701 H17
st. Melton S 268 H11
st. Richmond 26 L6
st. Richmond 371 A13
st. Sunshine W 364 H10
BENNETTS
la. Melbourne 2 L6
la. Melbourne 24 F3
rd. Mornington 640 J18
BEN NEVIS
gr. Bulleen 329 F16
BENNIE
st. Brunswick 325 H13
BENNISON
st. Croydon 380 F6
BENNY
pl. Berwick 554 A19
BENO
ct. Thomastown 241 L12
BENONG
pl. Frankston 600 F20
BENOR
ct. Pakenham 584 G1
BENSAM
cl. Rowville 463 E12
BENSON
av. Toorak 415 J8
ct. Narre Warren 539 E18
dr. Yering 252 E20
dr. Yering 294 E1
la. Melbourne 24 H7
st. Belgrave 466 E15
st. Coburg 325 G5
st. Emerald 509 E4
st. Richmond 26 J15
st. Surrey Hills 373 J15
st. Geelong, off Myers St 703 B10
BENSTON
st. Craigieburn 150 H19
BENT
av. Brighton 454 H6
ct. Wantirna S 423 A13
pde. Black Rock 529 E2
rd. Wandana Ht 701 D19
st. Altona 409 D20
st. Bentleigh 456 B18
st. Blackburn 375 H12
st. Brighton 455 B16
st. Brunswick W 324 K11
st. Bundoora 284 H1
st. Caulfield S 455 L8
st. Cremorne 32 A1
st. Cremorne 414 F1
st. Elsternwick 454 K3
st. Kensington 34 D11
st. Malvern East 416 F20
st. Moonee Pnd 324 D11
st. Northcote 326 E12
st. St Albans 320 C10
st. Westmeadows 236 K14
BENTICK
st. Frankston 626 K3
BENTLEY
av. Dandenong N 501 H20
av. Roxburgh Pk 194 B7
cr. Hoppers Csg 448 F3
ct. Mulgrave 500 G2
ct. Warranwood 334 J14
ct. Watsonia N 243 F20
pl. Frankston 627 B4
rd. McCrae 684 H18
st. Surrey Hills 374 E20
st. Wantirna 422 G7
st. Williamstn N 410 C12
wy. Mill Park 243 A2
BENTLY
la. Ringwood 378 E12

BENTON
av. Seaford 599 C11
ct. Doncaster 331 B18
rd. Healesville 214 B17
wy. Taylors L 275 G5
BENTON GRANGE
dr. Mornington 657 E7
BENTONS
rd. Moorooduc 657 H8
rd. Mornington 656 G5
rd. Mornington 657 A6
rd. Mt Martha 656 C4
rd. Mt Martha 656 G5
BENWERREN
la. Yarra Jctn 347 F14
BENWERRIN
dr. Burwood E 419 F10
dr. Wantirna 422 B14
rd. Surrey Hills 374 D18
BENZ
cl. Mill Park 242 L2
cl. Mill Park 243 A2
ct. Keilor Dn 276 B14
BERALA
ct. Keysborough 534 E8
ct. Ringwood 335 B20
pl. Mill Park 242 E1
BERBERIS
cr. Frankston 600 B17
pl. Hoppers Csg 405 E16
BEREA
ct. Ringwood 378 G6
BEREAN
pl. Sorrento 679 B15
BEREMBONG
dr. Keilor East 278 B19
BEREND
st. Hampton E 495 L9
BERENDS
dr. Dandenong S 549 F8
BERENICE
tce. Toorak 415 B3
BERESFORD
cl. Doncaster E 331 H15
cr. Darley 222 C11
cr. Gladstone Pk 237 B17
dr. Boronia 424 J3
rd. Lilydale 338 A3
st. Caulfield N 415 E17
st. Kew East 372 C5
st. Mont Albert 374 B16
st. Pascoe Vale S 324 H6
BERGAMOT
pl. Berwick 580 B3
BERGEN
cl. Keilor Ldg 276 A3
st. Keysborough 534 K13
BERGER
st. Dallas 238 H10
BERGINS
rd. Rowville 502 H4
BERGLUND
rd. Beaconsfld Up 558 B1
rd. Pakenham Up 558 B1
BERGMAN
rd. Langwarrin 629 G15
BERGNER
ct. Lysterfield 464 D19
BERINGA
av. Grovedale 705 L15
BERKEFELD
ct. Cheltenham 497 B20
ct. Templestowe 331 H10
BERKELEY
av. Heidelberg 329 E4
av. Point Cook 450 H8
cl. Broadmeadows 238 J12
cr. Altona North 409 J9
ct. Kew 371 E10
ct. Mt Eliza 626 F16
ct. Seabrook 450 L3
gr. Brighton East 455 E16
st. Carlton 17 K16
st. Doncaster 331 A20
st. Hawthorn 372 A20
st. Hawthorn 416 A3
st. Huntingdale 458 E14
st. Melbourne 17 K16
BERKERLEY
ct. Watsonia N 243 F20
BERKLEY
ct. Endeavour Hl 537 B2
ct. Glen Waverley 460 C3
ct. Greenvale 237 B6
pl. Chirnside Pk 337 K3
pl. Melton W 226 D15
rd. Ringwood 379 A2
ri. S Morang 198 L8
st. Wantirna S 422 L14
st. Wantirna S 423 A14

BERKSHIRE
av. Cranbourne 603 E8
pl. Nar Warrn S 579 A3
rd. Sunshine N 321 D13
BERL
ct. Blackburn S 419 H2
BERMER
ct. Nar Warrn S 552 E17
BERMUDA
ct. Oakleigh S 497 G1
dr. Blackburn S 419 J6
BERNADETTE
ct. Doncaster E 332 H8
BERNARD
cr. Bundoora 285 B1
ct. Keilor East 278 E20
ct. Nar Warrn S 552 H16
ct. Somerville 645 C17
dr. Melton S 268 G5
rd. Rye 696 E9
st. Balwyn N 373 E1
st. Bayswater 423 B7
st. Cheltenham 496 L15
st. Maidstone 366 D3
st. Mt Waverley 458 J5
st. Reservoir 283 A11
st. Spotswood 411 C2
BERNARD HAMILTON
wy. Rowville 462 L20
wy. Rowville 463 A20
BERNARRA
ct. Donvale 333 B11
BERNAY
ct. Springvale S 499 J20
BERNBANKS
av. St Albans 320 J4
BERNBOROUGH
av. Balwyn 373 C8
av. Cranbourne W 577 F18
ct. Bacchus Msh 221 G18
ct. Keilor Dn 275 L13
pl. Mill Park 242 J10
BERNHARDT
av. Hoppers Csg 448 H9
BERNICE
ct. Coburg N 282 B18
st. Doncaster 330 C15
BERRABRI
dr. Scoresby 462 A6
BERRAMONGO
ct. Belmont 706 G2
BERRIDALE
ct. Hampton Pk 551 E11
BERRIE
rd. Gisborne S 141 A1
BERRIGAN
ct. Oakleigh S 498 A8
ct. Werribee 447 J8
BERRIMA
av. Malvern East 456 L3
cl. Craigieburn 150 G10
rd. Donvale 332 K20
rd. Rosanna 329 B2
st. Oakleigh E 458 L11
BERRINGA
ct. Bundoora 243 A20
ct. Meadow Ht 238 C4
rd. Pk Orchards 334 C20
rd. Ringwood N 378 C2
st. Frankston 599 L18
st. Parkdale 531 J9
BERRY
av. Edithvale 546 J15
av. Mitcham 377 E15
av. Somerton 194 G11
cl. Mornington 640 K16
ct. Doveton 536 J8
ct. Highton 705 H3
ct. Keysborough 534 F13
ct. Lilydale 338 J1
ct. Mill Park 242 E9
ct. Safety Bch 669 C11
la. Dandenong 535 K7
rd. Bayswater N 379 G15
rd. Silvan 384 F7
st. Box Hill N 374 J9
st. Clifton Hill 20 E3
st. Coburg 325 D4
st. E Melbourne 25 K11
st. Essendon N 323 G2
st. Fawkner 281 H10
st. Richmond 26 F11
st. Sunshine N 321 C13
st. Yarraville 367 D13
BERRYDALE
ct. Notting Hill 459 K14
rd. Sunbury 144 D7
BERRYS
rd. Emerald 509 D2
BERRYWOOD
wk. Warranwood 335 C16
BERTHA
st. Springvale 499 F16

BERTHANDRA
ct. W Footscray 366 D7
BERTHON
cr. Hillside 232 F18
BERTIE
st. Port Melb 368 H20
BERTRAM
rd. Bayswater 423 J7
st. Elsternwick 455 C10
st. Glen Iris 417 G10
st. Mordialloc 532 A19
BERTRAND
av. Mulgrave 500 K6
cl. Berwick 553 K5
ct. Craigieburn 150 H14
rd. Chelsea 546 L17
BERTY
st. Newport 410 G10
BERWEN
st. Chelsea 546 H16
BERWICK
cl. Frankston 600 G19
ct. Sunshine W 364 L5
pl. Greenvale 193 C20
pl. Melton W 226 D15
rd. Campbellfield 239 D11
rd. Nar Warrn E 506 K17
ri. Templestowe 331 G14
st. Brighton 454 J13
st. Camberwell 372 J18
st. Lilydale 338 F6
st. Reservoir 282 K13
BERWICK-CRANBOURNE
rd. Clyde North 579 L19
rd. Cranbourne 579 L19
rd. Cranbourne E 604 H5
rd. Cranbourne N 579 L19
BERWICK SPRINGS
prm. Nar Warrn S 579 F3
BERWYN
cr. Templestowe 331 H11
BERYL
av. Oakleigh S 457 K20
cl. Greensbrgh 244 B17
ct. Clarinda 498 C12
ct. Narre Warren 539 F14
ct. Rye 697 A12
ct. Skye 575 H15
pl. Rye 696 H10
st. Croydon 380 E3
st. Essendon W 322 L6
st. Glen Iris 417 H10
st. Nunawading 376 H10
BESANKO
cl. Mordialloc 532 D18
BESANT
st. Hampton E 495 L10
BESGROVE
st. Rosebud 699 K2
BESLEY
st. Dandenong 536 E9
BESS
ct. Dandenong 536 E7
BESSA
ct. Wonga Park 291 J16
BESSAZILE
av. Forest Hill 376 E20
BESSELL
ct. Jacana 237 K18
BESSEMER
rd. Bayswater N 380 H14
st. Springvale 499 L10
BESSIE
st. Oakleigh S 497 G2
BESSIE CREEK
rd. Gembrook 512 K20
BESSIERE
pl. St Kilda 414 A16
BEST
cl. Epping 241 K4
st. Belgrave 466 D16
st. Fitzroy N 19 E1
st. Fitzroy N 326 C20
st. Oakleigh 457 L15
st. Reservoir 282 G9
st. Ringwood 378 G13
BESWICK
st. Clayton S 499 F9
st. Deer Park 318 K17
BESWICKE
ct. Dandenong S 535 H14
BETCHWORTH
cl. Caroline Spr, off Great Barr Cr 317 J3
BETH
ct. Hampton Pk 552 A9
ct. Rosebud 684 H17
BETHANGA
ct. Taylors L 276 D7
st. Mt Eliza 641 J1
BETHANY
cl. Rye 697 L9
ct. S Morang 199 J19

BETHEL
cl. Nar Warrn N 539
BETHELA
st. Camberwell 417
BETHELL
av. Parkdale 531
st. Ormond 455
BETHELLE
ct. Rowville 463
BETHS
st. Bentleigh 456
BETHUNE
ct. Seaford 573
rd. Gruyere 342
rd.w, Gruyere 342
st. Hawthorn E 416
st. Queenscliff 708
BETHWYN
st. Bentleigh E 456
BETLEIGH
st. Anglesea 713
BETSON
ct. Kealba 276
BETTER BOY
ct. Skye 575
BETTINA
ct. Ascot Vale 323
ct. Berwick 554
ct. Templstw Lr 330
st. Burwood E 419
st. Clayton 459
BETTON
cr. Warrandyte 333
BETTS
wy. Burwood E 420
BETTSONS
ct. Whittington 703
BETTY
av. Mt Eliza 626
cl. Rowville 463
ct. Mt Waverley 459
st. Bulleen 329
st. Rye 696
BETULA
av. Bundoora 242
av. Bundoora 242
av. Mill Park 242
av. Nunawading 376
av. Vermont 376
av. Vermont 420
ri. Hoppers Csg 405
st. Doveton 536
tce. Sunbury 143
BEULAH
st. Broadmeadows 238
BEURON
rd. Altona North 409
BEVAN
av. Clayton S 499
ct. Pakenham 584
st. Albert Park 29
st. Albert Park 413
st. Balwyn 373
st. Ormond 455
BEVERAGE
dr. Tullamarine 278
BEVERIDGE
ct. Point Cook 450
st. Warrandyte 289
BEVERLEY
cl. Frankston 599
cr. Blackburn 375
ct. Balwyn N 374
ct. Heathmont 379
ct. Hoppers Csg 405
ct. Langwarrin 601
dr. Healesville 213
gr. Mt Waverley 458
pl. Keysborough 534
rd. Heidelberg 329
rd. McCrae 685
rd. Rosanna 329
st. Cheltenham 530
st. Doncaster E 375
st. Dromana 686
st. Glen Huntly 456
st. Kings Park 275
st. Scoresby 462
st. Yarraville 367
BEVERLY
ct. Narre Warren 553
BEVERLY HILLS
dr. Templestowe 332
BEVERSTONE
pl. Werribee 446
BEVINGTON
ct. Highton 701
BEVIS
st. Bentleigh E 456
st. Mulgrave 500
BEVNOL
rd. Langwarrin 629

WDLEY
Ormond 456 F14
WLEY
/. Berwick 553 H14
WSELL
Scoresby 462 E7
KLEY
Werribee 446 K11
Footscray 367 D9
KSARM
Rowville 463 B14
ZZELL
Brunswick 325 G14
ANGOO
Sydenham 274 J4
K
Keilor Park 277 L13
Croydon N 335 L15
LA
Mooroolbark 337 D11
NCA
Mornington 656 J1
Rowville 503 A4
Aspendale Gdn 546 H4
NCHI
Mill Park 242 K1
Keilor Dn 276 A16
NCO
Cranbourne N 577 L6
Langwarrin 629 D3
ARRITZ
Beaumaris 530 F4
Frankston 628 D12
ASIN
Brookfield 268 B5
BY
Albanvale 319 B3
Moorabbin 497 B10
LE
Eltham 287 H12
Ripponlea 454 J3
URY
Kilsyth S 424 L1
CENTENNIAL
Meadow Ht 194 B17
Doncaster E 332 K14
CKERTON
Rowville 502 G1
/. Roxburgh Pk 193 J13
CKFORD
Tullamarine 278 K1
Beaumaris 530 G6
Hallam 537 F15
Grovedale 706 A17
CKHAM
St Kilda E 414 L18
CKLEIGH
Croydon Hl 335 E17
Glen Iris 416 H9
Glen Iris 416 G9
CKLEIGH-VALE
Mooroolbark 381 H1
CKLEY
Thomastown 241 K14
Thomastown 242 A12
Sunshine W 365 B9
CKNELL
Broadmeadows 237 L20
Broadmeadows 280 A1
TON
Greensbrgh 286 E5
Mt Waverley 419 C17
DDICK
Werribee 448 A12
DEY
Prahran 414 L12
Prahran 415 A12
DGEE
Frankston 628 B1
DSTON
Ringwood 335 A19
ENIAS
Tootgarook 698 D8
ESKE
Grovedale 706 D16
GELOW
Rye 696 K3
GGS
St Albans 320 B1
GMORE
Geelong West 702 G6
GNELL
Roxburgh Pk 194 B12
Bentleigh E 497 C5
Moorabbin 497 B10
Flemington 34 C1
Flemington 324 G20
Pascoe Vale 280 K18
OLA
Ringwood 378 H7
PATS CREEK
E Warburton 350 K2

BILBUL
av. Rosebud 700 K7
BILBUNGRA
dr. Keysborough 534 C9
BILBY
la. Highton 701 H10
st. Templstw Lr 330 F10
BILGOLA
ct. Mt Eliza 642 A7
BILL
pl. Hampton Pk 552 D12
BILLABONG
cl. Croydon Hl 335 F13
cl. Mornington 656 K2
ct. Burnside 318 H6
ct. Greensbrgh 244 K15
ct. Wantirna S 421 L18
BILLANOOK
wy. Chirnside Pk 336 H7
BILLARA
cl. Wantirna S 422 L10
cl. Wantirna S 423 A10
BILLAROY
rd. Beaconsfld Up 541 H2
BILLING
pl. Brookfield 267 K10
st. Mt Waverley 458 J1
st. Springvale 500 A18
BILLINGHAM
rd. Deer Park 319 B11
BILLINGSLEYS
rd. Tooradin 652 F9
BILLS
st. Hawthorn 416 B4
tr. Kangaroo Grnd 249 A9
tr. Watsons Ck 249 A9
BILLSON
st. Brighton East 455 D20
BILLUNGAH
pl. Burnside 318 G8
BILLY TEA
ct. Greensbrgh 244 K16
BILOCLA
av. Cockatoo 471 H17
BILSTON
ct. Highton 705 G6
st. Seddon 367 D10
BILTRIS
ct. Jacana 237 J19
BIMBADEEN
cr. Yallambie 286 B13
ct. Bayswater 423 B9
ct. Wheelers Hl 460 J8
dr. Mooroolbark 337 E13
st. Burnside 318 G7
BIMBI
ct. Mooroolbark 337 D13
st. Clayton 499 C2
BIMBIANG
cr. Rye 696 L3
cr. Rye 697 A3
BIMBLE
st. Rye 697 H3
BINALONG
av. Chadstone 418 C20
ct. Burnside 318 F6
ct. Grovedale 705 K12
ct. St Albans 320 L6
ct. St Albans 321 A6
ct. Yallambie 286 B12
BINBROOK
ct. Highton 705 K6
dr. Croydon 335 F18
BINDA
ct. Patterson L 573 K7
BINDEA
rd. Yellingbo 388 C13
BINDI
cl. Frankston 600 D17
cl. Hallam 538 B20
cl. Springvale S 499 H19
cl. Templestowe 332 A13
st. Glenroy 280 C1
st. Wantirna S 422 L13
BINDING
av. Cranbourne 604 C3
BINDTS
rd. Wollert 198 A9
BINDY
st. Blackburn S 420 A4
st. Forest Hill 420 A4
BINGHAM
ct. Bundoora 284 L2
BINGIN
pl. Craigieburn 150 H14
BINGLEY
av. Hurstbridge 202 H9
av. Notting Hill 459 J13
pde. Anglesea 713 H2
BINGO
st. Preston 327 E5

BINNAK
ct. Meadow Ht 194 D19
dr. Watsonia N 243 E19
wy. Moorooduc 643 H11
BINNIE
st. Brighton East 495 B2
BINNS
st. Altona North 409 E2
st. Montmorency 286 J9
BINOWEE
av. Yallambie 286 C14
BINYA
ct. Dandenong N 501 F14
ct. Sunshine W 364 E7
BIOLOGY
dr. Bundoora, off Science Dr 284 C11
BIRALEE
ct. Berwick 554 G11
BIRAN
ct. Reservoir 283 C8
BIRBANK
ct. Doncaster 331 B14
BIRCH
av. Dandenong N 501 H18
av. Emerald 509 B6
av. Tullamarine 278 J6
ct. Bangholme 549 H13
ct. Campbellfield 239 F13
ct. Craigieburn 150 C13
ct. Grovedale 706 B16
ct. Langwarrin 629 J1
ct. Mill Park 242 D9
ct. Narre Warren 553 G9
ct. Pascoe Vale 280 L10
ct. Wyndham Va 446 F10
ct. Wyndham Va 446 F9
gr. Frankston 600 C18
la. Kensington 33 E9
rd. Wonga Park 336 D6
sq. Richmond 371 A15
st. Bayswater 423 E6
st. Caulfield S 455 G8
st. Mentone 530 K7
st. Mt Waverley 419 B16
st. Preston 326 C3
st. Springvale 499 J8
BIRCHBANK
cl. Lysterfield S 503 L15
BIRCHFIELD
cr. Wantirna 422 G13
ct. Narre Warren 538 J14
BIRCHGROVE
cr. Templestowe 331 F14
BIRCHMORE
ct. Taylors L 275 F7
BIRCHWOOD
av. Templstw Lr 330 E9
bvd. Deer Park 319 B10
bvd. Hoppers Csg 405 D17
dr. Mooroolbark 337 F9
dr. Preston 283 H18
pl. Sunbury 143 E17
st. Fawkner 239 F20
st. Nar Warrn S 553 E17
wy. Delahey 275 C11
BIRD
av. Northcote 326 E10
av. Thornbury 326 E10
av. Thornbury 326 E10
ct. Williamstown 410 K15
rd. Avonsleigh 470 K12
st. Deer Park 319 A17
st. Eltham 287 D8
st. Mt Eliza 642 E8
st. Springvale 500 D12
BIRDIE
av. Anglesea 713 A6
st. Mt Waverley 459 A6
BIRDROCK
av. Mt Martha 656 C6
BIRDS
rd. Ferny Creek 466 A1
BIRDSALL
pl. Carlton N 18 H4
BIRDSEY
st. Thomson 703 G16
BIRDUM
st. Moorabbin 496 J12
BIRDWOOD
av. Brighton 454 F9
av. Cockatoo 511 D3
av. Dandenong 535 F6
av. Ferntree Gly 424 L20
av. Healesville 212 L15
av. Macleod 285 A14
av. Melbourne 4 F18
av. Melbourne 24 K19
av. Melbourne 30 L1
av. Melbourne 31 A1
av. Melbourne 414 A1
av. Mornington 640 H11
av. Upwey 465 H11

rd. Croydon 380 A6
st. Aspendale 546 E8
st. Balwyn 372 K8
st. Balwyn 373 A8
st. Bentleigh E 457 G15
st. Box Hill S 374 L20
st. Box Hill S 375 A20
st. Box Hill S 418 L2
st. Essendon N 279 D20
st. Frankston 627 E1
st. Kew East 372 E4
st. Maribyrnong 367 A2
st. Parkdale 531 D13
st. Reservoir 282 G16
BIRGITA
ct. Langwarrin 601 J17
BIRKBY
st. Box Hill N 375 C7
BIRKDALE
av. Cranbourne 603 F7
cl. Anglesea 713 C6
cl. Wantirna 422 B12
ct. Frankston 599 J16
ct. Sunbury 144 F13
BIRKENHEAD
av. Wantirna 422 G11
dr. Grovedale 706 E11
dr. Kilsyth 381 C5
st. Fitzroy N 326 C19
BIRKETT
ct. Altona Mdw 451 J4
BIRKLEY
ct. Noble Park N 501 A7
ct. Rosebud 700 A2
BIRMINGHAM
rd. Mt Evelyn 338 K16
rd. Mt Evelyn 339 A17
st. Spotswood 410 J2
st. Springvale 500 C10
st. Yarraville 367 B15
BIRNAM
ct. Belmont 702 D20
BIRRAKAY
ct. Greensbrgh 244 B19
BIRRALEE
sq. Keilor Dn 276 G16
st. Mt Waverley 458 K2
st. Wantirna S 422 K12
BIRRALI
wy. S Morang 198 L9
BIRRARRUNG
ct. Bulleen 329 J8
BIRRELL
ct. Altona Mdw 451 F6
ct. Kew 372 H9
BIRRILEE
ct. Grovedale 706 E9
BIRRONG
av. Noble Park 534 H6
BIRTINYA
ct. Frankston 600 F16
BIRTLES
ct. Balwyn 372 L8
ct. Balwyn 373 A8
st. Balwyn 372 L8
st. Balwyn 373 A8
BIRTLEY
ct. Greenvale 192 K15
BISCAY
ct. Boronia 424 G4
ct. Dingley Vill 532 L8
ct. Melton W 226 C12
BISCAYNE
dr. Mt Waverley 419 J15
BISCHOFF
st. Preston 326 D2
BISCOP
rd. Moorabbin 496 E10
BISHOP
av. Diamond Ck 246 C11
cl. Tarneit 447 J1
ct. Mt Waverley 459 C3
ct. Wantirna 422 E13
pl. Epping 242 A1
pl. Melton W 226 D18
rd. Moorooduc 658 G10
st. Box Hill 375 B15
st. Brunswick 325 H10
st. Coburg 281 B19
st. Kingsville 366 H13
st. Oakleigh 457 L15
st. Yarraville 366 H14
BISHOPS
ct. Seabrook 450 L5
rd. Panton Hill 204 G16
BISLEY
ct. Craigieburn 149 L16
BISMARCK
ct. Bundoora 284 G6
BISSET
ct. Hoppers Csg 448 A2
BITHEL
st. Glen Waverley 420 B19

BITTERN
ct. Werribee 448 B5
dr. Endeavour Hl 536 L4
dr. Endeavour Hl 537 A4
st. Broadmeadows 237 H14
st. Melton 226 F17
BITTERN-DROMANA
rd. Merricks N 688 L11
BIZANA
st. W Footscray 366 D9
BIZLEY
st. Mt Waverley 419 G15
BLABY
st. Noble Park 534 L1
BLACK
ct. Avondale Ht 322 G8
ct. Noble Park 534 L3
st. Brighton 454 H17
st. Brunswick 325 E17
st. Chelsea 546 J16
st. Essendon 323 H7
st. Lilydale 338 B7
st. Mont Albert 374 E16
st. Oakleigh E 458 K16
st. Reservoir 283 E8
st. Watsonia 285 D7
st. Westmeadows 237 B14
BLACKBIRD
ri. Avondale Ht 322 E12
BLACKBURN
dr. Cheltenham 531 H1
rd. Blackburn 375 K16
rd. Blackburn S 419 K7
rd. Burwood E 419 K10
rd. Clayton 459 F19
rd. Doncaster E 332 B19
rd. Doncaster E 376 B6
rd. Glen Waverley 459 G10
rd. Mooroolbark 337 J18
rd. Mt Waverley 459 G10
rd. Notting Hill 459 F19
rd. Templestowe 332 B19
st. Lalor 241 G10
st. Surrey Hills 374 B16
BLACKBURNE
sq. Berwick 554 E7
BLACKBUTT
ct. Frankston N 599 K11
BLACK CAMERON
rd. St Andrews 205 H1
rd. Smiths Gly 205 H1
BLACK DOG
dr. Brookfield 268 A3
BLACKERS
la. Yarrambat 201 G14
BLACK FALCON
st. S Morang 199 H11
BLACK FOREST
rd. Mambourin 445 A13
rd. Werribee 445 A13
rd. Wyndham Va 445 A13
BLACKFRIARS
cl. Toorak 415 C4
cl. Wantirna 422 H10
la. Chirnside Pk 337 E1
BLACKGATE
rd. Torquay 712 G1
BLACK GULLY
rd. Diamond Ck 245 K1
rd. Yarrambat 201 G19
rd. Yarrambat 245 K1
BLACKHAM
ct. Wantirna S 462 A3
BLACKHEATH
av. Frankston 599 K16
BLACK HILL
pde. Selby 467 E14
rd. Menzies Ck 467 K14
rd. Selby 467 F14
rd. Selby 467 K14
BLACKHILL
rd. Diggers Rest 141 A14
rd. Diggers Rest 187 A13
BLACK HOLE
tr. Olinda 427 D5
BLACKLEY
ct. Deer Park 319 C12
BLACKMAN
av. Mill Park 242 K6
av. Mill Park 243 A7
cl. Sunbury 142 G9
cr. Taylors L 233 A19
cr. Taylors L 233 B20
BLACKMORE
cl. Pakenham 584 H9
ct. Bundoora 284 H4
st. Chum Creek 212 L11
st. Dandenong N 501 G8
st. Sunshine N 321 E17
BLACK NIGHT
st. Mordialloc 532 C16
BLACKS
rd. Wandin East 386 D10

BLACKSCAMP
rd. Somerville 644 H17
BLACKSHAW
st. Ormond 456 G15
BLACKSHAWS
rd. Altona North 409 C1
rd. S Kingsville 410 C3
BLACKSMITH
av. S Morang 199 L17
dr. Attwood 236 L11
dr. Attwood 237 A11
pl. Sydenham 274 L4
BLACK SPRINGS
rd. Chirnside Pk 336 F5
rd. Wonga Park 336 E5
BLACKSTON
st. Footscray 367 E7
BLACKSTONE
la. Nar Warrn E 506 H15
BLACK WALLABY
dr. Langwarrin 628 J6
BLACK WATTLE
pl. Somerville 644 D14
wy. Carrum Downs 575 C14
BLACKWELLS
la. Bulla 190 J15
BLACK WOOD
wk. S Morang 243 L3
BLACKWOOD
av. Mentone 531 G7
av. Warburton 349 K1
cl. Eltham North 245 F18
cr. Campbellfield 239 F13
ct. Cairnlea 319 F9
ct. Frankston S 627 K14
ct. Mt Martha 657 D8
ct. Nunawading 376 K11
ct. Werribee 447 J9
dr. Hampton Pk 551 L5
dr. Melton S 268 H3
dr. Narre Warren 538 J17
dr. Rosebud W 699 C3
dr. Wheelers Hl 460 E14
dr. Wonga Park 291 K19
pde. Heidelberg W 328 A2
pl. Sunbury 143 F15
ri. Somerville 645 C20
st. Carnegie 456 L5
st. Lalor 241 H12
st. N Melbourne 17 G16
st. Tecoma 466 C8
st. Yarraville 366 L16
wy. Delahey 275 D11
BLACKWOOD PARK
rd. Ferntree Gly 464 B11
rd. Rowville 464 B11
BLACKWOODS
rd. Chum Creek 213 C3
BLADEN
av. Brunswick E 325 L11
pl. Gladstone Pk 237 A18
st. Wheelers Hl 461 E16
BLADIN
st. Laverton 407 C17
BLADON
st. Wantirna 422 H14
BLAGDON
st. Cheltenham 530 J2
BLAIR
av. Frankston S 626 L7
ct. Altona North 409 J6
ct. Grovedale 706 E14
ct. Keilor 277 B14
ct. Portsea 677 J2
ct. Thomastown 240 J15
ct. Warranwood 334 L15
pl. N Melbourne 17 E19
rd. Belgrave 466 G16
rd. Glen Waverley 420 C20
rd. Portsea 677 K2
st. Bentleigh 456 A18
st. Broadmeadows 238 D17
st. Brunswick 325 G15
st. Coburg 325 G7
st. Doncaster 375 C1
st. Lilydale 337 K3
st. Maribyrnong 322 J17
st. Moonee Pnd 324 B10
st. Warrandyte 333 J2
BLAIRGOWRIE
av. Blairgowrie 679 H17
ct. Brighton 454 F14
pl. Melton W 226 C17
BLAKE
cl. Delahey 275 F13
ct. Mt Eliza 626 K18
ct. Scoresby 462 A6
ct. Truganina 405 F13
st. Berwick 553 K18
st. Blackburn N 375 F10
st. Caulfield 455 L5
st. Mornington 640 E13
st. Reservoir 283 H16
BLAKENEY
pl. Southbank 23 J20
BLAKEVILLE
dr. Caroline Spr 318 B3
BLAKISTON
av. Mt Evelyn 383 D7
gr. Rye 698 A3
BLAMEY
av. Mill Park 242 J12
ct. Boronia 424 D5
dr. Melton S 268 J13
pl. Mornington 640 F14
rd. Yallambie 285 F12
st. Ascot Vale 324 A19
st. Bentleigh E 497 B7
st. Noble Park 535 C4
BLANCH
st. Preston 326 J3
BLANCHARD
ct. Greensbrgh 243 J20
BLANCHE
av. Parkdale 531 G12
cl. Cranbourne 578 A14
ct. Coburg N 282 B17
ct. Doncaster E 376 B3
ct. Kilsyth S 381 A19
dr. Vermont 421 G2
st. Ardeer 320 B19
st. Brighton East 455 C16
st. Collingwood 19 H11
st. Cremorne 25 L18
st. Elsternwick 455 D3
st. St Kilda 414 D16
st. Yarraville 367 A15
BLAND
st. Dandenong N 501 H15
BLANDFORD
cr. Bayswater N 380 F19
cr. Nar Warrn S 579 C5
ct. Carrum Downs 574 H15
st. W Footscray 366 J7
BLANNIN
st. Healesville 213 K20
BLANTON
dr. Mulgrave 501 K6
BLANTYRE
av. Chelsea 546 K18
BLATCH
ct. Forest Hill 420 G1
BLAU
st. Bundoora 242 E16
BLAXLAND
av. Cranbourne N 577 L9
av. Frankston S 627 E10
av. Thomastown 240 E19
ct. Mooroolbark 337 K15
dr. Dandenong N 501 G8
dr. Rowville 463 G16
dr. Sunbury 143 C13
pl. Taylors L 275 K1
rd. Melton S 268 G12
st. Wyndham Va 446 G9
BLAZEY
rd. Croydon S 379 L12
st. Richmond 371 B15
wk. Croydon S 379 K13
BLEACHES
la. Wesburn 347 K15
la. Yarra Jctn 347 K15
BLEAKHOUSE
la. Albert Park 29 D17
BLEASES
la. Dixons Ck 210 G7
la. Yarra Glen 210 G7
BLEAZBY
av. Brighton 454 K18
st. Bentleigh 456 A19
BLENCAIRN
av. Caulfield N 455 H2
av. Mt Martha 655 H15
BLENDON
av. St Albans 320 H3
BLENHEIM
av. Glen Waverley 460 L1
av. Mont Albert 374 F17
pl. Frankston S 628 C15
rd. Altona North 410 D9
rd. Newport 410 D9
st. Balaclava 414 H18
st. Bentleigh E 457 B15
st. Glenroy 280 A6
st. Heathmont 422 H2
wy. Caroline Spr 317 K4
BLESSINGTON
ct. St Kilda 414 B19
st. Newtown 702 E8
st. St Kilda 414 B19
wy. St Kilda 414 E18
BLETCHLEY
pl. Kealba 276 L20
pl. Kealba 277 A20
rd. Hughesdale 457 G9
BLIBURG
st. Jacana 237 J19
BLIGH
cl. Cranbourne N 578 A9
ct. Endeavour Hl 537 D6
ct. Heathmont 422 G1
ct. Lilydale 338 J2
pl. Melbourne 1 L17
pl. Melbourne 24 C10
pl. Wyndham Va 446 G8
st. Melton S 268 E10
BLIND BIGHT
rd. Blind Bight 650 F8
BLIND CREEK
la. Wantirna S 422 A20
la. Wantirna S 462 A2
BLINKER
ri. Endeavour Hl 504 B20
BLISS
ct. Derrimut 363 G10
st. Burnley 371 A18
BLISSINGTON
st. Springvale 499 L6
BLOCK
ct. Melbourne 2 B15
ct. Melbourne, off Block Pl 24 D8
pl. Melbourne 2 B14
pl. Melbourne 24 D8
BLODORN
ct. Keysborough 534 C11
BLOMBERG
rd. Altona North 409 F9
BLOOM
st. Frankston 627 H3
st. Moonee Pnd 324 A10
BLOOMBURG
st. Abbotsford 26 B1
BLOOMFIELD
av. Maribyrnong 323 A15
av. Nar Warrn S 553 E17
rd. Ascot Vale 324 A17
rd. Keysborough 534 J11
rd. Noble Park 534 J11
BLOOMINGDALE
av. Albanvale 319 A5
ct. Point Cook 451 D10
BLOOMS
rd. N Warrandyte 290 A14
BLOOMSBURY
dr. Taylors Hill 274 J11
la. Wyndham Va 446 F9
st. Newtown 702 G13
BLOSSOM
ct. Doncaster 374 H3
ct. Glen Waverley 459 J6
dr. Doveton 536 H10
gr. Knoxfield 423 B19
la. Werribee 447 L10
st. Mitcham 377 J16
st. Parkdale 531 K8
wk. Croydon S 380 C14
BLOSSOM PARK
dr. Mill Park 243 B9
dr. Mill Park 243 C13
BLOXHAM
ct. Hoppers Csg 448 D2
BLUCHER
st. Ferntree Gly 464 E9
st. Glenroy 280 A7
tce. Williamstown 411 F12
BLUEBELL
cr. Gowanbrae 279 C6
ct. Berwick 539 G17
ct. Hoppers Csg 405 C16
ct. Melton W 225 H17
ct. The Patch 467 L6
dr. Epping 198 G19
gld. Somerville 645 D18
la. Launching Pl 346 C15
BLUEBERRY
cl. Cranbourne N 578 B10
ct. Bundoora 242 K15
ct. Werribee 447 J10
la. Monbulk 428 G16
rd. Mooroolbark 337 C12
BLUEBIRD
av. Cockatoo 471 D19
dr. Berwick 554 A1
wy. Roxburgh Pk 194 A6
wy. Roxburgh Pk 194 A7
BLUEBUSH
ct. Sunbury 143 J7
BLUECHIP
ct. Point Cook 451 B8
BLUEGRASS
cl. Waterways 547 E1
cr. Pakenham 585 E7
wk. Frankston 599 L16
BLUE GUM
ct. Chelsea 547 B19
ct. Greensbrgh 286 K1
ct. Narre Warren 553 G13
mw. Langwarrin 601 H15
pl. Grovedale 706 F9
BLUEGUM
av. Wheelers Hl 460 L11
cl. Templstw Lr 330 K12
ct. Mill Park 242 F11
ct. Upwey 466 A9
dr. Altona 409 C16
dr. Badger Creek 258 E12
la. Croydon S 379 L14
wy. Hampton Pk 552 A16
wy. Hampton Pk 552 B16
wy. Sunbury 143 F16
BLUE HILLS
av. Mt Waverley 419 F20
av. Nunawading 376 E11
cl. Wantirna 422 C11
BLUE HOUSE
rd. Panton Hill 205 C8
BLUE JAY
ct. Nar Warrn S 578 K4
BLUE MIST
dr. Croydon S 379 G11
BLUE MOON
wy. Sydenham 275 D8
BLUE RANGE
cr. Lynbrook 551 G17
BLUE RIDGE
dr. Mooroolbark 338 A15
la. Mt Eliza 625 L17
rd. Dewhurst 510 D20
BLUESTAR
ri. Bundoora 284 F9
BLUESTONE
ct. S Morang 199 K16
st. Kensington 33 G5
wk. Delahey 274 L16
BLUE WREN
ct. Mt Evelyn 382 K2
pl. Diamond Ck 245 C11
ri. Carrum Downs 601 A7
BLUFF
av. Elwood 454 B4
ct. Highett 495 H13
ct. Rosebud W, off Allambi Av 699 E3
rd. Black Rock 529 F5
rd. Cannons Creek 649 D9
rd. Hampton 495 H12
rd. Hampton E 495 H12
rd. Sandringham 495 F20
st. Hawthorn E 416 E7
st. Lalor 240 G9
BLUMM
rd. Belgrave S 507 D6
BLUSHING
wy. Bundoora 242 E14
BLYTH
ct. Croydon N 335 K11
ct. Gladstone Pk 279 C4
pl. Mulgrave 500 H1
st. Altona 408 H20
st. Altona 409 A19
st. Altona 452 F1
st. Brunswick 325 G12
st. Brunswick E 325 G12
st. St Albans 320 L6
st. Vermont 377 F20
BLYTHE
av. Boronia 424 G6
ct. Dingley Vill 533 B1
st. Murrumbeena 457 D12
st. Thornbury 326 J7
BLYTHES
rd. Mt Dandenong 382 J19
BLYTHSWOOD
ct. Kew 371 E12
BLYTON
cr. Sunbury 142 K9
ct. Highton 705 K9
ct. Templestowe 332 B11
BOA
ct. Sunshine W 364 D6
BOADLE
rd. Bundoora 284 E5
BOAKE
st. Carnegie 456 K13
BOANDYNE
ct. Toorak 415 G3
BOARD
pl. Geelong, off Little Malop St 703 C8
st. Doncaster 331 B17
tr. Olinda 428 B5
BOARDMAN
cl. Box Hill S 418 K5
st. Malvern East 416 C20
BOARDWALK
bvd. Point Cook 450 B6
BOASE
st. Brunswick 325 F13
BOATHOUSE
dr. Melbourne 4
dr. Melbourne 24
rd. Kew 371
BOB
st. Nar Warrn N 539
BOBBORA
ct. Taylors L 275
BOBCAT
tr. Olinda 427
BOBERRIT
wyn. Sydenham 274
wyn. Sydenham 274
BODALLA
ct. Frankston 628
BODKIN
av. Bundoora 243
BODLEY
st. Beaumaris 530
st. Clarinda 498
BODMIN
ct. Craigieburn 194
BODYCOATS
rd. Wollert 153
BOEING
ct. Forest Hill 420
rd. Strathmr Ht 279
BOGAN
ct. Boronia 424
BOGART
cl. Dingley Vill 533
BOGER
rd. Watsonia 285
BOGEY
ct. Dingley Vill 533
BOGIE
ct. Anglesea 713
BOGNOR
av. Seaford 573
BOGONG
av. Glen Waverley 460
av. Glen Waverley 460
cl. Hallam 552
ct. Bangholme 549
ct. Broadmeadows 238
ct. Doncaster E 332
ct. Forest Hill 420
ct. Frankston 600
ct. Lalor 240
ct. Reservoir 282
BOHAN
gr. Belmont 702
BOILEAU
st. Keysborough 535
BOISDALE
av. Sunshine N 320
st. Surrey Hills 418
BOKHARA
rd. Caulfield S 455
BOKISSA
dr. Frankston 599
BOLAC
ct. Taylors Hill 274
st. Bayswater 423
BOLAN
st. Glen Waverley 419
BOLAND
st. Burnley 371
BOLCH
pl. Oakleigh 458
BOLDEN
st. Heidelberg 328
BOLDREWOOD
pde. Kingsbury 283
pde. Reservoir 283
BOLGER
cr. Hoppers Csg 448
cr. Hoppers Csg 449
BOLINA
ct. Mill Park 242
BOLINDA
pl. Vermont 421
rd. Balwyn N 373
rd. Campbellfield 239
st. Bentleigh 456
BOLINGBROKE
st. Pascoe Vale 280
BOLITHO
st. Sunshine 365
BOLOKA
ct. Patterson L 573
BOLTE
ct. Frankston S 627
BOLTON
av. Hampton 494
ct. Avondale Ht 322
ct. Greenvale 192
ct. Langwarrin 629
ct. Mulgrave 460
rd. Selby 467
rd. Wyndham Va 446
st. Beaumaris 529

Box Hill 375 D14
Eltham 287 C15
Lower Plenty 287 B18
Spotswood 411 A1
.WARRA
Cranbourne W 577 K16
Chadstone 458 C2
.WELL
Werribee 447 H17
.YN
Vermont S 420 G10
N
Nar Warrn N 539 F9
NA
Healesville 257 F3
Oak Park 279 J11
Ashburton 417 E13
Ringwood E 379 B10
Tootgarook 698 F2
N AIR
Anglesea 713 H6
NANG
Meadow Ht 238 A3
NANZA
Beaumaris 530 G9
Beaumaris 530 G9
NAPARTE
Rowville 463 L12
NAR
Brunswick W 324 L7
Endeavour Hl 503 G17
Heidelberg Ht 328 D2
NA VISTA
Aspendale 546 C6
Surrey Hills 374 A19
Bayswater 423 C8
ND
Blackburn S 419 K5
St Albans 320 F11
Cranbourne 578 A19
Croydon 380 H5
Keilor East 322 B3
Lalor 241 L10
Meadow Ht 238 B2
Montrose 382 E8
Taylors L 275 F5
Newport 411 A10
Abbotsford 26 L3
Altona North 365 J20
Caulfield N 456 A1
Clayton S 498 G4
Doncaster 375 B3
Ferntree Gly 423 E16
Hadfield 281 A9
Hoppers Csg 405 A19
Ivanhoe 327 J10
Maddingley 264 B2
Melbourne 1 K19
Melbourne 24 C11
Mordialloc 532 E12
Mt Waverley 459 E2
Newtown 702 H11
Preston 282 H20
Ringwood 378 B12
South Yarra 32 D10
South Yarra 414 H5
w,Mordialloc 532 C12
NDI
Frankston 627 G5
Bonbeach 545 F14
Bonbeach 573 A3
Ringwood E 379 C12
NDS
Research 288 L5
Greenvale 192 G18
Lower Plenty 330 F6
NEO
Boneo 699 H11
Boneo 699 H20
Rosebud 683 H20
Rosebud 699 H11
Rosebud W 699 H11
NESHAKER
Carlton 18 H9
NFIELD
Hawthorn E 416 F6
Keilor 277 D14
NHAM
Oakleigh E 458 J15
Monbulk 468 D4
The Patch 468 D4
NICA
Tarneit 405 A8
NITA
Dandenong N 502 D19
NITO
Mt Eliza 641 K4
NLEIGH
Brighton 454 E9
NNER
Surrey Hills 417 K2

BONNEY
ct. Melb Airport 235 J12
ct. Taylors Hill 274 K10
pl. Roxburgh Pk 194 C10
st. Wyndham Va 446 B7
BONNIE
ct. Ferntree Gly 464 C6
BONNIE DOONE
st. Briar Hill 286 G3
BONNIE VIEW
rd. Croydon N 336 D16
rd. Mt Dandenong 426 E1
BONNY
ct. Nar Warrn S 579 G1
st. Bentleigh E 496 K5
BONNYBRAE
ct. Sunbury 144 G13
BONNYVIEW
rd. Mt Eliza 626 D11
st. Glen Iris 417 J10
BONO
cl. Blackburn S 419 D4
BONSEY
rd. Highton 705 G2
BONUS
ct. Werribee 446 H19
BONVIEW
av. Herne Hill 701 H1
av. Ringwood 377 L13
cr. Burwood E 419 H8
ct. Knoxfield 463 C2
rd. Ferny Creek 465 L2
rd. Malvern 416 A11
st. Reservoir 282 E12
BONVILLE
ct. Camberwell 417 D5
BON VUE
rd. Balwyn N 329 E19
BONWICK
st. Fawkner 281 G6
BONZA VIEW
Kalorama 382 K13
BOOBYALLA
st. Doveton 536 J10
BOOKER
st. Cheltenham 530 L4
st. Cheltenham 531 A4
st. Spotswood 411 D2
BOOKHAM
wy. Cranbourne W 577 F16
BOOLARONG
dr. Belmont 706 H5
BOOLOORA
rd. Springvale 499 G11
BOOM
pl. Carlton 18 J9
BOOMERANG
av. Braybrook 366 C6
ct. Nar Warrn S 578 K1
ct. Tootgarook 698 G7
BOONAH
ct. Templstw Lr 330 K8
st. Springvale 499 K16
wy. Forest Hill 420 E2
BOONDARA
gr. St Kilda E 414 K15
rd. Mont Albert N 374 E9
BOONGARRY
av. Blackburn 375 H18
BOONONG
av. Seaford 599 D11
BOORAHMAN
st. Balwyn N 373 E6
BOORAL
ct. Grovedale 705 L14
dr. Sunshine W 364 J7
BOORAN
av. Glen Waverley 460 B10
pde. Tootgarook 698 D9
rd. Caulfield 456 A4
rd. Caulfield E 456 A4
rd. Glen Huntly 456 A12
rd. Ormond 456 A12
BOORLEE
ct. Bundoora 284 K4
BOORMANII
dr. Mornington 656 J4
BOOROOL
rd. Kew East 372 J7
BOORT
st. Dallas 238 F13
BOOTH
cr. Dandenong N 501 J17
ct. Eltham 288 F3
ct. Gladstone Pk 236 L17
ct. Gladstone Pk 237 A17
st. Coburg 326 B1
st. Parkdale 531 J13
st. Preston 326 B1
st. Sunshine W 364 L10
st. Sunshine W 365 A10
wy. Taylors L 275 F6

BOOTHBY
st. Northcote 327 C15
BOOTIE
ct. Endeavour Hl 537 B6
ct. Roxburgh Pk 194 E15
BOOTTEN
ct. Hoppers Csg 449 E1
BOOYAN
cr. Greensbrgh 243 J18
BORADINO
pl. Rowville 464 A12
BORANG
av. Mt Evelyn 339 F20
av. Mt Evelyn 383 F1
av. Selby 467 A14
st. Coburg N 281 J12
BORCHART
st. Guys Hill 541 H15
BORDEAUX
av. Blackburn 375 H11
av. Glen Waverley 460 G11
cr. Frankston 628 D10
dr. Waurn Ponds 705 E15
gr. Nar Warrn S 579 E4
st. Avondale Ht 322 C9
st. Doncaster 330 H18
BORDER
bvd. Sunbury 142 J16
cl. Wantirna S 462 F5
dr. Keilor East 322 A1
dr. Mill Park 198 G20
dr. Mill Park 242 G1
pl. Meadow Ht 237 K7
BOREE
av. Clarinda 498 E3
ct. Berwick 553 F4
ct. Frankston 628 H1
BOREHAM
st. Sunshine 364 L9
st. Sunshine 365 A8
BORELA
ct. Clarinda 498 C8
BORG
cr. Scoresby 462 D8
BORISKA
ct. Glen Waverley 460 A8
BORLASE
st. Yallambie 285 E17
BORNEO
ct. Heidelberg W 328 C1
BORODA
ct. St Albans 320 H10
BOROLA
ct. Croydon N 336 B16
BORONIA
arc. Boronia 424 E11
av. Belgrave Ht 466 J18
av. Croydon S 379 J13
av. Dandenong N 501 G18
av. Rosebud W 699 B1
cl. Frankston 628 A7
cr. Cockatoo 511 C5
ct. Altona Mdw 451 B5
ct. Bellfield 327 L5
ct. Carrum Downs 575 D18
ct. Keysborough 534 A13
ct. Mt Martha 656 F6
dr. Glen Waverley 420 G19
dr. Hillside 273 J4
dr. Hillside 273 J5
gr. Doncaster E 375 L6
rd. Bayswater 422 L9
rd. Bayswater 423 A9
rd. Boronia 423 J12
rd. Vermont 421 D2
rd. Wantirna 422 A6
rd. Wantirna S 423 A9
rd. Warburton 349 K7
st. Bentleigh E 457 E17
st. Canterbury 373 E17
st. Dromana 686 F7
st. Newcomb 703 L15
st. Pascoe Vale 281 A19
st. Surrey Hills 418 C1
st. Thomastown 241 G14
wy. Wyndham Va 446 G9
BOROONDARA
rd. Sorrento 678 H7
BORRACK
sq. Altona North 409 J4
BORRELL
st. Keilor 277 B11
BORRIE
st. Reservoir 283 E6
BORROWDALE
ct. Cranbourne W 603 H3
ct. Mill Park 242 F5
BORVA
dr. Keilor East 278 C19
BOSANQUET
av. Newtown 701 J4
BOSC
ct. Templestowe 331 E3

BOSCARNE
av. Torquay 712 F2
BOSCO
cl. Narre Warren 539 B17
st. Chadstone 458 B3
tce. Keilor Ldg 276 A4
BOSISTO
st. Richmond 26 E10
BOSQUET
st. Maidstone 322 H20
st. Maidstone 366 G1
BOSSINGTON
st. Oakleigh S 457 H18
BOSTOCK
av. Manifold Ht 702 C1
ct. Lysterfield 463 L16
ct. Thomastown 241 F20
BOSTON
av. Malvern East 456 K4
av. Seaford 600 B5
cr. Keilor Dn 276 C14
ct. Narre Warren 539 G17
ct. Sorrento 678 F6
pl. Fitzroy N 19 B3
rd. Balwyn 373 D13
rd. Bundoora 243 C20
rd. Lalor 241 L11
rd. Torquay 711 L9
st. Ashwood 418 F14
st. Fawkner 281 F3
BOSWELL
av. Newtown 702 H13
ct. Dandenong N 502 B11
ct. Greenvale 237 B3
BOTANIC
ct. Bundoora 284 F6
dr. Cranbourne 604 F15
dr. Doncaster 331 C17
dr. E Geelong 703 G8
dr. Glen Waverley 460 D7
dr. Hillside 232 B18
dr. Junction Vill 604 F15
ri. Craigieburn 150 A14
wk. Mont Albert N 374 G11
wy. Wyndham Va 446 E11
BOTANICA
bvd. Bundoora 242 F13
bvd. Bundoora 242 F14
wy. Keysborough 534 G16
BOTANICAL
gr. Doveton 536 J5
gr. Doveton 536 K5
gr.n, Doveton 536 K5
gr.s, Doveton 536 K5
BOTANY
ct. Clarinda 498 F6
ct. Dingley Vill 533 A8
ct. Wantirna 422 E4
st. Albanvale 319 D6
wk. Mornington 656 L3
BOTHA
av. Reservoir 282 H5
BOTHERAMBO
st. Richmond 26 B16
BOTHWELL
st. Balaclava 414 G19
st. Pascoe Vale 280 C15
BOTTE
ct. Diamond Ck 245 F12
BOTTINGS
la. Dixons Ck 210 D4
la. Yarra Glen 210 D4
BOTTLE
bnd. Forest Hill 420 E2
BOTTLE BRUSH
dr. Doveton 536 J10
BOTTLEBRUSH
ct. Langwarrin 601 J14
ct. Sunshine W 363 K8
ct. Werribee 448 E18
ct. Wheelers Hl 460 G15
dr. Mill Park 243 B5
BOTTOMLEY
dr. Emerald 469 J19
BOUCHER
la. Olinda 427 B18
BOUGAINVILLE
pl. Princes Hill 325 J18
BOUGAINVILLEA
dr. Point Cook 450 G14
BOUGANVILLE
st. Boronia 424 E3
BOULTON
ct. Greensbrgh 286 F2
rd. Blackburn 376 C20
rd. Blackburn 420 C1
st. Springvale 499 L10
BOUNDARY
rd. Braeside 532 E19
rd. Carrum Downs 574 G12
rd. Coburg N 281 A11
rd. Coldstream 296 E20
rd. Coldstream 296 F9
rd. Coldstream 340 C10
rd. Derrimut 363 A14
rd. Dingley Vill 498 G20
rd. Dingley Vill 532 G9
rd. Dromana 686 B8
rd. E Geelong 703 K20
rd. Emerald 510 E3
rd. Grovedale 705 F18
rd. Gruyere 296 F9
rd. Harkaway 540 L1
rd. Heatherton 498 G20
rd. Kew 371 G6
rd. Laverton N 363 A14
rd. Lilydale 296 E20
rd. Lilydale 340 C10
rd. Marshall 706 G19
rd. Moorabbin Aprt 532 G9
rd. Mordialloc 532 E19
rd. Mt Duneed 705 F18
rd. Nar Warrn E 505 H19
rd. Nar Warrn E 506 E20
rd. Nar Warrn E 540 L1
rd. Nar Warrn E 541 A2
rd. Nar Warrn N 505 J19
rd. Newcomb 703 K20
rd. N Melbourne 34 G10
rd. Olinda 427 G6
rd. Pascoe Vale 280 H11
rd. Sunshine W 364 K16
rd. Thomson 703 K20
rd. Truganina 363 A14
rd. Wandin N 340 C10
rd. Whittington 703 K20
rd. Wollert 153 A15
rd.e, Emerald 509 D5
rd.w, Emerald 509 C5
st. Port Melb 29 A1
st. Port Melb 368 J18
st. Southbank 368 J18
st. S Melbourne 368 K20
st. S Melbourne 413 A1
tr. Frankston N 600 F10
tr. Frankston N 600 G14
tr. Warrandyte 334 D3
BOUNTY
cl. Highton 701 G10
ct. Lilydale 338 H3
pl. Melton W 225 F20
wy. Berwick 553 K19
BOURBON
st. Silvan 385 A19
wy. Waurn Ponds 705 C14
BOURCHIER
st. Glenroy 280 H4
BOURCHIERS
rd. Kangaroo Grnd 290 K4
rd. Kangaroo Grnd 291 A5
BOURKE
cr. Geelong 703 D11
cr. Hoppers Csg 448 F1
ct. Dandenong N 501 F7
pl. Melbourne 1 B10
pl. Melbourne 23 H9
rd. Clarinda 497 L9
rd. Cranbourne 578 A19
rd. Melton S 268 D12
rd. Oakleigh S 497 L9
rd. Pakenham 585 L20
rd. Red Hill 686 K19
rd. Red Hill 687 A19
st. Brunswick 325 H13
st. Bulla 190 C16
st. Bulleen 329 J11
st. Coburg 281 D20
st. Darley 222 D8
st. Docklands 23 B12
st. Essendon W 323 A8
st. Melbourne 1 B12
st. Melbourne 2 G12
st. Melbourne 2 H12
st. Melbourne 23 G10
st. Melbourne 24 G6
st. Mentone 530 J6
st. Mt Evelyn 339 G15
st. Reservoir 282 E14
st. Ringwood 378 B12
st. Seddon 367 C11
BOURKES
rd. Darley 221 A12
rd. Pentland Hl 221 A12
BOURKES CREEK
rd. Dewhurst 510 D20
rd. Pakenham Up 559 J1
BOURKE STREET
ml. Melbourne 24 C7
BOURNE
rd. Glen Iris 416 K12
BOURNEMOUTH
av. Springvale 499 F16
BOURNEVALE
dr. Berwick 554 C3
BOURNEVILLE
av. Brighton East 495 G5

BOURNIAN
av. Strathmore 280 B19
BOUVARDIA
cr. Frankston N 600 E6
BOUVERIE
pl. Carlton 18 A20
pl. Epping...............198 B16
pl. Skye..................601 G1
st. Carlton 18 A20
BOVARD
cl. Caroline Spr.......273 L7
BOVEC
ct. Bentleigh E 497 B3
BOW
cr. Camberwell........373 B19
BOWDEN
ct. Wheelers Hl 460 J11
la. Roxburgh Pk......194 E14
st. Ascot Vale 324 A17
st. Preston.............283 A17
BOWEN
av. The Basin..........425 G13
cl. Melton S............268 C10
cr. Burwood E.........419 F12
cr. Carlton N...........325 G18
cr. Melbourne 30 K6
cr. Melbourne 413 L3
cr. Princes Hill 325 G18
ct. Berwick 553 H4
ct. Bundoora............284 K1
ct. Mentone.............531 G6
ct. Sunbury 142 G11
la. Melbourne 30 K6
la. Melbourne 413 L3
rd. Aspendale Gdn...546 E1
rd. Aspendale Gdn...547 A3
rd. Doncaster E 376 B6
rd. Lilydale.............337 K6
rd. Pt Lonsdale........710 J1
rd. Sorrento 678 J11
st. Balaclava 414 G19
st. Camberwell........416 K7
st. Cranbourne........578 E18
st. Ferntree Gly 424 G20
st. Hawthorn...........372 A15
st. Hughesdale........457 G13
st. Kew..................371 F12
st. McCrae.............685 C13
st. Malvern East 457 E5
st. Melbourne.............2 G4
st. Melbourne 24 C1
st. Moonee Pnd 323 J15
st. Prahran 414 L12
st. Richmond............26 C8
st. Rye 697 F3
BOWER
ct. Emerald.............510 C2
ct. Ferntree Gly 463 K7
ct. Gladstone Pk 236 K20
ct. Langwarrin 629 H1
dr. Werribee............447 K6
st. Northcote 327 A19
BOWERBIRD
pl. Carrum Downs...601 A2
BOWERY
ct. Werribee............448 B15
BOWES
av. Airport W...........278 L18
pl. Craigieburn........194 E2
st. Frankston S 626 G9
BOWLER
st. Hawthorn E........372 D19
BOWLERS
av. Geelong West 702 G6
wy. Malvern East......456 L3
BOWLES
av. Caulfield N 455 L1
BOWLEY
av. Balwyn 373 B13
BOWLING GREEN
la. Mitcham 377 B11
st. Windsor 414 G12
BOWMAN
cl. Nar Warrn S.......552 G13
ct. Frankston 600 G17
dr. Mill Park............241 L5
dr. Mill Park............242 A4
dr. Mornington........657 B4
dr. Mornington........657 C4
gln. Craigieburn........150 F9
la. Keysborough 548 E7
rd. Beaconsfield 556 B4
rd. Guys Hill.............556 B4
st. Aspendale...........545 K1
st. Mt Waverley 419 A18
st. Noble Park..........501 B19
st. Werribee............448 A15
BOWMANS
pde. Oakleigh E 458 D10
BOWMORE
av. Pk Orchards.......333 L17
rd. Noble Park.........500 J17
st. Hughesdale........457 E11

BOWN
ct. Brighton East.....455 E19
BOWNANG
st. Sandringham 495 B13
BOWNESS
ct. Croydon Hl 335 H13
BOWOOD
ct. Derrimut............363 B5
ct. Seabrook 451 A4
BOWRAL
ct. Bundoora...........284 K3
BOWRINGS
rd. Red Hill..............688 B13
BOWYER
av. Kew..................372 G10
BOX
av. Forest Hill 420 F6
cl. Wheelers Hl 460 G14
ct. Altona North 410 C6
ct. Baxter................644 C1
ct. Bentleigh E 496 G1
ct. Kings Park 275 E18
ct. Templstw Lr 330 H13
la. Ringwood N.......378 C6
pl. Hoppers Csg......448 A2
pl. Mont Albert.........374 E15
rd. Briar Hill 286 J4
st. Dandenong........536 E13
st. Doveton.............536 G12
st. Reservoir...........283 E7
BOX FOREST
rd. Hadfield.............281 B5
BOX HEDGE
ct. S Morang 199 F11
BOX HILL
cr. Mont Albert N 374 G9
BOXLEIGH
gr. Box Hill N 375 A6
BOXMOOR
ct. Mt Eliza.............642 A4
BOXSHALL
st. Brighton 454 J16
BOXTREE
rd. Montrose...........382 A11
BOYANA
cr. Croydon 380 H2
BOYANDA
rd. Glen Iris............416 G13
BOYANICH
ct. Hoppers Csg......405 A19
BOYANNA
rd. Glen Waverley....420 G20
BOYCE
av. Briar Hill 286 J5
rd. Selby.................467 E14
BOYD
av. Chelsea.............547 C14
av. Oakleigh E 458 K14
cl. Mooroolbark.......337 C10
cr. Coburg N...........282 A18
cr. Heidelberg W.....284 A19
ct. Dandenong N.....502 A19
ct. Kealba 277 B20
ct. Melton S............268 K7
ct. Scoresby 462 A7
ct. Sunbury 143 A9
ct. Werribee............448 C8
ct. Wheelers Hl 460 G17
la. Dandenong........536 A8
pl. Mill Park............198 K20
pl. Mill Park............242 K1
rd. Gembrook 512 L18
st. Albert Park...........29 H18
st. Albert Park.........413 D9
st. Altona................408 J18
st. Bacchus Msh......222 B14
st. Blackburn S........419 L3
st. Dandenong N.....501 L19
st. Docklands..........368 J13
st. Doncaster..........374 J4
st. Greensbrgh.........285 J2
st. N Warrandyte.....290 A12
st. Richmond............26 L14
st. Richmond..........371 A17
st. Thornbury..........327 C8
BOYDEN
sq. Roxburgh Pk......194 C10
BOYDS
rd. Doreen 202 D6
rd. Hurstbridge 202 D6
rd. Nutfield..............202 D6
BOYLAND
ct. Box Hill N 375 B6
BOYLE
cl. Wantirna S.........462 F1
cr. Mill Park............242 F8
ct. Sunshine W 364 J10
st. Ashburton..........417 C16
st. Forest Hill 376 E19
tce. Burnside............318 D7
BOYNE
av. E Geelong..........703 H13
cl. Epping...............198 A20

st. Coburg N...........282 A17
st. Rowville.............463 A18
BOYNTON
pl. Berwick 554 K19
st. Bentleigh E 496 L3
BOYS
rd. Warrandyte........289 D16
BOYSE
ct. Tullamarine........236 G20
BOYS FARM
tr. Lysterfield.........504 L5
BOYS FARM HERITAGE
wk. Lysterfield.........504 K10
BRABHAM
dr. Mill Park............242 K3
BRACELET
st. Pakenham 584 K4
BRACK
av. Brooklyn............365 G18
ct. Mooroolbark......337 H11
ct. Sunbury 143 A9
BRACKEN
av. Maribyrnong......367 E3
av. Montrose...........382 A17
ct. Ferntree Gly 463 F9
ct. Highton 701 J18
ct. Wheelers Hl 461 B19
gr. Altona................452 G1
pl. Lyndhurst...........551 B20
rd. Caulfield S 455 F9
rdg. Arthurs Seat.......685 K10
rdg. Dromana 685 K10
wy. S Morang 199 G11
BRACKENBURY
st. Warrandyte........290 B18
st. Warrandyte........333 J2
BRACKLEY
ct. St Albans...........275 H20
BRACKNELL
ct. Vermont S 421 B10
pl. Deer Park...........318 J8
st. Keysborough 534 L12
st. Keysborough 535 A12
BRACY
av. Springvale S 534 B2
BRAD
ct. Cranbourne N 578 H11
dr. Mt Martha...........655 J17
st. Bentleigh E 496 L5
BRADANO
la. Roxburgh Pk......194 D7
BRADDON
ct. Hillside 274 G1
BRADEN BRAE
dr. Warranwood.......335 A12
BRADFIELD
la. Kensington 33 H5
BRADFORD
av. Greenvale 192 K17
av. Kew..................372 J11
av. Preston.............326 L5
cl. Gladstone Pk 278 L1
ct. Braybrook..........322 C20
ct. Braybrook..........366 C1
dr. Carrum Downs...575 C14
rd. Mt Martha...........668 J8
rd. Mt Martha...........669 A8
st. Oakleigh S 497 F3
BRADINA
ct. Chelsea Ht 547 E11
BRADLEY
av. Thornbury..........326 E10
av. Vermont 420 L5
ct. Clarinda.............498 D11
ct. Hampton Pk.......551 L7
dr. Hillside 274 E2
dr. Mill Park............243 B3
pl. Boronia..............423 J14
st. Broadmeadows..238 A20
st. Newport 410 G8
st. Pascoe Vale 280 J18
st. Sunshine N........321 D18
tce. Narre Warren.....553 C8
wy. Cranbourne W ...603 G2
BRADLEYS
la. N Warrandyte.....289 F19
BRADMAN
av. Mt Evelyn...........339 D14
bvd. Keilor East 322 C1
ct. Boronia..............424 F16
dr. Meadow Ht.........237 J7
dr. Sunbury 142 G14
dr. Sunbury 142 H15
st. Sunshine N........321 C15
tce. Epping...............198 H16
BRADSHAW
cr. Hillside 232 E17
dr. Healesville 213 K16
st. Essendon...........323 C6
st. Essendon...........323 C7
st. Frankston 599 F14
st. Kingsbury 283 L10
st. Mordialloc 532 B15

BRADSTREET
rd. Mt Waverley 458 G5
BRADWELL
st. Kealba 276 K20
BRADWORTH
st. Craigieburn........150 A14
BRADY
av. Clayton S...........499 D9
cl. Lynbrook...........551 E16
cl. Waterways.........532 L19
la. Kew..................371 H6
rd. Bentleigh E 497 A7
rd. Dandenong N.....501 K14
rd. Endeavour Hl 502 E15
st. Richmond............26 K13
st. Southbank 23 C19
st. S Melbourne 23 A18
st. S Melbourne 368 L19
BRAE
ct. Chadstone 458 E6
ct. Eltham North 245 B18
ct. Greenvale 193 F18
ct. Montmorency 287 A9
ct. Rye 697 B2
ct. Sherbrooke.......426 L20
ct. Sherbrooke.......427 A20
gr. Nunawading 376 G11
gr. Point Cook.........450 H4
rd. Lysterfield..........504 H4
BRAEDUKE
la. Hillside 232 E18
BRAELANDS
cl. Caroline Spr.......318 D3
BRAEMAR
cl. Gladstone Pk 236 L17
ct. Newtown 702 B13
ct. Sunbury 143 B6
ct. Wheelers Hl 461 D14
st. Croydon 380 F1
st. Essendon...........323 F5
st. Mont Albert N 374 E11
st. Pascoe Vale S 324 L4
st. Seaford.............599 H10
BRAEMER
ct. Endeavour Hl 503 J19
BRAESIDE
av. Camberwell........417 L7
av. Ringwood E 378 J10
av. Rosanna 284 L17
av. Sherbrooke........426 L20
av. Sherbrooke........427 A20
dr. Braeside 532 H15
dr. Doncaster 330 F19
dr. Launching Pl......345 D16
st. Pascoe Vale 281 B12
tce. Malvern East......457 F1
BRAESWOOD
rd. Kings Park.........275 C19
BRAEWOOD
av. Ringwood E 379 C15
pl. Melton W...........226 A14
BRAGGE
st. Frankston 599 C15
BRAHAM
st. Donvale 376 F6
BRAHE
pl. E Melbourne 25 L9
BRAHMAN
cl. Belmont.............706 B6
ct. Dandenong N.....501 E13
BRAHMIN
av. Wheelers Hl 460 J17
BRAID
st. W Footscray 366 J10
BRAIDHILL
rd. Macleod 285 C17
BRAIDWOOD
av. Rosebud............683 F19
av. Rosebud W........683 F19
BRAILSFORD
rd. Bentleigh 496 C5
BRAIM
st. Sunshine N........321 E15
BRAIMTON
cl. Ringwood N.......378 D2
BRAITHWAITE
st. Reservoir...........282 H3
BRAMALL
pl. Caroline Spr.......317 H2
BRAMBER
ct. Templestowe 331 L7
BRAMBLE
cl. Lyndhurst...........551 A20
cr. Bundoora...........242 D15
cr. Bundoora...........242 E15
wy. Point Cook.........450 H15
BRAMBLEBERRY
la. Chirnside Pk 337 C6
BRAMCOTE
dr. Westmeadows 236 L15
BRAMERTON
rd. Caulfield 455 K4

BRAMLEY
cr. Wheelers Hl 461
ct. Hallam...............537
ct. Kew..................372
dr. Ringwood N.......378
st. Dandenong.........535
BRAMPTON
cct. Delahey 275
cl. Craigieburn........150
cl. Craigieburn........194
cl. Point Cook..........450
ct. Narre Warren.....538
ct. Vermont 421
st. Cheltenham 497
BRAMTON
ct. Mulgrave 500
BRAMWELL
cl. Endeavour Hl 537
st. Lilydale.............339
BRANAGAN
dr. Aspendale Gdn...547
BRANCA
ct. Nar Warrn N 538
BRANCH
rd. Bayswater N 379
st. Moonee Pnd 324
BRAND
ct. Melton S............268
dr. Thomastown.......241
rd. Knoxfield 463
st. Hampton 495
st. Menzies Ck 468
st. Mt Waverley 418
BRANDON
cl. Brighton 454
ct. Briar Hill 286
ct. Craigieburn........194
ct. Endeavour Hl 537
ct. Springvale S 499
st. Glen Iris.............417
wy. Clayton S...........499
BRANDON PARK
dr. Wheelers Hl 460
dr. Wheelers Hl 460
dr. Wheelers Hl 460
BRANDT
rd. Lysterfield..........505
BRANIGAN
ct. Sunbury 143
BRANKSOME
gr. Blackburn S 375
gr. Blackburn S 419
BRANSDALE
cl. Mooroolbark......338
BRANSGROVE
st. Preston.............327
BRANSON
st. Rosebud............699
BRANSTON
rd. St Albans...........320
BRANTON
dr. Hampton Pk.......551
dr. Hampton Pk.......551
rd. Hoppers Csg......448
rd. Hoppers Csg......449
BRASSER
av. Dromana 686
ct. Rosebud............700
BRASSEY
av. Highton 705
av. Rosanna 285
BRAVO
cl. Keilor Dn 275
ct. Lilydale.............294
BRAW
st. Williamstown......411
BRAY
ct. Bentleigh E 457
ct. Templestowe 332
st. Reservoir...........240
st. South Yarra 32
st. South Yarra 414
BRAYBROOK
dr. Nar Warrn S.......579
BRAYFORD
nk. Craigieburn........194
BRAYSHAY
rd. Newcomb..........704
BRAYWOOD
dr. Bangholme 549
tce. Cairnlea 319
BRAZEEL
st. Blackburn S 419
BRAZIL
ct. Epping...............198
BRAZILIA
av. Kealba 276
dr. Glen Waverley....460
BREAD
st. Geelong West 702
BREADALBANE
av. Cairnlea 319
ct. Sydenham 274

Newport 411 A10
Newcomb 703 L14
EAKADAY
Chirnside Pk 337 J2
EAKNECK
Yarra Glen 208 B20
EAKWATER
Point Cook..........450 F3
Belmont.............706 K2
Breakwater 703 F19
Breakwater 703 D20
Breakwater 706 K2
Thomson...........703 E19
EAM
Maribyrnong......322 L12
Maribyrnong......323 A12
EAM BAY
Patterson L........573 F7
EAMLEA
Dandenong N.....501 K9
Meadow Ht........237 K6
Cranbourne W ...577 F19
EAR
Springvale 499 G10
EARLEY
Anglesea............713 J1
Rowville.............502 J5
e. Pascoe Vale S 324 J2
Roxburgh Pk......194 D11
ECHIN
Greenvale 237 A2
Narre Warren 552 L4
ECON
Craigieburn........194 B3
St Albans...........320 J7
EE
Berwick 553 L18
Kurunjang..........226 H14
Rowville.............463 E12
EEN
Brighton East 495 H2
Braybrook..........366 B5
Preston.............282 F18
Ferny Creek.......426 A15
EENS
Cranbourne W ...577 F13
EES
Keilor East 322 H3
EESE
Langwarrin 629 L6
Brunswick..........325 F11
EEZE
Bonbeach 573 A5
EEZEWAY
Bangholme 549 J13
EFFNA
Preston.............327 B4
EMEN
Keilor Dn 276 D12
EMNER
Altona Mdw 451 E5
Mill Park............243 B3
ENBEAL
Balwyn 373 H12
Balwyn 373 H12
ENCHLEY
Prahran 32 A17
Prahran 414 F9
ENDA
Mt Waverley 419 A12
Croydon 336 K17
Narre Warren.....538 K15
Nunawading 376 F16
Tecoma 466 C9
Research 288 J7
Nunawading 376 E17
ENDALE
Blackburn N.......376 C9
ENDAN
Doncaster..........330 J17
Highton 701 H13
Greenvale 192 L15
Greenvale 193 A15
Mernda..............156 A13
ENDEL
Rosebud W........683 F18
ENDON
Hallam...............538 A15
ENNAN
Beaconsfld Up....541 G13
Altona Mdw 451 G2
Sydenham 274 K4
Wantirna S........462 C4
Bentleigh 455 J17
McKinnon 455 J17
Melton S............268 G9
ENNAND
Fitzroy N..............20 C1
ENOCK PARK
Ferntree Gly 464 G7

BRENS
dr. Parkville...............17 A3
dr. Parkville...............17 A5
rd. Smiths Gly.........205 L3
BRENT
cl. Berwick 554 K19
ct. Doncaster E........332 J14
mw. Sunshine W.......364 C5
st. Glen Waverley....420 E20
st. Mornington........640 H19
BRENTANI
av. Elsternwick 455 A8
BRENTFIELD
ct. Mill Park 242 E9
BRENTFORD
ct. Noble Park N......501 F17
sq. Forest Hill 420 L2
BRENT LAUREN
ct. Anglesea............713 E3
BRENTLEIGH
ct. Vermont S 420 K8
BRENTLEY
cl. Point Cook.........450 G8
BRENTLY
cl. Nar Warrn N 538 K11
BRENTNALL
ct. Hampton Pk.......551 E8
rd. Croydon 379 E3
BRENTVALE
ct. Doncaster..........331 B12
BRENTWICK
dr. Greensbrgh........244 D17
BRENTWOOD
av. Lalor..................240 K9
av. Pascoe Vale S ...324 F4
cl. Clayton S 498 J6
cl. Dewhurst............510 D20
cr. Frankston 600 B18
dr. Avondale Ht 321 L15
dr. Cranbourne N 578 F10
dr. Glen Waverley....460 F12
dr. Wantirna............422 H12
dr. Werribee............447 G2
pl. Roxburgh Pk.......194 F11
ri. Eltham 287 E14
st. Bentleigh 496 E6
wy. Waurn Ponds.....705 B16
BRETBY
wy. Montrose...........381 J9
BRETONNEUX
sq. Malvern East 456 L3
BRETT
ct. Cheltenham 497 C18
ct. Lalor..................240 H4
ct. Sunbury 143 A8
dr. Carrum Downs...574 C16
dr. Keysborough 534 C12
mw. Mt Martha.........656 C9
pl. Endeavour Hl 537 K7
pl. Ferntree Gly 464 B5
pl. Wyndham Va 446 C13
rd. Warburton 349 G1
st. Brunswick...........325 H13
st. Murrumbeena 457 B14
st. Warrandyte 333 J3
BRETTON
ct. St Albans 275 J19
BREW
rd. Croydon 336 F15
BREWER
ct. Keysborough 534 F14
rd. Bentleigh 495 J1
rd. Brighton East.....455 H20
rd. Brighton East.....495 J1
BREWIS
la. Geelong..............703 B11
BREWSTER
rd. Rye 696 L15
rd. Rye 697 A14
st. Berwick 579 L1
st. Essendon............323 L6
st. Essendon............324 B6
wy. Taylors Hill.........274 K11
BREX
ct. Reservoir............282 A7
BREYDON
ct. St Albans 320 H6
pl. Hampton Pk.......552 D10
BREYLEIGH
dr. Pakenham 559 A17
BREYNIA
wy. Cranbourne W ...577 K16
BRIAN
ct. Dingley Vill.........533 B8
ct. Mt Eliza..............642 D2
ct. Niddrie 322 L3
st. Bentleigh E 496 G2
st. Fawkner..............281 G1
st. Mitcham..............377 A17
st. Safety Bch 668 K19
BRIAR
cl. Gladstone Pk 236 L20
cl. Narre Warren.....553 F9

cl. Somerville 644 J13
ct. Doncaster..........374 K1
ct. Grovedale 706 C16
ct. Langwarrin 629 H1
ct. S Morang 243 H1
ct. Tarneit................405 A8
gr. Mulgrave 500 E2
la. Templestowe 331 L1
pl. Pascoe Vale S 324 E6
st. Boronia...............424 E18
st. Oakleigh S 497 E1
wk. Blackburn S 420 A5
wy. Sunshine W 364 D8
BRIARCREST
dr. Cranbourne E......578 J20
dr. Cranbourne E......604 J1
BRIARDALE
dr. Werribee............446 L17
BRIARFIELD
ct. Forest Hill 420 J4
ct. Templestowe 331 D13
rd. Noble Park N......501 E17
BRIARHURST
av. Dandenong N......502 D15
BRIARLEY
ct. Hampton Pk........552 C14
BRIAR ROSE
wk. Croydon S 380 B14
BRIAR VIEW
la. Briar Hill 286 G5
BRIARWOOD
ct. Croydon 336 E17
ct. Doncaster E........332 E12
ct. Sunbury 144 C10
BRICE
av. Mooroolbark.......337 B18
av. Newtown 702 B10
gr. Knoxfield 463 A7
BRICK
ct. Pearcedale.........646 L3
ct. Pearcedale.........647 A3
BRICKENDON
dr. Rosebud W........699 D2
BRICKER
st. Cheltenham 497 D14
BRICKWOOD
st. Brighton 454 J10
BRICKWORKS
la. Northcote 326 L13
BRIDE
av. Hampton Pk........551 F8
st. Malvern 415 K10
BRIDGE
cr. Montmorency 286 K9
ct. Croydon S 379 G12
gr. Kalorama 383 F10
rd. Burnley...............371 A16
rd. Keysborough 535 C11
rd. Melton S.............268 H13
rd. Richmond.............26 B10
rd. Richmond...........371 A16
st. Brighton 454 L8
st. Bulleen 329 F9
st. Eltham................287 D10
st. Essendon............324 E3
st. Hampton 494 L11
st. Hampton 495 A11
st. Newtown 702 D14
st. Northcote 326 F17
st. Northcote 326 G17
st. Port Melb..............29 A8
st. Port Melb............412 H1
st. Port Melb............413 A4
st. Queenscliff..........709 C16
st. Spotswood 411 D1
st. Werribee.............447 H16
tr. Olinda.................427 H4
BRIDGEFORD
av. Blackburn N 376 C9
cr. Melton S.............268 H12
ct. Heidelberg W 328 D2
BRIDGE INN
rd. Doreen 156 C19
rd. Doreen 201 A1
rd. Mernda..............155 A17
rd. Wollert 153 J16
BRIDGES
av. Coburg N...........281 B13
av. Edithvale............546 K11
av. Mooroolbark.......381 E1
rd. Healesville 212 H15
st. Glen Iris..............417 A15
st. Melton S.............268 J9
BRIDGET
ct. Kings Park 319 C3
ct. Warranwood 334 K16
st. Glen Waverley....460 B4
BRIDGETON
st. Reservoir............283 G2
BRIDGE VIEW
st. Belmont..............702 B18

BRIDGEWATER
ct. Langwarrin 630 B12
dr. Dingley Vill.........532 L9
gr. Thomastown......241 K16
rd. Craigieburn 194 C6
rd. Roxburgh Pk.......194 D8
rd. Seville E.............343 A15
tce. Caroline Spr......317 L6
wy. Rowville.............462 K20
wy. Truganina 405 E13
BRIDGEWOOD
ct. Wantirna S.........423 A16
BRIDLE
ct. Endeavour Hl 503 L19
ct. Epping................198 D19
pl. Pakenham 585 F6
BRIDLE PATH
Chirnside Pk 337 F7
BRIDLINGTON
dr. Greenvale 193 B17
BRIDPORT
st. Albert Park...........29 H11
st. Albert Park.........413 D6
st. S Melbourne........29 H11
st. S Melbourne......413 D6
st.w,Albert Park 29 D13
st.w,Albert Park 413 B7
BRIEN
la. Melbourne.............2 L11
BRIENS
la. Croydon, off
Main St 380 A5
BRIERLY
ct. Sunbury 142 K6
BRIGALO
ct. Keysborough 534 G11
BRIGANTINE
ct. Frankston 628 E7
ct. Patterson L........573 H8
BRIGDEN
ct. Mill Park 242 J4
BRIGETTE
ct. Lalor..................240 H10
BRIGGS
cr. Noble Park..........500 K20
dr. Derrimut.............363 G13
st. Caulfield 455 H5
st. Laverton 407 F12
st. Mont Albert N 374 D6
st. Mt Waverley 458 G9
st. Reservoir............283 C2
BRIGHT
cr. Mt Eliza..............626 G15
pl. Blackburn S 375 F20
pl. Blackburn S 419 F1
pl. Geelong..............703 B9
rd. Montrose............381 K16
st. Brighton East 455 B18
st. Camberwell.........417 E8
st. Campbellfield 239 A9
st. Kew....................372 C8
st. Southbank 24 D14
BRIGHTON
av. Preston..............326 L4
av. Wyndham Va.....446 E8
cr. Mt Eliza..............642 C9
ct. Avondale Ht 322 C7
pl. Taylors Hill.........274 J8
rd. Balaclava 414 F19
rd. Dandenong 535 G10
rd. Elsternwick 454 G1
rd. Elwood 454 G1
rd. St Kilda 414 F19
rt. Berwick 539 K16
st. Flemington 33 L2
st. Frankston S 626 G10
st. Glen Waverley....420 G17
st. Oakleigh 458 A15
st. Richmond.............32 G3
st. Sandringham 495 D13
BRIGHTS
dr. Rye 697 J8
dr. Tootgarook 698 B7
pl. Melbourne.............1 C6
pl. Melbourne............23 H6
BRIGHTWELL
rd. Lilydale..............338 L11
rd. Lilydale..............339 A11
BRIM
ct. Westmeadows ...237 E11
BRIMAR
cl. Diamond Ck........246 A8
ct. Mt Waverley 418 K18
BRIMBANK
bvd. St Albans 275 K18
rd. Keilor East 277 G19
BRIMPTON
gr. Wyndham Va 446 B15
BRINAWA
dr. Greensbrgh.........243 J17
BRINBAAL
ct. Kurunjang...........227 D15

BRINDALEE
mw. Chadstone 458 D2
pl. Cranbourne E......578 J17
wy. Hillside 274 E5
BRINDISI
st. Mentone 530 L8
st. Mentone 531 A8
BRINDY
cr. Doncaster E 375 F4
ct. Croydon 336 G14
BRINE
st. Hughesdale.........457 E15
st. Mt Waverley 459 C2
BRINGA
av. Camberwell.........417 C3
BRINKHILL
ct. Cairnlea 319 L13
BRINKKOTTER
rd. Research 288 G5
BRINSLEY
rd. Camberwell.........373 A20
rd. Camberwell.........417 A1
BRINTON
la. Caroline Spr 317 K2
BRIODY
dr. Torquay..............711 E3
BRISBANE
la. Wantirna, off
Capital City Bvd..422 K17
pde. Warburton 349 H1
rd. Beaconsfld Up....542 G14
rd. Cockatoo 511 F12
st. Albion.................320 H19
st. Ascot Vale 324 F16
st. Beaconsfield 555 A16
st. Berwick 554 F6
st. Eltham................287 D9
st. Murrumbeena 457 B5
st. Strathmore 280 B17
tce. Parkdale 531 L11
BRISBANE HILL
rd. Warburton 349 H1
BRISCOE
ct. Endeavour Hl 537 J9
la. Melbourne.............1 K14
la. Melbourne...........24 B9
pl. Roxburgh Pk......194 C15
BRISLINGTON
st. Sunshine 365 F2
BRISTOL
av. Edithvale............546 H15
cr. Lilydale...............338 K10
ct. Epping................197 J17
ct. Forest Hill 420 E9
ct. Glen Iris..............416 G7
ct. Glen Waverley....459 H7
ct. Kilsyth 381 G6
ct. Noble Park..........534 J7
mw. Craigieburn 194 B4
pl. Rowville..............463 E17
rd. Pascoe Vale 280 H10
rd. Torquay..............711 L9
st. Airport W 279 C16
st. Bentleigh E 457 C20
st. Heidelberg 329 E3
st. Surrey Hills.........417 H1
BRISTOW
cl. Rowville..............463 F17
dr. Forest Hill 376 J20
st. Footscray............367 F11
st. Seddon...............367 F11
BRITANNIA
st. Geelong West 702 E1
wy. Lilydale..............338 H3
BRITANNIA CREEK
rd. Wesburn.............347 L14
rd. Wesburn.............348 E19
BRITANNIA STREET
ml. Mitcham, off
Maroondah Hwy 377 B13
BRITISH
pl. Hoppers Csg......448 A1
BRITT
ct. Keilor East 322 G4
ct. Newport 410 L6
BRITTEN
ct. Bundoora............242 H17
st. Glen Iris.............416 K12
BRITTINGHAM
ct. Macleod 284 K10
BRITTON
rd. Seville.................341 L14
BRIXTON
av. Eltham North 287 C2
pl. Melton 226 K16
rd. Cheltenham 495 L17
ri. Glen Iris..............416 K13
st. Bonbeach 545 F15
st. Bonbeach 573 A4
st. Flemington 324 E20
BROAD
st. Greensbrgh.........286 A5
st. W Footscray 366 H6

st. Westmeadows ...237 A13
st. Westmeadows ...237 B14
BROAD ACRES
rd. Panton Hill ...205 D14
rd. Smiths Gly ...205 D14
BROADACRES
ct. Narre Warren ...538 K20
BROADBEACH
rd. Jan Juc ...711 A20
BROADBENT
ct. Chelsea Ht ...547 E14
wy. Pakenham ...584 D3
BROADCHAPEL
pl. Clarinda ...498 D7
BROADFORD
cr. Macleod ...284 K11
BROADGREEN
av. Wantirna ...422 A12
BROAD GULLY
rd. Diamond Ck ...202 C11
rd. Diamond Ck ...245 J8
rd. Hurstbridge ...202 C11
rd. Wattle Glen ...246 A3
rd. Yarrambat ...202 C11
BROADHURST
av. Reservoir ...282 B6
rd. Pakenham ...585 E4
wy. Caroline Spr ...317 J4
BROADIES
rd. Coldstream ...295 K10
BROADLAND
wy. Nar Warrn S ...579 B5
BROADLANDS
ct. Hoppers Csg ...448 F9
st. Dandenong S ...535 L11
BROADLEA
cr. Viewbank ...285 K16
BROADMEADOWS
rd. Gladstone Pk ...236 L15
rd. Gladstone Pk ...237 A15
rd. Tullamarine ...278 H7
rd. Westmeadows ...236 L15
rd. Westmeadows ...237 A15
BROADOAK
st. Noble Park ...534 B3
st. Springvale S ...534 B3
BROADWALK
gr. Endeavour Hl ...537 D1
BROADWATER
dr. Waterways ...547 D1
BROADWAY
Belgrave ...466 E17
Bonbeach ...545 F12
Bonbeach ...573 A2
Camberwell ...372 K18
Camberwell ...372 L18
Camberwell ...373 A18
Elwood ...454 D3
Reservoir ...283 B10
Rosebud W ...698 K2
Rosebud W ...699 A1
bvd. Wyndham Va ...446 D11
gdn. Bonbeach ...547 D19
st. Roxburgh Pk ...193 K4
BROADWAY EAST
Point Cook ...450 A5
BROADWAY WEST
Point Cook ...449 L5
BROCK
pl. Richmond ...26 C13
st. Thomastown ...241 F18
BROCKA
av. Belmont ...702 A19
BROCKENSHIRE
st. Clifton Hill ...20 G7
BROCKLEY
rd. Fawkner ...281 G10
BROCKS
rd. Doreen ...201 J1
rd. Nutfield ...202 A1
BRODERICK
rd. Carrum Downs ...600 H1
BRODIE
ct. Meadow Ht ...238 D1
mw. Derrimut ...363 C5
mw. Officer ...555 J20
st. Seaford ...599 C3
BRODRIBB
st. Bentleigh ...495 L4
BROGDEN
ct. Rowville ...503 F2
BROGIL
rd. N Warrandyte ...289 J13
wk. Sydenham ...274 K7
BROKEN
ct. Werribee ...447 H8
BROLGA
av. Chelsea Ht ...547 G17
cr. Wandana Ht ...701 E20
ct. Carrum Downs ...600 J5
ct. Melton ...226 H18
ct. Werribee ...448 C10
pl. S Morang ...243 K4

st. Mt Waverley ...419 A18
st. Westmeadows ...236 H14
BROMAGE
cl. Hoppers Csg ...405 G20
ct. Grovedale ...706 B10
ct. Wantirna S ...462 C4
BROMBY
st. Gembrook ...512 J11
st. Melbourne ...31 A5
st. Melbourne ...414 A3
st. South Yarra ...31 A5
st. South Yarra ...414 A3
BROME
st. St Albans ...320 G5
BROMHAM
pl. Richmond ...26 F7
BROMLEY
av. Cranbourne E ...578 K18
cl. Chirnside Pk ...336 G7
cl. Ferntree Gly ...463 E3
cl. Heathmont ...379 A20
cl. Toorak ...415 G8
pl. Epping ...198 F15
st. Rosebud ...699 J2
st. Thomson ...703 H16
st. Wyndham Va ...446 F9
BROMPTON
cl. Frankston S ...627 G16
ct. Kilsyth ...380 L8
BROMWICH
ct. Mill Park ...242 H3
BROMYARD
st. Yarraville ...366 G16
BRONALDI
st. Heathmont ...379 C20
BRONCO
ct. Meadow Ht ...193 L20
BRONHILL
ct. Cranbourne W ...577 G18
rd. Ringwood E ...379 D4
BRONSDON
ct. Mill Park ...242 E2
BRONTE
av. Burwood ...418 K7
ct. Croydon N ...336 A11
ct. Delahey ...275 E15
ct. Hampton ...495 G9
ct. Williamstown ...411 G12
ct. Wyndham Va ...446 E10
ri. Templestowe ...332 B11
st. Heidelberg ...328 J4
BRONWYN
ct. Anglesea ...713 E9
ct. Blackburn S ...419 K4
ct. Clayton S ...499 D16
ct. Deer Park ...319 B11
ct. Research ...288 K4
ct. Wheelers Hl ...461 C17
st. Coldstream ...295 D14
BRONZE WING
ct. Cannons Creek ...649 C6
BRONZEWING
st. S Morang ...199 H10
BROOK
cl. Montmorency ...287 B7
cr. Box Hill S ...418 K5
ct. Hampton Pk ...551 H7
dr. Altona ...408 K15
st. Hawthorn ...371 E14
st. Jacana ...237 K17
st. Sunbury ...143 H12
st. Yarraville ...367 B14
BROOKDALE
av. Emerald ...469 F17
BROOKE
cl. Noble Park ...534 K5
cr. Blairgowrie ...679 G20
ct. Ashwood ...418 B15
ct. Eltham ...288 A2
ct. Hoppers Csg ...447 K3
ct. Pakenham ...585 G3
ct. Scoresby ...462 C6
dr. Doncaster E ...332 F8
st. Albert Park ...29 F10
st. Albert Park ...413 C5
st. Eaglemont ...328 J13
st. Northcote ...326 K17
st. S Melbourne ...29 F10
st. S Melbourne ...413 C5
BROOKEDGE
ct. Craigieburn ...194 A3
BROOKER
ct. Sunshine N ...321 F16
BROOKES
cr. Fitzroy N ...19 A3
ct. Mill Park ...242 H4
ct. Mooroolbark ...381 F1
st. Pt Lonsdale ...710 F4
BROOKFIELD
ct. Berwick ...539 F18
ct. Hawthorn E ...416 G2
pl. Warranwood ...335 C17

BROOKGLEN
bvd. Cairnlea ...320 A12
ct. Epping ...197 E20
BROOKING
st. Upwey ...465 L15
BROOKLAND
ct. Mulgrave ...501 D4
gr. Thomastown ...240 J11
BROOKLAND GREENS
bvd. Cranbourne ...603 D7
BROOKLYN
av. Caulfield S ...455 G9
av. Dandenong S ...535 F13
av. Frankston ...627 J9
ct. Campbellfield ...239 D14
rd. Brookfield ...267 B5
BROOKLYN BAY
cl. Rowville ...502 L7
cl. Rowville ...503 A7
BROOKLYN PARK
dr. Brookfield ...266 L6
dr. Brookfield ...267 A6
BROOKS
av. Blairgowrie ...680 A19
cr. Diamond Ck ...245 L11
dr. Dandenong S ...549 G4
st. Bentleigh E ...457 E18
st. Burnley ...371 C18
st. Fawkner ...281 K6
BROOKSIDE
ct. Caroline Spr ...318 B6
ct. Craigieburn ...150 C14
st. Upwey ...465 J17
BROOKVALE
cl. Beaconsfield ...555 A18
ct. Roxburgh Pk ...193 L5
BROOKVILLE
av. Werribee ...447 G2
ct. Nar Warrn S ...578 E3
dr. Craigieburn ...150 K5
rd. Toorak ...415 B7
BROOKWOOD
dr. Mt Eliza ...626 C9
st. Glen Waverley ...460 C8
BROOME
av. Mentone ...531 H7
cl. Lynbrook ...551 H16
cr. Cranbourne N ...578 J9
ct. Epping ...241 J4
BROOMFIELD
av. Alphington ...327 F19
rd. Hawthorn E ...372 D20
BROOMHILL
av. Blackburn ...375 G14
BROOMPARK
cr. Olinda ...427 E14
BROSA
av. Bentleigh E ...496 G5
BROSNAN
cr. Strathmore ...280 A15
rd. Bentleigh E ...497 A5
BROTHERS
cl. Scoresby ...462 D6
BROTT
ct. Dandenong N ...502 B15
ct. Keysborough ...534 D7
BROUGH
st. McKinnon ...456 D17
st. Springvale ...500 F9
BROUGHAM
av. Wyndham Va ...446 C14
cl. Eumemmerring ...537 D11
pl. Geelong, off Mercer St ...702 L5
sq. Mulgrave ...501 D6
st. Box Hill ...374 H16
st. Eltham ...287 D11
st. Geelong ...703 A6
st. Kew ...371 J10
st. N Melbourne ...34 J9
st. Richmond ...26 G13
BROUGHTON
av. Croydon ...335 J19
av. Reservoir ...282 J13
dr. Highton ...705 K7
pl. W Melbourne ...23 E5
rd. Surrey Hills ...374 C19
st. Seaford ...599 C1
BROULA
ct. Taylors L ...276 B7
BROWN
al. Melbourne ...1 B9
al. Melbourne ...2 C14
al. Melbourne ...23 H8
al. Melbourne ...24 D8
av. Altona Mdw ...451 F6
av. Ascot Vale ...323 H19
la. N Melbourne ...17 F18
pl. Geelong, off Ginn St ...702 K3
rd. Officer ...556 D14
rd. Officer ...557 C15
rd. Pakenham ...557 C15

st. Avondale Ht ...321 L15
st. Boronia ...424 E10
st. Brighton East ...455 D12
st. Coburg ...325 G4
st. Collingwood ...25 K1
st. E Geelong ...703 F12
st. Heidelberg ...328 H5
st. Heidelberg ...329 A6
st. Lilydale ...338 G4
st. Newport ...411 A7
st. Preston ...283 D19
BROWNBILL
st. Geelong ...703 E11
BROWNE
av. St Albans ...320 C12
la. Red Hill ...688 B12
st. McCrae ...685 B11
BROWNELL
rd. Glen Iris ...417 C12
BROWNES
cr. Eltham ...287 J9
BROWNFIELD
st. Cheltenham ...530 L1
st. Cheltenham ...531 A1
st. Mordialloc ...531 L13
st. Parkdale ...531 L13
BROWNHILL
st. Bundoora ...284 F2
BROWNING
av. Clayton S ...499 D8
cr. Avondale Ht ...322 F10
ct. Watsonia N ...285 E3
dr. Glen Waverley ...420 H14
dr. Templestowe ...332 A13
rd. Boronia ...423 J10
st. Elwood ...454 E1
st. Kilsyth ...380 K6
st. Kingsbury ...283 K11
st. Moonee Pnd ...324 C15
st. Seddon ...367 B12
wk. South Yarra ...32 F15
wk. South Yarra ...414 J8
BROWNLEE
cr. Wheelers Hl ...460 F17
BROWNLOW
cr. Epping ...198 A20
dr. Diamond Ck ...245 K5
BROWNS
av. Ringwood ...378 C11
ct. Clayton ...459 A18
la. Aspendale ...546 C1
la. Maddingley ...264 L10
la. Parwan ...265 A7
la. Plenty ...244 E3
la. S Melbourne ...29 K2
la. Glenroy, off Argyle St ...280 A6
rd. Bentleigh E ...496 J2
rd. Boneo ...698 K14
rd. Boneo ...700 K13
rd. Clayton ...499 A3
rd. Cranbourne S ...602 G19
rd. Cranbourne S ...604 J20
rd. Fingal ...697 E13
rd. Keilor ...277 A5
rd. Montrose ...382 F12
rd. Noble Park N ...500 K14
rd. N Warrandyte ...289 L16
rd. Nunawading ...376 L19
rd. Rye ...696 G11
rd. Rye ...697 A11
rd. Werribee ...446 E20
BROWN THORNBILL
ct. Langwarrin ...628 J7
BROWTOP
rd. Narre Warren ...539 F15
rd. Narre Warren ...539 G16
BROXBOURNE
br. Mornington ...656 L3
br. Mornington ...657 A3
BROXBURN
ct. Berwick ...554 E16
BRUARONG
cr. Frankston S ...626 H5
BRUCE
av. Rye ...696 E8
cr. Ferntree Gly ...464 E2
ct. Berwick ...554 G16
ct. Elsternwick ...455 C6
ct. Pakenham ...558 L20
ct. Ringwood E ...379 C11
ct. Springvale S ...500 B19
ct. Sunbury ...143 F3
dr. Somerville ...644 K16
rd. Frankston ...627 G7
rd. Mt Martha ...669 B11
rd. Mt Martha ...669 B11
rd. Safety Bch ...669 B11
rd. Safety Bch ...669 B11
st. Albion ...364 H1
st. Balwyn ...373 K9
st. Beaumaris ...529 K9
st. Bentleigh ...456 C18
st. Box Hill ...374 K14

st. Brighton East ...455
st. Brunswick ...325
st. Bulleen ...330
st. Coburg ...325
st. Cranbourne ...604
st. Dandenong ...536
st. Diamond Ck ...246
st. Fawkner ...281
st. Greensbrgh ...244
st. Greensbrgh ...286
st. Kensington ...34
st. Lalor ...241
st. Laverton ...407
st. Malvern East ...457
st. Mitcham ...376
st. Moonee Pnd ...323
st. Mornington ...641
st. Mt Waverley ...459
st. Newport ...410
st. Preston ...326
st. Preston ...326
st. Preston ...326
st. Rye ...697
st. Seaford ...599
st. Strathmore ...324
st. Toorak ...415
st. W Footscray ...366
st.s, Altona Mdw ...407
wy. Taylors L ...233
BRUCEDALE
cr. Pk Orchards ...333
BRUFORD
av. Wheelers Hl ...461
st. Diamond Ck ...246
BRULU
cl. Mt Eliza ...642
BRUMBY
ct. Cranbourne ...578
BRUMBYS
rd. Carrum Downs ...575
rd. Warrandyte S ...334
BRUMFIELD
rd. Healesville ...257
BRUNDAGE
ct. Heidelberg W ...328
BRUNDRETT
rd. Nar Warrn N ...539
BRUNEI
cr. Heidelberg W ...284
gr. Frankston ...600
BRUNEL
ct. Aberfeldie ...323
ct. Hampton Pk ...551
rd. Seaford ...573
rd. Seaford ...599
st. Aberfeldie ...323
st. Aberfeldie ...323
st. Malvern East ...416
st. S Kingsville ...410
BRUNET
st. Dandenong N ...535
BRUNNING
cr. Frankston N ...600
ct. Somerville ...644
st. Balaclava ...414
st. Upwey ...465
BRUNNINGS
rd. Carrum Downs ...575
BRUNSDON
st. Bayswater ...424
BRUNSWICK
gr. Taylors Hill ...274
pl. Fitzroy ...19
rd. Brunswick ...325
rd. Brunswick E ...325
rd. Brunswick W ...325
rd. Mitcham ...377
st. Coburg ...325
st. Fitzroy ...25
st. Fitzroy N ...19
st. Fitzroy N ...19
st. W Footscray ...366
st.n, Fitzroy N ...19
st.n, Fitzroy N ...326
BRUNT
rd. Officer ...581
st. Cranbourne ...604
BRUNTON
av. E Melbourne ...25
av. Melbourne ...25
cr. Tullamarine ...278
st. Ascot Vale ...324
wy. Ferntree Gly ...463
BRUSCO
pl. Rowville ...462
BRUSELL
cl. Taylors L ...233
BRUSH
gr. Glen Waverley ...420
rd. Epping ...197
BRUSHWOOD
cct. Roxburgh Pk ...193
cl. Somerville ...644

Bangholme...549 K13
Frankston...600 A16
USHY PARK
Chirnside Pk...292 A19
Wonga Park...336 B1
UTHEN
Brookfield...268 D5
Highton...701 K16
Moorabbin...496 H8
Preston...327 J3
UTON
Cheltenham...530 L4
Yallambie...285 G12
UTUS
Hampton Pk...551 E13
UXNER
Taylors L...233 F20
Taylors L...233 G20
YAN
Altona North...409 K9
Eltham...287 H6
Melton...226 F18
Pascoe Vale...280 L12
Sunshine N...321 F14
Frankston...627 G1
Northcote...327 C17
Reservoir...282 E15
YANT
Rye...696 J13
Brunswick...325 E11
Flemington...34 B2
YANTS
Dandenong S...536 A13
YDEN
Ferntree Gly...463 G9
YDIE
Tarneit, off
Pandelis Bvd...447 J2
YDON
Mornington...657 D3
YMPTON
Pk Orchards...333 G16
YNMAWR
Camberwell...416 J7
YNOR
Glen Waverley...460 J1
Preston...283 K17
YSON
Brighton...454 K18
Bundoora...242 H15
Endeavour Hl...537 J11
Langwarrin...601 L17
Sydenham...274 K4
Templstw Lr...330 F11
Canterbury...373 F20
YSONS
Warranwood...334 L13
Warranwood...335 A13
Wonga Park...335 D4
CH
Epping...241 F4
CHAN
Highton...701 F19
Keilor...276 L14
Keilor...277 A14
Taylors Hill...274 J15
Wantirna S...422 J19
n. Pakenham...583 L5
Dandenong N...501 L10
Meadow Ht...238 A3
Moorabbin...496 H8
CHANAN
Balwyn N...373 D7
Taylors L...233 G20
Greenvale...236 L2
Beaconsfield...556 A1
Berwick...554 H7
Brooklyn...365 C19
Guys Hill...556 A1
Boronia...424 E16
Ivanhoe...328 A15
St Albans...319 G5
CHER
Rosebud...684 D14
CKEYE
Hallam...552 D1
Narre Warren...552 E1
CKHURST
Richmond...26 L10
Richmond...371 A15
S Melbourne...29 F1
S Melbourne...29 C3
S Melbourne...413 B2
CKINGHAM
Bentleigh...456 F19
Springvale...499 L14
Narre Warren...539 F16
Somerville...644 H16
Doncaster...330 D18
Sunshine W...365 A9
Thomastown...241 H14
Heidelberg...329 E5
Rosanna...329 E5

dr. Rowville...502 J4
dr. Werribee...446 J11
pl. Frankston S...627 K11
rd. Newtown...701 L12
st. Footscray...367 C9
st. Richmond...26 H6
st. Richmond...371 A13
st. Sydenham...232 K20
BUCKLAND
av. Newtown...702 H9
cr. Epping...197 L17
cr. Keilor...276 L14
ct. Endeavour Hl...503 B20
st. Clayton...499 C4
st. Travancore...324 G20
wy. Sunbury...187 E7
BUCKLE
rd. Kurunjang...227 E12
BUCKLEIGH
la. Beaconsfld Up...542 D19
la. Guys Hill...542 D19
BUCKLEY
av. Sunshine N...321 B11
gdn. Avondale Ht...322 B7
pl. Melbourne...2 D10
pl. Melbourne...24 D6
rd. Diggers Rest...187 E8
st. Aberfeldie...323 D8
st. Avondale Ht...322 A6
st. Carnegie...456 G5
st. Essendon...323 C8
st. Essendon W...322 D7
st. Footscray...367 C10
st. Keilor East...322 A6
st. Noble Park...534 G6
st. Noble Park...534 H4
st. Point Cook...449 L4
st. Safety Bch...669 C13
st. Seddon...367 B10
wy. Lynbrook...551 D16
BUCKLEY FALLS
rd. Highton...701 E9
BUCKLEYS
la. Noble Park...500 H20
rd. Merrimu...222 J4
rd. Merrimu...223 A4
rd. Pt Lonsdale...710 E7
BUCKMASTER
dr. Mill Park...242 K9
dr. Mt Evelyn...339 F17
st. Sunbury...142 L10
st. Sunbury...143 A10
BUDD
st. Brighton...454 K13
st. Collingwood...19 H13
BUDDLE
dr. Toorak...415 C2
BUDDS
st. Coburg...325 J3
BUDERIM
rt. Berwick...553 J2
BUDGE
st. Noble Park...500 D17
BUDGIE
ct. Werribee...448 B10
BUENA VISTA
dr. Montmorency...286 K12
dr. Montmorency...287 A13
BUFFALO
ct. Berwick...580 A1
dr. Lalor...240 J9
BUFFER BREAK
tr. Wesburn...348 F20
BUGATTI
ct. Mill Park...242 L3
BUGAY
ct. Hillside...274 G6
BUGGATTI
ct. Keilor Dn...276 B16
BUGGY RIDE
la. Chirnside Pk...337 K2
BUICK
cr. Mill Park...242 K2
ct. Keilor Dn...276 C17
BULBAN
rd. Werribee...447 A18
BULDAH
st. Dandenong N...501 L9
BULEY
st. Hawthorn E...416 E6
BULGA
st. Mooroolbark...336 K14
BULLA
rd. Bulla...190 E17
rd. Essendon N...323 H1
rd. Strathmore...323 H1
BULLA-DIGGERS REST
rd. Bulla...189 A13
rd. Diggers Rest...187 K16
BULLANOO
ct. Greensbrgh...244 C18
BULLARTO
st. Chadstone...458 A2

BULLDOG
av. Olinda...427 H5
la. Long Forest...224 A19
BULLDOG CREEK
rd. Dromana...670 L16
BULLEEN
rd. Balwyn N...373 B3
rd. Bulleen...329 D20
BULLEN
av. Mitcham...377 D17
st. Doncaster E...375 J2
BULLENS
la. Melbourne...2 J11
la. Melbourne...24 F5
BULLER
ct. Hoppers Csg...449 B2
dr. Glen Waverley...420 D15
pde. Lalor...240 H7
tce. Templstw Lr...330 E12
BULLI
ct. Torquay...712 A3
st. Moorabbin...496 H12
BULL MALLEE
rd. Long Forest...224 C1
BULLOCK
ct. Donvale...332 K15
BULLRUSH
ct. Meadow Ht...193 K19
BULMANS
rd. Melton W...225 J20
rd. Melton W...225 K14
BULOKE
av. Wyndham Va...446 B5
cl. Mt Eliza...641 K8
BULONG
st. Dandenong...535 H8
BUNA
av. Seaford...599 C10
ct. Ashburton...417 G17
ct. Boronia...424 E3
ct. Herne Hill...702 A2
st. Heidelberg W...284 A19
wy. Keilor Dn...276 D13
BUNALBO
av. South Yarra...32 H11
av. South Yarra...414 K6
ct. Greensbrgh...286 L1
BUNANGIB
ct. Frankston S...626 H6
BUNARONG
cl. Keilor Dn...276 H17
ct. Dandenong N...501 G13
dr. Frankston...628 B3
BUNBURY
av. Narre Warren...538 E18
av. Narre Warren...538 F17
ct. Gladstone Pk...237 A16
st. Footscray...367 G9
st. Newport...411 C10
BUNCLE
st. N Melbourne...34 G11
st. N Melbourne...34 J7
BUNCLES
pl. N Melbourne...17 G15
BUNDALEER
rd. Wesburn...348 D20
BUNDALOHN
ct. St Kilda...414 E18
BUNDAMBA
rd. Noble Park N...501 C8
BUNDANOON
av. Sunbury...142 L1
av. Sunbury...143 A2
BUNDARA
cr. Mt Eliza...642 C5
ct. Frankston...627 D1
st. Fitzroy N...326 E18
BUNDARRA
ct. Vermont S...421 E11
BUNDEENA
av. Kealba...276 L18
av. Keysborough...534 H10
BUNDEERA
rd. Caulfield S...455 K9
BUNDJIL
ct. Cranbourne...578 A18
BUNDOORA
cr. Highton...705 G3
ct. Nar Warrn S...579 G2
BUNDORA
pde. Mentone...532 A8
pde. Moorabbin Aprt...532 A8
BUNDORAN
ct. Sunbury...144 G12
pde. Mont Albert N...374 C11
BUNDY
ct. Frankston N...600 D6
ct. Hillside...274 B1
ct. Yallambie...286 B11
dr. Melton S...269 D8
pl. Mill Park...243 B5
st. Frankston S...628 B16

BUNERONG
ct. Nar Warrn S...552 K20
wy. Mt Martha...656 C15
BUNGADOOL
st. Warneet...649 E13
BUNGALEEN
ct. Dandenong S...549 K10
BUNGALOOK
rd. Bayswater N...379 E20
rd. Bayswater N...423 G1
rd.w,Heathmont...379 D20
BUNGALOW
ct. Brighton...454 L9
la. Nar Warrn S...578 G3
BUNGARIM
wyn.Sydenham...274 J8
BUNGARRA
ct. Kurunjang...227 B14
BUNGAY
st. Fawkner...281 J2
st. Watsonia...285 C4
BUNGOWER
rd. Moorooduc...642 D18
rd. Mornington...641 B14
rd. Somerville...643 B18
BUNINYONG
st. Yarraville...367 B17
wy. Delahey...275 A11
BUNKER
av. Kingsbury...283 J9
cr. Glen Waverley...459 K3
ct. Dingley Vill...533 F8
ct. Frankston...599 J17
BUNNERONG
cr. Noble Park...534 G7
BUNNETT
rd. Knoxfield...463 D2
rd. Knoxfield...463 D3
st. Sunshine N...321 F13
BUNNEY
rd. Clarinda...498 C6
rd. Oakleigh S...498 A6
BUNNYS
la. Heatherton...497 L11
BUNTING
ct. Altona North...409 H6
ct. Lalor...241 J9
rd. Brooklyn...365 E13
st. Burnley...371 B19
BUNTON
ct. Werribee...447 C10
BUNURONG
pl. Cranbourne...578 B20
tr. Arthurs Seat...685 F11
BUNYA
ct. Narre Warren...538 J18
ct. Taylors L...276 A10
dr. Albanvale...319 D4
pl. Hampton Pk...551 K5
BUNYARRA
ct. Greensbrgh...244 D18
BUNYIP
ct. Werribee...447 F7
BURBANK
av. Gladstone Pk...279 C1
ct. Wheelers Hl...461 A8
dr. Reservoir...283 F2
st. Ashburton...417 E17
BURBERRY
ct. Carrum Downs...601 F2
BURBIDGE
cl. Bacchus Msh...221 F13
dr. Williamstown...410 L15
wy. Bacchus Msh...221 G13
BURBRIDGE
dr. Greenvale...237 D4
BURCH
st. Blackburn N...376 A9
BURCHALL
cr. Rowville...463 H18
gr. Dandenong N...501 J8
BURCHETT
la. E Melbourne...25 L8
st. Brunswick...325 G13
st. Monbulk...428 E19
BURCOTE
st. Blackburn N...376 A8
BURDEKIN
av. Bayswater N...380 G17
rd. Highton...705 F4
BURDEN
st. Springvale...499 H9
BURDETT
st. Frankston N...600 B8
st. Tootgarook...698 H1
BURDON
ct. Forest Hill...376 G20
BURDOO
dr. Grovedale...706 B15
st. Rye...697 C7
wy. Mt Martha...668 L4

BURGAN
ct. Cranbourne W...577 J17
pl. Meadow Ht...193 H20
BURGE
ct. Doncaster E...332 F18
BURGESS
cl. Bayswater N...380 D14
cl. Gladstone Pk...237 C18
ct. Frankston...599 J16
dr. Langwarrin...629 J1
rd. Bayswater N...380 E15
st. Beaumaris...530 A13
st. Bentleigh...496 B1
st. Brooklyn...365 E19
st. Hawthorn...416 C5
st. Hawthorn E...416 C5
st. Preston...326 D5
st. Richmond...32 G1
st. Tullamarine...278 F4
BURGI HILL
rd. Seville...341 E12
rd. Wandin N...341 E12
BURGOYNE
ct. Williamstown...411 A15
la. Williamstown...411 C13
BURGUNDY
cr. St Albans...320 F8
dr. Doncaster...330 H18
dr. Waurn Ponds...705 D14
dr. Waurn Ponds...705 E14
dr. Wyndham Va...446 H9
st. Heidelberg...328 H7
st. Heidelberg...329 B7
st. Pascoe Vale...280 E17
wy. Nar Warrn S...579 E4
BURILLA
av. Doncaster...375 E1
BURKE
av. Hawthorn E...372 H20
ct. Cranbourne N...577 L9
ct. Grovedale...706 B12
ct. Laverton...407 C17
rd. Balwyn...372 H20
rd. Balwyn N...372 J11
rd. Camberwell...416 G9
rd. Canterbury...372 H20
rd. Ferntree Gly...463 K1
rd. Glen Iris...416 G9
rd. Ivanhoe...328 K17
rd. Ivanhoe East...328 K17
rd. Kew...372 J11
rd. Kew East...372 J11
rd. Malvern East...456 F1
rd. Sunbury...142 L13
rd. Sunbury...143 A13
rd.n, Ivanhoe East...328 K14
st. Braybrook...321 J16
st. Montmorency...286 G11
st. Werribee...447 G19
BURKITT
ct. Preston...283 J17
BURLEIGH
ct. Frankston...627 H8
ct. Nunawading...376 D15
dr. Grovedale...706 H15
dr. Nar Warrn S...552 F19
dr. Templestowe...331 K13
rd. Melton...226 L15
st. Spotswood...411 B4
BURLES
ct. Kurunjang...227 F7
BURLEY
ct. Mulgrave...500 H1
st. Montrose...382 C9
BURLEY GRIFFIN
cl. Avondale Ht...321 L6
cl. Keilor East...321 L6
pl. Eaglemont...328 J12
BURLINGTON
ch. Hampton Pk...552 C11
cl. Wyndham Va...446 E8
cr. Wantirna...422 H9
st. Oakleigh...458 A12
BURLOCK
av. Ringwood N...378 B6
BURLORN
ct. Carrum Downs...601 D5
BURN
ct. Craigieburn...150 E17
BURNE
ct. Kew...371 L13
BURNELL
st. Brunswick W...324 L12
st. Mt Eliza...641 K2
BURNET
la. Point Cook...450 D5
st. Mulgrave...460 C18
wy. Point Cook...449 K6
BURNETT
av. Braybrook...321 J20
av. Braybrook...365 K1
cl. Taylors L...275 F2
cr. Frankston S...626 L12

cr. Reservoir 283 K3
ct. Altona Mdw 451 F5
ct. Mill Park 242 H5
ct. Ringwood 378 J15
st. Mitcham 377 D11
st. Mornington 640 E20
st. St Kilda 414 C14
BURNEWANG
st. Albion 364 H1
BURNHAM
dr. Hoppers Csg 448 E9
rd. Belgrave 466 C15
BURNIE
st. Toorak 415 B3
BURNISTON
av. Craigieburn 150 D8
BURNLEIGH
dr. Gladstone Pk 279 A1
BURNLEY
ct. Greenvale 192 L18
ct. Greenvale 193 A18
gr. Taylors Hill 274 J8
st. Burnley 371 A19
st. Frankston 627 H2
st. Laverton 407 F12
st. Point Cook 450 E6
st. Richmond 371 A19
BURNLEY TUNNEL
Melbourne 24 J16
Southbank 24 J16
BURNS
av. Clayton S 499 D8
av. Murrumbeena 457 A9
av. St Albans 320 J2
cl. Dromana 686 A10
cl. Mt Eliza 641 L7
ct. Eltham North 245 D20
ct. Heidelberg Ht 284 F18
ct. Templestowe 332 B12
gr. Kingsbury 283 J11
rd. Altona 407 K11
rd. Dromana 685 L9
st. Elwood 454 H4
st. Frankston 627 F2
st. Maidstone 366 G2
st. Moonee Pnd 323 H13
st. Prahran 31 K18
st. Prahran 414 E9
st. Yarraville 367 A13
wy. Delahey 275 E16
wy. Monbulk 468 K2
BURNSIDE
av. Canterbury 373 D20
av. Canterbury 417 D1
ct. Wantirna S 422 E16
pl. Greenvale 193 C17
st. Deer Park 319 C17
BURNT
st. Nunawading 376 F13
BURONG
ct. Mt Eliza 641 L3
BURONGA
av. Ringwood E 379 E13
BURR
ct. Laverton N 364 E16
rd. Woori Yall 344 A18
BURRAMINE
ct. Frankston S 627 F13
rd. Glen Waverley 460 F4
BURRANEER
cl. Ferntree Gly 463 H8
dr. Keysborough 534 G9
BURRAPIKE
av. Springvale 500 B16
BURRAWANG
ri. Eltham North 245 F18
tce. Mt Martha 669 B5
BURRAWONG
av. Seaford 573 D12
BURREEL
av. Elsternwick 455 D6
BURRELL
st. McCrae 685 A11
BURR HILL
ct. Berwick 554 H6
BURRIDGE
cl. Mill Park 242 A8
BURRILL
ct. Taylors Hill 274 G13
BURRINDI
rd. Caulfield S 455 K9
BURROUGHS
rd. Balwyn 373 K9
BURROW
st. Frankston 599 F17
BURROWES
st. Ascot Vale 323 L18
BURROWS
av. Dandenong 536 D5
pl. Geelong, off
Little Malop St..703 C8
st. Brighton 454 H20
BURROWYE
cr. Keilor 276 F8
cr. Taylors L 276 E9
BURSARIA
av. Ferntree Gly 423 H19
cr. Frankston N 600 C6
BURSTON
ct. Mt Martha 656 J6
pl. Brighton 494 H2
rd. Boronia 424 J13
BURSWOOD
cl. Frankston S 627 F13
ct. Seabrook 450 L6
BURT
cr. Hampton E 495 K10
st. Altona 408 K16
st. Northcote 326 L14
BURTON
av. Clayton 498 H3
av. Hawthorn 371 K19
av. Laverton 407 E16
cl. Keilor Dn 276 D13
cr. Ascot Vale 324 C19
cr. Ivanhoe East 328 J14
cr. Maribyrnong 323 E15
ct. Bayswater 423 J6
ct. Greenvale 192 J16
rd. Beaconsfld Up 542 H12
rd. Lilydale 338 H8
st. Balwyn N 373 J8
st. Chadstone 418 E20
st. Dromana 685 D9
st. Lalor 241 G8
st. Melbourne 24 H2
BURUNDA
rd. Rosebud 684 J19
BURVALE
ct. Tullamarine 278 F3
BURVILLE
cl. Berwick 554 B1
BURVILLES
rd. Mt Duneed 706 F20
BURWAH
av. Brighton East 495 G1
BURWOOD
av. Hawthorn E 372 H18
av. Ringwood 378 A13
av. Sunshine N 321 E12
av. Sunshine N 321 E9
ct. Narre Warren 553 A10
ct. Thomastown 240 H14
hwy. Belgrave 466 A12
hwy. Burwood 418 B9
hwy. Burwood E 419 B9
hwy. Camberwell 416 E7
hwy. Camberwell 417 H8
hwy. Ferntree Gly 463 J1
hwy. Hawthorn E 416 E7
hwy. Knoxfield 423 A18
hwy. Tecoma 466 B12
hwy. Up Fntree Gly 465 A7
hwy. Upwey 465 E8
hwy. Vermont S 420 H11
hwy. Vermont S 421 A11
hwy. Wantirna 422 A14
hwy. Wantirna 423 A18
hwy. Wantirna S 422 A14
hwy. Wantirna S 422 J17
hwy. Wantirna S 423 A18
rd. Burwood 418 D8
rd. Burwood E 419 F9
rd. Hawthorn 371 E16
rd. Hawthorn 372 F18
rd. Hawthorn E 371 F16
rd. Vermont S 421 D12
BUSANA
wy. Nunawading 376 F9
BUSCH
st. Sunshine N 321 D14
st. W Footscray 366 H7
BUSH
bvd. Mill Park 243 D2
ct. Frankston 599 L15
ct. Langwarrin 629 H1
mw. Gowanbrae 279 D4
pl. Sunbury 142 J8
st. Coburg N 281 G12
BUSHBURY
ct. Hughesdale 457 F7
ct. Somerville 644 C19
BUSHBY
ct. Darley 221 G4
ct. Kealba 276 K20
BUSHFIELD
cr. Coolaroo 238 E7
BUSHLAND
av. Clarinda 498 F10
ct. Eltham 287 D15
ct. Wheelers Hl 460 L10
BUSHLARK
dr. Carrum Downs 600 J1
dr. Carrum Downs 600 K2
BUSHMANS
wy. S Morang 199 L16
BUSHVIEW
gld. Boronia 424 E2
BUSHY
ct. Somerville 645 F18
BUSHY PARK
av. Caroline Spr 317 K1
av. Caroline Spr 318 A2
la. Wantirna S 421 F17
BUSINESS
dr. Nunawading 376 K16
BUSINESS PARK
dr. Notting Hill 459 B12
BUSSELL
ct. S Morang 243 H4
BUSST
dr. Watsonia N 285 E2
BUSTER
pl. Nar Warrn S 552 H17
BUTCHER
cr. Laverton 407 D12
ct. Nar Warrn S 552 D17
BUTE
st. Murrumbeena 457 C9
st. Seddon 367 D10
BUTLER
av. Mornington 640 L12
av. Mornington 641 A12
ct. Cheltenham 497 B20
ct. Cranbourne 577 K19
ct. Highton 705 F6
gr. Coburg 326 A6
la. Parkville 17 H10
la. Roxburgh Pk 194 C11
pl. Mill Park 198 H20
pl. Mill Park 242 H1
st. Braybrook 321 K19
st. Brighton 494 J1
st. Camberwell 416 J1
st. Essendon 324 C4
st. Eumemmerring ...537 A14
st. Northcote 326 J16
st. Preston 327 B5
st. Richmond 26 C3
st. Rye 680 G20
st. St Albans 319 H2
BUTLERS
cr. Panton Hill 248 K5
rd. Ferntree Gly 464 J3
rd. Plenty 244 H10
BUTMAR
cl. Werribee 446 H16
BUTTERCUP
gr. Bundoora 242 F16
la. Point Cook 450 J14
BUTTERFIELD
rd. Emerald 469 G9
BUTTERFLY
gdn. Doncaster E 332 H14
BUTTERMANS
tr. Christmas Hills ...207 C1
tr. St Andrews 207 C1
tr. Smiths Gly 207 C1
BUTTERS
st. Reservoir 282 H14
BUTTERWICK
tce. Cranbourne E 578 J17
BUTTERWORTH
cr. Anglesea 713 E4
BUTTLER
st. Kilsyth 381 E11
BUTTONWOOD
ct. Nar Warrn S 553 F19
BUTTRESS
cr. S Morang 199 J9
BUVELOT
ct. Chirnside Pk 336 K7
pl. Mill Park 243 A8
pl. Sunbury 143 C8
st. Yallambie 285 K14
wyn. Doncaster E 332 F16
BUXTON
cr. Frankston 628 D9
ct. Meadow Ht 193 K17
ct. Wheelers Hl 461 B9
ct.n, Mt Martha 655 L17
ct.s, Mt Martha 655 K17
pl. Sunbury 143 D11
rd. Herne Hill 701 J2
rd. Mitcham 377 J14
st. Elsternwick 455 D6
st. W Footscray 366 J7
BYAHAMEE
st. Rye 697 A6
BYAMBEE
ct. Grovedale 706 D15
BYFIELD
cl. Gladstone Pk 236 L17
cl. Gladstone Pk 237 A17
st. Reservoir 282 K10
BYNG
av. Heatherton 497 G14
BYRD
ct. Mt Waverley 459 C6
BYRNE
av. Elwood 454 C5
cl. Berwick 539 L20
cr. Watsonia N 243 G19
ct. Campbellfield 239 G11
ct. Cheltenham 497 C19
rd. Bayswater N 379 G15
st. Belgrave 467 A16
st. Deer Park 319 C18
st. Fitzroy N 326 D19
st. Mt Martha 669 A2
st. Port Melb 412 H4
BYRON
av. Keilor East 322 F4
av. Lower Plenty 286 H14
cl. Rye 696 G3
cl. Templestowe 332 B12
ct. Bundoora 242 J20
ct. Frankston 600 D18
ct. Glenroy 279 F6
ct. Grovedale 706 E11
ct. Heidelberg Ht 284 G20
ct. Mooroolbark 337 F19
ct. Nar Warrn S 552 E18
ct. Wyndham Va 446 F10
pl. Taylors Hill 274 H13
rd. Christmas Hills ...207 H16
rd. Kilsyth 380 K7
st. Blairgowrie 680 A19
st. Box Hill S 418 G1
st. Brighton 455 B15
st. Canterbury 373 C20
st. Canterbury 417 C1
st. Carnegie 456 F5
st. Clayton S 498 K6
st. Collingwood 25 J1
st. Cremorne 26 D17
st. Cremorne 370 H19
st. Elwood 454 D2
st. Footscray 367 F8
st. Kew 372 B12
st. Moonee Pnd 324 C15
st. Mt Martha 655 K16
st. N Melbourne 17 D16
st. Ringwood 378 G5
st. Williamstn N 410 C12
BYSOUTH
ct. Pakenham 584 D3
BYWAYS
dr. Ringwood E 379 D13

C

CABAL
ct. Mulgrave 500 E2
CABARITA
ct. Keysborough 534 F9
CABENA
cr. Chadstone 458 A6
st. Donvale 376 G7
CABERNET
cr. Bundoora 242 F17
ct. Frankston S 628 A16
ct. Waurn Ponds 705 F14
CABINDA
dr. Keysborough 534 J14
CABOT
dr. Epping 198 A18
CADBURY
ct. Truganina 405 L15
CADBY
av. Ormond 456 C15
ct. Caulfield 456 A5
pl. Frankston S 627 H10
st. Brighton 454 G15
CADD
la. Dandenong 535 J7
CADDICK
gdn. Caroline Spr 318 C5
CADDY
ct. Reservoir 283 J16
CADELL
ct. Sunbury 143 A14
pl. Berwick 553 K13
CADIZ
pl. Keilor Dn 276 F13
CADLE
ct. Bayswater 423 J9
st. Dandenong 535 K9
CADLES
rd. Carrum Downs ...575 B19
CADMAN
st. Brunswick W 325 A9
CADOGAN
pl. Altona Mdw 451 D5
CADORNA
st. Box Hill S 418 F5
CADOW
st. Kew East 372
CADRONA
ct. Hillside 274
CADROSS
av. Melton 226
CAERLEON
ct. Eaglemont 328
CAESAR
st. Mulgrave 500
CAHILL
cl. Mill Park 242
ct. Highton 705
dr. Brookfield 268
st. Bulla 190
st. Dandenong S 549
CAHILLTON
rd. Gruyere 341
CAIN
av. Keilor East 278
av. Northcote 327
ct. Altona 409
ct. Keilor East 322
rd. Rye 696
rd. Rye 697
st. Darley 222
st. Rosebud 699
st. Rosebud W 699
st. Sunbury 143
CAINE
ct. Endeavour Hl 536
CAIRN
cl. St Albans 320
ct. Frankston 600
ct. Wyndham Va 446
gr. Glen Waverley 420
rd. McCrae 685
rd. Rosebud 685
CAIRNCROFT
av. Launching Pl 345
CAIRN CURRAN
tce. Caroline Spr 317
CAIRN CURREN
cl. Rowville 462
CAIRNES
cr. Brighton 494
cr. Malvern East 416
gr. Bentleigh 455
CAIRNLEA
dr. Cairnlea 319
dr. Cairnlea 319
CAIRNS
av. Newtown 702
av. Rosebud 683
dr. Darley 221
pl. Diggers Rest 187
rd. Hampton Pk 551
st. Greensbrgh 244
st. Greensbrgh 286
st. Rosebud 684
CAIRNVIEW
ct. Launching Pl 345
CAIRO
rd. Mont Albert N 374
CAITHNESS
cl. Sunbury 143
cr. Glen Waverley 460
ct. Jan Juc 711
CAITHWILL
ct. Nar Warrn N 504
CAITLYN
ct. Bundoora 242
ct. Cranbourne N 578
ct. Wantirna S 422
CAKEBREAD
mw. Kensington 33
CALA
st. W Footscray 366
CALADENIA
cct. Frankston S 627
cct.s, ...Frankston S
D11
st. Wesburn 348
CALAIS
ct. Sydenham 274
CALBOURNE
st. Preston 326
CALCUTTA
cl. Altona Mdw 451
st. Mitcham 377
st. Sorrento 679
CALDER
ct. Sunshine W 364
ct. Sunshine W 365
fwy. Airport W 278
fwy. Calder Park 231
fwy. Diggers Rest 141
fwy. Diggers Rest 187
fwy. Gisborne S 141
fwy. Keilor 276
fwy. Keilor East 277
fwy. Keilor Ldg 275
fwy. Keilor N 275

y. Keilor Park.........277 D11
y. Sunbury............141 E2
y. Taylors L...........233 A13
Nangana............472 G3
Manifold Ht........702 B6
/. Wantirna S........422 A19
LDERA
Mooroolbark......337 C9
LDER PARK
Calder Park........232 J16
Hillside............232 H20
. Sydenham.........274 H4
Taylors Hill.........274 F15
LDERWOOD
. Wheelers Hl.......460 L15
Bulleen..............330 B15
Doncaster...........330 B15
LDWELL
Endeavour Hl.....538 A6
Melb Airport, off
North Dr...........235 K11
. Arthurs Seat.......685 L11
. Dromana...........685 L11
Vermont............421 J1
Glenroy.............280 G8
Mornington........640 J13
LEB
Bentleigh E........496 J1
LEDONIA
Mulgrave...........500 C4
Berwick.............539 H19
LEDONIAN
Hillside..............231 K16
Keysborough.....534 B8
Melbourne............2 E10
Melbourne...........24 D5
/. Point Cook.........450 G6
LEMBEENA
. Hughesdale........457 G14
LENDONIA
Eltham North.....245 D18
LENDULA
t. Epping..............198 F20
LEY
Frankston N.......600 D10
LGARY
Glen Waverley....461 A2
LIFORNIA
d. Pt Lonsdale........710 E1
Ferntree Gly.......423 H16
LISTA
. Oakleigh E.........458 L13
. Elsternwick........455 D3
LIVIL
Dallas...............238 F11
LK
Coburg N...........282 B15
LLAGHAN
. Glen Waverley....459 L9
. Cheltenham.......531 G2
. Frankston..........627 B4
. Noble Park.........534 L1
LLAM
Endeavour Hl.....537 E10
LLAN
Mill Park...........242 F1
LLANAN
. Melton S...........268 E3
LLANANS
Pearcedale.........647 E10
LLANDER
. Lysterfield.........464 D17
. Noble Park.........500 J18
. Pascoe Vale.......280 E12
. Hughesdale........457 E11
Reservoir............240 F20
Thomson...........703 H17
LLANDRA
/n.Upwey...............465 G12
LLANISH
. Camberwell........417 H7
LLANTINA
. Frankston..........628 C9
. Hawthorn..........415 K2
LLAS
Dromana...........686 F6
LEMONDAH
Ferntree Gly.......424 A20
LLENDER
Frankston..........628 B6
/. Hillside.............231 J17
LLER
Forest Hill.........420 J1
LLIBRIS
Keysborough.....534 A14
LLISTEMON
. Keysborough.....534 A14
. Narre Warren.....553 C1
. Springvale.........500 K13
Doncaster E.......332 F18
Mt Martha..........656 G7
Mill Park............243 B11

CALLUM
av. Somerville.........644 F19
CALMSDEN
st. Kilsyth S...........424 J1
CALOLA
ct. Ringwood E.......379 D6
st. Heidelberg W.....328 B2
CALOOLA
av. Oakleigh...........457 K7
ct. Rowville............463 G13
dr. N Warrandyte.....290 A12
CALROSSIE
av. Montmorency....286 K8
cl. Endeavour Hl.....537 G1
rd. Blackburn S.......419 F2
CALSHOT
gr. Gladstone Pk.....237 B18
CALTHORPE
grn. Caroline Spr.......317 J2
CALTOWIE
ct. Research...........288 G1
CALVERTON
rd. Kealba...............276 K20
CALVIN
cr. Doncaster E.......375 H2
ct. Watsonia N........285 F1
ct. Wheelers Hl.......461 E14
st. Hawthorn...........371 E14
CALVO
ct. Werribee............446 H16
CALWELL
ct. Mill Park............242 L5
ct. Mill Park............243 A5
ct. Skye..................601 D9
rd. Bend of Islands..249 G16
rd. Christmas Hills...249 G16
rd. Kangaroo Grnd..249 G16
st. Kensington..........33 J5
CALYPSO
ct. Forest Hill..........420 G6
pl. Thomastown......240 F16
CAM
st. Burwood E.........419 E11
st. Greensbrgh........286 A8
CAMARA
st. St Albans...........320 G10
CAMBALA
av. Lalor.................240 G9
CAMBARA
ct. Vermont S.........420 F9
CAMBDEN PARK
pde. Ferntree Gly.......463 E2
pde. Ferntree Gly.......463 E2
CAMBER
av. Pk Orchards.......334 C19
CAMBERLEY
ri. Ringwood N.......334 J20
CAMBERWELL
dr. Narre Warren.....553 C9
gr. Hawthorn E, off
Burke Av...........372 H20
rd. Camberwell.......416 J1
rd. Camberwell.......417 A5
rd. Hawthorn E.......372 F18
CAMBORNE
av. Mt Eliza............625 L16
CAMBRA
rd. Belmont.............706 D3
CAMBRIA
rd. Keysborough.....535 B11
CAMBRIAN
av. Preston.............282 K17
cr. Wheelers Hl.......461 A7
ct. Eltham North.....287 B1
wy. Melton W...........225 L16
CAMBRIDGE
cl. Cranbourne E.....578 K17
cl. Croydon Hl........335 D17
cl. Rowville............463 L17
cr. Roxburgh Pk......194 A9
cr. Taylors L..........233 D18
cr. Werribee...........446 K15
cr. Wyndham Va.....446 J12
ct. Mornington........657 A4
ct. Thomastown.......241 J16
dr. Berwick.............554 B1
dr. Glen Waverley....459 H7
dr. Springvale S......533 K7
gdn. Mooroolbark......381 B1
rd. Bentleigh E.......456 H18
rd. Kilsyth..............381 B1
rd. Montrose...........381 J5
rd. Mooroolbark......381 B1
rd. Mt Dandenong....426 F3
rd. Mt Martha..........669 K1
st. Armadale............415 E13
st. Belgrave S.........506 J1
st. Belmont.............706 E1
st. Box Hill.............374 J15
st. Brighton East.....455 B14
st. Caulfield N.......415 C15
st. Collingwood........25 G2
st. Frankston..........627 E4
st. Hawthorn E.......372 G17
st. Laverton N........364 A16
st. Maidstone..........366 G1
st. Oakleigh............457 L13
st. Port Melb..........412 J3
st. Seaholme..........409 J17
wy. Bundoora..........284 J2
wy. Campbellfield.....239 G13
wyn.Sorrento..........678 D8
wyn.Templstw Lr.......330 L13
CAMBRO
rd. Clayton.............459 G20
CAMBUS
rd. Yering...............253 E19
CAMDALE
cl. Hampton Pk........552 D9
pde. St Albans.........275 H19
st. Clarinda............498 H10
CAMDELL
ct. Belmont.............706 E6
CAMDEN
ct. Berwick.............553 G4
ct. Frankston..........600 B18
ct. Glen Waverley....420 L20
rd. Hawthorn...........372 A18
rd. Hughesdale........457 G11
rd. Newtown............701 K10
st. Balaclava..........414 G17
wy. Wyndham Va.....446 J9
CAMDON
gdn. Berwick...........554 B3
st. Pascoe Vale.......280 F17
CAMEELO
ct. Ferntree Gly.......423 K18
CAMELIA
cl. Lalor.................240 K10
cr. The Basin..........424 K10
ct. Croydon S..........379 E11
ct. Doveton.............536 J12
ct. Mornington.........641 B10
gr. Cheltenham........531 F2
st. Box Hill.............375 E14
st. Kings Park.........275 E19
CAMELLIA
av. Noble Park N......501 C18
ct. Tarneit..............447 J1
ct. Wheelers Hl.......460 G13
st. Blackburn N.......375 J8
CAMELOT
cl. Research...........289 F5
ct. Doncaster E.......331 L16
ct. Mooroolbark.......337 J14
ct. Mt Eliza.............626 K20
dr. Albanvale..........319 E4
dr. Glen Waverley....420 J17
dr. Springvale S......499 F19
pl. Hillside.............232 B20
CAMEO
ct. Bulleen.............329 J11
ct. Narre Warren.....553 F9
CAMERON
av. Altona Mdw.......407 E19
av. Oakleigh S.........497 J2
cl. Bayswater..........423 D8
cl. Burwood............418 A5
cl. Donvale.............332 J17
ct. Eltham...............246 F20
ct. Eltham...............288 F1
ct. Greenvale..........237 B4
ct. Kew..................371 G9
ct. Kilsyth..............381 A6
ct. Kurunjang..........227 F14
ct. Somerville.........644 F17
ct. Wantirna...........422 G12
la. Dandenong, off
Thomas St.........535 L10
pde. Bundoora.........284 J2
pde. Watsonia..........284 J2
pde. Watsonia N.......285 A2
pl. Albert Park...........29 A15
pl. Albert Park.........413 A8
pl. Keysborough......534 K13
rd. Anglesea............713 K3
rd. Box Hill N..........375 C11
rd. Croydon.............336 J19
rd. Essendon...........324 D4
rd. Mt Evelyn..........338 K14
rd. Ringwood N.......378 D5
st. Airport W...........278 L17
st. Brunswick.........325 F9
st. Cheltenham........530 K2
st. Coburg..............325 F9
st. Cranbourne........604 G7
st. Cranbourne E.....604 G7
st. Mt Waverley.......419 G19
st. Reservoir...........282 H15
st. Richmond............26 D8
st. Rosebud............684 J15
st. Sunshine...........365 F2
wy. Mt Eliza.............641 K7
wy. Pakenham.........585 D7

CAMERONS
cl. Sorrento...........679 F14
rd. Darley...............222 A1
rd. Healesville.........214 A14
CAMEROUN
ct. Berwick.............554 F7
CAMILLE
ct. Avondale Ht.......322 D9
CAMINO
ct. Glen Waverley....420 E16
tce. Malvern East.....457 D1
CAMINOLE
wyn.Templestowe......332 D6
CAMIRA
cl. Doncaster E.......332 G8
ct. Berwick.............553 H1
ct. Grovedale..........706 D13
st. Malvern East......457 J7
CAMLARNI
cl. Avondale Ht.......322 F15
CAMLEY
ct. Berwick.............554 D4
ct. Rowville............463 H12
CAMMS
rd. Cranbourne........577 L17
rd. Monbulk............467 K1
rd. The Patch..........467 K1
rd. The Patch..........468 A1
wy. Meadow Ht........237 J5
CAMP
ct. Mornington........656 G4
rd. Anglesea............713 H2
rd. Broadmeadows..238 B17
rd. Campbellfield.....239 B18
rd. Langwarrin S.....630 A16
st. Chelsea.............546 J18
CAMPASPE
cr. Brookfield..........268 D5
cr. Keilor................276 K14
dr. Croydon Hl........335 J15
st. Box Hill N..........375 A10
CAMPBELL
arc. Melbourne............2 C20
av. Deer Park..........318 K18
av. Mt Dandenong...426 G4
ct. Altona...............409 A16
ct. Brookfield..........268 A8
ct. Darley...............221 F9
ct. Warrandyte........333 B2
dr. Hampton Pk.......551 G11
gr. Dingley Vill.........533 A6
gr. Hawthorn E........416 E2
gr. Mornington........640 H15
gr. Northcote..........326 H17
pde. Box Hill S.........419 C6
pde. Cranbourne.......604 A3
pl. Geelong............703 C12
rd. Balwyn.............372 K13
rd. Briar Hill............286 G5
rd. Hawthorn E........416 G2
rd.s, Hawthorn E.......416 G2
st. Bentleigh...........495 L1
st. Berwick.............554 J8
st. Brighton............454 G11
st. Burnley..............371 C17
st. Campbellfield.....239 D13
st. Coburg..............325 H7
st. Collingwood........19 K18
st. Dandenong.........535 F5
st. Diamond Ck.......245 G13
st. E Geelong..........703 E14
st. Epping..............241 J1
st. Frankston..........599 J20
st. Glen Waverley....420 F17
st. Healesville.........258 C1
st. Heathmont.........378 J14
st. Kew..................372 F7
st. Kingsbury..........283 J11
st. Laverton............407 F13
st. Mooroolbark.......337 F20
st. Pakenham..........585 D9
st. Sandringham.....495 C16
st. Tecoma.............466 C13
st. Westmeadows....237 D15
st. Yarraville..........367 D17
CAMPBELLS
rd. Portsea.............678 B5
rd. Sorrento............678 B5
rd. Wandin East......385 D3
CAMPERDOWN
av. Sunshine N........320 K14
st. Brighton East.....455 B19
CAMPHOR
cl. Lysterfield..........503 L1
st. Doveton.............536 J6
CAMPHORA
ct. Plenty...............244 H11
pl. St Albans..........320 K8
CAMPION
wk. Lynbrook..........551 E18

CAMPUS
ct. Wheelers Hl.......460 D15
gte. Chirnside Pk......337 J5
pl. Thomastown......240 J12
CAMRIC
ct. Mt Evelyn..........339 E18
CAMROSE
ct. Jan Juc.............711 C13
CAMS
la. Caroline Spr.......274 B17
CANADA
la. Carlton................18 C17
CANADIAN
ct. Meadow Ht........238 B5
CANADIAN BAY
rd. Mt Eliza.............625 K13
CANANGA
ct. Mill Park............243 C11
CANARA
ct. Bayswater..........423 A4
ct. Greensbrgh........244 K19
st. Doncaster E.......375 L4
CANARY
ct. Mill Park............242 B10
CANBERRA
av. Dandenong S.....535 J13
av. Hoppers Csg......448 G6
gr. Beaumaris.........530 D6
gr. Brighton East.....495 C5
gr. Lalor.................242 A11
gr. Malvern.............416 A14
mw. Port Melb, off
Canberra Pde.....412 G5
pde. Port Melb.........412 H5
rd. Toorak...............415 B3
st. Brunswick..........325 C9
st. Carrum..............573 F7
st. Patterson L.........573 F7
st. Port Melb...........367 H20
CANDLEBARK
cl. Diamond Ck.......245 B15
cl. Hampton Pk........551 L6
cr. Frankston N.......600 A9
ct. Research...........288 K1
ct. Rosanna............329 E4
la. Nunawading......376 F16
qd. Rowville............502 C5
CANDOVER
st. Geelong West....702 H4
CANDWINDARA
ct. Langwarrin........601 K13
CANDY
cl. Seville...............341 K12
cr. Braybrook.........366 C6
st. Northcote..........326 H18
CANDYTUFT
cl. Cranbourne N.....578 C10
CANE
av. Seaford.............600 B1
mw. Seaford............600 C1
CANES
pl. Geelong............703 D11
CANET
gr. Nar Warrn S.......579 E4
CANN
pl. Rowville............463 C17
CANNA
st. Dromana...........686 F7
CANNERY
pl. Dingley Vill.........533 C7
CANNES
av. Avondale Ht.......322 E9
av. Bonbeach..........573 A4
ct. Greenvale..........237 E4
ct. Highton.............701 H9
gr. Beaumaris.........530 F5
CANNI
ct. Broadmeadows..238 B9
CANNING
dr. Berwick.............554 G13
st. Avondale Ht.......321 L15
st. Brunswick E.......325 L20
st. Carlton................18 J15
st. Carlton N.............18 K7
st. Frankston S.......626 H11
st. N Melbourne.......34 H11
CANNON
ct. Noble Park N......501 D13
st. Sunshine...........365 A8
CANNONS CREEK
rd. Cannons Creek...649 E4
CANNY
ct. Altona Mdw........451 F4
CANONBURY
cir. Seabrook...........451 A6
CANOPUS
cct. Long Forest.......224 C2
cct. Long Forest.......224 C3
dr. Doncaster E.......332 C17
pl. Melton W...........226 B16
CANORA
st. Blackburn S.......419 E4

CANOVA
dr. Glen Waverley....420 C14
CANOWINDRA
cl. Vermont S.........421 D7
pl. Grovedale..........706 D11
CANROBERT
st. Caulfield N.........415 F18
CANTALA
av. Caulfield N.........415 E16
av. Rosanna............285 D19
cr. Ringwood N.......377 L5
ct. Endeavour Hl.....538 A7
ct. Vermont S.........420 F9
ct. Wheelers Hl.......461 B17
dr. Doncaster...........331 A16
dr. Jan Juc..............711 C18
st. Clayton..............459 B19
st. Pascoe Vale S....324 E6
CANTER
st. Rowville.............502 D6
CANTERBURY
av. Sunbury............143 A1
cl. Melton S............268 B11
cl. Narre Warren......553 C10
cl. Rowville.............502 L8
cl. Rowville.............503 A8
ct. Bayswater N......379 G20
ct. Wandana Ht.......701 D20
la. Sydenham.........275 D8
pl. Brighton............494 F3
pl. Hawthorn E........416 G7
pl. Middle Park.........30 A15
pl. Werribee............446 K11
rd. Albert Park..........30 A13
rd. Bayswater N......379 K19
rd. Blackburn..........375 F20
rd. Blackburn S.......420 A1
rd. Box Hill..............374 D18
rd. Box Hill S...........375 A20
rd. Braeside............532 E19
rd. Camberwell........372 K16
rd. Canterbury.........372 K16
rd. Canterbury.........373 B17
rd. Forest Hill..........420 G2
rd. Kilsyth...............381 A14
rd. Kilsyth S............381 A14
rd. Middle Park.........30 A13
rd. Middle Park.......413 G8
rd. Montrose...........381 A14
rd. Ringwood..........377 L20
rd. Ringwood E.......379 C17
rd. St Kilda W.........413 G8
rd. Surrey Hills........374 D18
rd. Toorak..............415 B9
rd. Vermont............377 L20
rd. Vermont............421 A2
st. Cranbourne........578 E19
st. Deer Park..........319 C16
st. Flemington........324 C20
st. Hughesdale........457 G13
st. Moonee Pnd......323 L15
st. Mornington.........640 D13
st. Richmond...........371 A18
st. Sorrento...........678 E8
st. Yarraville...........367 B15
CANTERBURY JETTY
rd. Blairgowrie........696 C8
rd. Rye..................680 D20
rd. Rye..................696 C8
CANTLE
cl. Epping..............198 F18
cl. Pakenham.........585 F5
CANTLEY
la. Vermont............421 B3
CANTON
ct. Diamond Ck.......245 H16
CANTRELL
pl. Nar Warrn S.......552 E19
CANTS CREEK
rd. St Andrews........206 B1
rd. Smiths Gly.........206 B1
CANTWELL
rd. Nar Warrn N......539 F10
CANTY
la. Pakenham.........586 A5
CANUNGRA
cl. Hampton Pk.......552 C8
ct. Bundoora...........243 B20
CANYON
st. Balwyn.............373 A9
CAPE
st. Eaglemont.........328 L10
CAPEL
av. Rosebud W........683 D19
pl. N Melbourne........17 G19
st. N Melbourne........17 H20
st. W Melbourne.......17 G20
CAPELLA
cl. Doveton............537 C10
cr. Moorabbin.........497 D10
pl. Carrum Downs...575 B15
pl. Doncaster E.......332 E18
st. Balwyn N...........329 B20
st. Balwyn N...........373 B1
CAPER
ct. Mulgrave...........500 E1
ct. Werribee...........447 J10
CAPES
ct. Mill Park............241 L5
CAPESTHORNE
dr. Derrimut...........363 A7
CAPITAL
av. Glen Waverley....420 H14
ct. Braeside............532 G13
dr. Dandenong S.....550 D2
wy. S Morang..........198 J13
CAPITAL CITY
bvd. Wantirna S.........422 K16
CAPITAL LINK
dr. Campbellfield.....239 C2
dr. Campbellfield.....239 F3
CAPITOL
arc. Melbourne.............2 D14
av. McKinnon..........455 K15
CAPLE
pl. Gladstone Pk.....237 C17
CAPON
st. Malvern East......457 J6
CAPORN
av. Belgrave............466 H12
CAPP
st. Reservoir...........283 D15
CAPPELLA
ct. Glen Waverley.....460 D8
CAPRI
cl. Seville................341 J12
cl. S Morang..........198 J13
cl. S Morang..........198 K14
cr. Avondale Ht........322 E8
ct. Carrum Downs....600 L5
ct. Carrum Downs....601 A5
ct. Deer Park...........319 D10
ct. Doncaster...........330 D17
ct. Jan Juc..............711 B19
ct. Notting Hill.........459 H13
ct. Pakenham.........584 J4
ct. Reservoir...........282 B4
ct. Westmeadows....237 D15
dr. Mt Martha..........668 L6
gr. Sorrento............678 H11
wy. Point Cook.........450 E8
CAPRICE
av. Port Melb...........368 B19
cl. Wantirna............422 H8
ct. Frankston..........600 C17
ct. Keilor Dn...........275 K14
ct. Templestowe.....331 F12
pl. Narre Warren.....538 K15
CAPRICORN
av. Doncaster E.......332 D18
ct. Taylors L...........233 E19
CAPTAIN
st. Aspendale..........546 C3
CAPTAIN COOK
cl. Skye.................575 H14
CAPTAIN PEARSON
dr. Mickleham.........150 B2
CAPULET
st. Moonee Pnd......324 F11
CARA
cr. Berwick.............554 L5
ct. Berwick.............554 J20
rd. Highton.............701 K16
CARAAR CREEK
la. Mornington........640 L7
la. Mornington........641 A8
CARABEEN
wy. Lyndhurst..........551 B19
CARABOTT
pl. Berwick.............553 K16
CARADON
dr. Truganina..........405 K16
CARAMAR
av. Brighton East.....455 G17
dr. Oakleigh S.........497 H8
CARAMUT
ct. Warranwood......334 H15
rd. Brighton.............455 A13
rd. Ringwood E.......379 D5
wy. Seabrook..........450 L5
CARAVAN
st. Balwyn.............373 L9
CARAVEL
la. Docklands..........368 J14
CARAVELLE
cr. Strathmr Ht........279 C8
ct. Berwick.............540 C20
CARAWA
ct. Bundoora...........285 B1
dr. Reservoir...........282 A12
st. Cockatoo...........471 D20
st. Mooroolbark.......337 A15
wy. Skye.................601 G3
CARAWAH
rt. St Albans...........320 L7
rt. St Albans...........321 A7
CARAWATHA
rd. Doncaster..........374 H2
CARBEEN
dr. Bundoora...........242 G14
CARBEENA
pde. Heidelberg W.....328 A2
CARBERRY
dr. Kurunjang..........227 D14
CARBERY
ct. Grovedale..........706 E10
CARBINE
av. Clarinda.............498 D10
ct. Mill Park............242 K10
pl. Bundoora...........284 E4
st. Doncaster E.......332 G17
st. Donvale.............332 G17
wy. Keilor Dn...........275 K15
wy. Mornington.......641 D18
CARBON
cr. Mill Park............241 L6
ct. Werribee...........447 G12
CARBONI
cr. Lynbrook...........551 C16
ct. Mulgrave...........501 D4
CARBOOR
st. Tootgarook.........698 F9
CARBORA
dle. Greensbrgh........244 E18
CARBOST
ct. Macleod............284 L11
ct. Macleod............285 A11
CARCOOLA
ct. Ormond.............456 E14
ct. Rosebud............684 F19
rd. Monbulk............428 C16
rd. Ringwood E.......379 C5
st. Cockatoo...........471 G17
CARDAMON
dr. Hallam...............538 C17
CARDER
av. Seaford.............599 D12
CARDERRY
dr. Hopetoun Park...266 C8
CARDIFF
cl. Viewbank...........329 J2
ct. Craigieburn........194 C3
ct. Glen Waverley....459 J7
st. Bentleigh E........457 A20
st. Boronia..............423 L10
st. Thomastown......240 C11
st. Vermont............421 H4
CARDIGAN
cl. Melton S............268 C11
cr. Taylors L...........275 J2
pl. Albert Park...........29 F11
pl. Albert Park.........413 C6
rd. Montrose...........382 C2
rd. Mooroolbark......337 E20
st. Carlton................18 C20
st. Endeavour Hl.....536 K3
st. Geelong.............703 B12
st. St Kilda E..........414 K16
tce. Carlton................18 C20
CARDINAL
cl. Mill Park............242 K13
ct. Dingley Vill.........532 L3
ct. Narre Warren......552 F1
rd. Glenroy.............280 D10
CARDINIA
cl. Dandenong N.....502 F14
cr. Taylors Hill.........274 J13
ct. Menzies Ck........468 B12
rd. Officer...............583 B19
rd. Officer S............582 G20
rd. Officer S............583 B19
st. Berwick.............554 L11
wy. Rowville.............463 A18
CARDINIA CREEK
rd. Emerald.............507 G14
CARDORE
ct. Noble Park.........501 A19
CARDS
la. Olinda...............426 K8
CARE
cl. Meadow Ht........194 A19
CAREL
ct. Pk Orchards.......333 D19
CAREN
ct. Sunshine W.......364 J6
CAREW
ct. Brookfield..........268 B5
st. Sandringham.....495 A12
CAREX
wy. S Morang..........199 H9
CAREY
cl. Grovedale..........706 G11
cl. Werribee...........446 K11
cr. Bacchus Msh.....221 G14
ct. Blackburn..........376 A19
ct. Coldstream........295 F12
ct. Keilor East.........322 B4
ct. Keysborough.....534 D11
ct. Sunbury............144 F10
gr. Preston.............327 C5
grn. Point Cook.........449 K9
st. Bentleigh E........456 L15
st. Cranbourne N....578 G10
CARGO
dr. Campbellfield.....194 E18
dr. Coolaroo...........194 E18
rd. Melb Airport.......235 L18
CARIBBEAN
dr. Scoresby...........462 B11
CARIBOU
ct. Wheelers Hl.......460 J16
pl. Point Cook.........449 L5
CARINA
cl. Wantirna S.........422 K13
ct. Kilsyth...............381 G7
dr.n, Melton...............226 F19
dr.s, Melton...............226 F19
tce. Cranbourne W....577 H15
CARINDA
rd. Canterbury.........373 C20
CARINGA
st. Pascoe Vale.......281 A11
CARINGAL
av. Doncaster..........374 G2
ct. Clayton S...........498 H8
CARINISH
rd. Clayton..............458 F18
rd. Oakleigh S.........458 F18
CARINYA
av. Aspendale..........546 E4
av. Newcomb..........704 C13
bvd. Burnside............318 G8
cr. Caulfield N.........415 E16
ct. Mt Waverley.......459 C4
rd. Greensbrgh........285 L10
rd. Oakleigh S.........497 F1
rd. Vermont............421 B1
CARINZA
av. Altona Mdw.......450 J2
CARISBROOK
cr. Lower Plenty......286 D14
ct. Doncaster E.......332 D20
ct. Langwarrin........629 H2
CARISBROOKE
ct. Wantirna............422 G13
CARL
ct. Hallam...............537 J18
ct. Ringwood...........378 H7
pl. Diggers Rest.......232 H7
CARLA
ct. Aspendale Gdn...546 K4
ct. Somerville.........644 F15
vw. Sunbury............142 E8
CARLING
ct. Altona Mdw.......451 J9
CARLINGA
ct. Gladstone Pk.....279 B4
dr. Vermont............421 F4
CARLINGFORD
cl. Rowville.............503 D6
st. Caulfield S.........455 E7
st. Elsternwick........455 B7
CARLISLE
av. Balaclava..........414 J18
cl. Derrimut............363 C5
cr. Hughesdale........457 E10
ct. Campbellfield.....239 G13
ct. Frankston..........628 B6
dr. Epping...............197 J17
dr. Officer...............555 H19
rd. Ferntree Gly......463 E1
rd. Hallam...............537 E15
st. Balaclava..........414 C17
st. Coburg..............325 L4
st. Craigieburn........150 G20
st. Preston.............327 A6
st. St Kilda.............414 C17
tce. Point Cook.........450 H9
CARLITA
cl. Mill Park............242 L10
cl. Mill Park............243 A10
CARLO
ct. Greensbrgh........244 K15
CARLOGIE
ct. Burwood...........418 B3
pl. Darley...............221 G1
CARLOW
pl. Carlton................18 H14
rd. St Albans...........320 J7
st. Bentleigh E........457 B20
CARLSBERG
rd. Eaglemont.........328 J11
CARLSON
av. Clayton.............459 A13
st. Sunbury............143 C15
CARLSRUHE
pl. Caroline Spr.......318 D10
CARLSSON
ct. Brooklyn...........365 G19
CARLTON
ct. Braybrook..........321 K
ct. Craigieburn........150 G
ct. Rye...................698
ct. Taylors Hill.........274
ct. Templestowe.....331
pl. Carlton................18 B
rd. Dandenong N.....501 J
st. Braybrook..........321 J
st. Carlton................18 H
st. McKinnon..........456 A
st. Prahran................32 D
st. Prahran..............414
CARLUKE
cl. Berwick.............554 C
CARLY
cl. Nar Warrn S.......552 F
ct. Croydon N.........336 E
pl. Tootgarook........698
tce. Werribee...........447 L
CARLYLE
cl. Hurstbridge.......203 D
cr. Balwyn.............374 B
cr. Bellfield.............327
pl. Melton W...........226 C
st. Ashwood...........418 A
st. Croydon............380
st. Hawthorn E........372 H
st. Maidstone.........366
st. Moonee Pnd......324 A
st. Pakenham.........584
wy. Malvern East......416 H
CARLYON
ct. Springvale.........500 E
st. Ormond.............456 C
CARMANS
la. Geelong.............703 D
CARMARTHEN
cl. Werribee............446 L
CARMEL
av. Ferntree Gly.......424 F
av. Mt Waverley......418 L
cl. Greensbrgh........244 J
cl. Greenvale..........192 J
ct. Balwyn.............373 K
ct. Bentleigh E........496
ct. Forest Hill..........420
ct. Frankston..........600 D
ct. Sydenham.........274
CARMELA
cl. Narre Warren.....539 E
wy. Carrum Downs...601
CARMELLA
cl. Chirnside Pk......336
ri. Chirnside Pk......336
CARMELO
av. Malvern East......457
CARMEN
cl. Doncaster E.......332 J
cl. Eltham...............288
cr. Nar Warrn N......538
ct. Glen Waverley....460 E
ct. Hampton Pk.......552 C
ct. Lilydale.............339 A
ct. Ringwood..........379
st. Dandenong.........535
st. Newport............410
CARMICHAEL
av. Newtown...........701
ct. Glen Waverley....419 L
rd. Oakleigh E.........458 G
st. Ivanhoe East......328 H
st. Tootgarook........698
st. W Footscray......366
CARMINE
ct. Carrum Downs...575 F
CARMODY
dr. Cairnlea.............319 J
st. Burwood............418 E
CARMYLE
av. Toorak...............415
ct. Avondale Ht.......322 C
ct. Bundoora...........284
CARN
av. Ivanhoe............328 E
CARNABY
ct. Somerville.........645 E
pl. Wantirna............422 F
wy. Springvale S......499 J
CARNARVON
av. Jan Juc..............711 F
av. The Basin...........425 A
cl. Taylors L...........233 E
ct. Sunbury............144 E
dr. Grovedale..........706 A
pl. Melton W...........226 C
rd. Caulfield N.........415 J
rd. Essendon...........323
rd. Strathmore........323
st. Brunswick..........325 J
st. Doncaster..........330 K
st. Hawthorn E........372 E

RNATION
Endeavour Hl.....537 F5
Springvale S......534 A1
NE
Pakenham.........558 G1
Pakenham Up....559 D1
NEA
Frankston S......627 D10
RNEGIE
Kew East...........372 A5
Pt Lonsdale........710 G7
RNELL
Balwyn N...........374 A3
RNEY
Pakenham.........584 G6
RNON
Greensbrgh.......244 F20
RNOUSTIE
Jan Juc.............711 F16
Chirnside Pk......292 J10
Frankston..........599 J15
Rowville............462 D19
Sunbury............144 E12
Mornington........656 D3
. Heatherton.........497 G16
NSWORTH
Kew..................371 G9
ROBEN
Vermont............421 D5
ROL
Cranbourne........604 C3
Frankston..........600 C17
Newcomb..........704 A17
Ringwood N........378 H2
Warrandyte........333 E1
Tullamarine........278 J7
Mornington........656 F4
Scoresby...........462 C9
ROLANNE
Mooroolbark......337 H17
ROLE
Chirnside Pk......336 L6
Aspendale Gdn...546 K7
Cranbourne........577 L16
Seabrook...........450 K3
Templestowe.....331 C6
ROLE-JOY
Reservoir..........282 J12
ROL HANCOCK
Croydon N.........335 L13
ROLINA
Mt Waverley......419 F15
ROLINE
Cockatoo...........511 C5
Blackburn N.......375 G7
Cranbourne W...577 E20
Emerald............469 F16
Hurstbridge........203 G12
Kalorama...........382 L18
Bayswater..........423 C10
Blairgowrie........680 C19
Mt Martha..........656 L8
Preston.............327 A5
Rosebud............700 F4
Tootgarook.........698 B9
Templstw Lr.......330 E12
Hampton Pk........551 K5
Gowanbrae.........279 D7
Aberfeldie..........323 C10
Box Hill N..........375 D11
Clayton..............498 F1
Clifton Hill...........20 F5
Dandenong.........536 E10
Hawthorn E........372 D20
Highton..............701 K20
Kilsyth...............381 C5
Pt Lonsdale.........710 E4
Ringwood...........378 F14
Selby.................467 F15
South Yarra..........31 K8
South Yarra.........414 E4
Thomastown.......240 L14
Thomastown.......241 A14
ROLINE SPRINGS
. Caroline Spr.....274 A16
. Caroline Spr.....318 A5
ROLYN
Nar Warrn N......538 C6
Bundoora...........285 C2
Frankston...........600 G18
Keilor Park.........278 B13
Langwarrin.........629 J5
Hampton............495 H9
ROMAR
Croydon............336 K20
RON
Hallam...............537 L14
ROOL
Tootgarook.........698 E7
Ashburton..........417 G15
Carnegie............456 L9
ROUSEL
Epping...............198 F17

CARPENTARIA
ct. Aspendale Gdn...547 B3
CARPENTER
ct. Chelsea.............547 B19
rd. Beaconsfld Up....557 B1
rd. Officer...............557 B1
st. Brighton............454 H18
st. Noble Park.........500 L17
CARR
ct. Altona Mdw.......451 F3
ct. Bundoora...........284 L6
pl. Roxburgh Pk......194 D14
pl. Geelong, off Maud St............702 L10
st. Belmont.............706 E1
st. Breakwater........703 F16
st. Brighton East.....495 J4
st. Coburg N...........281 G17
st. Geelong.............702 L11
st. Thomson...........703 F16
CARRABIN
ct. Knoxfield...........463 B4
CARRADALE
st. Waurn Ponds.....705 D14
CARRAJUNG
st. Rosebud............700 K5
CARRAMAR
av. Camberwell........417 D3
av. Glen Waverley....460 A1
cr. Belgrave............466 L15
ct. Bayswater..........423 B9
ct. Emerald.............469 J15
ct. Highton.............701 G19
ct. Keysborough.......534 E8
ct. Rosebud............684 F19
ct. Vermont.............421 E6
dr. Frankston..........600 E18
rd. Cranbourne S.....630 K3
st. Chadstone.........458 C1
st. Mornington.........641 B16
st. Rye...................696 L6
st. Rye...................697 A6
CARRANYA
ct. Nar Warrn S.......579 A2
CARRARA
rd. Rowville.............502 E7
CARRATHOOL
st. Bulleen.............329 H11
CARRAWE
ct. Anglesea............713 D4
CARR BOYD
rd. Cranbourne S.....602 G15
CARRE
st. Elsternwick........454 L6
st. Elsternwick........455 A6
CARRERA
cl. Lysterfield..........464 F17
CARRIBEAN
dr. Keysborough.....534 C11
CARRICK
dr. Gladstone Pk.....237 B16
dr. Gladstone Pk.....278 K5
dr. Gladstone Pk.....279 A3
dr. Tullamarine........278 K5
st. Balwyn.............374 B11
st. Mont Albert.......374 B11
CARRIER
av. Parkdale............531 J14
CARRIGAL
st. Balwyn.............374 A9
CARRIGG
st. Dromana...........686 D3
CARRINGTON
av. Hawthorn E........372 H18
av. Seaford.............599 L3
bvd. Thomastown.......240 C14
cl. Chelsea Ht.........547 D8
cl. Wyndham Va.....446 H12
cr. Carrum Downs.....601 F1
ct. Burwood E.........420 C13
ct. Chirnside Pk......337 J3
ct. Nar Warrn S.......552 H14
ct. Seaford.............599 L4
ct. Tecoma.............466 D8
dr. Albion...............320 F17
dr. Rosebud............700 K3
gr. Brighton East.....455 D20
gr. St Kilda E..........414 L20
gr. St Kilda E..........415 A20
pl. Berwick.............553 L5
pl. S Melbourne........29 E4
rd. Box Hill.............374 H15
rd. Niddrie..............279 A20
rd. Niddrie..............323 A1
rd. Reservoir...........282 D13
st. Balwyn N...........373 G8
st. Edithvale............546 F11
st. Hampton E.........496 A8
st. Hawthorn...........372 A15
st. Pascoe Vale S....324 L6
st. Sydenham.........274 J2
st. Thomson...........703 F15

CARROL
gr. Mt Waverley......458 F7
st. Reservoir...........283 B8
CARROLL
av. Croydon............336 G18
av. Dandenong.........536 D5
cr. Glen Iris.............416 D9
cr. Mill Park............242 A7
ct. Greensbrgh........285 J3
ct. Narre Warren......538 H14
la. Dandenong.........535 J10
la. Greenvale..........192 F19
rd. Highton.............701 G10
rd. Oakleigh S.........497 L8
st. Deer Park..........318 L16
st. Launching Pl.......345 H15
st. N Melbourne........17 A11
st. Richmond............26 C16
st. Woori Yall...........344 B14
CARROLLS
la. N Melbourne........17 A11
rd. Fyansford...........701 C7
CARRON
st. Balwyn N...........329 J18
st. Coburg..............325 F6
CARRONSHORE
cl. Balwyn.............373 D14
CARRONVALE
rd. Mooroolbark......337 G18
CARRS
la. N Melbourne........17 A11
CARRUM
cl. Berwick.............539 J17
st. Malvern East......457 H7
CARRUM BELLA
dr. Carrum Downs....601 B6
CARRUM WOODS
dr. Carrum Downs...575 C14
CARRUP
pl. Somerville.........644 L20
pl. Somerville.........645 A19
CARRUTHERS
ct. Altona...............409 A16
ct. Altona Mdw.......451 D3
ct. Ringwood..........378 E20
ct. Thomson...........703 H16
CARSHALTON
ct. Hoppers Csg......405 D13
CARSLAKE
av. Blairgowrie........696 C7
CARSON
av. Keysborough.....533 K11
av. Mont Albert........374 C13
cr. Hawthorn...........371 J18
ct. Rowville.............502 K2
ct. Watsonia N........243 F20
ct. Watsonia N........285 F1
la. Roxburgh Pk......194 A14
pl. Melbourne.............2 D14
pl. Melbourne...........24 D8
rd. Seville...............387 B5
st. Dandenong.........535 H8
st. Kew..................371 E12
st. Mulgrave............500 C3
st. Reservoir...........282 K2
CARSONS
rd. Officer...............556 J10
CARSTAIRS
cl. Grovedale..........706 K11
CARTER
av. Nunawading......376 J13
av. Werribee............447 J18
cr. Werribee............447 K17
ct. Frankston...........628 D3
ct. Portsea.............678 A3
dr. Berwick..............554 A17
rd. Melton...............268 H2
st. Albert Park...........29 K15
st. Launching Pl.......345 G15
st. Middle Park.........29 K15
st. Noble Park.........535 B2
st. Sunshine W.......364 H4
wy. Dandenong S.......550 L5
wy. Dandenong S.......551 A5
CARTERS
av. Toorak..............415 B6
la. Kangaroo Grnd ..248 F17
la. Seville...............386 G8
la. Seville...............386 J14
CARTHEW
gr. Preston..............326 E5
CARTHY
st. Altona North......409 E1
CARTIER
wk. Point Cook.........451 D10
wy. S Morang..........198 K12
CARTLEDGE
st. Laverton............407 C16
CARTMELL
st. Heidelberg..........328 L7
CARTWRIGHT
st. Oak Park...........280 A10

CARUANA
cl. Epping...............198 B18
dr. Dingley Vill.........533 D1
CARVER
st. Burwood E.........419 G12
CARVEY
ct. Endeavour Hl.....538 A6
dr. Mt Martha..........656 J6
CARWARP
st. Macleod............285 A15
CARWEEN
av. Brighton East.....455 H13
av. Mitcham............377 A18
av. Upwey..............465 K8
CARWELL
ct. Oakleigh S.........497 L1
CARY
st. Sunshine N........320 L15
CASABLANCA
ri. Greenvale..........237 E5
CASALE
ct. Frankston..........628 B12
CASCADE
ct. Montrose............382 H8
ct. Noble Park N......501 E10
dr. Kew East............372 K2
dr. Vermont S.........420 F8
dr. Wyndham Va.....446 D10
rd. Emerald.............469 A19
st. Balwyn N...........372 L2
st. Balwyn N...........373 A2
st. Frankston..........599 G13
st. Oakleigh S.........498 A7
wy. Hallam..............538 F14
CASCADES
vw. Yallambie..........286 A11
CASCAM
ct. Rowville.............463 F13
CASCO
pl. Dingley Vill.........532 K9
CASDAR
ct. Nar Warrn N......539 C7
CASE
st. Maribyrnong......367 C1
CASELLA
st. Mitcham............377 F11
CASERTA
dr. Berwick.............540 B20
CASEY
av. Sunbury............143 E6
cl. Springvale S......499 E18
cr. Viewbank...........285 K17
ct. Clarinda.............498 F10
ct. Melton...............227 B16
ct. Wantirna............422 F4
dr. Berwick.............554 E2
dr. Lalor.................241 L10
st. Healesville.........258 A8
CASH
cl. Hampton Pk.......551 G12
gr. Mt Waverley......458 F7
st. Balwyn N...........329 H19
st. Coburg..............325 H5
st. Kingsbury...........284 A9
CASHEL
ct. Berwick.............553 H14
CASH FUES
pl. Wantirna............422 A4
CASHIN
ct. Melton...............227 B17
CASHINS MILL
pl. Lilydale.............338 H10
CASHMERE
cr. Berwick.............554 G20
ct. Wyndham Va.....446 H9
st. Travancore.........324 G18
CASHMORE
ct. Bacchus Msh.....221 G16
ct. Bundoora...........285 A1
pl. Roxburgh Pk......194 A13
CASINO
ct. Torquay.............712 C2
CASLEY
pl. Hoppers Csg......405 B13
CASON
st. Doncaster..........330 H17
CASPIAN
pl. Nar Warrn S.......552 J20
tce. Williamstown......410 H14
CASS
av. Croydon............336 F19
st. Rosebud............684 D16
CASSAB
mw. Sunbury............142 G7
CASSANDRA
cl. Somerville..........644 F13
cl. Ringwood..........378 L4
dr. Gladstone Pk.....279 B3
dr. Mt Martha..........656 E9
CASSAR
pl. Princes Hill........325 J18
CASSAVA
ct. Dingley Vill.........533 D10

CASSELDEN
pl. Melbourne...........24 H2
CASSELL
st. South Yarra.........32 K13
st. South Yarra.......414 L6
st. Werribee............447 H2
CASSELLS
rd. Research...........246 K20
rd. Research...........288 K1
rd. Research...........289 A1
CASSELS
rd. Brunswick..........325 E9
CASSIA
ct. Endeavour Hl.....502 L20
ct. Keysborough.....534 A14
ct. Mill Park............243 C10
ct. Newcomb..........704 D15
ct. St Albans...........276 B18
ct. Wantirna............422 B4
gr. Frankston..........627 J5
rd. Melton...............226 J17
st. Doncaster E.......332 E18
st. Doveton.............536 H9
st. Notting Hill.........459 G12
CASSIN
ct. Dandenong N.....502 B13
CASSINIA
av. Ashwood...........418 E15
cl. Knoxfield...........463 B2
cr. Meadow Ht.........237 J2
ct. Delahey.............275 C10
ct. Diamond Ck.......245 D13
pl. Frankston S.......627 G20
rd. Templstw Lr......330 K14
CASSIOBURY
av. Mt Eliza.............626 D11
CASSOWARY
av. Werribee............447 K5
cl. Carrum Downs...600 L2
cl. Taylors L............275 G2
rd. S Morang..........198 L10
st. Doncaster E.......375 K4
CASTAWAY
cr. Jan Juc.............711 A19
ct. Patterson L........573 G10
ct. Point Cook.........451 A13
CASTELLA
ct. Meadow Ht........238 A6
pl. Hampton Pk.......551 L16
st. Ivanhoe East......328 L17
st. Lilydale.............338 E5
CASTILLON
sq. Frankston..........628 B9
CASTLE
av. Greenvale..........237 E2
cl. Eaglemont..........328 L9
cl. Glen Waverley....421 A19
ct. Beaconsfield......555 D13
ct. Eltham North.....245 C18
rd. N Warrandyte.....290 B17
st. Dandenong S......535 L14
st. Eaglemont..........328 J9
st. Ferntree Gly.......424 B18
st. Williamstown.....411 B14
st. Yarraville...........366 K16
CASTLEBAR
rd. Malvern East......457 G6
wy. Templestowe.....332 A8
CASTLEBURY
pl. Craigieburn........193 L2
CASTLECRAG
cl. Endeavour Hl.....537 G3
CASTLEFIELD
sq. Wantirna............422 B10
CASTLEGATE
pl. Berwick.............555 A10
CASTLE HILL
dr. Bundoora...........243 C13
CASTLEHILL
av. Greenvale..........193 F17
ri. Langwarrin........629 H3
CASTLEMAINE
st. Yarraville...........367 B14
wy. Caroline Spr.......318 F8
CASTLEREAGH
ct. Mt Waverley......418 K12
pl. Watsonia...........285 D4
CASTLERIDGE
ct. Nar Warrn S.......579 C4
CASTLEROCK
dr. Wyndham Va.....446 D7
CASTLES
rd. Bentleigh...........496 C6
CASTLETON
ct. Gladstone Pk.....237 D17
rd. Herne Hill...........701 J2
rd. Viewbank...........285 J16
CASTLEWELLAN
bvd. Hillside.............273 J2
bvd. Hillside.............273 K3
CASTLEWOOD
dr. Boronia.............424 H14
pl. Point Cook.........450 F8

pl. Templestowe 331 G13
st. Bentleigh E 457 A18
CASTLEY
cr. Braybrook..........366 B1
CASTRICUM
pl. Ferntree Gly 423 K17
CASUARINA
av. Boronia..............424 J7
av. Torquay.............711 G10
cl. Langwarrin 629 J4
cl. Maribyrnong......322 H15
cl. Mornington..........656 J3
ct. Hampton Pk.......551 C5
ct. Narre Warren 553 D1
ct. Pascoe Vale 280 K10
ct. Sunbury 143 J8
dr. Frankston S 627 F13
rdg. Eltham North 245 G18
tr. Lysterfield..........504 G17
tr. Nar Warrn N 504 G19
CASULA
pl. Ringwood N.......378 E2
CATALINA
av. Ashburton..........417 K17
av. Dromana 686 H5
ct. Eltham...............287 D6
ct. Frankston 600 E17
ct. Point Cook.........450 A4
dr. Thomastown......240 F14
dr. Tullamarine.......236 H19
pl. Melton W...........226 C19
st. Heidelberg W 283 L20
CATALPA
pl. Lysterfield..........463 K20
st. Doveton.............536 J11
CATANI
bvd. Bend of Islands..291 H2
ct. Broadmeadows..237 J14
mw. Caroline Spr.......274 C16
CATANIA
av. Point Cook.........450 D9
st. Mentone 530 L8
CATERINA
pl. Carrum Downs...601 F4
CATERPILLAR
dr. Tullamarine........278 L8
CATESBY
cl. Mulgrave 501 K6
ct. Boronia..............423 J10
CATHAY
ct. Diamond Ck.......245 F15
la. N Melbourne........17 J20
st. Ferntree Gly 424 L19
st. Ferntree Gly 425 A19
CATHCART
st. Maidstone..........366 K1
CATHEDRAL
arc. Melbourne.............2 E18
cl. Pakenham 583 L1
ct. Tarneit...............405 D11
mw. Caroline Spr.......317 J8
pl. E Melbourne 25 A4
CATHERINE
av. Chelsea.............547 A18
av. Doncaster E 332 E13
av. Mt Waverley 458 H8
av. Tullamarine........278 G3
ct. Eltham...............287 L7
ct. Forest Hill 420 A6
ct. Kilsyth 381 B5
ct. Langwarrin 601 H19
dr. Hillside 274 D6
dr. Hillside 274 E3
pde. Frankston 599 F20
pl. Croydon Hl 335 F15
pl. Pakenham 584 B3
rd. Bentleigh E 496 H3
rd. Seabrook 450 J4
st. Boronia...............424 C10
st. Box Hill..............374 K18
st. Canterbury..........417 D1
st. Caulfield N 415 H20
st. Coburg N............281 D15
st. Footscray............367 D6
st. Geelong West 702 D3
st. McCrae...............684 L13
st. Ringwood............378 B16
st. Southbank..............3 A12
st. Southbank............23 L19
wy. Tecoma 466 C14
CATHERINE EDEY
pl. Hampton Pk.......552 A12
CATHIE
ct. Narre Warren 539 C19
CATHIES
la. Scoresby 461 L1
la. Wantirna S.........421 L16
CATHKIN
cl. Sunbury 143 C11
CATHY
st. Werribee............448 A11
CATIONS
ct. Altona Mdw 451 C4
CAT JUMP
rd. Donvale.............376 H1
CATO
la. Hawthorn E........416 C6
la.n, Hawthorn E........416 C6
pky. Lynbrook...........551 E19
st. Hawthorn E........416 C6
st. Prahran 32 C17
st. Prahran 414 G8
CATON
av. Coburg 326 A6
st. Ferny Creek.........465 K3
CATRON
st. Seaford..............573 E19
CATTANACH
cr. Werribee............447 L15
CATTERICK
ct. Greenvale 193 C17
CAULFIELD
cr. Roxburgh Pk......194 F14
ct. Narre Warren 553 B9
ct. Wantirna............422 A11
CAULSON
cl. Maribyrnong......322 K16
CAUSON
ct. Noble Park.........534 L7
CAVALIER
ct. Epping...............198 G16
st. Bentleigh E 457 G17
st. Doncaster E 331 L20
CAVANAGH
cl. Cairnlea 320 B13
rd. Lower Plenty......286 D14
rd. Millgrove 348 B2
rd. Wesburn.............347 K8
st. Cheltenham 497 A20
st. Cheltenham 497 B17
CAVE
st. Beaumaris 530 F5
CAVE HILL
rd. Lilydale..............338 A7
CAVELL
ct. Beaumaris 530 E6
ct. St Albans 320 F13
st. St Kilda..............414 A18
st. Scoresby 462 H5
CAVENDISH
av. Wantirna............422 E14
ct. Endeavour Hl 537 F3
dr. Deer Park...........318 L14
dr. Heatherton.........497 H14
dr. Point Cook..........450 G9
dr. Templstw Lr 330 E9
pl. Brighton 494 K4
pl. South Yarra 32 G16
st. Broadmeadows..237 K14
st. Geelong.............702 L5
CAVERSHAM
ct. Nunawading 376 G17
dr. Mornington........656 J3
tce. Lynbrook...........551 G17
CAVES
gr. Forest Hill 376 G20
gr. Forest Hill 420 G1
CAVESSON
ct. Epping...............198 F17
CAVEY
rd. Monbulk............468 L1
rd. Monbulk............469 A1
CAVILL
cl. Langwarrin 629 D9
ct. Vermont S 420 J11
CAWARRA
ct. Doncaster E 331 K15
st. Mornington.........656 H3
CAWDOR
av. Pk Orchards.......334 B19
CAWKWELL
st. Malvern 416 B12
CAWL
ct. Sunbury 144 F13
CAWLEY
ct. Mill Park............198 G20
ct. Mill Park 242 G1
ct. Wantirna S.........462 D3
rd. Yarraville 366 B19
CAWOOD
dr. Sunshine W 364 F10
CAXTON
ct. Kings Park 275 B20
st. Blairgowrie 696 B4
CAYLEYS
rd. Werribee S.........488 C17
CAYTRE
cr. N Melbourne........34 G10
CECELIA
dr. Keilor East 321 K5
CECIL
cct. Croydon 379 G7
ct. Mitcham 377 E17
ct. Newcomb 703 L17
ct. S Morang 243 H3
ct. Sydenham 274 K5
ct. Tecoma 466 B8
pl. Prahran 32 D19
pl. Prahran 414 H10
pl. S Melbourne 30 B9
pl. S Melbourne 413 G4
st. Bentleigh E 457 C20
st. Brighton East 455 D18
st. Eltham...............287 H7
st. Fitzroy 19 A9
st. Frankston 627 C4
st. Kew...................372 F11
st. Sorrento 679 A11
st. Southbank 29 J1
st. Southbank 413 E1
st. S Melbourne 29 J1
st. S Melbourne 413 F3
st. Warburton 349 D4
st. Williamstown 411 F15
st. Wonga Park.......336 D7
st. Yarraville 366 K15
CECILIA
ct. Tarneit...............405 A8
CECILIE
ct. Doncaster..........374 E2
CECILINA
la. S Melbourne........30 D4
CECILY
st. Springvale S 533 L6
CEDAR
av. Eltham North 245 H20
cl. Chadstone 458 C6
cl. Deer Park...........318 L14
cl. Jan Juc..............711 B16
cr. Boronia..............424 D17
ct. Altona Mdw 451 K1
ct. Campbellfield 239 F11
ct. Forest Hill 420 G4
ct. Frankston 599 L18
ct. Glen Waverley 420 B15
ct. Keysborough 534 F13
ct. Monbulk.............468 K2
ct. Oakleigh S 497 L9
ct. Pascoe Vale 280 K11
ct. Werribee............447 E10
dr. Maribyrnong......322 G17
dr. Dandenong, off David St............536 D5
gr. Highton 701 L16
gr. Selby.................466 K18
pde. Moolap..............704 L16
ri. Warrandyte........332 L8
ri. Warrandyte........333 A8
st. Caulfield S 455 G7
st. Doveton.............536 J11
st. Langwarrin 628 K2
st. Mentone 531 F5
st. Thomastown......241 C14
CEDARVIEW
cl. Rowville.............463 K17
CEDARVILLE
cl. Highton 705 G9
CEDARWOOD
cr. Berwick 580 B2
cr. Berwick 580 B3
ct. Mill Park............242 L3
wy. Roxburgh Pk......193 L5
CEDMAR
av. Highton 705 G1
CEDRIC
st. Ivanhoe East......328 G15
st. Mordialloc 531 L14
st. Parkdale 531 K14
CEDUNA
cl. Torquay.............712 G1
cl. Wantirna S.........422 B16
ct. Keilor Park.........277 L13
ct. Yarrambat..........202 B9
CEILTERRE
av. Ringwood N.......378 A9
CELEBRATION
ct. Cranbourne W ...577 G18
CELESTE
ct. Berwick 553 L5
ct. Chirnside Pk 336 L5
ct. St Kilda E...........415 B15
pl. S Morang 199 A14
st. Doncaster E 331 J20
CELESTIAL
av. Melbourne.............2 G10
av. Melbourne...........24 E5
ct. Rowville.............463 F16
CELESTINE
pl. Narre Warren 539 D13
CELIA
cl. Yarra Glen 208 L19
cl. Yarra Glen 209 A19
ct. Bangholme 549 H14
ct. Chadstone 458 E4
ct. Doncaster E 332 H8
st. Bentleigh E 496 K6
st. Glen Iris.............417 E12
st. Rye 696 L5
CELTIS
pl. Endeavour Hl 536 K1
CEMALOMA
ct. Highton 705 G2
CEMETERY
la. Bulla..................191 A17
rd. Brooklyn............366 B16
rd. Cranbourne.........603 L7
rd. Kangaroo Grnd ..248 F13
rd. Keilor East 277 K17
rd. Maddingley.........263 F3
rd. Pakenham 557 K18
rd. Warrandyte.........333 J1
rd. Werribee............448 B11
rd. Yarraville 366 B16
rd.e, Carlton 18 E8
rd.e, Carlton N 18 E8
rd.w,Carlton N 17 L6
rd.w,Parkville..............17 L6
tr. Warburton 349 B15
CEMETERY FIRELINE
Warburton 348 K12
Wesburn............348 J12
CENTALLA
grn. Rowville............463 B16
CENTAUR
ct. Bayswater..........423 L9
gr. Doncaster E 332 E18
wy. Hoppers Csg......448 G5
CENTAURUS
av. Roxburgh Pk......194 F10
CENTELLA
pl. Launching Pl......345 H13
CENTENARY
av. Kurunjang..........226 F14
av. Kurunjang..........227 A15
av. Melton...............226 F14
av. Melton...............227 A15
av. Melton W...........226 D14
cr. Werribee............447 F9
ct. Keysborough 535 A11
ct. Kings Park 275 A17
dr. Mill Park 242 J3
dr. Mill Park 243 A4
dr. Port Melb...........412 J5
st. Blairgowrie 679 F18
st. Seaford..............600 A3
CENTENARY BREAK
Frankston N 600 J11
CENTENNIAL
av. Brunswick W 325 A16
st. W Footscray 366 H10
CENTOFANTI
pl. Thomastown......241 J20
CENTRAL
av. Altona Mdw 451 A1
av. Balwyn N 329 G19
av. Bayswater N 379 J13
av. Black Rock.........529 H8
av. Blairgowrie 679 E20
av. Boronia.............424 B9
av. Box Hill S...........374 G19
av. Burwood............418 A8
av. Croydon S 379 J13
av. Dandenong N.....501 K15
av. Footscray...........367 D6
av. Ivanhoe 328 B16
av. Manifold Ht.........702 B5
av. Moorabbin 496 C7
av. Mooroolbark.......336 L19
av. Preston..............282 L20
av. Seaholme 409 G19
av. Sunshine 365 D8
av. Thomastown......241 A13
av. Torquay.............711 L6
bvd. Port Melb...........368 B18
dr. Bonbeach 547 E20
gr. Broadmeadows..238 F17
pky. Caroline Spr......274 D18
pky. Cranbourne W ...577 F16
pl. Box Hill..............374 J16
rd. Blackburn 375 L16
rd. Hampton Pk........551 E13
rd. Hampton Pk........551 E12
rd. Nunawading 376 C17
CENTRAL PARK
av. Maribyrnong......322 H16
av. Point Cook.........450 C5
rd. Malvern East......416 C17
CENTRAL PIER
Docklands..........368 L15
CENTRE
av. Mt Evelyn...........383 C1
av. Port Melb...........412 B4
av. Werribee............447 F12
ct. Avondale Ht 322 A7
ct. Burwood.............418 J8
ct. Highett 496 G12
ct. Torquay..............711 L4
dr. Rye 696 J3
gr. Healesville 213 A16
pl. Melbourne.............2 C17
pl. Melbourne...........24 E9
rd. Bentleigh 456 A19
rd. Bentleigh E 456
rd. Berwick 553
rd. Brighton East.....455
rd. Broadmeadows..238
rd. Carnegie 456
rd. Clarinda.............497
rd. Clayton.............499
rd. Clayton S...........497
rd. Clayton S...........499
rd. Hallam...............552
rd. Hampton Pk.......552
rd. Langwarrin 602
rd. Langwarrin 629
rd. Melb Airport.......235
rd. Menzies Ck 467
rd. Monbulk.............428
rd. Narre Warren 552
rd. Narre Warren 552
rd. Nar Warrn S........553
rd. Oakleigh S 497
rd. Olinda...............383
rd. Scoresby 462
rd. Springvale 499
rd. Upwey...............466
rd. Vermont 421
rd. Yellingbo 387
st. Reservoir...........283
st. Sunshine 365
st. Seddon, off Windsor St........367
wy. Balwyn N 373
wy. Croydon S 380
wy. Glenroy..............279
CENTRE DANDENONG
rd. Cheltenham 496
rd. Dingley Vill.........533
rd. Heatherton.........531
rd. Moorabbin Aprt..531
CENTRE KIRKHAM
rd. Dandenong S.....535
CENTREWAY
Bundoora............284
Keilor East 278
Mordialloc 531
Mt Waverley 459
arc. Melbourne.............2
CENTURION
ct. Epping...............197
CENTURY
dr. Braeside 532
dr. Mt Martha..........657
rd. Nar Warrn S.......579
CERAM
ct. Heidelberg W.....284
CERBERUS
cr. Williamstn N......410
rd. Baxter...............644
st. Donvale 376
CERCIS
ct. Doveton.............536
CERES
ct. Meadow Ht........237
st. Rosebud............700
CERISE
ct. Clarinda............498
pl. Mulgrave 501
CERNAN
ct. Whittington........704
CERUTTY
wy. Wantirna S.........462
CERVARA
st. Mentone 531
CESUNA
ct. Deer Park...........319
CEYLON
st. Nunawading 376
CEZANNE
cr. Wheelers Hl.......460
CHABLIS
cl. Croydon 335
cr. Vermont S 421
CHADACRE
pl. Mornington........656
CHADBOURN
pl. Nar Warrn S.......552
CHADDESLEY
av. St Kilda E...........415
CHADREE
ct. Dingley Vill.........533
ct. Highton 705
CHADSTONE
rd. Malvern East......457
CHADWELL
gr. Chelsea.............545
la. Chelsea, off Chadwell Gr 545
pl. Kings Park 319
CHADWICK
cl. Langwarrin 629
la. Attwood.............237
pl. Vermont S 421
rd. Harkaway..........540

Harkaway 541 A5
Newtown 702 F8
AFFER
Chum Creek 212 K11
AFFEY
Thomastown 240 K19
AFFMILL
Sydenham 275 A5
GALL
Scoresby 462 C8
IM
Donvale 377 H8
AIN
Nar Warrn S 578 K3
LCOT
Endeavour Hl 537 B2
LDRON
Dingley Vill 533 A2
LET
Badger Creek 258 E10
Olinda 427 C9
Olinda 427 J12
Silvan 427 J12
LEYER
Glen Iris 417 H13
Reservoir 283 E15
LICE
Wantirna 422 C14
LLAMBRA
Highton 701 H13
LLENGE
Frankston 628 F8
LLENGER
Chelsea Ht 547 D12
Diamond Ck 245 F13
LLIS
Rosebud 699 J2
Newport 410 G10
LLOTE
Keilor Ldg 275 L3
LMERS
Sandringham 494 L14
Sandringham 495 A14
Ferntree Gly 464 G9
Up Fntree Gly 464 G9
Taylors L 233 C17
McKinnon 456 E15
LON
Templstw Lr 331 A12
S Morang 198 J13
MBERLAIN
Kilsyth S 380 K19
Ashburton 417 C17
Olinda 427 K2
MBERLAINS
Sandringham, off Station St 495 A13
MBERLIN
Blackburn S 419 K6
MBERS
Darley 221 E1
Altona North 409 G8
Brunswick 325 J18
Coburg 325 H4
Footscray 367 F8
South Yarra 32 D10
South Yarra 414 H5
MNEY
Roxburgh Pk 194 C12
MOUNI
Frankston 628 C10
Alphington 327 L19
MP
Coburg 281 H19
MPAGNE
Nar Warrn S 579 E4
Chirnside Pk 336 K3
Hillside 274 F7
MPION
Bundoora 285 D1
Glen Waverley 421 A18
Lysterfield 464 E16
Newport 410 H10
Williamstn N 410 H10
Black Rock 529 H5
Blairgowrie 695 K3
Brighton 494 L4
Brighton 495 A4
Doncaster E 331 J20
NAK
Kurunjang 227 E7
Malvern East 416 B19
NCELLOR
Wheelers Hl 460 K19
Highton 701 F20
Airport W 278 J16
NDLER
Boronia 424 E11
Burwood 418 D12
/.Alphington 371 G1
/.Kew 371 G1
Boronia 424 D12
Glen Waverley 420 H19

rd. Gruyere 342 F6
rd. Keysborough 534 L15
rd. Noble Park 534 L11
st. Blackburn S 419 G1
st. Keilor East 322 D5
st. Parkdale 531 J11
st. Sunshine W 364 C2
st. Williamstown 411 C11
CHANDLERS
la. Kilsyth S 425 C4
rd. Malvern 415 K16
CHANDON
ct. Waurn Ponds 705 C17
CHANDOR
ct. Notting Hill 459 H14
CHANDOS
pl. Attwood 236 L10
pl. Langwarrin 601 F19
st. Cheltenham 496 D17
st. Coburg 325 E5
st. Sydenham 232 J20
CHANDRA
av. Kilsyth S 380 K18
CHANELLE
ct. Springvale S 534 C4
CHANNEL
cr. Blind Bight 650 C8
rd. Mt Evelyn 339 A19
rd. Silvan 384 F9
st. Mornington 640 L11
tr. Lysterfield S 503 D13
wk. Lysterfield S 503 B11
CHANNELLE
cl. Hampton Pk 551 H4
CHANTAL
cl. Thomastown 240 K16
CHANTELL
av. Endeavour Hl 537 K3
CHANTELLE
ri. St Helena 244 L20
ri. St Helena 245 A20
CHANTILLY
av. Avondale Ht 322 C9
ct. Frankston 628 C8
la. Craigieburn 150 B19
st. Mt Waverley 458 J8
CHAPARRAL
ct. Mooroolbark 337 D10
CHAPEAU
tce. Mt Martha 669 G5
CHAPEL
ct. Doncaster 331 E19
la. Nutfield 202 H1
rd. Keysborough 548 B4
rd. Moorabbin 496 F11
st. Blackburn 375 K14
st. Brunswick 325 G15
st. Cremorne 26 D18
st. Fitzroy 19 D14
st. Glen Waverley 420 H18
st. Lilydale 338 E5
st. Prahran 32 C20
st. Prahran 414 G11
st. St Kilda 414 F17
st. South Yarra 32 C20
st. South Yarra 414 H8
st. Taylors Hill 274 C8
st. Windsor 414 G11
CHAPLIN
ct. Templestowe 331 L6
CHAPMAN
av. Glenroy 279 J6
av. Seaford 599 C2
av. Thomastown 241 K15
bvd. Glen Waverley 461 A5
ct. Mooroolbark 337 J20
la. N Melbourne 17 C12
rd. Silvan 385 B14
st. Blackburn N 375 G7
st. Brighton East 495 C4
st. Carrum Downs 575 C15
st. Diamond Ck 246 C12
st. Macleod 285 A16
st. Malvern East 457 G4
st. N Melbourne 17 B11
st. Seddon 367 B12
st. Sunshine 365 B6
st. Oakleigh, off Palmerston Gr 457 K10
CHAPPELL
ct. Sunbury 142 G14
dr. Wantirna S 462 F2
dr. Watsonia N 243 D17
pl. Keilor East 322 C1
rtn. Meadow Ht 237 H6
st. Thomastown 241 A12
CHAPROWE
ct. Cheltenham 496 K18
CHAPTER HOUSE
la. Melbourne 2 G19
la. Melbourne 24 F9

CHARDONNAY
ct. Waurn Ponds 705 D15
dr. Mt Martha 657 B8
dr. Skye 601 G1
gr. Chirnside Pk 336 K4
CHARINGA
dr. Werribee 446 K15
CHARING CROSS
pl. Narre Warren 539 C14
pl. Wyndham Va 446 F9
CHARL
cl. Nar Warrn N 539 B10
CHARLBER
la. St Andrews 204 H1
CHARLBURY
gr. St Albans 275 G18
CHARLEMONT
la. Olinda 426 L8
CHARLES
av. Hallam 537 E15
av. Springvale 500 F7
ct. Melton S 268 J4
ct. Sydenham 275 B6
ct. Wandin East 384 L4
ct. Wandin East 385 A4
ct. Wantirna S 422 D17
ct. Warranwood 334 K14
dr. Pearcedale 646 K6
la. Torquay 711 K10
pde. Wesburn 348 C18
pl. Fitzroy 19 F17
rd. Altona 408 K13
rd. Lilydale 382 G3
st. Abbotsford 26 C3
st. Anglesea 713 E6
st. Ascot Vale 323 G20
st. Belmont 706 F4
st. Bentleigh E 456 J19
st. Blairgowrie 679 K19
st. Brighton East 455 E13
st. Brunswick 325 G16
st. Carlton 18 J10
st. Cheltenham 530 L3
st. Coburg N 281 B17
st. Dandenong 535 L3
st. Dromana 686 B6
st. E Melbourne 25 E10
st. Elsternwick 455 C4
st. Fitzroy 19 D17
st. Glen Iris 417 K10
st. Greensbrgh 286 A7
st. Hadfield 280 K7
st. Hampton 495 C9
st. Hawthorn 371 J16
st. Kew 371 L11
st. Kew 371 L13
st. Kew 372 A11
st. Kilsyth 381 D6
st. Lower Plenty 286 K15
st. McCrae 685 A12
st. Mooroolbark 337 A19
st. Mornington 640 C19
st. Mt Waverley 419 D19
st. Newcomb 703 L13
st. Northcote 326 F17
st. Northcote 326 G17
st. Nunawading 376 G10
st. Pakenham 584 L9
st. Prahran 31 L19
st. Prahran 414 F10
st. Preston 282 D19
st. Richmond 26 H17
st. Ringwood E 378 L8
st. Ringwood E 379 A8
st. Rye 697 B5
st. St Albans 276 A20
st. St Kilda 414 D15
st. Seaford 599 E1
st. Seddon 367 A11
st. Selby 467 C15
st. S Melbourne 30 A3
st. Sunbury 142 C13
st. Sunshine N 321 C17
st. Surrey Hills 374 F18
st. Thomastown 241 D15
st. Werribee 448 A15
st. Williamstown 411 D15
CHARLES CONDER
pl. Berwick 554 H18
CHARLES FARRER
ct. Mornington 656 J2
CHARLES GREEN
av. Endeavour Hl 537 B7
CHARLES GRIMES
ct. Williamstown, off Norval Cl 411 H18
pl. Seabrook 450 L7
CHARLES GRIMES BRIDGE
rd. Docklands 23 C16
CHARLES SMITH
dr. Wonga Park 335 G11
CHARLES STURT
dr. Doreen 201 H10
dr. Yarrambat 201 H10

CHARLES SWANSTON
wy. Seabrook 450 L7
CHARLESVILLE
rd. Plenty 244 B2
CHARLES WILSON
cl. Eltham North 245 F17
CHARLESWORTH
cr. Burnside 318 E7
pl. Mitcham 377 E9
st. Laverton 407 E15
st. McCrae 685 C11
CHARLEVILLE
ct. Carrum Downs 601 C4
CHARLNET
dr. Vermont S 420 J12
CHARLOTTE
av. Melton W 226 B13
av. Newcomb 704 A16
cr. Wyndham Va 446 E7
ct. Cranbourne W 603 G2
ct. Frankston S 627 H14
ct. N Warrandyte 289 L14
pl. St Kilda 414 G13
rd. Beaumaris 530 C7
rd. Boronia 423 C14
rd. Mill Park 242 C3
st. Blackburn S 375 H20
st. Blackburn S 419 H2
st. Brighton East 455 G19
st. Clayton S 498 K7
st. Collingwood 19 K11
st. Glenroy 280 B10
st. Glen Waverley 460 E1
st. Newport 410 E6
st. Richmond 26 G16
st. Springvale S 533 K5
st. Sunshine W 363 L4
st. Yarraville 366 F14
CHARLTON
av. Cheltenham 496 C19
bvd. Darley 222 C5
cr. Reservoir 283 F11
ct. Endeavour Hl 537 K9
ct. Portsea 677 L1
ct. Wantirna S 462 F3
pl. Frankston 627 B4
pl. Thomastown 240 E13
rd. Eaglemont 328 G11
st. Bentleigh 495 L1
st. Blackburn N 375 K9
st. Broadmeadows 238 F16
st. Mt Waverley 459 A3
st. Springvale 500 D6
CHARLTONIAN
cl. Bacchus Msh 221 E18
CHARLWOOD
ct. Donvale 376 H1
dr. Mooroolbark 337 L20
CHARM
ct. Mt Martha 669 G4
CHARMAINE
av. Avondale Ht 322 C9
pl. Melton W 226 C17
st. Dromana 686 A9
CHARMAN
av. Emerald 469 F17
rd. Beaumaris 530 H9
rd. Cheltenham 496 J20
rd. Mentone 530 H9
CHARMIAN
cl. Ivanhoe 328 F10
CHARMING
st. Hampton E 495 L7
CHARMOUTH
pl. Nar Warrn S 579 D4
CHARNFIELD
cr. Noble Park 534 L5
ct. Thomastown 241 E18
CHARNWOOD
cr. St Kilda 414 E14
ct. Narre Warren 552 K1
gr. St Kilda 414 E14
la. Cheltenham 496 L15
rd. St Kilda 414 D13
CHAROLAIS
ct. Belmont 706 B7
CHARON
ct. Frankston 600 D18
CHARTER
cl. Berwick 553 D4
rd. Sunbury 142 J12
rd.w, Sunbury 142 F12
st. Ringwood 378 B12
CHARTERIS
dr. Craigieburn 150 C6
dr. Ivanhoe East 328 J16
gr. Epping 197 L15
rd. Wandin East 386 A12
CHARTWELL
cr. Derrimut 363 A6
dr. Wantirna 422 J9

CHASE
la. Woori Yall 344 L17
rd. N Warrandyte 289 L10
CHASE VIEW
ct. N Warrandyte 290 B8
CHASTA
cr. Mitcham 377 F17
CHASTLETON
av. Toorak 415 C2
CHAT
pl. Werribee 448 C6
CHATEAU
av. Narre Warren 552 J1
cl. Croydon 335 E20
ct. Thomastown 240 E14
gr. Beaumaris 530 G9
ri. Bulleen 329 H9
CHATEAUX
cl. Mt Martha 657 B8
CHATFIELD
av. Balwyn 373 A13
av. Rosebud W 683 D19
st. Kingsville 366 J13
CHATHAM
av. Ferntree Gly 424 G19
cl. Cranbourne E 578 K17
pl. Kings Park 319 C1
rd. Canterbury 373 H17
st. Flemington 324 D20
st. Footscray 367 C5
st. Prahran 32 C17
st. Prahran 414 G9
CHATSWOOD
av. Langwarrin 601 B20
cl. Glen Waverley 420 J18
dr. Anglesea 713 D2
dr. Nar Warrn S 578 F3
gr. Chirnside Pk 336 H6
pl. Wyndham Va 446 E8
CHATSWORTH
av. Ardeer 320 C18
av. Brighton 454 F11
av. Derrimut 363 B4
cl. Cheltenham 496 K13
ct. Officer 555 J20
ct. Rowville 503 E4
ct. Springvale S 499 F20
qd. Templstw Lr 330 B10
rd. Prahran 415 A11
CHATTAN
ct. Greenvale 237 E1
CHATTERLEY
ct. Frankston 628 E5
dr. Noble Park N 501 C12
CHATTERTON
dr. Delahey 275 E11
CHAUCER
av. Frankston 600 C19
av. Malvern East 456 K2
cl. Delahey 275 C16
cr. Bundoora 242 J20
cr. Canterbury 373 C17
st. Blairgowrie 680 A20
st. Box Hill S 418 G2
st. Moonee Pnd 324 B14
st. Mooroolbark 337 G20
st. St Kilda 414 B18
CHAUMONT
dr. Avondale Ht 322 B8
CHAUNCY
wy. Lynbrook 551 E17
CHAUNDY
rd. Belgrave S 506 B4
st. Ferntree Gly 464 G3
CHAUVEL
pl. S Morang 198 K15
st. Ascot Vale 323 J20
st. Bentleigh E 457 G16
st. Heidelberg Ht 328 G2
st. Melton S 268 J11
st. Reservoir 282 H5
CHAVASSE
st. Brighton 454 H18
CHAVE
ct. Laverton 407 D14
CHEADLE
cr. Bundoora 243 D20
CHEAM
st. Dandenong N 502 C18
wk. Highton 701 H15
CHEASLEY
pl. Altona Mdw 452 A5
CHEDDAR
rd. Reservoir 283 D4
rd.e, Reservoir 283 B8
rd.w, Reservoir 283 B7
CHEDGEY
dr. St Albans 320 E9
CHEDWORTH
ct. Kilsyth S 424 L2
CHEEL
st. Armadale 415 E12
st. Oakleigh E 458 D10

CLAYTON
ct. Mill Park 242 B5
ct. Springvale S 534 B4
rd. Balwyn 373 L9
rd. Clarinda 498 H15
rd. Clayton 458 K18
rd. Clayton S 498 H15
rd. Cranbourne 603 K2
rd. Oakleigh E 458 K18
rd. Strathmr Ht 279 C9
st. Sunshine N 320 K15
st. Sunshine N 321 A14
CLAYTON HILL
rd. Langwarrin S 629 K18
CLEAL
ct. Noble Park 535 B1
CLEAR BROOK
rd. Clematis 508 J5
CLEARVIEW
cl. Ashwood 418 C15
ct. Eltham 288 B2
dr. Wantirna 422 D10
CLEARWATER
cl. Eltham 287 E14
cl. Mt Martha 669 C5
dr. Lilydale 338 D12
dr. Pakenham 583 J2
vw. S Morang 199 A16
CLEARWOOD
cl. Warranwood 335 B16
CLEARY
ct. Clayton S 498 K7
dr. Braybrook 366 A6
st. Springvale S 499 L19
CLEE
st. McKinnon 455 J15
CLEEK
av. Oakleigh S 457 J17
cr. Rosebud 700 A8
CLEELAND
cl. Epping 197 L20
ct. Rosebud 699 J3
ct. Roxburgh Pk 194 F15
rd. Oakleigh S 498 A5
st. Dandenong 536 A6
st. Reservoir 282 K10
CLEEVE
ct. Toorak 415 F6
CLEGG
av. Croydon 379 G5
gr. Ringwood 378 H10
rd. Mt Evelyn 339 H20
rd. Wandin East 340 G17
rd. Wandin N 340 G17
CLEGHORN
av. Altona North 410 C4
CLELAND
ct. Kurunjang 226 H14
st. Ringwood E 379 D13
CLELLAND
rd. Brooklyn 365 C19
CLEMANTINE
cl. Wonga Park 335 J4
CLEMATIS
av. Altona North 365 K20
av. Ferntree Gly 464 J1
av. Rosebud W 683 C20
ct. Langwarrin 629 J1
ct. Long Forest 224 F10
ct. Meadow Ht 193 L19
ct. Patterson L 573 J9
ct. Rye 696 F8
ct. Warrandyte 333 C10
dr. Taylors L 275 H2
pl. Sunshine W 363 L8
rd. Mt Evelyn 338 L19
rd. Mt Evelyn 339 A19
ri. Eltham North 245 F19
st. Belgrave 466 K15
st. Glen Waverley 420 J20
st. Vermont 421 E4
CLEMATIS PARK
rd. Clematis 509 A2
rd. Emerald 509 A2
CLEMENT
cr. Croydon 336 C18
ct. Altona Mdw 451 G7
ct. Mill Park 241 L5
ct. Nar Warrn S 552 H20
st. Dandenong 536 D8
CLEMENTINE
cl. Lysterfield 463 L20
CLEMENTS
av. Belgrave S 506 J2
av. Bundoora 285 B4
av. Donvale 377 A7
dr. Bundoora 242 J14
gr. Reservoir 283 F9
st. Bentleigh E 456 K16
st. Highett 495 J15
CLENDON
cl. Mt Eliza 641 L6
ct. Carrum Downs 601 A3
ct. Cheltenham 496 K14
ct. Hoppers Csg 405 D20
ct. Templestowe 332 B7
ct. Toorak 415 E7
ct. Vermont S 421 B14
pl. Melton W 226 C16
rd. Armadale 415 D10
rd. Ferntree Gly 423 L20
rd. Ferntree Gly 463 L1
rd. Mulgrave 501 F6
rd. Toorak 415 D6
CLEREHAN
ct. Wantirna S 462 B4
CLERY
av. Donvale 377 E4
CLEVE
av. The Basin 425 E11
gr. Heidelberg 328 J5
la. Melbourne 23 G8
rd. Pascoe Vale S 280 E19
CLEVEDON
rd. The Basin 425 F12
CLEVELAND
av. Lower Plenty 330 C2
cl. Nar Warrn N 539 G11
ct. Dandenong N 501 J9
ct. Lower Plenty 286 F18
ct. Rowville 503 D4
rd. Ashwood 418 D18
st. Northcote 326 K12
st. St Albans 319 H5
st. Thomastown 241 J13
CLIFF
ct. Narre Warren 538 K14
gr. Beaumaris 530 G10
pl. Hoppers Csg 405 L18
rd. Frankston 626 J4
rd. Frankston S 626 J4
st. Brunswick 325 D12
st. Essendon 323 K9
st. Laverton 407 E10
st. South Yarra 32 B13
st. South Yarra 414 G7
st. Torquay 712 B9
CLIFFE
la. Edithvale 546 L13
CLIFFER
pl. Taylors L 275 G9
CLIFFORD
cl. Ashburton 417 E19
cl. Mill Park 242 B4
ct. Forest Hill 376 G20
dr. Wonga Park 291 L11
gr. Healesville 214 C15
gr. Tecoma 466 B13
pl. Clifton Hill 20 H8
st. Bayswater 423 D9
st. Frankston 627 G1
st. Glen Waverley 460 E1
st. Huntingdale 458 E15
st. Port Melb 412 J5
CLIFFORD PARK
rd. Endeavour Hl 503 B14
CLIFFORDS
rd. Somerton 194 G16
rd. Werribee S 488 G3
CLIFFTOP
ct. Dromana 685 D9
CLIFT
ct. Altona North 409 A7
ct. Avondale Ht 322 C15
CLIFTON
av. Clifton Hill 20 E7
ct. Keilor Ldg 275 L2
ct. Mulgrave 500 E1
dr. Bacchus Msh 221 J13
gr. Carrum Downs 574 K16
gr. Coburg 281 D20
gr. Hawthorn E 416 F7
gr. Ivanhoe 328 C11
gr. Lalor 241 J9
gr. Preston 326 K3
la. Caroline Spr 274 D15
rd. Greenvale 193 D19
rd. Hawthorn E 416 F6
st. Aberfeldie 323 B10
st. Balwyn N 374 B4
st. Balwyn N 374 B7
st. Blackburn 376 C19
st. Box Hill S 374 J20
st. Caulfield E 456 D4
st. Clifton Hill 20 K2
st. Northcote 327 A13
st. Oakleigh S 497 F5
st. Prahran 32 E20
st. Prahran 414 H10
st. Richmond 26 D16
wy. Endeavour Hl 537 D1
CLIFTON PARK
dr. Carrum Downs 574 J16
CLINCH
av. Preston 282 J20
av. Preston 282 K19
CLINE
ct. Hampton Pk 551 H12
CLINGIN
st. Reservoir 283 J15
CLINNICK
st. Reservoir 282 H12
CLINTON
ct. Wollert 153 G12
la. Chirnside Pk 336 G6
st. Brighton East 455 G18
st. Heidelberg Ht 328 E5
wy. Toorak, off Winifred Cr 415 C2
CLINTONS
rd. Smiths Gly 205 E6
CLIPPER
ct. Ringwood 378 L1
ct. Ringwood 379 A1
CLIPPER ISLAND
Patterson L 573 H8
CLISBY
ct. Box Hill 374 K15
CLISSOLD
st. Ascot Vale 324 C18
CLITHEROE
ct. Glen Iris 417 J9
dr. Wyndham Va 446 D15
grn. Derrimut 363 A7
CLITUS
av. Glen Iris 417 H12
st. Glen Waverley 460 E8
CLIVE
av. Healesville 213 G17
ct. Avondale Ht 322 F7
ct. Balwyn N 329 J19
ct. Bundoora 284 F6
ct. Melton 227 A16
ct. Mooroolbark 337 H18
rd. Hawthorn E 372 F20
rd. Hawthorn E 416 F2
st. Alphington 327 H18
st. Brighton East 455 F18
st. Hampton Pk 551 C9
st. Mitcham 377 D15
st. Mt Waverley 418 J20
st. Murrumbeena 457 D6
st. Springvale 499 K6
st. W Footscray 366 G7
CLIVEDEN
av. Frankston 599 H17
cl. Nar Warrn S 578 K1
ct. Greenvale 237 A6
ct. Seabrook 451 A2
ct. Templestowe 332 B1
ct. Thomastown 241 C17
CLIVEDON
pl. Gladstone Pk 237 C17
CLIVEJAY
st. Glen Waverley 420 A14
CLOCKTOWER
ct. Berwick 553 L20
CLONAIG
st. Brighton East 455 C14
CLONARD
av. Elsternwick 455 A9
av. Geelong West 702 G2
CLONARG
st. Glen Iris 417 J12
CLONDARA
dr. Rowville 502 B4
CLONMORE
st. Beaumaris 530 B6
CLONMULT
av. Highett 496 B15
CLONTARF
cr. Templestowe 332 C6
CLORIS
av. Beaumaris 530 B8
CLOSE
av. Dandenong 535 J7
ct. Pakenham 584 G6
CLOSEBURN
av. Prahran 414 L13
av. Prahran 415 A13
CLOSTER
av. Ashwood 417 L15
av. Nunawading 376 G11
ct. Bacchus Msh 222 A20
ct. Lilydale 338 G8
CLOTA
av. Box Hill 375 C14
CLOUD
ct. Eltham 288 B2
st. Arthurs Seat 686 A14
CLOUGH
pde. Reservoir 283 J2
st. Avondale Ht 322 A7
st. Williamstown 411 F12
CLOVELLY
av. Glenroy 279 H7
av. Rosebud 684 F18
cl. Portsea 678 D8
ct. Balwyn N 374 B5
ct. Hawthorn 371 K14
ct. Mt Waverley 419 G15
ct. Viewbank 285 J16
ct. Portsea, off Hotham Rd 678 C6
dr. Craigieburn 150 C19
pde. Seaford 573 D15
pl. Berwick 554 C1
CLOVER
av. St Albans 320 G10
cl. Berwick 554 L8
ct. Altona Mdw 407 K19
ct. Boronia 424 J6
ct. Frankston 600 A18
ct. Gowanbrae 279 C6
ct. Grovedale 705 J13
ct. Keilor East 322 G6
ct. Thomastown 240 E18
la. Mornington 656 K5
la. Wyndham Va, off Greengables Dr 446 E9
pl. Carrum Downs 601 D6
CLOVERDALE
av. Toorak 415 A3
cl. Burwood E 419 L7
ct. Mulgrave 501 G6
la. Chirnside Pk 337 D2
la. Lysterfield S 504 D15
rd. Glen Iris 417 C12
tr. Lysterfield 504 G15
CLOVERFIELD
cl. Berwick 554 K1
CLOVERLEA
ct. Blackburn 376 B19
dr. Kilsyth S 381 B16
dr. Wantirna 422 J10
CLOVERLEIGH
av. Emerald 509 J5
CLOVERSET
av. Narre Warren 538 J19
CLOVIS
st. Oakleigh E 458 H15
CLOW
av. Up Fntree Gly 464 J8
st. Dandenong 535 L8
st. Dandenong 536 B8
CLOWES
st. Melton S 268 J10
st. South Yarra 31 H1
st. South Yarra 414 D1
CLOWS
la. Pt Lonsdale 707 A17
CLOYNE
st. Highett 496 B16
CLUB
av. Kingsbury 283 J9
ct. Dingley Vill 533 F8
la. Melbourne 24 J6
CLUBHOUSE
pl. Keilor Dn 276 J16
CLUB POINT
dr. Chirnside Pk 337 G5
CLUDEN
st. Brighton East 455 B17
CLUES
ct. Sunshine W 364 A8
CLUNES
av. Dallas 238 C11
pl. Epping 197 J19
st. Kingsbury 284 A10
CLUNEY
ct. Blackburn S 419 G3
CLUNIES ROSS
cr. Mulgrave 460 B18
CLYDE
cl. Taylors Hill 274 L12
ct. Croydon S 380 A12
ct. Frankston S 626 F7
ct. Heidelberg 329 A4
ct. Oak Park 280 A9
ct. Sunbury 144 F10
ct. Werribee 447 G6
rd. Berwick 580 B5
rd. Safety Bch 668 J19
st. Belmont 702 J18
st. Box Hill N 374 K10
st. Diamond Ck 245 G9
st. Ferntree Gly 463 H1
st. Frankston 599 C18
st. Glen Iris 416 F14
st. Highett 495 L12
st. Kew East 372 G5
st. Lilydale 338 A6
st. Maribyrnong 323 E14
st. Newport 410 E8
st. Oakleigh 458 A10
st. Rosebud W 683 C19
st. St Kilda 414 B17
st. Surrey Hills 373 J14
st. Thornbury 327 A10
CLYDEBANK
av. Endeavour Hl 503 J18
av. Greensbrgh 286 B5
ct. Rowville 503
rd. Edithvale 546
rd. Essendon W 323
CLYDEN
ct. Burwood E 419
CLYDESDALE
cr. Belmont 706
ct. Mt Martha 657
rd. Airport W 278
rd. Airport W 278
st. Box Hill 374
wy. Highton 701
wy. Sunbury 143
CLYNDEN
av. Malvern East 416
CLYNE
ct. Tullamarine 278
pl. Rowville 463
rd. Seville 386
CLYNO
ct. Keilor Dn 276
CLYVE
av. Mentone 530
COACH
ct. Kings Park 274
COACH HOUSE
dr. Attwood 236
la. Skye 601
COACHMAN
wy. S Morang 199
COACHMANS
ct. Chirnside Pk 337
ct. Vermont S 421
sq. Wantirna 422
COACHWOOD
cr. Narre Warren 539
cr. Narre Warren 553
COADY
ct. Vermont 377
COALDRAKE
ct. Carrum Downs 575
COALMINE
rd. Anglesea 713
COANE
st. Oakleigh E 458
st. Ormond 456
st. Pascoe Vale 280
COAPE
st. Cheltenham 530
COATE
av. Alphington 327
COATES
ct. Sunbury 142
la.e, Melbourne 24
st. Bentleigh 496
wk. Seaford 599
COATS
st. Moonee Pnd 324
COB
cl. Broadmeadows 238
pl. Clayton 459
COBAIN
ct. Ringwood 335
sq. Wantirna 422
st. Clayton 459
st. Keysborough 534
COBAR
ct. Mooroolbark 336
pl. Kings Park 275
st. Bentleigh E 457
COBB
jnc. Sydenham 275
rd. Mt Eliza 641
COBBITTY
ct. Boronia 424
COBBLER
gra. Lynbrook 551
st. Werribee 448
COBBLESTONE
av. Nar Warrn S 553
dr. Attwood 237
dr. S Morang 199
grn. Caroline Spr 318
la. Sunbury 144
COBBY
ct. Roxburgh Pk 194
st. Laverton 407
COBDEN
cr. Lilydale 338
st. Campbellfield 238
st. Caulfield N 415
st. Highton 701
st. Kew 371
st. N Melbourne 17
st. S Melbourne 30
st. S Melbourne 30
st. S Melbourne 413
COBHAM
ct. Mt Martha 669
rd. Langwarrin S 629
rd. Mitcham 377
st. Altona 408
st. Balwyn N 373

COMMONWEALTH
ct. Craigieburn 150 E16
COMMUNITY
dr. Greensbrgh 286 F2
pde. Nar Warrn S 578 F2
wy. Lilydale 338 D12
wy. Lilydale 338 D13
COMMUNITY HUB
Hillside 274 C5
Sydenham 274 C5
COMO
av. Rye 698 A8
av. South Yarra 32 K9
av. South Yarra 414 K5
av. Surrey Hills 373 J13
cl. Croydon 380 C10
ct. Dandenong N 502 A16
ct. Dromana 686 J4
ct. Mt Eliza 626 E17
ct. Mt Waverley 458 K9
ct. Springvale 499 J17
ct. Thomastown 240 G15
gln. Caroline Spr 274 C16
pde. Maribyrnong 323 D15
pde.e,Mentone 531 C9
pde.e,Parkdale 531 C9
pde.e,Parkdale 531 G13
pde.w,Mentone 531 A7
pde.w,Mordialloc 531 G13
pde.w,Parkdale 531 A7
pl. Campbellfield 239 G12
rd. Lilydale 338 L3
rd. Lilydale 339 A1
st. Alphington 327 K20
st. Alphington 371 K1
st. Doncaster 374 K3
st. Emerald 509 D3
st. Malvern 415 J16
COMPARK
cct. Mulgrave 459 L18
COMPASS
ct. Somerville 645 D18
COMPORT
st. Beaumaris 530 C12
COMPTON
pde. Sunshine N 321 C15
st. Canterbury 417 G1
st. Glen Waverley 420 F19
st. Mitcham 376 L8
st. Nunawading 376 L8
st. Reservoir 282 J10
COMRIE
ct. Bayswater 423 E7
COMTE
cl. Cranbourne W 577 G19
CONARGO
ct. Greensbrgh 244 J20
CONCORD
cct. Albanvale 319 A6
cr. Carrum Downs 574 G20
pl. Cranbourne 603 J4
pl. Ferntree Gly 423 J17
ri. Templestowe 332 C2
st. Preston 326 D3
CONCORDE
cr. Werribee 487 H2
CONDAH
ct. Ashwood 418 F17
CONDELL
st. Fitzroy 19 C16
CONDEN
ct. Vermont 421 B4
CONDER
av. Burwood 419 B7
cl. Yallambie 286 A14
pl. Caroline Spr 273 L7
st. Donvale 376 F6
CONDON
ct. Keysborough 535 A12
CONDONS
la. Darley 221 A10
CONDOR
ct. Frankston 628 F8
ct. Werribee 447 L9
pl. Mill Park 242 L8
pl. Mill Park 243 A8
pl. Sunbury 142 G8
pl. Taylors L 275 J9
st. Hawthorn E 372 F15
CONDOS
ct. Wantirna S 422 E19
CONE
cl. Ringwood N 334 H20
pl. Pakenham 585 K8
st. Bulleen 330 B17
st. Eumemmerring 537 D12
CONEY HURST
cr. Mornington 656 F2
CONFAIT
ct. Berwick 553 L4
CONFERTA
cl. Hillside 274 A4
cr. Doveton 536 K7
ct. Cranbourne W 577 K17
CONGO
ct. Roxburgh Pk 194 F6
CONGRAM
st. Broadmeadows 238 E18
CONICA
ct. Hallam 552 C2
CONIFER
av. Brooklyn 365 G18
cl. Gladstone Pk 279 B1
cl. Hampton Pk 551 E4
cl. Hoppers Csg 405 E16
cl. Mill Park 242 E11
cr. Dingley Vill 532 H5
ct. Dandenong N 501 K16
ct. Frankston S 627 J14
ct. Lysterfield 464 A20
ct. Nar Warrn S 553 E20
ct. Ringwood N 334 J20
dr. Pakenham 584 K3
pl. Hillside 274 D5
pl. Templstw Lr 330 J12
st. Hampton 495 F12
CONISTON
av. Airport W 278 K18
av. Berwick 554 A8
cl. Croydon Hl 335 J13
ct. Springvale S 533 L3
dr. Wheelers Hl 461 C15
st. Diamond Ck 246 A12
CONLEY
st. Noble Park 534 K6
CONN
st. Ferntree Gly 463 K3
CONNAL
dr. Frankston 599 J17
CONNAM
av. Clayton 459 F19
CONNAUGHT
pl. Glen Waverley 461 A3
CONNELL
cl. Dingley Vill 533 C8
cl. Hopetoun Park 265 K7
ct. Balwyn 373 L13
dr. Melton S 268 F10
rd. Oakleigh 458 B13
st. Glenroy 280 D5
st. Hawthorn 371 G15
st. Mordialloc 531 L18
wk. Roxburgh Pk 194 A10
CONNELLY
st. Brunswick 325 G11
st. Flemington 33 F1
st. Flemington 324 C20
CONNEMARA
cl. Highton 701 B17
CONNEMARRA
cct. Melton 227 H18
CONNERS FLAT
rd. Wandin N 340 K14
CONNEWARRA
av. Aspendale 546 E4
CONNEWARRE
av. Wyndham Va 446 B5
av. Wyndham Va 446 C6
CONNIE
ct. Cranbourne 603 K5
st. Bentleigh E 457 E20
CONNOLLY
av. Coburg 282 A19
cr. Bayswater N 380 A20
CONNOR
pl. Kangaroo Grnd 247 G11
st. Bacchus Msh 221 H16
st. Brighton East 495 D1
st. E Geelong 703 F10
st. Kew East 372 B4
CONNORS
la. Melbourne 17 K19
la. Seville 386 G4
st. Highett 496 H15
CONOS
ct. Donvale 377 D1
CONQUEST
dr. Werribee 447 K11
wy. Hallam 537 D19
CONRAD
ct. Blackburn N 376 A7
ct. Pakenham 585 E1
ct. Whittington 704 D19
pl. Wheelers Hl 460 K17
st. St Albans 276 A19
CONRAN
av. Endeavour Hl 537 L6
ct. Box Hill S 419 B5
CONROY
pl. Roxburgh Pk 194 D11
CONSERVATION
dr. Bangholme 549 J14
CONSERVATORY
dr. Burwood 418 A11
CONSIDE
cr. Torquay 712 A2
CONSIDEN
cl. Mill Park 242 E3
CONSIDINE
ct. Bayswater N 379 L15
CONSORT
av. Vermont S 420 G10
pl. Craigieburn 150 F7
CONSTABLE
ct. Scoresby 462 A7
CONSTANCE
cl. Lysterfield 464 B14
ct. Healesville 257 F2
ct. Narre Warren 539 E16
st. Alphington 327 L19
st. Blackburn S 419 K2
st. Hawthorn E 416 E4
st. St Albans 319 L1
CONSTANCE STONE
la. Melbourne 2 H8
CONSTELLATION
ct. Taylors L 275 K6
CONSTITUTION
ri. Berwick 554 H17
CONSTITUTION HILL
rd. Sorrento 678 K9
CONTESSA
ct. Point Cook 450 G11
CONTI
ct. Mentone 530 J4
CONTINENTAL
wy. Prahran 32 A18
CONTOUR
cl. Research 288 K2
ct. Chirnside Pk 337 F6
CONTRACTORS
la. E Melbourne 25 J3
CONTURSI
dr. Sydenham 274 H7
CONVENT
ct. Coburg N 281 G16
CONVENTION
av. Belgrave Ht 506 E1
CONVERY
cl. Gladstone Pk 237 D17
CONWAY
av. Donvale 377 A3
cr. Balwyn 373 H13
ct. Altona North 409 J2
ct. Boronia 424 A12
ct. Chelsea Ht 547 D10
ct. Cranbourne 577 L18
ct. Hampton Pk 551 H12
ct. Highton 705 F5
ct. Somerville 644 G15
st. Cranbourne N 578 F9
st. Dandenong S 535 H13
st. Mt Eliza 641 L4
CONYERS
st. The Basin 425 B11
COOBA
ct. Mornington 640 L15
ct. Mornington 641 A15
ct. Mulgrave 500 G2
pl. Frankston 628 C6
st. Canterbury 417 E1
COODE
rd. W Melbourne 367 J12
COOEE
ct. Diamond Ck 244 L13
COOGEE
av. Frankston 627 H6
la. Williamstown 411 D16
pl. Burnside 318 F6
pl. Port Melb 412 E5
st. Boronia 424 C9
wy. Yallambie 286 A13
COOINDA
cl. Burnside 318 G7
cr. Clarinda 498 D7
cr. Watsonia 285 J8
ct. Burwood E 419 F9
ct. Frankston S 627 B6
ct. Mt Waverley 459 C3
dr. Aspendale 546 F5
pl. Malvern East 457 A2
rd. Beaconsfield 555 K7
rd. Woori Yall 344 K15
rd. Woori Yall 345 A14
st. Warneet 649 E12
COOK
av. Kealba 277 A20
av. Rosebud 700 D1
ct. Cranbourne N 577 L8
ct. Dandenong N 502 A19
ct. Ferntree Gly 463 E2
ct. Springvale S 534 B1
ct. Sunbury 143 B12
dr. Pakenham 584 L8
pl. Westmeadows 237 E14
rd. Melton S 268 F13
rd. Mitcham 377 F12
st. Blairgowrie 696 C5
st. Brunswick W 325 A11
st. Bundoora 284 G1
st. Hawthorn 371 L17
st. Ivanhoe 327 K9
st. McCrae 685 B17
st. Mornington 640 E11
st. Newtown 702 A10
st. Port Melb 368 D20
st. Port Melb 412 A1
st. Preston 282 K20
st. Southbank 3 J5
st. Southbank 24 C14
st. Sunshine W 364 H14
COOKE
av. Hampton E 495 J10
av. Sunshine N 321 A12
ct. Richmond 26 G4
st. Abbotsford 26 J3
st. Clayton 498 J3
st. Essendon 324 A4
st. Sandringham 495 J18
COOKES
rd. Doreen 156 B18
rd. Doreen 201 B1
rd. Yuroke 192 H1
COOKS
cr. N Warrandyte 289 F14
mw. Point Cook 450 L9
wy. Taylors Hill 274 K12
COOKSON
st. Camberwell 372 J18
COOL
st. Reservoir 282 C14
COOLABAH
av. Glen Waverley 460 A11
cr. Hoppers Csg 405 D17
ct. Kurunjang 227 D15
dr. Eltham 287 K3
dr. Grovedale 705 L14
gr. Berwick 553 H4
st. Doncaster 375 D2
st. Mentone 531 J8
st. Mooroolbark 337 A15
COOLABINDI
ch. Eltham 287 B6
COOLAC
st. Chadstone 458 E1
st. Cheltenham 497 B20
COOLALIE
ct. Grovedale 705 L13
COOLAMON
st. Albion 320 K20
COOLANGATTA
rd. Mt Martha 655 K12
st. Menzies Ck 468 H18
tce. Dromana 685 L9
COOLARN
st. Mt Waverley 459 G5
COOLAROO
av. Hurstbridge 203 F13
ct. Mooroolbark 337 F12
COOLART
rd. Moorooduc 644 B19
rd. Somerville 644 B19
COOLAVIN
rd. Noble Park N 501 D16
COOLEY
av. Macleod 285 E11
COOLGARDIE
av. Malvern East 456 L1
st. Frankston N 600 A11
COOLIBAH
cr. Bayswater 423 G6
pl. Keysborough 534 F8
COOLIBAR
av. Seaford 573 D14
COOLIDGE
ct. Dandenong N 501 J8
COOLOCK
ct. Rosanna 285 D20
COOLOMON
cl. Wantirna S 422 K11
COOLONG
av. Berwick 553 E4
pl. Viewbank 286 C15
COOLOOLI
ct. Ringwood E 379 D14
COOLOONGATTA
rd. Camberwell 417 D5
rd. Sassafras 426 E14
COOLSTORE
rd. Croydon 380 B3
COOLULLAH
av. South Yarra 32 K11
av. South Yarra 414 L6
COOMA
ct. Berwick 553 J1
ct. Dandenong 536 F5
ct. Lalor 240 H8
la. Craigieburn 150 F10
st. Broadmeadows 238
st. Moorabbin 496
st. Preston 326
COOMALIE
cr. Heidelberg W 328
COOMBAH
ct. Mooroolbark 337
COOMBE
av. Hampton 495
COOMBES
ct. Rye 697
rd. Torquay 711
COOMBS
av. Kew 371
av. Oakleigh S 458
COOMGARIE
tce. Cairnlea 319
COOMLEIGH
av. Glen Waverley 420
COOMOORA
rd. Springvale S 533
COONAC
pl. Frankston 600
COONAMAR
st. Tullamarine 278
COONAN'S
rd. Pascoe Vale S 324
COONARA
av. Mt Eliza 642
av. Seaford 573
ct. Narre Warren 553
ct. Olinda 427
COONAWARRA
dr. Thomastown 240
dr. Vermont S 421
COONEY
cl. Berwick 554
st. Moolap 704
COONIL
cr. Malvern 415
st. Oakleigh S 498
COOP
rd. Pakenham 586
st. Werribee 447
COOPER
av. Altona North 409
av. Glen Waverley 460
ct. Cranbourne 604
ct. Dandenong 536
ct. Delahey 275
ct. Hallam 538
gr. Sorrento 678
rd. Bulla 232
rd. Bulla 233
rd. Rowville 463
st. Broadmeadows 238
st. Brunswick W 325
st. Campbellfield 195
st. Epping 195
st. Epping 241
st. Epping 241
st. Essendon 323
st. Hoppers Csg 405
st. Melton S 268
st. Preston 282
st. Somerton 195
st. Springvale S 500
st. Sunshine 365
COOPERS
la. Gruyere 341
la. Kensington 33
rd. Macclesfield 471
COOPERS HILL
dr. Westmeadows 236
dr. Westmeadows 237
COORA
ct. Frankston 600
rd. Oakleigh S 458
COORABONG
av. Rosebud 683
COORAMINTA
pl. Diamond Ck 245
rd. Rye 696
st. Brunswick 325
COORIE
av. Bayswater 423
cr. Rosanna 329
COORIGIL
rd. Carnegie 456
COORNONG
ct. Kurunjang 227
COORONG
ct. Meadow Ht 194
ct. Taylors Hill 274
ct. Taylors L 275
ct. Wantirna 422
la. Doncaster 374
pl. Burnside 318
COOROOMBONG
st. Werribee 447
COOTAMUNDRA
av. Rosebud W 699
cr. Blackburn 375

Mornington 656 J4
Werribee 448 G18
Wheelers Hl 460 F13
Doveton 536 J6
OTE
Blairgowrie 695 F1
Kensington 33 K7
S Melbourne 29 H5
S Melbourne 413 D3
OWARRA
Ferntree Gly 464 C8
. Berwick 553 F4
PE
Wheelers Hl 461 D17
Broadmeadows 238 A8
Airport W 278 K12
Coburg 281 F19
Preston 327 H5
PELAND
Point Cook 450 F6
Montrose 382 D9
Westmeadows 236 F14
PELEN
South Yarra 32 G6
South Yarra 414 J3
PERNICUS
/. Keilor Dn 275 J12
PNAL
Glen Waverley 460 K3
PPABELLA
. Vermont S 420 F11
PPARD
Burwood 418 G9
PPARDS
Moolap 704 F20
Newcomb 704 F20
PPEL
Blackburn S 419 J3
PPELIA
Wantirna S 462 B1
PPELIUS
Sunbury 143 D4
PPER
Clifton Hill 19 L9
PPERFIELD
Delahey 275 B10
PPICE
Boronia 424 K5
PPIN
Fitzroy N 20 A1
Hampton Pk 551 K6
Mitcham 377 D15
Glen Waverley 460 B11
Roxburgh Pk 194 B9
Hawthorn 371 E17
Sorrento 678 J11
Malvern East 416 C18
Richmond 26 J20
Richmond 32 J1
PROSMA
Frankston 628 A1
PSE WOOD
d. Caroline Spr 317 L3
PTFOLD
Glen Waverley 459 K9
QUETTE
Geelong West 702 G6
RA
. Altona 407 G15
Mt Waverley 458 K6
RAL
Beaumaris 529 L11
Footscray 366 L4
Lilydale 338 L10
Rosebud 700 J5
Avondale Ht 322 A16
Boronia 424 E4
Cheltenham 531 F3
Clarinda 498 F4
Craigieburn 150 E17
Glen Waverley 420 G17
Lalor 241 G6
Lower Plenty 286 H15
Vermont S 420 G13
Hampton Pk 551 K10
v. Skye 575 J18
Mornington 640 B20
Brunswick W 325 B8
Frankston 599 K19
Heidelberg W 328 C2
RAL GUM
Narre Warren 538 K19
RAL ISLAND
Patterson L 573 H11
RAM
Nar Warrn N 538 E11
Keysborough 534 D14
Meadow Ht 237 J6
RAMA
Sydenham 274 L9
RANDIRK
Yallambie 286 B14
Warneet 649 G11

CORANG
av. Grovedale 706 B11
CORBEN
st. Reservoir 282 D15
CORBENS
la. McCrae 685 B11
CORBERT
ct. Ferntree Gly 423 F20
CORBETT
st. Grovedale 706 G10
CORBETTS
rd. Launching Pl 346 C14
CORBIE
pl. Yallambie 285 H14
st. Bentleigh 496 B6
wy. Yallambie 285 H15
CORBIN
pl. Mill Park 242 D2
CORBY
ct. Deer Park 318 L9
st. Balwyn N 373 F3
CORD
cl. Berwick 554 G9
cl. Keilor Dn 276 A13
CORDELIA
gr. St Albans 275 H18
CORDITE
av. Maribyrnong 322 H14
CORDOVA
ct. Dandenong N 501 J10
CORDUROY
rd. Launching Pl 346 J13
rd. Yarra Jctn 346 J13
COREEN
av. Beaumaris 530 D7
st. Croydon 379 D2
CORELLA
av. Melton 226 F15
ct. Berwick 579 L1
ct. Carrum Downs 600 L4
ct. Carrum Downs 601 A4
ct. Doncaster 331 C19
ct. Ferntree Gly 464 D8
ct. Mornington 641 C15
pl. Werribee 447 K5
rd. Sunshine W 364 C5
st. Doncaster 331 C19
COREY
av. Dromana 686 H4
CORHAMPTON
rd. Balwyn N 372 L7
rd. Balwyn N 373 A7
CORHANWARRABUL
cl. Rowville 462 F17
CORIANDER
ct. Langwarrin 601 K14
CORINE
ct. Epping 241 L2
CORINELLA
cr. Dallas 238 D9
sq. Wantirna 422 H13
CORINGA
cl. Vermont 377 J20
ct. Knoxfield 463 A6
CORINNE
cl. Springvale S 499 K19
CORIO
av. Frankston 627 F7
dr. Springvale S 499 D18
pl. Geelong 703 F8
st. Belmont 702 G20
st. Geelong 703 A6
st. Geelong 703 C7
st. Glenroy 279 L7
st. Moonee Pnd 323 G11
st. Sunshine 365 C4
CORIS
pl. Epping 198 B16
CORIYULE
ct. Cranbourne N 578 D10
CORK
pl. Mt Martha 657 A9
CORKER
cl. Narre Warren 538 G16
CORLESS
cl. Mt Evelyn 339 J16
CORLETT
st. Frankston 599 E14
st. Mont Albert N 374 F9
CORMAC
st. Preston 327 C4
CORMILIO
dr. Wandin N 340 E5
CORMISTOM
rd. Ringwood N 378 E2
CORMORANT
cl. Blind Bight 650 E8
cl. Endeavour Hl 536 L3
cr. Werribee 448 C10
dr. Cairnlea 319 G10
pl. Dingley Vill 532 L7
pl. Mt Eliza 641 L4

CORNBOROUGH
ct. Frankston S 627 E9
CORNELIA
cl. Kilsyth 381 H8
CORNELIUS
cr. Healesville 213 G13
dr. Wantirna S 422 L19
dr. Wantirna S 423 A19
st. Dandenong 536 E2
CORNELL
ct. Broadmeadows 238 H12
ct. Bundoora 284 H4
ct. Frankston 600 B17
pl. Carlton 18 C19
pl. Hampton Pk 552 D12
st. Camberwell 417 J4
st. McCrae 685 B11
st. Mt Waverley 419 F19
CORNER
av. Ferny Creek 425 G19
CORNETTA
wy. Epping 197 E17
CORNFIELD
gr. Box Hill S 419 C6
CORNFORTH
wy. Mill Park 242 J1
CORNHILL
st. Ferntree Gly 464 G7
st. St Albans 319 K5
CORNISH
av. Belmont 706 J3
la. Kensington 33 D10
rd. Burwood E 419 G10
rd. Emerald 469 F20
rd. Emerald 509 F1
rd. Healesville 258 A2
rd. Lysterfield 504 C1
rd. Warburton 349 K1
st. Sunbury 143 C10
CORNS
pl. Richmond 26 C10
CORNUS
ct. Narre Warren 539 C20
tr. Olinda 427 D7
CORNUTA
wk. Vermont S 420 L11
wk. Vermont S 421 A11
CORNWALL
av. Keysborough 534 K9
cl. Gladstone Pk 237 C18
cr. Mt Martha 669 J1
rd. Pascoe Vale 280 G13
rd. Sunshine 365 F5
st. Avondale Ht 322 A12
st. Blackburn S 420 A2
st. Brunswick W 325 A9
st. Hallam 537 H15
st. Northcote 326 H19
CORNWELL
cr. Cranbourne E 578 J17
COROLLA
av. Bentleigh E 496 H4
COROMANDEL
ct. Knoxfield 463 C4
cr.s, Knoxfield 463 C5
ct. Bulleen 329 H15
pl. Melbourne 2 K13
pl. Melbourne 24 G6
CORONA
ct. Doncaster E 332 E17
pl. Roxburgh Pk 194 F9
st. Balwyn N 373 A1
st. Ivanhoe 328 C14
CORONADO
ct. Highton 705 J5
CORONAL
av. Newtown 701 H5
CORONATA
ct. Narre Warren 553 G11
CORONATION
ct. Bundoora 284 K6
st. Brighton East 455 B12
st. Brunswick W 324 L16
st. Geelong West 702 J7
st. Kingsville 366 K13
st. Mt Waverley 418 L12
st. Sunshine N 321 C17
CORONET
ct. Epping 198 F18
ct. Cranbourne 603 L4
gr. Beaumaris 529 J9
st. Flemington 33 F4
COROWA
cr. Burnside 318 H7
cr. Greensbrgh 244 A17
ct. Grovedale 705 L13
ct. Mooroolbark 337 E16
ct. Mt Waverley 419 G13
pl. Frankston 600 H18
CORPORATE
av. Rowville 502 A1
dr. Heatherton 497 G13

CORPORATION
la. Melbourne 2 L18
la. Melbourne 24 H9
CORR
gr. Melton 226 G18
st. Hughesdale 457 G9
st. Moorabbin 497 C9
CORRAN
ct. Endeavour Hl 503 K19
CORREA
av. Cheltenham 496 E19
cl. Delahey 275 C11
cl. Wantirna S 421 L14
ct. Doncaster E 332 E19
ct. Langwarrin 629 K4
ct. Mt Martha 656 G6
ct. S Morang 199 G10
ct. W Footscray 366 E11
gr. Frankston S 627 J12
pl. Endeavour Hl 536 K1
st. Edithvale 546 H15
wy. Sunbury 143 K4
CORRELL
wy. Roxburgh Pk 193 J16
CORRIB
ct. Melton W 225 F19
CORRIEDALE
cr. Pk Orchards 333 G18
ct. Belmont 706 C5
rd. Melton W 226 B17
CORRIGAN
av. Brooklyn 365 G17
pl. Attwood 237 B10
pl. Mill Park 242 J9
rd. Keysborough 534 D11
rd. Noble Park 534 D11
rd. Springvale 500 F20
st. Burwood 418 F11
st. Glenroy 279 L4
CORRINGHAM
rd. Beaconsfld Up 542 L15
CORRIS
st. Yarraville 366 J16
CORROBOREE
pl. Templstw Lr 330 D9
CORRONG
cr. Mooroolbark 337 B14
ct. Eltham 288 A15
CORRS
la. Melbourne 2 K10
la. Melbourne 24 F4
CORRYONG
cr. Taylors L 276 D8
CORSAIR
gr. Sorrento 679 A12
rd. The Basin 425 H12
st. Richmond 26 L14
st. Richmond 371 A17
wy. Torquay 712 B3
CORSEWALL
cl. Hawthorn 372 D14
CORSICAN
av. Doncaster E 332 G8
st. Frankston N 600 B7
CORTINA
pl. Avondale Ht 322 D7
CORTLAND
rd. Highton 705 K5
CORUNNA
av. St Albans 275 F19
ct. Glen Waverley 420 C14
CORVETTE
cl. S Morang 198 J14
st. Heidelberg W 284 B20
CORVEY
rd. Reservoir 283 B6
CORVI
ct. Dandenong 535 F4
CORY
ct. Kings Park 275 D17
pl. Berwick 554 L20
CORYULE
av. Mentone 531 A11
rd. Mt Martha 655 J19
COSDOWN
cl. Gladstone Pk 237 C20
COSGRAVE
la. Melbourne 1 A11
la. Melbourne 23 H9
COSGROVE
ct. Meadow Ht 238 A5
st. Rye 696 J6
st. Vermont 421 G3
COSHAM
ct. Greensbrgh 244 J15
st. Brighton 454 F14
COSIER
dr. Noble Park 534 L7
COSMA
ct. Albanvale 319 B7
COSMO
ct. Kilsyth 380 K9

COSMOS
ct. Doncaster E 332 G13
ct. Whittington 704 E20
st. Dromana 686 E8
st. Glenroy 280 H6
COSSAR
pl. Patterson L 547 H20
COSTA
dr. Hoppers Csg 449 F2
COSTAIN
ct. Gladstone Pk 236 L16
ct. Gladstone Pk 237 A16
COSTATA
ct. Narre Warren 553 G12
COSTELLO
cl. Bacchus Msh 222 B13
ct. Endeavour Hl 537 K5
la. N Melbourne 34 J11
st. Mont Albert N 374 G8
COSY GUM
rd. Carnegie 456 G4
COSY VALLEY
rd. Langwarrin 629 G6
COTHAM
ct. S Morang 198 J14
rd. Kew 371 K10
sq. Hampton Pk 551 J6
COTONEASTER
ct. Wheelers Hl 460 G15
wy. Langwarrin 601 J15
COTSWOLD
cl. Vermont 421 H5
cr. Springvale S 534 B4
ct. Chirnside Pk 337 G2
ct. Glen Waverley 459 K4
ct. Grovedale 706 C13
COTTAGE
cl. Mooroolbark 381 K3
cl. Roxburgh Pk 194 A7
ct. Hampton Pk 551 H8
pl. Mornington 657 C6
pl. Ringwood N 334 L20
pl. St Helena 245 B19
st. Blackburn 376 A15
COTTER
ct. Rowville 462 H17
st. Richmond 32 F1
st. Richmond 414 J1
COTTERELL
wy. Seabrook 450 L6
COTTERIDGE
pl. Caroline Spr 318 A2
COTTERS
rd. Epping 196 J14
COTTESLOE
ct. Doncaster E 332 B16
COTTESMORE
ct. Boronia 424 G14
COTTINGLEA
Ringwood N 378 F5
COTTLES BRIDGE-STRATHEWEN
rd. Cottles Br 203 J1
COTTONWOOD
av. Vermont S 420 F12
ct. Narre Warren 553 F10
ct. Templestowe 331 J5
COTTRELL
ct. Delahey 275 A12
ct. Nunawading 376 E8
st. Werribee 447 F15
st.e, Werribee 447 G14
COTTSWOLD
av. Narre Warren 553 D12
pl. Wantirna S 422 J15
ri. Templestowe 331 F14
COUCH
st. Sunshine 365 B6
COULL
cl. Boronia 424 F8
COULSON
av. Eumemmerring 536 L15
av. Eumemmerring 537 A15
rd. Monbulk 428 L14
rd. Monbulk 469 G1
COULSTOCK
st. Epping 197 D20
COULTER
st. Newcomb 704 F16
COULTON
ct. Werribee 446 K20
COUNCIL
la. Williamstown 411 H17
st. Clifton Hill 19 H7
st. Doncaster 331 A20
st. Hawthorn E 372 G20
COUNIHAN
av. Caroline Spr 274 A9
st. Sunbury 142 K10
COUNITHAN
pl. Lysterfield 464 E17
COUNSEL
ct. Sunbury 143 D5

COUNTRY
la. Viewbank 285 K20
COUNTRY CLUB
ct. Safety Bch 669 C19
dr. Chirnside Pk 337 F4
dr. Safety Bch 686 K2
dr. Safety Bch 687 A1
COUNTY
cl. Wheelers Hl 461 B14
dr. Berwick 554 B14
tce. Croydon Hl 335 H15
tce. Templestowe 331 G12
COUPER ANGUS
gr. Sunshine 364 L8
COURAGE
ct. Glen Waverley 420 L15
COURAGEOUS
ct. Frankston 628 E7
st. Taylors L 275 H8
COURANG
rd. Glen Iris 417 B14
COURBRANT
ct. Mont Albert N 374 F8
COURSE
cl. Forest Hill 420 E3
COURT
st. Blairgowrie 696 C2
st. Box Hill 374 L14
st. Essendon 323 J9
st. Yarraville 366 K16
COURTENAY
av. Cranbourne N 578 B8
COURT HOUSE
pl. Carlton 18 F12
pl. Bacchus Msh, off Bacchus Marsh Rd 222 A17
COURTIS
st. Williamstown 411 C12
COURTNAY
pl. Epping 197 K20
COURTNEY
av. Hoppers Csg 405 B19
pl. N Melbourne 17 E15
sq. Wantirna 422 F9
st. Bundoora 284 F4
st. Cheltenham 530 K2
st. N Melbourne 17 E14
COURTNEYS
rd. Belgrave S 506 C12
COUSEN
pl. Gladstone Pk 237 D18
COUSIN
dr. Bayswater 423 A9
COUTIES
rd. Kangaroo Grnd 248 C4
rd. Panton Hill 248 C4
COUTTS
ct. Blairgowrie 679 J20
st. Safety Bch 668 L18
COVAL
ct. Vermont S 420 K7
COVALA
ct. St Helena 244 L19
ct. St Helena 245 A19
COVE
av. Portsea 666 G20
ct. Endeavour Hl 503 L19
la. Seaford 573 F13
pl. Portsea 666 G19
COVEN
av. Heathmont 379 E18
COVENT
gdn. Point Cook 450 F10
COVENTRY
cr. Mill Park 242 L12
ct. Frankston 599 K16
ct. Grovedale 706 C12
dr. Werribee 446 L12
pl. Bayswater 423 E10
pl. Chirnside Pk 336 H7
pl. Melton S 268 C10
pl. S Melbourne 29 H4
rd. Narre Warren 553 C5
st. Burwood E 420 A13
st. Montmorency 286 G12
st. Southbank 3 G20
st. Southbank 30 E1
st. Southbank 413 H1
st. S Melbourne 3 A20
st. S Melbourne 29 E5
st. S Melbourne 413 C3
st. S Melbourne 413 H1
st. Tullamarine 279 A8
COVERLID
pl. Melbourne 2 K11
pl. Melbourne 24 G5
COWANS
la. Parwan 265 H11
rd. Hopetoun Park 223 L20
rd. Hopetoun Park 265 L4
COWARD
st. Footscray 367 F6

COWDEN
rd. N Warrandyte 289 J10
COWDEROY
pl. St Kilda, off Canterbury Rd 413 L12
st. Hoppers Csg 405 D20
st. St Kilda W 413 K13
COWELL
st. Fitzroy 18 L18
COWES
pl. Taylors L 275 H9
st. Craigieburn 150 A15
COWIE
la. Albert Park 29 E14
pl. Hoppers Csg 448 B2
COWIN
cl. Rowville 463 J19
st. Diamond Ck 245 H9
COWLEY
ct. Mooroolbark 337 H18
st. Delahey 275 A11
st. McCrae 684 J16
COWPER
av. St Albans 320 K4
cr. Sunbury 142 K11
ri. Berwick 554 D3
st. Blairgowrie 695 K3
st. Brighton 454 K13
st. Essendon N 279 F20
st. Footscray 367 F12
st. Footscray 367 H8
st. Hawthorn E 372 H15
st. Preston 327 A6
st. St Kilda 414 B20
st. Sandringham 495 C16
COWRA
av. St Albans 320 F12
st. Altona 408 J17
st. Brighton 455 B14
st. Vermont 421 F5
COWRIE
ct. Tootgarook 698 F7
rd. Torquay 711 L6
st. Glen Waverley 460 L5
COX
cr. Carrum Downs 574 H16
ct. Altona Mdw 451 J9
ct. Endeavour Hl 537 E9
st. Cheltenham 497 D19
st. St Albans 320 D11
COXS
gdn. Williamstown 411 F14
COZENS
cl. Frankston S 627 J11
st. Brunswick 325 F8
CRABAPPLE
cl. Glen Waverley 420 D14
cl. Lyndhurst 577 C1
rd. S Morang 199 J12
CRABBE
ct. Delahey 275 D12
CRABILL
wk. Nar Warrn S 552 F20
CRABTREE
ct. Bundoora 284 J5
ct. Reservoir 283 J16
CRACKNELLS
rd. Panton Hill 248 G3
CRADDOCK
av. Caulfield N 455 G1
ct. Sunshine N 321 E16
CRADLE
rd. Diggers Rest 187 A10
CRADLEY
av. Kew 371 F10
ct. Kilsyth 381 C3
CRAFT
wk. Nar Warrn S 578 G1
CRAIG
av. Camberwell 372 K19
av. Craigieburn 150 E17
av. Ferntree Gly 464 F3
av. Mt Dandenong 382 J16
ct. Altona North 409 E2
ct. Burwood 418 F12
ct. Carrum 573 E10
ct. Cheltenham 531 G1
ct. Chirnside Pk 337 H6
ct. Heathmont 378 J20
dr. Berwick 553 J9
rd. Cranbourne 604 H19
rd. Devon Mdw 648 E3
rd. Donvale 377 H8
rd. Junction Vill 604 H19
rd. Pearcedale 648 E3
rd. Plenty 244 G10
st. Blackburn S 375 E20
st. Frankston 627 J1
st. Keilor East 322 J4
st. Noble Park 534 F2
st. Spotswood 411 B2
CRAIGAVAD
st. Carnegie 456 F4

CRAIG AVON
la. Merricks N 688 L11
CRAIGAVON
ct. Deer Park 318 J10
CRAIGDARROCH
av. Anglesea 713 E7
CRAIG HILL
dr. Wheelers Hl 461 D16
CRAIGIE
av. Chelsea 546 H15
av. Edithvale 546 H15
ct. Hampton Pk 551 L9
rd. Mt Martha 656 A9
rd. Mt Martha 656 H10
rd. Mt Martha 657 A11
rd. Newtown 701 K11
CRAIGIEBURN
bps. Craigieburn 150 H9
bps. Epping 196 D19
bps. Epping 240 B6
bps. Lalor 240 B6
bps. Thomastown 240 B11
bps. Wollert 196 A2
rd.e, Craigieburn 150 K19
rd.e, Wollert 197 B1
rd.w, Craigieburn 149 C16
rd.w, Craigieburn 149 J17
CRAIGIELEA
av. St Albans 320 C2
CRAIGLEA
ct. Doncaster E 331 J15
CRAIGMORE
av. Mentone 531 J7
pl. Melton W 226 C16
CRAIGROSSIE
av. Coburg 325 D6
rd. Mornington 640 K10
CRAIGS
la. Cannons Creek 648 D7
la. Pearcedale 648 D7
CRAIGTON
ct. Cranbourne N 578 D10
CRAIK
rd. Beaconsfld Up 542 H16
CRAILEEN
st. Donvale 376 F4
CRAINE
st. S Melbourne 30 B2
CRAITHIE
av. Pk Orchards 334 C17
CRAMER
st. Coburg 325 B1
st. Preston 282 D20
wk. Brighton 454 H16
CRAMOND
pl. Greenvale 193 F16
CRAMPTON
cr. Mill Park 242 C7
cr. Rosanna 285 A17
ct. Hoppers Csg 405 B18
ct. Rowville 502 K6
CRANA
ct. Chadstone 458 A1
ct. Hoppers Csg 405 A17
gr. Greensbrgh 244 C16
CRANBERRY
pl. Bundoora 242 D14
CRANBOURNE
av. Sunshine N 321 B15
dr. Cranbourne 604 A2
pl. Cranbourne 578 D17
rd. Frankston 599 D20
CRANBOURNE-FRANKSTON
rd. Cranbourne 602 H13
rd. Cranbourne S 602 H13
rd. Cranbourne W 603 A11
rd. Langwarrin 628 K4
CRANBROOK
ct. Doncaster 330 J19
ct. Gladstone Pk 237 D20
ct. Gladstone Pk 279 D1
st. Yarraville 366 H19
CRANE
st. Berwick 580 A2
CRANESBILL
la. Mickleham 149 D2
CRANHAM
st. Caulfield 455 K5
st. Noble Park 500 D18
CRANHAVEN
rd. Langwarrin 629 A4
rd. Langwarrin 629 D5
CRANLEIGH
gr. Mt Waverley 458 L2
pl. Craigieburn 150 C20
CRANLEY
ct. Grovedale 706 A15
pl. Thomastown 240 J11
st. Springvale 500 A12
CRANMERE
av. Belmont 706 B7

CRANSTON
ct. Nar Warrn N 539 A6
ct. Rosebud 684 C20
CRANSTOUN
ct. Thomson 703 K16
CRANSWICK
ct. Mornington 656 L3
ct. Mornington 657 A3
CRANWELL
av. Strathmore 323 J1
ct. Bundoora 284 K1
ct. Highton 705 J8
ct. Mulgrave 500 D1
mw. Skye 575 J17
st. Braybrook 321 K19
CRATHIE
ct. Frankston 627 K8
CRATLOE
rd. Cockatoo 511 G9
rd. Mt Waverley 419 A14
CRAVEN
st. Noble Park 500 G17
st. Prahran 414 L12
CRAVENS
rd. Mernda 199 C4
CRAWFORD
av. Dandenong N 501 E20
rd. Clarinda 498 C5
rd. Doncaster 330 J16
rd. Templstw Lr 330 J16
st. Braeside 532 G18
st. Cheltenham 530 F3
st. Moonee Pnd 324 C10
st. Mt Eliza 626 C12
st. Newport 411 C9
wy. Sunbury 142 F9
CRAWLEY
ct. Craigieburn 149 L15
ct. Vermont S 421 A10
ct. Viewbank 285 J18
gr. Ringwood N 334 H20
rd. Nar Warrn N 539 E9
st. Reservoir 282 J14
CREA
ct. St Helena 245 A19
CREAL
av. Braybrook 366 A7
CREAN
ct. Mill Park 243 A4
CREASEY
ct. Bulla 190 A16
CRECY
ct. Heidelberg W 284 D18
CREEDMORE
dr. Rye 697 E8
CREEDON
st. Fawkner 281 H10
CREEK
ct. Eumemmerring 537 C12
pde. Northcote 20 E1
pl. Clyde North 581 G14
rd. Belgrave 466 J16
rd. Lilydale 338 E4
rd. Mitcham 377 D15
rd. Mornington 640 J15
st. Melton S 268 H8
st. Ringwood 378 D11
st. Spotswood 367 A20
CREEKBANK
pl. Caroline Spr 318 C8
st. Upwey 465 J17
vw. Pakenham 584 B4
CREEKVIEW
dr. Cairnlea 319 G14
wy. Wyndham Va 446 D8
CREEKWOOD
av. Pakenham 584 A4
ct. Tarneit 405 A9
dr. Craigieburn 149 L13
CREIGHTON
st. Narre Warren 538 K13
wy. Doreen 202 A9
wy. Mornington 657 C3
wy. Yarrambat 202 A9
CRELLIN
av. Laverton 406 J20
av.s, Altona Mdw 450 J1
cr. Watsonia 285 F6
gr. Camberwell 417 F5
st. Doncaster E 331 K18
CREMEAN
av. Ivanhoe 328 A10
CREMIN
cl. Kew 371 G4
cl. Mill Park 242 C5
cl. Mt Waverley 458 L8
ct. Rosanna 284 L20
ct. Rosanna 285 A20
ct. Rowville 502 L6
ct. Rowville 503 A6
dr. Pakenham 559 F15
CREMONA
st. Mentone 531 B9

CREMORNE
ct. Dingley Vill 532 L6
pl. Fitzroy 18 L15
st. Balwyn 373 E11
st. Braybrook 322 B20
st. Cremorne 26 A20
st. Cremorne 32 A1
st. Fitzroy 18 L15
CREPE MYRTLE
cr. S Morang 199 G11
CRERAR
rd. Kallista 467 K
rd. The Patch 467 K
CRESCENT
la. Ringwood 378 F1
rd. Camberwell 416 K
rd. Yarra Jctn 346 J1
st. Noble Park 500 F1
CRESMONT
ct. Kings Park 275 D1
CRESPIN
pl. Roxburgh Pk 194 B1
st. Niddrie 323 B
CRESSER
st. Altona North 409 K
CRESSIDA
cr. Sydenham 275 B
cr. Sydenham 275 B
CRESSONIERRE
ct. Hallam 537 K1
CRESSWELL
cr. Mitcham 377 A
CRESSWOLD
av. Avondale Ht 322 D1
CRESSY
ct. Broadmeadows 237 H1
pl. Geelong, off Malop St 703 C
st. Malvern 416 C1
st. Montmorency 287 A1
CREST
av. Balwyn 373 B1
av. Hampton E 495
ct. Mornington 656 L
ct. The Basin 425 E
dr. Rosebud 700 K
gr. Nunawading 376 K
rd. Research 247 A
rd. Research 289 A
st. Greensbrgh 244 G2
CRESTA
ct. Berwick 554 G
ct. Keilor East 322 H
ct. Lalor 240
ct. Mulgrave 500 G
CRESTDALE
rd. Wantirna 422 E
CRESTHAVEN
bvd. Berwick 580
ct. Donvale 332 K
CRESTMONT
ct. Doncaster E 332
ct. Toorak 415
dr. Glen Waverley 460
dr. Melton S 268
tce. Craigieburn 150
CRESTMOOR
dr. Highton 705
CRESTVIEW
cl. Montrose 381 K
cl. Roxburgh Pk 193 K
ct. Croydon N 336 A
ct. Frankston S 627 K
ct. Rye 697
dr. Beaconsfield 555 F
CRESTWAY
Lilydale 338
CRESTWOOD
la. Craigieburn 150 G
CRESWELL
av. Airport W 279 A
ct. Altona Mdw 451
rd. Marcus Hill 707 A
rd. Pt Lonsdale 707 A
CRESWICK
ct. Roxburgh Pk 194 D
dr. Point Cook 450
gr. McKinnon 456 E
la. Mont Albert 374 F
st. Balwyn 372
st. Brighton East 495
st. Donvale 376
st. Footscray 367
st. Glen Iris 416 L
st. Glen Waverley 460
st. Hawthorn 371 L
st. Laverton 407
CRETE
av. Ashburton 417
rd. Tremont 425
CREVELLI
st. Reservoir 283

CURRAWONG
av. Lalor 241 B5
ct. Rosebud W 699 F4
ct. Up Fntree Gly 465 G8
ct. Werribee 447 J5
dr. Carrum Downs 575 A20
gr. Cannons Creek 649 D7
la. Greensbrgh 286 D3
rd. Healesville 258 A1
rd. Montrose 382 B13
st. Keysborough 534 K8
st. Mornington 641 A15
CURRIE
av. Endeavour Hl 537 H7
av. Tecoma 466 D11
dr. Delahey 275 D10
st. Box Hill N 374 K8
tce. Glen Waverley 461 A6
CURRINGA
cl. Berwick 553 F6
CURRONG
gr. Croydon 379 H6
CURRUMBIN
ct. Taylors L 276 B9
ct. Tootgarook 698 C6
CURRUNGHI
ct. St Albans 320 L8
ct. St Albans 321 A8
CURRY
rd. Pk Orchards 333 J20
CURTAIN
rd. Hurstbridge 203 A16
st. Carlton N 18 G4
st. Kingsbury 284 A8
CURTAYNE
ct. Noble Park N 501 E12
CURTIN
av. Brunswick W 324 H8
av. Hadfield 280 L7
av. Lalor 241 E7
cr. Dandenong N 501 J20
ct. Altona 409 F17
ct. Maidstone 366 F2
dr. Sunbury 143 H4
pl. Fitzroy N 19 B7
st. Bentleigh E 457 A17
st. Bundoora 243 D20
st. Maidstone 366 E2
st. St Albans 320 C8
CURTIS
av. Mt Waverley 458 G7
av. Sunbury 144 B7
av. Watsonia 285 C9
ct. Cranbourne 578 B15
ct. Jan Juc 711 E15
la. Roxburgh Pk 194 E15
pl. Brunswick, off Stewart St 325 G11
rd. Emerald 509 D6
st. Belmont 706 K1
st. Essendon 324 C5
CURZON
av. Healesville 258 B3
pl. N Melbourne 17 C18
st. Brighton East 495 D1
st. Ivanhoe 327 K8
st. N Melbourne 17 B20
st. Reservoir 282 K1
st. W Melbourne 17 B20
CUSDIN
st. Glen Iris 417 B9
CUSH
pl. Hampton Pk 551 K16
CUSHING
av. Bentleigh 456 E20
CUSTER
gr. Bayswater N 380 J17
CUSTOM
pl. Werribee 487 G2
rd. Tullamarine 278 H1
CUSTOM HOUSE
la. Melbourne 1 D19
la. Melbourne 23 L12
CUTHBERT
av. Highton 705 J2
av. Truganina 405 F15
ct. Wantirna S 462 E2
ct. Wheelers Hl 460 K9
dr. Hillside 231 K18
dr. Mill Park 242 E8
pl. Burnside 318 D7
rd. Reservoir 283 B10
st. Broadmeadows 238 A16
st. Bulleen 329 J15
st. Heathmont 378 F20
st. Heathmont 422 F1
st. Niddrie 278 K20
st. Seddon 367 C10
CUTHBERTSON
ct. Bacchus Msh 221 K12
ct. Chelsea 547 B19

CUTLER
cl. Ferntree Gly 464 A6
ct. Lalor 241 D7
ct. Ringwood N 334 J19
CUTTER
st. Burnley 371 B19
CUTTRISS
rd. Werribee S 488 G20
CUTTS
av. Croydon 379 E4
av. Dromana 685 L10
st. Sunshine N 321 E17
CUZENS
pl. Geelong, off Fenwick St 702 L8
CYANAMID
st. Laverton N 408 B3
CYCADE
av. Altona North 409 L1
CYCLAMEN
av. Altona North 409 K1
CYGNET
av. Templstw Lr 330 A8
ct. Eltham 287 D8
ct. Frankston 600 C16
ct. Queenscliff 707 L19
CYNGA
ct. Grovedale 706 C10
st. Preston 327 E3
CYNISCA
ct. Wheelers Hl 460 J17
CYNTHIA
ct. Hillside 274 G3
ct. Wantirna S 423 B14
gr. Woori Yall 344 F13
CYPRESS
av. Boronia 424 C14
av. Brooklyn 365 H18
av. Burwood 418 L10
av. Glen Waverley 419 K14
av. Templstw Lr 330 J12
cl. Hampton Pk 552 A16
ct. Chelsea 547 B19
ct. Chirnside Pk 337 G6
ct. Cranbourne N 578 E8
ct. Hillside 273 K3
ct. Macleod 284 J13
ct. Noble Park 500 H17
ct. Oakleigh S 498 A9
ct. Portsea 678 B3
gr. Dandenong N 501 H20
la. Torquay 711 K3
st. Heidelberg W 327 L1
wy. Maribyrnong 322 L12
wy. Maribyrnong 323 A12
CYPRESS HILL
dr. Nar Warrn S 553 C19
CYPRESS POINT
ct. Sunbury 144 B11
dr. Mt Eliza 626 B9
pde. Heatherton 497 H17
CYPRUS
av. Nunawading 376 J10
ct. Bundoora 284 H6
ct. Wyndham Va 446 E11
pl. Melton W 226 A15
pl. Pakenham 584 H3
st. Eumemmerring 537 C12
st. Lalor 241 E11
CYRENE
st. Noble Park 534 F3
CYRIL
ct. Belmont 706 G2
gr. Noble Park 535 D5
st. Ashburton 417 K15
st. Box Hill S 418 H3
st. Elwood 454 G2
st. Lilydale 338 J5
st. Windsor 414 J12

D

DABCOR
cl. Hallam 552 B3
DACE
ct. Pascoe Vale S 280 J19
DACELO
av. Broadmeadows 238 A18
DACEY
st. Brighton East 495 G4
DACTYL
rd. Moorabbin 496 D9
DADSWELL
ct. Sunbury 142 L5
DAFF
av. Hampton E 496 A11
DAFFODIL
ct. Gowanbrae 279 C6
rd. Boronia 424 E16
st. Bentleigh E 496 J2
wy. Point Cook 450 G14
DAFIELD
ct. Rosanna 285 C18
DAGOLA
av. Nunawading 376 K18
DAGONET
st. Strathmore 279 K16
DAHLEN
pl. Berwick 553 K14
DAHLENBURG
st. W Melbourne 367 J12
DAHLIA
ct. Endeavour Hl 537 E5
ct. Nar Warrn S 579 D1
st. Dromana 686 E8
st. Dromana 686 E8
DAHMEN
st. Carrum 573 E7
DAI
ct. Mt Waverley 458 K8
DAIMLER
av. Keilor Dn 276 A16
ct. Epping 197 J14
ct. McCrae 684 K18
DAINA
ct. Diamond Ck 245 J6
ct. Skye 601 G4
DAINTREE
av. Pk Orchards 334 A17
gr. Narre Warren 539 F20
ri. St Helena 245 B19
DAIRY
cl. Sydenham 274 L5
ct. Viewbank 285 K20
la. Ferntree Gly 463 F6
pl. Skye 575 G17
rd. Werribee 448 E14
DAIRYFARM
tce. Hampton Pk 551 L12
DAISY
ct. Box Hill N 374 J6
ct. Braybrook 366 B1
ct. Nar Warrn S 552 H15
dr. Bundoora 242 F15
dr. Point Cook 450 H16
st. Essendon 323 J8
st. Heathmont 378 D18
st. Murrumbeena 457 D12
st. Newtown 702 C11
st. Warranwood 334 J13
wy. Carrum Downs 574 L19
DAKAR
ct. Keilor Dn 276 D14
DAKARA
cl. Meadow Ht 194 C20
ct. Mooroolbark 337 C16
ct. Wyndham Va 446 H13
pl. Sunshine W 364 K7
DAKOTA
ct. Forest Hill 420 D9
ct. Tullamarine 236 H20
dr. Thomastown 240 D17
pl. Point Cook 450 D4
DALBEATTIE
dr. Clarinda 498 C7
DALBURY
pl. Mill Park 242 F10
pl. Narre Warren 539 F17
DALBY
cl. Rowville 463 G15
DALE
av. Pascoe Vale 280 J18
av. Safety Bch 668 K19
cl. Highton 701 D16
ct. Balwyn N 374 A1
ct. Blackburn N 375 F10
ct. Dandenong N 501 J16
ct. Mt Martha 657 A7
ct. Scoresby 462 E8
ct. Seville 341 J12
st. Balwyn 372 K11
st. Bulleen 330 A17
st. Cremorne 32 D3
st. Cremorne 414 H2
st. Doncaster 330 A17
st. Eltham North 287 C2
st. Maribyrnong 323 A12
DALEGLEN
st. Reservoir 283 E2
DALEHEAD
ct. Croydon Hl 335 D16
DALENE
st. Essendon 324 A3
DALEY
ct. Brookfield 268 C4
st. Bentleigh 496 B2
st. Elwood 454 G4
st. Glenroy 279 L2
st. Pascoe Vale 280 H14
st. Preston 327 F5
st. Sunshine W 364 E2

DALGAN
st. Oakleigh S 457 H19
DALGARNO
st. Williamstown 411 E11
DALGETTY
rd. Beaumaris 530 B13
DALGETY
la. St Kilda 414 C14
pl. Carlton 18 J9
st. Brunswick W 324 K11
st. Dandenong S 535 J12
st. Oakleigh 457 K7
st. Preston 326 K1
st. St Kilda 414 C14
DALGLEISH
av. Rosebud 683 G18
st. Flemington 324 E20
DALI
ct. Keilor East 321 K3
ct. Wheelers Hl 460 L14
DALKEITH
av. Tullamarine 278 H5
cl. Wheelers Hl 460 L10
cr. Belgrave 466 H15
ct. Doncaster E 332 B16
ct. Frankston 628 B10
ct. Sunbury 142 L6
dr. Dromana 686 K5
dr. Point Cook 450 F10
rd. Wantirna 422 K7
DALLAS
av. Hughesdale 457 F13
cr. Watsonia N 285 E3
ct. Kilsyth 381 D4
dr. Broadmeadows 238 G15
dr. Dallas 238 G10
dr. Lalor 242 A10
st. Emerald 469 J19
st. Mentone 532 A7
st. Mt Waverley 458 J3
DALLAS BROOKS
dr. Melbourne 31 B4
dr. Melbourne 414 A2
DALLEY
st. Hawthorn 372 A19
DALLIMORE
ct. Noble Park 535 E5
DALLY
st. Clifton Hill 20 F7
st. Northcote 326 J12
DALMAHOY
st. Footscray 367 G8
DALMANY
av. Point Cook 450 G7
DALMATIA
ct. Rowville 503 D4
DALMONT
st. Highett 495 J14
DALMONTE
gr. Kallista 467 G3
DALMOR
av. Mitcham 377 D10
av. Ormond 456 B13
ct. Pakenham 585 D4
st. Parkdale 531 G14
DALMORE
dr. Scoresby 462 A13
rd. Dalmore 652 J7
rd. Tooradin 652 J7
DALNY
rd. Murrumbeena 457 A12
st. Malvern 415 L13
DALPURA
cct. Frankston 600 F16
ct. Berwick 553 K3
ct. Notting Hill 459 J13
ct. Werribee 446 K15
dr. Bayswater 423 A4
dr. Sunshine W 364 G7
DALRAY
cl. Mill Park 242 J11
cr. Kurunjang 227 E7
ct. Cranbourne 604 B5
ct. Keilor Dn 275 L15
pl. Lilydale 294 C20
DALRIADA
st. Toorak 415 E5
DALROY
cr. Vermont S 420 G10
DALRY
av. Pk Orchards 334 C18
cl. Endeavour Hl 503 K19
ct. Mt Eliza 641 L4
rd. Badger Creek 257 J12
rd. Don Valley 345 F5
rd. Healesville 257 J12
rd. Launching Pl 344 F2
rd. Launching Pl 345 F5
rd. Woori Yall 344 F2
DALSTEN
gr. Mt Eliza 626 B17
DALSTON
rd. Hughesdale 457 G11

DALTON
ct. Meadow Ht 238
ct. Mulgrave 500
dr. Melton S 268
pl. Gladstone Pk 237
rd. Epping 197
rd. Epping 241
rd. Lalor 241
rd. Thomastown 241
st. Eltham 287
st. S Geelong 703
st. Sunshine W 364
DALVANA
ct. Hampton Pk 551
DALVEEN
rd. Ivanhoe 327
DALVEY
st. Heidelberg 329
DALVIDA
ct. Eltham North 245
DALVISTA
ct. Werribee 446
DALWOOD
ct. Oakleigh S 498
ct. Vermont S 421
pl. Avondale Ht 322
DALWORTH
av. Dromana 686
st. Albion 320
st. Albion 364
DALY
av. Rye 697
bvd. Highton 705
cl. Sunbury 142
ct. Darley 221
ct. Mentone 531
ct. Rowville 463
dr. Cannons Creek 649
pl. Bundoora 284
rd. Sandringham 495
st. Brunswick W 324
st. Doncaster E 375
st. Frankston 600
st. Oakleigh E 458
st. S Melbourne 29
st. South Yarra 32
st. South Yarra 414
DALYSTON
st. Grovedale 706
DALZIEL
la. Northcote 326
DALZIELL
rd. Cockatoo 510
DAM
rd. Olinda 427
DAMALA
ct. Blackburn S 419
ct. Doncaster E 375
DAMAR
av. Boronia 424
DAMASK
pl. Niddrie 322
DAMELIO
ct. Rowville 503
DAME MARY GILMORE
pl. Oakleigh E, off Baynton St 458
DAME PATTIE
av. Pakenham 584
DAMIAN
cl. Mornington 641
cl. Cranbourne 578
ct. Dandenong 535
ct. Glenroy 279
pl. Wantirna S 421
st. Melton 226
DAMIEN
ct. Pakenham 585
ct. Watsonia N 243
DAMMANS
rd. Warburton 349
DAMON
cl. Nar Warrn S 552
cl. S Morang 199
ct. Millgrove 348
rd. Mt Waverley 458
DAMOSH
av. Carrum Downs 574
DAMPIER
cl. Skye 575
ct. Endeavour Hl 537
ct. Epping 198
ct. Grovedale 706
ct. Mornington 641
ct. Wyndham Va 446
gr. Mitcham 377
gr. Ringwood 377
DAMTE
pl. St Albans 275
DANA
av. Blairgowrie 695
ct. Dandenong S 536
ct. Keilor Ldg 276

st. Port Melb 29 B7
st. Preston 326 G6
st. Rosanna 284 J18
st. Safety Bch 669 C14
st. Sandringham 495 H19

DAVIESIA
dr. Plenty 244 G11

DAVINGTON
ct. Wantirna 422 G14

DAVIS
av. Avondale Ht 322 A10
av. Camberwell 416 H6
av. South Yarra 32 A11
av. South Yarra 414 F5
ct. Altona Mdw 451 G4
dr. Mt Eliza 642 E5
rd. Diggers Rest 187 A9
rd.e, Wonga Park 291 K12
rd.w, Wonga Park 291 G11
st. Belmont 706 A3
st. Burwood E 419 G8
st. Carlton N 18 J7
st. Coburg 325 B2
st. Doncaster 374 H4
st. Elsternwick 454 J4
st. Ferntree Gly 464 B3
st. Kensington 34 A6
st. Kew 372 D13
st. Reservoir 283 L17
st. Richmond 26 G19
st. Richmond 414 K1
wy. Springvale 500 C13

DAVISON
cr. Ferntree Gly 464 B7
ct. Maddingley 263 D5
dr. Coldstream 293 L3
pl. South Yarra 32 D12
pl. South Yarra 414 H6
pl. Geelong, off Myers St 703 D10
st. Brunswick 325 D11
st. Mitcham 377 H18
st. Mt Waverley 418 H14
st. Richmond 371 A15
wy. Berwick 554 G17

DAVISONS
pl. Melbourne 2 L6
pl. Melbourne 24 F3

DAVISSON
st. Epping 241 H1

DAVITT
dr. Deer Park 318 L12

DAVOR
ct. Burwood E 419 L8

DAVROSS
ct. Seville 342 K19

DAVY
ct. Nar Warrn S 579 F1
la. Forest Hill 420 G6

DAWAYNE
st. Burwood E 420 B8

DAWE
rd. Mitcham 377 E11

DAWES
ct. Ferntree Gly 464 B6
ct. Mill Park 242 C4
rd. Wonga Park 335 E1

DAWN
av. Dandenong S 535 G13
ct. Epping 198 A19
ct. Glen Waverley 420 C15
ct. Sunbury 142 J7
ct. Viewbank 285 J18
dr. Narre Warren 552 G1
st. Boronia 424 G8
st. Highett 496 J15
st. Mt Evelyn 339 E16
st. Rye 696 K8
st. Up Fntree Gly 465 E7

DAWS
ct. Taylors L 233 A20
rd. Doncaster E 331 K19

DAWSON
av. Brighton 454 F8
av. Footscray 367 D5
ct. Aspendale Gdn 546 J3
ct. Clayton 498 F1
ct. Endeavour Hl 537 C4
ct. Noble Park N 501 D9
dr. Glen Iris 416 K11
pl. Roxburgh Pk 194 B13
rd. Briar Hill 286 F6
rd. Kangaroo Grnd 248 B9
rd. Nar Warrn E 507 H18
st. Brunswick 325 A14
st. Brunswick W 324 J14
st. Brunswick W 325 A14
st. Coburg N 281 D18
st. Doncaster 331 E19
st. E Geelong 703 G13
st. Reservoir 282 C1
st. Sunshine 365 D1
st. Tullamarine 278 G4
st. Up Fntree Gly 465 A7

DAWSONS
gln. Heathmont 379 A18

DAX
rd. Kangaroo Grnd 248 D6

DAY
cr. Bayswater N 380 G17
rd. Clarinda 498 F12
st. Braybrook 366 B5
st. Dandenong 535 K6
st. E Geelong 703 J11
st. South Yarra 31 D5
st. Sunshine W 364 H4
st. Upwey 466 A8
st. Yarraville 366 H16

DAYAN
dr. Wantirna S 422 A17

DAYLESFORD
tce. Caroline Spr 318 C7

DAYMAR
ct. Hillside 274 F1
dr. Mooroolbark 337 E13

DAYS
pl. Geelong, off Garden St 703 F8

DEAKIN
av. Lalor 241 J10
av. Waurn Ponds 705 C10
cr. Baxter 644 C3
cr. Dandenong N 501 K19
ct. Berwick 554 G18
ct. Broadmeadows 238 E16
ct. Mill Park 243 C5
ct. Waurn Ponds, off Deakin Av 705 B10
dr. Mt Martha 655 D18
st. Bentleigh E 456 L17
st. Bentleigh E 457 A17
st. Brunswick E 325 L15
st. Coburg 325 D4
st. Essendon 323 B7
st. Maidstone 366 E3
st. Malvern East 416 C16
st. Mitcham 377 A12
st. Pt Lonsdale 710 E5
st. St Kilda W 413 L13
st. Sunbury 142 L14
st. Sunbury 143 A14
st. Yarraville 366 K14
st.n, Hampton 495 A9
st.s, Hampton 495 A10

DEAKINWOOD
ct. Waurn Ponds 705 E15

DEAKON
ct. Wantirna S 462 L1
ct. Wantirna S 463 A1

DEAL
av. Jan Juc 711 F14
cl. Moorabbin 496 G7

DEALBATA
av. Endeavour Hl 502 K19
pl. Croydon Hl 335 J13
rd. Upwey 465 J7

DEALING
ct. Bundoora 242 F20
dr. Oakleigh S 498 A7

DEALS
rd. Clayton S 498 K13

DEAN
al. Melbourne 2 H11
al. Melbourne 24 F6
av. Hawthorn 372 B18
av. Mt Waverley 459 F2
av. St Kilda E 415 B16
cl. Nar Warrn S 552 G15
cl. Templstw Lr 330 H13
cr. Launching Pl 345 F16
ct. Altona North 409 F2
ct. Carrum Downs 601 D1
ct. Coolaroo 238 D6
ct. Cranbourne W 577 F20
ct. Epping 198 D16
ct. Rowville 503 C2
ct. Sunshine W 364 F8
ct. Wantirna 422 H5
rd. Christmas Hills 207 K14
st. Belmont 706 F1
st. Fitzroy N 326 C18
st. Hoppers Csg 448 J3
st. Kew 372 H14
st. Moonee Pnd 324 E14
st. Preston 283 D20
st. Yarraville 366 L17

DEANE
st. Blackburn N 375 L9
st. Frankston 627 H2

DEANLEA
ct. Hawthorn E 416 C4

DEANS
rd. Upwey 465 H16
st. Coburg 281 H19

DEANSIDE
cl. Seabrook 450 L3

DEANS WOOD
rd. Forest Hill 420 B3

DEANSWOOD
cl. Keysborough 534 F11
cl. Wantirna S 422 J14
ct. Cheltenham 531 G4
dr. Somerville 645 B19
pl. Brookfield 268 A6
rd. Hampton Pk 551 H8
wy. Narre Warren 538 H13

DEANY
st. Springvale 500 B10

DEARING
av. Cranbourne 604 B1

DEARNLEY
st. Manifold Ht 702 B3

DEAUVILLE
ct. Berwick 554 C3
ct. Wantirna 422 J12
grn. Craigieburn 193 L2
st. Beaumaris 530 F10
st. Forest Hill 420 G5

DEAVEY
ct. Altona 408 K14

DEBANNE
ct. Narre Warren 538 L17

DEBBIE
cl. Clarinda 498 C9
cl. Doveton 536 L7
cl. Doveton 537 A7
ct. Dingley Vill 533 A6
ct. Mill Park 242 L8
pl. Ringwood N 378 B5
st. Mt Waverley 419 E13

DEBENHAM
dr. St Albans 320 E7

DEBLIN
dr. Narre Warren 552 J6

DEBLONAY
cr. Greensbrgh 286 C7

DEBORAH
av. Bentleigh E 496 K1
av. Boronia 424 G7
ct. Mt Waverley 459 F8
ct. Noble Park 534 D4
ct. Skye 575 H18
ct. Somerville 644 F17
dr. Baxter 644 C4
st. Kilsyth 381 F9
st. Werribee 447 G11

DEBRA
ct. Berwick 554 B16
ct. Lalor 241 J10
ct. Tootgarook 698 B6
ct. Yallambie 285 E16
st. Rowville 502 C6
wy. Doncaster E 331 G18

DE BRUN
ct. Laverton 407 C16

DEBSON
cl. Boronia 424 D7

DE BURGH
ct. Viewbank 285 F20

DE CARLE
la. Brunswick 325 G10
st. Brunswick 325 G11
st. Coburg 325 H7

DE CASTELLA
cl. Mill Park 198 H20
cl. Mill Park 242 H1

DECATHLON
st. Bundoora 284 J3

DECCO
dr. Campbellfield 239 C14

DE CHENE
pde. Coburg N 281 H16

DECONTRA
cl. Donvale 376 K3

DECOR
dr. Hallam 537 G17

DECORE
dr. S Morang 198 L13

DEDERICK
gr. Braybrook 365 J1

DEDICATION
ct. Carrum Downs 574 H16

DEE
ct. Endeavour Hl 503 H19
pl. Rowville 463 E18
st. Balwyn 373 E8
st. Heidelberg 328 K4

DEED
ct. Sunshine W 364 J10
dr. Pakenham 584 H2
st. Belmont 706 A5

DEEP CREEK
dr. Doncaster E 332 F7
rd. Mitcham 377 H13
rd. Pakenham 560 B20

DEEPDALE
gr. Mooroolbark 337 D8
st. Dandenong S 535 L15

DEEPDENE
pl. Balwyn 372 K13
rd. Balwyn 372 K13
st. Caroline Spr 274 C17

DEER
st. Deer Park 318 J15

DEERING
av. Badger Creek 258 E19

DEERY
rd. Emerald 509 J10

DEE WY
rd. Nar Warrn S 552 F9

DE FELICE
ct. Forest Hill 420 F3

DEFELICE
pl. Mooroolbark 337 K16
pl. Wantirna 422 B10

DEFENCE
rd. Portsea 665 A15
rd. Portsea 665 J16

DE FEU
st. N Melbourne 34 K16

DE FREDERICKS
la. Yarrambat 201 F13
rd. Yarrambat 201 C15

DEGA
av. Bentleigh E 496 G4

DE GARIS
pl. Werribee 447 B6

DEGARIS
la. Roxburgh Pk 194 E9

DEGAS
ct. Skye 601 G2
ct. Wheelers Hl 460 K16

DEGG
ct. Aspendale Gdn 546 J2

DEGOLDIS
rd. Fyansford 701 A8

DEGRAVES
pl. Melbourne 2 D18
pl. Melbourne, off Degraves St 24 E10
st. Flemington 323 K20
st. Melbourne 2 C19
st. Melbourne 24 E10
st. Parkville 17 J9

DE GRUCHYS
la. N Melbourne 17 A9

DEHAVILAND
av. Forest Hill 420 D9

DE HAVILLAND
av. Strathmr Ht 279 E9
rd. Mordialloc 532 D10

DEHNERT
st. Doncaster E 331 H20
st. Doncaster E 375 H1

DEIDRE
ct. Airport W 278 F15

DEIGHTON
dr. Rosebud 700 B1

DEIRDRE
ct. Montmorency 286 J7
st. Glen Waverley 459 L3

DELACEY
st. Maidstone 366 K2

DELACOMBE
ct. Cheltenham 497 C16
dr. Hampton Pk 551 K7
dr. Mill Park 243 F4
dr. Vermont S 421 F8

DELAGE
cl. Keilor Dn 276 A13

DELAHUNTY
ct. Altona Mdw 451 L6

DELAMARE
dr. Albanvale 318 L4

DELAMERE
cl. Mulgrave 501 H5
dr. Chirnside Pk 336 J7
mw. Ringwood N 378 G4

DELANCEY
rd. Wandin East 340 K19
rd. Wandin East 341 A17

DELANEY
ct. Keilor 276 G9

DELANEYS
rd. Warranwood 334 K10

DELANY
av. Burwood 418 J8
cl. Canterbury 373 F17

DELATITE
cl. Epping 197 K20
ct. Hallam 538 B19
ct. Rowville 463 E16
ct. Vermont 421 A5
ct. Warranwood 334 H14
ct. Werribee 448 B18
ct. Yallambie 286 A11
wy. Skye 601 F2

DELAWARE
dr. Dingley Vill 533 D10
st. Reservoir 283 A12

DELBRIDGE
dr. Sydenham 274
st. Fitzroy N 19

DELEWARE
st. Yarraville 366

DELFI
ct. Balwyn 373

DELFIN
cr. Greensbrgh 286
ct. Glen Waverley 460
ct. Rowville 502

DELGANY
av. Portsea 677
ri. Langwarrin 629

DELHI
ct. Travancore 324
st. Bentleigh 496
st. Glenroy 280
st. Mitcham 377

DELHUNTLY
ri. Nar Warrn S 579

DELIA
ct. Dandenong N 501
st. Oakleigh S 457

DE LISLE
av. Sunbury 143

DELL
ct. Mt Waverley 419
la. Maribyrnong, off William Cooper St 367
rd. Frankston 627
st. Narre Warren 553

DELLA
cl. St Helena 244
pl. Sunshine W 364
st. Scoresby 462

DELLAS
av. Templestowe 330

DELLA TORRE
cr. Ivanhoe 327

DELLFIELD
dr. Templstw Lr 330

DELL VIEW
cl. Nar Warrn N 538

DELLVIEW
ct. Donvale 332

DELLWOOD
ct. Templestowe 331

DELMA
av. Cairnlea 319
st. Bentleigh E 496

DELMAR
ct. Keilor Ldg 276

DELMARE
ct. Nar Warrn S 552
st. Lalor 241

DEL MONACO
la. Carlton 18

DELMONT
av. Altona 408
cl. Epping 241
ct. Cranbourne 578
ct. Endeavour Hl 537
ct. Mooroolbark 381
st. Albion 320
st. Werribee 446
st. Werribee 447

DELMORE
cr. Glen Waverley 419

DELMUIR
cl. Eltham 288

DELORAINE
cl. Doncaster E 332

DELOS
ct. Endeavour Hl 536
st. Oakleigh S 457

DELPHIN
av. Altona North 409
ct. Narre Warren 553

DELPHINIUS
cr. Roxburgh Pk 194

DELPURA
gln. Greensbrgh 244

DELTA
av. Ashwood 418
av. Coburg N 281
cl. Lilydale 294
ct. Cranbourne 604
ct. Narre Warren 539
ct. Rowville 502
ct. Thomastown 241
pl. Keilor Dn 275
rd. Greensbrgh 285
rd. Macleod 285
rd. Watsonia 285
st. Surrey Hills 417

DELVIEW
dr. Jan Juc 711

DELVILLE
av. Mentone 531
st. Mooroolbark 337

Yarra Jctn 346 J11
Prahran 31 K18
Prahran 414 E9
ONA
Kew 372 B11
ONAHA
Cockatoo 511 G10
ONBRAE
Noble Park N 501 D18
ONDOO
Burwood E 419 F11
ONE
Aberfeldie 323 D9
ONGA
Moorabbin 496 E9
ONGALLA
The Basin 425 G8
ONKUNA
Camberwell 417 D4
ONSIDE
Lilydale 338 G12
Richmond 371 B14
ORAWARRAH
Mt Waverley 459 D4
OWI
Greensbrgh 244 B17
PEL
Docklands 368 K14
RA
Blackburn 375 E15
Somerville 645 D17
Templestowe 331 E5
Braybrook 322 B19
Heidelberg 329 B9
Epping 198 F19
RADO
Balwyn N 329 D19
RAN
Frankston 600 E16
Southbank 23 E19
Delahey 275 B12
RCAS
S Melbourne 29 E7
Taylors Hill 274 D7
Boronia 424 D1
Newcomb 704 B12
Southbank 30 B4
Southbank 413 H1
S Melbourne 29 D7
S Melbourne 413 C3
RCHAP
Hoppers Csg 449 B2
RCHESTER
Montrose 382 F8
Carrum Downs 601 B5
Frankston 628 C9
Nar Warrn S 579 D4
Carlton 18 G15
Cockatoo 511 E10
Craigieburn 149 L17
RDOGNE
Roxburgh Pk 194 E5
RE
Nr Nr Goon N 560 H8
Pakenham 560 E20
Tooradin 651 D5
REEN
Montrose 381 L8
REEN ROGEN
S Morang 243 H2
RENE
Vermont S 420 H7
RGAN
Endeavour Hl 503 J20
Caulfield N 415 E18
Mt Waverley 459 G1
RIAN
Ferntree Gly 464 H3
RIS
Scoresby 462 H8
Springvale S 499 G18
Wheelers Hl 460 K16
Hoppers Csg 447 K3
Greensbrgh 285 H5
Murrumbeena 457 D11
RKING
Craigieburn 150 C19
Box Hill 375 B13
Box Hill N 375 C9
RLTON
Roxburgh Pk 194 C16
RMAN
Mill Park 242 A4
RNIE
w. Endeavour Hl 503 K18
RNING
Nar Warrn E 507 E16
RNOCH
Croydon 336 H20
Sunbury 144 D11
ROTHEA
Dromana 686 A9
Bundoora 242 F17

st. Canterbury 417 F1
st. Highett 496 A14
DOROTHEA MACKELLAR
av. Oakleigh E 458 H11
DOROTHY
av. Belmont 706 F1
av. Glen Huntly 456 C10
av. Ormond 456 C10
av. Sunshine 365 G1
av. Thomastown 241 C15
cr. Mornington 640 H20
ct. Clayton S 499 E16
ct. Dandenong N 501 K17
ct. Hampton Pk 551 F11
ct. McCrae 685 C14
gr. Ferntree Gly 464 H1
rd. Mt Evelyn 383 L5
st. Brunswick 325 J12
st. Burwood E 419 G10
st. Croydon 380 B9
st. Doveton 537 A8
st. Fawkner 239 G20
st. Healesville 213 G15
st. Pascoe Vale 281 A11
st. Rye 696 E10
st. Tullamarine 278 G4
DORR
ct. Belmont 706 H6
DORRIGO
dr. Boronia 424 K6
DORRINGTON
av. Glen Iris 416 G15
av. Reservoir 283 F14
ct. Bundoora 243 D19
ct. Dingley Vill 533 G7
ct. Mill Park 242 A2
dr. Mt Waverley 459 F1
st. Point Cook 450 E6
DORRIT
st. Carlton 18 E14
st. Springvale S 499 L20
DORSET
arc. Boronia 424 E11
av. Heidelberg 329 F4
av. Keilor East 322 G5
ct. Keysborough 534 J8
dr. Greenvale 237 F5
pl. Melton W 226 C15
rd. Bayswater N 380 D19
rd. Boronia 424 D9
rd. Croydon 380 D8
rd. Croydon S 380 D19
rd. Dandenong N 502 C14
rd. Ferntree Gly 464 C3
rd. Mt Martha 655 J19
rd. Pascoe Vale 281 A14
sq. Boronia 424 E11
st. Glen Waverley 459 H11
DORTAD
ct. Hampton Pk 551 H9
DORWARD
av. Newcomb 704 A15
DOTTEREL
cl. Blind Bight 650 B8
cl. Doveton 536 J5
ct. Chelsea Ht 547 D8
ct. Rosebud W 699 E5
ct. Werribee 448 B5
DOUBELL
bvd. Truganina 405 G13
bvd. Truganina 405 G15
cl. Glen Waverley 461 B6
ct. Mill Park 242 G8
DOUCH
st. Williamstown 411 B11
DOUG
ct. Narre Warren 538 L15
DOUGAL
ct. Highton 701 G19
ct. Kurunjang 227 E10
DOUGAND
ct. Dingley Vill 533 B8
DOUGHARTY
rd. Heidelberg Ht 284 B17
rd. Heidelberg W 284 B17
DOUGHERTY
ct. Mulgrave 501 E4
DOUGHTYS
rd. Kalorama 383 A19
rd. Olinda 383 A19
DOUGLAS
av. Box Hill S 418 H2
av. Chelsea 546 H17
av. Doncaster E 376 F3
av. Donvale 376 F3
av. St Albans 319 F2
cr. Monbulk 428 F17
ct. Altona Mdw 451 D3
ct. Cranbourne W 577 F19
ct. Nar Warrn N 539 F10
ct. Pt Lonsdale 710 G1
ct. Rye 697 B14
ct. St Helena 244 L19

ct. St Helena 245 A19
ct. Strathmr Ht 279 D9
ct. Thomastown 241 G15
ct. Westmeadows 236 H15
gr. Frankston 599 D15
pde. Croydon 335 L20
pde. Don Valley 346 E9
pde. Newport 411 D8
pde. Spotswood 411 D7
pde. Williamstown 411 D10
pde. Yarra Jctn 347 D18
pl. Geelong, off Maud St 702 K10
ri. Endeavour Hl 503 K18
st. Altona North 409 J8
st. Ashwood 417 L15
st. Balwyn N 373 C6
st. Beaumaris 530 F7
st. Blackburn N 375 L7
st. Boronia 424 D15
st. Malvern East 416 E20
st. Noble Park 500 H20
st. Pascoe Vale 280 C14
st. Port Melb 368 D19
st. Rosanna 328 L1
st. Rosanna 329 A1
st. Southbank 29 G1
st. Southbank 413 D1
st. Sunshine N 321 G13
st. Toorak 415 B4
st. Upwey 466 B9
DOUGLAS MAWSON
dr. Roxburgh Pk 193 J14
DOUGLASS
st. Herne Hill 701 L1
st. Manifold Ht 701 L1
DOULTON
av. Heathmont 378 H18
rd. Blackburn 375 F11
DOUTHIE
rd. Seville 342 K14
rd. Seville 387 E7
rd. Seville E 342 K14
rd. Seville E 387 E7
DOUTNEY
ct. Sunbury 142 J3
DOVAVALLEY
rd. Wandin East 340 H18
DOVE
av. Altona 408 F19
ct. Coolaroo 238 F7
ct. Pakenham 584 L2
ct. Pearcedale 646 K4
ct. Templstw Lr 330 D9
ct. Werribee 448 A8
pl. Burnley, off Type St 371 B17
st. Cremorne 26 A18
st. W Footscray 366 K7
tce. S Morang 199 H11
DOVER
ct. Diamond Ck 245 L6
ct. Dromana 686 E9
ct. Ferntree Gly 463 G3
ct. Mulgrave 500 H2
la. Williamstown 411 F12
pl. Melton W 226 E15
pl. Parkdale 531 D12
pl. Geelong, off Little Malop St 703 D8
rd. Williamstown 411 F11
st. Albanvale 319 D4
st. Bentleigh E 457 C20
st. Caulfield S 455 G9
st. Cremorne 32 A2
st. Flemington 33 G1
st. Flemington 324 C20
st. Oakleigh E 458 L15
DOVETON
av. Eumemmerring 537 C15
DOVETTE
ct. Wheelers Hl 460 K17
DOW
st. Port Melb 412 K6
st. Port Melb 413 A5
st. S Melbourne 30 A7
DOWD
ct. Pakenham 584 E5
pl. Glenroy 279 L5
rd. Healesville 214 L16
DOWDING
cl. Fawkner 281 F2
DOWELL
ct. Dandenong N 502 C15
DOWER
st. Camberwell 417 L3
DOWLE
st. Macleod 285 C13
DOWLING
av. Springvale 500 E7
ct. Sunbury 142 G11
gr. Doncaster E 332 F15
pl. N Melbourne 17 G16
rd. Oakleigh S 498 A8

st. Fawkner 281 H6
st. Kealba 321 A1
DOWMAN
st. Newport 411 D10
DOWN
st. Collingwood 19 J17
st. Reservoir 282 K14
DOWNARD
cr. Dandenong N 501 L17
st. Braeside 532 G12
DOWNE
pl. Wantirna 422 J7
DOWNES
av. Brighton 454 J11
la. Geelong, off Little Malop St 703 A7
pl. Geelong, off Little Malop St 703 A7
st. Strathmore 324 D1
DOWNEY
rd. Dewhurst 510 D20
rd. Yarrambat 201 C18
DOWNHAM
wy. Wyndham Va 446 D13
DOWNIE
st. Melbourne 23 H13
DOWNING
av. Glen Iris 416 K10
st. Blackburn 375 G15
st. Oakleigh 457 L12
st. Sunshine N 321 F16
DOWNLAND
pl. Dingley Vill 533 C4
sq. Avondale Ht 322 D10
DOWNS
rd. Lalor 240 C9
rd. Seaford 599 L2
rd. Thomastown 240 C12
st. Brunswick 325 D8
st. Pascoe Vale 280 J15
DOWNSHIRE
cl. Wantirna S 422 J20
rd. Belmont 702 C17
rd. Elsternwick 455 A7
DOWNTON
cr. Pt Lonsdale 707 H20
gr. Kew 372 G10
DOWNWARD
st. Mornington 640 D18
DOWSETT
st. S Geelong 703 D16
DOY
st. Dallas 238 L9
DOYLE
pl. Endeavour Hl 537 H5
rd. Pakenham Up 559 J1
st. Avondale Ht 322 A9
st. Bulleen 329 J14
st. Sunshine N 321 E14
DOYNTON
pde. Hoppers Csg 448 J6
pde. Mt Waverley 459 H2
DOYSAL
av. Ferntree Gly 424 G19
DOZEY
ct. Roxburgh Pk 194 D15
pl. Endeavour Hl 537 C6
DRAGON
wy. Kings Park 274 L18
DRAIN RESERVE
rd. South Yarra 32 G11
DRAKE
cl. Gladstone Pk 237 A16
ct. Avondale Ht 322 A13
ct. Carrum Downs 601 B5
ct. Lilydale 338 H3
ct. Melton 226 L16
pl. Pakenham 584 K8
st. Brighton 454 G10
st. Ferntree Gly 464 E8
st. Mornington 640 E11
st. Newport 411 B5
st. Spotswood 411 B5
st. Sunshine N 321 B14
DRAKES
la. N Melbourne 34 K10
DRANSFIELD
wy. Epping 198 E15
DRAPER
ct. Keilor Dn 276 D12
sq. Wheelers Hl 461 B8
st. McKinnon 456 F16
st. Ormond 456 F16
st. S Melbourne 29 G9
st. S Melbourne 413 D5
DRASKA
ct. Oak Park 279 G10
DRAYTON
cr. Pk Orchards 333 G18
ct. Baxter 644 B2
st. Sunshine 365 E5
DRAYTONS
pl. Wyndham Va 446 F13

DREADNOUGHT
st. Sandringham 495 F15
DREAM
pl. Melton S 268 F5
DREAMHAVEN
ct. Epping 197 D18
DREDGE
st. Reservoir 282 F1
DRESDEN
av. Heathmont 378 H17
st. Heidelberg Ht 328 G6
wy. Sunshine W 364 C8
DRESSAGE
pl. Epping 198 D17
DRESS CIRCLE
la. Mooroolbark 337 D7
DREW
st. Keilor East 322 E1
st. Yarraville 366 F15
DREWE
cl. Donvale 332 K17
DREWERY
al. Melbourne 2 D7
al. Melbourne 24 C4
la. Melbourne 2 E8
la. Melbourne 24 C4
pl. Melbourne 2 D7
pl. Melbourne 24 C5
DREWETT
st. Surrey Hills 374 D20
DREWS
rd. Marshall 706 L13
DRIFFIELD
cr. Sassafras 426 H12
DRIFTWOOD
av. Rye 696 E2
cl. Seabrook 450 J7
ct. Frankston 599 L16
ct. Mt Martha 656 K7
ct. Narre Warren 538 L20
dr. Glen Waverley 460 H1
mw. Carrum Downs 601 D6
DRILL
st. Hawthorn 371 J17
DRINA
st. Strathmore 280 B17
DRINAN
rd. Chelsea 546 L17
DRINKWATER
cr. Sunshine W 364 G7
DRISCOLLS
rd. Kealba 276 K17
rd. Kealba 277 A20
DRISHANE
st. Coburg 325 D5
DRIVER
la. Melbourne 2 B10
la. Melbourne 24 C6
st. Kingsbury 283 K8
st. Portsea 678 E2
DROITWICH
cr. Deer Park 318 J9
DROMANA
av. Airport W 279 A10
av. Bentleigh E 457 B16
av. Pascoe Vale 280 G17
av. Reservoir 282 D11
pde. Safety Bch 686 G2
st. Glenroy 279 H8
DROMSALLY
ri. Warranwood 334 K16
DROOP
st. Footscray 367 D5
DROUIN
ct. Melton S 268 E5
st. Dallas 238 F10
DROVERS
ct. Vermont S 421 B13
la. Somerville 645 F15
rt. Nar Warrn S 552 E17
wk. Chirnside Pk 337 E6
DRUCE
la. N Melbourne 34 J10
DRUITT
st. Oakleigh S 497 G5
DRUM
cl. Frankston 600 H16
st. Rye 696 H9
DRUMDOUNE
dr. Mt Eliza 626 C11
DRUMMARTIN
st. Albion 364 K1
DRUMMER
ct. Hoppers Csg 449 D2
la. Narre Warren 538 J12
DRUMMER HILL
la. Mooroolbark 337 D10
DRUMMOND
cl. Donvale 377 B2
cr. Rowville 462 E19
ct. Melton W 226 F11
la. Carlton N 18 H4
pl. Carlton 18 F18

NVEGAN
Dandenong 535 H1
Macleod 285 A10
Kurunjang 227 D11
NWOLD
Vermont 421 C4
OSA
Altona North 365 H20
PONT
S Morang 199 B14
RACK
Lynbrook 551 C16
Point Cook 449 L8
Sunbury 143 A15
Mill Park 242 H6
RANG
Croydon N 335 L14
Endeavour Hl 538 A7
Selby 467 B14
Upwey 466 A9
RBAN
Epping 198 B16
Grovedale 706 D12
Keilor Dn 276 E14
Emerald 509 J1
Bentleigh 496 F3
RCELL
Portsea 678 A4
RHAM
Craigieburn 150 G20
Craigieburn 194 G1
Hoppers Csg 448 F2
Croydon N 336 A11
Dandenong N 502 D12
Epping 197 L17
Mt Martha 655 L20
Narre Warren 538 K16
Somerville 644 G16
Mornington 657 B5
Clayton S 499 E10
Melton W 225 K14
Rosebud 684 C14
Sorrento 678 D9
Kilsyth 381 D6
Sunshine 365 B3
Surrey Hills 373 J20
Surrey Hills 417 J2
Albert Park 29 D11
Albert Park 413 B6
Eaglemont 328 J10
Kensington 33 K11
Richmond 32 G3
Richmond 414 J2
KIN
Templestowe 331 C8
Newport 410 K7
LEY
Frankston 600 B20
NESS
Endeavour Hl 503 K19
NSTAN
Wheelers Hl 460 J18
RANT
Endeavour Hl 538 A5
Brighton 454 L15
Brighton 455 A15
WARD
Glen Waverley 459 K7
Malvern East 457 G3
K
Hampton Pk 552 A15
KY
Safety Bch 669 B16
TER
Brookfield 268 B4
TIN
Sydenham 275 B6
CH
Melton 269 D1
CHMAN
Taylors L 275 H5
ON
Wheelers Hl 460 L7
TON
Lynbrook 551 D15
Meadow Ht 237 L2
AL
Albanvale 318 L3
Wheelers Hl 461 E14
SON
Templestowe 331 A9
ER
Reservoir 282 E13
Donvale 332 K16
Greensbrgh 243 H18
Blackburn 375 F20
Clifton Hill 20 H1
Macleod 284 K14
R
Clarinda 498 G11
Epping 197 K19
Hoppers Csg 448 J3

DYFFRYN
ct. Kilsyth 380 L4
DYLAN
ct. Berwick 539 G19
DYMOCK
ct. Craigieburn 194 B4
DYNES
st. Ringwood E 379 C6
DYNON
rd. Footscray 33 A17
rd. W Melbourne 33 A17
rd. W Melbourne 367 L8
DYSART
pl. Mooroolbark 381 H3
DYSON
ct. Mooroolbark 337 F11
dr. Lynbrook 551 E16
dr. Sunbury 142 G10
rd. Carrum 573 D9
st. Dromana 686 D7
st. Reservoir 282 D9
st. W Footscray 366 G12

E

EADES
ct. Templestowe 331 C8
pl. W Melbourne 17 E20
st. E Melbourne 25 D3
st. Laverton 407 F14
EADIE
av. Healesville 214 A16
st. Sunbury 144 A12
EAGLAND
rd. Cheltenham 531 E3
EAGLE
al. Melbourne 1 B6
al. Melbourne 23 H6
av. Anglesea 713 B5
av. Kingsbury 283 K9
ct. Blind Bight 650 C10
ct. Craigieburn 193 L2
ct. Dingley Vill 532 L7
ct. Eaglemont 328 H10
ct. Mt Waverley 458 K9
ct. Vermont S 420 G13
dr. Noble Park N 501 D10
dr. Pakenham 584 J2
dr. Pakenham 584 J3
pl. Melton 226 G15
rch. Wyndham Va 446 B8
ri. Templstw Lr 330 A8
st. Mornington 641 B11
st. Werribee 447 J18
tce. Taylors L 275 G3
EAGLEFARM
ct. Keilor Park 277 L12
EAGLEHAWK
cct. Cairnlea 319 H15
EAGLEMONT
cr. Eaglemont 328 H11
EAGLE NEST
rd. Olinda 427 J1
EAGLENEST
wy. Point Cook 450 A7
EAGLE RIDGE
ri. Burwood 418 B3
EAGLESCLIFF
cr. Cranbourne 603 D8
EAGLET
ct. Mill Park 242 J12
EAGLEVIEW
pl. Point Cook 451 B8
wy. Craigieburn 150 C7
EAGLING
st. Keilor 277 B13
EALING
cl. Craigieburn 150 E20
cl. Epping 197 K17
cr. Springvale S 499 H20
ct. Glen Waverley 460 L6
EAMA
ct. Bulleen 330 A15
EAMES
av. Brooklyn 365 H18
EAMON
ct. Kew 371 E10
dr. Viewbank 285 H19
EAMONT
cl. Chelsea Ht 547 D9
EARIMIL
dr. Mt Eliza 625 G16
EARL
ct. Hallam 538 B17
ct. Werribee 447 A10
gr. Craigieburn 150 F7
pl. Melton W 226 B14
st. Airport W 279 A16
st. Carlton 18 D20
st. Carlton N 18 K4
st. Doncaster 331 D17
st. Kew 371 K4
st. Kew East 371 K4
st. Upwey 465 G9
st. Windsor 414 H11
st.e, Windsor 414 J11
EARLBY
ct. Greenvale 193 D19
EARLE
cl. Mont Albert 374 C15
cl. Pakenham 559 A17
st. Preston 282 K20
EARLING
cl. Wyndham Va 446 G13
EARLINGTON
bvd. Burnside 318 E7
EARLS
ct. Balwyn N 373 L1
ct. Endeavour Hl 537 D1
ct. Mulgrave 500 D1
ct. Pascoe Vale 280 K12
ct. Point Cook 450 F9
ct. Wantirna S 422 E18
rd. Moolap 704 H20
EARLSFIELD
ct. Deer Park 319 B11
dr. Berwick 554 K20
dr. Berwick 554 L19
rd. Hampton 495 E8
EARLSTON
cct. Cranbourne 604 F9
sq. Berwick 554 G16
EARLSTOWN
rd. Hughesdale 457 H11
EARLSWOOD
cl. Caroline Spr, off Copse Wood Bnd 317 L3
EARLWOOD
ct. Thomastown 240 K16
dr. Wheelers Hl 460 H15
st. Dingley Vill 532 L6
st. Nar Warrn S 578 F2
EARLY
pl. Boronia 424 J4
EARNSHAW
dr. Carrum Downs 601 E3
EARSDON
st. Yarraville 367 E16
EASEY
st. Collingwood 19 G12
EAST
av. Mt Evelyn 383 D1
cct. Sunshine W 364 H11
cnc. Beaumaris 530 B10
cr. Springvale 500 K10
ct. Braybrook 366 C3
ct. Camberwell 417 L4
ct. Keysborough 534 E13
ct. Lalor 241 F9
ct. Mooroolbark 336 K20
ct. Newcomb 703 L16
gwy. Wyndham Va 446 F12
lk. Chirnside Pk 337 D5
rd. Pearcedale 630 L10
rd. Pearcedale 647 B11
rd. Seaford 599 J1
rd. Vermont S 421 G8
st. Ascot Vale 324 E18
st. Coburg 325 L8
st. Hadfield 281 A10
st. Heidelberg W 328 C1
st. Malvern 416 B11
st. Melb Airport 235 K10
st. Northcote 326 K19
st. Point Cook 450 C7
st. Reservoir 283 B13
EASTAWAY
st. Elsternwick 455 C3
EASTBANK
pky. Caroline Spr 273 L18
EAST BOUNDARY
rd. Bentleigh E 496 J6
rd. Scoresby 462 F11
tr. Lysterfield 505 D16
EASTBOURNE
ct. Frankston 599 J15
ct. Glen Waverley 460 F10
rd. Rosebud 683 J20
rd. Rosebud W 683 D20
st. Windsor 414 H11
wy. Nar Warrn S 579 B4
EASTBRIDGE
ct. Nunawading 376 L17
EASTBURY
ct. Nar Warrn S 552 K19
EASTCOTE
ct. Vermont S 420 H13
st. Sunshine N 321 C17
EASTERLEIGH
ct. Dandenong 535 K1

EASTERN
av. Doncaster 330 E19
fwy. Abbotsford 20 D10
fwy. Abbotsford 371 B4
fwy. Balwyn N 328 J20
fwy. Balwyn N 329 A20
fwy. Blackburn N 375 C5
fwy. Box Hill N 375 C5
fwy. Clifton Hill 371 B4
fwy. Collingwood 20 D10
fwy. Doncaster 374 B1
fwy. Donvale 375 C5
fwy. Fairfield 371 B4
fwy. Kew 371 B4
fwy. Kew 372 A3
fwy. Kew East 372 A3
fwy. Mont Albert N 374 B1
fwy. Nunawading 375 C5
hwy. Clifton Hill 19 F9
hwy. Fitzroy 19 F9
hwy. Fitzroy N 19 F9
pl. Hawthorn E 372 D17
rd. S Melbourne 3 C20
rd. S Melbourne 30 D2
rd. S Melbourne 413 H2
rd. S Melbourne 413 J3
st. Craigieburn 150 H16
EASTERN BEACH
Geelong 703 C6
Geelong 703 D7
EASTERN PARK
cct. E Geelong 703 G8
sq. Nar Warrn S 553 D20
EAST ESPLANADE
St Albans 275 L17
St Albans 320 B3
EASTFIELD
rd. Croydon 379 K10
rd. Croydon S 379 K10
rd. Ringwood E 379 C9
EASTGATE
ct. Wantirna S 423 A17
dr. Greensbrgh 243 G18
rd. Craigieburn 194 G1
st. Oakleigh 457 J15
st. Pascoe Vale S 280 G19
EAST GLIDE
rd. Melb Airport 235 F6
EASTHAM
st. Fitzroy N 326 D20
EAST INDIA
av. Nunawading 376 G17
EAST KIRKBY
ct. Highton 705 K7
EASTLEIGH
av. Keilor East 321 L4
dr. Glen Waverley 460 L2
EAST MADDINGLEY
rd. Maddingley 263 L16
rd. Maddingley 264 A9
rd. Parwan 263 L16
EASTMEAD
rd. Croydon 380 C8
EASTMENT
st. Northcote 326 H16
EASTON
av. Seaford 599 F9
ct. Dandenong N 501 F11
ct. Ferntree Gly 463 K6
EAST SPUR
ct. Kilsyth S 381 B15
EAST VIEW
cr. Bentleigh E 496 L2
tce. Jan Juc 711 D16
EASTVIEW
av. Seville E 343 D12
pde. Belmont 702 G16
EASTWAY
av. Donvale 376 H7
EAST-WEST
brk. Lysterfield 504 G6
EASTWOOD
av. Preston 282 H20
cr. Mooroolbark 337 G9
st. Kensington 33 L5
st. Kensington 34 A11
st. Seddon 367 F11
EATON
cl. Diamond Ck 245 L6
ct. Albanvale 319 D6
pde. Laverton 407 D13
pl. Baxter 644 C2
pl. Narre Warren 538 F20
pl. Wheelers Hl 461 E14
st. Melton S 268 J5
st. Oakleigh 457 K11
EATONS CUTTING
rd. Dromana 687 B11
rd. Red Hill 687 B18
EBB
st. Aspendale 546 C3
EBBELS
pde. Olinda 427 B10

EBBYS
wk. Mt Evelyn 339 A16
EBDALE
st. Frankston 599 C16
EBDEN
av. Black Rock 529 G5
ct. Broadmeadows 237 L9
st. Brighton 454 J6
st. Moorabbin 497 A9
st. Noble Park N 501 C17
EBELI
cl. Nar Warrn N 504 D19
cl. Nar Warrn N 538 F1
EBLANA
av. Mentone 531 B10
EBON
ct. Doncaster 374 G3
EBONY
cl. Wandana Ht 701 C18
dr. Bundoora 242 J15
dr. Langwarrin 601 K14
dr. Pakenham 585 F1
pde. Heidelberg W 328 A2
EBRO
ct. Roxburgh Pk 194 F5
ECCLES
cl. Mill Park 242 H2
ECHIDENA
cl. Langwarrin 628 J6
ECHIDNA
pl. S Morang, off Kangaroo Tce 243 J2
rd. Eltham 288 F2
ECHO
av. Balwyn N 373 G1
ct. Whittington 704 F19
ECHUCA
rd. Greensbrgh 286 D6
st. Dallas 238 H9
ECHUNGA
cl. Forest Hill 420 E7
ECKERSALL
st. Brunswick 325 G11
ECKERSLEY
ct. Blackburn S 419 K1
ECKFORD
st. Dandenong 536 D11
ECLIPSE
cr. Watsonia 285 H9
ct. Hampton Pk 552 A15
pl. Hoppers Csg 405 A13
EDALE
cl. Kings Park 319 A2
EDAM
ct. Balwyn 373 F10
EDAN
ct. Pakenham 559 A20
EDDIE
st. Highett 496 A15
st. Pascoe Vale 280 H16
st. St Albans 276 H19
EDDIE BARRON
tce. Pakenham 558 J20
EDDINGTON
pl. Endeavour Hl 537 E1
EDDISON
cl. Altona Mdw 451 K7
EDDY
ct. Abbotsford 20 B18
st. Brunswick E 325 K11
st. Camberwell 417 C8
st. Moonee Pnd 324 B12
EDDYS
gr. Bentleigh 455 K20
EDDYSTONE
rd. McCrae 684 K12
EDEBOHLS
rd. Nar Warrn E 506 L18
rd. Nar Warrn E 507 A17
EDELMAIER
st. Bayswater 423 K6
EDEN
av. Box Hill S 419 C5
av. Heathmont 422 J1
av. Springvale 500 C17
av. Watsonia 285 D6
cl. Mulgrave 501 A6
ct. Ascot Vale 323 G16
ct. Camberwell 417 K8
ct. Doncaster 375 C2
ct. Forest Hill 420 C3
ct. Noble Park 535 B3
ct. Toorak 415 H7
gr. Knoxfield 463 A8
gr. Nar Warrn S 553 A18
pl. Greenvale 237 F4
st. Cheltenham 530 K3
st. Croydon 379 G3
st. Footscray 366 L5
st. Heidelberg Ht 328 D5
wy. Kilsyth 381 G8
EDENBRIDGE
ct. Carrum Downs 601 B5

EDENHOPE
st. Kilsyth 381 G7
EDENMONT
rd. Emerald 468 L20
rd. Emerald 469 A20
rd. Emerald 508 L2
EDEN PARK
dr. Mornington 641 C18
EDEN VALLEY
cl. Vermont S 421 D10
rd. Cairnlea 319 K12
rd. Warranwood 335 C11
EDEYS RUN
Hampton Pk 551 K11
EDGAR
av. Wonga Park 335 J6
ct. Ferntree Gly 464 C2
pl. Mt Eliza 626 B13
st. Brighton 455 B17
st. Glen Iris 416 D13
st. Hadfield 280 L7
st. Heidelberg 329 A4
st. Kingsville 366 J13
st. Moonee Pnd 324 B15
st. Reservoir 282 L16
st. Rye 696 G1
st. Werribee 447 C14
st.n, Glen Iris 416 E9
EDGARS
rd. Lalor 240 K6
rd. Thomastown 240 J19
EDGBASTON
cct. Berwick 554 D19
pde. Caroline Spr 317 J3
EDGECOMBE
ct. Moorabbin 497 D10
st. Kew 371 F11
st. Oak Park 280 B13
wy. Roxburgh Pk 194 C13
EDGERTON
ct. Hampton Pk 551 H4
rd. Mitcham 377 F11
rd. Mitcham 377 H12
st. Hawthorn 371 H13
EDGEVALE
rd. Bulleen 329 J16
rd. Kew 372 C13
EDGEWARE
cl. Kealba 276 L19
ct. Wantirna 422 F14
EDGEWATER
bvd. Maribyrnong 367 C1
cct. Cairnlea 319 H6
cl. Queenscliff 707 L18
EDGEWOOD
av. Burwood E 419 L12
cl. Nar Warrn S 552 F6
cl. Thomastown 240 F15
ct. Cairnlea 319 K13
ct. Wantirna S 422 J19
rd. Dandenong 535 G3
rd. Roxburgh Pk 194 B4
st. Carnegie 456 G5
EDGOOSE
av. Mont Albert N 374 F10
EDGWARE
ct. Epping 197 J15
EDI
ct. Coolaroo 238 E7
EDINA
av. Port Melb 412 C5
cl. Port Melb 412 G5
ct. Blairgowrie 679 L20
gr. Altona Mdw 452 A3
pl. Torquay 712 D4
rd. Ferntree Gly 424 A18
st. Williamstn N 410 L13
EDINBOROUGH
st. Hallam 537 J15
EDINBURGH
av. Caulfield 455 E3
av. Glen Waverley 420 G18
av. Herne Hill 701 L4
ct. Frankston S 628 B15
ct. Greenvale 237 F6
ct. Werribee 446 L11
dr. Officer 555 J20
la. Caroline Spr 274 B16
pl. Melton W 226 D16
rd. Bayswater 423 F11
rd. Blackburn S 419 E3
rd. Lilydale 338 F20
rd. Springvale 500 F7
st. Bentleigh E 457 B19
st. Box Hill S 374 J20
st. Clayton 458 G18
st. Diamond Ck 245 F11
st. Flemington 33 E2
st. Hampton 495 E10
st. Oakleigh S 458 G18
st. Richmond 26 L17
st. Richmond 371 A18
wy. Derrimut 363 B5
EDINBUROUGH
dr. Skye 601 G1
EDINGTON
wy. Craigieburn 194 D4
EDIS
ct. Endeavour Hl 537 C2
EDITH
av. Croydon 379 E5
av. Nunawading 376 J18
ct. Belmont 706 D6
ct. Bentleigh E 497 B2
ct. Doncaster 374 G2
ct. Mt Dandenong 426 G5
ct. Olinda 426 G5
la. Box Hill N 375 E10
pl. Dromana 685 K9
rd. Ferny Creek 425 K14
ri. Hampton Pk 552 B12
st. Beaumaris 530 A10
st. Beaumaris 530 B9
st. Caulfield N 415 G18
st. Dandenong 536 B6
st. Glen Waverley 419 K20
st. Heathmont 378 K17
st. Mordialloc 531 K16
st. Noble Park 534 K4
st. Oak Park 280 C13
st. Preston 326 J1
EDITHVALE
rd. Aspendale Gdn 547 A10
rd. Chelsea Ht 547 A10
rd. Edithvale 546 H12
EDLINGTON
st. Hawthorn 372 D18
EDMANSON
av. Brighton 454 K7
EDMENDS
st. Brunswick 325 G12
EDMILL
ct. Belmont 706 D3
EDMOND
cr. Wandin N 340 J15
ct. Rowville 503 B5
st. Balwyn 373 D11
st. Parkdale 531 H9
st. Springvale 500 A11
EDMOND RICE
pde. Bundoora 243 C19
EDMONDS
av. Ashwood 418 A14
ct. Pascoe Vale 281 A15
st. Diamond Ck 245 G9
st. Narre Warren 539 A14
EDMONDSON
st. Lalor 241 F7
EDMONSON
pl. Geelong, off Fitzroy St 703 E10
EDMONTON
pl. Doncaster E 332 F5
EDMUND
rd. Silvan 385 C19
st. Clifton Hill 20 K3
st. Dallas 238 J9
st. Maidstone 366 H1
EDMUND RICE
pde. Watsonia N 243 D18
EDMUNDS
rd. Cockatoo 511 E10
EDNA
av. Dandenong N 501 F20
ct. Melton S 268 J6
ct. Wantirna 422 C3
gr. Coburg 326 A3
st. Frankston 626 L3
st. Heathmont 378 H17
st. Malvern East 457 A3
st. Mt Waverley 419 H20
st. Sunshine N 321 F16
st. Thomastown 241 E15
EDNA WALLING
la. Mooroolbark 381 J1
EDNEY
ct. Noble Park 501 A17
EDRINGTON PARK
dr. Berwick 554 G12
EDRO
av. Brighton East 495 B3
ct. Bundoora 284 H4
EDSALL
cl. Hampton Pk 551 E5
cl. Rowville 502 J3
st. Highett 496 H16
st. Malvern 415 K14
EDWARD
av. Altona North 409 H2
av. Dandenong 535 L4
ct. Berwick 554 L19
ct. Croydon 380 G7
ct. Ivanhoe 327 K13
ct. Taylors Hill 274 H14
gr. Mt Martha 655 C20
rd. Chirnside Pk 293 D16
rd. Chirnside Pk 337 C5
rd. Wandin East 384 L3
rd. Wandin East 385 A4
st. Anglesea 713 D7
st. Armadale 415 E9
st. Balaclava 414 G17
st. Bayswater 423 G10
st. Belgrave 466 E15
st. Brighton East 455 D13
st. Brunswick 325 F16
st. Brunswick E 325 F16
st. Bundoora 284 F2
st. Camberwell 416 L5
st. Chadstone 418 E20
st. Cheltenham 530 K2
st. Coburg 325 H5
st. Deer Park 319 A18
st. Donvale 377 C2
st. Elsternwick 455 C4
st. Essendon 323 K6
st. Fawkner 281 F8
st. Hawthorn 372 B15
st. Healesville 213 K20
st. Healesville 257 K1
st. Kew 372 H12
st. Langwarrin 628 J3
st. Macleod 285 B13
st. Mitcham 377 B13
st. Mordialloc 532 B16
st. Noble Park 534 D1
st. Northcote 326 K19
st. Oakleigh 458 A13
st. Rye 696 K2
st. Sandringham 495 E19
st. Seddon 367 A10
st. Somerville 644 K14
st. Toorak 415 B8
st. Up Fntree Gly 465 D9
st. Wattle Glen 246 G8
st. Wesburn 348 B9
EDWARDES
st. Berwick 554 G8
st. Reservoir 282 C9
EDWARD FREETH
dr. Endeavour Hl 537 J10
EDWARD HENTY
av. Doreen 201 E9
av. Yarrambat 201 E9
EDWARDS
arc. Altona 409 C19
av. Port Melb 412 D4
ct. Darley 222 A10
dr. Altona Mdw 451 F7
la. Blind Bight 650 F1
la. Werribee S 488 G12
rd. Diggers Rest 232 H8
rd. Werribee 448 C18
st. Burwood 418 B9
st. Lower Plenty 286 H15
st. Thomastown 240 L16
st. Thomastown 241 A16
EDWARDSTOWN
rd. Wesburn 348 E17
EDWIN
ct. Clarinda 498 D6
pde. Highett 496 E13
rd. Templestowe 331 D5
st. Box Hill N 374 K7
st. Fairfield 327 E14
st. Heidelberg Ht 328 E8
st. Nar Warrn S 553 G20
st. Preston 327 D6
EDWINA
ct. Croydon Hl 335 D15
EDYVEAN
st. Surrey Hills 374 D20
EDZELL
av. Toorak 415 E2
rd. Menzies Ck 468 H20
EEL RACE
rd. Carrum 573 B11
EFFIE
av. Upwey 465 L15
ct. Springvale S 499 F20
EFFINGHAM
rd. Newport 411 B8
EFFRON
ct. Frankston 600 E18
EFRON
ct. Box Hill N 375 D6
st. Dandenong N 501 J18
st. Nunawading 376 H10
EGAN
cl. Werribee 448 A6
ct. Darley 221 E2
dr. Bulleen 329 J13
pl. Richmond 26 C7
rd. Dandenong S 535 D13
st. Brighton East 455 H15
st. Carnegie 456 J5
st. Deer Park 318 J14
st. Diamond Ck 245 L12
st. Richmond 26 A7
st. Springvale 499 F16
EGANLEE
ct. Wantirna 422 B10
EGERTON
av. Cheltenham 531 C2
gr. Epping 198 G15
rd. Armadale 415 G15
st. Blairgowrie 695 K1
st. Pt Lonsdale 710 D4
wy. Delahey 275 B12
EGGINTON
st. Brunswick W 324 J10
EGGLETON
ct. Preston 283 G17
ri. Rowville 463 F18
EGLINTON
cl. Berwick 553 H14
st. Kew 371 K7
st. Moonee Pnd 323 J14
EGREMONT
st. Fitzroy N 326 C20
EGRET
cr. Cairnlea 319 G6
ct. Blind Bight 650 E8
ct. Mornington 657 B1
ct. Rosebud W 699 E4
ct. Werribee 447 K6
EGTON
ct. Craigieburn 150 E19
EIGHTH
av. Anglesea 713 E11
av. Chelsea Ht 547 E13
av. Rosebud 684 B19
av. Springvale 500 J9
av. Springvale 500 L9
av. Springvale 501 A9
bvd. Springvale 500 B13
st. Parkdale 531 F11
EILA
cl. Cheltenham 497 D20
EILDON
av. Wyndham Va 446 B6
cct. Taylors Hill 274 J14
ct. Meadow Ht 194 A19
ct. St Albans 320 C11
ct. St Kilda 414 B15
dr. Keysborough 534 C10
pde. Rowville 463 A18
rd. Ashwood 418 E14
rd. Endeavour Hl 503 E20
rd. St Kilda 414 B15
st. Doncaster 374 K4
st. Ferntree Gly 463 G1
EILEEN
av. Kalorama 382 L17
cl. N Warrandyte 289 L10
ct. Langwarrin 601 J18
ct. Werribee 447 G13
gr. Woori Yall 344 E15
rd. Clayton S 499 D13
st. Armadale 415 D10
st. Hadfield 280 H7
st. Mt Waverley 458 K10
st. Viewbank 285 F17
EINSTEIN
av. Mulgrave 500 K5
EIRENE
st. Yarraville 366 K18
EISE
ct. Brighton East 455 E20
EISEMANS
rd. Yarrambat 201 E12
rd. Yarrambat 201 E13
EISENHOWER
st. Reservoir 283 G16
EISNER
st. St Albans 276 F20
EKARI
ct. Yallambie 286 C12
EKERT
ct. Mt Martha 657 C8
ELAINE
cl. Epping 241 G5
ct. Bentleigh E 497 D2
ct. Cranbourne 603 K3
ct. Glen Waverley 460 F9
ct. Mooroolbark 336 K13
ct. Richmond 371 D13
ct. Somerville 644 E14
ct. Springvale 500 A17
pl. Rowville 503 B4
rd. Rye 696 F10
st. St Albans 320 B3
ELAMO
rd. Healesville 214 A17
ELANA
ct. Croydon N 336 A14
ct. Langwarrin 629 D7
ct. Langwarrin 629 D7
ELANDRA
ct. Seaford 600 C3
ct. Wantirna 422 F12
wy. Cranbourne W 603 E1
ELANORA
ct. Aspendale 546
ct. Mornington 641
ct. Rosebud W 683
ct. Torquay 712
wy. Hampton Pk 551
ELAROO
av. Camberwell 417
cl. St Helena 244
ct. Werribee 446
st. Chadstone 458
ELATA
dr. Tullamarine 278
pl. Endeavour Hl 502
st. Donvale 376
st. Oakleigh S 458
ELBA
cl. Rowville 463
pl. Keilor Dn 276
ELBE
cl. Werribee 447
ELBENA
gr. Carnegie 456
ELBERTA
av. Templstw Lr 330
ELCAN
av. Cranbourne W 603
EL CENTRO
Chirnside Pk 337
ELCHO
st. Newtown 702
ELDA
ct. Cranbourne N 578
ELDALE
av. Greensbrgh 286
ct. Wantirna 422
ELDAN
dr. Werribee 447
ELDENE
ct. Toorak 415
ELDER
cl. Hallam 538
cl. Meadow Ht 193
ct. Sunshine N 321
ct. Templstw Lr 330
ct. Thomastown 240
gr. Boronia 423
pde. Essendon 323
st. Blackburn 376
st. Clarinda 498
st. Clarinda 498
st. Greensbrgh 285
st. Watsonia 285
st.s, Heatherton 498
ELDERBERRY
pl. Frankston S 628
ELDERGREEN
cct. Craigieburn 193
ELDERSHAW
dr. Lynbrook 551
ELDERSLIE
tce. Newtown 702
ELDERWOOD
ct. Taylors Hill 274
ct. Taylors Hill 275
ELDINE
ct. Grovedale 705
ELDO
st. Keysborough 535
ELDON
ct. Hampton E 496
st. Broadmeadows 239
EL DORADO
ct. Noble Park N 501
ELDORADO
cr. Meadow Ht 237
ct. Frankston 628
ct. Wyndham Va 446
st. Strathmore 279
ELDRIDGE
ct. Point Cook 450
pl. Belmont 706
st. Footscray 367
ELEANOR
ct. Donvale 376
ct. Pakenham 585
gr. Kallista 468
st. Ashburton 417
st. Broadmeadows 279
st. Footscray 367
st. Jacana 237
st. Preston 326
ELEANORE
cr. Hallam 538
ELECTRA
av. Ashwood 418
ct. Forest Hill 420
st. Williamstown 411
ELECTRIC
av. Glenroy 280
pl. Melbourne 1
pl. Melbourne 23
st. Broadmeadows 237

Cremorne ... 32 D2
Cremorne ... 414 H1
EBANA
Hughesdale ... 457 G14
GAN
Hillside ... 273 J3
MHEIM
Blackburn S ... 419 L2
NYA
Frankston ... 600 H16
SBURY
Brunswick E ... 326 A13
VA
Healesville ... 213 A16
VENTH
Anglesea ... 713 C13
Y
Blackburn S ... 419 A6
Box Hill S ... 418 K6
Burwood ... 418 K6
Burwood E ... 419 A6
N
Chirnside Pk ... 337 J2
Kings Park ... 319 E2
ORD
Cairnlea ... 319 L13
AN
Rye ... 697 C3
AR
Kew East ... 372 J6
Doncaster ... 374 K1
Portsea ... 678 A4
Caroline Spr ... 274 D17
Box Hill ... 374 F20
Box Hill N ... 374 H9
Box Hill S ... 374 F20
Box Hill S ... 418 E8
Burwood ... 418 E8
Doncaster ... 374 H9
Mont Albert ... 374 F20
Mont Albert N ... 374 H9
Surrey Hills ... 418 F3
ATA
Meadow Ht ... 238 B1
Diamond Ck ... 245 F8
IN
Armadale ... 415 C12
Hillside ... 274 E6
Pk Orchards ... 334 B19
Belgrave S ... 506 H1
Pt Lonsdale ... 710 E4
. Cranbourne ... 603 E7
Carlton ... 18 D12
Hawthorn ... 371 H16
Greenvale ... 237 B3
Berwick ... 554 H8
Carlton ... 18 E12
Hawthorn ... 371 H16
Newport ... 411 B8
Pascoe Vale S ... 324 L4
OLEA
. Keilor Dn ... 275 J13
RECO
Scoresby ... 462 C8
Wheelers Hl ... 460 L14

Healesville ... 258 E4
Rowville ... 502 H1
NA
Kilsyth S ... 380 L20
Melton W ... 225 K13
Rowville ... 503 B4
Warranwood ... 334 J16
AS
. Endeavour Hl ... 537 J3
DA
Wheelers Hl ... 460 G17
DON
Point Cook ... 450 G6
MATTA
Carnegie ... 456 J13
Warneet ... 649 D14
NBANK
Grovedale ... 706 E11
NDA
Reservoir ... 283 F2
NGA
Albanvale ... 319 A4
Frankston ... 600 E17
OT
Bundoora ... 242 K20
Mooroolbark ... 337 E20
SABETH
Springvale S ... 499 L20
SDON
Seaford ... 600 A3
SSA
Cheltenham ... 497 F19
St Albans ... 275 K18
TE
S Morang ... 198 L10

ELIZA
cl. Bayswater ... 423 C5
cl. Greensbrgh ... 286 K3
cl. Warranwood ... 334 L12
cl. Williamstn N ... 410 G12
ct. Gladstone Pk ... 237 B20
ct. Hillside ... 232 H18
ct. Nunawading ... 376 G10
ct. Seaford ... 600 A4
dr. Mt Eliza ... 642 C4
pl. Somerville ... 644 F13
st. Black Rock ... 495 E20
st. Blairgowrie ... 679 E18
st. Keilor Park ... 277 K14
st. Newport ... 411 B9
st. Rosebud W ... 698 L2
st. Rosebud W ... 699 A2
tce. Mt Eliza ... 626 E11
ELIZABETH
arc. Melbourne ... 2 A14
av. Dromana ... 686 E7
av. Rosebud W ... 683 A19
av. Rosebud W ... 699 B4
av. Werribee ... 447 B14
cr. Carnegie ... 456 F8
ct. Altona Mdw ... 451 J7
ct. Dandenong ... 535 L5
ct. Donvale ... 377 H4
ct. Emerald ... 470 A20
ct. Mooroolbark ... 337 H15
ct. Narre Warren ... 539 D19
ct. Pakenham ... 585 A4
ct. Reservoir ... 283 E2
ct. Ringwood E ... 379 B5
ct. Rowville ... 462 G18
dr. Lalor ... 240 H5
dr. Rosebud ... 700 F2
dr. Sunbury ... 142 L14
gr. Bundoora ... 284 H3
gr. Torquay ... 711 G11
la. Woori Yall ... 344 B15
rd. Portsea ... 677 J5
rd. Red Hill ... 687 A19
st. Anglesea ... 713 K1
st. Bayswater ... 423 G10
st. Belmont ... 702 G20
st. Bentleigh E ... 496 G1
st. Box Hill N ... 374 K6
st. Braybrook ... 366 B3
st. Brighton East ... 455 E15
st. Brunswick ... 325 H13
st. Bulleen ... 329 G9
st. Burwood ... 418 A12
st. Coburg ... 326 A2
st. Coburg N ... 282 C17
st. Cranbourne N ... 578 B8
st. Croydon ... 380 A1
st. Diamond Ck ... 245 K10
st. Doncaster E ... 375 G3
st. Elsternwick ... 454 K4
st. Fawkner ... 281 K5
st. Ferntree Gly ... 464 F4
st. Frankston ... 627 D1
st. Geelong West ... 702 E4
st. Glen Iris ... 417 C9
st. Hawthorn ... 371 K17
st. Highton ... 701 J17
st. Kensington ... 34 B12
st. Kooyong ... 416 A10
st. Malvern ... 416 A10
st. Melbourne ... 2 B16
st. Melbourne ... 17 K17
st. Melbourne ... 23 L1
st. Melton S ... 268 J5
st. Mentone ... 530 L7
st. Mentone ... 531 A7
st. Mitcham ... 377 A14
st. Montmorency ... 286 J12
st. Moonee Pnd ... 324 D15
st. Mornington ... 640 G16
st. Mt Evelyn ... 339 B17
st. Newport ... 410 J5
st. Newport ... 410 J6
st. Northcote ... 326 E17
st. Oakleigh E ... 458 E10
st. Pt Lonsdale ... 710 G4
st. Richmond ... 26 B4
st. St Albans ... 319 J3
st. South Yarra ... 32 C15
st. South Yarra ... 414 G7
st. Westmeadows ... 237 D14
st. Yarraville ... 366 L16
st.n, Kooyong ... 416 A5
ELK
trn. Cranbourne ... 603 J5
ELKA
pl. Frankston ... 628 G1
rd. Springvale S ... 533 L4
ELKINS
ct. Wheelers Hl ... 460 G16
ELLA
cl. Newtown ... 701 L7
cr. Doncaster ... 374 F2
cr. Rosebud W ... 683 E19

ct. Hoppers Csg ... 405 A14
ct. Kurunjang ... 227 D12
ct. Lalor ... 240 L9
ct. Lalor ... 241 A9
ct. Narre Warren ... 538 L13
ct. S Morang ... 199 A10
gr. Chelsea ... 546 L15
gr. Chelsea ... 547 B12
gr. Edithvale ... 547 B12
pl. Langwarrin ... 629 L1
pl. Rowville ... 463 F19
st. Murrumbeena ... 457 D8
ELLABELLA
wy. Mornington ... 657 E3
ELLAD
cl. Vermont ... 421 F2
ELLAM
ct. Meadow Ht ... 237 J3
ELLAND
av. Box Hill ... 374 K14
ELLASWOOD
cl. Berwick ... 554 A2
ct. Hampton Pk ... 551 G5
ELLE
pl. Mt Martha ... 656 F9
ELLEMAREE
ct. Keilor East ... 322 F7
ELLEN
av. Keilor East ... 322 E6
ct. Burwood ... 419 A11
ct. Greensbrgh ... 286 G2
gr. Don Valley ... 346 D8
gr. Templestowe ... 330 J5
rd. Mooroolbark ... 337 D18
rd. Nar Warrn S ... 579 G2
st. Balwyn ... 373 F11
st. Bentleigh E ... 456 H19
st. Parkdale ... 531 J11
st. Springvale ... 499 G16
ELLENDALE
rd. Noble Park ... 500 L19
st. Balwyn N ... 373 J2
st. Hughesdale ... 457 E12
ELLENVALE
av. Pascoe Vale S ... 324 J4
dr. Narre Warren ... 539 F15
ELLERINA
rd.w, Mt Martha ... 669 A9
ELLERSLIE
ct. Bacchus Msh ... 222 B19
ct. Mill Park ... 242 K11
ct. Noble Park N ... 501 B9
pl. Toorak ... 415 A7
pl.e, Toorak ... 415 A7
st. Kingsbury ... 284 A10
ELLERTON
ct. Donvale ... 332 G16
sq. Wantirna ... 422 H14
ELLERY
ct. Cranbourne N ... 577 K9
ct. Mulgrave ... 460 C17
st. Bundoora ... 284 L1
st. Chadstone ... 458 A5
ELLESMERE
av. Croydon ... 379 L3
av. Mt Martha ... 655 F17
cr. Gladstone Pk ... 237 B17
ct. Frankston ... 628 B11
ct. Truganina ... 405 F14
pde. Rosanna ... 284 K20
rd. Burwood E ... 419 L10
rd. Windsor ... 414 K13
st. Blairgowrie ... 679 L20
st. Northcote ... 326 L16
st. Oakleigh S ... 497 H7
ELLESMORE
ct. Kew ... 371 K8
ELLESSE
wy. Berwick ... 554 G20
ELLETSON
ct. Dandenong ... 535 G3
ELLETT
ct. Grovedale ... 705 G13
ELLIMATTA
rd. Anglesea ... 714 B1
ELLIMINYA
ct. Clarinda ... 498 C7
ELLIN
st. Doncaster E ... 376 C4
ELLINDALE
av. McKinnon ... 456 D16
cl. Hampton Pk ... 552 B10
ELLINGBANK
cr. Mornington ... 657 C2
ELLINGSWORTH
st. Brunswick ... 325 H14
ELLINGTON
st. Caulfield S ... 455 F8
ELLINGWORTH
pde. Box Hill ... 374 L16
ELLIOT
cl. Donvale ... 377 D2
ct. Greenvale ... 237 A6

ct. Pt Lonsdale ... 707 H19
dr. Braeside ... 532 L15
la. Melbourne ... 1 A7
pl. Ringwood ... 378 A16
st. Fitzroy ... 19 E13
st. Kings Park ... 319 E3
st. Knoxfield ... 462 K3
st. Mordialloc ... 531 L14
st. Parkdale ... 531 K14
st. Reservoir ... 282 G5
ELLIOTT
av. Balwyn ... 373 C10
av. Broadmeadows ... 238 E20
av. Carnegie ... 456 K8
av. Highton ... 705 J3
av. Parkville ... 34 K5
cl. Epping ... 197 J19
cr. Dingley Vill ... 533 D9
ct. Burnside ... 318 H11
ct. Hoppers Csg ... 448 F1
ct. Whittington ... 704 C18
la. Melbourne ... 23 G7
pde. Lynbrook ... 551 F20
rd. Dandenong S ... 549 J5
rd. Upwey ... 466 A6
st. Ascot Vale ... 323 J20
st. Ashwood ... 417 L19
st. Boronia ... 424 E13
st. Cheltenham ... 531 C3
st. Coburg N ... 281 F16
st. Heidelberg Ht ... 328 E3
st. Seaford ... 599 H9
ELLIS
av. Sassafras ... 426 E16
cl. Point Cook ... 451 B10
ct. Braybrook ... 366 B2
ct. Grovedale ... 705 J16
ct. Mooroolbark ... 337 J19
la. Dandenong ... 535 H7
la. Diamond Ck ... 246 F11
rd. Glen Iris ... 416 E14
rd. Yarra Glen ... 208 L16
rd. Yarra Glen ... 209 A16
st. Dandenong S ... 535 L13
st. Frankston ... 600 A20
st. Richmond ... 26 D8
st. South Yarra ... 32 D13
ELLISON
st. Blackburn ... 376 C13
st. Malvern East ... 417 A19
st. Preston ... 283 B17
st. Ringwood ... 378 D14
ELLISYUM
pl. Frankston S ... 627 G18
ELLSA
cl. Keysborough ... 534 J14
st. Balwyn N ... 373 L5
ELLT
cr. Noble Park ... 500 G14
ELLWOOD
dr. Pearcedale ... 646 J3
ELM
av. Elsternwick ... 454 L8
av. Elsternwick ... 455 A8
cr. Eltham North ... 287 D5
cr. Emerald ... 469 H14
cr. Ivanhoe East ... 328 H13
ct. Altona North ... 410 D6
ct. Coolaroo ... 238 E3
ct. Frankston N ... 599 J10
ct. Mt Eliza ... 626 C9
ct. Nar Warrn S ... 553 C20
ct. Ringwood N ... 378 C5
ct. Rosebud ... 700 G1
ct. Scoresby ... 462 F6
ct. Templestowe ... 331 L14
ct. Waurn Ponds ... 705 E16
ct. Wyndham Va ... 446 E9
ct. Dandenong, off
David St ... 536 E4
gr. Armadale ... 415 E10
gr. Balaclava ... 454 J1
gr. Brighton ... 454 K12
gr. Brunswick E ... 326 A15
gr. Coburg ... 325 H1
gr. Essendon N ... 279 F20
gr. Kew East ... 372 D2
gr. Langwarrin ... 628 K1
gr. McKinnon ... 456 B16
gr. Mooroolbark ... 337 C8
gr. Mt Waverley ... 419 H17
gr. Parkdale ... 531 G13
gr. Richmond ... 26 G16
gr. Springvale ... 500 A14
pl. N Melbourne ... 17 A17
pl. Windsor ... 414 H13
rd. Glen Iris ... 416 J11
st. Airport W ... 278 K17
st. Bayswater ... 423 E6
st. Blackburn ... 376 B13
st. Elsternwick ... 454 K2
st. Flemington ... 33 J1
st. Hawthorn ... 371 E13
st. Northcote ... 326 E13

st. N Melbourne ... 17 A18
st. N Melbourne ... 34 L18
st. Preston ... 283 J18
st. St Albans ... 320 F9
st. Surrey Hills ... 418 D2
st. Thomastown ... 241 G12
ELMA
dr. Cheltenham ... 497 D14
rd. Cheltenham ... 497 D14
st. Keilor Park ... 278 C15
ELMAN
rd. Cheltenham ... 530 K2
ELMAR
ct. Campbellfield ... 239 H11
ELMBANK
dr. Keysborough ... 534 J9
ELMDON
dr. Scoresby ... 462 C11
ELMES
ct. Hoppers Csg ... 448 E1
ELM GROVE
ct. Torquay ... 712 B3
ELMHURST
ct. Melton S ... 268 F14
rd. Bayswater N ... 423 G1
rd. Blackburn ... 375 F13
rd. Caulfield N ... 415 G20
rd. Gladstone Pk ... 278 L1
rd. Gladstone Pk ... 279 A1
st. Noble Park N ... 501 E18
ELMIE
st. Hawthorn ... 372 C19
tce. Mt Martha ... 655 G16
ELMO
rd. Montmorency ... 287 A7
ELMORE
av. Croydon ... 336 D18
ct. Endeavour Hl ... 537 F3
ct. Ferntree Gly ... 463 H9
wk. Blackburn ... 375 G15
ELM PARK
dr. Hoppers Csg ... 449 G1
ELMS
ct. Dandenong N ... 502 C16
ct. Gowanbrae ... 279 B6
rd. Bangholme ... 575 C2
rd. Mooroolbark ... 337 G18
rd. Wandin East ... 384 H4
ELMSFORD
ct. Highton ... 705 G9
ct. Keysborough ... 534 E14
ELMSTEAD
ct. Ferntree Gly ... 423 L19
dr. Wheelers Hl ... 461 G15
ELMSTED
ct. Cairnlea ... 319 K12
ELM TREE
cl. Taylors Hill ... 274 H12
dr. Dingley Vill ... 532 J7
pl. Carlton ... 18 F20
ELMTREE
pl. Chadstone ... 458 E3
rd. Doncaster ... 375 B3
tce. Chadstone ... 458 E3
ELMWOOD
cr. Glen Waverley ... 460 A9
pl. Craigieburn ... 193 L3
pl. Cranbourne W ... 603 J2
ri. Eltham North ... 245 G19
ELNA
ct. Moorabbin ... 496 J11
EL NIDO
gr. Carnegie ... 456 E7
ELOERA
st. Upwey ... 465 H17
ELONARA
ct. Wheelers Hl ... 460 K8
rd. Vermont S ... 420 G9
ELONERA
av. Greensbrgh ... 286 B11
av. Yallambie ... 286 C11
rd. Noble Park N ... 501 C17
ELORA
ct. St Albans ... 320 C12
rd. Oakleigh S ... 497 J3
ELOUERA
cl. Eltham ... 288 D5
ELOURA
av. Brighton East ... 455 G17
ELPARA
pl. Skye ... 601 D7
wy. Hampton Pk ... 551 K16
ELPHIN
gr. Canterbury ... 417 D1
gr. Hawthorn ... 372 C15
st. Ivanhoe ... 328 B17
st. Newport ... 411 A7
ELPHINSTONE
bvd. Greenvale ... 236 K1
ct. Kew ... 371 H10
st. W Footscray ... 366 G6
wy. Caroline Spr ... 318 D10

ELPIS
ct. Oak Park...279 G10
ELRAY
av. Dandenong...535 E3
ct. Tullamarine...278 L3
EL RENO
cr. Airport W...278 K16
ELRONA
ct. Pakenham...585 A3
ELSA
ct. Eltham...287 H6
pl. Narre Warren...539 E18
st. Fawkner...281 K5
st. Templestowe...330 L8
ELSAN LEA
ct. Langwarrin...629 D2
ELSEY
rd. Reservoir...283 B5
ELSIE
av. Seaford...599 D5
gr. Chelsea...546 J15
gr. Edithvale...546 J15
gr. Healesville...258 A5
gr. Mt Evelyn...339 A19
mw. Brunswick E, off Elesbury Av...326 A13
st. Boronia...424 D10
st. Greensbrgh...286 A8
st. Wandin East...340 L20
st. Wandin East...341 A20
ELSTAR
dr. Carrum Downs...575 E16
rd. Narre Warren...538 H15
ELSTER
av. Elsternwick...455 B10
av. Gardenvale...455 B10
ELSTERNWICK
pl. Elsternwick...454 L5
ELSTONE
av. Airport W...279 A18
ELSTREE
ct. Kealba...276 K19
ELSUM
av. Bayswater N...380 A16
av. Deer Park...319 C8
ELSVERN
av. Belmont...702 A18
ELSWILL
st. Bentleigh E...497 A5
ELSWORTHY
ct. Endeavour Hl...502 L20
ct. Endeavour Hl...503 A20
ELTHAM
st. Dallas...238 D12
st. Flemington...33 K1
ELTHAM-YARRA GLEN
rd. Christmas Hills...205 K20
rd. Christmas Hills...249 C8
rd. Eltham...287 H5
rd. Eltham North...287 H6
rd. Kangaroo Grnd...247 J20
rd. Kangaroo Grnd...289 C2
rd. Lower Plenty...286 G13
rd. Montmorency...287 A15
rd. Panton Hill...248 D17
rd. Research...289 C2
rd. Smiths Gly...248 D17
rd. Watsons Ck...249 C8
rd. Yarra Glen...208 C18
ELTON
cl. Watsonia N...243 G19
rd. Ferntree Gly...463 H6
ELVA
ct. Braybrook...366 B3
ct. Mitcham...377 C10
ELVARA
ct. Mulgrave...460 F19
ELVIAN
rd. Woori Yall...344 A17
ELVIE
st. Doncaster E...376 D2
st. Rye...697 C5
ELVIN
cl. Gladstone Pk...237 C20
st. Macleod...285 F10
ELWERS
rd. Rosebud...684 G18
st. Watsonia N...285 F2
ELWICK
ct. Noble Park N...501 C7
ELWOOD
av. Sunshine N...321 F10
st. Brighton...454 G12
st. Notting Hill...459 H12
st. Surrey Hills...418 C2
ELWYN
st. Bentleigh E...456 J16
ELY
ct. Dingley Vill...533 B7
ct. Keilor East...277 K16
st. Eltham...287 C13
ELYSEE
av. S Morang...198 J11
ct. Noble Park N...501 E9
ct. Strathmr Ht...279 D9
ELYSIUM
cr. Oakleigh E...458 G11
ELYSTAN
rd. Altona Mdw...451 E6
EMANUEL
dr. Seaford...599 J1
EMARY
ct. Yarra Glen...208 L17
EMBANK
ct. Kealba...276 J17
EMBANKMENT
gr. Chelsea...546 K17
EMBERSON
st. Kallista...467 B2
EMBLEY
gld. Endeavour Hl...537 H6
EMBLING
rd. Malvern...415 K10
EMBREY
ct. Pakenham...585 E11
EMDEN
cr. Mulgrave...500 E2
ct. St Albans...320 H6
EMERALD
cct. Craigieburn...150 G14
cl. Emerald...469 G20
cl. Mornington...656 L2
ct. Belmont...706 J1
ct. Boronia...424 K11
ct. Caroline Spr...318 E9
ct. Hampton Pk...551 C10
ct. Langwarrin...629 G5
ct. Narre Warren...539 D14
dr. Springvale...499 H16
pl. Geelong, off Corio St...703 B7
st. Collingwood...19 J15
st. Dallas...238 E8
st. Essendon W...323 A7
st. Geelong West...702 J7
st. Mt Waverley...419 C14
st. Oakleigh S...497 J8
st. Preston...327 D2
st. Ringwood...378 G15
st. S Melbourne...29 H6
st. S Melbourne...413 D3
tce. Werribee...447 F3
wk. Bundoora...284 G8
wy. S Melbourne...30 C3
EMERALD CREEK
rd. Monbulk...428 F13
EMERALD HILL
pl. S Melbourne...30 A4
EMERALD LAKE
rd. Emerald...509 H2
EMERALD-MONBULK
rd. Emerald...469 G19
rd. Kallista...469 A7
rd. Monbulk...428 C20
rd. Monbulk...468 E1
rd. Monbulk...469 A7
EMERSON
cl. Frankston...600 F18
ct. Berwick...553 J3
ct. Roxburgh Pk...194 C11
pl. Rowville...503 C3
st. Glen Waverley...460 B8
EMERY
ct. Altona...408 L16
ct. Altona Mdw...451 D3
dr. Dingley Vill...533 F10
la. Montrose...382 B6
st. Port Melb...412 E4
st. Preston...326 J2
EMIL
ct. Melton...226 J18
EMILTON
av. St Kilda...414 C15
EMILY
cl. Pakenham...559 E19
cr. Point Cook...449 L4
ct. Burwood E...419 H7
ct. Clarinda...498 C11
ct. Coldstream...295 F15
ct. Cranbourne W...577 F14
ct. Croydon...336 A20
ct. Mulgrave...500 F4
ct. Springvale S...499 L20
dr. Hallam...538 E16
dr. Hallam...538 F15
dr. Narre Warren...538 F14
dr. Narre Warren...538 F17
pl. Aspendale Gdn...546 K2
pl. Mill Park...243 D5
st. Beaumaris...530 B10
st. Brighton...454 J17
st. Carnegie...456 L8
st. Pt Lonsdale...710 C1
st. St Albans...319 K4
EMMA
av. Reservoir...282 E9
ct. Berwick...553 F3
ct. Coburg N...281 H12
ct. Ferntree Gly...463 F7
ct. Hampton Pk...552 D13
ct. Mt Waverley...458 H9
ct. Taylors L...275 E6
ct. Thomastown...240 E16
ct. Woori Yall...344 G15
pl. Dingley Vill...532 L3
rd. Croydon...380 E1
st. Carrum...573 D9
st. Caulfield S...456 A8
st. Collingwood...19 H11
st. Fawkner...281 K5
st. Seddon...367 B10
EMMALINE
st. Northcote...326 E11
EMMAUS
ct. Rye...697 B14
EMMERSON
ct. Mill Park...242 H4
la. Croydon...380 G5
st. Keysborough...534 D7
EMMERTON
pl. South Yarra...31 G5
EMMS
st. Bundoora...284 E1
EMMY
ct. Burwood...418 C5
ct. Grovedale...705 K13
EMO
ct. Clarinda...498 F11
rd. Malvern East...456 G3
EMORA
ct. Frankston...628 A3
st. Croydon...380 E8
EMOU
cl. Cranbourne...578 G17
EMPEROR
pl. Rowville...464 B13
rd. Berwick...580 A1
EMPERY
ct. Donvale...332 K18
EMPIRE
av. Jan Juc...711 D17
ct. Torquay...712 A3
dr. Hoppers Csg...405 A12
st. Footscray...367 C4
st. Mornington...640 E14
st. Preston...283 D19
wy. Hallam...551 K1
EMPRESS
av. Kingsville...366 K13
ct. Sunshine W...363 L5
rd. St Kilda E...414 K18
rd. Surrey Hills...373 J15
wy. Melton W...226 B18
EMSLIE
st. Sunshine W...364 F9
EMU
av. Altona...408 G19
ct. Badger Creek...258 G12
ct. Dandenong N...501 H15
ct. Melton...226 H15
gr. Frankston...599 A18
pde. Jacana...237 H18
rd. Maidstone...322 H19
rd. Mt Eliza...625 J17
EMVILLE
ct. Cheltenham...497 G19
ENA
rd. Belgrave...466 G13
st. St Albans...320 A5
ENBROOK
ct. Grovedale...706 D9
ENCORE
av. Somerton...195 A14
ENDEAVOUR
av. Thomastown...240 F15
cr. Endeavour Hl...537 D3
cr. Westmeadows...237 E14
ct. Bundoora...284 K6
ct. Keilor Ldg...276 A3
dr. Chelsea Ht...547 D13
dr. Cranbourne N...577 H8
dr. Maribyrnong...322 J15
dr. Torquay...712 D3
dr. Williamstn N...410 F12
la. Williamstown, off Osborne St...411 D17
pl. Melton W...225 J20
pl. Wantirna S...462 B1
st. Mitcham...377 D9
wy. Braeside...532 K16
wy. Wyndham Va...446 C15
ENDERBY
ct. Boronia...424 G14
ct. Braybrook...365 K6
ENDERLY
av. Reservoir...283 D2
ENDSLEIGH
av. Bundoora...284 H3
ENEA
pl. Hoppers Csg...448 J1
ENFIELD
av. Pk Orchards...333 G20
av. Pk Orchards...377 G1
av. Preston...327 E1
av. Werribee...446 K10
cl. Endeavour Hl...537 J8
ct. Wheelers Hl...461 B7
dr. Bayswater...423 E9
pl. Craigieburn...150 C19
pl. Forest Hill...420 E3
rd. Brighton...455 A13
st. Albanvale...318 L7
st. Eltham...287 L8
st. St Kilda...414 B15
ENGELKE
rd. Belgrave S...506 G14
rd. Belgrave S...506 H8
rd. Nar Warrn E...506 G14
ENGINEERING
rd. Clayton...459 C15
ENGLAND
rd. Diamond Ck...201 K12
rd. Glen Waverley...459 H8
rd. Yarrambat...201 K12
st. Bentleigh E...496 J2
st. Bulleen...329 G9
st. Dandenong S...550 C8
st. Geelong, off Eastern Beach...703 D7
wk. Nar Warrn S...552 H20
ENGLEFIELD
ct. Werribee...446 J18
ENGLEWOOD
ct. Belmont...706 G4
ct. Hillside...231 L18
pl. Eltham...288 F2
ENGLISH
av. Scoresby...462 F8
ct. Kings Park...274 L17
st. Airport W...279 C15
st. Seville...341 L11
ENID
ct. Heatherton...497 H15
ct. Hillside...274 G7
ENMORE
cl. Berwick, off Milparinka Wy...554 F11
ct. Chelsea Ht...547 E12
ENNERSDALE
ct. Templestowe...331 L7
ENNGONIA
cr. Clayton S...498 G9
ENNISMORE
cr. Pk Orchards...333 K19
dr. Keysborough...534 A8
ENNISS
av. Bentleigh E...497 A4
ENOCH
ri. Hallam...538 B20
ENRICA
pl. Wheelers Hl...460 K16
ENRIGHT
st. Highett...496 H16
ENROB
ct. Grovedale...706 E13
ENSAY
ct. Endeavour Hl...537 E1
ct. Vermont S...420 K12
ENSBY
st. E Geelong...703 H15
st. Thomson...703 H15
ENSIGN
cl. Wantirna...422 G9
gr. Taylors L...275 J9
st. Maribyrnong...323 F13
ENTALLY
dr. Albanvale...318 L3
dr. Albanvale...319 A3
dr. Wheelers Hl...460 H11
ENTERPRISE
av. Berwick...554 B10
av. Hampton Pk...551 J9
av. Port Melb...412 B5
ct. Mulgrave...460 C20
pl. Thomastown...241 L18
wy. Bayswater N...380 A17
wy. Mitcham...377 B13
ENTERPRIZE
av. Chelsea Ht...547 D10
rd. W Melbourne...368 F13
ENTRANCE
rd. Seaford...573 C19
EOTHEN
la. Kilsyth...381 D6
EPACRIS
ct. Langwarrin...629 K3
ct. Ringwood...379 B2
pl. Keysborough...534 A14
EPALOCK
cr. St Albans...320
EPHCRIS
ct. Endeavour Hl...502
EPPALOCK
cct. Caroline Spr...318
ct. Noble Park N...501
dr. Wyndham Va...446
EPPING
rd. Epping...197
rd. Lalor...241
rd. Thomastown...241
rd. Wollert...197
rd. Woodstock...153
st. Hadfield...281
st. Malvern East...416
EPSOM
av. Epping...198
cl. Bacchus Msh...221
ct. Craigieburn...150
ct. Donvale...376
ct. Fawkner...281
ct. Noble Park N...501
pl. Caroline Spr...317
rd. Ascot Vale...323
rd. Flemington...33
rd. Flemington...323
rd. Flemington...368
rd. Kensington...33
rd. Mordialloc...531
st. Caulfield E...456
st. Laverton...407
st.s, Altona Mdw...407
EPSTEIN
st. Reservoir...282
EPWORTH
ct. Glen Waverley...420
EQUITABLE
pl. Melbourne...2
pl. Melbourne...24
ERA
ct. Donvale...332
ERAM
rd. Box Hill N...375
ERAMOSA
rd.e, Somerville...645
rd.w, Moorooduc...642
rd.w, Moorooduc...643
rd.w, Somerville...644
ERAMU
pl. Kurunjang...227
ERANG
cl. Greensbrgh...244
ct. Mooroolbark...337
dr. Mt Eliza...626
ERASMUS
st. Surrey Hills...374
ERAWAN
av. Notting Hill...459
ERCILDOUNE
av. Hawthorn...416
st. Caulfield N...415
EREBUS
st. Keilor Park...278
ERIC
av. Mordialloc...531
av. Templstw Lr...329
cr. Mornington...656
ct. Langwarrin...629
ct. Oakleigh S...458
ct. Pearcedale...646
ct. Wheelers Hl...460
st. Belgrave...466
st. Brighton East...455
st. Croydon...336
st. Essendon...324
st. Hawthorn...371
st. Preston...282
ERICA
av. Boronia...424
av. Glen Iris...416
av. St Albans...320
cl. Endeavour Hl...537
cr. Heathmont...378
cr. Kilsyth...381
ct. Bellfield...328
ct. Blackburn N...375
ct. Bundoora...285
ct. Heathmont...378
ct. Hoppers Csg...405
ct. Lalor...240
ct. Langwarrin...629
ct. Mt Martha...656
st. Canterbury...373
st. Dandenong N...501
st. Frankston...627
st. Mt Waverley...458
st. Pascoe Vale...280
st. Springvale...499
st. Windsor...414
ERICKSEN
st. Springvale...499

RIC McDONALD
i. Nar Warrn S...552 J13
RIDEN
l. Glen Waverley...420 G15
RIE
v. Rowville...462 K15
v. Rowville...463 A16
RIKSSON
y. *Nunawading, off Walkers Rd...376 H15*
RILYN
t. Vermont...377 F20
t. Vermont...421 F1
RIN
t. Coolaroo...238 F7
t. Doncaster...331 A18
t. Frankston...627 C4
t. Hampton Pk...552 B13
l. Keysborough...534 C7
l. Wantirna...422 A12
t. Hillside...274 G6
t. Preston...326 F4
t. Richmond...26 A9
RINBANK
r. Attwood...237 D11
r. Westmeadows...237 G12
RINDALE
v. Deer Park...319 B10
v. Ripponlea...454 H2
t. Grovedale...706 G14
nw. Point Cook...450 G7
l. Craigieburn...193 J3
l. Murrumbeena...457 C9
RINKA
r. Patterson L...573 K8
RINNE
t. St Helena...245 D15
RITH
. Kalorama...383 A12
RLANDSEN
v. Sorrento...679 B12
RLDUNDA
t. Lilydale...337 L2
RLI
t. Blackburn...375 L13
RMINGTON
l. Kew...372 B10
RNE
t. Balwyn...374 B11
RNEST
l. Melton W...225 K20
r. Nar Warrn S...552 F18
r. Nar Warrn S...552 G18
r. Portsea...678 B5
d. Croydon...336 D19
d. Kalorama...383 A17
t. Bayswater...423 B5
t. Blackburn...375 F12
t. Broadmeadows...238 D20
t. Mt Martha...655 L13
t. Sunshine...321 G20
t. Sunshine...365 G1
RNEST JONES
r. Macleod...284 H11
RNST
t. Doncaster...330 E16
RNST WANKE
d. Berwick...539 E13
d. Narre Warren...538 H12
d. Narre Warren...539 E13
d. Nar Warrn N...538 H12
d. Nar Warrn N...539 A12
ROWAL
t. Beaumaris...530 B3
RRINGTON
d. St Albans...320 H4
RROL
v. Brunswick...325 J12
t. Aspendale Gdn...547 A5
t. Greensbrgh...286 D8
l. N Melbourne...17 C19
t. Braybrook...321 L18
t. Footscray...367 B9
t. N Melbourne...17 C18
t. Prahran...32 L18
t. Prahran...414 L9
t. Prahran...415 A9
RSKINE
v. Cheltenham...496 E19
v. Reservoir...283 F13
r. Wheelers Hl...461 C15
t. Greenvale...237 A1
r. Rowville...463 B13
. N Melbourne...17 A10
l. N Melbourne...34 K10
d. Emerald...510 D11
d. Macleod...285 B15
dg. Mooroolbark...337 A11
t. Albert Park...29 K16
t. Armadale...415 G10
t. Frankston...599 D17
t. Middle Park...29 K16
t. N Melbourne...34 J10

st. Nunawading...376 J17
wy. Sydenham...274 H1
ERSWELL
ct. Montmorency...287 B10
ERUTTA
pl. Frankston S...627 H12
ERVAL
av. Preston...327 B3
ERVIN
rd. Kilsyth...380 L6
rd. Mooroolbark...380 L6
ERVINE
cl. Sunbury...143 F5
ERWIN
dr. Seaford...599 F3
ESCABON
gr. Frankston...600 H19
ESCARPMENT
dr. Frankston S...627 L17
ESCOTT
gr. Berwick...554 C15
ESDALE
st. Blackburn...376 B12
st. Nunawading...376 F12
ESHER
ri. Mt Martha...669 J3
ESK
ct. Dandenong...536 F6
ct. Forest Hill...376 E19
ESKAY
rd. Epping...198 A15
rd. Oakleigh S...497 L3
ESKDALE
ct. Eltham North...245 C19
ct. Mornington...657 B4
ct. Narre Warren...539 A15
dr. Croydon Hl...335 H12
rd. Caulfield N...455 H1
ESKHOLME
ri. St Helena...245 B20
ESLA
dr. Roxburgh Pk...194 D7
ESMALE
st. Strathmore...279 L16
ESME
ct. Mt Eliza...642 G1
ESMOND
st. Ardeer...320 A19
st. Preston...282 F18
ESPER
av. Oakleigh S...497 H4
ESPERANCE
av. Brighton...454 G17
ct. Mt Martha...656 L6
rd. Mt Waverley...419 G14
ESPERANTO
ct. Glenroy...280 C9
ESPLANADE
Altona...409 A20
Altona...452 L1
Brighton...454 F18
Brighton...494 G5
Frankston...626 L1
Mitcham...377 C13
Mornington...640 B19
Mornington...640 C13
Mt Martha...655 L11
Mt Martha...656 B6
Mt Martha...668 K4
Mt Martha...668 K9
Mt Martha...669 A2
Queenscliff...708 J19
Seaholme...409 G20
Sorrento...678 K8
Williamstown...411 D18
av. Brighton...494 G4
la. *Edithvale, off The Esplanade...546 G13*
pl. Port Melb...29 A8
w. Port Melb...412 L5
ESPLANADE EAST
Port Melb...29 A10
Port Melb...412 L7
Port Melb...413 A5
Port Melb...413 A6
ESPLANADE WEST
Port Melb...412 K7
Port Melb...413 A5
Port Melb...413 A6
ESSEX
cl. Avondale Ht...322 G10
ct. Bayswater...423 G9
ct. Cranbourne E...578 H18
ct. Epping...197 K16
ct. Heidelberg...329 F3
ct. Somerville...644 H16
ct. Tarneit...405 C12
ct. Templstw Lr...330 G11
dr. Melton...226 L17
pl. Carlton...18 C20
rd. Mt Martha...656 A20
rd. Mt Waverley...418 G14
rd. Surrey Hills...373 K20

rd. Surrey Hills...417 K2
st. Blackburn N...376 B10
st. Box Hill N...375 D9
st. Briar Hill...286 H5
st. Brunswick...325 H16
st. Dandenong N...502 E13
st. Footscray...366 L6
st. Glen Iris...416 J14
st. Moolap...704 J16
st. Pascoe Vale...280 G15
st. Prahran...32 E18
st. Prahran...414 H9
st. Sandringham...494 L13
st. Sandringham...495 A13
st. Sunshine N...321 G18
st. W Footscray...366 D5
ESSEX PARK
dr. Endeavour Hl...536 K1
ESSINGTON
ct. Mulgrave...460 C18
st. Grovedale...706 G10
ESSUE
ct. Mill Park...242 C2
ESTA
ct. Doncaster...374 H4
st. Blackburn N...375 F7
st. Melton...268 F1
ESTATE
rd. Don Valley...346 B6
ESTEEMED
ct. Tootgarook...698 C9
ESTELLA
ct. Narre Warren...539 F15
st. Glen Iris...416 L15
ESTELLE
ct. Altona North...409 H2
ct. Noble Park N...501 C13
st. Bulleen...329 J17
st. Oakleigh...458 C8
st. Sunshine W...364 F3
ESTER
cl. Endeavour Hl...537 H6
cr. Clayton S...498 F7
dr. Mill Park...242 A3
st. Greensbrgh...285 L5
ESTHER
cr. Mooroolbark...336 J14
ct. Boronia...424 C17
ct. Fawkner...281 H10
ct. Mt Waverley...458 F4
ct. Noble Park...500 F19
ct. Seabrook...450 J4
ct. Preston...326 J4
st. Templstw Lr...330 B11
ETHEL
av. Lalor...241 F9
ct. Pt Lonsdale...707 H19
ct. Springvale...499 H17
gr. Reservoir...283 C15
st. Bentleigh...496 B4
st. Boronia...424 F14
st. Brunswick E...325 L15
st. Greensbrgh...286 B7
st. Malvern...416 A8
st. Oak Park...279 L14
st. Sunshine...364 J2
st. Thornbury...326 J7
ETKA
av. Keilor East...278 F20
ETNA
cl. Keilor Ldg...276 A4
ct. Coolaroo...238 C7
st. Glen Huntly...456 C7
ETNAM
st. Preston...326 E4
ETON
cl. Sunbury...144 D10
ct. Balwyn...373 J9
ct. Dandenong...536 G5
ct. Frankston...627 D5
ct. Gladstone Pk...237 B19
ct. Heathmont...378 G18
ct. Heidelberg...329 F4
ct. Hoppers Csg...405 A14
pl. Portsea...677 L2
pl. Springvale S...499 H19
rd. Belmont...702 C20
sq. Wantirna...422 H9
st. Mt Waverley...419 C13
st. Preston...327 E2
ETTRICK
pl. Berwick...554 F16
ETZEL
st. Airport W...278 G13
EUCALYPT
av. Springvale...500 K11
av. Templstw Lr...330 K13
ct. Altona Mdw...407 L20
ct. Langwarrin...601 L16
dr. Lilydale...338 B14
dr. Mill Park...243 B6

EUCALYPTUS
ct. Sunshine W...364 C8
pl. Meadow Ht...194 A17
rd. Eltham...288 B12
st. Richmond...26 F11
wk. Carrum Downs...575 D18
EUCRA
st. Hadfield...280 K5
EUCUMBENE
dr. Berwick...580 A3
EUGENE
st. Viewbank...286 A16
tce. Ringwood...378 A17
EUGENIA
ct. Boronia...424 K7
st. Doveton...536 K11
st. Nunawading...376 J19
st. Rye...696 H8
EULA
ct. Chadstone...458 F2
ct. Frankston...628 H1
EULINGA
av. Aspendale...546 B3
rd. Clarinda...498 D5
EUMARELLA
st. Tullamarine...278 H7
EUMEMMERRING
dr. Eumemmerring...537 B12
EUMERALLA
av. Templestowe...330 L11
av. Templstw Lr...330 L11
ct. Frankston S...626 L13
gr. Mt Eliza...642 F8
rd. Caulfield S...455 L11
EUMONG
ct. Mornington...641 C14
EUNEVA
av. Glen Waverley...460 C1
EUNICE
ct. Kilsyth S...381 A19
ct. Pascoe Vale S...280 J19
dr. Cheltenham...531 F1
EUNSON
av. Northcote...326 E16
EURABBIE
ct. Eltham...288 A6
EURAH
pl. Eltham...288 C6
EUREKA
cr. Nar Warrn S...552 F7
ct. Bangholme...549 J13
ct. Kings Park...275 C17
rd. Diggers Rest...187 A10
st. Geelong West...702 E6
st. Richmond...26 H4
st. Rye...698 A6
EURELLA
cr. Rowville...502 E8
EUROA
av. Berwick...539 J20
av. Sunshine N...321 B13
wk. Kurunjang...226 J15
EUROKA
ct. Grovedale...705 K16
st. Chadstone...458 C1
EUROLIE
st. Balwyn N...373 E6
EUROPA
ct. Wheelers Hl...460 J17
EURORA
ct. Taylors L...276 A8
EURYTHMIC
st. Mordialloc...531 K16
EUSTACE
st. Blackburn...375 K19
EUSTON
av. Pk Orchards...334 B18
ct. Berwick...553 K14
pl. Springvale S...499 J19
pl. *Wyndham Va, off Mayfair St...446 F9*
rd. Hughesdale...457 F8
st. Malvern...416 B12
EVA
cr. Box Hill N...374 K8
ct. Croydon...335 L20
ct. Donvale...332 G20
ct. Fawkner...239 E20
ct. Hallam...537 J14
ct. Kilsyth...381 C11
ct. Mulgrave...500 E5
ct. Seabrook...450 J3
pl. Epping...241 L1
st. Clayton...498 G3
st. Malvern...416 A12
st. Parkdale...531 K14
st. Research...288 J5
st. Rye...697 C4
st. Sunshine W...364 D4

EVA BUHERT
cl. *Brunswick, off Albert St...325 G14*
EVAN
ct. Keilor...276 L10
ct. Keilor...277 A10
st. Berwick...554 C9
st. Box Hill N...375 D13
st. Parkdale...531 H10
EVANDALE
av. Nunawading...376 F11
rd. Malvern...415 J16
EVANS
av. Hampton E...496 B10
cl. Burnside...318 F10
cr. Laverton...407 E14
cr. Northcote...326 J19
cr. Reservoir...283 E9
ct. Broadmeadows...238 D20
ct. Darley...222 B10
ct. Toorak...415 H6
ct. Vermont...421 G2
gr. Wandin N...340 D14
la. Melbourne...24 G2
pl. Hawthorn E...372 H20
rd. Cockatoo...472 A19
rd. Cranbourne W...603 E2
rd. Kew...372 G13
rd. Lynbrook...577 F11
rd. Lyndhurst...577 F11
st. Anglesea...713 L4
st. Belmont...706 H1
st. Braybrook...322 C19
st. Brunswick...325 G14
st. Burwood...418 B9
st. Burwood...418 C11
st. Chadstone...458 A3
st. Fairfield...327 G16
st. Lalor...241 F9
st. Moonee Pnd...324 G11
st. Pearcedale...646 L3
st. Pearcedale...647 A3
st. Port Melb...29 A3
st. Port Melb...412 J4
st. Port Melb...413 A2
st. Rye...696 J10
st. Safety Bch...669 B13
st. Scoresby...462 G6
st. Sunbury...143 G13
st. Tooradin...651 G7
wy. Werribee...448 F17
EVANSDALE
rd. Hawthorn...371 G17
EVATT
ct. Mill Park...243 A4
EVE
cl. Nar Warrn S...553 A17
ct. Craigieburn...150 H17
ct. Dandenong N...502 A15
ct. Forest Hill...420 C3
ct. Ringwood...378 H6
ct. Springvale...500 F6
EVELINA
rd. Toorak...32 L15
rd. Toorak...414 L8
rd. Toorak...415 A8
st. Balwyn...374 C9
st. Mont Albert N...374 C9
EVELINE
av. Maribyrnong...367 C2
av. Parkdale...531 G13
rd. Selby...467 D16
st. Brunswick...325 G15
st. Selby...467 D15
EVELL
st. Glenroy...280 H2
EVELYN
cl. Melton W...225 L17
cr. Sunshine W...364 D3
ct. Dingley Vill...533 C1
ct. Hampton Pk...551 E11
ct. Narre Warren...538 L17
gr. Healesville...214 A17
pl. E Melbourne...24 K2
rd. Ringwood N...378 C5
rd. Ringwood N...378 C8
st. Bentleigh...456 F19
st. Clayton...459 C20
st. Frankston...599 B17
st. Glen Waverley...460 E2
st. Manifold Ht...702 C1
st. Pascoe Vale...280 L18
st. Preston...282 E20
st. Rye...696 F1
st. St Kilda E...414 H16
wy. St Helena...245 A20
EVELYNE
av. Cranbourne...577 L17
EVENING
cl. Point Cook...451 A8
EVERAGE
st. Moonee Pnd...324 C13
EVERAISE
ct. Laverton N...407 H7

EVERARD
dr. Warrandyte 289 E19
gr. Woori Yall 344 J14
pl. Hoppers Csg 449 B2
rd. Ringwood E 379 A7
st. Diamond Ck 246 C11
st. Footscray 367 A7
st. Glenroy 280 H3
EVEREST
cr. Olinda 426 K10
ct. Burwood 418 D12
ct. Lalor 240 G7
dr. Cheltenham 496 K15
EVERETT
ct. Macleod 284 J10
ct. Thomastown 240 D14
st. Brunswick W 324 K9
EVERGLADE
av. Forest Hill 420 H5
ct. Viewbank 285 L20
EVERGLADES
ct. Rowville 463 A17
EVERGOLD
cl. Nar Warrn S 553 F19
EVERGREEN
av. Albanvale 318 K5
av. Balwyn 373 H14
ct. Cranbourne N 578 A7
ct. Taylors Hill 274 L9
dr. Bangholme 549 K13
dr. S Morang 199 H14
dr. Wyndham Va 446 D7
dr. Wyndham Va 446 D8
ri. S Morang 198 L9
wy. Langwarrin 601 L20
EVERINGHAM
ct. Greenvale 193 A16
rd. Altona Mdw 451 K4
EVERITT
st. Hadfield 280 J9
EVERLEIGH
dr. Diamond Ck 245 H6
EVERTON
cl. Hallam 537 G16
cl. Mulgrave 501 G2
ct. St Albans 275 J19
gr. Surrey Hills 374 D19
rd. Mt Evelyn 339 D14
EVERWIN
dr. Werribee 447 A13
EVESHAM
rd. Cheltenham 531 B2
EVILLE
st. S Melbourne 29 G4
st. S Melbourne 413 C2
EVITA
tce. Westmeadows 236 G15
EVON
av. Ringwood E 379 D7
EVONNE
ct. Endeavour Hl 537 F1
EVRAH
dr. Hoppers Csg 405 A15
pl. Greensbrgh 243 J18
EVWICK
cr. Highton 701 H16
EWAR
st. Moorabbin 496 B8
EWART
ct. Burwood E 419 L10
la. Dandenong 535 L9
st. Malvern 416 A18
EWARTS
rd. Don Valley 346 D1
EWEN
st. Coburg 325 E4
st. Parkdale 532 A9
EWING
st. Brunswick 325 H17
EXAMINER
st. Maribyrnong 367 D2
EXCALIBUR
av. Glen Waverley 420 L18
EXCELSA
ri. Hoppers Csg 405 D15
wy. Hillside 274 C3
EXCELSIOR
dr. Frankston N 600 C6
hts. Craigieburn 150 D6
st. Reservoir 282 H14
EXCHANGE
cl. Keilor East 277 K16
dr. Pakenham 585 C17
EXECUTIVE
mw. Hampton Pk 552 C11
EXELL
av. Melton S 268 J7
ct. Wantirna S 422 J20
dr. Dandenong N 501 L10
mw. Berwick 554 J10
EXETER
cl. Sorrento 678 D9
cl. Templstw Lr 330 L13
ct. Dandenong 535 K3
ct. Heidelberg W 284 B18
ct. Wheelers Hl 460 H15
gr. Belmont 702 D17
pl. Nar Warrn S 578 D1
rd. Croydon N 336 A12
rd. Croydon N 336 B12
st. Hadfield 281 A8
EXFORD
cl. Craigieburn 149 L17
cl. Carrum Downs 601 C2
dr. Mornington 641 D14
pl. Berwick 554 L20
pl. Donvale 376 K6
rd. Melton S 268 G13
st. Coolaroo 238 C7
EXHIBITION
pde. Taylors Hill 274 G8
st. Fitzroy 19 C15
st. McKinnon 456 A17
st. Melbourne 24 G2
st. W Footscray 366 H11
EXLEY
ct. Endeavour Hl 537 K8
dr. Moorabbin 496 B9
rd. Hampton E 496 A8
EXMOOR
cl. Highton 701 B15
EXMOUTH
rd. Craigieburn 150 B20
rd. Craigieburn 194 B2
EXNER
dr. Dandenong N 501 K13
EXON
st. Brighton 494 J1
st. Hampton 494 L7
EXPLORATION
la. Melbourne 2 L6
la. Melbourne 24 F2
EXPLORERS
ct. Vermont S 420 L12
ct. Vermont S 421 A12
EXPO
ct. Meadow Ht 194 A20
ct. Mt Waverley 459 B8
rd. Craigieburn 150 K19
EXPORT
dr. Brooklyn 366 A18
la. Kensington 33 G7
EXTON
cl. Epping 198 A18
ct. Ferntree Gly 463 J7
EYCOT
st. Kilsyth S 424 J2
EYEBRIGHT
sq. Hallam 538 C17
EYMARD
st. Deer Park 319 B15
EYNON
ct. Mill Park 242 B4
EYRE
cl. Rowville 463 B17
cl. Taylors L 275 K2
ct. Cranbourne N 577 K10
ct. Frankston S 627 G10
ct. Templstw Lr 330 J9
rd. Caulfield N 455 E1
rd. Mt Dandenong 426 D1
st. Balwyn 372 K9
st. Burwood 418 B9
st. Melton S 268 G12
st. Reservoir 282 L2
st. Sunbury 143 A13
st. Westmeadows 237 E14
EYRIE
ct. Hopetoun Park 266 D9
EYTAN
st. Ferntree Gly 423 J20
EYTON
cl. Chirnside Pk 336 J7
EZARD
cl. Berwick 553 K7
EZIO
ct. Diamond Ck 245 A14

F

FABIAN
ct. Keysborough 534 D13
ct. Maribyrnong 323 C16
FABIO
ct. Campbellfield 239 B13
FABRIANO
pl. Nar Warrn S 553 G19
FACEY
ct. Narre Warren 539 B18
ct. Noble Park N 501 D13
FACTORIES
rd. S Geelong 703 B17
FADARO
cr. Ringwood N 334 F12
FADDEN
gr. Sunbury 143 E6
st. Dandenong N 501 J18
FAELEN
st. Burwood 418 E7
FAGAN
ct. Cranbourne 577 K19
FAGG
st. Thomson 703 J15
FAGGS
pl. Geelong, off Gheringhap St 702 L10
FAHEY
cr. Yallambie 285 E15
pl. Donvale 332 J19
FAHY
ct. Yarra Jctn 346 L17
FAIGH
st. Mulgrave 500 A2
FAILLA
av. Campbellfield 239 E4
FAIR
cr. Dandenong N 502 D18
la. Bayswater N 379 H15
FAIRBAIRN
av. Mt Martha 668 K7
av. Mt Martha 669 A7
dr. Kensington 33 C12
gr. Sunbury 143 B5
rd. Cranbourne 604 A2
rd. Sunshine W 364 J11
rd. Toorak 415 B8
st. Springvale 500 C9
wy. Caroline Spr 274 C17
FAIRBANK
av. Gladstone Pk 237 A17
av. Heathmont 378 G18
cr. Templstw Lr 330 J11
ct. Rosebud 700 B1
la. Box Hill 374 H14
pl. Melton W 226 A16
rd. Bentleigh 496 C6
rd. Clayton S 498 K9
wy. Viewbank 286 A17
FAIRBOURNE
wy. Keysborough 533 K9
FAIRBRAE
av. Belmont 702 A19
FAIRCHILD
st. Abbotsford 26 H3
st. Heatherton 497 G11
st. Heatherton 497 H12
FAIRCROFT
av. Glen Iris 416 F8
FAIRDALE
ct. Eltham 287 L7
FAIRDELL
cr. Hurstbridge 203 C14
FAIRFAX
cct. Albanvale 318 K6
st. Blairgowrie 680 D20
FAIRFIELD
av. Belmont 706 F5
av. Camberwell 416 H5
gr. Caulfield S 455 E11
rd. Alphington 327 E19
rd. Fairfield 327 E17
rd. Fairfield 327 E19
st. Cranbourne 578 C19
wk. Cairnlea 319 J10
FAIRFIELD PARK
dr. Fairfield 371 C1
FAIRFORD
ct. Bayswater N 380 E18
FAIRHAVEN
bvd. Cranbourne W 577 F15
ct. Mulgrave 501 G2
rd. Carrum Downs 601 C3
rd. Mt Dandenong 426 J3
FAIRHAZEL
ct. Beaconsfld Up 542 L15
FAIRHILLS
dr. Rye 697 D8
pde. Glen Waverley 420 E20
FAIRHOLM
gr. Camberwell 372 J20
FAIRHOLME
bvd. Berwick 554 G12
bvd. Berwick 554 G13
FAIRLAM
la. Cheltenham, off Elman Rd 530 K1
FAIRLAND
av. Oakleigh E 458 K12
FAIRLANE
ct. Blackburn N 376 E8
FAIRLAWN
pl. Bayswater 423 L8
FAIRLEIGH
av. Beaumaris 529 K4
av. Black Rock 529 K4
ct. Narre Warren 553 B11
st. Glenroy 281 C5
FAIRLIE
av. Macleod 285 D12
ct. South Yarra 31 H3
ct. South Yarra 414 D2
st. Yarraville 367 D14
FAIRMEAD
pl. Nar Warrn S 552 G19
FAIRMONT
av. Belgrave Ht 506 C1
av. Camberwell 417 A4
ct. Nar Warrn N 538 C5
rd. Newtown 702 B11
st. Kings Park 275 D17
FAIRMOUNT
rd. Hawthorn E 416 D3
st. Hadfield 281 B10
st. Hadfield 281 B9
FAIRSEA
gr. Rye 696 E1
FAIRVIEW
av. Camberwell 417 K8
av. Cheltenham 497 A17
av. Croydon N 336 B13
av. Mt Martha 655 J18
av. Narre Warren 539 G20
av. Newtown 702 D10
av. Ringwood E 379 C10
av. Wheelers Hl 460 K7
cr. Diamond Ck 245 G11
ct. Hillside 231 K16
dr. Roxburgh Pk 194 A5
gr. Glen Iris 416 H16
gr. Watsonia 285 E9
rd. Chum Creek 213 D8
rd. Mt Waverley 418 G16
st. Belmont 706 C1
st. Hawthorn 371 J20
st. Springvale 499 K6
FAIRWAY
av. Cheltenham 530 D2
av. Hoppers Csg 448 J7
av. Mt Waverley 459 B7
cir. Safety Bch 687 B1
cr. McCrae 684 K18
ct. Darley 221 F1
ct. Pakenham 585 K5
dr. Anglesea 713 B5
dr. Bundoora 284 A6
dr. Dingley Vill 533 G10
dr. Kew East 372 F3
dr. Rowville 463 L10
dr. Rye 696 J4
dr. Safety Bch 668 L20
dr. Safety Bch 669 A20
dr. Safety Bch 687 A1
gr. Rosebud 684 G19
la. Safety Bch 668 K20
rd. Doncaster 330 E19
rd. Emerald 470 D17
st. Frankston 599 F15
st. Ivanhoe 327 K11
FAIRWAYS
bvd. Craigieburn 193 J2
FAIRWEATHER
dr. Burnside 318 E5
FAIRWYN
cl. Mill Park 242 E10
FAIRY
st. Ivanhoe 328 A17
FAIRY DELL
rd. Monbulk 468 F4
rd. Tecoma 466 B15
rd. The Patch 468 F4
FAITH
ct. Langwarrin 629 L12
st. Ferntree Gly 463 K6
FAKENHAM
rd. Ashburton 417 G14
FALCON
cl. Blind Bight 650 C10
cst. Craigieburn 149 G17
ct. Carrum Downs 601 B1
ct. Doncaster E 375 K3
dr. Keysborough 535 C8
dr. Melton 226 F15
pl. Pakenham 584 L10
rd. Macleod 285 C17
st. Thomastown 240 E14
st. Werribee 448 C9
wk. Kings Park 319 A1
FALCON CREST
Wheelers Hl 461 C14
FALCONER
cr. Bayswater N 380 F17
ct. Keilor 276 G10
ct. Mornington 641 B15
rd. Boronia 423 H11
rd. Pk Orchards 334 A13
st. Fitzroy N 19 G1
st. Fitzroy N 326 E20
st. Glen Waverley 459 J2
FALCONHURST
ct. Eltham 245 K
FALDO
ct. Mill Park 242
ct. Rowville 463 H
FALFIELD
pl. Templestowe 332 A
FALK
av. Reservoir 283
rd. Wandin East 340 L
FALKINER
cr. Dandenong 536
ct. Carrum Downs 574 J
ct. Carrum Downs 600
st. Eltham 287 E
FALKINGHAM
rd. Mt Evelyn 339 B
rd. Mt Evelyn 383
FALLON
st. Brunswick 325 C
st. Caulfield 455
FALLONS
wy. Bayswater 423
FALLS
rd. Kalorama 382 J
rd. Kalorama 383 A
rd. Mt Dandenong 382 J
rd. Mt Dandenong 426
rd. Mt Dandenong 427
rd. Mt Evelyn 383
rd. Olinda 426
rd. Olinda 426
rd. Olinda 427
rd. Olinda 427
FALMER
pl. Craigieburn 150 D
FALMOUTH
ct. Craigieburn 194
rd. Nar Warrn S 578
st. Hawthorn 372 C
FALSHAM
pl. N Melbourne 17 D
FALSHAWS
la. N Melbourne 17 C
FAME
st. Coburg N 281 F
FAMECHON
rd. Chelsea 547 B
rd. Edithvale 547 B
FANECO
rd. Plenty 244
FANKHAUSER
dr. Vermont S 420 H
FANNING
st. Heidelberg 328
st. Heidelberg 329
st. Southbank 4
st. Southbank 24 E
FANNY
st. Moonee Pnd 324 F
FANTAIL
ct. Carrum Downs 600
ct. Taylors L 275 G
pl. S Morang 243 K
ri. Warburton 349
tce. Healesville 258
FAORO
ct. Keysborough 534 D
FARADAY
ct. Glen Waverley 460
ct. Taylors Hill 274
la. Carlton 18 E
rd. Croydon S 379 J
st. Boronia 423 J
st. Carlton 18 D
FAREY
av. Dromana 685
FARLEIGH
av. Burwood 418
gr. Brighton 454 F
FARLEY
ct. Gladstone Pk 237 C
FARLEY GREEN
ct. Vermont 421
FARM
cl. Greensbrgh 286 D
la. Berwick 540 L
la. Berwick 541 A
la. Don Valley 345
rd. Alphington 327 L
rd. Cheltenham 497 E
rd. Coburg 281 J
rd. Cocoroc 487 A
rd. Heatherton 497 E
rd. Oakleigh S 498
rd. Werribee 447 C
st. Newport 411
FARMER
ct. Melton W 226 A
st. Ashwood 418 E
st. Brighton East 495
st. Burnley 371 A
st. St Kilda 414 E

MERS
Cairnlea 319 K12
Narre Warren 552 K5
MHOUSE
Nar Warrn N 538 D12
Sydenham 274 L7
MILLO
Lysterfield 464 B16
MINGTON
Wheelers Hl 460 G14
Cairnlea 319 J13
NAN
Northcote 326 L18
'NBOROUGH
Craigieburn 150 B20
Berwick 553 K19
NCOMB
Ascot Vale 324 B20
NDONS
Mt Dandenong 382 J18
NHAM
Wheelers Hl 460 H16
Mill Park 242 G2
Bundoora 284 K1
Craigieburn 150 B20
Flemington 324 F20
Mornington 657 A1
Bayswater 423 J7
Healesville 214 B19
Caulfield 456 A5
Flemington 324 E20
NLEY
Croydon 380 H5
NSWORTH
Footscray 367 E4
Portsea 677 K4
Berwick 553 L3
Sunshine 321 E19
QUHARSON
Belgrave 466 H15
Mt Waverley 419 A19
RANT
Altona Mdw 451 J3
RAR
Wandin N 340 L13
Wandin N 341 A13
RELL
Yarra Glen 252 L2
Pakenham 584 G5
Williamstown 411 A16
Williamstown 411 A18
. Williamstown 411 A18
Frankston 599 F13
Niddrie 322 L1
Niddrie 323 A1
Port Melb 412 J3
Port Melb 412 K4
Safety Bch 668 L18
RELLY
Epping 197 L19
RER
Cranbourne 603 K1
Diamond Ck 246 A12
Wandana Ht 705 D1
Doncaster E 331 H15
Mill Park 242 L6
Mill Park 243 A6
Warranwood 334 K13
Berwick 553 D2
RIER EDWARDS
Port Melb, off Rouse St 412 J7
RINGDON
Kalorama 383 C12
Pascoe Vale 280 D15
RINGTON
Rosebud 684 C20
SKIENE
Hampton Pk 551 G12
VIEW
Rowville 503 A6
Glenroy 280 G8
AN
Ringwood N 334 F13
HION
. Broadmeadows 239 A19
HODA
Hawthorn 371 H15
TNET
Taylors L 275 F8
MAH
Torquay 712 J2
LKINER
Clayton 498 J2
LKNER
Bentleigh 496 C6
Blackburn S 420 A3
Forest Hill 420 B3
Hampton 495 G6
LL
Croydon N 335 L18

FAUNA
av. Badger Creek 258 E12
av. Dingley Vill 533 H10
ct. Narre Warren 538 J20
ct. Werribee 447 E6
FAUSSETT
la. Albert Park 29 J12
st. Albert Park 29 H12
st. Albert Park 413 D6
FAVARO
pl. Hillside 274 D3
FAVERSHAM
ct. Greenvale 237 C6
rd. Canterbury 373 G17
sq. Ferntree Gly 463 F4
FAVOURITE HILL
rd. Pearcedale 630 F15
FAVRIL
st. Hampton 495 B6
FAWCETT
pl. Sunbury 143 B11
st. Mitcham 377 C9
st. Sunshine N 321 E15
FAWKNER
av. Blairgowrie 679 F16
cr. Hurstbridge 202 H12
cr. Keilor East 322 C6
ct. Mill Park 242 J4
ct. Mooroolbark 337 K14
la. Southbank 3 L7
pl. Caroline Spr 274 B16
rd. Pascoe Vale 280 E16
st. Aberfeldie 323 D11
st. Aberfeldie 323 D12
st. St Kilda 414 B17
st. Southbank 3 G8
st. Southbank 3 K7
st. Southbank 3 G9
st. Southbank 24 C16
st. South Yarra 31 J11
st. South Yarra 414 E6
st. Sunbury 143 A13
st. Sunshine N 321 F18
st. Westmeadows 236 K14
wy. Seabrook 451 A7
FAWN
ct. Langwarrin 629 F3
FAY
ct. Croydon 380 H7
ct. Noble Park 534 C6
ct. Somerville 644 E14
st. Balwyn N 373 J1
st. Brunswick 325 G15
st. Eltham 287 E8
st. Fawkner 281 K4
st. Heidelberg 329 D4
st. Melton 268 H1
st. Scoresby 462 D8
st. Seaford 599 J9
FAYE
cr. Keilor 276 L10
cr. Keilor 276 L9
cr. Keilor 277 A10
cr. Keilor 277 A9
ct. Tootgarook 698 C8
pl. Hampton Pk 551 K6
st. Burwood E 420 B8
st. Moorabbin 496 J8
st. Reservoir 283 H15
FAYETTE
ct. Wheelers Hl 461 E18
FAYGATE
ct. Frankston 628 F4
FEAR
st. Richmond 26 A13
FEATHER
cr. Diamond Ck 245 J13
FEATHERBY
wy. Altona Mdw 451 G9
FEATHERPARK
tce. S Morang 199 J14
FEATHERTOP
av. Templstw Lr 330 D12
ch. Burwood E 419 F12
dr. Keilor 277 B14
dr. Noble Park N 501 D10
dr. Wyndham Va 446 C12
ri. Wheelers Hl 461 D17
FEDERAL
rd. Ringwood E 378 L10
st. Footscray 367 E6
st. Mt Waverley 418 L13
st. Williamstown 411 C12
FEDERATION
ct. Altona 409 A16
ct. Nar Warrn S 553 F20
ct. Pakenham 584 G8
dr. Melton 227 G19
gln. Croydon Hl 335 K15
la. Abbotsford 20 D11
la. Berwick 553 L16
st. Ascot Vale 324 A16
st. Box Hill 374 G17

trl. Brooklyn 365 B17
trl. Hoppers Csg 449 C4
trl. Laverton 406 H11
trl. Laverton N 364 G20
trl. Laverton N 407 B6
trl. Truganina 406 H11
trl. Werribee 487 H3
wk. Cairnlea 319 H7
wk. Hughesdale 457 F7
wy. Caroline Spr 318 A6
wy. Moorabbin Aprt 532 D3
wy. Sunshine W 364 E9
FEDERICO
ct. Ringwood 335 A18
FEDRA
st. Mt Martha 657 A10
FEEHAN
cr. Nar Warrn S 578 E2
FEENEY
ct. Hampton Pk 551 E11
FEHON
st. Yarraville 367 A16
FEIJOA
ct. Werribee 447 L12
FELDSPAR
cl. St Albans 320 J9
ct. Narre Warren 539 F13
FELECIA
st. Rye 696 J8
FELGATE
cl. Tullamarine 278 K3
pde. Vermont S 420 L7
pde. Vermont S 421 A8
FELICIA
gr. Forest Hill 420 K1
ri. Diamond Ck 246 D9
st. Mordialloc 532 B12
wy. Sydenham 275 E9
FELICITY
ct. Narre Warren 552 G1
FELIX
cr. Ringwood N 377 L8
cr. Torquay 712 B7
ct. Woori Yall 344 E14
gr. Mooroolbark 336 L18
la. St Kilda W, off Loch St 414 A14
st. Grovedale 706 E13
st. Surrey Hills 373 L20
FELL
cr. Malvern East 416 H19
ct. Altona Mdw 451 G2
rd. Cockatoo 471 F18
FELLMONGERS
rd. Breakwater 703 D20
FELLOWES
ct. Tullamarine 278 G9
st. Seaford 599 K6
FELLOWS
rd. Pt Lonsdale 707 G20
rd. Queenscliff 707 G20
rd. Swan Bay 707 G20
st. Hughesdale 457 F6
st. Kew 371 G7
st. Mitcham 377 B12
FELLOWSHIP
gr. Kilsyth 381 A8
FELSTEAD
av. Sunshine W 364 H10
FELTHAM
ct. Rosebud 699 L1
st. Pearcedale 646 L6
FELTON
av. Sunbury 142 H10
FENACRE
st. Strathmore 280 A17
FENCHURCH
st. Sunbury 144 C9
FENECH
cl. Mill Park 241 L7
FENFIELD
st. Altona 408 H16
st. Cranbourne 578 B14
FENLAND
ct. Highton 705 L5
FENNELL
st. Port Melb 412 J1
FENTON
av. Kew 371 J11
av. Rosebud 700 G6
cr. Frankston S 626 J5
ct. Keysborough 534 G14
pl. Nar Warrn S 552 E20
st. Ascot Vale 324 E16
st. Huntingdale 458 F16
st. Mt Dandenong 426 H2
wy. Kew, off High St 371 K10
FENWICK
ct. Bundoora 284 G5
pl. Avondale Ht 322 D10

pl. Geelong, off Little Ryrie St 702 L8
st. Carlton N 18 G3
st. Clifton Hill 20 G2
st. Frankston 627 E6
st. Geelong 702 K9
st. Kew 371 F10
st. Malvern East 457 E3
st. Thornbury 326 K10
st.s, Geelong 702 K9
FEODORE
st. Caulfield S 456 A11
FERDINAND
av. Balwyn N 373 K4
st. Nunawading 376 K8
FERDINANDO
la. Sandringham, off Abbott St 495 A13
FERGIE
st. Fitzroy N 19 F1
st. Fitzroy N 326 D20
FERGUS
ct. Sydenham 274 K4
FERGUSON
ct. Eumemmerring 537 C14
ct. Ferntree Gly 463 H2
rd. Kilsyth 381 E5
st. Abbotsford 26 B2
st. Albion 320 L19
st. Ascot Vale 323 K17
st. Belgrave 466 H12
st. Black Rock 529 H2
st. Brighton East 455 B16
st. Glen Iris 416 J16
st. Kew 371 G4
st. Macleod 285 B17
st. Maribyrnong 367 A2
st. Mitcham 377 J15
st. Spotswood 366 G19
st. Upwey 465 E12
st. Williamstown 411 D14
FERMANAGH
gr. Sorrento 679 A16
rd. Camberwell 372 K20
FERMONT
ct. Clarinda 498 D7
FERMOY
la. Narre Warren 553 F7
FERN
av. Ferny Creek 466 B3
av. Guys Hill 556 B2
av. Windsor 414 K12
cl. Broadmeadows 238 A12
cl. Seaford 599 L4
ct. Campbellfield 239 E13
ct. Craigieburn 150 D17
ct. Eltham North 287 B4
ct. Launching Pl 345 F17
ct. Mill Park 242 F12
ct. Rosebud 700 H7
ct. Werribee 447 B11
gr. Ferny Creek 466 C2
gr. Rye 696 E3
la. Dandenong, off David St 536 E4
mw. Langwarrin 601 K15
rd. Up Fntree Gly 464 L9
st. Beaconsfld Up 542 G15
st. Black Rock 495 G20
st. Newcomb 703 L15
st. Oakleigh E 458 D10
st. Pearcedale 646 G3
st. Sunshine W 364 B2
st. The Basin 425 G13
tce. Footscray 367 D5
wy. Nar Warrn S 553 C16
FERNALD
av. Anglesea 713 F4
FERNBANK
cr. Mulgrave 501 H6
ct. Kilsyth 381 E10
rd. Healesville 212 H16
FERNBERG
pl. Melton W 226 C15
FERNBROOK
rd. Ferny Creek 466 B2
ri. Knoxfield 463 C1
wy. Templestowe 331 D13
FERNCROFT
av. Malvern East 416 H17
ct. Berwick 554 K20
ct. Cranbourne N 578 C9
st. Vermont 420 L5
FERNDALE
av. Upwey 465 J16
cl. Dingley Vill 532 K6
cl. Werribee 447 B18
cr. Dandenong N 501 K16
dr. Frankston 628 F5
pde. Highton 701 L17
rd. Glen Iris 417 B11
rd. Sassafras 425 J14
rd. Silvan 385 F20
rd. Silvan 428 L3

rd. Sunshine N 321 C14
rd. Up Fntree Gly 464 L9
st. Surrey Hills 418 D3
FERNDELL
cr. Templestowe 331 J14
ct. Belgrave Ht 506 E3
FERNE
pl. Mt Martha 655 E20
FERNEAUX
pl. Melton W 226 B16
FERNERY
gr. Newtown 702 D9
la. Frankston 626 K2
rd. Upwey 465 J16
FERNGLADE
dr. Emerald 510 D3
FERNGLEN
av. Mt Dandenong 426 J1
FERNGULLY
gr. Kalorama 383 E9
rd. Cockatoo 510 L10
rd. Don Valley 346 D1
FERNHILL
av. Cranbourne 603 E6
ct. Albanvale 319 A4
dr. Dingley Vill 532 L4
dr. Highton 701 L16
rd. Caulfield S 455 E9
rd. Mt Evelyn 339 F14
rd. Sandringham 495 C15
rd.n, Sandringham 495 C15
st. Ascot Vale 324 G18
st. Glen Waverley 420 B20
FERNHURST
cl. Keysborough 534 B9
dr. Glen Waverley 420 B18
gr. Kew 371 H10
FERNIE
pl. Attwood 237 D11
FERNLEA
av. Rowville 463 H14
cl. Watsonia N 243 G19
cr. Doncaster E 332 E5
ct. Sunshine W 364 D5
FERNLEIGH
ct. Langwarrin 629 J6
dr. Mooroolbark 381 K3
st. Newtown 702 H13
FERNLEY
av. Macleod 285 C12
FERNLY
ct. Wheelers Hl 461 F15
FERNSHAW
gdn. Hallam 552 B1
pl. Mt Eliza 642 G4
pl. Sunbury 143 B10
rd. Monbulk 428 D20
st. Thomastown 240 F13
FERNSIDE
av. Briar Hill 286 H5
FERNTREE
av. Warburton 350 B3
ct. Ferntree Gly 463 H7
gr. Aspendale Gdn 547 C5
wk. Roxburgh Pk 194 A5
wy. Keysborough 534 A9
FERNTREE GULLY
rd. Clayton 459 C10
rd. Ferntree Gly 463 G4
rd. Glen Waverley 459 C10
rd. Knoxfield 463 A8
rd. Mt Waverley 459 C10
rd. Notting Hill 459 C10
rd. Oakleigh 458 B9
rd. Oakleigh E 458 B9
rd. Scoresby 462 A11
rd. Wheelers Hl 459 C10
rd. Wheelers Hl 460 H13
rd. Wheelers Hl 461 B13
FERNVALE
cr. Wheelers Hl 460 H15
FERNWOOD
av. Ringwood E 379 D17
dr. Langwarrin 629 J2
rd. Narre Warren 538 K20
FERNWREN
pl. Carrum Downs 600 E5
FERNY
ct. Bangholme 549 H14
ct. Nar Warrn S 553 E17
FERNY CREEK
av. Up Fntree Gly 465 D7
FERNYHILL
ct. Greenvale 193 D17
FERRARO
cl. Epping 198 F16
FERRARS
pl. S Melbourne 29 K7
pl. S Melbourne 413 E4
st. Albert Park 413 D2
st. Southbank 23 F18
st. Southbank 29 G1
st. Southbank 413 D1

st. S Melbourne........29 G1
st. S Melbourne......413 D1
st. S Melbourne......413 D2
FERRERO
gr. Mt Martha.........655 G18
FERRES
bvd. S Morang..........198 L19
ct. Glen Waverley....420 J15
rd. Emerald............469 E19
FERRIER
ct. Rosanna............284 L20
ct. Rosanna............285 A19
ct. Rowville............502 J5
FERRIMAN
st. Brunswick W.....324 L14
FERRIS
av. Box Hill N..........374 J8
av. Deer Park..........319 B10
av. Mitcham............377 E17
rd. Melton..............269 G8
rd. Melton S............269 E18
FERRY
cl. Wyndham Va.....446 G14
cr. Brunswick W.....325 A12
gr. Newcomb..........703 L16
FESCUE
pl. Delahey............274 L14
FESTIVAL
cr. Keysborough.....535 B10
gr. Lalor.................240 L5
pl. The Basin...........425 B8
tce. Berwick............553 E2
FETHERSTON
st. Armadale..........415 E12
FETLOCK
dr. Cranbourne E.....578 K19
pl. Epping..............198 D16
FETTLING
st. Preston.............282 G19
FEVERSHAM
av. Pk Orchards......334 B18
FEWSTER
dr. Wantirna S.........462 D3
rd. Hampton...........495 D8
FIANDER
av. Glen Waverley....459 J1
FIAT
ct. Keilor Dn...........276 C15
FICIFOLIA
dr. Doveton.............536 G12
FIDDAN
ct. Altona Mdw.......451 J6
FIDDES
st. Moorabbin.........496 F8
st. Reservoir...........282 D5
FIDGE
cr. Breakwater........703 H20
ct. Jacana...............237 J19
FIDLER
ct. Altona Mdw.......451 K7
FIELD
av. Edithvale............546 H12
ct. Berwick..............553 K17
ct. Dandenong N......502 A12
ct. Gladstone Pk......237 D18
ct. Montrose...........382 E10
st. Bentleigh............456 C17
st. Caulfield S..........455 K6
st. Clifton Hill...........20 J8
st. Craigieburn........150 F17
st. Croydon............379 J8
st. Hampton...........495 F12
st. McKinnon..........456 C17
st. Moonee Pnd.......324 A10
st. Rye...................697 J4
FIELDEN
cl. Mooroolbark......381 K1
FIELDER
rd. Cockatoo...........511 G9
FIELDERS
wk. Westmeadows...236 G15
FIELDING
dr. Chelsea Ht.........547 H18
dr. Gisborne S.........141 A2
rd. Diamond Ck.......245 B8
rd. Rosebud W........683 B20
st. Yarraville...........367 B13
wy. Templestowe.....331 L9
FIELDLARK
ct. Carrum Downs...600 K3
ct. Werribee............447 L6
FIELDSTONE
bvd. Beaconsfield......555 B12
FIESTA
ct. Thomastown......240 F17
FIFE
ct. Belmont.............702 H20
ct. Mulgrave...........500 J1
FIFER
ri. Bundoora...........242 C20
FIFESHIRE
dr. Hoppers Csg......405 C13
FIFTH
av. Altona North......409 K7
av. Anglesea............713 C11
av. Aspendale..........546 F10
av. Brunswick..........325 E9
av. Chelsea Ht.........547 F13
av. Cockatoo...........510 H6
av. Dandenong........535 H7
av. Edithvale...........546 F10
av. Hadfield.............281 D9
av. Pakenham..........584 L2
av. Point Cook.........451 C10
av. Rosebud............684 A18
av. Rowville.............462 E19
rd. Springvale.........500 L10
st. Black Rock.........529 H8
st. Parkdale............531 E11
FIG
ct. Cranbourne N....578 C5
st. Dromana...........686 E6
FIGTREE
ct. Mill Park............242 C10
gr. Bayswater..........422 J5
la. Burwood, off
College Wy........419 C7
FIJI
ct. Mulgrave...........500 C3
FILBERT
ct. Cranbourne N....577 L4
st. Bentleigh E........456 H20
st. Caulfield S.........455 G7
FILER
ct. Keysborough.....534 C9
FILIPPIN
ct. Werribee............447 K18
FILLMORE
rd. Dandenong N.....501 J10
FILLO
dr. Somerton..........195 C16
FILMER
cr. Nar Warrn S.......552 G17
ct. Rowville.............462 K20
FILMONT
dr. Werribee............448 D18
FILOMENA
ct. Cranbourne N....578 E10
FILSON
st. Ascot Vale.........324 D18
FINAL
la. Endeavour Hl.....502 L17
FINBAR
ct. Nar Warrn S.......552 E15
FINCH
cl. Wyndham Va.....446 B9
ct. Pakenham.........584 L2
pl. Blackburn S........419 K6
pl. Melton...............226 G15
st. Altona...............408 F20
st. Bayswater..........423 C5
st. Berwick.............539 J18
st. Burwood............418 K11
st. Doncaster E.......375 K4
st. Frankston..........599 D15
st. Glen Iris.............416 D15
st. Malvern East......416 C20
st. Mt Martha..........656 B8
st. Notting Hill.........459 G12
st. Thomastown.......240 G16
FINCHAVEN
av. Keysborough.....535 A11
st. Herne Hill...........701 L4
FINCHFIELD
la. Belmont.............706 A7
FINCHLEY
av. Glenroy.............279 K5
ct. Endeavour Hl.....503 B20
ct. Epping...............197 K18
ct. Hawthorn...........371 L18
ct. Springvale S......499 K20
pl. Kealba..............276 K19
rd. Point Cook.........450 J10
FINCHS
rd. Melton..............228 B10
rd. Plumpton...........228 B10
FINDEN
ct. Craigieburn........150 B15
FINDLAY
gr. Belmont.............702 G17
la. Altona...............409 C19
st. Northcote..........326 G11
FINDON
av. Caulfield N.........415 E16
cr. Kew...................371 F12
ct. Highett..............496 D12
ct. Point Cook.........450 D6
ct. Seaford.............573 F13
ct. Wantirna S.........462 C2
rd. Epping..............197 G15
rd. S Morang..........198 G17
st. Hawthorn..........371 F13
st. Malvern East......416 B19
st. S Geelong..........703 A14
wy. Berwick............554 G19
wy. Melton W..........226 D15
FINGAL
dr. Frankston..........600 B16
FINHAVEN
ct. Kew...................371 D11
FINISTERRE
ct. Frankston..........628 D10
dr. Keysborough.....534 G12
FINK
ct. Donvale............376 F7
st. Kensington..........34 C13
st. Preston.............327 H6
st. Williamstn N.......410 B12
FINKEL
rd. Harkaway...........540 L11
rd. Harkaway...........541 A11
FINLAY
al. Melbourne.............1 J7
al. Melbourne...........23 L5
cl. Gladstone Pk.....237 B17
pl. Carlton...............18 E18
st. Albert Park..........29 G14
st. Albert Park.........413 E7
st. Frankston..........599 E18
st. Yarraville...........366 H17
FINLAYSON
av. Mt Martha..........669 B2
st. Doncaster..........374 D2
st. Forest Hill..........420 C2
st. Malvern.............416 A18
st. Ringwood E.......379 E17
st. Rosanna............284 L20
st. Rosanna............285 A20
FINLEY
ct. Endeavour Hl.....538 B4
ct. Wantirna S.........422 D17
rd. Altona...............408 K14
FINMERE
cr. Up Fntree Gly.....464 J9
FINN
ct. Maddingley........264 E3
ct. Templstw Lr......330 F10
st. Rosanna............329 C2
FINNBARR
wy. Seabrook...........450 L6
FINNIGAN
st. Research...........288 J5
FINNINGLEY
ct. Highton.............705 L7
dr. Tullamarine........278 K2
FINSBURY
cl. Caroline Spr.......317 J1
cl. Rowville.............503 H2
ct. Dandenong N.....501 F10
rd. Devon Mdw.......604 J20
st. Flemington..........33 L2
wy. Camberwell........417 A4
FINSTALL
cl. Caroline Spr.......317 K2
FINTON
cl. Glen Waverley....461 A5
ct. Pakenham.........585 E4
gr. Gladstone Pk.....279 A2
gr. Reservoir...........283 C1
FINTONA
ct. Coldstream........295 F13
FINTONIA
rd. Noble Park.........501 A19
st. Balwyn N...........373 K1
st. Hughesdale........457 E13
FINUCANE
pl. Fawkner............281 F2
FIOCCHI
av. Frankston..........599 B15
FIONA
ct. Blairgowrie........679 C18
ct. Cheltenham.......531 D1
ct. Eltham..............288 A1
ct. Ferntree Gly.......463 E2
ct. Gladstone Pk.....279 B2
ct. Glen Waverley....419 K18
ct. Kealba..............276 H18
ct. Keysborough.....534 F11
ct. Mooroolbark......337 A11
ct. Mt Martha..........656 J7
ct. Narre Warren.....553 D8
ct. Ringwood..........379 B3
ct. St Kilda.............414 F16
ct. Somerville.........645 B16
ct. Vermont............377 F20
ct. Warrandyte........333 B6
ct. Werribee............447 H10
dr. Cranbourne S.....603 K20
pl. Pakenham.........559 F19
FIR
cl. Broadmeadows..237 L12
ct. Kilsyth..............381 K7
ct. Mt Waverley.......419 B16
gr. Cheltenham.......496 F19
st. Blackburn..........376 A13
st. Bulleen.............330 A17
st. Dingley Vill.........532 H6
st. Thomastown.......241 C13
FIRA
ct. Narre Warren.....539 A20
FIRBANK
cl. Langwarrin.........601 G19
tce. Albanvale...........319 A5
FIREBALL
ct. Taylors L...........275 H5
FIREBELL
la. Richmond............26 C13
FIRE STATION
rd. Melb Airport.......235 B10
FIRESTONE
ct. Sunbury............144 C10
grn. Cranbourne.......603 H8
FIRETAIL
ct. Carrum Downs...600 L1
ct. Carrum Downs...601 A1
FIRMAN
st. Springvale S......500 A20
FIRST
av. Altona North......410 A6
av. Anglesea............713 F8
av. Aspendale..........546 F9
av. Box Hill N..........375 E6
av. Brunswick..........325 D8
av. Chelsea Ht.........547 D14
av. Cockatoo...........510 J4
av. Craigieburn........150 G17
av. Dandenong N.....501 J15
av. Hadfield.............281 E11
av. Hoppers Csg......448 K6
av. Kew...................372 H7
av. Melton S............268 E6
av. Moorabbin Aprt..531 L4
av. Murrumbeena....457 A11
av. Pakenham.........584 K3
av. Rosebud............683 K20
av. Springvale.........500 G10
av. Strathmore........279 H19
av. Sunshine...........365 E7
cr. Hadfield.............281 D9
ct. Cranbourne........603 J6
ct. Preston.............282 C19
dr. Springvale.........500 G10
st. Black Rock.........529 G6
st. Clayton S...........499 D6
st. Geelong West....702 H3
st. Moorabbin Aprt..532 A5
st. Parkdale............531 D8
st. Warrandyte........333 F1
st. W Footscray.......366 F7
FIRST SETTLEMENT
dr. Sorrento............679 C15
FIRTH
la. Doncaster..........330 K20
la. Doncaster..........374 J1
pl. Point Cook.........450 G3
rd. Moorooduc.........643 L16
st. Doncaster..........374 J1
wy. Greenvale..........193 G19
FISCHER
st. Coburg..............281 C19
st. Torquay.............712 A9
FISCOM
ct. Croydon N..........336 A14
ct. Mill Park............242 J12
FISHBURN
ct. Mill Park............242 D3
pl. Cranbourne W...603 H3
FISHER
av. Belmont.............706 J3
av. Lalor.................241 J10
cl. Berwick..............554 G16
cr. Dandenong N......535 K1
ct. Altona...............409 E17
ct. Bayswater N......380 F17
ct. Bentleigh E........456 L17
ct. Sunbury............143 G4
ct. Werribee............448 A6
gr. Tullamarine........278 E7
mw. Waterways.........547 F3
pde. Ascot Vale.........367 G3
pde. Flemington.........367 G3
pde. Footscray..........367 G3
pl. Kurunjang..........227 D12
st. Footscray...........366 L6
st. Forest Hill..........376 H20
st. Maidstone...........322 K18
st. Malvern East......456 J4
FISHERIES
rd. Devon Mdw.......649 D2
FISHERMANS
dr. Blind Bight.........650 D8
FISHERS
la. Fitzroy................19 B16
FISHLEY
st. S Melbourne........29 L5
FISKEN
pl. Kensington.........33 G11
pl. Kensington........368 D6
st. Bacchus Msh.....222 D20
st. Maddingley........264
st. Maddingley........264
FITHIE
st. Blackburn N.......375
FITTIS
st. Newport............410
FITZGERALD
ct. Mooroolbark......337
ct. S Morang..........199
ct. Taylors L...........233
rd. Derrimut............363
rd. Essendon...........324
rd. Hallam..............538
rd. Laverton N.........407
rd. Sunshine W.......363
rd.n, Hallam............538
ri. Arthurs Seat.......685
st. Balwyn..............374
st. Ferntree Gly.......464
st. Mornington.........641
st. Ringwood E........379
st. South Yarra..........32
st. South Yarra........414
FITZGIBBON
av. Brunswick W......324
cr. Caulfield N.........455
st. Cremorne............26
st. Parkville...............17
FITZJOHNS
ct. Portsea.............677
FITZPATRICK
dr. Altona Mdw.......450
st. S Melbourne........30
FITZROY
av. Frankston..........599
cl. Caroline Spr.......274
ct. Endeavour Hl.....536
ct. Endeavour Hl.....537
gr. Chadstone.........418
pl. Taylors Hill.........274
st. Darley...............222
st. Fitzroy................24
st. Fitzroy................25
st. Footscray...........367
st. Geelong............703
st. Geelong............703
st. Geelong............703
st. Hadfield.............281
st. Laverton............407
st. McKinnon..........456
st. Preston.............282
st. St Kilda.............414
st. Sunbury............142
st.s, Altona Mdw.......407
FITZSIMONS
la. Eltham..............287
la. Lower Plenty......287
la. Templestowe.....331
FITZWILLIAM
st. Kew..................372
FIVE CROWN
gr. Doncaster E.......332
FIVE MILE
rd. Pakenham.........586
FIVEWAYS
bvd. Keysborough.....533
FLAG
st. Kingsbury..........283
FLAGSTAFF
la. Taylors Hill.........274
la. W Melbourne.......23
FLAKE
ct. Diggers Rest......187
FLAM
st. Frankston..........600
FLAME
cl. Delahey............275
cr. S Morang..........199
st. Mt Waverley......419
FLAME ROBIN
dr. Langwarrin........628
FLAMINGO
ct. Nar Warrn S.......552
dr. Wantirna S.........422
pt. S Morang..........199
rd. Rosebud W........698
rd. Rosebud W........699
FLANDERS
la. Geelong, off
Swanston St......703
FLANIGAN
la. Melbourne.............1
la. Melbourne...........23
FLANNERY
av. Bundoora...........284
ct. Brunswick W......324
ct. Oak Park............279
ct. Warrandyte........332
ct. Warrandyte........333
FLATROCK
rd. Hurstbridge.......203
rd. Kangaroo Grnd..247
rd. Panton Hill........247

.AVIA
Mt Waverley 459 E3
Keysborough 534 B17
AX
Cranbourne N 578 A4
Werribee 447 E12
AXEN HILLS
Doreen 156 L12
Doreen 156 L14
EAY
Badger Creek 258 D14
ECKNEY
Keysborough 534 G8
EET
Fitzroy 18 L18
Laverton N 407 H8
Mornington 640 G17
Mt Waverley 419 D18
Somerton 195 D18
EETWOOD
ct. Melton W 225 H19
ct. Melton W 225 H20
Frankston S 626 G7
Gladstone Pk 236 K20
Greenvale 192 L16
Greenvale 193 A16
Narre Warren 553 B11
EMING
Seabrook 451 A7
Endeavour Hl 538 A6
Oakleigh S 497 H6
Research 288 L5
Seaford 600 A1
Pascoe Vale 281 A15
Melbourne 1 L15
Melbourne 24 B9
Mill Park 242 L6
Mill Park 243 A6
Altona 408 K17
Brunswick W 324 L16
Mornington 640 A17
Safety Bch 686 G1
e. Pakenham 558 K20
EMINGTON
Werribee 446 H19
Mill Park 242 H9
N Melbourne 17 A8
Parkville 34 J5
Travancore 324 G20
EMMING
Burnside 318 D7
Maribyrnong 322 H16
Keilor 277 A14
ETCHER
Mt Waverley 458 J3
Carlton N 18 J1
e. Burwood 418 F8
Cranbourne S 603 K20
Dandenong N 502 C17
Frankston 599 B17
Frankston 599 C19
Mooroolbark 337 A8
Essendon 324 B8
Forest Hill 376 E20
Hawthorn E 372 D19
Moorabbin 496 G8
ETE
Armadale 415 G11
ETT
Preston 326 L4
EUR
Tootgarook 698 D9
Boronia 424 H10
Nar Warrn S 552 J17
IGHT
Thomastown 240 H17
Tullamarine 277 K8
INDERS
Canterbury 373 G16
Rosebud 700 D3
Pakenham 583 K1
Boronia 424 G7
Wyndham Va 446 G8
Bundoora 242 L20
Cranbourne N 577 L8
Kilsyth 381 J9
Lalor 240 J8
Melbourne 2 A19
Melbourne 24 D10
Mornington 640 D12
Glenroy 280 L3
Melbourne 1 A17
Melbourne 23 H12
Torquay 712 E2
Melton S 268 D11
Bulleen 329 L12
Coburg 281 C20
Docklands 23 G14
Heidelberg Ht 284 F19
Keilor Park 277 K14
McCrae 684 K17
Melbourne 1 B19
Melbourne 23 G14
Mentone 530 J5
st. Mentone 531 A5
st. Mitcham 377 E9
st. Noble Park 500 D16
st. Queenscliff 708 G19
st. Rye 696 H4
st. Sunbury 143 B13
st. Taylors Hill 274 F9
st. Thornbury 326 K7
st. Thornbury 327 C8
wk. Melbourne 24 C12
FLINDERS WAY
arc. Melbourne 2 D17
FLINT
cr. Delahey 275 A16
st. Eltham 287 C13
FLINTOFF
av. Burnside 318 F9
ct. Mill Park 241 L7
st. Greensbrgh 286 C4
FLINTOFT
av. Toorak 415 C2
FLOCKHART
st. Abbotsford 371 A12
st. Kensington 33 D11
FLODDEN
wy. Briar Hill 286 G4
FLOODS
rd. N Warrandyte 289 L10
FLORA
av. Badger Creek 258 G13
cl. Cockatoo 511 J1
cr. Smiths Gly 205 E2
ct. Chelsea Ht 547 E16
ct. Cranbourne N 578 B6
ct. Narre Warren 538 J19
ct. Ringwood 379 A4
gr. Forest Hill 420 C3
gr. Ivanhoe East 328 E16
la. Craigieburn 150 F14
rd. Clayton 458 H19
rd. Donvale 333 A20
rd. Donvale 377 B1
rd. Mt Martha 656 G7
st. Keilor 277 D14
st. Ringwood E 379 E14
FLORAL
ct. Warranwood 334 J12
gdn. Nar Warrn S 579 D1
FLORA PARK
wy. Carrum Downs 601 B7
FLOREAT
ct. Glen Waverley 419 L18
pl. Melton W 226 D17
FLORENCE
av. Berwick 553 J5
av. Clayton 459 A13
av. Donvale 376 J7
av. Emerald 469 G17
av. Frankston 599 C20
av. Kew 372 E10
av. Ringwood N 378 E3
av. Rosebud W 698 K1
av. Sassafras 426 G15
av. Upwey 466 B7
cl. Cranbourne 603 K1
cl. Reservoir 282 B3
ct. Dandenong 535 G1
ct. Wandana Ht 701 D20
ct. Werribee 447 F18
dr. Rye 696 G6
la. Sunbury 143 G19
pl. Port Melb 412 K5
rd. Cottles Br 202 K1
rd. Surrey Hills 374 B20
st. Bentleigh E 497 C2
st. Blackburn 376 D19
st. Brighton East 455 F19
st. Brunswick 325 F10
st. Burwood 418 F12
st. Coburg 325 E6
st. Essendon 323 J7
st. Glen Iris 416 L13
st. Glen Waverley 460 A3
st. Kilsyth 381 C5
st. Mentone 530 L8
st. Mentone 531 A8
st. Niddrie 278 H20
st. Noble Park 534 D3
st. Nunawading 376 D19
st. Ormond 456 G13
st. Prahran 415 B11
st. Seddon 367 A12
st. Williamstn N 410 H12
FLORET
pl. Narre Warren 553 D3
FLOREY
cr. Mulgrave 460 C18
pl. Mill Park 242 L6
FLORIANA
av. Doveton 536 J4
FLORIDA
av. Beaumaris 529 L10
av. Dingley Vill 533 B8
ct. Mitcham 377 F18
ct. Moorabbin 496 C10
dr. Ferntree Gly 423 H16
st. Mt Waverley 419 H15
wy. Seaford 573 D18
FLORISTON
gr. Eltham 288 C4
rd. Boronia 424 E13
FLORIZEL
st. Ashburton 417 E13
FLOWER
ct. Grovedale 706 E13
st. Essendon 323 L8
st. Ferntree Gly 424 B19
st. Pakenham 584 J8
FLOWERDALE
cr. Roxburgh Pk 194 C6
ct. Nar Warrn S 579 F1
rd. Cairnlea 319 F11
rd. Glen Iris 417 C12
rd. Hampton E 496 A10
FLOWERDRUM
cl. Templestowe 332 A6
FLOWERFIELD
dr. Coldstream 294 A11
FLOWERING GUM
gr. S Morang 199 J12
FLOWERS
cl. Roxburgh Pk 194 C14
st. Caulfield S 455 K7
FLOWERVALE
pl. Brookfield 267 L8
rd. Noble Park 534 E2
FLYGER
la. Edithvale, off Bank Rd 546 G13
FLYING FOX
tce. S Morang 199 J13
FLYING STAR
wk. Skye 575 H15
FLYNN
cr. Coolaroo 238 E5
ct. Frankston 628 G1
ct. Nar Warrn S 552 E15
st. Ferntree Gly 424 J19
st. Springvale 500 B12
st. Springvale 500 C10
FOAM
av. Blairgowrie 679 E20
av. Torquay 712 C3
rd. Fingal 697 L20
st. Aspendale 546 C3
st. Elwood 454 F7
st. Hampton 495 B9
st. Mornington 640 G16
st. Parkdale 531 E14
st. Rosebud 684 D20
FOCH
av. Coburg 325 D7
rd. Silvan 384 L9
rd. Silvan 385 A10
st. Box Hill S 418 K3
st. Ormond 456 B11
st. Reservoir 283 B16
FODEN
av. Campbellfield 194 H20
st. Brunswick W 325 A15
FOGARTY
av. Highton 705 D9
av. Highton 705 E8
av. Yarraville 366 F19
ct. Oakleigh 458 C9
pde. Blairgowrie 679 H20
st. N Melbourne 34 G14
FOKKER
st. Strathmr Ht 279 D9
FOLEY
av. Preston 327 D6
pl. Bentleigh E 497 A3
pl. Mill Park 243 E5
st. Eltham 287 D16
st. Kew 371 H13
FOLEYS
rd. Deer Park 318 G20
rd. Deer Park 363 A1
rd. Derrimut 363 A1
FOLKESTONE
cr. Beaumaris 530 F8
cr. Springvale S 499 H20
rd. Glen Waverley 419 K13
FOLKSTONE
cr. Ferntree Gly 463 E5
FOLLET
st. Torquay 712 B6
FOLLETT
ct. Carrum Downs 575 C15
rd. Cheltenham 531 C3
FONCECA
st. Mordialloc 532 E12
FONTAIN
ct. Werribee 448 D18
FONTAINE
st. Grovedale 706 B10
st. Pascoe Vale S 324 H1
tce. Nar Warrn N 538 D6
FONTAYNE
ct. Frankston S 627 B14
FONTEIN
st. W Footscray 366 D9
FONTEYN
dr. Wantirna S 462 B1
FOORD
la. Dromana 685 D9
FOOT
st. Frankston 627 D7
st. Frankston S 627 D7
st. Frankston S 627 D9
FOOTE
la. Albert Park 29 D13
st. Albert Park 29 B15
st. Albert Park 413 A8
st. Brighton 454 H11
st. Dromana 685 J7
st. Templestowe 330 G7
st. Templstw Lr 330 G7
FOOTHILLS
av. McCrae 684 K13
FOOTSCRAY
rd. Docklands 368 K12
rd. W Melbourne 367 L11
rd. W Melbourne 368 K12
FOOTT
rd. Beaconsfld Up 541 G7
FORAN
gr. Oakleigh S 458 F19
FORBES
av. Lynbrook 551 D16
cl. Knoxfield 463 C9
ct. Attwood 237 E11
ct. Bayswater N 380 E18
ct. Mill Park 242 D8
dr. Aspendale Gdn 546 H2
gr. Oak Park 280 D12
pl. Balwyn N 374 A3
st. Essendon 324 B9
st. Rye 697 B13
st. Safety Bch 686 H2
st. Warrandyte 289 J19
FORD
av. Oakleigh 458 A14
av. Sunshine N 321 B12
cr. Thornbury 327 H11
ct. Mill Park 242 D7
ct. Noble Park N 501 C13
ct. Truganina 405 G14
rd. Altona 408 K14
rd. Emerald 510 D6
st. Brunswick 325 D11
st. Clifton Hill 20 F6
st. Footscray 367 F7
st. Ivanhoe 327 J11
st. Newport 410 H8
st. Preston 282 F20
st. Ringwood 378 G15
st. Rye 680 F20
st. Southbank 23 D19
FORDE
ct. Narre Warren 539 F16
ct. Sunbury 143 H8
FORDHAM
av. Camberwell 417 C2
ct. Richmond 26 D12
ct. Rowville 503 C1
ct. Springvale S 534 B1
rd. Reservoir 283 C10
st. Newtown 702 B10
FORDHAMS
rd. Eltham 287 G15
FORDHOLM
rd. Hampton Pk 551 D9
rd. Hawthorn 371 K20
rd. Hawthorn 415 K2
FORDS
rd. Gruyere 342 H2
FORDSON
rd. Campbellfield 239 D12
FORDYCE
rd. Mt Dandenong 426 J3
rd. Olinda 426 J3
st. Cheltenham 497 B20
FORENSIC
dr. Macleod 284 H13
FORESHORE
st. Frankston 599 A20
FOREST
ct. Croydon 379 J3
ct. Gladstone Pk 237 A17
ct. Glen Waverley 459 J8
ct. Ringwood 335 A18
ct. Templestowe 332 C13
dr. Frankston N 599 K9
dr. Mt Martha 669 D9
dr. Somerville 644 K17
pl. Templestowe 332 B13
rd. Belgrave 466 J10
rd. Blackburn 376 D20
rd. Boronia 424 H13
rd. Boronia 424 H14
rd. Boronia 424 J13
rd. Ferntree Gly 424 J18
rd. Ferntree Gly 464 G4
rd. Ferntree Gly 464 H2
rd. Forest Hill 376 D20
rd. Mt Evelyn 340 D19
rd. The Basin 425 A12
rd. Wesburn 348 D17
st. Collingwood 20 A11
st. Greensbrgh 244 H19
st. Monbulk 428 E20
st. Monbulk 468 E1
st. Yarra Glen 208 K17
st. Yarra Glen 209 A17
tr. Kallista 467 H9
vw. Bundoora 284 E9
wk. Ringwood N 377 L4
wy. Kilsyth 380 K5
FOREST GLEN
av. Blackburn S 419 L6
FOREST OAK
dr. Up Fntree Gly 464 K7
FOREST PARK
rd. Dingley Vill 533 C8
rd. Upwey 465 E13
FOREST RED GUM
dr. Mickleham 149 B3
FORGE
cl. Maribyrnong 322 J16
la. Heidelberg 329 A8
rd. Mt Evelyn 339 F16
FORMAN
st. Westmeadows 236 K14
FORMBY
cl. Wantirna 422 C11
pl. Cranbourne 603 E7
FORMOSA
ct. Narre Warren 553 G11
st. Newtown 702 C8
FORREST
av. Sorrento 679 C16
ct. Anglesea 713 G7
ct. Endeavour Hl 538 A8
ct. Sandringham 495 K17
ct. Toorak 415 G5
hill, South Yarra 32 E7
hill, South Yarra 414 H4
pl. Taylors L 233 D18
st. Albion 364 F1
st. Ardeer 364 A1
st. Ardeer 364 F1
st. Bentleigh E 457 F18
st. Geelong 703 D14
st. Melton S 268 J12
st. Spotswood 411 A1
st. Sunbury 142 L12
st. Sunbury 143 A12
st. Sunshine 364 F1
st. Sunshine 365 A2
st. Sunshine W 364 A1
st. Yarraville 367 A14
FORRESTER
st. Essendon 323 B6
st. Essendon 323 G7
wk. Nar Warrn S 578 H1
FORREST HILL
gr. Lysterfield S 503 L14
FORSHAW
ct. Rosebud 700 H5
FORSTER
av. Frankston N 600 C11
av. Malvern East 416 L20
ct. Bentleigh E 456 L17
ct. Pascoe Vale S 324 F1
ct. Sunbury 143 F2
rd. Mt Waverley 459 B10
st. Heidelberg Ht 328 E7
st. Mitcham 377 J15
st. Noble Park 500 D17
st. South Yarra 32 E11
st. South Yarra 414 H5
st. Williamstown 411 D17
FORSYTH
cl. Burnside 318 D7
ct. Cranbourne N 578 F8
ct. Narre Warren 552 G1
pl. Rowville 502 H4
rd. Hoppers Csg 406 A18
rd. Hoppers Csg 450 B1
rd. Laverton 406 A18
rd. Point Cook 450 B1
rd. Truganina 406 B16
st. Frankston 599 K19
FORT
st. Mt Waverley 419 H16
FORTESCUE
av. Seaford 599 D10
ct. Wantirna 422 F10
gr. Vermont S 420 H11

FORTUNA
av. Balwyn N 373 D3
av. Croydon 379 J8
st. Clayton 459 B19
FORTUNE
av. Lilydale 339 B11
av. Mt Evelyn 339 B11
st. Box Hill N 375 E11
FORUM
pl. Tullamarine 278 K4
FORWOOD
wy. Roxburgh Pk 194 D16
FOSBERY
av. Caulfield N 415 C20
cr. Viewbank 285 G16
FOSSICKERS
wy. Warrandyte 333 G3
FOSTER
av. Glen Huntly 456 B9
av. St Kilda 414 C18
cr. Knoxfield 462 L3
cr. Knoxfield 463 A3
ct. Thomastown 240 F13
la. Aspendale, off Foster St 546 D7
pl. Richmond 26 L11
rd. Eltham 288 C4
rd. Olinda 427 J18
st. Anglesea 713 F6
st. Aspendale 546 D7
st. Dallas 238 G10
st. Dandenong 535 K10
st. Dandenong 536 A10
st. Elsternwick 455 C5
st. McKinnon 456 C17
st. St Kilda 414 D17
st. S Geelong 702 L13
st. S Geelong 703 A13
st. Werribee 446 J16
st.e, Dandenong 536 C9
FOSTERS
ct. Cranbourne N 578 G9
rd. Keilor Park 277 K15
FOTINI
gdn. Bundoora 242 L20
FOTIS
ct. Oak Park 279 G11
FOULDS
ct. Berwick 553 L8
ct. Montrose 382 A8
FOULKES
st. Alphington 327 K19
FOUNDRY
la. Maribyrnong 367 C2
rd. Sunshine 321 C19
FOUNTAIN
ct. Kew 371 H5
ct. Werribee 446 H19
dr. Narre Warren 538 H20
FOUNTAINE
av. Malvern East 457 A3
FOURTH
av. Altona North 409 K7
av. Anglesea 713 C10
av. Aspendale 546 F10
av. Brunswick 325 D9
av. Chelsea Ht 547 E13
av. Cockatoo 510 H5
av. Hoppers Csg 448 L5
av. Pakenham 584 K2
av. Rosebud 683 L18
av. Rowville 462 E19
av. Sunshine 365 E9
cr. Hadfield 281 C10
cr. Hadfield 281 C8
dr. Springvale 500 J12
st. Beaumaris 529 H7
st. Black Rock 529 H7
st. Parkdale 531 D10
FOWLER
cr. Newport 410 H9
ct. Mill Park 242 B5
ct. Rosebud 684 F14
rd. Dandenong S 536 F16
rd. Rowville 502 L7
st. Bonbeach 573 B1
st. Box Hill S 418 G3
st. Breakwater 703 F20
st. Chelsea 547 A19
st. Coburg 325 J3
st. Hoppers Csg 405 A19
FOWLERS
la. Geelong 703 D12
FOX
cl. Hampton Pk 551 D9
cl. Highett 496 E15
ct. Dandenong S 535 J13
ct. Jacana 237 K19
ct. Sunbury 143 B9
ct. Sunshine W 364 G8
rd. Beaconsfld Up 542 L9
rd. Nar Warrn N 538 K9
rd. Smiths Gly 206 G5
st. Dandenong 536 D12
st. St Albans 276 A19
FOXCROFT
ct. Sunshine W 364 B9
FOXDALE
pl. Cairnlea 319 K12
FOXEYS
rd. Dromana 670 G11
rd. Tuerong 670 G11
FOXGLOVE
ct. Cranbourne N 578 C5
ct. Viewbank 285 K20
la. Craigieburn 150 E14
pl. Epping 198 F20
FOXLEY
st. Glen Waverley 420 F15
FOXTAIL
tce. S Morang 199 H9
FOXTON
la. Melbourne 1 G19
la. Melbourne 24 B11
pl. Roxburgh Pk 194 A13
st. St Albans 320 D5
FOXWOOD
dr. Point Cook 450 E7
pl. Somerville 645 A16
FOXZAMI
cr. Epping 198 C20
cr. Epping 242 C1
FOY
av. Chelsea 546 H16
ct. Glen Waverley 420 J15
la. Chelsea 546 H16
la. Yellingbo 387 F12
FRALLON
cr. Frankston 600 A15
FRAME
av. Tecoma 466 D11
FRAMPTON
st. St Kilda 414 E15
FRAN
cr. Viewbank 329 G1
ct. Glen Waverley 420 D19
ct. Ringwood 378 L5
ct. Templstw Lr 330 D7
ct. Werribee 446 K16
st. Glenroy 279 G6
FRANCES
av. Greensbrgh 286 D10
av. Montrose 382 C11
av. Vermont 421 E2
av. Yarra Glen 209 C19
cr. Cranbourne N 578 F10
ct. Cranbourne 604 B5
dr. Sunshine N 321 A15
st. Heathmont 378 H19
st. Highett 495 H15
st. Springvale S 499 G18
st. The Basin 425 A11
FRANCES BROWNE
wy. Tarneit 405 C11
FRANCESCA
ct. Frankston 628 E9
st. Mont Albert N 374 D9
FRANCESCO
dr. Dandenong N 502 B12
st. Bentleigh E 456 J20
FRANCINE
ct. Narre Warren 538 F16
FRANCIS
av. Newcomb 704 B16
bvd. Sunbury 144 D14
cr. Ferntree Gly 424 D19
cr. Glen Iris 417 A16
cr. Mt Evelyn 338 K14
ct. Narre Warren 538 L17
dr. Mt Martha 656 F9
gr. Thornbury 326 L11
gr. Thornbury 327 A11
la. Kensington 33 C10
st. Ascot Vale 324 A18
st. Belmont 706 H6
st. Blackburn 375 L14
st. Brighton East 455 D15
st. Brooklyn 366 A16
st. Clayton 498 L1
st. Coburg 281 B20
st. Cockatoo 471 F17
st. Collingwood 20 A14
st. Dandenong S 535 J13
st. Dromana 686 A7
st. Frankston 599 G17
st. Hadfield 280 J9
st. Heidelberg Ht 328 E6
st. Keilor Park 277 L15
st. Melbourne 1 A15
st. Melbourne 23 G11
st. Melton S 268 H4
st. Mordialloc 532 A16
st. Mt Waverley 419 G20
st. Oak Park 279 K12
st. Prahran 32 H17
st. Prahran 414 K9
st. Richmond 26 K11
st. Rye 696 K10
st. Sandringham 495 C13
st. Seaford 599 H2
st. S Melbourne 29 L4
st. Tecoma 466 D12
st. Warrandyte 333 F2
st. Werribee 447 H17
st. Yarraville 366 A16
st. Yarraville 366 K17
FRANCIS BRIGGS
rd. Melb Airport 235 K14
FRANCISCAN
av. Frankston 628 B12
FRANCIS WALTON
rd. Mill Park 242 D3
FRANCONIA
ct. Mulgrave 501 D5
FRANGIPANI
cl. Endeavour Hl 537 G6
ct. Port Melb 412 H3
la. Maribyrnong 322 H16
wy. Bundoora 242 F14
FRANK
av. Clayton S 498 J4
ct. Rowville 463 K19
st. Balwyn N 373 K5
st. Belmont 702 H16
st. Box Hill S 418 H5
st. Coburg 325 E3
st. Dallas 238 L10
st. Doncaster 374 L3
st. Eltham 288 B5
st. Frankston 599 H18
st. Glen Waverley 460 C5
st. Lalor 241 B8
st. Mornington 640 J19
st. Newtown 702 D12
st. Noble Park 500 H20
st. Safety Bch 686 H1
st. Sunshine W 364 C2
st. Vermont 421 H2
FRANKCOM
st. Blackburn 375 G15
FRANK FORD
st. Northcote 326 J15
FRANKLAND
ct. Wyndham Va 446 G8
FRANKLIN
av. Chelsea 546 J17
av. Roxburgh Pk 194 A10
bvd. Hoppers Csg 449 A4
ct. Craigieburn 150 C17
ct. Frankston 599 G19
ct. Glen Waverley 459 J4
la. Chelsea 546 J17
pde. Lynbrook 551 E19
pl. Caroline Spr 318 B4
pl. Delahey 275 B11
pl. Mornington 640 F12
pl. W Melbourne 23 D5
rd. Doncaster E 375 K1
rd. Lalor 240 H10
rd. Portsea 677 L7
st. Coburg 325 K5
st. Eltham 287 G11
st. Maddingley 263 K1
st. Melbourne 1 G1
st. Melbourne 1 K1
st. Melbourne 23 H3
st. Mentone 531 B6
st. Moorabbin 496 H9
st. Newport 411 B9
FRANKLYN
st. Huntingdale 458 G16
st. Oakleigh E 458 G16
FRANKS
gr. Kew 372 A11
wy. Cranbourne N 578 E10
FRANKSTON
dr. Endeavour Hl 502 L12
fwy. Frankston 599 G18
fwy. Frankston N 599 G18
fwy. Seaford 599 G7
st. Reservoir 282 H14
FRANKSTON-DANDENONG
rd. Bangholme 549 K20
rd. Bangholme 575 A14
rd. Carrum Downs 574 J18
rd. Dandenong S 536 A20
rd. Dandenong S 549 K20
rd. Frankston 599 G12
rd. Frankston N 599 G12
rd. Lyndhurst 549 K20
rd. Lyndhurst 575 A14
rd. Seaford 599 G12
FRANKSTON-FLINDERS
rd. Frankston 627 G6
rd. Frankston S 627 G6
rd. Frankston S 627 K17
rd. Somerville 644 G7
FRANKSTON GARDENS
dr. Carrum Downs 574 D19
FRANK WORRELL
dr. Mornington 657 B2
FRANLEIGH
dr. Narre Warren 539 A17
FRASER
av. Anglesea 713 D3
av. Beaconsfld Up 541 G11
av. Edithvale 546 H13
cl. Mill Park 242 F7
cr. Wantirna S 462 E1
ct. Cranbourne N 578 G8
ct. Jacana 237 H16
ct. Sunbury 143 C13
pl. Forest Hill 420 G3
rd. Clayton S 498 J11
st. Airport W 278 K14
st. Airport W 279 A14
st. Bentleigh E 456 L19
st. Brunswick 325 C11
st. Coburg 281 E20
st. Dandenong N 502 C19
st. Diamond Ck 245 K12
st. Glen Waverley 460 A8
st. Herne Hill 701 J3
st. Hoppers Csg 448 J1
st. Malvern 416 A13
st. Melton S 268 J6
st. Middle Park 413 J12
st. Ormond 456 A12
st. Queenscliff 708 G19
st. Richmond 371 A17
st. Sunshine 364 J2
st. Sunshine 365 A2
st. Yarraville 367 D18
FRASERBURGH
cr. Greenvale 193 F18
FRATER
ct. Doncaster E 332 F16
pl. Mill Park 242 L8
st. Kew East 372 J3
FRAWLEY
ct. Tarneit 447 G1
rd. Eumemmerring 537 A12
rd. Hallam 537 G14
st. Frankston 599 L20
FRAXINUS
tr. Olinda 427 E8
FRAYNE
ct. Highton 705 K7
FRAZER
av. Altona 408 L14
FREAME
st. Yarraville 366 H17
FREDA
av. Cheltenham 496 L18
ct. Blackburn S 419 G5
ct. Eltham North 245 E19
ct. Narre Warren 539 B14
ct. St Albans 320 F11
ct. Wheelers Hl 460 L17
st. Broadmeadows 238 D19
st. Hughesdale 457 E10
FREDERIC
dr. Ringwood 379 A3
FREDERICK
ct. Werribee 448 H9
ri. Nar Warrn S 552 H7
st. Anglesea 713 E7
st. Balwyn 373 E10
st. Blackburn 375 H14
st. Brunswick 325 E11
st. Bulleen 329 L17
st. Caulfield S 455 L12
st. Croydon 380 C9
st. Dandenong S 536 A14
st. Doncaster 374 L2
st. E Geelong 703 H10
st. Fawkner 281 J8
st. Ferntree Gly 424 J15
st. Heidelberg Ht 328 G5
st. Malvern 416 B12
st. Northcote 326 J15
st. Thomastown 241 D15
st. Tottenham 365 J9
st. Windsor 414 H12
st. Yarraville 367 D17
st. Hawthorn, off Wakefield St 372 A16
FREDERICO
st. Highett 495 J11
FRED McCUBBIN
cl. Diamond Ck 245 A13
FREDMAN
ct. Dingley Vill 532 K6
FREE
st. Yarraville 367 A15
FREEBURGH
ct. Meadow Ht 238 B4
FREEDMAN
av. Boronia 424 B8
FREELAND
gr. Jacana 237 K20
FREELANDS
dr. Mt Eliza 642
FREEMAN
av. Burnside 318
cr. Mill Park 242
ct. Endeavour Hl 538
dr. Glenroy 280 G
dr. Pakenham 584 H
pl. Langwarrin 629
st. Balwyn 373 D
st. Campbellfield 239
st. Caulfield 455
st. Fitzroy N 19
st. Hawthorn E 372 F
st. Richmond 26
st. Ringwood E 378 L
st. Ringwood E 379 A
st. Sunshine 365
st. Wheelers Hl 461
st. Yarraville 366 H
FREEMANS
rd. Altona North 409
rd. Mt Eliza 626
FREEMANTLE
dr. Wantirna S 421 L
FREESIA
ct. Hoppers Csg 405 D
FREGON
rd. Clayton 458 L
FREIGHT
dr. Somerton 195 D
rd. Tullamarine 278
FREIGHTER
rd. Moorabbin 497 E
FREMANTLE
cl. Point Cook 449
rd. Sunbury 142 J
FREMONT
cl. Bulleen 329
pde. Sunshine W 364
st. Heathmont 378 K
FRENCH
av. Brunswick E 325 L
av. Edithvale 546 H
av. Northcote 327 C
cl. Mooroolbark 337 J
ct. Watsonia 285
rd. Greenvale 192 K
st. Camberwell 417
st. Coburg N 281 E
st. Croydon 336 G
st. Elsternwick 454
st. Footscray 367
st. Geelong West 702
st. Lalor 241 D
st. Mt Waverley 459
st. Noble Park 500 L
st. Ringwood E 378 L
st. Rye 696
st. Thomastown 241 D
FRENSHAM
rd. Macleod 285 F
rd. Watsonia 285 F
FRESHFIELD
av. Mooroolbark 337 L
av. Wantirna 422 A
FRESHWATER
pt. Point Cook 451
FRESNO
st. Altona 409 D
FREW
av. Frankston 599 L
FREY
st. Pascoe Vale 280 E
FREYER
st. Williamstown 411 C
FREYNE
st. Wonga Park 335
FRIAR
pl. Melton W 226 D
st. Blairgowrie 696
FRIAR PARK
pl. Point Cook 450
FRIARS
ct. Doncaster E 331 L
rd. Moorabbin 496 L
FRIBOURG
ct. Ivanhoe East 328 K
FRICKER
av. Greensbrgh 286
FRIEDA
ct. Ferntree Gly 464
st. Dromana 686
FRIEND
ct. Mill Park 242
st. Balwyn N 374
st. Mont Albert N 374
FRIENDLY
ct. Kilsyth 381
FRIENDSHIP
av. Mill Park 242
cl. Cranbourne W 603

G

cr. Cheltenham 531 F2
cr. Frankston N 600 E7
cr. Dandenong, off David St 536 E4
ct. Mt Martha 657 C9
ct. Nar Warrn S 579 D1
ct. Somerville 645 D15
pl. Cairnlea 319 G13
rd. Balwyn N 330 A20
rd. Balwyn N 374 A1
rd. Gardenvale 455 B11
rd. Lalor 240 L12
rd. Thomastown 240 L12
st. Blackburn 375 J17
st. Croydon S 379 J13
st. Pakenham 585 A2

GARDENS
rd. Rosebud 700 L7

GARDENVALE
rd. Caulfield S 455 B11
rd. Gardenvale 455 B11

GARDENVIEW
cl. Mill Park 243 B7
ct. Templestowe 331 E12
gr. Westmeadows 236 F15

GARDINER
av. Anglesea 713 G7
av. Dandenong N 501 F20
ct. Mill Park 242 L7
ct. Mill Park 243 A7
la. Rockbank 317 A7
pde. Glen Iris 416 K12
rd. Clayton 459 B13
rd. Hawthorn 415 L3
rd. Notting Hill 459 B13
rd. Seville 387 B5
st. Berwick 554 E4
st. Brunswick 325 D13
st. Bundoora 284 D4
st. Lilydale 338 F3
st. N Melbourne 17 F19
st. Pakenham 584 G6

GARDINERS
ps. Caroline Spr 274 D17

GARDINI
av. Ringwood 378 F16

GARDNER
ct. Albanvale 319 A6
ct. Altona Mdw 451 H5
ct. Balwyn N 373 D5
la. Kensington 33 F8
pde. Mt Evelyn 339 D17
pl. S Melbourne 29 L6
st. Box Hill S 374 K20
st. Richmond 26 L11
st. Richmond 371 A15

GAREM GAM
wyn. Nar Warrn S 552 J20

GARETH
av. Beaumaris 530 A7
ct. Glen Waverley 420 L16
dr. Burwood E 419 H12

GARFIELD
av. Ormond 456 G13
cl. Melton S 268 C11
ct. Dandenong N 501 H8
ct. Hampton Pk 551 J4
pl. Wheelers Hl 460 H18
st. Cheltenham 496 H18
st. Fitzroy 18 L15
st. Richmond 26 B5
st. St Albans 319 F5
wy. Craigieburn 150 C8

GARGENEY
ct. Berwick 580 A2

GARGOR
ct. Kurunjang 227 D13

GARIBALDI
st. Badger Creek 258 J14

GARIE
ct. Grovedale 706 B11
st. Blackburn 375 F17

GARLAND
ct. Noble Park N 501 E18
ri. Rowville 463 F20

GARLEPP
st. Coldstream 295 E14

GARLICK
av. Newtown 701 L6

GARNAR
la. Dandenong 535 L9

GARNER
ct. Blackburn S 419 E1
ct. Endeavour Hl 537 G5
pde. Dallas 238 L10
st. Dromana 685 K11

GARNET
cl. Narre Warren 539 F14
ct. Hampton Pk 551 B7
st. Brunswick 325 C9
st. Essendon W 323 A7
st. Ferntree Gly 464 E4
st. Niddrie 323 A7
st. Preston 326 J3
st. Sunshine N 321 C17

GARNET-LEARY
av. Black Rock 495 G20

GARNETT
rd. Wheelers Hl 461 F20
st. Huntingdale 458 E12

GARNOOK
gr. Badger Creek 258 F14

GARNSWORTHY
pl. Newport 411 A11
st. Springvale 500 C8

GARONNE
cct. Roxburgh Pk 194 E5

GARRELL
st. Caulfield N 455 F2

GARRETT
cr. Bellfield 327 K6
ct. Mill Park 242 J8
ct. Narre Warren 539 A14

GARRETTS
la. Box Hill 374 L15

GARRICK
ct. Wheelers Hl 461 A7

GARRISON
gr. Wantirna 422 E6

GARRISSON
dr. Glen Waverley 460 G1

GARRY
ct. Kings Park 275 F18
ct. S Morang 243 G3
st. Melton S 268 H6

GARRYLAWN
ct. Frankston 600 B20

GARRYOWEN
cr. Narre Warren 539 A20
tce. Tullamarine 278 K1

GARSIDE
st. Dandenong 536 F5

GARSTON
ct. Wantirna 422 B11

GARTH
st. Ivanhoe 328 C8

GARTON
st. Carlton N 325 G20
st. Port Melb 29 C5
st. Port Melb 413 B2
st. Princes Hill 18 B1
st. Princes Hill 325 G20

GARVEY
st. Bentleigh E 457 E20

GARVOC
ct. Meadow Ht 238 A7

GARWAIN
pde. Glen Waverley 420 K17

GARY
av. Hampton E 496 A10
ct. Croydon 336 H13
ct. Lilydale 338 L12
ct. Lilydale 339 A12
ct. Mt Martha 656 J9
st. Mt Waverley 419 H15

GARYTH
ct. Belmont 706 D4

GASCOYNE
ct. Frankston 628 D11
st. Canterbury 372 J16

GASKELL
av. Mt Eliza 641 K5
ct. Altona Mdw 451 K8

GASKETT
ct. Nar Warrn S 552 L13

GASTONS
rd. Eltham 287 K3

GATCUM
ct. Noble Park 500 L19

GATEHOUSE
dr. Attwood 237 B11
dr. Kensington 33 C9
la. Albert Park 29 F15
pl. Maribyrnong 322 K16
st. Parkville 17 E11

GATES
ct. Altona Mdw 451 J5
ct. Roxburgh Pk 193 K16

GATESHEAD
dr. Wantirna S 422 J15

GATEWAY
bvd. Epping 196 G20

GATH
ct. Rowville 463 C15

GATHERCOLE
la. Panton Hill 204 H18

GATHRAY
ct. Roxburgh Pk 194 C17

GATHREY
ct. Endeavour Hl 537 C6

GATIS
st. Glen Iris 417 K12

GATLEY
ct. Dandenong N 501 J10

GATTERS
la. Box Hill 374 L14
rd. Wonga Park 335 D8

GATTINARA
dr. Frankston 628 D8

GATUM
ct. Frankston 600 J19

GATWICK
cl. Wantirna 422 H11
ct. Craigieburn 150 B16
ct. Cranbourne E 578 J17
ct. Keilor Park 278 A12
rd. Bayswater N 380 G15

GAUDIN
ct. Werribee 446 H18

GAUDION
rd. Doncaster E 331 J15
rd. Wandin East 341 D19

GAUNTLET
av. Glen Waverley 420 K16
rd. Malvern East 457 H4

GAUSSBERG
wk. Roxburgh Pk 193 J14

GAUTIER
wy. S Morang 198 L14

GAVAN
ct. Frankston 599 H17
ct. Werribee 447 G10
dr. Springvale 499 G17
st. Camberwell 417 L8
st. Portsea 678 D4

GAVIN
st. Jacana 237 H18
st. Moorabbin 496 F11

GAVINTON
pl. Berwick 555 A6

GAWALLA
st. Rye 696 L9
st. Rye 697 A9

GAWITH
ct. Toorak 415 F2

GAWLER
ct. Cheltenham 497 C19
ct. Mont Albert 374 E13

GAY
st. Blackburn N 375 L11

GAYBRE
ct. Cheltenham 497 D18

GAYDON
st. Ferntree Gly 463 H5

GAYE
ct. Hoppers Csg 447 L2

GAYLARD
av. Newtown 701 K6
ct. Berwick 554 B4

GAYLE
ct. Clayton S 499 D16
st. Watsonia 285 C7

GAYNERS
rd. Olinda 426 H9

GAYNESS
ct. Werribee 446 J19

GAYNOR
cr. Gladstone Pk 237 C19
cr. Glen Waverley 420 J15
ct. Boronia 423 K11
ct. Frankston 600 D18
ct. Malvern 416 A16
st. Maddingley 263 L3
st. Noble Park 534 E1

GAZANIA
tce. Bundoora 242 E14

GAZE
ct. Mill Park 241 L7

GAZLEY
ct. Altona Mdw 451 D2

GEACH
st. Dallas 238 J11

GEAKE
st. Coburg 281 F20

GEAR
av. Mt Evelyn 339 E19

GEARON
av. Rowville 503 C5

GEDDES
cr. Hoppers Csg 448 F4
la. Melbourne 1 B17
la. Melbourne 23 K11
st. Ascot Vale 323 L18
st. Mulgrave 459 L14

GEDYE
ct. Wantirna S 422 B17
st. Doncaster E 375 H6

GEE
ct. Nunawading 376 G19
st. Sunshine N 321 B13

GEEBUNG
av. Frankston S 627 L16
rd. Cranbourne W 577 H16

GEEL
st. Bentleigh 496 E3

GEELONG
rd. Altona 407 F18
rd. Altona Mdw 407 F18
rd. Altona North 408 D5
rd. Brooklyn 366 A15
rd. Footscray 366 K10
rd. Kingsville 366 K10
rd. Laverton 407 F18
rd. Laverton N 408 D5
rd. Point Cook 449 L3
rd. Torquay 711 K8
rd. Tottenham 366 A15
rd. Werribee 447 A20
rd. W Footscray 366 A15
rd. W Footscray 366 K10
st. Kingsville 366 K10
st. W Footscray 366 K10

GEELONG-BACCHUS MARSH
rd. Maddingley 264 F20
rd. Parwan 264 F20

GEER
ct. Bentleigh E 497 C3
st. Ravenhall 318 G13

GEES
ct. Lower Plenty 286 J16

GEEWAN
ct. Greensbrgh 244 D19

GELA
ct. Tullamarine 278 F5

GELEA
cr. Vermont S 421 D9

GELL
ct. Noble Park 500 K19
st. Bacchus Msh 222 B17

GELLIBRAND
cl. Seabrook 450 L8
cr. Reservoir 282 J6
ct. Berwick 580 C1
pl. Plenty 244 C13
rd. Port Melb 412 D5
st. Kew 371 K11
st. McCrae 684 K12
st. Queenscliff 709 B19
st. Williamstown 411 B17

GELLIES
rd. Bulla 144 J13
rd. Sunbury 144 J13

GELLION
pl. Roxburgh Pk 194 F15

GEM
cl. Altona Mdw 451 L2
cl. Ringwood 335 A20
ct. Rosebud 700 B2
ct. Tootgarook 698 D7
st. Williamstn N 411 A12
st. Wyndham Va 446 D14

GEMBROOK
rd. Gembrook 512 K20
rd. Pakenham Up 559 E4

GEMBROOK-LAUNCHING PLACE
rd. Launching Pl 345 J14

GEMINI
cl. Doncaster E 332 D17
ct. Keysborough 535 A8
ct. Wheelers Hl 460 H9

GEMMA
ct. Carrum Downs 575 F16
ct. Langwarrin 629 K5

GENERAL JOSHUA
dr. Hampton Pk 551 G11

GENETICS
la. Parkville 17 K13

GENEVA
ct. Frankston 600 F19
rd. Alphington 327 L20
rd. Alphington 371 L1

GENEVIEVE
ct. Ferntree Gly 463 G6

GENINE
av. Heatherton 497 H15

GENISTA
av. Boronia 424 B12
av. Springvale 500 J12
rd. Cranbourne W 577 H18
st. Frankston S 627 E8

GENOA
av. Bonbeach 573 B3
av. Reservoir 283 F12
ct. Bangholme 549 H14
ct. Coolaroo 238 D7
ct. Frankston 600 D18
ct. Mt Waverley 459 G3
ct. Templstw Lr 329 K8
pl. Deer Park 319 D11
st. Dandenong N 502 A10
st. Moorabbin 496 J10
st. Parkdale 531 D13
wy. Cranbourne W 577 F15

GENT
st. Yarraville 366 G16

GENTLE
st. Clayton 498 G1

GENTLE ANNIE
dr. Blind Bight 650

GENTLES
av. Campbellfield 239 A

GENTZEN
dr. Wyndham Va 446 G

GEOFFREY
ct. Cranbourne 577 L
ct. Frankston 626
ct. Lower Plenty 287 B
ct. Narre Warren 538 J
dr. Kilsyth 381
st. Blairgowrie 696
st. Thomastown 241 C

GEOFREY
st. Frankston 626

GEORDY
cl. Wantirna S 462

GEORGE
av. Hallam 537 F
ct. Greensbrgh 286
ct. S Morang 243
la. St Kilda 414 B
pde. Melbourne 2 L
pde. Melbourne 24
rd. Healesville 257
rd. Silvan 385 B
rd. Vermont S 421
st. Anglesea 713
st. Ashwood 417 L
st. Bacchus Msh 222 B
st. Beaconsfield 555 C
st. Belmont 702 H
st. Bentleigh E 456 J
st. Blackburn 375 L
st. Brunswick 325 H
st. Camberwell 417
st. Caulfield N 415 C
st. Clifton Hill 20
st. Cockatoo 511
st. Cranbourne 578 D
st. Dandenong 535
st. Diamond Ck 245 L
st. Doncaster 330 L
st. Doncaster E 331 G
st. Dromana 686
st. E Melbourne 25
st. Ferntree Gly 464
st. Fitzroy 25
st. Fitzroy N 19
st. Flemington 33
st. Flemington 324 D
st. Frankston 627
st. Geelong West 702
st. Glenroy 279
st. Gruyere 342
st. Hampton Pk 551 D
st. Hawthorn 372 B
st. Highett 495 L
st. Lilydale 338
st. Maidstone 322 J
st. Malvern East 416 E
st. Mont Albert 374 F
st. Moonee Pnd 323 J
st. Mooroolbark 337 B
st. Mordialloc 531 H
st. Mornington 640 C
st. Mt Evelyn 338 L
st. Mt Evelyn 339 A
st. Murrumbeena 457 D
st. Newtown 702
st. Niddrie 322
st. Noble Park 500 G
st. Northcote 326 G
st. N Melbourne 34
st. Oakleigh 458 C
st. Olinda 426
st. Preston 282 C
st. Reservoir 282 H
st. Richmond 26 G
st. Rye 697
st. Safety Bch 686
st. St Albans 276 A
st. Sandringham 495 K
st. Scoresby 462
st. Somerton 194 G
st. Somerville 644 K
st. Sorrento 678
st. S Melbourne 29
st. Spotswood 410
st. Sunshine 365
st. Sunshine 365
st. Templstw Lr 330 J
st. Up Fntree Gly 465 C
st. Upwey 466 A
st. Wandin N 340 J
st. Windsor 31
st. Windsor 414 D
st. Yarra Jctn 346
st. Yarraville 367 A

GEORGE BASS
av. Endeavour Hl 537 H
ct. Skye 575 H

RGE BENJAMIN
Seabrook 450 K8
RGE CHUDLEIGH
Hallam 538 D14
RGE GREEVES
Hoppers Csg 447 K1
RGE KNOX
Rowville 502 B6
RGE RAE
Harkaway 540 E12
RGES
Taylors Hill 274 L11
Olinda 427 G4
Ringwood 378 G9
Sherbrooke 466 J1
The Patch 467 L5
RGETTE
Endeavour Hl 537 J3
RGIA
Ferntree Gly 463 L6
Kealba 276 J19
RGIA MAE
Rowville 503 B6
RGIAN
Roxburgh Pk 193 L4
Balwyn 373 D13
Ringwood 334 L20
Ringwood 335 A20
. Wantirna 422 F12
Melton W 226 B15
RGIANA
Chelsea Ht 547 E12
McCrae 685 A13
Sandringham 495 A12
RGINA
. Camberwell 417 D6
Berwick 554 L19
Wheelers Hl 461 E12
P
Healesville 213 H16
A
Wantirna S 421 L19
ALD
Chelsea Ht 547 E16
Langwarrin 629 C2
Blackburn 376 D19
Ferntree Gly 464 H1
Murrumbeena 457 B10
Sunshine N 321 C17
Werribee 446 L11
Werribee 447 A10
ALDINE
Kilsyth S 424 L2
Wheelers Hl 461 E19
Hampton Pk 552 C15
Rye 696 G11
ANG
Rowville 463 A16
ANIUM
Berwick 580 B3
ARD
Croydon N 336 D13
Pakenham 585 A3
Caulfield 455 F3
Dandenong 535 J2
Templstw Lr 330 H14
BER
Monbulk 468 H2
BERA
Blackburn N 375 J8
BERT
Broadmeadows 238 D18
DA
Scoresby 462 H9
LACH
Clayton S 498 H9
MAIN
Keilor Dn 276 B16
Oakleigh S 458 D16
MAN
Thomastown 240 L14
MANDER
Hillside 274 C4
Hoppers Csg 405 C14
Meadow Ht 193 J19
ONA
Keilor 277 C11
Keilor 277 B10
RARD
Glen Waverley 459 H6
Watsonia N 243 H19
RATTS
Upwey 465 L7
RY ANNA
Epping 198 E20
TONIA
Boronia 423 F15
TRUDE
Noble Park 535 B7
Tarneit 405 A10
Fitzroy 18 L19
Frankston 627 G1
Geelong West 702 D6

st. Preston 326 J4
st. St Albans 319 K2
st. Sunshine 365 F3
st. Templstw Lr 330 B11
st. Windsor 414 J12
GERTZ
av. Reservoir 283 H3
GERVASE
av. Glenroy 279 J2
GERVES
st. Torquay 711 G11
GEUM
st. Hadfield 280 H7
GEZA
ct. Baxter 643 L2
GEZIREH
st. Pascoe Vale S 324 H1
GHAZEEPORE
rd. Grovedale 705 C20
rd. Waurn Ponds 705 C20
GHERA
ct. Greensbrgh 244 C17
GHERINGHAP
st. Geelong 702 L10
GHIRAN
cl. Aspendale Gdn 546 H3
GHOST GUM
ct. Bundoora 242 F15
GIANA
ct. Ringwood N 377 L6
GIANNARELLI
dr. Brunswick E 325 K18
GIANNI
ct. Keysborough 534 C13
GIBB
ct. Pakenham 584 F3
rd. Red Hill 688 C5
st. Berwick 554 D9
st. Dandenong N 502 A16
st. Maidstone 366 F4
GIBBO
ct. Coolaroo 238 G7
GIBBON
av. Vermont S 420 J7
ct. St Albans 275 G18
GIBBONS
dr. Epping 198 G20
pl. Carlton 18 D18
st. Richmond 26 F20
st. Sunbury 142 J13
st. Werribee 447 J16
st. W Melbourne 367 K14
GIBBS
rd. Ferntree Gly 423 L19
rd. Healesville 258 H2
rd. Montrose 382 G11
rd. Yarra Glen 209 A11
st. Balaclava 414 G19
st. Balaclava 414 G20
st. Beaumaris 530 C10
st. Newcomb 703 L16
GIBCOE
st. Greensbrgh 286 B6
GIBDON
st. Burnley 371 B20
GIBLIN
la. Melton W 225 B7
GIBNEY
cl. Roxburgh Pk 194 C12
st. Hawthorn 371 H17
GIBSON
av. Brunswick W 324 J17
ct. Altona Mdw 451 D3
ct. Essendon 323 C2
ct. Ringwood 378 D20
ct. Sunbury 142 G9
ct. Sydenham 274 K4
rd. Ringwood N 335 A10
rd. Warranwood 335 A10
st. Alphington 327 K19
st. Box Hill S 374 H20
st. Broadmeadows 238 A19
st. Caulfield E 456 F3
st. Dromana 686 A5
st. Hallam 537 J13
st. Lalor 241 E5
st. Mitcham 376 L16
st. Northcote 326 L15
GIBSONS
pde. Warburton 349 H1
GIDEON
cl. Boronia 423 J14
GIDGEE
av. Templstw Lr 330 G13
ct. Cranbourne W 577 K15
ct. Forest Hill 420 F4
ct. Keilor Dn 276 H15
ct. Wantirna S 423 B11
GIFFARD
st. Williamstown 411 F18

GIFFORD
av. Ferntree Gly 464 C4
cl. Berwick 554 E16
rd. Doncaster 375 A2
GIFFORDS
rd. E Warburton 350 C2
rd. Warburton 350 C2
GILARTH
st. Highett 495 K14
GILBA
pl. Lilydale 338 G17
GILBANK
st. Reservoir 282 F13
GILBERT
ct. Keysborough 534 C11
ct. Lalor 240 J7
ct. Mt Waverley 458 F6
ct. Parkdale 531 J10
ct. Scoresby 462 H7
gr. Bentleigh 495 L1
gr. Carnegie 456 K12
la. Dandenong 535 L10
pde. Camberwell 417 D6
pl. Berwick 580 L1
rd. Ivanhoe 328 D15
rd. Preston 326 D5
rd. Reservoir 282 E20
st. Braybrook 321 L19
st. Bulleen 330 B16
st. Coburg 325 D4
st. Mont Albert 374 G13
st. Torquay 712 B9
GILBERT PARK
dr. Knoxfield 463 C8
GILBERTSON
rd. Laverton N 363 K18
st. Essendon 323 D2
wk. Kensington 33 E8
GILBY
rd. Mt Waverley 459 E11
GILCHRIST
cr. Sunbury 143 D9
wy. Aspendale Gdn 547 B7
GILDA
ct. Mulgrave 460 A17
ct. Ringwood 378 K5
ct. Rowville 503 A5
st. Maidstone 366 G3
GILDAN
ct. Hoppers Csg 449 C4
st. Balwyn N 373 A7
GILES
ct. Cranbourne N 577 J8
ct. Frankston S 627 F10
ct. Mill Park 242 L5
ct. Werribee 448 B8
rt. Endeavour Hl 537 J6
GILFORD
gr. Cheltenham 496 G19
GILGA
st. Mornington 640 L16
st. Mornington 641 A16
GILGANDRA
st. Warneet 649 F11
GILGUY
pl. S Morang 198 L8
GILJA
ct. Boronia 424 K7
ct. Cranbourne W 577 J16
GILL
ct. Rowville 463 J19
pl. Hoppers Csg 405 A14
pl. Mooroolbark 337 D11
pl. Sunbury 143 C8
rd. Pt Lonsdale 710 A4
st. Belmont 706 B1
st. Cranbourne 604 D2
st. Doncaster E 376 E1
st. Reservoir 282 D9
GILLAN
rd. Belgrave S 506 K10
rd. Belgrave S 507 B6
GILLARD
pl. Ringwood N 334 K20
st. Brighton East 455 F17
st. Burwood 418 G11
GILLARDS
rd. Mt Eliza 626 C15
rd. Mt Eliza 626 E16
GILLESPIE
ct. Cranbourne N 577 J9
pl. Epping 241 J5
rd. Kings Park 275 A19
rd. St Albans 275 G20
GILLIAN
pl. Pakenham 584 H9
rd. Mt Waverley 419 A16
st. Springvale S 534 A7
GILLIES
ct. Nar Warrn S 552 J12
st. Essendon N 323 G2
st. Fairfield 327 D17
st. Fairfield 327 D19

st. Hampton 495 B10
st. Mitcham 377 A12
st. Thornbury 327 E14
GILLIGAN
ct. Brunswick W 324 K8
rd. Altona North 409 L9
rd. Gisborne S 141 A2
GILLIGANS
ct. Rowville 502 F2
GILLINGHAM
cr. Craigieburn 150 D20
st. Preston 326 F5
st. Watsonia N 243 G19
GILLIS
ct. Diamond Ck 246 A16
st. Millgrove 348 E2
GILLMAN
st. Cheltenham 530 J3
st. Hawthorn E 372 F18
st. Malvern East 416 C16
GILLON
ct. Oakleigh 458 D7
ct. St Albans 320 G11
GILLS
al. Melbourne 1 L13
al. Melbourne 24 B8
rd. Watsons Ck 249 E4
GILLWELL
rd. Lalor 240 F10
GILMORE
cr. Lynbrook 551 D15
ct. Belgrave S 506 H3
dr. Attwood 237 B12
la. Caroline Spr 318 E10
pl. Gladstone Pk 279 D1
rd. Doncaster 375 B2
st. Pakenham 584 H9
GILMOUR
ct. Greensbrgh 243 K20
ct. Greensbrgh 285 K1
ct. Meadow Ht 237 L2
ct. Pascoe Vale 281 A15
rd. Bentleigh 496 D6
rd. Camberwell 417 K5
rd. Sunshine N 320 L16
rd. Sunshine N 321 A15
st. Burwood 418 B10
st. Coburg 325 F1
GILROY
cr. Mill Park 242 F2
GILSLAND
rd. Murrumbeena 457 D6
GILSTON
wy. Ringwood 335 A18
GILWAY
ri. Greensbrgh 244 B20
GIMCRACK
wy. Mt Martha 657 C8
GIMLET
cl. Meadow Ht 193 L18
GINA
ct. Doncaster E 332 G5
ct. Hallam 537 H15
GINGHAM
pl. Berwick 553 J1
GINGKO
tr. Olinda 427 E7
GINIFER
av. Altona North 409 H5
ct. St Albans 320 H12
GINN
cl. Mill Park 242 B6
st. Geelong 702 L3
GINNIE
ct. Mornington 640 J20
GINNIVANS
rd. Smiths Gly 206 D3
GINO
ct. Diamond Ck 246 D9
GIPPS
av. Mordialloc 532 A19
cr. Cranbourne N 577 H7
ct. Epping 197 A19
st. Abbotsford 20 B19
st. Collingwood 19 J18
st. E Melbourne 25 G6
st. Richmond 26 C15
st. Rosebud 684 C16
GIPSON
st. Diamond Ck 245 L9
GIPSY
wy. Sandringham 495 B13
GIRDWOOD
av. Carnegie 456 F4
rd. Boronia 424 D10
GIRGARRE
st. Broadmeadows 238 A9
GIRRALONG
ct. Greensbrgh 244 D19
GIRRAWEEN
dr. Eltham 245 K20
GIRTON
cr. Manifold Ht 702 B5

GIRVAN
cct. Endeavour Hl 503 H17
gr. Pt Lonsdale 710 E3
pl. S Morang 199 D10
GISBORNE
cr. Reservoir 283 F11
rd. Bacchus Msh 222 A16
rd. Darley 222 A16
st. Bulleen 329 L10
st. E Melbourne 24 L3
st. E Melbourne 25 A3
st. Elsternwick 454 L6
st. Elsternwick 455 A6
GISBORNE-MELTON
rd. Kurunjang 227 E15
rd. Melton 227 E17
GISELLE
av. Wantirna S 462 B1
ct. Frankston 600 F19
GISH
ct. Hadfield 281 A8
GISSARA
ct. Wonga Park 291 F14
GISSING
st. Blackburn S 419 K3
GITTUS
st. S Melbourne 368 K20
GIULIANO
ct. Keilor East 322 G7
GIVERNY
cl. Highton 701 E14
GIVVENS
av. Wantirna S 422 F17
GLADE
av. Altona North 409 F1
av. Craigieburn 150 D18
ct. Berwick 554 H20
dr. Bangholme 549 K14
GLADESVILLE
bvd. Patterson L 573 H10
bvd. Patterson L 573 J4
cl. Lysterfield S 504 B15
ct. Dandenong N 501 J16
dr. Bentleigh E 497 D5
dr. Kilsyth 381 F10
GLADESWOOD
dr. Mulgrave 501 D5
GLADHALL
av. Thornbury 327 E8
GLADIGAU
cr. Carrum Downs 575 G14
GLADMAN
st. Greensbrgh 286 A10
GLADSTONE
av. Armadale 415 G15
av. Aspendale 546 C6
av. Northcote 326 E12
gr. Melton 226 K18
gr. S Melbourne 29 G5
la. S Melbourne 29 B2
pde. Elsternwick 455 B8
pde. Glenroy 279 J7
pl. S Melbourne 29 E2
pl. Werribee 447 K15
rd. Briar Hill 286 E5
rd. Dandenong 535 H3
rd. Dandenong N 501 H20
st. Cairnlea 319 F5
st. Coburg 325 L3
st. Glen Iris 416 L14
st. Kew 372 B8
st. Lilydale 338 A4
st. Moonee Pnd 324 B14
st. Reservoir 283 A8
st. St Albans 319 F5
st. Sandringham 495 D16
st. Southbank 29 C2
st. Southbank 413 B1
st. S Melbourne 29 C3
st. S Melbourne 413 B1
st. Surrey Hills 374 F18
st. Thomastown 240 G13
st. Windsor 414 D11
st. Yarraville 367 B16
GLADSTONE PARK
dr. Gladstone Pk 236 K19
GLADSWOOD
st. Ascot Vale 324 A17
GLADWELL
st. Rye 696 H7
GLADWYN
av. Bentleigh E 456 J16
av. Frankston 599 J19
ct. Eltham 288 B4
GLADYS
ct. Coburg N 281 J15
ct. Mt Dandenong 426 G4
gr. Croydon 379 G2
st. Nunawading 376 G11
GLAISDALE
ct. Greenvale 237 C5
GLAMA
ct. Roxburgh Pk 194 D6

GLAMIS
av. Hampton 495 F9
ct. Balwyn N 373 L1
ct. Croydon 380 F3
ct. Derrimut 363 B5
ct. Endeavour Hl 537 L5
ct. Glen Waverley 460 A9
dr. Avondale Ht 321 L8
pl. Melton W 226 D15
rd. W Footscray 366 H11
ri. Officer 555 G19
st. Beaumaris 530 D4
st. Greensbrgh 285 L2
st. Mt Martha 655 L18
st. Newtown 701 K12
st. Warrandyte 333 A9
GLAMORGAN
av. Werribee 446 L12
av. Werribee 447 A12
cr. Mt Martha 656 A18
GLAN AVON
rd. Hawthorn 371 G18
GLANCE
st. Flemington 33 G4
GLANEUSE
av. Torquay 712 D2
rd. Pt Lonsdale 710 E6
GLANFIELD
ct. Ringwood N 334 H19
st. Northcote 327 A15
GLASGOW
av. Reservoir 282 C5
ct. Endeavour Hl 503 J19
rd. Kilsyth 381 E17
rd. Montrose 381 K19
rd. Mt Dandenong 381 K19
st. Collingwood 25 J1
GLASS
rd. Up Fntree Gly 465 A5
st. Essendon 323 K4
st. Kew East 372 J4
st. N Melbourne 17 C17
st. Richmond 26 L17
st. Richmond 371 A18
GLASSCOCKS
rd. Lyndhurst 575 K1
GLASSFORD
av. Springvale S 533 L5
av. Up Fntree Gly 465 G7
st. Armadale 415 F10
GLASSHOUSE
rd. Collingwood 19 J19
st. Burnley 371 B17
GLASSON
ct. Greenvale 193 A17
sq. Mt Waverley 419 D20
st. Rosebud 700 A1
GLASTONBURY
cct. Point Cook 450 H9
cct. Point Cook 450 J10
dr. Highton 705 J8
GLAZEBURY
ct. Langwarrin 629 B3
GLEADELL
st. Richmond 26 J10
GLEBE
av. Cheltenham 530 H2
ct. Wantirna 422 G5
pl. Melton W 226 D17
pl. Thomastown 240 K11
pl. Wheelers Hl 461 E15
st. Forest Hill 420 C4
st. Forest Hill 420 C1
GLEDHAN
cl. Altona Mdw 451 E6
GLEDHILL
st. Seddon 367 C11
GLEDITSIA
wy. Bundoora 242 E13
GLEESON
av. Camberwell 417 L5
av. Lysterfield 464 F18
ct. Langwarrin 602 A19
dr. Bundoora 285 B6
wk. Roxburgh Pk 193 L15
GLEGHORN
rd. Kallista 467 C1
GLEN
av. Belmont 706 K1
av. Croydon 379 K2
av. E Geelong 703 J10
ct. Frankston 627 C4
ct. Glen Waverley 460 F2
ct. Hampton Pk 551 E7
ct. Keilor East 322 H6
ct. Narre Warren 538 K16
ct. Templestowe 331 C12
dr. Eaglemont 328 J12
dr. Rye 697 F7
rd. Ashburton 417 B20
rd. Belgrave 466 D18
rd. Belgrave Ht 466 D18
rd. Cockatoo 510 K4
rd. Glen Waverley 460 D2
rd. Lysterfield 504 F4
rd. Melton 226 H19
rd. Mitcham 377 C11
rd. Silvan 385 A16
rd. Toorak 415 H5
st. Aspendale 546 E6
st. Blackburn N 376 C10
st. Essendon 323 L6
st. Glenroy 280 D5
st. Hawthorn 371 L20
st. Hawthorn 415 L2
st. Werribee 447 J13
tr. Lysterfield 504 D10
tr. Lysterfield 504 D13
GLENAIR
ct. Templstw Lr 330 G8
st. Templstw Lr 330 G10
GLENAIRE
cr. Cranbourne W 577 H14
GLEN ALLAN
st. Broadmeadows 238 A20
GLENALVA
pde. Cannons Creek 649 D8
GLEN ALVIE
av. Keysborough 533 J10
st. Seaford 599 K8
GLENANN
ct. Boronia 424 A8
GLENARA
ct. Belmont 702 H19
ct. Bundoora 285 A3
ct. Endeavour Hl 537 L8
dr. Bulla 190 E18
GLENARA FORD
Seabrook 451 A2
GLENARD
dr. Eaglemont 329 A11
dr.e, Eaglemont 329 B9
dr.w, Eaglemont 329 B9
GLENARM
pl. Mt Waverley 419 J16
rd. Glen Iris 416 F11
GLENAUBURN
ct. Sunbury 143 B6
rd. Lower Plenty 286 E14
GLEN AVIS
gr. Dingley Vill 532 K7
GLENBAR
ct. Kealba 276 L19
ct. Kealba 277 A20
GLENBARRY
rd. Campbellfield 239 C7
rd. Wantirna 422 K6
GLENBERVIE
dr. Somerville 645 B19
rd. Strathmore 323 K1
rd. Toorak 415 K6
GLENBOURNE
rd. Cranbourne 577 L15
GLENBRAE
ct. Belmont 706 G6
ct. Berwick 553 L4
GLENBROOK
av. Bonbeach 547 C20
av. Cairnlea 319 H14
av. Chelsea 547 C20
av. Clayton 458 L15
av. Malvern East 416 H17
cl. Frankston S 627 G18
cl. Mooroolbark 337 L19
ct. Greenvale 237 F5
gdn. Brookfield 267 L6
rd. Clematis 508 H4
rd. Warburton 349 E5
GLENBRUAR
dr. Hillside 232 F19
dr. Hillside 232 G18
GLENBURN
ct. Bangholme 549 H13
dr. Hallam 538 C19
rd. Boronia 424 H15
st. Newcomb 704 E16
st. Thomastown 240 C13
GLENBURNIE
rd. Mitcham 377 E20
rd. Vermont 377 E20
GLENCAIRN
av. Brighton East 495 F5
av. Camberwell 417 F8
av. Coburg 325 D7
av. Deer Park 319 E15
av. Hallam 552 B2
av. Ringwood 378 K6
cr. Broadmeadows 238 A9
ct. Eltham North 245 C17
dr. Greenvale 193 A19
pl. Mill Park 242 F10
st. Mulgrave 500 D4
GLENCANNON
cr. Clayton S 498 H7
GLENCAPEL
ct. Hillside 232 E16
GLENCAPLE
ct. Endeavour Hl 503 H16
GLENCARA
cl. Westmeadows 236 H15
st. Avondale Ht 322 D14
GLEN CENTRE
arc. Hawthorn, off Glenferrie Rd 371 L15
GLENCESTER
ct. Bulleen 329 H12
GLENCOE
av. Truganina 405 L14
cr. Mt Martha 655 L20
ct. Epping 198 C20
dr. Diggers Rest 188 D12
gr. Dandenong N 501 L16
pl. Lilydale 294 D19
pl. W Melbourne 23 B1
st. Caulfield N 455 E2
GLENCROFT
tce. Wheelers Hl 461 B19
GLENDA
cl. Clarinda 498 E11
ct. Boronia 424 J8
ct. Vermont S 420 J8
st. Doncaster 330 C19
st. Werribee 447 G10
GLENDALE
av. Epping 198 D17
av. Templestowe 331 B8
cl. Langwarrin 601 L17
cr. Berwick 553 H3
ct. Boronia 424 G15
ct. Kilsyth 381 D8
ct. Werribee 448 C5
dr. Chirnside Pk 337 A4
gr. McCrae 684 J15
pl. Gladstone Pk 237 C18
rd. Briar Hill 286 G4
rd. Springvale 499 J7
st. Glen Waverley 460 C2
st. Nunawading 376 G14
st. Surrey Hills 418 B2
GLENDALOUGH
ct. Watsonia N 243 E18
GLENDARRAGH
rd. Templestowe 332 B9
GLENDEARG
gr. Malvern 415 L17
GLENDEN
rt. Cheltenham 496 J13
GLENDENE
av. Kew 372 G10
ct. Doncaster 375 E5
ct. Werribee 447 A19
GLENDENNING
ct. Frankston 628 C13
ri. Templestowe 331 F4
st. St Albans 320 A5
GLEN DHU
rd. Kilsyth 381 A6
GLENDINNING
ri. Mornington 656 G2
GLENDOON
rd. Junction Vill 604 H14
GLENDORA
av. Brighton 454 K6
la. Doncaster E 331 L16
GLENDOWAN
rd. Mt Waverley 418 L18
GLENDOWER
ct. Mooroolbark 337 D8
GLENDYE
ct. Toorak 415 F5
GLENEADIE
av. Badger Creek 258 B11
cl. Hampton Pk 552 B9
GLENEAGLE
wy. Eltham 287 B7
GLEN EAGLES
ct. Burwood 418 B3
GLENEAGLES
av. Mornington 656 B1
ct. Croydon 380 J7
ct. Darley 221 G1
ct. Rowville 462 D19
dr. Endeavour Hl 503 J20
dr. Melton W 225 G19
dr. Sunbury 144 F13
GLEN EBOR
av. Blackburn 376 A16
GLEN EIRA
av. Balaclava 454 H1
rd. Caulfield 455 F2
rd. Caulfield N 455 A2
rd. Caulfield S 455 F2
rd. Elsternwick 454 H1
rd. Ripponlea 454 H1
rd. St Kilda E 454 H1
GLENELG
av. Frankston 627 J7
bvd. Taylors Hill 274 K12
ct. Brookfield 268 D6
ct. Dingley Vill 532 K7
ct. Rowville 462 J17
dr. Clayton S 498 F8
dr. Mentone 531 F5
pl. Taylors L 233 E18
st. Coolaroo 238 E3
st. Dandenong N 501 K8
wy. Seabrook 450 L5
GLENFERN
av. Doncaster 330 C17
av. Upwey 465 K15
cl. Upwey 466 A14
ct. Blackburn S 419 J7
pl. Glenroy 280 G9
rd. Ferntree Gly 464 E5
rd. Healesville 213 G18
rd. Lysterfield 465 B14
rd. Upwey 465 B14
GLENFERRIE
pl. Hawthorn, off Glenferrie Rd 372 A17
rd. Hawthorn 371 L20
rd. Hawthorn 415 L3
rd. Kew 371 L20
rd. Kooyong 415 K8
rd. Malvern 415 J15
st. Caulfield N 415 J17
GLENFIELD
cl. Cairnlea 319 H11
ct. Lalor 240 C9
GLENGALA
ct. Greensbrgh 286 B10
ct. Mentone 531 L8
dr. Sunshine W 364 H11
rd. Sunshine 364 H4
rd. Sunshine W 363 L3
rd. Sunshine W 364 G4
rd. Sunshine W 365 A3
GLENGARIFF
dr. Mulgrave 500 G2
GLENGARRIFF
cr. Montmorency 286 J8
GLENGARRY
av. Burwood 418 H6
dr. Torquay 712 B2
GLEN GULLY
rd. Eltham North 245 F19
GLENGYLE
st. Coburg 325 K7
GLEN HARROW
rd. Belgrave 466 H10
GLENHAVEN
ct. Thomastown 240 E16
rd. Diamond Ck 202 E19
GLENHELEN
pl. Wonga Park 336 E8
GLEN HOLME
av. Mt Evelyn 383 E2
GLEN HUNTLY
rd. Carnegie 456 E7
rd. Caulfield 455 B5
rd. Caulfield 456 A6
rd. Caulfield S 455 B5
rd. Elsternwick 454 G4
rd. Elwood 454 C4
rd. Glen Huntly 456 A6
GLENICE
av. Blackburn S 419 D6
st. Greensbrgh 286 B9
GLENIFER
av. Scoresby 462 G8
GLENIFFER
av. Brighton East 495 L5
GLEN INNES
cl. Wonga Park 336 E8
GLEN IRIS
rd. Camberwell 417 B7
rd. Glen Iris 417 A14
GLENISLA
dr. Mt Martha 655 G18
wy. Berwick 553 K14
GLENISTER
dr. Eltham 287 L10
GLEN KATHERINE
dr. St Helena 245 A18
GLENLEA
cl. Rowville 463 J14
ct. Mill Park 242 E10
GLENLEIGH
ct. Cranbourne N 578 G8
ct. Glen Waverley 420 H19
GLENLEITH
av. Geelong 702 K1
ct. Geelong 702 K1
GLENLITTA
av. Broadmeadows 238 L19
GLENLOTH
av. Lilydale 294 B18
ct. Epping 198 D19
GLENLUSS
st. Balwyn 373 K9
st. Werribee 447 J13
GLENLYON
rd. Brunswick 325
rd. Brunswick E 325
GLEN MAGGIE
pl. Wyndham Va 446
GLENMAGGIE
ch. Caroline Spr 317
cl. Berwick 554
ct. Meadow Ht 238
ct. Wantirna S 422
dr. St Albans 320
GLENMANOR
cl. Templestowe 332
GLENMARK
av. St Kilda 414
GLENMER
st. Bentleigh 496
GLENMIRE
st. Highton 701
GLEN MOIDART
dr. Berwick 540
GLENMORE
cr. Black Rock 529
ct. Seaford 600
gr. Mt Waverley 418
pl. Greenvale 237
st. Box Hill 374
st. Macleod 284
GLENMORGAN
cl. Clayton S 499
st. Brunswick E 325
GLENMOYNE
sq. Werribee 447
GLENMURRAY
pl. Wonga Park 336
GLENN
cl. Cranbourne W 577
cr. Bundoora 242
cr. Bundoora 284
ct. Clayton S 499
ct. Mooroolbark 336
ct. Rowville 503
dr. Bundoora, off College Dr 284
GLENNDEN
ct. Bundoora 285
GLENN ERIN
wy. Berwick 553
GLENNIE
av. Oakleigh S 497
GLENNIS
st. Frankston 627
GLENNON
la. Carlton 18
GLENOLA
rd. Chelsea 545
rd. Chelsea 547
GLENONE
av. Dromana 685
GLENORA
av. Coburg 325
av. Croydon 379
ct. Frankston 628
dr. Vermont 421
st. Chadstone 458
GLEN ORCHARD
cl. Templestowe 332
GLEN ORME
av. McKinnon 456
av. Ormond 456
GLEN PARK
av. Glenroy 279
dr. Selby 467
rd. Bayswater N 379
rd. Eltham North 287
GLENPARK
dr. Wonga Park 336
GLENROBE
st. Deer Park 319
GLENROSA
ct. St Albans 275
GLENROY
rd. Glenroy 280
rd. Hawthorn 371
rd. Hawthorn 415
GLENSCOTT
cr. Strathmr Ht 279
GLENSHEE
dr. Lynbrook 551
GLEN SHIAN
cr. Mt Eliza 625
la. Mt Eliza 625
GLENSIDE
cl. Lilydale 339
st. Avondale Ht 322
wk. Berwick 539
GLENTHORN
av. Balwyn N 373
GLENTHORNE
dr. Keysborough 534
GLENTILT
rd. Glen Iris 416

EN TOWER
Glen Waverley 460 J2
ENVALE
Mulgrave 460 B20
Donvale 377 K9
Glen Iris 416 H13
Reservoir 282 D12
Ringwood N 377 K9
EN VALLEY
Greensbrgh 285 J3
Forest Hill 376 E20
ENVALLEY
Seville E 343 C13
ENVERN
Kangaroo Grnd 248 J8
Panton Hill 248 D2
Panton Hill 248 J8
EN VIEW
Glen Waverley 460 H2
Monbulk 428 L17
Monbulk 469 D1
ENVIEW
Malvern 416 A11
Frankston 628 A4
Avondale Ht 322 F9
Croydon N 335 L12
Hillside 231 L16
Lysterfield 464 C14
Doncaster E 376 B5
Launching Pl 345 L13
Mt Evelyn 339 D18
Strathmore 280 B19
Yarra Glen 252 D9
Roxburgh Pk 194 A5
ENVILL
Templestowe 332 B8
ENVILLE
Glen Waverley 460 L2
Highton 701 G10
Highton 701 H11
EN VISTA
Nar Warrn N 538 D10
ENVISTA
Emerald 469 G15
Templestowe 332 C8
ENVUE
Rye 696 L10
Rye 697 A10
ENWAY
Dingley Vill 532 L7
ENWERRI
Vermont S 421 A14
ENWOOD
Altona 408 L17
Beaumaris 529 L9
Dromana 686 A9
Glen Waverley 460 A6
Donvale 377 K4
Cranbourne 578 C15
Croydon 379 G7
Greensbrgh 244 D15
Springvale S 499 L19
Knoxfield 423 B20
Nar Warrn N 538 H11
ENWRIGHT
Woori Yall 344 G13
ENYS
Airport W 278 G15
Belmont 706 D5
Clarinda 498 E10
Dandenong S 535 L13
Wantirna S 422 E17
EW
Brunswick E 325 L17
DER
S Morang 243 K2
KA
Donvale 376 E4
NDEN
Ardeer 320 B18
SMANN
Beaconsfield 555 E16
TTER
, Diggers Rest 187 D12
s, Diggers Rest 187 C12
OAMING
Mill Park 242 L12
AMING RIDE
Kurunjang 226 G11
BAL
Westmeadows 236 H16
Westmeadows 236 H17
OBE
Melbourne 2 F10
Melbourne 24 D5
Epping 241 G4
Yarraville 367 D18
MAR
Dandenong S 536 A17
RIA
Dandenong N 501 L20
Bundoora 285 B2

GLOUCESTER
av. Berwick 554 E10
ct. Eltham 287 K9
ct. Murrumbeena 457 B12
ct. Seaholme 409 H17
ct. Sydenham 274 K1
ct. Templestowe 331 F14
ct. Werribee 446 L12
dr. Heidelberg 329 E4
rd. Ashburton 417 J17
st. Grovedale 705 L12
st. Hadfield 281 A10
st. Mt Waverley 418 G12
st. Reservoir 282 G13
wy. Epping 197 K16
wy. Melton W 226 A14
GLOVER
cl. Mooroolbark 337 C11
ct. Berwick 554 A2
ct. Ferny Creek 466 B3
ct. Skye 601 G2
ct. Taylors L 275 A1
ct. Toorak 415 A2
st. Heidelberg Ht 284 E19
st. Newcomb 704 A14
st. Oakleigh S 497 G3
st. S Melbourne 29 C10
st. S Melbourne 413 B5
GLYN
ct. Cheltenham 496 L16
st. Belmont 706 D4
st. Jan Juc 711 E15
GLYNDA
st. Dandenong S 535 L13
st. Fawkner 281 G4
GLYNDEBOURNE
av. Toorak 415 H5
GLYNDON
av. Brighton 454 E12
av. Coburg N 281 E13
av. St Albans 320 H4
ct. Burwood E 419 F8
ct. Seaford 573 F13
rd. Camberwell 417 E6
GLYNELEA
cr. Skye 575 H16
GLYNNE
rd. Warranwood 334 H15
GLYNNS
rd. N Warrandyte 289 D16
GNARWIN
st. Mt Waverley 458 L4
GNARWYN
rd. Carnegie 456 K8
GNOORONG
st. Warneet 649 D13
GNOTUK
av. Aspendale 546 E8
GOA
ct. Keilor Dn 276 C14
GOATHLANDS
st. St Kilda E 414 L18
GOBLE
st. Laverton 407 C17
st. Niddrie 278 H19
GOBUR
ct. Meadow Ht 237 J6
GODALMIN
st. Eltham 287 D14
GODBEHEAR
ct. Ringwood 335 B18
GODBER
ct. Upwey 466 A16
rd. Diamond Ck 246 A16
GODDARD
ct. Mont Albert N 374 G10
GODFREY
av. St Kilda E 414 H15
av. Sunshine N 321 B12
av. Warrandyte 334 F1
cr. Dandenong 536 A3
ct. Surrey Hills 374 F19
la. Officer 557 C9
la. Pakenham 557 C9
st. Bentleigh 456 C19
st. Blairgowrie 679 L19
st. E Geelong 703 H14
st. Melbourne 23 G10
st. Thomson 703 H14
GODINGS
rd. Moorooduc 658 K14
GODLEY
st. Reservoir 282 D4
GODWIN
av. Narre Warren 539 E16
cr. Cranbourne N 578 E8
st. Blairgowrie 696 A2
GOE
st. Caulfield S 455 K7
GOEGAN
st. Werribee 448 A16

GOFF
st. Beaconsfield 555 C16
st. Coburg 282 B20
GOGOLL
cr. Torquay 712 A6
GOLCONDA
av. Frankston 599 L18
cl. Hoppers Csg 405 D14
GOLD
st. Brunswick 325 C16
st. Cheltenham 496 L20
st. Clifton Hill 19 L9
st. Collingwood 19 K13
GOLDBOROUGH
ct. Frankston S 627 H13
GOLDEN
av. Bonbeach 545 F11
av. Bonbeach 547 A20
av. Chelsea 545 F11
av. Chelsea 547 A20
av. Werribee 447 D11
ct. Doncaster 331 E18
ct. Doveton 536 J6
ct. Frankston N 600 F9
gr. Glen Waverley 420 G19
gr. Mill Park 242 E4
gr. Ringwood 378 K5
gr. The Basin 425 G12
qd. Glen Iris 416 G12
wy. Bulleen 329 F12
wy. Hillside 231 L20
wy. Hillside 273 L1
GOLDEN ASH
ct. Meadow Ht 238 B1
gr. Hoppers Csg 405 C14
wk. Croydon N 335 L13
GOLDEN BEACH
wy. Torquay 712 G2
GOLDEN FLEECE
al. Melbourne 2 K11
al. Melbourne, off Coverlid Pl 24 F5
GOLDENFLEECE
pl. Hoppers Csg 448 A1
GOLDEN GLEN
rd. Forest Hill 420 B6
GOLDEN GROVE
ct. Keilor Ldg 275 L3
GOLDEN LEAF
av. Nar Warrn S 553 C20
GOLDEN RIDGE
dr. Croydon Hl 335 G17
GOLDEN SQUARE
cr. Hoppers Csg 447 K2
GOLDENTREE
dr. Chirnside Pk 336 H6
GOLDEN VIEW
ct. Wheelers Hl 460 K8
GOLDERS
st. Heidelberg 328 J5
GOLDERS GREEN
wk. Caroline Spr 317 L3
GOLDFIELD
ct. Wheelers Hl 461 C11
GOLDFINCH
ct. Carrum Downs 600 H2
pl. Rowville 503 D3
GOLDIE
pl. Melbourne 1 K10
pl. Melbourne 24 A6
GOLDING
av. Rowville 503 B7
av. Rowville 503 C7
ct. Dandenong N 502 B15
ct. Scoresby 462 J6
ct. Springvale S 499 G19
st. Canterbury 373 G19
st. Hawthorn 371 K17
GOLDLANG
st. Dandenong 535 E4
GOLDMANS
rd. Cottles Br 204 G1
rd. Panton Hill 204 G1
rd. Smiths Gly 204 G1
GOLD MEMORIAL
rd. Warrandyte 333 H4
rd. Warrandyte 334 A4
GOLD NUGGET
ri. Warrandyte 333 F4
GOLDRUSH
ct. Beaconsfield 555 G15
GOLDSACK
cl. Cockatoo 471 G18
GOLDSBOROUGH
la. Melbourne 1 D11
la. Melbourne 23 K8
GOLDSMITH
av. Delahey 275 C13
av. Preston 283 A17
av. Ringwood N 378 E4
cl. Endeavour Hl 537 F7
gr. Northcote 326 D13

st. Elwood 454 D3
st. Elwood 454 E2
GOLDSWORTHY
ct. Kings Park 275 B18
la. Plenty 243 J9
GOLDTHORNS
av. Kew 372 H8
GOLEEN
st. Coburg N 281 G15
GOLF
av. Kingsbury 283 K9
av. Mt Waverley 418 K17
av. Rosanna 285 A19
la. Rye 697 H5
pde. Rye 697 D7
rd. Coburg N 281 K17
rd. Oakleigh S 457 J20
GOLF CLUB
rd. Cranbourne N 577 K3
rd. Hampton Pk 577 K3
GOLF COURSE
cir. Safety Bch 669 B20
la. Safety Bch 668 L18
la. Safety Bch 669 A18
GOLFERS
dr. Malvern East 417 E20
GOLF HILL
av. Doncaster 374 E1
GOLF LINKS
av. Oakleigh 457 K15
cr. Dingley Vill 533 G9
ct. Doncaster 330 D20
ct. Doncaster 374 D1
dr. Mill Park 242 C4
dr. Sunbury 143 G16
dr. Yarrambat 201 B11
rd. Anglesea 713 D4
rd. Baxter 628 B13
rd. Berwick 553 G13
rd. Croydon 336 F16
rd. Frankston 627 H8
rd. Frankston S 627 H8
rd. Frankston S 628 B13
rd. Glenroy 280 C8
rd. Langwarrin S 645 A2
rd. Narre Warren 553 A12
GOLF VIEW
dr. Craigieburn 193 K1
rd. Heatherton 497 J15
GOLFWOOD
cl. Dingley Vill 533 B6
GOLIGHTLY
st. Pt Lonsdale 710 D5
GOMAN
rd. Moorooduc 658 C10
GOMI
ct. Frankston 600 H20
GOMMS
rd. Somerville 644 G13
GONA
ct. Ashburton 417 H17
st. Heidelberg W 327 L2
GONGFLERS
dr. Bend of Islands 292 A5
GOOCH
cl. Sydenham 274 L3
st. Prahran 414 L12
st. Thornbury 326 K9
GOODALL
ct. Berwick 554 E20
dr. Lilydale 338 K4
st. Hawthorn 372 C19
GOODE
ct. Sunshine W 365 B10
st. Malvern East 457 B4
GOODENIA
cl. Meadow Ht 193 K20
pl. Hillside 274 E3
GOODENOUGH
ct. Heidelberg W 283 L19
GOOD GOVERNS
st. Mitcham 377 J16
GOODIN
gr. Glen Waverley 420 C20
GOODING
ct. Dandenong 536 D3
st. St Albans 320 C6
GOODJOHN
ct. Endeavour Hl 537 E4
GOODLET
pl. Eltham 288 F5
GOODMAN
dr. Noble Park 535 B5
st. Brunswick 325 D16
GOODRICH
ct. Craigieburn 194 E4
st. Bentleigh E 457 E16
GOODSON
st. Doncaster 331 A20
GOODWIN
cl. Hoppers Csg 448 B3
st. Blackburn 376 C14
st. Glen Iris 417 B9

st. Preston 326 B4
st. Richmond 26 G20
st. The Basin 424 L9
GOODWOOD
cr. Gladstone Pk 236 L19
cr. Gladstone Pk 237 A19
ct. Glen Waverley 460 G10
dr. Keilor Dn 275 L16
dr. Springvale 500 A18
st. Richmond 26 B11
st. Surrey Hills 418 C2
GOOLAGONG
rd. Blind Bight 650 G6
wy. St Albans 275 K18
GOOLD
st. Burwood 418 H11
GOOLGOWIE
st. Rosebud 700 K7
GOOLGUNG
gr. Greensbrgh 243 H18
GOONDAH
la. Healesville 214 C15
GOONYAH
ct. Greensbrgh 244 B18
GOORNA
ct. Rye 697 A9
GOOYONG
av. Chadstone 418 D20
GORAE
ct. Westmeadows 237 F12
GORDON
av. Elwood 454 E1
av. Frankston 599 J18
av. Geelong 702 K6
av. Geelong West 702 H6
av. Kew 372 A12
av. Laverton 406 K20
av. Montrose 381 L17
av. Oakleigh E 458 H13
av. Tecoma 466 C8
av.s, Altona Mdw 450 K1
bvd. Waurn Ponds 705 B11
cl. Nar Warrn S 552 F9
cr. Blackburn 375 K17
cr. Black Rock 529 E4
cr. Boronia 423 G15
cr. Kensington 33 J7
ct. Glenroy 280 B3
ct. Mooroolbark 381 G3
ct. Ringwood 422 D1
ct. Viewbank 285 F20
ct. Woori Yall 344 G15
gr. Malvern 415 J15
gr. Menzies Ck 467 L19
gr. Montmorency 287 C9
gr. Northcote 326 F16
gr. Preston 283 E20
gr. South Yarra 31 K4
gr. South Yarra 414 E2
pde. Yarraville 366 L18
pl. Carlton 18 H15
pl. Melbourne 24 J3
rd. Mt Waverley 419 C16
rd. Pakenham Up 559 J8
st. Balwyn 372 L10
st. Balwyn 373 A10
st. Beaumaris 530 G4
st. Bentleigh 495 L4
st. Brunswick W 325 A10
st. Bundoora 285 C2
st. Clifton Hill 20 D7
st. Coburg 281 B20
st. Coburg 325 A6
st. Cranbourne 604 F1
st. Cremorne 32 E2
st. Cremorne 414 H1
st. Croydon 380 E6
st. Elsternwick 454 K3
st. Elsternwick 454 K4
st. Essendon 324 G8
st. Fairfield 327 F17
st. Footscray 367 B8
st. Hampton 494 J5
st. Hawthorn E 372 F19
st. Lalor 241 E8
st. Malvern East 457 E4
st. Maribyrnong 323 C20
st. Maribyrnong 367 B4
st. Mont Albert 374 B16
st. Mornington 640 F12
st. Newport 410 E6
st. Noble Park 534 L4
st. Officer 555 K16
st. Rye 696 G1
st. Sunbury 142 F11
st. Toorak 32 L13
st. Toorak 414 L7
st. Toorak 415 A7
st. Tullamarine 278 G7
GORDONIA
cr. Narre Warren 539 C19
GORDON LUCK
av. Altona North 408 G4

GORDONS
rd. S Morang..........198 L9
rd. S Morang..........199 A9
rd. Templstw Lr......330 C8
GORE
pl. Geelong, off Corio St...........703 B7
ri. Endeavour Hl.....537 D5
st. Fitzroy................25 E2
GORENKOS
dr. Maidstone..........322 H17
GORGE
rd. S Morang..........199 H20
rd. S Morang..........243 H1
GORHAM
av. Epping...............197 H17
GORI
ct. Nar Warrn N......539 D12
GORMAN
al. Melbourne...........24 H2
GOROKE
ct. Croydon S.........380 A13
ct. Eltham...............288 A6
GORONG
wk. Delahey............275 A11
GORRIE
ct. Wantirna S.........462 D1
pl. Glenroy..............279 H5
GORST
rd. Diamond Ck.......202 E20
rd. Wattle Glen........202 E20
GORTON
ct. Sunbury............143 H3
GOSFIELD
rd. Hurstbridge.......203 G11
rd. Hurstbridge.......204 A11
rd. Panton Hill.........204 A11
GOSFORD
cr. Broadmeadows..238 C15
cr. Pk Orchards.......334 A19
ct. Pk Orchards.......334 C20
gdn. Derrimut...........363 B8
GOSHAWK
ct. Carrum Downs...600 J2
GOSNEYS
la. Geelong, off Mercer St..........702 K4
GOSS
tce. Williamstown.....411 F13
GOSSAMER
st. Werribee...........447 E11
GOSSE
ct. Sunbury............142 J11
GOTCH
la. E Melbourne........25 G4
GOTHA
st. Heidelberg Ht.....328 D5
GOTHIC
ct. Sunshine W.......364 B5
dr. Bacchus Msh.....221 G16
rd. Aspendale..........546 E6
rd. Rye..................697 E9
GOTTARD
ct. Keilor Dn..........276 D13
GOUDIESDALE
rd. Menzies Ck........467 F18
rd. Selby................467 F18
GOUGH
al. Melbourne.............1 A7
al. Melbourne...........23 H7
pl. Cremorne.............25 K19
st. Cremorne.............25 K20
st. Cremorne.............31 L1
st. Elsternwick.........455 B10
GOULBURN
av. Reservoir...........283 E12
cct. Caroline Spr.......318 C7
ct. Croydon Hl........335 K14
ct. St Albans...........320 D13
ct. Werribee............447 D7
dr. Rowville............463 B17
gr. Yallambie..........285 L11
pl. Clayton S...........498 G8
st. Box Hill N..........374 L10
st. Broadmeadows..238 F17
st. Cheltenham.......496 K19
st. Yarraville..........367 B15
wy. Craigieburn........150 F11
wy. Taylors L...........233 F20
GOULD
cl. Wantirna S.........462 F1
ct. Mt Waverley......459 G3
pl. Burnside............318 F8
pl. Mill Park.............242 F8
pl. Mooroolbark.......337 E11
st. Balwyn N...........329 G19
st. Brighton............494 F2
st. Coburg N............281 G15
st. Deer Park...........319 D9
st. Frankston..........599 A18
wk. Truganina..........405 G13
GOULDTHORP
av. Mentone............531 D7

GOURLAY
rd. Caroline Spr.......274 B13
rd. Taylors Hill.........274 B13
st. Balaclava...........414 H19
GOUROCK
st. Reservoir...........283 J3
GOVAN
ct. Footscray...........366 L4
st. Footscray...........366 L4
st. Langwarrin.........629 D3
st. Langwarrin.........629 D3
st. Seaford.............599 E7
GOVE
st. Springvale.........500 B9
GOVERNMENT
rd. Essendon...........324 D5
rd. Frankston..........627 F1
rd. Rye..................697 K4
rd. The Basin...........425 D14
rd. Tremont............425 D14
rd. Wesburn............347 K13
GOVERNMENT HOUSE
dr. Melbourne.............4 G17
dr. Melbourne...........24 J18
GOVERNOR
rd. Braeside............532 F19
rd. Mordialloc.........532 A20
rd. Waterways.........532 F19
GOVERNOR ARTHUR
dr. Patterson L........547 H20
GOVERNORS
rd. Coburg..............281 J20
GOW
ct. Hallam...............537 H13
GOWAN
rd. Mt Waverley......419 G18
GOWANBRAE
dr. Gowanbrae........279 C8
dr. Gowanbrae........279 D6
GOWAR
av. Camberwell........417 D4
GOWDIE
pl. Caroline Spr.......318 D4
GOWER
st. Kensington..........33 J11
st. Preston.............326 K1
GOWRIE
av. Frankston S.......626 L7
ct. Seabrook...........451 A4
ct. Sunbury............143 F4
pl. Cranbourne W...577 G19
rd. Clematis............508 F3
st. Bentleigh E.........457 E18
st. Glenroy.............280 H2
GOWRIE PARK
dr. Melb Airport.......235 K11
GOYA
ct. Gladstone Pk.....279 A3
ct. Scoresby...........462 C7
ct. Wheelers Hl.......460 L13
GOYARRA
ct. Grovedale..........706 D14
st. Rye..................696 L8
st. Rye..................697 A8
GRACE
av. Dandenong........536 D6
av. Mooroolbark.......337 J16
cl. Wyndham Va......446 G15
ct. Frankston..........600 G19
ct. Kew...................371 H4
ct. Lalor..................240 J5
ct. Mitcham............376 L16
ct. Mont Albert.........374 E12
ct. Nar Warrn N......539 G10
ct. Sunshine W.......365 C11
ct. Viewbank...........285 L15
la. Fitzroy N..............19 D7
st. Camberwell.........416 J6
st. Cranbourne.........578 E20
st. Essendon N........279 C20
st. Glen Waverley.....460 A1
st. Laverton............407 E18
st. Malvern.............416 A14
st. Melton S............268 E5
st. Mont Albert........374 D12
st. Moonee Pnd......323 L13
st. Rye..................697 G2
st. St Albans...........276 F20
st. Springvale..........500 D8
st. Watsonia............285 D7
st. Yarraville...........367 A13
st. Hawthorn, off Glenferrie Rd.....371 L16
st.s. Altona Mdw.......407 D20
GRACEBURN
av. Carnegie...........456 H7
av. Healesville.........214 E18
gr. St Albans...........276 A17
rd. Healesville.........214 C20
GRACEDALE
av. Eltham North.....287 D1
av. Ringwood E.......379 F13
ct. Strathmore........323 J1

GRACEFIELD
av. Dromana...........686 B9
dr. Box Hill N..........374 J8
GRACEHILL
av. Burwood............418 L11
mw. Cranbourne........603 F6
GRACEMERE
dr. Pearcedale.........646 H4
GRACE PARK
av. Springvale........499 L15
GRACIE
av. Chelsea.............546 H15
av. Edithvale............546 H15
la. N Melbourne........17 F19
st. Northcote...........326 F13
st. N Melbourne........34 F13
GRACILIS
ct. Endeavour Hl.....536 J1
GRADUATE
cr. Wheelers Hl.......460 D15
GRADY
cl. Mill Park............242 B5
ct. Frankston S.......627 H9
la. Mornington........641 B11
GRAEME
av. Montmorency....286 H7
av. Ringwood...........378 J4
cl. Doncaster..........331 A15
ct. Bulleen..............329 H15
st. Dromana...........686 E4
st. Frankston...........600 B19
st. Vermont.............421 H3
GRAF
ct. Point Cook.........450 G11
rd. Somerville.........644 H16
rd. Somerville.........644 J19
GRAFTON
st. Coburg..............325 D4
st. Elsternwick........455 B4
GRAGWEN
ct. Keysborough.....533 H17
GRAHAM
av. Kilsyth...............381 B9
av. McKinnon...........456 C16
ct. Altona Mdw.......451 G2
ct. Hampton Pk........551 J14
ct. Hoppers Csg......449 L1
ct. Keysborough......534 J8
ct. Macleod............285 C13
ct. Preston..............282 G18
ct. Thomastown......241 G15
pl. Box Hill..............375 A14
pl. Hawthorn E.........372 G19
rd. Carrum..............573 D8
rd. Clayton S...........499 D14
rd. Highett..............496 D16
rd. Kangaroo Grnd..247 F16
rd. Knoxfield...........462 L6
rd. Silvan................385 A9
rd. Viewbank...........285 E20
rd. Wandin East.......385 A9
st. Albert Park...........29 A12
st. Albert Park.........413 A7
st. Bacchus Msh.....222 A19
st. Braybrook...........366 B6
st. Broadmeadows..237 L19
st. Fitzroy................19 B20
st. Glen Waverley....419 K19
st. Kensington..........33 E9
st. Melton...............269 A1
st. Newport.............410 F6
st. Pascoe Vale S....324 K6
st. Port Melb............29 A12
st. Port Melb............368 F18
st. Port Melb............412 G1
st. Port Melb............413 A7
st. Sunshine...........365 B4
st. Surrey Hills........374 A20
st. Surrey Hills........418 A2
st. W Footscray.......366 K6
GRAHAM-MICHELE
cl. Keysborough.....534 H13
GRAIL
ct. Glen Waverley....420 K15
GRAINGER
ct. Mulgrave...........460 C16
st. Sunshine N........321 H13
GRAINGERS
rd. W Footscray......366 K10
GRAIN STORE
ct. Langwarrin........602 B17
GRAMAN
wy. Sydenham.........274 J8
wy. Taylors Hill.........274 J8
GRAMATAN
av. Beaumaris.........529 L8
GRAMMAR
cl. Truganina..........405 J13
st. Strathmore........280 B20
GRAMPIAN
st. Preston.............282 D19

GRAMPIANS
ct. Taylors L...........276 B9
wy. Caroline Spr.......317 K7
GRANARD
av. Pk Orchards.......333 J17
GRANARY
la. Mentone............531 A7
GRANBY
cr. Highton.............705 J8
cr. Highton.............705 K8
ct. Endeavour Hl.....537 C2
GRAND
av. Macleod............284 H12
bvd. Montmorency....287 A13
ct. Bangholme.........549 J14
pde. Epping.............241 F3
GRAND ARCH
wy. Berwick............553 H14
GRAND CANAL
bvd. Point Cook.........450 K13
GRANDEUR
ct. Cranbourne........603 L5
GRANDIFLORA
ct. Dingley Vill.........533 E10
gr. Bundoora...........242 G15
pky. Hoppers Csg......405 C14
GRANDISON
gr. Oak Park............279 K10
st. Moonee Pnd......324 A10
GRAND PANORAMA
ct. Launching Pl......345 G13
GRAND VALLEY
ct. Lysterfield S.......504 C16
tce. Lysterfield.........464 C14
GRANDVALLEY
dr. Chirnside Pk......337 G6
GRANDVIEW
av. Beaumaris.........529 L7
av. Croydon............336 A19
av. Dandenong.........536 D7
av. Emerald............469 G13
av. Glen Iris............417 G10
av. Maribyrnong......323 C16
av. Mulgrave...........499 K3
av. Pascoe Vale S....324 K3
av. Point Cook.........450 D6
av. Ringwood E.......379 C14
av. Rye..................697 K5
av. Rye..................697 L8
bvd. Craigieburn.......150 E7
cr. Healesville.........257 H1
cr. Hillside..............232 B20
cr. Tecoma..............466 D8
cr. Up Fntree Gly....464 L8
ct. McCrae.............685 E12
gr. Baxter...............644 K1
gr. Bayswater..........423 F6
gr. Carnegie...........456 J12
gr. Frankston..........626 K3
gr. Hawthorn E.........372 H17
gr. Menzies Ck........467 K17
gr. Moorabbin.........496 E11
gr. Northcote..........327 D16
gr. Oakleigh...........458 E8
gr. Prahran.............415 B9
gr. Rosanna............328 J2
gr. Sassafras..........426 E14
gr. Selby................467 J17
pde. Moolap............704 L15
rd. Belgrave Ht........506 D3
rd. Box Hill S...........418 H3
rd. Brighton............455 A13
rd. Chadstone.........418 E20
rd. Glen Iris.............416 H15
rd. Niddrie..............279 A20
rd. Niddrie..............323 A1
rd. Preston..............282 D20
rd. Torquay.............712 A5
rd. Warrandyte........333 K7
rd. Wheelers Hl.......461 B16
rd. Wheelers Hl.......461 D19
st. Glenroy.............279 J8
st. Moonee Pnd......323 L14
tce. Kew.................371 K4
tce. Mt Martha.........669 B10
tce. Nar Warrn S.......553 D19
GRANEBY
ri. Mt Evelyn...........338 K15
GRANEEL
gr. Berwick............554 G5
GRANGE
av. Canterbury.........373 E15
bvd. Bundoora...........284 E1
cct. Beaconsfield......555 D11
cr. Torquay.............712 E2
ct. Dandenong N.....501 J12
ct. Hoppers Csg......448 E8
ct. Notting Hill..........459 J13
dr. Lysterfield...........464 C16
pl. Melbourne.............2 K3
pl. Melbourne...........24 E1
pl. Westmeadows...236 H13
rd. Airport W...........278 K18

rd. Alphington.........327
rd. Blackburn S.......419
rd. Carnegie...........456
rd. Cheltenham.........531
rd. Dingley Vill.........498
rd. Fairfield.............327
rd. Frankston S.......626
rd. Kalorama...........383
rd. Kew...................372
rd. Moorabbin Aprt..531
rd. Mornington........640
rd. Ormond............456
rd. Rye..................696
rd. Sandringham.....495
rd. Sorrento............678
rd. Toorak...............415
ri. Craigieburn.........150
st. Mont Albert.........374
st. Oakleigh S.........458
st. Preston..............282
tce. Croydon Hl........335
tce. Taylors Hill.........274
GRANGE MOUTH
pl. Greenvale..........193
GRANGEMOUTH
dr. Point Cook.........450
GRANGE PARK
av. Doncaster..........375
dr. Waurn Ponds.....705
GRANITE
dr. Langwarrin.........601
tr. Lysterfield...........505
wy. Delahey.............274
GRANT
av. Altona................408
av. Balwyn..............373
av. Seaford..............599
av. Toorak...............415
av. Werribee............447
cl. Berwick..............553
cl. Wantirna S...........421
cr. Healesville.........214
cr. Ringwood...........377
ct. Beaconsfld Up....542
ct. S Morang...........243
dr. Bayswater N......380
gr. Keilor East.........322
la. Melbourne...........24
rd. Belgrave S.........506
rd. Mt Eliza..............641
rd. Pt Lonsdale.........710
rd. Somerville..........644
rd. Somerville..........645
st. Blairgowrie.........696
st. Brighton East......455
st. Brunswick..........325
st. Clifton Hill.............20
st. Coburg...............326
st. Cranbourne..........604
st. Dandenong.........536
st. Dromana............685
st. Fitzroy N..............19
st. Maddingley........263
st. Malvern East......416
st. Newtown.............702
st. Oakleigh.............458
st. St Albans............319
st. Southbank..............3
st. Southbank............24
st. Watsonia N.........243
st. Watsonia N.........285
GRANTCHESTER
av. Keilor East.........321
rd. Nar Warrn N......538
rd. Wheelers Hl.......461
GRANTDEE
ct. Mt Martha..........656
GRANTER
st. Brighton East.....455
GRANTHAM
cr. Berwick............554
ct. Brighton............454
pde. St Albans..........320
rd. Viewbank...........285
st. Brunswick W.....325
tce. Mulgrave...........501
GRANTLEY
cl. Hampton Pk.......552
dr. Gladstone Pk.....237
dr. Glen Waverley....420
GRANT OLSON
av. Bulleen..............329
GRANTON
av. Endeavour Hl....537
cl. Keysborough.....534
GRANTS
rd. Melb Airport.......235
GRANTULLA
rd. Kallista..............467
rd. Menzies Ck........467
rd. The Patch..........467
GRANTULLY
st. Mt Evelyn...........339

RANVILLE
r. Clayton S 498 G5
. Camberwell 417 L4
. Glenroy 280 B4
. Mentone 531 C11
RANYA
. Blackburn S 420 A3
r. Mt Eliza 625 H16
RAPE
t. Safety Bch 669 F18
RAPEVIEW
l. Sunbury 144 B10
t. Frankston S 627 L16
r. Sunbury 144 B9
RASMERE
v. Doncaster E 331 L18
t. Greenvale 192 K18
. Wantirna 422 G14
RASSLAND
v. Coburg 281 K20
. Cairnlea 319 J8
RASSLANDS
l. Boneo 700 D13
l. Bundoora 284 A8
RASSMERE
. Hallam 537 E13
. Bundoora 243 C13
l. Langwarrin 630 D4
l. Point Cook 450 F10
RASSWREN
. Langwarrin 629 C4
RASSY FLAT
l. Diamond Ck 245 H7
RASSY POINT
l. Cairnlea 319 E12
RASSY SPUR
k. Lysterfield 503 K9
RATLEA
. Carrum Downs 601 C3
RATTAN
. Carlton 18 E15
. Caroline Spr 274 C15
l. Carlton 18 D16
. Richmond 25 L13
. Carlton 17 H14
. Hawthorn 371 E15
. Melbourne 17 H14
t. Parkville 17 H14
t. Prahran 32 B18
t. Prahran 414 G8
RATTEN
l. Montrose 381 L11
RATWICK
. Lalor 241 D9
RATZ
. St Albans 320 B6
RAVEL PITS
l. S Geelong 703 C19
RAVENSTEIN
r. The Basin 424 K8
RAVES
t. Essendon 323 D2
RAVLIER
y. S Morang 198 H12
RAY
. Endeavour Hl 537 D4
t. Beaumaris 529 K9
t. Bundoora 242 K20
. Mooroolbark 337 G20
. Rockbank 317 A3
. St Albans 320 F12
. Williamstown 410 L15
. Albert Park 29 G13
l. Gruyere 342 B10
t. Bentleigh E 496 H1
. Brighton 494 J3
. Brunswick 325 C17
. Clifton Hill 20 G9
. Cranbourne N 577 L10
. Doncaster 374 D2
. Mt Martha 669 D3
. Northcote 326 L17
. Preston 283 D20
t. Ringwood E 379 E17
t. Rye 696 E9
t. Seaford 599 E6
t. Springvale 500 A7
. Wheelers Hl 461 D20
. Yarraville 367 D16
RAYDEN
. Berwick 554 G20
RAYDENS
l. Moorooduc 658 G19
l. Tuerong 658 G19
RAYDON
. Rosebud 700 A1
RAYLEA
v. Herne Hill 701 H1
RAYLING
. Croydon 379 C3
. Keysborough 534 F12
. Belmont 706 K3

GRAYLINGS
av. St Kilda E 414 G15
gr. St Kilda E 414 G15
GRAYSON
dr. Scoresby 462 J6
GRAZIER
cl. Werribee 447 K7
GRAZING
ct. Epping 198 E19
GREAT BARR
cr. Caroline Spr 317 H4
GREAT BRITAIN
st. Herne Hill 701 J3
GREAT OAK
ct. Mooroolbark 337 E8
GREAT OCEAN
rd. Anglesea 713 A14
rd. Jan Juc 711 A13
rd. Torquay 711 A13
GREAT RYRIE
st. Heathmont 378 H14
st. Ringwood 378 H13
GREAT VALLEY
rd. Glen Iris 416 H11
GREAT WESTERN
dr. Vermont S 421 C9
GREAVES
ct. Pakenham 584 E3
ct. Seaford 599 H1
rd. Berwick 553 B19
rd. Nar Warrn S 552 L19
rd. Nar Warrn S 553 B19
st. Cranbourne 604 D3
st. Dandenong 535 K11
st. Dandenong S 535 K11
st. Werribee 446 L10
st. Werribee 447 A10
st.s, Werribee 447 F17
GREBE
ct. Carrum Downs 600 J4
ct. Mornington 657 B1
GREEG
pl. Kew 371 H4
GREEN
av. Kingsbury 283 J9
av. Mulgrave 500 B2
cl. Delahey 275 D11
cl. Roxburgh Pk 193 L16
ct. Altona 408 L16
dr. Bangholme 549 J13
pde. Sandringham 495 H18
pl. E Melbourne 25 J3
rdg. Ringwood N 334 G13
st. Airport W 279 A16
st. Boronia 424 D9
st. Bulla 190 C16
st. Camberwell 417 L4
st. Cremorne 26 D17
st. Cremorne 32 C2
st. Doveton 536 F14
st. Healesville 213 J19
st. Ivanhoe 327 J11
st. Mooroolbark 337 K19
st. Noble Park 534 C1
st. Northcote 326 L19
st. N Melbourne 34 F14
st. Ringwood E 378 L14
st. Ringwood E 379 A14
st. St Kilda E 414 L20
st. St Kilda E 415 A20
st. Selby 467 D18
st. Sunshine 365 F8
st. Thomastown 241 L20
st. Windsor 414 F11
wk. Forest Hill 420 C6
GREENACRE
cr. Narre Warren 539 A19
gr. Gladstone Pk 236 L20
GREEN ACRES
ct. Langwarrin 602 A17
GREENACRES
st. Craigieburn 150 F16
GREENAWAY
dr. Ferntree Gly 463 F2
st. Bulleen 329 F11
st. Greensbrgh 285 G5
st.n, Bulleen, off
Bridge St 329 F9
GREENBANK
av. Box Hill S 418 K6
av. Endeavour Hl 502 K14
cr. Pascoe Vale S 324 F1
ct. Lysterfield 464 B18
dr. Mooroolbark 337 D8
GREENBELT
av. Preston 283 K18
GREENBRIAR
av. Wheelers Hl 460 L10
wy. Cranbourne W 603 J1
GREENBRIER
ct. Frankston 599 J17
GREENBROOK
dr. Epping 197 J20

GREENDALE
ct. Narre Warren 553 D11
pl. Mt Martha 656 J6
rd. Bentleigh E 497 B3
rd. Doncaster E 376 B5
rd. Glen Iris 417 B12
GREENE
ct. Darley 221 L9
st. S Kingsville 410 F3
GREENEY
st. Altona 408 L14
GREENFIELD
ct. Craigieburn 193 L3
ct. Werribee 447 F6
la. Truganina 405 K13
wy. Mt Martha 656 C17
GREENFIELDS
tce. Bundoora 243 E14
GREENFINCH
wy. Wandana Ht 705 D3
GREENGABLE
ct. Croydon Hl 335 G12
GREEN GABLES
av. Malvern East 457 J1
GREENGABLES
dr. Wyndham Va 446 E9
GREENGLADE
ct. Bayswater 423 F8
ct. Blackburn N 376 C9
ct. Epping 198 B17
ct. Noble Park 534 J7
GREENGLADES
ct. Wandin N 340 K16
GREEN GULLY
cl. Keilor Dn 276 G13
ct. St Helena 244 H17
rd. Kealba 276 J17
rd. Keilor 276 J17
rd. Keilor 277 A14
GREENHAM
cr. Mt Waverley 459 C5
pl. Footscray 367 E8
pl. Kensington 33 D8
st. Maidstone 366 H3
GREENHAVEN
ct. Rowville 464 A12
tce. Berwick 580 C2
GREEN HILL
pl. Craigieburn 150 F10
GREENHILL
cr. Wyndham Va 446 D12
ct. Bulleen 329 H12
ct. Dandenong N 501 J13
ct. Sunbury 142 J2
rd. Bayswater N 379 G18
rd. Greensbrgh 244 F19
rd. Rosebud 700 J6
rd. Selby 467 D20
ri. Hampton Pk 552 C12
ri. Ringwood N 377 L3
st. Melb Airport 236 C16
GREEN HILLS
rd. Pakenham 584 F17
GREENHILLS
av. Montrose 382 C8
dr. Kurunjang 226 H14
rd. Bundoora 242 G19
GREENHOOD
cr. Rosebud W 699 B3
ct. Long Forest 224 G8
GREEN ISLAND
av. Mt Martha 656 F5
GREENKNOWE
av. Frankston 628 C11
ct. Toorak 415 F5
GREENLAND
pl. Dandenong 535 L10
GREENLAW
cr. Berwick 554 D15
cr. Mt Martha 656 A18
GREENLEA
gr. Hampton Pk 551 F12
GREENLEAF
ct. Eltham North 245 C19
ct. Keysborough 534 D13
GREENLEES
ct. Lilydale 338 D15
GREENLOW
av. Wantirna 422 J7
GREENMANTLE
cl. Cranbourne W 577 E18
GREENMEADOWS
la. St Kilda E 414 L20
la. St Kilda E 415 A20
GREENMEYER
ct. Greensbrgh 286 D3
GREENMOUNT
av. McCrae 684 K14
cl. Narre Warren 538 F19
GREENOCH
ct. Keilor Dn 276 C12

GREENOCK
cr. Cranbourne E 604 H1
cr. Wantirna 422 K8
ct. Greenvale 236 K4
pl. Templestowe 331 G15
st. Reservoir 283 E4
GREENPATCH
dr. Bangholme 548 D13
GREEN RIDGE
av. Narre Warren 538 H19
GREENRIDGE
av. Templestowe 331 G14
ct. Chirnside Pk 336 J7
ct. Wesburn 347 K14
ct. Yarra Jctn 347 K14
la. Croydon S 380 B13
GREENS
ct. Mentone 530 K6
rd. Dandenong S 535 D20
rd. Keysborough 534 H20
rd. Keysborough 535 A19
rd. Mambourin 445 G7
rd. Wyndham Va 445 G8
GREENSBOROUGH
bps. Greensbrgh 243 K19
hwy. Diamond Ck 244 H15
hwy. Diamond Ck 245 D11
hwy. Greensbrgh 244 B19
hwy. Heidelberg 329 B4
hwy. Macleod 285 D16
hwy. Rosanna 285 D16
hwy. Rosanna 329 B4
hwy. Watsonia 285 G6
hwy. Watsonia N 243 J20
hwy. Yallambie 285 D16
rd. Greensbrgh 285 H6
rd. Watsonia 285 H6
GREENSHANK
ct. Carrum Downs 600 J5
ct. Werribee 448 A5
GREENSLADE
ct. Mt Martha 655 H16
GREENSLOPES
dr. Carrum Downs 601 C5
dr. Mooroolbark 337 G16
dr. Templstw Lr 330 D7
rd. The Patch 467 L6
GREENSTEAD
wy. Cairnlea 319 L11
GREENSTEAD AMBLE
Kurunjang 226 K11
GREENSTED
gr. Roxburgh Pk 194 B17
GREENSTONE
ct. Thomastown 240 E14
pl. Bundoora 284 F8
GREENTHORPE
rd. Olinda 427 E17
GREENVALE
dr. Greenvale 192 J17
GREEN VALLEY
cr. Hampton Pk 551 G7
gr. Meadow Ht 194 B18
GREENVIEW
cl. Dingley Vill 533 C7
cl. Lysterfield S 503 L15
ct. Bentleigh E 497 E7
ct. Epping 198 B19
ct. Greensbrgh 286 J2
ct. Rowville 463 G11
wy. Point Cook 450 L11
GREENVILLE
dr. Grovedale 706 D10
st. Mooroolbark 381 B2
GREENWAY
ct. Wandana Ht 705 D4
dr. Mill Park 242 L5
dr. Mill Park 243 A6
GREENWAYS
ct. Parkdale 531 D11
rd. Glen Waverley 459 K3
GREENWELL
rd. Selby 466 L13
rd. Selby 467 A13
GREENWICH
cl. Wyndham Va 446 F8
cr. Caroline Spr 317 K4
ct. Glen Waverley 460 G11
gra. Highton 701 F11
pl. Campbellfield 239 H13
pl. Viewbank 329 J3
GREENWOOD
av. Ringwood 378 E13
av. Sorrento 678 H6
dr. Bundoora 284 G6
dr. Carrum Downs 601 A6
dr. Launching Pl 345 E16
dr. Watsonia 285 A6
la. Forest Hill 420 K2
la. Mooroolbark 381 K2
st. Abbotsford 26 B1
st. Briar Hill 286 L5
st. Burwood 419 B9

st. Doncaster 330 F18
st. Newcomb 704 B16
st. Pascoe Vale S 281 A20
st. Wyndham Va 446 E11
GREENWOODS
cl. Dingley Vill 533 C4
GREER
st. Footscray 367 J7
GREEVES
dr. Kilsyth 381 A9
st. Anglesea 713 E7
st. Fitzroy 19 A14
st. St Kilda 414 D17
GREG
ct. Narre Warren 538 G15
GREGG
ct. Hillside 274 G4
st. Diamond Ck 246 A11
GREG NORMAN
dr. Point Cook 451 A11
GREGORY
av. Frankston S 627 G10
av. Newtown 702 E14
cl. Endeavour Hl 538 A1
cr. Mulgrave 500 G3
ct. Carrum Downs 574 H16
ct. Cranbourne N 577 J9
ct. Doncaster 330 B20
ct. Pakenham 585 A3
ct. Sunbury 142 L14
ct. Sunbury 143 A14
ct. Werribee 447 E7
dr. Carrum Downs 574 L18
gr. Preston 283 C20
la. Kensington 33 E7
mw. Forest Hill 376 D20
pl. Melton W 225 L19
rd. Boronia 423 J14
st. Brunswick 325 D12
st. Hillside 274 D6
st. Mt Martha 656 B12
st. Oak Park 279 L14
st. Sunshine W 364 J5
GREIG
ct. Elwood 454 F2
pl. Werribee 447 B10
st. Albert Park 29 D12
st. Albert Park 413 B6
st. Reservoir 282 B1
st. Seddon 367 C12
st. Sunshine 321 G19
GREIGS
rd. Melton S 268 H20
rd. Rockbank 270 G20
GREIGS-CAVALOT
rd. Bangholme 548 H14
GREIVE
st. Balwyn N 373 J6
GREMEL
rd. Reservoir 283 J13
GRENADIER
gr. Hillside 231 J15
GRENDA
ct. Dandenong S 535 H15
dr. Mill Park 242 B7
la. Dandenong, off
George St 535 K10
GRENFELL
rd. Mt Waverley 418 G19
ri. Nar Warrn S 552 F7
wy. Rosebud 699 J4
GRENHILDA
rd. Rosanna 329 A2
GRENOBLE
ct. Highton 705 H5
GRENVILLE
ct. Berwick 554 A5
ct. Blackburn S 419 L2
gr. Rosebud W 698 K1
pl. Melton W 226 D18
st. Box Hill N 374 J10
st. Cockatoo 510 L6
st. Hampton 494 K7
st. Newtown 702 F13
tce. Roxburgh Pk 194 A9
GRESFORD
rd. Wantirna 422 G7
st. Sunshine N 321 D15
GRESHAM
cl. Endeavour Hl 537 J7
pl. Blackburn 375 K20
st. Melbourne 1 C11
st. Melbourne 23 J8
wy. Sunshine W 364 B9
wy. Sunshine W 364 C9
wy. Sunshine W 364 E9
GRESSWELL
rd. Bundoora 284 K9
rd. Macleod 284 J9
GRESSWELL PARK
dr. Macleod 285 C7
dr. Watsonia 285 C7

GRETA
av. Ferntree Gly 463 F7
ct. Broadmeadows 238 A9
ct. Highett 496 J15
ct. Templstw Lr 330 B12
st. Greensbrgh 285 J6
st. Oakleigh E 458 J16
GRETAL
ct. Taylors L 275 J8
GRETANA
cr. Frankston 600 E18
st. Dandenong S 535 J15
GRETEL
ct. Croydon 336 J16
ct. Frankston 628 E10
ct. Hampton Pk 552 D16
ct. Scoresby 462 F8
gr. Melton 268 J2
pl. Berwick 554 K7
ps. Chirnside Pk 337 B4
GRETNA
cl. Westmeadows 236 F14
ct. Greenvale 193 D18
st. Mt Waverley 459 D7
GRETTON
ct. Highton 701 H17
GREVILLE
rd. Ferny Creek 466 C1
rd. Rosanna 329 C3
st. Essendon N 279 D20
st. Huntingdale 458 E13
st. Prahran 31 H17
st. Prahran 414 E9
GREVILLEA
av. Boronia 423 L11
cl. Eltham North 245 F16
cl. Hillside 274 B6
cr. Hoppers Csg 405 E16
ct. Forest Hill 420 K1
ct. Long Forest 224 G10
ct. Mornington 640 L17
ct. Mornington 641 A17
ct. Patterson L 573 H10
ct. Dandenong, off David St 536 E4
dr. Croydon N 335 L12
pl. Pakenham 584 K9
rd. Doncaster E 376 D6
rd. Kings Park 275 C17
rd. Langwarrin 601 K16
GREVILLIA
ct. Altona Mdw 451 K1
ct. Frankston 599 K15
ct. Glen Waverley 460 D9
dr. Mill Park 243 A11
gr. Plenty 244 J11
rd. Oak Park 280 D12
st. Doveton 536 G13
GREY
ct. Coburg 282 A19
ct. Sunbury 143 A16
st. Balwyn 372 L10
st. Belgrave 466 C16
st. Caulfield S 455 H11
st. Darley 221 F9
st. E Geelong 703 E13
st. E Melbourne 25 G4
st. Eltham 287 J10
st. Parkdale 531 L10
st. Ringwood E 379 B9
st. St Kilda 414 B14
st. South Yarra 32 D15
st. South Yarra 414 H8
st. Vermont 377 D20
GREYBOX
ct. Hillside 274 B1
GREY FANTAIL
ct. Langwarrin 628 J7
GREYFERN
ct. Highton 701 L17
GREY GUM
ct. Tecoma 466 D8
ri. Diamond Ck 245 E12
GREYGUM
ct. Launching Pl 345 E12
tce. Croydon Hl 335 F14
GREYLEA
gr. Seabrook 450 L3
GREYSHARPS
rd. Hurstbridge 202 L15
rd. Hurstbridge 203 A14
GREYSTANES
cr. Endeavour Hl 502 L13
GREYSTOKE
ct. Berwick 554 A8
GREYTHORN
ct. Chirnside Pk 337 J4
rd. Balwyn N 374 A7
GREYTHORNE
ct. Narre Warren 538 J13
GRICE
al. Melbourne 1 E11
al. Melbourne 23 K8
av. Fitzroy N 20 A1
av. Mt Eliza 641 L5
cr. Essendon 324 A6
qd. Pakenham 584 H10
GRICES
rd. Berwick 580 B7
rd. Clyde North 580 B7
GRIERSON
dr. Kilsyth 380 K9
GRIEVE
pde. Altona 408 K20
pde. Altona North 409 A10
st. Bayswater 423 D8
st. Launching Pl 345 G16
st. Macleod 284 J15
GRIEVES
st. Newport 410 F7
st. Newport 410 F8
GRIFFIN
cl. Surrey Hills 418 C2
cr. Port Melb 412 H3
ct. Eltham 288 F4
ct. Lalor 241 L11
la. Melbourne 24 J2
st. Brighton East 495 C4
GRIFFITH
av. Bentleigh E 457 A15
pl. Carrum Downs 575 E15
st. Endeavour Hl 536 K3
st. Grovedale 706 B12
st. Knoxfield 463 C8
st. Maddingley 263 F2
st. Noble Park 534 K2
st. Werribee 447 K13
GRIFFITH PARK
rd. Eltham 287 H17
GRIFFITHS
ct. Dandenong N 501 L13
ct. Mt Waverley 459 A6
gr. Brighton East 455 F16
gr. Kew 372 J9
la. Warrandyte 332 K2
rd. Upwey 465 E15
st. Beaumaris 530 C9
st. Bellfield 328 B5
st. Caulfield S 455 L7
st. Reservoir 282 G9
st. Richmond 26 J10
GRIGG
av. Vermont 421 B2
GRIGGS
ct. Mornington 641 B14
GRIGORIEVA
ct. Burnside 318 E5
GRIMES
av. Taylors L 275 L7
rd. Pt Lonsdale 707 G20
GRIMSBY
ct. Doncaster E 332 A17
GRIMSHAW
st. Bundoora 284 J2
st. Greensbrgh 285 C3
st. Greensbrgh 286 C4
st. Watsonia 285 C3
st. Watsonia N 285 C3
GRIMWADE
cr. Frankston 599 J16
ct. Caulfield N 415 B20
ct. Epping 242 C1
pl. Melton W 226 C17
st. Reservoir 282 K4
GRINDLAY
st. Newport 411 A8
GRINSTEAD
ct. Craigieburn 194 E2
GRINTER
st. Moolap 704 K19
GRIOTTE
st. Canterbury 373 F20
st. Canterbury 417 F1
GRIST
st. St Albans 319 J5
GROGAN
ct. Bayswater 423 C10
GRONG GRONG
ct. Toorak 415 H6
GRONN
pl. Brunswick W 324 J9
st. Reservoir 283 K4
GROOM
ct. Glen Waverley 420 F19
la. Fitzroy N 19 F6
st. Clifton Hill 20 E9
GROOME
ct. Altona Mdw 451 J11
GROSE
ct. Croydon Hl 335 D16
GROSS
ct. Grovedale 705 J13
ct. Mt Waverley 418 K15
GROSSMANS
rd. Torquay 711 A4
GROSVENOR
av. Mulgrave 500 G1
ct. Bundoora 284 J5
ct. Melton W 226 C12
ct. Portsea 678 A1
ct. Toorak 415 K7
dr. Wandana Ht 701 D17
dr. Wandana Ht 705 B1
pde. Balwyn 373 E10
pl. Carlton 18 F18
pl. Wantirna S 422 J14
pl. Werribee 447 B19
rd. Glen Iris 416 G7
rd. Rowville 463 J12
st. Abbotsford 371 A12
st. Balaclava 414 H20
st. Balaclava 414 G20
st. Blackburn N 376 A8
st. Brighton 454 F16
st. Doncaster 331 A19
st. Frankston S 626 H10
st. Moonee Pnd 324 A13
st. Niddrie 278 J20
st. South Yarra 32 B14
st. South Yarra 414 G7
wk. Lilydale 338 K1
wk. Lilydale 339 C6
GROUNDSBERRY
st. S Morang 199 H8
GROUSE
ct. Werribee 448 C10
GROUT
st. Hampton 495 C7
st. Mentone 530 K8
GROVE
ct. Carrum Downs 574 J15
gdn. Berwick 554 C19
rd. Grovedale 706 C8
rd. Hawthorn 371 G13
rd. Marshall 706 G8
rd. Rosanna 329 A3
st. Eltham 287 J7
st. Vermont 421 D1
GROVEDALE
cct. Cairnlea 319 J12
cl. Thomastown 240 F11
ct. Clayton 458 K18
rd. Surrey Hills 373 L14
GROVE END
rd. Endeavour Hl 537 D3
GROVE HALL
pl. Caroline Spr 317 L3
GROVELANDS
dr. Mulgrave 500 L5
GROVER
ct. Warranwood 334 K14
rd. Doncaster 331 E18
st. Pascoe Vale 280 E17
GROVES
st. Aspendale 546 D8
st. Keilor East 322 C4
GRUCHY
av. Chelsea Ht 547 F16
GRUMONT
rd. The Basin 425 H10
GRUNDY
st. Pascoe Vale S 324 J6
st. Westmeadows 236 L13
GRUNER
st. Sunbury 142 L10
st. Sunbury 143 A10
GRUYERE
cr. Ivanhoe East 328 L18
la. Ivanhoe East 328 K18
rd. Gruyere 341 C4
GRYLLS
st. Brunswick 325 H12
GRYPHON
wk. Kings Park 319 A2
GUAM
ct. Lalor 241 K8
GUAVA
cl. Sunshine W 364 A8
GUBBAH
ct. Ashwood 418 D18
GUELPH
st. Somerville 644 L13
st. Somerville 645 A13
GUERNSEY
av. Hampton E 496 A9
rd. Wandin East 340 K17
GUEST
av. Albanvale 319 B5
cl. Ringwood E 378 J10
rd. Oakleigh S 458 A16
rd. Pakenham 584 F3
st. Hawthorn 371 K17
st. Tootgarook 698 C5
GUESTS
la. Melbourne 1 D9
la. Melbourne 23 J7
GUIDEHOUSE
rd. Wesburn 348 B19
GUILA
ct. Epping 241 J3
GUILD
av. Noble Park 500 G13
GUILDFORD
av. Coolaroo 238 E7
av. Springvale 499 J18
cl. Frankston 627 K9
cr. Narre Warren 538 E19
ct. Keilor Dn 276 D13
dr. Doncaster E 332 G9
la. Melbourne 1 J5
la. Melbourne 23 L5
rd. Surrey Hills 373 J16
GUILFOYLE
av. Coburg N 281 C15
dr. Sassafras 426 H13
GUINANE
av. Hoppers Csg 448 G3
GUINEA
ct. Epping 198 E18
GUINESS
dr. Berwick 553 H13
GUINEVERE
pde. Glen Waverley 420 L17
GUINNESS
la. Kensington 33 F12
GULF
rd. Yarra Glen 209 A9
GULL
ct. Blind Bight 650 C9
ct. Patterson L 573 J10
ct. Rye 696 L14
la. Williamstown 410 J14
wy. Nar Warrn S 552 F12
wy. Nar Warrn S 552 F13
GULLANE
dr. Sunbury 144 D12
GULLINE
cl. Bacchus Msh 221 K18
GULLINES
rd. Maddingley 263 J13
GULLQUIST
wy. Pakenham 584 C4
GULLS
wy. Frankston S 626 E8
wy. Sorrento 679 C17
GULLY
cr. Belgrave 466 G9
mw. Chirnside Pk 336 J8
tr. Lysterfield 505 D5
GULWA
av. Frankston 627 L6
GUM
cl. Broadmeadows 237 L12
cl. Hoppers Csg 405 F16
ct. Cranbourne N 578 B7
ct. Doveton 536 K8
ct. Knoxfield 463 D2
ct. Montrose 381 L8
ct. Werribee 448 H18
gld. Eltham North 287 G4
gr. Bundoora 242 G14
rd. Kings Park 319 D3
st. Cockatoo 511 A8
st. Frankston N 600 C9
st. Sunshine W 364 H4
GUMBOW
cl. Bayswater N 380 J17
GUMBRAE
st. Reservoir 282 D11
GUMBRI
rd. Coburg 281 K20
GUMBUYA
cl. Eumemmerring 537 B14
GUM HILL
dr. Langwarrin 629 D13
GUMHILL
ct. Eltham 288 D7
GUM LEAF
pl. Craigieburn 150 C13
GUMLEAF
ct. Cairnlea 319 F10
la. Mitcham 377 A15
la. Officer 582 G1
GUMLEY
ct. Dingley Vill 532 L5
GUM NUT
dr. Langwarrin 601 H16
GUMNUT
ct. Berwick 553 E4
la. Lynbrook 551 D18
ri. Bundoora 284 G8
GUM RIDGE
cl. Templestowe 332 A7
GUMS
av. Belgrave 466 D14
GUM TIP
ct. Mornington 656 J4
GUM TREE
rd. Research 288 F9
GUMTREE
cl. Croydon 380 C
cl. St Albans 320 G
cl. Viewbank 285 L
cl. Wheelers Hl 460 L
ct. Campbellfield 239 F
ct. Carrum Downs 575 F
ct. Highton 705
gr. Belgrave Ht 466 C
gr. Hampton Pk 551 E
pl. Moorooduc 643 L
GUMVIEW
ct. Beaconsfield 555 G
GUMVISTA
wk. Skye 575 G
GUN BARREL
wy. Bangholme 548 L
wy. Bangholme 549 A
GUNBOWER
cl. Thomastown 240 E
cr. Meadow Ht 194 D
GUN CLUB
tr. Lysterfield 505 B
GUNDARA
ct. Epping 241
GUNDAROO
sq. Werribee 448 A
GUNDOWRING
dr. Seabrook 451
GUNDRY
gr. Watsonia N 243 D
GUNGARLAN
dr. Keilor East 278 B
GUNIDA
ct. St Andrews Bch 697 F
GUNN
ct. Westmeadows 236 F
st. Murrumbeena 457 B
GUNNAWARRA
rd. Kurunjang 227 B
GUNNEDAH
st. Albion 320 K
GUNNII
nk. Mill Park 243 C
GUNNS
rd. Hallam 537 H
GUNSYND
cl. Thomastown 240 H
ct. Bacchus Msh 221 F
ct. Keilor Dn 275 K
GUNTHER
av. Springvale 500 B
ct. Mt Waverley 459
GUNYAH
ct. Kurunjang 227 D
mw. St Albans 320
mw. St Albans 321
rd. Blackburn N 376 C
st. Rye 697
GURLEY
ct. Grovedale 706 C
GURNER
ct. Endeavour Hl 538
la. Roxburgh Pk 194 A
st. St Kilda 414 C
GURNERS
la. Melbourne 1 F
la. Melbourne 23 L
la. Mt Martha 656
la. Sunbury 143 J
la. Taylors Hill 274 F
GURR
st. E Geelong 703 G
GURRBORRA
wy. Bundoora 284
GUSTAVIS
ct. Nar Warrn S 552 G
GUTHRIE
st. Brunswick W 324 K
GUY
ct. Fawkner 239 G
ct. Montrose 382
ct. Nar Warrn N 538 L
ct. Sunshine W 364
ct. Wantirna 422 D
st. Upwey 465 E
GUYMER
ct. Montmorency 287 A
GUYRA
ct. Werribee 447 E
GWALIA
ct. Rowville 463 H
GWELO
st. W Footscray 366
GWEN
ct. Taylors L 275
rd. Cranbourne W 577 C
GWENDA
av. Blackburn 376 B
av. Canterbury 373 B
av. Moorabbin 496
ct. Lower Plenty 286 J
ct. Nar Warrn S 553 A

Box Hill S 418 G2
Dandenong 535 K4
WENDOLINE
Bentleigh 455 J18
WENETH
Highton 701 J16
WENMAY
Ringwood N 378 F3
WENNETH
Sassafras 426 F16
WENO
Frankston 626 K3
WENT
Springvale S 533 K6
WENTON
Cranbourne E 604 H5
WILT
Westmeadows 237 E13
WINGANA
Glen Waverley 460 G5
WYDIR
Werribee 447 E7
WYN
Boronia 424 F14
Vermont S 420 L8
Vermont S 421 A8
WYNNE
Cremorne 32 B2
Mt Waverley 419 C18
WYTHER
Highton 705 F3
YLES
Pascoe Vale 280 G16
YMEA
Rowville 502 C6
Glen Waverley 420 D16
Keysborough 534 G8
YMKHANA
Endeavour Hl 504 A18
Keilor Park 277 H13
YMPIE
Aspendale Gdn 547 A3
Bulleen 329 J14
YPSY
Mill Park 243 C12
YRA
Bundoora 285 A2
YTON
Glen Waverley 420 C15

H

AAG
Seville 341 G12
ACKETT
Delahey 275 E10
Pascoe Vale S 324 F1
ACKETTS
Point Cook 449 F20
Olinda 427 B18
Yarrambat 201 F17
ACKWORTH
Rye 696 D7
ADDINGTON
Greenvale 237 A3
ADDON
Meadow Ht 238 C5
Mitcham 377 G12
ADDON HILL
Attwood 236 K11
ADFIELD
Broadmeadows 238 D20
ADKINSON
Clayton S 499 A6
ADLEY
ct. Nar Warrn S 578 D2
Kealba 276 K19
Glen Iris 416 F7
Templestowe 332 A5
Seaford 599 G10
ADLOW
Wantirna 422 G7
AERING
Boronia 423 J9
AFEY
Hoppers Csg 448 E4
AFFENDEN
St Andrews 205 E1
AGAN
Belmont 702 J18
Keysborough 534 C7
AGEN
Hoppers Csg 449 B2
Diamond Ck 245 K13
Berwick 553 L2
Lalor 240 H7
AGGARDS
Woori Yall 344 C13

HAIDEH
ct. Hoppers Csg 449 D2
pl. Wantirna S 462 A5
HAIG
av. Coburg 325 C7
av. Edithvale 546 J12
av. Healesville 257 G2
av. Monbulk 428 F18
ct. Doncaster E 376 B6
la. Southbank 23 K19
pl. Attwood 237 C12
rd. Mt Evelyn 339 B13
st. Balwyn 373 A10
st. Box Hill S 374 L20
st. Box Hill S 375 A20
st. Box Hill S 418 L2
st. Burwood 417 L13
st. Croydon 380 C2
st. Heidelberg Ht 328 D3
st. Mornington 640 G14
st. Reservoir 282 F15
st. Ringwood 378 D15
st. Southbank 23 J19
HAIGH
ct. Altona Mdw 451 G4
st. Oakleigh S 497 F4
HAILES
ct. Carrum Downs 574 L16
ct. Carrum Downs 574 L17
st. Greensbrgh 285 L2
st.e, Greensbrgh 286 B3
HAILEY
ct. Taylors L 275 H2
ct. Templestowe 332 C10
HAILEYBURY
ct. Keysborough 534 E11
ct. Sunbury 144 G10
ct. Wantirna 422 J9
st. Brighton 494 H4
HAILSHAM
ct. Mulgrave 501 G3
HAINES
ct. Sunbury 143 F6
st. Cheltenham 530 L1
st. Hawthorn 372 B15
st. Mitcham 377 B12
st. N Melbourne 17 A13
st. N Melbourne 34 K14
HAINTHORPE
gr. Mulgrave 500 L5
gr. Mulgrave 501 A5
HAIR
ct. Beaconsfield 554 L16
HAITE
ct. Endeavour Hl 537 B4
pl. Roxburgh Pk 194 A15
HAKATERE
st. Northcote 327 B13
HAKEA
av. Rosebud W 699 B1
ct. Altona Mdw 407 L20
ct. Langwarrin 601 H20
ct. Mt Waverley 459 B2
ct. Thomastown 240 K12
ct. Werribee 447 K10
dr. Montrose 381 L17
dr. Mt Martha 656 E7
pl. Meadow Ht 193 J20
pl. Rowville 502 E5
rd. Keilor 276 F7
st. Doveton 536 G12
st. Frankston 627 D5
st. Tecoma 466 B11
st. Templestowe 331 B7
st. Watsonia N 243 G20
st. Watsonia N 285 G1
HAKEA RIDGE
tr. Frankston N 600 F13
HAKEVILLE
av. Nunawading 376 H8
HALBERT
rd. Bayswater N 380 E14
HALCOT
cl. Mulgrave 501 D5
HALCYON
av. The Patch 467 J3
ct. Doncaster E 332 C15
dr. Wheelers Hl 460 J8
gr. Cockatoo 510 K10
ri. Mornington 657 D5
wy. Nar Warrn S 552 H9
HALDANE
ct. Doncaster E 332 G8
rd. Eltham 287 G17
rd. Niddrie 278 J19
st. Beaumaris 530 C11
st. Bonbeach 573 B5
st. Keysborough 535 A11
HALE
ct. Burwood E 419 F7
st. Kew East 372 E4

HALES
cr. Jacana 237 K17
cr. Jacana 237 L18
ct. Keysborough 534 C9
ct. Mill Park 242 H9
ct. Northcote 326 H20
HALESWORTH
st. St Albans 320 G5
HALEY
ct. Noble Park 535 B6
st. Diamond Ck 245 K11
HALEYS GULLY
rd. Hurstbridge 202 C10
HALF MOON
tce. Point Cook 451 E9
HALFMOON
pl. Pt Lonsdale 707 H18
HALFORD
la. Kensington 33 D8
st. Beaconsfld Up 542 F15
HALIDAY
ct. Greensbrgh 243 L20
ct. Greensbrgh 285 L1
HALIDON
cl. St Helena 245 A18
HALIFAX
av. Heidelberg 329 E2
cl. St Albans 275 J19
ct. Ashburton 417 K18
ct. Point Cook 449 K6
st. Brighton 454 K20
st. Brighton 455 A18
st. Dandenong 535 L1
st. Mont Albert N 374 E10
st. Mulgrave 500 D5
HALINKA
ct. Noble Park 534 D4
HALL
av. Altona Mdw 407 H18
av. Cockatoo 511 A5
ct. Berwick 554 F17
ct. Dandenong S 535 L13
ct. Meadow Ht 237 J2
ct. Thomastown 242 A13
rd. Carrum Downs 574 J19
rd. Cranbourne W 602 B1
rd. Gladstone Pk 237 D20
rd. Gladstone Pk 279 E1
rd. Healesville 214 H18
rd. Nar Warrn E 506 K18
rd. Ringwood N 334 E13
rd. Skye 575 G20
rd. Warrandyte S 334 E13
st. Braeside 532 G12
st. Brighton 454 L19
st. Brighton 455 A19
st. Brunswick 325 B11
st. Cheltenham 496 H20
st. Clifton Hill 20 H5
st. Coburg 325 E7
st. Epping 197 E17
st. Fairfield 327 F15
st. Hawthorn E 416 C7
st. Hoppers Csg 448 L4
st. McKinnon 456 E17
st. Moonee Pnd 324 B13
st. Mt Martha 669 B1
st. Newport 411 A5
st. Ormond 456 E16
st. Port Melb 368 E17
st. Spotswood 411 A5
st. Sunshine W 363 L4
st. Yarraville 367 E15
HALLADALE
av. Wyndham Va 446 G7
HALLAM
bps. Berwick 553 C3
bps. Endeavour Hl 537 K13
bps. Hallam 537 K13
bps. Narre Warren 537 K13
bps. Nar Warrn N 537 K13
gr. Anglesea 713 H3
rd. Hallam 537 L20
rd. Hampton Pk 551 H18
rd. Lynbrook 551 H18
HALLAM NORTH
rd. Endeavour Hl 538 B3
rd. Lysterfield S 504 C17
rd. Nar Warrn N 504 C20
rd. Nar Warrn N 538 B9
HALLAM VALLEY
rd. Dandenong S 536 H20
rd. Dandenong S 551 A1
HALLCROFT
pl. Hawthorn E 372 H17
HALLETTS
wy. Bacchus Msh 221 G13
wy. Darley 221 F8
HALLEUR
rd. Harkaway 540 A10
HALLEY
av. Camberwell 417 B7
cr. Campbellfield 194 L20

ct. Bentleigh 496 F1
rd. Ferntree Gly 424 G19
rd. Panton Hill 204 H9
st. Blackburn 376 B20
HALLIDAY
ct. Hughesdale 457 E13
st. Mt Waverley 458 F3
HALLIFAX
ct. Doncaster E 332 H8
st. Seaford 573 E17
HALLINAN
ct. Cheltenham 531 B4
HALLIS
ct. Torquay 712 H2
HALLMARK
cl. Mill Park 242 L10
dr. Nar Warrn S 578 E3
pl. Keilor Dn 276 A12
rd. Mordialloc 532 C16
HALLOW
st. Bentleigh E 457 F16
HALLOWS
st. Glen Waverley 420 F14
HALLS
pde. Mitcham 377 E18
pde. Vermont 377 E18
tr. Kallista 467 B2
HALLSTON
ct. Meadow Ht 238 A4
HALPIN
st. Brunswick W 324 L14
HALSBURY
cl. Doncaster E 332 D13
ct. St Helena 245 D15
dr. Rowville 502 J3
st. Hadfield 280 J9
HALSEY
rd. Airport W 278 H12
st. Box Hill S 375 A20
st. Ferntree Gly 424 E19
st. Reservoir 282 C4
HALSHAM
ct. Greenvale 192 K18
HALSTEAD
ct. Cranbourne 578 B15
ct. Hillside 232 F20
pl. Geelong West 702 H6
st. Caulfield N 455 H1
st. Maidstone 366 E1
HALSTON
rd. Lalor 241 A5
HALTER
cr. Epping 198 E19
HALTON
rd. Dandenong N 501 D15
rd. Noble Park N 501 D15
HALWYN
cr. Preston 326 B5
HAM
pl. S Geelong 703 A14
rd. Ferny Creek 466 C4
HAMAL
st. Donvale 376 E3
HAMBLEDON
ct. Craigieburn 150 D20
rd. Hawthorn 415 J2
HAMBLETON
ct. Lysterfield 464 C17
st. Albert Park 29 K15
st. Albert Park 413 E8
st. Middle Park 29 K15
st. Middle Park 413 E8
HAMBLINGS
la. Geelong 703 B12
HAMEL
st. Albion 320 L20
st. Box Hill S 418 F4
st. Hampton 495 A6
HAMER
st. Brunswick E 325 L13
st. Moorabbin 496 D10
HAMERSLEY
ct. Mt Eliza 642 E2
ct. Reservoir 239 L20
HAMILTON
av. Blackburn 375 G12
cl. Endeavour Hl 537 E2
cl. Kilsyth 381 G10
cl. Malvern 415 L8
cr. Bacchus Msh 221 K13
cr. Doncaster E 375 K3
ct. Lalor 241 H7
ct. Pearcedale 647 J1
ct. Watsonia N 243 G19
dr. Cranbourne N 578 H9
dr. Ringwood N 378 H2
gr. Frankston S 627 B7
hwy. Fyansford 701 B5
hwy. Geelong West 702 D6
hwy. Herne Hill 702 D6
hwy. Manifold Ht 702 D6
pl. Mornington 640 H19
pl. Mt Waverley 419 A20

rd. Bayswater N 379 L19
rd. Bayswater N 423 L1
rd. Emerald 509 H5
rd. Malvern 415 L8
rd. N Warrandyte 290 E13
st. Alphington 327 G18
st. Balwyn 373 E11
st. Bentleigh 456 A18
st. Brighton 454 L10
st. Broadmeadows 237 L11
st. Brunswick W 325 A10
st. Craigieburn 150 H15
st. Deer Park 319 B17
st. Diggers Rest 141 L11
st. Elsternwick 455 A7
st. Kew East 372 E6
st. Mont Albert 374 D16
st. Niddrie 279 A20
st. Niddrie 322 L2
st. Oakleigh 458 C14
st. Safety Bch 669 C14
st. Seddon 367 A13
st. Yarraville 367 A13
wk. Mt Waverley 419 A20
wk. Mt Waverley 459 A1
HAMILTON HUME
pde. Craigieburn 150 F10
HAMISH
ct. Greensbrgh 244 B16
HAMLAN
pl. Newtown 702 G12
HAMLET
pl. Dingley Vill 533 D3
st. Cheltenham 496 D17
HAMLYN
ct. Meadow Ht 237 K4
st. Aberfeldie 323 E9
HAMMEL
ct. Hallam 537 J18
HAMMENCE
st. Glen Waverley 420 F19
HAMMER
ct. Hoppers Csg 449 J2
HAMMERDALE
av. St Kilda E 414 H15
HAMMERSLEY
ct. Kilsyth 381 J6
ct. Lalor 240 H7
ct. Taylors L 276 C9
pl. Caroline Spr 317 K7
HAMMERWOOD
av. Derrimut 363 B5
grn. Officer 555 G20
HAMMOND
av. Airport W 279 B16
cct. Hopetoun Park 265 L6
cct. Hopetoun Park 266 A7
ct. Altona Mdw 451 C2
dr. Epping 197 G17
pl. Roxburgh Pk 194 E10
rd. Dandenong S 535 J20
rd. Dandenong S 549 G11
st. Altona 408 L15
st. Brighton 455 A19
st. Ringwood 378 C18
st. Sunshine N 321 C15
st. Thornbury 327 B11
HAMPDEN
av. Frankston 600 D18
ct. Rowville 463 H12
ct. Templestowe 331 F12
rd. Armadale 415 D13
rd. Kensington 33 K12
st. Braybrook 366 B3
st. Dallas 238 K10
st. Mornington 640 E17
HAMPSHIRE
cr. Sunshine 321 D20
ct. Bayswater N 380 F16
ct. Rowville 502 L6
ct. Rowville 503 A6
ct. Tarneit 405 C12
dr. Nar Warrn S 552 E18
rd. Doncaster 375 D4
rd. Forest Hill 420 J5
rd. Glen Waverley 459 H11
rd. Sunshine 365 C2
rd. Sunshine 365 C6
HAMPSON
pl. Caroline Spr 318 A4
HAMPSTEAD
cr. Glen Waverley 460 E12
ct. Thomastown 240 K11
dr. Hoppers Csg 448 H6
grn. Caroline Spr 317 L4
rd. Maidstone 322 G19
rd. Noble Park N 501 E17
HAMPTON
av. Sunshine 365 C7
cl. Narre Warren 539 F17
ct. Dandenong N 502 D13
ct. Glen Waverley 459 J8
ct. Hoppers Csg 405 B19

ct. Ivanhoe 328 D10
ct. Lilydale 338 K1
ct. Lilydale 339 C6
ct. Officer 555 J19
ct. Rosebud 684 F16
ct. Thomastown 241 K15
dr. Hampton Pk 551 F7
gr. Camberwell 417 F3
pde. W Footscray 366 E11
rd. Essendon W 322 K7
st. Brighton 455 B20
st. Brighton 495 A10
st. Hampton 494 L10
st. Newtown 702 F13

HAMS
rd. Waurn Ponds 705 A17

HAMSTEAD
ct. Endeavour Hl 503 C20

HAMSTERLEY
sq. Wantirna 422 F14

HANBURY
cl. Point Cook 450 H8
ct. Carrum Downs 575 E18
ct. Keysborough 534 B9

HANBY
st. Brighton 494 L3

HANCE
st. Yarraville 367 B17

HANCOCK
cl. St Helena 245 E16
cr. Braybrook 366 B1
dr. Berwick 553 J14
dr. Ferntree Gly 463 J7
st. Altona 409 A18
st. Southbank 3 A12
st. Southbank 23 L19
st. Vermont S 420 K8

HAND
st. Warburton 349 G1

HANDASYDE
av. Kilsyth S 425 A1
pl. Burwood, off Abrahams Ct 419 B7

HANDEL
ct. Blackburn 375 J19
ct. Bundoora 242 L20

HANDFIELD
st. Eltham 287 F8

HANDFORD
la. Officer 581 J6

HANDLEY
cr. Dandenong S 535 D11
ct. Blackburn N 376 B9
ct. Frankston S 626 L8

HANDS
rd. Kalorama 383 A11

HANDSCOMBE
ct. Croydon Hl 335 D14

HANDSWORTH
cr. Tullamarine 278 L3

HANI
ct. Torquay 712 G2
pl. Grovedale 706 F15

HANKE
pl. Sunbury 142 G7
rd. Doncaster 374 K3

HANLETH
av. Springvale 499 H17

HANLEY
ct. Pakenham 584 E3
st. Avondale Ht 321 L10
st. Narre Warren 553 F8

HANLON
cl. Mordialloc 532 E18

HANMER
st. Williamstown 411 G17

HANN
cl. Endeavour Hl 537 J5
st. Pearcedale 647 A6

HANNA
cr. Doreen 156 L14
ct. Braybrook 366 C1
dr. Endeavour Hl 537 K3
la. S Melbourne 3 D20
la. S Melbourne 30 D2
st. Melbourne 31 B14
st. Melbourne 414 A7
st. Noble Park 535 B4
st. Point Cook 450 F5

HANNAGAN
st. Aspendale Gdn 546 G2

HANNAH
av. Hillside 274 G5
cl. Glen Waverley 459 J9
cl. Melton W 225 L18
ct. Cranbourne 578 A11
st. Cheltenham 497 D16
st. Preston 283 H19
st. Seaford 599 G10
st. Southbank 3 A8
st. Southbank 23 L17

HANNAH PASCOE
dr. Gowanbrae 279 D7

HANNALORE
wy. Patterson L 573 H2

HANNAM
ct. Roxburgh Pk 193 J13

HANNAN
st. Williamstown 411 B18

HANNASLEA
st. Box Hill 374 K18

HANNORA
cr. Croydon 335 E20
cr. Croydon 379 E1

HANNOVER
rd. Badger Creek 258 E8

HANOVER
ct. Avondale Ht 322 F8
ct. Endeavour Hl 536 L2
ct. Endeavour Hl 537 A2
rd. Vermont S 420 L10
rd. Vermont S 421 A9
st. Brunswick 325 C11
st. Fitzroy 18 L17
st. Oakleigh 457 L12

HANRAHAN
st. Thomastown 241 G20

HANS
av. Ringwood N 378 G1
ct. Mulgrave 500 B3

HANSA
wk. Heidelberg W 284 A20

HANSEN
cl. Burwood 419 B7
ct. Mt Martha 656 E8
ct. Narre Warren 539 A13
dr. Grovedale 706 G15
rd. Boronia 424 J15
rd. Kilsyth 381 E6
st. Altona North 410 D6
st. Brighton East 495 H1
st. Forest Hill 376 E20
st. Kew 371 L13
st. Mt Waverley 458 H3
st. W Footscray 366 H12

HANSFORD
cl. Kilsyth 381 G10
ct. Narre Warren 553 C11

HANSLOPE
av. Alphington 327 F19

HANSLOW
wy. Taylors L 275 F8

HANSON
ct. Taylors L 233 C17
rd. Craigieburn 150 F15
st. Darley 222 D9
st. Niddrie 278 H18

HANSWORTH
st. Mulgrave 500 F4
st. Mulgrave 501 B6

HANWELL
ct. Croydon N 336 A14
ct. Glen Waverley 460 K6

HAPPY HOLLOW
dr. Plenty 244 B13

HAPPY VALLEY
av. Blairgowrie 696 C1
ct. Doncaster E 332 F11
ct. Rowville 502 L2
ct. Rowville 503 A2
ri. Diamond Ck 245 G10

HARBARD
st. Thomastown 240 G13

HARBER
ct. Glen Waverley 419 L15

HARBERTS
rd. Don Valley 346 B8

HARBINGER
ct. Wheelers Hl 460 H16

HARBORNE
st. Macleod 285 F10

HARBOUR
dr. Patterson L 547 H20
dr. Patterson L 547 J20
esp. Docklands 23 A8
la. Dandenong, off David St 536 D4
st. Beaconsfield 555 D13
st. Queenscliff 709 D16
wy. Blind Bight 650 E8

HARBURY
mw. Hampton Pk 551 F4
st. Reservoir 282 H10

HARCOMBE
dr. Sunbury 142 F9

HARCOURT
av. Caulfield 455 F3
av. Frankston S 626 K7
av. Mulgrave 500 A4
av. St Albans 320 K4
cl. Hampton Pk 551 K5
cl. Sunbury 142 H8
cr. Gladstone Pk 237 B20
cr. Gladstone Pk 279 C1
pde. Cremorne 25 K20
pde. Cremorne 31 L1

pl. Lower Plenty 286 H19
rd. Altona 407 H12
rd. Boronia 424 H11
sq. Wyndham Va 446 J9
st. Ashwood 418 E17
st. Blackburn N 375 L9
st. Doncaster 374 F2
st. Hawthorn E 372 E15
st. Newtown 702 B10
st. N Melbourne 17 E14
wy. Berwick 554 D2

HARDEEP
pl. Heathmont 422 E1

HARDHAM
st. Belgrave 466 G18

HARDIDGE
ct. Doncaster 375 A4
st. Croydon 336 B19

HARDIE
rd. Brooklyn 366 B16
rd. Yarraville 366 B17
st. Hampton 494 J6

HARDIMAN
ct. Mill Park 242 A8
st. Bundoora 284 B8
st. Kensington 34 B11

HARDING
av. Bonbeach 545 E14
la. Bonbeach, off Harding Av 545 F14
rd. Macclesfield 471 C8
rd. Warrandyte 334 E3
st. Ascot Vale 324 D19
st. Bentleigh 495 L4
st. Coburg 326 A3
st. Highett 496 B12
st. Surrey Hills 374 D19
st. Thomastown 240 L15
st. Thomastown 241 A15

HARDINGE
st. Beaumaris 530 A10

HARDMAN
ct. Endeavour Hl 537 B5

HARDNER
rd. Mt Waverley 459 A8

HARDWARE
la. Melbourne 1 K11
la. Melbourne 24 A5
la. Taylors Hill 274 F8

HARDWICK
la. Kensington 33 F7
st. Coburg 325 J5

HARDWICKE
ct. Frankston 628 D11
st. Balwyn 373 B11
st. N Melbourne 17 B13

HARDWOOD
ct. Mitcham 376 L11

HARDY
av. Cannons Creek 649 G8
av. Craigieburn 150 G19
cl. Gladstone Pk 236 L16
cr. Heathmont 422 F2
ct. Bentleigh 455 H19
ct. Berwick 553 K6
ct. Oakleigh S 498 E2
gr. Beaumaris 530 E7
st. Brunswick 325 H11
st. Lilydale 338 E7
st. Mornington 641 B16
st. Preston 282 F18
st. Rye 696 G2
st. Selby 467 A13
st. South Yarra 31 L15
st. South Yarra 414 F8
tce. Ivanhoe East 328 F16

HARDYS
rd. Clyde North 580 A20
rd. Melton W 224 L12
rd. Melton W 225 A12
rd. Tooradin 652 D1

HARE
ct. Darley 221 K10
st. Fawkner 281 L6

HAREEBA
ct. Mornington 657 C5

HAREFIELD
cr. Kealba 320 L1

HARESTA
av. Dandenong S 535 J15

HAREWOOD
cl. Boronia 424 E6
st. Tooradin 651 K8

HAREWOOD MAINS
rd. Tooradin 652 B4

HAREWOOD PARK
rd. Gembrook 512 C16

HARFLEUR
av. Beaumaris 530 G10

HARFORD
cl. Lynbrook 551 F19

HARGRAVE
cr. Wandana Ht 705 D2
ct. Cranbourne 603 L2
ct. Mill Park 242 J5
st. Airport W 279 D16

HARGREAVES
cr. Braybrook 365 L2
st. Cremorne 32 D3
st. Fitzroy 19 F15
st. Huntingdale 458 E15
st. Mornington 640 C16

HARICOT
ct. Keilor Dn 275 J11
ct. Seabrook 450 K6
wy. Lilydale 293 L19

HARKAWAY
dr. Cheltenham 497 H20
rd. Berwick 554 E1
rd. Harkaway 540 G8
rd. Nar Warrn N 540 G8
ri. Doncaster E 332 D14

HARKER
st. Alphington 327 J18
st. Burwood 418 C10
st. Healesville 257 G1
st. N Melbourne 17 C13
st. Sunbury 143 G14

HARKIN
av. Mentone 531 A10

HARKNESS
rd. Melton W 225 C17

HARLAND
sq. Wantirna 422 H12

HARLAW
ct. Wheelers Hl 460 H18

HARLEIAN
st. Blairgowrie 695 L1

HARLESTON
rd. Mt Eliza 626 D11
st. St Albans 320 G5

HARLEY
cr. Mooroolbark 381 A1
ct. Berwick 554 A4
ct. Keilor East 322 B3
ct. Thomastown 240 D15
pl. Wheelers Hl 460 H15
st. Dingley Vill 533 F9
st. Knoxfield 462 L7
st. Knoxfield 463 A7
st. Sunshine N 321 E14
st.n, Knoxfield 462 L4
st.n, Knoxfield 463 A4

HARLINGFORD
ct. Wheelers Hl 461 D15

HARLINGTON
av. Eltham 287 K10
st. Clayton 498 G3

HARLOW
ct. Deer Park 319 B8
ct. Keysborough 535 B11
ct. Moorabbin 496 G11

HARMAN
av. Eltham 288 C4
cl. Doncaster E 332 H7

HARMER
rd. Hallam 537 F16
st. Reservoir 283 B3

HARMON
av. St Albans 320 J3
cl. Berwick 553 K16

HARMONY
cl. Lilydale 338 D14
ct. Pakenham 585 H1
ct. Roxburgh Pk 194 B7
ct. Springvale S 534 B3
dr. Tarneit 447 F1
ri. Mornington 657 C4

HARMSWORTH
av. Wantirna 422 D10
st. Collingwood 19 L16

HARNESS
ct. Sydenham 274 L4
pl. Pakenham 585 F6

HARNETT
st. Boronia 424 J15

HAROLD
av. Glen Iris 416 G16
ct. Baxter 644 B3
pl. Thornbury 326 J8
rd. Keysborough 533 K4
rd. Noble Park 533 K4
rd. Rye 696 E9
rd. Skye 602 C10
rd. Springvale S 533 K4
st. Ascot Vale 323 F16
st. Ashwood 418 A15
st. Blackburn 375 H13
st. Bonbeach 573 D1
st. Briar Hill 286 G3
st. Bulleen 330 A17
st. Cockatoo 471 F17
st. Glenroy 280 C6
st. Hawthorn E 372 G19

st. McKinnon 455 J15
st. Middle Park 29 L20
st. Middle Park 413 F10
st. Olinda 426 J9
st. Preston 327 A4
st. Sandringham 495 D18
st. Seaford 599 E1
st. Seddon 367 A1
st. Thornbury 326 D7
st. Wantirna 422 C9

HAROLD KEYS
dr. Nar Warrn S 552 F
dr. Nar Warrn S 552 G

HAROS
av. Nunawading 376 G18

HARP
rd. Kew 372 F
rd. Kew East 372 F

HARPER
av. Bentleigh E 496 H
cl. Craigieburn 194 H
ct. Port Melb 412 H
la. Melbourne 1 G1
la. Melbourne 24 A1
pl. Mill Park 242 L
pl. Mill Park 243 A
st. Abbotsford 20 E1
st. Kensington 33 J
st. Northcote 326 K1
st. Werribee 447 B1

HARPFIELD
rd. Beaconsfld Up 542 C1

HARPLEY
st. Cheltenham 531 C

HARPTREE
cl. Rowville 503 C

HARPUR
ct. Oakleigh E 458 H1

HARRA
ct. Oak Park 280 D1

HARRAP
ct. Diamond Ck 245 K
rd. Mt Martha 656 H
rd. Mt Martha 657 A

HARRICKS
cr. Attwood 237 C
rd. Keilor Park 277 G

HARRIDGE
st. Rosebud 700 A

HARRIER
cl. Blind Bight 650 E
ct. Dingley Vill 533 C
ct. Mornington 640 L1
st. Werribee 448 C

HARRIES
ct. Nar Warrn N 539 F

HARRIET
st. Heathmont 379 D
st. Seddon 367 B
st. Werribee 448 E

HARRIETT
cr. Mont Albert 374 F

HARRINGTON
av. Balwyn N 373 K
dr. Melton W 225 G
dr. Nar Warrn S 578
dr. Nar Warrn S 578
pl. Doncaster E 332 H
rd. Airport W 278 F
st. Altona 408 J
st. Diamond Ck 246 C

HARRIS
av. Glen Iris 416
av. Hoppers Csg 448
cr. Glen Waverley 460
ct. Clarinda 498 G
ct. Pakenham 584
gr. Bayswater 423
pl. N Melbourne 17 D
rd. Beaconsfld Up 542 H
rd. Donvale 377
rd. Wonga Park 335
st. Altona North 365 E
st. Blackburn N 375 K
st. Brunswick 325 G
st. Footscray 367 F
st. N Melbourne 17 C
st. St Albans 320
st. Springvale 499 J

HARRIS GULLY
rd. Warrandyte 333 E

HARRISON
av. Burwood 418 A
cr. Hawthorn 371 D
ct. Altona Mdw 451
ct. Carrum Downs 574 K
ct. Highton 701 K
ct. Mornington 640 L
dr. Cranbourne 603
mw. Mitcham 377 D
pl. Fitzroy 19 A
rd. Montrose 382
st. Bellfield 327

HAYWOOD
gr. Melton W.......225 G20
st. Beaumaris.......530 E6
HAZEL
av. Dandenong S.....535 F11
av. Edithvale.......546 J15
av. Highett.......495 L11
av. Thomastown......240 J15
cr. Healesville.......258 A4
ct. Ashwood.......418 D12
ct. Hampton Pk.......551 K14
dr. Templstw Lr......330 D14
gr. Frankston.......627 G1
gr. Pascoe Vale.......280 J17
gr. Tecoma.......466 C9
st. Belmont.......706 C1
st. Camberwell.......416 L6
st. Camberwell.......417 A6
st. Cockatoo.......510 L6
st. Melton S.......268 F7
st. Mt Evelyn.......383 G5
st. Seaford.......599 D2
HAZELDEAN
av. Brighton East.....455 D17
ct. Hampton Pk.......551 F5
HAZELDENE
ct. Berwick.......554 F5
pl. Langwarrin.......629 H4
st. Meadow Ht.......237 L7
HAZELDINE
rd. Glen Iris.......417 B12
HAZELDON
pl. South Yarra.......32 E14
pl. South Yarra.......414 H7
HAZEL GLEN
dr. Doreen.......156 L12
HAZELMERE
av. Cranbourne W...603 J2
av. Cranbourne W...603 J3
HAZEL ROSE
ct. Montmorency....286 H7
HAZEL VALE
rd. Tecoma.......466 A18
HAZELVIEW
pkt. Croydon N.......336 A13
HAZELWOOD
av. Cranbourne N....578 D9
cl. Dingley Vill.......533 B10
ct. Bundoora.......242 F19
ct. Kings Park.......275 D18
rd. Boronia.......424 A16
HAZFORD
st. Healesville.......212 K17
HAZLITT
ct. Cranbourne.......578 A15
HEACHAM
rd. Eltham North.....287 A3
HEAD
ct. Vermont S.......421 B9
rd. Wandin East......385 D10
st. Balwyn.......372 K8
st. Blairgowrie.......680 B19
st. Brighton.......454 E8
st. Brighton.......454 G8
st. Elwood.......454 E8
st. Rosebud.......684 A16
st. Strathmore.......280 B20
HEADINGLEY
rd. Mt Waverley......419 D17
HEADINGLY
ct. Endeavour Hl.....537 J7
HEADLAND WATERS
Mt Martha.......669 B3
HEADLEY
cl. Caroline Spr.......317 H4
st. Coburg N.......281 G16
HEADLINE
ct. Heathmont.......379 C19
HEADS
rd. Donvale.......377 C5
HEALES
st. Dromana.......685 L7
HEALESVILLE-KINGLAKE
rd. Chum Creek.......213 B2
rd. Healesville.......213 C18
HEALESVILLE-KOO WEE RUP
rd. Badger Creek.....257 G8
rd. Healesville.......257 H8
rd. Nangana.......472 D1
rd. Woori Yall.......343 L19
rd. Yellingbo.......387 G14
rd. Yellingbo.......387 J7
HEALESVILLE-YARRA GLEN
rd. Healesville.......212 D20
rd. Tarrawarra.......210 G20
rd. Yarra Glen.......253 F2
rd. Yarra Glen.......254 A1
HEALEY
dr. Epping.......197 K15
rd. Dandenong S.....550 A7
st. Craigieburn.......150 G19
st. Moorabbin.......496 C7
HEALEYS
la. Melbourne.......1 C7
la. Melbourne.......23 H7
HEALS
rd. Mernda.......156 A17
HEALY
av. Sunbury.......142 J15
ct. Watsonia N.......243 D17
HEANY
ct. Thomastown......240 G11
st. Mt Waverley......458 J3
HEANY PARK
rd. Rowville.......503 B9
HEAPE
ct. Melbourne.......2 A7
ct. Melbourne.......24 A5
wy. Ringwood N.......334 H20
HEARD
av. Plenty.......244 K9
av. Yarrambat.......200 L20
cl. Berwick.......553 K8
HEARLE
av. Aspendale.......546 A2
HEARN
rd. Mt Martha.......669 B1
st. Altona North......410 B5
st. Dromana.......685 E10
HEARNE
pde. E Geelong.......703 H6
HEARSE
rd. Millgrove.......348 E4
HEART
st. Dandenong S.....535 L11
HEARTHSIDE
ct. Ringwood.......378 A10
HEARTY
st. Blackburn S.......419 K4
HEATH
av. Ferntree Gly.......424 L16
av. Frankston.......627 E1
av. Mt Evelyn.......339 E16
av. Oakleigh.......458 A12
cl. Altona Mdw.......407 L19
cr. Hampton E.......495 K8
ct. Darley.......221 L9
ct. Doveton.......536 H9
ct. Heathmont.......379 B18
ct. Mornington.......656 K4
ct. Noble Park N.......501 D13
la. Arthurs Seat.......686 G18
la. Red Hill.......686 G18
mw. Langwarrin.......601 K15
pl. E Geelong.......703 E11
pl. Geelong.......703 E11
pl. Meadow Ht.......193 L18
rd. Belgrave Ht.......506 C3
rd. Dromana.......686 E7
rd. Mt Eliza.......642 L4
st. Blackburn.......375 J18
st. Glen Waverley....460 D10
st. Pascoe Vale.......280 E17
st. Port Melb.......29 A6
st. Port Melb.......412 L4
st. Port Melb.......413 A3
st. Sandringham.....495 E16
st. Templstw Lr.......330 F9
st. Thomastown......241 C13
HEATHCOTE
ct. Endeavour Hl.....537 L6
dr. Forest Hill.......420 E3
gr. Lilydale.......339 J3
st. Pascoe Vale.......280 L13
HEATHDALE
rd. Nar Warrn N.......538 G12
HEATHER
av. Ashwood.......418 F18
av. Brooklyn.......365 J17
av. Emerald.......510 E4
av. Hurstbridge.......203 D20
av. Keilor East.......322 E3
av. Pascoe Vale.......281 A13
av. Sorrento.......678 L13
av. Thomastown.......240 K15
ct. Anglesea.......713 J3
ct. Glenroy.......279 L2
ct. Hampton Pk.......551 L13
ct. Hawthorn E.......416 C4
ct. Hoppers Csg.......405 B19
ct. Ringwood N.......378 B2
gr. Belgrave S.......506 G5
gr. Black Rock.......529 G2
gr. Briar Hill.......286 J4
gr. Cheltenham.......496 G19
gr. Cranbourne E.......579 F20
gr. Kew.......372 J9
gr. Nunawading.......376 G17
gr. Ringwood.......378 B17
gr. Springvale.......499 H16
gr. Templstw Lr.......330 D8
rd. Caulfield S.......455 E9
st. Balwyn N.......373 F8
st. Bentleigh E.......456 K20
st. S Melbourne.......30 D4
st. S Melbourne.......413 H3
HEATHERBRAE
av. Caulfield.......456 A6
av. Ringwood.......377 L12
cr. Sunbury.......143 B4
HEATHERDALE
rd. Mitcham.......377 K14
rd. Ringwood.......377 K14
rd. Vermont.......377 K20
rd. Vermont.......421 K1
HEATHERDEW
cl. Endeavour Hl.....537 G2
HEATHER GLADE
pl. Melton W.......226 C19
HEATHERHILL
rd. Frankston.......627 G5
HEATHERLEA
cr. Keilor East.......321 J5
cr. Narre Warren.......539 A19
ct. Blackburn N.......376 A11
dr. Wheelers Hl.......461 A10
HEATHERLEE
cl. Somerville.......644 J18
HEATHERLEIGH
ct. Carrum Downs...601 B4
pl. Malvern East.......456 L1
HEATHERMONT
av. Belgrave.......466 H14
HEATHERTON
rd. Clayton S.......498 H16
rd. Dandenong.......501 E20
rd. Dandenong N.....501 E20
rd. Endeavour Hl.....537 A2
rd. Nar Warrn N.......538 D4
rd. Noble Park.......500 G19
rd. Springvale.......499 B17
rd. Springvale S......499 B17
HEATHERWOOD
ct. Cranbourne W...603 J1
gr. Langwarrin.......629 G4
HEATHFIELD
ct. Croydon.......335 J19
ct. Newtown.......701 L9
gr. Montrose.......382 E10
rd. Brighton East.....495 B4
ri. Box Hill N.......375 D7
HEATHLAND
tr. Frankston N.......600 G12
wy. Dingley Vill.......533 B10
HEATHLAND BOARDWALK
Frankston N.......600 F11
HEATHMERE
cr. Endeavour Hl.....537 G1
HEATHMONT
cl. Frankston.......627 L7
rd. Heathmont.......378 L19
rd. Heathmont.......379 A20
rd. Ringwood.......378 H14
HEATHS
ct. Mill Park.......243 E3
la. Geelong, off
Swanston St.......703 E7
rd. Hoppers Csg.......447 K3
rd. Hoppers Csg.......449 A5
rd. Werribee.......446 J9
rd. Werribee.......447 A9
rd. Wyndham Va.....446 J9
HEATHWOOD
cl. Craigieburn.......150 E13
st. Ringwood E.......379 D17
HEATHWREN
cl. Frankston S.......628 B16
HEATON
av. Elwood.......454 H4
av. Glen Iris.......416 E15
cl. Sunshine W.......364 A5
ct. Burwood E.......419 H10
ct. Caroline Spr.......317 J5
HEBB
st. Braybrook.......321 L20
HEBDEN
st. Greensbrgh.......244 F19
HEBE
ct. Frankston N.......600 F9
pl. Sunshine W.......364 A8
HECTOR
ct. Glen Waverley....420 L18
ct. Moorabbin.......496 K9
st. Brighton.......455 A17
st. Geelong West....702 D1
HEDDERWICK
rd. Dandenong S.....550 J1
st. Balwyn N.......374 A7
st. Essendon.......323 E7
HEDDON
ct. Eltham.......288 C4
HEDENPARK
dr. Hillside.......232 G17
HEDGE END
rd. Mitcham.......376 L9
rd. Nunawading.......376 L9
HEDGELEY
av. Malvern East......416 J17
cl. Wantirna S.......462 A1
dr. Berwick.......554 C20
rd. Kealba.......276 J18
rd. Keysborough.....534 J11
HEDGELY
ct. Langwarrin.......629 G4
HEDGEROW
ct. Albanvale.......319 B5
ct. Keilor East.......321 J5
ct. Nar Warrn S.......553 C16
HEDGES
ct. Mt Martha.......656 C12
HEDLAND
pl. Kings Park.......275 B18
HEDLEY
ct. Narre Warren.....538 K14
pl. Hampton Pk.......551 L9
st. Anglesea.......713 L4
st. Fawkner.......239 E20
st. Hoppers Csg.......449 C3
HEDLINE
pl. Macleod.......285 H11
HEDWIG
dr. Mooroolbark.......336 L11
HEFFERNAN
la. Melbourne.......2 H10
la. Melbourne.......24 E5
st. Laverton.......407 B17
HEGGIES
la. Marcus Hill.......707 A13
HEIDELBERG
ct. Badger Creek.....258 F7
rd. Alphington.......327 H19
rd. Clifton Hill.......20 D2
rd. Clifton Hill.......327 C20
rd. Fairfield.......327 C20
rd. Ivanhoe.......327 H19
rd. Northcote.......326 K20
HEIDELBERG-KINGLAKE
rd. Cottles Br.......203 E12
rd. Hurstbridge.......202 L19
rd. Hurstbridge.......203 E12
rd. Hurstbridge.......246 J5
rd. St Andrews.......205 D1
rd. Wattle Glen.......246 J5
HEIDELBERG-WARRANDYTE
rd. Doncaster E.......331 L5
rd. Templestowe.......331 K5
rd. Warrandyte.......289 J20
rd. Warrandyte.......332 H3
rd. Warrandyte.......333 A3
HEIDI
ct. Pakenham.......585 F4
HEIN
rd. Pakenham.......557 L4
rd. Pakenham Up.....558 C1
HELD
st. Vermont.......377 H20
HELDER
ct. Melton W.......226 A19
HELEN
av. Croydon S.......380 C12
cl. Yarra Glen.......208 L20
cl. Yarra Glen.......209 A20
ct. Cheltenham.......497 J20
ct. Diamond Ck.......245 K8
ct. Lalor.......240 J7
ct. Melton W.......225 K20
ct. Narre Warren.....539 B16
ct. Noble Park.......534 F1
rd. Chadstone.......458 C5
rd. Ferntree Gly.......423 F17
rd. Ferny Creek.......425 L14
rd. Mt Dandenong...382 H18
st. E Geelong.......703 E15
st. Frankston.......626 K3
st. Heidelberg W.....284 F18
st. Mt Dandenong...382 H20
st. Mt Martha.......656 L8
st. Northcote.......326 H16
st. St Albans.......276 B17
vw. Glenroy.......280 G10
HELENA
av. Kallista.......467 D3
ct. Frankston.......600 C18
ct. Rowville.......503 B3
ct. Rye.......696 E2
rd. Lilydale.......338 H6
st. Belmont.......701 K20
st. Clayton S.......498 L6
st. Highton.......701 K20
st. Mt Martha.......656 A10
HELENE
ct. Boronia.......424 D18
st. Ardeer.......320 D19
st. Bulleen.......329 G11
st. Eltham.......287 J5
HELENS
wy. Langwarrin.......602 A19
HELENSLEA
rd. Caulfield N.......455 C2
HELEUS
ct. Mt Waverley......419
HELIA
ct. Burwood E.......419
HELIOPOLIS
st. Pascoe Vale S....324
HELLENIC
ct. Carrum Downs...601
HELLER
st. Brunswick.......325
st. Brunswick W.......325
HELLIER
dr. Mill Park.......242
HELLION
ct. Keilor Dn.......275
HELLYER
st. Noble Park.......534
wy. Endeavour Hl.....537
HELM
ct. Carrum Downs...601
ct. Epping.......197
st. Aspendale.......546
HELMER
cr. Thomson.......703
HELMICH
ct. Aspendale Gdn...546
HELMS
st. Newcomb.......704
HELMSDALE
cr. Greenvale.......193
ct. Cranbourne W.....577
rt. Templestowe.....332
HELMSLEY
av. Lysterfield.......464
HELPMAN
cr. Epping.......197
HELPMANN
st. Wantirna S.......462
HELSAL
ct. Frankston.......628
dr. Wantirna S.......422
HELSTON
ct. Croydon Hl.......335
st. Balwyn N.......329
st. Balwyn N.......373
HELVETIA
ct. Frankston.......627
HELWIG
av. Montmorency....286
HEMAR
cr. Hillside.......232
cr. Hillside.......232
HEMBURROW
st. Preston.......282
HEMEL
cl. Deer Park.......318
ct. Vermont S.......421
HEMINGFORD
rd. Bentleigh E.......456
HEMINGWAY
av. Templestowe.....332
HEMMING
st. Brighton East.....495
HEMMINGS
st. Dandenong.......535
HEMMINGWAY
la. Wyndham Va.....446
HEMPHILL
rd. Sunshine.......365
HEMPSTEAD
av. Vermont S.......421
HEMSTON
av. Portsea.......678
av. Sorrento.......678
av. Sorrento.......678
HEMSWELL
ct. Highton.......705
HEMSWORTH
ct. Roxburgh Pk.......194
HENBURY
wy. Taylors L.......276
HEND
st. Mt Waverley.......458
HENDER
ct. Balwyn.......373
st. Doncaster.......374
st. Mt Martha.......669
st. Ringwood E.......379
HENDERS
st. Forest Hill.......420
HENDERSON
av. Malvern.......415
ct. Bundoora.......243
ct. Glen Waverley....420
dr. Wandana Ht.......701
dr. Wandana Ht.......701
rd. Avonsleigh.......471
rd. Baxter.......644
rd. Clayton.......459
rd. Cockatoo.......471
rd. Keysborough.....534
rd. Knoxfield.......463

IDMARSH
Cranbourne N 577 J7
Wyndham Va.....446 B6
Wyndham Va.....446 B5
Rowville.....463 B17
. Taylors Hill.....274 J14
IDON
Blackburn 375 H15
.E
Darley.....221 K7
IKINS
Moonee Pnd 324 D14
IKLER
Bentleigh E 496 G6
Macleod 285 C11
Mill Park.....242 H5
Glen Waverley.....460 D1
Mordialloc 532 C11
e, Glen Waverley....460 H2
Braybrook.....365 K3
Mt Martha.....656 A9
IKLEY
Croydon 379 F2
IRICHSEN
Hallam.....538 B19
Hallam.....538 D20
ITON
Gladstone Pk 236 L17
Prahran 32 A17
Glen Huntly.....456 D6
Rosebud.....699 L2
ST
Sunbury 143 A4
Blackburn 375 E19
SCOCK
Boneo.....698 J6
Boneo.....699 A6
Rosebud W.....698 J6
Rosebud W.....699 A6
Chadstone 458 B4
KENS
Sorrento 678 K10
SLOP
Doncaster E 375 G2
Keilor.....277 B13
PANO
Keilor Dn 276 A17
TECH
Rowville.....462 L15
Rowville.....463 A14
Seaford.....599 H7
OR MISS
Healesville 212 J18
AD
Mulgrave 500 J4
Wantirna.....422 E4
Sunshine N.....321 C14
ADLEY
Frankston S 626 K6
Burwood E.....420 E13
Footscray.....367 E5
BAN
Montmorency 286 G10
Keilor Dn 276 G17
BART
Wantirna S.....422 K16
Murrumbeena....457 B6
Bentleigh 496 E3
Ringwood.....378 F8
BBS
Reservoir.....282 K6
Endeavour Hl 537 E6
Geelong.....703 D11
Wyndham Va.....445 L1
Altona North 409 K7
Seddon.....367 C11
BLER
Darley.....221 L7
BSON
Mill Park.....242 B3
Sunbury 142 L16
Sunbury 143 A16
Greensbrgh.....285 J4
Newport 411 A6
Queenscliff.....709 A17
Sandringham 495 D13
South Yarra 32 J16
South Yarra 414 K8
Thornbury.....326 F8
BSONS
Dingley Vill.....532 L9
Kensington 33 B12
BSONS BAY
e. Port Melb.....412 G5
CKEY
St Kilda.....414 A12
CKING
Mt Waverley 458 J2
Coburg N.....281 C15
Footscray.....367 A8
CKNELL
Canterbury.....417 G1

HOCTOR
cl. Gladstone Pk 237 C18
HODDE
ct. Sydenham 274 L4
HODDER
st. Brighton East.....455 G16
HODDLE
ct. Cranbourne.....577 L15
ct. Melton W.....225 H20
ct. Mill Park 242 K4
hwy. Cremorne 25 K18
hwy. E Melbourne 25 L8
hwy. Melbourne 25 K18
hwy. Richmond.....25 L8
hwy. South Yarra 31 H14
hwy. South Yarra 31 K4
hwy. South Yarra 414 E4
hwy. Windsor 414 D12
pl. Diamond Ck.....245 K13
st. Abbotsford 20 A20
st. Clifton Hill.....20 C8
st. Collingwood 20 A20
st. E Melbourne 25 L9
st. Elsternwick 455 D7
st. Essendon.....324 C9
st. Richmond.....25 L9
st. Yarra Jctn.....346 L16
st. Yarra Jctn.....347 A16
st. Yarra Jctn.....347 A17
wy. Altona Mdw 451 J8
HODGE
ct. Millgrove 348 F1
la. Armadale.....415 F12
st. Werribee.....447 F19
HODGES
cl. Rowville.....463 D20
rd. Chum Creek.....213 A7
st. Seaford.....599 L6
HODGINS
cr. Frankston N 600 D9
ct. Brunswick W 324 D6
HODGKINSON
ct. Springvale 500 E10
st. Clifton Hill.....19 H7
st. Dromana 685 L6
HODGSON
gr. Bentleigh E 497 D4
la. Kensington 33 D13
st. Brunswick.....325 C17
st. Darley.....221 L10
st. Fitzroy 19 F16
st. Geelong West 702 H1
st. Heidelberg 329 B5
st. Kew.....371 D11
st. Mitcham.....377 F17
st. Rosanna.....329 B5
st. Templstw Lr 330 B12
tce. Richmond.....26 F11
HODSON
rd. Warrandyte.....333 H4
st. Preston.....282 C19
HOEBERGIN
la. Hurstbridge 203 G19
HOFERT
la. Burnley, off
Type St.....371 B18
HOFFMAN
cct. Brunswick.....325 B14
la. Brunswick.....325 C14
st. Brunswick W 324 J13
st. Cheltenham 530 K2
tce. Williamstown.....410 L17
HOFFMAN'S
rd. Essendon.....323 B7
rd. Essendon W 323 B7
rd. Niddrie 323 B7
HOGAN
av. Warrandyte.....334 F2
ct. Box Hill N 375 C6
ct. Darley.....221 L4
ct. Wantirna S.....422 D20
dr. Rye 696 H6
gr. Werribee.....447 G13
pl. Mill Park 242 H9
rd. Glen Waverley.....460 D2
st. Deer Park.....319 A17
st. Fawkner.....281 H1
st. Sunbury 143 G9
HOGANS
rd. Hoppers Csg.....405 A18
HOHNES
rd. Eltham.....287 D17
HOIKI
dr. Mornington.....657 B6
HOILES
rd. Wandin East 385 H3
HOLBEACH
st. Burwood E.....420 A12
HOLBEIN
ct. Grovedale 705 K14
ct. Scoresby 462 C9
HOLBERG
st. Moonee Pnd 324 F15

HOLBERRY
st. Broadmeadows..238 E20
st. Nunawading 376 G19
HOLBOURNE
dr. Junction Vill.....604 H12
HOLBROOK
cr. Brunswick W 324 J14
HOLBURN
wy. Epping.....198 A16
HOLCOURT
rd. Laverton N.....364 G17
HOLDEN
av. Avondale Ht.....322 A10
ct. Fitzroy N, off
Holden St 326 E19
rd. Diggers Rest.....187 A13
rd. Diggers Rest.....231 A7
rd. Kallista.....427 G20
rd. Olinda.....427 G20
rd. Olinda.....467 G1
rd. Plumpton.....231 A7
rd. Rye 696 D5
rd. Seville.....386 A13
rd. Silvan 386 A13
rd. Wandin East 386 A13
st. Fitzroy N 326 B18
HOLDER
pl. Berwick 554 G18
HOLDING
st. Beaumaris 530 A12
HOLDSWORTH
st. Ascot Vale 323 J16
HOLEHOUSE
st. Sunshine N.....321 C16
HOLGATE
la. Kensington 33 G11
la. Kensington 368 D6
HOLLAND
av. Burwood.....418 G8
av. Dingley Vill.....533 A9
ct. Flemington 34 C4
ct. Highton 705 J2
ct. Maidstone.....366 F2
ct. Newport 411 D9
ct. Oakleigh 458 A11
dr. Melton.....269 D1
gr. Caulfield N 415 J20
rd. Blackburn S 419 J5
rd. Burwood E.....419 J8
rd. Ringwood E.....379 A8
st. Healesville 213 L17
HOLLICK
st. Richmond.....26 L4
HOLLINGSWORTH
av. Hawthorn.....415 K1
HOLLINGTON
cr. Point Cook.....450 C5
cr. Point Cook.....450 D5
st. Berwick 580 L1
HOLLOWAY
cl. Sandringham.....495 J17
cl. Sunbury 143 F4
ct. Noble Park.....500 J17
dr. Bayswater 424 B8
rd. Brunswick.....325 C12
rd. Croydon N 335 J9
rd. Sandringham 495 H17
rd. Wonga Park.....335 J9
st. Newport 410 G10
st. Ormond.....456 E12
HOLLOWS
cr. Grovedale 706 G12
HOLLSMOOR
rd. Camberwell.....417 K5
HOLLY
av. Dandenong N.....501 H19
cl. Mill Park 242 E11
ct. Bayswater 423 C7
ct. Campbellfield 239 E13
ct. Mitcham.....377 E14
dr. Dingley Vill.....532 J6
dr. Point Cook.....450 H16
pl. Narre Warren 539 B15
st. Camberwell.....372 J18
st. Preston.....283 H18
HOLLYDALE
cl. Berwick 554 C15
ct. Melton W.....225 H17
HOLLYDENE
ct. Narre Warren.....538 G19
dr. Bangholme 549 J14
HOLLY GREEN
cl. Donvale 376 K6
cl. Rowville.....503 D3
ct. Keilor East 321 K4
dr. Wheelers Hl 460 H12
HOLLYHOCK
ct. Cranbourne N 578 D8
wk. S Morang 199 H9
HOLLYOAK
ct. Ferntree Gly 424 J18
ri. Eltham North 245 H19

HOLLYOAK HAVEN
Chirnside Pk 337 H1
HOLLYVIEW
ct. Rowville.....463 K16
HOLLYWOOD
bvd. Pt Lonsdale.....710 E2
cl. Templestowe 332 C7
HOLM
cl. Broadmeadows..238 A12
HOLMAN
rd. Emerald.....469 F8
HOLMBURY
bvd. Mulgrave 501 G1
HOLMBY
rd. Cheltenham 530 K1
HOLME
rd. Ferntree Gly 463 H5
HOLMES
ct. Bayswater N 379 H17
rd. Moonee Pnd 323 J13
rd. Mooroolbark.....381 D2
rd. Red Hill.....687 C17
rd. Yarra Jctn 346 H16
st. Ardeer 364 B1
st. Brunswick.....325 K10
st. Brunswick E.....325 K10
st. Frankston 627 G4
st. Noble Park.....535 B2
st. Northcote 326 L20
wy. Caroline Spr.....318 B4
wy. Glen Waverley....459 L3
HOLMESDALE
cl. Werribee.....446 L17
cl. Werribee.....447 A17
HOLMHURST
ct. Brighton East.....495 E5
HOLM PARK
rd. Beaconsfield 555 C10
HOLMWOOD
av. Anglesea.....713 G5
av. Brighton 454 G14
brk. Dingley Vill, off
Albert Pl 532 K6
ct. Brighton 454 G14
pl. Carlton 18 D11
rd. Tottenham 366 B14
HOLOHAN
pl. Dandenong N.....502 C19
HOLOWKO
ct. Taylors L 276 E8
HOLROYD
av. St Kilda E.....415 B16
ct. Blackburn S 419 H6
ct. St Kilda E.....415 A16
dr. Epping.....241 J4
st. Coburg 281 D19
st. Kew.....371 G8
st. Seaford.....599 K5
HOLSKAMP
st. Mt Waverley 419 A19
HOLSTEIN
ct. Rowville.....502 C4
HOLSTEN
la.n, Kensington 33 C10
la.s, Kensington 33 C11
HOLSTOCK
ct. Jan Juc.....711 E14
HOLT
ct. Mordialloc 532 A16
ct. Springvale S 499 D18
pde. Bundoora.....283 K1
pde. Thomastown.....283 G1
pde. Thomastown.....283 G1
pl. Pakenham 584 L9
rd. E Geelong 703 J10
st. Ardeer 320 B18
st. Sunbury 143 D6
HOLTOM
st.e, Princes Hill 325 J19
st.w, Princes Hill 325 G19
HOLTON
ct. Hillside 232 F19
HOLTS
la. Darley.....221 D11
HOLYHEAD
dr. Torquay 712 E4
HOLYROOD
av. Newtown 702 A13
av. Sorrento 679 B12
av. Strathmore 279 H20
cr. Ringwood 378 L2
cr. Ringwood 379 A2
ct. Watsonia N 243 D19
dr. Vermont 421 H4
st. Camberwell.....417 F3
st. Hampton 494 J6
st. Highett 496 B12
HOLYWOOD
gr. Carnegie 456 F5
HOLZER
st. Sandringham.....495 E12
HOLZGREFE
ct. Altona Mdw 451 E3

HOMAN
ct. Ringwood N.....334 G12
HOME
rd. Newport 411 B7
st. Bayswater N 379 J14
st. Reservoir.....283 D15
st. Sorrento 679 A11
HOMEBUSH
cr. Hawthorn E.....372 H17
ct. Ringwood E 379 B16
la. N Melbourne.....17 A12
rd. Cairnlea 319 G7
HOMELEIGH
rd. Keysborough 534 D19
HOMER
av. Croydon S 380 B13
ct. Ferntree Gly 463 F9
st. Moonee Pnd 324 C12
HOMESTEAD
av. Tarneit.....405 A9
ct. Croydon S 380 D14
cl. Melton W.....226 A17
ct. Highton 705 E3
ct. Pakenham 584 F8
dr. Bangholme 548 D14
dr. Keilor Dn 276 H16
dr. Wheelers Hl 461 C11
pl. Mill Park 242 L7
rd. Berwick 553 G17
rd. Chirnside Pk 292 A18
rd. Eltham.....287 C18
rd. Langwarrin 602 C17
rd. Templestowe 287 L19
rd. Wonga Park.....335 J2
tr. Greenvale 191 E16
trl. Bundoora.....284 C6
wy. Narre Warren 552 K4
HOMESTEAD RUN
Roxburgh Pk.....193 K14
Seabrook 450 K7
HOMEWOOD
bvd. Hallam.....538 B17
cl. Ferntree Gly 463 H9
ct. Meadow Ht.....237 L4
ct. Rosanna.....285 E20
la. Highton 705 K6
rd. Cranbourne S.....630 G5
ri. Warrandyte.....288 K20
st. Nunawading 376 F17
HONDA
dr. Mill Park 242 K2
HONE
av. Blackburn S 375 F20
av. Blackburn S 419 F1
ct. Mill Park 242 A2
HONEY
ct. Epping.....241 K4
gr. St Albans 276 H20
HONEY EATER
ct. Tarneit.....405 B10
HONEYEATER
cl. Diamond Ck.....245 D11
cr. Craigieburn.....149 F17
cr. Taylors L 275 F2
pl. Carrum Downs...600 L5
tce. Cairnlea 319 J9
tce. S Morang 243 J4
HONEY MYRTLE
ct. Langwarrin 601 K14
ri. Eltham North 245 E18
HONEYPOT
cl. Knoxfield 423 C19
HONEYSUCKLE
av. Hillside 274 E4
av. Wheelers Hl 460 F14
cl. Pakenham 584 A4
ct. Altona Mdw 407 K20
ct. Cranbourne N 578 E8
ct. Meadow Ht.....238 C1
ct. Mill Park 242 C9
pl. Hoppers Csg.....405 B15
st. Frankston N 600 F10
wk. Croydon S 380 C13
wy. Chirnside Pk 293 J20
HONNI
ct. Fawkner.....239 G20
mw. Doncaster E 331 K16
HONOUR
av. Wyndham Va.....446 F14
av. Hawthorn, off
Wood St.....371 E16
ct. Mt Martha.....657 B7
HONYBUN
ct. Donvale 377 D3
HOOD
cr. Caulfield N 455 C2
cr. Fawkner.....281 L6
cr. Sunbury 143 B9
ct. Berwick 553 K6
st. Airport W.....279 A15
st. Balwyn N 373 B6
st. Belgrave Ht.....466 B19
st. Collingwood 20 A18

st. Elwood 454 B1
st. Frankston 599 G13
st. Hampton 495 B8
st. Mont Albert 374 E14
st. Yarraville 367 B13

HOOK
ct. Craigieburn 150 A16
st. Altona Mdw 407 H20
st. St Albans 319 J4

HOOKER
av. Springvale 499 F17
rd. Ferntree Gly 423 E20
rd. Werribee 446 L13
rd. Werribee 447 A13

HOOKS
rd. Warburton 348 K4

HOOP
ct. Frankston N 600 B8
ct. Mill Park 242 B9

HOOPER
cr. Brunswick W 324 J15
dr. Skye 575 H14
gr. Mt Martha 669 E2
rd. Wonga Park 291 A20
st. Macleod 285 B10
st. Murrumbeena 457 E6

HOOP PINE
ct. Cranbourne N 578 B9

HOPBUSH
av. Sunbury 143 J4

HOPE
av. Donvale 377 B8
av. Montrose 382 A11
ct. Delahey 275 E14
ct. Doncaster E 332 D6
ct. Ferntree Gly 464 B11
ct. Frankston 599 E14
ct. Kew 371 H4
ct. Mill Park 242 G6
ct. Noble Park N 501 E13
pl. Seabrook 450 K4
st. Brighton East 455 C15
st. Brunswick 325 A11
st. Brunswick W 325 A11
st. Camberwell 416 L3
st. Camberwell 417 A3
st. Fitzroy N 326 B18
st. Geelong 703 D12
st. Geelong West 702 D4
st. Glen Iris 416 F15
st. Greensbrgh 244 H19
st. Preston 282 C20
st. Rosebud 683 H18
st. South Yarra 31 D7
st. South Yarra 414 B4
st. Spotswood 411 A2
st. Springvale 499 K7
st. W Footscray 366 G5

HOPES
ri. Frankston S 626 G5

HOPETOUN
av. Brunswick W 324 G7
av. Canterbury 373 D17
av. Mt Martha 656 A17
av. Reservoir 282 D15
cr. Coburg N 282 B13
ct. Altona Mdw 451 C5
ct. Bentleigh E 456 L17
ct. Westmeadows 236 J15
gr. Eaglemont 328 G13
gr. Ivanhoe East 328 G13
gr. South Yarra 32 G12
gr. South Yarra 414 J6
pde. Box Hill 374 H15
rd. Pk Orchards 333 L18
rd. Tooradin 651 G3
rd. Toorak 415 J9
st. Dandenong 535 H7
st. Elsternwick 455 C5
st. Kensington 33 J8
st. Mitcham 377 G16
st. Moonee Pnd 323 K13
st. Northcote 326 L14

HOPETOUN ACCESS
rd. Mt Martha 656 B19

HOPETOUN PARK
rd. Hopetoun Park 266 C4
rd. Hopetoun Park 266 C5

HOPETOWN
cr. Richmond 26 C5
pl. Fitzroy N 19 C2

HOPKINS
av. Heidelberg Ht 328 G4
av. Keilor 276 L11
av. Keilor 276 L12
av. Keilor 277 A12
cl. Rowville 462 H16
ct. Altona Mdw 451 J10
ct. Clayton S 498 G9
ct. Werribee 447 D7
ps. Pakenham 584 B4
rd. Rockbank 317 A9
rd. Truganina 317 A9
st. Dandenong 536 A3
st. Footscray 367 J8
st. Greensbrgh 286 C7
st. McKinnon 455 J16
st. S Geelong 702 K13
wy. Meadow Ht 194 B18

HOPMAN
cl. Wantirna S 462 F2

HOPPER
ct. Mill Park 243 C3

HOPPERS
la. Werribee 448 L8
la. Werribee 449 A8
la. Werribee S 449 A19
la. Werribee S 488 L3

HOPWOOD
ct. Nar Warrn S 552 H19

HORACE
st. Malvern 416 B15

HORATIO
cl. Rowville 503 E2
ct. Lilydale 338 J1
st. Noble Park 534 F4

HORDER
cr. Darley 221 K4

HORDERN
rd. Mt Evelyn 339 F19

HORFIELD
av. Box Hill N 374 H7

HORHAM
ct. St Albans 320 H5

HORIZON
bvd. Hampton Pk 551 J14
ct. Highton 701 F10
rd. Selby 507 B1
vw. Macleod 284 K11

HORKINGS
st. Blackburn S 419 J2

HORNBUCKLE
cr. Melton 227 C16
ct. Ferntree Gly 463 H7

HORNBY
st. Beaumaris 529 J7
st. Brighton East 455 F18
st. Windsor 414 H13

HORNE
ct. Chelsea Ht 547 D14
ct. Langwarrin 629 C2
ct. Pakenham 584 H3
st. Brunswick 325 J16
st. Campbellfield 239 F14
st. Clifton Hill 20 F7
st. Elsternwick 454 K5
st. Frankston 599 C17
st. Hoppers Csg 405 J20
st. Sunbury 143 E14
st. Thomastown 240 J19

HORNEMAN
rd. Gisborne S 141 A5

HORNER
cl. Knoxfield 462 K4
st. Beaconsfield 555 C15

HORNERS
la. Rye 697 A2
rd. Warburton 349 L4

HORNSBY
av. Westmeadows 236 G15
ct. Greenvale 193 C18
dr. Langwarrin 629 J3
la. Kensington 33 D10
st. Malvern 416 B9

HORNSEA
ct. Noble Park N 501 E13

HORONDA
st. Greensbrgh 285 L4

HORSBURGH
gr. Armadale 415 G10

HORSCROFT
pl. Moorabbin 496 D7

HORSEMAN
ct. Nar Warrn S 552 J20

HORSESHOE
cr. Epping 198 D17

HORSESHOE BEND
rd. Keilor 277 E15
rd. Marshall 706 L19
rd. Torquay 712 G2

HORSFALL
st. Templstw Lr 330 H12

HORSFIELD
st. Cranbourne N 577 L5

HORSHAM
dr. Cranbourne E 578 J19

HORSLEY
st. Bentleigh 456 C19

HORSMUNDEN
rd. Moorabbin 496 F9

HORSWOOD
rd. Lysterfield 505 A19
rd. Nar Warrn N 505 A19

HORTENSE
st. Glen Iris 417 F12
st. Maribyrnong 323 C14

HORTON
cl. Brighton 454 G8
dr. Hampton Pk 551 G13
dr. Hampton Pk 551 G13
st. Reservoir 282 C13

HOSES
la. Grovedale 706 H14

HOSIE
st. Altona Mdw 451 J10
st. Bayswater N 380 B17
st. Richmond 26 J12

HOSIER
la. Melbourne 2 H19
la. Melbourne 24 G9

HOSKEN
st. Altona Mdw 451 G2
st. Balwyn N 373 H6
st. Balwyn N 373 J8
st. Reservoir 282 C15
st. Springvale S 500 C20

HOSKIN
st. Bayswater 423 D2

HOSKING
ct. Pakenham 584 G5
ct. Williamstown 410 K14
st. Williamstown 411 D13

HOSKINS
st. Tremont 465 J3

HOSSACK
st. Coburg N 281 D17

HOTCHKISS
wy. Keilor Dn 276 A15

HOTHAM
cl. Deer Park 319 A9
cr. Hoppers Csg 449 A3
ct. Diamond Ck 245 L12
ct. Lalor 240 G8
ct. Melton S 268 C13
ct. Mont Albert 374 E12
ct. Sunbury 143 H6
gr. Ripponlea 454 H3
pl. Cremorne 26 E20
pl. E Melbourne 25 G6
pl. N Melbourne 17 F15
pl. Geelong, off La Trobe Tce 702 K9
rd. Niddrie 278 H19
rd. Niddrie 279 A20
rd. Portsea 677 J5
rd. Sorrento 677 J5
rd. Sorrento 678 J7
rt. Burwood E 419 F11
st. Balaclava 414 J19
st. Balaclava 454 J3
st. Beaumaris 530 B7
st. Braybrook 365 J5
st. Collingwood 19 G11
st. Cranbourne 578 G20
st. E Melbourne 25 G7
st. Elsternwick 454 J3
st. Frankston S 626 H10
st. Hughesdale 457 F13
st. Mont Albert 374 E13
st. Moonee Pnd 323 K15
st. Preston 326 L6
st. Ripponlea 454 J3
st. St Kilda E 414 K19
st. Seddon 367 C12
st. S Melbourne 29 L4
st. Templstw Lr 330 E14
st. Williamstown 411 E12

HOTHLYN
dr. Craigieburn 194 D3

HOUDINI
dr. Diggers Rest 187 A9

HOUGHTON
rd. Warrandyte 333 E2
st. Balwyn N 373 D4

HOUGHTONS
la. Tarrawarra 211 D19

HOULDEN
ct. Narre Warren 539 F19

HOULDER
av. Junction Vill 604 H12

HOULIHAN
ct. Pakenham 584 G7

HOUNDSFORTH
st. Cranbourne E 578 J20

HOUNDSWOOD
cl. Doncaster E 332 C13

HOUNSLOW
grn. Caroline Spr 317 H4

HOURIGAN
av. Clayton 458 L18

HOUSDEN
st. Broadmeadows 238 E20

HOUSMAN
cl. Burnside 318 G9

HOUSTON
av. Strathmore 279 L20
av. Strathmore 323 L1
ct. Box Hill S 419 B6
ct. Brooklyn 365 H19
ct. Reservoir 283 J17
st. Epping 197 E19
st. Mentone 531 L8

HOVE
pl. Craigieburn 150 C20
rd. Mt Martha 669 J2
rd. Rosebud 684 G20
rd. Rosebud 684 L20

HOVEA
ct. Boronia 424 K7
ct. Mill Park 243 C7
ct. Mt Waverley 419 D17
ct. Springvale S 534 B5
pl. Meadow Ht 237 J1
st. Mitcham 377 E10
st. Templestowe 331 B8

HOVELL
ct. Cranbourne 578 B18
ct. Grovedale 706 A12
st. Deer Park 319 C9

HOWARD
av. Mt Waverley 458 H3
av. Ormond 455 J13
av. Ringwood E 379 A15
ct. Bayswater N 380 G20
ct. Clayton 459 C19
ct. Dandenong N 502 A16
ct. Doncaster 330 G16
ct. Glenroy 280 C1
la. N Melbourne 17 G19
pl. Berwick 553 L14
rd. Dingley Vill 532 L9
rd. Olinda 427 B12
st. Altona Mdw 451 G5
st. Box Hill 374 J16
st. Brunswick 325 J11
st. Epping 197 G20
st. Glen Iris 416 K11
st. Greensbrgh 286 B5
st. Kew 371 G11
st. Maidstone 366 H3
st. Malvern East 456 G2
st. Mitcham 376 L16
st. Mitcham 377 A16
st. N Melbourne 17 F20
st. Reservoir 283 A11
st. Richmond 32 F3
st. Richmond 414 J2
st. Seville 341 H12
st. South Yarra 32 B13
st. South Yarra 414 G7
st. W Melbourne 17 F20

HOWARD ROAD
trl. Braeside 532 L12
trl. Braeside 533 A12

HOWARDS
rd. Panton Hill 204 L11
rd. Panton Hill 205 A11

HOWARTH
st. Brunswick 325 G13

HOWDEN
cr. Braybrook 321 L20
ct. Mill Park 243 B3
st. Oakleigh E 458 C10

HOWE
av. Dandenong N 501 K11
cr. S Melbourne 29 L7
cr. S Melbourne 30 A9
cr. S Melbourne 413 F4
cr. S Melbourne 413 F5
ct. Geelong West 702 G1
ct. Melton S 268 C10
ct. Thomastown 240 G16
pde. Port Melb 411 H3
pde. Port Melb 412 C4
st. Fitzroy N 19 L3
st. Murrumbeena 457 D9

HOWELL
av. Beaumaris 530 G6
av. Surrey Hills 374 D20
ct. Doncaster E 332 H13
ct. Research 288 H4
dr. Berwick 554 J6
dr. Mt Waverley 459 A6
pl. Braybrook 365 J6
rd. Plenty 244 H8
st. Bentleigh 496 A5
st. Brighton East 455 E16
st. Lalor 241 A10
st. Rye 696 J10

HOWES
st. Airport W 279 A10

HOWEY
pl. Melbourne 2 D14
pl. Melbourne 2 D14
pl. Melbourne 24 D8
rd. Mt Martha 655 H15
st. Pakenham 584 F2

HOWGATE
ct. Eltham 287 L11

HOWIE
st. Glen Iris 417 C11

HOWITT
av. Hampton E 495
cr. Sunshine W 364
cr. Sunshine W 365
ct. Berwick 553
ct. Werribee 448
dr. Templstw Lr 330
la. Melbourne 24
la. Roxburgh Pk 194
pl. Burwood E 419
rd. Caulfield N 455
st. Dromana 685
st. Glen Iris 416
st. McCrae 685
st. Northcote 327
st. South Yarra 32
st. South Yarra 414

HOWLETT
st. Kensington 33

HOWLEYS
rd. Notting Hill 459

HOWQUA
ct. Epping 198
ct. Glen Waverley 420
ct. Vermont 421
ct. Warranwood 334
dr. Rosebud W 698
dr. Rosebud W 699
pl. Cranbourne 578
pl. Pakenham 583
wy. Taylors Hill 274

HOWSHIP
ct. Ringwood E 378

HOWSON
cl. Endeavour Hl 537
ct. Mont Albert 374
pl. Roxburgh Pk 194
st. Brunswick W 325

HOY
ct. Delahey 275

HOYA
cr. Frankston N 600
ct. Cranbourne N 577
pl. Sunbury 143

HOYLAKE
av. Jan Juc 711
ct. Sunbury 144
gr. Mornington 656

HOYLE
ct. Clayton S 498
ct. Cranbourne 578

HOYSTED
av. Cranbourne N 578
cl. Mordialloc 532

HOYT
st. Hampton 494

HUB
arc. Melbourne 2

HUBBARD
av. Mulgrave 500
rd. Yarra Glen 209

HUBBLE
ct. Altona Mdw 451

HUBERT
av. Glenroy 280
st. Mt Martha 668
st. Mt Martha 669
st. Preston 282
st. Upwey 466

HUCKERBY
st. Cremorne 25

HUCKSON
ri. Dandenong N 502

HUDDERSFIELD
rd. Deer Park 319

HUDSON
av. Frankston 599
cct. Meadow Ht 238
ct. Ashburton 417
ct. Avondale Ht 322
gr. Brunswick W 324
pl. Carlton 18
pl. Melton 226
pl. Rowville 463
st. Beaconsfield 554
st. Caulfield N 455
st. Coburg 325
st. Cranbourne 604
st. Fawkner 281
st. Hampton 495
st. McKinnon 456
st. Moonee Pnd 323

HUDSONS
rd. Spotswood 410

HUEGILL
dr. Burnside 318
dr. Caroline Spr 318

HUFF
st. Glen Waverley 459

HUGGINS
ct. Altona Mdw 451
rd. Donvale 377

I

st. Clayton S..........499 F9
st. Coburg N..........281 G16
st. Fitzroy N..........326 D17
st. Niddrie..........322 L4
st. Niddrie..........323 A4
IDEAL
av. Aspendale..........546 C5
ct. Rowville..........502 B5
IDINIA
ct. Doncaster..........330 J20
st. Kilsyth..........381 A4
IDON
av. Frankston S..........627 A8
IDONIA
ct. Carrum Downs...601 B3
IDRIESS
ct. Mill Park..........242 G5
IDWALL
ct. Highton..........705 K8
IENA
st. Dandenong S.....535 K15
IERINA
ct. Wantirna S..........422 A15
IEVERS
pl. Carlton..........18 D19
st. Parkville..........325 E19
st. Upwey..........465 K13
tce. Carlton..........18 D18
IFFLA
st. S Melbourne..........29 D11
st. S Melbourne..........29 E6
st. S Melbourne..........413 B5
IFFLEY
ct. Ivanhoe..........328 B8
IGLOO
ct. Mornington..........641 K18
pl. Keilor Dn..........275 G10
IKARA
cl. Kings Park..........319 E1
ct. Cheltenham..........496 K16
ct. Frankston..........600 E17
st. Mornington..........656 J3
IKO
wy. Werribee..........446 H18
ILA
st. Glenroy..........280 G7
ILANA
ct. Nar Warrn S..........553 D19
ILANA VIEW
dr. Diamond Ck..........246 E9
ILANI
st. Epping..........197 L14
ILARI
ct. Mt Martha..........655 K20
ILFORD
ct. Craigieburn..........194 E5
rd. Heathmont..........422 H1
ILIAS
ct. Bundoora..........242 G19
ILINGA
ct. Eltham..........246 E20
ILIOS
cl. Forest Hill..........420 D6
ILLALONG
ct. Tootgarook..........698 F6
ILLAROO
st. Rosebud..........683 F20
st. Rosebud W..........699 F1
ILLAWARA
cr. Bayswater N..........379 L14
ILLAWARRA
av. Rowville..........502 C7
cl. Chadstone..........458 E3
cl. Frankston..........628 D4
cr. Dandenong N.....501 G15
cr. Toorak..........415 F4
rd. Balwyn N..........373 F6
rd. Flemington..........33 G2
rd. Hawthorn..........372 B20
rd. Hawthorn..........416 B3
st. Glenroy..........280 A8
st. Williamstown.....411 F19
ILLAWONG
ct. Patterson L..........573 L5
dr. Donvale..........332 K19
dr. Torquay..........711 H4
gr. Werribee..........446 K15
mw. Langwarrin..........601 J15
tce. Burnside..........318 H7
ILLIRA
av. Frankston..........600 H15
ILLONA
ct. Bulleen..........329 H14
ILLOUERA
av. Grovedale..........705 L14
ILLOURA
av. Ringwood E..........378 L12
cl. Noble Park N..........501 D10
ct. Olinda..........426 J5
st. Watsonia..........285 G10
ILLOWA
cl. Frankston..........600 E17
st. Malvern East..........416 K18

st. Mornington..........640 L15
st. Mornington..........641 A15
ILLOWRA
ct. Berwick..........553 H3
wk. Blackburn S..........419 J5
ILLUKA
cr. Mt Waverley..........459 G5
ILLUMINATE
ct. Kilsyth S..........425 A1
ILMA
ct. Bulleen..........329 E12
ct. Parkdale..........531 H14
ct. Seaford..........599 F2
gr. Bonbeach..........573 B6
gr. Northcote..........326 K15
ILORA
ct. Glen Waverley....460 A10
ILTON
av. Frankston..........599 H18
ILUKA
av. Aspendale..........546 F5
ct. Altona..........408 J17
ct. Bundoora..........242 C19
ct. Ferntree Gly..........424 E20
ct. Jan Juc..........711 B18
ct. Sunshine W..........364 F6
dr. Werribee..........446 J14
pl. Mornington..........640 E17
pl. Ringwood N..........378 C4
rd. Rye..........697 K5
st. Black Rock..........529 J5
st. Safety Bch..........669 C13
st. Warneet..........649 E12
ILUKA ISLAND
Patterson L..........573 J3
ILYUKA
ct. Portsea..........678 G3
wy. S Morang..........198 L8
IMAROO
st. Fawkner..........281 L11
IMBROS
st. Hampton..........495 C5
IMES
st. Parkdale..........531 H11
IMLACH
ct. Dingley Vill..........533 F7
IMMARNA
rd. Camberwell..........417 D5
IMMERSET
dr. Chelsea Ht..........547 G18
IMPARA
ct. Scoresby..........462 D9
IMPERIA
ct. Nar Warrn S..........553 F18
IMPERIAL
av. Bayswater..........423 D7
av. Caulfield S..........455 E6
av. Mt Waverley..........418 F20
av. Sunshine N..........321 E8
av. Wandin East..........340 L20
av. Wandin East..........341 A20
ct. Hillside..........231 H20
pl. Hoppers Csg..........405 B13
tce. S Morang..........198 J10
IMPRESSA
cl. Langwarrin..........601 J19
IMRE
ct. Baxter..........643 L2
ct. Clarinda..........498 E11
INALA
ct. Burwood E..........419 F9
ct. Frankston..........600 G17
ct. Mulgrave..........500 H3
ct. Yallambie..........286 C11
st. Rye..........696 L9
st. Rye..........697 A8
INCANA
cl. Hoppers Csg..........405 C15
ct. Cranbourne W...577 J18
ct. Meadow Ht..........193 K19
dr. Mill Park..........243 D8
la. Mornington..........656 F1
pl. Rowville..........502 D4
INCE
ct. Frankston..........600 C17
pl. Melton W..........226 D14
INCHCAPE
av. Wantirna..........422 E5
pl. Melton W..........226 B15
INCINERATOR
rd. Melb Airport..........235 B13
INDEPENDANCE
ri. Kilsyth S..........381 A20
INDEPENDENCE
st. Moorabbin..........496 K11
INDIGO
ct. Broadmeadows..238 A10
ct. Frankston N..........600 E10
st. Wesburn..........348 C20
wy. Bundoora..........242 E13
INDIGOFERA
wy. Langwarrin..........629 L4

INDRA
rd. Blackburn S..........419 E5
INDURA
st. Mt Martha..........656 E6
INDUSTRIAL
av. Hoppers Csg..........405 K20
av. Notting Hill..........459 B13
av. Thomastown..........239 L19
dr. Braeside..........532 F17
dr. Melton..........269 E2
dr. Somerville..........645 B13
dr. Sunshine W..........364 G13
INDUSTRY
cct. Kilsyth S..........380 L15
ct. Lilydale..........338 E2
pl. Bayswater..........423 K4
INDUSTRY PARK
dr. Brooklyn..........365 J15
INDWE
st. W Footscray..........366 D10
INEZ
av. Eltham..........287 E6
av. Ringwood..........378 B16
ct. Doncaster..........330 C15
ct. Melton..........268 J1
INGA
ct. Berwick..........554 J19
ct. Chadstone..........458 D2
ct. Chelsea..........547 C14
ct. Frankston..........628 C1
pde. Mt Martha..........656 B10
pde. Mt Martha..........656 E10
st. Burwood E..........419 E10
st. Oakleigh E..........458 H11
INGAMELLS
st. Cranbourne..........578 D18
INGARA
pl. Delahey..........275 A9
INGERSOLL
rd. Baxter..........645 G7
INGLEBRAE
ct. Essendon..........323 L10
ct. Noble Park N..........501 D10
INGLENOOK
cr. Frankston..........600 H18
INGLES
st. Port Melb..........29 A3
st. Port Melb..........368 H18
st. Port Melb..........413 A2
INGLESBY
rd. Camberwell..........416 H2
INGLESIDE
cr. Glen Waverley....459 H4
INGLETON
ct. Baxter..........644 C2
ct. Narre Warren.....539 A15
INGLEWOOD
av. Forest Hill..........420 H5
av. Noble Park N..........501 E17
cl. Doncaster E..........331 H15
cr. Rosebud..........700 C3
ct. Gladstone Pk.....237 A17
ct. Mill Park..........243 E6
ct. Wheelers Hl..........460 L8
dr. Thomastown..........241 J18
INGLIS
av. Frankston..........599 C13
ct. Doncaster..........330 H18
ct. Glen Waverley....420 A17
rd. Beaconsfield..........554 H4
rd. Berwick..........554 H4
st. Box Hill N..........374 L8
st. Diamond Ck..........245 J10
st. Maddingley..........263 H1
st. Mornington..........640 L12
st. Mornington..........641 A12
st. Sunshine N..........321 G18
st. Williamstn N..........410 J13
INGLISBY
rd. Mont Albert..........374 C13
INGOLDSBY
ct. Delahey..........275 B12
INGOT
rd. Diggers Rest..........187 A9
INGRAM
av. Glen Waverley....460 D3
av. Sunshine W..........364 G7
cl. Narre Warren..........539 B15
rd. Anglesea..........713 G3
rd. Coldstream..........295 C16
rd. Gruyere..........296 F17
rd. Lilydale..........295 C16
st. Brunswick..........325 H17
INGRAMS
rd. Research..........288 H3
INGRID
ct. Herne Hill..........701 H2
st. Dandenong..........536 C3
st. Scoresby..........462 D7
INK
la. N Melbourne..........34 E11

INKERMAN
gr. St Kilda, off Inkerman St......414 D16
rd. Camberwell..........416 J3
rd. Caulfield N..........415 C17
st. Balaclava..........414 D16
st. Maidstone..........366 K2
st. St Kilda..........414 D16
st. St Kilda E..........414 D16
INLET
pde. Tooradin..........651 K7
st. Aspendale..........546 D4
INMAN
st. Thornbury..........327 H8
INN
ct. Gladstone Pk.....236 K16
INNELLAN
rd. Murrumbeena....457 B8
INNER
cr. Brighton..........454 J16
INNER HARBOUR
dr. Patterson L..........573 H6
INNERLEVEN
ct. Frankston..........599 J16
INNES
ct. Berwick..........554 J18
ct. Taylors L..........276 B9
ct. Tootgarook..........698 E8
INNICHEN
cl. Frankston S..........627 C15
INNIS
ct. Deer Park..........318 K12
INNISFAIL
dr. Point Cook..........449 L9
INNISFALLEN
av. Templestowe.....331 J6
INNKEEPER
pl. Hoppers Csg..........447 K1
pl. Sydenham..........274 L5
INNKEEPERS
wy. Attwood..........236 L10
INNS
pl. Hoppers Csg..........447 K1
INSAF
ct. Hampton Pk..........551 F12
INSIGNIA
cr. Berwick..........553 D3
INTERLAKEN
pde. Rosanna..........285 C18
INTERMAN
rd. Boronia..........424 F14
INTERNATIONAL
ct. Scoresby..........462 C11
dr. Westmeadows....236 H18
sq. Tullamarine..........278 E2
INTERVALE
dr. Avondale Ht..........321 L7
dr. Wyndham Va..........446 F12
INTREPID
st. Berwick..........554 B10
INVERARY
ct. Portsea..........678 D1
INVERAY
av. Jan Juc..........711 D13
INVERBERVIE
ct. Wonga Park..........291 G18
INVERELL
av. Mt Waverley..........419 H19
INVERIE
ct. Greenvale..........193 G19
pl. Point Cook..........450 G4
INVERLEIGH
ct. Meadow Ht..........237 L5
INVERLEITH
ct. St Kilda..........414 A15
st. Hawthorn..........372 C20
st. Hawthorn..........416 C1
INVERLOCH
cr. Dallas..........238 D10
dr. Point Cook..........450 F6
st. Box Hill S..........418 G5
st. Preston..........327 C1
INVERLOCHY
st. Anglesea..........713 L3
INVERMAY
ct. Frankston..........628 D11
gr. Hawthorn E..........416 D1
gr. Rosanna..........328 J2
rd. Monbulk..........427 K16
st. Reservoir..........283 H5
INVERNESS
av. Armadale..........415 G13
av. Armadale..........415 H14
av. Blairgowrie..........679 L18
av. Burwood..........418 J6
av. The Basin..........425 F14
cl. Pakenham..........584 J2
ct. Cairnlea..........319 J13
ct. Croydon..........379 G7
ct. Somerville..........645 A20
dr. Kew East..........372 K3
mw. Greenvale..........192 L20
rd. Kalorama..........383 C8

rd. Kalorama..........383 D
rd. Kalorama..........383 E
rd. Montrose..........383 A
rd. Mt Evelyn..........383 A
st. Brunswick E..........325 L
st. Clarinda..........498 E
st. Endeavour Hl.....503 J
st. Reservoir..........283 H
st. Seaford..........599 H
wy. Balwyn N..........372 L
wy. Balwyn N..........373
INVESTIGATOR
gr. Altona Mdw..........452 A
IOLANDA
st. Rye..........696 H
IOLANTHE
cl. Pk Orchards..........334 C
IONA
av. Belmont..........705
av. Brighton..........455 A
av. Highton..........705
av. Toorak..........415
ct. Frankston..........600 F
ct. Macleod..........285 C
ct. Mt Waverley..........419 B
ct. Wantirna S..........423 A
ct. Westmeadows.....237 E
st. Black Rock..........529
st. Clayton..........459 B
IPSWICH
ct. Wantirna..........422
pl. Craigieburn..........150 D
st. St Albans..........320
IPYDENE
ct. Chadstone..........457
IRAMOO
cct. Rockbank..........270 B
ct. Albanvale..........318
la. Yarraville..........366 G
st. Balwyn..........373 G
IRANDA
st. Frankston..........628
IREDALE
ct. Watsonia N..........243 G
IRELAND
av. Doncaster E..........376
av. Mitcham..........377 D
av. Narre Warren.....553 A
av. Wantirna S..........422 K
av. Wantirna S..........423 A
rd. Clayton S..........499 D
st. Burwood..........418 D
st. Ringwood..........378 E
st. Seaford..........573 D
st. W Melbourne..........23
st. W Melbourne..........34
st. W Melbourne..........368 L
IRENE
av. Up Fntree Gly.....465
cr. Mitcham..........377
ct. Chelsea..........547 E
ct. Cheltenham..........497 D
ct. Dandenong..........536
ct. Diamond Ck..........244
ct. Doncaster..........330 E
ct. Wheelers Hl..........460 L
gr. Selby..........467 D
pde. Cannons Creek...649
pl. Prahran..........32
pl. Prahran..........414
pl. Prahran..........415
st. Coburg N..........281 E
st. Preston..........326
IRILBARRA
rd. Canterbury..........373
IRIS
av. Brooklyn..........365
cl. Cranbourne N.....577
cl. Keilor Dn..........276
cl. Mulgrave..........501
cl. Tootgarook..........698
cr. Boronia..........424
ct. Blackburn N..........375
ct. Cannons Creek...649
ct. Doncaster E..........332
ct. Gowanbrae..........279
ct. Melton S..........268
ct. Mooroolbark..........337
pl. Point Cook..........450
rd. Glen Iris..........416
st. Bellfield..........327
st. Burwood..........418
st. Dromana..........686
wy. Bundoora..........242
IRISH
ct. Bonbeach..........573
IRMA
gr. Pascoe Vale..........280
IRONBARK
cl. Eltham..........288
cl. Hampton Pk..........552
cl. Keysborough.....534
ct. Frankston N..........599
ct. Meadow Ht..........193

JAMIE
cl. Cranbourne 578 F17
ct. Pakenham 559 G20
mw. Berwick 554 K18
JAMIESON
av. Footscray 367 J7
av. Rowville 463 C17
cl. Roxburgh Pk 194 C12
ct. Diamond Ck 244 K13
ct. Epping 242 B1
ct. Langwarrin 629 H10
ct. Pakenham 584 K9
ct. Werribee 446 L9
ct. Werribee 447 A9
dr. Yallambie 286 A11
rd. Wonga Park 335 E3
st. Cheltenham 496 J18
st. Coburg 325 B4
st. Dromana 686 F11
st. Fitzroy N 19 F7
st. Northcote 326 K18
st. St Albans 319 H3
st. Thomson 703 J18
tce. Taylors Hill 274 L12
tce. Taylors Hill 274 L13
wy. Berwick 579 L2
wy. Point Cook 450 F12
JAMIL
ct. Endeavour Hl 538 A4
JAMISON
av. Endeavour Hl 537 E10
st. Laverton 407 E18
st.s, Altona Mdw 407 E20
JAN
ct. Greensbrgh 286 B9
ct. Lalor 240 H4
ct. Mt Eliza 626 J19
JANCOL
ct. Berwick 554 H12
JANDA
ct. Box Hill N 374 J6
JANDEN
cl. Knoxfield 463 B7
JANDO
ct. Rowville 463 J15
JANE
av. St Albans 275 K19
ct. Boronia 424 D2
ct. Dingley Vill 533 B7
ct. Kilsyth S 381 C14
ct. Langwarrin 629 C7
ct. Meadow Ht 238 D3
ct. Mernda 156 A16
st. Bentleigh E 496 L6
st. Berwick 554 B9
JANE BELL
la. Melbourne 2 H7
JANEFIELD
dr. Bundoora 243 A14
JANELAINE
ct. Springvale S 499 E19
JANE-MAREE
pl. Cranbourne 578 A14
JANESDELL
av. Ferny Creek 425 G17
JANET
cr. Bundoora 242 J18
ct. Hampton Pk 552 A13
ct. Heathmont 422 H2
ct. Narre Warren 539 A15
ct. Newcomb 704 B15
ct. Portsea 677 H5
ct. Yallambie 286 C12
st. Blackburn 375 E18
st. Boronia 424 G7
st. Brighton East 495 J5
st. Dandenong N 501 K18
st. Keilor East 322 F5
st. Templstw Lr 330 B12
JANET BOWMAN
bvd. Beaconsfield 555 F16
JANETTE
ct. Carrum Downs 575 E14
JANFOURD
ct. Mt Waverley 459 C5
JANG
pl. Kurunjang 227 C13
JANICE
av. Cheltenham 497 F18
ct. Fawkner 239 F19
gr. Dandenong 535 G2
pl. Ringwood N 334 G16
rd. Glen Waverley 459 J8
st. Macleod 285 H11
JANIESLEIGH
rd. Tremont 465 E6
rd. Up Fntree Gly 465 E6
JANINA
ct. Vermont S 420 J11
ct. Wheelers Hl 461 B17
JANINE
ct. Doncaster E 332 D8
ct. Newcomb 704 E13
ct. Somerville 645 A18
rd. Nar Warrn N 538 H11
rd. Springvale S 500 B20
st. Scoresby 462 F10
JANKE
ct. Carrum Downs 575 F14
JANMAR
ct. Grovedale 705 G15
JANMARA
ct. Dandenong N 501 H13
ct. Endeavour Hl 504 A19
JAN MAREE
ct. Pakenham 584 G2
JANNA
pl. Berwick 553 H12
JANNALI
dr. Dingley Vill 533 E9
JANOS
cl. Narre Warren 538 H15
JANSON
cl. Nar Warrn S 552 G12
ct. Croydon N 335 J9
st. Maidstone 366 F2
JANUS
st. Tullamarine 278 F3
JANVILLE
st. Boronia 423 J12
JAPADDY
st. Mordialloc 532 E10
JAPONICA
ct. Cairnlea 319 E8
ct. Newcomb 704 D14
dr. Yarra Glen 209 C11
gr. Frankston S 627 D8
st. Bundoora 242 K16
JAQUES
gr. Forest Hill 420 E5
st. Hawthorn E 372 G15
JARDIER
tce. S Morang 198 L12
JARDINE
cr. Sunbury 143 G15
ct. Nar Warrn S 578 L2
rd. Macclesfield 471 F8
tce. Waterways 547 E1
JARED
rd. Altona Mdw 451 C5
JARLO
dr. Lilydale 338 C9
JARMA
cov. Doncaster E 331 K17
rd. Heathmont 378 F18
JARMAN
ct. Hoppers Csg 405 A16
ct. Sorrento 679 A15
dr. Langwarrin 602 A20
st. Mordialloc 532 E17
JARRAH
ct. Boronia 424 K6
ct. Delahey 275 C10
ct. Frankston N 599 L9
ct. Glen Waverley 460 B10
ct. Greensbrgh 243 J18
ct. Hoppers Csg 405 D18
ct. Montrose 382 E6
ct. Narre Warren 553 C8
ct. Pakenham 585 G1
ct. Templstw Lr 330 J13
dr. Braeside 532 G17
dr. Carrum Downs 575 D18
pl. Belmont 706 G6
pl. Waurn Ponds 705 D16
ps. Deer Park 319 B9
JARRAHDALE
st. Cheltenham 497 C20
JARRANG
rt. Nar Warrn N 538 E1
JARRETT
ct. Rowville 463 E19
JARROD
pl. Croydon N 335 L9
JARROT
ct. Meadow Ht 238 B2
JARRYD
cr. Berwick 554 K18
JARVIE
st. Brunswick E 325 K15
JARVIS
av. Croydon 380 H5
cr. Dandenong N 536 C1
rd. Waurn Ponds 705 A12
JASA
cr. Cranbourne W 577 G17
JASERFOLD
st. Balwyn N 373 F3
JASMIN
cl. Mt Martha 656 B9
ct. Narre Warren 539 B15
ct. Waurn Ponds 705 E14
JASMINE
cl. Hoppers Csg 405 B14
ct. Blackburn S 419 G4
ct. Cranbourne N 578 C8
ct. Dingley Vill 532 K4
ct. Eltham North 245 D18
ct. Frankston 600 B17
ct. Meadow Ht 238 C1
ct. Rowville 463 J16
dr. Mill Park 242 C11
pl. Melton W 226 C14
rd. Bayswater N 379 J14
rd. Cairnlea 319 L12
st. Caulfield S 455 H8
wy. Glenroy 281 D4
JASON
cl. Berwick 554 B18
ct. Balwyn N 329 G20
ct. Donvale 332 J16
ct. Noble Park 500 J17
ct. Viewbank 285 J19
pl. Frankston 600 G20
pl. Hampton Pk 551 D12
pl. Melton W 225 L15
rd. Carrum Downs 575 E14
st. Oakleigh S 458 E19
JASPER
ct. Hampton Pk 551 C9
ct. Mt Martha 655 E20
rd. Bentleigh 496 C6
rd. Kalorama 382 L11
rd. Kalorama 383 A11
rd. McKinnon 456 C20
rd. Ormond 456 C20
st. Noble Park 500 H18
st. Point Cook 450 E3
tce. Frankston 627 A5
tce. Frankston S 627 A5
JASSA
st. Bentleigh E 457 E16
JAY
ct. Werribee 447 L8
ri. Berwick 554 K19
JAYA
ct. Hallam 552 C1
JAYBREE
ct. Grovedale 706 A9
JAYCEE
cr. Carrum Downs 574 H16
JAYCO
ct. Mulgrave 500 E5
JAYDEE
ct. Rowville 502 B2
JAYE
pl. Cranbourne W 577 G18
JAYNE
ct. Dandenong S 551 A9
st. Frankston 600 A20
JAYSON
av. Eltham 287 D18
st. Burwood E 420 B7
JEAN
av. Clayton 498 L3
ct. Keysborough 534 L12
ct. Mooroolbark 337 B10
ct. Nar Warrn S 579 G1
pl. Grovedale 705 H14
st. Aberfeldie 323 C11
st. Cheltenham 496 G18
st. Forest Hill 376 D20
st. Lalor 241 G11
st. McKinnon 455 L16
st. Reservoir 282 H7
st. Templstw Lr 330 G10
st. Up Fntree Gly 464 L5
JEANBART
ct. Wantirna S 422 B19
JEANETTE
cl. St Helena 244 L17
ct. Mulgrave 501 H7
ct. Ringwood E 379 C11
st. Bayswater 423 D10
st. Clayton S 498 G4
st. Woori Yall 344 E15
JEANETTE MAREE
ct. Kilsyth 381 D16
JEANINE
cr. Fawkner 281 E2
JEANNE
st. Cockatoo 510 L9
JEANNINE
ct. Mt Martha 656 C7
JEAVONS
ct. Altona Mdw 451 G5
JEDAN
ct. Rowville 503 G2
JEDBURGH
pl. Greenvale 236 L2
wy. Point Cook 450 G5
JEDDA
ct. Cheltenham 497 A20
st. Rye 696 L11
JEDEM
cl. Viewbank 286 B16
JEEVES
av. Kalorama 383 C13
JEFF
ct. Oakleigh S 498 A10
ct. Sunshine N 320 L11
ct. Sunshine N 321 A11
JEFFCOTT
pl. W Melbourne 23 E5
st. W Melbourne 1 A2
st. W Melbourne 23 D6
JEFFERS
st. Noble Park 501 B18
JEFFERSON
gr. Doncaster E 332 H12
rd. Croydon S 379 G12
st. St Albans 319 G5
JEFFERY
av. Noble Park 534 E3
ct. Greensbrgh 286 D8
st. Blackburn 375 L19
JEFFREY
av. Altona North 410 D3
cl. St Albans 320 E13
ct. Clayton S 499 D15
ct. Epping 241 L4
dr. Ringwood 378 K5
dr. Yarrambat 201 B11
gr. Bayswater 423 B6
st. Bentleigh 496 F1
st. Campbellfield 239 E18
st. Dandenong N 536 A1
st. Hampton Pk 551 D10
st. Keilor East 322 C4
st. Mt Waverley 459 E6
st. Northcote 327 B20
st. Reservoir 283 A16
st. Templstw Lr 330 C12
JEFFREYS
ct. Bacchus Msh 221 J14
JEFFRIES
pde. Melbourne 4 H5
pde. Melbourne 24 K12
JEFFS
ct. Endeavour Hl 537 B6
JEJANA
tce. Rowville 503 B8
JELBART
ct. Eltham 288 A9
ct. Rosebud 699 L2
JELF
ct. Fawkner 281 J11
JELIMAR
ct. Sunbury 142 J8
JELLICO
dr. Scoresby 462 A8
JELLICOE
av. Monbulk 428 G17
ct. Werribee 447 L13
st. Box Hill S 375 A20
st. Cheltenham 496 K18
st. Ivanhoe 327 L8
st. Noble Park 535 B2
st. Werribee 447 K14
JELLINDALE
ct. Highton 702 A16
JELLS
rd. Cheltenham 531 G1
rd. Mulgrave 461 A19
rd. Wheelers Hl 461 B11
JEM
cl. Brunswick E 326 B14
JEMA
cl. Nar Warrn S 552 E11
ct. Boronia 424 B9
JENELLE
ct. Baxter 644 C1
JENHILL
ct. Rowville 463 J18
JENKENS
st. Frankston N 600 C11
JENKIN
st. Brunswick E 325 L16
st. Reservoir 282 C13
JENKINS
cl. Ringwood N 377 L4
ct. Kealba 276 K20
ct. Wantirna 422 G12
dr. Templestowe 332 A10
st. Caulfield S 455 H10
st. Mordialloc 532 D18
st. Noble Park 500 J16
st. Northcote 327 A12
JENNA
cl. Greensbrgh 285 L8
ct. Rowville 464 B12
JENNER
cl. Mornington 656 L6
cl. Mornington 657 A6
ct. Hampton Pk 551 B8
st. Blackburn S 419 D5
JENNI
ct. Hoppers Csg 447 L3
JENNIFER
av. Parkdale 532 A10
cr. Bayswater N 380 D17
cr. Pt Lonsdale 710
ct. Avondale Ht 322
ct. Grovedale 706
ct. Keilor 276
ct. Keilor 277
ct. Langwarrin 601
ct. Macleod 285
ct. Mt Waverley 459
ct. Narre Warren 539
ct. Ringwood 378
ct. Vermont S 420
ct. Warrandyte 333
rd. Lilydale 338
st. Cheltenham 497
st. Fawkner 281
st. Junction Vill 604
st. Noble Park N 501
JENNINGS
ct. Rosebud W 699
rd. Bayswater N 380
rd. Monbulk 468
st. Laverton 407
st. Moonee Pnd 323
st. Noble Park 500
st. Sandringham 495
JENNISON
ct. Chelsea Ht 547
JENNY
ct. Cranbourne N 578
ct. Ferny Creek 465
ct. Hillside 274
ct. Mooroolbark 336
ct. Scoresby 462
JENOLA
pde. Wantirna S 422
JENOLAN
av. Grovedale 706
JENSEN
ct. Wheelers Hl 460
rd. Broadmeadows 238
rd. Preston 283
rd. Up Fntree Gly 465
st. Hadfield 280
JENSZ
rd. Parwan 264
JEPHSON
st. Blairgowrie 696
JEPSON
st. Yarraville 366
JEREMIC
ct. Croydon N 336
JEREMY
ct. Mornington 640
JERICHO
ct. Berwick 553
JERILDERIE
dr. Berwick 539
JEROME
ct. Frankston 628
JERRIBRY
pl. Blackburn 376
JERROLD
st. Footscray 367
JERSEY
cl. Endeavour Hl 537
ct. Belmont 706
ct. Tarneit 405
pde. Carnegie 456
rd. Bayswater 424
st. Balwyn 373
st. Coburg 281
JERULA
av. Mt Eliza 626
JERVIS
st. Camberwell 417
JERVOIS
st. St Kilda E 414
JESMOND
rd. Croydon 380
JESS
ct. Ringwood E 379
st. Reservoir 282
JESSAMBER
ct. Diamond Ck 246
JESSAMINE
av. Prahran 414
JESSE
ct. Altona Mdw 451
ct. Nar Warrn N 539
st. Glen Iris 417
JESSICA
cl. Wantirna S 421
ct. Mt Evelyn 338
dr. Hampton Pk 552
mw. Berwick 554
pl. Delahey 275
rd. Campbellfield 239
JESSICAS
la. Eltham North 287
JESSIE
st. Blackburn N 376
st. Coburg 325
st. Cranbourne N 578

Cremorne 26 A18
Noble Park.........534 L6
Northcote 326 K19
Oak Park...........280 B10
Preston..............326 G2
Sunshine 365 G5
SSON
Dandenong........536 F6
SSOP
Gladstone Pk 279 A2
Greensbrgh........285 L4
SSUP
Mulgrave 501 F1
STER
Kings Park.........274 L19
SKE
Dingley Vill.........532 K6
TI
Torquay.............711 J2
TY
Boneo...............700 F6
Dromana 686 C8
Rosebud............700 D4
Rosebud............700 F6
Sandringham.....494 K12
NE
Berwick 553 J14
WELL
Brunswick W 324 H14
Yarraville 366 J17
ABEEL
Flemington 33 J2
KELL
Glen Iris.............417 E9
A
Werribee...........446 K15
Richmond............26 A7
Coburg 281 K20
Heidelberg 329 B8
BA
Tootgarook........698 C7
L
Ringwood..........378 J6
LARD
Hoppers Csg......448 A1
LIAN
Highett 495 H13
Rye 697 C13
Cranbourne........604 A3
Dandenong N.....501 J18
Mooroolbark......337 H16
Tullamarine........278 F4
Mt Martha..........657 D9
MAX
Forest Hill 376 E19
PANGER
Donvale 332 G19
Berwick 554 A19
BA
Viewbank..........286 C16
CHILLA
Frankston S 627 G17
DA
Melton W...........225 J18
DABYNE
Chadstone 418 C20
Dandenong N.....502 B17
Taylors Hill........274 L10
Taylors Hill.........274 L11
Lysterfield..........464 B16
DALEE
Yallambie...........286 B14
Rowville.............462 L18
Bulleen 329 H12
Frankston 628 D6
Nar Warrn S........553 B18
n. Cranbourne W ...603 F1
DARA
Gladstone Pk 279 C2
DIVICK
Maribyrnong......322 J15
GAI
Frankston 600 H16
GELLA
Ashwood 418 A19
GHI
Reservoir...........283 B5
JELLA
Highton 701 K14
KANA
Eltham...............288 C6
RAH
Aspendale..........546 H7
ING
Doncaster E.......375 F2
SU
Mt Evelyn...........339 E12
TULLY
Doncaster..........331 C20
AMI
Cheltenham 497 C17

JOAN
av. Dromana 686 D3
av. Ferntree Gly 424 K16
cr. Burwood E.........420 A8
ct. Campbellfield 239 H12
ct. Heathmont.........378 E19
ct. Mulgrave 501 E2
ct. Noble Park N......501 D19
ct. Reservoir...........239 K20
ct. St Albans...........276 G18
ct. Werribee............448 A16
ct. Woori Yall..........344 H14
st. Melton...............226 G20
st. Moorabbin.........496 G10
st. Sunshine W........363 L4
st. Sunshine W........364 A4
st. Sunshine W........364 C4
JOAN KIRNER
dr. Newport 411 A11
JOANNA
ct. Mt Waverley 459 B4
ct. Torquay.............712 F2
st. Nunawading 376 J20
JO-ANNE
pl. Kings Park.........319 E2
JOANNE
av. Chirnside Pk 336 K6
ct. Bayswater N 380 E17
ct. Epping...............197 H14
JOBERT
ct. Blackburn S.......419 J3
st. Springvale 500 A16
JOBSON
st. Williamstown.....411 D14
JOCELYN
av. Balwyn N...........374 D4
ct. Doncaster E.......331 J19
ct. Forest Hill..........376 H20
st. Lalor..................240 J7
st. Surrey Hills........373 K16
JODI
av. Wheelers Hl 460 K18
pl. Hampton Pk........552 D14
st. Cheltenham 531 H1
JODIE
cl. Doveton.............536 L7
ct. Campbellfield 239 H12
ct. Diamond Ck.......244 L14
pl. Kilsyth S.............381 A20
JOEL
av. Altona North 409 G7
ct. Bayswater..........423 B6
ct. Heathmont.........378 F19
ct. Moorabbin.........497 C9
pl. Gladstone Pk 279 A3
wy. Hampton Pk.......551 L7
JOELLE
ct. Aspendale Gdn...546 L6
JOFFRE
av. Edithvale............546 H12
pde. Cockatoo 511 C2
rd. Pascoe Vale 280 H12
rd. Silvan 384 K11
st. Broadmeadows..238 E17
st. Camberwell.........417 K6
st. Croydon 380 B2
st. Healesville 257 H2
st. Noble Park.........535 B1
st. Reservoir............283 B16
JOHANN
av. Scoresby 462 H8
JOHANNA
ct. Dingley Vill.........532 K5
ct. Pakenham 585 L3
JOHANSEN
pl. Darley................221 L7
JOHANSONS
rd. Warrandyte........334 G3
rd. Warrandyte S.....334 G3
JOHN
ct. Bundoora...........243 B20
ct. St Albans............320 C12
ct. Somerville 645 A15
ct. Newtown 702 G12
pl. Geelong, off
Little Malop St ..703 D8
st. Altona North 409 E2
st. Balwyn 373 E12
st. Bayswater...........423 G6
st. Beaumaris 530 B10
st. Bentleigh E 456 J20
st. Blackburn 375 J12
st. Box Hill...............374 L16
st. Brunswick E........326 A16
st. Clifton Hill............20 D5
st. Collingwood 19 J17
st. Dandenong S.....536 B14
st. Eltham................287 G11
st. Elwood 454 E3
st. Emerald..............469 E15
st. Fitzroy 19 A15
st. Flemington 33 J1
st. Frankston 599 G18
st. Geelong West 702 E2
st. Glenroy..............280 H1
st. Glen Waverley....419 K20
st. Hawthorn...........372 B17
st. Ivanhoe 328 C14
st. Kew....................372 F12
st. Lalor...................240 J4
st. Langwarrin 629 B6
st. Lilydale..............338 A6
st. Malvern East......416 B20
st. Mordialloc 531 H17
st. Oakleigh 458 C13
st. Oak Park.............279 K13
st. Pakenham 584 K7
st. Pascoe Vale 280 K18
st. Ringwood N.........378 E6
st. St Albans............319 H2
st. Sandringham 495 E12
st. Seddon...............367 B10
st. S Melbourne 30 A4
st. Sunbury 143 K11
st. Templstw Lr 330 G13
st. Tootgarook.........698 C4
st. Wandin N 340 H14
st. Werribee............448 D16
st. Williamstown......411 D12
st. Geelong, off
Little Malop St ...703 A7
JOHN AUGUST
wk. Seabrook...........450 L6
JOHN BALL
pl. Werribee............447 B7
JOHN BARR
ct. Berwick, off
Keith Taylor Dr...554 D9
JOHN BATMAN
dr. Melton W...........225 H20
JOHN BERTRAM
dr. Sorrento 679 C17
JOHN COOKE
tce. Seabrook 450 L7
JOHN EDGCUMBE
wy. Endeavour Hl 537 E7
JOHN FAWKNER
dr. Endeavour Hl 537 H8
JOHN FISHER
dr. Berwick 554 F13
JOHN HOLLAND
ct. Blackburn 375 K11
JOHN HUNTER
ct. Mill Park............242 D4
dr. Endeavour Hl 537 G11
JOHN JOSEPH
ct. Nar Warrn N 539 H11
JOHN LECKY
rd. Seabrook...........450 L8
JOHN LISTON
dr. Newport 411 A11
la. Newport 411 A11
JOHN MONASH
dr. Skye 575 G15
JOHN PAUL
dr. Hillside 274 E2
JOHN PHELPS
ct. Seabrook...........451 A8
JOHN ROWELL
la. Mornington.........640 K10
JOHN RYAN
dr. S Morang 243 K2
JOHNS
cr. Mt Evelyn............338 K20
dr. Rye 696 L1
gr. Doncaster E 332 D8
la. Panton Hill..........205 D10
rd. Mornington.........640 B20
rd. Selby..................467 D15
st. Up Fntree Gly.....465 C8
JOHNSON
av. Carrum...............573 A9
av. Hoppers Csg.......448 C2
av. Rye 680 G20
bl. Meadow Ht 237 J7
ct. Rosebud W..........683 F18
ct. Roxburgh Pk.......194 D15
dr. Ferntree Gly 423 F18
dr. Glen Waverley.....460 B8
la. Albert Park...........29 H15
pl. Endeavour Hl 537 C5
st. Avondale Ht 322 B16
st. Avonsleigh...........470 F17
st. Belmont..............706 B3
st. Footscray............367 D6
st. Hawthorn............372 A14
st. Moonee Pnd 324 H12
st. Noble Park..........534 L7
st. Northcote 326 H11
st. Oakleigh 457 J12
st. Pascoe Vale S 324 E6
st. Reservoir............283 A4
st. Richmond.............26 L6
st. Richmond............371 A13
st. Rosebud W.........683 E19
st. St Kilda E 414 K14
st. S Melbourne 29 A2
st. S Melbourne 413 A1
st. Sunshine N 321 F15
st. Thomastown........240 L15
st. Thomastown.......241 A15
st. Thornbury..........326 H11
JOHNSONS
rd. Mernda..............156 A14
JOHNSTON
av. Eumemmerring..536 L15
av. Eumemmerring..537 A15
av. Newcomb 704 A16
ct. Dandenong S.....536 B17
pde. Ferny Creek........465 H1
st. Abbotsford 20 D14
st. Ashburton...........417 D14
st. Burwood.............419 B8
st. Collingwood 19 A13
st. Fitzroy 19 A13
st. Mentone 531 C6
st. Newport 410 H6
st. Port Melb 29 A13
st. Port Melb............412 L7
st. Port Melb............413 A7
st. Wandin East 340 K17
wy. Taylors Hill.........274 D9
JOHNSTONE
st. Broadmeadows..237 H15
st. Jacana 237 H15
st. Malvern 416 A18
st. Pt Lonsdale.........707 J20
st. Seaford...............599 E3
st. Westmeadows ...237 D14
JOHN WEDGE
pl. Seabrook 450 K7
wyn. Skye 575 H16
JOHN WILLIAM
dr. Mt Martha...........657 A7
JOINER
la. Seaholme 409 G19
st. Williamstown.....410 J14
JOLEN
ct. Donvale 332 K13
JOLIE
gr. Box Hill...............375 B18
JOLIE VUE
rd. Balwyn N 329 E19
JOLIMONT
av. Mulgrave 501 D6
la. E Melbourne 25 C10
pl. Dingley Vill.........499 B20
pl. Narre Warren 539 F15
rd. E Melbourne 25 C10
rd. Forest Hill 420 H5
rd. Vermont 420 H5
rd. Vermont 421 A6
st. E Melbourne 25 C11
tce. E Melbourne 25 E10
JOLLEY
st. Brunswick W 324 L9
JOLLIFFE
cr. Rosanna.............328 L1
cr. Rosanna.............329 A1
JOLLY
ct. Roxburgh Pk.......193 L8
pl. Sydenham 274 K3
st. Dandenong 535 F5
st. Frankston 599 G19
tce. S Morang 243 H3
JOMARY
ct. Berwick 554 G10
JON
pl. Keysborough 534 D9
st. Laverton N..........408 A4
JONAS
st. Richmond..............26 B4
JONATHAN
av. Burwood E..........419 J8
cl. Bayswater N 380 H17
ct. Eumemmerring..537 B15
ct. Noble Park..........534 K4
pl. Pakenham 559 F19
JONATHON
ct. Mornington.........656 J1
ct. Taylors L 275 G5
ct. Wantirna S..........422 E17
ct. Werribee............447 A16
dr. Darley.................221 L10
JONES
av. Up Fntree Gly.....465 G7
cr. Rosanna.............285 C19
cr. Smiths Gly..........206 E6
ct. Aspendale Gdn...547 A6
ct. Beaconsfield 555 F16
ct. Bundoora............242 H20
ct. Darley.................221 L8
ct. Endeavour Hl 537 A6
ct. Laverton 407 F12
ct. Mt Waverley 458 F9
ct. Sunshine W 364 H10
la. Melbourne 2 L8
la. Melbourne 24 G3
la. N Melbourne.........17 E17
la. Roxburgh Pk......194 C14
pl. Caroline Spr 318 E9
pl. Geelong..............703 B11
pl. Richmond...........371 C16
pl. W Melbourne 23 B1
rd. Brooklyn 365 C17
rd. Dandenong 535 G6
rd. Kangaroo Grnd ..247 G11
rd. Somerville 644 K20
st. Brunswick...........325 G10
st. Lilydale..............338 E4
st. Thornbury...........327 F8
st. Oakleigh, off
Chester St..........457 J11
JONESFIELD
cnr. Cairnlea 320 B13
JONQUIL
cl. Diamond Ck.......245 J6
ct. Doncaster E 332 E13
JONSON
av. Melton W...........225 J19
JORDAN
ct. Beaconsfield 555 F16
ct. Boronia...............423 G15
ct. Endeavour Hl 537 C3
gr. Glen Waverley.....460 E5
pl. Roxburgh Pk.......194 C17
rd. Monbulk..............428 C17
rd. Pt Lonsdale.........710 F2
st. Ashwood 418 C18
st. Brunswick W 324 K15
st. Clayton S 498 J4
st. Malvern 416 B15
st. Somerville 645 C15
JOROMA
pl. Wonga Park........336 D8
JOSEF
av. Bundoora............242 G16
JOSEPH
ct. Pakenham 585 B6
ct. Pk Orchards........334 D19
ct. Wantirna S..........462 A4
dr. Hillside 274 F3
rd. Footscray.............33 A14
rd. Footscray...........367 K7
st. Blackburn N 375 G6
st. Broadmeadows..238 B17
st. Bundoora.............284 G2
st. Ringwood E 379 C6
st. Templstw Lr 330 G14
JOSEPH BANKS
cr. Cranbourne.........603 K2
cr. Endeavour Hl 537 B4
JOSEPHINA
ct. Carrum Downs...601 E4
JOSEPHINE
av. Cranbourne N 578 G10
av. Mt Waverley 419 F17
av. Narre Warren 538 H16
cl. Rowville..............464 A13
ct. Melton W............225 L13
ct. Plenty 244 J11
gr. Preston...............283 C18
st. Langwarrin 601 H19
st. Oak Park.............279 L12
JOSHUA
cl. Springvale S 499 G18
ct. Bundoora............242 G20
ct. Kings Park...........319 C2
ct. Narre Warren.....539 A14
pl. Kurunjang...........227 C9
JOSIE
ct. Lilydale..............338 G14
ct. Pk Orchards........377 H1
pl. Rosebud 700 H5
JOSLYN
dr. Research 289 D8
JOULES
ct. Deer Park............319 C9
ct. Macleod 285 F11
JOUSTING
pl. Glen Waverley....420 K16
JOVIC
rd. Epping................241 D3
JOWETT
av. Sunshine W........364 J9
JOY
av. Mt Evelyn...........383 E1
cl. Werribee............447 F3
ct. Lilydale..............338 E12
ct. Narre Warren.....539 E18
mw. Pakenham 584 F2
pde. Noble Park..........500 F19
st. Balwyn N 329 K19
st. Bentleigh E 456 H18
st. Braybrook............365 L4
st. Donvale 376 G4
st. Frankston 599 E20
st. Melton S.............268 E5
st. Mt Waverley 419 J14
st. South Yarra 32 H15

st. Alphington 327 J15
st. Beaumaris 530 H4
st. Coburg 325 L2
st. Hampton E 495 L9
st. Maidstone 322 G20
st. Oakleigh E 458 H16
st. Parkdale 531 J12
st. Tootgarook 698 E5
st. Yarra Jctn 347 K16
KEITH CAMPBELL
ct. Scoresby 462 F10
KEITH TAYLOR
dr. Berwick 554 D9
KEIWA
pl. Rowville 463 D17
pl. Taylors Hill 274 J15
KELBA
st. Balwyn N 373 F8
KELBOURNE
gr. Sunbury 143 A5
KELBOW
cl. St Helena 245 B16
KELBURN
rd. Berwick 553 L16
st. Caulfield N 415 D16
KELDALE
ct. Noble Park 500 H17
KELL
ct. Greensbrgh 286 A7
pl. Templestowe 332 D5
st. Greensbrgh 286 A7
KELLAND
av. Hillside 232 E19
KELLAWAY
av. Moonee Pnd 324 C12
cr. Mill Park 242 G5
ct. Wantirna 422 F8
st. Maribyrnong 322 L20
st. Maribyrnong 323 A20
st. Maribyrnong 366 L1
st. Mt Waverley 419 F14
KELLBOURNE
dr. Rowville 463 G14
KEL LEMON
ct. Mt Martha 656 C15
KELLER
cl. Greenvale 237 C4
ct. Hampton Pk 551 K12
KELLERHER
st. Lalor 241 E9
KELLET
wy. Roxburgh Pk 194 A12
KELLETT
gr. Kew 372 A3
st. Cranbourne N 577 L4
st. Northcote 327 A13
st. Reservoir 283 D15
KELLETTS
rd. Lysterfield 463 L16
rd. Rowville 462 J15
rd. Rowville 463 A15
KELLEY
gr. Preston 326 C5
KELLIE
ct. Hampton Pk 551 C9
KELLS
av. Herne Hill 702 A4
KELLY
av. Hampton E 495 J6
cl. Rye 697 K9
ct. Broadmeadows 238 A20
ct. Pakenham 559 F20
ct. Somerville 645 C17
ct. Warranwood 335 B14
dr. Langwarrin 629 L1
la. Nunawading, off Oval Wy 376 G15
mw. Berwick 554 L18
pl. Mill Park 243 A6
rd. Cranbourne S 603 K20
st. Bayswater 423 B3
st. Chadstone 457 L4
st. Diamond Ck 246 B12
st. Doncaster 330 L17
st. Sunbury 143 D12
st. Werribee 447 K14
KELLYBROOK
cl. Delahey, off Ryland Cct 275 C11
KELLYS
av. Burnside 318 F9
la. Sandringham 495 B14
rd. Warburton 349 L2
KELMAN
ct. Westmeadows 237 D15
st. Frankston 599 H20
KELMAR
st. Albanvale 318 L3
st. Cheltenham 497 A18
KELMSCOTT
ct. Armadale 415 G11
KELRINDA
cl. Oakleigh S 498 A7
KELSALL
ct. Hampton E 495 L10
KELSBY
st. Reservoir 282 H9
KELSEY
ct. Craigieburn 194 D1
ct. Pt Lonsdale 710 D3
KELSO
ct. Wheelers Hl 461 D15
pl. Berwick 554 D15
pl. Wantirna 422 J7
st. Coldstream 295 E14
st. Cremorne 25 L19
st. Frankston 599 E19
st. Mentone 530 K9
wy. Point Cook 450 G6
KELSON
st. Coburg 325 C2
KELSTERN
ct. Highton 705 J9
KELTIE
ri. Endeavour Hl 537 G10
st. Glen Iris 417 J12
KELVAN
gr. Doncaster E 332 E6
KELVERNE
st. Reservoir 282 B9
KELVIN
av. Montmorency 286 H7
av. Seaford 599 D2
cl. Niddrie 322 L4
ct. Prahran 415 B12
ct. Ringwood N 378 F2
dr. Ferntree Gly 463 K1
gr. Ashburton 417 F14
gr. Chelsea 546 J17
gr. Langwarrin 602 E16
gr. Prahran 415 B12
gr. Preston 282 L20
gr. S Morang 199 H20
gr. S Morang 243 H1
gr. Springvale 500 A12
gr. Thornbury 326 K11
gr. Werribee 447 A13
pl. Carlton 18 C18
rd. Alphington 327 J17
rd. Bayswater N 380 F14
st. Ascot Vale 324 A17
KELVINSIDE
dr. Templestowe 330 L9
rd. Noble Park 500 G15
st. Balwyn N 329 K19
st. Hughesdale 457 E11
KELWAY
cr. Eltham North 287 B4
KELWIN
ct. Hoppers Csg 449 E1
KEMBLA
st. Cheltenham 531 H4
st. Hawthorn 416 B2
KEMERTON
cl. Point Cook 450 H10
KEMP
av. Mt Evelyn 339 E15
av. Mt Waverley 459 A3
av. Thomastown 240 H15
ct. Rowville 463 J19
grn. Caroline Spr 274 B7
pl. Sunbury 142 H9
rd. Portsea 678 G3
rd. Sorrento 678 G3
st. Burwood 418 B6
st. Carrum 573 E11
st. Northcote 326 G10
st. Springvale 500 A7
st. Thornbury 326 G10
st. Upwey 465 G8
KEMPS
st. Ringwood E 378 L7
st. Ringwood E 379 A7
KEMPSON
ct. Keysborough 535 A14
wk. Berwick 554 E8
KEMPSTON
ct. Croydon N 335 K10
ct. Rowville 502 J3
st. Greensbrgh 285 J2
KEMPTON
ct. Epping 198 A16
ct. Seabrook 450 L4
KEMSLEY
ct. Hawthorn E 372 E14
KENARRA
ct. Hurstbridge 203 G13
KENAUD
av. Mt Eliza 626 B18
KENBRY
rd. Heathmont 422 L1
KENDAL
ct. Croydon Hl 335 K13
KENDALE
ct. Bayswater N 380 J20
st. Airport W 278 K18
KENDALL
av. Parkville 17 H1
cl. Templestowe 331 L10
ct. Oakleigh E 458 J12
ct. Rosebud 699 K3
ct. Sunbury 142 L9
dr. Narre Warren 538 L14
rd. Ringwood N 334 E12
rd. Warrandyte S 334 E12
rd. Yallambie 285 J13
st. Canterbury 373 E18
st. Coburg 325 E3
st. Elwood 454 G3
st. Essendon 324 F9
st. Hampton 495 H7
st. Mt Waverley 419 J14
st. Nunawading 376 E10
st. Preston 326 B4
st. Ringwood 378 E13
KENDALLS
la. Hurstbridge 202 F13
KENDARI
av. Balwyn N 373 B7
ct. Hampton Pk 552 B9
KENDON
cl. Wheelers Hl 460 L7
KENDRA
pl. Keysborough 534 J11
KENEALLY
dr. Point Cook 449 K9
KENILWORTH
av. Beaconsfield 555 A16
av. Frankston 627 K4
av. Officer 581 G1
av. Wonga Park 335 G4
cr. Glen Waverley 419 K13
gr. Glen Iris 416 F10
pde. Ivanhoe 327 L13
st. Balwyn 374 A9
st. Reservoir 282 K9
KENJI
st. Mornington 640 K18
KENJULIE
dr. Bentleigh E 497 A5
KENLEIGH
gr. Prahran 414 L13
gr. Prahran 415 A13
KENLEY
ct. Burwood E 419 H11
ct. Frankston 628 G4
ct. Meadow Ht 237 K7
ct. Toorak 415 G8
KENLON
st. Bentleigh E 497 C7
KENMAN
cl. Templestowe 331 F8
KENMARE
av. Croydon 379 J2
st. Mont Albert 374 C11
st. Mont Albert N 374 C11
st. Watsonia 285 D8
KENMORE
ct. Frankston 628 C7
KENNA
dr. Lalor 241 F6
st. Macleod 284 J15
st. Moonee Pnd 324 D12
KENNARD
pl. Burwood E 420 C12
KENNAUGH
st. Oakleigh E 458 K16
KENNEALY
st. Surrey Hills 373 J20
KENNEDIA
av. Springvale 500 K12
KENNEDY
av. Chelsea Ht 547 G17
av. Nar Warrn N 539 J5
av. Ringwood 378 E8
ct. Cranbourne N 577 J9
gr. Highton 705 J1
pde. Roxburgh Pk 194 B9
rd. Avonsleigh 470 L11
rd. Pakenham 559 C19
rd. St Andrews 206 D1
st. Bentleigh E 457 E20
st. Blairgowrie 696 C1
st. Fairfield 327 G15
st. Glenroy 279 J9
st. Glen Waverley 420 E20
st. Keilor 277 C13
st. Reservoir 282 D13
st. Richmond 26 L6
st. Sunshine 365 D2
KENNETH
av. Emerald 469 G17
av. Sassafras 426 G16
cl. Hoppers Csg 405 E18
ct. Pearcedale 646 L3
ct. Pearcedale 647 A3
rd. Bayswater 423 J8
st. Anglesea 713 J1
st. Belmont 702 D18
st. Braybrook 365 L1
st. Bulleen 329 K17
st. Noble Park 534 K6
st. Preston 327 E1
st. Rosanna 329 B1
st. Sandringham 495 G12
st. Thomastown 240 K18
KENNETT
st. Ashwood 417 L16
KENNEY
st. Sunshine W 364 H7
KENNINGTON
rd. Rosebud 684 F17
KENNINGTON PARK
dr. Endeavour Hl 503 A20
KENNON
st. Doncaster E 331 L20
KENNY
la. Monbulk 428 G20
pl. Geelong 703 C12
st. Attwood 237 A12
st. Attwood 237 C13
st. Balwyn N 373 J7
st. Richmond 26 F8
st. Westmeadows 237 A12
st. Westmeadows 237 C13
KENRICK
mw. Caroline Spr 317 L2
KENROSS
cl. Point Cook 450 G7
ct. Braybrook 365 H5
ct. Wantirna 422 G6
dr. Wheelers Hl 461 D18
KENSINGTON
av. Frankston S 628 C16
cir. Derrimut 363 A7
cr. Altona Mdw 451 D5
ct. Greenvale 237 F6
ct. Hampton Pk 551 H4
ct. Mulgrave 500 D2
ct. Thomastown 241 J15
gdn. Vermont S 420 G6
pl. Mooroolbark 381 D1
pl. Narre Warren 539 B14
pl. Wantirna S 422 F18
rd. Kensington 33 A16
rd. Kensington 368 A8
rd. South Yarra 32 J9
rd. South Yarra 414 K5
rd. W Melbourne 33 A16
rd. W Melbourne 368 A8
KENSLEY
st. Up Fntree Gly 465 G7
KENSWICK
dr. Hillside 232 G20
dr. Hillside 232 H20
KENT
av. Brighton 454 F10
av. Croydon 335 K20
cl. Blackburn N 376 B7
ct. Avondale Ht 322 F8
ct. Belmont 706 E2
ct. Bulleen 329 G12
ct. Bundoora 284 L6
ct. Craigieburn 194 D3
ct. Cranbourne N 577 J5
ct. Deer Park 318 K8
ct. Doncaster E 332 E7
ct. Eltham 287 K9
ct. Glen Waverley 420 F16
ct. Heidelberg 329 F3
ct. Keysborough 534 L9
ct. Toorak 415 F9
ct. Werribee 446 J11
gr. Caulfield N 415 D19
gr. Frankston 627 L4
la. Hawthorn 372 A17
la. Prahran 414 L11
mw. Cranbourne N 577 J5
pl. Somerville 644 H17
pl. S Melbourne 29 J2
rd. Box Hill 374 J17
rd. Lalor 241 L11
rd. Launching Pl 345 E17
rd. Narre Warren 553 C7
rd. Pascoe Vale 280 H12
rd. Rye 697 F7
rd. Surrey Hills 373 J19
st. Ascot Vale 324 D19
st. Braybrook 365 J5
st. Clifton Hill 19 J7
st. Clifton Hill 370 E4
st. Dromana 686 D9
st. Fitzroy 19 C16
st. Glen Iris 416 E12
st. Hawthorn 372 A17
st. Kew 372 B10
st. Knoxfield 463 C3
st. Mornington 640 F17
st. Richmond 26 H7
st. Richmond 371 A14
st. Seddon 367 D11
st. Windsor 31 K20
st. Windsor 414 E10
st. Yarraville 367
wy. Tullamarine 278
KENT-HILL
cl. Wandana Ht 701
KENT-HUGHES
rd. Eltham 287
KENTHURST
ct. Lilydale 338
ct. Mill Park 242
KENTIA
ct. Aspendale Gdn 547
KENTISH
pl. Chirnside Pk 336
KENTMERE
ct. Greenvale 193
KENTON
pl. Gladstone Pk 237
pl. Kealba 276
wk. Nar Warrn S 578
KENTUCKY
cl. Narre Warren 539
ct. Notting Hill 459
rd. Red Hill S 688
KENTWOOD
rd. Macleod 285
KENVARRA
cr. Jan Juc 711
KENWAY
st. Sunbury 143
KENWITH
gr. Newtown 702
KENWOOD
cr. Ringwood 379
ct. Preston 326
grn. Derrimut 363
la. Hawthorn 371
KENWORTH
ct. Rowville 463
KENWORTHY
ri. Mornington 657
KENWYN
ct. Ferntree Gly 464
ct. Greensbrgh 244
KEOGH
ct. Box Hill S 419
ct. Meadow Ht 238
ct. Pascoe Vale 280
st. Burwood 418
st. Rosebud 684
KEOL
st. Clayton S 499
KEON
cr. Sunshine W 364
ct. Balwyn N 329
pde. Reservoir 283
pde. Thomastown 241
st. Thornbury 326
KEOWN
ct. Campbellfield 239
pl. Geelong, off McKillop St 702
KEPPEL
dr. Hallam 551
st. Carlton 18
st. Carlton 18
KEPPLER
cct. Seaford 574
KERABOITE
ct. Mt Eliza 626
KERAM
cr. Highton 701
KERANG
av. Reservoir 283
ct. Broadmeadows 238
ct. Taylors L 276
pl. Thomastown 240
KERBY
st. Eltham 287
KEREFORD
pl. Sunbury 143
KERFERD
av. Sorrento 678
cl. Melton S 268
la. Albert Park 29
pl. Albert Park 29
pl. Albert Park 413
rd. Albert Park 29
rd. Albert Park 413
rd. Glen Iris 416
rd. Glen Iris 416
rd. Glen Waverley 460
rd. Hampton 495
st. Coburg 281
st. Essendon N 279
st. Malvern East 416
KERFORD
cr. Point Cook 450
KERGER
ct. Grovedale 705
KERGO
pl. Wantirna S 462

RLEY
Geelong, off
Mercer St.........702 L5
RMEEN
Sunshine W.......364 F8
RN
Donvale............332 L17
RNAN
Pascoe Vale.......280 E19
Moonee Pnd......324 B9
Strathmore.......279 K20
RNOT
Mulgrave...........460 D17
Noble Park N......501 C15
Westmeadows...237 G13
Parkville..............17 L14
E Geelong..........703 G11
S Kingsville........410 G3
Spotswood........410 G3
RR
Oak Park............279 J10
Aspendale Gdn...546 J5
Camberwell........416 H6
Montrose...........382 D10
Box Hill N..........374 H8
Patterson L........573 H2
Bacchus Msh.....221 K14
Beaumaris.........530 F5
Blackburn..........375 F11
Fitzroy.................19 A11
Kingsville...........366 G13
Lilydale.............337 K3
Preston.............327 F7
S Melbourne........29 F1
S Melbourne......413 C1
RRI
Sunbury............143 B8
Bundoora...........284 G1
RRIBEE
Clayton S...........498 H9
RRIE
Eltham..............287 D6
Grovedale..........706 E12
Springvale S.......533 K2
Glen Waverley....420 H20
RRIE ANNE
Skye..................575 G18
RRILEA
Kilsyth S...........424 L3
RRIMUIR
Box Hill N..........375 D9
RRINS
Highton.............705 F5
Templestowe.....331 K3
RRISDALE
Sunbury............142 L8
RRISON
Noble Park........500 E18
St Albans..........275 J18
Hampton Pk.......551 D9
RRS
Lysterfield.........505 J18
Nar Warrn E.......505 J18
N Melbourne.......34 L13
Maddingley........263 B8
St Andrews........205 C1
RRY
Mt Martha..........656 F5
Berwick.............554 K6
Doncaster E.......331 G19
Viewbank...........285 F20
St Albans...........320 D12
e. Balwyn...........374 C10
e. Mont Albert N....374 C10
Warranwood......335 E12
Langwarrin........601 F19
Seaford.............599 H4
RRY ANNE
Wonga Park.......336 D6
RRYLIN
Blackburn..........376 D13
RSEY
Doncaster..........331 C13
RSHAW
Nar Warrn S.......552 E20
Nar Warrn S.......578 E1
Mordialloc.........531 L14
Oakleigh S.........497 F4
Parkdale............531 L14
RTA
Greensbrgh........243 K18
Hoppers Csg......405 A18
RYN
Templestowe.....331 L9
STREL
Blind Bight.........650 B9
Chelsea Ht.........547 C9
Baxter...............644 D1
Carrum Downs...575 A20
Carrum Downs...601 A1
Mornington........640 K16
Taylors L...........275 G2
Werribee...........447 K4

rd. S Morang.........199 A10
wy. Craigieburn.......149 F16
KESWICK
av. Belgrave Ht........506 E1
cr. Bayswater N......380 F20
ct. Delahey.............275 B14
ct. Nar Warrn S........579 A4
gln. Greensbrgh.......244 F20
ri. Eltham...............287 L6
ri. Sunbury.............142 L1
st. Bentleigh E........457 B16
KETNOR
st. Cranbourne........604 B5
KETT
pl. Kensington..........33 H6
st. Blackburn N.......376 D8
st. Lower Plenty......286 H12
st. Nunawading......376 F9
KETWICK
ct. Ferntree Gly......424 A17
ct. Sydenham.........274 J3
KEVERELL
rd. Caulfield N.........455 G1
KEVIN
av. Blackburn..........375 G11
av. Ferntree Gly.......464 A4
cl. Beaconsfield.......554 L17
ct. Cheltenham.......497 D20
ct. Donvale.............376 K6
ct. Kilsyth...............381 B9
ct. Melton S............268 G4
ct. Somerville.........645 B15
gr. Kew...................371 D10
st. Bundoora...........284 G1
st. Mt Waverley.......458 F9
st. Pascoe Vale......280 K18
st. Sunshine...........365 F4
st. Tootgarook........698 E2
KEVINGTON
st. Werribee............448 B18
KEVLAR
cl. Braeside............532 K12
ct. Wonga Park.......291 L18
KEW
ct. Donvale.............376 K7
ct. Narre Warren.....553 B10
pl. Wantirna............421 L12
KEY
la. Pakenham.........583 L17
KEYES
ct. Wantirna S.........462 L1
ct. Wantirna S.........463 A1
pl. Gladstone Pk.....237 E16
st. Ashburton..........417 C16
KEYLANA
bvd. Mt Waverley......459 E7
KEYNES
ct. Deer Park...........319 A9
KEYS
av. Brighton East.....455 D15
ct. Narre Warren.....553 C6
rd. Cheltenham.......496 L12
rd. Keysborough......547 H4
rd. Moorabbin..........496 L12
st. Beaumaris.........530 D12
st. Dandenong.........535 K8
st. Frankston..........599 B18
KEYSBOROUGH
av. Keysborough......533 J10
st. Craigieburn........150 D15
KEYSTONE
cr. Kew East............372 K1
ct. Lynbrook............551 F16
KHALIL
av. Dandenong N......536 E1
KHARTOUM
ct. Frankston..........628 C11
st. Burnley..............371 C18
st. Caulfield N.........415 G17
st. W Footscray.......366 J5
KHASSA
pde. Ringwood..........378 F11
KIA
ct. Preston..............327 K2
ri. Frankston S.......627 H15
KIAH
ct. Patterson L........573 K2
mw. Eltham...............288 D7
st. Glen Waverley....420 C16
KIAKA
la. Rowville.............462 K18
KIALLA
av. Glen Iris.............416 H14
ct. Noble Park N.......501 C14
pl. Langwarrin.........629 B8
KIALOA
ct. Narre Warren.....539 B17
ct. Taylors L...........275 K10
KIAMA
cl. Montmorency.....286 G11
cl. Scoresby............462 C6
cl. Vermont S..........420 L11
ct. Mooroolbark......336 J13

ct. Oakleigh E.........458 K11
ct. Rye...................697 C5
dr. Lalor.................241 B6
pl. Cairnlea.............320 A13
rd. Flemington..........33 H2
rd. Werribee............447 G20
st. Glenroy..............280 A9
st. Moorabbin..........496 J9
KIANDRA
cl. Aspendale..........546 B4
cl. Greensbrgh........244 J19
cl. Noble Park..........534 K5
ct. Doncaster E.......331 J18
ct. Frankston...........627 K4
mw. Hampton Pk.......552 B11
st. Mornington.........656 H5
wy. Wyndham Va......446 H14
KIA ORA
av. Mt Martha..........656 C11
av. Upwey...............465 L12
KIA-ORA
pde. Ferntree Gly......464 K3
rd. Reservoir...........282 D12
KIATA
ct. Coolaroo............238 E5
ct. Mt Eliza..............641 K3
ct. Seabrook...........451 A5
KIBO
ct. Cranbourne N....578 B4
KIDDERMINSTER
dr. Wantirna............422 E8
KIDDLE
st. Fawkner.............281 J10
KIDDS
rd. Doveton.............536 G9
KIDGELL
st. Lilydale.............337 L3
KIDMAN
av. Belmont.............706 D4
st. Yarraville...........366 D14
KIELY
av. Werribee...........447 L20
KIERAN
ct. Carrum Downs...575 A15
KIERENS
wy. Chadstone.........458 D4
KIERNAN
av. Ivanhoe.............328 B14
cl. Mill Park............242 J1
rd. Macclesfield.......471 H1
KIERS
av. Mt Waverley......419 H18
ct. Caulfield N.........415 E19
ct. Viewbank...........285 F17
KIEV
wk. Delahey.............275 B14
KIEWA
cl. Croydon Hl.........335 K15
cr. Dallas................238 E12
cr. Keilor................276 L13
ct. Aspendale..........546 H6
ct. Dandenong N......501 L8
ct. Werribee............448 B19
st. Ashwood............418 F14
st. Clifton Hill...........20 G7
st. Clifton Hill...........20 G8
st. Doncaster..........375 E1
KILA
st. Heidelberg W.....284 A19
KILANDER
ct. Ferntree Gly.......464 E6
KILANI
ct. Eltham...............288 F1
KILARA
ct. Croydon.............379 H7
pl. Clarinda.............498 E8
rd. Mentone............531 A10
KILBERRY
av. Springvale S......533 K1
bvd. Hampton Pk.......552 C10
cr. Hallam...............537 H13
KILBIRNIE
cl. Mt Eliza..............641 K7
KILBORN
ct. Kilsyth...............381 G9
ct. Mill Park............242 F7
KILBRIDE
st. Keysborough......535 A12
KILBURN
cr. Frankston..........628 E6
ct. Keysborough......534 D8
ct. Wheelers Hl.......461 D15
gr. Mt Martha..........655 G16
st. Strathmore........280 B17
KILBY
cl. Epping...............241 H4
ct. Campbellfield.....239 A9
ct. Noble Park..........534 L5
rd. Kew East............372 C3
KILCATTEN
ri. Rowville.............503 B7
KILCUNDA
dr. Rowville.............463 G12

KILDAIRE
vw. Cranbourne........603 G8
KILDARE
ct. Frankston..........628 A6
st. Burwood............418 E7
st. Geelong West.....702 E2
st. Hawthorn E........372 F16
KILDRUMMIE
ct. Sorrento............678 H5
KILEE
pl. Avondale Ht.......322 E8
KILEEN
av. Brighton East.....495 B4
KILFERA
ct. Narre Warren.....539 G15
KILGERRON
ct. Nar Warrn S.......553 A15
KILGOUR
ct. Geelong, off
La Trobe Tce......702 K10
st. E Geelong..........703 E12
st. Geelong.............702 K10
st. S Geelong..........702 K10
KILKENNY
ct. Dandenong S.....549 H3
KILLARA
ct. Belmont.............702 A20
ct. Noble Park..........534 G7
ct. Rosebud............684 F18
ct. Werribee............487 A1
mw. Bulleen.............329 E13
rd. Campbellfield.....239 F8
rd. Coldstream........295 E11
rd. Gruyere.............296 B10
rd. Gruyere.............342 L2
st. Box Hill N..........375 B9
st. Lalor..................240 C9
st. Reservoir...........283 A16
st. Sunshine W.......364 K4
KILLARNEY
ct. Berwick.............554 J7
dr. Melton..............227 F17
rd. Templstw Lr......330 B14
st. Rye...................680 E20
KILLARRA
av. Camberwell........417 D5
KILLEARN
av. Pt Lonsdale........710 F3
rd. Launching Pl......345 K20
KILLEEN
av. Blackburn N.......376 B9
st. Sunshine W.......364 K8
KILLERTON
cr. Heidelberg W.....284 A20
KILLIBURY
ct. Templestowe.....331 J11
KILLINGHOLME
dr. Mornington........657 A3
KILLOP
st. Alphington.........327 K19
KILMARNOCK
ct. Hoppers Csg......449 K3
KILMARTIN
pl. Nar Warrn S.......579 B4
st. Essendon...........324 B6
KILMISTON
ct. Frankston S.......627 G20
KILMORE
av. Reservoir...........283 G11
cr. Dallas................238 C12
KILMUIR
ct. Macleod............284 L12
ct. Macleod............285 A12
pl. Melton W...........226 B14
rd. Malvern East......456 F2
KILMUR
rd. Hoppers Csg......449 K2
KILORAN
av. Kilsyth...............380 L3
ct. Templestowe.....330 L5
KILPA
rd. Moorabbin.........497 D13
KILPARA
ct. Mornington........640 H20
KILRUSH
st. Brighton............494 H2
KILSYTH
av. Burwood............418 J6
av. Kilsyth...............381 C8
av. Toorak...............415 C6
KILTO
dle. Greensbrgh........286 C1
st. Box Hill N..........375 C9
KILVINGTON
ct. Berwick.............554 L11
dr. Emerald.............509 E3
dr. Emerald.............509 E6
KILWINNING
ct. St Kilda E..........414 K18
KILWORTH
ct. Noble Park.........534 L5

KIM
cl. Bulleen.............329 E10
cl. Frankston S.......627 F11
cl. Meadow Ht........238 A7
cl. Narre Warren.....539 E19
cl. Wheelers Hl.......461 E18
ct. Altona................408 L14
ct. Seabrook...........450 H6
ct. Sunshine W.......364 B8
st. Diamond Ck.......245 F13
KIMBA
av. Frankston..........628 B4
KIMBARRA
dr. Berwick.............554 D20
st. Clayton S...........498 J5
KIMBER
cl. Ferntree Gly.......463 H5
ct. Dingley Vill........533 C5
st. Burnley.............371 C19
st. Preston.............326 J6
KIMBERLEY
cl. Eltham...............287 C6
ct. Blairgowrie........679 G20
ct. Mt Waverley......418 J12
dr. Chirnside Pk......336 L8
dr. Ferntree Gly......464 B11
rd. Cairnlea.............319 G14
rd. Werribee............446 J13
st. Lalor..................240 G9
wy. Bulleen.............329 J8
KIMBERLY
ct. Berwick.............554 C18
rd. Dandenong S......549 H8
KIMBOLTON
dr. Lysterfield.........464 B15
KIMBURRA
ct. Kurunjang..........227 C12
KIMPTON
ct. Carrum Downs...574 H16
st. Cheltenham.......497 E20
KIMTARA
ct. Somerville.........644 E16
KINANE
st. Brighton............494 G1
KINARRA
ct. Mooroolbark......337 D16
ct. Springvale S......533 L5
KINBRAE
dr. Research...........289 D10
KINCAID
ct. Ferntree Gly.......464 A6
KINCUMBER
dr. Croydon.............380 G2
dr. Glen Waverley....420 G20
KINDALE
ct. Avondale Ht.......322 E7
ct. Highton.............705 J6
KINDER
st. Campbellfield.....239 E7
KINDRA
cl. Portsea.............678 B5
ct. Vermont S.........420 F10
KING
cct. Caroline Spr.......318 B8
dr. Hillside.............231 J20
la. St Kilda, off
Albert St...........414 C17
pde. Knoxfield...........463 D4
rd. Emerald.............469 A19
rd. Harkaway...........539 L13
rd. Harkaway...........541 A15
st. Airport W...........278 K14
st. Bacchus Msh.....221 K18
st. Balwyn.............372 L10
st. Balwyn.............373 A10
st. Bayswater..........423 G2
st. Belmont.............706 D1
st. Blackburn..........376 C15
st. Braybrook..........366 C1
st. Brunswick E.......326 C17
st. Bulleen.............329 G10
st. Camberwell........416 L3
st. Camberwell........417 A3
st. Coburg..............325 E3
st. Croydon S.........379 L12
st. Dallas................238 J11
st. Dandenong.........536 B7
st. Doncaster..........331 B13
st. Doncaster E.......331 J14
st. Elsternwick........455 B4
st. Eltham...............288 C13
st. Essendon...........323 F4
st. Fitzroy N...........326 C17
st. Glen Iris.............416 G11
st. Glenroy..............279 L3
st. Hawthorn E........416 G1
st. Ivanhoe East......328 H14
st. Lalor..................241 F9
st. Melbourne.............1 A18
st. Melbourne............23 F4
st. Mentone............530 J9
st. Montrose...........382 E9
st. Mornington........640 C14

STREETS

st. Mt Evelyn 339 J14
st. Nunawading 376 C15
st. Oakleigh 458 B13
st. Pakenham 585 A7
st. Prahran 32 D18
st. Prahran 414 H9
st. Queenscliff.........708 G18
st. Richmond 25 L14
st. Ringwood E 379 A8
st. St Kilda E..........414 G16
st. Sandringham 495 B12
st. Somerton 194 G16
st. Sorrento 678 J14
st. Templestowe 331 B13
st. Werribee 447 H18
st. W Melbourne 1 A18
st. W Melbourne 23 D1
st. Yarra Glen 208 G20
st. Yarra Glen 252 L2
KINGAROY
rd. Sunshine 365 F5
KING ARTHUR
dr. Glen Waverley 420 L18
KINGBURN
ct. Templestowe 332 C15
KING DAVID
ct. Hampton Pk 551 H10
KINGDOM
av. Kings Park 274 L20
ct. Roxburgh Pk 194 B4
KING EDWARD
av. Albion 364 J1
av. Albion 365 A1
KINGFIELD
ct. Camberwell 417 K3
KINGFISHER
av. Rosebud W 698 K3
ct. Carrum Downs ...600 L2
ct. Kings Park 274 L16
ct. Werribee 447 L4
dr. Diamond Ck 245 D12
dr. Doveton 536 J4
dr. Seabrook 450 J7
gdn. Brunswick E 326 C12
pl. S Morang 243 J4
KING GEORGE
av. Mornington 640 B17
pde. Dandenong 535 F5
KINGHAM
st. Newport 410 G4
KINGLOCH
pde. Wantirna 422 H6
KING ORCHID
dr. Langwarrin 601 D19
KINGS
arc. Armadale, off
High St 415 F12
cl. Frankston N 600 C8
ct. Cranbourne 577 L17
ct. Frankston 600 B16
ct. Jan Juc 711 D15
ct. Oakleigh E 458 L11
ct. Pt Lonsdale 707 G19
ct. Wantirna S 422 C19
la. Geelong West 702 J3
pl. S Melbourne 30 G4
pl. S Melbourne 413 J2
rd. Delahey 275 E10
rd. Delahey 275 E9
rd. Emerald 509 F3
rd. Kangaroo Grnd 248 D9
rd. Kings Park 319 E3
rd. Panton Hill 248 D9
rd. St Albans 319 E3
rd. Sydenham 275 E9
rd. Taylors L 233 G20
rd. Taylors L 275 E6
wy. Melbourne 3 A4
wy. Melbourne 30 H5
wy. Melbourne 413 J2
wy. Southbank 3 A8
wy. Southbank 23 K15
wy. Southbank 30 C1
wy. Southbank 413 J2
wy. S Melbourne 3 A4
wy. S Melbourne 30 C1
wy. S Melbourne 30 H5
wy. S Melbourne 413 J2
wy. Waurn Ponds 705 B9
KINGSBRIDGE
cct. Cairnlea 319 K13
ct. Croydon Hl 335 G15
KINGSBURGH
la. Lilydale 293 L18
la. Lilydale 294 B19
KINGSBURY
ct. Diamond Ck 245 L7
dr. Bundoora 284 C10
dr. Heidelberg Ht 284 C10
dr. Heidelberg W 284 C10
dr. Macleod 284 C10
la. Dandenong 536 A10

KINGSCLERE
av. Keysborough 534 F7
st. Vermont 421 D3
KINGS COLLEGE
dr. Bayswater 423 D10
KINGS DOMAIN
Caroline Spr 274 B15
KINGSFIELD
wy. Truganina 405 E13
KINGSFORD
av. Coburg N 281 C14
av. Melton S 268 H5
st. Bayswater 422 L9
st. Braybrook 365 L4
st. Lalor 241 D6
st. Laverton 407 C15
wy. Roxburgh Pk 194 C11
KINGSHOTT
cl. Williamstown 410 K16
KINGSLAND
cl. Dingley Vill 533 G10
KINGSLEY
av. Point Cook 450 C6
av. Vermont 420 L4
cl. Rowville 462 H14
cr. Mont Albert 374 F13
ct. Mt Eliza 626 D17
ct. Thomastown 241 G15
ct. Toorak 415 D3
dr. Sunbury 143 A16
gr. Kew East 372 E4
gr. Mt Waverley 458 L10
pde. Carnegie 456 E11
pl. Delahey 275 E16
pl. Melton W 226 A15
rd. Airport W 278 G15
rd. Reservoir 282 D12
st. Camberwell 372 L19
st. Camberwell 373 A19
st. Elwood 454 F7
st. Ivanhoe 327 L17
st. St Albans 320 C8
KINGS LYNN
pl. Wheelers Hl 461 B9
KINGSMEAD
cl. Sunshine N 321 C7
ct. Dingley Vill 533 D4
KINGSMERE
cl. Gladstone Pk 237 A16
dr. Berwick 554 K19
KINGSMILL
tce. Berwick 554 C18
KINGSNORTH
st. Doncaster 374 C1
KING SOUND
cl. Waterways 547 E3
KINGSTON
av. Ascot Vale 367 G1
av. Nar Warrn S 578 D1
av. Nar Warrn S 578 D2
av. Pakenham 585 D7
bvd. Hoppers Csg 405 A14
cl. Mornington 657 B6
cl. Thomastown 240 E17
ct. Chelsea 547 B15
dr. Dingley Vill 532 J5
hts. Frankston 628 D7
pl. Richmond 26 B7
rd. Clarinda 498 B16
rd. Heatherton 497 G15
rd. Langwarrin 630 B4
rd. Surrey Hills 373 H17
st. Ferntree Gly 463 J5
st. Glen Iris 416 E17
st. Grovedale 706 D12
st. Hampton 495 D7
st. Keilor Park 278 A14
st. Malvern East 416 E17
st. Moolap 704 K17
st. Mordialloc 532 A13
st. Mt Waverley 418 H13
st. Richmond 26 F20
st. Yarraville 366 K15
KINGSTON HEATH
ct. Craigieburn 150 C15
KINGSTON TOWN
cl. Oakleigh 458 B8
cr. Mill Park 242 H11
KINGSVALE
ct. Cranbourne 577 L11
KINGSVILLE
st. Kingsville 366 J13
KINGSWAY
Armadale 415 F12
Glen Waverley 460 C2
Melton 226 K17
Moorabbin 497 E8
dr. Lalor 240 H7
KINGSWOOD
av. Mt Waverley 458 L9
cr. Noble Park N 501 D17
dr. Chirnside Pk 337 F3
dr. Craigieburn 150 G15

dr. Dingley Vill 533 E7
rd. Cheltenham 496 K17
KING WILLIAM
st. Broadmeadows ..238 B14
st. Fitzroy 18 L16
st. Reservoir 283 A14
KINKA
ct. Bulleen 329 J12
pl. Greensbrgh 243 H18
KINKEAD
ct. Endeavour Hl 537 H5
KINKORA
rd. Blackburn 375 G13
rd. Hawthorn 371 J14
rd. Melton 268 F2
rd. Reservoir 283 D16
KINLEY
pl. Hillside, off
Kanmore Cr 232 G19
KINLOCH
av. Jan Juc 711 D13
av. Mont Albert 374 C13
cl. Wheelers Hl 461 C14
ct. Craigieburn 150 L1
ct. Wyndham Va 446 E7
gdn. Eltham 287 L9
gdn. Endeavour Hl 503 H17
gr. Greenvale 193 G17
rd. Melton 268 F2
KINLOCK
av. Murrumbeena 457 A13
st. Macleod 284 L12
st. Macleod 285 A12
KINLORA
av. Epping 197 G15
ct. Springvale S 534 A6
dr. Somerville 645 B16
KINNAIRD
st. Jacana 237 K18
KINNANE
cr. Sunshine 321 E20
KINNARD
ct. Taylors L 233 B18
KINNEAR
ct. Montmorency 286 L11
st. Footscray 367 C4
KINNEIL
st. Sorrento 679 C12
KINNON
av. Belmont 706 J3
KINNOUL
av. Caulfield N 415 C17
av. Keysborough 534 L10
KINNOULL
gr. Glen Waverley 459 L2
KINRADE
st. Hughesdale 457 E14
KINROSS
av. Caulfield N 415 G20
av. Edithvale 546 K9
ct. Greenvale 237 D2
ct. Pakenham 584 K1
rd. Tecoma 466 E8
st. Belmont 706 D2
st. Hampton E 495 J7
st. Mt Martha 655 L19
st. Pascoe Vale 280 J19
KINSALE
cr. Balwyn 374 C11
cr. Mont Albert N 374 C11
st. Reservoir 282 G13
st. Seaford 600 B3
vw. Berwick 553 G14
KINSELLA
ct. Pakenham 584 G6
KINSLEY
ct. Belmont 706 C6
KINSMEAD
st. Waurn Ponds 705 D15
KINTA
cl. Berwick 554 D18
cl. Yallambie 286 C12
ct. Croydon N 336 D12
KINTAL
ct. Frankston 600 D16
KINTBURY
cl. Wantirna 422 F15
KINTERBURY
dr. Kings Park 318 L2
KINTHER
ct. Highton 705 H3
KINTON
ct. Ringwood 379 A4
KINTORE
cl. Sunbury 143 E4
cr. Box Hill 374 G16
st. Camberwell 372 J17
st. Springvale 500 A13
KINTYRE
ct. Greenvale 193 A20
KINWAL
ct. Moorabbin 496 H11

KINWENDY
rd. Boneo 700 K12
KIONGA
st. Clayton 499 C3
KIORA
st. Altona Mdw 407 F20
st. Essendon 324 C6
st. Pt Lonsdale 710 E5
KIPARRA
cl. St Albans 320 L6
cl. St Albans 321 A6
KIPEN
dr. Hawthorn E 416 C5
KIPLING
av. Mooroolbark 337 E19
av. Mooroolbark 337 G19
ct. Bundoora 242 K20
ct. Burwood E 420 C8
pl. Carrum Downs 574 K18
pl. Delahey 275 D16
pl. Frankston 600 C19
st. Carrum 573 B7
st. Cremorne 26 C17
st. Cremorne 370 G19
st. Moonee Pnd 324 F15
st. N Melbourne 34 J11
st. St Kilda 414 F16
KIPPAX
ct. Mt Waverley 458 L3
KIPPENROSS
dr. Nar Warrn S 553 E20
dr. Nar Warrn S 553 F20
dr. Nar Warrn S 579 E1
KIPPING
ri. S Morang 243 G3
KIRA
cl. Frankston 600 F20
ct. Forest Hill 420 C5
KIRAMI
ct. Wandana Ht 701 D20
KIRBISTER
st. Pascoe Vale 280 L17
KIRBY
cl. Greenvale 192 K17
ct. Ferntree Gly 463 L4
ct. St Albans 320 C7
ct. Werribee 447 C18
st. Reservoir 283 H16
KIRCALDY
ct. Greenvale 193 D20
KIREEP
rd. Balwyn 373 J12
KIRK
ct. Tullamarine 278 F6
pl. Geelong, off
Little Malop St ..703 C8
rd. Cockatoo 471 H10
rd. Pt Lonsdale 710 D4
st. Ascot Vale 323 J19
st. Kensington 33 C12
st. Noble Park 534 J1
st. Ringwood 378 C15
KIRKBRIDE
wy. Craigieburn 194 F1
KIRKBY
ct. Frankston S 626 K14
st. Coburg 326 A7
KIRKDALE
st. Brunswick E 326 B14
KIRKFELL
ct. Berwick 554 A7
KIRKFORD
dr. Mooroolbark 337 C8
KIRKHAM
ct. Berwick 554 J5
dr. Greenvale 193 D20
dr. Greenvale 193 G19
rd. Belgrave S 506 B11
rd. Dandenong S 535 G14
rd. Murrumbeena 457 C12
rd.w, Keysborough 535 A13
KIRKMORE
av. Jan Juc 711 D14
KIRKPATRICKS
rd. Macclesfield 470 F1
KIRKS
la. Melbourne 1 K11
la. Melbourne 24 A7
KIRKSTALL
cl. Frankston S 627 B19
KIRKSTONE
rd. Point Cook 450 H12
rd. Point Cook 450 H12
KIRKTON
dr. Kurunjang 227 C10
dr. Kurunjang 227 E11
KIRKWALL
ct. Glen Waverley 460 F11
KIRKWELL
ct. Greenvale 237 E3
KIRKWOOD
av. Sandringham 495 E17
av. Seaford 599 E10

cr. Hampton Pk 552 C1
ct. Montrose 381 K1
dr. Camberwell ....417 C
st. Beaumaris ....530 D
KIRRA
cl. Nar Warrn S 552 F1
ct. Croydon ....379 F
ct. Kurunjang 227 E1
ct. Pakenham ....584 H
ct. Springvale S 499 G2
KIRRAWEE
av. Wantirna S 422 L1
av. Wantirna S 423 A1
ct. Noble Park ....534 H
KIRRI
st. Rye ....697 C
KIRRIBILLI
av. Keysborough .....534 F
cl. Craigieburn 193
cl. Langwarrin 602 C1
KIRRILEE
ct. Berwick 553 L1
KIRRUM
cl. Wantirna S 422 K2
KIRSTEN
ct. Mooroolbark 337 B1
KIRSTIN
cl. Oakleigh S ....497 H
KIRSTINA
rd. Glen Waverley ....460 D
KIRTAIN
dr. Croydon ....335 H
KIRTON
ct. Doncaster 331 B1
KIRWAN
av. Lalor ....241 J
av. Roxburgh Pk ......194 B
KIRWANA
gr. Montmorency ......287 B
KIRWIN
av. Eltham 288
KIRWOOD
st. Blairgowrie ....695 H
KISMET
cl. Ringwood 379
rd. Sunbury 143
KITARA
ct. Frankston 628
KITCHEN
rd. Beaconsfld Up ....542 L
rd. Dandenong S 550
KITCHENER
gr. Preston ....283 C
pde. Cockatoo 511
rd. Croydon 380
rd. Pascoe Vale ....280 H
rd. Silvan ....384 K
rd. Tecoma ....466 E
st. Balwyn ....372 K
st. Balwyn ....373 A
st. Box Hill S ....375 A
st. Box Hill S 419
st. Broadmeadows ....238 B
st. Brunswick W 324
st. Kew East 372
st. Mentone ....530 L
KITCHIN
rd. S Morang ....199 B
KITE
av. Bayswater N ....380 D
ct. Werribee 447
KITEROA
st. Belmont ....702 C
KITMONT
st. Murrumbeena 457
KITSON
cr. Airport W 278
cr. Templstw Lr 330
ct. Altona Mdw 451
ct. Rowville 503
rd. Clayton S 498
st. Frankston ....599 C
st. Ringwood ....378 H
KITTY
st. Clematis 508
KITTYHAWK
rd. Laverton ....406 C
st. Airport W ....278 D
KITZ
la. Melbourne 1
la. Melbourne 23
KIUNA
rd. Keilor N 276
KIWI
ct. Chelsea Ht 547
ct. Mill Park 242
rt. Keilor Dn 275
KLAUER
st. Frankston 599
st. Seaford 599
KLEAD
ct. Ringwood N 378

EIN
Roxburgh Pk......194 A10
EINE
Noble Park.........534 F2
EINERT
. Boronia.............423 D15
EMKE
Grovedale 706 A12
IM
Burnside............318 D6
AITH
Ringwood E.......378 L12
Ringwood E.......379 A12
APDALE
Greenvale 193 H18
APP
Altona North 409 E1
Preston.............282 E20
APTON
. Beaconsfld Up....541 J11
EALE
Box Hill N 375 A9
EE
Croydon N 335 K12
EEN
Fitzroy N 326 E20
EES
Pk Orchards.......333 L13
Pk Orchards.......334 A15
Warrandyte........333 L13
ELL
Mulgrave 500 F4
IGHT
. Herne Hill............701 L4
. Sunshine N........321 D9
Roxburgh Pk......193 L15
Donvale 333 B10
Endeavour Hl 537 F9
Ferntree Gly 463 F7
Hillside 231 J19
Meadow Ht........238 B3
Geelong, off Malop St...........703 F8
v. Williamstown.....411 A15
Dandenong N.....501 G12
Newcomb..........704 E18
Aberfeldie 323 E8
Blairgowrie 696 A3
Clayton S...........498 H5
Coburg N............281 G16
Elwood 454 F3
Watsonia 285 G5
Williamstown.....411 B16
IGHTON
Airport W...........278 D16
Mornington........656 J3
IGHTS
Glen Waverley....421 A17
Gembrook 512 K11
Mannerim 707 A1
Pt Lonsdale........707 G4
. Kings Park.........274 L18
IGHTSBRIDGE
Altona Mdw 451 E5
Nunawading 376 K12
Glen Waverley....420 B16
Narre Warren.....539 A14
Somerville 645 B18
OLE
Hadfield.............281 A10
OLLBROOK
Highton 701 F20
OTT
Langwarrin 629 D3
Safety Bch 669 C13
OWING
Cranbourne W ...577 H18
OWLE
Hurstbridge 202 K15
OWLES
Dandenong S.....550 K7
Dandenong S.....551 A7
Northcote 326 J19
OWSLEY
Wantirna............422 B12
OX
Altona Mdw 451 C4
Kurunjang..........227 F8
Sunbury 143 G9
Melbourne...........2 D6
Melbourne..........24 C4
Knoxfield 463 B7
Melbourne............2 E5
Melbourne..........24 C4
Blairgowrie 695 L5
Canterbury.........372 L15
Canterbury.........373 A15
Carrum Downs...574 K16
Malvern East......416 F17
Noble Park.........534 G3
Reservoir...........282 D14
Yarraville 367 D15

KNUTSFORD
st. Balwyn 373 D14
KOALA
av. Badger Creek.....258 F13
av. Nunawading 376 K18
cr. Westmeadows...236 G13
ct. Chelsea..............547 B15
ct. Doncaster E.......375 G2
ct. Frankston S 627 E9
ct. Keysborough 534 E7
ct. Somerville 645 D17
rd. Seville...............385 G1
rd. Wandin East 385 G1
wk. S Morang 243 K4
KODRE
st. St Albans...........319 J4
KOEL
ct. Carrum Downs...600 J3
pl. Werribee............447 L5
KOETONG
ct. Mulgrave 500 J3
pde. Mt Eliza.............625 K19
KOGARAH
ct. Keysborough 534 G9
KOGIA
st. Mt Eliza..............641 J3
KOHRY
la. Newport 410 K4
KOHURAU
ct. Taylors L 276 D10
KOITAKI
ct. Heidelberg W.....284 B20
KOKARIBB
rd. Carnegie 456 J7
KOKODA
ct. Boronia..............424 D3
ct. Lalor..................241 F6
rd. Williamstown.....411 A15
st. Heidelberg W.....328 C3
st. Sorrento 679 D16
KOLAN
ct. Werribee............447 G7
KOLINDA
cr. Rosebud W........683 E20
KOLIVAS
ct. Hillside 274 E2
KOLONGA
ct. Greensbrgh........285 L10
ct. Vermont S 420 F11
KOLOR
wy. Templestowe 331 E14
KOLORA
cr. Mt Eliza..............641 L3
rd. Heidelberg W.....284 C17
KOMBI
rd. Clayton S...........499 E6
KONAC
ct. Berwick 553 G2
KONAGADERRA
rd. Oaklands Jctn 191 E1
KONG
ct. Hampton Pk.......551 L8
KONRAD
ct. Ferntree Gly 463 E6
ct. Bentleigh E 497 A3
KONRADS
cr. Highton 705 H4
cr. Mill Park 242 D9
ct. Truganina 405 G14
KONTEK
wy. Sydenham 274 J4
KOOKABURRA
av. Tecoma 466 D10
av. Werribee............448 B10
la. Mt Evelyn...........339 D11
la. Yellingbo 387 J18
st. Altona................408 F20
st. Frankston 599 D14
wk. S Morang 243 K3
KOOKABURRA DELL
Upwey...............465 K10
KOOLENA
cl. Clayton S...........499 F11
KOOLKUNA
av. Doncaster...........374 G2
la. Hampton 494 L8
KOOLUNA
ct. Frankston 600 F15
KOOLYA
ct. Rye 697 A7
ct. Yallambie...........286 C12
KOOMALOO
ct. Carrum Downs...574 K18
KOOMBA
rd. Wantirna............421 L9
KOOMBAHLA
ct. Rowville.............503 A6
ct. Werribee............448 G18
KOOMBOOLOOMBA
ct. Lilydale..............337 L2
KOOMEELA
dr. Torquay.............712 B1

KOONALDA
av. Glen Waverley....460 B9
gr. Dandenong N.....501 G20
rd. Gladstone Pk 279 A1
KOONAWARRA
st. Clayton 458 L16
wy. Diamond Ck.......245 G8
KOONUNG
ct. Doncaster..........330 B19
rd. Blackburn N.......375 K10
st. Balwyn N 374 A1
st. Dandenong N.....501 F14
KOONYA
av. Blairgowrie 679 D19
KOORA
ct. Yallambie...........286 C11
KOORALI
cl. Noble Park.........534 D5
st. Keilor.................276 F9
KOORANG
pl. Berwick 553 G6
KOORINGA
cr. Wheelers Hl 460 H16
ct. Rosebud.............684 F18
pl. Torquay.............711 K6
rd. Carnegie 456 F11
KOORINGAL
gr. Brighton 454 L9
rd. Blairgowrie 680 C20
rd. Upwey...............465 E14
KOORNALLA
cr. Mt Eliza..............625 G17
KOORNANG
rd. Carnegie 456 H13
rd. Ormond.............456 H13
rd. Scoresby 462 E10
KOORNONG
cr. N Warrandyte.....290 F13
KOORONG
av. Bayswater N 380 J19
av. Rosebud............683 K20
ct. Highton 705 G4
KOOROORA
ct. Vermont 421 A6
KOOS
rd. Kangaroo Grnd ..248 D7
KOO WEE RUP
rd. Pakenham 585 B19
KOO WEE RUP NORTH-NAR NAR GOON
rd. Nr Nr Goon 586 L18
KOOYONG
cl. Hampton Pk.......551 J11
cl. Hawthorn E.........416 D8
ct. Taylors Hill.........274 C8
pl. Highton 701 E9
rd. Armadale 415 F11
rd. Caulfield 455 D10
rd. Caulfield N 415 E20
rd. Caulfield S 455 D10
rd. Elsternwick 455 D10
rd. Gardenvale 455 D10
rd. Geelong.............702 K2
rd. Toorak...............415 F11
KOOYONGA
gr. Mornington........656 D3
KOOYONGKOOT
rd. Hawthorn...........372 B20
rd. Hawthorn...........416 A3
KORIELLA
dr. Sunbury 143 C11
KORINA
ct. Langwarrin 629 C7
KOROIT
av. Dallas 238 D11
pl. Geelong.............703 D11
pl. Taylors L 276 B8
st. Nunawading 376 D14
KORONG
ct. Broadmeadows..238 C15
ct. Mornington........640 L17
ct. Mornington........641 A17
rd. Heidelberg W.....284 D17
KORONIS
rd. Keilor.................276 K5
KOROROIT
app. Caroline Spr.......318 B3
ct. Kurunjang..........227 G12
st. Albion.................364 L2
st. Albion.................365 A2
st. W Footscray 366 D13
KOROROIT CREEK
rd. Altona................407 L9
rd. Altona................409 C10
rd. Williamstown.....410 A12
rd. Williamstn N 410 A12
KOROWA
st. Rye 697 C7
st. Sunshine W........364 J3
KORRA
ct. Blairgowrie 696 B7

KOSCIUSKO
ct. Lalor..................240 H9
ct. Wheelers Hl 460 K9
rd. Balwyn N 329 G18
KOSKY
st. Sunshine W.......364 K3
KOSSECKS
pl. Belmont.............706 J6
KOTOR
cl. Mt Martha..........656 B14
KOVAL
ct. Springvale S 533 K7
KOWA
ct. Greensbrgh........244 B17
KOWHAI
cl. Altona Mdw 452 A3
KRAFT
ct. Pakenham 584 G4
KRAMBRUK
st. Sunshine W.......364 J4
KRAMER
dr. Berwick 554 D6
st. Werribee............448 A9
KRIEGEL
wy. Dandenong N.....502 C10
KRIS
ct. Doncaster E.......332 G7
ct. Melton W...........226 A19
KRISHNA
ct. Noble Park.........535 B5
KRISTEN
cl. Frankston S 627 D20
cl. Frankston S 643 D1
cl. Glen Waverley....421 A20
ct. Boronia..............423 K11
KRISTIAN
ct. Mt Martha..........656 H6
KRISTINA
ct. Pakenham 584 H1
KRISTINE
ct. Cheltenham 497 G20
KRISTY
ct. Jan Juc..............711 C15
KRITHIA
st. Coburg N............281 G12
KRONA
ri. Keilor Ldg...........276 B3
KRONE
st. Mordialloc 531 L16
KROWERA
st. Mooroolbark......337 A14
KRUSES
rd. N Warrandyte.....290 D11
KRYSTAL
ct. Mooroolbark......336 K12
KRYSTAL GLENN
gdn. Boronia.............424 G14
KUALA
cl. St Albans...........275 J19
KUBBA
rd. Ringwood N.......377 L6
KUBIS
av. Aspendale..........546 D4
cr. Dingley Vill.........533 A6
dr. Ringwood N.......377 L5
KUBURA
pl. St Albans...........321 A6
KUEBLER
st. Glen Waverley....420 B18
KULANDA
ct. Patterson L........573 L6
KULIN
cl. Cranbourne........578 C19
KULNINE
av. Mitcham 377 J17
KULPA
ct. Kurunjang..........227 E13
KULSI
ct. Croydon Hl 335 G13
KUMALA
dr. Somerville 644 E19
rd. Bayswater..........423 C8
KUMALI
ct. Noble Park.........534 K5
KUMARA
pl. Clayton 459 A18
KUMBA
ct. S Morang 198 L9
KUMBADA
av. Upwey...............466 A12
KUNAT
st. Deer Park...........318 J16
KUNDY
cl. Greensbrgh........244 C19
KUNYUNG
rd. Mt Eliza..............625 G17
KUNZEA
cl. Meadow Ht........193 K19
ct. Mt Waverley 419 C20
KURANDA
cr. Berwick 553 K3
cr. Oakleigh E 458 K11

ct. Wattle Glen 246 G9
st. Lalor..................240 F10
st. Langwarrin 629 D9
KURANGA
ct. Mornington........640 B20
rd. Viewbank...........285 K17
KURDIAN
ct. Yallambie...........286 D12
KURINGAI
rd. Tootgarook 698 D7
KURINGGAI
cr. Noble Park.........534 F6
KURNAI
av. Reservoir...........282 C12
KURNEH
pl. South Yarra.........31 G4
pl. South Yarra 414 D2
KURNWILL
pl. Berwick 553 K14
KURONG
av. Frankston 628 A1
KURRAJONG
av. Croydon 380 J3
av. Glen Waverley....460 A7
av. St Kilda E...........414 L16
av. St Kilda E...........415 A16
cl. Viewbank...........285 K19
cr. Melton S............268 F7
cr. Watsonia N 285 H2
ct. Cranbourne N 578 B4
ct. Frankston S 627 H12
ct. Grovedale 706 F9
dr. Altona Mdw 407 K20
rd. Delahey 275 C10
rd. Narre Warren.....539 D20
st. Bentleigh E 457 F17
vw. Mill Park 243 E10
wy. Blackburn N.......375 G10
KURRAK
rd. Plenty 200 C20
rd. Yarrambat..........200 C20
rd. Yarrambat..........244 C1
KURRAWA
cr. Patterson L........573 K10
KURRUP
st. Mt Martha..........655 L16
KURT
pl. Cranbourne........603 K3
pl. Noble Park.........534 K6
KURUNG
dr. Kings Park.........275 A18
KURUNJANG
dr. Kurunjang..........227 A15
KUTCHER
ct. Sunshine W.......364 B8
KUYURA
rd. Mt Evelyn...........383 D3
KWINANA
ct. Campbellfield 239 F18
ct. Ivanhoe 328 B8
st. Glen Waverley....419 L17
KYA
cl. Ferntree Gly 423 K19
KYABRAM
st. Coolaroo.............238 F4
KYAK COURSE
Delahey 275 F12
KYA-LAMI
ri. Mooroolbark......337 L18
KYAMBA
ct. Bayswater N 379 K14
KYARRA
rd. Glen Iris.............416 H11
st. Hampton 495 C11
KYBERD
ct. Chelsea..............547 B19
KYBROLYDE
ct. Research 289 B4
KYEAMBA
gr. Toorak...............415 H6
KYEEMA
av. Highton 701 C16
av. Highton 701 E16
KYILLA
ct. Frankston S 627 B5
KYLE
av. Belmont.............702 F17
la. Hopetoun Park....224 D19
pl. Croydon N 335 L11
rd. Altona North 410 A2
wy. Bacchus Msh......221 J12
KYLIE
cl. Mooroolbark......337 K18
cl. Mornington........641 D16
ct. Hallam...............537 K13
ct. Hampton Pk.......551 K12
ct. Pakenham 585 B3
la. Seville E.............343 A5
pl. Cheltenham 496 L13
pl. Gladstone Pk 279 A3
pl. Montmorency 287 A9
KYLTA
rd. Heidelberg W.....284 C17

KYM
pl. Melton...269 A2
KYME
pl. Port Melb...412 L5
KYMME
ct. Glen Waverley...421 A20
KYNE
pl. Eltham...288 F4
KYNETON
av. Reservoir...283 F11
cct. Caroline Spr...318 C8
la. Caroline Spr...318 C8
KYNOCH
la. Maribyrnong...322 J16
st. Deer Park...319 C14
KYNUNA
st. Nar Warrn S...578 L2
KYORA
ct. Melton...268 G2
dr. Kew East...372 K2
pde. Balwyn N...372 L1
pde. Balwyn N...373 A1
KYOTO
ct. Rowville...463 B14
KYRA
cl. Lilydale...338 J13
KYRELI
cl. Donvale...333 C11
KYRENIA
ct. Warrandyte...333 B6
KYRIE
ct. Carrum Downs...601 B3
KYUP
st. Mt Eliza...625 K20

L

LAANE
av. Rosanna...329 B2
LAANECOORIE
dr. Lysterfield...464 A16
LABASSA
ct. Narre Warren...539 E15
gr. Caulfield N...415 C18
wy. Seabrook...451 A4
LABILLIERE
st. Maddingley...263 G1
LABRENT
ct. Mt Martha...655 E20
LABUAN
pl. Wantirna...422 D12
st. Sorrento...679 E16
LABURNUM
ct. Brighton...455 A19
gr. Doveton...537 B10
pl. Hillside...273 J7
pl. Rockbank...273 J7
st. Blackburn...375 G15
st. Brighton...455 A20
st. Parkdale...531 H13
LACE
st. Eumemmerring...536 J15
LACEBARK
ct. Oakleigh S...498 A9
rd. Delahey...275 B10
st. Doveton...536 K8
LACENET
av. Frankston N...600 D11
LACEY
pl. Melbourne...2 L10
pl. Melbourne...24 G4
st. Croydon...380 B3
st. Lalor...241 J11
LACEYS
rd. Cottles Br...203 J10
rd. Hurstbridge...203 J10
rd. Panton Hill...203 J10
LACHAN
pl. Keysborough...534 C7
LACHLAN
cl. Cranbourne N...577 L7
cr. Roxburgh Pk...194 C7
ct. Keilor Park...278 A13
ct. Pakenham...558 K20
ct. Sunbury...143 B5
ct. Werribee...447 F8
dr. Endeavour Hl...537 G1
gra. Bulleen...329 H9
la. Taylors Hill...274 K12
rd. Boronia...424 K13
rd. Melton S...268 D10
rd. Sunshine W...364 F5
st. Bundoora...284 E2
st. Mentone...531 F5
LACKENHEATH
ct. Dingley Vill...533 C4
dr. Tullamarine...278 K1

LACY
st. Avondale Ht...322 C16
st. Braybrook...322 B19
st. Selby...467 D16
LADBROKE
st. Epping...197 L16
LADD
ct. Bacchus Msh...221 K13
rd. Emerald...510 D11
sq. Emerald...510 E13
st. Bundoora...285 C7
st. Watsonia...285 C7
LADDS
la. Melbourne...17 K18
LADE
av. Kilsyth...381 C12
ct. Ringwood...378 G7
ct. Rowville...463 E20
LADNER
ct. Chadstone...458 E4
LADONGA
pl. Rowville...462 K17
LADY BARLOW
ct. Patterson L...547 H19
LADY BETTY
pde. Viewbank...285 G18
LADY BEVERLEY
cct. Somerville...644 E17
LADY BRASSEYS
dr. Kew...372 J8
LADY EMILY
wy. Skye...601 G6
LADY HASTINGS
la. E Melbourne...25 J5
LADY LOCHS
dr. Kew...372 H8
LADY NELSON
cr. Altona Mdw...451 L3
dr. Sorrento...679 A14
wk. Patterson L...547 G20
wy. Taylors L...275 F8
LADY PENRHYN
av. Mill Park...242 E3
ct. Cranbourne W...603 H1
dr. Wyndham Va...446 G6
LADY ROSE
cr. Sydenham...275 C7
LADYS
wk. Ferntree Gly...464 K3
wk. Tremont...464 K3
LADY WELLINGTON
ct. Patterson L...547 H19
LAE
ct. Ashburton...417 H17
ct. Herne Hill...702 A2
st. Heidelberg W...327 L3
st. W Footscray...366 E13
LAEMMLE
st. Dandenong N...501 G17
LAFFAN
ct. Broadmeadows...238 D19
LAFITTE
ct. Lalor...240 F10
LAFRANK
st. Burwood...419 A10
LAGARNA
dr. Kurunjang...226 G13
dr. Kurunjang...226 G14
LAGEN
ct. Bundoora...283 L1
LAGGAN
ct. Endeavour Hl...503 H17
LAGNICOURT
st. Hampton...495 C6
LAGO
cl. Keilor Dn...276 A14
LAGOON
la. Port Melb...29 A9
pl. Patterson L...573 G11
LAGOONA
ct. Blackburn...376 B20
LAGUNA
cl. Keilor Ldg...276 C4
pl. Grovedale...706 E8
LAHA
cr. Preston...283 G18
LAHINCH
dr. Fingal...698 C14
st. Broadmeadows...238 B19
st. Broadmeadows...280 B1
st. Preston...327 D3
LAHONA
av. Bentleigh E...496 G3
LAHY
st. St Albans...319 G5
LAIDLAW
ct. Keysborough...534 C7
ct. Vermont...377 J20
LAING
ct. Forest Hill...420 E6
pl. Macleod...285 B11
st. Mont Albert...374 E13

LAINIE
av. Keysborough...534 C12
ct. Wantirna S...422 B17
LAIRA
st. Geelong West...702 F6
LAIRD
cl. Aspendale Gdn...546 H5
ct. Heidelberg...328 L7
dr. Altona Mdw...451 K2
pl. Narre Warren...539 A15
st. Croydon...336 J19
LAITY
st. Richmond...26 H6
LAKALA
cl. Hampton Pk...552 D9
rd. Seville...342 B15
LAKE
av. Mitcham...377 F14
av. Pascoe Vale...280 G11
dr. Dingley Vill...532 H6
dr. Waurn Ponds...705 D9
gr. Coburg N...281 H18
rd. Blackburn...376 A17
rd. Forest Hill...376 C19
rd. Nunawading...376 C19
st. Avondale Ht...322 A9
st. Burnside...274 E18
st. Carnegie...456 E7
st. Caroline Spr...274 B20
st. Geelong...703 F9
st. Reservoir...282 E10
st. Geelong, off Park St...703 F9
tr. Lysterfield...504 J13
tr. Lysterfield...504 L18
LAKE BOGA
av. Deer Park...318 K16
LAKE EDGE
dr. Keysborough...533 L12
LAKE EYRE
pl. Caroline Spr...317 K7
LAKEFIELD
wy. Cairnlea...319 F11
LAKE KING
cir. Waterways...547 E1
LAKELAND
ct. Dingley Vill...533 B1
ct. Pt Lonsdale...707 F19
dr. Doreen...156 K13
LAKE LOGAN
wy. Caroline Spr...317 K5
LAKE PARK
ct. Lysterfield S...504 B15
LAKER
dr. Pt Lonsdale...710 D7
LAKES
dr. Craigieburn...193 K3
dr. Sunbury...144 D13
dr. Taylors L...275 J4
LAKES ENTRANCE
dr. Pt Lonsdale...707 G18
LAKESFIELD
dr. Lysterfield...464 A17
LAKESIDE
av. Reservoir...282 D8
bvd. Pakenham...583 L3
bvd. Rowville...462 K16
cr. Croydon Hl...335 F13
ct. Melton W...226 D12
ct. Safety Bch...669 C19
dr. Albert Park...30 J9
dr. Albert Park...413 K5
dr. Broadmeadows...239 A18
dr. Burwood E...420 D11
dr. Emerald...469 H18
dr. Lower Plenty...286 E19
dr. Melbourne...30 H9
dr. Melbourne...31 A17
dr. Melbourne...413 K5
dr. Point Cook...450 J12
dr. Roxburgh Pk...194 E12
dr. Roxburgh Pk...194 E12
dr. St Kilda...414 B10
pl. Williamstown...410 H16
LAKE VIEW
bvd. Keysborough...533 L12
ct. Emerald...470 A20
dr. Nar Warrn S...552 F11
dr. Nar Warrn S...552 F13
dr. Safety Bch...668 L19
dr. Safety Bch...669 A19
la. Safety Bch...668 L20
la. Safety Bch...669 A20
LAKEVIEW
av. Rowville...462 E18
ct. Glen Waverley...459 K4
dr. Lilydale...338 B14
dr. Mickleham...149 F3
dr. Scoresby...462 C12
gr. Wyndham Va...446 C8
tce. Beaconsfield...555 B11
tce. Melton W...225 J18

tce. Templstw Lr...330 B13
tce.n,Beaconsfield...555 C11
LAKEWAY
cl. Caroline Spr...318 B8
LAKEWOOD
bvd. Braeside...532 J16
bvd. Cairnlea...319 G13
ct. Macleod...284 H10
dr. Knoxfield...463 C1
LALA
av. Warburton...349 J3
LALANI
tce. Templestowe...331 L11
LALBERT
cr. Prahran...415 C12
ct. Lysterfield...463 L15
LALEHAM
ct. Eltham...288 A9
ct. Frankston...599 K16
LALINA
cl. Frankston...600 F14
LALLA
ct. Kew...372 F9
st. Kew...372 E8
LALOMA
ct. Templstw Lr...330 K11
LALOR
cl. Mulgrave...501 F2
cr. Sunbury...142 L17
cr. Sunbury...143 A17
ct. Caroline Spr...318 E10
ct. Springvale S...499 D18
pl. E Melbourne...25 H6
st. Dallas...238 C10
st. Port Melb...412 L4
wy. Williamstown...410 H14
LALORS
la. Healesville...257 J2
rd. Healesville...257 H3
LALUMA
st. Essendon...323 G6
LALWA
st. Blackburn...375 J20
LALWINYA
st. Delahey...275 B10
LA MAMA
pl. Carlton...18 F14
LAMANA
st. Mordialloc...532 C18
LAMAR
ct. Dandenong N...502 C18
LAMARK
ct. Greenvale...236 K3
LAMART
st. Strathmore...279 G12
LAMAT
ct. Frankston...628 H2
LAMB
ct. Bundoora...242 K20
st. Cranbourne...604 D4
st. Moonee Pnd...324 D14
LAMBASSA
gr. Reservoir...283 D2
LAMBECK
dr. Melb Airport...277 J7
dr. Tullamarine...277 K8
dr. Tullamarine...277 K8
LAMBERT
av. Newtown...702 E13
av. Sunbury...142 L11
ct. Blairgowrie...680 D20
ct. Endeavour Hl...537 H10
ct. Rosebud...699 K2
gr. St Kilda E...414 K16
pl. Doncaster E...332 F14
pl. Roxburgh Pk...193 J16
rd. Caulfield N...415 E17
rd. Pearcedale...630 J15
rd. Toorak...415 C8
st. Diamond Ck...245 F10
st. Frankston N...600 C9
st. Richmond...26 J7
LAMBERTS
tr. Lysterfield...504 E11
LAMBETH
av. Armadale...415 H13
ct. Epping...197 K18
ct. Keysborough...534 B8
ct. Point Cook...450 F9
pl. St Kilda...414 E15
st. Kensington...34 C8
st. Kings Park...319 A1
wk. Balwyn, off Barnsbury Rd...372 L12
LAMBHILL
cr. Highton...701 G16
LAMBIE
wy. Roxburgh Pk...194 D5
LAMBOLE
ct. St Albans...275 G19
LAMBOURNE
av. Rowville...463 J15
rd. Watsonia...285 D8

st. Surrey Hills...374
st. Surrey Hills...418
LAMBRUK
ct. Yallambie...286
LAMELLAH
st. Caulfield...455
LAMIN
la. Toorak...415
LAMINA
av. Mill Park...242
LAMING
rd. Deer Park...319
LAMMAS
ct. Mulgrave...501
LAMOND
ct. Greenvale...237
LAMONT
av. The Patch...467
cr. Cranbourne...577
ct. Wantirna S...421
LAMORNA
ct. Eltham...287
LAMOUR
av. S Morang...198
LAMPLIGHT
wy. Attwood...237
LAN
av. Altona Mdw...451
LANA
ct. Airport W...278
pl. Narre Warren...538
st. Blackburn S...419
wy. Maribyrnong...367
LANAGHAN
av. Caroline Spr...318
LANARK
ct. Glen Waverley...420
ct. Point Cook...450
st. Brunswick...325
st. Brunswick E...325
st. Clayton S...498
st. Epping...197
wy. Gowanbrae...279
LANCASHIRE
la. N Melbourne...17
LANCASTER
av. Avondale Ht...322
av. Narre Warren...553
av. Newcomb...704
av. Newtown...701
ct. Greenvale...192
ct. Greenvale...193
ct. Keysborough...534
ct. Somerville...644
dr. Point Cook...450
pl. Chirnside Pk...337
rd. Mooroolbark...337
st. Ashburton...417
st. Bentleigh E...456
st. Sunshine N...321
wy. Melton W...226
LANCE
cl. Aspendale Gdn...547
rd. Bayswater...423
rd. Diggers Rest...187
rd. Sunshine N...321
LANCEFIELD
ct. Endeavour Hl...537
LANCELEY
grn. Caroline Spr...274
LANCELOT
cl. Wantirna S...462
cr. Glen Waverley...420
ct. Hillside...231
ct. Kings Park...275
LANCEWOOD
av. Heidelberg W...328
LANCIA
ct. Epping...197
ct. Ferntree Gly...464
dr. Keilor Dn...276
dr. Tootgarook...698
LANCING
ct. Wheelers Hl...460
LANCOM
ri. Rowville...503
LANDALE
av. Croydon...380
rd. Toorak...415
st. Box Hill...374
LANDARA
ct. Mooroolbark...337
LANDAU
ct. Cranbourne N...578
ct. Taylors L...275
dr. Warranwood...334
pl. Avondale Ht...322
pl. Melton W...226
LANDBURY
rd. Bundoora...242
LANDCOX
st. Brighton East...455

ANDELL
t. Ringwood E.......379 D14
ANDELLS
d. Pascoe Vale.......280 K16
ANDEN
v. Balwyn N...........374 B6
v. Glen Waverley....460 L1
l. Toorak..............415 F3
ANDERS
t. Caroline Spr.......318 A4
ANDEX
t. Diamond Ck.......246 A7
ANDHILL
l. Langwarrin 629 F7
t. Hallam...............538 B16
ANDLES
. Roxburgh Pk......193 L12
t. McKinnon.........456 E17
ANDO
l. Springvale S 533 J6
ANDON
l. Carrum Downs...601 F2
ANDOR
l. Hoppers Csg......405 A18
t. Narre Warren.....539 D15
ANDRA
v. Reservoir...........283 C2
t. Berwick 554 H19
t. Grovedale 705 L16
l. Greensbrgh.........243 L19
t. Rye 696 G8
ANDRIDGE
t. Glen Waverley....420 E18
ANDSBOROUGH
v. Rowville.............463 E13
v. Taylors L 275 D1
v. Wheelers Hl.......460 H19
l. Endeavour Hl.....537 F6
r. Sunbury 142 L12
ANDSCAPE
t. Eltham...............245 L18
t. Wheelers Hl 461 F15
r. Boronia..............424 D5
r. Doncaster E.......332 E14
r. Hillside 231 K18
r. Mooroolbark......337 G11
ANDSDALE
r. Wantirna S.........422 H18
ANDSDOWNE
t. Frankston 628 C13
t. Blairgowrie 680 A20
ANDSIDE
d. Melb Airport.......235 J14
ANDSTEAD
t. Carrum Downs...601 B3
ANDSTROM
d. Kilsyth 380 K8
ANDY
v. Highton 705 H3
l. Mill Park............242 F9
t. Burnside............318 H11
t. Kilsyth...............381 F11
t. Pt Lonsdale.......707 H19
t. Wantirna S.........462 E3
t. Wheelers Hl.......460 L9
d. Jacana...............237 K19
t. Reservoir...........282 E8
ANE
r. Reservoir...........283 C10
t. Darley.................221 L4
d. Ferntree Gly.......424 F19
t. Blackburn N.......376 D10
y. Cranbourne........578 D17
ANENA
t. Frankston 600 H14
ANE NO 10
Geelong, off
Moorabool St.....703 A10
ANE NO 11
Geelong.............703 A11
ANE NO 20
Geelong, off
Maud St.............702 K10
ANE NO 25
Geelong, off
Little Ryrie St.....703 C9
ANE NO 28
Geelong, off
Yarra St.............703 C7
ANE NO 29
Geelong, off
Fenwick St.........702 L8
ANE NO 5
Geelong.............702 L11
ANES
. Lysterfield..........505 H4
ANG
t. Malvern East......457 D2
d. Langwarrin 629 E4
d. Melton S...........268 G3
d. Mt Waverley......458 G4
t. Beaumaris 529 L11
t. Clifton Hill............20 A8

st. Princes Hill 325 G18
st. South Yarra 31 J11
st. South Yarra 414 E6
LANGBOURNE
ct. Greenvale 193 G18
ct. Point Cook...........450 H4
dr. Nar Warrn S.......552 D18
LANGDALE
dr. Croydon Hl 335 J13
LANGDON
av. Blairgowrie 679 F16
cr. Craigieburn 194 E1
rd. Caulfield N 455 G2
st. Lalor..................240 D10
LANGEWAN
rd. Langwarrin 629 K6
LANGFORD
av. Mitcham 377 F19
cr. Donvale 377 A7
ct. Tecoma 466 B11
rd. Sorrento 678 G4
st. N Melbourne..........34 E11
st. Surrey Hills.........374 A14
st. Williamstown.......411 E17
LANGFORDS
la. N Melbourne........34 L9
LANGHAM
ct. Grovedale 706 D9
pl. Hawthorn E.........372 H18
st. Avondale Ht 322 A16
LANGHORNE
cr. Rowville.............463 J12
st. Altona Mdw 451 K5
st. Dandenong.........536 B9
LANGLEY
cr. Dandenong S.....535 H14
pl. Roxburgh Pk......194 A10
pl. S Morang 243 G1
rd. Cranbourne S.....630 G3
st. Ardeer 320 C19
st. Ringwood E.......379 B12
LANGLI
av. Warranwood.......334 K12
LANGMORE
dr. Hillside 232 E17
la. Berwick 554 D8
LANGOLD
ct. Noble Park.........535 D1
LANGRIDGE
st. Abbotsford 25 K1
st. Collingwood 19 G20
st. Fairfield..............327 F17
st. Hoppers Csg.......448 K2
st. Middle Park 413 H12
LANGRIGG
av. Edithvale............546 G10
av. Mt Martha..........655 H15
LANGS
la. Melbourne 23 H9
rd. Ascot Vale 323 J20
rd. Flemington 323 J20
rd. Ivanhoe 327 L12
LANGSHAW
st. Altona North 365 J20
LANGSLOW
rd. Aspendale Gdn...546 G3
st. Bentleigh E 456 L19
LANGSTON
st. Northcote 327 A19
LANGTON
st. Glenroy.............279 K2
st. Glenroy.............279 K4
st. Jacana...............237 K20
wy. Greenvale 192 L18
LANGTREE
av. Pascoe Vale S....324 H5
ct. Blackburn 376 B11
LANGVALE
ct. Mill Park............242 E2
LANGVILLE
ct. Malvern East.....456 H4
LANGWARRIN
cr. Langwarrin 601 H20
LANGWELLS
pde. Northcote 326 J13
LANGWITH
av. Boronia..............424 A12
LANHAM
st. Oakleigh E 458 H16
LANIER
cr. Croydon N 335 K9
LANIGAN
st. Fawkner.............281 K4
LANKESTER
st. Templestowe 330 K7
LANNING
cr. Seville...............342 B15
LANOMA
ct. Wheelers Hl 460 J19
pl. Sorrento 679 C16
LANSBURY
cr. Highton 701 F15
dr. Nar Warrn S.......578 E3

LANSDOWN
st. Balwyn N 373 E5
st. Brighton East 455 D13
st. Hampton 495 D11
LANSDOWNE
ct. Grovedale 706 J13
pl. Carlton 18 A19
rd. Cairnlea 320 A12
rd. Endeavour Hl 503 B14
rd. St Kilda E...........415 A16
st. E Melbourne 25 B7
st. Pascoe Vale S 281 A20
LANSELL
av. Highett 495 H15
av. Safety Bch 669 C15
av. Safety Bch 669 C17
cl. Nar Warrn S........553 A16
cl. Ringwood N.......378 D4
cr. Camberwell.........417 A3
ct. Carrum Downs...600 L3
ct. Carrum Downs...601 A3
ct. Rowville.............463 F18
ct. Thomastown......241 F15
ct. Toorak...............415 D5
dr. Cranbourne N 578 G11
dr. Doncaster 331 A18
dr. Highton 701 F20
pl. Melton W...........226 D16
pl. Mt Martha...........656 E7
rd. Glen Waverley.....460 H5
rd. Mooroolbark.....337 F14
rd. Toorak..............415 D5
rd. Toorak..............415 E2
rd. Wyndham Va 446 D10
LANSOR
st. Springvale S 533 K6
LANSVALE
ct. Frankston 627 K9
LANTANA
av. Hoppers Csg......448 F6
av. Thomastown......240 K14
cl. Greensbrgh........244 J20
ct. Dandenong N.....501 H17
ct. Frankston 600 C16
ct. St Albans 320 G10
ct. Wantirna............422 C3
dr. Narre Warren.....553 G10
dr. Wonga Park........291 H14
rd. Gardenvale 455 C11
st. Blackburn N.......375 J9
st. Clayton 459 B20
st. Doncaster E.......332 D19
st. Ivanhoe 328 D8
LANTERN
cl. Epping...............198 C19
ct. Cairnlea 319 F8
pl. Lilydale..............294 B18
LANVOS
dr. Diamond Ck.......245 K7
LANYON
ct. Lysterfield..........464 B18
st. Dandenong S.....550 C3
LA PEROUSE
cl. Sunbury 144 C10
LAPSTONE
cr. Yallambie...........285 L14
LAPWING
ct. Langwarrin 629 C5
LARA
cl. Thomastown......240 E12
ct. Deer Park...........319 C8
ct. Doncaster 374 E3
ct. Frankston 599 L16
ct. Hallam...............537 G13
ct. Mt Evelyn...........338 L18
ct. St Helena 244 L17
ct. St Helena 245 A17
pl. Melton W...........226 B20
pl. Patterson L.........573 J1
st. Malvern..............416 B8
st. South Yarra 32 B14
wy. Campbellfield 239 G5
LARADO
pl. Clayton S...........499 E15
LARAINE
ct. Bonbeach 573 D1
pl. Melton W...........226 C16
LARAMIE
rd. Nar Warrn S.......552 L20
LARBERT
av. Balwyn N 329 H18
rd. Mooroolbark......337 J17
rd. Noble Park.........500 H17
LARCH
cr. Diamond Ck.......245 A11
cr. Mt Waverley 419 G15
la. Dingley Vill.........532 H5
st. Blackburn 376 A12
st. Caulfield S 455 G6
st. Langwarrin 628 K2
st. Thomastown.......241 E13
LARCOM
ct. Greensbrgh........244 D15

LARCOMBE
st. Highton 705 J2
LARDNER
rd. Frankston 627 G5
LARGE
st. Springvale 499 G16
LARGS
ct. Greenvale 193 B20
st. Seaford.............573 D16
LARISA
rd. St Albans...........320 H7
LARISSA
av. Ringwood 378 G11
av. Tullamarine........278 F7
ct. Croydon 380 G7
st. Heidelberg W 328 A1
LARK
rd. Exford...............267 C13
st. Altona...............408 F20
LARKIN
av. Airport W...........279 C15
cl. Mt Martha...........656 J6
ct. Bundoora...........242 H15
ct. Doncaster E 332 H8
dr. Croydon 335 G20
pde. Queenscliff.........709 D16
pl. Hoppers Csg......449 H3
LARK RISE
ct. Narre Warren.....538 H19
LARKSONG
ct. Springvale S 534 A5
LARKSPUR
av. Doncaster 375 B4
cct. Glen Waverley....460 D5
cl. Epping...............198 G20
dr. St Albans............320 E8
LARKWOOD
la. Craigieburn 193 L2
LARLAC
st. Hadfield 280 J5
LARMAN
st. Bentleigh E 456 L20
LARMOUR
rd. Pakenham 557 G15
LARNACA
ct. Templestowe 331 L13
LARNACH
rd. Baxter...............645 G3
rd. Langwarrin S 645 G3
rd. Pearcedale.........645 G3
rd. Pearcedale.........646 D4
LARNARK
ct. Chelsea Ht 547 F11
LARNE
av. Bayswater..........423 B4
av. Donvale 376 L3
cl. Berwick 553 H13
gr. Preston..............326 L6
LARNOO
av. Brunswick W 325 A12
dr. Doncaster E 332 H7
LARNOOK
cl. Greensbrgh........244 A20
cr. Aspendale..........546 E4
cr. Mooroolbark......337 B16
st. Prahran 415 B12
LA ROCHELLE
bvd. Point Cook.........450 F12
LAROOL
av. St Helena 244 K17
cl. Doncaster E 331 K15
cr. Seaford..............573 D13
cr. Sunshine W 364 F6
LA ROSE
st. Brunswick...........325 E10
LAROSE
pl. Werribee............447 L14
LARPENT
st. Glen Waverley....420 E17
LARRA
ct. Seabrook...........450 L4
LARRY
ct. Noble Park.........500 D19
LARSON
rd. Diamond Ck.......202 A17
LARTER
ct. Bundoora...........242 G18
ct. Hoppers Csg......449 D1
ct. Kurunjang..........227 D10
ct. Mt Martha..........656 L10
ct. Mt Martha..........657 A10
ct. Wantirna S.........462 B4
LA RUE
pl. S Morang 199 B15
LARWOOD
cl. Avondale Ht 322 F16
LA SCALA
av. Maribyrnong......323 C20
LASCELLE
dr. Vermont S 421 B13
LASCELLES
av. Toorak...............415 C5
av. Viewbank...........285 H18

ct. Frankston 628 C12
dr. Lalor.................240 J8
pl. Highton 701 F19
sq. Kensington 33 B10
st. Carnegie 456 J11
st. Coburg 325 B4
st. Springvale 500 A10
LASER
ct. Taylors L 275 J5
dr. Rowville.............462 L15
dr. Rowville.............463 A14
LASIANDRA
av. Forest Hill 376 K20
av. Nunawading 376 K20
cct. Narre Warren.....553 D2
LASPEZIA
ct. Point Cook.........450 D10
LASSA
ct. Dandenong N.....501 F10
LASSITER
ct. Nar Warrn S.......552 G6
st. Sunbury 143 A13
LASSWADE
ct. Brighton 494 G3
LATHAM
cl. Mill Park............243 C6
cr. Dandenong N.....501 K19
ct. Doncaster E.......331 J18
ct. Forest Hill 376 J20
ct. Glen Waverley....419 K18
dr. Portsea..............677 H6
st. Bentleigh E 457 A17
st. Ivanhoe 328 B15
st. Mornington........641 B19
st. Northcote 326 G13
st. Tarneit...............447 F6
st. Werribee.............447 F6
LATHAMS
rd. Carrum Downs...574 B19
rd. Seaford.............574 B19
LATIMER
pl. Gladstone Pk 236 K19
st. Noble Park.........534 G3
LATINA
ct. Nar Warrn N 538 C10
LATONA
av. Knoxfield 462 K6
av. Preston.............326 E3
st. Mentone 530 K9
LA TROBE
bvd. Newtown 702 J14
bvd. S Geelong 702 J14
ct. Sunbury 143 H6
pl. Melbourne.............2 G11
pl. Melbourne...........24 E5
st. Melbourne.............1 A4
st. Melbourne...........23 A8
st. W Melbourne.........1 A4
tce. Belmont.............702 K19
tce. Geelong 702 K19
tce. Geelong West 702 K19
tce. Newtown 702 K19
tce. S Geelong..........702 K19
LATROBE
av. Alphington 327 H20
av. Alphington 371 H1
av. Bundoora...........284 C1
av. Pakenham 583 K5
av. Portsea..............677 J4
cr. Keysborough 533 K15
ct. Caulfield S 455 L8
ct. Craigieburn 150 G15
ct. Croydon Hl 335 J14
ct. Rowville.............463 B19
ct. Werribee.............447 G8
ct. Wheelers Hl 461 B10
dr. Mt Martha..........655 L15
pde. Dromana 685 F8
rd. Yarrambat...........200 G18
st. Box Hill S...........374 L20
st. Brunswick...........325 K10
st. Bulleen 329 J10
st. Bulleen 329 L10
st. Caulfield S 455 L7
st. Cheltenham 530 J4
st. Cranbourne.........578 E19
st. Footscray...........367 B7
st. Hughesdale.........457 H13
st. Mentone 530 J4
st. Mentone 531 A4
st. Moonee Pnd 323 K15
st. Newport 411 B9
st. Windsor 31 L20
st. Windsor 414 F11
tce. Taylors Hill..........274 G9
LATROSE
st. Keilor Park.........278 C14
LATS
av. Carrum Downs...575 E20
LATURNS
ct. Vermont S 420 L14
ct. Vermont S 421 A14

LAUBES
rd. Ferny Creek 465 L1
LAUDER
ct. Gowanbrae 279 D4
dr. Bundoora 242 E20
pl. Berwick 554 F15
LAUDERDALE
dr. Tarneit 447 H1
rd. Narre Warren 553 B4
LAUER
st. Doncaster 331 E20
LAUFFRE
wk. Caroline Spr 318 B3
LAUGHING WATERS
rd. Eltham 288 F14
LAUGHLIN
av. Nunawading 376 F16
LAUGHTON
ct. Altona Mdw 451 K3
LAUNCHING
wy. Carrum 573 C7
LAUNDER
st. Hawthorn 372 A18
LAUNDERS
av. Wonga Park 291 G18
LAURA
av. Belmont 705 L1
ct. Bayswater N 380 G20
ct. Box Hill N 375 B7
ct. Greensbrgh 285 J2
ct. Sunshine N 321 B10
dr. Hampton Pk 552 D11
gr. Avondale Ht 322 C15
gr. Mt Waverley 419 G16
la. Mooroolbark 381 J1
pl. Fitzroy N 19 A7
rd. Knoxfield 462 J7
rd. Knoxfield 463 A6
rd. Wantirna S 462 J7
st. Aspendale 546 B3
st. Brunswick 325 G14
st. Caulfield S 456 A8
st. Clayton S 499 A6
st. Fitzroy N 19 B7
st. Moonee Pnd 323 L14
st. Tootgarook 698 B2
LAURAVILLE
av. Werribee 448 B19
LAUREATE
cl. Sunbury 143 D4
LAUREL
av. Boronia 423 K11
av. Doveton 536 L10
av. Doveton 537 A10
av. Tarneit 405 B10
cr. Campbellfield 239 F12
cr. Carrum Downs 574 J20
cr. Carrum Downs 574 K20
cr. Carrum Downs 600 J1
ct. Frankston N 599 K10
ct. Glen Waverley 460 E11
ct. Hawthorn E 372 E15
ct. Heidelberg Ht 284 G19
ct. Maidstone 366 J3
ct. Olinda 427 G17
ct. Sunbury 144 F12
gr. Belgrave 466 L16
gr.n, Blackburn 375 H18
gr.s, Blackburn 375 G20
st. Ashburton 417 F17
st. Bentleigh E 456 K20
st. Preston 283 H17
st. Rye 696 E6
st. St Albans 320 H8
st. St Albans 320 J9
LAUREL BANK
pde. Newtown 702 H9
LAUREL HILL
dr. Eltham North 245 H19
LAUREN
cl. Dingley Vill 532 J5
ct. Epping 198 D15
ct. Frankston S 627 L15
dr. Hampton Pk 551 L8
LAURENCE
av. Airport W 278 J17
gr. Ringwood E 379 A12
LAURENCIA
ct. Mont Albert 374 F16
LAURENS
st. N Melbourne 34 H19
st. Rosebud 684 H14
st. W Melbourne 34 H19
st. W Melbourne 368 K10
LAURENTEN
ct. Langwarrin 629 B8
LAURI ANN
st. Templstw Lr 330 D14
LAURICELLA
av. Keilor East 322 B4
pl. Caroline Spr 318 A3

LAURIE
av. Sunshine N 320 L14
av. Sunshine N 321 A14
av. Tecoma 466 C13
rd. Doncaster E 332 D11
rd. Wandin N 340 D12
st. Newport 410 G8
st. Reservoir 283 H6
st. Yarrambat 201 B7
LAURINA
cr. Frankston N 600 C6
ct. Doveton 536 H8
ct. Hillside 274 B5
trn. Mill Park 243 D11
LAURISON
rd. Eltham North 287 D3
LAURISTON
av. Selby 467 E19
ct. Cheltenham 496 K17
ct. Mulgrave 500 B3
ct. Ringwood 378 F7
dr. Coldstream 295 E16
dr. Endeavour Hl 537 L7
qy. Caroline Spr 317 K6
wk.n, Sunbury, off Belleview Dr 143 F16
wk.s, Sunbury, off Belleview Dr 143 F16
wy. Sunbury 143 F15
LAURUS
ct. Dandenong N 501 G17
ct. Narre Warren 539 D20
LAUTOKA
dr. Wonga Park 291 J19
LAUTREC
av. Wheelers Hl 460 K14
ct. Doncaster E 331 K15
st. Frankston 628 D9
LAVARACK
st. Melton S 268 J10
LAVELLE
st. Blackburn S 420 A1
LAVENDER
ct. Bayswater 423 C6
ct. Glenroy 281 C4
ct. Mill Park 242 D11
ct. Newcomb 704 C15
la. Baxter 643 K3
la. Carrum Downs 574 L19
la. Sunbury 143 E18
pl. Berwick 539 H19
st. Ringwood 378 G14
LAVENDER FARM
rd. Emerald 509 B9
LAVENDER PARK
rd. Cairnlea 319 K11
rd. Eltham 287 G17
LAVER
cl. Mulgrave 500 J4
ct. Mill Park 242 J4
ct. Wantirna S 422 D20
st. Kew 371 C11
LAVEROCK
ct. Taylors L 275 K7
LAVERTON
st. Williamstown 411 C16
LAVERY
cl. Mornington 641 C14
pl. Attwood 237 C12
LAVIAH
ct. Templestowe 332 D5
LAVIDGE
rd. Ashwood 418 E15
st. Hawthorn 371 H17
LAVINGTON
ct. Craigieburn 150 B20
LAW
ct. Rowville 502 K1
ct. S Morang 243 H2
ct. Sunshine W 364 H12
st. Blairgowrie 696 B4
st. Briar Hill 286 G3
st. Heidelberg Ht 328 D3
st. S Melbourne 30 E4
LAWANNA
dr. Templestowe 331 C12
st. Noble Park N 501 D15
LAWBOROUGH
av. Parkdale 531 L10
LAWERENCE
pl. Geelong, off Little Ryrie St 703 A8
LAWES
st. Hawthorn 371 F14
LAWFORD
st. Box Hill N 374 L7
st. Doncaster 330 J20
LAWLER
la. Coldstream 295 A9
LAWLESS
dr. Cranbourne N 578 A7
LAWLEY
st. Reservoir 282 E2

LAWN
cr. Braybrook 322 C20
cr. Braybrook 366 B1
ct. Craigieburn 150 L20
ct. Frankston 599 J16
rd. Noble Park 500 D19
LAWNCLIFFE
ct. Rowville 503 G1
LAWNHILL
rd. Malvern 416 A8
LAWRANCE
gr. Portsea 678 B5
st. Murrumbeena 457 E6
LAWRENCE
av. Aspendale 546 E7
av. Sunbury 142 K4
cr. Noble Park N 501 E16
ct. Altona North 409 H3
ct. Bayswater 423 D2
ct. Bundoora 242 H20
ct. Cranbourne N 577 K6
ct. N Warrandyte 290 A11
ct. The Patch 467 J4
dr. Berwick 554 B2
rd. Mt Waverley 459 F2
rd. Panton Hill 204 L20
rd. Panton Hill 205 A20
rd. Pt Lonsdale 707 G20
st. Ardeer 320 C20
st. Ardeer 364 C1
st. Blackburn S 419 H2
st. Brighton 454 K18
st. Brunswick 325 J12
st. Doncaster E 375 H3
st. Eaglemont 328 L11
st. Hadfield 280 K8
st. Kew East 372 K6
st. Seddon 367 A11
st. Somerville 645 B15
LAWRENNY
ct. Toorak 415 F2
LAWREY
rd. Diamond Ck 245 L1
st. Frankston 599 E20
LAWRY
ct. Keilor East 322 C1
pl. Meadow Ht 237 K7
st. Northcote 326 J14
LAWSON
av. Frankston S 627 E10
cl. Cranbourne 603 K1
cr. Rosebud 684 D17
cr. Thomastown 240 D19
ct. Croydon N 336 A12
ct. Grovedale 706 G12
ct. Mornington 656 G1
ct. Mulgrave 460 D17
ct. Taylors L 275 J1
ct. Watsonia N 243 H20
gr. South Yarra 32 A4
pde. Heidelberg Ht 328 F2
pde. Highett 495 H15
pl. Footscray 367 F10
rd. Melton S 268 F11
rd. Merrimu 222 H11
rd. Mooroolbark 381 F3
st. Albion 320 K18
st. Balwyn N 373 A7
st. Bentleigh 496 F1
st. Blackburn 376 A13
st. Braybrook 366 A7
st. Brighton East 495 G3
st. Elwood 454 B2
st. Essendon 324 F11
st. Footscray 367 F10
st. Hampton 495 G6
st. Hawthorn E 416 E7
st. Moonee Pnd 324 F11
st. Oakleigh E 458 H13
st. Reservoir 283 C11
st. Sunbury 143 B14
wy. Endeavour Hl 537 H4
wy. Endeavour Hl 537 J4
LAWSONS
ct. Templestowe 332 B8
rd. Emerald 469 L20
LAWTON
av. Geelong West 702 G3
st. Braybrook 365 H5
LAXDALE
rd. Camberwell 417 H7
LAYARD
st. Dromana 685 H7
LAYER
la. Cannons Creek 648 E8
la. Pearcedale 648 E8
LAYFIELD
st. Croydon Hl 335 K12
st. S Melbourne 30 A5
LAYTON
av. Greensbrgh 286 K2
cr. Mt Martha 656 J8
cr. Newtown 702 A8

ct. Glen Waverley 420 F16
pl. Mill Park 242 E10
LAZAR
gr. S Morang 199 A15
LEA
cr. Bundoora 285 A6
rd. Mulgrave 500 F3
st. Ferntree Gly 464 B4
st. Mt Martha 656 B9
wy. Rosebud 684 B18
LEABURN
av. Caulfield N 415 E19
LEACH
av. Box Hill N 375 C12
st. Briar Hill 286 H2
st. Briar Hill 286 H4
LEADER
st. Campbellfield 194 J18
LEAFIELD
st. Watsonia 285 C8
LEAGH
ct. Scoresby 462 J8
LEAH
av. Upwey 465 L15
ct. Rowville 503 B3
ct. Rye 697 K9
ct. Werribee 448 B14
gr. Carrum Downs 574 D19
LEAHE
wy. Chirnside Pk 336 G7
LEAHY
st. Maddingley 263 C5
LEAKE
ct. Altona Mdw 451 H9
st. Essendon 323 J4
LEAKES
rd. Laverton N 407 A7
rd. Plumpton 228 L17
rd. Rockbank 270 L14
rd. Tarneit 405 A5
rd. Truganina 405 G6
LEAMINGTON
cr. Caulfield E 456 E4
cr. Glen Waverley 460 J2
st. Reservoir 282 F8
LEAMON
ct. Ferntree Gly 463 L6
LEAN
av. Herne Hill 701 J3
LEANDER
st. Footscray 366 L7
LEANE
dr. Eltham 246 B20
dr. Eltham 288 A2
LEANNA
ct. Cranbourne W 577 K19
LEANNE
cr. Keysborough 534 C8
ct. Cranbourne 578 C16
ct. Doncaster E 332 G6
LEAR
ct. Greensbrgh 244 B16
LEARMONTH
cr. Sunshine W 365 B9
ct. Caroline Spr 318 B7
rd. Carrum Downs 574 B8
rd. Patterson L 574 B8
st. Heidelberg 328 J4
st. Moonee Pnd 324 A13
st. Queenscliff 709 A18
st. Sunbury 142 F12
st. Tullamarine 278 G4
LEARMOUTH
st. Belmont 706 C4
LEASON
st. Kew East 372 H3
LEATHERS
ct. Altona Mdw 451 H6
LEATHERWOOD
cl. Rowville 502 D4
cr. Wheelers Hl 460 H14
dr. Hoppers Csg 405 A11
gr. Meadow Ht 193 K17
st. Frankston S 627 K16
LEAVESDON
av. Kealba 276 L20
LEAWARRA
cr. Doncaster E 331 K15
dr. Heathmont 378 K17
pde. Frankston 627 L3
st. Rye 697 A5
LEBANON
cr. Mulgrave 500 B4
st. Dandenong 536 E8
st. Strathmore 279 H14
st. Strathmore 280 B16
LEBER
st. Warrandyte 333 E4
LEBUNYA
cl. Mooroolbark 337 E15
ct. Greensbrgh 244 C19
LE CATEAU
st. Pascoe Vale S 324 H3

LECHLADE
av. South Yarra 32
av. South Yarra 414
LECHTE
rd. Mt Waverley 419 C
LECKIE
dr. Albanvale 319
pl. Geelong West 702
st. Bentleigh 496
LECKY
rd. Officer 582 E
rd. Officer S 582 E
st. Cranbourne 604
LEDBURY
cr. Bundoora 285
ct. Toorak 415
LEDDY
st. Forest Hill 420
LEDGER
av. Fawkner 281
LEDUC
tce. Nar Warrn S 552
LEE
av. Mt Waverley 419 H
av. Springvale 500
ct. Heathmont 378 E
pde. Mitcham 377 E
st. Altona North 365 H
st. Arthurs Seat 686 A
st. Brunswick E 326 C
st. Carlton N 18
st. Craigieburn 150 D
st. Deer Park 318 J
st. Fawkner 281 F
st. Flemington 33
st. Frankston 628
st. Noble Park 535
st. St Albans 319
LEE ANDY
ct. Ferntree Gly 463
LEE-ANDY
ct. Dingley Vill 533
LEE ANN
cr. Croydon 336 G
LEE-ANN
st. Blackburn S 420
st. Forest Hill 420
LEE ANNE
cr. Bundoora 284
LEECH
ct. Jacana 237 G
ct. Nar Warrn N 538 L
LEED
st. Dandenong 536
LEEDS
ct. Greenvale 193 B
dr. Kilsyth S 381 C
pl. Campbellfield 239 H
rd. Mt Waverley 419 E
st. Canterbury 373 G
st. Doncaster E 375
st. Footscray 367
st. Richmond 26
LEEK
st. Yarraville 367 E
LEEMAK
cr. Berwick 540 A
LEENA
ct. Warranwood 335 B
LEES
ct. Epping 241
ct. Rosanna 285 E
pl. Melbourne 24
rd. Lower Plenty 286 E
st. McKinnon 456 A
st. Northcote 327 A
LEESIDE
st. Dandenong N 501 G
LEESON
gr. Lalor 240
pl. Keysborough 534
LEEWARRA
dr. Glen Waverley 420 G
LEFERN
ct. Carrum Downs 601
LE FEVRE
st. Sandringham 495 E
LEFEVRE
ct. Frankston 628 C
st. Spotswood 366 J
LE FEY
ct. Glen Waverley 420 L
LEFLAN
cl. Ringwood N 378
LEGACY
dr. Mt Martha 655 H
LE GALLIENNE
cr. Mulgrave 460 C
LEGANA
ct. Endeavour Hl 537
ct. Patterson L 573
ct. Werribee 446 K

t. Mt Waverley 459 C7
t. St Albans 320 H9
EGEND
v. Glen Waverley 420 K17
t. Hallam 538 B16
t. Rowville 503 B8
EGERWOOD
d. Nar Warrn N 538 K10
EGG
t. Endeavour Hl 537 C7
d. Emerald 509 E5
d. Macclesfield 470 D4
EGGATT
r. Mt Martha 655 E18
t. Melton S 268 H9
EGGETT
r. Mt Evelyn 339 K19
y. Sorrento 679 F13
EGGO
Richmond 26 E10
EGH
t. Reservoir 282 C4
EGON
d. Oakleigh S 458 E19
t. Port Melb 412 L6
E GRAND
l. Mt Eliza 642 C1
t. Wheelers Hl 461 C17
hw. Mt Eliza 642 D2
EHEM
v. Oakleigh S 497 H3
EHHONG
Rowville 502 H1
EHMANN
v. Grovedale 705 H16
r. Frankston N 600 A9
Croydon Hl 335 J17
EHMANNS
d. Wollert 197 J2
EICESTER
v. Glen Waverley 459 H5
v. Mt Eliza 626 B19
r. Melton 227 A16
t. Somerville 645 C19
t. Wantirna S 422 J14
hw. Kensington 33 E12
l. Carlton 18 A17
l. Wyndham Va 446 E9
q. Malvern 415 K7
q. Seaholme 409 H17
q. Tullamarine 279 A8
t. Balwyn N 374 B2
t. Carlton 17 L20
t. Fitzroy 19 A10
t. Heidelberg Ht 328 G4
t. Melbourne 17 L20
t. Preston 326 E2
EICHARDT
l. Taylors L 275 K1
r. Reservoir 282 L2
t. Mill Park 242 J6
t. McCrae 684 K16
t. Sunbury 142 L13
EIGH
Lilydale 338 K10
t. Craigieburn 149 L15
t. Dallas 238 E12
t. Doveton 536 L6
t. Eltham North 245 G16
t. Macleod 285 G11
r. Pakenham 559 E20
Richmond 26 C10
d. Croydon 380 C7
d. Highton 701 D15
t. Footscray 366 L5
t. Huntingdale 458 E13
t. Mt Waverley 418 H20
t. Oakleigh S 497 F5
t. Werribee 447 D10
EIGHTON
v. Emerald 509 B4
r. Deer Park 318 L11
r. Fawkner 239 F20
t. Frankston 600 A15
t. Toorak 415 C7
rn. Derrimut 363 B8
d. Bayswater N 380 G16
EILA
St Albans 320 K7
t. Bacchus Msh 222 B12
t. Endeavour Hl 537 J3
t. Thomastown 241 J13
d. Carnegie 456 D11
d. Carnegie 456 J12
d. Murrumbeena 456 J12
d. Ormond 456 D11
d. Warburton 349 J5
t. Deer Park 318 K16
t. Essendon 324 G9
t. Mt Waverley 418 J20
t. Prahran 32 G18
t. Prahran 414 J9

LEILANI
ct. Highton 701 E10
ct. Keilor Dn 275 L16
ct. Mornington 641 J17
gr. Thomastown 240 G17
LEINDAN
ct. Mt Eliza 626 J18
LEINSTER
gr. Brunswick E 325 K15
gr. Northcote 326 D11
gr. Thornbury 326 D10
st. Ormond 456 E14
LEISCHA
ct. Greensbrgh 244 B16
st. Langwarrin 602 E12
LEISHA
ct. Wonga Park 291 G14
LEISURE
wy.n,Rosebud 700 E3
wy.s,Rosebud 700 E4
LEISURELAND
dr. Langwarrin 630 B11
LEITCH
st. Ferntree Gly 464 G3
LEITH
av. Sunshine 365 B5
cr. Hampton E 495 K11
cr. Port Melb 412 D4
ct. Endeavour Hl 503 H18
ct. Frankston 599 H17
ct. Rye 697 B14
ct. Sunbury 144 F11
rd. Macleod 285 A14
rd. Montrose 382 C9
wk. Macleod 285 B14
LEITHEAD
st. Brunswick 325 J10
LE JOHN
st. Rowville 503 B2
LELAND
st. Altona 408 J18
st. Blairgowrie 696 D1
LEMAIR
av. Glen Waverley 420 A18
LEMAL
av. Boronia 423 D13
LEMAN
cr. Noble Park 500 L20
LEMANA
cr. Mt Waverley 459 G5
ct. Mornington 641 C16
LE MANS
ct. Doncaster 330 D15
LEMCO
wk. Delahey 275 C15
LEMINS
rd. Waurn Ponds 705 A16
LEMMING
pl. N Melbourne 17 B10
LEMMON
av. Keilor East 278 B17
st. Williamstn N 411 A13
LEMNIAN
ct. Langwarrin 629 F8
LEMNOS
av. Pascoe Vale S 324 H3
st. Croydon 379 L5
LEMON
gr. Bayswater 423 D5
gr. Mt Waverley 459 H4
gr. Nunawading 376 K10
rd. Balwyn N 374 B3
LEMONGRASS
ct. Baxter 643 L3
LEMONGROVE
cr. Croydon Hl 335 E17
LEMONGUM
rd. Yellingbo 387 K20
LEMONT
av. Mt Waverley 459 F7
st. Endeavour Hl 537 J11
LEMPRIERE
av. Mt Martha 655 E18
av. St Kilda E 414 L19
av. St Kilda E 415 A19
cl. Templestowe 331 D3
ct. Altona Mdw 451 G6
LENA
ct. Berwick 554 D20
ct. Hoppers Csg 447 L3
ct. Thomastown 240 K15
gr. Kilsyth 380 L9
gr. Ringwood 378 J14
la. Roxburgh Pk 194 D6
pl. Carrum Downs 601 F4
st. Viewbank 285 H20
LENARO
st. Dandenong S 535 J14
LENDOR
ct. Cheltenham 497 H20
LENHAM
cl. Ferntree Gly 463 G3

LENKUNYA
ct. Eltham North 245 E18
LENNA
ct. Chadstone 458 D2
st. Burwood E 419 D10
LENNE
ct. Camberwell 417 F4
rd. Beaconsfld Up 542 F11
LENNON
av. Flemington 323 K20
bvd. Point Cook 450 D10
cct. Nar Warrn S 578 J3
st. Parkville 34 H3
st. W Melbourne 33 L16
st. W Melbourne 368 F8
LENNOX
av. Glen Waverley 421 A19
cr. Bundoora 242 E19
ct. Scoresby 462 C9
gr. Sassafras 426 G13
st. Hawthorn 371 G16
st. Moonee Pnd 323 J15
st. Moorabbin 497 B10
st. Northcote 326 K15
st. Richmond 26 C16
st. Yarraville 367 D15
LENOAK
st. Gladstone Pk 279 C3
LENOLA
st. Macleod 285 F10
st. Watsonia 285 F10
LENORE
cr. Williamstown 411 E14
st. Springvale 500 A8
LENS
st. Coburg N 281 B17
LENTARA
cr. Wyndham Va 446 H14
ct. Cheltenham 496 A19
LENTELL
av. Sorrento 678 H4
LEN THOMAS
pl. Narre Warren 552 G3
LENTINI
pl. Keilor Ldg 275 L4
st. Hoppers Csg 449 K2
LENTON
rd. Keysborough 534 G12
LEO
cl. Wantirna S 423 A19
pl. Aspendale Gdn 546 E1
st. Bentleigh E 496 L3
st. Fawkner 281 F7
LEO FINK
ct. St Kilda E 414 K15
LEON
av. Rosanna 329 A2
av. Rosebud 684 E17
ct. Donvale 376 E3
ct. Ferntree Gly 464 D8
st. Cheltenham 496 L18
st. Wheelers Hl 461 D12
LEONARD
av. Aspendale 546 F8
av. Berwick 553 F3
av. Glenroy 280 E6
av. Noble Park 534 J3
av. St Albans 320 G4
cl. Clarinda 498 E8
cr. Ascot Vale 367 H2
cr. Bundoora 243 C20
cr. Eltham 287 F16
cr. Flemington 367 H2
ct. Doncaster 330 K17
ct. Pakenham 585 A4
ct. Sorrento 678 J6
ct. Vermont S 420 L8
ct. Wandana Ht 701 C20
dr. Langwarrin 601 L17
dr. Somerville 644 K18
rd. Kilsyth 381 A7
rd. Lilydale 339 G5
st. Ashwood 418 F16
st. Balwyn 373 A11
st. Bayswater 422 L7
st. Bayswater 423 A7
st. Belmont 702 B18
st. Burwood 418 K11
st. Dandenong 536 D3
st. Fawkner 281 L6
st. Frankston 599 J19
st. Hampton E 495 L8
st. Heidelberg Ht 328 F4
st. Northcote 327 C19
st. Parkville 17 J4
st. Preston 282 H18
st. Ringwood 378 J8
st. Sunshine 321 D20
st. Tootgarook 698 B2
st. Upwey 465 E13
st. Werribee 447 C13
LEONI
av. Heathmont 378 J18

LEONIE
av. Bentleigh E 497 A2
av. Mt Waverley 458 K5
ct. Brighton 455 B18
ct. Narre Warren 539 D13
LEONINA
ct. Somerville 644 H19
LEONIS
av. Balwyn N 329 D19
LEONNE
ct. Hampton Pk 551 J8
LEONOR
ct. Reservoir 283 J2
LEONS
ct. Blackburn 376 C20
rd. Springvale S 533 L5
LEOPOLD
av. Springvale S 534 A4
cr. Hampton Pk 551 K14
cr. Mont Albert 374 C17
la. Point Cook 450 D6
st. Burwood 418 A13
st. Caulfield S 456 A12
st. Glen Iris 416 C13
st. Maribyrnong 323 F14
st. Melbourne 31 A11
st. Melbourne 414 A6
st. Preston 282 H18
st. South Yarra 31 F7
st. South Yarra 414 C4
LE PAGE
st. Moorabbin 496 C10
LEPPITT
rd. Beaconsfld Up 557 E3
rd. Pakenham 557 E3
LEPROSA
cl. Endeavour Hl 502 L19
la. Tecoma 466 E8
LERDERDERG
st. Bacchus Msh 222 B16
LERDERDERG GORGE
rd. Darley 222 B1
LERDERDERG PARK
rd. Merrimu 222 G8
rd. Merrimu 223 A10
LERINA
pl. Wheelers Hl 461 G16
st. Oakleigh E 458 H16
LERNES
st. Forest Hill 420 J2
LEROUX
st. Oakleigh 458 D9
LEROY
pl. Doncaster E 331 K16
LERWICK
ct. Frankston 628 B7
LESA
ct. Mt Martha 657 A10
LESAY
ct. Mt Waverley 458 H7
ct. Rowville 502 K3
dr. St Helena 245 E15
LESDEN
st. Bentleigh E 496 H7
LESDON
av. Cranbourne 578 A13
LESLEIGH
st. Fawkner 281 K11
LESLEY
dr. Hampton Pk 552 D13
gr. Noble Park 500 F18
st. Camberwell 417 L7
LESLIE
av. Boronia 424 J14
av. Coburg N 281 B16
ct. Burwood 418 G13
ct. Clayton S 498 G5
ct. Hillside 274 F2
ct. Lower Plenty 286 E12
gr. Brighton 494 G3
gr. Ringwood N 378 F3
rd. Clarinda 498 G12
rd. Essendon 323 L10
rd. Laverton N 364 J17
st. Belgrave 466 G11
st. Brunswick 325 E13
st. Bulleen 329 L16
st. Croydon 336 G17
st. Dandenong S 535 F11
st. Donvale 332 G18
st. Elsternwick 455 C4
st. Frankston S 626 K8
st. Hawthorn 372 C20
st. Newport 410 F6
st. Newtown 702 C9
st. Richmond 371 A13
st. St Albans 320 E1
st. St Kilda E 414 J16
st. Thomastown 241 L15
st. Woori Yall 344 G14
LESNEY
st. Richmond 26 G18

LESPRAY
av. Bentleigh E 496 H3
LESS
la. Coburg 326 A8
LESTER
av. Ringwood E 379 E14
av. St Albans 320 F4
st. Moolap 704 H18
st. Woori Yall 344 K18
LESTWICK
ri. Wantirna S 421 L15
LETCHWORTH
av. Brighton East 495 H5
pl. Epping 197 K20
pl. Wheelers Hl 461 A7
LETHBRIDGE
st. Moonee Pnd 324 D10
LEUMEAR
st. Oakleigh E 458 J14
LEUNIG
pl. Footscray 367 J7
LEURA
av. Rosanna 285 D19
cr. Rosebud 700 F1
ct. Gladstone Pk 237 E20
ct. Werribee 448 B18
gr. Hawthorn E 416 E3
st. Doncaster E 332 A20
st. Murrumbeena 457 C12
st. Surrey Hills 373 H19
LEVANSWELL
rd. Moorabbin 497 A11
LEVANTO
st. Mentone 531 E7
LEVENDALE
av. Mooroolbark 381 H4
ct. Vermont 421 B6
LEVENIA
st. St Albans 320 B10
LEVER
av. Blairgowrie 679 H20
st. Coburg 325 A5
st. Oakleigh 458 B9
LEVESON
st. N Melbourne 17 D19
LEVIEN
st. Essendon 323 J9
LEVIN
st. Springvale S 534 B1
LEVUKA
st. Seaford 599 E5
LEWANA
st. Rye 697 B6
LEWELLIN
gr. Carrum 573 C9
gr. Rosanna 285 D17
LEWES
dr. Malvern East 456 L1
LEWIN
ct. Altona Mdw 451 G2
st. Carrum Downs 600 L1
st. Deer Park 318 J16
st. Sunbury 143 A15
LEWIN'S RAIL
S Morang 199 F11
LEWIS
av. Burnside 318 F10
cl. Mill Park 242 J9
ct. Anglesea 713 D3
ct. Delahey 275 D15
ct. Grovedale 706 F11
ct. Nunawading 376 F17
ct. Richmond 26 F4
ct. Sunshine W 364 J8
gr. Mt Waverley 458 G7
pl. Hoppers Csg 449 B4
rd. Beaconsfld Up 542 L3
rd. Emerald 542 L3
rd. Healesville 258 D5
rd. Montrose 382 G10
rd. N Warrandyte 290 C17
rd. Silvan 384 H5
rd. Wandin East 384 H5
rd. Wantirna S 423 A17
st. Brighton 454 G13
st. Camberwell 417 L6
st. Coburg N 281 F18
st. Darley 221 H7
st. Flemington 33 L3
st. Frankston 599 D18
st. Glenroy 280 A7
st. Kingsville 366 H13
st. Mordialloc 531 K17
st. Mt Waverley 418 K14
st. Ormond 456 D15
st. Pearcedale 646 L4
st. Pearcedale 647 A4
st. Springvale 499 K9
st. Thornbury 326 D8
LEWISHAM
cl. Hampton Pk 552 C8
rd. Windsor 414 J12

v. Melbourne...24 J15
t. Frankston...628 C8
t. Greenvale...193 F19
t. Narre Warren...539 B20
de. Caroline Spr...317 K6
d. Toorak...415 H7
t. Mitcham...377 G16
ce. Waterways...547 F2
vy. Melton W...226 A15
NMAC
t. Hampton Pk...552 A16
NMAX
t. Point Cook...450 D2
NN
t. Ivanhoe East...328 L15
t. Ivanhoe East...329 A15
'NNEL
t. Rowville...502 F1
'NNET
v. Hurstbridge...202 G12
t. Mornington...640 K16
t. Altona...408 H19
NO
t. Whittington...703 L20
NOAK
v. Lalor...241 B7
NSEY
t. Coburg...325 C2
'NSLEY
t. Box Hill...375 A15
vy. Wantirna...422 C9
NTHWAITE
l. Highton...705 F3
NTON
v. Templstw Lr...330 J10
l. Chelsea Ht...547 F16
t. Berwick...554 G6
t. Hawthorn E...416 G2
r. Thomastown...240 F10
a. Highton...701 J13
t. Balaclava...414 G17
t. Ivanhoe...328 D14
t. Moorabbin...496 D9
vy. Meadow Ht...237 J4
NTOT
t. Mt Eliza...641 L1
NUM
t. Blackburn...375 G17
NWOOD
d. Seville...342 D20
ON
t. Hawthorn...371 F15
'ONEL
r. Croydon...380 J1
d. Mt Waverley...459 E10
t. Airport W...279 C14
t. Doncaster E...376 B4
t. Rosanna...329 D2
t. Thomastown...241 J15
ONHEART
v. Taylors L...275 J9
t. Epping...241 G5
PARI
t. Frankston S...627 D17
PIZZANER
t. Highton...701 D15
PSCOMBE
t. Reservoir...283 J3
PTON
r. Dandenong N...501 K10
r. Frankston...628 B4
r. Thomastown...240 E18
t. Taylors L...275 H10
QUIDAMBAR
a. Mt Evelyn...383 C1
'QUIDAMBER
t. Doveton...536 J7
vy. Sunbury...143 E17
RA
t. Thomastown...241 L16
RATA
l. Langwarrin...629 J4
RIS
t. Ringwood...335 D19
RREWA
r. Caulfield...455 G3
SA
l. Doncaster E...332 G7
l. Ringwood N...377 L6
l. Wantirna S...422 A18
t. Avondale Ht...322 E7
t. Braybrook...365 L4
t. Caulfield S...455 D9
t. Frankston...600 E18
t. Glen Waverley...461 A2
t. Langwarrin...629 B7
t. Mordialloc...532 A10
t. Mt Eliza...641 K5
t. Noble Park...534 L5
t. Thomastown...242 A13
l. Berwick...554 C18
l. Coolaroo...238 H4
l. Melton W...226 D15

LISA BETH
mw. Skye...575 J17
LISABRITT
ct. Mt Martha...656 F9
LISBAN
ct. Sunshine W...364 A6
LISBETH
av. Donvale...377 B7
LISBON
ct. Doncaster E...332 J12
ct. Kings Park...275 D18
st. Glen Waverley...420 B20
LISBUOY
ct. Toorak...415 E9
LISBURN
wy. Berwick...553 J13
LISCARD
st. Elsternwick...455 A2
LISDALE
st. Geelong West...702 G4
LISGOOLD
st. Heathmont...378 K19
LISHEEN
rd. Cockatoo...511 F11
LISMORE
st. Dallas...238 F10
LISSON
ct. Berwick...554 G19
gr. Hawthorn...371 H19
LISTER
av. Sorrento...679 C14
cr. Sunbury...143 A4
ct. Ringwood...378 G8
st. Kew East...372 J2
st. Oakleigh...458 D8
st. St Albans...320 C9
LISTON
av. Reservoir...283 B1
rd. Glenroy...281 B4
st. Glen Iris...417 H13
LITCHFIELD
av. Ferntree Gly...424 A17
wy. Lynbrook...551 D17
LITHGOW
av. Blackburn...375 H14
av. Warburton...350 A3
st. Abbotsford...26 F3
st. Glen Iris...417 F9
LITTEL
st. Up Fntree Gly...465 E6
LITTLE
av. Hampton E...495 J9
ct. Bacchus Msh...221 L15
ct. Frankston...628 D7
ct. Melton W...226 A16
la. Roxburgh Pk...194 C9
st. Altona North...410 B5
st. Anglesea...714 A4
st. Box Hill S...418 H4
st. Deer Park...319 D11
st. Glen Waverley...460 E2
st. Werribee...447 F12
LITTLE ABBOT
st. Collingwood...19 K12
LITTLE ACRE
cl. Langwarrin...629 F9
LITTLE ALFRED
st. Richmond...26 A13
LITTLE BAILLIE
st. N Melbourne...17 A16
LITTLE BAKERS
st. Northcote, off Charles St...326 F17
LITTLE BANK
st. S Melbourne...30 G3
LITTLE BARKLY
st. Carlton...18 H14
LITTLE BAY
st. Port Melb...412 K6
LITTLE BENDALL
st. Kensington...33 F6
LITTLE BERRY
st. Yarraville...367 E13
LITTLE BOND
st. Newtown...702 H11
LITTLE BOUNDARY
rd. Laverton N...364 K16
st. S Melbourne...29 C10
LITTLE BOURKE
pl. Melbourne...24 J3
st. Melbourne...1 A10
st. Melbourne...23 G9
LITTLEBOY
ri. Endeavour Hl...537 C7
LITTLE BREESE
st. Brunswick...325 F12
LITTLEBROOK
cl. Mt Evelyn...339 H18
LITTLE BROUGHAM
st. Geelong, off Brougham St...703 A5
LITTLE BUCKINGHAM
st. Richmond...26 H6

LITTLE BURWOOD
hwy. Wantirna S...422 K17
LITTLE BUTLER
st. Richmond...26 C3
LITTLE CARDIGAN
st. Carlton...18 D19
LITTLE CHAPEL
st. Prahran...32 D18
st. Prahran...414 H9
LITTLE CHARLES
cl. Abbotsford...26 D2
st. Abbotsford...26 D3
st. Fitzroy...19 D17
LITTLE CHELMSFORD
st. Kensington...34 B11
LITTLE CHIPPING
dr. Chirnside Pk...336 J6
LITTLE CHURCH
st. Hawthorn...371 F14
LITTLE COBDEN
st. N Melbourne...17 J19
LITTLE COLENSO
st. Carrum...573 B8
LITTLE COLLINS
st. Melbourne...1 A14
st. Melbourne...23 G11
LITTLECROFT
av. Nar Warrn S...578 L3
av. Nar Warrn S...579 A3
LITTLE CRUIKSHANK
st. Port Melb...29 B11
LITTLE CURRAN
st. N Melbourne...34 J7
LITTLE CURZON
st. N Melbourne...17 C19
LITTLE DAVID
st. Yarraville...366 K15
LITTLE DERHAM
st. Port Melb...412 K2
LITTLE DOW
st. Port Melb...412 K6
LITTLE DRYBURGH
st.n, N Melbourne...34 L17
st.s, N Melbourne...34 K18
LITTLE EASTMENT
st. Northcote...326 H14
LITTLE ELGIN
st. Carlton...18 E12
LITTLE ERROL
st. N Melbourne...17 D18
LITTLE FENWICK
st. Geelong, off La Trobe Tce...702 K10
LITTLE FERGUSON
st. Williamstown...411 C14
LITTLE FINLAY
st. Albert Park...29 G14
st. Albert Park...29 J14
LITTLE FLEET
st. Fitzroy...18 L18
LITTLE FYANS
st. S Geelong...702 K14
LITTLE GEORGE
st. Fitzroy...25 D1
st. N Melbourne...17 F14
LITTLE GLOVER
st. S Melbourne...29 C10
LITTLE GOLD
st. Brunswick...325 E16
LITTLE GORE
st. Fitzroy...19 E19
st. Fitzroy...25 D1
LITTLE GRAHAM
st. Albert Park...29 C14
LITTLE GRATTAN
st. Carlton...18 B15
LITTLE GREIG
st. Albert Park...29 D12
LITTLE GREY
st. St Kilda...414 B14
LITTLE HANOVER
st. Fitzroy...19 A17
LITTLE HARDIMAN
st. Kensington...34 B11
LITTLE HIGH
st. Northcote, off Cunningham St..326 H20
LITTLE HODDLE
st. Richmond...26 A5
LITTLE HOWARD
st. N Melbourne...17 G19
LITTLE HYDE
st. Yarraville...367 E17
LITTLE IFFLA
st. S Melbourne...29 D10
LITTLE INGLES
st. Port Melb...29 C6
LITTLE JAMES
st. Richmond...26 G18
LITTLE JEAN
st. Up Fntree Gly...464 L5

LITTLE JOE
ct. Wesburn...348 B7
LITTLE JOHN
ct. Vermont...421 J4
ct. Werribee...448 D17
st. Footscray...367 H9
LITTLEJOHN
av. Mt Evelyn...339 L18
rd. Warranwood...334 H16
LITTLE JONES
st. Brunswick...325 G10
LITTLE KENT
st. Richmond...26 H7
st. Richmond...371 A14
LITTLE KILGOUR
st. Geelong...703 A11
LITTLE LA TROBE
st. Melbourne...2 B3
st. Melbourne...24 A3
LITTLE LEICHARDT
st. Melbourne...24 H2
LITTLE LESNEY
st. Richmond...26 G17
LITTLE LEVESON
st. N Melbourne...17 E19
LITTLE LITHGOW
st. Abbotsford...26 F3
LITTLE LONSDALE
st. Melbourne...1 A6
st. Melbourne...23 F7
LITTLE LOTHIAN
st.n, N Melbourne...17 A16
st.s, N Melbourne...34 L18
LITTLE LYELL
st. S Melbourne...29 D7
LITTLE MALOP
st. Geelong...702 K7
LITTLE MARION
st. Fitzroy...18 L18
LITTLE MARY
st. Spotswood...366 L20
LITTLE MAUD
st. Geelong...703 B11
LITTLE MERCER
st. Geelong, off Mercer St...702 K4
LITTLE MERTON
st. Albert Park...29 H12
LITTLE MILLER
st. Brunswick E...326 A17
LITTLE MORAY
pl. S Melbourne...3 A19
pl. S Melbourne...30 B2
LITTLE MOUNTAIN
st. S Melbourne...29 D8
LITTLE MYERS
st. Geelong...702 K9
LITTLE NAPIER
st. Fitzroy...19 C20
LITTLE NELSON
pl. Williamstown...411 H16
LITTLE NEWMARKET
st. Northcote...326 L17
LITTLE NICHOLSON
st. Abbotsford...26 E3
LITTLE O'GRADY
st. Albert Park...29 G13
LITTLE OPIE
st. Ferntree Gly...424 K19
LITTLE OSBORNE
st. Williamstown...411 C17
LITTLE OXFORD
st. Collingwood...19 G19
LITTLE PAGE
st. Albert Park...29 E15
st. Middle Park...29 K18
LITTLE PALMERSTON
st. Carlton...18 F11
LITTLE PARK
st. South Yarra...31 E7
LITTLE PARKER
st. Williamstown...411 G16
LITTLE PELHAM
st. Carlton, off Leicester St...18 A16
LITTLE PESCOTT
st. Newtown...702 F7
LITTLE PRINCES
st. Flemington...34 E1
st. Travancore...324 H20
LITTLE PROVOST
st. N Melbourne...17 A17
LITTLE QUEEN
st. Melbourne...1 G11
st. Melbourne...23 L8
LITTLE QUEENSBERRY
st. Carlton...18 C19
LITTLER
ct. Altona Mdw...451 J3
LITTLE RICHMOND
st. Geelong...703 E12

LITTLE ROSE
st. Richmond...26 G19
LITTLE RUBY
st. Preston...327 C2
LITTLE RYRIE
st. Geelong...702 K8
LITTLE ST VINCENT
st. Albert Park...29 C12
LITTLE SMITH
st. Fitzroy...25 E1
st. Kensington...34 A8
st. Yarraville...367 B13
LITTLE SMYTHE
st. Geelong, off Brougham St...703 A5
LITTLE SWALLOW
st. Port Melb...412 G6
LITTLE TRIBE
st. S Melbourne...29 D9
LITTLE TURNER
st. Abbotsford...20 D14
LITTLE UNION
st. Brighton East...455 C15
LITTLE VALLEY
rd. Templestowe...331 C9
LITTLE VICTORIA
st. Fitzroy...25 C1
LITTLE WALKER
la. Clifton Hill...20 H3
LITTLE WEBB
st. N Melbourne...17 D19
LITTLE WELLINGTON
st. Collingwood...19 H15
LITTLE WILLIAM
st. Melbourne...1 F11
st. Melbourne...23 K8
LITTLE WITHERS
st. Albert Park...29 F13
LITTLEWOOD
st. Hampton...495 A7
LITTLE YARRA
rd. Yarra Jctn...347 B17
LITTLE YORK
st. S Melbourne...29 L2
LITTON
ct. Craigieburn...150 G20
LIVERMORE
cl. Vermont S...421 G7
LIVERPOOL
cct. Craigieburn...150 G10
ct. Nar Warrn S...578 H2
dr. Keysborough...534 A10
rd. Boronia...425 B6
rd. Kilsyth...381 C7
rd. Kilsyth...381 D14
rd. Kilsyth...425 B6
rd. Kilsyth S...381 D14
rd. The Basin...425 B6
st. Bentleigh E...457 C20
st. Coburg...325 C4
st. Fitzroy N...326 A19
st. Footscray...366 K7
st. Melbourne...24 J4
LIVESTOCK
rd. Pakenham...585 B16
LIVIANA
dr. Rowville...502 L6
dr. Rowville...503 A6
LIVINGSTON
st. Deer Park...318 K10
st. Highett...496 C12
LIVINGSTONE
cl. Burwood...418 E5
ct. Mt Eliza...626 J16
dr. Greenvale...191 K15
pde. Preston...327 A3
rd. Eltham...287 J6
rd. Malvern East...456 K2
rd. Vermont S...420 J10
ri. Lynbrook...551 H17
sq. Point Cook...450 G9
st. Coburg N...282 A14
st. Ivanhoe...327 K12
LIVONIA
pl. Dandenong N...501 J11
LIVORNO
la. Point Cook...450 E8
LIZA
ct. Glenroy...280 G10
L L
rd. Officer...555 L12
LLANEAST
st. Armadale...415 H14
LLANOS
av. Malvern East...457 K1
LLEWELLYN
av. Aspendale Gdn...547 B6
ct. Cranbourne N...577 L7
ct. Noble Park...535 B4
pl. Eumemmerring..537 A15
st. Beaumaris...530 H4

LLOYD
av. Epping...197 G19
av. Narre Warren...553 D7
av. Reservoir...283 B2
ct. Blackburn S...419 L5
ct. Brookfield...268 B4
ct. Templestowe...332 B14
rd. Research...289 A9
st. Balwyn N...373 E6
st. Belmont...706 G1
st. Deer Park...319 C18
st. Heidelberg Ht...328 D2
st. Kensington...33 L17
st. Knoxfield...463 C5
st. Langwarrin...629 B4
st. Malvern East...416 H19
st. Mont Albert N...374 G11
st. Newport...410 E10
st. Northcote...327 C17
st. Rye...696 J7
st. Strathmore...279 K19
st. W Melbourne...33 L17
st. W Melbourne...368 F8
st.n, Knoxfield...463 C4
LLOYDS
av. Caulfield E...456 D5
pl. Attwood...237 A12
LLOYD WEBBER
dr. Carrum Downs...575 D16
LOATTA
st. Rye...697 B7
LOBATOR
st. Frankston N...600 D8
LOBB
st. Brunswick...325 G13
st. Coburg...325 G1
LOBELIA
ct. Blackburn N...375 H8
ct. Cranbourne N...578 A6
ct. Dingley Vill...532 K5
ct. S Morang...243 K1
gr. Cairnlea...319 E9
st. Reservoir...282 B10
LOBOSCO
ct. Kilsyth...425 E1
LOCAN
ct. Altona Mdw...451 F2
LOCARNO
av. Kallista...467 G5
ct. Mulgrave...501 B6
LOCH
av. Monbulk...468 J2
av. St Kilda E...414 L20
av. St Kilda E...415 A20
av. St Kilda E...454 L1
cr. Strathmore...280 A17
ct. Bentleigh E...497 D2
ct. Glen Waverley...460 F11
rd. Dandenong N...502 A15
st. Camberwell...372 K18
st. Coburg...325 F5
st. Cranbourne...578 E19
st. E Geelong...703 F13
st. Ferntree Gly...463 F1
st. Hawthorn E...372 E20
st. Kew...372 B6
st. Kilsyth...381 A5
st. Pt Lonsdale...710 G4
st. St Kilda W...413 L13
st. Surrey Hills...374 E18
st. Yarraville...366 L14
LOCHABAR
ct. Ivanhoe...328 F9
LOCHABER
av. Frankston...628 B7
LOCHALSH
ct. Endeavour Hl...503 H19
LOCH ARD
dr. Williamstn N...410 G12
LOCHARD
dr. Torquay...712 D3
tce. Nar Warrn S...552 G5
LOCHARN
cr. Keysborough...534 J12
ct. Kealba...276 J17
LOCHER
av. Reservoir...283 F2
LOCH FYNE
ct. Sorrento...679 B14
LOCHGOIN
mw. Highton...701 E11
LOCHGREEN
vw. Cranbourne...603 H7
LOCHIEL
av. Edithvale...546 F10
av. Mt Martha...655 H15
ct. Greenvale...237 C2
LOCHINVAR
rd. Glen Waverley...460 B9
st. Pascoe Vale S...324 L5
LOCHMABEN
ct. Clarinda...498 E8
ct. Greenvale...237 D2

LOCHNORRIES
gr. Reservoir...283 A16
LOCH RAE
ct. Hawthorn...371 J19
LOCHTON
ct. Greenvale...193 B18
LOCINDA
st. Highett...495 L12
LOCK
av. Werribee...447 J19
ct. Sunbury...143 J3
st. Airport W...278 J17
st. Fawkner...281 H8
LOCKE
st. Brighton East...455 D18
st. Essendon...323 K10
st. Rye...696 H4
LOCKENS
av. Glen Waverley...459 K9
LOCKERBIE
ct. Greenvale...193 C20
ct. St Kilda E...415 B18
LOCKEY
av. Arthurs Seat...685 J14
LOCKHART
av. Attwood...237 B11
ct. Hoppers Csg...448 F9
ct. Kilsyth...381 E9
dr. Rosebud...699 K4
rd. Ringwood N...378 D4
st. Camberwell...417 J3
st. Caulfield...455 G4
LOCKHEED
st. Strathmr Ht...279 D10
LOCKIE
pl. Taylors Hill...274 H15
LOCKINGTON
cr. Dandenong...535 H1
cr. Pt Lonsdale...710 B5
LOCKLEY
cl. Endeavour Hl...537 L9
st. Hadfield...280 J5
LOCKS
wy. Belgrave S...506 L5
wy. Belgrave S...507 A5
LOCKSLEY
av. Kew...372 H9
av. Reservoir...282 G13
ch. Vermont...421 C4
cl. Bayswater...423 A9
cl. Dingley Vill...533 D10
cl. Heathmont...379 D19
rd. Eaglemont...328 E14
rd. Ivanhoe...328 E14
rd. Ivanhoe...328 E15
rd. Rye...697 H4
LOCKTON
av. Reservoir...282 B1
LOCKWOOD
av. Brighton East...455 D12
dr. Roxburgh Pk...194 A6
gr. Thomastown...240 C12
rd. Belgrave Ht...506 D1
rd. Belgrave Ht...506 F1
rd. Belgrave S...506 E3
st. Bentleigh...496 C5
st. Pt Lonsdale...710 E3
LOCKWOODS
rd. Boronia...424 F6
LOCUM
ct. Wheelers Hl...460 K19
LODDEN
st. Sunshine N...321 D16
LODDON
av. Keilor...276 K13
av. Reservoir...283 G12
cl. Caroline Spr...318 B5
cl. Rowville...463 C17
cl. Clayton S...498 F8
ct. Croydon Hl...335 J15
ct. Thomastown...241 K16
ct. Werribee...447 G8
dr. Taylors Hill...274 H12
st. Box Hill N...375 B10
LODE
ct. Diggers Rest...187 D13
LODERS
rd. Moorooduc...658 G11
LODGE
cl. Rowville...502 H3
cr. Berwick...553 L7
ct. Viewbank...285 K19
rd. Camberwell...417 E7
st. Greensbrgh...286 D9
st. Maddingley...221 K20
st. Noble Park...501 A18
LOEMAN
ct. Burwood E...419 H10
st. Essendon...324 D9
st. Strathmore...280 B19
st. Strathmore...280 B19

LOEMANS
rd. Bulla...189 J19
rd. Bulla...232 L8
rd. Bulla...233 C7
LOFTS
av. Kew...372 B13
LOFTUS
ct. Keysborough...534 D8
st. E Geelong...703 G14
LOFTY
av. Camberwell...417 F5
LOGAN
av. Altona...409 A15
av. Kalorama...382 L15
av. Kalorama...383 A14
av. Ormond...456 G14
av. Pk Orchards...333 L9
av. Warrandyte...333 L9
ct. Lysterfield...464 F17
ct. Mentone...531 F6
ct. Noble Park...535 C3
ct. Sunbury...143 A18
pl. Berwick...553 L1
st. Canterbury...373 E20
st. Frankston...599 J20
st. Glenroy...280 C6
LOGANBERRY
cl. Cranbourne N...577 K4
LOGAN PARK
tr. Lysterfield...504 L20
tr. Nar Warrn N...504 L20
LOGIE
ct. Oakleigh...457 L9
st. Oakleigh...457 J8
LOGISTICS
wy. Altona North...409 C8
LOG SCHOOL
rd. Doncaster...374 G4
LOHSE
st. Laverton...407 D17
LOIS
ct. Bentleigh E...497 D2
ct. Langwarrin...602 A19
ct. Thomastown...240 L15
pl. Mt Eliza...626 B12
st. Ringwood E...379 B11
st. St Albans...276 F19
LOJOSA
ct. Ferntree Gly...423 J19
LOLA
st. Mulgrave...500 H4
LOLLER
st. Brighton...454 L18
st. Springvale...499 L7
LOLLIPOP
dr. Wyndham Va...446 C9
LOLOMA
ct. Glen Iris...417 K11
LOMA
ct. Tootgarook...698 C8
st. Noble Park...500 D19
st. Ringwood E...379 C12
LOMA LINDA
gr. Balwyn N...373 L8
LOMANDRA
ct. Bundoora...242 E14
ct. Nar Warrn S...553 D19
wy. Cairnlea...319 F8
LOMAR
ct. Frankston...628 F1
LOMATIA
cl. Frankston S...628 A16
ct. N Warrandyte...289 L18
LOMBARD
ct. Nar Warrn N...538 D7
rd. Vermont...377 J20
st. Roxburgh Pk...193 K5
wy. Seaford...600 A6
LOMBARDY
av. Dromana...686 G7
LOMIC
ct. Templestowe...332 B4
LOMOND
av. Kilsyth...381 A5
ct. Endeavour Hl...537 L6
ct. Lalor...240 G8
ct. Warrandyte...332 K4
ct. Werribee...446 K13
dr. Glen Waverley...420 J18
st. Glen Iris...416 K9
tce. E Geelong...703 G14
tce. Malvern East...417 F20
tce. Thomson...703 G14
LONDON
cr. Narre Warren...539 B12
cr. Narre Warren...539 B13
ct. Blackburn N...376 A9
ct. Craigieburn...150 B15
ct. Dandenong N...501 G14
ct. Greensbrgh...286 B10
ct. Hoppers Csg...405 E19
ct. Kurunjang...227 D10
dr. Bayswater...424 A5

rd. Broadmeadows...238 C17
st. Bentleigh...496 D2
LONDON BRIDGE
rd. Portsea...677 D4
LONDRES
wy. S Morang...199 A14
LONDREW
av. Springvale S...499 F18
ct. Maribyrnong...323 A12
ct. Tullamarine...278 J1
LONG
dr. Sunbury...142 J3
pl. Hughesdale...457 F15
st. Elsternwick...455 A2
st. Frankston...627 H3
st. Langwarrin...629 C2
st. Mentone...531 F9
st. Reservoir...240 G20
st. Williamstown...411 A15
LONGACRES
rd. Yallambie...285 G16
LONG BEACH
cr. Mt Waverley...458 K8
LONGBEACH
cl. Aspendale...546 E3
LONGBOURNE
av. Notting Hill...459 K13
LONGBRAE
av. Forest Hill...420 K4
ct. Forest Hill...420 J6
LONG CRESCENT NORTH
Langwarrin...628 L11
LONG CRESCENT SOUTH
Langwarrin...628 L12
LONGFELLOW
av. Mooroolbark...381 G2
dr. Delahey...275 D16
LONGFIELD
ct. Watsonia N...243 D19
st. Burnley...371 C17
LONGFORD
cl. Hampton Pk...551 E4
cr. Coolaroo...238 C6
ct. Kealba...320 L1
ct. Kealba...321 A1
ct. Springvale...499 J4
LONGFOREST
rd. Long Forest...224 D17
LONG GULLY
rd. Healesville...212 C17
rd. Panton Hill...204 J14
rd. Panton Hill...249 B4
LONGHURST
cr. Hillside...274 D1
LONG ISLAND POINT
Patterson L...573 H7
LONGLAND
rd. Mitcham...377 J14
LONGLEAF
gr. Mitcham...377 A15
st. Frankston N...600 B10
LONGMORE
st. St Kilda W...413 K12
LONGMUIR
rd. Watsonia...285 G7
LONG POCKITT
la. Belgrave...467 B16
la. Selby...467 B16
LONGS
rd. Lower Plenty...286 D13
rd. Yellingbo...388 C5
LONGSTAFF
ct. Doncaster E...332 E15
ct. Vermont...421 J4
rd. Bayswater...424 C1
st. Carnegie...456 K13
st. Ivanhoe East...328 L15
st. Kew East...372 G3
wy. Sunbury...142 G6
LONGTOWN
ct. Craigieburn...194 G3
LONGUEVILLE
la. Grovedale...706 F12
LONG VALLEY
wy. Doncaster E...332 G12
wy. Eltham...288 A1
LONGVIEW
av. Bentleigh E...456 L20
av. Manifold Ht...702 B5
ct. Thomastown...242 B18
pde. Rosanna...284 J17
rd. Balwyn N...373 D3
rd. Croydon S...379 F10
rd. Mt Evelyn...339 J18
st. Pascoe Vale...280 F14
LONGWOOD
av. Cairnlea...319 G8
cl. Rowville...464 B12
ct. Meadow Ht...238 C3
dr. Epping...198 E15
dr. Epping...198 G17
dr. Mornington...657 B4

LONHILL
ct. Endeavour Hl...537
LONIE
st. N Melbourne...34
LONSDALE
av. Hampton E...495
av. Rowville...463
cct. Hoppers Csg...449
cr. Cranbourne N...577
ct. Caroline Spr...318
la. Melbourne...1
la. Melbourne...23
st. Bulleen...329
st. Caulfield S...456
st. Coburg...281
st. Dandenong...536
st. Geelong...703
st. McCrae...684
st. Melbourne...1
st. Melbourne...23
st. Pt Lonsdale...710
st. Rosebud...684
st. S Geelong...703
LONSDALE PARK
la. Launching Pl...344
LOOKER
rd. Montmorency...286
st. Murrumbeena...457
LOOKOUT
rd. Kalorama...383
rd. Red Hill...687
LOOKOVER
rd. Donvale...377
LOOMAI
cl. Greensbrgh...244
LOONGANA
av. Glenroy...279
st. Rye...697
LOOP
rd. Werribee...487
LOOREA
ct. Greensbrgh...244
LORAC
av. Brighton...454
ct. Sydenham...274
LORACK
cl. Mulgrave...500
LORAINE
av. Box Hill N...374
LORAM
ct. Blackburn S...419
ct. Glen Waverley...420
LORANNE
st. Bentleigh...496
LORD
av. Dingley Vill...533
pl. Braybrook...365
pl. Braybrook...366
pl. Richmond...26
rd. Gruyere...342
st. Bacchus Msh...222
st. Brunswick E...325
st. Caulfield E...456
st. Doncaster E...375
st. Fawkner...281
st. McKinnon...456
st. Richmond...26
st. Richmond...371
LORDING
st. Ferntree Gly...424
LORD RODNEY
dr. Patterson L...547
wy. Patterson L...547
LORDS
ri. Berwick...554
LORD SOMERS
rd. Ferny Creek...425
rd. Tremont...425
LORD WEAVER
gr. Bonbeach...545
LOREEN
st. Oakleigh S...457
LORENA
cl. Hoppers Csg...447
LORENSEN
av. Coburg N...281
LORENZ
st. Sunshine...321
LORENZO
wy. Aspendale Gdn...547
LORETTA
av. Wheelers Hl...461
ct. Seabrook...450
pl. Sunshine W...364
st. Carrum Downs...601
LORETTAS
wy. Anglesea...713
LORETTO
av. Ferntree Gly...423
st. Cremorne...26
LORGROVE
ct. Avondale Ht...322

ORI
l. Glen Waverley....460 J3
ORICA
Broadmeadows..238 A19
ORIENNE
Heathmont.........378 E18
ORIKEET
Boronia..............424 A11
Diamond Ck.......245 D12
Frankston 628 C5
Mornington.........640 K16
Werribee...........447 K6
Berwick 553 L1
Nunawading 376 J18
Bundoora...........284 B3
RIMER
Wattle Glen........246 H15
Wattle Glen........247 B10
Greensbrgh........285 K3
Melton..............268 G2
Port Melb...........367 G20
Port Melb...........411 G1
Southbank..........23 A17
Southbank.........368 F17
RINDA
Sydenham 274 J5
RIS
Grovedale 706 E14
Blackburn 375 G20
Silvan 384 E13
Springvale S 533 L2
RMER
Yarraville 367 C18
RNA
Northcote 327 C14
Sunshine W 364 B3
Aspendale Gdn...546 K6
Mooroolbark........337 H16
Templstw Lr 330 J10
The Basin...........425 A10
Melton W...........225 L17
Bacchus Msh.......222 A13
Cheltenham 497 C20
Clematis 508 K4
Cranbourne........604 C3
Seaford..............599 H9
RNE
Camberwell........372 L19
de. Mont Albert........374 C16
Hawthorn E........372 F17
Prahran 415 A10
Caulfield E..........456 E3
Fawkner.............281 G10
Lalor..................241 G11
Melbourne 31 D19
Melbourne 414 B10
Moonee Pnd 324 A15
Yarraville 366 L18
RRAINE
Langwarrin 601 C20
Warrandyte........333 F3
Jacana..............237 G16
Hampton 494 J6
Hampton Pk.......551 E10
Pakenham 585 D7
Sunshine 364 K2
Warranwood......334 H13
Wheelers Hl.......460 K17
Briar Hill 286 K6
Burwood E.........419 G8
le. Viewbank..........285 G20
Bacchus Msh.....222 B14
Boronia.............424 G8
Cheltenham 531 B4
Dandenong........535 F5
Essendon..........323 K9
Frankston 599 F16
Hampton 494 J6
RRAINE LEE
Sydenham 275 B8
RREAN
Brighton East.....455 G13
RRIMORE
Mt Eliza.............642 J1
S ANGELES
Ripponlea 414 G20
SSI
Keilor Ldg..........276 B3
THAIR
Pascoe Vale S 324 H6
THIAN
N Melbourne........34 L20
W Melbourne.......34 L20
TIS
Keilor Dn 276 B16
TRIEL
Mt Martha...........655 J13
TUS
Cairnlea 319 G10
Mulgrave 500 H4
Cheltenham 531 F2
Diamond Ck.......245 L6
Epping...............197 J15

ct. Meadow Ht........237 J1
ct. Wantirna............422 F6
LOUDEN
pl. Melbourne.............2 E10
pl. Melbourne...........24 D6
LOUDON
rd. Burwood............418 A8
LOUGHIES
tr. Ringwood N........378 A4
LOUGHNAN
pl. Ringwood N........378 E7
rd. Ringwood..........377 L10
rd. Ringwood N........377 L10
st. Richmond............26 A13
LOUIS
av. Dandenong........536 D2
ct. Newtown...........701 L8
st. Airport W...........279 A12
st. Doveton............537 A8
st. Glen Iris.............416 E15
st. Greensbrgh........286 B7
st. Heathmont.........379 D19
st. Reservoir............282 J7
wy. Sunbury............143 H6
LOUISA
ct. Narre Warren.....539 B16
ct. Oakleigh S.........497 G7
pl. Templestowe......331 L8
st. Brunswick..........325 G12
st. Coburg..............325 G3
st. Croydon............380 J5
st. Kilsyth...............380 J5
st. Mt Evelyn..........339 C17
LOUIS BUVELOT
wyn. Diamond Ck.......245 A13
LOUISE
av. Mont Albert........374 D17
ct. Doncaster..........330 B20
ct. Glen Waverley....419 L17
ct. Hallam...............538 B14
ct. Rowville.............463 L17
ct. Seaford..............599 K2
ct. Skye..................575 G18
ct. Springvale S.......499 F20
st. Brighton East......455 F13
st. Clifton Hill............20 H7
st. Heidelberg..........329 C5
st. Lalor..................241 G9
st. Melbourne............31 B13
st. Melbourne..........414 A7
st. Rye....................696 H6
LOUISE BAILLE
av. Narr Warrn S.......553 G20
LOUISE MACK
wk. Lynbrook...........551 E19
LOUISVILLE
av. Pascoe Vale S.....324 H6
LOUPIE
st. Mooroolbark......381 H3
LOURIE
ct. Ringwood..........377 L10
LOUVAIN
st. Coburg N...........281 B17
LOVAT
ct. Coolaroo............238 E3
pl. Melton...............268 L2
LOVE
cl. Maddingley........264 C3
st. Black Rock.........529 E1
st. Camberwell........417 D7
st. Yarraville...........366 J18
LOVELACE
st. Preston..............327 D2
LOVELL
cl. Rowville.............463 J15
ct. Whittington........704 C20
dr. St Albans...........320 E13
la. Nunawading, off Wood St..........376 H15
st. Hawthorn E.........416 E6
LOVELY
st. Fawkner.............281 E3
wy. S Morang..........199 B15
LOVERIDGE
wk. Berwick.............554 E7
wy. S Morang..........198 K10
LOVETT
dr. Avondale Ht........322 G8
LOVITT
cl. Diamond Ck.......246 E9
LOWALDE
dr. Epping...............197 L19
LOWAN
av. Templstw Lr......329 L8
av. Yallambie...........286 D11
ct. Dallas.................238 D12
ct. Ferntree Gly.......463 G10
ct. Frankston...........600 D16
ct. Werribee.............446 K15
st. Brunswick E........326 C15
LOWANA
cr. Forest Hill..........420 E6

LOWDEN
ct. Nar Warrn S.......552 H19
LOWE
av. Altona...............408 L15
cr. Sunshine............365 H3
ct. Bayswater N.......379 G16
ct. Doncaster E.......375 H2
st. Ivanhoe.............328 B12
st. Mt Eliza.............642 K1
LOWELL
av. Kingsbury..........283 J11
LOWEN
av. Heathmont.........378 J20
rd. Cockatoo...........510 K9
rd. Glen Waverley....419 L16
LOWENPARK
dr. Hoppers Csg......449 G2
LOWER
cr. Mt Eliza.............642 F6
ct. Nunawading......376 L19
ct. Nunawading......377 A19
dr. Kew...................371 H5
esp. St Kilda.............414 A17
la. Melbourne...........25 B20
rd. Eltham North.....287 H1
rd. Wattle Glen........246 J4
LOWER DANDENONG
rd. Braeside............531 H8
rd. Dingley Vill.........531 H8
rd. Mentone.............531 H8
rd. Moorabbin Aprt..531 H8
rd. Mordialloc..........531 H8
rd. Parkdale............531 H8
LOWER GRIEVE
rd. Avonsleigh.........470 F20
LOWER HEIDELBERG
rd. Eaglemont.........328 J14
rd. Heidelberg.........328 J14
rd. Ivanhoe.............328 C14
rd. Ivanhoe East......328 C14
rd. Ivanhoe East......328 J14
LOWER HOMESTEAD
rd. Chirnside Pk......292 B15
rd. Chirnside Pk......292 D14
rd. Wonga Park........292 B15
rd. Wonga Park........292 D14
LOWER PAPER MILLS
rd. Fyansford..........701 D6
LOWER PLENTY
rd. Heidelberg.........328 H3
rd. Rosanna............328 H3
rd. Viewbank...........285 J15
LOWER SOMERVILLE
rd. Baxter...............645 E6
rd. Somerville..........645 H14
LOWER TERRACE
cr. Noble Park N......501 C13
LOWER VIEW
rd. Montrose............382 B15
rd. Mt Dandenong...382 B15
LOWES
rd. Chum Creek.......213 D8
rd. Healesville.........213 H1
rd. Yarra Jctn..........347 D14
LOWESS
la. Point Cook.........451 B7
LOWRY
ct. Nar Warrn N......539 C11
LOWSON
st. Fawkner.............281 F2
LOWTHER
ct. Cranbourne N....578 D10
st. Alphington.........327 H18
LOXFORD
ct. Nar Warrn S.......552 H18
LOXLEY
bvd. Nar Warrn S.......553 D15
ct. Doncaster E.......331 H15
ct. Hoppers Csg......405 A17
LOXTON
av. Wantirna S.........462 C2
st. Kew...................372 J14
tce. Epping..............198 H16
LOXWOOD
av. Keysborough.....534 B10
LOYOLA
av. Brunswick..........325 J15
ct. Watsonia............285 E4
gr. Burnley...............371 C20
rd. Werribee............448 A19
LUAIN
av. Oakleigh S.........497 H2
LUANA
la. Sunbury.............143 F16
LUANDA
st. Keysborough......534 J13
LUBBROOK
cl. Ferntree Gly.......463 G8
LUBECK
ct. Meadow Ht.........238 A6
LUBEL
st. Anglesea............713 K1

LUBRANO
st. Brighton East.....455 F14
LUBY
ct. Melton...............268 G2
LUCALBYN
ct. Wandana Ht.......701 D18
LUCAN
st. Caulfield N.........415 C15
LUCANIA
cl. Ringwood E.......379 F17
LUCAS
av. Kilsyth...............381 B12
cl. Boronia..............424 E7
cr. Seaford..............599 K1
ct. Nar Warrn S.......552 G14
ct. Noble Park.........500 L16
ct. Sunshine W.......364 F8
pl. Tullamarine........278 K3
st. Brighton East.....495 B2
st. Caulfield S.........455 E11
st. Newcomb...........704 C14
st. Reservoir...........282 E15
LUCERNE
av. Mornington........640 K14
cr. Alphington.........371 K1
cr. Frankston..........628 G1
ct. Narre Warren.....538 L20
rd. Ferntree Gly.......463 F8
st. Ashburton..........417 E18
st. Campbellfield......239 F14
st. Mentone.............531 C10
st. Mt Waverley......419 J13
st. Vermont.............421 E4
LUCETTA
wy. Sydenham.........275 C7
LUCIA
ct. Carrum Downs...601 D3
ct. Blackburn S.......419 G5
LUCIAN
av. Springvale.........500 A9
LUCIEER
ct. Templestowe......331 H9
LUCIELLA
ct. Dandenong N.....502 C18
LUCIEN
rd. Rye...................696 L3
LUCIFER
st. Balwyn N...........373 G1
LUCILIA
pl. Bundoora...........242 K15
LUCILLE
av. Croydon S.........379 G11
av. Reservoir...........283 E3
LUCINDA
cl. Heathmont.........379 D18
ct. Warranwood......335 C14
LUCK
st. Eltham...............287 H7
LUCKIE
st. Nunawading......376 D13
LUCKINS
rd. Bentleigh...........496 E5
LUCKNOW
ct. Mitcham.............377 A17
st. Mitcham.............377 A17
st. Travancore........324 G18
LUCON
gln. Point Cook.........450 E11
LUCY
cl. Rowville.............463 H15
ct. Bundoora...........242 F20
ct. Narre Warren.....539 B13
pl. Carrum Downs...575 D16
pl. Ringwood N.......334 H20
st. Gardenvale........455 B10
wy. E Geelong.........703 K5
LUCY HILL
ri. Rowville.............503 D4
LUDBROOK
av. Caulfield S........455 D11
LUDEMAN
ct. Reservoir...........282 H2
LUDLOW
ct. Derrimut............363 C6
ct. Officer...............555 J19
LUDSTONE
st. Hampton............495 B6
LUDWELL
cr. Bentleigh E........497 D2
LUDWIG
st. Springvale S......534 A1
LUENA
rd. Balwyn N...........374 B8
LUGANO
av. Dromana............686 H5
st. Lalor.................240 D9
LUGARNO
ct. Keysborough.....534 E7
LUGG
st. Altona...............408 L13
LUGO
ct. Tullamarine........278 E5

LUGTON
st. Alphington.........371 H1
LUISA
av. Dandenong S.....549 H11
ct. Brookfield..........268 C4
ct. Montmorency.....286 L9
LUKE
av. Blackburn..........376 D13
ct. Frankston S.......627 K12
ct. Hampton Pk.......551 D11
ct. Keysborough.....534 B7
ct. Mill Park............243 A3
pl. Guys Hill............541 H20
st. Clayton..............459 B20
st. Reservoir...........282 E7
LUKEDENN
dr. Beaconsfield......555 E8
LUKIN
ct. Mill Park............242 B8
LULIE
st. Abbotsford..........20 C14
LULWORTH
pl. Frankston..........600 H17
st. Blackburn N.......376 B10
LULY
st. Altona North......409 J6
LUM
rd. Wheelers Hl.......460 J16
rd. Wheelers Hl.......460 J19
rd. Wheelers Hl.......460 J19
LUME
ct. Noble Park.........535 A3
LUMEA
pl. Melton W...........225 L15
LUMEAH
av. Olinda...............426 J10
cr. Ferntree Gly.......463 G7
ct. Dingley Vill.........533 A2
rd. Caulfield N.........455 D2
LUMLEAH
ct. Greensbrgh........286 D10
LUMLEY
ct. Prahran.............414 L12
LUNAN
pl. Frankston S.......627 G12
LUNAR
cr. Vermont............421 D4
LUND
ct. Highton.............705 J3
LUNE
ct. Torquay.............712 B3
LUNETTE
av. Preston..............282 L17
LUNIK
ct. Whittington........704 B20
LUNN
ct. Altona Mdw........406 L20
ct. Narre Warren.....539 B18
LUNTAR
rd. Oakleigh S.........497 H4
LUPIN
ct. Cranbourne N....578 A4
ct. St Albans...........320 G8
st. Blackburn N.......375 J8
st. Dromana............686 F8
LUPTON
st. Geelong West....702 F6
wy. Boronia.............424 E11
LURG
av. Sunshine N........320 L13
LURLINE
st. Bundoora...........284 E4
st. Cranbourne........604 B3
LURNEA
rd. Glen Iris............417 B14
LUSATIA PARK
rd. Woori Yall..........345 A19
LUSCANDER
ct. Hillside..............232 E19
LUSCOMBE
av. Carrum Downs...574 L16
ct. Kilsyth...............381 C9
st. Brunswick..........325 J17
LUSH
ct. Altona Mdw........451 C1
la. Melbourne.............2 H17
la. Melbourne...........24 G8
LUSHER
rd. Croydon............379 L9
LUSK
dr. Vermont.............421 F3
LUTANA
ct. Frankston..........628 C4
ct. Mooroolbark......381 J4
ct. Mt Martha..........656 E5
ct. Wheelers Hl.......461 C18
st. Rosebud W........699 E2
LUTEA
ct. Mill Park............243 D7
LUTHER
av. Grovedale..........706 G11
pl. Frankston..........600 J18
st. Box Hill N..........375 D7

Rosanna 329 D1
Dandenong 536 B9
Elwood 454 F2
Maddingley 263 J1
Reservoir 283 A6
CREDDEN
Box Hill S 418 J2
CRORY
Coburg 325 H3
CUBBIN
Mill Park 243 A7
Sunbury 142 H10
Taylors L 233 A19
n. Caroline Spr 274 B8
Burwood 419 A10
Footscray 367 A4
Ivanhoe East 328 L13
Ivanhoe East 329 A13
Kew East 372 J1
e. Doncaster E 332 E16
y. Berwick 554 H18
CULLOCH
Seaford 599 D9
Dromana 685 L7
Essendon N 323 F2
Nunawading 376 J14
k. Point Cook 449 L9
CULLOCK
Warrandyte 333 K1
CULLY
Ascot Vale 324 B17
CURDY
Herne Hill 701 H2
CURE
Ringwood E 379 F17
CUTCHEON
Mt Eliza 626 E15
Northcote 326 J13
y. Collingwood 19 L17
DERMOTT
Mooroolbark 337 B16
ACDHUI
Eltham North 245 B18
ACDONALD
Altona North 410 B5
Mornington 640 H16
Sunbury 143 A5
Taylors Hill 274 G13
Glen Iris 416 G8
DONALD
Ivanhoe 327 L14
Templestowe 331 J7
Boronia 424 J9
Bacchus Msh 221 K19
Nar Warrn S 552 J14
Carlton 18 E20
Roxburgh Pk 194 A10
Sunshine 365 C2
Glenroy 279 J4
Brooklyn 365 J15
Queenscliff 707 L16
Rye 697 H5
Beaumaris 530 B4
Belmont 702 G18
Coburg N 281 F18
E Geelong 703 E14
Melton S 268 H7
Mordialloc 531 K17
Northcote 327 B19
Preston 282 F20
Werribee 447 H17
Williamstown, off
Madigan Ct 410 L16
DONALDS
Mulgrave 460 A15
Epping 197 J18
Mill Park 199 B20
Mill Park 243 D1
S Morang 199 B20
S Morang 243 E1
DONALDS DRAIN
Pakenham 585 K19
ACDONNELL
Kilsyth 381 J6
Taylors L 275 K1
DONNELL
Coburg N 281 H15
DONOUGH
Vermont 421 L2
ACDOUGAL
Blairgowrie 679 G17
DOUGAL
Kurunjang 227 E6
DOUGALL
Sunbury 143 C16
Anglesea 713 K2
Brunswick 325 F17
Fawkner 281 F5
Geelong West 702 D3
DOWALL
Hampton Pk 551 D12
Mitcham 377 C12

McDOWELL
st. Greensbrgh 285 K6
st. Rosebud 684 C15
MACE
ct. Mt Evelyn 339 A20
ri. Hallam 538 C18
MACEDON
av. Balwyn N 373 B3
av. Dallas 238 J10
av. Dromana 686 D7
cl. Caroline Spr 317 J7
ct. Nunawading 376 K9
ct. Templstw Lr 330 G8
rd. Templstw Lr 330 F14
st. Hoppers Csg 449 A1
st. Keilor 277 D13
st. Maribyrnong 322 L19
st. Maribyrnong 323 A19
st. Sunbury 143 H10
McELROY
st. Sunshine W 364 K8
McEVOY
cl. Highton 705 E8
st. Kew 371 C10
McEWAN
rd. Heidelberg Ht 284 F20
rd. Heidelberg Ht 328 F1
rd. Pk Orchards 334 D17
McEWEN
dr. Sunbury 143 G4
MACEY
av. Avondale Ht 322 D12
gr. Ringwood N 378 E5
st. Cranbourne 578 G20
st. Croydon S 380 A12
McFADZEAN
av. Reservoir 282 G3
av. Reservoir 282 G8
st. Coldstream 295 F14
MACFARLAN
av. Blairgowrie 679 F17
la. South Yarra 31 L10
la. South Yarra 414 F5
st. South Yarra 31 K10
st. South Yarra 414 E5
MACFARLAND
st. Brunswick 325 E10
McFARLAND
st. Bacchus Msh 222 B15
McFARLANE
cr. Dandenong 536 A7
cr. Epping 197 L19
ct. Highett 496 F13
ct. Lysterfield 464 A17
la. Albert Park 29 F13
st. Keilor East 322 D4
st. Montmorency 286 K10
st. Northcote 326 J13
McFEES
rd. Dandenong N 501 J18
McGAHY
ct. Templestowe 332 A14
st. Templstw Lr 330 G14
McGEE
pl. Burnside 318 E4
McGEORGE
ct. Sunbury 142 G8
McGHEE
av. Mitcham 377 D14
McGILL
ct. Pakenham 558 L20
ct. Sunbury 144 D11
McGINESS
av. Roxburgh Pk 194 D10
McGIVERN
ct. Bayswater N 424 H1
McGLONE
st. Mitcham 377 A14
McGLYNN
av. S Morang 243 G2
McGOUN
st. Richmond 26 D9
MACGOWAN
av. Glen Huntly 456 B9
McGOWAN
av. Preston 282 C19
ct. Altona Mdw 451 H7
st. Southbank 3 E12
st. Southbank 24 C18
McGOWANS
la. Burwood 418 L7
pl. Carlton 18 D13
rd. Donvale 376 J4
McGOWN
rd. Mt Eliza 626 E16
McGRATH
cl. Kealba 276 L20
ct. Richmond 26 G15
pl. Sunshine N 321 J16
rd. Werribee 446 G19
rd. Wyndham Va 446 G19
rd. Wyndham Va 446 H10
st. Bacchus Msh 222 C19
st. Bellfield 328 B5
st. Caulfield 455 J6
st. Sunshine 365 G3
McGRATHS
la. Melbourne 24 J6
MACGREGOR
av. Portsea 678 B2
ct. Rowville 463 E12
st. Malvern East 456 H3
st. Parkdale 531 J11
McGREGOR
av. Beaumaris 529 J8
av. Brunswick W 324 K7
av. Healesville 214 A15
av. Mt Martha 669 C3
av.e, Healesville 214 E15
ct. Bacchus Msh 221 K19
ct. Dingley Vill 533 C6
ct. Mt Evelyn 339 D15
ct. Sunshine W 364 A7
rd. Pakenham 584 E20
st. Canterbury 373 G19
st. Clayton 498 J1
st. Fairfield 327 F14
st. Middle Park 30 E20
st. Middle Park 413 H11
st. Pascoe Vale 281 A12
McGRETTONS
rd. Healesville 257 D1
McGUIGAN
dr. Cranbourne W 603 F1
gr. Ferntree Gly 464 H8
McGUINNESS
rd. Bentleigh E 497 E3
McGUIRE
cr. Williamstown 410 J14
st. Cheltenham 497 E15
st. Greenvale 237 C1
McHALE
ct. Essendon 323 J6
McHENRY
st. St Kilda E 414 K20
MACHINERY
dr. Point Cook 450 A3
McILRAITH
ct. Croydon 380 L2
McILROYS
rd. Red Hill 687 K13
McILWAITH
ct. Berwick 554 J19
McILWRAITH
pl. Melbourne 24 J5
st. Princes Hill 18 F1
st. Princes Hill 325 J20
McILWRICK
st. Windsor 414 G12
McINDOE
pde. Parkdale 531 F16
McINNES
cl. Sunbury 143 A9
ct. Pakenham 584 J1
McINTOSH
av. Hoppers Csg 448 G4
ct. Aspendale Gdn 546 K4
pl. Monbulk 428 F16
rd. Altona North 409 K8
st. Airport W 278 K13
st. Northcote 326 G16
st. Oakleigh 458 B15
st. Sunshine 364 J2
MACINTYRE
la. Yering 252 C18
McINTYRE
al. Melbourne 2 D6
al. Melbourne 24 C4
av. Point Cook 449 K6
av. Roxburgh Pk 194 D11
cl. Ferntree Gly 463 L7
dr. Altona 409 A14
rd. Kealba 321 D5
rd. Sunshine N 321 B17
st. Burwood 418 C9
st. E Geelong 703 J12
McINTYRES
rd. Pk Orchards 333 D17
McIVER
pl. Kensington 33 J5
st. Brunswick 325 G14
st. Ferntree Gly 464 D7
McIVOR
ct. Melton W 225 H19
rd. St Albans 320 C3
st. Cheltenham 496 K19
st. Dallas 238 F12
st. Reservoir 283 C14
wy. Attwood 237 B12
MACK
cr. Clarinda 498 G10
ct. Belmont 706 H3
rd. Nar Warrn S 552 K14
st. Reservoir 283 B4
MACKA
av. Greensbrgh 287 A1

MACKAY
av. Glen Huntly 456 D10
av. Mooroolbark, off
Reay Rd 337 C20
rd. Yallambie 285 G14
st. Essendon 323 L6
st. Greenvale 236 L5
st. Prahran 32 H18
st. Prahran 414 K9
st. Springvale S 533 K3
st. Yarraville 367 C12
wk. Roxburgh Pk 193 K15
McKAY
av. Black Rock 529 G1
cl. Berwick 554 J11
ct. Dandenong N 502 C19
ct. Ringwood 378 D19
pl. Attwood 237 A11
rd. Rowville 462 L20
rd. Rowville 463 A20
st. Alphington 327 J13
st. Brunswick 325 D17
st. Coburg 325 G1
st. Mordialloc 531 L13
st. Parkdale 531 L13
st. Richmond 26 K4
st. Sunshine 365 E4
McKAYS
rd. Langwarrin 602 A18
McKEAN
st. Box Hill N 375 C12
st. Fitzroy N 20 A2
McKECHNIE
st. St Albans 320 B5
MACKEITH
ct. Mt Eliza 626 D20
McKELL
av. Sunbury 143 E6
MACKELLAR
av. Wheelers Hl 460 E16
cl. Nar Warrn N 538 B11
dr. Roxburgh Pk 194 A9
la. Point Cook 449 L7
McKELLAR
st. Bayswater 423 A7
st. Watsonia 285 E4
MACKELROY
rd. Plenty 244 D10
McKELVIE
ct. Glen Waverley 459 J9
McKENDRICK
la. W Melbourne 23 C3
McKENNA
rd. Forest Hill 420 E3
rd. Glen Waverley 459 J11
st. Avondale Ht 322 D14
MACKENNEL
st. Ivanhoe East 328 L14
McKENRY
pl. Dandenong N 501 K14
MACKENZIE
cl. Taylors L 233 H20
ct. Croydon S 379 J11
rd. W Melbourne 367 J16
st. Brunswick 325 E11
st. Cheltenham 530 H3
st. Cockatoo 511 B9
st. Melbourne 2 K2
st. Melbourne 24 E1
st. Reservoir 282 C5
McKENZIE
av. Healesville 214 J16
cr. Hoppers Csg 448 B3
cr. Roxburgh Pk 194 B10
cr. Roxburgh Pk 194 C10
ct. Greensbrgh 286 B8
ct. Merrimu 222 H7
ct. Oakleigh E 458 G12
gr. Montrose 382 D13
gr. Mt Dandenong 382 D13
la. Nar Warrn N 539 A9
rd. Beaconsfld Up 542 L17
st. Belmont 702 E17
st. Doncaster E 332 D18
st. Geelong 703 B11
st. Melton 226 J20
st. Richmond 26 K8
st. Seaford 599 E1
wy. Langwarrin 629 C1
McKENZIE-KING
dr. Millgrove 348 F2
McKEON
av. Pascoe Vale S 324 J5
cct. Dandenong N 502 B13
rd. Donvale 377 D9
rd. Mitcham 377 D9
McKEOWN
cr. Roxburgh Pk 194 C5
McKERCHAR
st. Glenroy 281 B5
McKERRAL
pl. Croydon N 335 K11

MACKERRAS
ct. Wheelers Hl 460 G18
MACKEY
st. Lalor 241 E9
MACKIA
ct. Niddrie 322 K2
MACKIE
ct. Blairgowrie 680 A18
ct. Kew 371 F10
gr. Brighton East 455 G15
rd. Bentleigh E 457 D19
rd. Mulgrave 500 B2
McKILLOP
la. Fitzroy N 326 E19
pl. Endeavour Hl 537 K4
pl. Geelong, off
McKillop St 702 K9
rd. Mt Evelyn 383 J3
rd. Mt Evelyn 384 E1
rd. Wandin East 384 E1
st. E Geelong 703 G12
st. Geelong 702 K9
st. Melbourne 1 K13
st. Melbourne 24 B8
st. South Yarra 32 J16
McKIMMIES
rd. Bundoora 242 C12
rd. Lalor 241 K12
rd. Mill Park 242 C12
McKINLEY
av. Malvern 415 K16
ct. Dandenong N 501 H8
dr. Roxburgh Pk 194 E15
MACKINNON
ct. Attwood 237 E11
ct. Keysborough 534 D9
gr. Glenroy 280 B9
McKINNON
ct. Melton W 226 B19
rd. Bentleigh E 456 A16
rd. McKinnon 455 J16
st. Blackburn 375 L18
st. Thomastown 240 J14
tce. Christmas Hills 207 H18
MACKINOLTY
st. Braybrook 366 A5
MACKINTOSH
rd. Wheelers Hl 460 H8
McKIRDY
st. Springvale 499 F16
McKITTRICK
rd. Bentleigh 496 D4
MACKLIN
wy. Caroline Spr 318 C4
MACKS
la. Geelong, off
Brougham St 703 B6
pl. Hoppers Csg 447 L1
MACLACHLAN
ct. Greenvale 193 E20
McLACHLAN
st. Northcote 326 G19
st. Templestowe 330 L7
MACLAGAN
cr. Reservoir 282 K6
MACLAINE
ct. Nar Warrn N 538 E7
MACLAREN
ct. Greenvale 193 F20
ct. Greenvale 237 F1
McLAREN
av. Cranbourne 604 D2
ct. Rosebud 685 A20
pl. Mornington 640 F13
st. Mt Waverley 458 G3
st. Tullamarine 278 F6
st. Upwey 465 L13
McLARTY
la. S Melbourne 29 D9
pl. Geelong, off
Little Malop St 703 A7
McLAUCHLIN
av. Sandringham 495 F16
McLAUGHLAN
av. Eumemmerring 537 B15
McLAUGHLANS
la. Plenty 244 D12
McLAUGHLIN
cr. Mill Park 242 K5
st. Ardeer 320 B20
st. Ardeer 364 C1
McLAURIN
av. Roxburgh Pk 194 D12
rd. Carnegie 456 K8
MACLEAN
ct. Seaford 573 E19
st. Williamstown 411 F14
McLEAN
al. Melbourne 1 K6
al. Melbourne 23 L5
av. Bentleigh 455 H18
cr. Dandenong N 501 L20
ct. Frankston S 627 F20

st. Blackburn S.......419 F1
st. Thornbury..........326 K8
MANSION
pl. Chirnside Pk......337 G3
MANSION HOUSE
la. W Melbourne.......23 D2
MANSON
dr. Melton S............268 J7
MANSTON
wy. Fawkner.............281 F2
MANTAURA
av. Taylors L...........276 D9
MANTELL
st. Coburg N...........281 F17
st. Doncaster E.......376 B3
st. Moonee Pnd......323 L13
MANTON
ct. Thomastown......240 K15
la. Melbourne............1 B7
la. Melbourne...........23 H7
pl. Roxburgh Pk......194 B12
rd. Clayton..............458 G17
rd. Moolap..............704 G18
rd. Oakleigh S.........458 G17
st. Burnley..............371 B18
st. Heidelberg.........328 L5
st. Heidelberg.........329 A5
MANTOVA
dr. Wheelers Hl.......460 J18
MANTUNG
cr. Rowville.............462 L19
cr. Rowville.............463 A18
MANUELA
ct. Dingley Vill.........533 A5
st. Croydon N..........336 C11
tce. Ringwood N.......378 A5
MANUKA
av. Belgrave............466 J19
ct. Frankston S.......627 K17
ct. Mill Park............243 B9
dr. Boronia..............423 G16
dr. Ferntree Gly.......423 F16
mw. Langwarrin........601 K15
pl. Meadow Ht.........193 J18
rd. Berwick..............554 K11
rd. Hurstbridge........203 L14
rd. Panton Hill.........203 L14
rd. Panton Hill.........204 C14
st. Bentleigh E........457 F18
st. Somerville.........645 C16
MANUS
ct. Lalor..................241 G6
st. Sorrento............679 E16
MANYUNG
ct. Keilor East.........321 L3
ct. Mt Eliza.............641 G3
ct. Mulgrave............500 J2
ct. Seaford.............573 E19
MAORI
st. Rye...................697 C2
MAPITI
ct. Frankston..........600 F15
MAPLE
av. Belgrave............466 J18
av. Selby.................466 J18
cr. Camberwell........417 B5
cr. Hoppers Csg.......405 C16
cr. St Albans...........320 F8
ct. Campbellfield......239 F12
ct. Cheltenham.........531 G3
ct. Doncaster...........375 A3
ct. Doveton.............536 G13
ct. Heidelberg W......328 B2
ct. Keilor.................276 K9
ct. Kilsyth...............381 K6
ct. Mornington.........641 E13
ct. Ringwood E........379 D15
ct. Taylors Hill.........274 L10
ct. Taylors Hill.........275 A10
dr. Altona North.......410 D7
gr. Bundoora............284 K5
gr. Mitcham.............377 A17
gr. Toorak...............415 E8
pl. Craigieburn.........150 A13
pl. Waurn Ponds.......705 E16
st. Bayswater..........423 F6
st. Blackburn...........376 A14
st. Box Hill...............375 A18
st. Caulfield S.........455 G9
st. Glenroy..............280 B2
st. Lalor..................241 H12
st. Langwarrin.........628 L1
st. Mt Waverley.......419 H17
st. Seaford.............599 J1
st. Springvale.........500 B12
st. Dandenong, off
David St............536 E4
tce. Glenroy.............281 D3
MAPLEDENE
ct. Sunshine W.......364 D6
ct. Templestowe.....332 B6
MAPLEHURST
av. Hoppers Csg......405 C20
MAPLE LEAF
av. Nar Warrn S.......579 C1
MAPLES
la. Prahran...............32 C20
la. Prahran.............414 G10
MAPLESON
ct. Hallam...............537 E14
MAPLETREE
gr. Mill Park............242 L3
MAPLEWOOD
cl. Brookfield..........267 K10
cl. Brookfield..........267 L10
ct. Carrum Downs....601 D1
rd. Kings Park.........275 D19
MARA
cl. Wantirna S.........422 B16
ct. Taylors L...........276 C8
MARABOU
cl. Nar Warrn S.......579 G4
mw. Mt Martha..........656 H8
pl. Aspendale..........546 F7
MARAGLE
av. Brighton............455 A18
MARAIS
gr. S Morang...........198 L10
MARALBER
rd. Highett..............496 A12
MARALEE
ct. Berwick..............554 D20
dr. Mooroolbark........337 G12
pl. Doncaster...........330 G16
MARALINE
rd. Skye..................602 F8
MARALINGA
av. Keysborough.......535 A8
tce. Mooroolbark.......337 B15
MARAMA
dr. Frankston S.......627 A6
rd. Belgrave Ht........466 D20
st. Blackburn S.......419 K4
st. Box Hill N..........375 C8
st. Coburg N...........281 D12
MARAMBA
av. Grovedale..........705 L15
dr. Narre Warren.....538 J14
MARANA
cl. Lilydale..............338 L5
MARANOA
cr. Coburg..............325 D6
MARAQUITA
gr. Hawthorn E.........416 D7
MARARA
rd. Caulfield S.........455 K10
MARATHON
dr. Mt Eliza.............626 C9
MARBERT
ct. N Warrandyte.......290 C10
MARBRAY
cl. Sorrento............679 C15
dr. Glen Waverley....459 K3
MARCEL
ct. Ringwood N........378 H3
MARCELLA
av. Dandenong N......501 F19
ct. Glen Waverley....459 H6
ct. Oakleigh E.........458 K11
pl. Carrum Downs....601 D3
MARCELLE
st. Cockatoo...........511 A8
MARCELLIN
ct. Deer Park...........319 B15
rd. Bulleen..............329 H13
MARCHAIR
dr. Point Cook.........450 H7
MARCHANT
av. Reservoir...........283 B9
av. Upwey...............465 L11
cr. Sunshine W........364 F9
ct. Croydon.............335 F19
st. Highett..............495 J14
MARCHINGTON
av. Mornington.........640 H12
MARCHIORI
rd. Blackburn N.......376 C11
MARCIA
av. Rye...................696 D8
cl. Ringwood...........335 A20
ct. Glen Waverley....460 A8
st. Sunshine W.......364 G5
st. Thomastown......241 D15
MARCONI
ct. Research...........288 K5
MARCO POLO
st. Essendon...........323 K4
MARCUS
av. Mt Waverley.......419 F17
av. W Footscray.......366 H5
cr. Coolaroo............238 F4
ct. Dromana............686 B6
ct. Forest Hill..........376 E20
ct. Narre Warren......538 G16
rd. Croydon............379 D2
rd. Dingley Vill.........533 D7
rd. Frankston S.......626 L9
rd. Templstw Lr.......330 C14
st. Dromana............686 B5
st. Highton.............701 G17
st. Mt Evelyn...........338 L19
st. Mt Evelyn...........339 A19
MARDEN
dr. Briar Hill............286 H2
st. Canterbury.........373 C19
MARDENE
ct. Mulgrave...........501 H4
MARDI
cl. St Helena...........244 K17
ct. Clayton S...........499 D16
MARDION
dr. Nunawading......376 E11
MARDIS
pl. S Morang...........198 H13
MAREE
ct. Kurunjang..........227 D11
ct. Rowville.............503 B5
ct. Warrandyte.........333 E1
st. Bentleigh E........456 J17
MAREEBA
cr. Bayswater..........423 C9
ct. Glen Waverley....420 C15
MARELLA
pl. Nar Warrn S.......579 B1
MARENDAZ
rd. Waurn Ponds.....705 A15
MARENO
rd. Tullamarine........277 K7
MARETIMO
ct. Frankston S.......627 G13
MARFELL
ct. Highton.............705 H5
MARGARET
av. Bayswater..........423 G11
av. Chirnside Pk......336 K4
av. Montmorency......287 B10
av. Seaford.............573 F19
av. Yarra Glen.........209 D19
cl. Somerville..........644 D17
cr. Braybrook...........366 C3
cr. Dandenong.........535 L5
cr. Menzies Ck........467 H11
ct. Bundoora............242 C19
ct. Hampton Pk........551 D10
ct. Kurunjang..........227 E11
ct. Warrandyte.........332 H1
dr. Bacchus Msh.....221 K19
gr. Alphington..........327 F20
gr. Preston.............283 C19
la. Nar Warrn N.......539 F10
pl. Rowville.............502 H3
pl. Taylors Hill.........274 H14
rd. Avonsleigh..........470 F18
rd. Healesville..........213 E15
rd. Mt Evelyn...........383 L5
st. Berwick..............554 C9
st. Blackburn S.......419 L1
st. Blairgowrie........679 K18
st. Box Hill..............375 C13
st. Box Hill N..........375 C13
st. Brighton East.....495 C1
st. Canterbury.........373 G18
st. Carnegie............456 L8
st. Clayton..............458 G18
st. Doncaster E.......376 B6
st. Fawkner............281 F4
st. Jan Juc..............711 C17
st. Kilsyth...............381 B5
st. Langwarrin.........629 C4
st. McCrae..............685 B11
st. Moonee Pnd......324 B12
st. Moorabbin..........496 E7
st. Newport.............410 E5
st. Newtown............702 D8
st. Oakleigh S.........458 G18
st. Oak Park............280 A14
st. Parkdale............531 L9
st. Research...........246 E19
st. Richmond............26 A15
st. Ringwood...........377 K12
st. Rosanna............329 B1
st. Seddon..............367 A10
st. South Yarra.........31 K15
st. South Yarra.......414 E7
st. Werribee............447 G11
MARGARET GRAY
cl. Glen Waverley....459 L10
MARGARETTA
av. Murrumbeena....457 C14
st. Bentleigh E........496 K3
MARGARITA
cl. Berwick..............554 C17
st. Hampton............494 K6
MARGATE
av. Frankston..........627 G6
cr. Glen Waverley....459 J6
st. Beaumaris..........530 G8
MARGIE
sq. Nar Warrn S.......578 G3
MARGO
st. Dromana............686 C7
MARGOT
av. Doncaster..........331 A14
ct. Cranbourne N....578 H10
st. Chadstone..........458 A2
st. Ferntree Gly.......464 D3
st. W Footscray......366 G12
MARGRAVE
st. St Albans...........319 K1
MARGTMARY
av. Preston.............282 F19
MARGUERITA
av. Mt Martha..........655 D20
MARHAM
pl. Tullamarine........278 K2
MARI
cl. Greensbrgh........244 B20
tce. Croydon Hl........335 H13
MARIA
av. Nunawading......376 J12
cr. Pakenham..........585 B5
ct. Cranbourne N....578 F9
ct. Hadfield.............280 K6
dr. Langwarrin........601 J18
st. Laverton N.........407 H6
MARIAN
ct. Blackburn..........375 E19
ct. Eltham North.....245 F16
st. Hawthorn...........372 A20
MARIANA
av. Croydon S.........379 G11
MARIANNE
av. Rye..................696 D8
wy. Doncaster..........330 E16
wy. Mt Waverley......419 C16
MARIBYRNONG
bvd. Footscray..........367 G4
ct. Werribee............447 F8
rd. Ascot Vale.........323 J15
rd. Moonee Pnd.......323 J15
st. Footscray...........367 H12
st. Footscray...........367 J8
MARIDA
ct. Berwick..............554 B16
MARIE
av. Heidelberg Ht....284 E20
av. Springvale.........500 F6
cl. Tullamarine........278 F4
ct. Bundoora............285 B5
ct. Mt Eliza.............626 F20
ct. Mt Waverley.......458 G9
st. Boronia.............424 E14
st. Doveton.............536 L9
st. Doveton.............537 A9
st. Oak Park............279 L11
st. Vermont.............377 H20
MARIE DALLEY
dr. Kew, off
Coombs Av.......371 E10
MARIEMONT
av. Beaumaris.........530 F8
av. Wantirna...........422 H10
MARIE WALLACE
wy. Bayswater, off
Valma St...........423 E8
MARIGOLD
av. Altona North......365 K20
cr. Gowanbrae........279 E4
pl. Lyndhurst..........551 C20
st. S Morang...........199 J13
MARIGOLDS
rd. Yallambie..........285 G15
MARILLA
cl. Mt Eliza.............641 L9
MARILLAC
ct. Frankston..........628 C11
MARILYN
cr. Ringwood..........379 B3
ct. Blackburn N.......376 D9
ct. Watsonia...........285 C8
st. Doncaster..........330 C16
MARIN
la. Braybrook..........321 L17
la. Maribyrnong......322 J15
MARINA
av. Frankston..........628 A3
av. McCrae.............684 L18
cl. Gladstone Pk.....279 B3
ct. Berwick.............554 F18
ct. Notting Hill.........459 K15
dr. Melton...............226 K18
gr. Bonbeach..........545 F15
rd. Mentone............530 J9
st. Vermont............421 E4
st. Werribee...........447 F5
MARINDA
dr. Skye.................601 D8
MARINE
av. Mornington........640 D16
av. St Kilda.............414 B20
dr. Mt Martha..........668 L10
dr. Mt Martha..........669 A10
dr. Roxburgh Pk......194
dr. Safety Bch.........686
pde. Abbotsford..........20 F
pde. Elwood.............454
pde. St Kilda............414 B
MARINER
cl. Cranbourne N....578
ct. Mt Martha..........656
ct. Taylors L...........275
st. Williamstown.....411 G
vw. Patterson L........573
MARINERS ISLAND
Patterson L........573
MARINGA
cl. Wantirna S.........422 B
ct. Keilor Dn...........276 G
st. Bulleen..............329 H
MARINIQUE
dr. Aspendale Gdn...547
MARINO
ct. Mornington.........657
la. Caroline Spr.......318
wy. Diamond Ck.......244 L
wy. Greensbrgh........244 L
MARION
av. Balwyn..............373 E
av. Brunswick W.....324 K
av. Cockatoo...........511
av. Kilsyth..............380
av. Mooroolbark......380
ct. Craigieburn........150 B
ct. Keysborough.....534 C
la. Fitzroy.................18 L
rd. Rosebud............700
st. Altona North......409
st. Altona North......410
st. Bentleigh...........456 F
st. Brighton............454 L
st. Brighton............455 A
st. Coburg N...........281 B
st. Dandenong.........535
st. Fitzroy.................19 A
st. Footscray...........367
st. Pt Lonsdale........710
st. Seaford..............599
wk. Hoppers Csg......447
wy. Eltham...............246 A
MARIPOSA
ct. Wantirna S.........422 C
pl. Port Melb...........412
MARISA
cr. Berwick.............554 H
ct. Carrum Downs...601
MARISSA
cr. Greensbrgh........244 K
ct. Langwarrin........601 K
MARITA
ct. Cheltenham.......497 A
MARITANA
av. Reservoir...........282 H
cr. Thomastown......240 H
ct. Balwyn..............373 J
MARJON
st. Attwood.............236 K
MARJORAM
cl. Hallam...............538 C
MARJORIE
av. Belmont.............706
av. Dingley Vill.........533
av. Sunbury............142 F
cl. Bulleen..............330 A
ct. McCrae..............684 K
st. Preston.............327
MARJORY
pl. Tullamarine........278
st. Fawkner............281
st. Thomastown......241 E
st. Yarraville...........367 A
MARK
ct. Chadstone.........458
ct. Dandenong N.....501 K
ct. Diggers Rest......187 G
ct. Epping...............241
ct. Hampton Pk.......551
ct. Noble Park.........500 D
ct. Seabrook...........450
ct. Wollert..............153 F
dr. Hillside..............274
pl. Melton W...........225 K
pl. Nunawading......376 F
st. Bayswater..........423
st. Fitzroy N..............19
st. Fitzroy N............326 D
st. Keilor East.........278 E
st. Mooroolbark......337 F
st. Mt Martha..........656 E
st. N Melbourne........34
st. N Melbourne........34
st. Rosebud............684 D
st. St Albans...........319
st. Sunshine W.......363
st. Viewbank...........285 L
st. Warrandyte........290 G
st. Warrandyte........334

ARK ANTHONY
Dandenong S 549 E11
ARKER
Melb Airport 235 L8
ARKET
Reservoir 283 B5
Skye 575 G17
Melbourne 2 L11
Melbourne 24 G5
N Melbourne 17 E15
Braybrook 321 J19
Camberwell 372 J20
Port Melb 412 K5
S Melbourne 29 K2
Brooklyn 365 E11
Sunshine 365 E11
Werribee 447 F11
Boronia 424 F7
Box Hill 374 K15
Dandenong 536 A7
Essendon 323 C2
Essendon 323 F3
Keilor Park 277 L13
Kensington 33 H7
Lilydale 338 D6
Melbourne 1 G18
Melbourne 24 A10
Newport 410 H10
Nunawading 376 H15
Ringwood 378 C12
Rye 696 J3
St Kilda 414 D17
Southbank 3 A16
Southbank 29 J2
Southbank 413 E1
S Melbourne 3 A16
S Melbourne 29 J2
S Melbourne 413 E1
South Yarra 32 C15
South Yarra 414 G8
W Footscray 366 J7
Geelong, off Myers St 703 A9
e. Taylors Hill 274 E8
ARKEY
Altona Mdw 451 K6
ARKHAM
Ashburton 417 F18
Altona Mdw 451 C6
Keysborough 534 B8
y. Altona Mdw 451 D6
ARKHILL
Heathmont 422 H1
Knoxfield 423 D20
ARKLIN
Cranbourne 578 F20
ARKS
Heidelberg Ht 284 E18
Rosebud 683 G18
Harkaway 540 F17
Emerald 510 G16
Footscray 367 K6
Brunswick 325 J13
Coburg 325 D5
Pascoe Vale 280 B15
Strathmore 279 K19
ARKSTONE
Sunshine 321 F19
ARLA
Frankston 600 E19
ARLAND
Boronia 424 G10
ARLBOROUGH
Camberwell 417 B3
Hoppers Csg 448 E9
Noble Park 534 J5
Bayswater 423 C2
Heathmont 378 E20
Heathmont 422 E1
Balaclava 414 G18
Bentleigh E 457 B19
Caulfield N 415 D16
Fawkner 281 G11
Glenroy 280 A5
Herne Hill 701 J3
Mont Albert 374 C14
Sydenham 232 K20
Sydenham 274 K1
Sydenham 274 L1
ARLEE
Grovedale 706 C11
ARLEIGH
Vermont 420 K5
RLENE
Doncaster E 332 F7
Cheltenham 497 F20
Hampton Pk 551 E9
Lysterfield 464 A17
Springvale 500 E7
RLESFORD
Wantirna 422 F14
Berwick 554 D18

MARLEY
cl. Rowville 463 F20
mw. Cranbourne E 604 H5
MARLEYBOURNE
ct. Greenvale 237 F4
MARLIN
tce. Seabrook 450 J7
MARLIN BAY
Patterson L 573 G8
MARLINO
av. Warburton 349 E1
MARLO
ct. Broadmeadows 238 B15
ct. S Morang 199 K16
dr. Melton W 225 L13
gr. Beaumaris 530 E5
gr. Mt Eliza 641 L5
pl. Frankston 600 H17
pl. Hallam 537 E17
sq. Wyndham Va 446 J9
st. Wantirna 422 E11
MARLOCK
cl. Thomastown 240 J12
st. Frankston N 600 F9
wy. Delahey 275 C10
MARLOO
ct. Croydon Hl 335 F15
MARLOW
pl. Eltham 288 B8
st. Mooroolbark 337 B16
MARLOWE
st. Canterbury 373 D18
MARLTON
cr. St Kilda 414 F13
MARLYN
ct. Highton 701 K17
MARMA
ct. Grovedale 706 C16
rd. Murrumbeena 457 B12
MARMAL
ct. Tullamarine 236 E19
MARMARA
dr. Elsternwick 454 L8
dr. Elsternwick 455 A8
MARMION
st. Rye 696 G10
MARMONT
pl. Lysterfield 464 A14
MARNA
ct. Noble Park 535 C1
st. Dromana 686 D5
st. Healesville 257 G4
MARNE
av. Wyndham Va 446 D15
ct. Bundoora 284 F6
rd. Mt Evelyn 382 J1
st. St Kilda E 415 A17
st. South Yarra 31 G8
st. South Yarra 414 D4
st. Surrey Hills 417 L2
MARNEBECK
ct. Cranbourne 578 B19
MARNEY
ct. Brookfield 268 C5
MARNGO
ct. Kurunjang 227 C13
MARNI
st. Dandenong S 549 H7
MARNIE
dr. Cranbourne W 577 F20
pl. Hallam 538 D14
MARNOCK
rd. Newtown 702 C15
MARNOO
ct. Tootgarook 698 B7
st. Braybrook 365 H4
MAROCK
pl. Balwyn 373 D14
MARON
cl. Seabrook 450 K7
MARONEY
ct. Doncaster E 332 H14
MARONG
ct. Boronia 424 L4
ct. Broadmeadows 238 D15
ct. Greensbrgh 244 J19
gr. Balwyn 373 L13
tce. Forest Hill 420 D1
MAROO
st. Hughesdale 457 F7
MAROOCHY
pl. Burnside 318 H6
MAROONA
rd. Brighton 455 A12
rd. Carnegie 456 E6
rd. Highett 496 A11
MAROONDAH
ct. St Albans 320 F13
hwy. Blackburn 375 C15
hwy. Box Hill 374 C13
hwy. Chirnside Pk 337 A8
hwy. Coldstream 295 A19
hwy. Croydon 379 B5
hwy. Croydon N 335 J20
hwy. Gruyere 254 F20
hwy. Healesville 257 B10
hwy. Lilydale 295 A19
hwy. Lilydale 337 A8
hwy. Lilydale 339 A3
hwy. Mitcham 376 G14
hwy. Mont Albert 374 C13
hwy. Mooroolbark 337 A8
hwy. Nunawading 376 G14
hwy. Ringwood 379 B5
hwy. Ringwood E 379 B5
hwy. Ringwood N 379 B5
hwy. Surrey Hills 374 B13
pde. Healesville 214 E13
rd. Ashwood 418 F15
tce. Bundoora 242 C19
MAROONG
dr. Eltham 288 G1
dr. Research 246 G20
dr. Research 288 G1
MAROORA
st. Malvern East 456 J3
MAROUANDS
rd. Truganina 405 K10
MAROUBRA
av. Noble Park 534 G7
MARQUET
ct. Hillside 274 F1
MARQUIS
av. Mornington 657 A5
rd. Bentleigh 496 E5
st. Ashburton 417 E14
MARRA
ct. Endeavour Hl 537 D7
MARRAKAI
ct. Eltham North 287 C3
MARRAROO
cl. Bayswater N 380 J16
MARRBRIDGE
rd. Moorabbin 496 K9
MARRIAGE
rd. Brighton East 455 B20
MARRIOT
rd. Bentleigh 496 C5
rd. Keilor Dn 275 L11
MARRIOTT
cr. Skye 575 H15
dr. Mt Martha 656 L7
pde. Glen Waverley 460 C3
st. Caulfield 455 J3
st. Oakleigh 458 A8
st. Parkdale 531 H10
st. St Kilda 414 E16
MARRITA
ct. Pt Lonsdale 710 D3
MARROO
st. Doncaster 374 H3
MARROWIE
pl. Taylors Hill 274 L11
pl. Taylors Hill 275 A11
MARRSON
pl. Glenroy 279 H3
MARS
ct. Newcomb 704 D13
st. Caulfield S 455 E9
MARSDEN
av. Pascoe Vale S 324 G6
cr. Doncaster E 331 J17
cr. St Albans 320 A4
ct. Cranbourne N 578 A9
ct. Kilsyth S 424 L1
ct. Mill Park 242 E1
pde. Braybrook 366 A6
wk. Roxburgh Pk 194 C12
MARSEILLES
wy. Point Cook 450 F11
MARSH
cr. Sunbury 142 J14
ct. Wantirna S 462 D5
gr. Berwick 579 L4
gr. Berwick 580 A1
st. Altona North 409 F3
st. Maidstone 322 K20
MARSHALL
av. Clayton 459 A16
av. Doncaster 375 C2
av. Highett 495 K15
av. Kew 372 D10
av. Montmorency 286 L13
av. St Albans 320 L3
av. St Albans 321 A4
cl. Carrum Downs 600 J1
cl. Sunbury 143 D2
ct. Hampton Pk 551 C6
dr. Mill Park 242 G6
dr. Reservoir 283 G3
pl. Clifton Hill 20 F4
pl. Hallam 537 F14
rd. Airport W 278 J11
rd. Box Hill N 375 D8
st. Flemington 33 G3
st. Ivanhoe 328 D16
st. Moonee Pnd 324 A12
st. Mt Evelyn 339 G19
st. Newtown 702 G12
st. Noble Park 501 C20
st. Rye 698 A2
st. S Melbourne 29 L4
st. Sunshine N 321 F13
st. Tootgarook 698 A2
st. Wheelers Hl 461 D20
tce. Montrose 382 D14
tce. Mt Dandenong 382 D14
wy. Glen Waverley 459 K10
MARSHALLS
rd. Christmas Hills 207 D1
rd. St Andrews 207 D1
MARSHALLTOWN
rd. Grovedale 706 G9
rd. Marshall 706 G9
MARSHAM
rd. Mt Waverley 419 C14
st. Noble Park N 501 F16
MARSH MAYS
rd. Cairnlea 319 L12
MARSON
cr. Hallam 538 B16
ct. Pakenham 584 E6
MARSTON
st. Bentleigh 496 D2
MARTELL
st. Broadmeadows 238 B17
MARTENS
ct. Sunbury 142 G9
ct. Taylors L 275 B1
pl. Dingley Vill 532 L3
MARTHA
ct. Craigieburn 150 H17
st. Donvale 376 F5
st. Seaford 599 F5
MARTI
ct. Sunshine W 364 E7
MARTIN
cl. S Morang 199 E11
cr. Glen Iris 416 E14
ct. Bentleigh E 497 C7
ct. Berwick 554 C17
ct. Doncaster 331 B15
ct. Fairfield 327 G18
ct. Forest Hill 420 G4
ct. Montrose 382 B13
ct. Seaholme 409 J16
ct. Toorak 415 C6
pl. Bayswater 423 C5
pl. Cranbourne 578 A16
pl. Glen Waverley 420 C16
pl. Pakenham 585 A1
rd. Glen Iris 416 J10
st. Beaumaris 530 C12
st. Belgrave 466 C17
st. Box Hill N 375 C7
st. Brighton 454 F10
st. E Geelong 703 E15
st. Heathmont 379 C20
st. Heidelberg 328 J7
st. Mt Martha 669 A2
st. Notting Hill 459 G14
st. Pascoe Vale 280 L13
st. Preston 327 B1
st. Rosebud 684 G16
st. St Kilda 414 E17
st. Seaford 599 F5
st. S Melbourne 29 L8
st. S Melbourne 413 F4
st. Springvale S 534 B3
st. Sunshine 365 D3
st. Thomson 703 E15
st. Thornbury 326 J10
MARTINDALE
pl. Templestowe 331 L7
MARTINE
ct. Hoppers Csg 447 K3
MARTINGALE
ct. Epping 198 F17
pl. Pakenham 585 E5
MARTINS
la. Portsea 677 K3
la. Viewbank 285 G16
MARTYR
rd. Warburton 349 D2
MARVIL
av. Narre Warren 539 E13
MARVILLE
ct. Boronia 423 H13
MARVIN
av. Rye 697 C3
MARWAL
av. Balwyn N 373 B4
MARWARRA
st. Ringwood E 378 J13
MARWEN
dr. Derrimut 363 G14
MARWICK
st. Flemington 324 F20

MARY
av. Edithvale 546 J10
av. Heidelberg Ht 328 E4
av. Highett 496 B16
av. Werribee 447 K17
av. Wheelers Hl 461 D12
cl. Woori Yall 344 B13
ct. Berwick 554 L8
ct. Croydon N 336 A12
ct. Epping 241 C1
ct. Mornington 640 H16
ct. Noble Park 535 C7
ct. St Albans 320 B11
ct. Somerville 645 B15
pl. Hurstbridge 246 K1
st. Balwyn N 374 B6
st. Beaumaris 529 L5
st. Blackburn 375 L15
st. Box Hill N 375 C13
st. Brighton 454 J17
st. Carlton 18 D16
st. Carlton N 325 K19
st. Clayton 498 K1
st. Coburg 325 G2
st. Dromana 686 E8
st. Emerald 469 J20
st. Essendon 323 B5
st. Ferny Creek 426 B15
st. Footscray 367 D6
st. Frankston 599 A16
st. Hampton Pk 551 B6
st. Hawthorn 371 J15
st. Kew 372 A10
st. Malvern 416 A8
st. Melton S 268 G5
st. N Melbourne 17 E14
st. Officer 582 L7
st. Officer 583 A7
st. Pakenham 558 B20
st. Preston 282 K20
st. Preston 326 K2
st. Richmond 32 H3
st. Richmond 414 K2
st. Ringwood 377 K13
st. Safety Bch 668 K20
st. St Kilda W 413 L14
st. Spotswood 366 J20
st. Springvale 500 A10
st. Upwey 465 C10
st. Wandin East 340 L18
st. Wandin East 341 A18
st. Windsor 414 J11
MARYBOROUGH
av. Kingsbury 283 L10
rd. Boronia 423 K15
MARY BRYANT
ct. Mill Park 242 E5
MARYFIELD
la. Dromana 687 B3
MARYGATE
pl. Berwick 554 G8
MARYKIRK
dr. Wheelers Hl 461 C16
MARYLAND
cl. Thomastown 240 E15
st. Caulfield S 455 K8
MARYLEBONE
st. Sunbury 144 F8
MARYLIN
ct. Bentleigh E 496 H6
MARYLOU
ct. Delahey 275 D10
MARYLYN
pl. Cranbourne 578 A12
MARYN
cl. Berwick 553 L6
MARY ROSE
st. Blairgowrie 679 J19
MARYROSE
cr. Endeavour Hl 537 L1
MARYSTON
st. Yarraville 366 J14
MARYVALE
st. Sunshine 365 E2
MARYVILLE
st. Ripponlea 454 H1
wy. Boronia 424 D14
MARY WALSH
st. Maribyrnong 367 C2
MASARYK
ct. Vermont 421 A3
MASCHES HILL
rd. Monbulk 427 L20
rd. Monbulk 467 L1
MASCOMA
st. Ascot Vale 324 F17
st. Strathmr Ht 279 C9
MASCOT
av. Bonbeach 573 A7
MASEFIELD
av. Mooroolbark 381 F1
av. Sandringham 495 C17
ct. Delahey 275 E15

MASERATI
dr. Epping...............197 J14
MASHIE
ct. Rosebud............700 B9
MASHOOBRA
st. Coburg N...........281 C13
MASKED OWL
rd. S Morang..........199 H13
MASKELL
cr. Lower Plenty......286 F14
st. Brighton............454 L16
st. Selby.................467 B17
MASKELLS HILL
rd. Selby.................467 A19
MASLEN
cl. Frankston..........599 H18
MASON
av. Elwood.............454 F1
av. Safety Bch.........686 G1
ct. Bayswater N......379 H19
ct. Highett..............496 G13
ct. Highton.............705 J3
ct. Melton...............268 J1
ct. Mt Waverley......458 H9
ct. Queenscliff.........707 K18
ct. Templstw Lr......330 G10
dr. Braeside............532 G15
gr. Sassafras...........426 G11
la. Mont Albert........374 D15
mw. Pakenham.........584 H10
pl. South Yarra.........31 E7
st. Altona North......409 K5
st. Braybrook...........366 A6
st. Campbellfield.....239 G12
st. Collingwood........25 F1
st. Dandenong.........535 L9
st. Ferntree Gly.......464 G7
st. Hawthorn...........371 E14
st. Mt Eliza.............642 E5
st. Newport.............410 H6
st. Northcote..........326 K18
st. Reservoir............282 L15
st. South Yarra.........31 E7
wy. Berwick.............553 L8
MASONIC
av. Warrandyte........290 D20
MASONS
la. Abbotsford..........20 F15
la. Bacchus Msh.....221 H13
la. Melbourne.............2 E13
la. Melbourne...........24 D7
la. Mernda..............154 D10
la. Mernda..............155 A11
la. Mernda..............156 A12
la. Werribee S.........488 C18
la. Wollert..............153 J10
la. Wollert..............154 D10
rd. Blackburn..........376 A20
MASSEY
av. Reservoir...........282 E3
st. Box Hill S...........419 A5
st. Doncaster...........374 E3
MASSON
rd. Parkville...............18 B13
MASTERS
cct. Roxburgh Pk.......194 A9
st. Caulfield.............455 H6
st. Dandenong........536 D10
MASTERTON
pl. Cranbourne E.....578 H19
MAST GULLY
rd. Ferny Creek........466 B5
rd. Upwey...............465 J10
MASTOS
pl. Rowville.............502 L8
MATEO
cl. Dandenong N.....502 B11
MATER
st. Collingwood........19 H10
MATHER
cl. Croydon............380 C1
rd. Mt Eliza.............642 G2
rd. Noble Park.........534 K3
MATHERS
av. Kew East...........372 C4
av. Launching Pl......345 E16
MATHESON
ct. Berwick.............554 D2
ct. Wheelers Hl.......460 L18
rd. Forest Hill..........420 F6
MATHEW
ct. Langwarrin........629 F4
pl. Mt Evelyn, off Camric Ct..........339 E18
MATHEWS
ct. Reservoir...........283 K16
la. S Melbourne........30 H4
st. Melton S............268 F11
MATHIAS
rd. Olinda...............427 A3
MATHIESEN
tce. Hillside.............232 G18
MATHIESON
pl. Burwood............418 E5
st. Coburg N...........281 G12
MATHILDE
rd. Surrey Hills........374 B20
MATHIS
av. Keilor Dn...........276 B13
av. Tootgarook........698 B7
MATHOURA
cl. Noble Park N.......501 C11
rd. Toorak...............415 A8
MATILDA
av. Wantirna S.........422 B15
ct. Belmont.............706 H3
ct. Eltham North......287 C4
rd. Moorabbin.........496 K10
MATIPO
st. Doveton.............536 H12
MATISI
st. Thornbury..........327 H7
MATISSE
dr. Templestowe.....332 C9
MATLOCK
av. Mulgrave...........500 F1
ct. Bangholme........549 H13
ct. Caulfield N.........415 G16
ct. Jan Juc..............711 B16
ct. Thomastown.......240 E12
rd. Boronia..............423 B11
rd. Wantirna S.........423 B11
st. Canterbury.........373 C19
st. Hoppers Csg.......449 D1
st. Preston..............326 C3
MATONG
rd. Mt Eliza.............625 H18
MATSON
dr. Upwey...............465 L16
MATTEA
ct. Lilydale..............338 F3
ct. Reservoir............283 K17
MATTERS
rd. Pakenham Up....511 E20
MATTHEW
cl. Hoppers Csg......448 A3
cl. Keysborough.......534 G13
ct. Hampton Pk........551 F10
ct. Sunshine W.........363 L7
ct. Taylors L............275 F5
rt. Endeavour Hl......537 K3
st. Carnegie.............456 F7
st. Glen Waverley.....419 J19
st. McCrae..............685 B15
st. Mt Martha..........656 B12
st. Tooradin.............651 G6
MATTHEW FLINDERS
av. Endeavour Hl.....537 E8
MATTHEWS
av. Airport W...........279 A18
cr. Roxburgh Pk.......194 B15
ct. Brighton East.....455 E16
ct. Ferntree Gly.......464 H4
ct. Launching Pl......345 F17
ct. Mill Park............242 F7
ct. Pakenham..........584 D3
ct. Toorak...............415 C2
mw. Kensington..........33 E10
pl. Dandenong N.....501 L13
rd. Bentleigh E........497 D4
st. Sunshine...........365 F6
MATTHIESON
st. Highett..............496 G15
MATTINGLEY
cr. Brunswick W.....325 A8
MATTINGLY
la. N Melbourne........17 C17
MAUCHLINE
ct. Noble Park N......501 E11
MAUD
rd. Dromana............685 K9
st. Balwyn N...........372 L4
st. Balwyn N...........373 A4
st. Geelong.............702 K10
st. Ivanhoe.............327 L13
st. Ormond..............455 L13
MAUDE
av. Doncaster E.......376 C3
av. Glenroy..............280 G6
ct. Narre Warren.....538 F15
st. Box Hill N..........375 A9
st. Chadstone.........418 E19
st. Cheltenham.......496 J20
st. Mt Martha..........655 L13
st. Murrumbeena....457 D12
MAUGHAN
pde. Balwyn N...........373 L6
rd. Mt Eliza.............642 C9
MAUGIE
st. Abbotsford..........20 C11
st. Abbotsford..........20 D11
MAUREEN
cl. Cranbourne W...603 E2
cr. Noble Park.........534 G4
ct. Dandenong N.....501 G19
ct. Heatherton.........497 H15
ct. Melton W............225 L19
ct. Narre Warren.....538 F15
st. Mt Waverley......419 A13
MAUREVA
ct. Bundoora...........285 C2
MAURICE
av. Ringwood..........378 B15
av. Somerton...........194 H11
ct. Keilor East.........278 G20
ct. Nar Warrn N......538 H10
ct. Nunawading.......376 L16
ct. Wantirna S.........422 J17
rd. Gruyere.............340 L4
rd. Gruyere.............341 A4
st. Cockatoo............510 L9
st. Dandenong.........535 E2
st. Hawthorn E........372 E14
MAURINE
ct. Ringwood N.......378 G1
MAURY
la. Chelsea.............546 K20
rd. Chelsea.............546 K20
MAUS
st. Highton.............701 K20
MAVERICK
cl. Doncaster..........331 A15
st. Sorrento............679 B12
MAVERSTON
st. Glen Iris.............417 E10
MAVHO
st. Bentleigh...........456 A20
MAVIS
av. Beaconsfield......555 J9
av. Brighton East.....455 D14
cr. Kings Park..........275 E20
ct. Broadmeadows..238 E19
ct. Yallambie...........285 E16
st. Coburg..............325 D5
st. Footscray...........367 A4
MAVISTA
av. Glen Waverley....420 C15
MAVRON
st. Ashwood...........418 D17
MAWARRA
av. Rosebud W.......699 E2
cr. Chadstone.........458 D1
ct. Highton.............701 K15
MAWBEY
st. Kensington..........33 F6
MAWBY
rd. Bentleigh E........496 G4
MAWSON
av. Anglesea............713 G4
av. Deer Park...........319 C10
cl. Mill Park............243 A6
cl. Taylors L............275 H4
cl. Wantirna S.........462 C3
ct. Cranbourne N....577 L10
ct. Mulgrave............460 C17
ct. Sunbury.............143 B13
ct. Vermont.............421 F4
st. Kew...................372 H13
st. Melton...............226 G18
MAX
cl. Rowville.............463 H15
ct. Noble Park.........500 D19
MAXFLO
ct. Highett..............495 L15
MAXIA
rd. Doncaster E.......375 L5
MAXINE
ct. Mentone............531 G5
ct. Mt Waverley.......458 F4
ct. Noble Park.........535 D1
dr. St Helena...........245 A16
MAXWELD
st. Ardeer...............320 B20
MAXWELL
av. Altona North......410 D6
av. Belmont.............706 K1
ct. Attwood.............237 C10
ct. Blackburn S.......419 G1
ct. Langwarrin........629 D9
ct. Millgrove...........348 F1
ct. Moorabbin.........496 F11
ct. Noble Park.........535 B4
ct. Point Cook.........449 K5
ct. Seaford..............599 L1
ct. Toorak...............415 E3
gr. Caulfield.............455 K4
gr. Glen Waverley....420 A18
pl. Croydon N.........335 J11
st. Ashburton..........417 B17
st. Blairgowrie.........679 K19
st. Dandenong S.....536 C15
st. Kew...................372 D11
st. Lalor.................241 F10
st. Mornington........656 F4
st. Mornington........656 H1
st. Northcote..........327 C15
st. Springvale S......534 C4
MAY
av. Altona Mdw.......451 D4
av. Rye...................697 E3
ct. Bundoora...........284 F2
ct. Dandenong........536 C2
ct. Ferntree Gly.......463 F6
ct. Glen Waverley....459 K9
ct. Grovedale..........706 B10
ct. Mitcham............377 J11
gr. South Yarra..........32 H11
gr. South Yarra........414 K6
gr. Sunbury.............142 H10
pl. Port Melb...........412 J3
rd. Beaconsfield......555 H17
rd. Junction Vill.......604 H12
rd. Lalor.................241 C11
rd. Mooroolbark.......337 J17
rd. Officer..............555 H17
rd. Toorak.................32 L16
rd. Toorak...............414 L8
rd. Toorak...............415 A8
st. Aberfeldie..........323 B11
st. Altona North......409 K3
st. Balwyn..............373 B11
st. Bentleigh E........456 G19
st. Brighton............454 K10
st. Bundoora...........284 E2
st. Cannons Creek...649 G9
st. Cheltenham.......496 H18
st. Coburg..............281 F19
st. Doncaster E.......332 B19
st. Elsternwick........454 L4
st. Elwood..............454 G2
st. Fitzroy N...........326 C17
st. Footscray...........366 L3
st. Frankston S.......626 K4
st. Glenroy.............280 K4
st. Hampton...........495 D8
st. Kew...................372 C13
st. Macleod............285 A14
st. Mornington........640 E14
st. Newport............410 E4
st. Northcote..........327 C19
st. Preston..............282 F17
st. Silvan................384 F14
st. Sunshine...........365 G3
st. Tullamarine........278 G4
MAYA
ct. Somerville.........645 E16
MAYBERRY
la. Cairnlea............319 J12
MAYBURY
ct. Berwick.............554 L20
ct. Rowville.............463 J20
dr. Mill Park............242 F10
MAYEGLEN
ct. Cockatoo............511 C7
MAYFAIR
av. Templstw Lr......330 G11
cl. Gladstone Pk......237 B18
cl. Narre Warren.....539 B14
cr. Narre Warren.....539 C14
ct. Chirnside Pk......336 J6
ct. Croydon............335 K20
ct. Frankston..........600 C17
ct. Keysborough......534 K8
ct. Mulgrave............500 L4
dr. Ferntree Gly.......464 C6
dr. Newtown...........701 K10
la. Mont Albert N, off Scarborough Sq 374 E7
st. Wyndham Va.....446 E9
MAYFIELD
av. Brunswick..........325 B16
av. Camberwell........417 F4
av. Malvern.............415 K7
ct. Croydon............335 H19
ct. Grovedale..........706 H14
ct. Montrose............381 K11
dr. Mill Park............242 L11
dr. Mt Waverley.......458 H5
gr. Altona Mdw.......450 J1
gr. Caulfield N.........415 K18
pl. Rowville.............463 L13
rd. Cranbourne E.....579 D20
rd. Cranbourne E.....604 L6
st. Abbotsford..........26 G1
st. Coburg..............325 F3
st. Greensbrgh........285 K2
st. St Kilda E...........414 K20
MAYFIN
ct. Sunbury.............143 C4
MAYFLOWER
ct. Brighton East.....455 C18
mw. Point Cook.........451 C9
MAY GIBBS
cir. Point Cook.........449 L8
cr. Lynbrook...........551 C18
MAYGRAND
pl. Kilsyth S............425 A1
MAYGROVE
wy. Mulgrave...........501 E4
MAYLANDS
av. Balwyn N...........372
av. Balwyn N...........373
cr. Glen Waverley....460
st. Albion................320
MAYLING
ct. Watsonia...........285
MAYNARD
pl. Kings Park.........319
st. Preston..............327
MAYNE
st. Cheltenham.......497
st. Sunshine W.......364
st. Sunshine W.......365
MAYO
cl. Templestowe.....332
ct. Chelsea Ht.........547
ct. Wandin N..........340
ct. Wandin N..........341
st. Sunshine...........364
st. Sunshine...........365
MAYONA
rd. Montmorency....286
MAY PARK
av. Ashwood...........417
MAYRAH
ct. Grovedale..........706
MAYROSE
cr. Brighton East.....495
MAYRUCK
ri. Hampton Pk.......551
MAYS
rd. Eltham...............288
MAYSBURY
av. Brighton............494
av. Elsternwick........455
av. Rosebud............683
MAYSIA
st. Canterbury.........417
MAYSTON
st. Hawthorn E........372
MAYSWOOD
ct. Moorabbin.........496
MAYTON
ct. Grovedale..........706
MAYUNE
ct. Cranbourne........578
MAYVIEW
dr. Monbulk............468
MAYWOOD
dr. Epping...............241
rd. Cranbourne S.....630
MAZDA
ct. Southbank...........23
ct. S Melbourne........23
MAZEEPA
st. Healesville.........257
MAZZEI
wy. Sydenham.........274
MEABY
st. Jan Juc..............711
MEAD
ct. Oakleigh............457
ct. Wantirna S.........462
MEADE
wy. Sydenham.........274
MEADEN
st. Ashburton..........417
st. Southbank...........23
st. Southbank...........29
st. Southbank.........413
MEADER
st. Doncaster..........330
MEADOW
av. Rye...................698
cr. Badger Creek.....258
cr. Montmorency....286
cr. Mt Waverley......459
ct. Blackburn S.......419
ct. Dingley Vill.........533
ct. Viewbank...........285
ct. Wandin N..........340
gr. Balwyn..............372
gr. Balwyn..............373
la. Ferntree Gly.......463
la. Mt Eliza.............626
pl. Nar Warrn S.......553
pl. Templestowe.....331
rd. Croydon N.........336
st. St Kilda E...........415
MEADOWBANK
av. Chirnside Pk......336
av. Doncaster..........375
cl. Lysterfield S.......504
ct. Craigieburn........194
ct. Kings Park.........275
dr. Sunshine N........320
la. Craigieburn, off Meadowbank Ct..194
st. Glenroy..............281
MEADOWBROOK
dr. Wheelers Hl.......460
pl. Keysborough.....534

MEREWEATHER
av. Frankston 599 C15
MERIBAH
cl. Mornington........656 G4
ct. Frankston 627 K5
ct. Noble Park.........534 E6
ct. Parkdale 531 J9
MERIBEL
wy. Lynbrook..........551 G15
MERIBIL
cl. Mt Eliza.............626 J19
MERIDIAN
ct. Langwarrin 601 F18
ct. Mooroolbark......337 B13
dr. S Morang 199 A7
pde. Wantirna S.........422 D19
wy. Mornington........657 D5
MERILYN
wy. Frankston S 627 E20
wy. Rosebud............700 A1
MERIMBULA
ct. Taylors L 276 B7
rd. Ferny Creek........425 K20
MERINDA
ct. Frankston 628 C3
ct. Grovedale 706 D15
MERINGER
ct. Nunawading 376 K11
MERINO
av. Dallas 238 D10
ct. Highton 701 G16
mw. Kensington 33 B10
st. Laverton N.........364 G19
st. Reservoir...........283 J6
MERION
ct. Rowville.............462 C20
ct. Sunbury 144 H13
vst. Cranbourne........603 H7
MERITON
pl. Clayton S...........498 K6
MERIVALE
dr. Wantirna............422 F9
MERLE
st. Blackburn N......375 K10
MERLEWOOD
ct. Bundoora...........242 E18
MERLIN
al. Melbourne.............1 H10
al. Melbourne...........23 L7
cr. Ferntree Gly 463 G7
ct. Frankston 600 B18
ct. Notting Hill.........459 J15
st. Chum Creek........213 A13
st. Doncaster..........374 L2
st. Healesville 213 A13
MERLINS
tr. Warrandyte.........334 D1
MERLOT
ct. Frankston S 628 A17
ct. Yarra Glen 209 A18
gr. Sunbury 144 C6
st. Waurn Ponds.....705 G15
MERLOW
st. Albion...............320 G20
st. Altona...............408 H16
MERLYN
av. Clayton S..........498 J7
st. Coburg N...........281 E12
st. Maribyrnong......367 A1
MERMAID
ct. Patterson L........573 K11
MERNA
dr. Templestowe 331 F7
MERNDA
av. Ashburton..........417 K14
av. Bonbeach 573 A6
av. Burwood.............417 K14
av. Carnegie 456 F8
av. Cheltenham 496 E17
av. Glen Iris............417 K14
pde. Belmont.............706 F3
rd. Kooyong.............415 L6
rd. Olinda...............427 F17
st. Rye 696 G10
st. Sunshine W.......364 L3
st. Sunshine W.......365 A3
MEROLA
wy. Campbellfield.....239 C2
MERON
ct. Greensbrgh........286 B9
MERRAFIELDS
ct. Taylors L 276 F8
MERRALYN
st. Belmont.............706 K2
MERRAN
ct. Wheelers Hl 461 E18
MERRANG
ct. Wheelers Hl 460 H12
MERRANS
rd. Healesville 214 J15
MERRETT
av. Flemington 323 L20
av. Hoppers Csg......448 G2
dr. Williamstown.....410 K14
MERRETTS
pl. Melbourne.............1 B10
pl. Melbourne...........23 H8
rd. Avonsleigh.........471 B8
rd. Macclesfield.......471 B8
MERRI
ct. Campbellfield.....239 H8
dr. Campbellfield.....239 H9
dr. Waterways.........547 F2
pde. Northcote 326 E17
st. Brunswick..........325 F15
st. Templstw Lr 330 F9
MERRIANG
rd. Woodstock 153 H1
MERRIBAH
wy. Cranbourne W ...577 F17
MERRIBELL
av. Coburg 326 A3
dr. Waurn Ponds.....705 F15
dr. Waurn Ponds.....705 F15
MERRICK
cr. Glen Waverley....460 B9
ct. Highton 705 H4
st. Keysborough 534 L11
MERRICKS
cl. Ferntree Gly 464 D6
st. Broadmeadows..237 H15
MERRIFIELD
st. Brunswick..........325 F13
MERRIGAL
ct. Frankston S 626 J13
MERRIGAN
ct. Roxburgh Pk......194 A13
MERRIGUM
cr. Clarinda............498 D8
ct. Doncaster..........331 F18
ct. Highton 701 E11
la. Belgrave 466 C16
la. Launching Pl.......345 E17
wy. Roxburgh Pk......194 B5
MERRIJIG
av. Cranbourne........578 G16
MERRILANDS
rd. Reservoir...........282 K1
MERRILL
cr. Croydon Hl 335 D12
cr. Warranwood......335 D12
ct. Mooroolbark.......337 A11
dr. Epping..............198 C18
st. Mulgrave 500 F4
MERRILONG
st. Ringwood E.......379 A13
MERRIMAN
la. Melbourne...........23 G7
MERRIMU
ct. St Albans...........320 E12
la. Sherbrooke........466 H2
st. Murrumbeena....457 E6
MERRINDALE
dr. Croydon S 380 E11
dr. Kilsyth 380 E11
MERRION
gr. Kew, off Merrion Pl.........371 H11
pl. Kew..................371 H11
MERRITS
rd. Panton Hill.........204 H15
MERRITT
ct. Altona................408 K14
MERRIVALE
av. Sunshine W.......364 A5
pl. Roxburgh Pk......194 A7
wy. Bundoora...........284 G8
MERRIWEE
cr. Toorak..............415 J6
gr. Nar Warrn S.......579 G5
MERRIWOOLA
st. St Kilda E...........455 A1
MERRY
st. Ringwood E.......378 L12
MERRYLANDS
av. Portsea.............678 G3
MERRYN
cl. Bundoora...........242 G15
cl. Endeavour Hl 537 G5
ct. Templestowe 331 H7
gr. Wantirna S.........422 B16
MERSEY
cl. Rowville.............463 E18
cr. Seaford.............573 E15
ct. Werribee............447 H7
la. Caroline Spr.......317 J2
rd. Kilsyth 381 C13
st. Box Hill N 375 B12
st. Bundoora...........284 B1
st. Ringwood N.......378 D7
MERSO
ct. Carrum Downs...600 K1
MERTHER
rd. Ivanhoe 327 L8
MERTHYR
pl. Aspendale Gdn...547 B7
MERTON
av. Brighton 454 G10
cl. Cheltenham 531 D2
cl. Mt Waverley 419 H16
cl. Sunbury 143 B11
ct. Coldstream 295 F16
ct. Endeavour Hl 503 C20
gr. Healesville 213 G17
gr. Manifold Ht........702 C4
pl. Albert Park..........29 H15
pl. Albert Park.........413 D7
pl. Mill Park 243 F4
st. Albert Park..........29 G11
st. Albert Park.........413 D6
st. Altona................407 G16
st. Altona Mdw 451 F6
st. Box Hill.............374 L17
st. Camberwell.........417 G7
st. Caulfield N 455 B1
st. Ivanhoe 328 B16
st. St Albans...........320 D7
st. S Melbourne........29 F8
st. S Melbourne......413 C5
st. Springvale 500 B13
MERTZ
wy. Point Cook.........450 E4
MERUKA
dr. Eltham...............287 C8
MERVILLE
av. Malvern East.....457 A4
MERVIN
st. Bentleigh E 496 H5
MERVYN
cr. Ivanhoe 328 D15
rd. Belgrave S 506 A11
st. Doncaster..........374 J3
st. Newtown 702 F11
MERYL
st. Armadale 415 G13
st. Doncaster E 375 J5
MERYTON
la. Ivanhoe 328 E10
MERZ
pl. Roxburgh Pk......194 C8
MESETA
st. Mooroolbark......337 D9
MESKILL
cr. Viewbank...........286 A15
MESSINA
cr. Keilor Ldg..........276 A4
cr. Point Cook.........450 D8
cr. Kurunjang..........227 C11
MESSMATE
ct. Berwick 553 G4
ct. Emerald.............470 A17
ct. Mt Martha...........656 F7
pl. Rosebud.............700 L9
rd. Ferntree Gly 423 F19
rd. Torquay.............711 D3
ri. Eltham North 245 F18
st. Frankston N 599 L11
st. Lalor..................241 C11
MET
rd. Melb Airport.......235 B9
METCALF
cr. Rowville.............463 D18
pl. Epping..............197 K19
METELMAN
ct. Broadmeadows..238 F19
METEOR
ri. Kealba 321 A2
st. Mt Waverley 419 A12
METERY
rd. Eltham..............287 H13
METHERALL
st. Sunshine N.........320 K13
st. Sunshine N.........321 A13
METHVEN
st. Brunswick E.......325 K15
st. Coburg 325 G4
METROPOLITAN
av. Craigieburn........150 C14
av. Nunawading 376 D15
ct. Burwood............418 B4
ct. Keilor................276 H8
METROPOLITAN RING
rd. Bundoora...........242 C17
rd. Bundoora...........243 B16
rd. Fawkner.............239 F19
rd. Greensbrgh........243 B16
rd. Thomastown.......239 F19
METROPOLITAN RING
rd. Watsonia N........243 B16
METTERS
st. Maribyrnong......367 B2
METUNG
ct. Dingley Vill.........532 L8
st. Balwyn 373 B10
METYLENE
av. Springvale 499 F13
METZ
pl. Keilor Dn 276 A15
MEW
ct. Mill Park 242 A3
MEYER
cl. Blackburn 375 L11
ct. Brighton East 455 C13
rd. Burwood............418 A11
st. Cockatoo 511 B8
MEYERS
pl. Melbourne...........24 J5
MEYRICK
cr. Viewbank...........285 G19
MEYTAN
wy. Albanvale...........319 B4
MIA
cl. Reservoir...........282 A3
ct. Sunshine W........364 J7
ct. Werribee............448 D16
pl. Meadow Ht........194 A17
st. Clarinda............498 G11
MIAMI
ct. Oakleigh S 497 G1
st. Hawthorn E........416 D2
MICA
ct. Kings Park.........275 B18
ct. Narre Warren.....539 D13
MICHAEL
av. Glen Waverley....460 F3
av. St Albans...........276 G18
ct. Altona North 365 L20
ct. Berwick 554 K6
ct. Eltham North 245 G17
ct. Forest Hill 420 J5
ct. Hillside 274 F2
ct. Niddrie 322 K3
ct. Noble Park..........535 B6
ct. Seaford..............599 G3
ct. Springvale 500 G7
ct. Woori Yall..........344 F14
la. Melbourne.............1 H12
la. Melbourne...........24 A8
la. Mt Evelyn...........339 K15
pl. Ringwood N.......378 J1
st. Beaumaris 530 F6
st. Brunswick...........325 E15
st. Dromana 685 L10
st. Fitzroy N 326 E20
st. Lalor..................241 J8
st. Pakenham 558 B20
st. Rye 696 J3
st. Scoresby 462 D8
st. Templstw Lr 330 E13
wy. Somerville 644 J15
MICHAELIA
cl. Cranbourne W ...577 H17
MICHEALA
ct. Langwarrin 601 L19
MICHELE
ct. Rye 696 K1
dr. Scoresby 462 E5
MICHELINE
st. Tullamarine........278 G4
MICHELLAN
ct. Bayswater..........422 K4
ct. Donvale 332 H18
MICHELLE
av. Watsonia N 243 G20
cl. Thomastown......240 G17
ct. Carrum Downs...574 J16
ct. Cranbourne W ...577 J19
ct. Hoppers Csg.......405 F18
ct. Noble Park..........534 D6
ct. Oakleigh S 498 A6
ct. Rosanna 285 D20
dr. Berwick 554 A19
dr. Hampton Pk........551 L14
pl. Melton W...........226 C18
pl. Wheelers Hl 460 J10
MICHIGAN
av. Broadmeadows..238 K12
pl. Rowville.............462 L16
tce. Thomastown......240 G11
MICKLE
st. Dandenong S.....549 H8
st. Tooradin............651 G9
MICKLEHAM
rd. Attwood.............236 J18
rd. Craigieburn........149 A16
rd. Craigieburn........192 J1
rd. Gladstone Pk 236 J18
rd. Greenvale 192 H20
rd. Tullamarine........278 J3
rd. Westmeadows 236 J18
rd. Yuroke..............192 J1
MICKLETON
gr. Point Cook.........450 G10
MIDAS
ct. Meadow Ht........237 K5
MIDDLE
cr. Brighton 454
ct. Thomastown.......242
rd. Camberwell........416
rd. Derrimut............363
rd. Malvern East......457
rd. Maribyrnong......323
rd. Pearcedale........630
rd. Pearcedale........646
st. Ascot Vale 324
st. Hadfield 280
wy. Yellingbo 387
MIDDLEBOROUGH
rd. Blackburn 375
rd. Blackburn N.......375
rd. Blackburn S.......419
rd. Box Hill..............375
rd. Box Hill N 375
rd. Box Hill S..........419
rd. Burwood............419
rd. Burwood E.........419
MIDDLEBROOK
dr. Ringwood N.......334
MIDDLEFIELD
dr. Blackburn N.......375
MIDDLEHAM
cl. Cranbourne W ...577
cl. Lysterfield..........464
MIDDLE HUT
rd. Doreen 201
rd. Nutfield.............201
MIDDLESEX
rd. Surrey Hills........373
rd. Surrey Hills........417
st. Sunshine N........321
MIDDLETON
ct. Greenvale 193
dr. Woori Yall..........344
pl. W Melbourne.......23
st. Black Rock.........529
st. Braybrook..........366
st. Highett 496
st. Lalor..................241
st. Watsonia N........285
MIDHOLM
ct. Thomastown......240
MIDHURST
ct. Craigieburn........149
rd. Croydon 335
MIDLAND
wy. Taylors L 233
MIDLOTHIAN
ct. Point Cook.........450
pl. Glen Waverley....460
st. Malvern East......457
MIDVALE
av. Balwyn N 373
MIDWAY
cl. Gladstone Pk 279
cr. Lalor..................241
ct. Keilor Park.........278
st. Heidelberg W.....328
st. Mt Waverley 418
MIGA
cl. Greensbrgh........244
MIGHTY APOLLO
la. W Melbourne.......23
MIHAN
ct. Pakenham 559
st. Noble Park.........501
MIHIL
st. Preston.............327
MIKADO
rd. Mt Evelyn...........339
st. Hadfield 280
MIKKELL
ct. Pakenham 585
MILAN
ct. Bonbeach 573
ct. Dandenong N.....502
ct. Sunbury 142
st. Doncaster E 376
st. Mentone 530
st. Wantirna............422
MILANO
ct. Bundoora...........242
pl. Cranbourne N 578
MILAS
ct. Keilor Dn 276
MILBORNE
cr. Eltham...............288
MILBREY
cl. Wantirna S.........422
MILBURN
cct. Caroline Spr.......318
ct. Endeavour Hl 538
gr. St Kilda E...........415
pl. Craigieburn........150
rd. Keilor................277
st. Keilor................277
MILDARA
st. Vermont S 421

MILDENHALL
ct. Altona Mdw 451 J2
MILDURA
av. Sandringham 494 L13
av. Warburton 348 K3
cr. Dallas 238 F8
cr. Endeavour Hl 537 D2
MILE
la. Parkville 17 J5
la. Parkville 325 E20
MILE END
rd. Carnegie 456 G5
MILES
cl. Mill Park 243 B4
ct. Bacchus Msh 221 J18
ct. Cranbourne 577 L19
gr. Seaford 599 E5
pl. Roxburgh Pk 194 D14
rd. Parwan 264 G16
rd. Parwan 265 D17
st. Bentleigh 495 K1
st. Deer Park 319 C16
st. Ivanhoe 327 L13
st. Mulgrave 499 K1
st. Newtown 702 F10
st. Richmond 26 B12
st. Southbank 3 F16
st. Southbank 24 D19
st. Southbank 413 H1
MILES FRANKLIN
bvd. Point Cook 449 K8
MILEWA
ct. Mornington 656 G3
MILFAY
av. Kew 371 F9
av. Moonee Pnd 324 B13
ct. Balwyn N 374 A2
MILFORD
av. Burwood 418 H8
av. Wheelers Hl 461 A9
cl. Albanvale 318 L6
cr. Frankston 600 F18
ct. Kings Park 319 A1
ct. Meadow Ht 237 K2
gr. Rosanna 285 B20
pl. Belmont 706 A7
pl. Bundoora 284 L1
st. Bentleigh E 496 J5
st. Kilsyth 381 G6
st. Moolap 704 K20
st. Newport 410 J9
st. Thomastown 242 A12
MILFUL
cl. Rowville 463 J18
MILFULL
ct. Narre Warren 539 H16
MILGATE
ct. Forest Hill 376 J20
ct. Mooroolbark 337 G11
st. Oakleigh S 458 F17
tce. Sunbury 142 H2
wy. Avondale Ht 322 C12
MILINA
ct. Frankston 600 H17
MILITARY
rd. Avondale Ht 322 B8
rd. Avondale Ht 322 C11
tr. Langwarrin 628 G13
MILKWORT
tr. Frankston N 600 G10
MILL
av. Forest Hill 420 E4
av. Yarraville 366 G18
ct. Viewbank 285 K17
ct. Wesburn 348 A12
ct. Wheelers Hl 461 C19
la. Williamstown 411 D18
pl. Coburg 326 A7
pl. Melbourne 1 L18
rd. Oakleigh 457 J11
rd. Yarra Glen 208 L17
st. Aspendale 546 B1
st. Pakenham 584 D1
MILLAH
rd. Balwyn 373 E14
MILLAN
ct. Glen Waverley 460 B11
MILLAR
rd. Tullamarine 278 G1
MILLARD
st. Bentleigh E 497 A3
st. Frankston 627 F3
st. Templstw Lr 329 L8
MILLAWA
av. St Albans 320 D4
MILLBANK
dr. Deer Park 319 A12
dr. Mt Eliza 626 G20
pl. Cranbourne 578 H17
st. Bacchus Msh 221 L17
MILLEARA
rd. Avondale Ht 322 C8
rd. Keilor East 278 D19
st. The Basin 425 H8
MILLENNIUM
ct. Knoxfield 462 J10
wy. Torquay 711 H12
MILLER
cl. Eltham North 287 H3
cr. Mt Waverley 418 K19
ct. Bundoora 284 L1
ct. Cranbourne 577 L10
ct. Dandenong N 536 D1
ct. Hoppers Csg 405 C18
gr. Kew 371 F12
gr. Ringwood E 379 B9
la. S Melbourne 30 H4
pl. Doncaster 331 D17
pl. W Melbourne 17 A20
rd. Heathmont 379 E19
rd. Macclesfield 471 H1
rd. The Basin 424 J8
st. Alphington 327 J18
st. Berwick 554 G6
st. Blairgowrie 696 A3
st. Box Hill 375 B15
st. Brighton 454 E13
st. Brunswick E 326 A17
st. Carnegie 456 E10
st. Coburg 325 J5
st. Elsternwick 454 J4
st. Epping 241 D1
st. Essendon 323 J7
st. Fawkner 281 J6
st. Fitzroy N 326 A17
st. Healesville 213 L20
st. Heidelberg Ht 328 E5
st. Highett 495 L14
st. Newcomb 704 B13
st. Prahran 32 J17
st. Prahran 414 L9
st. Preston 326 D5
st. Preston 326 J6
st. Richmond 26 A13
st. Sandringham 495 H16
st. Sunbury 143 D12
st. Thornbury 326 D5
st. W Melbourne 34 L20
MILLERS
rd. Altona 409 F20
rd. Altona North 409 J3
rd. Brooklyn 365 K18
rd. Kangaroo Grnd 247 E11
rd. Seaholme 409 F20
rd. Wattle Glen 247 E11
MILLETT
rd. Gisborne S 141 A1
MILLEWA
av. Malvern East 457 D4
cr. Dallas 238 D12
wy. Wyndham Va 446 F13
MILLGATE
dr. Mornington 641 C20
MILLGROVE
av. Thomastown 240 E11
st. Scoresby 462 B6
wy. Berwick 554 C20
MILLIARA
gr. Brighton East 455 E16
st. Mt Waverley 419 G17
MILLICENT
av. Balwyn N 329 G20
av. Bulleen 329 L17
av. Toorak 415 D8
ct. Mornington 640 L8
st. Burwood 418 C9
st. Carrum 573 D8
st. Rosanna 329 A1
MILLIE
ct. Rowville 503 D3
MILLIGAN
pde. Sydenham 274 K3
MILLIS
av. Bentleigh E 497 A4
MILLOO
cr. Mt Waverley 419 D13
MILL PARK
dr. Mill Park 242 J10
MILLPERRA
ct. Frankston 600 H14
MILLPORT
ct. Endeavour Hl 503 K17
ri. Greenvale 237 G2
MILLS
av. Sassafras 426 J12
av. Somerton 194 G17
cl. Footscray 367 F5
la. Geelong, off Bellerine St 703 C10
rd. Belgrave Ht 466 H20
rd. Braeside 532 G12
rd. Dandenong 535 E10
rd. Hurstbridge 203 G14
st. Albert Park 29 J19
st. Albert Park 413 D10
st. Altona North 410 A8
st. Cheltenham 497 E16
st. Glen Iris 417 G10
st. Hampton 495 A7
st. Middle Park 29 H19
st. Middle Park 413 D10
st. Sunshine N 321 F15
MILLSON
cl. Bundoora 242 G16
ct. Pascoe Vale 281 A14
MILLSTREAM
av. Point Cook 450 B4
cct. Cairnlea 319 F6
MILLSWYN
av. Hampton Pk 551 G5
pl. South Yarra 31 E5
st. South Yarra 31 D7
st. South Yarra 414 B4
MILLWARD
st. Brunswick 325 B17
MILLWOOD
av. Berwick 554 B8
ct. Templestowe 331 G13
MILNE
av. Seaford 599 D8
ct. Delahey 275 D15
ct. Langwarrin 629 D7
ct. Pt Lonsdale 710 C6
pl. Eltham North 245 C17
pl. Ringwood N 378 G3
rd. Mont Albert N 374 F7
rd. Pk Orchards 334 D18
st. Mitcham 376 L13
st. Point Cook 450 A5
st. Templestowe 330 L8
st. Thomastown 241 D18
MILNER
av. Anglesea 713 G6
cl. Templestowe 331 F7
ct. Cranbourne 577 L14
MILNERS
rd. Yarra Jctn 347 C20
MILOJEVIC
ct. Cranbourne 578 E17
MILONE
ct. Werribee 447 F19
MILORA
ct. Pt Lonsdale 710 C5
MILPA
ct. Rye 697 G9
MILPARINKA
st. Safety Bch 669 D11
wy. Berwick 554 F11
MILPERA
cr. Wantirna 422 A13
MILPORT
ct. Point Cook 450 G7
MILROY
cr. Seaford 573 F14
ct. Wheelers Hl 461 F17
st. Brighton East 455 C14
MILSOM
av. Templstw Lr 330 F10
pl. S Melbourne 29 D3
MILTHORPE
rd. Diamond Ck 201 K19
rd. Yarrambat 201 K19
MILTON
av. Clayton S 499 C8
av. St Albans 320 J2
cl. Warrandyte 333 G4
cr. Box Hill S 418 G2
cr. Heidelberg Ht 328 D2
cr. Mulgrave 500 G5
cr. Preston 326 K5
ct. Aspendale Gdn 546 H3
ct. Mooroolbark 381 F2
dr. Wyndham Va 446 D14
pde. Bundoora 242 J20
pde. Glen Iris 416 D10
pde. Malvern 416 B7
pl. Cremorne 26 F17
pl. Gladstone Pk 279 E1
pl. Nar Warrn S 552 J15
rd. Rye 696 G3
st. Ascot Vale 324 C16
st. Bentleigh 455 J19
st. Canterbury 373 E20
st. Carnegie 456 F6
st. Elwood 414 E20
st. Elwood 454 C1
st. Ferntree Gly 464 F4
st. Glenroy 280 B9
st. Heathmont 379 A18
st. Macleod 285 C12
st. Nunawading 376 D18
st. Pascoe Vale S 280 J20
st. W Footscray 366 K7
st. W Melbourne 23 G1
wy. Hurstbridge 203 D14
MILVERTON
ct. Grovedale 706 H13
st. Camberwell 417 G8
st. Melton 226 J16
st. Moonee Pnd 323 L14
MIMI
ct. Somerville 644 E16
MIMOSA
av. Campbellfield 239 F12
av. Emerald 510 E4
av. Kilsyth 381 C8
av. Mt Evelyn 383 B1
av. Oakleigh S 458 B17
ct. Croydon S 379 E12
ct. Doncaster E 332 F18
ct. Frankston 628 F7
rd. Carnegie 456 G8
rd. Carnegie 456 H5
rd. Mill Park 242 F11
rd. Selby 467 C15
st. Doveton 536 L8
st. Glen Waverley 420 K20
st. Newcomb 704 A15
MINAK
rd. Selby 467 C14
MINAKI
av. Doncaster E 332 C20
MINATO
pl. Taylors L 275 H3
MINCHA
av. Templstw Lr 329 L9
st. Brunswick W 324 K16
st. Frankston 627 E6
MINCHINBURY
dr. Vermont S 421 E9
MINDAH
ct. Vermont S 421 C8
MINDANAO
ct. Armadale 415 G11
MINDARA
av. Rowville 502 E7
ct. Diamond Ck 245 K6
ct. Hoppers Csg 448 G8
MINDORO
cr. Lalor 241 J6
MINE
rd. Cottles Br 202 H1
rd. Nutfield 202 H1
st. Greensbrgh 244 G19
MINER
ct. Werribee 447 K10
MINERS
ct. Diggers Rest 187 A12
ct. Mulgrave 501 F3
MINERVA
av. Balwyn N 373 G1
cr. Keilor Dn 276 B11
cr. Vermont S 420 H12
ct. Wheelers Hl 460 D14
dr. Williamstn N 410 F12
rd. Herne Hill 702 A5
rd. Manifold Ht 702 A5
rd. Newtown 702 A5
rd. Newtown 702 A6
MINES
rd. Ringwood E 378 K9
MINE SHAFT
rd. Macclesfield 470 K1
rd. Smiths Gly 206 F11
MINETT
ct. Narre Warren 552 F2
MINETTE
ct. Ormond 455 J13
MINGANA
rd. Wantirna S 422 L11
rd. Wantirna S 423 A11
MINGAY
pl. Cranbourne W 577 G15
MINGETA
av. Blackburn S 419 K6
MINGOS
ct. Werribee 447 A15
MINIATA
wk. Vermont S 420 L10
wk. Vermont S 421 A10
MINIFIE
av. Anglesea 713 G6
MINIMBAH
ct. Frankston S 626 K12
MINJAH
ct. Dingley Vill 533 D6
MINKA
pl. Skye 601 D7
MINKARA
ct. Croydon 380 G7
MINKELL
ct. Wantirna 422 A9
MINLYA
av. Mt Waverley 459 D4
MINNA
st. Blackburn 375 E15
MINNIE
st. Brunswick 325 J15
st. Sandringham 495 D12
st. Yarraville 367 F17
MINNIMURRA
rd. Rye 697 B3
MINNO
ct. Frankston 600 J19
MINNS
la. Geelong, off Little Malop St 703 A7
pl. Geelong, off Little Malop St 703 A8
rd. Kurunjang 226 H5
rd. Melton W 226 B4
MINOGUE
cr. Hoppers Csg 448 F3
st. Kew East 372 G2
MINONA
st. Fawkner 281 J4
st. Hawthorn 372 C18
MINT
ct. Chelsea Ht 547 H18
st. Wantirna 422 C3
MINTARO
ct. Templestowe 331 E14
wy. Seabrook 450 L4
MINTBUSH
cl. Keysborough 534 A14
rd. Wesburn 348 D16
MINTER
ct. Pk Orchards 333 H10
st. Belgrave 466 E14
MINTLEAF
ct. Mitcham 377 A16
MINTO
st. Kew East 372 E4
MINTON
cl. Boronia 424 J4
dr. Frankston 599 J17
wk. Nar Warrn S 579 F2
MINVI
tce. Cairnlea 319 H13
MINYA
ct. Rowville 463 F13
MIOWERA
grn. Greensbrgh 244 D14
MIRA
st. Blackburn S 419 G6
MIRABEL
av. Ringwood E 379 C8
MIRABELLA
cl. Werribee 447 J3
cr. Box Hill S 419 C4
ct. Warrandyte 333 C7
dr. Tullamarine 278 L5
dr. Tullamarine 279 A5
MIRAGE
wk. Point Cook 450 D5
wy. Port Melb 367 H20
wy. Port Melb 411 H1
wy. S Morang 198 L11
MIRALIE
wy. Cranbourne W 577 F16
MIRAM
ct. Westmeadows 237 H12
MIRAMA
ct. Mitcham 377 C13
MIRAMAH
cl. Rowville 502 J2
MIRAMAR
ct. Donvale 332 G16
MIRAMS
st. Ascot Vale 323 K17
MIRANDA
cl. Clayton S 499 E11
cl. Torquay 712 E4
ct. Noble Park 534 H6
gdn. Hampton Pk 552 D10
pl. Frankston 627 K10
rd. Reservoir 283 D6
st. Sorrento 678 F9
MIRANG
av. Croydon 380 E9
av. Mt Martha 655 H14
ct. Frankston 599 K16
MIRBELIA
cr. Mill Park 243 B8
MIRBOO
ct. Brookfield 268 C6
ct. Dallas 238 C12
st. Dandenong N 501 F13
MIRCELLA
pl. Melton W 226 D19
MIRIAM
cl. Narre Warren 538 L15
cl. Wantirna S 421 L15
cl. Wheelers Hl 461 B20
ct. Airport W 278 G16
ct. Bundoora 285 C2
ct. Somerville 644 F16
ct. Templestowe 331 G8
dr. Yarra Glen 208 L19

fwy. Safety Bch 687 A2
fwy. Tuerong 657 A19
fwy. Tuerong 670 A11
MORNINGTON-TYABB
rd. Moorooduc 658 B4
rd. Mornington 640 H19
MOROBE
st. Heidelberg W 283 L20
st. Sorrento 679 D16
MOROCCO
ct. Glen Waverley 420 B15
MOROKAI
gr. Lilydale 337 L2
MORONEY
cr. Menzies Ck 468 B20
st. Boronia 424 G13
st. Oakleigh 458 C15
st. St Kilda, off Brighton Rd 414 E18
MOROTAI
av. Ashburton 417 F16
pde. Heidelberg W 328 B3
st. Sorrento 679 E15
MORPETH
st. Newcomb 704 D17
MORPHETT
av. Ascot Vale 323 H19
MORRAH
st. Parkville 17 G10
MORRES
st. Bentleigh 456 B19
st. Ripponlea 454 H1
MORRICE
st. Caulfield N 455 B2
MORRIE
cr. Blackburn N 375 G9
MORRIS
av. Mont Albert N 374 G6
ct. Dandenong N 501 L15
ct. Epping 198 F15
ct. Frankston 627 J7
ct. Meadow Ht 237 J3
ct. Springvale 500 G7
ct. Sunbury 142 J15
ct. Wandin N 340 K13
dr. Beaconsfld Up 541 H6
dr. Keilor Dn 276 B14
la. Williamstown 411 D11
rd. Beaconsfld Up 542 H12
rd. Croydon 379 J9
rd. Hoppers Csg 448 L5
rd. Hoppers Csg 449 A5
rd. McCrae 684 J17
rd. Tarneit 405 B12
rd. Upwey 465 G17
st. Ashwood 417 L16
st. Balwyn N 373 D8
st. Belmont 702 D19
st. Blairgowrie 696 A1
st. Coburg N 281 H16
st. Doncaster 374 H4
st. Melton S 268 F5
st. Parkdale 531 L12
st. Reservoir 282 K2
st. S Melbourne 29 G4
st. Sunshine 365 B5
st. Tootgarook 698 F4
st. Williamstown 411 H19
MORRISON
cr. Doncaster 374 K3
cr. Kilsyth 381 F5
cr. Sunshine W 364 L10
cr. Sunshine W 365 A10
ct. Mont Albert N 374 D7
ct. Mt Waverley 459 G2
dr. Darley 221 L9
pl. E Melbourne 25 A2
rd. Pakenham Up 560 B2
st. Clayton 498 F2
st. Hawthorn 415 J2
st. Geelong, off Maud St 703 B10
MORRISONS
av. Mt Martha 656 B8
MORROW
pl. Hoppers Csg 448 C2
st. Altona 408 F15
st. Brunswick W 324 F7
st. Melton W 225 L17
MORSHEAD
av. Mt Waverley 459 G1
st. Ascot Vale 324 B20
st. Melton S 268 H11
MORTIMER
st. Heidelberg 328 H5
st. Huntingdale 458 E12
st. Kew 372 D11
st. Werribee 447 D15
MORTIMORE
st. Bentleigh 496 D3
MORTLAKE
av. Dallas 238 K11

MORTON
av. Carnegie 456 J5
gr. Chelsea 546 H16
la. Flemington 324 C19
pl. Chirnside Pk 336 H7
pl. Rowville 463 D19
rd. Ashwood 418 B15
rd. Burwood 418 B12
rd. Burwood 418 B15
st. Bacchus Msh 222 D15
st. Box Hill S 418 J4
st. Clayton 459 E18
st. Elsternwick 455 C4
st. Essendon 324 B4
MORTON BAY
dr. Highton 705 H1
MORTONS
rd. Pentland Hl 221 A14
MORUYA
dr. Grovedale 705 J14
MORVAL
ct. Deer Park 318 L13
MORVAN
ct. Ferntree Gly 463 H7
MORVEN
av. Tecoma 466 E9
ct. Highton 701 H20
st. Mornington 640 J13
st. Yarraville 367 A18
MORWELL
av. Bundoora 284 H4
av. Dandenong S 535 H13
av. Watsonia 285 C5
cr. Dallas 238 F9
gdn. Caroline Spr 317 K8
pde. Springvale 500 B11
MOSEL
pl. Roxburgh Pk, off Wisla Cct 194 C6
MOSELEY
dr. Mt Eliza 626 F19
MOSELLE
ct. Doncaster 330 H17
st. Mont Albert N 374 E9
MOSER
rd. Wonga Park 291 F15
MOSIG
ct. Hampton Pk 551 D11
ct. Noble Park N 501 E15
MOSMAN
cl. Wantirna S 422 D19
wy. Craigieburn 193 J3
MOSRAEL
pl. Rowville 462 J13
MOSS
cl. Hoppers Csg 448 D1
ct. Croydon N 336 D15
ct. Glenroy 280 B3
ct. Rowville 463 H19
pl. N Melbourne 17 F19
st. Fitzroy N 326 B19
st. Melton S 268 E11
st. Prahran 31 L17
st. Prahran 414 F9
MOSSDALE
ct. Templestowe 331 F13
MOSSFIEL
dr. Hoppers Csg 448 H2
MOSSFIELD
av. Ferntree Gly 463 L1
mw. Tullamarine 278 K1
MOSSGIEL
av. Greenvale 237 C3
MOSSGIEL PARK
dr. Endeavour Hl 537 G2
MOSSMAN
cr. Lalor 240 E9
dr. Eaglemont 329 A11
MOSSTROOPER
ct. Mill Park 242 H12
MOSSVALE
cl. Endeavour Hl 537 H1
MOSSY CREEK SLOPE
Warrandyte 333 H4
MOTEL
ct. Launching Pl 345 H13
MOTHERWELL
av. Greenvale 193 A20
st. South Yarra 32 G14
st. South Yarra 414 K7
MOTON
pl. Carlton 18 G14
MOTSCHALLS
rd. Panton Hill 205 D14
MOTT
ct. Chelsea Ht 547 F18
ct. Glen Waverley 459 J2
MOTTO
ct. Hoppers Csg 449 F2
MOUBRAY
ct. Werribee 448 A18
la. Albert Park 29 G13
st. Albert Park 29 F12

st. Albert Park 413 C6
st. Melbourne 31 E17
st. Melbourne 414 C9
MOULE
av. Balwyn N 374 B6
av. Brighton 454 E14
st. Brunswick W 324 K15
MOUNSEY
ct. Sunbury 143 D13
st. Sunshine W 364 K10
MOUNT
ct. Mill Park 242 D11
dr. Sunbury 142 D7
rd. Kalorama 382 K17
rd. Yarra Glen 209 A16
st. Altona 409 E20
st. Eaglemont 328 J11
st. Glen Waverley 460 D3
st. Kew 372 F14
st. Prahran 32 E20
st. Prahran 414 H10
st. Preston 326 D2
MOUNTAIN
av. Emerald 510 B9
av. Frankston S 643 D2
cr. Montrose 382 L5
cr. Montrose 383 A8
cr. Mulgrave 500 A3
dr. Mooroolbark 381 J3
gr. Kew 372 J13
hwy. Bayswater 423 B5
hwy. Bayswater 423 J3
hwy. Boronia 424 E2
hwy. Ferny Creek 425 J13
hwy. Sassafras 425 J13
hwy. The Basin 425 B8
hwy. Wantirna 421 J12
hwy. Wantirna 422 F6
rd. Cockatoo 471 F19
st. Essendon 323 F6
st. S Melbourne 29 D8
st. S Melbourne 413 B4
MOUNTAIN ASH
av. Ashwood 418 D14
ct. Up Fntree Gly 464 K6
dr. Sunbury 143 F17
MOUNTAIN FLAT
rd. Nar Warrn E 506 D17
MOUNTAIN GATE
dr. Ferntree Gly 463 L3
MOUNTAIN HEATH
wk. Croydon S 380 C14
MOUNTAIN VIEW
av. Avondale Ht 321 L10
cct. Beaconsfield 555 F11
cir. Safety Bch 669 D18
cr. Seaford 600 C4
la. Mickleham 150 E4
pde. Rosanna 328 H2
rd. Balwyn N 373 E4
rd. Briar Hill 286 F2
rd. Greensbrgh 286 F2
rd. Hurstbridge 202 G10
rd. Kalorama 383 E11
rd. Kilsyth 381 B7
rd. Montmorency 286 J7
rd. Mt Eliza 642 C6
rd. Nunawading 376 F11
MOUNTAIN-VIEW
rd. Heathmont 378 K20
MOUNTAINVIEW
cl. Croydon Hl 335 G11
MT AITKEN
rd. Diggers Rest 141 A14
rd. Diggers Rest 141 K20
MT ALEXANDER
rd. Ascot Vale 324 E15
rd. Essendon 323 K5
rd. Flemington 34 E1
rd. Flemington 324 E15
rd. Moonee Pnd 323 K5
rd. Travancore 324 D15
MT ARARAT
rd. Nr Nr Goon 586 K14
MT ARARAT NORTH
rd. Nr Nr Goon N 586 K1
MT ARTHUR
av. Rosebud 700 H5
rd. Rosebud 683 L17
MOUNT BATTEN
wy. Sydenham 274 K1
MOUNTBATTEN
ct. Oakleigh E 458 L11
ct. Reservoir 239 L20
st. Grovedale 706 B14
MT BRIDE
rd. Warburton 349 C9
MT BURNETT
rd. Mt Burnett 511 K20
MT COOPER
dr. Bundoora 284 D4
dr. Bundoora 284 F4

MT COOPER SCENIC
dr. Bundoora 284 C3
MT COTTRELL
rd. Melton 270 C6
rd. Melton S 270 A20
rd. Rockbank 228 C20
rd. Rockbank 270 A20
MT DANDENONG
rd. Croydon 379 G6
rd. Kilsyth 380 D5
rd. Montrose 381 A6
rd. Montrose 381 L10
rd. Ringwood E 378 H11
MT DANDENONG TOURIST
rd. Ferny Creek 465 J3
rd. Kalorama 382 H19
rd. Kalorama 383 A12
rd. Montrose 382 C10
rd. Montrose 383 A9
rd. Mt Dandenong 382 H19
rd. Olinda 426 G2
rd. Olinda 427 A11
rd. Sherbrooke 426 B19
rd. Tremont 465 D5
MT DERRIMUT
rd. Deer Park 319 D20
rd. Derrimut 363 C13
MT EAGLE
rd. Ivanhoe East 328 L13
wy. Wyndham Va 446 C12
MT ECCLES
pl. Caroline Spr 317 J8
MT EIRENE
rd. Gembrook 512 L20
MT ELIZA
wy. Mt Eliza 626 A17
wy. Mt Eliza 626 A18
MT ERIN
cr. Frankston S 627 H10
rd. Ferny Creek 425 F18
MOUNTFIELD
av. Malvern East 457 J1
rd. Kilsyth 381 E4
rd. Mitcham 376 L10
st. Brunswick 325 H11
st. Canterbury 372 K14
MOUNTFORD
dr. Springvale 500 K8
MT GRAND VIEW
rd. Pearcedale 630 F17
MT HILDA
rd. Pearcedale 630 E14
MT IDA
av. Hawthorn E 416 E4
av. Rosanna 328 J2
MT KOROIT
rd. Rockbank 270 L14
MT KOROROIT
rd. Melton 228 B4
rd. Toolern Va 228 B4
MT LEBANON
rd. Chum Creek 213 A11
MOUNTLEIGH
ct. Glen Waverley 460 L3
MT MARTHA
rd. Mt Martha 669 A10
MT MORTON
rd. Belgrave 466 C18
rd. Belgrave Ht 466 B19
rd. Belgrave Ht 506 B3
rd. Belgrave S 506 F4
MT PIPER
ri. Craigieburn 150 F10
MT PLEASANT
dr. Mt Waverley 459 C4
gr. Armadale 415 D11
rd. Belmont 702 B17
rd. Belmont 702 C17
rd. Eltham 287 G14
rd. Eltham 288 G12
rd. Forest Hill 376 J20
rd. Highton 701 F16
rd. Monbulk 428 D17
rd. Nunawading 376 H17
rd. Preston 326 B3
rd. Research 288 G12
rd. Research 289 A11
MT RIDDELL
rd. Healesville 257 C8
rd. Healesville 257 H6
rd. Healesville 258 C2
MT RIDLEY
rd. Craigieburn 149 A3
rd. Mickleham 149 A3
MT SHAMROCK
rd. Pakenham 558 K10
MOUNT VIEW
ct. Burwood 418 A9
MOUNTVIEW
av. Parkdale 531 J13
ct. Frankston 627 D4
rd. Highett 496 J15

rd. Malvern 415
st. Aspendale 546
MT VIEW
av. Hallam 537 K
gr. Balwyn N 372
gr. Balwyn N 373
pde. Croydon 336 G
pde. Mooroolbark 337 A
rd. Boronia 424 H
rd. Ferny Creek 425 G
rd. Rosebud 684 G
rd. Templestowe 331 E
rd. Thomastown 240 L
rd. Thomastown 241 A
rd. Up Fntree Gly 464
st. Croydon 380
MOUNT VUE
rd. Healesville 212 J
MT WISE
rd. Yarra Glen 208 E
MOURELL
st. Sunshine W 364 G
MOURIK
ct. Wantirna 422 C
MOUSHALL
av. Niddrie 323
MOWAT
st. Geelong West 702
MOWBRAY
cr. Kurunjang 226 L
ct. Carrum Downs 601
ct. Doncaster E 332 B
ct. Noble Park N 501
ct. Sunbury 143
dr. Wantirna S 462
st. Hawthorn E 416
MOXHAMS
rd. Monbulk 468
rd. Monbulk 468
MOYA
cl. Endeavour Hl 537
cr. Noble Park 500 F
ct. Yallambie 285 F
MOYANGUL
dr. Keilor East 278 B
MOYLAN
la. Kensington 33 D
rd. Glen Waverley 420 B
st. Bentleigh E 456 H
MOYLANS
la. Melbourne 1 H
la. Melbourne 24 A
MOYNE
cr. Coolaroo 238
MOYSEYS RUN
Beaumaris 530
MOYSTON
cl. Vermont S 421
ct. Meadow Ht 237
la. Waurn Ponds 705 B
MOZART
cir. Donvale 332 G
cr. Bundoora 242 E
pl. E Melbourne 25
st. St Kilda 414 E
MUCHELL
gr. Coburg 326
MUDDY CREEK
rd. Nar Warrn E 507 E
MUDDY GATES
la. Tooradin 651
MUDFORD
st. Sunshine W 364
MUDGEE
ct. Chadstone 458
st. Burwood E 419 E
MUDIE
av. Sunbury 142
MUDLARK
ct. Carrum Downs 600
ct. Berwick, off Allardice Pde 539 H
MUDO
ct. Rowville 503
MUELLER
ct. Endeavour Hl 537
MUES
st. Keilor East 322
MUGAVIN
rd. Mt Evelyn 339 L
MUGG
la. N Melbourne 34 L
MUHALLS
rd. Emerald 470
rd. Macclesfield 470
MUIR
ct. Chelsea Ht 547 G
ct. Ringwood 378 D
ct. Rosebud W 683 D
la. Hawthorn 371 D
rd. Christmas Hills 251
st. Bacchus Msh 221 K
st. Frankston 626

. Hawthorn...371 D14
. Highett...496 B12
. Mt Waverley...419 E17
. Richmond...26 A8
. Spotswood...366 H20
JIRFIELD
/. Jan Juc...711 F14
. Heatherton...497 J15
. Burwood...418 B4
. Frankston...599 J17
. Rowville...462 C19
. Sunbury...144 F13
w. Chirnside Pk...292 H10
JIRHEAD
. Werribee...447 F13
. Greenvale...237 F2
ln. Caroline Spr...317 K6
JIRKIRK
. Endeavour Hl...537 H1
JIRS
. Taylors L...233 F20
JIR SMYTH
. Mt Evelyn...339 F14
JLAWA
Croydon N...336 A16
JLBERRY
. Frankston N...600 D6
. Cranbourne N...578 D8
. Eltham...287 K10
. Cairnlea...319 J10
de. Heidelberg W...328 A2
. Craigieburn...149 L13
. Doreen...156 L11
. Richmond...26 B11
e. Werribee...447 L12
JLCAHY
Altona Mdw...451 H7
. Pakenham...557 L18
JLDOWNEY
Aberfeldie...323 D10
ULDURI
. Croydon S...379 L14
JLGA
. Carrum Downs...575 F18
. Narre Warren...553 F11
. Altona...408 J19
. Thomastown...241 E13
JLGOA
/. Dandenong N...501 H19
. Keysborough...534 E10
. Brighton...454 E13
JLGOWRIE
. Greensbrgh...244 J20
. Greensbrgh...286 J1
JLGRA
. Frankston S...626 L14
JLGRAVE
Ashwood...418 C17
Elsternwick...455 B2
Glen Waverley...420 C17
Kensington...34 A7
. Reservoir...283 F10
/. Croydon N...335 L15
JLGUTHRIE
Hallam...537 L16
JLHALL
. St Albans...320 G10
JLHOLLAND
Grovedale...705 J17
JLKARRA
. Chelsea...547 B16
JLLANE
. Pakenham...559 F16
JLLENGER
. Braybrook...321 K17
JLLENS
. Vermont S...420 F9
. Warrandyte...290 C19
JLLER
Heathmont...422 L1
JLLIN
. Cranbourne...577 L18
JLLINS
Williamstown...411 A17
w. Williamstown...411 A18
JLLOCK
. Diggers Rest...187 C12
JLLUM
Springvale S...534 B6
. Donvale...332 K17
. Doncaster E...332 J10
JLLUM MULLUM
. Ringwood...378 F8
JLQUINEY
. Highton...705 F6
JLSANE
/. Mornington...656 F2
JLSANNE
Bentleigh E...457 C15
. Donvale...376 J5
. Warranwood...334 J14

MULWALA
ct. Wyndham Va...446 B5
gdn. St Albans...321 B6
pl. Taylors Hill...274 H12
MUMMERY
st. Mt Waverley...459 B3
MUNCH
pl. Sunbury...142 H6
MUNDARA
ct. Glen Waverley...460 J1
dr. Ringwood...334 L19
dr. Ringwood...335 A19
MUNDARING
dr. Cranbourne...604 D2
MUNDAY
ct. Skye...575 G20
st. Torquay...712 A12
MUNDOORA
ct. Mornington...641 C15
MUNDY
st. Geelong...703 A12
st. Mentone...530 J9
st. Watsonia...285 D6
MUNGALA
cr. Blairgowrie...696 B7
MUNGANA
ct. Taylors L...276 A9
MUNGARI
st. Dingley Vill...533 D5
MUNICA
ct. Frankston...627 F6
MUNICH
dr. Keilor Dn...276 F16
MUNJONG
pl. Delahey...275 B11
MUNRO
av. Ashburton...417 D18
av. Carnegie...456 F8
av. Cheltenham...496 E17
av. Edithvale...546 J12
av. Lilydale...338 L11
av. Mt Waverley...419 G20
av. Sunshine N...321 C10
cl. Hampton Pk...551 J4
ct. Altona Mdw...451 H9
ct. Bacchus Msh...221 H14
ct. Meadow Ht...237 K3
sq. Footscray...367 H6
st. Armadale...415 F11
st. Ascot Vale...323 K17
st. Black Rock...529 G2
st. Blairgowrie...695 L4
st. Brighton...454 H19
st. Brunswick...325 B15
st. Coburg...325 A2
st. Cremorne...32 B2
st. Cremorne...414 G1
st. Hawthorn E...372 E20
st. Kew East...372 K3
st. Lalor...241 E11
st. Macleod...285 C16
st. Mitcham...377 G18
st. Northcote...327 A14
st. Port Melb...29 A2
st. Port Melb...413 A1
st. Ringwood...378 B10
st. Southbank...23 B20
st. Southbank...413 A1
st. S Melbourne...29 A2
st. S Melbourne...413 A1
MUNROS
la. N Melbourne...17 E15
MUNSTER
av. Carnegie...456 F4
ct. Endeavour Hl...537 B2
tce. N Melbourne...34 J18
MUNTZ
av. Glenroy...279 J3
st. Caulfield N...415 F16
MURA
cl. Greensbrgh...244 A19
ct. Grovedale...706 C15
MURAWA
dr. Rosebud...700 K5
st. Frankston...627 F5
MURCH
cr. Anglesea...713 J3
MURCHISON
av. Taylors L...275 E1
av. Vermont S...421 E8
cr. Clayton S...499 E11
ct. Herne Hill...702 A3
ct. Werribee...447 G7
dr. Roxburgh Pk...194 F15
st. Carlton...18 K14
st. St Kilda E...414 L15
st. St Kilda E...415 A15
wy. Thomastown...241 L17
MURDO
rd. Clayton...459 F19
MURDOCH
av. Mulgrave...460 C17
av. Narre Warren...539 D16
ct. Altona North...365 F20
ct. Ferntree Gly...463 H7
ct. Keilor East...322 B1
ct. Sunbury...144 G10
st. Camberwell...417 C5
MURDOCK
ct. Maddingley...263 G4
st. Brunswick...325 E9
st. Clayton S...498 K6
MURENE
ct. Boronia...423 J9
MURIEL
ct. Coburg N...282 B18
ct. Epping...197 H19
ct. Reservoir...283 H3
st. Glen Iris...417 J10
st. Niddrie...322 L3
st. Niddrie...323 A3
st. Northcote...327 C17
MURIEL REIDY
st. Maribyrnong, off Eveline Av...367 C2
MURILLO
ct. Doncaster...331 B14
ct. Wheelers Hl...460 L15
MURNDAL
ct. Berwick...554 B14
ct. Frankston S...627 G13
dr. Donvale...376 L5
MURNONG
st. Maribyrnong...322 J17
st. Point Cook...450 B6
MURPHY
gr. Preston...283 D20
pl. Roxburgh Pk...194 C9
rd. Doncaster E...331 G20
rd. Pakenham...559 E20
st. Altona North...409 H4
st. Brighton...454 J11
st. Chadstone...457 L3
st. Clarinda...498 H10
st. Deer Park...319 B11
st. Kew...371 D11
st. N Melbourne...17 E13
st. Oak Park...279 L11
st. Preston...282 C16
st. Richmond...26 L10
st. Richmond...371 A15
st. South Yarra...32 A8
st. South Yarra...32 B6
st. South Yarra...414 F4
MURPHYS
rd. Exford...267 A19
rd. Parwan...265 K18
wy. Emerald...509 F3
MURRA
ct. Ashwood...418 C18
st. Bentleigh E...456 L14
st. Burwood...419 A8
MURRABIT
gr. Taylors L...276 D7
MURRAC
st. Coldstream...295 C12
MURRAGONG
av. Bundoora...284 L4
MURRAJONG
ct. Sunshine...321 K6
MURRALINGA
pl. Mt Eliza...642 B8
MURRAY
av. Braybrook...366 B7
cl. Frankston...628 F5
cl. Noble Park...534 K5
cr. Rowville...463 A19
ct. Carrum...573 D10
ct. Cranbourne...578 B17
ct. Greenvale...237 A4
ct. Tootgarook...698 B7
ct. Vermont S...420 H6
ct. Werribee...447 C10
dr. Burwood...418 B7
dr. Wattle Glen...246 J7
la. Caulfield...455 F5
la. Seville E...343 C12
pl. Ringwood...378 C13
rd. Coburg...281 K19
rd. Croydon...379 F2
rd. Dandenong N...501 L10
rd. Diamond Ck...245 G7
rd. Heidelberg W...327 G1
rd. McKinnon...455 J14
rd. Ormond...455 J14
rd. Preston...282 G19
rd. Queenscliff...707 J17
rd. Reservoir...281 K19
rd. Rockbank...270 G13
rd. The Patch...467 K2
st. Abbotsford...26 G2
st. Anglesea...713 F4
st. Armadale...415 G10
st. Brighton East...455 H14
st. Brunswick W...324 K10
st. Caulfield...455 C5
st. Caulfield S...455 C5
st. Clayton...458 L19
st. Coburg...281 A20
st. Coburg...325 D1
st. Elsternwick...455 C5
st. Fawkner...281 F5
st. Glenroy...280 C7
st. Highton...701 G17
st. McCrae...684 L16
st. Melton S...268 G11
st. Mentone...531 F7
st. Moonee Pnd...324 D10
st. Mornington...640 F13
st. Newcomb...704 E17
st. Prahran...32 G19
st. Prahran...414 J9
st. Richmond...26 K13
st. Rye...696 E3
st. St Albans...319 G3
st. Sunshine W...363 L3
st. Sunshine W...364 B3
st. Thornbury...326 G7
st. Yarraville...367 B15
wk. Roxburgh Pk...194 D6
wy. Narre Warren...538 H15
MURRAY-ANDERSON
rd. Rosebud...684 E14
MURRAYS
pl. Eltham North...245 G18
MURRELL
ct. Narre Warren...539 A19
st. Glenroy...280 A5
MURRINDAL
cl. Eltham North...245 F17
dr. Rowville...463 H14
MURRONG
av. Bentleigh E...456 K15
MURROWONG
av. Rosebud...683 J19
MURRUMBEENA
cr. Murrumbeena...457 A11
rd. Murrumbeena...456 L14
MURRUMBUNG
rd. Mt Evelyn...383 D4
MURTOA
pl. Cranbourne W...603 F1
st. Dallas...238 F13
MURTON
ct. Rosebud...699 J3
MURTONS
wy. Port Melb, off Stokes St...412 J6
MURUMBA
dr. Oakleigh S...497 L1
st. Greensbrgh...244 K19
MUSCA
st. Balwyn N...373 A1
MUSCAT
ct. Sunbury...144 D9
MUSGRAVE
wk. Yallambie...285 L13
MUSGROVE
ct. Greensbrgh...244 E15
ct. Nar Warrn S...579 B3
mw. Kensington...33 D8
MUSK
ct. Melton...268 J1
ct. Westmeadows...237 F10
gr. Up Fntree Gly...464 L5
st. Blackburn...376 A14
MUSKET
pl. Waurn Ponds...705 F15
MUSSELBURGH
ct. Frankston...599 K17
MUSSERT
av. Dingley Vill...533 C8
MUSTANG
av. Narre Warren...538 K19
ct. Ashburton...417 J15
pl. Sunbury...143 K16
MUSTER
ct. Vermont S...421 A13
MUSWELL
hill, Glen Iris...416 L13
MUTIMER
st. Preston...327 B1
MUTTON
rd. Fawkner...281 H10
MUTUAL
ct. Forest Hill...420 E2
rd. Balwyn N...374 B5
MUXWORTHY
av. Herne Hill...702 A1
MYALL
pl. Frankston S...627 B5
tce. Mt Martha...669 A6
MYALLA
ct. Wantirna S...462 H1
st. Braybrook...365 J3
MYAMBERT
av. Balwyn...373 B14
MYAMIN
cl. Selby...467 B16
MYAMYN
st. Armadale...415 J12
st. Braybrook...365 J4
MYDDLETON
dr. Viewbank...285 L15
MYER
pl. Rowville...502 A2
MYERS
av. Glen Waverley...420 B20
ct. Bundoora...242 C20
ct. Doncaster...375 A3
ct. Hoppers Csg...448 C1
ct. Melton...227 B16
ct. Noble Park...500 J17
pde. Altona Mdw...451 E3
rd. Footscray...367 F3
st. Darley...221 C5
st. E Geelong...703 F10
st. Geelong...702 L8
st. Mt Eliza...626 B15
st. Pascoe Vale S...280 J20
st. Sunshine W...364 G5
MYERS CREEK
rd. Healesville...213 J8
MYLES
pl. S Geelong...702 L14
MYNA
ct. Carrum Downs...600 G3
MYOLA
st. Carrum...573 E8
MYOORA
ct. Greensbrgh...243 G17
dr. Mooroolbark...337 C15
rd. Toorak...415 F6
MYORA
ct. Chadstone...417 L20
MYRA
cl. Montmorency...287 B8
ct. Gladstone Pk...237 C20
ct. Kalorama...383 A17
ct. Rye...696 K14
st. Seaford...599 D3
MYRIONG
av. Vermont S...420 L10
av. Vermont S...421 A9
ct. Clayton...459 B18
st. Clayton...458 L17
MYRNIONG
gr. Hawthorn E...416 G4
st. Glen Iris...417 L10
MYRNONG
cr. Ascot Vale...324 G16
cr. Toorak...415 H4
MYRON
pl. Doncaster...331 B13
MYROSS
av. Ascot Vale...323 G19
MYRTLE
av. Heathmont...378 K14
av. Kew...372 G9
av. Newcomb...704 A12
cr. Ferntree Gly...464 J1
ct. Doncaster E...376 C3
ct. Frankston...628 B5
ct. Oakleigh S...458 D19
ct. Watsonia N...285 H1
gr. Airport W...278 K17
gr. Altona...452 H1
gr. Blackburn...375 F17
gr. Doveton...536 L11
gr. Doveton...537 A11
gr. Guys Hill...555 L2
gr. Preston...282 H17
gr. Reservoir...282 H17
gr. Tecoma...466 B8
rd. Canterbury...373 B17
rd. Ferny Creek...426 B17
rd. Hampton...495 D10
st. Bayswater...423 F5
st. Bentleigh...456 D19
st. Brunswick E...325 L13
st. Campbellfield...239 E13
st. Clifton Hill...20 E7
st. Glen Waverley...460 B5
st. Hawthorn...371 E13
st. Heidelberg Ht...328 E8
st. Langwarrin...628 J3
st. Langwarrin...628 K1
st. Melton S...268 E7
st. Mordialloc...532 D16
st. Noble Park...500 D19
st. St Kilda E...454 K1
st. South Yarra...31 L10
st. Springvale S...500 A19
st. Thomastown...241 H13
st. Werribee...447 D10
st. Williamstn N...410 K13
MYSTIC
ct. Eumemmerring...537 C14
rd. Tremont...425 C15
MYTTON
cl. St Albans...320 C11
gr. Brighton...454 E15

ORMANBY
v. Caulfield N......415 K18
v. Sunshine W......364 H14
v. Thornbury......326 B8
t. Heidelberg W.....284 A18
r. Greenvale......237 C3
Richmond......26 B10
Windsor, off
Newry St......414 K11
d. Bentleigh E......497 B4
d. Caulfield E......456 B1
d. Caulfield N......415 L18
d. Clayton......459 D13
d. Kew......372 G11
d. Kew East......372 G11
d. Notting Hill......459 D13
d. Port Melb......29 A2
d. Sorrento......678 E10
d. Southbank......29 A2
d. Southbank......413 A1
d. S Melbourne......29 A2
d. S Melbourne......413 A1
Brighton......454 F17
Cranbourne......578 F19
E Geelong......703 F12
Hughesdale......457 H13
Moonee Pnd......323 L15
S Melbourne......29 D6
S Melbourne......413 B3
Sydenham......274 L2
Windsor......414 K11
e. Mt Martha......655 G17
ORMANDY
d. Elwood......454 C5
Ashburton......417 E17
ORMANTON
Berwick......554 F12
ORM CLARK
k. Rosebud, off
Wannaeue Pl......684 B15
ORMDALE
d. Bentleigh E......497 B5
ORMLEITH
r. Boronia......424 H10
ORRAY
v. Mt Waverley......419 C15
ORRIS
Bundoora......284 A1
Healesville......258 B8
Thomastown......284 A1
Blackburn......375 L19
Noble Park N......501 G15
Lilydale......338 H7
N Melbourne......34 L12
d. Pakenham......560 C13
d. Rowville......463 A20
Coburg N......281 F14
Noble Park......534 L3
Surrey Hills......373 H15
ORTH
Altona Mdw......407 F18
v. Belmont......706 J2
v. Bentleigh......496 A4
v. Bulleen......329 J9
v. Mt Evelyn......339 C20
v. Mt Evelyn......339 D20
v. Strathmore......324 D2
nc. Beaumaris......530 A9
Heidelberg W......284 C20
Forest Hill......420 E3
Highett......496 G12
Surrey Hills......418 A2
Melb Airport......235 K11
Springvale......500 J10
wy. Langwarrin......629 H2
wy. Wyndham Va......446 C11
Chirnside Pk......337 D5
d. Avondale Ht......321 K10
d. Bentleigh E......456 B13
d. Brighton......454 F11
d. Brighton......454 G11
d. Carnegie......456 B13
d. Caulfield S......455 C12
d. Clayton......457 G15
d. Cranbourne S......630 F9
d. Gardenvale......455 C12
d. Hughesdale......457 G15
d. Huntingdale......457 G15
d. Kilsyth......381 D6
Langwarrin......628 J6
Lilydale......338 H5
Lilydale......339 A6
Menzies Ck......467 L15
Murrumbeena......456 B13
Newport......411 A8
d. Oakleigh S......457 G15
d. Ormond......456 A13
Reservoir......283 B13
Airport W......278 G12
Ardeer......364 E1
Ascot Vale......324 C17
Brunswick......325 K10
Hadfield......280 H5
Preston......282 C18

st. Richmond......371 B14
st. Seddon......367 D11
tce. Clifton Hill......20 A5
NORTHA
ct. Langwarrin......629 C8
NORTHAM
av. Highton......705 K4
ct. Mill Park......242 D9
rd. Bentleigh E......497 A1
rd. Wantirna......422 H5
st. Glen Waverley......461 B6
NORTHAMPTON
cr. Caroline Spr......318 D8
cr. Caroline Spr......318 E8
pl. South Yarra......31 K7
NORTH BOUNDARY
tr. Lysterfield S......503 A10
NORTHBOURNE
rd. Campbellfield......195 B20
NORTH BOX
ct. Hadfield......281 A5
NORTHBROOK
av. Malvern......415 L12
NORTH CIRCULAR
rd. Gladstone Pk......237 A17
NORTHCLIFFE
rd. Edithvale......546 J14
NORTH CLUSTER
Pakenham......584 K2
NORTHCORP
bvd. Broadmeadows..238 J14
bvd. Broadmeadows..238 L17
bvd. Broadmeadows..239 A18
NORTHCOTE
av. Balwyn......373 H15
av. Caulfield N......455 J2
rd. Armadale......415 E10
st. Northcote......327 A16
st. Richmond......26 F20
st. Richmond......32 F1
st. Seaford......573 F17
tce. Mornington......640 D13
NORTHCOTT
av. Croydon......336 G18
st. Melton S......268 H10
NORTHERN
av. Brighton East......455 E12
av. Moorabbin Aprt..531 K3
cr. Craigieburn......150 G15
rd. Heidelberg Ht......284 C15
rd. Heidelberg W......284 C15
NORTHERNHAY
st. Reservoir......283 A14
NORTHEY
cl. Thomastown......240 H11
cr. Hoppers Csg......405 A19
NORTHGATE
dr. Springvale S......533 K7
dr. Thomastown......241 H18
dr. Thomastown......242 A19
st. Pascoe Vale......280 F18
st. Pascoe Vale S......280 E19
NORTH GATEWAY
Coldstream......295 C13
NORTH GLIDE
rd. Melb Airport......235 B6
NORTH HAVEN
dr. Epping......197 K15
NORTH HIDDEN VALLEY
cct. Beaconsfield......555 F13
NORTHLEIGH
av. Craigieburn......194 D1
NORTH OATLANDS
rd. Yarrambat......200 F16
NORTHROCK
ct. Craigieburn......149 L17
NORTHROP
ct. Strathmr Ht......279 C9
NORTHUMBERLAND
dr. Epping......197 L16
rd. Pascoe Vale......280 F17
rd. Sunshine N......321 F18
st. Collingwood......25 J1
st. S Melbourne......29 J2
NORTH VALLEY
rd. Highton......701 J17
rd. Pk Orchards......333 J14
NORTHVIEW
ct. Beaconsfield......555 F12
NORTH WEALD
wy. Fawkner......281 F1
NORTH WHARF
rd. Docklands......23 A14
rd. Docklands......368 H16
NORTHWOOD
dr. Viewbank......285 K19
st. Ringwood E......379 B13
NORTON
cl. Carrum Downs...574 L17
dr. Melton......269 E3
pl. Roxburgh Pk......194 A12
rd. Croydon......380 C6
rd. Kallista......467 C2

st. Pascoe Vale......280 G16
st. Sunshine W......364 D2
NORTONS
la. Wantirna S......461 F1
rd. Parwan......265 J20
NORVAL
cl. Williamstown......411 H18
cr. Coolaroo......238 D4
ct. Wheelers Hl......460 G17
pl. Langwarrin......629 C9
tce. Altona Mdw......451 L3
NORVEL
rd. Ferntree Gly......423 J17
st. Blackburn......375 J20
NORVILLE
st. Bentleigh E......497 B6
NORWARRAN
wy. Langwarrin......629 C8
NORWAY
av. Blackburn......375 G11
NORWEENA
st. Doncaster......330 C18
NORWEGIAN
ct. Mt Martha......656 L9
wy. Nar Warrn S......578 H3
NORWICH
av. Thomastown......240 G19
cl. Chirnside Pk......336 G7
cr. Campbellfield......239 G13
pl. Templestowe......331 H14
st. Boronia......423 L10
st. St Albans......320 F6
st. Werribee......447 H19
NORWOOD
av. Brighton......494 G1
cr. Moonee Pnd......324 A12
ct. Bundoora......284 H5
ct. Cranbourne......577 L12
ct. Wheelers Hl......460 H12
dr. Keilor East......321 K5
pl. Flemington......33 L3
rd. Caulfield N......415 C14
rd. Mill Park......242 E12
st. Albion......320 G20
st. Flemington......33 L3
st. Glen Iris......417 F10
st. Herne Hill......701 K4
st. Oakleigh S......497 J8
st. Sandringham......495 D18
NOSKE
st. Newtown......702 A5
NOTLEN
st. Ringwood......378 D9
NOTRE DAME
dr. Sunbury......144 D10
NOTT
av. Frankston......627 D1
st. Balwyn......373 D10
st. Belmont......706 D4
st. Malvern East......416 E17
st. Nunawading......376 L19
st. Port Melb......29 A5
st. Port Melb......412 J6
st. Port Melb......413 A3
NOTTAGE
st. St Kilda E......415 B16
NOTTINGHAM
av. Somerville......644 G16
ct. Viewbank......329 J3
sq. Wantirna......422 G11
st. Glen Waverley......419 L16
st. Kensington......34 B6
st. Prahran......31 L16
st. Prahran......414 E9
st. Sunshine N......321 H18
wy. Sydenham......232 H18
NOTTINGWOOD
st. Doncaster E......331 L19
NOUMEA
ct. Mulgrave......500 C3
NOURELL
ct. Meadow Ht......238 A7
NOUVELLE
gr. S Morang......198 L12
NOVA
av. Deer Park......319 A9
ct. Craigieburn......150 K19
ct. Safety Bch......669 D15
ct. Wheelers Hl......461 E16
dr. Dandenong......536 E9
st. Oakleigh S......458 E20
NOVARA
pde. St Albans......320 H7
NOVELLO
ct. Eltham......287 L10
NOVIAN
st. Coburg N......281 E12
NOWA
ct. Frankston......628 C1
ct. Werribee S......488 D10
NOWELL
ct. Endeavour Hl......537 E8
ct. Roxburgh Pk......194 C15

NOWIE
cl. Kurunjang......227 B11
NOWINGI
ct. Vermont......421 A6
NOWRA
ct. Mornington......656 G3
st. Moorabbin......496 H7
NOYES
st. Highett......495 J15
NUGENT
ct. Endeavour Hl......537 D1
st. Monbulk......428 D18
st. Preston......283 B19
NUGONG
pl. Lynbrook......551 G17
NUKARA
ct. Frankston......600 A18
NULGARRAH
cr. Greensbrgh......244 J20
NULLAWARRE
av. Rosebud......700 L5
NULLAWIL
st. Springvale......500 D6
NULLICA
ct. Berwick......553 H4
NUMERALLA
st. Mooroolbark......337 A14
NUMERING
ct. Kurunjang......226 L13
NUMINBAH
ct. Taylors L......276 A9
NUMIRA
pl. St Albans......321 B7
NUNAN
pl. Reservoir......283 H15
st. Brunswick E......326 B10
NUNANA
ct. Ferntree Gly......464 D9
NUNDAH
dr. Eltham......288 D6
NUNGA
ct. Mt Eliza......626 H15
NUNGERNER
st. Balwyn......373 B10
NUNGEROO
ct. Eltham North......286 L3
NUNKERI
st. Vermont......421 B4
NUNN
av. Truganina......405 G14
cl. Mill Park......242 B7
ct. Whittington......704 B18
pl. E Melbourne......25 J6
NUNNEY
ct. Craigieburn......150 A14
NUNNIONG
st. Werribee......448 B20
NUNNS
rd. Mornington......640 B18
NURAGI
ct. Werribee......447 C12
NURAYLIA
av. Croydon......380 K2
NURLA
ct. Frankston......628 D6
ct. Sunshine W......364 J7
pl. St Helena......244 L17
NURLENDI
rd. Vermont......421 B6
NURSERY
av. Frankston......627 J1
av. Frankston......628 A2
ct. Dingley Vill......533 E10
ct. Rowville......503 A8
dr. Croydon......335 G20
la. Blind Bight......650 G1
wy. Burwood......418 A12
NURTEN
pde. Aspendale Gdn...546 K6
NUSPAN
ct. Kurunjang......227 F6
NUTALL
la. Mont Albert......374 C16
NUTTALL
ct. Sunshine W......365 B10
NUTWOOD
st. Reservoir......283 J7
NYADALE
dr. Scoresby......462 B10
NYAH
ct. Dallas......238 G8
pl. Cranbourne W...577 E18
st. Keilor East......278 E20
NYALA
ct. Keysborough......534 J13
NYANDA
cl. Keilor Dn......276 H17
ct. Croydon......380 F10
NYARRIN
pl. Cranbourne W...577 G16
NYE
rd. Swan Bay......708 C5

NYLAND
ct. Portsea......678 G2
NYM
ct. Greensbrgh......243 K18
NYMPH
st. Mitcham......377 J16
NYON
pl. Berwick......554 D4
NYORA
av. Boronia......424 L13
cl. Endeavour Hl......537 G5
cl. Frankston......600 H19
cl. Taylors L......275 J2
ct. Westmeadows......237 G11
gr. Caulfield N......455 B1
la. Mt Eliza......626 A20
rd. Eltham......288 C10
rd. Glen Iris......417 D14
st. Malvern East......416 F17
NYORIE
ct. Ivanhoe......328 C18
NYRANG
st. Chadstone......458 E3

O

OAK
av. Boronia......424 D11
av. Cheltenham......531 B4
av. Doveton......536 K13
av. Elsternwick......454 L7
av. Emerald......469 J14
av. Mentone......531 B4
av. Warburton......348 K3
cr. Caulfield N......455 L3
cr. Templstw Lr......330 H13
ct. Altona North......410 C7
ct. Box Hill S......375 B20
ct. Braybrook......365 L3
ct. Gowanbrae......279 D5
ct. Heidelberg W......328 B1
ct. Kew......371 G6
ct. Lalor......240 G8
ct. Mitcham......377 A17
ct. Mt Waverley......419 B15
ct. Somerville......645 D19
gr. Brighton......454 K12
gr. Langwarrin......628 L2
gr. Malvern East......456 J1
gr. Mt Eliza......626 A13
gr. Mt Evelyn......383 B4
gr. Mt Martha......669 G1
gr. Ripponlea......454 J1
gr. Springvale......500 A15
la. Croydon S......379 H13
pl. Melton W......226 D14
pl. South Yarra......32 E14
pl. South Yarra......414 J7
st. Airport W......278 K17
st. Beaumaris......530 D11
st. Bentleigh......456 A19
st. Canterbury......372 J14
st. Dingley Vill......532 G7
st. Flemington......33 J1
st. Hawthorn......371 E13
st. Herne Hill......701 H2
st. Parkville......34 H1
st. Parkville......324 K20
st. Pascoe Vale......280 C13
st. Preston......283 H18
st. Surrey Hills......418 E2
OAKBANK
av. Highton......701 H12
av. Mill Park......242 H11
cl. Berwick......539 J18
ct. Mooroolbark......337 H10
ct. Roxburgh Pk......194 B8
ct. St Helena......245 C20
ct. Wheelers Hl......461 G15
gr. Pascoe Vale......280 K17
pl. Somerville......644 H13
rd. Keilor N......276 C2
rd. Melton S......268 F14
rd. Mornington......641 D11
rd. Mt Eliza......641 D11
st. Newport......411 C9
OAKDALE
av. Balwyn......373 B14
ct. Springvale......499 K8
la. Sunbury......144 G4
pl. Thomastown......240 F15
rd. Upwey......465 C11
OAKDEN
dr. Bundoora......284 D4
pl. Cranbourne W...603 H2
st. Pearcedale......646 L3
OAKDENE
cr. Carnegie......456 L6
ct. Mt Waverley......459 C2
ct. Noble Park N......501 E11
ct. Rowville......463 E13

rd. Tuerong.............657 G16
rd. Tuerong.............657 G20
rd. Tuerong.............670 D12
OLD MORNINGTON
rd. Mt Eliza.............626 B15
OLD MOUNTAIN
rd. Kalorama...........382 H13
OLD ORCHARD
dr. Wantirna S.........422 D17
wy. Doncaster..........331 E18
OLD PARA
ct. Montmorency....286 F8
OLD PARK
rd. Melton...............227 G18
OLD PLENTY
rd. Mernda..............155 K18
rd. Mernda..............156 A6
rd. S Morang...........199 H19
rd. Yan Yean...........156 A6
OLD POST OFFICE
la. Carrum..............573 A9
OLD PRINCES
hwy. Beaconsfield......555 B13
OLD RESERVOIR
rd. Belgrave............466 G17
OLD RIDDELL
rd. Sunbury.............142 F1
OLD SNEYDES
rd. Werribee............449 A8
OLD SOLDIER
rd. Cockatoo...........472 H15
rd. Gembrook..........472 H15
OLDSTEAD
rd. Greensbrgh........244 H16
OLD STUD
rd. Wantirna S.........422 G16
OLD TARRANGO
rd. Yarra Jctn..........347 K18
OLD TOM MORRIS
la. Fingal................698 C17
OLDTRACK
pl. Hoppers Csg......447 L2
OLD TRAFFORD
ct. Berwick.............554 C19
OLD VINEYARD
rd. Sunbury.............187 A7
OLD WARBURTON
rd. Seville...............341 L12
rd. Seville E.............343 B13
rd. Warburton...........348 G12
rd. Warburton...........349 A10
rd. Wesburn.............348 B12
OLD WARRANDYTE
rd. Donvale.............376 G2
rd. Ringwood N.......334 F14
rd. Ringwood N.......334 G20
OLD WHITE HILL
rd. Dromana...........687 F9
OLD WINERY
rd. Sunbury.............144 C9
OLD YARRA
rd. Wonga Park.......291 G18
OLEA
ct. Mill Park............243 B8
OLEANDA
cr. Nunawading......376 K19
OLEANDER
ct. Skye..................601 E9
dr. St Albans...........320 E7
st. Doveton.............536 J13
st. Glen Waverley....460 C10
st. Rye...................698 A5
OLEARIA
cl. Endeavour Hl.....502 L20
cr. Langwarrin........601 K20
OLEOSA
ct. Frankston..........628 H1
OLGA
ct. Ringwood E.......379 C5
pl. Mt Martha..........656 H9
st. Coburg..............325 D5
st. Scoresby............462 H7
OLIN
ct. Wheelers Hl.......461 C17
OLINDA
av. Beaumaris.........529 K9
av. Olinda................426 H9
av. Springvale.........499 H17
cl. Thomastown......240 E12
cr. Olinda................426 K10
cr. Vermont.............421 F5
ct. Broadmeadows..237 H14
ct. Cheltenham........497 H20
gr. Oakleigh S.........458 F19
pl. Frankston...........628 E4
rd. Mt Evelyn...........339 A20
st. Caulfield S.........455 J10
st. Glen Waverley....460 F6
OLINDA CREEK
rd. Kalorama...........383 A14
rd. Olinda................383 D17
OLINDA-MONBULK
rd. Monbulk............427 E17
rd. Olinda................426 L10
rd. Olinda................427 A9
OLIPHANT
ct. Mulgrave...........460 C17
st. W Melbourne.....367 K15
wy. Seaford.............573 L18
OLIVE
av. Harkaway...........540 D14
av. Mt Waverley.......458 F4
ct. Campbellfield.....239 E12
ct. Chelsea Ht.........547 G17
ct. Epping...............198 B17
gr. Airport W...........278 G15
gr. Boronia..............424 E9
gr. Frankston..........599 D19
gr. Heidelberg.........328 K5
gr. Keysborough......534 L14
gr. Keysborough......535 A14
gr. Lilydale..............382 H2
gr. Mentone.............531 G9
gr. Parkdale.............531 G9
gr. Pascoe Vale........280 J16
gr. Ringwood...........378 B14
gr. Sunbury.............142 J8
gr. Tecoma.............466 C9
la. Ringwood E........379 B11
pl. Melton W...........226 E15
rd. Eumemmerring..537 A15
rd. Eumemmerring..537 B12
rd. Hampton Pk.......551 E15
rd. Lynbrook............551 E15
st. Blairgowrie........679 J17
st. Caulfield S.........455 F6
st. Clayton S...........498 K4
st. Dandenong.........536 B6
st. Hampton.............495 G7
st. Malvern East......416 K20
st. Mornington........640 D20
st. Reservoir............282 K11
wy. Wyndham Va.....446 E14
OLIVEBANK
rd. Ferntree Gly.......424 J18
OLIVER
av. Blackburn..........376 C16
ct. Fawkner.............239 E19
ct. Ferntree Gly.......463 L7
ct. Greensbrgh........286 A7
ct. Kilsyth S.............380 K19
ct. Mulgrave............501 L6
ct. Nar Warrn S.......552 J16
rd. Templestowe......331 K8
st. Ashburton..........417 C16
st. Manifold Ht........702 D2
st. Ringwood...........378 G8
st. Yarra Glen.........252 K3
OLIVERS
la. Melbourne.............2 K19
la. Melbourne...........24 H9
rd. Mickleham.........149 A10
OLIVETREE
cl. Werribee............447 C9
OLIVETTE
av. Up Fntree Gly.....465 H7
OLIVIA
ct. Rowville.............462 F17
OLLEY
wy. Mornington........657 A6
OLNEY
av. Thomson............703 J18
ct. Knoxfield............462 K2
O'LOUGHLAN
st. Ormond..............455 L14
O'LOUGHLIN
pl. S Morang...........199 K18
OLRON
ri. Doncaster E........331 L17
OLSEN
cl. Mooroolbark......337 H12
ct. Werribee............448 D8
pl. Broadmeadows..238 D19
st. Frankston...........599 B18
OLSON
pl. Sunbury.............142 H9
OLSTEAD
dr. Baxter................644 B2
OLTON
ps. Caroline Spr.......317 J4
OLVER
st. Preston...............282 K18
OLWEN
av. Belmont..............706 D6
st. Nunawading.......376 H9
OLYMPIA
ct. Ormond..............455 J13
pl. Melton W...........226 E16
st. Tottenham..........366 A9
OLYMPIAD
cr. Box Hill N...........374 J9
OLYMPIAN
av. Mt Waverley.......458 G1
OLYMPIC
av. Cheltenham........496 E18
av. Frankston...........627 L3
av. Montmorency.....287 A11
av. Springvale S.......534 A1
ct. Forest Hill...........420 C3
ct. Glen Waverley.....420 G18
ct. Montmorency.....286 L12
pde. Dromana...........686 H8
st. Bundoora............284 J3
wy. Wyndham Va......446 E10
OLYMPUS
dr. Croydon S..........380 B13
dr. Templstw Lr.......330 J16
OLYVE
ct. Surrey Hills.........418 B2
O'MALLEY
cr. Dandenong N......501 J19
ct. Sunbury.............143 G8
OMAMA
rd. Murrumbeena.....457 C6
OMANIA
dr. Badger Creek......258 K15
OMAR
st. Caulfield S..........455 F7
st. Maidstone...........366 F1
st. Rye.....................696 F9
st. Templstw Lr........330 G7
O'MARA
st. Fawkner.............281 J7
OMAROO
rd. Frankston...........600 A19
OMARU
ri. Greensbrgh.........244 C19
OMEGA
ct. Mitcham.............377 F11
ct. Thomastown.......241 L14
st. Sunshine............321 D19
OMEO
ct. Bentleigh E.........496 K1
ct. Blackburn S........419 F1
ct. Mulgrave............500 J4
pde. Warranwood......334 L13
pde. Warranwood......335 A13
st. Dallas..................238 C11
st. Noble Park N......501 D9
OMUNA
ct. Safety Bch..........669 C11
ONCIDIUM
gdn. Keilor Dn...........275 J13
ONDEAN
ct. Frankston...........628 E10
ONDELLA
wy. Sydenham..........275 E9
ONDINE
ct. Keysborough......534 L10
dr. Wheelers Hl.......460 H18
ONE CHAIN
rd. Somerville..........645 A16
O'NEIL
rd. Beaconsfield......542 C20
rd. Beaconsfield......555 F16
rd. Beaconsfield......556 C1
rd. Officer...............555 F16
rd. Officer...............556 A11
rd. Officer...............556 D4
O'NEILL
av. Elsternwick........454 L8
av. Elsternwick........455 A8
av. Hoppers Csg.......448 L1
av. Hoppers Csg.......449 A1
pl. Sunbury.............142 H14
wy. Warranwood......335 C11
O'NEILLS
rd. Melton...............226 H17
ONE TREE
hill, Donvale.............332 L18
ONE TREE HILL
rd. Christmas Hills...206 H9
rd. Ferny Creek.......425 G19
rd. Smiths Gly..........206 C6
ONKARA
ct. Eltham...............288 D6
st. Frankston...........600 G16
ONSLOW
av. Campbellfield.....239 F18
ct. Noble Park.........534 E3
ONTARIO
pl. Rowville.............462 L15
pl. Rowville.............463 A15
st. Caulfield N.........415 D18
ONYX
ct. Narre Warren.....539 D13
OONAH
cl. Eltham North......287 A3
st. Cockatoo............471 H19
OORINDI
cl. Kurunjang..........227 C12
OPAL
ct. Bayswater..........423 G7
ct. Bentleigh E.........497 C2
ct. Dromana............685 J10
ct. Eltham North......287 C3
ct. Lilydale..............338 L10
ct. Meadow Ht.........238 D2
ct. Mulgrave............500 G1
ct. Narre Warren......539 E14
ct. Skye...................601 G3
pl. St Albans............320 K9
st. Forest Hill...........420 H3
st. Preston...............327 D2
OPALA
ct. Donvale.............332 L19
ct. Kings Park..........319 E1
ct. Wyndham Va......446 H15
OPAWA
st. Brighton.............454 G14
OPERATIONS
rd. Melb Airport.......235 B10
OPHELIA
st. Ferntree Gly.......463 F1
OPHIR
rd. Mt Waverley.......459 F2
st. Broadmeadows..238 F20
st. Moonee Pnd......324 A10
OPIE
rd. Albanvale...........318 K5
rd. Deer Park...........318 J9
st. Ferntree Gly.......424 K20
OPLOO
ct. Dingley Vill.........532 J5
OPOSSUM
ri. Warrandyte.........333 F6
OPPY
cr. Hoppers Csg......448 G3
ORA
ct. Rye....................696 L7
ct. Rye....................697 A7
st. Hampton Pk........551 F9
ORAMA
av. Carrum Downs...575 D14
ct. Templestowe......332 B13
dr. Carrum Downs...575 E15
st. Deer Park...........318 L15
ORAN
cl. Keilor Dn............276 D15
ct. Doncaster E.......332 D7
ORANA
cr. Chelsea..............547 A15
cr. Rosebud W.........699 G1
ct. Belgrave S..........506 G3
ct. Bundoora............284 L3
ct. Frankston...........628 C1
ct. Moorabbin..........496 C8
ct. Sunshine W........364 H7
dr. Mt Martha...........655 J19
dr. Watsonia............285 H8
pl. Chelsea Ht..........547 D11
pl. Epping................197 E17
pl. Melton W...........226 D16
rd. Highton..............701 A11
st. Blackburn...........375 F19
st. Wyndham Va......446 C11
ORANGE
av. Reservoir............283 B8
ct. Bellfield..............328 C7
ct. Doveton..............536 J9
gr. Balaclava............414 J18
gr. Bayswater..........423 D6
gr. Camberwell.........417 A6
gr. Essendon N........323 G1
gr. Werribee.............447 L11
st. Bentleigh E.........457 F19
st. Braybrook...........365 L1
st. Williamstn N.......410 E12
ORANNA
ct. Glen Waverley.....420 C15
ORARI
av. Brunswick E........326 A12
ORAVEL
av. Malvern East......457 C2
st. Balwyn N...........329 L20
st. Balwyn N...........373 L1
ORBEL
ct. Eltham...............288 B6
ORBIT
dr. Whittington........704 C19
ORBITAL
dr. Kealba...............321 A2
ORBOST
ct. Vermont.............421 K3
ORCA
st. Mt Eliza..............641 J2
ORCADES
av. Rye....................696 E2
mw. Port Melb...........412 G6
pl. Diamond Ck........245 F15
ORCHARD
av. Eltham North......287 E2
cr. Mont Albert N.....374 C6
ct. Gladstone Pk......237 E20
ct. Gladstone Pk......279 E1
ct. Somerville..........645 D14
dr. Croydon.............379 G9
gr. Blackburn S........375 H20
gr. Blackburn S........419 H4
gr. Emerald.............469 F19
gr. Heathmont.........422 K1
gr. Warrandyte.........332 J4
la. Avonsleigh..........470 J9
la. Mt Eliza..............626 B10
rd. Bayswater..........423 D3
rd. Doreen...............201 A3
rd. Gembrook..........512 C12
ri. Pk Orchards.........334 D20
st. Armadale.............415 G13
st. Brighton..............454 H12
st. E Geelong............703 G11
st. Frankston S.........626 G5
st. Glen Waverley.....419 K18
st. Kilsyth.................381 A10
wy.n,Rowville.............503 C4
wy.s,Rowville.............503 C4
ORCHARDVIEW
gr. Sunbury..............144 C10
ORCHID
av. Boronia...............424 B12
av. Dandenong N......501 F18
av. Mornington.........640 E18
av. Rosebud W.........699 B2
ct. Hoppers Csg.......405 G17
ct. Lalor...................240 K9
ct. Pk Orchards.........333 L15
rd. Belgrave S..........506 D8
sq. Sydenham...........274 L8
st. Heathmont..........422 L1
st. Heathmont..........423 A1
st. Launching Pl.......346 C16
st. Nar Warrn S.......579 C1
ORD
ct. Mentone.............531 F5
ct. Werribee.............447 H9
pl. Rowville..............462 H16
ORDISH
rd. Dandenong S......549 D6
ORDNANCE
res. Maribyrnong......322 K15
ORDSALL
cl. Caroline Spr.......317 J4
ORDUNA
pl. Wheelers Hl.......460 K18
OREGAN
cl. Wheelers Hl.......460 J13
OREGON
cl. Cheltenham........496 J13
cl. Frankston S........627 L15
cl. Cranbourne N.....578 C9
ct. Nar Warrn S.......552 E14
dr. Doncaster E........376 E3
dr. Donvale..............376 F3
pl. Mill Park.............243 B5
O'REILLY
ct. Lynbrook............551 C17
ct. Sunbury.............142 H15
ORFORD
av. Kew....................372 F13
rd. Ashburton..........417 L14
rd. St Albans............320 F6
st. Moonee Pnd.......323 G14
ORGAN PIPES
rd. Keilor N.............232 K12
ORGILL
st. Dandenong.........536 D11
ORIANA
ct. Flemington.........324 F20
gr. Skye...................601 D9
wy. Sydenham..........275 B7
ORIEL
rd. Bellfield.............327 L12
rd. Heidelberg W.....328 B4
rd. Ivanhoe..............327 L12
ORIENT
av. Mitcham.............377 D18
gr. Brunswick...........325 E11
gr. Preston...............326 E3
pl. Heidelberg..........328 K8
ORIFLAMME
ct. Aspendale Gdn...546 G3
ORIOLE
ct. Carrum Downs...575 A20
dr. Werribee............447 L5
ORION
av. St Albans...........275 G17
cl. Ferntree Gly.......424 C19
cl. Taylors L.............275 G1
ct. Eltham North......245 J17
ct. Lilydale..............338 H1
ct. Mulgrave............460 D20
ct. Springvale S.......499 H19
mw. Port Melb...........412 G5
pl. Doncaster E........332 C18
st. Balwyn N............329 A20
st. Hoppers Csg.......448 H6
st. Vermont.............377 D20
wy. Roxburgh Pk......194 F10
ORKNEY
cl. Endeavour Hl.....503 J18
ORLANDA
ct. Mornington........640 L17

ORLANDO
cl. Wantirna S 421 K18
dr. Roxburgh Pk 194 B5
st. Hampton 494 K7
ORLEANS
rd. Avondale Ht 322 B9
ORLI
ct. Wheelers Hl 461 A18
ORLIT
cl. Cranbourne N 577 J5
ct. Epping 198 F16
ORLOFF
cl. Clayton S 499 D17
ct. Burwood E 419 C11
ct. Sunshine N 320 L10
st. Bentleigh E 497 A6
st. Keysborough 535 A8
ORME
rd. Diamond Ck 246 A15
st. Diamond Ck 246 F16
ORMEAU
rd. Mt Evelyn 383 H3
ORMISTON
cl. Wantirna 422 G14
pl. Nar Warrn S 578 G2
st. Mt Waverley 419 G14
ORMOND
av. Mitcham 376 L11
av. Sunshine 365 D7
esp. Elwood 454 C6
pl. Carlton 18 E17
pl. Kilsyth S 380 K17
rd. Ascot Vale 324 E16
rd. Clayton 498 G3
rd. Eaglemont 328 H13
rd. E Geelong 703 F11
rd. Elwood 454 D4
rd. Hampton Pk 551 J15
rd. Lynbrook 551 C14
rd. Moonee Pnd 324 E16
rd. Nar Warrn S 552 E16
rd. Nar Warrn S 578 G1
rd. Newcomb 703 F11
rd. Ormond 456 E13
rd. Thomson 703 F11
rd. W Footscray 366 G12
ri. Roxburgh Pk 193 L12
st. Brunswick 325 D10
st. Healesville 257 K1
st. Kensington 33 J14
st. Mordialloc 531 L17
st. Pascoe Vale 280 J15
ORMONDE
ct. Diamond Ck 245 H16
rd. Ferntree Gly 464 B7
rd. Ferntree Gly 464 D8
ORMSBY
cl. Carrum Downs 575 E18
cl. Gladstone Pk 237 E20
gr. Toorak 415 B6
ORMSKIRK
st. Newtown 702 A11
ORNA
st. Ferntree Gly 463 J1
ORNATA
rd. Mt Dandenong 426 D1
ORONSAY
cr. Diamond Ck 245 G15
ORR
ct. Laverton 407 E13
la. Montmorency 286 L14
pl. Roxburgh Pk 194 E15
st. Carlton 18 D20
st. Heidelberg Ht 284 G16
st. Heidelberg W 284 G16
st. Manifold Ht 702 C1
st. Strathmore 279 J20
st. Strathmore 323 K1
ORRELL
ct. Mt Waverley 458 J4
ORRONG
av. Frankston 599 A17
av. Reservoir 283 A9
cr. Camberwell 417 B5
cr. Caulfield N 415 C16
cr. Mornington 656 J1
gr. Caulfield N 415 D17
gr. Mt Eliza 642 F8
pde. Caroline Spr 274 D17
rd. Armadale 415 C13
rd. Caulfield N 415 B20
rd. Elsternwick 455 A3
rd. Elsternwick 455 A7
rd. Mooroolbark 337 E14
rd. St Kilda E 415 B20
rd. Toorak 415 D5
ORSETT
ct. Carrum Downs 601 F1
ct. Mill Park 242 F11
ORSINO
st. Springvale 500 A9
ORSON
st. Scoresby 462 E7
ORSOVA
cl. Eltham North 245 H17
ct. Bundoora 284 G6
ORTHLA
av. Heidelberg W 284 C17
ORTOLAN
av. Broadmeadows 238 A17
ORTON
pl. Roxburgh Pk 194 B16
ri. Endeavour Hl 537 H8
ORUNGAL
ct. Torquay 712 D4
ORVIETO
st. Coburg N 281 D12
ORVILLE
st. Altona Mdw 407 G20
st. Coolaroo 238 F7
st. Malvern East 456 K1
ORWIL
st. Frankston 599 E16
OSBERT
st. Sunshine 321 F20
OSBORN
gr. Pakenham 559 C19
OSBORNE
av. Belgrave Ht 466 C20
av. Bentleigh 456 F19
av. Clayton S 498 J10
av. Clayton S 499 D11
av. Gladstone Pk 236 L16
av. Glen Iris 416 E13
av. McKinnon 456 F19
av. Mt Waverley 458 G8
av. Springvale 499 G11
cl. Brighton 454 K11
cl. Deer Park 318 K11
cl. Williamstown 411 G18
ct. Hawthorn 371 D14
dr. Mt Martha 655 L12
gr. Preston 326 L4
rd. Christmas Hills 207 G17
rd. N Warrandyte 290 F14
st. Brunswick 325 E11
st. Dandenong 535 J4
st. Maddingley 263 G8
st. Northcote 326 E14
st. Safety Bch 669 B14
st. South Yarra 32 A15
st. South Yarra 414 F7
st. Williamstown 411 B16
tce. Roxburgh Pk 194 B12
OSBURN
av. Balwyn N 373 C4
OSCAR
ct. Berwick 553 G4
st. Seddon 367 A12
O'SHANASSY
st. N Melbourne 17 A15
st. Sunbury 143 G14
O'SHANNASSY
st. Essendon N 323 F1
O'SHANNESSY
ct. Altona Mdw 451 J7
st. Nunawading 376 H14
st. Pakenham 584 G3
O'SHAUGHNESSY
st. Kew 371 H12
O'SHEA
rd. Berwick 580 C1
O'SHEAS
rd. Christmas Hills 206 J15
OSIER
pl. Cockatoo 471 H20
OSLO
wy. Keilor Dn 276 E17
OSMENT
st. Armadale 415 E11
OSMINGTON
cir. Nar Warrn S 579 D4
OSMOND
pl. Caroline Spr 317 J7
OSNEY
av. Ivanhoe 328 A9
OSPREY
av. Mt Eliza 625 G18
ct. Carrum Downs 601 B1
ct. Torquay 712 C4
st. Vermont 421 J1
st. Werribee 447 K8
OSRIC
ct. Ashburton 417 F13
OSSETT
st. Sorrento 678 F10
OSTEND
ct. Clayton S 498 K5
OSTERLEY
cl. Caroline Spr 317 J1
st. Werribee 447 H19
OSTIA
ct. Thomastown 240 C13
O'SULLIVAN
ct. Fawkner 281 F6
rd. Glen Waverley 420 B20
st. Pakenham 585 D12
O'SULLIVANS
rd. Lilydale 339 F5
OSWALD
st. Cheltenham 497 D16
st. Dandenong 536 B3
st. Elsternwick 455 C10
OSWAY
st. Broadmeadows 237 L20
OSWIN
ct. Kilsyth 381 E4
st. Kew East 372 H5
OTARIA
st. Mt Eliza 641 H2
OTFORD
cl. Moorabbin 496 G7
OTIRA
rd. Caulfield N 415 C20
rd. Knoxfield 462 K6
OTIS
ct. Mulgrave 501 A5
pl. Eltham 288 C5
OTLEY
wy.s,Cranbourne E 578 K17
O'TOOLES
rd. Cranbourne 604 A5
OTTAWA
av. Blackburn 376 C20
rd. Toorak 415 F8
OTTER
st. Collingwood 19 G15
OTTERBURN
dr. Berwick 553 L3
OTTERINGTON
gr. Ivanhoe East 328 G16
wy. Lilydale 338 K2
wy. Lilydale 339 C6
OTTERY
ct. Craigieburn 150 B20
OTWAY
ct. Doncaster E 331 J17
ct. Lalor 240 J7
ct. Werribee 447 H9
pl. Keilor 276 K11
pl. Roxburgh Pk 193 K5
st. Knoxfield 463 B7
OULTON
cr. Reservoir 283 H15
st. Caulfield N 415 F20
st. Fawkner 281 J2
OUTCROP
cr. S Morang 199 H8
OUTER
cr. Brighton 454 H15
OUTHWAITE
av. Doncaster 330 B19
rd. Heidelberg Ht 284 C20
rd. Heidelberg W 284 C20
OUTLOOK
av. Yarra Jctn 347 B16
cr. Briar Hill 287 A6
ct. Chadstone 458 C6
ct. Ferntree Gly 464 B8
ct. Keilor East 322 H5
ct. Mornington 656 L5
dr. Berwick 554 D5
dr. Camberwell 417 K8
dr. Dandenong N 501 L8
dr. Doncaster 375 C2
dr. Eaglemont 328 J13
dr. Glenroy 279 E7
dr. Gowanbrae 279 E7
dr. Hampton Pk 551 G8
dr. Kalorama 383 B17
dr. Nunawading 376 J9
dr. Werribee 447 B10
rd. Coburg N 281 L18
rd. Emerald 509 F7
rd. Frankston 627 K6
rd. McCrae 685 D11
rd. Mt Waverley 418 G15
rd. Tremont 425 C17
ri. Bundoora 284 E2
wy. Sunbury 143 F18
OUTLOOK RIDE
Kurunjang 227 A12
OUYEN
ct. Dallas 238 G8
OVAL
wy. Nunawading 376 G15
OVAL VIEW
st. Point Cook 450 C7
OVANDO
st. Preston 327 D3
OVATA
cl. Yallambie 286 A11
ct. Frankston S 627 L16
dr. Tullamarine 278 C8
pl. Cranbourne W 577 J16
OVENS
ct. Broadmeadows 238 A9
ct. Clayton S 498 G8
ct. Croydon Hl 335 J16
ct. Dandenong N 502 A9
ct. Keilor 276 L12
ct. Mentone 531 G5
ct. Sunbury 142 L13
ct. Sunshine W 364 H14
ct. Werribee 448 B19
pl. Rowville 463 A19
st. Box Hill N 374 L10
st. Brunswick 325 F12
st. Moonee Pnd 324 D14
st. Yarraville 367 B16
OVERALL
dr. Skye 575 H14
OVERBANK
rd. Eltham 288 H13
rd. Eltham 289 A14
rd. N Warrandyte 289 A14
st. Roxburgh Pk 194 B6
OVERBAY
av. Dromana 686 D9
OVEREND
cl. Hampton E 495 H10
st. Brunswick 325 K12
OVERLAND
dr. Doreen 156 K14
dr. Narre Warren 552 L3
dr. Vermont S 420 L14
dr. Vermont S 421 A14
pl. Keilor East 321 L3
OVERLEA
av. Rosebud 684 H15
OVERMAN
ct. Essendon 324 C8
OVERNEWTON
cl. Keilor 276 J7
rd. Keilor 276 J7
OVERPORT
rd. Frankston S 627 A17
OVERS
ct. Hoppers Csg 405 H20
st. Airport W 278 K18
OVERSEAS
dr. Noble Park N 501 A15
OVERTON
cl. Greenvale 192 K18
cl. Rowville 463 L14
rd. Frankston 599 D12
rd. Seaford 599 D12
OVERTON LEA
bvd. Sydenham 274 L6
bvd. Sydenham 275 A3
bvd. Sydenham 275 A8
OVINGTON
ct. Mill Park 243 C5
pl. Altona Mdw 451 E6
OWARRA
st. Rye 697 B9
OWEN
cl. Frankston 600 C20
cl. Keilor Dn 276 B12
ct. Pakenham 584 E5
ct. Rye 696 J2
ct. Somerville 645 C15
ct. Thomastown 241 K14
ct. Werribee 448 D7
st. Boronia 424 G13
st. Brunswick W 324 J13
st. Carlton 18 K15
st. Footscray 367 C3
st. Kallista 466 L2
st. Kallista 467 A2
st. Kew 372 G7
st. Maribyrnong 367 C3
st. Mitcham 377 A17
st. Mordialloc 531 J19
OWENS
av. Glen Waverley 460 B7
ct. Hampton Pk 551 F12
rd. Woori Yall 345 A20
rd. Woori Yall 388 K12
st. Doncaster E 331 H16
OWERS
pl. Cockatoo 471 H13
OXENFORD
ri. Nar Warrn S 552 K19
OXFORD
cl. Croydon Hl 335 D16
cl. Sunbury 144 E9
cl. Templestowe 332 A2
ct. Dandenong N 502 C13
ct. Ivanhoe 328 D10
ct. Mt Martha 669 K1
ct. Sydenham 232 H18
dr. Bundoora 284 K2
dr. Nar Warrn S 553 F15
dr. Thomastown 241 J15
gr. Vermont S 420 G6
la. South Yarra 32 F11
rd. Laverton N 363 L17
rd. Sorrento 678 D7
ri. Bayswater 423 E11
st. Belmont 706 D1
st. Box Hill 374 J16
st. Brighton East 455 C13
st. Camberwell 417 K6
st. Collingwood 25 G1
st. Frankston 627 E5
st. Hadfield 280 L5
st. Kew East 372 K5
st. Malvern 415 L14
st. Mt Waverley 459 E3
st. Newport 410 J6
st. Northcote 327 A17
st. N Melbourne 17 G15
st. Nunawading 376 K8
st. Oakleigh 457 L12
st. South Yarra 32 D10
st. South Yarra 414 H5
st. Sunshine N 321 G15
st. W Footscray 366 H5
st. Whittington 703 L19
wy. Wyndham Va 446 C13
OXFORD DOWNS
rd. Macclesfield 470 B1
OXLEY
av. Bundoora 242 H18
av. Nar Warrn S 578 E3
cl. Glen Waverley 460 F11
ct. Broadmeadows 238 A16
ct. Chirnside Pk 336 J8
ct. Cranbourne N 577 J8
ct. Langwarrin 601 G16
ct. Melton S 268 E12
ct. Wyndham Va 446 H8
pl. Keilor 276 J10
rd. Bend of Islands 291 F2
rd. Hawthorn 372 A18
rd. Kangaroo Grnd 291 F2
st. Sunbury 143 A13
wy. Endeavour Hl 537 E7
OZAN
cr. Jan Juc 711 C14
OZONE
av. Aspendale 546 C5
av. Beaumaris 530 D6
av. Emerald 510 A9
av. Mt Martha 656 B10
av. Seaford 599 C8
av. Sorrento 678 E10
rd. Bayswater 423 F8
st. Hampton 495 F8
st. Port Melb 412 B5
st. Rye 697 H4
OZZIMO
dr. Hillside 274 F5
wy. Werribee 447 A16

P

PAAS
pl. Williamstown 410 J14
PACE
cct. S Morang 199 J19
cr. Chelsea 547 B14
PACES
la. Maddingley 263 A13
PACH
rd. Wantirna S 422 L10
PACIFIC
av. Sorrento 679 C17
bvd. Beaumaris 529 L10
cl. Wantirna 422 C12
dr. Aspendale Gdn 547 B4
dr. Heidelberg W 284 A19
dr. Mooroolbark 337 L17
pl. Taylors L 275 E2
tce. Mt Martha 668 L4
tce. Mt Martha 669 A4
wy. Forest Hill 420 C2
PACKARD
st. Keilor Dn 276 C16
PACKARD COURSE
Mill Park 242 J3
PACKER
st. Murrumbeena 457 E7
PACKHAM
cr. Glen Waverley 419 K16
ct. Darley 222 B10
pl. Wonga Park 335 J10
st. Box Hill N 375 C10
PACKINGTON
pl. Prahran 414 L12
pl. Prahran 415 A12
st. Prahran 414 L12
st. Prahran 415 A12
PADDINGTON
av. Carrum Downs 600 G3
rd. Hughesdale 457 H9

PADDLEWHEELER
pkt. Croydon N 336 A13
PADDOCK
ct. Ferntree Gly 463 F6
PADDYS
la. Nar Warrn N 538 H12
la. Pk Orchards......377 F1
PADGHAM
ct. Box Hill N 375 A5
PADLEY
st. Pearcedale 646 L4
st. Pearcedale 647 A4
PADSTOW
ct. Nar Warrn S......579 C3
PADSTOWE
ct. Craigieburn......194 G4
PADSTUM
av. Lalor......240 D9
PADUA
ct. Gladstone Pk 279 C2
ct. Glen Waverley......420 B13
ct. Vermont 421 H4
dr. Mornington......641 D12
PADULA
ct. Hillside 274 G7
PAGE
av. Kew East......372 D3
av. Port Melb......412 E4
cl. Noble Park......500 H18
ct. Dandenong N......501 L20
ct. Lalor......242 A11
ct. Mulgrave 501 E2
ct. Wonga Park......291 H17
pl. Sunbury 143 H7
st. Albert Park......29 F15
st. Albert Park......413 C8
st. Balwyn N 373 E8
st. Beaumaris 529 K8
st. Cheltenham 530 L2
st. Clifton Hill......19 K7
st. Coburg 325 H3
st. Middle Park 29 K18
st. Middle Park 413 C8
st. Mitcham 376 L12
PAGEANT
wk. Kings Park......274 L19
PAGEBROOK
rd. Berwick 540 J20
rd. Berwick 554 J1
PAGET
av. Glenroy......280 C5
st. Hughesdale......457 F8
PAGETT
rd. Carrum Downs...574 J14
PAGNOCCOLO
st. Werribee......447 G19
PAGODA
ct. Doncaster 330 L16
PAIGE
st. Nar Warrn S......553 G20
PAINE
st. Blairgowrie 680 B20
st. Newport 411 B10
PAINSDALE
pl. Carlton 18 D11
PAINTED HILLS
rd. Doreen 156 J14
PAISLEY
av. Boronia......424 H11
cl. Templestowe 332 A9
ct. Gowanbrae 279 C6
ct. Mulgrave 500 H1
ct. Werribee......448 D17
dr. Frankston 599 L20
st. Balwyn 372 L8
st. Balwyn 373 A8
st. Box Hill N 374 K9
st. Coolaroo......238 D5
st. Footscray......367 D8
PAJO
ct. Doncaster E 332 F19
PAKENHAM
rd. Cockatoo 511 B3
rd. Cockatoo 511 B6
rd. Mt Burnett 511 B6
rd. Pakenham 584 E2
st. Blackburn 375 E20
PAKINGTON
st. Geelong West 702 H6
st. Kew......371 L9
st. Newtown 702 G14
st. St Kilda......414 E16
PALACE
ct. Kings Park 275 A18
PALAGIA
ct. Somerville 645 E17
ct. Strathmr Ht......279 C8
PALAIS
cr. S Morang 198 H12
PALAMINO
ct. Belmont......706 B6
ct. Lower Plenty......330 G1
PALAMINO VALLEY
ct. Greenvale 237 B6
PALANA
ct. Springvale S 534 C3
st. Glenroy......279 G8
PALARA
ct. Montmorency 286 F11
st. Delahey 275 A10
PALAZZO
ct. Greenvale 237 D3
PALERMO
st. Mentone......531 B11
st. South Yarra 32 E11
st. South Yarra 414 H6
PALFREY
grn. Caroline Spr......317 H3
PALFREYMAN
st. South Yarra 32 F14
st. South Yarra 414 J7
PALINGA
st. Greensbrgh......244 K20
PALJAN
ct. Cheltenham 497 H19
PALKANA
st. Frankston 600 G16
PALL
ml. Mt Waverley 418 L20
ml. Wandana Ht......701 E18
PALLANT
av. Reservoir......282 E2
PALLETT
st. Coburg N......281 D16
PALLIDUS
wy. Narre Warren 553 C2
PALM
av. Caulfield N 415 D15
av. Reservoir......283 B8
cl. Hillside 274 D3
cl. St Albans......320 G8
ct. Campbellfield 239 F13
ct. Croydon S 379 H11
ct. Frankston 599 A16
ct. Lysterfield......464 B14
ct. Mt Waverley 419 A17
ct. St Kilda E......414 J14
ct. Templstw Lr 330 A9
gr. Balwyn 372 L13
gr. Balwyn 373 A13
gr. Dromana 686 F4
gr. Kilsyth 381 D7
plz. Dandenong......536 A8
st. Deer Park......318 L17
st. Fairfield......327 F14
st. Hoppers Csg......405 F17
st. Thomastown......241 F13
wy. Nar Warrn S......552 G13
rd. Lysterfield......464 A14
rd.e, Ringwood 378 A17
rd.w, Ringwood 377 L17
st. Berwick 554 H8
st. Camberwell......373 A20
st. Camberwell......417 A1
st. Carlton 18 E11
st. Melton 268 L1
st. W Footscray 366 E6
PALMA
ct. Frankston S 627 L18
PALM BEACH
cr. Mt Waverley 458 K10
dr. Patterson L 573 F11
PALMER
av. Balwyn 373 A9
av. Brighton East 455 E17
av. Croydon N 336 C14
cl. Darley......221 F1
cl. Rowville......462 E20
ct. Hoppers Csg......405 C17
ct. Mt Waverley 459 A8
ct. Roxburgh Pk......194 A9
la. Dandenong N......501 H18
pde. Cremorne 32 B3
pde. Cremorne 32 C2
pde. Cremorne 414 G1
pl. Hawthorn......371 D16
st. Braybrook......365 H5
st. Collingwood 19 L16
st. E Melbourne 25 D10
st. Fawkner......239 E20
st. Fitzroy 18 L18
st. Footscray......367 H7
st. Northcote 327 A17
st. Oakleigh 457 K9
st. Richmond......26 K10
st. Richmond......371 A15
st. S Melbourne 30 C5
st. S Melbourne 413 G3
st. Upwey 465 K16
PALMERS
rd. Truganina 406 E13
PALMERSTON
av. Dromana 686 B7
av. Templstw Lr 330 J16
cr. Frankston S 626 H8
cr. S Melbourne 30 F6
cr. S Melbourne 413 K2
cr. Taylors L 233 F18
cr. Wheelers Hl 461 E14
ct. Greensbrgh......285 K4
gr. Oakleigh 457 K10
pl. Carlton 18 D11
pl. Highton 701 F15
pl. S Melbourne 30 H5
PALM GROVE
bvd. Aspendale Gdn...546 K3
PALM ISLAND
ct. Patterson L......573 J10
PALM TREE
ct. Safety Bch 669 A18
dr. Safety Bch 669 A18
PALMTREE
pl. Aspendale Gdn...547 B5
PALM VISTA
dr. Safety Bch 669 C18
PALMWOOD
ct. Jan Juc......711 C19
PALMYRA
ct. Greensbrgh......244 G18
PALOMA
ct. Boronia......424 L5
ct. Hoppers Csg......448 E5
pl. Melton W......226 E15
st. Bentleigh E 457 E18
PALOMINO
dr. Sunbury 143 K17
PALPERA
tce. Greensbrgh......244 B15
PALTARA
ct. Eltham......288 D7
ct. Meadow Ht 194 E20
PALTARRA
ct. Croydon 380 H7
ct. Doncaster E 332 F7
PAM
av. Balwyn N......374 B5
ct. Bentleigh E 456 J19
ct. Kilsyth S......381 C14
ct. Mooroolbark......337 D17
PAMAY
rd. Mt Waverley 419 H13
PAMBARA
ct. Donvale 333 C12
PAMBURRA
ct. Greensbrgh......244 C20
PAMELA
av. Keilor East 322 J3
av. Rye 696 J2
ct. Blackburn S 419 K6
ct. Bundoora......243 C20
ct. Clarinda 498 C12
ct. Darley......221 G1
ct. Frankston S 626 L10
ct. Melton W......225 L18
ct. Millgrove 348 G1
ct. Narre Warren 539 A16
ct. Scoresby 462 F7
ct. Somerville 644 F14
ct. Springvale S 499 K20
ct. Thomastown......240 F15
ct. Warrandyte......332 J2
ct. Werribee......447 A10
gr. Templstw Lr 330 D8
pl. Langwarrin 629 B1
pl. Mornington......656 E2
pl. Ringwood N......378 B4
st. Mt Waverley 458 J6
st. Noble Park......535 B3
PAMIR
st. Dandenong N......502 A16
PAMPAS
la. Cairnlea 319 J9
st. N Melbourne......34 H10
PAMPERO
ct. Mooroolbark......337 C9
PANAMA
st. Williamstown......411 G16
PANAMUNA
av. Taylors L 275 K7
PANDAN
pl. Aspendale Gdn...547 B5
PANDANUS
ct. Heidelberg W 328 C2
PANDELIS
bvd. Tarneit 447 J1
PANDORA
av. Thomastown......240 C16
cr. Croydon S 380 A11
ct. Whittington......704 A18
PANEL
st. Mitcham 377 K18
PANFIELD
av. Ringwood 378 H4
PANGBOURNE
av. Melton W......226 B13
PANKINA
ct. Dingley Vill......533 F10
PANMURE
st. Frankston 599 J14
PANNAM
dr. Hoppers Csg......405 A20
PANNELL
ct. Grovedale 705 J13
PANORAMA
av. Highett 496 A12
av. Lower Plenty......286 J15
av. Officer 555 H19
av. Ringwood N......378 C8
cl. Bundoora......284 D2
ct. Bulleen 329 F13
ct. Glenroy......279 F7
ct. Lysterfield S......503 J14
dr. Chelsea Ht 547 F18
dr. Croydon N 335 J10
dr. Forest Hill 420 D8
dr. Hillside 274 C3
dr. Mt Martha......669 E3
dr. Tootgarook 698 E6
rd. Herne Hill......702 A2
rd. Kalorama 382 K16
ri. Lilydale 338 L6
ri. Lilydale 339 A6
st. Clayton 459 B20
tr. Frankston N 600 F11
wy. Point Cook......451 A13
PANORAMIC
av. Dromana 686 D8
dr. Langwarrin 601 L20
gr. Glen Waverley......460 E3
rd. Balwyn N 373 E4
PANTE
pl. Werribee......447 E3
PANTEG
rd. Sassafras......426 D17
PANTHER
pl. Eltham......287 G9
pl. Fairfield......327 C20
pl. Fairfield......371 C1
pl. Northcote 327 D20
PANTON
dr. Melb Airport......234 J11
PANTONS SPUR
rd. Healesville 212 G19
PAOA
pl. Templestowe 331 K11
PAOLA
cct. Point Cook......450 E8
PAPAS
la. Wattle Glen 247 B5
PAPERBARK
av. Sunbury 143 E17
dr. Mt Martha......656 K8
dr. Mt Martha......657 A9
pl. Knoxfield 463 C2
pl. Plenty 244 H12
st. Doveton......536 L12
tr. Langwarrin 628 K14
PAPHOS
ct. Plenty 244 F13
PAPROTH
gr. Altona North 409 K8
PAPUA
st. Watsonia 285 G7
PAPWORTH
ct. Meadow Ht 237 L2
PAR
ct. Darley......221 G1
pl. Mornington......641 C10
st. Anglesea......713 B6
PARA
ct. Doncaster 330 K19
ct. Wheelers Hl 460 L19
ct. Wheelers Hl 461 A19
rd. Briar Hill 286 C4
rd. Greensbrgh......286 C4
rd. Lower Plenty......286 E13
rd. Montmorency 286 E13
st. Balwyn 373 A8
PARABURDOO
la. Kings Park 275 A17
PARADE
ct. Sunbury 144 E10
sq. Maribyrnong 322 K16
PARADISE
av. Clematis 508 J4
gr. Emerald......509 D2
PARAGRENE
ct. Montmorency 286 E12
PARAM
st. Grovedale 706 D9
PARAMOUNT
av. Blackburn S 419 H6
av. Kilsyth 381 C11
cr. Mt Martha......669 C9
ct. Tullamarine......278 K4
rd. Tottenham 366 C12
rd. W Footscray 366 C12
wy. Pakenham 585 E5
PARAN
cl. Endeavour Hl 537 L9
pl. Glen Iris......416 J13
PARANA
gr. Roxburgh Pk......194 G6
st. Aspendale......531 K20
PARANDA
ct. Vermont 421 J2
PARAS
dr. Carrum Downs...601 D6
PARATEA
av. Frankston S 627 D19
ct. Greensbrgh......244 L20
dr. Rowville......502 H1
PARATTAH
ct. Rosebud 700 G2
PARAWEENA
ct. Greensbrgh......244 H19
pl. Epping......198 C17
PARDALOTE
av. Carrum Downs...601 B2
cl. Queenscliff......707 L18
cl. Werribee 447 K4
PARDELLA
pl. Mt Martha......657 B7
PARDELOTE
ct. Mornington......640 K16
PARDIN
ct. Bayswater N 380 J18
PARDON
pl. Geelong, off Maud St 702 K10
PARDONER
rd. Rye 696 E6
PARDY
st. Pascoe Vale 280 E18
PAREIRA
ct. Mill Park 241 L4
PAREORA
av. Brunswick E......326 A12
PARER
rd. Airport W......278 E14
st. Burwood......418 C9
st. Frankston 599 H19
st. Mt Martha......656 A9
st. Oakleigh 458 B15
st. Reservoir......282 B7
wy. Roxburgh Pk......194 C9
PARFAIT
ct. Wantirna S......462 C2
PARFREY
av. Lalor......240 G10
PARGETER
ct. Pakenham 584 D4
PARHAM
ct. Altona Mdw 451 K4
PARHNAM
ct. Carrum Downs...601 D2
PARINGA
bvd. Meadow Ht 238 A1
cr. Anglesea......713 E4
ct. Chadstone 418 B19
ct. Frankston 628 B3
dr. St Albans 321 A7
rd. Altona North 365 H20
rd. Portsea 677 J6
wy. Burnside......318 H8
PARIS
av. Croydon S 380 C12
cl. Carrum Downs......575 D14
ct. Mooroolbark......337 L17
rd. Broadmeadows...238 D17
PARK
av. Alphington 327 J19
av. Burnley......371 D17
av. Burwood......418 A11
av. Doncaster 330 B19
av. Glen Huntly......456 D9
av. Mornington......657 E4
av. Preston......282 G20
av. Rosebud W......683 C19
av. Sandringham 495 G17
av. Wattle Glen 246 L7
bvd. Ferntree Gly 423 G16
bvd. Pakenham 584 G10
cl. Heathmont......379 F18
cl. Vermont 421 B2
cr. Aberfeldie 323 F11
cr. Bentleigh 495 L1
cr. Boronia......424 C14
cr. Caulfield N 415 L19
cr. Fairfield......327 D20
cr. Kew......372 A6
cr. Moonee Pnd 323 F11
cr. S Geelong......702 J13
cr. Williamstn N 410 J12
dr. Belgrave 466 H18
dr. Bundoora......284 G14
dr. Clifton Hill......20 K4
dr. Dandenong S......550 C9
dr. Keilor East 321 L5
dr. Maribyrnong 322 L12
dr. Maribyrnong 323 A12

ATRICIA
v. Blairgowrie 679 D19
v. Bundoora 285 B3
v. Montrose 382 D11
l. Werribee 448 C16
t. Berwick 554 C8
t. Hampton Pk 551 K13
t. Yallambie 285 G16
r. Fawkner 281 E2
l. Melton W 226 C15
d. Blackburn 375 E13
t. Box Hill 374 L18
t. Keilor East 322 G4
t. Oakleigh S 497 E2
ATRICK
v. Croydon N 336 C14
l. Greensbrgh 244 L15
t. Airport W 278 F14
t. Boronia 423 J15
t. Melton W 226 A14
t. Mitcham 377 J15
t. Seaford 599 F7
t. Wheelers Hl 461 A10
l. Beaconsfield 555 E14
t. Box Hill N 375 D13
t. Campbellfield 239 J10
t. Glenroy 280 B9
t. Oakleigh E 458 K15
t. St Albans 275 K19
t. Thomastown 241 J13
t. Whittington 703 L20
t. Woori Yall 344 C13
ATRICK NORTHEAST
r. Narre Warren 552 K2
ATRONA
t. Dandenong 536 E14
t. Thomastown 240 F11
ATTANGA
t. Mornington 641 A17
ATTEN
t. Newtown 701 K6
t. Sunshine W 364 H9
ATTERDALE
t. Croydon Hl 335 H11
ATTERSON
v. Burwood 418 D5
v. Hoppers Csg 448 F4
v. Keilor 276 K12
v. Sunshine 365 D8
l. Caroline Spr 318 B4
t. Endeavour Hl 537 H8
l. S Melbourne 29 G5
l. S Melbourne 413 D3
d. Bentleigh 495 K2
t. Bacchus Msh 221 L15
t. Bayswater 423 B8
t. Bonbeach 573 A5
t. Brunswick 325 C9
t. Carnegie 456 K13
t. Coburg 325 K5
t. E Geelong 703 K12
t. Middle Park 413 H12
t. Mill Park 242 H5
t. Nunawading 376 D17
t. Preston 327 A3
t. Ringwood E 378 K12
t. Ringwood E 379 B10
t. Safety Bch 669 C15
ATTERSONS
d. Clyde North 579 K20
ATTISON
t. Moonee Pnd 324 G15
t. St Kilda 414 C13
ATTON
t. Altona Mdw 451 G7
Hoppers Csg 449 B4
Mt Martha 669 F5
ATTY
t. Mentone 530 J5
t. Mentone 531 A6
ATULLOS
Craigieburn 194 J8
Somerton 194 J8
d. Cottles Br 203 B6
ATYAH
Diamond Ck 245 L12
AU
Coburg N 281 F16
Noble Park 500 K20
AUL
. Box Hill N 374 J5
. Keilor East 322 D1
. Wantirna S 422 K14
Mt Evelyn 339 K15
Epping 197 H14
Bundoora 285 B1
Dandenong 535 G9
Endeavour Hl 537 G9
Frankston S 627 G14
Hampton Pk 551 F10
Melton W 225 L17
Beaconsfld Up 542 F14
Langwarrin 629 C1
Forest Hill 420 D4

st. Cheltenham 496 F20
st. Croydon 380 L1
st. Doncaster 374 C1
st. Malvern East 457 C3
st. Rye 697 A12
PAULA
cl. Sunshine W 364 B9
cr. Doncaster E 376 E6
ct. Langwarrin 629 E7
ct. Oakleigh S 458 F19
tce. Endeavour Hl 537 F1
wy. Chirnside Pk 336 F7
PAULETTE
cl. St Helena 244 L20
ct. Blackburn S 419 H3
ct. Scoresby 462 A6
PAULINE
av. Dingley Vill 533 D8
av. Tecoma 466 C10
ct. Hallam 552 C2
ct. Hampton Pk 552 C14
ct. Mt Martha 656 C5
PAULKA
ct. Epping 198 D15
PAULS
ct. Ringwood N 378 E5
la. Dixons Ck 211 D11
PAULSON
rd. Campbellfield 239 E14
PAVEY
ct. Macleod 285 J11
pl. Vermont S 420 J10
PAVIOUR
ct. Dandenong N 502 C17
PAVITT
la. Kilsyth 425 E5
la. The Basin 425 E5
PAVLEKA
st. Hillside 274 E6
PAVO
st. Balwyn N 329 C20
st. Balwyn N 373 C1
st. Belmont 705 L2
PAWLEENA
cct. Cairnlea 319 H14
PAW PAW
rd. Brooklyn 365 D18
PAX
ct. Noble Park N 501 D15
st. Frankston 599 E19
PAXCROFT
av. Kalorama 383 B12
PAXTON
cl. Berwick 580 L1
dr. Glen Waverley 460 K5
st. Malvern East 416 F18
st. Ringwood 378 F7
st. S Kingsville 410 F3
PAY
dr. Werribee 487 J2
PAYDON
ct. Dandenong N 502 B12
wy. Hampton Pk 552 B8
PAYNE
ct. Berwick 553 K6
pl. S Morang 199 J20
rd. Beaconsfield 555 G6
rd. Officer 556 C9
st. Brunswick 325 H9
st. Caulfield N 455 L2
st. Gladstone Pk 236 K18
st. Glen Iris 416 F14
st. Surrey Hills 373 H19
st. Torquay 712 A10
PAYNES
la. Box Hill, off Watts St 374 L14
pl. Melbourne 2 L10
pl. Melbourne 24 G5
rd. Chirnside Pk 292 E15
rd. Mt Waverley 458 J4
rd. Seville 341 K16
rd. Wonga Park 292 E15
PAYNTERS
rd. Wonga Park 291 K15
PAYWIT
ct. Pt Lonsdale 707 H19
st. Preston 282 G18
PEACE
ct. Doveton 536 H12
st. Box Hill S 374 L20
st. Glen Iris 416 L15
st. Highett 496 G14
st. Springvale 499 L6
PEACEDALE
gr. Blackburn 376 D13
gr. Nunawading 376 D13
PEACH
ct. Doveton 536 J8
st. Pearcedale 646 H2
wy. Templestowe 332 C13
PEACH BLOSSOM
ct. Nar Warrn S 553 C20

PEACHEY
ct. Pascoe Vale 280 H10
PEACHTREE
pl. Heatherton 497 H16
PEACHWOOD
pl. Croydon Hl 335 F17
ri. Doncaster E 332 F12
PEACOCK
cl. Mill Park 242 L5
st. Brighton 495 A1
st. Brunswick W 324 J8
st. Burwood 418 H11
st. Hoppers Csg 448 F9
PEAK
ct. Blackburn 376 C20
dr. Harkaway 540 B15
pl. Werribee 447 G15
st. Malvern East 457 J2
PEAR
ct. Burwood E 419 K8
ct. Wonga Park 335 H11
PEARCE
ct. Altona Mdw 451 J2
ct. Niddrie 322 L4
ct. Noble Park N 501 D12
ct. Pearcedale 647 A4
la. Dandenong 535 L9
st. Bacchus Msh 222 E17
st. Burwood 419 A11
st. Caulfield S 455 J7
st. Laverton 407 F13
st. Yarraville 366 L17
PEARCEDALE
pde. Broadmeadows 237 K16
rd. Cranbourne S 630 L5
rd. Pearcedale 646 J11
PEARCEY
gr. Pascoe Vale 280 L16
PEARL
ct. Cranbourne W 577 J20
ct. Mill Park 242 G5
ct. Mt Evelyn 339 J17
ct. Noble Park 534 D4
ct. Tootgarook 698 C8
pl. Ferntree Gly 423 L20
pl. Ferntree Gly 463 L1
st. Brooklyn 365 D19
st. Essendon W 323 A6
st. Glenroy 280 D8
st. Niddrie 323 A6
st. Northcote 326 H18
st. N Melbourne 34 H9
st. Torquay 712 B10
PEARSE
rd. Blairgowrie 696 A6
st. Bellfield 328 C6
PEARSON
cr. Coolaroo 238 E5
ct. Rosebud 699 J3
gr. Caulfield N 415 C18
pl. N Melbourne 17 E17
st. Brighton 455 A15
st. Brunswick W 325 A14
st. Cremorne 26 E18
st. Dandenong N 501 L18
st. Mornington 640 G14
st. Rosebud W 683 A20
st. Williamstown 411 G13
PEART
ct. Brookfield 268 B3
PEARTREE
ct. Doncaster E 332 D11
ct. Roxburgh Pk 193 K5
pl. Knoxfield 423 A20
wy. Glen Waverley 420 C15
PEARWOOD
st. Ringwood 378 G15
PEARY
st. Belmont 702 F19
PEASHOLM
cnr. Craigieburn 150 D8
PEATE
av. Glen Iris 416 K9
PEBBLE BEACH
ct. Sunbury 144 G13
PECAN
ct. Epping 241 L2
ct. Frankston N 600 F7
ct. Lysterfield 503 J1
ct. Oakleigh S 498 A7
ct. Templstw Lr 330 J14
PECHAM
st. Glenroy 279 J2
PECK
av. Strathmore 279 L16
av. Strathmore 280 C17
rd. Pakenham 557 D15
st. Bayswater 423 B5
st. Flemington 323 L19
st. Vermont S 420 L7
st. Vermont S 421 A7
PECKOVER
ct. Endeavour Hl 537 E5

PECKS
rd. Sydenham 275 A8
PECKVILLE
st. Clifton Hill 20 A8
st. N Melbourne 34 K11
st. Port Melb 412 H3
PECOS
pl. Roxburgh Pk 194 F7
PEDDER
ct. Dandenong N 502 C14
PEDEN
st. Chirnside Pk 337 J4
PEDERSEN
av. Reservoir 283 J2
wy. Montmorency 287 C11
PEDLEY
wy. Lynbrook 551 E19
PEEBLES
st. Endeavour Hl 503 J20
PEEL
ct. Gladstone Pk 237 B15
gr. Mt Martha 656 B11
la. Caroline Spr 317 K2
pl. S Melbourne 29 H4
st. Berwick 554 F7
st. Collingwood 19 G19
st. Eltham 287 D11
st. Kew 371 K9
st. Melbourne 23 H3
st. Mitcham 377 A13
st. Newport 411 C8
st. Northcote 327 C17
st. N Melbourne 17 H20
st. The Patch 467 L4
st. W Melbourne 23 H3
st. Windsor 414 D12
PEELMANS
la. Maddingley 222 A20
PEERLESS
ct. Avondale Ht 322 F10
PEERS
st. Brunswick E 326 B15
st. Richmond 26 B6
PEET
st. Pakenham 585 C12
PEGASUS
ct. Roxburgh Pk 194 F10
PEGGIE
ct. Narre Warren 539 C18
PEGGY
st. Sunbury 142 G12
PEJARO
ct. Knoxfield 463 A6
pl. Endeavour Hl 537 K6
PEKINA
ct. Carrum Downs 600 F5
pl. Wheelers Hl 460 H19
sq. Sorrento 679 D16
PELHAM
cr. Wyndham Va 446 E7
ct. Armadale 415 F15
ct. Epping 198 F19
ct. Pt Lonsdale 710 G1
dr. Vermont S 420 L10
pl. Balwyn 372 L14
pl. Carlton 18 C17
st. Carlton 17 K16
st. Carlton 18 C17
st. Melbourne 17 K16
PELICAN
ct. Chelsea Ht 547 C9
ct. Nar Warrn S 552 F13
pl. Mt Eliza 625 L11
pl. Werribee 448 C9
pt. Hopetoun Park 266 G9
st. Westmeadows 236 J14
PELICAN POINT
rd. Point Cook 451 B15
PELL
st. Bentleigh E 457 F16
PELLA
ct. Coolaroo 238 D5
PELLATT
st. Beaumaris 530 E8
PELLET
st. Greensbrgh 286 B7
PELLEW
st. Reservoir 282 H14
st. Sandringham 495 E15
st. Sunshine W 364 H5
PELLEY
pl. Geelong 703 A9
PELLING
rd. Murrumbeena 457 D11
PELLITA
wy. Langwarrin 629 L2
PELLONG
ct. Bayswater N 380 J18
PELMET
cr. Thomastown 240 L18
PELSON
ct. Dandenong S 550 H7

PELUSO
pl. Richmond 26 E11
PEMBERLEY
dr. Notting Hill 459 K14
PEMBERTON
dr. Narre Warren 538 F20
PEMBREY
rd. Cairnlea 319 L13
PEMBROKE
av. Frankston 628 G1
cl. Taylors L 233 H20
cr. Cheltenham 497 B17
cr. Craigieburn 194 B1
ct. Berwick 553 L2
ct. Ringwood 378 B9
dr. Somerville 644 G14
pl. Portsea 678 C7
pl. Wyndham Va 446 F9
rd. Balwyn 373 E14
rd. Mooroolbark 381 G4
st. Epping 197 L16
st. Greensbrgh 244 F20
st. Surrey Hills 374 E20
PEMBROOKE
rd. Portsea, off Hotham Rd 678 C6
PEMBURY
ct. Nar Warrn S 579 E1
PENALGA
rd. Mooroolbark 381 H4
PENANG
pl. Geelong, off Alexandra Av 703 E7
st. McKinnon 456 D16
PENARTH
ct. Craigieburn 150 B14
PENDA
cl. Doncaster 331 C14
PENDER
al. Melbourne 23 G8
av. Mornington 656 D2
pl. Melbourne 2 L10
pl. Melbourne 24 G4
st. Preston 282 L19
st. Thornbury 326 K7
PENDEREL
ct. Wonga Park 292 A16
wy. Bulleen 329 K10
PENDLE
cl. Gladstone Pk 279 B1
cl. Nar Warrn S 579 B5
ct. Jan Juc 711 C16
pl. Kilsyth 381 G8
st. Box Hill 375 D14
PENDLETON
pl. Lysterfield 464 A19
PENDRAGON
cr. Derrimut 363 B4
PENDULA
ct. Narre Warren 553 G11
PENDULUM
pl. Berwick 553 L19
PENFOLD
pl. Albanvale 318 K4
pl. Melbourne 1 J13
pl. Melbourne 24 B8
PENGANA
av. Glenroy 279 G8
st. Rosebud 684 G14
PENGELLY
ct. Sunshine 365 E1
st. Werribee 447 D18
PENGHANA
pl. Kings Park 275 C18
PENGUIN
cl. Blind Bight 650 C8
st. Melton 226 F16
PENHURST
ct. Glen Waverley 460 K5
st. Narre Warren 538 J14
PENHYRN
av. Croydon 379 H3
PENINA
ct. Sunbury 144 E11
PENINGTON
st. Glen Waverley 460 L6
PENINSULA
av. Rye 696 L5
av. Rye 697 A5
bvd. Seaford 599 H6
cr. Langwarrin 629 G2
pl. Mt Eliza, off Nepean Hwy 641 L4
PENLEIGH
cr. Mt Martha 655 L18
ct. Moonee Pnd 323 L11
ct. Mt Waverley 418 K14
ct. St Kilda E 415 A14
PENLOW
ct. Hillside 274 D1
PENLYNNE
av. Vermont 421 G4

PENMAN
st. Blairgowrie 696 B5
PENN
cl. Werribee 448 B15
ct. Fawkner 281 G4
ct. Rowville 463 L18
ct. Tootgarook 698 C8
pl. Dingley Vill 533 F10
st. Balwyn N 373 F2
st. Clayton 498 F2
PENNA
av. Sunshine N 321 F10
ct. Ferntree Gly 423 E20
PENNELL
av. St Albans 319 L5
ct. Rowville 502 K4
st. Eltham North 287 C5
PENNINGTON
cl. Mt Eliza 626 E20
ct. Baxter 644 C2
dr. Mt Martha 657 B12
st. Keilor East 322 D4
PENNY
la. Berwick 539 G19
la. McCrae 685 B10
la. Moonee Pnd 324 C14
la. Mt Eliza 626 A15
la. South Yarra 32 D10
la. South Yarra 414 H5
la. Mont Albert N, off Scarborough Sq 374 E7
wk. Mont Albert N, off Sewell St 374 E7
PENNYCROSS
ct. Rowville 503 F2
PENNYROYAL
cr. Kurunjang 227 A15
PENOLA
cl. St Albans 320 L8
cl. St Albans 321 A8
ct. Noble Park N 501 D10
dr. Seville 341 J15
pl. Wheelers Hl 460 J17
st. Preston 326 G4
st. Torquay 712 F3
PENOLE
wy. Wyndham Va 446 C14
PENRHYN
av. Glen Iris 417 L12
ct. Keilor Ldg 275 L2
PENRITH
cl. Bayswater N 380 D19
cr. Bundoora 242 D18
ct. Berwick 554 A8
ct. Eltham 287 L6
st. Boronia 423 L11
PENROSE
ct. Croydon N 336 E11
ct. Mill Park 243 E5
st. Box Hill S 419 B5
PENRYN
pl. Craigieburn 150 F20
PENSBURY
av. Mill Park 242 G11
PENSBY
ct. Ringwood 335 C18
PENSHURST
ct. Hillside 274 E4
pl. Warranwood 335 B12
PENTAL
rd. Caulfield N 415 G17
PENTATHLON
st. Bundoora 284 J3
PENTECOST
rd. Mornington 640 J17
PENTLAND
ct. Glen Waverley 460 K4
dr. Epping 198 A16
dr. Narre Warren 553 B12
pde. Seddon 367 C14
pde. Yarraville 367 C14
rd. Pt Lonsdale 710 E3
st. Ascot Vale 323 G16
st. Williamstown 411 C13
PENTLAND HILLS
rd. Pentland Hl 221 A14
PENTLOWE
av. Templstw Lr 330 C7
rd. Wantirna S 423 A13
st. Hoppers Csg 448 E10
PENTON
ct. Diamond Ck 245 L7
ct. Somerville 644 K18
PENTRIDGE
bvd. Coburg 281 J20
bvd. Coburg 325 J1
PENZA
ct. Keilor Dn 276 F15
PENZANCE
pl. Sydenham 232 H19
rd. Pascoe Vale 280 H13
PEONY
ct. Nar Warrn S 579 C2

PEPE
ct. Frankston 628 H2
PEPINO
ct. Werribee 447 K11
PEPPER
ct. Templestowe 332 B14
ct. Wattle Glen 246 G8
PEPPERCORN
ct. Avondale Ht 322 E11
ct. Cranbourne N 578 B9
ct. Hillside 274 F5
ct. Point Cook 451 B7
la. S Melbourne 30 F5
la. Sunbury 143 G20
pde. Epping 241 K1
pl. Surrey Hills, off Canterbury Rd 374 A18
tce. Pascoe Vale S 324 E5
PEPPERDINE
wy. Highton 705 E2
PEPPERELL
av. Glen Waverley 459 K2
PEPPERMINT
ct. Altona Mdw 407 K19
ct. Ashwood 418 C16
ct. Doncaster E 332 B15
ct. Emerald 509 D4
ct. Glenroy 281 D4
ct. Hampton Pk 551 J5
ct. Rosebud 700 L8
gr. Box Hill S 375 B20
gr. Cairnlea 320 A12
gr. Eltham 288 C9
gr. Knoxfield 463 C1
gr. Langwarrin 601 J14
gr. Meadow Ht 194 A18
pl. Croydon Hl 335 E13
pl. Somerville 644 E14
st. Doveton 536 G11
wk. S Morang 243 K3
PEPPERTREE
av. Nar Warrn S 579 D2
wy. Lilydale 338 B13
PEPPIN
st. Camberwell 416 L2
PERADON
wy. Hillside 232 G20
PERCEVAL
cl. Caroline Spr 274 A8
cr. Taylors L 233 A20
ct. Lysterfield 464 D18
st. Sunbury 143 C9
wy. Doncaster E 332 G15
wy. Mill Park 242 K9
PERCIVAL
st. Bayswater 423 K8
st. Brighton East 495 H1
st. Oak Park 279 J10
st. Preston 282 L17
st. Rosebud W 683 E18
PERCIVALE
av. Glen Waverley 420 L17
PERCY
pl. Prahran 32 A19
pl. Prahran 414 F10
st. Balwyn 373 C12
st. Black Rock 495 E19
st. Brunswick 325 E13
st. Croydon S 379 K11
st. Fawkner 281 K8
st. Fitzroy N 19 B6
st. Hawthorn 372 B14
st. Heidelberg W 284 E16
st. Kensington 33 H7
st. Mitcham 377 C14
st. Mordialloc 532 B19
st. Newport 410 F3
st. Newtown 702 F12
st. Noble Park 534 E1
st. Prahran 32 A19
st. Prahran 414 F10
st. Rye 696 J7
st. St Albans 320 C6
PERCY JONES
ct. Highton 705 G5
PEREGRINE
pl. Carrum Downs 601 B1
PERENNIAL
ri. Grovedale 705 H13
PERICLES
ct. Sorrento 679 A13
PERICOE
st. Frankston 627 K5
PERIMETER
rd. Melb Airport 234 E8
rd. Melb Airport 234 G6
rd. Melb Airport 235 A9
rd. Melb Airport 235 K15
PERITON
pl. Vermont 421 C5
PERKIN
av. Pascoe Vale 280 E11
ct. Dandenong 535 H3

PERKINS
av. Bellfield 327 L7
av. Bellfield 328 A7
cl. Delahey 275 F11
dr. Carrum Downs 575 E15
gr. Burnside 318 F9
pl. Torquay 711 J7
st. Mornington 640 E17
PERMIEN
st. Dromana 685 K6
PERON
ct. Boronia 424 K4
ct. Narre Warren 538 F19
PERONNE
st. Pascoe Vale S 324 H1
PEROVIC
pl. Chelsea Ht 547 D15
PERRA
st. Ferntree Gly 424 K19
PERRET
wk. Sydenham 274 K7
PERRETT
av. St Albans 320 G1
st. Brunswick W 325 B8
st. Grovedale 706 F14
PERRINS
st. S Melbourne 30 A6
st. S Melbourne 413 F3
PERRINS CREEK
rd. Olinda 427 A12
rd. Olinda 427 B16
PERRI RASO
ri. Rowville 503 B8
PERROMBA
av. Eaglemont 328 J9
PERRON
cl. Craigieburn 150 C19
PERRONE
wk. Yallambie 286 A14
PERROTT
ct. Mill Park 242 K5
PERRUMBA
st. Greensbrgh 286 L1
PERRY
cl. Breakwater 703 H19
cl. Croydon S 380 B12
cl. Melton 226 F18
ct. Brighton East 455 G17
ct. Herne Hill 702 A3
ct. Kew 372 J10
ct. Roxburgh Pk 194 B16
ct. Tullamarine 278 K3
rd. Bangholme 549 A6
rd. Dandenong S 549 A6
rd. Keysborough 534 G19
st. Alphington 327 F20
st. Collingwood 19 G14
st. Fairfield 327 G17
st. Moorabbin 496 C8
st. St Albans 320 D5
st. Seddon 367 C12
st. South Yarra 32 B14
st. South Yarra 414 G7
st. Williamstown 411 D15
PERSHING
st. Reservoir 282 F14
PERSHORE
ct. Westmeadows 236 K15
PERSICA
pl. Niddrie 322 K2
PERSIMMON
ct. Doncaster 331 E19
PERTAKA
cl. Montmorency 286 G11
PERTH
av. Albion 320 H19
ct. Frankston 599 H16
ct. Gowanbrae 279 D4
ct. Wantirna S 422 L16
st. Belmont 706 H1
st. Blackburn S 419 D1
st. Heidelberg W 284 B18
st. Murrumbeena 457 B5
st. Prahran 31 K19
st. Prahran 414 E10
PERU
ct. Mt Waverley 459 F3
PERVERSI
av. Diamond Ck 246 D10
PERYMAN
st. Pearcedale 646 J5
PESARO
pl. Point Cook 450 C10
PESCARA
pl. Donvale 376 J2
pl. Wantirna 422 A9
PESCOTT
st. Newtown 702 F8
PETA
ct. Blairgowrie 679 D18
PETAIN
rd. Silvan 384 J11

PETALNINA
cl. Somerville 645 D17
cr. Wantirna 422 A9
PETCHAM
la. Caroline Spr 317 H3
PETER
av. Anglesea 713 F6
av. Blackburn N 375 L11
av. Parkdale 531 H14
ct. Dandenong 536 C2
ct. Lalor 240 K6
ct. Langwarrin 601 K18
ct. Mooroolbark 337 A10
ct. Narre Warren 538 L14
ct. Pakenham 585 B4
ct. St Albans 276 A18
ct. Seaford 600 A3
dr. Ferntree Gly 424 D19
dr. Sunshine W 364 C8
pl. Melton W 226 D16
st. Box Hill N 374 J6
st. Croydon S 379 K11
st. Doncaster E 375 G4
st. Dromana 686 B5
st. Eltham 287 E7
st. Footscray 367 E6
st. Grovedale 706 C13
st. Oakleigh S 458 D19
st. Preston 326 H3
st. Rye 696 J7
st. South Yarra 31 L12
st. Springvale 500 B18
PETERBOROUGH
cr. Deer Park 318 J9
PETER BUDGE
av. Templestowe 331 H13
PETER CHANEL
ct. Deer Park 319 B14
PETERHO
bvd. Pt Lonsdale 707 E19
PETERHOUSE
ct. Sunbury 144 G11
PETER KENT
dr. Somerville 645 D18
PETER LALOR
wk. Lalor 241 C11
PETERLEE
ct. Craigieburn 194 F1
PETERLEIGH
gr. Essendon 324 B6
PETER PAN
pl. Bacchus Msh 221 F16
PETERS
av. Mulgrave 459 L20
cl. Maddingley 263 D4
dr. Cheltenham 497 F19
la. Abbotsford 20 B15
rd. Belgrave 466 F9
rd. Seville E 343 B14
st. Airport W 278 J17
st. Cannons Creek 649 C8
st. Watsonia 285 G4
PETERSFIELD
ct. Boronia 424 J5
PETERSON
av. Coburg N 282 A18
rd. Officer 556 K11
rd. Officer 557 A9
st. Highett 495 J12
st. Seaford 599 J1
PETER THOMSON
dr. Fingal 698 G17
PETHAJOHN
pde. Grovedale 705 G15
PETHYBRIDGE
cl. Dingley Vill 533 E8
PETINA
wy. Sunshine W 364 C9
PETLEY
ct. Carrum Downs 601 E3
PETRA
ct. Epping 241 G3
PETRE
av. Altona Mdw 451 F2
ct. Roxburgh Pk 194 D10
PETREL
av. Sorrento 679 D15
cl. Blind Bight 650 C10
cl. Mt Eliza 641 K5
cl. Torquay 712 C2
ct. Carrum Downs 601 B2
ct. Werribee 448 A10
pl. Berwick 580 A1
st. Geelong West 702 G2
PETRIANA
ct. Torquay 712 E3
PETRIE
st. Frankston 599 E18
PETRIK
dr. Keilor 276 E7
PETRONELLA
av. Wheelers Hl 461 C11

PETT
ct. Heathmont 423 B1
PETTER
st. Glen Waverley 460 B3
PETTYS
la. Doncaster 374 F2
PEUGEOT PURSUIT
Mill Park 242 J2
PEVENSEY
cr. Geelong 703 E9
dr. Nar Warrn S 579 D5
la. Geelong, off Alexandra Av 703 F8
st. Geelong 703 F8
PEVERIL
ct. Kings Park 319 A2
cr. Cranbourne N 578 F9
ct. Narre Warren 538 K13
st. Brunswick 325 F8
st. Glen Waverley 459 K7
PEVERILL
st. Balwyn 372 K13
st. Malvern East 457 J2
PEYTON
dr. Mill Park 242 K3
PEZZIMENTI
pl. Wonga Park 336 E7
PHAIR
ct. Altona 408 H17
PHALARIS
ct. Delahey 275 A14
PHAR LAP
pl. Kurunjang 227 E
PHARLAP
cl. Mill Park 242 J1
PHEASANT
ct. Berwick 554 A
pde. Warburton 350 C
st. Burwood 418 L1
PHELAN
ct. Kurunjang 226 J1
ct. Tullamarine 278 H
dr. Cranbourne N 577 J
pl. Narre Warren 539 F1
st. Preston 283 B1
PHILIP
av. Doncaster 330 E1
ct. Pakenham 584 L
ct. Thomastown 241 H1
rd. Hallam 537 D1
st. Altona Mdw 451 H
st. Cheltenham 496 D1
st. Dandenong N 502 A2
st. Heathmont 378 E1
st. Lower Plenty 286 K1
st. Manifold Ht 702 D
st. Mornington 640 F1
st. Vermont 421 D
PHILIPPA
ct. Viewbank 285 H1
rd. Boronia 424 K1
PHILIPSON
st. Albert Park 29 E1
st. Albert Park 413 C
PHILLIP
av. Box Hill N 375 C1
av. Springvale 500 G
ct. Cranbourne N 578 A
ct. Greensbrgh 286 C
dr. Sunbury 142 H
dr. Wonga Park 336 D
rd. Avonsleigh 470 G1
rd. Keilor East 322
rd. Knoxfield 462 L
rd. Knoxfield 463 A
rd. Woori Yall 344 H1
st. Bentleigh 496 A
st. Dallas 238 C1
st. Frankston 599 G1
st. Melton S 268
st. Mentone 530
st. Mentone 531 A
st. Reservoir 239 K
st. Rosebud 684 H
PHILLIPA
st. Blairgowrie 696
PHILLIPDALE
ct. Ferntree Gly 463
PHILLIPPS
rd. W Melbourne 368 B
PHILLIPS
av. Carnegie 456
cr. Rosanna 285 A
ct. Northcote 326 G
la. Geelong, off Little Ryrie St 703
st. Alphington 327 K
st. Coburg 325
st. St Kilda E 414 G
PHILLIS
st. Elwood 454
PHILPOTT
st. E Geelong 703 J

PIVOT
ct. Doncaster 375 E4
ct. Keilor Dn 276 A12
pl. Mill Park 242 J2

PIZER
st. Geelong West 702 G6

PIZZEY
st. Sunshine 365 F4

PLAIN
st. Tootgarook 698 D2

PLAISTED
st. Coburg N 281 F13

PLAISTOW
ct. Cranbourne N 578 C10

PLANE
ct. Altona North 410 C7
ct. Campbellfield 239 F13
ct. Templestowe 331 L14
la. Melb Airport 234 F9
st. Lalor 241 F13
st. Thomastown 241 F13

PLANET
ct. Whittington 704 D19

PLANE TREE
av. Dingley Vill 532 H4

PLANT
rd. Melb Airport 235 A11
st. Malvern 415 L10
st. Northcote 326 J18

PLANTATION
av. Brighton East 495 B1
av. Frankston N 599 J10
dr. Rosebud 700 G6
la. Briar Hill 286 F7
st. Maribyrnong 323 D13

PLANTE
ct. Sunbury 143 C14

PLATANI
gr. Roxburgh Pk 194 F6

PLATEAU
cr. Hampton Pk 551 J15
rd. Reservoir 282 C9

PLATH
cl. Delahey 275 F13

PLATINA
pl. Chelsea Ht 547 F12

PLATO
cr. Wheelers Hl 460 C14
ct. Thomastown 240 J16

PLATYPUS
al. Melbourne 1 K10
al. Melbourne 24 B7
ct. Maribyrnong 322 H15
pl. S Morang 243 K2

PLAYER
cl. Hoppers Csg 405 C18
cl. Wantirna S 462 D4

PLAYFIELD
gr. Mornington 656 L3

PLAYFORD
ct. Berwick 554 H18

PLAYGROUND
dr. Bundoora 284 D7

PLAYNE
st. Frankston 599 B20

PLAZA
cr. Dingley Vill 532 L8
ct. Lilydale 338 B1
ct. Wantirna S 422 F18

PLEASANCE
st. Bentleigh 455 J20
st. Fitzroy N 326 C16

PLEASANT
av. Doncaster 375 D1
av. Kew 372 H9
cl. Mill Park 242 D12
dr. Heathmont 379 C19
pl. Wyndham Va 446 D12
rd. Bulleen 329 K12
rd. Ferntree Gly 464 K1
rd. Hawthorn E 416 E2
rd. Templstw Lr 329 K12
rd. Thomastown 241 A13
ri. Croydon S 379 F11
st. Kilsyth 381 B8
st. Newtown 702 G10
st. Pascoe Vale 280 G15

PLEASANT VIEW
av. Preston 283 E19
cr. Wheelers Hl 460 J7
ct. Diamond Ck 245 F12
ct. Mt Martha 655 D17

PLEDGER
cl. Diamond Ck 245 K12
cl. Nar Warrn S 552 G18

PLENTY
cl. Caroline Spr 318 C5
cl. Taylors L 233 F18
ct. Altona Mdw 451 C2
la. Greensbrgh 286 B8
rd. Bundoora 283 K12
rd. Bundoora 284 E7
rd. Kingsbury 283 E15
rd. Mernda 155 J19
rd. Mill Park 242 L14
rd. Preston 326 K5
rd. Reservoir 283 E15
rd. S Morang 243 E2
rd. Yan Yean 156 A9

PLENTY RIVER
dr. Greensbrgh 244 A19

PLEONE
ct. Werribee 446 K18

PLESSEY
la. N Melbourne 34 G6

PLIMSOLL
gr. Fairfield 327 F16

PLOUGH
ri. Nar Warrn S 552 H20

PLOVER
ct. Frankston 600 G20
ct. Endeavour Hl 537 A3
ct. Mt Eliza 641 K6
ct. Patterson L 573 H10
pl. Carrum Downs 600 L5
pl. Craigieburn 149 F17
st. Melton 226 F16

PLOW
st. Thornbury 326 J8

PLOWMAN
ct. Epping 242 A1
pl. Frankston 627 A1
st. Olinda 427 C13

PLUM
ct. Gembrook 512 C12
st. Doveton 536 K7

PLUMBS
la. Geelong, off McKillop St 703 C10

PLUME
ct. Glen Waverley 421 A17

PLUMER
st. Croydon 380 D2

PLUMLEY
st. Mont Albert 374 D12

PLUMMER
av. Flemington 323 K20
av. Frankston S 626 H4
ct. Mentone 530 K9
rd. Laverton N 364 G16
rd. Mentone 530 K10
st. Port Melb 412 C3

PLUMPTON
av. Craigieburn 150 F18
av. Glenroy 280 B8
ct. Endeavour Hl 537 L8
rd. Diggers Rest 187 A12
rd. Diggers Rest 231 A6
rd. Plumpton 231 A19
rd. Plumpton 273 A13

PLUMTREE
ct. Eltham 287 K11
ri. Croydon Hl 335 E17

PLUNKET
st. Brighton East 495 E1

PLUNKETT
av. Carnegie 456 E11
rd. Dandenong 536 D14
st. Bellfield 328 B7
st. Cheltenham 497 A20
st. Geelong West 702 G6

PLUTO
ct. Newcomb 704 E14
pl. Hoppers Csg 405 D13

PLYM
st. Bentleigh 496 B5

PLYMOUTH
cl. Sunshine N 321 B8
ct. Craigieburn 150 B16
ct. Dandenong N 502 B12
ct. Epping 197 J17
ct. Nunawading 376 J12
rd. Croydon Hl 335 D17
rd. Ringwood 335 A17
rd. Ringwood 335 D17
rd. Warranwood 335 A17
st. Bentleigh E 457 B20
st. Geelong West 702 G4
st. Glen Waverley 420 G15
st. Heidelberg 329 F5
st. Pascoe Vale 280 J13

PLYMTREE
ct. Nar Warrn S 579 C3

POA
ct. Delahey 275 A14

POATH
rd. Hughesdale 457 D14
rd. Murrumbeena 457 D14

POCKETT
la. Healesville 257 K2
rd. Healesville 257 K1

PODBURY
cr. E Geelong 703 G7

PODMORE
st. Dandenong S 536 A13

POET
ct. Keilor Dn 275 L10
rd. Bentleigh E 457 D16

POETS
ct. Glen Waverley 421 A19
gr. Elwood 454 F3
la. Sherbrooke 426 J20
la. Truganina 405 F13

POHLMAN
av. Fitzroy N 20 B1
cl. Pakenham 583 L5
la. Prahran, off Grandview Gr 415 B9

POINCIANA
ct. Werribee 447 K9
st. Frankston S 627 D8

POINT
av. Beaumaris 529 L11

POINT COOK HOMESTEAD
rd. Point Cook 451 A20

POINT HENRY
rd. Moolap 704 L14

POINT KING
rd. Portsea 678 G3
rd. Sorrento 678 G3

POINT LONSDALE
rd. Pt Lonsdale 707 J20

POINT NEPEAN
rd. Blairgowrie 679 J17
rd. Dromana 685 A11
rd. McCrae 685 A11
rd. Portsea 666 H20
rd. Rosebud 683 J16
rd. Rosebud W 683 C18
rd. Rye 696 K1
rd. Rye 697 B1
rd. Sorrento 678 H5
rd. Tootgarook 698 A2

POINT ORMOND
av. Elwood 454 B4

POINT PLEASANT
wy. S Morang 199 B14

POINT SIDE
ct. Glen Waverley 460 G2

POINTSIDE
av. Bayswater N 380 A19

POKOLBIN
ct. Bangholme 549 H13

POLARIS
ct. Carrum Downs 575 B14
dr. Doncaster E 332 D17
wy. Chirnside Pk 337 F1

POLAT
ct. Mt Evelyn 339 K16

POLE
st. Seddon 367 E11

POLICE
rd. Dandenong N 502 C8
rd. Endeavour Hl 502 G8
rd. Mulgrave 500 B5
rd. Mulgrave 501 C7
rd. Mulgrave 501 L8
rd. Noble Park N 501 C7
rd. Rowville 502 C8
rd. Springvale 500 B5

POLK
ct. Dandenong N 501 G9

POLLARD
ct. Altona 409 F17
pde. Healesville 213 H16
pl. Sunbury 143 H8
st. Braybrook 366 B5

POLLEY
ct. Grovedale 705 K13

POLLINA
cl. Hampton Pk 551 E5
st. Bentleigh E 496 G3

POLLINGTON
st. St Kilda 413 L16

POLLOCK
ct. Delahey 275 A11
dr. Mill Park 242 J1
pl. Roxburgh Pk 193 L15

POLLY KELLY
pl. Frankston S 627 J10

POLLY WOODSIDE
dr. Altona Mdw 452 A4

POLO
pde. Caulfield N 455 E1

POLTAVA
wk. Delahey 275 B15

POLWARTH
cr. Belmont 706 B7

POLYDOR
ct. Epping 197 L16
pl. Blackburn N 375 J9

POMMEL
cr. Epping 198 F17
st. Pakenham 585 F4
st. Pakenham 585 F5

POMORA
av. Torquay 712 D1

PONDEROSA
pl. Dromana 686 J3

PONSFORD
av. Wantirna S 422 E20
av. Wantirna S 462 E1
pl. Epping 198 H17
pl. Sunbury 142 H14

PONT
ct. Keysborough 533 L8

PONTFORD
ct. Wheelers Hl 461 E16

PONTIN
ct. Burwood E 419 H12

PONTING
st. Williamstown 410 B13

PONTO
ct. Endeavour Hl 537 G8

PONYARA
rd. Mt Martha 668 L4
rd. Mt Martha 669 A4

POOL
st. Port Melb 412 L4

POOLE
av. Hampton 495 F10
ct. Endeavour Hl 537 J4
st. Burwood 419 A7
st. Deer Park 319 A17
st. McCrae 685 C14

POOLEY BRIDGE
rd. Mordialloc 532 D17

POOLMAN
st. Port Melb 412 F3

POORINDA
ri. Narre Warren 553 G10

POPE
av. Boronia 424 H5
ct. Mooroolbark 337 E19
pl. Greensbrgh 286 D3
rd. Blackburn 375 K13

POPES
rd. Keysborough 535 A7

POPLAR
av. Ashwood 418 D14
av. Hawthorn 372 A18
cl. Rowville 463 J16
cr. Bellfield 327 K5
cr. Emerald 469 H13
ct. Belmont 706 H6
ct. St Albans 320 J8
dr. Rosebud 700 G2
gr. Carnegie 456 L5
gr. Langwarrin 629 A2
rd. Parkville 324 L18
st. Box Hill 374 H14
st. Campbellfield 239 F13
st. Caulfield S 455 F7
st. Frankston N 600 B9
st. Newcomb 704 A14
st. Thomastown 241 F13
tr. Olinda 427 F10

POPPY
dr. S Morang 199 H8
pl. Carrum Downs 574 L19

POPPYS
ct. Warrandyte 333 C4

PORCHESTER
bvd. Officer 555 G19

PORENA
ct. Ferntree Gly 423 L20

POROSA
ct. Langwarrin 629 L3

PORSCHE
ct. Epping 197 J14

PORT
la. Plenty 244 A9
st. Highett 496 J15
st. Newport 410 E10

PORTAL
pl. Patterson L 547 J20
st. Ascot Vale 324 A19

PORTARLINGTON
rd. Moolap 704 A11
rd. Newcomb 704 A11

PORTARLINGTON-QUEENSCLIFF
rd. Pt Lonsdale 707 G12
rd. Swan Bay 707 G12

PORTEOUS
rd. Melton W 225 G1
rd. Toolern Va 225 G1

PORTER
av. Highton 705 J2
av. Roxburgh Pk 194 E15
ct. Deer Park 319 D11
ct. Mill Park 242 G8
la. Kensington 33 J6
pl. Croydon N 336 A13
rd. Balwyn 373 K10
rd. Bentleigh 496 D6
rd. Carnegie 456 J9
rd. Heidelberg Ht 328 G2
st. Briar Hill 286 J6
st. Eltham 287 D16
st. Fitzroy N 326 C
st. Hampton 495 G
st. Hawthorn E 372 H
st. Melton S 268 H
st. Prahran 32 A
st. Prahran 414 F
st. Templestowe 330
st. Templestowe 331 E
st. Templestowe 332 A

PORTERS
rd. Wesburn 348 A

PORTLAND
la. Melbourne 2 J
la. Melbourne 24
pde. Seaford 573 E
pl. Endeavour Hl 537
pl. Roxburgh Pk 194 E
pl. South Yarra 32 B
pl. South Yarra 414 C
pl. Thomastown 240 F
st. Carnegie 456 H
st. Coburg 325 E
st. Mulgrave 501 G
st. Richmond 26 D

PORTMAN
rd. The Patch 468 C
st. Oakleigh 457 K

PORT MARNOCK
ct. Sunbury 144 H

PORTO
ct. Cranbourne N 578 G

PORTOBELLO
pl. Wheelers Hl 461 D
tce. S Morang 199 A

PORTOFINO
cr. Point Cook 450 E
dr. Cranbourne N 578 J

PORT PHILLIP
arc. Melbourne 2 D
cr. Williamstown, off Anchorage Av 411 D
dr. Mornington 640 H
dr. Mornington 656 H
vw. Frankston S 627 G

PORTREE
ct. Sunbury 144
pl. Nar Warrn S 578 L
st. Macleod 285 A

PORTRUSH
av. Mornington 656 D
tce. Cranbourne 603

PORTSEA
pl. Narre Warren 539 F

PORTSMOUTH
cr. Grovedale 706 B
pl. Epping 241 H
st. Heathmont 422
st. Mt Waverley 419 D

PORTVIEW
sq. Port Melb, off Rouse St 412

POSEIDON
cl. Mill Park 242 J

POSITARNO
wy. Point Cook 450

POSSUM
la. Heathmont 422
pl. Berwick 553 K
pl. S Morang 243 K

POSSUM TAIL
run. Sunbury 143 A

POST OFFICE
la. Parkville 17 H
pl. Carlton 18 F
pl. Glenroy 279
pl. Port Melb 412 K
pl. Malvern East, off Dandenong Rd 416 C
pl. St Kilda, off Inkerman St 414 E

POTOMAC
cl. Werribee 447 G

POTTAGE
cct. Macleod 284 J

POTTENGER
wy. St Albans 320 B

POTTER
ct. Northcote 326 F
ct. Templstw Lr 330 C
st. Armadale 415 D
st. Black Rock 495 E
st. Craigieburn 194
st. Dandenong 535
st. Geelong West 702

POTTERY
ct. Brunswick 325 C
dr. Blackburn N 375 G

POTTON
av. Rosebud 684 D

POTTS
rd. Langwarrin 601 J
rd. Skye 601 H
st. Parkdale 531

rd. Narre Warren 538 H18
rd. Surrey Hills 373 H20
rd. Surrey Hills 417 H1
PROSPECTOR
ct. Wheelers Hl 461 C12
dr. Cairnlea 319 H7
PROSPER
pde. Glen Iris 417 G13
PROSPERITY
rd. Lower Plenty 286 F14
PROSPERO
wy. Truganina 405 F14
PROSSORS
la. Red Hill 687 J20
PROTEA
cr. St Albans 320 F8
ct. Langwarrin 601 L16
ct. Mill Park 242 C10
ct. Newcomb 704 C16
ct. Sunbury 143 D18
st. Carrum Downs 575 B18
PROTON
ct. Whittington 704 C20
PROUDFOOT
st. Mont Albert 374 E16
PROUSE
pl. Werribee 447 E12
PROVAN
dr. Wyndham Va 446 F15
PROVENCE
pl. Nar Warrn S 578 J2
PROVIDENCE
rd. Greenvale 191 L14
PROVIS
cl. Burnside 318 D6
PROVOST
st. N Melbourne 17 A16
PROWSE
av. Balwyn 373 D13
la. Bundoora 284 E4
st. Brunswick 325 F9
PRUDENCE
cr. Carrum Downs 574 L17
ct. Lilydale 338 D14
PRUE
ct. Fawkner 281 G9
ct. Warranwood 334 H15
PRUNELLA
cl. Doncaster 330 J18
PRUNUS
ct. Bellfield 327 L6
gr. Doveton 536 K13
PRYDE
ct. Wheelers Hl 460 J12
PRYOR
st. Eltham 287 H8
PRYTON
ct. Balwyn 374 B10
PUCKLE
la. Moonee Pnd 324 C13
st. Moonee Pnd 324 B13
st. Taylors Hill 274 C7
PUEBLA
st. Torquay 711 L7
PUERTA
st. Burwood 418 C6
PUFFIN
cl. Chelsea Ht 547 G19
ct. Endeavour Hl 537 A4
PUFFING BILLY
pl. Emerald 509 E3
PUKAKI
ct. Taylors L 276 E10
PULFORD
cr. Mill Park 242 K3
ct. Melton W 225 K17
PULI
st. Werribee 447 F18
PULLAR
st. Maidstone 366 G1
PULLEN
ct. Springvale 500 A8
dr. Hurstbridge 246 L1
dr. Hurstbridge 247 A1
PULLMAN
ct. St Kilda E 455 B1
PULLYN
st. Clayton 498 L3
PULSAR
pl. Kealba 321 B1
PULTNEY
st. Dandenong 536 B10
PUMMEROY
la. St Kilda, off St Kilda Rd 414 E15
PUMP
st. Heathmont 379 A17
PUMPKIN
la. St Kilda, off Blessington St 414 C19
PUMPS
la. Wantirna S 421 F17
rd. Wantirna S 421 H17
PUNARI
ct. Seaford 600 B5
mw. Eltham 287 C7
PUNCH
la. Melbourne 24 H4
PUNJEL
dr. Diggers Rest 187 F13
PUNKERRI
cct. Greensbrgh 244 C14
PUNT
la. W Footscray 366 F6
rd. Cremorne 25 K19
rd. E Melbourne 25 K19
rd. Melbourne 25 K19
rd. Melbourne 31 G20
rd. Melbourne 414 D11
rd. Prahran 31 G20
rd. St Kilda 414 D11
rd. South Yarra 31 H14
rd. South Yarra 414 D7
rd. Windsor 414 D11
PURBECK
pl. Nar Warrn S 579 D3
PURCELL
cr. Roxburgh Pk 194 A14
ct. Bundoora 243 A20
ct. Werribee 447 F18
st. N Melbourne 17 C17
PURCHAS
st. Werribee 447 D6
PURCHES
av. Pascoe Vale S 324 J4
st. Mitcham 377 H18
st. Vermont 377 H20
PURDY
av. Dandenong 535 H7
PURINUAN
rd. Reservoir 283 B6
PURLEY
ct. Hillside 232 E16
dr. Dandenong N 501 L14
PURNELL
st. Altona 408 F19
st. Anglesea 713 L3
PURRI
cl. Greensbrgh 244 B20
PURRUMBETE
av. Manifold Ht 702 B1
PURSE
st. Mt Waverley 418 L14
PURSELL
av. Blackburn S 419 L2
PURSER
av. Ringwood E 378 L9
av. Ringwood E 379 A9
PURTEL
cl. Mordialloc 532 E16
PURTELL
st. Bentleigh E 496 G3
PURTON
rd. Pakenham 584 C1
PURVES
rd. Arthurs Seat 685 J16
PUSHKIN
ct. Doncaster E 331 L16
PUTNEY
ct. Endeavour Hl 537 L7
cl. Wantirna 422 E8
la. Frankston 627 K9
PUTT
gr. Keysborough 534 C9
PYALONG
av. Rosanna 285 A19
cr. Broadmeadows 238 H12
cr. Dallas 238 H12
PYCNANTHA
ct. Endeavour Hl 502 L19
PYE
st. Port Melb 412 B4
PYGMALION
ri. Warrandyte 333 A2
PYINGERRA
cr. Cheltenham 530 E2
PYKE
ct. Mulgrave 500 H1
dr. Gladstone Pk 237 E19
pl. Kurunjang 227 B14
st. Dandenong 535 E3
st. Werribee 447 G18
PYMBLE
gdn. Craigieburn 193 J3
PYMM
av. Eltham North 287 C1
PYNE
st. Caulfield 455 G5
PYRAMID
pl. Lyndhurst 551 A19
PYRAMUS
pl. Altona Mdw 451 K5
PYRENEES
ct. Beaconsfield 555 E12
PYRUS
ct. Doveton 536 J7
pl. Donvale 377 C1
PYTCHLEY
rd. Croydon 380 F1
PYTHIAS
ct. Millgrove 348 E4

Q

QUADRAT
cl. Berwick 553 E2
QUAIL
cl. Chelsea Ht 547 G18
cr. Melton 226 F15
ct. Carrum Downs 600 H3
ct. Nar Warrn S 552 F14
ct. Werribee 448 D9
pl. Craigieburn 149 F16
wy. Rowville 503 D4
wy. Rowville 503 D4
QUAILLE
ct. Darley 221 K5
QUAINTANCE
st. Mt Waverley 418 K15
QUALITY
dr. Dandenong S 549 J6
st. Frankston 599 D19
wy. Mitcham 377 C14
QUAMBY
av. Frankston 628 E6
av. Guys Hill 555 L2
av. South Yarra 32 L12
av. South Yarra 414 L6
ct. Viewbank 285 L18
ct. Werribee 446 J15
pl. Donvale 332 K19
rd. Guys Hill 555 K2
rd. Ringwood N 334 H17
QUANDOLAN
cl. Ivanhoe East 328 L17
QUANDONG
ct. Frankston 628 B4
st. Thomastown 241 C12
QUANTOCK
st. Canterbury 373 E20
st. Canterbury 417 E1
QUANTUM
cl. Dandenong S 550 K7
QU'APPELLE
st. Pt Lonsdale 710 E6
QUARBING
st. Werribee 447 C12
QUARRION
dr. Carrum Downs 600 J3
la. Northcote 326 K15
QUARRY
cct. Coburg 281 J19
cl. Belmont 702 G16
rd. Ferntree Gly 464 J5
rd. Langwarrin 601 B12
rd. Lilydale 338 H1
rd. Melb Airport 235 L11
rd. Mitcham 377 C10
rd. Mitcham 377 F8
rd. Narre Warren 539 G16
rd. Tottenham 365 L9
rd. Up Fntree Gly 464 J5
tr. Lysterfield 504 A6
QUARRY HILLS
dr. Berwick 553 L6
QUARTOK
av. Werribee 447 C12
QUARTZ
pl. Narre Warren 539 F13
st. Bulla 190 B14
st. Delahey 275 A15
QUAT QUATTA
av. Ripponlea 454 J2
QUAYLE
rd. Seville 341 D19
rd. Wandin East 341 D19
QUEEN
rd. Lilydale 338 H6
st. Altona 452 D2
st. Altona Mdw 451 H1
st. Belmont 706 D1
st. Blackburn 375 J15
st. Brunswick E 325 K12
st. Burnley 371 C19
st. Coburg 325 A7
st. Dandenong 535 F2
st. Essendon 323 H3
st. Fitzroy N 326 C17
st. Footscray 367 C8
st. Frankston 599 F18
st. Kew 371 K11
st. Lalor 241 G8
st. Melbourne 1 J18
st. Melbourne 23 K3
st. Melbourne 23 K3
st. Mornington 640 D14
st. Nunawading 376 K14
st. Ormond 456 A14
st. Parkdale 531 D9
st. Queenscliff 708 H18
st. Reservoir 283 A15
st. St Kilda E 414 G16
st. Seaholme 409 G20
st. S Melbourne 29 H6
st. Surrey Hills 417 H2
st. Williamstown 411 D12
st. Yarra Jctn 347 E17
QUEEN BEATRIX
dr. Carrum Downs 575 A14
QUEENS
av. Ascot Vale 324 D18
av. Caulfield E 456 D5
av. Doncaster 375 C1
av. Hawthorn 372 C17
av. Mont Albert 374 F13
av. Oakleigh 457 J13
av. Springvale 499 H10
av. Springvale 499 K12
cr. Bacchus Msh 221 K17
ct. Berwick 554 C6
ct. Jan Juc 711 D15
ct. Rye 697 E8
ct. Werribee 448 B12
la. Melbourne 30 L6
la. Melbourne 31 A6
la. Melbourne 31 C16
la. Melbourne 413 L3
la. Melbourne 414 B8
pde. Ashwood 418 A17
pde. Clifton Hill 19 D8
pde. Fawkner 281 G11
pde. Fitzroy N 19 D8
pde. Glen Iris 417 K11
pde. Hillside 232 B19
rd. Albert Park 31 C16
rd. Melbourne 30 L6
rd. Melbourne 30 L8
rd. Melbourne 31 A9
rd. Melbourne 31 C16
rd. Melbourne 413 L3
rd. Melbourne 413 L4
rd. Newtown 702 A9
rd. Pearcedale 646 E8
rd. Seville 385 F5
rd. Silvan 384 L9
rd. Sorrento 678 G11
rd. Wandin East 384 L9
rd. Wandin East 385 F5
sq. Sandringham 495 B12
wy. St Kilda 414 E12
wy. Windsor 414 E12
QUEENSBERRY
ct. Hillside 231 J19
pl. Carlton 18 C19
pl. N Melbourne 17 C17
st. Carlton 17 L18
st. Keilor Park 278 A14
st. Melbourne 17 L18
st. N Melbourne 17 A17
st. N Melbourne 34 J17
QUEENSBRIDGE
sq. Southbank 3 F3
sq. Southbank 24 B13
st. Southbank 3 B8
st. Southbank 24 A16
QUEENSBURY
wy. Werribee 446 K10
QUEENSCLIFF
rd. Moolap 704 E18
rd. Newcomb 704 E18
rd. Thomastown 240 E11
QUEENSFERRY
pl. Greenvale 236 K1
QUEENS PARK
rd. Highton 701 H8
rd. Newtown 701 H8
QUEENSPOINT
cr. Queenscliff 707 J18
QUEENSTOWN
rd. Boronia 423 E15
QUEENSVILLE
st. Kingsville 366 L13
QUEENS WHARF
rd. Melbourne 1 B20
rd. Melbourne 23 K13
QUEEN VICTORIA
cr. Taylors L 275 J6
QUELLTALER
pl. Vermont S 421 D11
QUENGO
ct. Seaford 573 E19
QUENTIN
rd. Malvern East 457 G3
st. Forest Hill 420 F5
st. Scoresby 462
wy. Eltham 288
QUERCUS
ct. Camberwell 417
ct. Mt Waverley 419
QUEST
ct. Craigieburn 150
ct. Glen Waverley 420
ct. Mooroolbark 337
QUICK
st. Pascoe Vale 280
QUICKSILVER
dr. Torquay 711
QUIET
dr. Bangholme 549
QUILAN
ct. Caroline Spr 318
QUILL
ct. Mt Martha 656
QUINELLA
cl. Keilor Park 278
QUINLAN
ct. Werribee 447
QUINN
cr. Mt Evelyn 338
cr. Mt Evelyn 338
cr. Mt Evelyn 339
cr. Mt Evelyn 339
cr. Mt Evelyn 383
ct. Altona Mdw 451
ct. Rowville 463
gr. Keilor East 322
st. Dandenong 536
st. Deer Park 318
st. Heidelberg 329
st. Preston 327
st. Seaford 599
wy. Montmorency 287
QUINNS
pde. Mt Eliza 642
rd. Bentleigh E 456
QUINTON
ct. Mt Eliza 626
ct. Mt Waverley 419
rd. Camberwell 417
QUIRK
ct. Endeavour Hl 537
QUIST
ct. Dandenong S 550
ct. Mill Park 242
QUIXLEY
gr. Wantirna 422

R

RAAF
st. Whittington 703
RABAUL
ct. Boronia 424
RACECOURSE
dr. Springvale 500
rd. Altona 409
rd. Flemington 33
rd. Flemington 34
rd. Kensington 33
rd. Mornington 641
rd. Mt Martha 656
rd. Mt Martha 657
rd. Noble Park 500
rd. N Melbourne 34
rd. Pakenham 585
rd. Sunbury 143
rd. Werribee 446
rd. Werribee 447
rd.n, Pakenham 585
RACHAEL
ct. Pakenham 585
ct. Seabrook 450
dr. Mooroolbark 381
RACHAL
cl. Mt Evelyn 339
RACHEL
ct. Sydenham 275
dr. Cranbourne N 577
st. Dandenong N 501
RACHELLE
dr. Wantirna 422
rd. Keilor East 322
RACING CLUB
la. Melbourne 1
RADCLIFF
av. Cheltenham 496
RADCLIFFE
mw. Glen Waverley 420
st. W Melbourne 34
st. W Melbourne 368
RADE MACUT
ct. Nar Warrn N 538

)ESIN
Nar Warrn N 539 B6
)FORD
Brookfield 268 B4
Reservoir...........282 B9
Williamstown.....411 A16
)IANT
Forest Hill 420 E5
)IATA
Ringwood N.......334 H20
Mill Park 242 A9
Narre Warren 539 E20
Frankston N 600 A8
)IO
Maidstone..........322 E19
)LEIGH
Wheelers Hl 460 K16
)LEY
Mornington........640 G17
NOR
Mt Dandenong ...426 F5
Camberwell.........416 K7
Heidelberg 328 K4
)OVIC
Cranbourne N 577 J5
)STOCK
Craigieburn........194 D2
UETT
Endeavour Hl 503 D20

Edithvale............546 G11
Bundoora...........285 C2
Darley................221 K4
Melton S............268 H3
Pakenham 584 E3
Prahran 414 L12
Bentleigh E 497 C7
Chadstone 457 K5
Fitzroy N 19 B8
Hawthorn............372 C14
Mt Waverley 419 H13
Rosebud W........683 E19
Templstw Lr 330 B10
BURN
Newcomb 704 A15
Pascoe Vale 280 K16
MUR
Hoppers Csg......449 C4
WYN
Langwarrin 601 K17
Springvale S 534 A5
FINDALE
Mill Park............242 H10
TER
St Albans 275 K19
LAN
Kurunjang...........227 A14
Maidstone.........366 H1
Research 288 H3
S Melbourne........30 C8
S Melbourne......413 H4
Research 288 H4
Avondale Ht.......322 C15
Caulfield N 415 F18
Darley................222 B8
Diggers Rest......142 A13
Maidstone.........366 H1
Newtown 702 J8
N Melbourne........17 D19
Port Melb 29 A5
Port Melb...........412 L2
Port Melb...........413 A3
Preston.............326 L5
Queenscliff.........708 K19
St Kilda E..........414 H16
S Melbourne........30 A8
S Melbourne......413 F4
LIN
Somerville 644 G14
EEN
Wantirna............422 D14
Vermont S 421 A13
Kew....................371 E9
Craigieburn........150 B20
Melton W...........226 E15
NSTON
Vermont 421 K1
TON
Preston..............327 A5
WAY
Boronia..............424 E11
Hawthorn............372 A17
Armadale 415 H16
Ashwood 418 E17
Beaconsfield 555 B16
Brighton 454 H20
Laverton 407 A19
Oakleigh 458 C15
Pakenham 585 A8
Ringwood E 378 K12
Up Fntree Gly 465 A6
Werribee............447 K13
Bentleigh 496 B3
cr. Broadmeadows..238 B15
cr. Croydon 380 B2
cr. Dallas 238 B12
cr. Hampton 494 L9
cr. Moonee Pnd 324 A11
cr. Williamstown 411 C15
gr. Croydon 380 A3
gr. Mornington........640 E12
la. Fitzroy N 326 A19
pde. Bayswater 423 G3
pde. Camberwell........372 J19
pde. Dandenong........535 C4
pde. Deer Park...........319 B19
pde. Eltham...............287 G5
pde. Healesville 213 E20
pde. Highett 496 C12
pde. Menzies Ck 468 C18
pde. Murrumbeena 457 B7
pde. Newport 410 F10
pde. Noble Park.........535 C4
pde. Pascoe Vale 280 C14
pde. Seaford..............573 C13
pde. Wandin N 340 K14
pde. Wandin N 341 A14
pde.n,Glen Waverley ..460 C1
pde.s,Chadstone 418 C19
pde.s,Deer Park 319 A18
pde.w,Northcote 326 H12
pl. Balaclava 414 H19
pl. Belgrave 466 H14
pl. Brunswick...........325 E16
pl. Coburg 325 F4
pl. Cremorne 26 D17
pl. Fairfield..............327 D18
pl. Footscray.............367 H7
pl. Preston...............326 H5
pl. Ringwood............378 D13
pl. Southbank.............29 G1
pl. South Yarra 32 G13
pl. South Yarra 414 J7
pl. W Melbourne.......23 A4
pl. W Melbourne.......34 A17
pl. W Melbourne.......34 J20
pl. W Melbourne......368 F9
pl. W Melbourne.....368 K11
pl. Williamstown.....411 C15
pl. Fitzroy N, off
Byrne St 326 D19
pl. Hawthorn, off
Evansdale Rd.....371 G17
pl.e, Ascot Vale 324 D18
pl.e, Preston..............326 J6
pl.n, Williamstown.....411 G17
pl.w, Flemington 324 D19
rd. Baxter.................644 C3
rd. Blackburn 375 H15
rd. Blackburn 375 L14
rd. Briar Hill 286 E5
rd. Carnegie 456 H7
rd. Cheltenham 530 J1
rd. Eltham 287 H4
rd. Emerald 509 F4
rd. Epping.................241 E3
rd. Ferntree Gly 464 H4
rd. Mt Evelyn............339 B20
rd. Mt Evelyn............382 L2
rd. Mt Evelyn............383 A2
rd. Seville..................342 A10
rd. Sunshine N 321 E6
rd. Wesburn..............347 E12
rd. Yarra Jctn 347 E12
st. Fitzroy N 326 C19
st. Northcote 326 G17
st. Yarra Jctn 347 C15
st.n, Altona...............408 L18
st.s, Altona...............408 L18
tce. Geelong..............702 L6
tce. Williamstown.....411 J18
wk. Cheltenham 496 J20
wk.s,Hampton 494 L9
wk.s,Hampton 495 A9
RAIMENO
st. Lalor...................241 G9
RAIN
ct. Doveton..............536 L8
RAINBIRD
ct. Epping................198 C20
ct. Keilor Dn 275 L16
RAINBOW
al. Melbourne...............2 F13
al. Melbourne 24 E7
ct. Mt Waverley 418 J17
ct. Pearcedale...........646 K3
ct. Rye 696 E3
ct. Sunbury 143 H15
ct. Taylors L 275 H6
RAINBOW VALLEY
rd. Pk Orchards.........333 C15
RAINE
ct. Delahey 275 E12
RAINER
rd. S Morang 199 A14
st. Pascoe Vale S 324 H5
RAINHAM
cl. Greensbrgh........244 D20
cl. Greensbrgh........286 D1
RAINIER
av. Dromana 686 H9
RAINONE
pl. Tarneit...............447 J1
RAINSFORD
ct. Dingley Vill.........532 L5
dr. Noble Park N.......501 E9
pl. Viewbank............286 A17
st. Elwood 454 G2
st. Werribee.............447 F19
tce. Campbellfield 239 G12
RAINTREE
rd. Templestowe 332 D5
RAINY HILL
rd. Cockatoo 471 E14
RAISELL
rd. Cranbourne W ...577 H20
RAITERI
ct. Croydon 335 D20
ct. Croydon 379 E1
RAITH
av. Sandringham 495 C17
ct. St Kilda E...........414 K15
tce. Newtown 701 K5
RAKAIA
wy. Docklands..........368 K14
RALEIGH
ct. Werribee............446 L11
dr. Nar Warrn S.......552 G19
gr. Essendon N 323 G1
rd. Maribyrnong 322 L14
rd. Maribyrnong 323 A15
st. Blackburn S 420 A3
st. Clarinda 498 F5
st. Essendon...........324 B7
st. Footscray...........367 D9
st. Forest Hill 420 A3
st. Malvern 415 L17
st. Melbourne 31 F20
st. Melbourne 414 D10
st. Seville................341 J14
st. Spotswood 411 B2
st. Thornbury...........326 J9
st. Westmeadows ...237 B13
st. Windsor 31 F20
st. Windsor 414 D10
RALEIGHS
rd. Melton...............227 A17
RALEON
av. Frankston S 627 K11
RALPH
av. St Albans...........320 L4
av. St Albans...........321 A4
cr. Hampton Pk.......552 C11
ct. Altona Mdw 451 G8
ct. Ferntree Gly 463 L5
ct. Mt Waverley 418 K12
st. Blackburn S 419 J1
st. Bulleen 330 A15
st. Hampton 495 D11
st. Reservoir 282 K9
st. Sunshine W 364 B6
RALPHS
av. Sorrento 678 L13
RALRON
ct. Pakenham 584 L1
RALSTON
av. Sunshine N........321 D10
st. South Yarra 31 J10
st. South Yarra 414 E5
RALTON
av. Glen Waverley....460 F5
RALUND
rd. Doncaster 330 D17
RAMADA
ct. Lilydale 338 K3
RAMAGE
ct. Kings Park.........275 B20
la. Gembrook 512 L15
rd. Mt Dandenong ...426 E3
st. Bayswater 424 B4
RAMBLE
cr. Croydon 379 F3
RAMBLERS
wy. Doreen 156 L11
RAMLEH
rd. Reservoir 283 H6
RAMLER
mw. Portsea.............677 J3
RAMONA
av. Malvern East......457 E1
ct. Boronia..............424 L4
pl. Melton W...........226 C16
RAMPART
av. Glen Waverley....420 L14
RAMPTONS
rd. Eltham North 287 B5
rd. Eltham North 287 D3
RAMSAY
av. Kew East............372 D5
cl. Doncaster E 332 D15
cr. Darley................221 G6
ct. Cheltenham 497 C20
ct. Endeavour Hl 537 C4
ct. Mt Martha...........655 H17
ct. Sunbury 142 H8
la. Melbourne 1 C11
la. Melbourne 23 J8
st. Aberfeldie 323 B9
st. Anglesea............714 A4
st. Bayswater N 379 L19
st. Brighton 454 G20
st. Spotswood 411 B3
RAMSBURY
st. Craigieburn........194 B2
RAMSDEN
st. Clifton Hill.............20 D5
RAMSEY
cl. Gladstone Pk 237 D16
ct. Mulgrave 500 H2
st. Burwood E..........419 E8
RAMSON
ct. Altona Mdw 451 D3
RAMU
av. Tremont 425 D19
gr. Ashburton..........417 H18
pde. Heidelberg W 284 A20
RANCEBY
cl. Rowville.............463 H12
RANCH
ct. Mornington........656 F4
ct. Narre Warren 552 H1
RANCHER
pl. Mornington........657 B6
RAND
st. Greensbrgh........286 E4
RANDALL
av. Chelsea.............547 A12
av. Edithvale............547 A12
ct. Mt Waverley 418 J16
pl. South Yarra 31 E6
st. Maribyrnong 323 A13
RANDELL
cr. Hampton E.........495 J6
ct. Doncaster E 331 K16
ct. Mill Park 242 E2
st. Parkdale 531 H15
RANDLE
ct. Nar Warrn N 539 C7
RANDO
ct. Frankston S 627 A6
RANDOLF
ct. Templstw Lr 330 E8
RANDOLPH
st. Hawthorn...........371 F14
RANDOM
st. Frankston 627 J3
RANDWICK
av. Bacchus Msh......221 D14
ct. Epping...............197 J17
ct. Noble Park N.......501 B9
dr. Keilor Park 278 A13
RANEEN
dr. Langwarrin 602 B16
pl. Berwick 554 B19
RANELAGH
ct. Glen Iris 417 H9
dr. Mt Eliza..............626 A18
RANFURLIE
av. Point Cook..........449 L6
cr. Glen Iris.............416 G14
ct. Forest Hill 420 J4
dr. Glen Waverley....460 D8
rd. Forest Hill 420 G4
RANGE
rd. Burwood E.........419 L9
rd. Mt Martha...........670 D2
rd. Olinda................426 E9
rd. Sassafras............426 G10
st. Camberwell.........416 L7
st. Camberwell.........417 A7
RANGER
ct. Seaford..............573 F13
RANGE VIEW
ct. Croydon 380 F2
tce. Bulleen 329 K11
RANGEVIEW
av. Malvern East......457 F4
ct. Glen Waverley....460 H3
ct. Viewbank...........285 J16
dr. Skye 575 G20
gr. Balwyn N...........373 B5
rd. Boronia..............424 E11
rd. Diamond Ck.......245 L9
rd. Donvale 377 E8
rd. Lower Plenty......286 K10
rd. Mt Evelyn...........339 F17
st. Cairnlea 319 G11
RANGOON
ct. Mulgrave 500 C2
RANKIN
av. Sunshine N........321 G10
la. Albert Park...........29 H14
rd. Boronia..............423 J16
rd. Ferntree Gly 423 J16
rd. Herne Hill...........702 A4
st. Altona................408 J19
st. Panton Hill 204 F18
RANKINS
la. Melbourne 1 L11
la. Melbourne 24 B7
rd. Kensington 34 A9
rd. Monbulk 468 J2
rd. Monbulk 468 J2
RANLEIGH
ct. Moorabbin.........496 K10
ri. Sunbury 143 B4
ri. Templstw Lr 330 G13
RANMORE
gr. Caroline Spr.......317 K2
RANNOCH
av. Mt Eliza.............625 J13
RANSOM
av. Altona...............409 A15
RAOUL
ct. Yarrambat..........201 B12
RAPALLO
wy. Cranbourne N 578 H11
RAPANEA
av. Templstw Lr 330 H14
ct. Endeavour Hl 536 K1
RAPHAEL
cr. Frankston 628 B10
ct. Grovedale 705 J15
ct. Scoresby 462 C7
dr. Wheelers Hl 460 K14
ri. S Morang 198 H13
st. Abbotsford 26 C1
st. Caulfield N 415 E18
st. Hallam...............538 D19
RAQUEL
cl. Carrum Downs...601 C5
RASHEDA
st. Watsonia 285 F9
RASHU
ct. Clarinda 498 G11
RASMAY
ct. The Patch 467 L4
RASMUSSEN
ct. Coburg 282 A19
dr. Templestowe 331 C11
RASON
ct. Keilor Dn 276 E14
RASSAY
ct. Frankston 600 J16
RATA
st. Wheelers Hl 461 B19
RATCLIFFE
cl. Mill Park 242 D5
ct. Keysborough 535 A10
wy. Lynbrook 551 B15
RATHCOWN
rd. Reservoir 283 C7
RATHDOWN
st. Coburg 281 A20
RATHDOWNE
cct. Melton W...........226 D15
pl. Carlton 18 H14
st. Brunswick E........325 K20
st. Carlton 18 G20
st. Carlton N 18 H7
RATHGAEL
av. Mt Martha...........655 J14
RATHGAR
rd. Lysterfield..........464 C13
RATHMINES
gr. Hawthorn E........372 E15
rd. Hawthorn E........372 E16
rd. Toorak...............415 A4
st. Fairfield..............327 D17
st. Fairfield..............327 D19
st. Newtown 702 F13
st. Thornbury...........327 D14
RATHMULLEN
qd. Doncaster 330 H19
rd. Boronia..............423 E15
RATHO
av. Brighton East 495 A4
RATTEN
av. Kew East............372 A5
RATTRAY
ct. Altona Mdw 451 G5
rd. Montmorency 286 G10
RAU
ct. Broadmeadows..238 B9
ct. Grovedale 706 A11
RAUTMAN
cr. Sunshine W 365 A10
RAVA
ct. Aspendale Gdn...546 H2
RAVELL
mw. Langwarrin 629 G3

STREETS

rd. Kallista 468 F12
rd. Kalorama 382 E19
rd. Mt Dandenong 426 E1
rd. Oak Park 279 L10
rd. Olinda 426 E1
rd. Wantirna S 462 E5
rd. Yan Yean 156 L4
tr. Lysterfield S 503 F11
RIDGEMONT
dr. Berwick 580 C3
RIDGE VIEW
ct. Somerville 644 G13
RIDGEVIEW
av. Chirnside Pk 336 J7
st. Eltham 288 A2
tce. Lysterfield 464 D14
RIDGEWAY
Melton W 225 G19
Sunbury 143 E20
av. Glenroy 279 H3
av. Kew 372 A10
ch. Nar Warrn S 552 G7
pde. Sunshine W 364 B1
pde. Sunshine W 364 G2
st. Templstw Lr 330 K11
RIDGWAY
av. Croydon 379 L5
pl. Melbourne 24 J6
RIDING
wy. Ferntree Gly 463 F6
RIDING BOUNDARY
rd. Ravenhall 317 L20
rd. Truganina 317 A19
RIDLEY
av. Avondale Ht 322 A11
cl. Carrum Downs 600 F4
ct. Doncaster E 332 G10
st. Albion 364 L1
st. Albion 365 A1
st. Blairgowrie 695 J3
st. Burwood E 419 E8
RIDOUT
ct. Bulleen 329 H14
RIFLE RANGE
dr. Williamstown 410 L16
rd. St Andrews 206 C1
rd. Smiths Gly 206 E2
rd. Smiths Gly 207 A3
RIFLE RANGE GULLY
rd. Olinda 427 C2
RIGANI
ct. Blackburn N 375 J9
RIGBY
av. Carnegie 456 H12
ct. Nar Warrn S 578 H3
ct. Taylors L 233 A20
la. Kensington 33 G7
mw. Rowville 502 G1
st. Carrum 573 E8
st. Warneet 649 D13
RIGEL
st. Melton 226 J16
RIGGALL
st. Broadmeadows 238 A12
st. Broadmeadows 238 C12
st. Dallas 238 C12
RIGO
st. Belmont 706 B1
RILEY
ct. Braybrook 366 C3
ct. Burnside 318 C6
ct. Glen Waverley 460 A3
ct. Keilor Dn 276 B12
ct. Pakenham 584 A4
dr. Mill Park 243 D6
pl. Hampton Pk 551 H11
rd. Upwey 465 G15
st. McCrae 684 J18
st. Murrumbeena 457 D7
st. Oakleigh S 457 L20
st. Oakleigh S 497 L1
st. Thornbury 327 E8
RILL
st. Heidelberg 328 J4
RIMBANDA
ct. Kurunjang 227 B12
RIMBOOL
rd. Grovedale 706 E15
RIMCROSS
dr. Avondale Ht 321 L6
dr. Keilor East 321 L6
RIMES
ct. Cranbourne W 603 H1
RIMFIRE
cl. Thomastown 240 H16
cr. Cranbourne 604 C5
ct. Lilydale 294 B20
ct. Melton W 226 C13
dr. Hallam 552 A2
RIMINGTON
av. Kew 372 J10
ct. Hampton Pk 551 E6

RIMMER
pl. Doncaster E 332 H12
st. Mentone 530 L4
RIMU
cl. Doveton 536 J5
RINELLA
ct. Frankston S 627 E17
RING
ct. Dandenong N 501 L14
rd. Bundoora 284 D10
rd. Bundoora 284 D13
rd.n, Clayton 459 C14
rd.s, Clayton 459 C16
RINGO
pl. Nar Warrn S 578 G3
RING ROAD WEST INNER
Clayton 459 B16
RING ROAD WEST OUTER
Clayton 459 B16
RINGS
rd. Moorabbin 496 K11
RINGWOOD
bps. Ringwood 378 D10
ct. Gladstone Pk 237 B17
st. Ringwood 378 D9
RINGWOOD-WARRANDYTE
rd. Pk Orchards 334 E13
rd. Ringwood N 334 E13
rd. Warrandyte 290 D18
rd. Warrandyte S 334 E13
RIO
ct. Ferntree Gly 464 E10
ct. Torquay 712 B3
pl. Campbellfield 239 G18
RIO GRANDE
dr. Roxburgh Pk 194 E8
RIORDAN
ct. Mornington 656 C1
pl. Templstw Lr 330 D10
RIO VISTA
ct. Cheltenham 497 D20
ct. Rye 697 L8
RIPLEY
cl. Derrimut 363 C4
ct. Narre Warren 553 D11
ct. Ringwood 378 L2
ct. Ringwood 379 A2
gr. Caulfield N 455 H2
st. Geelong West 702 K4
st. Mt Waverley 458 H6
st. Oakleigh S 498 A7
RIPON
cl. Diamond Ck 245 H7
ct. Forest Hill 376 F19
ct. Noble Park N 501 C8
gr. Brighton 494 G4
gr. Elsternwick 454 K3
st. Sunshine 364 K2
RIPPER
st. Montmorency 286 K10
RIPPLEBROOK
dr. Broadmeadows 237 G15
RIPPON
ct. Templestowe 331 L14
st. Footscray 367 E4
RIPS
ct. Dingley Vill 532 J6
RISDALE
cl. Diamond Ck 245 H8
RISDON
ct. Wantirna S 422 D16
dr. Notting Hill 459 J14
RISELEY
ct. Keysborough 534 E14
RISHON
av. Blackburn S 419 J7
RISING
ct. Hillside 232 A17
st. Pascoe Vale 281 B12
RISLEY
cl. Caroline Spr 317 L2
st. Richmond 26 G6
RISSON
la. Hawthorn E 372 G20
st. Melton S 268 H11
RITA
ct. Endeavour Hl 537 L2
ct. Epping 197 G15
ct. Hoppers Csg 448 J1
st. Aberfeldie 323 C11
st. Preston 283 G19
st. St Albans 319 K5
st. Upwey 465 K15
RITCH
pl. Geelong, off Storrer St 703 D11
RITCHIE
av. Blairgowrie 695 J4
bvd. Geelong 703 D7
ct. Sunshine 365 D3
st. Gembrook 512 L16
RITZ
st. Vermont S 420 H10

RIVER
av. Ascot Vale 323 F19
av. Plenty 243 J6
av. Plenty 244 A7
bvd. Richmond 371 C13
dr. Avondale Ht 321 L7
la. South Yarra 32 F8
la. South Yarra 414 J4
rd. Millgrove 348 B1
rt. Kew 371 F7
st. Briar Hill 286 F5
st. Greensbrgh 286 F5
st. Healesville 213 E19
st. Maribyrnong 322 L19
st. Maribyrnong 323 A19
st. Newport 411 A6
st. Richmond 371 C16
st. South Yarra 32 F9
st. South Yarra 414 J5
tce. Hallam 538 E14
wk. Maribyrnong 322 L12
RIVERBANK
dr. Maribyrnong 322 L12
dr. Maribyrnong 322 L13
RIVERBEND
cr. Werribee 447 B8
RIVERBRAE
ct. Alphington 371 K1
RIVERDALE
rd. Seville E 387 G5
RIVEREND
rd. Bangholme 547 J12
RIVEREX
pl. Hoppers Csg 447 K1
RIVERFRONT
wy. Maribyrnong 322 L11
wy. Maribyrnong 323 A11
RIVERGLADES
dr. Point Cook 451 E8
RIVER GLEN
ct. Belmont 702 D16
RIVERGLEN
dr. Werribee 446 L10
rd. Berwick 580 A1
RIVER GUM
ct. Cairnlea 319 E13
RIVERGUM
dr. Croydon N 335 L13
dr. Mill Park 243 B6
pl. Hillside 231 L19
pl. Keysborough 533 L9
RIVERHILL
dr. Lower Plenty 287 A19
RIVERINA
rd. Montmorency 287 C14
RIVER PARK
tce. Maribyrnong 322 H15
RIVERPARK
ct. Werribee 447 D6
dr. Wantirna S 422 F18
RIVER REDGUM
pl. S Morang 243 L4
RIVER RESERVE
rd. Anglesea 713 G3
RIVER RUN
dr. Werribee 447 E4
RIVERS
dr. Bundoora 243 B14
RIVERSDALE
av. Carrum 573 D7
av. Eltham North 287 D1
av. Seaford 599 H4
cr. Darley 221 F2
ct. Hawthorn 371 H20
ct. Mt Waverley 418 K19
dr. Tarneit 447 E1
dr. Werribee 447 E2
rd. Box Hill S 418 G3
rd. Burwood 417 D2
rd. Camberwell 372 A20
rd. Hawthorn 371 J19
rd. Hawthorn 372 A20
rd. Hawthorn E 371 J19
rd. Hawthorn E 372 A20
rd. Newtown 702 C14
rd. Surrey Hills 417 D2
rd. Yarra Jctn 347 E19
st. Craigieburn 150 F14
RIVERSIDE
av. Avondale Ht 322 A14
av. Balwyn N 372 L2
av. Balwyn N 373 A2
av. Keilor 277 C15
av. Port Melb 368 B17
av. Werribee 487 H1
dr. Kew East 372 K2
dr. S Morang 243 K1
dr. Torquay 712 A4
dr. Warburton 349 L3
dr. Warburton 350 C2
pl. Keilor East 321 L6
qy. Southbank 3 J4
qy. Southbank 24 C14

rd. E Warburton 350 G1
rd. Ivanhoe 328 A19
RIVERSIDE WEST
Patterson L 573 H2
RIVER VIEW
tce. Belmont 702 G17
RIVERVIEW
cr. Eumemmerring 537 B12
ct. Maribyrnong 323 A12
dr. Hopetoun Park 266 A9
dr. Werribee 447 E13
gr. Alphington 327 J19
pde. Launching Pl 346 F14
rd. Balwyn N 373 D2
rd. Essendon 323 K10
rd. Montmorency 286 G10
st. Avondale Ht 322 E13
tce. Bulleen 329 L15
tce. Sunbury 142 L1
tce. Sunbury 143 A1
RIVER WALK
dr. Point Cook 451 E9
RIVETT
cr. Mulgrave 460 C17
RIVETTE
ct. Cranbourne 604 B5
ct. Keilor Dn 275 L15
st. Mordialloc 532 B10
st. Scoresby 462 G6
RIVETTE ROUND
Mill Park 242 J11
RIVIERA
av. Doncaster 330 D15
cl. Mt Eliza 641 L8
ct. Fawkner 239 F19
ct. Reservoir 240 A20
ct. Thomastown 240 F14
dr. Berwick 554 G20
dr. Jan Juc 711 A18
la. Blackburn 375 H16
rd. Avondale Ht 322 C8
st. Mentone 531 D7
st. Mt Waverley 419 B13
st. Seaford 573 C14
RIVINGTON
av. Kallista 467 A1
ct. Highton 701 G14
RIVOLI
ct. Dingley Vill 532 L4
ct. Mt Waverley 458 L5
pl. Keilor Ldg 276 B4
st. Mentone 530 J8
RIVULET
pl. Warrandyte 332 L1
pl. Warrandyte 333 A1
RIX
rd. Officer 581 F2
st. Glen Iris 416 F8
ROACH
av. Aberfeldie 323 D9
dr. Altona Mdw 451 G6
pl. Roxburgh Pk 194 E14
rd. Lilydale 339 B8
ROAD
lk. Sunshine W 364 E7
ROADHOUSE
wyn. Sydenham 274 L8
ROANOKE
ct. Epping 197 L17
ct. Sorrento 679 B14
grn. Craigieburn 193 K2
ROB
cl. Hoppers Csg 448 A3
ct. Berwick 554 F1
ct. Boronia 424 F8
ROBB
cl. Bulleen 329 E12
ct. Hampton Pk 551 H10
st. Essendon 323 J10
st. Reservoir 283 D16
st. Spotswood 411 B2
ROBBIE
cl. Rowville 463 J20
ROBBIES
rd. Yarrambat 201 K10
ROBBINS
ct. Bundoora 242 L20
st. Ivanhoe 328 B10
st. Keilor 277 B14
wy. Hampton Pk 551 H11
ROBBS
la. Geelong, off Bayley St 703 A6
pde. Northcote 326 J13
rd. W Footscray 366 J10
ROBDON
ct. Donvale 377 C5
ROBE
ct. Glen Waverley 460 K2
st. St Kilda 414 A17
ROBERN
pde. Viewbank 285 G19

ROBERNA
ct. Langwarrin 601
st. Moorabbin 497
ROBERT
ct. Croydon 336
ct. Hampton Pk 551
ct. Kurunjang 226
ct. Viewbank 285
st. Balwyn N 373
st. Bentleigh 496
st. Bulleen 329
st. Burwood E 419
st. Chadstone 458
st. Collingwood 19
st. Dandenong 536
st. Elwood 454
st. Lalor 240
st. Lilydale 338
st. Montmorency 286
st. Parkdale 531
st. Sassafras 426
st. Somerville 644
st. Somerville 645
st. Spotswood 411
ROBERTA
ct. Bundoora 285
gr. Frankston 599
st. Dandenong 535
ROBERT LYALL
pl. Hoppers Csg 447
ROBERT MOLYNEUX
av. Endeavour Hl 537
ROBERT RUSSELL
la. E Melbourne 25
ROBERTS
av. Airport W 279
av. Box Hill S 418
av. Hoppers Csg 405
av. Hoppers Csg 448
av. Hoppers Csg 449
av. Mulgrave 499
cr. Sunshine W 364
ct. Brighton East 495
ct. Endeavour Hl 537
ct. Sunbury 142
rd. Airport W 278
rd. Belmont 702
rd. Christmas Hills 207
rd. Cranbourne 577
rd. Cranbourne 577
rd.n, Mornington 641
rd.s, Mornington 657
st. Brunswick E 326
st. Essendon 323
st. Ferntree Gly 464
st. Frankston 627
st. Glen Waverley 460
st. Keilor East 322
st. Noble Park 500
st. Northcote 326
st. Rye 697
st. W Footscray 366
st. Yarraville 366
wy. Doncaster E 332
wy. Richmond, off Crown St 371
ROBERTSON
av. St Kilda 414
cr. Boronia 424
cr. Laverton 407
ct. Pt Lonsdale 707
dr. Mornington 640
dr. Mornington 641
pde. Aspendale 546
st. Kensington 34
st. Preston 283
st. Thomson 703
st. Toorak 415
st. Williamstown 410
ROBERTSONS
rd. Darley 221
rd. Taylors L 275
ROBERTSWOOD
cl. Doncaster E 332
ROBESON
st. Preston 326
ROBHILL
ri. Templestowe 331
ROBIN
cl. Doveton 536
ct. Doncaster 331
ct. Keysborough 534
ct. Pakenham 584
ct. Wantirna 422
dr. Carrum Downs 574
gr. Mt Waverley 419
pde. Healesville 213
pde. Rye 696
pl. Craigieburn 149
pl. S Morang 243
st. Altona 408
st. Hoppers Csg 448
st. Melton 226

OBINA
t. Dingley Vill 533 C9
t. Rowville 502 L3
d. Eaglemont 328 G10
d. Monbulk 428 D20
d. Sydenham 275 A9
OBIN HILL
r. Mornington 656 L5
OBIN HOOD
t. Doncaster E 332 A17
d. Ivanhoe East 328 H16
OBINIA
. Hillside 274 B5
t. Nar Warrn S 579 C1
t. Werribee 446 L9
. Sunbury 143 E18
t. Frankston 627 K7
OBINLEE
v. Burwood E 420 A9
OBINS
v. Reservoir 283 G3
. Mt Martha 656 D16
OBINSON
r. Hampton Pk 551 G9
t. Bayswater N 424 H1
t. Delahey 275 F10
. Donvale 376 L6
r. Burwood E 420 D12
r. Bulleen 329 J15
. Portsea 677 J4
d. Carrum Downs 574 A12
d. Footscray 367 E4
d. Harkaway 539 L13
d. Hawthorn 372 C20
d. Hawthorn 416 B4
d. Nar Warrn N 539 E6
d. Reservoir 282 K15
d. Surrey Hills 373 K17
. Brighton East 455 F20
. Clayton 458 F19
. Croydon 379 D3
. Dandenong 535 K9
. Jacana 237 J17
. Malvern 415 L8
. Moonee Pnd 324 B9
. Mt Martha 669 D4
. Prahran 32 L17
. Prahran 414 L9
. Prahran 415 A9
. Sunshine 365 E4
OBINSONS
k. Langwarrin 628 J14
d. Deer Park 318 H15
d. Deer Park 318 H20
d. Derrimut 363 A14
. Frankston 627 J12
. Frankston S 627 J12
d. Langwarrin 628 G14
d. Langwarrin S 628 G14
. Langwarrin S 629 D15
. Langwarrin S 630 A16
. Pearcedale 630 A16
d. Pearcedale 647 D1
d. Ravenhall 318 H20
. Seaford 599 E3
d. Truganina 363 A14
OBINSWOOD
le. Nar Warrn S 579 A4
OBINVALE
. Thomastown 240 D11
. Endeavour Hl 503 F20
OBJANT
. Hampton Pk 551 B8
OBLYN
. Tootgarook 698 C6
OBOROUGH
. Mt Eliza 626 A19
OBROSS
. Cheltenham 497 C19
OB ROY
. Malvern East 457 F2
. Smiths Gly 206 A11
. Glen Waverley 459 J6
OBSON
. Avondale Ht 322 A13
. Point Cook 451 D10
. Sunshine N 321 G14
BUSTA
. Bundoora 242 D14
BY
. Greensbrgh 244 D16
OBYN
. Albanvale 319 D4
. Carrum 573 E11
. Dandenong N 501 K11
. Hampton Pk 551 D10
. Mooroolbark 337 A13
. Oakleigh S 497 G7
. Rye 696 K5
. Nunawading 376 E10
. Doncaster 331 B19
CCO
. Scoresby 462 A8

ROCHDALE
dr. Burwood E 419 F7
sq. Lalor 241 E8
ROCHE
ct. Chelsea Ht 547 G16
ct. Epping 198 A19
ct. Oakleigh S 497 J7
st. Hawthorn 371 H17
st. St Albans 275 K19
ROCHELL
ct. Clarinda 498 D11
ROCHELLE
ct. Aspendale Gdn 547 C7
ct. Doncaster E 332 J13
ct. Nar Warrn S 552 E14
ct. Wantirna S 462 H1
ct. Wheelers Hl 460 H10
ROCHE'S
tce. Williamstown 411 E13
ROCHESTER
dr. Thomastown 241 H16
rd. Balwyn 373 F14
rd. Canterbury 373 F17
rd. Somerville 644 G15
st. Braybrook 365 L5
st. Fitzroy 19 D13
st. Kew 371 C11
vst. Derrimut 363 B6
vst. Officer 555 G19
ROCHFORD
pl. Nar Warrn S 552 F7
st. Bentleigh E 456 J15
ROCHUSSEN
ct. Mt Eliza 641 L7
ROCK
ct. Pakenham 558 K7
gdn. Dromana 686 B10
st. Craigieburn 150 D17
st. Werribee 447 F12
tr. Olinda 427 C9
ROCKAWAY
dr. Viewbank 285 K16
ROCKBANK
ct. Meadow Ht 237 L5
ct. Tarneit 405 A10
rd. Ardeer 320 B19
ROCKBANK MIDDLE
rd. Burnside 318 D6
rd. Caroline Spr 317 J5
ROCKBEARE
ct. Clayton 458 K17
gr. Ivanhoe 327 L16
ROCKBROOK
rd. St Kilda E 414 K20
ROCKCLIFF
ct. Mornington 640 C14
ROCKCLIFFE
st. Eltham 287 K13
ROCKE
st. Ivanhoe 328 A15
ROCKEFELLER
wy. Point Cook 451 D9
ROCKFORD
ct. Noble Park 534 L4
ROCKINGHAM
cl. Kew 371 E12
st. Kew 371 E12
ROCKLAND
ct. Taylors Hill 274 K9
ROCKLANDS
rd. Ashwood 418 F15
ri. Meadow Ht 194 A20
ROCKLEA
cr. Skye 575 H16
ct. Port Melb 412 C2
dr. Torquay 711 J9
rd. Bulleen 329 F13
ROCKLEIGH
dr. Mt Martha 669 C4
ROCKLEIGH PARK
rd. Nar Warrn N 538 E4
ROCKLEY
cl. Diamond Ck 245 J7
rd. South Yarra 32 H9
rd. South Yarra 414 K4
ROCK LODGE
ct. Frankston S 627 A13
ROCKMAN
ct. Nar Warrn N 538 H11
ROCK O'CASHEL
la. Geelong, off Little Malop St 703 B8
ROCKSLEIGH
av. Tecoma 466 D13
ROCKWALL
cl. Sydenham 275 A7
ROCKWOOD
pl. Hillside 232 D17
st. Ardeer 320 B18
ROCKY
la. South Yarra 32 D12

ROCKYS
wy. Lilydale 338 D11
wy. Lilydale 338 D11
ROD
st. Herne Hill 701 J1
RODD
rd. Airport W 279 A10
st. Dandenong 535 K8
RODDA
ct. Gladstone Pk 237 D18
pde. Eltham 287 F16
st. Coburg 325 J2
RODDICK
gr. Queenscliff 708 A19
RODEN
ct. Doncaster E 331 K17
st. W Melbourne 23 A3
RODEO
ct. Endeavour Hl 504 A19
RODERICK
cl. Viewbank 285 L17
dr. Kurunjang 227 E12
st. Doncaster E 375 K1
RODGER
ct. Bundoora 284 D1
rd. Panton Hill 204 H17
rd. Wandin N 340 G10
RODGERSON
st. Box Hill 374 H12
RODINGS
st. Hadfield 281 B7
ROD LARNI
cr. Berwick 553 J13
RODLEIGH
st. Croydon 336 G14
RODMAN
st. Reservoir 282 L3
RODMAR
cl. Hillside 274 F1
ct. Sorrento 679 B14
RODNEY
av. Coburg N 281 C13
cl. Blackburn S 419 H4
cl. Wheelers Hl 461 D12
ct. Broadmeadows 238 E15
ct. Frankston 599 D16
ct. Hoppers Csg 405 C20
ct. Mornington 640 B17
ct. Skye 575 G17
ct. Springvale S 500 C19
ct. Viewbank 285 H16
dr. Keilor Dn 276 A16
dr. Knoxfield 462 J3
pl. Carlton 18 F17
st. Bayswater 423 B6
st. Moorabbin 496 G10
st. Rye 696 F7
RODWELL
pl. Gladstone Pk 236 L16
pl. Gladstone Pk 237 A16
ROE
ct. Mt Waverley 419 C17
wy. Mill Park 242 G1
ROEBOURNE
cr. Campbellfield 239 F18
ROEBUCK
st. Newtown 702 H8
ROEHAMPTON
av. Wantirna 422 H11
cr. Mt Eliza 625 K15
ROEMER
cr. Alphington 371 J1
ROESZLER
la. Melbourne 1 G14
la. Melbourne, off Bank Pl 24 A9
ROFF
ct. Altona Mdw 451 C3
st. Reservoir 283 G2
ROGAN
ct. Langwarrin 601 K18
la. Kensington 33 F8
ROGER
ct. Nunawading 376 F10
ct. Rowville 502 J2
st. Belmont 702 C20
st. Doncaster E 376 A3
ROGERS
av. Brighton East 455 F16
av. Carrum Downs 574 H16
cl. Burnside 318 F9
rd. Bentleigh 496 D5
st. Coburg 281 G19
st. Dandenong 535 K2
st. Eumemmerring 536 L15
st. Eumemmerring 537 A15
st. Mentone 531 C9
st. Pakenham 584 H7
st. Port Melb 368 J18
st. Richmond 26 B13
ROGERSON
ct. Balwyn 373 H10
st. Avondale Ht 322 A12

ROHAN
ct. Fawkner 281 K1
ct. Hampton Pk 551 K7
st. Viewbank 285 J20
ROJIM
ct. Wattle Glen 246 G8
ROKEBY
cl. Hallam 538 B18
cr. Craigieburn 150 A17
st. Collingwood 25 J2
ROKEWOOD
cr. Meadow Ht 237 H5
ct. Endeavour Hl 537 E2
ROLA
cl. Endeavour Hl 538 A1
ROLAIN
tce. S Morang 198 L14
ROLAINE
cl. Lilydale 338 J9
ROLAND
av. Mt Evelyn 339 J18
av. Strathmore 279 K18
st. Mt Waverley 418 H13
ROLEX
ct. Noble Park 535 D5
ROLLAND
ct. Brookfield 268 C4
ct. Endeavour Hl 537 H7
ct. Montmorency 287 A11
st. Coburg 281 E20
ROLLING HILLS
rd. Chirnside Pk 337 E1
ROLLING MEADOWS
dr. Sunbury 144 C8
ROLLINGS
cl. Rosebud 700 J4
rd. Up Fntree Gly 465 B8
ROLLINGTON
dr. Ringwood 378 L4
ROLLO
st. Coburg N 281 B13
ROLLOWAY
ri. Chirnside Pk 337 D1
ROLLS
ct. Glen Waverley 460 G1
ct. Rye 696 L13
st. Coburg 325 H5
ROLORAN
av. Croydon 336 J19
ROLSTONE
ct. Narre Warren 553 E7
ROMA
av. Badger Creek 258 J14
av. Cranbourne 578 A16
ct. Eumemmerring 537 C13
ct. Springvale S 534 A6
ct. Templstw Lr 330 E13
ct. Thomastown 240 C14
ct. Tullamarine 278 F5
pde. Upwey 465 G12
st. Bentleigh 496 D3
st. Hoppers Csg 448 H5
st. Scoresby 462 F6
tce. Mooroolbark 337 L17
ROMALYN
ct. Werribee 447 L16
ROMANO
av. Mill Park 242 E1
ROMANY
ct. Mt Martha 657 D7
ROMAWI
st. Altona 409 A19
ROME
ct. Glen Waverley 419 K17
ROME BEAUTY
av. The Basin 424 K9
ROMEO
ct. Mill Park 242 L3
ct. Mill Park 243 A3
ct. Torquay 712 E4
rd. Healesville 258 J2
ROMERIL
ct. Altona Mdw 451 K6
ROMFORD
ct. Doncaster E 331 L18
ROMILLY
av. Templstw Lr 330 L12
cr. Mulgrave 501 A6
ROMINA
wy. S Morang 199 L16
ROMME
ct. Frankston 628 B10
ROMNEY
av. Tootgarook 698 D2
cl. Moorabbin 496 F9
ct. Mt Waverley 458 F9
ROMOLY
dr. Forest Hill 420 C6
ROMSEY
av. Sunshine N 320 L13
av. Sunshine N 321 A13
cr. Dallas 238 F12
pl. Langwarrin 601 H15

ri. Doncaster E 331 G18
st. Noble Park 500 F20
st. Reservoir 283 D1
ROMY
ct. Altona Mdw 451 D5
RONA
av. Yarraville 367 F16
ct. Baxter 643 L2
st. Ferntree Gly 424 J19
st. Reservoir 282 H15
RONALD
av. Altona North 409 K8
av. Bulleen 329 J11
av. Frankston S 626 G8
av. Noble Park 500 G14
av. Selby 467 B18
av. Sorrento 678 H12
av. S Morang 243 G3
cl. Gladstone Pk 279 C3
cr. Boronia 424 H10
ct. Pakenham 584 G5
ct. Somerville 644 J15
ct. Sunbury 142 L11
ct. Sunbury 143 A11
ct. Watsonia N 285 E2
gr. Keilor East 322 D1
gr. Millgrove 348 G2
rd. Croydon 379 J9
rd. Emerald 470 B17
st. Box Hill N 375 A7
st. Clematis 508 K3
st. Coburg N 282 A16
st. Dandenong 536 D9
st. Essendon N 279 D20
st. Mitcham 377 B18
st. Moorabbin 496 E7
st. Ringwood 378 K5
st. Tootgarook 698 G3
RONALDSAY
pl. Point Cook 450 H8
RONANS
rtn. Lynbrook 551 B17
RONCLIFFE
rd. Highton 701 H17
RONDE
ct. Healesville 257 F2
RONDELL
av. W Footscray 366 F7
RONDOR
cl. Westmeadows 236 H15
RONDU
pl. Eltham 288 A7
RONLEY
st. Blackburn 375 J20
RONLYN
st. Rosebud W 683 F19
RONSTON
ct. Wheelers Hl 461 C16
ROODING
st. Brighton 454 K13
ROOKE
ct. Sunshine W 364 F9
ROOKERY
rd. Point Cook 450 H9
ROOKS
rd. Mitcham 376 L15
rd. Nunawading 376 L15
rd. Vermont 376 L19
rd. Vermont 377 A19
rd. Vermont 420 L1
rd. Vermont 421 A1
ROOKWOOD
st. Balwyn N 373 F3
ROONEY
st. Maidstone 366 F1
st. Richmond 26 K20
st. Templstw Lr 330 E13
ROONEYS
la. Richmond 26 B13
ROOSEVELT
ct. Brighton East 495 E4
ct. Dingley Vill 532 L7
st. Coburg N 281 C17
ROPE
wk. Brunswick, off La Rose St 325 E9
ROPER
ct. Gladstone Pk 237 C19
ct. Taylors L 275 K2
pl. Doncaster E 332 E15
st. Moorabbin 496 J11
ROPLEY
av. Balwyn 372 L10
av. Balwyn 373 A10
gra. Frankston 599 F12
gra. Upwey 465 E10
RORY
ct. Lilydale 338 D12
ct. Werribee 446 L10
ct. Werribee 447 A10

ROSA
av. Springvale 500 C17
st. Scoresby 462 G7
st. Templstw Lr 330 F14
ROSALA
av. Altona North 409 G2
ROSALEEN
ct. Narre Warren 539 D19
ROSALIE
av. Cranbourne 578 A17
av. Dromana 686 G4
ct. Hampton Pk 551 K8
ct. Pakenham 584 H8
ct. Wantirna S 422 C17
rd. Mornington 657 B3
st. Springvale 500 A10
ROSALIND
cr. Blackburn 376 A19
st. Queenscliff 707 K19
ROSALINE
av. Mt Waverley 419 B18
ROSAMOND
av. Tarneit 405 A8
cr. Doncaster E 332 C20
rd. Footscray 366 L2
rd. Maidstone 322 L20
rd. Maidstone 323 A20
rd. Maribyrnong 322 L20
rd. Maribyrnong 323 A20
rd. Maribyrnong 366 L2
st. Balaclava 414 G18
ROSAMUNDE
st. Rye 696 E4
ROSANNA
ct. Badger Creek 258 E8
ct. Carnegie 456 K11
ct. Craigieburn 150 E15
rd. Heidelberg 329 A7
rd. Rosanna 329 A7
st. Carnegie 456 J10
ROSAPENNA
cl. Sunbury 144 F12
ROSCIUS
pl. Sorrento 679 B13
ROSCO
dr. Templestowe 332 A6
ROSCOE
ct. Noble Park N 501 E12
ROSCOMMON
pl. Herne Hill 702 A4
ROSCREA
ct. Werribee 447 C13
rd. Melton 226 J16
ROSDALE
pl. Sunshine 365 A3
ROSE
al. Melbourne 23 G8
av. Boronia 423 K12
av. Bulleen 330 A13
av. Croydon 380 C2
av. Dandenong N 501 G18
av. Glen Waverley 420 A20
av. Hurstbridge 202 L16
av. Hurstbridge 203 A16
av. Niddrie 322 K5
av. Rosebud 683 J17
av. Surrey Hills 374 A20
av. Surrey Hills 418 A1
av. Templstw Lr 330 A13
ct. Brighton 454 G20
ct. Croydon 379 K1
ct. Gowanbrae 279 D5
ct. Greenvale 237 C3
ct. Jacana 237 G16
ct. Lilydale 338 L9
ct. McCrae 684 K13
ct. Newcomb 703 L15
ct. Reservoir 282 H13
ct. Somerville 644 F13
ct. Sydenham 275 E9
ct. Thomastown 240 J16
dr. Doveton 536 G11
la. Cranbourne 578 C14
st. Altona 408 K20
st. Armadale 415 D10
st. Bentleigh 455 L19
st. Box Hill 375 A17
st. Braybrook 365 K1
st. Brighton 455 A11
st. Brunswick 325 B9
st. Burnley 26 K19
st. Burnside 318 G9
st. Clayton 498 L1
st. Clifton Hill 20 E3
st. Coburg 324 L4
st. Doncaster 374 J2
st. Essendon 323 L7
st. Fitzroy 19 A10
st. Frankston S 626 H7
st. Hawthorn E 372 F20
st. Highett 496 A14
st. Ivanhoe 328 B15
st. McKinnon 455 L17
st. Pascoe Vale 280 K10
st. Richmond 26 G19
st. Richmond 26 J19
st. Rosebud W 683 A19
st. Sandringham 495 F17
st. Sorrento 679 A11
st. Tecoma 466 E12
st. Up Fntree Gly 465 B7
ROSEBANK
av. Clayton S 499 B8
av. Ringwood N 378 E5
av. Strathmore 324 C2
ct. Rowville 463 L14
dr. Cranbourne N 578 E10
dr. Cranbourne N 578 F8
dr. Point Cook 451 B7
la. Beaconsfld Up 542 F13
tce. Templstw Lr 330 B14
ROSEBERRY
av. Brighton East 455 C16
av. Cairnlea 319 H14
av. Chelsea 546 H16
av. Keilor Dn 275 K14
av. Preston 282 L20
gr. Glen Huntly 456 B6
st. Ascot Vale 323 K17
st. Hawthorn E 372 E19
ROSEBERY
st. Altona Mdw 451 H1
ROSEBROOK
st. Rosebud 683 J18
ROSEBUD
av. Moorabbin 496 F9
av. Rosebud 700 H4
cr. Broadmeadows 237 G15
pde. Rosebud 684 C20
pde. Viewbank 285 G19
ROSEBUD-FLINDERS
rd. Boneo 699 H10
rd. Boneo 699 H17
rd. Rosebud 699 H10
rd. Rosebud W 699 H10
ROSEBURN
ct. Lower Plenty 286 E18
ROSEDALE
av. Glen Huntly 456 D7
cr. Dallas 238 F9
cr. Ringwood E 378 K11
ct. Endeavour Hl 537 F2
dr. Lalor 240 K10
gr. Frankston S 627 D20
gr. Frankston S 627 G16
gr. Frankston S 643 C1
gr. Ivanhoe 328 A11
pl. Wyndham Va 446 H11
rd. Glen Iris 417 B12
ROSE GARDENS
pl. Hoppers Csg 448 A1
ROSE GRANGE
bvd. Tarneit 405 A8
ROSE HEDGE
dr. Sydenham 275 C9
ROSEHILL
av. Caulfield N 455 G2
ct. Mill Park 242 K10
ct. Narre Warren 539 G14
ct. Noble Park N 501 B7
dr. Bacchus Msh 221 E13
rd. Essendon W 322 H5
rd. Essendon W 323 A5
rd. Keilor East 322 H5
rd. Lower Plenty 286 F18
rd. Lower Plenty 286 H18
rd. Niddrie 322 H5
rd. Niddrie 323 A5
st. Scoresby 462 H6
ROSELAND
cr. Hoppers Csg 448 E8
gr. Doncaster 331 B17
gr. Ivanhoe 328 D9
ROSELANDS
ct. Langwarrin 629 H3
gr. Bundoora 243 C13
ROSELEA
ct. Sunshine 321 E19
st. Box Hill N 375 C7
st. Caulfield S 455 H7
ROSELEIGH
bvd. Sydenham 275 B8
bvd. Sydenham 275 C8
ROSELILLIAN
ct. Warrandyte 332 H3
ROSELLA
av. Boronia 424 D11
av. Clarinda 498 C10
av. Werribee 447 L8
av. Werribee 448 A9
cr. Healesville 257 L1
ct. Blackburn S 419 K6
ct. Pearcedale 646 K4
ct. Westmeadows 236 J14
rd. Parkdale 531 G17
rd. Wesburn 347 D4
ri. Eltham North 287 B3
st. Doncaster E 375 K4
st. Frankston 599 C13
st. Murrumbeena 457 C8
tr. Frankston N 600 E11
wk. S Morang 243 K2
ROSELYN
cr. Bentleigh E 456 J18
cr. Boronia 423 C14
ROSEMAN
rd. Chirnside Pk 337 J3
ROSEMAR
cct. Viewbank 285 J19
ROSEMARY
av. Croydon Hl 335 G16
av. Springvale 499 L16
cl. Hoppers Csg 447 K3
cr. Frankston N 600 B10
ct. Berwick 580 C2
ct. Campbellfield 239 E11
ct. Carrum Downs 601 C5
ct. Mulgrave 460 A13
ct. Viewbank 285 K16
dr. Lalor 240 H5
gr. Glen Iris 417 L10
pl. Woori Yall 344 D15
rd. Beaumaris 530 C7
st. Chadstone 458 D4
st. Templstw Lr 330 H8
ROSEMONT
av. Caulfield N 455 F1
cr. Kalorama 382 L16
ct. Dandenong N 501 F19
dr. Bulleen 329 J8
dr. Narre Warren 553 D11
rd. Lilydale 295 B20
st. Surrey Hills 374 D18
wy. Roxburgh Pk 194 B6
ROSEMORE
st. Rosebud 684 G14
ROSEN
st. Blackburn S 419 K3
ROSENE
ct. Keysborough 534 G13
ROSENEATH
pl. S Melbourne 29 K2
st. Clifton Hill 20 E7
ROSEN FRASER
cl. Epping 197 H16
ROSENTHAL
cr. Reservoir 282 J3
ROSER
dr. Altona Mdw 451 D3
ROSETTA
av. Sorrento 679 D14
ROSETTI
la. Elwood 454 C3
ROSEVILLE
av. Blairgowrie 695 H1
av. Doncaster 331 A19
ROSEWALL
ct. Wantirna S 462 D5
pl. Clarinda 498 E7
pl. Greenvale 193 G18
st. Sunshine N 321 D14
ROSEWARNE
av. Cheltenham 496 L17
ROSEWIN
ct. Berwick 539 J17
ct. Carrum Downs 575 E14
ROSEWOOD
bvd. Lysterfield 464 C19
ct. Frankston 627 J9
ct. Grovedale 705 L15
ct. Mulgrave 500 J2
ct. Nar Warrn S 579 C2
la. Cairnlea 319 E7
pl. Chirnside Pk 336 G8
pl. Craigieburn 150 D14
pl. Tarneit 405 B11
ROSHERVILLE
pl. S Melbourne 29 F2
ROSICA
ct. Roxburgh Pk 194 C6
ROSIE
ct. Aspendale Gdn 547 C8
ROSINA
dr. Melton 268 E1
st. Bentleigh 496 E6
st. Rye 696 F9
ROSINE
ct. Doncaster 330 F17
ROSINGS
ct. Notting Hill 459 K12
ROSLYN
av. Rye 696 G1
ct. Dandenong N 502 A10
ct. Donvale 376 K3
ct. Eltham North 287 C4
rd. Belmont 701 F18
rd. Cranbourne S 602 J15
rd. Highton 701 F18
st. Brighton 454 L20
st. Brighton 455 A20
st. Brighton 494 L4
st. Brighton 495 A4
st. Burwood 418 C8
st. Montrose 381 J10
st. Mt Martha 655 J19
st. Newport 410 K9
st. Rye 697 B15
st. Somerville 645 B15
st. Strathmore 279 L16
ROSLYN PARK
dr. Melton W 226 F10
ROSNEY
pl. Torquay 712 D4
st. Hawthorn, off Evansdale Rd 371 G17
ROSNY
pl. Mooroolbark 381 H3
pl. Williamstown 411 D14
st. Port Melb 412 D4
ROSS
av. The Basin 425 E11
cr. Heathmont 378 F19
cr. Skye 575 J17
ct. Brookfield 268 C3
ct. Mill Park 242 D4
ct. Mt Waverley 459 F8
ct. Niddrie 279 B19
ct. Springvale 500 C17
ct. Sunbury 143 D8
ct. Yallambie 286 D11
pl. S Melbourne 29 L2
rd. Altona North 409 G9
rd. Croydon 379 F5
rd. Gruyere 341 J4
st. Alphington 327 H15
st. Aspendale 546 E8
st. Belgrave 466 E16
st. Bentleigh 456 D19
st. Coburg 281 G19
st. Dandenong 536 E8
st. Doncaster E 375 G2
st. Elsternwick 454 K5
st. Ferntree Gly 463 G3
st. Heatherton 532 E2
st. Huntingdale 458 E14
st. Kew 372 H14
st. Mitcham 377 A17
st. Mornington 640 E12
st. Newport 410 K5
st. Niddrie 279 B20
st. Northcote 326 J20
st. Port Melb 412 H4
st. Port Melb 412 J4
st. Reservoir 282 D1
st. St Albans 320 D6
st. S Melbourne 3 A17
st. S Melbourne 30 A1
st. S Melbourne 413 F1
st. Surrey Hills 373 K14
st. Tecoma 466 D11
st. Toorak 415 B6
ROSSACK
dr. Grovedale 705 G12
dr. Waurn Ponds 705 G12
ROSSCOMMON
pl. Seabrook 450 L4
ROSSDALE
ct. Glen Waverley 420 F15
st. Craigieburn 150 H16
st. Oakleigh E 458 L15
ROSSEAU
st. Williamstown 411 G15
ROSSER
st. Brunswick 325 F13
ROSSERDALE
cr. Mt Eliza 625 J13
ROSSETTI
ct. Pakenham 584 D4
ROSSFIELD
av. Kew 372 B13
ROSS GREGORY
dr. Albert Park 414 A11
dr. St Kilda 414 A11
ROSSHIRE
rd. Newport 410 E10
ROSSI
st. Ivanhoe 328 B11
ROSSITER
av. Endeavour Hl 537 G9
av. Roxburgh Pk 194 C13
av. Roxburgh Pk 194 C16
ct. Rowville 464 B11
ct. Seaford 573 H20
rd. Carrum Downs 574 F11
ROSSLARE
ct. Hoppers Csg 405 E18
pde. St Albans 320 H7
ROSSLYN
av. Seaford 599 D10
ct. Seaford 599 D11
st. Blackburn S 419 K1
st. Hawthorn E 416 D
st. W Melbourne 23
ROSSMITH
av. Beaumaris 530 G
ROSSMOYNE
st. Thornbury 326 K
ROSS PINCOTT
dr. Mooroolbark 337 B1
ROSS SMITH
av. Frankston 599 B
ROSSTOWN
rd. Carnegie 456
ROSSTREVOR
cr. Mitcham 377 A1
ROSTELLA
av. Wheelers Hl 460 H1
cr. Keilor East 321
ROSTILL
ct. Toorak 415
ROSTO
ct. Tullamarine 236 J
ROSTRATA
vw. Mill Park 243 D
ROSTREVOR
pde. Mont Albert 374 D
pde. Mont Albert N 374 D
ROSTRON
wy. Roxburgh Pk 193 L
ROSWELL
st. Glen Waverley 460
ROSYTH
rd. Rye 697
ROTARY
ct. Box Hill S 418
dr. Keilor East 322
ROTHAN
av. Boronia 424
ROTHBURY
ct. Wantirna 422 F
ROTHERHAM
st. Belmont 702 B
ROTHERWOOD
av. Mitcham 377
av. Ringwood E 379 D
cl. Wantirna 422 E
dr. Malvern East 457
pl. Lilydale 338 K
rd. Ivanhoe East 328 E
st. Richmond 26 A
ROTHESAY
av. Brighton 454 G
av. Elwood 454
av. Malvern East 416 H
av. Mornington 640 K
ct. Noble Park N 501 E
ct. Templestowe 332 C
pl. Greenvale 193 A
pl. Melton W 226 A
ROTHRAY
av. Sunshine N 321 C
ROTHSAY
av. Burwood 418
la. Melbourne 2 B
la. Melbourne 24 D
ROTHSBY
wy. Greenvale 193 G
ROTHSCHILD
st. Caulfield S 456
st. Glen Huntly 456
ROTHWELL
ct. Epping 197 H
ct. Mitcham 377 H
st. Ascot Vale 324 F
ROTOROA
ct. Taylors L 276 E
ROTORUA
st. Caulfield S 455
ROUEN
rd. Cockatoo 511
st. Hampton 495
ROUGET
rd. Wandin East 341 E
ROUKE
st. Lilydale 337
ROULSTON
ct. Noble Park N 501
ROUNDHAY
ct. Berwick 554
ROUND TOWER
rd. Dandenong S 550
ROURKE
la. Kensington 33
st. Bayswater 423
ROUSE
st. Cranbourne 577
st. Port Melb 412
ROUSSAC
ct. Sunshine N 321
ROUT
st. Cremorne 25

VER
Keilor Dn ...276 C12
Sunbury ...142 F11
W
Portsea ...677 K1
WALLAN
Harkaway ...540 H10
Harkaway ...541 A9
Balwyn N ...374 B4
Doncaster E ...332 D20
WAN
Bentleigh E ...496 H4
Boronia ...424 J11
Brooklyn ...365 F18
The Basin ...424 J11
Belmont ...706 D7
Carrum Downs ...600 K1
Frankston N ...600 F9
Mt Waverley ...459 G4
Doveton ...536 H8
Kealba ...276 K17
Kealba ...276 L18
Kealba ...277 A18
Bayswater ...423 E5
Dingley Vill ...533 G7
Springvale S ...533 H6
Croydon ...380 C8
Doncaster E ...331 J17
Elsternwick ...455 A6
Glenroy ...279 L3
Preston ...326 D4
Vermont ...421 J2
WANS
Port Melb, off Lalor St ...412 L4
Highett ...496 F13
Moorabbin ...496 G11
WAN TREE
Viewbank ...285 L18
WCROFT
Lynbrook ...551 F19
WDON
Aspendale Gdn ...547 B5
WE
Avondale Ht ...322 F9
Alphington ...327 K18
Fitzroy N ...19 H3
Maribyrnong ...323 A20
Montrose ...381 L19
WELL
Camberwell ...416 J7
Melton S ...268 H11
Taylors L ...233 A18
Rosanna ...285 C20
WELLYN
Carrum Downs ...601 E1
WEN
Cranbourne N ...578 G9
Glen Iris ...417 H12
Thomastown ...242 A14
WENA
Keysborough ...534 F10
e. Richmond ...26 A12
Mt Martha ...656 E9
Malvern East ...457 H4
Wantirna S ...422 C20
Caulfield N ...415 J20
WERN
Box Hill N ...375 E12
WES
Werribee ...446 K9
Werribee ...447 A11
WITTA
Glen Waverley ...420 C16
WLAND
Ivanhoe East ...328 F16
Hampton Pk ...551 E4
Ferntree Gly ...464 B7
Glen Waverley ...419 L16
Wonga Park ...336 C8
Point Cook ...449 L6
Bentleigh E ...496 K7
Kew ...372 F12
Mont Albert ...374 F16
WLANDS
Noble Park ...534 D3
Blairgowrie ...679 E18
WLANDSON
Taylors L ...233 C17
WSLEY
Mt Eliza ...625 H19
WSLEY-EXFORD
Maddingley ...263 A13
Parwan ...264 A20
Parwan ...264 G20
Parwan ...265 B20
Parwan ...265 J20
WSLEY STATION
Maddingley ...263 A13
WSON
Altona Mdw ...451 G5
Clarinda ...498 H12

rd. Chum Creek ...212 G6
st. Boronia ...423 L11
ROXANNE
cl. Scoresby ...462 G8
pl. Newcomb ...704 D18
ROXBURGH
ct. Epping ...197 L17
rd. Wantirna ...422 J8
st. Ascot Vale ...324 A17
st. Preston ...326 K6
ROXBURGH PARK
dr. Roxburgh Pk ...193 L13
ROXBY
cl. Eltham ...287 L10
ct. Berwick ...553 L2
st. Epping ...241 D3
st. Manifold Ht ...702 C3
ROXLEY
pl. Mulgrave ...501 G3
ROXY
cl. Berwick ...554 K20
mw. Deer Park ...318 K13
ROY
cl. Nar Warrn N ...539 B12
ct. Boronia ...423 D12
ct. Keysborough ...534 L11
ct. Mt Eliza ...626 A16
rd. Olinda ...427 E17
st. Donvale ...376 E5
st. Geelong ...702 K5
st. Geelong ...702 L5
st. Glenroy ...280 E2
st. Melbourne ...31 C15
st. Melbourne ...414 B8
st. Oakleigh E ...458 J16
ROYA
ct. Hoppers Csg ...449 D2
ct. Mt Martha ...656 L10
ROYADIE
rd. Blairgowrie ...695 L5
ROYAL
arc. Melbourne ...2 B13
arc. Melbourne ...24 C8
av. Bonbeach ...573 C2
av. Essendon N ...279 G20
av. Glen Huntly ...456 C9
av. Heathmont ...378 L16
av. Heathmont ...379 A16
av. Mooroolbark ...337 F18
av. Portsea ...678 A2
av. Sandringham ...495 D17
av. Springvale ...499 J15
av. Wandin East ...341 A19
cr. Armadale ...415 F11
cr. Camberwell ...372 K19
cr. Hillside ...232 A19
cr. Hillside ...232 A20
cr.e, Officer ...555 F19
cr.w, Officer ...555 F19
ct. Ivanhoe ...328 A9
ct. Jan Juc ...711 D17
ct. Mt Waverley ...418 H14
ct. Nar Warrn S ...578 D3
ct. Seabrook ...450 L3
dr. Bangholme ...549 K14
la. Fitzroy ...18 L19
la. Melbourne ...2 G13
la. Melbourne ...24 E6
la. Surrey Hills ...374 C20
pde. Carlton N ...17 K7
pde. Caulfield S ...455 E6
pde. Emerald ...469 L20
pde. Emerald ...509 L1
pde. Melbourne ...17 J15
pde. Parkdale ...531 G15
pde. Parkville ...17 J15
pde. Pascoe Vale S ...324 L4
pde. Reservoir ...283 A9
pl. Cremorne ...26 E17
pl. S Morang ...198 L13
rd. Bonbeach ...573 C2
rd. Croydon S ...379 J12
st. Mornington ...640 D13
st. Up Fntree Gly ...465 F9
tce. Craigieburn ...150 C7
tce. Highett ...496 E12
ROYAL CHARLOTTE
dr. Patterson L, off Harbour Dr ...547 H19
ROYALDEN
cl. Boronia ...424 J8
ROYAL MELBOURNE
bvd. Burwood ...418 B4
ROYAL OAKS
dr. Tarneit ...405 A11
ROYAL PALMS
bvd. Aspendale Gdn ...547 B5
ROYAL PARK
av. Caroline Spr ...274 C17
ROYAL PINES
pl. Burwood ...418 B4

ROYAL TROON
av. Heatherton ...497 H16
pl. Heatherton ...497 H16
ROYALTY
av. Highett ...496 E16
st. Clayton ...458 L18
ROYAN
mw. Point Cook ...450 F11
ROYCLIFF
ct. Box Hill N ...374 H9
ROYCROFT
av. Aspendale ...546 D8
av. Burnside ...318 E8
av. Highton ...705 K3
av. Mill Park ...242 E8
av. Wantirna S ...422 D20
cl. Glen Waverley ...461 A5
ct. Endeavour Hl ...503 L20
rd. Roxburgh Pk ...194 A7
ROYDEN
rd. Warrandyte ...334 E6
ROYD GRANGE
ct. Belmont ...702 E17
ROYDON
st. Hampton E ...495 J7
ROYENA
ct. Warranwood ...334 K12
rd. Moorabbin ...496 J9
ROYLE
av. Kallista ...467 C2
st. Frankston ...599 H19
ROYLSTON
ri. Hurstbridge ...203 D14
ROYMAR
ct. Wonga Park ...336 D8
ROYSTON
av. Berwick ...554 D2
av. Malvern East ...416 C16
cl. Mill Park ...242 F10
ct. Boronia ...423 H14
ct. Brookfield ...268 B6
ct. Carrum Downs ...601 F1
ct. Kew ...372 H9
ct. Mt Eliza ...641 D4
pl. Caroline Spr ...318 C5
pl. Gladstone Pk ...237 C19
pl. Melbourne ...2 D18
pl. Melbourne ...24 E10
st. Diamond Ck ...246 B13
st. Viewbank ...285 J20
ROYTON
st. Burwood E ...419 G7
ROZELLE
av. Ringwood E ...379 F14
ROZZY
pde. Narre Warren ...539 D16
RUA
ct. Oakleigh ...458 C7
RUABON
rd. Toorak ...415 B8
RUAIRI
ct. Kurunjang ...226 G14
RUBBER
la. Carrum Downs ...574 J14
RUBEN
dr. Sydenham ...274 J7
RUBENS
ct. Grovedale ...705 J15
ct. Scoresby ...462 C8
ct. Wheelers Hl ...461 A15
gr. Canterbury ...372 L16
gr. Canterbury ...373 A16
pl. Templestowe ...332 B9
RUBEO
dr. Altona Mdw ...451 F3
RUBICON
av. Taylors Hill ...274 K13
cr. Doncaster ...375 E2
ct. Hallam ...538 B20
ct. Sunbury ...143 C11
pl. Epping ...198 A20
pl. Werribee ...448 C20
st. Dallas ...238 C10
st. Reservoir ...283 D14
RUBICON VALLEY
Montrose ...381 L18
RUBIDA
ct. Boronia ...424 E14
ct. Endeavour Hl ...536 J1
dr. Langwarrin ...629 K4
pl. St Albans ...320 L8
RUBINA
ct. Noble Park N ...501 D17
RUBUS
ct. Meadow Ht ...193 J20
RUBY
cl. Rowville ...503 B7
ct. Lalor ...240 H6
ct. Meadow Ht ...237 J5
pl. Berwick ...554 J6
pl. Dingley Vill ...533 A4
pl. Werribee ...447 H9
pl. Springvale, off Eighth Bvd ...500 B13
rd. Montrose ...381 L13
st. Balwyn ...373 D9
st. Burwood E ...420 A9
st. Donvale ...376 K5
st. Essendon W ...322 L7
st. Hawthorn ...371 K16
st. Ormond ...455 L14
st. Preston ...327 D3
RUBY JOY
dr. Somerville ...645 C17
RUCKER
st. Northcote ...326 F19
RUDA
st. Doncaster ...374 D2
RUDD
av. Torquay ...711 L11
RUDDUCK
la. Coldstream ...295 A7
st. Dromana ...685 E11
st. McCrae ...685 E11
RUDLOE
pl. Hampton Pk ...551 F4
RUDOLF
ct. Dingley Vill ...533 A6
ct. Ringwood N ...378 A5
RUDOLPH
st. Hoppers Csg ...448 L3
st. Hoppers Csg ...449 A3
RUDSTONE
bnd. Greenvale ...192 J18
RUDYARD
ct. Lilydale ...338 G13
st. Oakleigh S ...497 F3
RUE DE GARE
Wandin N ...340 K15
RUFFEY
st. Templestowe ...330 H7
st. Templstw Lr ...330 H7
RUFFINS
la. Geelong West ...702 J6
RUFFLES
cl. Nar Warrn S ...552 G15
ct. Cranbourne W ...577 F17
RUFFORD
st. Sunshine N ...321 D15
RUFFY
dr. Cranbourne ...578 B18
RUFUS
ct. Narre Warren ...539 D20
st. Epping ...197 E20
RUGBY
ct. Doncaster E ...332 B17
ct. Mt Eliza ...625 L20
rd. Hughesdale ...457 H8
st. Belmont ...706 D1
RUHBANK
av. Balwyn ...373 C13
RULE
cl. Mill Park ...243 B4
st. Richmond ...26 F7
RULLA
ct. Ferntree Gly ...464 A7
RUMANN
av. Scoresby ...462 H7
RUMBRIAH
rt. St Albans ...321 B6
RUMPF
av. Balwyn N ...374 A3
RUNCORN
cr. Deer Park ...319 B13
RUNDELL
wy. Pakenham ...584 D2
RUNDLE
dr. Carrum Downs ...575 E14
dr. Carrum Downs ...575 E15
RUNNYMEDE
la. Brookfield ...267 J9
rd. Belgrave ...466 E18
st. Doncaster E ...331 L17
st. Mt Waverley ...419 A13
RUNYAN
ct. Ringwood N ...378 D2
RUPERT
ct. Broadmeadows ...238 C20
ct. Thomastown ...241 J14
dr. Mulgrave ...500 J4
st. Brunswick E ...326 B15
st. Collingwood ...25 K2
st. Doncaster E ...376 B2
st. Elsternwick ...455 D10
st. Highett ...496 B13
st. Mitcham ...377 E15
st. Newport ...411 C8
st. Parkdale ...531 H12
st. Ringwood ...378 H9
st. W Footscray ...366 D7
RUPERTSDALE
rd. Sunbury ...144 F6
RUPERTSWOOD
dr. Brookfield ...267 J8
ri. Nar Warrn S ...578 J1

RUPICOLA
ct. Hillside ...274 B2
ct. Rowville ...502 D5
RUSDEN
st. Brighton ...454 J6
st. Elsternwick ...454 J6
RUSH
ct. Altona ...408 L15
pl. Carlton ...18 D18
pl. Warrandyte ...333 A1
RUSHALL
cr. Fitzroy N ...326 F20
st. Fairfield ...327 F17
RUSHCLIFFE
ct. Frankston ...599 J15
RUSHDALE
ct. Kings Park ...319 B1
ct. Mill Park ...243 E7
st. Knoxfield ...463 D7
RUSHFORD
la. Werribee ...447 J15
RUSHMEAD
st. Malvern ...415 L17
RUSHWOOD
dr. Craigieburn ...194 L4
RUSHWORTH
st. Watsonia ...285 F5
RUSKIN
av. Croydon ...380 G5
cl. Templestowe ...332 A12
ct. Bundoora ...242 H17
ct. Eltham ...288 A10
ct. Glen Iris ...417 C8
rd. Glen Iris ...417 C9
st. Elwood ...454 C3
RUSS
ct. Wantirna S ...423 A11
RUSSDANN
ct. Springvale S ...533 L1
RUSSEL
st. Sunshine ...365 C2
RUSSELL
av. Anglesea ...713 D3
av. Berwick ...554 E6
av. Mooroolbark ...337 G18
cr. Boronia ...423 D14
cr. Doncaster E ...376 D4
cr. Mt Waverley ...459 B5
cr. Sorrento ...678 K12
ct. Altona Mdw ...451 H5
ct. Brookfield ...268 A7
ct. Dandenong S ...536 C15
ct. Mentone ...530 J6
ct. Woori Yall ...344 H13
la. Newcomb ...704 B15
pl. Melbourne ...2 H13
pl. Melbourne ...24 F6
pl. Williamstown ...411 D12
rd. Hawthorn E ...372 G20
rd. Seville ...341 H15
rd. Warrandyte ...290 D20
st. Abbotsford ...20 B20
st. Brunswick ...325 E13
st. Bulleen ...329 L9
st. Camberwell ...372 L18
st. Campbellfield ...239 A9
st. Caulfield S ...455 H12
st. Coburg ...325 H3
st. Cranbourne ...604 F4
st. Darley ...222 B9
st. Emerald ...509 D4
st. Essendon ...324 A9
st. Greensbrgh ...286 A10
st. Ivanhoe ...328 C16
st. McCrae ...684 L15
st. Melbourne ...2 J17
st. Melbourne ...2 J20
st. Melbourne ...24 E2
st. Mt Evelyn ...339 H16
st. Newtown ...702 H11
st. Northcote ...327 C17
st. Nunawading ...376 E14
st. Prahran ...414 L11
st. Preston ...282 J18
st. Springvale ...500 D8
st. Surrey Hills ...374 B20
st. Toorak ...415 J8
st. Tootgarook ...698 B3
st. Werribee ...447 H19
st. W Footscray ...366 H8
RUSSELL DRYSDALE
pl. Diamond Ck ...245 A13
RUSSELLS
pl. Hawthorn E ...372 E18
RUSSELTON
st. Keilor Park ...278 B14
RUSSET
ct. Keysborough ...534 K11
ct. Lalor ...241 A5
rd. Ringwood E ...379 A12
RUSSETT
ct. Frankston ...628 C8

RUSSIA
mw. Lilydale 337 L1
RUSSLIE
ct. Glen Waverley 460 G11
RUSSO
pl. Kilsyth 381 B6
RUSTIC
ct. Thomastown 240 F17
dr. Bangholme 549 K14
dr. Boronia 424 E7
ri. Croydon N 336 A17
ri. Nar Warrn N 538 D10
RUTH
av. Sorrento 678 K8
ct. Bayswater 422 L8
ct. Glen Waverley 460 K5
ct. Melton S 268 J4
ct. Newcomb 704 E14
ct. Springvale S 499 F18
rd. Mornington 656 E3
st. Balwyn N 373 H1
st. Donvale 376 E5
st. Lalor 241 H10
st. St Albans 319 J2
st. Sunshine N 321 D16
RUTHERFORD
ct. Maddingley 263 C7
pde. Warneet 649 D15
pde. Warneet 649 G11
rd. Seaford 573 L19
rd. Tecoma 466 A11
rd. Viewbank 285 H20
wy. Roxburgh Pk 194 A13
RUTHERGLEN
cr. Gowanbrae 279 C4
ct. Rowville 463 K12
rd. Vermont S 421 E9
st. Noble Park 534 G5
wy. Taylors L 276 C7
RUTHVEN
cl. Hillside 232 G18
cr. Lalor 241 G7
st. Launching Pl 345 H17
st. Macleod 284 J16
st. Newtown 702 B7
st. Rosanna 284 J16
st. Sunbury 143 F8
wy. Ringwood E 379 E7
RUTLAND
av. Mt Eliza 625 J15
av. Templestowe 331 F7
ct. Keysborough 534 A8
rd. Berwick 554 F7
rd. Box Hill 374 L15
st. Braybrook 366 B4
st. Clifton Hill 20 D9
st. Newtown 702 G13
st. Niddrie 278 J20
RUTLEDGE
la. Melbourne 2 H18
la. Melbourne 24 G9
RUTMAN
cl. Werribee 447 L6
RUTTER
av. Healesville 213 K18
RUVINA
st. Aspendale 546 B2
RUXTON
wy. Hopetoun Park 266 B8
RUYTON
ct. Sunbury 144 F10
dr. Rosebud W 698 L4
dr. Rosebud W 699 A4
st. Burwood 417 G6
st. Camberwell 417 G6
RYALL
ct. Doncaster 331 F18
RYAN
cl. Hoppers Csg 448 C2
ct. Bacchus Msh 221 L13
ct. Berwick 554 H12
ct. Ferntree Gly 463 K7
ct. Melton 268 K1
ct. Sunshine N 321 F18
gr. Blackburn S 419 K4
la. Altona 409 A18
la. Caroline Spr 318 B5
mw. Dingley Vill 533 C2
pl. Geelong, off Myers St 703 A9
rd. Delahey 275 D11
rd. Pakenham 585 K12
rd. Seville E 343 C10
st. Brunswick E 326 B13
st. Coburg 281 F19
st. Diamond Ck 245 J8
st. Footscray 367 F7
st. Northcote 326 E15
st. Reservoir 282 H3
st. Seaford 600 A1

RYANS
la. Melton 227 L17
la. N Melbourne 17 E17
la. Toolern Va 228 A3
la. Williamstown 411 G14
rd. Belgrave Ht 505 K3
rd. Belgrave S 505 J11
rd. Clayton S 498 J13
rd. Diamond Ck 245 E17
rd. Eltham 287 D8
rd. Eltham North 245 E17
rd. Eltham North 287 D2
rd. Healesville 213 C14
rd. Lysterfield 505 J11
rd. St Helena 245 E17
RYBURNE
av. Ashburton 417 C20
RYDAL
pl. Wheelers Hl 460 J16
RYDALDENE
wy. Berwick 554 E4
RYDE
av. Mt Eliza 625 K17
st. Preston 326 C5
RYDEN
cl. Greensbrgh 244 E16
RYDER
ct. Doncaster E 332 H10
ct. Frankston 628 F5
ct. Mt Waverley 458 L9
ct. Rowville 463 L11
pl. Sunshine 365 E4
st. Lalor 241 B9
st. Niddrie 279 A20
st. Niddrie 322 L2
st. Niddrie 323 A2
st. Noble Park 501 D20
st. Sunshine W 364 K4
RYE
ct. Delahey 275 A13
ct. Glen Waverley 420 F15
st. Box Hill N 375 B6
st. Dallas 238 C9
st. Mitcham 377 D10
RYEBURNE
av. Hawthorn E 372 H16
RYECROFT
ct. Noble Park N 501 B12
ct. Vermont 421 B5
st. Brunswick W 324 J11
RYEFIELD
ct. Diamond Ck 246 A7
RYELANDS
dr. Berwick 553 D1
dr. Narre Warren 539 C20
dr. Narre Warren 553 D1
RYE OCEAN BEACH
rd. Rye 697 C15
RYLAND
av. Croydon 379 G1
cct. Delahey 275 C11
pl. Thomastown 240 G11
st. Ashburton 417 F14
st. Coburg N 281 F15
RYLANDES
dr. Gladstone Pk 236 K17
RYLANDS
pl. Wantirna 422 H8
rd. Dandenong 535 G4
RYLETT
ct. Frankston S 627 H16
RYLIE
la. Maribyrnong 322 J15
RYLSTON
ct. Mt Eliza 642 G1
RYLSTONE
st. Ferntree Gly 424 J19
RYMER
av. Safety Bch 669 D17
RYMILL
ct. Altona North 409 G3
RYONG
st. Grovedale 706 E15
RYRIE
ct. Lilydale 338 J8
ct. Montmorency 286 K11
la. Melbourne 1 J17
la. Melbourne 24 B10
pl. Vermont S 420 L13
pl. Wheelers Hl 461 G18
st. E Geelong 702 K7
st. Geelong 702 K7
st. Geelong 703 A8
st. Healesville 257 G1
RYTHDALE
ct. Glen Waverley 460 L4

S

SABASON
ct. Doncaster E 332 F20
SABATO
st. Croydon 380 J1
st. Rye 696 J10
SABINE
av. Dandenong N 501 H14
SABO
pl. Mt Martha 657 B9
SABOT
ct. Taylors L 275 H7
SABRE
ct. Ferntree Gly 463 G7
ct. Narre Warren 553 C12
ct. Tullamarine 236 H20
pl. Point Cook 450 E4
wy. S Morang 199 B10
SACHIKO
pl. Berwick 553 K17
SACKVILLE
st. Collingwood 19 G13
st. Heidelberg Ht 328 D4
st. Kew 372 E12
st. Mernda 198 L1
st. Montmorency 286 L14
st. Safety Bch 668 L18
SACRAMENTO
av. Coburg 281 L20
SACRAS
ct. Sydenham 275 A4
SADDLE
cr. Cranbourne E 578 K19
SADDLEBACK
rdg. Chirnside Pk 337 H6
SADDLERS
ct. Epping 198 D18
la. Geelong, off Mercer St 702 K3
SADIE
ct. Noble Park 535 D1
st. Glenroy 280 J4
st. Mt Waverley 458 J6
SADLER
ct. Dingley Vill 533 A3
st. Williamstown 410 L14
SAFFRON
ct. Burwood E 420 B10
dr. Hallam 538 C16
dr. Narre Warren 538 C16
dr. Narre Warren 538 G17
st. Newtown 702 H10
SAGAMORE
ct. Caulfield N 415 D17
SAGAN
ct. Glen Waverley 420 A15
SAGE
av. St Albans 321 A5
cl. Hillside 231 K18
ct. Langwarrin 601 J16
dr. Frankston S 627 B10
pl. Rowville 502 H4
st. Oakleigh E 458 G12
st. Pascoe Vale 280 L11
SAGES
rd. Baxter 643 G2
rd. Frankston S 643 G2
rd. Glenroy 281 D4
SAGOE
la. Box Hill 375 C15
SAGRAMORE
ct. Glen Waverley 420 L16
SAHARA
ct. Portsea 678 B4
SAHRA
ct. Epping 198 A15
SAINSBURY
av. Greensbrgh 285 L7
av. Hillside 274 D3
ct. Greenvale 237 C6
ST AGNES
cl. Craigieburn 194 A2
ct. Avondale Ht 322 D9
ct. Carrum Downs 601 C4
ct. Glenroy 280 C5
ST ALBANS
rd. Breakwater 703 F13
rd. E Geelong 703 F13
rd. Kealba 276 K16
rd. Keilor 277 A11
rd. St Albans 320 D7
rd. Sunshine N 320 G12
rd. Thomson 703 F13
st. Mt Waverley 419 B19
ST AMBROSE
gr. Lilydale 338 K2
gr. Lilydale 339 C6
ST ANDREW
st. Sunshine W 364 J4

ST ANDREWS
av. Rosanna 285 A19
av. Rosebud 700 L2
cl. Carrum Downs 575 C15
cl. Croydon 380 J7
cr. Bulleen 329 F12
ct. Black Rock 529 G1
ct. Burwood 418 B4
ct. Chirnside Pk 292 H9
ct. Eltham North 245 D20
ct. Mt Waverley 458 J10
ct. Nar Warrn S 552 E20
ct. Rowville 502 B1
ct. Sunbury 144 E14
dr. Chirnside Pk 337 H5
dr. Craigieburn 193 K2
dr. Heatherton 497 H16
dr. Jan Juc 711 F13
dr. Rye 696 H5
dr. Sunshine N 321 H16
dr. Werribee 446 J17
pl. E Melbourne 24 L5
pl. E Melbourne 25 A5
rd. Bayswater 423 D10
rd. Panton Hill 248 A8
st. Brighton 454 H17
st. N Melbourne 17 F19
st. Queenscliff 709 A19
wy. Darley 221 H1
ST ANDRIES
st. Camberwell 417 B7
ST ANNES
cr. Berwick 554 F19
ST ANNS
ct. Hoppers Csg 405 C19
ST ANTHONY
ct. Seabrook 450 H5
ST ANTHONYS
pl. Kew 371 L11
ST AUBIN
st. Beaumaris 530 G9
ST AUBINS
av. Caulfield N 415 B20
wy. Sorrento 678 J6
ST AUSTELL
ct. Craigieburn 194 H4
ct. Croydon Hl 335 G16
rd. Belgrave S 506 G5
ST BERNARDS
cr. Lynbrook 551 G18
ct. Wantirna S 422 L19
ct. Wantirna S 423 A19
dr. Keilor East 322 H5
rd. Alphington 327 L19
ST BOSWELLS
av. Berwick 554 C19
ST BRIDGETS
ri. Balwyn N 374 C5
ST CATHERINES
ct. Mornington 657 A2
dr. Highton 701 F20
la. Toorak 415 F4
ST CLAIR
av. Point Cook 450 E11
bvd. Roxburgh Pk 194 A13
cr. Mt Waverley 419 H19
rd. Wantirna S 422 L10
rd. Wantirna S 423 A10
ST CLAIRE
av. S Morang 198 K15
wk. Doncaster E 332 B18
ST CLEMS
rd. Doncaster E 376 C6
st. Eltham North 245 C20
st. St Helena 245 B19
ST CLERE
ct. Frankston 628 F2
ST CLOUD
ct. Highton 701 H9
ct. Mt Waverley 458 J9
ST COLUMBS
st. Hawthorn 372 B18
ST CRISPIN
st. Richmond 26 G17
ST CUTHBERTS
av. Dingley Vill 533 D9
ST DAVID
st. Fitzroy 19 C15
st. Northcote 326 L12
st. Thornbury 326 L12
st. Thornbury 326 L9
ST DAVIDS
dr. Wantirna 422 F5
ST DENYS
cr. Wonga Park 291 J18
ST DUTHUS
st. Preston 282 F19
ST EDMONDS
gr. Glen Iris 416 F10
rd. Prahran 32 B20
rd. Prahran 414 G10

ST ELMO
av. Ferntree Gly 424
cr. Highton 701
pl. S Morang 198
rd. Ivanhoe 328
ST ELMOS
cl. Rosebud W 699
ST FAITHS
rd. Montmorency 286
ST FILLANS
ct. Frankston 628
ST FINBARS
cr. Brighton East 455
ST FORT
ct. Harkaway 540
ST GABRIELS
pl. Highton 701
ST GEORGE
av. Montrose 382
ct. Frankston 600
ST GEORGES
av. Bentleigh E 456
av. Caroline Spr 317
av. Caroline Spr 317
av. Mont Albert 374
av. Templestowe 331
av. Templstw Lr 331
cr. Ashburton 417
cr. Croydon 380
ct. Brighton East 455
ct. Glen Waverley 461
ct. Greensbrgh 244
ct. Highton 701
ct. Hoppers Csg 448
ct. Parkdale 531
ct. Toorak 415
ct. Fitzroy N, off St Georges Rd 326
gr. Parkville 34
rd. Armadale 415
rd. Beaconsfld Up 541
rd. Elsternwick 454
rd. Elsternwick 455
rd. Fitzroy N 19
rd. Fitzroy N 326
rd. Nar Warrn S 578
rd. Northcote 326
rd. Preston 326
rd. Thornbury 326
rd. Toorak 415
rd.s, Fitzroy N 19
ST GOTHARDS
rd. Alphington 327
ST HELENA
pl. Rowville 464
rd. Briar Hill 286
rd. Eltham North 245
rd. Greensbrgh 244
rd. Greensbrgh 286
rd. St Helena 244
rd. St Helena 245
ST HELENS
cr. Nar Warrn N 538
ct. Vermont 421
rd. Hawthorn E 416
ST HELIERS
st. Abbotsford 20
ST HELLIER
st. Heidelberg Ht 328
ST HUBERT
rd. Ivanhoe East 328
ST HUBERTS
rd. Carnegie 456
rd. Yering 253
ST IVES
av. Frankston S 627
ct. Croydon Hl 335
ct. The Basin 425
dr. Nar Warrn S 579
gr. Mt Martha 656
pl. Craigieburn 193
pl. Melton W 226
rd. Bentleigh E 456
ST JAMES
av. Bentleigh 456
av. Kallista 467
av. Mont Albert 374
av. Montrose 382
av. Springvale 499
cl. Brighton 454
cr. Mt Eliza 641
ct. Blackburn S 419
ct. Doncaster E 332
ct. Narre Warren 553
ct. Wantirna S 422
ct. Watsonia 285
la. Melbourne 1
la. Melbourne 23
mw. Brighton 454
pde. Elsternwick 455
pl. Kew 371
pl. Toorak 415
rd. Armadale 415

Heidelberg 328 J3
Heidelberg 329 A3
Rosanna 329 A3
Rosanna 329 C3
Geelong West 702 F6
Hadfield 281 B6
Moonee Pnd 324 A10
Hawthorn, off
Isabella Gr 371 E17
Caroline Spr 317 K3
JAMES PARK
Brighton 454 J13
Mooroolbark 381 D1
JAMES WOOD
Tarneit 405 D12
JOHN
Chirnside Pk 292 G10
Melton W 226 E17
Rowville 462 L17
Rowville 463 A17
Windsor 32 A20
Windsor 414 F10
JOHNS
Camberwell 416 K2
Croydon 380 F4
Frankston 627 G5
Mont Albert 374 E17
Springvale 499 J16
Narre Warren 553 D9
Reservoir 283 G2
Melbourne 1 H10
Melbourne 23 L7
Mt Eliza 626 D15
Toorak 415 A9
Kew 372 A11
N Melbourne 17 F17
Bulla 190 H8
Oaklands Jctn 190 H8
Warburton 349 E2
Wonga Park 335 G4
Caroline Spr 317 K1
Mulgrave 500 C5
JOHNS WOOD
Skye 575 G16
Blairgowrie 695 H3
Mt Waverley 418 K17
Berwick 554 C19
KILDA
Upwey 465 J9
Melbourne 2 E20
Melbourne 4 D19
Melbourne 24 G13
Melbourne 31 B8
Melbourne 413 L1
Prahran 31 B8
Prahran 414 C10
St Kilda 414 C10
Baxter 644 L3
Brighton 454 F15
Elwood 454 F15
Mt Eliza 642 C8
Taylors Hill 274 C9
KILIAN
Hampton 494 L5
KINNORD
Aberfeldie 323 F10
KYRILLOS
Hallam 538 E17
LAURENCE
Eltham 287 G8
LAURENT
Knoxfield 463 A8
LAWRANCE
Rowville 463 E16
LAWRENCE
Werribee 447 G6
LEGER
Epping 198 E18
Bundoora 284 E4
LEONARD
Pakenham 583 K1
LEONARDS
St Kilda 414 A16
Yarraville 366 H18
Yarraville 366 J18
Noble Park 534 C3
South Yarra 31 H1
South Yarra 370 D20
South Yarra 414 D1
St Kilda, off
St Leonards Av ..414 B15
Ascot Vale 323 J16
Healesville 213 L17
Selby 467 E16
LOUIS
Thomastown 240 E13
Burnley, off
Cherrill St 371 B20
LUKE
S Melbourne 30 B3
LUKES
Tarneit 405 C11

SAINTLY
gr. Berwick 553 J15
ST MALO
av. Doncaster 330 D17
st. Prahran 32 K20
st. Prahran 414 L10
SAINT MANGOS
la. Docklands 368 K14
ST MARGARETS
pl. Berwick 554 G10
rd. Healesville 258 E4
ST MARK
ct. Montrose 382 H7
ST MARKS
cl. Dingley Vill 533 E7
ST MARTINS
cl. Kooyong 415 L5
ct. Wantirna S 462 C5
la. South Yarra 31 E6
pl. S Morang 198 K13
pl. South Yarra 31 E5
ST MARYS
pl. Dromana 686 B9
ST MATTHEWS
la. Geelong, off
Walls St 703 D12
wy. Prahran 32 C19
ST MAXIMIN
ct. Nar Warrn S 578 K2
ST MICHAEL
dr. Tarneit 405 D12
ST MICHAELS
wk. Melbourne 2 L15
wk. Melbourne 24 G7
ST MICHEL
cl. Avondale Ht 322 C7
ST MITCHELL
cct. Mornington 641 D16
ST MUIR
dr. Warrandyte 332 K4
ST NEOTS
av. Northcote 326 J16
ST NICHOLAS
ct. Tarneit 405 D11
ST NINIANS
ct. Brighton 454 E14
rd. Brighton 454 E13
ST PATRICKS
al. Melbourne 1 H11
al. Melbourne, off
Little Bourke St 23 L7
pl. Lilydale 338 K2
pl. Lilydale 339 C6
pl. Tarneit 405 C11
ST PAULS
ct. Wantirna S 462 A4
rd. Sorrento 678 H14
ST PETER
ct. Tarneit 405 C12
ST PETERS
cl. Carrum Downs 575 D14
ct. Bentleigh E 497 A2
ST PHILLIP
st. Brunswick E 325 K17
ST PHILLIPS
pl. Box Hill N 374 L7
st. Abbotsford 20 D19
ST RAPHAEL
st. Avondale Ht 322 B9
ST REMO
pl. Dromana 686 H8
ST RONANS
ct. Eltham 287 C6
ct. Sunbury 144 F1
gr. S Morang 198 J11
rd. Glen Waverley 460 G9
SAINTSBURY
cr. Dandenong N 501 J13
ST SHENOUDA
ct. Hallam 538 E16
ct. Hallam 538 F16
ST THOMAS
av. Wantirna 422 E5
ST VIGEONS
rd. Reservoir 283 D5
ST VINCENT
pl. Albert Park 29 G10
pl. Albert Park 413 D5
pl.n, Albert Park 29 G9
pl.n, Albert Park 413 D5
pl.s, Albert Park 29 G10
pl.s, Albert Park 413 D5
st. Albert Park 29 C11
st. Albert Park 413 B6
st. Caulfield E 456 E5
wy. Caroline Spr 274 C16
ST VINCENTS
plz. E Melbourne 25 A2
plz. Fitzroy 25 A2
ST WARDEN
ct. Keilor Dn 275 L13
SALADIN
av. Glen Waverley 459 K7

SALAMANDER
av. Thomastown 240 H16
dr. Taylors L 275 G1
SALCOMBE
ct. Craigieburn 194 D2
SALDANNA
wy. Sorrento 679 B15
SALE
ct. Dallas 238 H8
SALEM
av. Oakleigh S 497 H2
ct. Vermont S 420 J7
SALERINO
ct. Point Cook 450 E9
SALERNO
wy. Rowville 502 H5
SALESIAN
ct. Sunbury 144 C9
SALFORD
av. Balwyn 373 E14
ct. Grovedale 706 F9
ct. Mulgrave 500 H1
la. Caroline Spr 317 J3
SALI
ct. Oakleigh S 497 K8
SALIBA
ct. Sunshine W 364 H8
SALICINA
ct. Endeavour Hl 502 K19
SALICKI
av. Epping 241 E4
SALIGNA
ct. Langwarrin 629 K1
dr. Tullamarine 278 C9
wk. Vermont S 420 L11
wk. Vermont S 421 A11
SALIGNUS
ct. Narre Warren 539 C20
SALINA
wk. Caroline Spr 318 B3
SALISBURY
av. Blackburn 375 E17
av. Cockatoo 511 D11
av. Ivanhoe 328 A16
av. Mont Albert 374 D16
bnd. Lilydale 338 K2
bnd. Lilydale 339 C6
cr. Fitzroy N 19 B2
ct. Glen Waverley 459 H10
ct. Heathmont 378 L19
ct. Heathmont 379 A19
ct. Hillside 231 J18
ct. Sydenham 274 J2
ct. Wantirna 422 G15
gr. Hawthorn 372 A14
gr. Northcote 326 K12
rd. Ashwood 418 C18
rd. Beaconsfld Up 542 G16
st. Balwyn 373 C14
st. Brighton 454 J6
st. Caulfield N 415 G18
st. Coburg 325 K3
st. Essendon N 279 F20
st. Glenroy 280 A4
st. Moonee Pnd 324 E10
st. Newport 410 H9
st. Richmond 26 G6
st. Sandringham 495 F13
st. Sunshine N 321 G13
st. Thomastown 241 J15
st. Up Fntree Gly 465 D7
st. Werribee 447 K15
st. Yarraville 366 L18
SALLY
cl. Mt Eliza 642 A9
cl. Wantirna S 422 C17
ct. Newcomb 704 E13
ct. Warranwood 334 J14
ct. Woori Yall 344 G13
SALLYBROOK
cct. Narre Warren 553 G8
SALLY FRANCIS
ct. Scoresby 462 C9
SALMON
av. Essendon 323 L3
rd. Boronia 423 F15
st. Mentone 530 L6
st. Mentone 531 A6
st. Port Melb 368 C18
SALMON BAY
Patterson L 573 G8
SALMOND
st. Deer Park 319 A12
SALONIKA
st. Sorrento 679 A12
SALSBURG
ct. Vermont S 421 C14
SALTA
dr. Altona North 408 J10
SALTAIR
ct. Berwick 554 H20
st. Hampton E 495 J10

SALTAIRE
la. Mornington 640 G20
SALTAU
st. Keilor East 322 C5
SALTBUSH
ct. Rowville 502 L2
ct. Sunshine W 364 D8
gld. Frankston 600 A16
st. Point Cook 450 K11
SALTER
st. Essendon 324 A5
SALTERS RUSH
rd. Smiths Gly 206 B5
SALTLEY
st. S Kingsville 410 E3
SALTMARSH
pl. Cairnlea 319 F6
SALTRAM
ct. Carrum Downs 575 D20
SALTWATER
cr. Maribyrnong 322 G16
SALUATORE
ct. Sunshine W 364 B8
SALURN
ct. Vermont S 420 L13
ct. Vermont S 421 A13
SALVANA
av. Mitcham 376 L10
ct. Taylors L 233 B19
SALVIA
ct. Rosebud 700 G2
ct. Warranwood 334 H14
st. St Albans 320 G8
SALWEEN
cr. Roxburgh Pk 194 D7
SAM
cl. Endeavour Hl 537 J2
SAMADA
st. Frankston 627 G4
st. Notting Hill 459 H13
SAMAHER
ct. Endeavour Hl 537 L1
SAMANTHA
cl. Wheelers Hl 461 C13
cr. Cranbourne N 578 H8
ct. Frankston 628 D9
ct. Knoxfield 463 C10
ct. Templestowe 331 J13
dr. Mornington 641 C17
SAMARA
gr. Gladstone Pk 279 A2
SAMARI
cl. Keilor 276 K13
SAMARIA
st. Dandenong N 501 H14
SAMARINDA
av. Ashburton 417 G16
SAMBELL
la. Parkdale 531 E13
st. Kensington 33 E11
wk. Kensington 33 E12
SAMBUCO
ct. Sydenham 274 J3
SAMOS
ct. Whittington 704 D19
SAMPSON
dr. Mt Waverley 459 C7
la. Melbourne 1 H6
la. Melbourne 23 K5
SAMS
wy. Toorak 32 L16
SAMSON
st. Hadfield 281 A7
SAMUEL
cl. Berwick 539 H19
cl. Mt Martha 656 C9
cl. Wheelers Hl 461 E12
ct. Bentleigh E 497 C2
ct. Bundoora 242 F19
ct. Werribee 447 K7
dr. Campbellfield 239 J12
la. Melbourne 1 H17
la. Melbourne 24 B10
rd. Blackburn S 419 G7
st. Blairgowrie 679 D18
st. Brunswick 325 K14
st. Croydon 336 A20
st. Ringwood 378 G10
wy. Mornington 657 D4
SAMUEL BEAVIS
pl. Croydon Hl 335 G15
SAMUEL EVANS
ct. Seabrook 450 L8
SAN ANGELO
rd. N Warrandyte 289 E11
SAN ANTONIO
ct. Mentone 531 C13
SAN CARLOS
wk. Croydon, off
Main St 380 B4
SANCTUARY
cl. Balwyn 373 H11
cl. Werribee 447 D18

ct. Lilydale 338 C13
dr. Bundoora 284 F8
pl. Aspendale Gdn 546 F2
pl. Templestowe 332 F2
ri. Mickleham 150 B1
ri. Narre Warren 538 G15
tce. S Morang 199 G10
wy. Beaconsfield 555 B12
wy. Beaconsfield 555 D13
SANCTUARY LAKES
bvd. Point Cook 450 K12
SANCTUARY LAKES SOUTH
bvd. Point Cook 451 A13
SANCTUARY PARK
dr. Rosebud W 699 C4
SANDALA
ct. Dandenong N 502 A18
SANDALONG
ct. Bonbeach 573 C5
SANDALWOOD
av. Hillside 232 E19
dr. Narre Warren 553 C2
dr. Oakleigh S 498 A8
dr. Pakenham 584 J10
gr. Carrum Downs 575 C16
rt. Frankston S 628 A17
SANDARA
ct. Mt Eliza 625 K12
SANDAY
st. Glen Waverley 460 G4
SAND DUNE
ri. Torquay 712 G1
SANDELLS
rd. Tecoma 466 C12
SANDEMAN
pl. Fitzroy 19 E17
SANDERLING
cr. Mornington 640 L16
ct. Rosebud W 699 F4
st. Werribee 448 A10
SANDERS
av. Sunshine W 364 K6
av. Sunshine W 365 A5
ct. Narre Warren 553 B11
pl. Richmond 26 F19
rd. Box Hill 375 C17
rd. Doncaster E 332 F19
rd. Frankston S 627 F11
rd. Frankston S 627 G11
SANDERSON
st. Yarraville 366 E15
SANDFIELD
dr. Carrum Downs 601 B2
SANDFORD
av. Sunshine N 320 L13
av. Sunshine N 321 A13
cl. Rowville 503 D7
ct. Meadow Ht 237 K5
gr. Yarraville 367 D16
st. Highett 496 F13
SANDGATE
av. Croydon 335 G18
av. Frankston 627 J7
av. Glen Waverley 459 H7
bvd. Ferntree Gly 463 E4
pl. Berwick 554 J8
rd. Blackburn S 419 H3
SANDHAM
ct. Elsternwick 455 B4
rd. Westmeadows 236 F14
st. Elsternwick 454 L4
st. Elsternwick 455 A4
SANDHURST
av. Doncaster E 331 H18
cr. Bundoora 284 K1
cr. Jan Juc 711 B19
ct. Eltham 245 K19
ct. Wheelers Hl 461 B7
gr. Warranwood 335 A13
mw. Hampton Pk 552 B11
rd. Wantirna 422 G13
tce. Mt Martha 656 K6
SANDILANDS
ct. Narre Warren 539 H15
st. S Melbourne 30 G7
st. S Melbourne 413 J4
SANDLEFORD
ct. Sunbury 142 F10
pl. Dingley Vill 533 B10
SANDLEWOOD
ct. Grovedale 706 C8
ct. Kings Park 275 D17
la. Point Cook 450 L10
SAN DOMINO
av. Point Cook 450 D9
SANDON
cct. Forest Hill 420 D2
SANDOVER
dr. Roxburgh Pk 194 C5
dr. Roxburgh Pk 194 D5
wy. Taylors L 233 G19
SANDOWEN
av. Burwood E 419 L11

SANDOWN
cl. Mill Park 242 L13
ct. Somerville 644 H14
rd. Ascot Vale 33 C1
rd. Ascot Vale 324 A20
rd. Springvale 500 A13
st. Brighton 454 E15
SANDPIPER
cl. Blind Bight 650 E8
cl. Chelsea Ht 547 F19
ct. Boronia 424 A11
ct. Rosebud W 699 E4
dr. Taylors L 275 H3
gr. Maribyrnong 322 H15
pl. Frankston 628 B2
pl. Williamstown 410 K17
st. Cairnlea 319 G9
st. Werribee 448 D10
wy. Mt Eliza 641 K5
wy. S Morang 199 J13
SANDRA
av. Eltham 287 D7
av. Fawkner 281 E1
av. Noble Park 534 E2
ct. Croydon 336 H14
ct. Donvale 332 K17
ct. Knoxfield 462 K5
ct. Langwarrin 601 L19
ct. Rye 696 L4
ct. Somerville 645 B14
ct. Wheelers Hl 460 E15
gr. Bentleigh 496 E6
st. Balwyn N 329 J19
st. Bulleen 329 F17
st. Doveton 537 B8
st. Forest Hill 420 B4
st. Kings Park 275 E19
st. Melton 268 G1
SANDRIDGE
av. Port Melb 412 B5
ct. Patterson L 573 K10
SANDRINGHAM
pde. Newtown 701 L13
rd. Sandringham 495 B14
st. Wantirna 422 C5
SANDS
pl. Williamstown 411 D17
SANDSTONE
av. Seabrook 450 K7
ct. Delahey 275 A15
SANDTOFT
ct. Highton 705 K8
SANDVYK
ct. Scoresby 462 B8
SANDWELL
grn. Caroline Spr 317 J3
SANDWICH
av. Jan Juc 711 G15
SANDY
ct. Cannons Creek 649 D8
ct. Dandenong N 501 F18
ct. Noble Park 534 C6
ct. Portsea 678 D3
ct. Taylors L 275 K7
pl. Maribyrnong 323 A13
rd. St Andrews Bch 697 F20
st. Nunawading 376 D12
wyn. Kilsyth S 381 A20
SANDYGATE
ct. Cairnlea 320 A13
SANDY POINT
rd. Point Cook 450 J13
SANG
ct. Ringwood 378 J4
SANGLEN
tce. Belmont 701 K20
SANICKI
ct. Bentleigh E 497 F8
SANIKY
st. Notting Hill 459 H12
SAN LEANDRO
dr. Reservoir 283 F2
SAN MARCO
la. W Melbourne 17 G20
SAN MARTIN
dr. Croydon N 335 K16
SAN REMO
ct. Nar Warrn S 553 F18
dr. Avondale Ht 322 E9
dr. Werribee 447 C8
rd. Ringwood N 378 D6
SANSOM
ct. Taylors L 233 D17
SANTA BARBARA
dr. Frankston 600 C16
SANTA CRUZ
bvd. Roxburgh Pk 194 D7
SANTA MONICA
bvd. Pt Lonsdale 710 D1
dr. Keilor Ldg 276 C4
SANTARAM
st. Bentleigh E 457 G17
SANTA ROSA
bvd. Doncaster E 332 G11
SANTED
ct. Rowville 462 E20
SANTIAGO
st. Doncaster 374 F2
st. St Albans 320 H10
SANTLEY
cl. Mill Park 242 G10
SANTOLIN
dr. Hillside 274 F3
SANTON
st. Greensbrgh 285 J5
SANTORINI
ct. Mt Martha 656 K6
SANTOS
st. Keilor Dn 276 F17
SAPLING
tce. Cairnlea 319 G6
SAPPHIRE
av. Boronia 424 K11
cl. Point Cook 451 B13
ct. Glen Waverley 420 G17
ct. Lower Plenty 286 H14
ct. Narre Warren 539 G13
ct. Werribee 446 L15
ct. Werribee 447 A15
dr. Hampton Pk 551 C10
st. Essendon W 323 A6
st. Forest Hill 420 H3
st. Niddrie 323 A6
st. Preston 327 D1
SARA
av. Brighton East 495 F1
ct. Bayswater N 380 F20
ct. Fawkner 239 G20
ct. Noble Park 534 C6
dr. Wheelers Hl 461 C17
gr. Tottenham 365 K9
pl. Aspendale Gdn 546 F2
rd. Scoresby 462 G9
st. Pt Lonsdale 707 H20
st. Rye 696 G9
SARABANDE
cr. Torquay 711 J8
SARAH
cl. Clayton S 499 D15
cr. Templestowe 331 F9
ct. Eltham North 245 G18
ct. Kurunjang 226 H13
ct. Montrose 381 L10
ct. Nar Warrn S 552 L14
ct. Pakenham 559 F19
ct. Vermont 420 L4
ct. Vermont 421 A4
ct. Wantirna S 462 A4
pl. Carrum Downs 575 C16
pl. Frankston S 627 J10
pl. Hampton Pk 551 L9
st. Black Rock 529 F1
st. Campbellfield 239 H10
SARAH-LOUISE
pl. Berwick 553 J12
SARATOGA
cr. Keilor Dn 275 J12
SARAZEN
st. Rye 696 J3
SARDINE
st. Port Melb 411 G2
SARGASSO
av. Keysborough 534 G16
SARGENT
st. Doncaster 374 J5
st. Geelong West 702 F2
SARGON
gr. Brighton 454 L9
gr. Brighton 455 A9
SARGOOD
ct. Endeavour Hl 537 K8
st. Altona 409 C19
st. Coburg 325 G4
st. Hampton 495 D11
st. Toorak 415 D8
SARI
la. Hampton E 496 A6
SARIC
ct. Plumpton 273 D13
SARNIA
ct. Narre Warren 539 D15
SARNO
ct. Cranbourne 603 K2
SARONA
st. Dandenong 536 E8
SARONG
st. Watsonia 285 F10
SARONVALE
cr. Hillside 274 F1
SAROSE
ct. Dingley Vill 532 L5
SARSHAS
wy. Mt Martha 657 B7
SARTON
rd. Clayton 499 G1
SARTORI
st. Burwood E 419 G8
SARTRE
ct. Glen Waverley 420 A14
SARZANA
st. Mentone 531 E5
SASH
cl. Carrum Downs 601 E4
SASHA
ct. Hallam 538 D20
ct. Langwarrin 629 K5
ct. Tullamarine 278 H1
ct. Werribee 446 L10
pl. Noble Park N 501 B10
pl. S Morang 199 A10
SASKIA
ct. Greensbrgh 243 L20
SASSAFRAS
cl. Pakenham 583 K1
ct. Boronia 424 H16
dr. Frankston 600 J19
dr. Sunbury 143 D17
dr. Templstw Lr 330 H13
SASSAFRAS CREEK
rd. Olinda 426 H14
rd. Olinda 427 A18
rd. Sassafras 426 H14
rd. Sherbrooke 426 H14
rd. Sherbrooke 427 A18
SASSARI
ct. Point Cook 450 D10
SASSELLA
st. Deer Park 319 C13
st. Oakleigh S 497 E3
SASSES
av. Bayswater 423 D10
SATELBERG
ct. Heidelberg W 328 A2
SATIN
st. Bundoora 242 D15
SATINWOOD
ct. Langwarrin 601 E19
wy. Lyndhurst 551 A19
SATORI
ct. Ferntree Gly 464 A7
SATTERLEY
cl. Endeavour Hl 537 B5
SATTERLY
wy. Roxburgh Pk 194 B14
SATURN
ct. Wheelers Hl 460 L19
st. Balwyn N 373 F2
st. Caulfield S 455 E10
st. Newcomb 704 D15
tce. Doncaster E 332 E17
SAUL
ct. Greensbrgh 285 J10
SAUNDERS
cl. Rowville 463 K18
cr. Epping 197 L15
ct. Roxburgh Pk 193 L14
st. Clayton S 499 F9
st. Coburg 325 B7
SAUNTON
dr. Cranbourne 603 F7
SAUVAGE
wy. S Morang 198 J13
SAVAGE
ct. Nunawading 376 K10
ct. Werribee 446 J18
st. Belmont 701 L20
st. Pakenham 584 J9
SAVANNA
ct. Berwick 554 C3
dr. Mooroolbark 337 C10
SAVANNAH
cr. Epping 197 L19
ct. Frankston 599 K15
ct. Hillside 231 L16
pl. Chadstone 458 E4
SAVARIS
ct. Donvale 377 B6
SAVERNAKE
ct. Doncaster E 332 D7
SAVIGE
av. Mt Waverley 459 H2
rd. Yallambie 285 G13
st. Ascot Vale 324 B19
st. Newport 410 F6
SAVILLE
ct. Rowville 463 L12
ct. Rye 697 G3
ct. Templestowe 330 L9
pl. S Morang 198 K14
st. Ferny Creek 466 B1
SAVIO
st. Chadstone 458 C3
SAVONA
st. Mentone 531 D7
SAWLEY
gr. Wyndham Va 446 E13
SAWREY
pl. Mill Park 242 L9
pl. Mill Park 243 A9
SAXBY
ct. Burnside 318 D6
ct. Wantirna S 422 K13
rd. Glen Iris 416 L15
SAXIL
ct. Seaford 599 K1
gr. Healesville 212 H14
SAXON
av. Wantirna 422 F12
ct. Oakleigh 458 D8
dr. Mooroolbark 337 J18
st. Brunswick 325 F15
st. Burwood E 419 H12
st. Doncaster 331 A18
st. Rye 696 D7
SAXON WOOD
dr. Vermont S 420 F7
SAXONWOOD
ct. Ferntree Gly 424 J17
ct. Frankston 628 C12
dr. Doncaster E 331 K17
dr. Narre Warren 553 B8
dr. Sunbury 142 K2
la. Sunbury 142 K1
SAXONY
ct. Mulgrave 500 J2
SAXTON
st. Box Hill N 374 J9
SAYCE
la. Hawthorn E 372 D20
la. Hawthorn E 416 D1
SAYERS
la. Brighton 454 H19
rd. Ferny Creek 465 K5
rd. Hoppers Csg 405 A12
rd. Laverton 406 D13
rd. Laverton N 406 D13
rd. Tarneit 405 A12
rd. Truganina 405 G12
rd. Upwey 465 K5
SAYLE
st. Yarra Glen 252 L3
SAYVEL
cl. Hillside 274 D6
SAYVON
ct. Dromana 686 C9
SCAMMEL
st. Campbellfield 194 J20
SCAMMELL
cl. Mt Waverley 459 F4
cr. Torquay 712 D3
SCAMPTON
cr. Tullamarine 278 J2
ct. Highton 705 J7
SCANLAN
st. Bentleigh E 497 C7
st. Berwick 554 G8
SCARBOROUGH
av. Craigieburn 149 K17
av. Cranbourne W 603 G3
av. Cranbourne W 603 H1
cl. Pt Lonsdale 707 H18
cr. Melton W 226 B14
ct. Tarneit 405 A11
dr. Hampton E 495 H10
dr. Heidelberg 329 G2
dr. Nar Warrn S 552 G18
dr. Patterson L 573 G6
gr. Beaumaris 530 G7
pl. Kensington 34 C7
rd. Epping 197 K18
rd. Vermont S 420 H8
sq. Mont Albert N 374 E7
tce. Craigieburn 150 D8
wy. Kings Park 319 C2
SCARLET
dr. Bundoora 242 D13
dr. Doveton 536 H6
st. Mordialloc 532 A11
SCARLET ASH
ct. Eltham 288 C10
dr. Templstw Lr 330 G14
SCARLET OAK
ct. Blackburn S 420 B6
SCARLETT
av. Carrum Downs 575 G14
st. Geelong West 702 F3
SCENIC
av. Ringwood E 379 B14
cr. Eltham North 287 E4
cr. Kalorama 383 C10
ct. Croydon N 335 K14
ct. Dandenong N 501 K11
ct. Ferntree Gly 463 G6
dr. Ashwood 418 C15
dr. Beaconsfield 555 E11
dr. Launching Pl 345 G14
dr. Point Cook 451 A8
pl. Arthurs Seat 685 L13
pl. Kealba 276 L19
pl. Kealba 277
pl. Maribyrnong 323
rd. Highton 701
rd. Wandana Ht 701
ri. Doncaster 330
ri. Eltham North 245
tce. Craigieburn 150
tce. S Morang 199
SCENIC VIEW
dr. Mt Martha 669
SCENTBARK
ct. Launching Pl 345
SCEPTRE
ct. Taylors L 275
SCHAEFFER
rd. Hurstbridge 203
SCHAFTER
dr. Doncaster E 332
SCHANCK
pl. Endeavour Hl 537
SCHEELE
st. Surrey Hills 374
SCHERMAN
dr. Altona Mdw 451
SCHILD
st. Yarraville 367
SCHMIDT
ct. Seaford 600
SCHNAPPER POINT
dr. Mornington 640
SCHNEIDER
cr. Clarinda 498
st. Ferntree Gly 424
SCHOFIELD
st. Essendon 323
st. Moorabbin 496
SCHOLTZ
rd. Christmas Hills 206
SCHONING
ct. Croydon N 335
SCHOOL
ct. Glenroy 280
ct. Nar Warrn S 552
la. Brunswick W 324
la. Bulla 189
la. Christmas Hills 250
la. Diggers Rest 187
la. Ferny Creek 466
la. Maddingley 264
la. Tarrawarra 211
la. Yarra Jctn 346
rd. Ferny Creek 465
rd. Menzies Ck 467
rd. Olinda 426
rd. Olinda 427
rd. Seville 342
rd. Silvan 384
rd. Tremont 465
rd. Up Fntree Gly 465
st. Blackburn S 375
st. Blackburn S 419
st. Geelong 703
wk. Croydon S 380
SCHOOLHALL
st. Oakleigh 457
SCHOOL HOUSE
rd. Woori Yall 344
rd. Woori Yall 345
SCHOOLHOUSE
la. Sunbury 143
SCHOONER BAY
dr. Frankston 628
dr. Patterson L 573
SCHOTTERS
rd. Mernda 155
SCHULER
ct. Narre Warren 552
SCHULZ
st. Bentleigh E 496
SCHUTT
ct. Williamstown 410
dr. Rye 696
st. Newport 410
SCIENCE
dr. Bundoora 284
SCOBLE
ct. Vermont 420
pl. Narre Warren 539
st. Frankston S 626
SCONE
cl. Eltham North 245
SCORESBY
rd. Bayswater 423
rd. Ferntree Gly 463
SCOTCH
cct. Hawthorn 416
ct. Sunbury 144
pde. Bonbeach 547
pde. Bonbeach 573
pde. Chelsea 547
SCOTCHMANS CREEK
rd. Warburton 349

SCOTCHMER
st. Fitzroy N...326 A20
SCOTIA
cr. Keysborough...534 C7
gr. South Yarra...32 C13
gr. South Yarra...414 G7
st. Moonee Pnd...323 H14
st. N Melbourne...17 C16
st. Preston...326 E4
SCOTLAND
av. Greensbrgh...285 L3
st. Braybrook...366 B5
SCOTSBURN
av. Clayton...498 F2
av. Oakleigh S...498 F2
cl. Mulgrave...501 E6
ct. Grovedale...706 G15
ct. Mornington...657 C2
gr. Toorak...415 G6
gr. Werribee...447 H13
st. Hawthorn...415 J1
wy. Endeavour Hl...537 G2
SCOTSGATE
wy. Berwick...554 K9
SCOTSMORE
rd. Springvale S...534 A5
SCOTT
al. Melbourne...2 D18
al. Melbourne, off Flinders La...24 E10
av. Clayton S...499 E12
av. St Albans...319 L5
cl. Hallam...537 K14
cl. Templestowe...332 C12
ct. Altona Mdw...451 K4
ct. Patterson L...547 G20
ct. Wantirna S...422 L20
ct. Wantirna S...423 A20
gr. Burwood...418 A10
gr. Glen Iris...416 F13
gr. Kingsbury...283 H10
gr. Somerville...644 L13
rd. Cranbourne S...603 C20
rd. Cranbourne S...630 L5
rd. Laverton N...407 J5
rd. Yarra Glen...208 K10
st. Anglesea...713 L3
st. Beaumaris...530 C11
st. Belmont...702 E19
st. Blairgowrie...696 A2
st. Canterbury...373 E20
st. Caulfield S...455 K12
st. Cranbourne...604 C4
st. Dandenong...535 J8
st. Dromana...686 B10
st. Elwood...454 F3
st. Essendon...323 H11
st. Hampton E...496 B11
st. Hawthorn...416 C2
st. Heathmont...422 E3
st. Keilor...276 L10
st. Kew...372 C12
st. Melton...226 H15
st. Mitcham...377 F20
st. Moonee Pnd...323 H11
st. Mornington...640 G19
st. Northcote...326 G13
st. Seaford...599 E3
st. Seddon...367 A10
st. Sunbury...143 A12
st. Tarneit...447 H1
st. Thomastown...241 C12
st. Vermont...377 F20
st. Werribee...447 L12
wyn. Blairgowrie...679 J18
SCOTT LEE
dr. Beaconsfield...555 G17
SCOTTS
pde. Ivanhoe...328 D16
pl. Carlton...18 B16
st. Bentleigh...456 E20
SCOTTS ANGLE
rd. Wattle Glen...246 K3
SCOTTSDALE
st. Surrey Hills...374 B20
SCOVELL
cr. Maidstone...366 J1
SCREEN
rd. Diggers Rest...187 B11
st. Frankston...627 H5
SCULLIN
ct. Mill Park...242 L4
ct. Mill Park...243 A4
ct. Sunbury...143 G3
st. Altona...409 E17
st. Dandenong N...501 L19
st. Maidstone...366 F3
SCURRAH
ct. Keilor East...322 J4
SEA
ct. Craigieburn...150 G18
pde. Mentone...530 H9
tce. Mentone...530 J9

SEABIRD
ct. Torquay...712 C4
wy. Portsea...678 A5
SEA BREEZE
la. Williamstown...410 H16
SEABREEZE
av. Ferny Creek...425 G18
SEABROOK
av. Rosebud...700 J3
bvd. Seabrook...450 L2
wy. Seaford...573 E13
SEABY
av. Up Fntree Gly...465 A6
SEACH
st. Caulfield S...455 F12
SEACHANGE
ct. Mt Martha...656 K7
SEACOMBE
gr. Brighton...454 E14
pl. Cranbourne...578 H17
st. Dromana...686 E3
st. Fawkner...281 H8
st. Fitzroy N...19 D1
st. Fitzroy N...326 B20
SEACREST
av. Seaford...599 K3
SEAEAGLE
av. Point Cook...450 D4
SEAFARER
ct. Patterson L...573 G10
SEAFOAM
st. Hampton E...496 A9
SEAFORD
rd. Seaford...599 F4
rd. Seaford...599 H4
SEAFORTH
rd. Wantirna S...423 A10
SEAGULL
av. Altona...408 G19
cl. Blind Bight...650 E9
la. Maribyrnong...322 J15
SEA HAZE
ct. Mt Eliza...641 L7
SEAHAZE
st. Arthurs Seat...686 A14
SEAHOLME
av. Seaholme...409 H17
SEAL
st. Rosebud...684 C18
SEAL ROCK
av. Arthurs Seat...685 H14
SEAMER
rd. Monbulk...428 J15
SEAMISTS
dr. Arthurs Seat...685 F19
SEAMONS
ct. Endeavour Hl...537 K10
SEAN
cl. Wheelers Hl...461 D13
ct. Kurunjang...226 H14
SEAQUESTA
ct. Frankston...628 E10
SEAQUINN
cl. Dromana...686 D3
SEARCH
rd. Diggers Rest...187 C11
SEARES
dr. Ringwood E...379 B6
pl. S Morang...198 L12
SEARLE
ct. Dandenong N...501 L14
ct. Werribee...447 D18
st. Geelong West...702 E6
SEASCAPE
cl. Ferntree Gly...424 K18
cl. Ferntree Gly...424 L17
pl. Safety Bch...669 B16
st. Clayton...459 B18
SEASIDE
cl. Seabrook...450 J6
pde. Mt Martha...668 L5
pde. Mt Martha...669 A5
SEATHORPE
st. Bentleigh E...496 J4
SEATON
ct. Mt Waverley...459 H3
ct. Somerville...644 L13
dr. Dingley Vill...533 D5
pl. Rowville...463 F19
rd. Highett...496 A11
rd. Mornington...656 C2
ri. Hallam...552 B1
st. Glen Iris...417 B16
SEATTLE
ct. Knoxfield...463 D6
sq. Narre Warren...539 F16
st. Balwyn N...329 H19
SEAVER
gr. Reservoir...282 E9
SEA VIEW
av. Ferny Creek...466 C1

SEAVIEW
av. Bentleigh...456 D18
av. Brighton...494 H5
av. Mornington...640 G19
av. Safety Bch...669 A17
cl. Rosebud...700 K5
cr. Black Rock...529 E3
cr. Mulgrave...500 A3
cr. Seaholme...409 G19
ct. Dandenong N...501 J14
pde. Belmont...702 G17
pde. Dromana...686 B8
pde. Williamstown...410 A13
rd. Cockatoo...510 K8
rd. Frankston S...626 K11
st. Blairgowrie...679 F16
st. Caulfield S...455 F9
st. Dromana...686 F10
st. Emerald...510 A9
st. Mt Waverley...418 J13
SEAWIND
la. Arthurs Seat...685 J14
SEBAN
ct. Wantirna S...462 F5
SEBASTION
st. Epping...197 G16
SEBASTOPOL
st. Caulfield N...415 F18
st. St Kilda E...414 J16
SEBIRE
av. Wandin N...341 A15
SEBROFF
st. Frankston...627 C5
SEC
brk. Langwarrin...628 J8
SECCULL
dr. Chelsea Ht...547 G16
SECOMB
ct. Glen Waverley...420 A17
pl.n, Footscray...367 J7
pl.s, Footscray...367 J7
SECOND
av. Altona North...409 L7
av. Anglesea...713 C9
av. Aspendale...546 F9
av. Box Hill N...375 E7
av. Brunswick...325 D8
av. Chelsea Ht...547 E14
av. Cockatoo...510 H4
av. Craigieburn...150 G17
av. Dandenong N...501 J15
av. Hadfield...281 C11
av. Hoppers Csg...448 K6
av. Kew...372 J8
av. Melton S...268 G6
av. Moorabbin Aprt...531 K5
av. Murrumbeena...457 B11
av. Pakenham...584 K3
av. Rosebud...683 L19
av. Rowville...462 E18
av. Springvale...500 H10
av. Sunshine...365 E8
cr. Hadfield...281 D10
ct. Cranbourne...603 J6
ct. Preston...282 C18
dr. Springvale...500 G11
rd. Springvale...500 J10
st. Black Rock...529 G6
st. Clayton S...499 D5
st. Geelong West...702 G3
st. Moorabbin Aprt...531 L4
st. Parkdale...531 D9
st. Warrandyte...333 F1
SECRETS
wy. Mt Martha...657 C8
SECTION
rd. Greenvale...192 E20
SEDDON
st. Ivanhoe...328 C13
st. Olinda...427 B17
st. Seddon...367 A12
SEDGE
cl. Braybrook...321 L18
SEDGEFIELD
pl. Craigieburn...194 G3
tce. Cairnlea...319 G7
SEDGMAN
ct. Mill Park...242 H4
st. Brunswick E...325 K14
SEDGWICK
rd. Boronia...423 E14
SEEBECK
dr. Nar Warrn S...552 F17
dr. Nar Warrn S...552 H17
rd. Rowville...502 C5
SEEBREEZE
dr. Aspendale...546 D4
SEFTON
ct. Mt Waverley...419 F15
la. Caroline Spr...317 K3
pl. Camberwell...373 A18
st. Bulleen...329 K17
st. Pascoe Vale...280 D14

SEGARTA
cct. Ferntree Gly...464 A6
SEGTOUNE
st. Kew...372 F7
SEINE
cl. Werribee...447 H6
SEISMAN
st. Port Melb...412 L5
SEISMIC
ct. Rowville...462 L13
ct. Rowville...463 A13
SELBORNE
cl. Wantirna...422 H9
rd. Toorak...415 C7
SELBOURNE
av. Werribee...447 J2
pl. Hampton Pk...551 L16
rd. Kew...372 A12
st. Ascot Vale...324 A16
st. Coburg...325 C6
st. Hawthorn...372 C16
wy. Mulgrave...501 E6
SELBY
av. Noble Park...500 G14
ct. Berwick...554 D20
ct. Croydon N...336 E10
ct. Hopetoun Park...265 K6
pl. Craigieburn...150 G20
rd. Woori Yall...344 C16
st. Dallas...238 D8
st. Mt Waverley...458 G7
st. Preston...283 D18
SELBY-AURA
rd. Menzies Ck...467 K19
rd. Selby...467 D16
SELET
st. Mt Evelyn...383 K7
SELINA
av. Mooroolbark...337 F15
ct. Frankston...628 F4
st. Footscray...367 H8
SELKIRK
av. McKinnon...456 F17
av. Wantirna...422 E4
ct. Berwick...554 D16
SELL
st. Doncaster E...376 A2
st. Keilor Park...278 C15
SELLARS
rd. Emerald...509 L3
st. Watsonia N...285 H3
SELLERS
st. Glen Waverley...420 B18
SELLICK
dr. Croydon...380 E10
SELLWOOD
rt. Cheltenham...496 J13
SELMA
cl. Lynbrook...551 H19
SELMAN
av. Ferntree Gly...464 G4
SELOLA
ct. Fawkner...281 G2
SELSDON
ct. Greensbrgh...244 E16
tce. Donvale...376 K4
SELSEY
ct. St Albans...275 J20
st. Seaford...573 D18
SELWOOD
ct. Berwick...554 B2
ct. Mill Park...243 E6
ct. Mornington...640 L12
ct. Mornington...641 A12
ct. Rowville...462 H20
ct. Watsonia N...243 D18
pl. Altona Mdw...451 F7
st. Hawthorn E...416 G3
SELWORTHY
av. Oakleigh S...457 H18
SELWYN
av. Craigieburn...150 D18
av. Elwood...454 D6
ct. Mulgrave...500 G1
ct. Templestowe...330 L8
ct. Toorak...415 G6
la. Mt Dandenong...426 F1
st. Albion...320 G20
st. Blackburn...375 F11
st. Brighton...454 G13
st. Canterbury...373 G20
st. Elsternwick...454 K4
SEMILLON
ct. Sunbury...144 D9
ct. Yarra Glen...209 B18
SEMINARY
cr. Scoresby...462 D6
SENAR
st. Kilsyth...381 H6
SENBIN
ct. Greensbrgh...243 J18
SENGA
st. Noble Park...534 D1

SENIOR
cl. Mill Park...242 C5
ct. Watsonia N...243 G20
SENNA
ct. Thomastown...240 J12
SENNITTS
rd. The Patch...468 C6
SENTRY
pl. Maribyrnong...322 K16
rd. Coburg...281 J20
SEPARATION
st. Alphington...327 H15
st. Fairfield...327 A14
st. Mornington...640 F17
st. Northcote...326 J14
SEPIK
va. Mt Evelyn...339 E11
SEPPELT
av. Mt Martha...656 B14
SEPTEMBER
st. Moolap...704 L17
SEPTIMUS
cl. Mill Park...242 K6
SEQUOIA
ct. Nar Warrn S...553 C19
tr. Olinda...427 E9
SERAFINI
ct. Eltham North...287 G3
SERCOMBE
gr. Hawthorn...372 A14
SERENDIP
ct. Narre Warren...539 D15
SERENITY
wy. Mornington...657 D3
wy. Pt Lonsdale...707 G17
wy. S Morang...199 J20
SERGEANT
st. Blackburn...375 F15
SERICA
ct. Grovedale...706 A16
ct. Keilor Dn...276 G15
pl. Wheelers Hl...460 H16
SERJEANT
ct. Seaford...573 J18
SERONG
st. Kensington...33 G5
SERPELLS
la. Hawthorn...372 A17
rd. Doncaster E...332 F12
rd. Templestowe...331 A9
tce. Donvale...332 H15
SERPENS
ct. Roxburgh Pk...194 F8
SERPENTINE
ct. Lalor...240 H9
ct. Waterways...547 D2
ct. Werribee...447 H8
rd. Keysborough...533 L8
st. Mont Albert...374 F15
SERRATA
ct. Hillside...274 G7
st. Cranbourne W...577 H18
SERRELL
st. Malvern East...456 K4
SERVANTE
st. Sunshine...365 E3
SERVICE
rd. Blackburn...375 F14
rd. Melb Airport...235 H12
st. Caulfield N...415 K20
st. Coburg...281 F20
st. Essendon N...323 H2
st. Hampton...495 B9
st. Sunshine...365 D1
SESAME
st. Mt Waverley...419 H15
SESTON
st. Reservoir...283 K17
SETANI
cr. Heidelberg W...284 B19
SETH
pl. Mt Evelyn...339 L16
SETON
cl. Greenvale...193 B20
SETTE
ct. Greensbrgh...244 J16
SETTLEMENT
rd. Belmont...706 E3
rd. Bundoora...284 D1
rd. Thomastown...241 C17
rd. Wesburn...347 E12
rd. Yarra Jctn...346 J12
rd. Yarra Jctn...347 A12
SETTLER
ct. Glen Waverley...459 L6
ct. Werribee...447 K8
SETTLERS
ct. Pakenham...584 G10
ct. Rowville...463 J15
ct. Vermont S...420 L12
ct. Vermont S...421 A12
wy. Cairnlea...319 G8
wy. Frankston S...627 J11

wy. Mt Martha..........656 J6
wy. St Helena...........245 B20
SETTLERS HILL
cr. Croydon Hl.........335 G15
pl. Nar Warrn N.......538 F12
ri. Pakenham..........584 H1
SEVENOAKS
av. Croydon............335 J18
av. Heidelberg.........329 F2
rd. Burwood E.........420 A12
st. Balwyn..............373 C10
SEVENTH
av. Altona North......409 J7
av. Anglesea............713 C13
av. Chelsea Ht..........547 D14
av. Dandenong..........535 H5
av. Hadfield..............281 D5
av. Rosebud..............684 A19
rd. Springvale..........500 L11
rd. Springvale..........501 A11
st. Parkdale............531 E11
SEVERINO
pl. Sunbury............142 J12
SEVERN
cr. Rowville.............463 E17
ct. Dandenong N.......501 G14
ct. Mt Waverley.......418 H15
ct. Roxburgh Pk......194 G6
st. Balwyn N...........373 A6
st. Box Hill N..........374 H12
st. Epping..............198 B18
st. Moonee Pnd.......323 J11
st. Newport............410 G9
st. Yarraville...........366 K17
SEVES
st. Altona...............409 F20
SEVILLA
pl. Hampton Pk.......551 L16
SEVILLE
cl. Thomastown......240 E15
ct. Cheltenham.......497 H20
ct. Kings Park.........275 C19
ct. Meadow Ht........238 C4
gr. Scoresby...........462 B7
st. Camberwell........417 A6
SEWART
cl. Vermont S.........421 C13
SEWELL
ct. Frankston S.......627 J11
dr. Harkaway..........541 E17
ri. Bundoora...........284 E4
st. Mont Albert N....374 E6
SEXTON
ct. Altona Mdw.......451 E2
ct. Endeavour Hl.....537 L7
st. Airport W..........278 J12
SEYMOUR
av. Armadale...........415 H13
av. Carnegie............456 F6
av. Mt Eliza.............626 A16
cl. Grovedale..........706 H14
cl. Wantirna............422 J10
dr. Plenty................245 A3
gr. Brighton............494 J4
gr. Camberwell.........416 J3
rd. Elsternwick.........455 B3
rd. Nr Nr Goon N.....560 G14
rd. Viewbank............286 B17
st. Belgrave.............466 E14
st. Broadmeadows..238 B16
st. Preston...............326 K4
st. Ringwood...........378 B13
st. Seville................341 J11
SHABA
ct. Meadow Ht........194 B17
SHACKELL
st. Coburg..............325 B2
st. Kingsville...........366 K11
SHACKLETON
st. Belmont.............702 C18
SHADFORTH
st. Westmeadows...237 C14
SHADI
ct. Cranbourne W...577 H20
ri. Yarra Glen.........209 B18
SHADOWPLAY
rd. Mooroolbark......337 C13
SHADWELL
ct. Whittington........704 A18
st. Cheltenham.......497 B20
SHADY
gr. Forest Hill..........420 H1
gr. Rowville.............463 F17
pl. Noble Park.........534 C5
wy. Croydon S.........380 A14
SHAE
ct. Kings Park.........319 D2
SHAFER
ct. Endeavour Hl.....537 G5
rd. Blackburn N.......375 G9
SHAFT
ct. Hoppers Csg......449 J2
SHAFTESBURY
av. Malvern.............416 B11
av. St Andrews........205 H1
ct. Keysborough.....534 B7
dr. Berwick.............539 L20
pde. Thornbury.........326 E9
st. Coburg..............325 C7
st. Essendon............324 C6
st. Frankston...........627 H4
SHAFTON
st. Huntingdale.......458 E16
SHAFTSBURY
av. Berwick.............553 J14
bvd. Point Cook.........450 E8
dr. Mulgrave...........460 E20
SHAH
ct. Torquay.............712 H2
SHAKESPEARE
av. Mooroolbark......337 G20
av. Mooroolbark......381 G1
av. Preston..............283 A17
dr. Bundoora............242 G17
dr. Delahey.............275 D16
dr. Templestowe.....332 A11
gr. Hawthorn...........371 E17
gr. Heidelberg Ht.....284 G19
gr. Northcote..........326 E13
gr. St Kilda..............414 B18
gr. Truganina...........405 F14
pl. Cremorne............26 E17
st. Carlton N.............18 G4
SHALBURY
av. Eltham...............287 L5
SHALE
ct. Delahey.............274 L16
SHALIMAR
cr. Boronia..............424 J7
cr. Dandenong N......501 L15
ct. Sorrento.............679 A13
ct. Vermont S..........420 H11
pl. Melton W...........225 L15
SHALLESS
dr. Camberwell........417 C3
SHALLOT
cl. Glen Waverley....420 K16
SHAMROCK
cl. Nar Warrn S.......553 D18
dr. Mill Park............243 F5
pl. Melton W...........225 A16
pl. S Melbourne.......29 F2
pl. Roxburgh Pk, off Brushwood Cct..193 L4
st. Abbotsford........371 A12
st. Brunswick W......325 B9
st. Essendon...........323 L7
st. Richmond............26 F18
SHANAHAN
cr. McKinnon..........456 G17
SHAND
ct. Berwick.............553 K4
rd. Reservoir...........283 D13
st. Safety Bch.........669 A15
SHANDEAU
av. Clayton..............458 K19
SHANDEEN
ct. Meadow Ht........237 L4
SHANDFORD
av. Brighton............454 E13
SHANDON
st. Mornington........640 J13
st. Mornington........641 A13
SHANDS
la. N Melbourne........34 K11
st. Beaumaris..........530 H4
SHANE
av. Seabrook...........450 H5
cl. Lilydale..............338 L12
cr. Croydon S..........379 E10
ct. Avondale Ht.......322 G10
ct. Berwick..............553 L1
ct. Carrum Downs....601 D3
ct. Gladstone Pk......279 D2
SHANHUNS
rd. Panton Hill.........204 C8
SHANKLAND
bvd. Meadow Ht........193 L20
SHANKLIN
st. Box Hill N..........375 A6
st. Hurstbridge.......202 L13
SHANLEY
st. Pascoe Vale.......280 J12
SHANNON
av. Ferntree Gly.......424 E19
av. Geelong West....702 C6
av. Manifold Ht........702 C6
av. Newtown............702 B14
cl. Werribee.............447 H6
cr. Watsonia............285 H10
ct. Clarinda.............498 E8
ct. Dingley Vill.........532 L4
ct. Mooroolbark......336 K11
ct. St Albans...........275 G19
gr. Roxburgh Pk......194 D7
pl. Langwarrin........601 L19
pl. Mill Park............242 L12
st. Box Hill N..........374 H10
st. Frankston..........599 B19
wy. Berwick.............554 J7
wy. Sydenham.........275 B8
SHANNS
av. Mt Martha..........656 B7
SHAPIRO
ct. Reservoir...........283 J2
ri. S Morang..........198 J11
SHARA
ct. Belmont.............706 H5
ct. Narre Warren.....539 A17
SHARAN
av. Mentone............531 K8
SHAREN
ct. Rosebud............684 H16
SHARLAND
cl. Mt Evelyn...........338 J19
SHARMAN
ct. Bentleigh...........496 G1
ct. Bundoora...........242 G16
SHARNA
ct. Ferntree Gly.......463 J7
SHARNALEE
ct. Lilydale.............338 D12
SHARNE
ct. Cranbourne N....578 G11
ct. Doncaster E.......375 J2
SHARON
ct. Mooroolbark......336 L12
ct. Taylors L...........275 E5
rd. Springvale S......500 C20
st. Doncaster..........331 E19
SHARP
gr. Coburg N...........281 E13
st. Bulla..................190 E17
st. Hoppers Csg.......448 F3
st. Newtown............702 H12
st. Northcote..........326 L16
SHARPE
ct. Berwick.............553 L19
st. Cranbourne........578 C17
st. Reservoir...........282 J14
SHARPES
rd. Watsonia N........285 D3
SHARPLEY
av. Safety Bch.........669 B12
SHARPS
ct. Heathmont.........378 L18
ct. Heathmont.........379 A18
rd. Melb Airport.......278 C7
rd. Tullamarine........278 C7
SHARRA
ct. Clarinda.............498 C10
SHARROCK
av. Cheltenham.......531 G1
cl. Caroline Spr.......318 C5
dr. Dingley Vill........533 B7
SHARROW
rd. Mitcham............377 G11
SHARYN
st. Cranbourne W...577 H17
SHASTA
av. Brighton East.....455 B19
av. Ringwood E.......378 L13
av. Ringwood E.......379 A13
wy. Portsea.............677 J3
SHAUN
av. Blackburn S.......419 K7
ct. Croydon N.........336 A12
ct. Springvale.........499 K17
ct. Templestowe.....331 D7
SHAW
cl. Dandenong N.....501 F12
ct. Altona Mdw.......451 K8
ct. Coburg N...........281 B12
ct. Delahey.............275 C14
ct. Sunbury............143 C9
rd. Junction Vill.......604 H13
st. Ashwood............417 L17
st. Dromana............686 F3
st. Fawkner.............281 F1
st. Ivanhoe.............327 L13
st. Niddrie..............322 L1
st. Niddrie..............323 A2
st. Richmond............26 H13
st. Springvale S......534 B4
SHAWLANDS
av. Blackburn S.......419 J2
rd. Tullamarine........278 J3
SHAWNEE
ct. Narre Warren.....552 F1
SHAWS
rd. Werribee............447 C9
SHAXTON
cir. Frankston..........628 D11
SHAYLOR
ct. Greensbrgh........285 L7
SHEA
st. Bacchus Msh.....221 J15
st. Newport............410 K11
SHEAHAN
cr. Hoppers Csg......448 L1
cr. Hoppers Csg......449 A1
rd. Rockbank..........317 A7
SHEAHANS
rd. Bulleen.............329 K10
rd. Templstw Lr......329 K10
SHEALES
st. Dandenong........536 A3
SHEARER
cl. Hoppers Csg......405 B18
cl. Sydenham.........275 A8
ct. Frankston S.......627 H9
ct. Mill Park............242 B5
ct. Mornington........641 E12
ct. Narre Warren.....553 F13
dr. Rowville.............502 K6
pl. Roxburgh Pk......194 B11
SHEARERS
ct. Pakenham.........584 G9
ct. Vermont S.........420 L12
ct. Vermont S.........421 A12
SHEARGOLD
ct. Reservoir...........239 L20
SHEARMAN
cr. Mentone............530 K6
ct. Keysborough.....535 A9
SHEARSON
cr. Mentone............531 H5
SHEARWATER
ct. Cairnlea.............319 H10
ct. Mornington........640 K17
ct. Pt Lonsdale........707 G18
ct. Taylors Hill.........274 L9
dr. Carrum Downs...600 H2
dr. Pakenham.........583 L3
pl. Craigieburn........194 A4
pl. Rosebud W.........698 L3
pl. Rosebud W.........699 A3
SHEBLER
pl. Melton...............226 L17
SHEDDEN
st. Pascoe Vale.......281 A18
SHEEDY
rd. Hoppers Csg......448 E4
st. Richmond............26 J12
SHEEHAN
ct. Dandenong N.....502 B20
rd. Heidelberg W.....284 B17
SHEEHANS
rd. Blackburn..........375 G20
rd. Red Hill.............687 E19
SHEEPFOLD
ct. Melton W...........226 A18
SHEEPRUN
pl. Hoppers Csg......447 L1
SHEEPSTATION CREEK
rd. Hoddles Ck........388 E14
rd. Yellingbo...........388 C6
SHEFFIELD
cl. Pakenham.........584 H2
ct. Cairnlea.............319 L12
ct. Nar Warrn S.......553 E15
ct. Thomastown......240 L15
ct. Thomastown......241 A15
rd. Kilsyth...............425 G5
rd. Montrose...........425 G5
rd. The Basin...........425 F9
rd.n, Montrose.........382 F11
rd.s, Montrose.........381 K18
st. Bentleigh E........457 C20
st. Brunswick W......325 B10
st. Caulfield S.........455 G10
st. Coburg..............325 H4
st. Eltham...............287 K5
st. Preston.............282 F17
SHEFFIELDS
la. Heidelberg.........328 L7
SHEILA
ct. Thomastown......240 G17
st. Preston.............283 G20
st. Rye...................697 L4
SHELAGH
ct. Warrandyte........333 B5
SHELBOURNE
ct. Meadow Ht........238 C5
ct. Mornington........640 G12
SHELBURY
pl. Frankston S.......627 G17
SHELDON
av. Darley...............221 L8
av. Mooroolbark......337 F20
ct. Gladstone Pk.....237 D19
pl. Clayton S...........499 D10
pl. Sunshine W.......364 D6
pl. Wheelers Hl.......461 A7
SHELDRAKE
cl. Frankston..........628 D3
st. Keysborough.....534 G15
SHELDUCK
pl. Craigieburn........149 G17
SHELFORD
cr. Kallista..............468 F1
ct. Cheltenham.......531 D
ct. Ferntree Gly.......424 A1
gr. Dingley Vill........533 B
SHELL
ct. Patterson L........573 K1
SHELLARD
st. Newport............410 E
SHELLEY
av. Bundoora..........242 K2
av. Kilsyth..............380 K
av. Newtown...........702 A
cl. Grovedale..........706 A1
cl. Torquay.............711 G1
ct. Ashwood...........418 B1
ct. Hampton Pk.......551 D1
ct. Kilsyth..............380 K
ct. Templestowe.....332 C1
st. Elwood.............454 C
st. Heidelberg Ht....328 E
st. Keilor East........322 D
st. Mornington.......640 D1
st. Richmond...........26 C
SHELLY
av. Boronia.............424 D
ct. Bacchus Msh.....221 L1
st. Footscray..........367 G
st. Noble Park.........534 D
SHELTER
tr. Lysterfield S.......503 C1
SHELTON
cr. Noble Park N......501 D
SHENFIELD
av. Bonbeach..........545 E1
av. Chelsea.............545 E1
la. Bonbeach, off Shenfield Av......545 E1
SHE OAK
ct. Melton W...........226 E1
SHEOAK
av. Rosebud W........699 C
ct. Highton.............705 F
ct. Hoppers Csg......405 F1
ct. Meadow Ht........238 C
gr. Cairnlea............319 F1
gr. Mt Martha..........668 L
gr. Mt Martha..........669 A
la. Maribyrnong......322 H1
mw. Cheltenham.......496 J1
pl. Plenty...............244 G1
rd. Frankston S.......627 J1
st. Doveton.............537 E
tr. Frankston N.......600 F1
SHEOKE
gr. Sorrento...........679 C1
SHEPHERD
av. Roxburgh Pk......194 E1
ct. Dingley Vill........533 E
ct. Williamstn N......411 A1
rd. Glen Waverley....460 K
st. Braybrook..........365 L
st. Footscray...........367 E
st. Glenroy.............279 J
st. Surrey Hills........374 D2
st. Surrey Hills........418 D
SHEPHERDS
gr. Kings Park.........274 L2
la. Sunbury............188 H
SHEPHERDS FLAT
la. Cottles Br..........204 E
SHEPHERDS HUT
la. Langwarrin S.....629 J1
SHEPPARD
ct. Altona Mdw.......451 L
dr. Scoresby...........462 E
st. Coburg N...........281 E1
st. Moorabbin.........496 E
st. Thornbury..........327 H
SHEPPARDS
la. Chirnside Pk......337 D
SHEPPARSON
av. Carnegie...........456 J
SHEPPERD
wy. Cairnlea............319 H1
SHEPRETH
av. Noble Park.........534 K
st. Surrey Hills........373 K1
SHERATON
cl. Burwood E.........420 B1
cr. Ferntree Gly.......463 H
SHERBOURNE
av. Bayswater N......380 E1
dr. Carrum Downs...575 C1
rd. Briar Hill...........286 G
rd. Eltham..............287 A
rd. Gladstone Pk.....279 E
rd. Montmorency....286 G
st. Essendon...........323 L1
tce. Newtown...........701

SHERBROOK
av. Ringwood 378 A13
tce. Lilydale 338 K2
tce. Lilydale 339 C6
SHERBROOKE
av. Elsternwick 454 L6
av. Oakleigh S 497 G8
cr. Taylors L 276 B10
ct. Doncaster E 376 C6
ct. Nar Warrn S 553 E16
mw. Somerville 645 D18
rd. Kallista 466 K1
rd. Sassafras 426 D19
rd. Sherbrooke 426 D19
rd. Sherbrooke 467 A2
st. Eltham North 287 F3
SHERBROOKE LODGE
rd. Sherbrooke 466 H2
SHERDLEY
grn. Caroline Spr 317 L4
SHERGOLDS
la. Dromana 687 C9
SHERIDAN
av. Frankston 599 C15
av. Mooroolbark 337 A12
av. Rowville 503 D5
cl. Kilsyth S 380 K18
ct. Brighton 454 J13
ct. Dingley Vill 532 K5
ct. Endeavour Hl 537 L7
ct. Heathmont 379 D20
gr. Caulfield S 455 D11
rd. Rosebud 684 H15
wy. Roxburgh Pk 194 B11
SHERIE
ct. Keysborough 534 E11
SHERINGA
cr. Grovedale 705 K15
ct. Mornington 641 C16
SHERINGHAM
dr. Werribee 448 A16
dr. Wheelers Hl 460 K11
SHERLOCK
dr. Mornington 657 B4
rd. Croydon 336 H19
rd. Mooroolbark 336 L18
SHERLOWE
cr. Viewbank 285 L16
ct. Bentleigh E 497 D2
SHERMAN
ct. Berwick 554 F12
dr. Bayswater N 380 H19
st. Forest Hill 420 J3
SHERRIFF
cl. Millgrove 348 B1
rd. Emerald 509 H1
ri. Pakenham 585 C6
SHERRIN
ct. Werribee 448 C7
SHERRY
ct. Bacchus Msh 221 G16
SHERWIN
ct. Melton 227 G18
pl. Roxburgh Pk 194 F15
st. Kensington 33 E9
SHERWOOD
av. Chelsea 546 L19
av. Ringwood E 378 K13
av. Rosebud 700 G6
av. Warburton 350 C1
cl. Albanvale 319 A4
cr. Dandenong N 502 C14
cr. Mt Martha 656 A20
ct. Croydon 379 F7
ct. Doncaster E 331 L18
ct. Highton 705 G3
ct. Langwarrin S 628 G15
ct. Sunbury 143 J10
ct. Wantirna S 423 A16
dr. Thomastown 240 D15
rd. Eaglemont 328 E12
rd. Ivanhoe 328 E12
rd. Junction Vill 604 J15
rd. Mt Waverley 458 L1
rd. Nar Warrn S 578 E1
rd. Nar Warrn S 578 E3
rd. Rye 697 H7
rd. Surrey Hills 418 C1
rd. Tooradin 651 F1
ri. Vermont S 420 G13
st. Glen Iris 417 C16
st. Hadfield 281 B9
st. Ormond 455 J13
st. Richmond 26 A11
wy. Lysterfield 464 E19
wy. Lysterfield 464 F18
SHERWOOD FOREST
dr. Rye 696 J8
SHETLAND
av. Brunswick W 324 L8
cl. Highton 701 C16
cl. Vermont S 420 F7
ct. Belmont 706 C6
ct. Pakenham 558 L19
dr. Wantirna 422 K7
st. Endeavour Hl 503 G19
wy. Sunbury 143 K16
SHEVLINS
la. Woori Yall 344 E17
SHIBOR
dr. Vermont 421 K2
SHIEL
st. N Melbourne 34 J12
SHIELA
st. Blackburn N 376 A8
SHIELD
ct. Glen Waverley 421 A18
ct. Kilsyth 381 A5
rd. Yellingbo 386 K17
SHIELDS
ct. Altona Mdw 451 F4
ct. Bacchus Msh 221 L19
ct. Blackburn S 419 G1
ct. Sydenham 274 J7
st. Flemington 34 B4
st. Sunbury 143 F15
st. Sunbury 143 H16
SHIELS
la. Carlton 18 J14
SHIERLAW
av. Canterbury 373 G17
SHIERS
st. Alphington 327 J16
st. Reservoir 240 B20
SHILLING
la. Melbourne 2 G8
SHILO
ct. Thomastown 240 F16
SHIMMERLAKE
cl. Point Cook 451 B14
SHINE
ct. Narre Warren 539 C15
SHINNERS
av. Berwick 539 E19
av. Narre Warren 539 E19
SHINYRUBY
ct. Vermont S 420 G6
SHIPLEY
ct. Sunshine N 320 L11
st. Box Hill 374 J14
st. South Yarra 31 K6
st. South Yarra 414 E3
SHIPMAN
st. Blairgowrie 696 C5
SHIPSTON
rd. Cheltenham 531 C3
SHIPTON
ct. Campbellfield 239 G15
ct. Noble Park N 501 D14
SHIRALEE
ct. Wheelers Hl 461 C15
SHIRAZ
cl. Mt Martha 657 B9
cr. Narre Warren 539 A18
ct. Bundoora 242 J17
ct. Noble Park N 501 E9
ct. Sunbury 144 E9
dr. Waurn Ponds 705 F14
SHIRE
ct. Highton 701 D16
rd. Dromana 685 G9
SHIRLEY
av. Glen Waverley 419 J20
av. Seaford 573 F18
av. Sorrento 678 H12
cr. Woori Yall 344 G13
ct. Boronia 424 F16
ct. Brighton East 455 E15
ct. Croydon 380 B9
ct. Doncaster E 375 G4
ct. Mitcham 377 A12
gr. Heidelberg 328 J4
gr. St Kilda E 414 L14
gr. St Kilda E 415 A14
st. Altona Mdw 451 J1
st. Fawkner 281 E4
st. Mooroolbark 337 A15
st. Noble Park 500 E18
st. St Albans 319 J2
wy. Epping 196 G19
SHIRLIAN
st. Cheltenham 531 F1
SHIRLOW
av. Rye 697 L4
SHIRRA
pl. Attwood 237 E12
SHIRVINGTON
pl. Donvale 376 H3
SHOAL
ct. Dingley Vill 532 K9
SHOALHAVEN
st. Bundoora 284 E3
st. Werribee 447 G8
SHOALWATER
dr. Waterways 547 F1
SHOEMAKER
st. Attwood 237 A11
SHOEMARK
rd. Cranbourne W 577 D10
SHOGAKI
dr. Melton S 269 G9
SHOLDEN
ct. Wandana Ht 705 B1
SHOOBRA
rd. Elsternwick 455 B7
SHOPPERS
la. Taylors L 276 B6
SHORE
gr. Coburg N 281 J17
nk. Doncaster E 332 G14
SHORING
rd. Diggers Rest 187 A11
SHORT
av. Oak Park 279 K10
cr. The Basin 425 C13
cr. Tremont 425 C13
la. Pakenham 558 A12
rd. Eltham North 287 H2
rd. Hampton Pk 551 G14
st. Airport W 279 C13
st. Altona North 410 A8
st. Belmont 702 B18
st. Boronia 424 C10
st. Box Hill 375 C15
st. Camberwell 416 J6
st. Canterbury 373 G19
st. Dandenong 535 G9
st. Doncaster 375 A1
st. Footscray 367 E9
st. Glen Waverley 460 B3
st. Hampton E 495 J8
st. Keilor East 322 G4
st. Macleod 285 A10
st. Maidstone 366 H2
st. Malvern East 417 A20
st. Murrumbeena 457 D7
st. Northcote 326 J20
st. Ringwood E 379 C10
st. Springvale 500 C12
st. Torquay 711 L7
st. Vermont 421 B2
SHORT CUT
rd. Eltham 287 G15
wk. Lysterfield 504 H13
SHORTHORN
wk. Nar Warrn S 578 H1
SHORTLANDS
rd. Ringwood 422 A1
SHORTRIDGE
cct. Roxburgh Pk 194 B9
SHORTS
pl. Geelong, off Little Malop St 703 A8
rd. Coburg N 281 C13
rd. Eltham 289 A11
rd. N Warrandyte 289 A11
rd. Research 289 A11
SHOTTON
rd. Mt Eliza 641 F10
SHOUBRA
ct. Highton 701 G20
dr. Highton 701 H20
SHOWERS
av. Chelsea 546 J18
st. Braybrook 365 K5
st. Preston 326 H4
SHOW JUMP
cr. Endeavour Hl 503 L19
SHREWSBURY
ct. Frankston 628 D12
rd. Nunawading 376 K8
st. Bentleigh E 456 J17
st. Malvern East 457 J2
SHRIDAN
pl. Richmond 26 E11
SHRIMPTON
ct. Balwyn 374 B11
SHRIVES
rd. Hampton Pk 552 D7
rd. Narre Warren 552 D7
rd. Nar Warrn S 552 D7
SHROPSHIRE
st. Heidelberg 329 E4
SHRUBBY
wk. Croydon S 380 A14
SHUTE
av. Berwick 554 D5
cl. Templestowe 332 A11
SHUTER
st. Moonee Pnd 324 B14
SIAN
ct. S Morang 199 A10
pl. Point Cook 450 F8
SIANDRA
pl. Berwick 554 G13
SIBELLA
ct. Greensbrgh 243 L20
SIBERIA
la. Kensington 33 H7
SIBLEY
st. Werribee 448 B9
SIBTHORPE
st. Mordialloc 532 D9
SIBYL
av. Frankston S 627 B20
SICA
ct. Sydenham 274 J7
SIDDELEY
ct. Dingley Vill 532 L5
st. Docklands 23 F15
SIDDONS
wy. Hallam 537 D19
SIDGEWICK
st. Attwood 236 H11
SIDING
rd. Parwan 266 H18
SIDNEY
ct. Narre Warren 539 B13
pl. Caroline Spr 318 C9
st. Cranbourne 577 L15
st. Warrandyte 334 E1
SIDWELL
av. St Kilda E 415 A18
ct. Lower Plenty 286 H20
ct. St Kilda E 415 A18
SIEBEN
cl. Mill Park 242 C9
ct. Truganina 405 G13
SIEDE
ct. Cheltenham 496 F17
SIENNA
cr. Endeavour Hl 537 K7
ct. Rowville 463 G16
pl. Point Cook 450 H12
SIERRA
ct. Hoppers Csg 448 F5
pl. Chirnside Pk 337 J1
pl. Doncaster E 331 K20
SIGVARD
bvd. Hallam 538 B15
SILAS
av. Frankston 599 G19
SILBER
ct. Melton W 225 L19
SILFLAY
ct. Warranwood 335 C11
SILICON
pl. Tullamarine 278 F10
SILK
av. Manifold Ht 702 B6
ct. Dandenong N 502 D20
ct. Epping 198 F16
ct. Werribee 447 F13
la. Wesburn 347 L7
pl. W Melbourne 34 K19
st. Rosanna 285 C17
SILKHORN
cr. Mt Martha 656 C16
SILKWOOD
av. Berwick 539 F18
la. Craigieburn 150 E14
wy. Rowville 503 C2
SILKY OAK
dr. Bundoora 242 D13
gr. Sunbury 143 F17
SILVAN
av. Springvale 499 H17
ct. Emerald 510 E5
ct. Rowville 463 B19
ct. St Albans 320 D12
ct. Taylors Hill 274 K15
ct. Werribee 448 A19
gr. Hampton Pk 551 J8
gr. Mornington 640 K10
rd. Hurstbridge 246 L2
rd. Monbulk 428 D15
rd. Mt Evelyn 383 J3
rd. Olinda 383 L20
rd. Olinda 427 G11
rd. Silvan 384 C12
rd. Silvan 385 A19
rd. Silvan 428 H8
rd. Wattle Glen 246 L2
rd. Wattle Glen 247 A2
st. Oakleigh S 497 J8
SILVANA
ct. Doncaster E 332 F6
ct. Wheelers Hl 460 H17
wy. Hillside 274 F7
SILVAN VIEW
st. Kalorama 382 J15
SILVER
av. Frankston N 600 D7
gr. Nunawading 376 G15
st. Cheltenham 497 A20
st. Collingwood 19 J20
st. Eltham 287 D9
st. Malvern 416 A9
st. Newcomb 704 A18
st. Werribee 447 F11
SILVER ASH
av. Ashwood 418 D14
SILVER BIRCH
av. Dingley Vill 532 H5
cl. Croydon N 335 L13
ct. Nar Warrn S 553 C20
SILVERBIRCH
ri. Mill Park 242 L4
SILVER CREEK
dr. Lynbrook 551 F15
SILVERDALE
cl. Rowville 503 A7
ct. Doncaster E 331 H19
ct. Springvale S 534 C4
rd. Eaglemont 328 F12
ri. Bundoora 284 F8
wk. Cairnlea 320 A13
SILVERDENE
av. Sydenham 275 B7
SILVERENE
ct. Vermont S 421 C11
SILVEREYE
cr. Werribee 448 B4
pl. S Morang 243 J5
SILVER LEAF
ct. Forest Hill 376 D20
SILVERLEAF
pl. Healesville 214 D17
SILVERLEAVES
bvd. Berwick 539 H17
wy. Roxburgh Pk 193 J5
SILVERLEY
rd. Croydon 380 G4
SILVER RIDGE
rd. Pt Lonsdale 707 F18
SILVERTHORN
ct. Mill Park 242 E3
SILVERTON
cl. Laverton N 364 L16
dr. Ferntree Gly 463 K4
dr. Noble Park N 501 D12
pl. Craigieburn 150 A16
st. Malvern East 456 J2
SILVERTOP
cl. Lynbrook 551 G16
cr. Frankston N 600 A11
ct. Mill Park 243 B6
st. Frankston N 599 L11
SILVERTREE
av. Delahey 274 L13
av. Delahey 275 A14
av. Taylors Hill 274 L13
SILVER WATTLE
av. Maidstone 366 E3
cl. Rosebud W 699 B4
st. Yallambie 285 K14
SILVERWATTLE
dr. Lyndhurst 551 C20
rd. Launching Pl 346 A13
SILVERWOOD
ct. Hillside 231 L20
wy. Glen Waverley 420 K20
SILVESTER
cr. St Albans 320 A1
pde. Roxburgh Pk 193 L12
SIM
ct. Box Hill S 418 J4
st. Glenroy 279 L9
st. Mitcham 377 D15
st. Mt Waverley 419 F14
SIMCOCK
av. Spotswood 411 B1
st. Somerville 644 L13
st. Somerville 645 A13
SIMETO
wy. Roxburgh Pk 194 G6
SIMLA
cl. Viewbank 329 F1
ct. Heathmont 378 K20
st. Mitcham 377 B15
SIMMIE
st. Sunshine W 364 J5
SIMMINGTON
cct. Greenvale 192 L18
cct. Greenvale 193 A18
SIMMONDS
ct. Bentleigh E 457 A19
ct. Wantirna S 422 E16
pl. Endeavour Hl 537 B5
pl. Roxburgh Pk 194 C14
st. Hughesdale 457 F14
SIMMONS
av. Olinda 427 E9
cl. Cockatoo 471 H19
ct. Anglesea 713 L3
ct. Greensbrgh 286 F3
ct. South Yarra 32 F15
ct. South Yarra 414 J8
dr. Seaholme 409 J16
la. Belgrave S 506 K3
st. Box Hill N 374 K10
st. South Yarra 32 E14
st. South Yarra 414 H7
st. Tecoma 466 B7

SIMMS
rd. Greensbrgh 286 E7
SIMON
av. Noble Park 534 D4
av. Rowville 462 K20
ct. Brookfield 268 B4
ct. Darley 221 L10
ct. Epping 197 G15
ct. Hampton Pk 552 A14
ct. Rosanna 329 E1
ct. Werribee 448 F17
ct. Wheelers Hl 460 E15
dr. Pakenham 585 C6
st. Blackburn N 375 L8
st. Clayton S 498 H6
SIMONE
cr. Doncaster E 332 F5
ct. Hallam 538 C14
rd. Bacchus Msh 221 L13
SIMPSON
av. Sunbury 142 K14
av. Yallambie 285 F11
ct. Hallam 537 J13
ct. Meadow Ht 237 J7
ct. Werribee 446 J17
dr. Dandenong N 536 B1
dr. Mt Waverley 419 C15
la. Kensington 33 B11
pl. Hawthorn 371 F15
pl. Keilor East 322 B1
rd. Ferntree Gly 424 B20
st. Bacchus Msh 222 C18
st. E Melbourne 25 K9
st. Kew 372 F8
st. Mitcham 377 C16
st. Moorabbin 497 E12
st. Noble Park 500 E20
st. Northcote 326 L19
st. Pt Lonsdale 710 F7
st. Sunshine N 321 F14
st. Thomastown 240 H14
st. Yarraville 367 B16
wk. Kensington 33 B11
wy. Seabrook 450 K8
SIMPSONS
ct. Heathmont 422 G3
rd. Box Hill 375 C14
rd. Christmas Hills 206 B19
rd. Christmas Hills 250 B1
rd. Clayton S 498 K15
rd. The Basin 425 J8
SIMS
ct. Carrum Downs 575 D15
sq. Kensington 33 E7
st. Braybrook 365 L6
st. Pascoe Vale 280 J14
st. Reservoir 282 L3
st. Sandringham 495 B15
st. W Melbourne 367 J10
SINATRA
wy. Cranbourne E 604 J5
SINCLAIR
av. Edithvale 546 F12
av. Glen Iris 416 F9
av. Rye 697 E3
av. Templstw Lr 330 J10
cr. Macleod 285 D11
ct. Attwood 237 D10
ct. Hampton Pk 551 D6
ct. Mill Park 242 C3
ct. Mt Martha 655 J16
la. Edithvale, off Sinclair Av 546 F12
rd. Bayswater 423 J8
rd. Dandenong 535 E10
rd. Hurstbridge 204 A13
rd. Panton Hill 204 A13
st. Blairgowrie 695 J2
st. Cheltenham 496 H19
st. Elsternwick 454 K4
st. Oakleigh S 458 E20
st. Somerville 644 K16
SINCLAIRS
rd. Plumpton 273 A20
rd. Rockbank 317 A5
SINGER
av. Glen Waverley 420 H16
av. Keilor Dn 276 B12
SINGERS
la. Melbourne 1 F4
la. Melbourne 23 J4
SINGLETON
dr. Endeavour Hl 537 K6
dr. Mulgrave 500 G5
la. E Melbourne 25 H5
pl. Noble Park N 501 F16
rd. Balwyn N 329 J20
st. Collingwood 19 J18
tce. Kalorama 382 E14
tce. Montrose 382 E14
tce. Mt Dandenong 382 B18
tce. Mt Dandenong 382 E14
SINNOTT
st. Burwood 418 F11
st. Preston 327 B2
SINNS
av. Werribee 447 L15
SION
cl. Eltham 288 A11
SIRACUSA
av. Point Cook 450 E10
SIRDAR
st. Melton 226 K16
SIRENS
pl. Hallam 538 E15
SIRET
ct. Roxburgh Pk 194 D5
SIR GARNET
rd. Surrey Hills 373 H16
SIR HAROLD
cl. Endeavour Hl 537 H4
SIRI
ct. Kings Park 319 E3
SIRIUS
ct. Keilor Dn 275 J13
ct. Mill Park 242 K12
ct. Yallambie 285 G16
pl. Nar Warrn S 552 H11
SIR JOHN MONASH
dr. Caulfield E 456 C1
SIR LAURENCE
dr. Seaford 599 J6
SIROCCO
la. Newport 411 A12
SIR THOMAS
dr. Pakenham 585 F3
SIR WILLIAM
st. Kew 371 H9
SISKA
ct. Frankston 628 F7
SITAR
ct. Burwood E 419 J11
SITELLA
ct. Carrum Downs 600 J3
SITTELLA
ct. Werribee 447 K4
SIXTH
av. Altona North 409 K4
av. Altona North 409 K7
av. Anglesea 713 C11
av. Aspendale 546 F8
av. Burwood 418 B12
av. Chelsea Ht 547 F13
av. Cockatoo 510 H6
av. Dandenong 535 H6
av. Hadfield 281 C7
av. Rosebud 684 A20
av. Springvale 500 H10
av. Springvale 500 K10
av. Springvale 501 A10
st. Parkdale 531 E11
SIYAN
ri. Diamond Ck 246 A13
SKARDONS
rd. Cottles Br 204 G1
SKEFFINGTON
st. Bellfield 328 A6
SKEHAN
bvd. Altona Mdw 451 C1
pl. Epping 197 K15
SKELTON
pl. Sorrento 678 K9
rd. Craigieburn 194 G2
SKENE
ct. Greenvale 237 D2
pl. Fitzroy N 19 C2
st. Burwood E 419 C12
st. Flemington 367 L1
st. Newtown 702 D7
SKEWES
st. Avondale Ht 322 A9
st. Braybrook 365 K2
SKINNER
ct. Grovedale 705 K16
SKIPPER
la. Seddon, off Admiral St 367 D10
SKIPTON
cl. Keilor Dn 275 K13
ct. Mill Park 242 J11
ct. Wantirna 422 D11
pl. Endeavour Hl 504 A20
rd. Hughesdale 457 F10
rd. Olinda 427 G19
st. Box Hill 375 D13
st. St Albans 320 K6
SKUA
ct. Blind Bight 650 E8
SKUSE
ct. Greenvale 237 F1
SKY
ct. Jan Juc 711 B16
ct. Werribee 447 A10
la. Ashburton 417 G17
vw. Wonga Park 291 J16
SKYE
cr. Endeavour Hl 503 H19
ct. Bayswater N 380 J16
ct. Bayswater N 380 J16
ct. Chelsea Ht 547 G18
ct. Glen Waverley 460 J6
ct. Sunbury 143 B4
pl. Doncaster E 331 H16
rd. Frankston 599 H13
rd. Langwarrin 600 C16
rd. Wantirna 422 J8
st. Macleod 285 B10
SKYLINE
dr. Keilor 277 C14
dr. Maribyrnong 367 D2
dr. S Morang 199 B9
rd. Bend of Islands 250 C20
rd. Christmas Hills 250 C20
rd. Christmas Hills 251 H7
rd. Yarra Glen 208 B20
rd. Yarra Glen 208 F7
rd. Yarra Glen 251 H7
rd.n, Christmas Hills 208 B19
rd.n, St Andrews 208 E5
rd.n, Steels Ck 208 E5
rd.n, Yarra Glen 208 B19
ri. Craigieburn 150 D8
wy. Berwick 580 C3
SLADE
ct. Bundoora 285 C1
SLADEN
cl. Thomastown 240 D16
st. Cranbourne 603 K3
SLATER
av. Blackburn N 376 B9
ct. Narre Warren 553 D11
ct. Seaford 599 K1
ct. Sunbury 142 J14
pde. Keilor East 321 K1
pl. Burwood, off Livingstone Cl 418 E6
st. Melbourne 31 B9
st. Melbourne 414 B5
st. Northcote 327 C16
SLATTERY
ct. Maddingley 263 D5
st. Werribee 448 A15
SLEETH
av. Dandenong 536 C8
ct. Melton W 225 L18
SLESSOR
av. Lynbrook 551 D16
dr. Delahey 275 E13
SLEVIN
st. Lilydale 338 A4
SLIM
ct. Sunbury 143 E2
SLINGSBY
av. Beaconsfield 554 K16
SLOAN
ct. Sunbury 141 L8
SLOANE
ct. Altona Mdw 451 D6
ct. Keysborough 533 L8
st. Maribyrnong 322 L17
SLOANS
rd. N Warrandyte 290 A10
rd. Warrandyte 290 A19
SLOSS
rd. Healesville 258 B2
SLOUGH
rd. Altona 408 E15
st. Deer Park 319 C14
SLYM
ct. Springvale S 533 L5
SMALE
ct. Noble Park N 501 C17
ct. Seaford 599 K1
SMALL
ct. Mill Park 241 L4
rd. Bentleigh 496 C5
st. Hampton 494 L9
SMART
ct. Delahey 275 D12
ct. Grovedale 705 K15
st. Sunshine W 364 H2
st. Hawthorn, off Elgin St 371 H14
SMEATON
av. Dallas 238 C10
av. Hoppers Csg 448 H2
ct. Craigieburn 150 D19
ct. Frankston S 627 H13
SMEDLEY
la. Yarra Glen 209 H10
rd. Pk Orchards 377 K2
rd. Pk Orchards 378 A1
rd. Ringwood N 378 A1
SMEED
st. Black Rock 529 E1
SMETHURST
av. Pakenham 584 E6
st. Cranbourne 604 F1
SMETHWICK
grn. Caroline Spr 317 J3
SMIKE
st. Yallambie 285 H15
SMILEY
cr. Essendon W 323 A9
rd. Broadmeadows 238 F19
SMITH
av. Croydon 336 F19
av. Thomastown 241 H14
av. Williamstown 411 A16
cr. Footscray 367 E4
ct. Nar Warrn S 552 H13
ct. Sunbury 142 H2
rd. Camberwell 417 B7
rd. Springvale 500 E8
st. Albert Park 29 E11
st. Albert Park 413 C6
st. Alphington 327 J14
st. Bentleigh 456 D19
st. Brooklyn 365 E19
st. Brunswick W 324 K13
st. Burwood E 419 C11
st. Carrum 573 C8
st. Caulfield E 456 B1
st. Caulfield N 456 B1
st. Clifton Hill 19 F14
st. Coburg N 281 F16
st. Collingwood 25 F2
st. Fitzroy 19 F20
st. Fitzroy N 19 F14
st. Grovedale 706 G11
st. Hampton 495 H7
st. Healesville 257 F2
st. Kensington 34 A7
st. Maddingley 263 G3
st. Maidstone 322 J19
st. Marshall 706 L12
st. Melton 226 L18
st. Moonee Pnd 324 A11
st. Mt Martha 656 B9
st. Noble Park 501 B19
st. Port Melb 412 C3
st. Queenscliff 708 G19
st. Reservoir 283 B4
st. Richmond 26 C5
st. St Kilda 414 C18
st. S Melbourne 29 E10
st. S Melbourne 29 E5
st. S Melbourne 413 C3
st. S Melbourne 413 C5
st. Thornbury 326 C8
st. Williamstown 411 H19
SMITHACRES
rd. Montrose 381 K9
SMITHDENE
av. Ringwood E 379 D11
SMITHFIELD
ct. Keysborough 534 D12
rd. Flemington 33 B9
rd. Flemington 368 B4
rd. Kensington 33 B9
sq. Wantirna 422 K9
wk. Vermont 421 K1
SMITHS
la. Clyde North 581 F20
la. Pearcedale 647 F5
la. Smiths Gly 205 L3
rd. Parwan 263 J16
rd. Parwan 264 D16
rd. Templestowe 331 J11
rd. Yellingbo 387 K20
SMITHS GULLY
rd. Smiths Gly 205 F6
rd. Smiths Gly 206 B5
SMITHSON
ct. Dandenong S 535 G14
SMOKEY
ct. Somerville 644 E17
SMOLIC
ct. Tullamarine 236 E18
SMORGAN
ct. Kew 371 H5
SMORGON
sq. Kensington 33 E8
SMOULT
dr. Kurunjang 226 J14
SMYTH
pl. Geelong, off Little Ryrie St 703 B9
st. Chelsea Ht 547 H17
st. Frankston 599 D19
st. Mt Waverley 458 K6
st. Toorak 32 L14
st. Toorak 414 L7
st. Toorak 415 A7
SMYTHE
av. Balwyn 374 B13
la. Melbourne 24 G4
st. Geelong 703 A5
SNAEFELL
cr. Gladstone Pk 236 K16
SNAKE GULLY
dr. Bundoora 284 D
dr. Bundoora 284 E
SNAPPER POINT
dr. Patterson L 573 G
SNEAD
cl. Hoppers Csg 405 B1
ct. Dingley Vill 533 A
ct. Mt Waverley 458
SNEDDEN
dr. Glen Waverley 420 D2
SNEDDON
ct. Mulgrave 501 E
dr. Nar Warrn S 552 H1
SNELL
gr. Oak Park 280 B1
gr. Oak Park 280 D1
gr. Pascoe Vale 280 D1
SNEYDES
rd. Point Cook 449 H1
rd. Werribee 448 C1
rd. Werribee S 449 A1
rd. Werribee S 449 C1
SNIDERS
la. Melbourne 2 D
la. Melbourne 24 C
SNIPE
cl. Chelsea Ht 547 F
ct. Werribee 448 B
tr. Nar Warrn N 538 H
SNODGRASS
st. Pakenham 584
SNOOKS
ct. Brighton 454 J1
SNOW
ct. Darley 222 B
ct. The Basin 424
st. Keilor Park 278 B
SNOWBALL
av. Mt Evelyn 339 C
rd. Eltham North 287 E
SNOWBERRY
pl. Nar Warrn S 579 D
SNOWBUSH
lk. Langwarrin 601 E
tce. Point Cook 450 H
SNOWDEN
dr. Glen Waverley 460
pl. Canterbury 373 D1
pl. Vermont 420
pl. Vermont 421 A
pl. Wantirna S 422 J1
st. Laverton 407 D
st. Sunshine 321 E1
SNOWDON
av. Caulfield 455 H
cl. Keilor Dn 276 D1
dr. Cheltenham 531 G
SNOW GUM
pl. Somerville 644 D
rd. Doncaster E 332 E
SNOWGUM
cl. Rowville 463 J
ct. Bundoora 242 F
ct. Keysborough 534 A
ct. Mulgrave 501
ct. Nar Warrn S 553 D2
la. Beaconsfield 555 F
la. Brookfield 267
wk. Mornington 656
SNOWVIEW
dr. Yarra Jctn 346 K
SNOWY
ct. Clayton S 498
ct. Werribee 447
st. Dandenong N 501
SOAME
st. Deer Park 319 D
SOANES
dr. Mooroolbark 336 K
SOBAR
ct. Keilor Dn 275 L
SOCIETY
ct. Kilsyth 380
SODEN
rd. Bangholme 547
SODERLUND
dr. Doncaster 330 G
SOFIA
ct. Sunshine N 321 E
SOKLENG
cl. Rowville 502
SOLAIRE
wy. S Morang 198 L
SOLANDER
ct. Roxburgh Pk 194 A
st. Dromana 686
SOLAR
ct. Glen Waverley 460
ct. Nunawading 376
dr. Whittington 704 B

SOLDIERS
rd. Berwick 554 J20
rd. Berwick 580 J5
rd. Clyde North 580 J5
SOLELL
pl. Nar Warrn S 579 F5
SOLENT
cr. Taylors L 275 G8
SOLFERINO
cl. Mt Waverley 419 F13
wy. Carrum Downs 575 G15
SOLITACE
wk. Glen Waverley 459 K1
SOLLEY
ct. Carrum Downs 600 F4
SOLLY
av. Princes Hill 325 H18
SOLLYA
ct. Narre Warren 553 E11
SOLOMON
ct. Sunbury 142 K3
dr. Cairnlea 319 E10
dr. Keilor 277 A14
la. Truganina 405 J14
st. Mt Waverley 458 F5
SOLOMONS
tce. Mt Martha 656 C15
SOLSON
ct. Springvale S 533 K7
pl. Donvale 376 J5
SOLWAY
cl. Ferntree Gly 463 J8
cl. Patterson L 547 H18
ct. Epping 197 L18
ct. St Helena 245 A18
dr. Glen Waverley 420 F15
gdn. Werribee 446 K9
st. Ashburton 417 C20
SOLWOOD
ct. Somerville 644 G17
la. Blackburn 375 K15
SOMALI
cl. Diamond Ck 245 H16
st. Pascoe Vale S 324 H2
SOMERLAYTON
cr. Fawkner 281 J1
SOMERLEIGH
cr. Greensbrgh 244 E20
cr. Greensbrgh 286 E1
rd. Laverton N 364 H16
SOMERS
av. McCrae 684 L17
av. Macleod 285 A13
av. Malvern 415 K9
av. Mt Martha 655 G20
cl. McCrae 685 A17
cl. Mill Park 242 B5
ct. Avondale Ht 322 F9
ct. Glen Waverley 459 J1
pde. Altona 408 G20
rd. N Warrandyte 289 L16
st. Balaclava 414 G20
st. Bentleigh 455 H18
st. Burwood 418 B9
st. Mitcham 377 G16
st. Newtown 702 G9
st. Noble Park 500 D17
st. Sunshine N 321 G12
SOMERSET
cl. Werribee 446 L11
cr. Croydon 379 L1
ct. Blackburn S 419 H6
ct. Mulgrave 500 K4
ct. Nar Warrn S 579 A4
ct. Rowville 503 D6
dr. Dandenong N 502 B11
dr. Dromana 686 D10
dr. Keysborough 534 L9
dr. Mt Martha 669 K3
dr. Portsea 678 F2
dr. Sunshine N 321 A9
dr. Viewbank 329 H3
pl. Melbourne 2 A11
pl. Melbourne 24 B7
pl. Safety Bch 669 C16
pl. Windsor 414 H12
rd. Campbellfield 239 D14
rd. Frankston S 627 B15
rd. Glen Iris 417 D9
st. Avondale Ht 322 B11
st. Box Hill N 375 B6
st. Elsternwick 455 B3
st. Epping 197 L17
st. Pascoe Vale 280 D17
st. Richmond 26 H8
st. Richmond 371 A14
st. St Kilda 414 E15
st. Sunbury 142 B13
st. Wantirna S 422 K12
st. Wantirna S 423 A13
SOMERTON
cr. St Albans 275 G19
ct. Darley 222 B11
rd. Bulla 190 D14
rd. Bulla 190 E12
rd. Greenvale 192 B14
rd. Greenvale 193 B15
rd. Greenvale 193 G16
rd. Oaklands Jctn 190 H12
rd. Oaklands Jctn 191 B13
rd. Roxburgh Pk 193 G16
rd. Somerton 193 B15
SOMERTON PARK
dr. Campbellfield 194 K20
SOMERVILLE
cr. Somerville 645 D15
rd. Brooklyn 365 B11
rd. Footscray 367 G15
rd. Hampton Pk 551 D8
rd. Kingsville 366 J13
rd. Sunshine W 364 J11
rd. Sunshine W 364 K11
rd. Sunshine W 365 B11
rd. Tottenham 366 A13
rd. W Footscray 366 A13
rd. Yarraville 366 H13
st. Coburg 325 E5
st. Doncaster 330 G17
SOMES
st. Wantirna S 462 A4
SOMME
av. Frankston 626 J3
pde. Edithvale 546 G14
SOMMERS
dr. Altona Mdw 451 H10
pl. Geelong 703 E9
st. Belmont 702 H16
SOMMERSBY
ct. Lysterfield 464 B20
rd. Point Cook 450 F11
rd. Point Cook 450 F11
SOMMEVILLE
dr. Roxburgh Pk 194 E14
SONG
st. Narre Warren 539 C20
SONGBIRD
av. Chirnside Pk 337 A3
SONGLARK
cr. Werribee 447 K4
SONIA
cl. Lilydale 338 C15
ct. Cranbourne W 577 F14
ct. Werribee 446 L11
ct. Werribee 447 A11
st. Carrum Downs 574 E18
st. Dandenong S 549 K8
st. Donvale 376 E4
st. Ringwood 378 H7
SONJA
ct. Narre Warren 553 B12
SONLEY
st. Maidstone 366 G3
SONNET
wy. Truganina 405 F14
SOPHI
ct. Mulgrave 500 E4
SOPHIA
av. Aspendale 546 C6
ct. Campbellfield 239 H12
ct. Carrum Downs 601 D4
gr. Parkdale 531 E13
gr. Tecoma 466 B12
pl. Melton W 226 B17
SOPHIE
ct. Hallam 537 H14
ct. Mornington 641 C20
st. Kilsyth 381 F8
SOPHORA
ct. Templstw Lr 330 K14
SORBONNE
dr. Sunbury 144 E10
SORBUS
cl. Endeavour Hl 536 L2
SORELL
ct. Keilor Dn 276 F13
SORGHUM
wy. Delahey 275 A13
SORREL
cr. Warranwood 334 J12
SORRELL
ct. Altona Mdw 451 J5
SORRENTO
av. Berwick 539 J17
av. Point Cook 450 E8
pl. Epping 197 E17
st. Broadmeadows 237 H15
SORRETT
av. Malvern 415 K11
SOTTILE
dr. Cranbourne 603 K5
SOUDAN
rd. W Footscray 366 J5
st. Coburg 325 A1
st. Malvern 415 K16
SOUHAIL
ct. Berwick 554 B19
ct. Cranbourne W 577 J19
SOUTER
st. Beaconsfield 555 B16
st. Eltham 287 D16
st. Springvale 499 G13
SOUTH
av. Altona Mdw 451 F6
av. Bentleigh 496 A5
av. Mt Evelyn 383 C2
brk. Lysterfield 504 F17
cnc. Beaumaris 530 A10
cr. Heidelberg W 328 C1
cr. Northcote 326 J19
ct. Highett 496 G13
ct. Surrey Hills 418 A2
dr. Werribee S 488 A9
gwy. Langwarrin 629 H1
lk. Chirnside Pk 337 D6
pde. Blackburn 375 H15
rd. Airport W 278 H14
rd. Bentleigh 496 B6
rd. Bentleigh E 497 A7
rd. Braybrook 365 J4
rd. Brighton 494 H4
rd. Brighton East 495 B5
rd. Hampton E 495 B5
rd. McCrae 684 J13
rd. Menzies Ck 467 L16
rd. Moorabbin 496 B6
rd. Rosebud 684 F15
rd. Werribee 448 F16
st. Ascot Vale 324 D18
st. Belmont 702 B19
st. Hadfield 280 H9
st. Hawthorn 415 L1
st. Preston 327 A3
st. Seddon 367 D11
tce. Avondale Ht 322 A6
tce. Clifton Hill 20 A7
tce. Seabrook 451 B6
SOUTHAM
ct. Bulleen 329 H15
st. Brunswick W 324 F7
SOUTHAMPTON
cr. Abbotsford 26 L2
cr. Abbotsford 371 A11
dr. Point Cook 450 E5
st. Footscray 367 A7
SOUTH ANDERSON
ct. Cranbourne 577 L11
SOUTH AUDLEY
st. Abbotsford 26 K3
st. Brunswick 325 J13
SOUTHBANK
bvd. Southbank 3 H5
bvd. Southbank 24 C14
prm. Southbank 24 C13
wk. Taylors Hill 274 G8
SOUTH BOUNDARY
rd.e, Pearcedale 646 D7
rd.e, Somerville 646 D7
rd.w, Pearcedale 645 K4
SOUTHBOURNE
av. Dandenong S 535 J13
SOUTH BOX
ct. Hadfield 281 A6
SOUTH CAROLINE
st. South Yarra 31 K10
st. South Yarra 414 E5
SOUTH CENTRE
rd. Melb Airport 235 L20
rd. Melb Airport 277 L2
SOUTH CHARLES
ct. Cranbourne 577 L12
SOUTH CIRCULAR
rd. Gladstone Pk 236 L19
rd. Gladstone Pk 237 A20
SOUTH CORPORATE
av. Rowville 502 A1
SOUTH DALY
st. Brunswick W 324 K15
SOUTHDEAN
Melton W 225 G19
st. Dandenong 535 L2
SOUTHDOWN
av. Glen Waverley 460 B3
cr. Belmont 706 C7
SOUTHDOWNE
cl. Springvale 500 B14
SOUTHERN
bvd. Nar Warrn S 579 B1
cr. Craigieburn 150 E16
ct. Forest Hill 420 E3
dr. Dingley Vill 533 F9
rd. Heidelberg Ht 328 A1
rd. Heidelberg W 328 A1
rd. Mentone 531 K8
rd. Moorabbin Aprt 531 K8
SOUTHERN CROSS
dr. Roxburgh Pk 194 F10
st. Chirnside Pk 337 G1
SOUTHERNHAY
st. Reservoir 283 A14
SOUTHEY
ct. Elwood 454 E1
gr. Elwood 454 E1
rd. Boronia 424 G4
st. Blackburn N 375 K10
st. Brighton 455 A15
st. Elwood 454 D1
st. Kensington 34 A13
st. Sandringham 495 C16
st. Williamstn N 410 D12
SOUTHFORK
dr. Kilsyth S 381 B15
SOUTHGATE
av. Southbank 3 L5
av. Southbank 4 D4
av. Southbank 24 D13
av. Southbank 24 F13
st. Parkville 34 J5
SOUTH GATEWAY
Avondale Ht 321 K9
Coldstream 295 C14
SOUTH GIPPSLAND
fwy. Dandenong S 551 B7
fwy. Doveton 537 C19
fwy. Eumemmerring 537 C19
fwy. Hallam 537 C19
fwy. Hampton Pk 551 B7
hwy. Cranbourne 578 C11
hwy. Cranbourne E 604 E5
hwy. Cranbourne N 577 H1
hwy. Dandenong S 536 F16
hwy. Dandenong S 550 H1
hwy. Hampton Pk 551 D12
hwy. Hampton Pk 577 H1
hwy. Junction Vill 604 E5
hwy. Lynbrook 551 D12
hwy. Lynbrook 577 H1
hwy. Tooradin 650 J1
hwy. Tooradin 651 A3
SOUTH HIDDEN VALLEY
cct. Beaconsfield 555 G14
SOUTH HILL
tr. Warrandyte 334 D5
SOUTHLAND
st. Glen Iris 417 A12
SOUTH LOCALISER
rd. Melb Airport 235 E19
SOUTH MADDINGLEY
rd. Maddingley 263 K8
SOUTH PARK
cl. Keysborough 533 J9
dr. Dandenong S 549 G2
st. Northcote 326 F18
SOUTH RIDGE
ct. Beaconsfield 555 F15
SOUTH RING
rd. Werribee 487 L1
SOUTH SHORE
av. Point Cook 450 L14
SOUTH VALLEY
rd. Highton 705 H7
rd. Pk Orchards 333 J15
SOUTHWARD
av. Port Melb 412 H3
SOUTHWELL
cl. Endeavour Hl 537 G10
SOUTH WHARF
rd. Southbank, off Lorimer St 23 E17
SOUTHWICK
bvd. Altona Mdw 451 E1
SOUTHWOLD
st. St Albans 320 F6
SOUTHWOOD
cl. Wantirna 421 L12
SOVEREIGH
ct. Templestowe, off Oakwood Ct 331 L14
SOVEREIGN
cl. Patterson L 547 G19
ct. Epping 198 A17
ct. Mornington 641 F12
pl. Wantirna S 422 F18
ri. Diamond Ck 245 J6
rt. Hoppers Csg 448 D1
wy. Avondale Ht 322 B10
wy. Hillside 231 J20
SOVEREIGN MANORS
cr. Rowville 463 J13
SOVEREIGN POINT
ct. Doncaster 330 K19
SOVEREIGN CREST
bvd. Rowville 463 L12
SOWTER
ct. Donvale 376 K1
SPAIN
ct. Northcote 326 F16
SPALDING
av. Sunshine N 321 E7
ct. Rowville 502 J4
SPANIEL
ct. Mill Park 242 K3
SPANISH GULLY
rd. Smiths Gly 205 K9
SPARK
ct. Vermont S 420 L8
gr. Preston 327 C5
la. Melbourne 24 K8
st. Murrumbeena 457 C11
SPARKFORD
rd. Craigieburn 150 B15
st. Ivanhoe 327 K11
SPARKS
av. Burwood 418 L11
av. Fairfield 327 F14
av. Thornbury 327 G10
st. Beaumaris 530 C13
SPARROW
av. Anglesea 713 D7
st. S Morang 199 J11
SPARROWHAWK
rd. Doreen 156 L12
SPARTA
pl. Brunswick, off Tripovich St 325 F13
SPAVIN
dr. Sunbury 143 B4
SPEAKMEN
st. Kensington 33 B10
SPEAN
ct. Endeavour Hl 503 H17
SPEAR
ct. Altona 408 K15
ct. Bulleen 329 G12
ct. Glen Waverley 420 L16
SPEARFELT
ct. Cairnlea 319 F6
SPEARGRASS
dr. Hillside 231 K15
st. Maribyrnong 367 E2
SPEARWATER
wy. Burwood 418 B4
SPEEDIE
st. Coburg N 281 J15
SPEEDWAY
dr. Calder Park 232 K14
SPEEDWELL
st. Somerville 645 B11
SPEERS
ct. Warrandyte 332 G2
SPEIGHT
st. Newport 410 H7
st. Thornbury 327 A10
SPELLMAN
av. Sydenham 274 K5
SPENCE
av. Roxburgh Pk 194 B9
st. Burwood 418 E10
st. Keilor Park 277 K13
SPENCER
av. Avonsleigh 470 C17
av. Dromana 686 F2
ct. Berwick 554 F17
ct. Melton S 268 C12
dr. Carrum Downs 575 E15
pl. Richmond 26 H12
rd. Camberwell 373 B20
rd. Camberwell 373 C19
rd. Olinda 427 G15
rd. Parkville 18 B12
st. Blairgowrie 680 B20
st. Docklands 23 E5
st. Essendon 323 C4
st. Essendon 323 F4
st. Hawthorn 371 G15
st. Heidelberg Ht 284 F20
st. Melbourne 23 E5
st. Mentone 531 A6
st. Mt Martha 669 D3
st. Northcote 326 H11
st. Nunawading 376 H9
st. Preston 282 K18
st. Sunshine W 364 G15
st. Thomastown 241 G16
st. Thornbury 326 H11
st. W Melbourne 23 A1
st. W Melbourne 34 L20
SPENSER
st. St Kilda 414 B18
SPENSLEY
st. Clifton Hill 20 D4
st. Rosebud 684 G14
SPERO
av. Mt Eliza 626 C19
SPERRY
dr. Tullamarine 278 G2
SPICE
ri. Hallam 538 C18
SPICER
bvd. Altona Mdw 451 B4
ct. Aspendale Gdn 546 J5
st. Beaumaris 530 G6

SPIKE
cl. S Morang 199 H8
SPILLERS
rd. Macclesfield 471 F1
SPINDRIFT
ct. Carrum Downs 600 L5
wy. Point Cook 450 H7
SPINEBILL
ct. Healesville 258 A1
SPINIFEX
st. Cairnlea 319 F8
SPINK
st. Brighton 455 A11
SPINNAKER
ct. Aspendale Gdn 546 L3
ri. Mornington 640 H20
ri. Mornington 656 H1
SPINNINGDALE
cl. Seabrook 450 K6
SPINOSA
cl. Endeavour Hl 536 L1
SPLENDENS
wk. Narre Warren 553 C2
SPLIT ROCK
rd. Beaconsfld Up 542 L17
SPOLETO
cl. Keilor Ldg 275 L4
SPOONBILL
ct. Carrum Downs 601 A1
st. Berwick 579 L2
st. Doreen 156 L13
SPORING
ct. Endeavour Hl 537 K10
ct. Roxburgh Pk 194 D14
SPORTSMANS
dr. Pakenham 584 A2
SPOTTED GUM
cr. Bundoora 242 F13
SPRATLING
st. Reservoir 282 G11
SPRAY
av. Mordialloc 532 D20
st. Elwood 454 E4
st. Frankston 599 F15
st. Mornington 640 H16
st. Parkdale 531 F14
st. Rosebud 684 B20
SPRAY POINT
rd. Blairgowrie 679 D20
SPRING
cct. Caroline Spr 318 B6
cct. Pakenham 583 L4
cl. Melton W 226 D12
ct. Ringwood 335 C18
dr. Hoppers Csg 448 J2
dr. Hoppers Csg 449 A2
la. Coldstream 254 H19
la. Gruyere 254 H19
rd. Belgrave S 505 L11
rd. Caulfield S 455 K12
rd. Dingley Vill 533 D2
rd. Hampton E 495 L12
rd. Highett 495 L12
rd. Junction Vill 604 G12
rd. Malvern 415 L12
rd. Monbulk 428 J20
rd. Monbulk 468 J1
rd. Silvan 428 K3
rd. Springvale S 533 D2
ri. Glen Waverley 459 L2
sq. Hallam 537 J16
st. Belmont 706 H2
st. Box Hill 374 H13
st. Bulleen 329 L9
st. Coburg 282 A19
st. Doveton 536 J7
st. E Melbourne 24 J2
st. Ferntree Gly 464 F4
st. Fitzroy 18 L12
st. Frankston 627 B2
st. Geelong West 702 H6
st. Greensbrgh 244 F19
st. Melbourne 24 J2
st. Mt Evelyn 339 G17
st. Niddrie 278 G18
st. Prahran 32 L19
st. Prahran 414 L10
st. Prahran 415 A10
st. Preston 282 H18
st. Reservoir 282 J14
st. Rye 696 J2
st. Sandringham 495 G18
st. Thomastown 240 J15
st. Thomastown 241 A15
st. Torquay 711 L8
st. Tullamarine 278 G5
st.e, Port Melb 29 A7
st.e, Port Melb 413 B4
st.n, Port Melb 29 A6
st.s, Port Melb 29 A7
st.w, Port Melb 412 L3
st.w, Port Melb 413 A3
SPRINGBANK
ct. Bulleen 329 G14
ct. Point Cook 450 K12
pl. Viewbank 329 G1
ri. Nar Warrn N 538 D3
st. Tullamarine 236 E18
wy. Brookfield 267 L9
SPRINGBROOK
pl. Point Cook 451 D8
SPRINGFIELD
av. Camberwell 417 F5
av. Clayton S 498 H4
av. Croydon 380 D4
av. St Kilda E 414 L19
av. St Kilda E 415 A19
av. Toorak 415 C7
cl. Caroline Spr 318 E4
cr. Hampton Pk 551 K12
ct. Bundoora 243 E13
ct. Mill Park 242 K6
ct. Noble Park N 501 E18
dr. Narre Warren 552 F1
rd. Blackburn 376 B11
rd. Blackburn N 375 D10
rd. Boronia 423 L15
rd. Box Hill N 375 D10
rd. Mitcham 376 J11
rd. Nunawading 376 J11
rd. Springvale S 499 G19
st. Briar Hill 286 H4
SPRING GARDENS
st. South Yarra 31 H13
SPRINGHALL
pde. Pascoe Vale S 324 K3
SPRING HILL
ct. Queenscliff 707 K19
SPRINGHILL
rd. Hurstbridge 202 G14
SPRINGHURST
cr. Grovedale 705 L17
SPRINGLAKE
av. Caroline Spr 317 K7
av. Caroline Spr 317 L8
av. Caroline Spr 318 A8
SPRINGS
rd. Clarinda 498 F9
rd. Clayton S 498 F9
st. Cockatoo 510 L6
SPRINGSIDE
cr. Keysborough 535 B9
dr. Grovedale 706 E10
SPRINGSONG
ps. Chirnside Pk 337 G1
SPRINGTHORPE
bvd. Macleod 284 K10
SPRINGVALE
rd. Aspendale Gdn 547 D7
rd. Bangholme 547 D7
rd. Braeside 533 G20
rd. Burwood E 420 E11
rd. Chelsea Ht 547 D7
rd. Dingley Vill 533 J10
rd. Donvale 376 H3
rd. Forest Hill 376 F20
rd. Forest Hill 420 E11
rd. Glen Waverley 460 C7
rd. Keysborough 547 D7
rd. Mulgrave 500 A8
rd. Nunawading 376 F20
rd. Springvale 499 K19
rd. Springvale S 533 H10
rd. Vermont S 420 E11
rd. Waterways 547 D7
rd. Wheelers Hl 460 B20
SPRING VALLEY
av. Craigieburn 150 G16
dr. Clayton S 499 E12
dr. Templestowe 331 L6
dr. Torquay 711 H12
SPRINGVALLEY
cr. Keysborough 534 B11
wy. Nar Warrn S 552 E14
SPRINGVIEW
bvd. Taylors Hill 274 L9
SPRING WATER
cr. Cranbourne 603 D6
SPRINGWATER
sq. Point Cook 450 K12
SPRINGWOOD
av. Narre Warren 552 J4
cl. Donvale 332 K15
ct. Brookfield 267 J8
vw. Bundoora 284 G7
SPRINGYBARK
tr. Langwarrin 629 B11
SPRINT
st. Keilor Park 278 B15
SPROUL
st. Sunshine N 321 B9
SPRUCE
ct. Frankston N 600 E7
ct. Gladstone Pk 237 D19
ct. Narre Warren 538 J19
dr. Rowville 463 H18
SPRUZEN
av. Kew East 372 A4
SPRY
st. Coburg N 281 F14
SPRYS
la. Hurstbridge 203 C17
SPUNNER
ct. Sorrento 678 F8
SPUR
la. Carlton 18 J15
SPURGEON
cl. Rye 697 C14
SPURLING
cl. S Geelong 702 L13
cl. S Geelong 703 A13
st. Maidstone 366 H1
SPURR
av. Bacchus Msh 221 F13
st. Craigieburn 150 F17
SPURWAY
la. Brunswick 325 D17
SPYGLASS
cl. Heatherton 497 G16
ct. Sunbury 144 B10
SQUATTER
ct. Werribee 447 J7
SQUATTERS
tr. Cairnlea 319 L11
SQUIRE
ct. Glen Waverley 420 L18
st. Blairgowrie 696 A3
SQUIRES
ct. Caroline Spr 318 C5
SREDNA
st. W Footscray 366 C9
STABLE
ct. Endeavour Hl 504 A20
gr. Skye 575 G17
STABLEFORD
av. Glen Waverley 459 J4
ct. Rowville 463 H20
STABLES
pl. Sydenham 274 L5
STACEY
ct. Endeavour Hl 538 B2
STACKPOLE
cr. Sunbury 142 H15
STACKPOOLE
st. Noble Park 534 L6
STADAN
pl. Hillside 232 F18
STADIUM
dr. Docklands 23 C12
dr. Keilor Park 277 J10
dr. Tullamarine 277 J10
STAFF
st. Seddon 367 C10
STAFFORD
ct. Bayswater N 380 E19
ct. Doncaster E 332 B18
ct. Ivanhoe East 328 G14
pl. Chirnside Pk 336 G6
pl. Narre Warren 539 B16
pl. Williamstown 411 J16
rd. S Morang 198 K10
st. Abbotsford 20 B15
st. Blackburn S 419 E2
st. Footscray 366 L7
st. Herne Hill 701 K3
st. Hoppers Csg 405 D14
st. Huntingdale 458 D15
st. Melton S 268 G10
st. Northcote 327 D17
st. Preston 326 C3
st. Richmond 371 A17
STAG
la. Yarra Glen 210 B15
STAGECOACH
bvd. S Morang 199 K16
cl. Hoppers Csg 447 L1
cr. Sydenham 274 L6
STAINSBY
cl. Endeavour Hl 537 C4
cr. Roxburgh Pk 194 D16
STAKE
rd. Diggers Rest 187 B10
STALEY
st. Brunswick 325 G13
st. Junction Vill 604 G12
STALLARD
ct. Watsonia N 243 D18
STALLION
ct. Nar Warrn S 578 K1
STAMFORD
cl. Bacchus Msh 221 L16
cr. Rowville 462 G19
ct. Broadmeadows 238 J12
ct. Eltham 288 D4
ct. Ringwood N 334 L19
gr. Caroline Spr 317 J4
rd. Oakleigh 458 C9
STANBURY
ct. Sunshine W 364 B5
STANDALE
ct. Highton 701 L16
STANDARD
av. Box Hill 374 G17
STANDEN
ct. Warranwood 335 B13
STANDFIELD
st. Bacchus Msh 222 A19
STANDRING
ct. Donvale 332 G18
STANE BRAE
ct. Wonga Park 291 C15
STANFIELD
ct. Glen Waverley 420 D18
dr. Wandana Ht 705 C1
STANFORD
av. Keysborough 533 J16
cl. Fawkner 281 F1
cl. Werribee 446 K11
ct. Frankston 600 C17
ct. Sunbury 144 E10
ct. Whittington 704 A19
st. Ascot Vale 323 G18
st. Sunshine 365 D6
STANGER
st. Yarraville 366 D16
STANHILL
dr. Cranbourne S 602 L12
STANHOPE
ct. Ringwood 378 C18
ct. South Yarra 32 J10
ct. South Yarra 414 K5
gr. Camberwell 372 L19
gr. Camberwell 373 A19
st. Armadale 415 J13
st. Black Rock 529 G2
st. Broadmeadows 238 E17
st. Dandenong S 535 H13
st. Eltham 287 E8
st. Geelong West 702 D6
st. Malvern 415 K13
st. Mont Albert 374 D16
st. Upwey 465 K14
st. W Footscray 366 D6
STANILAND
av. Malvern 415 L16
gr. Elsternwick 454 L4
gr. Elsternwick 455 A5
STANIS
st. Eumemmerring 536 L15
st. Eumemmerring 537 A15
STANLAKE
ri. Templstw Lr 330 E8
st. Footscray 366 L5
st. Reservoir 282 K13
STANLEY
av. Cheltenham 530 J1
av. Eltham 287 J5
av. Hawthorn E 372 F17
av. Mt Waverley 458 H9
av. Ringwood E 379 B11
cr. Brookfield 268 A4
cr. Mt Martha 668 K6
cr. Mt Martha 669 A6
ct. Deer Park 318 L11
ct. Hoppers Csg 405 C18
ct. Thomastown 241 K14
dr. Doncaster 331 A14
dr. Somerton 194 H11
gr. Blackburn 375 F12
gr. Canterbury 372 L16
gr. Canterbury 373 A16
pde. Caulfield N 415 G19
pl. Hawthorn E 372 H20
rd. Healesville 258 D5
rd. Keysborough 534 F18
rd. Laverton N 364 E18
rd. Monbulk 428 D20
rd. Vermont S 420 H10
st. Altona 408 H19
st. Belgrave 466 H12
st. Black Rock 529 G4
st. Box Hill S 374 J19
st. Brighton 455 A18
st. Brunswick 325 K12
st. Bulleen 329 G16
st. Carrum 573 B8
st. Chirnside Pk 336 H5
st. Collingwood 19 G16
st. Cranbourne 578 A17
st. Dandenong 535 H8
st. Don Valley 346 E6
st. Elsternwick 454 L5
st. Elsternwick 455 A5
st. Essendon 323 L9
st. Frankston 599 E18
st. Glenroy 279 K9
st. Hampton Pk 551 F10
st. Ivanhoe 327 K10
st. Kew 371 L12
st. Malvern East 416 J16
st. Newtown 702 E12
st. Northcote 327 B19
st. Olinda 426 J4
st. Pascoe Vale 280 K19
st. Richmond 26 D16
st. Somerville 645 D15
st. Somerville 645 D16
st. South Yarra 32 H10
st. South Yarra 414 K5
st. The Basin 425 A9
st. W Footscray 366 G5
st. W Melbourne 23 A4
st. Williamstown 411 F12
tce. Surrey Hills 373 H18
STANLEY GROSE
dr. Malvern East 417 A18
STANLEY JONES
dr. S Morang 243 J2
STANSELL
st. Kew 372 C13
STANSFIELD
ct. Frankston S 628 D16
STANTON
cl. Mt Martha 656 K10
cl. Nar Warrn S 552 G13
cr. Rosanna 285 A16
ct. Darley 222 C11
ct. Glen Waverley 461 B3
ct. Pakenham 584 H11
ct. Seabrook 450 K3
ct. Westmeadows 236 L15
ct. Westmeadows 237 A15
dr. Diamond Ck 245 K13
gr. Lilydale 339 L5
pl. Mill Park 242 E5
st. Abbotsford 20 B18
st. Doncaster 374 E3
st. Highett 496 J15
STANWORTH
ct. Preston 282 J19
STAPLES
ct. Hadfield 281 B6
wy. Seabrook 450 L8
STAPLEY
cr. Altona North 410 D5
cr. Chadstone 458 A6
STAR
al. Melbourne 2 F11
al. Melbourne 24 E6
cr. Hallam 551 H1
ct. Fawkner 281 F6
gr. Bundoora 242 D15
st. Geelong, off Myers St 703 A8
STARBOARD
la. Patterson L 547 H20
STARCHENKO
ct. Carrum Downs 575 E16
STARCROSS
av. Croydon 379 K5
STARFLOWER
wy. Sunbury 143 E19
STARK
pl. Sunshine 365 C2
STARLING
rd. Diamond Ck 245 D8
rd. Officer 556 H20
st. Burwood 419 A10
st. Montmorency 286 G7
st. S Morang 199 H10
STATE
st. Oakleigh E 458 E11
STATEN
wy. Point Cook 451 C10
STATEN ISLAND
Patterson L 573 J7
STATESMAN
av. Burwood E 419 J9
av. Roxburgh Pk 194 A4
cr. Mill Park 242 L9
cr. Mooroolbark 337 H10
STATION
av. Ascot Vale 324 C17
av. Ashwood 418 D18
av. Emerald 509 K5
av. Glen Iris 417 E9
av. McKinnon 456 C16
av. St Albans 320 E3
cr. Baxter 644 D3
la. Mernda 155 K17
la. Williamstown 411 C13
pl. Glen Huntly 456 D6
pl. Sunshine 365 D4
pl. Malvern, off Princes Hwy 415 J16
rd. Albanvale 319 E11
rd. Cairnlea 319 E11
rd. Cheltenham 530 J1
rd. Cockatoo 510 K4
rd. Deer Park 319 D18
rd. Gembrook 512 H10
rd. Glenroy 280 A9
rd. Launching Pl 346 K9
rd. Marshall 706 L9

STREETS

STOOKE
st. Yarraville 366 D16
STORE
st. Melb Airport.......235 B11
STOREN
cl. Ferntree Gly 424 G18
STORER
dr. Dromana 685 K10
STORES
ct. Braybrook..........366 B5
STOREY
av. Hampton 495 D9
av. Research 288 H2
ct. Tootgarook.........698 E8
dr. Pakenham 584 H9
rd. Reservoir 283 B13
st. Yarraville 367 B14
STORK
av. Belmont.............706 F2
STORNOWAY
dr. Baxter................644 C1
gln. Viewbank...........286 B16
pl. Camberwell.........417 H7
rd. Camberwell.........417 H6
STORRER
st. Geelong.............703 D10
STORRINGTON
av. Hoppers Csg......405 B20
STORTFORD
av. Ivanhoe 327 K10
STORY
rd. Warburton 349 H6
st. Parkville...............17 F11
STOTT
st. Box Hill S...........418 F5
st. Northcote 326 H12
st. Preston..............326 G4
st. Thornbury...........326 H9
STOTTS
la. Frankston S 628 A20
STOW
cl. Epping...............198 E19
STOWE
av. Greensbrgh.........286 B6
STOWHEAD
la. Caroline Spr........317 L3
STRABANE
av. Balwyn 374 C9
av. Mont Albert N 374 C9
wy. Hampton Pk.........551 F12
wy. Hampton Pk.........551 G12
STRACHAN
av. Manifold Ht.........702 B2
cl. Taylors L 233 A19
la. Melbourne 24 J7
pl. Melton S.............268 G13
st. Oak Park.............280 A11
STRACHANS
rd. Mornington.........640 B18
STRACHEN
ct. Sunbury 142 K4
STRADA
cr. Wheelers Hl........460 E13
cr. Wheelers Hl........460 F16
STRADBROKE
av. Brighton East.....455 E17
av. Frankston S 627 B8
av. Heidelberg..........328 J7
av. Toorak...............415 D7
cl. Berwick 539 G19
cr. Mulgrave 500 D1
ct. Noble Park N.......501 B7
dr. St Albans............320 E7
rd. Boronia..............424 B15
rd. Montrose.............382 A10
st. Oakleigh S 458 D17
st. W Footscray 366 J9
wy. Wyndham Va.......446 F11
STRADBROOK
ct. Carrum Downs...601 D1
STRADELLA
av. Vermont S 420 H13
cl. Mill Park.............242 G11
ct. Mt Eliza..............642 J1
STRADISHALL
wy. Tullamarine.........278 K2
STRADLING
av. Geelong.............702 K2
STRADMORE
av. Templestowe 331 C7
STRAFFORD
av. Cranbourne.........577 L13
STRAHAN
ct. Boronia..............423 E14
ct. Keilor Dn 276 E13
STRAKER
st. N Melbourne.........34 E12
STRAND
cl. Glen Waverley....460 L4
ct. Templestowe 332 A14
STRANG
st. Hoppers Csg......448 K2
STRANGER
st. Brunswick..........325 G18
STRANKS
av. Brunswick W 325 A10
STRANRAER
cl. Greenvale 193 G17
STRASBOURG
rd. Rosanna 328 L3
rd. Rosanna 329 A3
STRATFORD
av. Bentleigh E 457 A19
av. Kew...................371 J11
cl. Somerville 644 J20
ct. Grovedale 706 E14
ct. Mulgrave 460 E20
pl. Bundoora............284 L2
rd. Rye 696 L12
rd. Rye 697 A12
sq. Wantirna 422 C9
st. Hadfield 281 B7
wy. Point Cook..........450 G8
STRATHAIRD
cl. Diamond Ck.......245 F16
dr. Nar Warrn S.......578 E1
st. Strathmore 279 G13
STRATHALBYN
st. Kew East...........372 F6
STRATHALLAN
la. Brighton, off
Male St 454 L18
rd. Macleod 285 B13
STRATHALLYN
rd. Ringwood 378 F7
STRATHAVAN
dr. Berwick 554 G16
STRATHAVEN
pl. Lilydale..............338 K2
pl. Lilydale..............339 C6
STRATHBOGIE
ct. Kilsyth 381 J8
wk. Blackburn S, off
Feathertop Ch....419 F12
STRATHCAIRN
av. Jan Juc..............711 D13
STRATHCONNAN
pl. Wheelers Hl 461 B12
sq. Tullamarine........236 E18
STRATHDON
pl. Point Cook.........450 H7
STRATHEARN
av. Coburg 325 D7
av. Murrumbeena 457 B14
ct. Carrum Downs...601 D1
dr. Sunbury 143 B6
STRATHEDEN
ct. Rye 696 E1
ct. Sydenham 274 K2
pl. Mooroolbark......337 J20
STRATHFIELD
pde. Croydon 335 D20
pde. Croydon 379 D1
STRATHFORD
ct. Werribee............446 K10
st. Epping................198 B16
STRATHMERTON
st. Reservoir 283 C8
STRATHMIGLO
ct. Bayswater N 380 G19
STRATHMORE
cr. Hoppers Csg......448 F6
dr. Jan Juc..............711 A14
st. Bentleigh 456 D18
st. Rye 697 F5
STRATHNAVER
av. Strathmore 279 G12
STRATHWYN
pl. Kew East............372 F6
STRATTON
cl. Kings Park.........319 A1
ct. Bayswater..........423 B8
STRATUS
ct. Hampton Pk.......551 L15
STRAUGHAN
st. Glen Iris............417 E9
STRAW
st. Brunswick W 325 A11
STRAWBENT
ri. Narre Warren 552 J4
STRAWBERRY
cl. Grovedale 705 H13
rd. Kurunjang...........227 E9
STREAM
wk. Hallam...............538 E16
STREETLY
ct. Tullamarine.........278 J3
STREETON
cct. Mill Park 242 L9
cct. Mill Park 243 A8
cr. Ivanhoe East 328 L14
cr. Ivanhoe East 329 A14
ct. Burwood E.........419 G7
ct. Mont Albert.........374 F17
ct. Rowville.............502 G4
ct. Skye 601 G4
ct. Sunbury 142 K5
ct. Taylors L 275 A1
la. Doncaster E.......332 D16
rd. Bayswater 424 C1
wy. Berwick 554 G18
wy. Caroline Spr.......274 B7
STRELDEN
av. Oakleigh E 458 K13
STRELDON
av. Strathmore 279 J14
STRETTLE
st. Kensington 33 E8
st. Thornbury...........326 C7
STRETTON
ct. Mt Waverley 458 G6
pl. Wyndham Va.....446 D6
STREZLECKI
av. Sunshine W 364 L13
av. Sunshine W 365 A12
gr. Laverton 406 K19
gr.s, Altona Mdw.......450 K1
STRICKLAND
av. Highton 705 J3
av. Hoppers Csg......449 C2
av. Mill Park 242 E7
cl. Pakenham 583 K1
cr. Burnside............318 E6
ct. Blackburn N.......376 A10
ct. Greensbrgh........286 F4
dr. Wheelers Hl 460 L8
STRICTA
ct. Frankston N 600 C6
STRIMON
ct. Roxburgh Pk, off
Garonne Cct......194 E5
STRINGER
rd. Blairgowrie 679 F18
STRINGERS
pl. Geelong.............703 C12
ri. Donvale 332 L18
STRINGY BARK
pl. S Morang 243 L4
ri. Croydon N 336 B12
STRINGYBARK
bvd.n,Mt Evelyn 339 K17
bvd.s,Mt Evelyn 339 J17
cl. Forest Hill 376 D20
cr. Frankston N 599 K9
ct. Berwick 553 H5
ct. Hillside 274 F4
ct. Ringwood N........334 J20
la. Seville E.............343 D11
pl. Meadow Ht.........193 L17
rd. Cockatoo 511 A8
rd. Eltham...............288 B13
STRINGYLEAF
gr. Mitcham 377 B15
STRODE
pl. Richmond............26 A11
st. Richmond............26 A11
STROMA
av. Balwyn N 329 H20
STRONER
av. Keilor East 322 F6
STRONG
av. Thomastown.......240 J19
dr. Hampton Pk........551 L9
st. Breakwater 703 F16
st. S Geelong...........703 A11
st. S Geelong...........703 C14
st. S Geelong...........703 E16
st. Spotswood 366 F19
STROUD
ct. Kilsyth S 424 L2
st. Balwyn 373 D8
STRUAN
av. Endeavour Hl 503 K18
av. Mooroolbark.......337 E16
st. Toorak 415 C3
STRUTT
pl. Caroline Spr 274 A8
STRZELECKI
ct. Cranbourne N 577 K9
ct. Kilsyth 381 H7
ct. Taylors L 275 K3
STUART
av. Cheltenham 496 E18
av. Hampton Pk........551 H9
av. Jan Juc..............711 D17
cl. Bayswater N 380 G18
cl. Frankston 626 L3
cr. Nunawading 376 H11
ct. Balwyn N 374 C4
ct. Keilor.................276 K10
rd. Lilydale 337 K6
rd. Seville E.............343 A13
st. Armadale.............415 H13
st. Bayswater N 380 G17
st. Dandenong 536 B8
st. Greensbrgh........245 B20
st. Moonee Pnd 324 F16
st. Noble Park..........534 J2
st. St Helena 245 B20
st. Sorrento 678 K9
st. The Basin............425 A10
st. Balaclava, off
William St 414 H18
STUBB
st. Somerton 195 D18
STUBBS
av. Mt Evelyn...........339 A15
st. Kensington 34 D10
STUBER
rd. Altona North 408 K6
STUBLEY
ct. Greensbrgh.........286 B4
STUD
ct. Lower Plenty......330 H1
ct. Skye..................575 G19
rd. Bayswater..........422 K8
rd. Dandenong.........536 C8
rd. Dandenong N......536 C8
rd. Knoxfield 462 H11
rd. Rowville.............462 G20
rd. Scoresby 462 G1
rd. Wantirna............422 K8
rd. Wantirna S.........462 G1
STUDD
rd. Pakenham 558 C19
STUDLEY
av. Kew...................371 G10
ct. Doncaster 330 G17
ct. Laverton 407 C17
ct. Mill Park 242 K13
pl. Mt Martha...........656 D7
rd. Brighton East 495 H5
rd. Eaglemont 328 G10
rd. Heidelberg 328 G10
rd. Ivanhoe 328 E11
st. Abbotsford 20 B15
st. Craigieburn 150 B17
st. Doncaster 330 F18
st. Maidstone...........366 J4
st. Mulgrave 500 C5
STUDLEY PARK
rd. Kew.....................20 L15
rd. Kew...................371 B9
wy. Caroline Spr.......274 B16
STUMBLERS
la. Tooradin 651 F7
STUMPY GULLY
rd. Moorooduc.........643 F20
rd. Moorooduc.........658 L6
STURDEE
rd. Black Rock.........495 G20
rd. Donvale 377 D8
st. Ascot Vale 324 C19
st. Box Hill..............375 A19
st. Chelsea..............547 C18
st. Coburg N............281 F16
st. Reservoir 283 A4
st. Seaford..............600 B3
STURIO
pde. Mt Eliza..............625 G18
STURIS
ct. Westmeadows ...237 D15
STURNS
la. Geelong.............703 C12
STURROCK
ct. Altona Mdw 451 H10
ct. Berwick 553 K6
ct. Mill Park 198 F20
ct. Mill Park 242 F1
st. Brunswick...........325 L9
STURT
ct. Cranbourne N 577 K7
ct. Grovedale 706 A13
ct. Taylors L 233 J20
pl. Diamond Ck.......246 A13
pl. Frankston S 627 F10
rd. Melton S............268 E12
st. Collingwood 19 L18
st. Essendon...........323 K5
st. Flemington 33 H1
st. Flemington 324 D20
st. Southbank 3 F19
st. Southbank 30 D1
st. Southbank 413 H1
st. Sunbury 143 C12
st. Sunshine 321 G20
st. Yarraville 366 J14
st.n, Croydon 380 D3
st.s, Croydon 380 C4
STUTT
av. Doncaster 374 D1
STUTZ
cl. Keilor Dn 276 A10
STYLES
ct. Wonga Park.......291 K14
STYMIE
st. Kingsbury 283 H9
STYNES
wy. Cranbourne W ...577 F14
SUAAD
ct. Cranbourne W ...577 H19
pl. Langwarrin 602 B16
SUBIACO
ct. Glen Waverley....419 L17
SUBZERO
cl. Rowville.............503 A2
st. Kurunjang..........227 E8
SUCCESS
av. Coburg 281 L20
SUDA
av. Ringwood 378 F10
ct. Avondale Ht 322 F7
SUDHOLZ
st. Docklands..........368 J13
SUE
ct. Hampton Pk.......551 L8
pl. Berwick 554 K18
pl. Carrum Downs...600 K4
SUEMAR
st. Mulgrave 500 E4
SUERULLA
ct. Rowville.............503 C8
SUFFERN
av. Bayswater..........423 B3
SUFFOLK
av. Coburg 325 D1
av. Cockatoo 511 D5
cr. Mt Martha...........669 L2
ct. Grovedale 706 A14
pl. Campbellfield 239 H14
rd. Dandenong N......502 C11
rd. Sunshine N.........321 C16
rd. Surrey Hills.........373 K20
st. Blackburn 375 H12
st. Maidstone...........366 K4
st. Nunawading 376 K8
st. Reservoir 283 A6
st. Wantirna S..........422 L14
st. W Footscray 366 E4
SUGAR BUSH
dr. Lynbrook............551 G15
SUGAR GUM
ct. Nar Warrn S.......552 F12
ct. Up Fntree Gly 464 K6
dr. Bundoora............284 E3
dr. Hillside 273 L5
dr. Hillside 274 A3
SUGARGUM
ct. Nunawading 376 F16
ct. Viewbank............285 L18
dr. Altona................409 B17
dr. Mulgrave 501 E2
gr. Cairnlea 319 G11
wk.n,Point Cook.........450 C4
wk.s,Point Cook.........450 C4
wy. Sunbury 143 G17
SUGARLOAF
av. Lynbrook............551 G16
bnd. Brookfield 267 J7
cl. Burwood E.........419 F11
dr. Chirnside Pk 337 B6
la. Berwick 554 J17
rd. Beaconsfld Up....542 K16
ri. Doreen 156 L15
tr. Christmas Hills...249 K10
SUGDEN
pl. Melbourne.............2 D13
pl. Melbourne...........24 D7
SUJAMA
pl. E Melbourne 25 G6
SULBY
pl. Gladstone Pk 237 C15
SULKY
ct. Endeavour Hl 538 B1
SULLIVAN
av. Rowville.............463 K18
ct. Belmont.............706 B1
ct. Wantirna............422 H5
dr. Somerville 645 C14
pl. Footscray...........367 E9
rd. Cairnlea 319 F7
st. Bellfield..............328 C6
st. Moorabbin.........497 A8
st. Preston..............327 H5
st. Rye 697 G3
st. Sorrento 678 G12
st. Springvale ....499 L
SULVA
rd. Warrandyte S.....334 J
SUMAK
rd. Mt Martha..........656 H
SUMERS
st. Laverton 407 C1
SUMERSETT
av. Oakleigh S 457 J1
SUMMER
la. Ringwood..........378 A1
pl. Mooroolbark......337 J
st. E Geelong..........703 G1
SUMMERFIELD
dr. Mornington........657 C

rd. Lilydale 338 H9
rd. Lilydale 382 E8
rd. Montrose 382 C9
rd. Mt Evelyn 338 H9
rd. Mt Evelyn 382 E8
SWANSFIELD
ct. Warrandyte 332 L3
ct. Warrandyte 333 A3
SWANSON
cr. Chadstone 458 B6
SWANSTON
ct. Taylors Hill 274 E9
pl. Geelong, off Little Malop St 703 D8
st. Bulleen 330 A12
st. Carlton 18 B20
st. Geelong 703 D8
st. Heidelberg Ht 284 F19
st. Melbourne 2 E15
st. Melbourne 2 E3
st. Melbourne 24 B1
st. Mentone 531 B7
st. Parkville 18 B20
st. Preston 327 K4
st. Queenscliff 708 J19
st. S Geelong 703 B15
st. Templstw Lr 330 A9
st. Williamstown 411 B14
SWARAN
ct. Oakleigh S 498 A6
wy. Werribee 447 L6
SWAYFIELD
rd. Mt Waverley 419 A14
SWEENEY
ct. Highton 705 F8
dr. Narre Warren 553 B7
SWEENEYS
la. Eltham 288 A18
SWEENY
dr. Doreen 156 L12
SWEETFERN DELL
Frankston S 626 J6
SWEET GUM
av. Narre Warren 538 J20
SWEETLAND
rd. Box Hill 375 C17
rd. Mooroolbark 337 B17
SWEETLANDS
ct. Mt Martha 656 L8
SWEETWATER
dr. Frankston S 627 C9
SWEET WATTLE
pl. Somerville 645 C17
SWEYN
st. Balwyn N 374 A5
st. Balwyn N 374 D3
SWIFT
ct. Carrum Downs 601 C2
ct. Keilor Dn 276 A11
dr. Glen Waverley 460 G11
st. Frankston 599 G16
st. Hoppers Csg 448 L4
st. Hoppers Csg 449 A4
st. Northcote 327 D13
st. Preston 327 A2
st. Thornbury 327 D13
wy. Dandenong S 549 H10
SWILK
st. Templestowe 330 K7
SWINBORNE
st. Box Hill S 418 L6
SWINBURNE
av. Hawthorn 372 A18
av. Mooroolbark 381 E1
pl. Hawthorn, off Railway Arc 372 A17
SWINDEN
av. Cheltenham 531 A3
SWINDON
av. Glen Waverley 460 L3
cr. Keilor Dn 276 D12
ct. Lalor 241 J6
gr. McKinnon 456 D16
mw. Westmeadows 237 H12
rd. Hughesdale 457 H10
rd. St Albans 320 K7
SWINTON
av. Kew 371 E11
ct. Baxter 644 C3
wy. Greenvale 237 A5
SWISS
ct. Endeavour Hl 503 B20
SWISS CHALET
rd. Badger Creek 258 G10
SWITCHBACK
rd. Chirnside Pk 293 D20
SWORD
wk. Kings Park 274 L19
SWORDS
st. Dandenong 535 K9
SWORD SEDGE
tr. Frankston N 600 H12
SWYER
st. Hampton 495 G12
SYBIL
ct. Keilor Dn 275 J10
st. Hampton E 496 B9
SYCAMORE
av. Emerald 469 K14
av. Mentone 531 H7
av. Tullamarine 278 J5
cr. Boronia 424 E17
cr. Campbellfield 239 E12
ct. Nar Warrn S 553 E20
gr. Balaclava 454 J1
gr. Mt Evelyn 383 C5
rd. Frankston S 627 D9
st. Box Hill S 418 L3
st. Camberwell 417 H4
st. Caulfield S 455 E7
st. Langwarrin 628 L1
st. Malvern East 457 B3
st. Mill Park 242 B9
SYDARE
av. Malvern East 457 D4
SYDENHAM
av. Manifold Ht 702 B5
la. Surrey Hills, off Balmoral Cr 374 C18
rd. Delahey 275 G11
rd. Sydenham 275 C5
st. Highett 495 J15
st. Moonee Pnd 324 A13
st. Seddon 367 A10
wy. Surrey Hills, off Beatrice Av 374 B18
SYDNEY
av. Emerald 469 D18
av. Geelong 703 D10
av. Mt Evelyn 383 G3
cr. Lalor 241 E8
ct. Geelong, off Admiral Pl 703 D9
pde. Geelong 703 D9
pl. Port Melb 412 L3
rd. Bayswater 423 A7
rd. Brunswick 325 F17
rd. Campbellfield 239 C11
rd. Coburg 325 G3
rd. Coburg N 281 G18
rd. Fawkner 239 C11
rd. Fawkner 281 F9
rd. Hadfield 281 F9
st. Albion 364 K1
st. Ascot Vale 324 E16
st. Avondale Ht 322 B15
st. Bacchus Msh 222 A19
st. Cheltenham 530 H3
st. Clayton S 498 J4
st. Collingwood 20 A14
st. Footscray 367 A7
st. Macleod 285 D13
st. Murrumbeena 457 B6
st. Nar Warrn S 579 G3
st. Newport 410 F10
st. Prahran 415 C10
st. Rye 697 B15
st. Somerville 644 K16
SYDNEY NOLAN
pl. Diamond Ck 245 B13
SYDNEY PARKINSON
av. Endeavour Hl 537 G8
SYDNEY WILSON
ct. Bundoora 284 D5
SYKES
av. Ferntree Gly 423 L18
ct. Pakenham 584 H5
la. N Melbourne 17 D13
SYLEHAM
st. St Albans 320 G6
SYLPHIDE
wy. Wantirna S 462 C1
SYLVAN
av. Keysborough 534 G16
av. Warburton 349 K6
cr. Ashwood 418 F16
ct. Kew 371 E10
ct. Dandenong N 502 F14
ct. Forest Hill 420 K3
ct. Ivanhoe 328 A19
ct. Newtown 701 K10
dr. Rosebud 700 F5
gr. Pascoe Vale 280 J17
st. Balwyn N 373 E6
st. Montmorency 286 J12
wy. Campbellfield 239 H11
SYLVANA
st. Wantirna S 421 L17
SYLVANDALE
ct. Yarrambat 201 C10
SYLVANDER
st. Balwyn N 373 K2
st. Clayton S 498 H8
SYLVANWOOD
cr. Narre Warren 538 H17
SYLVERLY
gr. Caulfield 455 G3
SYLVESTER
cr. Malvern East 457 B1
gr. Preston 283 C19
st. Oak Park 279 K13
SYLVIA
cl. Hillside 274 F6
cr. Black Rock 529 F4
ct. Thomastown 241 L12
ct. Whittington 703 L20
gr. Ringwood 378 B17
la. Narre Warren 553 A6
rd. Beaconsfield 555 C14
st. Blackburn S 419 G6
st. Dandenong N 501 J17
st. Ferntree Gly 464 B2
st. Templstw Lr 330 B12
st. Viewbank 285 F18
SYME
ct. Sunbury 142 K11
rd. Pakenham 558 E19
rd. Woori Yall 344 B14
st. Brunswick 325 C14
st. St Albans 319 G1
st. Williamstown 411 H16
SYMES
st. Lower Plenty 286 K15
SYMINGTON
rd. Long Forest 224 F1
SYMON
cr. Greensbrgh 244 K15
cr. Thomastown 240 L16
cr. Thomastown 241 A16
SYMOND
st. Yarra Glen 208 L17
st. Yarra Glen 209 A18
SYMONDS
st. Hawthorn E 372 F20
st. Queenscliff 709 A16
SYMONS
rd. Avonsleigh 470 E20
rd. Avonsleigh 510 E1
st. Healesville 213 H20
st. Preston 282 D16
SYNDAL
st. Fawkner 281 K9
SYNNOT
st. Werribee 447 F18
SYON
cl. Deer Park 318 K12
SYPHON
wk. Lysterfield S 503 F14
SYTHNEY
ct. Surrey Hills 374 A19
SZER
wy. Carrum Downs 600 J2

T

TABBITA
st. Moorabbin 496 L11
TABILK
ct. Wantirna 422 G6
st. Fawkner 281 F10
TABOR
ct. Sunbury 144 D10
mw. Frankston 628 E4
TABULAM
ct. Grovedale 705 L13
TACABERRY
av. Nar Warrn N 539 H5
TACOMA
st. Pk Orchards 333 E19
TAD
ct. Cranbourne N 578 A5
TADDOR
dr. Cranbourne 578 F17
TADEDOR
ct. Forest Hill 420 F5
TADEMA
cr. Eltham 288 B6
ct. Noble Park N 501 D11
TADJI
cl. Croydon N 335 L15
ct. Mornington 641 D15
st. Sorrento 679 E15
TADOR
dr. Somerville 644 G18
TADSTAN
ct. Clayton S 499 D16
dr. Hampton Pk 551 C8
dr. Tullamarine 278 H2
pl. Donvale 376 J2
TAEGTOW
wy. Altona Mdw 451 G8
TAFT
cl. Dandenong N 501 H8
TAGELL
rd. Heathmont 378 K15
TAGGART
la. Elwood 454 C4
TAGGERTY
cr. Meadow Ht 238 A6
ct. Keilor 276 L12
TAHARA
ct. Thomastown 240 J12
ct. Werribee 447 E2
rd. Toorak 415 E4
TAHBILK
ct. Vermont S 421 F9
TAHITI
ct. Mulgrave 500 C3
ct. Rye 696 F2
TAHLEE
pl. Montmorency 287 B8
pl. Vermont S 421 C7
TAINTON
rd. Burwood E 420 A8
st. Wandin N 340 K13
st. Wandin N 341 A13
TAISHO
ct. Werribee 446 H18
TAIT
ct. Bundoora 242 K17
ct. Oakleigh S 498 A6
la. W Melbourne 23 A2
st. Fitzroy N 326 D20
st. Footscray 367 E4
st. Newport 411 A7
st. Ringwood N 378 E7
TAITS
la. Geelong, off Mundy St 703 A11
la. Geelong, off Mundy St 703 B12
TAKAPUNA
st. Caulfield S 455 J11
TAKETA
cr. Frankston 628 H1
TALAB
ct. Chelsea Ht 547 H17
TALARA
ct. Cranbourne 578 G17
ct. Frankston 628 B1
TALARNO
av. Vermont S 421 D7
TALASKIA
rd. Up Fntree Gly 465 C9
TALBA
ct. Carrum Downs 601 A6
TALBETT
st. Burwood 418 J10
TALBOT
av. Balwyn 373 G15
av. Belgrave 466 C14
av. Bentleigh 495 K1
av. Oakleigh S 458 D20
av. Oakleigh S 498 D2
av. St Kilda E 414 K20
av. Thomastown 241 H14
cl. Keilor Dn 276 A16
cr. Kooyong 416 A5
ct. Frankston 600 G20
ct. Hampton Pk 551 D10
ct. Noble Park 534 K7
gr. McCrae 684 J17
pl. Sunbury 143 H5
rd. Mt Waverley 458 L6
rd. Strathmore 324 E2
st. Altona Mdw 451 J1
st. Brunswick 325 D12
st. Footscray 367 G9
st. Greensbrgh 286 D7
st. Hadfield 281 A9
st. Hampton 494 L7
st. Keilor East 322 G5
st. Mitcham 377 H14
st. Newtown 702 E10
st. Sunshine N 321 F14
st. Templstw Lr 330 D14
TALDRA
cr. Seaford 600 A3
ct. Belmont 706 F6
dr. Ferntree Gly 463 K8
dr. Ferntree Gly 463 L6
pl. Cranbourne W 577 H15
st. Box Hill N 375 C9
TALFORD
st. Doncaster E 376 C2
TALGARNO
cl. Taylors L 276 D8
st. Broadmeadows 237 L13
TALIA
ct. Melton S 268 E5
ct. Rowville 462 L18
ct. Werribee 447 D11
TALI-KARNG
cl. Rowville 462 K15
TALINA
cl. Hoppers Csg 447 K2
TALINGA
ct. Berwick 580 J
ct. Mornington 641 C1
rd. Cheltenham 495 L1
rd. Sandringham 495 L1
TALISMAN
pl. Lysterfield 464 C1
ri. Glen Waverley 460 F
TALLANGATTA
pl. Berwick, off Tallara Sq 553 A
TALLANT
av. Sorrento 679 D1
TALLARA
sq. Berwick 553 E
TALLAROOK
ct. Croydon Hl 335 F1
st. Blairgowrie 680 B1
TALLAROON
ct. Greensbrgh 286 L
TALLAWARRA
ri. Donvale 377 G
TALLENT
st. Croydon 380 A
TALLERK
cl. Greensbrgh 244 B1
ct. Kings Park 319 A
TALLINTYRE
rd. Sunshine W 364 F
TALLIS
cl. Camberwell 372 J1
dr. Mornington 640 L1
dr. Mornington 641 A1
TALLOW WOOD
dr. Greensbrgh 244 L2
dr. Greensbrgh 286 K
TALLOWWOOD
st. Frankston N 599 K1
TALLY
ct. Berwick 539 H2
TALLY HO
ct. Burwood 420 B1
TALMA
cl. Eltham 287 K1
pl. Cranbourne W 577 F
TALMAGE
st. Albion 321 A
st. Albion 365 A
TALMARA
ct. Mt Martha 657 D
TALOFA
av. Brighton East 455 C
av. Ringwood E 378 L
av. Ringwood E 379 A
TAL TALS
cr. Mt Martha 656 C
TALWONG
ct. Research 246 G2
ct. Research 288 G
TALWOOD
cl. Wantirna S 422 A
ct. Burwood E 420 B
TAMA
ct. Grovedale 705 J1
TAMALA
av. Marshall 706 L1
av. Notting Hill 459 J1
TAMAR
ct. Keilor 276 L1
ct. Mentone 531 G
ct. Narre Warren 539 H
dr. Deer Park 318 K
dr. Melton S 268 K
gr. Oakleigh 458 A
rd. Springvale S 534 E
st. Aberfeldie 323 E
st. Bayswater 422
st. Bayswater 423 A
st. Bundoora 284 E
st. Ringwood N 378
TAMARA
cl. Berwick 540 C
ct. Bundoora 242 F
ct. Thomastown 240 D
st. Albanvale 319 D
st. Wantirna S 462 C
TAMARIND
cr. Werribee 447
TAMARISK
av. Glen Waverley 460 D
dr. Frankston N 600
rd. Narre Warren 553 E
TAMBET
st. Bentleigh E 457 C
TAMBO
av. Reservoir 283 D
cl. Clayton S 498
cl. Croydon Hl 335 H
cr. Taylors Hill 274 K
ct. Dandenong N 501
ct. Dingley Vill 533
ct. Glen Waverley 419 J
ct. Keilor 276 L

THE BLOCK
arc. Melbourne 2 C15
THE BOARDWALK
Waterways 547 D2
THE BOULEVARD
Aberfeldie 323 B11
Aberfeldie 323 E12
Balwyn N 372 L1
Eaglemont 329 B9
Glen Waverley 420 D16
Hawthorn 372 A19
Heathmont 379 A19
Ivanhoe 328 A17
Ivanhoe 328 E15
Ivanhoe East 328 D16
Ivanhoe East 328 E15
Ivanhoe East 328 K17
Ivanhoe East 329 A17
McCrae 685 D12
Malvern East 417 H19
Montrose 382 F7
Nar Warrn S 553 B20
N Warrandyte 289 G12
Pascoe Vale S 324 E4
Pascoe Vale S 324 H4
Patterson L 573 E6
Point Cook 450 B4
Port Melb 412 B5
Thomastown 241 C13
Yarraville 366 J19
THE BOULEVARDE
Doncaster 331 B16
Warrandyte 289 G14
THE BRENTWOODS
Chirnside Pk 337 G1
THE BRIARS
Lysterfield 503 H2
Mooroolbark 337 H8
Seabrook 451 A2
THE BROADWAY
Altona North 410 C3
THE BULLOCK
tr. Melton W 225 A18
THE CAUSEWAY
Melbourne 2 C13
Melbourne 24 C7
Taylors Hill 274 F9
THE CENTREWAY
Preston 282 J20
Ringwood 378 F9
THE CHANCERY
Lilydale 338 K2
Lilydale 339 C7
THE CIRCLE
Altona North 410 D5
THE CIRCUIT
Gladstone Pk 279 A4
Greensbrgh 286 A4
Lilydale 338 C14
THE CLOSE
Beaumaris 530 F10
Caroline Spr 317 L6
Frankston S 626 L6
Hampton Pk 551 E12
Hoppers Csg 448 K5
Langwarrin 629 J2
Mt Waverley 418 K17
Scoresby 462 G8
Somerville 645 A19
Thomastown 240 F16
THE COMMON
Croydon S 380 C14
Macleod 284 J12
Nar Warrn S 578 E1
cl. S Morang 199 B14
THE CONCORD
Bundoora 284 L4
THE CONDER
Ivanhoe East 328 L14
Ivanhoe East 329 A14
THE CORSO
Parkdale 531 D12
THE COTSWOLDS
Sunbury 144 C8
THE COURT
Hoppers Csg 448 E2
THE COVE
Port Melb 412 E5
THE CREEK
pp. Craigieburn 150 F13
THE CRESCENT
Ascot Vale 324 B16
Belgrave Ht 466 D19
Footscray 367 D5
Highett 496 F12
Kensington 33 C10
Kew 371 J5
Mt Evelyn 339 H19
Nar Warrn S 579 C1
Point Cook 450 G9
Port Melb 412 F5
Rosebud 683 J19
Sandringham 494 L13
Sandringham 495 A13
Sassafras 426 F16
Springvale 499 K15
Wesburn 348 B7
Waurn Ponds, off
Nicol Dr 705 A9
THE CRESENT
Ferntree Gly 464 E2
THE CREST
Attwood 236 L12
Attwood 237 A12
Bulleen 329 J16
Frankston S 627 A6
Highton 701 H12
Hillside 232 A16
Langwarrin 629 K2
Melton W 226 E13
Watsonia N 285 G2
Wonga Park 291 J19
Yarra Glen 208 H5
THE CROFT
Croydon N 336 A10
Lysterfield 503 H2
Ringwood N 378 A4
THE CROFTS
Richmond 25 L12
THE CROSSING
Caroline Spr 274 A20
Caroline Spr 318 B1
THE CROSSOVER
Carnegie 456 J8
THE CROSSWAY
Avondale Ht 321 L7
Keilor East 322 A5
Strathmore 324 C2
THE CUTTING
Portsea 666 J20
THE DELERY
Cranbourne 603 F7
THE DELL
Croydon N 336 A9
Nar Warrn N 538 D10
THE DEVIATION
Wheelers Hl 461 A14
THE DRIVE
Rosebud 683 H18
THE ELMS
Donvale 332 H15
Hillside 273 K4
Narre Warren 553 D1
THE ENTRANCE
Burnside 274 E16
Mt Evelyn 339 J17
THE ESPLANADE
Clifton Hill 20 J1
Clifton Hill 371 A1
Edithvale 546 F12
Fairfield 327 E20
Geelong 702 K1
Maribyrnong 323 C13
Nar Warrn S 579 H1
Research 288 J1
St Kilda 413 L16
St Kilda 414 A17
Sydenham 274 L2
Torquay 712 B12
s. Geelong 702 K2
THE ESTUARY
pl. Hallam 538 E15
THE EYRIE
Eaglemont 328 G11
Eltham 245 K20
Hampton Pk 551 E12
Lilydale 338 F5
McCrae 685 C10
THE FAIRWAY
Bonbeach 573 C5
Hampton Pk 551 F9
Kingsbury 283 H8
Rowville 462 D20
THE FRED HOLLOWS
wy. Mill Park 242 H1
THE GABLES
Albion 321 A20
Lysterfield 503 J1
S Morang 199 C10
THE GALLEY
Rosebud W 683 B20
THE GATEWAY
Berwick 553 E3
Croydon S 380 B14
Lilydale 293 L20
THE GEORGIAN
rd. Olinda 427 A8
THE GLADE
Bonbeach 545 F15
Dandenong 536 E11
Ferntree Gly 464 J2
Fingal 698 H20
Hampton Pk 551 E14
Langwarrin 629 K2
Lysterfield 503 H2
Lysterfield 503 J1
Mitcham 377 E10
Mooroolbark 337 G18
Ringwood N 378 A8
Viewbank 286 A17
Wheelers Hl 461 B7
THE GLADES
Doncaster 331 A18
Hoppers Csg 448 D2
THE GLEN
Carrum Downs 575 B17
Donvale 376 J6
Ferntree Gly 464 H2
Frankston 599 J18
Hurstbridge 202 L18
Hurstbridge 203 A18
Rye 698 A3
THE GLENN
Hoppers Csg 448 D2
THE GOATS
la. Eaglemont 328 K11
THE GRANARY
Sunbury 144 B6
THE GRANGE
Hampton Pk 551 J5
Malvern East 416 G20
Ringwood N 334 K20
Templestowe 331 F13
Wantirna 422 A13
Yallambie 286 A13
THE GREAT EASTERN
wy. S Morang 199 C16
THE GREEN
Endeavour Hl 537 B2
Mill Park 243 E4
Somerville 645 A19
THE GREENWAY
Craigieburn 193 K2
Heathmont 423 B1
THE GROVE
Boronia 424 F9
Camberwell 416 H7
Caroline Spr 318 A3
Coburg 325 G6
Dromana 685 L9
Frankston S 626 G6
Glen Waverley 459 K1
Hampton Pk 552 D8
Hillside 273 J4
Langwarrin 629 J2
Mt Dandenong 426 H1
Plenty 244 F13
Reservoir 283 B2
THE GUMS
S Morang 199 L18
THE HAVEN
Bayswater 423 F11
THE HEADS
Mt Martha 669 B4
THE HEATH
Croydon N 336 A10
THE HEIGHTS
Frankston S 627 A5
Hillside 232 A18
Somerville 644 K19
Sorrento 678 G4
Sunbury 143 F19
THE HELM
Frankston S 627 C14
Rosebud W 699 B1
THE HIGHWAY
Bentleigh 456 E20
Mt Waverley 459 B1
Upwey 465 K9
THEILE
ct. Truganina 405 G13
THE KNOLL
Ferntree Gly 463 G6
Langwarrin 629 K2
Mt Eliza 626 G14
Somerville 645 F15
THE LAIRIDGE
Kensington 33 G6
THE LAKES
bvd. S Morang 198 K15
bvd. S Morang 198 K15
bvd. S Morang 199 H12
THE LANE
Ferny Creek 466 A3
Pascoe Vale S 324 F1
Toorak 415 E4
THE LINK
Keilor Park 277 L12
Mill Park 243 B4
Rosebud 684 B18
Sunbury 144 D5
Taylors Hill 274 L10
THELMA
av. Boronia 424 F15
av. Essendon N 279 C20
ct. Werribee 447 L18
ri. Hampton Pk 552 D12
st. Beaconsfield 555 C13
st. Carrum 573 D10
st. Noble Park 535 B6
st. Nunawading 376 F11
THE LOCH
Croydon Hl 335 F13
THE LODGE
Langwarrin 602 B18
THE LOOKOUT
Lysterfield 503 J2
THE LOOP
Blairgowrie 679 K17
Hadfield 280 K6
THE LOUGH
ct. Nar Warrn N 539 L11
THE MALL
Boronia 424 E12
Croydon S 379 J10
Frankston 627 C6
Point Cook 450 G10
Templstw Lr 330 F14
Wantirna 422 F7
THE MAPLES
Narre Warren 553 E1
THE MEARS
Epping 198 D15
THEMEDA
ct. Delahey 275 A14
ct. Meadow Ht 193 L18
la. Maribyrnong 367 E2
THE MEWS
Frankston 628 A7
Hampton Pk 552 A14
Hawthorn 371 J19
Highton 705 E1
Hoppers Csg 448 D2
Somerville 645 B14
Sunshine W 364 E6
Torquay 711 G12
Vermont 421 J3
Viewbank 285 J17
Wantirna 421 L12
THE MIDWAY
Lilydale 338 C14
THE MOOR
Balwyn N 373 C2
THE MOUNT
Croydon S 379 F10
THE NOOK
Balwyn N 373 C2
Bayswater N 379 L18
Doncaster E 332 F12
Ferntree Gly 464 C8
Langwarrin 629 D1
Viewbank 285 J19
Watsonia N 285 H3
THE OAKS
Croydon 380 H6
Hillside 273 J4
Ivanhoe East 328 F14
Narre Warren 553 D1
Sunbury 144 B8
THEOBALD
st. Thornbury 327 H8
THEODORE
av. Noble Park 534 F3
ct. Toorak 415 G3
st. St Albans 320 A2
st. Surrey Hills 374 F18
tce. Berwick 553 F4
THE OLD FORD
Werribee 447 B8
THE OLD STOCK RUN
Sunbury 144 D7
THE OUTLOOK
Glen Waverley 460 F4
Heathmont 422 L1
Heathmont 423 A1
Lysterfield S 503 L14
Somerville 644 L19
Waterways 547 D3
THE OVAL
Berwick 554 D19
THE PANORAMA
Eaglemont 328 K11
Mickleham 150 F5
THE PARADE
Ascot Vale 323 J15
Caroline Spr 274 B20
Clarinda 498 C4
Northcote 326 J20
THE PARK WAY
Chirnside Pk 337 C4
Diamond Ck 246 C10
THE PARKWAY
Caroline Spr 317 J6
Hampton Pk 552 A17
Patterson L 547 H20
Templestowe 332 D3
THE PASS
Croydon 379 F9
Rosebud 684 B17
THE PATCH
rd. The Patch 467 J5
THE PEAK
Hillside 231 K17
THE PINES
Doveton 536 H13
Kew 372 F14
out. Doncaster E 332 D7
THE PLACE
Croydon S 380 A15
Toorak, off
Toorak Rd 415 B5
THE POINT
Point Cook 451 B7
S Morang 198 K15
THE PONDS
S Morang 199 A12
THE PORTAL
Lilydale 338 F14
THE PRIORY
Templestowe 331 L12
THE PROMENADE
Nar Warrn S 553 D20
Nar Warrn S 579 B2
Nar Warrn S 579 B3
Point Cook 450 C4
S Morang 198 K15
THE QUADRANGLE
Glen Waverley 460 A10
THE QUADRANT
Nar Warrn S 553 F20
THE QUARTERDECK
Portsea 678 D2
THE QUAYS
Nar Warrn S 579 G2
THE RAMEO
Bundoora 285 A1
THE RANGE
Frankston S 627 A5
THE REGENCY
Hillside 231 J20
Hillside 231 J20
THERESA
av. Langwarrin 629 B1
gdn. Endeavour Hl 537 K2
st. Bentleigh 496 F1
st. Richmond 26 K13
st. Sunshine N 321 D13
st. Tullamarine 278 H4
THERESE
av. Mt Waverley 458 H8
THE RETREAT
Hampton Pk 551 E13
THE RIALTO
Malvern East 457 D1
w. Malvern East 457 C2
THE RIDGE
Blackburn 376 A19
Canterbury 372 L16
Frankston S 626 L4
Glen Waverley 420 D17
Hampton Pk 552 C12
Highton 701 F14
Knoxfield 463 C4
Lilydale 338 E14
Mt Eliza 642 D4
Roxburgh Pk 193 L15
Somerville 644 K19
Templestowe 288 F20
Templestowe 332 F1
rd. Fingal 698 G19
THE RIDGEWAY
Ivanhoe 328 C16
Kensington 33 G11
Pakenham 585 A1
THE RIDGE WEST
Knoxfield 463 B3
THE RIGHI
Dromana 686 H5
Eaglemont 328 G13
Eaglemont 328 H11
South Yarra 31 J3
South Yarra 414 E2
Wyndham Va 446 C14
THE RISE
Diamond Ck 246 D9
Frankston 628 A7
Glen Waverley 459 L1
Narre Warren 539 G13
Somerville 644 L19
Somerville 645 A19
Sunbury 144 F4
Wantirna 422 A13
Warrandyte 332 L4
Warrandyte 333 A4
THE ROBBINS
Seabrook 450 K5
THERRY
st. Coldstream 295 F12
st. Melbourne 23 K1
THE SANDS
Aspendale Gdn 546 K3
THE SEEKERS
cr. Mill Park 242 H1

THE SERPENTINE
Tecoma 466 D9
THE SILO
Viewbank 329 K1
THE SKYLINE
Sunbury 144 B7
THE SPINNEY
Belmont 706 A7
THE SPRINGS
cl. Nar Warrn S 579 H2
THE SPUR
Frankston S 626 L5
Frankston S 627 A5
Hampton Pk 551 L15
THE STRAND
Belgrave S 506 A12
Chelsea 546 J19
Keilor East 321 L3
Lysterfield 503 J2
Melton 268 L2
Moonee Pnd 324 C11
Nar Warrn S 578 L4
Nar Warrn S 578 L5
Newport 411 E8
Newport 411 E9
Point Cook 450 C5
Point Cook 450 G5
Preston 282 J20
S Morang 198 L9
Wandana Ht 701 C18
Williamstown 411 F11
THE SUMMIT
Ringwood N 378 A3
THE TERRACE
Armadale 415 G14
Blackburn 375 F15
Croydon 379 L3
Lysterfield 503 H2
Melton 268 L2
Nar Warrn S 553 E20
Seabrook 451 B6
Somerville 644 L19
S Morang 198 L8
THE TROSSACHS
Frankston 628 B7
THE TRUMP
cl. Sunbury 143 E5
THE VAUCLUSE
Richmond 26 E13
South Yarra 32 H12
THE VIEW
Rosebud 700 J5
THE VILLAGE
grn. Sunbury 144 E7
THE VINE
Chirnside Pk 336 K5
THE VINEYARD
Fingal 698 H19
Waurn Ponds 705 E16
THE WALK
Taylors Hill 274 F9
THE WALLABY RUN
Chirnside Pk 337 D3
THE WATER COURSE
Keysborough 533 L11
THE WELKIN
trl. Kurunjang 226 G10
THE WILLOWS
Hillside 231 J16
THEWLIS
rd. Pakenham 557 J19
THE WOODLAND
Wheelers Hl 460 K12
THE WRIDGEWAY
Mt Evelyn 384 A5
THEXTONS
rd. Yellingbo 387 J8
THEYER
st. Eumemmerring 536 K15
THICKINS
st. Pascoe Vale 280 F14
THIELE
ct. Blackburn 375 E15
st. Doncaster 331 C20
THIRD
av. Altona North 409 L5
av. Altona North 409 L7
av. Anglesea 713 C9
av. Aspendale 546 F9
av. Box Hill N 375 E6
av. Brunswick 325 D8
av. Chelsea Ht 547 E14
av. Cockatoo 510 H5
av. Dandenong N 501 J15
av. Hadfield 281 B11
av. Hadfield 281 D10
av. Hoppers Csg 448 K5
av. Pakenham 584 K2
av. Rosebud 683 L19
av. Rowville 462 E18
av. Springvale 500 H10
av. Sunshine 365 E8
cr. Hadfield 281 C10
ct. Cranbourne 603 J6
dr. Springvale 500 H11
rd. Springvale 500 K10
st. Black Rock 529 G7
st. Clayton S 499 D5
st. Moorabbin Aprt 531 K4
st. Parkdale 531 D10
st. Warrandyte 289 E20
THIRLMERE
ct. Berwick 554 A8
THISTLE
cl. Hoppers Csg 405 B15
ct. Delahey 275 A16
ct. Meadow Ht 194 B18
gr. Highett 496 D14
st. Brunswick 325 B9
st. Essendon 323 K6
st. Pascoe Vale S 324 G1
st. Surrey Hills 418 A1
THISTLE BROOK
ct. Gowanbrae 279 F6
THISTLEDOWN
ct. Cairnlea 319 J8
THISTLETHWAITE
st. S Melbourne 29 D4
st. S Melbourne 413 B2
THISTLEWOOD
pl. Cranbourne E 604 J1
THOMAS
av. Hampton E 495 L7
av. Melton S 268 G4
av. Warburton 349 F2
cl. Mt Eliza 626 C18
cr. Cranbourne 603 L2
cr. Lilydale 382 F2
ct. Doncaster 375 A3
ct. Eaglemont 328 H10
ct. Glen Waverley 460 C9
ct. Hallam 537 K13
ct. Parkdale 531 H14
dr. Mt Martha 657 C9
pl. Pakenham 584 K10
pl. Prahran 32 A16
pl. Prahran 414 F8
rd. Healesville 214 B20
rd. Healesville 258 C1
rd. Laverton N 364 E18
rd. Red Hill S 688 F20
rd.n, Emerald 469 F8
rd.s, Emerald 469 F10
st. Airport W 278 H13
st. Baxter 644 D1
st. Belmont 706 J1
st. Box Hill S 418 J4
st. Braybrook 366 B5
st. Brighton East 455 H20
st. Brunswick 325 H14
st. Camberwell 417 L5
st. Clayton 498 K3
st. Croydon S 379 J11
st. Dandenong 535 L8
st. Doncaster E 376 C4
st. Dromana 686 A7
st. Eltham 288 B5
st. Ferntree Gly 464 C3
st. Geelong West 702 F6
st. Hampton 495 A9
st. Hawthorn 371 J17
st. Kew 372 E12
st. Laverton 407 D17
st. Malvern East 457 C4
st. Mitcham 377 E12
st. Moonee Pnd 324 D12
st. Mordialloc 531 L17
st. Mornington 640 L14
st. Mornington 641 A14
st. Noble Park 534 J3
st. Officer 581 F1
st. Pakenham 584 L9
st. Preston 283 B18
st. Richmond 26 E9
st. Ringwood 378 F15
st. Rosebud 683 K18
st. Roxburgh Pk 193 K15
st. St Albans 319 J1
st. Selby 467 D17
st. S Morang 243 H2
st. Thomastown 240 L12
st. Thomastown 241 A12
st. Williamstown 411 E11
st. Yarraville 366 L19
st. Port Melb, off Ross St 412 H4
st. Port Melb, off Ross St 412 J4
st.n, Windsor 32 B20
st.n, Windsor 414 F11
st.s, Windsor 414 F11
THOMAS ARNOLD
av. Glen Waverley 459 K10
THOMAS BREW
la. Croydon, off Lacey St 380 B3
THOMAS BRUNTON
pde. Roxburgh Pk 194 D13
pde. Roxburgh Pk 194 F16
THOMAS CARR
dr. Tarneit 405 B10
THOMAS HARDY
dr. Templestowe 332 C11
THOMAS HOLMES
st. Maribyrnong 367 C1
THOMASINA
st. Bentleigh E 456 J16
THOMAS LAWFORD
pl. Croydon Hl 335 G14
THOMAS MITCHELL
dr. Endeavour Hl 537 K7
THOMASZ
pl. Kurunjang 227 C9
THOMPSON
cct. Mill Park 242 F5
cr. Research 288 G6
cr. Roxburgh Pk 194 B10
ct. Altona Mdw 451 K9
ct. Endeavour Hl 537 D9
ct. Werribee 448 E11
dr. Wantirna 422 A8
rd. Bangholme 574 G5
rd. Carrum Downs 574 G5
rd. Patterson L 573 H6
rd. Upwey 465 J14
st. Abbotsford 26 K3
st. Avondale Ht 321 L10
st. Campbellfield 239 C16
st. Clayton 458 H19
st. Frankston 599 B19
st. Glen Waverley 420 F16
st. Kensington 34 C9
st. Ormond 455 K14
st. Watsonia 285 H6
st. Williamstown 411 G19
tr. Lysterfield 504 L13
THOMPSONS
ct. Balwyn N 329 F18
rd. Balwyn N 329 E17
rd. Bulleen 329 E17
rd. Carrum Downs 575 F7
rd. Clyde North 580 A13
rd. Cranbourne 578 D11
rd. Cranbourne E 578 D11
rd. Cranbourne E 579 A12
rd. Cranbourne N 578 D11
rd. Cranbourne W 577 A9
rd. Diggers Rest 232 B6
rd. Kalorama 382 H12
rd. Kalorama 383 A11
rd. Keilor N 232 B6
rd. Lyndhurst 575 F7
rd. Montrose 382 H12
rd. Skye 575 F7
rd. Templstw Lr 330 B12
THOMSON
av. Laverton 407 E12
av. Murrumbeena 457 A10
av. Olinda 427 H17
ct. Rowville 462 L16
ct. Rowville 463 A16
dr. Rosanna 285 A16
rd. Beaconsfld Up 542 F9
ri. Parkdale 531 G16
st. Belmont 702 F19
st. Brighton 454 K11
st. Essendon 323 F7
st. Maidstone 366 H3
st. Melbourne 1 F10
st. Melbourne 23 L8
st. Northcote 327 A18
st. Pt Lonsdale 710 G2
st. Seddon 367 C12
st. S Melbourne 30 B9
st. S Melbourne 413 G5
st. Sunshine 365 G2
tce. Dromana 686 K5
tce. Rye 696 J5
wy. Taylors Hill 274 K14
THOONA
gr. Greensbrgh 286 D6
THOONEN
ct. Keysborough 534 D13
THOR
ct. Bundoora 284 L5
ct. Keilor East 277 K17
st. Strathmore 280 A15
THORBURN
rd. Hampton 495 G10
THORESBY
gr. Ivanhoe 328 E12
THORN
st. Camberwell 372 J18
st. Essendon 323 J6
THORNBILL
cct. Pakenham 584 H11
cl. Healesville 214 A20
dr. Carrum Downs 600 L4
dr. Werribee 447 L10
pl. Craigieburn 149 G17
THORNBURY
cr. Malvern East 417 A20
la. Highton 701 J15
THORNCOMBE
wk. Doncaster E 332 D14
THORNDON
dr. St Albans 320 D7
THORNE
pl. Geelong, off Swanston St 703 D9
st. E Geelong 703 G10
THORNHILL
dr. Forest Hill 420 F2
dr. Keilor Dn 276 B15
rd. Highton 705 F4
THORNLEIGH
pl. Templestowe 331 G13
pl. Westmeadows 236 F14
THORNLEY
cl. Ferntree Gly 463 E4
ct. Greenvale 193 A16
dr. Berwick 554 F19
THORNS
rd. Wattle Glen 247 C7
THORNTON
av. Bundoora 284 L5
av. Sunbury 143 B10
av. Surrey Hills 373 J14
cl. Hallam 538 B19
cr. Mitcham 376 L15
ct. Dandenong N 502 A12
ct. Mooroolbark 337 J8
ct. The Basin 425 B9
rd. Mt Eliza 626 G11
st. Eltham 287 C15
st. Kew 371 F11
st. Lalor 240 H6
st. Macleod 284 L10
st. Macleod 285 A10
st. Oakleigh S 497 F4
THORNYCROFT
st. Campbellfield 194 J20
THOROGOOD
ct. Grovedale 706 F10
ct. Taylors L 275 F7
THOROUGHBRED
av. Werribee 446 J19
dr. Highton 701 C17
THORPDALE
av. Coolaroo 238 E4
THORPE
av. Hoppers Csg 448 L4
av. Hoppers Csg 449 A4
ct. Altona Mdw 451 G4
pl. Burnside 318 E6
st. Lilydale 338 D16
st. Newport 410 E9
st. Sunshine 365 C5
THREADBOW
cr. Wheelers Hl 460 J12
THREADNEEDLE
st. Attwood 236 H11
st. Balwyn 374 A12
THREDBO
ct. Dandenong N 502 C16
ct. Epping 198 A20
THRICE
la. Kurunjang 226 J12
THROSBY
cr. Deer Park 319 C10
ct. Endeavour Hl 537 H6
THROSSELL
la. Melbourne 24 L8
THROUGH
rd. Camberwell 417 H8
rd. Noble Park 500 J15
rd. Ringwood N 378 E6
st. Hawthorn 371 J19
THROWER
st. Reservoir 282 D8
THRUSH
ct. Werribee 448 D8
st. S Morang 199 G10
THULE
ct. Brighton 454 H10
THURBRO
dr. Keysborough 535 A9
THURLEIGH
av. Croydon S 379 J13
THURLING
st. Mentone 530 K9
THURLOO
dr. Safety Bch 669 C12
st. Chadstone 457 L1
THURMAID
ct. Roxburgh Pk 194 D15
THURMOND
ct. Endeavour Hl 537 E4
THURRA
ct. Dandenong N 502 B10
THURSO
ct. Endeavour Hl 503 K19
st. Malvern East 417 F20
THURSTON
st. Box Hill 374 J16
THURZA
ct. Wheelers Hl 461 C15
THWAITES
rd. Pakenham 559 B20
rd. Pakenham 585 A1
st. Albion 320 F18
THYER
rd. Ivanhoe 328 B17
THYME
ct. Croydon Hl 335 H16
rd. Campbellfield 239 E12
THYRA
st. Sunshine 365 A6
TIAMO
ri. Sydenham 275 C8
TIARA
dr. S Morang 198 K11
TIBARI
ct. Croydon 380 C9
TIBARRI
ct. Mooroolbark 337 D12
TIBBLES
st. Beaumaris 530 B3
TIBER
cl. Werribee 447 H4
TIBIR
st. Blairgowrie 696 B6
TIBROCKNEY
st. Highett 496 A15
TICHBORNE
pl. S Melbourne 3 C19
pl. S Melbourne 30 C1
TIDAL
pl. Torquay 712 H1
TIDCOMBE
cr. Doncaster E 332 E7
TIDE
st. Elwood 454 F5
TIE
st. Mont Albert N 374 E5
TIEMEN
rd. Yarrambat 201 A18
TIERNAN
st. Footscray 367 E5
st. Glen Waverley 460 L4
st. Preston 327 D5
TIERNEY
ct. Highton 705 E9
ct. Werribee 447 G4
TIFFANY
av. Cheltenham 531 G3
cr. Roxburgh Pk 194 B7
ct. Doncaster 330 L18
ct. Keilor 277 B14
ct. Montrose 382 J4
gr. S Morang 198 K13
gr. Templestowe 331 J8
pl. Sydenham 275 C8
wk. Point Cook 451 C10
TIGRIS
cl. Werribee 447 F5
ct. Roxburgh Pk 194 E5
TIKALARA
pl. Templestowe 332 F
TIKANTI
ct. Chelsea Ht 547 D1
TIKI
ct. Wheelers Hl 461 B2
TILBA
ct. Berwick 553 H
pl. Wantirna S 423 B12
st. Aberfeldie 323 D1
TILBURN
rd. Deer Park 319 F2
TILBURY
ct. Cranbourne E 578 J1
ct. Kings Park 319 C
st. Thomastown 240 G1
TILIA
ct. Frankston N 600 E1
TILLBROOK
ct. Noble Park N 501 C1
gr. Cairnlea 319 H
TILLBUSH
cl. Hoppers Csg 405 A1
TILLER
la. Patterson L 547 H2
st. Burwood E 419 G1
TILLEY
rd. Maddingley 263 C
st. Cheltenham 531 D
st. Coburg N 282 B1
wk. Roxburgh Pk 194 D1

TILLEYS
rd. Maddingley 264 B6
TILLOTSON
tce. Armadale, off Orrong Rd 415 C9
TILLS
dr. Warrandyte 290 D16
TILLY
ct. Newcomb 704 B16
TILMOUTH
pl. Nar Warrn S 578 L3
TILNEY
cl. Mulgrave 500 L5
TILSON
dr. Vermont 421 C2
TIM
ct. Hampton 494 K6
TIMARA
ct. McCrae 685 E12
TIMARRON
ct. Langwarrin 630 A7
TIMARU
av. Brunswick E 325 L12
cl. Sorrento 679 D15
ct. Wheelers Hl 460 H18
pl. S Morang 198 K10
TIMBARRA
ct. Grovedale 706 D11
TIMBER
la. Glen Waverley 459 L1
rdg. Doncaster 330 C16
TIMBERGLADE
dr. Noble Park N 501 C12
TIMBERGLADES
Pk Orchards 333 L20
dr. Bundoora 284 G7
rd. Montrose 382 B12
TIMBERLINE
rd. Launching Pl 344 F5
rd. Woori Yall 344 G5
TIMBERSIDE
dr. Beaconsfield 555 E13
TIMBERTOP
ct. Frankston N 600 A12
ct. Mooroolbark 337 F7
dr. Rowville 502 C4
dr. Vermont 421 A5
rd. Ringwood N 377 L10
rd. Sunbury 144 D11
rdg. Warrandyte 333 E5
TIMBERVIEW
tce. Croydon Hl 335 F12
TIMBOON
cr. Broadmeadows 237 H14
TIME
ct. Torquay 712 E3
la. South Yarra 32 G9
TIMELE
dr. Hillside 274 E7
TIMES
sq. Point Cook 451 C9
st. Cheltenham 497 D17
TIMEWELL
cr. Boronia 424 J10
TIMINS
st. Sunbury 143 G14
TIMMINGS
st. Chadstone 457 L4
TIMMINS
cr. Rye 697 D5
ct. Mill Park 242 C4
ct. Wheelers Hl 460 J11
st. Northcote 326 H18
TIMMIS
av. Cheltenham 530 D2
TIMMOTHY
cl. Pakenham 559 E19
dr. Wantirna S 422 D17
TIMMS
av. Croydon 380 H3
av. Kilsyth 380 K3
cr. Dingley Vill 533 A7
ct. Kilsyth 380 K3
ct. Sunbury 142 L10
pl. Doncaster E 332 D6
st. Nar Warrn S 552 H20
TIMOK
la. Roxburgh Pk 194 D6
TIMOR
cl. Burwood 418 D6
ct. Boronia 424 D4
ct. Coolaroo 238 F7
pde. Heidelberg W 328 C1
pl. Highton 701 C15
TIMOTHY
ct. Hallam 537 H14
ct. Kings Park 319 D2
ct. Templestowe 331 K2
la. Melbourne 1 L7
la. Melbourne 24 A5
TIN
al. Parkville 17 L11
TINA
cl. Carrum Downs 601 E3
cl. Fawkner 239 G20
ct. Clarinda 498 D10
ct. Mulgrave 500 H4
TINAGEL
wy. Mornington 656 L4
TINAPHER
dr. Rye 696 K5
TINARA
ct. Cranbourne N 578 D9
TINAROO
gr. Lilydale 337 L3
TINARRA
ct. Kilsyth 381 C12
ct. Wantirna S 422 A17
TINDAL
ct. Frankston S 627 G16
ct. Greensbrgh 244 C16
TINDALE
ct. Attwood 237 E10
TINDALS
rd. Donvale 333 B15
rd. Pk Orchards 333 B15
rd. Warrandyte 333 D4
TINGARA
ct. Patterson L 573 K4
TINGLE
cl. Narre Warren 553 B8
TINKS
rd. Narre Warren 538 G20
TINNING
st. Brunswick 325 C9
TINTAGEL
ct. Mt Eliza 626 A9
TINTALDRA
dr. Taylors L 276 E9
TINTERN
av. Bayswater N 379 G14
av. Preston 282 D19
av. Ringwood E 379 G14
av. Toorak 414 L6
av. Toorak 415 A6
cr. Wantirna S 462 C4
ct. Frankston S 627 J15
ct. Seabrook 450 L5
dr. Springvale S 499 H19
gr. Cheltenham 496 K15
gr. St Albans 275 J19
mw. Cheltenham 496 L14
ri. Glen Waverley 460 K3
TINTINARA
cr. Belmont 706 E6
TINTO
cl. Deer Park 318 K12
ct. Mt Waverley 418 J14
gr. Tecoma 466 C10
TINWORTH
pl. Ringwood N 378 J2
TIPPET
st. Clayton S 499 D5
TIRA
ct. Mornington 641 C17
TIRANA
st. Mitcham 377 A10
TIRHATUAN
dr. Rowville 502 J2
TIRO
ct. Bundoora 285 A5
ct. Hawthorn E 372 D14
TIRRAY
cl. Greensbrgh 243 K18
TISDALL
dr. Langwarrin 629 K5
st. E Geelong 703 G14
TITAN
dr. Carrum Downs 574 G20
st. Whittington 704 B20
TITANIA
cr. Ferny Creek 425 F19
cr. Ferny Creek 465 G1
cr. Tremont 425 F19
tce. Ferny Creek 465 H2
tce. Tremont 465 J2
TITCH
st. Footscray 367 C3
TITCHER
rd. Noble Park N 501 D16
TITIAN
ct. Grovedale 705 J14
TI TREE
av. Bayswater 422 J4
ct. Viewbank 285 L18
dr. Doveton 536 K10
TI-TREE
av. Blairgowrie 695 G1
av. Bonbeach 545 F15
cr. Seaford 600 C4
ct. Kilsyth 381 L7
gr. Mornington 656 C1
gr. Seaford 573 C16
gr.e, Parkdale 531 E14
gr.w, Parkdale 531 E13
la. Mt Eliza 626 C13
TITUS
av. Hoppers Csg 448 L2
ct. Reservoir 283 G3
TIUNA
ct. Glen Waverley 460 L5
gr. Elwood 454 C5
TIVENDALE
rd. Officer 556 F19
TIVERTON
ct. Bayswater N 380 F20
dr. Mulgrave 500 H1
st. Belmont 702 A18
TIVEY
pde. Balwyn 373 B9
st. Reservoir 282 J5
TIVOLI
arc. Melbourne 2 F13
ct. Eumemmerring 537 C13
ct. Keilor Ldg 275 L4
gdn. Rowville 503 B8
pl. S Morang 198 K11
pl. South Yarra 31 J6
pl. South Yarra 414 E3
rd. South Yarra 32 G9
rd. South Yarra 414 J5
st. Point Cook 450 F5
TOAGARA
st. Rye 697 B6
TOBIAS
av. Glen Waverley 460 E6
ct. Carrum Downs 575 E14
la. Mont Albert 374 C13
TOBIN
av. Northcote 326 J17
dr. Queenscliff 709 B18
TOBRUK
av. Heidelberg W 328 A4
av. Tremont 425 D15
cr. Williamstown 411 A16
ct. Lalor 241 G7
rd. Ashburton 417 J16
st. Bulleen 330 B18
TODD
ct. Cranbourne W 603 E2
ct. Croydon 380 K1
ct. Darley 221 K8
ct. Mentone 531 F5
ct. Roxburgh Pk 194 G5
gr. Somerville 645 D14
rd. Port Melb 367 K19
rd. Port Melb 411 L1
st. Bentleigh 495 J1
TODMAN
cl. Bacchus Msh 221 E17
cl. Mill Park 242 L9
ct. Melton W 226 C14
st. Watsonia 285 F8
TOINETTE
ct. Doncaster E 331 L19
TOIRRAM
cr. Cranbourne 577 K11
rd. Mt Waverley 458 K3
TOKOL
ct. Kurunjang 227 C13
TOLEDO
rd. St Albans 320 K6
TOLGA
cl. Carrum Downs 575 C14
ct. Bayswater 423 C8
TOLHURST
av. Boronia 424 K4
pl. Mt Martha 656 D7
TOLL
dr. Altona North 409 B10
TOLLHOUSE
rd. Kings Park 275 C20
TOLLINGTON
av. Malvern East 416 G17
TOLLKEEPERS
pde. Attwood 236 L11
pde. Attwood 237 A11
TOLLS
av. Mentone 531 C6
TOLMIE
av. Gruyere 342 J8
av. Werribee 447 L19
ct. Broadmeadows 237 L9
pl. Geelong, off Gheringhap St 703 A7
ri. Hallam 538 B18
wy. Glen Waverley 420 E15
wy. Mt Martha 656 H6
TOLSON
ct. Roxburgh Pk 194 A12
TOLSTOY
ct. Doncaster E 331 L15
TOM
st. Anglesea 714 A3
TOMAH
ct. Grovedale 706 C10
TOMAR
cl. Croydon 379 F8
ct. Cheltenham 497 C19
TOMASETTI
cr. Narre Warren 538 F18
TOMASINA
ct. Langwarrin 601 B20
TOM BEGG
ct. Wheelers Hl 460 K9
TOMBOLO
ct. Mooroolbark 337 C9
TOM GEARON
ct. Nar Warrn N 539 J11
TOM HILLS
ct. Port Melb, off Webb Rd 412 H5
TOMINTOUL
ct. Clarinda 498 D8
TOM JONES
ct. Nar Warrn N 539 D5
TOMKIN
ct. Altona Mdw 451 D1
TOM MAW MEMORIAL
dr. Rosebud 699 J5
TOM RIGG
st. Cairnlea 319 H11
TOM ROBERTS
cr. Yallambie 285 J15
gld. Diamond Ck 245 B13
rd. Kallista 467 B3
TONBRIDGE
st. Carrum 573 B9
TONELLI
cr. Mill Park 242 D8
pl. Burnside 318 F8
TONGE
st. Anglesea 713 J6
TONGIO
ct. Broadmeadows 238 A11
TONGOLA
ct. Cranbourne 578 B18
TONGUE
st. Yarraville 367 C14
TONI
ct. Wantirna 422 C4
st. Doncaster 331 B18
TONIA
ct. Pakenham 559 G19
TONKIN
av. Balwyn 373 H9
av. Coburg N 281 B12
st. Safety Bch 668 L16
st. Safety Bch 669 A16
TONKINS
la. Richmond 26 A12
TONMAR
ct. Forest Hill 420 G6
TONNANT
ct. Lilydale 294 J20
TONY
pl. Mooroolbark 337 K18
st. Warrandyte 333 E4
TONYL
ct. Greensbrgh 286 D9
TOOAN
ct. Westmeadows 237 J11
TOOGOOD
ct. Pakenham Up 560 B5
TOOGOODS
ri. Box Hill N 375 D7
TOOHEY
cl. Hampton Pk 551 E14
ct. Bellfield 328 A5
st. Bellfield 328 A6
st. Footscray 367 H9
TOOLAMBOOL
rd. Carnegie 456 H5
TOOLANG
ct. Mt Waverley 459 G6
rd. Selby 467 C13
TOOLANGI
gr. Preston 327 E6
rd. Alphington 327 J17
TOOLEBEWONG
rd. Badger Creek 257 L16
TOOLERN
av. Dromana 686 F9
st. Melton S 268 H9
TOOLIM
wk. Sydenham 274 K7
TOOLIMERIN
av. Bayswater N 380 H20
TOOLONDO
cl. Caroline Spr 317 L5
TOOLOOMBA
ct. Frankston 600 F16
TOOMAH
st. Nar Warrn S 578 K1
TOOMBAH
st. Mt Waverley 459 F7
TOOMBAK
wk. Sydenham 274 L7
TOOMBARRA
pl. Greensbrgh 287 A1
TOOMEY
st. Vermont 377 J19
TOOMUC VALLEY
rd. Pakenham 558 C4
rd. Pakenham 558 D13
rd. Pakenham Up 558 D3
TOON
ct. Dandenong N 501 K13
TOONGABBIE
ct. Keysborough 534 H8
ct. Werribee 447 C12
pl. Craigieburn 150 E11
TOORA
ct. Badger Creek 258 D7
cr. St Albans 320 G13
dr. Westmeadows 237 E11
st. Ivanhoe 328 D13
TOORAC
dr. Briar Hill 286 K6
rd. Upwey 465 L18
TOORADIN
av. Dallas 238 C8
TOORADIN STATION
rd. Tooradin 651 H6
TOORAK
av. Baxter 644 L2
av. Croydon 379 L2
av. The Basin 425 E12
av. Toorak 415 J5
ct. Greensbrgh 244 J15
dr. Dingley Vill 533 D6
pde. Geelong 702 K2
rd. Camberwell 417 A8
rd. Hawthorn E 416 A7
rd. Kooyong 416 A7
rd. Malvern 415 B5
rd. Melbourne 414 B4
rd. Mt Dandenong 426 F2
rd. South Yarra 31 C7
rd. South Yarra 32 A9
rd. South Yarra 414 B4
rd. Toorak 415 B5
st. Tootgarook 698 F6
TOORANG
av. Balwyn N 373 D1
TOORONGA
ct. Ashwood 418 F18
rd. Glen Iris 416 C10
rd. Hawthorn E 416 C10
rd. Malvern East 416 B18
rd. Ringwood E 378 K13
st. Dandenong N 502 B19
TOOROURRONG
rd. Upwey 466 B6
TOOTAL
rd. Dingley Vill 532 L3
rd. Springvale S 499 B20
TOOTH
ct. Mill Park 241 K7
TOOTLES
ct. Hoppers Csg 405 D20
TOOYAL
st. Frankston 599 D14
TOPAROA
la. Mt Martha 656 J7
TOPAZ
av. Wyndham Va 446 E14
ct. Mulgrave 500 F1
ct. Wantirna S 421 L16
dr. Hillside 231 J18
pl. Narre Warren 539 D14
pl. St Albans 320 J9
st. Blairgowrie 696 A4
wy. Hampton Pk 551 C9
TOPE
st. S Melbourne 3 B20
st. S Melbourne 24 C20
st. S Melbourne 30 C1
st. S Melbourne 413 G1
TOPPINGS
rd. Wonga Park 291 J18
TOPTANI
dr. Nar Warrn S 579 E2
TOR
rd. Belgrave Ht 506 C2
TORANA
ct. Doveton 537 B10
ct. Hoppers Csg 448 E6
TORBAY
ct. Werribee 446 K13
st. Macleod 285 B12
TORBRECK
cl. Hoppers Csg 449 C2
st. Glen Waverley 460 A9
TORCA
tce. Mornington 641 A20
TORI
pl. Patterson L 547 J20
TORINA
ct. Mt Eliza 626 C20

TORINO
- st. St Albans 320 K5

TORLEY
- rd. Emerald 509 F9

TORMEY
- st. Balwyn N 373 J4
- st. Reservoir 282 G1

TORMORE
- rd. Boronia 424 A12

TORMORVEY
- av. Hillside 232 E20

TOROA
- rd. Mt Dandenong ...426 E3

TORONTO
- av. Doncaster 374 F3

TORORO
- ct. Croydon N 336 D11

TOROWATTA
- pl. Burnside 318 H9

TORQUATA
- ct. Hoppers Csg 405 D16

TORQUAY
- av. Chadstone 458 E4
- av. Seaford 573 D17
- bvd. Jan Juc 711 D16
- cl. Dingley Vill 532 K7
- ct. Endeavour Hl 503 E20
- rd. Belmont 706 F10
- rd. Grovedale 706 E19
- st. Dallas 238 H11
- wy. Wyndham Va 446 H10

TORQUITA
- ct. Hillside 274 C3

TORRBAY
- ct. Frankston S 627 B6

TORRENS
- av. Boronia 424 D14
- st. Werribee 447 G7

TORRES
- ct. Grovedale 706 B13
- ct. Sunbury 142 L11

TORRESDALE
- ct. Toorak 415 F3
- dr. Boronia 424 K3
- rd. Toorak 415 F3

TORRING
- rd. Hawthorn E 416 G2

TORRINGTON
- pl. Canterbury 372 K16
- st. Canterbury 372 J15
- st.e, Canterbury 372 K15

TORRO
- wk. Sydenham 274 K8

TORRODUN
- st. Mt Waverley 459 E6

TORRY HILL
- rd. Upwey 465 J15

TORTEVAL
- pl. Clayton 499 E3

TORTICE
- av. Nunawading 376 F10
- dr. Ringwood N 334 H20

TORULOSA
- ct. Highton 705 J1

TORWOOD
- av. Glen Waverley 461 A1
- cl. Narre Warren 539 E20
- dr. Vermont S 420 J13

TOSARI
- rd. Kalorama 382 L15

TOTARA
- ct. Templstw Lr 330 K13
- ct. Werribee 447 K9

TOTTENHAM
- pde. Tottenham 366 C14
- pde. W Footscray 366 C14

TOTTINGTON
- ri. Berwick 554 B15

TOUHEY
- av. Epping 197 K20

TOULON
- ct. Bonbeach 573 B3
- dr. Templstw Lr 331 A12

TOULOUSE
- rd. S Morang 199 A10
- tce. Nar Warrn S 579 F4

TOUMLIN
- gr. Viewbank 285 H17

TOURELLO
- av. Hawthorn E 416 G4
- rd. Mt Eliza 625 H17
- st. Mitcham 377 E10

TOURMALINE
- cr. Wheelers Hl 461 E19

TOURNAMENT
- dr. Point Cook 450 K9
- ri. Craigieburn 193 H2

TOVA
- ct. Epping 198 A15
- ct. Wantirna S 422 F19
- dr. Carrum Downs ...574 F19

TOVAN-AKAS
- av. Bentleigh 495 J1

TOVELL
- st. Brighton 454 H13

TOVEY
- st. Balwyn N 373 H7
- st. Reservoir 282 H3

TOWARD
- st. Murrumbeena 457 B8

TOWE
- st. Avondale Ht 322 A16

TOWER
- av. Alphington 327 F20
- av. Frankston 599 E16
- av. Nar Warrn S 578 D3
- ct. Armadale 415 H11
- ct. Bayswater N 379 J15
- ct. Noble Park 535 C7
- ct. Sunbury 142 J14
- dr. Briar Hill 286 H3
- pl. Hawthorn E 416 G5
- rd. Balwyn N 373 D7
- rd. Beaconsfld Up 542 J13
- rd. Melb Airport 235 A11
- rd. Mt Eliza 641 J6
- rd. Werribee 447 K15
- st. Ardeer 364 F1
- st. Doncaster 330 L20
- st. Kilsyth 381 F6
- st. Surrey Hills 374 E18

TOWER HILL
- rd. Dromana 685 K9
- rd. Glen Iris 417 D16

TOWERHILL
- bvd. Lynbrook 551 G17
- dr. Ringwood 378 L2
- rd. Frankston 627 C6
- rd. Frankston S 627 C6

TOWERS
- la. Toorak 415 E2
- rd. Lilydale 338 G5
- rd. Toorak 415 D2
- st. Beaumaris 530 G5

TOWN
- la. Patterson L 573 H2
- rd. Gembrook 512 J11

TOWNER
- dr. Knoxfield 462 L5

TOWN HALL
- av. Preston 327 A1

TOWNHALL
- av. Preston 282 L20

TOWNLEY
- pl. Up Fntree Gly 465 B8

TOWNSEND
- av. Gladstone Pk 237 D18
- ct. Lalor 240 H9
- gr. Montrose 382 D10
- la. Mornington 640 C14
- st. Glen Waverley 460 F3
- st. Ivanhoe 328 E13
- st. Ivanhoe East 328 E13

TOWNSING
- ct. Altona Mdw 451 F4

TOWNSINGS
- rd. Diggers Rest 141 J20

TOWNSVILLE
- cl. Scoresby 462 D6

TOWNVIEW
- cl. Wantirna S 422 G20

TOWNVILLE
- cr. Hoppers Csg 405 E18

TOWONG
- ct. Dallas 238 F13
- ct. Doncaster E 331 J17
- st. Dandenong N 502 A9

TOWT
- ct. Rowville 502 F1

TOWYN
- cl. Lower Plenty 286 D13

TOXTETH PARK
- st. Coburg N 282 C15

TRACEY
- cl. Keysborough 534 K10
- cr. Brighton 494 K1
- ct. Cheltenham 531 E2
- ct. Ferny Creek 426 A15
- ct. Wheelers Hl 461 B11
- dr. Cranbourne W ...577 G19
- dr. Vermont S 420 G13
- pl. Greensbrgh 244 B15
- st. Bayswater 423 E9
- st. Doncaster E 331 J19
- st. Reservoir 282 G3
- st. Tullamarine 278 H4
- st. Werribee 447 L12
- st. Werribee 448 A12
- st. Werribee 448 A12

TRACIE
- ct. Sunbury 142 L7

TRADE
- pl. Brooklyn 365 K15
- pl. Coburg N 281 J14
- pl. Vermont 420 L2
- pl. Vermont 421 A2
- pl. Werribee 487 G2
- wy. Kilsyth S 380 K16

TRADE PARK
- dr. Tullamarine 278 E1

TRADERS
- ct. Boronia 424 F2

TRADES HALL
- pl. Carlton 2 L1
- pl. Carlton 18 E20

TRADEWINDS
- la. Patterson L 573 F11

TRAFALGAR
- av. Altona Mdw 451 F3
- cr. Bundoora 242 L20
- cr. Lilydale 294 J20
- ct. Blackburn S 419 E6
- ct. Nar Warrn S 553 E15
- pl. Greenvale 237 F5
- pl. N Melbourne 17 D19
- rd. Camberwell 372 L20
- rd. Camberwell 416 L2
- sq. Wandana Ht 701 D18
- st. Albanvale 319 C3
- st. Brighton 454 L18
- st. Ferntree Gly 464 E9
- st. Mont Albert 374 C15
- wy. Cranbourne E 578 J18

TRAFFORD
- av. Brighton 454 K6
- cl. Lilydale 338 K2
- cl. Lilydale 339 C7
- ct. Wheelers Hl 460 L13
- rd. Carrum Downs ...574 J15
- st. Brunswick 325 J14
- wy. Epping 197 L16

TRAILL
- st. Northcote 326 E15

TRAIN
- dr. Bangholme 549 J13
- st. Highett 496 C13

TRAINOR
- ct. Noble Park 500 G15
- pl. Burwood E 420 D13
- st. Box Hill N 374 J8

TRAK
- *ctr. Toorak, off Toorak Rd 415 B5*

TRALEA
- pl. Frankston 628 A6

TRALEE
- cct. Narre Warren 553 F8
- ct. Pk Orchards 333 B16
- la. Fingal 698 H19

TRAM
- rd. Doncaster 374 L1

TRAMELAND
- ct. Langwarrin 629 K5

TRAMINER
- dr. Mt Martha 657 A9

TRAMLINE
- wk. Lysterfield 504 E13

TRAMOO
- st. Lalor 241 A10

TRAMORE
- cl. Templestowe 332 C5
- tce. Cranbourne 603 F6

TRAMWAY
- la. Darley 221 A5
- pde. Beaumaris 530 B13
- rd. Mt Evelyn 383 C3

TRANMERE
- av. Carnegie 456 K8
- st. Fitzroy N 19 D1
- st. Fitzroy N 326 B20

TRANQUIL
- ct. Pt Lonsdale 707 G18
- pl. Thomastown 240 G16

TRANQUILITY
- ct. Portsea 678 D3
- dr. Bangholme 549 J14
- pl. Beaconsfield 555 F13

TRANQUIL WINTER
- ct. Viewbank 329 J2

TRANSIT
- *pl. Geelong, off Gheringhap St ...703 A6*

TRANSLINK
- dr. Keilor Park 277 H14

TRANSPORT
- dr. Somerton 195 A16
- st. Braybrook 322 C20
- st. Braybrook 366 C1

TRANTER
- sq. Lynbrook 551 E16

TRANTINO
- av. Somerton 194 K11

TRAP
- st. Bulla 190 A15

TRAPANI
- av. Point Cook 450 C10

TRAPHINA
- ct. Oakleigh S 497 H8

TRASK
- st. Braybrook 366 A7

TRAVELLYN
- ct. Blackburn S 375 G20
- ct. Blackburn S 419 G1

TRAVERS
- cr. Burwood E 419 L10
- st. Thomastown 241 A11

TRAVIS
- cl. Clarinda 498 C10
- ct. Berwick 554 C2
- ct. Hoppers Csg 405 A16

TRAWALLA
- ct. Thomastown 239 K17
- av. Toorak 415 C5
- ct. Hampton Pk 551 H6
- rd. Croydon 380 J7
- st. Aspendale Gdn 546 H4

TRAWOOL
- st. Box Hill N 375 C9

TRAYDAL
- cl. Wantirna 421 L13

TREACY
- *pl. Geelong, off Yarra St 703 B7*

TREADWELL
- rd. Essendon N 279 C20
- rd. Niddrie 279 C20

TREASURY
- pl. E Melbourne 24 L6
- pl. E Melbourne 25 A6
- pl. Taylors Hill 274 G9

TREBORYN
- ct. Rowville 463 G20

TRECASTLE
- ct. Craigieburn 149 L14

TREE
- st. Waurn Ponds 705 E17

TREEBY
- bvd. Mordialloc 532 D17
- ct. Springvale S 534 A3

TREECREEPER
- pl. Frankston S 628 B16

TREEFERN
- dr. Sunbury 143 E17

TREEHAVEN
- pl. Somerville 644 E15

TREELEAF
- la. Melton S 269 H9

TREELINE
- pl. Pk Orchards 334 F20

TREEMONT
- ct. Cairnlea 319 F11

TREES
- ct. Clarinda 498 B10

TREESBANK
- av. Springvale 500 C18

TREETOP
- cl. Roxburgh Pk 194 B6
- ct. Heathmont 378 L16
- ct. Nar Warrn S 553 F19
- dr. Kilsyth 381 G7
- tce. Plenty 244 H12

TREETOPS
- cl. Eltham 288 B3

TREE VIOLET
- ct. Sunbury 143 J4

TREFOIL
- st. Ferntree Gly 463 F9

TREFOREST
- dr. Clayton 459 D20

TREGARRON
- av. Kew 372 J11

TREGENNA
- ct. Brighton East 455 C14

TREGUNTER
- st. Ascot Vale 323 F19

TREGUTHA
- wy. Newport 411 A12

TREHERNE
- ct. Carrum Downs ...601 E2

TRELAWNY
- pl. Kings Park 275 C20

TRELOAR
- av. Eltham 288 A11
- cr. Braybrook 365 J2
- la. Pakenham 584 L8
- st. Coburg N 281 G14

TREMAINE
- av. Kings Park 275 A20
- ct. Carrum Downs ...600 L4
- ct. Mulgrave 500 L6

TREMBATH
- ct. Altona Mdw 452 A5

TREMONT HILL
- tr. Tremont 465 H4

TRENCH FARM
- rd. Healesville 213 J5

TRENDE
- st. Dandenong 535 H5

TRENERRY
- cr. Abbotsford 20 F11

TRENHAM
- ct. Mitcham 377 G1

TRENOWETH
- st. Brunswick W ....324 L

TRENT
- cl. Greensbrgh 244 C1
- cl. Werribee ....447 J
- ct. Bonbeach 547 D2
- ct. Burwood E ....419 F
- ct. Keilor East ....322 G
- ct. Notting Hill 459 H1
- st. Glen Iris ....417 F
- st. Ivanhoe ....328 C
- st. Mont Albert 374 C1
- st. Moorabbin 497 E1

TRENTHAM
- ct. Thomastown 240 D1
- ct. Wantirna 422 E1
- dr. Gladstone Pk ....279 B
- st. Blairgowrie ....696 C
- st. Sandringham 495 B1
- wy. Langwarrin ....629 C

TRENTON
- av. Glen Waverley 460 K1
- cl. Albanvale ....319 B
- ct. Nar Warrn S ....578 D
- pl. Mooroolbark ....337 J

TRENTWOOD
- av. Balwyn N ....373 L
- av. Melton W 225 H1
- dr. Highton ....701 H
- rd. Narre Warren 538 K1

TRESCO
- ct. Mulgrave ....500 L
- ct. Mulgrave ....501 A
- st. Dallas ....238 G

TRESISE
- av. Wantirna S 422 A1

TRETHOWAN
- av. Melton W 225 K1
- st. Broadmeadows ..238 E1

TREVALLYN
- rd. Montrose ....382 B

TREVALYAN
- ct. Airport W 278 H1

TREVANNION
- st. Glenroy ....280 A

TREVASCUS
- st. Caulfield S 455 K1

TREVATT
- av. Templstw Lr 330 J1

TREVELYAN
- st. Caulfield S ....455 E
- st. Elsternwick ....455 C

TREVENA
- cl. Rowville 463 C1

TREVENEN
- ct. Jan Juc 711 E1

TREVETHIC
- rd. Springvale ....499 L

TREVINDEN
- cl. Templestowe 331 J1

TREVINO
- cl. Hoppers Csg 405 B1

TREVOR
- ct. Herne Hill ....702 A
- ct. Keysborough ....534 E
- ct. Mt Waverley 419 F1
- ct. Nunawading ....376 J
- ct. Warranwood 335 A1
- rd. Nr Nr Goon N 560 L1
- st. Upwey 465 K1

TREVOSE
- ct. Albanvale ....319 B

TREWEEK
- pde. Ferny Creek ....465 L

TREWHITT
- ct. Dromana ....686 K

TREWIN
- ct. Narre Warren 539 D1
- st. Dandenong S 535 L1

TREZISE
- st. Warrandyte ....333 J

TRIBE
- st. S Melbourne ....29 D
- st. S Melbourne ....413 B
- st. Sunshine 321 G2
- st. Sunshine ....365 G

TRIBUTE
- ct. Hoppers Csg 405 C1

TRIBUZI
- cl. Pakenham 559 B2

TRICIA
- av. Springvale 499 H1
- ct. Burwood E 419 J1

TRICKEY
- av. Sydenham ....275 A
- ct. Altona Mdw ....451 H
- ct. Sunshine N ....321 B

TRICKS
- ct. Glen Waverley 419 J1

TRIDENT
cl. Diamond Ck......245 K13
cl. Keilor Dn......275 H11
TRIESTE
wy. Point Cook......450 D10
TRIGG
st. Geelong West......702 E1
TRIGGER PLANT
tr. Frankston N......600 H11
TRIHOLM
av. Laverton......406 J20
TRIMBLE
dr. Langwarrin......629 B7
TRINACRIA
ct. Deer Park......319 E15
TRINAFOUR
st. Moonee Pnd......324 A11
TRINDALL
pl. Taylors L......233 E17
TRINIAN
st. Prahran......32 J20
st. Prahran......414 K10
st. Vermont......421 E3
TRINITY
bvd. Attwood......236 H13
ct. Bentleigh E......497 D8
ct. Berwick......554 D2
ct. Brighton East......455 G16
ct. Patterson L......547 G20
ct. Patterson L......573 G1
ct. Rye......696 L14
ct. Rye......697 A14
ct. Sunbury......144 F10
dr. Langwarrin......629 D4
la. Keysborough......533 K16
pl. E Melbourne......25 F7
st. Brunswick......325 D16
wy. S Morang......198 J13
TRIPOLI
ct. Hallam......537 G14
TRIPOVICH
st. Brunswick......325 F13
TRISH
wk. Werribee......448 F18
TRISHA
dr. Rowville......503 A5
TRIST
st. Watsonia N......285 G3
TRISTAN
ct. Eltham North......245 G18
ct. Hadfield......281 B9
TRISTANA
hts. S Morang......198 J14
TRISTANIA
st. Doncaster E......375 G3
st. Doveton......536 L12
st. Frankston S......627 D9
TRISTRAM
ct. Glen Waverley......420 K16
TRISTRON
ct. Melton W......226 C13
TRITON
ct. Gladstone Pk......279 C3
ct. Ringwood......335 B20
dr. Keysborough......534 F10
TRIUMPH
cl. Glen Waverley......460 A3
ct. Highton......701 E16
TROEDEL
st. Pearcedale......646 L6
st. Pearcedale......647 A6
TROLLABY
cl. Gladstone Pk......236 L16
TROODOS
ri. Eltham......288 G2
ri. Research......288 G2
TROON
av. Jan Juc......711 F15
av. Mornington......656 D3
cr. Sunshine N......321 H16
ct. Endeavour Hl......537 H1
ct. Rowville......462 D19
ct. Sunbury......144 F13
pl. Frankston......600 F18
rd. McCrae......684 K19
rd. Rosebud......684 K19
TROOPER
ct. Wheelers Hl......461 B13
TROTT
pl. Keilor East......278 A20
TROTTING
pl. Epping......198 D16
TROUP
ct. Werribee......447 G12
TROVE PARK
dr. Vermont......421 B4
TROY
cl. Sunshine W......364 C6
ct. Forest Hill......420 C4
ct. Werribee......447 L8
st. Bonbeach......573 C1
st. Glen Waverley......420 H15
tce. Lysterfield......463 K20
TRUCK CITY
dr. Campbellfield......194 L20
TRUDGEON
av. Reservoir......282 K16
TRUDI
ct. Donvale......377 A2
TRUDY
pl. Mt Evelyn......339 J20
TRUE
av. Carrum......573 D7
TRUEMANS
rd. Boneo......698 G11
rd. Boneo......698 J15
rd. Fingal......698 G11
rd. Fingal......698 G11
rd. Fingal......698 L20
rd. Fingal......699 A18
rd. Rosebud W......698 G11
rd. Tootgarook......698 G11
TRUGANINA
av. Seabrook......450 K8
wy. Truganina......405 J14
TRUGANINI
rd. Carnegie......456 H8
TRUGO
la. Footscray......367 F9
TRUMAN
ct. Altona Mdw......451 F4
st. S Kingsville......410 F3
TRUMPER
cr. Sunbury......142 J16
pl. Epping......198 G15
st. Camberwell......416 K4
TRUMPINGTON
gr. Kallista......468 C16
gr. Menzies Ck......468 C16
tce. Attwood......236 J11
TRUNCATA
ct. Mill Park......243 D8
TRURO
cr. Keilor Ldg......275 K4
st. Abbotsford......20 C12
TRUSCOTT
av. Roxburgh Pk......194 C8
ct. Mill Park......243 A5
ct. Wheelers Hl......460 F16
st. Brunswick E......325 L18
st. Glenroy......280 G8
st. Whittington......703 L18
TRUSLOVE
ct. Endeavour Hl......537 L9
TRYTHALL
ct. Altona Mdw......451 G3
st. Beaconsfield......555 A15
TSCHAMPIONS
rd. Macclesfield......470 H2
TUANS
tr. Yarra Glen......208 F6
TUBE
st. Sunshine N......321 F11
TUCK
ct. Narre Warren......539 B15
st. Cheltenham......530 K3
st. Moorabbin......496 B7
wk. Fawkner......281 F1
TUCKER
av. Brighton......455 A17
av. Port Melb......412 G4
rd. Bentleigh......456 G20
rd. Bentleigh......496 F6
rd. McKinnon......456 G20
rd. Ormond......456 G20
rd. Vermont......421 E5
st. Bundoora......242 K20
st. Cranbourne......578 C20
st. Fawkner......281 H8
st. W Footscray......366 J4
wy. Macleod......285 E12
TUCKERS
rd. Templestowe......331 K14
TUCKETT
st. Alphington......327 G19
st. Murrumbeena......457 C7
TUCKEY
st. Sorrento......679 C13
TUCKFIELD
ct. Macleod......285 D11
TUDAWALI
cr. Wheelers Hl......460 G18
TUDBALL
ct. Bacchus Msh......221 L14
TUDOR
cr. Noble Park N......501 D17
ct. Balwyn N......374 A2
ct. Blackburn S......419 J6
ct. Craigieburn......150 B18
ct. Edithvale......546 K9
ct. Frankston......600 A17
ct. Glen Waverley......459 H10
ct. Heathmont......378 K15
ct. Hoppers Csg......405 B20
ct. Ivanhoe......328 D9
ct. Keilor East......322 H6
ct. Narre Warren......539 E13
ct. Wantirna......422 F12
dr. Mooroolbark......338 A16
pl. Melton W......226 E15
rd. Doncaster......330 E18
rd. Rosebud......700 K3
rd. Sunshine N......321 C14
st. Bentleigh E......457 E19
st. Burnley......371 C17
st. Burwood......418 E10
st. Glenroy......280 A7
TUDOR COURT
rd. Yellingbo......387 H9
TUDOR ROSE
cr. Sydenham......275 D9
TUDOR VILLAGE
dr. Lilydale......338 L5
dr. Lilydale......339 A5
TUERONG
rd. Moorooduc......657 H16
rd. Tuerong......657 G17
rd. Tuerong......657 H16
st. Rye......697 B5
TUFFS
gr. Grovedale......705 K12
TUFNEL
ct. Endeavour Hl......537 A1
TUGAN
pl. Ringwood N......334 K19
TUGUN
rd. Lilydale......338 H8
TUHAN
st. Chadstone......457 L3
TUHANS
rd. Mt Waverley......458 G4
TUILERIES
ri. Nar Warrn S......578 J2
TULAR
av. Oakleigh S......497 H3
TULIP
cl. Hoppers Csg......405 B16
cr. Boronia......424 B15
ct. Doncaster E......332 F13
ct. Hillside......274 D4
ct. Lalor......240 L9
ct. Notting Hill......459 J14
ct. Warranwood......334 J13
gr. Cheltenham......496 F20
st. Black Rock......495 G19
st. Cheltenham......495 G19
st. Silvan......428 L5
TULKARA
gr. Vermont......421 K2
TULLAMARINA
av. Tullamarine......278 K7
TULLAMARINE
fwy. Airport W......279 B17
fwy. Essendon N......279 C19
fwy. Gladstone Pk......236 E15
fwy. Gladstone Pk......278 L2
fwy. Gladstone Pk......279 A4
fwy. Gowanbrae......279 A4
fwy. Melb Airport......236 E15
fwy. Niddrie......279 C19
fwy. Strathmore......279 C19
fwy. Tullamarine......236 E15
fwy. Westmeadows......236 E15
TULLAMARINE PARK
rd. Tullamarine......278 B10
TULLAMORE
av. Doncaster......330 D20
TULLAROOP
ct. Lysterfield......464 A14
ct. St Albans......320 E13
TULLIDGE
st. Melton......269 B1
TULLIMBAR
cct. Vermont S......420 F11
TULLIUS
av. Oakleigh E......458 K12
TULLO
pl. Richmond......26 G11
TULLOCH
av. Kurunjang......227 C15
ct. Bacchus Msh......221 F15
ct. Keilor Dn......275 K10
ct. Mill Park......242 J11
gr. Glen Waverley......459 K10
st. Deer Park......319 C17
st. Millgrove......348 D1
wy. Roxburgh Pk......194 A11
wy. Roxburgh Pk......194 B12
TULLUS
ct. Kings Park......274 L17
TULLY
ct. Doncaster......330 L18
ct. Ivanhoe......327 L8
ct. Werribee......447 H9
rd. Clarinda......498 G11
st. E Geelong......703 E13
TULLYVALLIN
cr. Sorrento......679 B16
TULONG
cl. Mooroolbark......337 E16
st. Hurstbridge......203 F13
TULSA
dr. Sunbury......144 E11
TULSK
ct. Hampton Pk......551 G13
TULUM
ct. Frankston......599 F17
TUMBLE TREE
ct. Highton......705 F3
TUMUT
cl. Epping......198 A19
ct. Berwick......554 C20
ct. Keilor......276 L13
ct. Patterson L......573 K3
ct. Wantirna S......422 D16
ct. Werribee......447 H8
TUNA
la. Pt Lonsdale......707 F14
TUNALEY
pde. Reservoir......283 F1
TUNBERRY
ct. Rowville......462 C19
TUNBRIDGE
cr. Lalor......241 J8
mw. Westmeadows......237 H13
rd. Cairnlea......319 H13
st. Flemington......324 D19
wy. Ferntree Gly......463 F4
TUNBURY
av. Ringwood......378 L3
av. Ringwood......379 A3
cl. Ringwood......378 L3
ct. Highton......701 F15
TUNLEY
cl. Endeavour Hl......537 F8
pl. Roxburgh Pk......194 C15
TUNNECLIFFE
ct. Keilor East......277 L16
TUNNEL
st. Warrandyte......334 B2
TUNSTALL
av. Boronia......424 B9
av. Nunawading......376 H13
rd. Donvale......376 E7
sq. Doncaster E......376 E2
TUPPAL
pl. Keilor East......278 C18
TUPPEN
st. Yarraville......366 J15
TURAKINA
av. Edithvale......546 G13
TURANA
st. Doncaster......331 B19
TURANGA
pl. Hallam......537 L15
TURANO
ct. Roxburgh Pk......194 F5
TURBO
dr. Bayswater N......379 L17
TURELLA
ct. Berwick......553 L14
ct. Lalor......240 D9
ct. Mooroolbark......337 D13
TURFAN
cl. Keilor Dn......276 E16
TURIA
gr. Roxburgh Pk......194 E6
TURIN
pl. Keilor Ldg......276 B5
TURKEITH
av. Herne Hill......702 A1
cr. Croydon N......336 D11
TURNBERRY
av. Nar Warrn S......578 L2
ct. Frankston......628 B6
ct. Heatherton......497 G15
dr. Sunbury......144 G12
la. Chirnside Pk......292 J11
rd. Sunshine N......321 H14
TURNBULL
al. Melbourne......24 J4
av. Oakleigh E......458 K12
av. Toorak......415 H4
ct. Brunswick W......324 G10
ct. Carrum Downs......601 B6
ct. Ringwood......378 F9
dr. Pascoe Vale S......324 G4
gr. Northcote......326 H14
st. Clifton Hill......20 B4
st. Mornington......640 E16
TURNER
al. Melbourne......2 E11
al. Melbourne......24 D6
av. Glen Huntly......456 B9
cl. Springvale......500 C6
cr. Braybrook......365 K5
ct. Dandenong......536 E3
ct. Glen Waverley......459 J3
ct. S Morang......243 H1
ct. Sunbury......143 F6
pl. S Geelong......703 A13
rd. Boronia......424 E12
rd. Highett......496 G14
rd. Langwarrin......629 B2
st. Abbotsford......20 C13
st. Abbotsford......20 D13
st. Armadale......415 E10
st. Bacchus Msh......221 L18
st. Berwick......554 J10
st. Briar Hill......286 H4
st. Croydon......380 C5
st. Glen Iris......416 H8
st. Malvern East......416 D20
st. Moonee Pnd......324 H11
st. Pascoe Vale S......280 L20
st. Port Melb......368 C18
st. Thornbury......327 H10
st. Westmeadows......236 L14
TURNERS
la. Healesville......211 K8
la. Officer......557 A4
TURNHAM
av. Rosanna......328 L1
TURNLEY
st. Balwyn N......329 H20
st. Balwyn N......373 H1
TURNSTONE
ct. Carrum Downs......600 E4
st. Doncaster E......376 A4
TURNUNG
rd. Panton Hill......205 E19
rd. Watsons Ck......249 C2
TURQUOISE
cl. St Albans......320 K9
TURRAMURRA
dr. Keysborough......534 F9
dr. Rowville......502 H1
TURRANA
st. Rye......697 A5
TURTUR
cl. Mill Park......242 B7
TURVILLE
pl. Port Melb......412 J5
TUSANNE
pl. Doncaster E......331 K18
TUSCAN
ct. Thomastown......240 K17
ct. Waurn Ponds......705 B16
TUSCANY
ct. Roxburgh Pk......194 B7
ri. Templestowe......331 G5
TUSCORORA
grn. Craigieburn......193 K2
TUSKAR
pl. Carrum Downs......601 E3
TUSMORE
ri. Craigieburn......193 J3
TUSSOCK
cr. Sydenham......274 K8
ct. Frankston......599 L15
gr. Cairnlea......319 E12
st. Narre Warren......553 F10
TUTA
cl. Croydon Hl......335 G15
ct. Greensbrgh......244 A18
TUTTAWATTA
rd. Selby......467 B14
TUXEN
av. Carrum Downs......574 K17
ct. Brighton East......495 K4
ct. Highton......701 H9
st. Balwyn N......373 G6
st. Balwyn N......373 H4
TWAKURRA
st. Rye......697 F8
TWEED
ct. Glen Waverley......420 K18
ct. Langwarrin......629 B5
ct. Werribee......447 H5
pl. Hawthorn, off Tweed St......371 J17
st. Hawthorn......371 J17
st. Highett......495 K12
st. Ringwood E......378 L13
st. Vermont......421 J1
TWEEDIE
ct. Box Hill N......375 B6
pl. Richmond......26 F7
TWEEDSIDE
st. Essendon......323 G8
TWELFTH
av. Anglesea......713 D13
TWENTYMAN
ct. Seaholme......409 J15
TWICKENHAM
cr. Burnley......415 C1
TWILIGHT
pl. Safety Bch......669 B16
TWIN
ct. Ferntree Gly......423 L17
TWINING
av. Bundoora......242 D13
TWIN RIVER
dr. S Morang......198 L11

TWISDEN
rd. Bentleigh 495 L2
TWITT
st. Moolap 704 H18
TWOBAR
pl. Kilsyth 381 F12
TWO BAYS
cr. Mt Martha 655 D18
cr. Selby 467 E16
rd. Mt Eliza 642 J7
TWOFOLD
cl. Dingley Vill 532 K8
TWOHIG
ct. Dandenong N 501 J17
TWYFORD
cl. Doncaster E 332 J13
cl. Hillside 232 E18
st. Box Hill N 375 C9
st. Fawkner 281 K2
st. Williamstown 411 F18
TYABB
ct. Broadmeadows 237 G15
ct. Frankston 600 F17
gr. Aspendale 546 G6
TYALLA
cl. Lower Plenty 286 H14
cr. Toorak 415 G4
ct. Hampton Pk 551 G10
ct. Mulgrave 500 F2
gr. Mornington 640 F17
TYAS
pl. Carrum Downs 601 E3
TYBURN
cl. Werribee 446 J13
TYE
av. Selby 467 B16
TYERS
cr. Rowville 463 B18
ct. Dallas 238 D10
ct. Frankston 628 C1
la. Keysborough 534 D18
wk. Caroline Spr 317 L6
TYLDEN
ct. Grovedale 706 D11
ct. Mentone 531 J7
pl. Westmeadows 236 L14
TYLER
ct. Epping 197 K19
dr. Carrum Downs 575 E17
st. Preston 282 L16
st. Preston 283 A16
st. Reservoir 283 A16
st. Sunshine 365 E3
TYLOID
sq. Wantirna 422 E14
TYMON
rd. Cockatoo 511 F10
TYNAN
st. Preston 282 E19
TYNDALL
st. Surrey Hills 373 H20
wy. Mill Park 243 D5
TYNE
cl. Deer Park 318 L12
cl. Nunawading 376 G16
ct. Frankston 599 J18
ct. Mt Waverley 418 H15
st. Box Hill N 374 K11
st. Camberwell 417 G7
st. Carlton 18 E13
TYNEFIELD
ct. Brighton 454 G9
TYNEHEAD
pl. Geelong, off Maud St 702 L10
TYNER
rd. Wantirna S 422 J19
TYNHAM
cl. Ferntree Gly 463 F2
ct. Mornington 656 K3
TYNONG
st. Box Hill N 375 C9
st. Croydon 335 L19
TYNTYNDER
cl. Berwick 554 C16
dr. Carrum Downs 601 C4
TYPE
st. Burnley 371 B17
TYQUIN
st. Laverton 407 F14
TYREE
av. Springvale 499 L16
pl. Dandenong S 550 A6
TYRELL
ct. Altona Mdw 451 H3
ct. Keilor 276 L12
ct. Keilor 277 A12
ct. Meadow Ht 194 C18
ct. Rowville 463 D18
pl. Berwick 580 B3
wy. Caroline Spr 317 L8
TYRES
ct. Sunshine N 321 C9

TYRO
ct. Montrose 382 F9
TYROL
ct. Doncaster E 331 G16
ct. Epping 197 L18
st. Dandenong N 502 D17
TYRONE
av. Macleod 285 C12
av. Rye 680 G20
ct. Avondale Ht 322 F7
ct. St Helena 245 B16
ct. Wheelers Hl 460 L19
dr. Eltham 288 F1
st. Camberwell 417 C6
st. Langwarrin 629 C6
st. N Melbourne 17 G16
st. Ormond 456 E14
st. Seaford 599 H4
st. South Yarra 31 K14
st. South Yarra 414 E7
st. Werribee 448 B12
TYRRELL
av. Blackburn 375 H13
cr. Fawkner 281 J9
pl. Wyndham Va 446 A6
st. Mont Albert N 374 F9
tce. Waterways 547 F1
TYSON
ct. Darley 221 L10
ct. Lalor 240 H9
ct. Ringwood 378 L3
ct. Ringwood 379 A3
ct. Wantirna S 422 F20
ct. Wantirna S 462 E1
st. Fawkner 281 J4
st. Richmond 26 A14
wy. Sydenham 274 H5
TYSSEN
ct. Doncaster E 331 G15

U

UGANDA
st. Burwood 418 D6
ULAH
ct. Scoresby 462 B6
ULLARA
ct. Frankston 600 G14
ULM
cl. Mill Park 243 A6
st. Coburg N 281 C14
st. Laverton 407 C15
ULMARA
pl. Greensbrgh 244 A20
pl. Greensbrgh 286 A1
pl. Keilor Dn 276 G16
ULMER
rd. Emerald 510 C7
ULRIC
ct. Frankston 628 F5
ULRICH
ct. Viewbank 285 E19
ULSTER
ct. Hoppers Csg 448 E8
la. Melbourne 24 K6
ULTIMO
pl. S Morang 198 J11
pl. Toorak 415 E3
ULUPNA
rd. Ormond 456 D13
ULYSSES
av. Croydon S 380 D12
UNA
st. Mt Waverley 419 F19
st. Sunshine 365 G1
st. Tootgarook 698 E2
st. Watsonia N 285 G2
UNAVALE
cr. Boronia 423 H11
UNDERA
ct. Fawkner 281 K9
UNDERBANK
bvd. Bacchus Msh 221 E17
UNDERHILL
ct. Sunbury 142 F10
UNDERWOOD
cl. Mill Park 242 F3
dr. Donvale 376 G5
la. Lilydale 338 L8
rd. Ferntree Gly 464 G1
UNGARA
cl. Eltham North 245 E17
UNGARIE
ct. Hampton Pk 551 F12
UNIACKE
ct. Melbourne 1 A10
ct. Melbourne 23 H8
UNICORN
wy. Kings Park 275 A18

UNION
av. Pakenham 558 K20
dr. Bundoora, off College Dr 284 E13
gr. Springvale 499 L14
la. Melbourne 2 D13
la. Melbourne 24 D7
pl. Carlton 18 D12
pl. Newtown 702 H11
pl. S Melbourne 30 C4
rd. Ascot Vale 323 L19
rd. Balwyn 374 A17
rd. Balwyn 374 A20
rd. Dandenong S 535 F18
rd. Langwarrin 629 G2
rd. Lilydale 338 K7
rd. Parkville 18 A12
rd. Somerton 194 J17
rd. Surrey Hills 374 A17
rd. Surrey Hills 417 L2
rd. Wandin N 340 L16
st. Armadale 415 G13
st. Belmont 702 E20
st. Brighton East 455 C15
st. Brunswick 325 A15
st. Brunswick W 324 J16
st. Kew 371 L10
st. Melbourne 414 C11
st. Melbourne 414 C11
st. Northcote 326 F18
st. N Melbourne 17 A18
st. Port Melb 412 J3
st. Preston 282 D16
st. Reservoir 282 D16
st. Richmond 26 C11
st. S Melbourne 29 L3
st. Sunshine 365 G4
st. Templstw Lr 330 F7
st. Williamstown 411 E12
st. Windsor 414 C11
st. Geelong, off Ryrie St 703 B8
UNION LOOP
rd. Clayton 459 D15
UNITING
la. Bulla 190 L18
la. Bulla 191 A18
UNITT
ct. Broadmeadows 237 L12
st. Melton 226 J18
UNITY
ct. Warburton 349 K6
wy. Kilsyth 381 A7
UNIVERSE
ct. Whittington 704 D19
UNIVERSITY
dr. Highton 705 E8
dr. Mill Park 243 C4
dr. Taylors Hill 274 D9
pl. Carlton 18 G14
pl. Clayton 459 H16
rd. Bayswater 422 L3
rd. Bayswater 423 A3
st. Carlton 18 F14
UNLEY
ct. Vermont 420 K6
gr. Ascot Vale 324 C16
UNO
st. Belmont 702 B19
UNSWORTH
rd. Ringwood N 378 E6
UNTHANK
ct. Somerville 644 F18
UNWIN
st. Templestowe 330 K5
UONGA
rd. Bentleigh 496 C4
UPALONG
rd. Mt Dandenong 382 G20
UPLAND
ct. Eltham North 287 B2
rd. Strathmore 324 B1
UPLANDS
ct. Meadow Ht 237 K7
ct. Narre Warren 538 H19
pl. Thomastown 240 D12
rd. Balwyn N 372 L7
rd. Chirnside Pk 336 E5
rd. Wonga Park 336 E5
rd. Yarra Glen 208 G6
UPMINSTER
ct. Frankston 599 K17
UPPER
ct. Nunawading 376 L19
ct. Nunawading 377 A19
rd. Wattle Glen 246 J4
UPPER COONARA
rd. Kallista 427 C19
rd. Olinda 427 C19
rd. Olinda 427 G20
UPPER CRESCENT
rd. Yarra Jctn 346 H15

UPPER GRIEVE
rd. Avonsleigh 470 G19
UPPER HEIDELBERG
rd. Heidelberg 328 G8
rd. Heidelberg Ht 328 F8
rd. Ivanhoe 328 B14
UPPER PAPER MILLS
rd. Fyansford 701 B6
UPPER SKENE
st. Newtown 702 A7
UPSNDOWNS
rd. Dromana 670 C14
UPTON
cl. Diamond Ck 245 L6
cr. Narre Warren 553 D8
ct. Burwood E 419 H11
ct. Mulgrave 501 G2
ct. Ringwood 335 B19
ct. Werribee 448 D7
ct. Wonga Park 291 F17
dr. Hillside 232 B17
pl. Prahran 414 L11
pl. Prahran 415 A11
rd. Emerald 509 E5
rd. St Kilda 414 E12
rd. Windsor 31 L20
rd. Windsor 414 E12
st. Altona 409 A18
st. Altona 409 A19
st. Roxburgh Pk 193 L5
UPTONS
la. Geelong, off Maud St 703 B10
UPWEY
av. Springvale 499 J17
URAL
ct. Dandenong N 502 D17
URALLA
ct. Mooroolbark 337 A13
pl. Yallambie 286 B13
rd. Mt Martha 656 B15
st. Vermont 421 G3
URANA
av. Sunshine N 320 L14
av. Sunshine N 321 A14
dr. Keilor East 278 B19
st. Kilsyth 381 C10
st. Newtown 702 J12
st. Newtown 702 J13
URANDALINE
gr. Caulfield 455 K3
URBAN
pl. Albanvale 319 C7
st. Braeside 532 H14
URE
rd. Cockatoo 472 L13
rd. Gembrook 512 G8
rd. Nangana 472 K1
UREN
ct. Altona Mdw 451 K3
ct. Thomastown 241 J14
ct. Williamstown 410 K15
rd. Emerald 469 H8
URQUHART
ct. Darley 221 K7
ct. Greenvale 193 D20
ct. Hampton Pk 551 K6
st. Coburg 325 L1
st. Hawthorn 372 A19
st. Northcote 20 E1
URSA
st. Balwyn N 329 C20
st. Balwyn N 373 C1
st. Belmont 706 C3
URSULA
cl. Wheelers Hl 461 D13
st. Box Hill N 375 B7
URWIN
st. Yarraville 366 D16
USHER
ct. Dandenong S 535 H15
UTAH
ct. Dandenong N 501 L9
rd. Glen Waverley 419 J17
UTOPIA
pl. Burnley 371 B20
UTRECHT
ct. Donvale 377 B3
ct. Warranwood 334 J15
UTRILLO
cl. Scoresby 462 A7
UVADALE
gr. Kew 372 D10
UXBRIDGE
av. Doncaster 330 C20

V

VABIRO
ct. Greensbrgh 243 K1
VADLURE
av. St Kilda E 414 L1
VAIL
pl. Cranbourne S 603 J1
st. Prahran 415 B1
VAIN
cl. Mill Park 242 J1
VAINA
st. Werribee 447 D1
VAL
ct. Dandenong 536 E
VALADERO
ct. Mill Park 242 H1
VALANNE
st. Brighton East 455 G1
VALDA
av. Mont Albert N 374 G
av. Ringwood E 379 D
cl. Berwick 554 K
ct. Cranbourne 577 K1
gr. Brighton 454 K1
st. Anglesea 713 K
st. Watsonia 285 C
VALDALE
ct. Heathmont 379 D1
VALDEMAR
ct. Brighton East 495 J
VALDOONE
ct. Oak Park 279 H1
VALE
rd. Belgrave Ht 506 E
st. Albanvale 319 C
st. Bentleigh 496 C
st. E Melbourne 25 K1
st. Glen Iris 417 C1
st. Heathmont 378 E1
st. Mornington 640 F1
st. N Melbourne 17 F1
st. Pascoe Vale 280 C1
st. Reservoir 282 D1
st. Rosebud W 698 K
st. St Kilda 414 C1
VALENCIA
ct. Kings Park 275 C1
la. Werribee 447 J1
rd. Lilydale 338 L1
rd. Lilydale 339 A1
st. Aberfeldie 323 E1
st. Glenroy 280 G
tce. Templestowe 331 L
VALENCY
ct. Mitcham 377 F1
rd. Glen Iris 416 G1
VALENTE
st. Altona Mdw 407 K1
VALENTINE
av. Kew 371 K1
av. Thomastown 241 J1
cr. Sunshine W 364 G1
ct. Glen Waverley 459 J
gr. Armadale 415 H1
rd. Langwarrin 601 C2
st. Bayswater 423 G
st. Bulleen 330 A1
st. Ivanhoe 327 J1
st. Rye 696 F
VALENTINO
dr. Croydon 379 F
VALEPARK
cl. Noble Park N 501 C1
cr. Cranbourne 603 L
dr. Donvale 332 H1
dr. Donvale 332 J1
VALERIAN
av. Altona North 409 K
st. Hampton 495 G1
VALERIE
cl. Mt Martha 656 L
ct. Hampton Pk 551 E1
ct. Heathmont 378 F1
ct. Melton S 268 J
ct. Seaford 599 G
ct. Vermont S 420 G
dr. Cranbourne 603 L
dr. Wonga Park 335 J
st. Bentleigh E 496 G
st. Boronia 423 H1
st. Kew East 372 E
st. Lalor 241 H
st. Noble Park 534 K
st. Pascoe Vale 280 H1
st. Templstw Lr 330 D1
VALERO
pl. Thomastown 240 K1

VALETTA
cr. Knoxfield 463 B3
st. Carrum 573 B8
st. Malvern 415 K13
VALEWOOD
ct. Narre Warren 538 G19
dr. Kealba 276 L19
dr. Kealba 277 A19
dr. Launching Pl 345 F16
dr. Mulgrave 500 E1
dr. Wyndham Va 446 G11
VALIANT
ct. Glen Waverley 421 A16
sq. S Morang 198 K12
st. Abbotsford 20 F15
VALIAS
st. N Warrandyte 289 G13
VALKSTONE
st. Bentleigh E 456 H17
VALKYRIE
cr. Ringwood 335 C20
VALLENCE
rd. Maddingley 264 E2
rd. Maddingley 264 E5
VALLEY
cr. Glenroy 279 G4
ct. Craigieburn 150 C16
ct. Croydon S 380 A15
ct. Dandenong N 502 B11
ct. Diamond Ck 245 G11
ct. Mt Eliza 641 H4
dr. Rye 697 G7
mw. Wyndham Va 446 D9
pde. Glen Iris 416 J10
rd. Bundoora 284 A1
rd. Frankston 627 L6
rd. Langwarrin 601 E10
rd. Mt Waverley 459 C1
rd. Research 288 H3
rd. Seville 341 L12
rd. Skye 601 E10
rd. Wattle Glen 246 L7
rd. Wattle Glen 247 A6
rd. Wonga Park 336 B5
rd. Yarra Glen 208 H5
st. Oakleigh S 458 D19
wy. Warrandyte 333 H5
VALLEY FAIR
dr. Narre Warren 552 J4
VALLEY FARM
rd. Healesville 213 J9
VALLEY HO
rd. Chirnside Pk 337 J3
VALLEY PARK
dr. Mooroolbark 337 L18
gr. Eltham 287 D15
VALLEY VIEW
cr. Berwick 553 H2
ct. Bulleen 329 G14
ct. Glen Waverley 460 H3
ct. Lilydale 338 D14
ct. Niddrie 322 L3
ct. S Morang 199 L18
gr. Melton W 226 D12
rd. Glen Iris 416 H16
rd. Hurstbridge 202 G13
ri. Hampton Pk 552 A12
tr. Lysterfield 504 B10
VALLEYVIEW
dr. Rowville 463 B13
VALLOTA
cr. Noble Park 534 D5
VALMA
av. Cranbourne 577 L15
ct. Forest Hill 376 H20
st. Bayswater 423 E8
VALMONT
av. Beaumaris 530 G9
VALNERE
st. Maribyrnong 367 A1
VALONIA
av. Surrey Hills 374 C18
ct. Craigieburn 150 B17
dr. Eltham 288 B6
VAN
ct. Gladstone Pk 237 D16
ct. Melton W 226 A20
ct. Narre Warren 539 A16
VANBERG
rd. Essendon 324 E7
VANBROOK
dr. Mill Park 243 F5
st. Forest Hill 420 G3
VANCE
cl. Darley 222 D11
ct. Keysborough 534 C9
ct. Narre Warren 538 L12
st. Lilydale 338 K5
VANCOUVER
st. Mornington 640 D12
VAN DER HAAR
av. Berwick 553 K7
VANDEVEN
ct. Ferntree Gly 423 L17
VAN DIEMAN
av. Nunawading 376 F9
VANESSA
av. Highton 705 H1
av. Keysborough 534 K8
av. Lalor 241 A6
cr. Wheelers Hl 460 L18
ct. Frankston 600 A17
ct. Oakleigh S 498 A9
ct. St Helena 244 L19
ct. Somerville 645 B16
ct. Warranwood 334 L12
dr. Hampton Pk 551 C7
rd. Campbellfield 239 C4
wy. Delahey 275 D11
VAN HAASTER
ct. Rowville 502 B6
gr. Skye 575 G19
VANILLA
st. Bundoora 242 F15
VANITY
ct. Dandenong 535 L9
VANNAM
dr. Ashwood 418 C16
VAN NESS
av. Glen Iris 417 A9
av. Maribyrnong 323 C17
av. Mornington 656 E1
VAN UNEN
ct. Doncaster E 332 G9
VAN WYK
ct. Springvale S 534 A2
VARCOE
cl. Burwood 418 E6
ct. Frankston 628 F6
VARDON
av. Beaumaris 530 D4
st. Springvale 500 A17
VARGA
cl. Mill Park 242 F1
rd. St Andrews 205 C5
rd. Smiths Gly 205 C5
VARLEY
ct. Ferntree Gly 464 D6
VARMAN
ct. Nunawading 376 F15
VARNA
ct. Hillside 274 E3
pl. Keilor Dn 276 E14
VARSITY
ct. Albanvale 319 A7
mw. Wyndham Va 446 A6
VARYDALE
av. Torquay 712 A6
VARZIN
av. Surrey Hills 374 A20
VASA
pl. Keilor Ldg 276 A3
VASEY
av. Lalor 241 D8
av. Mt Waverley 459 G2
cl. Mt Martha 656 C15
cnc. Croydon 379 E6
cnc. Croydon 379 F8
cnc. Ringwood E 379 E6
ct. Melton S 268 H11
gr. Donvale 377 E8
ri. Endeavour Hl 537 G4
st. Ascot Vale 324 A19
st. Bentleigh E 497 A6
st. Ivanhoe East 328 H17
VASTO
lp. Point Cook 450 D8
VAUCLUSE
av. Gladstone Pk 279 C2
ct. Wheelers Hl 460 H14
ri. Highton 701 E15
st. Berwick 579 L3
st. Brighton 454 H13
VAUGHAN
av. Canterbury 373 G17
cr. Kew 371 G4
ct. Pakenham 584 H10
rd. Ferntree Gly 424 F17
st. Airport W 279 C14
st. Richmond 371 B15
st. Sunbury 143 K14
tce. N Melbourne 34 H11
VAUTIER
pl. S Morang 198 K14
st. Elwood 454 E6
VAUX
st. Pascoe Vale S 324 H2
VAUXHALL
rd. Balwyn 373 F14
rd. Northcote 327 B17
VAYNOR
st. Niddrie 322 L4
st. Niddrie 323 A4
VEAR
st. Heidelberg W 284 G17
VEARINGS
rd. Epping 196 B19
rd. Wollert 196 C6
VEARS
rd. Ashburton 417 J15
rd. Glen Iris 417 J15
VEDA
av. Mt Martha 656 H9
ct. Templestowe 331 E14
VEEMA
av. Croydon 379 K5
VEGA
cl. Lilydale 338 L6
cl. Noble Park 534 D5
ct. Newcomb 704 D14
st. Balwyn N 329 C20
st. Balwyn N 373 C1
VEGAS
ct. Narre Warren 553 D12
VEITCH
pl. Geelong, off Corio St 703 D7
st. Ivanhoe East 328 J16
VELA
pl. Roxburgh Pk 194 F8
VELDEN
av. Ferntree Gly 464 B2
VELLA
ct. Ferntree Gly 464 F2
ct. Springvale S 499 F20
dr. Sunshine W 365 A11
VELLVUE
ct. Tootgarook 698 D5
VELMA
gr. Ringwood E 379 D8
VELRA
av. Murrumbeena 457 D14
VELVET
av. Bundoora 242 E13
VENABLES
ct. Berwick 554 B17
VENETIAN
ct. Croydon 380 G6
VENEZIA
wy. Skye 601 H3
VENICE
av. Mitcham 377 A10
ct. Avondale Ht 322 E8
ct. Frankston 600 F19
ct. Glen Waverley 420 B14
gdn. Endeavour Hl 537 J2
st. Box Hill S 374 G20
st. Box Hill S 418 G1
st. Mentone 530 L9
st. Mentone 531 A9
st. Mornington 640 C17
VENN
mw. Templstw Lr 330 D10
VENTICH
st. Glen Iris 417 J11
VENTNOR
cr. Coolaroo 238 E3
pl. Keilor Dn 276 C12
st. Balwyn N 329 K19
st. Chadstone 458 B6
st. Mitcham 377 B18
st. Preston 326 C5
VENTOR
ct. Craigieburn 194 D3
VENTOSA
wy. Werribee 447 H9
VENTURA
ct. Keilor Ldg 276 B4
pl. Dandenong S 550 G7
pl. Point Cook 450 D5
st. Ashburton 417 K16
st. Blackburn N 376 A7
wy. S Morang 198 L12
VENTURE
dr. Berwick 554 B10
wy. Braeside 532 J15
VENUE
cl. Eltham 288 B9
VENUS
ct. Dingley Vill 533 A9
ct. Hillside 232 B18
ct. Newcomb 704 D13
ct. Thomastown 240 G14
st. Caulfield S 455 D10
VERA
cr. Rye 696 L8
cr. Rye 697 A8
ct. Dandenong 535 H2
st. Bulleen 330 B16
st. Frankston 627 F4
st. Murrumbeena 457 D13
st. Oakleigh S 497 G2
st. Werribee 448 C12
st. Williamstown 411 C17
VERBENA
av. The Basin 425 A11
cr. Noble Park 534 D6
ct. Cairnlea 319 K12
ct. Frankston S 627 G12
rd. Springvale 500 J12
st. Blackburn N 375 J7
st. Mordialloc 532 B12
st. Templestowe 331 B7
VERDAL
ct. Grovedale 706 C10
VERDALE
cl. Mitcham 377 H18
VERDANT
av. Ardeer 320 C18
av. Toorak 415 A3
ct. Glen Waverley 460 K1
dr. Keysborough 534 G17
pl. Dingley Vill 533 C3
VERDELHO
ct. Sunbury 144 C6
VERDEN
pl. Keilor Dn 276 E13
VERDI
ct. Bundoora 242 L20
ct. Templestowe 332 C9
VERDON
st. Dromana 685 K7
st. Williamstown 411 D15
VERDUN
dr. Narre Warren 553 C5
dr. Narre Warren 553 C5
gr. Reservoir 282 J15
st. Maidstone 322 K20
st. Surrey Hills 417 L2
VERE
ct. Plumpton 273 A13
st. Abbotsford 20 B16
st. Collingwood 19 J16
st. Richmond 26 E6
VERENE
av. Templstw Lr 330 G12
VERES
la. Geelong West 702 J4
VEREY
ct. Dandenong 535 G9
VERGESS
ct. Ringwood 378 H15
VERINA
wy. Lilydale 338 G14
VERITY
ct. Altona Mdw 451 E3
st. Richmond 26 B11
VERMAY
av. Frankston 599 L19
VERMEER
ct. Grovedale 705 K14
VERMILION
pl. Mt Waverley 419 G13
VERMONT
av. Bundoora 242 D19
av. Sunshine N 321 G10
ct. Blackburn S 420 A5
pde. Greensbrgh 285 L5
st. Blackburn S 420 A6
st. Glen Waverley 460 B8
VERNA
pl. St Albans 320 E12
VERNAL
av. Mitcham 377 D18
rd. Oakleigh S 497 H4
VERNE
cl. Delahey 275 E15
ct. Templestowe 332 A10
VERNER
av. Frankston 627 E6
st. E Geelong 703 C13
st. Geelong 703 C13
st. S Geelong 703 A12
VERNIER
st. Spotswood 366 J20
VERNON
av. Heidelberg W 284 E17
cl. Jan Juc 711 C16
cr. Sunshine W 364 B3
ct. Epping 241 J4
ct. Hoppers Csg 449 C1
ct. Noble Park 534 D2
rd. Beaconsfield 555 K9
st. Blackburn S 420 A2
st. Blairgowrie 696 C7
st. Brighton East 495 G1
st. Croydon 379 K7
st. Donvale 377 D1
st. Glen Iris 417 C15
st. Huntingdale 458 E13
st. S Kingsville 410 G3
st. Spotswood 366 G20
st. Strathmore 280 B18
st. Up Fntree Gly 465 G8
VERONA
ct. Bayswater 423 A9
dr. Hampton Pk 551 E5
dr. Keilor Ldg 275 L4
st. Belgrave S 506 H1
st. Box Hill S 374 G20
st. Box Hill S 418 G1
st. Dromana 686 H8
st. Vermont S 421 E7
VERONICA
av. Chirnside Pk 337 B3
av. Newcomb 704 C16
cr. Mill Park 243 A10
ct. Noble Park 534 D5
ct. Werribee 447 G13
dr. Skye 601 F6
pl. Sunshine W 363 L8
st. Ferntree Gly 424 G20
st. Langwarrin 629 A3
st. Northcote 326 D11
st. Oakleigh S 497 E2
VERSAILLES
pl. Narre Warren 539 F16
VERT
st. Keilor 277 B11
VERVALE
av. Fawkner 281 K9
VERWOOD
ct. Craigieburn 194 G4
VESPER
dr. Narre Warren 552 H3
st. Burnley, off Tudor St 371 C17
VESTA
la. Newport 411 A12
VIADUCT
rd. Sunbury 143 D20
VIALLS
av. Parkdale 531 J12
VIA MEDIA
Box Hill 375 C17
VICARAGE
wy. Watsonia N 243 D19
VICARS
st. Balwyn N 373 H2
st. Hawthorn 372 A15
VICKERS
av. Strathmr Ht 279 D9
dr. Richmond 371 C13
la. Roxburgh Pk 194 D10
st. Reservoir 282 B8
VICKERY
st. Bentleigh 456 C18
st. Bentleigh 456 C19
st. Malvern East 416 F20
VICKI
ct. Doncaster E 375 H4
pl. Langwarrin 629 L1
st. Blackburn S 420 A4
st. Croydon 336 H14
st. Forest Hill 420 A4
VICKIE
ct. Rosebud 684 H17
VICTOR
av. Cheltenham 530 F3
av. Dandenong N 501 K15
av. Guys Hill 541 H20
av. Kew 372 J9
av. Rye 697 J8
av. Seaford 573 C20
cr. Forest Hill 420 D5
cr. Narre Warren 553 C3
ct. Hampton Pk 552 A9
ct. Hoppers Csg 448 F5
ct. Lalor 240 L9
ct. Melton S 268 G5
pl. Attwood 237 D11
rd. Bentleigh 455 H20
rd. Brighton East 455 H20
rd. Clematis 508 J2
rd. Glen Iris 417 A15
rd. Oakleigh S 497 F5
st. Beaumaris 530 B9
st. Olinda 426 K12
st. Pt Lonsdale 710 D6
st. Sunshine N 321 G19
VICTORIA
av. Albert Park 29 D17
av. Albert Park 413 B8
av. Canterbury 373 D16
av. Cremorne 26 A20
av. Glen Waverley 460 E4
av. Mitcham 377 A12
av. Monbulk 428 F19
av. Ripponlea 454 H1
av. Rosanna 284 K18
av. Springvale 499 J14
cl. Carlton 18 F15
cl. Eltham 246 B20
cl. Eltham 288 B1
cr. Abbotsford 20 F20
cr. Mont Albert 374 C14
cr. Mont Albert 374 D13
cr. Mt Martha 655 J13
cr. Safety Bch 668 J20
cr. St Albans 320 B3
ct. Dandenong N 501 J17
ct. N Melbourne 17 D19
ct. Springvale 499 J15
dr. Thomastown 240 E12

dr. Tottenham 366 A12
gr. Brunswick 325 J11
gr. Ferny Creek 466 B4
gr. Hawthorn E 372 E17
la. Albert Park 29 G13
pde. Carlton 24 L2
pde. Carlton 25 B2
pde. Collingwood 24 L2
pde. Collingwood 25 B2
pde. E Melbourne 24 L2
pde. E Melbourne 25 B2
pde. Fitzroy 24 L2
pde. Fitzroy 25 B2
pde. Frankston 627 D4
pde. Melbourne 24 L2
pde. Melbourne 25 B2
pl. Carlton 18 J8
pl. Richmond 26 H4
rd. Bayswater 423 F9
rd. Camberwell 372 J17
rd. Chirnside Pk 293 L19
rd. Chirnside Pk 337 J7
rd. Coldstream 294 A7
rd. Gruyere 341 A10
rd. Hawthorn E 372 E17
rd. Langwarrin S 629 L20
rd. Lilydale 293 L19
rd. Lilydale 337 J7
rd. Narre Warren 538 J18
rd. Northcote 327 B19
rd. Seville 341 E10
rd. Sydenham 232 K20
rd. Thornbury 327 B11
rd. Wandin N 340 F10
rd. Wandin N 341 A10
rd. Yering 252 B20
rd. Yering 294 A7
rd.n, Malvern 416 B18
rd.s, Malvern 416 B19
sq. St Albans 320 B3
st. Abbotsford 26 B3
st. Altona Mdw 451 F8
st. Box Hill 375 B17
st. Brighton 454 F18
st. Brunswick 325 G13
st. Brunswick E 325 K13
st. Brunswick W 324 K12
st. Bulleen 329 L10
st. Carlton 2 J1
st. Carlton 17 K20
st. Coburg 325 D2
st. Darley 222 C7
st. Diamond Ck 246 A12
st. Doncaster 331 F20
st. Doncaster E 331 F20
st. Elsternwick 455 C6
st. Ferntree Gly 464 G2
st. Fitzroy 19 A13
st. Flemington 34 C4
st. Footscray 367 C10
st. Glenroy 279 J9
st. Greensbrgh 286 C10
st. Hurstbridge 202 K10
st. Launching Pl 346 G16
st. Melbourne 2 J1
st. Melbourne 17 K20
st. Melbourne 24 B1
st. Melb Airport 236 D13
st. Moonee Pnd 323 L11
st. N Melbourne 34 L19
st. Parkdale 531 J11
st. Preston 327 D6
st. Richmond 26 B3
st. Ringwood E 379 C11
st. Safety Bch 669 A15
st. St Kilda 413 L16
st. Sandringham 495 E16
st. Seddon 367 C10
st. S Geelong 703 A14
st. S Melbourne 30 E3
st. Sunshine 365 E4
st. Templestowe 331 F20
st. Up Fntree Gly 465 B10
st. Wandin N 340 B13
st. Westmeadows 236 D13
st. W Melbourne 34 J19
st. Williamstown 411 B18
st. Windsor 414 H11
st. Yarra Jctn 346 H14
tce. Belmont 702 C16
tce. South Yarra 32 G6
tce. South Yarra 414 J3
wy. Caroline Spr 317 L7
wy. Caroline Spr 318 A7

VICTORIA HOTEL
la. N Melbourne 17 H20

VICTORIA KNOX
av. Rowville 463 K12

VICTORY
av. Wandin East 340 L17
bvd. Ashburton 417 G18
ct. Brighton East 455 H17
ct. Narre Warren 538 L17
pde. Ascot Vale 323 J19
pl. Mt Eliza 642 F8
pl. S Geelong 703 A14
rd. Airport W 278 J11
rd. Clarinda 498 F14
rd. Langwarrin 630 A15
st. Croydon 336 D17
st. Fawkner 281 H5
st. Keilor Park 277 K15
st. Mitcham 377 G14
st. Murrumbeena 457 A12
st. Sandringham 495 D15
wy. Carrum Downs 575 D14
wy. Highton 701 E15

VIDA
ct. Wantirna S 462 C4
st. Aberfeldie 323 E12

VIDOTTO
ct. Pearcedale 647 G1

VIENNESE
wy. Mooroolbark 337 L18

VIEW
cr. Montrose 382 E10
ct. Brighton 494 G3
ct. Dandenong N 502 B10
ct. Heathmont 379 E19
ct. Hillside 232 B17
pt. Kew 371 L4
rd. Bayswater 423 F3
rd. Belgrave 466 E10
rd. Epping 197 D17
rd. Glen Waverley 420 E17
rd. Lower Plenty 286 L17
rd. Rye 697 B3
rd. Springvale 500 B18
rd. Tecoma 466 E10
rd. The Basin 425 C11
rd. The Patch 467 G2
rd. Vermont 421 F2
rd. Yarra Jctn 346 H16
st. Alphington 371 J1
st. Avonsleigh 470 E17
st. Belmont 702 G16
st. Canterbury 373 D16
st. Clayton 498 F1
st. Coburg N 281 J15
st. Croydon 380 H3
st. Essendon W 322 L8
st. Glenroy 280 A1
st. Hampton Pk 551 E9
st. Hawthorn 372 D15
st. Healesville 213 J20
st. Highett 496 E14
st. Mentone 530 J8
st. Mornington 640 C16
st. Mt Evelyn 339 D20
st. Pascoe Vale 280 D15
st. Reservoir 282 E11
st. St Albans 320 C4
st. Surrey Hills 374 E18
st. Upwey 465 J12
st. Wandin East 340 L17
st. Warburton 350 C2
st. Werribee 447 E4
st. W Footscray 366 G5
st. Woori Yall 344 B14
tce. Sunbury 142 D7

VIEWBANK
cct. Roxburgh Pk 194 E11
ct. Aspendale 546 E5
ct. Point Cook 451 C7
dr. Keilor East 322 H5
pl. Mill Park 243 C7
rd. Glen Iris 416 G13
rd. Mt Waverley 458 J10
ri. Beaconsfield 555 D11

VIEW GRAND
rd. Maribyrnong 322 L13

VIEWGRAND
wy. Greensbrgh 244 H15

VIEW GULLY
rd. Hopetoun Park 266 F6

VIEW HILL
cr. Eltham 287 L12
rd. Cockatoo 511 A11

VIEWHILL
rd. Balwyn N 373 H3

VIEWMONT
ct. Croydon N 335 L14
st. Doncaster E 332 H9

VIEW MOUNT
ct. Eltham 288 E8
rd. Glen Waverley 460 G12
rd. Wheelers Hl 460 G12

VIEWMOUNT
ct. Nar Warrn S 553 F18

VIEW PARK
cct. Nar Warrn S 579 G2

VIEW POINT
rd. McCrae 685 B10

VIEWPOINT
av. Glen Waverley 460 F5
av. Mt Eliza 626 B16
dr. Chirnside Pk 337 B5
rd. Balwyn N 329 F18

VIEWSIDE
wy. Hampton Pk 552 B15

VIEWTECH
pl. Rowville 502 C3

VIGANO
ct. Mooroolbark 337 G12

VIGGERS
pde. Glen Waverley 460 F10

VIGIL
av. Glen Waverley 420 J16

VIGILANT
av. Nunawading 376 E12

VIGO
st. Seddon 367 C11

VIGOR
ct. Darley 221 G4

VIKA
av. Monbulk 428 J19

VIKING
ct. Carrum Downs 575 B15
ct. Cheltenham 497 B14
ct. Epping 198 A17

VILA
ct. Mt Waverley 458 F6

VILLA
rd. Springvale 499 F12
st. Heidelberg 329 A8
wk. Werribee 447 C8

VILLAGE
av. Doncaster 330 D18
av. Taylors L 276 A5
cl. Carrum Downs 575 B17
cl. Mt Martha 656 A16
cl. Westmeadows 237 H12
cr. Chelsea 547 A14
ct. Mulgrave 460 B13
ct. Rowville 502 H5
dr. Dingley Vill 532 K5
dr. Hampton Pk 551 J7
dr. Pakenham 584 K3
dr. Reservoir 283 J14
grn. Chirnside Pk 336 L4
la. Carrum 573 B8
la. Mt Eliza 626 A16
wk. Box Hill 374 J16
wk. Mooroolbark 381 K4
wk. Vermont S 421 D7
wk. Toorak, off Toorak Rd 415 B5
wy. Maribyrnong 322 J15
wy. Toorak, off Toorak Rd 415 B5

VILLAGE GREEN
dr. St Kilda 414 A12

VILLAMANTA
pl. Geelong West 702 H6
st. Geelong West 702 H7

VILLANOVA
ct. Pk Orchards 334 D12

VILLAWOOD
av. Roxburgh Pk 193 K4
cl. Berwick 539 J18
ct. Highton 705 G4

VILLEA
av. Grovedale 705 K16
ct. Bundoora 284 L6

VILLEROY
st. Hampton 495 A5

VILLERS
sq. Malvern East 456 L4

VILLIERS
st. Elsternwick 454 L3
st. Elsternwick 455 A3
st. Frankston S 626 H11
st. N Melbourne 17 E15

VILLOSA
cl. Langwarrin 629 J3
ct. Mill Park 243 D8

VIM
st. Melton 268 J2

VIMINALIS
ct. Endeavour Hl 536 K1

VIMY
ct. Pascoe Vale S 324 H3
rdg. Healesville 257 H1
st. Reservoir 282 C7

VINCENT
av. Geelong 702 K1
av. St Albans 320 E4
cr. Noble Park 500 K17
cr. Werribee 447 F10
ct. Cranbourne N 578 E9
ct. Greensbrgh 243 J20
ct. Whittington 704 A19
mw. Chirnside Pk 336 G7
pl. Kensington 33 D9
rd. Pk Orchards 334 E15
st. Bayswater 423 C3
st. Brighton East 495 J3
st. Brunswick 325 C16
st. Coburg 325 D2
st. Cockatoo 511 C8
st. Deer Park 319 B18
st. Edithvale 546 H12
st. Glen Iris 416 D15
st. Macleod 285 A11
st. Mulgrave 500 D4
st. Oak Park 279 H11
st. Sandringham 495 C13
st. Surrey Hills 374 A16
st. Tootgarook 698 F5

VINCE STELLA
cl. Cairnlea 319 F8

VINCT
cl. Keilor Dn 276 C11

VINE
cr. Wonga Park 291 G17
ct. Braybrook 366 A1
ct. Doncaster 330 K18
ct. Glen Waverley 460 K3
ct. Hillside 274 C5
ct. Narre Warren 553 G9
gr. Carnegie 456 E8
st. Blackburn 375 H15
st. Braybrook 366 A1
st. Eltham 287 E6
st. Heidelberg 329 B8
st. Moonee Pnd 324 E14
st. Ringwood 378 C16
st. W Footscray 366 D6
st. Windsor 414 G13

VINEN
rd. Scoresby 462 B6

VINES
ct. Mill Park 242 B6

VINEY
st. Clarinda 498 D9

VINEYARD
la. Tuerong 670 L4
rd. Diggers Rest 187 A12
rd. Sunbury 187 A5

VINNY
ct. Langwarrin 629 C3

VINTAGE
ct. Kilsyth S 381 A20
ct. Waurn Ponds 705 F14
gr. Chirnside Pk 336 K4

VINTER
av. Croydon 379 K8

VIOLA
av. Brooklyn 365 F18
av. Mt Dandenong 426 F5
av. Olinda 426 F5
cr. Highett 496 D12
ct. Frankston 600 G17
ct. Keysborough 534 A15
ct. Mill Park 243 A11
ct. Reservoir 282 K11

VIOLEN
st. Bayswater 423 E4

VIOLET
cr. Brighton East 455 E18
ct. Blackburn S 419 L4
ct. Doncaster 330 G16
ct. Noble Park 534 D5
ct. Wonga Park 292 B14
gr. Hawthorn 372 B20
gr. Kew East 372 H7
st. Belmont 701 L20
st. Essendon 323 K8
st. Frankston S 626 J4
st. Glen Iris 416 H10
st. Rosebud W 698 L1
st. Williamstn N 410 H11
wy. Point Cook 450 H16

VIPONT
st. Footscray 367 H7

VIRGILIA
ct. Rowville 502 L2
st. Doveton 536 H13

VIRGILLIA
st. Blackburn N 375 J8

VIRGINIA
cr. Bundoora 242 B19
ct. Bulleen 329 K11
ct. Caulfield S 455 K8
ct. Mentone 532 A7
ct. Montmorency 287 C10
gr. Malvern East 457 H4
st. Cranbourne 578 A17
st. Mornington 640 J18
st. Mt Waverley 458 K1
st. Newtown 702 H8
st. Pascoe Vale 280 K10
st. Springvale 500 A11
wy. Ferntree Gly 423 J16

VIRGO
pl. Wantirna S 422 L19

VIRIDIS
pl. Endeavour Hl 502 K20

VISAGE
dr. S Morang 198 K11

VISCOUNT
dr. Doncaster 331 A14
wy. Forest Hill 420 D8

VISION
av. Sorrento 679 E14
ct. Wyndham Va 446 D11
dr. Burwood E 420 E12
st. Chadstone 458 A1
st. Strathmore 279 H13

VISTA
av. Kew 372 H10
av. Mt Waverley 418 G14
av. Ringwood E 379 B14
cr. Rowville 463 C20
cr. Rowville 503 C1
ct. Altona Mdw 451 B6
ct. Berwick 553 L6
ct. Box Hill N 375 E7
ct. Forest Hill 420 F2
ct. Frankston S 626 L8
ct. Ringwood E 379 B15
ct. Yarrambat 200 K15
dr. Chirnside Pk 337 A5
dr. Emerald 510 C1
dr. Keilor East 322 B5
dr. Melton 226 G19
gr. Sherbrooke 426 J18
gr. Toorak 415 A3
pl. Beaconsfield 555 B13
rd. Belgrave Ht 506 B3
rd. Hampton 494 K5
rd. Newtown 702 B11
st. Bulleen 330 A17
st. Doncaster 330 A17
st. Olinda 426 K12
st. St Albans 320 D6
wy. Wyndham Va 446 D13

VISTAWAY
ct. Donvale 332 H18

VISTULA
ct. Springvale S 533 K6

VITIS
av. Noble Park 534 C6
dr. Bundoora 242 F14

VITTORIO
ct. Lilydale 293 L19

VIVA
st. Glen Iris 416 C14

VIVALDI
ct. Templestowe 332 C9

VIVI
ct. Skye 601 E7

VIVIAN
ct. Doncaster 374 F3
ct. Oakleigh S 458 G19
gr. Hawthorn 371 H18
st. Belmont 702 C17
st. Blackburn N 375 G7
st. Ivanhoe 327 J10
st. Mt Waverley 418 H20
wy. Mt Martha 656 J7

VIVIANI
cr. Heathmont 378 G20

VIVIANNE
av. Mont Albert N 374 F6

VIVIANNES
wy. Melton 268 K3

VIVIEN
st. Bentleigh E 496 K3
st. Dandenong S 535 K16

VIVIENNE
av. Boronia 423 L14
ct. Doncaster E 332 H7
ct. Healesville 212 J13
st. Seaford 599 J
wy. Berwick 554 F1

VIZARD
st. Dandenong 536 A2

VOCE
ct. Belmont 706 F4

VOCKLER
st. Yarraville 367 D18

VOGEL
av. Mt Martha 656 J9

VOGUE
av. Vermont S 420 H

VOLANT
rd. Rockbank 270 C

VOLANTIS
cr. Roxburgh Pk 194 G

VOLGA
st. Hadfield 280 J

VOLITANS
av. Mt Eliza 641 J

VOLK
rd. Cranbourne W 577 D1

VOLTRI
st. Cheltenham 531 E
st. Mentone 531 E
st. Mentone 531 H

VOLUM
st. Manifold Ht 702 B

VONADAWN
av. Ringwood E 379 A1

VON GUERARD
pl. E Melbourne 25 H

VON NIDA
cr. Rosanna 284 L19
cr. Rosanna 285 A19
ct. Dingley Vill 533 A6
ct. Mill Park 242 D5
ct. Rowville 502 L6
dr. Hoppers Csg 405 C19
VOSGES
st. Selby 467 D13
VOSTOK
ct. Whittington 704 E19
VOUMARD
st. Oakleigh S 458 A17
VOWELL
dr. Pearcedale 648 A8
VUE
ct. Rowville 503 H1
rd. Mt Eliza 626 E12
VULCAN
gr. Williamstown 411 D16
VULE
st. St Albans 319 J5
VUNABERE
av. Bentleigh 495 J2

W

WACHTER
ct. Noble Park 501 B20
WACKETT
st. Laverton 407 C12
WADDELL
ct. Altona Mdw 451 H5
st. Bacchus Msh 222 A18
WADDINGTON
cr. Springvale S 533 K5
ct. Highton 705 J6
WADE
ct. Cheltenham 497 F19
ct. Langwarrin 601 K20
WADESON
rd. Diamond Ck 202 D17
rd. Hurstbridge 202 D17
WADEY
st. Southbank 4 C15
st. Southbank 24 H18
WADHAM
ct. Endeavour Hl 503 A20
pde. Mt Waverley 419 A18
rd. Ivanhoe 328 A8
st. Pascoe Vale S 324 F6
WADHURST
dr. Boronia 423 C15
WADI
st. Boronia 424 B16
WADSLEY
av. Pakenham 584 J7
rd. Carrum Downs 574 A8
rd. Patterson L 574 A8
WAGGA
ct. Keysborough 534 E6
rd. Reservoir 283 C3
WAGNER
st. Blackburn S 419 K5
WAGON
rd. Templestowe 332 A8
WAGSTAFF
ct. Brighton 454 J14
dr. Mill Park 243 D6
la. Dandenong 536 A10
st. Mt Waverley 459 B5
st. Rye 696 E7
WAGTAIL
ct. Langwarrin 628 J6
WAHGOO
rd. Carnegie 456 L9
WAHGUNYAH
cr. Langwarrin 629 D9
dr. St Albans 320 L6
dr. St Albans 321 A6
WAHINE
ct. Templestowe 331 L10
WAHRONGA
av. Highton 701 H16
WAHROONGA
av. Keysborough 534 G8
cr. Greensbrgh 244 K19
ct. Glen Iris 416 L13
ct. Rowville 463 H13
WAHROONGAA
cr. Murrumbeena 457 D6
rd. Murrumbeena 457 C6
WAIGANI
av. Ravenhall 318 G14
WAIGO
wy. Diamond Ck 245 K11
WAIHI
av. Brunswick E 326 A12
WAIMARIE
dr. Mt Waverley 459 C1
WAIMEA
gr. Selby 466 L14
WAINEWRIGHT
av. Mooroolbark 337 E11
ct. Sunbury 142 F10
WAINTREE
ct. Endeavour Hl 537 H6
WAINUI
av. Heathmont 378 K18
WAIORA
av. Beaumaris 529 L6
cl. Wantirna S 422 D19
ct. Pt Lonsdale 707 J20
pde. W Footscray 366 E10
rd. Caulfield N 415 D15
rd. Heidelberg Ht 328 H3
rd. Macleod 284 J15
rd. Rosanna 328 H2
WAIROA
av. Brighton East 455 D13
WAIROU
st. Taylors L 276 D10
WAITARA
av. Keysborough 534 E8
ct. Lalor 240 E9
ct. Wheelers Hl 460 K17
WAITE
ct. Mill Park 242 L3
ct. Sunshine W 364 H8
WAITES
ct. Brooklyn 365 H19
ct. Templestowe 331 E8
WAKANUI
st. Northcote 327 A13
WAKATIPU
ct. Taylors L 276 C10
WAKE
ct. Lalor 241 H6
WAKEFIELD
av. Frankston S 627 B8
cl. Eltham North 287 C4
ct. Cranbourne N 577 L9
ct. Point Cook 450 C4
la. Sherbrooke 466 J2
pl. Templestowe 331 E6
ri. Endeavour Hl 537 G7
st. Blackburn N 376 D10
st. Hawthorn 372 A16
st. Kensington 33 E12
st. Nunawading 376 D10
WAKEFIELDS
gr. Camberwell 417 J6
WAKEFUL
pl. Mill Park 242 L9
pl. Mill Park 243 A9
WAKELIN
cr. Taylors L 275 A1
WAKEMAN
ct. Dingley Vill 533 A3
WAKENSHAW
cr. Pakenham 584 G7
WAKLEY
cr. Wantirna S 421 L17
WAKOOL
av. Deer Park 319 B18
av. Mentone 530 H8
av. Rosebud 700 J7
cl. Frankston 628 E6
WALA
pl. Greensbrgh 244 B18
WALARA
dr. Mt Martha 655 J19
WALBROOK
dr. Vermont S 420 J6
rd. Rye 696 F6
st. Watsonia N 285 G1
WALBUNDRY
av. Balwyn N 372 L3
av. Balwyn N 373 A3
av. Ferntree Gly 464 L1
av. Frankston 599 G12
dr. Kew East 372 K3
WALCHA
ct. Chadstone 458 B2
WALCOTT
pl. Nar Warrn S 578 L2
WALDAU
ct. Doncaster 331 F17
WALDEMAR
rd. Eaglemont 328 G10
WALDEN
av. Wheelers Hl 460 L8
ct. Bundoora 284 L2
ct. Springvale S 499 H19
gr. Carnegie 456 J11
pl. Lalor 241 J7
rd. Mentone 530 L10
rd. Mentone 531 A10
st. W Footscray 366 G6
WALDHEIM
rd. Bayswater 423 A4
WALDORF
ct. Bentleigh E 497 D5
WALDRON
pl. Geelong 703 E12
WALER
ct. Highton 701 C15
WALERNA
rd. Glen Iris 417 A12
WALES
ct. Hallam 537 H15
ct. Hillside 231 J17
st. Brunswick W 324 K9
st. Hampton 495 E12
st. Kingsville 366 K13
st. Northcote 327 A12
st. Springvale 500 B11
st. Thornbury 327 A11
WALHALLA
ct. Beaconsfield 555 G15
ct. Mooroolbark 337 F16
dr. Ringwood E 379 D14
st. Pascoe Vale S 324 K6
WALKER
av. Hampton 495 G8
av. Mitcham 377 D19
av. Preston 327 B2
cl. Altona North 409 J3
ct. St Albans 320 F12
ct. Sunbury 142 H4
ct. Viewbank 329 H2
gr. Cheltenham 531 A1
pl. Braybrook 366 A1
rd. Montrose 382 B9
rd. Mt Waverley 419 E14
rd. Seville 342 B12
rd. Wonga Park 335 E2
st. Anglesea 713 J3
st. Balwyn 373 D11
st. Belmont 706 K3
st. Braeside 532 F14
st. Brunswick W 324 K13
st. Clifton Hill 20 H3
st. Coburg 325 G3
st. Dandenong 535 L9
st. Doncaster 375 A3
st. Healesville 213 K20
st. Healesville 257 K1
st. Moonee Pnd 324 D13
st. Murrumbeena 457 C9
st. Newport 410 L6
st. Northcote 326 G20
st. Parkville 17 J1
st. Prahran 32 D17
st. Prahran 414 G9
st. Southbank 3 A7
st. Southbank 23 L16
st. The Basin 425 E11
st. Torquay 712 B9
WALKERS
la. Healesville 213 K17
rd. Carrum 573 B10
rd. Mt Eliza 626 E20
rd. Nunawading 376 H15
WALL
ct. Chadstone 457 L3
pl. Richmond 26 J14
st. Beaumaris 530 F6
st. Noble Park 534 G1
st. Richmond 26 J14
WALLABAH
st. Mt Waverley 459 F6
WALLABY
av. Sassafras 426 F13
tr. Lysterfield 504 A8
wk. S Morang 243 J1
wk. Sunbury 143 A2
wy. Badger Creek 258 F13
WALLACE
av. Bayswater 423 F7
av. Dandenong 535 E4
av. Donvale 332 J16
av. Frankston 627 K4
av. Murrumbeena 457 A13
av. Oakleigh S 458 D19
av. Point Cook 450 C2
av. Toorak 415 A5
cr. Beaumaris 530 G5
cr. Strathmore 324 E2
dr. Greenvale 237 D1
gr. Brighton 494 J1
la. Bundoora 284 D4
pde. Healesville 258 E2
pl. Caroline Spr 318 A8
pl. Mill Park 242 G4
pl. Mt Martha 656 D8
rd. Burwood 418 A7
rd. Christmas Hills 207 K12
rd. Cranbourne 603 K1
rd. Seville 341 F15
rd. Wantirna S 422 J20
rd. Wantirna S 423 A20
rd. Wantirna S 463 A1
sq. Melton 226 L18
st. Balwyn 373 E10
st. Beaconsfield 555 C14
st. Bentleigh E 496 H2
st. Brunswick W 324 L11
st. Delahey 275 A12
st. Ivanhoe 328 A13
st. Maidstone 366 H3
st. Newtown 702 E10
st. Preston 326 E2
st. S Geelong 703 A13
wy. Mooroolbark 336 L14
WALLACES
rd. Dromana 669 J19
WALLAN
ct. Dallas 238 C8
WALLARA
cl. Doncaster E 332 H10
cr. Bundoora 284 K4
cr. Croydon 380 B10
dr. Kings Park 275 D20
rd. Aspendale 546 G7
rd. Werribee 446 J16
WALLARANO
dr. Noble Park 534 F5
WALLAROO
av. Narre Warren 538 J20
sq. Werribee 447 L19
wy. Highton 701 F10
WALLEN
rd. Hawthorn 371 G19
rd. Ormond 456 G13
st. Brighton East 455 E19
WALLER
ct. Ascot Vale 324 C20
ct. Cheltenham 530 K4
ct. Mooroolbark 337 E10
ct. Sunbury 143 D8
pl. McCrae 685 B12
WALLINGFORD
pl. Nar Warrn S 579 E5
pl. Rowville 503 A9
st. Cheltenham 531 A2
WALLIS
av. Glen Iris 417 B11
av. Ivanhoe East 328 G16
ct. Heathmont 422 J1
ml. Niddrie 279 B20
st. Anglesea 713 G7
WALLMAH
ct. Templestowe 330 J7
WALLOWA
cr. Frankston N 600 D7
cr. Narre Warren 538 J18
rd. Eltham North 245 D16
rd. St Helena 245 D16
WALLS
rd. Werribee 446 L15
st. Geelong 703 D11
WALLUM
rd. Edithvale 546 H15
WALLY
ct. Altona North 365 L20
WALMER
av. St Albans 320 D4
st. Abbotsford 371 B12
st. Kew 371 B11
st. Ringwood 378 D17
WALNUI
gr. Beaconsfield 542 D20
gr. Beaconsfld Up 542 D20
WALNUT
av. Emerald 509 D2
cr. Noble Park 534 D6
ct. Cranbourne N 578 C8
ct. Kings Park 275 F19
ct. Mulgrave 500 D1
dr. Kilsyth 381 K7
rd. Balwyn N 373 J3
rd. Greensbrgh 286 K2
st. Carnegie 456 L5
st. Cremorne 26 D20
st. Cremorne 32 D2
st. Malvern 416 A9
st. Ormond 456 F15
wy. Hoppers Csg 405 E16
WALNUT TREE
ct. Viewbank 285 L17
WALPA
ct. Westmeadows 237 E12
WALPOLE
av. Belmont 706 C5
av. Rosebud 683 G19
av. Rosebud W 683 G19
ct. Watsonia 285 C9
st. Kew 371 K10
st. Mt Martha 656 C11
WALSAL
av. Reservoir 283 C16
WALSH
av. Moorabbin 496 G11
av. Scoresby 462 B6
av. Thornbury 327 F8
ct. Mill Park 243 A5
ct. Pakenham 584 G5
rt. Berwick 553 J8
st. Balwyn 372 L13
st. Balwyn 373 A13
st. Broadmeadows 238 B20
st. Coburg 325 H4
st. Eltham 287 C16
st. Kew 372 H14
st. Noble Park 500 F19
st. Ormond 456 D12
st. Preston 327 D4
st. South Yarra 31 H8
st. South Yarra 414 D4
st. Sunshine N 321 E16
st. W Melbourne 23 F2
WALSHAM
ct. Wheelers Hl 461 B8
rd. Blackburn 375 K19
WALSHE
ct. Altona Mdw 451 C4
WALSINGHAM
cr. Kurunjang 227 C14
WALSTAB
st. Brighton East 495 B1
WALTER
cr. Tullamarine 277 J7
st. Ascot Vale 323 H15
st. Bulleen 330 A14
st. Cranbourne 578 C19
st. E Geelong 703 K12
st. Glen Waverley 420 D17
st. Hadfield 280 H8
st. Mitcham 377 G14
st. Moorabbin 497 A9
st. Noble Park 534 L4
st. Port Melb 412 G3
st. Preston 282 L18
st. Safety Bch 686 H2
st. St Albans 320 D1
st. Seddon 367 D10
st. South Yarra 32 K11
st. South Yarra 414 L6
st. Sunshine 365 G5
st. Tecoma 466 D12
st. Williamstn N 410 H12
WALTER LYNCH
wy. Chirnside Pk 336 G6
WALTERS
av. Airport W 278 L18
ct. Altona Mdw 451 D2
ct. Rowville 503 D1
la. Dixons Ck 211 A7
st. Brunswick 325 D10
st. Craigieburn 150 H18
WALTER WITHERS
ct. Viewbank 329 K1
WALTHAM
dr. Mornington 657 A3
pl. Avondale Ht 322 E12
pl. Richmond 26 F12
rd. Newport 411 B8
st. Flemington 33 K1
st. Richmond 26 E12
st. Sandringham 495 A13
WALTON
av. Preston 327 B4
cl. Craigieburn 194 F1
ct. Bacchus Msh 221 J16
ct. Narre Warren 553 E7
st. Airport W 279 B11
st. Brunswick 325 G16
st. Kew 371 K9
st. Melton S 268 G14
WALTON HEATH
cr. Mt Waverley 458 J8
ct. Sunbury 144 G12
WALWA
pl. Werribee 448 A20
st. Mitcham 377 K16
WALWORTH
av. Caulfield N 455 G2
ct. Keysborough 534 C8
WAMBA
av. Rye 697 J6
rd. Bentleigh E 496 H6
rd. Ivanhoe East 328 F15
WANAKA
cl. Rowville 462 L16
cl. Rowville 463 A16
dr. Taylors L 276 D10
WANALTA
rd. Carnegie 456 E6
WANAWONG
cr. Camberwell 417 D6
WANBANNA
av. Greensbrgh 243 K17
WANBROW
av. Balwyn N 373 K8
WANDA
av. Wandin N 340 F12
cl. Portsea 678 A5
ct. Aspendale 546 G6
ct. Greensbrgh 243 J17
ct. Hallam 537 J13

rd. Caulfield N.........415 F17
rd. Cranbourne S.....602 L19
rd. Cranbourne S.....603 A17
st. Mulgrave...........500 E5
WANDANA
cr. Mooroolbark......336 K13
ct. Frankston S.......627 B12
dr. Wandana Ht.......705 B4
st. Mooroolbark......336 K14
WANDARRA
wy. Warranwood......335 C15
WANDARRI
ct. Cheltenham.......496 A19
WANDEEN
rd. Glen Iris............416 H13
st. Balwyn N...........330 A20
WANDELLA
ct. Albanvale...........319 C6
rd. Frankston..........627 J5
rd. Mornington........656 G3
WANDERER
ct. Berwick.............539 H19
ct. Werribee............448 B5
WANDIN
ct. Forest Hill..........420 H4
ct. Meadow Ht..........238 D3
ct. Werribee............448 A19
rd. Camberwell........373 B20
rd. Camberwell........417 B1
WANDIN CREEK
rd. Seville...............386 A6
rd. Wandin East......386 A6
WANDIN EAST
rd. Wandin East......385 E5
rd. Wandin East......385 E6
WANDO
gr. St Kilda E...........415 B14
WANDOO
av. Clarinda.............498 E4
cl. Hurstbridge.......203 H17
ct. Wheelers Hl.......460 F13
WANDSWORTH
av. Deer Park...........319 B13
rd. Surrey Hills........373 K15
WANG
ct. Cranbourne.........578 C20
WANGANUI
ct. Taylors L...........276 D9
WANGARA
rd. Cheltenham.......495 K17
rd. Sandringham.....495 K17
WANGARATTA
st. Richmond............26 B16
WANGARRA
rd. Frankston..........600 A19
WANKE
cr. Dandenong.........535 J1
WANNAEUE
pl. Rosebud............684 C15
WANNAN
ct. Clayton S...........498 G9
ct. Kilsyth...............381 C7
st. Highett..............496 H13
WANNAWONG
rd. Sassafras...........426 D14
WANNON
ct. Brookfield..........268 D6
ct. Keysborough.....534 G10
ct. Rowville.............463 D16
ct. Toorak...............415 G4
pl. Taylors Hill.........274 J13
st. Gladstone Pk.....279 A2
WANRUA
st. Cheltenham.......496 C17
WANTIRNA
rd. Ringwood..........378 D14
rd. Wantirna............422 D5
WANTIRNA-SASSAFRAS
rd. Bayswater..........423 K2
rd. Boronia.............424 H4
rd. Ferny Creek........426 A12
rd. Sassafras...........426 A12
rd. The Basin...........425 D10
rd. Wantirna............422 C8
WAPITI
st. Maribyrnong......322 J15
WARA
cl. Noble Park N......501 B12
WARADGERY
dr. Rowville.............462 C19
dr. Rowville.............462 D20
WARAIN
ct. Werribee............446 J14
WARANA
ct. Glenroy..............279 H6
dr. Hampton Pk........551 L8
wy. Mt Eliza..............642 B1
WARANGA
cl. Caroline Spr.......317 L8
cr. Broadmeadows..238 D15
cr. St Albans...........320 C12
rd. Bayswater..........423 H8
st. Box Hill N..........375 B8

st. Dandenong N.....501 L9
wy. Taylors Hill.........274 K15
WARATAH
av. Bayswater N......379 L20
av. Beaumaris.........529 L6
av. Belgrave............466 J17
av. Belgrave............467 A17
av. Burwood............418 A6
av. Glen Huntly.........456 D8
av. Mordialloc..........532 B12
av. Mornington........640 L9
av. Selby.................466 J17
av. The Basin...........424 L11
av. Tullamarine........278 J5
cr. Blackburn...........375 G18
ct. Langwarrin.........629 E9
ct. Lilydale..............338 A13
dr. Altona Mdw........451 B5
dr. Dandenong N.....501 H16
dr. Templstw Lr.......330 F9
la. Taylors Hill.........274 L13
mw. Keysborough.....534 A15
pl. Grovedale..........706 F9
pl. Melbourne.............2 J10
pl. Melbourne...........24 F5
rd. Werribee............448 E17
st. Ascot Vale..........324 E16
st. Bentleigh E........457 E16
st. Campbellfield.......239 F12
st. Doveton..............536 L8
st. Geelong West....702 D2
st. Glen Waverley....420 J20
st. Melton S............268 E7
st. Pascoe Vale.......281 A18
st. Rye....................697 L4
st. Seaholme..........409 G18
st. Thomastown......241 E13
st. W Footscray......366 F13
wy. Cockatoo...........511 H1
WARBLA
st. Dandenong N.....501 G20
WARBLER
cl. Werribee............447 K6
ct. Boronia..............424 B11
ct. Carrum Downs...600 L4
wk. S Morang...........243 J3
WARBURTON
al. Melbourne.............1 L10
al. Melbourne...........24 B6
ct. Endeavour Hl......537 F6
ct. Mill Park............242 J6
hwy. Launching Pl......346 C13
hwy. Lilydale.............339 C3
hwy. Millgrove...........348 C4
hwy. Seville...............341 G15
hwy. Seville E.............343 A13
hwy. Wandin East......341 B16
hwy. Wandin N..........340 A9
hwy. Wandin N..........341 B16
hwy. Warburton.........348 C4
hwy. Wesburn............347 L13
hwy. Woori Yall..........344 H16
hwy. Woori Yall..........345 A18
hwy. Yarra Jctn..........347 E15
la. Melbourne.............1 L11
la. Melbourne...........24 B7
rd. Camberwell........373 C18
rd. Canterbury.........373 C18
st. Brunswick...........325 J16
trl. Gruyere.............342 E6
trl. Launching Pl......345 C11
trl. Lilydale..............338 H4
trl. Millgrove...........348 A6
trl. Mt Evelyn...........339 D16
trl. Seville...............341 C14
trl. Seville E.............343 A5
trl. Wandin N..........340 C16
trl. Warburton..........349 F2
trl. Wesburn............347 F11
trl. Woori Yall...........344 C13
trl. Yarra Jctn...........347 F11
WARD
av. Caulfield N.........455 K2
av. Oakleigh S.........457 H17
ct. Altona Mdw.......451 J10
ct. Wonga Park........292 A17
dr. Mill Park............243 D4
gr. Heidelberg..........328 K4
gr. Pascoe Vale S....324 J5
rd. Berwick..............553 H18
rd. Kallista...............467 J8
rd. Queenscliff..........707 L20
rd. The Patch...........467 J8
st. Ashburton...........417 F16
st. Beaumaris...........530 B12
st. Bentleigh............456 B18
st. Brighton East.....455 E19
st. Cheltenham.......531 C3
st. Diamond Ck.......246 D11
st. Glenroy..............280 K2
st. Preston..............326 B2
st. S Melbourne........29 K4
st. S Melbourne......413 E2

WARDALE
rd. Springvale S......534 A1
WARDE
st. Footscray...........367 J8
WARDENS
wk. Coburg..............281 J19
WARDLE
cl. Blackburn S.......419 F2
WARDLOW
ct. Croydon Hl........335 E14
WARDROP
gr. Northcote..........326 K15
WARDS
gr. Bentleigh E........496 L3
rd. Monbulk............469 D1
rd. Monbulk............469 G1
WARE
cr. Ringwood E.......379 C8
WAREE
st. Lilydale..............338 L4
WAREHAM
ct. Hillside..............232 E19
st. Springvale.........500 A8
WARES
rd. Wesburn............347 J10
WARGUNDY
av. Rye...................697 F9
WARIANNA
ct. Kurunjang..........227 C12
WARIBA
la. Mornington........640 C15
WARIDA
av. Malvern East......457 A2
WARILDA
ct. Mornington........656 H3
WARINA
rd. Carnegie............456 K10
WARLAND
rd. Hampton E.........496 A8
WARLEIGH
gr. Brighton............454 L14
gr. Brighton............455 A14
rd. Footscray...........366 J8
rd. W Footscray......366 J8
WARLEY
rd. Malvern East......456 F2
WARMINGTON
rd. Sunshine W.......364 K9
rd. Sunshine W.......365 A9
WARNCLIFFE
rd. Ivanhoe East......328 H17
WARNE
gr. Epping...............198 G16
pl. Berwick.............554 J9
st. Brunswick...........325 E10
st. Coolaroo............238 G7
st. Eaglemont.........328 K12
WARNEET
rd. Blind Bight.........650 F7
rd. Warneet............649 G12
WARNER
av. Ashburton..........417 H17
av. Mornington........640 L13
av. Mornington........641 A13
ct. Donvale.............377 H7
la. Melbourne...........23 G7
pl. Geelong, off Little Ryrie St.....703 A8
rd. Nr Nr Goon N.....560 L13
st. Coburg N............281 C15
st. Essendon...........323 K4
st. Malvern.............416 B10
st. Oakleigh............458 D15
WARNES
rd. Mitcham............377 J13
WARNGAR
cl. Carrum Downs...575 E13
WARNOCK
st. Broadmeadows..238 F18
WARNOO
ct. Frankston S.......627 B5
WAROONA
ct. Pakenham.........585 A4
WARRA
ct. Thomastown......240 D11
rd. Upwey...............465 L18
st. Toorak...............415 J5
WARRABEL
rd. Ferntree Gly.......464 D2
WARRABURRA
av. Rosebud............683 J20
WARRADALE
ct. Noble Park N......501 D11
WARRAGAMBA
ct. Keysborough.....534 E10
WARRAGUL
st. Dallas................238 F10
WARRAH
ct. Gladstone Pk.....279 B1
st. Mornington........640 L15

WARRAIN
av. Mornington........640 K8
av. Rosebud............700 K6
st. Frankston..........627 E5
WARRALONG
av. Greensbrgh........285 K10
ct. Langwarrin.........629 D8
WARRAMUNGA
rd. Bundoora...........284 E2
WARRANDYTE
brk. Langwarrin........629 C14
rd. Langwarrin.........629 D9
rd. Langwarrin S......645 B2
rd. Pk Orchards.......378 F5
rd. Ringwood..........378 E8
rd. Ringwood N.......378 F5
WARRANILLA
av. Rosebud............683 J18
WARRANWOOD
rd. Warranwood......335 B16
WARRAWEE
av. Beaconsfield.......555 K8
av. Noble Park.........534 F7
cct. Frankston..........600 E15
dr. Bundoora...........285 A2
rd. Mt Evelyn...........383 C6
rd. Wantirna S.........422 L11
WARRAWEE CIRCUIT
wk. Frankston N.......600 F13
WARRAWEENA
rd. Clayton S...........498 H9
rd. Sorrento............678 G5
WARRAWITUR
ct. Bonbeach..........573 C5
WARRAWONG
dr. Berwick.............553 H1
WARREENA
gr. Chum Creek.......213 A8
WARREGO
pl. Taylors L...........233 F20
WARREN
av. Yarrambat..........201 C10
cl. Mill Park............242 A8
cl. Narre Warren.....553 C8
ct. Altona Mdw.......451 F3
ct. Dandenong N.....502 D19
ct. Keilor East.........322 C2
ct. Mooroolbark......337 F17
ct. Mt Waverley......418 L15
ct. Thomson...........703 G16
la. Yarra Jctn..........346 L16
la. Yarra Jctn..........347 A16
pl. Gladstone Pk.....279 D1
rd. Cheltenham.......497 C15
rd. Mordialloc.........531 L15
rd. Parkdale...........531 L15
rd. Viewbank..........285 F19
st. Bonbeach..........573 A4
st. Burwood............418 B8
st. Doncaster..........374 F3
st. Pascoe Vale S....324 H5
st. Thomson...........703 G16
WARREN PARK
pl. Nar Warrn S.......552 J10
WARRENS BROOK
rd. Hillside..............231 J15
WARRENWOOD
av. Hoppers Csg......448 K7
cl. Ferntree Gly.......464 J3
pl. Bundoora...........283 L1
pl. Narre Warren.....553 F12
WARRICK
ct. Avondale Ht.......322 H8
dr. Bangholme.........549 K13
gr. Templestowe.....331 L8
st. Ascot Vale..........324 F17
WARRIEN
ct. Bayswater..........423 H8
rd. Croydon N.........336 B17
WARRIGAL
ct. Keysborough......534 E9
hwy. Bentleigh E........497 F14
hwy. Cheltenham........497 F14
hwy. Heatherton........497 F14
hwy. Moorabbin.........497 F14
hwy. Oakleigh S.........497 F14
rd. Ashburton..........417 K20
rd. Ashwood............417 K20
rd. Bentleigh E........457 H20
rd. Bentleigh E........497 G7
rd. Burwood............417 K20
rd. Burwood............418 A7
rd. Camberwell........418 A7
rd. Chadstone.........457 J6
rd. Cheltenham.......497 E20
rd. Cheltenham.......531 D6
rd. Glen Iris............417 K20
rd. Heatherton.........497 E20
rd. Hughesdale........457 H13
rd. Malvern East......457 J6
rd. Mentone............531 C11
rd. Moorabbin..........497 E20
rd. Oakleigh............457 H13

rd. Oakleigh S.........457 H2
rd. Oakleigh S.........497 G
rd. Parkdale...........531 C1
rd. Surrey Hills.........374 A2
rd. Surrey Hills.........418 A
WARRIN
ri. Langwarrin.........629 E
WARRINA
ct. Burwood E.........419 F1
dle. Greensbrgh........244 D1
st. Chadstone.........418 D1
WARRINDALE
cl. Langwarrin.........629 C
WARRINER
ct. Oakleigh E.........458 G1
WARRINGA
cr. Hoppers Csg......448 F
rd. Frankston..........626 J
rd. Frankston S.......626 J
WARRINGAH
cr. Eltham...............287 B
cr. Eltham North.....287 B
rd. Chum Creek.......213 F
WARRINGAL
pl. Heidelberg.........328 G
st. Bulleen..............329 H
WARRINGTON
av. Vermont S.........421 B1
cl. Narre Warren.....538 H1
cr. Deer Park...........318 K1
cr. Wattle Glen........246 H
WARRIOR
ct. Lilydale..............293 L2
WARRIPARRI
cr. Greensbrgh........244 A2
WARRISS
ct. Gladstone Pk.....237 C1
WARRISTON
st. Brighton............455 B1
WARROCK
av. Donvale.............376 L
ct. Berwick.............554 B1
ct. Frankston S.......627 H1
WARROOL
ct. Greensbrgh........244 B1
WARRS
rd. Maribyrnong......323 C1
rd. Maribyrnong......323 C1
st. Preston..............326 J
WARRUGA
av. Bayswater..........423 B
ct. Croydon............336 K1
pl. Greensbrgh........285 K
WARSAW
ct. Clarinda.............498 H1
WARTOOK
gld. Caroline Spr.......317 K
wy. Rowville.............463 B1
WARUKA
cl. Endeavour Hl.....537 K
ct. Mornington........641 B1
WARWICK
av. Springvale.........499 L1
av. Surrey Hills........374 A2
cl. Wantirna............422 F
ct. Berwick.............554 E1
ct. Dandenong N.....502 C1
ct. Glen Waverley....460 G1
ct. Rye...................697 A1
ct. Surrey Hills........374 A2
ct. Thomastown......241 K
ct. Vermont S.........421 B
pl. Croydon N.........335 J
pl. Tullamarine........278 L
pl. Tullamarine........279 A
rd. Greensbrgh........286 E
rd. Kalorama...........382 L
rd. Kalorama...........383 A
rd. Montrose...........382 A
rd. Olinda...............426 L
rd. Olinda...............427 A
rd. Pascoe Vale.......280 J
rd. Sunshine N........321 C
st. Bentleigh E........457 B
st. Box Hill N..........375
st. Newtown...........701 L
st. N Melbourne........17 F
WARWICK FARM
rd. Olinda...............426 L
WARWICK HILL
dr. Pt Lonsdale........710 D
WARWICKSHIRE
ct. Narre Warren.....539 F1
WASHFORD
la. Cairnlea............319 K1
WASHINGTON
av. Malvern East......456
dr. Frankston..........600 D1
dr. Oakleigh S.........497 H
la. Malvern East......456
pl. Point Cook.........450 D
st. Dallas................238
st. Essendon...........323

st. St Albans 319 J5
st. Toorak 415 A4
WASHUSEN
rd. Heathmont 422 J1
WASLEY
st. Albion 320 F19
WASTELL
st. Northcote 327 A18
WATCHET
ct. Craigieburn 150 B14
WATCHTOWER
rd. Coburg 281 K20
WATER
rd. Officer 555 E20
rd. Preston 327 J2
st. Camberwell 417 D7
wy. Frankston S 627 F11
WATERBURY
trn. Craigieburn 193 L4
WATERBUSH
cr. Lyndhurst 551 B20
WATERDALE
cl. Melton W 225 J19
dr. Cranbourne S 603 C20
dr. Cranbourne S 630 L5
pl. Aspendale Gdn 546 J4
rd. Bellfield 328 C12
rd. Bundoora 284 D20
rd. Heidelberg Ht 328 D5
rd. Heidelberg W 284 D20
rd. Heidelberg W 328 D5
rd. Ivanhoe 328 B18
rd. Ivanhoe 328 C12
ri. Craigieburn 193 K4
WATERFALL GULLY
rd. Arthurs Seat 685 K20
rd. Rosebud 700 E4
WATERFIELD
rd. Kallista 468 H8
rd. Monbulk 468 H8
rd. The Patch 468 H8
st. Coburg 325 G2
WATERFORD
av. Craigieburn 194 A3
av. Maribyrnong 322 J16
cl. Caroline Spr 317 L7
cl. Nar Warrn N 504 D19
ct. Point Cook 451 B14
ri. Pakenham 583 K1
tce. Keysborough 533 L12
wy. Melton W 225 H18
WATERFRONT
bvd. Werribee 447 E4
pl. Port Melb 412 G6
WATERGUM
av. Lyndhurst 551 C19
WATERHOUSE
ct. Greenvale 193 D17
WATERLILLY
ct. Waterways 547 D3
WATERLILY
cl. Point Cook 450 H14
la. Lilydale 338 J11
WATERLOO
av. Warburton 349 E2
cr. St Kilda 414 D15
ct. Keysborough 534 B7
pl. Mornington 640 E13
pl. Richmond 26 G12
pl. Richmond 370 J16
pl. Rowville 464 A12
pl. S Melbourne 29 K3
rd. Collingwood 19 J20
rd. Glenroy 280 A7
rd. Northcote 326 K16
rd. Oak Park 280 A7
st. Belmont 702 G19
st. Brighton 454 L18
st. Camberwell 372 K20
st. Camberwell 416 K1
st. Carlton 18 E10
st. Geelong West 702 J2
st. Heathmont 378 G20
st. Williamstown 411 F12
WATERMAN
dr. Wantirna 422 C9
pl. Frankston 627 B4
WATERMANS
ct. Pt Lonsdale 707 F20
WATERMARK
wy. Point Cook 450 B4
WATERMILL
ct. Mill Park 242 H9
WATERMOOR
av. Kilsyth S 424 L2
WATER RESERVE
rd. Rockbank 270 K8
WATERS
av. Up Fntree Gly 464 H9
ct. Clarinda 498 H11
ct. Seaholme 409 J14
rdg. Williamstown 411 A17
dr. Heathmont 422 F3
WATERSEDGE
cl. Knoxfield 463 B2
tce. Highton 701 J9
WATERSIDE
cl. Hoppers Csg 405 E15
dr. Cranbourne E 578 J20
dr. Waterways 547 D1
pl. Rosebud 700 G4
WATERSPRITE
bvd. Sunbury 143 E19
WATERSUN
ct. Point Cook 450 L14
rd. Jan Juc 711 B19
WATERVALE
bvd. Taylors Hill 274 J14
WATERVIEW
cl. Dandenong S 550 L3
cl. Dandenong S 551 A3
cl. Queenscliff 707 L18
ct. Croydon Hl 335 F12
dr. Cairnlea 319 F12
la. Cairnlea 319 G12
tce. Lilydale 338 H9
wk. Docklands 23 B12
WATERVILLE
vst. Cranbourne 603 F7
WATERWAYS
bvd. Waterways 547 F2
WATERY GULLY
rd. Kangaroo Grnd 247 A8
rd. Wattle Glen 247 A8
WATFORD
cr. Craigieburn 149 L16
ct. Epping 197 K17
ct. Somerville 644 K19
rd. St Albans 320 F6
WATKINS
cr. Mt Evelyn 383 H2
ct. Ferntree Gly 463 G10
ct. Springvale 500 D10
gr. Werribee 447 D19
la. Gembrook 512 L14
pl. Langwarrin 601 L17
st. Aspendale 545 L1
st. Diamond Ck 245 H12
st. Fawkner 281 L3
st. Fitzroy N 19 C3
wy. Kensington 33 E8
WATLING
tce. Doncaster E 332 F15
WATSON
av. Belmont 706 C1
av. Dromana 686 F3
av. Mont Albert N 374 F6
cl. Rowville 462 E19
ct. Altona 409 E17
ct. Clarinda 498 C8
ct. Lalor 242 B10
ct. Melton 226 H17
gdn. Berwick 553 K9
gr. Braybrook 365 J1
gr. Glen Huntly 456 D6
pl. Melbourne 2 G17
pl. Melbourne 24 F9
pl. S Geelong 702 K14
rd. Mt Martha 655 H14
rd. Noble Park N 501 C10
rd. Officer S 583 C20
rd. Sorrento 678 J11
ri. Keilor 277 B13
st. Armadale 415 D9
st. Bacchus Msh 221 K17
st. Brunswick 325 E17
st. Dandenong N 501 J20
st. Frankston S 627 G8
st. Glen Iris 417 D11
st. Macleod 285 F11
st. Malvern East 416 J18
st. Preston 327 C3
st. S Kingsville 366 F20
WATSONIA
rd. Watsonia 285 E9
st. Oakleigh 458 A15
WATSONS
bnd. Fingal 698 J19
rd. Diggers Rest 187 B7
rd. Glen Waverley 460 E12
rd. Newcomb 703 L14
rd. Sunbury 187 B7
wk. Kensington 33 H7
WATT
av. Oak Park 280 D13
ct. Bacchus Msh 221 G15
rd. Mornington 640 K18
rd. Mornington 641 A18
st. Airport W 278 J18
st. Bentleigh E 457 C15
st. S Kingsville 410 H3
st. Spotswood 410 H3
st. Springvale 499 L10
st. Sunshine 365 B4
st. Thornbury 326 G7
WATTAMOLLA
av. Werribee 447 D12
rdg. Donvale 377 G3
WATTERS
rd. Officer 556 J6
WATTIES
rd. Templestowe 287 L20
WATTLE
av. Balwyn N 372 L3
av. Balwyn N 373 A3
av. Beaumaris 529 L8
av. Belgrave 466 E12
av. Emerald 509 B5
av. Glen Huntly 456 D9
av. Kings Park 275 E18
av. Montmorency 286 J8
av. Mt Evelyn 339 C20
av. Mt Martha 655 J14
av. Ringwood 378 F9
av. Werribee 448 A14
av. Werribee 448 D15
cl. Meadow Ht 193 J17
cl. Rowville 463 J17
ct. Emerald 510 D2
ct. Forest Hill 376 E19
ct. Grovedale 706 A16
ct. Jan Juc 711 B17
ct. Long Forest 224 G11
ct. Templstw Lr 330 A8
dr. Bundoora 243 B15
dr. Doveton 536 G13
dr. Frankston 628 A7
dr. Sunbury 143 J5
dr. Watsonia 285 C9
dr. Watsonia 285 D10
gr. Coburg 325 D6
gr. Eltham 288 A12
gr. Hawthorn 371 J18
gr. McKinnon 456 A16
gr. Malvern East 456 K2
gr. Mulgrave 500 B5
gr. Nar Warrn S 579 C2
gr. Point Cook 450 B4
gr. Portsea 678 A3
gr. Portsea 678 A4
gr. Reservoir 282 F13
gr. Seaholme 409 G18
pl. McCrae 684 J13
pl. Melton S 268 D7
pl. Somerville 644 J13
rd. Bayswater N 379 G16
rd. Hawthorn 371 H18
rd. Kew East 372 D2
rd. McCrae 684 J15
rd. Maidstone 322 J18
st. Box Hill N 374 J11
st. Prahran 32 C16
st. Prahran 414 G8
st. Springvale 500 B13
st. Thomastown 241 G13
st. W Footscray 366 G11
WATTLE BIRD
pl. Knoxfield 423 B19
wy. Langwarrin 601 K16
WATTLEBIRD
ct. Burwood 418 B6
ct. Diamond Ck 245 C12
ct. Dingley Vill 533 C10
ct. Narre Warren 553 G8
ct. Werribee 447 L6
st. Roxburgh Pk 193 L5
wk. S Morang 243 H4
wy. Healesville 258 A1
WATTLE-BLOSSOM
rd. Warrandyte 290 D19
WATTLEBRAE
st. Reservoir 282 E11
WATTLEGLADE
ct. Wheelers Hl 461 A10
WATTLEGLEN
st. Craigieburn 150 C17
WATTLE GLEN-KANGAROO GROUND
rd. Kangaroo Grnd 247 G12
WATTLE GROVE
rd. Cairnlea 319 J11
WATTLE GULLY
cl. Somerville 645 B20
WATTLEPARK
av. Moolap 704 H16
st. Caroline Spr 274 D16
WATTLES
ct. Healesville 214 A16
WATTLE TREE
la. Croydon N 336 A13
la. Frankston 628 C4
rd. Boronia 424 A20
rd. Ferntree Gly 424 A18
WATTLETREE
av. Wonga Park 291 L19
cl. Lysterfield S 503 L16
ct. Glen Waverley 460 H1
rd. Armadale 415 E14
rd. Eltham 287 H1
rd. Eltham North 245 F18
rd. Hurstbridge 202 G9
rd. Malvern 415 F14
rd. Malvern East 416 A15
wk. S Morang 243 L3
WATTLE VALLEY
dr. Hillside 231 K19
rd. Belgrave 466 D18
rd. Brunswick W 324 K14
rd. Camberwell 417 F8
rd. Canterbury 417 F5
rd. Mitcham 377 G10
rd. Mt Evelyn 339 H14
WATTLEVIEW
rd. Roxburgh Pk 194 B7
ri. Scoresby 462 J5
WATTON
cl. Clayton S 499 D15
st. Werribee 447 F17
WATTS
cr. Mt Eliza 625 L13
ct. Melton W 226 A16
pde. Mt Eliza 625 L12
rd. Doreen 156 C17
rd. Healesville 257 C1
rd. Sorrento 678 K8
rd. Yan Yean 156 F11
st. Box Hill 374 L13
st. Box Hill N 374 L14
st. Laverton 407 F16
tce. Pakenham 584 J9
WAU
st. Heidelberg W 328 A3
WAUCHOPE
av. Narre Warren 553 D6
la. Dandenong 535 G10
WAURN PARK
ct. Belmont 705 L9
WAURNVALE
dr. Belmont 705 L8
WAVE
av. Mt Waverley 459 A6
st. Elwood 454 F5
st. Frankston 599 F14
st. Hampton 495 A9
WAVELL
av. Kilsyth 380 K5
st. Bentleigh 456 D18
st. Box Hill 375 A19
WAVENEY
rd. Mt Eliza 626 D9
st. St Albans 320 F5
WAVENHOE
av. St Kilda E 414 L15
WAVERLEY
av. Ivanhoe 328 A14
av. Kew 372 C9
cl. Narre Warren 553 C10
ct. Craigieburn 150 C15
ct. Gladstone Pk 237 C18
pde. Pascoe Vale S 324 J3
rd. Chadstone 457 H1
rd. Glen Waverley 460 E6
rd. Malvern East 456 E1
rd. Malvern East 457 C2
rd. Mt Waverley 458 F3
rd. Wheelers Hl 460 E6
st. Aberfeldie 323 H12
st. Brighton East 495 B1
st. Broadmeadows 237 L20
st. Essendon 323 H12
st. Moonee Pnd 323 H12
st. Richmond 26 E16
st. Upwey 465 K14
WAVERLEY PARK
dr. Cranbourne N 577 K5
WAVERLY
st. Sandringham 495 F16
st. Sorrento 678 K14
WAVERTREE
av. Caroline Spr 317 J3
WAVISH
ct. Werribee 448 A6
WAXMAN
pde. Brunswick W 324 G9
WAY
dr. Bangholme 549 J13
WAYAMBA
pl. Templestowe 331 H12
WAYCOTT
wy. Mt Evelyn 339 G14
WAYGARA
st. Eumemmerring 537 B14
WAYLAND
ct. Diamond Ck 245 J6
WAYLETT
ct. Deer Park 318 K12
WAYNE
av. Boronia 423 G15
ct. Aspendale 546 A1
ct. Clarinda 498 E6
ct. Dandenong 535 E10
ct. Heathmont 379 E19
ct. Rye 696 L15
ct. Rye 697 A15
ct. Wheelers Hl 460 E15
rd. Wonga Park 292 D7
WAYSIDE
ct. Hampton Pk 551 E7
dr. Bangholme 549 K13
WEABRA
ct. Chadstone 458 C2
WEAFGREEN
ct. Camberwell 417 K3
WEALD
ct. Frankston 628 E5
WEALTHILAND
dr. Mill Park 243 D1
WEATHERALL
rd. Cheltenham 530 C3
WEATHERLAKE
st. Watsonia 285 F4
WEATHERLY
ct. Rye 696 L4
ct. Rye 697 A4
gr. Brighton 454 L19
gr. Brighton 455 A19
st. Melton 268 K2
WEATHERSTON
st. Seaford 599 E4
WEAVER
ct. Altona Mdw 451 H2
tce. Cairnlea 319 F7
WEBB
av. Springvale 500 B7
av. Taylors Hill 274 H15
cl. Meadow Ht 237 L7
cl. Warrandyte 334 C3
ct. Bellfield 327 K6
ct. Hopetoun Park 265 L5
ct. Rowville 463 K10
ct. Vermont 421 C2
la. E Melbourne 25 L11
pl. Doncaster E 376 C1
rd. Airport W 279 A11
rd. Port Melb 412 H5
st. Altona 408 L20
st. Anglesea 714 A1
st. Brighton 454 F17
st. Burwood 418 D11
st. Caulfield 455 H4
st. Coburg 281 D19
st. Fitzroy 19 D18
st. Glen Iris 417 A9
st. Kingsville 366 K12
st. Mornington 640 B17
st. Narre Warren 552 L6
st. Seaford 599 K7
st. Warrandyte 290 A18
WEBBER
pde. Keilor East 277 L20
WEBBS
rd. Ferny Creek 465 L4
WEBER
cr. Burwood E 419 E11
ct. Altona Mdw 451 K5
dr. Mornington 656 E2
st. Brighton East 455 G13
WEBSTER
av. Croydon 379 H4
cr. Watsonia 285 G10
ct. Bayswater 423 C3
ct. Carrum Downs 574 J16
ct. Highton 705 G5
dr. Patterson L 573 H2
rd. Armadale, off Fulton St 415 D11
st. Camberwell 417 L3
st. Dandenong 535 L12
st. Dandenong S 535 L12
st. Malvern East 457 J6
st. Seddon 367 A12
st. Sorrento 678 L12
WEBSTERS
rd. Templestowe 331 J3
WEDD
st. Cheltenham 530 L1
WEDDERBURN
cr. Mt Evelyn 339 B18
WEDDING
ct. Broadmeadows 238 D19
WEDGE
cr. Rowville 463 C15
ct. Darley 221 L9
ct. Glen Waverley 459 J3
ct. Seaford 573 J18
rd. Carrum Downs 575 B13
rd. Skye 575 B13
rd. Skye 576 D15
st. Dandenong 536 C12
st. Epping 241 D1
st. Kingsbury 283 J8
st. Werribee 447 F14
st. Werribee 447 G16

WIGHT
st. Kensington 33 K9
WIGHTMAN
st. Footscray 367 H8
WIGSTONE
st. Noble Park 534 L1
WIGTON
st. Ascot Vale 324 E19
WILAM
ct. Cranbourne 578 B18
WILANA
st. Ringwood 378 F13
WILBERTON
dr. Springvale 499 G13
WILBRAHAM
ct. Frankston 628 F1
WILBUR
cr. Hughesdale 457 G8
WILBURTON
pde. Balwyn N 329 L19
WILBY
ct. Broadmeadows 237 L10
ct. St Albans 320 E6
st. Sorrento 678 E10
WILCOX
ct. Noble Park 500 D19
st. Preston 282 L19
WILD
cr. Roxburgh Pk 193 K13
ct. Endeavour Hl 537 E6
st. Parkdale 531 J11
st. Reservoir 282 K15
WILDBERRY
cl. Croydon Hl 335 F16
ct. Knoxfield 463 C1
WILD CHERRY
dr. Eltham 288 C15
la. Diamond Ck 201 E19
la. Yarrambat 201 E19
rd. Montrose 382 C12
rd. Ormond 456 F13
st. Maribyrnong 322 J16
WILDCOAST
av. Blairgowrie 696 B6
rd. Portsea 678 C8
WILDCROFT
ct. Carrum Downs 601 A4
WILD DUCK
wy. Beaconsfield 555 E13
wy. Blind Bight 650 B10
WILDE
ct. Mooroolbark 337 F19
WILDFIRE
ct. Mill Park 243 C12
WILDFLOWER
cr. Hoppers Csg 405 B16
ct. Hillside 274 E5
ct. Warrandyte 333 D5
la. Cairnlea 319 K9
WILD-LIFE
pde. Balwyn N 373 L6
WILDOER
dr. Aspendale Gdn 547 C7
WILDWOOD
av. Vermont S 420 F13
cl. Knoxfield 423 B19
ct. Albanvale 319 A5
ct. Cranbourne N 578 A6
gr. Ringwood 378 C10
pl. Mulgrave 501 F6
rd. Bulla 190 G16
rd.s, Bulla 190 B2
rd.s, Wildwood 190 B2
wk. Croydon S 380 B14
WILELA
ct. Noble Park 535 B2
WILEMAN
rd. Sunbury 142 A9
WILFRED
ct. Glen Waverley 460 B9
rd. Ivanhoe East 328 G16
st. Rosebud 684 H13
WILGA
av. Altona 452 H1
av. Selby 467 D18
ct. Meadow Ht 193 K17
ct. Narre Warren 538 E19
ct. Noble Park N 501 F15
ct. Wantirna S 423 B12
st. Mt Waverley 459 C6
WILGAH
rd. Rosebud 684 H20
st. St Kilda E 414 L17
st. St Kilda E 415 A17
st. Thomastown 241 D13
WILGRA
av. Ashburton 417 J14
cr. Caulfield 456 A4
WILGUL
wy. Mornington 640 F17
WILHELMA
av. Bayswater 423 G11
WILHELMINA
ct. Croydon 379 E3
WILKENS
la. Silvan 428 L3
WILKES
ct. Mernda 154 H8
pl. Blackburn S 419 D4
st. Ferntree Gly 464 C2
st. Narre Warren 552 H2
WILKILLA
rd. Mt Evelyn 383 E7
WILKIN
ct. Endeavour Hl 537 A1
WILKINS
av. Beaumaris 530 H6
gr. Ringwood E 379 A8
st. Anglesea 713 J1
st. Newport 411 C9
st. Yarraville 366 G16
WILKINSON
cr. Bellfield 327 L5
ct. Roxburgh Pk 194 B14
pl. Glen Waverley 459 L9
rd. Sunshine 365 F1
st. Brunswick 325 F13
st. Burwood E 420 A8
st. Hoppers Csg 448 F2
st. Macleod 285 G11
st. Reservoir 283 D14
st. Tootgarook 698 G1
wy. Endeavour Hl 537 D6
wy. Pk Orchards 334 D20
WILKS
av. Malvern 415 L9
la. Caulfield N, off Wilks St 415 D15
rd. Officer 557 A8
st. Caulfield N 415 D15
WILL
st. Forest Hill 420 H1
WILLA
av. Viewbank 285 F17
WILLANDRA
av. Canterbury 373 G18
ct. Taylors L 275 L10
ct. Werribee 448 C15
lp. Caroline Spr 317 L8
WILLANJIE
ct. Bundoora 284 E1
WILLANSBY
av. Brighton 455 A15
WILLARD
ct. Lalor 241 A6
wy. Chirnside Pk 337 B5
WILLATON
st. St Albans 320 D8
WILLAURA
pl. Yallambie 286 A13
WILLCYRUS
st. Surrey Hills 374 E18
WILLEN
st. Cheltenham 497 D15
WILLESDEN
dr. Waurn Ponds 705 E15
rd. Hughesdale 457 F9
WILLETT
av. Oak Park 279 K10
WILLEY
st. Sunshine N 321 D16
WILLGILSON
ct. Oakleigh 457 L13
WILLIAM
av. Dandenong S 535 L14
av. Hallam 537 E15
cct. Caroline Spr 318 C9
cr. Millgrove 348 G1
cr. Rosebud W 683 D20
ct. Werribee 448 G9
pl. Balaclava, off William St 414 H19
rd. Berwick 553 L5
rd. Blairgowrie 695 L2
rd. Carrum Downs 574 K18
rd. Carrum Downs 575 A18
rd. Croydon 336 C20
rd. Lilydale 338 F17
rd. Red Hill 686 K18
rd. The Patch 468 A9
st. Abbotsford 26 E3
st. Armadale 415 G12
st. Bacchus Msh 222 A15
st. Balaclava 414 H19
st. Belmont 706 A1
st. Boronia 424 C11
st. Box Hill 375 A17
st. Brighton 454 L15
st. Brighton 455 A17
st. Brunswick 325 F10
st. Bulleen 329 L12
st. Clifton Hill 20 H7
st. Cranbourne 578 C20
st. Cremorne 26 E19
st. Donvale 376 K7
st. Emerald 510 A4
st. Essendon 323 F3
st. Fawkner 281 G6
st. Ferntree Gly 464 B3
st. Glenroy 279 H6
st. Greensbrgh 285 K3
st. Hawthorn 372 B17
st. Kalorama 383 C10
st. Keilor Park 277 K13
st. Lalor 241 E11
st. McCrae 684 L13
st. Melbourne 1 E18
st. Melbourne 23 H4
st. Melton 227 C20
st. Mernda 154 L19
st. Mernda 155 A19
st. Mitcham 377 C11
st. Moorabbin 496 E11
st. Mt Waverley 458 K2
st. Murrumbeena 457 E8
st. Newcomb 704 A16
st. Newport 410 K6
st. Newtown 702 D7
st. Northcote 327 C18
st. Oakleigh 458 D13
st. Preston 282 J19
st. Ringwood 378 B9
st. St Albans 276 A20
st. Seddon 367 B11
st. Somerton 194 H16
st. South Yarra 32 C11
st. South Yarra 414 G5
st. Sunshine 365 F9
st. Up Fntree Gly 465 B7
st. W Melbourne 1 E18
st. W Melbourne 17 G20
st. W Melbourne 23 H4
st.e, Lilydale 338 B6
st.w, Lilydale 338 B6
WILLIAM ANGLISS
dr. Laverton N 363 F19
dr. Laverton N 363 G17
WILLIAM BUCKLEY
ct. Seabrook, off Cotterell Wy 450 L6
wy. Sorrento 679 A16
WILLIAM CLARKE
wyn. Nar Warrn S 578 H1
WILLIAM COOPER
st. Maribyrnong 367 C2
WILLIAM CROOK
pl. E Melbourne 25 K6
WILLIAM GILL
pl. Croydon Hl 335 G14
WILLIAM GOOD
ct. Sorrento 679 A12
WILLIAM HOVELL
dr. Endeavour Hl 537 F6
ps. Craigieburn 150 F11
WILLIAM HUNTER
ct. Rosebud 700 G3
WILLIAM LEAKE
av. Seabrook 450 L7
WILLIAM LEONARD
ct. Nar Warrn S 579 F2
WILLIAM McPHERSON
cr. Seabrook 450 L8
WILLIAM PERRY
cl. Endeavour Hl 537 D7
WILLIAMS
av. Keilor East 278 A18
cl. Dingley Vill 533 E10
cr. Woori Yall 344 G16
ct. Richmond 26 F4
gr. Bonbeach 545 E13
la. Ferntree Gly 464 F1
pl. S Melbourne 29 F3
rd. Blackburn 375 J13
rd. Briar Hill 286 F6
rd. Coburg N 281 E18
rd. Dandenong S 550 D1
rd. Don Valley 346 D7
rd. Laverton 407 F16
rd. Mooroolbark 337 F18
rd. Mornington 640 C16
rd. Mt Eliza 625 L11
rd. Olinda 426 L6
rd. Olinda 427 A7
rd. Pk Orchards 378 D1
rd. Pt Lonsdale 710 F2
rd. Prahran 32 K20
rd. Prahran 414 K13
rd. Ringwood N 378 D1
rd. South Yarra 32 K20
rd. South Yarra 414 L8
rd. South Yarra 415 A6
rd. Toorak 32 K20
rd. Toorak 414 L8
rd. Toorak 415 A6
rd. Windsor 414 K13
rd.n, South Yarra 414 L2
rd.n, South Yarra 415 A2
rd.n, Toorak 414 L2
rd.n, Toorak 415 A2
st. Dromana 686 E3
st. Frankston 626 L2
st. Mentone 531 B6
st. S Melbourne 29 F3
WILLIAM SALTHOUSE
wy. Patterson L 547 H19
WILLIAMS BAY
gr. Williamstown 410 H16
WILLIAMSBROOK
tce. Bundoora 243 C14
WILLIAMSON
av. Strathmore 323 L1
cl. Mordialloc 532 E16
rd. Ferntree Gly 424 F19
rd. Gembrook 512 L16
rd. Maidstone 322 J17
rd. Maribyrnong 322 J17
rd. Mont Albert N 374 E6
st. Berwick 554 H9
st. Tootgarook 698 B3
WILLIAMSONS
rd. Doncaster 330 L16
rd. S Morang 199 E17
rd. Templestowe 331 B12
rd. Templstw Lr 330 L16
WILLIAMSTOWN
rd. Kingsville 366 K18
rd. Port Melb 411 H5
rd. Seddon 366 K18
rd. Yarraville 366 K18
WILLIAM WRIGHT
wyn. Hoppers Csg 447 L1
WILLIS
cl. Hampton Pk 551 B7
ct. Altona Mdw 451 F5
ct. Darley 221 J9
ct. Vermont 421 B1
la. Hampton 494 L8
la. Hampton 495 A8
pl. Delahey 275 D10
pl. S Geelong 702 L14
rd. Kallista 469 A6
rd. Menzies Ck 468 H18
rd. Monbulk 469 A6
st. Armadale 415 J12
st. Balwyn N 373 F4
st. Frankston 599 E19
st. Greensbrgh 286 F1
st. Hampton 494 L8
st. Heatherton 497 L15
st. Kensington 33 C9
st. Prahran 415 A12
st. Richmond 26 F20
st. Richmond 32 F1
st. St Albans 320 C8
st. Yarraville 367 C15
WILLISON
st. Bayswater 423 G8
WILLJOHN
dr. Mt Martha 657 A10
WILLMETTE
ct. Lilydale 338 B2
WILLMOTT
dr. Craigieburn 150 B13
dr. Hoppers Csg 448 E8
st. Aspendale 546 B2
WILLOBY
av. Glen Iris 416 G16
st. Junction Vill 604 G11
WILLONGA
st. Rye 697 C4
st. Strathmore 279 L15
WILLORA
cr. Cranbourne W 577 F20
ct. Frankston S 626 L15
WILLORNA
ct. Doncaster E 332 E8
WILLOUGHBY
av. Caroline Spr 318 C3
st. Reservoir 282 G11
WILLOW
av. Cheltenham 531 G2
av. Glen Waverley 419 L15
av. Mitcham 377 G15
av. Rowville 463 H16
av. St Albans 320 F8
bnd. Bulleen 330 A18
bnd. Doncaster 330 A18
ct. Bellfield 327 K6
ct. Keysborough 534 E13
ct. Kilsyth 381 L6
ct. Narre Warren 552 L7
ct. Whittington 704 A19
dr. Avondale Ht 321 K7
dr. Hampton Pk 551 G4
gr. Canterbury 417 C1
gr. Coburg 325 D5
gr. Kew East 372 D2
la. Carlton 18 H12
la. Richmond 32 F2
rd. Bangholme 549 H13
rd. Frankston 628 D4
rd. Up Fntree Gly 464 J9
st. Box Hill N 374 H10
st. Dingley Vill 532 H7
st. Elsternwick 454 K2
st. Essendon 324 A8
st. Malvern 416 B9
st. Preston 326 B3
st. Werribee 447 E11
wy. Craigieburn 150 B12
WILLOW BANK
gr. Ivanhoe 327 L17
WILLOWBANK
ct. Glen Waverley 420 E18
ct. Templestowe 331 K10
pkt. Pakenham 584 B3
rd. Fitzroy N 326 C16
wy. Attwood 237 A11
WILLOWDENE
cl. Somerville 645 D20
WILLOWFIELD
ct. Highton 701 F9
WILLOW-GLEN
ct. Dingley Vill 533 A10
WILLOWGREEN
wy. Point Cook 450 G7
WILLOWOOD
ct. Taylors Hill 274 K9
WILLOW TREE
la. Glenroy 281 D5
wy. Chirnside Pk 337 H6
WILLOWTREE
cr. Niddrie 322 K2
dr. Werribee 448 C15
WILLS
av. Mt Waverley 459 E1
av. Pakenham 584 F10
ct. Cranbourne N 577 J7
ct. Endeavour Hl 537 J8
ct. Grovedale 706 B12
ct. Mooroolbark 337 L16
ct. Taylors L 275 K1
rd. Dixons Ck 209 L2
rd. Melton S 268 D12
st. Balwyn 372 K10
st. Boronia 423 H10
st. Glen Iris 416 G11
st. Hawthorn E 416 H1
st. Kew 371 G6
st. Melbourne 1 G4
st. Melbourne 23 K4
st. Mornington 640 E20
st. Pascoe Vale S 280 J20
st. Sunbury 143 A12
st. Westmeadows 237 B15
WILLSLIE
cr. Berwick 554 C18
WILLSMERE
rd. Kew 371 K6
WILLSMORE
st. Williamstn N 410 E12
WILLUNGA
ct. Berwick 554 A16
wy. Bundoora 242 F13
WILLURAH
st. Forest Hill 420 J3
WILLY
ct. Dingley Vill 533 C5
WILLYS
av. Keilor Dn 275 K12
WILMA
av. Dandenong 535 G6
av. Mulgrave 499 L3
av. Seville E 343 C13
ct. Beaconsfield 555 D14
ct. Doncaster 375 D3
st. Bentleigh 496 D3
WILMOT
dr. Delahey 275 F14
st. Macleod 285 D17
st. Malvern East 456 G3
WILMOTH
av. Carnegie 456 L12
st. Northcote 327 D13
st. Thornbury 327 D13
WILMOTT
ct. Berwick 553 L19
WILNA
st. Pascoe Vale 280 H17
WILONA
wy. Berwick 554 G14
WILONG
cl. Kurunjang 227 A1
WILPENA
ct. St Albans 321 A
pl. Vermont S 420 L
pl. Vermont S 421 A
WILRAY
st. Grovedale 706 H
WILSHIRE
ct. Endeavour Hl 537 K
WILSON
av. Brunswick 325 E1
av. Montmorency 286 H1
av. Parkville 18 A14

WITHAM
dr. Coldstream 295 E13
WITHERS
av. Mulgrave 500 H6
cl. Sunbury 142 L9
cl. Sunbury 143 A9
st. Albert Park 29 C16
st. Albert Park 413 B8
st. Ivanhoe East 328 K14
st. Sunshine 365 D3
wy. Eltham 287 D12
WITKEN
av. Wantirna S 462 K2
WITNEY
ct. Darley 222 D10
wy. Bundoora 284 L3
WITNISH
st. Yarra Jctn 346 H14
WITT
ct. Box Hill N 375 D6
st. Mitcham 377 H14
WITTENBERG
ct. Narre Warren 552 F2
WITTERNBERG
av. Frankston 628 E11
WITTICK
st. Darley 221 G8
WITTIG
st. Doncaster 374 J3
WITTON
ct. Greenvale 192 J18
st. Deer Park 319 D17
WOBURN
cl. Kealba 276 L20
st. Heidelberg 328 J4
WODALLA
ct. Mill Park 242 L10
ct. Mill Park 243 A10
WODONGA
cr. Thomastown 240 D13
st. Broadmeadows 238 F17
WOFF
st. Beaumaris 530 B5
WOIWURUNG
cr. Coburg 281 K19
WOKING
st. Craigieburn 194 C4
WOLAI
av. Bentleigh E 457 F20
WOLANGI
ct. Greensbrgh 244 D19
WOLBERS
rd. Dingley Vill 533 D5
WOLF
ct. Endeavour Hl 537 D9
st. Wantirna S 422 G19
WOLFDENE
ct. Mornington 640 D16
WOLFE
rd. Melton 227 B16
WOLLAHRA
pl. Heathmont 379 C17
ri. Wyndham Va 446 D3
WOLLERT
st. Rye 697 B7
WOLLOMBI
rd. Exford 267 G19
WOLMAN
dr. Frankston 628 D11
WOLSELEY
av. Glen Waverley 460 G1
cl. Mont Albert 374 C15
cr. Balwyn 372 L10
cr. Blackburn 375 K17
gr. Brighton 494 J3
pde. Kensington 33 K12
pl. Rowville 502 H3
pl. Thomastown 240 H18
st. Coburg 325 G7
st. Hawthorn E 372 D18
st. Highett 496 C12
st. S Melbourne 29 G2
WOLSELY
cl. Werribee 447 G2
WOLSLEY
av. Frankston 600 G19
st. Bentleigh 495 L3
WOLVERHAMPTON
st. Footscray 367 C7
WOLVERTON
dr. Gladstone Pk 237 B19
WOLVISTON
av. Hillside 232 E19
av. Hillside 232 G17
WOMBALANA
rd. Selby 467 B15
WOMBALANO
rd. Mt Evelyn 383 E5
WOMBAT
cr. Emerald 510 C3
ct. Eltham 246 C19
ct. Greensbrgh 286 B10
ct. Westmeadows 236 J13
dr. Eltham 246 A19
pl. S Morang 243 J1
rd. Mt Dandenong 382 H16
WOMBELANO
st. Menzies Ck 468 J18
WONDALEA
cr. Wantirna 422 A11
cr. Wantirna 422 A12
WONDALGA
st. Dandenong N 502 B17
WONDAREE
st. Rye 697 A9
WONDERLAND
tce. Mt Martha 668 L4
tce. Mt Martha 669 A4
WONDOORA
av. Ferny Creek 465 K3
WONGA
av. Pascoe Vale 280 L12
ct. Bentleigh E 457 B15
gr. McCrae 685 D10
la. McCrae 685 D10
mw. S Morang 199 J9
pl. Gowanbrae 279 F5
rd. Millgrove 348 F1
rd. Ringwood 334 L19
rd. Ringwood 335 A19
rd. Ringwood 378 G5
rd. Ringwood 378 K2
rd. Ringwood N 334 L19
rd. Ringwood N 378 G5
rd. Ringwood N 378 K2
rd. Warranwood 334 J11
rd. Warranwood 335 A14
WONGALA
wy. Mooroolbark 337 C16
WONGANELLA
dr. Keilor East 278 C19
WONGELLA
ct. Aspendale 546 F7
WONG HEE
rd. Emerald 509 F10
rd.w, Emerald 509 E10
WONTHULONG
dr. Bayswater N 380 H18
WONUKA
ct. Croydon Hl 335 H16
ct. Doncaster E 331 J15
WOOD
ct. Cranbourne 577 L19
gr. Burnside 318 F8
rd. Nar Warrn S 553 E16
st. Avondale Ht 322 A14
st. Beaconsfield 555 B15
st. Beaumaris 530 B5
st. Bentleigh 496 E2
st. Deer Park 319 C18
st. Fitzroy 19 D16
st. Hawthorn 371 E16
st. Mornington 640 H19
st. N Melbourne 17 A12
st. Nunawading 376 H16
st. Preston 282 L18
st. Ringwood E 379 A14
st. Rosebud 684 B16
st. Sandringham 495 D13
st. S Geelong 703 C18
st. Springvale 500 B10
st. Strathmore 323 J2
st. Templestowe 330 J6
st. Templstw Lr 330 G6
st. Thomastown 241 G20
WOODALL
st. Black Rock 529 J5
WOODBINE
cl. Craigieburn 150 G13
ct. Wantirna 423 B16
gr. Chelsea 546 L19
rd. Cranbourne N 578 C10
WOODBRIDGE
pl. Burnside 318 D6
WOODBURN
av. Berwick 539 G18
av. Cairnlea 319 K13
cr. Meadow Ht 237 J5
pl. Craigieburn 194 H1
rd. Hawthorn 416 C3
WOODBURY
ct. Avondale Ht 321 L15
ct. Nar Warrn S 552 F12
WOODBYNE
cr. Mornington 641 E19
WOODCHASE
ct. Cranbourne E 604 J1
WOOD-CHURCH
cl. Ringwood 335 C19
WOODCOCK
cl. Flemington 33 D3
ct. Dandenong N 536 C1
wk. Aspendale Gdn 546 G2
WOODCREST
rd. Vermont 420 L4
WOODCUTTERS
pl. Nar Warrn S 553 E18
WOODDALE
gr. Donvale 377 B9
gr. Mitcham 377 B9
WOODED
wy. Montmorency 286 K12
WOODFERN
ct. Highton 705 K5
WOODFIELD
pl. Sunbury 143 B10
WOODFORD
av. Kew, off Princess St 371 J10
cl. Ringwood E 379 G8
WOODFULL
ct. Keilor East 322 B1
rd. Lower Plenty 286 J17
st. Prahran 415 B10
wy. Epping 198 H17
WOODGATE
st. Southbank 29 B2
st. Southbank 413 A1
st. S Melbourne 29 B2
st. S Melbourne 413 A1
WOODHALL
wyn. Donvale 376 K4
WOODHEAD
st. Fitzroy N 326 D20
WOODHENGE
dr. Cranbourne E 578 J20
WOODHILL
cl. Research 288 K6
pl. Mill Park 243 C6
WOODHOUSE
gr. Box Hill N 374 J8
rd. Doncaster E 332 C19
rd. Donvale 332 G20
WOODHURST
gr. Kalorama 383 E14
WOODINGTON
dr. Wheelers Hl 461 B18
WOODLAKE
pl. Wyndham Va 446 D8
WOODLAND
av. Croydon 379 H3
av. Mt Eliza 626 B12
cl. Blairgowrie 696 A5
ct. Dingley Vill 533 E6
dr. Albanvale 319 A5
dr. Cheltenham 496 K16
gr. Briar Hill 286 K4
gr. Montmorency 286 L8
gr. Selby 467 C17
ri. Melton W 226 E11
st. Doncaster 330 F18
st. Essendon 323 K2
st. Essendon 324 E3
st. Strathmore 323 K2
st. Strathmore 324 E3
wk. Lysterfield S 503 J11
wy. Eltham 288 C3
wy. Fingal 698 F20
wy. Gruyere 341 L5
WOODLAND PARK
ri. Croydon S 379 L13
WOODLANDS
av. Camberwell 417 C2
av. Clematis 509 B4
av. Cockatoo 511 D2
av. Emerald 509 B4
av. Kew East 372 H6
av. Pascoe Vale S 324 J5
av. Sassafras 426 G14
cl. Pk Orchards 378 A1
cr. Narre Warren 553 G9
ct. Craigieburn 150 D16
ct. Mordialloc 532 A15
dr. Braeside 532 K10
dr. Braeside 532 K15
dr. Greenvale 191 C18
dr. Somerville 644 D14
edg. Templestowe 332 B7
gr. Bundoora 284 G7
gr. Frankston 627 A4
gr. Frankston S 627 A4
gr. Malvern East 457 H7
gr. Mitcham 377 A16
gr. Safety Bch 686 H1
pl. Lalor 240 F9
rd. Cranbourne S 602 K13
rd. Cranbourne S 603 A14
rd. Heathmont 378 G18
ri. Macleod 285 K11
st. Clematis 508 L3
WOODLAWN
cct. Macleod 284 J13
st. Richmond 26 A14
WOODLEA
cr. Craigieburn 150 D13
cl. Frankston 599 H14
dr. Glen Waverley 460 A11
pl. Ferntree Gly 463 F9
pl. Langwarrin 629 B10
st. Doncaster E 331 H15
WOODLEE
ri. Lilydale 338 J11
st. Dandenong 535 L4
WOODLEIGH
av. Upwey 466 B7
cr. Vermont S 420 L10
cr. Vermont S 421 A10
ct. Launching Pl 345 F16
pl. Gladstone Pk 237 B16
st. Thomastown 240 F14
WOODLEY
ct. Highton 701 H17
st. Narre Warren 553 F7
WOODLOT
la. Tooradin 652 E10
WOODLYN
cl. Mt Eliza 626 C18
mw. Mt Eliza 626 D17
WOODMASON
av. Somerville 645 C19
rd. Boronia 424 A8
st. Malvern 415 K10
WOODPECKER
ps. Chirnside Pk 337 G6
WOODRIDGE
cl. Montrose 381 J11
ct. Eltham 288 C7
WOODROW
ct. Cockatoo 511 B10
ct. Narre Warren 553 F12
WOODRUFF
av. Maribyrnong 367 E3
ct. Point Cook 451 B8
rd. S Morang 199 G8
st. Kensington 33 F8
st. Port Melb 412 K1
WOODRUSH
ct. Nar Warrn S 553 E19
WOODS
av. Mordialloc 532 A17
cl. Meadow Ht 194 D20
la. Ferny Creek 426 B16
pl. Rowville 463 K10
pl. Roxburgh Pk 193 L12
rd. Pearcedale 645 K6
rd. Truganina 405 G6
rd. Yan Yean 156 H6
st. Ascot Vale 323 F16
st. Balwyn 373 H9
st. Laverton 407 D17
st. Newport 410 E8
st. St Albans 276 F20
st. Yarraville 367 C15
WOODSDALE
ct. Cairnlea 319 H12
WOODSIDE
av. Clayton 458 L15
av. Frankston S 627 J15
av. Ringwood 378 E10
cl. Hampton Pk 551 L16
cl. Somerville 645 B15
cr. Toorak 32 L12
cr. Toorak 414 L6
cr. Toorak 415 A6
ct. Werribee 447 J2
dr. Rowville 503 E1
mw. Roxburgh Pk 194 A8
rd. Seville 342 C12
st. Fitzroy N 19 K1
st. Fitzroy N 326 F20
WOODS POINT
dr. Beaconsfield 555 F15
rd. Warburton 350 B2
WOODSTOCK
cl. Sunbury 143 C6
ct. Doncaster E 332 A18
dr. Doreen 156 L11
dr. Gladstone Pk 236 K20
pl. Springvale S 534 B2
rd. Mt Waverley 458 K1
st. Balaclava 414 G19
st. Canterbury 372 J15
st. Newtown 702 H13
WOODTHORPE
av. Rosebud W 683 C19
WOODVALE
cl. Essendon 324 B3
ct. Forest Hill 420 D10
ct. Mill Park 242 E11
dr. Carrum Downs 601 C2
gr. Essendon 324 B3
gr. Rosebud 684 H16
rd. Boronia 423 L15
rd. Wesburn 348 A7
WOODVIEW
ct. Dandenong N 501 K11
ct. Wheelers Hl 461 B18
pl. Knoxfield 423 C20
WOODVILLE
av. Ormond 456 B10
rd. Mooroolbark 337 C17
st. Balwyn N 373 K2
WOODVILLE PARK
dr. Hoppers Csg 448 G6
WOODWARD
la. Dandenong 535 G6
st. Springvale 500 B17
WOODWORTH
cl. Endeavour Hl 537 E9
ct. Roxburgh Pk 194 B15
WOODY
lk. Croydon S 380 B13
WOODYARD
ct. Altona Mdw 451 H4
WOOLACOTT
st. Coburg 325 G5
WOOLART
st. Strathmore 279 H12
WOOLBOARD
rd. Port Melb 412 D1
WOOLCOCK
av. Kew East 372 D5
WOOLERT
st. Ashwood 418 C18
WOOLERTON
ct. Donvale 377 H7
WOOLHOUSE
st. Northcote 326 D13
WOOLLAHRA
av. Keysborough 534 E7
WOOLLEY
st. Essendon 323 F6
WOOLMER
ct. Croydon Hl 335 D16
ct. Frankston S 628 D15
WOOLNOUGH
dr. Epping 242 A
dr. Mill Park 242 A
WOOLPACK
rd. Bacchus Msh 264 H
rd. Maddingley 264 H
st. Hoppers Csg 447 L
WOOLRICH
rd. Olinda 427 D1
WOOLSCOUR
la. Marshall 706 L
WOOLSHED
av. Cairnlea 319 H1
rd. Nar Warrn S 579 G
WOOLSTON
dr. Frankston S 627 A
WOOLSTONE
cl. Kealba 320 L
cl. Kealba 321 A
WOOLTANA
rd. Keysborough 535 A1
WOOLTON
av. Thornbury 326 E1
WOOLVET
av. Belmont 706 J
WOOLWICH
dr. Mulgrave 500 D
WOOMBI
av. Rosebud 683 K1
WOOMERA
av. Keysborough 535 B
st. Rye 696 L
st. Rye 697 A
st. Viewbank 285 H1
WOONA
ct. Yallambie 286 B1
pl. Keilor Dn 276 H1
WOONAH
st. Chadstone 418 A2
WOONGARRA
ct. Eltham 246 D1
WOONSOCKET
ct. St Kilda 414 C1
WOONTON
cr. Rosebud 684 E1
st. Rosebud 684 G1
WOORABINDA
cl. Ringwood N 378 D
WOORAL
ct. Notting Hill 459 H1
WOORALLA
dr. Mornington 642 C1
dr. Mt Eliza 642 B
WOORARA
ct. Chirnside Pk 292 J
WOORARRA
av. Doncaster E 332 C
WOORAYL
st. Carnegie 456 J
WOORIGOLEEN
dr. Keilor East 278 B2
rd. Toorak 415
WOORILL
ct. Vermont 421 F
WOORILLA
ct. Frankston 599 L1
WOORITE
pl. Keilor East 278 D1
pl. Wyndham Va 446 F1
WOORI YALLOCK
rd. Avonsleigh 471 C
rd. Cockatoo 471 C
rd. Cockatoo 471
rd. Nangana 471

X

Y

AIRPORTS / AIRFIELDS

BAYS, BEACHES, ETC

INFORMATION

CARAVAN, TOURIST & MOBILE HOME PARKS

GOLF COURSES & DRIVING RANGES

Chirnside Park Country Club 337 E2
Churchill Park 503 F16
City of Kingston Municipal 532 G7
Coburg North Driving Range 281 K17
Commonwealth 497 J4
Craigieburn 150 A19
Cranbourne 578 D5
Croydon 336 F17
Dandenong Workers 536 F11
Devil Bend 658 K16
Dorset Public 380 H8
Dromana (par 3) 687 B2
Eagle Ridge 699 B14
Eastern 330 G20
Eastwood 425 C1
Elsternwick Park Public 454 J5
Emerald Golf & Country Resort 470 A15
Epping Driving Range 197 A14
Essendon Municipal 323 F18
Frankston 627 L10
Golf Park Driving Range 497 G9
Goonawarra 144 D14
Green Acres 372 D1
Heathmont Golf Park (Par 3) 379 F20
Heidelberg 286 E16
Huntingdale 458 B19
Ivanhoe 328 F18
Keilor 233 K18
Kew 372 E2
Keysborough 533 K20
Kingsbury Driving Range 283 L12
Kingston Heath 497 J16
Kingston Links 462 B19
Kingswood 533 B5
Kooringal 452 D2
Lalor 239 L7
Latrobe 328 A20
Long Island Country Club 599 H11
Lonsdale 710 D4
Malvern Valley 417 F20
Medway 322 F17
Melbourne Golf Academy & Driving Range 532 E2
Melton Golf Driving Range 269 J5
Melton Valley 227 D18
Metropolitan 457 K16
Montuna 555 H1
Moonah Links 698 F17
Moorabbin Driving Range 532 G7
Morack 421 G8
Mornington Country 641 B9
Mt Martha Municipal 670 A4
Mt Martha Valley Country Club 669 B19
Northcote Municipal 326 C9
Northern 280 E7
Oakleigh Public 458 A7
Olinda 427 B9
Pakenham & District 585 J2
Patterson River Country Club 573 D5
Peninsula Country Club 600 C13
Portsea 677 H1
Queenscliff 709 D11
Queens Park 701 J8
RACV Country Club 213 D18
Ranfurlie 603 B7
Richmond 371 C20
Ringwood 422 C1
Riversdale 418 H18
Rosanna 330 C2
Rosebud 700 H9
Rosebud Country Club 700 A5
Rosebud Park 700 L2
Rossdale 546 F8
Royal Melbourne 529 L3
Royal Park 325 D20
Sanctuary Lakes 451 A12
Sandhurst Club North Course 576 A10
Sandringham Driving Range 495 L18
Sandringham Municipal 529 L1
Seaford Driving Range 599 K7
Skye 602 A6
Sorrento 678 G4
Southern 533 G11
Spring Park 533 H9
Spring Valley 499 D14
Strathallan 284 H9
Studley Park (9 Holes, Par 3) 371 A9
Sunshine 363 K6
The Dunes 697 G15
Tirhatuan Lakes Public 502 F9
Torquay 711 J13
Torquay Sands 712 K1
Tullamarine Country Club 277 E1
Underbank Country Club 221 F15
Victoria 530 E1
Von Nida Golf Academy Driving Range 533 H19
Warburton 349 C3
Wattle Park 418 C4
Waverley 502 J6
Waverley Municipal 461 C6
Werribee Park 488 A11
Westgate 367 A20
Woodlands 532 D15
Yarra Bend 371 B6
Yarrambat Park 201 A10
Yarra Valley Country Club 329 F6
Yarra Valley Driving Range 336 H9
Yarra Valley Golf Park (9 Holes, Par 3) 336 J9
Yarra Yarra 497 E5

HOTELS & MOTELS

Abbotsford Inn Hotel/Motel (Golden Chain) Abbotsford 26 B1
Abbotswood Motor Inn Belmont 706 B5
Adelphi Hotel Melbourne 2 G18
Admiral Motor Inn Rosebud 684 F14
Airport Motel Attwood 236 L12
Albany Motel South Yarra 31 D7
Alexander Motor Inn Essendon 323 L7
All Nations Backpackers Hotel Melbourne 23 H13
All Seasons Crossley Hotel Melbourne 24 J4
Alphington Quest Lodging Alphington 327 G20
Ambassador Frankston Frankston 599 C14
Anglesea Homestead Motor Lodge Anglesea 713 H5
Arden Motel North Melbourne 17 E16
Aristocrat Waurnvale Motel Waurn Ponds 705 A14
Aspendale Shore Motel Aspendale 545 L2
Astoria City Travel Inn Melbourne 23 F7
Avenue Motel Bacchus Marsh 222 E17
Barkly Quest Lodging St Kilda 414 C18
Batmans Hill Melbourne 23 H12
Baxter Tavern Hotel/Motel Baxter 644 E2
Bayside St Kilda Motel St Kilda 414 A15
Bayview on the Park Hotel Melbourne 31 C17
Beacon Resort Motel Point Lonsdale 707 L20
Beaconsfield Lodge Motel Beaconsfield 555 B15
Beaumaris Bay Motel Beaumaris 530 D12
Beau Monde International Hotel/Motel Doncaster East 375 L1
Beaumont Hotel/Motel Kew 371 H10
Bell Motor Inn Preston 327 B3
Bells Hotel South Melbourne 3 A20
Berwick Springs Hotel Berwick 554 B20
Big Country Melton Motel Melton 226 K19
Billanook Country Motor Inn Lilydale 338 G6
Blue Dolphin Motel Dromana 686 G2
Boathouse Motel & Conference Centre Blairgowrie 679 L18
Box Hill Motel Burwood 418 K5
Brighton Savoy Motel Brighton 454 F19
Brooklands of Mornington Mornington 640 H14
Bruce County Motor Inn Mt Waverley 459 G8
Brunswick Tower Motel Brunswick 325 F8
Buckingham Motor Inn Highett 496 F14
Bulla Hotel/Motel Bulla 190 C17
Bull & Bear Tavern Melbourne 1 K18
Burnham Beeches Country House Sherbrooke 426 H18
Burvale Hotel/Motel Vermont South 420 F10
Burwood East Motel Burwood East 419 K10
Cabana Court Motel St Kilda West 413 L14
California Motel Hawthorn 371 J13
Carlisle Motor Lodge St Kilda 414 C17
Carlton Crest Hotel Melbourne 31 C18
Carlton Hotel Melbourne 2 H12
Carron Tavern West Melbourne 23 E5
Carrum Downs Motel Carrum 600 G2
Causeway Hotel Melbourne 2 D14
Causeway Inn On The Mall Melbourne 2 C13
Centra Melbourne Airport Melbourne Airport 235 K11
Chadstone Executive Motel Hughesdale 457 H8
Charnwood Motel St Kilda 414 D14
Chelsea Heights Hotel Chelsea Heights 547 E7
Ciloms Airport Motor Lodge Tullamarine 236 D18
City Limits Motor Inn Melbourne 24 J4
City Park Motel South Melbourne 30 G5
City Square Motel Melbourne 2 E16
Clarendon on York South Melbourne 30 A2
Clocktower Quest Inn Carlton 18 F15
Coburg Coach House Motel Coburg North 281 G15
Coburg Motor Inn Coburg 281 G17
Como Hotel South Yarra 32 E8
Copper Lantern Motel Rosebud West 683 E18
Cosmopolitan Motor Inn (Best Western) St Kilda 414 C17
Court House Hotel North Melbourne 17 D17
Crest On Barkly Hotel Melbourne St Kilda 414 D13
Crown Towers Hotel Southbank 3 D4
Croydon Hotel Croydon 379 E1
Daisy Club Hotel Ringwood East 378 J11
Dandenong Motel Dandenong 535 H4
Dingley International Motor Inn Dingley Village 532 H6
Disabled Motorists Motel Coburg 325 F7
Donview Heights Motel Doncaster 331 F20
Dorset Gardens Hotel/Motel Croydon 380 E7
Downtowner On Lygon Carlton 18 E19
Dromana Beach Motel Dromana 686 E2
Duke of Kent Hotel Melbourne 1 L5
Duke of Wellington Hotel Melbourne 2 K19
Duxton Hotel Melbourne 1 L19
Eastern Town House East Melbourne 25 K4
Eden On The Park Motel Melbourne 30 L7
Elizabethan Lodge Motel Blackburn North 375 F6
Elizabeth Tower Motel Melbourne 17 K15
Elms Family Hotel Melbourne 24 J2
Eltham Gateway Motel (Best Western) Eltham 288 C3
Essendon Motor Inn Essendon North 279 G20
Evancourt Motel Malvern East 456 G3
Excelsior Hotel/Motel Thomastown 240 H20
Exford Hotel Melbourne 2 J10
Explorers Inn Melbourne 23 H13
Fawkner Airport Motel Fawkner 281 F8
Ferntree Gully Motor Inn Ferntree Gully 464 H5
Flag Inn Eltham Motel Eltham 288 F3
Flag Inn St Georges Motel Thornbury 326 G9
Flagstaff City Motor Inn West Melbourne 23 E4

INFORMATION

Footscray Motor Inn
Footscray....367 D6
Formule 1 Motel
Melbourne Airport....235 K11
Fourth Furlong Motel
Cranbourne....604 F5
Frankston Motel
Frankston....627 H13
Gateway on Monash
Motor Inn
Notting Hill....459 G12
Gazebo Lodge Motel
Arthurs Seat....685 H15
George Powlett Motel
East Melbourne....25 H8
Glenferrie Hotel
Hawthorn....371 L17
Golden Gate Hotel
South Melbourne....30 A3
Golden Palms Motel
Grovedale....706 G11
Golden Sophie's Inn Hotel
Melbourne....1 A6
Gordon Place Hotel
Melbourne....24 J4
Grand Hyatt Melbourne
Melbourne....2 K16
Great Western Hotel
Melbourne....1 A10
Greensborough Motor Inn
Greensborough....285 E11
Grosvenor Tavern
Melbourne....1 L14
Grovedale Motel
Grovedale....706 G8
Healesville Maroondah
View Motel
Healesville....257 H4
(Budget)
Healesville....214 J16
Heritage Toorak Manor Hotel
(Flag)
Toorak....32 L14
Hilton Melbourne Airport Hotel
Melbourne Airport....235 J11
Hilton On The Park Melbourne
East Melbourne....25 F8
Holiday Inn Melbourne
Melbourne....23 H15
Holiday Inn on Flinders Hotel
Melbourne....23 H13
Holiday Inn St Kilda Rd
South Melbourne....30 J3
Hotel Bak Pak
Melbourne....1 K1
Hotel Cavalier
Wantirna South....422 G17
Hotel Enterprize
Melbourne....23 H12
Hotel Francis
Melbourne....1 L8
Hotel Grand Chancellor
Melbourne....2 L9
Hotel Ibis
Melbourne....24 A1
Hotel Lindrum
Melbourne....24 K8
Hotel Saville
South Yarra....31 J15
Hotel Sofitel
Melbourne....24 K7
Hume Villa Motor Inn
Fawkner....281 E1
Imperial Hotel
Melbourne....24 K4
Jika International
Alphington....327 G19
Keilor Motor Inn
Keilor....277 D13
Keysborough Hotel/Motel
Keysborough....534 D12
Kimberley Gardens
St Kilda East....414 L17
Kingston Lodge
Carrum Downs....575 A16
Kingsway Motel
South Melbourne....30 E5
King Village Resort Motel
Wantirna....422 A10
Lamplighter Apartment Hotel
Malvern East....457 J7
Lamplighter Motor Inn
Oakleigh....458 A9
Le Meridien At Rialto
Melbourne....1 C16
Lilydale Motor Inn
Lilydale....338 J4
Lims Garden Inn
Melbourne....24 J3
Linley Estate Motel
Kilsyth....381 G8
McKinnon Hotel....456 D16
Magnolia Court Boutique
Hotel/Motel
East Melbourne....25 H6
Mahogany Park Motel
Cranbourne....604 B4
Mahoneys Motor Inn
Reservoir....240 J20
Manor House Apartments
South Yarra....32 B6
Manor Motor Inn
(Best Western)
Mitcham....377 J13
Maori Chief Hotel
South Melbourne....3 A17
Marriott Hotel
Melbourne....24 J3
Matthew Flinders
Hotel/Motel
Chadstone....417 L20
Medina Executive Hotel
Melbourne....24 J9
Medina Grand Hotel
Melbourne....1 H10
Melaleuca Lodge Motel
Officer....555 K19
Melbourne Bar
Melbourne....2 B12
Mentone Hub Inn
Mentone....531 D8
Menzies Tavern
Melbourne....1 C14
Mercure Grand Hotel
Melbourne....1 L18
Mercure Grand Hotel on Swanston
Melbourne....2 E11
Mercure Hotel
Melbourne....24 L8
Mercure Welcome Hotel
Melbourne....2 D10
Metro Hotel & Suites Melbourne
East Melbourne....25 C10
Metro Inn Apartment Hotel
Melbourne....1 H14
Metropole Hotel
Fitzroy....19 B20
Metropolitan Hotel
Melbourne....1 D6
Mid Gate Motor Lodge
Footscray....367 E6
Mitre Tavern
Melbourne....1 G15
Monte Villa Motor Inn
Hoppers Crossing....449 C5
Motel Formule 1
Dandenong....535 G3
Fawkner....239 D19
Motel Maroondah
Mont Albert....374 F14
Motel Melbourne
Craigieburn....194 L8
Motel Ringwood
Croydon....379 D4
Mt Victoria Motel
Warburton....349 J3
Moylans Hotel
Melbourne....1 H17
Mulgrave Court Motor Inn
Mulgrave....499 L4
Nepean Country Club Resort
Boneo....699 B15
Nepean Hotel
Bentleigh....496 A6
Novotel Hotel
Glen Waverley....460 D2
St Kilda....414 A17
Novotel Melbourne On Collins
Melbourne....2 C15
Nunawading Motor Inn
Blackburn....376 C14
Oceanic-Whitehall
Guest House & Motel
Sorrento....678 F11
Oxford Scholar Hotel
Melbourne....2 E2
Ozone Hotel
Queenscliff....709 B18
Pacific International Apartments
Melbourne....2 B10
Pacific International
Suites Melbourne
Melbourne....1 G10
Pakenham Park Motel
Pakenham....584 D1
Palm Motel
Footscray....367 D7
Park Hyatt Melbourne
East Melbourne....25 A5
Parkroyal On St Kilda Road
Melbourne....31 D15
Parkside Inn Motel
Kingsbury....284 B9
Park Squire Motor Inn
Parkville....34 J5
Parkville Motel
Brunswick....325 D18
Parkville Place Motor Inn
(Budget)
Brunswick....325 G18
Pathfinder Motel
(Best Western)
Kew....372 J11
Penthouse
Coolaroo....238 J8
Peppers Delgany
Portsea....677 J1
Phoenix Hotel
Melbourne....24 J9
Plough Hotel/Motel
Footscray....367 C8
Poets Lane Motel
Sherbrooke....426 J20
Point Lonsdale
Guesthouse Motel
Point Lonsdale....710 G7
Point Lonsdale Motel
Point Lonsdale....710 G6
Portsea Village Resort
Portsea....677 K1
Prince Mark Motor Inn
Doveton....536 H15
Princes Highway Hotel
Pakenham....584 D1
Princes Park Motor Inn
Brunswick....325 F17
Pugg Mahones Irish Pub
Melbourne....1 L7
Quality Hotel Laureate
Parkville....325 E20
Queensbridge Hotel
Southbank....3 F3
Queenscliff Hotel
Queenscliff....709 B17
Quest Fairfax House
Melbourne....1 K13
Quest Flemington - A Quest Inn
Flemington....33 E5
Quest Kew - A Quest Inn
Kew....371 K9
Quest on Bourke Hotel
Melbourne....2 K12
Quest on Flinders
Melbourne....2 H18
Quest On Lygon
Carlton....18 F6
Quest On St Kilda Rd
St Kilda....414 D13
Quest On William
Melbourne....1 E11
Quest Williamstown - A Quest Inn
Williamstown....411 H16
Racecourse Hotel/Motel
Flemington....33 E4
Railway Hotel
West Melbourne....34 J20
Ramada Inn
Parkville....325 E18
Ramada Melbourne
Melbourne....2 B19
Redan Quest Lodging
St Kilda....414 F14
Richmond Hill Hotel
(Golden Chain)
Richmond....26 G15
Richmond Quest Lodging
Cremorne....25 L19
Ringwood Lake Motor Inn
Ringwood....378 H10
Ringwood Regent Motor Inn
Ringwood....378 L8
Rowville Tourist Park
Rowville....502 G5
Rydges Carlton
Melbourne Hotel
Carlton....18 C16
Rydges Melbourne
Melbourne....24 J4
Rydges on Flemington
North Melbourne....17 D12
Rydges Riverwalk
Richmond....371 D16
Rye Motel
Rye....698 F1
St James Motel
South Yarra....32 B7
St Kilda Quest Inn
St Kilda....414 A15
Saltair Motel
Sorrento....678 J11
Sanctuary House
Healesville Motel
Healesville....258 D9
Sandown Heritage Motor Inn
Noble Park....500 L16
Sandown Park Hotel/Motel
Noble Park....500 H12
Sandown Regency Motor Inn
Noble Park....500 K15
Saville On Russell
Melbourne....2 K9
Saville Park Suites Hotel
Melbourne....24 F2
Savoy Park Plaza
International Melbourne
Melbourne....23 G10
Seaford Hotel/Motel
Seaford....600 B5
Settlement Hotel
Cranbourne....578 E18
Shannon Motor Inn
Newtown....702 C7
Sheraton Towers Southgate
Southbank....4 A4
Shoan Heights
City Apartment Hotel
Melbourne....24 J4
Shoppingtown Hotel/Motel
Doncaster....330 K20
Skyways International
Hotel/Motel
Airport West....279 A9
Sofitel Grand Hotel
Melbourne....23 G12
Sorrento on the Park Motel
Sorrento....678 J8
South Melbourne
Quest Lodging
South Melbourne....30 H4

LIBRARIES

PLACES OF INTEREST

RACECOURSE & TROTTING TRACKS

SHOPPING COMPLEXES - MAJOR

SPORTING VENUES

SPORTING VENUES

St Kilda Cricket Ground
Junction Oval ... 414 C12
St Kilda Football Club Ground
Moorabbin ... 496 D8
Sandown Motor Racing Circuit
Springvale ... 500 E13
Sir D Nicholls Sporting Complex
Thornbury ... 326 G6
State Hockey Centre
Parkville ... 17 B2
State Netball Centre
Parkville ... 17 A2
Sydney Pargeter
Recreation Reserve
Endeavour Hills ... 503 A18
Telstra Dome
Docklands ... 23 C9
Trevor Barker Oval
Sandringham ... 494 L11
Trinity Grammar
Sporting Complex
Bulleen ... 329 E14
Victorian Baseball &
Softball Centre
Altona ... 407 H16
Victoria Park
Abbotsford ... 20 D12
Vodafone Arena
Melbourne ... 25 E14
Waverley Football Ground ... 460 C6
Waverley Park ... 501 B2
Waverley Womens
Sports Centre
Wheelers Hill ... 461 C7
Werribee Recreation Centre .. 447 A14
Whitten Oval
Footscray ... 367 A8
Williamstown
Cricket Ground ... 411 H20

TERTIARY & OTHER INSTITUTIONS

AUSTRALIAN CATHOLIC
UNIVERSITY
Fitzroy ... 25 C1
BARTON INSTITUTE OF TAFE
Richmond Campus
70 Gwynne St ... 26 B20
Richmond Campus
Cremorne St ... 26 A19
BOX HILL INSTITUTE OF TAFE
Doncaster Campus ... 332 H6
Elgar Rd Campus ... 374 G12
Mitcham Campus ... 377 A14
Nelson Campus ... 374 J14
Whitehorse Campus ... 374 L15
CENTRAL GIPPSLAND
INSTITUTE OF TAFE
Chadstone Campus ... 457 L4
CHISHOLM INSTITUTE
Berwick Campus ... 554 D13
Cranbourne Campus ... 604 H4
Dandenong Campus ... 536 B3
Moorabbin Campus ... 496 G7
Noble Park Campus ... 534 K1
Rosebud Campus ... 699 H7
DEAKIN UNIVERSITY
Geelong Campus ... 705 B10
Melbourne Campus ... 418 G7
Rusden Campus ... 459 G13
Toorak Campus ... 415 K9
ENGLISH LANGUAGE CENTRE
Blackburn
120 Eley Rd ... 419 H8
Broadmeadow
Blair St ... 238 D15
Brunswick
406 Victoria St ... 325 D13
Collingwood
Cambridge St ... 25 G1
Debney Meadows
Victoria St
Flemington ... 34 D3
Footscray
Primary School, Hyde St ... 367 F11
Maribyrnong
River St ... 323 B18
Travancore
Flemington St ... 324 G19
HOLMES COLLEGE &
JAMES COOK UNIVERSITY
185 Spring St
Melbourne ... 24 J4
HOLMESGLEN INSTITUTE OF TAFE
Chadstone Campus ... 417 K20
Waverley Campus ... 459 L4
JOHN BATMAN INSTITUTE OF TAFE
Coburg North Campus ... 281 E17
Fitzroy Campus ... 19 J1
Watsonia Campus ... 285 H6
KANGAN INSTITUTE OF TAFE
Avondale-Brimbank
Campus ... 322 B13
Broadmeadows Campus ... 237 K14
Mooney Valley Campus ... 324 C9
Moreland Campus ... 325 G6
LA TROBE UNIVERSITY
Melbourne ... 1 H1
Bundoora Campus ... 284 D11
MELBOURNE COLLEGE
OF TEXTILES
Pascoe Vale Campus ... 280 H19
MONASH MT ELIZA
BUSINESS COLLEGE
Kunyung Rd
Mt Eliza ... 625 H19
MONASH UNIVERSITY
Berwick Campus ... 554 B11
Caulfield Campus ... 456 E1
Clayton Campus ... 459 C16
Parkville Campus ... 17 K1
NORTHERN MELBOURNE
INSTITUTE OF TAFE
Collingwood Campus ... 19 J14
Epping Campus ... 241 H2
Fairfield Campus ... 371 B2
Greensborough Campus ... 244 E17
Heidelberg Campus
Heidelberg West ... 328 C4
Parkville Campus ... 324 K19
Preston Campus ... 326 H1
ROYAL MELBOURNE
INSTITUTE OF TECHNOLOGY
Brunswick Campus ... 325 E15
Bundoora Campus ... 242 H14
Bundoora East Campus ... 243 B12
City Campus ... 2 F1
Fishermans Bend
Campus ... 367 H20
TAFE Sector
Carlton ... 18 D20
ST LEOS INTERNATIONAL COLLEGE
Hay St
Box Hill South ... 419 C1
ST PAULS MISSIONARY
Nortons La
Wantirna South ... 461 E2
SWINBURNE UNIVERSITY OF
TECHNOLOGY
Hawthorn Campus ... 372 A17
Lilydale Campus ... 338 C9
Prahran Campus ... 414 G11
Wantirna Campus
Wantirna South ... 422 G18
SWINBURNE UNIVERSITY OF
TECHNOLOGY - TAFE DIVISION
Croydon Campus ... 380 C6
Hawthorn Campus ... 372 A17
Healesville Campus ... 213 J18
Lilydale Campus ... 338 C9
Prahran Campus ... 414 G11
Wantirna Campus
Wantirna South ... 422 G18
THEOLOGICAL COLLEGE
Salvation Army Training,
Eastern Victoria
cnr Canterbury & Elgar Rds
Box Hill South ... 374 G19
Tabor
222 Oban Rd
Ringwood North ... 378 C2
Whitley
271 Royal Pde
Parkville ... 17 K4
THE UNIVERSITY OF MELBOURNE
Facility of Agriculture,
Forestry & Horticulture
Werribee ... 448 E15
Institute of Early
Childhood Development ... 371 E11
Parkville ... 17 L14
Veterinary Science Clinical Centre
Werribee ... 448 J9
Victorian College of
Agriculture & Horticulture
Burnley Campus ... 371 F19
Victorian College of
Agriculture & Horticulture
Gilbert Chandler Campus
Werribee ... 448 E15
Victorian College of The Arts
Southbank ... 4 D11
Whitley College
Parkville ... 17 K4
VICTORIA UNIVERSITY
City Campus
Melbourne ... 2 A18
City Flinders Campus
Melbourne ... 1 L19
City King Campus
Melbourne ... 1 A9
City South Melbourne
Campus ... 3 C10
Footscray Park Campus
Footscray ... 367 E5
Melton Campus ... 268 E10
Newport Campus ... 410 K10
Nicholson Campus
Footscray ... 367 F10
St Albans Campus ... 320 B9
Sunbury Campus ... 143 H18
Sunshine Campus ... 321 D18
Werribee Campus ... 448 L10
Yarraville Campus ... 367 E14
VICTORIA UNIVERSITY -
TAFE DIVISION
Melton Campus ... 268 E10
WESTALL ARTS &
LANGUAGE CENTRE
Rosebank Av
Clayton ... 499 E9
WILLIAM ANGLISS
INSTITUTE OF TAFE ... 23 F6

THEATRES, CINEMAS & DRIVE-IN THEATRES

AIRPORT WEST
Airport West, Village 8
Westfield Shoppingtown ... 278 L10
ALBERT PARK
Gasworks (Anthill)
21 Graham St ... 29 B14
BALWYN
Balwyn Cinema
233 Whitehorse Rd ... 373 D12
BEAUMARIS
Beaumaris Theatre
82 Wells Rd ... 530 G8
BELGRAVE
Cameo Belgrave
550 Monbulk Rd ... 466 F14
BORONIA
Village Boronia
216 Dorset Rd ... 424 D13
BRIGHTON
Brighton Bay Cinemas
294 Bay St ... 454 L14
Dendy Brighton Twin
26 Church St ... 454 H17
BROADMEADOWS
Broadmeadows Hoyts
48 Pearcedale Pde ... 238 A14
BUNDOORA
Agora Cinema
La Trobe University,
Kingsbury Dr ... 284 D12
BURWOOD
Phoenix
Deakin University ... 418 G8
CARLTON
Comedy Club
380 Lygon St ... 18 F13
Courthouse
349 Drummond St ... 18 G12
Dancehouse
Community Centre,
150 Princes St ... 18 H8
IMAX
Rathdowne St ... 18 H17
La Mama
205 Faraday St ... 18 F14
Movie House
235 Faraday St ... 18 E13
Nova Cinema
Lygon Court,
380 Lygon St ... 18 F13
CAULFIELD
Caulfield Arts Complex
cnr Glen Eira &
Hawthorn Rds ... 455 G3
CHELTENHAM
Village Southland 16
1239 Nepean Hwy ... 496 H17
CLIFTON HILL
Organ Factory
6 Page St ... 19 K7
COBURG
Progress
236 Reynard St ... 325 B4

COBURG NORTH
- Village Triple Drive-In Newlands Rd 281 J13

COLLINGWOOD
- Collingwood College Theatre Vere St 19 L16
- Last Laugh 64 Smith St 19 F20

CRANBOURNE
- Century 4 Cinemas Cranbourne Park Shopping Centre 604 D3

CROYDON
- Croydon Hoyts 3 Hewish Rd 380 B4

DANDENONG SOUTH
- Lunar Drive-In South Gippsland Hwy 536 H19

DONCASTER
- Doncaster Village Twin Westfield Shoppingtown 330 L20
- Playhouse Theatre Doncaster Rd 331 A20

DROMANA
- Dromana Twin Drive-in Theatre Nepean Hwy 687 B3

EAST MELBOURNE
- Cinemedia at Treasury Theatre 1 Macarthur St 24 L6
- Dallas Brooks Hall 300 Victoria Rd 25 E3
- State Film Theatre St Andrews Pl 25 A5

ELSTERNWICK
- Classic Cinema 9 Gordon St 454 K4

EPPING
- Anderson Cinema Epping Plaza 241 D2

FAIRFIELD
- Northcote Amphitheatre Fairfield Park 371 C1

FOOTSCRAY
- Footscray Community Arts Centre 45 Moreland Rd 367 J9

FOREST HILL
- Forest Hill Hoyts 10 Forest Hill Chase 420 D2

GEELONG WEST
- Pix 23 Elizabeth St 702 E4

GLEN WAVERLEY
- Village Century City Walk 10 285 Springvale Rd 460 D2

GREENSBOROUGH
- Greensborough Hoyts Greensborough Plaza 286 B3

HAWTHORN EAST
- Village Rivoli 200 Camberwell Rd 372 H20

HEIDELBERG
- Banyule Theatre Buckingham Dr 329 E5

HOPPERS CROSSING
- Werribee 10 cnr Heaths & Derrimut Rds 448 D4

LILYDALE
- Athenaeum Theatre Castella St 338 E5

MALVERN
- Stonnington Theatre Deakin University 336 Glenferrie Rd 415 K9

MALVERN EAST
- Chadstone , Hoyts 8 Chadstone Shopping Centre 457 G5
- Malvern Community Arts Centre 29a Burke Rd 416 F20
- Malvern Theatre Burke Rd 416 F20

MARIBYRNONG
- Highpoint, Hoyts 10 Highpoint City Shopping Centre 323 B17

MELBOURNE
- Athenaeum Theatre 188 Collins St 2 G15
- Capitol Theatre 113 Swanston St 2 E14
- Chinatown 200 Bourke St 2 H11
- Comedy 240 Exhibition St 24 J4
- Forum The Old State Theatre 154 Flinders St 2 J18
- George Fairfax Studio, Victorian Arts Centre 100 St Kilda Rd 4 D7
- Glasshouse Theatre RMIT, 360 Swanston St 2 F3
- Her Majestys 219 Exhibition St 24 J4
- Hoyts Cinema Centre 140 Bourke St 2 L11
- Kino Collins Place, 45 Collins St 24 J7
- Lumiere 108 Lonsdale St 24 J3
- Melbourne Concert Hall Victorian Arts Centre, 100 St Kilda Rd 4 D4
- Playhouse, Victoria Arts Centre 100 St Kilda Rd 4 D7
- Princess 163 Spring St 24 J4
- Regent 186 Flinders La 2 G17
- Rialto 24/525 Collins St 1 B17
- Russell, Greater Union 131 Russell St 2 J13
- Sidney Myer Music Bowl Alexandra Av 24 L15
- State, Victorian Arts Centre 100 St Kilda Rd 4 E6
- Village Centre 206 Bourke St 2 H11

MELTON
- Melton Twin cnr McKenzie & Alexandra Sts 226 K20

MOONEE PONDS
- Incinerator 180 Holmes Rd 323 G12

MORDIALLOC
- Shirley Burke Parkers Rd 531 F13

MORNINGTON
- Mornington Cinema 1 Main St 640 D12

MT WAVERLEY
- Waverley, Pinewood Pinewood Dr 459 G7

MULGRAVE
- Village Waverley Gardens Waverley Gardens Shopping Centre 501 B6

NORTHCOTE
- Westgarth Theatre 89 High St 326 H18

NUNAWADING
- Nunawading Arts & Entertainment Centre 379 Whitehorse Rd 376 K13

PRESTON
- Northland, Hoyts 8 Northland Shopping Centre 283 J20

RESEARCH
- Eltham Little 1605 Main Rd 288 K2

RINGWOOD
- Eastland Hoyts Eastland Shopping Centre 378 D11

RINGWOOD EAST
- Karralyka Mines Rd 378 K9

ROSANNA
- Heidelberg Theatre Company 37 Turnham Av 328 L2

ROSEBUD
- Rosebud Twin Cinema 3 Rosebud Pde 684 C15

ST KILDA
- Astor Theatre cnr Chapel St & Dandenong Rd 414 G13
- George Cinema 133-137 Fitzroy St 414 B14
- National cnr Barkly & Carlisle Sts 414 C17
- Palais Lower Esplanade 414 A17

SORRENTO
- Athenaeum Theatre Ocean Beach Rd 678 J8

SOUTHBANK
- Grant Street Grant St 4 D13
- Malthouse (Playbox) 113 Sturt St 3 K15
- Village Megaplex Crown Casino, Clarendon St 23 K16

SOUTH MELBOURNE
- Napier Street (Arena) 199 Napier St 30 B7
- State Film Theatre Park St 30 B6

SOUTH YARRA
- Como Cinema Toorak Rd 32 F9
- Longford 59 Toorak Rd 31 L8
- Polyglot 27a Cromwell Rd 32 H14
- St Martins 44 St Martins La 31 E5
- Village Jam Factory 500 Chapel St 32 E12

SUNSHINE
- Village Sunshine Megaplex 20 Harvester Rd 321 B20

TAYLORS LAKES
- Hoyts Watergardens Watergardens Shopping Centre Melton Hwy 275 D4

THE BASIN
- The Basin Theatre Doongalla Rd 425 J8

TOORAK
- Trak 445 Toorak Rd 415 B5

UPPER FERNTREE GULLY
- 1812 Theatre Rose St 465 B7

WANTIRNA SOUTH
- Village Knox 10 Knox Tower Point, Burwood Hwy 422 J16

WEST MELBOURNE
- Festival Hall Dudley St 23 A5

YARRAVILLE
- Sun Theatre 8 Ballarat St 367 C15

WINERIES

- Ainsworth Estate 342 G17
- Andraos Bros 187 B1
- Barak Estate 658 C8
- Barrymore Estate 657 K17
- Bianchet 294 A9
- Craiglee 144 B14
- Darling Park 688 K19
- De Bortoli 210 E1
- Domaine Chandon 254 L11
- Dromana Estate 687 J5
- Dromana Valley Wines 669 J18
- Elmswood Estate 386 E7
- Ermes Estate 658 L13
- Evelyn County Estate 289 E2
- Fergussons 210 A1
- Five Oaks 386 C7
- Goona Warra 144 B13
- Henkell 210 D1
- Hickinbotham of Dromana 669 K17
- Hills of Plenty 200 H20
- Karina 687 J6
- Long Gully Estate 212 D14
- Lovegrove of Cottles Bridge 204 E4
- McWilliams Lilydale 342 L19
- Main Ridge Estate 686 K20
- Moorooduc Estate 658 F12
- Morning Star Estate 641 E7
- Mt Eliza Estate 641 F8
- Mt Martha Vineyard on Checkingurk Run 670 J3
- Myrtaceae 686 G19
- Parwan Estate 267 A13
- Paternoster 510 E9
- Port Philip Estate 688 L17
- Prince Albert (Off Map) 705 A16
- Punt Road Cellar Door 254 E18
- St Huberts 254 F19
- Seville Estate 342 E19
- Shadowfax 488 B10
- The Briars 656 G16
- The Tallarida Winery & Boneo Estate 699 L13
- Turramurra Estate 670 H19
- Vermont 421 C11
- Vintina Estate 641 H7
- Wantirna Estate 421 F19
- Wildwood 190 L3
- Yarra Burn 347 H13
- Yarra Edge 293 E9
- Yarra Glen 253 A2
- Yarra Ridge 252 E3
- Yarra Track 211 F14
- Yarra Valley Hills 334 K10
- Yering Farm Wines 253 J17
- Yering Station 253 D8

PUBLISHING DATES

- 1st Edition 1991
- 2nd Edition 1993
- 3rd Edition 1997
- 4th Edition 1999
- 5th Edition 2001
- 6th Edition 2004

SUBURBS and LOCALITIES INDEX

Listed below are Melbourne suburbs and localities together with their postcodes and map references.
Suburbs and are differentiated in the index as follows:

Altona — Suburb
Hawksburn — Locality shown on maps

Note: Streets are indexed to suburbs only, not localities.

	Postcode	Map	Ref
Fairfield	3078	327	F16
Fawkner	3060	281	J7
Ferntree Gully	3156	464	A9
Ferny Creek	3786	425	L16
Fingal	3941	698	D18
Fishermans Bend	3207	368	A20
Fitzroy	3065	370	C9
Fitzroy North	3068	326	D17
Flemington	3031	367	K3
Footscray	3011	367	D3
Forest Hill	3131	420	C5
Frankston	3199	599	E17
Frankston North	3200	600	G11
Frankston South	3199	626	K11
Fyansford	3221	701	C6
Gardenvale	3185	455	C10
Geelong	3220	703	A9
Geelong West	3218	702	G5
Gembrook	3783	512	F4
Gladstone Park	3043	237	A18
Glen Huntly	3163	456	C9
Glen Iris	3146	416	L11
Glenroy	3046	280	F4
Glen Waverley	3150	420	G17
Gowanbrae	3043	279	C7
Greensborough	3088	244	G14
Greenvale	3059	193	E19
Grovedale	3216	706	C18
Guys Hill	3807	541	H19
Hadfield	3046	280	K8
Hallam	3803	537	J17
Hampton	3188	495	C7
Hampton East	3188	495	K8
Hampton Park	3976	552	A10
Harkaway	3806	540	L8
Hawksburn	3142	414	J6
Hawthorn	3122	371	K14
Hawthorn East	3123	372	F19
Healesville	3777	257	J8
Heatherton	3202	497	K12
Heathmont	3135	378	H19
Heidelberg	3084	328	J6
Heidelberg Heights	3081	284	F19
Heidelberg West	3081	284	B16
Herne Hill	3218	701	L2
Highett	3190	496	C14
Highton	3216	705	E10
Hillside	3037	274	C5
Hoddles Creek	3139	388	J14
Holmesglen	3148	417	K19
Hopetoun Park	3340	266	D6
Hoppers Crossing	3029	405	A16
Hughesdale	3166	457	G12
Huntingdale	3166	458	F14
Hurstbridge	3099	202	H16
Ivanhoe	3079	328	C10
Ivanhoe East	3079	328	G15

	Postcode	Map	Ref
Jacana	3047	237	G17
Jan Juc	3228	711	C13
Jolimont	3002	370	D15
Junction Village	3977	604	G14
Kallista	3791	467	H6
Kalorama	3766	383	H14
Kangaroo Ground	3097	247	J12
Kealba	3021	276	K18
Keilor	3036	277	B8
Keilor Downs	3038	276	D15
Keilor East	3033	321	F3
Keilor Lodge	3038	276	A2
Keilor North	3036	234	D19
Keilor Park	3042	277	J12
Kensington	3031	368	D7
Kew	3101	372	F10
Kew East	3102	372	G4
Keysborough	3173	534	K15
Kilsyth	3137	381	E9
Kilsyth South	3137	381	B17
Kingsbury	3083	283	J10
Kings Park	3021	275	E19
Kingsville	3012	366	J12
Knoxfield	3180	462	K10
Kooyong	3144	416	A5
Kurunjang	3337	227	D7
Lalor	3075	241	H8
Langwarrin	3910	629	J7
Langwarrin South	3910	629	G18
Launching Place	3139	346	E15
Laverton	3028	407	B13
Laverton North	3026	407	E3
Lilydale	3140	338	B12
Long Forest	3340	224	F7
Lower Plenty	3093	286	J17
Lynbrook	3975	551	D20
Lyndhurst	3975	550	H14
Lysterfield	3156	464	H17
Lysterfield South	3156	503	K13
Macclesfield	3782	470	J5
Macleod	3085	285	C14
McCrae	3938	684	L13
McKinnon	3204	455	K15
Maddingley	3340	263	J6
Maidstone	3012	366	J3
Malvern	3144	416	B13
Malvern East	3145	457	D3
Mambourin	3024	445	C11
Manifold Heights	3218	702	C3
Mannerim	3222	707	J3
Marcus Hill	3222	707	A12
Maribyrnong	3032	322	H12
Marshall	3216	706	K7

	Postcode	Map	Ref
Meadow Heights	3048	237	K1
Melbourne	3000	413	K4
Melbourne Airport	3045	235	B8
Melton	3337	228	B15
Melton South	3338	269	J10
Melton West	3337	224	L14
Mentone	3194	531	J6
Menzies Creek	3159	468	E17
Merlynston	3058	281	C12
Mernda	3754	155	K16
Merricks North	3926	688	L7
Merrimu	3340	223	F11
Mickleham	3064	150	E2
Middle Park	3206	413	F9
Millgrove	3799	348	B3
Mill Park	3082	242	L1
Mitcham	3132	377	D12
Monbulk	3793	428	H13
Mont Albert	3127	374	D14
Mont Albert North	3129	374	D8
Montmorency	3094	286	J11
Montrose	3765	382	E12
Moolap	3221	704	J18
Moonee Ponds	3039	323	J13
Moorabbin	3189	496	F8
Moorabbin Airport	3194	532	C4
Moorooduc	3933	658	D7
Mooroolbark	3138	337	F10
Mordialloc	3195	532	D12
Mornington	3931	641	B18
Mt Burnett	3781	511	K17
Mt Dandenong	3767	426	J2
Mt Duneed	3216	705	F19
Mt Eliza	3930	626	A11
Mt Evelyn	3796	383	D2
Mt Martha	3934	656	C6
Mt Waverley	3149	419	E14
Mulgrave	3170	500	J3
Murrumbeena	3163	457	B13
Nangana	3781	472	H1
Nar Nar Goon	3812	586	H7
Nar Nar Goon North	3812	560	H11
Narre Warren	3805	553	J10
Narre Warren East	3804	506	H18
Narre Warren North	3804	538	E2
Narre Warren South	3805	552	F16
Newcomb	3219	704	C10
New Gisborne	3438	79	H3
Newport	3015	410	J5
Newtown	3220	702	A11
Niddrie	3042	278	J19
Noble Park	3174	500	J16
Noble Park North	3174	501	B15
Northcote	3070	327	B12
North Melbourne	3051	368	J8
North Warrandyte	3113	290	B14
Northcote	3070	327	B12
Notting Hill	3168	459	D12
Nunawading	3131	376	J16
Nutfield	3099	202	E1